D0024794

Encyclopedia of
Eastern Europe

Garland Reference Library of Social Science (Vol. 751)

Advisory Board

Paul J. Best
Southern Connecticut State University

Frederick B. Chary
Indiana University Northwest

Stephen Fischer-Galati
University of Colorado

Sarah A. Kent
University of Wisconsin—-Stevens Point

Thomas Sakmyster
University of Cincinnati

Joseph Frederick Zacek
State University of New York at Albany

Maps prepared by

Jeffrey Bradley
Northwest Missouri State University

Encyclopedia of Eastern Europe

From the Congress of Vienna to
the Fall of Communism

Edited by
Richard Frucht
Northwest Missouri State University

Garland Publishing, Inc.
A member of the Taylor & Francis Group
New York & London
2000

R
947.003
E56

Published in 2000 by
Garland Publishing, Inc.
A member of the Taylor & Francis Group
29 West 35th Street
New York, NY 10001

Copyright © 2000 by Garland Publishing, Inc.

All rights reserved. No part of this book may be reprinted or reproduced or utilized in any form or by any electronic, mechanical, or other means, now known or hereafter invented, including photocopying and recording, or in any information storage or retrieval system, without permission in writing from the publishers.

10 9 8 7 6 5 4 3 2 1

Library of Congress Cataloging-in-Publication Data
Encyclopedia of Eastern Europe : from the Congress of Vienna to the fall of communism
/ edited by Richard Frucht.
     p. cm. — (Garland reference library of social science ; v. 751)
   Includes bibliographical references and index.
   ISBN 0-8153-0092-1 (alk. paper)
   1. Europe, Eastern—Encyclopedias.   I. Frucht, Richard.   II. Series.
DJK6 .E53 2000
947'.0003   00-021517

Printed on acid-free, 250-year-life paper
Manufactured in the United States of America

AQUINAS COLLEGE LIBRARY
1607 ROBINSON RD.
GRAND RAPIDS MICH 49506

45.43
9-11-01

Contents

Introduction

In 1989, to the surprise of many, Communist governments throughout Eastern Europe collapsed. In a matter of months, a world that had existed since the end of World War II in 1945 was overturned. The infamous "Iron Curtain"—a term coined by British prime minister Winston Churchill in 1946 to describe the barriers that had arisen between the nations of the West and those in Eastern Europe that were under the influence of the Soviet Union—suddenly ceased to exist. For the first time in decades, people traveled freely across borders throughout Europe. Nations that had long been in the Soviet sphere of influence were now free to create democratic governments and market economies.

Despite the profound changes that have taken place since those climactic events, many textbooks often ignore that vast region that lies between Berlin and Vienna in the west and Moscow and St. Petersburg in the east—the area that is popularly referred to as Eastern Europe.

In 1990 I was asked by the American Association for the Advancement of Slavic Studies to direct a national project aimed at increasing awareness of Eastern Europe in the public schools, where little—if any—time has been devoted to the study of this part of the world. For many, knowledge of Eastern Europe, especially of its rich and diverse past, rarely went beyond mere Cold War stereotypes. Over the next three years, my colleagues and I attended numerous meetings and workshops speaking to dedicated professionals who often themselves had been taught very little about Eastern Europe. In discussions with teachers, one thing became instantly clear: They lacked

accessible information, and we were repeatedly told that the essential material that teachers needed was a reference guide. Thus, when Garland Publishing offered me the opportunity to edit this encyclopedia, I could not refuse. Despite the daunting nature and challenge of the project, to have done so would have been to turn my back on those who were asking for assistance.

The term "Eastern Europe" is itself somewhat imprecise, and some scholars argue that the region should be called East Central Europe or Central and Southeastern Europe. However, since "Eastern Europe" is more commonly used in the West, the decision was made to use that term throughout the book. We further decided to focus on the states of the former Eastern bloc, save for East Germany, an area more properly discussed by reference works on Germany. Clearly, the entire scope of the region's past could not be included in one volume. We focus our attention on developments over the past two centuries—the period roughly from the Congress of Vienna to the fall of Communism.

The cornerstones of the volume are the seven long articles on each of the primary countries/regions—Poland, Czechoslovakia, Hungary, Yugoslavia, Romania, Bulgaria, and Albania. These comprehensive entries provide an introduction to the major developments that have transpired over the course of the past two centuries. The remainder of the entries deal with geography, history, government, economics, culture, trends and ideas, as well as outside forces and individuals that have affected developments in Eastern Europe. References for further reading are also provided (although some of them, of necessity, are not in English). In addition, the reader is directed to other articles in the volume for further information on related topics. Obviously, given the limitations of space it would be impossible to cover everything and everyone we would have liked to have included. We have tried to be as comprehensive as possible and any and all slights to a potential topic were never intentional.

Putting together a volume such as this would be impossible without the assistance of distinguished scholars. My sincerest thanks go to Paul Best, Frederick Chary, Stephen Fischer-Galati, Sarah Kent, Thomas Sakmyster, and Joseph Zacek for all their advice in putting the entry list together as well as their critical reading of the articles. Their suggestions and input were, to say the least, invaluable. Likewise, words can never convey my gratitude to all the scholars whose professionalism, patience, support, and understanding made this all possible. The words are theirs but the appreciation is mine.

Thanks must also go to a number of students at Northwest Missouri State University who aided with the mountain of paperwork, copying, filing, and myriad computer-related problems that arise with a project of this magnitude: Jennifer Gump (Beekman); Jenifer Harr; Amy Bertoldie; Melissa Fletchall; Brian Stanfield; Seth Hofstetter; Sinan Atahan; and Matt Johnson.

And finally, as always, thanks to my wife Sue and my daughter Kristin for their support and good humor. They are and always will be the rudder that guides my ship.

Contributors

Philip J. Adler
East Carolina University

Hugh Agnew
George Washington University

Catherine Albrecht
University of Baltimore

June Granatir Alexander
University of Cincinnati

Josef Anderle
University of North Carolina

Gerasimos Augustinos
University of South Carolina

Olga Augustinos
University of South Carolina

Robert Austin
University of Toronto

Walter M. Bacon Jr.
University of Nebraska—Omaha

Douglass W. Bailey
University of Wales

Eugene F. Bales
Bethany College

George Barany
University of Denver

Enikő Molnár Basa
Library of Congress

Ann Marie Basom
University of Northern Iowa

Kenneth E. Basom
University of Northern Iowa

Margaret H. Beissinger
University of Wisconsin

Joel D. Benson
Northwest Missouri State University

William H. Berentsen
University of Connecticut

Dagmar Berry
Salisbury State University

Robert A. Berry
Salisbury State University

Paul J. Best
Southern Connecticut State University

Christina Y. Bethin
State University of New York at Stony Brook

Mark Biondich
Columbia University

William Lee Blackwood
Yale University

Milka T. Bliznakov
Virginia Polytechnic Institute and State University

Edward Bojarski
Cherokee County Health Dept.

Melissa Bokovoy
University of New Mexico

Vera Bolgár
University of Michigan

Michael Boll
San Jose State University

András Boros-Kazai
Beloit College

Andrei Brezianu
Voice of America

Gregory L. Bruess
University of Northern Iowa

Maria Bucur
Indiana University

Alice-Catherine Carls
University of Tennessee—Martin

Charles M. Carlton
University of Rochester

Magda Carneci
Institutul de istoria artei
Bucharest, Romania

David Cassens
St. Louis University

Frederick B. Chary
Indiana University Northwest

Koji Chikugo
Chiro International

Anna M. Cienciala
University of Kansas

Lee Congdon
James Madison University

Deborah S. Cornelius
Rutgers University

John K. Cox
Wheeling Jesuit College

Richard F. Crane
Greensboro College

Gerald W. Creed
Hunter College, CUNY

Darrick Danta
California State University, Northridge

Zdeněk V. David
The Woodrow Wilson International Center for Scholars

Elinor Murray Despalatović
Connecticut College

Nicholas Dima
Voice of America

Alex N. Dragnich
Vanderbilt University

N.F. Dreisziger
Royal Military College of Canada

Tanya L.K. Dunlap
Rice University

Ĺubomír Ďurovič
University of Lund, Sweden

Alexandru Duţu
Institutul de studii sud-est europene
Bucharest, Romania

Donald L. Dyer
University of Mississippi

Thomas Eekman
University of California—Los Angeles

James Eiswert
Northwest Missouri State University

Judith Fai-Podlipnik
Southern Louisiana University

Brigit Farley
Washington State University, Tri-Cities

James Felak
University of Washington

Mario D. Fenyo
Bowie State University

Gregory C. Ference
Salisbury State University

Richard Field
Northwest Missouri State University

John A. Fink
New York, New York

Clemansa Liliana Firca
Bucharest, Romania

Mari A. Firkatian
University of Hartford

Mary Ellen Fischer
Skidmore College

Lawrence J. Flockerzie
University of Dayton

Radu Florescu
Boston College

Victor A. Friedman
University of Chicago

Richard Frucht
Northwest Missouri State University

Richard Fulton
Northwest Missouri State University

Michal Gáfrik
Slovak Academy of Sciences
Bratislava, Slovakia

Bruce M. Garver
University of Nebraska—Omaha

Katherine Gyékényesi Gatto
John Carroll University

John Georgeoff
Purdue University

Susan Glanz
St. John's University

James Glapa-Grossklag
University of Chicago

Eagle Glassheim
Columbia University

Jonathan A. Grant
Florida State University

Charles E. Gribble
Ohio State University

Lyubomira Parpulova Gribble
Ohio State University

Marie J. Hall
Bar Harbor, Maine

Richard C. Hall
Mankato State University

Joseph F. Harrington
Framingham State College

Yana Hashamova
Union College

Peter I. Hidas
Dawson College

Robert Hislope
Grinnell College

Jiří Hochman
Ohio State University

Beth Holmgren
University of North Carolina

Peter Hruby
Curtin University of Technology

Todd Huebner
Office of Special Investigations
Washington, D.C.

Dennis P. Hupchick
Wilkes University

Dina Iordanova
Leicester University

Russell L. Ivy
Florida Atlantic University

Conrad Jarzebowski
Institute for East-West Studies

Charles Jelavich
Indiana University

Owen V. Johnson
Indiana University

Pieter Judson
Swarthmore College

Milenko Karanovich
University of the United States and Nasson University

Stanislav Kavka
University of Ostrava

T. Mills Kelly
Texas Tech University

Sarah A. Kent
University of Wisconsin—Stevens Point

Jo Ellen Kerksiek
Lindenwood College

Charles King
Georgetown University

Anto Knezevic
Albanian Catholic Institute

John Kolsti
University of Texas—Austin

Michael J. Kopanic Jr.
Indiana University of Pennsylvania

Andrzej Korbonski
University of California—Los Angeles

Jiří Kořalka
Hussite Museum
Tabor, Czech Republic

William B. Kory
University of Pittsburgh—Johnstown

Boian Koulov
George Mason University

Ladis K.D. Kristof
Portland State University

James P. Krokar
DePaul University

Andrzej Kulczycki
University of Michigan

Alexandros K. Kyrou
Salem State College

Ernest H. Latham Jr.
American Romanian Academy

Michael J. Lavelle
John Carroll University

Peter Lavelle
Warsaw, Poland

Paul D. Lensink
Washington, D.C.

Madeline G. Levine
University of North Carolina

André Liebich
Insitut Universitaire de Hautes Études Internationales

Irina Livezeanu
University of Pittsburgh

Barbara Łobodzińska
New Brighton, Minnesota

Christopher Long
University of Texas

Andrew Ludanyi
Ohio Northern University

Radomír V. Luža
Tulane University

James M.B. Lyon
Sarajevo, Bosnia

David MacKenzie
University of North Carolina—Greensboro

Paul Robert Magocsi
University of Toronto

Victor S. Mamatey
University of Georgia

Joseph M. McCarthy
Suffolk University

Kate L. McCarthy
University of Dubuque

Abraham Melezin
City College of New York

Paul E. Michelson
Huntington College

Daniel E. Miller
University of West Florida

Mirvet S. Muca
Riverhill, New York

Nicholas M. Nagy-Talavera
California State University—Chico

Robert Nemes
Colgate University

Remus Niculescu
Institutul de istoria artei
Bucharest, Romania

James P. Niessen
Texas Tech University

Claire E. Nolte
Manhattan College

Petra Orálková
University of Ostrava

Cynthia Paces
The College of New Jersey

Philip Pajakowski
Saint Anselm College

Aleksandar Panev
University of Toronto

Gregory J. Pano
Dean College

Peter Pastor
Montclair State University

Neal A. Pease
University of Wisconsin—Milwaukee

Jolanta T. Pękacz
University of Saskatchewan

William A. Pelz
Institute of Working Class History

Mártha Pereszlényi-Pintér
John Carroll University

Duncan M. Perry
Central Washington University

Barbara A. Peterson
University of Hawaii

Timothy Pogacar
Bowling Green State University

Robert M. Ponichtera
The Woodrow Wilson
International Center for Scholars

Ruzica Popovitch-Krekic
Mt. St. Mary's College

Thomas M. Poulsen
Portland State University

Tom Priestly
University of Alberta

Theophilus C. Prousis
University of North Florida

Paul D. Quinlan
Providence College

George Tivadar Radân
Villanova University

Spas T. Raikin
East Stroudsburg University

Svetlana Rakić
Franklin College

Miloslav Rechcigl Jr.
Czechoslovak Society of Arts & Sciences

Barbara K. Reinfeld
New York Institute of Technology

Carole Rogel
Ohio State University

Ignác Romsics
Eötvös Lóránd Tudományegyetem
Budapest, Hungary

Norma L. Rudinsky
Oregon State University

Nancy Lee Ruyter
University of California—Irvine

Konrad Sadkowski
University of Northern Iowa

Thomas Sakmyster
University of Cincinnati

Mark Sand
Northwest Missouri State University

Ben Slay
Middlebury College

Biljana Šljivić-Šimšić
University of Illinois—Chicago

Ronald Smelser
The University of Utah

William Smialek
Jarvis Christian College

Steven W. Sowards
Michigan State University

Robert Mark Spaulding
University of North Carolina—Wilmington

Thomas Spira
University of Prince Edward Island

Irina G. Stakhanova
Bowling Green State University

John Stanley
Ministry of Training, Colleges and Universities
Toronto

David Stefancic
Saint Mary's College

Ştefan Stoenescu
Ithaca, New York

Gale Stokes
Rice University

M. Mark Stolarik
University of Ottawa

Željan E. Šuster
University of New Haven

Richard Tempest
University of Illinois

Frank W. Thackeray
Indiana University Southeast

Marta Tobolczyk
Warsaw University of Technology

Glenn E. Torrey
Emporia State University

Albert M. Tosches
Salem State College

Pál Péter Tóth
Demographic Research Institute of the
Central Statistical Office
Budapest, Hungary

John D. Treadway
University of Richmond

Kurt W. Treptow
The Romanian Cultural Foundation
Iaşi, Romania

Daniel D. Trifan
Missouri Western State College

Frances Trix
Wayne State University

Stefan Troebst
University of Leipzig

Teddy J. Uldricks
University of North Carolina—Asheville

George R. Ursul
Emerson College

Barbara J. VanDrasek
University of Minnesota

Steven Béla Várdy
Duquesne University

Balint Vazsonyi
The Potomac Foundation

Gabor Vermes
Rutgers University

Ioana Vlasiu
Insitutul de istoria artei "G. Oprescu"
Bucharest, Romania

Piotr S. Wandycz
Yale University

Robert Weiner
University of Massachusetts—Boston

Nancy M. Wingfield
Northern Illinois University

Stanley B. Winters
New Jersey Institute of Technology

Andrew Kier Wise
University of Virginia

Peter Wozniak
Montgomery Academy

Piotr Wróbel
University of Toronto

Joseph Frederick Zacek
State University of New York at Albany

Lucie Zacharová
University of Ostrava

Katarzyna Zechenter
University of London

Encyclopedia of
Eastern Europe

Abakanowicz, Magdalena (1930–)

Polish artist who creatively explores many areas and techniques of art, chiefly sculpture and tapestry. Abakanowicz graduated from the Academy of Fine Arts in Warsaw in 1954. In the 1960s she created monumental three-dimensional gobelins, called *Abakans,* which opened a new era in the history of tapestry. In the 1970s she turned her interest to sculpture. Her cycle of *Alternations* consisted of groups of humanlike corpses shaped out of stiffened burlap. Her significant achievement is the outdoor environmental composition *Katharsis,* a group of thirty-three bronze figures referring to prehistoric megalithic structures (1985), and the stone sculpture *Negev* for the Israel Museum in Jerusalem.

In the 1990s Abakanowicz created two intriguing architectural visions: the memorial tower (2,112 feet [640 m] high), designed in the form of a human hand, for the city of Hiroshima, and a concept for an ecological housing complex in La Défense in Paris, called *Arboreal Architecture* for its forestlike shape.

Through her creations, she searches for problems related to human existence and the identity of an individual within a mass. In her opinion, an artist "should seek new solutions to make the human condition easier. If the artist does not become the shaman of the human herd, he will be rejected as a superfluous decorator." She ranks among the most outstanding and innovative contemporary creators. Her works are in collections of about 80 world museums. Abakanowicz was a professor at the Academy of Fine Arts in Poznań (1979–90) and has lectured abroad. She has received many international awards including titles of the *doctor honoris causa* from the Royal College of Art in London and the Rhode Island School of Design in the United States.

Marta Tobolczyk

Further reading

Abakanowicz, Magdalena and Jasia Reinchardt. *Magdalena Abakanowicz. Museum of Contemporary Art, Chicago and Abbeville.* New York, 1982.

Constantine, Mildred and Jack L. Larsen. *The Art Fabric: Mainstream.* New York, 1980.

Rose, Barbara. *Magdalena Abakanowicz.* New York, 1994.

See also Polish Art

Abdul Hamid II (1842–1918)

Ottoman sultan. The son of Abdulmecid I (r. 1839–61), Abdul Hamid II came to the Ottoman throne following the deposition of his mentally incompetent brother, Murad V (r. 1876), on August 31, 1876. Initially, he was generally praised for being industrious and sober in contrast to many of his predecessors. During his rule, the Ottoman state reform movement of the *Tanzimat* (Reorganization) reached its climax. Indeed, on December 23, 1876, Abdul Hamid promulgated the first Ottoman constitution. However, the favorable attitude that accompanied his ascension to the throne quickly disappeared. In fact, his reign was to be marked by a series of military and diplomatic disasters, as well as domestic instability.

Throughout the period of his reign, pressure from the subject Christian populations, the Balkan

A successor states, and the Great Powers increased, and sometimes converged, to further weaken and reduce the empire. After a disastrous war with Russia in 1877–78, Abdul Hamid dismissed the Ottoman parliament and suspended the constitution in February 1878. Thereafter, he ruled as an autocrat assisted by a system of secret police, arbitrary state brutality, and severe censorship.

Discontent with Abdul Hamid's despotic rule, as well as the continued decline of the empire and resentment against foreign intervention in the Balkans, aroused considerable Ottoman Turkish opposition. Inspired by intellectuals and politicians who had been forced to emigrate owing to Abdul Hamid's repression, the growing opposition groups gradually came together in a loosely formed coalition known as the Young Turks. Members of one of the Young Turk groups, the Committee of Union and Progress (CUP), led a military revolt in Ottoman Macedonia that forced Abdul Hamid to restore the parliament in 1908. After a short-lived counterrevolution in April 1909, Abdul Hamid was deposed by the CUP, and his brother was proclaimed sultan.

Alexandros K. Kyrou

Further reading

Haslip, Joan. *The Sultan: The Life of Abdul Hamid.* London, 1958.

Pears, Sir E. *Life of Abdul Hamid.* London, 1917.

Wittlin, A. *Abdul Hamid: The Shadow of God.* London, 1939.

See also Great Powers; Russo-Turkish War of 1877–78; *Tanzimat;* Young Turks

Adrianople, Treaty of (1829)

Treaty ending the Russo-Turkish War of 1828–29, which reflected Russia's decision to dominate rather than destroy its defeated opponent. Shortly before the signing of the treaty, a special commission met in St. Petersburg and discussed Russia's strategy in the peacemaking. The commission decided that the Russian government should not oust the Ottomans from the Balkans, but rather establish a dominant profile there. The treaty well expressed the commission's sentiments.

Signed at Adrianople, a Turkish city within two–three days' march of Istanbul, the treaty guaranteed Russia unprecedented influence in the Ottoman Empire's European possessions. Russian merchants received free passage in the Balkans and the right to deal with Russian rather than Ottoman officials. The merchants' ships would enjoy free access to the Turkish Straits and thence to the Danube and the Black Sea, an important advantage.

In the 1774 Treaty of Kuchuk Kainardji, Russia had received the right to intervene in Ottoman domestic affairs if the welfare of Balkan Christians was threatened. In the Adrianople treaty, it got much more. The Russian government received a protectorate over the Danubian Principalities, including the right to install a new administrative system and veto power over the appointment of the administrators, or *hospodars*. The treaty also contained a guarantee of Serbian autonomy, which had been violated repeatedly during the Greek revolt, and a provision for an autonomous Greek kingdom. It also made eastern Armenia and Georgia part of the Russian Empire.

The Treaty of Adrianople determined Russia's stance vis-à-vis the Ottoman Empire for the next twenty-five years. Some of Russia's neighbors, notably Austria, felt that the agreement gave Russia too much power in the Balkans; if the empire collapsed, the Russians could easily scrap the treaty and conquer the Ottoman Balkan possessions. Austria and the other powers would make haste to force Alexander II (1818–81) to abandon this privileged position in the Ottoman Empire following the Crimean War in (1853–56).

Brigit Farley

Further reading

Anderson, M.S. *The Eastern Question, 1774–1923.* London, 1966.

Lincoln, W. Bruce. *Nicholas I, Emperor and Autocrat of All the Russias.* Bloomington, Indiana, 1980.

Jelavich, Charles and Barbara Jelavich. *The Establishment of the Balkan National States, 1804–1920.* Seattle, Washington, 1977.

Stavrianos, L.S. *The Balkans since 1453.* New York, 1958.

See also Alexander II; Crimean War; Danubian Principalities; Eastern Question; Greek Revolution; Kuchuk Kainardji, Treaty of; Russo-Turkish War of 1828–29

Ady, Endre (1877–1919)

Poet who set the tone for modern, twentieth-century Hungarian poetry. Ady was the son of petty noble smallholders in Transylvania. In 1896 he enrolled at the law school of the University of Debrecen but did not complete his studies. In 1898 Ady turned to a career in journalism, writing mostly for the opposition. He distinguished himself with a flair for colorful language and biting sarcasm. By 1900, he was on the staff of a newspaper in Nagyvárad, along with other writers who were to acquire fame (such as Lajos Biró [1856–1931]). In 1901 he was tried and sentenced to three days in jail for a piece of "seditious" writing.

In 1903 he became involved with a married woman of Jewish background, Adél Brüll (n.d.), who figured in his poetry as "Léda." In addition to serving as his inspiration, Léda funded his travels and other endeavors.

Ady's first volume of poems was published in 1899, under the title *Versek* (*Poems*). His second volume of poetry appeared in 1903. Ady traveled to Paris in 1904 as a correspondent for a number of dailies in Budapest. He was to visit Paris and other parts of France several times, as well as Italy. In Paris, he had the opportunity to become acquainted with the works of Baudelaire (1821–67), to whom he has been compared, and the *symboliste* poets. In 1906 he published another volume of poetry titled *Uj versek* (*New Poems*), successful enough to give rise to long-lasting polemics surrounding his poetry and politics. In 1907 his volume *Vér és arany* (*Blood and Gold*) was published.

Ady became the leading poet of the literary review *Nyugat* from 1908, since its inception the only contributor on the journal's payroll. It was during this period that he became truly productive, publishing seven volumes of poetry between 1908 and 1918. Although he won an official prize from the municipality of Budapest in 1909, his poetry was still rejected by the establishment.

Like many of Hungary's (and East Central Europe's) eminent poets, Ady's poetry, and his journalistic writings all the more, had an impact beyond the realms of aesthetics and of the purely literary. While Ady's poetry is by now generally accepted and appreciated by all who read Hungarian, the controversies surrounding his role have not been settled; they center on Ady's politics, beginning with whether or not he was a "political poet." There is no denying, however, that some of his poetry and journalism was a powerful statement against the "semi-feudal" regime that still prevailed in the country, against oppression and arbitrary rule, and, after 1914, however cautiously, against World War I; Ady also spoke out for the landless peasant and the proletariat, especially at the time of mass worker demonstrations in the spring of 1912. At the beginning of the revolution of 1918, which swept Hungary after Austria-Hungary's defeat in World War I, Ady was elected president of the Vörösmarty Literary Academy, before his alcoholism, nicotine poisoning (he smoked a hundred or more cigarettes daily), and other infirmities caught up with him.

Mario D. Fenyo

Further reading

Horváth, Zoltán. *Die Jarhhundertwende in Ungarn.* Berlin, 1966.

Király, István. *Ady Endre,* 2 vols. Budapest, 1970.

Nyerges, Anton N. *Poems of Endre Ady.* Buffalo, New York, 1969.

Vezér, Erzsébet. *Ady Endre élete és pályája,* 2d ed. Budapest, 1977.

See also Hungarian Literature; *Nyugat*

Aehrenthal, Alois Baron Lexa von (1854–1912)

Austro-Hungarian diplomat and foreign minister (1906–12). Aehrenthal served as ambassador to Russia (1899–1906) before succeeding Count Agenor Gołuchowski (1849–1921) as foreign minister. Although politically conservative and generally desirous of maintaining good relations with the Great Powers, including Russia, Aehrenthal was determined to conduct a more dynamic policy than his predecessor, particularly in the Balkans. He hoped to consolidate the monarchy's position in relation to the South Slavs by formally annexing Bosnia and Hercegovina and by undertaking an extensive project of railroad construction to link Serbia to the Adriatic through Habsburg territory. In 1908, however, the Young Turk revolution induced Aehrenthal to rush the annexation of Bosnia and Hercegovina, and a diplomatic crisis ensued. The annexation provoked strong protests from France, Great Britain, and Italy; severely antagonized the Russian government; and led to a war scare with Serbia. Although Aehrenthal followed a conciliatory policy in the following years, relations with Serbia continued to deteriorate, and Russian diplomats distrusted Austro-Hungarian intentions in the Balkans. Advancing leukemia forced Aehrenthal to retire in 1912.

Philip Pajakowski

A

Further reading

Bridge, F.R. *From Sadowa to Sarajevo: The Foreign Policy of Austria-Hungary, 1866–1914.* London, 1972.

Wank, Solomon, ed. *Aus dem Nachlass Aehrenthal: Briefe und Dokumente zur österreichisch-ungarischen Innen- und Aussenpolitik 1885–1912.* Graz, 1993.

Williamson, Samuel R. Jr. *Austria-Hungary and the Origins of the First World War.* London, 1991.

See also Agenor Gołuchowski; Great Powers; Young Turks

Agrarian Parties

Agrarian (or peasant) parties have represented Eastern European rural interests since the nineteenth century. Agrarian parties advocated land reforms to distribute land on large estates among those who work it, village cooperatives to keep the profit from crop sales in local hands, and credit institutions to underwrite needed improvements. Many peasant parties were also nationalist parties, because peasants often worked their land for the benefit of landlords of different ethnicity. Nationalism sometimes eclipsed agrarianism as the focus of party identity. Agrarianism included elements of socialism, but peasant parties rarely allied with Communists. The Communist emphasis on industrialization and collectivized agriculture conflicted with agrarian support for rural traditions and family farms.

Peasant parties appeared across Eastern Europe between 1860 and 1910, when commercialized agriculture and world market forces disrupted traditional rural society. During the same years, expanded suffrage allowed peasants to vote for new mass parties. Peasant parties had little power before World War I, but some were influential in the interwar parliamentary states. A "Green International," comprising representatives from these peasant parties, operated for a few years in the 1920s. The Depression and the spread of right-wing regimes, however, again reduced agrarian influence. After World War II, Communist governments suppressed or co-opted the agrarian parties, but several were reestablished following the revolutions of 1989.

The Polish Peasant Party, Piast, became Poland's largest party in 1922 after the merger of several prewar parties. The party stood for agrari-

anism, Catholic values, and Polish nationalism but opposed the conservative regime of Józef Piłsudski (1867–1935) in the 1930s. After 1947, the Communists replaced the party with a puppet United Peasant Party. In the 1980s Rural Solidarity organized peasant opposition to communism. The Polish Peasant Party reappeared in 1989.

Czech and Slovak peasant parties merged after 1918 to form Czechoslovakia's Republican Party of Farmers and Peasants. This agrarian party shared power during most of the interwar period as a partner in the five-party *pětka* coalition. Party leader Antonín Švehla (1873–1933) was prime minister several times. The party was banned in 1945.

In Romania, pre–World War I parties from Transylvania and the Regat (Moldavia and Wallachia) merged as the National Peasant Party. Iuliu Maniu (1873–1953) presided over an agrarian cabinet from 1928 to 1930, but the Great Depression undercut reforms. The Iron Guard fascist movement had peasant roots but was not an agrarian party. The National Peasant Party joined the 1944 anti-Nazi coalition and became a major rival of the Communist Party. Forcibly dissolved in 1947, the party reformed in 1989.

Founded in 1899 to resist taxes and build cooperatives, the Bulgarian Agrarian National Union (BANU) came to power in 1919. The BANU introduced economic, social, and legal reforms. Alarmed conservatives crushed BANU in a 1923 coup and murdered its party leader, Aleksandur Stamboliiski (1879–1923). BANU joined the anti-Nazi Fatherland Front in 1945 and survived as a Communist puppet group until 1989, when it reorganized.

Serbia and Croatia each had important pre-1918 peasant parties. In both, agrarianism was soon overshadowed by nationalism. Nikola Pašić (1845–1926) and the Radical Party dominated Serbian politics after 1903 and monopolized power in Yugoslavia from 1918 to 1929; during the royal dictatorship of the 1930s, the party still furnished the prime minister. The Croatian Peasant Party originated during prewar Hungarian rule. Its leader, Stjepan Radić (1871–1928), was the leading advocate of Croatian separatism in interwar Yugoslavia until his assassination in 1928. The party never held real power. Banned under the Communists, the Croatian Peasant Party reappeared in 1989.

Hungary and Albania lacked significant peasant parties. In Hungary leftist rural reform was discredited after the collapse of the regime of Béla Kun (1886–1938), the de facto leader of the short-lived Hungarian Soviet Republic in 1919 (during the chaotic period that followed Austria-Hungary's defeat in World War I). Hungarian fascism appealed to some peasants, but its leaders pursued nonagrarian goals. Albania's political development never granted peasants enough power to sustain a peasant party.

Steven W. Sowards

Further reading

Bell, John D. *Peasants in Power: Alexander Stamboliski and the Bulgarian Agrarian National Union, 1899–1923.* Princeton, New Jersey, 1977.

Mitrany, David. *Marx Against the Peasant: A Study in Social Dogmatism.* Chapel Hill, North Carolina, 1951.

Narkiewicz, Olga A. *The Green Flag: Polish Populist Politics, 1867–1970.* London, 1976.

Roberts, Henry L. *Rumania: Political Problems of an Agrarian State.* New Haven, Connecticut, 1951.

See also Agriculture; Bulgarian Agrarian National Union; Fatherland Front; Great Depression; Green International; Hungarian Soviet Republic; Iron Guard; Béla Kun; Iuliu Maniu; Nationalism; Nikola Pašić; Peasants; *Pĕtka;* Józef Piłsudski; Stjepan Radić; Socialism; Aleksandur Stamboliiski; Antonín Švehla

Agriculture

Eastern Europe comprises two major agricultural zones. The northern region extends from the latitude of the Alps through the Polish plain. This area has heavy, fertile soil and plenty of precipitation. Farther south, mountain chains and rocky outcrops break up the landscape. Soils are light and thin; rainfall is sparse.

Eastern Europe is a source of grain and livestock products. Wheat grows throughout the region and is the dominant grain in districts along the Danube River. Oats, barley, and especially rye are grown in the northern zone. Maize corn is the principal cereal in most of the Balkans. Potatoes and sugar beets are major crops in Poland. Eastern Europe also supports forest products and fruit.

Cattle, horses, sheep, and pigs are the principal farm animals. War, depression, and the transfer of grazing land to cultivation have often reduced the livestock population. Pigs, less dependent on pasture, have outnumbered cattle in the Balkans for centuries; after World War II, swine also became the most numerous farm animals in Poland and Czechoslovakia. In the mountainous Balkans, sheep remain the most common stock.

Because horses and cattle function as draught animals and sources of fertilizer, their scarcity has curbed productivity and crop yields. Modern alternatives came slowly. Fertilizer use has gradually approached Western European levels, but even in the 1980s Eastern European farmers employed only one-sixth to one-half as many tractors per hectare as their Western European counterparts.

As early as the 1700s, large estate owners raised commercial crops, while subsistence farms operated in remote areas. During the 1800s, improved transportation spread commercial influences, and most peasants began raising some crops for cash sale. Entrepreneurs among the Serbian peasantry and the Romanian notables (*boiars*) provided financial backing for national cultural and political revivals.

Peasant farms were inefficient. As families divided land among their sons, many farms fell below five hectares (12.4 acres) in size, considered the minimum for viable farms. Peasants used traditional techniques of field rotation, paid exorbitant taxes, and could not afford modern tools. Large landowners, on the other hand, benefited from peasant dues and inequities in land tenure. Estates in Romania, Austria-Hungary, and divided Poland produced profitable grain and sugar-beet crops.

After World War I, reforms distributed land to some needy families, but productivity remained low. The successor states preserved small peasant farms for political reasons; the lack of industrial jobs led to rural overpopulation and underemployment. Over 70 percent of the population continued to work in agriculture. Eastern European products were too costly to compete on the world market, and the Great Depression of the 1930s worsened conditions.

Under communism, the Eastern European states began collectivizing agriculture in the late 1940s. Nearly all arable land came under state control in Czechoslovakia, Hungary, Albania, and Bulgaria, primarily through village collective cooperatives, with smaller numbers of state enterprise farms. In Romania farm acreage was divided roughly between collectives and state farms. In

Poland and Yugoslavia, peasant resistance and de-Stalinization brought a restoration of private farm ownership in the 1950s. In the 1980s private holdings exceeded 70 percent of farmland in Poland and 80 percent in Yugoslavia. Agriculture remained inefficient under communism. Workers on collectives lacked incentives, while private farmers lacked land, credit, and machinery. In the 1980s most socialist regimes increased agricultural investments and decreased state control. Plots leased for personal use provided from one-third to one-half of the vegetables and dairy products in much of Eastern Europe. After the revolutions of 1989, the redistribution of collectivized land back to farm families became a major issue.

Steven W. Sowards

Further reading

Mitrany, David. *The Land and the Peasant in Rumania: The War and Agrarian Reform (1917–21).* London, 1930.

Sanders, Irwin T., ed. *Collectivization of Agriculture in Eastern Europe.* Lexington, Kentucky, 1958.

Tomasevich, Jozo. *Peasants, Politics, and Economic Change in Yugoslavia.* Stanford, California, 1955.

See also Agrarian Parties; *Boiars;* Collectivization; De-Stalinization; Great Depression; Peasants; Revolutions of 1989

Ajdukiewicz, Kazimierz (1890–1963)

Member of the Warsaw School of Philosophy and Logic and a major contributor to semantics and the understanding of the relationship between language and knowledge. Under the influence of his teachers Kazimierz Twardowski (1866–1938) and Jan Łukasiewicz (1878–1956), Ajdukiewicz focused on the manner in which language is responsible for determining what is valid knowledge. Rejecting the notion that meaning in language can be merely derived from the syntax, vocabulary, and associated mental images, Ajdukiewicz argued in favor of semantic rules that govern the acceptance or rejection of a given proposition in a particular linguistic situation. These "meaning rules" could be either from within the language or extralinguistic. These extralinguistic rules are evidenced by the fact that knowledge has been transmitted over generations and languages; this led Ajdukiewicz to the belief in an existing universe of meaning.

Distinguishing between natural and artificial languages on the basis that a given natural language is a composite of a family of languages that resisted logical perfectibility, Ajdukiewicz argued that only with an artificial language can the rules of meaning be clearly specified. Scientific knowledge always occurs, he further argued, within the framework of some language and thereby necessarily includes certain a priori elements. These elements could be eliminated only if one allowed for the possible rejection of any axiom of meaning in the same manner that any given hypothesis is subject to rejection.

James Eiswert

Further reading

Ajdukiewicz, Kazimierz. *Pragmatic Logic,* trans. by Olgierd Wojtasiewicz. Boston, 1974.

———. *Problems and Theories of Philosophy,* trans. by Henryk Skolimowski and Anthony Quinton. London, 1973.

See also Philosophy; Kazimierz Twardowski

Alba Iulia

Small city located on the edge of the Apuseni Mountains in south-central Transylvania and a symbol of modern Romanian nationalism. Originally fortified in Roman times, for much of the sixteenth and seventeenth centuries Alba Iulia (German: Karlsburg; Hungarian: Gyulafehérvár) served as the capital of the autonomous Principality of Transylvania. In 1784 an uprising by local Romanian peasants against Hungarian landlords was crushed and the peasant leaders executed outside the citadel, an event later hailed as an early expression of Romanian national consciousness.

On December 1, 1918, leaders of ethnic Romanian communities in Transylvania and other regions then under the control of Hungary elected a Grand National Council (Marele Sfat Naţional) in Alba Iulia and proclaimed the union of these territories with the Kingdom of Romania. In October 1922 a ceremony was held in Alba Iulia crowning the Romanian king, Ferdinand (1865–1927), as ruler of the enlarged Greater Romania.

The declaration signed by the participants in the 1918 assembly set out six principles on which the new Greater Romania would be built: full national liberty for all races; regional autonomy; democracy and free elections; freedom of press and association; radical agrarian reform; and equitable conditions for industrial workers. However, few of these reforms were ever fully implemented in the interwar period. The date of the Alba Iulia assembly is now celebrated as Romania's national day.

Charles King

Further reading
Anghel, Gheorghe. *Alba Iulia.* Bucharest, 1987.
Seton-Watson, R.W. *A History of the Roumanians.* Cambridge, 1934.

See also Ferdinand I; Greater Romania

Albania (Geography)

Approximately one-half of the six million ethnic Albanians of southeastern Europe are included within the territory of the national state, located in the central portion of the Adriatic coastland of the Balkan Peninsula. The smallest of the East European states, with an area of 11,100 square miles (28,748 sq km), it is mostly rugged and mountainous with a largely rural population and few large towns.

North of the river Drin the terrain is dominated by the North Albanian Alps. Deeply cut by river and glacial erosion, the limestone mountains exceed 6,000 feet (1,820 m) and exhibit the typical karst landscape of the western Balkans. Largely forested, the region has a sparse population distributed in hamlets and villages and supported by pasture and valley cultivation. Recent developments in mining and manufacturing have been based on the exploitation of chromium and copper ores in the northeast, with Kukës as a major center. Hydropower development along the Drin is represented by the stations at Koman, Vau i Dejës, and Fierza, which produce about 80 percent of Albania's electricity needs.

The more moderate elevations and rounded mountains of the Mirditë and the Cermenikë are typical of the region south of the Albanian Alps and east of the coastal plain, though some peaks in the Korab range on the eastern frontier are among the highest in Albania. To the southeast are the tectonic basins occupied by lakes Pogradec (Ohrid) and Prespa and the Korçë basin, where the cultivation of grain, sugar beet, potatoes, and fruit is possible. Together, these areas contain the highest population densities in the region, with Pogradec and Korçë as major centers. Especially around Elbasan and Berat, mining and metallurgy have become important owing to deposits of iron and nickel ores as well as chrome and local sources of petroleum, natural gas, and lignite.

In southern Albania the extension of the Pindus range of northern Greece continues the rugged character of the interior to the southwest coast. Around Sarandë and along the coast, vineyards, as well as olive and citrus orchards, are cultivated on terraced slopes. The Mediterranean climate of the coastal zone extending to Vlorë combines with pebble and sand beaches bordered by rugged cliffs to form the Albanian Riviera, an area of great potential for tourism. Gjirokastër and Sarandë are major regional centers.

From the Bunë River in the north to the Bay of Vlorë in the south is a coastal lowland, interrupted by a succession of low hills into a series of smaller plains (Myzeqë, Durrës, Nenshkodra). This region includes large areas of reclaimed marshland and swamp and concentrates most of the arable land of Albania. Supported by substantial irrigation schemes, a complex agricultural production of maize, wheat, and fodder crops is combined with specialized production of rice, olives, and vines. Apart from its agricultural potential, the central portions of the lowland contain oil and natural gas together with lignite and soft coal. Within or adjacent to the lowland zone is more than two-thirds of the population and most of the larger towns of Albania—among them Tirana, the capital and dominant economic center, Shkodra, Durrës, and Vlorë.

Albert M. Tosches

Further reading
Osborne, R.H. *East Central Europe.* New York, 1967.
Pounds, Norman J.G. *Eastern Europe.* Chicago, 1969.
Pushka, Asllan. *Albanija.* Zagreb, 1978.
Zickel, R.E., and W.R. Iwaskiw, eds. *Albania: A Country Study,* 2d ed. Washington, D.C., 1994.

See also Lake Ohrid; Tirana

Albania (History)

Albania is in many ways the most overlooked nation in southeastern Europe. The Albanians are descendants of some of the oldest inhabitants of the Balkan Peninsula, the Illyrians and Thracians, whose influence stretched along the Adriatic Sea. During the third century B.C., their center was located at Shkodër. Conquered by the Romans, the region became an important and prosperous part of the empire. Under Roman rule, many of the inhabitants were romanized. Illyrian recruits proved to be some of the empire's best soldiers.

Albania before the Nineteenth Century

After the collapse of Roman authority, most of the tribes in the region either disappeared, were reduced in size, or were assimilated by others. Some took to the mountains (especially as Slavs expanded into the region), and there the Albanians took on a pastoral lifestyle, herding sheep in the mountains and occasionally raiding settlements in the plains. Very little has been written about their early existence. References to the people come not from native Albanian sources but rather from others with whom they came in contact.

Throughout most of the early Middle Ages, the Albanians were under the nominal control of the Byzantine Empire. For the Byzantines, the region was both a trade route and a key defensive area. The mountainous terrain offered an excellent line of defense against any invaders from the northwest. The Albanian people divided into two groups, the Gegs, located in the northern, more mountainous area, and the Tosks, who came to inhabit the southern and coastal regions, especially after the ebbing of Byzantine rule. The Gegs maintained a self-governing tribal organization well into the twentieth century based around the clan, while the Tosks often inhabited small villages (and later cities). Some feudal landowners also came into prominence during this era, while a few medieval towns, such as Durrës and Shkodër, became important for trade.

Unlike many of their neighbors, the Albanians never developed their own independent, sovereign state (other than a short-lived principality located at Krujë during the twelfth century). Instead they were dominated by others, especially the Venetians, the Serbs, and the Bulgars. In the mid-1300s the land became part of the Serbian empire of Stephan Dušan (r. 1331–1355). Venice, which took Durrës in 1205, traded heavily in Albania in the thirteenth and fourteenth centuries. The papacy also viewed the region as important for extending Roman Catholicism into the Orthodox Balkans.

However, it was the coming of the Ottoman Turks that most stamped the history of the Albanians. In the late fourteenth century, Ottoman forces began to penetrate southeastern Europe. In 1389 the Ottoman army destroyed its Serbian counterpart—the ranks of which included Albanian soldiers—at the battle of Kosovo. By the mid-1400s, most of the Balkans, including much of Albania (save for parts of the Dalmatian coast) had fallen under Ottoman control.

Perhaps the key personality in all of Albanian history was Gjergi Kastrioti (1405–1468), better known as Skanderbeg (even though little is recorded about him, thus making him as much a legendary figure as a historical one). The son of a minor noble, Kastrioti was sent as a hostage to the sultan's court. There he converted to Islam and served with distinction in the Ottoman army. However, after a Hungarian army led by János Hunyadi (1407–1456) defeated the Turks at Niš in 1443, Kastrioti deserted, converted to Christianity, and organized others to follow his lead in defending Albanian lands against the Turks. He organized a League of Lezhë, an often loose-knit alliance of Albanian lords who temporarily put aside their tribal blood feuds that were to so plague the Albanians well into the twentieth century, and for the next twenty-five years skillfully used the terrain to hold the Turkish forces at bay. To Albanians, Skanderbeg was not only a national hero, but also a European one, a warrior who defended Europe against what seemed like an inexorable Ottoman tide.

With the death of Skanderbeg, Albanian resistance collapsed. The Ottomans found that controlling Albania in a manner similar to other areas of the empire, however, was not always easy because of both terrain and local tribal structure. Although troops were garrisoned in key towns, the Ottomans granted certain areas self-governing status, even permitting some hereditary nobles to remain as long as taxes—including the *devshirme,* or child tax—were collected. Albanian leaders in turn often dealt directly with Istanbul.

The advent of Ottoman rule also witnessed the conversion of a majority of the population to Islam. By the nineteenth century, 70 percent of Albanians had converted. The majority became

Sunni (traditionalist) Muslims, while a smaller group (approximately 20 percent of Albanian Muslims) were from the Bektashi sect, a mystic and tolerant offshoot of the Shia, the other main branch of Islam. (In 1929 Albania became the world headquarters of the Bektashi after the movement was suppressed in Turkey.) Another 20 percent of the population, primarily in the South, was Orthodox, while 10 percent remained Roman Catholic.

The fact that such a sizeable portion of the population became Muslim was in many ways a result of initially favorable Ottoman taxation policies and the fact that a great deal of local control remained in the hands of the tribes. As such, local customs and traditions were preserved rather than threatened by the new overlords. Albanian soldiers became valuable recruits in the sultan's armies. Others served the state. At least thirty Albanians became grand viziers, the most powerful individual in the empire after the sultan. Most notable among these were the Körprülüs. Able administrators, the Körprülüs are credited with the revival of the empire's fortunes in the seventeenth century, bringing the Turkish armies for the second and final time to the gates of Vienna in 1683. Another notable figure of Albanian origin, Mohammed Ali (c. 1769–1849), became the governor of Egypt in the nineteenth century, and even challenged the sultan himself. But, although born of Albanian ancestry, none saw themselves as Albanian nationalists; Albanian self-identity remained nonexistent.

1815–1914

By the nineteenth century, the mountainous nature of Albania befit the isolated nature of the country; Albania seemed almost immune from the major developments taking place in Europe. At the dawn of the 1800s, conditions in the region had changed little in centuries: Turks dominated many areas of life; tribal customs remained; a backward peasant economy predominated; and cultural and educational isolation was almost universal. While nationalist stirrings would soon be felt throughout the rest of the Balkans, Albanian nationalism remained dormant; while revolts in neighboring Serbia and Greece would lead to autonomy, Albania was both quiet and loyal. For decades, the intellectual awakening that took place throughout the region was not to be found in Albania. Instead of a nationalist movement in Albania, local lords, such as Ali Pasha of Yannina (c. 1750–1822), asserted greater personal independence from Istanbul.

Ironically, it was Ottoman attempts at reform that caused the greatest anti-Turkish unsettlement in the Albanian lands. As the empire attempted to awaken from its own backwardness and isolation, the needed changes in the system brought the first stirrings against Ottoman rule. Scattered revolts greeted both Ottoman mismanagement and the reforms that aimed to diminish the power of local authorities who had for the most part run the region for almost a century. The laws of the reform period known as the *Tanzimat* in fact had little tangible effect on the region. Revolts against the proposed changes were aimed not against Turkish rule, but rather changes to it.

The Albanian national awakening, and ultimately the independence of Albania itself, was therefore not born out of a desire to break with Istanbul. Rather, its genesis was based on a fear that the empire was incapable of defending Albanian lands against the territorial aspirations of its neighbors—the Serbs, the Greeks, and the Montenegrins. As such, Albanians at first grew more supportive of the empire. In the end, however, it was the realization that the lands of the Ottoman Empire were disintegrating that caused the Albanians to seek independence in order to avoid being carved apart by their neighbors.

With the outbreak of war between the Russians and Turks in 1877, eighty delegates from the four Albanian *vilayets* (provinces) of Yannina, Monastir (Bitola), Üskub and Shkodër gathered in Prizren. While they were creating a central committee to serve as a voice for Albanian concerns, events elsewhere quickly determined their ultimate objectives. Following Russia's victory over the Turks, the resulting treaty of San Stefano rewarded the Bulgarians by granting them lands occupied by Albanians. The League of Prizren, at first dominated by conservative landowners, now grew more vocal in its defense of the integrity of Albanian territory and advocated autonomy for the four *vilayets*. By the time of the Congress of Berlin, called to discuss and revise the San Stefano provisions, the danger to the Albanian lands was readily apparent. Not only did their neighbors seek to gain at the expense of the Albanians but the Great Powers cared little for Albanian wishes.

The sultan himself, believing the Albanians to be loyal, did not see the danger in dealing

A

Albanian lands; Albanian concerns were of little importance to Istanbul since those lands were considered to be Turkish—not Albanian—territory. As such, the League of Prizren's advocacy of autonomy was not a concept bound to win the sultan's favor. For a brief moment the league proved to be a useful tool in preventing an even greater loss of territory, and Istanbul provided the Albanians arms to resist territorial concessions. However, once the Great Powers ordered the Porte to cede the territory, Istanbul had little use for the league.

In April 1881 the Turks crushed the league and arrested its leader, Abdul Frashëri (1839–1892), who had earlier led Albanian troops into southern Albania to resist Greek moves into the area. At first sentenced to death, Frashëri was released in 1885 and later sent into exile.

Although the league had failed in its aim of gaining autonomy for Albania within the Ottoman Empire, it had provided a spark for Albanian nationalism (even though most national leadership for the moment disappeared) and provided Albania's first semblance of a national organization. A cultural awakening—especially concerned with language—now emerged that looked to discover Albania's roots. In 1879 a Society for the Printing of Albanian Writings formed in Istanbul under the leadership of Sami Frashëri (1850–1904), the brother of the noted poet Naum Frashëri (1846–1900); the organization's aim was to produce a standard Albanian language. After the society was suppressed by the sultan following the crackdown on the League of Prizren, it moved its activities to Bucharest, Romania, in 1884.

Devising and agreeing upon a standard language proved to be a daunting challenge. Most Albanians were illiterate and the few schools that did exist were either taught in Greek or Turkish, save for two Catholic schools in which Albanian was used. In 1885 a school for boys was opened in Korçë; six years later a similar school was created for girls. Finally, in 1908, it was decided upon at a meeting in Monastir to adopt the Latin alphabet for the language (over the objections of many Muslims who preferred the Koranic script).

At the dawn of the twentieth century, much of the work of the Albanian awakening had been carried out by émigrés in places such as Romania, Italy, and the United States. It was also outside Albania that the movement for independence had any real following. Within Albania only the desire to safeguard institutions held sway.

In the early 1900s conditions within Albanian lands, as throughout the Ottoman Empire, continued to deteriorate. Anarchy abounded. The Young Turk revolution of 1908 provided only a fleeting hope that things would improve and that Albanian territory would be safeguarded. Twenty-six Albanians were elected to the empire's first parliament. Clubs sprang up in a number of cities promoting the concept of nationality and language. But, hopes for protection of Albanian lands and rights were quickly dashed. With the annexation of Bosnia-Hercegovina by Austria-Hungary in 1908, the Young Turks undertook a crackdown on nationalism throughout the empire. Schools, for example, were closed. Rebellions in Albania and Kosovo were put down in 1909–1910. And even though the regime loosened its grip in 1911 by allowing schools to reopen, the onset of the Balkan Wars (1912–13) led not only to the further dismemberment of the Ottoman Empire but also to a reluctant move by Albanians for independence.

There had already been limited moves toward greater independence outside of the country. In 1904 representatives of various Albanian émigré groups met in Bucharest. The following year, a secret society—the Committee for the Liberation of Albania—formed in Monastir. Three years later, émigrés in the United States declared the autonomy of the Albanian Orthodox Church. An anti-Turkish newspaper was created in Brussels. Although these movements attracted few adherents among the Albanian population, they were the seeds of anti-Ottoman rule.

The onset of the First Balkan War, the rapid collapse of the Ottoman army, and the obvious desire of Serbia, Montenegro, and Greece to acquire Albanian lands moved some Albanians to abandon their decades-long advocacy of autonomy and support full independence. On November 28, 1912, a national assembly, led by Ismail Kemal Bey (1844–1919), met in Vlorë and declared the nation's independence. Kemal in turn journeyed to London to obtain the backing of the Great Powers for the creation of an independent Albanian state. Italy and Austria-Hungary both supported the Albanian movement, not out of altruism but because an independent Albania served the best interests of Rome and Vienna. For the Italians, Albania represented a potential foothold in the Balkans, a mere 58 miles (93 km) across the Straits of Otranto. For the Austrians, it served as a block to Serbia's outlet to the sea. In December 1912 the

Great Powers took up the Albanian issue and by July 1913 they formally supported independence. They also declared that they would determine the new nation's borders (while forcing the Serbs and Montenegrins to retreat from some of the lands they had occupied during the Balkan Wars).

The Great Powers set up the International Control Commission, which was composed of their own representatives plus one Albanian. The commission created a general territory of approximately 11,000 square miles (28,748 sq km) with 800,000 inhabitants, by far the smallest nation of southeastern Europe. Only slightly more than half of ethnic Albanians in the region were included within the borders of the new state.

While blessed with ethnic homogeneity and few religious tensions, the fledgling country had few advantages. Its neighbors—especially Greece, which considered southern Albania (northern Epirus) to be rightfully Greek—still had territorial claims on Albanian lands. Albania was overwhelmingly rural (90 percent) with 90 percent illiteracy. Devoid of capital and infrastructure (it had only about 110 miles [185 km] of paved roads), the new country faced economic challenges that were overwhelming, certainly more than the chosen prince—William of Wied (1876–1945)—could realistically be expected to handle, even in the best of times.

William, a German officer, was appointed prince in April 1914 by the International Control Commission (which also created a legislature for the country). William, however, had no real credibility in the country and soon found himself challenged for political leadership by Esad Pasha Toptani (1863–1920). A conservative, William quickly alienated many young Albanians by favoring the interests of the large landowners. Faced with the absence of a political base, peasant unrest, avaricious neighbors, competition by Italy and Austria-Hungary for influence in the country, and the onset of World War I, William left the country on September 3, 1914.

World War I and Interwar Albania

By the time war broke out in the summer of 1914, Albania's borders were still in dispute, a symbol of its weakness and vulnerability. During World War I, the country was beset by political anarchy and was quickly overrun. Never officially a combatant, Albania now became a pawn among the Great Powers and its neighbors. By mid-1915, Montenegro had seized Shkodër, Serbia had occupied the central portion of the country (including Tirana), and Greece had seized lands in the south. No united opposition formed in Albania to combat occupation or promote Albanian interests. And when Serbia's forces were defeated (retreating across Albania into Greece), it merely meant that Austrian occupation took their place. In 1918, as the Habsburg armies retreated, Greek, Serbian, and Italian forces filled the void.

Although the hostilities further impoverished and imperiled the country, of greater danger were the secret plans of the Allies, who in the London Pact of 1915 agreed to dismember Albania and leave only a small autonomous rump state under Italian directorship. Serbia, Montenegro, and Greece were to partition the rest of the country. Albania's fate therefore rested on the decisions of the Paris Peace Conference in 1919. In December 1919 the Great Powers outlined the projected settlement of the Albanian question, essentially granting Italy a mandate over most of the country.

In a delicate position internationally, Albania was also fractured internally. However, as had happened in 1878 and again in 1912, the threat to Albanian lands pulled the country's leaders together. For the moment putting aside their competing interests and the bloodletting among the clans, in January 1920 Albanian representatives replaced the government in Durrës that had been formed in 1918 (but which was now discredited since it had acquiesced to the Italian occupation) and convened a congress in Lushnjë to support the territorial integrity of the nation and to demand an end to the Italian presence. In March 1920 the National Legislative Assembly convened in Tirana. Attacks on Italians and others considered to be allied to Italian interests took place.

In Paris, Albanian representatives successfully argued for independence. There they found an unlikely ally in the American president, Woodrow Wilson (1856–1924), who opposed the secret agreements decided upon in London in 1915. In November 1921 a conference of ambassadors recognized Italy's special interests in the country but reaffirmed Albanian interests and its borders. Italy agreed to abandon most of its claims in Albania in return for Fiume and Istria. Albania was also admitted to the League of Nations despite the objections of Italy, France, and Yugoslavia.

As difficult as it was to avoid dismemberment, the challenge of forming a new and stable

A government was far more daunting. The economy was in shambles. Most of the land remained non-arable. Peasants were not only illiterate, their high land payments left them impoverished. Industrialization was almost nonexistent. It was in this bleak atmosphere that a regency council consisting of one representative from each of the four religious groups (Sunni, Bektashi, Orthodox, and Roman Catholic) was created.

Parties in Albania were little more than factions representing unique interests. The two principal parties were the Popular party headed by Fan S. Noli (1882–1965) and the Progressive party of Ahmed Zogu (1895–1961). In 1908, Noli became bishop of the Albanian Orthodox Church. He served as the representative of the Albanian émigré community in the United States at the Congress of Leshnjë, having founded the Vatra (Hearth) cultural organization and served as the publisher of the newspaper *Dielli* (*The Sun*). Zogu, although perhaps lacking the credentials of Noli, was a young and ambitious man who represented the interests of the southern landholding areas. In the new government, Noli became foreign minister while Zogu took the post of minister of the interior.

Governments in Albania changed at an almost dizzying pace during the first years of the 1920s. Unrest was commonplace. No party could obtain a working majority in the assembly. In the elections of 1924, for example, forty seats went to the Progressives, thirty-five to the Popular party, and the remaining twenty seats were split among the other parties. Without clear political leadership, the nation grew more restless.

In February 1924, Zogu was wounded by a member of a radical opposition group. Five months later, he fled to Yugoslavia and Noli became premier. In a twenty-point program of reforms, Noli called for an end to feudalism, assistance for peasants, education, and health care. However, without foreign assistance (he criticized the League of Nations for failing to come to the country's aid) he had little chance to carry out his ambitious program. Moreover, he never developed a base of popular support. His overtures regarding land reform alienated the landowners while failing to gain much support from the peasants. Noli alienated others by his contacts with the Soviet Union; many, both in Albania and in neighboring states, feared that Albania might become a base for bolshevism. Instead of holding elections, he arrested political opponents and imposed censorship. Although Noli's government did balance the budget, a not insignificant achievement, its tenure was brief.

In December 1924, Zogu, who had organized a personal army in Yugoslavia aided by his hosts, invaded Albania, forcing Noli to flee. Although Noli and his followers formed an opposition in exile (*Konare*), it was of little consequence; Noli himself would return to Boston in 1930 after losing his own influence within the organization. Zogu had become the master of the nation.

For the next fifteen years, Zogu attempted to consolidate his power. On January 31, 1925, he was elected president of a newly proclaimed republic for a seven-year term. His broad powers included an absolute veto and the sole authority to call elections, initiate changes in the new constitution, and make appointments. Many of Noli's followers were quickly arrested or killed. Zogu attempted to disarm the tribes in the north (save for his own *Mati* tribe), end the blood feuds, and promote order.

Despite his sometimes good intentions, Zogu was never secure in power—even after having himself named the "King of the Albanians" (King Zog I) in 1928. He faced a number of uprisings and assassination attempts, and the country remained both illiterate and poor. Continued use of primitive agricultural techniques meant that food often had to be imported, while life expectancy in 1938 was only thirty-eight years of age. Although Zogu was nominally the head of a constitutional monarchy, he ruled as little more than an interesting hybrid of tribal chieftain and would-be despot. His regime was better than the previous anarchy that had plagued the country in the early 1920s, but corruption at the court was commonplace. And worse, Zogu was often little more than a mere puppet of Italy.

Albania desperately needed foreign aid. As such, Zogu quickly abandoned the Yugoslavs (who sought territorial concessions for their assistance in bringing him to power) for the Italians. While essential, funds from Rome proved to be like ropes, binding the country to the wishes of fascist Italy. In 1926, Zogu entered into a treaty of friendship with Rome (the Treaty of Tirana). A year later, after Yugoslavia and France entered into a military pact, Rome and Tirana drew up a new twenty-year defensive alliance. In return for what amounted to little more than subsidies, Italy received extensive privileges (such as the right to exploit Albania's mineral resources and form a national bank in the country). Italy also sent a military mission to train Albanian forces. Italian aid, often at high interest rates, became a needed economic lifeline (what little industrialization and development of infrastructure that took place in the country was a result primarily of Italian capital), but with it came Italian domination of the economy and a humiliating dependency.

In the early 1930s Rome began to call in some of the debts. In 1932 it demanded that Tirana form a customs union with Italy that would give Italians (including Italian colonists) even greater control over the economy. When Zogu balked at renewing the Treaty of Tirana and attempted to distance himself from his erstwhile benefactors (by among other things closing Italian schools) by turning back to Yugoslavia for economic support, Mussolini (1883–1945), the Italian dictator, was clearly irritated. Italian aid stopped. In 1934 an Italian fleet arrived in the port of Durrës as a reminder of Italy's power. Zogu had little, if any choice but to buckle to the pressure; he needed the Italians.

For the last five years of his reign, Zogu proved to be little more than a prisoner of Italian aid. Albania had become a source of raw materials for Italy and a prize simply waiting to be plucked. Italian economic penetration increased. The king was forced to support Mussolini's invasion of Ethiopia in 1935. Even though Zogu tried to make some moves internally, such as pursuing a limited policy of liberalization in 1935–36, his hands were tied.

Seeking to emulate the successes of Adolf Hitler (1889–1945) in Austria and Czechoslovakia, Mussolini presented Albania with an ultimatum on March 25, 1939: accept occupation and the creation of a protectorate or face invasion. Realizing the futility of resisting, Zogu and his family fled to Greece. On April 7, Italian troops landed; there was almost no opposition. On April 12, the Albanian assembly voted to accept union with Rome. Four days later a delegation presented Victor Emmanuel III (1869–1947), the Italian king, with the Albanian crown.

World War II
Italian occupation of the country lasted until 1943, when German troops replaced their Italian allies following the collapse of Mussolini's regime. A year after occupying Albania, Italy used it as a staging area for its failed invasion of Greece. After Greek forces pushed the Italians back across the border into land long claimed by Athens (northern Epirus [southern Albania]), German forces were dispatched in 1941 to drive the Greeks out. Five puppet governments dominated by large landowners represented Italian interests for the next three years. After Germany's occupation of most of Yugoslavia in 1941, the Yugoslav province of Kosovo was annexed to Albania.

Two major Albanian groups formed in opposition to Italian rule: the communist-led Partisan movement, known as the National Liberation Movement, patterned after the Partisan movement led by Tito (1892–1980) in Yugoslavia, and the *Balli Kombëtar* (National Union, also known as the BK), composed primarily of southerners who were as much anticommunist as they were antifascist and anti-Zog. Not only did both groups harass the Italians, they also attacked each other.

In the summer of 1943 the two groups met at Mukaj and temporarily declared a truce; however, when the Germans occupied the country in 1943, their tenuous cooperation broke down. The BK did not view the Germans in the same way as they viewed the Italians. German rule, they believed, was more benign than that pursued by Rome. The Germans even left the door open regarding the future disposition of Kosovo, where they expelled or killed many Serbs. This left the mantle of antifascism solely to the newly renamed National Liberation Front, led by the communists.

The communists now established an Anti-Fascist Council of National Liberation and by October 1944 were in control of much of the country, including Tirana. At a congress held in Berat, a new provisional government was created, led by Enver Hoxha (1908–1985). A month later, German troops left the country leaving Hoxha's government in complete control. Albania had been liberated by a communist-led "war of liberation" (and without any direct Soviet assistance).

Communist Albania
Like most other areas in Eastern Europe during the interwar period, there were few communists in Albania; unlike their neighbors, there was not even a formal party. An illiterate peasant country was hardly fertile ground for a party based on the teachings of Marxism. A handful of Albanian communists were trained in Moscow, but by the time of the Italian invasion, there was no party

A structure and fewer than a couple hundred communists in the entire country.

The formal creation of the Albanian party (consisting of 130 members) took place in November 1941 under the organizational guidance of two Yugoslavs sent to Albania by Tito. An eleven-man central committee was created, communist works were translated into Albanian, a youth organization was established, and a resistance movement created, all under the tutelage of Yugoslavia; Yugoslav advisors guided most facets of the party and the resistance movement. The leaders of the newly created party were Enver Hoxha, a thirty-three-year-old former teacher of French who was elected provisional head of the party, and Koci Xoxe (1911–1949), a tinsmith who had the best contacts with the Yugoslav party.

After the German occupation of the country in 1943, the party became identified with liberation while its rival, the *Balli Kombëtar,* was seen as collaborationist. The Communists thus enjoyed a greater sense of legitimacy, and, when German troops retreated in 1944, Hoxha's communist-led NLF took control. In December 1945 the newly renamed Democratic Front received 93 percent of the vote for a new assembly. Meeting in January, the parliament proclaimed the creation of the People's Republic of Albania. Dominated by the Tosks, the assembly adopted a new constitution modeled after that of Yugoslavia.

Despite gaining power, Hoxha faced innumerable internal problems: a devastated economy; opposition by many Gegs in the north who maintained pro-Zog loyalties; high illiteracy; few, if any rights for women; and both Yugoslav domination (through a Treaty of Friendship, Cooperation, and Mutual Aid) and machinations (especially over the future of Kosovo). Externally, Albania was an afterthought, especially for the Western Allies; even though the Allies refused to recognize Zog as the legitimate head of a government-in-exile, the very nature of Albania itself was never raised during the wartime conferences. Relations with the Western Allies quickly became strained. Although Hoxha had promised cordial relations with the West, the United States and Great Britain were wary of Albania's ties to Yugoslavia and its domination by the communists. In 1945 they withdrew their missions to Tirana and opposed Albania's admission to the United Nations. In 1946 two British ships hit mines in Albanian waters and forty-four sailors were killed. In the early 1950s the West tried to recruit anti-Hoxha forces to send into Albania; however, the plan failed after moles within the British Secret Service tipped off Albanian officials.

Hoxha had ambitious plans to protect the territorial integrity of the country while promoting a rapid plan of modernization—under the leadership of the party—to end the almost feudal nature of Albanian society. In attempting to carry out his objectives, Hoxha became a masterful manipulator of power. For the moment, he turned to Yugoslavia for much needed economic assistance. However, in 1948 he used the split between Tito and Stalin (1879–1953) to order Yugoslav officials and advisors from the country and to isolate and purge his opponents (most notably Koci Xoxe, one of the founders of the Albanian party, who was executed in 1949). The 1946 constitution was quickly changed to conform to the Soviet model. All difficulties in the country were blamed on Yugoslavia and Xoxe; Albanians were warned to be vigilant against traitors.

Hoxha now embarked on the creation of a highly centralized Stalinist state. Policies of Sovietization were undertaken. He subjected the economy to rigid planning and a policy of rapid industrialization. Large estates were confiscated (by the 1960s collectivization would be complete) and the size of private plots reduced. In 1952 the government enacted a new penal code that included a provision for the death penalty for anyone over the age of twelve who engaged in economic sabotage or was deemed to be conspiring against the state. One could also be jailed for even criticizing the Soviet Union.

In order to maintain his power, Hoxha pursued a policy of rapid government turnover and recurring purges. By the end of 1953, only Hoxha and two others remained from the original central committee. And, whereas a thaw took place in many areas of life in the Soviet bloc following the death of Stalin in 1953, Hoxha steadfastly refused to engage in any policy of de-Stalinization. To him, the Hungarian Revolution of 1956 was the result of a move away from orthodox Stalinism. He refused to rehabilitate Xoxe or to follow Moscow's lead in making overtures to Belgrade aimed at healing the breach. Hoxha also balked at following the edicts of Comecon—the Soviet-led economic organization—aimed at keeping Albania a producer of agricultural products. Rather, Hoxha became more determined to speed the process of industrialization and collectivization.

This independence from Moscow's dictates led to a rift with the Soviet Union by 1960. The Soviet leader Nikita Khrushchev (1894–1971) began to attack Hoxha, even hinting that he might need to be overthrown. At the same time, relations between Moscow and Beijing soured, leading to a Sino-Soviet split. In December 1961 Hoxha decided to break with the Soviet Union and shift Albanian ties to China.

The loss of vital Soviet aid to Albania was now offset by assistance from China. Beijing provided needed technical assistance and also opened its doors to Albanian students. Hoxha in turn began to emulate China's Cultural Revolution to "cleanse" the nation of deviationists. He withdrew Albania from the Warsaw Pact military alliance in 1968. Most important, Hoxha isolated the nation from the rest of Europe; contact with the outside world was essentially limited to China and North Korea.

Hoxha declared Albania to be the first atheist state in the world after he outlawed organized religion in 1967. Clerics were persecuted by the regime. And with the crackdown on religion and culture came a cult of the leader; Hoxha's words and deeds were glorified in the media.

However, during the 1970s, as China improved its relations with the United States and Europe (including Yugoslavia), actions steadfastly opposed by the virulently anti-West Albanian leader, ties between Tirana and Beijing began to fray. By the late 1970s, Beijing broke off the relationship.

Hoxha now became even more determined to pursue a policy of self-reliance. He cracked down again on all perceived deviation at home. Another round of purges took place in 1973 against those who advocated easing educational and cultural restrictions. Executions of a number of high-ranking military officials (including the defense minister, Beqir Balluku [1916–1976]), who hoped to relax the ideological control over the army, took place. In 1981 he even turned against his oldest ally—Mehmet Shehu (1913–1981), who it would later be reported "committed suicide"—in favor of his younger protégé, Ramiz Alia (1925–).

By the time of his death in 1985, Hoxha had guided Albania with an iron fist for over forty years. His secret police—the Sigurimi—was the equal of any in the region. Even though he had made some positive contributions—the regime had ended illiteracy, provided better health care, and granted women greater rights—the nation was still impoverished and isolated.

His successor, Ramiz Alia, was more pragmatic than Hoxha. He allowed missions from Western Europe to reopen in Tirana and even permitted a few limited joint ventures to operate. In 1990 he announced that Albania was willing to reestablish contacts with Washington and Moscow. Economic reforms included the encouragement of private plots to supplement food sales. Restrictions on religion eased.

While those were positive steps, trade deficits continued to mount and the inflation rate climbed. Albania, with the highest birth rate in Europe, had the lowest standard of living. Moreover, the dam of change that had burst across the rest of the region in 1989 could not be kept from the people. Large numbers of Albanians began to cram aboard ships in an attempt to reach Italy. News from the outside made what Alia was proposing seem to be half measures at best.

In December 1990 demonstrations broke out in a number of cities. Statues of Hoxha were torn down. An opposition party was now created and a new constitution established, one that permitted civil liberties and a multiparty system. A year after the fall of communism in Romania, the last bastion of communism in Eastern Europe had begun to crumble. Albania was now left to discover its place in Europe with numerous questions yet unsettled—economic, political, and geographic (the future of Kosovo—90 percent ethnic Albanian—still within the boundaries of Yugoslavia)—and the answers far from apparent.

Richard Frucht

Further reading

Glenny, Misha. *The Rebirth of History: Eastern Europe in the Age of Democracy.* London, 1990.

Hall, Derek. *Albania and the Albanians.* London, 1994.

Jelavich, Barbara. *History of the Balkans,* 2 vols. Cambridge, 1983.

Jelavich, Charles, and Barbara. *The Establishment of the Balkan National States 1804–1920.* Seattle, Washington, 1974.

Pano, Nicholas. *The People's Republic of Albania.* Baltimore, Maryland, 1968.

Pano, Nicholas C. "Albania," in *The Columbia History of Eastern Europe in the Twentieth Century,* ed. by Joseph Held. New York, 1992.

Prifti, Peter R. *Socialist Albania since 1944: Domestic and Foreign Development.* Cambridge, Massachusetts, 1978.

Rothschild, Joseph. *East Central Europe between the Two World Wars.* Seattle, Washington, 1974.

Rothschild, Joseph. *Return to Diversity: A Political History of East Central Europe since World War II.* New York, 1989.

Sedlar, Jean W. *East Central Europe in the Middle Ages 1000–1500.* Seattle, Washington, 1994.

Skendi, Stavro. *The Albanian National Awakening, 1878–1912.* Princeton, New Jersey, 1967.

Sugar, Peter. *Southeastern Europe under Ottoman Rule 1354–1804.* Seattle, Washington, 1977.

Wolff, Robert Lee. *The Balkans in Our Time.* New York, 1956.

See also Agriculture; Albania (Geography); Albanian Art; Albanian Culture; Albanian Émigrés; Albanian Language; Albanian Literature; Ali Pasha; Ramiz Alia; Antifascism; Balkan Wars; Collectivization; Comecon; Communist Party of Albania; Congress of Berlin; De-Stalinization; Economic Development in Albania; Gegs; Great Powers; Enver Hoxha; Fiume; Abdul Frashëri; Adolf Hitler; Hungarian Revolution of 1956; Islam; Kosovo; League of Nations; League of Prizren; London Pact; Media; Montenegro; Muslims; Fan S. Noli; Ottoman Empire; Paris Peace Conference; Peasants; Revolutions of 1989; Russo-Turkish War of 1877–78; San Stefano; Sovietization; Stalin; Tirana; Tito; Tito-Stalin Split; Esad Toptani; Tosks; *Tanzimat;* Warsaw Pact; William of Wied; Woodrow Wilson; World War I; World War II; Koci Xoxe; Ahmed Zogu

Albanian Art

The quest for national self-identity and the maintenance of the existing Stalinist model was a pillar of Albania's artistic awakening in the Communist era. Owing to centuries of foreign rule, all facets of Albanian life were in a state of neglect and the country's national renaissance in the late nineteenth century affected only a small minority of patriots. While twentieth-century patriots had made some important gains, especially in terms of translating Western classics into Albanian, the arts were by no means considered vital for a country that was often dealing with the more pressing concerns of nation building. As a result, a sustained attempt at a vitalization of the arts occurred only in the Communist period.

In keeping with the need to make party interests primary, artistic developments in the Communist period were intensely politicized. Despite this, the period witnessed some remarkable achievements. Since folklore had been a pillar of the country's cultural legacy, a regular folk festival was inaugurated in the southern city of Gjirokastër in 1968. Events related to the Albanian national awakening, the legacy of the Albanian hero Skanderbeg (1405–68), who resisted the Turks, as well as a wealth of party achievements were also marked by national festivals. The concept of national festivals was supplemented by a marked increase in artistic venues such as ballet, opera, and theater. On November 29, 1953, the National Theater of Opera and Ballet was opened in Tirana, and in 1966 a much larger Palace of Culture, which housed the Theater of Opera and Ballet and the National Library, was opened. The Communist regime used theater as a means to glorify the wartime partisan struggle and the virtues of Albanian socialism. The State Opera performed many of the classics such as *Madama Butterfly* and *La Traviata,* but also was a venue for the small but significant domestic operas such as Kristo Kono's (n.d.) *Agimi* (*The Dawn*), first performed in 1954, Prenkë Jakova's (1917–69) *Mrika,* performed in 1959, and Tish Daiia's (n.d.) *Pranvera* (*The Spring*), which premiered in 1960. Skanderbeg's struggle against the Ottoman forces was eulogized in Jakova's *Skenderbeu.* Ballet performances were also deeply influenced by party dogma. Nikolla Zoraqi's (n.d.) *Cuca e maleve* (*The Mountain Maiden*) chronicles the true story of a woman who rebels against tradition in the northern highlands. In 1972 a Philharmonic Society was established in Tirana.

Painting and sculpture also underwent a remarkable renaissance. As was the case throughout the Soviet bloc, the end product was an Albanian variant of socialist realism. The opening of a Gallery of Fine Arts in Tirana in 1954 was a milestone in Albanian artistic life, and the new institution had a superb collection of Albanian art. The vast majority of the holdings glorified the party's wartime struggle in a way that could be understood by the people. As well, the gallery held a wealth of both paintings and sculptures of Skanderbeg and other pillars of the Albanian national struggle. Albania's transition witnessed a flowering of previously scorned art, and, by 1991, the gallery had already allocated considerable space to new forms of artistic expression; by 1995, much of the socialist realist material had been quietly swept away.

Socialist realist trends also predominated in the vast array of monuments that dotted the countryside. While Skanderbeg's statue dominates the main square in Tirana and overlooks the city of Krujë, the rest of the country has a valuable collection of monuments to the partisan struggle, milestones of the twentieth century such as the 1912 proclamation of independence, and nineteenth-century awakeners. Most major centers also have a martyr's cemetery for victims of the war for liberation (1944–45), which is usually dominated by impressive monuments depicting strong and battle-worn young men with clenched fists in the air. The most impressive monument is *Mother Albania,* which overlooks Tirana, and a martyr's cemetery that until recently held the remains of Enver Hoxha (1908–85), the Albanian Communist leader. As well, the socialist realist mural was an important vehicle for socialist propaganda. The most impressive one, which dominates the main entrance to the National Museum in Tirana, depicts the Albanian struggle through the ages until the new socialist order. Other murals can be found throughout the country, with especially intriguing ones on the roadside near the industrial city of Elbasan. Finally, three impressive monuments to Hoxha were erected. The most massive overlooked Tirana's main square until demonstrators toppled it in February 1991; another was in Gjirokastër, Hoxha's birthplace; while a third was in the pyramid-shaped Hoxha Museum in Tirana.

Finally, film in the Communist era also became an important vehicle for party propaganda. With Soviet assistance, by 1952 Albania had a massive film studio in the suburbs of Tirana. In keeping with Skanderbeg's vital role in Albanian history, the first major production, released in 1953, was on Skanderbeg. Other, less significant films were produced throughout the Communist era and all fell within the strict limits of party control. By the mid-1970s, the studio was releasing some ten feature films a year.

Robert Austin

Further reading

Grothusen, Klaus-Detlev, ed. *Albanien.* Südosteuropa Handbuch, Band 7. Göttingen, 1993.

See also Albanian Culture; Cinema; Communist Party of Albania; Folklore; Enver Hoxha; Theater

Albanian Culture

Like every aspect of Albanian life during the Communist period, culture was politicized and under the strict control of the ruling Party of Labor (Communist party). Despite this, Albania's Communist rulers attached great significance to promoting and sustaining a truly national culture. While developments were kept well within the framework of Marxism-Leninism-Stalinism, artistic achievements still were made. Albanians emerged from the Stalinist system more aware of the nation's varied and rich cultural heritage.

One of the main legacies of the nearly five hundred years of Ottoman rule was that Albanian culture was effectively submerged. The result was that Albanian patriots not only had to fight for an independent existence but also had to overcome notions that there was no such thing as an Albanian nation. Thus, the main aim of cultural developments in the Communist period was fourfold: encourage and enhance national unity; overcome the notion that Albania was a backward and primitive nation; promote the concept that Albanians fought a long and difficult battle against foreign threats to further both their sovereignty and their national identity; and, finally, create dependable socialist citizens. Efforts to prove that as a small nation Albanians struggled to survive, first as a their nationality and later as an independent nation, have left a deep imprint on cultural norms and mentalities.

In the years before the Communist seizure of power, Albanian patriots were forced to concentrate on the more grassroots component of national awareness. For this vastly illiterate society, the main agenda was to shape a concept of national consciousness. Even after independence in 1912, little was done in terms of promoting cultural awareness. In the first place, the problem of language was a major obstacle. A litany of dialects was used, and it was only in 1908 that Albanians finally selected an alphabet. However, patriots such as Fan S. Noli (1882–1965) and Faik Konitza (1875–1942) worked diligently at promoting Albanian culture in the interwar years, as well as simultaneously undermining the impact of foreign culture, especially Greek. Both Konitza and Noli were pillars of the Albanian-American community, located primarily in Boston. The American diaspora, through its organization Vatra (The Hearth) and the community newspaper *Dielli* (*The Sun*), accomplished much in terms of attempting to

A promote Albania's past achievements and enhance the link between Albanian and Western culture. However, the interwar years, which were dominated primarily by Ahmed Bey Zogu (1895–1961), who became king in 1928, were devoid of any real achievements. The Albanian people remained illiterate, and although Zogu did make some important inroads in attempting to undermine regional and religious cleavages, Albanians for the most part were unaware of the existence of a national culture.

Albania's Communist rulers were determined to reverse this trend and embarked on an ambitious program to resurrect the country's cultural heritage. Not surprisingly, the main thrust of the effort was the glorification of the wartime partisan struggle.

With the establishment of a network of local museums, an extraordinary number of monuments, regular festivals marking the anniversary of past successes, and a wealth of published material, the government attempted to secure for the party the leading role in Albanian society. Aside from furthering the party's agenda, the Communists went to great lengths to uncover the nation's cultural legacy. The national hero, Gjergi Kastrioti or Skanderbeg (1405–68), continued to assume the paramount position. Skanderbeg's battle against the Ottoman forces in the fifteenth century was interpreted as a national struggle of the Albanian people. Operas, film, poetry, song, and historical literature focused on exploring Skanderbeg's legacy. A modern museum was also opened at one of Skanderbeg's castles in Krujë. The Skanderbeg family emblem—a black double-headed eagle on a red background—remains the Albanian flag and national symbol.

While Skanderbeg had always been a major component of Albanian national culture, possibly the most important development in the Communist period was the emphasis on the link between Albanians and Illyrians. Efforts to explore and enhance the idea that Albanians are descendants of the Illyrians were important not only from a cultural point of view but were considered just as useful in terms of proving that Albanians were a historic nation and thus the first inhabitants of the Balkan Peninsula. Extensive archaeological work was conducted in the main Illyrian centers in Durrës, Pojan, and most important, Butrint. The latter, located near the southern port of Sarandë, is possibly the nations's most intriguing archaeological site and in the aftermath of communism the subject of tremendous interest from Western specialists. The Illyrian connection remains the most important element of both the Albanian mentality and the national culture. In keeping with the desire to create a national culture that was both Albano-centric and subject to the Communist desire to create and sustain an Albanian siege mentality, the period of national renaissance also received considerable attention. The 1878 League of Prizren, formed to halt Albania's partition after the Russo-Turkish War of 1877–78, was enshrined in the national culture.

As for twentieth-century developments, the Communists were selective. Fan Noli's "bourgeois-democratic revolution" of June 1924 was eulogized and its eventual failure was blamed on outside interference. Zogu, on the other hand, was branded a national traitor and scorned for his alleged subservience to Yugoslavia and Italy and his "antinational" and "reactionary policies." Regular festivals marked the anniversaries of Noli's seizure of power, the League of Prizren, and Skanderbeg's death. A Palace of Culture opened in Tirana in 1966, and a massive National Museum dominates Tirana's Skanderbeg Square. In 1960 the government established the Institute of Folklore, which published several scholarly works and collected thousands of folk songs. The regime also went to great lengths to bring culture to the countryside, where the vast majority of Albanians lived, by building regional museums, cinemas, and small-scale cultural houses.

The most significant development in the Communist period, however, was the Albanian Cultural Revolution (1966–69). This extraordinary development, undertaken during the Chinese phase of Albanian communism, sought to limit the impact of Western culture, eliminate what were deemed as vestiges of backwardness, and destroy obstacles to national unity and modernization. Modeled on its Chinese counterpart but by no means as severe, the Party of Labor led an all-out attack on the state bureaucracy, clan-based habits, and educational and religious institutions. Feeling confident that the economic basis of Stalinism was laid, Albanian Communist leader Enver Hoxha (1908–85) pursued an agenda that reflected not only the need to undercut the impact of Soviet leader Nikita Khrushchev's (1894–1971) revisionism but to further the cause of national integration. The most significant outcome was certainly the destruction of religious institutions and the proclamation in 1967 that Albania was the world's first atheist state. According to official thinking, Albania's three religions were harbingers of backwardness and obstacles to national unity but also competing centers of loyalty.

As in the rest of the former Soviet bloc, the transition years and the accompanying economic austerity hit the cultural sectors hard. In part owing to the extreme isolation during the Communist period, Albanians in the aftermath of communism were all too willing to embrace Western cultural norms and abandon, or at least question, the distorted cultural norms established by the Communists. While the legacies of Illyria, Skanderbeg, and the late-nineteenth-century awakening have remained important parts of national culture during the transition, the siege mentality component of the previous regime's cultural agenda has been eroded.

Robert Austin

Further reading

Konitza, Faik. *Albania—the Rockgarden of Southeastern Europe and Other Essays,* ed. by G.M. Panarity. Boston, 1957.

Pano, Nicholas. "The Albanian Cultural Revolution." *Problems of Communism* 23 (July–August 1974): 44–57.

Prifti, Peter. *Socialist Albania since 1944.* Cambridge, 1978.

See also Albanian Art; Albanian Language; Albanian Literature; Communist Party of Albania; Education; Folklore; Enver Hoxha; League of Prizren; Fan S. Noli; Russo-Turkish War of 1877–78; Ahmed Zogu

Albanian Émigrés

Before the nineteenth century, Albanian emigration was principally directed toward Italy. The Albanian community in Italy, known as Arbëresh, played an important role in the cultural development of the Albanian people as a whole. Important literary figures such as Jeronim De Rada (1814–1903) contributed to the formation of Albanian literature and inspired the creation of a national consciousness in the Albanian lands. The Arbëresh community in Italy continues to be important, and many Albanians again emigrated to Italy after the collapse of the Communist regime in Albania in 1991.

During the last two centuries, important Albanian communities were established in many parts of the world. Of these, the most important were in Romania and the United States. At the beginning of the nineteenth century, Romania became the principal center of activity for Albanian intellectuals. The most outstanding personality was Naum Veqilharxhi (1797–1854), a lawyer in Brăila, who published the first Albanian primer in Bucharest in 1844. During the second half of the nineteenth and early twentieth centuries, Bucharest became the leading center of the Albanian national movement. After the suppression of the League of Prizren, Albania's first major nationalistic manifestation, by the Ottomans in 1881, the center of Albanian activities moved to Bucharest, where, in 1884, the Drita literary society was established. Leading Albanian intellectuals, such as Naum Frashëri (1846–1900), carried out their activities in Romania and published numerous Albanian books that were sent to Albania.

The first Albanians arrived in the United States in the latter half of the nineteenth century. Most settled in New England, with the center of Albanian activities being in Boston. The first Albanian newspaper, *Kombi* (*Nation*), appeared in 1906, edited by Sotir Peci (1873–1932). One of the most remarkable Albanian-American leaders, Fan S. Noli (1882–1965), established the Albanian Autocephalous Orthodox Church in 1908 and became its first priest; in 1919 he was elevated to the rank of bishop. He returned to Albania after World War I and served briefly as prime minister in 1924. After he returned to the United States in the 1930s, Noli withdrew from politics and carried out a variety of cultural activities. Faik Konitza (1875–1942) became another important Albanian leader in the United States. In 1912 the various Albanian associations that had been founded joined together to form Vatra, the Pan-Albanian Federation of America, with the newspaper *Dielli* (*The Sun*) as its principal organ. Konitza became the first secretary-general of this organization and later its president. In 1926 he became Albanian minister to Washington. Other important Albanian-American leaders included Constantine Chekrezi (1892–1959) and Christo Dako (1878–1941), who wrote works to support the Albanian cause at the Paris Peace Conference in 1919. Chekrezi also served as the first Albanian high commissioner to Washington. Remarkable Albanian-American scholars include Stavro

Skendi (n.d.), Nelo Drizari (b. 1900), and Arshi Pipa (1920–87).

Kurt W. Treptow

Further reading

Chekrezi, Constantine A. *Albania: Past and Present.* New York, 1919.

Elsie, Robert. *History of Albanian Literature,* 2 vols. Boulder, Colorado, 1995.

Federal Writers' Project of the Works Progress Administration of Massachusetts. *The Albanian Struggle in the Old World and New,* Boston, 1939.

Konitza, Faik. *Albania—The Rock Garden of Southeastern Europe and Other Essays,* ed. by G.M. Panarity. Boston, 1957.

See also League of Prizren; Fan S. Noli; Paris Peace Conference

Albanian Language

Albanian is an Indo-European language, but, like Greek, it is within its own subgroup. Albanian is spoken by approximately seven million people in Albania, Kosovo, Montenegro, Macedonia, Greece, and European Turkey. Outside the Balkans, there are vibrant Albanian communities in Canada, Italy, the United States, and Ukraine.

The origins of the language are subject to debate, although most scholars agree that it descended from Illyrian. Other scholars argue that it derives from Thracian. The link with Illyrian is important, as it established Albanians as the first inhabitants of the Balkans. As a result, the origin of the language is deeply politicized. In any case, there have been several borrowings from other languages, including Greek, Latin, Turkish, and Italian, as well as the Slavic languages. The oldest Albanian text dates as recently as 1462. With the onset of the Ottoman occupation, official proscriptions banned the use of written Albanian. It was only in the nineteenth century that patriots, both in Albania and abroad, made serious inroads in reviving the written language.

An alphabet for Albanian was decided in 1908 at the Congress of Monastir (Bitola), which adopted the Latin script. The selection of Latin script, as opposed to Arabic, was considered vital in linking Albania's future to the West and a rejection of Ottoman influence. Prior to 1908, there were as many as half a dozen alphabets in use. The thirty-six–letter Albanian alphabet includes nine two-consonant digraphs (dh, gj, ll, nj, rr, sh, th, xh, and zh) and two accented single letters (ë and ç).

There are principally two main dialects. Geg is spoken primarily by Albanians in the north, including Kosovo, while Tosk is the dialect of Albanians living south of the Shkumbin River. There were numerous other dialects throughout Albanian-inhabited lands, for example, by the Arberesh, an Albanian community in southern Italy who settled there after the Ottoman conquest. While the Monastir Congress finally fixed the alphabet, it was also accepted that patriots would work toward a common literary Albanian. In 1916, at a meeting in Shkodër, a first attempt was made to create a common literary Albanian. The participants chose the Geg idiom from the town of Elbasan as the basis for the gradual convergence of the Geg and Tosk dialects. No further progress was made, however, and nothing else was undertaken in the interwar period to unify the principal dialects.

The major efforts to standardize the language came during the Communist era. In 1952 an outline for a unified language was established. But it was not until 1972, at the Congress of Orthography, that a Unified Literary Albanian was adopted by the Communist regime. It represented a fusion of both Geg and Tosk, although roughly 80 percent is based on Tosk.

Robert Austin

Further reading

Pipa, Arshi. *The Politics of Language in Socialist Albania.* Boulder, Colorado, 1989.

Skendi, Stavro. *The Albanian National Awakening, 1878–1912.* Princeton, New Jersey, 1967.

Zymberi, Isa. *Colloquial Albanian.* London, 1991.

See also Gegs; Tosks

Albanian Literature

Because of Albania's difficult geographic position, which ensured a history of foreign domination, all facets of Albanian life faced severe developmental obstacles. This resulted from a series of foreign invaders, subsequent division between Rome and Constantinople, and the impact of Ottoman conquest. The development of a national literature came late, as Ottoman policy prohibited the use of written Albanian and banned its teaching. Orthodox Albanians, who fell under the sway of the Patriarchate of Constantinople, were forced to learn Greek. As a result, the activities of the Albanian diaspora in Romania, Italy, and Bulgaria were vital in keeping alive an Albanian literary tradition. It was only in 1908, with the Young Turk revolution in Istanbul, which overthrew Sultan Abdul Hamid II (1842–1918), that Albanians gained constitutional guarantees to allow for the unrestricted use of their language.

The first written document, a Geg baptismal formula, dates from 1462. In the sixteenth century religious literary texts began to appear, such as Gjon Buzuku's (n.d.) Missal in 1555. It was only in the mid-nineteenth century that a national literature began to emerge as a result of the national awakening of the Albanian people and the desire to assert greater independence from the Ottoman Empire. The period of national revival, which culminated in Albanian independence in 1912, led to a flowering of romantic national literature. It extolled the achievements of Skanderbeg (1405–1468), Albania's national hero, who battled the Ottoman armies between 1443 and 1468. The principal figure in this agenda was Naum Frashëri (1846–1900). In addition, Faik Konitza (1875–1942) was a central figure outside Albania who began publishing the journal *Albania* in Brussels in 1897.

In the aftermath of independence, and in the interwar period, Albanian literature grew considerably. Figures like Konitza, Fan S. Noli (1882–1965), and the Franciscan father Gjergj Fishta (1871–1940) were influential, although a truly grassroots growth was hindered by Albania's material condition between 1918 and 1939. The country was overwhelmingly poor and 80 percent of the population was illiterate, numerous dialects and subdialects were in use, and the major figure in the period, Ahmed Bey Zogu (1895–1961), who ruled as prime minister, president, and finally king, attached little significance to the growth of a national literature.

With the victory of the Albanian Communists in 1944, literature was made to serve the ideological wishes of Albania's ruling Party of Labor. Communist leader Enver Hoxha (1908–85) moved quickly to eliminate any intellectual freedom through a variety of methods. Albanian literature became desperately conformist and tedious. The main agenda of literature was thus to reflect socialist realism while reminding the Albanian people of their centuries-long battle to survive in the face of far more powerful neighbors. Particular emphasis was placed on the War of National Liberation (World War II), the growth of class consciousness, the liberation of the peasantry, and patriotism. Literature, like art and culture, served to glorify the partisan struggle. Owing to Albania's extreme isolation, foreign trends had little impact inside Albania.

Shackled by the demands of party ideology, and with the most influential literary figures of the prewar period totally discredited, little literature of any substantive value appeared in Albania prior to the 1960s. Experimentation with new approaches in literature emerged only as a result of the break with the Soviet Union. A liberal movement emerged in the late 1960s and early 1970s that sought to breathe new life into Albanian literature, art, and culture. As a result, liberal trends were encouraged in literature, art, and music. Yet the gains were short-lived, as the liberal movement was crushed in 1973 and its main leaders jailed.

The key figure in Albanian literature, and the best-known author outside of Albania, remains Ismail Kadare (1936–), whose works have been widely translated. Kadare was born in Gjirokastër and later studied at the University of Tirana and at the Gorky Institute of World Literature in Moscow. Despite his often veiled criticism of the regime, Kadare remained relatively protected by the country's Communist rulers until 1990, when he fled Tirana and sought exile in France, fearing that Albania's leaders were planning a major assault on him. His departure had a major impact on the course of political developments and did much to hasten the demise of Albanian communism.

Kadare's major works include poetry, historical novels, and short stories. His major historical novels include *Gjenerali i ushtrisë së vdekur* (*The General of the Dead Army,* 1970); *Keshtjella Tirana* (*The Castle,* 1970); *Dimri i Madh* (*The Great Winter,* 1977), which told of the break in relations with the Soviet Union; and the epic *Koncert në fund të dimrit* (*The Concert at the End of Winter,* 1988), which chronicled the bizarre end to Albania's alliance with China and was openly critical of the socialist system.

While Kadare remained the major figure in postwar Albanian literature, others include Dritëro Agolli (1931–), Sabri Godo (1924–), Teodor Laço (1936–), Teodor Kako (1958–), and Neshat Tozaj (1943–). Tozaj's *Thikat Tirana* (*The Knives,* 1989) was considered a major attack on the Albanian security forces (Sigurimi) and vital to the widening disenchantment that led to the collapse of Communist rule in the country.

Robert Austin

Further reading

Elsie, Robert. "Literature," in Grothusen, Klaus-Detlev, ed. *Albania—Handbook on South Eastern Europe,* vol. 7. Göttingen, 1993.
———. *Studies in Modern Albanian Literature and Culture.* Boulder, Colorado, 1996.
Pipa, Arshi. *Contemporary Albanian Literature.* Boulder, Colorado, 1991.

See also Abdul Hamid II; Albanian Art; Albanian Culture; Communist Party of Albania; Fan S. Noli; Patriarchate; Young Turks; Ahmed Zogu

Aleksandrov, Todor (1881–1924)

Macedonian revolutionary. Aleksandrov was born in Shtip, Macedonia; studied in the schools of the Bulgarian Exarchate in Skopje and Salonika; and joined the Internal Macedonian Revolutionary Organization (IMRO), which looked to create an autonomous Macedonian state. In and out of Turkish prisons, he saw the Young Turk revolution of 1908, which sought to reform the Ottoman Empire, as a farce that would not bring real reforms, and at the same time opposed the Supreme Committee of IMRO sponsored by the Bulgarian government in Sofia. He was elected as a member of the Central Committee of IMRO operating in Macedonia, but during the Balkan Wars (1912–13) and World War I he sided with Bulgaria. After the defeat of the latter and the partitioning of Macedonia, confirmed by the postwar Treaty of Neuilly, he resumed his activities as an underground leader of the Macedonian organization, which in the meantime had split: the left wing, supported by the Communist Third International (Comintern), Yugoslav intelligence services, and the Agrarian government of Aleksandur Stamboliiski (1879–1923); and the right wing, led by Aleksandrov and supported by the rank and file of IMRO. He continued to send armed bands into Macedonia from his Bulgarian bases, and Belgrade threatened Bulgaria with occupation. To accommodate Yugoslavia, Stamboliiski in turn threatened IMRO, which retaliated by assassinating Interior Minister Aleksandur Dimitrov (1878–

1921). Aleksandrov negotiated an agreement with the Comintern but repudiated it and on August 31, 1924, was assassinated by his left-wing confederates led by General Aleksander Protogerov (1867–1928), who in turn were executed by Aleksandrov's successor, Ivan Mikhailov (1896–1990).

Spas T. Raikin

Further reading

Anastassov, Christ. *The Tragic Peninsula: A History of the Macedonian Movement for Independence since 1878.* St. Louis, Missouri, 1938.
Mikhailov, Ivan. *Spomeni,* vol. 3. Louvain, Belgium, 1967.

See also Balkan Wars; Comintern; IMRO; Macedonia (History); Ivan Mikhailov; Neuilly, Treaty of; Aleksandur Stamboliiski; Young Turks

Alexander I (1777–1825)

Tsar of Russia. Alexander originally came to the aid of Austria against Napoléonic France by joining the Third Coalition in 1805; this effort failed, however, when Napoléon (1769–1821) defeated the allies at the Battle of Austerlitz that same year. Alexander next joined the Fourth Coalition in 1806, this time with Prussia, but French victories in the campaigns of 1806–7 forced the tsar to abandon his Prussian ally and seek peace with Napoléon through the Treaties of Tilsit (July 1807); these effectively gave Russia a dominant position in Eastern Europe as France's junior partner. Under the terms of the treaties, Russia gained the province of Białystok from Prussian Poland, while the remainder of Prussia's Polish provinces were consolidated into the Duchy of Warsaw, which was garrisoned by French forces and effectively functioned as a French satellite. French control in Poland was a source of constant irritation for Alexander, and it contributed to the seemingly inevitable conflict between the two powers when Napoléon invaded Russia in 1812. Meanwhile, Alexander's forces had moved into the principalities of Wallachia and Moldavia in 1806, thus initiating a war with the Ottoman Empire; Russian forces remained there until May 1812, when, under provisions of the Treaty of Bucharest, Russia annexed the territory of Bessarabia to establish the new frontier between the Ottoman and Russian Empires.

Alexander's pivotal role in pushing Napoléon back to France and ultimately defeating the French emperor in 1814 made the tsar an important player in the diplomatic negotiations among the European Great Powers in the postwar years. As a result of the Congress of Vienna in 1815, Alexander was named king of the Congress Kingdom of Poland, a political entity that had its own constitution and army but existed within the boundaries of the Russian Empire and for which Alexander determined foreign policy. This new Poland comprised most of the land of the former Duchy of Warsaw, and Alexander thus gained a territorial buffer for Russia on the western frontier. Alexander favored close relations with the other conservative monarchies, Prussia and Austria, and together the three powers worked to suppress revolutionary movements throughout Europe including the Greek uprising in the Danubian Principalities against Ottoman rule in 1821.

Jonathan A. Grant

Further reading

Hartley, Janet M. *Alexander I.* London, 1994.
Jelavich, Barbara. *Russia's Balkan Entanglements, 1806–1914.* Cambridge, 1991.
Thackeray, Frank W. *Antecedents of Revolution: Alexander I and the Polish Kingdom, 1815–1825.* Boulder, Colorado, 1980.
Zawadzki, W.H. *A Man of Honour: Adam Czartoryski as a Statesman of Russia and Poland 1795–1831.* Oxford, 1993.

See also Bessarabian Question; Congress of Vienna; Danubian Principalities; Duchy of Warsaw; Great Powers; Greek Revolution; Napoléon; Polish Congress Kingdom; Russia

Alexander II (1818–81)

Tsar of Russia. Alexander ascended the throne during the Crimean War (1853–56) and ended the conflict through the Treaty of Paris in March 1856. Under terms of this treaty, Russia gave up the southern part of Bessarabia to Moldavia, and the position of Russia as sole protector over the Danubian Principalities and Serbia ended. Also, Russia and the Ottoman Empire were each forbidden to have arsenals or warships in the Black Sea region. This left Russia vulnerable to the threat of naval attack, and the loss of control over the mouth of the Danube River further weakened Russia's strategic position in the Balkans. In general,

Alexander pursued a defensive policy in foreign affairs and concentrated on domestic reforms including the emancipation of Russian serfs in 1861. Alexander's public discussion of reform projects, however, raised expectations among Polish leaders that their old rights would be restored. Polish nobles, hoping to restore an independent Poland, revolted and threatened Russian control in 1863, but the tsarist army easily suppressed the uprising. As punishment, Alexander granted favorable emancipation terms to the Polish peasantry at the expense of the Polish nobility, and approximately one-tenth of noble land was confiscated. Additionally, the Congress Kingdom of Poland was formally abolished and Polish land was incorporated directly into the Russian Empire.

In the 1870s Alexander's foreign policy became more assertive. In October 1870 he unilaterally revoked the Black Sea clauses in the Treaty of Paris. After revolts against Ottoman rule in Bosnia and Hercegovina in 1875, and the outbreak of war between the Ottomans and Serbia in 1876, Alexander declared war against the Ottoman Empire. After the Russo-Turkish War of 1877–78, Russian gains caused an international crisis and led to the Congress of Berlin in June 1878. The Berlin settlement was generally considered disappointing for Russia, although it established an autonomous Bulgaria between the Balkan Mountains and the Danube River as a Russian sphere of influence. Under Russian administration, Bulgaria received a liberal constitution with a strong legislative branch, and a Russian general held the post of Bulgarian minister of war even after the Russian army withdrew in 1879. Alexander was assassinated by revolutionaries in 1881.

Jonathan A. Grant

Further reading

Jelavich, Barbara. *Russia and the Formation of the Romanian National State, 1821–1878.* Cambridge, 1984.
———. *Russia's Balkan Entanglements, 1806–1914.* Cambridge, 1991.
Jelavich, Charles. *Tsarist Russia and Balkan Nationalism; Russian Influence in the Internal Affairs of Bulgaria and Serbia, 1876–1886.* Berkeley, California, 1958.
Milojkovic-Djuric, Jelena. *Panslavism and National Identity in Russia and the Balkans 1830–1880, Images of Self and Others.* Boulder, Colorado, 1994.

See also Bessarabian Question; Congress of Berlin; Crimean War; Danube Question; Danubian Principalities; Eastern Question; January Uprising; Pan-Slavism; Paris, Treaty of; Polish Congress Kingdom; Polish Question; Russo-Turkish War of 1877–78; Serbo-Turkish War of 1876

Alexander III (1845–94)

Tsar of Russia, whose personal animosity toward the Bulgarian ruler, Alexander of Battenberg (1857–93), cost Russia its friendly strategic outpost in the Balkans. Within Bulgaria, army officers developed a hostile attitude toward Russia because all ranks in the Bulgarian army from captain and above were the exclusive preserve of Russian officers. The Bulgarian crisis began in 1883 when the Bulgarian liberal and conservative parties united behind their prince in opposition to Russian direction in Bulgarian affairs. Next, the Bulgarian prince restored the constitution against the wishes of the Russian tsar. In 1885 Alexander of Battenberg violated the Berlin settlement of 1878 and accepted the unification of Bulgaria and Eastern Rumelia. The tsar opposed such a unification because it would strengthen the prince's position and further weaken Russian dominance in Bulgaria. Alexander III had become so vehement in his opposition to the Bulgarian prince that he actively sought to remove Alexander of Battenberg as the Bulgarian ruler. To that end, the Russian government supported a conspiracy against the Bulgarian prince that succeeded in removing him in August 1885. By 1886, Alexander III was demanding the formal abdication of the Bulgarian prince, and in October the tsar broke off relations with Bulgaria. Russian relations with Bulgaria remained broken for the rest of Alexander III's life, and they were not restored until 1896 under Nicholas II (1868–1918). Britain and Austria supported the unification against the interests of Russia, effectively ending Russia's role as the protecting power over Bulgaria. Russia's loss of control over Bulgaria dealt a blow to Russian prestige in the Balkans and fostered a growing estrangement between Russia and Austria. In fact, Russia had no allies left in the Balkans. Serbia and Romania had both allied themselves with Austria prior to the Bulgarian crisis.

Meanwhile, Alexander III pursued an official policy of Russification in tsarist Poland. The Russian language replaced Polish at all levels of administration and in the local courts. Also, all associations, including the Catholic Church in Poland, were required to use Russian internally. The language policy accompanied a general removal of Poles from positions in the upper and middle administrative ranks.

Jonathan A. Grant

Further reading

Jelavich, Barbara. *Russia's Balkan Entanglements, 1806–1914.* Cambridge, 1991.

Jelavich, Charles and Barbara. *The Establishment of the Balkan National States, 1804–1920.* Seattle, Washington, 1977.

Rogger, Hans. *Russia in the Age of Modernisation and Revolution, 1881–1917.* London, 1983.

See also Alexander of Battenberg; Congress of Berlin; Eastern Question; Eastern Rumelia; Nicholas II; Russification

Alexander Karadjordjević (1806–85)

Prince of Serbia (1842–58). The son of the leader of the revolt against the Turks in 1804, Black George (1768–1817), Alexander came to the throne in 1842, thanks in part to anti-Obrenović leaders who conspired with the Turks to recognize him in place of Prince Miloš Obrenović (1780–1860). In a sense, Alexander owed everything to the council that had been established under the Turkish-granted constitution of 1838. Although Alexander shared power with the council in theory, the council's oligarchy, who styled themselves as defenders of the constitution, was dominant. By the mid-1850s, however, the prince began to assert his power, and the Turkish authorities chose not to interfere. The resulting conflict with the council in turn was sharpened by the prince's appointment of his wife's relatives to high office. By 1858, each party thought that a popular assembly would resolve the issue in its favor, and agreed to call one. To the surprise of both Alexander and the council, the Skupština (parliament) ousted both in a peaceful revolution that returned the once-deposed Miloš to the Serbian throne.

Alex N. Dragnich

Further reading

Dragnich, Alex N. *The Development of Parliamentary Government in Serbia.* Boulder, Colorado, 1978.

Jovanović, Slobodan. *Ustavobranitelji i njihova vlada, 1838–1858*. Belgrade, 1912.

Petrovich, Michael B. *A History of Modern Serbia*, 2 vols. New York, 1976.

See also Black George; Miloš Obrenović; Skup-ština

Alexander I Karadjordjević (1888–1934)

King of Yugoslavia. The son of Peter Karadjord-jević (1844–1921) and Princess Zorka (1864–90), Alexander (who was educated in Switzerland, Russia, and Belgrade) replaced his elder brother George (1887–1972) as crown prince of Serbia in 1909, after the latter renounced his right of suc-cession. Shortly before the outbreak of World War I, he was named regent and assumed most of his aging father's royal responsibilities. Refusing to surrender to invading Austro-German forces in 1915–16, Peter and Alexander withdrew with the army to the Adriatic coast and eventually ended up on the Allied Salonika Front in Greece.

Alexander's relations with certain military subordinates proved strained, and in 1917 a Ser-bian military court in Salonika convicted a group of officers of conspiring to assassinate the regent. Among those executed was Dragutin Dimitrijević-Apis (1876–1917), founder of the notorious Ujed-injenje ili smrt, the nationalist organization better known as the Black Hand.

In 1918 the South Slav components of the defunct Austro-Hungarian Empire joined with Ser-bia and Montenegro to form the Kingdom of Serbs, Croats, and Slovenes, a constitutional monarchy under the house of Karadjordjević. Alexander served as prince regent until August 16, 1921, when he succeeded his father as king.

In the 1920s ethnic and territorial disputes between the country's two largest national groups, the Serbs and the Croats, and a related political dispute between the proponents of centralism and federalism spawned prolonged political and social disorder. After the 1928 assassination of Stjepan Radić (1871–1928), the leader of the Croatian Peasant Party, Alexander instituted his "personal rule" on January 6, 1929, dissolving parliament, abrogating the constitution of 1921, outlawing existing political parties, and renaming the country Yugoslavia. In 1931 he granted a new constitution, but political opponents saw only a continuation of royal dictatorship. Alexander's policies earned him the hatred of such diverse groups as Serbian liberals, Yugoslav Commu-nists, as well as Croatian and Macedonian sepa-ratists (groups supported by Italy, Hungary, and Bulgaria).

Under Alexander, Yugoslavia became a mem-ber of the Little Entente in the 1920s and the Balkan Entente in 1934, two regional alliance sys-tems. Attempting to buttress ties with France later in 1934, Alexander traveled to Marseilles, where he and French Foreign Minister Louis Barthou (1862–1934) were assassinated by agents of the ultranationalist Croatian Ustaša and the Internal Macedonian Revolutionary Organization (IMRO), the radical organization that sought the creation of an autonomous Macedonia. Alexander was suc-ceeded by his eleven-year-old son, the last king of Yugoslavia, who reigned as Peter II (1923–70).

John D. Treadway

Further reading

Graham, Stephen. *Alexander of Yugoslavia: The Story of the King Who Was Murdered at Mar-seilles*. New Haven, Connecticut, 1939.

Roberts, Allen. *The Turning Point: The Assassina-tion of Louis Barthou and King Alexander I of Yugoslavia*. New York, 1970.

See also Apis; Balkan Entente; Black Hand; IMRO; Kingdom of Serbs, Croats, and Slovenes; Little Entente; Petar Petrović Njegoš; Peter Karad-jordjević; Stjepan Radić; Salonika Front; Ustaša; Vidovdan Constitution

Alexander Obrenović (1876–1903)

King of Serbia (1889–1903) and last monarch in the Obrenović dynasty. Alexander's childhood was joyless and troubled. His parents were in a state of constant marital discord that brought shame to the monarchy both domestically and internation-ally. Alexander came to the throne at the age of thirteen. Three years later (1893), he presided over a palace coup that was engineered by his father, King Milan (1854–1901), against his regency.

From 1893 to 1901, Alexander oscillated be-tween the influence of his father and mother. Both exploited the affections of their son in their quest for power and advantage. Under the sway of Milan, Alexander stifled Serbia's political progress. The liberal constitution of 1888 was replaced by the conservative constitution of 1896, and a nonparty

A personal regime that relied on police terror was installed in 1897.

Alexander broke with his parents over his love for his mother's lady-in-waiting, Draga Mašin (1866–1903). Draga brought controversy to the court; ten years older than Alexander, she was a commoner and a widow rumored to be barren and a former prostitute. Still, Alexander was prepared to sacrifice his throne and his family for her hand. His efforts to win popular support for his wife were undermined when it was discovered that Draga feigned a pregnancy in an attempt to gain public favor. Elements in the military, convinced Alexander brought nothing but dishonor to Serbia, assassinated the royal couple on June 10, 1903.

Alexander's reign is commonly recognized as an unhappy, scandalous, and tragic episode in modern Serbian history. His rule also represented a transitional period in Serbia's political evolution; his assassination marked the end of the Obrenović dynasty, the resolution of the perennial struggle between the Obrenović and Karadjordjević royal families, and the beginning of a constitutional parliamentary monarchy.

Robert Hislope

Further reading
Dragnich, Alex N. *The Development of Parliamentary Government in Serbia.* New York, 1978.
Mijatović, Čedomilj. *A Royal Tragedy: Being the Story of the Assassination of King Alexander and Queen Draga of Serbia.* London, 1906.
Petrovich, Michael Boro. *A History of Modern Serbia, 1804–1918,* 2 vols. New York, 1976.
West, Rebecca. *Black Lamb and Grey Falcon: A Journey through Yugoslavia.* New York, 1984.

See also Milan Obrenović

Alexander of Battenberg (1857–1893)

First prince of modern Bulgaria. Alexander of Battenberg was born in Verona, the second son of a morganatic marriage between Prince Alexander of Hesse (1823–88) and Julie Haucke (1825–95), a commoner. He was elected prince by the Bulgarian National Assembly (*Subranie*) on April 29, 1879, following the Treaty of Berlin, which ended the Russo-Turkish War of 1877–78 and established Bulgaria as a principality.

Because Alexander attempted to develop an independent Bulgarian foreign policy, he shortly found himself at odds with Russia, which considered Bulgaria totally within its sphere of influence. Internally, he also soon discovered that Bulgaria's new democratic constitution produced constant parliamentary deadlocks, a situation favored by Russia because it kept Bulgaria weak and dependent. In 1880, to end this constitutional crisis, Prince Alexander dissolved the National Assembly, suspended the constitution, and personally assumed certain powers of government. Although he restored the constitution two years later under a coalition government, his actions alienated Bulgarians.

In 1885 Eastern Rumelia, a territory that was primarily Bulgarian ethnically but under Turkish suzerainty, united with Bulgaria—a move contrary to the Berlin Treaty and strongly opposed by the new Russian tsar, Alexander III (1845–94). In retaliation, the tsar withdrew the Russian officers who at the time headed the Bulgarian army. Seizing the opportunity, neighboring Serbia attacked Bulgaria in November 1885 but was soundly defeated by the Bulgarian troops commanded by Alexander. Only intervention by the Great Powers, most notably Austria, saved the Serbs.

Such Bulgarian independence further alienated the tsar, and in a coup d'état on August 21, 1886, led by pro-Russian Bulgarian army officers, the prince was kidnapped, forced to abdicate, and turned over to Russia. Released, he returned to Bulgaria briefly, set up a provisional government, and officially abdicated on September 7, 1886. He spent the last years of his life as an officer in the Austrian army.

John Georgeoff

Further reading
Corti, Egon Caesar. *Alexander von Battenberg,* trans. by E.M. Hodgson. London, 1954.
———. *Alexander von Battenberg: Sein Kampf mit den Zaren und Bismarck.* Vienna, 1920.
———. *Leben und Liebe Alexanders von Battenberg.* Graz, 1950.
Dimitrov, Ilcho Ivanov. *Knazut, konstitutsiiata i narodut.* Sofia, 1972.
Hajek, Alois. *Bulgariens Befreiung und staatliche Entwicklung unter seinem ersten Fürsten.* Munich, 1939.

See also Alexander III; Bulgarian-Serb War of 1885; Congress of Berlin; Eastern Rumelia; Russo-Turkish War of 1877–78

Alia, Ramiz (1925–)

Albanian Communist. Born in the city of Shkodër, Alia completed his high school studies in Tirana and earned a university degree in philosophy at Moscow University in 1954. At the age of sixteen, Alia joined the Communist Youth, before becoming a member of the Communist Party two years later. In 1944 he was appointed the political commissar of the Fifth Brigade and fought with Tito's (1892–1980) Partisans against the Germans and their allies in Kosovo and other parts of Yugoslavia. At the First Congress of the Union of Anti-Fascist Youth of Albania (BRASH), held in 1944, Alia was elected a member of the secretariat, and five years later he became the first secretary of the Central Committee of the Union of Communist Youth of Albania.

After the Albanian-Yugoslav split in 1948, Alia became a close collaborator of Albanian Communist leader Enver Hoxha (1908–85). He was elected to the Central Committee of the Party of Labor of Albania at the First Party Congress held in 1948, and served as a minister of culture from 1955 to 1958. At the Third Party Congress, held in 1956, Alia became a candidate of the Politburo, becoming a full member in 1961. At the Fourth Party Congress, held in the same year, he also became a member of the party's Central Committee. Two days after the death of Hoxha in April 1985, the Eleventh Plenum of the Central Committee named Alia first secretary of the Central Committee. At Hoxha's funeral, Alia vowed to continue his predecessor's work in the construction of socialism in Albania.

Alia will be remembered not only as a man who remained loyal to Communist ideology but also as one who made possible the peaceful transition from Communist totalitarianism. When the first free national elections were held in Albania in March 1992, Alia's Socialist Party lost and he resigned soon afterward as president. In 1994 he was arrested for "abusing his presidential powers" and spent a year in jail.

Mirvet S. Muca

Further reading

Dilo, Jani. *The Communist Party Leadership in Albania.* Washington, D.C., 1961.

Zeri i Popullit. "Ramiz Alia's Speech at the Eleventh Plenum of the Central Committee of the Party of Labor," April 13, 1985.

See also Communist Party of Albania; Enver Hoxha; Tito

Ali Pasha (c. 1750–1822)

Provincial notable in the Ottoman-dominated western Balkans. Born in Tepelen, a village in southern Albania, into a prominent family deriving its power from brigandage and local government posts, Ali Pasha ruled over a large area including present-day southern Albania and western Greece from his capital at Yannina (Ioannina) in Epiros. After the death of his father when Ali was thirteen, he was initiated as a youth into the struggle for power in the local world of tribal feuds under the tutelage of his mother. Soon he became a bandit chieftain redoubtable for his ruthlessness, cunning, and rapacity. His ambition led him to seek political power. He acquired his first post in 1778 as deputy guardian of the passes in northern Epiros. In 1782 he became governor of Yannina, an office he kept until the end of his life and from which he launched forays of expansion and extermination against his enemies. During the Napoleonic campaigns into southeastern Europe, Ali was involved in the diplomatic and military activities centered on the Ionian Islands. He was courted by European states and the Ottoman government alike because they recognized his influence in the westernmost outpost of the Ottoman Empire. But his success, the product of his intrigues, duplicity, and negotiating skills, brought about his downfall. At the height of his power (1810–20), his dominions, along with those of his sons, extended from Albania to the Peloponnisos. Sultan Mahmud II (1785–1839) saw this as a threat to his reforming and centralizing interests. In 1820 Ali was stripped of all his possessions except for Yannina and an army was sent against him. Ali, who had been kept informed of the activities of the Filiki Etairia (Friendly Society), the Greek organization that looked to overthrow Ottoman rule, sought the support of the Christian chieftains whom he at one time had suppressed and urged Greek chieftains to revolt and prepare to resist. After a two-year siege of Yannina, Ali was killed on January 17, 1822. His severed head was sent to Istanbul, where it was displayed at the palace. Ali's powerful personality combining cruelty, greed, and sensuality with charm, a penetrating intelligence, and astuteness fascinated his European visitors and captivated the

AQUINAS COLLEGE LIBRARY
1607 ROBINSON RD.
GRAND RAPIDS MICH 49506

imagination of such writers as Lord Byron (1788–1824), Alexander Dumas (1802–70), and Victor Hugo (1802–85). His harsh rule, imposed by instilling fear and meting out punitive justice, however, allowed Yannina to become a center of commerce and education in the western Balkans.

Olga Augustinos

Further reading

Baggally, J.W. *Ali Pasha and Great Britain.* Oxford, 1938.

Plomer, William. *The Diamond of Jannina.* New York, 1970.

Skiotis, Dennis N. "From Bandit to Pasha: First Steps in the Rise to Power of Ali of Tepelen, 1750–1784." *International Journal of Middle East Studies* 2 (1971): 219–44.

See also *Filiki Etairia;* Mahmud II; Ottoman Empire

Andrássy, Count Gyula, Jr. (1860–1929)

Hungarian politician, writer, and historian. The son of Count Gyula Andrássy Sr. (1823–90), Andrássy was born in Töketerebes in 1860 and was elected to parliament on the Liberal Party ticket. In 1896 he published a book, entitled *The 1867 Compromise,* which gained considerable attention as a cogent defense of that constitutional arrangement between Austria and Hungary (the *Ausgleich*), which created the Dual Monarchy. Andrássy's next major work, *The Causes of the Hungarian State's Preservation and Constitutional Liberty,* published in 1901, received the Grand Prize of the Hungarian Academy of Sciences. He was a corresponding member of the academy after 1898 and a regular member after 1904. Andrássy also displayed a keen interest in the fine arts. He was president of both the Fine Arts Association and the National Salon.

Protesting Prime Minister Count István Tisza's (1861–1918) violation of parliamentary rules, Andrássy left the Liberal Party in 1904 and founded the Constitutional Party in 1905. This party joined the coalition that governed Hungary between 1906 and 1910. Andrássy held the position of minister of interior. He introduced the idea of a pluralistic franchise, apportioning the right to vote on a sliding scale of literacy and wealth. This plan never materialized, however. With the coalition's loss in the election of 1910, Andrássy again found himself in the opposition. On October 25, 1918, he was appointed foreign minister, the last one in the monarchy.

At the time of the Hungarian Soviet Republic of 1919 under Béla Kun (1886–1938), which followed in the wake of the Habsburg Monarchy's defeat in World War I, Andrássy organized anti-Communist activities in Vienna. Following the victory of the counterrevolution in the same year, Andrássy's support of Habsburg restoration landed him briefly in jail. After his release, he remained active as a leader of the pro-Habsburg legitimists until his death on June 11, 1929.

Gabor Vermes

Further reading

Hegedüs, Lóránt. *Két Andrássy és Két Tisza.* Budapest, 1941.

See also Gyula Andrássy, Sr.; *Ausgleich;* Dual Monarchy; Hungarian Soviet Republic; Béla Kun; István Tisza

Andrássy, Count Gyula, Sr. (1823–90)

Hungarian politician, prime minister (1867–71), and foreign minister (1871–79). Born in Kassa (Kosice), Andrássy was elected to the last feudal diet in 1847, where he joined the radical reformers under Lajos Kossuth's (1802–94) leadership. He fought in the 1848–49 War of Independence against Austria (during the revolutions of 1848), and accepted, in the summer of 1849, the diplomatic task of representing the revolutionary government first in Istanbul, then in Paris and London.

Following the Hungarian defeat in 1849, he was sentenced to death in absentia by an Austrian military court. However, upon receiving amnesty, Andrássy returned to Hungary in 1858. He broke with the intransigent nationalist position and joined Ferenc Deák (1803–76) in a search of a peaceful solution to the conflict with Austria. Such a solution was predicated on resurrecting the right, first obtained in April 1848, to a freely elected Hungarian parliamentary government. When this right was granted in 1867, Andrássy, whom Deák called a providential statesman, was appointed prime minister of Hungary. His major aim was to set up functioning state machinery and protect the gains accrued to Hungary by the terms of the 1867 Compromise (*Ausgleich*), which created the Dual Monarchy of Austria-Hungary.

On November 14, 1871, he was appointed minister for foreign affairs, probably the most prestigious position in Austria-Hungary's Council of Ministers for Joint Affairs, which was established after 1867 to coordinate affairs between the two halves of the empire. In this capacity, Andrássy shifted the monarchy's foreign policy direction from primarily German affairs to dealing with the volatile region of the Balkan Peninsula. He played a key role at the Congress of Berlin in 1878, where he succeeded in gaining a foothold for the monarchy in the Balkans through the military occupation of Bosnia-Hercegovina. Andrássy was also instrumental in sealing the Dual Alliance with Germany in 1879. After his resignation in the same year, he participated in politics only sporadically.

Gabor Vermes

Further reading

Ábrányi, Kornél. *Gróf Andrássy Gyula; Politikai Élet és Jellemrajz.* Budapest, 1878.

Decsy, Janos. *Prime Minister Gyula Andrássy's Influence on Habsburg Foreign Policy during the Franco-German War of 1870–1871.* Boulder, Colorado, 1979.

Hegedüs, Lóránt. *Két Andrássy és Két Tisza.* Budapest, 1941.

Wertheimer, Ede. *Gróf Andrássy Gyula és Kora,* 3 vols. Budapest, 1910–13.

See also *Ausgleich;* Congress of Berlin; Dual Alliance; Ferenc Deák; Dual Alliance; Dual Monarchy; Hungarian War for Independence; Lajos Kossuth; Revolutions of 1848

Andrić, Ivo (1892–1975)

Yugoslav writer. Andrić was born of Catholic parents in Travnik in Bosnia. He finished elementary school in Višegrad, a small town with a mixed Catholic, Orthodox, Muslim, and Jewish population, which later became the setting for many of his works, and attended high school in Sarajevo. He later studied Slavic languages and literatures in Zagreb, Vienna, Kraków, and Graz. After the assassination of Archduke Franz Ferdinand (1863–1914), which led to the outbreak of World War I, Andrić returned to Bosnia but was imprisoned as a member of the radical student organization, Young Bosnia. He was interned in Bosnia until 1917. *Ex Ponto* (1918) and *Nemiri* (*Anxieties,*

1920) refract his experience during this period. In 1920 Andrić accepted a position in the Ministry of Foreign Affairs of the new Kingdom of Serbs, Croats, and Slovenes and moved to Belgrade. As a diplomat, he served in Vatican City, Bucharest, Trieste, Graz, Marseilles, Madrid, Geneva, and Berlin. Unwilling to cooperate with the Yugoslav government after the German invasion of 1941, he resigned his post. After World War II, he became a major cultural figure in socialist Yugoslavia.

Andrić's fiction is marked by three major characteristics—an intimate link with folk ballads and legends, a strong interest in the history and culture of Bosnia, and an appreciation of storytelling and imagination as a means of transcending restrictions and brutality. They first appeared in *Put Alije Djerzeleza* (*The Journey of Ali Djerzelez,* 1920) and continued to be present in the short stories he wrote throughout his life. The culmination of his literary achievements is *The Bridge on the Drina* (1945), which was awarded the Nobel Prize in literature in 1961. In 1945 he published two other novels: *Bosnian Chronicle* and *Woman from Sarajevo.* Andrić also wrote a number of essays, travelogues, and memoirs. Most of his fiction and a substantial number of his other works have been translated into English.

Lyubomira Parapulova Gribble

Further reading

Hawkesworth, Celia. *Ivo Andrić: Bridge between East and West.* London, 1984.

Mukerji, Vanita Singh. *Ivo Andrić: A Critical Biography.* Jefferson, North Carolina, 1990.

Popović, Radovan. *Ivo Andrić: A Writer's Life.* Belgrade, 1989.

See also Franz Ferdinand; Yugoslav Literature

Andropov, Yuri (1914–84)

General Secretary of the Communist Party of the Soviet Union, 1982–84. Born in Stavropol, Andropov entered the political arena by heading the Communist Youth League (Komosol) in the Karelia Republic. During World War II, he organized guerrilla forces behind German lines and by 1947 was named party secretary of Karelia. In 1953 Andropov was assigned to the foreign service and sent to Hungary, where, as the USSR's ambassador from 1954 to 1957, he became a key figure in the Hungarian uprising of 1956. Andropov

A assured Hungarian leader Imre Nagy (1896–1958) that the Soviet Union would not interfere in Hungary's national reform movement. However, on October 31, 1956, Soviet tanks entered Budapest and suppressed the rebellion. In 1957 Andropov returned to Moscow to head the Department of Relations with Communist Parties in Power and in 1967 began a fifteen-year reign as director of the Committee for State Security (KGB). Following the death of Leonid I. Brezhnev (1906–82), Andropov was elected general secretary of the Communist Party. Andropov initiated reforms to improve a stagnant economy and actively strove to strengthen ties with the West by negotiating arms reduction treaties. But owing to a fatal kidney ailment, he remained in office for too short a time to achieve his goals.

Conrad Jarzebowski

Further reading

Ebon, Martin. *The Andropov File: The Life and Ideas of Yuri V. Andropov, General Secretary of the Communist Party of the Soviet Union.* New York, 1983.

Frankel, Benjamin, ed. *The Cold War: Leaders and Other Important Figures in the Soviet Union, Eastern Europe, China and the Third World.* Detroit, Michigan, 1992.

Medvedev, Zhores A. *Andropov.* Oxford, 1983.

See also Hungarian Revolution of 1956; Imre Nagy

Anschluss

German annexation of Austria on March 12, 1938, which set the stage for Nazi Germany's expansion into Eastern Europe. After the collapse of the Habsburg Empire in 1918, many Austrians wanted their newly truncated state to merge with the German Republic, but the Versailles peace treaty prohibited the integration of the two Germanic states. By 1938, however, few Austrians wanted to join Nazi Germany, yet Hitler (1889–1945) was intent on annexing his Austrian homeland, both to gain territory and population for the Third Reich and to outflank his next intended victim, Czechoslovakia. Hitler had made an earlier attempt to take over Austria in 1934, but he had been thwarted by Mussolini's opposition. In contrast, by 1938, Mussolini (1883–1945), now a partner in the Rome-Berlin Axis, sanctioned the *Anschluss.*

At the beginning of 1938, Hitler accused the Austrian government of violating its agreements with Germany and behaving hostilely toward Berlin. This pressure forced Chancellor Kurt von Schuschnigg (1897–1977) to legalize the Austrian Nazi Party and to include Austrian Nazi leader Artur von Seyss-Inquart (1892–1946) in his cabinet. Further concessions followed that gravely compromised Austria's sovereignty. In a desperate attempt to save his state, Schuschnigg scheduled a nationwide plebiscite on the question of *Anschluss* for March 9. He hoped that a resounding rejection of annexation would make it too embarrassing politically for Hitler to take Austria by force. Hitler could not afford to let the plebiscite take place, for the vote would certainly have gone against him. He therefore ordered German troops to cross the border. Seyss-Inquart gave the invasion an aura of legitimacy by "requesting" German assistance in quelling internal disorder. The Western powers, anxious to avoid war at almost any price, offered no effective resistance to Hitler's aggression.

Teddy J. Uldricks

Further reading

Low, Alfred D. *The Anschluss Movement,* vol. 2, *1931–1938, and the Great Powers.* Boulder, Colorado, 1985.

Luža, Radomír. *Austro-German Relations in the Anschluss Era.* Princeton, New Jersey, 1975.

Rich, Norman. *Hitler's War Aims,* vol. 1, *Ideology, the Nazi State, and the Course of Expansion.* New York, 1973.

Weinberg, Gerhard. *The Foreign Policy of Hitler's Germany: Starting World War II, 1937–1939.* Chicago, 1980.

See also Axis; Adolf Hitler; St. Germain, Treaty of

Antall, József (1932–93)

Hungarian post-Communist prime minister. Antall was born into a politically active family. His father played a role in the Independent Smallholders' Party, as well as trying to protect Jews during World War II. Antall was determined to follow his father's commitment to both Christian and democratic values. In so doing, he faced many obstacles. The Hungarian Revolution of 1956 saw him arrested and deprived of his teaching position because of his founding role in the Christian Youth

Federation and his role in the revived Independent Smallholders' Party. This convinced him to switch his career to the less visible area of library administration, where he excelled as a diligent and skilled researcher.

In the late 1980s Antall emerged from relative obscurity to become Hungary's first freely elected prime minister after the collapse of communism in East Central Europe. Despite his lack of name and face recognition outside Hungary, he played a pivotal role in the region. As criticism of the regime of János Kádár (1912–1989) grew, Antall committed himself to the forces that challenged the status quo. He became a founding member of MDF (Hungarian Democratic Forum) and after October 1989 served as the new party's chairman. He was the opposition's negotiator in the "roundtable discussions" with the Communist government, acting as an architect of the peaceful transition from the one-party dictatorship to a multiparty parliamentary democracy. In the international realm, he was the first to propose the disbanding of the Warsaw Pact at a meeting in Moscow in 1990. His name is also closely linked to the statement that "in spirit" he is "Prime Minister of fifteen million Hungarians." This gave assurance to Hungarian minorities outside of Hungary that they would no longer be ignored, but it aroused fears in neighboring countries of a resurgence of Hungarian territorial revisionism.

In domestic affairs, he prepared Hungary for a reunion with Western Europe. He committed Hungary to the repayment of its foreign debt and began to implement a far-reaching program of privatization. But probably his most important contribution to post-Communist Hungary was the establishment of a strong constitutional foundation and the institutionalization of the rule of law. Yet he was unable to keep the former Communist managers from gaining advantageous positions in the privatization process and to control their influence in the media. The latter, in particular, contributed to the defeat of his party in the elections of 1994.

Andrew Ludanyi

Further reading

Borbandi, Gyula. *Emigració és magyarország: 1985–1995.* Zurich, 1996.

Kurtán, Sándor et al., eds. *Magyarország politikai évkönyve.* Budapest, 1990, 1991, 1992.

Molnár, Éva, ed. *Hungary: Essential Facts Figures & Pictures.* Budapest, 1995.

Tökés, Rudolf L. *Hungary's Negotiated Revolution: Economic Reform, Social Change and Political Succession, 1957–1990.* Cambridge, 1996.

See also Hungarian Revolution of 1956; János Kádár; Law and Codification; Warsaw Pact

Anti-Comintern Pact

Agreement among Japan, Germany, and Italy, initially directed against the USSR, that evolved into the World War II–era Axis alliance. Germany and Japan concluded the Anti-Comintern Pact on November 25, 1936. The pact was aimed against the Communist International (Comintern) and indirectly against the USSR. In a secret protocol, both parties pledged neutrality if either were attacked by the Soviet Union. Several multinational anti-Communist commissions were to be set up under the terms of this agreement, but none were ever created. The pact also gave its signatories some potential leverage in their relations with the Western democracies, especially Britain. Italy adhered to the pact on November 6, 1937. At various times the Germans tried to interest Great Britain in joining the pact and, in 1939, Hitler sought to impose membership on Poland. Both London and Warsaw refused these offers. Hungary adhered to the pact at the end of 1938, and Spain subsequently joined in March 1939. Manchukuo (Japanese-occupied Manchuria) joined that year as well. In November 1941 Bulgaria, the collaborationist Nanking regime in Japanese-occupied China, Nazi-occupied Denmark, Finland, Romania, and Slovakia also subscribed to the pact.

Teddy J. Uldricks

Further reading

Weinberg, Gerhard L. *The Foreign Policy of Hitler's Germany,* vol. 1, *Diplomatic Revolution in Europe, 1933–36,* and vol. 2, *Starting World War II, 1937–1939.* Chicago, 1970, 1980.

See also Axis; Comintern; World War II

Antifascism

An important component of resistance to the Axis powers before and during World War II. Antifascism originated in the Soviet Union's reaction to the rise of Nazi Germany in the 1930s. In the 1920s Soviet leaders directed European

A Communists to oppose "bourgeois" parties and promote the goals of communism. But the rise of Nazi Germany and its explicitly anti-Communist ethos forced a reconsideration of this tactic. Following the 1933 burning of the German Reichstag in Berlin, for which Bulgarian Communist Georgi Dimitrov (1882–1949) was tried and convicted in absentia, the 1935 Comintern (Communist Third International) congress decreed that henceforth Communists were to support the leadership of those capitalist states committed to the defeat of Nazism and Italian fascism. After 1935, "popular front," or antifascist, coalitions formed against Germany and Italy, notably in France and Spain.

Although antifascism proved ineffectual in Europe, it played a crucial role in the outcome of the war in the Balkans, especially in Yugoslavia. Upon the 1941 Axis invasion of Yugoslavia and the creation of Ante Pavelić's (1889–1959) "independent" Croatian state, two resistance movements emerged. One was the Chetnik forces, led by Dragoljub Mihailović (1893–1946). As Serbs who had supported King Alexander (1888–1934) in prewar Yugoslavia, they did not include non-Serbs in their ranks and maintained close ties with King Peter's (1923–1970) government-in-exile in London.

The other group, the Partisans, made the antifascist/popular front strategy the centerpiece of their recruitment. Although the leadership was primarily Communist, they welcomed all political persuasions and, most significantly, all nationalities. Traveling through Croatia listening to Serbian peasants tell of Pavelić's execution squads in the villages, Partisan stalwart Milovan Djilas (1911–95) gradually became aware of "the extraordinary bond between my ideas and the destinies of my people—a bond not against the bourgeoisie but against the aggressors whose killing of 'aliens' and of innocents was a confirmation of the 'idea,' if not indeed its real aim." The Partisans' leader, Josip Broz Tito (1892–1980), was of mixed Croat-Slovene origin; their rallying cry, "Death to fascism, Freedom to the people," captured the spirit of the movement and its appeal in a war-torn land.

Partisan tactics reflected a similar commitment to the antifascist concept. The Chetniks shrank from attacking the enemy on a large scale because they feared the impact of massive reprisals on the Serb population; Tito ordered all-out attacks on the enemy whenever and however possible. In the Partisan ranks, it was understood that no nationality's lives were more valuable than others in fighting to expel the occupiers.

As the Axis powers weakened, the key question for all Yugoslavs concerned the movement that represented the best foundation for postwar Yugoslavia. Here the Partisans' antifascism again had a crucial impact. The Partisan administrative body, the Anti-Fascist Council (AVNOJ), had representatives of all nationalities and parties. At its first meeting in November 1942, it declared itself in favor of free elections and a federal Yugoslavia after the war. By contrast, the Chetniks promised more Serbian centralist rule, an unacceptable future for most non-Serbs. Only the inclusive character of the Partisans' activities promised the creation of a truly new Yugoslavia.

No one doubted that the Communist Party would dominate postwar Yugoslav politics; it had predominated in the Partisan leadership. But the national component of Yugoslav antifascism had always been most important, and only the Communists offered an end to national hostilities.

Brigit Farley

Further reading

Djilas, Milovan. *Wartime.* New York, 1977.
Jackson, Julian. *The Popular Front in France: Defending Democracy, 1934–1938.* Cambridge, 1988.
Jelavich, Barbara. *History of the Balkans,* vol. 2. Cambridge, 1983.
Tomasevich, Joso. *The Chetniks: War and Revolution in Yugoslavia, 1941–1945.* Stanford, California, 1975.

See also Alexander I Karadjordjević; Axis; Chetniks; Comintern; Communist Party of Yugoslavia; Georgi Dimitrov; Milovan Djilas; Dragoljub Mihailović; Ante Pavelić; Tito; World War II

Antonescu, Ion (1882–1946)

Romanian military officer and dictator during World War II. Born in Piteşti, Antonescu served as a major in World War I, and as military attaché to France and Britain in the 1920s. Chief of the general staff in 1934–35 and minister of national defense in 1937–38, he earned credibility as a capable officer opposed to court corruption. On September 4, 1940, Carol II (1893–1953) endowed him with unlimited political powers to deal with the crisis wrought by the Vienna Award, in which

Romania was forced to turn over part of Transylvania to Hungary. Antonescu formed an authoritarian government with himself as *Conducător* (leader) and the bulk of posts given to members of the Iron Guard, the ultranationalist/right-radical organization. Hoping to persuade Hitler to revise the Vienna Award, Antonescu, an ardent anti-Slav, led Romania into the Tripartite Pact in November 1940 and accepted German oversight of key areas of the Romanian economy. Annoyed by the Iron Guard's pogroms and political assassinations, he suppressed the order in February 1941 and made himself sole dictator. He joined the German invasion of the Soviet Union in June 1941 to restore Romanian control of Bessarabia and Northern Bukovina, commanding the Antonescu Army Group with the aid of a German staff. After the Battle of Stalingrad, he realized that Germany would lose the war and he opened secret contacts with the Allies. They proved fruitless. He was arrested and deposed on August 23, 1944, tried for treason, and shot at Jilava Prison on June 1, 1946.

Joseph M. McCarthy

Further reading

Buzatu, Gheorghe. *Mareşalul Antonescu in faţă istoriei,* 2 vols. Iaşi, 1990.

Hillgruber, Andreas. *Hitler, König Carol und Marschall Antonescu: Die deutsch-rumänischen Beziehungen, 1938–1944.* Wiesbaden, 1954.

Lauen, K. *Marschall Antonescu.* Essen, 1943.

Watts, Larry L. *Romanian Cassandra: Ion Antonescu and the Struggle for Reform, 1916–1941.* Boulder, Colorado, 1993.

See also Carol II; Adolf Hitler; Iron Guard; National Legionary State; Right-Radicalism; Transylvania; Transylvanian Dispute; Vienna Awards; World War II

"Apis" (Dragutin T. Dimitrijević) (1876–1917)

Serbian General Staff officer who organized the May 1903 coup d'état that returned the Karadjordjević family to power and was involved in the assassination of Archduke Franz Ferdinand (1863–1914) in Sarajevo in 1914. Of peasant origin, Dimitrijević was born in Belgrade in August 1876 and obtained his higher education at the military academy there. As a junior officer, "Apis" ("the Bull"), nicknamed for his powerful build and dynamic energy, organized an officer conspiracy against the Obrenović rulers, leading to their murders on May 29/June 11, 1903, and the enthronement of Peter Karadjordjević (1844–1921) as king of Serbia. Dominating the junior conspirators by personal magnetism and winning friends in high places, Dimitrijević spurred essential army reforms and remained from 1906 to 1914 Serbia's unofficial war minister and chief of the intelligence division of the General Staff (1913–15). As a revolutionary nationalist, he and his friends in the Serbian guerrilla movement in Macedonia organized the secret society Unification or Death! (Black Hand) to liberate and unite all Serbs by any means. In 1914 Dimitrijević helped direct the conspiracy by Young Bosnia, the revolutionary group that assassinated Franz Ferdinand in Sarajevo in Bosnia. He fought in several World War I campaigns and served on the Salonika Front, the Allied southern flank, as Third Army's chief of staff. In December 1916 the Serbian exile regime of Prince Regent Alexander Karadjordjević (1888–1934) suddenly imprisoned Dimitrijević and his chief colleagues in the Black Hand. Accused at a trial in Salonika (March–May 1917) of attempting to murder the prince regent and overthrow the Serbian regime, he and two colleagues were sentenced to death and executed near Salonika, Greece, in June 1917. In 1953, after the chief witnesses recanted their 1917 testimony, the Supreme Court of Serbia exonerated Dimitrijević and the others.

David MacKenzie

Further reading

Bogićević, Miloš. *Le Procès de Salonique.* Paris, 1927.

Jovanović, Slobodan. *Moji savremenici.* Windsor, Canada, 1962.

MacKenzie, David. *Apis: The Congenial Conspirator.* Boulder, Colorado, 1989.

Živanović, Milan Ž. *Pukovnik Apis. Solunski proces 1917.* Belgrade, 1955.

See also Black Hand; Franz Ferdinand; Alexander I Karadjordjević; Peter Karadjordjević; Salonika Front

Apostol, Gheorghe (1913–)

Member of the Romanian Communist Party (RCP) leadership until 1969 and an early rival of Nicolae Ceauşescu. Born in Galaţi County,

Apostol was a railroad worker like his father and became a Communist in 1930. He was imprisoned in Romania from 1936 to 1944, spending the war with Gheorghe Gheorghiu-Dej (1901–65), Ceauşescu (1918–89), and others in an internment camp at Tîrgu Jiu. This group formed the core of the Gheorghiu-Dej leadership, dominating the RCP from the early 1950s to the late 1960s.

When Gheorghiu-Dej died in 1965, most observers expected Apostol to succeed him. A longtime head of the trade unions, Apostol had served briefly as party first secretary in 1954–55, when Gheorghiu-Dej gave up the post temporarily. Although Apostol was evidently his mentor's choice as successor, the Political Bureau members chose the younger and apparently more pliable Ceauşescu. Thereafter Ceauşescu's clever personnel strategies continuously weakened Apostol as others were promoted around him, and in 1969 he was not reelected to the party Central Committee. He lived quietly until January 1989, when he publicly repudiated Ceauşescu in an early indication of the dictator's pending demise. Apostol and five other respected Communists demoted by Ceauşescu signed an open letter condemning the president for betraying both communism and the Romanian nation.

Mary Ellen Fischer

Further reading

Behr, Edward. *Kiss the Hand You Cannot Bite: The Rise and Fall of the Ceauşescus.* New York, 1991.

Fischer, Mary Ellen. *Nicolae Ceauşescu: A Study in Political Leadership.* Boulder, Colorado, 1989.

Ionescu, Ghita. *Communism in Rumania 1944–1969.* New York, 1964.

See also Nicolae Ceauşescu; Communist Party of Romania; Gheorghe Gheorghiu-Dej; Trade Unionism

Apponyi, Count Albert (1846–1933)

Hungarian politician. Born in Vienna, Apponyi was elected as a member of the parliament on the Deák Party ticket in 1872, but after 1875 participated in the short-lived Conservative Party. After 1878, he became a leader of a new opposition party, first called the United Opposition. This group aimed at defending landed interests, and it also gradually moved in the direction of enhancing Hungarian influence and power in the monarchy without however abandoning the fundamental tenets of the 1867 *Ausgleich* (Compromise), which created the Dual Monarchy of Austria-Hungary. During those years, Apponyi acquired the reputation of a spellbinding orator. In 1899 he joined the Liberal Party and became speaker of the parliament in 1901. In 1903, protesting Prime Minister Count István Tisza's (1861–1918) violation of parliamentary rules, he left the Liberal Party and joined the Party of Independence in 1904. This party was the prime force in the coalition that came to power in 1906. Apponyi held the position of minister for religious and educational affairs between 1906 and 1910. Although his controversial educational bill of 1907 instituted the system of free public schools and raised teachers' salaries, its emphasis on magyarization—the promotion of Magyar language and culture on the non-Hungarian minorities—provoked strong resentment, primarily on the part of the ethnic minorities. After World War I, Apponyi led the Hungarian delegation to the Paris Peace Conference (1919). From 1923 until his death in 1933, he represented Hungary at the League of Nations.

Gabor Vermes

Further reading

Gajzágó, László. *Le Comte Apponyi, juriste international.* Budapest, 1943.

Kornis, Gyula. *Apponyi Világnézete.* Budapest, 1935.

Pethő, Sándor. *Gróf Apponyi Albert.* Budapest, 1926.

See also *Ausgleich;* Ethnic Minorities; League of Nations; Magyarization; Paris Peace Conference; István Tisza

April Uprising (1876)

Bulgarian revolt (May 1876 [new calendar]). The Bosnian crisis of 1875 incited the Bulgarian Revolutionary Central Committee (BRCC) in its Romanian exile to wage warfare against the Turks. By that time, the BRCC had managed to set up a network of military structures in some one hundred settlements of what it called the "revolutionary districts" of Turnovo, Vratsa, Sliven, and Plovdiv. At a clandestine meeting of April 10–13 in the Sredna Gora Mountains in central Bulgaria, a large-scale uprising was scheduled for mid-May. Owing to a lack of coordination within the group, however, fighting broke out on April 20 in the town of Koprivshtitsa.

The poorly organized revolt received little support from the Bulgarian population, but it triggered a brutal reaction by regular and irregular Ottoman troops. For example, in the Rhodope mountain villages of Bratsigovo, Perushtitsa, and Batak, massacres against the civilian Bulgarian population—with several thousand casualties—took place. Within four weeks, Ottoman security forces were again in full control of all Bulgarian *vilayets* (provinces). Nevertheless, the April Uprising became a prominent topic in Bulgarian patriotic historiography and literature, a striking example of nationalist distortion by exaggeration for chosen glory and chosen trauma at the same time.

In political terms, the April Uprising (and especially the subsequent atrocities by the Ottomans) was instrumental in promoting the Bulgarian national cause on the international level, particularly in Great Britain and Russia. Relying on eyewitness accounts of the massacre at Batak, the Liberal British ex-prime minister William E. Gladstone (1809–98) published his famous brochure "Bulgarian Horrors." Within weeks, it sold tens of thousands of copies, and by influencing European public opinion, it brought about a change in Britain's pro-Ottoman policy in the Eastern Question.

Stefan Troebst

Further reading

"Aprilsko vustanie 1876 g.," in Veska Nikolova and Milen Kumanov, eds., *Kratuk istoricheski spravochnik,* vol. 3, *Bulgariia.* Sofia, 1983, 23–29.

Gladstone, William Ewart. "Bulgarian Horrors and the Question of the East." London, 1876.

K'osev, Aleksandar. "Historische Tatsachen, Nationalideologie und Nationalliteratur oder zum Thema der Befreiung Bulgariens in der bulgarischen Literatur," in K.D. Grothusen, ed., *110 Jahre Wiedererrichtung des bulgarischen Staates 1878–1988.* Munich, 1990, 47–55.

Stoyanoff, Zachary. *Pages from the Autobiography of a Bulgarian Insurgent,* trans. and intro. by M.W. Potter. London, 1913.

See also Bulgarian Massacres; Eastern Question; Rhodope Mountains

Architecture

Although Eastern Europe has produced a rich and distinguished architectural legacy over the past two centuries, until very recently the standard histories of architecture largely ignored the region or portrayed it as both provincial and backward. Since the 1970s, however, scholars in the West have begun to show increasing interest in the area's architecture, especially in the ongoing search for regional and national identity, which has been one of the hallmarks of its history.

Despite the diversity of architectural forms and ideas in the countries of Eastern Europe, some common themes and directions can be charted. In the period immediately after the Congress of Vienna in 1815, the monumental architecture of the region was dominated by the attempt to forge a new, purified aesthetic based on classical forms and motifs. In Poland, for example, Jakub Kubicki (1758–1833) and Florence-born Antonio Corazzi (1792–1877) transformed Warsaw with a series of neoclassical works, including the Staszic Palace (1820–23), the Wiełki Theater (1826–33), and the palaces in Dzierzynski Square (1823–30). Similar buildings, often drawing inspiration from the Austrian and German Biedermeier (understated neoclassicism), were also constructed in Prague, Budapest, and other large cities.

By the middle of the nineteenth century, however, architects throughout the region, like their counterparts in the West, began to revive other historical styles, beginning with the Gothic and Romanesque and moving on to the Renaissance and Baroque. In some instances these works—such as the Czech National Theater (1868–83) in Prague designed by Josef Zítek (1832–1909), the Hungarian Parliament (1885–1902) in Budapest designed by Imre Steindl (1839–1902), or the Slowacki-Theater (1881–93) in Kraków designed by Jan Zawiejski (1854–1922)—were closely linked with attempts to forge new national identities and to assert independence from Austrian, German, Russian, or Turkish domination. Leading local artists and sculptors were enlisted to decorate the buildings with scenes and symbols celebrating past and present national achievements. But in most cases the architectonic language of these monumental buildings remained that of historicism, barely distinguishable from similar works in other parts of Europe.

A During the 1880s and 1890s, however, architects throughout Eastern Europe began to revive local folk forms and motifs. Perhaps the most striking example of this trend can be found in the works of Hungarian architect Ödön Lechner (1845–1914), who combined brightly colored Magyar folk ornament with historical and Jugendstil (Art Nouveau) forms to forge a unique architectural expression. Comparable experiments with folk motifs were also found in the works of many other architects after 1900, including Stanisław Witkiewicz (1885–1935), Czesław Domaniewski (1861–1936), and Jarosław Wojciechowski (1874–1942) in Poland; Dušan Jurkovič (1868–1947) in Slovakia; and Aladár Árkay (1868–1932), Károly Kós (1883–1977), István Medgyaszay (1877–1959), Móric Pogány (1878–1942), and Ferenc Pfaff (1878–1945) in Hungary. Other architects explored the possibilities of a pure, unalloyed Art Nouveau idiom. In Prague, just prior to the turn of the century, for example, Bedřich (Friedrich) Ohmann (1858–1927) and Jan Kotěra (1871–1923) introduced a new figurative language that featured highly stylized vegetal and human forms. Similar Art Nouveau works—inspired by French, Belgian, German, and Austrian examples—were built in cities throughout the region. In many instances, these buildings displayed a marked unity of style, with every element—from the ornament to the fixtures to the furnishings—subordinated to a single design concept. After 1904, Art Nouveau decorative style became simpler, with a greater emphasis on the use of geometric forms and patterning. This trend reflected a new spirit of rationalism that had a potent influence on younger architects of the time, especially in Hungary and the Czech lands.

The period between 1900 and 1914 witnessed a continued turn away from Austrian, German, and Russian influences as architects throughout Eastern Europe sought new sources of inspiration as a means to assert their independence. One of the best examples of this trend can be found in the work of the Czech cubists, including Josef Gočár (1880–1945), Josef Chochol (1880–1956), and Pavel Janák (1882–1956), who looked to French cubist painting for creative stimulus, melding it with local late medieval vaulting and Bohemian ornamental patterns to generate a singular and resonant brand of modernism. Other leading architects, among them the Hungarians Béla Lajta (1873–1920) and József Vágó (1877–1947) and

the Czechs Otakar Novotný (1880–1959) and Emil Králík (1880–1946), rejected decorative elements altogether, seeking to create an architecture that would better reflect the spirit of the rapidly expanding and modernizing cities of the region. By gradually stripping away traditional ornamental motifs, they produced a sleek new modern aesthetic that in many ways anticipated the functionalist architecture of the 1920s and 1930s.

Not all architects in the region, however, took such radical steps. Many continued to work within the historical framework, combining traditional motifs with modernist concepts of design to foster a new but more widely acceptable brand of architecture. One notable example of this impulse was a modernized classicism popular throughout the region from the turn of the century to the advent of World War II.

The period after World War I brought sweeping changes for the architecture of the region. With the collapse of the Russian, Austrian, German, and Ottoman Empires, architects in the newly established nations of Eastern Europe redoubled their efforts to forge their own distinct identities. In Czechoslovakia, the most industrialized country in the region, this search for national identity led to a radical rejection of the past. Inspired by the work and ideas of Le Corbusier (1887–1965), the German Bauhaus, Russian constructivism, and the Dutch de Stijl movement, many of the country's leading architects adopted what came to be known as the International Style, and Brno and Prague became important centers of the new aesthetic. Between 1925 and 1940, Czech and Slovak architects, including Bohuslav Fuchs (1895–1972), Josef Kranz (1901–68), Arnošt Wiesner (1890–1971), and Jiří Kroha (1893–1974), produced a broad range of innovative buildings widely admired in progressive circles in the rest of Europe, while theorists such as Karel Teige (1900–51) published in many of the leading avant-garde journals. In Hungary, too, the International Style took firm hold, particularly in Budapest, where architects such as Farkas Molnár (1897–1945), Fred Forbát (1897–1972), and József Fischer (1901–95) erected numerous examples of the style. Romania was also a fertile field for modernist experiments during the interwar years. But while a number of International Style works were erected in Bucharest and the other large cities of the country, Romanian architects, led by Marcel Iancu (Jancu) (1895–1984) and Horia Creangă

(1892–1943), investigated the possibilities of a wide array of modern ideas, and Romanian architecture of the period—to a greater degree than was the case in either Czechoslovakia or Hungary—continued to be characterized by a complex blending of various styles and themes.

Yet not all the region's architects subscribed to the new aesthetic currents. Architects working in Bulgaria, Yugoslavia, and Poland were slower to reject historical and peasant traditions, and much of what they produced seemed, in the context of the times, badly outdated. An exception among these more conservative architects was the Slovene Jože Plečnik (1872–1957), who was able to blend classical, vernacular, and modern elements to create a unique form-language that has been widely admired in recent years.

Despite the reluctance of conservative architects in some regions to adopt the language of modernism, by the eve of World War II International Style buildings could be found throughout Eastern Europe. Although some examples of the monumental classicism popular in Stalinist Russia were erected after the war, most notably the Palace of Culture in Warsaw (1952–56), designed by Lev Rudnev (1885–1956), the International Style and its offshoots remained the dominant architectural expression through the 1970s. Beginning in the 1960s, however, younger architects, influenced by the growing dissatisfaction with modernism that manifested itself throughout the architectural world, began to seek alternatives, attempting to find a new aesthetic that combined the best of past and present. Architects such as Hungary's Imre Makovecz (1935–), whose works draw on folk and local historical traditions, have helped to forge new regional and national expressions. This trend continued into the 1990s and has led to an explosion of new architectural forms and ideas.

Although many buildings in Eastern Europe fell into disrepair during the decades of Communist rule, the architectural heritage in many parts of the region was actually better preserved than in the cities of Western Europe and the United States, where speculation and urban renewal took their toll on older buildings. Several Communist governments—most notably in Poland, Czechoslovakia, and Hungary—also undertook extensive programs to restore older works. In the period after World War II the central core of Warsaw, which had been almost completely destroyed during the war, was meticulously rebuilt, and much of the old city in Prague was documented and preserved in the 1960s and 1970s. The notable exception to this trend was Romania, where during the last years of the regime of Nicolae Ceauşescu (1918–89) many towns and villages were systematically destroyed in an ill-conceived effort to revitalize the cities and resettle much of the rural population.

Christopher Long

Further reading

Beldiman, Alexandru, ed. *Bucharest in the 1920s–1940s: Between Avant-garde and Modernism*. Bucharest, 1993.

Bichev, Milko. *Architecture in Bulgaria from Ancient Times to the Late 19th Century*. Sofia, 1961.

Gerle, János, Attila Kovács, and Imre Makovecz. *A századforduló magyar építészet*. Budapest, 1990.

Gerö, Lászlo. *Magyar építészet a XIX. század végéig*. Budapest, 1954.

Giurescu, Dinu C. *The Razing of Romania's Past*. New York, 1989.

Ionesco, Grigore. *Histoire de l'architecture en Roumanie de la préhistoire à nos jours*. Bucharest, 1972.

Knox, Brian. *The Architecture of Poland*. London, 1971.

Leśnikowski, Wojciech, ed. *East European Modernism: Architecture in Czechoslovakia, Hungary and Poland between the Wars, 1919–1939*. New York, 1996.

Lisowski, Bohdan. *Modern Architecture in Poland*. Warsaw, 1968.

Moravánszky, Ákos. *Die Architektur der Donaumonarchie*. Berlin, 1988.

———. *Die Erneuerung der Baukunst: Wege zur Moderne in Mitteleuropa 1900–1940*. Salzburg, 1988.

Švácha, Rostislav. *The Architecture of New Prague, 1895–1945*. Cambridge, Massachusetts, 1995.

Vegesack, Alexander von, ed. *Czech Cubism: Architecture, Furniture, and Decorative Arts 1910–1925*. New York, 1992.

See also Albanian Art; Belgrade; Bratislava; Bucharest; Budapest; Bulgarian Art; Nicolae Ceauşescu; Croatian Art; Czech and Slovak Art; Hungarian Art; Macies Nowicki; Polish Art; Prague; Romanian Art; Serbian Art; Sofia; Tirana; Warsaw

Arghezi, Tudor (1880–1967)

One of the greatest Romanian poets of the twentieth century. As a young boy, Arghezi left home permanently after an argument with his father. All his life, beset by existential uncertainties, he pursued new self-definitions. Between 1900 and 1905, he tried the monastic life, whereupon in 1905 he went to Switzerland for five years, serving as a watchmaker's apprentice. Returning home in 1910, he embarked on an ambitious writing career. His poetry was recognized for its originality. Arghezi edited journals, the most important of which was *Bilete de papagal* (*Parakeet's Slips*).

His *Cuvinte potrivite* (*Matched Words,* 1927) remains perhaps his most important volume. In his other most significant collection, *Flori de mucigai* (*Flowers of Mildew,* 1931), Arghezi speaks frankly of the ugly. His sketches of the monk's life, the fauna of a prison, the denizens of politics attest to his talent as a social critic in a language both lyrical and satirical.

His personal life was marked by political perturbations, notably imprisonment in World War I in Văcărești monastery (which had been turned into a prison); during World War II he was jailed for a time at Tîrgu Jiu for protesting the German occupation.

In 1947 Arghezi received the National Prize for poetry. The authorities responded by placing him under house arrest and banning his works (1948–55), until on a state visit, the Indian vice president cited Arghezi as one of the greatest poets in the world.

Charles M. Carlton

Further reading

Academia Republicii Socialiste România. *Dicționarul literaturii romăne de la origini pînă la 1900.* Bucharest, 1979.

Bantaş, A. trans. *Tudor Arghezi: Poems.* Bucharest, 1983.

Călinescu, G. *Istoria literaturii romăne de la origini pînă în prezent,* 2d ed., Bucharest, 1982.

Selected Poems of Tudor Arghezi, trans. by M. Impey and B. Swann. Princeton, New Jersey, 1976.

See also Romanian Literature

Armia Krajowa

Clandestine military force operating in German- and Soviet-occupied Poland during World War II.

The *Armia Krajowa* (AK, Home Army) had its origins in the waning days of the September 1939 campaign in the Poles' effort to continue the fight against the invading Germans. A secret military organization, *Służba Zwycięstwu Polski* (Service for Poland's Victory), was created. This was supplanted at war's end by the Związek Walki Zbrojnej (ZWZ, Union for Armed Struggle), which was formed by General Władysław Sikorski (1881–1943), premier of the Polish government-in-exile. To give the impression of a united front (although many different armed groups were active in occupied Poland), Sikorski ordered the name of the ZWZ changed to Home Army on February 14, 1942.

At its peak, the Home Army numbered more than 380,000 members. Lacking adequate weaponry, it still hampered the German war effort by disrupting supply lines and transport services. Its intelligence branch also obtained vital information about the development of German V-weapons, the rockets used against Great Britain.

With the approach of Soviet forces in 1943, the Home Army made plans for cooperation with the Red Army, provided that the latter recognized the Polish government-in-exile's authority within the boundaries of prewar Poland. In November the AK's leadership ordered the beginning of Operation Burza (Tempest), which called for increased diversionary activity in anticipation of a general uprising. In the spring and summer of 1944, AK units collaborated with Soviet forces, yet after the local defeat of the Germans, Home Army members were detained and officers deported by the Soviets. Against this background the AK launched the controversial Warsaw Uprising of August–October 1944. Intended to liberate the capital in the name of the government-in-exile before the arrival of the Soviets, the uprising failed and the Germans destroyed what was left of the city. The best AK soldiers and some 200,000 civilians also perished. Although Tempest continued in some western areas of Poland, the AK leadership dissolved the formation on January 19, 1945. Some 50,000 Home Army members who reported to the Soviet authorities were arrested and deported, while others remained underground as partisan detachments, operating through mid-1945.

The activities of the Armia Krajowa remain among the most sensitive issues in the historiography of Poland during World War II. Material abounds in Polish, although much of it is tendentious, apologetic, or tainted by ideological considerations.

Robert M. Ponichtera

Further reading

Armia Krajowa w dokumentach, ed. by Studium Polski Podziemnej, 6 vols. London, 1970–1989.

Documents on Polish-Soviet Relations, 1939–1945, ed. by the General Sikorski Historical Institute, 2 vols. London, 1961–1967.

Komorowski, Tadeusz. *The Secret Army.* New York, 1951.

Korbonski, Stefan. *The Polish Underground State.* New York, 1981.

Polskie Siły Zbrojne w drugiej wojnie światowej, vol. 3. *Armia Krajowa.* London, 1950.

See also Nazi–Polish War; Red Army; Władysław Sikorski; Warsaw Uprising; World War II

Arrow Cross

The most popular movement of the radical right in Hungary during the interwar period. The movement was inseparable from its leader, Ferenc Szálasi (1891–1946), who as Pártvezető (Party-Leader) determined its ideology of "Hungarism." An eccentric who consulted a clairvoyant, Szálasi was shocked by the Great Depression. Out of that shock arose the Arrow Cross. Szálasi's Kárpát-Duna-Nagy-Haza (KNDH, Carpatho-Danubian-Great-Fatherland) movement stood for the premises of historic Hungary, including Croatia and Bosnia-Hercegovina. Although he was willing to grant the nationalities greater autonomy than other rightist movements, Szálasi was convinced that all would wish to live under Hungarian supremacy. His movement was to be a one-party, corporate, authoritarian state. Moreover, Hungarism espoused a classless society consisting of workers, peasants, and the intelligentsia. Other parties and movements professed similar ideas. What made this more dynamic was Szálasi's sincerity. Although the strongest support for the Arrow Cross came from workers, miners, and the officer corps, Szálasi was concerned about all poor, destitute people. Thus, he drew mass support as a Hungarian nationalist even though he himself was of Armenian-Ruthenian origin.

Although Szálasi was a racist and an anti-Semite who considered Jews a people not "capable of having roots in the soil, capable of having a homeland," he was not a fanatic (unlike many of his followers). He rejected Jews passively. Jews should merely leave. He even opposed the 1944 deportations of Jews to concentration camps. He was also suspicious of the Nazis. His inflexible adherence to the idea of Hungarism alienated not only the Germans but other Right-Radical allies of his. As a result, the Arrow Cross lost many allies and followers. In 1944 those views changed dramatically.

In October 1944, with the Russians 60–80 miles (100–135 km) from Budapest, the Germans put Arrow Cross in power in Hungary. Szálasi and Arrow Cross followed the Germans unconditionally, and the organization's supporters unleashed an anti-Semitic reign of terror upon the country.

Nicholas M. Nagy-Talavera

Further reading

Kállay, Nicholas. *Hungarian Premier.* New York, 1954.

Lackó, Niklós. *Nyilasok, Nemzetiszocialisták, 1935–1944.* Budapest, 1966.

Nagy-Talavera, Nicholas. *The Green Shirts and the Others.* Stanford, California, 1970.

See also Right Radicalism; Ferenc Szálasi

Askenazy, Szymon (1865–1935)

Historian, publicist, and Poland's first plenipotentiary to the League of Nations (1920–23). A professor of history at the University of Lemberg in the years before World War I, Askenazy is best known for creating his own school of historical thought. Rejecting the pessimistic scholarship of the Kraków school of historians, which maintained that setbacks in Polish history were the result of the Poles' own arrogance or incompetence, Askenazy instead stressed the heroic character of his country's past. Since he believed that the early nineteenth century was a particularly patriotic epoch, Askenazy also insisted that Polish historians begin researching the postpartition history of the Polish lands. His own work on this period included biographies of Prince Józef Poniatowski and the revolutionary Walerian Łukasiński, monographs that emphasized the abilities and heroism of Poles.

Askenazy's writings appealed to the intelligentsia of Austrian Galicia and contributed to the growth of Polish patriotism in that region in the early twentieth century. Several of his students were closely associated with the various Polish paramilitary organizations then based in Galicia.

Askenazy lived in Switzerland during World War I, where he copublished a journal dedicated to Polish affairs. After the war, he wrote *Gdańsk a Polska (Danzig and Poland,* 1921), a work translated into several European languages. It aimed to influence Western opinion for the assignment of the port of Danzig (Gdańsk) to Poland.

Conflicts with the younger generation of Polish historians and attacks by the Polish political right (because of his Jewish heritage) prevented Askenazy from receiving a full professorship and severely restricted his activity in post-1918 Poland.

Robert M. Ponichtera

Further reading

Dutkiewicz, Józef. *Szymon Askenazy i jego szkoła.* Warsaw, 1958.

Rose, William J. "Szymon Askenazy." *Slavonic and East European Review* 14 (January 1936): 425–28.

Zahorski, Andrzej. Introduction to Szymon Ashkenazy, *Napoléon a Polska.* Reprint. Warsaw, 1994.

See also Walerian Łukasiński

Auschwitz

German name for the Polish town of Oświęcim (located thirty-seven miles [sixty km] west of Kraków), near which the largest and most infamous Nazi concentration and extermination camp was established during World War II. On April 27, 1940, SS chief Heinrich Himmler (1900–1945) ordered the establishment of a large concentration camp near Oświęcim. In June 1940 the first transport of Polish political prisoners was brought to the camp. In March 1941 its population reached 10,900. Until the fall of 1941, Poles constituted a majority among the prisoners of Auschwitz.

In March 1941 Himmler ordered the establishment of an additional, larger camp in the area. The construction of Auschwitz II began 1.9 miles (3 km) west of the original camp. The Germans destroyed several Polish villages, among them Brzezinka (German, Birkenau) and enclosed a large area of about 15.5 square miles (40 sq km) with a system of barbed-wire fences. In 1942 the Germans started the construction of Auschwitz III, a labor camp producing synthetic oil and rubber for I.G. Farben and other German enterprises. The Auschwitz complex cooperated with and controlled forty-five subcamps built in Upper Silesia. In August 1944 the total population of Auschwitz I, II, and III reached 105,168 prisoners plus 50,000 inmates in the satellite camps.

This constituted only a fraction of those who were brought to Auschwitz. In September 1941 the first victims were killed with Zyklon B in a small experimental gas chamber in Auschwitz I. In August 1942 the systematic killing of Jews started in four large gas chambers of Birkenau. The chambers resembled shower rooms and each of them had a capacity to kill 6,000 prisoners a day. Auschwitz became the main Nazi center of mass extermination of the Jews. Between one and two million people perished there. Most of them were Jews but also about 20,000 Gypsies, over 100,000 Poles, and thousands of representatives of other nations died in Auschwitz. About one-quarter of European Jewry was murdered there.

Trains transported Jews from the countries of German-occupied Europe to the railroad platform of Birkenau. After the "selection," a vast majority of the inmates, the so-called non-able-bodied, mainly children and older people, went directly to the gas chambers. The able-bodied were registered and given striped prisoners' garb. Altogether 405,000 prisoners of various nationalities were registered by 1945. From March 1943, numbers were tattooed on the left forearms of adults and left thighs of children, while Soviet POWs were tattooed on their chests. Most of the prisoners were sent to forced work to the subcamps. Beginning in 1941, a Polish resistance movement operated inside the camp, and in the spring of 1943, it developed into an international organization. On January 18, 1945, the Germans ordered the evacuation of the remaining 58,000 inmates to escape the Soviet offensive. The camp—with 7,500 remaining prisoners—was liberated by the Red Army nine days later.

Piotr Wróbel

Further reading

Encyclopedia of the Holocaust, ed. by Israel Gutman, vol. 1. New York, 1990, pp. 107–19.

Gutman, Yisrael and Michael Berenbaum, eds. *Anatomy of the Auschwitz Death Camp.* Bloomington, Indiana, 1994.

Sehn, Jan. *Oświęcim-Brzezinka Concentration Camp.* Warsaw, 1957.

See also Gypsies; Holocaust; Jews; Red Army; World War II

Ausgleich

Compromise in 1867 creating the Dual Monarchy of Austria-Hungary. Vienna exacted harsh reprisals and imposed an absolutist regime on Hungary following the revolution and war of 1848–49. The reigning "forfeiture theory" stated that Hungary had forfeited its constitutional rights by rebelling and deserved to be treated as a conquered country. Baron Alexander von Bach (1813–93), Austrian minister of the interior, subjected Hungary to a centralizing, Germanizing rule, but military losses in Italy, financial crisis in Vienna, and resistance in Hungary led to his dismissal in 1859. Ferenc Deák's (1803–76) "Easter article" of 1865 indicated Hungary's willingness to negotiate and, after Franz Joseph (1830–1916) reconvened the diet, negotiations began in 1866. Gyula Andrássy (1823–90) formed a government for Hungary in February 1867, and in May the Hungarian diet passed the "Compromise" law (1867: XIII). On June 12, four days after being crowned in Budapest, Franz Joseph signed the law.

Under the terms of the *Ausgleich,* the monarch was at once the "Emperor of Austria" and "Apostolic King of Hungary." The monarch retained significant powers, especially over the army. Both halves of the monarchy had their own prime ministers, cabinets, bicameral legislatures, and territorial armies. The *Ausgleich* gave Hungary full internal independence while still allowing for common affairs. "Pragmatic affairs," based on the Pragmatic Sanction of 1722–23, the succession law that recognized the unity of the Hungarian lands, created common foreign and defense ministries, as well as a finance ministry responsible for their budgets. While the common ministers were in theory accountable only to "delegations" from the Austrian and Hungarian parliaments, in practice they answered to the monarch. "Affairs of common concern" covered economic policy, trade, customs, and taxes. The "quota" determined the contribution of each half to the financing of the common affairs. The economic provisions of the *Ausgleich* were to be renewed every ten years, giving rise to long and painful negotiations. With the *Ausgleich,* Vienna abandoned its vision of a unitary empire, while Hungary abandoned its dream of full independence. Although the *Ausgleich* had

no shortage of critics, the Dual Monarchy lasted for over half a century.

Robert Nemes

Further reading
Barany, George. "Ungarns Verwaltung: 1848–1918," in *Die Habsburgermonarchie,* vol. 2, ed. by Adam Wendruszka and Peter Urbantisch. Vienna, 1975, 304–468.

László, Péter. "The Dualist Character of the 1867 Hungarian Settlement," in György Ránki, ed. *Hungarian History—World History.* Budapest, 1984, 85–164.

Szabad, György. *Hungarian Political Trends between the Revolution and the Compromise (1849–1867).* Budapest, 1977.

See also Gyula Andrássy, Sr.; Baron Alexander von Bach; Ferenc Deák; Dualism; Dual Monarchy; Franz Joseph; Hungarian War for Independence; Revolutions of 1848

Austroslavism

A political movement in the Austro-Hungarian Empire, the aim of which was to achieve equality of the empire's Slav peoples (Czechs, Slovaks, Poles, Ukrainians, Serbs, Croats, and Slovenes) with its dominant peoples—Germans and Hungarians (Magyars). The movement originated in the year of the "springtime of nations"—1848—as a response of the Slavs to the movement for German national unification and also to the movement for Hungary's independence. Its ideological basis was provided by the Czech historian František Palacký (1798–1876) in his letter of April 11, 1848, to the promoters of German national unification, who had invited the peoples of the states of the German confederation to elect representatives to a constituent German National Assembly at Frankfurt. The confederation, which had been established at the Congress of Vienna in 1815, included Austria with its Slav peoples. Palacký declined the invitation on the grounds that the Germans, who claimed the right to unite on the basis of the principle of national self-determination, could not deny it to the Czechs and other Austrian Slavs who did not wish to be incorporated in a united Germany. The Austrian Empire, if democratized and federalized, would provide a safe haven to the Austrian Slavs against the threat to them of both Pan-Germanism and Russian

Pan-Slavism, he argued. "If the Austrian state did not long exist, we would have to create it in the interest of Europe, indeed, of humanity itself," he concluded.

To counter the convocation of the German National Assembly at Frankfurt, Palacký and his collaborator, journalist Karel Havlíček (1821–56), took the lead in calling a Slav congress in Prague to propose reform of the Austrian Empire, giving the Slavs due representation in it. Before it completed its resolutions, however, the revolutions of 1848 in the empire were crushed, the congress was dispersed, and a repressive imperial dictatorship was established.

Although Austroslavism failed as a concrete program, it continued to animate Austrian politics as an idea. The adoption of universal (male) suffrage in the Austrian half of the empire in 1907 raised the Slavs' hopes of gaining equality through the ballot box, since of the empire's population of about fifty-one million (according to the census of 1910), they numbered about twenty-four million (against twenty-two million Germans and Magyars). In 1908 a "Neo-Slav" Congress met in Prague, but the hopes it raised for greater cultural and economic cooperation among the empire's Slavic subjects foundered, perhaps because of the tensions raised between the empire's peoples by the approach of World War I.

Victor S. Mamatey

Further reading

Beneš, Edvard. *Úvahy o slovanství. Hlavní problémy slovanské politiky.* London, n.d. Trans. into French as *Où vont les Slaves.* Paris, 1948.

Vyšný, Paul. *Neo-Slavism and the Czechs, 1898–1914.* Cambridge, 1977.

See also Congress of Vienna; Karel Havlíček; Neo-Slavism; František Palacký; Pan-Germanism; Pan-Slavism; Prague Slav Congress; Revolutions of 1848; Trialism

Averescu, Alexandru (1859–1938)

Romanian marshal, hero of World War I, and premier. Averescu rose from humble origins, through the ranks, to become an officer, taking his higher military education in Italy. His outstanding ability brought him rapid advancement: general staff (1888); command of the War College (1894); military attaché in Berlin (1895–98); minister of war (1907–9); and army chief of staff in the Second Balkan War (1913). He was generally acknowledged as Romania's most able general in World War I for his success in the battles of Mărăşti and Oituz (1917). Immensely popular among soldiers and civilians as the "people's general," he was not well liked by the government of Ion I.C. Brătianu (1864–1927) and many of his peers, who considered him arrogant and vain. He became premier briefly in February 1918 in an unsuccessful attempt to obtain more lenient terms when peace became inevitable. Unsuccessful, he gave way to Alexandru Marghiloman (1854–1925) and founded a political coalition, the League of the People, which continued after the war as the Peoples Party. He returned as premier twice briefly in the 1920s. Commentators generally dismiss his political career as an attempt to exploit his military reputation for the benefit of personal power. Nevertheless, Averescu remains one of Romania's preeminent military heroes.

Glenn E. Torrey

Further reading

Averescu, Alexandru. *Notiţe zilnice din război,* 2 vols. Bucharest, 1937; reprint, 1992.

Cioroui, N. Stefan. *O viaţă prestigiu, Al. Averescu, mareşal al Românei.* Bucharest, 1938.

Vlădescu-Mihail, C. *General Averescu. Semănătorul de ofensive.* Bucharest, 1923.

See also Balkan Wars; Ion I.C. Brătianu; Mărăşti-Mărăşeşti-Oituz; Alexandru Marghiloman; World War I

Axis

Alliance of Germany, Italy, and Japan (as well as satellite states later) in World War II. The Axis evolved gradually. When Adolf Hitler (1889–1945) first came to power, Italy stood with Britain and France in opposing any expansion of Germany. By 1936, however, a combination of events, including Western opposition to the Italian invasion of Ethiopia and a growing personal affinity between the Nazi and Fascist dictators, caused Benito Mussolini (1883–1945) to reverse his policy. In the fall of that year, Germany and Italy agreed to cooperate in European affairs, a step that Mussolini characterized as a new Rome-Berlin Axis around which the politics of Europe would revolve in the future.

Germany and Japan concluded the Anti-Comintern Pact on November 25, 1936, aimed against the Communist International (Comintern) and indirectly against the USSR. In a secret protocol, both parties pledged neutrality if either were attacked by the Soviet Union. Italy subscribed to the pact on November 6, 1937, and, at various times subsequently so, too, did Bulgaria, the collaborationist Nanking regime in Japanese-occupied China, German-occupied Denmark, Finland, Hungary, Romania, Slovakia, and Spain.

Germany and Italy signed the Pact of Steel on May 22, 1939, each promising assistance if the other were attacked by a third power. Japan declined to join the mutual assistance pact at this time, but Germany's stunning victories over Poland, Denmark, Norway, Belgium, Holland, and France in the first year of the war changed Japan's thinking. Japanese leaders concluded that the moment was auspicious for a more aggressively expansionist policy and for closer cooperation with Germany. The Tripartite Pact was signed on September 27, 1940, by Germany, Italy, and Japan, mainly to forestall American entry into the war. This pact failed to intimidate the United States into dropping either its support for the British war effort or its resistance to Japanese advances in the Far East. In November 1940 the Germans offered participation in the pact, and thus membership in the Axis alliance, to the USSR. Stalin (1879–1953) flirted with the idea but only on terms unacceptable to Berlin. Both sides knew that their cooperation, under the provisions of the Nazi-Soviet Pact, was no more than a temporary truce before an inevitable conflict. However, Soviet Russia continued to be a major supplier for the German war effort until the Nazi attack on the USSR in June 1941. Hungary, Romania, and Slovakia signed the Tripartite Pact in November 1940. In March 1941 Bulgaria adhered to the pact, as did Yugoslavia (though that act sparked a military coup in Belgrade, repudiation of the pact, and a German invasion in quick succession). Croatia joined on June 15, 1941.

The Axis was never a closely cooperative alliance. Although the Germans treated the Italians and Japanese with diplomatic courtesy, Nazi doctrine viewed these Axis partners as racial inferiors. Moreover, none of the three main Axis allies pursued a concerted wartime strategy. Just the opposite; each presented the others with a series of unpleasant surprises. Hitler attacked Poland in 1939, barely three months after telling Mussolini there would be no war before 1943, and, with the Nazi-Soviet Pact, he astonished the Japanese, who had thought that their cooperation with Germany was directed against the USSR. Tokyo repaid this betrayal by signing a nonaggression treaty with Moscow on April 13, 1941, just two months before the German attack on the Soviet Union. Similarly, Mussolini's botched invasion of Greece in the winter of 1940 forced Hitler to delay his attack on the USSR to campaign in the Balkans, a delay that fatally compromised Operation Barbarossa. In the same vein, Japan permitted American aid for the Soviet war effort to cross the Pacific largely unhindered, in exchange for a tacit agreement that Moscow would not let the Americans bomb Japanese cities from bases in the Soviet Far East.

Teddy J. Uldricks

Further reading

Mack Smith, Denis. *Mussolini's Roman Empire.* New York, 1976.

Meskill, Johanna. *Hitler and Japan: The Hollow Alliance.* New York, 1966.

Steinberg, Jonathan. *All or Nothing: The Axis and the Holocaust, 1941–1943.* New York, 1990.

Weinberg, Gerhard L. *The Foreign Policy of Hitler's Germany,* vol. 1, *Diplomatic Revolution in Europe, 1933–36,* and vol. 2, *Starting World War II, 1937–1939.* Chicago, 1970, 1980.

———. *A World at Arms: A Global History of World War II.* Cambridge, 1994.

See also Anti-Comintern Pact; Barbarossa; Comintern; Molotov-Ribbentrop Pact; Stalin; World War II

B

Babits, Mihály (1883–1941)

Hungarian poet, novelist, essayist, translator, and key figure in the poetic revival of the early twentieth century. Education helped to form Babits's humanism in a world of political conflicts, misery, and alienation. A student of the classics, languages, philosophy, and literature, Babits worked as a high school teacher in a number of provincial towns, until he was called to Budapest to help edit *Nyugat* (*West*), the foremost Hungarian literary journal of the time. His poems and translations had already begun to be published while he was at the university, but it was Babits's association with *Nyugat* that would have the greatest influence on his life and career as a writer. In 1929 he became its chief editor, a position that gave him tremendous power and influence as an arbiter of literary taste.

Babits's literary output was broad and prolific. His works reflected his classical education, the *l'art pour l'art* (art for the sake of art) aesthetic, and the eclecticism prevalent at the turn of the century. His philosophical and intellectual attitude was a by-product of the shocking and alienating effects of war, the turbulent political times in which he lived, as well as his own painful suffering from disease. Perhaps no other Hungarian writer was as familiar with world literature as was Babits. His artistry with the word has remained unmatched. At the same time, he uniquely captured the humanistic traits of the Hungarians that transcended politics and nationalism. Some of Babits's more important collections of verse are *Levelek Írisz koszorújából* (*Leaves from Iris' Wreath,* 1909); *Herceg, hátha megjön a tél is* (*Prince, What If Winter Comes,* 1911); *Nyugtalanság völgye* (*The Valley of Unrest,* 1920); *Sziget és Tenger* (*Island and Sea,* 1925); *Versenyt az esztendőkkel* (*Racing with the Years,* 1933); and *Jónás könyve* (*Book of Jonah,* 1941). His novels *Timár Virgil fia* (*The Son of Virgil Timar,* 1922) and *Halálfiai* (*The Sons of Death,* 1927) are literary classics, the former noted for its subtlety of plot, economy of style, and keen psychological observations, the latter depicting the decay of the traditional Hungarian gentry. Of his many translations of ancient and modern poetry, Dante's *Divina Commedia* excels in quality and beauty and was duly awarded the San Remo Prize by the Italian government in 1940 as the best foreign translation of Dante. Finally, out of his many critical essays on literature, *Európai irodalom története* (*A History of European Literature,* 1934) stands out as a synthesizing journey through European literature in which Babits makes clear his belief in the superiority of European civilization and exhibits his remarkable knowledge and culture.

Katherine Gyékényesi Gatto

Further reading

Babits, Mihály. *Összegyűjtött versei.* Budapest, 1961.

Czigány, Lóránt. *The Oxford History of Hungarian Literature.* Oxford, 1984.

Hegedüs, Géza. *A magyar irodalom arcképcsarnoka.* Budapest, 1976.

Klaniczay, Tibor, ed. *A History of Hungarian Literature.* Budapest, 1982.

Reményi, Joseph. *Hungarian Writers and Literature: Modern Novelists, Critics, and Poets.* New Brunswick, New Jersey, 1964.

See also Hungarian Literature; *Nyugat*

B

Bach, Baron Alexander von (1813–93)

Austrian statesman who, as minister of the interior from 1849 to 1859, oversaw the implementation of neoabsolutist rule throughout the Habsburg Empire. As a prominent Viennese lawyer with liberal leanings, Bach was initially sympathetic to the Revolution of 1848 but soon grew disenchanted as the revolution became more radical. He entered Prince von Schwarzenberg's (1800–52) cabinet as minister of justice in late 1848 and was subsequently named minister of the interior in May 1849. Distancing himself from his liberal past, Bach countenanced the monarchy's unilateral nullification of the federalist, democratic Kremsier constitution and went on to serve Emperor Franz Joseph's (1830–1916) absolutist regime until 1859. As minister of interior, Bach was instrumental in centralizing and modernizing the empire's administrative and judicial systems, emancipating the peasantry, and placing the entire Habsburg realm under unitary rule from Vienna. Commonly known as the "Bach system," this attempt to govern the empire in a centralized, absolutist fashion not only irked traditional, conservative sensibilities but also disregarded the national and constitutional aspirations that had been awakened throughout the empire in 1848. It was abandoned in 1859 when, following the empire's defeat in Italy in the Austro-Sardinian War, the emperor was forced to grant political concessions. Bach was dismissed from his ministerial post. From 1859 until his retirement in 1865, he served as Habsburg representative to the Holy See in Rome. Although many of Bach's administrative and judicial reforms remained in place until 1918, his ideal of a unitary, absolutist state soon gave way to the dualistic *Ausgleich* (Compromise) of 1867, which established the Austro-Hungarian Empire.

Lawrence J. Flockerzie

Further reading

Macartny, C.A. *The Habsburg Empire, 1790–1918.* New York, 1969.

Walter, Friedrich. *Österreichishe Verfassungs- und Verwaltungsgeschichte von 1500–1955.* Vienna, 1972.

Wandruszka, Adam and Peter Urbanitsch, eds. *Die Habsburgermonarchie, 1848–1918,* vol. 2, *Verwaltung und Rechtswesen.* Vienna, 1975.

See also *Ausgleich;* Dualism; Franz Joseph; Kremsier-Kroměříž Parliment; Neoabsolutism; Peasants; Revolutions of 1848; Prince Felix zu Schwarzenberg

Badeni, Count Kazimierz (1846–1909)

Austro-Polish official and minister-president. A member of a Galician aristocratic family, Badeni studied law at Kraków University and entered the imperial civil service. He was appointed Galician viceroy in 1888. A staunch conservative, Badeni belonged to the Stańczyk faction in Galician politics, which emphasized administrative efficiency and advocated limited concessions to the Ukrainian minority of the province. He thus inaugurated a "new era" in Galician administration by cooperating with Ukrainian National Populists and encouraging educational development, including the establishment of a chair for Ukrainian history at Lvov (Ukrainian, L'viv) University. His forceful administrative style also included harassment of the growing socialist and radical peasant movements in the province.

Reputed to be a tough, capable administrator, Badeni was appointed Austrian minister-president in 1895 and implemented aggressive responses to the political problems facing the imperial government. He extended the suffrage to nearly all adult men in a new fifth electoral curia for limited representation in parliament. To attain the support of the Young Czechs and resolve conflict over language rights, he issued language ordinances for the administrative offices of Bohemia and Moravia. The extension of the official use of Czech provoked extreme resistance from German politicians, who obstructed parliamentary proceedings. Desperate to enact legislation to renew the economic union with Hungary in the fall of 1897, Badeni approved a revision of parliamentary procedure to allow the expulsion of delegates who refused to come to order. Amid wild scenes in parliament and unrest among the populace of Vienna, the Habsburg emperor, Franz Joseph (1830–1916), dismissed Badeni in November 1897.

Philip Pajakowski

Further reading

Garver, Bruce. *The Young Czech Party, 1874–1901, and the Emergence of the Multiparty System.* New Haven, Connecticut, 1978.

Łazuga, Waldemar. *"Rządy polskie" w Austrii: Gabinet Kazimierza Hr. Badeniego, 1895–1897.* Poznań, 1991.

Sutter, Berthold. *Die Badenischen Sprachverordnungen von 1897: Ihre Genesis und ihre Auswirkungen vornehmlich auf die innerösterreichischen Alpenländer.* Graz, 1960–65.

See also Curial System; Franz Joseph; Young Czechs

Bagrianov, Ivan (1891–1945)

Bulgarian politician. The son of a teacher, Bagrianov graduated from military school in 1910 and served as an artillery officer in the Balkan Wars (1912–13) and World War I. Appointed by King Ferdinand (1868–1948) as his adjutant officer in the royal court, he continued to serve Boris III (1894–1943) and shared the most critical moments of the coup d'état of June 9, 1923—which overthrew the government of Aleksandur Stamboliiski (1879–1923)—at his side. After these events, he retired to his farm. Called out of retirement in 1935, he became president of the government-sponsored Agrarian Associations. Elected to the National Assembly, on June 22, 1938, he delivered a devastating attack on the existing social, economic, and political order of the royal regime in the country. He later served as minister of agriculture.

On June 1, 1944, Bagrianov was appointed prime minister, in the vain hope of preventing Soviet occupation. Overtaken by events and rebuffed by the Allies, he resigned on September 1, 1944. Arrested and tried by a Communist People's Court, he was executed, together with twenty-eight regents and cabinet ministers, on February 1, 1945. Royalists in 1938 and Communist writers of recent times have branded him as a demagogue, while others view him as a true statesman wasted by his association with the royal court.

Spas T. Raikin

Further reading

Dimitrov, Ilcho. *Ivan Bagrianov.* Sofia, 1995.
Dimov, I. "Vunshnata politika na Pravitelstvoto na Ivan Bagrianov—1 iuni–1 septemvri, 1944," in Filiosofsko-Istoricheski facultet. *Godishnik na Sofiyskia Universitet* 61 (1967): Kn. 3, Istoria. Sofia, 1968.
Groueff, Stephane. *Crown of Thorns: The Reign of King Boris III of Bulgaria, 1918–1943.* Lanham, Maryland, 1987.
Stamenov, Mitre. *Ivan Bagrianov.* Sofia, 1992.

See also Balkan Wars; Boris III; Ferdinand I; Aleksandur Stamboliiski

Bajcsy-Zsilinszky, Endre (1886–1944)

Hungarian politician and publicist, and a leading figure of Hungary's resistance movement in World War II. Zsilinszky (he took the name Bajcsy-Zsilinszky in 1925) studied law in Hungary and Germany, and started his career as a county official. In World War I he served as a cavalry officer and was severely wounded. During the postwar revolutionary turmoil brought on by Hungary's defeat, he sided with the forces of the counter-revolution. Later he was active in various right-radical organizations and journalistic ventures. In the 1930s he gradually parted with the Right and by 1939 he had joined the opposition Independent Smallholders Party. As a parliamentarian and newspaper editor, he warned against the spread of Nazi influence. After June 1941, he campaigned against the German alliance and the mistreatment of war resisters and Jews. When Gestapo agents came to arrest him during the March 1944 German occupation of Hungary, he was captured only after being wounded in an exchange of gunfire. In early October the Hungarian government expedited his release from captivity. After the unsuccessful attempt by Miklós Horthy (1868–1957), the Hungarian regent, to defect from the Axis, Bajcsy-Zsilinszky assumed the leadership of the underground group that planned to take up arms against the government of the right-radical leader Ferenc Szálasi (1891–1945). However, he was betrayed and arrested. On Christmas eve 1944, a military tribunal of the Arrow Cross, the Hungarian right-radical organizaton, condemned him to death and he was promptly hanged.

N.F. Dreisziger

Further reading

Vigh, Károly. *Bajcsy-Zsilinszky Endre külpolitikai nézeteinek alakulása.* Budapest, 1979.
———, ed. *Kortársak Bajcsy-Zsilinszky Endréről.* Budapest, 1969.

See also Arrow Cross; Miklós Horthy; Right Radicalism; Ferenc Szálasi

Balázs, Béla (1884–1949)

Hungarian man of letters, best known as a librettist and film theorist. Born Herbert Bauer to a family of assimilated Jews, Balázs had earned a reputation as a poet and dramatist by the time he collaborated with the composer Béla Bartók (1881–1945) on *Duke Bluebeard's Castle* (1911) and *The Wooden Prince* (1914–16). After seeing action in World War I, he played a leading role in

B the literary-philosophic circle that gathered around noted Hungarian philosopher György Lukács (1885–1971), and like Lukács he embraced communism at war's end. To that "religion," as he invariably characterized it, he dedicated the remainder of his life.

When the post–World War I Hungarian Soviet Republic led by Béla Kun (1886–1938) collapsed in August 1919, Balázs fled to Austria, where, among other things, he reviewed films and, in 1924, published the first full-blown theory of film: *The Visible Man.* What he professed to admire the most about what was then silent film was its purported ability to make the soul visible in the body, in much the same way, he argued, that communism infused material being with spiritual consciousness. That was important to him because of his own soul's alienation from his body, his spiritual detachment from his (obsessive) sex life.

By the time he published his book on sound film, *The Spirit of Film,* in 1930, Balázs had moved on to Berlin to work as a scenarist with G.W. Pabst (1885–1967), Leni Riefenstahl (b. 1902), and others. In 1931 he emigrated to the Soviet Union, where he prostituted his talent to survive Stalin's (1879–1953) purges. He returned to Hungary in 1945, exhausted by years of fear and creative sterility.

Lee Congdon

Further reading

Congdon, Lee. *Exile and Social Thought: Hungarian Intellectuals in Germany and Austria, 1919–1933.* Princeton, New Jersey, 1991.
Nagy, Magda K. *Balázs Béla világa.* Budapest, 1973.
Zsuffa, Joseph. *Béla Balázs: The Man and the Artist.* Berkeley, California, 1987.

See also Béla Bartók; Cinema; Hungarian Soviet Republic; Béla Kun; György Lukács; Stalin

Bălcescu, Nicolae (1819–52)

Liberal politician and historian from Wallachia. After his studies, Bălcescu enlisted in 1838, serving as an instructor in military schools and participating in revolutionary activity. In 1840 he was sentenced to prison, where he contracted the tuberculosis that would eventually kill him. Amnestied in 1843, in 1845 he published a historical journal, *Magazinul istoric pentru Dacia* (*Historic Magazine for Dacia*), that included his important study on the sources of Romanian history. From 1846 until the outbreak of revolution in the Danubian Principalities in 1848, Bălcescu lived in Paris, associating with other Romanian émigrés, attending the history lectures of French historian Jules Michelet (1798–1874), and conducting research in libraries and archives. Returning home with his compatriots in 1848, he helped write the Proclamation of Islaz (a call for independence and rights for Romanians) and was a leader of the revolutionary committee in Bucharest. From June until September 1848, he was foreign minister and commissioner for peasant affairs. With the fall of the government, he was captured by Turkish forces and exiled. In 1849 he worked to bring about peace between the forces of the Hungarian revolutionary Lajos Kossuth (1802–94) and Avram Iancu (1824–72), the leader of Romanian armed resistance to the revolution in Hungary and Transylvania, during the final months before the defeat of the Hungarian War of Independence in 1849. In London, Paris, and Italy he collaborated with democratic émigrés from other countries and completed his greatest works: an article arguing that the Romanian Revolution of 1848 was a product of indigenous tendencies in Romanian history, and a major study of the unification of Wallachia, Moldavia, and Transylvania under Michael the Brave (1557–1601) in 1600.

James P. Niessen

Further reading

Bălcescu, Nicolae. *Opere,* ed. by G. Zane and Elena G. Zane, 4 vols. Bucharest, 1974–90.
Stan, Valeriu. *Nicolae Bălcescu 1819–1852.* Bucharest, 1977.
Tóth, Zoltán I. *Bălcescu Miklós élete (1819–1852).* Budapest, 1958.
Zane, G. *N. Bălcescu: Opera, omul, epoca.* Bucharest, 1975.

See also Avram Iancu; Danubian Principalities; Hungarian War for Independence; Islaz Proclamation; Lajos Kossuth; Revolution of 1848; Romanian Émigrés

Balicki, Zygmunt (1858–1916)

Leading Polish political theoretician. Together with Roman Dmowski (1864–1939) and Jan Ludwik Popławski (1854–1908), Balicki belonged to the triumvirate that guided the evolution of Polish right-wing political thought during the period that witnessed the emergence of modern political parties in the Polish lands. Balicki exerted considerable influence on the organization of the national democratic movement during the critical phase prior to the creation of an independent state. His doctrine of "national egoism" helped lay the groundwork for Polish national democracy's subordination of individual rights to collective interests. In 1902 Balicki popularized his theories through his work *Egoizm narodowy wobec etyki* (*National Egoism in Relation to Ethics*), his most significant contribution to Polish political thought.

Balicki's ideological searchings reflected the intellectual ferment among his generation of the Polish intelligentsia. Initially affiliated with socialism, he broke with this movement because he believed that left-wing internationalism was detrimental to the stateless nation's cause. In the late 1880s Balicki was instrumental in the establishment of the Union of Polish Youth (Zet), a conspiratorial formation committed to propagating Polish independence. He brought this organization under the authority of the Polish League, the most significant nonsocialist political entity in the Polish lands, and he subsequently played a central role in the league's transformation into the National League in the early 1890s. This latter organization then provided an infrastructure for the growing national democratic movement. After 1905, Balicki supported efforts to cooperate with the Russian state. In this vein, he became a member of the pro-Russian Polish National Committee at the beginning of World War I and tried to raise a Polish legion for the Russian army.

William Lee Blackwood

Further reading

Fountain, Alvin Marcus. *Roman Dmowski: Party, Tactics, Ideology 1895–1907*. Boulder, Colorado, 1980.

See also Roman Dmowski; Intelligentsia; Polish League; Zet

Balkan Entente

Interwar Balkan regional pact. The pact signed in Athens on February 9, 1934, by the foreign ministers of Greece, Romania, Turkey, and Yugoslavia called into being the Balkan Entente. Roots for such regional cooperation went back to the nineteenth century, and several Balkan conferences were held in the early 1930s with a view toward a Balkan Union. The entente, however, was a product of the worsening international situation, revisionism becoming a real threat to the smaller states. Partly inspired by the Little Entente, the interwar alliance to which two of the signatories belonged, the Balkan Entente provided for mutual guarantees of Balkan frontiers, consultations (a Permanent Council and an Economic Advisory Council were established, and a secret annex stipulated military cooperation in the defense of existing borders), and an engagement to refrain from political acts against or in agreement with another Balkan state. This meant Bulgaria. Having shown interest in cooperation to strengthen security, and figuring together with Albania as a potential member in the early negotiations, Bulgaria refused to join a pact that stressed territorial status quo.

Represented as complementing the Little Entente, the Balkan bloc really strained it by diverting attention to southeastern Europe. The diplomatic offensive of Nazi Germany and Fascist Italy, combined with Western appeasement, made the Balkan Entente increasingly ineffective. Both the 1937 Yugoslav-Bulgarian treaty and the July 1938 accord between the entente and Bulgaria (providing for nonaggression and abolishing Bulgarian disarmament clauses) weakened its cohesion. With the outbreak of World War II, the Balkan Entente was unable to create a neutral security bloc protecting the area. In 1940–41 it could not prevent Romania's partial dismemberment under German-Italian aegis. When Greece and Yugoslavia faced Italian and German invasions, they did not coordinate their military defenses and were defeated separately.

Piotr S. Wandycz

Further reading

Campus, Eliza. *The Little Entente and the Balkan Alliance*. Bucharest, 1978.

Kerner, R.J. and H.N. Howard. *The Balkan Conferences and the Balkan Ententes 1930–1935*. Berkeley, California, 1936.

Stavrianos, L.S. *Balkan Federation: A History of the Movement toward Balkan Unity in Modern Times*. Hamden, Connecticut, 1964.

See also Little Entente; Revisionism; Vienna Awards

B

Balkan League(s)

A series of regional anti-Ottoman alliances. Between 1865 and 1912, two Balkan Leagues were formed among the successor states of southeastern Europe. Both leagues were initiated largely by Serbian diplomacy, and both had as their goal the destruction of Ottoman rule in the Balkans and the liberation of the region's subject Christian populations. At the center of the first Balkan League was the prince of Serbia, Mihailo Obrenović (1823–68). Taking advantage of favorable domestic and international conditions between 1865 and 1868, Mihailo concluded a series of alliances with Greece, Montenegro, and Romania. The members of the alliance undertook to arm the Christians in Ottoman Europe, to oppose any Great Power that might seek to annex southeast European lands, and to coordinate a united Balkan revolt against the Ottoman Empire. The allies' ambitious plans, however, were not realized, and the league disintegrated following the assassination of Mihailo in June 1868.

The second, and decidedly more important, Balkan League was as much the product of Russian involvement in southeastern Europe as it was the handiwork of Serbian foreign policy. To create a regional counterweight against the expanded presence and influence of the Habsburg Empire in the Balkans after 1878, and especially after Vienna's annexation of Bosnia in 1908, Russia encouraged the Balkan states to form an alliance among themselves. Although the Russian aim was not to organize for a war or the final partition of the Ottoman lands in southeastern Europe, the Balkan governments concluded a series of agreements that were in fact war alliances against the Ottoman Empire. Thus, albeit promoted and assisted by Russian diplomats, the secret negotiations between the Balkan states progressed completely beyond the planning and control of St. Petersburg.

Although the first series of negotiations for an alliance in 1909 between Serbia and Bulgaria foundered on the issue of competing claims in Macedonia, a strong stimulus for Balkan unity was provided by the Ottoman army's poor performance in the Italo-Turkish War of 1911, which saw Italy acquire Libya. Encouraged by signs of Ottoman weakness, Serbia and Bulgaria signed an alliance in March 1912 that included a provisional accord for the partition of Macedonia. Two months later, Greek negotiations with Bulgaria resulted in an

expansion of the anti-Ottoman alliance, and in September Montenegro also joined the Balkan League. Despite warnings from the Great Powers, the Balkan allies launched an attack on the Ottoman Empire in October 1912. The First Balkan War was a decisive and rapid victory for the Balkan states, which by March 1913 had occupied virtually all the Ottoman territories in southeastern Europe outside Constantinople.

Once the Ottomans were defeated, however, there was nothing left to hold the Balkan League together. The allies had not planned an inter-Balkan organization, nor had they established any foundations for cooperation to extend beyond their immediate war goals. Moreover, the allies had not definitively settled their divergent territorial claims. Consequently, dissension among them over territorial spoils in Macedonia led to the collapse of the Balkan League. Indeed, the alliance system was shattered when Bulgaria attacked Greece and Serbia in June 1913, provoking the Second Balkan War.

Alexandros K. Kyrou

Further reading

Geshov, Ivan E. *The Balkan League.* London, 1915.

Helmreich, Ernst C. *The Diplomacy of the Balkan Wars, 1912–1913.* Cambridge, Massachusetts, 1938.

Jelavich, Barbara. *Russia's Balkan Entanglements, 1806–1914.* Cambridge, Massachusetts 1991.

Rossos, Andrew. *Russia and the Balkans: Inter-Balkan Rivalries and Russian Foreign Policy, 1908–1914.* Toronto, 1981.

Thaden, Edward C. *Russia and the Balkan Alliance of 1912.* University Park, Pennsylvania, 1965.

See also Balkan Wars; Great Powers; Habsburg Empire; Macedonia (History); Mihailo Obrenović; Ottoman Empire; Russia

Balkan Mountains

Name for the Stara Planina mountain chain system in Bulgaria. The name "Balkan" is of Turkic origin, and it is used to denote the southeast peninsula of Europe, the Balkan Peninsula. The mountain chain is 318 miles (530 km) long and runs approximately along the 43rd parallel north from the Belogradchik Pass to Cape Emine on the Black Sea. To the north it borders the Lower Danubian

Plain, and to the south the Podbalkan valleys. The highest peak, Mount Botev, is 7,795 feet (2,376 m), but many peaks are above 6,600 feet (2,000 m). Structurally and morphologically the mountain is divided by the Zlatitsa and Vratnik Passes.

The mountain chain is an important physical-geographic boundary. The generally continental climate is strongly diversified by the chain's height and the exposition of its slopes. The warmest month is August; below-freezing temperatures last four or five months. Snow cover varies from one to seven months a year. At least twelve rivers spring from this mountain range. There are many endangered species in Stara Planina, including numerous endemites.

Anthracite and black coal, and ferrous and copper ores are mined, and water power is extensively used. Industry is the main branch of the economy in the area, but agriculture, forestry, and tourism are also developed. Despite its average height of 2,383 feet (722 m), three railroads and over ten roads cross the chain. This is the most densely populated mountain range in Bulgaria (22.4 people per square kilometer), but the towns and villages are relatively small. One of its dialects served as a basis for the modern official Bulgarian language.

Boian Koulov

Further reading
Bulgarian Academy of Sciences. *Entsiklopedia Bulgaria,* vol. 6. Sofia, 1988.
Nenov, T. and G. Chorponov. *Stara Planina: Meditsina i Fizkultura.* Sofia, 1987.

Balkan Pact (1954)

Security treaty among Greece, Turkey, and Yugoslavia. After the break with the Soviet Union in 1948, Yugoslavia felt isolated and vulnerable because of its position in the Balkans between Soviet-allied Albania, Bulgaria, and Romania and U.S.–allied Greece and Turkey. In the early 1950s Tito (1892–1980) attempted to end this isolation by a policy of affiliation with Greece and Turkey. On February 28, 1953, Greece, Turkey, and Yugoslavia signed a Treaty of Friendship in Ankara. This was followed the next year by a Treaty of Alliance, Political Cooperation, and Mutual Assistance signed in Bled, Yugoslavia, on August 9, 1954. This Balkan Pact provided for mutual military aid in the event of an attack against any one of the signatories. It was to remain in force for twenty years and was renewable. It also provided for the establishment of a Balkan Consultative Assembly for an economic conference to increase future cooperation. This Balkan Pact appeared to replicate the earlier Balkan Entente of 1934 in that it placed Bulgaria in the position of the most likely enemy, although all three signatories to the 1954 treaty also feared Soviet aggression in the Balkans.

The Balkan Pact did not succeed. Mutual antipathy between Greece and Turkey over Cyprus gravely weakened it. Also, by 1955 Yugoslavia's foreign policy had changed. Belgrade's relations with the Soviet Union and its allies began to improve after the death of Stalin (1879–1953), and increasingly Tito pursued a policy of nonalignment. Although the signatories never formally repudiated the Balkan Pact, in 1960 both Yugoslavs and Greeks indicated that they considered it defunct.

Richard C. Hall

Further reading
Braun, Aurel. *Small State Security in the Balkans.* London, 1983.
Grenville, J.A.S. *The Major International Treaties 1914–1973.* New York, 1974.
Junkovic, Branimir M. *The Balkans in International Relations.* London, 1988.

See also Balkan Entente; Nonaligned Movement; Stalin; Tito; Tito-Stalin Split

Balkans

Region that includes the states in the southeastern peninsula of Europe. The predominantly mountainous relief prompted its naming after the Balkan Mountains (Stara Planina) in Bulgaria. The northern boundary of the Balkan Peninsula begins at the mouth of the river Idria in the North Adriatic Gulf of Trieste and follows the southeast foothills of the Julian Alps and the Sava and Danube Rivers. The Black Sea borders the region on the east, the Marmara and Aegean Seas on the south, and the Ionian and Adriatic Seas on the west.

The physical and political boundaries of the region do not coincide. Romania and Turkey, with only about 3 percent of their territory within the

B

peninsula, are considered Balkan countries, along with Albania, Bosnia-Hercegovina, Bulgaria, Croatia, Greece, Macedonia, Slovenia, and Yugoslavia. They have a combined territory of 576,000 square miles (1.6 million sq km) and a population of 130 million. Despite ethnic, cultural, and geopolitical links to the Balkans, Cyprus is generally not regarded a Balkan state.

Industry dominates most Balkan economies, but agriculture still plays a significant role. Transportation and international tourism are two sectors of increasing importance.

The Balkans are a cradle of diverse ancient civilizations. The Slavic ethnicity is predominant, and all official languages belong to the Indo-European family. The majority of the population is Eastern Orthodox, with significant groups of Roman Catholics and Muslims present. The diverse ethnic composition and strategic position of the Balkans placed the Eastern Question, the issue of national liberation for the Balkan peoples and competing interests of the Great Powers, high on the European political agenda. For years, the Balkans carried the infamous title of "powder keg" of Europe, since several wars were waged among the Balkan states and regional conflicts threatened to spark a wider European conflict. This eventually occurred in 1914, as the assassination of Archduke Franz Ferdinand (1863–1914) led to World War I.

Boian Koulov

Further reading

Balkanite. Sofia, 1982.
Bulgarian Academy of Sciences. *Entsiklopedia Bulgaria,* vol. 1. Sofia, 1981.
Lazarov, P. *Zheleve Zh. Geografia.* Sofia, 1994.

See also Balkan Mountains; Balkan Wars; Eastern Question; Franz Ferdinand; Great Powers; Industrialization; Muslims; Orthodoxy; Slavs

Balkan Wars (1912–13)

Consecutive and interlocking conflicts resulting in the expulsion of the Ottoman Empire from most of southeastern Europe (thus putting to rest the Balkan component of the long-standing Eastern Question, that is, the diplomatic issue concerning the disintegration of the Ottoman Empire), the creation of an independent Albania, and the territorial aggrandizement of the other Balkan states, mostly at Ottoman expense. The First and Second Balkan Wars set the stage for considerable future regional strife, including a third Balkan conflict that quickly developed into World War I.

In the First Balkan War (October 1912–May 1913), Bulgaria, Serbia, Greece, and Montenegro, recently united in the Balkan League, sought to expel the Ottomans from Turkey-in-Europe, a sizable swath of the Balkan Peninsula still under Turkish control. On October 8, 1912, tiny Montenegro initiated hostilities against the Ottomans, with Serbia and Bulgaria declaring war on October 17, followed by Greece on October 19. In short order, Bulgarian and Serbian forces inflicted major defeats on the Turks at Kirk-Kilisse and Kumanovo, Greece occupied Salonika (Thessaloniki), and units of the Bulgarian army reached the gates of Constantinople (Istanbul).

Peace talks opened in London on December 16 but were soon interrupted by a resumption of hostilities. With the surrender of the long-besieged Turkish fortresses of Yannina (Ioannina), Adrianople (Edirne), and Scutari (Shkodër) in March–April 1913, the Ottoman government felt compelled to give up the fight.

By the terms of the Treaty of London (May 30, 1913), the Ottoman Empire surrendered all its European possessions west of the Enos-Media (Enez-Midye) line. The issue of how the spoils of war were to be divided was complicated by the decision of the Conference of (Great Power) Ambassadors in London, acting under pressure from Austria-Hungary and Italy, to provide for the creation of an independent Albanian state, thus depriving Serbia, Montenegro, and Greece of anticipated territorial gains.

A related dispute over the partition of Macedonia led directly to the Second Balkan War (June–August 1913). On the night of June 29–30, 1913, Bulgaria, which coveted most of north-central Macedonia and demanded adherence to the original Serb-Bulgarian partition agreement of March 1912, launched an attack against Serbia and Greece, which were seeking territorial compensation in Macedonia for the aforementioned losses in Albania. Montenegro immediately entered the new war on the side of Serbia and Greece, and they were soon joined by Romania and the Ottomans. Surrounded on all sides, Bulgaria was quickly defeated and obliged to capitulate.

By the terms of the Treaty of Bucharest (August 10, 1913), Serbia and Greece maintained control of those parts of Macedonia they had occupied during the Balkan Wars, while Romania annexed southern Dobrudja (Dobruzha). Bulgaria was permitted to retain only a sliver of Macedonia, as well as a short stretch of the Aegean coastline between the Mesta and Marica Rivers. The following month, the Treaty of Constantinople returned most of Eastern Thrace, including Adrianople, to Turkish control.

The Balkan Wars saw Serbia double in size. In addition to northern and central Macedonia (subsequently called South Serbia), it acquired Kosovo, the historic "cradle of Serbdom," but also a region occupied by a sizable Albanian population. Serbia and Montenegro divided the Sanjak of Novi Pazar between them, acquiring a common frontier in the process. In addition to Aegean Macedonia and part of the Epirus region, Greece also assumed formal control of Crete.

John D. Treadway

Further reading

Helmeich, Ernst C. *The Diplomacy of the Balkan Wars 1912–1913.* Cambridge, Massachusetts, 1938.

International Commission to Inquire into the Causes and Conduct of the Balkan Wars. *The Other Balkan Wars: A 1913 Carnegie Endowment Inquiry in Retrospect.* Washington, D.C., 1993.

Rossos, Andrew. *Russia and the Balkans: Inter-Balkan Rivalries and Russian Foreign Policy, 1908–1914.* Toronto, 1981.

See also Balkan League; Bucharest, Treaty of (1913); Dobrudja; Eastern Question; Kosovo; Macedonia; Montenegro; Sanjak of Novi Pazar

Balta Liman, Convention of (1849)

Agreement between Russia and the Ottoman Empire to restore order and control in the Danubian Principalities following the suppression of the Revolution of 1848 in Moldavia and Wallachia. The revolt that began in Paris in February 1848 spread east to the Balkans. In Romania, a revolutionary committee formed in May 1848. The issuance of the Islaz Proclamation on June 21, which, among other things, called for a liberal program and an end to the Russian protectorate in the principalities, brought a swift reaction from St. Petersburg. The Russians demanded that the Porte suppress the revolution, and by late September Russian and Ottoman forces entered Moldavia and Wallachia. In May 1849 St. Petersburg and the Porte signed the Convention of Balta Liman, which called for the appointment of *hospodars* (princes) with seven-year terms for Moldavia and Wallachia. It also replaced the assemblies with *divans* (councils) composed of loyal *boiars*. Grigore Ghica (1807–57) and Barbu Ştirbei (1799–1869) were named the princes of Moldavia and Wallachia, respectively. In addition, Russian and Ottoman troops remained until 1851 to ensure compliance with the provisions of the convention, and commissioners were named to oversee the actions of the princes.

Richard Frucht

Further reading

Hitchins, Keith. *The Romanians 1774–1866.* Oxford, 1996.

Jelavich, Barbara. *History of the Balkans,* vol. 1, *The Eighteenth and Nineteenth Centuries.* Cambridge, Massachusetts, 1983.

———. *Russia and the Formation of the Romanian National State 1821–1878.* Cambridge, Massachusetts, 1984.

See also Danubian Principalities; Eastern Question; Grigore Ghica; Islaz Proclamation; Porte; Revolutions of 1848; Barbu Ştirbei

Banat

An historic province of Hungary centered on the city of Temesvar (Romanian, Timişoara) that was divided between Romania and the Kingdom of Serbs, Croats, and Slovenes (Yugoslavia) following World War I. The Banat is bounded by the Mureş, Tisa, and Danube Rivers and the slopes of the Western Carpathian mountains. The Yugoslav segment contains 3,500 square miles (9,720 sq km) with 700,000 inhabitants; the Romanian section embraces 3,200 square miles (8,900 sq km) with a population of 1,500,000. The Banat is a remarkably level region with warm, rainy summers. Most of its exceptionally fertile soils are developed on thick beds of mineral-rich loess deposited by winds during the last ice age.

The sixteenth-century advance of Ottoman armies through the Banat resulted in its nearly complete depopulation. Planned resettlement occurred following recapture by Austrian forces in

B the following century. Particularly significant was a Habsburg colonization program during the years from 1765 to 1772 that created homes and farms for 42,000 individuals. Banat villages remain noted for their rectangularity and uniform architectural styles. House lots generally have frontages of 75 feet (23 m) along streets. Buildings are stretched along western or northern lot lines, leaving intervening courtyards that discourage the spread of fires.

The planned colonization brought settlers to the Banat from all parts of the Habsburg domains. Germans were recruited extensively because authorities deemed them more likely to be stable and loyal, particularly in comparison with Hungarians. Many so-called Swabian Germans remain in the Romanian Banat, but virtually all German families on the Yugoslav side were expelled at the end of World War II.

Thomas M. Poulsen

Further reading

Bertić, Ivan. *Veliki geografski atlas Jugoslavije.* Zagreb, 1987.

Clissold, Stephen, ed. *A Short History of Yugoslavia: From Early Times to 1966.* Cambridge, 1968.

Rugg, Dean S. *Eastern Europe.* London, 1985.

Bánffy, Dezsö (1843–1911)

Hungarian prime minister. Born in Kolozsvár (today Cluj-Napoca, Romania), Bánffy was sent as a commissioner to the frontier region with Romania, where he firmly opposed non-Magyar nationalist forces. Many considered him to be a typical representative of Hungarian chauvinism in action. An ardent supporter of Kálmán Tisza (1830–1902), the Hungarian prime minster (1875–1890), Bánffy opposed the policies of Lajos Kossuth (1802–94), Hungarian revolutionary leader in 1848–49, and his followers. His refusal to attend Kossuth's funeral in 1894 endeared him to the monarchy. Franz Joseph (1830–1916) appointed him prime minister of Hungary in 1895, a post he would retain until 1899. Bánffy believed in a strongly centralized government in alliance with the crown but also under Magyar domination. He strongly opposed the socialists and the political aspirations of the nationalities. In 1899 parliamentary filibustering forced him to resign. In 1904 Bánffy was reelected to parliament, where he remained as head of the New Party, which he founded. By 1906 he had become an isolated and generally inconsequential politician.

Peter I. Hidas

Further reading

Magyar Életrajzi Lexikon, ed. by Ágnes Kenyeres. Budapest, 1981.

See also Franz Joseph; Lajos Kossuth; Kálmán Tisza

Banking

A wide range of financial institutions emerged in Eastern Europe reflecting the diverse economic needs of the region during the nineteenth and twentieth centuries. The western half of the Habsburg Monarchy, which experienced significant industrialization in the nineteenth century, also saw the emergence of sophisticated financial institutions to provide credit to these new businesses. The Balkan Peninsula, by contrast, experienced relatively little growth in industry or commerce and therefore had less well-developed financial sectors.

The origins of banking in Eastern Europe are found in the urban setting among private banking houses, which provided credit to the nobility, large merchants, and governments, and smaller pawn brokerages and *monte pietatis,* which made loans to artisans and workers. Rural areas had their own system of credit, usually grain funds, which provided relief during times of bad harvest or simply to tide peasants over from the late spring to the early fall. Likewise, itinerant peddlers often offered some credit as they made their rounds in rural districts.

By the early nineteenth century, modern banking began to emerge with the establishment of government banks, like the Austrian National Bank (founded in 1816 and renamed the Austro-Hungarian Bank in 1877). The Austrian National Bank was the bank of issue and the main conduit through which government loans were placed with creditors. It also made private loans to well-established firms and to the nobility. By the mid-1850s, a variety of other financial institutions had been established in Austria, ranging from commercial banks such as the Niederösterreichische Escomptegesellschaft and the Creditanstalt für Handel und Gewerbe in Vienna to provincial mortgage banks specializing in agricultural credit to local financial institutions like credit cooperatives and savings banks.

In the Balkan Peninsula, banking emerged with the newly independent states of Greece, Romania, Serbia, and Bulgaria. As these countries established their own currencies, they also formed national banks of issue. Likewise, economic development created a demand for commercial and agricultural banks, including small, local savings and loan institutions. In the Polish territories, the banking systems were tied closely to the economic role each partition played in the German, Austrian, and Russian Empires. Russian Poland had the most highly developed credit system before World War I.

Given the national complexity of Eastern Europe and the variety of levels of economic development in different regions, access to financial resources was often fraught with ethnic tension. As a result, financial institutions sometimes became symbols of ethnic pride and autonomy, as, for example, among the Ukrainians in Galicia and Russian Poland or the Slovenians and Czechs in the Habsburg Monarchy. Cases of financially motivated nationalism can be observed from the late nineteenth century through the interwar period in all the countries of the region, from Romania and Yugoslavia to Poland and Czechoslovakia. The association of financial questions and nationalism was one factor that fueled anti-Semitism in Eastern Europe in the interwar era, since Jews were often identified in the popular imagination with both local moneylending and high finance. Likewise, foreign investments in commercial banking in the region tended to exacerbate xenophobia between the wars.

Communist governments in Eastern Europe simplified the financial sector by consolidating the myriad of different financial institutions into a few state-run banks, each oriented to particular purposes like savings or credit for agriculture, industry, and foreign trade. Since 1989, many state banks have been privatized and new private banks have been founded.

Catherine Albrecht

Further reading

Lampe, John R. "Financial Consequences of Political Independence," in John R. Lampe and Marvin R. Jackson. *Balkan Economic History, 1550–1950: From Imperial Borderlands to Developing Nations.* Bloomington, Indiana, 1982, 202–36.

———. "Serbia, 1878–1912," in Rondo Cameron, ed. *Banking and Economic Development: Some Lessons of History.* New York, 1972, 122–67.

Michel, Bernard. *Banques et banquiers en Autriche au début du 20ᵉ siècle.* Paris, 1976.

Rudolph, Richard. *Banking and Industrialization in Austria-Hungary: The Role of Banks in the Industrialization of the Bohemian Crownlands, 1873–1914.* New York, 1976.

See also Industrialization; Jews; Kreditanstalt; Nationalism; Privatization

Barbarossa

Code name for the German invasion of the Soviet Union on June 22, 1941. The destruction of the USSR had always been Hitler's intent. The Soviet Ukraine and Russian heartland, together with Poland, made up the Lebensraum (living space) he coveted. The Nazi-Soviet Pact of 1939 had never been more than a temporary expedient for Hitler (1889–1945), protecting his rear while fighting in the West and allowing him to harness the Soviet economy to the German war machine.

The invasion was originally scheduled for April 1941 but was delayed until late June by operations in the Balkans. On June 22 approximately 120 German divisions and allied forces (including Italian, Spanish, Finnish, Hungarian, Slovak, and Romanian troops) struck from three points, attacking toward Leningrad, Moscow, and Kiev. Their objective was not merely to capture territory but to encircle and destroy the Soviet armies. German forces achieved almost complete tactical surprise. Although Soviet intelligence had given ample warning of the impending attack, Stalin (1879–1953) refused to permit Soviet armed forces to prepare adequately. He refused to consider the nightmare scenario of a German attack, preferring instead to believe that the Wehrmacht buildup along his border was merely Hitler's gambit to extract diplomatic concessions from the USSR.

Soviet forces, stretched along the border from the Arctic Ocean to the Black Sea and forbidden to mobilize fully beforehand, were quickly overwhelmed. The fighting was unusually savage. Hitler ordered his commanders to disregard the usual rules of war, because he considered the Slavs of Eastern Europe virtually Untermenschen (subhumans) and because he wanted to exterminate much of the population in the land he claimed as

B

Lebensraum. By December, German troops had surrounded Leningrad, captured Kiev, and were within twenty miles (thirty-three km) of Moscow. Yet German forces had reached the limits of their capabilities. The Wehrmacht ground to a halt owing to a combination of exhaustion, roads turned to rivers of mud by the fall rains, then brutal winter weather, and much greater Soviet resistance than the Germans had expected.

On December 6, the Soviet army counterattacked with fresh troops who, unlike the Germans, were properly dressed and well equipped for the severe winter conditions. Stalin could afford to transfer his reserves from the Far East because in April 1941 he had negotiated a neutrality treaty with Japan. The Wehrmacht lines were now forced back as much as 100 miles (167 km) in some sectors before the Soviet counteroffensive stalled. Operation Barbarossa conquered vast territories and inflicted staggering losses on the Soviets, but it failed to achieve its ultimate aim—the rapid and complete destruction of the Soviet armed forces. The war in the east would now become a protracted battle of attrition that Germany did not have the resources to win.

Teddy J. Uldricks

Further reading

Bartov, Omer. *The Eastern Front, 1941–45: German Troops and the Barbarization of Warfare.* New York, 1986.

Erickson, John. *The Road to Stalingrad.* London, 1975.

Erickson, John and David Dilks, eds. *Barbarossa: The Axis and the Allies.* Edinburgh, 1994.

Glantz, David M. and Jonathan House. *When Titans Clashed: How the Red Army Stopped Hitler.* Lawrence, Kansas, 1995.

Whaley, Barton. *Codeword Barbarossa.* Cambridge, Massachusetts, 1973.

See also Adolf Hitler; Molotov-Ribbentrop Pact; Stalin; World War II

Bárdossy, László (1890–1946)

Hungarian diplomat and politician, one of the chief architects of Hungary's involvement in World War II. A lawyer by training, Bárdossy first found employment in the Ministry of Culture and Education. After World War I, he joined his country's newly established Ministry of External Affairs and, from 1924 to 1926, headed its Press Bureau. Later he held diplomatic postings in London and Bucharest. In January 1941 he was appointed minister of external affairs and, in early April, prime minister. Soon, after Hungary became Germany's ally, in mid-April 1941 the Bárdossy administration dispatched troops to some of the former Hungarian areas of Yugoslavia and, on June 27, 1941, it declared the existence of "a state of war" between Hungary and the Soviet Union. Following the Japanese attack on Pearl Harbor, Bárdossy declared war on the United States. In March 1942 the Hungarian regent, Miklós Horthy (1868–1957), dismissed Bárdossy. At war's end, he fled to Germany, from where American authorities returned him to Hungary to face charges of war crimes before a "People's Tribunal." He was convicted and was executed by a firing squad.

N.F. Dreisziger

Further reading

Pritz, Pál. *Bárdossy László a Népbíróság elött.* Budapest, 1991.

Tilkovszky, Loránd. "The Later Interwar Years and World War II," in Peter F. Sugar et al., eds. *A History of Hungary.* Bloomington, Indiana, 1990.

See also Miklós Horthy

Baritiu, George (1812–93)

Transylvanian journalist, historian, and cultural leader. The founder and editor of *Gazeta de Transilvania* (*Transylvanian Gazette*) and its literary supplement, *Foaia pentru minte, inima şi literatura* (*Paper for Mind, Heart, and Literature*), Baritiu was a supporter of modernization, commerce, manufacturing, and Western-style bourgeois development. Such economic development, he believed, could only help Romanians in Transylvania. He therefore attacked the privileges of the landed aristocracy and advocated an end to guilds; the latter, he believed, only locked out Romanians and thus prevented the rise of a Romanian middle class. Although *Gazeta* had few subscribers, Baritiu was an intellectual leader in Transylvania who advocated the teaching of Romanian culture, language, and history as a means of defense against repression; he felt it was imperative that nationalities in the Habsburg Empire have the right to use their native tongue in education and in government.

When news of the Revolutions of 1848 hit Transylvania, Bariţiu was at first optimistic that change would follow. He became one of the leaders of the Romanian national assembly that announced a sixteen-point program calling for equality and national consciousness to thirty thousand gathered at Blaj. Frustrated by Vienna's failure in the wake of revolution to recognize the loyalty of Romanians, Bariţiu later turned against cooperation with the monarchy.

Richard Frucht

Further reading

Hitchins, Keith. *The Romanians 1774–1866.* Oxford, 1996.

Jelavich, Barbara. *History of the Balkans,* vol. 1, *The Eighteenth and Nineteenth Centuries.* Cambridge, 1983.

Netea, Vasile. *George Bariţiu. Viaţa şi activitatea sa.* Bucharest, 1966.

See also Blaj; Revolutions of 1848; Romanian Culture

Bărnuţiu, Simion (1808–64)

Outstanding representative of the Transylvanian Latinist school who eloquently formulated the program of the Romanian Transylvanian revolutionaries in 1848. Having studied philosophy, Bărnuţiu taught the first course on the subject in Romanian at the Blaj Uniate seminary. When the Transylvanian diet attempted to introduce Hungarian in all Transylvanian schools, Bărnuţiu's protest resulted in his dismissal in 1845. Bărnuţiu played a leading role during the Revolution of 1848, when forty thousand Romanians from all sections of Transylvania (including the leaders of the Orthodox and Uniate Churches), assembled at the Field of Liberty, near Blaj. In a stirring speech, he demanded equality for the Romanian nation with the three so-called historic nations: the Hungarians, the Germans, and the Szeklers. He also demanded representation in the Transylvanian diet. Because these demands were not met, the Romanian Transylvanian revolutionaries sided with the Austrian and Russian reactionary forces in helping quell the Hungarian revolution in 1849, even though they received little gratitude from the restored (Alexander) Bach (1813–93) regime in Vienna. Disillusioned, Bărnuţiu resumed his legal studies begun earlier at Sibiu, studying in Vienna and Pavia,

where he received a doctorate in law. He ended his career as a law professor at Iaşi University, where he taught and wrote texts on jurisprudence, acquiring a deserved reputation as a jurist. He was criticized, however, for his exaggerated "latinism" (an emphasis on Romania's ties to ancient Rome), his republicanism, and traces of anti-Semitism.

Radu Florescu

Further reading

Bodea, Cornelia. *The Romanians Struggle for Unification 1834–1849.* Bucharest, 1970.

Duica, Bodgan. *Viaţa şi ideile lui Simeon Bărnuţiu.* Bucharest, 1924.

Pantazzi, Radu. *Simeon Bărnuţiu. Opera si gândirea.* Bucharest, 1967.

See also Alexander von Bach; Blaj; Hungarian War for Independence; Revolutions of 1848; Uniate Church

Bartók, Béla (1881–1945)

Hungarian composer, pianist, and ethnomusicologist. Bartók is recognized as the greatest Hungarian composer and one of the greatest composers of the twentieth century. At first under the strong influence, in turn, of the composers Ernő Dohnányi (1877–1960) and Richard Strauss (1864–1949), Bartók found his unique voice at thirty in his opera, *Duke Bluebeard's Castle* (1911). Although by this time he had begun (with Zoltán Kodály [1882–1967]) to explore the wealth of Hungarian folk music, it was to be but one—though important—component in his output, which drew on all great musical traditions.

A pianist of distinction and a man of outstanding character, Bartók's difficulty in communicating verbally may explain the concentration of immense power in his music. His personal integrity was matched by meticulous care in composition. In the 1920s he again accommodated the influence of contemporaries—this time Igor Stravinsky (1882–1971) and Arnold Schoenberg (1874–1951)—but, by the 1930s, he embarked on a series of large-scale compositions that have stood the most rigorous test of time.

Recognition was slow, and his unyielding personality, though admired, did not always win friends. But Dohnányi kept Bartók's music before the public, and, in time, many outstanding musicians came to commission works. The six string

B

quartets, three piano concertos, *The Miraculous Mandarin, Cantata Profana,* Divertimento, Concerto for Orchestra, and the Second Violin Concerto place Bartók in the mainstream of the European succession.

Deeply interested in nature and the traditions of all nations, he collected folk songs in more places than anyone else. He devoted considerable time to the organization of his collections, first in Hungary, then in New York City, where he chose to relocate when news of the outbreak of World War II reached him, and where he died.

Balint Vazsonyi

Further reading
Bónis, Ferenc. *Béla Bartók.* Budapest, 1972.
Sadie, Stanley, ed. *The New Grove Dictionary of Music and Musicians.* London, 1980.
Ujfalussy, József. *Bartók Béla.* Budapest, 1976.

See also Ernő Dohnányi; Folk Music; Zoltán Kodály; Music

Baťa, Tomáš (1876–1932)

The major representative of welfare capitalism in prewar Czechoslovakia. By profession a shoemaker, Baťa started the A. & T. Baťa Shoe Company in 1924, and by 1928 he became the leading shoe manufacturer in the world. After 1904, he visited the United States on several occasions. It was especially the Ford Motor Company that served as Baťa's model of technological advancement. Between 1923 and 1924, he carried out experimental studies based on Taylorite hypotheses (using efficiency of motion to maximize productivity) and installed the first conveyers in his company. The gradual intensification of mass production was accompanied by the gradual reduction of shoe prices. As a result, many countries erected high tariff walls to protect their shoe industries against Baťa's competition. In 1924 the workshop-autonomy system was put into effect, resulting in the decentralization of Baťa's management. The profit-sharing incentive was also introduced to improve employee work performance. Although Baťa was often referred to as "Europe's Henry Ford," his welfare program points to the example of labor loyalty as practiced at the Endicott Johnson Shoe Company in New York City. After 1923, Baťa served until his death as the mayor of Zlín. Through the symbiotic union of nature and indus-try, he developed his native town of Zlín as Czechoslovakia's first garden city.

Koji Chikugo

Further reading
Baťa, Tomáš. *How I Began,* trans. by Jan Baroš, 2d ed. Batanagar, India, 1942.
Cekota, Antonín. *Entrepreneur Extraordinary: The Biography of Tomáš Bata.* Rome, 1968.
Chikugo, Koji. *Tomáš Baťa: The Czech Example of Welfare Capitalism.* Ann Arbor, Michigan, 1991.
Lehár, Bohumil. *Dějiny Baťova koncernu 1894–1945.* Prague, 1960.

See also Economic Development in Czechoslovakia; Industrialization

Batthyány, Count Lajos (1806–49)

Hungarian aristocrat, statesman, and first constitutional prime minister of Hungary. Born in Pozsony, Batthyány became a soldier at the age of sixteen. After leaving the army in 1827, he made use of his experiences gained in trips abroad to promote the development of the Hungarian economy, especially the creation of new economic unions and enterprises. A politician of liberal, progressive attitudes, he opposed the privileges of the nobility. In the elections of 1847 he became the leader of the National Oppositionist Party and was one of the members of the deputation that handed the address of the parliament to the emperor in Vienna on March 15, 1848. Batthyány was nominated to be president of the Hungarian government on March 17, 1848. His principal ambition was to achieve the country's political independence. He played an important role in organizing the National Guard, the Honvéd Army. On August 29, 1848, he went to Vienna to entreat Baron Josip Jelačić (1803–59), the *ban* (governor) of Croatia, and the Austrian emperor, Ferdinand (1793–1875), to stop the offensive against Hungary. Ferdinand refused to receive him. Following Jelačić's offensive against Hungary on September 9, 1848, Batthyány resigned. He was later charged with creating a new cabinet by the palatine of Hungary (the highest administrative dignity in feudal Hungary before 1848), but because he was not confirmed by the king, he returned his commission and resigned on October 2, 1848. He retired to his estates in the country for a while before fighting as a member of the national guard, later serving in the diet. In the interest of peace, he sought to negotiate with the commander in chief of the Austrian troops, Count Windischgrätz (1787–1862); the latter not only refused to receive him but also had Batthyány arrested on January 8, 1849. Though the military court rejected the absurd accusations of high treason and murder, he was nonetheless sentenced to prison. Under pressure from Felix Schwarzenberg (1800–1852), the Austrian prime minister and minister of foreign affairs, the court sentenced him to death but also left open the possibility of pardon. Batthyány was taken to Pest, where Baron Julius Haynau (1786–1853), the commander-in-chief of the imperial troops, who was vested with full power by the king, ignored the pardoning procedure and sentenced him to be hanged, accusing Batthyány of promoting the upheaval in the monarchy. Batthyány tried to take his own life but failed. He was shot the following day. In Budapest a sanctuary lamp on the place of his execution preserves his memory.

Pál Péter Tóth

Further reading

Horváth, S. *Graf Ludwig Batthyány, ein politischer Martyrer.* Hamburg, 1850.

Spira, György. *Négy magyar sors.* Budapest, 1983.

Szinnyei, József. *Magyar írók élete és munkái,* vol. 1. Budapest, 1894.

Urbán, Aladár. *Batthyány miniszterelnöksége.* Budapest, 1986.

See also *Honvéd;* Hungarian War for Independence; Josip Jelačić; Revolutions of 1848; Prince Felix zu Schwarzenberg; Alfred Windischgrätz

Beck, József (1894–1944)

Polish statesman. Born into a Polish intelligentsia family in Warsaw, Beck was raised in Austrian Poland. He joined József Piłsudski's (1867–1935) Polish Legions (Polish volunteers who fought against the Russians in World War I) in 1914, was wounded, and was decorated for bravery. After serving in military intelligence and several special missions, Beck served as military attaché in Paris and Brussels, and was awarded the French Legion of Honor in May 1923. He became chief of Piłsudski's war ministry cabinet from 1926 until 1930. He later became deputy premier (August–December 1930), deputy foreign minister (December 1930–December 1932), and foreign minister (December 1932–September 1939).

Piłsudski handpicked Beck to continue his foreign policy, which was based on two axioms: Poland must always balance between Germany and the USSR, maintaining good relations with both, but alliance with neither, because the disparity in strength would make Poland a satellite at best. While distrusting Moscow, both Piłsudski and Beck rejected German proposals for a common attack on the USSR and of Polish territorial acquisitions in Ukraine, because they believed Poland would be swallowed by Germany. Moreover, assuming that France and Britain would not fight Germany for Austria or Czechoslovakia, they believed Poland must try to secure the return of the economically important and mostly Polish-speaking western Teschen, taken by the Czechs in January 1919 and awarded to them by the Western powers in July 1920. If the Western powers did fight Germany, however, Beck believed that Poland must join them, for not only was it allied to France but it could never be on Germany's side in a European war. When the first assumption was proved correct by the 1938 Munich Conference, which handed the Sudetenland to Germany, Poland demanded western Teschen, annexing it in early October 1938, and later obtained other small pieces of Czechoslovak territory.

In 1938–39 Beck and the Polish cabinet refused to negotiate on Hitler's (1889–1945) demands for Danzig (Gdańsk) and a German corridor through the Polish Corridor (territory Germany had been forced to cede to a reconstituted Poland after World War I), and concluded a treaty of mutual assistance with Britain. Despite French and British commitments to help Poland, the nation fought alone when the Germans invaded on September 1, 1939. After the Red Army entered Poland from the east on September 17, the Polish government with Beck crossed into Romania, intending to proceed to France and form a new Polish government and army. They were interned in Romania, but a new Polish government and armed forces were nevertheless established in London. Beck died of tuberculosis on June 5, 1944. He was buried in a military cemetery in Bucharest; in May 1992 his remains were reburied with honors in a sector reserved for distinguished Poles in the Powązki cemetery in Warsaw.

Anna M. Cienciala

B

Further reading

Cienciala, Anna M. "Poland in British and French Policy in 1939: Determination to Fight or Avert War?" *Polish Review* 34, no. 3 (1989): 199–226.

———. "Polish Foreign Policy, 1926–1939: 'Equilibrium,' Stereotype and Reality," *Polish Review* 20, no. 1 (1975): 42–58.

———. "The View from Warsaw," in Maya Latynski, ed. *Reappraising the Munich Pact: Continental Perspectives.* Baltimore, 1992, 79–102.

Roberts, Henry L. "The Diplomacy of Colonel Beck," in Gordon A. Craig and Felix Gilbert, eds. *The Diplomats: 1919–1939,* Princeton, New Jersey, 1953, 579–614.

Wandycz, Piotr S. *The Twilight of French Eastern Alliances 1926–36: French-Czechoslovak-Polish Relations from Locarno to the Remilitarization of the Rhineland.* Princeton, New Jersey, 1988.

See also Gdańsk; Adolf Hitler; Munich Pact; Nazi-Polish War; Józef Piłsudski; Polish Corridor; Polish Legions; Red Army; Sudeten Crisis; Teschen

Belcredi, Richard (1823–1902)

Moravian noble and conservative politician, governor of Bohemia, and Austrian prime minister. In the state service of the Habsburg Empire, Belcredi rose from being a subordinate official to head of the provincial administration of Austrian Silesia in 1861 and vice governor and (later) governor of Bohemia from 1863 to 1865. As a member of the Moravian diet he was also sent to the House of Deputies of the Imperial Council in Vienna. An adherent of conservative monarchism, Belcredi maintained a neutral position in the ethnic struggle in the Czech lands and did not join either of the two national parties. An opponent of modern liberalism, he wished to strengthen the position of the emperor by an extensive decentralization of representative bodies to crownlands and districts. In February 1865 Franz Joseph (1830–1916) approached him as a prospective successor to State Minister Anton von Schmerling (1805–93). Although he at first hesitated, Belcredi was appointed state minister and chairman of the Council of Ministers in July 1865. His most important task, he felt, was an agreement with Hungary. In September 1865 he put through the suspension of the Imperial Council and the reinforcement of the diets in the crownlands. Belcredi asserted equal rights for the German and Czech languages in public functions in Bohemia and Moravia. This movement toward greater federalism in Belcredi's program, however, met resistance from German-Austrian liberals and the Hungarian opposition. That opposition was reinforced by the results of the Austro-Prussian War of 1866. He was forced to resign on February 7, 1867, warning against the one-sided hegemony of the Germans and Hungarians in the empire. He retired from public life until 1881, when he returned as a member of the upper house and president of the Administrative Law Court.

Jiří Kořalka

Further reading

Brettner-Messler, Horst. *Die Protokolle des österreichischen Ministerrates (1848–1867): Abteilung VI: Ministerium Belcredi,* 2 vols. Vienna, 1971–73.

Mertal, Walter. "Graf Richard Belcredi (1823–1902): Ein Staatsmann aus dem Österreich Kaiser Franz Josefs." Ph.D. diss., University of Vienna, 1963.

Traub, Hugo. "Jak se stal hrabě Belcredi ministerským předsedou rakouským?" *Český časopis historický* 35 (1929): 105–29.

Zimprich, Arthur. "Belcredis Versuche einer Föderalisierung der Donaumonarchie." *Ungarn-Jahrbuch* 1 (1969): 99–138.

See also Franz Joseph

Belgrade

Capital city of Serbia since 1806 and of Yugoslavia since 1918. Belgrade is situated at the junction of the Danube and Sava Rivers, on the border between the Pannonian (Hungarian) Plain and upland terrain of the Balkan Peninsula. The city has a population of more than one million, with an additional five hundred thousand living in suburban areas.

Celtic tribes established the fortified settlement of Singedunum on the present site of Belgrade as early as the fourth century B.C. The community developed on a high hill at the strategic intersection with the Danube of the ancient route that extended northward through the Balkan

Peninsula from the shores of the Aegean to the Baltic coast. The Romans captured Singedunum at the end of the first century A.D., and the community became headquarters of a Roman legion in the fourth century.

Several states controlled the town during the Middle Ages, including the Byzantine Empire, Bulgaria, and Hungary. The Slavic name *Belgrad* first appeared in the ninth century while the region was under Bulgarian control. In 1521 Ottoman forces captured Belgrade. Its hilltop fortress, Kalemegdan, became the principal Turkish outpost facing the Austrian-held Pannonian Plain after the 1699 Treaty of Karlovac. Subsequently, during the 1720s, Austrian engineers under terms of a peace treaty modernized Kalemegdan's fortifications.

Serbian rebels made Belgrade their capital after seizing it in 1806 and again in 1830; the Ottoman sultan recognized the town as capital of an autonomous Serbian principality. Belgrade's population then was barely seven thousand. Turkish troops did not leave Kalemegdan until 1867, however. The town remained the capital following Serbian independence in 1878, its population at that time being sixty thousand. Belgrade became the capital of the Kingdom of Serbs, Croats, and Slovenes upon the latter's establishment in 1918.

The Germans bombed the city on Easter Sunday 1941 to begin their occupation of Yugoslavia. It lost more than thirty thousand structures during the course of the war. In 1944 Tito (1892–1980) made Belgrade the capital of the Yugoslav federation and also capital of the internal Socialist Republic of Serbia. After World War II, Belgrade expanded westward to incorporate the old Austro-Hungarian border town of Zemun lying across the Sava River. The residential community of Novi Beograd (New Belgrade) later developed along the Sava adjacent to Zemun.

In addition to its administrative role, Belgrade is a significant industrial and commercial center. It contains more than two hundred major manufacturing enterprises producing a wide range of goods, including metals, textiles, chemicals, and processed foods. The city became a major river port following construction in the 1960s of the Djerdap Dam on the lower Danube between Yugoslavia and Romania at the entrance to the Iron Gates canyon.

Thomas M. Poulsen

Further reading

Bertić, Ivan. *Veliki geografski atlas Jugoslavije.* Zagreb, 1987.

Hamilton, F.E. Ian. *Yugoslavia: Patterns of Economic Activity.* New York, 1968.

Pavić, Radovan and Nikola Stražičić. *Ekonomska geografija Jugoslavije,* 3d ed. Zagreb, 1970.

See also Great Hungarian Plain; Iron Gates; Kingdom of Serbs, Croats, and Slovenes; Serbia; Tito

Bem, Józef Zacharjasz (1794–1850)

Polish military and revolutionary leader. Bem's military career began as a cadet in 1809 in a school of artillery and engineers. He advanced rapidly, was assigned to an artillery regiment in Gdańsk in 1811, and attained the rank of lieutenant in 1812. During this period, he fought in the Baltic and East Prussian theaters during the Napoleonic Wars and was awarded the Knight's Cross of the French Legion of Honor in 1813. In 1822 his flirtation with Freemasonry led to his arrest, trial, and imprisonment with a recommendation for dismissal. Only the intervention of Grand Duke Constantine (1779–1831) prevented his discharge.

Following the outbreak of the 1830 November Uprising against the Russians, Bem made his way to Warsaw. His ability, audacity, and successes led to rapid promotion. On August 22, 1831, he was named brigadier general. In the subsequent defense of Warsaw, Bem's dissatisfaction with the scheme of deployment led to his personally taking charge of the artillery and subsequently of overseeing its withdrawal. In later actions and war councils, Bem remained a staunch advocate of continuing the war against Russia at all costs.

Joining other Polish émigrés in France, Bem believed he could create Polish legions to continue the struggle for Polish independence. He organized the passage of defeated Polish columns through Germany to France, collecting the funds to make it possible. Bem also joined the organization of Prince Adam Czartoryski (1770–1861), the émigré leader with whom he remained tied until 1848.

With the outbreak of the Revolutions of 1848, he returned to the political-military stage. Bem had hopes of being named commander of the Hungarian army by Lajos Kossuth (1802–94), the

Hungarian revolutionary leader. Though this did not come to pass, Bem took charge of the army in Transylvania, where, despite the odds against him, he was able to seize control over that region by the end of March 1849. Ill-supplied and with a poorly trained force, Bem attempted invasions of the Banat and Wallachia in April and May. Forced to retreat to Transylvania, he now faced overwhelming odds. A few minor tactical successes and a desperate attempt to draw the Ottomans into the war failed to turn the tide. Finally named commander of the Hungarian army in August 1849, Bem fought General Haynau (1786–1853) at Temesvar under hopeless conditions.

With the failure of the Hungarian revolution, Bem went into exile. His death in 1850 left a legacy as a military hero not only to Poland, but also to Hungary.

Robert A. Berry

Further reading

Chudzikowski, Jadwiga. *Generał Bem*. Warsaw, 1990.

See also Constantine; Adam Czartoryski; Freemasonry; Hungarian War for Independence; Lajos Kossuth; November Uprising; Polish Émigrés; Revolutions of 1848

Beneš, Edvard (1884–1948)

Czech politician, diplomat, and second president of Czechoslovakia (1935–38; 1940–48). The son of a small farmer and entrepreneur, Beneš earned two doctorates in 1908, in law from the University of Dijon, France, and philosophy from the University of Prague. He aspired to distinction in both academia and politics, attaining both in 1912 with his *Stranictví: Sociologická studie* (*Political Parties: A Sociological Study*). After the outbreak of World War I, he joined his fellow professor, Tomáš G. Masaryk (1850–1937), in organizing a political movement at home and abroad with the aim of achieving the dissolution of the Habsburg Empire into a number of independent states, including Czechoslovakia. During the war, Beneš served as secretary of the Czechoslovak National Council in Paris. After the proclamation of the new state in 1918, he served as minister of foreign affairs until 1935. His goal was to safeguard the security of the nation through alliances with the principal continental powers of Europe, as well as

Romania and Yugoslavia. He was a strong believer in the supposed guarantor of international peace, the League of Nations, and served the organization as a member of its Executive Committee (1924–27) and chair of its Security Committee (1927–29).

In December 1935 Masaryk resigned the presidency because of illness and age and Beneš was elected his successor. He soon found himself confronting a resurgent Germany, which, in 1938, threatened to destroy Czechoslovakia by invasion under the pretext of securing self-determination for its German minority in the Sudetenland. Faced with a war for which they were not prepared, France and Britain declined Beneš's appeals for military help, instead signing an agreement in Munich in September 1938 that turned over nearly 29 percent of Czechoslovak territory to Germany, Poland, and Hungary. Faced with abandonment by his allies and the silence of the League of Nations, Beneš and his government had little choice but to turn over the claimed areas. In protest and under pressure from his domestic critics, Beneš resigned and moved to the United States.

With the dismemberment of the rest of Czechoslovakia in 1939, Beneš assumed leadership of a resistance movement at home and abroad aimed at restoring an independent Czechoslovakia to its prewar borders. By the end of World War II, the allies approved of the Czechoslovak plan. Beneš returned to Prague in May 1945, hailed by his people as a liberator. But the prospects for his second presidency were bleak. The Soviet Union looked upon East Central Europe as a buffer zone of satellite states. In 1948 Czechoslovak Communists skillfully used a government crisis to bypass the leadership of the non-Communist parties and assumed full control of the country. With his health shattered after several strokes, Beneš felt himself unable to find an alternative to a civil war with Soviet interference and no assurance of help from the West. On February 25, 1948, he accepted the new Communist government. He resigned three months later. Following another stroke in late summer, he died on September 3.

Beneš's life was a witness to the turbulent times that were the fate of Central Europe during the first half of the twentieth century, a fact reflected in his memoirs (including *Mnichovské dny* [*The Munich Days*, 1968] and *Memoirs: From Munich to New War and New Victory* [1954]) and essays (such as *Democracy Today and Tomorrow*

[1939] and *Úvahy o novém Slovanství [Contemplations on the New Slavdom,* 1946]). All displayed his hopes for a better world, where all nations, small and large, would live together peacefully in spite of their political differences.

Josef Anderle

Further reading

Hanzal, Josef. *Edvard Beneš.* Prague, 1994.

Korbel, Josef. *The Communist Subversion of Czechoslovakia, 1938–1948.* Princeton, New Jersey, 1959.

———. *Twentieth Century Czechoslovakia.* New York, 1977.

Taborsky, Edward. *President Beneš between East and West, 1938–1948.* Stanford, California, 1981.

Weinberg, Gerhard L. *The Foreign Policy of Hitler's Germany,* vol. 2. Chicago, 1980.

See also Communist Party of Czechoslovakia; League of Nations; Tomáš G. Masaryk; Munich Pact; Sudeten Crisis; Sudetenland

Beran, Rudolf (1887–1954)

Czech politician and statesman. Born in Pracejovice in Bohemia, Beran was a prominent member of the right-of-center Agrarian Party. A close collaborator of Antonín Švehla (1873–1933), the party's founder, he served successively as the party's secretary-general (1915–33), acting chairman (1933–35), and chairman (1935–38), as well as deputy in the Czechoslovak National Assembly (1918–39). Beginning in the mid-1930s, Beran favored a policy of conciliation with the Sudeten German Party (Sudetendeutsche Partei) of Konrad Henlein (1898–1945) in Bohemia and Moravia and normalization of Czechoslovakia's relations with Nazi Germany. The most conspicuous portion of his political career followed the Munich Agreement (September 30, 1938), which saw the loss of the Sudetenland to Germany, when he was appointed prime minister of Czechoslovakia's Second Republic (December 1, 1938–March 15, 1939). He also founded and chaired the Party of National Unity (Strana národní jednoty), dedicated to conciliating the Third Reich. After the establishment of the Protectorate of Bohemia and Moravia following German occupation of the country, Beran served briefly as the prime minister of the first Protectorate government (March 16–April 27, 1939). After retiring from political life, he was jailed by the German authorities from 1941 to 1943. With the restoration of Czechoslovakia in May 1945, he was arrested, tried in April 1947, and received a twenty-year prison sentence for wartime collaboration with the enemy. He died in a penitentiary in Leopoldov in Slovakia in 1954.

Zdeněk David

Further reading

Jindra, V. *Rudolf Beran, dokumenty zrady.* Prague, 1946.

Mamatey, Victor S. and Radomír Luža, eds. *A History of the Czechoslovak Republic, 1918–1948.* Princeton, New Jersey, 1973.

Procházka, Theodore. *The Second Republic: The Disintegration of Post-Munich Czechoslovakia, October 1938–March 1939.* Boulder, Colorado, 1981.

See also Agrarian Parties; Konrad Henlein; Munich Pact; Protectorate of Bohemia and Moravia; Antonín Švehla

Berchtold, Count Leopold von (1863–1942)

Austro-Hungarian diplomat. Berchtold served as Austria-Hungary's foreign minister from 1912 to 1915. As foreign minister, Berchtold directed the monarchy's final efforts to reverse its deteriorating position in the Balkans. These efforts culminated in the July crisis of 1914 and the outbreak of World War I.

Berchtold inherited a diplomatic situation made tense by his predecessor's (Count Alois Aehrenthal [1854–1912]) annexation of Bosnia-Hercegovina in 1908, an event that intensified Serbian irredentist claims on southern sections of the Dual Monarchy and deepened Russian suspicions of Austro-Hungarian intentions in the Balkans. The First and Second Balkan Wars (1912–1913) exacerbated international tensions in this region and further eroded Serbian-Habsburg relations. Alleged Serbian complicity in the assassination of Archduke Franz Ferdinand (1863–1914) at Sarejevo on June 28, 1914, afforded Berchtold an opportunity to confront directly the Serbian threat. During July, Berchtold embarked on a series of diplomatic initiatives aimed at crushing Serbia. After succeeding on July 5 in gaining unequivocal support from the monarchy's principal ally, Germany, and after overcoming the reluctance of Hungarian Minister-President István Tisza (1861–

B

1918) by July 14, Berchtold moved against Serbia. On July 26, as a prelude to military action, Berchtold sent a harsh, forty-eight–hour ultimatum to the Serbian government containing items designed to assure its rejection. Belgrade's subsequent failure to accept the ultimatum resulted in an Austro-Hungarian declaration of war on July 28. Berchtold's rather sanguine hope that an armed confrontation with Serbia would remain a localized conflict proved illusory as Germany, Russia, France, and ultimately Great Britain all entered the conflict in early August. The resulting European-wide war lasted for four years and ended with the destruction of the Habsburg Empire in late 1918.

Berchtold continued in office until early 1915, when he resigned after his failure to secure the benevolent neutrality of the monarchy's erstwhile ally, Italy.

Lawrence J. Flockerzie

Further reading

Bridge, F.R. *The Habsburg Monarchy among the Great Powers, 1815–1918.* New York, 1990.

Hantsch, Hugo. *Leopold Graf Berchtold: Grandseigneur und Staatsmann,* 2 vols. Graz, 1963.

Williamson, Samuel R., Jr. *Austria-Hungary and the Origins of the First World War.* New York, 1991.

See also Alois Aerenthal; Balkan Wars; Dual Monarchy; Franz Ferdinand; István Tisza

Berg, General Count Teodor Fryderyk Wilhelm Rembert (Feodor Feodorovich) (c. 1790–1874)

Russian general, geographer, cartographer, and last viceroy of the Congress Kingdom of Poland. Born in Sagnitz, Estonia, Berg was a member of an impoverished gentry family. After completing his education at the University of Dorpat, he entered the military in 1812, enrolling in a foot regiment. He soon transferred to the quartermaster corps and took part in the campaigns of 1813–14 against Napoléon (1769–1821). In 1820, having reached the rank of colonel, he entered the Russian civil service. Shifting between military and diplomatic roles, he led a diplomatic mission to Constantinople in 1825, returned to the army as a major general, and fought the Ottomans in the Russo-Turkish War of 1828–29. Following this, he headed a surveying expedition to northeast Bulgaria, Rumelia, and the Balkan Mountains.

Berg participated in the military campaigns against the Poles in the November Uprising of 1831 and, during the storming of Warsaw, was sent to the Polish commander to negotiate the surrender of the city. For the next twelve years, he remained on active duty in Warsaw. In 1843 Berg was promoted to the rank of general and appointed as quartermaster general of the general staff. For the next twenty years, his career primarily encompassed geography and cartography, with a brief diplomatic interlude during 1848–49 to Prussia and Austria relating to Polish affairs. As a reward for his services defending the Baltic from the British during the Crimean War (1853–56), Berg was raised to the rank of count of the Great Kingdom of Finland and named governor-general of Finland in 1860.

At the close of his career, Berg was named viceroy of the Congress Kingdom of Poland just as the 1863 uprising against the Russians broke out. While viceroy, he invoked severe measures to quell the uprising, but once it was over, he advocated leniency and economic development for the region. Berg died in St. Petersburg.

Robert A. Berry

Further reading

"Berg, Graf Feodor Feodorovich." *Russkii biograficheskii slovar,* vol. 2, pt. 2. St. Petersburg, 1908.

See also Crimean War; January Uprising; Napoléon; November Uprising; Polish Congress Kingdom; Russo-Turkish War of 1828–29

Berlin Wall

Fortified barrier that divided the city of Berlin and came to represent the Cold War. Following World War II, Berlin was governed by France, Great Britain, the Soviet Union, and the United States. Lying geographically in the Soviet sphere of influence in the German Democratic Republic, Moscow considered the Western Allied presence in the city as a direct threat to its authority in the region. Of equal concern was the fact that Berlin served as an escape route that saw over three million East Germans flee to the West. With negotiations between U.S. President John F. Kennedy (1917–1963) and Soviet leader Nikita Khrushchev (1884–1971) proving inconclusive, on August 13, 1961, the East German government began erecting a thirteen-foot (four m) wall to seal off West Berlin. Aside from preventing a further migration of people, the Berlin Wall solidified the East German regime, which then pursued more repressive domestic policies. By highlighting the geographic and ideological division in postwar Europe, a fact confirmed by Kennedy's historic visit to Berlin in 1963, the Berlin Wall came to serve as the most recognizable symbol of the Cold War. In the summer of 1989, with the liberalization of political regimes in Eastern Europe, Hungary opened its borders with Austria, thereby providing East Germans with an alternate escape route to the West. On November 9, the East German government dissolved its borders with West Germany, which precipitated German unification in October 1990 and the dismantling of the Berlin Wall.

Conrad Jarzebowski

Further reading

Elper, Doris M. *The Berlin Wall: How It Rose and It Fell.* Brookfield, Connecticut, 1992.

Gelb, Norman. *The Berlin Wall: Kennedy, Khrushchev and a Showdown in the Heart of Europe.* New York, 1986.

Read, Anthony and David Fisher. *Berlin Rising: Biography of a City.* New York, 1994.

See also Cold War; Iron Curtain; Revolutions of 1989

Bernolák, Anton (1762–1813)

Catholic priest and first codifier of the Slovak language. Born in Slanica (Orava county) to a family of the small landed gentry, Bernolák entered the seminary in 1778 and studied in Trnava, Vienna, and Bratislava. Ordained in 1787, he was appointed chaplain in Čeklís, served in the vicar's office in Trnava, and in 1797 became pastor in Nové Zamky, where he remained until his death.

While studying at the Bratislava general seminary, Bernolák anonymously printed *Dissertatio philogico-critica de literis Slavorum (Dissertation on the Philological Critique of the Slavic Literary Language,* 1787), a justification for a Slovak literary language. He also authored *Linguae slavonicae per regnum hungariae usitatae compendiosa simul et facilis orthographia (A Contemporary Compendium and Orthography of the Customary Slavic Language during the Hungarian Reign,* 1787), a Slovak orthography. In 1790 he published *Grammatica slavica,* a Slovak grammar. His *Etymologia vocum slavicarum (Etymology of the Slavic Voice),* an etymology of Slovak words, appeared in 1791. Bernolák's six-volume dictionary, *Slowár slowenski, česki-lat'insko-ňemecko-uherskí,* was published posthumously (1825–27).

Bernolák codified the language used by educated Slovaks of the Trnava region and, hence, based his codification on the Western Slovak dialect. Later known as bernolákovčina, this literary language received its most advantageous support from the Slovak Learned Society, founded in 1792 in Trnava. Although short-lived, the society, whose membership comprised primarily Catholic priests and included Bernolák, printed literature in bernolákovčina and disseminated it.

Catholic intellectuals and clergymen adopted bernolákovčina, but Slovak Protestants shunned it. In 1851 Bernolákovites and Protestant supporters of štúrovčina, a Slovak literary language developed in the 1840s, reached a compromise. A modified version of štúrovčina that incorporated elements of bernolákovčina was published in 1852 and became the foundation for modern literary Slovak.

June Granatir Alexander

Further reading

Kirschbaum, Joseph M. *Anton Bernolák: The First Codifier of the Slovak Language (1762–1813).* Cleveland, n.d.

Trylčová, Elena. *Anton Bernolák (1762–1813).* Martin, Slovakia, 1962.

See also Slovak Language

Bessarabia *See* Bessarabian Question

Bessarabian Question

International dispute surrounding the status of Bessarabia, an area of southeastern Europe bounded by the Prut River to the west, the Dniester River to the north and east, and the Danube River and Black Sea to the south. Until 1812, Bessarabia formed the eastern half of the Principality of Moldavia (Moldova), but under the Treaty of Bucharest, which ended the Russo-Turkish War of 1806–12, Alexander I (1777–1825) annexed Bessarabia and transformed it into a province of the Russian Empire. Local nobles in the truncated Moldavian principality (which remained a vassal state of the Ottoman Empire) argued that the sultan had no right to cede the territory to Russia without their consent.

In 1859 truncated Moldavia united with the Principality of Wallachia to form the precursor of modern Romania (which achieved independence from the Ottomans in 1878). Since it was populated mainly by Romanian speakers, Bessarabia remained a contentious issue between Russia and the new Romanian state. After the Bolshevik revolution, a "national assembly," or Sfatul Ţării,in the Bessarabian capital of Chişinău initially declared an autonomous Bessarabian republic and then, on March 27, 1918, voted for union with the Kingdom of Romania.

While Romanian leaders welcomed the 1918 union as the realization of Romanian national unity, the Soviets argued that Bessarabia's rightful place was within the new Soviet Union, the successor state to the tsarist empire. Moreover, Moscow held that Bessarabia's majority population—the Romanian-speaking "Moldovans"—formed a distinct nation whose uniqueness Romanian nationalists were ostensibly ignoring. The region's status remained unresolved throughout the interwar period since neither the Soviet Union nor the Western powers ever recognized the 1918 Romanian-Bessarabian union.

Under the Molotov-Ribbentrop Pact of August 1939, Bessarabia was assigned to the Soviet sphere of interest, and on June 28, 1940, Red Army troops crossed the Dniester River into Bessarabia and declared the region's union with the Soviet state inside a newly created Moldovan Soviet Socialist Republic (MSSR). During the war, Bessarabia again came briefly under Romanian control, but by 1944, the Soviets had shored up their control over the region and reaffirmed its place inside the MSSR. In February 1947 Romania recognized the Soviet incorporation of Bessarabia as part of the postwar territorial settlements.

Although Romania itself became a Communist state in 1947, the Bessarabian question remained a source of tension between Bucharest and Moscow. Especially under the regime of Nicolae Ceauşescu (1918–89), Communist leaders in Romania used veiled references to Bessarabia to distance themselves from the Soviet Union and to portray the Romanian Communist Party as the defender of Romanian national interests.

Charles King

Further reading

Cioranesco, George et al. *Aspects des relations russo-roumaines:Rétrospectives et orientations.* Paris, 1967.

Jewsbury, George F. *The Russian Annexation of Bessarabia: 1774–1828.* Boulder, Colorado, 1976.

van Meurs, Wim P. *The Bessarabian Question in Communist Historiography.* Boulder, Colorado, 1995.

See also Alexander I; Bessarabian Question; Nicolae Ceauşescu; Chişinău; Greater Romania; Irredentism; Molotov-Ribbentrop Pact; Nationalism; Red Army

Bethlen, Count István (1874–1946)

Hungarian politician and scion of an old and influential Hungarian aristocratic family. Bethlen was born in a small Transylvanian village located in an ethnically mixed area, close to Tîrgu Mureş (Hungarian: Marosvásárhely). He attended high school at the prestigious Theresianum in Vienna and later studied law in Budapest and agronomy in Magyaróvár. His political career began in 1901, when he was elected to parliament. As a member of different parties, he remained a representative from 1901 to 1918. During this period, he was interested primarily in Transylvanian issues, especially in light of a fledgling Romanian separatism and irredentism.

During the revolutions of 1918–19 that followed in the wake of Austria-Hungary's defeat in World War I, he became a leading figure of the conservative forces. In 1921 he was appointed prime minister. As holder of this post for over a decade, he became the creator of the so-called (Miklós) Horthy (1868–1957) regime. His political philosophy was a type of old-fashioned liberal conservatism that continued to assign to the aristocracy and the gentry a natural leadership in political and social life. Accordingly, the political system he created was a kind of authoritarian parliamentarism based on limited pluralism. By 1923–24, he was able to stabilize the internal political situation, and by 1926–27, the country's desperate financial and economic conditions improved as well. His primary foreign political goal was the revision of the Treaty of Trianon, which cost Hungary two-thirds of its prewar territory, and thus the establishment of a great and powerful Hungary dominating the Danube basin.

As a consequence of the Great Depression, economic conditions in the country worsened and the political situation was shaken again. Bethlen was forced to resign his office on August 19, 1931. He remained, however, one of the country's most influential politicians up to 1944. From 1931 to 1939 he was a representative in parliament; in 1939 he was appointed as a permanent member of the Upper House. Operating mostly behind the scenes, he opposed the growing Nazi influence in the country and the attempts to establish a one-party dictatorship.

After the German army occupied Hungary in March 1944, Bethlen became the most hunted man in his own country. On December 7 he emerged from hiding and reported to the advancing Red Army. He was taken into custody and transferred to the Soviet Union in April 1945, where he died in a prison hospital in Moscow.

Ignác Romsics

Further reading

Macartney, C.A. *October Fifteenth: A History of Modern Hungary, 1929–1945.* Edinburgh, 1961.

Romsics, Ignác. *István Bethlen. A Great Conservative Statesman of Hungary, 1874–1946.* Boulder, Colorado, 1995.

See also Great Depression; Miklós Horthy; Irredentism; Red Army; Revisionism; Transylvanian Dispute; Trianon, Treaty of

Beust, Count Friedrich Ferdinand von (1809–86)

Habsburg statesman and foreign minister from 1866 to 1871. A Saxon and previously Saxony's foreign minister, Beust was appointed Habsburg foreign minister by Emperor Franz Joseph (1830–1916) following the empire's defeat in the Austro-Prussian War of 1866. As minister-president from 1866 to 1868 and thereafter chancellor until 1871, Beust also exerted significant influence in the empire's domestic affairs. As a precondition to conducting a foreign policy that would revive the empire's international fortunes, Beust had first to set its troubled domestic arrangements on a firm foundation and especially to reconcile the Hungarian opposition to Habsburg rule. Working effectively as an outsider unencumbered by past entanglements in Habsburg domestic politics,

Beust successfully facilitated the crown's final negotiations with the Hungarians, which resulted in the *Ausgleich* (Compromise) of 1867, which established the Dual Monarchy of Austria-Hungary. In foreign affairs, Beust cultivated close relations with the remaining independent states in southern Germany and attempted to construct a tripartite alliance with Italy and France. He also engaged Russia across a number of issues as relations with that power became increasingly strained, owing to the rise of Pan-Slavism (which promoted the unity of the Slavic peoples) and growing Habsburg-Russian competition in the Balkans.

Beust's ultimate goal may have possibly aimed at recapturing the Habsburg dynasty's leading role in German affairs, which had been lost as a result of its defeat to Prussia in 1866. At the very least, he probably wished to limit Prussia to its 1866 gains in north Germany. Any such hopes were dashed, however, by Prussia's quick and decisive victory over France in 1870 and in the subsequent proclamation of the German Empire. Recognizing that Vienna's loss of influence over Germany was now irreversible and concerned with the growing Russian and Pan-Slav threat, Beust steered the empire toward reconciliation with Berlin, a policy that reached its culmination in the 1870s under his successor, Gyula Andrássy (1823–90).

Lawrence J. Flockerzie

Further reading

Bridge, F.R. *The Habsburg Monarchy among the Great Powers, 1815–1918.* New York, 1990.

Potthoff, Heinrich. *Die deutsche Politik Beusts.* Bonn, 1968.

Schoenhals, Kai Peter. *The Russian Policy of Count Friedrich Ferdinand von Beust, 1866–1871.* Ann Arbor, Michigan, 1964.

See also Gyula Andrássy, Sr.; *Ausgleich;* Dual Monarchy; Franz Joseph; Pan-Slavism

Białystok

City in northeastern Poland, a large center of textile production, with a population of 265,000, some three times larger than the prewar figure. Originally a village located south of a large forested complex (Knyszyn Forest) at the intersection of the Warsaw-Grodno and several local roads, Białystok served as a residence of a Polish

B

magnate who introduced handicraft woolen mills. It started to grow and received an urban charter in 1749. Russia annexed it after the partitions of Poland in the late eighteenth century.

The first textile-woolen factory appeared in 1824, but the developmental takeoff was in 1831, after Russia established the customs boundary with the Congress Kingdom of Poland, effectively removing competition with the Polish woolen industry. The St. Petersburg-Warsaw railroad increased accessibility to Russian markets and facilitated further development. In 1879 Białystok had 47 textile factories; that number grew to 81 in 1890 and 113 in 1922, employing 5 percent of the city's population. The loss of Russian markets and the Depression (1929) undercut further growth. In 1937 only 68 factories were active, accounting for 8 percent of Poland's woolen production. Besides the textiles, Białystok also had light industry (tobacco, tanneries, brewery, and agricultural implements).

German occupation during World War II destroyed most of the industries. After the war, old industries were restored, consolidated, and modernized, and new ones were added (light metal, electronics, building materials, and food processing). Białystok became a transportation hub based on the network of railroads that traversed the region. The functional profile of the city was enriched by the addition of a medical school, a college (a branch of Warsaw University), and several cultural institutions.

Abraham Melezin

Further reading

Janiszewski, Michał. *Geograficzne warunki powstawania miast polskich.* Lublin, 1991, 81–83.
Werwicki, Andrzej. "Białostocki przemysł włókienniczy." *Przegląd Geograficzny,* 29, no. 3 (1957): 583–94.

See also Polish Congress Kingdom; Railroads

Bibescu, Gheorghe (1804–73)

Prince of Wallachia. The son of a wealthy *boiar* family, Bibescu served as an adviser to Count Paul Kiselev (1788–1863), the administrator of the Russian protectorate in the Danubian Principalities, before being elected prince of Wallachia in 1842 in accordance with the provisions of the Organic Statute, the document that administered the principality. As prince, Bibescu was influential in promoting economic reforms, most notably a customs union with Moldavia in 1847 and improvements in roads. Nevertheless, his association with the Russians was antithetical to the growing nationalism among young Romanian intellectuals. Such opposition only made Bibescu rely more heavily on Russian support and ignore the advice of moderates. When the Revolutions of 1848 broke out, the Wallachian revolutionaries declared a liberal agenda in June (Islaz Proclamation) aimed at ending the Russian protectorate and the Organic Statute. Although he first endorsed the Islaz program, an assassination attempt a few days later caused Bibescu to abdicate and leave for Transylvania. When order was restored, his brother, Barbu Ştirbei (1799–1869), was named prince in his stead. After the Crimean War, Bibescu was looked upon as a possible prince of a United Principalities, but familial rivalry with Ştirbei helped lead to the election of Alexandru Ioan Cuza (1820–73).

Richard Frucht

Further reading

Hitchins, Keith. *The Romanians 1774–1866.* Oxford, 1996.
Jelavich, Barbara. *History of the Balkans,* vol. 1, *The Eighteenth and Nineteenth Centuries.* Cambridge, Massachusetts, 1983.
———. *Russia and the Formation of the Romanian National State 1821–1878.* Cambridge, Massachusetts, 1984.

See also Alexandru Ioan Cuza; Crimean War; Danubian Principalities; Islaz Proclamation; Count Pavei Dimitrievic Kiselev; Organic Statutes; Revolutions of 1848; Barbu Ştirbei; United Principalities

Bierut, Bolesław (1892–1956)

Polish Communist and leader of the Polish United Workers Party. Bierut joined one of the predecessors of the Polish Communist Party (KKP) in 1912. During the interwar period, following his training in Moscow, he became an agent of the Comintern (Communist International) in Austria, Bulgaria, and Czechoslovakia. Jailed in 1935, he escaped the fate of the top leaders of the KKP, who, after the dissolution of the KKP by Stalin (1879–1953), were executed in the late 1930s in the Soviet Union as part of the Moscow purges.

After the outbreak of the Polish-German war in September 1939, Bierut escaped to the USSR, where he remained until 1943. On the Comintern's orders, in the summer of 1943 Bierut was sent to Warsaw, where he became a member of the Central Committee of the underground Communist Party, known at that time as the Polish Workers Party (PPR), created a year earlier as a successor to the KKP. In 1944 he was appointed chairman of the National Council of the Homeland (KRN), a bogus underground parliament organized by the PPR.

Following Western recognition of the new Communist-led Polish government in July 1945, Bierut continued as chairman of the KRN until January 1947, when he was elected president of the Republic of Poland. Until then, his position in the PPR was overshadowed by Władysław Gomułka (1905–82), secretary-general of the party. In 1948, after the birth of the Cominform (Communist propaganda organization), the Stalin-Tito conflict, and the beginning of the Stalinization of Poland, Gomułka was ousted and Bierut took over as party leader, which after its merger with the Polish Socialist Party (PPS) in December 1948 became known as the Polish United Workers Party (PZPR).

The new Polish constitution of 1952 abolished the office of the presidency and, in accordance with the new practices introduced in the Soviet Union in the wake of Stalin's death, Bierut became prime minister of Poland, the job he held until 1954. He died in March 1956, while attending the Twentieth Congress of the Communist Party of the Soviet Union in Moscow.

Details of Bierut's life were long kept under wraps. New studies, however, show how an otherwise obscure Comintern functionary, elevated by Stalin to the top position in Poland, remained a faithful disciple of the Kremlin, being primarily responsible for the rule of terror that, although somewhat muted in Poland as compared with that in the other satellites of Moscow, proved to be costly in terms of human lives and suffering.

Andrzej Korbonski

Further reading
Garlicki, Andrzej. *Boleslaw Bierut.* Warsaw, 1994.
Kozlowski, Czeslaw. *Namiestnik Stalina.* Warsaw, 1993.
Rechowicz, Henryk. *Boleslaw Bierut 1892–1956.* Warsaw, 1974.

See also Cominform; Comintern; Communist Party of Poland; Władysław Gomułka; Nazi-Polish War; Stalin; Tito-Stalin Split

Bismarck, Prince Otto von (1815–98)

Adviser to William I (1797–1888) from 1862 to 1870 and chancellor of Germany from 1871 to 1890. Born into an aristocratic Prussian German family, Bismarck remained an arch-conservative throughout his long political career. He is best known for his achievements between 1866 and 1871, bringing together thirty-eight states of the German Confederation into a unified German Empire. As the architect of German foreign and domestic policies from the 1860s to 1890, Bismarck's actions profoundly affected Eastern Europe.

Like many other Prussian Germans, Bismarck understood that Prussia's (and later Germany's) position required the continued suppression of any Polish national state. In response to the Polish rebellion of 1863 against the Russians, Bismarck established the Alvensleben Convention with St. Petersburg, an understanding of cooperation against the Polish insurrection. Prussia closed its eastern border against Polish insurgents and prevented pro-Polish European volunteers from entering Poland from Prussia while allowing Russian soldiers to cross into Prussian territory when in pursuit of Polish insurgents.

After 1871, Bismarck sought to maintain good relations with both Austria-Hungary and Russia, despite steadily worsening relations between those two empires. At the Congress of Berlin in 1878, Bismarck successfully mediated the Balkan rivalries that threatened to produce conflict between Russia and Austria-Hungary. With difficulty, Bismarck managed to maintain satisfactory relations with both empires through the 1880s by using a complex web of overlapping agreements and alliances, including the Dreikaiserbund (Three Emperors League), the Dual Alliance, and the Reinsurance Treaty.

Robert Mark Spaulding

Further reading
Gall, Lothar. *Bismarck, the White Revolutionary,* trans. by J.A. Underwood. Boston, 1990.
Pflanze, Otto. *Bismarck and the Development of Germany,* 3 vols. Princeton, New Jersey, 1990.

B

See also Congress of Berlin; Dual Alliance; Germany; January Uprising; Kulturkampf; Prussia; Reinsurance Treaty; Three Emperors League

Black George (Karadjordje) (1768–1817)

The leader of the first Serbian uprising (1804–13) and the founder of the Karadjordjević dynasty. Born in the Šumadija region of Serbia, Black George (Karadjordje Petrović) joined the Austrian Free Corps and participated in campaigns against the Ottoman Turks during the Austro-Turkish War of 1788–90. After the war, he became a local notable in the Šumadija as a livestock merchant. As conditions worsened in the Belgrade *pashalik* (province) under the tyrannical rule of the local janissaries (Turkish military forces), a group of Serbian notables elected Karadjordje as their leader in February 1804. He amassed almost thirty thousand armed men, thus initiating the Serbian uprising. Karadjordje's role in the uprising was crucial, for he managed to raise the Serbian question from an internal Ottoman issue to a matter of European diplomatic discussion by appealing for support to Russia and in 1807 to both France and Austria.

Although his leadership was eventually challenged by other Serb notables, he held the insurrectionary movement together in spite of many conflicting interests and insurmountable odds. In 1808 he declared himself the hereditary supreme ruler of the country. He maintained his leading position in the uprising until his final military defeat in 1813, when the Ottoman armies recaptured virtually all of the *pashalik*. The Serbian revolt thus ended in failure and Karadjordje fled to the Austrian Empire. He returned to Serbia in 1817 but was murdered on the orders of the newly appointed prince of Serbia, Miloš Obrenović (1789–1860).

Mark Biondich

Further reading

Desnica, Gojko. *Karadjordje: Celokupna istorija vožda Srbije 1768–1817*. Belgrade, 1977.
Perović, Dušan. *Iz istorije prvog srpskog ustanka*. Belgrade, 1979.
Petrovich, Michael B. *A History of Modern Serbia, 1814–1918,* vol. 1. New York, 1976.

See also Janissaries; Miloš Obrenović

Black Hand

Secret Serbian national revolutionary society founded in Belgrade in May 1911 as Unification or Death!, but soon dubbed the Black Hand. Founded at the initiative of civilian national activists, Bogdan Radenković (1875–1917) and Ljubomir Jovanović-Čupa (1877–1913), Black Hand was soon dominated by officers under Colonel Dimitrijević-Apis (1876–1917). Jovanović-Čupa drew up its formidable constitution and rules justifying the use of all means outside of Serbia to make Serbia the magnet for a South Slav state. Run by a ten-man central executive committee, its membership has been estimated variously from several hundred to about 2,500. During 1911–12, Black Hand worked in close cooperation with the Serbian government to promote Balkan cooperation. However, in May 1914 Black Hand feuded with the Serbian regime. Many Black Hand leaders died heroically in World War I, and their remnants, led by Colonel Dimitrijević, served in the Serbian army on Corfu and on the Salonika Front, the Allied southern flank, in 1915–16. The Serbian exile regime, after arresting Black Hand leaders in December 1916, tried them before a military court in Salonika in March–May 1917. They were accused of seeking to overthrow the Serbian monarchy and replace it with a military oligarchy and of attempting to assassinate Prince Regent Alexander (1888–1934) in August 1916. Among the accuseds' personal effects were found the organization's chief documents, which were utilized to obtain its leaders' convictions. Dimitrijević, Major Ljubomir Vulović (1876–1917), and Rade Malobabić (1881–1917) were sentenced to death and shot near Salonika in June 1917. The Serbian Supreme Court at the Belgrade retrial of June 1953 exonerated the Black Hand and Salonika defendants.

David MacKenzie

Further reading

Bogićević, Miloš. *Le procès de Salonique*. Paris, 1927.
MacKenzie, David. *Apis: The Congenial Conspirator.* Boulder, Colorado, 1989.
———. "The 'Black Hand' and Its Statutes." *East European Quarterly* 25, no. 2 (June 1991): 179–206.
———. *The "Black Hand" on Trial: Salonika 1917.* Boulder, Colorado, 1995.
Živanović, Milan Ž. *Pukovnik Apis: Solunski proces 1917.* Belgrade, 1955.

See also Alexander I Karadjordjević; Apis; Franz Ferdinand; Gavrilo Princip; Salonika Front

Black Sea

Large body of water forming much of the eastern margins of the Balkan Peninsula. The sea occupies 160,000 square miles (444,500 sq km), with maximum dimensions of 380 miles (633 km) north/south and 700 miles (1,170 km) east/west. It has an average depth of more than 4,000 feet (1,200 m), with the deepest portion exceeding 7,300 feet (2,200 m). The Black Sea is fed principally by the Danube, Dniester, Dnieper, Rion, and Chorokh Rivers, with half the total coming from the Danube. Surface layers of the sea have noticeably low salinity, ranging from 18 parts per thousand in the center to fewer than 3 parts per thousand at the mouths of rivers. In comparison, sea depths below 500 feet (152 m) average about 23 parts per thousand.

The freshwater intake of the Black Sea is nearly matched by evaporation from it. A continuous interchange exists with the Mediterranean Sea, however. A surface current of relatively fresh water flows westward through the Sea of Marmara, and a lower-level countercurrent brings substantial amounts of salty Mediterranean water back. Surface temperatures in January range from 46° F (8° C) in the center and south to 32° F (0° C) in the northwest. A belt of ice up to a half-mile wide forms adjacent to shore there in winter. July temperatures reach 75° F (24° C).

Because of weak vertical circulation due to the difference between salt- and fresh-water layers, oxygen is confined principally to the upper 150 feet (45 m) of the sea, with none present below 650 feet (197 m). At greater depths, waters are characterized by the presence of hydrogen sulfide and are devoid of life except anaerobic bacteria.

A substantial continental shelf that lies within 650 feet (197 m) of the surface extends seaward from Bulgaria and Romania. It supports up to 140 species of fish, including such commercial species as sturgeon, herring, mackerel, sardines, and tuna. The Black Sea is also noted for large numbers of dolphins.

Thomas M. Poulsen

Further reading

Degens, Egon and David Ross, eds. *The Black Sea: Geology, Chemistry and Biology*. Tulsa, Oklahoma, 1974.

Blagoev, Dimitur (1856–1924)

The father of the Bulgarian Communist Party. Blagoev was born in the village of Zagorichanie, in Macedonia. In 1878 he received a scholarship to study at a seminary in Odessa, Russia, which was a center of revolutionary ideas and activities. Blagoev quickly became a convert to Marxism and actively began to write and speak on social revolution. He was expelled from Russia in 1885 for his revolutionary associations and returned to Bulgaria.

In 1903 Blagoev became the leader of the "Narrow" faction of the Bulgarian Social Democratic Party. This faction of Marxists preferred to split the small socialist party rather than dilute its class purity by encouraging the membership of the peasantry. Blagoev even refused to aid the Agrarian government of Aleksandur Stamboliiski (1879–1923) when it was violently overthrown in June 1923 by conservative elements in the military and units of the Internal Macedonian Revolutionary Organization (IMRO), the Macedonian national liberation organization. When Blagoev was ordered by the Central Committee of the Soviet Union to launch a worker-and-peasant uprising in September 1923, he again opposed supporting the peasantry. Blagoev remained a strict and dedicated Marxist until his death on May 27, 1924.

David Cassens

Further reading

Bell, John D. *The Bulgarian Communist Party from Blagoev to Zhivkov*. Stanford, California, 1987.
———. *Peasants in Power: Alexander Stamboliski and the Bulgarian Agrarian National Union, 1899–1923*. Princeton, New Jersey, 1977.
Crampton, Richard J. *Bulgaria 1878–1918: A History*. Boulder, Colorado, 1983.
Oren, Nissan. *Revolution Administered: Agrarianism and Communism in Bulgaria*. Baltimore, 1973.
Rothschild, Joseph. *The Communist Party of Bulgaria: Origins and Development 1883–1936*. New York, 1959.

See also Communist Party of Bulgaria; IMRO; Marxism; Aleksandur Stamboliiski

Blaj

Central Transylvanian town that played a preeminent role in the Romanian national movement. Although it never exceeded five thousand in

B

population before the twentieth century, Blaj owed its influence to the schools, writers, and bishops of the Greek Catholic (Uniate) Church who were based there. Clerics returning from studies in Vienna and Rome became the propagators of the theory of Daco-Romanian continuity (that is, tracing the origins of the nation to the ancient Dacians) in the Romanian lands (including Transylvania) and of national rebirth (the Transylvanian School) in their writings and teaching. Over ten thousand studied in the high school, normal school, and seminary of Blaj in the century following their founding in 1754. Blaj was isolated from Hungarian culture; however, its scholars carried on an extensive correspondence with their Hungarian counterparts. Nevertheless, in the decades before 1848, militant professors and students sparked the first resistance to Hungarian political nationalism. Twice in 1848, popular assemblies on the "Field of Liberty" in Blaj galvanized Romanian resistance to the Hungarian government.

The Uniate bishop attained the dignity of metropolitan in 1854, and the schools of Blaj were the leaders of Romanian education in the province until 1918. As political leadership shifted to the laity and more Romanians gained access to higher education elsewhere, however, the political role of Blaj declined. It retained tremendous national symbolism and still led the church of half of Transylvanian Romanians. In 1948 the Uniate Church was suppressed and the metropolitan joined his colleagues in prison. After the church was restored to legality in 1990, the metropolitan returned to Blaj and its seminary was reestablished. In May 1991 the church regained control of its eighteenth-century cathedral.

James P. Niessen

Further reading

Chindriş, Ioan and Ferenc Kovács, eds. *Kelt Balózs-falván . . . A román-magyar levelezés multjából 1746–1916*. Bucharest, 1985.

Hitchins, Keith. *The Rumanian National Movements in Transylvania, 1780–1849*. Cambridge, Massachusetts, 1966.

See also Revolutions of 1848; Uniate Church

Bleiweis, Janez (1808–81)

Influential Slovene editor and political figure. In 1843 the Carniolan Agricultural Society received government approval to launch the first Slovene-language newspaper in almost half a century, the *Kmetijske in rokodelske novice* (*Peasants' and Craftsmens' News*). As its editor, Bleiweis fashioned a politically moderate, business-oriented, and culturally weak organ. Bleiweis's Slovene skills at the outset were poor, and he never truly appreciated the language's artistic potential. Thus, he was at odds with poet Francè Prešeren (1800–1849) in the 1840s and writer and critic Fran Levstik (1831–87) in the 1860s. Nonetheless, by adopting the orthographic conventions of Croatian writer Ljudevit Gaj (1809–72) for the newspaper, Bleiweis aided the cause of a uniform literary language. He occupied leadership posts during the national cultural upsurge of the 1850s and 1860s but failed to grasp language's role in defining national identity. He helped organize the German-language paper *Triglav* (1865–70), directed at a Germanized, patriotic audience. Differences with Levstik over this action led to a split between more nationalistic Young Slovenes and the more cautious Old Slovenes. Bleiweis has found disfavor with many cultural historians because of his cautious politics, unappealing personality, and mediocre literary tastes, though by the end of the 1850s some of the better poetry of the period was published in *Novice*.

Irina G. Stakhanova

Further reading

Batis, Janez and Peter Vodopivec, eds. *Bleiweisov zbornik: Zbornik za zgodovino, naravoslovja in tehnike,* vol. 7. Ljubljana, Slovenia, 1983.

Kovač, Tita. *Slovenski oratar: Dr. Janez Bleiweis.* Ljubljana, Slovenia, 1990.

Rupel, Dmitrij. *Svobodne besede: Od Prešerna do Cankarja.* Koper, Slovenia, 1976.

See also Ljudevit Gaj; Francè Prešeren; Press

Bobrzyński, Michał (1849–1935)

Austro-Polish conservative historian and politician, and viceroy of Galicia (1908–13). Born and educated in Kraków, Bobrzyński attained an appointment as professor of Polish and German law at the University of Kraków in 1877. His *Dzieje Polski w zarysie* (*Survey of Polish History*), published in 1879, is a monument of Polish historiography. The book presents the "pessimistic" view of the Kraków historical school, which placed primary blame for the decline and partition of the Polish state on the Poles themselves, particularly on the undiscipline and egoism of the Polish nobility. Bobrzyński drew political lessons from the Polish past and called on his compatriots to learn the discipline of state building through cooperation with the Habsburg authorities. Though sharply criticized by many Poles for his critical view of his country's history, Bobrzyński undertook political activity that reflected his historical view of the need for social order and strong government.

Elected to the Austrian parliament and the Galician diet in 1885, he joined the Polish delegation in parliament and became a prominent representative of the Stańczyk faction in Galician politics, which stood for loyalty to the Habsburg Empire and moderate reforms in provincial administration. Appointed viceroy of Galicia in 1908, Bobrzyński sought to extend the suffrage for the provincial diet to all adult men. However, his efforts to improve relations between Poles and Ukrainians in the province earned him the animosity of the chauvinistic Polish National Democratic Party. Together with the Catholic bishops of Galicia, the National Democrats engineered the defeat of Bobrzyński's electoral reform proposal and brought on his resignation as viceroy. Although he served as Austrian minister for Galician affairs in 1917, Bobrzyński's political importance subsequently waned, and, regarded as a diehard Habsburg loyalist, he attained little political influence in independent Poland.

Philip Pajakowski

Further reading

Bobrzyński, Michał. *Z moich pamiętników,* ed. by A. Galos. Wrocław, 1957.

Davies, Norman. *God's Playground: A History of Poland,* vol. 2, *1795 to the Present.* New York, 1982.

Łazuga, Waldemar. *Michał Bobrzyński: Myśl historyczna a działalność polityczna.* Warsaw, 1982.

Bodnaraş, Emil (1904–76)

Member of the Romanian Communist Party Politburo. Born in Suceava of Ukrainian and German parents, Bodnaraş's real name may have been Bodnarenko or Bodnariuk. He took courses in law at the University of Iaşi and completed Artillery Officers' School in Timişoara. During the 1930s,

he became a revolutionary and went to Moscow, where he fought in the Red Army during World War II. He returned to Romania in early 1944 and was involved in helping Gheorghe Gheorghiu-Dej (1901–65), the future Communist leader of Romania, escape from prison. Generally viewed as an agent of the Kremlin, he became minister of national defense in 1947 and reorganized the Romanian army according to Soviet standards. In 1952 he became a member of Gheorghiu-Dej's Politburo and participated in the execution of Lucreţiu Pătrăşcanu (1900–1954), the Communist intellectual and minister of justice, in 1954. In 1965 he joined the Presidium of Nicolae Ceauşescu (1918–89), Gheorghiu-Dej's successor, and shortly thereafter became a first vice president of the Council of Ministers. He survived the April 1968 plenum, which denounced those involved with Pătrăşcanu's death, probably because he had differed from Moscow and supported Ceauşescu's view of a national, industrial Romania. Upon his death, he and Ceauşescu were the only important figures remaining from the 1965 Politburo.

Joseph F. Harrington

Further reading

Fischer, Mary Ellen. *Nicolae Ceauşescu: A Study in Political Leadership.* Boulder, Colorado, 1989.

Fischer-Galati, Stephen. *The New Rumania: From People's Democracy to Socialist Republic.* Cambridge, Massachusetts, 1967.

Wolff, Robert Lee. *The Balkans in Our Times.* New York, 1967.

See also Nicolae Ceauşescu; Communist Party of Romania; Gheorghe Gheorghiu-Dej; Lucreţiu Pătrăşcanu; Red Army

Bogomilism

A heretical branch of Eastern Orthodoxy emanating from Bulgaria in the tenth century, concentrated primarily in Bulgaria and Bosnia. Bogomilism, named for its supposed founder, the priest Bogomil, tried to explain the obvious existence of evil coupled with the belief in a loving God. It attempted to answer the question: How can God be the creator of an obviously imperfect world?

The Bogomils held a dualist position that two forces operate in the world: God and the devil. In contradistinction to many dualist theologies and

B

philosophers, the two forces, good and evil, are not equal in Bogomilism. The devil is inferior and subject to God. However, the devil, also called the elder son of God, created all material things; therefore, the material world is evil.

This heresy had both theological and social consequences. On the moral level, to avoid evil one must avoid contact with the world as far as possible. Extreme adherents of Bogomilism shunned sexual contact, were abstemious in diet, and even condemned the physical and material sacramentality of the church.

On a social level, the doctrine was used to explain the existence of vast differences in wealth and power between nobility and higher clergy on the one hand, and the peasantry on the other. The heresy, which is an attempt to explain evil and which helped its followers to provide a rationale for striving for social justice, nonetheless did not involve itself in the reform of social or religious structures. Since the world was created by the devil, it was to be shunned rather than reformed. This led to a withdrawal from political life and an espousal of disobedience to civil and religious authority.

When the Byzantine Empire took final control over the Kingdom of Bulgaria in the eleventh century, Bogomilism spread throughout the empire. Bogomilism, together with its related heresies, Manichaeanism, Albigensianism, and Catharism, influenced Byzantine, Mediterranean, and southeastern Europe for centuries, and adherents could be found throughout the region.

After the seventeenth century, Bogomilism seems to have had little formal impact in Eastern (Slavic) society, except insofar as dualism continues as a vestige in present-day cosmology. But during Communist times, the *Great Soviet Encyclopedia* stressed Bogomilism's rejection of church order and its antimaterialism—the former to underpin the antichurch position of communism, the latter not to condemn materialism itself but feudalism and capitalist accumulation of wealth.

Michael J. Lavelle

Further reading

Hussey, J.M. *The Orthodox Church in the Byzantine Empire.* Oxford, 1986.

Obolensky, Dimitri. *The Bogomils: A Study in Baltic Neomanichaeism.* Cambridge, Massachusetts 1948.

———. *The Byzantine Commonwealth.* New York, 1971.

See also Orthodoxy

Bogorov, Ivan Andreev (1818–92)

Bulgarian doctor and journalist. Born to a craftsman's family in Karlovo, Bogorov studied in Kuru Çesme at the Greek National School. Later, he transferred to the Richelieu Lyceum in Odessa, Russia, and remained there until 1843. From 1845 to 1847, he studied chemistry in Leipzig; his studies were sponsored by Bulgarian businessmen from Bucharest. He published the first Bulgarian newspaper during his stay in Leipzig: *Bûlgarski Orel* (*Bulgarian Eagle,* 1846–47). When his support from Bucharest expired, he left for Constantinople, where he opened a print shop. There he began publishing *Tvarigradski Vestnik* (*Constantinople Newspaper,* 1848–50).

After the Crimean War (1853–56), with support from the Russian government, he successfully completed a degree in medicine in Paris in 1858. Returning to Constantinople, he supported himself in a variety of ways: by practicing medicine, as a publisher, and as a translator. He edited the magazine *Bûlgarski knizhitsi* (*Bulgarian Letters*). Bogorov was the sole Bulgarian participant at the Slav Congress in Moscow in 1867, which promoted Pan-Slav unity. In Bucharest he edited the newspaper *Narodnost* (*Nationality,* 1867–69). In Plovdiv he founded the first Bulgarian business publication, *Zhurnal za nauka, zanaiat i tûrgoviia* (*Journal of Science, Trade, and Business,* 1862).

After the liberation of Bulgaria, Bogorov remained active in publishing and journalism. His work appeared in *Bûlgarski knizhitsi, Turtsiia* (*Turkey*), *Sûvetnik* (*Adviser*), *Gaida* (*Bagpipes*), *Chitalishte* (*Reading Room*), and *Letostrui* (*Chronicle*). He also translated scientific works as well as folk songs and sayings, a grammar, a French-Bulgarian dictionary, and foreign works of literature.

Mari A. Firkatian

Further reading

Bogorov, Ivan. *Materiali, svûrzani sûs 150-godishniia iubilei ot rozhdenieto mu,* ed. by M. Ivanov. Plovdiv, 1972.

Nedialkov, Khr. *Doktor Ivan Bogorov.* Sofia, 1977.

See also Crimean War; Pan-Slavism

Bohemia

The western third of the Czech Republic and the cradle of Czech culture. The region occupies a gently rolling landscape skirted by mountainous borders with Poland, Germany, and Austria. This highland fringe is made up of the Sudeten Mountains, the Ore Mountains, and the Bohemian Forest. A lowland plain to the east connects the region with Moravia.

Inside the mountainous fortress is an area of high soil fertility that has long been used for grain and sugar-beet production. The best agricultural region of the interior is the northern plain that lies below the Ore and Sudeten Mountains. The Central Bohemian Hills are a dissected upland region through the middle, and the southern portion of interior Bohemia is an extensive plateau. The interior is drained by the Vltava, Labe, and Ore Rivers. Thermal springs are also abundant in western Bohemia, resulting in the development of spas such as Karlovy Vary, Mariánské Lázně, and Františkovy Lázně.

Bohemia's central location within Europe has had both positive and negative impacts. Bohemia prospered from (and contributed to) the cultural wealth and diversity of Central Europe. But the area has been the site of a great deal of religious, ethnic, and national conflict, ranging from the Hussite Wars of the fifteenth century to the Nazi takeover prior to World War II. It was also the westernmost province of the Habsburg Empire before World War I.

Bohemia is highly industrialized. Prague, Plzeň, and the northern fringes of the region provided most of the industrial output that made Czechoslovakia the tenth-richest nation in the world before 1939 and had supplied 90 percent of the industrial production of the Habsburg Empire. While contributing to the economic growth of Czechoslovakia, these industrial regions (a combination of light industries such as textiles and heavier ones such as steel) also became a major contributor to environmental problems for the nation. The acid rain destruction of Bohemia's forests, which developed under communist rule, has been among the worst in the world.

Russell L. Ivy

Further reading

Berentsen, William, ed. *Europe in the 1990s: A Geographical Analysis,* 7th ed. Chicago, 1997.
Pounds, Norman. *Eastern Europe.* Chicago, 1969.
Rugg, Dean. *Eastern Europe.* London, 1985.
UNIDO. *Czechoslovakia: Industrial Transformation and Regeneration.* Oxford, 1992.

See also Czech Culture; Economic Development in Czechoslovakia; Environment; Industrialization; Plzeň; Prague

Boiars

Slavic term generally used to describe the upper-class landowners in Eastern Europe who dominated economic, social, and political life in the region. In the Romanian lands, for example, the *boiars* were looked upon by some as a feudal aristocracy, by others as court nobility. The *boiars'* claim to represent a native aristocracy predated the formation of the Romanian principalities and was associated with land tenure. Such tenure was later conferred and extended to a handful of families in both Moldavia and Wallachia in recognition of military service. Thus, they constituted the traditional families of both lands. These *boiars,* known from the fourteenth century by their given names and court titles, had considerable power: they sat in the assembly (*divan*); elected (and could themselves be elected) the prince; formed the highest judicial court; signed edicts; and had to raise levies proportionate to their landed estates. Their titles were borrowed from Byzantine and Slavic courts, *ban* (governor) being the highest in Wallachia, and *spathar,* the highest military title in Moldavia. Surnames began in the fifteenth century and were associated with location of properties, such as the Florescu's at Floreşti or Golescu's at Goleşti. Beyond court functions, titles (with the exception of prince) were unknown in the Romanian lands, although some *boiars* received Western titles from the eighteenth century onward from Habsburg emperors or Hungarian kings. During the rule of the Phanariot Greeks in the eighteenth century, Turco-Byzantine court titles sold by Greek princes proliferated and conferred *boiar* status of first, second, or third class. This lowered the prestige of the term. There were no fewer than thirty thousand *boiars* by 1739, and the title was abolished that year. With the restoration of native rule in 1822, however, the old order returned, and the traditional *boiar* families played an important role in Romania's national regeneration and in the formation of the modern Romanian state, up to the period of Communist rule.

Radu Florescu

B

Further reading
Cernovodeanu, Dan. *Ştiinţa şi arta heraldică în România*. Bucharest, 1977.
Florescu, George. *Divanurile domneşti din Muntenia în secolul al XV-lea dregatori şi boeri 1496–1601*. Bucharest, 1929.
Giurescu, Constantin. *Despre boeri*. Bucharest, 1920.
Stoicescu, Nicolae. *Dicţionar al marilor dregători din ţara romanească şi Moldova*. Bucharest, 1971.
Sturdza, Mihai. *Grandes Familles de Grece, d'Albanie et de Constantinople*. Paris, 1893.

See also Danubian Principalities; Golescu Family; Phanariots

Bolyai, Janos (1802–60)

Hungarian mathematician who published the first exposition of non-Euclidean geometry to be widely read in Europe. An officer in the Habsburg army, Bolyai was interested in the efforts of the time to prove Euclid's fifth postulate—"Given a line and a point not on the line, there is exactly one line passing through the given point and parallel to the given line"—as a consequence of the first four postulates. By 1823, he became convinced that the fifth postulate was independent of the first four, and that by using a different fifth postulate, an entirely new geometric system could be created. As he wrote to his father, Wolfgang (1775–1856), "out of nothing I have created a strange new world."

By 1829, this was written in complete detail, then included as an "Appendix Explaining the Absolutely True Science of Space" at the end of a mathematics textbook published in 1832 by Wolfgang Bolyai. Disappointed by the lack of fame he thought would accompany such new and exciting mathematics, Bolyai never published again, even though he left behind a large collection of original manuscripts.

Mark Sand

Further reading
Boyer, Carl B. and Uta C. Merzbach. *A History of Mathematics*, 2d ed. New York, 1989.
Burton, David M. *The History of Mathematics: An Introduction*. Boston, 1984.
Eves, Howard W. *An Introduction to the History of Mathematics*, 5th ed. New York, 1982.

Boris III (1894–1943)

Tsar of Bulgaria during the politically turbulent interwar period. Boris was born on January 30, 1894, the son of Tsar Ferdinand I (1861–1948) and Princess Marie-Louise of Italy (1870–99). Ironically, Ferdinand named his son Boris to commemorate the medieval tsar who had converted the Bulgarians to Orthodox Christianity, yet his marriage agreement stipulated that any children be raised Roman Catholic. In early 1896, however, Ferdinand's desire to earn diplomatic recognition from Russia resulted in Boris's rebaptism into Orthodoxy, with Nicholas II (1868–1918) as godfather. In October 1918 Boris ascended the throne when his father, who had allied with the Central Powers, abdicated and left Bulgaria at the insistence of the victorious Allies and Bulgarian political parties. The political disquiet of the 1920s nearly claimed his life in April 1925, when a bomb exploded in Sofia Cathedral during a service he was to have attended. In the interests of Bulgarian foreign policy, Boris married Princess Ioanna (1907–), daughter of Victor Emmanuel III of Italy (1869–1947), in October 1930. In April 1935 Boris restored a civilian form of government heavily dependent on his personal power (termed "controlled democracy"), which lasted until his death. In March 1941 he signed the Tripartite Pact with Italy, Japan, and Germany. During World War II, he stubbornly refused Soviet and German entreaties to fight in the war, successfully protected Bulgaria's fifty thousand Jews from deportation, and extended Bulgaria's borders. Boris died of a heart attack on August 28, 1943, and was buried at Rila Monastery.

Gregory L. Bruess

Further reading
Crampton, R.J. *A Short History of Modern Bulgaria*. Cambridge, Massachusetts, 1987.
Dimitroff, Pashanko. *Boris III of Bulgaria: Toiler, Citizen, King, 1894–1943*. Sussex, England, 1986.
Goueff, Stephane. *Crown of Thorns: The Reign of King Boris III of Bulgaria, 1918–1943*. Lanham, Maryland, 1987.

See also Axis; Ferdinand I; Ioanna; Nicholas II; Orthodoxy; World War II

Bosnia-Hercegovina

A historic territory serving as a frontier between Christian and Muslim Europe and between Western and Eastern Christianity. The state of Bosnia-Hercegovina, which declared its independence from the Yugoslav federation in 1991, has an area of 19,135 square miles (53,150 sq km) and a population of 4,200,000. In 1992 it was home to three Serbo-Croatian–speaking national groups: Bosnian Muslims (40 percent), Serbs (32 percent), and Croats (18 percent).

The term *Bosnia* (Serbo-Croatian, *Bosna*) derives from the Bosna River, which flows northward from the Sarajevo-Zenica basin to the Sava River. The designation *Hercegovina* (Dukedom) dates from the fifteenth century, when Stephen Vuksić (d. 1466) seized control of southern Bosnia and declared himself *herzog* (duke) of the region. Hercegovina mainly occupies the drainage basin of the Neretva River and constitutes 20 percent of the area and 10 percent of the population of Bosnia-Hercegovina.

The republic is generally mountainous, with only 8 percent of lands lying below the elevation of 500 feet (150 m); most of the low-lying areas are on the northern boundary and along the lower Neretva River. The southern mountains are composed almost entirely of folded limestone layers that have eroded into a distinctive terrain known as karst topography. Precipitation in the region generally does not coalesce into surface streams but enters cracks in the soluble rock to form caves and underground channels. Interspersed nonlimestone layers have generally been eroded away, resulting in flat-floored, fertile *poljes* between the limestone block mountains.

Bosnia-Hercegovina is virtually landlocked. It has only thirteen miles (twenty-two km) of coastline, established in the eighteenth century through manipulations by Dubrovnik diplomats to ensure that the city republic bordered only with the Ottoman Empire, and not with Venetian-controlled Dalmatia. The small coastal strip lacks a suitable natural harbor, however, and in modern times Bosnia-Hercegovina has utilized the Croatian port of Ploče, near the mouth of the Neretva, as its outlet to the sea.

The climate of Bosnia-Hercegovina is modified continental. Summers are warm and winters are cold, especially in the heart of the republic. Annual rainfall ranges between 30 and 60 inches (76–152 cm). Areas closer to the Adriatic Sea have notably dry summers and rainy winters, while in the north dual maxima occur in the late spring and the fall. About half the land is in forest, 70 percent being deciduous.

Turmoil has characterized Bosnia-Hercegovina since the first Slavic tribes moved into the region in the seventh century, displacing the native Illyrians. In the twelfth century many nobles and peasants adopted the heretical Bogomil form of Christianity that had evolved in Bulgaria. They were persecuted for their beliefs by both Roman Catholics to the west and Orthodox believers to the east. In 1463 Ottoman forces seized Bosnia. The faiths of Catholic and Orthodox inhabitants were tolerated during the first centuries of Ottoman rule, but Christians could not own land.

A series of Christian serf uprisings occurred during the early nineteenth century. At length, in 1850 the Ottoman regime took power away from the Bosnian aristocracy and established a centrally controlled administration. Christian serfs continued to rebel, however, and by 1875 were in general revolt. Serbia and Montenegro supported the insurrection and were joined by Russia in 1877. A Russian-dictated peace treaty signed in San Stefano in March 1878 provided for recognition of an autonomous Bosnia-Hercegovina, but the Congress of Berlin four months later placed the territory temporarily under Austro-Hungarian rule. In 1908 Austria-Hungary formally annexed Bosnia-Hercegovina, mainly to frustrate Serbian ambitions to seize the territory. On June 28, 1914, a Serbian nationalist assassinated the heir to the Habsburg throne, Franz Ferdinand (1863–1914), in Sarajevo, thereby precipitating World War I.

Following the war, Bosnia-Hercegovina became a component of the Kingdom of Serbs, Croats, and Slovenes. It disappeared as an administrative entity in 1929, when it was apportioned among three *banovine* (provinces) as part of antinationalist redistricting in Yugoslavia, as the state was renamed. Following Yugoslavia's capitulation to Axis forces in April 1941, all of Bosnia-Hercegovina became part of the new Independent State of Croatia.

Bosnia-Hercegovina once again appeared in 1945 as a multicultural republic within the postwar Communist federal republic of Yugoslavia. Ethnic rivalries were suppressed until 1991, when Bosnia-Hercegovina declared its independence

B

from the federation. Fighting broke out among the three principal ethnic groups that ended formally only in 1996 by accords signed in Dayton, Ohio. Under terms of the settlement, Serbs were allotted an autonomous area amounting to half the total territory. The remainder was under joint authority of Bosnia-Hercegovina's Muslim and Croatian communities. Although Bosnia's Serbs received a disproportionately large territory in relation to their total numbers, the other two groups generally were beneficiaries of the better farming lands and developed industrial regions.

The Communist era witnessed substantial economic development in Bosnia-Hercegovina, financed principally by transfer payments from the richer Yugoslav republics of Croatia and Slovenia. The territory's rich reserves of coal, iron ore, and bauxite became the backbone of a significant metallurgical industry, particularly in the Sarajevo-Zenica basin.

About half of the republic is cultivated, principally in corn and other grains. A third of the land is used for grazing, and 15 percent is in meadows. Cattle predominate on territories peripheral to the Pannonian (Hungarian) Plain, sheep in the karst region, and swine in the northern borderlands with Serbia. Farming has remained largely on a subsistence basis, although commercial production of tobacco and wine grapes is notable in Hercegovina.

Thomas M. Poulsen

Further reading

Bertić, Ivan. *Veliki geografski atlas Jugoslavije.* Zagreb, 1987.
Clissold, Stephen, ed. *A Short History of Yugoslavia: From Early Times to 1966.* Cambridge, 1968.
Sugar, Peter. *The Industrialization of Bosnia-Hercegovina.* Seattle, 1963.

See also Bogomilism; Bosnia-Hercegovina, Birth of the Republic of; Congress of Berlin; Franz Ferdinand; Great Hungarian Plain; Muslims; Peasant Revolts; Russo-Turkish War of 1877–78; San Stefano, Treaty of; Sarajevo; Ustaša

Bosnia-Hercegovina, Birth of the Republic of (1992)

Independent state created following the breakup of Yugoslavia. Serbian propaganda (controlled by Slobodan Milošević [1941–]), which so effectively

radicalized and alienated Croatia's Serbs, was equally effective among the Serbs in Bosnia-Hercegovina. In 1990 equally strident Croatian nationalist propaganda joined Milošević's. By mid-1990, old antagonisms were artificially rekindled; relations among Bosnia's Serbs, Croats, and Muslims rapidly deteriorated under the barrage of nationalist propaganda and rhetoric. Following December 1990 elections, three ethnically based political parties dominated Bosnia's political scene: the Serbian Democratic Party (SDS); the Muslim-based Party for Democratic Action (SDA); and the Croat-based Croatian Democratic Community (HDZ). Beginning in early 1990, Radovan Karadžić (1945–)—a Milošević surrogate and head of the SDS—indicated his party had no intention of remaining part of a multi-ethnic Bosnia and was interested only in union with Serbia.

In March 1991 Milošević and Croat leader Franjo Tudjman (1922–1999) met to discuss the partition of Bosnia between Serbia and Croatia, followed by a May meeting between their surrogates to work out the details. In April 1991 fourteen Serbian-dominated regions in northwest Bosnia proclaimed a "Municipal Community of Bosnian Krajina," effectively seceding from Sarajevo's control. Following the Croatian and Slovenian declarations of independence in June 1991, Bosnia-Hercegovina occupied a tenuous position amid reports of active Bosnian Serb participation in the war in Croatia. The Serb-Croat antagonism spilled into Bosnia as the Serb-dominated Yugoslav People's Army (JNA) used Bosnian territory to mount offensive operations against Croatia, and the Croatian Interior Ministry conducted maneuvers inside Bosnia. In September the JNA created borders for a "Serbian Autonomous Region of Hercegovina," used to launch attacks on Dubrovnik and Dalmatia, and for autonomous regions around Banja Luka and Romanija. The JNA covertly armed Bosnian Serbs while disarming Bosnia's local defense forces. Simultaneously, Serbian paramilitary forces began terrorizing Croats and Muslims in Serb-controlled regions.

Following a Serb walkout from the parliament on October 14, 1991, the Croat and Muslim delegates passed a resolution demanding sovereignty. In response, Karadžić established a Serb National Assembly in Banja Luka and held a referendum in which more than 100 percent of the Serbs voted for independence. Karadžić called for taking two-thirds of Bosnian territory and making Sarajevo the Serb capital. In December the Bosnian parliament voted for sovereignty, and on December 21, 1991, Bosnian Serbs held a formal vote for independence. During the winter of 1991–92, the JNA and Serbian paramilitary organizations constructed artillery emplacements around many Bosnian government-controlled regions, including Sarajevo. Hoping to secede peacefully, Alija Izetbegović's (c. 1925–) SDA government turned to the European Community, which established formal criteria for recognition. The Bosnian government held free elections on February 29 and March 1, 1992. Although Karadžić's SDS boycotted the referendum and the JNA blocked voting in Serb-controlled regions, approximately 64 percent of the electorate voted, including many Serbs. The vote was nearly unanimous for independence. On March 2, when election results were announced, Serb paramilitary groups began to set up barricades throughout Sarajevo and take control of large regions of Bosnia. On April 6, 1992, the European Community officially recognized Bosnia-Hercegovina as an independent state.

James M.B. Lyon

Further reading

Cohen, Lenard. *Broken Bonds: Yugoslavia's Disintegration and Balkan Politics in Transition,* 2d ed. Boulder, Colorado, 1995.
Donia, Robert J. and John V.A. Fine. *Bosnia and Hercegovina: A Tradition Betrayed.* New York, 1994.
Malcolm, Noel. *Bosnia: A Short History.* New York, 1994.
Thompson, Mark. *Forging War: The Media in Serbia, Croatia, and Bosnia-Hercegovina.* London, 1994.

See also Alija Izetbegović; Slobodan Milošević; Muslims; Franjo Tudjman

Botev, Khristo Petkov (1848–76)

Bulgarian writer, poet, and revolutionary. The son of a teacher, Botev was accepted, with the help of Bulgarian writer Naiden Gerov (1823–1900), to the Odessa, Russia, high school; his tuition was paid by the Russian government. During this time, he was influenced by Russian revolutionary democrats and Polish émigrés who fled to that city after the failed 1863 Polish uprising against Russian domination.

He emigrated to Romania and worked on the newspaper *Dunavska Zora* (*Danubian Dawn,* 1867–68). In 1871 he published the newsletter *Duma na bûlgarskite emigranti* (*The Word of Bulgarian Émigrés*). Later that year, he collaborated with writer Liuben Karavelov (c. 1834–79) on the newspapers *Svoboda* (*Freedom*) and *Nezavisimost* (*Independence*).

In the 1870s Botev became a member of the Bulgarian Revolutionary Central Committee but left after a failed revolt in Stara Zagora in 1875. He and Karavelov parted ways and Botev organized a *cheta* (armed band). He and his men boarded the ship *Radetski* at Giurgevo on May 16, 1876. When they landed on the Bulgarian side of the Danube, the *cheta* headed for the Vratsa region, where a few days later Botev died in a battle with Turkish forces.

Botev left a legacy of a small body of poetry that has been unmatched by his countrymen both for its technical perfection and its evocative nature. His work can be classified as romantic, a reflection of the age—passionaate, profound, and evocative.

Mari A. Firkatian

Further reading

Burmov, Al. *Hristo Botev prez pogleda na sûvremenntsite si.* Sofia, 1943.
Dimitrov, M. *Hristo Botev: Biografiia.* Sofia, 1948.
Natan, Zh. *Ideologiata na Hristo Botev.* Sofia, 1955.
Undzhiev, Ivan and Tsv. Undzhieva. *Hristo Botev: Zhivot i delo.* Sofia, 1975.

See also Bulgarian Literature; *Cheta*

Bozveli, Neofit (c. 1785–1848)

Leading figure in the Bulgarian national awakening. After receiving his early education in the local school, Bozveli trained at the Khilendar Monastery on Mount Athos in Greece. Around 1810, he decided to become a monk. From about 1814 to 1834, he served as teacher and priest in the city of Svishtov. There he organized a school that, in addition to the usual courses in religion that formed the curricular content of the schools of the time, also included secular subjects. During 1834–35, he traveled to Serbia to arrange for the publication of textbooks he had prepared in the Old Church Bulgarian (Slavonic) language, the language of use

B

in the schools. In addition to using these texts in his teaching at his new position in the town of Kalofer, he also distributed them in many other parts of Bulgaria. During 1839 in Constantinople, he became involved in the movement for the establishment of a Bulgarian Orthodox Church independent from the Greek hierarchy. At the same time, he laid plans to organize a printing house in Gabrovo to publish books in Bulgarian. His efforts in the Bulgarian cause gained him a reputation among Greek clerical officials as an agitator, and he was banished to Mount Athos, where he remained from March 1840 until August 1844. Managing to flee Athos, he again went to Constantinople, where he became active once more in the movement for a separate Bulgarian church. He shortly presented a memorandum to Ottoman authorities in which he outlined the movement's proposals for a separate church. His attempt was unsuccessful, and he again was arrested and banished to Mount Athos a second time, where he remained until his death in 1848.

John Georgeoff

Further reading

Arnaudov, Mikhail Petrov. *Neofit Hilendarski-Bozveli: Zivot, delo, epokha: 1785–1848,* 2 vols. Sofia, 1971.

Atanasov, Zhecho. *Neofit Bozveli.* Sofia, 1974.

Neofit, Archimandrite. *Nepoznatiyat Bozveli.* Sofia, 1942.

Smokhovska-Petrova, Vanda. *Neofit Bozveli i bulgarskiiat tsurkoven vupros.* Sofia, 1964.

See also Education; Exarchate

Brancuşi, Constantin (1876–1957)

Romanian sculptor who became one of the most celebrated sculptors of the twentieth century and is considered the father of modern sculpture. Born in Hobiţa, Brancuşi began his studies in Craiova in 1894–98 at the School of Arts and Crafts. In 1902 he left for Paris, arriving in 1904 after a lengthy journey. There, he studied for a year at the École des Beaux-Arts. His earliest works (1904–7) were portraits, mostly of children or suffering children, fashioned in part after Rodin's (1840–1917) sculpture. In 1907 Brancuşi sculpted two stone works, *The Wisdom of the Earth* and *The Kiss,* which signified a departure from traditional European sculpture. Brancuşi stressed the importance of direct carving as a way of access to the true nature of the material. Many of the bases of his works are wood carvings becoming themselves sculptures. The principle of direct carving assumed a polemical value synonymous with modernity. It is also direct carving, which related Brancuşi's sculpture in wood to Romanian folk sculpture (as well as to African sculpture), greatly admired in Paris at the beginning of the century. In the same year (1907), *The Prayer,* part of a funerary monument in Buzău, Romania, that recalled Byzantine formal reduction, made conspicuous his move toward a new language of forms. The process of essentializing the form became more and more radical, free from influences and cultural suggestions in the series of works in marble and bronzes such as *Sleeping Muse, Mlle Pogany, Măiastra,* and *Bird in Space,* themes that are known in different variants, striving to an ideal of purity and geometrical perfection. The climax of this direction could be seen in the marble egg shape called *The Beginning of the World.*

In 1913 Brancuşi took part in the famous Armory Show in New York City and had one-man shows there in 1926 and again in 1933. He found faithful collectors in the United States. Later, in 1927, the process credited to him by the U.S. Customs Court, which considered *Bird in Space* an industrial object, led to an important debate concerning the status of modern art. In 1933 he projected a temple for the maharaja of Indor for three of his *Birds in Space* already in the maharaja's possession. The project remained unrealized, however. His only large-scale sculptural ensemble was erected in 1937–38 in Tîrgu-Jiu, Romania. Composed of three pieces—*Table of Silence, Gate of the Kiss,* and *Endless Column*—as a war memorial, the ensemble is considered his opus magnum, his artistic testament.

Brancuşi conceived his own studio as a total work of art, which he willed to the Museum of Modern Art of the City of Paris with the condition that it be kept in its original state. The studio is now part of the Musée d'Art Moderne at Centre Pompidou. Brancuşi died in March 1957 in Paris.

Ioana Vlasiu

Further reading

Bach, Teja. *Brancuşi: Metamorphosen plastischer Form.* Cologne, 1987.

Brezaniu, B. *Brancuşi în România.* Bucharest, 1974.

Chave, A. *Constantin Brancuşi: Shifting the Bases of Art.* New York, 1993.

Fontaine, S. Geist. *Brancuşi photographe.* Paris, 1977.
Gienion-Welcker, C. *Constantin Brancuşi.* Basel, 1958.

See also Romanian Art

Braşov

Romanian city. With a population of over two hundred thousand, a rail and highway junction, and an old manufacturing tradition, Braşov (German, Kronstadt; Hungarian, Brasso) is today a leading industrial (and not heavily polluted) city of Romania. Its aircraft industry, developed in the interwar period, continues to build light planes for domestic and foreign markets. Tourism and especially winter sports also play an important economic role. One of the oldest cities in Romania, known as a town even prior to the great Tatar invasion of 1241, Braşov owes its early and rapid development mainly to two factors. First, exploiting its location as the most southern and eastern outpost of Transylvanian culture and economy, it developed a lively trade with its immediate neighbors east of the Carpathians by playing up the complementary character of its products and skills and gradually extending the geographic range of this trade to become the gateway for commerce from the Near East to Central Europe. Second, German craftsmen and merchants who began to settle in the city as early as 1200 brought know-how and connections that were virtually unique in this part of Europe; they gradually helped build Braşov culturally and economically into a still recognizable European center of civilization. However, practically all German residents have emigrated since 1945. In the early 1960s the city was briefly called Oraşul Stalin (Stalin City).

Ladis K.D. Kristof

Further reading
Iancu, Mihai et al. *Judeţul Braşov.* Bucharest, 1971.
Ionescu, Grigore. *Istoria Arhitecturii în Romînia.* Bucharest, 1963.
Magocsi, Paul Robert. *Historical Atlas of East Central Europe.* Seattle, Washington, 1993.
România: Atlas istoric-geografic. Bucharest, 1996.

Brătianu, Ion C. (1821–91)

Romanian politician, prime minister, and founder of a political dynasty that spanned three generations, and a significant contributor to the economic, institutional, political, and constitutional shape of modern Romania. From a lesser *boiar* family, Brătianu received a basic education at home before joining his brother in Paris. There, he came to work with émigré leaders of other East European nationalities and participated in the French Revolution of February 1848, before returning to Bucharest in April. In June he led a street uprising in Bucharest that toppled the Russian-backed regime of Prince Gheorghe Bibescu (1804–73). He became first secretary of the provisional government. At several critical junctures, he utilized the "streets" to support the revolution.

Arrested and exiled by the Turkish and Russian forces that ended the revolution in September 1848, Brătianu and his longtime political collaborator C.A. Rosetti (1816–85) became the leaders of efforts to promote the Romanian national cause in France. In 1859 he was a deputy to the Wallachian Elective Assembly that chose Alexandru Ioan Cuza (1820–73) as prince, creating a de facto Romanian state.

Brătianu soon became a bitter opponent of Cuza, however, and was a leader in forcing his abdication in 1866. He and Rosetti headed the more radical wing of the National Liberal group and were responsible for the 1866 Constitution of Romania, a relatively democratic document. He became the principal confidant of Prince Carol (1839–1914), the moving force behind the 1867–68 liberal governments and the architect of important reforms of the army and finance. Although he turned against Carol in 1870, by 1876 Brătianu had recovered both the support of the prince and his leadership role, becoming prime minister from 1876 to 1888 (except for a brief period in 1881). Carol's desire was to achieve Romanian independence; Brătianu spearheaded this effort, which culminated in a declaration of independence in 1877 and the establishment of the Romanian kingdom in 1881. Brătianu became increasingly autocratic, and under his leadership the National Liberal faction became firmly established as part of the ruling oligarchy through control of the national bank and other important institutions.

Brătianu dominated the formative era of Romanian politics between 1848 and 1888. The fiery, youthful 1848 radical became the domineering and pragmatic *"vizier"* of the 1880s. He also created a virtual family dynasty, which saw his

B

sons and other Brătianus following in his footsteps. [The most notable was Ion I.C. Brătianu [1864–1927], who was to become prime minister seven times.)

Paul E. Michelson

Further reading

Hitchins, Keith. *Rumania 1866–1947*. Oxford, 1994.

Stan, Apostal. *Ion C. Brătianu: Un promotor al liberalismului în România*. Bucharest, 1993.

Stan, Apostal and Mircea Iosa. *Liberalismul politic în România*. Bucharest, 1996.

See also Gheorghe Bibescu; Ion I.C. Brătianu; Carol I, Alexandru Ioan Cuza; Revolutions of 1848; C.A. Rosetti

Brătianu, Ion I.C. (1864–1927)

Romanian statesman, prime minister, and principal architect of Greater Romania, the post–World War I unification of the Romanian lands. The eldest son of Ion Brătianu (1821–91), Ion I.C. Brătianu followed his father in the National Liberal Party, frequently serving as a cabinet minister. Upon becoming premier in 1908, Brătianu led his party in the direction of electoral and land reform as a prerequisite to the modernization and industrialization of the country.

Dedicated to the union of all Romanians, he initiated a reorientation of Romania from the Central Powers to the Entente during the first years of World War I. Skillfully and secretly during Romania's neutrality (1914–16), he gradually drew the Entente into an agreement (the Treaty of Bucharest, 1916) recognizing Romania's territorial wishes vis-à-vis Austria-Hungary (Transylvania, Banat, and Bukovina) while at the same time deceiving the Central Powers as to his true intentions. This cleverness seemed to backfire with the quick defeat of the Romanian army in the campaign of 1916 and its retreat with the government into Moldavia.

The Russian Revolution and collapse of the eastern front forced Romania to accept the harsh Treaty of Bucharest (May 1918), which took Romania temporarily out of the war and brought Brătianu to the nadir of his political career. But the Allied victory in November 1918 allowed him to return to power and represent Romania at the Paris Peace Conference. His uncompromising and abrasive insistence on the complete fulfillment of the promises of the agreements of 1916 angered the Great Powers, but they could do little but acquiesce as the Romanian army had already occupied the territories in question. After the war, Brătianu dominated Romanian politics until his death in 1927. His authoritarian and partisan political style made him either adored or hated by his contemporaries.

Glenn E. Torrey

Further reading

Bănescu, N. *Ion I.C. Brătianu*. Craiova, 1931.

Discursurile lui Ion I.C. Brătianu, 4 vols. Bucharest, 1933–40.

Duca, I. Gheorghe. *Amintiri politice,* 3 vols. Munich, 1981.

Scurtu, Ioan. *Ion I.C. Brătianu*. Bucharest, 1992.

See also Ion C. Brătianu; Bucharest, Treaty of (1918); Greater Romania; Paris Peace Conference; World War I

Bratislava

The major urban center and capital of Slovakia. Bratislava (Hungarian, Poszony; German, Pressburg) has played an important role in the histories of Hungary, Czechoslovakia, and the newly formed state of Slovakia. Originally the site of a Celtic settlement and a Roman outpost (Posonium), Bratislava gained status as a royal free city in 1291. It served as Hungary's capital from the sixteenth to the eighteenth century, later was a regional administrative and major economic center both within the Hungarian portion of the Austro-Hungarian Empire and within the state of Czechoslovakia, was the capital of independent Slovakia from 1939 to 1945, and is again a capital after Slovakia's reestablishment in 1993. The city occupies a strategic location at a historic ford on the north bank of the Danube River, where it cuts through the Little Carpathian Mountains.

Bratislava was incorporated into Hungary in the tenth century, and its role within that state reached an apogee with its designation as capital from the early sixteenth to the late eighteenth century, when much of Hungary, including Budapest, was occupied by Ottoman forces. The city was also the meeting site of the Hungarian diet from 1526 until 1848. During the revolutionary years of 1848–49, Bratislava was a stronghold of Hungarian nationalists. Owing to its location, the city served as a key link in trade between Austria and

Hungary in general and Vienna and Budapest in particular.

Since 1918, Bratislava has been the capital and major urban center for the region, now the country, of Slovakia. The city was originally populated primarily by Germans (largely expelled after World War II), later Hungarians, and since 1918 by Slovaks. Bratislava is an important river port and rail junction, a service center for the rich farm country around it, and a diversified manufacturing center, with notable production of textiles, metals, and chemicals. The chemical industry is supported by its connection to the Soviet-era "Friendship" oil pipeline from Russia.

Contemporary Bratislava (population 441,000 in 1991) is a modern, industrialized center punctuated by socialist-era housing blocks, but it also contains a number of historic structures near its city center. The city is the home of numerous educational and cultural institutions including Comenius University, museums, and the Slovak National Theater.

William H. Berentsen

Further reading

Burghardt, A.F. *Borderland.* Madison, Wisconsin, 1962.

See also Revolutions of 1848; Slovak Republic, Birth of the

Brauner, František August (1810–80)

Leading Czech lawyer, statesman, and deputy of the Bohemian diet and the Austrian parliament. Among the leaders of the Czech national movement in the midnineteenth century, Brauner was esteemed as the foremost specialist on the peasant question and economic problems of agriculture. He acquired this knowledge as a lawyer in state service in the rural districts of Bohemia before 1845. Brauner's discussions of the economic and living conditions of peasants (*Böhmische Bauernzustände* [*Bohemian Farmers' Conditions,* 1847]) and of the abolition of feudal duties (*Von der Robot und deren Ablösung* [*On the Robot and Relief,* 1848]) offered a well-balanced position between the rights of property and necessary reforms. He was very popular among the Czech and German peasants of Bohemia and was elected in both Czech and German districts to the Imperial Parliament in Vienna in 1848.

As a student, Brauner helped to smuggle Polish refugees out of the country after the failed Polish uprising of 1830–31 against the Russians, and at the University of Vienna he shared the national ardor of his South Slav colleagues. He was the principal author of the first petition of the citizens of Prague to the Austrian government in March 1848, and he was a more consistent defender of the rights and unity of the lands of the Bohemian crown than many other Czech deputies in 1848 (as well as in the Parliament of 1861). Together with František Palacký (1798–1876) and František Ladislav Rieger (1818–1903), Brauner belonged to the close circle of the Old Czech leadership in the 1860s and 1870s.

Jiří Kořalka

Further reading

Král, Václav. "F.A. Brauner za revoluce a reakce." *Sborník archivních prací,* 2, no. 1 (1952): 123–90.

Rieger, František Ladislav, ed. *Ottův Slovník naučný,* vol. 4, Prague, 1891.

———, ed. *Slovník naučný,* vol. 1, Prague, 1860.

Tobolka, Zdeněk. *Politické dějiny československého národa od roku 1848 až do dnešní doby,* vol. 1, Prague, 1932; vol. 2, 1933.

Urban, Otto. *Česká společnost 1848–1918.* Prague, 1982.

See also Agriculture; November Uprising; Old Czechs; František Palacký; Peasants; Revolutions of 1848; František L. Rieger

Brauner, Victor (1903–66)

Romanian surrealist painter. Brauner began painting in 1917–18. Between 1919 and 1921, he studied at the Fine Arts School in Bucharest, but, dissatisfied, he quit school to attend courses at the Free Painting Academy. Brauner became active in the Romanian avant-gardist milieu during the 1920s and 1930s. In 1924 he opened his first one-man show in Bucharest, where he exposed figurative/realist paintings of an expressionist tendency. He participated in the first international art show organized by *Contimporanul* (*The Contemporary Man*) magazine in 1924, as well as in those organized in 1929 and 1930. Beginning in 1929, and continuing through the 1930s, he composed poetic-fanciful drawings for *Unu* (*One*), *Meridian,* and *Pinguin* magazines of surrealist and

B modernist orientation. He created numerous drawings for poetry books by a number of Romanian avant-garde poets. In 1936 he opened his second one-man show in Bucharest, where his personal surrealist style—nourished by bodily and psychic obsessions and by a mythology of archaic roots—was defined in large canvases such as *Composition* and *Passivité courtoise*. In 1930 he was introduced in the French surrealist circle. During the 1930s, he took part in surrealist shows in New York, San Francisco, London, Paris, and Japan. During that time, he became a close friend with Constantin Brancuşi (1876–1957), who taught him photography, and André Breton (1896–1966), the founder of surrealism. Brauner left Romania for Paris in 1938; there he became a renowned surrealist artist (primarily after World War II).

Magda Carneci

Further reading

Alexandrian, Sarane. *Les Dessins magiques de Victor Brauner.* Paris, 1965.
Catalogue Victor Brauner. Paris, 1972.
Jouffroy, Alain. *Victor Brauner.* Paris, 1959.
Semin, Didier. *Catalogue Victor Brauner.* Paris, 1996.
———. *Victor Brauner.* Paris, 1990.
Vanci-Perahim, Marina. "Surréalisme et renouveau de l'image plastique (1928–1948)," in *Bucharest in the 1920s–1940s: Between Avant-Garde and Modernism.* Bucharest, 1994.

See also Constantin Brancuşi; Romanian Art

Brest-Litovsk, Treaty of (1918)

Treaty signed March 3, 1918, between Russia and Germany and its allies, which ended Russian involvement in World War I. Lenin (1870–1924) and the Bolsheviks came to power in Russia in November 1917 promising "peace, land, and bread." On November 8, Lenin sued for peace with the Germans, and negotiations opened in December. The resulting treaty allowed the Bolsheviks to consolidate their power and create the USSR by 1922.

The Germans attempted to divide the Soviet delegation by granting independence to the former Russian Baltic states, Poland, and the Ukraine. At the same time, Leon Trotsky (1879–1940), the chief Soviet negotiator, hoped to stall the talks to gain better terms, but the Ukrainian delegation bolted and signed a separate peace with Germany on February 9, 1918. To compel Lenin to accept their demands, the Germans briefly resumed fighting on February 18, 1918, forcing his government to terms by February 26, 1918. The treaty was signed at a fortress in Brest-Litovsk in Belorussia (which later became eastern Poland). It surrendered all Russian claims to the territories west of a line running from Riga, Latvia, to the northwest corner of the Ukraine. Russia was to evacuate all regions taken from Turkey during the war. The Germans occupied the Ukraine and went as far as Baku in Azerbaijan. Russia's military forces were to be demobilized and anti-German propaganda was to cease. As a result of the treaty, Bolshevik Russia lost Estonia, Latvia, Lithuania, Poland, the Ukraine, and Finland. The treaty detached 34 percent of Russia's population, 54 percent of its industrialized regions, 32 percent of its agricultural land, and 89 percent of its coal mines. Lenin accepted the treaty knowing the alternative was revolutionary war and erroneously believing that he could get the lost territories back eventually through worldwide revolution. Russia and the Ukraine subsequently abrogated the Treaty of Brest-Litovsk on November 11, 1918, and Lenin's government recovered the Ukraine in 1919 during the Russian Civil War.

Barbara Peterson

Further reading

Baumgart, Winfried. *Deutsche Ostpolitik 1918: Von Brest-Litovsk bis zum Ende des Ersten Weltkrieges.* Munich, 1966.
Wheeler-Bennett, John W. *Brest-Litovsk: The Forgotten Peace.* New York, 1956.

See also Lenin; World War I

Brezhnev Doctrine

Soviet foreign policy pronouncement for Eastern Europe. In 1968 the Soviet Union and most of its Warsaw Pact allies invaded Czechoslovakia to stop the reform movement known popularly as the Prague Spring. Leonid Brezhnev (1906–82), the Soviet premier, and his associates feared that liberalization in Czechoslovakia might ultimately bring an end to Communist control of the country. In a series of statements shortly after the invasion, Brezhnev attempted to reconcile the action with Marxist principles by claiming that the Soviet

Union had an obligation to intervene wherever socialism was threatened. Collectively, these statements became known as the Brezhnev Doctrine.

The doctrine provided the basic justification for Soviet military intervention and it also set clear limits on how far Eastern European satellite states could challenge Soviet orthodoxy. Although the doctrine made claims to socialist internationalism, in reality it was a thinly veiled tool of Soviet hegemony intended to preserve Soviet state power and security objectives in Eastern Europe. The policy dashed hopes that the Soviet Union would allow meaningful reform in Eastern Europe and contributed to a period of stagnation there in the 1970s. The doctrine was used to justify the Soviet occupation of Afghanistan in 1979 and Soviet pressure on Poland during the Solidarity trade union uprising in 1980.

In the late 1980s, however, Soviet policy shifted when Mikhail Gorbachev (1931–), the dynamic new leader of the Soviet Union, began to encourage reform in the USSR as well as in Eastern Europe. In 1989 the Soviet Union took no action when popular revolts toppled successive East European Communist regimes. The revolutions signaled the end of the practical application of the Brezhnev Doctrine.

Paul D. Lensink

Further reading
Dawisha, Karen. *The Kremlin and the Prague Spring.* Berkeley, California, 1984.

Hutchings, Robert L. *Soviet–East European Relations: Consolidation and Conflict 1968–1980.* Madison, Wisconsin, 1983.

Jones, Robert A. *The Soviet Concept of "Limited Sovereignty" from Lenin to Gorbachev: The Brezhnev Doctrine.* London, 1990.

See also Mikhail Gorbachev; Prague Spring; Revolutions of 1989; Solidarity; Warsaw Pact

Brno

Major city of Moravia, a region in the Czech Republic. Brno (German, Brünn) was incorporated as a free city in 1243 and has since been Moravia's major political-administrative and economic center. It is the Czech Republic's second-largest city (estimated population, 392,000 in 1990) and the administrative center for the South Moravian region. The city has been a major industrial center since the nineteenth century and also serves as an important educational and cultural center.

Brno and nearby areas seem to have been inhabited for tens of thousands of years. Remains and artifacts of Cro-Magnon humans have been found in the area, and Brno itself was the site of a Celtic settlement. The importance of the city increased after it became the seat of the margraves of Moravia (1621–1857), and it was an important center for trade fairs and manufacturing within the Habsburg Empire. The city's population was dominated by Germans until after World War II, when most of those residents were expelled. Brno's inhabitants are now mostly Czech.

Dramatic events in the city's history include its siege by Swedish troops during the Thirty Years War (1618–48) and Napoléon's (1769–1821) use of it for his headquarters during the decisive battle of Austerlitz (Slavkov) just east of Brno. Špílberk (Spielberg) castle, a twelfth-century bastion on one of the city's twin hills, served as a notorious Austrian political prison during much of the eighteenth and nineteenth centuries.

Modern Brno remains important for the manufacture of textiles and machinery, as a site for international trade fairs, and as an educational and cultural center. The city is home to Masaryk University as well as several colleges and museums. Numerous historic buildings survive near the city center, but much of Brno's outskirts has contrasting, contemporary architectural styles, including socialist-era high-rise apartment complexes.

William H. Berentsen

Further reading
Pounds, N.J.G. *Eastern Europe.* London, 1969

Brusilov Offensive (June–August 1916)

Russian offensive against Austro-Hungarian positions in 1916. Launched on June 5, 1916, on the southwest front, the so-called Brusilov Offensive was initially successful because of the innovative tactics of its architect, General Aleksey Brusilov (1853–1926). He emphasized probing attacks, close coordination of infantry and artillery, and surprise, in contrast to the heretofore Russian reliance on massive frontal assault. During June and July, Brusilov forced an Austro-Hungarian retreat to the Carpathians, inflicting more than five hundred thousand casualties, and threatened to break into the Hungarian plain before being

B

stopped in August by the exhaustion of his reserves and the arrival of German reinforcements. The importance of the Brusilov Offensive lies in the relief it gave Russia's allies on the Western and Italian fronts, the impetus its heavy losses gave to disaffection with the war among Russians, and the catalytic effect it had on Romania's entry into the war. The latter, surrounded on three sides by the Central Powers, had long been planning to attack Austria-Hungary; the Brusilov Offensive seemed to insure a reasonable chance of doing so successfully. At the same time, it suggested that speed was necessary lest a dispirited Dual Monarchy seek peace and thereby end the Romanian hope of occupying and annexing Bukovina and Transylvania.

Glenn E. Torrey

Further reading

Brusilov, A.A. *A Soldier's Notebook 1914–1918.* London, 1930; reprint, Westport, Connecticut, 1971.

Rostunov, Ivan I. *General Brusilov.* Moscow, 1964.

Stone, Norman. *The Eastern Front 1914–1917.* New York, 1975.

See also Dual Monarchy; World War I

Bucharest

Capital of Romania. Bucharest is a city of over two million inhabitants located in the southeastern part of Romania. It lies in a low area in the middle of the Danubian plain, 36 miles (60 km) north of the Danube River, 60 miles (100 km) south of the Carpathian Mountains, and 120 miles (200 km) west of the Black Sea. Inside the city, the former hills are almost imperceptible. Unlike other capital cities in the region, Bucharest lacks a big river, and it is divided only by two small streams, the Dâmbovița and the Colentina. Hundreds of years ago, the entire area was covered by a big forest, Codrul Vlăsiei, which in time was replaced by farms and settlements. Owing to its continental climate, vegetation consists of remains of the former forest and of various other plants typical of the region. The city also has many parks filled with flowers, such as roses and lilacs, as well as streets shaded by rows of linden and chestnut trees.

According to legend, the city was founded by a shepherd, Bucur, and from him was derived the name București. Archaeological evidence shows that the area was occupied by various early settlements, but the first historic document referring to the city dates only to 1459, when Wallachia was ruled by Vlad Țepeș (the Impaler) (1429–76), the historical Dracula. Bucharest became the capital of the principality under Prince Constantin Brâncoveanu (r. 1688–1714), and the capital of modern Romania in 1862. Thereafter, the city grew rapidly, especially between the two world wars, when its population increased from 472,000 in 1927 to about one million toward the end of World War II.

Bucharest is the political, social, economic, and cultural center of Romania. Before the Communist takeover in 1947, the city developed freely at a natural pace, but during the last decades, it was changed according to a central plan of industrialization with all the consequences that entailed. Currently, for example, with less than 10 percent of Romania's population, the city produces about 25 percent of Romania's industrial output. To accommodate the additional one million people who moved to Bucharest after 1945, huge housing projects were built without proper regard for the necessary infrastructure. As a result, Bucharest is now a big city struggling to survive, and this is probably most evident in the political and cultural arenas.

From a cultural point of view, Bucharest was the birthplace of the first Romanian translation of the Bible in 1688, which coincided with the moment when Brâncoveanu moved the last institutions of his government from Târgoviște, the old capital, to Bucharest. In 1695 he endowed Bucharest with its first institution of higher education, where disciplines were taught in Greek, the language of the Romanian Orthodox Church at that time. A major revamping of the curricula took place in 1776 under the reign of Prince Alexandru Ypsilanti (r. 1796–97), who tried to apply to the instruction process ideas borrowed from the French Enlightenment. It was not until 1864, however, that a university patterned after western European models began to function in Bucharest.

Throughout the nineteenth century, a move toward Europeanization took place in Bucharest. By the middle of the century, Bucharest boasted a widely admired Opera House. But Bucharest achieved cultural stature during the first half of the twentieth century when the city earned its reputation as Little Paris. In Bucharest during those decades some of the century's world-renowned cultural personalities made their debut, among them playwright Eugen Ionescu (1912–94), sculptor Constantin Brancuşi (1876–1957), historian of religions Mircea Eliade (1907–86), and composer George Enescu (1881–1955). Among the noteworthy architectural monuments in the neoclassic tradition that escaped Communist-era destruction were the Royal Palace, the Arch of Triumph, the Romanian Atheneum, the University Library, the Old Post Office, the Savings and Loans Palace, and the Old Parliament.

Nicholas Dima and Andrei Brezianu

Further reading

Caselli, Domenico. *Cum au fost Bucureşti odinioara*. Bucharest, 1994.

Cucu, V. and D. Ghinea. *Die Städte Rumäniens.* Bucharest, 1992.

Enciclopedia Geografică a României. Bucharest, 1982.

Giurescu, Dinu. *The Razing of Romania's Past.* New York, 1989.

Morand, Paul. *Bucharest.* Paris, 1935.

See also Architecture; Constantin Brancuşi; Mircea Eliade; George Enescu; Eugen Ionescu

Bucharest, Treaty of (1913)

Peace treaty concluding the Second Balkan War. After the First Balkan War (1912–13), the Great Powers compelled the Balkan states to accept the London Peace Treaty, an agreement that did not grant Serbia an outlet to the Adriatic Sea. Consequently, Serbia demanded a revision of its treaty of alliance with Bulgaria and refused to relinquish a part of Macedonia that had been assigned to Bulgaria. The two states failed to find a peaceful solution, and on June 29, 1913, Bulgaria attacked Serbia. Greece, Romania, Montenegro, and the Ottoman Empire subsequently entered into the war on the Serbian side. Bulgaria was defeated and compelled to seek a cease-fire, which was established on July 30, 1913. The combatants shortly thereafter gathered in Bucharest and concluded a treaty on August 10, 1913, which defined the borders of Bulgaria with Romania, Serbia, and Greece and sanctioned the partition of Macedonia. It also called for the demobilization of the Bulgarian army, release of prisoners of war, and compensation to the victors. Romania gained southern Dobrudja (Dobruzha). The Serbian-Bulgarian border was established more or less at the present Serbian-Bulgarian and Bulgarian-Macedonian frontiers, except for the districts of Pirot and Strumica, which were given to the Kingdom of Serbs, Croats, and Slovenes (Yugoslavia) after World War I. The Greek-Bulgarian border established by the treaty ran from the Serbian-Bulgarian border at Belasica to the area in which the Mesta River flows into the Aegean Sea.

Aleksandar Panev

Further reading

Hristov, Aleksandar and Jovan Donev. *La Macédoine dans les traités internationaux 1875–1919.* Skopje, 1994.

Hurst, Michael. *Key Treaties for the Great Powers 1870–1914.* New York, 1972.

See also Balkan Wars; Dobrudja; Great Powers; Macedonia

Bucharest, Treaty of (May 1918)

Peace treaty between Romania and the Central Powers during World War I. Although the final version of the treaty was the work of the government of Alexander Marghiloman (1854–1925) (March–October 1918), the basic contours of the agreement were determined by the armistice of Focşani (December 9, 1917) and the preliminary Peace of Buftea (March 5, 1918), which were the work of the governments of Ion I.C. Brătianu (1864–1927) and Alexandru Averescu (1859–1938), respectively. The Romanian armies had suffered significant defeats in 1916 at the hands of the Central Powers. Despite some successes in the summer of 1917, an exhausted Romania signed an armistice in December. Faced with the Russo-German Peace of Brest-Litovsk, which took Russia out of the war, and an Austro-German threat to resume hostilities, the Marghiloman government had few cards in its negotiating hand except rivalries among the Central Powers. Despite battling hard for Romanian interests, the Romanian delegation was eventually forced to agree to onerous terms: handing over Dobrudja (Dobruzha) to the Central Powers; cession of the Carpathian passes to Hungary; unfavorable trade and financial agreements; and granting monopolies for up to ninety years on some of Romania's most important resources. The treaty was ratified by a parliament elected under enemy intimidation. However, King Ferdinand (1865–1927) withheld his signature until the

B

defeat of the Central Powers made the treaty irrelevant. Like the Treaty of Brest-Litovsk, the Treaty of Bucharest illustrated the extremity of German war aims.

Glenn E. Torrey

Further reading

Bornemann, Elke. *Der Frieden von Bukarest, 1918.* Frankfurt, 1978.

Iancovici, D. *La Paix de Bucarest (7 Mai 1918).* Paris, 1918.

Notovich, F.I. *Bukharestskii mir 1918g.* Moscow, 1958.

Moisuc, Viorica, "The Importance of the Bucharest 'Peace Treaty' of May 1918." *Romania: Pages of History* 2 (1983).

See also Alexandru Averescu; Ion I.C. Brătianu; Brest-Litovsk, Treaty of; Dobrudja; Ferdinand; Alexander Marghiloman; World War I

Budapest

Capital and largest city of Hungary. Budapest is located on the Danube River in the north-central part of Hungary. Founded by the Romans in the second century A.D. as Aquincum, the city fell into neglect until the thirteenth century. Budapest became the capital of Hungary in the fifteenth century under Matthias Corvinus (c. 1443–90) but was held by the Ottoman Turks from 1541 until 1686. Important events during the 1800s included its role in the 1848–49 Hungarian Revolution and as capital of Hungary in the Dual Monarchy with Austria (1867), unification in 1872 of the formerly separated Buda, Pest, and O'Buda, and the growth of industries, primarily textile and food processing, during the latter third of the century. The population of the city swelled from 54,000 in 1800 to 861,000 by 1900.

Budapest's growth in terms of population and industry continued to outstrip the rest of the country through the first half of the twentieth century. The city suffered considerable damage during World War II but was quickly repaired in the postwar period. Industrialization was accelerated under socialist planning despite explicit policies to spread development to other parts of the country. The city's rapid growth, which pushed totals from 1,232,000 in 1920 to 1,590,000 in 1949, slowed during the 1970s and 1980s. In 1990 the population stood at 2,016,774.

Buda, located on the west side of the Danube, is historically the royal part of town. Dominated by the Buda hills and the Castle District, this half remains the more prestigious residential location. Pest, located on the east, level, side of the Danube, is the commercial and industrial part of the city, although—since its completion in 1902—it has been the site of the neo-Gothic parliament building. Toward the south is Csepel Island, a major heavy industrial zone, while toward the north is Margaret Island, one of the city's many playgrounds. Transportation is facilitated by seven bridges linking the two sides of the city and one of Europe's oldest subway systems. The city is divided into twenty-two semiautonomous districts.

Darrick Danta

Further reading

Bencze, Imre and Erzsébet V. Tatji. *Budapest: An Industrial-Geographical Approach.* Budapest, 1972.

Enyedi, György and Viktória Szirmai. *Budapest: A Central European Capital.* London, 1992.

Gutkind, E.A. *International History of City Development,* vol. 7, *Urban Development in East-Central Europe: Poland, Czechoslovakia, and Hungary.* New York, 1972.

Hanák, Péter, ed. *One Thousand Years: A Concise History of Hungary.* Budapest, 1988.

Lukacs, John. *Budapest 1900: A Historical Portrait of a City and Its Culture.* New York, 1988.

See also Dual Monarchy; Hungarian War for Independence

Budapest Conventions of 1877

Two secret agreements between Russia and Austria-Hungary regarding the Balkans. After Russia, Austria-Hungary, and Germany failed to mediate the disputes resulting from the insurrection in Bosnia and Hercegovina that began in 1875, the crisis caused Serbia and Montenegro in June 1876 to declare war against the Turks. Austro-Hungarian Foreign Minister Gyula Andrássy (1823–90) and Russian Chancellor Aleksandr M. Gorchakov (1798–1883) held discussions in Reichstadt concerning the war and its aftermath. Turkish victories jeopardized the informal talks, however, and prompted an exchange of notes between Alexander II (1818–81) and Emperor Franz Joseph

(1830–1916) in an attempt to resolve the difficulties in the Balkans.

When domestic Pan-Slavic pressure forced Russia to make preparations for war, it had to secure Austro-Hungarian neutrality to fight the Ottomans. A series of secret negotiations conducted by Andrássy and Gorchakov from January to March 1877 resulted in two agreements that formalized the earlier Reichstadt conversations. They stated that in return for Austro-Hungarian benevolent neutrality in event of a Russo-Turkish war, Austria-Hungary could occupy at its wish and later annex Bosnia and Hercegovina with the exception of the Sanjak of Novi Pazar. The fate of the Sanjak would be determined at a later date, while it, Montenegro, Serbia, Romania, and Bulgaria were to become neutral zones for Austria-Hungary. Russia could take back southern Bessarabia, which it had lost in 1856, and agreed not to fight in Bosnia and Hercegovina, Serbia, and Montenegro. Serbia, Montenegro, and Greece would receive lands from the Ottoman Empire, and Bulgaria and Eastern Rumelia would become autonomous regions of the empire. Austria-Hungary and Russia further agreed to consult each other diplomatically if a general European crisis arose from their agreement. In essence, these actions divided the Balkans into Russian and Austro-Hungarian spheres of influence. Russia went to war in April 1877, but relations between the two powers remained edgy, and the conventions became moot with the Treaty of San Stefano (1878), in which Russia forced the creation of a new, large Bulgarian state.

Gregory C. Ference

Further reading

Hurst, Michael, ed. *Key Treaties for the Great Powers 1814–1914,* 2 vols. New York, 1972.

See also Gyula Andrássy, Sr.; Bessarabian Question; Eastern Question; Aleksandr Gorchakov; Pan-Slavism; Russo-Turkish War of 1877–78; Sanjak of Novi Pazar; San Stefano, Treaty of

Bug River

Major river in eastern Poland. The Northern or Western Bug River has its source in the foothills of the Carpathian Mountains (the Volyn Podolsk Upland) in L'viv province of western Ukraine,

about 20 miles (32 km) southeast of the city of L'vov (Ukrainian, L'viv). The river flows along a 516-mile (830 km) course and drains an area of 28,367 square miles (73,470 sq km).

In its upper course, the river flows rapidly northwestward out of the foothills following the general slope of the North European Plain. One hundred miles (160 km) from its source, the river reaches the flat, swampy lowlands and for 125 miles (200 km) forms the border between Poland on the west and Ukraine and Belarus on the east. This middle course of the Bug formed part of the line proposed in 1939 as a border between Germany and the Soviet Union. This stretch of the river flows along the western edge of the Pripet Marshes, the largest marshland on the European continent and one of the largest in the world. In this middle course through flat, swampy land, the river flows too slowly for navigation.

The only city of importance along the river is Brest, a rail node linking Moscow, Minsk, and Warsaw. In 1989 the population of Brest was 258,000.

The Bug enters Poland 30 miles (48 km) north of Brest. It is joined by the Narew River north of Warsaw, and then flows on to join the Vistula River 23 miles (37 km) downriver. The Bug becomes navigable, for the last 300 miles (500 km) of its 484-mile (779 km) course, starting 195 miles (314 km) upriver from its intersection with the Narew. It is connected to Warsaw by canal to avoid the complicated currents where it meets the Narew. The Bug empties into the Baltic Sea at Gdańsk.

Barbara VanDrasek

Further reading

Curtis, Glenn E., ed. *Poland: A Country Study.* Washington, D.C., 1994.

Gottmann, Jean. *A Geography of Europe,* 3d ed. New York, 1962.

Hoffman, George W. *Europe in the 1990s: A Geographic Analysis,* 6th ed. New York, 1990.

Bujak, Zbigniew (1954–)

Polish Solidarity union activist. Bujak studied electrical engineering before going to work at the Ursus factory complex in Warsaw. Involved in protecting workers' rights in the late 1970s, he played a major role in the Solidarity movement. With the start of workers' strikes in Gdańsk in August 1980, Bujak represented the Ursus workers on the Interfactory

B

Strike Committee, which signed the agreement establishing the Solidarity trade union. A delegate to the Solidarity National Delegate Conference in September 1981, he was elected to the National Coordinating Commission representing the Mazowsze (Warsaw) district. After the imposition of martial law on December 13, 1981, Bujak became the head of the Mazowsze underground organization and a member of the national Temporary Coordinating Commission (TKK), the main organ of Solidarity's underground structures. He was arrested in May 1986 and amnestied in August. Bujak—who was awarded the Robert Kennedy Memorial Prize in 1986—went on to participate in the "round table" negotiations (1989) between the Solidarity movement and the regime of Wojciech Jaruzelski (1923–). With the end of Communist rule in Poland, Bujak slowly moved away from the Solidarity trade union—first by not supporting Lech Wałęsa (1943–) for president and then cofounding a new political party, Unia Pracy (Union of Work).

Peter Lavelle

Further reading

Lopinski, Maciej et al. *Konspira: Solidarity Underground.* Berkeley, California, 1990.

Ramet, Sabrina P. *Social Currents in Eastern Europe: The Sources and Meaning of the Great Transformation.* Durham, North Carolina, 1991.

"Voices from the Underground." *Survey* 26 (Autumn 1982): 92–94.

See also Wojciech Jaruzelski; Solidarity; Lech Wałęsa

Bukovina

Northern Romanian province. The medieval Principality of Moldavia did not make a clear distinction between its eastern and western reaches, but rather between the upper and lower lands. The upper north, actually the cradle of the principality, is mountainous, beautiful, and full of history. After 1775, when Austria annexed the region as a prize for mediating a Russo-Turkish war, Vienna named the area Bukovina. At the time, the area was inhabited mostly by Romanians, but Austria pursued a policy of assimilation and took many measures to weaken the Romanian element.

Bukovina has a surface area of 3,750 square miles (10,442 sq km) representing over 10 percent of old Moldavia's territory. The area is mostly a forested highland with hilly regions cut by steep, narrow valleys. The Carpathian Mountains reach almost 6,270 feet (1,900 m), and the entire water drainage and geomorphological structure attach the area to the rest of Moldova. At the end of World War I, the province was returned to modern Romania, but this time its population was ethnically mixed.

According to the 1930 census, Bukovina had 830,000 inhabitants, of whom 380,000 were Romanians, 236,000 Ukrainians and Ruthenians, 92,000 Jews, and 76,000 Germans. In 1940, however, following the Nazi-Soviet Pact of 1939, the northern part of the province was forcibly annexed by the Soviet Union. Moscow claimed that it was the last missing piece of Ukraine, but neither Russia nor Ukraine had owned it previously. Ever since, the area has remained in contention, first between Romania and the USSR, now between Romania and Ukraine.

The southern part of Bukovina now in Romania is one of the most attractive regions of the country. It has numerous historic and cultural relics and monuments. Suceava is the provincial center and is one of the early capitals of Moldavia. Putna Monastery, where Prince Stephen the Great (Ştefan cel Mare [r. 1457–1504]) is buried, is a place of historic and religious pilgrimage. Suceviţa, Moldoviţa, Voroneţ, and Humor are among the fifteenth- and sixteenth-century monasteries internationally famous for their painted exteriors. These monasteries have been placed under the auspices of the United Nations agency UNESCO.

Nicholas Dima

Further reading

Dima, Nicholas. "Bukovina, Romania, and the Ukraine," in *The Tragic Plight of a Border Area: Bessarabia and Bukovina,* ed. by Maria Manoliu-Manea. Humboldt, California, 1983.

Nistor, Ion. *Bessarabia and Bukovina.* Bucharest, 1939.

Prothero, G.W., ed. *Bukovina.* London, 1920.

See also Carpathian Mountains; Moldavia; Molotov-Ribbentrop Pact

Bulgaria (Geography)

Bulgaria is a small state in the southeastern Balkan Peninsula fronting on the Black Sea, with an area of 42,850 square miles (119,000 sq km) and a population of nine million. It is bounded by Romania, Serbia, Macedonia, Greece, and Turkey, all of which hold territories deemed by Bulgarian nationalists rightfully to be parts of a Greater Bulgaria.

The east-west trending Stara Planina range (Balkan Mountains) effectively divides Bulgaria into two roughly equal parts. To the north is the Danubian Upland Plain, and to the south a complex of hills, mountains, and basins that include the fertile valley of the Maritsa River. The Stara Planina has ridge crests that range from 6,500 feet (1,970 m) elevation in the west to 2,500 feet (758 m) in the east. A number of passes, including two river gorges, permit relatively easy passage. The Danubian Upland Plain is characterized by rolling hills averaging 600 feet (182 m) in elevation. It has fertile soils but is relatively dry and treeless. The jumbled terrain lying south of the Stara Planina range includes several large lowlands and a section of the Rhodope Mountains rising to nearly 10,000 feet (3,030 m).

Bulgaria has hotter summers and colder winters than are found further west. July lowland temperatures average about 75° F (24° C), with January temperatures generally hovering around freezing (32° F [0° C]). Summers tend to be cooler and winters warmer along Bulgaria's southern margins, reflecting proximity to the moderating effects of winds coming off the Aegean Sea. Rainfall is typically 20 inches (51 cm) annually, distributed rather evenly throughout the year. Higher elevations receive 40 inches (102 cm) or more and exhibit a sequence of vegetation zones from oak and beech forests on lower slopes to conifers and alpine meadows near crests.

Bulgarians, numbering 85 percent of the population, speak a distinctive south Slavic language and share an Eastern Orthodox religious heritage. Up to 4 percent, mostly in the southwest Pirin region, identify themselves ethnically as Macedonians, with a distinctive language and traditions, but Bulgarian regimes have long refused to acknowledge them as a distinctive group. More than 8 percent of the population has a Muslim heritage, divided between 700,000 ethnic Turks in the northeast and 160,000 Slavic-speaking Pomaks living in the south-central border region. More than half a million Muslims have emigrated to Turkey in recent years because of discriminatory pressures. Bulgaria also has about 450,000 Gypsies. Two-thirds of the Bulgarian population is classified as urban. Half live in the eight cities having more than 100,000 inhabitants: Sofia, Plovdiv, Varna, Ruse, Burgas, Stara Zagora, Pleven, and Sliven. Before World War II, some 80 percent of Bulgarians were farmers.

Bulgaria produces a wide range of industrial and consumer goods. It is noteworthy in the production and export of lift equipment, computers, batteries, and farm machinery; 20 percent of its industrial production is concentrated in the Sofia basin, 10 percent in the western Maritsa valley, 7 percent in the eastern Maritsa valley, and 5 percent in the vicinity of the Black Sea port of Varna.

In agriculture, Bulgaria differs from its neighbors in the notably higher proportion of its territory devoted to crops (45 percent) than to grazing (7 percent). About two-thirds of farmland is in cereal production, mainly wheat but also a notable amount of corn (maize). The remainder is devoted to specialized crops, including fruits and vegetables, sugar beets, tobacco, vineyards, and herbs. Bulgaria ranks second in world per capita production of tobacco, grown mainly in the southwest. Its oriental tobacco is noted for low nicotine and high tar. The country leads the world in distillation of the perfume component attar of roses from petals grown in the Valley of Roses on the southern flank of the Stara Planina.

Thomas M. Poulsen

Further reading

Alisov, N.V. et al. *Economic Geography of the Socialist Countries of Europe.* Moscow, 1985.

Berentsen, William H. *Contemporary Europe: A Geographic Analysis,* 7th ed. New York, 1997.

Crampton, R.J. *A Short History of Bulgaria.* New York, 1987.

Curtis, Glenn E., ed. *Bulgaria: A Country Study.* Washington, D.C., 1993.

Lampe, J.R. *The Bulgarian Economy in the Twentieth Century.* New York, 1986.

See also Agriculture; Balkan Mountains; Burgas; Eastern Rumelia; Exarchate; Gypsies; Macedonia; Maritsa Valley; Muslims; Orthodoxy;

Pleven; Plovdiv; Pomaks; Rhodope Mountains; Ruse; Sofia; Turks; Varna

Bulgaria (History)

Bulgaria before the Nineteenth Century

Modern Bulgarians trace their history from 681, the supposed date when Asparuch (c. 644–c. 701), a leader of the Turkish Bulgars of the Ukrainian steppe, conquered the lands of the eastern Balkans north and south of the Danube River. This region, where human habitation has existed since the Old Stone Age (ca. 700,000 B.C.), was the home of the ancient Thracians in the Golden Age of Greece and the Persian Empire. In addition, a number of Greek colonies existed along the Black Sea coast.

In the fourth century B.C. Thrace was part of the empire of the Macedonian Philip II (382–336 B.C.) and his son Alexander the Great (356–323 B.C.). The Romans conquered the area 200 years later, and when their empire began to decline, European and Turkish peoples tried to force entry into Roman lands. The South Slavs settled in the Balkans in the fifth century.

Asparuch, with his Bulgar princes (*boiars*), established control over the eastern branch of these South Slavs. The Bulgars remained the ruling aristocratic caste, but their culture submerged into the Slavic. From 681 to 1018, under a succession of Bulgar khans, this first Bulgarian Empire became one of the powerful states of the region, challenging the Byzantine Empire for mastery of the peninsula.

In the ninth century, after the internal strife in the Greek Empire ended and the emperors could bring more energy and resources to bear on their European neighbors, Bulgaria had by this time become a fully integrated state, controlling the north Balkans. In 864, after negotiating with Rome and Constantinople, Prince Boris I (c. 826–907) adopted Christianity from the latter through the meditation of the disciples of the apostles to the Slavs, Saints Cyril (d. 869) and Methodius (d. 885). Since Bulgaria was the first Slavic nation to adopt Christianity, the Bulgarian language, known today as Old Church Bulgarian or Old Church Slavonic, became standard for all Slavic Orthodox liturgies.

Boris's son Simeon (863–927) defeated the Greek emperors in battle and claimed the throne for himself. He adopted the title tsar. His troops beat the Byzantine armies in the field and marched to the very walls of Constantinople, but he was unable to take the city.

When Simeon's son and heir Peter (d. 970) ascended the throne, Bulgaria fell into decline. Less of a military leader than his father, Peter sought accommodation with the Byzantine Empire through diplomacy, while the latter increased its strength. In the meantime, Peter was beset by other enemies, internal as well as external. Serbs, Bosnians, Croatians, Magyars, Russians, and Pechenegs challenged his borders. Internally, there was religious as well as civil strife. The *boiars* of the southwest pulled away from the tsar's control and eventually established de facto autonomy, and later the Bulgarian patriarch, established under Simeon, moved his seat from Preslav to Ohrid. Part of the reason for this change was the growth of the heretical Bogomil movement (which held a dualistic view of the world in which two forces—God and the devil—operated), but Peter's desire to hunt down his own citizens because of religious dissidence was as weak as his desire to fight foreign enemies.

The results of Peter's reign continued into those of his successors. Samuil (d. 1014), who came to the throne in 976, moved the capital to Ohrid. Now, however, Byzantine ruler Basil II (d. 1025) seized the opportunity to conquer his neighbor. He waged war against Samuil and in 1014 defeated the Bulgarian army near Thessaloniki. According to legend, Basil ordered every soldier blinded except for one in a hundred who was to be left with one eye to lead his comrades back to his king. Shortly after seeing the pitiful sight, Samuil died. Four years later, Bulgaria became part of the Byzantine Empire, and Basil added *Bulgarothronctus* (Bulgar Slayer) to his list of titles.

Byzantine success was short-lived, however. Within fifty years, the empire was in disarray, and during the chaos, losses to the Turks, Franks, and Western crusaders destroyed the once proud Byzantine state.

In 1185 two Bulgarian aristocratic brothers, Ivan Asen (d. 1196) and Peter (d. 1197), taking advantage of Byzantine weaknesses, raised the standard of revolt and declared a new, independent Second Bulgarian Empire. The capital of this empire was the luxurious city of Turnovo, located on the meandering Yantra River, a tributary of the Danube.

In 1204 the Fourth Crusade conquered Constantinople and put a Westerner, Count Baldwin of

Flanders (1171–1205), on the Byzantine throne. Baldwin's attempt to reconquer the rebellious Bulgarians failed, however, when the latter, led by King Kaloian (d. 1207), not only defeated the empire but captured Baldwin and took him prisoner. The Bulgarian king, according to legend, locked his illustrious captive in a tower of the palace overlooking the Yantra. The remains of the prison has remained a local curiosity to this day, and in recent years it has become the central piece of the reconstructed castle, now a tourist attraction.

While the Second Bulgarian Empire was more prosperous than even the first, the Balkans were now the site of a great many more successful states equal to or even surpassing Bulgaria in power. Serbia, the Despotate of Epirus, Bosnia, Hungary, expanding Venice, the other commercial city-states such as Dubrovnik and Split, and the vassal provinces of the Latin Empire all enjoyed a chance to take advantage of an expanding economy as the wealth of Eastern Europe, the Near East, and the Mediterranean passed through the Balkan markets.

Bulgaria, too, enjoyed the wealth of the new times. Turnovo was a bustling commercial metropolis, a miniature Constantinople, with a cosmopolitan population. In fact, thirteenth-century emperor Ivan Alexander (d. 1371) put away his wife and married the daughter of a Jewish merchant, Theodora (née Sara, n.d.). Intermarriage among faiths was not that unusual in those centuries, and Ivan and Theodora gave their daughter as a concubine to Bayezid (1347–1403), the heir to the Turkish sultanate, the strongest power in the region. Ivan divided his kingdom between his two sons, Ivan Shishman (d. 1395) and Ivan Stratsimir (d. c. 1398), but the Ottomans defeated both of them. Shishman's southern kingdom fell shortly after the battle of Kosovo (1389), in which Bayezid's father defeated the Serbs but was killed in the battle. His son followed up with a victory over Shishman and then, in 1396, consumed the remainder of Bulgaria.

Bulgaria under Ottoman Rule

For the next five centuries, Bulgaria was part of the Ottoman Empire, and as the closest state to the Turkish capital its lands were the most integrated. The Greeks had privileges and the Greek patriarch controlled the Orthodox *millet* (religious community). For an extended period, the Serbs had their own patriarch and the Romanians enjoyed semi-autonomous liberties. But the Bulgarians were directly under Ottoman rule. In the early years, when Ottoman strength allowed a measure of justice, this perhaps was not so bad in the context of the times, but beginning in the seventeenth century a chronic malaise of misrule struck the empire, which led to the worst injustices of all.

The long, five-century Ottoman period put Bulgaria in a state of national semiconsciousness. Although the judgment of some modern Bulgarian historians—who see the period as unrelenting tyranny—is too harsh, there is no doubt that the Bulgarians, of all the Balkan nations with the possible exception of the Albanians, had their national consciousness the most erased. The Romanians had their princes, the Greeks their nobility and church, the Serbs their patriarch and emigration in Austria, but Bulgaria, the closest to Istanbul, remained the most controlled. The Ottomans put Bulgarians in the Orthodox *millet* so that not only did the Turks control their politics but the Greeks their religion as well.

Yet Bulgarians never completely lost their identity. Bound together by their church and language, the communities continued to exist. Remembrances of their past were kept alive in isolated monasteries, such as the one most renowned in the Rila Mountains south of Sofia. In 1752 the Bulgarian monk Paissi (1722–73) of Hilendar Monastery on Mt. Athos wrote his landmark book, *History of the Slavic Bulgarians,* recounting the glory of the nation's medieval period. The book started a revival of Bulgarian nationalism spread especially by Paissi's disciple Stoiko Vladislavov (1739–1813), the Bishop Sofroni of Vratsa, who traveled through Bulgarian lands promoting self-consciousness and searching to replace the Greek clergy in Bulgaria with a native one. He was not successful, for while the Greek, Romanian, and Serbian population had native priests, the Bulgarians remained in the hands of Greek clergy, and while the Old Church Bulgarian liturgy was heard at Romanian and Serb masses, in its own land it was more and more replaced by Greek.

Bulgaria in the Nineteenth Century

In the early nineteenth century Bulgaria was divided into small territories dominated by Turkish landlords, rebel warlords, and powerful janissary (military) leaders. The sultan's authority had little effect outside of Istanbul. The Christian peasants (*rayah*), whom Muslims regarded virtually as

B cattle, were in a position of abject subjugation. However, the reforms of Mahmud II (1784–1839), including the destruction of the janissaries in 1826, began a period of change for the Balkan peoples including the Bulgarians. With the help of the Russians, who fought and defeated the Ottoman Empire in 1828–29, Greece gained its independence and Serbia its autonomy. In 1839 the new young sultan, Abdul Mejid (1823–61), announced the Hatt-i-Sharif of Gülhane, the Rose Garden decree, and began the *tanzimat* (reform) movement in the Ottoman Empire. The empire was now in the hands of reformers like Reshid Pasha (1799–1858) and his disciples, the pashas Fuad (1815–69), Ali (1815–71), and Midhat (1822–84). The reformers wished to modernize the empire and above all hold on to its remaining territory. Bulgaria and Macedonia benefited economically from these Turkish reforms, but nationalist independence movements were seriously watched. The reforms meant that Bulgarian Christians could work their own farms. Some became rich in the rose oil trade of the Balkan Mountains or raising sheep in the Rhodope Mountains. One merchant, Veselin Aprilov (1789–1847), established a secular school for Bulgarian youth in Gabrovo, the Balkan Mountain town that was becoming a center of local cloth weaving. Other schools followed and along with them a national system of reading rooms, a type of library where the new Bulgarian daily press could be read and discussed. Bulgaria became the most literate country in the Balkans.

After the Crimean War (1853–56), in which a number of Bulgarians fought as volunteers with the Russians, the ambitious Midhat Pasha became governor of northern Bulgaria. Committed to the modernization of the Ottoman Empire with opportunity for all citizens (but without secession of territory), he made Bulgaria a testing ground for his theories. He encouraged Bulgarian agriculture, establishing a peasant land bank for easy credit, the basis for an institution that exists to this day. Although the inefficient extended family farms, *zadrugi,* common among the other South Slavic nations, existed only in a small portion of Bulgaria, Midhat encouraged the dissolution of these and their replacement with single-family farms. He invested much in the province's infrastructure, including better roads and veterinary stations. Large estates were owned by Turks, but Bulgarians became small and middle farmers.

From the wealthier middle farmers and infant bourgeoisie, mainly rose oil and tobacco merchants and textile manufacturers, came a group of citizens derisively called the *chorbadzhii* (meat soup eaters). Representing the conservative elements, they sought Bulgarian cultural autonomy within the Ottoman Empire. They formed the background in a growing movement asking for an autonomous Bulgarian church. The Greek hierarchy resisted, but in 1868, when the Greeks of Crete, still under Ottoman rule, rose in revolt, the Kingdom of Greece aided the rebels, approaching the brink of war with the Ottomans. The Greeks lost, but the sultan (Abdul Aziz [1830–76]), in part in retaliation, granted a *firman* (decree) creating a Bulgarian autocephalous exarchate still part of the patriarchate, even though the Greek patriarch refused to recognize it. Atanas M. Chalukov (1816–88) was installed as the first exarch, Antim I. Even more controversial than the religious hierarchy was the geographical area of which the exarchate extended—not only the present Bulgarian lands but Thrace and Macedonia—including both sides of Lake Ohrid (although excluding Thessaloniki).

The *firman* allowed the exarchate to establish churches and elementary schools throughout its designated region, and over the next decades a generation of South Slavs in the exarchate's boundaries learned that they were Bulgarians. This was not controversial in the northern and eastern sections, where all South Slavic–speaking Christians were Bulgarians and a clear majority. However, in the south—Macedonia and Thrace—the situation was less clear. In the struggle for the region, Bulgaria's neighbors—Serbia, Turkey, and Greece—claimed large portions of the population as their nationals. There were also Albanians, Jews, Romanian-related Vlachs, Gypsies, and numerous smaller pockets of other natives. Very few claimed to be or were acknowledged to be Macedonians. In the decades to come, all the major groups sponsored rival guerrilla gangs (called *chetnik*s or *cheta* in the Slavic languages), which sought independence from the Turks (or if they were Turkish, to maintain Ottoman control) and to prevent their rivals from gaining ascendancy. To complicate matters, bands of outlaws, as in the past, roamed the area exploiting the political controversies for their own ends.

The religious autonomy satisfied the conservative elements in Bulgaria—the *chorbadzhii*—but a radical independence movement had been growing since the 1840s, spurred on by journalists such as Georgi Rakovski (1821–67) and Liuben Karavelov (1834–79) and daring romantic brigands, called *"haidutsi,"* like Hadzhi Dimitur (1840–68), Stefan Karadzha (1840–68), and Philip Tot'o (1830–1907), whom the patriots lauded as freedom fighters. Secret societies were formed in Odessa, Belgrade, Bucharest, and even Istanbul. Two of the most important were the Bulgarian Secret Central Committee (BSCC), based in Bucharest, and the even more influential Bulgarian Revolutionary Central Committee (BRCC), led by Karavelov and Vasil Levski (1837–73), the latter a radical activist who in the 1860s drew up plans for an armed uprising. The BRCC had branches in Belgrade and Bucharest, and hundreds of members in Bulgaria itself were enlisted. On one of his organizing trips in Bulgaria in 1872, Levski was betrayed and turned over to the authorities. The Porte hanged Levski, the George Washington of modern Bulgaria, early the next year.

In actual fact, the Bulgarian rebellion began earlier than planned in response to an uprising in Bosnia in 1875. In May 1876 (April in Bulgaria's Julian calendar), the Bulgarians fired the "first shot" of the revolution in the mountain town of Kaprivshtitsa, and soon hundreds of Bulgarian mountain men from the region joined the fray. Romantic poet and adventurer Khristo Botev (1848–76), twenty-eight years of age, hijacked a Danubian steamer and led a small *cheta* into Bulgaria, where he lost his life, thus becoming another martyr (along with Levski) to the cause. The most infamous event from the Bulgarian front took place in the south, in the Rhodope Mountains, where Christian and Muslim villages lay side by side. Many of these Muslims were Pomoks—Bulgarian in speech and Muslim in faith. In May a series of raids between villages occurred, and in one community, the village of Batak, irregular Turkish troops, the Bashi-Bazouks, massacred the entire Christian population, finally burning down the church in which they sought refuge. These horrors, reported by American journalist Januarius A. MacGahan (1844–78), determined the fate of Bulgarian history. After the diplomatic efforts of the Constantinople Conference of the winter of 1876–77 failed, Russia, mainly in response to the "Bulgarian horrors," declared war on Turkey in the spring.

The initial rapid advance of the Russian troops, however, bogged down in the summer in the unsuccessful attempts to take the fortress of Pleven. By the time the city finally fell, Great Britain was ready to face Russia at Constantinople, and Moscow wisely held back. On March 3, 1878, the Russians and the Turks signed the Treaty of San Stefano in the outskirts of the Ottoman capital. In addition to Russian gains in Bessarabia and the Caucuses and independence for Serbia, Romania, and Montenegro, the treaty created a large Bulgaria roughly along the lines of the exarchate. It also provided for Russian assistance in administering the new country. Yet Bulgaria was to be an autonomous region of the Ottoman Empire, not an independent state.

San Stefano contradicted treaties between Russia and Austria guaranteeing that no large Slavic state would be created in the Balkans, as well as other treaties with the Great Powers guaranteeing the integrity of the Ottoman Empire. German Chancellor Otto von Bismarck (1815–98), attempting to resolve the crisis without upsetting his alliances with both Russia and Austria, hosted the Congress of Berlin in June 1878. The congress kept most of San Stefano intact except for the border of autonomous Bulgaria, which was reduced to the northern third. Russian troops of occupation were to guide the new regime. A second, middle section around Plovdiv was given lesser autonomous status, and Macedonia and Thrace were handed back to the Porte. To preserve the European balance of power, other parts of the Ottoman Empire were distributed among the Great Powers.

The leaders of Bulgaria greeted the reduction of the new state with anger and threatened to boycott the proposed constitutional assembly. However, under the direction of Russian general Prince Aleksandr Mihailovich Dondukov-Korsakov (1820–93), the assembly—elected by direct universal manhood suffrage—met at the medieval capital of Turnovo. The radical nationalists who led the struggle for political independence dominated the body. Liuben and Petko Karavelov (1843–1903), Dragan Tsankov (1828–1911), and Petko Slaveikov (1827–95) led their delegation.

A number of conservatives, including Konstantin Stoilov (1850–1901), were also members. Although Prince Dondukov favored this latter group, he allowed the Liberals and Radicals in the assembly to capitalize on their victory and write

Europe's most democratic constitution up to that time. The delegates determined to make Sofia, located in the center of the San Stefano borders, the country's capital, rather than Turnovo. They gave the country a unicameral legislature, rejecting the conservative and Russian pressure to establish a senate. The delegates had no choice, however, but to establish a prince as head of state. The Great Powers by the Treaty of Berlin forbade a republic, the choice of many of the delegates.

The "Turnovo Constitution" was in many ways a model document for the ideals of Western civilization, the culmination of the highest goals of nineteenth-century liberalism. Slavery was outlawed. Education was free, universal, and compulsory. Elections were based on universal manhood suffrage. All citizens were equal regardless of religion or ethnicity (although Bulgarian Orthodoxy remained the state religion). But the provision for a monarch—whose interests and views were bound to run counter to the Liberals and Radicals who in Bulgarian circumstances would control the parliament—made the document difficult to operate. It would be suspended twice in its historic run (1879–1947) and violated by the monarchs in a number of other ways. Both the monarch and parliament had great, almost equal powers. The prince, not the parliament, chose the government. The parliament ultimately made the laws.

The Congress of Berlin had provided for the Russian military administration not only to establish the constitutional assembly but to remain in Bulgaria for nine months as government and military supervisors. Yet Russians continued to play major roles in the Bulgarian government and military for seven years. The first postconstitutional task was to find a prince—one had already been selected before the assembly finished. Dondukov recommended Alexander of Battenberg (1857–93), a prince of Hesse related to the English, German, and Russian royal houses. A popular choice, he met little opposition either inside or outside Bulgaria. However, among that opposition was his cousin, the tsarevich, the future Alexander III (1857–93), who saw his German relative and namesake as too pro-Western for his Pan-Slav tastes.

Battenberg appointed Tudor Burmov (1834–1906), a leader of the conservatives, as his first prime minister. In the first decade of independence, Bulgarian cabinets included ministers imported from Russia, such as generals Alexander Kaubeers (1844–1929) as minister of war and Casimir Ehrenroth (1833–1913) as minister of the interior. Both of these were more conservative and overbearing than the wise and moderate Dondukov, who left the country in 1879; moreover, their appointments caused a great deal of conflict with the Liberals of the parliament over sharing power in the new state. The years from 1879 to 1881, therefore, witnessed a struggle pitting the government and crown against the Liberals. Even minor items such as the title of the prince ("your excellency" or "your majesty") led to protest and confrontation. In 1881 the internal struggles gave Prince Alexander the chance he needed to suspend the constitution and prorogue parliament. His attempts to add a senate failed, however, and in 1883 he restored the assembly.

During the following years, the parliamentary leaders themselves began to fall out. Dragan Tsankov and Stefan Stambolov (1854–95) emerged as the leaders of the Liberals, but Stambolov formed his own National Liberal Party, and in 1896 Petko Karavelov formed his own party as well, the Democrats. The conservatives formed the National Party, and in 1899 Tsankov broke from the Liberals to create the Progressive Liberal Party.

The main order of business was the unification of the other sections of San Stefano Bulgaria. In Eastern Rumelia a "liberation" committee carried out a coup d'état with help from Sofia in the summer of 1885. The prince was presented with a fait accompli. Bulgarian nationalists arrested the governor of Eastern Rumelia in Plovdiv and elected to unify with Bulgaria. Stambolov told Alexander he had to choose between two paths— one that led to Plovdiv or one that led to exile. Alexander agreed to unite the provinces. The world reaction, however, judged the prince to be the author of the unification plot and the Russian tsar, now Alexander III, saw England's hand in it, as Battenberg's brother had just recently married British Princess Beatrice (1857–1944).

The tsar reacted with anger to the Bulgarian union, withdrawing the Russian officer corps from the country. Prince Alexander did not have a commander left above the rank of lieutenant colonel. Austria-Hungary as well sought to punish Bulgaria and pushed King Milan of Serbia (1854–1901), jealous and fearful of Sofia's gains, to attack the latter, which appeared weakened by the Russian move. Instead, however, the Bulgarians, led by

Prince Alexander in the field and Major Racho Petrov (1861–1942), surprisingly defeated the Serbs in a great victory at Slivinitsa. Vienna was forced to intervene to prevent a Bulgarian entry into Belgrade.

The Great Powers now acceded to Bulgarian wishes, allowing the union of the two Bulgarian provinces to stand. But within five months, in August 1886, Russophile officers linked to Tsankov's party kidnapped the prince and forced him to sign a note of abdication. Tsar Alexander rejected the activity of his Bulgarian supporters, but when Alexander offered to genuinely abdicate if the tsar so wished, the Russian monarch accepted the offer. Battenberg left the country.

Stambolov was now in complete control of Bulgaria, and through his rough-handed methods he was able to keep all rivals in tow. He followed an anti-Russian, pro-English policy, seeking a reconciliation with the Porte, much to the chagrin of those Macedonians hoping to unite with Bulgaria. Stambolov's first order of business, however, was to find a new prince. Russian resistance made the search difficult, but after ten months, in July 1887, Ferdinand of Saxe-Coburg (1861–1948) agreed to accept the post. It was not until 1896 that all of the Great Powers accepted him.

Ferdinand was not particularly fond of his new country, but his ambition led him to make the most of it. Yet for his first seven years, he was dominated by Stambolov, whose dictatorial methods of government overriding the civil liberties of the Turnovo constitution left neither his opponents nor the monarch little scope in Bulgarian politics. In one infamous case, Petrov, acting on Stambolov's orders, executed seven soldiers, officers, and enlisted men who were involved in a conspiracy.

By 1894, however, Ferdinand outmaneuvered Stambolov and established his personal control over Bulgarian politics. Macedonians, relatives of men who had fallen afoul of the former prime minister, murdered the ousted Stambolov shortly thereafter. By bribes and threats, the prince manipulated the politicians into doing his bidding. His first choice for governing was the conservative National Party under Stoilov. The national government gained recognition for Ferdinand, hastened by the death in 1894 of the prince's most adamant foe, Alexander III, and the monarch's agreement to have his new-born son and heir, Prince Boris (1894–1943), baptized in the Orthodox faith rather than the Catholic (Ferdinand's religion) in the face of family and papal opposition. In domestic affairs, the government had a rockier time, brought about by the confusion over its railroad program. The Bulgarian and Eastern Rumelian railroads were owned by both state and foreign interests. Attempts by Stoilov to unify the system without creating diplomatic problems led to confusion, duplication, and government waste. His seeking of foreign loans to bail out the country's ensuing financial difficulties raised the ire of the peasantry, whose taxes were increased to pay for them. There was further opposition when a French loan in 1898 was linked to the tobacco crop. In 1899 Ferdinand dismissed Stoilov and handed the government to Dimitur Grekov (1847–1901), Stambolov's successor in the National Liberal Party.

The decade witnessed—in response to the crises—the birth of two mass parties—the Social Democrats and the Bulgarian Agrarian Union. The former, begun in 1891, found its support in the new government unions (teachers, railroad workers, etc.), although the most orthodox Marxists looked forward to the growth of a Bulgarian proletariat. The latter, founded in 1899, avoided the term *party,* but it soon engaged in partisan politics and slated candidates. The Agrarian Union was founded by teachers at the country's agricultural schools and other peasant leaders. Hard times, brought about by increased taxation and a growing populist movement, fueled the founding of the organization.

Also in 1893, an independence movement in Macedonia, later called the Internal Macedonian Revolutionary Organization (IMRO), under Gotse (1872–1903) and Jane Sandanski (1872–1915), arose inside the province in European Turkey.

The depression at the end of the decade exacerbated matters. Many peasants fell into debt to village usurers, typically the local innkeeper. When the Grekov government introduced a tax in kind, previously used by the Ottomans, the peasants revolted and further fueled the initial growth of the Agrarian Union.

The tax protest led to large-scale demonstrations and riots in several cities in 1900. The prince responded by replacing the offending Liberal Party with the Russophile Progressives of Tsankov. The prince wanted his government to arrange a large loan from France (Russia's ally) based once again on the tobacco crop. But peasant and rival opposition stopped it. The prince turned to a nonparty

B government under Petrov, who, with a few more benefits to the tobacco farmers, was able to arrange the loans.

Bulgarian society continuously modernized throughout the nineteenth century by contacts with the Greek independence movement, the efforts of the Turkish reformers, and the influence of Bulgarian communities abroad and foreigners in the country. Foreign Christian ministries from America and Europe established schools in the country. After liberation, modernizing and Westernizing influences increased. Many Bulgarian students went to study abroad. The results of these efforts appeared chiefly in the major cities, however, as most of the country lagged two or three decades behind. The rapid growth of an urban middle class particularly accelerated the process of modernization.

Modernization especially affected the place of women in Bulgarian society. The general Ottoman attitudes toward the segregation and inferior position of women pervaded Bulgarian society well into the twentieth century, even during the Communist period. Modernization brought about the beginning of women's liberation in society. Some women in fact contributed to the country's liberation. Raina Popgeorgieva "Kniaginia" (1856–1917), the Betsy Ross of Bulgaria, sewed the liberation banner and carried it into battle. Female education was enhanced through new schools, including some sponsored by foreign countries.

Bulgarian women had a significant impact on the arts and in the theater. Women such as Sultana Petrova (n.d.) and Ekaterina Karavelova (1860–1947), both wives of prime ministers, emerged as social leaders. The wives and daughters of the monarchs played this role as well. But women played only a minimal role in politics. They could not even vote until 1936 and then only if they were married mothers. After World War I, Aleksandur Stamboliiski (1879–1923) employed a number of women in his government, but his reason for doing so was chiefly economical as women were paid less than men. There were no women cabinet members before the Communist period, and there has never been a female prime minister or president in the country (although the renowned author Blaga Dimitrova [1922–] served as vice president in the 1990s). Muslim women had an even more difficult time breaking through the established prejudices.

At the beginning of the twentieth century, the turmoil of the times and the further separation of Bulgaria into haves and have-nots doubled the number of parties—Radicals split from the Democrats, Young Liberals from the Liberals, and Social Democrats divided into the moderate union-oriented "broad course" and the orthodox Marxist "narrow course." The Bulgarian Agrarian National Union (BANU, BZNS)—to which it changed its name in 1901—managed to stay intact for the time being, although it suffered some individual losses and was badly shaken by divisions over the tax riots and the loan question. However, the leadership of the union fell to the brilliant orator and political strategist Aleksandur Stamboliiski, who soon turned it into the country's most popular and potent political force.

After the loan, the prince turned to the National Liberals once again, who used the same Draconian measures of its former leader, Stambolov, to maintain control over the country. The party remained in power from 1903 to 1908 doing Ferdinand's bidding. Those were the years of great conflict in Macedonia, a battleground for Greeks, Serbs, Bulgarians, and Turks. IMRO carried out daring actions such as kidnapping American schoolteacher Ellen Stone (n.d.) in 1901 and the St. Elijah's Day–Day of Assumption uprising in 1903. The Porte responded with brutal reprisals against Macedonian Slavic villages.

Opposition to Ferdinand grew among the peasantry, the socialists, the students, and intellectuals. Then he saw a chance for regaining popularity by supporting Bulgarian expansion in Macedonia. Thus, in 1908 he dismissed the Stambolovists and turned to the Democrats, who had by this time become the court favorite. Despite its relatively small size, the party won parliamentary elections by the usual Bulgarian tricks—gerrymandering, party jumping of local candidates, and pressure at the polls. The BZNS came in second. In the fall Ferdinand—suddenly and with the connivance of Austria—declared complete independence from the Ottoman Empire, which was then in the hands of the Young Turks (who had earlier in the year forced Abdul Hamid II [1842–1918] to restore the 1876 constitution). Austria annexed outright Bosnia and Hercegovina, and Crete declared its union with Greece at the same time, but Russian foreign minister Alexander Izvolskii's (1856–1919) attempt to join the action by forcing St. Petersburg's warships through the straits failed and thus began a crisis that would eventually lead to World War I.

At a grand national assembly called to amend the Bulgarian constitution (in order that the document reflect the country's new status), the Agrarians increased their number of representatives and staged a massive disruptive protest; however, with the power of the crown behind them, the Democrats were able to change the constitution and have Bulgaria's independence approved.

In 1912 the Italian victory over the Ottoman Empire in Libya inspired the Bulgarians to join in a Balkan coalition to drive the Turks from Europe. Ferdinand had already dismissed the Democrats and appointed Ivan Geshov (1849–1924) of the National Party as prime minister. Geshov put together a coalition government with the pro-Russian Progressives and prepared for an alliance of other Balkan states. The chairman of the National Assembly, Stoian Danev (1857–1949), met with Serbian prime minister Nikola Pašić (1845–1926), who also was foreign minister, in a railroad car in Belgrade. The two agreed to join forces and fight a war against the Porte. They divided the spoils in advance, with Bulgaria getting most of Eastern Thrace and Macedonia and Serbia a section of northwest Macedonia. The rest of Macedonia would be divided between the two after the war, with disputes to be resolved by the Russian tsar. Separate treaties without plans to divide territory brought the Greeks and Montenegrins into the alliance.

The First Balkan War, which pitted the Christian allies against the Ottoman Empire, began on October 10, 1912. The Bulgarians bore the brunt of the fighting as they faced the Turkish army stationed in Eastern Thrace. The Serbs and Greeks, therefore, moved into their rear and took the lion's share of the spoils. By the time the war ended at the insistence of the Great Powers, all of European Turkey except Istanbul itself was in the hands of the allies. The Great Powers, however, recognized Albania, which declared its independence during the war, effectively cutting Serbia out of some of its conquests. The Greeks furthermore occupied southern Macedonia (including Thessaloniki). Athens and Belgrade made a secret alliance to prevent Bulgarian action, and when Sofia learned of these plans, Bulgaria attacked its former allies. This Second Balkan War, fought in the summer of 1913, was a disaster. Romania and the Ottoman Empire joined in attacking Bulgaria on their borders away from the front. When the war was over, Bulgaria's territorial allotment was further diminished, although it included an outlet to the Aegean Sea. Romania was given southern Dobrudja (Dobruzha) as compensation.

Bulgarian nationalists and Bulgarian Macedonians seethed. Most of the country was simply beaten and turned to Stamboliiski, who had opposed the war, in protest. Ferdinand dismissed the government and appointed a Liberal coalition under Vasil Radoslavov (1854–1929). Then the unprecedented happened. The government failed to attain a majority. Stamboliiski put together a coalition that voted no confidence in Radoslavov. Ferdinand and the prime minister simply used the expedience of proroguing the assembly and gerrymandering enough districts to win a new victory.

World War I and the Interwar Period

When World War I broke out, Bulgaria's populace wished to stay neutral. Stamboliiski, now the obvious spokesman for the majority of the nation, agitated against Bulgarian entry into the war. He told a crowd filling Parliament Square that Ferdinand would be hanged from the statue of Alexander II (1818–81) in the square if he led Bulgaria to disaster once more. In 1915, when the parliament was about to approve Bulgarian entry on the German side and even the leaders of the pro-Western parties were joining the hawkish frenzy, he responded to a jibe from a representative who asked whether he was a Serb or a Bulgarian by stating "I am a Yugoslav [South Slav]."

Stamboliiski's protests were to no avail. Ferdinand called the leaders of the major parties except the Social Democrats, but including even Stamboliiski, to the palace to announce his decision to enter the war on the side of the Central Powers. Stamboliiski continued his objections. As the audience ended, the king turned specifically to the peasant leader and recalling his speech in the square warned him. "My head is old. Yours is young. Watch out for it." Shortly thereafter, Stamboliiski was arrested on the charge of Lèse-majesté. Ferdinand wished to execute Stamboliiski but was persuaded to commute his sentence to life imprisonment.

Bulgaria's fortunes on the battlefield followed the fortunes of its partners. The 1915 entry into Serbia met little opposition, and in 1916 a joint German-Bulgarian force occupied the important Fort Rupel. The conquest of Romania

B in 1917 established a condominium occupation of Dobrudja between Bulgaria and Germany. However, in the summer of 1918 the large force that the Allies gathered in Macedonia along the Salonika Front broke through the Bulgarian lines, and the army fled. Later gathering in Radomir, a small city some thirty miles (fifty km) south of Sofia, they declared a republic with Stamboliiski as president and marched on Sofia. But the loyal troops in the city defeated them.

The war devastated Bulgaria as the government raped the farms for the war effort. Much of the produce was sent off to Germany. Farm animals, horses, and oxen were sent to the front. Stamboliiski was right again. In the spring of 1918 the king dismissed Radoslavov and brought back the Democrats. By the end of the summer, they sought peace with the Allies, the first of the Central Powers to do so. However, King Ferdinand was forced to abdicate in favor of his son Boris III, and Stamboliiski's Agrarians attained power in 1919.

Stamboliiski ruled with a popular mandate. The Agrarians were the first party to govern without partners since Stambolov in 1894. Since postwar Europe was charged with an atmosphere of revolution, his government was portrayed in the same way. In fact, while his rhetoric was still inflammatory, the actual changes were less than revolutionary, even though he possibly thought of establishing a republic before his ouster.

His most significant programs included a modest land reform law (never really implemented); establishment of a civilian draft of young people; furthering the cooperative movement; and war-crimes trials of Radoslavov and other ministers of the wartime governments. In the civilian draft that replaced the military one, which was now illegal under the Treaty of Neuilly (which ended World War I for Bulgaria), boys worked on conservation projects while girls made uniforms for railroad workers and the small army that was permitted.

In 1923 a coup d'état ended Stamboliiski's government and brought the Sofia lawyers back to power. Stamboliiski, the great tribune of the Bulgarian people, was brutally tortured and murdered by his captors.

Stamboliiski's last effort to raise a peasant army before his capture had met with little success. His appeals for help from the Communists were rejected until later in the year; the Communist International (Comintern)—the umbrella organization of Communist parties led by Moscow—ordered the Bulgarian party to rise up against the new government in September, too late to help. Yet for the next two years Communist terrorism rocked Bulgaria, culminating in the bombing of the Holy Sunday Cathedral in downtown Sofia in a botched attempt to kill the king.

The Communists were outlawed, but only the most radical Agrarians were barred from politics, and a later amnesty allowed even them to return. The party was now split into several factions. The two main groups were the BZNS-Vrapcha 1 (Sparrow street No. 1—named after the party headquarters) and the BZNS–"Aleksandur Stamboliiski," the left-wing group that had been outlawed but allowed to return in the 1930s. The Communist Party remained outlawed despite amnesty so it formed a front party—the Bulgarian Workers' Party.

After the coup against Stamboliiski, former Social Democratic university professor Aleksandur Tsankov (1879–1959) became premier. He led a coalition of members of the old parties under the name Democratic Alliance. By 1926, Tsankov was replaced by the Alliance with Andrei Liapchev (1866–1933). Tsankov then made the complete political circuit and became a fascist leader, calling his party the Bulgarian National Socialist Party.

The Alliance governments followed a pro-monarchist, anti-Communist policy but were heavily influenced by IMRO. The minister of war, General Ivan Vulkov (1875–1962), supported Ivan Mikhailov (1896–1990), who had succeeded the assassinated Todor Alexandrov (1881–1924) as leader of IMRO in 1922. Mikhailov's IMRO moved right of center and finally into the fascist camp, with Mikhailov allying himself to the Italian fascist leader Benito Mussolini (1883–1945) and the Croatian (Right-Radical) Ustaša leader Ante Pavelić (1889–1959). IMRO followed its murder of Stamboliiski with the assassination of other Agrarian leaders both inside and outside Bulgaria. It conducted raids from Bulgarian Macedonia across the border into Yugoslavia. It taxed the Macedonian population and raised poppies for the manufacture of heroin used in its illegal drug traffic. In 1934 IMRO cooperated with the Ustaša in the murder of King Alexander of Yugoslavia (1888–1934) in Marseilles.

In 1926 Alexander Protogerov (1867–1928) broke from Mikhailov to form another branch of

IMRO. The rival factions conducted daily warfare in the streets of Sofia as well as elsewhere at home and abroad. Their bands fought battles in the provinces. In this struggle, other Bulgarian politicians were fair game if the Macedonians perceived them as enemies. Crowds of young toughs hung out near the parliament building offering their services to escort members of the assembly the three blocks to the café of the Hotel Bulgaria, their daily meeting place.

In 1931 an alliance of the Democrats and BZNS–Vrapcha 1, the Popular Bloc, defeated the Alliance at the polls, but the Macedonian terror did not decrease. Furthermore, the Great Depression brought new problems for Bulgaria. In May 1934 members of the Military League, a clandestine political organization of army officers, working with the intellectual political circle, Zveno, carried out another coup d'état. The leaders, Kimon Georgiev (1882–1969), Damian Velchev (1883–1954), and Dimo Kazasov (1886–1980), were left of center, but Boris was able to break the coalition and within a year was in control of the country, another Balkan royal dictator in the mode of Carol II of Romania (1893–1953) and Prince Paul (1893–1976), the regent of Yugoslavia.

During this period, the Bulgarian Communist leader Georgi Dimitrov (1882–1949) became an international figure, the world's best-known Bulgarian, by his successful defense at the Reichstag fire trial in Berlin and Leipzig; the German Nazis had accused him and several other Bulgarian and German Communists of acting as accessories of the Dutchman Marinus van der Lubbe (1909–34) in the arson attack on the German parliament building, the Reichstag. Afterward, he went to the Soviet Union and became the secretary-general of the Communist International.

In Bulgaria, after Boris took control, he named his chamberlain, Ivan Kioseivanov (1884–1960), premier. The latter remained the government chief until 1940. The Zveno camp had outlawed political parties, and Boris and Kioseivanov continued this policy. However, in 1938 the government conducted parliamentary elections with candidates running without party labels, declaring only whether they were government supporters or in opposition. Nevertheless, most of the candidates were the old politicians and former party members. Government supporters won by a substantial majority, but Ivan Bagrianov (1891–1945), an adventurer and a politician close to the royal court,

bolted the majority and brought a vote of no confidence against the government in the fall of 1938. He and the Bulgarian ambassador to Berlin, Purvan Draganov (1890–1945), rumored to be Ferdinand's illegitimate son (that is, Boris's half-brother), plotted to wrest real power from the king.

Boris dissolved the assembly, and Kioseivanov formed a caretaker government. When war broke out, Sofia immediately declared its neutrality. In December 1939 and January 1940 a new assembly was elected with a majority of 140 to 20. Almost half of the opposition were Communists. In February 1940 Boris appointed a new government, naming Bogdan Filov (1883–1945) as prime minister. The wily monarch had forced Bagrianov and Draganov off the stage of power. By May, Bulgaria's neutrality began to wane as German victories in Western Europe pulled the kingdom closer to Berlin. After the Soviet Union annexed Bessarabia in June, Moscow pressured Sofia to accept a treaty agreement, dangling a return of Dobrudja as bait. Boris asked Adolf Hitler (1889–1945) to arrange the return of the province to avoid a Soviet alliance. In August the German *führer* did just that, forcing Bucharest into the Treaty of Craiova. Boris was now in Hitler's debt, and the pro-German atmosphere in Sofia increased. In the fall and winter the assembly and the king introduced anti-Semitic legislation into the country.

World War II

The winter of 1940–41 witnessed Mussolini's disastrous attempt to invade Greece. Hitler was forced to bale his ally out. Operation Marita, the German Balkan campaign plan, required German troops to pass through Bulgaria, and Hitler called in Boris's debt. In March 1941 Bulgaria joined the Tripartite Pact (Germany, Italy, and Japan), the basic Axis treaty, and German troops entered the kingdom. Bulgaria played a role in occupying Greek Thrace and Yugoslav Macedonia and Pirot during the war, and the German embassy became a clearinghouse for Bulgarian policy.

In the spring of 1942 a government shift put an even more pro-German cabinet in power still under Filov. In the summer harsher laws were passed against the Jews and plans were made for Bulgaria's participation in the Holocaust by preparations for deporting the Jewish community to Poland.

Bulgaria declared "symbolic war" on the United States and Great Britain in December 1941,

B but never did declare war on the Soviet Union. However, Bulgarian Communists operating in the country and in the USSR began a resistance war shortly after Germany invaded the Soviet Union. Other antifascists joined in a coalition with them called the Fatherland Front, which included the BZNS–"Aleksandur Stamboliiski" and Zveno leaders, among others. The pro-Allied resistance grew during 1943 and 1944. In the meantime, Germany's losses on the eastern front caused a turn in Bulgarian policies as well. Opponents of the government's policies were able to prevent the deportation of Bulgarian Jews to the death camps (but not the Greek and Yugoslav Jews under Sofia's administration).

In August 1943 Boris suffered a fatal heart attack. The Germans wanted Filov and Boris's brother Kiril (1895–1945) on the regency council for the young king Simeon II (1937–) and persuaded the Bulgarians to select the council without following the constitution. Filov, despite his inadequacies now the strongest figure in the country, selected as his prime minister the ineffectual Dobri Bozhilov (1884–1945). In the fall the Allies began an intensive bombing campaign. Sofia responded by beginning secret peace negotiations. In June 1944 Filov recalled Bagrianov to take Bulgaria out of the war. But the Allies recognized Soviet preeminence in Bulgaria although the two countries were not yet at war. Moscow would deal only with a Fatherland Front government.

Filov installed a pro-Western government of members of the old Popular Bloc, but Moscow still refused to accept anything but a Fatherland Front government. Finally on September 6, 1944, a day after the USSR declared war on the kingdom, Bulgaria switched sides and joined the Allies. On September 9, the Fatherland Front took over. The regency was changed as well, the government changed over to the Allies, and Bulgarian troops fought the Germans in Yugoslavia and Hungary.

Fascist legislation was overturned and members of the previous governments (even those of the pro-Western Popular Bloc) were put on trial. The Fatherland Front placed the old Zveno prime minister Kimon Georgiev in the premier's chair, but soon the allies in the coalition began to fall out. Nikola Petkov (1893–1947), a leader of the BZNS–"Aleksandur Stamboliiski" was executed. Damian Velchev and George "Gemeto" Dimitrov (1903–72), another Agrarian leader, fled abroad. Georgiev, Dimo Kazasov, and several other prominent Bulgarian non-Communist politicians remained on, however, in minor roles.

Bulgaria under Communism

By 1947, the Communists were in complete control, and a new constitution changed the country to a republic. Georgi Dimitrov returned from the Soviet Union as prime minister. All parties except the Communists and a rump Agrarian Union, which had only secondary significance, were outlawed.

There was some move for Bulgaria to unite with Yugoslavia, but Soviet leader Josef Stalin (1879–1953) vetoed this. Dimitrov, in fact, died in Moscow while discussing the scheme with Stalin. The old Comintern functionary Vasil Kolarov (1877–1950) replaced him as Bulgarian prime minister. In the meantime, the new Communist government began nationalizing property and businesses. The split between Yugoslavia's leader, Josip Broz Tito (1892–1980), and Stalin led to a purge of Communists throughout Eastern Europe. In Bulgaria the wartime leader Traicho Kostov (1897–1949) was executed.

When Kolarov died in 1950, Dimitrov's brother-in-law Vulko Chervenkov (1900–1980) replaced him. Bulgaria became Moscow's most loyal ally in the East.

The early 1950s also witnessed a collectivization of Bulgarian agriculture. In 1954, reflecting changes in Moscow after Stalin's death, Chervenkov lost some of his power, and Sofia replaced him with a coalition at whose head stood the young (forty-two) and obscure functionary Todor Zhivkov (1911–98). He would lead Bulgaria for the next thirty-five years.

At the April Plenum Session of the Central Committee of the Communist Party in 1956, further liberalization took place reflecting the thaw of the Soviet Union. During his tenure, Zhivkov dismissed rivals like wartime leader Anton Yugov (1904–91), and conservatives like Mitko Grigorov (1920–) lost their power. Zhivkov also survived conspiracies against his leadership role in 1958, 1962, and 1974.

Under his direction, Bulgaria modernized and reached out to the world. Zhivkov reestablished relations with the United States (which had been broken off in 1953) and opened up trade with West Germany. In the 1970s the standard of living in the country began to rise and a modest liberalization in cultural affairs began. By 1981, when Bulgaria celebrated the 1,300th anniversary of the founding of the state, the country enjoyed one of the best economies in the Eastern bloc. Many of the restrictions on civil liberties that had marked the early years of Communist rule were eased. Foreign visitors from abroad visited the country including hundreds of thousands who went to enjoy the Black Sea sands in summer and the ski slopes in winter. Scholars and students from all over the world came to study. Furthermore, Bulgarians who could afford it were able to travel abroad as well. But politics remained tightly contained in Zhivkov's hands.

Modernization continued, but just as throughout the twentieth century, not at a rapid pace. Outside influences still concentrated in the major cities, although uniform government education programs spread the new ways to the provinces.

Women continued their active role in the country's cultural life, and they also began to enter the professions, but their political role remained limited, even in left-wing parties except for designated women's groups. Political inequality continued even into the Communist period despite the complete lifting of legal barriers. During the war, women played an active role in the partisan movement. Tsola Dragoicheva (1898–1993) was the head of the Fatherland Front. There were a number of partisan heroes, such as Violeta Iakova (1923–44), a member of the celebrated Sofia assassin group, Dark Angels. Women freely entered the professions and were prominent in the academy in a number of other fields, especially in the last decades of the period. However, their numbers were far less than those of men, and in many areas and departments their role was de facto inferior. Sexual harassment in the workplace was an accepted way of life. Furthermore, in the Communist period all women (as well as men) were expected to work. To be sure, there were generous maternity benefits and ample day-care centers even for the youngest children, but the prevailing attitude throughout society was that housework and raising children were women's work (effectively giving wives two jobs). Throughout the 1950s and 1960s, the accepted method of birth control was abortion. Women in the party hierarchy and government were rare, although Tsvetla Daskolava (n.d.), daughter of the BANU martyr, served for many years as minister of justice. The great feminist holiday, International Women's Day (May 8), became a Bulgarian socialist version of a combination of the American St. Valentine's Day and Secretary's Day as men brought their wives flowers and took their secretaries our for an extended (and often liquid) lunch. Ironically, women ultimately played major roles in bringing an end to the Zhivkov government, including renowned gymnastic coach and member of parliament Neshka Robeva (1946–) and author Blaga Dimitrova.

The 1980s saw a reversal to what had been steady progress and improvement. In 1981, shortly after the Grand Congress on Bulgarian Studies marking the founding of the state, Ludmilia Zhivkova (1942–81), the president's liberal daughter often mentioned as a successor to her father, died. Economic overspending linked with bad harvests and severe winters caused a downturn. Furthermore, the liberal policies of the 1970s whetted the populace's appetite for more. Bulgaria's attempt to improve its image abroad was also marred by two of the most publicized events involving the country—the murder of dissident Georgi Markov (1929–78) on a London street, allegedly by a biological weapon shot into him with an umbrella, and unsubstantiated assertions that Sofia was involved in an assassination plot against Pope John Paul II (1920–) in 1981. Negative publicity also surrounded the attempts by Zhivkov's government to force Bulgarian Muslims to adopt Christian and Slavic names.

The latter campaign led to a shooting war between Bulgarian Turks and the police. Thousands of Turks left Bulgaria, both voluntarily and under government pressure.

While some internal opposition to the name campaign existed in the country, far more serious for Zhivkov was the stagnating economy and the changes sweeping Eastern Europe and the Soviet Union. The pace of liberalization in other East bloc countries now surpassed that of Bulgaria. Soviet television available in Bulgaria revealed it all. In the fall of 1988 Zhivkov dismissed a number of scholars who objected to his policies, though he had promised open debate on the issues and the objections had been made in secret. The intelligentsia retaliated by voting against party slates in the academic and cultural congresses in the spring of 1989. Other Bulgarians joined the protests.

Zhivkov's problems mounted. The Chernobyl nuclear disaster of 1985 in the Soviet Union caused a great deal of concern over Bulgaria's own unsafe nuclear plants, leading to protests in

B

the following years. In 1989 protest broke out in the open. Members from the Ruse delegation in the assembly, whose district suffered from chemical pollution from a Romanian factory across the Danube, raised the environmental issue in parliament. In November 1989, while Bulgaria was hosting an environmental meeting, hundreds marched in protest against the government's own policies. That same week Germans began tearing down the Berlin Wall. On November 11, 1989, Zhivkov resigned.

Foreign minister Peter Mladenov (1936–), a loyal but popular member of Zhivkov's politburo, replaced him, but the Communist government's woes increased. Relations between the government and the Turkish-speaking minority remained a problem. Many unofficial human rights and public policy groups arose calling for more thorough and rapid change. In 1990 the country held its first free elections in over forty years. Following the lead of other parties in Eastern Europe, the Communists renamed themselves the Bulgarian Socialist Party. They faced a coalition of over a dozen parties and groups named the Union of Democratic Forces (UDF). Bulgaria was now an open political society with complete freedom of expression, although the Socialist government tried to limit the opposition against it through various nonlegal measures.

The division of the opposition allowed the Socialists to continue in power until 1991. They won a bare majority in the 1990 elections and offered to join the UDF in a coalition. The latter, however, refused. Nevertheless, the Socialists appointed a UDF leader, Zheliu Zhelev (1935–) as president until the elections for that office. Zhelev was a former Communist who had fallen from grace for publicly criticizing Zhivkov. He was very popular and subsequently won the presidential elections. The Socialists and UDF (along with a number of smaller parties) worked together to write a new democratic constitution. In the meantime, the Turkish issue continued to vex the country, remaining second only to the economic problem of privatization as the government's major crisis. The Turks and other Muslims formed the Rights and Freedom Party. (Parties with ethnic names were illegal.) Another less publicized minority issue concerned the country's Gypsies, who suffered discrimination in Bulgaria as in other countries but who, unlike the Turks, did not organize politically. (The Turks and non-Turkish Muslims who supported them represented about 10 percent of Bulgaria's population; the Gypsies, half of whom are Muslim, total about 8 percent.)

In foreign policy, both the Socialists and the UDF sought better relations with the West. They actively helped end the Warsaw Pact, sought membership in the North Atlantic Treaty Organization (NATO), sided with the American-led international alliance against Iraq in the Gulf War, enthusiastically embraced Israel, and followed other pro-Western policies. Both the Socialists and the UDF denounced the attempted August 1991 coup d'état against Mikhail Gorbachev (1931–) in the Soviet Union.

In 1991 the UDF won the parliamentary elections by a slight majority and formed a government with the Rights and Freedom Party under Philip Dimitrov (1955–). This lasted only until the end of 1992, when a ministry under economist Liuben Berov (1925–) was established. The Socialists were returned in the elections of 1994, putting in a Socialist prime minister, Zhan Videnov (1959–).

During this period of change and fragile balance, the Bulgarian economy wavered. At times it appeared to be improving, but generally it was mired in difficulties associated with privatization, shortages, harsh winters, and other difficulties. The country was plagued by strikes, protests, and demonstrations. In 1996 the old Bulgarian virus of political assassination once again reared its head when ex-Communist and former prime minister Andrei Lukanov (1938–96) was shot in front of his home. In the succeeding elections for president, the UDF candidate, Peter Stoianov (1952–), won a landslide victory. When the Socialists continued to control the government, however, massive riots forced them to hold early parliamentary elections in April 1997. The UDF won 137 of the 240 seats. The Socialists fell to under 60. The new parliament selected Democrat Ivan Kostov (1949–) as the new prime minister.

Frederick B. Chary

Further reading

Bell, John D. *The Bulgarian Communist Party from Blagoev to Zhivkov.* Stanford, California, 1986.
———. *Peasants in Power: Alexander Stamboliski and the Bulgarian Agrarian National Union, 1899–1923.* Princeton, New Jersey, 1977.
Black, Cyril E. *The Establishment of Constitutional Government in Bulgaria.* Princeton, New Jersey, 1943.

Boll, Michael M. *Cold War in the Balkans: American Foreign Policy and the Emergence of Communist Bulgaria, 1943–1947.* Lexington, Kentucky, 1984.

Chary, Frederick B. *The Bulgarian Jews and the Final Solution, 1940–1944.* Pittsburgh, 1972.

Clarke, James F. *Bible Societies, American Missionaries, and the National Revival of Bulgaria.* New York, 1971.

Crampton, Richard. *Bulgaria, 1878–1918: A History.* Boulder, Colorado, 1983.

Crampton, Richard. *A Short History of Modern Bulgaria.* Cambridge, 1987.

Firkatian, Mari. *The Forest Traveler: Georgi Stoikov Rakovski and Bulgarian Nationalism.* Baltimore, 1996.

Genchev, Nikolai. *The Bulgarian National Revival Period.* Sofia, 1977.

Genov, G.P. *Bulgaria and the Treaty of Neuilly.* Sofia, 1935.

Hupchick, Dennis P. *The Bulgarians in the Seventeenth Century: Slavic Orthodox Society and Culture under Ottoman Rule.* Jefferson, North Carolina, 1993.

Lampe, J.R. *The Bulgarian Economy in the Twentieth Century.* New York, 1986.

Miller, Marshall Lee. *Bulgaria during the Second World War.* Stanford, California, 1975.

Moser, Charles A. *Dimitrov of Bulgaria: A Political Biography of Dr. Georgi M. Dimitrov.* Ottowa, 1979.

———. *Revolution Administered: Agrarianism and Communism in Bulgaria.* Baltimore, 1973.

Oren, Nissen. *Bulgarian Communism: The Road to Power.* New York, 1971.

———. *Revolution Administered: Agrarianism and Communism in Bulgaria.* Baltimore, 1973.

Perry, Duncan M. *The Politics of Terror: The Macedonian Liberation Movement, 1893–1903.* Durham, North Carolina, 1988.

———. *Stefan Stambolov and the Emergence of Modern Bulgaria, 1870–1895.* Durham, North Carolina, 1993.

Rothschild, Joseph. *The Communist Party in Bulgaria.* New York, 1959.

See also Agrarian Parties; Agriculture; Alexander of Battenberg; Alexander I Karadjordjević; Alexander III; Todor Aleksandrov; Antifascism; April Uprising; Axis; Ivan Bagrianov; Balkan Wars; Berlin Wall; Otto von Bismarck; Bogomilism; Boris III; Khristo Botev; Bulgarian Agrarian National Union; Bulgarian Art; Bulgarian Culture; Bulgarian Émigrés; Bulgarian Language; Bulgarian Literature; Bulgarian Massacres; Bulgarian-Serb War of 1885; Vulko Chervenkov; *Cheta; Chitalishte;* Collectivization; Communist Party of Bulgaria; Crimean War; Georgi Dimitrov; Aleksandur Dondukov-Korsakov; Eastern Question; Eastern Rumelia; Economic Development in Bulgaria; Education; Environment; Exarchate; Fatherland Front; Ferdinand; Bogdan Filov; Folklife; Folklore; Kimon Georgiev; Mikhail Gorbachev; Great Depression; Great Powers; Green International; Gypsies; Holocaust; Ilenden Uprising; IMRO; John Paul II; Dimo Kazasov; Traicho Kostov; Vasil Levski; Andrey Liapchev; Macedonia; Ivan Mikhailov; Milan Obrenović; Military League; *Millet;* Muslims; Nationalism; Neuilly, Treaty of; Ottoman Empire; Paissi of Hilendar; Pan-Slavism; Patriarchate; Nikola Pašić; Ante Pavelić; Peasant Revolts; Peasants; Percentages Agreement; Nikola Petkov; Pleven, Battle of; Pomaks; Vasil Radoslavov; Georgi Rakovski; Rhodope Mountains; Neshka Robeva; Russia; Salonika Front; San Stefano, Treaty of; Simeon II; Petko Slaveikov; Slavs; Sofia; Aleksandur Stamboliiski; Stefan Stambolov; Sofronii Vrachanski; Konstantin Stoilov; Subranie; *Tanzimat;* Aleksandur Tsankov; Dragan Tsankov; Turks; Turnovo Constitution; Damian Velchev; Ivan Vulkov; Warsaw Pact; Women in Bulgaria; World War I; World War II; Young Turks; Antun Yugov; *Zadruga;* Zheliu Zhelev; Todor Zhivkov; Ludmila Zhivkova; Zveno

Bulgarian Agrarian National Union (BANU, BZNS)

A key political and social movement that played a central role in the evolution of twentieth-century Bulgarian history. Founded in 1899, the nascent Bulgarian Agrarian National Union (BANU [Bulgarian: BZNS]) adopted a program calling for peasant self-improvement, easy agrarian credit, promotion of cooperatives, and opposition to existing tax policies. It became a major political force by 1908. The ideology of the union was authored largely by Aleksandur Stamboliiski (1879–1923), editor of the main Agrarian paper. He maintained that society was composed not of classes but of estates based on broad occupational groups, the agrarian estate being the most important because of its members' greater sense of personal fulfillment.

In the aftermath of World War I, Stamboliiski was appointed prime minister, introducing land reform and compulsory labor service in 1920. In 1923 conservatives, aided by the military, overthrew the Agrarian government, murdered Stamboliiski, and produced a splintering of Agrarian unity. By the 1930s, a minimum of five distinct agrarian groups existed.

In 1942 Bulgarian Communists appealed for a common front against the pro-German government in Sofia and received support from the Agrarians, led by Nikola Petkov (1893–1947). The Fatherland Front government that took power in September 1944 included four Agrarian members, with Petkov becoming minister without portfolio. Shortly thereafter, two hundred delegates from all sectors of the agrarian movement proclaimed the rebirth of the united BANU at a national congress.

Prospects for an independent political movement were less than even in postwar, Communist-dominated Bulgaria, and the BANU under the leadership of Petkov soon found itself in opposition to the new regime. In 1945 Petkov was ousted by a new BANU congress and resigned from government, owing to his refusal to sanction a common list with the Fatherland Front in upcoming elections. In late 1946 Petkov and a bloc of opposition candidates received almost 30 percent of the ballots despite widespread fraud and violence. The following year, with America having approved a peace treaty with Sofia, Petkov was accused of treason, tried, convicted, and executed. The rump of the BANU now requested admission to the Fatherland Front, having finally conceded the leadership of the Communist Party.

Michael Boll

Further reading

Bell, John D. *Peasants in Power: Alexander Stamboliski and the Bulgarian Agrarian National Union, 1899–1923*. Princeton, New Jersey, 1977.

Boll, Michael M. *Cold War in the Balkans: American Foreign Policy and the Emergence of Communist Bulgaria, 1943–1947*. Lexington, Kentucky, 1984.

Crampton, R.J. *A Short History of Modern Bulgaria*. Cambridge, Massachusetts, 1987.

See also Agrarian Parties; Agriculture; Fatherland Front; Peasants; Nikola Petkov; Aleksandur Stamboliiski

Bulgarian Art

Bulgaria is a country of ancient cultures as testified by Thracian gold and silver treasures (thirteenth to third century B.C.), Greek colonies along the Black Sea shore (after the seventh century B.C.), and Roman towns on the plains (after the first century A.D.). Art and architecture continued to flourish during the First Bulgarian Kingdom (681–1018) and the Second Bulgarian Kingdom (1186–1396), especially after Christianity became the official religion in 865. These achievements were largely destroyed during the period of Ottoman domination (1396–1878), and returned to light only during the twentieth century.

After the Ottoman conquest, several monasteries secluded in the mountains, although raided and burned, continued to sustain and promote religious frescoes and icon paintings. During the eighteenth and nineteenth centuries, some of these monasteries were rebuilt, enlarged, or redecorated with new frescoes and murals. The Rila Monastery, for example, was founded in the tenth century, but was almost entirely rebuilt and decorated in the nineteenth century (1834–48). By that time, wealthy Bulgarian merchants, textile manufacturers, and craftsmen supported the building of churches, schools, clock towers, and bridges. Their large houses prominently displayed carved paneling and elaborately carved ceilings, colorfully painted rooms with decorative medallions, or wall paintings of figural compositions. Often, the facades were also covered with painted geometric and ornamental decorations. Many of these houses are preserved in provincial towns.

Secular paintings also emerged during the nineteenth century. Leading examples are the portraits of Zakharii Zograph (1810–53) and Nikola Obrazopisov (1828–1915), both trained in the Samokov Apprentices School (founded in the late eighteenth century). A few painters were educated abroad: Nikolai Pavlovich (1835–94) in Vienna and Munich; Stanislav Dospevskii (1823–78) in Moscow and St. Petersburg; and Anton Mitov (1862–1930) in Florence. Mitov was among the founders (1896) of Sofia's School for Painting (Art Academy, after 1908), together with Czech painters Ivan (Jan) Mrkvichka (1856–1938) and Yaroslav Veshin (1860–1915), and Russian sculptor Boris Schatz (1866–1932). The school cultivated an academic method focused on national and folk subjects. Yet, after the turn of the century, Western influences also became evident in Bulgarian art: impressionism in the work of Nikola Petrov (1881–1916), Khristo Kavarnaliev (1894–1951), and Boris Denev (1883–1969); expressionism in the work of Vladimir Dimitrov-Maistora (1882–1960); and symbolism-expressionism marked in the paintings of Ivan Milev (1897–1927), Nikolai Rainov (1889–1954), and Vasil Zakhariev (1895–1971).

Petrov, a student of Veshin, was the first Bulgarian landscape artist to work out of doors and to concentrate on Sofia's urban scenes. He was a founder of the Contemporary Art Society (1903), which also included architects Pencho Koichev (1876–1957), Kiro Marichkov (1875–1922), and Georgi Fingov (1874–1944). Their goal was to unite artists in all fields (architects and applied artists) in a quest for artistic renewal and to popularize contemporary artistic developments.

Several women painters also achieved prominence: Anna Iosifova (1872–1931), a member of the Contemporary Art Society; Elisaveta Konsulova-Vazova (1881–1965) and Elena Karamikhailova (1875–1961), both founding members of the Native Art Society. While they excelled in impressionist and postimpressionist portraits, art critic Sirak Skitnik (pseudonym of Panaiot Todorov, 1883–1943) explored the venues of expressionism and abstract art. Abstract art was not appreciated by the conservative Bulgarian public, however, and its promoters, Georges Papazoff (1894–1972) and Nikolai Diulgheroff (1901–1982), left the country to settle in France and Italy, respectively.

In contrast, modern architecture flourished, especially in cooperative apartment houses and country villas, since all architects were educated in Western Europe until the Sofia Polytechnic was established in 1943.

With the Communist takeover in September 1944 and the end of World War II, the development of art and architecture was constrained by the method of socialist realism and guided by the slogan "national in form and socialist in content." Professional organizations were abolished and all artists were forced to join the Union of Artists in Bulgaria. By 1989, it counted about five thousand members who were depicting "revolutionary struggles" of the past and the "socialist construction of the present" to educate and "mold a new type of mentality." Artists of the older generation,

Stoian Venev (1904–89), for one, developed during the 1930s a distinctive style based on folk art. He changed only the thematic content of his work (partisans, farming scenes, and village festivities). Dechko Uzunov (1899–1986) also produced large canvases dedicated to the partisan (antifascist) movement. Many artists participated in the decoration of important public buildings in Sofia, such as the Communist Party Headquarters (designed in 1950 by Petso Zlatev [1905–]), the Ministry of Electrification and attached Grand Hotel (by Ivan Danchov [1893–1972] and Dimiter Tsolov [1896–1970]), and the House of the Agrarian Union (now the opera house), designed by Lazar Parashkevanov (1890–1977), with Uzunov heading the team of artists and sculptors. Numerous statues of Stalin (1879–1953), Lenin (1870–1924), and Bulgarian Communist leader Georgi Dimitrov (1882–1949) (now destroyed) and several monuments to the Soviet army and Bulgarian heroes kept sculptors busy.

Monumental art—big sculptures, large frescoes and mosaics, and wood carvings—spread throughout the country during the 1970s and 1980s, as demonstrated by the 1972 monument *Ivalo,* near Kotel, by sculptor Liuben Dimitrov Stoichev (1904–); the 1983 monument *Simeon and His Chroniclers,* in Preslav, by sculptor Ivan Neshev (1927–) and architect Vera Kolarova (1931–); and the 1981 memorial *1300 Years Bulgaria,* in Shumen, by a team of sculptors, painters, and architects. Two monuments were hailed as the "total synthesis of art and architecture"—the memorial complex of the Bulgarian Communist Party at the Balkan Mountain peak Buzludzha and the National Palace of Culture in Sofia. Both were completed in 1981 for the celebration of the 1300th anniversary of the Bulgarian state. The first, a large auditorium for Communist celebrations, was designed by Georgi Stoilov (1929–), a former mayor of Sofia (1967–71), minister of architecture (1973), and president of the Union of Architects in Bulgaria (1977). Numerous artists filled the interiors with frescoes, mosaics, and sculptures. The second model, sponsored by Lyudmila Zhivkova (1942–81), daughter of Bulgarian head of state Todor Zhivkov (1911–98), was designed by Alexander Barov (1931–) and a large team of architects, sculptors, painters, wood carvers, and tapestry weavers. The wide variety of artistic expressions, techniques, personal styles,

B and the lavish display of the handicrafts transformed this building into numerous art galleries "designed to convey a strong emotional message to its visitors." Unlimited budgets were allocated to these and many other buildings with exceptional symbolic meaning.

Milka T. Bliznakov

Further reading

Bozhkov, Atanas. *Bulgarian Art.* Sofia, 1964.
Filov, Bogdan. *Geschichte der Bulgarischen Kunst.* Berlin-Leipzig, 1933.
Lvova, Evgeniia. *Iskusstvo Bolgarii.* Moscow, 1971.
Paskaleva, Kostadinka. *Bulgarian Icons through the Centuries.* Sofia, 1987.
Stoilov, Georgi. *Modern Bulgarian Architecture.* Sofia, 1987.

See also Architecture; Bulgarian Culture; Communist Party of Bulgaria; Georgi Dimitrov; Vladimir Dimitrov-Maistora; Folklife; Tsanko Lavrenov; Bencho Obreshkov; Dechko Uzunov; Vasil Zakhariev; Todor Zhivkov; Lyudmila Zhivkova

Bulgarian Culture

The rapid development of Bulgarian culture before the Ottoman conquest in 1396 owed much to the adoption of Christianity and the development of Slavic literacy, both events of the first Bulgarian Empire (681–1018). The Bulgarian church played a major role in the development of a Slavic language, literature, and, inseparably, culture. Schools of fresco painting (such as at Veliko Turnovo) document additional developments in the graphic arts in the twelfth and thirteenth centuries. Perhaps the most widely recognized Bulgarian cultural art form, the icon, is linked to the ritual of the Eastern Orthodox Church. Icon painting provided artists with a canonized style in an accepted medium in which they could express individual artistic creativity. The earliest icon, produced in glazed ceramic tiles in the image of St. Theodore, dates from 900. The finest icons were made of chased repoussé silver casings and frames. Popular subjects included the Virgin and child, the crucifixion, and the annunciation. Manuscript illumination also flourished toward the end of this period. Wood carvings decorated church doors with saintly and fantastic imagery. Architectural developments of the major cities of Bulgaria emphasized Byzantine styles. The influence of the Byzantine chant led eventually to the restoration of Slav chantbooks and a national school of liturgical chant developed in Veliko Turnovo.

While traditional cultural activities survived throughout the period of Ottoman rule (folk songs, epic poetry, and mural painting), a substantial growth in cultural activities accompanied weakening Ottoman power and the strengthening Bulgarian economy in the late eighteenth and nineteenth centuries. This cultural development, which occurred during the Revival Period (1762–1878), established a foundation, both intellectual and physical, for revolt against the Ottomans and served as a major source of cultural references for twentieth-century literature and art.

The first school to teach Bulgarian was established in Gabrovo in 1835, and the first Bulgarian grammar was produced in the 1820s. An important facility for the development of the emerging Bulgarian culture was the *chitalishte,* or reading room, the first of which was established in Svishtov in 1856. An amalgam of library, theater, auditorium, debating chamber, and school, the *chitalishte* became a focus for community cultural activity. Indeed, the *chitalishte* were later to become known as informal ministries of culture.

The publication of Bulgarian language books, journals, and newspapers increased dramatically through the nineteenth century. Religious and secular art were revitalized and schools of wood carving were established at Samokov, Razlog, and Turnavo producing iconostases, crosses, altars, thrones, icons, and more secular objects such as musical instruments and architectural features. The 1800s also witnessed the formation of the first Bulgarian music ensembles, which played the particular forms of church music that had developed at the close of the previous century.

Following the liberation of Bulgaria from Ottoman rule, the increased emphasis on establishing political and economic institutions and protocol was balanced by a reduction in the intensity of cultural activities. The attention to infrastructure produced institutions of cultural importance, most notably the National Library (1879) and the Bulgarian Academy of Sciences (moved in 1911 from Romania, where it had been founded as the Bulgarian Literary Society in 1869).

After 1878, a rapid development in professional music occurred. The first music school was formed in 1904, and the State Music Academy was founded in 1921. The Bulgarian National Philharmonic followed three years later. While the first Bulgarian opera dates from 1850, the first operatic company was founded in 1890, with regular opera seasons occurring after 1910. The Bulgarian Opera Society dates from 1907, and the first opera sung in Bulgarian was performed in 1909. The first completely Bulgarian opera, Emanuil Manolov's (1860–1902) *Siromakhkinya* (*The Poor Woman*), dates from 1900. Opera developed professionally during the 1920s (the Sofia National Opera was founded in 1921), and the 1930s witnessed an increase in the number of opera companies.

The first professional theater companies were established in the 1880s in Plovdiv and Sofia, and the National Theater Company formed in the early years of the twentieth century based on the Sulzi i Smiah (Tears and Laughter) company, which had been formed in 1892. By 1939, thirteen theaters had been established, with major municipal theaters in Plovdiv, Varna, and Ruse.

After World War II, the primary goal of Communist cultural policy was the creation of a unified, national, democratic culture accessible to all Bulgarians. Artists, writers, and museum curators worked together to help build socialism and develop Bulgarian society. Culture became part of every worker's life; artists worked alongside the people to advance a common social and cultural cause. Thus, the performing arts were not to entertain the privileged few but to awaken national consciousness and public social responsibility.

Many cultural institutions were nationalized in the 1940s. Cultural workers were organized into national and regional associations that coordinated and promoted the activities of their membership. Where education instilled knowledge and appreciation of artistic forms and styles among young Bulgarians, a plethora of amateur performing arts companies, competitions, and festivals (coordinated by bodies such as the National Center for Amateur Artistic Activities) promoted adult participation in unified cultural activities. Cultural activities were more than mere recreation; they helped to shape the new social citizen.

Cultural themes were explicitly detailed, having immediate relevance to working life, offering encouraging images of the construction of socialism, and representing edifying lessons from Bulgaria's heroic past of the struggle against foreign rulers and invaders. Cultural and artistic themes adhered to the principles of socialist realism, that is, to portray reality as revolutionary development in harmony with the ideological alteration and education of workers in the spirit of socialism.

After 1944, the number of music ensembles, schools, opera houses, and orchestras increased. Five national opera companies and more than twenty-five amateur groups existed, and festivals of opera and ballet took place on a regular basis. Modern Bulgarian opera produced a range of internationally respected talent, and the Sofia National Opera toured successfully throughout Europe.

The most widely recognized format of Bulgarian performing art is folk music. While the origins of folk music lie with the traditional village peasantry and preindustrial agricultural communities, political and social developments since 1944 elevated and transformed folk music to cater to socialist needs (such as songs praising the heroic actions of peasants and revolutionaries of the Revival Period). Bulgarian folk music is marked by great variety of rhythm, meter, and scale. Folk songs are grounded in peasant life and accompany a wide range of activities: agricultural harvest, important social and personal events, weddings, banquets, dances, feasts, funerals, and religious and secular holidays such as saints' days.

Folk musicians play instruments particular to their music. Wind instruments include the large and small rim-blown flute (*kaval* and *ovcharska srivka*), the single- and double-fipple flute (*duchik* and *droyan ka*), bagpipes (*gayda*), and the shawn (*zurnal*). Stringed instruments include the upright fiddle (*gadulka*) and the long-necked fretted lute (*tambura*). Percussion instruments include the double-headed drum (*tapan*) and the clay finger drum (*tarabuka*).

The importance of folk tradition in Bulgaria was provided by annual festivals of folksinging, dancing, and music making. The modernization and promotion of traditional folk music to suit modern needs though has left little room for the original spontaneity and simplicity of traditional folk music.

Although the origins of Bulgarian archaeology can be traced to the work of foreign scholars at the end of the nineteenth century and the establishment of a Bulgarian archaeological institute in 1923, it was in the post-1944 period that the study of the past accelerated. Museums hold a central role in the dissemination of Bulgarian culture to the people; exhibits illuminate the long struggle

B

for liberty and national independence. Towns of historical and national importance are preserved as historical monuments (such as Koprovishitsa), as are old quarters of more developed towns (Plovdiv and Nesebur).

By 1956, almost fifty theaters had been established, and annual festivals of contemporary Bulgarian drama now exist at both local and national levels. Likewise, an increase in the number of cinemas has accompanied an increase in Bulgarian film production. In the late 1960s the administration of cultural affairs was reorganized and a committee of culture assumed responsibility for directing cultural policy. The committee, chaired by a member of the government, was responsible for activities ranging from the publication and sale of books to research and conservation of cultural monuments.

Douglass W. Bailey

Further reading

Bix, R. *Bulgarsky Operen Teatr.* Sofia, 1976.
Brown, J.F. *Bulgaria under Communist Rule.* London, 1970.
Lang, David Marshall. *The Bulgarians: From Pagan Times to the Ottoman Conquest.* London, 1976.
Petrov, Stoyan and Nikolai Kaufmann. "Bulgaria," in *The New Grove Dictionary of Music and Musicians,* ed. by Stanley Sadie. London, 1980, 430–38.
Popov, Kostadine. *Cultural Policy in Bulgaria.* Paris, 1981.
Shaoulov, L. *The Bulgarian Theater.* Sofia, 1982.
Stamov, Stefan, ed. *The Architectural Heritage of Bulgaria.* Sofia, 1972.

See also Architecture; Bulgarian Art; Bulgarian Language; Bulgarian Literature; *Chitalishte;* Cinema; Dance; Education; Folklife; Folklore; Folk Music; Music; Orthodoxy; Peasants; Theater

Bulgarian Émigrés

Bulgarian émigrés began arriving in North America after the failed 1903 Illinden Uprising, which was unsuccessful in gaining autonomy for Macedonia. In those days, the Macedonian Slavs still identified themselves as ethnic Bulgarians, and they formed the core of the Bulgarian emigrant community in the United States and Canada, with colonies established in the Middle West—from Pennsylvania to Montana, and from Toronto and Detroit to Granite City and Madison, Illinois. They even established a settlement in New Mexico and appropriately named it "Sofia."

Bulgarian émigrés worked in steel mills and coal mines, laid railroad tracks, and engaged in small businesses serving their needs. Although they lived in squalid conditions and were often unemployed, they often sent their last pennies to their families still at home—wives, children, and parents. Their wages were pitifully low, but their perseverance and determination did not waver.

The second wave of emigrants began soon after World War I, when the Bulgarians in Greek and Yugoslav Macedonia were subjected to ethnic assimilation. They were followed by fugitives from Bulgaria itself after the right-wing coup in Sofia in 1923; this group included leftist intellectuals, workers, and peasants. The last group provided the leadership for numerous organizations and associations of socialist orientation, including a Communist Party led by Georgi Pirinski (1901–78), who would later be deported to Bulgaria in 1952, where his American-born son later became foreign minister of Bulgaria.

The third wave of Bulgarian émigrés was composed of displaced persons, escapees, and defectors after the Iron Curtain left Bulgaria in the Soviet orbit. Men of the professions, the better educated, but also peasants and laborers made up this group. They were bitter anticommunists and nationalists. Resented by the older communities, they scattered throughout North America and formed their own associations, represented mainly by the Bulgarian National Front and the Bulgarian National Committee. The political activists on the left and the right, missionary clergy of the Bulgarian Orthodox Church, and Protestant groups sought to establish religious congregations and to preserve the national heritage of their people. In 1937 the Holy Synod in Sofia constituted a Bulgarian Orthodox Diocese, led by Metropolitan Andrey (1884–1972) of New York, but it was plagued by a variety of political groups, mainly Bulgarian-Macedonian and Bulgarian nationalists seeking to transform the church into an instrument of their political agendas.

Estimating the number of Bulgarian immigrants in the United States and Canada is at best guesswork. The numbers vary from twenty-five thousand to one hundred thousand or more. Because of the scarcity of female émigrés, the widely scattered settlements, and mixed marriages, the Bulgarians were largely absorbed by the American melting pot. Here and there, in Granite City, Madison, and Chicago in Illinois; in Fort Wayne, Indianapolis, and Gary in Indiana; in Detroit, Toledo, Battle Creek, and Flint in Michigan; in Akron, Cleveland, and Cincinnati in Ohio; in Pittsburgh and Steelton in Pennsylvania; and Toronto in Canada, at times the Bulgarian communities numbered in the thousands, but more recently they seem almost on the verge of extinction, owing to loss of ethnic identity. The social, cultural, and political life of these communities centered primarily around their political associations and religious congregations. They published their daily and weekly papers—the Communist *Suznanie* (*Consciousness*) and *Narodna volya* (*People's Will*), the Bulgarian-Macedonian nationalist *Makedonska tribuna* (*Macedonian Tribune—* still published in Fort Wayne, Indiana), the Bulgarian nationalist *Borba* (*Struggle*) and *Svoboda* (*Freedom*), and the republican *Svobodna i nezavisima Bulgaria* (*Free and Independent Bulgaria*). The longest existing independent paper, *Naroden glas* (*People's Voice*), was published by pastor Tsvetko Bagrianov (n.d.).

Bulgarian émigrés have contributed little specific to American society except for the cheap labor they provided in building the great railroads in the Midwestern states, the mines, and the steel mills. They had little impact on politics, sports, or scholarship, although those that did enter the halls of academe served with distinction and honor. The most outstanding contribution, though little publicized, was the work of John V. Atanassov (1904–95), the father of computer technology. The best-known artist, although not known by the general public to be a Bulgarian émigré, is Christo (Yavashev) (1935–), who has wrapped mountains, valleys, and even the German Reichstag in Berlin in gigantic plastic sheets, stunning the world with his unusual art. But strangely, the almost minuscule Bulgarian emigration to the United States provided key leadership to some American émigré organizations. Pirinski became a leader of the Slavic Congress of the early 1940s, a Communist front in support of the Soviet Union against the Nazis that gained the approval of President Franklin D. Roosevelt (1882–1945); Ivan Dochev (1906–) served for many years as president of the American Friends of the Anti-Bolshevik Bloc of Nations, made up of former officials of the governments in Eastern Europe and the former Soviet Union.

G.M. Dimitrov (1903–72) served as president of the Assembly of Captive European Nations, another anticommunist organization supported by the American Free Europe Committee.

Spas T. Raikin

Further reading

Altankov, Nikolai G. *The Bulgarian-Americans.* Palo Alto, California, 1979.

Avramoff, Assen. "The Macedonian Immigrants in the United States and Canada." *Macedonia* 1 (February 1932).

Christowe, Stoyan. *My American Pilgrimage.* Boston, 1947.

Nizamov, Christo. *The Struggle for Freedom.* Indianapolis, 1985.

Pirinski, Georgi. *Kakvo vidiakh i prezhiviakh v Amerika.* Sofia, 1970.

Roucek, Joseph S. "The American Bulgarians," *Orientator,* 1937. United States Congress, House Committee on Un-American Activities. *Report on the American Slav Congress and Associated Organizations.* Washington, D.C., 1949.

Yankov, Peter D. *Peter Menikov: The Story of a Bulgarian Boy in the Great American Melting Pot.* Nashville, Tennessee, 1928.

See also Emigration

Bulgarian Language

A Slavic language with about nine million speakers, and the official language of the Republic of Bulgaria. Bulgarian and the closely related Macedonian language make up the eastern branch of the South Slavic languages.

The modern Bulgarian literary language, based on the northeastern dialects, was basically defined during the second half of the nineteenth century. Bulgarian uses a modern version of the Cyrillic alphabet; a major spelling reform took place in 1945. The main dialects are Eastern and Western, each with North and South subdivisions.

Modern Bulgarian differs from the other Slavic languages except Macedonian in several ways. Many of these innovations are shared by other languages of the Balkans. There is a definite article, which follows the noun (or first adjective in a phrase): *kniga* (book); *knigata* (the book); *nova kniga* (a new book); *novata kniga* (the new book). Nouns have lost declension, except for the vocative form, and prepositions in Bulgarian take

B on new meanings: *knigata za zhenata na moja brat* (the book about the wife of my brother).

Verbs have a large number of tenses. The present and two past tenses, the aorist, and the imperfect are simple tenses. Compound tenses made with auxiliaries from the verbs for "be" and "want" produce five other tenses: the future, future perfect, future in the past, perfect, and pluperfect. There are also an imperative, verbal adverb, and participles. These forms all interact with aspect, as in the other Slavic languages. The infinitive has been lost.

There is a set of verbal forms to indicate that an event has not been witnessed or is not vouched for: *Vladimir napisa tova* (Vladimir wrote that [I witnessed it or vouch for the truth of the statement]); *Vladimir napisal tova* (Vladimir is alleged to have written that [but I didn't witness the act or don't want to vouch for the truthfulness of the statement]). Another set of forms indicates disbelief or doubt: *Vladimir bil napisal tova* (Vladimir is supposed to have written that [but I doubt it]).

Charles E. Gribble

Further reading

Comrie, Bernard and Greville G. Corbett, eds. *The Slavonic Languages.* London, 1993.
Schenker, Alexander M. and Edward Stankiewicz, eds. *The Slavic Literary Languages.* New Haven, Connecticut, 1980.

See also Macedonian Language; Slavic Languages

Bulgarian Literature

Bulgarian literature has existed for more than eleven centuries. Although a written tradition (in Greek) is attested as early as the eighth century, its true beginning is believed to be connected with the conversion to Christianity in 863–864. The medieval literary language, Old Church Slavonic/Old Bulgarian, was codified by the brothers Cyril (d. 869) and Methodius (d. 884) in 863. The people understood it perfectly well, because it was based on the Slavic dialects around Thessaloniki and in the southern parts of the First Bulgarian Empire. After the demise of Slavic literacy in Moravia, disciples of Cyril and Methodius went to Bulgaria in 885 and, supported by Prince Boris (r. 852–889), established the Schools of Pliska/Preslav and of Okhrid. The former included prominent writers such as Ioan Ekzarkh (n.d.), Konstantin of Preslav (c. mid-tenth–mid-eleventh century), Chernorizets Khrabŭr (n.d.), as well as some members of the royal family. The main figures of the latter were Kliment (c. 840–916) and Naum (d. 910). During the reign of Simeon (c. 863–927), many new translations and original works (saints' lives, offices, polemical writing, apocrypha, etc.) were created. The heritage of Simeon's Golden Age laid the foundation for the literary traditions of medieval Serbia and Kievan Rus. A period of decline (1018–1187) was followed by a silver age that culminated in the activities of the School of Turnovo. After the Ottoman conquest in 1393–94, several disciples of Patriarch Evtimii of Turnovo (c. 1325–c. 1402)—Metropolitan Kiprian (c. 1330–1406), Grigorii Tsamblak (c. 1364–1420), and Konstantin Kostenechki (c. 1380–1430s)—became influential clerics in Muscovite Russia and Serbia, where they transplanted the legacy of the Turnovo school. The devastation of the cultural centers during Ottoman rule greatly delayed literary developments.

The transition from the medieval to the modern Bulgarian language and literature began during the National Revival (1762–1878). Its early landmarks are Paisii Hilendarski's (1722–73) *Istoriia slavianobolgarskaia* (*History of the Bulgarian Slavs,* 1762) and Sofronii Vrachanski's (1739–1813) *Zhitei stradanie* (*Life and Suffering,* 1804). Modern poetry (Dobri Chintulov [1823–86], Petko Slaveikov [1827–95], and Elena Muteva [c. 1825–54]); prose (Liuben Karavelov [c. 1834–79]); and drama (Dobri Voinikov [1833–78] and Vasil Drumev [c. 1841–1901]) developed during the next six decades. Their progress was facilitated by rich native folklore and by the influence of Russian and Western literature. The transition was completed during the 1870s, when two of the greatest modern Bulgarian authors appeared on the literary scene: Khristo Botev (1847–76), the romantic poet whose extraordinary talent and heroic death made him a national icon, and Ivan Vazov (1850–1921), whose poems, short stories, novels, plays, and travelogues, most of them written after the liberation of Bulgaria in 1878, display a unique blend of romanticism and realism.

During the 1890s and the 1900s, poet and literary critic Pencho Slaveikov (1866–1912) and poet and playwright Peio Iavorov (1878–1914) challenged Vazov's authority and modernized

Bulgarian literature. Iavorov became one of the most influential Bulgarian symbolists. Vazov's novel *Pod Igoto* (*Under the Yoke*, 1889–90), however, remained unsurpassed. The best young short-story writer of the 1900s, Elin Pelin (1877–1949), established his style without engaging in theoretical polemics. Some of the finest Bulgarian plays appeared during this period. Between the two world wars, new styles, frequently associated with radical political ideas, replaced the waning symbolism. Expressionism and futurism informed the poetry of Geo Milev (1895–1925), Nikola Furnadzhiev (1903–68), and Nikola Vaptsarov (1909–42). In contrast, Atanas Dalchev (1904–77) favored a deliberately reserved tone. The best Bulgarian poetess, Elisaveta Bagriana (1893–1991), also made her triumphant debut. The short stories and plays of Iordan Iovkov (1880–1937) combined external simplicity and psychological density.

The post–World War II period was dominated by socialist realism, a Soviet import that regarded art as means of reinforcing the goals of the Communist Party. Ironically, the best literary works were created by circumventing this officially imposed style. These include the novels of Dimitŭr Dimov (1909–66), Dimitŭr Talev (1898–1966), and Emilian Stanev (1907–79); the short stories and plays of Iordan Radichkov (1929–); the poetry and the plays of Valeri Petrov (1920–); the poetry and the novels of Blaga Dimitrova (1922–); and the satirical verse of Radoi Ralin (1923–). The fall of totalitarianism in 1989 finally released writers from the restrictions of socialist realism. At present, Bulgarian literature is undergoing major changes, but their full effect is still difficult to evaluate.

Lyubomira Parpulova Gribble

Further reading

Black, Karen L., ed. *A Biobibliographical Handbook of Bulgarian Authors*. Columbus, Ohio, 1981.

Moser, Charles. *A History of Bulgarian Literature, 865–1944*. The Hague and Paris, 1972.

Tsanev, Georgi et al., eds. *Rechnik na bŭlgarskata literatura*, 3 vols. Sofia, 1976, 1977, 1982.

See also Khristo Botev; Bulgarian Culture; Folklife; Folklore; Paisii of Hilendar; Elin Pelin; Petko Slaveikov; Sofronii Vrachanski; Ivan Vazov

Bulgarian Massacres

The slaughter of Bulgarians by Ottoman forces in 1876, an event tragically instrumental in the liberation of the country from the Ottomans Turks. In April 1876 the Bulgarian Revolutionary Central Committee launched a national uprising designed to free Bulgaria from Ottoman rule. Fearing that the uprising would lead to the murder of Ottoman civilians, Ottoman authorities reacted with a policy of deliberate atrocity. Irregular Ottoman forces known as *bashibazouks,* composed primarily of Pomaks and Circassians, roamed the countryside of southern Bulgaria, burning, looting, and killing. By the summer of 1876, the *bashibazouks* had killed many Bulgarians, with perhaps as many as five thousand dead in the village of Batak alone. Estimates of the real number of dead vary widely from three to one hundred thousand. These massacres succeeded in quelling the uprising but also provoked outrage throughout Europe. Reports filed by London *Daily News* journalist Januarius A. MacGahan (1844–78) and American consul in Constantinople Eugene Schuyler (1840–90) on the horrors they had encountered while traveling through Bulgaria revived the Bulgarian cause. In Great Britain, these reports undermined the pro-Ottoman policy of Benjamin Disraeli (1804–88) and led to the revival of the political fortunes of William Gladstone (1809–98). In Russia, news of the massacres in Bulgaria aroused further the Pan-Slavist sentiments of the government of Alexander II (1818–81). One year later, the Russians intervened militarily against the Ottoman Empire in the Russo-Turkish War of 1877–78, which led to the liberation of Bulgaria from Ottoman rule in 1878.

Richard C. Hall

Further reading

Harris, David. *Britain and the Bulgarian Horrors of 1876*. Chicago, 1939.

Jelavich, Charles and Barbara Jelavich. *The Establishment of the Balkan National States, 1804–1920*. Seattle, Washington, 1977.

Macdermott, Mercia. *A History of Bulgaria, 1393–1885*. London, 1962.

See also Alexander II; April Uprising; Pan-Slavism; Pomaks; Russo-Turkish War of 1877–78

B

Bulgarian-Serb War of 1885

Military conflict between Bulgaria and Serbia. The proclamation of the union of Eastern Rumelia with the Principality of Bulgaria in September 1885 caused Alexander III (1845–94) of Russia to break off relations with Bulgaria and to summon home Russian officers assigned to the Bulgarian army. Sensing an opportunity to gain land, King Milan of Serbia (1854–1901) proclaimed himself the champion of the Treaty of Berlin, which revised the boundaries of Bulgaria after the Russo-Turkish War of 1877–78 and the subsequent Treaty of San Stefano, and declared war on Bulgaria on November 13, 1885. The Serbs appeared to have the advantage because of the recall of the Russian officers of the Bulgarian army and because the Bulgarian forces were disposed mainly on the Turkish frontier. However, under the command of the Bulgarian monarch, Prince Alexander of Battenberg (1857–93), the Bulgarian forces marched rapidly to the western borders, covering on one occasion fifty-nine miles (ninety-nine km) in thirty-two hours. They established defensive positions around the narrow defiles of Slivnitsa, barring the road to Sofia. Serbian attacks on the Slivnitsa positions began on November 17, but within two days the Bulgarians had repulsed these attacks. The Bulgarians then counterattacked and started to advance through the Dragoman Pass (now Dmitrovgrad Pass) into Serbia. Fearing the complete defeat of their Serbian ally, Austria threatened military intervention against Bulgaria on November 28. This threat forced the Bulgarians to stop their advance and prevented them from obtaining any great advantage from their victory over the Serbs. The Treaty of Bucharest of March 2, 1886, restored the status quo ante between Bulgaria and Serbia. Nevertheless, the success against the Serbs secured the unification with Eastern Rumelia and imparted to the young Bulgarian state a tremendous sense of self-confidence.

Richard C. Hall

Further reading

Crampton, Richard. *Bulgaria 1878–1918.* Boulder, Colorado, 1983.

Istoriya na Sŭrbsko-bŭlgarskata voina na 1885 god. Sofia, 1939.

Mitev, Yono, ed. *Istoriya na Sŭrbsko-bŭlgarskata Voina, 1885.* Sofia, 1971.

See also Alexander III; Alexander of Battenberg; Congress of Berlin; Eastern Rumelia; Milan Obrenović; Russo-Turkish War of 1877–78; San Stefano, Treaty of

Burgas

Major port and industrial center on the southern Black Sea coast of Bulgaria. Burgas became a major port only in the twentieth century as a consequence of Bulgarian independence in 1878 and construction of a railroad from Sofia during the 1890s. Throughout most of the nineteenth century, the city was a fishing village with fewer than three thousand inhabitants, although four hundred years earlier it had been the site of a fortified town. The failure of Burgas to develop in the past is attributed to the long presence of malaria in the vicinity and the existence of small ports nearby. Port development also suffered before Bulgarian independence from a location away from major Ottoman Empire trading routes.

The population of Burgas is approximately 205,000. Burgas continues to be a center of fishing and fish processing, handling most of Bulgaria's commercial fish catch. It has also become notably specialized in importing and refining petroleum from Russia and the Middle East. Burgas has also developed a significant shipbuilding industry.

Thomas M. Poulsen

Further reading

Penkov, Ignat and Todor Khristov. *Ikonomicheska Geografiia na Bŭlgariia,* 2d ed. Sofia, 1965.

Shapira, P. and K. Paskaleva. "After Central Planning: The Restructuring of State Industry in Bulgaria's Bourgas Region." *European Planning Studies* 2 (1994): 131–57.

Zakhariev, Ivan, Dobri Bradistilov, and Petŭr Popov. *Ikonomichesko Raionirane na N.R. Bŭlgariia.* Sofia, 1963.

Burgenland

Austria's easternmost province located at the foothills of the Styrian Alps on the little Hungarian Plain and surrounding the Neusiedler See. The region was transferred from Hungarian to Austrian control by the Treaty of Trianon at the end of World War I. This was a rare case of territory taken from one defeated power and given to another.

The old boundary between Austria and Hungary had been the Leitha River (west of Burgenland), but pressure from the significant number of Germans in the population of Burgenland (75 percent) led to a plebiscite in 1921. Only Sopron (formerly Odenburg), which served as the region's traditional economic service center, voted to remain under Hungarian rule. This left Sopron almost completely surrounded by Austria and severed the economy of the region, particularly after World War II and the imposition of the Iron Curtain.

Burgenland has become an economically depressed region within Austria with a higher rate of unemployment than most of the rest of the nation. Ailing industries, heavy reliance on relatively inefficient, small-scale agriculture (especially grapes and grains), and lack of a regional service center have hindered economic growth and development. Only tourism is a high-growth sector of the economy. Burgenland was one of the targeted areas for assistance under the Alpe-Adria development program of 1978, which focused on regional development problems in national border areas.

Russell L. Ivy

Further reading

Berentsen, William, ed. *Europe in the 1990s: A Geographical Analysis,* 7th ed. Chicago, 1997.

Pounds, Norman, J.G. *Eastern Europe.* Chicago, 1969.

Rugg, Dean. *Eastern Europe.* London, 1985.

UNIDO, *Czechoslovakia: Industrial Transformation and Regeneration.* Oxford, 1992.

See also Cisleithania/Transleithania; Iron Curtain; Trianon

C

Cankar, Ivan (1876–1918)

Prominent Slovene writer of the modernist period (1899–1918). Cankar wrote in a wide variety of prose forms and styles. His early writings were published in a collection of sensual poems (*Erotika,* 1899), part of the Slovene poetic renaissance at the time, and a book of sketches with different fin-de-siècle styles and topics, *Vinjete* (1899). As a halfhearted student of engineering in Vienna (1896–1902), Cankar next attempted longer fiction and plays, such as the portrait of a destructive family man, *Jakob Ruda* (1900), and the political satire of governing Slovene politicians, *Za narodov blagor* (*For the Good of the People,* 1901).

Social mores and the psychology of power are the subjects of his next four plays; the seventh, *Lepa Vida* (1912), is a stylistic tour de force that tries to show the tension between the physical and the spiritual in life.

Cankar's best-known novel, *Hlapec Jernej in njegova pravica* (*The Servant Jernej and His Rights,* 1907), is the tragic story of a wronged farmworker in search of justice. This book expresses Cankar's thirst for social justice most powerfully. The fate of the downtrodden is also key to his symbolist *Hisa Marija Pomosnice* (*The House of Our Lady of Mercy,* 1904), which grew out of the artist's observations of child abuse, and the collection of stories *Za križem* (*Following the Cross,* 1909). Cankar's prose of the period combines elements of naturalism and realism with modernist features.

Cankar returned from Vienna to stand as a candidate to the imperial assembly in 1907. He stayed and wrote his final satirical works by 1910, after which he devoted himself to philosophical novels and autobiographical sketches. His last collection of stories, *Podobe iz sanj* (*Dream Visions,* 1917), are poetic glimpses into the horrors of World War I.

Timothy Pogacar

Further reading

Bernik, France. *Cankarjeva zgodnja proza.* Ljubljana, 1976.

Ožbalt, Irma. "Ivan Cankar," in *Dictionary of Literary Biography,* vol. 147. Detroit, 1995.

Slodnjak, Anton. "Ivan Cankar in Slovene and World Literature." *Slavonic and East European Review* 59 (April 1981).

Vidmar, Josip, Stefan Barbarič, and Franc Zadravec, eds. *Simpozij o Ivan Cankarju.* Ljubljana, Slovenia, 1976.

Zadravec, Franc. *Cankarjeva ironija.* Murska Sobota, Slovenia, 1991.

See also Slovene Literature

Čapek, Karel (1890–1938)

Czech writer. One of the most important and prolific writers of the interwar period in Czechoslovakia, Čapek, best known in the West for his science fiction plays and novels, was also a noted journalist, dramatist, stage director, novelist, and master of short fiction. Čapek was born in Malé Svatoňovice in northwestern Bohemia, the son of a country doctor and the youngest of three children. His older brother, Josef (1887–1945), was also a writer and painter of renown. Karel studied at Charles University, as well as in Berlin and Paris, completing his dissertation in 1915. Exempted from military service because of poor health, he began his career as a journalist, publishing sketches and aphorisms, and contributing to humorous journals. He never gave up journalism, considering it a matter of immense importance, and in 1922 joined the staff of *Lidové noviny* (*People's Gazette*), to which he contributed for the rest of his life. Reflected in his literary work are all his various interests, especially gardening, photography, phonograph records, folk music, and travel. He believed the intelligentsia was responsible for the social, political, and moral health of the nation. His *Conversations with T.G. Masaryk* (1928–1935) reflect his work along these lines. Among Čapek's short prose fiction, humorous stories of the everyday, his collections of police stories, *Povídky z jedné kapsy* (*Tales from One Pocket,* 1929) and *Povídky z druhé kapsy* (*Tales from the Other Pocket,* 1929), remain extraordinarily popular. Čapek died on December 25, 1938, only a few months before Nazi troops entered Prague on March 15, 1939. Gestapo agents, unaware of his death, came to arrest him shortly thereafter.

In 1920 Čapek's first play was staged at the National Theater in Prague, where he met Olga Scheinpflugová (1902–), an actress whom he later married in 1935. In 1921 he completed his most famous play, *R.U.R.* (*Rossum's Universal Robots*), for which he coined the term *robot* (from the Czech meaning hard, or slave, labor), a term that has since been adopted by many languages, including English. His other plays include *Ze života hmyzu* (*From the Insect World,* 1921 [coauthored with Josef]); *Věc Makropulos* (*Makropulos Secret,* 1922); and *Bílá nemoc* (*The White Plague,* 1937). Director at the Prague City Theater from 1921 to 1923, Čapek was increasingly dissatisfied with writing for the stage, because in the end too much depended on factors beyond the playwright's control (the director, the actors, and the facilities).

Many of Čapek's novels, like his plays, may be categorized as anti-utopian science fiction, including *Továrna na Absolutno* (*Factory of the Absolute,* 1922); *Krakatit* (1924); and the brilliant moral and political science fiction satire, *Válka s mloky* (*War with the Newts,* 1936). Čapek's science fiction is characterized by its reflection of contemporary life; the inclusion of imitations of genres of nonfiction, such as news clippings, interviews and statements from famous personalities, letters, and references to current events, creates the illusion of a documentary recording of real events.

Strongly influenced by Anglo-American pragmatism, Čapek's sympathies lie with the average person, not with the revolutionaries, dreamers, or saviors with grandiose plans for remaking the world. Opposed to general theories, principles, and ideologies, Čapek emphasizes the value of the individual, as well as personal moral responsibility. His trilogy of philosophical novels, *Hordubal* (1933), *Povětroň* (*Meteor,* 1934), and *Obyčejný život* (*An Ordinary Life,* 1934), concern the problem of self-identity.

Ann Marie Basom

Further reading

Černý, Václav. *Karel Čapek.* Prague, 1936.
Harkins, William E. *Karel Čapek.* New York, 1962.
Matuška, Alexander. *Karel Čapek: An Essay,* trans. by Cathryn Alan. Prague, 1964.

See also Charles University; Czech Literature; Intelligentsia

Capitulations

Commercial, financial, consular, juridical privileges granted by the Ottoman Empire to foreign governments. The capitulations represented an instrument of Western expansion and exploitation much resented by Ottoman reformers and Turkish nationalists.

Capitulation agreements between the Porte and European states, including England, France, Austria, Russia, Italy, and Germany, granted concessions to foreign nationals conducting business in Ottoman lands: unhindered trade and navigation; reduced customs duties; security of person and property; consular representation; immunity from Ottoman taxes, laws, and courts. Diplomatic envoys of capitulatory states distributed protection patents to traders, interpreters, agents, and household staff, all of whom received capitulatory status. Many of the protected were non-Muslim subjects with tax, labor, and other obligations to the Ottoman state. For a price that became a lucrative revenue source for the financially strapped Porte, protection patents were issued to foreign envoys, who in turn sold them to Ottoman subjects. Beneficiaries included Greek, Italian, Jewish, and Armenian traders who purchased patents, escaped Ottoman taxation, and expanded commerce as clients of foreign states.

European governments and companies exploited the capitulations to extend control over Ottoman ports, banks, mines, railroads, and virtually all public services. Reformers and nationalists in the nineteenth and twentieth centuries sought to curtail capitulations as a vital first step toward economic sovereignty. Abolished in September 1914 but restored in 1920, the capitulations were finally abolished by the Treaty of Lausanne (1923).

Theophilus C. Prousis

Further reading

Hurewitz, Jacob, ed. *The Middle East and North Africa in World Politics: A Documentary Record. Volume 1: European Expansion, 1535–1914.* New Haven, Connecticut, 1975.

Inalcik, Halil. "The Ottoman Empire," in J. Wansbrough et al., "Imtiyazat," *Encyclopaedia of Islam* 3 (1971): 1179–89.

Naff, Thomas and Roger Owen, eds. *Studies in Eighteenth-Century Islamic History.* Carbondale, Illinois, 1977.

Shaw, Stanford. *History of the Ottoman Empire and Modern Turkey,* 2 vols. New York, 1976–77.

Sousa, N. *The Capitulatory Regime of Turkey.* Baltimore, Maryland, 1933.

See also Lausanne, Treaty of; Ottoman Empire; Porte

Caragiale, Ion Luca (1851–1912)

The outstanding playwright and satirist of modern Romania, and the originator of social comedy. Caragiale was born in 1852 in a village near Ploieşti in south-central Romania. Though deprived of a suitable education, he was drawn as a child to literature; his early experiences working in the theater (as a prompter and copyist) to support his family made a deep impression on his creative energies. Caragiale worked as a freelance journalist until 1878, when he completed his first drama, a genre in which he then excelled for twelve years before turning more fully to fiction. His plays and prose are satirical portraits of late-nineteenth-century Romania turning from largely rural conditions to urban ways of life; he cleverly and critically exposed the comedy of these transitions. Caragiale's best-known plays include *O noapte furtunoasă* (*A Stormy Night*), a trenchant commentary written in 1880 ridiculing the corruptions of provincial life (a work so controversial that its performance was originally banned), and *O scrisoare pierdută* (*A Lost Letter,* 1884)—an astute parody of the rifts between the Romanian bourgeois and landowning parties. He was also known for his sharply satirical prose, especially short stories and anecdotes; "O făclie de Paşte" ("An Easter Torch," 1889),"Păcat" ("The Sin," 1892), and "Kir Ianulea" (1909) are masterpieces of Romanian fiction. Caragiale died in Berlin in 1912.

Margaret H. Beissinger

Further reading

Caragiale, Ion Luca. *The Lost Letter and Other Plays.* London, 1956.

Cioculescu, Şerban. *Viaţa lui I. L. Caragiale.* Bucharest, 1986.

Tappe, Eric Ditmar. *Ion Luca Caragiale.* New York, 1974.

See also Romanian Literature; Theater

Carol I (1839–1914)

Prince (1866–81) and later king of Romania (1881–1914). A descendant of the south German, Catholic branch of the Hohenzollern family, Carol was trained and educated in the Prussian army and served in the Danish War of 1864. A rigidly disciplined, methodical, proud, unbending, and moderately liberal man, he became prince of Romania in 1866 when the native ruler, Alexandru Ioan Cuza (1820–73), was forced to abdicate.

Carol's reign, the longest in Romanian history, can be divided into two major parts. The first of these, from 1866 to 1878, was a formative period of marked political crisis and upheaval that culminated in national independence after the Russo-Turkish War of 1877–78 (in which Romanian armies played an important role). The second period was one of consolidation and internal development, including the proclamation of the Romanian Kingdom in 1881 and the emergence of a kind of rotational system of governance between 1888 and 1914, in which power alternated between the National Liberals and the so-called Conservatives.

Internally, Carol's reign saw a flowering of Romanian culture, some movement in the economic sphere, and considerable Europeanization of Romania's educational and sociological structures. Steps taken under Carol's urging in regard to the army and transportation did contribute to making Romania less subject to external pressures. However, economic growth remained at a rudimentary level. His reign was also marred by the outbreak of a peasant uprising in 1907 that resulted in thousands of deaths and showed how shallow and tentative a good deal of this development had been.

The relative success of Carol's regime saw the affirmation of Romania in southeastern Europe in the early twentieth century. Romania became an adherent of the Triple Alliance (Germany, Austria-Hungary, Italy), despite the existence of an important Romanian irredenta in Transylvania, and an active participant in Balkan affairs, including the Second Balkan War of 1913.

The outbreak of World War I presented a dilemma for Carol. He wanted Romania to support Germany and Austria-Hungary, but the majority of the Romanian elite was opposed because of the Transylvanian issue. Carol acquiesced to the argument that the alliance's defensive character did not obligate Romania to join the Central Powers. He died in October 1914, two years before Romania entered the war on the side of the Allies.

Paul E. Michelson

Further reading

Hitchins, Keith. *Rumania 1866–1947*. Oxford, 1994.

Mamina, Ion and Ion Bulei. *Guverne şi governanţi, 1866–1916*. Bucharest, 1994.

Michelson, Paul E. *Conflict and Crisis: Romanian Political Development, 1861–1871*. New York, 1987.

See also Balkan Wars; Alexandru Ioan Cuza; Irredentism; Romanian Peasant Revolt of 1907; Russo-Turkish War of 1877–78; Transylvania; Transylvanian Dispute; World War I

Carol II (1893–1953)

King of Romania. Born in Sinaia, Carol was the eldest son of King Ferdinand (1865–1927) and Queen Marie (1875–1938). He became crown prince in October 1914. Carol eloped with Ioana (Zizi) Lambrino (1898–1953), a commoner, in September 1918. His shocked parents had the marriage annulled by the Romanian Supreme Court, despite Carol's renunciation of his rights to the throne, which his parents refused to recognize. With the blessing of his parents, he then married Princess Helen of Greece (1896–1982) in March 1921. They had one child, the future King Michael (1921–). But in 1925 Carol met another femme fatale, Magda Lupescu (1899–1977), and in December he abandoned his wife and child and left Romania to be with her. He subsequently renounced his rights to the throne again. Carol became known worldwide as a playboy and his affair with Lupescu was one of the great romances of the time.

In June 1930 Carol seized control of the throne from the regency council running the country in the name of Michael. His rule has remained a source of controversy. In February 1938 he replaced what was left of the country's beleaguered parliamentary government with an authoritarian royal dictatorship. Finally, in September 1940, as a result of the loss of Bessarabia and Northern Bukovina to the Soviets and a large part of Transylvania to the Hungarians in the Vienna Awards, he was forced into exile by Marshal Ion Antonescu (1882–1946). He died in Estoril, Portugal, in April 1953.

Paul D. Quinlan

Further reading

Hillgruber, Andreas. *Hitler, König Carol und Marschall Antonescu*. Wiesbaden, 1954.

Hohenzollern-Romania, Prince Paul of. *King Carol II: A Life of My Grandfather*. London, 1988.

Muşat, Mircea and Ion Ardeleanu. *România dupa Marea Unire, 1918–1933*. Bucharest, 1986.

———. *România dupa Marea Unire, noiembrie 1933–septembrie 1940*. Bucharest, 1988.

Quinlan, Paul D. *The Playboy King: Carol II of Romania*. Westport, Connecticut, 1995.

See also Ion Antonescu; Ferdinand; Elena Lupescu; Marie; Michael; Vienna Awards

Carp, Petre P. (1837–1919)

Romanian politician and cultural figure. Carp was the scion of a Moldavian *boiar* family. He was educated in Berlin and Bonn, returning to Iaşi, where he was a founding member—along with Titu Maiorescu (1840–1917)—of the Junimea Literary Society, the Romanian cultural association, in 1864. Carp became the political leader of the

Junimea/"young conservative" faction as a parliamentarian; served as diplomatic agent in Paris, Vienna, Berlin, and Rome; and was cabinet minister for foreign affairs, cults and education, agriculture and industry, finance, and, finally, prime minister in 1900–1901 and 1911–12.

Carp was unusual among Romanian politicians in his bluntness, ruthless logic, and refusal to countenance nationalistic myths (including anti-Semitism). This made him unpopular with both political friend and foe, including Carol I (1839–1914), but his undeniable talent was frequently sought out. In the dominant conservative cabinet of 1891–95, Carp was the animating spirit, proposing and often carrying a wide variety of laws relating to industry, finance, and education. His own prime ministerships were surprisingly ineffective, ad hoc, and even disoriented, partly because of the unremitting financial crises that faced Romania in the early 1900s and factionalism among the conservatives.

In 1914 Carp tenaciously argued for Romania's adherence to the Central Powers and opposed its 1916 alliance with the Entente, but his germanophilism owed largely to his fear of Russian expansionism.

Paul E. Michelson

Further reading

Bulei, Ion. *Sistemul politic al României moderne: Partidul conservator.* Bucharest, 1987.
Gane, C. *P.P. Carp şi locul său în istoria politică a ţării,* 2 vols. Bucharest, 1936.
Ornea, Z. *Junimea şi junimismul,* 2d ed. Bucharest, 1978.

See also Carol I; Junimea; Titu Maiorescu

Carpathian Mountains

A chain of mountains extending over 960 miles (1,600 km) in a semicircle. Starting from the Danube River near Vienna, the Carpathians extend eastward through Czech, Slovak, Polish, and Ukrainian lands. In Romania they turn first sharply southward, but after a second sharp turn they follow a westward course until they reach the Danube and its so-called Iron Gates on the border between Romania and Serbia. Thus, within Romania the Carpathians form an arch around Transylvania. Here, under the relative protection of the Carpathi-

ans and its forests, the Romanian nation was formed, culturally and politically. While providing some cover from the harsh continental climate blowing from the east and from invaders penetrating from the steppe, the Carpathian range is not an inhospitable environment. Its weathered old mountains are on average only 3,335 feet (1,000 m) high, and even its few high summits of 8,333 feet (2,500 m)—in Fagaraş and Maramureş in Romania and in the Tatras in Slovakia—are not solid rock or glacial peaks. Spruce forests climb in Romania to an elevation of 4,660–6,000 feet (1,400–1,800 m). With a median annual temperature at the lower elevations of about 50° F (10° C) (70° F [21° C] in July and roughly 23° F [minus 5 ° C] in January) and a median annual precipitation of around 31.5–55 inches (80–140 cm), life in this environment was never too harsh. Cut by rivers in many places, settled thousands of years ago, the Carpathians are a honeycomb of humanity with distinctive traditions and culture. The Romanian national culture, material and spiritual, has its roots in the Carpathian and sub-Carpathian ways of life, in the genius of the Romanian peasants' adaptation to and transformation of the surrounding nature. Of course, in time peasants began to move into the lowlands, where the soil was more fertile, or into the cities, where modern life beckoned. Still, it is telling that even today demographic maps of Romania show that the density of population is greater close to the Carpathians than it is in the Danube valley.

Ladis K.D. Kristof

Further reading

Magocsi, Paul Robert. *Historical Atlas of East Central Europe.* Seattle, Washington, 1993.
România: Atlas istoric-geografic. Bucharest, 1996.

See also Romanian Culture; Transylvania

Carpatho-Rusyns

East Slavic people also known in English as Ruthenes or Ruthenians (Latin, *Rutheni*). The ancestors of the Rusyns began to settle in the foothills and valleys of the north-central Carpathian Mountains as early as the fifth century A.D. The earliest Slavic settlers, who came in the wake of the Hunnic invasions, were followed in the sixth and seventh centuries by White Croats from the

C original Slavic homeland north of the Carpathians. These East Slavs in the Carpathians began to be called Rusyns after they received Christianity either directly from Byzantine missionaries Cyril (d. 869) and Methodius (d. 884) or from their disciples during the second half of the ninth century. In the centuries that followed, further immigration came from the north and east (Rusyns from Galicia and Podolia) and from the south (Romanian Vlach shepherds from Transylvania who were later assimilated by the Carpatho-Rusyns).

The land traditionally inhabited by Carpatho-Rusyns is today within the borderland regions of three countries: far western Ukraine (the Transcarpathian oblast), northeastern Slovakia, and southeastern Poland. Carpatho-Rusyns refer to these three areas as Subcarpathian Rus' (in Ukraine), the Prešov Region (in Slovakia), and the Lemko Region (in Poland). Until the nineteenth century, Carpatho-Rusyn settlement extended much farther south into what is today southeastern Slovakia, northeastern Hungary, and northern Romania. Most of those Rusyn settlements have since been assimilated.

There are no reliable statistics on the number of Carpatho-Rusyns, because after World War II they were not (at least until very recently) recorded as a distinct nationality in most of the countries where they lived. Reasonable estimates suggest there may be today as many as 900,000 Rusyns in the Carpathian homeland. The majority lives in Ukraine (650,000), followed by Slovakia (130,000), Poland (60,000), Romania (20,000), and Hungary (3,000). Outside the homeland, there are also Carpatho-Rusyn immigrant communities, some dating as far back as the eighteenth century, in Yugoslavia—the Vojvodina (25,000), the Czech Republic (12,000), Croatia (5,000), and a large group in the United States (620,000).

With few exceptions, Carpatho-Rusyns historically have not had their own state or distinct administrative entity. In such circumstances, it is through their language, culture, and Eastern-rite (Orthodox or Greek Catholic) variant of Christianity that they have retained a distinct identity. The Rusyn language consists of several East Slavic dialects that include as well a high number of archaic Slavic elements, borrowings from Hungarian, and vocabulary and other linguistic features from Slovak and Polish. There have been several attempts, mostly in the twentieth century, to codify a Carpatho-Rusyn literary language.

Written in the Cyrillic alphabet, Carpatho-Rusyn was widely used in public life and schools in the former Czechoslovak province of Subcarpathian Rus' before World War II and in Yugoslavia (the Vojvodina) since then.

Like most peoples in East Central Europe, the Carpatho-Rusyns experienced a national revival during the nineteenth century, as the intelligentsia "rediscovered" the cultural and linguistic distinctiveness of their own national group. They then set out to make the populace aware that it belonged to a distinct nationality and to have that distinctiveness recognized by the state or states in which the group lived. They generally carried out this task through teaching the native language in schools and by establishing newspapers, publications, libraries, and other national organizations.

It was not until the Revolutions of 1848 that a Carpatho-Rusyn national revival became a serious undertaking. It was associated, in particular, with two individuals: Greek Catholic priest Aleksander Dukhnovych (1803–65), who established the first Rusyn cultural organization and publications; and Adol'f Dobrians'kyi (1817–1901), a member of the Hungarian parliament who pressed for the establishment of an autonomous territory for Carpatho-Rusyns in Austria-Hungary.

From the outset of their national revival, Carpatho-Rusyn leaders confronted two questions. The intelligentsia first had to define what the term *Rusyn* meant and, in particular, its relationship to other East Slavic, or Rus' peoples—the Russians, Belorusans, and Ukrainians. They were also faced with the problem of defining their identity and adopting for it an appropriate literary language. Were the East Slavs living along the southern and northern slopes of the central Carpathian Mountain ranges part of the Russian nationality or the Ukrainian nationality, or did they represent a distinct Carpatho-Rusyn nationality? Analogously, should their literary language be Russian, Ukrainian, or a distinct Carpatho-Rusyn literary language based on the local dialects? Aside from debates about their specific East Slavic identity, Carpatho-Rusyns faced another reality: the inhabitants of many villages, in particular in the lowland areas of what is today southeastern Slovakia and northeastern Hungary, had gradually lost their Carpatho-Rusyn identity through assimilation with Slovaks or Hungarians.

Among those Carpatho-Rusyns who retained an East Slavic identity, the relative strength of the

Russian (Russophile), Ukrainian (Ukrainophile), and Rusyn (Rusynophile) orientations has varied during the past century and a half. This has had as much to do with the intervention of the governments under which Carpatho-Rusyns have lived as with the attractiveness and success of a given national orientation. The earliest leaders of the Carpatho-Rusyn national revival were Pan-Slavists who believed their people could survive only by identifying with Russian culture. As such, they believed that there existed a single, or "common Russian," nationality made up of three branches: the "Great Russian" (Russian), "Belo-russian" (Belorusan), and "Little Russian" (Ukrainian), with the Carpatho-Rusyns being part of the last group. Not surprisingly, by the final decades of the nineteenth century, the Russophile orientation was opposed by the Austro-Hungarian authorities, who by then had become concerned with the expansionist tendencies of the Russian Empire into East Central Europe and the Balkans. Consequently, the Hungarian government encouraged Carpatho-Rusyn writers to publish newspapers and school texts in the local Carpatho-Rusyn vernacular and to inform their readers that Rusyn constituted a fourth East Slavic nationality alongside of, but distinct from, Russians, Belorusans, and Ukrainians. This was the beginning of the Rusynophile movement.

Following World War I, three-quarters of the Carpatho-Rusyns united voluntarily with the new state of Czechoslovakia; the remainder (in the so-called Lemko Region north of the mountains) were annexed by Poland. In both of these states, the Russophile and Rusynophile orientations continued among Carpatho-Rusyns, although a new Ukrainian orientation came into being as well. Ukrainophiles believed that there was no such thing as a "common Russian" people and that Rusyns, whom they called Carpatho-Ukrainians, were part of a distinct Ukrainian nationality that lived in a compact territory from the Carpathian Mountains in the west to the Kuban River valley in the east. Analogously, Ukrainophiles argued that there could be no such thing as a "separate" Rusyn nationality or language and that Carpatho-Rusyns should adopt the Ukrainian literary language as their own.

After World War II, the largest Carpatho-Rusyn territory (Subcarpathian Rus') was annexed to the Soviet Ukraine, which together with other Rusyn-inhabited lands in Slovakia and Poland came under Communist rule. The Soviets and their satellite allies "resolved" the Carpatho-Rusyn nationality question by administrative decree. Regardless of what Carpatho-Rusyns may have called themselves or believed their national identity to be, they were henceforth to be considered "Ukrainians." The Lemko Region "Ukrainians" were between 1945 and 1947 either resettled in the Soviet Ukraine or forcibly deported to the western regions of Poland. In neighboring Slovakia, Rusyns were administratively transformed into Ukrainians during the early 1950s. In short, a Rusyn identity was banned in all countries where Carpatho-Rusyns lived, with the exception of the small group (ca. 25,000) in Yugoslavia. There, in the Vojvodina, the Yugoslav state provided support for Rusyn-language schools, publications, organizations, and, after 1974, a university department of Rusyn language and literature.

The revolutions of 1989 and the fall of communism brought in their wake a return of the Carpatho-Rusyn nationality question. New Rusyn organizations and Rusyn-language publications were founded in Ukraine, Slovakia, Poland, the Czech Republic, Yugoslavia, and even Hungary, where the last Rusyns were thought to have been assimilated before World War I. All of these organizations believe that Carpatho-Rusyns represent a distinct nationality that should have a newly codified Rusyn literary language taught in schools and used in the media and other cultural activity. Alongside the new Rusynophile movement there exist Ukrainian organizations and publications (in some cases under new names) that were established throughout the Carpatho-Rusyn homeland during the period of Communist rule, as well as a few new ones founded since 1989. The pro-Ukrainian organizations deny that a distinct Rusyn nationality "can or should exist," and they request that "separatist" Rusyn organizations should be denied state support or even be legally banned.

In a sense, the only thing that has changed about the Carpatho-Rusyn nationality question during the past century and a half is the elimination of the Russophile orientation. On the other hand, the Rusynophile and Ukrainophile orientations continue to exist. Each claims to be the "true voice" of the entire group, whether it is referred to as Carpatho-Rusyn or Carpatho-Ukrainian, and each continues to struggle against the other ongoing reality (in particular outside Ukraine)—assimilation to Slovak, Polish, or Serb culture or identity.

Paul Robert Magocsi

C

Further reading

Bonkáló, Alexander. *The Rusyns*. New York, 1990.

Magocsi, Paul Robert. "The Birth of a New Nation, or the Return of an Old Problem." *Canadian Slavonic Papers* 34, no. 3 (1992): 192–223.

————. *The Persistence of Regional Cultures: Rusyns and Ukrainians in Their Carpathian Homeland and Abroad*. New York, 1993.

————. *The Rusyns of Slovakia: An Historical Survey*. New York, 1993.

————. *The Shaping of the National Identity: Subcarpathian Rus', 1848–1948*. Cambridge, Massachusetts, 1978.

Makara, M.P. and I.I. Myhovych. "Karpats'ki rusyny v konteksti suchasnoho etnopolitychnoho zhyttia." *Ukraïns'kyi istorychnyi zhurnal*, no. 1 (1994): 117–28.

See also Carpathian Mountains; Ethnic Minorities; Orthodoxy; Pan-Slavism; Revolutions of 1848; Revolutions of 1989; Slavs; Subcarpathian Rus'; Vojvodina; World War II

Catargiu, Lascăr (1823–99)

Nineteenth-century Romanian conservative political leader and prime minister. Though scion of a Moldavian *boiar* family, Catargiu received little formal education and at the age of twenty entered the Moldavian administrative apparatus, becoming the chief magistrate in Neamţ in 1845. He later became an active participant in the movement that led to the union of the Romanian Principalities in 1859, serving as police chief of Iaşi in 1855–56 and as deputy in the assembly that elected Prince Alexandru Ioan Cuza (1820–73). (Catargiu was among those who received support for the throne but withdrew in favor of Cuza.) Catargiu soon came to be part of an anti-Cuza coalition that opposed the new prince's reformism and autocratic rule, a coalition that eventually overthrew Cuza in 1866.

Catargiu was instrumental in getting a restrictive voting franchise and veto powers for the prince included in the otherwise quite liberal Romanian constitution of 1866 and briefly served as the first prime minister under the new prince, Carol I (1839–1914). He was called back to power in 1871 during a dynastic crisis that nearly led to Carol's abdication. His conservative prime ministership (1871–76) was the first in modern Romania to serve through a complete legislative term. Catargiu became the leader of the Romanian conservatives and was prime minister again in 1889, and for a fourth time in 1891–95.

His rapport with Carol I was excellent and his stolid, deliberate character provided a contrast to the volatility of many of his rivals. His reputation for bulldog administrative abilities and lack of pretence was unusual in Romanian political life. He succeeded in preserving the political influence of the conservative wing of the Romanian oligarchy in the pre–World War I era but failed to turn it into a viable political party. In the long run, the means used to maintain the conservatives in power beyond their actual strength and their support of patronage politics proved disastrous both for Romanian political development and for the conservative interests that Catargiu represented.

Paul E. Michelson

Further reading

Bulei, Ion. *Sistemul politic al României moderne: Partidul conservator*. Bucharest, 1987.

Hitchins, Keith. *Rumania 1866–1947*. Oxford, 1994.

Iordache, Anastasie. *Sub zodia lui Strousberg. Viaţa politică din România între 1871–1878*. Bucharest, 1991.

Lungu, Traian. *Viaţa politică în România la sfîrşitul secolului al XIX-lea 1889–1900*. Bucharest, 1967.

See also Boiars; Carol I; Alexandru Ioan Cuza

Catholicism

The Roman Catholic Church, which is the majority faith in Poland, Hungary, Croatia, Slovenia, and the Czech and Slovak Republics, is the product of two distinct and separate historical processes. The first was the break from Eastern Orthodoxy in 1054, which established all of Western Catholic Christianity under the authority of the Bishop of Rome, the pope. The second was the Protestant Reformation, which arose in the sixteenth century. Roman Catholicism claims to have inherited the true form of Christianity from apostolic times. This inheritance is most distinctive in its emphasis on the authority of the pope, whose infallibility was solemnly proclaimed by the First Vatican Council in 1870. While the bishops are regarded collectively as the ordinary teaching authority of the church, the pope is understood as the extra-ordinary authority, whose infallibility in faith and morals is founded upon the general infallibility of the church itself.

Catholics recognize two sources of revealed truth: Scripture and tradition. On this point they are divided from many Protestants, who recognize only the former as a source of divine revelation. The significance of tradition can be found, for example, in the 1854 proclamation of the Immaculate Conception of the Virgin Mary, a doctrine nowhere to be found in Scripture but claimed to have been found in tradition from the earliest times.

In addition to a concern about the doctrinal significance of Mary, a concern that distanced Catholics from Protestants generally, Catholics also defend reason as a source of truth, claiming in particular that there are certain preambles to the faith, such as the existence of God, that can be established through philosophical reasoning. In making this argument, Catholic theologians sought to repudiate the strong emphasis on faith alone among their Protestant counterparts.

The heart of Catholic faith and piety lies in the system of seven sacraments—Baptism, Confirmation, Eucharist, Penance, Holy Orders, Marriage, Anointing of the Sick—that are understood as signs through which the grace of God is dispensed to the faithful. The sacraments—especially the Eucharist and Penance—are administered only by ordained priests, and hence there is a close tie between the reception of the sacraments and the hierarchical priestly system.

Catholics believe that Scripture is subject to the interpretation of papal authority and that private or individual interpretation is not allowed. Until recently, most did not have much exposure to Scripture except during the Eucharist, and that was in Latin, the universal language of the church not always understood by the faithful.

Catholicism has changed significantly since the Second Vatican Council of 1964. There, a wide range of documents thoroughly revamped the practice of the faith, as well as the dominant theology inherited since the sixteenth century. A call for liturgical renewal, the setting aside of Latin as the required language of the liturgy, an understanding of the church that is turned toward the outside world, an emphasis on the collegiality of bishops in harmony with papal authority, and a renewed emphasis on the involvement of the laity

set off major changes in the way Catholics understood themselves. Progress toward establishing a dialogue with the Eastern Orthodox Church has also been made.

In East Central Europe, Poland was and remained a bulwark of Catholicism. The role of the Habsburg ruler as Holy Roman Emperor, until the nineteenth century, also ensured that the lands under the control of Vienna would be strongly pro-Catholic. After the fall of the region to communism in the wake of World War II, the church remained a strong moral voice and force, one that often, as in the case of Hungarian Cardinal József Mindszenty (1899–1975), confronted the authorities. The power of the church forced many of the regimes to seek a rapprochement with the Vatican (such as Hungary in 1974) and/or leave the church relatively untouched (as in Poland, where 95 percent of the population is Catholic). The election of John Paul II (1920–), a native of Poland, the first non-Italian pope in centuries, gave an important boost to resistance to communism.

In the Balkans, Catholics make up but a small minority of the overall population.

Eugene F. Bales

Further reading

Adam, Karl. *The Spirit of Catholicism.* Garden City, New York, 1954.

Foy, Felician. *A Concise Guide to the Catholic Church.* Huntington, Indiana, 1984.

McBrien, Richard P. *Catholicism.* San Francisco, 1994.

Michel, Patrick. *Politics and Religion in Eastern Europe: Catholicism in Hungary, Poland, Czechoslovakia.* Oxford, 1991.

See also József Glemp; John Paul II; József Mindszenty; Orthodoxy; PAX; Protestantism; Uniate Church; Stefan Wyszyński

Ceauşescu, Elena (c. 1919–89)

Wife of Romanian President Nicolae Ceauşescu (1918–89). Born a peasant in the village of Petreşti, Elena Petrescu moved to Bucharest and met her future husband when both were teenagers involved in illegal Communist activities. A textile worker, she married Nicolae upon his release from prison after World War II. They had two sons and a daughter, and Elena eventually received a doctorate in chemistry, reportedly owing to political influence rather than intellectual labor. After Ceauşescu became head of the Romanian Communist Party (RCP) in 1965, his wife moved into politics: National Council on Scientific Research (1965); Bucharest Municipal Party Committee (1968); RCP Central Committee (1972); RCP Executive Committee (1973); RCP Bureau (1977); president of the National Council on Science and Technology (1979); first vice president of the Council of Ministers (1980). Her husband's informal assistant on all matters, by the late 1970s she was part of his personality cult; like his, her birthday became an occasion for public rejoicing, although her age was never announced. Portrayed as a wife, mother, and scientist—the perfect socialist woman—she was widely hated because of her unpleasant personality and her close association with Ceauşescu's policy of forced population growth that prohibited contraception and abortion. A devoted couple to the end, the Ceauşescus were tried and executed together on Christmas Day, 1989.

Mary Ellen Fischer

Further reading

Behr, Edward. *Kiss the Hand You Cannot Bite: The Rise and Fall of the Ceauşescus.* New York, 1991.

Fischer, Mary Ellen. *Nicolae Ceauşescu: A Study in Political Leadership.* Boulder, Colorado, 1989.

———. "Women in Romanian Politics: Elena Ceauşescu, Pronatalism, and the Promotion of Women," in Sharon L. Wolchik and Alfred G. Meyer, eds. *Women, State, and Party in Eastern Europe.* Durham, North Carolina, 1985.

Pacepa, Ion Mihai. *Red Horizons: Chronicles of a Communist Spy Chief.* Washington, D.C., 1987.

See also Nicolae Ceauşescu; Communist Party of Romania; Women in Romania

Ceauşescu, Nicolae (1918–89)

President of Romania until his execution on Christmas Day, 1989. Born a peasant in Scorniceşti, Ceauşescu became a shoemaker's apprentice in Bucharest at the age of eleven. Arrested and jailed for Communist activities in the 1930s, he spent the war with Gheorghe Gheorghiu-Dej (1901–65) and other Communists in Romanian prison camps.

Released in 1945, Ceauşescu rose rapidly in the Romanian Communist Party (RCP) under Gheorghiu-Dej. Deputy minister of the armed forces in 1950–54, then Central Committee secretary, and by 1955 a full member of the Political Bureau, he eventually was RCP cadre secretary.

Elected general secretary after Gheorghiu-Dej's death in 1965, Ceauşescu outmaneuvered rivals such as Gheorghe Apostol (1913–) and Alexandru Drăghici (1919–) and by 1969 dominated the RCP. In 1974 the post of president was created especially for him, and for the rest of his life a cult of personality centered on him and his wife, Elena (c. 1919–89). Together the couple ruled Romania in a highly personalized and arbitrary fashion, promoting many family members to high positions.

Despite his anti-Soviet foreign policy in the 1960s, during the 1970s, Ceauşescu introduced Stalinist economic policies of rapid industrial growth and low living standards. Frustrated by a growing foreign debt, he reduced imports and increased exports in the 1980s, making Romanians cold and hungry while the ruling couple lived in ostentatious luxury. Widespread hatred for the Ceauşescus was intensified by a policy of forced population growth, outlawing contraceptives and abortions. Nevertheless, Ceauşescu's shrewd political strategies, his appeals to nationalism, and his merciless use of the ubiquitous secret police kept him firmly in control until December 1989, when demonstrations forced him and his wife to flee Bucharest by helicopter. They were soon captured, tried, and executed, protesting to the end their innocence and their right to rule.

Mary Ellen Fischer

Further reading

Behr, Edward. *Kiss the Hand You Cannot Bite: The Rise and Fall of the Ceauşescus.* New York, 1991.

Fischer, Mary Ellen. *Nicolae Ceauşescu: A Study in Political Leadership.* Boulder, Colorado, 1989.

Pacepa, Ion Mihai. *Red Horizons: Chronicles of a Communist Spy Chief.* Washington, D.C., 1987.

Shafir, Michael. *Romania: Politics, Economics, and Society.* Boulder, Colorado, 1985.

See also Gheorghe Apostol; Elena Ceauşescu; Communist Party of Romania; Gheorghe

Gheorghiu-Dej; Nationalism; Revolutions of 1989; Systematization; Women in Romania

Censorship

Any official restriction imposed on free expression by governments or other authorities with the power to do so (military authorities, the church, the ruling political party, among others). In Eastern Europe, both main forms of censorship, preventive and punitive, existed with few and brief historical exceptions until 1989. Before religious tolerance prevailed in the eighteenth and nineteenth centuries in the whole area, secular powers traditionally exercised controls charted mainly by the church. In those parts of the Balkans still under Ottoman control until 1817, 1878, or 1912, the situation was different; religious controls were of secondary importance, and a military type of censorship was more typical. Under different circumstances and for different periods, Bohemia, Poland, Hungary, and Saxony enjoyed various degrees of freedom of expression and of the press between the fifteenth and eighteenth centuries. In Poland, the situation differed after the partitions; the heaviest controls were exerted by the tsarist secret police in the Russian-annexed lands. The most relaxed conditions existed in Galicia, held by the Habsburgs.

Censorship played a gradually diminishing role in most of these countries between 1848 and World War I, but it continued in different forms even after the territorial reconfigurations of 1918–19. Poland between 1918 and 1939 enjoyed the greatest degree of freedom of expression and of the press in East Central Europe during the interwar period. Totalitarian press controls were imposed on East European countries occupied by Nazi Germany during World War II. The countries allied with Germany (Bulgaria, Hungary, Romania, and Slovakia) practiced their own strict controls of the media and publishing.

Strict censorship on the Soviet model was introduced in Albania and Yugoslavia as early as 1944. The same system, in a less severe form, was then already applied in Bulgaria, Hungary, Poland, and Romania. In Czechoslovakia, after a relatively free period lasting fewer than three years, Soviet-type censorship was fully applied in 1948, as it was everywhere else in Eastern Europe. Yugoslavia, which broke away from the Soviet bloc in 1948, experienced an increasing relaxation of these controls after the late 1950s. In Hungary, censorship was briefly abolished in 1956, and in Czechoslovakia in 1968.

The contents and practice of the Soviet-type censorship were decided by the leading bodies of the Communist Parties and exercised by a hierarchical control system. At the top, each Communist Party maintained a department of its Central Committee apparatus to supervise the media. Auxiliary tools included the power to launch or close down any newspaper or radio/TV station, licensing of journalists through official journalists' unions, and power of appointment. All leading editorial positions were held by highly paid party bureaucrats. One official wire service monopolized the supply of political news. In addition, there was a formal censorship institution modeled on the Soviet GLAVLIT (Main Administration for the Protection of Official and Military Secrets). One or two representatives of these agencies worked directly in all editorial offices, and no story could be printed or broadcast without their explicit approval. Among journalists and writers, autocensorship became a generally accepted practice. In East Germany, where all journalists were subject to a special system of bribes, autocensorship was for years believed to be the most effective tool of press control. This system was completely abolished after the changes in 1989. Since 1990, the constitutions of all East European countries have at least formally guaranteed freedom of expression and freedom of the press, and censorship has been explicitly prohibited in most of them. Nevertheless, it has not quite disappeared. Continued and heavy-handed government interference with the workings of the media has taken place in Croatia, for example. The Slovak government, after the breakup of Czechoslovakia, is also reported to have muzzled the opposition press and to have harassed independent journalists. Limitations also exist in Albania, Romania, and Bulgaria. Commercialization and newsroom rules used by some new publishers, mainly foreign ones, are considered a factor limiting freedom of the press in Czechoslovakia, Hungary, and Poland.

Jiří Hochman

Further reading

Brash, Walter M. and Dana Ulloth. *The Press and the State.* New York, 1986.

C

Ebon, M. *The Soviet Propaganda Machine.* New York, 1987.

Ernst, M.L. *Censorship,* New York, 1964.

Yearly Reports of the Joint Congressional Committee on Cooperation and Security in Europe on Political Freedom in Albania, Bulgaria, the Czech Republic, Croatia, Hungary, Macedonia, Poland, Romania, Slovakia, Slovenia, and Yugoslavia, 1992–94.

See also Media; Press

Černý, Jan (1874–1959)

Czech bureaucrat who was close to President Tomáš G. Masaryk (1850–1937) and the Republican Antonín Švehla (1873–1933). Černý held key administrative posts in Moravia during the Habsburg monarchy. After the creation of Czechoslovakia, he headed the administration for Moravia (1918–28) and Moravia-Silesia (1928–39), and he served in numerous posts throughout the interwar period, including prime minister, interior minister, and minister of supplies.

Daniel E. Miller

Further reading

Klimek, Antonín. *Boj o Hrad,* vol. 1, *Hrad a Pětka: Vnitropolitický vývoj Československa 1918–1926 n půdorysu zápasu o prezidentské nástupnictví.* Prague, 1996.

See also Tomáš G. Masaryk; Antonín Švehla

Chamberlain, Neville (1869–1940)

British prime minister responsible for negotiating the Munich Pact of 1938, which turned Czechoslovakia's Sudetenland over to Germany. As prime minister of Britain from 1937 to 1940, Chamberlain did not invent the policy of appeasement, with which he is so commonly associated, but it became his personal guiding principle. Despite warnings from trained diplomats, Chamberlain made it clear to Adolf Hitler (1889–1945) that the British government was eager to maintain the European peace, even at the expense of other nations.

Following the *Anschluss,* the German annexation of Austria in 1938, Chamberlain called for Czechoslovakia to come to terms with its disaffected German minority, thereby removing the German "grievance" over the Sudetenland and helping Anglo-German relations. He bullied the French into supporting this policy, but the continued breakdown of Czech–Sudeten German negotiations led ultimately to Chamberlain's decision to go to the Munich Conference. The resulting agreement only sustained Hitler's basic demands, and although Germany's subsequent conquest of Czechoslovakia in March 1939 shocked Chamberlain, he refused to acknowledge the failure of his policy. Even the subsequent British guarantees of Polish, Romanian, and Greek independence were not seen by Chamberlain as a failure of the policy of appeasement, but only as a warning to Hitler of the limits of British patience. When Germany attacked Poland on September 1, 1939, Chamberlain delayed for two days, honoring the British promise. The policy of appeasement had failed, and Chamberlain's political career would soon end with the German invasion of France in 1940.

Joel D. Benson

Further reading

Dilks, David. *Neville Chamberlain.* Cambridge, Massachusetts, 1985.

Parker, R.A.C. *Chamberlain and Appeasement: British Policy and the Coming of the Second World War.* London, 1993.

Rock, William R. *British Appeasement in the 1930s.* New York, 1977.

See also Anschluss; Adolf Hitler; Munich Pact; Sudeten Crisis; Sudetenland

Charles I (1887–1922)

Emperor of Austria and king of Hungary, and the last ruler of Austria-Hungary, who presided over the dissolution of the monarchy in 1918. The great nephew of Franz Joseph (1830–1916), Charles became heir to the throne when his uncle Franz Ferdinand (1863–1914) accepted the removal of the children of his morganatic marriage from the line of succession. On assuming the throne in 1916, Charles sought to overcome the gathering unrest in the empire caused by World War I by negotiating a compromise peace with the Entente powers and introducing a federalist reform of the empire. His attempt to negotiate with France and Great Britain through his brother-in-law, Sixtus of Bourbon-Parma (1886–1934), failed, and the revelation of his offer of French annexation of Alsace-Lorraine forced Charles to agree to the subordination of Austria-Hungary to its German ally at a meeting with the German high command in May 1918. Plans for an internal political reform of the empire based on the extension of rights to the minorities faltered on Hungarian and German resistance, and Charles's proclamation of a federalist reorganization of the empire in October 1918 did not satisfy the empire's nationalities or delay the collapse of the monarchy. After renouncing his powers, Charles withdrew to Switzerland, from which he twice attempted to return as king of Hungary in 1921, but his regent, Admiral Miklós Horthy (1868–1957), blocked both attempts. Removed from Central Europe under British supervision, Charles died in exile on Madeira.

Philip Pajakowski

Further reading

Brook-Shepard, Gordon. *The Last Habsburg.* New York, 1968.
Lorenz, Richard. *Kaiser Karl und der Untergang der Donaumonarchie.* Graz, 1959.
May, Arthur J. *The Passing of the Hapsburg Monarchy, 1914–1918.* Philadelphia, 1966.

See also Franz Ferdinand; Franz Joseph; Miklós Horthy; World War I

Charles University

The first university in Central Europe, founded in 1348 by Emperor Charles IV (1316–78). Located in Prague, Charles University was best known in its early years as the center for Jan Hus's (1369–1415) protest against abuses in the Catholic Church. It lost some of its intellectual stature during the Counter-Reformation that accompanied and followed the Thirty Years' War (1618–48). In 1654 the original Carolinum was merged with the Jesuit Klementinum, and the university became known as Charles Ferdinand University.

During the second half of the nineteenth century, the University of Prague (as it was known at the time) served as the center of Czech intellectual life. Its four faculties (theology, philosophy, law, and medicine) began to regain their international prominence. Following the electoral victory of Prime Minister Eduard Taaffe's (1833–95) Iron Ring in 1879—a coalition of German conservative, Czech, and Polish politicians—Czechs received several concessions from the government, including the division of the University of Prague

into autonomous Czech and German sections in 1882. By 1890–91, the Czech University in Prague had 122 faculty and 2,507 students, only 4 of whom declared their nationality as German. The German University (excluding the theological faculty, which had not been divided) had 142 faculty and 1,468 students, 136 of whom declared their nationality as Czech. Rival student organizations and protests contributed to nationalist conflicts in Prague in the late nineteenth century.

With the founding of the Czechoslovak Republic in 1918, the university was renamed Charles University. It remained divided into Czech and German sections until 1939 and was the dominant university in Czechoslovakia. The Czech university was closed November 17, 1939, following the establishment of the German Protectorate of Bohemia and Moravia. University students and professors were among those targeted for arrest during the German occupation.

Charles University reopened in 1945; it was taken over by the Communists in 1948, and a number of students and faculty were expelled at that time. Charles University became the site of intellectual ferment in the 1960s, culminating in the Prague Spring of 1967–68, when students and faculty were among the most active supporters of "socialism with a human face." Intellectual freedoms were once again suppressed with the "normalization" that followed the Warsaw Pact invasion of Czechoslovakia in August 1968. By the mid-1980s, however, student dissatisfaction with the lack of intellectual freedom had begun to grow, and a student demonstration on November 17, 1989, commemorating the suppression of the universities under German rule, provoked police brutality and prompted the outbreak of the "velvet revolution" in Czechoslovakia, which overthrew the Communist regime.

Catherine Albrecht

Further reading

Connelly, John. "Creating the Socialist Elite: Communist Higher Education Policies in the Czech Lands, East Germany, and Poland." Ph.D. diss., Harvard University, 1994.
Kavka, František, ed. *Dějiny Univerzity Karlovy,* 4 vols. Prague, 1995–98.
———. *Stručné dějiny Univerzity Karlovy.* Prague, 1964.
Odložilík, Otakar. *The Caroline University, 1348–1948.* Prague, 1948.

C

Petráň, Josef. *Nástin dějin filozofické fakulty Univerzity Karlovy v Praze (do roku 1948)*. Prague, 1983.

Seibt, Ferdinand, ed. *Die Teilung der Prager Universität 1882 und die intellektuelle Desintegration in den böhmischen Ländern*. Munich, 1984.

Skilling, H. Gordon. "The Partition of the University in Prague." *Slavonic and East European Review* 27 (1949): 430–49.

See also Higher Education; Prague Spring; Protectorate of Bohemia and Moravia; Eduard Taaffe; Velvet Revolution

Charter 77

The human rights declaration of Czechoslovak dissidents submitted to the Czechoslovak government in January 1977, as well as the organization that reported on human rights violations by the Czechoslovak government in the 1970s and 1980s. In 1975 the Czechoslovak government agreed to the international Helsinki Accords, which guaranteed "human rights and basic freedoms, including those of thought, conscience, religion, and creed." The following year, on October 13, 1976, the Czechoslovak government passed Law No. 120, which incorporated the International Agreement on Civil and Political Rights and the International Agreement on Economic, Social, and Cultural Rights.

Soon after the passage of Law No. 120, a group of Czechoslovak dissidents banded together and wrote the Charter 77 document to petition the government to uphold the human rights that the new law guaranteed. The group of 617 original signatories included committed Marxists, who believed that their government did not uphold the ideals of socialism; Roman Catholic leaders, whose main concern was freedom of religion; and liberal intellectuals, who fought for freedom of expression.

Charter 77 was not a political organization with a specific program or platform. Three official spokespersons constituted the rotating leadership of Charter 77 and submitted reports to the government when human rights were violated. Topics of these reports included police brutality, artistic freedom, women's rights, and injustice in the educational system.

The leaders of Charter 77 were persecuted for their participation in the movement. Future president Václav Havel (1936–) was imprisoned

following the submission of the charter, and philosopher Jan Patočka (1907–77) died during police interrogation.

Cynthia Paces

Further reading

Laber, Jeri, ed. *A Decade of Dedication: Charter 77, 1977 to 1987*. New York, 1987.

Riese, Hans-Peter. *Since the Prague Spring: Charter '77 and the Struggle for Human Rights in Czechoslovakia*. New York, 1979.

Skilling, H. Gordon. *Charter 77 and Human Rights in Czechoslovakia*. Boston, 1981.

See also Civic Forum; Václav Havel; Velvet Revolution

Chelm

City and province in eastern Poland. Chelm province was established in 1975 and has an area of 1,493 square miles (3,866 sq km). The Bug River separates the province from Belarus and Ukraine on the east. Lublin province is to the west, Zamość province to the south; and Biała-Podlaska province to the north. Other rivers that flow through the province include the Wieprz, the Udal, and the Siennica, as well as the Wieprz-Krzna drainage canal.

Chelm province is a lightly settled agricultural district producing rye, potatoes, and sugar beets; coal extraction also plays a large part in the local economy. The 1991 population of the province was 247,200. The city of Chelm is located on the Uherka River, a tributary of the Bug, 15 miles (24 km) west of the Ukraine border. The city is a processing and trade center for the surrounding region.

The city and province fell under Austrian control with the third partition of Poland in 1795 and were restored as part of the Congress Kingdom of Poland under Russian rule in 1815; they have remained part of Polish territory since then.

During World War II, a Nazi extermination camp, Sobibór, was established by the village of the same name, near the Ukrainian border, where 250,000 Jews died. Another 90,000 people died in the two German prison camps near the city. In 1944 Chelm was the first Polish city taken by the Red Army. The new Polish Republic was proclaimed in Chelm on July 22, 1944.

Chelm has been important as an industrial center and capital of the province since the thirteenth century. The economic base of the city includes coal mining and other mineral extraction, food processing (flour milling), brewing (liquor distillery), textile processing (especially wool), glass, cement, furniture, and machinery production. Chalk is quarried in the surrounding area. Chelm is also an important rail junction. The city's population grew from 46,000 in 1974 to 64,800 by 1989.

Barbara VanDrasek

Further reading

Davies, Norman. *God's Playground: A History of Poland,* vol. 2, *1795 to the Present.* New York, 1982.

Held, Joseph. *Dictionary of East European History since 1945.* Westport, Connecticut. 1994.

Hoffman, George W., ed. *Europe in the 1990s: A Geographic Analysis,* 6th ed. New York, 1990.

See also Polish Congress Kingdom

Chervenkov, Vulko (1900–1980)

Leader of the Bulgarian Communist Party in exile and during the postwar reconstruction of Bulgaria. Chervenkov joined the party in 1919, rising quickly to a position of leadership. In 1923 he became secretary of the Sofia Communist Youth League, advancing to its Central Committee the following year. Two years later, following an abortive Communist uprising, Chervenkov began a twenty-year exile in the Soviet Union. There he underwent training with the Soviet secret police and served as a lecturer.

During World War II, Chervenkov was associated with Radio Khristo Botev, which directed propaganda toward Bulgaria from Moscow. In the fall of 1944, after an uprising installed the Fatherland Front government (a Communist-led coalition) in Sofia, Chervenkov returned to Bulgaria, becoming a full member of the Bulgarian Communist Party Politburo the following year. Now at liberty to implement his and Stalin's (1879–1953) ideas, Chervenkov's star rose rapidly. Taking advantage of the Tito-Stalin dispute of 1948, Chervenkov helped purge the Bulgarian Communist Party, becoming prime minister of the state and general secretary of the party after the death of Georgi Dimitrov (1882–1949). From these heights, he directed the course of Bulgaria's continuing socialization.

The death of Stalin and the rise of Nikita Khrushchev (1894–1971) in the Soviet Union brought troubles for Chervenkov, as it did for many old-line East European Communists. In 1954 he resigned as general secretary and in 1956 stepped down as prime minister following serious criticism of his own "cult of the individual." In 1961, following the Twenty-second Soviet Party Congress in Moscow, Chervenkov was expelled from the Bulgarian Politburo and the following year from the party itself.

Michael Boll

Further reading

Bell, John D. *The Bulgarian Communist Party from Blagoev to Zhivkov.* Stanford, California, 1977.

Crampton, R.J. *A Short History of Modern Bulgaria.* Cambridge, 1987.

Oren, Nisan. *Bulgarian Communism: The Road to Power.* New York, 1971.

See also Communist Party of Bulgaria; Georgi Dimitrov; Fatherland Front; Stalin; Tito-Stalin Split

Cheta

Small groups (pl. *cheti*) of armed revolutionaries, usually organized in Serbia or Romania, who launched raids against Ottoman forces to gain Bulgarian independence during the nineteenth century. In 1841 Bulgarian Vasil Hadzhivulkov (n.d.), along with a Serbian captain, organized a *cheta* in Brăila in Wallachia and crossed the Danube into Bulgaria to incite a rebellion among the peasantry. Although the incursion failed, other revolutionaries continued to organize *cheti* with the same dismal results until the late 1860s, when they began to focus on internal agitation. Georgi Rakovski (1821–67), who participated in the failed uprising of 1841, fought with the Russians in the Crimean War (1853–56) and formed the Bulgarian legion in Belgrade in 1862. Later that year, Rakovski moved to Bucharest after quarreling with the Serbs over the question of future national boundaries and a recent raid against the Turkish garrison in Belgrade. In Romania, Rakovski secured the political support of the government and the financial backing of the Bulgarian merchant communities for his activities. In the spring of 1866 he sent two contingents of *cheti* across the Danube and the Turks decimated them. Alarmed Bulgarian merchants subsequently

C refused to support future revolutionary movements, and Rakovski died of tuberculosis in 1867. The last significant attempt to foment mass rebellion with *cheta* tactics occurred in 1868. Hadzhi Dimitur (d. 1868) and Stefan Karadzha (n.d.) organized a *cheta* that was to cross the Danube, establish a revolutionary government in the Stara Planina (Balkan Mountains), and precipitate an uprising. In July 1868 over one hundred men crossed the Danube and were crushed.

Gregory L. Bruess

Further reading

Crampton, R.J. *A Short History of Modern Bulgaria.* Cambridge, 1987.

Genchev, Nikolai. *The Bulgarian National Revival Period.* Sofia, 1977.

Jelavich, Barbara. *History of the Balkans: Eighteenth and Nineteenth Centuries.* Cambridge, 1983.

See also Georgi Rakovski

Chetniks

Loosely organized group of Serbian guerrilla fighters formed in Yugoslavia during World War II. Remnants of the royal Yugoslav army retreated to the countryside after the German invasion in April 1941 and called themselves Chetnik Detachments of the Yugoslav Army in reference to similar armed bands that engaged in guerrilla warfare against Ottoman rule. Colonel Draža Mihailović (1893–1946), a member of the army general staff, became the supreme Chetnik commander. The Chetnik movement drew its members almost exclusively from the Serbian population and maintained units in Serbia, Montenegro, Bosnia-Hercegovina, and areas of Croatia inhabited by Serbs. Throughout the war, the Chetniks remained loyal to the king and the Yugoslav government-in-exile in London. Mihailović and his fellow Chetniks wanted to protect Serbian interests and to maintain the position of dominance Serbia had enjoyed in prewar Yugoslavia.

During the initial months of the war, the Chetniks cooperated on a limited basis with the Communist-led Partisans, another resistance movement in wartime Yugoslavia. However, the two movements split in November 1941 because of fundamental differences in philosophy and tactics. Mihailović was strongly anti-Communist and also opposed a mass insurgency because it might waste manpower and expose Serb civilians to brutal German reprisals. He decided to build Chetnik forces and to wait for the tide of war to turn against the Axis. In contrast, the Partisans favored immediate attacks on the German invaders. Ultimately, the Chetnik and Partisan differences degenerated into civil war, and the Chetniks subsequently considered the Partisans as their primary enemy. The Chetniks also attacked Croat villages in retaliation for the masscres of Serbs by the Ustaša (the Croatian ultranationalist organization) and, on several occasions, destroyed Muslim villages in southwestern Bosnia. In general, the Chetniks avoided direct confrontation with either Italian or German forces. On the contrary, they frequently cooperated with them in attacks on the Partisans.

In the first years of the war, the British supported the Chetniks as the official armed force of the Yugoslav government-in-exile. This situation changed in 1943 when the British determined that the Chetniks were not fighting the Germans but were instead collaborating with them to fight the Partisans. The British then withdrew support from the Chetniks and began aiding the Partisans, who were actively resisting the German occupation.

With this development, Chetnik fortunes quickly waned. Chetniks suffered a series of defeats to Partisan forces beginning in late 1943 and were no longer a credible fighting force by 1945. At war's end, the new Communist-dominated Yugoslav government imprisoned or executed the remaining Chetnik fighters. Mihailović was finally captured in March 1946, convicted of treason in a public show trial, and executed in July.

Paul D. Lensink

Further reading

Milazzo, Matteo. *The Chetnik Movement and the Yugoslav Resistance.* Baltimore, Maryland, 1975.

Roberts, Walter. *Tito, Mihailović, and the Allies, 1941–1945.* New Brunswick, New Jersey, 1973.

Tomasevich, Jozo. *War and Revolution in Yugoslavia, 1941–1945: The Chetniks.* Stanford, California, 1975.

See also Antifascism; Axis; Dragoljub Mihailović; Muslims; Ustaša; World War II

Chiftlik

Large private farms employing sharecropper labor that were a feature of the landed economy in certain areas of the Ottoman Empire by the eighteenth century. They were bound up with long-term developments in the empire including the decentralization of governmental authority, increasing state fiscal problems, commercialization of agriculture, and a decline in the economic and social status of the peasantry. *Chiftliks* as private estates existed in the sixteenth century. They were grants made by sultans as well as marginal land taken over for use in animal husbandry or cultivation of cotton and rice. During the seventeenth century in the Balkans, there was a decrease in rural population, grain prices tended to fall, animal husbandry became more prominent, social disorder in the form of banditry grew, the earlier feudal *timar* land system declined, and the state turned to leasing land as tax farms in an effort to raise needed revenue. Provincial notables took advantage of these developments to secure greater power locally and boost their economic standing by taking over tax farms. With the upswing in the Ottoman and world economies in the eighteenth century, the number of *chiftliks* grew as the cultivation of cotton, tobacco, cereals, and maize increased. Many *chiftliks* were devoted to livestock. The opening up of the Ottoman economy to the European market in the nineteenth century brought a pronounced rise in agricultural exports. In the Balkans, *chiftliks* were found in low-lying areas in Macedonia, Thrace, and Thessaly. But they were not the dominant form of agricultural unit. Located as they were on marginal land and with the lack of an abundant and cheap labor force, *chiftliks* never amounted to more than a small percentage of the land use system. Instead, smaller, upland peasant holdings predominated. Seen by some as characteristic of feudal society and others as part of the emerging world of bourgeois commerce, they reflected elements of both worlds but were really a response to particular developments in the Ottoman Empire.

Gerasimos Augustinos

Further reading

Adanir, Fikret. "Tradition and Rural Change in Southeastern Europe during Ottoman Rule," in *The Origins of Backwardness in Eastern Europe,* ed. by Daniel Chirot. Seattle, Washington, 1989.

Inalcik, Halil. "The Emergence of Big Farms, Chiftliks: State, Landlords and Tenants," in *Contributions à l'histoire économique et sociale de l'empire ottoman,* Collection Turcica 3. Louvain, 1984.

McGowan, Bruce. *Economic Life in Ottoman Europe: Taxation, Trade and the Struggle for Land, 1660–1800.* Cambridge, Massachusetts, 1981.

See also Agriculture; Ottoman Empire; Peasants; *Timar*

Chişinău

Capital and largest city of the Republic of Moldova and historic capital of the Bessarabia region. Situated on the Bîc River in south-central Bessarabia, Chişinău (Russian, Kishinev) had a 1989 population of 715,000, of which 51 percent were ethnic Romanians/Moldovans, 25 percent Russians, 14 percent Ukrainians, and 5 percent Jews.

The earliest reference to Chişinău as a settlement dates from 1466. Over the next four hundred years, it grew into a significant regional trading center but was repeatedly razed as warring parties passed back and forth between Russia and southeastern Europe. In 1818 it was named the administrative center of Bessarabia after the Russian Empire annexed the region from the Ottomans in 1812. Chişinău, like the Bessarabian province in general, remained a backward corner of the Russian Empire, an area to which Russian poet Alexander Pushkin (1799–1837) was exiled in the 1820s and that served as an out-of-the-way headquarters for the underground Russian socialist newspaper *Iskra* (*Spark*) after 1901. The city achieved international notoriety in 1903 as a result of a major anti-Jewish pogrom there. In 1940 it became the capital of the newly created Moldovan Soviet Socialist Republic.

Charles King

Further reading

Judge, Edward H. *Easter in Kishinev: Anatomy of a Pogrom.* New York, 1992.

Shukhat, M. *Moldavia: A Guide.* Moscow, 1986.

See also Bessarabian Question; Moldova, Birth of the Republic of; Pogrom

Chitalishte

Local Bulgarian cultural-educational organs of town and village community boards that played a

C

significant role in popularizing education, literacy, publishing, music, and drama during the later decades of the Bulgarian national revival. In Bulgarian, the term *chitalishte* can mean "reading room," "library," "literary/cultural club," and "community center," all of which were functions served by local community boards (which came to be denoted by the term as well).

The first *chitalishta* (pl.) were founded during 1856 in the towns of Svishtov, Shumen, and Lom as an outgrowth of the 1856 *Hatti hümayun* reform manifesto pressed on the Ottoman authorities by the European Great Powers following the Crimean War (1853–56). In part, the manifesto permitted the empire's subjects local self-administration of educational and cultural activities. Newly founded *chitalishta* supplemented the educational activities of Bulgarian school boards (first established in 1835) by offering weekend classes for those unable to attend ordinary primary and secondary institutions, and they disseminated cultural and nationalist books and periodicals through their libraries and reading rooms.

During the 1870s, many *chitalishta* served as underground Bulgarian revolutionary organs. By 1878, and the official creation of the autonomous Bulgarian Principality at the Congress of Berlin, 131 *chitalishta* operated in Bulgarian-inhabited areas. Following 1878, they continued operating in Bulgaria as literary-cultural centers, officially organized under the Union of National Chitalishta in 1911. There were 480 *chitalishta* in 1944, many of which were pro-socialist. During the Communist period, they were integrated institutionally into the Fatherland Front, the Communist-dominated coalition that seized power in 1944, and their number expanded.

Dennis P. Hupchick

Further reading

Chilingirov, Stiliian. *Bŭlgarskite chitalishta predi Osvobozhdenieto: Prinos kŭm istoriiata na Bŭlgarskoto vŭzrazhdane.* Sofia, 1930.

Genchev, Nikolai. *Bŭlgarsko vŭzrazhdane,* 3rd ed. Sofia, 1988.

Kosev, Dimitŭr, et al. eds. *Istoriia na Bŭlgariia,* vol. 6. Sofia, 1987.

See also Bulgarian Culture; Congress of Berlin; Crimean War; Education; Fatherland Front; *Tanzimat*

Chłopicki, Józef (1771–1854)

General and briefly dictator of Poland during the 1830 November Uprising against the Russians. Born into a minor Polish noble family, Chłopicki entered the Polish army in 1785 and participated in campaigns against Russia during the final partitions of Poland (1792, 1794). In 1797 Chłopicki joined the Polish Legions under Napoléon (1769–1821). He commanded the legions during the Peninsula War against the British in Spain, receiving the French Legion of Honor.

After the establishment of the Kingdom of Poland in 1815, Chłopicki commanded a Polish army division. In 1818 he resigned his commission after quarreling with Grand Duke Constantine (1779–1831), Alexander I's (1777–1825) brother and commander in chief of the Polish army. His principled stand won him popularity with the Poles, who hated the brutal Constantine.

The outbreak of the November Uprising distressed the politically conservative Chłopicki, and he distanced himself from the revolutionaries. After moderate elements led by Prince Adam Czartoryski (1770–1861) gained control of events in Warsaw, however, Chłopicki consented to become dictator on December 5, 1830. Nevertheless, Chłopicki was convinced that the uprising had no chance of success. He hoped for a negotiated settlement with Russia and did little to prepare the Polish army for battle. When Nicholas I (1796–1855) rejected Polish overtures for a negotiated settlement and the revolution's leadership passed into more radical hands, Chłopicki resigned as dictator on February 18, 1830. Yet he remained de facto commander in chief of the Polish army. Chłopicki was seriously wounded at the Battle of Grochów on February 25, 1831, and went into retirement at Kraków.

Frank W. Thackeray

Further reading

Davies, Norman. *God's Playground: A History of Poland,* 2 vols. New York, 1982.

Skowronek, Jerzy and Maria Żmigrodzka, eds. *Powstanie Listopadowe, 1830–1831.* Wrocław, 1983.

Tarczyński, Marek, *Generalicja Powstania Listopadowego.* Warsaw, 1980.

See also Alexander I; Constantine; Adam Czartoryski; Napoléon; Nicholas I; November Uprising; Polish Congress Kingdom

Chopin, Frédéric François (Fryderyk Franciszek) (1810–49)

Polish composer and pianist whose artistic creations exhibited the expressive strengths of his instrument and drew upon the folk idiom of his homeland. The son of a French tutor who had settled in Poland during the Napoleonic period, Chopin received his early musical training from Adalbert Żywny (1756–1842). In his youth he became the darling of Polish nobility and throughout his life was accepted into aristocratic circles. He studied composition in Warsaw from 1826 to 1829 with well-known musician Józef Elsner (1769–1854), who allowed him to develop an individual style. He left Warsaw on the eve of the November 1830 insurrection against the Russians, eventually settling in Paris. There he composed piano music suited to salon settings and taught aristocratic students. In 1837 Chopin began a decade-long romantic relationship with the writer George Sand (1804–1876). Long-term ill health from pulmonary disease led to his early death in 1849.

Chopin's music exhibits a balance of classical form and romantic inspiration with national motives. His Polish identity is found primarily in the mazurkas and polonaises. The influence of Polish folk music explains some of the defiance of melodic and harmonic convention in his music. Nevertheless, Chopin is viewed as a more cosmopolitan composer than strict nationalist in his artistic achievements. The mythic view of his short life and exile from martyred Poland received a sympathetic response in Western Europe. To this day, Chopin claims the musical soul of Poland.

William Smialek

Further reading

Atwood, William G. *Fryderyk Chopin: Pianist from Warsaw.* New York, 1987.

Kobylańska, Krystyna. *Frédéric Chopin: Thematisch-Bibliographisches Werkverzeichnis.* Munich, 1979.

Samson, Jim. *The Music of Chopin.* Oxford, 1988.

See also Folk Music; Music; November Uprising

Chorin, Ferenc (1879–1964)

Powerful Hungarian industrial magnate. Great-grandson of the learned Aaron Chorin (1766–1844), who migrated to Hungary in 1789, and son of the founder of the Chorin industrial dynasty of the same name, Ferenc Chorin earned a law degree in 1901 and later became the general manager (1918) and still later the president (1925) of the family-owned Salgótarján Coal Mines. In 1925 Chorin was elected vice president and in 1928 president of the National Association of Manufacturers [*GYOSZ*] (1928–42). In 1927 he was appointed a life member of the upper house of parliament. His Jewish background made him less than fully acceptable in the inner circles of Hungarian society, yet Chorin was still a close confidant and an ardent supporter of Admiral Miklós Horthy (1868–1957), the interwar Hungarian regent. Like the regime, he too lacked sensitivity to the needs of the rural poor and the urban proletariat. Although protected by Horthy, Nazi German pressure still forced him out of public life in 1942. Following Germany's occupation of Hungary in April 1944, Chorin was permitted to leave the country after transferring his property to the German Gestapo. Between 1947 and 1964, he lived in New York City, where he founded several businesses and was also active in Hungarian cultural and social life.

Steven Béla Várdy

Further reading

Braham, Randolph L. *The Politics of Genocide: The Holocaust in Hungary,* 2 vols. New York, 1982; rev. ed., 1994.

Macartney, C.A. *A History of Hungary, 1929–1945,* 2 vols. New York, 1956–57.

McCagg, William O. *Jewish Nobles and Geniuses in Modern Hungary.* New York, 1972; reprint 1986.

See also Miklós Horthy

Churchill, Winston (1874–1965)

British prime minister. Serving at the Admiralty during World War I, Churchill supported the 1915 Dardanelles campaign during World War I as a means to break the stalemate on the western front. This attempt to force the Turkish straits and open direct communication with Russia failed, and Churchill resigned from government under heavy political attack. As secretary of war in 1919, Churchill urged the British government to press Poland to attack the Bolsheviks.

Although out of office from 1929 to 1939, Churchill feared the Nazi German threat to Eastern

C Europe and severely criticized the Munich Agreement of 1938, which gave Czechoslovakia's Sudetenland to Germany. In 1940, after the outbreak of World War II in Europe, the failure of the British expedition to Norway and the German invasion of the Low Countries and France forged a coalition government under Churchill's commitment to the total defeat of Nazi Germany. With the German attack on the Soviet Union in June 1941 and the entrance of the United States into the war in December, Churchill argued for an early, full-scale attack through the Balkans, "the under-belly of the Axis," but failed to win acceptance from the Americans. In September 1944 Churchill flew to Moscow to discuss the political future of Eastern Europe. The resulting "Percentages Agreement," in which Stalin (1879–1953) and Churchill "divided" the interests of their respective countries in Eastern Europe, did not affect Poland, and following the Yalta Conference in February 1945, which dealt with the future of Europe, he urged the United States to allow Allied troops to thrust as far as possible into Eastern Europe to forestall Soviet gains in the region; however, he could not convince the Americans to support his views.

With the end of the war, the Labour Party won control of the British House of Commons. As leader of the parliamentary opposition, Churchill was still deeply concerned with foreign policy, and in March 1946, at Fulton, Missouri, he called for Britain and the United States to halt the spread of Soviet communism, which had already divided Europe with an "iron curtain."

Joel D. Benson

Further reading

Ashley, Maurice. *Churchill: As Historian.* New York, 1968.

Churchill, Randolph S. and Martin Gilbert. *Winston S. Churchill,* 8 vols. Boston, 1966–88.

Gilbert, Martin. *Churchill: A Life.* New York, 1991.

Stansky, Peter, ed. *Churchill: A Profile.* New York, 1973.

See also Iron Curtain; Munich Pact; Percentages Agreement; Stalin; World War II; Yalta

Cieszkowski, August (1814–94)

Polish philosopher and activist, prominent as a follower of German philosopher Hegel (1770–1831) and as author of *Ojcze Nasz* (*Our Father*), the summa of Polish messianism, a movement that appeared during the mid-nineteenth century linking Polish culture and history with the revolutionary processes calling for a rebirth of Poland. Born into an aristocratic family, Cieszkowski studied philosophy in Berlin. His *Prolegomena zur Historiosophie* (*Prolegomena to Historiosophy,* 1838) challenged Hegelianism to become a philosophy of action. Cieszkowski's call for praxis (the practical application of philosophy) was picked up by the radical Hegelian Left, by Russian thinkers such as Alexander Herzen (1812–70), and eventually by Karl Marx (1818–83), although Cieszkowski's own outlook, as a devout Catholic, was ideologically very distant from that of Marx.

Cieszkowski was closely connected with reformist/socialist groups in France throughout the 1840s, writing such works as *Du Crédit et de la circulation* (*Of Credit and Circulation,* 1839) and *De la Pairie et de l'aristocratie moderne* (*Of Peerage and Modern Aristocracy,* 1844). He also became increasingly active in Polish life in Posen (Polish, Poznań) Province. Arguing that the times called for "organic" construction and "association," he launched numerous initiatives in agriculture, education, and publishing. Cieszkowski represented Posen in the Prussian diet for many years and was prominent in the political events of 1848.

Cieszkowski's opus magnum, *Our Father,* is a multivolume reflection on the Lord's Prayer as the prophecy of an imminent third era where Christianity will acquire a social content. Cieszkowski worked on this book virtually all his life. Only a small part, however, was published (anonymously) in his lifetime, because of his fear of offending the church. *Our Father* is a striking combination of Christian millenarianism, utopian socialism, and Hegelian dialectics.

André Liebich

Further reading

Liebich, André. *Between Ideology and Utopia: The Politics and Philosophy of August Cieszkowski.* Dordrecht, Netherlands, 1979.

———, ed. *Selected Writings of August Cieskowski.* Cambridge, Massachusetts 1979.

Walicki, Andrzej. *Philosophy and Romantic Nationalism: The Case of Poland.* Oxford, 1982.

See also Philosophy; Polish Culture

Cinema

Throughout Central and southeastern Europe, the cinema industries began developing in the early twentieth century. Film art in turn enjoyed growing popularity. Early pioneers in the cinema included Gustav Machatý (1901–63) from Czechoslovakia, Alexander Ford (1908–80) and Wanda Jakubowska (1907–) from Poland, and Sándor (Alexander) Korda (1893–1956) and Mihály Kertész (Michael Curtiz) (1888–1962) from Hungary. Along with mainstream cinema, a specific tradition of Yiddish-language films peaked in Poland during the 1930s.

Although cinema was a popular art form before World War II, major developments occurred after the postwar Communist takeovers. The state viewed cinema as socially and culturally important art. As such, the film industries were nationalized, and centralized organizations were created to coordinate all spending related to the cinema: production, exhibition, distribution, import-export, and education. Film production was funded by the state. A centralized system of exhibition also came into being. Several film schools were also opened, including the Prague Film School (FAMU), the Budapest Academy of Film and Theater, and the Hungarian experimental studio named after film historian and theoretician Béla Balázs (1884–1949). Film departments were also established at theater schools in Belgrade, Sofia, and Bucharest. The centralized system also included censorship mechanisms that varied from country to country. As a result of censorship, some films were shelved and not released for years, usually owing to ideological considerations.

National film festivals were held in all countries. The most important international forums for filmmakers were Karlový Varý in Czechoslovakia and the Belgrade Film Fest, along with the Moscow International Film Festival. Filmmakers from Eastern Europe garnered international recognition and many received numerous prestigious international awards.

East European filmmakers have been preoccupied with major moral issues, displaying a preference for exploring the gloomiest sides of human life and social reality. They have largely ignored the entertainment conventions of Hollywood-style filmmaking. However, because of the vagaries of international distribution, some masterpieces of East European cinema, such as the Czech film *Daisies* (1966) and the Yugoslav film *I Even Met Happy Gypsies* (1966) have remained largely unknown, while others, such as *Shop on Main Street* (1965), are available at all levels of distribution around the world.

During the Communist period, some lavish productions that explored the historical past were created with significant state subsidies, such as Andrzej Wajda's *The Promised Land* (1975). East European cinema also was prominent in examining the Holocaust; notable films include *The Last Stage* (1947); *Border Street* (1948); *Samson* (1961); *Sweet Light in a Dark Room* (1962); *Transport from Paradise* (1963); *Diamonds of the Night* (1964); *Shop on Main Street* (1965); *Angry Harvest* (1986); *Korczack* (1990); *Europa, Europa* (1990); *Holly Week* (1996); and *To Speak the Unspeakable* (1996).

Meticulous explorations of painful moral problems by the totalitarian social order are found in the works of Polish filmmakers Andrzej Wajda (1926–): *Man of Marble,* 1976; *Without Anesthesia,* 1978; Krzysztof Zanussi (1939–): *The Structure of Crystal,* 1969; *Balance,* 1974; *Camouflage,* 1977; Agnieska Holland (1948–): *A Woman Alone,* 1981; and Krzysztof Kieslowski (1941–): *Camera Buff,* 1976; *Blind Chance,* 1981; *Decalogue,* 1988; *Three Colors,* 1993–95; as well as the Hungarians Karoly Makk (1925–): *Love,* 1971; *Another Way,* 1982; and Péter Bacsó (1928–): *Witness,* 1969.

The historical legacy and natural beauty of the Balkans have been major themes among southeastern European filmmakers (*Stone Wedding* [Romania, 1973]; *The Goat's Horn* [Bulgaria, 1972]; *Petra's Wreath* [Yugoslavia, 1975]; and *A Tale from the Past* [Albania, 1987]).

Some of the masterpieces of East European cinema have become classic examples of achievement in film language and form. One of the best-known works is Wajda's *Ashes and Diamonds* (1958), which depicts the fate of a young Polish anticommunist in the last days of World War II. Past and future collide in his personal life as he becomes a tragic victim of the coming postwar reality. The film is considered a cinematographic achievement in the field of montage and camera movement. A case study for students of film is the early work of Miklós Jancsó (1921–), especially his *The Round-Up* (1965) and *The Red and the White* (1967). These films explore episodes of Hungary's past, set respectively in 1848 and 1918, but the most important achievements of these films are the elements of film language and style—

the mise-en-scène and the prolonged shots taken mostly through a handheld camera, the complex scenes featuring hundreds of extras placed around complexly structured backgrounds. These have become classic examples of cinematography and have influenced the development of the non-Hollywood tradition in filmmaking. Another extremely popular and well-shot movie is Jiří Menzel's (1938–) *Closely Watched Trains* (1967), a humorous take on wartime life and bureaucracy. In his early period, Czech filmmaker Miloš Forman (1932–) worked with cameraman Miroslav Ondříček (1933–) to create films that remain masterpieces of dynamic camera work as a basic storytelling device. Their lighthearted comedy *Loves of a Blonde* (1965) has been particularly celebrated.

Other examples of innovative filmmaking can be found in the unique montage and collage techniques used by vanguard filmmakers such as Věra Chytilová (1929–) in her 1967 *Daisies* and by Dušan Makavejev (1932–) in his 1971 *WR: Mysteries of Organism,* a controversial take on human sexuality and ideology. In the 1980s and 1990s several East European films have been recognized at a number of international film festivals. These include Wajda's *Man of Iron* (1981), looking at the Solidarity movement in Poland; István Szabó's (1938–) *Mephisto* (1982), the story of a German actor and his concessions to Nazism, thus metaphorically examining the dilemmas of the artist under totalitarianism; Emir Kusturica's (1954–) *When Father Was Away on Business* (1985), the story of a Yugoslav family in the 1950s charmingly told through the eyes of a young boy; and *Underground* (1995), a unique take on recent Yugoslav history; Kieslowski's *Double-Life of Veronique* (1991), an enigmatic fable of love and creativity; and Lucian Pintilie's (1933–) *The Oak* (1992), which looks at the drabness of life in late-Communist Romania.

Feminist filmmaking is represented in the work of numerous artists, including Chytilová; Márta Mészáros (1931–): *The Girl,* 1967; *Adoption,* 1975; *Diary for My Children,* 1982; Ildikó Enyédi (1955–): *My Twentieth Century,* 1989; *The Magic Hunter,* 1995; Judit Elek (1937–): *Maria's Day,* 1985; *Memories of a River,* 1991; and Binka Zhelyazkova (1923–): *The Attached Balloon,* 1967.

In addition to feature films, state-subsidized animation productions flourished. Key figures in this genre include puppeteers Jiří Trnka (1912–70) and Karel Zeman (1910–) from Czechoslovakia; Walerian Borowczyk (1923–), Jan Lenica (1928–), and Daniel Szchechura (1930–) from Poland; Ion Popescu-Gopo (1923–) from Romania; and Todor Dinov (1919–) and Donio Donev (1929–) from Bulgaria. The Zagreb school of animation became particularly well known; key figures were Vatroslav Mimica (1923–), Dušan Vukotić (1927–), and Borivoj Dovniković-Bordo (1932–). Zagreb also became the site of a biannual international animation festival.

The major film studios in Eastern Europe were located in Łódź and Warsaw in Poland; Prague and Gotvaldov in Czechoslovakia; Budapest in Hungary; Buftea in Romania; Boyana in Bulgaria; and Tirana in Albania. In Yugoslavia there were studios in all the republics. Most state production companies were modeled after the Polish film units, a system established in the mid-1950s. These units consisted of teams that included several directors (one of whom was the leader), screenwriters, cinematographers, costume and set designers, and staff. The units had relative creative autonomy within the production system.

Poland

Film Polski was established in 1945, and the most prominent film units became X, Tor, Kadr, and Zodiak, producing thirty to fifty features yearly before 1989. Although many of the films dealt with Polish history, in the 1970s and 1980s the so-called school of cinema of moral anxiety focused on socioethical problems. Prominent film directors include Jerzy Kawalerowicz (1922–); Wajda; Jerzy Hoffman (1932–); Zanussi; Kieslowski; Janusz Zaorski (1947–); Holland; and émigrés Roman Polanski (1935–) and Jerzy Skolimowski (1938–).

Czechoslovakia

After World War II, the Czechoslovak film industry was nationalized. During the 1950s and 1960s, Alfred Radok (1914–), Ján Kadár (1918–79), Elmar Klos (1910–92), and Zbynek Brynych (1927–) worked on films dealing with the Holocaust. In the years immediately preceding the Prague Spring, the short-lived intellectual and political thaw of 1968, a cinematic style known as Czech New Wave emerged. Its most prominent personalities were directors Vojtěch Jasný (1925–), Chytilová, Forman, Ivan Passer (1933–), Jan Nemec

(1936–), and Menzel, as well as screenwriter Josef Škvorecky (1924–) and cinematographer Ondrříček. After the Soviet invasion of Czechoslovakia in 1968, some filmmakers chose exile, while still others were prohibited from making films for a decade.

Hungary

Hungarian film production dates to 1898. After 1945, the state-owned production company Mafilm, which consisted of several units, produced fifteen to thirty films annually. Notable directors include Zoltán Fábri (1917–), András Kovács (1925–); Makk; Bascó; Janscó; Mészáros; Szabó; and Sándor Pál (1939–). Other important personalities include actor György Cserhalmi (1948–) and cinematographer Lajos Koltai (1946–).

Yugoslavia

Before Yugoslavia's dissolution in 1991, the Yugoslav cinema was multicultural, reflecting a variety of Slovenian, Croatian, Bosnian, Serbian, and Macedonian films. Film studios were located in the various republics, with the best known in Belgrade (Avala Film) and Zagreb (Jadran Film). The most prominent filmmakers include Aleksandar Petrović (1929–93); Makavejev; Slobodan Sijan (1946–); Ademir Kenović (1948–); Kusturica; and Rajko Grlić (1947–).

Romania

In Romania, film industries established before World War II were quickly nationalized. The major production studio was at Buftea, outside Bucharest. Notable directors include Liviu Ciulei (1923–); Sergiu Nicolaescu (1930–); Pintilie; Dan Pita (1938–); and Mircea Daneliuc (1943–).

Bulgaria

The Bulgarian film industry began early in the twentieth century with the movies of cinema enthusiast Vassil Gendov (n.d.). After World War II, the nationalized film industry produced between fifteen to twenty-six features annually at Boyana studios near Sofia. Prominent directors include Vulo Radev (1923–); Zhelyazkova; Rangel Vulchanov (1927–); Lydmil Staykov (1937–); Eduard Zahariev (1938–); and Georgi Dyulgerov (1943–).

After 1989, like other enterprises across the region, the film industry underwent significant changes, especially in terms of ownership, production, and distribution. Postcommunist problems have been explored by most directors in a pessimistic light. However, the dependency on international funding for filmmaking has grown larger, and many of the filmmakers have emigrated to the West to work there temporarily or permanently.

Dina Iordanova

Further reading

Burns, B. *World Cinema: Hungary.* Cranbury, New York, 1996.

Goulding, Daniel. *Liberated Cinema: The Yugoslav Experience.* Bloomington, Indiana, 1985.

———. *Post New-Wave Cinema in the Soviet Union and Eastern Europe.* Bloomington, Indiana, 1989.

Hames, Peter. *The Czechoslovak New Wave.* Los Angeles, 1985.

Holloway, Ronald. *The Bulgarian Cinema.* London, 1984.

Liehm, Mira and Antonin J. Liehm. *The Most Important Art: Soviet and East European Film after 1945.* Los Angeles, 1977.

Michalek, Boleslaw and Frank Turaj. *Modern Cinema of Poland.* Bloomington, Indiana, 1988.

Paul, David, ed. *Politics, Art and Commitment in the East European Cinema.* New York, 1983.

Petre, G. *History Must Answer to Man (The Contemporary Hungarian Cinema).* Budapest, 1978.

Slater, Thomas, J., ed. *Handbook of Soviet and East European Films and Filmmakers.* New York, 1992.

See also Béla Balázs; Miloš Forman; Miklós Janscó; Krzystof Kieslowski; Emir Kusturica; Dušan Makavejev; Márta Mészáros; Josef Škvorecky; István Szabó; Rangel Vulchanov; Andrzej Wajda

Cisleithania/Transleithania

The Austrian and Hungarian portions of the Austro-Hungarian Empire as defined by the *Ausgleich* (Compromise) of 1867, which established administrative autonomy for most governmental functions for the two parts of the empire. The names of the regions derive from a combination of Latin terms, *"cis"* meaning "this side of" and *"trans"* meaning "the other side of," and the Leitha River, which served as part of the historic boundary between Austrian and Hungarian lands for over nine centuries. The Leitha is a small tributary of the Danube River that demarcated a key part of the Austrian-Hungarian border between the heartlands of the two halves of the empire. Cisleithania/Transleithania reflects an Austrian perspective; Cisleithania refers to the region "this side" of the Leitha (Austria) and Transleithania to the region "the other side" of the Leitha (Hungary).

The Austrian-Hungarian border was first established with the founding of the Hungarian state by Saint Stephen (975–1038) in the year 1000, and its demarcation changed only in detail until the fall of the empire in 1919, even though Hungary was occupied by the Austrians and Ottomans and ultimately absorbed within the Habsburg Empire after Hungary's catastrophic defeat at the hands of the Turks in 1526. The historic lands of Cisleithania include Austria, Bohemia, Moravia, Austrian Silesia, Austrian Poland, and Slovenia. Transleithania includes "Hungary," Transylvania, and Croatia. Historically "Hungary" contained areas in all the countries now surrounding it, including Burgenland (now in Austria), southern Slovakia, the Transcarpathian Rus' (presently in Ukraine), and the Banat (now in Serbia/Montenegro and Romania). The Leitha remains the basis of a border, albeit now a provincial border, within Austria between the provinces of Burgenland and Lower Austria. Burgenland, historically part of west Hungary (in Transleithania), was transferred to Austria after World War I based on political and linguistic factors, though its major city Sopron (Ödenburg), remains in Hungary. The transfer of the Sopron area was first prevented by local armed Hungarians who opposed it and was ultimately canceled by an internationally brokered compromise and associated, controversial plebiscite, which registered Sopron voters' preference to remain within Hungary.

William H. Berentsen

Further reading

Burghardt, A.F. *Borderland*. Madison, Wisconsin, 1962.
Pounds, N.J.G. *Eastern Europe*. London, 1969.

See also *Ausgleich*

Civic Forum

A coalition of Czech opposition groups that formed in Prague on November 19, 1989, during the course of the Velvet Revolution, whose leader, Václav Havel (1936–), emerged as the chief spokesman of the opposition and helped to negotiate a rapid end to the rule of the disintegrating Communist regime. The forum was a movement encompassing a wide range of opposition groups. Charter 77 dissidents (who reported on human rights violations by the Czechoslovak government) were the most prominent in its leadership, but it also included students, workers, Catholics, actors, and academics. Other than Havel, a playwright who had been in and out of jail since his leadership in Charter 77, the movement included Jiří Dienstbier (1937–), an intellectual and former coal stoker, and Václav Klaus (1941–), an economist with the Institute of Forecasting of the Czechoslovak Academy of Sciences.

The group chose the title "Civic" to emphasize that they represented society, the Czech people whom the Communist Party had long denied a role in government. Though participants in the forum had a variety of agendas, they were united in their belief that the Communist government should resign to make way for a democratically elected successor.

After a series of protests and a massive general strike, the Communist regime stepped down on December 10. The forum provided most of the leaders of the new government, including Havel, Dienstbier, and Klaus, who became president, foreign minister, and economics minister, respectively.

Civic Forum and its Slovak counterpart, Public Against Violence, remained united long enough to win the first post-Communist elections in June 1990. But even then, strains began to emerge as Catholics, free-marketeers, Slovaks, environmentalists, democratic socialists, and others pressed separate agendas. By 1992, Civic Forum had split up into a wide variety of political parties, the final proof that democracy had arrived in Czechoslovakia.

Eagle Glassheim

Further reading

Ash, Timothy Garton. *The Magic Lantern*. New York, 1993.
Banac, Ivo, ed. *Eastern Europe in Revolution*. Ithaca, New York, 1992.

Holy, Ladislav. *The Little Czech and the Great Czech Nation.* Cambridge, 1996.

Kavan, Zdeněk and Bernard Wheaton. *The Velvet Revolution: Czechoslovakia 1988–1991.* Boulder, Colorado, 1992.

See also Charter 77; Václav Havel; Revolutions of 1989; Velvet Revolution

Clementis, Vladimír (1921–52)

Slovak Communist lawyer, publicist, politician, and diplomat. Clementis studied law at Charles University in Prague (1921–25) then practiced in Bratislava (1925–38). He wrote pamphlets and articles for the Communist Party press. He came to public attention in 1931 when he defended Štefan Major (1887–1963), a Communist member of parliament who was tried for supposedly instigating a violent strike of farm workers in the village of Košuty during which gendarmes fired into the crowd and killed three workers. The Communists gave wide publicity to the trial in an effort to discredit the "bourgeois" Czechoslovak Republic. In 1935 Clementis was elected to parliament, principally as a result of the publicity he received from the Košuty trial.

After the destruction of the republic in 1939, Clementis went into exile, first in France and then in England. In 1939 he was excluded from the party for denouncing the Nazi-Soviet Pact. In 1945 he was readmitted to the party and appointed state secretary for foreign affairs to keep an eye on Foreign Minister Jan Masaryk (1886–1948), whose outlook and background were pro-Western. In 1948, when the Communists seized power in Czechoslovakia and Masaryk was either murdered or committed suicide, Clementis was promoted to foreign minister. But he remained suspect to the dyed-in-the-wool Stalinists. During the party's witch-hunt against Titoists (nationalist Communists), "rootless cosmopolites" (Jews), and sundry other heretics, Clementis was accused of bourgeois nationalism, arrested, condemned, and hanged on December 12, 1952.

Victor S. Mamatey

Further reading

Holotíková, Zdenka and Viliam Plevza. *Vladimír Clementis.* Bratislava, 1968.

See also Communist Party of Czechoslovakia; Jan Masaryk; Molotov-Ribbentrop Pact

Cluj-Napoca

City in Transylvania. A city of Western character located on a plateau (1,150 feet [345 m] in altitude) on the river Somesul Mic in northwest Transylvania, Cluj-Napoca (Napoca is the Roman name of Dacian origin; Latin, Claudiopoli; German, Klausenburg; Hungarian, Kolozsvar) has a population of 331,000, the majority of which is Romanian, but with a substantial Hungarian minority (as well as Gypsies and others). Cluj-Napoca is a major rail and highway junction and an important industrial, commercial, financial, scientific, and especially cultural center. It also plays a major role in Romanian national politics.

In Roman times, Cluj-Napoca was already a significant settlement. Mentioned in documents first in 1173, it was destroyed by the Tartars in 1241, but by 1316 it was again a functioning town and, in the next century, a fortified city. In 1541 Transylvania was organized under Ottoman suzerainty into an autonomous principality, with Cluj becoming its most important economic, cultural, and political center. A Franciscan academy, established in 1580, was transformed in 1776 into a collegium. The university, established in 1872, has 32 faculties and 29,000 students, and also has Hungarian- and German-language sections of course offerings. Several relatively large-scale museums offer additional opportunities for study and research: the National Museum of History of Transylvania; the Ethnographic Museum of Transylvania; the Museum of Art (which emphasizes Transylvanian art); and the Museum of Pharmacy. There is also a large botanical garden covering 34.6 acres (14 hectares), established in 1872, with 11,000 plants from all over the world. The beauty of the city is enhanced by various historical buildings, churches, and monuments. The Roman Catholic Cathedral, founded in 1349, is in the Gothic style, as is the Reformed Church, established in 1486 and rebuilt in 1644. The Franciscan Church, originally Gothic in style, was reconstructed in the baroque style. The Orthodox Cathedral, built in 1921–33, is constructed in a modern Byzantine style.

Ladis K.D. Kristof

Further reading

Hitchins, Keith. *Rumania 1866–1947.* Oxford, 1994.

Ionescu, Grigore. *Istoria Arhitecturii în Romînia.* Bucharest, 1963.

Magocsi, Paul Robert. *Historical Atlas of East Central Europe.* Seattle, Washington, 1993.

România: Atlas istoric-geographic. Bucharest, 1996.

See also Transylvania

Codreanu, Corneliu Zelea (1899–1938)

Romanian nationalist leader. Born into a high school teacher's family in Iaşi and raised in Huşi in northernmost Moldova, Codreanu studied law at the University of Iaşi, where he came under the influence of the rabidly anti-Semitic Professor A.C. Cuza (1857–1947). He became involved in anticommunist groups and a leader of the city's nationalist youth. He briefly studied in Germany in 1922 but quickly returned to Romania to participate in student demonstrations against the granting of citizenship to Jews. In 1923 he helped Cuza found the anti-Semitic League of National Christian Defense.

In the first half of the 1920s, the corrupt political system's failure to fulfill what he considered to be its national and Christian duty led to Codreanu's estrangement from Western democratic practices and toward the direct action (including assassination) favored by fascists.

After studying in France, Codreanu returned to Romania to found the Legion of the Archangel Michael (1927) and later its political offshoot, the Iron Guard (1930), a disciplined, hierarchically organized, religiously inspired national renewal movement. Codreanu's personal charisma attracted thousands of students and peasants to the legion. He became their "Captain."

Despite harassment by successive Romanian governments, Codreanu grew in popularity. Carol II (1891–1953), the epitome of the system that Codreanu detested, had him arrested, tried, and imprisoned (April–May 1938). On the night of November 29–30, 1938, Codreanu and thirteen of his followers were murdered by the king's secret police at the Jilava prison.

Walter M. Bacon Jr.

Further reading

Codreanu, Corneliu Zelea. *For My Legionaries.* Madrid, 1976.

Heinen, Armin. *Die Legion "Erzengel Michael" in Rumänien.* Munich, 1986.

Nagy-Talavera, Nicholas M. *The Green Shirts and Others.* Stanford, California, 1970.

Palaghiţă, Ştefan. *Istoria Mişcării Legionare.* Bucharest, 1993.

See also Carol II; Iron Guard; Right Radicalism

Cold War

Bilateral competitive relationship in the post–World War II era between the Communist and non-Communist system of states, with the Iron Curtain in Eastern Europe symbolizing the division. At the same time, an intra-Communist state system reflected its own Cold War rhythm, as the dimensions of ideology, power, culture, and economics played themselves out within the Soviet sphere as well as in the East-West arena. The image of a Communist monolith, which included the assumption of a Marxist universe exclusive of nationalism and culture-centered loyalties, was always a myth. Fundamental national differences drove ongoing power and economic conflicts within the system and led to the reformation of the so-called satellite countries in the post–Cold War era.

The Cold War within the Soviet empire consisted of five basic periods: Stalin's postwar empire building (1945–52); "normalization" through de-Stalinization (1953–64); doubt, dissent, and diversity (1964–79); stagnation and decline (1980–88); independence (1989–91).

Wherever the Red Army went during World War II, the political empire of the Soviet Union followed. As the bipolar world emerged, in which Washington and Moscow served as magnets for the different camps, Stalin (1879–1953) established "friendly" regimes in Eastern Europe. Internally, this took the form of step-by-step movements toward control and then Sovietization by "local" Communist parties directed by the Kremlin. Stalin used stringent centralization, an integrated planning for intrasystem trade and economic development and enforced coordinated foreign/military policies. The organizational reflections of this integrative effort were the Warsaw Pact and Comecon, the Moscow-led military and economic organizations, respectively. Stalin looked upon the satellite nations as not only a buffer between the USSR and the West but also as an empire to be exploited.

After Stalin's death, the Hungarian Revolution of 1956 and unrest in Poland and East Germany helped to define the new role of the Kremlin in satellite affairs. Some leeway was given to national leadership and localized public policy, but all had to adhere to a Marxist rationale, Soviet hegemony, and rule by the Communist Party. Change was balanced with continuity. Integration of the Soviet economy with that of Eastern Europe was seriously modified. Yet while liberalism in Poland and Hungary continued to compete with Soviet dominance, crackdowns in East Germany, Bulgaria, and Albania illustrated the continued existence of hard-line leadership where it was locally viable.

The period from 1964 to 1979 was dominated by the cautious pragmatism of Leonid Brezhnev (1906–82), who encouraged a concentration on national problems. Since economic growth became a significant element of the public policy needs of these nations, an opening of trade with Western Europe slowly emerged. Although most of the nations of the region maintained a cautious isolation from the West, Hungary and Czechoslovakia were particularly receptive to West German and French initiatives. However, when Czechoslovakia's Prague Spring, the liberal period of reform, was crushed by Soviet intervention in 1968, the mood of the satellite regimes changed. The optimism of the early 1960s lingered through the 1970s but only through exploitation of Brezhnev's dual policy of limited sovereignty with a commitment to the foundations of communism—the Brezhnev Doctrine. Still, movements emphasizing autonomous organizations emerged and, in the case of Poland, exploded.

The emergence of movements such as Solidarity, the trade union movement in Poland, and increased economic and political contacts with the West began to erode the bloc's cohesiveness. Economic stagnation within the Soviet Union encouraged further attempts at liberalization in Hungary, Poland, and Czechoslovakia and increased attempts at internal control in most of the other satellites, even as some, like Romania, found room to challenge Soviet foreign policy leadership.

After the death of Brezhnev, a leadership crisis emerged within the Kremlin. Uncertainty and unpredictability only fed the malaise that spread throughout the Soviet empire. The economy had stagnated, the debacle of Afghanistan weighed on the Soviet people, and the more active economies in the satellites were becoming weighted down by debt owed to the West. The emergence of Mikhail Gorbachev (1931–) as a reform leader in late 1985 merely signaled the end of the old guard in Moscow and loosened the dam of protest against a moribund society. Glasnost (openness) and perestroika (restructuring) were policies aimed at reform of the Communist system, but they served only to open up the politics of the Soviet Union and the satellites first to protest and then to active democratization. Thus, the remarkable collapse of the Soviet Union and the independence of its satellites was accomplished without significant force and relatively little political conflict. Only in the nations with the most stringent of Communist political leadership was the movement toward democratization difficult. Regardless of the process within each nation, the Soviet Union's East European empire had ended.

Richard Fulton

Further reading

Gati, Charles. *The Bloc That Failed: Soviet–East European Relations in Transition.* Bloomington, Indiana, 1990.

Shoptlin, G. *Politics in Eastern Europe.* New York, 1993.

Stokes, Gale. *From Stalinism to Pluralism: A Documentary History of Eastern Europe since 1945.* New York, 1996.

Walker, M. *The Cold War and the Making of the Modern World.* London, 1993.

See also Brezhnev Doctrine; Comecon; De-Stalinization; Glasnost/Perestroika; Hungarian Revolution of 1956; Iron Curtain; Soldiarity; Prague Spring; Red Army; Revolutions of 1989; Sovietization; Stalin; Truman Doctrine

Collective Security

Effort by states in East Central and southeastern Europe to band together for mutual protection during the interwar period (1918–39). The pursuit of collective security by Eastern European states resulted from insecurity after World War I. Many of these states were newly created out of former empires—Poland from the German, Austro-Hungarian, and Russian empires, and Czechoslovakia and Yugoslavia from Austria-Hungary; even Romania's territory had been enlarged at the expense of the former Austria-Hungary. These new states especially feared Hungary (though Bulgaria was also dissatisfied after the war), since Hungarian anger over lost territories dominated Budapest's domestic and foreign policy.

C

One perceived means of protection was to band together for mutual defense. The Little Entente, comprised of Czechoslovakia, Yugoslavia, and Romania, was created in 1920–21. Treaties provided for common defense against Hungarian attack, though Romania and Yugoslavia also had provisions regarding attacks by Bulgaria. Similarly, the Balkan Entente (1934) resulted from a Romanian and Greek desire for defense against Bulgaria. Yugoslavia and Turkey later joined the entente, but it never expanded beyond its initial purpose. Bilateral agreements were also made with the Great Powers, but these proved to be of little value in light of Nazi expansion in the late 1930s.

At best, these pacts offered protection only against small states of Eastern Europe, not against larger enemies such as Germany and the Soviet Union. No greater regional entente was created because Polish conflict with Czechoslovakia over Teschen left the Poles little inclined to join with Czechoslovakia for protection. These associations were moribund by 1938 regardless, as German economic penetration of Romania and Yugoslavia had left them little freedom of independent action.

Jo Ellen Kerksiek

Further reading

Palmer, Alan. *The Lands Between: A History of East-Central Europe since the Congress of Vienna.* New York, 1970.

Rothschild, Joseph. *East Central Europe between the Two World Wars.* Seattle, Washington, 1974.

Walters, E. Garrison. *The Other Europe: Eastern Europe to 1945.* New York, 1988.

See also Balkan Entente; Franco-Czechoslovak Alliance; Great Powers; Little Entente; Teschen; Trianon, Treaty of

Collectivization

The frequently brutal process by which Marxist-Leninist regimes in the Soviet Union, Eastern Europe, and elsewhere attempted to establish their new "socialist order" in the countryside. Collectivization meant the forced consolidation of small-scale peasant farms and larger holdings belonging to the landed classes, with the goal of creating larger, more "modern" farms owned (in theory) by their workers ("collective" farms) or the state.

Collectivization was pioneered by Josef Stalin (1879–1953) in the Soviet Union during 1929 and

the early 1930s, and was transplanted to other socialist countries after World War II. In addition to eradicating the inefficiencies associated with small-scale farming on discontiguous land holdings, collectivization had the political goal of removing the rural basis for resistance to communist regimes. Collectivization was also justified by the need to promote industrial development by facilitating the state's procurement of agricultural products and by transferring "surplus labor" from rural to urban areas.

Collectivization often met with strong resistance in the countryside; peasants frequently destroyed property and livestock rather than surrender them to the collectives. Such behavior was often provoked by the authorities' persecution of those landholders regarded as class enemies. While collectivization generally afforded the state more control over grain procurement and facilitated massive migrations of labor from rural to urban areas, it also inflicted significant damage on agriculture. Per capita rural incomes generally declined significantly during the first years of collectivization, and mass deportations and famines were not uncommon. In the Soviet Union, estimates of the lives lost because of collectivization range from one to ten million. The damage wrought by Soviet collectivization may have been so extensive as to have required a net inflow of resources into agriculture from other sectors during the ensuing years.

In part because of the problems created by collectivization, reforms in socialist economies frequently focused on agriculture. Agriculture was largely decollectivized in Poland in 1957 and in China after 1979; reform of agricultural cooperatives is generally viewed as one of the most successful aspects of the reforms introduced in socialist Hungary in the 1960s; and state and collective farms in the former Soviet Union and Eastern European countries underwent various forms of privatization after 1989.

Ben Slay

Further reading

Conquest, Robert. *The Harvest of Sorrow: Soviet Collectivization and the Terror-Famine.* Oxford, 1986.

Millar, J.R. "Mass Collectivization and the Contribution of Soviet Agriculture to the First Five Year Plan: A Review Article." *Slavic Review* 33, no. 4 (December 1974): 750–66.

Stuart, R.C., ed. *The Rural Soviet Economy.* Totowa, New Jersey, 1984.

Swain, N. *Collective Farms Which Work?* Cambridge, Massachusetts, 1985.

See also Agriculture; Peasants; Privatization

Comecon

Western name for the Council for Mutual Economic Assistance (CMEA), formed in January 1949 by Josef Stalin (1879–1953) in response to the U.S. Marshall Plan initiative as an economic control equivalent of the Warsaw Pact, the Soviet bloc's military alliance. Its founding members were the USSR, Bulgaria, Czechoslovakia, Hungary, Poland, and Romania, but this group was later expanded to include East Germany (1950), Mongolia (1962), Cuba (1972), and Vietnam (1978). Yugoslavia was admitted as an associate member in 1965. CMEA's purpose was to sponsor cooperation and coordination of member economies within a framework of integrative policies and of Soviet hegemony. It was never a supranational planning agency as member nations maintained sovereignty over their own economic development. Rather, its fundamental goals were coordination of the plans, production specialization, and establishment of a regional system of trade based on an "international socialist division of labor."

Stalin was content to preside over a Soviet-centered maze of bilateral trade within a dormant CMEA structure. By 1953, two-thirds of all European member trade was within the bloc, whereas in the prewar period these levels were only 20 percent. The post-Stalin Soviet leadership tried to energize CMEA with formal institutionalization through a charter finally formulated in 1959. Though summit meetings of member party secretaries maintained power, an annual council meeting set formal policy to be carried out by a Moscow-based Executive Committee. A Secretariat served as the core permanent administrative organ, augmented by several specialized commissions and standing committees. CMEA's secretary was always a high-ranking Soviet official. Permanent conferences and standing commissions were crucial to cooperative activities.

Nikita Khrushchev's (1894–1971) response to increased conflict within the Communist world was an attempt at strengthening the integration of CMEA through a single regional plan (1961) emphasizing national specialization in economic sectors (for example, Bulgaria and Romania in agriculture). Its East European members resisted and concentrated on domestic economic reforms, integrating largely only where trade patterns already existed.

By 1971 CMEA reformulated a "Comprehensive Programme" that brought cooperation on some large long-term investment projects and technology research but also a plethora of inefficient bureaucratic commissions covering over 130 sectors of the economy. Soviet limits to reform, demonstrated by the invasion of Czechoslovakia in 1968, combined with the oil crisis of the mid-1970s and the heavy hand of the bogus "transferable rouble" as the CMEA pricing mechanism, left Eastern Europe economically dependent on Soviet policy and energy supplies.

Détente and the growing idea of "different roads to socialism" in the 1980s led to expanded trade with the West for many CMEA members and consequent increased trade deficits in hard currencies. Mikhail Gorbachev (1931–) tried to attack the limits of CMEA ability to break out of inefficiencies and build a "unified socialist market," but with no success. The collapse of communism in 1989 doomed CMEA. Market policies and demands for hard currency trading (especially for Soviet gas and oil) brought the formal dissolution of CMEA in June 1991.

Richard Fulton

Further reading

Brine, Jenny. *Comecon: The Rise and Fall of an International Socialist Organization.* New Brunswick, New Jersey, 1993.

Kaser, Michael. *Comecon: Integration Problems of the Planned Economies.* London, 1967.

Smith, Alan H. *The Planned Economies of Eastern Europe.* London, 1983.

VanBrabant, Jozef. *Economic Integration in Eastern Europe: A Handbook.* London, 1989.

Zwas, Adam. *The Council for Mutual Economic Assistance: The Thorny Path from Political to Economic Integration.* London, 1990.

See also Mikhail Gorbachev; Industrialization; Marshall Plan; Stalin; Warsaw Pact

Cominform

Communist propaganda organ. Formally named the Information Bureau of the Communist and

Workers Parties (1947–56), Cominform was erroneously thought by many to be a successor organization to the Comintern, which Josef Stalin (1879–1953) dissolved in 1943. Rather, the Cominform was a weak organ permitted by Stalin as a means of communicating the Soviet "party line" to world (particularly satellite) Communist parties. Marshall Tito (1892–1980) of Yugoslavia had urged Stalin to reformulate a Communist International like the Comintern; instead, Stalin compromised with this organization, allowing it to provide party information without the ability to pass binding resolutions. Placing the bureau in Belgrade was a sop to Tito; when Yugoslavia was expelled in 1948, the center was moved to Bucharest, Romania. The fact that the Cominform was centered outside of Moscow in the midst of Stalinist centralization indicates that it was never meant to serve as a center of international communism or an activity center. Its permanent bureau never had high-level party functionaries, only fifty journalists (thirty of whom were in the Russian department) to assemble its main organ, *For Lasting Peace, For People's Democracy*. This clumsily titled journal (named personally by Stalin) was the main, almost exclusive activity of the Cominform. Every word was sent to Moscow for approval before publication.

The Cominform was inaugurated in Poland at a secret meeting of most of the leaders of European Communist parties. Only resolutions and selected speeches were ever published. Although it was to be a reflection of the fraternity and equality of these parties, in the end it was only a tool for Stalin to reassert central dominance and discourage nationalist communism.

Richard Fulton

Further reading

Brzezinski, Zbigniew. *The Grand Failure: The Birth and Death of Communism in the Twentieth Century.* New York, 1989.

Lowenthal, Richard. *World Communism: The Disintegration of a Secular Faith.* London, 1966.

See also Comintern; Stalin; Tito; Tito-Stalin Split

Comintern

Popular term for the Communist (Third) International (1919–43), specifically formed by V.I. Lenin (1870–1924) as an international Communist party upon principles of democratic centralism. Each national party was to constitute a territorial branch of a single party dedicated to world revolution. The Second Congress in 1920 created the organizational foundation on the contrary basis of Bolshevik domination. It became a tool of the Soviet party by giving power to internal CPSU (Communist Party of the Soviet Union) regional "commissions"; by organizing clandestine activities sections; by sponsorship of propaganda vehicles (*Communist International* and *World News and Views*); through leadership training; and by the creation of special-purpose organs such as the Youth International, aimed at organizing the young. Its "guest house" and insurgent training provided a beginning for many future leaders of East European Communist nations. All member parties were pledged to follow the directives of the Executive Committee of the Communist International (ECCI), the organization's leadership.

The early tactics of the ECCI concentrated on the formation of "united fronts" with socialist and peasant organizations. By the end of the 1920s, the transformation of control to committees of the Soviet party was complete. The mid to late 1930s brought tactics necessitated by the fascist threat in Europe. At the same time, Stalin's purges of the late 1930s included Comintern leadership, as the Comintern turned into Stalin's tool for displacing local leadership with Moscow-trained party leadership. In 1938, for example, Stalin (1979–1953) dissolved the entire Polish party. The necessities of the alliances with Western nations during World War II led Stalin to dissolve the Comintern by decree on May 15, 1943.

Richard Fulton

Further reading

Annals of Communism series. Yale University Press.

Carr, Edward H. *The Twilight of the Comintern.* New York, 1983.

Drachkovitch, Milorad and Branko Lazitch, eds. *The Comintern: Historical Highlights.* New York, 1966.

McKenzie, Kermit E. *COMINTERN and World Revolution, 1928–1943.* New York, 1964.

See also Georgi Dimitrov Lenin; Stalin

Communist Party of Albania

The Communist Party of Albania was founded on November 8, 1941. At a conference held in Tirana, four major political groups—the Korca, Shkodra, Tirana, and Fire groups—were unified into one national party—the Communist Party of Albania. At the first congress, a seven-member Provisional Central Committee was elected with Enver Hoxha (1908–85) named as its head. The party immediately set about consolidating its organization and preparing for an armed struggle aimed at liberating the country from Italian occupation. As part of that effort, the Organization of Communist Youth was established on November 23, 1941, and the Democratic Front of Albania was founded on September 16, 1942, organizations created and led by the Communist Party. At the conference of the Anti-Fascist National Liberation Front held at Peze on September 16, 1942—all patriotic forces in the country, regardless of class or political affiliation, were called on to engage in an armed struggle against the fascist occupiers. The leaders of the Albanian Communist Party at first considered the possibility of uniting all Albanians into a single national and democratic state, including the Albanian national minority in Yugoslavia. But in view of relations between Albania and Yugoslavia during the war, it was impractical and impolitic to pursue such a nationalist agenda.

After the Communist takeover of Albania in November 1944, the leadership headed by Hoxha sought to achieve two major objectives: to maintain and consolidate their grip on Albania and to preserve the independence and territorial integrity of the country. To realize the first objective, the Communist Party established the most extreme form of dictatorship, a system of totalitarianism designed by Hoxha himself. It consolidated its position through a campaign of terror. Many nationalist leaders fled to the West. Others were brought before so-called people's courts where they were charged with war crimes or as enemies of the people. It has been estimated that between 1944 and 1984 fifteen thousand individuals were executed or murdered without trial, while another estimated 27,000 were thrown into prisons and labor camps for various "political" offenses. Throughout this period, the party elite was also affected. One-third of Politburo members were removed and two-thirds of the members of the Central Committee lost their party positions. Many of them were executed as "Titoists," "traitors," and "revisionists," including Koci Xoxe (1911–49), former vice premier of Albania who was executed in 1949, and Beqir Balluku (1916–76), minister of

defense and member of the party's Central Committee who was executed in 1976.

Regarding the second objective, the preservation of Albania's independence and territorial integrity, the party enjoyed a large measure of success. The most dangerous threat to Albania's independence came during the period 1944–48. In 1947 Tito (1892–1980) considered incorporating Albania as the seventh republic of the Yugoslav Federated State. Albania's independence was secured only when Stalin (1879–1953), on June 28, 1948, expelled Yugoslavia from the Cominform, the Communist propaganda organization. The Albanians now took advantage of the Soviet-Yugoslav split to free themselves from domination by Belgrade.

The Soviet advocacy of de-Stalinization in the mid-1950s and Soviet-Yugoslav rapprochement, however, revived the anxiety of Albania's Communist leaders. Such a movement threatened Hoxha's hard-line policies, but Hoxha used the developing Sino-Soviet rift to avoid the tide of de-Stalinization. By late 1961, state and party ties between Albania and the Soviet Union were severed. A Beijing-Tirana axis then emerged within the socialist camp. China's ideological, material, and diplomatic support enabled Albanians to continue to defy the dictates of Moscow and to preserve their independence in the 1960s and early 1970s.

Yet the alliance between Albania and Communist China lasted only a decade. By 1978, the Albanian leadership began referring to the Chinese as social revisionists, social imperialists, and traitors to Marxist-Leninism.

In 1948 the Communist Party of Albania was renamed the Party of Labor of Albania at the First Party Congress held in Tirana. From 1978 through 1991, the party pursued a policy of self-reliance for the nation, which brought about national catastrophe. The party severed relations with most countries, pursued an independent and disastrous program of economic autarchy, and promoted harsh internal policies, including strict atheism.

From 1948 until Hoxha's death in 1985, the Party of Labor of Albania held eight congresses. The last party congress was held in Tirana in 1991 under the leadership of Ramiz Alia (1925–), Hoxha's successor. At this congress, the party changed its name for the last time, from the Party of Labor of Albania to the Socialist Party of Albania. During national elections in 1992, the new

Democratic Party of Albania won the majority of seats in the new government, displacing the Communists.

Mirvet S. Muca

Further reading

Dilo, Jani. *The Communist Party Leadership in Albania*. Washington, D.C., 1961.

Donald, Zagoria. *Sino-Soviet Dispute*. Cambridge, Massachusetts, 1963.

Hoxha, Enver. *Collected Works*, vols. 1–3. Tirana, 1968.

Prifti, Peter. *Socialist Albania since 1944*. Cambridge, Massachusetts, 1978.

See also Ramiz Alia; Cominform; De-Stalinization; Enver Hoxha; Stalin; Tito; Koci Xoxe

Communist Party of Bulgaria

As was true of many other such movements in Eastern Europe, the Bulgarian Communist Party had its origins in the late nineteenth century. In 1891 Dimitur Blagoev (1856–1924) founded the precursor of the Bulgarian Communist Party (BCP) under the name Bulgarian Social Democratic Party (BSDP). In 1903 its revolutionary Marxist offspring, the Bulgarian Workers' Social Democratic Party "Narrow Socialists" (BWSDP), adopted democratic centralism and declared itself a party of the proletariat, against private property and collaboration with bourgeois parties. By 1912, however, only one Socialist had been elected to the Bulgarian parliament.

In 1919 the party changed its name to Bulgarian Communist Party (BCP) and joined the Third Communist International (Comintern) in Moscow. From 1919 to 1923, the BCP was the second most powerful force in parliament. The Communists organized an uprising against the bloody coup of June 9, 1923, that overthrew the regime of Aleksandur Stamboliiski (1879–1923), but as a result of its failure, the party was outlawed. In 1924 BCP attempted to legalize itself under a different name, but the same year both were outlawed by the newly introduced Law for Protection of the State. In another attempt at legalization in 1927, BCP created the Workers Party. Both were strongly influenced by the emphasis of Soviet leader Josef Stalin (1879–1953) on underground armed struggle and relied exclusively on the Soviet Union, rather than internal allies. After the May 19, 1934,

military coup that took control in Sofia, all political parties were banned and BCP continued its underground activities.

In 1936 the party adopted the Comintern's "peoples' front" strategy to form an antifascist coalition. In 1937–38 it collaborated with the Bulgarian Agrarian People's Union "A. Stamboliiski" and the Social Democratic Party to create the Democratic Alliance parliamentary coalition. In 1938–39, following a Comintern decision, BCP merged with the Workers' Party to create the Bulgarian Workers' Party (BWP).

After the German invasion of the Soviet Union in June 1941, BWP turned to armed struggle against the pro-German government in Sofia. Soviet victories in 1942–43 facilitated the formation of a united antifascist front in Bulgaria. In August 1943 the BWP, Bulgarian Agrarian Peoples' Union (Pladne), the BWSDP, the political circle Zveno, and independent intellectuals formed the underground Fatherland Front. After the Soviet Union declared war on Bulgaria, the Fatherland Front established control over scores of towns and villages, and on September 8, 1944, it initiated a successful military coup in Sofia.

In the immediate postwar years the BWP secured its leading role through control of key ministries and the Fatherland Front's national and local committees. Its membership increased from about fourteen thousand (September 9, 1944) to five hundred thousand in 1946, the highest increase of any party in the country. BWP's power was secured also through mass political repression, that is, camps for the "politically dangerous" and "peoples' courts" against supposed war criminals. The party, led by Georgi Dimitrov (1882–1949), who served as Bulgaria's prime minister and secretary-general of the party from November 1945 until his death, also used the judicial system and state security forces for its political purposes. While the West was careful not to damage its relations with the USSR and its support for the opposition proved futile, BWP received decisive military, diplomatic, and economic help from Moscow.

The beginning of the Cold War expedited the adoption of the Stalinist totalitarian model of socialism. The Communists gradually became the majority in coalition governments and in the parliament, and established control over the army and the church. BWP imposed its ideology on the whole society, fused state institutions, liquidated the division of power, and carried out mass propaganda that included the creation of a cult of personality of its leader. It eliminated opposition parties and restructured the Fatherland Front into a sociopolitical organization. In December 1948 BWP renamed itself the Bulgarian Communist Party and embarked on a course of forced industrialization, formation of agriculture cooperatives, and cultural revolution. The private sector was nationalized and central planning introduced. Repression was widely used within the party itself. During the campaign against the "enemy with a party card," about one hundred thousand party members were discharged from the party's ranks.

After Stalin's death in 1953, the changes in BCP proceeded slowly and under pressure from Moscow. In 1954 Todor Zhivkov (1911–98) became first secretary of the BCP's Central Committee, and after the Twentieth Congress of the Soviet Communist Party (1956), he received Soviet support. A trend toward democratization emerged, illustrated by greater use of economic incentives and improved standard of living. Partial amnesty was granted to political prisoners and emigrants, and most labor camps were closed. Concern over political unrest in Poland and especially the Hungarian Revolution in 1956, however, terminated the democratization period.

In 1962 Zhivkov also assumed the position of prime minister. A series of economic experiments began, designed to restructure the Bulgarian economy through the introduction of market principles. At the same time, the new 1971 constitution stipulated BCP's "leading role" in society. It also instituted the merger of legislative and executive power in a state council, chaired by Zhivkov.

The policies of glasnost (openness) and perestroika (restructuring), initiated in the Soviet Union in the 1980s, produced a split in BCP's leadership. The faction around Zhivkov opposed the idea that new people had to realize the proposed fundamental changes in the socialist system. The 1987 "July Concept" and Decree No. 56 introduced market principles and stimulated private initiative. The other faction maintained closer relations with the Soviet leadership and accepted Mikhail Gorbachev's (1931–) model of transition. In 1988–89 the first unsanctioned opposition organizations appeared.

Within the framework of the sweeping changes in Eastern Europe, on November 9, 1989, BCP's ruling body demanded Zhivkov's resigna-

tion, and the next day the decision was confirmed by the Central Committee's Plenum. Peter Mladenov (1936–), Zhivkov's foreign minister for eighteen years, became the new party leader. This act released the simmering social discontent but allowed BCP to retain the political initiative until the fall of 1990. The party introduced political pluralism and negotiated free and democratic elections. It discarded its Communist program, the principle of democratic centralism, and adopted a new statute. BCP embraced democratic socialism and renamed itself the Bulgarian Socialist Party (BSP). BSP won the majority of seats in the 1990 and 1994 parliamentary elections.

Boian Koulov

Further reading

Baeva, I. "Bulgarskiyat prehod sled 1989 v istoricheski kontekst." *Istoricheski Pregled* 1 (1996): 90–113.

———. *Iztochna Evropa sled Stalin, 1953–1956.* Sofia, 1995.

Bell, John. *The Bulgarian Communist Party from Blagoev to Zhivkov.* Stanford, California, 1986.

———. "Post-Communist Bulgaria," *Current History* 89 (1991): 32–38.

Brown, J.F. *Bulgaria under Communist Rule.* New York, 1970.

Istoria na Bulgaria. vol. 7. Sofia, 1991.

Kumanov, M. *Politicheski partii, organizatsii i dvizheniya v Bulgaria i tehnite lideri, 1879–1949.* Sofia, 1991.

Oren, Nissan. *Bulgarian Communism.* New York, 1971.

Rothschild, Joseph. *The Communist Party of Bulgaria: Origins and Development, 1883–1936.* New York, 1959.

See also Dimitur Blagoev; Comintern; Georgi Dimitrov; Fatherland Front; Glasnost and Perestroika; Mikhail Gorbachev; Hungarian Revolution of 1956; Revolutions of 1989; Aleksandur Stamboliiski; Zheliu Zhelev; Todor Zhivkov; Zueno

Communist Party of Czechoslovakia

Representatives of the Czech Marxist Left and the Marxist Left in Slovakia and Ruthenia constituted the Czechoslovak Communist Party (Komunistická strana Československa [KSČ]) in May 1921. The Comintern (Communist International),

C however, denied the KSČ admission until it agreed to accept members from all ethnic groups, including the left wing of the German Social Democratic Party of Czechoslovakia, whose adherents had already accepted V.I. Lenin's (1870–1924) twenty-one points the previous March. A unification congress was held in October 1921, making the KSČ one of the last Communist parties formed in Europe. The longtime Czech Social Democratic Party functionary Bohumír Šmeral (1880–1941) became the first head of the party.

The attractiveness of the Communist Party, which had both urban and rural support and was the only party in Czechoslovakia to draw members from across the national spectrum, became clear with the communal elections of September 1923, when the KSČ made major gains at the expense of the Czechoslovak Social Democrats, who were committed to supporting the First Republic. The parliamentary elections of November 1925 confirmed this trend, as the KSČ, with 13.7 percent of the vote, became the second-largest party in parliament. The Czechoslovak Communist Party, whose electoral support was consistently higher than its membership, received just over 10 percent of the popular vote in the other parliamentary elections of the interwar period (1929: 10.2 percent; 1935: 10.3 percent).

Many of the original leaders of the KSČ were sensitive to the ethnic concerns of the working class, which remained difficult issues throughout the interwar period. As Czech and Slovak relations after 1948 would demonstrate, the KSČ failed to find an adequate solution to these problems. Ethnonational questions took second place on the KSČ political agenda, however, as Moscow increasingly dominated the party, first with its Bolshevization during the mid-1920s and then with its Stalinization in the late 1920s and early 1930s. The KSČ paid the price for Soviet domination; factional strife and purges resulting in mass defections and expulsions transformed the party into a Stalinist sect by the early 1930s.

The KSČ assumed a patriotic image and played an active role during the Munich crisis of September 1938, when Czechoslovakia was forced to turn over the Sudetenland to Germany. Under pressure from Berlin, the post-Munich government in Prague dissolved the KSČ in December 1938. Klement Gottwald (1896–1953), party secretary since 1929, and other Czechoslovak Communist leaders soon went into exile, primarily to Moscow.

Following its initial disarray after Munich, the KSČ evolved a wartime program reflecting Comintern policies. KSČ leaders first embraced the national front against the Germans during the spring of 1939 but changed course following the Nazi-Soviet Pact of August 23, 1939. Until June 1941, the KSČ interpreted the war as a conflict between two imperialist camps. After the Nazi invasion of the Soviet Union, the Czechoslovak Communists aligned themselves behind Edvard Beneš's (1884–1948) London-based government-in-exile.

As the Red Army began liberating Slovakia in early 1945, the Beneš government returned home by way of Moscow, where the KSČ played a major role in designing the program of Czechoslovakia's postwar government. The Košice program, named for the Slovak town where the government formally took office in April 1945, involved a National Front in which the non-Communists had a majority of government portfolios, while the Communists held most of the important ministries, including interior, information, and education. The KSČ was the most popular party in the first postwar parliamentary elections on May 1946, receiving 38 percent of the vote.

At first, the Communists had been relatively moderate in their demands concerning the distribution of portfolios as well as in domestic and foreign policy. However, confrontations between the KSČ and the other parties in the National Front, reflecting a variety of domestic and foreign issues, rendered the internal political situation increasingly tense by late 1947. In the wake of a cabinet crisis in mid-February 1948, the Communists seized power by formally legal means, free of violence, but not of the threat of violence, since they controlled the army and the security forces. The KSČ closed anti-Communist newspapers and periodicals and purged non-Communist ones. It also instituted mass purges of the civil service, the military, professional organizations, sports clubs, and universities. In April 1948 enterprises employing more than fifty workers were nationalized. There was a parallel effort to collectivize agriculture.

In the Tito-Stalin split—the expulsion of Yugoslavia from the Cominform (international Communist propaganda organization) for failing to support the Stalinist model—purge trials from 1949 through 1954 removed critics of Stalin (1879–1953) as well as any possible rivals to Gottwald. Victims included Jewish functionaries and intellectuals, Slovak autonomists, and Communists who had spent the war in the underground or London. These purges left Czechoslovakia among the most Stalinist of the so-called people's democracies. Czechoslovakia remained immune to de-Stalinization during the 1950s, not least because the KSČ leadership was directly implicated in the earlier purges. Antonín Novotný (1904–75), Gottwald's successor as party secretary in 1953, remained in power until his resignation in January 1968. The Novotný government's brutal response to domestic protest and growing calls for reform led to his demise. Alexander Dubček (1921–92), secretary of the Slovak section of the party, replaced him as party secretary.

With the support of the reformist majority, the party leadership drew up a comprehensive "action program" whose goals included more solid cultural, economic, and political foundations for the Communist system. Relaxed censorship played a major role, as popular calls for reform went further than the KSČ had anticipated. Czechoslovak citizens responded with requests ranging from permission to travel abroad to the creation of a new political system.

The authority and popularity of the reform Communists was the greatest in KSČ history. Thus, when Warsaw Pact armies invaded Czechoslovakia during the night of August 20–21, 1968, they met popular resistance. Initially there was no alternative conservative leadership to the reform Communists, creating a power vacuum. Dubček and other reform-Communist leaders were spirited to Moscow, where they could do little but accept Soviet interruption of the Czechoslovak experiment with "Socialism with a Human Face" and the end of the Prague Spring, the period of liberal reforms.

Gustáv Husák (1913–91), a longtime party member whose participation in the reform movement ceased with the Warsaw Pact intervention, replaced Dubček on April 17, 1969, later becoming president of Czechoslovakia as well as party secretary. His neo-Stalinist government imposed stability in Czechoslovakia and remained in place until the events of November 1989. Miloš Jakeš (1922–), who directed the post-1968 purges of Dubček supporters, replaced Husák as party secretary in December 1987. Neither he nor Husák showed much interest in the possibilities of reform that Soviet leader Mikhail Gorbachev (1931–) offered.

When protests began in Prague during 1989, the government responded with force. Mass demonstrations that autumn, under the auspices of Civic Forum, the coalition of Czech opposition groups, led to Jakeš's resignation on November 24. On December 10, Marián Čalfa (1946–) formed a new government whose participants were roughly balanced between party and nonparty members. Husák resigned as president that same day, marking an end to Communist rule in Czechoslovakia. Čalfa soon left the KSČ and joined Public Against Violence, the Slovak counterpart to Civic Forum. The elections of June 1990 reconfirmed Čalfa as prime minister, and he became head of Czechoslovakia's first non-Communist government since 1948.

Loss of its political monopoly in late 1989 meant change for the KSČ, including its federation into separate Czech and Slovak parties in autumn 1990, a division that soon became full separation. The Czech Communist Party of Bohemia and Moravia retained limited political support in the Bohemian lands during the first post-Communist years, getting 13.5 percent (second place) in the Czech parliamentary elections of 1990, the best showing up to that point for an East Central European Communist party in free elections. The Czech party split, however, in June 1993 when the reformists resigned from the rigid, doctrinaire parent body (the only post-Communist successor party in the region to retain the label "Communist") to found a more moderate organization. Alone in Eastern Europe the Czech left has been dominated (at least since 1995) by social democrats rather than ex-Communists, owing primarily to splits and dogmatism among the Communists. Generally more flexible than their Czech counterparts, the Slovak Communists, under pressure from their reform wing, soon transformed themselves into the Party of the Democratic Left and retained some support in Slovakia, gaining 13.8 percent (third place) in the Slovak parliamentary elections of 1990 and 10.4 percent in the 1994 elections, participating in the interim pre-election government of 1994.

Nancy M. Wingfield

Further reading

Kaplan, Karel. *Report on the Murder of the General Secretary.* Columbus, Ohio, 1990.
———. *The Short March.* New York, 1987.
Myant, M.R. *Socialism and Democracy in Czechoslovakia, 1945–1948.* Cambridge, Massachusetts, 1981.

Suda, Zdeněk. *Zealots and Rebels: A History of the Ruling Communist Party of Czechoslovakia.* Stanford, California, 1980.

See also Edvard Beneš; Censorship; Civic Forum; Comintern; De-Stalinization; Alexander Dubček; Mikhail Gorbachev; Klement Gottwald; Gustáv Husák; Lenin; Munich Pact; Antonín Novotný; Prague Spring; Red Army; Stalin; Warsaw Pact

Communist Party of Hungary

The Hungarian Communist Party was founded in Moscow on November 4, 1918, by former Hungarian prisoners of war. The party's precursor was the Russian Communist (Bolshevik) Party's Hungarian Section, which was set up on March 24, 1918. The dominant personality of the new party's Central Committee was Béla Kun (1886–1938), who along with two hundred of his comrades was repatriated to Hungary in November to bring about a revolution.

The party was reorganized in Budapest on November 24, 1918. On March 21, 1919, the party, numbering between four thousand and seven thousand members, fused with the Hungarian Social Democratic Party and formed a revolutionary government. The rise of the Hungarian Soviet Republic was brought about by the resignation of President Mihály Károlyi (1875–1955) and the occupation of part of Hungary by Romanian and Czechoslovak troops.

Kun remained the dominant personality of the united party, which took the name Party of the Socialist-Communist Workers of Hungary. With no help from Soviet Russia, however, Soviet Hungary was defeated by the invading Romanian army and the waning of internal support, owing to the government's nationalization of industry and agriculture and its aggressive antireligious policy. The Communist experiment collapsed on August 2, 1919, as did its unity with the socialists.

The Communist leaders, as well as many rank-and-file members, first sought asylum in Austria before most emigrated to Soviet Russia. In Hungary, a government decree of August 19, 1919, ordered the internment of Communists, and, on March 16, 1921, the Communist Party was officially outlawed. As an underground political party it was never able to attract more than about one thousand members, not only because of official repression but because the party and its exiled leadership were discredited in the eyes of the masses, owing to its actions in 1919.

A party in exile was organized, but an intra-party rift developed among its leaders over apportioning blame for the failure of the Communist experiment. A faction formed in Vienna, headed by Jenö Landrer (1875–1928), and one in Moscow, led by Kun. To end the squabbles, in March 1922 the Comintern (Communist International) ordered the dissolution of the party in exile.

In August 1925 there was a new attempt to revive the party in Hungary with a central committee of exiles and a secretariat that was to operate in Hungary. Earlier in the year, a legal cover party was also formed in Hungary, the Socialist Workers' Party of Hungary. The Communists, however, were unable to rebuild the movement because of the mass arrests in Hungary and because of the continuing infighting among the émigrés. In the summer of 1932 members of the secretariat were arrested, and under the provisions of martial law two of them, Imre Sallai (1897–1932) and Sándor Fürst (1903–32), were executed. Meanwhile in Moscow, the Comintern ordered the Central Committee of the Hungarian Communist Party to disband. The Comintern's decision doomed the party to a complete disorganization that lasted until the end of World War II. Stalin's purges of the late 1930s, moreover, caused immeasurable harm to the movement, as over fifty prominent Hungarian Communist exiles living in the Soviet Union were executed, including Kun.

In the shadow of an impending war in Europe, on June 10, 1939, the Comintern ordered the reestablishment of party organizations under centralized leadership. But in Hungary the arrest of hundreds of Communists in 1940 and 1942 stood in the way of party reorganization. In response to the dissolution of the Comintern in May 1943, the Hungarian Communist Party of 400–450 members dissolved itself in Hungary and repositioned itself as the Peace Party. The moment Soviet troops approached the Hungarian frontier in September, however, the party retook its old name.

The Communist Party was now backed by a major victor of the war, the Soviet Union. Since the party lacked mass support, its leadership, led by Mátyás Rákosi (1892–1971), who was imprisoned in Hungary from 1924 to 1940 and spent the war years in Moscow, favored a gradualist approach to power.

After joining the postwar coalition government, the party now began to expand its power base through mass recruitment and by getting key positions on the Trade Union Council and among the police; it also dominated the political police. In the postwar elections of October/November 1945, the Communist Party suffered a stunning defeat, which led it to intimidate the opposition. It resorted to fraudulent suffrage practices, thereby winning a plurality in the August 1947 elections. Soon, with the onset of the Cold War, the Communists abandoned all pretense of parliamentary niceties. The left wing of the Social Democratic Party was absorbed into the Communist Party in June 1948, and the party took the name Hungarian Workers' Party. All other political parties were eliminated and a totalitarian party-state on the Soviet model was established. The party even aped the Soviet show trials, as prominent—as well as rank-and-file—Communists were purged; some were executed, including stalwart László Rajk (1909–1949). The party's leadership fell into the hands of the Stalinists Rákosi, Ernö Gerö (1898–1980), Mihály Farkas (1904–65), and József Révai (1898–1959).

The death of Stalin (1879–1953) and the subsequent power struggle in Moscow had an impact on the Hungarian party as well. In June 1956 party leaders were summoned to Moscow and received new directives. Consequently, the "June Resolutions" outlined the party's errors and their causes and offered immediate political and economic solutions to the problems. Rákosi was forced to give up the premiership to Imre Nagy (1896–1958), though he remained party leader. Hence, the "New Course" abandoned forced collectivization and industrialization.

Although Rákosi came out on top in the power struggle, his success was short-lived, as Nikita Khrushchev (1894–1971), in his "Secret Speech" of February 1956, denounced Stalin's crimes and his "cult of personality." This led to Rákosi's downfall as the conflict within the party between the old guard and the reformers and the disaffection of the population led to an uprising on October 23, 1956. On the following day, Party Secretary Gerö was forced to cede his position to János Kádár (1912–89), a former victim of the purges. Kádár lorded over a phantom party, however, as members melted away during the revolution of 1956. The party of 850,000 was reduced to 37,818. Thus the old party was dissolved and the existence of its heir, the Hungarian Socialist Workers' Party, was announced by First Secretary Kádár on November 1, 1956. The massive Soviet intervention that began on November 4, 1956, crushed the revolution, and the new puppet government was headed by party leader Kádár.

Party dictatorship was reimposed as its structure was rebuilt. Party members who sided with the revolution, such as Nagy, minister of defense Pál Maléter (1917–58), and journalist Miklós Gimes (1917–58), were tried in secret before a kangaroo court and executed on June 16, 1958. Others were imprisoned.

But beginning in 1962, amnesty was given to those implicated in the revolution, and the party sought to rule by consensus with the slogan of "those who are not against us are with us." It also aimed to bring material well-being, the so-called "goulash communism," to Hungary.

By 1980, party membership again numbered eight hundred thousand, 74 percent of whom had not been members before 1956. Those in the party who sought further reforms welcomed a shift in the Soviet leadership, and the policy of perestroika (restructuring) pursued by Mikhail Gorbachev (1931–) gave an opportunity to push the aging Kádár aside, as nonparty dissent rose. In May 1988 Kádár was named to the ceremonial post of party president, as Károly Grósz (1930–96) became the party's last general secretary. During 1989, party reformers recognized that they would be unable to maintain power without a return to bloodshed. As such, on February 10–11, the Central Committee decided to negotiate with the still illegal opposition at the National Round Table about a transition to a multiparty system. In response to the new situation, at the Fourteenth Party Congress on October 7, delegates voted to dissolve the party and discharged rank-and-file members. The reformers then proceeded to form a new party, the Hungarian Socialist Party, which identified with the social democratic traditions of the West. Two months later, the general secretary of the defunct party, Grósz, and its ideologist, János Berecz (1930–), went on to form the Hungarian Socialist Workers' Party, which claimed the name and the mantle of the old party. The appearance of these two parties was the last blow for the party-state and signaled Hungary's return to a multiparty liberal democracy.

Peter Pastor

Further reading

Király, Béla, ed. *Lawful Revolution in Hungary, 1989–1994.* New York, 1995.

Kovrig, Bennett. *Communism in Hungary: From Kun to Kádár.* Stanford, California, 1979.

Molnár, Miklós. *From Béla Kun to János Kádár: Seventy Years of Hungarian Communism.* New York, 1990.

Pastor, Peter. "One Step Forward Two Steps Back: The Rise and Fall of the First Hungarian Communist Party, 1918–1922," in Ivo Banac, ed. *The Effects of World War I: The Class War after the Great War: The Rise of Communist Parties in East Central Europe, 1918–1921.* New York, 1983.

Stastny, Charles Ira. "The Hungarian Communist Party, 1918–1930: Days of Power, Years of Futility." Ph.D. diss., Harvard University, 1967.

Tökés, Rudolf L. *Hungary's Negotiated Revolution: Economic Reform, Social Change, and Political Succession, 1957–1990.* New York, 1996.

See also Cold War; Collectivization; Comintern; De-Stalinization; Ernö Gerö; Glasnost and Perestroika; Mikhail Gorbachev; Károly Grósz; Hungarian Revolution of 1956; Hungarian Soviet Republic; Industrialization; Mihály Károlyi; Béla Kun; Imre Nagy; NEM; József Pogány; Mátyás Rákosi; László Rajk; Revolutions of 1989; Stalin

Communist Party of Poland

The roots of Polish communism date to the 1880s, when two Marxist parties, the Socio-Revolutionary Party "Proletariat" (1882–93) and the League of Polish Workers (1889–93) merged in 1893 to form the Social Democracy of the Kingdom of Poland and Lithuania (SDKPiL). Among its leaders were Feliks Dzierzynski (1877–1926), Jozef Unszlicht (1879–1938), and Rosa Luxemburg (1871–1919), of whom the first two ended up occupying high posts in the Communist Party of the Soviet Union and the latter was assassinated in 1919 as one of the leaders of the Communist Party of Germany. SDKPiL was the first truly Marxist revolutionary party in Poland, and at the time of the 1905 revolution, which erupted in the area of Poland under Russian domination, it numbered about thirty thousand members. In December 1918 it merged with the Left Faction of the Polish Socialist Party (PPS-Lewica) to form the Communist Worker Party of Poland (KPRP), renamed the Communist Party of Poland (KKP) in 1925.

A member of the Comintern (Communist International), KPP was outlawed in 1919. During the interwar period, it went through several ideological and programmatic splits and never exerted much influence on Polish political life. The main reason for this was that throughout its existence it had given strong support to Poland's national minorities, thus antagonizing the majority of the population. As a result, its membership, estimated at about seven thousand, consisted mostly of Jews, Ukrainians, and Belorussians. In 1938, on Stalin's (1879–1953) orders, the Comintern announced the dissolution of the KPP, and nearly all its leaders were executed in the Soviet Union in the course of the Moscow purges. This unprecedented decision, justified by the Kremlin on the ground that KPP had been supposedly penetrated by the Polish intelligence services, has not been satisfactorily explained, though the KPP was officially rehabilitated by Moscow in 1956.

Some of the KPP leaders, who survived the purges because at that time they were in Polish jails, tried to rebuild the party. Ultimately, they succeeded in having the Comintern authorize the formation of a Polish Worker Party (PPR), which was formally established in Poland in January 1942 by a group of individuals parachuted from the Soviet Union. For the next two years, the party made little progress and never became a major actor in the anti-German resistance movement. On the eve of the Red Army's entry into Poland in the summer of 1944, PPR, led by its secretary-general, Władysław Gomułka (1905–82), numbered only a few thousand members. The Polish Communists, who spent the war years in the USSR, in 1944 organized a Central Bureau of Polish Communists in Moscow. The presence of two centers of Communist activities, one in Poland and the other in the Soviet Union, planted the seeds of a conflict between the "natives" and the "Moscovites" that erupted only four years later.

Initially, however, again on Stalin's orders, the two groups joined forces and Gomułka remained as secretary-general. The birth of the Cominform (propaganda organization designed to promote the Soviet party's agenda) at a meeting in Poland in 1947, followed by the Stalin-Tito split, the announced merger between PPR and PPS, and the beginning of the collectivization of agriculture, seen as the first step in the establishment of a

Soviet-led satellite system in Eastern Europe, brought the previously mentioned conflict to a head. Gomułka was expelled and later put under house arrest, and the leader of the new party, known as the Polish United Workers Party (PZPR), became Bolesław Bierut (1892–1956), a veteran Comintern agent who at that time held the office of the president of the republic.

Bierut presided over the party during the Stalinist period. Following the revelations of the 20th Congress of the Communist Party of the Soviet Union and the death of Bierut in March 1956, the new party leader, selected personally by Nikita Khrushchev (1894–1971), became Edward Ochab (1906–89). Ochab turned out to be only a transitional leader and ultimately paved the way for the return of Gomułka, who survived the Stalinist terror and assumed leadership on the wave of popular enthusiasm in October 1956. Despite granting some concessions, such as the abolition of collectivization and improving relations with the Catholic Church, Gomułka proved a major disappointment to his followers and was finally ousted in December 1970, in the wake of worker demonstrations on the Baltic coast.

His successor was Edward Gierek (1913–), the party leader of Silesia, the most industrialized region of Poland. Gierek performed reasonably well during the first few years of his rule, but, beginning in 1976, he lost control of the party and the country at large (in part owing to a series of worker riots). Following the success of the Solidarity trade union movement in achieving the status of an independent worker movement, Gierek resigned in favor of Stanisław Kania (1927–). Kania tried hard but failed to develop a modus vivendi with Solidarity, and in light of a rapidly deteriorating political and economic situation he was replaced as party leader by the minister of defense, General Wojciech Jaruzelski (1923–), who imposed martial law on the country in December 1981.

This proved to be the beginning of the end for the PZPR. Attempts to dissolve it and replace it with a new, reformed party were vetoed by Moscow. Faced with an increasingly restless country, Jaruzelski tried to preserve Communist rule by negotiating with the opposition, led by Lech Wałęsa (1943–), and an agreement to share power was reached at the so-called Round Table meeting in April 1989. Following its unexpected defeat in the semifree parliamentary elections in June 1989, the PZPR decided to dissolve itself in January 1990.

Under the new name Social Democracy of the Republic of Poland (SDRP), the party took part in the first truly free elections in 1991 and received about 10 percent of the popular vote. For the next two years it behaved as a loyal opposition, and in the September 1993 elections, under the leadership of Aleksander Kwasniewski (1954–), who also led the left-of-center coalition known as the Democratic Left Alliance (SLD), it gained the largest number of votes and formed a coalition government with the Polish Peasant Party. The alliance proved fragile and, in February 1995, the government was reorganized and the new prime minister became Jozef Oleksy (n.d.), until 1989 one of the regional secretaries of the PZPR.

The Polish Communist Party was never able to achieve full legitimacy. Also, despite some obvious achievements, it did not succeed in ensuring unity and in producing outstanding leaders. Gradually, the party managed to antagonize key segments of Polish society—workers, peasants, and intelligentsia—and it never recovered from the series of crises in 1956, 1968, 1970, 1976, and 1980–81—which ultimately destroyed its credibility. Its ability to survive the debacle of 1989 and to return to power in 1993 may be attributed less to its renewed popularity and more to the ineptness of the anti-Communist reforms.

Andrzej Korbonski

Further reading

de Weydenthal, Jan B. *The Communists of Poland,* 2d rev. ed. Stanford, California, 1986.

Dziewanowski, M.K. *The Communist Party of Poland,* 2d ed. Cambridge, Massachusetts, 1976.

Kowalski, Józef. *Komunistyczna Partia Polski 1935–1938.* Warsaw, 1975.

See also Bolesław Bierut; Collectivization; Comintern; De-Stalinization; Feliks Dzierzynski; Edward Gierek; Władysław Gomułka; Wojciech Jaruzelski; Rosa Luxemburg; Red Army; Solidarity; Tito-Stalin Split; Lech Wałęsa

Communist Party of Romania

The ruling party of Romania, 1948–89, named Romanian Workers' Party, 1948–65. Founded in 1921 as an offshoot of the larger Romanian Socialist

Party, the Romanian Communist Party (RCP) was outlawed in 1924 and never played an important role before World War II. It attracted some support during those years in the small Romanian working class and also among non-Romanian ethnic minorities, whose right to self-determination was accepted by the Soviet Union and imposed on the RCP. This nationality policy alienated most ethnic Romanians, however, and made fascism rather than communism the attractive ideology for interwar malcontents. Quarrels with Moscow and divisions within the RCP weakened it further. Only as the Soviet army occupied Romania at the end of World War II did the Communists begin to play a significant political role in the country.

Three groups of RCP leaders emerged in 1945: those who had spent the war in Romanian prisons, mostly uneducated Romanian workers and peasants such as Gheorghe Gheorghiu-Dej (1901–65) and Nicolae Ceauşescu (1918–89); those who managed to remain out of prison because of political or family connections, often educated Romanians such as Lucreţiu Pătrăşcanu (1900–1954); and those who spent the war in the Soviet Union, usually educated non-Romanians such as Ana Pauker (1893–1960) and Vasile Luca (1898–1952). All three groups cooperated to seize power by 1948; the king (Michael [1921–]) had abdicated, the Socialist Party was forced to unite with the RCP to form the Communist-dominated Romanian Workers' Party (RWP), other political parties were outlawed, and RWP membership had risen from a few thousand in 1944 to over a million. The party then proceeded to follow Lenin's (1870–1924) example in consolidating control: instituting a centrally planned and nationalized economy and placing the armed forces and police under RWP control.

Next came an internal struggle for power within the party reminiscent of Stalin's (1879–1953) strategies. The first to lose out was Pătrăşcanu, arrested in early 1948 but not executed until 1954. Then, in 1950–51 Pauker and Luca and their supporters were purged, reducing party membership from 1,060,000 in 1948 to 595,393 in 1955. Gheorghiu-Dej, general secretary since 1944, thereafter could dominate the leadership until his death from cancer in March 1965.

Under his guidance and that of Ceauşescu (party secretary for cadres by the late 1950s), party membership rose to 1,450,000 by 1965. Growth was particularly rapid in 1962–64, when Gheorghiu-

Dej sought greater autonomy from Moscow and redirected Romanian trade away from the Soviet bloc. To enhance his internal support he was willing to accept more members just as his more popular policies induced more Romanians to join. Ceauşescu continued and intensified both trends— autonomy from the USSR and growth in party membership. Elected to succeed Gheorghiu-Dej, he based his rule on his control of the party and its domination of society. Well known throughout Eastern Europe and in the West for his anti-Soviet and nationalist rhetoric, Ceauşescu returned the Romanian Workers' Party in July 1965 to its previous, more prestigious name, the Romanian Communist Party. By the late 1980s, he had made the RCP the largest Communist party in Eastern Europe, both in absolute terms and as a proportion of the population, with almost four million members representing about a third of the active population.

The party's social composition also shifted with regime priorities. Until 1948, almost anyone willing to join had been accepted, but the share of workers—supposedly the core of Communist support—dropped steadily from 54 percent in October 1945 to 37 percent in 1950. Former railroad worker Gheorghiu-Dej then stressed workers' recruitment, and by 1960 workers once more made up over 50 percent of party membership. Priorities soon shifted again. A campaign to complete the collectivization of agriculture saw the peasants' share jump from 22 to 34 percent in 1960–65. Notable in 1964–68, however, was the attempt to attract intellectuals, whose share rose from 9 to 23 percent. By 1969, however, the emphasis was once again on workers, and this would continue for the rest of Ceauşescu's rule; throughout the 1980s, workers made up about 55 percent of party membership.

The basic Leninist contradiction emerged between the RCP as an organization of the working class and as the leader of economic and social development. The RCP was expected simultaneously to be both revolutionary and ruling, egalitarian and elitist, a funnel of upward mobility and a stable group of policymakers and administrators presiding over economic development. These contradictory demands weakened the party even as it grew larger, reducing the quality of members and the rewards of membership while intensifying the demands placed on them. These factors—and Ceauşescu's nepotism and arbitrary circulation of personnel—contributed to the rapidity of the party's collapse in late 1989.

Mary Ellen Fischer

Further reading

Crowther, William E. *The Political Economy of Romanian Socialism.* New York, 1988.

Fischer, Mary Ellen. *Nicolae Ceauşescu: A Study in Political Leadership.* Boulder, Colorado, 1989.

Gilberg, Trond. *Nationalism and Communism in Romania.* Boulder, Colorado, 1990.

King, Robert R. *History of the Romanian Communist Party.* Stanford, California, 1980.

Shafir, Michael. *Romania: Politics, Economics, and Society.* Boulder, Colorado, 1985.

See also Elena Ceauşescu; Nicolae Ceauşescu; Collectivization; Gheorghe Gheorghiu-Dej; Lenin; Vasile Luca; Michael; Lucreţiu Patraşcanu; Ana Pauker; Revolutions of 1989; Stalin; Systematization

Communist Party of Yugoslavia (League of Communists of Yugoslavia)

The Communist Party of Yugoslavia (CPY) was founded during the aftermath of World War I in 1919. At that time the party played a major role in leading strikes and agitating for workers' rights. In 1920 the Communist Party gained the third-largest number of votes in elections for Yugoslavia's first constituent assembly. However, the State Security Act of 1921 made the party illegal shortly after a young Communist assassinated the minister of the interior. The Communists then continued their activities underground in trade union and youth organizations.

From its inception, internal divisions plagued the party. One faction favored a greater measure of autonomy for the nationalities in Yugoslavia, while the other faction, mainly Serbs, wanted to keep Yugoslavia centralized and insisted that the class struggle could not take place if workers were divided along national lines. Meanwhile, the Yugoslav regime harassed and imprisoned many party members. Consequently, during the 1920s and 1930s, the CPY remained weak and ineffectual, and many of its leading members went into exile in the Soviet Union.

The party's fortunes began to change in the late 1930s. Stalin (1879–1953) decided to support a united Yugoslavia, and he urged Yugoslav Communists to cooperate with other progressive parties in a popular front against fascism. In 1937 Josip Broz Tito (1892–1980) returned to Yugoslavia after a period in exile and took over leadership of the party. He was able to stop factional squabbling and to recruit many capable young leaders from all national groups.

When German armies invaded Yugoslavia in 1941, Tito and his fellow Communists established leadership over the Partisan resistance movement. Under their guidance, the Partisans appealed to patriotic Yugoslavs of all nationalities to form a popular front to fight against the German and Italian occupiers. The popular front idea was reflected in the creation of the Anti-Fascist Council for the Liberation of Yugoslavia (AVNOJ) in 1942. AVNOJ appealed to a broad political base, but Communists were the dominant force. As the war progressed the Partisans successfully fought and defeated internal rival factions such as the Serbian Chetniks and the Croatian Ustaša. After the Partisan army pushed the Germans from Yugoslavia in 1945, the Communists further consolidated their position by liquidating, often through brutal measures, all internal political opposition. AVNOJ became the de facto government of Yugoslavia. Thus, the Yugoslav Communist Party was able to turn the Partisan movement from an instrument of national liberation to one of social revolution.

From 1945 to 1948, the CPY followed Stalinist development models, creating a powerful central bureaucracy and emphasizing the expansion of heavy industry. But underneath the surface, tensions were growing between Yugoslavia and the Soviet Union. The Yugoslavs resented Soviet attempts to infiltrate their military and secret police, and they also complained that trade arrangements with the USSR were unfair. Perhaps most important, the Yugoslav Communist Party had gained power through its own efforts and hence did not owe its ruling position to Stalin and the Red Army. In 1948 the Cominform, an international Communist organization under Stalin's guidance, expelled Yugoslavia. The Cominform then imposed an economic and military blockade on Yugoslavia to topple the Tito regime.

Although the blockade put the Yugoslavs in an extremely precarious position, they obtained military and economic aid from the West and successfully resisted Stalin's pressure. The break with Stalin prompted important changes in the CPY's internal policies because Yugoslav Communists wanted to distinguish their policies from those of Stalin. In 1950 leading theorists in the CPY introduced the concept of "worker's self-management," which they believed more accurately reflected true Marxism. The new policy was to give workers' councils direct control over economic enterprises. The CPY also introduced other changes to create a more decentralized administrative system. At its Sixth Congress in 1952, the CPY changed its name to League of Communists of Yugoslavia (LCY). This action reflected the new role that the party was to have in society. Communists were expected to maintain a leading role but to influence policy through education and general programs rather than through direct administration.

Although the LCY retained its paramount position as the only legal party in Yugoslavia, it remained relatively pragmatic and allowed comparatively more freedom than other ruling Communist parties. When the economy of Yugoslavia slowed in the 1960s, the LCY attempted to spur productivity through the introduction of "market socialism." Market forces were to determine the production and distribution of goods as well as labor allocation.

Like many other LCY reforms, this policy did not work as intended when put into practice, and there remained considerable disagreement within the party over economic and national policies. Communist leaders from the wealthier republics such as Slovenia and Croatia demanded more autonomy, while others, particularly Serbian Communists, wanted to reestablish central authority. In the wake of a crisis provoked by Croatian nationalists in 1971, Tito did tighten control of the LCY and reaffirmed its importance as a unifying force in Yugoslav society. Nonetheless, the republics retained a great deal of autonomy, and economic decentralization remained in force. The party was caught squarely in a dilemma. Its survival depended on unity and enforced authority, yet the requirements of economic efficiency and national aspirations frequently pulled it in the opposite direction.

The problems facing the LCY intensified after Tito's death in 1980. With no leader of Tito's stature able to enforce discipline, the Communists from the various republics could not agree on a workable policy. National tensions heightened as the economy stagnated and communism began to lose authority elsewhere in Europe. In January 1990 an Extraordinary Congress of the LCY was convened to try to resolve the problems facing the party and the country. The Slovene delegation proposed that the LCY accept an end to its constitutionally protected status and allow multiparty elections. They also wanted to make the LCY into a loosely organized confederation of parties. When the Slovenes failed to win support for their proposal, they walked out of the congress. The remaining delegations could not agree to continue debate, and the congress collapsed in failure. This effectively marked the end of the LCY as the governing party of Yugoslavia. In 1991 open warfare erupted among the Yugoslav nations, destroying the Yugoslav Federation created by the Communists in 1943–45.

Paul D. Lensink

Further reading

Avakumović, Ivan. *History of the Communist Party of Yugoslavia.* Aberdeen, Scotland, 1964.

Banac, Ivo. *With Stalin against Tito: Cominformist Splits in Yugoslav Communism.* Ithaca, New York, 1988.

Cohen, Lenard J. *Broken Bonds: Yugoslavia's Disintegration and Balkan Politics in Transition,* 2d ed. Boulder, Colorado, 1995.

Johnson, A. Ross. *The Transformation of Communist Ideology: The Yugoslav Case, 1945–1953.* Cambridge, Massachusetts, 1974.

Rusinow, Dennison. *The Yugoslav Experiment, 1948–1974.* Berkeley, California, 1977.

See also Antifascism; Chetniks; Cominform; Vladimir Dedijer; Milovan Djilas; Self-Management; Stalin; Tito; Tito-Stalin Split; Ustaša

Conference on Security and Cooperation in Europe (CSCE)

Multilateral forum for dialogue and negotiation on matters of European security. Officially launched on August 1, 1975, the CSCE comprises fifty-one European and North American nations. Established during the period of détente between East and West during the Cold War, it fostered cooperation by introducing a code of behavior for international relations, promoting dialogue in an effort to identify and resolve potential conflicts, and developing confidence-building measures that encompass the principal areas of security, economics, and human rights. The process was aided by proceeding in stages where summits in Belgrade (1977–78), Madrid (1980–83), and Vienna (1987–89) addressed specific issues such as human rights, culture, and military disarmament. The Paris summit in November 1990 saw the successful contribution of the CSCE within East-West affairs with the signing of the Conventional Armed Forces Treaty, which substantially reduced the number of both NATO and Warsaw Pact armed forces. Reflecting the political changes of post–Cold War Europe and expanding to include nations of the former Soviet Union, the CSCE supports Eastern Europe's transformation while monitoring ethnic stability in the region through the High Commissioner on National Minorities. In January 1995 the CSCE changed its name to the Organization for Security and Cooperation in Europe.

Conrad Jarzebowski

Further reading

Berg, Rolf and Adam-Daniel Rotfeld. *Building Security in Europe.* New York, 1992.

Bloed, Arie, ed. *From Helsinki to Vienna: Basic Documents of the Helsinki Process.* The Hague, 1990.

Borawski, John. *From the Atlantic to the Urals: Negotiating Arms Control at the Stockholm Conference.* McLean, Virginia, 1988.

Mastny, Vojtech. *The Helsinki Process and the Reintegration of Europe, 1986–1991.* New York, 1992.

See also Cold War; Warsaw Pact

Congress of Berlin (1878)

International conference of Great Powers held from June 13 to July 13, 1878, with the immediate purpose of revising the Treaty of San Stefano (March 3, 1878), a bilateral agreement that had been imposed on the Ottoman Empire by the victorious Russians at the conclusion of the Russo-Turkish War of 1877–78. A concomitant goal of this meeting was to regulate the general affairs of the Balkans, which had been in a state of crisis since the Bosnian revolt against Ottoman rule in 1875. Attending the conference were representatives from Austria-Hungary, Russia, Germany, Britain, France, Italy, and the Ottoman Empire.

The Treaty of San Stefano had upset the fragile balance of power in the Balkans by creating an overextended Bulgarian state nominally under Ottoman suzerainty but in reality dominated by Russia. This situation evoked for the other Great Powers the specter of Russian hegemony in this region. Consequently, the statesmen assembled at Berlin, convening in the name of the European concert, significantly trimmed the dimensions of the new Bulgarian state, returning some of its territory directly to the Ottoman Empire and allowing for two autonomous but separate principalities with only limited Russian influence. At the same time, Austria attained the right to occupy and administer the Ottoman province of Bosnia-Hercegovina as well as the adjacent Sanjak of Novi Pazar, two strategic areas in the western Balkans. Serbia, Montenegro, and Romania, whose recent independence from Ottoman rule was confirmed by the congress, also received small accretions of territory. Russia's open dissatisfaction with the results of the congress and particularly its rancor at Germany's role precipitated an Austro-German defensive alliance, a diplomatic combination that would further complicate Great Power cooperation in the region.

The Congress of Berlin constitutes an important milestone in the history of the Eastern Question and the ongoing but often futile effort of the Great Powers to peacefully regulate affairs in the Balkans. The resurgence of crises in Bulgaria and in Bosnia-Hercegovina in later decades would progressively erode Great Power cooperation and eventually erupt into World War I.

Lawrence J. Flockerzie

Further reading

Hurst, Michael, ed. *Key Treaties for the Great Powers, 1814–1914,* vol. 1. New York, 1972, 551–77.

Medlicott, William N. *The Congress of Berlin: A Diplomatic History of the Near Eastern Settlement, 1878–1880,* 2d ed. London, 1963.

Novotny, A. *Quellen und Studien zur Geschichte der Berliner Kongresses, 1878.* Graz, Austria, 1957.

See also Bosnia-Hercegovina; Dual Alliance; Eastern Question; Great Powers; Russo-Turkish War of 1877–78; San Stefano, Treaty of; Sanjak of Novi Pazar; World War I

Congress of Lushnjë (1920)

Albanian nationalist protest against the proposed partition of Albania after World War I that organized a new Albanian government to preserve Albania's independence and territorial integrity.

The end of World War I saw a threat to Albania's existence. By the Treaty of London of 1915, Great Britain, France, and Italy had agreed to the postwar partition of Albania by Italy, Serbia, Montenegro, and Greece. At the Paris Peace Conference of 1919, Italy, Greece, and the new Yugoslavia put forward various territorial claims against Albania. On December 9, 1919, Britain, France, and the United States released a memorandum outlining the settlement of claims in Albania. Greece was to get the Gjirokastër district, while the fate of the Korçë district was left undecided. Yugoslavia was to be allowed to build a railroad across northern Albania. Italy was to annex Vlorë and its surrounding area and was to hold the remainder of Albania as a mandate.

This memorandum provoked Albanian nationalists. Since December 1918, an Albanian national government had existed at Durrës. The Durrës government, under Italy's control, was thoroughly discredited since it had accepted the idea of an Italian protectorate. Therefore, Albania's nationalists sought to replace it. During December 1919 and January 1920, nationalists traveled throughout Albania to encourage the selection of delegates to a congress to create a government that would be more aggressive in enunciating Albania's interests.

The Congress met in Lushnjë on January 28–31, 1920. It demanded a completely independent Albania within its "ethnic frontiers," rejecting any foreign mandate or protection. All representatives were sworn to defend Albania with their lives. Protests were sent to the Great Powers. For example, the Congress pleaded with the United States to "save Albania from the imperialistic pretention of the neighbor states." The delegates insisted that their only goal was to live in peace and harmony with their neighbors.

The congress also dissolved the Durrës government. By adopting a provisional statute, the congress rejected the system that had been imposed on Albania by a conference of the Great Powers in 1913. The rudiments of a new government were established, but many decisions regarding the form and particulars of that government were to be decided at some future date. For the moment, a Supreme Council, composed of four members, was to serve as the executive branch while a thirty-seven–member National Council would serve as the legislature. A prime minister was named, and a decision was made to hold general elections for a national parliament that would nominate a cabinet. Tirana (Albanian) was selected as the new national capital. Finally, the congress changed the Albanian delegation to the Paris Peace Conference to reflect its viewpoint.

Within the next few months, the new government, established in Tirana in March, was able to assert its control over Albania. When the French occupation ended, the areas claimed by Greece fell into Albanian hands. By the summer of 1920, Italy withdrew its troops from Vlorë, partly as a result of Albanian armed resistance. Italy renounced its claim to annex Vlorë and pledged to respect Albania's independence and territorial integrity.

The Congress of Lushnjë proved to be a turning point in modern Albanian history. The Albanians defied the Great Powers, saved their independence, and claimed the right to decide their own destiny.

Gregory J. Pano

Further reading

Frashëri, Kristo. *The History of Albania*. Tirana, 1964.

Pollo, Stefenaq and Arben Puto. *The History of Albania—from Its Origins to the Present Day*. London, 1981.

See also Great Powers; London Pact; Paris Peace Conference

Congress of Vienna (1814–15)

International conference that deliberated in Vienna from September 1814 to June 1815 with the central purpose of completing the post-Napoleonic reconstruction of Europe begun with the First Treaty of Paris of May 30, 1814. The congress dealt primarily with territorial and political issues pertaining to Germany, Italy, and Poland. Although all states of Europe sent representatives to Vienna, both the agenda and the major decisions of the congress were effectively controlled by the five Great Powers: Britain, Austria, Prussia, Russia, and France. Despite divergent aims and often acrimonious negotiations—particularly over the future dispositions of Saxony and Poland—the Great Powers maintained solidarity and steered the congress to a successful conclusion. The various decisions of the congress were incorporated into the so-called Final Act, dated June 8, 1815. The Congress of Vienna, which formed a central part of the general post-Napoleonic settlement negotiated between 1814 and 1818, is considered one of the most successful international conferences in modern history. The general spirit of restraint and cooperation in international affairs that emerged from the congress contributed to almost a half-century of peace in Europe.

In the course of reorganizing Central and East Central Europe, the leading statesmen at Vienna—Metternich of Austria (1773–1859), Castlereagh of Britain (1769–1822), Hardenberg of Prussia (1750–1822), Alexander I of Russia (1777–1825), and Talleyrand of France (1754–1838)—based their decisions primarily on strategic concerns, balance of power, and dynastic interests. Nonetheless, the results of their work had significant long-term impact on the political modernization and subsequent national development of this region. For example, much of the political consolidation and administrative modernization that had occurred in Germany during the Napoleonic era was retained and carried over to the new German Confederation, a loose union of thirty-four sovereign states and four free cities created at the congress and placed under the permanent presidency of the Austrian Empire. Moreover, although the congress repartitioned Poland among Austria, Prussia, and Russia, its largest section—that taken by Russia—was made into an autonomous, constitutional kingdom, linked to Russia through personal union with the tsar.

A most important "missed opportunity" for regulating the emerging Eastern Question occurred at the congress when the Great Powers considered, but failed to carry out, a guarantee of the integrity of the increasingly unstable Ottoman Empire.

Lawrence J. Flockerzie

Further reading

Griewank, Karl. *Der Wiener Kongress und die europäische Restauration, 1814–1815,* 2d ed. Leipzig, 1954.

Hurst, Michael, ed. *Key Treaties for the Great Powers, 1814–1914,* vol. 1. New York, 1972, 41–96.

Kraehe, Enno E. *Metternich's German Policy,* vol. 2, *The Congress of Vienna 1814–1815.* Princeton, New Jersey, 1983.

Schroeder, Paul W. "Did the Vienna Settlement Rest on a Balance of Power?" *American Historical Review* 97 (June 1992): 683–706.

Webster, C.K. *The Congress of Vienna 1814–1815.* New York, 1966.

See also Alexander I; Eastern Question; Great Powers; Clemens von Metternich Napoléon; Polish Congress Kingdom

Conrad, Joseph (1857–1924)

Polish-born novelist. Conrad was born in Berdichev in the Polish Ukraine to an educated landowner father with literary ambitions who was exiled with his family to northern Russia for participation in the Polish independence movement. Orphaned by the age of ten, Conrad was educated under the guardianship of a maternal uncle but early on began thinking of a life at sea, a remarkable ambition for a boy without nautical background in a country without a seacoast.

Conrad went to sea at seventeen, twice sailing to South America as an apprentice in French ships. During a twenty-year career at sea, he became a British merchant service captain and a British citizen in 1886. He began to turn his experiences at sea into literature during an ill-fated journey to Africa and up the Congo River in 1892. His first novel, *Almayer's Folly,* appeared in 1895, followed by a second, similar South Seas tale, *An Outcast of the Islands,* in 1896. *The Nigger of the "Narcissus"* (which in the United States was titled *The Children of the Sea*) followed in 1897 and led to his most popular work, *Lord Jim,* in 1900. The two dozen years until his death produced in fairly rapid succession—despite great creative difficulties aggravated by financial and physical problems—a stream of novels and short stories including such widely recognized masterpieces as *Nostromo* (1904), *The Secret Agent* (1907), *Under Western Eyes* (1911), *Chance* (1914), *Victory* (1915), *The Shadow Line* (1917), *The Arrow of Gold* (1919), and *Notes on Life and Letters* (1921). He produced thirteen novels, two volumes of memoirs, and twenty-eight short stories, many of considerable length, among them his most often studied novella, *Heart of Darkness* (1899). Conrad visited Poland with his English family in 1914 and was trapped in Europe by the outbreak of World War I, but he managed to return to England with the aid of the American ambassador in Vienna. He died at Canterbury in Kent, England, where he settled after his seagoing days were over.

Although Conrad's reputation in Poland declined after his death, it revived during World War II when his work seemed to speak so eloquently to the hopelessly embattled Poles.

Edward Bojarski

C

Further reading
Batchelor, John. *The Life of Joseph Conrad: A Critical Biography.* Cambridge, Massachusetts, 1994.
Palmer, John A. *Joseph Conrad's Fiction: A Study in Literary Growth.* Ithaca, New York, 1963.
Stallman, R.W., ed. *The Art of Joseph Conrad: A Critical Symposium.* East Lansing, Michigan, 1960.
Zyla, Wlodymyr. T. and Wendell A. Aycock. *Joseph Conrad: Theory and World Fiction.* Lubbock, Texas, 1974.

See also Polish Literature

Constanţa

An industrial city of over two hundred thousand inhabitants and Romania's only seaport. Built on the spot where the Romans had erected Tomis, a fortified town, Constanţa was a backward village inhabited by a mostly diverse population until 1878, when, after a successful war (waged jointly with Russia) against the Ottoman Empire (the Russo-Turkish War of 1877–78), Romania gained full sovereignty and was permitted to annex the coastal province of Dobrudja. The most important factor in linking Constanţa to Romania and building it up into a major port was the construction of the Cernavoda railroad bridge over the Danube in 1895. Industries began to move to the city and the port itself was built in 1909. Simultaneously, Constanţa slowly began to develop a tourist infrastructure. A casino and a large hotel were in place in the late 1930s, but large-scale hotel building did not begin until the 1950s and 1960s. In 1968 the administrative boundaries of Constanţa were enlarged to include several major tourist centers located in the vicinity. At the same time, as Romania's Communist regime forcefully developed its industry, including shipbuilding and international trade, the port's role grew. However, the Danube–Black Sea canal, which was built with enormous material and human sacrifices, and which was expected to affect Constanţa significantly, ultimately proved to be a major disappointment and had little impact on the city.

Ladis K.D. Kristof

Further reading
Magocsi, Paul Robert. *Historical Atlas of East Central Europe.* Seattle, Washington, 1993.
Rădulescu, I. and Athena Herbst-Rădoi. *Judeţul Constanţa.* Bucharest, 1974.
România: Atlas istoric-geographic. Bucharest, 1996.

See also Dobrudja; Russo-Turkish War of 1877–78

Constantine, Grand Duke Pavlovich (1779–1831)

Russian grand duke, grandson of Catherine II (1729–96), son of Paul I (1754–1801), younger brother of Alexander I (1777–1825), and elder brother of Nicholas I (1796–1855). Constantine (Konstanty Pawłowicz, Konstantin Pavlovich) took part in numerous campaigns against Napoléon (1769–1821). Appointed commander in chief of the army of the new Kingdom of Poland by Alexander I in 1815, he held the virtual powers of a viceroy. He introduced to the army the strict discipline of a martinet, which alienated the army, the Sejm (assembly), and eventually the population in general. To marry a Polish countess in 1820, he had to renounce his claims to the Russian throne. Although he—like his emperor-brothers—violated the Congress Kingdom's constitution on numerous occasions, he defended the autonomy of the Polish army and bureaucracy. He was thus completely surprised when the Polish army supported a revolt against the Russians, the November Uprising of 1830–31. He escaped from Warsaw in December 1830 and died before the uprising was suppressed.

John Stanley

Further reading
Leslie, R.F. *Polish Politics and the Revolution of November 1830.* London, 1956.
Thackeray, Frank. *Antecedents of Revolution: Alexander I and the Polish Kingdom, 1815–1825.* Boulder, Colorado, 1980.

See also Alexander I; Napoléon; Nicholas I; November Uprising; Polish Congress Kingdom; Sejm

Constantinople/Istanbul

Capital of the Byzantine and Ottoman Empires. The impact of more than a thousand years of Byzantine and Ottoman control and overlordship in the Balkans may be considered from three perspectives: the cultural legacy, social and economic development, and the landscape.

Orthodox Christianity became well established in the Balkans during the Byzantine period, and Ottoman policy helped to maintain its influence and authority, first, by strengthening the authority of the Ecumenical Patriarch at Constantinople (Istanbul), and, second, through the *millet* system. Organized on the basis of national churches, it is predominant among the peoples of the southern and southeastern Balkans (Slavs, Greeks, Romanians). Although the presence of Muslim Turk minorities is recognized in Bulgaria, Greece (Eastern Thrace), Romania (Dobrudja), and the regions of Bosnia, Kosovo, Macedonia, and southern Serbia, the major residual of the Ottoman past is in the number and extent of the Islamized population (Bosnians, Albanians, Bulgarian Pomaks).

Agriculture in the Balkans generally declined or stagnated during the Ottoman period, owing to poor land use management and an exploitative system of semifeudal organizations (*chiftliks*). Apart from the encouragement of crafts, textiles, and agricultural processing, there was little development of factory industry until late in the nineteenth century. Scores of villages and towns disappeared, and only centers of Ottoman administration grew in importance (Sofia, Bucharest, Novi Pazar, Skopje, Sarajevo). Railroad development in Ottoman territory did not begin until 1860 and was little advanced until later in the nineteenth century. This history of economic backwardness in the southern and southeastern Balkans continues to strain resources and impede development in the region.

The Byzantine and Ottoman traditions in the cultural landscape of southeastern Europe are distinctive, though often modified by local and national styles. The cluster of churches and monasteries in the vicinity of the Patriarchate of Pec are typical of the Serbian style, in contrast to the painted monasteries of northern Moldavia and the Rila Monastery in Bulgaria. Mosques in Bulgaria are often in the "Balkan" style, with decorated exteriors. The contrast in landscape to other parts of Europe is greatest in the largely Muslim areas: the minarets in both rural and urban areas, the typically arched stone bridges, and the caravansaries and bazaars of the larger towns.

Albert M. Tosches

Further reading
Lampe, John R. *Balkan Economic History, 1550–1950.* Bloomington, Indiana, 1982.
Mellor, Roy E.H. *Eastern Europe.* New York, 1975.
Pounds, Norman J.G. *An Historical Geography of Europe, 1800–1914.* Cambridge, 1985.
Rugg, Dean S. *Eastern Europe.* New York, 1985.

See also Agriculture; Architecture; *Chiftlik;* Dobrudja; Islam; *Millet;* Orthodoxy; Ottoman Empire; Patriarchate; Railroads; Thrace; Turks

Corfu Declaration

An agreement signed on July 20, 1917, between representatives of the Serbian government, then in exile on the island of Corfu, and the Yugoslav Committee, a group of émigré South Slav politicians from the Habsburg Monarchy. The declaration stated that the Serbs, Croats, and Slovenes were determined to create a united state after World War I.

The declaration consisted of fourteen specific articles relating to the organization of a common future South Slavic state. This state was to be a constitutional, democratic, and parliamentary monarchy headed by the Serbian Karadjordjević dynasty. The first point stated that the constitution of the new state was to be determined after the war by a constituent assembly. This constitution had to be accepted by a "numerically qualified majority," which is to say well over 50 percent of the deputies in the constituent assembly, and approved by the king. This provision for a qualified majority was never strictly defined or subsequently adhered to, however, and thus became a matter of dispute after 1918. Moreover, the declaration made no provisions for the continuation of historical territorial frontiers and institutions, and this had important future consequences. On a positive note, it did recognize in principle the equality of the Serbs, Croats, and Slovenes, the three national flags and two religions (Orthodoxy and Catholicism), and two alphabets (Cyrillic and Latin scripts). The declaration was, on the whole, a compromise among its signatories, but each interpreted the document differently. This was to cause important political problems in the postwar Yugoslav state because the terms of unification were not agreed to before that act took place. Nevertheless, this document is usually interpreted as

C an important step toward the creation of a Yugoslav state.

Mark Biondich

Further reading
Janković, Dragoslav. *Jugoslovensko piatnje i Krfska deklaracija 1917 godine.* Belgrade, 1967.

See also Yugoslav Committee

Corfu Incident

Italian dictator Benito Mussolini's first act of aggression in the Balkans. In September 1923 Italy seized the Greek island of Corfu, thus provoking a major diplomatic incident. This was done in reaction to the assassination on August 27 on Greek soil of four Italian officials working for an international commission delimiting the Greek-Albanian frontier. Although it was never determined who was responsible for the murders, Mussolini (1883–1945) issued a drastic ultimatum to the Greek government and demanded that it be accepted unconditionally. Greece accepted parts of the ultimatum and offered to submit the dispute to the League of Nations for arbitration. The refusal to accept the ultimatum unconditionally prompted Italian bombardment and occupation of the island.

This action presented the League of Nations with a difficult problem and tested its credibility. The league skirted the issue and let the Conference of Ambassadors resolve the matter. The conference came up with a compromise solution, the terms of which stipulated that Greece pay a large financial reparation to Italy. Mussolini's real intention was to annex Corfu, and only after the British issued a thinly veiled threat to use their Mediterranean fleet did Italy evacuate its troops from Corfu on September 27. Although Mussolini backed down, the crisis was resolved outside the league. As a result, the league was greatly weakened, whereas Mussolini's prestige had been enhanced.

Mark Biondich

Further reading
Barros, James. *The Corfu Incident of 1923: Mussolini and the League of Nations.* Princeton, New Jersey, 1965.
Blatt, Joel. "France and the Corfu-Fiume Crisis of 1923." *The Historian* 50, no. 2 (1988): 234–59.
Yearwood, Peter J. "'Consistently with Honour': Great Britain, the League of Nations and the Corfu Crisis of 1923." *Journal of Contemporary History* 21, no. 4 (1986): 559–79.

See also League of Nations

Cosić, Dobrica (1921–)

Serb writer and dissident. Ćosić was born in the Serbian village of Velika Drenova. Although he attended primary school, he received most of his education from his grandfathers. From one, he received a love of politics, politicians, elections, and deputies. From the other, he came to love village life, nature, and the soil. Ćosić continued his education in agriculture in secondary school, where he was introduced to Communist propaganda and books, which he read avidly, and in 1939 he became a member of the (illegal) Communist Youth Organization. In 1941 he joined the Partisan movement in the fight against the fascists and became a political commissar. He edited several propaganda journals, rising quickly through the ranks of the Yugoslav Communist Party, and held many important administrative, political, and cultural positions until 1968, when he openly became, in his own words, a "dissident." In the late 1960s Tito (1892–1980) himself dismissed Ćosić from all his functions. Many years later, Ćosić said that he was thankful to Tito for doing this because he was left with free time to write.

Ćosić never forgot his village and his Serbian roots. Numerous travels through Serbia added to his identification with Serbian national feeling, one of many things Tito did not tolerate. Both Ćosić and his literary characters were shaped by the events that confronted Serbia and Yugoslavia both during and after World War II. His prose grips the reader because all his works are full of action, containing stories within stories. His first important work, *Daleko je sunce: Far Away is the Sun* (1951), caused ripples in Yugoslav literary circles with its depiction of Partisans as men, not mythological heroes, as they had been portrayed in the literature of socialist realism. Ćosić's heroes are serious; they do not laugh, and they do not believe in either God or the devil. *Koreni* (*The Roots*, 1964) deals with a Serbian peasant society on the brink of destruction and the natural impulses of a family to survive. *Deobe* (*Divisions*, 1961) is a tragedy in which the victim is a village society trying to preserve its old moral codes and ethics. *Bajka* (*A Fairy Tale*, 1996) portrays a science fiction view of history, one of Ćosić's obsessions throughout his literary and political works. It is an absurdist story, written in the first person, about a nonexistent yet very real country called Kamonija, in which the people are happy and the machines are absolute. Some Yugoslav literary critics saw in this story a parody of Yugoslavia itself. Ćosić's anti-war stories have been hailed as "epic novels of the survival of the Serbian people" in Yugoslavia.

In 1989 Ćosić was accused by many within Yugoslavia of being the principal destroyer of the myth of Tito for his steadfast criticism of the decades of Tito's rule and the failure to resolve the nation's complex problems.

Ruzica Popovitch

Further reading
Bandić, Miloš. *Dobrica Ćosić.* Belgrade, 1968.
Ćosić, Dobrica. *Moć i strepnje.* Belgrade, 1971.
Đukić, Slavoljub. *Čovek u svom vremenu: Razgovori sa Dobricom Ćosićem.* Belgrade, 1989.
Palavestra, Predrag. "Obnova istorijskog romana." *Kritičke rasprave (Književne teme XI).* Belgrade, 1995, 215–22.

See also Antifascism; Communist Party of Yugoslavia; Tito; Yugoslav Literature

Creangă, Ion (1837–89)

Romanian writer. Creangă was born in Humulești, Moldavia, into the *răzeş* (free peasant) social class. As the eldest of eight children, he was expected to become a priest. After graduating from Socola Monastery in 1859, he continued his education at the theology seminary in Iaşi, but he could not adapt to an urban existence. Running afoul of the church, he trained as a teacher. As a school inspector, he met poet Mihai Eminescu (1850–89) who introduced him to the literary society Junimea in 1875.

Eminescu gave Creangă the impetus to write, finding in him a rich source of folk wisdom and an extraordinary linguistic talent. Creangă's masterpiece, *Amintiri din copilărie (Recollections of Childhood,* 1880–92), is remarkable for its close observation of human nature, enlivened by *"paremiologie"* (a style abounding in proverbs, anecdotes, etc.). It describes village life and traditional customs and records the rural speech of nineteenth-century Moldavians. Creangă wrote tales in the folk manner based on features stem-ming from the lives of country dwellers, including *Povestea lui Harap Alb (The Story of the White Moor,* 1877), and exploited the humor of ambiguous situations, as in the story *Moş Nichifor Coţcariul (Old Swindler Nichifor,* 1877).

Charles M. Carlton

Further reading
Academia Republicii Socialiste Romănia. *Dicţionarul literaturii romăne de la origini pînă la 1900.* Bucharest, 1979.
Călinescu, G. *Istoria literaturii romăne de la origini pînă în prezent,* 2d ed., Bucharest, 1982.
Cartianu, A. and R.C. Johnston, trans. *Memories of My Boyhood: Stories and Tales.* Bucharest, 1978.

See also Mihai Eminescu; Folklore; Junimea; Romanian Literature

Crimean War (1853–56)

War that pitted Russia against the armies of the Ottoman Empire, Britain, France, and Sardinia. The Crimean War originated in a dispute over access to Jerusalem's Holy Places. Orthodox Christians had lost certain privileges at the sites. Nicholas I (1796–1855) sent an envoy, Prince Alexander Menshikov (1787–1869), to obtain more favorable terms for the Orthodox. Menshikov insisted that Russia be granted a formal protectorate over all Orthodox Christians in the Ottoman Empire.

British officials recalled Nicholas's numerous references to the Ottoman Empire as the "sick man of Europe" in recent years and his suggestions for a Russo-British partition of the empire. They therefore urged the sultan to resist Menshikov's demands, which he did. Russia responded by sending troops into the Danubian Principalities.

Nicholas expected a show of loyalty for his assistance against rebellious Hungarians in 1849. However, Austria's Franz Joseph (1830–1916) wished to avoid a Russian presence near his South Slavic lands. He also feared alienating France, whose leaders could use their influence to cause trouble in the monarchy's Italian possessions. His foreign ministry therefore issued the Vienna Note of 1853, which called for reaffirming the conditions of two previous Ottoman-Russian treaties involving Orthodox Christians: Kuchuk Kainardji (1774) and Adrianople (1829).

The sultan refused to sign it without amendments, which Russia found objectionable. The Ottoman government demanded that Russian troops leave the Principalities; shortly thereafter, Ottoman troops entered Russian territory. In early November an Ottoman squadron of ships sailed into the Black Sea, hoping to create an incident. The Russian navy sank the Ottoman ships at Sinope.

At first, Russia's armies recorded several quick victories. In 1854, however, the conflict broadened to include Britain, France, and a contingent of Sardinian troops. Moreover, Franz Joseph ordered Russian troops out of the Principalities and negotiated an agreement with the Ottoman Empire to send his own occupation force there. Nicholas could only rage at Austria's ingratitude and brace for a wider conflict, which suddenly seemed unavoidable, even though Russia lacked a compelling reason to fight.

The conflict widened in September 1854 with a British and French landing in the Crimea. Although many of the battles were bloody and often inconclusive, the key engagement of the war proved to be the long siege at Sevastopol, which fell in September 1855, sealing Russia's fate.

The business of peacemaking fell to Nicholas's heir, Alexander II (1818–81). In the 1856 Peace of Paris, the Allies presented the new tsar with exacting terms. Russia would forfeit its right to intervene in Ottoman affairs on behalf of Orthodox Christians, a right it had claimed since 1774; now those Christians would have an international guarantee. Russia would lose its protectorate over Serbia and the Principalities and yield Bessarabia, a territory it had held since 1812. Perhaps most important, the Black Sea would henceforth be demilitarized, depriving Russia of the right to send warships forth from that strategic body of water. In essence, Russia lost the privileged position it had gained in the Treaty of Adrianople twenty-five years earlier.

The Peace of Paris marked a long withdrawal from foreign affairs for Alexander II and Russia, a period that would see significant internal reforms such as the liberation of the serfs in 1861. The Crimean defeat insured that when that nation returned to foreign affairs, it would seek change in the 1856 status quo.

Brigit Farley

Further reading

Anderson, M.S. *The Eastern Question 1774–1923.* New York, 1966.

Jelavich, Barbara. *The Habsburg Empire in European Affairs 1814–1918.* Chicago, 1969.

Lincoln, W. Bruce. *Nicholas I: Emperor and Autocrat of All the Russias.* Bloomington, Indiana, 1978.

See also Adrianople, Treaty of; Alexander II; Danubian Principalities; Eastern Question; Franz Joseph; Kuchuk-Kainardji, Treaty of; Nicholas I; Ottoman Empire; Paris, Treaty of; Russia

Cristea, Miron (1868–1939)

Leading ecclesiastical figure and first patriarch of interwar Romania, member of the regency (1927–39), and prime minister (1938–39). Born Elie Cristea in Topoliţa, Transylvania, Cristea was ordained into the Orthodox clergy and completed a thesis in Romanian literature. After becoming secretary to the Orthodox metropolitan in Sibiu, he took monastic vows as well as a second name—Miron—in 1902. Having become prominent in the Romanian national movement through his contributions in the press in Transylvania, he gained confirmation by the Hungarian government as bishop with some difficulty.

As primate and later patriarch, Cristea opposed (but failed to prevent) the postwar Romanian government's concordat (rapprochement) with the Vatican. He did not originate the idea of a patriarchate but presided ably over its establishment and championed the prior work of Andrei Şaguna (1809–73), outstanding Romanian religious leader of the nineteenth century, as the foundation of the reorganization of the church. He created a biblical institute that published a Romanian Bible in 1936, and secured considerable financial support from the state for construction. He defended the church against political interference, but as regent and prime minister he was not an independent political figure.

James P. Niessen

Further reading

Hitchins, Keith. *Rumania 1866–1947.* Oxford, 1994.

See also Orthodoxy; Patriarchate; Andrei Şaguna

Croatia, Birth of the Republic of (1991)

Newly independent state formed from the breakup of Yugoslavia. As the economic and constitutional system created by Tito (1892–1980) eroded during the late 1980s, Serbian President Slobodan Milošević (1941–) whipped up Serbian nationalist passions to gain broader power in the Yugoslav federation. After disrupting the federal constitutional order by removing Kosovo's autonomy (1988) and staging putsches in Vojvodina (October 1988) and Montenegro (January 1989), Milošević redirected Serbian nationalist rhetoric at Serbs in Croatia and Bosnia-Hercegovina, attacking Croatia's fascist Ustaša regime during World War II. The Serbs in Croatia's Knin region (approximately one-quarter of Croatia's Serbs) initially responded to Milošević's propaganda with an abortive attempt to establish an autonomous Serbian cultural society in 1988. Inflammatory Serbian rhetoric included Serbian writer Dobrica Ćosić's (1921–) call for a Greater Serbia and the removal of Zadar, Istria, and the Adriatic islands from Croatian control. As Croatia's first independent political parties formed after 1988, many reacted sharply to Serbian propaganda. Serbia's escalating anti-Croatian rhetoric and the destruction of the League of Communists of Yugoslavia (the country's Communist party) in January 1990 brought Franjo Tudjman's (1922–1999) Hrvatska Demokratska Zajednica (HDZ, Croatian Democratic Community) to power in May 1990 on a Croatian nationalist platform. For many Serbs, the HDZ's iconography confirmed Milošević's propaganda, as did HDZ attempts to alter Serb legal status. The Croatian Sabor (parliament) quickly declared the Republic of Croatia "sovereign," setting the stage for future secession from Yugoslavia, and the HDZ removed Communist references from official titles and symbols.

Croatia's Krajina Serbs—by now armed and financed directly from Belgrade through the Serb-dominated Yugoslav National Army (JNA) and a variety of paramilitary groups—responded with an autonomy referendum and began the *Balvan* (tree-trunk) revolution around Knin in August 1990 by blocking major roads and train tracks, severing Zagreb's main arteries with the tourist-rich Dalmatian seacoast. The Knin Serbs spoke of unifying Croatia's Serbian-populated regions with Serbia. Order deteriorated throughout Croatia as Tudjman's government attempted to disarm the republic's substantial Serbian minority and began to dismiss many Serbs from their jobs. In early December a crisis erupted between Croatia and Slovenia on the one hand and the JNA on the other over the issue of local defense units, which Tudjman refused to disarm. In mid-January 1991 the Yugoslav military police began arresting Croatian officials, while Tudjman met with the federal prime minister in an effort to avert full-scale civil war. By late January, these talks had broken down, and the JNA attempted to arrest Croatia's defense minister. During the first half of 1991, the JNA sided with Croatia's Serbs, as armed clashes occurred with increasing frequency. A series of meetings between republic leaders only emphasized the gap, as Milošević pressed for recentralization and stronger federal control, while Croatia and Slovenia pushed for decentralization and a confederation. Tensions simmered as U.S. Secretary of State James Baker (1930–) visited Yugoslavia on June 22, 1991, declared U.S. support for a unified Yugoslavia, and stated the U.S. would not recognize an independent Croatia or Slovenia.

On June 25, 1991, Croatia, along with Slovenia, declared independence from Yugoslavia, while promising full cultural autonomy and equal rights to Croatia's Serbs. Almost immediately, Serbs from Serbia and Croatia launched attacks on Croatian targets with artillery and air support from the JNA. The fighting escalated throughout the summer and fall of 1991. In October the Serbian and Montenegrin delegates officially expelled the Croatian and Slovenian delegates from Yugoslavia's rotating presidency, forming a rump Yugoslavia. Croatia's independent status was given international legitimacy by Germany's decision to recognize both Croatia and Slovenia, followed by official European Community recognition on January 15, 1992.

James M.B. Lyon

Further reading

Cohen, Lenard. *Broken Bonds: Yugoslavia's Disintegration and Balkan Politics in Transition,* 2d ed. Boulder, Colorado, 1995.

Glenny, Misha. *The Fall of Yugoslavia.* London, 1992.

Magaš, Branka. *The Destruction of Yugoslavia.* London, 1993.

Ramet, Sabrina. *Nationalism and Federalism in Yugoslavia, 1962–1991,* 2d ed. Bloomington, Indiana, 1991.

Stokes, Gale. *The Walls Came Tumbling Down.* Oxford, 1993.

Thompson, Mark. *Forging War: The Media in Serbia, Croatia, and Bosnia-Hercegovina.* London, 1994.

See also Communist Party of Yugoslavia; Dobrica Ćosić; Greater Serbia; Kosovo; Slobodan

Milošević; Sabor; Serbia and the Breakup of Yugoslavia; Slovenia, Birth of the Republic of; Tito; Franjo Tudjman; Ustaša

Croatia (Geography)

Newly independent state of East Central Europe and a historic part of the Habsburg Empire and Yugoslavia. Croatia has an area of 21,823 square miles (60,620 sq km) and a population of 4,600,000. A 1981 census, taken before massive refugee flows generated by the breakup of Yugoslavia, showed that 80 percent of the population identified itself as Croatian and 14 percent as Serbian. A significant portion of the Serbian population now has fled to Serbia and Bosnia-Hercegovina.

Croatia consists of three parts: a north-central core region around the capital city, Zagreb; an eastward-trending belt, Slavonia, extending between the Sava River and the Hungarian border to Serbia; and a coastal region, Dalmatia, lying between Bosnia-Hercegovina and the Adriatic Sea southward to the border with Montenegro.

North-central Croatia is a region of hills and low mountains descending from the flanks of the Alps to the alluvial plain of the Sava River. Few elevations are higher than 3,000 feet (910 m). Despite its rolling character, this region has some of the highest densities of rural population in Europe—descendants of refugees finding haven from Ottoman armies that advanced northward up the Balkan Peninsula in the fifteenth century. Slavonia is a generally more level region lying on the southern margin of the vast Pannonian (Hungarian) Plain, although ranges of hills separate the drainage basins of the eastward-flowing Sava and Drava Rivers, which are tributaries of the Danube. The Dalmatian coastal region is characterized by mountainous limestone karst topography of slopes generally devoid of vegetation and with few streams flowing above ground.

Dalmatia exhibits a typically Mediterranean climate of warm, dry summers and mild, rainy winters. Average temperatures are about 40° F (4° C) in January and 75° F (24° C) in July. Rainfall ranges from fewer than 24 inches (61 cm) annually on offshore islands in the Adriatic to more than 110 inches (262 cm) in the Gorski Kotar Mountains behind the coastal port city of Rijeka. The climates of northwestern Croatia and Slavonia are more continental in character. They have January temperatures near freezing and July averages about 72° F (22° C). Approximately 40 inches (102 cm) of precipitation falls in these interior regions, mainly in the summer months.

Croatia's economy has long been based on a productive agriculture, particularly in the favored terrain and climatic conditions of Slavonia. Grains—mainly corn—occupy three-fourths of the farmland. Other crops include sugar beets and sunflowers, the latter grown for their vegetable oils. Fruits, vineyards, and early vegetables characterize the limited areas of farming in Dalmatia, which has more than four million olive trees grown primarily for their oil. Tourism has become Dalmatia's principal industry in recent decades.

Industrial growth began in the 1860s with the building of railroads in the Austro-Hungarian Empire. It developed strongly after the formation of an independent Yugoslavia in 1918. Among Croatia's mineral resources are oil, natural gas, bauxite, and minor deposits of coal. These have given rise to several heavy industries, including petrochemicals, aluminum, and iron and steel production. Also playing a role are imported raw materials, such as cotton for Croatia's significant textile industry. About a quarter of industrial production is concentrated in Zagreb and its environs.

Thomas M. Poulsen

Further reading

Eterovich, Francis H. and Christopher Spalatin, eds. *Croatia: Land, People, Culture,* 2 vols. Toronto, 1970.

Hamilton, F.E. Ian. *Yugoslavia: Patterns of Economic Activity.* New York, 1968.

Lijepa naša Hrvatska, ed. by Boris Zdunić. Zagreb, 1991.

Pavić, Radovan and Nikola Stražičić. *Ekonomska geografija Jugoslavije,* 3d ed. Zagreb, 1970.

See also Dalmatia; Rijeka; Slavonia; Zagreb

Croatian Art

Influences from Austria and Italy were crucial in the development of Croatian art during the nineteenth century. The traditions of the late baroque were still alive in sacral art and portrait painting. However, classicism of the Vienna School also existed, and around the 1830s it turned into Biedermeier, an artistic trend in Germanic Europe ideologically opposed to academic and religious painting, which flourished in the 1850s in the works of Vjekoslav Karas (1821–58). The most important Croatian painter at the turn of the twentieth century was Vlaho Bukovac (1855–1922). In the 1890s his strong, bright colors influenced a generation of young painters who formed the Multicolored Zagreb School. Celestin Medović (1857–1920), who made historical and religious compositions in the style of academic realism, was another important artist of the period. After 1900, his plein air paintings brought him close to the Multicolored Zagreb School, which was active until the late 1920s.

The most prominent representatives of this school were Oton Iveković (1869–1939), who painted historical themes in the impressionist manner; Menci Clement Crnčić (1865–1930), who used the plein air technique and thick impasto; and Ferdo Kovačević (1870–1927), who composed landscapes in a more delicate mood. Ivan Tišov (1870–1928), with his decorative approach, and Branko Šenoa (1879–1939), with his plein air technique, also belonged to the circle of Bukovac's followers.

Early-twentieth-century art was also marked by the influences of the European secession movement (the most progressive trend in German-speaking Europe in the late nineteenth and early twentieth centuries, which supported avant-garde styles and challenged traditional art policies) and themes from classical mythology (Bela Čikoš-Sesija [1864–1931] and Bukovac's last phase). Before World War I, symbolism—as defined by the European secession—occurred in the works of Emanuel Vidović (1870–1953), Mirko Rački (1879–1982), and Tomislav Krizman (1882–1955). In the 1910s impressionist influences in the works of artists such as Vladimir Becić (1886–1954) further illustrated the diversity of artistic trends of the period.

The strong coloristic expressionism of Ljubo Babić (1890–1974), Zlatko Šulentić (1893–1971), and Marino Tartaglia (1894–1984) continued modernist trends during the interwar period. Milivoj Uzelac (1897–1977), Marijan Trepše (1897–1964), and Vilko Gecan (1894–1973) followed another direction and worked under Cézanne's (1839–1906) influence and the principles of cubism. Immediately before World War II, artists around Krsto Hegedušić (1901–75) formed a group called The Soil, which stressed the necessity of social criticism in art. Peasant artists Ivan Generalić (1914–)

and Franjo Mraz (1910–81), well-known representatives of the first generation of Croatian naive painters, also belonged to the group.

After World War II, current European trends quickly replaced a short period of social realism. They ranged from neo-impressionism to Picasso (1881–1973) and Ernst (1891–1976), and were followed by characteristically European and American lyrical abstraction, *art informel,* and abstract expressionism. Edo Murtić (1921–), Zlatko Prica (1916–), and Ferdinand Kulmer (1925–) were the first to follow this direction. Miljenko Horvat (1935–) added lyrical and poetical dimensions to this variant of abstract expressionism. The interest in naïve art was renewed in the 1960s in works of Ivan Rabuzin (1921–), Ivan Lacković-Croata (1932–), and Ivan Večenaj (1920–). On the other hand, Julije Knifer (1924–) represented art of geometrical abstraction, while Miljenko Stančić (1926–77) and Vasilije Jordan (1934–) followed the trend of postsurrealistic painting. At that time, Croatian painters began to explore possibilities of neoconstructivism and optical art. In the 1980s Boris Bućan (1947–), Sanja Iveković (1949–), and Mladen Stilinović (1947–) exploited conceptual art and performance.

At the turn of the twentieth century, the academic realism of sculptures by Ivan Rendić (1849–1932) heralded the beginnings of modern Croatian sculpture. Somewhat later, the impressionist tradition inspired Branislav Dešković's (1883–1939) exquisite series of canine figures. However, the greatest Croatian sculptor was Ivan Meštrović (1883–1962). Dynamic and realistic sculptures with social connotations by Antun Augustinčić (1900–1979) and Vanja Radauš (1906–92) dominated the interwar period. After World War II, aesthetic principles of socialist realism were much more visible in sculpture than in painting, especially in public monuments dealing with the socialist revolution. Only in the 1960s did Croatian sculpture depart from realistic forms and introduce metal as the main medium. Experiments in optical and kinetic sculpture by Dušan Džamonja (1928–) and Ivan Kožarić (1921–) in the 1970s led to the establishment of new avant-garde trends in Croatian art.

Svetlana Rakić

Further reading

Gamulin, Grgo. *Hrvatsko slikarstvo XX stoljeća.* Zagreb, 1987.

Ilić, Aleksandar et al. *EgoEast: Croatian Art Now.* Zagreb, 1992.

Neue Tendenz: 10 Künstler aus Zagreb. Mainz, 1971.

Protić, Miodrag B. *Slikarstvo XX veka.* Belgrade, 1982.

See also Ivan Meštrović

Croatian Culture

Although there is uncertainty and controversy about the ethnogeny of the Croats, as they settled in the territory of present-day Croatia, they brought with them their ancient Slavic culture, while at the same time falling under the influence of Rome. Thus, even though they became part of the Roman Catholic Church, Dalmatian monks continued to use the Glagolitic alphabet (one of the two alphabets used by the Byzantine Church to spread the holy scriptures among the Slavs) up to the nineteenth century. Preceding the invention and application of printing, illuminated books in Glagolitic were produced and transcribed by artists such as the Missal of Prince Novak (1368) and the Missal of Vojvoda (Duke) Hrvoje (early fifteenth century).

National Slavic culture manifested itself in a rich variety of lyrical and epic songs, the latter accompanied by the *gusle* (a one-string violin). A written literature (mainly poetry) in the vernacular began to appear in Dubrovnik in the fourteenth century. But exploitation by Venice along the coast and by the Habsburg Empire inland, as well as Turkish raids in the fifteenth through seventeenth centuries, were not propitious to the development of a rich cultural life, and many intellectuals and artists left the country, often settling in Italy. Nevertheless, humanism, the Renaissance, and the baroque were all represented in the Croatian lands in poetry, prose, drama, philosophy and science, architecture, painting, and sculpture. Džore Držić (1461–1501) and Šiško Menčetić (1457–1527) were the earliest known poets of Dubrovnik. Marko Marulić of Split (1450–1524) wrote poetry and moralistic treatises in Latin as well as poetry in Croatian, including his main work, the biblical epic *Judita* (*Judith,* 1507, printed in Venice in 1521). Among other plays, Marin Držić (1505–67) wrote *Dundo Maroje* (*Uncle Maroje*), which was staged in 1551. Ivan Gundulić (1588–1638), poet and playwright, was the author of the epic *Osman,* which pitted the Christian Polish prince Władysław against Turkish ruler Osman. A peculiar author

from the period of Counter-Reformation was Juraj Križanić (1618–83), who, inspired by the idea of returning the Orthodox Russians to the Holy Mother Church, went to Russia but was exiled by the suspicious Russian authorities to Tobolsk in Siberia, where he spent fifteen years and wrote his main work, *Politika* (1661–63). The most illustrious Croatian figure of the eighteenth century was Rudjer Bošković (1711–87), poet, philosopher, mathematician, and physicist (*Theoria philosophiae naturalis,* 1763).

By the first half of the nineteenth century, Croatia (under Hungarian rule) was politically, socially, and culturally in a sad state. Among intellectuals during the 1830s and 1840s, however, a revival known as the Illyrian Movement set in. The movement was led by Ljudevit Gaj (1809–72), who propagated the use of Croatian instead of Hungarian, published a *Brief Outline of Croatian-Slavic Orthography* (1830), and founded the first newspaper in Zagreb, with a literary supplement, *Danica* (*The Morning Star*). The most prominent poet of the Illyrian period was Ivan Mažuranić (1814–90), author of the epic poem *Smrt Smail-age Čengića* (*The Death of Smail-Aga Čengić,* 1846), written in the syllabic meter of heroic folk songs. In the same year, Petar Preradović (1818–72), an officer and later general in the Austrian army, published his first book of lyrical poetry, *Prvenci* (*Firstlings*). He sincerely believed in the greatness and great future of Croatia, the South Slavs, and Slavdom as a whole. Prose was represented by August Šenoa (1838–81), a prolific writer who wrote a series of historical and contemporary novels. The most distinguished poet at the end of the nineteenth century was Silvije S. Kranjčević (1865–1908), who expressed deep emotions with warmth and truthfulness.

With poet and playwright Ivo Vojnović (1857–1929) as a forerunner and poet, prose writer, and literary critic Antun G. Matoš (1873–1914) as its main promoter, the literary Moderna gave a new impulse to literature at the turn of the century, especially in lyrical poetry.

In the field of architecture and sculpture, Croatia displays, especially in the coastal towns, a rich variety of styles and periods: from antiquity (the amphitheater of Pula [first century A.D.] and Emperor Diocletian's [245–313] palace in Split [ca. A.D. 300]) through the Romanesque (thirteenth-century porch of the cathedral in Trogir), Renaissance, and baroque (cathedral of Hvar and many buildings in Dubrovnik) periods, to the various schools and trends of the nineteenth and twentieth centuries. Old churches and monasteries have also been preserved, like the Holy Cross church of Nin, built during the ninth century. Furthermore, Zagreb developed into a national center of culture, art, and learning.

Only in the second half of the nineteenth century did painting become a more prominent and recognized art form. An invaluable promotor of the arts was Bishop Josip Strossmayer (1815–1905), cofounder of the Yugoslav Academy of Sciences and Arts (1866). The fact that in the early twentieth century two promising young painters—Josip Račić (1885–1908) and Miroslav Kraljević (1885–1919)—moved from Munich to Paris points to a shift in artistic orientation from Austria and Germany to France. Cézanne (1839–1906) and van Gogh (1853–90) became models for the artists of the Croatian Moderna, Le Corbusier (1887–1965) for the architects. A leading figure of this trend in the first half of the twentieth century was internationally renowned sculptor Ivan Meštrović (1893–1962).

Music, chiefly in Italian style, was intensely created and performed in cities along the Adriatic. Ivan Mane Jarnović (1745–1804), famous throughout Europe as a violinist, composed many works, mostly for stringed instruments. Vatroslav Lisinski (1819–54) was a music teacher in Zagreb and Prague who composed operas. A prolific composer was Ivan Zajc (1832–1914), director and conductor of the first permanent opera in Zagreb. Theaters were also built in Zagreb, Split, Varaždin, Rijeka, and Osijek, and a national opera culture developed. The most renowned twentieth-century composer was Josip Štolcer Slavenski (1896–1955), for many years a professor at the Music Academy in Belgrade, who broke with the romantic tradition and created works inspired by the folk music of the Balkan Peninsula.

During the interwar years, the most forceful and original figure in a thriving literary world was Miroslav Krleža (1893–1981), poet, dramatist, prose writer, essayist-polemist, and author of a famed drama trilogy and novels such as *Povratak Filipa Latinovicza* (*Filip Latinovicz's Return,* 1932). Tin Ujević (1891–1955), a highly talented poet, should also be mentioned.

After Tito's (1892–1980) break with Moscow and Stalinism in 1948, the strict political-ideological supervision of cultural life by the Communist Party disappeared and an atmosphere of free creation gradually gained the upperhand. New forms of poetry flowered, notably in and around the Zagreb monthly *Krugovi* (*Circles,* 1952–58). The plethora of post–World War II writers includes author Ranko Marinković (1913–), whose works include the short story volume *Ruke* (*Hands,* 1953) and the novel *Kiklop* (*The Cyclops,* 1965); short-story writer Petar Šegedin (1909–); dramatist Mirko Božić (1919–); poet Vesna Parun (1922–); and storyteller and novelist Ivan Raos (1921–).

Thomas Eekman

Further reading

Baletić, Milovan, ed. *Croatia 1994.* Zagreb, 1994.
Hrašćanec, A. "Kriza kulture." *Marulić,* no. 6. Zagreb, 1990.
Majstorović, Stevan. *Cultural Policy in Yugoslavia: Self-Management and Culture.* Paris, 1980.
Matvejević, Predrag. *Jugoslavenstvo danas.* Zagreb, 1982.
Pusić, Eugen, ed. *Hrvatska, zadanosti i usmjerenja.* Zagreb, 1992.
Stallner, Robert and Jeanne Laurens. *Historical Dictionary of the Republic of Croatia.* Methuen, New Jersey, 1995.
Republika, no. 11/12. Zagreb, 1989.

See also Architecture; Croatian Art; Croatian Literature to 1918; Folklife; Folklore; Ljudevit Gaj; Illyrian Movement; Miroslav Krleža; Ivan Mažuranić; Ivan Meštrović; Petar Preradović; Josip Račić; August Šenoa; Bishop Josip Strossmayer; Tito; Tito-Stalin Split; Yugoslav Literature

Croatian Émigrés

Adverse political and economic circumstances have been the primary factors encouraging emigration from Croatia in the nineteenth and twentieth centuries. A small wave of Croats emigrated in the 1850s and 1860s because of political repression after the revolutions of 1848 and the imposition of neoabsolutism in the Habsburg Empire. More important, the period before World War I saw a massive economic migration caused by the phylloxera epidemic, the crash of the Viennese stock market (1873), a twenty-year European-wide agricultural depression, and the depletion of the Slavonian wood industry.

During the interwar period, Croats emigrated primarily for economic reasons, but after 1945, many emigrated because they feared political reprisals for wartime collaboration. Another wave of migration occurred in the 1970s—partly in response to the end of the Croatian Spring, the surge in nationalist sentiment (1967–72), and partly because young professionals began to seek better opportunities abroad. In 1990, after the first free elections since 1945, part of the post–World War II emigration returned to Croatia; most supported the newly elected Croatian Democratic Union (HDZ).

Emigrants left from every part of Croatia, but the majority came from traditionally impoverished areas—Dalmatia (until the advent of mass tourism in the 1960s) and some areas of the former Croatian Military Frontier such as Lika. Exact numbers of emigrants are difficult to establish, especially for the nineteenth century. In the records at Ellis Island, for example, country of origin, not nationality, was the category recorded; in addition, names were frequently altered, translated, or bastardized during migration.

In the period before World War I, the overwhelming majority of emigrants from Croatia came to the United States. The earliest communities were in Louisiana and California, but by the end of the nineteenth century the industrial and mining areas of the Midwest had significant communities of Croatian emigrants as well. In 1921, however, the United States embraced immigration limitations, which redirected emigrants from Croatia toward South America (especially Argentina, Uruguay, and Peru) and Canada; after World War II, many emigrants went to Australia as well as to parts of Europe.

To preserve their home culture, Croats established institutions such as benevolent societies, singing groups, newspapers, savings banks, and insurance unions. The most famous such institution in the United States is the Croatian Fraternal Union, founded in Pittsburgh in 1894. In many areas, the Catholic Church was also a powerful force in maintaining the bonds of community, and frequently Croatian parish priests came from the Old Country to serve emigrant communities.

The institutional organization of the émigré community has been supplemented since 1951 by Hrvatska Matica Iseljenika (Croatian Homeland Foundation) in Zagreb, which the Communist regime established to maintain and encourage ties with that part of the Croatian émigré community that was not anti-Communist. Much of Matica's work in the Communist period was primarily folkloric in nature, such as the Smotra folklora (Folklore Exhibition), which brought tamburica and dance troops from all over the world. Since the fall of communism, Matica has increased its ties with the anti-Communist and anti-Yugoslav émigré communities from Croatia.

Famous emigrants from Croatia include sculptor Ivan Meštrović (1893–1962), who taught at Syracuse University and Notre Dame; inventor Nikola Tesla (1856–1943), a Serb from Lika; and Vladko Maček (1879–1964), the interwar leader of the Croatian Peasant Party.

Sarah A. Kent

Further reading
Čizmić, Ivan. *Hrvati u životu Sjedinjenih Američkih Država: Doprinos u ekonomskom, političkom i kulturnom životu.* Zagreb, 1982.
Holjevac, Večeslav. *Hrvati izvan domovine.* Zagreb, 1967.
Prpić, George J. *The Croatian Immigrants in America.* New York, 1971.

See also Croatian Military Frontier; Croatian Spring; Dance; Emigration; Folk Music; Folklore; Vladko Maček; Ivan Meštrović; Neoabsolutism; Revolutions of 1848

Croatian Language *See* **Serbo-Croatian Language**

Croatian Literature to 1918
The modern period in Croatia witnessed a cultural renaissance distinguished by the development of a standard literary language and a revival of national literature. Modern Croatian literature generally followed from romanticism through realism and modernism.

Croatian literature in the first half of the nineteenth century was greatly advanced by the Illyrian Movement, a program founded by a group of young educated Croats who sought cultural unity among South Slavs. Led by Ljudevit Gaj (1809–72), the Illyrians fostered interest in native oral traditions and a revival of Croatia's rich heritage of secular literature from the Dalmatian Renaissance (sixteenth through eighteenth centuries); they also normalized literary Croatian in the Latin alphabet. Romanticism was promoted by the Illyrian writers, primarily through epic and lyric poetry. Ivan Mažuranić (1814–90) is regarded as the most distinguished poet of the Illyrian Movement. Greatly influenced by oral epic, Mažuranić's narrative poem *Smrt Smail-Age Čengića* (*The Death of Smail-Aga Čengić,* 1846) depicts the struggles between Cross and Crescent in Montenegro. Other romantic poets writing in the 1840s and early 1850s include Stanko Vraz (1810–51), a Slovene celebrated for his love lyrics, and Petar Preradović (1818–72), regarded as the foremost Croatian lyricist of the Illyrian Movement; both poets drew much inspiration from oral tradition.

Prose genres flourished in Croatia during the second half of the nineteenth century as realism emerged. By the mid-1860s, August Šenoa (1838–81)—considered the most prominent Croatian writer of his day—was an influential critic of the excessive romanticism of his contemporaries. Arguing for the social function of literature, he introduced realism in his short stories and historical novels, such as the well-known *Seljačka buna* (*The Peasant Uprising,* 1877). French and Russian literary influence increased considerably at this time. The prose of the 1880s and 1890s was imbued with various aspects of realism: naturalism (found in the novels of Evgenij Kumičić [1850–1904]), verism, and Russian realism. Croatian literary criticism also originated at this time, initially in discussions of the principles of realism. Ksaver Šandor Djalski (1854–1935) was the preeminent writer of realist short stories and the founder of the psychological novel in Croatia. Vjenčeslav Novak (1859–1905), also a prolific writer of realist fiction, was a master at depicting the Croatian petty bourgeoisie.

Modernism in Croatia—the Moderna—evolved in the early years of the twentieth century as writers sought more artistic freedom and favored bringing Croatian literature more in step with Western European trends. The Moderna prompted an expansion of literary influence and activity in Croatia. Lyrics became the chief genre of the period, represented by writers such as the great symbolist Silvije Strahimir Kranjčević (1865–1908), as well as poets Dragutin Domjanić (1875–1933) and Vladimir Vidrić (1875–1909). Ivo Vojnović (1857–1929) was a prominent modernist writer of drama, poetry, and novels; his drama *Dubrovačka trilogija* (*Dubrovnik Trilogy,* 1900) is his best-known work. Antun Gustav Matoš (1873–1914) excelled in essays and criticism. Vladimir Nazor (1876–1949) is regarded as the most important poet of the Moderna; his work

reflected a deep awareness of European literature and a personal, idiosyncratic style.

With the emergence of Yugoslavia after World War I, Croatian literature became part of a new, larger entity.

Margaret H. Beissinger

Further reading

Barac, Antun. *A History of Yugoslav Literature.* Ann Arbor, Michigan, 1976.
Despalatović, Elinor M. *Ljudevit Gaj and the Illyrian Movement.* New York, 1975.
Kadić, Ante. *From Croatian Renaissance to Yugoslav Socialism.* The Hague, 1969.

See also Ljudevit Gaj; Illyrian Movement; Ivan Mažuranić; Petar Preradović; Romanticism; August Šenoa; Serbo-Croatian Language; Yugoslav Literature

Croatian Military Frontier

Military system organized by Austria to defend the Habsburg monarchy from the Ottomans (1522–1881). The respective Latin, German, and Croatian names of the Frontier were Confinia militaris, Militärgrenze, and Vojna krajina. In 1102 independent Croatia entered a personal dynastic union with Hungary but retained its internal autonomy and authorities, including the Croatian Sabor (diet) and the *ban* (governor). By the sixteenth century, however, the local rulers were too weak to resist Ottoman attacks successfully. In 1527 Austrian Archduke Ferdinand I (1503–64) was elected Croatian king by the Sabor. Austria created an arch-shaped military zone with fortresses from the Adriatic Sea to the Banat region north of Belgrade. By 1538, two military areas had appeared. The larger one, Krabatische Gränitz (Croatian Frontier), stretched from Austria's southernmost posts along the Una River to fortified settlements located west of Zagreb; the other, in eastern Croatia, was the Slavonian Frontier. These two zones (called respectively the Karlovac and the Varaždin *Generalat*s) were united under the Austrian colonel commandant in Karlovac (1578). Many frontiersmen who came to Croatia from the Ottoman Empire (mainly Bosnia and Serbia) were Orthodox Christians, but the Croats remained a majority throughout the existence of the Frontier. Reluctantly, the Croatian authorities granted the settlers certain privileges in the "Vlach Law" (1629). Austrian Emperor

C

Ferdinand II (1578–1637) in his *Statuta Valachorum* (1630) guaranteed the frontiersmen internal autonomy. They were relieved of many feudal duties. Land, homes, cattle were the common property of large household family units (*zadruge*). The settlers in villages elected their local administrative and military leaders. Later their autonomy was restricted, and the *Statuta Valachorum* abolished (1737). In the eighteenth century many reforms were carried out to make the Frontier militarily stronger and economically self-sustaining. After 1767, the frontiersmen were used as Austria's professional soldiers in various fronts throughout Europe. In the nineteenth century the Basic Law (Grundgesetz,1807) specified that the land belonged to the ruler, while its goods could be used by the frontiersmen on duty. In 1809 Napoléon (1769–1821) replaced German with French as the administrative language, but retained the Frontier. In 1868 general military service was adopted in Austria-Hungary. Although de jure an inseparable part of the Kingdom of Croatia, the Frontier remained under Austria's control until the 1880s. The demilitarization of the Frontier ended in 1873, and it was reincorporated into Croatia in 1881.

Anto Knezevic

Further reading

Kaser, Karl. *Freier Bauer und Soldat.* Graz, 1986.

Nouzille, Jean. *Histoire de frontières l'Autriche et l'Empire ottoman.* Paris, 1991.

Rothenberg, Gunther Erich. *The Austrian Military Border in Croatia, 1522–1747.* Urbana, Illinois, 1960.

———. *The Military Border in Croatia 1740–1881: A Study of an Imperial Institution.* Chicago, 1966.

See also Krajina; Napoléon; Sabor; *Zadruga*

Croatian Spring (Croatian National Movement, 1967–72)

A surge of nationalist sentiment, variously referred to as the Croatian National Movement, Croatian Crisis, and Croatian Spring. During the 1960s, Yugoslavia began to decentralize its economy, government administration, and Communist Party organization. As a result, more authority passed to the governments and party organizations of the six Yugoslav republics. This brought national differences among the republics to the foreground.

The first public signs of renewed Croatian nationalism came in 1967 when a group of Croatian intellectuals published a declaration asserting that Croatian and Serbian were different languages and that only Croatian should be used in the schools of the republic. Croats also expressed dissent through cultural organizations such as Matica Hrvatska, which became a sort of nationalist political party.

Although cultural questions were important, the major Croatian complaint concerned the economy. Croats claimed that their republic was not receiving its fair share of foreign currency earnings and that 30 percent of the Croatian state income went to other parts of Yugoslavia. Even some leaders of the Croatian Communist Party such as Miko Tripalo (1926–), secretary of the party, and Savka Dabčević-Kučar (1923–), head of the Croatian government, called for further political decentralization and reform of currency regulations.

During 1971, some Croatian nationalists demanded that Croatia have a separate monetary policy and an autonomous territorial army. The situation reached a climax in November when students at the University of Zagreb went on strike and began demonstrating in favor of Croatian nationalist demands. These actions raised fears of violent nationalist conflict and even of the disintegration of Yugoslavia.

Several times in 1971 Tito (1892–1980), the longtime president of Yugoslavia, had warned Croatian officials about the dangers of extreme nationalism. After local authorities failed to respond to the student strikes, Tito and the federal authorities finally reacted decisively. In a nationwide television broadcast on December 1, Tito asserted that events in Croatia had gone too far. Within weeks, Dabčević-Kučar and Tripalo were forced to resign from their leadership positions. Troops and police also occupied Zagreb and arrested student leaders. In early 1972 most of the Croatian nationalists were purged from party and government positions. This marked the end of this Croatian national movement and also demonstrated that the Tito regime would not allow decentralization or nationalism to threaten the overall integrity of the Yugoslav state.

Paul D. Lensink

Further reading

Cuvalo, Ante. *The Croatian National Movement, 1966–1972.* New York, 1990.

Ramet, Sabrina. *Nationalism and Federalism in Yugoslavia, 1962–1991*. Bloomington, Indiana, 1992.

Schöpflin, George. "The Ideology of Croatian Nationalism," in *Survey* 19, no. 1 (1973): 123–46.

Tanner, Marcus. *Croatia: A Nation Forged in War*. New Haven, Connecticut, 1997.

See also Communist Party of Yugoslavia; Matica Hrvatska; Nationalism; Serbo-Croatian Language; Tito

Crownlands of St. Stephen

Historic Hungarian lands. Born in Esztergom, Vajk was baptized as Stephen (István) and lived his life as a devout Christian. Stephen (c. 975–1038), who was made a saint after his death in 1038, became Prince of Hungary in 997. On Christmas day 1000, he was crowned "King by the Grace of God" by the pope, who also gave a crown that remained the supreme symbol of authority in the country for centuries.

Stephen quickly consolidated royal authority over the clan chieftains, establishing a system of administration based on counties (*comitatus;* Hungarian, *megye*) protected by fortified castles (*vár*). He also established a system of church administration based on village churches, ten episcopal seats, and archbishoprics at Esztergom and Kalocsa. Furthermore, he established a royal seat at Székesfehérvár (white castle seat), which became the site where kings of Hungary were crowned and buried for the next five hundred years. By the time of Stephen's death, Hungary was a Christian, Western-looking nation.

Stephen's crownlands in 1038 formed a nearly circular territory extending in the west to present-day Austria, which at the time was part of the Holy Roman Empire; in the north to the Carpathian Mountains, today's Slovakia; in the east to the Transylvanian Alps, now within Romania; and in the south to the lands of Croatia and the Byzantine Empire. The geographical center of this territory was in present-day Szolnok County on the Great Hungarian Plain.

Darrick Danta

Further reading
Fügedi, Erik. *Castle and Society in Medieval Hungary (1000–1437)*. Budapest, 1986.

Hanák, Péter, ed. *One Thousand Years: A Concise History of Hungary*. Budapest, 1988.

Magocsi, Paul Robert. *Historical Atlas of East Central Europe*. Seattle, Washington, 1993.

Webster's New Geographical Dictionary. Springfield, Massachusetts, 1984.

Csángó

Designation for the Hungarians who inhabit settlements in Moldavia along the Seret River, particularly in Bacău (Hungarian, Bakó) County. Their settlements were probably much more extensive in this region prior to the sixteenth and seventeenth centuries. At present, most estimates place their numbers between 80,000 and 90,000. However, the official Romanian census lists approximately only 6,000 Hungarians in all of Moldavia. The discrepancy can be explained by purposeful undercounting and by the linguistic Romanianization of about 50 percent of the Csángó (Romanian, Ciangău) population. Besides their Hungarian language and unique folk culture, they are distinguishable from their Romanian neighbors by their Roman Catholic religion.

A number of theories exist concerning the origin of the Csángó inhabitants of Moldavia, one of which was that they were the rearguard of the Hungarian tribes when they entered the Carpathian basin in 895–896. More convincing is the theory that they were settled in that region by Béla IV (1206–70), who feared a second invasion of the Mongols after 1241. Thus, he placed military settlements as a screen, or "early-warning system," between the eastern slopes of the Carpathians and west of the Seret. These settlements were supplemented by Hungarian Hussites (followers of Czech religious reformer Jan Hus [c. 1370–1415]) fleeing persecution from the Catholic monarchs of the fifteenth century and later by Székely settlers who fled across the Carpathians to avoid governmental encroachment or taxation. The last major such Székely addition took place after 1764, but they settled further north in Bukovina and were resettled in southern Hungary during World War II. The Csángó settlements farther to the south have come under a great deal of pressure since the advent of modern nationalism. Since the 1880s, Romanian governments have followed an assimilationist policy toward them. Only in the late 1940s did they have a brief respite when the government of Petru Groza (1884–1958) allowed them to have Hungarian-language schools. However, subsequent Romanian governments returned to assimilationist objectives.

At the probable behest of the regime of Romanian Communist leader Nicolae Ceauşescu (1918–89), a book appeared in 1982 claiming that the Csángó people are merely Hungarianized Romanians. Yet, despite continued pressures to assimilate, the Csángó settlements cling to their distinctive culture and language.

Andrew Ludanyi

Further reading

Beke, György. *Csángó passió: Barangolások moldvai csángó-magyarok között.* Budapest, 1988.

Kos, Károly, Judit Szentimrei, and Jenö Nagy. *Moldvai csángó népmüvészet.* Bucharest, 1981.

Malonyay, Dezsö. *A magyar nep müveszete: A székelyföldi, a csángó és a torockói magyar nép müvészete,* vol. 2. Budapest, 1909.

Mikecs, Lászlo. *Csángók.* Pecs, 1989.

See also Nicolae Ceauşescu; Ethnic Minorities; Petru Groza; Nationalism; Székely

Csontváry, Koszta Tivadar (1853–1919)

Hungarian modern artist. Trained as a pharmacist, Csontváry decided to study art in Munich, Karlsruhe, and eventually at the Julian Academy in Paris. His travels took him to Italy, where in Pompeii his native realism underwent a change and his style became more hallucinatory. But it was in the Near East—especially Cairo and Jerusalem—where the sun and the blazing light vivified his colors and he found the total expression of plein air. His best period is considered to be during his travels in the Levant (*At the Entry to the Wailing Wall* [1904] and *Pilgrimage to the Cypresses of Lebanon* [1907]). His tableaux assumed unnatural hues and decorative lushness. A timeless air dominated his scenes. During that period, his paintings resembled the expressionistic and fauve avantgarde of Europe; however, the works of this solitary genius are well founded in classical art. His religious themes, although half-satirical and grotesque and half-saturated with spiritual passion, never became blasphemous. At times his magically entrancing, sophisticated, fresh observations created a mosaic-like poetry (as in *Baalbeck* [1906]). He was a solitary genius directed by his "inner principles," and in his writings he spoke of "Divine power which finds its fulfillment in creation."

Although international recognition came before the end of his life, it was not until 1958 that Csontáry made his entry into the European painter's apex when his *Horse Ride at the Sea Shore* (1909) received the Grand Prix posthumously at the international exhibit 50 Years of Modern Art in Bruxelles.

George Tivadar Radân

Further reading

Németh, L. *Csontváry.* Budapest, 1964.

———. "La vie et l'art de Tivadar Csontvary." *Acta Hist. Art.* 10 (1964): 125–69.

Ybl, E. *Csontváry.* Budapest, 1960.

See also Hungarian Art

Csoóri, Sándor (1930–)

Hungarian poet, essayist, cinema scriptwriter, and political activist. Csoóri was born to a peasant family in Zámoly in western Hungary. Educated at the Protestant school in Pápa and later at the Lenin Institute in Budapest, he made his debut around the time of the "thaw," the general easing of tensions after the death of Stalin (1879–1953). After returning to his home village because of illness, he witnessed not only social injustices but also bread shortages and poverty. Poetry being an indicator of political unrest in Hungary, Csoóri's works inspired others to declare their allegiance to "the people" rather than to inept party policies. He published his first volume of poetry, *Párbeszéd sötétben* (*Dialogue in the Dark*) in 1954, the same year he won the József Attila Prize for his poetry. That year also marked the publication of *Felröppen a madár* (*The Bird Takes Wing*), which was inspired by folk poetry and the poems of Sándor Petőfi (1823–49). Csoóri also became active in samizdat (underground) publications regarding the conditions of ethnic Hungarians in neighboring countries.

Csoóri served as a script reader, writer, and artistic adviser for MAFILM, formerly the state-run film studio. He collaborated on scripts for six feature films, including *Tízezer nap* (*Ten Thousand Days,* 1967), which won the Grand Prize at the Cannes Film Festival.

Mártha Pereszlényi-Pintér

Further reading

Czigány, Loránt. *The Oxford History of Hungarian Literature.* Oxford, 1984.

Klaniczay, Tibor, ed. *A History of Hungarian Literature.* Budapest, 1982.

Tezla, Albert. *Ocean at the Window: Hungarian Prose and Poetry since 1945.* Minneapolis, 1980.

Vajda, Miklós. *Modern Hungarian Poetry.* New York, 1977.

See also Cinema; De-Stalinization; Hungarian Literature; Sándor Petőfi

Curial System

System for the election of local and state institutions across Central Europe, in which groups of voters organized on the basis of social status or income elect candidates. Although clearly derived from traditional systems of electing feudal diets by estate (Stand), curial voting was also a product of the liberal age. In the Habsburg Empire, Anton Ritter von Schmerling (1831–1903) introduced curial voting for provincial diets and the Austrian parliament (Reichsrat) with the February Patent of 1861. Schmerling divided the eligible electorate into curias: great landowners, chambers of commerce, urban voters, and rural voters. This innovation differed significantly for the individual, although occasionally indirect voting systems elected the Austrian Reichstag and the Frankfurt Parliament in 1848. Most regional diets in 1848, however, had maintained a system of election that simply added new categories (like urban burgher or peasants) to the existing estates. The curial system was not fully elaborated or justified philosophically until 1861, when it was used specifically to balance social, economic, and national interests and to guarantee socially conservative constituencies.

During the second half of the nineteenth century, liberal political parties increasingly clung to this mode of election as a means of maintaining their social influence against new mass parties at all levels of government. In 1873, for example, when Austrian liberals reformed the electoral system to elect parliamentary deputies directly by individual constituencies rather than indirectly from the individual diets, they nevertheless maintained the curial system of voting within those constituencies. A 1907 law introducing universal manhood suffrage abolished curial voting for the Reichsrat but left it firmly in place for provincial and local institutions.

Pieter Judson

Further reading

Berghahn, Volker R. *Imperial Germany 1871–1914: Economy, Society, Politics.* Providence, Rhode Island, 1994.

Judson, Pieter. *Exclusive Revolutionaries: Liberal Politics, Social Experience, and National Identity in the Austrian Empire, 1848–1914.* Ann Arbor, Michigan, 1996.

Kolmer, Gustav. *Parlament und Verfassung in Österreich,* vol. 2. Vienna, 1902–5.

Redlich, Josef. *Das österreichische Staats- und Reichsproblem,* 2 vols. Leipzig, 1920–26.

Sheehan, James J. *German Liberalism in the Nineteenth Century.* Chicago, 1978.

See also February Patent; Liberalism

Curie, Marie Skłodowska (1867–1934)

Polish scientist and winner of the Nobel Prize for her research into radium. The youngest of six children, Marie Skłodowska, whose father was a professor of physics and mathematics, grew up in Warsaw in a Poland under Russian domination so strict that even the Polish language was suppressed, and for women there was no possibility of education beyond the gymnasium. Marie did not begin her academic career until she was almost twenty-four. She attended classes of the illegal "flying university," which, despite Russian prohibitions, met clandestinely and offered a rigorous program of instruction, before leaving for Paris to start classes at the Sorbonne in November 1891. In 1895 she married Pierre Curie (1859–1906), then a teacher at the School of Physics and Chemistry. They collaborated in studies of radioactivity, work for which they, jointly with Antoine H. Becquerel (1852–1908), were awarded the Nobel Prize in physics in 1903. In 1898 the Curies discovered both polonium and radium while studying uranium in pitchblende. Working in the courtyard of a school shed, Marie herself isolated and purified one gram of radium salts from approximately eight tons of pitchblende purchased with their own funds from a Czech mine.

In 1906 Pierre Curie died in a street accident. Marie, appointed to his chair at the Sorbonne, the first woman to teach there, continued her research as well as teaching at the normal school in Sèvres, where she introduced a new teaching method based on the demonstration of experiments. In 1910 (with André Debierne [1874–

1949]) she isolated metallic radium, and in 1911 was awarded the Nobel Prize in chemistry for the discovery of polonium and radium. During World War I, she organized the first fleet of twenty mobile radiological medical units and manned one as well, and installed two hundred radiology rooms. More than a million men were treated in these facilities. The Curies, who were scornful of personal gain, believed that scientific discoveries should belong to all and therefore never patented any of their work. Marie continued her work at the Radium Institute in Paris until shortly before her death.

In addition to the two Nobel Prizes, Marie Curie was the recipient of six major prizes, sixteen medals and decorations, and more than one hundred honors from governments, universities, and learned societies. She was also a fervent Polish patriot and the devoted mother of two daughters, Irene Joliot-Curie (1897–1956), who together with her husband, Frederic Joliot-Curie (1900–1958), was awarded the Nobel Prize in chemistry in 1935, and Eve Curie (1904–), a pianist and author.

Marie J. Hall

Further reading

Curie, Eve. *Madame Curie.* Garden City, New York, 1938.

See also Flying University

Curzon Line

Provisional eastern borderline for Poland established on December 8, 1919. In view of the absence of a regular Russian government whose cooperation the Allies deemed necessary to establish a definitive frontier, this declaration recognized territories west of the line as Polish while reserving Poland's rights to territories farther east. The line ran roughly from Grodno in the north to the former Austrian Galicia near Sokal. This line reappeared at the Allied Conference in Spa as a cease-fire line between the Polish and the Soviet armies. Extended through eastern Galicia (although in an inconsistent way), it figured in the dispatch of July 11, 1920, sent to the Bolshevik government and signed by the British foreign secretary, Lord Curzon (1859–1925). Accepted by the Poles, it was rejected by the Bolsheviks.

The Polish-Soviet peace treaty of 1921 established a frontier east of the Curzon Line. Following the division of Poland in 1939 between Germany and the USSR, a border, commonly referred to as the Ribbentrop-Molotov Line, named after the foreign ministers of Germany and the Soviet Union, respectively, emerged approximating the Curzon Line except in the north (the district of Białystok). Soviet demands for Allied recognition of this frontier usually invoked the Curzon Line as evidence of Western preference for such a settlement. The present-day eastern border of Poland comes close to the Curzon Line.

Piotr S. Wandycz

Further reading

Cienciala, Anna M. "The Question of the Polish-Soviet Frontier in British, Soviet and Polish Policy in 1940." *Polish Review* 33, no. 3 (1988).

Garliński, Józef. *Poland in World War II.* New York, 1985.

Wandycz, Piotr S. *Soviet-Polish Relations 1917–1921.* Cambridge, Massachusetts, 1969.

See also Molotov-Ribbentrop Pact; Peace of Riga; Polish-Soviet War

Cuza, Alexandru Ioan (1820–73)

First modern Romanian prince, elected by separate assemblies in Iaşi and Bucharest, which resulted in the union of Moldavia and Wallachia in 1859 and the establishment of a single Romanian government in 1862. A member of a *boiar* family of Moldavia, and educated in Paris, Padua, and Bologna, Cuza took part in the aborted Moldavian revolution of 1848 (during the Revolutions of 1848) and escaped to the West after its failure. He returned to Moldavia in 1849 and resumed an army career. As a liberal nationalist, he broke rank with his protector, the anti-unionist governor of Moldavia, and became a candidate for the combined throne of both principalities, winning a majority of the votes in the electoral assemblies of Bucharest and Iaşi. With the support of Napoléon III (1808–73), he overcame Austrian and Turkish opposition and convinced the sultan to accept personal union (1859) and effective union of the Romanian Principalities (1862). These years were marked by extensive and radical reform, particularly under the premiership of Mihail Kogălniceanu (1817–91) in 1863, the organization of the Romanian army by General Ion Emanoil Florescu (1819–93), a modern university system, the liberation of the serfs, the nationalization of the Greek monasteries, and fiscal and legal reform. Cuza's dismissal of parliament in 1864 and his corrupt, authoritarian regime, as well as scandal in his private life (although married, he kept a mistress and fathered two illegitimate sons), led to a conspiracy that forced his abdication in 1866. He died at Heidelberg in 1873 and was buried at his palace at Ruginoasa in Moldavia, which still stands.

Radu Florescu

Further reading

Berindei, Dan. *L'union des principautés roumaines.* Bucharest, 1967.

Bobango, Gerald. *The Emergence of the Romanian National State.* Boulder, Colorado, 1979.

Giurescu, Constantin. *Viaţa şi opera lui Cuza Voda.* Bucharest, 1970.

Henry, Paul. *L'Adbication du Prince Cuza et i'avenement de la dinastie des Hohenzollern au throne de Roumanie.* Paris, 1930.

See also *Boiars;* Mihail Kogălniceanu; Napoléon III; Revolutions of 1848; United Principalities

Cvetković, Dragiša (1893–1969)

Yugoslav prime minister. Cvetković made his mark as Yugoslavia's prime minister in the difficult years before the German invasion of 1941. As a member of Milan Stojadinović's (1888–1961) government, he had watched Yugoslavia's allies retreat in the face of Nazi German aggression. When he took office in March 1939, Germany had already annexed Austria and would soon invade Czechoslovakia. It had previously forged an alliance with Italy, a haven for Croat separatists. Cvetković intended that the nation close ranks and avoid entanglements with the Axis powers. To this end, he helped shape two fateful agreements. The first was the *Sporazum* (understanding) between the Yugoslav government and Croatian Peasant Party leader Vladko Maček (1879–1964). Signed in August 1939, it gave Croats some long-sought local autonomy and a legislature, and linked them with Belgrade only for common endeavors such as national defense. Although it displeased other nationalities, the *Sporazum* brought Croats back into the government and lessened the chance of an uprising in the Croatian lands. Cvetković's second agreement addressed Yugoslavia's international situation. By the beginning of 1941, German economic and military ascendance was complete in the Balkans. Cvetković agreed to adhere to the Tripartite Pact, the alliance among Germany, Italy, and Japan, with conditions. In return for neutrality in the invasion of Greece, Germany and Italy would agree to respect Yugoslav territorial integrity, seek no military assistance, and award the state an outlet to the Aegean Sea. Yugoslavia could not win a war with Germany, Cvetković reasoned. For him, the pact was the lone acceptable alternative.

In the end, Cvetković's efforts could not save Yugoslavia from catastrophe and, in fact, they hastened its demise. Cvetković's government perished in a coup staged by Serbian army officers who had vehemently opposed the prime minister's domestic and foreign policy. The ensuing German invasion on April 6, 1941, marked the end of the first Yugoslavia.

Cvetković's brief tenure as prime minister bears eloquent testimony to Yugoslavia's intractable and often intertwined foreign and domestic problems on the eve of World War II.

Brigit Farley

Further reading

Čulinovic, Ferdo. *Jugoslavija izmedju dva rata,* 2 vols. Zagreb, 1961.

Hoptner, Jacob. *Yugoslavia in Crisis, 1934–41.* New York, 1962.

Maček, Vladko. *In the Struggle for Freedom.* University Park, Pennsylvania, 1971.

See also Axis; Vladko Maček; *Sporazum* of 1939; Milan Stojadinović

Czartoryski, Prince Adam Jerzy (1770–1861)

Polish and Russian statesman. Czartoryski, or Prince Adam, as he was known, came from a wealthy and powerful Polish noble family. As a young man, Czartoryski traveled extensively throughout Western Europe, where he came to admire the British constitutional system. Returning to Poland, he participated in the 1792–93 Russo-Polish War. After the final partition of Poland in 1795, Czartoryski went to St. Petersburg to ransom the family estates that the Russians had confiscated.

While in St. Petersburg, Czartoryski joined the Russian government. He developed a close friendship with Grand Duke Alexander (1777–

C

1825), and when Alexander became tsar in 1801, Czartoryski was at his side. Alexander named Czartoryski deputy foreign minister in 1802 and foreign minister in 1804. In 1803 Alexander appointed him curator of the Wilno educational district, where he vigorously promoted Polish cultural and educational activities.

Although Alexander dismissed Czartoryski as foreign minister in 1806, the two men remained on good terms. With Napoléon's (1769–1821) defeat in 1815, Czartoryski accompanied Alexander to the Congress of Vienna, where he acted as the tsar's chief adviser and helped to create the Kingdom of Poland—the so-called Congress Kingdom—a constitutional monarchy under the tsar's rule.

Czartoryski expected to play a major role in the kingdom, but he was overshadowed by the tsar's brother, Grand Duke Constantine (1779–1831), and the Russian imperial commissioner, N.N. Novosil'tsov (1761–1836). Consequently, Czartoryski withdrew from public life. In 1824 Alexander ignominiously removed him as curator of the Wilno educational district.

At the time of the November Uprising in 1830 against the Russians, Czartoryski—who opposed the revolution—emerged as the leader of the moderate forces who wished to end the revolution without bloodshed and to maintain Poland's quasi independence. For a time he headed the provisional government. When it became apparent that Nicholas I (1796–1855) wanted to crush the Poles, Czartoryski backed the revolutionaries and worked earnestly but unsuccessfully to secure international support for Poland. When the revolution collapsed, Czartoryski emigrated to Paris; there he established the Hôtel Lambert, the headquarters for conservative Poles in exile.

Czartoryski's authority was great, and for many he became the de facto Polish king in exile. Relying on his vast resources, Czartoryski conducted extensive diplomatic activity at London, Paris, Rome, Constantinople, and among the Slavic peoples of the Balkans. He sought to weaken Russia and to reestablish an independent Poland. During the Crimean War (1853–56), Czartoryski organized Polish legions in Turkey to fight against Russia. Unsuccessful in his efforts, he died shortly before the outbreak of the January Uprising against the Russians in 1863.

Frank W. Thackeray

Further reading

Dziewanowski, M.K. "Czartoryski and His 'Essai sur la diplomatie,'" *Slavic Review* 30 (1971): 589–605.
Grimsted, Patricia Kennedy. *The Foreign Ministers of Alexander I.* Berkeley, California, 1969.
Kukiel, Marian. *Czartoryski and European Unity, 1770–1861.* Princeton, New Jersey, 1955.
Morley, Charles. "Czartoryski as a Polish Statesman." *Slavic Review* 30 (1971): 606–14.
Zawadzki, W. H. *A Man of Honour.* Oxford, 1993.

See also Alexander I; Congress of Vienna; Constantine; Crimean War; Hôtel Lambert; January Uprising; Napoléon; Nicholas I; November Uprising; Polish Congress Kingdom; Polish Émigrés

Czas

One of the premier Polish-language daily newspapers of the nineteenth century. Published in Kraków from 1848 to 1939, *Czas,* thanks to the quality of its articles, immediately rose to the position of the most authoritative newspaper in all of partitioned Poland. Its readership consisted primarily of landowners, richer members of the burgher class, and members of the intelligentsia. Subscriptions were delivered both within the Polish lands and abroad, wherever Polish émigrés were to be found.

Czas was founded in November 1848 by a group of noblemen, political leaders, and men of letters including such important figures as Adam Potocki (1822–72), Lucjan Siemieński (1809–77), Ludwik Wodzicki (1834–94), Paweł Popiel (1807–92), and Stanisław Tarnowski (1837–1917). From its inception, the editorial board of *Czas* took the position that Poles needed to "work" rather than to fight for their independence. This attitude would later develop into a full-fledged anticonspiratorial stance. Throughout the 1850s, the newspaper was often critical of the neoabsolutist Austrian government. Beginning in 1863, *Czas* began to identify itself more clearly with the conservative social and political viewpoints then crystallizing among the Kraków and west Galician educated elites. The daily came to be a mouthpiece for conservative politicians who preached loyalty to the Habsburg dynasty and opposition to revolution and socialism.

The widely read editorial pages of *Czas* attracted contributors from outside Galicia as well. Émigré statesmen, publicists, members of the intelligentsia, and clergymen all found opportunities to express themselves in these pages. Nineteenth-century newspapers, however, were not solely devoted to social and political issues. Literary scholars, poets, and novelists, among others, published in the popular feuilleton section. These literary works, along with periodic supplements, made the newspaper a focal point for Polish cultural development.

Peter Wozniak

Further reading

Bienarzówna, Janina and Jan Małecki. *Dzieje Krakowa: Kraków w latach 1796–1918,* vol. 3. Kraków, 1979.

Kras, Janina. *Życie umysłowe w Krakowie w latach 1848–1870.* Kraków, 1977.

Wandycz, Piotr. *The Lands of Partitioned Poland 1795–1918.* Seattle, Washington, 1974.

Wolff, Lawrence. "Czas and the Polish Perspective on the Austro-Hungarian Compromise of 1867." *The Polish Review* 27, nos. 1–2 (1982): 65–75.

See also Intelligentsia; Neoabsolutism; Press

Czech and Slovak Art

Together with the political and economic developments that influenced Europe at the beginning of the nineteenth century, nationalism became one of the driving forces for cultural change in the Czech lands and Slovakia. German and Hungarian art and culture influenced all spheres of cultural life there. By the late eighteenth century, Czech and Slovak artists had turned to national and folk traditions as sources of inspiration for their work. Following several decades of stagnation and dependence on Italian and German art styles and patterns of painting, Czech artistic life experienced dramatic changes during the second half of the eighteenth century with the emergence of uniquely local styles. The artists turned to folklore and took ordinary country people and local landscapes as their models.

Antonín Mánes (1784–1843), professor of landscape painting at the Czech Academy of Arts in Prague, was the first significant artist to incorporate these genres in his work. His son, Josef (1820–71), was among the artists who strongly influenced the so-called "generation of the National Theater," a group of nationalistically oriented artists whose work decorates the National Theater in Prague. Mánes's ethnographic portraits depicting people in folk costumes are considered among the very best of this period. Other significant contemporary artists included Vojtěch Hynais (1854–1925), who designed the curtain of the National Theater; Josef Navrátil (1798–1865), who continued to develop Czech landscape painting; and, most of all, Mikoláš Aleš (1852–1913), considered to be the most representative of the Czech national artists of the nineteenth century. Aleš's cycles *"Má vlast"* (*My Country*) in the National Theater, and *"Život starých Slovanů"* (*The Life of the Ancient Slavs*), are outstanding examples of the historically inspired nationalistic art of this period. He also produced numerous drawings, illustrations, and paintings of the common people of the Czech lands and Slovakia. Sculptor Josef V. Myslbek (1848–1922) was the leading exponent of monumental realism. His best-known work is the statue of Svatý Václav (St. Wenceslas), a powerful symbol of Czech nationalism, which stands at the top of Wenceslas Square in Prague.

By the twentieth century, the descriptive realism of the nineteenth century had given way to a variety of styles and schools. Many of the art groups that developed during the first four decades of the century turned away from the nationalism of the nineteenth century. Among the most renowned artists of this period is Alfons Mucha (1860–1939), whose many designs, illustrations, postcards, menus, and especially his posters depicting the actress Sarah Bernhardt (1844–1923) made him and the Art Nouveau style famous.

A group of artists loosely connected with the so-called proletarian and social art movement, which concentrated primarily on social themes, included Václav Špála (1885–1946); Bohumil Kubišta (1884–1918); Rudolf Kremlička (1886–1932); Václav Rabas (1885–1954); Josef Čapek (1887–1945); Jan Zrzavý (1890–1977); and František Tichý (1896–1961). After a time, most of the members of this group went their own artistic way, developing very different and distinct styles.

World War II ushered in a tragic setback in the development of Czech art. Many artists were imprisoned or died during this time; others were not allowed to exhibit their art. The brief period following the war prior to the Communist takeover in 1948 saw the arts flourish once more, as the artists expressed their joy of freedom and the end of war.

C The development of the arts in Slovakia paralleled in many respects that of the Czech lands. Through the end of the eighteenth century, Slovak art showed a heavy dependence on Italian and German examples and patterns, especially in the landscape and portrait genres. During the first half of the nineteenth century, as the Czechs were shedding Germanic influences, the emerging movement in Slovakia was similarly engaged in freeing itself from strong Hungarian influences in both art and literature. The leading figure in this nationalistic growth was writer and linguist Ľudovít Štúr (1815–56), whose impact can be seen in both literature and the arts. To create a literary Slovak language, Štúr focused on the central Slovak dialect around the town of Liptovský Svätý Mikuláš, which was declared the national language in 1844.

The establishment of the organization Matica slovenská in 1863 in support of Slovak language and culture was a major step in strengthening Slovak national identity, although it had little to do with art. During this period, no public art gallery or art school existed in Slovakia, and students had to study abroad. There were few wealthy collectors to support artists and few public exhibits (in Bratislava in 1853, 1854, and 1865, as well as in Košice in 1857) to allow artists to show their work. Despite these difficulties, the arts began to develop. Major Czech figures like Josef Mánes and Mikuláš Aleš (1852–1913) provided strong encouragement to the fledgling Slovak movement. Personal contacts and mutual visits among Czech and Slovak artists facilitated the growth of national art on both sides.

The portrait artist Kornel Bohúň (1858–1902), son and student of Peter M. Bohúň (1822–83), emerged as a bridge between the older "Štúr" generation and the new one at the turn of the century. Cyril Kutlík (1869–1900) was another talent, known not only for his portraits but also as a creator of historic compositions. Josef Hamuľa (1863–1944) strove to unite art with both national and folk traditions. His depictions of Slovak peasants are good examples of the realism of the period.

Early in the twentieth century, Martin Benka (1888–1971) emerged as an artist whose work was based on purely Slovak roots. He carried these themes further than his predecessors and is considered the founder of modern Slovak art. Ľudovít Fulla (1902–80) blended folk art and tradition with modern views. Although he was influenced by cubism, fauvism, and expressionism, he used these styles in his own unique way. After 1950, Fulla devoted himself exclusively to book illustrations, for which he is best known. Mikuláš Galanda (1895–1938) concentrated on social themes in his work, and his nationalism is less descriptive and more expressive. Gustáv Mallý (1879–1952) primarily depicted the fate of poor Slovak peasants, painting portraits with strong social overtones. From 1939 to 1945, during the time of the pro-Nazi Slovak Republic, all arts in Slovakia were subjected to strict state control.

Following the brief period of freedom between 1945 and 1948, both Czech and Slovak art, under Soviet influence, displayed a strong preference for socialist realism, in which all art had to be easy to understand, optimistic, and depict society in a positive light. After 1948, artists who did not adhere to that style were not allowed to display their work publicly, and many could show their art only in private. For a brief period in 1968, the Prague Spring, a cultural thaw, provided many artists with the freedom to create. The Warsaw Pact invasion of August 21, 1968, crushed this fledgling movement. From that time until the fall of communism in 1989, the government maintained a policy of strict state control over all forms of artistic expression.

Dagmar Berry

Further reading

Malý Encyklopedický Slovník A–Ž. Prague, 1972.
Šmatlák, Stanislav et al. *Slovensko-kultúra (I časť)*. Bratislava, 1979.
Vladár, Jozef. *Malá encyklopédia Slovenska*. Bratislava, 1984.

See also Architecture; Czech Culture; Folklore; Josef Mánes; Matica slovenská; Alfons Mucha; Nationalism; Prague Spring; Slovak Culture; Slovak Republic; Ľudovít V. Štúr; Warsaw Pact

Czech Culture

The second half of the eighteenth century brought many changes to the Czech lands. Following decades of German dominance in language and culture, a distinctly Czech culture and language reemerged. The upper classes and intellectuals who, to this time, had primarily used German, now also began to learn and use Czech. This transformation was a central focus of the Czech National

Renascence (1781–1848), marked by the abolition of serfdom and the failure of the 1848 revolution.

One of the most significant figures at the start of the Enlightenment was Václav Matěj Kramerius (1753–1808), publisher, journalist, writer, and proprietor of the bookstore Czech Expedition (*Česká expedice*), which was the center of the literary movement. A major goal of this movement—the dissemination of literature written in the Czech language—was made easier owing to the existence of a highly literate population. The establishment of a department of Czech Language and Literature at Charles University in Prague in 1781 was a major achievement of the movement.

The theater was another important source for spreading the use of Czech and advancing Czech culture to a higher plane. For example, Matěj Kopecký (1775–1847) traveled through the countryside with his puppet theater. His and similar theater groups performing in Czech were a significant link to the common people and a source of an emerging culture based on the language.

Music has always been an important aspect of cultural life in the Czech lands. Early exponents of the rich domestic musical tradition included Jan V. Stamic (1717–57), Karel Stamic (1746–1800), František X. Dušek (1731–99), and Josef Mysliveček (1737–81), known in Italy as Il divino Boemo (The divine Bohemian). Folksongs, a part of the oral tradition, were incorporated into the music being composed by an emerging generation of musicians. František Škroup (1801–62) composed the first original Czech opera *Dráteník* (*The Tinker*) in 1826 based on folk themes. Another of Škroup's operas, *Fidlovačka* (1834), includes the song "Kde domov můj" (Where Is My Home), which later became the Czech national anthem. Bedřich Smetana (1824–84), considered one of the geniuses of Czech music, continued this tradition. Among his major compositions are *Prodaná nevěsta* (*The Bartered Bride*) and the symphonic poem *Má vlast* (*My Country*). Antonín Dvořák (1841–1904) raised Czech music to new heights and became world renowned. His Symphony No. 9, *From the New World,* combines Czech and American themes in his unique style. Dvořák's operas, *Slavonic Dances,* and other works are still considered to be the epitome of Czech music. Although the twentieth century brought changes in style, music still retained close ties to its folk roots. Leoš Janáček (1854–1928) is a prime example. Bohuslav Martinů (1890–1959) followed in Janáček's footsteps. Both were closely connected to their Moravian roots, and their music was based on that folk music.

The development of Czech art also emphasized national and folk themes. Especially close ties can be seen between the period of the national enlightenment and the time of the construction of the National Theater in Prague (1868–83). The artists and musicians who participated in creating the decorations for the theater and in writing the music performed there are identified as "the generation of the National Theater."

Around the turn of the century, Czech art started to place less emphasis on nationalistic themes and began to explore different styles, as other European artists did. The most influential Czech artists of this period included Josef Mánes (1820–71), Vojtěch Hynais (1854–1925), and Mikoláš Aleš (1852–1913). Alfons Mucha (1860–1939) was best known for his development of the Art Nouveau style and his posters publicizing the performances of Sarah Bernhardt (1846–1923). Václav Špála (1885–1946), Josef Čapek (1887–1945), and Jan Zrzavý (1890–1977) were among those who based their work on national themes but did not limit themselves to any narrow nationalist cause and became modern European artists as well as a significant part of Czech culture.

A more modern aspect of Czech culture is film. Influenced by both American and Western European traditions, the Czech film industry gained world recognition in the 1960s with the release of the works of Jiří Menzel (1938–), Věra Chytilová (1929–), and Miloš Forman (1932–). In the European tradition, film is considered primarily an art form, not an entertainment medium.

Although the country is mostly Roman Catholic, the Czech Republic has a long tradition of other religions as part of the mainstream of culture. From the beginning of the Protestant Reformation in Bohemia, led by Jan Hus (1370–1415), Czech society emphasized the importance of literacy and religious and cultural tolerance, and many of these values have become a part of Czech culture. Jewish writers, musicians, and artists have contributed heavily to what is now considered Czech culture. Other national groups (Slovaks, Germans, Poles, Ukrainians, and Gypsies) have always been part of Czech national culture and continue to enrich it today.

Dagmar Berry

Further reading
Československá vlastivěda, díl IX-umění. Prague, 1971.
Malý encyklopedický slovník A-Ž. Prague, 1972.
Očadlík, Mirko. *Svět orchestru.* Prague, 1995.

See also Charles University; Cinema; Czech and Slovak Art; Czech Language; Czech Literature; Antonín Dvořák; Folk Music; Miloš Forman; Leoš Janáček; Josef Mánes; Alfons Mucha; Music; Revolutions of 1848; Bedřich Smetana; Theater

Czech Émigrés

Emigration from the Czech lands has occurred in almost every century, especially, however, with the beginning of the fifteenth century. The first massive emigration took place in the seventeenth century, following the disastrous defeat of the Bohemian Estates at the Battle of White Mountain at the hands of the Habsburgs on November 8, 1620. Because of the political and religious persecution that ensued, the Czech nation lost three-fourths of its native nobility, and its most eminent and wealthy citizens and noted scholars were forced to flee into exile. It is estimated that in 1628, 36,000 families left the Kingdom of Bohemia. Confiscated property exceeded 100 million gulden, and 500 of the 936 noble estates were forfeited. The exiles sought, at first, refuge in Saxony, Silesia, Hungary, and Poland; later, however, they scattered beyond the borders of those countries as well. The most eminent among the refugees condemned to perpetual exile by the Treaty of Westphalia, which ended the Thirty Years' War (1618–48), was Jan Ámos Komenský (Comenius) (1592–1670), leader of the condemned Unity of Bohemian Brethren, who settled in Leszno and later in the Netherlands. Some of the refugees migrated via Holland to New Amsterdam (New York) in the New World. The most prominent of them was Augustine Herman (1621–85), author of the first map of Maryland, who was granted the estate that he called the Bohemian Manor.

The mass emigration of non-Catholic nobles and burghers from the Kingdom of Bohemia was followed by at least six distinct waves of peasant migration, from the end of the seventeenth century until 1781—the year of the issuance of the Toleration Patent by Joseph II (1741–90). During this period, a group of Moravian Brethren from the Czech lands emigrated by way of Saxony to Georgia and later to Pennsylvania, where they established the town of Bethlehem. It is estimated that in the fifty-year period prior to 1781, some sixty thousand individuals emigrated from the Czech lands.

The Habsburg monarchy generally opposed emigration from its territories and severely punished those who tried to leave illegally. However, it encouraged internal migration for the purpose of colonizing the less populated regions of the monarchy. As a result of the increased unemployment and the worsened economic situation, more liberal imperial patents were adopted, based on the belief that emigration might lessen the number of unemployed. Nevertheless, emigration was always connected with the loss of Austrian citizenship, and frequent illegal emigration to avoid military draft was severely punished.

The large mass emigration from the Czech lands occurred following the Revolutions of 1848, primarily because of socioeconomic reasons. The combination of high fertility and reduced mortality led to increased population growth and consequently to higher unemployment. With the onset of industrialization, there was also a lesser need for skilled Czech artisans and craftsmen, who now were forced to seek employment abroad. Another important factor was the rural economic crisis, which was responsible for a large wave of migration among Czech farmers and peasants. It is estimated that 54,000 persons emigrated from 1841 to 1850, as compared with 177,000 who left the country during the 1860s and 250,000 during the 1880s. Although a considerable number of emigrants settled in Vienna, more than half moved to the United States where some settled in New York City, Chicago, and St. Louis; others headed west, attracted to wide-open spaces and the promise of owning their own land. They moved to wooded states such as Wisconsin, Michigan, and Minnesota as well as the prairie states of Iowa, Nebraska, Kansas, and the Dakotas.

During the interwar period, emigration from the Czech lands practically ceased. When World War II began, the Nazi onslaught precipitated a new emigration or escape of some 20,000 persons, of whom one-fourth were intellectuals. The greatest exodus occurred in 1948, after the Communist coup in Czechoslovakia. In the decade following the coup, over 60,000 people escaped to the West. Most of them found their way to the United States, Canada, and Australia, while others either remained in Western Europe or moved to Latin America. After the liberalized regime of Alexander Dubček (1921–1992) was crushed by Warsaw Pact forces in August 1968, another large exodus of refugees followed, a majority of whom stayed in Europe. After the overthrow of the Communists in 1989, a number of the post-1968 emigrants returned to their homeland.

Miloslav Rechcigl Jr.

Further reading

Aurhan, Jan and Rudolf Turčin. "Češi a Slováci za hranicemi," in *Českoslovanská vlastivěda,* vol. 5. Prague, 1931, 503.
Češi v cizině, nos. 1–7 and ff. Prague, 1986–93.
Ottův slovník naučný, vol. 8. Prague, 1894, 574–80.
Rechcigl, Miloslav, Jr. "In the Footprints of the First Czech Immigrants in America." *Czechoslovak and Central European Journal* 9 (1990): 75–90.

See also Alexander Dubček; Emigration; Prague Spring; Revolutions of 1848; Warsaw Pact

Czech Language

A Western Slavonic language, spoken by ten million people in the historical territories of Bohemia, Moravia, and Silesia that form the territory of the Czech Republic. Czech as a national language comprises several structural formations based primarily on the territorial spread: the top position is occupied by Literary, or Standard, Czech (*spisovná čeština*), codified in grammar, lexicon, texbooks, and official manuals. In its spoken norm, it is defined loosely as colloquial Czech (*hovorová čeština*). Common Czech (*obecná čeština*) is restricted primarily to the urban area of Prague, although it may be considered as an interdialect unifying all Bohemian dialects. In the territories of Moravia and Silesia, three main regional dialects still exist, although they are in the process of merging.

The tradition of genuine Standard Czech dates to the thirteenth century, although Old Church Slavonic, created by the missionaries Cyril (d. 869) and Methodius (d. 884) in the ninth century on a Macedonian-Bulgarian dialect, may as well be considered as the origin of the domestic language. Throughout the following centuries, Czech always existed in a spoken form, but as a literary language it had to struggle for its survival against Latin and German, being suppressed entirely by the former in the twelfth and thirteenth centuries and by the latter after the arrival of the Habsburgs in the sixteenth century. On the other hand, it became enriched considerably by those two languages, both in grammar and in lexis. The resurrection of Czech began in the eighteenth century, and principally after 1848, during the Czech National Renaissance. Since the creation of the independent Czechoslovak republic in 1918, it has been not only a national but also an official and state language of the people on the Czech territory, except during World War II (1939–45).

Standard Czech phonemics are represented by five short simple vocalic phonemes and their five long counterparts, three diphthongs, and twenty-five consonantal phonemes. Using the modern Latin alphabet of twenty-six letters, inclusive of one diagraph, and those with diacritics to denote length and palatalization, the written form is able to record all the phonemes and graphemes with the maximum possible direct correspondence between phonemes and graphemes. Its robust morpology displays a seven-case declension and five-class conjugation system, and has indicators also of gender, number, person, tense, aspect, voice, and mood. Although it is far from being an agglutinating language, its prevailing synthetic character allows for relatively loose word order. An abundant list of derivational morphemes, including infixes, adds to the possibilities of enlarging the vocabulary, also in terms of aspectual evaluation such as imperfectivity, perfectivity, multiplication, distributiveness, durativity, iterativity, and inchoativity.

Stanislav Kavka

Further reading

Barták, B. et al. *Encyklopedický slovník.* Prague, 1993.
Etymologický slovník jazyka českého. Prague, 1957.
Haller, J. *Český slovník věcný a synonimický.* Prague, 1969.
Havránek, B. et al. *Slovník spisovného jazyka českého.* Prague, 1989.
Havránek, B. and A. Jedlička. *Česká mluvnice.* Prague, 1988.
Hlavsa, Z. et al. *Pravidla českého pravopisu.* Prague, 1969.

See also Slovak Language

Czech Literature

The earliest Czech writings, dating from the ninth century, were written in two languages:

Czech-Church Slavonic, the Slavic liturgical and literary language brought to Morava by the scholars Cyril (d. 869) and Methodius (d. 884), and Latin (the Latin rite and language dominated by the eleventh century). Church literature, saints' lives (Cyril and Methodius; Václav and Ludmila), hymns ("Hospodine, pomiluj ny," "Svatý Václave"), and chronicles (in Latin, Kristián, c. 994; Kosmas, 1119–26) made up the literature of the Czech lands until the end of the thirteenth century. In the fourteenth century priests, the only writers of the earliest period, were joined by knights (court literature) and occasionally burghers. The most notable documents of the period included the Czech epic poem *Alexandreis* and the *Dalimil Chronicle,* which was noted for its anti-German tone.

Jan Hus (1370–1415), leader of the Czech Reformation, known for his eloquent sermons in both Czech and Latin as well as for many religious tracts and letters from prison, exerted a profound impact on Czech culture and literature. Following his death at the stake in Constance in 1415, the Czech lands were ravaged by the Hussite Wars. These wars ushered in a new era, changes in both the spoken and written language, including the orthographic reforms of Hus, and the severance of Czech culture from the Latin-Roman community. The literature of this period continued to be largely religious, with hymns the predominant genre. Among these writers was Petr Chelčický (c. 1390–c. 1460), known for his religious writings, one of the most radical moralists of the Middle Ages, and a direct predecessor of Russian writer Lev Tolstoy (1828–1910).

The religious wars continued into the seventeenth century with the Thirty Years' War (1618–1648). A significant turning point in Czech history and literature was marked by the 1620 defeat of Czech forces by the Habsburgs at the Battle of White Mountain. Jesuits arrived and imposed a militant Catholicism; Czech nobles (and other Protestants) fled or were executed, and entire libraries were destroyed. The Czech people lost their nobility, their best citizens, and their independence. The result was a decimation of the Czech language, literature, and culture. Books were burned, schools were Latinized, and culture Germanicized.

One last star of medieval Czech letters, compelled to emigrate from Bohemia in 1628, was Jan Ámos Komenský (Johann Amos Come-nius, 1592–1670), the last bishop of the Unity of the Bohemian Brethren. A man of universal stature and friend to English poet John Milton (1608–74) and Swedish statesman Count Axel Oxenstierna (1583–1654), Komenský was recognized as a European authority, partly because he wrote in Latin as well as in Czech. His work embodied the synthesis of humanism and the reformation in Bohemia, and his writings on education, science, and religion were surpassed by none of his contemporaries.

During the seventeenth and eighteenth centuries, the Czech language and traditions, abandoned by the educated elites and ruling classes, were preserved by the lower classes and rural population. Folk songs especially flourished. This tradition was rediscovered by German, and later Czech, romantics at the turn of the nineteenth century.

Habsburg Emperor Joseph II's (1741–90) Decree of Tolerance in 1781 set the stage for the revival of the Czech language and literature. A burning desire to re-create the Czech language and reclaim Czech history characterized the first half of the nineteenth century, referred to as the period of National Revival.

Literature drew its inspiration from history, specifically from the work of historians Pavel Josef Šafařík (1795–1861) and František Palacký (1798–1876), who reconstructed the ancient history of the Czechs. Karel Havlíček (1821–56), next to Palacký the most popular and important political leader of his time, founded *Národní Noviny* (*National Gazette*), the first independent political journal in the Czech language. Writers directed their energies to the creation of a poetic diction, and one of the earliest masterpieces of this period was the patriotic elegy *Slávy dcera* (*The Daughter of Sláva,* 1824) of Ján Kollár (1793–1852). An interest in folk stories and traditions, as representative of the Czech national heritage, also characterized this era. František Ladislav Čelakovský (1799–1852) created original poetry in the spirit of folk songs, and Karel Erben (1811–70), a collector of folk songs and tales, created ballads on folk themes, *Kytice z pověstí národních* (*A Banquet of National Tales,* 1853). Karel Hynek Mácha (1810–36), the first great poet of modern Czech literature, composed his masterpiece *Máj* (*May,* 1836), a Byronic verse tale noted for its fine descriptions of nature, its musical language, and its romantic, melancholy tone. Božena Němcová

(1820–62), who also collected and published Czech folk tales, wrote her classic prose idyll, *Babička* (*Grandmother,* 1855), a description of happy childhood in the Bohemian countryside.

The national revival continued in the second half of the nineteenth century, but the emphasis of writers largely shifted to political and social reform. The group of writers who organized around the journal *Máj* in 1860 were generally oriented toward realism and concerned primarily with social problems. Advocates of literary cosmopolitanism, they insisted on the universal nature of poetry. The most influential figure of this period, Jan Neruda (1834–91), was a renowned journalist and poet. The Máj group, whose most successful genre was lyric poetry, included Vítězslav Hálek (1835–74) and Adolf Heyduk (1835–1923). The most renowned prose writer of this period was Karolina Světlá (1830–99), whose greatest works present contemporary moral problems set in the rural past. The Ruch group, the major literary school in the mid-1870s, emphasized political reform, rejecting the cosmopolitanism of the Máj group (many writers, including Neruda, joined this new movement) and returning to the romantic ideals of the National Revival. These writers emphasized a popular approach and native themes, appealing to the common reader. Historical novels, many written by historians, became the most popular genre, as the past provided support for the national political struggle. The most noted historical novelists of this period include Svatopluk Čech (1846–1908), Alois Jirásek (1851–1930), and Zikmund Winter (1846–1913). The greatest elegist in Czech poetry, Josef Václav Sládek (1845–1912), a leading organizer of Ruch, later became editor of *Lumír,* a journal founded by Neruda. In the 1880s the *Lumírovci,* contributors to this weekly (*Lumír*), set on a course to raise Czech literature to the level of other nations. They succeeded in greatly widening the horizon of Czech literature through translations of foreign literature, the development of new forms, and closer contact with the traditions of Western Europe. Chief among them were Jaroslav Vrchlický (1853–1912), a prolific poet, dramatist, critic, essayist, prose writer, and translator, and Julius Zeyer (1841–1901), an epic poet, dramatic poet, and novelist.

Czech realism flourished in the 1890s. Tomáš G. Masaryk (1850–1937), a philosopher and critic, led a group organized around the cultural and political journal *Čas* (*Time*). This group demanded realism in scholarship, reevaluation of the National Revival, and attention to the present, especially to social concerns. Representative of this period were Josef Machar (1864–1942), the poet of Czech realism, who was also a noted journalist, and Matěj Šimáček (1860–1913), leader of the Czech realists, who published in the exceptional weekly *Světozor.* The prose of Czech naturalism, with its graphic depictions of contemporary life, reflected its ties to the visual arts, especially impressionism. Its chief practitioners were K.M. Čapek-Chod (Karel Matěj Čapek, 1860–1927) and Vilém Mrštík (1863–1912).

The social, political, and moral tasks of literature became the predominant emphasis of many writers in the mid-1890s. During this period, literary criticism gained prestige and influence, and novelists and poets engaged in criticism. The champion of these new directions was František Xaver Šalda (1867–1937), critic and poet. A master of literary criticism whose work remains highly respected, he promoted a philosophy of art that viewed artistic creation as dependent on a gifted personality that was educated, disciplined, and morally responsible. Opposed to formalism, he advocated psychological criticism, examining the author, that author's society, and the validity of the ideas expressed in the work. Among contemporary authors, those he rated the most highly were two representatives of Czech symbolism, impressionist poet Antonín Sova (1864–1928) and metaphysical poet Otakar Březina (1868–1929).

Between the wars, when Czechoslovakia existed as an independent state, Czech literature flourished. In 1918 Masaryk became the first president of the Czechoslovak republic. As a writer and participant in the Fridays group (*Pátečníci*), along with Karel Čapek (1890–1938) and other prominent literary and political figures of the time, he set a high cultural standard for his new country. The 1920s saw an interest in a new proletarian, antibourgeois poetry published by such poets as Stanislav Neumann (1875–1947), Josef Hora (1891–1945), Jaroslav Seifert (1901–86), Jiří Wolker (1891–1945), Karel Teige (1900–1951), and Vítěslav Nezval (1900–1958). Čapek wrote his famous science fiction plays, including *R.U.R.* (*Rossum's Universal Robots,* 1921), and novels, including *Factory of the Absolute* (1922) and *War with the Newts* (1936), during this period, as well as numerous translations, essays, and short stories.

C In response to World War I, Jaroslav Hašek (1883–1923) produced the most famous Czech satiric antiwar novel, *The Adventures of the Good Soldier Švejk during the World War* (1920–23). Vladislav Vančura (1891–1942), best known for his masterly use of the Czech language, attempted to renew it in his stories and novels by using archaic words and images from ancient Czech chronicles, Hussite literature, and the Czech Brethren's sixteenth-century translation of the Bible. Ivan Olbracht (1882–1952), known for his adventure stories and novels set in the most eastern mountainous part of interwar Czechoslovakia (the Carpathians), wrote his best works in the 1930s.

The Prague Linguistic Circle, a major school of thought that contributed on an international level to theory in literature, linguistics, semiotics, art, folklore, and the social sciences in general, whose main tenets came to be known as Czech structuralism, flourished in the 1920s and 1930s, and briefly again after World War II, until the Communist seizure of power. Leading figures included Roman Jakobson (1896–1982), who emigrated to the United States after 1948; Jan Mukařovský (1891–1975); Vilém Mathesius (1882–1945); and Felix Vodička (1909–74).

The Communist seizure of power in 1948 ended the brief interval of Czech independence following the German occupation of 1939–1945. Many writers, now under the strict eye of the censor, turned to children's literature or translation. The government emphasized the value of literature as propaganda and the Soviet-imported doctrine of socialist realism. Criticism again became a dominant force, because of the official need to reevaluate the entire literary tradition in light of Marxist criticism. The cultural and political thaw began in Czechoslovakia only in the late 1950s, and the years 1963–68 witnessed great creativity in the arts. Censorship was abolished in June 1968. During that period, for virtually the first time in Czech history, the novel became the predominant genre. The influence of film on writing was also great because of the close collaboration of many writers with Czech New Wave Film in Prague in the 1960s. Milan Kundera (1929–) taught at the Film Faculty of the Prague Academy of Arts in the 1960s, and film directors such as Miloš Forman (1932–) and Jiří Menzel (1938–) directed film versions of contemporary writers' novels and plays. Among the best-known writers of this period are Josef Škvorecký (1924–), Bohumil Hrabal (1914–97), Ladislav Fuks (1923–), Kundera, Ludvík Vaculík (1926–), and playwrights Václav Havel (1936–), Ivan Klíma (1931–), and Pavel Kohout (1928–). The Prague Spring ended when tanks of Warsaw Pact members rolled into Prague in August 1968, halting the Czechoslovak experiment in "socialism with a human face."

In the years that followed, émigré literature played an increasingly important role in maintaining the Czech literary tradition. Škvorecký opened Sixty-Eight Publishers (named for the year Soviet tanks stopped the Prague Spring) in Canada in 1972 with his wife, actress and writer Zdena Salivarová (1933–), which became the major outlet for Czech literature in exile, as well as for many Czech writers who remained in Czechoslovakia. While many of these works could be classified as literature of protest, depicting the absurdities of life under Communist rule, others were anathema to the Czech authorities because their depiction of life, the world, and religion did not match that of the official ideology. In spite of repression during this period, poet Jaroslav Seifert won the Nobel Prize in literature in 1984; Kundera's novels were translated into many languages, and he was nominated for the Nobel Prize in literature in 1988; and Havel became famous for his plays, as well as his anti-Communist stance.

After the Velvet Revolution of 1989, which brought an end to Communist rule in the country, Havel, the playwright imprisoned several times for his antigovernment activities, became president of Czechoslovakia. Censorship was abolished, and works prepared in the West could now be published in the Czech Republic.

Ann Marie Basom

Further reading

Balajka, Bohumil and V. Tichý. *Stručné Dějiny české a slovenské literatury.* Prague, 1965.

Chudoba, František. *A Short Survey of Czech Literature.* New York, 1924.

Hrubý, Peter. *Daydreams and Nightmares: Czech Communist and Ex-Communist Literature 1917–1987.* New York, 1990.

Kovtun, George J. *Czech and Slovak Literature in English: A Bibliography,* 2d ed. Washington, D.C., 1988.

Měšťan, Antonín. *Geschichte der tschechischen Literatur im 19. und 20. Jahrhundert.* Cologne, 1984.

Novák, Arne. *Czech Literature,* trans. by Peter Kussi, ed. by William E. Harkins. Ann Arbor, Michigan, 1976.

Volková, Bronislava. *A Feminist's Semiotic Odyssey through Czech Literature.* Lewiston, New York, 1997.

See also Karel Čapek; Censorship; Cinema; Czech Culture; Czech Émigrés; Czech Language; Folklife; Miloš Forman; Jaroslav Hašek; Václav Havel; Karel Havlíček; Alois Jirásek; Ján Kollár; Milan Kundera; Karel Hynek Mácha; Tomáš G. Masaryk; Božena Němcová; František Palacký; Prague Spring; Romanticism; Jaroslav Seifert; Pavel Josef Šafárik; Josef Škvorecký; Velvet Revolution

Czech Mafia

Secret Czech political committee (*Česká Maffie*) during World War I that promoted Czechoslovak independence from Austria-Hungary. At the outset of the war, Czech—and a fortiori Slovak—politicians had no plan for independence and union in a common Czechoslovak state. The Czechoslovak independence movement arose gradually. The leaders of the Czech Social Democratic party and of the clerical Catholic People's parties, for different reasons, declared their support of the Habsburg monarchy. The leader of the middle-class, nationalist Young Czech Party, Karel Kramář (1860–1937), expected Russian liberation and was content to passively await the arrival of Russian troops in Prague. Professor Tomáš G. Masaryk (1850–1937), leader of the small but intellectually influential Realist Party, felt that Allied support for Czechoslovak independence had to be actively sought. After probing Allied opinion through his English friend R.W. Seton-Watson (1879–1951), he quietly slipped into exile in December 1914 and launched the Czechoslovak independence movement abroad (*zahraniční odboj*).

Meanwhile, Edvard Beneš (1884–1948), Masaryk's dedicated disciple, began to lay the basis of the independence movement at home (*domácí odboj*). In March 1915 he began quiet discussions with party leaders (other than the Social Democrats and Catholic clericals) to this effect. As a result, an informal secret steering committee was formed, which after the war was dubbed the Czech Mafia. Beneš was its guiding spirit until he was forced to flee abroad, in September 1915, to evade arrest. The leadership of the Mafia then passed to,

and was held until the end of the war by, Přemysl Šámal (1867–1942), a well-connected Prague lawyer with a flair for intelligence work and behind-the-scenes maneuvering.

The outbreak of the Russian Revolution and the American declaration of war in 1917 gave a new ideological dimension to the war and greatly energized the Czechoslovak independence movement at home and abroad. While the Czechoslovak National Council in Paris under Masaryk, Beneš, and Slovak astronomer, soldier, and diplomat Milan R. Štefánik (1880–1919) worked to secure Allied recognition, the Czech National Committee in Prague under Kramář, Antonín Švehla (1873–1933), and Alois Rašín (1867–1923) prepared the ground for independence and statehood at home. The Mafia coordinated the efforts of the two committees in the final year of the war so effectively that the Czechoslovak state could be established in a bloodless revolution. The Prague National Committee took over power from the Austrian authorities without an armed uprising or direct Allied military intervention.

Victor S. Mamatey

Further reading

Paulová, Milada. *Dějiny Maffie,* 2 vols. Prague, 1937.

———. *Tajný výbor (Maffie) a spolupráce s Jihoslovany v letech 1916–1918.* Prague, 1968.

See also Edvard Beneš; Karel Kramář; Tomáš G. Masaryk; Alois Rašín; R.W. Seton-Watson; Milan R. Štefánik; Antonín Švehla; Young Czechs

Czechoslovakia (Geography)

The Czechoslovak state was created in 1918 and was dismantled at the end of 1992 with the separation of the Czech and Slovak republics. Bohemia to the west, Moravia in the middle, and Slovakia to the east were the three major subdivisions of the state, and have had a long history of intertwined paths. In 1989 the population of the nation was 15.5 million, with 64 percent Czechs and 31 percent Slovaks. The remaining were minorities including Hungarians, Poles, Germans, and Ukrainians. A significantly higher representation of minorities existed before the post–World War II period.

The nation occupied a fortresslike physical area within Europe, with Bohemia flanked by

C mountainous borders and Slovakia engulfed by the Carpathians. Only Moravia has a central gateway that breaks the upland barrier. The Czechoslovak lands are drained by several rivers, including the Vltava, which runs northward through Prague, and the Danube, which forms part of the border between Slovakia and Hungary.

Czechoslovakia was initially carved out of the Austro-Hungarian Empire because of events during World War I and the skillful diplomacy of Czech statesmen. The Czech side of the state fell under Nazi German control from 1938–39 until 1945; during that same period, Slovakia was nominally independent. Following World War II, Czechoslovakia came under Soviet domination and remained firmly entrenched behind the Iron Curtain. The state was also aligned with the Warsaw Pact and the Council for Mutual Economic Assistance (CMEA), the Soviet bloc's military and economic umbrella organizations that were largely directed from Moscow.

Prior to the Soviet period, Czechoslovakia had grown to be an economic giant within Europe. Bohemia and Moravia housed major industrial regions with cities such as Prague, Plzeň, and Ostrava dominating the productivity. Slovakia remained largely rural and agricultural until after World War II. The economy of the nation was therefore complementary.

During the Communist era, a major shift in industrial production occurred. Most new industry was placed in Slovakia in an attempt to balance the distribution of wealth and to ensure that key CMEA industries were located away from the western borders of the bloc. The bulk of the manufactured exports for the Czechoslovak state in 1988 were clothing, footwear, and transport equipment.

Prague (population 1.2 million in 1990) served as the capital of Czechoslovakia and still maintains that role for the Czech Republic. The city grew up around a series of islands in the Vltava River. While the fourteenth century is referred to as the Golden Age of Prague, an era in which commerce, art, music, and literature flourished, the city remains the heart of the nation and a cultural and economic center in Europe.

Russell L. Ivy

Further reading

Berentsen, William, ed. *Europe in the 1990s: A Geographical Analysis,* 7th ed. Chicago, 1997.

Pounds, Norman J. G. *Eastern Europe.* Chicago, 1969.

Rugg, Dean. *Eastern Europe.* London, 1985.

UNIDO. *Czechoslovakia: Industrial Transformation and Regeneration.* Oxford, 1992.

See also Bohemia; Comecon; Industrialization; Iron Curtain; Moravia; Ostrava; Plzeň; Prague; Protectorate of Bohemia and Moravia; Slovak Republic; Slovakia; Vltava River; Warsaw Pact

Czechoslovakia (History)

In 1815 the state of Czechoslovakia did not exist. Its major constituent regions—Bohemia, Moravia-Silesia, and Slovakia—which had existed since the early Middle Ages, were all parts of the Austro-Hungarian Empire. As one of the "successor states" that replaced the defunct Habsburg monarchy after World War I, the First Czechoslovak Republic (ČSR) lasted from October 1918 through September 1938. The truncated, federated Second Republic of Czecho-Slovakia lasted only six months, from October 1938 to March 1939. During World War II, the Czech and Slovak lands were politically separated. In March 1939 Bohemia and Moravia became the Protectorate of Bohemia-Moravia, ruled by Nazi Germany. With the latter's encouragement, Slovakia declared its independence as the Slovak Republic (1939–1945). The Czechs and Slovaks were reunited at war's end in the Third Czechoslovak Republic, from May 1945 to February 1948. After the Communist takeover in February 1948, the country was renamed Czechoslovak People's Democracy, amended in 1960 to the Czechoslovak Socialist Republic (ČSSR). In 1969, as the sole remaining positive result of the unsuccessful reform movement of the 1960s called Prague Spring, the latter was federalized into two equal Czech and Slovak socialist republics. After the fall of the Berlin Wall in 1989 and the rapid subsequent collapse of communism in Central and Eastern Europe, the Czechs and Slovaks coexisted briefly—from April 1990 through December 1992—in a new democratic Czech and Slovak Federal Republic. On January 1, 1993, unable after extensive negotiations to agree on a joint political-economic future relationship, the two nations parted peacefully as two separate, fully sovereign states, the Czech Republic and the Republic of Slovakia.

The Czechs and Slovaks before 1815

The history of the Czechs and Slovaks is the history of two small kindred nations, closely similar ethnically and linguistically but markedly different in historical development, who first attempted to build a common state in the early twentieth century, after having lived almost totally separate lives since the original appearance of their ancestors in East Central Europe. Small in numbers and relatively nonaggressive but occupying an important geopolitical area of Europe, they have constantly had to defend themselves, their lands, and their cultures against their more powerful neighbors—the Czechs primarily against the Germans, the Slovaks against the Hungarians (Magyars). Until their union in 1918, they were separated politically and had to accommodate these threats and influences individually. After 1918, their repeated attempts at harmonious coexistence in a common state were fundamentally handicapped by a strong dissimilarity in their previous historical development and especially by the reluctance of the dominant and more numerous Czechs to grant the Slovaks a fully equal status.

Both peoples are members of the western branch of the Slavs, whose ancestors migrated from the common Slavic homeland southward across the Carpathian Mountains, about the fifth century A.D. Both were included, along with other peoples, in the brief, shadowy Great Moravian Empire in the ninth century. After it fell to the attacks of Germans and Magyars in 907, the paths of the Czechs and Slovaks diverged for a millennium. The Czechs succeeded in establishing their own independent kingdom of Bohemia-Moravia, before it fell to the control of the Habsburg dynasty by election in 1526 and again by conquest in 1620. The Slovaks were engulfed by the Kingdom of Hungary and enjoyed little self-rule for the next thousand years. They also passed, with Hungary, to Habsburg rule in 1526. Although they shared almost four centuries of Habsburg rule, the Czechs and Slovaks lived largely apart from each other, and the lives they experienced were drastically different.

The Czechs

Under their first and only native dynasty, the Přemyslids, and a number of imported dynasties (Luxemburgs, Jagellonians, Habsburgs), the Czechs had constructed an important medieval monarchy in East Central Europe by 1620. A flourishing commercial, mining, and manufacturing economy had made it prosperous, with a socially differentiated and heavily urbanized population. Prague, with its own university, Charles University founded in 1348, was a major center of learning. As a Christian people, the Czechs were deeply involved in the rich culture of Catholic Europe. Because their kingdom had accepted feudal ties with the Holy Roman Empire and because of heavy German immigration into it from the eleventh century onward, the Czechs also became fatefully embroiled very early with their powerful German neighbors. Growing difficulties with both Catholicism and Germandom led to the famous Hussite Reformation at the start of the fifteenth century, regarded by many as the most important forerunner of the Lutheran Reformation a century later. For two centuries, the Czechs successfully defended their own "Protestant" interpretation of Christianity, based largely on the revisionist theological ideas of the martyred Jan Hus (1370–1415). Forced to defend themselves constantly against unending attacks, the Hussite Czechs acquired, as part of their siege mentality, a sense of ethnic-linguistic uniqueness, a premodern version of national consciousness.

When their Catholic-German Habsburg rulers tried to encroach on their Reformation, the Czechs rebelled against them in 1618. The defeat of the Bohemian forces at the Battle of White Mountain in 1620 began three centuries of unsympathetic hereditary rule of the Czech lands by the Habsburgs. As a result of the Thirty Years' War (1618–1648), they lost two-thirds of their population through death and expulsion, including a large part of their native political and intellectual leadership. The acknowledged spokesman for the Czech diaspora forced to live in exile was renowned philosopher and pedagogue Jan Ámos Komenský (Comenius [1592–1670]). Those who remained at home were rigorously re-Catholicized and their language and culture increasingly marginalized under German pressure. Significant native resistance began only in the later eighteenth century, when the two Austrian "Enlightened Despots," Empress Maria Theresa (1717–80) and her son and successor Joseph II (1741–90), attempted to accelerate the political and cultural absorption of all the lands and peoples they governed into a more centralized and homogeneous empire. A coalition of Bohemian nobles, resentful of the threat to their inherited privileges, and a small Czech intelligentsia, bent on restoring the Czech language and

Czech national consciousness, joined forces to launch the Czech National Revival. Czech national aspirations received additional stimulation from the stirring events and the inspiring principles of the French Revolution and the Napoleonic period (1789–1815), both of which touched Bohemia and Moravia.

The Slovaks

After it was conquered and absorbed by the Magyars in the early tenth century, Slovakia became one of the principal parts of the Hungarian kingdom. Indeed, during the sixteenth and seventeenth centuries, when central Hungary was occupied by the Ottoman Turks, it was the center of the territory that remained to the Hungarians and their elected Habsburg rulers. But the large majority of Slovaks themselves, mostly smallholding peasants, shepherds, and serfs, lived in poverty and suffered a stunted political and cultural life. They acquired virtually no experience in self-governance, and their native culture, under attack both from within and without, was ultimately reduced to the status of a simple folk culture. Sharing a fervent Catholicism with their Magyar overlords, the Slovak masses were easily susceptible to the influence of their own Magyarone Catholic priests. The small minority consisting of the Slovak gentry, townsmen, and intellectuals centered in such places as Pressburg and Trnava felt the influence of the neighboring Czech Hussitism. They tended to use a Slovakized version of the sixteenth-century Czech written language or Latin in formal communication. The Slovak language increasingly became only a rough spoken vernacular. Those Slovaks who subsequently became Protestants, chiefly Lutherans, a comparatively small but extremely energetic and important group, were inclined to be Czechophiles and to accept the view that Czechs and Slovaks were parts of the same nation. They reacted unsympathetically to any attempts to develop a separate Slovak written language well into the nineteenth century. When, as part of modest Slovak national stirrings in the late eighteenth century, such an attempt was made in 1787 by a Slovak Catholic priest, Anton Bernolák (1762–1813), it failed. The French Revolution and the Napoleonic Wars had practically no impact on Slovak national life.

The Czechs and Slovaks, 1815–1914

Except for brief and minor contact with French and Russian troops who occupied or passed through the territory of the Habsburg monarchy, most Czechs and Slovaks experienced the French Revolution and the Napoleonic Wars only indirectly and reacted to them with moderation. The Czech upper classes generally gave their loyal support to the government, though the revolutionary propaganda appealed to the peasantry. Except for the tragic "Helvetian Rebellion" of 1797, when peasant military deserters fought government troops in the Bohemian-Moravian highlands, there was little open resistance. A number of Slovak intellectuals took part in the unsuccessful "Jacobin Conspiracy" in Hungary in 1794–95; its purpose was to transform Hungary into a republic and to make Slovakia an autonomous national unit within it. Nevertheless, after Napoléon's (1769–1821) fall, the Czech and Slovak lands were not spared the implacable "conservative reaction" loosed upon Europe by the victorious coalition led by Austria's Prince Clemens von Metternich (1773–1859). Indeed, as constituent parts of the Habsburg monarchy, they received a direct and heavy dose of Metternich's repressive system of governance, including political and religious censorship, police surveillance and espionage, and suppression of everything new, revolutionary, and nationalistic.

But even the rigors of Metternich's police state could not stop the growth of Czech and Slovak national consciousness. The Czech and Slovak "national revivals" had begun in the 1780s, largely in reaction to the attempt of the Austrian emperor, Joseph II, to modernize, completely centralize, standardize, and Germanize his realm. They were deeply stimulated by the powerful example of group identity and purpose presented by the French during the Revolutionary and Napoleonic periods. And drawing strength from the coming of the Industrial Revolution to the monarchy and the wave of modern nationalism that washed over the entire continent during the nineteenth century, they would steadily continue to grow and mature (the Czech national movement much more so than that of the Slovaks) to the very outbreak of World War I.

The Czechs

The first phase of the celebrated Czech National Revival (Awakening) in the late 1700s was the achievement of a coalition of two disparate groups. One was the Bohemian nobility, largely of foreign origins, who resented the imperial attack on their inherited privileges and cultivated a Bohemian-Moravian "territorial patriotism" (*Landespatrio-*

tismus). The other was a group of Czech linguistic and historical scholars, many of them of clerical calling, who served and were supported by the nobles. A leading example of such a learned retainer was the Abbé Josef Dobrovský (1753–1829), a celebrated philologist and master of critical historical methodology who dominated this phase of the Czech national movement. The second phase, which followed the Napoleonic era, was the work of a second generation of "Awakeners." These were a remarkable group of enthusiastic younger intellectuals, mostly with roots in the peasantry or lower middle class, of Moravian or Slovak extraction, and Lutheran in religion. They included such hallowed historical figures as Josef Jungmann (1773–1847), the "elder" among them, a linguist and literary scholar; the Czechophile Slovaks Ján Kollár (1793–1852), a Pan-Slav poet, and Pavel Josef Šafárik (1795–1861), a pioneer of Slavic ethnology; and the Moravian historian František Palacký (1798–1876). More ambitious than their predecessors, they intended nothing less than to instill a deep national consciousness in the broad masses of the Czech population. This was to be done through a linguistic and literary revival of major dimensions, by transforming the clumsy Czech vernacular into a sophisticated vehicle of a nationally oriented literature. They compiled grammars and dictionaries, authored works of belles lettres and scholarship, published periodicals and newspapers, and Czechicized existing Bohemian cultural institutions or created new ones. Their acknowledged leader was Palacký, who devoted his long life entirely to the cause of Czech national revival. His involvement with almost every important event, institution, issue, and program of the revival earned him the title of Father of the Czech Nation.

Palacký was primarily a historian, and his chief contribution to the revival was his monumental *History of the Czech Nation in Bohemia and Moravia* (1848–76). Although a model of modern scientific historiography, it was not meant to be merely a work of historical reference. In it, Palacký also expounded a stirring philosophy of Czech history that glorified the Czechs' past and justified their continued existence. He depicted them as an enlightened and heroic people whose destiny was to champion the rights of the individual against the absolute authority of church and state. Sometimes, as in the Hussite Reformation, it brought them martyrdom. Palacký's definition of

Czech national character and mission has been the one most widely accepted by Czechs ever since.

By 1848, the goals of the Awakeners—a revival of Czech culture and an aroused Czech national consciousness—had been achieved. In that year, the Revolution of 1848 brought a new political dimension to Czech national life as well. Deserted by the conservative nobility, the liberal intelligentsia was forced to assume the political leadership of the Czech nation. Here, too, Palacký was the chief spokesman and representative of the Czechs in 1848–49. As such, he did not demand complete independence for them. In his policy of Austroslavism, which he expounded at the Slavonic Congress (1848) in Prague, at the Imperial Constituent Assembly (1848–49) at Kremsier (Kroměříž), and in numerous publications, Palacký described the Habsburg Empire as an indispensable protective shield for the small nations of Central Europe against both German and Russian aggression. He did not wish to destroy the empire but to maintain it, requiring, however, that it be reorganized and democratized to guarantee complete political and cultural equality for all the nationalities within it—specifically, that the empire's loyal Slavic peoples be granted absolute parity with the dominant Germans and Magyars. At Kremsier, involved with drafting a constitution for the empire, he first proposed a federalistic arrangement based on traditional historical-political entities, then, instead, a federation of entirely new entities organized on ethnic principles. One of the latter was to be a "Czechoslovak" national unit.

When the Revolution of 1848 was suppressed by force and the monarchy placed under martial law, Palacký returned to his historical and cultural labors. He resumed political activity after 1860 to head—along with his son-in-law František Ladislav Rieger (1818–1903) and František Brauner (1810–80)—the "Old Czech" (National) Party. The latter was a liberal-conservative coalition of the noble landowners and the upper middle class, whose platform was a return to the defense of Bohemia's historic state rights (Böhmische Staatsrecht). After the creation of the Dual Monarchy (Austria-Hungary) in 1867, the Old Czechs resorted to a policy of passive resistance, boycotting the imperial diet. The *Ausgleich* (Compromise), which established the Dual Monarchy, destroyed Palacký's hope that the Czechs would ever receive justice from the Habsburgs, but he had no new political ideas to advance. He could only urge the Czechs to continue to strengthen and improve their society in every way and to wait for a suitable opportunity (a great European war?) to better their status.

In the 1890s, the "Old Czechs" were replaced by the "Young Czechs" as the dominant Czech political party. The latter was a group of younger urban professionals led by the brothers Edvard (1827–1907) and Julius (1831–96) Grégr. They pursued more active and radical tactics and concentrated on gaining piecemeal political and cultural concessions from Vienna, such as proportional Czech representation in the parliamentary bodies, greater self-government for Bohemia and Moravia, and the increased use of the Czech language in schools and in public administration.

At the turn of the century, especially after the granting of universal manhood suffrage in 1907, the two older political parties were joined by a host of new ones representing the peasantry, proletariat, and a variety of special interests. One of these was the small but hyperactive and influential Realist Party, headed by the perpetual political gadfly and ombudsman, Tomáš G. Masaryk (1850–1937), a philosopher and professor at Charles University. The result was the growth of a genuine multiparty system in the Czech lands and greater political participation and experience among the inhabitants, but also a splintering of the national political platform. Some Czechs hoped for a further political subdivision of the Habsburg monarchy that would grant the Kingdom of Bohemia-Moravia the same autonomous status as Austria and Hungary (Trialism). Others, such as the neo-Slav leader, Karel Kramář (1860–1937), sought to tie future Czech security to political and cultural solidarity with other Slavic nations in a variety of all-Slav (Pan-Slav) movements.

In the nonpolitical spheres—economic, social, cultural—Czech progress in the half-century preceding World War I was steady and impressive. It was grounded in the increasingly larger role the Czech lands were playing in the accelerating industrialization of the Dual Monarchy. By the turn of the century, Bohemia and Moravia-Silesia were the most economically advanced parts of the empire, boasting such industrial centers as Prague, Plzeň (Pilsen), Brno, and Ostrava. There was heavy growth in the coal and iron industries; in the production of sugar, flour, and beer; and in the manufacture of glass, porcelain, and textiles. Czechs participated in these not only as a blue-collar proletariat but increasingly also as gray-collar managers and even as independent entrepreneurs. Czech-owned banks, corporations, and cooperatives began to compete more successfully with older German enterprises.

Growing economic prosperity fueled social mobility and increased sophistication among the Czechs. The Czech population was not only becoming rapidly larger but more urbanized and—thanks to a free and compulsory system of primary education—better educated. It enjoyed an ever greater number of specifically Czech institutions, from fraternal and benevolent associations to the Sokols (a mass gymnastic society founded in 1862 by Miroslav Tyrš [1832–84]); an independent Czech university (split off from the German-dominated university in Prague in 1882); and a Czech National Theater in 1883 (built with funds collected by a mass popular subscription).

Czech women, especially those living in Prague, began to press for a greater role in public—including political—life. Led by two prominent women writers—at first, Božena Němcová (1820–62) and later, Eliška Krásnohorská (1850–1923)—and with support from the Young Czech and Realist Parties, they demanded improved access to higher and professional education. A fledgling feminist movement, under the leadership of Krásnohorská, also made its appearance at the end of the nineteenth century.

Perhaps nowhere was Czech national progress in the nineteenth century more strikingly evident than in Czech cultural achievements. In its second, culminating half-century, the Czech National Revival was shaped by a virtual pantheon of creative talents, men and women who not only enjoyed—and continue to enjoy—vast popularity and admiration at home but, in many cases, abroad as well. A basic listing would have to include at least artists Josef Mánes (1820–71) and Mikoláš Aleš (1852–1913), who together created the Czech national school of art; the beloved musical composers Bedřich Smetana (1824–84) and Antonín Dvořák (1841–1904); sculptor Josef Myslbek (1848–1922); Byronic poet Karel Hynek Mácha (1810–36); and several writers whose names are synonymous with Czech literature in the nineteenth century—Jan Neruda (1834–91), Karolina Světlá (1830–99), Jaroslav Vrchlický (1853–1912), and Alois Jirásek (1851–1930). Such striking multifaceted progress, together with the high

Czech birthrate, could not fail to alarm the ethnic German population of Bohemia and Moravia, which felt its historic dominance increasingly threatened.

The Slovaks

In every respect—in the growth of national consciousness and in political, economic, social, and cultural development—the Slovaks experienced markedly less improvement than the Czechs in the nineteenth century. They suffered from enormous handicaps. The Industrial Revolution made very slow progress among the Slovaks, and they remained largely an agricultural people. They also remained socially stagnant, essentially a population of a single social class, peasants and artisans, with practically no middle class and a small aristocracy co-opted and alienated by their Magyar counterparts. The masses, largely Catholic, were politically passive and powerless and subjected to increasingly intense attempts at Magyarization as the century wore on, especially after 1867. The small Lutheran minority offered political leadership. However, it was divided between those who were Czechophiles and accepted the belief that the Czechs and Slovaks constituted a single nation (like Kollár and Šafárik) and those who rejected that idea and were suspicious of Czech designs, like Ľudovít Štúr (1815–56). Deprived of all but the most meager educational opportunities, the Slovaks faced almost insurmountable difficulties in creating a broadly based high culture.

The most aggressive Slovak national and political activity in the nineteenth century was the work of Štúr and those, like Lutheran pastors Jozef Miloslav Hurban (1817–88) and Michal Miloslav Hodža (1811–70), who were affiliated with him (the so-called Štúrovci). In the 1840s a rising wave of Magyar nationalism accompanied by a fierce campaign to Magyarize the other nationalities of Hungary, spurred Štúr to seek a way to unite all Slovaks, both Catholics and Protestants, against the onslaught. He chose the path of linguistic unification. Though Bernolák's attempt in 1787 had failed, Štúr structured his codification on the more suitable central Slovak dialect and was successful. The new literary language was widely accepted by the Roman Catholic majority, and after 1852, Štúrovčina—a compromise between Bernolák's and Štúr's versions—became progressively used by Slovak writers and intellectuals, such as eminent poet Pavol O. Hviezdoslav (1849–1921) and prolific novelist Svetozár Hurban-Vajanský (1847–1916). The successful development of a separate Slovak literary language opened a cultural schism between them and the Czechs, however, and set the Slovaks firmly on their own path of national development.

Like their Czech counterparts, the Slovak Awakeners also had to speak and act for their nation in the Revolution of 1848. Through their Petition of Liptovský Svätý Mikuláš and at the Slavonic Congress in Prague, they demanded recognition of Slovak nationhood, self-government and official use of the Slovak language, Slovak schools and a university, universal suffrage, and freedom of assembly, association, and the press. Many Czech intellectuals and cultural figures had been encouraging and supportive of the Slovaks' attempts at national revival, and in 1848 Palacký and others attempted to cooperate with their leadership. But the suspicious Štúr rejected Palacký's proposal for a "Czech-Slovak Crownland," and in September 1848 he and his followers declared armed rebellion against the Magyars. They led small volunteer detachments in several military expeditions against the latter. In the end, however, the Slovaks gained practically nothing in 1848, except for the general abolition of serfdom.

Their situation worsened considerably after 1867, when the Magyars were given virtually unchecked control over them. In a brutal, systematic attempt to assimilate the Slovaks forcibly into a Magyar national state, the Hungarians closed their secondary schools and reduced the number of their elementary schools. In 1875 they abolished the Matica slovenská, a member-supported cultural society founded in 1863 to foster Slovak national identity through literature, the fine arts, and education. The chief Slovak political organization, the Slovak National Party, never managed to gain more than a tiny representation in the Hungarian parliament. Attempting to find a way out of their dilemma, some Slovaks stressed their linguistic and cultural affinity with other Slavs and looked to the Pan-Slav movement for assistance. (Before his death, Štúr himself had developed strong pro-Russian sympathies.) Others, such as the "Hlasists," revived the idea of Czechoslovak national unity. Some simply chose to emigrate. Before 1914, a half-million Slovaks abandoned their homeland, most of them going to the United States. A quarter of a million Czechs had preceded and accompanied them there. Both groups emigrated primarily for

C economic rather than political reasons. In the coming war, however, both would turn to organized political activity in an attempt to help their beleaguered kinsmen back home achieve their independence.

World War I

The outbreak of World War I in 1914 found most Czechs and Slovaks still passively loyal to the Habsburg monarchy, and their political leaders focused on improving the lot of their constituents within it, not rebellion against it. Plans for the secession of the Czechs and Slovaks and their union in an independent state developed piecemeal and gradually as the war progressed. Karel Kramář, the Russophile Young Czech, looked to the Russians to liberate the Czechs and restore the old Bohemian kingdom with a Russian incumbent on the throne. On the other hand, Realist Party member Tomáš G. Masaryk went surreptitiously abroad in December 1914 to seek the diplomatic support of the Entente Powers for a free and united Czechoslovak republic. In 1915 Masaryk's close friend, the young lawyer Edvard Beneš (1884–1948), organized the "Czech Mafia," a domestic group that was to work covertly within the monarchy for Czechoslovak independence, and directed it until he, too, had to flee abroad to avoid arrest. Ultimately, the Mafia became the link between two separate groups planning and working for Czechoslovak independence, one at home, the other abroad. In Paris, London, Washington, D.C., and St. Petersburg, Masaryk, Beneš, and Milan R. Štefánik (1880–1919), a Slovak astronomer and a general in the French air force, set up and operated the Czechoslovak National Council. In Prague, Kramář presided over the Czech National Committee.

Valuable assistance for their efforts came from other sources abroad. Czech and Slovak emigrants in the West, especially members of such groups as the Bohemian National Alliance and the Slovak League of America in the United States, volunteered for military service in the Allied armies and raised the funds needed to finance the activities of Masaryk and his collaborators. They also pressured the Allied governments and propagandized Western public opinion to back the cause of Czechoslovak independence. Masaryk signed a formal agreement with representatives of Czech and Slovak Americans during the course of the war—the Pittsburgh Agreement (May 30, 1918). In it, the signatories expressed their support for a new joint Czech and Slovak state in which the Slovaks were to enjoy autonomy, the official use of their own language, and full equality with the Czechs.

Equally important for the Czechoslovak cause were the famous Czechoslovak military legions, composed of deserters, prisoners of war, and volunteers, which fought alongside the Allied armies in France, Italy, and Russia from the end of 1915 on. Numbering almost one hundred thousand men, they provided Masaryk with valuable diplomatic leverage as the commander of a major force of "fellow-combatants." Especially dramatic were the exploits of the legionnaires in Russia between May 1918 and September 1920. Under a triumvirate of leaders of their own choosing, including the colorful "Czechoslovak Napoléon," Radola Gajda (1892–1948), and against heavy Bolshevik opposition, they fought their way successfully along the entire length of the Trans-Siberian Railroad, through Siberia to Vladivostok on the Pacific Ocean. They were the most important Allied military presence on the eastern front during this period.

As the end of the war approached, and with it the impending defeat of the Central Powers and the disintegration of the Habsburg Empire, Czech and Slovak leaders were spurred to make formal declarations of independence on behalf of their peoples. In this, they belatedly received the encouragement and support of the Western powers, especially the United States. Finally abandoning his persistent reluctance to promote the dismemberment of Austria-Hungary, in his celebrated Fourteen Points in January 1918, the American president, Woodrow Wilson (1856–1924), gave his blessing to the self-determination of the peoples of the multinational empire. Later that year, the United States, Great Britain, and France all came out specifically in favor of Czech and Slovak independence and recognized the Czechoslovak National Council as the Provisional Government of a new Czechoslovak Republic. On October 18, 1918, Masaryk in Washington, D.C., and on October 28, 1918, the Czech National Committee in Prague proclaimed the birth of an independent, sovereign Czechoslovak state. The committee also moved swiftly to assume power from the Habsburg authorities at home. It promulgated its own provisional constitution and set up its own administrative system. Two days later, on October 30, about one hundred prominent Slovaks assembled at Turčiansky Svätý Martin in Slovakia. Speaking and acting for a largely passive Slovak population, they elected a twelve-member Slovak National Council and officially proclaimed the right of the Slovaks to withdraw their allegiance from Hungary and to unite with the Czechs. On November 14, 1918, a new provisional parliament in Prague elected Masaryk the first president of the new Czechoslovakia.

The First Czechoslovak Republic, 1918–38

The first Czechoslovak state included the territory of Bohemia, Moravia, part of Silesia, and Slovakia, as well as Subcarpathian Ruthenia, the latter allocated to it by the Allied peacemakers for strategic reasons. Of a total population of some fourteen million, the Czech and Slovak "state peoples" amounted to about 67 percent. The remaining one-third was composed of "national minorities," including Germans (an alarming 24 percent) and small percentages of Hungarians (Magyars), Ruthenes, Jews, and Poles.

Politically, the First Republic was a Western-style democratic republic with universal suffrage. Its parliament, elected by equal, direct, secret balloting, gave proportional representation to a broad range of political parties that, in turn, reflected a large variety of nationalities, ideologies, and viewpoints. During its short life span, it had only two presidents—the idolized "President-Liberator" Masaryk, from 1918 to 1935, and his handpicked successor, Beneš, from 1935 to 1938. Despite the preponderance of Roman Catholics, there was no established state religion, and public life was kept fastidiously secular. The first Czechoslovakia was internationally recognized as a genuine democracy, the most democratic state in Central and Eastern Europe, where the fundamental human rights of all citizens—state peoples as well as national minorities—were constitutionally guaranteed and routinely respected in everyday life. With the wealth of economic resources it had inherited from the Habsburg monarchy, a highly trained and disciplined workforce, and prudent fiscal policies, the new state provided its inhabitants with a well-balanced and well-managed economy, a high standard of living, and an extensive program of social benefits. Since its national boundaries were largely historically delineated, and since there were no significant groups of Czechs, Slovaks, or other ethnic groups anywhere that it wished to incorporate, it had no incentives to pursue revisionist or irredentist policies against neighboring states.

Under such promising conditions, Czechoslovakia should have enjoyed a long, trouble-free existence. But it was endangered from its very beginning by its exposed and important geographic location and a combination of powerful threats from within and without. The Czech-Slovak majority was a slim one and the coalition shaky. The constitution of 1920 established a unitary, centralized "Czechoslovak state," not the promised federal one that was supposed to provide autonomy for the Slovaks and Ruthenes (Carpatho-Rusyns). Masaryk's deep personal antipathy for the Roman Catholic Church and his insistence on a completely secular society alienated the Slovaks, who were mostly devout Catholics. Such widespread grievances played into the eager hands of Slovak separatist politicians. Other ethnic groups were also seriously dissatisfied. Though their civic and cultural rights were fully protected, the Germans, Magyars, and Poles had not wanted to be part of the new Czechoslovak state and resented their "minority" status. Real or imaginary, the grievances of the non-Czech nationalities led them to withhold their full loyalty and support for the building of a broad state patriotism. Several were manipulated by their mother countries—Germany, Hungary, and Poland—which were determined to recover their "lost" countrymen and to destroy the "synthetic" Czechoslovak state. Neither the patient, sincere attempts the latter made to accommodate its minorities nor the elaborate web of defensive diplomatic and military treaties it signed with other European states proved able to save Czechoslovakia from complete destruction in the end.

Nevertheless, during its two decades of existence, Czechoslovakia was a stable and well-functioning polity. This was largely due to the spirit of interparty cooperation and compromise that permeated its political atmosphere. President Masaryk and his capable foreign minister, Beneš, themselves presided over an impromptu body called the "Hrad" (Castle). This was a group of influential leaders from major walks of public life whom they consulted to help them formulate government policies and build supportive coalitions. The most important of these coalitions was the "Pětka," an informal committee composed of the leaders of the five major Czech political parties. Its most influential member was Antonín Švehla

C (1873–1933), who headed the centrist Agrarian (Republican) Party and himself served three times as prime minister. The Slovaks and the national minorities also had their political parties and representatives in parliament. The forces of the extreme left and right—a fledgling Communist Party founded in 1921, and a small native fascist movement centered about the charismatic general Radola Gajda and the flamboyant politician Jiří Stříbrný (1880–1955)—never acquired strong popular strength or parliamentary representation.

Though it had to face the same challenges of postwar economic dislocation and worldwide economic depression after 1929 as the rest of Europe, Czechoslovakia was comparatively prosperous during the interwar period. Its inhabitants enjoyed an eight-hour workday and the same standard of living as the French. The country grew steadily into one of the largest manufacturing economies in the world, shifting its labor force from agriculture into metallurgy and the production of machinery and quality consumer goods. Tomáš Bat'a (1876–1932) became one of the world's foremost manufacturers of footwear and one of its best-known "welfare capitalists." By far the largest share of industrial production took place in Bohemia and Moravia. Though the government made major capital investments in the less developed regions of Slovakia and Subcarpathian Ruthenia, these remained almost entirely providers of agricultural products and raw materials.

The stable, pluralist democracy and the well-developed economy provided a secure foundation for noteworthy achievements in social welfare, education, and culture. The state regulated and subsidized a broad range of public social services and health benefits, including low-income housing, health and accident insurance, and unemployment compensation. The legal status of women, in particular, improved enormously. From the onset, they were constitutionally guaranteed the same rights to vote, hold public office, gain an education, and enter the workforce as men. Encouraged and supported by such prominent personalities as Václav Klofáč (1868–1942), Czech radical-nationalist politician, and Charlotte Garrigue Masaryk (1850–1923), the American wife of the president, women moved steadily from domestic and farm occupations to nonagricultural employment, the professions, and political office. This was partially the result of their greater participation in the country's postelementary educational system. Drawing on the Czechs' traditional regard for learning, interwar Czechoslovakia constructed a comprehensive, secular, and open system of education that was the envy of its neighbors. It practically eliminated illiteracy among its inhabitants. Members of the national minorities were guaranteed the right to be educated in their own languages. Intellectual and cultural life flourished, in many branches and ethnic colorations (Czech, Slovak, German, Jewish). It could claim a large number of thinkers and artists with world reputations. These included artist Alfons Mucha (1860–1939), of Art Nouveau fame; Moravian composers Leoš Janáček (1854–1928) and Bohuslav Martinů (1890–1959); and a bevy of famous novelists and playwrights, such as Franz Kafka (1883–1924), Jaroslav Hašek (1883–1923), and Karel Čapek (1890–1938).

Despite its overwhelmingly positive balance sheet, the First Czechoslovak Republic did not manage to exist more than twenty years. Unable to dispel the alienation of its Slovaks and Sudeten Germans or to counter the machinations of Hungary and Nazi Germany, it became one of the first casualties of Adolf Hitler's preparations for another great European war.

The Slovaks were a "state people" and part of the governing coalition. Some of their more moderate political leaders, such as Vavro Šrobár (1867–1950) and Milan Hodža (1878–1944), worked effectively with their Czech counterparts and rose to ministerial posts in the government. But relations between Czechs and Slovaks in general were not cordial. The Slovaks charged that Masaryk had reneged on the promises he had made to their American kinsmen in the Pittsburgh Agreement of 1918, that they would enjoy home rule and the official use of their own language in the postwar state. The new Czechoslovakia had not become the contemplated Swiss-like federation. Rather, everything about it seemed dedicated to "Czechoslovakism." Its constitution described it as the domain of a single "Czechoslovak nation" speaking an official "Czechoslovak language" in two dialects. The Slovaks also resented the official anticlericalism of the Czech-dominated administration and the Czechs' patronizing, paternalistic attitude toward their Slovak "country cousins." The latter was particularly manifested by the members of the Czech "ruling complex" of administrators and other professionals sent to aid and tutor the "underdeveloped" Slovaks until they were deemed ready to manage their own affairs. Slovak grievances and Slovak demands for autonomy and even secession were articulated most effectively by the Slovak People's Party. Its leader, Father Andrej Hlinka (1864–1938), was a Roman Catholic priest and an ardent Slovak nationalist. While Hlinka generally limited himself to passionate denunciations of the secularism of the "godless" Czechs and eloquent appeals for the promised autonomy, some of his more radical lieutenants, especially those with ties to Hungary, wanted nothing less than "self-determination" for the Slovaks, that is, their outright secession from Czechoslovakia.

The large Sudeten German minority, almost three million strong and concentrated in northwest Bohemia and north-central Moravia, posed an equally formidable problem. Once a dominant ethnic elite when the Czech lands were part of Austria-Hungary, they now had to face the practical and psychological problems of being a national minority in a state they had not wished to join. To make matters worse, the Sudeten German industrial areas suffered particularly harsh effects of the Great Depression. Some Sudeten German political parties, notably the Social Democrats, participated regularly in Czechoslovak politics and even assumed places in the government. But most Sudeten Germans were ready for a more radical solution to their unhappy situation, and the rise of the Nazis to power in neighboring Germany in the early 1930s supplied it. From 1935 on, they rallied to the militant Sudeten German Party headed by Konrad Henlein (1898–1945), a former gymnastics instructor who openly sought Germany's assistance for Czechoslovakia's "persecuted" German minority. Following Hitler's instructions, Henlein began a long process of negotiation with the Czechoslovak government over Sudeten grievances and German self-rule in the country. Though the government offered him major concessions, Henlein refused them and continued to escalate his demands. In their most drastic form, they would have required the complete restructuring of Czechoslovakia along nationality lines, the placing of its German population under Hitler's personal protection, and even major changes in the conduct of Czechoslovakia's foreign affairs and its alliances. The negotiation process entered a particularly tense phase after Germany's annexation of Austria (*Anschluss*) in March 1938. Henlein himself soon fled to Germany.

In early September Hitler (1889–1945) publicly declared his support for the self-determination of the Sudeten Germans and threatened military action on their behalf. Great Britain and France, fearing the outbreak of a major war for which they were not adequately prepared, pressured Czechoslovakia to be conciliatory and to yield to Germany all of its territories in which the population was at least 50 percent German. Although the Czechoslovak armed forces responded efficiently when ordered to mobilize for action, and although there were mass popular demonstrations calling for resistance to Hitler, President Beneš, fearful of risking his small country's annihilation, decided to entrust its fate to the good offices of the Western powers that had acted as "godfathers" at its birth.

At a conference in Munich on September 29–30, 1938, the specific terms and boundaries were drawn up. The infamous Munich Agreement was worked out by Prime Minister Neville Chamberlain of Great Britain (1869–1940), Premier Édouard Daladier of France (1884–1970), Italy's duce, Benito Mussolini (1883–1945), and Hitler himself. There were no Czechoslovak representatives involved. The results were simply presented to them for their acceptance, and the devastating losses were compounded by the opportunistic seizure of smaller, long-disputed border areas by Poland and Hungary. In all, Czechoslovakia gave up almost 34 percent of its territory and about five million people, of whom a quarter were Czechs and Slovaks. It lost its elaborate system of border fortifications and natural defenses, together with a large part of its economic resources. The First Czechoslovak Republic was technically still in existence but no longer very viable. What remained of it was restructured into the emasculated Second Republic.

Ironically, the "Munich crisis" was precisely the sort of threat that Beneš, the master diplomat, had foreseen and worked exhaustively to meet. As Czechoslovakia's foreign minister from 1918 to 1935, he had publicly stated that the political and territorial integrity of his small country was primarily dependent on its foreign policy, not on its armed forces. Accordingly, he made Czechoslovakia a dedicated participant in the activities of the League of Nations and a host of other international bodies, movements, and conferences designed to deter aggression and ensure peace. Czechoslovakia also entered into a number of specific mutual-defense military alliances with Romania and Yugoslavia (the Little Entente) in 1920–21 and with France and the Soviet Union in 1935. But when it was challenged by Hitler's diktat in 1938, only the Soviet Union offered, under specific conditions, its military assistance.

The Second Czechoslovak Republic, 1938–39

The so-called Second Czechoslovak Republic lasted a mere six months. Beneš resigned at German insistence and left the country in October 1938. He was replaced in November by Emil Hácha (1872–1945), an eminent jurist of conservative leanings who had been prominent in the Austro-Hungarian and Czechoslovak legal worlds but was inexperienced as a practicing political executive. His new prime minister was Rudolf Beran (1887–1954), a prominent Agrarian politician well known for his pro-German sentiments. Hácha, Beran, and a new right-wing government took power, hoping to save what remained of Czechoslovakia's independence by accommodating all of Germany's demands, as well as the complaints of major domestic critics. Slovakia and Subcarpathian Ruthenia were granted home rule. In December, at Germany's insistence, the Czechoslovak Communist Party was declared illegal. Klement Gottwald (1896–1953) and other Communist leaders left the country and took refuge in the Soviet Union, where they continued their antifascist activities during World War II.

At the other end of the political spectrum, Czech fascist leader Gajda first offered to organize a rigorous Czechoslovak national defense against an attack by Nazi Germany. When that was rejected by the government, he then offered to facilitate Czechoslovakia's subjection for Hitler, who also refused him.

During the six-months of the Second Republic, the Czech lands also witnessed a remarkably swift, comprehensive, and largely voluntary restructuring and simplification of public life. The large number of political parties and public and private institutions and organizations of every description dissolved or consolidated themselves into larger groups, as the Czechs braced to withstand the further onslaught they feared was coming—all to no avail.

On March 15, 1939, contradicting Hitler's assertion after the signing of the Munich Pact that he had no further territorial demands on Czecho-

slovakia, German military forces invaded and occupied the country. The new Protectorate of Bohemia-Moravia was described as an autonomous territory within the Third Reich. One day earlier, on March 14, responding to Germany's promptings and pressures, Slovakia's political leaders declared it an independent state. The clericofascist Slovak Republic, headed by a Roman Catholic priest, Father Jozef Tiso (1887–1947), assumed its place as an obedient puppet and military ally of the Third Reich. Subcarpathian Ruthenia was annexed by Hungary. The promising Czechoslovak political experiment, so long desired and with such promising beginnings, had lasted just two decades.

World War II

The Protectorate of Bohemia and Moravia

The wartime Czech government of the ailing and ineffective Emil Hácha possessed only very restricted powers and functions of internal governance and only a limited police force to enforce its decisions. With the Czech army demobilized and the protectorate under heavy German military occupation, Hácha's administration had to work under the watchful surveillance of a series of German "Reich Protectors" and "State Secretaries." These included Konstantin von Neurath (1873–1956), Karl Hermann Frank (1898–1946), and the dreaded Reinhard Heydrich (1904–42). The Czech lands experienced the same treatment as other territories conquered by Nazi Germany. Universities were closed, and Czech cultural-intellectual life was closely monitored and censored. Intellectuals considered particularly dangerous were killed or imprisoned in concentration camps. Some were sent to the "model" camp of Terezín (Theresienstadt), which the Nazis maintained as an elaborately "humane" and aesthetic showroom for international propaganda purposes. About eighty thousand Jews had their property confiscated and were sent to Czech or Polish camps, where most of them died.

Though the Nazis had their detailed "racial" plans for the postwar assimilation, deportation, and extermination of the entire Czech population, they were mindful of the importance of Bohemia-Moravia's impressive industrial resources and its highly skilled workers for Germany's war effort. To that end, they used both the carrot and the stick. They kept cooperative Czech workers well supplied with food and other basic creature comforts and punished acts of sabotage and violence against the German military with harsh reprisals. In general, these techniques proved successful. The Czech industrial establishment, including the famous Škoda munitions works, was fully maintained and even expanded, contributing significantly to German war production. Czech wartime resistance was comparatively modest. The Czech underground generally eschewed guerrilla activity and other forms of armed violence, concentrating on work delays and especially intelligence collection. Until his exposure and execution in 1942, General Alois Eliáš (1890–1942), prime minister of the protectorate, was a pivotal figure in the collection of such intelligence data and their secret transmission to the Czechoslovak government-in-exile in London.

On two occasions, the Czechs did resist their occupiers violently, and it cost them dearly. In 1941 Heydrich, a cold-blooded "prototype Nazi," was named Reichsprotector of Bohemia-Moravia. Beneš's government in London, criticized by its allies for the passivity of its Czech countrymen at home, decided to have Heydrich assassinated, as a testament to the Czechs' commitment to the anti-German war effort. Despite the strenuous objections of the Czech underground leadership, the London government selected and trained a special team of Czech and Slovak soldiers attached to the British armed forces and parachuted them into the protectorate. Though badly mismanaged, the scheme was ultimately successful and Heydrich was attacked and killed in May 1942. In response, the German occupiers unleashed a reign of terror on the Czechs of the protectorate. The villages of Lidice and Ležáky, allegedly implicated in the assassination, were razed to the ground. Their men were shot, their women sent to concentration camps, and their children sent to camps or German orphanages. Except for the continuing underground activity of the Communists, Czech resistance was virtually exterminated, and some have charged the Czechs with excessive passivity and even large-scale collaboration thereafter. The Czechs did rise up at the very end of the war, in Prague, in May 1945. Various poorly coordinated groups armed themselves and attacked the departing German forces. Taking heavy casualties, the Czechs called for outside assistance. American general George S. Patton (1885–1945) was bound by Allied political agreements not to take his troops farther east than Plzeň and could not respond, but Soviet forces did fight their way westward to Prague, at the cost of many lives. The apparent "reluctance" of the Americans to risk their lives for the Czechs and the "willingness" of the Soviets to do so was not lost on Czech popular opinion once the war was over.

In all, the Czech lands suffered considerably less during the war than most of the rest of Central and Eastern Europe. There was comparatively little physical damage to the country, and probably no more than fifty-five thousand Czechs lost their lives. But the psychological damage resulting from the humiliating capitulation at Munich and the largely docile acceptance of the wartime occupation was enormous and would remain with the Czechs for a long time.

The Slovak Republic

The independent Slovak state was ruled by the Slovak People's Party and led by a group of officials with a long interwar record of strong Catholic and nationalist-separatist convictions. Its president, later Vodca (*führer*), was Monsignor Jozef Tiso, a comparatively moderate Roman Catholic priest who had become chairman of the Slovak People's Party in 1938, when Hlinka died. Much more radical was the prime minister, later also foreign minister, Vojtěch Tuka (1880–1946). Tuka, a legal scholar, was a magyarized Slovak, a Czech-hater with strong fascist leanings and ties to Germany. The ruling hierarchy, equipped with its own paramilitary group, the Hlinka Guards, regimented the small country into an obedient puppet of Hitler's Germany. Its official ideology, Slovak National Socialism, aped that of the Reich, and its foreign and domestic policies were dictated by it. Slovak troops fought alongside Hitler's armies on the eastern front, and between 60,000 and 100,000 Slovak Jews were sent to be murdered in Nazi death camps in Poland. Slovakia's industry served the German war effort and benefited from extensive German financial and technological investment.

As the war progressed, increasing German military setbacks and defeats generated widespread Slovak dissatisfaction with their alliance. In August 1944 a coalition of right- and left-wing dissidents, including Communists and elements of the Slovak army, tried to topple the Tiso regime. The Slovak National Uprising, centered at Banská Bystrica in central Slovakia, managed to last two months before it was crushed with the help of

German troops. Nazi Germany then took direct control of Slovakia and prepared to make a major defensive stand there against the approaching Soviet armies.

The ill-chosen collaboration with Hitler brought great physical devastation to Slovakia and cost the lives of many thousands of Slovaks. Postwar Slovaks have not universally renounced it, however. Some continue to maintain a certain pride in the six-year-long "first independent Slovak state." Others dispute whether Slovak leaders really had any practical choice but to abandon the Czechs and join Germany in 1939, and whether, in any event, the Slovak popular masses were given any meaningful voice in the decision.

The Czechs and Slovaks in Exile

As in World War I, the Czechs and Slovaks had their political representatives abroad and supplied troops to fight as members of the military forces of the Western powers on both the western and eastern fronts in Europe. From 1940 to 1945, the Allied governments recognized a legitimate Czechoslovak government-in-exile, headed by President Beneš and Foreign Minister Jan Masaryk (1886–1948), son of the interwar president. Eager to preserve Allied support for a revived, independent Czechoslovak state at war's end, Beneš tried hard to keep the Czechs as actively combatant as possible. But he remained deeply disillusioned with the abandonment of his country by the West in 1938. In making his postwar plans, he decided to reorient the foreign and domestic policies of the future Czechoslovak state eastward, toward a greater reliance on and cooperation with the Soviet Union. In 1943 he traveled to Moscow where, with the active participation of Czechoslovak Communist leaders who had taken refuge in the Soviet Union, he signed a twenty-year treaty of Czechoslovak-Soviet friendship.

In April 1945 the first postwar Czechoslovak government was reestablished on native soil in Kosice, in eastern Slovakia. It included a large contingent of Communists, and the Kosice Agreement signed there, which outlined the future Czechoslovak state, reflected major concessions to them. It also promised the Slovaks recognition as a separate nation and a large degree of home rule. Communists were also very active in the "action committees" that took control of the local administration of Czech and Slovak territories as the retreating Germans abandoned them.

The Third Czechoslovak Republic, 1945–1948

The first order of business of the postwar Czechoslovak government under the restored (1946) President Edvard Beneš was to settle old scores with those who had allegedly delivered the First and Second Republics to Hitler and ruled the protectorate for him. Considered "collectively guilty," some three million Sudeten Germans were expelled from the country, mostly to neighboring West Germany. They suffered considerable violence and many deaths in the process. A number of Czechs, Germans, and Slovaks were quickly arrested and placed on trial as collaborators, traitors, and war criminals. These included Hácha, Beran, Gajda, Stříbrný, Frank, Tiso, and Tuka. Some died awaiting trial. Others were convicted and sentenced to long prison terms or execution.

The Third Republic's political structure did not differ greatly from that of the First. To be sure, Subcarpathian Ruthenia was no longer part of it, having been ceded to the Soviet Union in 1945. But the crucial and vexing political arrangement between the Czech and Slovak regions remained essentially the same. Power and control were centralized in Prague. At various times during the war—for example, in the Moscow Treaty of 1943, the Slovak National Uprising of 1944, and the Kosice Agreement of 1945—Slovak spokesmen had declared the willingness of their people to rejoin the Czechs in a postwar state on the basis of full national equality. After 1945, however, the Slovaks again received only the minimal trappings of regional autonomy.

In other respects, however, the postwar Czechoslovak state underwent significant political, economic, and social change. Beneš, reacting to the West's indifference to and abandonment of Czechoslovakia in 1938–39, was determined to reorient his state's foreign policy eastward, toward the "brotherly" Soviet Union. As he had agreed in the Kosice Agreement of 1945, Czechoslovakia would reflect a compromise between Communists and non-Communists and would be a political-economic "bridge between East and West." This was in accord with strong and widespread Czech feelings of disenchantment with the West and gratitude toward the Soviet "liberators" in the immediate postwar period. Such sentiments were abetted by a general Western apathy toward Eastern Europe and a continuing strong Soviet military presence in the area after the end of hostilities.

Exploiting this favorable climate, the Czechoslovak Communist Party (KSČ) moved rapidly and effectively to increase its power and influence in the organs of local and central government. In the first postwar parliamentary elections in May 1946, the KSČ garnered about 38 percent of the popular vote and one-third of the seats in parliament. Its chairman, Klement Gottwald, a founding member of the KSČ and its leader since 1929, became the country's prime minister in 1946. The Communists also moved swiftly to gain control of such crucial ministries as education, communications, interior, and the military (defense). A number of prewar political parties of the right and center, including the once-powerful Agrarians, were labeled collaborationist and disloyal and were banned from political activity. Major industries and sectors of the economy were nationalized.

By late 1947, however, the Communists' heavy-handed tactics and obvious intentions appeared to be losing them popular support, and their relations with their competitors became increasingly hostile. Their attempts to terrorize and assassinate leading opponents and to pack the police ranks with their own followers provoked a governmental crisis in February 1948. In an attempt to force an immediate special election and prevent an anticipated Communist coup, twelve non-Communist ministers resigned from the government. The parliamentary stratagem failed. The Communists responded with a massive show of force by armed workers' militias and loosed a threatening propaganda barrage throughout the country. Beneš, ill and fearful of unleashing civil war and even attracting outright Soviet military intervention, capitulated to the Communist demands. He agreed to accept a new government dominated by the Communists and their political allies, thus allowing them to claim later that they had come to power "peacefully." On February 25, 1948, they proclaimed the birth of a new People's Republic of Czechoslovakia. Beneš resigned as president in June (he died soon afterward, on September 3) and was replaced by Gottwald himself. The last of the so-called "Soviet satellites" had fallen into place.

Communist Czechoslovakia, 1948–89

The victorious Communists moved rapidly to solidify their newfound power. Though public opinion expected them to adopt a moderate, "national" way to achieve socialism, they immediately set about a drastic internal transformation of the country into a Soviet-style totalitarian state. Czechoslovak Communist leaders were largely people with plebeian or proletarian backgrounds and strong antibourgeois biases, doctrinaire Marxists whose loyalty was deeply committed to the Soviet Union. They made Communist Czechoslovakia into one of the most Stalinist members of the Soviet bloc and one that supported the Soviet Union's foreign policy without question, especially after Czechoslovakia joined the Warsaw Pact in 1955.

Though the constitution of the new Czechoslovak People's Democracy assured the Communist Party a predominance of legal political power, the KSČ showed no leniency to its vanquished political opponents. Mass purges swept anti-Communists and non-Communists from all major sectors of life—the government bureaucracy, the military, educational institutions, the professions, and sports associations. Many of them were condemned as conspirators and subversives and sent to labor camps and prisons. Foreign Minister Jan Masaryk may have been the victim of a Communist plot to assassinate him in the fall of 1948. (His body was found beneath his apartment window.) Nor were the new Czechoslovak Communist masters of the country any more willing than the preceding Beneš government had been to grant Slovak desires for genuine autonomy. The Czechoslovak People's Democracy (renamed Czechoslovak Socialist Republic in 1960 to manifest that all power had passed securely into the hands of the "working people") was officially "a unitary state of two equal nationalities, the Czechs and Slovaks." But the formal organs of national political power—the unicameral legislature, the prime minister and his cabinet, and the presidency—were all centralized in Prague. An awkward, asymmetrical arrangement gave the Slovaks their own Slovak National Council, which nominally administered Slovakia's affairs but was only empowered to apply national legislation to Slovak conditions. This situation did not change until the reforms of the Prague Spring period in 1968.

Of course, actual political power was always completely in the hands of the Czechoslovak Communist Party (at its zenith boasting about two million members) and its junior, likewise asymmetrical partner, the Slovak Communist Party. Almost without exception, its general (or first) secretaries (some of whom, in Soviet fashion, simultaneously held the state presidency) were a dogmatic and unimaginative lot. Gottwald, who had held the position through World War II, was succeeded by Rudolf Slánský (1901–52) until 1952. After their respective deaths in 1953 and 1952, Gottwald and Slánský were replaced by Antonín Zápotocký (1884–1957) as president (1953–57) and Antonín Novotný (1904–75) as party secretary (1953–68) and later also as president (1957–68). During the Prague Spring reform period, popular Slovak Communist Alexander Dubček (1921–92) served as secretary (1968–69) and respected Czech general Ludvík Svoboda (1895–1979) as president (1968–75). Another Slovak, Gustáv Husák (1913–91), presided over the subsequent "normalization" of Czechoslovakia as party secretary (1969–87) and as state president (1975–89), until he was forced to resign both positions by the impending collapse of the Communist system. His last-minute replacement as secretary, the nondescript Miloš Jakeš (1922–), was quickly swept away by the Velvet Revolution in 1989.

In the early 1950s, following the open split of the Yugoslav Communist leader Tito (1892–1980) with the Soviet Union, the Czechoslovak Communist Party, as did all its satellite counterparts, obeyed the order of Josef Stalin (1879–1953) to rid its ranks of covert "bourgeois nationalists." A great number and variety of its high-ranking members—especially Jews, Slovak autonomists, and those with extensive Western contacts—were arrested, interrogated, brainwashed, tortured, and tried in garish public show trials where they confessed to a wide spectrum of antistate crimes and were convicted and sentenced to imprisonment or death. Most prominent among the victims were the general secretary, Slánský (a founding member of the Communist Party and one of the executors of its coup in 1948, who was Jewish), and the Slovak Vladimír Clementis (1921–1952), who had succeeded Jan Masaryk as Czechoslovak foreign minister. The purges ended with Stalin's own death in 1953, when the harshness of the Czechoslovak Communist police state was somewhat lessened as part of the ensuing blocwide thaw. But after the Polish and Hungarian uprisings against Soviet rule in 1956, the old familiar Stalinist conditions returned and remained until the onset of Prague Spring.

Immediately after their takeover, the Communists nationalized and took complete control of all major sectors of the economy—industrial, agricultural, commercial, financial, transportation. Following hallowed Communist practices, they placed heavy emphasis on the development of the manufacturing and engineering branches (iron and steel, chemicals, glass and ceramics, textiles and shoes) and mining. Far less of the state's capital investment and labor force were allocated to the production of consumer goods. Slovakia, less economically developed than Bohemia and Moravia, was strongly favored with government investments and subsidies and became a center of heavy industry (metallurgy and armaments production). Although about 95 percent of the country's agricultural establishment was forcibly collectivized into cooperatives and state farms, Czechoslovakia did not achieve self-sufficiency in basic foodstuffs.

Despite a wealth of inherited resources, skills, and experience and continued heavy state investment, Communist Czechoslovakia's economic balance sheet showed mixed results. Within the Soviet bloc, it achieved the highest standard of living after that of the German Democratic Republic. The government's policy of adjusting wage levels to favor blue-collar workers and its disproportionately large economic investments in Slovakia worked successfully to diminish income inequalities between social classes and geographic regions. All Czechoslovak citizens were entitled to a wide range of state-subsidized benefits. These included free comprehensive medical care and education, low-cost housing, cheap transportation and food, and inexpensive recreational and cultural facilities. But there were also constant and widespread complaints about the poor quality and limited availability of these benefits and their biased allocation by Communist Party bureaucrats. There were perpetual shortages of basic consumer goods and services, with the result that an extensive black market developed to help provide them. Ultimately, Czechoslovakia's required membership in the Soviet-dominated Council for Mutual Economic Assistance (CMEA, Comecon) forced it to orient its economic production and foreign trade eastward, primarily to meet the needs of the Soviet bloc, and to lose Western and other desirable world markets. Government-guaranteed employment, manipulated wage levels, and the almost complete elimination of private profit-making enterprises encouraged slipshod work habits and resulted in shoddy products that lacked competitive quality.

The interwar republic, when Czechoslovakia had prided itself on manufacturing world-class products and had enjoyed a high European standard of living, remained only a memory.

In a state determined to exercise totalitarian control, religion, education, and cultural-intellectual life could not escape heavy regulation. In Communist Czechoslovakia, they were all rigorously restructured and censored on the basis of Marxist ideology and Soviet models. The officially atheistic state declared some religions illegal. The remainder were placed under close governmental supervision, though they also received limited financial support from the state. The largest religious establishment, the Roman Catholic Church, received especially harsh treatment, losing much of its property, including theological schools and seminaries. The other legal Christian denominations were merged in the so-called Ecumenical Council of Churches. The public pronouncements and activities of all religious congregations and their leaders were sharply restricted and zealously monitored by a governmental Department of Church Affairs.

The Ministry of Education supervised a comprehensive, unified educational structure extending from nursery schools to universities and professional and technical institutes. Education at all levels was officially free for all eligible citizens with the "correct social and economic class origins." Its purpose was to train them to enjoy and contribute to a socialist society. The KSČ hierarchy's deep anti-intellectual biases meant that institutions of higher learning, considered suspect, were comparatively neglected, thus leaving much of the country's intellectual elite perpetually dissatisfied and restless. The latter were also bored and frustrated by the regime's unremitting Marxist policing of high and popular culture. Cultural endeavors that failed to meet governmental norms (such as socialist realism) or defied them and went underground (such as rock music) brought severe restrictions and punishments (except in such rare and brief periods of ideological loosening as the early 1960s). A sizable number of leading Czechoslovak cultural/intellectual figures left to work in the West, some of them achieving international reputations. These included Academy Award–winning film director Miloš Forman (1932–); prizewinning novelists Josef Škvorecký (1924–) and Milan Kundera (1929–); and renowned symphony conductor Rafael Kubelik (1914–96).

But the worldwide recognition accorded the plays of Václav Havel (1936–) and the poems of Jaroslav Seifert (1901–86), a Nobel Prize winner, showed that even the dead hand of Czechoslovakia's Marxist regime could not completely stifle the creativity of its people at home.

The needs and rights of women and children received special consideration by the Communist state. Women were constitutionally guaranteed full equality with men across the board, including parity in such vital areas as education, employment, social welfare benefits, health care, and eligibility to hold public office. They grew into almost one-half of the total workforce, moving especially into agriculture, commerce, transportation, office bureaucracies, and the health and medical services. The national health-care system provided them with legal abortions, generous maternity leaves, extensive pre- and postnatal care, and a network of state-supported nurseries and day-care facilities. Czechoslovakia could claim the lowest rate of infant mortality in the Soviet bloc. On the debit side, female professionals generally occupied lower ranks and received lower pay than their male counterparts. They were badly underrepresented in the ranks of the Communist Party and in higher-level positions in the government. Married women had to work a "double shift"— as employees outside the home and as wives and mothers within it.

Prague Spring, 1963–68

By the early 1960s, there was deep and broad disenchantment with the Communist system in Czechoslovakia. Led by the cultural-intellectual elite and with growing boldness, the public expressed its displeasure with the stagnant economy, the depressed standard of living, and the stubborn refusal of the Novotný regime to permit greater personal freedom. At the same time, the Slovak Communist leadership began to press forcefully for a formal recognition of the Slovaks as a totally separate nation and a genuine federalization of the Czechoslovak state. By 1968, the accumulated pressures had convinced a majority of the KSČ that major reforms were necessary to prevent an open confrontation with the masses.

In January 1968 Novotný was replaced as KSČ secretary by Alexander Dubček (who had become first secretary of the Slovak Communist Party in 1963) and in March as president of

Czechoslovakia by Ludvík Svoboda, a popular hero of World War II. In the next seven months of Prague Spring, under the slogan of "socialism with a human face," Communist reformers began a thorough liberalization and de-Sovietization of Czechoslovakia. Their "action program" reaffirmed the basic rights of free speech, press, assembly, and religious observance; allowed greater public activity on the part of non-Communist parties and organizations; agreed to a modernization of the economy by decentralizing controls and permitting private enterprises; and started the process of legally "rehabilitating" all persons unjustly convicted of political crimes between 1949 and 1954. The Slovaks were recognized as a separate "brotherly" nation and promised a federal status fully equal to that of the Czechs.

Dubček and other reform leaders enjoyed mass support and great personal popularity at home. But their ambitious reform program aroused apprehension in the Soviet Union and some of the other satellites, who feared that such dangerous "contagion" might spread to them. They threatened Czechoslovakia through stern official warnings and consultations, attacks in the media, and military maneuvers on its frontiers. Under unremitting domestic pressure to continue his reform program, Dubček could only assure his external critics of his country's pledged loyalty to the socialist commonwealth. Unconvinced, some five hundred thousand Soviet-led troops of the Warsaw Pact invaded Czechoslovakia on August 20–21, 1968, allegedly to help put down a West-backed, right-wing counterrevolution. Popular resistance was minor, but Dubček and several others were briefly abducted to the Soviet Union. Czechoslovakia and the Soviet Union signed a treaty permitting the stationing of Soviet troops on Czechoslovak soil. In April 1969 Dubček was replaced as party secretary by Gustáv Husák, who later also assumed the presidency. Although himself a victim of the bloody purges of the 1950s, Husák willingly assumed his dictated task of re-Sovietizing and re-Stalinizing his conquered and demoralized country.

From Prague Spring to the Velvet Revolution, 1969–89

With the aid of a legion of Soviet civilian and military advisers, Husák devoted himself zealously to the "normalization" of Czechoslovakia—returning it to orthodox Marxism, total party control, and full subordination to the Soviet Union. The reforms of Prague Spring were almost entirely rescinded, with the notable exception of the rectification of the formal relationship between Czechs and Slovaks. In October 1968 a new constitution federalized the country into two separate and equal socialist republics, each with its own parliament and government. (But the Czechoslovak Communist Party continued to exist and to wield more power than its Slovak counterpart.) The new egalitarian power-sharing agreement went into effect on January 1, 1969.

Dubček and his assistants were purged from the party's ranks and public life, and they received various punishments. All signs of continued resistance were harshly repressed. But an underground dissident movement developed soon, and in January 1977 it went public with a group calling itself Charter 77. In 1975 Czechoslovakia had been one of many countries that signed the Helsinki Accords, in which the signatories guaranteed their citizens basic human rights and freedoms. Charter 77 publicly accused the Czechoslovak Communist regime of violating its Helsinki pledges. The government responded with shocking brutality, but it could not succeed in destroying the organization. Originally numbering about 250 members, Charter 77 was a broadly representative group, including men and women from all walks of life, Marxists and non-Marxists, Czechs and Slovaks. Their triumvirate of official spokespersons, drawn and continuously replenished from the ranks, included such prominent individuals as playwright Václav Havel and philosopher Jan Patočka (1907–77). Charter 77's heroic persistence in the face of appalling persecution provoked a massive sympathetic response and denunciation of the Husák regime around the world.

Nevertheless, communism ultimately disappeared from Czechoslovakia primarily because of a terminal internal crisis within the Soviet Union that had its effect on the entire Soviet bloc. When Mikhail Gorbachev's (1931–) attempt, in the 1980s, to revitalize communism in the Soviet Union failed, the latter was forced to withdraw its support for the East European regimes crucially dependent on it. A rising tide of public criticism and open resistance (symbolized by the toppling of the Berlin Wall in 1989) quickly swept away one Communist regime after another.

In the Czech and Slovak lands, the anti-Communist rebellion was led by the (Czech)

Civic Forum and the (Slovak) Public Against Violence groups. The unresponsive Husák was replaced as party secretary by a virtual unknown, Miloš Jakeš, in 1987. In late 1989 the government met mass protests and demonstrations with a final, ineffective show of force. Soon afterward, it began to disintegrate quickly and peacefully, in what has come to be called the Velvet Revolution. By the end of 1989, Jakeš had resigned as party secretary and Husák as president.

In June 1990 free elections created the first non-Communist government in Czechoslovakia since 1948. Václav Havel became the first president of the new, democratic Czech and Slovak Federated Republic. Alexander Dubček, who had spent most of the previous two decades in retirement and under house arrest, returned briefly to public life as president of the new National Assembly.

The Velvet Divorce (1993)
Having successfully freed themselves from four decades of Communist rule, Czechs and Slovaks were unable to surmount centuries of divergent historical development and create a joint state acceptable to both. For almost two years, they negotiated over its political and economic nature. The Czechs, represented by Prime Minister Václav Klaus (1941–), favored a tightly centralized federation and rapid progress toward a capitalist, free-market economy. The Slovaks, led by Prime Minister Vladimír Mečiar (1942–), insisted on a loose federation, with both republics fully sovereign and possessing separate international personalities. They also wanted a slower rate of decentralization of economic controls and privatization of nationalized resources. Unable to reach agreement, the two peoples decided to live apart. The Velvet Revolution had led to a Velvet Divorce. On January 1, 1993, the joint Czech and Slovak state was peacefully dissolved and replaced by two entirely independent Czech and Slovak republics. After so many centuries of foreign domination and domestic discord, the two peoples were free, at last, to chart their own destinies.

Joseph Frederick Zacek

Further reading
Bokes, František. *Dejiny Slovenska a Slovákov od najstarších čias po oslobodenie.* Bratislava, 1946.

Gogolák, Ludwig von. *Beiträge zur Geschichte des slowakischen Volkes.* 3 vols., Munich, 1963–1972.

Kirschbaum, Stanislav J. *A History of Slovakia: The Struggle for Survival.* New York, 1995.

Kořalka, Jiří. *Češi v Habsburské Říši a v Evropě, 1815–1914.* Prague, 1996.

Korbel, Josef. *Twentieth-Century Czechoslovakia: The Meanings of Its History.* New York, 1977.

Leff, Carol Skalnik. *National Conflict in Czechoslovakia: The Making and Remaking of a State, 1918–1987.* Princeton, New Jersey, 1988.

Mamatey, Victor S. and Radomír Luža, eds. *A History of the Czechoslovak Republic, 1918–1948.* Princeton, New Jersey, 1973.

Odložilík, Otakar. *Nástin československých dějin,* 5th ed., Prague, 1946.

Sayer, Derek. *The Coasts of Bohemia: A Czech History.* Princeton, New Jersey, 1998.

Stone, Norman and Eduard Strouhal, eds. *Czechoslovakia: Crossroads and Crises, 1918–1988.* New York, 1989.

Thomson, S. Harrison. *Czechoslovakia in European History,* 2d enlarged ed., Hamden, Connecticut, 1965.

Wallace, William V. *Czechoslovakia.* London, 1976.

Zacek, Joseph F. "Nationalism in Czechoslovakia," in Peter F. Sugar and Ivo John Lederer, eds. *Nationalism in Eastern Europe.* Seattle, Washington, 1994, 166–206.

See also Agrarian Parties; *Anschluss; Ausgleich;* Austroslavism; Banking; Tomáš Baťa; Edvard Beneš; Rudolf Beran; Berlin Wall; Anton Bernolák; Bohemia; František Brauner; Brno; Karel Čapek; Carpatho-Rusyns; Catholicism; Censorship; Neville Chamberlain; Charles University; Charter 77; Civic Forum; Vladimír Clementis; Collectivization; Comecon; Communist Party of Czechoslovakia; Czech and Slovak Art; Czech Culture; Czech Émigrés; Czech Language; Czech Literature; Czech Mafia; Czechoslovak Legion; Czech Republic, Birth of; De-Stalinization; Josef Dobrovský; Dual Monarchy; Alexander Dubček; Antonín Dvořák; Economic Development in Czechoslovakia; Education; Alois Eliáš; Emigration; Ethnic Minorities; Family; Miloš Forman; Fourteen Points; Franco-Czechoslovak Alliance; Karl Frank; Radola Gajda; Charlotte Garrigue; Mikhail Gorbachev; Klement Gottwald; Great Depression; Edvard Grégr; Julius Grégr; Habsburg Empire; Emil

Hácha; Jaroslav Hašek; Václav Havel; Konrad Henlein; Reinhard Heydrich; Higher Education; Adolf Hitler; Andrej Hlinka; Milan Hodža; *Hrad;* Gustáv Husák; Svetozár Hurban-Vajanský; Pavol O. Hviezdoslav; Industrialization; Intelligentsia; Leoš Janáček; Alois Jirásek; Josef Jungmann; Franz Kafka; Václav Klofáč; Ján Kollár; Karel Kramář; Kremsier/Kroměříž; Milan Kundera; Law; League of Nations; Lidice; Little Entente; Karel Hynek Mácha; Magyarization; Josef Mánes; Manuscripts; Martin Declaration; Jan Masaryk; Tomáš G. Masaryk; Matica Slovenská; Clemens von Metternich; Moravia; Alfons Mucha; Munich Pact; Napoléon; Nationalism; Božena Němcová; Neo-Slavism; Jan Neruda; Antonín Novotný; Old Czechs; Ostrava; František Palacký; Pan-Slavism; Peasants; *Pětka;* Pittsburgh Agreement; Plzeň; Prague; Prague Slav Congress; Prague Spring; Press; Privatization; Protectorate of Bohemia and Moravia; Revolutions of 1848; Revolutions of 1989; František L. Rieger; Right-Radicalism; Pavel Šafárik; Jaroslav Seifert; Škoda; Josef Škvorecký; Rudolf Slánský; Slavs; Slovak Culture; Slovak Émigrés; Slovak Language; Slovak League; Slovak Literature; Slovak Republic; Slovak Republic, Birth of; Slovakia; Bedřich Smetana; *Sokol;* Vavro Šrobár; Stalin; Milan R. Štefánik; Jiří Stříbrný; Ľudovít Štúr; Subcarpathian Rus'; Sudeten Question; Antonín Švehla; Ludvík Svoboda; Theater; Jozef Tiso; Tito; Trialism; Vojtěch Tuka; Miroslav Tyrš; Velvet Revolution; Warsaw Pact; Women in Czechoslovakia; Woodrow Wilson; World War I; World War II; Young Czechs

Czech Republic, Birth of (1993)

New state created by the formal separation of Czechoslovakia on January 1, 1993, into the Czech and Slovak Republics. Most of the population of Czechoslovakia insisted in public opinion polls that they wanted to preserve the nation. The political leaders of the governments in Prague and Bratislava, Václav Klaus (1941–) and Vladimír Mečiar (1942–), however, after protracted discussions during which they could not agree on the forms of an eventual federal or confederate entity, decided to create two independent states. The country had become in many respects ungovernable, with different political cultures and aspirations of Czechs and Slovaks, divergent views on future economic programs (primarily concerning

the speed or even fate of privatization of socialized enterprises), and a divided parliament. Although no referendum was held—and separation was considered regrettable—the peaceful nature of the split was widely appreciated.

Václav Havel (1936–) was elected the first president of the Czech Republic. The new constitution did not grant him much power, but it was hoped that he would represent some of the better traditions of prewar Czechoslovakia, namely, its democratic ethos and humanism. Although often disagreeing with him, Prime Minister Klaus, a more pragmatic and realistic politician, maintained another positive tradition: that of keeping a solid and stable coalition government and the astute management of economic affairs.

The new state was admitted into the Council of Europe and began to seek membership in both the European Common Market and NATO. Holding many economic advantages over its neighbors, the Czech Republic quickly became a magnet for foreign investment.

Peter Hruby

Further reading

Ash, Timothy Garton. "Prague: Intellectuals and Politicians." *New York Review of Books* 12 (January 1995): 34–41.

Havel, Václav. *Toward a Civil Society: Selected Speeches and Writings,* ed. and trans. by Paul Wilson. Prague, 1992.

Staff of the Commission on Security and Cooperation in Europe. *Implementation of the Helsinki Accords: Human Rights and Democratization in the Czech Republic.* Washington, D.C., September 1994.

See also Václav Havel; Privatization; Slovak Republic, Birth of

Czechoslovak Legion

Allied volunteer force during World War I and the Russian Civil War. Shortly after the outbreak of the war, the Czech community in Russia organized a unit, the Družina,within the Russian army. Recognizing the usefulness of armed troops, the leaders of the Czechoslovak independence movement lobbied successfully for permission to organize units in France and Italy as well. Czech and Slovak prisoners constituted a large potential pool, but recruitment was only modestly successful. By the end of the war, the Russian force numbered about sixty thousand, the Italian about twenty-five thousand, and the French roughly eleven thousand. The Slovaks were underrepresented in all three. Despite its small size, the legion played a crucial role in the achievement of Czechoslovak independence. In May 1918 the troops in Russia revolted against the Bolshevik government (and initially against their own civilian leadership as well), quickly seizing control of the strategic Trans-Siberian Railroad. Czechoslovak leaders in London and Paris, under pressure to assist with Allied intervention against the Bolsheviks, exploited the new situation to win official Allied recognition of their movement. Once entangled in intervention, however, Czechoslovak forces remained discontentedly in Russia until September 1920.

The legion has always been controversial. Its adventures are a source of Czech and Slovak national pride, but since the force was recruited primarily from prisoners of war, its very existence represented a violation of international law. The legionnaires enlisted for motives ranging from idealism to opportunism, and their conduct varied from courageous to contemptible, enabling historians to sustain widely diverging interpretations.

Once home, the legionnaires obtained various legal privileges, especially in the new Czechoslovak army (although integration with nonlegion troops was not always achieved smoothly). Legionary veterans groups constituted a significant political lobby in the first Czechoslovak republic.

Todd Huebner

Further reading

Bradley, J.F.N. *The Czechoslovak Legion in Russia, 1914–1920.* New York, 1991.

Thunig-Nittner, Gerburg. *Die tschechoslowakische Legion in Russland: Ihre Geschichte und Bedeutung bei der Entstehung der 1. Tschechoslowakischen Republik.* Wiesbaden, 1970.

See also Radola Gajda

Czernin, Count Ottokar (1872–1932)

Austro-Hungarian diplomat and statesman. A Bohemian noble who served in the Austro-Hungarian embassies in Paris and The Hague before entering the Bohemian diet in 1903, prior to World War I Czernin sat in the Austrian upper house and served as an adviser to Archduke Franz Ferdinand (1863–1914). He urged the archduke, upon accession to the throne, to end Magyar dominance in Hungary, while in Austria, he opposed the notion of universal suffrage. Instead, he believed that the crown should act decisively, particularly in Bohemia, to end the nationality problems. In October 1912 Czernin became ambassador to Romania. At the onset of World War I, he in vain urged Vienna to grant Romania territory in return for neutrality.

Appointed as foreign minister on December 22, 1916, Czernin remained a firm proponent of the Dual Alliance, which linked Germany and Austria-Hungary, but he attempted to convince the Germans of the need for peace. He led the Austro-Hungarian delegation to the peace talks with the Bolsheviks at Brest-Litovsk from December 1917 to March 1918, where he unsuccessfully proposed a Romania, enlarged by Transylvania, as an Austro-Hungarian satellite and the Congress Kingdom united with Galicia as an independent Poland closely tied with Germany. He angered Austrian Poles, however, by ceding the Chelm district, claimed by them, to independent Ukraine.

In April 1918, Czernin gave a speech in which he referred to French overtures for peace. French Premier Georges Clemenceau (1841–1929) and Czernin then leveled accusations until Clemenceau suggested Emperor Charles's part in the negotiations. Czernin denied these allegations, not being fully aware of the talks from March to May 1917 between Charles (1887–1922) and his brother-in-law, Prince Sixtus (1886–1934). Consequently, when Clemenceau published the "Sixtus Letter," in which the emperor supported French claims to Alsace and Lorraine, Czernin was forced to resign on April 16, 1918.

Gregory C. Ference

Further reading

Czernin, Ottokar. *In the World War.* New York, 1920.

Singer, Ladislaus. *Ottokar Graf Czernin: Staatsmann einer Zeitenwende.* Graz, 1965.

See also Brest-Litovsk; Charles; Chelm; Dual Alliance; Franz Ferdinand; Polish Congress Kingdom

D

Dalmatia

Province along the eastern coastland of the Adriatic Sea from south of the Velebit range to the Gulf of Kotor, where historical traditions are combined with unique physical attributes to produce a distinctive regional identity.

The coastal zone of Dalmatia is a region of submergence, characterized by a highly irregular coastline and numerous small islands. Small areas of coastal lowland are interspersed with limestone hills and typical karst topography and bordered by the steep slopes of the Dinaric Alps. The northwestern region represents the only significant lowland zone between the karst and the coast and, from Zadar to Split, is the most intensely developed and densely settled portion of Dalmatia. In the central portion, the Neretva River cuts through the karst through a narrow valley and enters the Adriatic through an alluvial plain. Southern Dalmatia offers some isolated patches of lowland on which coastal settlements such as Dubrovnik, Herceg Novi, and Kotor are found. As a result of the attraction of a Mediterranean climate regime, combined with a distinctive historical and cultural tradition, the importance of manufacturing and commerce to economic development has gradually been surpassed by tourism as the major economic activity of the region.

Much of Dalmatia had been under the political control and cultural influence of Venice for nearly four hundred years before its acquisition by Austria in 1797. The impact of the classical Italian tradition in the organization and structure of Dalmatian cities, evident in areas of former Venetian political control, also extends to Dubrovnik, which, as the Republic of Ragusa, contended with Venice for control and influence in Dalmatia and the Adriatic. After briefly forming part of the Illyrian Provinces during the Napoleonic period, Dalmatia remained part of Austria-Hungary until the end of World War I. By the Treaty of Rapallo (1920), Italy obtained the district of Zadar together with the offshore islands of Cherso, Lošinj, and Lastovo. The entire region was united with Yugoslavia as part of Croatia after World War II.

Albert M. Tosches

Further reading

Albrecht-Carrie, Rene. *Italy at the Paris Peace Conference.* Hamden, Connecticut, 1966.
Pounds, Norman J.G. *Eastern Europe.* Chicago, 1969.
Rugg, Dean S. *Eastern Europe.* New York, 1985.

See also Dinaric Alps; Dubrovnik

Dance

Dance has been an important element in the cultural life of the many different nationalities of Europe. As a participatory activity, Eastern European traditions include most prominently a great variety of peasant communal dances—often referred to as "folk dance"—and an array of urban social dances, many part of the international repertoire. Theatrical dance in the region includes theatricalized folk dance, ballet, modern dance (a genre of concert dance that developed in the twentieth century), and popular stage genres. More information existed on fashionable urban social and theatrical dance than on village and rural traditions until well into the twentieth century, when

D dance scholars both in Eastern Europe and outside began to make systematic studies of folk dance in its original settings and also of popular urban social and theatrical dance forms.

Eastern European folk dance cultures have gained international visibility in the twentieth century because of the many professional ensembles—"folk ballets"—that have toured under Communist government sponsorship. Modeled on the work of Igor Moiseyev (1906–), founder and director of the Soviet Union's State Folk Dance Ensemble, the dances and music presented by such groups have been adapted (as folk material must be) for the stage and greatly edited and changed to provide officially approved images of the given nation, its culture, and its supposedly "happy peasants." The dancers in such ensembles are professionals, trained in ballet as well as the adapted folk dance vocabulary, and the choreographies follow models found in ballet and other Western theater dance.

The actual folk dances of Eastern Europe have a greater range than that presented by the folk ensembles. They are varied in their expressive, rhythmic, and technical range and integral to all serious as well as recreational aspects of life from birth to death. Dance and music have traditionally been a part of church festivals and private ceremonial occasions such as baptisms, weddings, and funerals, which at the same time fulfill religious and social functions. Comparably rich peasant dance cultures existed all over Europe until well past the Middle Ages, but with modernization, urbanization, and mechanization, the old ways of life that supported the development of folk arts began to change. In Eastern Europe, peasant traditions have persisted longer because the lifestyles of the rural populations stayed much the same whether under the Habsburgs or the Ottomans. But much has disappeared since World War II under the managed Communist economies, the increasing urbanization of the populations, and the adaptation of folklore for political purposes.

Folk dances may be done by groups or couples or as solos. Group dances in connected lines or opened or closed circles date from antiquity, exist throughout Europe, and both reflect and reinforce an individual's relationship to the community. They are particularly common in the lands of southeastern Europe that were under the Ottoman Empire. In fact, most of the traditional dances of Albania, Bulgaria, Romania, and the Yugoslav republics of Macedonia, Bosnia, and Serbia are in single-sex or mixed lines. Couple dances are related to courtship practices and the accepted societal roles for men and women. They exist in two forms: one with physical contact, the other without. In the former Habsburg areas of Czechoslovakia, Hungary, Poland, and Yugoslav Croatia and Slovenia, most of the couple dances are done with the man and woman holding each other and some include such patterns as the man twirling the woman, swinging her away and back again, or lifting her. A few couple dances in which the partners do not touch can be found in the southern and eastern areas of the region. The dancers begin facing each other and perform the step or rhythmic pattern independently as they move close, then apart, circle each other, follow each other, and so on. Solo folk dances are relatively rare in Eastern Europe. Notable examples include the Hungarian Lads' Dance performed by men with sharp movements and slapping of the boots and thighs, and the sensuous *Čoček* of Macedonian Gypsies.

Urban social dance in nineteenth-century Eastern Europe followed the trends of the rest of Europe and added to the international social dance repertoire of America as well as Europe with dances such as the Bohemian polka and the Polish mazurka and polonaise. An interesting intersection of urban and rural dance occurred during the Illyrian South Slav nationalist movement. In 1842, at a fashionable Illyrian ball in Zagreb, a group of young nationalists introduced the *dvoransko kolo*. This dance made a political statement by incorporating steps from folk dances of various South Slavic regions into the form of the pan-European quadrille (a figure dance). Into an elitist urban society that had traditionally looked on the peasantry with contempt, the South Slav patriots introduced elements such as this dance to encourage a feeling of solidarity among all classes. In the twentieth century Eastern European urban social dance practices have closely following Western European and American fashions. In some areas, however (particularly in the south and east), an evening's dancing includes both traditional folk and modern international social dances.

In theater dance as well as urban social dance, Eastern Europe has been part of the international scene. From its beginnings in the Renaissance and baroque eras, ballet increasingly developed into an international art form. In the late eighteenth and nineteenth centuries, major cities of Eastern

Europe began establishing permanent theaters, and as soon as opera was introduced the ballet came as well, as it was an integral part of opera production. The opera and the ballet experienced the same kinds of buffeting from the political situation as did dramatic theater, but both managed to survive and create significant works. By the late twentieth century, there were at least the following number of major ballet companies, most of which were associated with opera: Albania (1), Bulgaria (5), Czechoslovakia (6), Hungary (4), Poland (4), Romania (1), and Yugoslavia (8). As part of the international ballet circuit—and depending on the political climate—Eastern Europe received visits from foreign ballet companies and personnel and also sent their own artists traveling to other places. One of the most important venues of exchange has been the annual international ballet competition in Varna, Bulgaria.

The other major theatrical dance art—modern dance, or contemporary dance—developed in the early twentieth century in the United States and Germany. From those beginnings, it too grew into an international dance genre with a network of contacts through touring and exchange programs.

German modern dance began to spread eastward well before World War II, but under the Communist regimes that took over after the war, it was not an approved genre, so its development in Eastern Europe was for the most part arrested until the strictures were eased. By 1989, there were modern dance companies at least in Czechoslovakia, Hungary, Poland, and Yugoslavia. Many of the modern dance performances were given by amateurs partly because heretofore there has been no official support and subsidy for the art.

In considering the Eastern European region, one sees that the countries under Habsburg rule and closer to Western Europe were predictably more influenced by Western fashions and practices than those under the Ottoman Empire. By 1989, however, influences had become global. While the former Ottoman territories have probably retained more of their traditional folk dance and music in close to original contexts than have the former Habsburg areas, international dance culture has invaded the entire region. Theatricalized folk dance, ballet, modern dance, and popular theater dance genres appear nearly everywhere in Eastern Europe, while in the social dance realm, Western fashions prevail.

Nancy Lee Ruyter

Further reading

Ballet International; Dance Chronicle; Dance Studies; UCLA Journal of Dance Ethnology (formerly *Journal of the Association of Graduate Dance Ethnologists*); *Viltis.*

Dunin, Elsie Ivancich and Nancy Lee Chalfa Ruyter. *Yugoslav Dance: An Introduction and List of Sources Available in United States Libraries.* Palo Alto, California, 1981.

Katzarova-Kukudova, Raina and Kiril Djenev. *Bulgarian Folk Dances,* trans. by Nevena Geliazkova and Marguerite Alexieva, 2d ed. Cambridge, Massachusetts, 1976.

Martin, György. *Hungarian Folk Dances.* Budapest, 1974.

See also Folklife

Danilo I Petrović Njegoš (1826–60)

Montenegrin prince. Danilo succeeded his uncle, Prince-Bishop (*vladika*) Petar II (1813–51). In 1852 he secularized the Montenegrin state, separating the offices of prince and bishop (retaining the former for himself) and transforming the country into a hereditary monarchy. Danilo laid the foundations of modern state government in Montenegro, resisted tribal separatism, and sought to eliminate blood feuds. He reorganized the army and founded the Order of Prince Danilo (*Orden knjaza Danila*). In 1855 he issued a major law code (*Obšti zakonik crnogorski i brdski*). In 1852–53 he fought the traditional Turkish enemy, defeating the Turks at the Battle of Ostrog, but his decision not to become involved in the Crimean War (1853–56) provoked some of his Russophilic subjects to open rebellion. At the Congress of Paris in 1856, he petitioned unsuccessfully for territorial adjustments and for formal recognition of his country's independence. In 1858 troops led by his brother inflicted a major defeat on the Ottomans at the Battle of Grahovo, resulting in the delimitation of the Turco-Montenegrin frontier and the transfer of some additional territory to Montenegro. Fatally wounded by an assassin's bullet on August 12, 1860, Danilo died the following day.

John D. Treadway

Further reading

Pavićević, Branko. *Danilo i Petrović njegoš: Knjaz crnogorski i brdski, 1851–1860.* Belgrade, 1990.

See also Crimean War; Montenegro; Paris, Treaty of; Petar II; Petrović Njegoš

D

D'Annunzio, Gabriele (1863–1938)

Italian poet, writer, and nationalist political leader who precipitated a clash with the Yugoslavs over the city and port Rijeka. D'Annunzio's novels presented ruthless, selfless men serving great causes and devoted to passion and beauty. His literature and his politics idealized war and Italian national greatness. As Italy's most famous contemporary writer, D'Annunzio became a cultural icon for the early fascists.

D'Annunzio's politics were shaped by humiliating Italian military defeats in Ethiopia in 1896. He blamed these losses on the lack of heroism inherent in democracy and parliamentary government, while he ardently supported Italian aggression in Libya and organized large and often violent pro-war demonstrations.

At the Paris Peace Conference (1919) after World War I, Italy gained Trent, South Tirol, and Istria, but not Dalmatia or Rijeka. Thus, many Italian nationalists viewed the peace as "mutilated." In September 1919 D'Annunzio led a group of war veterans to Rijeka and occupied it with the support of some generals and industrialists. The Italian government, fearing military mutiny, did nothing to counter D'Annunzio. Rijeka remained in D'Annunzio's control until December 1920, when Italians elected a new government that dispatched the navy to demand D'Annunzio's surrender.

D'Annunzio's occupation of Rijeka greatly influenced Mussolini (1883–1945) and the development of Italian fascism. In Rijeka, D'Annunzio pioneered the politics of theater by organizing a private, uniformed army with parades and mass meetings. He roused crowds to a frenzy by peppering his balcony speeches with slogans and eliciting the crowd to roar them back at him. Mussolini drew on many of D'Annunzio's techniques in his own rise to power, including the use of symbols, ritual, myth, and theatrics to generate a mass following.

Katherine McCarthy

Further reading

Ledeen, Michael A. *D'Annunzio at Fiume.* Baltimore, 1977.

Rhodes, Anthony. *D'Annunzio: The Poet as Superman.* New York, 1960.

Rusinow, Dennison. *Italy's Austrian Heritage, 1919–1946.* Oxford, 1969.

See also Paris Peace Conference; Rijeka

Danube Delta

Mouth of the Danube River. The Danube empties into the Black Sea through three main arms, which form a typical delta. It is a low area of about 864,850 acres (350,000 hectares), created in recent geological times by alluvial deposits on a previous gulf. The three arms of the river are Chilia to the north, Sulina (the chief maritime channel) in the middle, and Sfântul Gheorghe (St. George) to the south.

The average altitude of the delta is only half a meter, with the highest hills reaching 43 feet (13 m) and the deepest water being 63 feet (19 m). Half of the delta's area is neither dry land nor under water, but fluctuates in between, depending on the season and precipitation. The climate is dry and rather moderate for this latitude and the vegetation is very rich. The delta has the largest area of reeds in the world, and on Letea Island there is a primeval forest dominated by centennial oak trees covered by vines. On various lakes are many floating islands made of aquatic vegetation.

The delta is an ornithological paradise with some three hundred different species of birds of which about eighty nest in this area. It is the home of sea eagles, swans, and the largest colony of pelicans in Europe. The area is also an important stopover for many birds migrating between the polar circle and the equator.

Traditionally, the delta was a reliable source of fish and the home of the much-prized caviar. The fish, however, have suffered gravely as a result of water pollution, and the caviar-producing sturgeons, reaching over 300 pounds (136 kg) each, have diminished to an alarming degree.

The delta has been populated since ancient times. Its inhabitants, living in small villages along rivers and lakes, make a living by fishing, sheep herding, and farming. The only large city and tourist center here is Tulcea, at the beginning of the delta, while Sulina is an old but small maritime port.

Over the last decades, some 25 percent of the area was drained for permanent agriculture, but the results have been mixed. Ecologically, the delta also suffered severely. The construction of several dams on the Danube has caused dangerous alluvial changes. The industrial, urban, and agricultural discharges have also polluted the waters. And the intense exploitation of various reed areas for pulp has changed the balance of the ecosystem.

Recently, however, the delta was declared a natural monument and was taken under the protection of the United Nations. A special international fund was also established to clean up the Danube and its delta.

Nicholas Dima

Further reading
Brătescu C. "Delta Dunării." *BSSRG* 16 (1922).
Enciclopedia Geografică a României. Bucharest, 1982.
Geografia României. Bucharest, 1983.

See also Danube River; Environment

Danube Question

An international dispute concerning jurisdiction over the Danube River. In 1856, with the end of the Crimean War (1853–56), Europe's statesmen sought to create an international body to regulate commerce and disputes along the Danube. But like the larger Eastern Question which centered on the future of southeastern Europe in the wake of the disintegration of the Ottoman Empire), which so vexed the capitals of Europe, the formulas proposed to resolve the Danube Question consistently failed. Originally the Treaty of Paris of 1856 called for the creation of a River State Commission, composed of the river-bordering states, to serve as the administrative organ for the waterway. When it became clear, however, that this body would be dominated by Vienna, the other Great Powers refused to recognize its authority. That left the European Commission of the Danube, originally formed to clear the Danube delta of debris left from the Crimean conflict, as the river's sole functioning agency. Instead of its duties being absorbed by the now defunct River State Commission, the European Commission continued to be renewed by the Great Powers. Although successful in its goal of improving conditions along the lower Danube, the area between the Black Sea and the Romanian ports of Galați and Brăila, the agency, which included representatives of all the Great Powers and Romania, quickly ran afoul of the wishes of Bucharest. The existence of an autonomous agency on Romanian soil was an affront to Romanian nationalism. In 1920–21 a special Danube Conference finally created an International Commission of the Danube for the Upper Danube but once again renewed the European Commission to govern maritime commerce. Throughout the 1920s, Romanian nationalists pointed to the European Commission as a symbol of imperialism, and Romanian diplomats continued to challenge the authority of the organization to operate on Romanian soil. In 1938, with the admission of Germany to the commission, the Danube fell into the Nazi German orbit. In 1948 the Belgrade Conference, called to deal with the question of the river's governance, created a single agency, a new International Commission under the jurisdiction of the riverine states, to regulate the entire length of the river. This legitimized the domination of the Danube by the Soviet Union.

Richard Frucht

Further reading
Frucht, Richard. *Dunărea Noastră. Romania, the Great Powers and the Danube Question 1914–1921.* Boulder, Colorado, 1982.
Gorove, Stephen. *Law and Politics of the Danube.* The Hague, 1964.

See also Crimean War; Danube River; Eastern Question; Great Powers; Paris, Treaty of

Danube River

Europe's longest river. Formed by the confluence of two streams near Donaueschingen in the Black Forest, the Danube flows 1,770 miles (2,950 km) before emptying into the Black Sea. The waterway either traverses or borders Romania, Moldova, Bulgaria, Yugoslavia, Croatia, Hungary, the Slovak Republic, Austria, and Germany. In addition, four capitals—Belgrade, Budapest, Bratislava, and Vienna—are situated along the river's banks. Although the Danube is navigable from the Black Sea to Ulm in Bavaria, physical conditions confine oceangoing ships to the lower or maritime Danube, the portion of the river comprising the delta to the Romanian port of Brăila. Goods are then transshipped to shallower draft vessels for passage along the upper (or fluvial) Danube.

Long an important European trade route, the Danube served as the northern boundary of the Roman Empire and an avenue for the migration of the peoples of East Central Europe. With numerous tributaries—including the Drava, Sava, Tisza, and Morava Rivers—throughout the region, the Danube served as a highway for expanding European trade during the nineteenth century, especially vital shipments of grain to an industrializing Western Europe. As a result, control of Danubian

D trade during the nineteenth century became a thorny diplomatic issue known as the Danube Question.

Immortalized in Johann Strauss's (1825–99) "Blue Danube Waltz," the river's swift-moving currents present a recurring problem of silting in the delta. Similarly, the narrow passage between Romania and Yugoslavia known as the Iron Gates represented a constant hazard to shipping before the construction of a massive hydroelectric facility built by Romania and Yugoslavia.

Richard Frucht

Further reading

Hajnal, Henry. *The Danube: Its Historical, Political and Economic Significance.* The Hague, 1920.
Magocsi, Paul Robert. *Historical Atlas of East Central Europe.* Seattle, Washington, 1993.
Magris, Claudio. *Danube.* New York, 1989.
Pounds, N.J.G. *Eastern Europe.* London, 1969.

See also Danube Delta; Danube Question; Iron Gates

Danubian Principalities

Term designating the Principalities of Moldavia and Wallachia, which was not used in Romania but was rather an invention of nineteenth-century European diplomats. The term "Danubian Principalities" was actually first used in the eighteenth century when Austria penetrated the Ottoman sphere of influence, first in Hungary and Transylvania, then in 1716 the territory of Oltenia, the western part of the Principality of Wallachia. In 1775 Austria constrained the Ottomans to cede outright the northern part of the Principality of Moldavia, which became known as Bukovina. Russia followed suit in 1812 by annexing the eastern part of Moldavia (so-called Bessarabia, most of which today forms the Republic of Moldova). Briefly, it was clear that these two Great Powers were competing to see who would gain more of the Ottoman inheritance, while the rest of Europe was worried by this disturbance of the continental balance of power and favored either propping up the "sick" Ottoman Empire or at least preventing its dismemberment (thereby unduly strengthening rival powers). Thus, following the Congress of Vienna (1815), which tried to restore "normalcy" to the European international scene, innumerable conferences, consultations, and diplomatic maneu-

vers took place, many of them instigated and controlled by Prince Metternich (1773–1859), the Austrian chancellor who largely dominated the European scene until 1848. The disposition of the Ottoman inheritance that proved the least upsetting to the European balance of power was to permit the emergence of independent states in the Balkan area. The Danubian Principalities availed themselves of this opportunity and, both being inhabited by people of Romanian nationality, first aimed at unification, a goal that they gradually achieved de facto in 1859–66, the core of the future Romania. Full, internationally recognized sovereignty was obtained in 1878 after one last armed struggle with the Turks, the Russo-Turkish War of 1877–78.

Ladis K.D. Kristof

Further reading

Hitchins, Keith. *Rumania 1866–1947.* Oxford, 1994.
Magocsi, Paul Robert. *Historical Atlas of East Central Europe.* Seattle, Washington, 1993.
România: Atlas istoric-geographic. Bucharest, 1996.

See also Bessarabian Question; Bukovina; Congress of Vienna; Eastern Question; Clemens von Metternich; Moldavia; Moldova; Paris, Treaty of; Revolutions of 1848; Russo-Turkish War of 1877–78; United Principalities; Wallachia

Darányi, Kálmán (1886–1939)

Hungarian prime minister (1936–38) who, although generally expected to reverse the trend toward totalitarianism, served through his policies to promote German National Socialist and indigenous fascist influence in Hungary. The illegitimate son of a distinguished noble family, Darányi began his political career in Pest County in 1909. From 1910 to 1917, he was a government official in Transylvania. Darányi helped organize the counterrevolution against the short-lived Soviet Republic of Béla Kun (1886–1938) in 1919. Between 1920 and 1927, he held various offices in the provincial administration in northwestern Hungary. In 1927 he was elected to parliament on the ticket of the Unified Party. He became political undersecretary in the prime minister's office from 1928 to 1935.

In 1935 Darányi was appointed minister of agriculture in the right-wing cabinet of Gyula Gömbös (1886–1936); the following year, after the death of Gömbös, he was appointed prime minister, while retaining the post of minister of agriculture. Ostensibly, his mission was to steer away from the trend toward fascism. Indeed, still under the influence of Count István Bethlen (1874–1946), the "grand old man" of Hungarian politics, he adopted a more conservative line in domestic affairs. In foreign affairs, however, he continued Gömbös's policy of friendship with Italy and Germany. Even internally he fell increasingly under the sway of Nazi Germany and the indigenous extreme right-wing movements in Hungary, to the point where he was ready to appoint representatives of the latter into a coalition cabinet. He was also responsible for the first anti-Jewish law, passed in 1938. Darányi was forced to resign on May 13, 1938, in part because he lost the trust of the regent, Miklós Horthy (1868–1957). He was elected speaker of the House that same year, but died shortly thereafter.

Mario D. Fenyo

Further reading

Juhasz, Gyula. *Hungarian Foreign Policy, 1919–1945*. Budapest, 1979.
Macartney, Carlyle Aylmer. *October Fifteenth: A History of Modern Hungary, 1929–1945,* vol. 1. Edinburgh, 1956–57.
Sakmyster, Thomas. *Hungary, the Great Powers, and the Danubian Crisis, 1936–1939*. Athens, Georgia, 1980.

See also István Bethlen; Gyula Gömbös; Miklós Horthy; Hungarian Soviet Republic; Béla Kun; Right Radicalism

Daszyński, Ignacy (1866–1936)

Founder and leader of the Polish Social Democratic Party in Galicia. Daszyński emerged as one of the most prominent Polish political leaders before the creation of the independent state. From 1897 to 1918, he served as a delegate to the Austrian Reichsrat (parliament), where he established his reputation as an adept parliamentary politician and an accomplished orator. Daszyński consistently supported the pro-independence faction within Polish socialism and worked closely with his fellow socialist Józef Piłsudski (1867–1935). In November 1918 Daszyński became the first premier and foreign minister of independent Poland in the short-lived Lublin government consisting of socialists and radical peasant politicians. During the Soviet advance on Warsaw in the Polish-Soviet War of 1919–21, Daszyński served as vice premier in the multiparty Government of National Defense from July 1920 to January 1921. His second and last tenure in the government attested to Poland's political consolidation in the face of a grave external threat to the state's existence. From 1919 to 1930, he served as a representative in the Polish Sejm (parliament), and from 1922 to 1927, he was the vice marshal and then from 1928 to 1930 the marshal of this body. Daszyński, who belonged to the inner circle of the Polish Socialist Party's leadership in the interwar period, supported Piłsudski's coup in May 1926, which toppled the government, but he later grew disillusioned with the new regime and subsequently became one of the main figures in the antigovernment opposition. Because of his contacts in European socialist circles, Daszyński enjoyed a degree of international recognition unusual for a Polish politician.

William Lee Blackwood

Further reading

Daszyński, Ignacy. *Teksty*. Warsaw, 1986.
Kto był kim w Drugiej Rzeczypospolitej. Warsaw, 1994.
Najdus, Walentyna. *Ignacy Daszyński 1886–1936*. Warsaw, 1988.

See also Józef Piłsudski; Polish-Soviet War

Davidović, Ljubomir (Ljuba) (1863–1940)

Leading politician in Serbia and in the first Yugoslavia, widely respected for his uncommon civility and commitment to parliamentary and constitutional government. Davidović pursued an academic career before entering politics. In 1901 he was one of the founders of the Independent Radical Party, which championed a liberal constitution. He implemented educational reforms as minister of education in 1904 before becoming president of the national assembly the following year. He was the minister of education in the coalition government of Nikola Pašić (1845–1926) from February 1914 to June 1917.

After World War I, Davidović merged political parties from several regions of the emerging Yugoslav state to form the Democratic Party. He served as minister of education from February 1918 to August 1919, and was president of a coalition

D

government with the Socialist Party from August 1919 to February 1920. He supported the 1921 Vidovdan Constitution but saw the need to revise it and abandon its extreme centralism. In keeping with this view, he opened discussions with the supporters of Stjepan Radić (1871–1928), the Croatian Peasant Party leader, in 1922, which led to an open break in the Democratic Party between Davidović and Svetozar Pribičević (1875–1936).

Davidović put together a broad coalition government in July 1924 that included four Slovenes, three Bosnian Muslims, and reserved four places for representatives of Radić's Croatian Republican Peasant Party. Radić's intemperate speeches and King Alexander's displeasure ended this government in October 1924.

During the 1927 elections, Davidović championed parliamentary government, while his opponents within the Democratic Party favored more authoritarian rule. He opposed the royal dictatorship imposed in Yugoslavia in 1929 and became one of the leaders of the opposition until his death in 1940.

Kenneth E. Basom

Further reading

Dragnich, Alex N. *The First Yugoslavia: Search for a Viable Political System.* Stanford, California, 1983.

Lampe, John R. *Yugoslavia as History: Twice There Was a Country.* New York, 1996.

Petrovich, Michael Boro. *A History of Serbia 1804–1918.* New York, 1976.

Spomenica Ljubomira Davidovića. Belgrade, 1940.

See also Alexander I Karadjordjević; Nikola Pašić; Svetozar Pribičević; Stjepan Radić; Vidovdan Constitution

Deák, Ferenc (1803–76)

Architect of the *Ausgleich* (Compromise) of 1867 and a leading figure in Hungarian political life for four decades. Deák was born in Söjtör in western Hungary, where his father was a gentry landowner. In 1833 his native Zala County sent him to the national diet in Pozsony (Bratislava), where his masterful knowledge of the law, political acumen, and personal probity quickly made him a leader of the liberal opposition. His skillful negotiations at the diet of 1839–40 led Vienna to abandon its open persecution of liberals. He rejoined the diet again

only in March 1848 and helped to draft the April Laws transforming Hungary into a constitutional monarchy and ending serfdom. As minister of justice in the government of Prime Minister Lajos Batthyány (1806–49), he worked to clarify and extend the April Laws. He took part in fruitless negotiations with Vienna during the summer of 1848 and resigned with Batthyány in September.

In the years following the Revolutions of 1848–49, Deák led "passive resistance" against the occupying absolutist regime, which he considered illegal because of its refusal to recognize the April Laws. In 1861 Deák's firm adherence to the validity of the laws of 1848 led Franz Joseph (1830–1916) to prorogue the diet after only a few weeks. Deák left the door open to compromise, and his famous "Easter Article" of 1865 argued that the Pragmatic Sanction of 1722–23 (which dealt with the matter of succession within the empire) allowed for common military, foreign, and financial affairs between Austria and Hungary. Over the objections of Lajos Kossuth (1802–94), leader of the Hungarian War for Independence (1848–49), and his supporters, Deák guided Hungary through the negotiations that led to the *Ausgleich,* creating the Dual Monarchy of Austria-Hungary. Deák remained active in politics through 1873, and although his followers called themselves the "Deák Party," he saw himself representing national rather than party interests. Deák refused all honors, never married, and led a puritanical lifestyle. His unimpeachable political and personal integrity earned him the title Sage of the Nation.

Robert Nemes

Further reading

Ferenczi, Zoltán. *Deák élete,* 3 vols. Budapest, 1904.

Király, Béla. *Ferenc Deák.* London, 1975.

Tajács, Péter. *Deák Ferenc politikai pályája, 1849–1865.* Budapest, 1991.

See also *Ausgleich;* Lajos Batthyány; Dual Monarchy; Franz Joseph; Hungarian War for Independence; Lajos Kossuth; Revolutions of 1848

Debrecen

Second-largest city of Hungary. Debrecen is located 140 miles (226 km) east of Budapest in the Great Hungarian Plain (*Nagy Alföld*). The city is the seat of Hajdú-Bihar County, site of a major university (founded in 1912), and a center of industry, especially food processing, pharmaceuticals, and printing. Debrecen is located in a rich agricultural area known especially for cattle raising on the nearby plain. The population of the city has climbed from an 1870 total of 43,048 to 212,235 in 1990.

The area around Debrecen had been for centuries the site of settlement by various groups prior to the arrival of the Hungarians in the ninth century. The city grew in wealth and importance during the Middle Ages as a center of trade, mainly in salt, furs, and cattle. The town remained relatively free during Ottoman times, which lasted from the 1520s until the 1660s, and even swelled with population displaced from other areas. In the 1560s Debrecen became a center of Calvinist thought. The Great Church, built in 1823, is the largest Protestant church in Hungary and still the symbol of the city. A theological college has operated in Debrecen since the Middle Ages.

Debrecen, along with several other towns, became impoverished during the late 1600s under Habsburg domination. In 1848–49 the city became the center of the Hungarian War for Independence (during the Revolutions of 1848); Lajos Kossuth (1802–94), leader of the revolution, delivered his proclamation against the Habsburgs in the Great Church, and a provisional independent government operated there for a time. Debrecen also acted as the seat of the Provisional National Government of Hungary after liberation from the Germans in 1944.

Darrick Danta

Further reading

Gutkind, E.A. *International History of City Development*, vol. 7, *Urban Development in East-Central Europe: Poland, Czechoslovakia, and Hungary.* New York, 1972.

Hanák, Péter, ed. *One Thousand Years: A Concise History of Hungary.* Budapest, 1988.

Webster's New Geographical Dictionary. Springfield, Massachusetts, 1984.

See also Hungarian War for Independence; Lajos Kossuth; Revolutions of 1848

Dedijer, Vladimir (1914–)

Prominent Yugoslav writer and historian. A native of Montenegro, Dedijer began his professional career as a journalist, covering the Spanish Civil War for the Belgrade newspaper *Politika* (*Politics*). In 1937 he lost his job at the newspaper because of his leftist-oriented articles and sympathetic accounts of republican Spain. He completed a law degree in 1937 in Belgrade and became active in the Communist Party in late 1930s. During World War II, he rose to the rank of lieutenant colonel in the Communist-led Partisan army and was severely wounded. Dedijer's diaries recounting his wartime experiences became a classic account of the Partisan war effort.

After the war, he became the editor of the Communist Party newspaper *Borba* (*Struggle*) and eventually a member of the party's Central Committee. He fell from favor in 1955 after he defended Milovan Djilas (1911–95), a member of the leadership who publicly advocated greater democracy. Dedijer was ultimately expelled from the party and, after enduring much official harassment, allowed to go abroad. In exile, he taught at various British and American universities and devoted himself to writing history. He returned to Yugoslavia in the late 1960s when the political climate improved.

Among his best-known works are his study of the Young Bosnia revolutionary movement, *The Road to Sarajevo,* his *War Diaries,* and his biography of Tito (1892–1980). He has also compiled and edited volumes of documents on numerous aspects of twentieth-century Yugoslav history. Dedijer has actively supported various human rights causes and defended the right to free expression and freedom of the press.

Paul D. Lensink

Further reading

Dedijer, Vladimir. *War Diaries of Vladimir Dedijer,* 3 vols. Ann Arbor, Michigan, 1990.

Gligorijević, Milo, *Rat i mir Vladimira Dedijera: Sećanja i razgovori.* Belgrade, 1986.

See also Antifascism; Communist Party of Yugoslavia; Milovan Djilas; Press; Tito

Dembowski, Edward (1822–46)

Polish philosopher, literary critic, and social and revolutionary leader. The son of a senator and educated on the family estate, Dembowski concentrated on philosophy and literature. Inherited wealth made him one of the richest landowners in

D the country. After moving to Warsaw in 1836, Dembowski turned against his father's social and political environment and gravitated toward democratic revolutionary circles.

In 1842 Dembowski began publication of the periodical *Scientific Review*. As publisher and editor, he continually faced problems with Russian censorship. He wrote numerous articles on philosophy, literature, art, and nature, while publishing poems in translation as well as his own. In his philosophical writings, he fought against those who were conciliatory toward the tsar, and strove to create a particularly Polish philosophical terminology.

As a revolutionary leader, Dembowski became involved in a plot to stage a simultaneous uprising in all three parts of partitioned Poland in the spring of 1844. When the tsarist police learned of the scheme and arrested some of the leaders in the fall of 1843, Dembowski fled to Poznań in Prussian Poland, where he continued with his writing, sharpening his attacks against the aristocratic order. He continued to agitate for revolution, goading the Polish Democratic Society, a group that coordinated revolutionary activities from outside Poland, to accelerate its timetable for an uprising. Dembowski's advocacy of communist ideas led to his expulsion from Poznań in the fall of 1844. He went to Galicia as an emissary of the Polish Democratic Society and began a career as agitator and spy. He continually pressed for an uprising and undertook bold acts of espionage, often in disguise, to elicit information useful to revolutionary planning.

With the outbreak of the uprising in the Kraków Republic in February 1846, Dembowski rushed to Wieliczka, organized a revolutionary council, and proceeded to Kraków to join the government. There, he refused to allow any legislation that would punish peasants for acts of murder or brigandage against landowners. In February he organized a procession of peasants, priests, and revolutionaries to go to the countryside to engage the peasants to support the rising. Leaving Kraków on the afternoon of February 27, the procession returned after dark as Austrian troops entered the city. In the skirmish that followed, Dembowski was killed almost immediately. The authorities failed to recognize him and, having quelled the uprising, continued to search for him for several months afterward.

Robert A. Berry

Further reading

Grzybowski, Konstanty. "Edward Dembowski," *Poland* 8, no. 120 (August 1964): 21–23.
Szpowski, Maria. *Edward Dembowski, 1822–1846.* Warsaw, 1973.

See also Republic of Kraków

De-Stalinization

The gradual abandonment of Stalinist political and economic measures in the Soviet Union and Eastern Europe following the death of Josef Stalin (1879–1953). This process defined the USSR's relations with its satellites in the 1950s and 1960s and exposed cracks in the facade of unity among the Soviet bloc states.

Stalin's death in March 1953 brought substantial changes in the USSR and its relations with its satellites. Within the Soviet Union, the emergence of Nikita Khrushchev (1894–1971) coincided with the execution of Stalin's chief lieutenant, Lavrentii Beria (1899–1953), and the release of some prisoners from forced-labor camps. In Eastern Europe, Khrushchev accepted Tito's (1892–1980) "separate road" to socialism by making an official visit to Belgrade, and prominent East European Communists purged by Stalinist leaders were posthumously rehabilitated. These developments preceded the dramatic revelations in the so-called Secret Speech at the Twentieth Party Congress in February 1956, in which Khrushchev accused Stalin of numerous crimes against the USSR and the Communist Party. Khrushchev's speech, however, did not result in any major structural changes in the USSR; it condemned Stalin's excesses as the fault of one individual rather than the system that produced him.

Nevertheless, the speech reverberated in Eastern Europe, where local Communists struggled to manage their own transition from Stalinism. Confronted with persistent disorders among workers in Poznań, Polish officials decided to follow Khrushchev's example, making some changes to appease the public while retaining the essential features of the Stalinist system. They replaced their Stalinist-era leader with Władysław Gomułka (1905–82), a victim of Stalin's purges. Subsequently, the least popular Stalinist measures, such as repression of the Catholic Church and collectivization, were relaxed or abandoned, and the crisis passed. It appeared that Poland would remain a reliable ally of the USSR.

In Hungary, where reformers and Stalinists had waged a difficult, seesaw battle, the autumn of 1956 brought Polish-style disturbances. In contrast to their Polish counterparts, Hungarian demonstrations soon took on a distinctly anti-Russian tone. Protestors gathered in Budapest around a statue of Polish General Bem (1794–1850), who had led Hungarian revolutionaries against the invading Russian army in 1849 (during the Revolution of 1848–49); some organized in honor of Sándor Petőfi (1823–49), who had written anti-Russian verse. When executed Hungarian leader László Rajk (1909–49) was given a solemn reburial on October 24, an eyewitness noted, it seemed that Hungarians considered both Stalinism and socialism dead. In the midst of the tumult, Imre Nagy (1896–1958) became Hungarian prime minister by popular demand. A victim of the Hungarian purges, he appeared poised to assume the role of Gomułka in Hungary. However, Nagy soon found himself powerless to stem the popular tide and went over to the revolutionaries. He called for Hungary's exit from the Warsaw Pact and the withdrawal of Soviet troops from the country.

Although Khrushchev had accepted independent initiative from Polish Communists, he would not preside over Hungary's exit from the Soviet bloc. Soviet troops returned to Budapest on November 4, quelled the disturbances, and installed János Kádár (1912–89) as Hungary's new leader. Nagy was later arrested and shot.

Other nations were quick to learn from the Hungarian and Polish episodes. It seemed that Moscow would tolerate separate roads to socialism as long as they did not lead out of the Soviet orbit. Tito continued to take Yugoslavia on its own way with Khrushchev's tacit blessing. In Romania, Gheorghe Gheorghiu-Dej (1901–65) forged a divergent path in economic and foreign policy in the 1960s. He rejected Romanian participation in the revived Council for Mutual Economic Assistance (Comecon), the Moscow-dominated economic planning organ, maintaining that it would kill Romania's chances to create a diversified economy. Meanwhile, the Albanian government refused to accept Khrushchev's un-Stalinist détente with unfriendly neighbor Yugoslavia. Albania allied itself with China following that state's break with the USSR in 1957. Yugoslav, Romanian, and Albanian leaders were careful not to jeopardize the leading role of the Communist parties in their states or to renounce their ties to the socialist world.

By 1967, the process of de-Stalinization in the USSR had ended. Khrushchev's successor, Leonid Brezhnev (1906–82), made it clear with the prosecution of dissident writers that criticism of Stalin was no longer permitted. In fact, some observers have characterized Brezhnev's domestic policy in the late 1960s as neo-Stalinist. He did not return the country to unrelenting terror but cracked down on those who had led condemnations of Stalin and conducted sporadic repressions elsewhere to frighten others.

By contrast, Czechoslovakia was embarking on a long-delayed journey away from Stalinism in 1967. It had escaped the tumult of the 1950s because of its rigid leadership and the country's high level of general prosperity. Only in 1962, when an economic slump coincided with the zenith of de-Stalinization in the USSR, did the Czechoslovak leader, Antonín Novotný (1904–75), seem vulnerable. Novotný's decline occurred gradually, but by December 1967, Alexander Dubček (1921–92) had replaced him and ushered in a remarkable period of domestic reform known as the Prague Spring.

Mindful of the experience of other East European countries, Czechoslovak reformers proceeded with caution. A graduate of the Moscow Higher Party School, Dubček permitted neither official rival parties nor talk of leaving the Soviet orbit. Indeed, he took great pains to emphasize his country's loyalty to the USSR.

Inevitably, however, the formation of potential opposition groups and the lifting of censorship in Czechoslovakia angered the Brezhnev government. Access to information about Czechoslovak postwar controversies, such as the death of Foreign Minister Jan Masaryk (1886–1948), could produce revelations damaging to the USSR. Such revelations could lead to serious disturbances in the heart of the Soviet bloc; the leaders of Czechoslovakia's neighbors, ironically including Poland's Gomułka, protested the probable impact on their peoples. Finally, the unfolding Czechoslovak reform had caught the attention of dissidents in the USSR, who drew unflattering comparisons between Soviet socialism and Czechoslovakia's "socialism with a human face."

All these considerations influenced Brezhnev's decision to put down the Prague Spring by force in August 1968. A few months later, the

Soviet government issued the Brezhnev Doctrine, in which it declared its right to intervene wherever socialism was threatened. This represented the foreign policy variant of "anti-Soviet agitation" in its vague wording and was intended to prevent any future reforms likely to threaten Soviet hegemony in Eastern Europe.

De-Stalinization did not proceed smoothly or predictably in Eastern Europe. The process had clear winners and losers, Czechoslovakia most prominently among the latter. Yet it succeeded insofar as no country returned to the coercive regime of the Stalin era after 1956. Moreover, it helped to define the shifting limits of dissent within the Soviet bloc in the 1950s and 1960s and forever altered the previously monolithic face of socialism in Eastern Europe.

Brigit Farley

Further reading

Fejto, François. *A History of the People's Democracies: Eastern Europe since Stalin,* trans. by Daniel Weissbort. New York, 1971.

Medvedev, Roy. *Khrushchev,* trans. by Brian Pearce. Garden City, New York, 1983.

Mićunović, Veljko. *Moscow Diary.* New York, 1980.

Rothschild, Joseph. *Return to Diversity: A Political History of East Central Europe since World War II.* Oxford, 1989.

Zubok, Vladislav and Constantine Pleshakov. *Inside the Kremlin's Cold War: From Stalin to Khrushchev.* Cambridge, Massachusetts, 1996.

See also Józef Bem; Brezhnev Doctrine; Collectivization; Comecon; Alexander Dubček; Gheorghe Gheorghiu-Dej; Władysław Gomułka; Hungarian Revolution of 1956; János Kádár; Jan Masaryk; Imre Nagy; Antonín Novotný; Sándor Petőfi; Prague Spring; László Rajk; Stalin; Tito; Warsaw Pact

Dimitrov, Georgi (1882–1949)

Prominent activist of the international and Bulgarian workers' and socialist movement. In 1902, as a printer, Dimitrov joined the Bulgarian Workers' Social Democratic Party (BWSDP), which later became the Bulgarian Communist Party (BCP). In 1904–5 he became secretary of the Sofia party branch of the BWSDP and in 1909 was elected to its Central Committee. In 1913 Dimitrov became a member of parliament.

Dimitrov led a Communist-organized uprising against the bloody June 9, 1923, coup that overthrew the regime of Aleksandur Stamboliiski (1879–1923). After its failure, Dimitrov was forced to emigrate. In 1924 he became a candidate member of the Executive Committee of the Comintern (the Communist International). From 1929 to 1933, he chaired the organization's West European Bureau.

Dimitrov's most distinguishing moment was his self-defense in the Reichstag (Parliament) fire trial in Germany in 1933. Although acquitted, Bulgaria denied him reentry; he assumed Soviet citizenship and moved to Moscow. There, Dimitrov persuaded the Comintern to abandon Stalin's previous antisocial democracy position and accept his proposal of a "united, antifascist front." In 1935 he was unanimously elected secretary-general of the Comintern and held this post until the organization's dissolution in 1943.

During World War II, Dimitrov helped establish the Fatherland Front, a political coalition that organized antifascist resistance in Bulgaria. From November 1945 until his death in 1949, he was prime minister of Bulgaria and secretary-general of the BCP. Dimitrov authored the concept of "people's democracy," which outlined a different road, compared with the Soviet experience, to socialism in postwar Eastern Europe. After Stalin (1879–1953) created the Cominform, the Communist propaganda organ, in September 1947, Dimitrov was forced to abandon his concept and present people's democracy as a new form of proletarian dictatorship.

Dimitrov was instrumental in consolidating the BCP's control in Bulgaria. He directed the policies to abolish the monarchy through a referendum, as well as the political purges that resulted in the dissolution of the multiparty system and the imprisonment and execution of many politicians. He died in 1949 while meeting with Stalin in Moscow.

Boian Koulov

Further reading

Delev, P. et al. *Istoria na Bulgaria.* Sofia, 1996.

Kratka Bulgarska Entsiklopedia, vol. 2. Sofia, 1964.

Kumanov, M. *Politicheski partii, organizatsii I dvizheniya v Bulgaria I tehnite lideri, 1879–1949.* Sofia, 1991.

See also Antifascism; Cominform; Comintern; Communist Party of Bulgaria; Fatherland Front; Stalin; Aleksandur Stamboliiski

Dimitrov-Maistora, Vladimir (1882–1960)

The most accomplished and popular representative of Bulgarian painting between the world wars. Dimitrov-Maistora was born into a family of Macedonian emigrants and began working as a house painter when the family moved to the town of Kiustendil in 1889. With the support of the local community, he enrolled in the Sofia School of Painting, where he was called "The Master" for his talent. During the Balkan Wars (1912–13) and World War I, Dimitrov-Maistora served as a military painter for the army. His etchings of this period are remarkable examples of symbolism's and expressionism's influence on his work. After World War I, he refused a teaching appointment and retreated to the village of Shishkovtsi in the Kiustendil valley to dedicate his life to painting.

Like Leo Tolstoy (1828–1910), whom he admired, Dimitrov-Maistora lived the simple life of his people. He spent his days observing the villagers' activities, sketching his impressions, and translating them into paintings, usually during the evening hours. Rooted in Bulgarian folklore and village imagery, his two-dimensional style resembles icon paintings, the inception of his artistic life. He used bold, clearly outlined forms painted with broad brush strokes. His constructive composition of bright hues, flat planes of abstracted landscape forms, and peasant figures represented as decorative elements are personal interpretations of reality. Humans and nature are linked in a cosmic rhythm magnified by the creative power of the artist. American art collector John Oliver Crane (1899–1982) placed Dimitrov-Maistora under contract for over four years (1923–28) and secured about two hundred of his paintings. Dimitrov-Maistora traveled to and exhibited in Europe and the United States but always returned to his beloved village to paint and ultimately developed a style compatible with expressionism. A member of the Contemporary Art Society, Dimitrov-Maistora usually exhibited with this group in Sofia or at local markets in Shishkovtsi and the surrounding villages. He was awarded the Dimitrov Prize (1950) and the title People's Artist (1952). Maistora died in Sofia on September 29, 1960.

Milka T. Bliznakov

Further reading

Avramov, Dimitur. *Maistora I negovoto vreme*. Sofia, 1989.

Kolev, Boris. *Vladimir Dimitrov-le Maître*. Sofia, 1955.

See also Balkan Wars; Bulgarian Art; Folklore

Dinaric Alps

Mountain range fronting the Adriatic Sea and including the western margins of Slovenia, Croatia, Bosnia and Hercegovina, Serbia, Montenegro, Macedonia, and Albania. Its highest peaks range from 4,200–8,900 feet (1,273–2,700 m), with greatest elevations to be found in the Prokletije region along the border zone between Montenegro and Albania. The mountain region is characterized by two distinctive belts roughly equal in size. To the southwest, adjacent to the Adriatic, is a belt of massively folded limestone rocks that forms a distinctive landscape termed karst. Because the limestone is soluble, precipitation characteristically does not generate surface streams but penetrates deeply into the rocks through cracks and fissures, forming caverns and underground rivers. Valleys form mainly where erosion has reduced exposed folded layers of sandstone and shale lying between the formerly horizontal beds of limestone. Northwest of the karst zone, the Dinaric Alps contain far less limestone and are characterized by more normal erosion patterns of ridges and valleys.

The mountains pose a significant climatic barrier between the Mediterranean basin and the interior of the Balkan Peninsula. Moisture-laden air brought by passing storms is abruptly forced to rise, resulting in abundant precipitation. Rainfall in the Prokletije range averages 160 inches (406 cm) annually. The village of Crkvice above Kotor Bay received 212 inches (539 cm) in one year—the highest ever recorded in Europe. However, vegetation tends to be sparse throughout most of the karst region because of the internal penetration of rainfall and also past removal of forests, which was followed by erosion of soil accumulations.

The relatively young Dinaric Alps contain few mineral resources, though some sections contain layers of coal and lignite. The central portion has surface deposits of bauxite, a principal raw material in the manufacture of aluminum.

Thomas M. Poulsen

Further reading

Ager, D.V. *The Geology of Europe*. London, 1980.

Bertić, Ivan. *Veliki Geografski Atlas Jugoslavije*. Zagreb, 1987.

D

Bonacci, Ognjen. *Karst Hydrology with Special Reference to the Dinaric Karst.* Berlin, 1987.
"Dinarsko Gorje." *Enciklopedija Jugoslavije,* vol. 2. Zagreb, 1956: 709–12.

Djilas, Milovan (1911–95)

Yugoslav Communist leader, author, and dissident. A close associate of Tito (1892–1980) for over fifteen years (before his ouster from the party in 1954), Djilas had a colorful and, some would say, inconsistent career that spanned all the key periods of the former Yugoslavia. Djilas changed in his lifetime from loyal party Stalinist to novelist and gadfly of the Tito regime. He left behind an important body of history, political commentary, and literature that is both provocative and readable. His most important works include *The New Class* (1957), *Land without Justice* (1958), *Conversations with Stalin* (1962), *The Unperfect Society* (1969), and *Tito: The Story from Inside* (1980).

Djilas was born in 1911 in Podbišće, Montenegro. Like his brother, he became a Communist activist in his student days. He was imprisoned in Belgrade during the period of dictatorship in Yugoslavia in the 1930s.

Djilas was involved in some of the most controversial activities of the Yugoslav Communists: negotiations with the Nazis during World War II, the diplomatic altercations with Stalin (1879–1953) after the war, and the scramble to find and justify a new set of ruling principles for the country as it set off on its independent path. Djilas insistently criticized the Soviet Union's Leninist principles and called on the Yugoslav Communists to allow political pluralism. This led to his fall from the inner circle of power, which he shared with men such as Edvard Kardelj (1910–79) and Aleksandar Ranković (1909–83). In the decade after 1956, Djilas was jailed several times. He remained active as a publicist in Yugoslavia and Serbia until his death, critical of both aggressive Serbian nationalism and the Western media's "demonization" of Serbia as the sole culprit in the bloody wars in Croatia and Bosnia.

John K. Cox

Further reading

Clissold, Stephen. *Djilas: The Progress of a Revolutionary.* New York, 1983.
Reinhartz, Dennis. *Milovan Djilas: A Revolutionary as a Writer.* Boulder, Colorado, 1981.

Sulzberger, C.L. *Paradise Regained: Memoir of a Rebel.* New York, 1989.

See also Communist Party of Yugoslavia; Edvard Kardelj; Aleksandar Ranković; Tito; Tito-Stalin Split

Dmowski, Roman (1864–1939)

Polish nationalist and political figure. After initial activity within the nascent Polish nationalist movement, Dmowski assisted in founding the National Democratic Party in 1893, quickly becoming its acknowledged leader and theorist. His program of integral nationalism, articulated in such books as *Thoughts of a Modern Pole* (1903), foresaw an independent Poland, expressed hostility toward Jews and national minorities, and identified Germany as the chief enemy of the Poles. He led the "Polish Circle," a group of National Democrats, in the third Russian duma (parliament).

During World War I, Dmowski founded the Polish National Committee in Paris in 1915, calling for restored Polish statehood in conjunction with Allied victory. Although the Allies recognized him as their favored Polish spokesman, his lifelong rival Józef Piłsudski (1867–1935) assumed leadership of the Second Polish Republic after the war. Dmowski served as Polish delegate to the Paris Peace Conference of 1918–19.

Following the recovery of Polish statehood, he served briefly as foreign minister (1922) but largely avoided official or electoral pursuits and focused on advancing the interests of the National Democrats and their political allies. Permanently relegated to opposition upon Piłsudski's return to power by coup d'état in 1926, he founded the Camp of Great Poland, an oppositionist group, in the same year in hopes of consolidating and reviving the Polish right. In his later years, he grew increasingly attracted to fascism but stopped short of embracing the doctrine. Dmowski remains the classic exponent of modern Polish nationalism.

Neal A. Pease

Further reading

Dmowski, Roman. *Myśli nowoczesnego polaka.* Lvov, 1907.
Fountain, Alvin Marcus. *Roman Dmowski: Party, Tactics, Ideology, 1895–1907.* Boulder, Colorado, 1980.
Micewski, Andrzej. *Roman Dmowski.* Warsaw, 1971.
Wapiński, Roman. *Roman Dmowski.* Lublin, 1988.

See also Duma; Nationalism; Paris Peace Conference; Józef Piłsudski; World War I

Dniester River

Important river in Eastern Europe. The total drainage area, in Ukraine and Moldova, of the Dniester River (in antiquity known as Tyras or Danastris; Ukrainian, Dnister; Romanian, Nistru; Russian, Dniester) extends over 25,950 square miles (72,100 sq km). Its total length is 811 miles (1,352 km). The Dniester flows from the sub-Carpathian area in western Ukraine, cuts through the Ukrainian and Moldovan plateaus creating deep canyons in some places, and reaches the Black Sea at Bilhorod in Ukraine, just south of Odessa. It receives a number of affluents, especially in its upper reaches. At Tighina, in Moldova, its water flow is calculated at 11,500 cubic feet (310 cu m) per second, but the flow varies greatly with the seasons and from year to year. In 1954 a water storage lake of 25 square miles (68 sq km) was built in Moldova for purposes of irrigation, generating electricity, and supplying the cities of Chişinău and Tiraspol with water.

The Dniester was never a waterway, but along its banks routes for commerce developed in antiquity. In the Middle Ages immigrant Armenian merchants created a lively trade between the Middle East and East Central Europe. Many cities along (or in the vicinity of) this trade route—including Iaşi, Suceava, Kamenets Podilskii, and Lvov—owed their development and prosperity primarily to this commerce.

Politically, the role of the Dniester, from the fourteenth through the nineteenth centuries (and even today), has been to form the frontier between the Romanian and Ukrainian societies that, by and large, coexisted on friendly terms.

Ladis K.D. Kristof

Further reading

Magocsi, Paul Robert. *Historical Atlas of East Central Europe.* Seattle, Washington, 1993.
România: Atlas istoric-geografic. Bucharest, 1996.

Dobrogeanu-Gherea, Constantin (1855–1920)

Major figure in the Romanian Social Democratic Party, who introduced Marxist analysis to the conditions that existed in Romania. Dobrogeanu-Gherea was a prominent literary critic who observed that socialism was like an exotic plant when it was first introduced in Romania. He is most known for his theory of *neoiobăgia* (neoserfdom), in which he argued that the Romanian system was a hybrid mixture of bourgeois-liberal political reforms and neofeudal economic substance. He believed that this was due to the fact that the effort to introduce Western political institutions after the French Revolution of 1848 had failed because relations between the governing oligarchy and the peasantry were still characterized by a condition of servitude. Dobrogeanu-Gherea stressed that neoserfdom as it existed in Romania was an absurd condition in which society was marked by a profound gap that separated the legal country from the real country, as laws and administration were not really implemented. He argued that the large farms, or the latifundia of the oligarchy, should be broken up, and that a genuinely free peasantry should be created through property reform and such political reforms as universal suffrage. He also believed that Romania, which had been kept backward and exploited by the more advanced, Western industrialized countries, should go through the historical stage of liberal-bourgeois industrial development before it could realize the goal of becoming a socialist state.

Robert Weiner

Further reading

Dobrogeanu-Gherea, Constantin. *Neoiobăgia.* Bucharest, 1977.
Fischer-Galati, Stephen. *Twentieth Century Rumania.* New York, 1991.
Hitchins, Keith. *Rumania: 1866–1947.* Oxford, 1994.
Ionescu, Ghita. *Communism in Rumania.* Westport, Connecticut, 1976.
Roberts, Henry L. *Rumania.* New Haven, Connecticut, 1951.
Shafir, Michael. *Romania.* Boulder, Colorado, 1985.

See also Marxism; Peasants

Dobrovský, Josef (1753–1829)

Czech scholar, philologist, and historian, founder of modern Slavic studies, and dominant figure in the first generation of the Czech national renascence. Dobrovský spent nearly all of his career as a private tutor and scholar, supported by

D various members of the Bohemian nobility. He published actively in a wide variety of disciplines between 1778 and the 1820s. From first to last, Dobrovský's work was permeated with the Enlightenment's rationalism and criticism.

His earliest publications commented critically on various aspects of contemporary intellectual life in Bohemia and Moravia, but his major works involved history, literary history, and philology. He subjected many traditional sources for Bohemian history to critical methodology, attacking hearsay and fable. He applied a similar approach in his history of the Czech language (1792, 1818), where he sketched the interpretation of Czech history later developed by František Palacký (1798–1876). Dobrovský also pioneered comparative Slavic studies, his crowning achievement a grammar of Old Church Slavonic published in 1822.

Dobrovský wrote in Latin or German but contributed greatly to the Czech linguistic revival through grammatical studies and especially his Czech-German dictionary (1821). In 1791, before Leopold II (1747–92), Dobrovský described the Slavs as the strongest pillar of the monarchy and called for Leopold to support the development and public use of the Czech language. Nevertheless, Dobrovský's enlightened outlook differed from the romanticism of younger Czech patriots. When he declared as fakes the manuscripts containing fragments of early medieval Czech epic verse "discovered" in 1817 at Dvůr Králové and Zelená Hora, it cost him their admiration. Later generations recognized his tremendous contribution to the Czech national renascence.

Hugh Agnew

Further reading

Brandl, Vincenc. *Život Josefa Dobrovského*. Brno, 1883.

Československá akademie věd, Sekce jazyka a literatury. *Josef Dobrovský, 1753–1953: Sborník studii k dvoustému výročí narození*. Prague, 1953.

Machovec, Milan. *Josef Dobrovský: Studie s ukázkami z díly*. Prague, 1964.

Universita Karlova, Seminář pro slovanskou filologii. *Josef Dobrovský, 1753–1829: Sborník stati k stému výroči smrti Josefa Dobrovského*. Prague, 1929.

See also Czech Language; Manuscripts; Romanticism; Slavs

Dobrudja

Historical-geographic region in the northeast part of the Balkan Peninsula. In ancient times Dobrudja (Dobruzha) was called Scythia Minor. The current name is derived from the Turkish pronunciation of the Slavic *Dobrotitsa* (see below). To the north and northeast it borders the Danube River, to the east the Black Sea, and to the south the Batova River. Its southwest border is not delimited. North Dobrudja is located in Romania and South Dobrudja is in Bulgaria.

In the 1330s the relaxation of central power in the Bulgarian kingdom turned Dobrudja into a separate feudal principality under the leadership of the *boiar* Balik (n.d.), and later his brother Dobrotitsa (n.d.), after whom the region was named. In 1395 it was taken over by the Ottoman Empire.

The Congress of Berlin in 1878 gave southern Dobrudja to Bulgaria, while its northern part was bequeathed to Romania. After the Balkan Wars (1912–13), Romania annexed the town of Silistra and the southern part of Dobrudja. Although Bulgarian troops retook the region during World War I, the Treaty of Neuilly (1919) restored the region to Romania. South Dobrudja was returned to Bulgaria in 1940. The current Bulgarian-Romanian boundary was confirmed with a bilateral treaty in 1947.

Dobrudja has a hilly relief. Near the Black Sea it is low and marshy, with many lakes; karst relief is typical. The region has a temperate continental climate. The average January temperature is 29° F (–1.8° C) and the average July temperature is 70° F (21° C). The average annual precipitation is 19–26 inches (48.3–66 cm). Currently most of Dobrudja is agricultural land; wheat, maize, industrial and forage crops, vegetables, melons, grapes, and fruits are grown. Irrigation systems have been built using water from the Danube and other rivers and lakes. Stockbreeding is also developed. Typical industries are machine building, electronics, timber processing, and textiles.

Boian Koulov

Further reading

Bulgarian Academy of Sciences. *Dobruja: Etnografski, Floklorni i Ezikovi Prouchvaniya*. Sofia, 1974.

———. *Entsiklopedia Bulgaria,* vol. 2. Sofia, 1981.

See also Balkan Wars; Congress of Berlin; Neuilly, Treaty of; Transdanubia; Vienna Awards

Dohnányi, Ernő (1877–1960)

Hungarian pianist, composer, and conductor. The first major talent to choose Budapest's Liszt Academy for his studies, Dohnányi's world career of six decades as a pianist began in London in 1898 with a single performance of Beethoven's Fourth Piano Concerto. Brahms's (1833–97) unreserved admiration for his Piano Quintet, op.1, established his reputation as the leading Hungarian composer of the day. While he rarely broke new ground, his sizable output shows unfailing mastery and invention.

Dohnányi's formal teaching career began in Berlin, continued in Budapest (from 1934 serving as director of the Liszt Academy), and ended at Florida State University. He became the principal architect of Hungary's musical culture. As chief conductor of Hungary's Philharmonic Society for twenty-five years (interrupted to direct the New York State Symphony for one season), as Hungarian Radio's first music director, and as the idol of concert audiences, Dohnányi used his position to forge a lasting bond between the great masters and the Hungarian public. He was also the first to champion the music of his countrymen Béla Bartók (1881–1945) and Zoltán Kodály (1882–1967). Hungarian musicians for half a century have learned to hear and feel music by absorbing his influence.

During World War II, he largely succeeded in shielding Hungarian musical life from Nazi influence. When he found he was no longer able to do so, he resigned his posts and, to escape Soviet occupation, left Hungary. For many years, his existence was completely ignored there. A reevaluation of his legacy is currently underway.

Balint Vazsonyi

Further reading

Sadie, Stanley. *The New Grove Dictionary of Music and Musicians.* London, 1980.

Vázsonyi, Balint. *Dohnányi Ernő.* Budapest, 1971.

See also Béla Bartók; Zoltán Kodály; Music

Dondukov-Korsakov, Prince Aleksandur Mihailovich (1820–93)

Russian military leader and supervisor of the establishment of the first Bulgarian government. Dondukov-Korsakov had a generally undistinguished career in the Russian army. He took command of Russia's Thirteenth Army at the start of the Russo-Turkish War of 1877–78. After the signing of the Treaty of San Stefano, he was named the commissioner in Bulgaria and headed the ruling council. The first Bulgarian government was established under his supervision; his duties included drafting a constitution that instituted a strong executive. He also oversaw the creation of a national Bulgarian army before relinquishing his duties on the ascension to the throne of Prince Alexander of Battenberg (1857–93).

Mari A. Firkatian

Further reading

Entsiklopediia Búlgariia, vol. 2. Sofia, 1981.

See also Alexander of Battenberg; Russo-Turkish War of 1877–78; San Stefano, Treaty of

Drava River

Important tributary of the Danube. This eastward-flowing river has its source in the Carnic Alps on the eastern boundary of Italy and Austria. After flowing through the Klagenfurt basin, it proceeds through eastern Slovenia and Slavonia (eastern Croatia) to join the Danube near Osijek.

The steep gradients of the upper and middle Drava, with their great potential for hydroelectric power development, contrast with the broader profile and landscape of the lower portions of the stream. The valley and lowlands of the lower Drava are part of the southwestern portion of the Pannonian (Hungarian) Plain, one of the most fertile and productive cereal-growing areas of southeastern Europe. As the gradient becomes extremely gentle, a wide floodplain develops, with meanders and ox-bow lakes, bordered by alluvial terraces rising to the level plains known as the Posavina and Podravina. Near its confluence with the Danube is an area of marsh and swamp (the Osijek Marshes).

The valley of the Drava, together with that of the Sava River, connects with the Danube and the Vardar-Morava corridor to form a natural route between Central Europe and the Mediterranean. After World War I, Austria retained the upper portion of the Drava with its small Slovene minority, while the middle portion became part of the international boundary between Hungary and Yugoslavia.

Albert M. Tosches

D

Further reading

Hoffman, George W. *Regional Development Strategy in Southeast Europe.* New York, 1972.

Nyrop, Richard F., ed. *Yugoslavia: A Country Study,* 2d ed. Washington, D.C., 1982.

Pounds, Norman J.G. *Eastern Europe.* Chicago, 1969.

Drucki-Lubecki, Prince Franciszek Ksawery (1778–1846)

Polish statesman and minister of the treasury. Prince Drucki-Lubecki came from a wealthy and powerful Polish family living in what is now Belarus. Reflecting his family's pro-Russian orientation, Lubecki joined the corps of cadets at St. Petersburg and served in General Alexander Suvorov's (1729–1800) Russian army that fought Napoléon (1769–1821) in Italy and Switzerland.

In 1813 Lubecki joined the Provisional Supreme Council of the Russian-occupied Duchy of Warsaw. After the Kingdom of Poland was established in 1815, Lubecki successfully settled Poland's debt with Prussia and Austria. In 1821 Alexander I (1777–1825) named him Poland's minister of the treasury. Poland's finances were so chaotic at that time that Alexander hinted at terminating the kingdom's independence and merging it with Russia. Under Lubecki's guidance, Polish finances recovered and the threat to Poland's continued existence passed.

As treasury minister, Lubecki inaugurated an ambitious plan for economic growth that placed heavy emphasis on industrialization. He developed new industry for Poland, especially mines, foundries, and textile factories at Łódź. He also negotiated a tariff agreement that opened the Russian Empire to Polish goods, and established a Land Credit Society and the Bank of Poland.

Lubecki, a political conservative, disapproved of the 1830 November Uprising against the Russians. Shortly after its outbreak, he went to St. Petersburg to seek a negotiated settlement with Nicholas I (1796–1855). When the tsar rejected his overtures, Lubecki elected to remain at St. Petersburg and was appointed to the Russian State Council in 1832, where he concentrated on Russian legal and financial matters until his death.

Frank W. Thackeray

Further reading

Ajzen, Mieczysław. *Polityka Gospodarcza Lubeckiego, 1821–1830.* Warsaw, 1932.

Smolka, Stanisław. *Polityka Lubeckiego przed Powstaniem Listopadowym,* 2 vols, 2d ed. Warsaw, 1984.

Wandycz, Piotr S. *The Lands of Partitioned Poland, 1795–1918.* Seattle, Washington, 1974.

See also Alexander I; Duchy of Warsaw; Industrialization; Nicholas I; November Uprising; Polish Congress Kingdom

Dual Alliance

Alliance of 1879 between Germany and Austria-Hungary. Originally, the Austro-German alliance was a defensive alliance directed against Russia in which each power promised the other active support if attacked by Russia. By these terms, Germany was not required to support Austria-Hungary if the German government viewed the Austrians as aggressors in a Russian-Austrian conflict. Because Austria-Hungary could not fight Russia without German support, the alliance allowed Germany to deter any reckless Austro-Hungarian moves against Russia. Together with the Reinsurance Treaty, the Dual Alliance allowed the German chancellor, Otto von Bismarck (1815–88), to restrain both Austria-Hungary and Russia, allowing Germany to maintain good political relations with both empires.

After 1906, Germany's political relations soured with all other important European powers except Austria-Hungary. In the following few years the original, purely defensive nature of the Dual Alliance was lost. In the crisis that followed Austro-Hungarian annexation of Bosnia in 1908, Germany promised full military support for Austria against Russia not only in the annexation of Bosnia by Austria-Hungary but also in Austrian contingency plans for an attack on Serbia. These German promises of support for expansionist and aggressive Austrian actions transformed what had been originally a defensive alliance into an offensive one. As a result, Germany lost its ability to restrain Austria in the Balkans. That, in turn, increased the likelihood of Austrian-Russian confrontation. These developments contributed greatly to the disastrous outbreak of war in July 1914.

Robert Mark Spaulding

Further reading

Bridge, F.R. *The Great Powers and the European States System, 1815–1914.* New York, 1980.

———. *The Habsburg Monarchy among the Great Powers, 1815–1918.* New York, 1990.

Craig, Gordon. *The Politics of the Prussian Army, 1660–1945.* Oxford, 1955.

See also Otto von Bismarck; Reinsurance Treaty

Dualism

The fragile balance between the two halves of the Dual Monarchy (Austria-Hungary) created by the *Ausgleich* (Compromise) of 1867. The *Ausgleich* gave Hungary more independence than it had enjoyed since the fifteenth century; nevertheless, disputes over the its economic and military provisions dominated Hungarian political life through the end of the monarchy. After 1867, the government of Gyula Andrássy (1823–90) reincorporated Transylvania, negotiated a "mini-compromise" with Croatia (the *Nagodba,* which granted political autonomy and language rights to Croatians), and passed liberal education and nationality laws. At the same time, Hungary's adamant resistance to "Trialism" undermined Vienna's attempts to grant equal status to Bohemia. In 1875 Kálmán Tisza (1803–1902) brought a period of political uncertainty to an end by creating the Liberal Party. Tisza supported the *Ausgleich,* renewing it twice, and his policy of *quieta non movere* (let sleeping dogs lie), together with rigged elections, political patronage, and oppression of nationalities, brought domestic stability. After Tisza's fall from power in 1890, a succession of short-lived Liberal governments stood by the *Ausgleich,* but they faced a growing opposition, especially from the Independence Party. The opposition was variegated but united in 1903 against the government's defense bill. While outwardly objecting to the exclusive use of German as the language of command in the common army, in reality the opposition was challenging the monarch's absolute control of the army, a pillar of the *Ausgleich.* Their obstructionism brought down the government and sparked a political crisis. In January 1905 the Liberals lost their parliamentary majority for the first time in thirty years, but Franz Joseph (1830–1916) let the opposition form a government only after they had secretly promised not to press for revision of the *Ausgleich.* With its hands tied, the opposition's "coalition government" failed miserably. It won minimal concessions from Vienna concerning the common army, customs and tariffs, and the National Bank. István

Tisza (1861–1918), Kálmán's son, reorganized the Liberals as the Party of National Work, and they won a large majority in the 1910 elections. As prime minister, Tisza rejected calls for wider suffrage but firmly supported the Compromise and guided Hungary through World War I.

Robert Nemes

Further reading

Gerő, András. *Modern Hungarian Society in the Making: The Unfinished Experience.* Budapest, 1995.

Jászi, Oskár. *The Dissolution of the Habsburg Monarchy.* Chicago, 1961.

Vermes, Gábor. *István Tisza: The Liberal Vision and Conservative Statecraft of a Magyar Nationalist.* New York, 1985.

See also Gyula Andrássy, Sr.; *Ausgleich;* Franz Joseph; *Nagodba;* Nationality Law of 1868; István Tisza; Kálmán Tisza; Trialism

Dual Monarchy

The Austro-Hungarian Empire created by the *Ausgleich* (Compromise) of 1867. The major effects of the creation of the Dual Monarchy were seen in the Hungarian half of the empire, which witnessed rapid population growth, great economic development and a fin-de-siècle cultural flowering, but sharp national and social conflicts as well. The *Ausgleich* gave Hungary its own parliamentary government and a free hand in its internal affairs. Hungary quickly created an independent judiciary and reformed its administration, but the political system remained archaic and only one out of four adult males could vote in 1914. Hungary's large Jewish population was emancipated in 1867 and church-state relations took a decisive turn with the introduction of civil marriage in the 1890s. József Eötvös's (1813–71) elementary education act of 1868 made schooling compulsory, and by 1914 the illiteracy rate had fallen to 31 percent.

The population of Hungary grew from 15.5 million in 1867 to 21 million in 1914. Hungary was foremost an agricultural country, and in 1910 agriculture still accounted for two-thirds of national income. Some nine thousand large landowners, including aristocrats with vast estates, dominated the rural economy and politics. They owed their prosperity to the secure Austrian market, a growing railroad network, and modern

D farming methods. While some medium and small landowners flourished, the peasantry was increasingly landless or clinging to small plots. Peasants made up 99 percent of all landowners yet owned only 56 percent of arable land. During this period, almost 1.5 million peasants emigrated, most of them to the United States.

The other path for the rural poor led to the city, and by 1910 almost one-third of the population lived in cities with more than ten thousand inhabitants. Urbanization reflected the rapid growth of industry and commerce, which was helped by state subsidies, foreign and domestic capital, and the Austrian market. No city could compare with Budapest, whose population exploded from 250,000 in 1867 to 900,000 in 1913. Budapest had only 5 percent of the country's population but two-thirds of its heavy industry. Workers first attempted to organize themselves in the 1870s; a lasting organization came only in 1890 with the founding of the Hungarian Social Democratic Party. The Socialists never achieved their goal of universal suffrage, although they showed increased muscle after 1900 in strikes and demonstrations. Budapest was also the center of government and culture. The monumental new parliament building (built 1885–1904) stood as a symbol of the city's political importance, while social reforms under Mayor István Bárczy (1866–1943) led to improved housing and health services. Across the country, universities, colleges, theaters, museums, and libraries contributed to the development of cultural life. This was also a period of great national pride, as seen in the grandiose Millennial Celebration of 1896.

Robert Nemes

Further reading

Berend, Iván and György Ránki. *Hungary: A Celebration of Economic Development.* New York, 1974.

Hoensch, Jörg K. *A History of Modern Hungary, 1867–1986.* London, 1986.

Janos, Andrew. *The Politics of Backwardness in Hungary, 1825–1945.* Princeton, New Jersey, 1982.

Lukacs, John. *Budapest 1900: A Historical Portrait of a City and Its Culture.* New York, 1988.

See also Agriculture; *Ausgleich;* Budapest; Dualism; Emigration; József Eötvös; Hungarian Émigrés; Magyarization; Peasants

Dubček, Alexander (1921–92)

First secretary of the Communist Party of Czechoslovakia (KSČ) during the Prague Spring and its aftermath, (1968–69). Dubček was born in Uhrovec, Slovakia, shortly after his parents returned from years in the United States. Before he was four, they took him to the Soviet Union, where they lived and worked until 1938. He returned to Slovakia after the Munich crisis (in which Czechoslovakia was forced to cede the Sudetenland to Nazi Germany). During World War II, Dubček worked in the armaments complex in Dubnica, Slovakia. In 1944 he fought in the Slovak national uprising against the Germans and was twice wounded.

In 1947 Dubček became a professional KSČ worker, and in 1955 he was sent to study in Moscow. After his return in 1957, his party career developed rapidly, and he became a Politburo member in 1962. In the mid-1960s Dubček adopted reformist views, and in January 1968 he took over as the KSČ first secretary. He played a key role in the Prague Spring, the short-lived period of reform in 1968. After the Soviet-led Warsaw Pact invasion in August 1968, he was kidnapped and sent to Moscow, where he reluctantly signed an act of surrender called the Moscow Protocol; he was then reinstalled. After eight months of inconsistent resistance to Soviet pressures to abrogate previous reforms, Dubček was removed from office; in 1970 he was expelled from the KSČ. He then held manual jobs and, after 1981, lived in retirement. He took no part in the dissident movement. After the fall of communism, he made a political comeback, and until June 1992, served as president of the National Assembly. He died in November 1992, several weeks after a car accident.

Jiří Hochman

Further reading

Dubček, Alexander. *Hope Dies Last: The Autobiography of Alexander Dubček.* New York, 1993.

Shawcross, William. *Dubček.* New York, 1970.

Tigrid, Pavel. *Le Printemps de Prague.* Paris, 1968.

See also Brezhnev Doctrine; Communist Party of Czechoslovakia; Prague Spring; Warsaw Pact

Dubrovnik

Picturesque medieval walled city on the southern Dalmatian coast of Croatia. The community of

Ragusa was founded on an offshore limestone island in the seventh century by refugees from the nearby Roman colony of Epidaurus after its sacking by Avars and Slavs. In time, a Slavic-speaking community of Dubrovnik developed in the wooded area (*dubrava*) across the coastal marshland from Latin-speaking Ragusa. The two communities were united in the thirteenth century. The intervening marshland was drained and today is the site of Dubrovnik's main street, Stradun.

Dubrovnik's encircling walls were begun in the seventh century and completed in their present form in the sixteenth. They are more than 6,300 feet (1,910 m) long and in places stand more than 80 feet (24 m) high. They are 5–16 feet (1.5–5 m) wide.

The medieval city-state flourished as a center of trade and culture. Dubrovnik (Ragusan) ships calling on London gave rise to the English term "argosy." Merchants of the Dubrovnik Republic established an accord with the Ottoman sultan giving them overland trading access to Bosnia, Macedonia, Serbia, and even Bulgaria. During this time, however, the city faced constant attempts at domination by Venice.

Dubrovnik's decline followed a severe earthquake in 1667 that killed 20 percent of its population and destroyed most of its structures. The 1815 Congress of Vienna made it part of the Austrian Empire. In 1918 Dubrovnik entered the Kingdom of Serbs, Croats, and Slovenes (Yugoslavia).

The city became a major Mediterranean tourism center during the twentieth century, annually hosting more than seven hundred thousand foreign visitors before severe damage by Yugoslav naval and artillery bombardment in 1991 during the conflicts following the breakup of Yugoslavia.

Thomas M. Poulsen

Further reading

Carter, F.W. *Dubrovnik (Ragusa): A Classic City-State.* London, 1972.

Lijepa naša Hrvatska. ed. by Boris Zdunić. Zagreb, 1991.

Duchy of Warsaw (1807–15)

Rump Polish state established by Napoléon (1769–1821) as part of the Treaty of Tilsit in 1807, which reflected the French emperor's desire to have a buffer state between Prussia and Russia. The duchy comprised lands taken by Prussia during the partitions (excepting the cities of Gdańsk and Bia-łystok), totaling 36,988 square miles (102,744 sq km) with a population of 2.5 million. Its borders did not correspond to those of any past Polish state. The duchy was nominally ruled by the king of Saxony, Frederick August (1750–1827) but was actually run on the basis of a French-inspired centralized constitution dictated by Napoléon. After Napoléon's defeat, the duchy was formally liquidated at the Congress of Vienna (1814–15).

Variously viewed as a gift of Napoléon to the Poles for their loyal support, or as a cynical power play on the part of the emperor, the duchy has a special place in the political history of Poland in the nineteenth century. Never truly independent or sovereign, it nevertheless provided Poles with the hope that one day their state would be restored. Polish was the language of administration, troops wore Polish uniforms, and traditional Polish titles and coats-of-arms were in use. The constitution established a bicameral parliament and an independent judiciary. Opportunities to serve the state abounded and provided many Poles with valuable practical administrative experience. In particular, the landless Polish nobility came to play increasingly important roles in the growing bureaucracy and intelligentsia. In short, this period witnessed the initiation of a number of the processes of modernization in Polish society that would continue to unfold long after the duchy was gone.

At the same time, the state was beset by virtually insurmountable economic and social difficulties from the outset. Forced to participate in Napoléon's unsuccessful Continental System, the French-dominated trading system, the economy could not rely on exports to stimulate growth. Although serfdom was ended, the state failed to address adequately the issue of peasant rights to land. Costs of administration were extremely high, and Napoléon's continued need for troops further depleted the meager financial and physical resources available. Furthermore, Napoléon saddled the state with the so-called Bayonne sums—an attempt at paying off mortgages owed to the former partitioning power Prussia. Napoléon assumed the debt as a spoil of war and set a short, four-year term for repayment. As the monies were irrecoverable owing to depressed economic conditions and the ravages of war, the end result was that the duchy soon fell behind in its payments to France.

One point on which all analysts agree is that the army of the duchy was an effectively run institution

D and, as a result, played an important role in the state. Under Prince Józef Poniatowski (1763–1813), the duchy provided the emperor with a sizable army in the 1809 campaign against Austria, which brought further territorial acquisitions. In 1812 the duchy raised one hundred thousand troops for the invasion of Russia, and Polish units played an important role in covering the flanks of the remnants of the Grande Armée in its disastrous retreat from Moscow. Poniatowski served with distinction to his death at the battle of Leipzig in 1813.

The legacy of the Duchy of Warsaw is twofold. One aspect lies in the main political debate in Polish society during the nineteenth century: how best could a resurrected Poland be achieved. Many patriotic Poles strove for an independent state by looking abroad for a "man of action," or an outside power, as the only possible source for a solution to their predicament. For them, Napoléon was that man, and the Duchy of Warsaw represented a first step in a new chapter in Polish history. There was also an opposite view. As early as 1796, Polish patriot Tadeusz Kościuszko (1746–1817) recognized that Napoléon's policies were neither designed to help the Poles nor likely to do so. In his pamphlet "Can the Poles Win Their Independence?" Kościuszko argued that only by relying on inner strength and resources—and not by looking abroad—would Poland find redemption.

The second aspect of the duchy's legacy is the important role played by the state in strengthening Polish national consciousness. The existence of statehood, however, circumscribed, provided Poles with concrete experience in running a modern state—something they lacked under the partitioning powers. In addition, in the pantheon of military heroes, songs, and traditions, the duchy offered a wealth of cultural material for the important processes of the creation of national consciousness so typical for nineteenth-century Europe.

Peter Wozniak

Further reading

Davies, Norman. *God's Playground: A History of Poland,* 2 vols. New York, 1984.
Gieysztor, Aleksander. *History of Poland.* Warsaw, 1979.
Wandycz, Piotr. *The Lands of Partitioned Poland.* Seattle, Washington, 1974.

See also Congress of Vienna; Tadeusz Kościuszko; Napoléon

Duma

The elected legislative assembly established in tsarist Russia after the humiliating defeat in the Russo-Japanese War (1904–05) and the ensuing 1905 revolution. First established in August 1905 with merely consultative powers, the Duma's mandate was extended by the October Manifesto, which granted it legislative powers. Although liberals hoped this would mean the beginning of true parliamentary government in Russia, the tsar intended the Duma to be a compliant, conservative assembly. With representation based on increasingly restricted suffrage, the Duma actually had only limited powers. Its main purpose was to discuss and approve proposals that had originated in government ministries. Also, the Duma could question ministers, but the latter were not obliged to respond and were in no way responsible to the assembly. In all, four Dumas sat between 1906 and 1917. The fourth Duma rose to unexpected political prominence during 1915 when it began to question government handling of the war effort, but the tightly controlled electoral system insured that the Duma would continue to favor the landed nobility. In March 1917 the Duma selected a Provisional Government and accepted Nicholas II's (1868–1918) abdication.

In Russian Poland, socialist parties boycotted the elections to the first Duma. As a result, the majority of the Polish delegates to the Duma came from the National Democratic Party, whose platform included municipal self-government and Polonization of the administration and school system. The "Endeks," as members of the party were known, were led by Roman Dmowski (1864–1939) and believed that Poles should look to Russia for support against the perceived German menace to Polish society. The history of Polish participation in the Dumas is largely the history of the rise of the National Democratic Party in the Kingdom of Poland. In terms of actual political concessions from the government, however, the National Democrats made little progress.

The Polish representatives during the first Duma planned to form a club, much as Galician Poles had done to great effect in the Viennese Reichsrat (parliament). They were unsuccessful in this endeavor and obtained only minor administrative concessions for their constituents. The second Duma at first proved to be more promising for the Poles. The National Democrats succeeded in forming a Polish Circle and submitted a proposal for autonomy in April 1907, which, however, brought no results. The second Duma was dissolved and the government amended suffrage laws to weaken non-Russian parties. Dmowski and the National Democrats softened their demands in the third Duma, but once again made no concrete gains. By the time of the fourth Duma (1912), Dmowski's politics of conciliation toward the regime had bankrupted his position sufficiently to lead to his electoral defeat in the Warsaw district.

Peter Wozniak

Further reading

Chmielewski, E. *The Polish Question in the Russian State Duma.* Knoxville, Tennessee, 1970.
Rogger, Hans. *Russia in the Age of Modernisation and Revolution 1881–1917.* London, 1983.

See also Roman Dmowski

Dunaújváros

Hungarian industrial city, representative of the Communist period. Dunaújváros is located 41 miles (67 km) south of Budapest on the Danube River. Like many locations in Eastern Europe, the city is a "new industrial town," the result of government planning schemes adopted in the immediate post–World War II period to increase overall industrial capacity (especially iron and steel) in the country and disperse activity away from Budapest. Although not the first choice of planners, the village of Dunapentele, which had a population of only 3,949, was selected in 1949 as the site for construction of an integrated iron and steel plant and associated town. Declared a town in 1951, the name was changed initially to Sztalinváros (Stalin Town) but was changed again in 1961 to Dunaújváros (Danube New Town).

From the 1950s until the late 1980s, the Dunai Vasmű (Danube Ironworks) operated as a vertically integrated open-hearth plant that received iron ore from the USSR and coal from southern Hungary. The plant produced significant amounts of crude iron, steel, and rolled sheet. In addition, Dunaújváros has a paper mill, textile plant, shoe factory, and dairy.

The city incorporates socialist planning concepts in its design. Rectangular in shape, the residential areas of the city are separated from the industrial zone by a mile-wide greenbelt. From 1965 to 1980, eleven thousand dwellings were built, most of them eleven-story "panel"-type construction utilizing the neighborhood unit concept of planning. Population totals rose to 26,918 in 1960, 45,129 in 1970, 60,736 in 1980, but dropped slightly to 59,028 in 1990.

Darrick Danta

Further reading

Ádám, László and Boros Ferenc, eds. *Dunaújváros Földrajza.* Budapest, 1979.
Compton, Paul A. "The New Socialist Town of Dunaujvaros." *Geography,* 50, no. 3 (1965): 288–91.
Danta, Darrick, "Hungarian Urbanization and Socialist Ideology." *Urban Geography* 8, no. 1 (1987): 1–13.

See also Economic Development in Hungary; Industrialization

Dvořák, Antonín (1841–1904)

Czech composer of international renown who instilled his program and instrumental music with Bohemian and Moravian folk influences (*Slavonic Dances*). Dvořák studied violin and piano as a youth and entered the Prague Organ School in 1857. He worked in Prague as a musician, mostly playing viola in the National Theater Orchestra (1862–71). He had an early interest in composing opera, and his eleven works in this genre—*Rusalka* (1900) is his best known—concentrate on Slavic folklore and history. He married Anna Čermaková (1854–1931) in 1873 and soon afterward became the organist at St. Adalbert's Church in Prague. Dvořák won an Austrian State Scholarship in 1875–78. Johannes Brahms (1833–97), a member of the jury, recommended his work for publication. Dvořák was honored with a professorship at the Prague Conservatory in 1891 and later received honorary doctoral degrees from Charles University and Cambridge University.

In June 1891 Dvořák was invited to New York City to serve as artistic director of the National Conservatory of Music. During his American period (September 1892 to April 1895), Dvořák developed an interest in American Indian and African American music. There, in 1893 he wrote the symphony for which he is most known, *From the New World.* In 1895 Dvořák returned to Bohemia, and after November taught at the Prague Conservatory and resumed his creative work.

E Dvořák's well-crafted music is classical in style with the warmth of romantic melodic inventiveness. Many of his works, including the last five symphonies, the Cello Concerto, and the *Stabat Mater* have become staples of the repertory.

William Smialek

Further reading
Burghauser, Jarmil. *Antonín Dvořák: Thematický Katalog.* Prague, 1960.
Chapham, John. *Dvořák.* New York, 1979.
Šourek, Otakar. *Antonín Dvořák.* Prague, 1956.

See also Music

Dzierzynski, Feliks Edmundovich (1877–1926)

Prominent Bolshevik and founder of the Soviet secret police, leading Polish revolutionary, and founder of the Social Democratic Party of the Polish Kingdom and Lithuania (SDKPiL). Dzierzynski was born in the Wilno Province of Russian Poland, a member of the petty Polish nobility. He joined the Lithuanian Social Democratic Party in Wilno in 1895 and was arrested and exiled to Siberia for revolutionary activities in 1897. He escaped in 1899, traveling to Warsaw, where in 1900 he helped form the SDKPiL from Rosa Luxemburg's (1870–1919) Social Democratic Party of the Kingdom of Poland and several Lithuanian socialist organizations. During the 1905 revolution, which erupted after Russia's disastrous participation in the Russo-Japanese War, Dzierzynski led antiwar demonstrations in Warsaw and actively sought to incite revolution in Poland.

An advocate for close cooperation of the SDKPiL with the Russian Social Democrats, Dzierzynski was elected a member of the Bolshevik Central Committee in 1917. He played a major role in the Bolshevik coup in October 1917 and was later assigned the task of heading the All-Russian Extraordinary Commission for Combatting Counter-Revolution and Sabotage (Cheka). In March 1919 he was appointed people's commissar of internal affairs, and in April 1921 he became people's commissar for transport.

Dzierzynski disagreed with V.I. Lenin (1870–1924) and Bolshevik policy during the Polish-Soviet War. He did not believe a social revolution was imminent in Poland. Nevertheless, Dzierzynski was given a command in the Soviet forces on the southwest front and was included in a Provisional Revolutionary Committee for Poland established in July 1920. In January 1924 Dzierzynski was named chairman of the Supreme National Economic Council and in June of that year became a candidate member of the Politburo. Dzierzynski died of a heart attack in July 1926.

Andrew Kier Wise

Further reading
Blobaum, Robert. *Feliks Dzierzynski and the SDKPiL: A Study of the Origins of Polish Communism.* Boulder, Colorado, 1984.
Dzerzhinskii, F.E. *Biographia,* 3d ed. Moscow, 1987

See also Lenin; Rosa Luxemburg; Polish-Soviet War

E

East Prussia

Historic area of Prussia and Germany, lying on the Baltic Sea, now divided between Poland and Lithuania. This large region (population 2,331,000 in 1939) was under the control of the Teutonic Knights, Prussia, and then Germany from the thirteenth century until 1945. The collapse of the Third Reich and the subsequent Potsdam Agreement led to its division between Poland and the Soviet Union, in which the northern half became a detached portion of Russia—Kaliningrad Oblast. The Polish southern portion became Olsztyn Province in northeastern Poland.

In the thirteenth century the Poles invited the Teutonic Knights to occupy East Prussia to eliminate the constant threat of raids from the Prussi, a Baltic tribe who long inhabited the region and for whom Prussia is named. Thereafter, German settlement and Germanization also largely obliterated Baltic and Slavic ethnicity among the populace. The region became politically and economically dominated by a relatively small number of conservative landowners, the Junkers. Though for centuries at least tacitly ruled by Poland, from 1701 to 1945 the region was part of Prussia then Germany. East Prussia was the scene of heavy fighting between Russian and German imperial forces at the outset of World War I. Between 1919 and 1939 the area was detached from less-well-known West Prussia; the Polish Corridor and the free state of Danzig (Gdańsk) lay between East Prussia and the rest of Germany. Briefly reannexed to Germany during World War II, the region was overrun by Soviet forces in 1944–45 and most Germans fled, died, or were later expelled. The northern part of East Prussia that has become the Russian exclave of Kaliningrad Oblast was the only territory directly taken from prewar Germany and added to any part of the former Soviet Union. Beyond this symbolic value, the region has had strategic significance, particularly because of the shipyards, port, and naval base at Kaliningrad (Königsberg).

Most of East Prussia is heavily glaciated hill country. Its economy is dominated by primary-sector activities, though manufacturing, shipbuilding, and port activities are especially important at Kaliningrad.

William H. Berentsen

Further reading
Pounds, N.J.G. *Eastern Europe.* London, 1969.

See also Gdańsk; Polish Corridor; Potsdam Conference

Eastern Question

The international question centering on the disintegration of the Ottoman Empire from the mid-eighteenth century to the establishment of the Turkish Republic in 1923. The Eastern Question concerned three major problems: internal instability in the Ottoman Empire, the growth of nationalism, and territorial and strategic designs by the Great Powers on Ottoman lands. By 1700, the sultans were no longer effective rulers, which meant that social and economic instability grew. Anxious to exploit this condition and determined to expel the Ottomans from the European continent, Austria and Russia fought the Turks, with Russia imposing the decisive Treaty of Kuchuk Kainardji in 1774. The sultan lost the Crimea, opened the Black Sea to

Russian ships, and agreed to an ambiguous provision that Russia would interpret as granting it the right to speak on behalf of Orthodox Christians in the Ottoman Empire's European territories. In the French Revolution, the Ottoman Empire, at different times, found itself at war with Russia, Austria, Britain, and France. At the same time, the Serbs revolted (1804–15) and created an autonomous principality under Russian protectorship. Thus, by 1815, internal Ottoman weakness, the first stirrings of nationalism, and Great Power interference in Ottoman affairs had been joined and would play themselves out until the end of World War I.

The successful Greek revolution (1821–33) was achieved largely because the Great Powers defeated Ottoman forces. However, it brought into sharp focus the British-Russian rivalry over the closure of the Turkish Straits—Bosphorus and Dardanelles—to all naval ships. If implemented it would effectively confine Russia's fleet to the Black Sea, thereby protecting Britain's naval forces in the Mediterranean. The issue of the Straits was the center of numerous treaties and conferences—1833, 1841, 1849, 1856, 1870, 1878, 1881, 1908, 1914–15, and 1923. For example, in the 1833 Treaty of Unkiar Skelessi, the Porte, under Russian duress, agreed to the closure of the Straits to foreign ships, but not Russian. In 1841, following unrest in his domains, the sultan yielded sovereignty over the Straits and agreed to an international treaty that closed them to all naval ships, a provision that, however, was violated in 1849, 1854–56, 1878, and 1914.

The Straits issue was a symptom of the decline of the empire. The reforms introduced in the nineteenth century by the sultans, with the expectation that they would pacify their restless subjects, were instead interpreted as evidence of weakness. Thus, in the 1830s, Mohammed Ali (c. 1769–1849), the sultan's vassal in Egypt, led a revolt against Constantinople. Following its defeat in the Crimean War (1853–56) and finding itself diplomatically isolated and saddled with humiliating peace terms, Russia joined France in supporting the unification of the United Principalities (Romania) in 1857–61. A major Balkan crisis in 1875–78 led to the Congress of Berlin in 1878, which further dismembered the empire. Romania, Serbia, and Montenegro were recognized as independent. Bulgaria became an autonomous principality and independent in 1908. Britain gained Cyprus and in 1882 occupied Egypt. In 1908

Austria-Hungary annexed Bosnia-Hercegovina, which it had occupied since 1878. In 1913, following the two Balkan Wars (1912–13), Albania gained its independence and the Ottoman Empire was expelled from the European continent save Constantinople and its immediate hinterland. Thus, in 1914 there were six independent Balkan states—Albania, Bulgaria, Greece, Montenegro, Romania, and Serbia.

In the secret agreements of World War I, Britain, France, Italy, and Russia agreed to partition the Ottoman Empire, leaving the Turks only the northwest portion of the Anatolian Peninsula. At the end of the war, Kemal Atatürk (1881–1938) rallied the Turks, deposed the sultan, and united the entire Anatolian Peninsula, creating the modern Turkish Republic in 1923. The other Ottoman lands—Syria, Iraq, Kuwait, Lebanon, Palestine, and Jordan—were established as mandates by the League of Nations administered by Britain and France.

Charles Jelavich

Further reading

Anderson, M.S. *The Eastern Question 1774–1923.* London, 1966.

Goriainov, S.M. *Le Bosphore et les Dardanelles.* Paris, 1910.

Jelavich, Barbara. *The Ottoman Empire, the Great Powers and the Straits Question, 1870–1887.* Bloomington, Indiana, 1973.

Lewis, Bernard. *The Emergence of Modern Turkey.* Oxford, 1961.

Macfie, A.L. *The Eastern Question 1774–1923.* London, 1989.

See also Balkan Wars; Crimean War; Congress of Berlin; Danube Question; Great Powers; Greek Revolution; Kuchuk Kainardji, Treaty of; London Pact; Nationalism; Ottoman Empire; Paris, Treaty of; Porte; Russo-Turkish War of 1828–29; Russo-Turkish War of 1877–78; San Stefano, Treaty of; Turks; United Principalities

Eastern Rumelia

Autonomous administrative district in the territory of South Bulgaria created by the 1878 Treaty of Berlin. The name Eastern Rumelia comes from the Turkish *"Rumili,"* meaning land of the Romans (that is, Byzantines), to denote the former Ottoman lands in Europe. To the north, it borders Stara Planina's crest; to the east, the Black Sea; to the south, the Rhodope Mountains; and to the west, the Ihti-manska Sredna Gora Mountain. In 1878 Eastern Rumelia had a territory of 11,872 square miles (32,978 sq km) and a population of approximately one million people. Plovdiv was its capital city.

According to the Treaty of Berlin, Eastern Rumelia maintained administrative autonomy but remained under the political and military authority of the Ottoman sultan. The head of the district was to be a Christian governor general, appointed with the approval of the Great Powers. The sultan had the right to keep troops on the territory and to defend its borders. The Bulgarian population protested emphatically against the treaty. No Ottoman troops were allowed in the district, and the government was overtaken by Bulgarians. The de facto official language became Bulgarian. Internal order and external security were maintained by Bulgarian militia and gendarmerie.

On April 14, 1879, the European Commission for Eastern Rumelia (1878–79), appointed by the Great Powers, agreed on an Organic Statute, which served as the district's constitution. The statute guaranteed the political autonomy and parliamentary character of the district government. The sultan, however, retained various measures of control over Eastern Rumelia.

At the beginning of 1885, on the initiative of Zakhari Stoyanov (1850–89) and other revolutionaries, the Bulgarian Secret Central Revolutionary Committee was established. It planned and carried out the unification of Eastern Rumelia with the Principality of Bulgaria on September 6, 1885.

Boian Koulov

Further reading
Bulgarian Academy of Sciences. *Entsiklopedia Bulgaria,* vol. 3, Sofia, 1982.

See also Congress of Berlin; Great Powers; Plovdiv; Zakhari Stoyanov

Eckhardt, Tibor (1888–1972)
Hungarian lawyer, politician, and, after 1941, prominent figure of the Hungarian émigré community in the West. Eckhardt received his university training in Budapest, Berlin, and Paris, and began his career as a county official. In 1918–19, during the unsettled period following Austria-Hungary's loss in World War I, he sided with the opponents of Hungary's revolutionary governments and continued his involvement in rightist causes in the 1920s. In 1930 he joined the Independent Smallholders Party and became its leader two years later. In 1934–35 he was Hungary's delegate at the League of Nations. During the late 1930s, he became an advocate of a pro-British orientation in Hungarian foreign policy. He also came out in favor of Habsburg restoration and a federal union of Austria, Hungary, and Czechoslovakia. In the early spring of 1941 the government of Pál Teleki (1879–1941) sent him to the West to prepare the ground for the establishment of a government-in-exile should Hungary lose its independence. Following his arrival in the United States in August, Eckhardt launched the Movement for an Independent Hungary but failed to gain recognition from Allied governments. After the war, Eckhardt became a leading figure in the anti-Soviet Hungarian emigration. He headed the Hungarian National Council (a quasi government-in-exile) and was the Hungarian representative in the Council of Captive Nations, remaining in close contact with Otto Habsburg (1912–), the claimant to the Hungarian throne.

N.F. Dreisziger

Further reading
Borbándi, Gyula. *A magyar emigráció élatrajza, 1945–1985.* Munich, 1985.
Dreisziger, N.F. "Bridges to the West: The Horthy Regime's Reinsurance Policies in 1941." *War and Society* 7, no. 1 (May 1989): 1–23.

See also Hungarian Émigrés; Pál Teleki

Economic Development in Albania
With the death of the Albanian hero Skanderbeg (1405–68) and the effective end of Albanian resistance to Turkish domination, Albania was integrated into the Ottoman *vilayet* (province) system. For almost five centuries, the Albanian economy was characterized by the growth of a large landowning class (*beys*) and a mass of peasantry that worked the land at little more than subsistence level. Albanian historians have made much of the legacy of Ottoman rule, insisting that from an economic point of view the Ottomans left the country almost as they found it. Economic development, even by Ottoman standards, was marginal at best, and when independence was proclaimed in 1912, Albania found itself the most backward country in Europe.

E Independence, however, did not alleviate any of the country's pressing economic problems, as World War I postponed progress; only in the war's aftermath, with independence reconfirmed, could economic development be confronted at all. As a primarily agricultural country, with the peasantry making up some 90 percent of the population in the interwar period, the most pressing need was substantial land reform. While the landowners, who naturally rose to the top in the new state, remained reluctant to change the status quo, their dominance was challenged by progressives led by Bishop Fan Noli (1882–1965). By 1923, Noli's faction, which included substantial support from a vocal Albanian-American community, was emerging as a key force seeking radical change in the country. Seizing power by force in June 1924, Noli's government promulgated an ambitious agrarian reform plan that would have confiscated the large estates and redistributed their land to the largely landless peasantry, according to family size. Unable to find either domestic or foreign support for the program, however, Noli was pushed out of power by a resurgent Ahmed Zogu (1895–1961), who would declare himself king in 1928.

While the early 1920s witnessed a grassroots agenda to transform the country's agricultural system, there was also considerable interest in Albania's mineral resources, especially petroleum. A heated battle took place among American, British, French, and Italian concerns for a piece of what were considered to be large oil reserves. It was not until 1925 that exploitation of this resource got underway. Exploitation of Albania's other resources, such as copper, chromium, and iron-nickel, remained largely undeveloped throughout the entire interwar period.

Zogu's rule, first as president (1925–28) then as king (1928–39), witnessed Albania's slow but inexorable drift toward dependence on fascist Italy, which did lead to some, albeit limited, advances in the economy. However, Italian investment was primarily geared to serving military aims, so that by the onset of World War II, Albanian industry was virtually nonexistent and the vast majority of Albanians still worked on the land.

The Communist "liberation" of the country in November 1944 inaugurated what was the country's first real attempt at eliminating the vestiges of feudalism. The Communist leaders, especially the party's general secretary, Enver Hoxha (1908–85), were all too aware of the pitfalls of foreign dependence. Determined to transform the backward agrarian nation into an industrialized one that was also self-sufficient in agriculture, they immediately set about nationalizing the country's means of production and imposing Stalinist-style central planning. Priority was attached to the exploitation of the country's natural resources. As for the peasantry, Albania's first policy was "land to those that till it," while at the same time it implemented cooperatives. Not until the Second Five-Year Plan (1956–60) were real efforts to completely collectivize agriculture put in place. By 1960, the lion's share of agricultural production was completely socialized in the form of cooperative or collective farms, with the majority falling into the latter category.

Albania's somewhat impressive economic development during the Communist period (1944–91) was closely linked to external support—first Yugoslav (1944–48), then Soviet (1948–61), and finally Chinese (1961–78). In the aftermath of the break with China, Hoxha implemented a peculiar and economically devastating policy of self-reliance. Up until then, owing to foreign assistance, the Albanian economy had been able to meet the main needs of the country and had grown rapidly. Without foreign aid, the economy slid into a deep crisis.

The cumulative effect of nearly fifty years of Soviet-style command planning was not entirely negative, although the bad far outweighed the good. The country remained primarily rural (65 percent), but both agricultural and industrial production had increased substantially, and by 1971 the electrification of the entire country was completed. By 1992, with the election of the Albanian Democratic Party and the effective end of Communist control, Albania faced a myriad of economic problems. The legacy of self-reliance was disastrous, having almost completely removed Albania from the world economy. The country's new government was committed to a "shock therapy" transformation to a market-based economy and by 1995 seemed to show some already significant gains, especially in agricultural productivity as a result of the breakup of the collective farm system and a redivision of land to the peasants. Industry, especially heavy industry, remained stagnant, and foreign investment was slow in coming owing to conflicts in the Balkans and internal obstacles embodied in poorly drafted legislation, bureaucratic intransigence, and general confusion over property ownership.

Robert C. Austin

Further reading

Biberaj, Elez. *Albania—a Socialist Maverick.* Boulder, Colorado, 1990.

Grothusen, Klaus-Detlev, ed. *Albanien.* Sudosteuropa Handbuch, vol. 7. Göttingen, 1993, 289–451.

Prifti, Peter. *Socialist Albania since 1944.* Cambridge, Massachusetts, 1978.

Schnytzer, Adi. *Stalinist Economic Strategy in Practice—the Case of Albania.* Oxford, 1982.

See also Agriculture; Collectivization; Communist Party of Albania; Enver Hoxha; Industrialization; Fan S. Noli; Ahmed Zogu

Economic Develpment in Bulgaria

Historically, Bulgaria has provided agricultural products both to its own people and to its neighbors. The country chiefly grew grains, principally wheat, and in modern times corn (maize). In addition, the farms have produced barley, rye, oats, rape seed, sugar beets, fruits, and vegetables. Furthermore, the country's agricultural renown included the cash export crops tobacco and rose oil for the perfume industry. Bulgaria has also developed a successful viticulture industry. Livestock has concentrated on sheep, goats, swine, and poultry. Yogurt originated in the Bulgarian mountains made from the milk of sheep and goats as well as cows.

Under Ottoman rule, Muslim governors and landlords controlled large estates (*timars, chiftliks*), reducing the Christian population to a condition of servitude similar to Western European serfdom. In the nineteenth century most of these estates fell into private Muslim hands and produced wheat and corn. The reforms of the *tanzimat* period, the Turkish reform era that began in 1839, led to the creation of small and middle-size farms that the native Bulgarian population worked for their own profit. Some small handicraft industry developed based on agricultural products (such as wool and linen), wood carving, metalworking, and ceramics. A few successful Bulgarian farmers, particularly in rose oil production, appeared. In the town of Gabrova, the first textiles mill opened in the 1830s. As other Balkan nations—Serbia, Greece, Romania—gained their independence, the Bulgarian economy assumed a greater share of the Istanbul market.

After liberation from the Ottoman Empire in 1878, the Turkish landlords left and Bulgarian farmers absorbed their land. Much of it was in small, nonadjacent strips, however, which both rural (80 percent of the population) and urban Bulgarians bought up to grow compact products, particularly grapes and tobacco, as a fruitful cash supplement. Most Bulgarians remained small and middle farmers. There were relatively few subsistence or large farmers and no great estates at all.

Liberation brought opportunity in other areas, although agriculture continued as the mainstay of the kingdom's economy. The new government and its bureaucracy called for an ever increasing number of civil servants, and railroad development in the 1880s and the national public school system provided further opportunities for economic development. Industries related to agriculture prospered. Government contracts for the uniforms for military and state officials supported textile and clothing manufacturers. Sugar-beet refineries also established a lucrative production, and canning, food processing, candy manufacturing, and the like earned their share of the Bulgarian market. In addition to agriculture, forestry, mining, and quarrying emerged as staples of the Bulgarian economy. Local manufacturing increased: breweries, bakeries, dyers, soap manufactures, to name a few. In general, however, before World War II, heavy industry occupied only a small percentage of the Bulgarian scene.

With liberation, Bulgaria integrated into the modern European world. Within the first decade of independence, it witnessed rapid growth of railroad construction and other means of transportation and communication. Foreign capital and enterprises accomplished much of this, but Bulgarians were active as well. The sons of peasants opened insurance agencies and banks. Franchises and agents of international companies, especially those that handled mechanized farm equipment, surfaced. Import/export merchants, especially in tobacco, established profitable enterprises.

In the beginning of the twentieth century Bulgarian politicians debated the best way to develop the country's natural resources. Most agreed that Bulgaria should remain a breadbasket for the rest of Europe. The farmers' party (Bulgarian Agrarian National Union [BANU]—Bulgaria's dominant political organization) sought to maintain the character of the country by preserving small farms. They promoted the cooperative movement and in the 1920s implemented a modest land reform. Extensive reform was hardly necessary.

After the brutal coup d'état against the Agrarian government in 1923, the new rulers adopted policies that benefited large-scale farming and even more the manufacturers and merchants whose industry and trade were based on agriculture.

The Great Depression hit Bulgaria exceptionally hard, especially with the collapse of agricultural prices. The German policy of supporting the agricultural trade of southeastern European countries partially compensated for this. But Berlin bought these goods with credits valuable only in exchange for German products—a practice that helped bring Bulgaria into World War II on the Axis side. When the Allies defeated the German Reich, the Bulgarian economy completely collapsed. More important, defeat brought the Communist era, as it did in the rest of Eastern Europe.

Orthodox Marxist ideology emphasized the need for industry and an industrial proletariat. Therefore, Bulgaria's Communist governments devoted much of the country's resources to creating new factories, some of which (such as the great Kremokovtsi metallurgical works outside of Sofia) were notoriously unproductive. Indeed, in the 1950s, for the first time the industrial sector of the economy outstripped the agricultural.

However, the Communist leadership incorporated Bulgaria into the Council of Mutual Economic Assistance (CMEA, Comecon)—the Soviet bloc's economic alliance. At first, the Kremlin required Bulgaria, like other countries under Communist Party control, to sign trade agreements with the Soviet Union highly favorable to the latter. Moscow still regarded Bulgaria as an agricultural source, although it permitted Sofia to develop modest industrial targets. One of these, Balkankar, made industrial equipment for the Soviet bloc. Since Bulgaria's main economic task was to provide agricultural goods for export, grain, vegetables, fruit, industrial plants, livestock and poultry, rose oil, and tobacco, either raw or processed, remained the basis of Bulgarian exports.

In the 1970s Bulgaria increased its foreign trade. Bulgarplod products (vegetables and fruits) appeared in supermarkets throughout Europe. Sofia engaged in the lucrative trade of supplying the heavy-smoking Soviet Union with cigarettes, and tobacconists around the continent stocked the popular Stuardesa brand (which was very high in tars and nicotine). In the 1980s Bulgaria's high-quality yet inexpensive wines captured the public's enthusiasm in both Europe and America. Bulgarian feta cheese (made from sheep's milk) also had a significant market on both continents. Bulgaria exported services to Third World countries. For example, Bulgarian engineers traveled to the Middle East and North Africa working on construction projects. Furthermore, Western concerns such as Coca-Cola established plants inside the country, and Sofia actively sought tourists to enjoy its beaches and ski slopes.

The economic explosion reached a peak around 1980, but a series of bad harvests and over-borrowing caused a subsequent downturn. Disasters like the Kremokovtsi works and Bulgaria's poor nuclear plants drained the country. Furthermore, the poor quality of many Bulgarian manufactured goods dampened the previous success of Sofia's trade. In the mid-1980s the government introduced partial privatization by allowing individual entrepreneurs in small enterprises such as taxicabs and restaurants.

After the introduction of multiparty democracy in 1989, Socialist and Democratic governments alternated. Economic issues, particularly the question of privatization, vexed the entire society. The country's leaders debated whether to introduce the voucher system giving every citizen a portion of state property, to return property to former owners, or to employ some other formula. The new independent labor unions showed their muscle by organizing one strike after another. In some years the economy fared better than in others. Some Bulgarians were able to make fortunes, while others suffered deprivation. Those in previous Communist governments or high in the nomenklatura (Communist bureaucracy) who had stored away money and goods now had the advantage, and persons dependent on government pensions and subsidies were most seriously affected.

Frederick B. Chary

Further reading

Berov, Liuben. *An Outline of Bulgaria's Geography and Economy.* Sofia, 1984.

Bristow, John A. *The Bulgarian Economy in Transition.* Cheltenham, United Kingdom, 1996.

Bulgaria: Crisis and Transition to a Market Economy. Washington, D.C., 1991.

Bulgarian Economy of Today and Tomorrow. Sofia, 1992.

Lampe, John R. *The Bulgarian Economy in the Twentieth Century.* New York, 1986.

Lampe, John R. and Marvin R. Jackson. *Balkan Economic History, 1550–1950*. Bloomington, Indiana, 1982.

Miller, Jeffrey B. and Stefan Petranov. *Banking in the Bulgarian Economy*. Sofia, 1996.

Rule of Law and Transition to a Market Economy: Proceedings of the UniDem Seminar Organised in Sofia on 14–16 October 1993. Strasbourg, France, 1994.

See also Agriculture; Bulgarian Agrarian National Union; *Chiftlik;* Comecon; Communist Party of Bulgaria; Education; Great Depression; Industrialization; Peasants; Privatization; Railroads; *Tanzimat; Timar*

Economic Development in Czechoslovakia

Throughout its history, Czechoslovakia has had a strong mixed industrial economy, ranking among European leaders in both agricultural and industrial productivity. The foundations for this impressive performance were laid during the final thirty years of the Habsburg monarchy. Beginning in 1880, industrialization of the Czech lands accelerated rapidly, and by 1900 agricultural workers represented only 41 percent of the labor force in Bohemia and Silesia. Only the Midlands of England and the Ruhr valley of Germany had higher concentrations of industrial workers at the turn of the century. During this era, cities in Bohemia, Moravia, and Silesia experienced rapid and sometimes spectacular growth, with the most rapid growth occurring in the new industrial suburbs of Prague.

By the turn of the century, the Czech lands were the most economically advanced region of the Habsburg monarchy. This success was the result of strong coal and steel industries and a highly productive agricultural sector capable of supplying the food requirements of a large industrial workforce. The Czech lands, especially Bohemia and Silesia, were blessed with extensive and high-quality coalfields, and the adoption of the Thomas-Gilchrist process facilitated the exploitation of the large phosphoric iron deposits of Bohemia and Moravia. By 1910, the Czech lands were producing more than 85 percent of the monarchy's coal and one-third of its iron ore. Rapid development of the rail net plus river traffic that flowed north into the Elbe improved connections with the rapidly growing German economy.

The growth of the sugar refining industry in Bohemia, combined with gains in metallurgy, increased the demand for machinery. Companies in the Czech lands produced approximately half of all beer, liquor, and flour in the monarchy, as well as dominating the production of porcelain, china, and glass. Bohemia and Moravia held a similarly dominant position in the Austrian textile industry, with 84 percent of all Austrian cotton mills and an annual cotton consumption half that of France. By 1902, 56 percent of all Austrian industrial workers were employed in the Czech lands. Feeding off one another, these factors helped produce an economic growth curve in the Czech lands that was among the most sustained in late-nineteenth and early-twentieth-century Europe.

While Czech ownership of the means of production was increasing, the bulk of industry in the Czech lands was controlled by Germans. Only in the final decade before World War I did Czech owners begin to make inroads into some of the most important industrial sectors, in part as a result of the *svůj k svému* movement for national economic separation. This campaign received strong support from the increasingly successful Czech banks.

The new Czechoslovak state emerged from the war with a strong economy but faced challenges that included severe market dislocation, the need for currency stabilization, and most of all, the need to incorporate the less developed Slovak and virtually undeveloped Carpatho-Ruthenian economies into the much more developed economy of the Czech lands. Under the guidance of Finance Minister Alois Rašín (1867–1923), Czechoslovakia avoided the wild currency fluctuations experienced in the other new states of East Central Europe. Restrained intervention in the economy by the government helped to fuel continued private-sector growth. One of the challenges faced by the new state was its dependence on exports. Without the Habsburg free-trade area, Czech exporters faced stiff competition from larger European states, especially in the markets of southeastern Europe.

The Czechoslovak economy adapted only slowly to the new circumstances in Europe and failed to capitalize on its advantageous position. Although the First Republic was among the world's ten-largest manufacturing economies and its growth rate in the 1920s was among the highest in Europe, its dependence on exports (industrial and

E agricultural) was not significantly reduced. This dependency meant that Czechoslovakia was hit particularly hard by the world economic crisis of the 1930s. By 1932, exports had fallen to two-thirds of their 1929 level, and unemployment soared from 38,600 in 1928 to 738,000 in 1933.

The greatest challenge, however, remained integration of the two eastern regions into the new state. For example, when Czechoslovakia was founded in 1918, Slovakia represented some 36 percent of the land area and 23 percent of the population but only 8 percent of the industrial output. Moreover, agricultural productivity in the Slovak lands was substantially lower than in the Czech lands. The unequal relationship between the two regions was not substantially improved during the First Republic. In fact, the First Republic was a period of deindustrialization in Slovakia, where less developed industries found it all but impossible to compete with their more developed Czech counterparts. This unequal competition all but destroyed the nascent Slovak iron industry and forced Slovakia into an almost total emphasis on agriculture and raw material extraction. As a result, most industrial development that did occur in Slovakia was an adjunct to the more advanced Czech industries. Finally, with the virtual withdrawal after 1919 of Hungarian and German capital from Slovakia, Czech financial institutions stepped in, leaving much of the Slovak industry that survived Czech competition under Czech financial control. This situation greatly exacerbated Slovaks' unhappiness with their nation's position in the new state and helped to fuel the desire among many Slovaks for greater autonomy and later for independence.

During World War II, the Czech lands were integrated completely into the German economy. This situation resulted in economic exploitation during the war and severe hardship after the collapse of the Third Reich. The expulsion of the German population from the heavily industrialized border regions of Bohemia also caused great dislocation in the immediate postwar years. By contrast, the Slovak state experienced strong economic growth as a result of direct German wartime investment in its economic development, especially the heavy industrial sector. Although much of Slovakia was devastated by fighting in late 1944–45, it emerged from the war in a much more competitive position vis-à-vis the Czech lands than had been the case prior to the war.

After the war, the differences between the two economies were greatly reduced. A succession of postwar governments emphasized economic growth in the Slovak lands so that between 1948 and 1989, industrial output in Slovakia increased almost thirty-three times, while in the Czech lands output grew by only twelve times during the same period. Over those same forty-plus years, net income in Slovakia increased by seven and one-half times, while in the Czech lands it increased only five times. The result of the rapid growth in the Slovak economy was that by the end of the 1970s the disparity between the two economies had been reduced to the point where, by many conventional measures, it had all but disappeared. For example, by the end of the 1980s, average wages and levels of personal consumption were virtually identical in the two halves of the federation.

Although per capita income in Czechoslovakia remained well above that in the other states of East Central Europe, per capita economic growth in Czechoslovakia lagged behind its neighbors. All but 5 percent of Czechoslovak industry had been nationalized after 1948, and much of the emphasis in industrial development shifted from consumer goods to heavy engineering products and chemicals. A fair amount of decentralization in the decision-making apparatus was retained; thus, unlike some other members of the Soviet bloc, the Czechoslovak economy never made the transition to a command economy. However, like its socialist neighbors, after 1949 Czechoslovakia was forced to orient its trade almost entirely eastward, to the point that by the mid-1950s the country had all but broken its economic ties with the West. By the end of the decade, state investment in heavy industry resulted in strong growth in employment, wages, and productivity, but despite the apparent success of the transformation to a socialist economy, by the mid-1960s, it was clear that these early gains could not be sustained and the economy was stagnating. Frustration over this situation in the Communist Party hierarchy played an important role in the Prague Spring movement. While crushing the Prague Spring—the liberal period in the spring and summer of 1968—resulted in political stability, this stability did little to improve the underlying economic problems faced by the state. As productivity slowed and as the Soviet economy likewise began to decline, in the late 1970s the Czechoslovak economy began a long, slow decline in competitiveness. By 1988, Czechoslovakia, like its socialist neighbors, was finding it increasingly difficult to supply consumer goods of all types and to avoid the structural problems brought on by extensive external debt. Just as in 1968, these economic problems contributed to the revolutionary events of 1989 that brought the socialist era to a close.

T. Mills Kelly

Further reading

Čapek, Aleš. "The Past and Future of Czecho-Slovak Economic Relations." Program on Central and Eastern Europe Working Papers Series #22 (Prague, March 1992).

Krejčí, Jaroslav and Pavel Machonin. *Czechoslovakia 1918–92: A Laboratory for Social Change.* New York, 1996.

Myant, Martin. *The Czechoslovak Economy, 1948–1988.* Cambridge, Massachusetts, 1989.

Prinz, Friedrich. "Der Aufbau der modernen Industriegesellschaft Schlussbetractung," in *Handbuch der Geschichte der böhmischen Länder,* vol. 3, ed. by Karl Bosl. Stuttgart, 1968, 202–35.

Průcha, Václav, ed. *Hospodářské dějiny Československa v 19. a 20. století.* Prague, 1974.

Statistická ročenka Republiky československé/Statistická ročenka ČSSR. Prague.

Teichová, Alice. *The Czechoslovak Economy 1918–1980.* New York, 1988.

See also Agriculture; Banking; Tomáš Baťa Bohemia; Comecon; Communist Party of Czechoslovakia; Environment; Great Depression; Industrialization; Moravia; Old Czechs; Peasants; Prague Spring; Alois Rašín; Revolutions of 1989; Silesia; Slovakia; Trade Unionism; Young Czechs

Economic Development in Hungary

The history of the Hungarian economy in the nineteenth century was directly tied to the Habsburg monarchy. Although Hungary had become an integral part of the economy of the Austrian Empire, it had been relegated to an inferior role. Having a common currency permitted a division of labor in the empire based on location, natural resources, and level of development. At the same time, it allowed the monarchy to introduce economic policies that favored the western part of the empire. Hungary, in the eastern part, was an agrarian nation. Landed aristocracy intent on maintaining its political and economic privileges kept many medieval institutions alive.

Napoléon's (1769–1821) Continental Blockade (1806) increased the demand for and the price of wheat throughout Europe. This encouraged many landowners in the empire to modernize their operations. At the end of the Napoleonic Wars, the price of wheat fell, but the demand for wool increased. To take advantage of this new market, Hungarian landlords enclosed their land to graze sheep. In 1848 serfs were emancipated and the land worked by them became their property, while manorial estates remained in the hands of landlords. With emancipation, serfs gained small strips of land, but they could not become self-sufficient, thus leaving them no other choice but to become wage laborers. The area under cultivation by landlords and the use of machinery on their farms increased rapidly. The transformation of these manorial estates to capitalist farms was also aided by the introduction of railroads and the new banking system. The first banks, which were opened in the 1830s, were savings banks; the first commercial bank opened its doors in 1841 (Pesti Magyar Külkereskedelmi Bank [Hungarian Commercial Bank of Pest]).

During the first half of the nineteenth century, industry, predominately handicraft, was organized within the guild system. The spreading of the rail network, the creation of a common customs area (1850s), and new commercial laws encouraged the establishment of factories. The Industrial Revolution, which had already taken hold in Western Europe, took off only after the creation of the Dual Monarchy (Austria-Hungary) in 1867. One of the major industries became flour milling (only Minneapolis produced more). Other industries that thrived were sugar, distilleries and breweries, iron manufacture, and some branches of machine production. Exponential growth came about with government intervention beginning in the 1880s. In 1881 tax exemption was granted to all new factories producing goods with new technologies. In 1890, 1899, and 1907 interest-free loans were offered by the state for establishing new companies. To protect its industries, the monarchy also imposed high tariffs at its borders, but this mostly protected the industrially more advanced western part of the monarchy.

To reduce competition and as a reaction to the panic of 1873, many industries established cartels. In areas where Hungarian industry was viewed as a competitor to Austrian companies, the creation of common cartels was encouraged. However,

E where Hungarian products were not competitive, Austrian firms rejected all Hungarian proposals to establish such cartels.

World War I interrupted the process of modernization in the monarchy. By the end of the war, the Hungarian economy was in a shambles. It was on these ruins that Hungary declared itself an independent democracy in 1918. Separating itself from the monarchy was not only a political event but an economic one as well. Hungary lost its supply of raw materials and a natural market for its products as a result of its new borders. As a result of deepening economic crisis a Soviet republic came to power, peacefully, in 1919. The regime immediately nationalized industry and commerce, and expropriated land. But that republic lasted only a few months. In August 1919 a right-wing government took over.

The Treaty of Trianon not only established the new borders of Hungary, it also required a new Hungarian currency, (authorized by the Hungarian parliament in November 1925) to be separate from Austria's currency. Hungary was also obligated to pay part of its prewar debt and heavy reparation payments to the Allied powers. This set off an inflationary spiral. With the help of the League of Nations, a loan in 1926 made it possible to fight the hyperinflation and a new currency was introduced. While the Austro-Hungarian monarchy was a closed economy, the new state of Hungary now had to become an open one. Hungary's situation was precarious; as an agrarian economy it needed to earn foreign exchange by exporting its produce, but at the same time, other European nations imposed protectionist tariffs, causing a great reduction in exports.

The impact of the Great Depression was more devastating than in most other countries and lasted longer in Hungary. The nation lost income because of falling agricultural prices, which in turn caused the domestic demand for industrial products also to decline. Furthermore, a recall of all foreign loans started a bank run, bringing the state close to bankruptcy. Loans from the Bank for International Settlements and from other European banks and a domestic bank holiday averted a crisis, and the country entered into a series of bilateral agreements with Germany, which allowed the export of Hungarian agricultural products in exchange for German industrial products. Similar agreements were reached with Austria and Italy.

During World War II, Hungary was allied with Germany. To meet the demand of a war economy, the government introduced rationing of consumer goods and regulated the use of capital. As the Hungarian economy became increasingly incorporated into the German war effort, payments made for Hungarian goods declined.

World War II destroyed 40 percent of the nation's wealth. After the war, Hungary fell within the Soviet orbit. It was obligated to pay reparations for war damages, and trade negotiations with the victorious Allies were dependent on government guarantees of repayment of its prewar debt. As a result of this drain on the economy, inflation skyrocketed between August 1945 and August 1946. In an attempt to jump-start the economy, the coalition government introduced radical land reform that expropriated and redistributed land. Furthermore, industry was helped by direct government awards of contracts and rationing of raw materials, labor, credit, and transportation. Since firms worked to fulfill state orders and were financed by state credit, the government also felt that the best way to achieve its production goals was to take over the management of these firms. In this case state management meant expropriation; as a result, nearly 50 percent of employees became employees of the state. In 1946 a new currency, the forint, was introduced. To prevent inflation from reappearing, both wages and prices were centrally planned. Owing to this deflationary monetary policy, capital formation was extremely limited.

In 1946 Stalinist economic strategy was accepted as a guiding economic policy. In 1947 the First Three-Year Plan was introduced and with it came the creation of the National Planning Office (Országos Tervhivatal). On March 25, 1948, all firms employing more than 100 persons were nationalized. On December 28, 1948, all firms employing more than ten persons were nationalized. The majority of small businesses that remained private were taxed or harassed out of existence by 1952.

A fully centralized economy was introduced in 1950 with the First Five-Year plan—a set of detailed, binding directives spelled out in figures for every year and for every enterprise. Companies were told how much raw materials, energy, and labor power they could use (and of what quantity and quality), as well as the assortment of goods they had to produce. Foreign trade became a monopoly of the state. Distribution of produced goods was directed by the National Planning Office using a centrally calculated demand analysis. Nearly all resources designated for industry were allocated to heavy industry. Agricultural output declined as the system of forced deliveries at low prices and high taxes discouraged production. As a result of decreased consumer supplies, inflationary pressures grew and real wages fell. Social tension rose to the point that in 1953, after the death of Stalin (1879–1953), economic reforms were introduced. The government of Imre Nagy (1894–1958) permitted resignations from agricultural cooperatives, and a mass exodus resulted from the co-ops. In industry, the government tried to put the planning process on a more rational footing. A new incentive plan was introduced where bonuses were tied directly to maximizing quantitative production requirements and at the same time to meeting the cost of production directives as well. But to meet these new requirements, companies cut corners and used cheaper inputs. As a result, lower-quality goods were produced and unsalable inventory accumulated rapidly.

In the summer of 1956 a reassessment of the planning process began, but the Hungarian Revolution of 1956, in the fall, closed this chapter of economic planning. The Second Three-Year Plan (1958–60) and the Second Five-Year Plan (1961–65) continued the emphasis on industrialization but lowered the rate of capital accumulation and investment. The rate of investment in heavy industry still exceeded that in other industries, but by a smaller margin, and emphasis was placed on the modernization of other industries as well. Similar changes occurred in agriculture. The compulsory delivery system and sowing plans were abolished. The state was still the buyer of commodities but it paid close to market prices. Planting decisions by the farmers were influenced by price and tax incentives. To encourage the conversion of individual farms to cooperatives in order to take advantage of economies of scale, a new program was initiated to help cooperatives purchase machinery. Peasants were also given the right to elect the cooperatives' management and to keep small private plots.

The revision of the industrial planning process was not as successful as efforts to revamp the agricultural sector. Individual ministries were allowed to decide on the number of compulsory directives that they were to give to enterprises. In negative correlation to the number of directives issued, the uncertainties at the enterprise level rose. Instead of less government interference, enterprises demanded more government direction. Cost of production and selling prices still remained unconnected. As an experiment to bring world market prices closer to domestic prices, the state's foreign trade monopoly was broken, when four firms received the right to trade on their own accounts.

Despite all of these changes, fundamental problems still plagued the economy. A negative balance of payments and a lack of surplus labor hampered the modernization of the economy to postwar standards. The New Economic Mechanism (Új gazdasági mechanizmus, NEM) was introduced on January 1, 1968, to solve these problems. The "new" mechanism was the use of market prices as the guiding basis for all production. The NEM was to be introduced gradually over a number of years. In 1973, however, a change in the political arena brought about a slowdown in implementing the NEM. Its architects were fired and recentralization reappeared. Rising import prices and the deterioration in the terms of trade for Hungary resulted in an increasing balance-of-payments deficit.

In 1978 the Sixth Five-Year Plan was introduced and the industrial ministries were merged. The new ministries became policy-making entities with no say over production quotas. The price setting of goods was transferred to the National Board for Material and Price (Országos Anyag-és Árhivatal). To increase competition, the large horizontal industrial and mining trusts were broken up into smaller firms. In addition, companies were given more leeway in their investment decision making and were granted permission to trade for their own account and to set wages.

On January 1, 1980, subsidies to industry were cut to achieve parity between domestic and world prices. As a result, consumer prices rose by 20 percent. To improve the standard of living, small groups of employees were allowed to subcontract to their company. Small-scale private industry, mainly in the service sector, was again permitted to operate. As a result, the second economy grew very rapidly.

In January 1983 enterprises, cooperatives, and local government entities were given the right to issue and purchase bonds, and a fledgling bond market was born. Some bonds were traded on an intra-enterprise market and had no guarantees to either principal or interest. Other bonds were traded on an exchange and had government guarantees for both principal and interest.

In 1985 managerial reform was introduced, thus permitting enterprises to make hiring and firing decisions. In 1986 a bankruptcy law was passed, the first in Eastern Europe, and unemployment compensation was introduced. Value-added taxes were introduced the same year. In 1987 the functions of the central bank and commercial banks were separated as a result of reform of the banking system. The stock market opened for business in 1988 (another first in Eastern Europe). Empowered by a 1989 law, enterprises began their conversion to joint-stock companies, and the arduous task of privatization and moving to a market economy began.

Susan Glanz

Further reading

Berend, Ivan T. and György Ránki. *Economic Development in East-Central Europe in the 19th and 20th Centuries.* New York, 1974.
———. *The European Periphery and Industrialization, 1780–1914.* Cambridge, Massachusetts, 1982.
———. *The Hungarian Economy in the Twentieth Century.* London, 1985.
———. *Hungary: A Century of Economic Development.* New York, 1974.
Swain, Nigel. *Hungary: The Rise and Fall of Feasible Socialism.* London, 1992.

See also Agriculture; Banking; Communist Party of Hungary; De-Stalinization; Dual Monarchy; Great Depression; Hungarian Revolution of 1956; Hungarian Soviet Republic; Industrialization; Law; League of Nations; Imre Nagy; NEM; Peasants; Privatization; Railroads; Trianon, Treaty of

Economic Development in Poland

In a historical context, economic development in Poland is closely linked to the political, military, and social forces that have determined the modern shape of Central and Eastern Europe. These include development under Russian, German, and Austrian rule from the latter part of the eighteenth century until the end of World War I, the regaining of independence during the interwar period, the tragedy of World War II, and the crucible of Soviet-type socialism during the 1949–89 period. Polish economic development since 1989 has been characterized by the transition from socialism to capitalism, and Poland is generally considered to be one of the more successful transitional economies.

The development of industrial capitalism in what is now Poland began largely during the nineteenth century, following a series of partitions of the Polish-Lithuanian Commonwealth (also known as the First Republic) by the Russian, Austrian, and Prussian (later German) empires. (Although Poland is considered to have been one of the most important European states before the partitions, little firm information or statistical data concerning economic development prior to the nineteenth century exist.) Poland's initial industrial development was therefore closely linked to trends in the economies of the imperial overlords, which served to strengthen the connection between the socioeconomic tensions unleashed by the Industrial Revolution and political movements on behalf of Polish independence. Likewise, economic policy during the interwar Second Republic (1918–39) emphasized the development of a national Polish economy through integrating what had been disparate territories of the three empires. Prime Minister Władysław Grabski's introduction of the Polish złoty, the currency of the nation, in 1924 is credited with ending the postwar hyperinflation and creating a unified national monetary system. The relatively conservative economic policies dating from Grabski (1874–1938) gave way in the 1930s to a greater emphasis on state direction of, and intervention in, the economy, associated with the policies of Deputy Prime Minister Eugeniusz Kwiatkowski (1888–1974) during the second half of the decade. Many of the Second Republic's economic achievements were obliterated during World War II, when the brutalities of the German and Soviet occupations significantly reduced Poland's population and national wealth.

The Poland that emerged from World War II in 1945 moved some 400 miles (670 km) to the West. This was due to the acquisition of former German lands in Silesia, Eastern Prussia, and Pomerania, and to the ceding of some of Poland's prewar eastern territories to the Ukrainian, Byelorussian, and Lithuanian Soviet republics. This re-drawing of borders on the one hand worked to

Poland's economic advantage, since the industrial and agricultural potential of the lands acquired from Germany generally exceeded that of the lands ceded to the USSR. On the other hand, the border redrawing also produced millions of refugees and migrants, and helped ensure that Poland would be closely tied to the Soviet bloc that had formed by the late 1940s. Along with this came the transplanting of Soviet-style forced industrialization at the end of the 1940s.

The Soviet development model proved to be a recipe for economic and political instability in Poland. Economic performance in "People's Poland" during the 1949–89 period was inferior to many of Poland's neighbors (both East and West), while strikes, rebellions, and uprisings during 1956, 1968, 1970–71, 1976, 1980–81, and 1988 underscored the political weakness of the Polish United Workers' Party. The 1979–82 period, for example, saw a 25 percent decline in national income, triple-digit inflation, Poland's failure to service its international debt, the emergence of democratic, anti-Communist opposition movements, and the declaration of martial law. Poland's seemingly insurmountable economic problems played a major role in the Communist government's decision to permit semidemocratic elections in June 1989, which led to the creation in September 1989 of Eastern Europe's first non-Communist government since 1949.

Leszek Balcerowicz (1947–), deputy prime minister in the new government, introduced on January 1, 1990, a program calling for a rapid transition from socialism to capitalism. The so-called Balcerowicz Plan, which subsequently became identified with the phrase "economic shock therapy," was the first of its kind. It was closely watched by Poland's neighbors and the international community, and was supported by Western governments, the World Bank, and the International Monetary Fund. Following sharp declines during 1990–91, Poland's gross domestic product during 1992–95 recorded one of the highest growth rates in the world, and inflation, which had been surging out of control in late 1989, had been brought down to around 30 percent per year by 1995. Poland effectively became an associate member in the European Union in 1991, and much of Poland's foreign debt had been renegotiated on favorable terms by 1994.

Largely for these reasons, Poland came to be generally regarded as one of the most successful cases of post-Communist economic transition, and the Polish approach to transition was emulated after 1990 in other post-Communist countries—including Russia—with varying degrees of success. Still, Poland's economic successes were something of a mixed blessing, as they were accompanied by rapid increases in unemployment rates, insolvency of many state-owned banks and enterprises, a fiscal crisis that decimated social services, and widespread public perceptions of declines in public safety. Within Poland, the socio-political ramifications of the economic changes introduced after 1989 were extremely controversial, and the political parties most closely associated with the Balcerowicz Plan were soundly defeated during the 1993 parliamentary elections. However, the parties in power during 1993–95, who were themselves descended from the pre-1990 political order, did not deviate significantly during that time from the economic course established during 1990–91.

Ben Slay

Further reading

Jezierski, A. and B. Petz. *Historia gospodarcza Polski Ludowej.* Warsaw, 1988.
Kemme, D., ed. *Economic Reform in Poland: The Aftermath of Martial Law, 1981–1988.* Greenwich, Connecticut, 1991.
Slay, Ben. *The Polish Economy: Crisis, Reform, and Transformation.* Princeton, New Jersey, 1994.
Taylor, J. *The Economic Development of Poland, 1919–1950.* Ithaca, New York, 1952.

See also Agriculture; Comecon; Communist Party of Poland; Environment; Władysław Grabski; Great Depression; Industrialization; Peasants; Polish Congress Kingdom; Silesia

Economic Development in Romania

Although the Romanian lands were divided for centuries, and often under the influence of foreign powers, economic relations contributed to strengthening the ties among them before the founding of the modern nation-state. At the beginning of the nineteenth century, a feudal economy predominated throughout the Romanian lands. There was little urban development, and large landowners, called *boiars,* dominated the agrarian economy. The peasants, who formed the majority of the population, lived in poverty. The Ottoman system of taxation and the commercial monopoly exercised by the empire over the Romanian Principalities strengthened this system, which resulted in a lack of economic development in these territories compared with countries in the West. As a result of these conditions and the decline of Ottoman power, during the nineteenth century efforts were directed toward overcoming this underdevelopment. Beginning with the revolt of 1821 led by Tudor Vladimirescu (1780–1821), numerous plans for economic reform were drafted by members of the national parties in Moldavia and Wallachia. In 1829 the Treaty of Adrianopole opened the way for the development of a market economy by eliminating the Ottoman economic monopoly over Wallachia and Moldavia. Customs taxes between the principalities were eliminated on January 1, 1848, and strong economic ties to Transylvania, evidenced by the fact that 97.8 percent of its exports and 91.8 percent of its imports were with Moldavia and Wallachia and provinces of the Ottoman Empire, helped to lay the basis for the future development of a national market.

The reforms proposed by Romanian intellectuals during the revolutions of 1848 concentrated on land reform and stipulated measures concerning the development of industry, commerce, banking, and transportation. After the formation of Romania through the union of Moldavia and Wallachia under the rule of Alexandru Ioan Cuza (1820–73) in 1859, the land reform of 1864 abolished feudal relations and distributed land to the peasants; 515,422 peasants received 4,682,365 acres (1,894,927 hectares) of land, and another 106,714 peasants bought 1,350,630 acres (546,593 hectares). This promoted the development of capitalist relations in general, especially in agriculture. Legislation was adopted to promote industrial development in 1887 and again in 1912, and a mining law adopted in 1895 opened the way for the development of oil production, which was to become one of Romania's most important economic resources during the first half of the twentieth century. Because of the agricultural basis of the country, food-processing industries remained the most important, and agricultural products continued to be Romania's principal export.

Oil production increased so that by 1943 Romania was the third-largest oil producing country in the world after the United States and the Soviet Union. Chemical, wood, textile, and heavy industries developed, especially after the estab-lishment of the Romanian National Bank in 1880. Agricultural products continued to be Romania's principal export. Despite the progress that had been made, the agrarian problem continued to plague the Romanian economy. Peasants lacked the land resources needed to maintain a viable farm. The land problem led to continued peasant unrest, culminating in the great peasant uprising of 1907. Most peasants had too little land to make ends meet (424,000 had fewer than 7.4 acres [3 hectares], while for a farm to be self-sufficient a minimum of 12.4 acres [5 hectares] were required). In addition, many peasants had no land at all.

The formation of Greater Romania, with the union of the Regat (Moldavia and Wallachia) with Transylvania, Bukovina, and Bessarabia at the end of World War I, led to the development of a national economy. The liberal doctrine, expressed by the formula "by ourselves alone," which supported the growth of a native bourgeoisie, dominated political life after World War I. Large private factories began to appear. Traditional economic relations between the historic provinces facilitated the rapid integration of the newly acquired provinces in Romania, bringing about a reorganization of industry and agriculture, as well as of the transportation and communication networks. The results were seen immediately. Stimulated by the agrarian reform of 1921, agricultural production increased by 168.4 percent from 1921 to 1938. Oil, coal, and ore production also increased. The number of manufacturing plants increased from 2,747 in 1921 to 3,767 in 1938, an evolution slowed somewhat by the Great Depression at the end of the 1920s. Nevertheless, problems remained in agriculture, which lacked government support to stimulate modernization and depended heavily on manual labor.

During World War II, the economy continued to grow despite the exactions of the war, until the occupation of the country by the Red Army in 1944. The looting of the country by Soviet forces and the demands of the Soviet authorities devastated the economy. After the installation of the Communist regime in Bucharest, systematic nationalization of the economy began. Agriculture was collectivized and every aspect of the economy was centrally controlled. The Communists concentrated on the development of heavy industry, neglecting the needs of the agricultural sector, which did not experience significant development.

In addition, collectivization failed to stimulate production. Lack of investment led to rapid decline in the oil industry, and by the 1970s Romania was forced to import oil to meet its domestic consumption needs. To carry out the program of industrialization, the regime incurred a large foreign debt. This concentration on heavy industry, such as steel production, created further problems as they depended on the import of raw materials. At the beginning of the 1980s, the government of Nicolae Ceauşescu (1918–89) adopted a draconian policy to repay the foreign debt; most goods were exported and the population suffered from a lack of basic goods.

After the fall of the Communist regime in December 1989, the process of establishing a market economy began. Foreign investment began to enter the country and by 1995 totaled over $1.3 billion. The difficulties of reorganization led to a steady decline in productivity from 1990 to 1992, but gross domestic production began to recover in 1993 and has steadily risen in following years.

Kurt W. Treptow

Further reading

Adăniloaie, Nichita and Dan Berindei. *La Réforme agraire de 1864 en Roumanie et son application.* Bucharest, 1966.

Crowther, William. *The Political Economy of Romanian Socialism.* New York, 1988.

Pearton, Maurice. *Oil and the Romanian State.* London, 1971.

Treptow, Kurt W., ed. *A History of Romania.* Iasi, 1995.

Tsantis, Andreas C. and Roy Pepper. *Romania: The Industrialization of an Agrarian Economy under Socialist Planning.* Washington, D.C., 1979.

See also Adrianople, Treaty of; Agriculture; Alexandru Ioan Cuza; Banking; *Boiars;* Nicolae Ceauşescu; Collectivization; Communist Party of Romania; Great Depression; Greater Romania; Industrialization; Ottoman Empire; Peasants; Red Army; Revolutions of 1848; Romanian Peasant Revolt of 1907; SovRoms; Systematization; Tudor Vladimirescu; United Principalities

Economic Development in Yugoslavia and the Yugoslav Lands

The process of nation building that occurred throughout the nineteenth and twentieth centuries was accompanied by the rapid economic transformation of traditional societies. This was especially apparent in the case of the Balkan countries and regions that unified and formed the common country Yugoslavia in 1918. At the beginning of the nineteenth century, the "Yugoslav" lands—Croatia-Slavonia, Dalmatia, Vojna Krajina (Military Frontier), Slovenia, Bosnia-Hercegovina, and parts of Macedonia—were divided between the Ottoman and Habsburg Empires. The vast differences between the two empires heavily affected the economic development of the respective states and regions. The economy of the lands under Habsburg domination was characterized by the large estates owned by the Hungarian and Austrian nobility. On the other hand, a special sort of the Ottoman feudalism known as the *chiftlik* was the dominant feature in the lands under Turkish occupation. Another Yugoslav country—the tiny but independent principality of Montenegro—shared all the common characteristics of the Ottoman lands in southeastern Europe. Finally, the economy of autonomous Serbia differed from both Habsburg and Ottoman feudalism.

The end of the second Serbian insurrection against the Turks (1815–16) saw the beginning of Serbia's emancipation from the Turks and the formation of the national economy. Prince Miloš's (1780–1860) Serbia was an overwhelmingly peasant country. But unlike the Yugoslav lands under Habsburg rule—characterized by large estates, a privileged landed aristocracy, and a peasantry of serfs—rural Serbia was a land of small family homesteads. This feature of Serbian society played a distinctive role in the path of Serbia's economic development in the nineteenth century. Given the large number of small-size farms, Serbia's agriculture was able neither to enjoy advantages of economies of scale nor to take advantage of capital-intensive production. Although a peasant country with fertile soil, Serbia's main nineteenth-century economic activity was not the sale of crops but the sale of livestock, such as pigs, oxen, sheep, and goats. Consequently, trade, and especially foreign trade, became a major force in the economic development of nineteenth-century Serbia.

The political support that Serbia received from Austria-Hungary in its struggle against the Ottoman Empire, as well as its proximity to the Austro-Hungarian market, determined the direction of Serbia's foreign trade. Moreover, the Austrophile policy of King Milan Obrenović (1854–

1901) further amplified Serbia's economic dependence on its powerful northern neighbor. Trade treaties between the two states from 1881 and 1892 resulted in Serbia's complete economic dependence on Austria-Hungary.

This dependence on Austria-Hungary was interrupted by the fall of the Obrenović dynasty in 1903 and the subsequent Pig War between Serbia and Austria-Hungary. During this tariff war, which lasted from 1906 to 1911, both the geographic and product composition of Serbia's foreign trade changed substantially. The Austro-Hungarian share of Serbia's exports fell from 90 percent in 1905 to 18 percent in 1911, while its import share dwindled from 60 percent to 19 percent. Additionally, semifinished and manufactured goods began to replace live animals as Serbia's principal exports. The establishment of an independent tariff system enabled Serbia to use the infant industry argument in designing its foreign trade policy. Thus, almost a century after its Western European counterparts such as the Netherlands and Belgium, Serbia finally entered into industrialization at the outset of World War I.

The situation in the rest of the Yugoslav lands did not substantially differ. The agricultural production per capita in Slovenia, Croatia-Slavonia, and Vojvodina did not significantly exceed that in Serbia. On the other hand, Macedonia and Bosnia-Hercegovina were still feudal societies and economically among the most backward in Europe. Accordingly, contrary to certain conceptions today, the core of the "Yugoslav" lands was at a similar level of economic development when the common country was formed in 1918. The major difference was not the level of development but Serbia's establishment of its national economy while the other regions had been part of the Habsburg and Ottoman economic systems.

The fact that at the moment of unification, Croatia and Slovenia had not yet developed their national economies became a source of continuous friction within the new state of Yugoslavia after 1918. The principal problem arose over the strategy of economic development that the unified state should pursue. Anxious to continue rapid industrialization, Serbia encouraged protectionism and state intervention. These measures, combined with a restrictive monetary policy, enhanced development of industry and stabilized both the external and the internal finances of Yugoslavia. The establishment of over two thousand new factories increased industrial employment by 145,000 workers, while the expansion of the mining sector and the rapid growth of railroads and of commercial activities created an additional 200,000–300,000 jobs. Formerly part of the Habsburg financial and commercial network, Croatia and Slovenia strongly opposed protectionism and state intervention. The comprehensive land reform in 1919, by which the large estates in Croatia-Slavonia and Vojvodina were broken up, further heightened the discontent of the northern regions.

The overall results of economic development of the first Yugoslavia were mixed. The average growth rate of net national product between 1921 and 1939 was an annual 3.33 percent. There was a substantial expansion of railroads, a considerable increase in urban population, a noticeable increase in the literacy rate, and a significant decrease in the rate of mortality. Despite progress toward modernizing the economy, however, Yugoslavia remained one of Europe's least-developed countries. Its exports were labor-intensive, consisting mainly of crops, forestry, livestock, and minerals. Finally, the pattern of development and underlying economic policies chosen by Yugoslav policymakers between 1918 and 1941 did not address regional imbalances.

The new Yugoslav state that emerged in 1945 had to face the tremendous destruction of all basic factors of economic development brought about by the world war and the concomitant civil war. The economically active population was decimated while various categories of capital equipment were more than 80 percent destroyed. The Communists, who emerged victorious from the war, began to nationalize the economy in 1946. The economic policies closely followed those of the Soviet Union's centrally planned economy. The First Five-Year Plan was inaugurated in 1947. Despite its ambitious targets—national income was to be doubled as compared to the prewar level—the plan was not successfully carried out until after the Cominform economic sanctions, brought on by the break between Marshall Tito (1892–1980) and Soviet dictator Stalin (1879–1953), were launched in 1948–49.

The Soviet-led economic blockade prompted Yugoslav decision makers to radically change the strategy of economic development. In 1950 the system of self-management began to replace the centralized-planning scheme. The transformation of the economic system, based on the increased role of workers in the decision-making process, yielded substantial results during the 1950s. Between 1952 and 1960, industrial production rose by 12.8 percent, while the rate of growth of the entire economy exceeded 10 percent annually.

This vigorous economic growth came to a halt in the early 1960s. The reform instituted in 1965 was supposed to embark on the beginning of "market socialism," yet another phase of Yugoslav economic development. The reform, however, did not yield the expected results. Price liberalization had resulted in inflationary pressures, while the overvalued currency and liberalized foreign trade created a current account deficit. This internal and external disequilibrium prompted yet another change in the economic system. The new system, inaugurated by the constitution of 1974, resulted in the decentralization of the Yugoslav economy. Autarkhic tendencies continuously grew while growing budget and trade deficits led to rapid increases in foreign borrowing.

The death of Tito in 1980 was followed by the rapid deterioration of overall economic conditions. In the late 1980s a two-digit inflation rate turned into a hyperinflation of 1,000 percent per year; the trade balance further deteriorated; and internal debt exceeded $20 billion. Faced with total unraveling of the existing economic structure while pressured by international creditors, the government launched a comprehensive economic reform in 1989.

That reform was essentially an orthodox stabilization package designed by the International Monetary Fund. It hinged on drastic cuts in government expenditures, reduction in the money supply, liberalization of prices and foreign trade, and currency depreciation. While the measures yielded some positive results, they adversely affected importers, a majority of whom were located in Bosnia-Hercegovina, Serbia, and Macedonia. Serbia, as the major energy supplier in Yugoslavia, bitterly opposed the government's decision not to liberalize energy prices. The economic reform inaugurated in 1989 intensified Yugoslavia's problems of economic development—that is, the severe regional imbalances and diverse economic and political interests of various regions in a highly decentralized country.

Between 1945 and 1990, Yugoslavia made significant economic progress. With a gross national product per capita of $2,480, it joined the ranks of middle-income countries. With respect to life expectancy, education, and health and nutrition, Yugoslavia was on a par with the highly developed Western countries. However, the absence of the market mechanism and an apparent voluntarism in designing developmental policies heightened regional differences and intensified autarkhic tendencies in the Yugoslav economy. Consequently, the creation of severe regional disparities epitomized the principal feature of economic development in Yugoslavia.

Željan E. Šuster

Further reading

Đorđević, D. *Carinski rat Austro-Ugarske i Srbije 1906–1911.* Belgrade, 1962.

Lampe, John and Marvin Jackson. *Balkan Economic History, 1550–1950.* Bloomington, Indiana, 1982.

Petrovich, Michael B. *History of Modern Serbia, 1804–1918,* 2 vols. New York, 1976.

Šuster, Željan E. *Historical Dictionary of the Federal Republic of Yugoslavia.* Metuchen, New Jersey, 1997.

Vucinich, Wayne. *Serbia between East and West: The Events of 1903–1908.* Stanford, California, 1954.

See also Agriculture; Banking; *Chiftlik;* Cominform; Communist Party of Yugoslavia; Great Depression; Industrialization; Milan Obrenović; Miloš Obrenović; Peasants; Pig War; Railroads; Self-Management; Tito; Tito-Stalin Split; *Zadruga*

Education

Until the eighteenth century, education in areas of Eastern Europe other than the Balkans compared well in extent and quality with that in most areas of Western Europe. In the eighteenth century, rapid industrialization and political liberalization in the West fostered curricular changes and experiments in mass education that outstripped educational efforts in the East.

In 1815 the map of East Central Europe was dominated by the Austrian Empire. Its educational legislation mandated compulsory one-year schools teaching the trivium (grammar, logic, rhetoric) in each parish, main schools in each district seat, and normal schools in the capitals of the various crown lands. There were three types of secondary schools: Gymnasia, which emphasized classical languages in a conservative curriculum; Realschulen, which taught modern languages, mathematics, and sciences; and the Bürgerschulen, emphasizing practical subjects. The first two of these were exam schools, graduates of which could apply to universities; the latter was open to all graduates of grade schools but did not lead to university-level study. The Catholic Church had the right to see that the curriculum of these schools didn't conflict with religious instruction. In 1869 education was secularized and each community was required to maintain an elementary school taught in the language of the district and compulsory for children aged six to twelve. Roman Catholic religious education was normative, with Protestant instruction provided for groups of more than twenty students. In the Hungarian portion of the empire, the spread of Magyar language and culture was vigorously pursued after the *Ausgleich* (Compromise) of 1867, which established the Dual Monarchy of Austria-Hungary, resulting in insufficient emphasis on basic instruction and enforced cultural backwardness of non-Magyar populations, such as the Slovaks and the Romanians. Thus, at the turn of the twentieth century the Austrian portion of the empire had achieved a 62 percent literacy rate, while the rate in the Hungarian portion was only about 50 percent.

Bulgaria in the nineteenth century had seen education as a way of asserting Bulgarian cultural claims against Greek and Turkish influences. By the beginning of the twentieth century, 3,060 national primary schools existed as well as 1,284 Turkish, Greek, and Jewish schools (along with 175 secondary schools, 8 Gymnasia, and 20 specialized schools). The overall literacy rate was 24 percent, but the literacy rate of the army in 1912 was 75 percent (compared to 70 percent for Greece, 59 percent for Romania, and 50 percent for Serbia).

Elsewhere, the educational situation was bleak. In Albania, education was almost nonexistent before 1908, with instruction in the Albanian language prohibited by the Turkish authorities. Tsarist Poland had a 3 percent literacy rate, with church and peasant schools showing a 3.5 percent completion rate as compared with 10 percent in European Russia as a whole. Jewish children received no instruction except in Jewish schools. The proportion of primary schools to the general population declined, while there was twice as much demand for secondary schooling as could be accommodated. The only university, at Warsaw, was a Russian-language institution. Although Romania inaugurated free and compulsory primary education for ages seven to eleven in 1864, by the turn of the century, the country had only a 15 percent literacy in rural areas (6 percent in Bessarabia). In 1907, 4,463 primary schools served 515,000 students, but only a tiny fraction passed on to the Gymnasia and Lycea, or from there to the universities at Bucharest or Iaşi. Serbia also had free compulsory education, Realgymnasia in large towns, five secondary schools for girls, and a university at Belgrade, but only a 17 percent literacy rate in 1910.

After World War I, the states of Central and southeastern Europe had daunting educational problems. Poland had to piece together an educational system from the remainders of German, Austrian, and Russian efforts. Czechoslovakia had to reverse the effects of forced Magyarization of Slovaks. Romania had to modify and extend its educational system to assimilate a huge population of Hungarians. Yugoslavia had to merge highly effective Austrian schools in the north and rudimentary Turkish education in the south with the Serbian system. Throughout Eastern Europe, extending educational opportunity, developing literacy, cultivating national sentiment, and dealing with minorities were at the top of the agenda.

Yugoslavia's 49.5 percent literacy rate embraced extremes of 91.8 percent in Slovenia and 16.2 percent in Macedonia. A rigidly centralized system expanded elementary schools from 5,600 to 9,169, pupils from 650,000 to 1,493,000, and teachers from 11,000 to 31,000; but, by 1940, 250,000 children were still not attending school, and the literacy rate in the country had climbed to only 60 percent. Bulgaria achieved 50 percent literacy by the 1920s and extended the period of compulsory education to seven years. Yet 61 percent of Bulgarian school buildings were inadequate. From 1934 to 1944, many Turkish schools were closed and 75 percent of Turkish children in Bulgaria could not go to school. Turkish-language instruction was deemphasized, while Bulgarian was made compulsory. Albania built from virtually nothing an educational system in which Albanian-language study was required. Many French teachers were imported to counteract the influence of Italian schools. In 1933 all Albanian schools were nationalized and all Italian schools closed. Thus, though progress had been made, the educational program of most East European nations was far from being effectively implemented at the advent of World War II.

After 1945, the growing political ascendancy of communism in Eastern Europe resulted in an education policy that sought to purge a largely bourgeois teaching profession, remove private education as an element of civil society by nationalization of schools, replace religion in the curriculum with Marxist-Leninist ideology, and import Russian paradigms and Russian-language instruction. Even so, unresolved prewar problems continued to be vexatious. In Bulgaria, the remaining Turkish schools were nationalized in 1946 and Koranic instruction ended in 1952. By 1960, Turkish schools had been closed or merged with Bulgarian-language schools. The project of creating socialist citizens had served as an excuse for suppressing Turkish language and culture even to the point of attempting to coerce ethnic Turks into accepting Bulgarian names. The greatest success of Bulgarian education in the period 1944–89 lay in achieving almost universal literacy and in massive promotion of scientific and technical education. Romania nationalized education in 1948, abolished all schools under foreign sponsorship, and established a highly centralized educational system with polytechnicalization of the curriculum. After 1964, the growing personality cult of Communist Party leader Nicolae Ceauşescu (1918–89), with its strong emphasis on Romanian nationalism, brought a particularly stultifying curricular emphasis on Marxist-Leninist ideology as reflected in the writings of Ceauşescu and his wife Elena (1919–89), readings from which often substituted for subject matter instruction even in the sciences. Persistent attempts to eradicate Hungarian culture, schools, and language instruction were ineffective and contributed to the fall of the regime. In 1949 Albania decreed compulsory schooling of all illiterate men under forty to combat its 50 percent illiteracy rate. In 1960 curriculum in schools was changed to integrate study with work in farms and factories. By 1965, Albania's literacy rate was estimated to have risen to 98 percent. Poland established a state monopoly of education in 1948, with strictly centralized controls. But the tradition of Roman Catholic resistance to Russian and German authority in the nineteenth century provided a powerful model for a resistant civil society and frustrated efforts to make education an instrument of state policy. Thus, the church was able to have religious instruction removed from the state schools and conduct its own catechetical centers, the number of which grew from 384 in 1960 to about 23,000 in 1990.

Overall, nationalization and centralization were useful in modernizing Eastern European nations by making universal primary and secondary instruction available, maximizing literacy rates, and steering students away from preparation for "the briefcase professions" and into technical/scientific careers. However, the emphasis on ideological conformity, refusal to permit schooling that was not state-sponsored and controlled, and the capture of the educational agenda by the ethnic nationalistic agenda in many nations of the area all were profoundly antimodern in their effects.

Joseph M. McCarthy

Further reading

Apanasewicz, Nellie and Seymour N. Rosen. *Education in Czechoslovakia.* Washington, D.C., 1953.

Apanasewicz, Nellie and William K. Medlin. *Educational Systems in Poland.* Washington, D.C., 1959.

Braham, Randolph L. *Education in Romania: A Decade of Change.* Washington, D.C., 1972.

Glenn, Charles L. *Educational Freedom in Eastern Europe.* Washington, D.C., 1995.

Jelavich, Charles. *South Slav Nationalisms: Textbooks and Yugoslav Union before 1914.* Columbus, Ohio, 1990.

Tchakurov, Naiden and Zetcho Atanassov. *History of Bulgarian Education.* Sofia, 1976.

See also Elena Ceauşescu; Nicolae Ceauşescu; Chitalishte; Ethnic Minorities; Higher Education; Magyarization; Nationalism

Eleonore von Reuss-Kostritz (1860–1917)

Bulgarian queen. Tsar Ferdinand (1861–1948) had been a widower for nine years before he decided to select a new queen. His queen would be the royal palace administrator and housekeeper, and his children's stepmother and chaperon. Neither love nor physical attraction figured in his search or in the final selection of a forty-eight-year-old German princess, Eleonore von Reuss-Kostritz, daughter of the late Prince Henry IV of Reuss (n.d.). Her name was suggested by matchmakers in the Russian imperial family, and she was an excellent choice. Neither beautiful nor an intellectual, she was earnest, educated, and had an impressive record of voluntary Red Cross work in Manchuria during the Russo-Japanese War. The couple were married in 1908 and Eleonore became a devoted and useful queen to Ferdinand. He treated her as a member of the royal household, realizing that in a short time she had won the respect of the country and the love of his children. The heir apparent to the Bulgarian throne, Boris (1894–1943), son of Marie Louise (1870–99), became especially devoted to Eleonore. It was a commonly held opinion that she had consented to marry Ferdinand from a spirit of self-sacrifice and because of the opportunities offered in Bulgaria for hospital and charitable work, in which she actively engaged.

David Cassens

Further reading

Black, Cyril E. *The Establishment of Constitutional Government in Bulgaria.* Princeton, New Jersey, 1943.

Corti, Egon C. *Alexander von Battenberg: Sein Kampf mit dem Zaren und Bismarck.* Vienna, 1920.

Kennan, George F. *The Decline of Bismarck's European Order: Franco-Russian Relations, 1875–1890.* Princeton, New Jersey, 1979.

See also Boris III; Ferdinand I; Marie Louise

Eliade, Mircea (1907–86)

Romanian writer and historian of religions. Eliade is one of the best-known figures from a whole generation of Romanian thinkers whose outlook took shape during the interwar years. His work became seminal in the development of hermeneutics in Romania throughout the twentieth century and played an essential role in establishing the history of religions as an academic discipline.

Eliade matured intellectually as European civilization was coming apart in the aftermath of World War I. His early writings were marked by an existential hunger for new signs of meaning and the freedom to create a new hierarchy of values. Eliade's studies in philosophy at the University of Bucharest greatly influenced his intellectual development, as he turned from writing prose and disparate encyclopedic articles to a systematic analysis of philosophy. He studied under Nae

Ionescu (1888–1940), a philosopher whose charisma turned him into an idol of the postwar generation. Prompted by Ionescu's encouragement and his own intellectual curiosity, Eliade gained interest in Eastern religions during the 1928–31 period, when he traveled to India to study the theories and practices of yoga.

During the 1930s, Eliade forged closer ties with Ionescu as his assistant in teaching philosophy at the university. At the same time, Eliade became established as a talented and controversial writer of prose, especially with his novels *Maitreyi* (1933) and *The Hooligans*. He also continued to publish political articles in various periodicals endorsed by Ionescu. In some of these essays, Eliade expressed interest in the Iron Guard, the foremost Romanian fascist movement. Since he later passed over in silence this aspect of his life, Eliade's disciples have continuously struggled to defend his moral and intellectual integrity against accusations of support for the Iron Guard.

After the war, Eliade sought refuge in Paris. There, he published his *Traité d'histoire des religions* (1949), a work that brought him academic notoriety. In 1955 he moved to Chicago, where he continued to work as a professor in history of religions at the University of Chicago until his death. Although his academic writings have come under criticism since the 1970s, even his detractors acknowledge Eliade's valuable contribution to the development of history of religions.

Maria Bucur

Further reading

Cave, David. *Mircea Eliade's Vision for a New Humanism.* New York, 1993.

Olson, Carl. *The Theology and Philosophy of Eliade: A Search for the Centre.* New York, 1992.

Ricketts, Mac Linscott. *Mircea Eliade: The Romanian Roots. 1907–1945.* Boulder, Colorado, 1988.

See also Nae Ionescu; Iron Guard; Philosophy

Eliáš, Alois (1890–1942)

Czech general and statesman. Born in Prague, Eliáš fought as an officer during World War I in the Czechoslovak legion, first in Russia and later in France. In 1919 he participated in military actions to secure the territory of Slovakia for the Czechoslovak Republic. After attending the military academy in Paris in 1921–23, he headed the section for organization of the general staff of the Czechoslovak army in 1924–29 and led the Czechoslovak delegation at the League of Nation's Commission for Disarmament in Geneva in 1929–31. He held command positions successively at the brigade, division, and army corps levels in Litoměřice, Bohemia, and Trenčín, Slovakia, from 1931 to 1938. On April 27, 1939, Eliáš succeeded Rudolf Beran (1887–1954) as prime minister of the government of the recently created Protectorate of Bohemia and Moravia (following the occupation of Prague by the Germans in March 1939). While holding this position until his arrest on September 27, 1941, he maintained contacts with the underground anti-German resistance, particularly the military group *Obrana národa* (Nation's Defense), as well as the Czechoslovak government-in-exile under President Edvard Beneš (1884–1948). In less than a year after his arrest, Eliáš was executed by German authorities in Prague under the martial law imposed in retribution for the assassination of the acting Reich protector, Reinhard Heydrich (1904–42).

Zdeněk David

Further reading

Mamatey, Victor S. and Radomír Luža, eds. *A History of the Czechoslovak Republic, 1918–1948.* Princeton, New Jersey, 1973.

Mastny, Vojtech. *The Czechs under Nazi Rule: The Failure of National Resistance, 1939–1942.* New York, 1971.

Pasák, Tomáš. *Generál Alois Eliáš a odboj: Slovo k historii.* Prague, 1991.

See also Edvard Beneš; Rudolf Beran; Czechoslovak Legion; Reinhard Heydrich; Protectorate of Bohemia and Moravia

Elin Pelin (Dimitur Ivanov Stoyanov) (1877–1949)

Bulgarian writer. Elin Pelin, the pseudonym of Dimitur Ivanov Stoyanov, was born in the village of Baylovo, near Sofia. He pursued his education in various Bulgarian schools, but his love of literature and writing caused him to leave school before he completed his secondary education. In 1903 Pelin was appointed to work in the library of Sofia University and was sent to France in 1906 to further his studies. Between 1926 and 1944, he was the curator of the Ivan Vazov Museum.

Pelin was one of Bulgaria's greatest classic fiction writers and a master of the Bulgarian short story. He was the author of two short novels and humorous sketches. He also composed poems and humorous stories for children and a novel for children, written in two parts, *Yan Bibiyan* (1921) and *Yan Bibiyan na lunata* (*Yan Bibiyan on the Moon,* 1922). His greatest works, however, were written before 1920 and his subjects are characteristically peasants from small backward villages buried under taxes, the tithe, and poverty. Philosophically he was humanistic, a trait best seen in his stories of fantasy, *Pod manastirskata loza* (*Under the Monastery Grapevine,* 1936). He also evoked a Christian philosophy in his writings. Many of his characters are poetic and gentle; yet as conflict and turmoil arise from the social inequality of peasant life in Bulgaria, vengeance is taken by his protagonists with a moral justification.

David Cassens

Further reading

Black, Karen L., ed. *A Biobibliographical Handbook of Bulgarian Authors.* Columbus, Ohio, 1981.

Manning, Clarence A. and Roman Small-Stocki. *A History of Modern Bulgarian Literature.* New York, 1960.

Moser, Charles. *A History of Modern Bulgarian Literature 865–1944.* The Hague, 1972.

See also Bulgarian Literature

Elisabeth (Carmen Sylva) (1843–1916)

Romanian queen and promoter of the arts. Pauline Elisabeth Ottilie Louise was the eldest child of Prince Hermann of Wied (1814–64) and Princess Marie of Nassau (1825–1902). Intellectual, generous, and sensitive, she was also often lonely and melancholy. She had an artistic personality, possessed a vivid imagination, and had a fondness for the occult. In 1869, at the age of twenty-six, she married Prince (later King) Carol of Romania (1839–1914). At first the marriage went well, but after the death of their four-year-old daughter, she became an intellectual workaholic. The death of her only child seemed to serve as the "supreme tragedy" of her life, from which she never recovered. In spite of her well-intentioned but often poorly-thought-out or unrealistic schemes, such as trying to build a city for the world's blind, her cultural contributions to Romania were significant.

Her books (which she wrote under the pen name Carmen Sylva) alone number over fifty volumes. It was through her efforts that many unknown Romanian artists, such as composer George Enescu (1881–1955), got their start. Her tireless promotion of the arts helped to put Romania on the cultural map of Europe.

Paul D. Quinlan

Further reading

Burgoyne, Elizabeth. *Carmen Sylva*. London, 1941.

Elisabeth, H.M. Queen of Roumania. *From Memory's Shrine: The Reminiscences of Carmen Sylva*, trans. by Edith Hopkins. Philadelphia, 1911.

Letters and Poems of Queen Elisabeth (Carmen Sylva), 2 vols. Privately printed for members of the Bibliophile Society of Boston, 1920.

Wolbe, Eugen. *Carmen Sylva: Der Lebensweg einer einsamen Königin*. Leipzig, 1933.

See also Carol I; George Enescu

Emigration

Although mass emigration from East Central Europe did not begin until the last decades of the nineteenth century, several waves of émigrés saw the need to leave their homelands earlier. One left Poland and settled mainly in France after the abortive revolution of 1830. Many of these nationalist Poles came from an elite group of revolutionaries who fled persecution, including cultural leaders who came to define the Polish character of resistance—including poet Adam Mickiewicz (1798–1855) and piano master Frédéric Chopin (1810–1849). Another wave left following the Revolutions of 1848, mainly from Bohemia, Hungary, and Galician Poland. Many came from the middle classes, fleeing largely for political reasons. They brought valuable business, artistic, and craft skills with them, often settling in the new world.

Largely owing to overpopulation and the lack of an industrial economy growing fast enough to absorb the surplus population, by the last third of the century many people had begun to leave their homelands to seek work elsewhere in Europe, or more frequently, made the distant trek to the lands of opportunity in the Americas. Overpopulation generated the most significant migration of peoples from 1871 to 1910. The population of Polish territories more than tripled between 1800 and 1910, from nine million to twenty-nine million. In Austria and Hungary, the figures more than doubled, from twenty-three million to forty-nine million. The Balkan lands grew more slowly at first, but more than doubled after 1860.

The highest rates of Austrian emigration occurred in provinces with large Slavic (or other ethnic) populations—Galicia, Bukovina, and Dalmatia. Over 1.8 million left the region. Even after allowing for the repatriation of one-half million, emigration resulted in a 28.4 percent decrease in population growth. Hungary lost nearly 1.4 million people, or close to one-fourth of its population growth. Over one-half million Slovaks emigrated out of a population of around two million. The Polish districts of Russia lost 1.1 million, and total Polish emigration before World War I approached 3.5 million. Less migration came from the more backward Balkan countries, but they still lost about half a million inhabitants. This migration continued after World War I until the Great Depression reversed the trend and retro-migration sent some peoples back eastward.

The more significant emigration to America began in the 1870s and peaked during the first decade of the twentieth century. Many left their homelands with the intention of working in America for a few years. Since wages were so much higher, they planned to save a nest egg then return home to buy a large plot of land and settle down to a life of middle-class farming. A significant number, as high as 20 percent, did just that. But the overwhelming majority stayed in America.

The impact of mass emigration can hardly be overstated. In some cases, nearly entire villages left the Old Country in a continual chain migration. As one Slovak newspaper put it, "only the old stayed behind." When loved ones did remain behind, those in America often brought them over later or sent money, which also contributed to the economies of their home country.

After World War I, movements resumed and over two million people from the defeated powers migrated across the newly created international borders. Over 750,000 ethnic Germans moved to Germany and Austria from areas partitioned to Poland and Czechoslovakia. About 400,000 Magyars left Slovakia and Transylvania, and another 100,000 Magyars fled the Kingdom of Serbs, Croats, and Slovenes (Yugoslavia) to resettle in adjacent Hungary. In terms of percentage, Bulgaria experienced the greatest migration, as

200,000 Bulgarians and Macedonians fled areas ceded to Greece; another 100,000 fled areas granted to Yugoslavia and Romania. At the same time, Bulgaria expelled large numbers of Turks to make room for the new arrivals.

During the interwar period, despite restrictions and discriminatory quotas placed on immigration by the United States in 1921 and 1924, over 400,000 people emigrated from East Central Europe to America. Over 200,000 of these came from Yugoslavia. The U.S. quotas were always filled.

World War II and its aftermath brought new waves of migration, both forced and free. Nazi policies herded Jews, Poles, and other "inferior peoples" to labor and death camps. Later, Soviet occupiers of Poland and other "liberated" countries exiled over two million people, many of whom wound up in Siberian hard labor camps. After the war, approximately one million displaced persons (DPs) found themselves homeless. Many emigrated to the United States, Israel, Canada, Australia, Great Britain, France, or South America.

In the postwar resettlement, the reconstituted countries expelled most of their German ethnic residents. Nearly three million Sudeten and Carpathian Germans were forced to leave Czechoslovakia. Likewise, large minorities of four million Germans in Poland and smaller German minorities in the Baltic countries, Hungary, Romania, and Yugoslavia had their homes and property confiscated and were forced to emigrate—mostly to West Germany.

When Czechoslovakia reoccupied areas of southern Slovakia that Hungary had seized in 1939, part of the local Magyar population found itself either compelled to go south to Hungary or transferred to other parts of the country. Bulgaria used ethnic purging to rid itself of 160,000 Turks. In general, the large population transfers made the expelling countries more homogeneous than before the war, even though many pockets of minorities continued to exist.

Relative to their numbers, more Jews left East Central Europe than any other peoples. A region that had once hosted a large number of Jewish urban dwellers lost nearly all its population between 1939 and 1948.

Several waves of political refugees also left East Central Europe during the Cold War. As the Communist regimes came to power, leading democratic leaders, some clergy, and businessmen fled their homelands. Another mass migration followed the Soviet occupation of Hungary in 1956, and a somewhat smaller wave of mostly intellectuals and skilled workers left Czechoslovakia in 1968. Polish émigrés left in increasing numbers after the declaration of martial law in Poland during the 1980s. While individual events caused spikes in emigration, émigrés seeking political asylum to escape the Iron Curtain countries continued to trickle into the West until the Revolutions of 1989.

Emigration has helped soften the impact of rising populations, and no doubt has defused some potential social and political unrest. It also exposed rural peoples to different cultures and technologies, and linked the Old Countries with new lands and new ideas. In another sense, emigration drained away some of the most productive people—ambitious youth—and rewarded host countries with much needed labor and potential talent.

Michael J. Kopanic Jr.

Further reading

Barton, Joseph. *Peasants and Strangers: Italians, Rumanians, and Slovaks in an American City, 1890–1950.* Cambridge, Massachusetts, 1975.

Berend, Iván T. and György Ránki. *Economic Development in East-Central Europe in the 19th and 20th Centuries.* New York, 1974.

Bodnar, John. *The Transplanted: A History of Immigrants in Urban America.* Bloomington, Indiana, 1985.

Kaser, M.C. and E.A. Radice, eds. *The Economic History of Eastern Europe 1919–1975,* 3 vols. Oxford, 1985–86.

Thomas, William I., and Florian Znaniecki. *The Polish Peasant in Europe and America.* Urbana, Illinois, 1984.

See also Albanian Émigrés; Bulgarian Émigrés; Frédéric Chopin; Croatian Émigrés; Czech Émigrés; Ethnic Minorities; Great Depression; Hungarian Émigrés; Hungarian Revolution of 1956; Jews; Adam Mickiewicz; November Uprising; Polish Émigrés; Prague Spring; Revolutions of 1848; Revolutions of 1989; Romanian Émigrés; Serbian Émigrés; Slovak Émigrés; Slovene Émigrés

Eminescu, Mihai (1850–89)

Romania's greatest poet. Influenced by both Western and Oriental thinking, yet rooted in the

Romanian native experience, Eminescu's philosophical lyrics express a vibrant meditation on life and death. He initiated the modern period of Romanian literature, profoundly affecting generations of writers.

Eminescu was born Mihail Eminovici in 1850 near Botoşani in Romanian Moldova. The folklore of his childhood surroundings made a profound impression on his artistic expression. His first poems were published in 1866 in a journal issued in Transylvania, *Familia* (*The Family*). Eminescu studied in Vienna from 1869 to 1872 and then in Berlin until 1874. While abroad, he absorbed German philosophical and Western literary trends. After settling in Iaşi in 1874, he became active in the influential literary circle Junimea (Youth) and edited the literary journal *Timpul* (*Time*). By the mid-1870s, Eminescu's artistic personality and genius were well established. His poetry regularly appeared in journals such as *Convorbiri literare* (*Literary Conversations*), the voice of the Junimea society. Among Eminescu's best-known works is his masterpiece *Luceafărul* (*The Evening Star*), a stylized folktale in verse published in 1883. The first large-scale volume of his poetry was published in 1884. Although primarily a poet, he also wrote prose, especially stories and essays. By the early 1880s, Eminescu was showing signs of mental disorder; he spent periods on and off throughout the decade in hospitals and sanatoriums and died in 1889 in Bucharest. Expressing deep romanticism, melancholy, and mysticism in his verse, Eminescu is regarded by Romanians as their most celebrated yet tragic national poet.

Margaret H. Beissinger

Further reading

Dumitrescu-Buşuleanga, Zoe. *Eminescu: viaţă, creaţie, cultură.* Bucharest, 1989.
Eminescu, Mihai. *Poems.* Cluj-Napoca, 1980.
Piru, Alexandru. *Eminescu azi.* Bucharest, 1993.

See also Folklore; Junimea; Romanian Literature

Enescu, George (1881–1955)

Romanian composer, violinist, and conductor. Enescu studied at the conservatories of Vienna (1888–94) and Paris (1895–99). He became the most important representative of Romanian composition in the first half of the twentieth century by synthesizing, in a deeply personal manner, basic elements of the European traditional and modern musical language with those deriving from Romanian folklore. The polyphonic and harmonic complexity of the musical texture, along with the simultaneously inspired melodism of the themes, created a certain asymmetry of rhythm and combination of the tonal with the modal character, which gives a special color to his music. His creations included symphonic music (two Romanian Rhapsodies; three symphonies; three symphonic suites; *Vox Maris*, a tone poem); chamber music (String Octet, *Dixtuor pour instruments à vent*, three sonatas for piano and violin [one of them the well-known Third Sonata "in Romanian Folk Character"], two sonatas for piano and cello, two piano sonatas, the *7 Chansons de Clèment Marot* song cycle, two string quartets, two quartets for strings and piano, a quintet for piano and strings, and the Chamber Symphony for Twelve Solo Instruments); and the opera *Oedipus*, which premiered in Paris in 1936. A violinist and conductor of world renown, Enescu gave concerts in numerous countries and cities in Europe and America. His artistry as a violin player is mainly preserved in the recordings of Bach's (1685–1750) sonatas and partitas for solo violin.

Clemansa Liliana Firca

Further reading

Bentoiu, Pascal. *Capodopere enesciene.* Bucharest, 1985.
Cosma, Octavian Lazăr. *Oedip-ul enescian.* Bucharest, 1977.
Firca, Clemansa Liliana. *Le Catalogue thématique de œuvres de Georges Enescu. I (1886–1900).* Bucharest, 1985.
Gavoty, Bernard. *Les Souvenirs de Georges Enescu.* Paris, 1955.
Malcolm, Noel. *George Enescu.* London, 1990.
Voicana, Mircea et al. *George Enescu: A Monograph,* 2 vols. Bucharest, 1977.

See also Music

Environment

The environmental disaster in Eastern Europe became well known after the fall of communism. Intense industrialization, coal-burning power plants, large-scale agriculture, industrial waste dumping, and pesticide runoff have scarred the landscape. The Black, Adriatic, and Baltic Seas have suffered from oil spills, hydroelectric power plants, and polluted tributaries. The major international waterways—the Danube and Elbe Rivers—are toxic waste flows. In the 1980s these conditions enabled environmental groups to become effective critics of Communist regimes. Activists raised awareness of the dangers and risks of pollution, and after 1990 these groups became well represented in government. Many expected that more stringent environmental laws, protection, and cleanup would help reverse the legacy of the previous forty-five years of industrial pollution.

All East European countries lack capital to retool or rebuild older industrial plants and develop new, "clean" industries. Chronic unemployment and conditions for obtaining aid put pressure on governments to keep polluting industries at full capacity. The worst pollution comes from the region's major industries, which cannot be shut down summarily. The coal, fuel, power, and nonferrous metal industries account for one-half to three-quarters of all pollution in East Central Europe. Many Western firms eagerly contract with polluting industries and negotiate for lax environmental standards because these operations produce goods more cheaply.

As in the West, most pollution in the region stems from heavy industry and raw materials processing. After 1945, Communist countries invested in those industries (steel and automobile manufacturing, power generation, chemical and oil production) that had enabled West European countries to dominate the world economy before World War II. Thus, the most polluted areas in East Central and southeastern Europe are also the most industrialized. The area with the most environmental damage, known as the "black triangle," includes southeastern Germany, southwestern Poland, and the western Czech Republic (Bohemia). This area represents the oldest and most intense industrial development in East Central Europe.

In addition to developing heavy industries, these states also took advantage of their natural resources and developed timber, food processing, coal mining, and nonferrous metal extraction. In the 1970s and 1980s these countries became major suppliers of processed raw materials to the West. These mining and processing industries severely damaged air, water, and soil quality, and posed serious health hazards. In fact, within the black triangle, the copper mining and smelting areas in Lower Silesia and Kraków have

suffered some of the most severe environmental degradation.

Most of the air pollution comes from coal-burning power plants that emit sulfur dioxide, the principal cause of acid rain. The Czech Republic, Romania, and Bulgaria are world leaders in sulfur dioxide production. These same power plants also spew out dust, carbon disulfide, fluoride, and chlorine into the air. In some areas, sulfur dioxide pollution has been linked to significantly shortened life spans as well as heart ailments and widespread childhood diseases. Vehicle-linked pollutants such as nitrogen oxide, carbon dioxide, and hydrocarbons remain low compared with levels in Western countries, but they rank high as a percentage of these states' populations and gross national products.

Water and soil pollution are less visible than smog but no less dangerous. Reaching international accords to enforce environmental regulations on common waterways is just as problematic as agreeing on air emissions standards. The Danube and Elbe Rivers transport highly toxic water through several countries before depositing it in the Black and Baltic Seas. The Danube's tributaries carry high levels of toxic waste, while the Elbe contains 250 times the European Community's limits on mercury. The main contributors to water and soil pollution include nitrates, pesticides, fertilizer residues, chlorinated hydrocarbons, solvents, untreated sewage, and phosphates. In addition, inadequate pesticide, chemical, and nuclear waste disposal, as well as unprotected uranium mining, buried oil, and diesel fuel deposits have allowed poisons to seep out of containers and to come into contact with ground water. All East European countries have problems with toxins contaminating ground water. It is estimated that only 17 percent of the water in the Czech Republic can be consumed and only 5 percent of the water in Poland is potable. Romania has no untreated water that is safe to drink, while Hungary provides no water treatment.

Between 1945 and 1990, the governments of Eastern Europe passed many laws to protect the environment. However, weak laws, inadequate penalties, and lax law enforcement allowed polluting industries to flourish. After the Communist regimes fell, many expected that the new regimes would enact a spate of stringently enforced environmental laws. Since 1990, some factories have been closed and governments have

E made commitments to reduce pollution to West European standards. But the effects of unemployment, inadequate resources, and the necessity of foreign investment have stalled progress on environmental regulation. Western industrialized countries have also helped prevent these new regimes from developing cleaner industries. Aid to the new governments proved to be far more meager and much slower in arriving than promised. Therefore, countries funded the complicated transitions from communism at a time when their economies were in collapse. Restructuring strategies focused on increasing short-term export earnings and production to pay debts and privatize their economies. The focus on short-term returns required using the same factories and industrial plants that had created the pollution and developing new industries that might better compete in a global market and help the environment. Pressure for earnings also pushed governments to accept contracts with Western companies that benefited from these polluting industries' cheap manufacturing. Faced with high unemployment and few resources, the new governments opted for more jobs and laxer environmental regulations.

Katherine McCarthy

Further reading

Carter, Francis W. and David Turnock, eds. *Environmental Problems in Eastern Europe.* London, 1993.

Höll, Otmar, ed. *Environmental Cooperation in Europe: The Political Dimension.* Boulder, Colorado, 1994.

Jancar-Webster, Barbara, ed. *Environmental Action in Eastern Europe: Responses to Crisis.* Armonk, New York, 1993.

Manser, Roger. *Failed Transitions: The Eastern European Economy and Environment since the Fall of Communism.* New York, 1993.

See also Health; Industrialization; Silesia

Eötvös, Baron József (1813–1871)

Hungarian writer, political thinker, statesman, and reformer. Eötvös was the noblest and most far-sighted representative of the generation of Hungary's Age of Reform, the era leading up to the Hungarian Revolution of 1848–49. Always on the side of the poor and the downtrodden, he was erudite and widely traveled. As a publicist, he wrote

on prison reform, Jewish emancipation, and poverty in Ireland. His first novel, *A karthausi (The Carthusian,* 1839–41), which reveals the human suffering inflicted by the egotism and lack of responsibility of young aristocrats, was inspired by Eötvös's travels in England, Western Europe, and especially France. The basis of his social critique was further broadened in two other major works, *A falu jegyzője (The Village Notary,* 1845) and *Magyarország 1514-ben (Hungary in 1514,* 1847), with which he established the critical realist novel in Hungary. Using a wealth of characters, Eötvös depicts corruption and misery in an imaginary Hungarian county in the former, while in the latter, published on the eve of the Revolution of 1848, the terrible early-sixteenth-century peasant uprising serves as a warning of what could happen if Hungary failed to emancipate the serfs.

As a member of the upper chamber of the diet after 1839, Eötvös became one of the leaders of the liberal opposition. A moderate Catholic, he championed religious equality for Protestants. He was also prominent in the formation of a working group of liberals called "centralists," who were critical of the outdated feudal county administration and advocated legal, administrative, and constitutional reforms to introduce a Western-style political system with a government responsible to an elected parliament. Eötvös and the centralists prepared the road for the institution of Parliament during the revolutionary year of 1848. He himself entered the government of Count Lajos Batthyány (1806–49) as minister of religion and education, but left the country on the eve of the armed conflict with Austria.

Eötvös believed that Hungary's place was within a constitutionally governed Habsburg state system. Deeply concerned about revolutionary violence and excesses of nationalism, he wrote in his self-imposed Munich exile *A XIX. század uralkodó eszméinek befolyása az álladalomra (The Influence of the Ruling Ideas of the Nineteenth Century on the State,* 1851), a critical analysis of the effect of national passions on individual liberty since the French Revolution of 1789. Although encouraged by French social philosopher Alexis de Tocqueville (1805–59) and French liberal Catholic Charles Forbes René de Montalembert (1810–70), Eötvös's critique of nationalism based on popular sovereignty met with hostility in Hungary. Nevertheless, he played an important role in negotiating the *Ausgleich* (Compromise) of 1867 with Austria and took charge of the portfolio of religion and public education in the government of Count Gyula Andrássy Sr. (1823–90). It was under the statesmanlike guidance of Eötvös that the legislation on Jewish emancipation and universal and compulsory primary education was enacted by parliament. He also played a major part in formulating the most progressive principles of the Nationalities Act of 1868.

George Barany

Further reading

Bödy, Paul. *Joseph Eötvös and the Modernization of Hungary, 1840–1870.* Philadelphia, 1972, in Transactions of the American Philosophical Society, N.S., vol. 62, Pt. 2.

Czigány, Lóránt. *The Oxford History of Hungarian Literature.* Oxford, 1984, 168–78.

Eötvös, József. *Báró Eötvös József Összes Művei,* 20 vols. Budapest, 1901–3.

Jones, D. Mervyn. *Five Hungarian Writers.* Oxford, 1966, 160–228.

Reményi, Joseph. *Hungarian Writers and Literature,* ed. by A.J. Molnar. New Brunswick, New Jersey, 1964, 117–26.

Sőtér, István. *Eötvös József,* 2d ed. Budapest, 1967.

See also Gyula Andrássy Sr.; *Ausgleich;* Lajos Batthyány; Nationality Law of 1868; Revolutions of 1848

Esterházy Family

Leading Hungarian family. The first known Esterházy ancestor is first mentioned in a document dating from 1186. The family rose to prominence in the late-sixteenth-century Habsburg Empire, which, in the eighteenth century, was a major power in Europe. One of the essential pillars of that political and social structure was the aristocracy. About one-third of the total land area of the monarchy was owned by a few hundred families. By the end of the century, one of them, the Esterházy family, owned 10 million acres (4.1 million hectares) of Hungary, including over 100 villages, 400 towns, and 30 castles. The first truly outstanding representative of the family was Nicholaus Esterházy (1582–1645), who through marriage became the proprietor of vast estates in Hungary. As a reward for championing the Catholic cause and faithfully serving the Habsburgs, he received more land—which included Eisenstad in north-

western Hungary, the eventual center of the Esterházy estates. Nicholaus's eldest son died fighting the Turks and the family leadership passed to Nicholaus's second son, Paul (1635–1713). In 1687 Paul became a prince of the Holy Roman Empire. The title was inherited by successive generations. In 1721 the titular leadership of the family devolved on Paul Anton (1711–62), who was ten years old at the time. He and his younger brother, Nicholaus (1714–90), were heirs to enormous wealth and a glittering array of family honors and titles until 1790, when Nicholaus died. Nicholaus is known primarily for his patronage of the arts and artists, including Franz Josef Haydn (1732–1809), and for his building of the Versailles-like palace of Estrháza in Fertöd, Hungary (1766–69). The family also nurtured the development of a Jewish community in an unequal partnership to assist in the craft and the trade aspects of estate management. Throughout the centuries, their political influence was marginal and never in proportion to their wealth and connections. Nevertheless, the Esterházys remained one of Hungary's preeminent families until 1945.

Peter I. Hidas

Further reading

Gates-Coon, Rebecca. *The Landed Estates of the Esterházy Princes: Hungary during the Reforms of Maria Theresa and Joseph II.* Baltimore, Maryland, 1994.

Esztergom

Hungarian ecclesiastical city. Esztergom (population 29,841 in 1990) is located 28 miles (46 km) north of Budapest on steep hills overlooking the Danube River. Castle Hill (Várhegy) is the site of a first-century Roman settlement called Solva Mansio. The city entered Hungarian history when it was selected as the capital during the reign of Prince Géza (940–997). However, the city is mainly associated with his son, Stephen (975–1038), who was born, received his baptism, and was crowned first king of Hungary in Esztergom. King (later Saint) Stephen built a basilica and founded one of two of the country's archbishoprics here; the archbishop of Esztergom is the primate of Hungary. Esztergom lost some of its significance, though, when the capital was moved to Buda following the Mongol invasion of 1241. The city declined further after capture by the Turks in 1543.

Hungarian Catholicism began to reassert itself in Esztergom in 1822 with the construction of a cathedral. Completed in 1856, Esztergom Cathedral is the largest in Hungary; the neoclassical building supports a 263-foot (72 m) high central dome, which is visible for miles. Notwithstanding its ecclesiastical functions, Esztergom has remained a small town on the northern border of Hungary. A bridge connecting the city with the Slovak industrial city of Štúrovo located directly across the Danube was never repaired following its destruction during World War II.

Darrick Danta

Further reading

Fügedi, Erik. *Castle and Society in Medieval Hungary (1000–1437).* Budapest, 1986.

Gutkind, E.A. *International History of City Development,* vol. 7, *Urban Development in East-Central Europe: Poland, Czechoslovakia, and Hungary.* New York, 1972.

Hanák, Péter, ed. *One Thousand Years: A Concise History of Hungary.* Budapest, 1988.

Webster's New Geographical Dictionary. Springfield, Massachusetts, 1984.

Ethnic Minorities

The situation concerning ethnic minorities is more visible and more of a "problem" in Eastern than in Western Europe or the United States. The reason for this is twofold. First, what are normally referred to as "ethnic groups" in the United States are not analogous to minority national communities in Eastern Europe. This distinction is related to a difference in the historic experiences of ethnic groups versus national communities. Ethnic groups and minority national communities are alike insofar as both are based on a sense of common identity derived from common cultural traits, certain common historical experiences, and a common language. These are acquired through socialization by family, peer groups, and institutions such as schools and churches. Unlike racial characteristics, ethnic and national identity are learned rather than genetic. However, ethnicity and nationality differ from each other in that national identity is more politicized and concerned with obtaining some level of self-determination or self-government for the national community. Ethnic identity is less politicized, hence more focused on identity mainly within a cultural context. This difference is due mainly to the different origins and developmental experiences of ethnic groups as opposed to national communities. The relationship of national communities is more directly linked to a territorial base that they tend to define as their "homeland." All nationalities lay claim to such a homeland on the basis of conquest, effective settlement, or appeal to international recognition or treaty agreement. As opposed to this, ethnic groups have existed and exist within national communities, and have acquired a distinct place in society as a subculture. In other words, nationalities have in the past had the opportunity to organize a state with their own governing institutions. Ethnic groups have not had such opportunities or capabilities. Most ethnic groups are a consequence of emigration from one part of the world to another (Armenians in Romania; Gypsies in Hungary or Romania; Greeks in Hungary; or Jews in Czechoslovakia, Hungary, or Romania). Conversely, minority national communities are a consequence of border changes, not of emigration or immigration. For example, the disintegration of the Ottoman and Austro-Hungarian Empires created not only new "states" controlled by new "nations" but also new national minority communities within these new political entities (for example, Hungarians in Romania, Czechoslovakia, or Yugoslavia; Germans in Romania or Czechoslovakia; or Turks in Bulgaria, Greece, or Yugoslavia).

Eastern Europe has been defined as a "shatter zone" in the twentieth century because of the collapse of the multinational empires that controlled the region until World War I. Unlike Western Europe, where the dominant nations were able to consolidate their control and assimilate most of their minority populations, Eastern Europe has remained ethnically and nationally heterogeneous. During the period of the Russian, Austro-Hungarian (prior to 1867, Habsburg), and Ottoman Empires, there were some "ruling nations" like the Russians, Turks, Germans, and Hungarians. After World War I, the former ruling peoples became the major minority nations. Thus, in the interwar period Germans constitutes the largest portion of people living in minority status, while Jews and Hungarians were the second- and third-largest minority peoples. Following World War II, because of the Jewish Holocaust and the expulsion of Germans from many successor states, Hungarians were left with the dubious distinction as the largest minority nationality population of Europe.

National minority communities vary greatly on the basis of their overall numbers, their relative numbers in relation to the ruling nation of the state they inhabit, and whether as a minority they live along borders with a state controlled by their own nationality or as "island settlements" surrounded by the majority nationality of the state, or, finally, whether they are scattered and interspersed in the general population. If minority nationalities find themselves in the first category, it may arouse irredentist sentiments if they are abused or oppressed. If they find themselves in significant numbers as "island" or "cluster" settlements, it leads to demands for local autonomy and self-government, while if they are scattered throughout the population—but in significant numbers—then there will be a demand for cultural autonomy and proportional representation in decision making. Ethnic groups usually do not have these options, since they are immigrants, relatively recent arrivals in the overall population, scattered throughout the majority, with few instances of settlements along borders or in clusters. Consequently, at most they want to be defended against discriminatory treatment. Where neither numbers nor settlement patterns reinforce group identity, and there is no realistic option for secession or local or cultural autonomy, this signifies "ethnic" rather than "national" communities.

Andrew Ludanyi

Further reading

Breuilly, John. *Nationalism and the State.* Chicago, 1993.

Cuthbertson, Ian M. and Jane Leibowitz, eds. *Minorities: The New Europe's Old Issue.* New York, 1993.

Janowsky, Oscar I. *Nationalities and National Minorities.* New York, 1945.

Jászi, Oscar. *The Dissolution of the Habsburg Monarchy.* Chicago, 1929.

King, Robert. *Nationalities under Communism.* Cambridge, Massachusetts, 1973.

Macartney, C.A. *National States and National Minorities.* London, 1934.

Olson, James Stuart. *The Ethnic Dimension in American History.* New York, 1979.

See also Carpatho-Rusyns; Csángó; Emigration; Gypsies; Holocaust; Irredentism; Jews; Lusatian Sorbs; Nationalism; Székely; Transylvania; Transylvanian Dispute; World War I

Ethniki Etairia (National Society)

Organization founded in 1894 by junior officers in the Greek army motivated by a decline in the army's size (half of what it was in 1885), the steep reduction in government funding, the poor state of the army's preparedness, the perception that political leaders did not value the professional military in defending the state's interests, and resentment at the country's political and economic dependence on foreign powers. As younger officers, they did not perceive any personal responsibility for the poor state of the military. The purpose of the organization as stated in its bylaws was the "revival of national self-confidence, vigilance for the interests of the enslaved Greeks, and preparation for their liberation by every sacrifice." In the beginning, membership was open only to men at the rank of lieutenant, but soon the society was recruiting senior officers. It also widened its membership to include civilians, among them political figures from various parties, intellectuals, academics, and state administrators. Reminiscent in its rites and organization of the Filiki Etairia (Friendly Society), the organization founded earlier in the century to overthrow Ottoman rule, the society placed its governance in the hands of a board made up equally of military and civilians. Within a couple of years the society had units in all Greek cities (thirty in Athens alone) and had established a network among Greek communities abroad. The object of the society's actions were the Greeks in the Ottoman-controlled regions of Epirus, Macedonia, and the island of Crete. With the Cretans already well organized and conditions not conducive for determined action in Epirus, the society concentrated on Macedonia. By 1896, the society had agents in Trikala organizing armed bands among chieftains who had crossed the border from Macedonia into Thessaly. In March 1897 a few thousand armed irregulars went into Macedonia inciting revolt among the Greeks there. They were no match for the regular Turkish forces and in April war broke out between Greece and the Ottoman Empire. Fighting ended in early May with Ottoman troops occupying much of Thessaly. Blamed for the humiliating defeat, the society dissolved. But some junior officers renewed their irredentist efforts in response to the military humiliation. Also the question of military-civilian relations continued to affect domestic politics in Greece into the twentieth century.

Gerasimos Augustinos

E

Further reading

Koliopoulos, John S. *Brigands with a Cause*. Oxford, 1987.

Lyritzis, G. Th. *The Ethniki Etairia and Its Activities*. Kozani, Greece, 1979.

Mazaraki-Ainianos, Alexander. *Historical Study 1821–1897*. Athens, n.d.

See also Filiki Etairia; Irredentism; Macedonia

Exarchate

The Bulgarian Orthodox Church, independent of the Greek Patriarchate of Constantinople, established by Ottoman decree in 1870 and existing until 1953. In 1856 Sultan Abdülmecid I (1823–61) issued a reform edict for the Ottoman Empire (*Hatti Hümayun*) that included an article for reorganizing the *millets*, the administrative units that governed the empire's non-Muslim subjects. An Orthodox Church council met in Istanbul (1860–61) to discuss the reorganization, but the Bulgarians were underrepresented. On Easter Sunday 1860, nationalist Bulgarian merchants in Istanbul, seeking to remove Bulgarians from Greek ecclesiastical authority within the Orthodox *millet,* declared that Bulgarians would no longer recognize the authority of the Greek Patriarchate. There ensued a decade of religious-national conflict between Bulgarians and Greeks over that issue known as the Bulgarian Church Question, with the Bulgarians ultimately demanding an independent church (thus an officially recognized separate *millet*). With the strong support of Russian Pan-Slavs, especially of the Russian minister to the Ottoman Empire, Count Nikolai Ignatiev (1832–1908), Bulgarian efforts to win ecclesiastical independence succeeded. On February 28, 1870, Sultan Abdülaziz (1830–76) issued an imperial decree establishing the independent Bulgarian Exarchate with jurisdiction over large tracts of three regions in the empire: Bulgaria, Thrace, and Macedonia. The decree was officially confirmed two years later (1872), when Antim I (1816–88), the metropolitan of Vidin, was named first exarch.

Bulgarian nationalists considered the boundaries of the new church's jurisdiction to delineate the borders of a future independent Bulgarian nation-state. Such ideas exacerbated nationalist tensions among the young modern Balkan states once an independent Bulgaria was established following the Russo-Turkish War of 1877–78. The Russian-imposed Treaty of San Stefano (1878), created a Bulgarian state whose borders reflected those of the Exarchate, but its terms were overturned by the Congress of Berlin (1878) and new Bulgaria was confined to a much smaller territory. Those regions lost were returned to Ottoman control. According to the Ottoman founding decree, the Exarchate could acquire further territories within the empire if two-thirds of their Orthodox population voted for membership. Taking advantage of this provision, Bulgaria agitated heavily for ecclesiastical elections in those territories stripped from the state at Berlin. This resulted in nationalist conflicts among Bulgaria, Greece, and Serbia over Macedonia, whose population predominantly voted to join the Exarchate. The Macedonian Question poisoned relations among the three states through the Balkan Wars (1912–13), and its tensions continue to resonate into the present.

The seat of the Exarchate lay in Istanbul even after Bulgaria won independence, a fact that the Bulgarian government used to its nationalist advantage until defeat in the Second Balkan War (1913) ended hopes of Bulgaria's territorial expansion into Macedonia and Thrace. After the death of Exarch Iosif I (1840–1915), the Exarchate was placed under the authority of the Holy Synod, which until that time had represented the Exarchate within Bulgaria, and its seat was relocated to Bulgaria's capital, Sofia. A deputy chairman from the synod headed the Exarchate until Stefan (1878–1957), metropolitan of Sofia, was elected exarch in 1945. On May 10, 1953, the Exarchate was transformed into the Bulgarian Patriarchate.

Dennis P. Hupchick

Further reading

Crampton, Richard J. *Bulgaria, 1878–1918: A History*. Boulder, Colorado, 1983.

Mach, Richard von. *The Bulgarian Exarchate: Its History and the Extent of Its Authority in Turkey*. London, 1907.

Markova, Zina. *Bŭlgarskata ekzarhiya, 1870–1879*. Sofia, 1989.

Meininger, Thomas A. *Ignatiev and the Establishment of the Bulgarian Exarchate, 1864–1872: A Study of Personal Diplomacy*. Madison, Wisconsin, 1970.

See also Balkan Wars; Congress of Berlin; Nikolai Ignatiev; Macedonia; *Millet;* Orthodoxy; Pan-Slavism; Patriarchate; Russo-Turkish War of 1877–78; San Stefano, Treaty of

F

Family

Numerous factors have affected the family in Eastern Europe over the centuries: loss of national independence, underdeveloped economies, high rates of rural population, biased gender ideology, uneven urbanization and industrialization, and a socialist system introduced in 1945. Family life patterns developed through links among family functions, gender-segregated employment, legislation, and state intervention. During periods of political unrest or economic instability (male emigration, migrant workers), women replaced men in nondomestic roles. Women occupied strong positions in the family. The family had the characteristics of a modified extended unit, where members maintain geographic mobility while exchanging services (noticeable between rural and urban relatives, and between older relatives and working mothers).

The traditional family structure—with both parents present and gender-specific division of roles—persisted. Dual-career couples and mothers employed full-time became a norm after 1945. Premarital pregnancy more often led to marriage or abortion than to the condition of single mother. A shortage of staples and family-oriented services made relatives an indispensable source of assistance (childcare, housekeeping, and care of the ailing and the elderly). Consequently, the economic/productive family function was not entirely eliminated. Family ties, shared values, an acceptance of parents' authority, mutual interdependence (gender and age), and housing shortages contributed to family unity and relatively low divorce rates (in 1988: Bulgaria, 1.4 per 1,000 population; Czechoslovakia, 2.5; Hungary, 2.4; Poland, 1.3; Romania, 1.4; Yugoslavia, 1.0). Low standards of living and shortages (and erratic supplies) of consumer goods limited family expenditures mostly to essentials and turned housekeeping into time-consuming chores. Socialist legislation protected family, mother, and child. Access to "education for all" resulted in increased educational levels. However, mothers maintained a strong influence on children's educational and occupational choices. The socialist efforts to reduce the family's socializing function by including ideological programs in school curricula therefore failed.

To bring married mothers into the workplace, a family benefits policy, job security for working mothers, and (almost) free-of-charge abortion on demand was implemented. A steady improvement in health and life expectancy was recorded. The number of children per family decreased, while the chances of the children's survival improved. But urban-rural residence and parents' education remained factors modifying family size and children's education; families thus continued to be larger in rural areas. Owing to the rapid migration of young people to the cities, an intensified demand for industrial labor force, and female employment, birth rates fell. During the 1960s, the demographic policy resulted in zero population, including negative natural increase (Czechoslovakia and Hungary). To compensate for the low birth rates, pronatal measures and protection of women's reproductive functions were implemented, and a system of privileges for families was introduced. Romania was a stark exception. Reproductive decisions were not accorded privacy by the state, abortion became illegal, and

F sex education and contraceptives were unavailable; this resulted in high infant mortality rates.

Barbara Łobodzińska

Further reading

Boh, Katja et al., ed. *Changing Patterns of European Family Life: A Comparative Analysis of 14 European Countries.* London, 1989, 265–98.

Borowczyk, Ewa. "State Social Policy in Favor of the Family in East European Countries." *International Social Security Review* 39, no. 2: 164–82.

Čermakova, Marie, ed. *Women, Work and Society.* Prague, 1995.

Hernes, Gudmund, and Knud Knudsen. "The Iron Law of Inequality: Different Paths, but Same Results? Some Comparison Between Lithuania and Norway." *European Sociological Review* 7, no. 3 (December 1991): 195–211.

Łobodzińska, Barbara, ed. *Family, Women and Employment in Central-Eastern Europe.* Westport, Connecticut, 1995.

———. "Women's Employment or Return to '*Family Values*' in Central-Eastern Europe." *Journal of Comparative Family Studies* 27, no. 3 (Fall 1996): 519–44.

McIntyre, Robert. "Pronatalist Programmes in Eastern Europe." *Soviet Studies* 27, no. 3 (July 1975): 366–80.

Millard, Frances L. "Social Policy in Poland," in *The New Eastern Europe: Social Policy Past, Present, and Future,* ed. by Bob Deacon. London, 1992.

Nowak, Stefan. "Value System of the Polish Society." *Warsaw: The Polish Sociological Bulletin* 50, no. 2 (1980): 45–53.

See also Women in Albania; Women in Bulgaria; Women in Czechoslovakia; Women in Hungary; Women in Poland; Women in Romania; Women in Yugoslavia; *Zadruga*

Fascism *See* **Right Radicalism**

Fatherland Front

Coalition of Bulgarian center and left political parties that seized power in September 1944. The Fatherland Front originated with a December 1941 appeal from Moscow by Bulgarian Communist leader Georgi Dimitrov (1882–1949) for a common front against the ruling pro-German government in Sofia. Concerted negotiations by the Bulgarian Communist Party (BCP) produced a National Committee of the Fatherland Front in 1943. The National Committee, uniting members of the Communist, Agrarian, and Social Democratic Parties with the promilitary Zveno movement (a sociopolitical organization that held that the party system was detrimental to the nation) supported termination of the alliance with Germany and withdrawal of Bulgarian troops from Serbia. The political crisis produced by the August 1944 Soviet invasion of Bulgaria's northern neighbor, Romania, led to unsuccessful negotiations with authorities in Sofia, while the September 5, 1944, Soviet declaration of war on Bulgaria prompted the Communist-led Fatherland Front's preparation to seize power by force. On the night of September 8–9, 1944, an armed uprising led to the creation of the First Fatherland Front Cabinet, composed of representatives from the four coalition partners.

The transition from opposition to power soon produced fierce conflict among the various claimants to political leadership. Under Communist Party direction, Fatherland Front committees outside the capital soon controlled the operations of local government and local economies. So-called peoples courts now emerged, purging representatives of parties and ideologies incompatible with that of the BCP.

In the spring of 1945 the First Congress of the Fatherland Front approved the use of a single list of candidates for the upcoming parliamentary elections, which the Front handily won that November. Elections for a constitutional assembly a year later produced similar results. In December 1947 a new constitution was passed, placing all power in the hands of the workers and peasants. That same month, the purged remnants of the Bulgarian Agrarian National Union (BANU) remaining in the Fatherland Front acknowledged the leadership of the Bulgarian Communist Party. The following fall, the Bulgarian Social Democrats merged with the BCP, while other political parties and movements renounced their independent status. The Fatherland Front, once a coalition of parties, had by now become simply a mass organization through which the BCP controlled the entire political life of the nation.

Michael Boll

Further reading

Bell, John D. *The Bulgarian Communist Party from Blagoev to Zhivkov.* Stanford, California, 1977.

Boll, Michael M. *Cold War in the Balkans: American Foreign Policy and the Emergence of Communist Bulgaria, 1943–1947.* Lexington, Kentucky, 1984.

Oren, Nissan. *Bulgarian Communism: The Road to Power.* New York, 1971.

See also Bulgarian Agrarian National Union; Communist Party of Bulgaria; Georgi Dimitrov; Zveno

February Patent (1861)

Habsburg imperial decree of 1861 that contributed to Austrian constitutional development. Promulgated as a response to the failure of the earlier October Diploma to satisfy the major political constituencies in the empire, the patent revised that document by allocating greater authority to the central legislative assembly (Reichsrat) and limiting the power of the provincial diets. The diets, which continued to select the representatives to the Reichsrat, were elected through a curial system, by which four groups of electors (great landowners, chambers of commerce, and urban and rural general curia) selected representatives in a manner that strongly favored wealthy voters and denied suffrage to women and the majority of men. Although substantially altered in 1873, 1882, and 1896, the curial electoral system remained in use in Austria until 1907.

Implemented by Minister of State Anton von Schmerling (1805–93), a liberal German official, the February Patent had the support of most German liberals. Hungarian, Czech, and Polish political leaders rejected the patent, however, and in 1865 it was suspended. In 1867 Hungary gained broad self-government and a new constitution; in Austria the December laws of 1867 revised the patent but retained many of its features.

Philip Pajakowski

Further reading

Fellner, Fritz. "Das 'Februarpatent' von 1861: Entstehung und Bedeutung." *Mitteilungen des Instituts für österreichische Geschichtsforschung* 63 (1955): 549–64.

Macartney, C.A. *The Habsburg Empire, 1790–1918.* London, 1969.

Rumpler, Helmut, ed. *Die Protokolle des österreichischen Ministerrates 1848–1867,* part 5, *Die Ministerien Erzherzog Rainer und Mensdorff,* vols. 1, 7, *Februar 1861–30. April 1861,* prepared by Herbert Brettner-Messler. Vienna, 1977.

See also Curial System; October Diploma

Ferdinand I (1861–1948)

Tsar of Bulgaria. Ferdinand I was born on February 14, 1861, in Vienna. His father was Prince August of Saxe-Coburg-Gotha (1818–81), and his mother, Princess Clementine of Orleans (1817–1907), was the daughter of Louis Philippe (1773–1850), the deposed king of France. In 1887, following the abdication of Alexander of Battenberg (1857–93), Bulgaria's first prince, and while Bulgaria was still nominally a suzerainty of Turkey, Ferdinand was called by the Bulgarian National Assembly (Subranie) to assume the throne. Ruling first as prince, he assumed the title of tsar in 1908, when Bulgaria declared its full independence.

Ferdinand's reign was a difficult one. Using at first Great Power rivalry to Bulgaria's advantage, he obtained the finances necessary to improve Bulgaria's communication system and its economy generally. However, ultimately this strategy failed. So too did his efforts to unite the Macedonian Slavs to Bulgaria. Internally, political assassinations and attempted coups plagued most of his reign. Ultimately, because of Bulgarian reverses in the Second Balkan War (a war that he initiated) and in World War I, Ferdinand was forced to abdicate in 1918 in favor of his eldest son, Boris (1894–1943).

John Georgeoff

Further reading

Constant, Stephen. *Foxy Ferdinand.* London, 1979.

Ganchev, Dobre. *Spomeni za kniazeskoto vreme na Ferdinand I.* Sofia, 1973.

Iovkov, Ivan. *Koburgut: Ferdinand I Saks-Koburg-Gotski: Monographiia.* Sofia, 1978.

Konigslow, Joachim V. *Ferdinand von Bulgarien.* Munich, 1970.

Kumanov, Milen. *Abdikatsiiata na Tsar Ferdinand: Dokumenti, spomeni, fakti.* Sofia, 1993.

Macdonald, John. *Czar Ferdinand and His People.* London, 1913.

Madol, Hans Roger. *Ferdinand of Bulgaria: The Dreams of Byzantium,* trans. by Kenneth Kirkness. London, 1933.

See also Alexander of Battenberg; Balkan Wars; Boris III; Great Powers; World War I

Ferdinand I (1865–1927)

King of Romania. Designated in 1889 by his uncle, Carol I (1839–1914), as Romania's crown prince, Ferdinand, who was born in Sigmaringen, Germany, assumed his new role with seriousness, studying Romanian and identifying with Romania's self-interest. Although slow of mind and speech himself, he profited from a clever and popular wife, Marie (1875–1938), an intelligent personal adviser (Marie's lover, Barbu Ştirbei [1873–1946]), and after his accession to power in October 1914, a masterful premier (Ion I.C. Brătianu [1864–1927]). He supported the latter's decision for war against Austria-Hungary in 1916, even though it estranged him from his Hohenzollern relatives. Ferdinand endured with dignity the agonizing defeat of 1917 and enhanced his stature among his people during the revolutionary stirrings of 1917 by agreeing to electoral and land reform, offering some of his own for the latter. The treaty of 1916 with the western Allies, which brought Romania into World War I, and the advance of Romania's armies into Hungary in 1918–19, allowed Ferdinand to be crowned king of Greater Romania, with the postwar union of the Regat (Moldavia and Wallachia) with Transylvania, Bukovina, and Bessarabia. While Ferdinand did not initiate any of the crucial decisions in 1914–18 that led to success, he supported those who did. His postwar reign was marred by the escapades of his son and heir, Carol II (1893–1953).

Glenn E. Torrey

Further reading

Hitchins, Keith. *Rumania 1866–1947.* Oxford, 1994.
Wolbe, Eugen. *Ferdinand I. der Begründer Grossrumäniens: Ein Lebensbild.* Leipzig, 1938.

See also Ion I.C. Brătianu; Carol I; Carol II; Greater Romania; Marie

Filiki Etairia (Friendly Society)

A secret organization founded in 1814 in the Russian port of Odessa by three Greeks engaged in commerce: Nikolaos Skoufas (1779–1819), Athanasios Tsakalov (1788–1851), and Emmanouil Xanthos (1772–1852). Taking ideas from other groups, they envisioned a conspiracy to overthrow Ottoman rule that would involve not only the Greeks but all Orthodox Christians in the Balkans. Initially they had little success in recruiting, although they managed to enlist Serbian leader Karadjordje Petrović (Black George [1768–1817]). In 1818 the organization was reorganized and headquarters moved to Istanbul, where the society recruited several hundred using a system of "apostles" who organized in specific areas. Eventually the Etairia included merchants and shipowners, who made up the majority of the members, professionals such as physicians, teachers and lawyers, community notables, clergy, and military men. Very few peasants, who were the largest social class, joined. In general, the more prosperous mercantile Greeks who were well established in European cities did not become members. The Etairia was not a broad national movement forged by a unified Greek bourgeoisie. The society was able to bind the disparate elements together in the name of a national cause in an oathing ceremony requiring initiates to sacrifice for God and compatriots.

In 1820 the society's leadership sought to recruit Count Ioannis Kapodistrias (1776–1831) as its leader. Kapodistrias, then sharing the post of foreign minister of Russia, would lend prestige to the organization by linking it with the Russian state. He refused, however, believing that European diplomacy and time rather than wild conspiracies would gain the Greeks' freedom. They then turned to Alexandros Ypsilantis (1792–1828), a Greek born in Istanbul, whose family had gone to Russia where he had joined the military and risen to the rank of general, serving as an aide-de-camp to the tsar. Ypsilantis accepted, and the Etairia promoted the myth of Russian support. When Ypsilantis learned of the armed resistance by Ali Pasha (c. 1750–1822) against the Ottoman government in 1820, he prepared plans for an uprising in the Peloponnesis in the fall of that year. It was soon evident that the military and political preparedness required was inadequate and Ypsilantis put off the revolt until the spring of 1821. The plan was to invade the Danubian principality of Moldavia, raise the standard of revolt among the Balkan Christians, and gain support from Tudor Vladimirescu (1780–1821), a Romanian who started a revolt against the rule of the Phanariots (the Greek princes of Moldavia and Wallachia) in January 1821, and from the Serbian leader Miloš Obrenović (1780–1860). Ypsilantis began the revolt in early March with a few thousand men, including a "Sacred Legion" of Greek students; however, the significant support he expected from the Serbs, Romanians, and Bulgarians did not materialize. Ypsilantis's invasion of the Danubian Principalities ended in failure, but supporters of the Etairia rose in the Peloponnesis, setting off the Greek struggle for independence. Many of the groups that fought did so for their particular local interests. But it was the Etairia that had provided the coordination and goal for the Greek national liberation movement.

Gerasimos Augustinos

Further reading

Dakin, Douglas. *The Greek Struggle for Independence 1821–1833.* London, 1973.

Frangos, George. "The Philike Etaireia, 1814–1821: A Social and Historical Analysis." Ph.D. diss., Columbia University, 1971.

See also Ali Pasha; Black George; Danubian Principalities; Greek Revolution; Miloš Obrenović; Phanariots; Tudor Vladimirescu; Alexandros Ypsilantis

Filov, Bogdan (1883–1945)

Bulgarian archaeologist, academician, and politician. Filov was born in Stara Zagora, and, after completing his primary and secondary education in Bulgaria, obtained a scholarship from the Ministry of Education in 1901 to study abroad. After attending universities at Wurzburg and Leipzig, he went on to Freiburg, where he completed his doctorate on the history and archaeology of ancient Rome. Following a short stay in Bulgaria, he resumed study in Bonn, Paris, and Rome. Returning to Bulgaria in 1909, he became curator of the National Museum and shortly after that, its director. During the following two decades, he produced several important pioneering works on Bulgarian antiquity. In 1920 he was appointed professor of archaeology and head of the newly established Department of Archaeology and Art History at Kliment Okhridski University in Sofia. The following year, he also became director of the newly established Bulgarian Archaeological Institute. Filov became president of the Bulgarian Academy of Sciences in 1937, a position he held until 1944.

Filov's scholarly achievements led to his being named minister of education in November 1938. A cabinet crisis in February 1940 resulted in his appointment as prime minister. In early March 1941 Filov negotiated a treaty with Germany making Bulgaria an ally of the Axis powers. General popular dissatisfaction with the alliance, however, forced Filov increasingly to adopt strongman tactics, vigorously suppressing all opposition. In September 1943 Tsar Boris (1894–1943) died unexpectedly, leaving his six-year-old son, Simeon II (1937–), as heir. A regency council was formed, with Filov resigning his prime ministership to become one of its three members. Barely a year later, the Fatherland Front, a coalition of left and center parties, came to power and the regents, including Filov, were removed from office. Charged with betrayal of his country, he was condemned to death by a People's Court and executed.

John Georgeoff

Further reading

Chary, Frederick, ed. "The Diary of Bogdan Filov," in *Southeastern Europe,* 1974–1977.

Filov, Bogdan. *Bulgariens Weg:Die Aussenpolitik der bulgarischen Regierung, Bulgariens Beitrag zur Errichtung der neuen Ordnung.* Sofia, 1942.

———. *Dnevnik,* ed. by Ilcho Dimitrov. Sofia, 1990.

———. *Geschichte der bulgarischen Kunst unter der türkischen Herrschaft und in der neueren Zeit.* Berlin, 1933.

———. *Ideitie i dielata na dneshniia bezpartien rezhim.* Sofia, 1942.

———. *L'Art antique en Bulgarie.* Sofia, 1925.

———. *Putuvaniia iz Trakiia, Rodopite i Makedoniia, 1912–1916.* Sofia, 1993.

See also Boris III; Fatherland Front; Simeon II

Fiume Resolution

Memorandum signed on October 3, 1905, by Croat politicians from Croatia-Slavonia (then an autonomous unit of the Kingdom of Hungary) and Dalmatia (which was under Austrian administration). The resolution addressed the emerging constitutional crisis in the Habsburg monarchy provoked by Hungarian demands for a looser, personal union with Austria.

The Croat politicians who signed the resolution expressed their solidarity with the demands articulated by the Hungarian opposition parties against Vienna. But this support was made conditional on Hungarian support for the unification of Dalmatia with Croatia and the introduction of a number of democratic and constitutional reforms in Croatia, such as a broader franchise and financial autonomy. In effect, they called for greater national freedoms in Croatia-Slavonia and Dalmatia. By expressing support for the Hungarians against Vienna, they hoped to gain the former's assistance in the realization of their national aspirations.

The Fiume Resolution was followed by the Zadar Resolution (October 17, 1905), which was signed by Serb politicians from Croatia and Dalmatia who pledged to cooperate with the Croats. The significance of the Fiume Resolution and its Serb counterpart lies in the fact that these memoranda initiated the so-called new course in Croatian politics after 1905. They also led to the creation of the Croato-Serb Coalition (December 1905), a political alliance between the majority of Croatia's Croat and Serb parties. The new course was a policy predicated on Croat and Serb political cooperation and the eventual destruction of the Habsburg monarchy.

Mark Biondich

Further reading

Gross, Mirjana. *Vladavina hrvatsko-srpske koalicije.* Belgrade, 1960.

Horvat, Josip. *Politička povijest Hrvatske,* 2d ed., vol. 1. Zagreb, Yugoslavia, 1989, 269–75.

Flying University

Informal name of TKN (Towarzystwo Kursów Naukowych [Society of Scientific Courses]), one of the institutions of Polish dissidence in the second half of the 1970s. The "Flying University" (Uniwersytet Latający) and TKN took their name from similar late-nineteenth-century initiatives at a time when there were no possibilities of instruction in the Polish language within the Russian-governed parts of Poland. It also harkened back to analogous experiences undertaken by the Polish resistance in German-occupied Poland during World War II. The founders of TKN invoked a historic name to suggest a continuing tradition of opposition to national oppression. As in the case of its historical predecessors, TKN consisted of informal seminars and lectures open to all. The clandestine or semiclandestine meetings regularly changed their venue, usually private homes, to avoid police disruption, but were often unsuccessful in this respect. The Flying University concentrated on social studies, humanities, and history, particularly modern Polish history. In all cases, TKN dealt with issues misrepresented or considered taboo in the official school and university curricula. TKN was closely connected to KOR—KSS (Komitet Obrony Robotników—Komitet Samoobrony Społecznej), the Committee for the Defense of Workers and for Social Self-Defense established by prominent Polish dissident intellectuals as a response to the repression that followed riots in June 1976. TKN was officially founded in January 1978 largely on the initiative of the Polish political activist and dissident Adam Michnik (1946–).

André Liebich

Further reading

Kuron, Jacek. *Maintenant ou jamais.* Paris, 1993.

Raina, Peter. *Independent Social Movement in Poland.* London, 1981.

See also KOR; Adam Michnik

Folklife

Folklife, or the general way of life for rural populations, is strongly influenced by particular local customs, history, and environment. However, it is also shaped by forces that cut across village localities. At this level the rural way of life can be seen as the interaction between economic activity and customs of social organization, with political forces overlapping both.

The economic situation for villagers in Eastern Europe prior to World War II depended on where they lived. Much of the Balkans, for example, was characterized by relatively smallholding subsistence equality; that is, most people in the region were agriculturalists in much the same predicament: barely producing their own basic needs with simple technology on too-small plots often scattered over large areas. To fill the widening gap between their needs and what they could grow, and to supply increasing cash needs, they sold agricultural products, expanded artisan activity, went to work temporarily for others, and migrated out of the region altogether (although these strategies too had their limits). The division of labor in the countryside was based on age and gender within the family, complemented by various customs of labor sharing among village households. The situation was somewhat different in Hungary, where agrarian estates accounted for a significant amount of agricultural land. A large number of landless or land-poor workers worked for estate owners, creating more extreme class divisions than found elsewhere. In areas of northeastern Europe, especially Poland, the so-called second serfdom provided another important distinction affecting peasant life. Legal measures binding peasants to the soil and requiring various labor services to the lord increased in severity, just as such feudal measures were declining in the West. The exploitation was often extreme and lasted into the nineteenth century.

The greatest transformation of East European rural life was set in motion by the collectivization of agriculture after World War II. Only two countries in the region, Poland and the former Yugoslavia, never collectivized agriculture. Rural life there remained statistically more predominant but became increasingly distinct from the more common East European pattern. This pattern included state control of agricultural production either through nationalization of land or de facto control over so-called cooperatives that villagers were forced to join. Villagers ended up working for the cooperatives much like state employees.

Since work was still hard and the rewards limited, it is not surprising that collectivization provoked massive migration of rural residents to towns and cities. This was exacerbated by socialist industrialization, which attracted villagers to new jobs beyond the village, and by the subsequent mechanization of agriculture, which reduced the need for rural workers. Villages were already feeling the impact of a decline in fertility evident in most places by the early twentieth century. These combined processes had a huge impact on rural life as the population of villages dropped significantly, families dispersed, and the city/town became the premier settlement form. Villagers remaining in the countryside were seen as old-fashioned, and rural life lost standing vis-à-vis the urban.

Disengagement from agriculture as an occupation eventually began to affect villagers who stayed behind as well. Increased possibilities for daily commuting to nearby towns and the subsequent dispersion of industrial workshops to rural areas brought nonagricultural employment to the village. However, rural workers remained strongly connected to agriculture as a sideline activity through the cultivation of so-called subsistence plots. These plots of land were allocated by the cooperative farm to village families for household subsistence cultivation. Nearly all villagers worked diligently on these plots, often providing most of their family's food needs and sometimes additional products for the market. This consumed much of their free time after work and on weekends and led many observers to characterize East European villagers under socialism as "peasant workers"—people who combine subsistence farming with wage labor. Women often bore a greater burden in this scheme. While they gained financial influence and independence through wage labor, they often maintained sole responsibility for domestic work as well, creating a double burden that became a triple threat when agricultural subsistence activity was included.

While labor consumed much of villagers' time and energy, the seasonality of farming and the intimacy of the village combined to maintain and encourage intense commensalism. Thus, folklife in Eastern Europe has always been characterized by extended sociability and ritual celebration. Daily socializing takes place in the context of visiting relatives and neighbors and during brief stops en route to chores. Politics, the progress of the crops, and village gossip are the most recurrent themes of conversation. For men, time before or after the evening meal may be passed in the village tavern drinking and talking with friends. Events in the life cycle (especially birth and marriage) are highly marked, bringing together family, friends, and neighbors for large festive banquets. Alcohol and food are important elements in this social intercourse.

Life cycle events are so important in part because of the significance of the family in rural social organization. Prior to socialism, the rural family often formed the major unit of production and consumption. While nearly all adult family members took jobs outside the household under socialism, the household remained an important economic unit coordinating the resources of its members. For example, a three-generation household was common in which retired grandparents provided their pensions and labor for childcare and gardening, while the younger couple went to work at state jobs, bringing home salaries and helping on subsistence plots or other profitable sidelines after work and on weekends. Even family members who no longer lived in the village continued to be significant as they returned to assist village relatives with subsistence production, especially during periods of peak labor demand. Of course, they also took much of the family produce back with them to their urban apartments. Kinship was also an important basis for the connections needed to acquire scarce goods or services in the shortage economy of socialism. Ultimately, the attempt of the socialist state to control all of society reinforced the family unit as the last bastion of defense against state intervention.

In some parts of Eastern Europe, kinship once provided the basis of political structure. In areas of Albania and Montenegro, for example, tribal structures continued to function into the twentieth century. The Balkans are also famous for a form of social organization known as the *zadruga*, or extended joint communal family. These large property-owning communal families, sometimes numbering over fifty members, administered their own affairs, and the heads of such units constituted the political leadership of villages. Some researchers believe that similar communal relations actually characterized entire villages in what is now Romania from the thirteenth to the sixteenth centuries, surviving in some places into the nineteenth and twentieth. In these communal villages, cultivation and economic activity were communally regulated. The complementarity of village and kinship relations was manifested explicitly in the customs of godparenthood. These ritual relations, common in many parts of the region, actually recast village connections in a kinship idiom.

Even among unrelated villagers, the rural context insured intense interaction among villagers, so that social sanction and pressure were effective forces, limiting variation or violation of custom and law. Under socialism, the administration of villages passed to the Communist Party, which was also not known for its tolerance. The party filled all the important posts of the village—mayor, cooperative farm president, party secretary—with its members. Still, the degree of central party control and local autonomy varied over time and across the region.

While many of the countries of Eastern Europe became predominantly urban and industrial under socialism, folklife continues to be more important than either statistics or cultural values would suggest. Modern nationalist rhetoric often draws heavily on folklife for its unifying themes.

More important, the economy continues to rely heavily on folk strategies rooted in the countryside, especially subsistence production and the movement of goods and services informally along kin lines between rural and urban contexts.

Gerald W. Creed

Further reading

Bell, Peter D. *Peasants in Socialist Transition: Life in a Collectivized Hungarian Village.* Berkeley, California, 1984.

Creed, Gerald W. *Domesticating Revolution: From Socialist Reform to Ambivalent Transition in a Bulgarian Village.* University Park, Pennsylvania, 1998.

Fél, Edit and Tamás Hofer. *Proper Peasants: Traditional Life in a Hungarian Village.* Chicago, 1969.

Halpern, Joel M. *A Serbian Village.* New York, 1956.

Kideckel, David A. *The Solitude of Collectivism: Romanian Villagers to the Revolution and Beyond.* Ithaca, New York, 1993.

Nagengast, Carole. *Reluctant Socialists, Rural Entrepreneurs: Class, Culture, and the Polish State.* Boulder, Colorado, 1991.

Salzmann, Zdenek and Vladimír Scheufler. *Komárov: A Czech Farming Village.* New York, 1974.

Verdery, Katherine. *Transylvanian Villagers: Three Centuries of Political, Economic and Ethnic Change.* Berkeley, California, 1983.

See also Agriculture; Collectivization; Dance; Family; Folklore; Folk Music; Peasants; *Zadruga*

Folklore

Folklore is a major part of the culture of all of today's Eastern European nations (Eastern Slavs: Belorussians, Russians, Ukrainians; Western Slavs: Czechs, Poles, Slovaks, Sorbs; South Slavs: Bulgarians, Bosnians, Croats, Macedonians, Montenegrins, Serbs, Slovenes; Romanians; Hungarians; and Albanians). The existence of folklore before the conversion of the early Slavic states to Christianity (ninth–tenth century) is inferred only on the basis of indirect evidence. References to folklore increase with the rise of literature, which followed Christianization. The clerics/writers were openly hostile if they perceived folklore as expression of pagan or heretical belief. However, if they saw it as a means of supporting Christian values and institutions, they were rather accommodating. Medieval (tenth-sixteenth centuries) and early-modern (seventeenth-eighteenth century) literatures, painting, and music preserved, although with various degrees of modification, some folklore texts and melodies. The first serious efforts to record the region's folklore were inspired by the ideas of Western romanticism. They started at the end of the eighteenth and the beginning of the nineteenth centuries. The view of folklore as an expression of "the spirit of the nation" informs the attitude of educated people and the artistic elite even today. During the last two centuries, national folklore has been a source of inspiration for all major East European writers, musicians, and artists. Western audiences find the folk art component of modern East European culture exotic; the native public, however, perceives it as symbol of self-identity.

All of the region's languages use "folklore" (or its synonyms "oral literature/tradition," "[oral] folk poetry," "[oral] folk art," "folk music") to refer to the traditional arts (singing, storytelling, dance, and instrumental music) and crafts (embroidery, weaving, wood carving, pottery, metalwork, etc.) of the rural population. Much less studied are urban folklore, the folklore of social groups other than peasants and blue-collar workers, as well as the contemporary themes and forms of expression (except for songs and narratives devoted to the workers' movement, class-struggle, antifascist resistance, and the socialist way of life).

The focus on the culture of the village folk is understandable. Until the middle of this century, the population of most of the countries was predominantly rural, and its rich traditional art was still thriving. Since folklore is tightly interwoven with traditional folklife, the major technological, social, and economic changes during the second half of the twentieth century could not but modify the entire folk tradition. As the old forms of social interaction (that is, village dances, manual harvesting of crops, various family and calendar celebrations) changed or disappeared, books, radio and television programs, records, compact discs, folk festivals, and professional or amateur folk ensembles became increasingly influential means for the preservation, transformation, and dissemination of folk art.

Folk songs, instrumental music, and dance are usually characterized either on the basis of their links to various customs and rituals or by their form and content. For example, all nationalities have special songs for religious/calendar holidays (the Christmas season, New Year, St. George's Day, St. John's Day, etc.) or for family rituals (weddings, funerals [mostly in the Balkans]). Other songs are sung at various ritual occasions as well as at village dances, festive dinners, autumn and winter working bees, or while working in the fields, tending sheep, and the like. In terms of form and content, the songs are usually divided into heroic epics (found only among Eastern and Southern Slavs and among the other groups in the Balkans); historical songs; mythical, religious, and rebel ballads; lyric songs; and humorous songs and couplets. There is a well-developed tradition of storytelling whose repertoire includes fairy tales, animal tales, tales of everyday life, anecdotes, historical and religious legends, and oral histories. Mythology has not been preserved in its entirety, but many elements of it have survived in epic songs, ballads, legends, healing and other magic charms, and fortune-telling customs. The short genres such as sayings and proverbs are still quite popular. The riddles have moved to the repertoire of children.

In the not-so-distant past there was a rather pronounced differentiation between the male and the female skills and repertoire in the folk traditions of East European peoples. For instance, embroidery and weaving were female crafts, while wood carving and metalworking were traditionally male occupations. Epic songs used to be primarily male songs, while wedding songs and funeral laments were and still are performed only by women. Musical instruments, especially winds, used to be played by men. Certain dances (solo, couples, chains, and circular-ones) were performed only by men, others only by women, and still others by mixed groups. Some restrictions concerning singing and dancing were based on age, sexual maturity, and marital status. There were special children's songs and games.

The folklore of the different peoples was modified to a certain extent because of their contacts with various other cultures. Thus, Western and some Southern Slavs (Slovenes, Croats) interacted with Germans, Austrians with Hungarians, Russians with various Baltic, Mongol, Tatar, and other ethnic groups, and the rest of the peoples of southeastern Europe with Greeks, Turks, and their other neighbors. Some specific features of the folklore of the predominantly

Roman Catholic, Eastern Orthodox, and Muslim nations resulted from the difference in their religious denomination.

Folk art has become part of the culture of today's "global village." For example, the unique rhythm of Slavic music and the elaborate steps of Slavic dance attract people all over the world. A record of a Bulgarian rebel ballad was placed in an American space capsule intended to represent present-day human civilization, and the producers of the television series *NOVA* used it as an opening theme song. Albert Lord's study of the epic tradition of the Bosnian Muslims gave rise to the theory of oral composition and kindled the interest in orality and literacy as means of cultural interaction.

Lyubomira Parpulova Gribble

Further reading

Jakobson, Svatava Pirkova. "Slavic Folklore," in *Funk & Wagnalls Standard Dictionary of Folklore, Mythology and Legend.* New York, 1950.

Lord, Albert B. *The Singer of Tales.* Cambridge, 1960.

Propp, V. *The Morphology of the Folktale.* Austin, Texas, 1971.

Romanska, Tsvetana. *Slavianski folklor.* Sofia, 1963.

See also Dance; Folklife; Folk Music; Romanticism

Folk Music

East European folk music, produced by diverse ethnic and linguistic groups (Slavic, Finno-Ugric, Romance), represents a great variety of traditions, styles, and practices. Most East European folk music is based on an equal-tempered tonal system (although irregular intervals can be found in the Balkans owing to the influence of the Near East). Narrow-ranged and pentatonic scales belong to the oldest repertory and are characteristic primarily of ritual songs; the majority of the scales are seven-tone. The general melodic contour is undulating, with a descending tendency.

Strophic structure of vocal music (that is, the same melody repeated several times with different words) is most typical of the region's folk music. The melody is divided into sections that correspond with the divisions of the text lines; the arrangement of phrases is usually symmetrical, with exceptions found mainly in the Balkans and the Baltic region.

Syllabic songs (in which one note is sung to each syllable of a text) predominate in the music of the Western Slavs (Poles, Slovaks, Czechs); more melisms (where a succession of different notes is sung upon a single syllable) are found in slower and ceremonial songs, and in the folk music of the Balkans. Monophony (where a single melody without harmonizing or accompaniment is used) characterizes Polish, Czech, Slovak, and Hungarian folk styles; while polyphony (utilizing two or more melodies) is frequent in Russian, Ukrainian, and Balkan ones. Most of East European folk music adheres to the concept of meter (a regularly occurring accent pattern) with double or triple meters predominating; irregular metric patterns, such as 5/4 or 7/4, may occur throughout the region, but Balkan countries have an unusual degree of metric and rhythmic complexity, including freely declaimed melodies, those with changing meter, and those with a dominant meter based on a prime number of beats: 5, 7, 11, 13, and so on. Absence of anacrusis (an upbeat) and "descendental" rhythms (progressively decreasing rhythms within a phrase or a bar) are predominant in East European folk music.

Folksongs can be classified into a number of categories: narrative (epics and ballads); ceremonial (accompanying weddings or funerals); and songs accompanying annual rituals, both religious and nonreligious (agricultural).

Instruments used in the music vary in type, design, and origin. The most frequently used instruments throughout the region include a variety of fiddles, bass chordophones, wooden flutes, drums, and bagpipes. There are also instruments typical only of certain regions, such as the large hammered dulcimer in Hungary, Poland, Moravia, and Slovakia; the zither and hurdy-gurdy used in Hungary; and the *tambura,* a long-neck fretted lute used in the Balkans. Clarinets, trumpets, cornets, and accordions are relatively new additions in folk music, first appearing at the end of the nineteenth century.

East European folk music can be divided into four main stylistic groups: Western Slavs (most influenced by West European art music); Russians, Ukrainians, and Caucasians (with highly developed polyphony); Balkan (with music of small intervals and strong influence of the Near East); and Hungarians and other Finno-Ugric peoples (with the prominence of the pentatonic scale and transposing as a part of the song structure).

Jolanta T. Pękacz

Further reading

Bartók, Béla. *Serbo-Croatian Folk Songs.* New York, 1951.

Czekanowska, A. *Ludowe melodie wąskiego zakresu w krajach słowiańskich.* Kraków, 1972.

Kodaly, Zoltán. *Folk Music of Hungary,* 2d ed. Budapest, 1971.

Krutsev, V. *Bulgarian Music.* Sofia, 1978.

Nettl, B. *Folk and Traditional Music of the Western Continents,* 3d ed. Englewood Cliffs, New Jersey, 1990.

Tiberiu, A. *Romanian Folk Music.* Bucharest, 1980.

See also Folklife; Folklore

Forman, Miloš (1932–)

Czech film director and screenwriter. Forman became one of the major representatives of the Czech New Wave of the 1960s. During his early period, he worked with cameraman Miroslav Ondříček (1933–) and coscreenwriters Ivan Passer (1933–) and Jaroslav Papoušek (1932–). His early style is characterized by a sensitivity to detail, a quasi-documentary style, and subtle humor. In 1969 Forman emigrated to the United States, where he has worked ever since. He chairs the film program at Columbia University. In the United States, Forman's directorial style gradually changed to accommodate the expectations of American audiences. In the 1970s he became concerned with specifically American topics and issues. By the 1980s, his interests were mostly in period psychological drama. His major recognitions were the Cannes Award for *Loves of a Blond* (*Lásky jedné plavovlásky,* 1965), and Academy Awards for *One Flew Over the Cuckoo's Nest* (1975) and *Amadeus* (1984). Apart from those, his other features included *Konkurs* (*The Competition,* 1963); *Kdyby ty muziky nebyly* (*If There Were No Music,* 1963); *Černý Petr* (*Black Peter,* 1963); *Hoři, má panenko!* (*The Fireman's Ball,* 1967); *Taking Off* (1971); *Decathlon* (1971); *Hair* (1979); *Ragtime* (1981); *Valmont* (1989); and *The People vs. Larry Flynt* (1996).

Dina Iordanova

Further reading

Forman, Miloš and Jan Novák. *Turnaround: A Memoir.* New York, 1994.

Hames, Peter. "Forman," in *Five Filmmakers.* Bloomington, Indiana, 1994.

Liehm, Antonin J. *Miloš Forman's Stories.* New York, 1975.

Slater Thomas J. *Miloš Forman: A Bio-Bibliography.* New York, 1987.

See also Cinema

Fourteen Points

Celebrated framework for World War I peace settlement proposed by U.S. president Woodrow Wilson (1856–1924). The origins of this American diplomatic initiative can be traced to 1917, the year of the American entry into the war on the side of the Allies and the outbreak of the Russian Revolution. Shortly after seizing power, the Russian Bolsheviks published the secret treaties of the deposed tsarist government, casting an embarrassing light on Allied war objectives. On January 8, 1918, President Wilson addressed a joint session of Congress in an effort to clarify U.S. war aims and to disassociate Washington from inter-allied agreements contracted before U.S. entry into the coalition. The Fourteen Points he set forth sketched a vision of an idealistic and enlightened settlement, hinging on creation of a League of Nations.

Four of these postulates dealt directly with East European issues. The sixth called for the evacuation of Russian territory and benevolence toward that country, then convulsed by revolution. The tenth promised "the freest opportunity of autonomous development" for the peoples of the Habsburg Empire. The eleventh demanded the restoration of Romania, Serbia, and Montenegro. The thirteenth urged the restoration of an independent Poland, comprising at least "the territories inhabited by indisputably Polish populations" and possessing "free and secure access to the sea," implying a rightful claim to the port city of Danzig (Gdańsk). Aside from enshrining the favored Wilsonian principle of self-determination, the statement reflected the growing Allied willingness to appeal to the restive national minorities of the Central Powers.

While Wilson's formula received widespread popular acclaim, other Allied governments accepted it only with considerable reservations. In the final days of the war, Germany came to terms for an armistice on the basis of the Fourteen Points.

F The degree to which the subsequent formal peace treaties truly reflected the substance and spirit of the Fourteen Points is a subject of controversy to this day.

Neal A. Pease

Further reading

Baker, Ray Stannard. *Woodrow Wilson and World Settlement,* 3 vols. Garden City, New York, 1922.

Ferrell, Robert H. *Woodrow Wilson and World War I, 1917–1921.* New York, 1985.

House, Edward M. *The Intimate Papers of Colonel House,* 4 vols. Boston, 1926–28.

Mamatey, Victor S. *The United States and East Central Europe, 1914–1918.* Princeton, New Jersey, 1957.

See also League of Nations; Paris Peace Conference; Woodrow Wilson; World War I

Franco-Czechoslovak Alliance

Bilateral alliance, representative of similar such alliances throughout East Central Europe during the interwar period. The Franco-Czechoslovak alliance had its roots in World War I, reached fruition in the mid-1920s, and suffered a long demise in the 1930s. During World War I, Czech and Slovak volunteers fought alongside French, Italian, and Russian troops against the Central Powers, while Edvard Beneš (1884–1948) and Tomáš Masaryk (1850–1937), the future presidents of interwar Czechoslovakia, campaigned for Allied recognition of a new Czechoslovak state. France supported an independent Czechoslovakia to contain Germany and stop the spread of bolshevism. In February 1919 French officers arrived to train, and for a time command, the infant republic's army.

A February 1924 Treaty of Alliance and Friendship limited itself to a general political accord, largely due to Czechoslovak reticence to go further. President Masaryk had frowned on France's occupation of the Ruhr in 1923 when Germany fell behind on its reparations, and Foreign Minister Beneš sought to maintain his country's freedom of maneuver within the League of Nations and the Little Entente, which allied Czechoslovakia with Romania and Yugoslavia. The 1925 Locarno Pact, which guaranteed the postwar borders in Western Europe, did not mark an end to the Franco-Czechoslovak alliance; indeed, it was accompanied by a formal reiteration of the 1924 agreement. But the return to a Great Power directorate can be seen in retrospect as an ominous sign, in part because Germany accepted only its western frontier as permanent. Moreover, in 1929 French politicians voted to build the Maginot Line, its defensive system along the German border, a development hardly compatible with supporting an eastern ally.

Hitler's (1889–1945) revisionist challenge after 1933 broke apart the Franco-Czechoslovak alliance. A consensus grew in French official circles that the relationship now constituted a liability rather than an asset. French and Czechoslovak treaties with the Soviet Union in 1935 meant little without military discussions, and French immobility in the March 1936 Rhineland crisis (when Germany reoccupied the region) furthered a diplomacy of drift in the face of Nazi German aggression. Germany outflanked Czechoslovakia with the March 1938 *Anschluss* (the German annexation of Austria) as it fomented increasing unrest in the Sudetenland. Though the Czechoslovaks showed their mettle by mobilizing against a perceived German invasion in May, the French endorsed British appeasement. The September Munich Pact among France, Britain, Germany, and Italy, which handed the Sudetenland to Hitler, postponed war but officially severed the Franco-Czechoslovak alliance.

Richard F. Crane

Further reading

Crane, Richard F. *A French Conscience in Prague: Louis Eugène Faucher and the Abandonment of Czechoslovakia.* Boulder, Colorado, 1996.

Jordan, Nicole T. *The Popular Front and Central Europe: The Dilemmas of French Impotence, 1918–1940.* Cambridge, 1992.

Komjathy, Antony T. *The Crises of France's East Central European Diplomacy, 1933–1938.* Boulder, Colorado, 1976.

Wandycz, Piotr S. *The Twilight of French Eastern Alliances, 1926–1936.* Princeton, New Jersey, 1988.

See also Edvard Beneš; Little Entente; Locarno; Tomáš Masaryk; Munich Pact; Sudeten Crisis

Frank, Josip (1844–1911)

Croatian nationalist politician. Trained as a journalist and a lawyer, Frank rose to prominence after writing a pamphlet in 1880 on the unfavorable financial aspects of the 1868 *Nagodba* (Compromise), the legal arrangement that regulated the constitutional position of Croatia within the Habsburg Empire. In 1884 he won a seat in the Sabor, the Croatian diet. He became a follower and friend of Ante Starčević (1823–96), the radical Croatian nationalist. Frank joined Starčević's Party of Rights, soon establishing his own faction. Shortly before Starčević died—and with his blessing— Frank in 1895 split off his group to form the Pure Party of Rights. By 1897, Frank had become the leader of the states' rights movement.

Unlike Starčević, Frank became a pro-Habsburg Austrophile. Under his tutelage, the party remained anti-Serbian, anti-Yugoslav, and nationalistic. He proposed a trialistic approach to the Habsburg lands by making the Kingdom of Croatia the third entity in the empire. He envisioned a Greater Croatia including Bosnia-Hercegovina, Carinthia, Carniola, Dalmatia, Fiume, the Littoral, and Styria. Despite Frank's Jewish extraction, his chief support came from the Roman Catholic clergy and students, but he enjoyed little following among the peasantry, who could not relate to his polemics.

When the various Croatian opposition parties created the Croato-Serb Coalition, a group consisting of Croat and Serb parties in 1905, Frank opposed their cooperation, attacking the coalition leaders with his mouthpiece, *Hrvatsko pravo* (Croatian Rights). After the parliamentary elections of 1910, Frank used his influence to keep the Croato-Serb Coalition from receiving a majority in the Sabor. By the time of his death, his party had declined because of his antics. Nonetheless, his followers honored him by calling themselves Frankists, and they later became the core of the Croatian Ustaša movement, the Croatian ultranationalist organization.

Gregory C. Ference

Further reading

Gross, Mirjana. *Povijest pravaske ideologije.* Zagreb, 1973.

See also Frankovici; *Nagodba;* Sabor; Ante Starčević; Trialism; Ustaša

Frank, Karl Hermann (1898–1946)

Sudeten German radical politician. With his roots in traditionally nationalistic western Bohemia, Frank, born in Karlsbad (Karlovy Vary) in January 1898, represented the most radical of Sudeten German nationalism during the 1930s. A frustrated book dealer and publisher manqué, after World War I, Frank gravitated from the Sudeten youth movement to the Bohemian National Socialist party, one venue where he could give expression to his rather primitive anti-Czech hatred.

In 1933 he joined Konrad Henlein's newly proclaimed German Heimatfront (later Sudeten German Party) and, consumed with ambition, became one of the organization's top leaders. Possessed of more "fire in the guts" than the more phlegmatic Henlein (1898–1945), Frank soon cultivated ties to the most radical organizations in Hitler's Germany, especially the SS, and helped those organizations to finance, influence, and infiltrate the party in the ensuing years. Indeed, Frank seems to have cast himself in the role of rival to party leader Henlein, and with his better contacts in Germany took the lead in radicalizing the party in the period before the Munich crisis of 1938 (in which Hitler [1889–1945] demanded and received the Sudetenland from Czechoslovakia). If Henlein eventually threw himself into Hitler's arms, it was in part an attempt to maintain his position vis-à-vis the well-connected Frank.

After the destruction of Czechoslovakia in March 1939, Frank, a protégé of Reinhard Heydrich (1904–1942) and the SS, came to overshadow Henlein as a major player in the Protectorate of Bohemia and Moravia. As SS-Gruppenführer (group leader) and Staatssekretär (state secretary) in the Protectorate administration, he gave full rein to his hatred of Czechs and became the very symbol of Nazi tyranny during the war years. After the war, Frank was tried by the newly reconstituted Czechoslovak government for his crimes and executed in Prague in March 1946.

Ronald Smelser

Further reading

Smelser, Ronald. *The Sudeten Problem: Volkstumspolitik and the Formulation of Nazi Foreign Policy, 1933–1938.* Middletown, Connecticut, 1975.

See also Konrad Henlein; Reinhard Heydrich; Munich Pact; Protectorate of Bohemia and Moravia; Sudeten Crisis

F

Frankovci

Croatian political party known as the Pure Party of Rights (Čista Stranka Prava) from 1895 to 1918, then revived as the Croatian Party of Rights (Hrvatska Stranka Prava) in 1919. ČSP/HSP members are often called "Frankovci" after their leader, Josip Frank (1844–1911), to differentiate them from the original Party of Rights (Stranka Prava) of Ante Starčević (1823–96), the most important Croatian opposition party in the 1880s and 1890s. Frank saw the Habsburgs as Croatia's natural allies against Magyar nationalism and Serbian expansionism. He wanted to found a Croatian political unit within the framework of the Habsburg monarchy that would include all South Slav Habsburg territories and be dominated by the Croats. The ČSP was openly anti-Serbian and was responsible for several waves of violence against the Serb minority in Croatia before and during World War I. The ČSP formally disbanded itself on October 29, 1918, when the Croatian parliament handed political power to the National Council, which took Croatia into the Kingdom of Serbs, Croats, and Slovenes.

The ČSP revived itself in 1919 as the HSP (Croatian Party of Rights) and played a minor role as an opposition party in the 1920s. The goal of the HSP was an independent Croatian republic. The HSP was a small extreme nationalist party with membership drawn from the intelligentsia, ex-Habsburg army officers, and the lower middle class. Ante Pavelić (1889–1959) soon became its outspoken leader. When King Alexander (1888–1934) imposed his dictatorship in January 1929, Pavelić and a group of HSP members went into exile, where they founded the Ustaša movement, the Croatian ultranationalist organization.

Elinor Murray Despalatović

Further reading

Banac, Ivo. *The National Question in Yugoslavia: Origins, History, Politics*. Ithaca, New York, 1984.

Boban, Ljubo. "Stranke političke Hrvatske," in Miroslav Krleža, ed. *Enciklopedija Jugoslavije*. Zagreb, 1971.

Gross, Mirjana. *Povijest pravaške ideologije*. Zagreb, 1973.

Lampe, John R. *Yugoslavia as History: Twice There Was a Country*. New York, 1996.

See also Alexander I Karadjordjević; Josip Frank; Kingdom of Serbs, Croats, and Slovenes; Ante Pavelić; Ante Starčević; Ustaša

Franz Ferdinand, Archduke (1863–1914)

Heir to the Austro-Hungarian throne, assassinated in Sarajevo, Bosnia, on June 28, 1914. The son of Archduke Karl Ludwig (1833–1896), brother of Emperor Franz Joseph (1830–1916), Franz Ferdinand began his military career in 1878 and remained in the military throughout his life. After the suicide of Franz Joseph's only son, Archduke Rudolph (1858–89), Karl Ludwig (1833–96) became heir to the Austrian throne. At his death in 1896, Franz Ferdinand, his eldest son, acquired that position. In 1900 he married Countess Sophia Chotek (1868–1914), but because this union was considered inappropriate at the conservative Habsburg court (owing to her family's stature), Franz Ferdinand had to renounce the throne for their children. For a time, as a conservative Catholic opposed to Hungarian pretensions to equality with the ruling Germanic element, he supported the idea of creating a third Habsburg kingdom by including the South Slavs as a third element. After 1903, he opposed the expansion of Serbia, regarding it as a threat to Austria-Hungary, but he opposed annexing its territory. In the summer of 1914 Franz Ferdinand ordered major military maneuvers in newly annexed Bosnia as a demonstration against Serbia and decided deliberately to visit Sarajevo, the Bosnian capital, on St. Vitus Day (Vidovdan), June 28, the Serbian national holiday. Regarding him as their most dangerous foe, Bosnian high school students organized loosely in the nationalistic and irredentist organization Young Bosnia (Mlada Bosna) decided to kill Franz Ferdinand. They received support and training from leaders of the Serbian Black Hand, the Serbian national revolutionary society, notably one of its leaders, Colonel Dimitrijević-Apis (1876–1917). Upon the archduke's return from Sarajevo city hall, Gavrilo Princip (1894–1918), one of several armed Bosnians, with two revolver shots fatally wounded the archduke and his wife. Austria-Hungary made the archduke's death the pretext for its decision to go to war against Serbia in July 1914, thus igniting World War I.

David MacKenzie

Further reading

Brook-Shepherd, Gordon. *Archduke of Sarajevo: The Romance and Tragedy of Franz Ferdinand of Austria*. Boston, 1984.

Dedijer, Vladimir. *The Road to Sarajevo*. New York, 1966.

Joll, James. *The Origins of World War I,* 2d ed. New York, 1992.

Lafore, Lawrence. *The Long Fuse: An Interpretation of the Origins of World War I.* London, 1965.

See also Apis; Black Hand; Franz Joseph; Irredentism; Gavrilo Princip; Trialism; World War I

Franz Joseph (1830–1916)

Reigning monarch of the multinational Habsburg Empire from 1848 to 1916. During his long, sixty-eight-year reign, Franz Joseph presided over the empire's final attempts at internal reform and international assertion. Although his ideal form of government remained that of a unitary state under an absolute monarch, he displayed the ability to adapt—tactically, if not intellectually—to modern circumstances. Consequently, he initiated a number of innovations aimed at satisfying, in a limited fashion, the political and national aspirations of his subjects. Some of these efforts included the introduction of constitutional government after 1860; reconciliation with his Hungarian subjects through the *Ausgleich* (Compromise) of 1867, which created the Dual Monarchy of Austria-Hungary; and the introduction of universal, equal male suffrage in Cisleithania, the Austrian half of the empire, in 1907. In foreign affairs, he worked to maintain the empire's Great Power status despite its limited resources and an increasingly hostile international environment.

Although conscientious in duty and personally popular with most of his fifty-one million subjects, Franz Joseph could not reverse the empire's decline with his policies. By the eve of World War I, the empire's long-term survival was in doubt. His death at age eighty-six, on November 21, 1916, came two years before the dissolution of the empire at the close of World War I. He was succeeded by his grand-nephew, Charles I (1887–1922).

Lawrence J. Flockerzie

Further reading

Bled, Jean-Paul. *Franz Joseph.* Oxford, 1992.

Redlich, Joseph. *Emperor Francis Joseph of Austria.* New York, 1929.

See also *Ausgleich;* Charles I; Dual Monarchy; Habsburg Empire; Hungarian War for Independence; Revolutions of 1848

Frashëri, Abdul (1839–92)

Nationalist leader, organizer of the League of Prizren, and proponent of autonomy for Albania within the Ottoman Empire. Frashëri was born in the southern Albanian village of Frasher to a family of Muslim beys and studied in a Greek gymnasium. In 1877 he was elected deputy from Yannina to the first Ottoman parliament.

When the Treaty of San Stefano (which ended the Russo-Turkish War of 1877–78) surrendered areas with Albanian populations to Montenegro and Serbia, Frashëri set up a Central Committee for the Defense of the Rights of the Albanian People in Istanbul. He was also a moving spirit behind the League of Prizren, which began meeting on June 10, 1878. There he argued for protests to the Congress of Berlin and the Ottoman government against any partition of Albanian territory. Since northern Albanians were much more willing to show resistance than their southern compatriots, Frashëri used his influence to organize branches of the league in the south. Under his guidance, southern Albanian leaders met in Frasher in November 1878 and drew up a plan for administrative autonomy. The plan called for all Albanians living in four *vilayet*s (provinces) of the Ottoman Empire to be united into a single province. It also demanded that this unit be run by Albanian officials and that Albanian be used as the language of administration. The southerners debated and approved the plan in principle; the northerners followed suit later. The finishing touches were put on the autonomy plan at an assembly at Gjirokastër in July 1880, but opinions differed on how to put the plan into action. It was finally decided to activate the plan if any overt moves were made against Albanian interests.

When the Turks sent an army in late 1880 to force the Albanians to relinquish territory, the League of Prizren resolved to implement the autonomy plan. In Dibër, an attempt to assassinate Frashëri failed. He used the incident to inflame the populace and the Turkish authorities were expelled from the area. Frashëri then went to Prizren, where he convinced the league to proclaim a provisional government and to assert control over territories in the north and the south. Despite initial Abanian successes, Turkish forces occupied Prizren in April 1881, and Frashëri was soon captured. Although he was sentenced to death for his activities, the sultan commuted his sentence to life imprisonment. Frashëri was released in a general amnesty in

F 1885. Ill and isolated during his later life, he died in Istanbul in 1892.

Gregory J. Pano

Further reading

Frashëri, Kristo. *Abdyl Frashëri*. Tirana, 1984.
Skendi, Stavro. *The Albanian National Awakening, 1872–1912*. Princeton, New Jersey, 1967.
————. "Beginnings of Albanian Nationalist and Autonomous Trends: The Albanian League (1878–1881)." *American Slavic and East European Review* 12 (1953): 219–32.

See also Congress of Berlin; League of Prizren; San Stefano, Treaty of

Freemasonry

Urban movement of secret, voluntary societies in eighteenth- and nineteenth-century Europe. The geographic base of Freemasonry was England, though "lodges" of freemasons were to be found throughout the length and breadth of the continent. In providing a forum for those wishing to discuss the texts of the Enlightenment philosophes, Freemasonry may be said to be one of the sources of modern political consciousness and of civil society.

In Eastern Europe, Freemasonry was most widespread in the lands of the Habsburg Empire, especially in Bohemia and in the Austrian lands. In addition, masons played a role in both Polish and Russian history, where, in addition to their "enlightening" role, they became closely associated with nationalism. In 1726 the first lodge was founded in Prague, which soon became the hub of Freemasonry in the empire. Masons were drawn from both the Czech and the German population. Socially, the majority were aristocrats, though there was some bourgeois representation. By making significant cultural and philanthropic contributions to Prague, such as funding for a theater, art galleries, libraries, orphanages, and hospitals, masons played an important role in developing cultural centers dedicated to spreading the ideas of the Enlightenment. Lodge members even lectured about such topics and the emancipation of Jews, Protestants, and peasants in Bohemia. By the 1760s, Prague Freemasonry was successful enough to expand and found sister lodges in other Bohemian urban centers, in the Austrian and Hungarian lands, and as far afield as Transylvania and Poland.

The main lodge of Vienna was established in 1742, where it played much the same role on the cultural scene as in Prague, though the focus tended to be on state reform. Masons wrote in favor of religious toleration, public education, and reform of criminal justice.

Freemasonry in Poland also had its start in the first half of the eighteenth century. The first lodge was founded in 1735 and the Warsaw Grand Lodge in 1769. In the reform period immediately prior to the partitions of the state, masonry was attractive to segments of the noble population for the same rationalist, reforming impulses noticeable in masonry throughout Europe. The last king of Poland, Stanisław August Poniatowski (1732–98), was himself a member. After the disappearance of the Polish state, however, masonry became associated with subversive, secret societies dedicated to the resuscitation of an independent Poland and thus became inextricably linked with Polish nationalism. Such societies were liberal on various social issues and were further united by the idea that they had to contribute to the "maintenance of the continuity of the nation, despite its partition." By 1817, Polish masonry had thirty-two lodges with over four thousand members.

The founder of the National Freemasonry (1819–25) was Major Walerian Łukasiński (1786–1868), a Napoleonic hero who was at first encouraged by the liberalizing policies of Alexander I (1777–1825) and then disgusted by factionalism among Polish and Russian lodge members. His National Freemasonry organization in Warsaw was dedicated to the unification of all Polish lands and eventually espoused the position of full independence from Russia. As the movement spread to other cities, the Russian regime became worried and ordered Łukasiński to disband. Łukasiński was eventually arrested and sentenced to nine years' incarceration. As a result of the 1830 uprising against the Russians, however, the unfortunate "founder" of Polish Freemasonry remained in the Schlüsselburg prison until his death in 1868. The movement itself took on a more conservative line and soon fractured. Active participation in the society declined and masonry became part of a network of other secret societies that permeated the society of the Congress Kingdom. In the second half of the nineteenth century, Freemasonry in Poland was most important for the model it provided for other secret groups, such as the Union of Polish Youth (Zet).

Peter Wozniak

Further reading

Gieysztor, Aleksander et al., eds. *History of Poland.* Warsaw, 1979.

Jacob, Margaret. *Living the Enlightenment: Freemasonry and Politics in Eighteenth-Century Europe.* New York, 1991.

Pienkos, Angela. *The Imperfect Autocrat: Grand Duke Constantine Pavlovich and the Polish Congress Kingdom.* New York, 1987.

Weisberger, William. *Speculative Freemasonry and the Enlightenment: A Study of the Craft in London, Paris, Prague and Vienna.* New York, 1993.

See also Alexander I; Walerian Łukasiński; Nationalism; November Uprisng; Polish Congress Kingdom; Zet

Freud, Sigmund (1856–1939)

Neurologist and founder of the psychoanalytic movement in psychology. Freud was born in May 1856 in Freiburg (Czech, Příbor) in Moravia. At the age of three, his family moved to Vienna, where he was educated and practiced until the German occupation forced his relocation to London in 1938, a year before his death. His early professional work during the 1880s and 1890s—in collaboration with Josef Breuer (1842–1925), an Austrian physician and Freud's early mentor—was devoted mainly to the treatment of hysteria. Freud became convinced that hysterical symptoms and other neuroses stemmed from psychological trauma of a sexual nature experienced early in life, the memories of which were repressed. Successful treatment required that the patient recover these memories to conscious awareness through a therapeutic method known as psychoanalysis.

From this work, Freud developed a general theoretical model of the mind that classified all psychical content into three categories: the conscious, consisting of all content of which at a given time a person is aware; the preconscious, content below the threshold of awareness that is available for conscious recall; and the unconscious, consisting of content that is actively repressed, and thus beyond volitional recall. Later, to explain more adequately the dynamic mechanisms of repression, Freud supplemented this schema with the tripartite division of the personality into the ego (*das Ich*), the id (*das Es*), and the superego (*das Über-Ich*), which may be roughly character-

ized as the rational, passional, and self-critical aspects of the self, respectively. Major works of Freud, a prolific writer, include *The Interpretation of Dreams* (1900); *The Psychopathology of Everyday Life* (1901); *Three Essays on the Theory of Sexuality* (1905); *Totem and Taboo* (1913); *Introductory Lectures on Psychoanalysis* (1917–18); *Beyond the Pleasure Principle* (1920); *The Ego and the Id* (1923); and *Civilization and Its Discontents* (1930).

Though Freud's ideas never garnered broad support in academic psychology, the psychoanalytic movement developed through the adoption of Freud's therapeutic methods by a growing number of psychotherapists in Europe and the United States during the first half of the twentieth century. Freudian theory has also had a profound impact on literature, the arts, and philosophy.

Richard Field

Further reading

Clark, Ronald William. *Freud: The Man and the Cause.* New York, 1980.

Gay, Peter. *Freud: A Life for Our Time.* New York, 1988.

Jones, Ernest. *The Life and Work of Sigmund Freud,* 3 vols. New York, 1953–57.

The Standard Edition of the Complete Psychological Works of Sigmund Freud, 24 vols., trans. by James Strachey et al. London, 1953–74.

Wollheim, Richard. *Sigmund Freud.* Cambridge, Massachusetts, 1990.

Friedjung Trial

Trial in Austria-Hungary involving alleged seditious activities by Habsburg Serbs and Croats with independent Serbia. The Friedjung affair pitted Habsburg Croat and Serbian politicians of the Croato-Serb Coalition—most notably Franjo Supilo (1870–1917) and Svetozar Pribičević (1875–1936)—against distinguished Austrian historian Heinrich Friedjung (1851–1920). In a March 1909 article for the Vienna *Neue Freie Presse,* Friedjung accused the politicians of conspiring with individuals from Serbia to undermine Habsburg rule in Bosnia-Hercegovina. The timing of the article raised eyebrows, since it appeared at a time of extreme tension between Austria-Hungary and Serbia over the annexation of Bosnia-Hercegovina. The politicians vehemently denied the allegations and sued the professor for libel,

F producing witness after witness able to discredit Friedjung's allegedly solid evidence. By the end of the trial, it had become obvious that Friedjung had based his article on forgeries and/or fabrications. Indeed, Friedjung had to admit he had erred and agreed to settle the case out of court.

The settlement cast a shadow over Friedjung and the sources of his information. It was widely supposed that the Austro-Hungarian Foreign Ministry and Friedjung had cooperated to produce a justification for military action against Serbia following the annexation of Bosnia-Hercegovina. Certain key details remained unclear, however, especially whether the Foreign Ministry had given Friedjung documents it believed to be authentic. If so, it exposed itself to charges of criminal negligence or stupidity since evidence of forgery was so plentiful. On the other hand, if it had knowingly passed off forgeries as authentic, it appeared craven and unscrupulous.

The Friedjung affair illustrated the degree of concern that the so-called South Slav question caused the Habsburg monarchy. In retrospect, it also previewed the fundamental cause of the coming world war: the feud between Austria-Hungary and Serbia over Bosnia-Hercegovina. The trial revealed the depth of anti-Serbian sentiment in the Austro-Hungarian government, which only intensified with the passage of time. Meanwhile, it undoubtedly emboldened Serbian nationalists, who agitated with renewed fervor against Austria-Hungary in Bosnia-Hercegovina after seeing their enemies in Vienna discredited. Finally, those Croats and Serbs whom Friedjung had libeled now viewed the Habsburg government with greater contempt. From their ranks emerged the Yugoslav Committee, dedicated to the creation of a Yugoslav state after 1914.

Brigit Farley

Further reading

MacCartney, C.A. *The Habsburg Monarchy 1790–1918*. London, 1968.

May, Arthur J. *The Habsburg Monarchy 1867–1914*. New York, 1951.

Seton-Watson, Robert W. *The Southern Slav Question and the Habsburg Monarchy*. New York, 1969.

See also Svetozar Pribičević; Yugoslav Committee

G

Gafencu, Grigore (1892–1957)

Romanian minister of foreign affairs and ambassador to Moscow, best known for his detailed diplomatic memoirs of the early years of World War II. After completing doctoral work in law in Geneva and Paris in 1914, Gafencu worked in Romania as a journalist and founded the first Romanian press agency, RADOR. From 1928, he played a leading role in the powerful National Peasant Party and held various posts in the Ministry of Foreign Affairs, the Ministry of Public Works and Communications, the Ministry of Industry and Commerce, and the Council of Ministers. In February 1939 he was named minister of foreign affairs and began an extensive series of diplomatic visits in Western Europe and the Balkans to shore up Romania's system of alliances. In July 1940 he was made ambassador to Moscow at a time when Romanian-Soviet relations were near their nadir.

After the outbreak of Soviet-German hostilities in June 1941, Gafencu left Moscow, returned briefly to Bucharest, and then left Romania to spend the rest of his life primarily in Switzerland and Paris. After 1947, he attempted unsuccessfully to rally Romanian émigrés against the newly installed Romanian Communist regime and carried out an active correspondence with Western scholars and political figures. In 1968 his remains were removed to Romania and reinterred in Bucharest.

Charles King

Further reading

Gafencu, Grigore. *The Last Days of Europe*, trans. by F. Allen. London, 1947.

———. *Prelude to the Russian Campaign, 1939–1941*, trans. by F. Allen. London, 1945.

Gaj, Ljudevit (1809–72)

Croatian writer, politician, and leader of the Illyrian Movement, the Croat national revival. Born in Krapina, Gaj studied law and philosophy in Vienna, Graz, and Pest, and received his doctorate from the University of Leipzig in 1834. In Graz he met his countrymen Mojsije Baltić (1804–79) and Dimitrije Demeter (1811–72), who helped him develop his national and Illyrian ideas, particularly Baltić, who taught him the Cyrillic alphabet and to speak and write in the štokavian dialect (which is composed of two principal sub-dialects: Serbian and Croatian). Since he was not an original thinker, Gaj took his ideas from various sources (including Johann Herder [1744–1803], Ján Kollár [1793–1852], Pavel Šafárik [1795–1861], Jernej Kopitar [1780–1844], Vuk Karadžić [1787–1864], and Josef Dobrovský [1753–1829], among others) and adapted them to his needs.

Gaj's principal contribution to the Illyrian movement was his advocacy of the linguistic, cultural, and political unity of the South Slavs and the need to resist Magyar influence. His ideas and works shaped the movement. In 1830 he published *Kratka osnova horvatsko-slavenskoga pravopisańa* (*Short Outline of a Croatian-Slavic Orthography*). The final version of his well-known *"Još Horvatska nij' propala"* (*"No, Croatia has not perished"*) was published in 1833 and soon became the Illyrian and national hymn. Because of his efforts, *Novine Horvatzke* (*Croatian News*) and its literary supplement, *Danicza Horvatzka,*

G *Slavonzka y Dalmatinzka* (*Morning Star of Croatia, Slavonia and Dalmatia*), began to be published in 1835. In the beginning both were published in the kajkavian dialect (the dialect in northern Croatia). However, *Danicza* contained some articles and poems in other South Slavic dialects. In the interest of Illyrian unity, Gaj changed the title of *Novine* to *Ilirske narodne novine* (*Illyrian National Newspaper*) and *Danicza* to *Danica ilirska* (*Morning Star of Illyria*) in January 1836. After 1836, both were published in the new literary language (Illyrian, štokavian dialect) and Gaj's new orthography. In the same year, *Danica* published the first Illyrian grammar, *Osnova slovnice Slovjanske narečja Ilirskoga* (*Basic Slavic Grammar of the Illyrian Dialect*). Gaj also wrote a brief dictionary.

In August 1841, as a leader of the newly founded Illyrian Party (after 1843 called the National Party), Gaj entered politics. Because of his political inexperience, however, he did not leave an important mark on the history of Croatia as a politician. In 1848 Gaj was accused of taking money from Prince Miloš Obrenović (1780–1860) of Serbia and later his *Narodne novine* became an official newspaper of the unpopular regime of Alexander Bach (1813–93). He never regained his lost popularity and lived out the rest of his life in relative obscurity. He died in Zagreb in April 1872.

Milenko Karanovich

Further reading

Despalatović, Elinor M. *Ljudevit Gaj and the Illyrian Movement.* Boulder, Colorado, 1975.

Horvat, Josip. *Ljudevit Gaj.* Belgrade, 1961.

Jonke, Ljudevit. *Hrvatski književni jezik 19. i 20. stoljeća.* Zagreb, 1971.

Šidak, Jaroslav. *Studije iz hrvatske povijesti XIX. stoljeća,* vol. 2. Zagreb, 1973.

Šišić, Ferdo. *Jugoslovenska misao: Istorija ideje jugoslovenskog narodnog ujedinjenja i oslobodjenja od 1790–1918.* Belgrade, 1937.

See also Alexander von Bach; Josef Dobrovský; Illyrian Movement; Vuk Karadžić; Ján Kollár; Jernej Kopitar; Magyarization; Miloš Obrenović; Pavel Šafárik; Serbo-Croatian Language

Gajda, Radola (1892–1948)

A commander of the Czechoslovak legion in Russia during World War I and a fascist adventurer in postwar Czechoslovakia. Rudolf Geidl, whose name was later Slavicized to Radola Gajda, was born in Kotor, Montenegro, the son of a noncommissioned officer in the Austro-Hungarian army. He also joined the latter, deserting it in World War I and ultimately joining the Czechoslovak volunteer brigade, an Allied force, on the Russian front in 1917. Charismatic and talented, he rose rapidly from captain to regimental commander. In May 1918 he was elected one of the triumvirate charged with leading the withdrawal of the Czechoslovak legion across Russia to the Pacific along the Trans-Siberian Railroad. Gajda also briefly joined the staff of White Russian leader Admiral Aleksandr Kolchak (1874–1920) as a lieutenant general and was given major command responsibilities against the Bolsheviks during the Russian Civil War. In 1919 he broke with the Russians and left for Europe.

The "Czechoslovak Napoléon," as he came to be known, became a dismal military and political failure in the new Czechoslovakia. Though achieving the status of acting chief of staff of the army, in 1926 he was convicted of planning a coup against the government, reduced to the rank of private, and cashiered. He became the most conspicuous Czechoslovak fascist, founding the *Národní obec fašistická* (National Fascist Community), and was repeatedly implicated in many unsuccessful fascist escapades. During the Munich crisis of 1938, which saw Czechoslovakia lose the Sudetenland to Germany, and the subsequent wartime protectorate in Bohemia and Moravia he opportunistically offered his cooperation to various Czechoslovak authorities as well as to Nazi Germany. In 1947 he was convicted of treason by the restored Czechoslovak government and imprisoned. He died on April 15, 1948.

Joseph Frederick Zacek

Further reading

Kelly, David. *The Czech Fascist Movement, 1922–1942.* Boulder, Colorado, 1995.

Klimek, Antonín and Petr Hofman. *Vítéz, který prohrál: Generál Radola Gajda.* Prague, 1995.

Zacek, Joseph F. "Radola Gajda: Czechoslovak Soldier-Statesman," in *East Central European War Leaders, Civilian and Military,* ed. by Béla K. Király and Albert A. Nofi. Boulder, Colorado, 1988, 319–30.

See also Czechoslovak Legion; Protectorate of Bohemia and Moravia; Right Radicalism

Galicia

Province of the Habsburg Empire, composed of territory annexed in the first partition of Poland of 1772. The Habsburg authorities derived the name for the new province by Latinizing *"Halich,"* a historical region in the east of the province. Bounded in the south by the Carpathian Mountains, most of Galicia comprised a plain, traversed by, among others, the Vistula, San, and Bug Rivers, which flow north, and by the Dniester River, which flows southeast to the Black Sea. Galicia contained a total area of 27,828 square miles (77,300 sq km). Galicia's principal city was Lwów (Lemburg). Its major resources included salt and petroleum, which was exploited beginning in the 1880s, but the primary economic activities of the province were forestry and agriculture, especially the production of meat and grain. Galicia was one of the poorest provinces in the Austro-Hungarian Empire, and its population increased rapidly, from 5,958,907 in 1880 to 7,980,477 in 1910. Approximately one million Galicians emigrated to the New World between 1895 and 1914.

The population of Galicia is divided into several religious and linguistic groups. In the 1880s, 46 percent of the population was Roman Catholic, 42 percent was Greek Catholic, and 12 percent was Jewish. By language, 52 percent spoke Polish; 43 percent, Ukrainian; and 5 percent, German. Yiddish was not included in Austrian imperial census records. The predominantly Greek Catholic Ukrainians were concentrated in the eastern part of the province; the Roman Catholic Poles inhabited western Galicia but also constituted most of the urban populace and rural great landowners in the east. Independent Poland absorbed all of Galicia in the 1920s and 1930s. In 1939 the Soviet Union annexed eastern Galicia and united it with the Ukrainian Soviet Republic.

Philip Pajakowski

Further reading

Samuel Koenig. "Geographic and Ethnic Characteristics of Galicia." *Journal of Central European Affairs* 1 (1941): 55–65.

Magocsi, Paul Robert. *Galicia: A Historical Survey and Bibliographic Guide.* Toronto, 1983.

Wandycz, Piotr S. *The Lands of Partitioned Poland, 1795–1918.* Seattle, Washington, 1974.

See also L'vov

Garašanin, Ilija (1812–74)

Serbia's major political leader in the midnineteenth century, best known for his *Načertanije* (Outline), the 1844 document proposing a foreign and national policy for Serbia. The son of a well-to-do farmer, Garašanin had a private tutor, some education, and travel abroad before beginning government service in 1834. He served as a member of the Council regime from 1838 to 1858 and was instrumental in the peaceful transition that overthrew it. He was minister of the interior from 1843 to 1852 and again in the mid-1850s. He served as prime minister (and often also as foreign minister) in the years from 1861 to 1867, when Serbia's de facto independence was strengthened and the Turks were forced to leave their fortresses in Serbia. Dismissed by Prince Mihailo (1823–68) in 1867 because of disagreements concerning the prince's marital problems, he nevertheless played a key role in saving the throne for the Obrenovićes at the time of Mihailo's assassination in 1868. Conservative in outlook, Garašanin did not believe that the Serbs were ready for self-government.

Garašanin foresaw the downfall of the Ottoman Empire in Europe and that Russia and Austria-Hungary would compete to fill the vacuum, a situation that would be detrimental to Serbia. In this view, he was influenced by Polish émigré circles. The best alternative was Western Europe, preferably France (although he later became disillusioned by the latter). The first Serbian politician realistically to comprehend the country's diplomatic problems, he spelled out his ideas in the *Načertanije,* the text of which was not made known to the Serbian public until 1906, even though Vienna had obtained a copy secretly as early as 1883.

Some historians have argued that the *Načertanije* was a blueprint for a Great Serbia, while others have maintained that it was a design for a South Slav (Yugoslav) state. Evidence indicates that Garašanin knew there were "brothers" who should be united with Serbia so as to create a larger and stronger state that would be in a position to ward off Russian and Austrian efforts at dominance in the Balkans.

Garašanin's great disappointment was that, with his dismissal and Mihailo's assassination, his and Mihailo's dream of forcing the Turks out of Europe would not soon be realized.

Alex N. Dragnich

G

Further reading

Jovanović, Slobodan. *Druga vlada Miloš i Mihaila, 1858–1868*. Belgrade, 1923.

MacKenzie, David. *Ilija Garašanin: Balkan Bismarck*. Boulder, Colorado, 1985.

———. "Ilija Garašanin: Man and Statesman." *Serbian Studies* 5 (Spring 1990): 41–55.

Petrovich, Michael B. *A History of Modern Serbia*, 2 vols. New York, 1976.

See also Greater Serbia; Mihailo Obrenović; *Načertanije*

Garrigue, Charlotte (1850–1923)

American-born wife of Tomáš G. Masaryk (1850–1937), who exerted great influence on him and on the Czech people in the areas of religion and feminism. Masaryk, who embraced her brand of Protestantism and accepted her firm belief in the equality of men and women, always acknowledged his debt. Charlotte believed that religion must further social justice and that it must be accompanied by a degree of puritanism. Charlotte was instrumental in the translation of the British economist John Stuart Mill's (1806–73) essay "On the Subjection of Women," which served as a stimulant for a fledgling Czech feminist movement at the end of the nineteenth century. She was among the founding members of the Ženský klub (Women's Club) in 1903 and pressed for greater educational opportunities for women. But she channeled most of her intellectual energy into collaboration with Masaryk on his manuscripts. In the process, Charlotte became a Czech patriot. A trained pianist, she studied Czech composers and wrote three essays about Bedřich Smetana (1824–84) for Masaryk's *Naše Doba* (*Our Time*). Two of her five children, Alice (1879–1966) and Jan (1886–1948), rose to prominence as public figures.

Barbara K. Reinfeld

Further reading

Lev, Vojtěch. *Památce Ch. G. Masarykové*. Prague, 1923.

Masaryková, Alice G. *Dětství a mládí*. Pittsburgh, 1960.

Reinfeld, Barbara K. "Charlotte Garrigue Masaryk (1850–1923)." *Czechoslovak and Central European Journal* 8 (1989): 90–104.

See also Jan Masaryk; Tomáš G. Masaryk; Bedřich Smetana; Women in Czechoslovakia

Gdańsk

Major Polish port and industrial center on the Vistula River and Baltic Sea. Gdańsk (German, Danzig) has played a prominent role in the histories of Poland, the Teutonic Knights, the Hanseatic League, and Germany. Over the past nine hundred years, political control over it has frequently changed, and struggle for it played a prominent role in the outbreak of World War II. Today, Gdańsk (population 461,000 [1989]) is a major Polish port and center of industry, culture, and administration.

Gdańsk was founded as a Slavic settlement approximately one thousand years ago but was seized and remained in the hands of the Teutonic Knights from 1308 to 1466. Thereafter, Gdańsk developed as a beautiful medieval city and flourishing Hanseatic port, greatly advantaged as the port of exit for products, especially wheat, moved by boat down the Vistula River. After 1466, Gdańsk became a Polish city, but its relative economic importance waned through time, in part owing to the declining importance of transport on the Vistula and to the city's separation from its economic hinterlands after the eighteenth-century partitions of Poland. From 1793 to 1919, Gdańsk became a Prussian, then German, city (excepting the 1807–14 Napoleonic period, when it was a free city).

Following World War I, Gdańsk was again a free city at the northern end of the Polish Corridor under League of Nations supervision. The city's inhabitants were mostly German, but its location and, at least initially, its port were deemed to be key factors for the survival of newly independent Poland. Distrusting Gdańsk's German population and political sympathies, the Polish government built a rival port, Gdynia, 12 miles (20 km) to the north. In 1939, when Hitler's (1889–1945) demands for unification of Gdańsk with Germany went unmet, the Germans launched an attack on Poland that marked the official beginning of World War II in Europe. Devastated during the war, in 1945 Gdańsk was reincorporated into the Polish state for the first time since 1772. Owing to riots in 1970 and to worker agitation in 1980 that resulted in the formation of the Solidarity trade union, Gdańsk has played an important, recent role in Polish internal politics.

Gdańsk's medieval grandeur has been partially restored at great cost, but today much of the city reflects postwar architecture and socialist planning. It remains a major transport hub, a center for a wide range of manufacturing activities, as well as an important cultural and administrative locale.

William H. Berentsen

Further reading
Pounds, N.J.G. *Eastern Europe*. London, 1969.

See also Adolf Hitler; League of Nations; Nazi–Polish War; Polish Corridor; Solidarity

Generalgouvernement

Nazi German administrative district in occupied Poland, 1939–1945. After defeating Poland in September 1939, Germany and the Soviet Union divided the country between them. Approximately 73,000 square miles (202,833 sq km) of Polish territory passed into German hands, the eastern portion of which was designated the General-gouvernement of Poland (39,000 square miles [108,333 sq km]). The Generalgouvernement consisted of four districts, centered in the cities of Kraków, Lublin, Radom, and Warsaw, with each district administered by a governor. Hans Frank (1900–1946) was appointed governor-general on November 8, 1939, with his headquarters at Kraków. A fifth district, centered on the city of L'vov, was added to the Generalgouvernement in July 1941.

In accordance with general instructions issued by SS Lieutenant General Reinhard Heydrich (1904–42) in September 1939, Jews from throughout occupied Poland, with the exception of those in the city of Łódź, were deported to the Generalgouvernement; along with the Jewish inhabitants of small villages and towns in the Generalgouvernement they were then concentrated into ghettos chiefly in Kraków, Lublin, Radom, and Warsaw. The process was largely completed by April 1941. To facilitate concentration and administration, each ghetto was ordered to form a Judenrat (Jewish Council), under German authority. Jews in the ghettos were subject to forced labor, limited food rations, and arbitrary violence from the SS. As a result, as many as five hundred thousand ghetto Jews died.

Between March 1942 and July 1943, the Jews of the Generalgouvernement were deported to various extermination camps established by the Germans in Poland. It is estimated that more than 1,440,000 Jews were murdered during this period.

Daniel D. Trifan

Further reading
Dawidowicz, Lucy S. *The War against the Jews 1933–1945*. New York, 1975.
Frank, Niklas. *In the Shadow of the Reich*. New York, 1991.
Trunk, Isaiah. *Judenrat: The Jewish Councils in Eastern Europe under Nazi Occupation*. New York, 1972.

See also Reinhard Heydrich; Holocaust; Jews; Nazi-Polish War; Warsaw Ghetto; Warsaw Uprising; World War II

Generation of 1848

Term for Romanian intellectuals who helped promote Romanian autonomy in 1856 and the subsequent unification of the principalities of Moldavia and Wallachia. Like many nationalists, the young men—including Mihail Kogălniceanu (1817–91), Ion C. Brătianu (1821–91), and Nicolae Bălcescu (1819–52)—drew inspiration from the romanticism of the first half of the nineteenth century and their contacts with nationalist movements elsewhere in Europe. They stressed the unique character and mission of both the Romanian "nation" and its people. Many were either schooled or lived in Paris in the decades before and after the Revolutions of 1848 engulfed Europe. Although their return to Moldavia and Wallachia in 1848 failed to bring about the hoped-for independence of the Danubian Principalities, their continued activities—especially their contacts with Napoléon III of France (1808–73)—helped lead first to recognition of the principalities in 1856 and later, despite the misgivings of the Great Powers, unification of Moldavia and Wallachia under Alexandru Ioan Cuza (1820–73).

Richard Frucht

Further reading
Bobango, Gerald. *The Emergence of the Romanian National State*. Boulder, Colorado, 1979.
Hitchins, Keith. *The Romanians 1774–1866*. New York, 1996.

See also Nicolae Bălcescu; Ion C. Brătianu; Alexandru Ioan Cuza; Danubian Principalities;

Great Powers; Mihail Kogălniceanu; Napoléon III; Revolutions of 1848; Romanticism; United Principalities

Georgiev Stoianov, Kimon (1882–1969)

Bulgarian officer and politician. A leading member of the Voenen Suiuz (Military League), the organization of Bulgarian army officers, and its political arm, the Naroden Sgovor (National Alliance), Georgiev actively participated in the June 9, 1923, coup against Aleksandur Stamboliiski (1879–1923) and his Agrarian government. From 1923 to 1931, he was a member of parliament, and during the period from January 4, 1926 to March 3, 1928, he served as minister for railroads, mail, and telegraphs. On May 19, 1934, together with the Military League's "mentor," Damian Velchev (1883–1954), Georgiev carried out another successful coup d'état and became prime minister. He was forced to resign, however, eight months later. Henceforth, Georgiev gradually moved to the left. Having become a member of the illegal pro-Communist Fatherland Front in June 1943, on September 9, 1944, Georgiev again was named Bulgarian prime minister. He maintained his position in the Communist-controlled coalition government until November 23, 1946. He stayed on in the cabinet in a number of capacities, including deputy prime minister (1946–47 and 1958–62), foreign minister (1946–47), and minister for electrification and irrigation (1947–59). In 1962 he was elected to be a member of the presidium of the parliament, a post he held until his death.

Stefan Troebst

Further reading

Georgiev, Kimon. *Izbrani proizvedeniia,* comp. and ed. by Gani Ganev and Nediu Nedev. Sofia, 1982.

See also Fatherland Front; Military League; Aleksandur Stamboliiski; Damian Velchev

Germanization

Promotion of German expansionist objectives in East Central Europe. Germanization in Eastern Europe began in the fourteenth century, primarily by Saxon settlers, and resumed after the Turkish occupation, in the early eighteenth century, mainly by Swabians from south Germany. The earlier arrivals founded new towns throughout the region; the later ones became and remained tillers of the soil. Most were Roman Catholics, the rest Lutherans or members of the Reformed Church. They resided largely in ethnic rural clusters and clung to their customs and language. After 1870, newly created countries with sizable German and other populations, such as Romania and Serbia (later Yugoslavia), as well as the autonomous Kingdom of Hungary, tried to assimilate their "alien" populations, which often defied their subject peoples' desires to maintain their ethnic integrity. These de-Germanization attempts alarmed the public and governments of Austria and Germany. They regarded the East as their commercial bailiwick and the German populations as potentially faithful assistants in the economic subjugation of these regions.

After the unification of Germany in 1871, Germanization efforts proceeded officially and unofficially in the Second Empire (1871–1918), especially after the alliance with the Habsburg monarchy (1873–1918) provided a common cause for preserving Germandom in the East. This still predominantly rural population of Germans numbered approximately two million people by 1918. The Second Empire maintained low-key Germanization policies, not wishing to offend the Austro-Hungarians, under whose rule most of these Germans resided. By 1914, some eighty-four private societies, discreetly supported by the government, assisted the subsidization activities and Germanizing efforts of the unofficial Alldeutscher Verband (Pan-German League) (1891). These combined influences proselytized the *Volksdeutsche,* who responded by founding a plethora of privately funded local cultural associations and a German-language press of their own.

During the Weimar era (1919–33), German public interest in the fate of the *Volksdeutsche* grew. Some 75 percent of them now lived in non-German states (Romania and Yugoslavia); the other 25 percent resided in Hungary, which, after the Treaty of Trianon, had become a nearly homogeneous Magyar country. (Czechoslovak Germans were almost exclusively Sudetenlanders.) With the Germanophile Habsburg protection eliminated, the entire region's Germans faced assimilation. German foreign minister (and later prime minister) Gustav Stresemann (1878–1929) reacted to this challenge. Masquerading as a "European" statesman, he surreptitiously funded *völkisch* associations in the Reich, such as the Verband der deutschen Volksgruppen (1922) and subsidized *völkisch* periodicals, such as *Der Auslandsdeutsche*. These organizations and publications urged total cultural autonomy for Eastern Europe's *Volksdeutsche*. Stresemann also funded and financed a business firm, the Vermittelungs-und Handelsgesellschaft, to promote economic deals and outright gifts made to *volksdeutsch* businesses and *völkisch* individuals abroad, without the German parliament's awareness. With the tacit encouragement of Weimar, small bands of young Germans, primarily *völkisch* high school and university youths, the Wandervögel, inundated Eastern Europe's German villages, especially in Hungary, where they spread the pan-German spirit and culture among a receptive Swabian population.

Increasingly, especially with the Great Depression, Weimar informed East European governments that continued purchase of their agricultural products depended on their "proper treatment" of their German minorities. These countries would have to maintain German-language schools, associations, publications, and all other public endeavors short of political autonomy. The regional governments resisted these pressures with all their might, and their German citizens found themselves caught between two fires.

The National Socialist regime (1933–45) exponentially magnified the relatively modest interventionist activities of Weimar. The Nazis rejuvenated languishing *völkisch* associations either through *Gleichschaltung* (subordination of autonomous centers of power) or through outright seizure. They also initiated an intricately and confusingly interlinked associational network with the single-minded purpose of Germanizing and Nazifying all *Auslandsdeutsche* (foreign Germans). This was particularly true in Eastern Europe, which the Nazis regarded as their rightful economic, social, and political preserve. The Nazis threatened noncooperative governments with cessation of diplomatic and economic support, or forcible occupation.

In 1917 the Deutsche Auslandsinstitut (DAI) began its modest operations to serve the cultural interests of Germans abroad. This innocuous organization continued operations throughout the Weimar period. In 1933 the Nazis transformed the DAI into an aggressive, powerful association that influenced the *Volksdeutsche,* especially those in the East, to become enthusiastic supporters of National Socialism. The DAI established connections with all kindred agencies in Germany, such as the Nazi Party's Auslands-Organisation der NSDAP in Hamburg, the Aussenpolitisches Amt der NSDAP in Berlin, and the academic NS-Lehrerbund and Deutscher Studentenschaft. The DAI also absorbed lesser organizations, such as the Volksbund für Deutschtum im Ausland (VDA), the Deutsche Akademie, and the Bund der Auslandsdeutscher. The DAI published *Die Auslandsdeutsche* (*The Foreign Germans*) jointly with the Volksbund der Deutschen im Ausland, and influenced the latter's publication, *Deutsche Arbeit*. The DAI also published the bimonthly newsletter *Pressekorrespondenz* and the popular calendar *Deutsche in aller Welt*. The DAI received large subventions from the Nazi regime, totaling at least five hundred thousand Reichsmarks annually. The organization played a major role in the Nazification of *Volksdeutsche*. The various host states greatly resented its efficiency, whereas the leaders of all *völkisch* associations abroad maintained close links with the DAI.

The Verein (later Volksbund) für das Deutschtum im Ausland (1908) paralleled the activities of the DAI. It had developed close links with the Nazis in the 1920s, and after 1933, the party commissioned it to coordinate the activities of all associations in Germany that dealt with *Auslandsdeutschtum*. In January 1937 Rudolf Hess (1894–1987) established still another organization, the Volksdeutsche Mittelstelle (VOMI), a special agency to promote ethnic German affairs. It maintained particularly close connections with the Volksbund der Deutschen in Ungarn (1939), headed by Volksgruppenführer Franz Basch (d. 1946), leader of Hungary's völkisch Swabians. The VOMI came under the direct supervision of Heinrich Himmler (1900–1945), who established the Reichskommissariat für die Festigung deutschen Volkstums (RKFDV) after Hess apparently lost interest in the VOMI. Himmler thereupon co-opted the latter to promote a vigorous German, that is, National Socialist, program in Eastern Europe.

The Auslands-Organisation (AO), founded in Hamburg in 1931, became the Nazi Party's highest-level special organization designed to coordinate the economic affairs of domestic associations and *Auslandsdeutsche*. Reorganized in 1933, the AO communicated with other Reich organizations through the Hauptamt für Volkstumfragen, the intermediary link with the RKFDV, in particular.

G The success of this elaborate network of organizations devoted to *Auslandsdeutschtum* hinged on the multiplying effects of satisfying personal ambitions, settling mutual jealousies, and pleasing Hitler (1889–1945) through outstanding achievements.

After World War II, the East and West German governments and their respective publics expressed little interest in the destiny of remaining *Auslandsdeutsche*. Their sole concern was to see their brethren from the East find a safe haven in Austria or in one of the two Germanies. The sole remaining major association, the Institut für Auslandsbeziehungen (the DAI's successor) has a strictly cultural agenda under new leadership.

Thomas Spira

Further reading

Komjathy, Anthony and Rebecca Stockwell. *German Minorities and the Third Reich: Ethnic Germans of East Central Europe between the Wars.* New York, 1980.

Macartney, C.A. *Problems of the Danube Basin.* Cambridge, 1942.

Paikert, G.C. *The Danube Swabians: German Populations in Hungary, Rumania and Yugoslavia and Hitler's Impact on Their Patterns.* The Hague, 1967.

Rothschild, Joseph. *East Central Europe between the Two World Wars.* Seattle, Washington 1974.

Spira, Thomas. *German-Hungarian Relations and the Swabian Problem: From Károlyi to Gömbös 1919–1936.* New York, 1977.

———. *The German-Hungarian-Swabian Triangle 1936–1939: The Road to Discord.* New York, 1990.

Tilkovszky, Loránt. *Die Sozialdemokratische Partei und die Frage der deutschen Nationalität in Ungarn 1919–1945.* Budapest, 1991.

See also Great Depression; Pan-Germanism; Sudeten Crisis

Germany

Great power whose influence on Eastern Europe dramatically affected the course of the twentieth century. Over the centuries, German boundaries have shifted dramatically in all directions. Since 1945, Germany has been bounded by the upper Rhine River on the west, the lower Oder River on the east, the Alps on the south, and the Baltic and North Seas on the north. Although the concept of Germany as a territory has existed for centuries, Germany as a modern nation-state came into existence only in 1871. Historically, Germany served as the transmitter of Western ideas and technology to the East and as a channel to the West for information about Eastern Europe.

By the second century B.C., the Romans had identified "Germanic" peoples among the barbarians north of the Danube and east of the Rhine. Their ultimate origins remain obscure. By the tenth century, the German tribes had come together in the Holy Roman Empire of the German Nation, located between the Rhine and the Elbe Rivers, although the empire was in fact a very loose confederation of states and princes that the emperor himself could not control. In the eleventh century, the German population began expanding eastward, crossing the Elbe and initiating a centuries-long process of injecting German population, culture, and technology into Eastern Europe. Major routes of the German advance were the Baltic littoral and the Danube valley, but German settlers moved broadly into Polish territory across the North European Plain as well.

In the eighteenth century, one of the German states, Prussia, joined with the Russian and Habsburg Empires in the three partitions of Poland (1772, 1792, 1795). This action, combined with the arrival of modern nationalist sentiments in the nineteenth century, provided the basis for a long period of German-Polish antipathy in the modern era. The unification of the German territories into a single nation-state in 1871 produced a powerful new Germany and considerable tension with the neighboring Russian Empire, despite a large volume of German-Russian trade.

German support for Austria-Hungary against Russia in the Balkans was a major factor leading to World War I. Before their own defeat by the Western Allies in 1918, the Germans defeated the Russians and made plans to annex vast Russian territories in the peace of Brest-Litovsk. German relations with Poland worsened in the 1920s as a result of the Versailles peace settlement that transferred some German-Prussian territory to Poland.

After 1933, the Nazi regime in Germany produced a new low point in German–East European relations. The Nazis launched a major war of conquest in Eastern Europe with plans to enslave, exterminate, or remove the existing populations and replace them with German settlers. Defeated by the Allies in 1945, Germany was divided into four occupation zones separately controlled by the Soviet Union, the United States, Britain, and France. In 1949 the three western zones became the Federal Republic of Germany (West Germany), a democratic state allied to the West; the Soviet zone became the German Democratic Republic (East Germany), a Communist state and member of the Soviet bloc. In 1990 Germany was reunited when East Germany was merged into West Germany.

Robert Mark Spaulding

Further reading

Craig, Gordon. *Germany 1866–1945.* Oxford, 1978.

Holborn, Hajo. *A History of Modern Germany, 1648–1945,* 3 vols. Princeton, New Jersey, 1969.

Sheehan, James. *German History 1770–1866.* Oxford, 1989.

See also Otto von Bismarck; Brest-Litovsk, Treaty of; Germanization; *Hakata;* Pan-Germanism; Paris Peace Conference; Polish Corridor; Prussia; World War I; World War II

Gerö, Ernö (1898–1980)

Hungarian Communist. Gerö was born in 1898 to a lower-middle-class Jewish family and joined the Hungarian Communist Party in 1918. An active participant in the short-lived Communist regime of Béla Kun (1886–1938), which was created in the tumultuous period following Austria-Hungary's defeat in World War I, he emigrated after its collapse and became an important Communist International (Comintern) operative during the interwar period. He served the Comintern in numerous capacities including as instructor with the French and Belgian parties and, under the alias of Pedro, as controller of the Catalan Communist Party during the Spanish Civil War.

When World War II began, the austere, ascetic, and abrasive Gerö was a major contender to lead the Hungarian Communists in exile. However, Stalin (1879–1953) selected Mátyás Rákosi (1892–1971) to serve in this position. Gerö accepted the decision gracefully and became one of Rákosi's most loyal acolytes. As the Red Army reached Hungary, Gerö set up the party's preliminary organizations in Szeged, Debrecen, and Miskolc. By the time Rákosi arrived in Budapest in February 1945, the party had coalesced under the "Muscovite" (trained in Moscow) leaders.

Gerö played a key role in the party's drive to gain control over Hungary. He was the negotiator responsible for setting up the first Soviet-Hungarian joint-stock companies and was one of the prime movers responsible for the country's transformation into a "people's democracy." Gerö initially served as minister of transportation. But more important than any of his government posts was his membership in all the important party organs. He contributed to both the Rákosi cult of personality and the reign of terror that followed the Communist consolidation of power. Gerö also had primary responsibility to orchestrate the First Five-Year Plan and the Stalinization of the Hungarian economy.

The Hungarians associated Gerö with all the worst features of Stalinism. It is therefore surprising that after the Soviet leadership deposed Rákosi, they selected Gerö to be the first secretary of the Hungarian Communists. In this post, he lasted from July 18 to October 25, 1956. Gerö is most remembered as the leader who called in Soviet troops to crush the Hungarian Revolution of 1956. He was soon replaced by the moderate "home" Communist János Kádár (1912–89). He remained an unreconstructed, doctrinaire Stalinist until his death. After a short exile in the Soviet Union, he returned to Hungary, where he died in 1980.

Andrew Ludanyi

Further reading

Kovrig, Bennett. *Communism in Hungary: From Kun to Kadar.* Stanford, California, 1979.

Csonka, Emil. *A Forradalom oknyomozó története, 1945–1956.* Munich, 1981.

Nagy, Ferenc. *The Struggle behind the Iron Curtain.* New York, 1948.

Vali, Ferenc A. *Rift and Revolt in Hungary.* Cambridge, 1961.

Zinner, Paul E. *Revolution in Hungary.* New York, 1962.

See also Comintern; Communist Party of Hungary; Hungarian Revolution of 1956; Hungarian Soviet Republic; János Kádár; Béla Kun; Mátyás Rákosi; Red Army; Sovietization; Stalin

Gerov, Naiden (1823–1900)

Bulgarian writer. Gerov (N.G. Hadzhidobrevich, Mchan, Mushek) was born in Koprivchitsa to Hadzhi Gerov Dobrevich-Muchek (n.d.), a teacher.

After attending his father's school, Gerov finished high school in Odessa, where he attended the Richelieu Lyceum. He returned to Bulgaria in 1846 with Russian citizenship. Gerov taught in Koprivchitsa from 1846 to 1849 before founding a school in Plovdiv in 1850. During the Crimean War (1853–56), he lived in St Petersburg. He was named vice consul to Plovdiv when he returned to Bulgaria in 1857. There, he was active in combatting Greek cultural and political influence in Bulgaria. Part of his efforts on behalf of his people included obtaining financial support for Bulgarian students who studied in Russia. After the April Uprising in 1876 aimed at overthrowing Turkish rule, he was named governor of Svishtov.

For the rest of his life, Gerov lived in Plovdiv and was principally preoccupied with writing. His most notable work was the *Rechnik na bûlgarskiia ezik* (*Dictionary of the Bulgarian Language*). He also published in the newspapers *Tsarigradski Vestnik* (*Constantinople Newspaper*), *Bûlgarska Pchela* (*Bulgarian Bee*), *Makedonaiia* (*Macedonia*), and *Vek* (*Century*). His poem "Stoian i Rada" (Stoian and Rada) was the first example of modern Bulgarian verse.

Mari A. Firkatian

Further reading

Georgiev, Em. *Naiden Gerov: Kniga za nego i negovoto vreme.* Sofia, 1972.
Panchev, T. *Naiden Gerov: Sto godini ot rozhdenieto mu. 1823–1923. Kûsi cherti ot zhivota i deinostta mu.* Sofia, 1923.

See also April Uprising; Bulgarian Literature; Crimean War

Gegs

Northern Albanian group. To the north of the Shkumbin River in Albania, as well as in Kosovo and adjacent areas of Macedonia, Montenegro, and southern Serbia, social and political traditions, as well as language, have historically distinguished the ethnic Albanian population from its counterpart to the south.

The Geg dialects, spoken by more than 70 percent of Albanians, evolved under the more isolated conditions of northern Albania and exhibit distinct differences from the southern (Tosk) dialects. South Geg, the dialect of the Tirana-Durrës-Elbasan region, was adopted as the official unified literary standard for Albanian in 1916 and remained so until after World War II. In 1972 the decision of the Albanian government to replace Geg with Tosk as the official standard language was accepted by the Albanians of Yugoslavia and the Albanian diaspora in southern and southeastern Europe. As a result, Geg has largely disappeared as a language of publication, although it continues to be widely spoken.

During the nineteenth century and until recent times, a tribal or clan system of social organization (*fis*), together with a traditional territorial-political organization (*bajrak*), continued among the Gegs. A system of customary law (Code of Leke Dukajini) formed the basis of social and political order within a region of difficult access and tenuous administrative control. The Gegs were largely Muslim, with important Catholic minorities concentrated in certain areas such as the Mirditë. Important among the leaders of the Albanian national movement before independence, as well as in the Albanian interwar governments of Ahmed Zogu (Zog I) (1895–1961), Gegs were much less prominent in Albanian politics under the regime of the Communist leader Enver Hoxha (1908–85), a Tosk, after World War II.

Albert M. Tosches

Further reading

Huld, Martin E. *Basic Albanian Etymologies.* Columbus, Ohio, 1984.
Pano, Nicholas C. *The People's Republic of Albania.* Baltimore, Maryland, 1968.
Repishti, Sami. *Albania in Brief: History, Language, Literature.* New York, 1992.
Skendi, Stavro. *The Albanian National Awakening: 1878–1912.* Princeton, New Jersey, 1967.

See also Albanian Language; Enver Hoxha; Muslims; Tosks; Ahmed Zogu

Gheorghiu-Dej, Gheorghe (1901–65)

Head of the Romanian government and Communist Party, 1952–65. Born on November 8, in Bârlad, Gheorghiu-Dej became a shoemaker's apprentice and later worked in textiles and on the railroad. In 1930 he joined the outlawed Communist Party and moved to Dej. At a general meeting of railroad workers in Bucharest, Gheorghiu attended as the representative from Dej, and there he decided to add "Dej" to his name. Arrested on

February 14, 1933, as a labor organizer, he was in prison during the most violent of the Griviţa demonstration, interwar Romania's most famous strike, but gained national publicity as one of its major instigators. He was incarcerated until his escape on August 9, 1944, whereupon he vied for control of the Communist Party against those Romanian Communists who had spent World War II in the Soviet Union. He built a power base in the government beginning as the minister of communications and public works in 1945, and in 1946 assumed responsibility for the Romanian economy. In 1948 he was elected general secretary of the new Romanian Workers Party. He continued to struggle against Romanian Communists who were loyal to Moscow and in 1952 purged his major opposition, including Vasile Luca (1898–1952) and Ana Pauker (1893–1960). In April 1954 he eliminated his final opponent, Lucreţiu Pătrăşcanu (1900–1954), and in compliance with Soviet demands of a separation of the top positions in party and state, Gheorghiu-Dej resigned as party general secretary but retained his position as president of the Council of Ministers. In 1961 he became chairman of the Council of State, a position that combined state and party leadership. Over the years, Gheorghiu-Dej moved from endorsing Moscow's political views to supporting national communism for Romania. He championed rapid industrialization, rather than Moscow's desire for an agrarian Romania, and in 1964 proclaimed Romania's independence, rejecting Soviet hegemony in the Communist bloc. Three years after his death, he was denounced by his successor, Nicolae Ceauşescu (1918–89) for his role in the execution of Pătrăşcanu.

Joseph F. Harrington

Further reading

Fischer, Mary Ellen. *Nicolae Ceauşescu: A Study in Political Leadership.* Boulder, Colorado, 1989

Fischer-Galati, Stephen. *The New Rumania: From People's Democracy to Socialist Republic.* Cambridge, Massachusetts, 1967.

Harrington, Joseph and Bruce Courtney. *Tweaking the Nose of the Russians: Fifty Years of American-Romanian Relations, 1940–1990.* Boulder, Colorado, 1991.

See also Nicolae Ceauşescu; Communist Party of Romania; Vasile Luca; Lucreţiu Pătrăşcanu; Ana Pauker

Ghica, Grigore (1807–57)

Prince (*hospodar*) of Moldavia. A leading *boiar*, Ghica broke with other members of his family in endorsing the aims of the reformers during the Revolutions of 1848. Under the provisions of the Convention of Balta Liman in 1849, Ghica was appointed prince of Moldavia for a seven-year term. A moderate, Ghica permitted some of the leaders of the 1848 revolution to return to Iaşi and serve in his administration. Ghica promoted economic development, but, like his counterpart in Wallachia, Barbu Ştirbei (1799–1869), he refused to move beyond limited agrarian reforms.

Ultimately, Ghica became a victim of the Crimean War (1853–56). Despite Austrian support in regaining his throne after the temporary occupation of the Danubean Principalities by Russian troops in 1853, Ghica looked to Napoléon III (1808–73) for backing and gave liberals greater freedom to publish their pro-autonomy program. That, combined with his pro-union stance, cost him the support of both Austria and the Ottoman Empire at the Paris conference of 1856.

Richard Frucht

Further reading

Hitchins, Keith. *The Romanians 1774–1866.* Oxford, 1996.

Jelavich, Barbara. *Russia and the Formation of the Romanian National State 1821–1878.* Cambridge, 1984.

See also Balta Liman, Convention of; Crimean War; Napoléon III; Paris, Treaty of; Revolutions of 1848; Barbu Ştirbei

Ghica, Ion (1817–97)

Romanian politician, prime minister, and influential writer. From a noble family that produced nine ruling princes, Ghica was born in Bucharest and educated at St. Sava school with politician and historian Nicolae Bălcescu (1819–52) and conservative prime minister C.A. Rosetti (1816–85). He studied law and literature in Paris, earning degrees in letters and mathematics from the Sorbonne and in engineering from the École Royale de Mines. He taught briefly at Iasi's Academia Mihaileană (1842), where he became Romania's first notable political economist.

Ghica became involved in many revolutionary and conspiratorial activities in the Danubian

G Principalities. Returning to Paris in the late 1840s, he was active in Romanian circles working for radical change in the Principalities and became a major participant in the Romanian revolution of 1848.

Exiled following the defeat of the revolution, Ghica served in the Ottoman provincial administration before returning in 1858 to participate in the unionist agitation that resulted in the eventual creation of the Romanian national state. He was numerous times prime minister (1859; 1859–60; 1866–67; 1870–71), cabinet member, deputy or senator, and ambassador, though his reputation for ambition and deviousness made him a mistrusted and somewhat unpopular figure. He was a key leader in the overthrow of Prince Cuza (1820–73) in 1866 and in the coalition governments that followed. After his ambiguous role in the near abdication of Prince Carol (1839–1914) in 1871, he never again was part of a cabinet, though he served as the Romanian kingdom's first ambassador to Great Britain (1881–90).

Ghica served as president of the Romanian Academy, was a reformist director general of the national theater (1877–81), and created an entire genre of Romanian literature with his elegant *Letters to Vasile Alecsandri* (1887), which dealt with the 1821–59 era in Romania. He was also noteworthy as one of the few major advocates of economic liberalism in Romania.

Paul E. Michelson

Further reading
Hitchins, Keith. *Rumania 1866–1947.* Oxford, 1994.
Iordache, Anastasie. *Ion Ghica: Diplomatul şi omul politic.* Bucharest, 1995.
Păcurariu, D. *Ion Ghica.* Bucharest, 1965.
Stan, Apostal and Mircea Iosa. *Liberalismul politic în România.* Bucharest, 1996.

See also Nicolae Bălcescu; Carol I; Alexandru Ioan Cuza; Revolutions of 1848; C.A. Rosetti

Gichev, Dimitur (1893–1964)

Bulgarian Agrarian politician. Born to teachers in Perushtitsa, Gichev graduated from a seminary before joining the Agrarian Party in 1911. He became a leader of the left Agrarians (1926–44) and a member of the National Assembly, serving four terms in office. He was also minister of agriculture (1931–33) and minister of commerce (1933–34). One of the founders of the *Petorka,* (Five), a coalition of five leaders and their supporters who represented every political group in opposition to the rightist government of Aleksandur Tsankov (1879–1959), his convictions led him in May 1936 to first join with the Communists immediately before the outbreak of World War II, only later to stand in opposition to the Fatherland Front, the Communist-led coalition of left and center parties. After the war, he joined the Nikola Petkov (1893–1947) faction of the Agrarians before eventually being persuaded to join the Fatherland Front.

Mari A. Firkatian

Further reading
Crampton, R.J. *A Short History of Modern Bulgaria.* Cambridge, 1987.

See also Agrarian Parties; Fatherland Front; Nikola Petkov; Aleksandur Tsankov

Gierek, Edward (1913–)

Leader of Poland (1970–80). Gierek spent his early life in France after the death of his Polish father. There, he became associated with the French and Belgian Communist Parties. During World War II he served in the Belgian underground army. He returned to Poland in 1948 to build up a power base in Silesia and was named to the party's Politburo in 1956. Gierek followed in the general line of adapting socialism/communism to Poland until 1970, when worker riots in Gdańsk led to Gierek's replacing Władysław Gomułka (1905–82) as first secretary of the party. Under Gierek's rule, Poland was brought closer into Moscow's orbit and greater economic centralization was introduced. Initially, social conditions improved, thanks to foreign loans, but by 1976 the economy began to slip back into stagnation. Workers responded with demonstrations in 1976, which resulted in the creation of the Workers Defense Committee (KOR), and finally the creation of Solidarity, the Polish trade union, in 1980. Gierek was blamed for all of Poland's ills and replaced as first secretary of the party in September 1980. He was expelled from the party the following year.

David Stefancic

Further reading
Blazynski, George. *Flashpoint Poland.* Oxford, 1979.
Bromke, Adam. *Gierek's Poland.* New York, 1973.
Karpinski, Jakub. *Countdown.* New York, 1973.

See also Communist Party of Poland; Władysław Gomułka; KOR; Solidarity

Giers, Nikolai Karlovich (1820–95)

Russian foreign minister (1882–94). Of Swedish-German background and a Lutheran, Giers entered the Russian Foreign Ministry in 1838, serving in Moldavia, Constantinople, Alexandria, Bucharest, Persia, Switzerland, and Sweden. In 1875 he was appointed head of the Asiatic Department and deputy to Aleksandr Gorchakov (1789–1883), the foreign minister, whom he replaced in 1882.

Given Russia's internal weaknesses, Giers was a moderate and compromiser, avoiding military adventures. He supported the Dreikaiserbund (Three Emperor's League, 1881–1887) with Germany and Austria-Hungary, because it guaranteed Russia peace and security. When the crisis over Bulgarian unification in 1885 strained relations with Austria and foreclosed renewal of the Dreikaiserbund, Giers negotiated the Reinsurance Treaty with Germany in 1887, because he considered Germany the key to preventing Russia's diplomatic isolation. In 1890 Wilhelm II (1859–1941) refused to renew the treaty; hence Giers turned to France. Initially this led to French loans and in 1892 a French-Russian consultative military agreement. It was followed by the Franco-Russian Alliance of 1894, thus avoiding Russia's diplomatic isolation, whose consequences Giers had witnessed in the Crimean War (1853–56) and at the Congress of Berlin in 1878.

Charles Jelavich

Further reading

Jelavich, Charles. *Tsarist Russia and Balkan Nationalism: Russian Influence in the Internal Affairs of Bulgaria and Serbia, 1879–1886.* Berkeley, California, 1958.

Jelavich, Charles and Barbara Jelavich, eds. *The Education of a Russian Statesman: The Memoirs of Nicholas Karlovich Giers.* Berkeley, California, 1962.

Kennan, George. *The Decline of Bismarck's European Order: Franco-Russian Relations, 1875–1890.* Princeton, New Jersey, 1975.

See also Congress of Berlin; Crimean War; Aleksandr Gorchakov; Reinsurance Treaty; Three Emperors' League

Glasnost and Perestroika

Terms meaning "openness" and "restructuring," respectively, whose application, together with *demokratizatsiia* (democratization), would destroy the Soviet empire. When Mikhail Gorbachev (1931–) took power in the Soviet Union during the 1980s, he believed that changes had to be made to save the system. Glasnost and perestroika became cornerstones of his policies aimed at reinvigorating the state by removing archaic controls.

The impact of these policies on Eastern Europe was uneven, at least at the beginning, but decisive toward the end. Hard-line party leaders in Czechoslovakia and East Germany were nervous from the start, hoping that Gorbachev would soon be replaced, and were losing self-confidence by the obvious lack of economic progress accompanied by revelations of corruption, dishonesty, systematic lying, and continuing degeneration of the system. The dissidents were encouraged by self-criticism of Soviet media and enjoyed the embarrassment of their hated masters.

In Hungary and Poland the liberalizing governments and the gradually winning opposition were so far ahead of Soviet developments that from their point of view, the Russians were just clumsily beginning to catch up with their own societies. Gorbachev's policies allowed them to press ahead with further reforms.

East European observers realized that Gorbachev and his advisers, ranging across the intelligentsia of liberal sociologists, economists, jurists, political scientists, and demographers, were worried about the worsening situation in the Soviet Union and its threatening collapse. They did not, however, share the illusion that Leninist and Stalinist communism could be saved by reform. They no doubt had the impression of déjà vu because their regimes had gone through similar processes from the 1950s to the 1980s. In spite of their semi-colonial status vis-à-vis the Soviet Union, their societies enjoyed not only a higher standard of living but also more advanced educational, cultural, and political institutions.

Peter Hruby

Further reading

Ash, Timothy Garton. *The Uses of Adversity.* Cambridge, 1989.

———. *We the People: The Revolution of '89. Witnessed in Warsaw, Budapest, Berlin and Prague.* London, 1990.

G

Freedom House. *Glasnost—How Open?* Lanham, Maryland, 1987.

Gwertzman, Bernard and Michael T. Kaufman, eds. *The Collapse of Communism.* New York, 1990.

Spring, D. W., ed. *The Impact of Gorbachev: The First Phase, 1985–1990.* New York, 1991.

See also Mikhail Gorbachev; Revolutions of 1989; Soviet Union

Glemp, Józef (1929–)

Roman Catholic primate of Poland. Ordained a Catholic priest in Poland and completing a doctoral degree in church law at the Lateran University in Rome in 1964, Glemp went on to become a close collaborator of Cardinal Stefan Wyszyński (1901–81) in church administration. From 1979 to 1981, Glemp served as bishop of the Warmiński diocese. After the death of Cardinal Wyszyński in April 1981, Glemp succeeded him as primate of Poland, the archbishop of the Warsaw-Gniezno diocese. At the same time, the Solidarity trade union movement and the Polish Communist regime were slowly moving toward an impasse. In an effort to save Poland from social and political deadlock, the church, under Glemp, attempted to mediate between Solidarity and the regime of Wojciech Jaruzelski (1923–), but to no avail. With the imposition of martial law on December 13, 1981, Glemp, under heavy criticism at times from underground Solidarity, continued to speak out against violations of civil and human rights while maintaining a certain distance from the current political debate. In 1983 he became a cardinal. Representing the church's interests and many of the ideals of the Solidarity movement, Glemp supported the "Round Table" negotiations in 1989 that ended Communist rule in Poland.

Peter Lavelle

Further reading

Hruby, Suzanne. "The Church in Poland and Its Political Influence." *Journal of International Affairs* 26, no. 2 (1982–83).

"Interview with Cardinal Glemp." *Survey* 26 (Summer 1982): 206–7.

Ramet, Sabrina P. *Social Currents in Eastern Europe: The Sources and Meaning of the Great Transformation.* Durham, North Carolina, 1991.

See also Catholicism; Wojciech Jaruzelski; Solidarity; Stefan Wyszyński

Gödel, Kurt (1906–78)

Austrian-born mathematician whose "incompleteness theorem" revolutionized modern mathematical logic. Gödel was born in Brünn, now Brno, in the Czech Republic. He received a doctorate in mathematics in 1930, with a dissertation that proved a certain small logical system to be "complete"—every statement that is representable in the system can be proved either true or false.

In 1931, while a faculty member at the University of Vienna, he published the paper "On Formally Undecidable Propositions of *Principia Mathematica* and Related Systems." In this landmark work, he showed the startling result that any reasonably large system of mathematical axioms and theorems, such as the *Principia Mathematica* of Bertrand Russell (1872–1970) and Alfred North Whitehead (1861–1947), must contain statements that cannot be proven true or false within the system. This provided an answer to a question posed by the great German mathematician David Hilbert (1862–1943) on the completeness of axiomatic systems.

Incorrectly identified as a Jew, Gödel and his wife fled Europe in 1940 to avoid persecution by Nazi Germany. The danger of crossing the Atlantic by ship forced them to ride the Trans-Siberian railroad to the Pacific, travel by boat to San Francisco, and finally arrive in New Jersey. Gödel was given a position at the Institute for Advanced Study in Princeton, New Jersey, where he worked until retirement. Although a recluse, he published in several areas, including finding a solution to the equations of general relativity that allows for the possibility of travel into the past.

Mark Sand

Further reading

Burton, David M. *The History of Mathematics: An Introduction.* Boston, 1984.

Holmes, Frederic L., ed. *Dictionary of Scientific Biography,* vol. 17. New York, 1990.

McMurray, Emily J., ed. *Notable Twentieth-Century Scientists,* vol. 2. Detroit, 1995.

Goga, Octavian (1881–1938)

Romanian poet and politician. Born in Sibiu in Hungarian-ruled Transylvania, Goga studied philosophy at the University of Budapest. His ten volumes of poetry, his plays, and his biographical essays extolled Romanian peasant values and faith.

His flowing translations of foreign poetry into Romanian, including those of fellow Transylvanian Sándór Petőfi (1823–49), are also worthy of note.

In politics, as in poetry, Goga was a nationalist. Before World War I, he was among the most prominent maximalists (those who would settle for nothing less than full integration of Transylvania with the rest of Romania) of the Romanian National Party. He spent the war agitating for Romanian national unity in the Old Kingdom. In 1920 he joined the People's League of General Alexandru Averescu (1859–1938) and served both as a parliamentary deputy and a government minister. Pulled toward the anti-Semitic right, Goga founded the National Agrarian Party in 1932. With German urging, Goga fused his party with the League of National Christian Defense of Professor A.C. Cuza (1857–1947), forming the National Christian Party (1935), which garnered 9 percent of the vote in the December 1937 elections. To undermine the traditional parties as well as the Iron Guard, the Romanian nationalist-fascist organization, Carol II (1893–1953) appointed Goga prime minister. The forty-four-day Goga-Cuza government (December 1937–February 1938) was the prelude to Carol's royal dictatorship. Shortly after his dismissal as prime minister, Goga died.

Walter M. Bacon Jr.

Further reading

Balan, Ion. *Octavian Goga.* Bucharest, 1966.
Fatu, Mihai. *Cu pumnii strînsi: Octavian Goga în viaţa politică a României, 1918–1938.* Bucharest, 1993.
Şeicaru, Pamfil. *Poezie şi politica: Octavian Goga.* Madrid, 1956.

See also Alexandru Averescu; Carol II; Iron Guard; Right Radicalism; Sándór Petőfi

Golescu Family

One of the oldest *boiar* families of Wallachia, among whose members rank some of the principal figures of the Revolution of 1848 in the Romanian lands and the makers of the modern Romanian state. Tracing their roots back to the sixteenth century, the Golescu family derived their name from their estates in Goleşti. Various family members held high office under a number of Wallachian princes (often as *ban,* or governor, of Oltenia [southwestern Romania]) and ranked among the most powerful *boiars* of the land, occasionally aspiring to the Wallachian throne. During the eighteenth century, Radu Golescu (1746–1818) supported the Habsburg occupation of Oltenia. Two Golescu brothers, Constantin (1777–1828), aptly called "the first modern Romanian," and Iordache (1763–1848), fathered six of the Romanian revolutionaries of 1848. They were all schooled in the Romanian language at the family estate school directed by Gheorghe Lazar (1779–1821), a Transylvanian professor. The eldest, Ştefan (1809–74), was born in 1809. Born a year later, Nicolae (1810–77) was elected to the Romanian Revolutionary Council in May 1848. Radu (1814–82) and Alexandru (1818–81), the latter nicknamed "the Black" (because of his complexion), were considered "radicals" during the revolution. Conversely, Dumitru (b. 1819) and Alexandru "the White" (1815–73) also joined the revolution but were considered moderates. The latter was one of the few *boiars* who understood the importance of agrarian reform and wrote on the subject.

The Golescu mansion in the village of Goleşti is presently one of the best organized family museums in Romania, full of mementos of important events in the history of Wallachia and that of the family with which it is closely intertwined.

Radu Florescu

Further reading

Anastase, Iordache. *Pe urmele Goleştilor.* Bucharest, 1982.
Berindei, Dan. "Legăturile genealogice dintre fruntaşii revoluţiei de la 1848 din ţara românească," in *Caietele Bălcescu,* 1984, 13–127.
Fotino, George. *Din vremea renasterii Naţional: Boerii Goleşti,* 4 vols. Bucharest, 1939.
Sebastian, Tudor, Oprea Radu, et al. *Complexul Muzeul Goleşti.* Sibiu, Romania, 1980.

See also Boiars; Revolutions of 1848

Gołuchowski von Goluchow, Count Agenor, Senior (1812–75)

Conservative Galician politician, appointed to three terms as *Statthalter* (governor) of Galicia (1849–59; 1866–68; 1871–75) and the first Pole to head an Austrian cabinet as minister of the interior (August 28, 1859–February 4, 1861) in the

G

so-called Rechberg-Gołuchowski cabinet. As interior minister, Gołuchowski developed the October Patent (1860), which envisioned a federalist constitutional structure for the monarchy as a whole. His failure to garner the necessary support for this reform from three critical groups—the Hungarians, the centralist bureaucracy, and German liberals—caused him to be replaced in 1861 and brought about a turn toward a more centralist and eventually dualist constitution. Gołuchowski's efforts gained Galicia a substantial degree of autonomy within the Habsburg Empire, often at the expense of Ruthene nationalist demands.

Pieter Judson

Further reading

Brandt, Harm-Hinrich. *Der österreichische Neoabsolutismus: Staatsfinanzen und Politik 1848–1860,* 2 vols. Göttingen, Germany, 1978.

Redlich, Josef. *Das österreichische Staats- and Reichsproblem,* 2 vols. Leipzig, 1920–1926.

Wandycz, Piotr. "The Poles in the Habsburg Monarchy." *Austrian History Yearbook* 3, no. 2 (1967).

See also Carpatho-Rusyns; Dualism; October Diploma

Goma, Paul (1935–)

Romanian writer and political dissident, exiled to France in 1977. Goma was born in Bessarabia and grew up in Sibiu and Făgăraş, where his parents taught in village schools. His 1956 arrest for subversive literary activity resulted in prison and forced domicile until 1962. Allowed to resume his university studies in 1965, he published his first novel, *Camera de alaturi (The Adjoining Room),* in 1968, when he also joined the Romanian Communist Party. The Romanian censors turned down his next two novels, *Ostinato* and *The Door,* both published in West Germany and in France, where he lived in the early 1970s. Returning to Romania in 1973, he criticized the authorities, was expelled from the party, and in early 1977 intensified his protests with open letters to Czech dissidents and to President Nicolae Ceauşescu (1918–89). He was warned, beaten up, briefly arrested, and harassed. Finally in November 1977 he went into exile in France, where he continued to criticize Ceauşescu and to publish works of fiction and autobiography. The Romanian regime tried and failed to assassinate him in 1982, but it had suc-

cessfully uprooted the only intellectual protest movement to appear under Ceauşescu. After 1989, Goma became quite critical of the government of Ion Iliescu (1930–), Ceauşescu's successor, and in 1995 he even announced his candidacy for the presidential race in 1996.

Mary Ellen Fischer

Further reading

Shafir, Michael. *Romania: Politics, Economics, Society.* Boulder, Colorado, 1985.

———. "Who Is Paul Goma?" *Index on Censorship* 7, no. 1 (January–February 1978): 29–39.

See also Nicolae Ceauşescu; Communist Party of Romania; Ion Iliescu

Gömbös, Gyula (1886–1936)

Leading representative of right-wing, fascist-type policies in interwar Hungary. Born into a middle-class German-Hungarian family, Gömbös became a General Staff officer in the Austro-Hungarian Army. After World War I, he cooperated closely with Admiral Miklós Horthy (1868–1957) to organize an independent Hungarian army. He played a major role in establishing the new Hungarian government and in securing the election of Horthy as regent. An indefatigable worker and an effective propagandist, Gömbös quickly became the spokesman for a radical right-wing movement that established contact with like-minded anti-Communist groups in Central and Eastern Europe. In the 1920s Gömbös was Hungary's most prominent and demonstrative anti-Semite; however, his ultranationalistic "Party of Race Defenders" had only limited political success.

Gömbös's influence increased greatly when the economic crisis that brought on the Great Depression struck Hungary in the late 1920s. In 1932 Regent Horthy, seeking more radical solutions to Hungary's economic problems, appointed Gömbös prime minister. Distrustful of the Western democracies, Gömbös moved quickly to establish close ties with Nazi Germany and Fascist Italy. In his oratory and political style he emulated Hitler (1889–1945) and Mussolini (1883–1945), even assuming the title "vezér" (like *duce* and *führer,* leader). His efforts to take action on the "Jewish question" and to create a totalitarian regime in Hungary were thwarted, however, by the conservative establishment. In 1936 Horthy, fearing that

Gömbös intended to violate the constitution and establish dictatorial rule, resolved to dismiss him. But before the regent could take action, Gömbös became ill and died. Although he had not succeeded in introducing Nazi institutions into Hungary, Gömbös left a lasting imprint on parliament and on the government party, which during World War II remained strongly pro-Nazi and anti-Semitic.

Thomas Sakmyster

Further reading

Kónya, Sándor. *Gömbös kisérlete totális fasiszta diktatúra megteremtésére.* Budapest, 1968.

Macartney, C.A. *October Fifteenth: A History of Modern Hungary, 1929–1945.* Edinburgh, 1961.

Pritz, Pál. *Magyarország külpolitikája Gömbös Gyula miniszter-elnöksége idején 1932–1936.* Budapest, 1982.

Sakmyster, Thomas. *Hungary, the Great Powers, and the Danubian Crisis.* Athens, Georgia, 1980.

See also Great Depression; Miklós Horthy; Right Radicalism

Gombrowicz, Witold (1904–69)

Polish novelist, playwright, and essayist. Born into an upper-middle-class family with aristocratic pretensions, Gombrowicz dutifully completed a law degree, yet soon after plunged into a life of writing. His youth in a vociferously nationalist Poland (he came of age with the winning of Polish independence in 1918) forged his fundamentally rebellious and individualistic art. In his prewar works—the short story anthology *Pamiętnik z okresu dojrzewania* (*Memoirs from a Time of Immaturity,* 1933), the play *Iwona, księzniczka Burgunda* (*Ivona, Princess of Burgundy,* 1935), the novels *Ferdydurke* (1937) and the unfinished *Opętani* (*Possessed*), and assorted shorter works—he established the major genres and topics of his œuvre. His masterpiece, *Ferdydurke,* explicitly spells out the philosophy he would variously reenact in his works. Gombrowicz maintained that the principle of form inheres in all human interaction and entails our involuntary acceptance and acting out of the ready self-images assigned us by any observing "other." Form can be eluded only temporarily through retreat into such formless states as inferiority and immaturity. Gombrowicz became one of the greatest and most original writers in modern European literature, and his genius lies in his provocative theatricality, stylistic virtuosity, and inventive iconoclasm.

When a 1939 trip to Buenos Aires exiled him for the next twenty-four years in Argentina, Gombrowicz reiterated and repackaged his antiform gospel for the world in his plays *Ślub* (*The Marriage,* 1947) and the unfinished *Historia* (*History*); the novels *Trans-atlantyk* (*Trans-Atlantic,* 1952), *Pornografia* (1957), and *Kosmos* (*Cosmos,* 1962); and his very public *Dziennik* (*Diary,* 1953–68). Indeed, the *Diary,* published in installments, served as his spokestext in which he played prophet, iconoclast, mentor, critic, and crank to a real audience. Overlapping with, but not imitative of, existentialism, structuralism, and the theatre of the absurd, Gombrowicz's works were well received in postwar Europe, and a 1963 Ford Foundation grant enabled his relocation to Berlin and then to France, where he died in 1969.

Beth Holmgren

Further reading

Gombrowicz i krytycy, ed. by Zdzisław Łapiński. Kraków-Wrocław, 1984.

Gombrowicz, Witold. *A Kind of Testament,* ed. by Dominique de Roux, trans. by Alastair Hamilton. London, 1973.

Holmgren, Beth. "Witold Gombrowicz within the *Wieszcz* Tradition." *Slavic and East European Journal* 4 (1989): 556–70.

Thompson, Ewa. *Witold Gombrowicz.* Boston, 1979.

See also Polish Literature

Gomułka, Władisław (1905–82)

Polish Communist leader. Born in 1905 in Krosno, in the Russian part of Poland, Gomułka became an activist in the interwar Polish Communist movement. He joined the socialist youth movement and the trade union of chemical workers in the 1920s. In 1926 he joined the Communist Party. Gomułka studied at the international Lenin School in Moscow from 1934 to 1936, and after his return to Poland, he was arrested many times for political activities. During World War II, he became a leader in the Communist resistance movement. Always viewed as a "Polish" Communist, particularly by those Polish Communists returning from Moscow with the Red Army in 1944, he was granted the post of secretary-general of the Polish Workers Party in 1945. Gomułka was accused of

G "nationalist deviation" in 1948 and was expelled from the party. Imprisoned for five years, he was quietly released after the death of Stalin (1879–1953) and in 1956 was named first secretary of the party after the death of Bolesław Bierut (1892–1956). Gomułka guided Poland through the turbulent events of the fall of 1956, which saw widespread demonstrations in the country, and he attempted liberal reforms in the late 1950s. He began to retreat from reform after 1960, which led to growing economic and social stagnation in Poland until 1970, when worker strikes in Gdańsk and elsewhere forced Gomułka to resign. He was replaced by Edward Gierek (1913–).

David Stefancic

Further reading

Bethell, Nicholas. *Gomułka, His Poland and His Communism.* London, 1969.

deWeydenthal, Jan. *The Communists of Poland.* Stanford, California, 1978.

Dziewanowski, M.K. *The Communist Party of Poland: An Outline History.* Cambridge, 1976.

See also Bolesław Bierut; Communist Party of Poland; Edward Gierek; Stalin

Gorbachev, Mikhail (1931–)

Soviet leader under whom the Communist system collapsed. Gorbachev's political career began in 1970, when he became the top party boss in the Stavropol region. In 1978 he became party secretary for agriculture. Two years later he joined the Politburo. When Gorbachev became Soviet leader in March 1985, he called for "revolutionary changes" and for "profound transformations in the economy and the whole system of social relations." He understood that not only the Soviet Union but also its satellite bloc of East European states showed "signs of disease," because of accumulated grievances. Many of his close advisers experienced the Prague Spring, the short-lived period of liberalization in Czechoslovakia in 1968, and hoped for similar progress in the Soviet Union. Therefore, it came as a surprise when, during a visit to Prague, Gorbachev disappointed the enthusiastic welcoming crowds by stressing his intention not to interfere in local politics. He stressed that "no party has a monopoly on the truth." This left it to the Czechs and Slovaks to get rid of their unpopular bosses.

In June 1989, every Communist candidate in Poland was defeated. When no Soviet military threats followed, this affirmed the Kremlin's positive side of noninterference. One month later, Gorbachev in a speech to the Council of Europe in Strasbourg proclaimed a policy of laissez-faire in Eastern Europe.

In September 1989 Hungarians opened their borders to Austria, and East German tourists streamed across as refugees. Others climbed the walls of the West German embassy in Prague and were allowed to flee from the Soviet bloc. After several Soviet warnings to East German leader Erich Honecker (1912–94) to make reforms were not heeded, he was replaced and demonstrators were allowed to break down the Berlin Wall. Although Gorbachev hoped only to see hard-line leaders replaced by reforming and more efficient Communists, he did not stop Czechoslovakia from becoming a democratic state with dissident Václav Havel (1936–) as president and East Germany reuniting with West Germany. There was no Soviet invasion and not a shot was fired. Gorbachev won the Nobel Peace Prize in 1990. Hard-liners in Moscow, in large part for his permitting the "loss" of Eastern Europe, attempted to remove him from power in August 1991. Although the coup failed, the Soviet Union was rapidly disintegrating, and in December 1991, Gorbachev resigned.

Peter Hruby

Further reading

Dawisha, Karen. *Eastern Europe, Gorbachev, and Reform.* New York, 1988.

Steele, Jonathan. *Eternal Russia: Yeltsin, Gorbachev and the Mirage of Democracy.* Cambridge, 1994.

Stokes, Gale. *The Walls Came Tumbling Down: The Collapse of Communism in Eastern Europe.* New York, 1993.

See also Berlin Wall; Glasnost and Perestroika; Václav Havel; Prague Spring; Revolutions of 1989

Gorchakov, Aleksandr Mikhailovich (1789–1883)

Russian foreign minister (1856–82). Gorchakov's goal was to escape Russia's diplomatic isolation following the Crimean War (1853–56) and to remove the humiliating provisions of the Treaty of Paris of 1856, which prohibited Russia from maintaining a Black Sea fleet and naval fortifications. He collaborated with France in the unification of the Romanian Principalities (Romania) in 1857–61 but lost French cooperation when Russia crushed the Polish revolt of 1863. His greatest success resulted from the diplomatic support he rendered Prussia in the Austro-Prussian War (1866), which led to Bismarck's (1815–1898) unification of Germany in 1871, after Prussia defeated France. While Europe was engaged with the Franco-Prussian War in 1870, Russia, with Bismarck's acquiescence, unilaterally abrogated the onerous provisions of the Treaty of Paris. Next Gorchakov entered into a loose conservative alliance with Germany and Austria-Hungary (Dreikaiserbund [Three Emperors' League]) in 1873, which later collapsed during the Balkan crisis of 1875–78. Notwithstanding his efforts, Pan-Slavism, a largely ill-defined movement that promoted the concept of Slavic unity, which Gorchakov opposed, helped push Russia into a war with the Ottoman Empire. Successful on the battlefield, Russia imposed harsh terms on the Turks in the Treaty of San Stefano. But the Great Powers, led by Britain, France, and Austria-Hungary, compelled Russia at the Congress of Berlin to dismember the Greater Bulgaria that it had created in the Treaty of San Stefano, which would have facilitated Russian control of the Turkish Straits. This was a bitter defeat for Gorchakov, because Russia was again diplomatically isolated, precisely the situation he had set out to overcome in 1856. Although he did not officially resign until 1882, others now actually conducted foreign affairs.

Charles Jelavich

Further reading

Khvostov, V. M. *Istoriia diplomatii,* vol 2. Moscow, 1963.

Mosse, W.E. *The Rise and Fall of the Crimean System, 1855–1871.* London, 1963.

Ragsdale, Hugh, ed. *Imperial Russian Foreign Policy.* Washington, D.C., 1993.

Semanov, S.A.M. *Gorchakov russkii diplomat XIX v.* Moscow, 1962.

Sumner, B.H. *Russia and the Balkans, 1870–1880.* Oxford, 1937.

See also Otto von Bismarck; Congress of Berlin; Crimean War; Eastern Question; Great Powers; January Uprising; Pan-Slavism; Paris, Treaty of; Russo-Turkish War of 1877–78; San Stefano, Treaty of; Three Emperors' League; United Principalities

Görgey, Artur (1818–1916)

General in the Hungarian War for Independence of 1848–49 and minister of defense. Görgey was descended from a landed gentry family. According to his father's wishes, at the age of fourteen, he was sent to the Army Cadet School at Tuln, Austria, and at the age of nineteen he became a lieutenant in the Hungarian Guards. After his father's death in the summer of 1845, he received his discharge and continued his chemical studies at Prague University, where he discovered the compound lauric acid.

As the events of 1848 unfolded, Görgey returned to Hungary and offered his services to the Hungarian government, quickly rising through the ranks. He played an important role in defeating the troops of Baron Josip Jelačić (1801–1859), the *ban* (governor) of Croatia. Görgey became a general on November 1, 1848. During the winter of 1848, he commanded the western territories of Hungary, as well as Buda, then capital of Hungary. After his successful campaign in western Hungary, on March 31, 1849, he became the commander in chief of the Hungarian army. In his Proclamation in Vác in January 1849, he declared his readiness to arrive at an agreement, based on the Laws of April 1848 (which established a constitutional monarchy in Hungary), as sanctioned by the king. Although he did not agree with the Declaration of Independence of 1849, which on April 14, 1849 declared the independence of Hungary and the dethronement of the Habsburgs, he nevertheless accepted the position of minister of military affairs in the new government. During the course of the spring campaign, he inflicted serious defeats on the imperial army, and on May 21 his troops recaptured Buda. On July 5, 1849, shortly after the Russian intervention army began its offensive, Lajos Kossuth (1802–94) relieved Görgey of his duty as commander in chief. A month later, on August 10, 1849, Kossuth resigned his commission as governor and granted Görgey supreme power. Facing an impossible situation, Görgey had no alternative but to surrender unconditionally to Russian forces on August 13, 1849, at Világos. Owing to the intervention of Nicholas I (1796–1855), Görgey was pardoned. He lived in Austria until 1867 and returned to Hungary only after the *Ausgleich* (Compromise) of 1867, which created the Dual Monarchy of Austria-Hungary. His memoirs, *Mein Leben und Wirken in Ungarn* (*My Life and Work in Hungary*),

G were published in Leipzig in 1852 but not in Hungary until 1911.

Pál Péter Tóth

Further reading

Handlery, Georg de Poór. *General Artur Görgey and the Hungarian Revolution of 1848–1849.* Ann Arbor, Michigan, 1974.

Kosáry, Domokos. *A Görgey-kérdés és története.* Budapest, 1936.

Szinnyei, József. *Magyar írók élete és munkái,* vol. 3. Budapest, 1894.

See also *Ausgleich;* Dual Monarchy; Hungarian War for Independence; Josip Jelačić; Lajos Kossuth; Nicholas I; Revolutions of 1848

Gottwald, Klement (1896–1953)

Leader of the Communist coup d'état in Czechoslovakia and the country's first Communist president. Gottwald was born to a Moravian peasant family. Sent to Vienna to be a woodworker's apprentice, he joined the Social Democratic youth movement there. He served honorably in the Austro-Hungarian army in World War I and afterward helped form the new Czechoslovak Communist Party in 1921. By 1929, he had become its secretary-general and, by 1935, leader of the Communist deputies in the Czechoslovak parliament. Gottwald bitterly opposed Czechoslovakia's capitulation to Hitler's (1889–1945) demands that the Sudetenland be turned over to Germany at Munich in 1938. He spent World War II in the Soviet Union, making propaganda broadcasts and organizing underground resistance in the Czech lands. In 1943, in Moscow, he and Edvard Beneš (1884–1948), the Czechoslovak president-in-exile, worked out a compromise governmental structure for postwar Czechoslovakia.

In liberated Czechoslovakia, Gottwald was elected chairman of the Czechoslovak Communist Party and, after the stunning showing of his party in the national elections, became prime minister in July 1946. In February 1948, exploiting a cabinet crisis, he mobilized his party and its adherents in a show of force, and on February 25, President Beneš permitted him to form a new government of Communists and sympathizers. In June Gottwald replaced Beneš himself as president, then presided over a drastic, Soviet-style communization of the country. He dutifully obeyed Stalin's (1879–1953) order to purge "potential Titoists" from Communist ranks by condemning some of his closest comrades to death or life imprisonment. He died in Prague on March 14, 1953, shortly after attending Stalin's own funeral in Moscow.

Joseph Frederick Zacek

Further reading

Kaplan, Karel. *The Short March: The Communist Takeover in Czechoslovakia, 1945–1948.* London, 1987.

Korbel, Josef. *The Communist Subversion of Czechoslovakia, 1938–1948.* Princeton, New Jersey, 1959.

Suda, Zdeněk L. *Zealots and Rebels: A History of the Ruling Communist Party of Czechoslovakia.* Stanford, California, 1980.

See also Edvard Beneš; Communist Party of Czechoslovakia; Munich Pact; Stalin; Tito-Stalin Split

Grabski, Stanisław (1871–1949)

Polish political activist. Born in the town of Borow, Grabski, along with his brother Władysław, was a political activist, publicist, and economist. Although he was a founder of the Polish Social Party (PPS), along with Roman Dmowski (1864–1939), Grabski was nonetheless also one of the founders of the National Democracy movement, which has been identified as one of the extreme right-wing Polish national political groupings of the nineteenth and twentieth centuries. Before World War I, Grabski was active in Galicia and looked to Russia for assistance in obtaining Polish independence. In post-1918 Poland he continued to support Dmowski's program, and he served as minister of religion and public education in 1923 and again in 1925–26, during which time he pursued pro-Catholic and pro-Polish nationalistic policies in the multinational interwar republic.

After Józef Piłsudski's (1867–1935) coup d'état of May 1926, Grabski withdrew into academic activity. He was already a professor at Lwów's Polish University from 1910, and he continued there until the outbreak of World War II.

In 1939 Grabski found himself in the Soviet-occupied zone of Poland, in Lwów (L'vov), and was able to leave the USSR only after General Władysław Sikorski obtained the consent of Stalin (1879–1953) in July 1941. From February 1942 to

June 1945, Grabski worked with Sikorski (1881–1943) and Stanisław Mikołajczyk (1901–66) in the Polish government-in-exile in London. He returned to Poland in 1945 (along with Mikołajczyk) and was in the interim government until 1947, when the Communists consolidated power. His last two years were spent at the Law School of Warsaw University.

Paul J. Best

Further reading

Grabski, Stanisław. *Ku Lepszei Polsce.* Warsaw, 1938.

———. *Polska gospodarka planowa.* Warsaw, 1947.

Maly Slownik historii Polski, 4th ed. Warsaw, 1967.

Schmitt, Bernadotte E., ed. *Poland.* Berkeley, California, 1945.

"Stanislaw Grabski," *Wielka Encyklopedia Powszechna,* vol. 4. Warsaw, 1964, 371.

See also Roman Dmowski; Władysław Grabski; May Coup; Stanisław Mikołajczyk; Józef Piłsudski; Władysław Sikorski

Grabski, Władysław (1874–1938)

Economist, scholar, premier of Poland (1920, 1923–25), and finance minister (1919–20, 1923–25). Although he held several important political positions in the early 1920s, Grabski is best known for inaugurating a series of economic reforms during his second term as premier. He began his political career as a deputy to the Russian Duma (1906–12). In 1919 he served as a member of the Polish delegation at the Paris Peace Conference as an expert in financial and economic matters.

His first term as premier (1920) came at a critical time. At the Spa Conference in Belgium (July 1920), Grabski accepted the unfavorable terms of the Allied Supreme Council to negotiate a conclusion to the Polish-Soviet War. The Poles soon repudiated this agreement after defeating the Red Army later in 1920.

Nominated as premier of a nonpartisan government in December 1923 and given extraordinary powers to issue economic decrees, Grabski gained control of Poland's runaway inflation rate and made great headway toward balancing the budget. In April 1924 he replaced the Polish mark with the złoty, which was based on gold and set at a value of 5.18 to the dollar. He also established a new central bank, the Bank of Poland. Although

Grabski's program restored some international confidence in the Polish state, his successes were temporary. In 1925 a decline in the world market price of some major Polish exports and a tariff war with Germany helped undermine his reforms and weakened the value of the złoty. The continued depreciation of the currency, along with public unrest, caused his government to fall in November 1925.

Grabski withdrew from political life after the coup led by Józef Piłsudski (1867–1935) in 1926 and devoted his energies to scholarly endeavors.

Robert M. Ponichtera

Further reading

Grabski, Władysław. *"Myśli o Rzecypospolitej."* Autonomia, Reforma, Edukacja obywatelska: Wybór myśli politycznych i społecznych, ed. by Maria Drozdowski and Marian Drozdowski. Kraków, 1988.

———. *Wybór pism,* ed. by Józef Wojnarowski. Warsaw, 1987.

Pease, Neal. *Poland, the United States, and the Stabilization of Europe, 1919–1933.* New York, 1986.

Tomaszewski, Jerzy. *Stabilizacja waluty w Polsce; z badań nad polityką gospodarczą rządu polskiego przed przewrotem majowym.* Warsaw, 1961.

See also Duma; Economic Development in Poland; Paris Peace Conference; Józef Piłsudski; Polish–Soviet War; Red Army

Great Depression

Worldwide economic decline beginning in 1929 and lasting throughout the 1930s. The Great Depression had a disastrous impact on the economies of East Central Europe. Many states had just begun to recover from the difficult adjustment to independent statehood and the effects of World War I. Reorienting the region's economies after the war had led to a severe economic crisis during the 1920s. However, by the late 1920s, most of the economies had stabilized and were even modestly growing.

After 1929, East Central Europe could not escape the disruption in the major financial and economic markets. While overall European industrial production (excluding the Soviet Union) dropped 27 percent, the corresponding figures in Poland and Czechoslovakia were 41 percent and

G 37 percent, respectively. Industrial decline was less pronounced in other regions because of the preponderance of agriculture.

Apart from pursuing a more nationalist based economic policy, the postwar reconstruction of most states in the region had depended on good prices for agricultural exports and the import of Western capital for investment and modernization. In 1929 agricultural prices dropped precipitously. By 1932–33, grain products fetched between one-third and one-half of their pre-Depression prices. Likewise, Western investment soon came to a virtual halt once credit markets collapsed. By 1931, sources of foreign capital ceased to look for opportunities in the region. Those countries that accumulated a large debt could pay their interest and amortization only by obtaining new loans; however, those, too, quickly dried up as new loans became rare.

Economic difficulties mounted, especially for debtors who could no longer finance their loans. Peasant smallholders, who predominated in the region, experienced the greatest hardships, as many poor farmers had borrowed heavily. Only Czechoslovakia had not run up a huge foreign debt and managed to continue to service its debts and slowly recovered after 1936. The more conservative Poland adhered to the gold standard and paid its amortization, at least until 1936, when circumstances forced more direct government intervention. Increasingly, Poland fostered the development of the state-owned sector of industry (63 percent of all investment by 1939).

The other East Central European countries managed to stave off total financial collapse by temporarily closing banks in 1931, devaluing national currencies, and imposing strict controls over currency exchange and private/public payment of debts owed to foreigners. Most of the controls remained in effect until World War II, and indeed were considerably expanded during the war years.

Romania handled the decline in agriculture by sharply accelerating oil production, leading to only an 11 percent decline in overall industrial product compared with the 1929 level. Industry in both Yugoslavia and Bulgaria fared better than in some of the other countries in the region. While mining production fell by 25 percent in Yugoslavia, employment and investments in industry rose by 10 percent between 1928 and 1933. Countries with more developed heavy industries, such as Poland and Hungary, suffered greater economic dislocation. Hungarian heavy industry and machine factories declined to 52 percent of their pre-Depression levels. Likewise Poland, heavily dependent on coal exports, saw a 40 percent decline in coal production by 1933. Only the electric power and chemical industries continued to expand steadily despite the overall decline.

Since Czechoslovakia was the most industrialized country in the region, it suffered some of the sharpest declines in production, especially in consumer goods industries such as textiles and glass-making. Likewise the metal industry produced 60 percent less than at its peak production levels in 1929.

In the social realm, this resulted in high unemployment, and underemployment skyrocketed throughout East Central Europe, as it did in the industrialized countries. It also exacerbated tensions with ethnic minorities.

Recovery came gradually in the late 1930s, accelerated by the economic policies of Nazi Germany. Germany reoriented its domestic economy around rearmament and formulated a foreign economic policy that reduced imports and assured economic autarky by negotiating favorable bilateral trade agreements. While the trade helped stimulate the economies of the region, it also placed a stranglehold on them once the German war machine had geared up for battle.

Michael J. Kopanic Jr.

Further reading

Berend, Iván T. and György Ránki. *Economic Development in East-Central Europe in the 19th and 20th Centuries.* New York, 1974.

Hertz, F. *The Economic Problem of the Danubian States: A Study on Economic Nationalism.* London, 1936.

Kaser, M.C. and E.A. Radice, eds. *The Economic History of Eastern Europe 1919–1975,* 3 vols. Oxford, 1985–86.

Lampe, John R. and Marvin R. Jackson. *Balkan Economic History, 1550–1950.* Bloomington, Indiana, 1982.

Spulber, N. *The State and Economic Development in Eastern Europe.* New York, 1966.

See also Agriculture; Banking; Economic Development in Albania; Economic Development in Bulgaria; Economic Development in Czechoslovakia; Economic Development in Hungary;

Economic Development in Poland; Economic Development in Romania; Economic Development in Yugoslavia; Emigration; Ethnic Minorities; Industrialization

Greater Romania

Denotes the creation of a single Romanian state by uniting ethnic Romanians in all the contiguous lands largely inhabited by the Romanian people. With the development of Romanian nationalism in the latter part of the eighteenth century and the first part of the nineteenth, the idea of a united, independent Romanian state gradually developed. In the 1830s and 1840s wealthy, often French-educated, sons of Romanian *boiars* first took up the call for uniting the so-called Danubian Principalities of Wallachia and Moldavia, which at that time were still part of the Ottoman Empire. In 1859 Wallachia and Moldavia were united, and the country's independence was recognized in 1878. In the decades that followed, the idea of uniting Romanians living in adjacent lands developed. This idea was especially championed by the National Liberal Party within the Romanian Kingdom.

With the collapse of the Central Powers and tsarist Russia at the end of World War I, Greater Romania became a reality. The Romanians in Transylvania, the Banat, Maramureş, Crişana, Bessarabia, and Bukovina, taking advantage of the chaotic times, joined with their brethren in the Romanian Kingdom in forming a large, or Greater Romanian, state. Thanks to the shrewd diplomacy of Ion I.C. Brătianu (1864–1927), these changes were recognized by the Allies at the Paris Peace Conference of 1919. As a result, the Romanian state more than doubled its territory and population. During World War II, however, Romania was forced to give up Bessarabia, Bukovina, and Southern Dobrudja (Dobruzha), which left the state with its present frontiers.

Paul D. Quinlan

Further reading

Fischer-Galati, Stephen. "Romanian Nationalism," in *Nationalism in Eastern Europe,* ed. by Peter F. Sugar and Ivo John Lederer. Seattle, Washington, 1969.

Hitchins, Keith. *The Romanians: 1774–1866.* Oxford, 1966.

———. *Rumania: 1866–1947.* Oxford, 1994.

Livezeanu, Irina. *Cultural Politics in Greater Romania.* Ithaca, New York, 1995.

See also Alba Iulia; Ion I.C. Brătianu; *Boiars;* Danubian Principalities; Dobrudja; Irredentism; Nationalism; Paris Peace Conference; United Principalities

Greater Serbia

Nationalist program that has informed Serb political discourse since 1844. Using Italian and German models for national unification, Ilija Garašanin's (1812–74) *Načertanje* (Outline) proposed that Serbia attempt to expand its territory to include all lands associated with the Serbian Orthodox Church. Garašanin's vision of Greater Serbia included Ottoman Bosnia, Hercegovina, northern Albania, and Montenegro, as well as Habsburg Srem, Bačka, and the Banat. By 1860, the Greater Serbian ideal also included Catholic Croat lands as well as Kosovo, Macedonia, and western Bulgaria, which had been part of a medieval Serb state but were not necessarily Serbian and Orthodox.

After World War I, the Paris Peace Conference dismembered the Ottoman and Habsburg Empires and gave substantial territory to the new Kingdom of Serbs, Croats, and Slovenes (later Yugoslavia). Nikola Pašić (1845–1926), the kingdom's new prime minister, used movements for both Serb nationalism and South Slav unity to advance Serb political aspirations. The Paris Peace Conference (1919) and the Vidovdan Constitution (1921) validated a centrally organized state headed by the Serbian monarchy, fulfilling the Greater Serbian ideal.

In 1945 Yugoslavia became a Communist state, divided into six politically equal republics (representing each of the six nations) and two autonomous provinces (representing substantial ethnic minorities within the Serbian republic). In 1974 the autonomous provinces, Kosovo and Vojvodina, were given federal power coequal with the other six nations, diminishing the Serbian republic's political influence. After Tito's death (1892–1980), Yugoslavia plunged into economic and political turmoil that fanned nationalist sentiments. In 1986 the Serbian Academy of Arts and Sciences circulated a memorandum arguing that Serbs had been the chief victim of Communist rule. The memorandum proclaimed their historic

G right to unite Serbs under Serb control and resurrected the idea of Greater Serbia.

Slobodan Milošević (1941–) used nationalism to unite old-line Communists and military officers and put the Greater Serbia idea into practice. Milošević rallied millions to the cause of Greater Serbia by using Kosovo as a symbol of Serbian decline under communism; Kosovo, the medieval cultural and religious center of Serbia, had become 90 percent Albanian. Milošević reasserted control over Kosovo and Vojvodina, making Serbia the most powerful republic in Yugoslavia. By subsequently claiming that Serbs' rights could be protected only by Serbia, Milošević called for unity of all Serbs within Yugoslavia. This campaign upset the precarious political balance within the ethnically diverse state and led to a bloody war among the various republics starting in 1990.

Katherine McCarthy

Further reading

Cohen, Lenard J. *Broken Bonds: Yugoslavia's Disintegration and Politics in Transition,* 2d ed. Boulder, Colorado, 1995.

MacKenzie, David. *Ilija Garašanin: Balkan Bismarck.* Boulder, Colorado, 1985.

Petrovich, Michael B. *A History of Modern Serbia, 1804–1918.* New York, 1976.

Stokes, Gale, ed. *From Stalinism to Pluralism: A Documentary History of Eastern Europe since 1945,* 2d ed. Oxford, 1996.

See also Ethnic Minorities; Ilija Garašanin; Kingdom of Serbs, Croats, and Slovenes; Kosovo; Slobodan Milošević; *Načertanje;* Nationalism; Nikola Pašić; Paris Peace Conference; Serbia; Tito; Vidovdan Constitution

Great Hungarian Plain

Agricultural heartland of Hungary. The Great Hungarian Plain (*Nagy Alföld*), accounting for 56 percent of the country's territory, is located east of the Danube River and south of the northern mountains. The plain's topography is uniformly flat, ranging in elevation from 280 feet (85 m) in the south to 610 feet (185 m) in the northeast. It is drained by the north–south-flowing Tisza River and its several tributaries, such as the Körös and Berettyó. The climate is temperate, with temperatures during the growing season averaging 64° F (18° C), and precipitation averages 21–24 inches (55–60 cm), although summer drought is common. Soils are generally good, though in places they can be either poorly drained or too sandy. Natural vegetation consists of short grasses and mixed forests along waterways.

Debrecen in the north and Szeged in the south are the major towns of the plain; other settlements include numerous market towns and the isolated farmstead (*tanya*). Much of the plain is characterized as *puszta,* barren land depopulated during Turkish times. The plain also contains smaller local regions, such as the Hortobágy, Kunság, Nyírség, and Hajduság.

The economy is dominated by large-scale agriculture, mainly extensive cultivation of cereals (wheat, barley, rice), seeds (sunflower, rape), tubers (sugar beets, potatoes), and cattle, pork, and poultry raising. The principal industry is grain milling and food processing, though some manufacturing, especially in Debrecen, also occurs. Despite its agricultural development, the Great Plain has traditionally been the poorest and least developed of Hungary's major regions.

Darrick Danta

Further reading

Bernát, Tivadar, ed. *An Economic Geography of Hungary.* Budapest, 1985.

Csizmadia, Ernő and Magda Székely. *Food Economy in Hungary.* Budapest, 1986.

Sárfalvi, Béla, ed. *The Changing Face of the Great Hungarian Plain.* Budapest, 1971.

See also Agriculture; Debrecen; Tisza River

Great Poland (Poznań) Uprising

Armed action of Polish inhabitants of the German province of Posen (Poznań) to secede from Germany at the end of World War I and join the newly re-created Polish state. In late 1918 the Polish inhabitants of Posen province (which was considered to be the area of Germany most animated by the Polish national movement) began to organize their own political institutions in anticipation of future unification with Poland. Experienced politicians planned to break away from Germany through a long-term process of organization and propaganda and with the help of the victorious Entente Powers. The younger generation of patriots preferred instead to take up arms. Ensuing events overtook the Polish plans. On December 26,

1918, Ignacy Jan Paderewski (1860–1941), world-renowned pianist and advocate of the Polish cause, visited the city of Poznań. His arrival caused an outburst of patriotic manifestations by the city's Polish inhabitants. The following day, a counter-demonstration by Germans prompted an exchange of gunfire, thus sparking the Polish uprising. Within five days, local Polish political and military organizations controlled the city. Spontaneous actions by Polish fighting units throughout the province also scored successes against German units, which were disorganized and weakened by revolutionary turmoil in Berlin. In mid-January 1919, however, German formations regrouped, striking against the province to overturn Polish gains and restore the German administration. Yet the Poles, in large part because of the growing strength of their military formation (the Army of Poznań), were able to defend against these attacks. Pressured by the Entente Powers, the Germans recognized Poland's incorporation of the duchy in February 1919, confirming it in the Treaty of Versailles (June 28, 1919).

Robert M. Ponichtera

Further reading

Blanke, Richard. *Orphans of Versailles: The Germans in Western Poland, 1918–1939*. Lexington, Kentucky, 1993.

Czubiński, Antoni. *Powstanie Wielkopolskie, 1918–1919*, 2d ed. Poznań, 1988.

Czubiński, Antoni and Bogusław Polak, eds. *Powstanie Wielkopolskie, 1918–1919: Wybór źródeł*. Poznan, 1983.

Komarnicki, Titus. *Rebirth of the Polish Republic*. London, 1957.

Łukomski, Grzegórz and Bogusław Polak. *Powstanie Wielkopolskie 1918–1919*. Koszalin-Warsaw, 1995.

See also Ignacy Jan Paderewski

Great Powers

The dominant powers—Russia (and later the Soviet Union), Habsburg Empire, Ottoman Empire, Great Britain, France, Prussia/Germany, Italy, and, after 1945, the United States—whose actions often determined (and even dominated) events in East Central and southeastern Europe.

Throughout the nineteenth century, there were four regional powers in Eastern Europe. The Habsburg Empire, which itself comprised much of East Central Europe and had joined with Russia and Prussia in the partitions of Poland in the late 1700s, spent much of its energies in the 1800s watching events in the Balkans. Although it judiciously avoided direct conflict in southeastern Europe after 1815, Vienna maintained an active (and often reactive) policy toward the region, which often found the empire at odds with Russian policy in the Balkans and especially with the emerging nations in the area, principally Serbia.

Russia, which in the early 1800s was the principal voice for stability in Europe (even interceding in 1848 to help put down revolts in Moldavia, Transylvania, and Hungary), was constantly confronted with vexing problems in both Poland and the Balkans. With regard to the former, St. Petersburg attempted to preserve and consolidate its hold, even in the face of major insurrections in 1830 and 1863; the question of the Balkans, however, presented a more difficult problem. Russia, which saw itself as the champion of Orthodoxy and the Slavic peoples of the Balkans, found itself drawn into three major wars with the Ottomans between 1815 and 1914 (the Russo-Turkish War of 1828–29, the Crimean War [1853–56], and the Russo-Turkish War of 1877–78). Despite its own internal weaknesses, and it own best interests notwithstanding, Russia was thus a prisoner of its own self-identity.

In contrast to the expanding power and influence of the other regional Great Powers, the Ottomans, who had dominated the Balkans since the late 1300s, witnessed their hold on southeastern Europe disappear in a series of wars and rebellions during the nineteenth century.

Finally, Prussia/Germany, the fourth regional power, usually pursued a policy of stability in the region, especially after unification in 1870–71; anything less represented a threat to its overriding goal of preventing the formation of an anti-German coalition in Europe. Thus, for two decades German Chancellor Otto von Bismarck (1815–98) sought to maintain peace between Russia and Austria-Hungary, two states whose policies often collided in the Balkans. However, after Bismarck's fall, Berlin pursued a dangerous policy in Eastern Europe that would ultimately draw Germany into World War I.

Two other European powers, Britain and France, also had active policies in Eastern Europe.

G Throughout much of the nineteenth century, London feared Russian actions and therefore opposed any potential Russian expansion toward the Mediterranean. As such, Britain saw stability in the region as vital to its own geopolitical interests. France, meanwhile, often saw itself as the champion of nationalist (especially Polish and Romanian) movements and served as a magnet for émigré organizations.

Despite the competing interests of the Great Powers in Eastern Europe and their general inability to control events, primarily in the Balkans, a general balance of power was maintained in the nineteenth century, one of the by-products of the Congress of Vienna (1815) and reconfirmed in later Great Power convocations such as the Congress of Berlin (1878). By the early 1900s, however, the creation of the alliance systems may have brought former adversaries (Britain, France, and Russia, on the one hand; Austria-Hungary and Germany on the other) together, but Great Power competition in the region, especially between Vienna and St. Petersburg, left Europe a tinderbox in which the assassination of Austrian archduke Franz Ferdinand (1863–1914) by a Serbian nationalist led to war in 1914.

World War I destroyed four empires (and the Austrians and Turks would never regain Great Power status) but not the influence of the Great Powers. In fact, Woodrow Wilson's (1856–1924) Fourteen Points set the stage for postwar decisions that stamped the interwar period. At the Paris Peace Conference in 1919 the peacemakers redrew the map of Eastern Europe, creating new states out of the former Habsburg, German, and Russian empires (Poland, Hungary, Czechoslovakia), enlarging others (Romania and the Kingdom of Serbs, Croats, and Slovenes [Yugoslavia]), and leaving behind regional tensions and animosities that went unchecked throughout the interwar period. Moreover, despite the emergence of a seemingly new and independent Eastern Europe after 1918, by the 1930s, the resurgent totalitarian states (Germany, Soviet Union, and Italy) had made the region again an area of Great Power machinations.

The demise of fascism in 1945 witnessed the end of the era of the European Great Powers but not the end of Great Power influence. The Cold War that followed World War II saw the Soviet Union exert a new domination (and dominion) over Eastern Europe. Like the Congress of Vienna, the Congress of Berlin, and the Paris Peace Con-

ference, the postwar decisions by the Powers at places like Yalta and Potsdam, and the 1946 speech by Winston Churchill (1874–1965) warning of a descending Iron Curtain, were fitting symbols of Great Power actions, reactions, and policy making that would continue until the collapse of the Berlin Wall in 1989. Despite its attempts (including invasions of Hungary in 1956 and Czechoslovakia in 1968) to maintain hegemony over the region, like the best-laid plans of other Great Powers before them, the Soviet Union too was unable in the end to dominate the diverse and often volatile region.

Richard Frucht

Further reading

Anderson, M.S. *The Eastern Question 1774–1923.* London, 1966.

Davis, Lynn Etheridge. *The Cold War Begins: Soviet-American Conflict over Eastern Europe.* Princeton, New Jersey, 1974.

Jelavich, Barbara. *The Habsburg Empire in European Affairs 1814–1918.* Chicago, 1969.

———. *St. Petersburg and Moscow: Tsarist and Soviet Foreign Policy 1814–1974.* Bloomington, Indiana, 1974.

Langer, William E. *European Alliances and Alignments 1871–1890.* New York, 1950.

Shaw, Stanford J. and Ezel Kural Shaw. *History of the Ottoman Empire and Modern Turkey,* vol. 2. Cambridge, 1977

See also Berlin Wall; Brezhnev Doctrine; Winston Churchill; Cold War; Congress of Berlin; Congress of Vienna; Crimean War; Danube Question; Eastern Question; Fourteen Points; Germany; Greek Revolution; Habsburg Empire; Hungarian Revolution of 1956; Iron Curtain; Kuchuk Kainardji, Treaty of; Ottoman Empire; Pan-Slavism; Paris Peace Conference; Paris, Treaty of; Polish Question; Potsdam Conference; Prague Spring; Prussia; Revolutions of 1989; Russia; Russification; Russo-Turkish War of 1828–29; Russo-Turkish War of 1877–78; Sovietization; Woodrow Wilson; World War I; Yalta Conference

Greek Civil War (1946–49)

Internecine conflict between Communists aided by Yugoslavia and nationalists aided by the West. The Greek Civil War may be viewed as the culmination of a longer struggle for the domination of Greek political life and the control of the state. Political divisions in postwar Greece were accentuated during World War II. The wartime government-in-exile did not enjoy popular support or legitimacy. Moreover, during the Axis occupation, fighting erupted between the Communist-led resistance and rival non-Leftist resistance organizations. A truce prior to the liberation of Greece from the Axis ended this first phase of civil war when a moderate coalition cabinet was formed with representatives from all parties, including the Communists.

In October 1944 the government entered Athens under the protection of British troops, while Communist armed bands seized control of most of the countryside on the heels of the German withdrawal from Greece. Cooperation between the government and the Left soon collapsed as Athens attempted to gain control of all the armed forces in Greece and to disarm the Communists. In early December fighting erupted in Athens between the Communist-led forces and the British and loyalists. This second phase of the civil war ended with the Agreement of Varkiza (February 1945), which specified that the defeated Communists would surrender their arms in exchange for a general amnesty and that a plebiscite would be held to decide the restoration of the monarchy.

The agreement did not bring stability. In December 1945 the Left abstained from parliamentary elections, and in September 1946 a plebiscite restored the monarchy. Frustrated, the Left prepared to resort to arms once more. With significant material support from Tito's (1892–1980) Yugoslavia, Greek Communists resumed military operations in March 1946. Within a year, the Greek government turned to the United States for support, as it became impossible for exhausted Britain to continue its assistance to Athens. Washington, fearing an expansion of Soviet influence in the Eastern Mediterranean, responded in March 1947 with the launching of the Truman Doctrine, aimed at containing global communism, beginning with Greece.

With massive military and economic aid from the United States, as well as the reorganization of the Greek armed forces, the initiative shifted to the government. The Communists' struggle was also hampered by a split in the party's leadership, the failure to form a consistent and viable strategy, and the lack of popular support. In the summer of 1949 Belgrade, reacting to the Greek Communists' support of Moscow in the Tito-Stalin dispute, closed the Yugoslav border and ceased delivery of supplies to the Greek insurgents. In August 1949 a series of offensives by government forces destroyed the remaining Communist strongholds in northwestern Greece.

Alexandros K. Kyrou

Further reading

Baerentzen, Lars, John O. Iatrides, and Ole L. Smith, eds. *Studies in the History of the Greek Civil War, 1945–1949.* Copenhagen, 1987.

Close, David H., ed. *The Greek Civil War, 1943–1950: Studies of Polarization.* London, 1993.

Iatrides, John O. *Revolt in Athens: The Greek Communist "Second Round," 1944–1945.* Princeton, New Jersey, 1972.

———., ed. *Greece in the 1940s: A Nation in Crisis.* Hanover, New Hampshire, 1981.

Iatrides, John O., and Linda Wrigley, eds. *Greece at the Crossroads: The Civil War and Its Legacy.* University Park, Pennsylvania, 1995.

Woodhouse, Christopher M. *The Struggle for Greece, 1941–1949.* London, 1976.

See also Tito; Tito-Stalin Split; Truman Doctrine

Greek Revolution (1820s)

The first successful Balkan struggle for national independence from the Ottoman Empire, which began in March 1821 with simultaneous insurrections in the Danubian Principalities and the Peloponnisus; it concluded in July 1832, when the Ottoman Empire formally recognized the legitimacy of the Kingdom of Greece as established and guaranteed by Russia, Great Britain, and France. The decrepit Ottoman administrative system, the shared religious beliefs and ecclesiastical structure of the Orthodox populations in the Balkans, a rising merchant class, an increasingly oppressed peasantry, national revival movements, and Great Power interests all ensured that the Greek revolt would profoundly affect not only Greece but the entire Balkans. The leadership of the Odessa-based Greek secret society, Filiki Etairia (Friendly Society), reflected this reality when it planned a Balkan-wide armed uprising, not just a Greek revolt, enlisted many non-Greek nationals to its cause, and actively sought the support of Serbian, Bulgarian, Romanian, and Montenegrin national leaders, merchants, and churchmen. Even though the Balkan leaders ignored these entreaties to join

G

the revolt, thousands of Balkan volunteers did fight alongside the Greek insurgents. Ultimately, however, the other Balkan nations did benefit from the Greek Revolution. Serbia gained complete autonomy from the Ottomans as a consequence of Russian intervention on behalf of Greece in 1828. Wallachia and Moldavia gained Russia as a protector in place of the Ottomans and, for the first time, native Romanians displaced Ottoman-appointed Greeks as governors. More important, the success of the Greek Revolution proved to the Balkan peoples that independence was possible.

Gregory L. Bruess

Further reading

Clogg, Richard, ed. *Balkan Society in the Age of Greek Independence.* Totowa, New Jersey, 1981.

Djordjevic, Dimitrije and Stephen Fischer-Galati. *The Balkan Revolutionary Tradition.* New York, 1981.

Jelavich, Barbara. *History of the Balkans: Eighteenth and Nineteenth Century.* Cambridge, 1983.

See also Danubian Principalities; Filiki Etairia; Phanariots; Philhellenism; Tudor Vladimirescu; Alexandros Ypsilantis

Green International

Loose international organization of East Central and southeastern European agrarian political parties that celebrated the virtues of rural life, championed peasant solidarity, advocated representative government, and called for the end of national rivalries. Aleksandur Stamboliiski (1879–1923), Bulgarian premier and leader of the Bulgarian Agrarian National Union (BANU), conceived the idea of a "Green International" in 1920 out of his sincere belief that traditional peasant desires for peace, social justice, equitable land distribution, egalitarian government, and individualism could be successfully articulated at the international level. Stamboliiski argued that a union of national peasant movements, a Green International, could effectively safeguard Eastern Europe from the anti-individualistic and labor-oriented Red International of Soviet Bolshevism and the equally pernicious White International of reactionary monarchists and landlords. Antonín Švehla (1873–1933), Czechoslovak Agrarian Party leader, enthusiastically endorsed Stamboliiski's proposal and suggested that Prague serve as the home for the

Green International's administrative body, the International Agrarian Bureau. From 1921 to 1925, the Green International consisted of the Bulgarian, Czechoslovak, Polish, and Serbian peasant parties and functioned primarily as an information center that spread the ideas of agrarianism. Unfortunately, Czechoslovak Agrarian Party leaders dominated the bureau in Prague and imbued it with a pronounced Pan-Slav orientation that alienated other peasant parties. The bureau sponsored annual congresses and published a trilingual quarterly, the *International Agrarian Bureau Bulletin.* Yet even these minor activities compelled the Comintern (Communist International) to create its own "red" peasant international, the Krestintern, in October 1923. In 1925 Karel Mečíř (n.d.) took command of the bureau, downplayed Pan-Slavism, and emphasized the moral reinforcement of peasants by forming new peasant parties in states where none had existed and coordinating the efforts of all member parties for greater international leverage and prestige. By May 1929, the Green International boasted seventeen member parties. The cumulative effects of the Great Depression and World War II diminished the Green International's social base and political prospects in Europe, but in 1947, several agrarian party émigrés reconstituted it as the International Peasant Union in Washington, D.C.

Gregory L. Bruess

Further reading

Bell, John D. *Peasants in Power: Alexander Stamboliski and the Bulgarian Agrarian National Union, 1899–1923.* Princeton, New Jersey, 1977.

Jackson, George D., Jr. *Comintern and Peasant in East Europe, 1919–1930.* New York, 1966.

Moser, Charles A. *Dimitrov of Bulgaria: A Political Biography of Dr. Georgi M. Dimitrov.* Ottawa, 1979.

See also Agrarian Parties; Agriculture; Bulgarian Agrarian National Union; Comintern; Great Depression; Pan-Slavism; Peasants; Aleksandur Stamboliiski; Antonín Švehla

Grégr, Edvard (1827–1907)

The principal Young Czech Party spokesman in the Bohemian diet and the Reichsrat (parliament) from 1874 to 1894 and a leader of the most outspokenly civil libertarian and anticlerical Young Czech delegates. Typical of the many Young Czechs who were trained in medicine or the sciences, Grégr believed that the extension of representative government and individual liberty was necessary and complementary to the advancement of scientific inquiry, technological innovation, and economic prosperity. After earning a medical degree in 1854, he worked as a research assistant to physiologist Jan Evangelista Purkyně (1787–1869) and helped popularize the natural sciences in published articles and as editor of *Živa* (*Nature*). Upon the advent of constitutional rule in Bohemia in 1861, he decided not to practice medicine but devote himself to politics, journalism, and publishing, as did his younger brother Julius (1831–96). In 1862 the Grégrs helped Jindřich Fügner (1822–65) and Miroslav Tyrš (1832–84) establish the Sokol (Slavic gymnastic club) organization. Subsequently both became prosperous entrepreneurs and advocates of free enterprise, with Edvard founding and building up a printing plant, a publishing house, and a bookstore.

In advocating the formation of an independent Young Czech party in 1874, Grégr contended that Old Czechs and Young Czechs were complementary parts of one national movement when he likened their proper relationship to that of the mainspring (Young Czechs) to the weights (Old Czechs) in a well-regulated clock: "If the weight were not present, the mainspring would run down too quickly; and if there were no mainspring as the driving force, the weight would stop the whole machine." In 1876 he asserted that both parties' program of "Bohemian state rights" was worthless without the representative governmental institutions and individual political rights necessary to implement and maintain it. He left most work of party organization and leadership to trusted colleagues and concentrated on serving the party as an eloquent publicist and "agitator." He thereby contributed mightily to the party's overwhelming victory in the elections of 1891 to the Reichsrat and in those of 1895 to the Bohemian diet.

Grégr belonged to the minority of Young Czechs who opposed their party's cooperation after 1894 with the Conservative Great Landowners. He continued his outspoken criticism of authoritarian Habsburg practices while supporting Young Czech efforts to extend the responsibilities of communal and district self-government. Moderate Young Czechs were critical of what they called Grégr's "theatrical radicalism." But they and most Czechs in other political parties respected his courage of conviction and the extensive knowledge of science, technology, and practical politics that informed his publications and speeches. His diary (*Denník*, two vols., 1908–14) is one of the most revealing records of his and other Young Czechs' aspirations, motivations, and opinions.

Bruce M. Garver

Further reading

Grégr, Edvard. *Naše politika: Otevřený list panu dru. Fr. L. Riegrovi,* 2d ed. Prague, 1874.
Znoj, Milan, Jan Havránek, and Martin Sekera, eds. *Český liberalismus: Texty a osobnosti.* Prague, 1995.

See also Julius Grégr; Old Czechs; Sokol; Miroslav Tyrš; Young Czechs

Grégr, Julius (1831–96)

Cofounder and editor-in-chief of the *Národní listy* (*National News*) and a leader of the Young Czechs. Within a year of its inception (January 1861), Grégr became the owner of *Národní listy* and built it into the Czech daily with the largest circulation and political influence. In doing so, he showed himself to be both a shrewd businessman and a courageous champion of civil liberties and greater Czech autonomy within the Habsburg monarchy. His outspoken defense of individual freedom and Czech national interests increased newspaper sales as well as provoking Habsburg fines, confiscation, and censorship. Throughout his life, he remained a bold advocate of civil liberties and freedom of the press. Unfortunately, his uncritical nationalism brought him into conflict with Czechs who sought to expose and correct injustices in Czech society and also led him to insist on the authenticity of Czech manuscripts "discovered" in the early 1800s and used by Czech nationalists to boost national consciousness, even after Czech scholars exposed them as forgeries.

Beginning in 1863, Grégr gave editorial support to the Young Czech faction within the National Party. From 1874 onward, *Národní listy* served as the principal organ of the independent Young Czech Party and contributed greatly to its electoral successes. Even after Grégr's death, the paper usually sided with the radically civil-libertarian and anticlerical factions within the party. This policy reflected not only the editors' political predilections but also their conviction that uncompromising advocacy of populistic and nationalistic programs would sell more newspapers and win more votes. This also accentuated differences with party moderates, particularly those who sought to make legislative compromises with other political groups. In 1908 the purchase of *Národní listy* by Karel Kramář (1860–1937) from Julius's son brought the paper under the control of moderates.

Bruce M. Garver

Further reading

Grégr, Julius et al. *Čtyři řeči pronešené na III. sjezdu národní strany svobodomyslné.* Prague, 1879.

Holeček, Josef. *Tragedie Julia Grégra.* Prague, 1914.

Tůma, Karel. *Život Dra. Julia Grégra. slavého obrance svobody české.* Prague, 1896.

See also Edvard Grégr; Karel Kramář; Manuscripts, The (Czech); Old Czechs; Press; Young Czechs

---

Grigorescu, Nicolae (1838–1907)

Founder of the modern Romanian school of painting. Grigorescu began as a church painter (1850–60), initially following the classicist trend prevalent in the Romanian Principalities throughout the first half of the nineteenth century. A long stay in France, particularly in Barbizon, acquainted him with French painting in one of its richest periods (1861–69). He soon abandoned the École des Beaux-Art but assiduously copied the Old Masters in the Louvre. Like many of his contemporaries, he was influenced by Corot (1796–1875), Courbet (1819–77), and the Barbizon painters, especially the work and style of Millet (1814–75). In the 1860s he was one of the pioneers of the plein air landscape and painted figures in a lyrical mood. After his return to Romania, he continued to develop his style, in portraits and in rustic subjects. His participation in some Bucharest exhibitions (1870, 1873) established him as the leading Romanian artist of his time. A trip to Italy (1873–74) and another sojourn in France (1876–77) contributed to the widening of his visual experience. During the Russo-Turkish War of 1877–78, he recorded in a series of canvases and in hundreds of drawings the maneuvres of the Romanian army. In 1883–84, in the Seine valley and in Brittany, his serene contemplation and his sense of light, as well as the vigor of his execution, reached their full maturity. Finally returning to Romania in 1885, and living principally in the region of his preferred motifs, Grigorescu became the most congenial interpreter of the Romanian rural world, to which he dedicated the largest part of his later work.

Remus Niculescu

Further reading

Niculescu, Remus. *William Ritter despre N. Grigorescu: Aspecte ale perioadei finale a pictorului. Studii și Cercetari de Istoria artei,* ser. *Arta Plastică,* vol. 31, 1984, 31–65.

Oprescu, G. and Remus Niculescu. *N. Grigorescu,* 2 vols. Bucharest, 1961–62.

Vlahoutza, A. *N.I. Grigorescu: Sa vie at son œuvre,* trans. by Léo. Bachelin. Bucharest, 1911.

See also Romanian Art; Russo-Turkish War of 1877–78

Grósz, Károly (1930–96)

Hungarian Communist. Born in Miskolc, Grósz was trained as a printer before joining the Communist Party in his twenties. After the Communist takeover in 1948, he was instrumental in subjugating Hungary's labor unions. By 1950, he was working for the Central Committee, also serving as a political officer in the army from 1950 to 1954. In 1959–61 he received advanced cadre training in Moscow and went on to hold a number of party and government positions.

Although he initiated political reforms that made Hungary more "open" than most of its neighbors, Grósz always remained a reluctant reformer, never quite making the move to establish a new social model. By the tumultuous summer of 1989, the tide of change he is credited with initiating had made him largely irrelevant. Thus, even though around that time Imre Nagy (1896–1958), the Communist reformer executed in the wake of the Hungarian Revolution of 1956, was exonerated and reburied, the Hungarian section of the Iron Curtain was dismantled, and a democratic constitution was created, Grósz had little to do with those developments. After 1988, he lived out his remaining years as a sickly and embittered pensioner in the town of Gödöllő.

András Boros-Kazai

Further reading
Banac, Ivo, ed. *Eastern Europe in Revolution.* Ithaca, New York, 1992.
Bozóki, András, A. Köröséy, and G. Schöpflin, eds. *Post-Communist Transition: Emerging Pluralism in Hungary.* New York, 1992.
East, Roger. *Revolutions in Eastern Europe.* New York, 1992.
Szakolczay, Árpád et al. *The Dissolution of Communist Power: The Case of Hungary.* New York, 1992.

See also Hungarian Communist Party; Iron Curtain; Imre Nagy; Revolutions of 1989

Groza, Petru (1884–1958)

Post–World War II premier of Romania. Born in Transylvania and educated in Budapest, Groza served in World War I in the Austro-Hungarian army. He became a wealthy businessman and joined the People's Party in 1919. He served in two cabinets under governments led by Alexandru Averescu (1859–1938), first as minister for national minorities and then as minister of communications. In 1933 he became the founder and leader of the Ploughman's Front, a leftist organization for poor peasants in Transylvania that advocated agrarian reform through land redistribution and improved relations between Hungarians and Romanians in Transylvania. While his leftist sympathies caused his arrest in April 1944 and a monthlong jail sentence, these same sympathies made him attractive to the Communists. On November 4, 1944, Groza was named vice premier of Romania. Five months later, on March 6, 1945, he was made premier, owing to the personal intervention of the Soviet deputy foreign minister, a post Groza held until 1952. In return for this appointment, the Soviets returned Transylvania to Romania. (It had been given to Hungary under the terms of the Vienna Award in 1940.) As premier, Groza supported socialist agrarian programs. In 1952 he became president of the Grand National Assembly, a post he held until his death in 1958.

Joseph F. Harrington

Further reading
Fischer-Galati, Stephen. *The New Rumania: From People's Democracy to Socialist Republic.* Cambridge, Massachusetts, 1967.
Quinlan, Paul. *Clash over Romania: British and American Policies towards Romania, 1938–1947.* Los Angeles, 1977.
Saiu, Liliana. *The Great Powers and Rumania, 1944–1946: A Study of the Early Cold War Era.* Boulder, Colorado, 1992.

See also Agrarian Parties; Alexandru Averescu; Ploughman's Front; Vienna Awards

Gymnastic Societies

Voluntary associations promoting physical culture. The Turnverein, the nationalist gymnastic society founded in Berlin in 1811, not only pioneered in inventing modern gymnastic practices; it also bequeathed the concept of politically charged physical training to Germany's eastern neighbors. Because nationalist clubs were not welcomed by the imperial regimes in the region, it was several decades before the Turnverein concept took root in Eastern Europe. The first gymnastic societies appeared in the Habsburg Empire in the 1860s and included the Sokol, the most successful gymnastic movement among the Slavs, as well as the Turnverein. Although these gymnastic associations all followed training programs based on the German system, they varied in other ways. For example, the Polish Sokol favored a militaristic style, the Ruthenian Sič undertook fire fighting in addition to gymnastics, and the Bulgarian Junak, unlike the other clubs, was founded at the impetus of the government. Further complicating the gymnastic picture, new clubs emerged at the turn of the century based on Social Democratic, Christian Socialist, Zionist, and other platforms. The Nazis were not immune to the political uses of gymnastics, as the example of Sudeten German gymnastic leader Konrad Henlein (1898–1945) demonstrates, and they persecuted the Slavic gymnastic societies in the areas under their control. After World War II, the new Communist leaders of the region attempted to harness the gymnastic idea to their own political programs, disbanding non-Communist clubs or merging them into government-run associations. These artificial constructs collapsed after 1989, paving the way for a new type of nonpolitical gymnastics in the post-Communist era.

Claire E. Nolte

G

Further reading

Blecking, Diethelm, ed. *Die slawische Sokolbewegung: Beiträge zur Geschichte von Sport und Nationalismus in Osteuropa.* Dortmund, 1991.

See also Konrad Henlein; Sokol

Győr

Hungarian city. Győr (population 129,338 in 1990) is an industrial city located on the *Kis Alföld* (Little Plain) at the confluence of the Danube and Rába Rivers in northwestern Hungary. The site has been settled by Celts, Romans (who called it Arrabona), Avars, and Magyars, who arrived in the early tenth century. A bishopric was established by King Stephen (975–1038) in the early eleventh century, a cathedral was constructed in the twelfth century, and the city was given a royal charter in the thirteenth century. After the Mongol invasion of the mid-1200s, the Hungarian king settled foreign "guests," mainly Germans, in Győr as well as several other castle towns.

The city gained fame as an outpost against the advancing Ottomans. Because of its location on water and its high protective walls, the castle at Győr held out against the Turks until 1594, sixty-eight years after the defeat of the Hungarians at Mohács. However, the castle was retaken only four years later.

The city preserves many elements of its history. At the river, the old walls still protect the Bishop's Castle and cathedral. The lanes in the old city are little changed from the seventeenth and eighteenth centuries, though farther south are realist-style buildings typical of socialist architecture. Finally, south of the rail tracks, lie the vast complexes typical of Hungarian industrial towns.

Darrick Danta

Further reading

Fügedi, Erik. *Castle and Society in Medieval Hungary (1000–1437).* Budapest, 1986.

Gutkind, E.A. *International History of City Development, vol. 7, Urban Development in East-Central Europe: Poland, Czechoslovakia, and Hungary.* New York, 1972.

Hanák, Péter, ed. *One Thousand Years: A Concise History of Hungary.* Budapest, 1988.

Webster's New Geographical Dictionary. Springfield, Massachusetts, 1984.

Gypsies

Gypsies, or Roma, have their roots in the mixed Rajput population of northeast India. They began their westward movement nearly one thousand years ago through Persia, Armenia, and the Asian provinces of the Eastern Roman, or Byzantine, Empire, reaching Europe in the thirteenth century. While continuous assimilation of changing neighbors along their migration routes produced both physical and linguistic differences in the Romani groups, the Roma to this day remain a genetically related people preserving some basic cultural beliefs and ritual practices that effectively separate "them" from "us," sharply dividing the world around them into *gadže* (non-Gypsies) and Roma. A common sense of "apartness" may be demonstrated in the foods that are eaten or avoided, in rules of behavior in the family and among other Roma, in personal hygiene, and in the identification and treatment of various illnesses. This apartness to some extent is a product of the hostility of non-Gypsy populations through which the Roma passed or were allowed to settle and to survive, and remains a factor contributing to the negative stereotypes that followed them into the heart of Europe.

Gypsy migration across Europe may be tracked north and west from Byzantium by the appearance of local laws directed against the dark-skinned "heathens," or "Saracens," or "Egyptians," whose arrival barely preceded that of Turkish invasions threatening first Eastern and then Western Christendom. By 1400, those allowed to settle in exposed Romanian borderlands because of their trade skills were treated as estate property and eventually enslaved, to be emancipated only in the 1860s (as were Russia's serfs and America's slaves). Caught up in the spirit of the national movements of the nineteenth century, particularly Zionism, Europe's Roma, whose only homeland was their shared feeling of "Gypsiness," in spite of some attempts to organize politically, tragically became in the 1930s the first "worthless" ethnic group in Germany to be targeted for extermination. Europe's Gypsies became the group that lost the highest percentage of its population in the 1940s in the *Porajmos,* or Romani Holocaust during World War II, when the Germans sent the Gypsies in enormous numbers to concentration and extermination camps. Since World War II, renewed efforts to reestablish regional, national, and international Romani organizations have been successful, despite continuing anti-Gypsy prejudices, social and legal pressures, and even acts of violence.

At the present time, Gypsy organizations in twenty-eight countries, including the German Sinti League, are represented in the International Romani Union (Romano Internacionalno Jekhethanibe) and have sponsored four world Romani congresses. Commissions have been appointed at these congresses to collect, record, and document the linguistic, historical, and cultural legacy of the world's Romani population, to seek justice for victims of the *Porajmos* and its aftermath, and to assure the preservation of Romani identity in a still hostile, non-Gypsy world in which policies of assimilation, not integration of the Roma into the society of host nations, are still in effect. It remains to be seen whether or not a standardized Romani language or common, transnational political goals will be realized at future world congresses.

John Kolsti

Further reading

Crowe, David. *The History of the Gypsies of Eastern Europe and Russia.* New York, 1994.
Crowe, David and John Kolsti, eds. *The Gypsies of Eastern Europe.* New York, 1991.
Fraser, Angus. *The Gypsies.* Oxford, 1992.
Hancock, Ian. *The Pariah Syndrome: An Account of Gypsy Slavery and Persecution,* 2d ed. Ann Arbor, Michigan, 1988.
Kendrick, Donald and Gratton Puxton. *The Destiny of Europe's Gypsies.* New York, 1972.

See also Holocaust

Gyurgevo Committee

Bulgarian planning committee for the April Uprising of 1876 against Ottoman rule. In November 1875 leading figures in the Bulgarian revolutionary movement met in the Romanian town of Giurgiu (Bulgarian, Gyurgevo), located across the Danube River from Ruse. They sought to continue the work of the Bulgarian Revolutionary Central Committee, which had originally formed in Bucharest in 1870 to plan revolutionary activity to liberate Bulgaria from the Ottoman Empire. The failure of an uprising earlier in 1875 had motivated nationalist-minded Bulgarians to renew their efforts to end Ottoman rule and establish an independent Bulgarian state. In attendance in Gyurgevo was the new head of the committee, Stefan Stambolov (1854–95), as well as Nikola Obretenov (1848–1939), Georgi Obretenov (c. 1849–76), Georgi Benkovski (1841/44–76), Stoyan Zaimov (1853–1932), Panaiot Volov (c. 1850–76), Ilarion Dragostinov (1850/52–76), Khristo Karaminkov (1825/32–88), Georgi Ikonomov (1846–76), Georgi Izmirliev (1851–76), and two others. The committee decided to organize another uprising to coincide with the anticipated fighting in Bosnia and Serbia the next spring. They concentrated their revolutionary activities on the Turnovo, Sliven, Vratsa, and Plovdiv regions of Bulgaria, choosing these particular areas because they were mountainous and did not have large Turkish populations. The committee hoped that the rest of the country would join in the uprising once it began. The meetings in Gyurgevo lasted until December 25, whereupon committee members dispersed into the four regions to carry out their preparations to collect funds and incite support for the new uprising. The Gyurgevo Committee was instrumental in the planning and organization of the April Uprising of 1876, an important step toward the eventual liberation of Bulgaria two years later.

Richard C. Hall

Further reading

Macdermott, Mercia. *A History of Bulgaria 1393–1885.* London, 1962.
Mitev, Iono. *Istoriya na Aprilskoto vŭstanie 1876,* vol. 1, *Predpostovki i podgotovka.* Sofia, 1986.
Perry, Duncan. *Stefan Stambolov and the Emergence of Modern Bulgaria 1870–1895.* Durham, North Carolina, 1993.

See also April Uprising; Georgi Obretenov; Nikola Obretenov; Stefan Stambolov; Panaiot Volov

H

Habsburg Empire

Also known as the Austrian Empire from 1804 to 1867 and thereafter as the Dual Monarchy, or Austria-Hungary, the Habsburg Empire refers to the sprawling multinational realm in Central and East Central Europe ruled by the Habsburg dynasty from the Middle Ages to its dissolution in 1918. Along with the multinational Russian and Ottoman Empires, the Habsburg Empire constituted the territorial and political framework from which much of independent Eastern Europe emerged.

By the end of the Napoleonic Wars in 1815, the frontiers of the Habsburg Empire extended from northern Italy and alpine Austria in the west to the borders of the Russian and Ottoman Empires to the east. By the early twentieth century, the Habsburg realm counted over fifty-one million inhabitants divided, according to language, into eleven principal national groups. The breakdown in approximate percentages was Germans 23.9, Magyars 20.2, Czechs 12.6, Poles 10.0, Ruthenians 7.9, Romanians 6.4, Croats 5.3, Slovaks 3.8, Serbs 3.8, Slovenes 2.6, and Italians 2.0. Jews, who made up an estimated 3.9 percent of the empire's population, were often counted as members of the other national groups, since Yiddish was not designated a national language. As a multinational, dynastic state in an age of nationalism, the Habsburg Empire experienced in the last century of its existence an increasingly debilitating series of national, centrifugal tensions as each constituent ethnic group evolved toward some form of national self-assertion. Consequently, the dynasty and its government expended much energy in the search for administrative and con-

stitutional solutions aimed at reconciling—or suppressing—the various and varying demands of the empire's constituent nationalities.

During the first half of the nineteenth century, the Habsburg monarchs ruled primarily in reaction to the French Revolution, staunchly preserving the absolutist institutions of the eighteenth century, while at the same time adhering to a strict conservatism and stifling all manifestations of political nationalism and liberalism. The national and liberal revolutions of 1848–49, although ultimately suppressed, clearly indicated a new approach to governing was necessary. After a brief flirtation with a genuine federal structure along national and liberal lines (the stillborn Kremsier constitution of 1849), the dynasty, now led by Franz Joseph (1830–1916), attempted once again to rule the empire as a centralized, albeit now economically progressive, absolutist regime during the 1850s. Military defeat in Italy in 1859, as well as continued Magyar resistance to Habsburg centralization, compelled Franz Joseph to abandon this neoabsolutist experiment. After further experimentation with various constitutional forms during the early 1860s, and in the wake of yet another lost war (against Prussia) in 1866, the crown finally produced what came to be known as the *Ausgleich* (Compromise) of 1867.

This controversial agreement, which endured until the empire's demise, divided the realm into two internally autonomous states: the Kingdom of Hungary, or "Transleithania," which was dominated by the Magyars and governed from Budapest, and Austria, or "Cisleithania," which was dominated (at least initially) by the Germans and governed from Vienna. Each state possessed its

H own constitution and parliament, and both were linked economically, with common commercial and tariff policies being negotiated between Budapest and Vienna every ten years. Overarching this dualistic structure was an imperial government that controlled defense, foreign policy, and imperial finances. The Habsburg monarch was simultaneously emperor in Austria and king in Hungary. The *Ausgleich* offered short-term stability to the empire by clarifying the crown's prerogatives in foreign and domestic affairs and by placing considerable power into the hands of the empire's two dominant ethnic groups, the Germans and the Magyars. Yet it failed to offer a long-term solution to the empire's growing ethnic difficulties, since other nationalities in both the Hungarian and the Austrian halves of the empire perceived the *Ausgleich* as inimical to their aspirations. This shortcoming, made worse by the crown's refusal to modify the arrangement to accommodate other national groups, had deepening consequences in the later decades of the nineteenth century as resentment against both Magyar and German domination and the tenor of ethnic politics became progressively acrimonious.

The problems arising out of the *Ausgleich* stand in contrast to the empire's impressive achievements in other areas at this time, such as constitutional protection of individual liberties, progressive social and political legislation, and a flourishing cultural and intellectual atmosphere. The empire as a whole also experienced steady economic growth in the decades following the 1870s. Impressive as these achievements were, they nevertheless did little to alleviate the centrifugal pull of national politics.

National tensions also unfolded at a time of slow but steady decline in the empire's international standing. Indeed, the two were often linked. Although the empire had emerged from the Congress of Vienna in 1815 as a leading great power, its heterogeneous makeup, limited resources, and unsteady finances soon caused it to fall behind the other great powers. As a result of two disastrous wars, against France and Sardinia-Piedmont in 1859 and against Prussia in 1866, the empire forfeited its traditional influence in northern Italy and Germany. These losses prompted Habsburg foreign policymakers to focus increasingly on the Balkans, which set the empire on a collision course with Russian ambitions in this region as well

as with the ambitions of the emergent Balkan national states, a number of which harbored irredentist claims against the southeastern territories of the empire. The Habsburg decision to launch a punitive war against Serbia in 1914 (for its alleged complicity in the assassination of Archduke Franz Ferdinand [1863–1914] in Sarajevo and as a desperate attempt to stem Serbian expansionism) plunged this area into a crisis that quickly escalated into World War I. During that war, the empire fought as a member of the Central Powers coalition and as Germany's principal ally.

The strains of four years of relentless warfare, Wilsonian appeals for the self-determination of peoples, and the empire's unequivocal defeat in late 1918 converged to escalate national programs for reform within the empire into demands for complete independence. During October and November, Habsburg authority dissolved as the empire broke into its national components. On November 11, 1918, the Habsburg monarch, Charles I (1887–1922), officially renounced participation in affairs of state. Out of the empire's wreckage emerged the successor states of Austria, Hungary, Czechoslovakia, Poland, and Yugoslavia. Italy and Romania also received areas belonging to the defunct empire.

The Habsburg Empire was little mourned at the time of its passing, being seen by many as an anachronism unsuitable to the postwar age of liberal democracy and national self-determination. With time, however, the empire's historical image improved, somewhat by default, as the newly independent states of East Central Europe left many political and economic expectations unfulfilled and as the entire region went on to endure the violent upheavals and repression of the Nazi and Soviet eras.

Lawrence J. Flockerzie

Further reading

Bridge, F.A. *The Habsburg Monarchy among the Great Powers, 1815–1918.* New York, 1990.

Good, David F. *The Economic Rise of the Habsburg Empire, 1750–1914.* Berkeley, California, 1983.

Kann, Robert A. *A History of the Habsburg Empire, 1526–1918.* Berkeley, California, 1974.

Österreichische Akademie der Wissenschaften. Kommission für die Geschichte der Österreichisch-Ungarischen Monarchie (1848–1918).

Die Habsburgermonarchie, 1848–1918, Adam Wandruszka and Peter Urbanitsch, eds., vols. 1–4. Vienna, 1973–93.

Sked, Alan. *The Decline and Fall of the Habsburg Empire.* London, 1989.

See also *Ausgleich;* Charles I; Cisleithania/Translerthania; Congress of Vienna; Dualism; Dual Monarchy; Eastern Question; Emigration; Ethnic Minorities; Fourteen Points; Franz Ferdinand; Franz Joseph; Great Powers; Hungarian War for Independence; Irredentism; Kremsier/Kroměříž Parliament; Magyarization; Nationalism; Neoabsolutism; Revolutions of 1848; St. Germain, Treaty of; Trianon, Treaty of; World War I

Hácha, Emil (1872–1945)

Prominent jurist and later president of the Second Czecho-Slovak Republic (1938–39) and Nazi-occupied Protectorate of Bohemia and Moravia (1939–45). Born in 1872 near České Budějovice (German, Budweis), Hácha served under the Austrian Empire as an official of the Bohemian Provincial Committee and later on the Supreme Administrative Court in Vienna. He continued to distinguish himself in jurisprudence in the Czechoslovak republic, both as a teacher and scholar and as president of the Supreme Administrative Court (1926–38). Though ailing, aging, and without political experience or affiliation, Hácha succeeded Czechoslovakia's president, Edvard Beneš (1884–1948), in November 1938. When Nazi Germany destroyed the republic in March 1939, Hácha signed a declaration placing Bohemia and Moravia in Hitler's hands. He remained on as president of the protectorate, a position he held until his arrest in May 1945. As president, Hácha first tried to maintain contacts with Beneš's Czechoslovak government-in-exile, providing intelligence and offers of clandestine cooperation. However, Nazi pressure drove him to abandon such efforts and resign himself to implementing Germany's will. In 1945 he was arrested and died in the hospital at Pankrác prison in Prague. To some, Hácha was a traitor to his nation and an obsequious servant to Hitler (1889–1945); to others, he was a Czech patriot who tried to spare his nation from destruction through accommodation with the Nazis.

James Felak

Further reading

Československý bibliografický slovník. Prague, 1992.

Kennan, George. *From Prague after Munich: Diplomatic Papers 1938–1940.* Princeton, New Jersey, 1968.

Mamatey, Victor S. and Radomír Luža, eds. *A History of the Czechoslovak Republic, 1918–1948.* Princeton, New Jersey, 1973.

See also Edvard Beneš; Adolf Hitler; Protectorate of Bohemia and Moravia

Haiduks

Slavic Christian bandits in Ottoman-ruled Serbia who fought Ottoman officials, symbolized resistance to oppression, inspired struggles for national freedom, and were revered as Robin Hood–style figures in epic poems and folk songs.

Brigands in the Ottoman-controlled Balkan Peninsula, known as *haiduks* (Serbs), *klephts* (Greeks), and *kirdjalis* (Bulgarians), engaged in guerrilla warfare against Ottoman administrative officials, military officers, tax collectors, landowners, and merchants. From safe havens in forests, hills, and mountains, bandits operated in bands of fifty to one hundred and often had the support of local Christians. With the collapse of Ottoman ruling institutions, attacks by *haiduks* escalated and contributed to the state of unrest that led to the 1804 Serb revolt.

Haiduks had a narrowly defined and locally rooted sense of patriotism, focusing primarily on their birthplaces and kinship groups rather than on broader concepts of nation-state and ethnicity. Yet the tradition of armed resistance to Ottoman oppression transformed the *haiduks* into symbols of freedom, champions of the oppressed, and icons of courage and bravery. *Haiduks* thus inspired and participated in Serb independence movements.

Serb epic poetry and folk song extolled the deeds of the *haiduks* by describing specific episodes of battle, death, and valor and by celebrating the *haiduk* code of honor and liberty. As chronicles of Balkan society, these epics and ballads constitute a rich source of historical, cultural, and ethnographic information. While sometimes marked by exaggeration and flight of imagination, these literary works illuminate daily life, custom, and tradition. *Haiduk* epics and ballads helped

Slavic Christians preserve their religious and cultural identity, in addition to echoing their hope of liberation, and became a vital source for Serb poetry and prose in the twentieth century.

Theophilus C. Prousis

Further reading

Barac, Antun. *A History of Yugoslav Literature.* Ann Arbor, Michigan, 1973.

Ibrovac, Miodrag. *Claude Fauriel et la fortune européenne des poésies populaires grecque et serbe.* Paris, 1966.

Jelavich, Barbara. *History of the Balkans: Eighteenth and Nineteenth Centuries.* New York, 1983.

Petrovich, Michael. *A History of Modern Serbia, 1804–1918,* 2 vols. New York, 1976.

Sugar, Peter. *Southeastern Europe under Ottoman Rule, 1354–1804* Seattle, Washington, 1977.

Vucinich, Wayne. *The Ottoman Empire: Its Record and Legacy.* Princeton, New Jersey, 1965.

See also Folklore; Serbian Literature to 1918

Hakata

German society to promote a policy of Germanization in Poland. In 1894 in Prussian Poland, three wealthy German landowners—Ferdinand von Hansemann (1861–1900), Hermann Kennemann (1815–1910), and Heinrich von Tiedemann (1843–1922)—organized what was officially known as the Deutscher Ostmarkverein (German East Mark Society). More popularly it was known as Hakata from the initials of its founders. Its chief purpose was the promotion of German colonization and a program of Germanization against the Poles in the east. Effectively an extension of the earlier Bismarckian Kulturkampf (struggle for culture), which attacked the Catholic Church, it had a more nationalistic twist: the Hakata had Bismarck's (1815–1898) blessing.

From the outset, Hakata strongly influenced German governmental policies in the east. It organized a land bank to subsidize German settlement and led the government to invest heavily in social and cultural institutions to promote German culture. Names of towns and villages were germanized, the use of Polish was proscribed, while the government encouraged officials to engage in nationalistic German activities by paying them bonuses for such acts. The society grew rapidly, reaching a membership of 21,500 in 1901 and by 1913, 54,000. Most of its members were middle class: government officials, teachers, army officers, new settlers, and Protestant ministers, that is, those who had a stake in promoting Germanization in the east.

Anti-Polish measures intensified, including the banning of Polish in religious instruction, restrictions on Poles' abilities to build permanent dwellings on land purchased from Germans, as well as attempts to limit the enrollment of Polish students beyond primary school and to restrict the circulation of the Polish press. After 1907, a new wave of discriminatory legislation, including laws permitting the confiscation of Polish-owned land and prohibiting the use of Polish for public purposes in communities where Poles constituted less than 60 percent of the inhabitants, affected the area.

These measures inflamed Polish nationalism. The response included school strikes and the boycotting of German shops and German culture. Poles established their own financial institutions and purchased land. Improvements in the banking system and the creation of peasant cooperatives resulted in significant economic progress among Poles, both in agriculture and in manufacturing. Hakata, in the prewar era, had succeeded in stimulating Polish consciousness, political activity, and social and economic development and had, in effect, failed in its aims.

Robert A. Berry

Further reading

Wandycz, Piotr. *The Lands of Partitioned Poland, 1795–1918.* Seattle, Washington, 1974.

See also Otto von Bismarck; Germanization; Kulturkampf; Nationalism

Haller, Józef (1873–1960)

Polish general. Born August 13, 1873, in Jurzyce, Haller served as an artillery captain in the Austrian army. With the inception of World War I, Haller was given command of the Second Polish Brigade, fighting under the auspices of the Austrian government. After losing faith in the Central Powers' assurances for Polish sovereignty, on February 15, 1918, Haller led his forces across the eastern front to Russia, where they were transported to serve with the Western Allies in France.

Once in Paris, Haller was responsible for organizing the "Blue Army." Named for their horizon-blue uniforms, this military force of fifty thousand Polish volunteers was repatriated to an independent Poland in the spring of 1919, where it reinforced the Galician front in the war against Russia. In the autumn of 1920 Haller commanded the northern front in the Battle of Warsaw during the Polish-Soviet War (1919–21). From 1920 to 1926, he held the position of inspector general of artillery and served as a member of the Polish War Council. In July 1926 Marshall Józef Piłsudski (1867–1935), following his takeover of the Polish government, forced Haller into retirement. Having long-standing political and religious differences with Piłsudski, Haller actively conspired with partisan organizations, and in February 1936 contributed to the Front Morges, a consolidated opposition to the Polish government. After Germany's attack of Poland in 1939, Haller made his way to France, where he mobilized Polish forces for the government-in-exile. Haller resided in London until his death on June 4, 1960.

Conrad Jarzebowski

Further reading

Aksamitek, Stefan. *General Jozef Haller: Zarys Biografii Politycznej.* Katowice, Poland, 1989.

Cienciala, Anna M. and Titus Komarnicki. *From Versailles to Locarno: Keys to Political Foreign Policy 1919–1925.* Lawrence, Kansas, 1984.

Komarnicki, Titus. *Rebirth of the Polish Republic: A Study in the Diplomatic History of Europe 1914–1920.* London, 1957.

Trawinski, Witold. *Odyseja Polskiej Armii Blekitnej.* Wrocław, Poland, 1989.

See also Nazi–Polish War; Józef Piłsudski; Polish-Soviet War; Warsaw, Battle of

Haraszti, Miklós (1945–)

Hungarian dissident writer. Born in Jerusalem, Haraszti studied philosophy and literature at the Eötvös Lóránd University in Budapest. As early as 1963, he published poems and articles in the literary press. Following his experiences as a youth counselor in the countryside from 1963 to 1964, he became one of the organizers of a democratic dissident movement among university students in Budapest and was placed under police surveillance.

After his expulsion from the university in 1970 for political activities, Haraszti became a fac-tory worker. In 1973 the authorities confiscated a manuscript of his describing workers' lives. During his detention, he initiated a hunger strike, and the resulting international attention may have led to the mild sentence he received. The manuscript was subsequently smuggled abroad and published in the West as *A Worker in the Workers' State,* repudiating the notion of socialism being built by and for the working class.

As restrictions on freedom of association eased, in 1988 Haraszti was instrumental in establishing the Alliance of Free Democrats, which became one of the major liberal parties after Hungary's return to parliamentary democracy in 1989. His vocal advocacy of liberal policies made him a target of Hungary's newly active nationalists.

András Boros-Kazai

Further reading

Haraszti, Miklós. *Darabbér.* Paris, 1980

———. *The Velvet Prison: Artists under State Socialism.* New York, 1987.

Hašek, Jaroslav (1883–1923)

Czech writer. Hašek, an eccentric nihilist, anarchist, and carouser, surrounded by thieves, pimps, prostitutes, and drunkards (sources for his fiction), was known for his cruelty, recklessness, irresponsibility, lies, and hoaxes. Before World War I, he wrote verse, folk anecdotes, burlesque humor, comic sketches, and caricatures of the lower working and middle classes. During this period, he became editor of the family journal *Animal World.* In 1915 he was drafted into the Habsburg army but was soon captured by the Russians and spent the war years writing for them and recruiting prisoners of war into the Družina (Czechoslovak Legion), an Allied force during World War I. After deserting from the Czechoslovak Legion in 1918, Hašek served as a Bolshevik commissar during the Civil War in Russia, returning to Prague in 1920.

His fame was established only after World War I with the 1920–23 serialization of his satiric masterpiece, *Osudy dobrého vojaka Švejka za světové války* (*The Adventures of the Good Soldier Švejk during the World War*), which has been translated into many languages and studied critically by scholars the world over. Švejk's adventures revolve around his doing whatever was necessary to avoid going to the front and to stay alive. He accomplishes his goal through ostensible stupidity,

H claiming he is an idiot, and at the same time appearing to try to please everyone. Yet behind this stupidity and obsequiousness possibly exists a clever rogue who simply does what he does to attain his goal (to stay alive). Critics have interpreted Švejk in many ways, viewing him as idiot or rogue, as cowardly buffoon or heroic anti-imperialist soldier, as fighter for a future Communist paradise or as pacifist, as life-loving, or as misanthropic. This monumental work remained unfinished because of Hašek's untimely death at the age of forty from pneumonia and heart failure, likely hastened by alcoholism.

Ann Marie Basom

Further reading

Ančík, Zdena. *O životě Jaroslava Haška.* Prague, 1953.

Hašek, Jaroslav. *The Good Soldier Švejk and His Fortunes in the World War,* trans. by Cecil Parrott. New York, 1973.

Parrott, Cecil. *The Bad Bohemian: A Life of Jaroslav Hašek, Creator of the Good Soldier Švejk.* London, 1978.

———. *Jaroslav Hašek: A Study of Švejk and the Short Stories.* New York, 1982.

Pytlík, Radko. *Zpráva o Jaroslavu Haškovi,* 2d ed. Prague, 1982.

See also Czech Literature; Czechoslovak Legion

Havel, Václav (1936–)

Czech playwright, dissident, political prisoner, and president of Czechoslovakia and the Czech Republic. Born into a rich family in Prague and guided by the humanistic ideals of President Tomáš Masaryk's (1850–1937) interwar Czechoslovakia, Havel experienced many hardships under the Communists. He was forced to work in a chemical laboratory cleaning test tubes, and he attended night high school classes with his fellow workers. This enabled him to see the world "from below," as he later commented. When he was finally admitted to the Academy of Dramatic Artists in Prague, he was already a known playwright.

He began as a stagehand in a small experimental theater in Prague. His successful plays, *The Garden Party* (1963), *The Memorandum* (1965), and *The Increased Difficulty of Concentration* (1968), ridiculed mechanized official language. The plays reflected the absurdity of the Czechoslo-vak version of Soviet communism in a growing impasse, and they became popular abroad.

At the Congress of Czechoslovak Writers in 1967, Havel attacked the bureaucratic system of the writers' union. Two one-act plays from 1975, *The Audience* (based on his experience as a worker in a brewery) and *Private View,* are dramatic studies of sections of Czech society as they attempted to deal with the demoralizing influence of post-Soviet invasion politics (after Prague Spring, the short-lived period of reform in 1968). The publication of his powerful indictment of life under the Communist regime, *Power and the Powerless* (1978), his essays devoted to the malaise (such as his lengthy "Letter to President Husák," 1975), and initiatives such as Charter 77 and the typewritten publication of forbidden books, brought the wrath of the police state upon him. He was tried four times and spent five years in prison. His prison epistles to his wife were published under the title *Letters to Olga* in 1985. In these and other essays he explored the modern crisis of human identity. Meanwhile, his new plays, such as *The Mountain Resort* (1976) and *Largo Desolato* (1984), could play only outside of Czechoslovakia.

In 1989 Havel managed to lead a successful people's movement from the Magic Lantern theater and, without any bloodshed, helped to oust the Communists from power in the so-called Velvet Revolution. In the ensuing elections, he was voted president of the republic.

Peter Hruby

Further reading

Goetz-Stankiewicz, M. *The Silenced Theatre.* Toronto, 1979.

Kriseová, Eda. *Václav Havel: The Authorized Biography.* New York, 1993.

Skilling, H. Gordon. *Charter 77 and Human Rights in Czechoslovakia.* Boston, 1981.

See also Charter 77; Czech Literature; Czech Republic, Birth of; Tomáš Masaryk; Prague Spring; Revolutions of 1989; Theater; Velvet Revolution

Havlíček, Karel (1821–56)

Prominent Czech national leader. A liberal editor of three journals—*Pražské noviny* (*Prague News*), with its literary supplement *Česká včela* (*Czech Bee,* 1846–48); *Národní noviny* (*National News*), with its satirical supplement *Šotek* (*The Wag,*

1848–49); and *Slovan* (*Slav,* 1850–51)—was a leading figure in the nineteenth-century Czech national renascence as it changed from a primarily cultural movement into a political one. Havlíček aimed to tie Czech nationalism to Western liberalism; he rejected forms of political romanticism, such as Pan-Slavism, a movement that emphasized cultural unity among the Slavic peoples, as well as any abstract patriotism in favor of a realistic assessment of issues facing the Czech people. During 1848, Havlíček advocated Austroslavism, a federal restructuring of the Habsburg Empire on the basis of national equality. In his editorials, he pressed for civil liberties, universal manhood suffrage, separation of church and state, and language rights for the Czechs. Havlíček was a master of Czech prose and poetry, and effectively using wit and satire to make his point. He was most interested in persuading the Czech people to work for the nation by using self-reliance to develop a communal spirit that would enable them to organize politically from the ground up.

Havlíček was a courageous editor who tested the limits of censorship until forced into exile in 1851. His death from tuberculosis shortly after his release turned him into a martyr in the eyes of many Czech patriots. Leaders of all political persuasions, but especially Tomáš G. Masaryk (1850–1937), the future president of Czechoslovakia, expressed their indebtedness to him.

Barbara K. Reinfeld

Further reading

Chalupný, Emil. *Havlíček: Prostředí, osobnost a dílo.* Prague, 1929.

Masaryk, Thomas G. *Karel Havlíček.* Prague, 1920.

Morava, Jiří. *C.k. disident Karel Havlíček.* Prague, 1991.

Reinfeld, Barbara K. *Karel Havlíček (1821–1856).* Boulder, Colorado, 1982.

———. "Masaryk and Havlíček." *East European Quarterly* vol. 25, no. 3 (September 1991): 307–24.

See also Austroslavism; Tomáš G. Masaryk; Pan-Slavism; Press; Revolutions of 1848

Health

The health status of a population is a key indicator of its social welfare. In contrast to the situation in northwestern Europe, however, little is known about the health of nineteenth-century populations in East Central Europe, then still mostly preindustrial. Endemic diseases such as typhus, smallpox, and syphilis killed and disabled many. In the early 1830s and again in the late 1840s and early 1850s, major cholera epidemics swept across Europe by way of Russia. The second pandemic turned out to be more virulent in the East, and cholera kept reasserting itself epidemically in parts of Poland and Russia during the second half of the nineteenth century. Death rates were particularly high among undernourished rural peasants, who also succumbed in large numbers to tuberculosis. The pace of industrialization and population growth quickened at the turn of the century, though, as elsewhere on the Continent, urbanization and exploitation of the laboring poor often brought on dismal living and working conditions. This situation changed only as public health reforms took root and housing and nutrition improved.

The destruction of World War I was followed by the deadly 1918–19 influenza pandemic and a severe famine. The rest of the interwar period was marked by uneven progress and, in the absence of a more egalitarian order, continued suffering among vulnerable groups, particularly as a result of the economic effects of the Great Depression. World War II produced enormous loss of life, especially among civilians of Eastern Europe. In Poland alone, one-sixth of the prewar population perished, amounting to six million Poles, half of whom were Polish Jews.

The health record since World War II can be divided into two periods. The first, connected to postwar reconstruction, lasted until the mid-1960s. This period saw sustained gains in health status, despite the political persecution and relatively low per capita income levels. The socialist economies offered free, universal access to health care and were well endowed with trained medical personnel. Life-expectancy levels rose throughout the region, attaining levels only several years behind those in Western Europe. During the 1950s, life expectancy at birth stood higher in Czechoslovakia than in Austria. Infant mortality rates declined sharply, converging rapidly in several countries (Poland, Hungary, Czechoslovakia) to Western levels until the mid-1970s.

By then, however, the overall health situation had begun to deteriorate, along with the economic outlook. During this second phase, which has lasted from the mid-1960s to the present, East-West

H differentials in survival widened owing to steady progress in the West and stagnant, or even declining, life expectancies in the East. Life expectancy at age one actually fell for males throughout Eastern Europe up to 1989, and rose by less than 1½ years for females. In Poland, Bulgaria, and especially Hungary, adult age-specific death rates rose, particularly for men of working age. The health records for the former Czechoslovak republics are slightly better. In more isolated and economically backward Romania, the regime of Nicolae Ceauşescu (1918–89) stopped training nurses and specialists in the 1980s, having earlier outlawed modern contraceptives. Most women resorted to clandestine abortions, leading to very high maternal mortality rates. Standards of maternal and child health care improved slowly after the regime changes of 1989–91 but inevitably deteriorated in the war-ridden countries of former Yugoslavia.

Some of the reasons for the poorer health in the region include harmful lifestyle practices such as heavy smoking and alcohol consumption, high dietary fat intakes, as well as a high number of industrial accidents. Levels of environmental pollution are generally higher than in the West, sociopolitical conditions have been more difficult, and the underfinanced health services have become dilapidated. The long-term health reversals represent a significant loss of human capital, making it more difficult to catch up with the countries of the European Union.

Andrzej Kulczycki

Further reading
Eberstadt, Nicholas. "Health and Mortality in Central and Eastern Europe: Retrospect and Prospect," in James R. Millar and Sharon L. Wolchik, eds., *The Social Legacy of Communism.* New York, 1994, 196–225.

Hertzman, Clyde. *Environment and Health in Central and Eastern Europe: A Report for the Environmental Action Programme for Central and Eastern Europe.* Washington, D.C., 1995.

See also Nicolae Ceauşescu; Environment; Family; Great Depression; Industrialization; Peasants; World War I; World War II

Hebrang, Andrija (1899–1949?)
Prominent Croat Communist who was purged from the Yugoslav Communist Party (League of Communists) after World War II. Hebrang joined the Communists in 1919 and acted as secretary of the Croat party from 1942 to 1944. He was made a member of the Politburo in 1944. In April 1946 he was dismissed from his position on the Politburo and in 1947 lost his posts as minister of industry and president of the economic council. He was imprisoned in early May 1948, on the eve of the formal Yugoslav-Soviet split in June. Hebrang was accused by the Yugoslav central party leadership of misinforming the Soviets about the party and of collaborating with the wartime German-sponsored Croat fascist regime. This latter charge was essentially groundless. The real bone of contention between Hebrang and the central leadership, headed by Tito (1892–1980), was the former's willingness to act independently of central directives during the war and his ability to build a firm regional power base in his native Croatia. Thus, the issue was Hebrang's "nationalist deviation" and his willingness to defend Croatian interests in the new Yugoslav Communist state. He died in prison under dubious circumstances, probably in early 1949. The official version of his death was that he committed suicide.

Mark Biondich

Further reading
Banac, Ivo. *With Stalin against Tito: Cominformist Splits in Yugoslav Communism.* Ithaca, New York, 1988.

Irvine, Jill A. *The Croat Question: Partisan Politics in the Formation of the Yugoslav Socialist State.* Boulder, Colorado, 1993.

———. "Tito, Hebrang, and the Croat Question, 1943–1944." *East European Politics and Societies* 5, no. 2 (1991): 306–40.

Supek, Ivan. *Krunski svjedok protiv Hebranga.* Chicago, 1983.

See also Communist Party of Yugoslavia; Tito–Stalin Split; Ustaša

Heliade Rădulescu, Ion (1802–72)
Romanian romantic poet, writer, and journalist. Heliade Rădulescu came to embody the spirit of change in the Danubian Principalities in the first half of the nineteenth century. A productive poet and author, and a man of unbounded energy, Heliade Rădulescu was involved in numerous cultural endeavors in the decades prior to the revolution of

1848 in Wallachia. Notable among these were the founding of a philharmonic society to promote theater and music and the promotion of the Romanian language. A romantic visionary, he was partly motivated by a desire to "modernize" Romanian culture, to bring his "nation" into the mainstream of European developments. As publisher of *Curierul Românesc* (*Romanian Courier*), he looked to the education of the people. In many ways, Heliade Rădulescu is correctly perceived as the father of modern Romanian literature, even though his attempts to elevate the intellectual life of the people (partially through the translation of great works of European literature into Romanian) for the most part failed.

In June 1848 Heliade Rădulescu read the Islaz Proclamation, which called for reforms in Wallachia. Its emphasis on the "nation" reflected Heliade Rădulescu's romantic yearnings. He became a member of the provisional government (as head of religious affairs) that superseded Prince Gheorghe Bibescu (1804–73), who had fled to Vienna. Like others within the revolutionary circles, Heliade Rădulescu was forced to confront the thorny matter of peasant emancipation. He opposed immediate action in the belief that it would produce a shock to the entire economy and lead to foreign intervention. After Russian and Ottoman forces entered the principalities in September 1848, Heliade Rădulescu went into exile in Paris alongside many of his compatriots. With the outbreak of the Crimean War (1853–56), he returned to Bucharest to the accolades of the young.

Richard Frucht

Further reading

Anghelescu, Mircea. *Ion Heliade Rădulescu.* Bucharest, 1986.
Hitchins, Keith. *The Romanians 1774–1866.* Oxford, 1996.
Jelavich, Barbara. *History of the Balkans,* vol. 1, *The Eighteenth and Nineteenth Centuries.* Cambridge, 1983.

See also Crimean War; Danubian Principalities; Islaz Proclamation; Revolutions of 1848; Romanian Literature; Romanticism

Henlein, Konrad (1898–1945)

Sudeten German politician and Gauleiter (district leader) in the Sudetenland. Born of mixed German extraction in Maffersdorf bei Reichenau (Czech,

Vratislavice nad Nisou) in Bohemia, Henlein served in the Austro-Hungarian army during World War I and after the war earned his living for a time as a bank clerk. After 1925, he devoted his time more and more to the Sudeten German gymnastics (Turner) movement, a nationalistic sport organization designed to preserve a collective German identity in the face of what was regarded as Czech onslaughts after 1918.

In the wake of Hitler's rise in Germany and the dissolution of the Bohemian-German National Socialist Party in October 1933, Henlein found himself propelled into the national spotlight when he took the leadership of a newly created Sudeten German Heimatfront (after 1935, the Sudeten German Party). It was a party in which traditional autonomist and more recent Nazi strains came together in uneasy coexistence. Henlein himself, an unassuming man of scant charisma, was over his head from the outset, although in the provincial, petit bourgeois milieu of the Sudetenland he enjoyed a high level of popularity.

His party quickly became a mass one, garnering the votes of 60 percent of the German electorate in the May 1935 elections and becoming the single-largest party in the Czechoslovak Republic. At the same time, however, it was increasingly infiltrated and financed by Nazi organizations located in Germany proper until, by 1937, much of the party and, finally, Henlein as well, came under the spell of Hitler (1889–1945) and the Third Reich. In November 1937 Henlein offered his services to Hitler, and in 1938, as he turned his attention to Czechoslovakia, Hitler availed himself of that offer. In the months preceding the Munich crisis of 1938, Henlein's party became what many had accused it of being from the outset—a Trojan horse for Hitler.

After the incorporation of the Sudetenland in the wake of the Munich Agreement, Henlein was named Gauleiter and Statthalter (governor) of the Sudetenland by a grateful Hitler. During the war, however, Henlein came to be overshadowed by his deputy, Karl Hermann Frank (1898–1946), who had close relations with the SS. Captured by American forces of the Seventh Army at the end of the war, Henlein committed suicide on May 10, 1945.

Ronald Smelser

Further reading

Smelser, Ronald. *The Sudeten Problem: Volkstumspolitik and the Formulation of Nazi Foreign*

H

Policy, 1933–1938. Middletown, Connecticut, 1975.

See also Karl Hermann Frank; Germanization; Gymnastic Societies; Adolf Hitler; Munich Pact; Right Radicalism; Sudeten Crisis

Herbert, Zbigniew (1924–)

Polish poet, playwright, and essayist. Although Herbert made his debut as a writer shortly after World War II, he refused to publish during the years when artists were forced to follow the dictates of socialist realism and resigned from the Polish Writers' Union. He survived by working at odd jobs until the post-Stalinist "thaw" in 1953. After his second debut, *Struna światła,* (*Chord of Light,* 1956), his fame grew rapidly (*Hermes, pies i gwiazda* [*Hermes, Dog and Star,* 1957]; *Studium przedmiotu* [*The Study of the Object,* 1961]), and it reached its peak in the 1970s and 1980s with the publication of *Pan Cogito* (*Mr. Cogito,* 1974) and *Raport z oblężonego miasta* (*Report from the Besieged City,* 1983). In both, the lyrical persona of Mr. Cogito, an average, common man, becomes a symbol of moral endurance and ethical heroism. Mr. Cogito remains faithful to the "upright attitude" of being human: "you were saved not in order to live,/ you have little time, you must give Testimony/ . . . / Be faithful. Go."

Herbert's poetry is marked by three major antinomies: the antinomy between Western tradition and "the experience of an inhabitant of Eastern Europe"; the antinomy between the present and the past (although the past is neither idealized nor simplified); and the antinomy between myth and experience. Tragic historical experiences exclude an East European from the Western world, which is often presented as a place for which Herbert's protagonist longs but which often brings disillusionment.

Herbert is also the author of two volumes of essays: *Barbarzyńca w ogrodzie* (*The Barbarian in the Garden,* 1962) and *Martwa natura z wędzidłem* (*Still Life with a Bridle,* 1993), which analyze the timelessness of art, its material aspects, and its connections with history.

Katarzyna Zechenter

Further reading

Barańczak, Stanisław. *A Fugitive from Utopia: The Poetry of Zbigniew Herbert.* Cambridge, Massachusetts, 1987.

Carpenter, Bogdana. "The Prose Poetry of Zbigniew Herbert: Forging a New Genre." *Slavic and East European Journal* 1 (1984).

———. "Zbigniew Herbert: The Poet as Witness." *Polish Review* 1 (1987).

Prokopczyk, Czesław. "Zbigniew Herbert's Poetry and Its Explication through Antinomies." *Polish Review* 1 (1987).

See also Polish Literature

Herder, Johann Gottfried (1744–1803)

German philosopher whose ideas, developed especially in his *Ideen zur Philosophie der Geschichte der Menschheit* (*Ideas toward the Philosophy of the History of Mankind,* 1784–91), greatly influenced the genesis and development of modern East European national consciousness. Critical of Enlightenment universalism, Herder formulated a philosophical anthropology that stressed self-expression and extolled human diversity. Of particular relevance to Eastern Europe was Herder's application of these ideas to society and history. Herder saw humanity as composed of natural national units, each endowed with its own unique spirit and assigned a particular part in the fulfillment of humanity's purpose. Each nation was defined in terms of its collective experience, cultural habits, and, above all, language. Moreover, Herder insisted that each language, even if not established as a literary or scientific tongue, is valuable both intrinsically and as a component of humanity's common spiritual wealth. Even more specifically, in his *Ideen* Herder drew an enthusiastic and idyllic portrayal of the Slavs as a people blessed with a bright future.

Although Herder was not a nationalist in any conventional sense, his work awakened pride and interest in local history, folklore, and languages throughout Eastern Europe, from the Baltic through the Balkans. In particular, Czech and Slovak philologists, such as Josef Jungmann (1773–1847) and Ján Kollár (1793–1852), and Czech political leaders, from František Palacký (1798–1876) to Tomáš Masaryk (1850–1937), drew inspiration from Herder, as did some Russian Slavophiles and the leading figures in other national revival movements.

André Liebich

Further reading

Barnard, F.M. *Herder's Social and Political Thought: From Enlightenment to Nationalism.* Oxford, 1965.

Ergang, Robert. *Herder and the Foundations of German Nationalism.* New York, 1931.

Janeff, Janko. "Herder und die Slaven," *Monatschrift für Höhere Schulen* 37 (1938): 91–97.

See also Folklore; Josef Jungmann; Ján Kollár; Tomáš Masaryk; František Palacký; Philosophy; Slavophilism

Heydrich, Reinhard (1904–42)

Head of the German Security Police and the Security Service (Sicherheitsdienst, or SD), organizer of the Final Solution of the "Jewish question," and acting Reich protector of Bohemia and Moravia. Born in Halle, Saxony, Heydrich entered the navy as a career officer in 1922 and became a first lieutenant in 1928. He was dishonorably discharged from the navy in April 1931 because of an alleged breach of promise to marry. He joined the SS and was invited by its chief, Heinrich Himmler (1900–1945), to Munich in 1931 to organize the SD, the secret intelligence section of the National Socialist Party. In 1936 Heydrich was named chief of the SD and Security Police, which included the State Secret Police (Gestapo) and the Criminal Police. At the outset of the war in September 1939, Heydrich combined all security forces in the Reich Security Main Office. On September 24, 1941, Hitler (1889–1945) promoted Heydrich to SS Obergruppenführer and general of the police. Because of the increased Czech underground activity during the summer of 1941, Hitler appointed Heydrich acting Reich protector in Prague. On his arrival in Prague on September 27, Heydrich declared a state of emergency, and subsequently over four hundred Czechs were sentenced to death by summary courts. Heydrich tried to balance the use of terror with an improvement in social services. While undertaking his police functions, he also carried out preparations for the Holocaust.

Heydrich was tall, blond, cold, amoral, cruel, without compassion and trusting no one, highly intelligent, introverted, and a loner. He displayed a multifaceted personality: an energetic organizer and ruthless policeman, a successful sportsman and fighter pilot, a good father and husband, a pas-

sionate musician, a fanatic National Socialist, and a pragmatic technocrat. He died from bomb injuries inflicted by two Czechoslovak military commandos who had parachuted into the protectorate from London for the purpose of assassinating him. In retaliation, the Nazis murdered the male population of the Czech town of Lidice and sent the women and children to concentration camps.

Radomír V. Luža

Further reading

Aronson, Shlomo. *Reinhard Heydrich und die Frühgeschichte von Gestapo und SD.* Stuttgart, 1971.

Calic, Edouard. *Reinhard Heydrich: Schlüsselfigur des Dritten Reiches.* Düsseldorf, 1982.

Deschner, Günther. *Reinhard Heydrich.* New York, 1981.

Kárný, Miroslav and Jaroslava Milotová, eds. *Protektorátní politika Reinharda Heydricha.* Prague, 1991.

MacDonald, Callum. *The Killing of SS-Obergruppenführer Reinhard Heydrich, 27 May 1942.* London, 1989.

See also Adolf Hitler; Holocaust; Lidice; Protectorate of Bohemia and Moravia

Higher Education

Historically, the development of higher education in Eastern Europe has been marked by uneventfulness. Generally, in the territories that at some point were independent countries or were subject to the Habsburg Empire or the German states, higher education developed as early as the fourteenth century. The beginnings of industrialization in this region during the eighteenth and nineteenth centuries resulted in the founding of other institutions of higher education, several of which were highly technical or specialized. But in those territories under the Ottoman Turks, modern forms of higher education were virtually nonexistent until at least the middle or latter part of the nineteenth century. The breakup of the Ottoman Empire and later of the Austro-Hungarian Empire spawned a number of higher educational institutions in the newly independent countries. However, it was after World War II that the greatest expansion of higher education in Eastern Europe took place. Several factors influenced this expansion: the need to replace the skilled and professional manpower decimated by the war, the Communist drive for economic development, and the desire of party officials to recruit new and younger personnel who could be considered politically reliable. In Romania alone, thirty-eight new institutions were formed by 1950.

There are several types of institutions of higher education in Eastern Europe. The first is the university. Most of these are modeled after German schools in terms of levels, curricular patterns, and administrative structure, although serious constraints in all three areas existed during the Communist period. The second consists of technological institutes for the training of students for work in industry, construction, and communication as the engineers and technicians. A third group is the teacher-training schools. These prepare young people to enter the teaching profession, generally at the elementary-school level. (Secondary-school teachers are usually prepared by the universities.) A fourth group consists of specialized agricultural institutes for instruction in forestry, horticulture, and general agriculture. A fifth group includes specialized veterinary or medical institutes for teaching and research. Other types are institutes for physical culture; conservatories of music; academies; and institutes for art, motion pictures, ballet, folk dancing, and the like. Lastly, some countries also have specialized institutes for instruction in law and economics.

Most institutions are government-financed and controlled, although within limits faculty generally have broad rights of self-governance and decision making. Often, the national ministry of education or a national ministry of higher education assumes this responsibility. A few private institutions exist, for instance, the Catholic University of Lublin, Poland, and the new American University in Blageovgrad, Bulgaria, but to date these are rare. The chief executive officers of a large university almost always include a rector and several vice rectors elected by members of the faculty, usually by professors and lecturers. The term of office for the rectors may be anywhere from one to four years. In some places an executive council, whose exact size varies, may oversee the work of the institution as an intermediate unit. A university is divided into faculties (departments) by disciplines or related areas of study. Each faculty has a dean and possibly one or more associate deans, elected by the members of the respective faculty. In a few institutions, students are included in the process, serving even as associate deans and vice rectors.

Since 1989, profound changes have taken place in the higher educational institutions of the former Soviet bloc. Student Communist organizations that existed in the universities have been disbanded. Curricula that espoused Marxist doctrines have been revised to include more comprehensive and more objective material. Books have had to be rewritten to keep up with these changes. Communist professors have either been forced to retire or to revamp their teaching orientation. These changes are still in progress, with time alone determining their direction in the final outcome.

John Georgeoff

Further reading

Altabach, Philip G., ed. *International Higher Education: An Encyclopedia,* 2 vols. New York, 1991.

Clark, Burton R. and Guy R. Neave, eds. *The Encyclopedia of Higher Education: National Systems of Higher Education,* 4 vols. Oxford, 1992.

Husen, Torsten and T. Neville Postlethwaite, eds. *The International Encyclopedia of Education,* 2d ed., 12 vols. Oxford, 1994.

International Association of Universities. *International Handbook of Universities,* 13th ed. Paris, 1993.

——. *Liste mondiale* (*World List*), 19th ed. Paris, 1992.

Knowles, Asa S., editor-in-chief. *The International Encyclopedia of Higher Education,* 10 vols. San Francisco, 1977.

Kurian, George Thomas, ed. *World Education Encyclopedia,* 3 vols. New York, 1988.

See also Charles University; Education; Industrialization; Jagiellonian University; Robert College

Hitler, Adolf (1889–1945)

Dictator of Nazi Germany whose foreign policy objectives in Eastern Europe precipitated World War II in Europe. Although Hitler did not rise to power in Germany until 1933, reacquisition of lands taken from Germany (including those inhabited by ethnic Germans) as well as Lebensraum (living space) in Eastern Europe were fundamental goals of Nazi policy. Toward that end, Hitler annexed Austria in early 1938, forced Czechoslovakia to turn over the Sudetenland in September

1938, and carved up the remainder of Czechoslovakia in early 1939. In September 1939, over the pretext of the failure of Poland to return the Polish Corridor and the city of Danzig (Gdańsk) to Germany, Hitler launched an invasion of Poland that brought on World War II.

Through the use of occupation (Poland, Bohemia), the creation of rump states (Slovakia, Croatia), and allies (Bulgaria, Hungary, Romania), Hitler came to dominate all of Eastern Europe by June 1941, save for the areas in Yugoslavia in which the Partisans continued to operate.

After his defeat of Poland, Hitler turned his attention temporarily to the West, but his eyes were always on the East. Italian defeats in Greece and Albania and defiance from Yugoslavia, however, forced Hitler to postpone the invasion of the Soviet Union, because an alliance of Greece and Yugoslavia, supported by Great Britain, posed a threat to his rear. In April 1941 the Germans attacked Yugoslavia, rapidly crushing the Yugoslav army and setting up a pro-Nazi state in Croatia. The Greeks and their British allies were pushed out of Albania, and Greece itself was subdued by the end of May 1941. Although these campaigns left Hitler in virtual control of Eastern Europe (since Romania, Bulgaria, and Hungary were German allies, and Czechoslovakia and Poland had been occupied or conquered in 1939), the operations in Eastern Europe led to a delay that was to prove fatal to Hitler's ultimate goal—conquest of the Soviet Union.

On June 22, 1941, the Germans launched Operation Barbarossa. Fighting alongside the German army were divisions from Hungary and Romania. The latter were important in conquering the southern Ukraine, including the cities of Odessa and Sevastopol. But the failure of these units to protect the flanks of the German advance at Stalingrad led to the encirclement of the German army there in early 1943.

In the areas controlled by the Germans, Hitler implemented his vision for the future of Europe, including the systematic liquidation of Jews, Gypsies, Communists, and Partisans. Four SS *Einsatzgruppen* (mobile action units) began operations in occupied Russia and the Baltic states, shooting and gassing in vans more than 500,000 people by the middle of 1942, the vast majority of whom were Jews.

Following their victory at Stalingrad in early 1943, the Soviets mounted an offensive, ultimately subduing Hitler's Eastern European allies one by one. By the beginning of 1945, all of Eastern Europe and the Balkans had been retaken by the Allies. By April 1945, Hitler's personal Lebensraum was confined to his Berlin bunker, where he committed suicide.

Daniel D. Trifan

Further reading

Dallin, Alexander. *German Rule in Russia: 1941–1945.* Boulder, Colorado, 1982.

Erickson, John. *The Road to Stalingrad: Stalin's War with Germany.* Boulder, Colorado, 1984.

Littlefield, Frank C. *Germany and Yugoslavia 1933–1941: The German Conquest of Yugoslavia.* Boulder, Colorado, 1988.

Lucas, James. *War on the Eastern Front: The German Soldier in Russia 1941–1945.* Portland, Oregon, 1991.

See also *Anschluss;* Antifascism; Axis; Barbarossa; Gdańsk; Generalgouvernement; Germany; Gypsies; Holocaust; Jews; Munich Pact; Nazi–Polish War; Polish Corridor; Protectorate of Bohemia and Moravia; Slovak Republic; Sudeten Crisis; Ustaša; Vienna Awards; World War II

Hlinka, Andrej (1864–1938)

Roman Catholic priest and one of the foremost Slovak nationalist leaders. Hlinka defended what he regarded as Slovak national interests during the first four decades of the twentieth century, first against Hungary, then, after 1918, Czechoslovakia. Born of humble origins in the north central Slovakian village of Černová in 1864 and ordained in 1889, Hlinka was the pastor of the nearby Ružomberok parish from 1905 until his death. Engaged in nationalist politics since the early 1900s, Hlinka helped found a Catholic Slovak nationalist faction that eventually became the Slovak People's Party (SPP). His condemnation to prison by a Hungarian court for political agitation led to a riot in Černová in 1907 in which fifteen Slovaks were killed; this gained him international fame. In the closing months of World War I, he and other Slovak leaders declared Slovakia's attachment to the new Czechoslovak Republic. Quickly disillusioned with Slovakia's status within Czechoslovakia, however, Hlinka and his SPP spearheaded the Slovak autonomy movement. His attempt to present Slovak nationalist complaints to

H the Paris Peace Conference in 1919 led to his brief imprisonment by the Czechoslovak regime and contributed to the aura of national martyrdom that surrounded him throughout his career. As SPP chairman, the charismatic Hlinka forcefully opposed Czechoslovak nationality and centralism in word and deed. Speaking the language of the Slovak peasant, he came to personify rural, conservative, Catholic Slovakia in the eyes of contemporaries. Hlinka died on August 16, 1938, in Ružomberok.

James Felak

Further reading

Bartlová, Alena. *Andrej Hlinka.* Bratislava, 1991.

Felak, James Ramon. *"At the Price of the Republic": Hlinka's Slovak People's Party, 1929–1938.* Pittsburgh, 1995.

Hoensch, Jörg K. *Dokumente zur Autonomiepolitik der Slowakischen Volkspartei Hlinkas.* Munich, 1984.

Kramer, Juraj. *Slovenské autonomistické hnutie v rokoch 1918–1929.* Bratislava, 1962.

Sidor, Karol. *Andrej Hlinka, 1864–1926.* Bratislava, 1934.

See also Paris Peace Conference

Hodža, Milan (1878–1944)

Czechoslovak prime minister (1935–38) and leading Slovak political figure from the early 1900s until his death in 1944. Born in 1878 near Turčiansky Svätý Martin and educated at the universities in Budapest and Vienna, Hodža was an agrarian activist, journalist, and parliamentarian (1905–10) in prewar Hungary. From 1908, he was part of the Belvedere Circle around Franz Ferdinand (1863–1914), which sought to reform the Habsburg Empire. Between the wars, Hodža sought to translate his influence in Slovakia into power in Prague. He organized and led the Slovak branch of the Czechoslovak Agrarian Party, sought cooperation with opposition parties in Slovakia, and advocated regionalism, that is, addressing the Slovak question through economic development and administrative autonomy. Despite some political setbacks, Hodža became Czechoslovakia's prime minister from 1935 until just before the Munich Agreement (1938), in which Czechoslovakia would be forced to turn over the Sudetenland to Nazi Germany. Hodža spent the war years in exile in Western Europe and the United States, where he advocated Central European federation and opposed Czechoslovak president-in-exile Edvard Beneš (1884–1948) on a number of issues, including the Slovak question. He died in Illinois in 1944. Despite a reputation as a political opportunist, Hodža was devoted in principle to agrarian and Central European cooperation. He advanced agrarianism through his support for land and tax policies that favored the development of a Slovak agrarian middle class and through his support for the Green International, the loosely tied organization of agrarian parties.

James Felak

Further reading

Hodža, Milan. *Články, reči a štúdie,* 7 vols. Prague, 1930–34.

Mikula, Susan. "Milan Hodža and the Politics of Power, 1907–1914," in *Slovak Politics: Essays on Slovak History in Honour of Joseph M. Kirschbaum.* Cleveland, Ohio, 42–62.

Milan Hodža, štatník a politik. Bratislava, 1992.

Slovenský biografický slovník, vol. 2. Martin, Slovakia, 1987.

See also Agrarian Parties; Edvard Beneš; Franz Ferdinand; Green International; Munich Pact; Sudeten Crisis

Hohenwart zu Gerlachstein, Count Karl Sigmund (1824–99)

Austrian bureaucrat. Among his many positions, Hohenwart headed an Austrian cabinet in 1871 and later built a strong coalition of conservative groups in the Austrian parliament. Hohenwart is best known for his attempts to reconcile Czech nationalists and Bohemian conservative nobles to the monarchy by granting Bohemia a degree of autonomy similar to that gained by Hungary in the 1867 *Ausgleich* (Compromise), which established the Dual Monarchy of Austria-Hungary. His project failed when centralist German liberals in Austria and Hungarian leaders blocked all attempts at federalization. Of equal importance, if less well known, were his cabinet's efforts under economics professor Albert Schäffle (1831–1903) to replace the laissez-faire liberalism of its predecessors with a sweeping conservative social and economic policy. In the 1870s Hohenwart forged an interregional Conservative Party coalition in the

Reichsrat (parliament) composed of Slovene nationalists, German clerics, and other social conservatives. This party constituted the backbone of Count Eduard Taaffe's (1833–95) antiliberal Iron Ring coalition government (1879–93). In 1893 Hohenwart abandoned Taaffe for a short-term coalition government with his erstwhile enemies, the German liberals, in an attempt to block electoral reform and to maintain the national status quo in the Windischgrätz cabinet (1893–95). The rise of mass parties organized increasingly around single issues of national, class, and regional identity weakened Hohenwart's coalition considerably in the 1890s.

Pieter Judson

Further reading

Garver, Bruce. *The Young Czech Party 1874–1901 and the Emergence of a Multiparty System.* New Haven, Connecticut, 1978.

Höbelt, Lothar. *Kornblume und Kaiseradler: Die deutschfreiheitlichen Parteien Altösterreichs 1882–1918.* Vienna, 1993.

Kolmer, Gustav. *Parlament und Verfassung in Österreich,* vol 2. Vienna, 1902.

Schäffle, Albert. *Aus meinem Leben,* 2 vols. Berlin, 1905.

See also *Ausgleich;* Dual Monarchy; Eduard Taaffe

Holocaust

Term for the Nazi persecution and destruction of the Jews (1933–45), derived from the Greek *holokauston* (Hebrew, *sho'ah*), which meant a sacrifice burned by fire. Later it indicated slaughter or destruction of masses of people. In 1940 it was used for the first time with reference to the persecution of the Jews in Poland. Since the 1950s, the term has applied primarily to the destruction of European Jews. It is also used in other contexts, such as the holocaust of the Gypsies, the Armenians, or the Poles.

The culmination of the Holocaust took place during World War II, when the Nazi leadership made a decision about the Final Solution (*Endlösung*) of the "Jewish question," but Adolf Hitler (1889–1945) had always been obsessed with the Jews, and anti-Semitism was one of the most important segments of his worldview. During 1919–32, in his speeches and articles, Hitler frequently mentioned "removal," "expulsion," and "exclusion" of the Jews and made their disposition the "pivotal question" of the Nazi Party. After he became chancellor in 1933, Hitler began a policy of systematic discrimination against the Jews of Germany, including the destruction of synagogues, seizure of property, and internment in camps.

In 1939, after the fall of Poland, an additional two million Jews found themselves in territories controlled by the Nazis. Hitler decided first that all the Jews living on these territories should be concentrated in the Generalgouvernement, the Nazi administrative district in occupied Poland. Then he planned to organize a Jewish reservation in the Lublin region, in the southeastern part of German-occupied Poland. In early 1940 a plan of sending the Jews to the island of Madagascar was discussed, but the German defeat in the Battle of Britain made this plan unfeasible. At that time, the first ghettos had already been established in Poland; the Nazis had also gained experience in the so-called euthanasia program against "undesirables" (e.g., the mentally ill) of their own population and liquidation of the Polish intelligentsia. In late 1940 and early 1941 the term *Endlösung* appeared in the orders and documents issued by Heinrich Himmler (1900–45), head of the Gestapo, and his staff. When the Germans invaded the Soviet Union, the Wehrmacht (regular German army) was followed by *Einsatzgruppen,* mobile killing units that murdered Jews in the Soviet territories. Mass murder by shooting and gas vans was not efficient enough so the Nazis developed new killing techniques in the fall of 1941. A system of extermination camps was created in which poison gas was used to kill Jews before cremation or other means of disposal. Since a majority of European Jews lived in Poland and elsewhere in East Central Europe, Hitler chose Poland as the place of mass murder. From 1941 and early 1942, millions of Jews shipped from all countries occupied by Hitler were killed in the camps of Chełmno, Bełżec, Sobibór, Treblinka, Majdanek, and Auschwitz-Birkenau. The plan of the Final Solution was finally elaborated and sanctioned during the Wannsee Conference of January 20, 1942, in Berlin. Then on November 26, 1944, with the Red Army approaching central Poland, Himmler ordered an end to gassing. The remaining Jews were murdered on the spot or shipped to camps in Germany. Altogether, the Nazis murdered about 5,750,000 Jews.

Piotr Wróbel

H

Further reading

Encyclopedia of the Holocaust, ed. by Israel Gutman, vol. 2. New York, 1990, 488–93, 681.

Reitlinger, Gerald. *The Final Solution.* New York, 1968.

Yahil, Leni. *The Holocaust: The Fate of European Jewry.* Oxford, 1990.

See also Auschwitz; Generalgouvernement; Gypsies; Adolf Hitler; Jews; Red Army; Raoul Wallenberg; Warsaw Ghetto

Holy Alliance

International treaty sponsoring peace and monarchical solidarity signed at Paris on September 26, 1815, by Alexander I of Russia (1777–1825), Francis I (1768–1835) of Austria, and Frederick William III of Prussia (1770–1840). The Holy Alliance had been conceived and drafted by Alexander I and amended—with a conservative emphasis—by Prince Metternich (1773–1859), foreign minister of Austria. The treaty called on all Christian monarchs to rule their subjects according to the precepts of Christianity and to work with one another in fraternal cooperation. The Holy Alliance was eventually signed by all reigning monarchs of Europe save for the prince regent of England and the pope. Because of its spiritual tone and idealistic goals, the Holy Alliance may be viewed not so much as a tangible instrument of international law but rather as a manifestation of the widespread desire among Europe's monarchs for repose and stability in the wake of the French Revolution and the Napoleonic Wars. After the 1820s, the Holy Alliance came to be more narrowly associated with the antirevolutionary, repressive policies of the conservative eastern monarchies of Russia, Austria, and Prussia, especially as they pertained to the revolutionary movements in Central and southeastern Europe.

Lawrence J. Flockerzie

Further reading

Bourquin, Maurice. *Histoire de la Sainte Alliance.* Geneva, 1958.

Hurst, Michael, ed. *Key Treaties for the Great Powers, 1814–1914,* vol. 1. New York, 1972, 96–98.

Näf, Werner. *Zur Geschichte der Heiligen Allianz.* Bern, 1928.

See also Alexander I; Clemens von Metternich

Hóman, Bálint (1885–1951)

Hungarian historian, historiographer, university professor, and politician. The son of a distinguished professor of classics and philology, Hóman received a doctorate from Péter Pázmány University in Budapest. From 1915 until 1931, he held a number of important academic positions, including director of the Hungarian National Museum. He also taught medieval Hungarian history at his alma mater. Hóman conducted valuable research into the Hungarian steppe-land traditions, the settlements of the Árpád period, and the origins of the Hungarian state. His most important work was the multivolume *Magyar történet* (*Hungarian History,* 1928–33), written with Gyula Szekfű (1883–1955).

During the 1930s, his shift toward the political right became marked. Nationalist tendencies gained ground in Hungary's educational system during his tenure as minister of religious and public education from 1932 to 1938. In 1946 he was indicted as a war criminal by the Communists, and a "people's tribunal" sentenced him to life in prison. He died in the infamous Vác prison.

András Boros-Kazai

Further reading

Hóman, Bálint. *A magyar hún hagyomány és hún monda.* Budapest, 1925.

———. *Magyar középkor.* Budapest, 1938.

Szekfű, Gyula, Bálint Hóman, and Károly Kerényi, eds. *Egyetemes történet I–IV.* Budapest, 1935–37.

Vardy, Steven B. *Modern Hungarian Historiography.* Boulder, Colorado, 1976.

See also Gyula Szekfű

Honvéd

Hungarian home army. The first part of the word, *"hon,"* (native land, fatherland, motherland, homeland) may be found as early as the thirteenth century among the written relics of the Hungarian language, while the second part, *"véd,"* comes from words *"védelem"* (defense) or *"véd"* (to defend). The word was revived during the period of language reform at the beginning of the nineteenth century, and more new derivatives, such as *honvédelem* (home defense) and *honvédelmi miniszter* (minister of defense), were created from it. The word itself, made up of two components, was created by writer Károly Kisfaludy (1788–1830). *"Honvéd"* was first used in one of his poems "Az élet korai" ("Ages of Life"), in the form of a soldier defending his homeland (*Nem csügged és honvéd tisztét teljesíti*—He does not lose faith and performs his *honvéd*-duty). After this, the word appeared in a German-Hungarian military vocabulary written by Károly Kiss (1793–1866), which appeared in Budapest in 1843. Following the initial victory of the Hungarian revolution in 1848, soldiers of the Hungarian army, recruited on the order of the Hungarian government on March 19, 1848, were called (on Kiss's initiative) *honvéd.* Later this became the name of those volunteers and Austrian soldiers who, supporting the Hungarian revolution, joined the Hungarian army. The Hungarian territorial army (*honvédség*), as a Hungarian military force, was disbanded after the defeat of the Hungarian revolution, following the capitulation at Világos on August 13, 1849. However, because of these events, the term *honvéd* has since become connected with the idea of a soldier fighting for Hungarian freedom. Following the *Ausgleich* (Compromise) of 1867 between Austria and Hungary, which created the Dual Monarchy, the state administrations of defense, finance, and foreign affairs were placed under joint administration. In spite of this, Hungary did not wish to give up claim to its own national army to defend the motherland. Between 1868 and 1918, according to the provisions of Law XLI of 1868, in addition to the common Austro-Hungarian army, the military force, which was recruited in Hungary, was called *honvédség.* Consequently, soldiers who after 1868 belonged to the Hungarian command were again called *honvéd.*

Pál Péter Tóth

Further reading

A magyar nyelv történeti-etimológiai szótára, vol. 2. Budapest, 1970.
Erdélyi magyar szótörténeti tár, vol. 5. Budapest-Bucharest, 1993.
Kiss, Károly. *Hadi Műszótár.* Pest, 1843.

See also *Ausgleich;* Dualism; Dual Monarchy; Hungarian War for Independence; Revolutions of 1848

Horthy, Miklós (1868–1957)

Hungarian regent and the dominant political figure in Hungary in the era of the two world wars. Born into a Protestant, gentry family, Horthy embarked on a successful career as an officer in the Austro-Hungarian navy. After World War I, he rose to power as a war hero and a "man on horseback" who vowed to suppress communism and overturn the hated Treaty of Trianon (in which Hungary lost over two-thirds of its prewar territory). In 1920 the parliament elected him regent, a post he was to occupy for twenty-four years.

During the 1920s, Horthy settled into the role of ceremonial head of state in an authoritarian but pluralistic regime. Notorious for his anti-Semitism, he now moderated his views and forged an informal alliance with prominent Jewish industrialists. The Great Depression and the coming of a new European war created problems for Hungary that Horthy was incapable of solving. He firmly rejected the idea that right-wing totalitarian principles be applied in Hungary but nonetheless respected German military power. His strategy when war came was to cling to armed neutrality while at the same time cooperating with Hitler's Germany to regain lost Hungarian territories. This policy ended in disaster in 1941 when Horthy approved Hungarian participation in German attacks on Yugoslavia and the Soviet Union.

Horthy came to despise the Nazis and tried to withdraw from the war, but he feared even more a Soviet occupation of Hungary. He thus continued a limited collaboration with Hitler (1889–1945) even after the Germans occupied Hungary in 1944. Horthy now gave his initial approval to the deportation of the Jews, though he intervened to save the Jews of Budapest when he finally realized the true nature of the Final Solution. In October 1944 the Germans forced his abdication and transported him as a prisoner to Bavaria. The victorious Allies chose not to try Horthy as a war criminal, and Horthy spent his remaining years as an exile in Portugal, never returning to his native land. He remained a bitter opponent of the Communist regime until his death in 1957. In 1993 Horthy's remains were returned to Hungary and reburied in Kenderes, his home village.

Thomas Sakmyster

Further reading

Gosztony, Péter. *Miklós von Horthy: Admiral und Reichsverweser.* Göttingen, 1973.
Macartney, C.A. *October Fifteenth: A History of Modern Hungary, 1929–1945.* Edinburgh, 1961.

H

Sakmyster Thomas. *Hungary's Admiral on Horseback: Miklós Horthy, 1918–1944.* Boulder, Colorado, 1994.

See also Great Depression; Adolf Hitler; Holocaust; Trianon, Treaty of; World War II

Hôtel Lambert

The palace of the Czartoryski family in Paris, synonymous with the center of political activity for Polish exiles from 1830 to 1865, particularly for the conservative camp of the (Polish) Great Emigration. Directed by Prince Adam J. Czartoryski (1770–1861), a representative of one of Poland's magnate families and often considered the "Polish king-in-exile," the conservatives hoped to win foreign support for the restoration of Poland after the failure of the November Uprising (1830–31) against the Russians and the abolition of the Congress Kingdom's constitution. The conservatives attempted to use diplomacy to divide England and France from Russia rather than depending on revolutionary conspiracies or insurrection to free Poland. They also encouraged the national movements in the Balkans. A diplomatic network throughout Europe, with unofficial representatives in Constantinople, Rome, and other European capitals, reported to the Hôtel Lambert, but its influence was not limited to the political. The Polish Library in Paris and the Towarzystwo Historyczno-Literackie (Historical-Literary Society) were also founded with its support, and it supported a number of Polish-language newspapers to propagate its point of view.

John Stanley

Further reading

Berry, Robert A. "The Hotel Lambert and French Foreign Policy in the Balkans 1840–1848," in Richard Frucht, ed., *Labyrinth of Nationalism, Complexities of Diplomacy: Essays in Honor of Charles and Barbara Jelavich.* Columbus, Ohio, 1992.

Kukiel, Marian. *Czartoryski and European Unity 1770–1861.* Princeton, New Jersey, 1955.

See also Adam Czartoryski; Emigration; November Uprising; Polish Congress Kingdom; Polish Émigrés

Hoxha, Enver (1908–85)

Albanian Communist leader. Hoxha received his primary and secondary education in his southern Albanian home of Gjirokastër and later was awarded a scholarship by the Albanian government to study in France. In the early 1930s he joined the Communist Party of France, which caused the Albanian government to suspend his scholarship in the spring of 1934. After returning to his country in 1936, Hoxha taught in Korçë before moving to Tirana in 1940. There, he worked in a tobacco shop named Flora, which became a center for underground Communist activities.

When the Communist Party was officially founded on November 8, 1941, Hoxha became the secretary of the Provisional Central Committee. In September 1942 he became the leader of the National Liberation Movement, and in March 1943 he was elected general secretary of the Communist Party of Albania. When the regular national liberation army was formed, he became commissar and later head of the general staff. At the Second Conference of the Anti-Fascist Council in Berat in October 1944, Hoxha was appointed head of the democratic government of Albania. In this capacity, he entered Tirana on November 28, 1944. A day later, Albania was declared liberated from fascist (Italian) and Nazi (German) occupiers.

For over forty years Hoxha held the most important party and government positions in Albania: from 1944 to 1954 he was premier; from 1954 until his death in 1985, he was the first secretary of the Communist Party, commander in chief of the armed forces, and president of the Democratic Front of Albania.

Hoxha did not trust anyone, especially Russian premier Nikita Khrushchev (1894–1971). At the World Conference of Communist Parties held in Moscow in November 1960, Hoxha publicly supported China in the Sino-Soviet dispute. After Khrushchev failed in his overtures to Hoxha, he remarked that it was easier to negotiate with the British than with Hoxha. In 1961 the Albanian leader broke all diplomatic and other relations with the Soviet Union.

The Cultural Revolution in China in 1966 served as Hoxha's inspiration. He immediately launched his own minicultural revolution aimed at revolutionizing the party and life in Albania. He made Albania the first atheist state in the world, closing 2,169 churches and mosques. Those who refused to follow the party directives were sent to concentration camps.

From 1978 (when Albania broke off relations with China) until the day he died, Hoxha isolated Albania from the rest of the world, in the process making Albania the poorest country in Europe.

Mirvet S. Muca

Further reading

Dilo, Jani. *The Communist Party Leadership in Albania.* Washington, D.C., 1961.

Griffith, William E. *Albania and the Sino-Soviet Rift.* Cambridge, Massachusetts, 1963.

Prifti, Peter. *Socialist Albania since 1944.* Cambridge, Massachusetts, 1978.

Ramadan, Marmullaku. *Albania and the Albanians.* Boston, 1975.

See also Communist Party of Albania

Hrad

Prague's Hradčany castle and an informal group around the president of the Czechoslovak First Republic. Once the residence of the kings of Bohemia and the presidents of Czechoslovakia, since 1993 the castle has been the seat of the president of the Czech Republic. Between 1918 and 1938, the *Hrad* also referred to those supporting the policies of presidents Tomáš G. Masaryk (1850–1937) and Edvard Beneš (1884–1948), whether they were employed in the Chancellery of the president of the republic at the *Hrad,* leading some of the country's most important political parties, or serving in the bureaucracy. The *Hrad* was an important factor in building political coalitions and setting government policy, especially during the interwar period.

Daniel E. Miller

Further reading

Bosl, Karl, ed. *Die "Burg": Einflussreiche politische Kräfte um Masaryk und Beneš,* 2 vols. Munich, 1973–74.

Klimek, Antonín. *Boj o Hrad,* vol. 1, *Hrad a Pětka: Vnitropolitický vývoj Československa 1918–1926 na půdorysu zápasu o prezidentské nástupnictví.* Prague, 1996.

See also Edvard Beneš; Tomáš G. Masaryk

Hungarian Art

At the turn of the nineteenth century, art in Hungary was, as everywhere else, dominated by the tradition of historicism and romanticism. Miklós Barabás (1811–98) provided a panoramic view of prerevolutionary Hungary, while the paintings of his contemporary Jozsef Molnár (1821–99) offered visions of low-key, bourgeois sentimentalism. The artist who best understood the spirit of contemporary French romanticism was Mihály Zichy (1827–1906). However, although his *Lifeboat* betrayed a dependence on Géricault's (1791–1824) *Raft of the Medusa* and Delacroix's (1798–1863) *Barge of Dante,* it lacked the vibrant brushwork of the French masters. His contemporary Mór Than (1828–99) was a voice against the stern absolutism that followed the defeat of the Hungarian revolution in 1848–49. In his repertory of Hungarian historical events, he depicted (on a monumental scale) frequently disguised insurgent themes in which the traumatic defeat of the revolutionaries was overcome. Victor Madarász (1830–1917), who fought in the 1848–49 revolution, became a darling of the Salon and of Parisian society; his highly dramatic masterpiece, *The Bewailing of László Hunyadi,* won a gold medal in Paris. Moody lights and deep shadows gave his innate romanticism full play and dominated his portraits, such as that of the hero Miklós Zrinyi. Interest in landscape painting and historical representation in Hungary was partially due to the school of Károly Markó (1791–1860), a painter of international reputation who spent most of his life in Florence and Pisa. Sándor Brodszky (1819–1901), a frequent exhibitor at the Kunstverein in Munich, Gustáv Keleti (1834–1902), a member of the Hungarian Academy of Sciences, and Károly Telepy (1828–1906), one of the original members of the National Hungarian Fine Arts Society, were also important romantics.

By the middle of the nineteenth century, Hungarian painters began to travel and absorb foreign influences. Most of them showed the emotional connotations of nature, implying the mystery and revery of the romantic spirit. Eventually, however, the younger generation of romantic painters turned with renewed interest to the Magyar historical past.

The most famous Hungarian artist of the last century, Mihály Munkácsy (1844–1900), was born of a simple and poor family. His academic background, handling of line, empiricism, and brilliant

H sense of tone and color never allowed him an impressionistic period, but the influence of the Barbizon painters is felt in his landscapes. His famous *Condemned Cell* was an early masterpiece, where his highly passionate, dramatic style, powerful composition, and masterful handling of color were manifested. A romantic Magyar irredentism, so important in the next century, marked his painting. In contrast to Munkácsy's humble beginnings, the somewhat younger Pál Szinyei Merse (1845–1920) was the offspring of wealthy gentry family. His *Majális Picnic in May* depicted big, flat areas locking into space as though they were suspended in the dazzling colors of impressionism.

By 1895, the most important Hungarian painting school, Nagybánya, reached its zenith. Avant-garde, it brought the most important achievements of modern schools within the grasp of the public's increasing artistic interests. Begun by Simon Hollosy (1857–1918), it eventually became a center of Hungarian painting. Hollosy turned toward the more progressive movements in France. The second generation of painters of the Nagybánya school included Oszkár Glatz (1872–1958) and the talented and versatile Béla Iványi-Grünwald (1867–1940), whose art displayed influences of the fauves, Art Nouveau, and cubism. The movement, sometimes called Hungarian impressionism, had little to do with the earlier romantic responses to nature (with their vague mysteries, romantic yearnings, and emotional connotations) but aimed rather to grasp *natura phenomena* as they were seen. Of this group, the one who may be called impressionist (and later postimpressionist) was István Csók (1865–1961), whose work used surfaces of shifting translucencies, thereby creating an impressionistic shimmering. He was the only Hungarian artist whose work was displayed in the Uffizi gallery in Florence.

The resistance of the academic establishment to nonacademic approaches lasted only a short time. Merse's *Majális* salvaged Hungarian painting from academic eclecticism. Merse eventually became the president of the MIENK (The Circle of Hungarian Impressionists and Naturalists). Soon other art colonies came into existence at Szolnok, Szentendre, and Kecskemét. One of the most interesting movements of the time was that of the Gödöllö colony, which aimed at the aesthetic resurrection of English pre-Raphaelitism.

At the beginning of the twentieth century, as the memory of Munkácsy was fading, the society of Nyolcak (the Eights) became devoted to modern art. Men such as Robert Berényi (1887–1953) and Béla Czobel (1883–1976) turned with great interest to the work of artists such as Cézanne (1839–1906), Matisse (1869–1954), and Picasso (1881–1973).

The most influential Hungarian painter at the turn of the century and the best artist of the Hungarian Art Nouveau was József Rippl-Rónai (1861–1927), who exhibited with Cézanne, Toulouse-Lautrec (1864–1901), and the Nabis, a group gathered around Gaughin (1848–1903) in the Breton village of Pont-Aven in the late 1880s. He won a silver medal at the 1900 Paris World Fair. Others, like Bertalan Por (1880–1964), became harbingers of socialist realism while supplying revolutionary dynamism to Hungary's short-lived Communist government in 1919. Those artists were welcomed in the Hungarian Socialist Republic after World War II.

National art also gained new strength, and the aims of the Hungarian artists of the fin de siècle were related to the avant-garde periodical *Nyugat* (*West*), the country's most important literary journal. The opening of Rippl-Rónai's most famous exhibit in 1906 coincided with the appearance of the poetry of Endre Ady (1877–1919) and may be regarded as a turning point in a new chapter in Hungarian art.

Reacting to the changing artistic scene around Europe, a group of expressionist painters, notably Béla Utiz (1887–1911), introduced a somewhat more nervous and brooding style frequently mirroring left-leaning political and social movements. Aurel Bernáth's (1895–1982) luminism created timeless scenes. István Szönyi's (1894–1960) expressionism frequently conveyed ominous, dark visions as sardonic social observations. János Vaszary's (1867–1941) lyrical vistas brought the Great Hungarian Plain into focus, while the ethnic characteristics of Hungarian peasants reached heroic proportions in József Koszta's (1864–1954) works. Many Hungarian painters also labored in the spirit of nationalism and irredentism after 1918. The deeply felt loss of the postwar Treaty of Trianon, which saw Hungary lose two-thirds of its prewar territory, found resonance and symbolic expression in the paintings of Gyula Rudnay (1878–1957), which became an apotheosis of the disinherited. Many artists were also motivated by the same agony that inspired Béla Bartók's (1881–1945) music and Ady's poetry.

An unusual painter, the source of whose pictures resided in his own imagination, was Tivadar Csontváry (1853–1919). His forms and unrealistic, passionate handling of color, immediacy, and naive approach cannot be associated with any Hungarian school.

Meanwhile, a group of artists calling themselves Activists were strongly associated with two periodicals, *Tett* (*The Deed*) and *Ma* (*Today*). They worked in various forms of expressionism and cubism and became the avant-garde of modern aesthetics. Of these artists, József Egry (1883–1951) was a late product of the Nagybánya school. In his paintings the plastic quality of cubism is softened by an airy, all-permeating atmosphere.

The compositions of Gyula Derkovits (1894–1934) remind one of Matisse's fauvism but with a lyrical touch. He presented the epic of the disinherited peasant class with naked reality. Another painter with a similar social consciousness was István Dési-Hubert (1895–1944). Crushed by poverty, he lived in obscurity. His compassionate observation of the working class was expressed by excellent draftsmanship, while his violent expressionist colors carry the message of his social convictions.

Some painters who left Hungary became internationally known. Philip de Lászlo (Fülöp László [1869–1937]) was honored in England for his portraiture. Lászlo Moholy-Nagy (1895–1946) joined the Bauhaus in Germany and founded the New School in Chicago (an extension of Bauhaus—which promoted new standards in art and architecture aiming at mass production with inventiveness).

During the Stalinist regime in Hungary after World War II, there was little encouragement to advance modern European or American movements such as abstract expressionism unless executed in the socialist realist spirit. Nevertheless the avant-garde was not dormant, and toward the end of the 1980s a reinvigorated, well-prepared new generation began to emerge.

George Tivadar Radân

Further reading

Fehér, Zs. and Ö.G. Pogány. *Twentieth-Century Hungarian Painting.* Budapest, 1975.
Kampis, A. *The History of Art in Hungary.* Budapest, 1966.
Kontha, S., ed. *Magyar Müvészet, 1919–1945,* vol. 7. Budapest, 1985.
Németh, L. *Modern Hungarian Art.* Budapest, 1972.
Vollmer, H. *Allgemeines Lexikon der Bildenden Kunst des 20.Jh.6 Bde.* Leipzig, 1953–62.

See also Endre Ady; Architecture; Béla Bartók; Koszta Tivadar Csontváry; Great Hungarian Plain; Hungarian Culture; Hungarian Soviet Republic; Hungarian War for Independence; Irredentism; Mihály Munkácsy; *Nyugat;* Romanticism; Trianon, Treaty of

Hungarian Culture

Hungarian culture is rooted in Western Christianity with undertones of Eastern motifs. The origin of the Magyars is lost in myth, but the seven tribes who, under the leadership of Árpád (d. 907), settled the Carpathian basin in 896 came from the region west of the Ural Mountains. Under Árpád's successor, King (Saint) Stephen (c. 975–1038), Roman Christianity was adopted and this tied the country to Western European traditions and culture. The Renaissance, inaugurated in Hungary by King Matthias (1443–90) in the fifteenth century, was short-lived; the Turks invaded Hungary in 1526 and effectively occupied one-third of the country until 1699. While this occupation had relatively little direct cultural influence, the loss of political and cultural autonomy led to Hungary's isolation from developments in the West. The western and northern parts of the country were subservient to Austria, while the central part was dominated by the Ottomans. Only in Transylvania did Hungarian culture and national tradition flourish, enjoying a flowering of the late Renaissance in the sixteenth and seventeenth centuries. Scholars of European reputation, such as Moravian churchman and educator Jan Comenius (1592–1670), spent time there, and freedom of religion and conscience was first made law in Transylvania in 1557. Constant wars among the three parts of the nation were finally resolved when Transylvania lost its independence and the Turks were driven out by the Habsburgs. The liberal cultural traditions of Transylvania, however, were stifled by Habsburg absolutism in the eighteenth century.

In the nineteenth century Hungarian national sentiment was revived by writers such as Ferenc Kazinczy (1759–1831), Jószef Katona (1792–1830), and Mihály Vörösmarty (1800–1855). In the works of Sándor Petőfi (1823–49), Hungarian folk traditions and European romanticism merged

H to produce one of the greatest lyric poets of the country. János Arany (1817–82) revived legends and old chronicles to create a rich Hungarian tapestry. In his vocabulary he drew heavily on the language of the countryside and the village—the Hungarian peasantry and gentry—thus contributing to the evolution of the language by reaching back to its roots. In music, Ferenc (Franz) Liszt (1811–86) rose to international prominence drawing on Hungarian themes and motifs for his romantic symphonies, and while he lived abroad much of his life, he closely followed events in Hungary. Ferenc Erkel (1810–93) expressed national, patriotic sentiments in his operas *Hunyadi László* and *Bánk Bán*. He also wrote the music to the words of Ferenc Kölcsey's (1790–1838) *"Hymnusz"* (Hymn) when it was chosen as the national anthem. Painters Miklós Barabás (1810–98) and Mihály Munkácsy (1840–1900) exemplified the same blend of traditional Hungarian values, often influenced by folk tradition and classical European style.

A cultural revival followed the *Ausgleich* (Compromise) of 1867, which created the Dual Monarchy of Austria-Hungary, and again writers like Endre Ady (1877–1919) reached back to folk songs while bringing in the styles and topics of Western literature. In prose, Dezső Koszlolányi (1885–1936) and the cosmopolitan Ferenc Molnár (1878–1952) emerged as leaders of the new generation. Women's voices were also heard in the novels of Margit Kaffka (1880–1918) at the turn of the century and the perceptive study of changes in Hungarian life under communism in the work of Erzsébet Galgóczi (1930–1989).

As in earlier decades, the cultural scene in the twentieth century continued to reflect a blend of the traditional and the innovative. The novel also became popular, challenging the primacy that poetry had enjoyed. Moreover, films, drama, and modern musical plays—including several successful rock operas—have gained Hungarian arts a European—if not international—reputation. As in literature, the innovative and the traditional often diverge in music; Béla Bartók (1881–1945) and Zoltán Kodály (1882–1967) began with like concerns, but while the former became an innovator in twentieth-century music, the latter gave modern interpretations to age-old musical traditions. The rock opera *István a király* (*Stephen the King*) turned to the legend of St. Stephen's consolidation of his reign to examine the clash of national values and foreign rule in a daring examination of Communist rule in Hungary a decade before its fall.

Hungarian culture continues to evolve out of the tension between the traditional "folk" styles and the cosmopolitan, international styles that influence all the world today. Under the impact of mass communication, which works to eradicate national differences, this tension is a creative force that enables writers, artists, musicians, filmmakers, and all other creative minds to give expression to the problems of human existence in a fresh, unique way.

Enikő Molnár Basa

Further reading

Bodolai, Zoltán. *The Timeless Nation: The History, Literature, Music, Art, and Folklore of the Hungarian Nation.* Sydney, 1978.

Czigány, Loránt. *The Oxford History of Hungarian Literature from the Earliest Times to the Present.* Oxford, 1984.

Magyar Tudományos Akadémia. Történettudományos Intézet. *A History of Hungary,* trans. by László Boros et al. London, 1975.

Sisa, Stephen. *The Spirit of Hungary: A Panorama of Hungarian History and Culture.* Morristown, New Jersey, 1990.

See also Endre Ady; Béla Bartók; Cinema; Folklore; Folk Music; Hungarian Art; Hungarian Literature; Ferenc Kazinczy; Zoltán Kodály; Franz Liszt; Ferenc Molnár; Mihály Munkácsy; Music; Sandor Petőfi; Romanticism; Mihály Vörösmarty

Hungarian Émigrés

Hungarians have been migrating to neighboring countries throughout the last five centuries. Major migrations did not take place, however, until the turn of the nineteenth and twentieth centuries, and then largely to the United States. These Hungarian migrations were motivated by three distinct considerations: a search for adventure, the need to escape political persecution, and the desire to find a better livelihood. The first of these causes produced only sporadic exoduses and was usually limited to individuals or individual families. The second resulted in numerically more significant political emigrations, usually after failed revolutions, civil wars, or military conquests. The third one brought about the mass migrations of peasants and workers, usually with the seldom-fulfilled hopes of repatriation.

Among the 2.3 million Hungarian citizens who have left Hungary during the past two centuries were about one million Magyars, or real Hungarians, 80 percent of whom (800,000) ended up in the United States. The rest settled in Western Europe, Canada, Australia, and several Latin American countries. The large majority of the Hungarian immigrants to the United States (650,000–700,000) came before 1914. Only about 118,000 entered after World War I—a third of these (47,000) during the interwar years, and nearly two-thirds (71,000) after World War II. They came in several waves, the first of which appeared after the revolution of 1848–49. The next wave was the great "economic emigration" that began in the 1880s, climaxed in 1907, and came to a halt in 1914. Most Hungarian emigrants settled in America during those three decades. This economic emigration was followed by a small political emigration in wake of the Socialist, Communist, and anti-Communist revolutions of 1918–20, and then by a reduced economic immigration during the interwar years. The 1930s again witnessed a small but powerful political immigration, consisting of top Hungarian intellectuals, scientists, and artists who left Hungary and neighboring states to escape the threat of Nazi Germany. They, in turn, were followed by two more political immigrations: that of the Displaced Persons (DPs) between 1948 and 1952, who represented the political and social elites of interwar Hungary, and that of the "Fifty-Sixers" or "Freedom Fighters," who came after the failed anti-Soviet Hungarian Revolution of 1956. A trickle continued through the next four decades—motivated during the 1960s and 1970s by political and in the 1980s and 1990s by economic considerations.

Ever since the appearance of the economic immigrants in the late nineteenth century, Hungarians in North America were socially polarized. Having transferred their class consciousness from Hungary to the New World, the educated segments (mostly political immigrants) did not wish to have anything to do with their compatriots' peasant and working-class background. Among the educated, the scientific intelligentsia possessed transferable skills, merged easily into American society, and kept only occasional contacts with Hungarian ethnic communities. The economic immigrants and those intellectuals with no transferable skills (the literary and administrative intelligentsia) usually started out in the mines, steel mills, and factories, but a number of the latter also managed to gain white-collar employment. It was their children who moved into the professional fields.

The most important institutions of the economic immigrants were their churches, fraternal associations, newspapers, and various cultural associations. The educated political immigrants rejected the economic immigrants' institutions and founded their own. They met their social inferiors only in church, but even there, social segregation prevailed. The economic immigrants generally stayed out of American political life for quite a while, partly because few of them became U.S. citizens until after World War I, and partly because they were reluctant to leave their own ethnic enclaves to experience Anglo-American society. Thus, not until the rise of the first native-born generation during the interwar years was there any meaningful involvement in domestic American politics. The foreign-born among the immigrants continued to be attached to Hungary, and their initial political activism usually consisted of demonstrating on the side of the mother country (except when under communism) or for other Hungarian causes. In the course of time, however, even they became active in American party politics. The economic immigrants usually voted Democratic, but the post–World War II political immigrants generally favored the Republicans because of their harder stance on communism.

Although the contributions of the turn-of-the-century economic immigrants were limited mostly to brawn power, the interwar and post–World War II political immigrants contributed significantly to American cultural, intellectual, and scientific life. They were involved in the creation of the American film industry (Adolf Zukor [1873–1948], William Fox [1879–1952], Michael Curtiz [1888–1962], and George Cukor [1899–1983]); captivated American popular culture (Harry Houdini [1874–1926] and Johnny Weissmuller [1904–84]); ruled America's great symphony orchestras (Fritz Reiner [1888–1963], George Széll [1897–1970], Eugene Ormándy [1899–1985], Antal Doráti [1906–88], and Sir George Solti [1912–97]); were in the forefront of nuclear research (Edward Teller [1908–] and Eugene Wigner [1902–95]), space technology (Theodore von Kármán [1881–1963] and Leo Szilárd [1898–1964]), and the computer industry (John von Neumann [1903–57] and

H Andrew Grove [1936–]); and more recently moved into American and international finance (George Soros [1930–]). At the same time, they won an impressive number of Nobel Prizes (George Békésy [1899–1972], Dennis Gábor [1900–1979], John Harsányi [1920–], George Hevesy [1885–1976], George Oláh [1927–], John Polányi [1891–1966], Albert Szent-Györgyi [1893–1986], and Wigner). They also occupied virtually thousands of prominent positions at America's major universities and scientific research institutions.

Steven Béla Várdy

Further reading

Lengyel, Emil. *Americans from Hungary.* Philadelphia, 1948; reprint, 1974.

Puskás, Julianna. *From Hungary to the United States, 1880–1914.* Budapest, 1982.

Tezla, Albert. *The Hazardous Quest: Hungarian Immigrants in the United States, 1895–1920.* Budapest, 1993.

Várdy, Steven Béla. *The Hungarian-Americans.* Boston, 1985.

———. *The Hungarian Americans: The Hungarian Experience in North America.* New York, 1990.

See also Emigration; Hungarian Revolution of 1956; Hungarian War for Independence; Intelligentsia; John von Neumann; Revolutions of 1848; Albert Szent-Györgyi; Leo Szilárd; Edward Teller

Hungarian Folk High School Movement

Movement to train a new national leadership from talented peasant youth. The Hungarian folk high school movement aimed to broaden the horizons of young peasant adults and create self-confident citizens capable of leading the agrarian population in modernization and reform. Based on the Danish midnineteenth-century model, residential sessions of several weeks were held during the late 1930s, first in Protestant secondary schools, then in Catholic folk high schools. In 1941 a National Folk High School Commission was established, the first major cooperative venture between Protestant and Catholic churches in interwar Hungary. The schools were initiated by local groups, financed by contributions, and taught by volunteers, an educated elite who lived and worked on a basis of social equality with peasant youth. The curriculum concentrated on history, literature,

geography, and Bible studies. Seminar discussions encouraged individual participation. Programs were geared to raising students' self-image and increasing their self-confidence and ability to deal with local conditions. Students elected their own officials to run their "model village" during each session.

The movement grew rapidly and by 1944 approximately ten thousand peasant youth had participated. In 1945 it was often graduates of folk high schools who presided over land reform. Cut short by the Communist takeover in 1948, the movement was revived in the mid-1980s as a means to repair the damage done to civil society. The focus today is education for local self-government and vocational training.

Deborah S. Cornelius

Further reading

Jagasics, Béla, ed. *Népfőiskola és Önkormányzat.* Budapest, 1994.

Kovács, Bálint. *Protestáns Népfőiskolai Mozgalom Magyarországon (1936–1948).* Budapest, 1994.

Ugrin, Jószef. *Emlékezéseim: A KALOT parasztifjúsagi mozgalomról, a népfőiskolákról, meg egy kicsit előbbről is.* Budapest, 1995.

See also Peasants

Hungarian Language

Finno-Ugric language and part of a larger language group known as Ural-Altaic, which includes Finnish and Turkish. Its closest relative languages are manysi (Vogul) and hanti (Ostyak). Hungarian is spoken by about sixteen million people and ranks thirtieth in the world in the number of speakers. It is an agglutinative and phonetic language; words are pronounced exactly as they are written. The stress is always on the first syllable of the word, and the language when spoken is very melodious. Two sound mutations, harmonization of vowels and assimilation of consonants, contribute greatly to its musicality. It is possible to distinguish eight regional dialects in Hungarian: western, Transdanubian, Great Plain, Tisza-Danubian, northwestern (Palóc), northeastern, Transkirályhág, and the Székely (Szekler).

During their long period of migration, the Hungarians were in contact with many other nations and assimilated from them new ideas along with new words. They learned agriculture from the

Turkish and Slavic peoples, religion from the Italian and Slavic missionaries, and trade and commerce from the Germans. In spite of the "loan" words from other languages, 80 percent of the Hungarian vocabulary used today belongs to the original Hungarian and Finno-Ugric language family. After its differentiation from Finno-Ugric, which occurred around the year 1000, the evolution of Hungarian is divided into the following stages: ancient Hungarian (before the year 1000), old Hungarian (up to the middle of the fourteenth century), middle Hungarian (until the end of the sixteenth century), and new Hungarian.

The oldest surviving Hungarian text is the *Funeral Oration,* which dates to the first third of the thirteenth century. *The Lamentation of Mary,* a thirteenth-century poem, is the oldest Hungarian poem. Other early writings in Hungarian include fragments from monastery charters. The first manuscript written in Hungarian is the *Jókai Codex,* from around 1400. The Hungarian literary language of today, a language of great expressiveness, has its roots in the sixteenth century and is a product of the language renewal that took place toward the end of the eighteenth and the beginning of the nineteenth century.

Katherine Gyékényesi Gatto

Further reading

Bánhidi, Zoltán, Zoltán Jókay, and Dénes Szabó. *Learn Hungarian,* 2d ed. Budapest, 1965.

Czigány, Lóránt. *The Oxford History of Hungarian Literature.* Oxford, 1984.

Sisa, Stephen. *The Spirit of Hungary,* 2d ed. Toronto, 1983.

Hungarian Literature

The origins of Hungarian literature can be traced to the folkloristic poetry of the pre-Christian epoch of the conquest of the country in A.D. 896. It is customary to refer to four major periods of Hungarian literary history. The first extends from the earliest manifestations to the end of the medieval period (marked by the 1526 defeat at Mohács at the hands of the Ottoman Turks), and is characterized by a strictly religious tone, reflected in the legends, epics, chronicles, and theological works, many of them directly translated from the common corpus of medieval Latin church literature. The second encompasses the period between 1526 and 1772 and exhibits (in addition to religious themes)

a freer, more worldly, independent, international spirit. In contrast to these earlier two periods, the year 1772 marks the beginning of the most fruitful era of Hungarian literature, which extends throughout the nineteenth century and is imbued with a national literary consciousness that recognizes its mission, its goals, and its role in describing, defining, and molding Hungarian cultural and ethnic identity. The final period, the writings of the twentieth century, includes literature of social and political commentary in addition to literature of literary and aesthetic concerns. The greatest influence on writers in the twentieth century was World War I and the Treaty of Trianon, which deprived historical Hungary of two-thirds of its territory and almost one-half of its population.

Because of the influence of monasteries, foreign preachers, and monks, Christian literature in Latin replaced the early popular, oral poetry. Important chronicles, sacred tales, and legends, especially those of Saints Stephen, Emery, Ladislaus, Margaret, and Elizabeth, hymns and songs, and collections of sermons are illustrative of this Latin literature. Early writings in Hungarian include fragments in the *Charter of the Benedictine Monastery at Tihany* (1055) and the *Funeral Oration* (ca. 1200), the oldest Hungarian language text. *The Lamentation of Mary,* a thirteenth-century poem, is the oldest Hungarian-language poem. Humanism stimulated Hungarian writers but they continued to write in Latin. The humanist court of King Matthias Corvinus (1443–90) was renowned for its Corvina Library and produced the first great Hungarian poet, Janus Pannonius (1434–92), who continued to compose in Latin. The catastrophe at Mohács in 1526 and the Reformation had powerful impacts on the character of Hungarian literature, which since then has reflected the preoccupation of writers and poets with the question of national and cultural survival.

The language of the Reformation was Hungarian, and the art of printing spread the new controversial ideas quickly in Hungarian. Polemical literature became the most important contribution of the first half of the sixteenth century. Bálint Balassi (1554–94), the first great lyric poet of the Hungarian language, cultivated flower, religious, and soldier songs, and was the first to develop a poetical attitude toward life. Péter Pázmány (1570–1637) was the intellectual leader of the Catholic revival. The first epic poem, *The Siege of Sziget* (1651), was written by Miklós Zrinyi

H (1620–64) about the defense of the town of Sziget against Turkish assault.

In 1686, with the liberation of Buda from the Turks, the Austrian economic and political burden replaced the Turkish one. Early-eighteenth-century literary contributions include the poetry of the Rákóczy wars (1703–11) of independence against Austrian rule.

Despite Habsburg opposition and censorship, the ideas of the French Enlightenment and Revolution spread in Hungary. Reformers demanded the establishment of Hungarian as a literary language. Among those reformers were György Bessenyei (1747–1811), a pioneer in the area of Hungarian drama; Ferenc Kazincy (1759–1831), leader of the great language controversy and reform; Mihály Csokonai Vitéz (1773–1805), the second-greatest lyric poet of Hungarian literature after Sándor Petőfi (1823–1849); Sándor Kisfaludy (1772–1844), a master of the lyric sentimental poem; and Ferenc Kölcsey (1790–1838), who wrote the Hungarian national anthem, the *Himnusz.*

The Golden Age of Hungarian literature, with its foundations laid by the reformers, produced some of Hungary's most gifted, prolific, and patriotic writers. Mihály Vörösmarty (1800–1855), literary critic and director of the Academy of Sciences, excelled in the genre of lyric poetry. Petőfi, the national poet, cultivated a poetry of beautiful simplicity, precise wording, and natural images to become the symbol of personal freedom and the nation's independence. János Arany (1817–82), famed for his ballads, epics, and meditative lyric poetry, knew the soul, language, and folklore of his peasant people. Imre Madách (1823–64) wrote the Hungarian Faust, *The Tragedy of Man,* wherein he explored the mystery of human perseverance. Baron József Eötvös (1813–71), Mór Jókai (1825–1904), and Kálmán Mikszáth (1847–1910) wrote mainly novels in the realist mode with romantic undertones.

The commencement of the modern period of Hungarian literature is associated with poet Endre Ady (1877–1919) and the publication of the periodical *Nyugat* (*West*) (1908–41). Characteristic of much of twentieth-century writing are the poem, short story, novel, and drama of political import. Contemporary writers are often critical of unresponsive governments and shed light on the trials and tribulations of the disenfranchised segments of society. Attila József (1905–37); Gyula Illyés (1902–83), considered by many to be Hungary's greatest poet of the twentieth century; Mihály Babits (1883–1941); Dezső Kosztolányi (1885–1936); Sándor Weöres (1913–88); János Pilinszky (1921–81); Géza Ottlik (1912–); István Örkény (1912–79); Miklós Radnóti (1909–44); Ágnes Nemes Nagy (1922–91); Sándor Csoóri (1930–); and Péter Esterházy (1950–) are among twentieth-century Hungarian literature's foremost creators.

Katherine Gyékényesi Gatto

Further reading

Basa, Enikő M., spec. ed. *Hungarian Literature.* Whitestone, New York, 1993.

Czigány, Lóránt. *The Oxford History of Hungarian Literature.* Oxford, 1984.

Klaniczay, Tibor, ed. *A History of Hungarian Literature.* Budapest, 1982.

Nagy, Moses M., ed. *A Journey into History: Essays on Hungarian Literature.* New York, 1990.

Nemeskürty, István. *Diák, Írj Magyar Éneket: A Magyar Irodalom Története,* 2 vols. Budapest, 1985.

See also Endre Ady; Mihály Babits; Sándor Csoóri; József Eötvös; Gyula Illyés; Hungarian Language; Mór Jókai; Attila József; Ferenc Kazinczy; Ágnes Nemes Nagy; *Nyugat;* Sándor Petőfi; Trianon, Treaty of; Mihály Vörösmarty

Hungarian Populist (*Népi*) Movement

The most influential intellectual/literary movement of the interwar period, urging radical agrarian reform to provide new direction for national development. In the *Népi* movement of the 1930s, populist writers described the stark reality of the living conditions of the agrarian population, which made up more than half the total population of 8.7 million in 1930. After Hungary's defeat in World War I and the signing of the punishing Treaty of Trianon, they believed it would be the peasantry (*nép,* or people) who would provide the strength for national renewal and the basis for a new agrarian middle-class leadership. In East Central Europe the concept *"nép"* generally designated the oppressed lower classes, particularly the peasantry, but the peasantry were also considered bearers of a unique national culture. In contrast to populist movements in neighboring countries, which concentrated on the political organization of the peasantry, populist writers focused their attention on the educated public, attempting to awaken public opinion to the need for radical land reform and democratization to incorporate the peasantry into the body politic.

Hungary had not carried out a major land reform after the war like those in Czechoslovakia and Romania. National condemnation of the Treaty of Trianon, in which the nation lost two-thirds of its territory as well as 3.2 million Hungarian citizens, and the blame placed on the 1919 Communist regime that followed in the wake of the collapse of Austria-Hungary after World War I, thoroughly discredited all liberal opposition and entrenched the anachronistic regime of Admiral Horthy (1868–1957). Half the land under cultivation remained in the hands of 7,500 large estate owners, while the agrarian population—600,000 farm laborers, 1.2 million landless day laborers, and 1.2 million "dwarf-holders"—were poorly educated and isolated in the countryside.

The effects of the Great Depression and the threat of German expansion intensified the national sense of crisis, and during the 1930s the movement attracted diverse individuals: peasant writers such as Péter Veres (1897–1970), Pál Szabó (1893–1970), and Pál Sinka (1897–1969); first-generation intellectuals of peasant origin, Ferenc Erdei (1910–71), Gyula Illyés (1902–83), Jozsef Darvas (1912–73); as well as other intellectuals such as László Németh (1901–1975), who proposed a third way for Hungarian development between Western modernization and Soviet collectivization. As the movement gained strength, it attracted people from all parts of the political spectrum who were united in criticism of the existing regime but who differed in their ideas on how to institute widespread reform. The high point of the movement came in 1936–38 with the publication of a number of populist writings describing agrarian problems that deeply affected public opinion and gave momentum to the reform movement. In 1937 the short-lived March Front movement, which pressed for democratic and agrarian reforms, swept the country, but the movement was quelled, and with the increased threat of war populist efforts turned to long-term planning to create a strong, independent peasantry after the war. Populist influence was strong in the immediate postwar period and again during the Hungarian Revolution of 1956.

Deborah S. Cornelius

Further reading

András, Emmerich. *The Rise and Development in Hungary of the So-Called "Popular Movement" [Populist Movement], 1920–1956.* Vienna, 1974.

Borbándi, Gyula. *A magyar népi mozgalom.* New York, 1983.

Tóth, Pál Péter. "A népi mozgalom mint a magyar társadalom megkésett fejlödésének eredménye." *Múltunk* 38. Budapest, 1993.

See also Collectivization; Great Depression; Miklós Horthy; Hungarian Revolution of 1956; Hungarian Soviet Republic; Gyula Illyés; Peasants; Trianon, Treaty of

Hungarian Revolution of 1956

Revolution in Hungary in 1956 against Soviet domination. Prepared during the thaw following the death of Soviet dictator Josef Stalin (1879–1953) and sparked by the government's harsh response to peaceful street demonstrations, the events in the autumn of 1956 brought Hungary to a break with Soviet-style leadership and a bloody conflict seen by many as the "first war between socialist countries." Hungarians resented the misuse of their country's resources, as exemplified by the emphasis on industrial growth, forced collectivization, and the unnatural trade relations with other members of the Soviet bloc. They also resented Hungary's appearance as a satellite of the Soviet Union.

During the afternoon of October 23, 1956, thousands of students, workers, and intellectuals took to the streets of Budapest to show their solidarity with striking Poles, who were protesting against similar conditions in their country. The crowd soon began to chant "Russians, go home!," toppled a huge statue of Stalin, and marched to the radio station to have their list of demands read. State security forces fired at the demonstrators, who now stormed the building and confronted the government with a full-fledged popular uprising. With most Hungarian soldiers refusing to shoot at the rebels, the authorities came to rely on the security forces (AVO) and units of the Soviet Red Army, neither of which was able to quell the revolt. Atrocities on the part of the troops (especially AVO) were answered by incidents of street justice. Still a compromise seemed possible. On October 27, a new government, still composed largely of

H

Communists, was formed by Populist-Communist Imre Nagy (1896–1958). Extensive reforms were promised, and on October 30 the Soviet Union gave its blessings to an independent Hungary.

However, Moscow was terrified of the revolution's implications. After Nagy announced the end of the one-party system, his fate was sealed. The outbreak of the crisis in the Suez that pitted Anglo-French forces against Egyptians and the West's reluctance to intervene on Hungary's behalf gave the green light to a Soviet invasion. In response to a "call for Soviet assistance," Red Army units prepared to reenter Hungary. By the 31st, a declaration of the new pro-Moscow government, to be headed by János Kádár (1912–89), had been drawn up.

On November 1, Soviet divisions entered Hungary. Kádár and his circle moved to the Soviet embassy compound while Nagy proclaimed Hungary's independence (from the Soviet bloc) and called, in vain, on the United Nations for protection. On November 4, even while Soviet-Hungarian negotiations were proceeding, the Red Army went into full action. The Hungarian army, crippled by Soviet control of communications and an indecisiveness of command, provided only limited defense. At dawn, Nagy left his office and at 8:07 A.M. Hungarian Radio went silent. By Christmas, the Kádár government was in full control, although sporadic resistance continued until spring.

Estimates of Hungarian casualties range from the official figure of 229 to over 2,000. Moreover, between October 1956 and May 1957, nearly 200,000 individuals (over 1.5 percent of the population) fled the country.

Western public opinion initially considered the uprising the internal affair of the Soviet bloc and paid less attention to it than to the Suez crisis or to the U.S. presidential elections. Nevertheless, the Hungarian Revolution of 1956 changed the relationship between the Soviet Union and its satellite states. After November 4, 1956, the political and spiritual influence of Soviet communism went into a decline that led to its eventual self-destruction.

András Boros-Kazai

Further reading

Felkay, Andrew. *Hungary and the USSR, 1956–1988: Kádár's Political Leadership.* New York, 1989.

Free Europe Committee. *The Revolt in Hungary: A Documentary Chronology of Events Based Exclusively on Internal Broadcasts by Central and Provincial Radios,* October 23–November 4, 1956.

Király, Béla et al., eds. *The First War between Socialist States: The Hungarian Revolution and Its Impact.* Brooklyn, New York, 1984.

Litván, György, ed. *The Hungarian Revolution of 1956: Reform, Revolt and Repression 1953–1963.* London, 1996.

Molnár, Miklós. *From Bela Kun to Janos Kadar: Seventy Years of Hungarian Communism.* New York, 1991.

Rainer, János. "The Yeltsin Dossier: Soviet Documents on Hungary." *Bulletin of the Woodrow Wilson Center for Scholars.* Washington, D.C., Spring 1995.

See also Collectivization; Communist Party of Hungary; De-Stalinization; Hungarian Émigrés; János Kádár; Imre Nagy; Red Army

Hungarian Soviet Republic (1919)

Short-lived Communist state formed during the chaotic period following the defeat of Austria-Hungary in World War I. In March 1919 the Hungarian government of Mihály Károlyi (1875–1955) was handed a note by the head of the French military mission in Budapest, Fernand Vix (1872–1941), demanding that Hungarian troops in the southeast pull back some sixty miles (one hundred km), which many believed signaled an indication of Hungary's future boundaries. On March 20, Károlyi resigned, and on the following day a Soviet republic was proclaimed.

Modeled along the lines of Soviet Russia, the Hungarian Soviet Republic would last but 133 days. Although nominally headed as president by a Social Democrat, Sándor Garbai (1879–1947), the so-called Republic of Councils was guided by Béla Kun (1886–1938), commissar of foreign affairs, who had only months earlier been arrested by the government for his political activities. Seen as the defender of the Hungarian lands, the Soviet Republic was initially greeted with general optimism. On April 7, elections were held for local and national councils. A week later the National Congress of Councils met.

To the consternation of Hungary's middle and upper classes, Kun's government issued a series of decrees virtually nationalizing the entire economy as well as regulating the media and culture. However, the government's failure to distribute land to the peasants proved to be a fatal error; collectivization and attacks on the church alienated the peasantry.

In the end, the Hungarian Soviet Republic was doomed by its isolation. The Bolsheviks in Russia could lend only verbal support. More important, the Allies, fearful of the spread of communism, stood by as Hungary was invaded by its neighbors: first on April 16 by Romanian forces, ten days later by Czechoslovak troops.

Although Hungary's army drove back the Czechoslovaks (while the Romanian advance slowed owing to pressures along Romania's eastern boundaries), shortages brought on by the Allied blockade and discontent among the peasants soon undermined the government's internal support. The fact that Kun and numerous other members of the government were Jews also fed the discontent, especially in the countryside. By June, a virtual state of civil war existed. Counterrevolutionary forces quickly formed including a "National Army" in Szeged, headed by the future Hungarian regent, Admiral Miklós Horthy (1868–1957).

In late July Hungarian troops, having evacuated Slovakia, attacked the Romanian positions along the Tisza River, a move doomed to fail. On July 29, Romanian troops crossed the Tisza approximately sixty miles (one hundred km) from Budapest. On August 1, the council resigned and a new trade union government under Gyula Peidl (1873–1943), head of the typographers' union, was formed. Although the new government dissolved the Red Guard (Communist-led military units), released political prisoners, and restored private property, its fate too was sealed with the occupation of Budapest by Romanian troops on August 3.

In the wake of the collapse of the Republic of Councils, a white terror ensued that saw the execution or imprisonment of numerous members of the government. Estimates of deaths range from 1,500 to 5,000, with another 60,000 imprisoned. Another 100,000 emigrated.

Richard Frucht

Further reading

Hajdú, Tibor and Zsuzsa L. Nagy. "Revolution, Counterrevolution, Consolidation," in Peter F. Sugar, Péter Hanak, and Tibor Frank, eds. *A History of Hungary*. Bloomington, Indiana, 1990.

Mayer, Arno J. *Politics and Diplomacy of Peacemaking: Containment and Counterrevolution at Versailles, 1918–1919*. New York, 1967.

Ormos, Mária. "The Hungarian Soviet Republic and Intervention by the Entente," in Béla K. Király, Peter Pastor, and Ivan Sanders, eds., *War and Society in East Central Europe*, vol. 6, *Essays on World War I: Total War and Peacemaking, a Case Study on Trianon*. New York, 1982.

Sakmyster, Thomas. *Hungary's Admiral on Horseback: Miklós Horthy, 1918–1944*. Boulder, Colorado, 1994.

See also Communist Party of Hungary; Miklós Horthy; Béla Kun; Mihály Károlyi; White Terror

Hungarian War for Independence (1848–49)

Largest and most significant national revolt in the Habsburg lands in 1848–49. When the general revolutionary agitation began in Europe in early 1848, the Kingdom of Hungary had been undergoing a national revival for twenty years. The 1825 restoration of the Hungarian diet coincided with efforts to promote appreciation of Hungarian culture and the use of the Hungarian language for official purposes. Led by Count István Széchenyi (1791–1860), who decried Hungary's backwardness and proposed numerous far-reaching programs for improving economic conditions, this movement won the support of prominent Hungarians. Lajos Kossuth (1802–94) was in substantial agreement with Széchenyi on the need for economic reform but insisted that liberal reforms must also be instituted to counter the detrimental influence of the autocratic Austrian government. The chief outlet for Kossuth's views was *Pesti Hirlap* (*Pest News*), which quickly became the most important newspaper in Hungary.

After events in Italy and France had created turmoil in Vienna sufficient to force the hated Prince Metternich (1773–1859), Austrian chancellor, into exile, Kossuth and others proposed the creation of an autonomous Hungary united with Vienna only in the person of the emperor. Highlights of subsequent legislation included the creation of a two-house parliament, expansion of the franchise, equality of all citizens before the law, and provisions for economic and technological improvements. This series of bills, known as the

April Laws, ushered in a liberal—and legal—revolution in Hungary. Pressured by revolutionary activity in Austria, Emperor Ferdinand (1793–1875) was forced to approve them.

Hungary was now transformed into a constitutional monarchy with Lajos Batthyány (1806–49) as prime minister. Kossuth, minister of finance, called on parliament to raise troops to defend Hungary.

Reaction among non-Hungarians to the April Laws soon complicated relations between the new Hungary and Austria. Autonomous Hungary proposed to erase historic boundaries, make Hungarian (Magyar) the official language of administration, and Hungarians the preeminent group in Hungary. The response was swift and predictable. Romanians protested a possible merger of Hungary with Transylvania. Slovak representatives demanded autonomy for themselves, while Serbs in the Vojvodina rejected Hungarian rule and staged a brief uprising. The Croats, who had experienced their own national ferment in the 1840s, elected Josip Jelačić (1801–59) as leader of their representative body (Sabor). By September 1848, Jelačić led troops into battle on his own initiative against the Hungarian leadership.

Because its members suspected that Vienna was intriguing with the protesters, the Hungarian parliament took a hard line during the summer of 1848. It demurred when Austrian authorities requested assistance in their war with Italian rebels but it later refused to support Austria in its conflict with the Frankfurt Assembly, which had convened to discuss possible German unification. This refusal rankled the Habsburgs because it appeared to be a violation of the Pragmatic Sanction, the eighteenth-century law regarding Habsburg succession, and because fiery rhetoric about the creation of a large Hungarian national army (honvéd) had accompanied it.

In August Batthyány went to Vienna in an attempt to halt the offensive against Hungary. Ferdinand, however, refused to meet with him. In September, after Jelačić and his frontier guard force launched an invasion of Hungary, Kossuth and some members of parliament formed a National Defense Committee to cope with the exigencies of war, which included printing money. Hoping to defuse this explosive situation, Vienna sent Count Francis Lamberg (1791–1848) to attempt negotiations with Jelačić. Shortly after arriving, Lamberg was denounced in the Hungarian radical press

and assassinated. The Habsburgs dissolved the Hungarian parliament on October 3. Jelačić was now appointed commander of Habsburg forces in Hungary.

The legal revolution in Hungary had now become a rebellion. Fresh from his triumph in Bohemia, General Alfred Windischgrätz (1787–1862) and the Habsburg army, which had remained loyal to the emperor throughout the events of 1848, prepared to fight the now rebellious Hungarians. The latter were ready for the Austrians, employing capable officers such as Artur Görgey (1818–1916) and Polish revolutionary veteran Józef Bem (1794–1850) to head their forces. Despite these preliminaries, there still had been no formal rupture between Hungary and Austria. When Ferdinand was forced to abdicate the throne in favor of his young nephew, Franz Joseph (1830–1916), in December, the Hungarian parliament insisted that Ferdinand would remain its sovereign until and unless Franz Joseph accepted the April Laws.

Neither side was able to gain an advantage in the ensuing hostilities during the first months of 1849. In January Habsburg forces inflicted a setback severe enough to force the rebels to abandon Budapest for Debrecen. In March, forces led by Görgey, who would be named commander in chief of the Hungarian army on March 31, counterattacked and pushed Austrian forces back toward the Danube and eventually out of Buda in May. These successes, combined with Franz Joseph's imposition of the highly centralized Stadion Constitution in March, encouraged Kossuth and his compatriots to sever ties with Austria. On April 14, 1849, they proclaimed the independence of Hungary in Debrecen, with Kossuth as its first president.

Independent Hungary's existence was short-lived. Kossuth hoped for foreign intervention, but none was forthcoming. Meanwhile, Franz Joseph turned to Nicholas I of Russia (1796–1855) to assist in annihilating the rebellion. The tsar had good reasons to come to the aid of his fellow monarch. He deplored the widespread successes of the revolutionaries in 1848–49 and appreciated the young emperor's right-mindedness. Nicholas also contemplated the implications of an independent Hungarian state on his Polish provinces. The sight of a victorious General Bem, rallying his oppressed countrymen against Russia, doubtless disturbed the tsar.

In June 1849 Russian troops arrived in Hungary; by August, they were able to inform Franz

Joseph that Hungary lay at his feet. Despite valiant efforts by the Hungarian army, on August 13, 1849, Görgey was forced to surrender at Világos. Several months of reprisals ensued, during which some one hundred prominent Hungarians, including Batthyány, were executed and many more imprisoned. Many others, including Kossuth, went into exile. Vienna now imposed strict control (neoabsolutism) over the empire, which drastically centralized power, thereby severely restricting Hungarian rights.

Although the Habsburg government solved its immediate problem with the rebellious Hungarians in 1849, in so doing it guaranteed itself more serious trouble in the future. Franz Joseph owed his victory to Nicholas, who would call in the debt sooner than later. When Franz Joseph declined to take the Russians' side in the Crimean War (1853–56), dooming St. Petersburg to defeat, he forfeited Russian goodwill. Furthermore, the victory over Hungary meant difficulties for the monarchy in the defense of its realm. When Camilio di Cavour (1810–61), premier of Sardinia, plotted the campaign for Italian unification, he correctly surmised that the Habsburg army included Hungarian troops whose loyalty was questionable. When war with Prussia threatened to decide the future of Germany, Nicholas's successor, Alexander II (1818–81), proclaimed Russia's neutrality. Franz Joseph thus faced the Prussian army without allies, with disastrous results. Before the 1866 war, Otto von Bismarck (1815–98) even planned machinations in Hungary so that Austria would potentially have to face two adversaries simultaneously. The unreconciled Hungarians constituted a fearsome security risk for the emperor. Thus, in many respects, the Hungarian War for Independence, and the Habsburg response to it, cost the monarchy its Italian lands and its leadership in Germany.

Ironically, the war eventually cost the Habsburgs unitary rule in their own state as well. Determined to restore the monarchy's standing as a great power following the disastrous reversals of 1859 and 1866, the emperor and his advisers realized that they would have to begin by reaching an agreement with the Hungarians. The terms of that agreement, the 1867 *Ausgleich* (Compromise), proved similar to the 1848 April Laws, with one notable exception: Austria would thereafter be a dual monarchy: Austria-Hungary.

Brigit Farley

Further reading

Deák, István. *A Lawful Revolution: Louis Kossuth and the Hungarians, 1848–1849*. New York, 1979.
Jelavich, Barbara. *The Habsburg Empire in European Affairs, 1814–1918*. Chicago, 1969.
MacCartney, C.A. *The Habsburg Empire, 1790–1918*. London, 1968.
Palmer, Alan. *Twilight of the Habsburgs: The Life and Times of Emperor Francis Joseph*. New York, 1994.
Sugar, Peter F., Peter Hanak, and Tibor Frank, eds. *A History of Hungary*. Bloomington, Indiana, 1990.

See also Alexander II; *Ausgleich;* Lajos Batthyány; Józef Bem; Otto von Bismarck; Crimean War; Dual Monarchy; Franz Joseph; Artur Görgey; *Honvéd;* Josip Jelačić; Lajos Kossuth; Clemens von Metternich; Neoabsolutism; Nicholas I; Revolutions of 1848; Sabor; István Széchenyi; Alfred Windischgrätz

Hungary (Geography)

Hungary is a small (35,919 square miles [93,030 sq km]) kidney-shaped, landlocked East Central European country surrounded by Austria, Slovakia, Ukraine, Romania, Serbia, Croatia, and Slovenia. Given its location in the Danubian, or Pannonian, basin, two-thirds of the country is flat plain lying below 650 feet (200 m) in elevation. A broad expanse of the southeast is covered by the Great Hungarian Plain (*Nagy Alföld*), while the Little Plain (*Kis Alföld*) occupies the northwest corner. An axis of low mountains (980–2,300 feet [300–700 m]) runs northeast-southwest from the Börzsöny, Mátra, and Bükk ranges along the northern border, into the Bakony and Vértes ranges of central Hungary, to the Mecsek range in the south-central area. The north-south flowing Danube River, after forming part of the northern border with Slovakia, splits the country into halves: the western Trans-Danubia, and the eastern plains, which in turn are drained by the Tisza River. Lake Balaton (230 sq mi [590 sq km]), located in west-central Hungary, is the largest lake in Central Europe and a major tourist site.

Hungary's midlatitude location (46°–48° north latitude) ensures a temperate climate. However, Mediterranean air masses frequently push summer temperatures well into the 90° F (middle 30° C) range, while continental air masses

H occasionally drop winter temperatures well below the freezing mark. Precipitation varies greatly from year to year, though on average around 20 inches (50 cm) falls on the Great Hungarian Plain while over 24 inches (60 cm) is received in the northern mountains, usually as snow in winter.

Hungary's 1990 population stood at 10,375,000, down from a 1980 total of 10.7 million. Since then, births per 1,000 population have dropped from 13.9 to 11.4, while deaths per 1,000 have risen from 13.6 to 14.6, resulting in natural decrease and aging of the populace. The country is overwhelmingly ethnic Hungarian (96 percent Magyar), and is 62 percent Roman Catholic and 23 percent Protestant.

Budapest, with a 1990 population of 2,016,774, is the capital and by far the largest city in Hungary; until recently, it was also the largest city in Eastern Europe. The rest of the settlement system comprises five regional centers—Debrecen, Miskolc, Szeged, Pécs, and Győr—plus another 161 recognized urban places. Hungary's population in 1990 was 62 percent urban.

Hungary's 1990 employment structure was composed of 10 percent primary employment, 35 percent secondary, and 54 percent tertiary. The generally fertile soil, especially on the Great Plain, coupled with the long growing season, allows for good yields of wheat, corn, barley, and vegetables. Although relatively resource poor, the country has some deposits of bauxite, coal, manganese, oil, and natural gas. Manufacturing is based on chemicals, metallurgy, textiles, instruments, engineering, and food processing. Per capita gross domestic product is approximately U.S. $6,100. Pollution of air, water, and soil is a major problem throughout Hungary, particularly in the predominantly industrial areas in the north.

Darrick Danta

Further reading

Bateman, Graham and Victoria Egan. *The Encyclopedia of World Geography.* New York, 1993.

Bernát, Tivadar, ed. *An Economic Geography of Hungary.* Budapest, 1985.

Enyedi, György. *Hungary: An Economic Geography.* Boulder, Colorado, 1976.

Magyar Statisztikai Évkönyv—Statistical Yearbook of Hungary 1993. Budapest, 1994.

Webster's New Geographical Dictionary. Springfield, Massachusetts, 1984.

See also Budapest; Debrecen; Great Hungarian Plain; Győr; Lake Balaton; Pécs; Tisza River

Hungary (History)

Whatever the period of Hungarian history, it is important to bear in mind that the histories of individual nations, much as centuries or "periods," are largely artificial constructs that may hinder objective understanding and reassessment. The historian, to paraphrase French philosopher Voltaire (1694–1778), should be of no religion, no epoch, and no nation, even when writing national history.

The Habsburg monarchy (which designated itself as the Austrian Empire in 1804, in emulation of Napoléon's France), comprised more than just one or two nations. This multinational empire included a large, likewise multinational unit referred to as the Kingdom of Hungary, which, at the beginning of the nineteenth century, could lay claim to a historic existence of nine hundred years. This kingdom encompassed, around 1800, all of what is now Hungary, Slovakia, Croatia, a corner of Ukraine (referred to as Carpatho-Ukraine or Ruthenia), parts of Romania (mainly Transylvania), and parts of Yugoslavia (mainly the Banat and Vojvodina). In many respects the interplay between those national groups (Magyars [as Hungarians refer to themselves], Slovaks, Croats, Romanians, Serbs, and others), the rising tide of nationalism, and the nature of the monarchy itself dominated and determined the course of Hungarian history in the nineteenth century.

The histories of the nations and peoples of Hungary—as well as the entire Danube (Carpathian) basin—are in fact inextricably interwoven. One has to look no further than their national heroes, who are often symbols to two or more nations. The Croatian hero of the struggle against the Ottoman Turks was Nikola Subić Zrinski (c. 1508–66), who, to Hungarians, is known as the Hungarian hero, Miklós Zrinyi, and whose great-grandson of the same name (1620–64) was to become a celebrated poet in Hungarian. The foremost Romanian hero in the struggle against the Turks was Iancu of Hunedoara, known to Hungarians as their own János Hunyadi (c. 1407–56). The leader and martyr of the great peasant uprising of 1514 was the Szekely-Hungarian György Dózsa (c. 1472–1514), claimed by Romanians (especially during the "socialist" period) as their own

Gheorghe Doja. Indeed, to this day many Hungarians may be surprised to learn that these figures, and others equally prominent, are heroes to be shared.

Hungary before the Nineteenth Century

According to a series of recent sociological surveys, Hungarian history, since its beginnings late in the ninth century, has had a deep impact on the consciousness and attitudes of those who consider themselves Hungarian. They tend to perceive themselves as belonging to a small nation, isolated among strangers or enemies, a nation that functions as the "easternmost bastion of Western civilization"; they also tend to exhibit feelings of self-pity and pride, of fatalism derived from a sense of tragic destiny.

The course of early Hungarian history may or may not validate such feelings. While the millennium of the existence of Hungary as a nation was celebrated in 1896 (and the "millecentenary" in 1996), all that can be said with assurance is that the Hungarian tribes, originating somewhere beyond the Ural Mountains of Russia, settled in the fertile Hungarian plains before the end of the ninth century, under the leadership of Árpád (d. 907). Since the plains were so fertile, it must be taken for granted that they were already inhabited by Slavs, Avars, and others. Hence, the Hungarian ethnic group absorbed these populations, as it was to absorb waves of settlers in subsequent centuries.

The plains may not have been their final destination; during the summers at least, the cavalry of the Hungarians forayed into western regions of Europe as far as the Pyrénées, until they were decisively defeated at Augsburg in 955 by troops under the command of German Emperor Otto I (912–973). Forced to settle, they finally received their reward; around Christmastime in the year 1000, Hungarian ruler Vajk donned a crown sent by the pope, accepted the Christian religion on behalf of himself and his people, and became István (Stephen) I (c. 975–1038). István, eventually Saint Stephen, was to become a powerful symbol, as was the crown with its bent cross (apparently dropped by a nervous ruler), which, in the eyes of Hungarians, assumed a mystical existence, beyond that of a mere object. Hungary itself became the "lands of the Crown of Saint Stephen."

Stephen was able to consolidate his rule in wars against foreign and internal adversaries—the two not easily distinguishable. The Árpád dynasty, as it was called, acquired international prestige; its female progeny were considered a desirable match, and Hungarian princesses married rulers across Europe and beyond.

In spite of the dynastic struggles and rebellions, the kingdom evolved into a centralized, near-absolute monarchy and expanded at least as far as the watershed of the Carpathian Mountains, thanks in part to its economic underpinnings, especially its mineral resources, including gold. Except for West Africa, Transylvania produced more gold than any other region of the globe.

The Crusades, however, proved to be a disaster for the Kingdom of Hungary. They enticed the Hungarian rulers away from their kingdom; worse, the country became a transit zone for crusading armies. The Golden Bull of 1222 (which some Hungarian historians like to compare to the British Magna Carta adopted a few years earlier) did indeed set limits on the power of the rulers and marked the ascendance of the aristocracy and of the feudal system.

The Mongol (Tatar) invasion in 1241–42 may be an indication of the reputation for wealth of the kingdom, as Hungary became its westernmost victim. The Mongols, led by a grandson of Genghis Khan (c. 1167–1227), did not come to stay, only to sack or destroy. Almost half of all settlements in the kingdom were burnt to the ground. Although the destruction left a deep mark on Hungarian consciousness, the kingdom recovered relatively quickly.

The fourteenth century was a period of further Hungarian expansion. Hungarian prestige is illustrated by the "Visegrád" agreement of 1335—a kind of economic summit with the participation of foreign rulers and delegations. The ruling house was the Anjou dynasty, signaling a Western orientation. For a while, Poland became part of their domain.

In 1453 the final remnant of the Byzantine Empire, Constantinople, was captured by the Ottoman Turks. Having gained a foothold in Europe, the Turks sought to penetrate the Continent. Although the main thrust of Turkish economic and military interests was in Asia and Africa, expedition after expedition was launched up the Balkan Peninsula with mixed results.

In 1526, however, Hungarian forces were annihilated by the Turks at Mohács, in southern Hungary. The Hungarians failed largely because the ruler and the ruling class had been unable and

H unwilling to resolve internal social conflicts. By far the most significant of these conflicts was the one pitting serfs against lords. There had been peasant uprisings in Hungary as elsewhere, the best known of these being the one led by György Dózsa, a petty noble of Transylvania, in 1514. Again, as elsewhere, the serfs were defeated and subjected to atrocious reprisals. At the same time, the nobility, through the work of the jurist István Verböczi (1458–1542), declared itself the "Hungarian nation." It was a nation of "estates" (much as in France), among whom the trend, however, was rather the opposite of that obtained in Western Europe, for feudal privilege was reinforced. The gap between haves and have-nots became an abyss, and the peasantry no longer felt a vested interest in "saving" the country.

The battle of Mohács, and the subsequent (1541) capture of the seat of the Hungarian kingdom, the town of Buda, introduced a century and a half of Ottoman rule. The long occupation left surprisingly little imprint on Hungarian culture and society. The population was not converted to Islam, thus enabling the Turkish overlords to exploit the country more fully. If anything, one may speak of the Hungarian impact on the Ottoman Empire, since the Turkish elite military force were the Janissaries, who had been kidnapped from Christian lands at a tender age; Egypt itself was ruled by Mamlukes, or former slaves. Traces of Hungarian folk art can be detected as far as the land of the Nubians, in southern Egypt and northern Sudan.

Turkish rule produced little positive in Hungary. A Hungarian Renaissance on the verge of flowering at the court of King Mátyás (1440–90) was nipped in the bud by the Turkish occupation. During much of the sixteenth and seventeenth centuries, Hungary remained cut off from Western and Central Europe. There was no intellectual ferment, no economic development, and little population growth.

Turkish rule did not cover all of Hungary. Although required to pay tribute, Transylvania enjoyed autonomy, while an arc of territory in the west and north fell under Habsburg and Austrian sway.

Although Buda was recaptured by a Christian alliance in 1686, for many Hungarians the struggle continued. The Protestant rulers of Transylvania had often sided with the Turks against the Catholic Habsburgs. As the Habsburgs were able to extend their control at the expense of the Ottoman Empire, the Protestants of Transylvania became Hungarian freedom fighters, known in Hungarian history as the *"kurucz,"* a term of uncertain origin. Hungarian patriotism was particularly alive in the Protestant and religiously mixed areas, that is, in Transylvania and eastern Hungary. In fact, Calvinism was sometimes referred to as the Hungarian creed.

Between 1703 and 1711, the most celebrated leader, albeit a Catholic, of the patriot *kurucz* forces was the prince of Transylvania, Ferenc II Rákoczi (1676–1735). As always, the patriotic movement had economic roots; Hungarian ores, especially gold and silver bullion, depreciated as a result of the inflation caused by the sudden influx of silver and gold from the Western Hemisphere. The decrease in the value of production of precious metals was compensated, to some extent, by the export of Tokaj wine produced in northeastern Hungary—"the king of wines, the wine of kings."

Although backed by the underprivileged masses, Rákoczi's cause was doomed to defeat once international, anti-Habsburg support was withheld. In 1717 Rákoczi was compelled to escape and settle in the Ottoman lands, where the sultan awarded him a small pension. Habsburg domination of Hungary was now uncontested.

From 1740 until 1780, Empress Maria Theresa (1717–80) ruled Hungary by confirming the social status quo. She had little choice in the matter, for she owed her throne partly to the Hungarian nobility. Indeed, the Hungarian diet, consisting of the nobility, had committed itself to accepting her eventual accession to the throne by approving the Pragmatic Sanction in 1722. On the one hand, serfdom was declared everlasting while, on the other, the empress explicitly recognized the privileges of the nobility, who continued to defend her empire. The second half of the seventeenth century was relatively free of conflict for Hungarians.

Ironically, it was the enlightened absolutism of her son Joseph II (1741–90) that antagonized certain strata of the Hungarian nobility, often members of Maria Theresa's Hungarian Guard, mainly because of its efforts to create a centralized bureaucracy that insisted on German as the official language for the sake of greater efficiency in administration. Joseph's reign in fact rekindled anti-Habsburg sentiment in Hungary.

The Era of National Awakening: The Age of Reform

Throughout much of Central Europe during the past two centuries, the determining factor in the history of individual nations and groups—with the possible exception of Jews and Gypsies—has been the language spoken, rather than the geographic origins of one's ancestors. The vernacular languages were endowed with a legitimate form—that is, a grammar—by a few literary pioneers. Thus it becomes understandable that in all areas of East Central Europe, including Hungary, nationalism was to a large extent simply a by-product of the literature of the romantic period.

It has also been argued that the ethnic groups of the lands that the Kingdom of Hungary comprised "awoke" in response to, or in reaction against, Hungarian nationalism. There were additional factors as well, such as modernization and the evolution of an indigenous middle class, or the stimulus of Pan-Slavism from outside the kingdom. Historicism contributed to the process. Some peoples of the empire—Poles, Czechs, Serbians, and Hungarians—could seek inspiration and enthusiasm from periods of extended national existence, of medieval glory. Spokespersons for other nations, including Slovaks, Slovenes, and even Romanians, came up with often fanciful yet equally powerful constructs, such as the unbroken "Daco-Romanian" tradition, or the existence of a Greater Moravian Empire.

Although education remained a privilege separating some social classes, literacy spread throughout the kingdom. During the eighteenth century, Maria Theresa decreed that there be a school in every village. If there was a school, it is safe to assume it attracted pupils, and those pupils had to learn to read in the vernacular. Hence romantic literature, the literature of nationalism, was never the exclusive, private property of the nobility or the gentry in Hungary.

According to statistics from 1839, the Kingdom of Hungary (excluding Transylvania) had a population of 11,187,288. The census of 1850–51 indicates that the population of Transylvania was around 2,070,000 (although these figures are open to question). Hungarians made up 37 percent of the total population of the Kingdom of Hungary (26 percent in Transylvania)—less than half the population of the entire kingdom. Although there were over twice as many Hungarians as any other nationality, the majority of the kingdom's population was non-Hungarian. They too were prone to national fermentations.

The first half of the nineteenth century saw the emergence of the Romanian principalities of Moldavia and Wallachia from Ottoman and Greek Phanariot domination, and from feudal relations as well. Fearing any manifestations of Romanian nationalism within Transylvania—the Romanians forming the second-largest group within the Kingdom of Hungary (17 percent) and the majority in Transylvania—Habsburg authorities intervened to ban the formation of a "Great Romanian Philosophical Society" in 1795. Nevertheless, Romanian scholars, mainly from Transylvania, published works on the Daco-Roman tradition, that is, the Latin, or Roman, roots of Romanian language and culture. A Romanian grammar was published in 1828 by yet another Transylvanian (Ion Heliade Rădulescu [1802–72]) and, ten years later, in 1838, George Barițiu (1812–93) launched a Romanian-language newspaper, *Gazeta de Transylvania* (*Transylvanian Gazette*), in Brașov.

Meanwhile, the Slovaks, who occupied the northern counties of the kingdom (termed by Hungarians the "Upper Region" rather than "Slovakia"), made up 13.1 percent of the total population in 1839. Like other ethnic groups within the kingdom, they had not objected to surrendering occasionally the use of their mother tongue, so long as it was to some "neutral" lingua franca such as Latin, or even German. The imposition of Hungarian as the official language in 1840, however, would elicit resentment and create practical difficulties for Slovaks and all other nationalities. The resentment was all the deeper as Slovak and Czech had already become not only a written language but one with a well-defined grammar and syntax, as early as the *Grammatica slavica* (*Slav Grammar Book*), compiled by Antonín Bernolak (1762–1813) in the late eighteenth century, albeit the standard was closer to Czech than to Slovak. In fact, the best-known Slovak poet, Ján Kollár (1793–1852), wrote in Czech. Moreover, in the first half of the nineteenth century Ľudovít Štúr (1815–56) consciously attempted to unite all Slovaks, across religious lines, against the program of Magyarization. Not surprisingly therefore, during the Hungarian War of Independence in 1848–49, there arose demands for Slovak nationhood and even an uprising against Hungarian domination.

H The people of Croatia had been bound to the Kingdom of Hungary since 1102, a relationship confirmed by Maria Theresa in 1779. Even though Croatians are seldom even mentioned in the context of the history of the Hungarians, it is not possible to excise their history entirely from the history of other nations in this multinational kingdom. A large part of the country, about one-half of present-day Croatia, was called the Military Frontier, the function of which was akin to that of medieval counties, that is, to defend the hinterland—Hungary, Austria, and Central Europe in general—from the Ottoman Turks. The total population of the frontier in 1815 stood at 941,000, overwhelmingly peasants, 136,000 of whom were liable for military service. Once the Ottoman danger subsided, these soldiers were used as an elite force to fight in foreign lands on behalf of the Habsburgs. A substantial portion of the Croatian nobility lent the remainder of the Hungarian nobility a helping hand in their resistance to the centralizing absolutist tendencies under Joseph II.

As in the case of the Slovak intellectuals, the national awakening of the Croats was prompted in 1830 not by industrialization or political modernization as in the West but by the imposition of the Hungarian language in the administration of the land. In that year, Ljudevit Gaj (1809–72), influenced by Pan-Slavism emanating from outside the kingdom, primarily from Bohemia and Serbia, published an essay on "The Elements of Croato-Slavonic Orthography"—creating a standardized spelling and grammar. The so-called Illyrian Movement, to unite South Slavs, was spearheaded by Gaj and other writers in 1835.

It came as no surprise therefore that in 1848 the Croatian elites, as well as a large segment of the general population, felt inclined to fight on the side of Austria against the Hungarian freedom fighters. Even so, the emperor had no mind to reward the Croatians for their loyalty in his war against the Hungarian rebels of 1848–49. On the contrary, the Austro-Russian victory over the Hungarians would result in nine years of repression against any manifestation of Croatian nationalism. In 1868, the year after the *Ausgleich* (Compromise) between Austria and Hungary, the Hungarian government in turn arranged a compromise settlement with Croatia. This autonomy, however, did little to defuse the nationalist ardor of Croatian writers and of the intelligentsia, especially in the period between 1883 and 1903, when the person appointed as *ban* (governor) of Croatia was a Hungarian nationalist, Count Khuen-Héderváry (1849–1918).

While the national awakening of the ethnic groups within Hungary occurred largely in reaction to Hungarian domination, the national consciousness of many Hungarians awakened in reaction to German-Austrian domination. At the conclusion of the Napoleonic Wars in 1815, when the peacemakers assembled in Vienna, few Hungarians cared. For some, like János Bacsányi (1763–1845), who spent many years in jail, the victory of the allies was unfortunate. During Napoléon's invasion of Hungary, Bacsányi had supported the French emperor, who, to him, still represented the ideals of the French Revolution. Much of the nobility, however, had forgotten that Austrian absolutism tried to deprive them of their language and political autonomy. They resented Napoléon (1769–1821), much as they had resented Joseph II, both for being a despot and for being enlightened; as such, in 1809 they fought and lost the battle of Győr against the French.

The Hungarian nobility had their own agenda, regarding themselves as *the* "nation." This was certainly a presumption, but not as outlandish as it might appear on the surface, since the nobility amounted to about 5 percent of the total population; only the Polish *szlachta* had been anything comparable in numbers and power. Nevertheless, it would be a mistake to assume that the nobility was united in defending its class interests, or even had a clear picture of what those interests were. To be sure, the politicians of the "Age of Reform" were generally more interested in reasserting their privileges vis-à-vis the crown than in bringing about social justice.

The number of "common nobles" was estimated at 618,000 in 1839. About one-fifth of them, the most well-to-do (including the few "magnates"), became referred to as the "gentry" class—a somewhat inappropriate application of the English term—while the remaining nobility, albeit titled and enjoying a few privileges, was economically and functionally often indistinguishable from the peasantry. The aristocracy, or higher nobility, was on the whole a cosmopolitan group, some of whom, gravitating around the court in Vienna, seldom had occasion to speak Hungarian; some, in fact, were not even familiar with the language.

In the first half of the nineteenth century the kingdom included half a million townspeople, burghers or bourgeois, as residents of sixty-one chartered royal towns; many of them spoke German as their mother tongue. This was true even of the largest town, Pest—hardly a city as yet. At the beginning of the century, some towns still banned Hungarians, Slovaks, or Romanians from settling in their midst; but the ethnic makeup of the population of the towns, including Pest, was soon to shift dramatically. By 1900, Pest had become part of Budapest, a metropolis of nearly one million, populated by Hungarian speakers (as were most towns in the kingdom).

The bulk of the population in nineteenth-century Hungary—as in the rest of the world—were peasants. The peasantry suffered from exploitation and various forms and degrees of discrimination, no matter what language they spoke. In Transylvania, for example, before emancipation, the serfs and cotters made up 54 percent of the population, as opposed to 31 percent "free peasants." Many of those free peasants were to swell the ranks of the agrarian proletariat; between the mid-nineteenth and the mid-twentieth centuries, their condition was seldom or hardly relieved by halfhearted attempts at land reform.

After the Napoleonic Wars, the Habsburg ruler attempted to restore the status quo ante bellum, a false sense of prewar normalcy in which the crown would dominate all. Forced by financial exigencies, in 1825 the ruler convoked the Hungarian diet, after thirteen years of absolute rule. Traditionally the diets met in Pozsony (Slovak, Bratislava), in the northeastern corner of the Kingdom of Hungary, not far from Vienna, for that area, unlike Buda or Visegrád, had never been under Turkish occupation.

The diet assembled in an atmosphere imbued with romanticism, which swept across Hungarian intellectual life as it had elsewhere in Europe. That movement would in fact soon galvanize Hungarian political and cultural life.

Ferenc Kazinczy (1759–1831) and other Hungarian writers discovered their own language and elaborated grammatical rules, even before the Slovaks, Serbs, or Romanians; and this language, the rules notwithstanding, proved to be flexible and expressive as few others. As statesman István Széchenyi (1791–1860) wrote, "The nation lives in its language." Consequently, from that period on, Hungarian poets, and poetry in Hungarian translation for that matter, became most effective in conveying ideas and emotions. As János Bac-

sányi wrote of the role of the poet: "Like a burning torch that blazes in the darkness, / And, itself consuming, casts a light for others." Indeed, the poet was more than a poet—the symbol and manifestation of the national spirit.

The transformation of pluralistic Hungarian patriotism into an exclusive Hungarian nationalism of the intelligentsia was probably hastened by the notion propounded by Johann Gottfried Herder (1744–1803), the German romantic who was an advocate for many different cultures but who predicted that Hungarians were doomed to be absorbed by their neighbors. Partly in response to this prophecy of doom, county and national leaders passed a series of measures in the 1830s imposing Hungarian as the new official language. While the ethnic groups may have had little problem with German or Latin as the official language—for they felt equal in their handicap—the imposition of Hungarian evidently gave a clear advantage to those who could speak it, especially to those who spoke it as their mother tongue, all the more so as Hungarian syntax and grammar are particularly daunting.

Henceforth literary production and national politics became fused. Poets sat or even led in the diet, while romantic love often became a secondary concern in their work. Kazinczy and others spent long terms in jail, a good measure of what the Austrian authorities perceived as a threat. Ferenc Kölcsey (1790–1838) gave Hungarians an anthem, in addition to other fine poetry. Mihály Vörösmarty (1800–1855) wrote fine drama in verse; but in what became his most popular poem ("Szozat" [Pronouncement]), he wrote: "There is no place for you anywhere on earth. Be you blessed or damned by fate, here must you live and here must you die!" But it was the young Sándor Petőfi (1823–49) who became not only the epitome of the romantic poet but, more important, a poet of the people, by writing in a manner all Hungarian speakers could understand.

Intellectual ferment was not confined to poetry. Széchenyi enhanced his reputation by publishing essays, including "Hitel" (Credit, 1830), which deplored the lack of credit available to the Hungarian farmer. Széchenyi was a pioneer in addressing the need for economic changes in the Hungarian lands (even if the bulk of the population remained untouched in the first half of the century by technological modernization). An aristocrat of means, Széchenyi undertook to

H modernize Hungary almost single-handedly, with marked success; he navigated up and down the Danube eight times, scanning the river with the eye of an engineer. Canals were constructed and rivers rendered navigable. In addition to improving navigation, he promoted the construction of a permanent bridge linking Buda and Pest, contributing to the evolution of these two cities as the national center, and he founded a National Academy of Science.

Clearly, a modern Hungarian consciousness had been born, based on cultural self-identity. That consciousness would soon dominate the country's political landscape. It was the contrasting style and ideas, between Széchenyi (and his emphasis on change within the Habsburg system) and the "radicals," especially the fiery Lajos Kossuth (1802–94), that would come to mark the decade of the 1840s.

In 1841 Kossuth, fresh out of jail for political activities, was ready to attack both foreign domination and the privileges of the aristocracy in the columns of the most important Hungarian newspaper of the day, *Pesti Hirlap* (*Pest News*). Aristocratic privileges and economic discussions and developments were about to give way to matters less tangible but certainly more volatile: nationalist yearnings.

War of Independence, 1848–49, and Its Aftermath

In 1848 a wave of revolutionary activity swept across Europe. On March 13, demonstrations took place in Vienna, prompted not only by the revolutionary events in France but also by a speech Kossuth delivered at the diet in Pozsony a few days earlier regarding the need for a constitution. Two days later, there were rallies in Pest. In Hungary, March 15 has become ever since a day for celebrations and protests (even though the Hungarian national holiday is August 20, St. Stephen's Day). In Paris and Vienna, workers and others were seeking social justice; in most other places, including Hungary, while social reforms were also on the agenda, the revolutions assumed the character of a liberation struggle, an anticolonial conflict, led by nationalist forces.

The radical youth of Pest rallied around the poet Sándor Petőfi. Already on March 11, they formulated their demands in twelve points, beginning with freedom of the press, annual parliaments to be held in Pest (instead of Pozsony), equal rights before the law, the end of serfdom, and, as the last point, the union of Hungary and Transylvania. The twelve points were rephrased in a proclamation issued on March 15. On this occasion, Petőfi recited a stirring poem, "National Song," from the steps of the National Museum in Pest; the refrain "the time has come, now or never/until now we were slaves" hit home. Crowds rallied around him on that day in increasing numbers, including most adult males in the city.

As the protagonists of the age of reform either dropped out, like the conservative Széchenyi, or became revolutionaries, like Kossuth, the Habsburg ruler, Ferdinand (1793–1875), gave in, perhaps too readily, to the demands of the radicals in Vienna and in Hungary. He granted extensive powers to a Hungarian government, as well as meeting at least some of the twelve demands. After three hundred years of subjection to Habsburg and Austrian domination, Hungary was granted substantial autonomy. Moreover, the emperor extended Hungarian jurisdiction to Transylvania and to areas between Hungary and Transylvania, known as "the Part."

Easily the most significant achievement of the movement of 1848 was the abolition of serfdom, promulgated in March; it was an altruistic undertaking, since the ranks of the Opposition Party, now in control, included serf-owning landholders. Because the cause of national rights was their cause, they (not unlike the French bourgeoisie in the midst of the revolution of 1789) were willing to grant the peasants far-reaching concessions to secure their support. The tragic flaw—or, as members of other nationalities might put it, the ignominy—of the Hungarian struggle for liberation was that it seemed exclusively for the benefit of Hungarians. Since it was primarily a nationalist struggle in a multinational state, contradictions were bound to arise.

The newly adopted laws (the April Laws) reaffirmed the special rights enjoyed by Hungarian speakers. Only a Hungarian speaker could be elected to parliament. Except in the case of Croatia, even the county assemblies were required to conduct their debates in the Hungarian language, regardless of the makeup of the population or of their representatives.

The attempts to rally other ethnic groups were too little and came too late. In any case, the new *ban* of Croatia, Baron Josip Jelačić (1801–59), would not have been swayed by Hungarian concessions, since he was loyal to the emperor, whose advisers were beginning to realize that Ferdinand had given in too quickly to the demands of the radicals. Jelačić appealed to the national feelings of the Croatian population and was able to muster a sizable military force to cross the Mura and Drava Rivers and march almost to Buda, before his troops were turned back.

Overall, the April Laws promulgated by the emperor, sometimes described as a Hungarian constitution, were progressive and satisfactory to the new leaders of Hungary, who had actually drafted them. Relations with Austria gradually deteriorated, however, reaching a breaking point in September. Among the relevant factors in the breakdown in relations was the armed revolt of the Serbs in southern Hungary, followed by the Croatian attack, both of which were blamed by Hungarians on Austrian manipulation. Hungarian discussion of the possibility of abolishing the monarchy and the withdrawal of conservative politicians from the Hungarian government or from the ranks of its sympathizers did not help matters. The king in turn withdrew his support from Lajos Batthyány (1806–49) and appointed a loyal officer, Count Franz Lamberg (1791–1848), as commander in chief of all troops in Hungary; the next day, Lamberg was lynched by a mob in Pest (and soon afterward the Austrian minister of war, General Theodor Latour [1780–1848], suffered the same fate in Vienna). As the crisis escalated, the ruler dismissed the Hungarian parliament and government. The first armed confrontation between Austrian troops and Hungarian militia occurred at Schwechat (the site of Vienna's present-day airport) late in October. The war was on.

Except for Croatia, Kossuth and Count Batthyány, the head of the new government, refused to recognize even the existence of nationalities other than Hungarians. Kossuth met the rather moderate and diplomatic demands of a Serbian delegation visiting him in Pozsony to their satisfaction, until the subject of a Serbian "nation" came up, at which point Kossuth shifted from diplomacy to confrontation: "I will never, but never recognize any nation other than the Hungarian under the holy Hungarian crown. There may be people and ethnic groups that speak different languages, but there is but one nation here!"

While the emancipation of the serfs and other progressive measures should have been of equal benefit to the masses of non-Hungarians, the government hedged on implementation; the majority of the peasants, Hungarian and non-Hungarian alike, former serfs or simply the agricultural proletariat, had been and remained landless; as in Russia or the United States twenty years later, this act meant freedom without land, the freedom to go hungry. Since the authorities, not to mention the landowners, were often dragging their feet in carrying out emancipation and a large fraction of the peasantry saw no improvement in their lot, peasants revolted at a hundred spots around the country, Hungarians arm-in-arm with non-Hungarians.

While the Hungarian government in Pest responded slowly, and not always effectively, to pacify the impatient peasants, the leaders of various ethnic groups stepped in to fill the vacuum. Even those Slovak leaders who had little interest in social reform soon realized that reform, or promises of reform, was the best means to their end; they had to rally peasants to the national (ethnic) cause.

In Transylvania, Simion Bărnuțiu (1808–64) called on the Romanians of Transylvania to be recognized as a political nation, with their own national assembly. The movement gained momentum when the Habsburg ruler approved the annexation (or, in Hungarian eyes, reannexation) of Transylvania to Hungary in April 1848; for Romanians, the revolution was now no longer exclusively a movement of the bourgeoisie or of intellectuals. Although the leaders of the Romanians of Transylvania did attempt to negotiate, both with the ruler in Vienna and with the Transylvanian diet in Kolozsvár (Romanian, Cluj)—which was dominated by Hungarians—a Romanian national guard was being formed.

While the Ottoman and Russian Empires intervened to put down social revolt in the Romanian Principalities, the Romanian leaders in Transylvania had better luck. A Romanian National Committee was organized in the fall. On December 16, 1848, a "National Assembly" of Romanians adopted a "national petition" in Sibiu (Hungarian, Nagyszeben), which, among other accomplishments, set up a land commission to examine conflicts between peasants and noble landowners. Romanian peasants were emancipated along with everyone else, but emancipation was not followed by land reform.

During the 1848–49 fight for freedom, some Romanians of Transylvania—no longer merely the intelligentsia—gained a consciousness of their

Hnational identity, of their distinctive culture. In May 1848, at a mass rally at Blaj (Balázsfalva), a "National Petition" was drafted calling for equal rights for the Romanian nation and the use of the Romanian language in administration and legislation. Romanians, with weapons in hand, now found themselves opposing the Hungarian freedom fighters.

The Hungarian forces, led by Polish general József Bem (1794–1850), pushed out the Austrians and their Romanian allies from Sibiu and most of Transylvania, although Romanian forces under Avram Iancu (1824–72) continued to resist in the Bihar (Apuseni) Mountains. On the other hand, a number of Romanian leaders, including Nicolae Bălcescu (1819–52), were willing to negotiate and find a common cause with Kossuth; on July 2, 1849, a draft of peace was signed by Kossuth, Bălcescu, and Cezar Bolliac (1817–81), granting Romanians the right to use their mother tongue in education and administration, while the Romanian side pledged itself to help defend Hungarian independence. It was too late for both Hungarians and Romanians, however; Russian forces marched into Transylvania and the Banat, and soon there was no Hungarian independence and no Romanian rights left to defend.

In late 1848, after a hesitant and ill-fated expedition to capture Vienna, Hungarian forces retreated to Buda. They were defeated near Buda on December 30, 1848, forcing the government to relocate in Debrecen, in eastern Hungary.

Henceforth, the Hungarian war effort was organized by Kossuth and General Artur Görgey (1818–1916). Initially at least they were successful. By April 1849, the Hungarian army (*honvéd*), numbering some 170,000 effectives, was strong enough to recapture most of the country. Rather than take advantage of the favorable military position to negotiate, however, Kossuth and the Hungarian government pressed their luck. They issued a declaration of independence, formally severing all constitutional ties with Austria. The young Austrian ruler, Franz Joseph (1830–1916), who had replaced the incompetent Ferdinand, appealed to Russia's Nicholas I (1796–1855), who, in the spirit of the Holy Alliance of 1815, had already offered to help. Russian and Austrian forces administered the Hungarians a series of defeats, leading to the surrender of August 13, 1849, at Világos, near Arad. It was at this battle that the twenty-eight-year-old Petőfi lost his life, under circumstances

he had predicted, only to be reborn as a symbol of romantic nationalism. A few days later, Kossuth and some Hungarian and Polish troops crossed the border to seek refuge within the Ottoman Empire.

Although Kossuth in exile became a living symbol of freedom, honored by the Congress of the United States and much of the rest of the world, and while some forts continued to hold out against Austrian forces, August 1849 marked the end of the Hungarian War for Independence—the longest military episode in the revolutionary "spring of nations" that had reached across Europe in 1848.

The defeat of the freedom fighters led to massive repression: over a hundred death sentences, including that of the Hungarian generals, who would now be revered by Hungarian patriots as the "13 martyrs of Arad." Among the victims was the moderate Count Batthyány, Hungary's first prime minister. Count Széchenyi, who took no part in the action, went mad.

In the eyes of the court, the Hungarians had forfeited their historic rights, and direct rule from Vienna was in order. Croatia and Transylvania were detached, but that did not mean they were administered more liberally, or that those Croatians and Romanians who had fought against the Hungarians were rewarded for their loyalty.

Nevertheless, the period of neoabsolutism, also known as the "Bach system" (named for Alexander Bach [1813–93], who masterminded the firm rule from Vienna), became something few Hungarians could accept. For one thing, the execution of thirteen Hungarian generals at Arad (in spite of the tsar's intervention on their behalf) and of the mild-mannered Count Batthyány, would not soon be forgotten. The name of the Austrian general who decreed the bloodbath in Hungary, Julius Haynau (1786–1853), was pronounced as "hyena." Outsiders (non-Hungarians) were now appointed to run the country, and Hungarian patriots were only too willing to relinquish their posts, even at the cost of being deprived of income. Others, including the nobility who had stood on the sidelines during the liberation struggle, adopted passive resistance to the absolutist regime within Hungary, while Kossuth and other exiles were drumming up international sympathy for the lost cause.

Although there was no Hungarian government and no self-government even at the county or municipal level, the major achievements of the revolution were not contested. The peasants remained free, all citizens remained equal before the law, and taxation became progressive. There was also notable economic progress. The railroad network expanded, and the food-processing industry got a boost—especially the construction of flour mills, fourteen of them in Pest alone.

Hungary under the Dual Monarchy (1867–1914)

It is an article of faith among historians of East Central Europe that one outcome of the war Austria lost to Prussia in 1866 was the *Ausgleich* (Compromise) with Hungary. The Austrian ruler needed subjects, and they might as well be to his east, since areas to the west or north were now blocked by the might of Prussia. Ferenc Deák (1803–76) and other Hungarian personalities who had the ear of the ruler suggested an honorable compromise, which became known by its German name as the *Ausgleich.* According to its terms, only foreign affairs, the military, and finances were to be conducted in common, under joint ministries; Hungary was to bear 30 percent of common expenses. All other matters were to be left in the hands of Austrian and Hungarian ministers, respectively. The emperor of Austria was now crowned king of Hungary. Henceforth the name of the country was the Austro-Hungarian Monarchy.

The Hungarian government in the period of the *Ausgleich* functioned well for a while, and Hungarians found little to complain about. Even joint affairs, such as the Ministry of Foreign Affairs, were in Hungarian hands much of the time, as under Count Gyula Andrássy Sr. (1823–90). What little disagreement remained between the Austrian and Hungarian sides centered on reducing Hungarian contributions to joint expenditures or on increasing Hungarian influence, by requiring the ruler to reside in Budapest.

The social history of Hungary in the period from 1867 to 1918 was hardly remarkable. Long after the emancipation of the serfs, as late as 1895, the distribution of wealth in Hungary remained among the most uneven in the world—and in Hungary, as in much of East Central Europe, wealth meant land. Thus large estates made up 32.3 percent of the land yet were owned by only 0.2 percent of the landowners. At the other extreme, 53.4 percent of all landowners owned but 5.8 percent of all land, in parcels often clearly insufficient in that period to maintain a family.

Nevertheless, in hindsight, after 1918 Hungarians and Austrians, young or old—unlike Romanians and most other ethnic groups—tended and still tend to recall the monarchy in nostalgic terms. In literature, in the arts, in operettas, in a number of scholarly works focusing on Vienna or Budapest, and in the psyche of many, it was "the good old days."

The growth of the gross national product approached 7 percent in the last two decades of the century, reaching 8.5 percent in the fifteen years preceding World War I—statistics comparable to the near-fantastic rates of development in Russia and Japan. Per capita income is estimated to have tripled between 1901 and 1913, the last year of peace, although the rate of inflation absorbed most of the growth. Moreover, economic relations with Austria had become even more symbiotic, with Austria absorbing 92 percent of Hungary's exports of wheat, 91 percent of its cattle, and 81 percent of the flour. Railroads were constructed, and industrial plants were built or expanded with the help of foreign capital. It was French capital at first, in the late nineteenth century; in 1881, 14 percent of all French foreign investment went to Austria-Hungary. Eventually, French capital was supplanted by German.

Already Széchenyi and Kossuth had demonstrated interest in railroad construction. The first railroad line, from Pest to Vác, meant as a segment of the Pest-Vienna line, was completed in 1846, about twenty years after the first such line in the world (Stockton-Darlington in England in 1825), and two years before the first railroad in Spain. By 1860, 90 percent of the railroad network of the advanced industrial countries was complete; while not matching those standards, in Hungary too, construction was accelerating. By 1913, the country had 13,200 miles (22,000 km) of railroad, or 62 miles (110 km) for every 100,000 population—placing Hungary sixth in Europe in terms of railroad per population and railroad density per area. These railroads were built, of course, with economic exploitation in mind; thus most lines ended in the capital city, which, in turn, was connected to the West, facilitating the export of foodstuff and raw materials, integrating Hungary into the Western European–dominated world economy. Between 1850 and 1913, the value of Hungarian exports jumped more than tenfold, much of it accounted for by grain. All in all, the Hungarian economy "fell relatively less far behind" than that of most other countries on the European periphery.

The reason the Hungarian economy performed relatively well was flour production. This implied processing in Hungarian mills, and the technology in these mills was ahead of the rest of the world. Among the imports, machinery was significant, as industrialization was well underway. Thus Hungarian industry employed 417,000 workers by 1913. Yet all this did not quite suffice to pull Hungary from the ranks of "peripheral" countries.

Despite the advantages accorded to Hungary by the *Ausgleich,* problems and dissatisfaction remained. Kossuth died in Turin in 1894, and the return of his remains to Budapest resulted in a mass funeral, fanning the flames of strong nationalist sentiment. Then, in 1896 Hungary celebrated its millennium, the day when the first Hungarians resettled from somewhere deep in Asia onto the fertile Hungarian plains. It was a lavish celebration, indicating, for one thing, that ample resources were available for mere display. The new neo-Gothic, monumental parliament building on the banks of the Danube, which has since become the symbol for Budapest in tourist pamphlets and commercials, was completed in 1901—yet another occasion for celebration, that of a parliamentary regime that fancifully claimed to be as old as that of England (that is, dating to the "Hungarian Magna Carta," the Golden Bull of 1222, which curtailed the powers of the monarch).

These events were also indicative of aspirations to greater control and independence. Never mind that Hungary had wrung out an advantageous deal from the Habsburg ruler, or that Austria was Hungary's number-one customer. At the turn of the century, most Hungarian politicians found reason to complain about one thing or another. Among the prominent political parties were the "Forty-eighters," the Kossuth Party, and the "Independence Party," whose very names intimated that the Compromise of 1867 with Austria was unsatisfactory, or that Hungary should demand even greater concessions—though few politicians went so far as to advocate a complete break with Austria or a rejection of the House of Habsburg. The issue of what languages should be used within the units of the Imperial and Royal Army was also hotly debated in parliament after 1890. So was the issue of a national bank. In a way this too was a positive sign, for it implied there were no issues considered more serious; however, although Hungarians demanded more, they would concede less to others.

Most Hungarians, including members of ethnic groups, were even more interested in the issue of suffrage, which was still very limited. This was certainly true about the progressive forces in the country, such as the Social Democratic Party, for whom democracy and universal suffrage were prerequisites to other demands. There were politicians, such as future prime minister Count István Bethlen (1874–1946), who, conservative as they may have been, were inclined to grant all Hungarian speakers suffrage, provided it could be withheld from non-Hungarians. Nevertheless, the ruling class, including the gentry, was able to hang on to their privileges.

Much of the politics from 1867 to 1918 was dominated by Kálmán Tisza (1830–1902) and his son, István (1861–1918), as prime ministers. Although respected and admired by many, including later historians, their conservatism, especially on the issue of suffrage, did not stand them in good stead with many Hungarians. Nevertheless, István Tisza took the initiative in attempting to negotiate a compromise with the Romanians of Transylvania. It was also Tisza who recoiled from the war with Serbia in the summer of 1914, justifiably fearful of the consequences, especially for Hungary.

As for social reform, while it was a period of relative and growing prosperity for many, workers and peasants gained but little—just enough to whet their appetite. Per capita income increased in real value, even for workers, at least until 1900, but workers' daily wage was still only about half of a worker's wage in Berlin. Foreign observers from the West, including American labor organizer Samuel Gompers (1850–1924), described the condition of the working class in Hungary as "one of the worst in the world." The industrial working class, nearly doubling in size between 1890 and 1910, was highly concentrated in Budapest and in a few major plants at that. It was relatively easy for them to organize and make their demands felt. Their demands were expressed through labor unions, which collectively had a membership of about 130,000 by 1900—the largest organization in Hungary—while Social Democrats numbered about half that. The legalization of the strike in 1904 was both an indication of the growing strength of labor unions and a factor furthering their growth.

The demands of the landless peasant, however, found little sympathy and little political support. While workers could meet and organize with relative ease, peasants were scattered all over the country. It is all the more remarkable that groups of peasants were able to take action and resort to violence, or rather respond to the actions of the authorities in the last years of the nineteenth century. They formed the National Union of Agrarian Laborers, mustering almost fifty thousand members.

For the rural proletariat, at least those with minimal resources, there was another escape: emigration. Between 1881 and 1914, 13 percent of all immigrants to the United States, Canada, and Australia came from Austria-Hungary, and at one point, one-fourth of all immigrants to the United States came from the monarchy. Even considering that most emigrants never intended to remain abroad permanently, and that many did indeed return, the net loss to the country was between 1.3 and 1.4 million, one-fourth of the population growth in the period 1870–1914. But here again, the numerical preponderance of Slovaks, Romanians, Serbians, and other "minorities" over the Hungarians is an indication of their even lower status and faint hopes for improvement. (Polish immigrants cannot be included here, since they came from the Austrian side, as well as from the Prussian or Russian territories of Poland.)

Although primary school attendance became compulsory in Denmark even before the end of the eighteenth century, soon followed by other Scandinavian and Western countries, the Austrian Empire lagged behind. A decree issued by Maria Theresa in 1774 required the establishment of schools in every village and parish, yet free, compulsory education was adopted in Hungary only in 1868, under a law sponsored by noted novelist and minister of education Baron József Eötvös (1813–71). At that point 68 percent of the population was still illiterate. Even then, it took many years before the law could be fully implemented; not more than 82 percent of school-age children were attending school by 1900, and in 1910, the illiteracy rate was still 33 percent. Nevertheless, in this respect, Hungarians were ahead of most other peoples of East Central and southeastern Europe. They were also ahead of some other groups within the kingdom, including Slovaks and Romanians, whose progress was adversely affected by the Trefort law of 1879 and other measures that, in contrast to the spirit of the Eötvös law, required not only that Hungarian be taught in all schools but that Hungarian become the language of instruction at most levels. It is not surprising that this policy of Magyarization was bitterly opposed by other ethnic groups in the Hungarian half of the empire. In vain did Hungarian poet Endre Ady (1873–1918) declare, "In Hungary, it is a patriotic thing to hate Germans, Serbs, Romanians, Slovaks, isn't it? If so, I solemnly declare I am no patriot!"

Not only had the majority of Hungarians become literate but they actually read. In the first decade of the twentieth century, one thousand periodicals were published in the country; the dailies alone numbered over one hundred. Of course, quantity does not imply quality; circulation of the more sophisticated newspapers and journals remained small. Still, this was the heyday of the progressive literary magazine *Nyugat* (*West*), founded in 1908, and of *Huszadik század* (*Twentieth Century*), a journal of the social sciences. Together they ushered in a modern age in scientific thought and creativity, allowing Western ideas of progress, liberalism, and democracy to gain some currency in the country. This was the age of Ady, Mihály Babits (1883–1941), and a host of other poets, and of Zsigmond Móricz (1879–1942), Frigyes Karinthy (1887–1938), and Gyula Krúdy (1845–1928) in prose. Their impact did not extend beyond the borders of the country, however, and Hungarian literature continued to flourish in isolation.

Isolation did not apply to music, philosophy, and especially the sciences, where the same generation, sometimes dubbed the "generation of 1900," comprised a plethora of key figures whose accomplishments became known outside the country (many made a career abroad): in music, Béla Bartók (1881–1945), Zoltán Kodály (1882–1967), Ernő Dohnányi (1877–1960), and, at a more popular level, Franz Lehár (1870–1948) and Imre Kálmán (1882–1953); in philosophy, György Lukács (1885–1971), Károly Mannheim (1893–1947), and Vilmos Szilasi (b. 1889); in the sociology of art Arnold Hauser (1892–1978); in economics Jenö Varga (1879–1964); in physics and other natural sciences, Todor Kármán (1881–1963), János von Neumann (1903–57), Leo Szilárd (1898–1964), György Hevesy (1885–1966), György Békesy (1899–1972), Eugen Wigner (1902–), Albert Szent-Györgyi (1893–1986), and Edward Teller (1908–); in art and architecture,

H László Moholy-Nagy (1895–1946); in cinema, Béla Balázs (1884–1949); and Arthur Koestler (1905–83) in world literature.

World War I

The rich culture and economic progress of the decades before the outbreak of war in 1914 notwithstanding, Hungary remained part of Austria-Hungary, which counted as a great power in a volatile Europe. Thus, when World War I broke out in the summer of 1914, "the most beautiful summer," according to the Bosnians in Ivo Andrić's (1892–1975) *Bridge on the Drina*, Hungary was in the midst of the maelstrom. In World War I as in World War II, East Central Europe was the powder keg. World War I started in Sarajevo, Bosnia-Hercegovina, the recently acquired province of the Austro-Hungarian monarchy, with "the shot heard around the world" that killed the heir to the Habsburg throne, Austrian Archduke Franz Ferdinand (1863–1914) and his wife. And the first to declare war was Austria-Hungary, on Serbia, Hungary's neighbor to the south.

Although the prime minister of Hungary had objected in the secret meetings of the joint cabinet to the belligerent stand the monarchy would adopt, he could not prevent the outbreak of war. In Hungary, as elsewhere, the war was welcomed with cheers; "Down with dog Serbia!" became the slogan of the day. "All that took place had the outer semblance of dignity and the attraction of novelty, a terrible, short-lived, and inexpressible charm which later disappeared so completely that even those who felt it so strongly could no longer evoke its memory," wrote Andrić, experiencing the events from the opposite side. It took a few months of slaughter and frustration, and the realization that the end of the war was not in sight, before the mood would change.

Although Hungary did not become a theater of operations during the conflict—except for Transylvania, and even there but briefly—the Great War, as it was called, or simply the World War, caused great suffering in Hungary. The death toll was high from the beginning; the number of widows and orphans soared. Ever greater numbers of seats had to be reserved for the amputees and disabled on the trams and trains of Hungary.

Save for rare occasions, the Austro-Hungarian armies advanced or retreated fewer than 50 miles (84 km), whether against Russia or Italy. Even the 1917 victory over Romania, after the latter

attacked the empire "in the rear," was due largely to a German rescue operation.

Although censorship was largely self-imposed, voices raised against the war were seldom heard before 1916; even then, they belonged not to political leaders but to writers or poets such as Babits and Ady and to feminist and ardent pacifist Margit Kaffka (1880–1918). Powerful as these voices may have been, they could not stop the carnage or preclude defeat.

It would be unfair to place the onus of deteriorating ethnic relations and the eventual dissolution of the monarchy entirely on the short-sightedness of Hungarian leadership, or on policies of repression against minorities. While manifestations of cultural autonomy were increasingly curtailed, the demands of minority groups were becoming more vociferous; in other words, repression and nationalism fed on each other. It is doubtful, however, that even the most farsighted, liberal concessions would have sufficed. While the bourgeois Radicals, a small group of intellectuals in opposition, advocated liberal policies with regard to the "nationalities," they could not have prevented the dissolution of the monarchy even if their ideas had been heard. Indeed, they proved impotent in 1918, when they actually attained leadership in the country; outside events controlled Hungary's destiny.

Hungary between the World Wars

Although an armistice with the Allied powers had already been negotiated at Padua, on the Italian front, the new Hungarian leader, Mihály Károlyi (1875–1955)—yet another count, albeit a progressive one—and his ministers felt it would be advisable to negotiate a military convention in Belgrade with the commander on the southern front, French General Louis Franchet d'Esperey (1856–1942). The revolutionary Hungarian government, which took over as a result of popular pressure in the waning days of the war, late in October 1918, insisted on Hungary's innocence as regards responsibility for the war. Although this argument was rejected by the Allies, the convention allowed Hungary to retain sovereignty over its lands, until the peace conference decided otherwise.

To the dismay of the new government in Budapest, it became increasingly obvious that Hungary (along with Austria and Germany) would be held responsible by the victors for the war's destruction. Moreover, it soon became clear that the multinational state hitherto known as the thousand-year-old "historic" Kingdom of Hungary, which celebrated its millenary in 1896, had ceased to exist.

To be sure, the radical Oszkár Jászi (1875–1957), the new minister of nationality affairs in the Károlyi cabinet, hoped to maintain the country's borders intact by negotiating privileges of autonomy with various ethnic groups within former Hungary. But the solution was not up to Hungary or even to the victorious Great Powers, far removed from local events.

Well before the end of the war, Czech and some Slovak leaders had already agreed to set up their own country—not without encouragement from the United States and the Entente. So too did the South Slavs; for them, there seemed to be little point in waiting for any peace treaty, or even a cease-fire. Similarly, the Romanians took matters into their own hands; in December 1918, soon after revolution broke out in Hungary, Romanian troops were able to penetrate and occupy all of Transylvania. The government of France under Georges Clemenceau (1841–1929) and the French commanders on the southern front merely sanctioned this fait accompli by their minor allies, that is, the reduction of Hungary to by and large its present size and population.

The principle of "Wilsonism," with its cornerstone of self-determination, on which the Károlyi government relied, was already widely disregarded by the victors and the newly created successor states arising from the ashes of the former Austro-Hungarian Empire. By January 1919, Hungary had de facto lost more than half its territory and population, including several million Hungarian speakers. On March 20, 1919, the head of the French military mission in Budapest handed Count Károlyi a note, which has become infamous in Hungarian history as the "Vix ultimatum," demanding that all Hungarian forces withdraw to a demarcation line that would have allowed the Romanians to occupy additional Hungarian territory.

In despair, the revolutionary regime resigned, leaving a void that the recently formed Communist Party of Hungary was poised to fill. Béla Kun (1885–1938), who once liberated from a Russian prisoner-of-war camp had gained admittance into Lenin's (1870–1924) inner circle, returned from Russia to organize the Communist Party of Hungary and agitate. Although arrested, beaten, and jailed, he felt that the opportunity presented by the chaotic political situation and the territorial losses was too good to allow to pass. From his cell, comfortably appointed by the guilt-ridden government that had arrested him, he made a deal with the Social Democrats. On March 21, 1919, the dictatorship of the proletariat and a Hungarian Soviet Republic (*Magyar Tanácsköztársaság*) modeled on Soviet Russia was proclaimed.

The next 133 days were eventful and remarkable in many ways. The Hungarian Soviet Republic would be the only postwar revolutionary state outside the USSR to last for any length of time. The new Hungarian regime was not strictly Communist, however; power was shared with the Social Democrats. Moreover, although the government became known as Kun's regime, he was not the president; that honor was bestowed on an actual member of the working class. Although committed to the principle of internationalism because of the parameters of Marxist-Leninist ideology, the government took up arms, in the name of the revolution, to defend the borders of Hungary, wherever these may have lain. In fact, the hastily set-up Hungarian Red Army defeated the Czechoslovak forces, also recently organized with Italian and French cadres, and reconquered most of Slovakia.

The new regime passed a number of measures that not only emulated what had recently taken place in Soviet Russia but in some ways went beyond what the Bolsheviks initially dared to attempt. Kun was eager to earn the praise of Lenin and the Bolsheviks. Among these measures, practically the entire economy except for land was nationalized. The failure to deal with the land question proved to be one of the government's undoings. The leadership, dogmatic as it was, made the mistake of neglecting the yearnings of the peasants who, after all, were still the majority of the population; Kun and his advisers were in no hurry to resolve the issue of land ownership and create what in their view would be a class of "petty bourgeois proprietors."

Even if they had carried out land reform, however, they could probably not have saved the Communist revolution for its survival depended on the international conjuncture, particularly the possibility of linking up with the Red Army in the Ukraine, which never occurred. But while the Allies could not muster the moral and material wherewithal for a permanent victory over the Bolsheviks in Russia, they certainly had sufficient

H unspent energy, using the Romanian army as a proxy, to defeat the Hungarian Bolshevik regime. Their cause was aided, furthermore, by a fifth column of counterrevolutionaries, partly inside Hungary, partly spreading propaganda from areas on the periphery not under the control of Kun's Republic of Councils—from Vienna, Szeged, and Transdanubia. These included troops under the leadership of a former admiral of the Austro-Hungarian navy, Miklós Horthy (1868–1957). Nor were Lenin's Red Army forces, under attack by several anti-Bolshevik armies, in a position to come to the rescue of the fledgling Communist state in Hungary at that moment. Short of direct Soviet intervention, the only chance of success for Kun and his regime would have been the spread of revolution in the region, beginning with Austria; although the regime did what little it could to promote workers' states in neighboring lands, the needed revolutions either did not materialize or promptly petered out. Kun's republic proved no exception.

Having evacuated Slovakia at the prompting of the Allies in Paris, the Hungarian Red Army advanced eastward, in the vain hope of pushing the Romanian forces out of eastern Hungary and in the expectation of rallying the support of most Hungarians. Within a few days, the Romanian forces counterattacked, and the Hungarian Soviet government was forced to resign on August 1, in favor of a moderate government of the labor unions. While the Romanian army entered Budapest, Kun and other Communist and Socialist leaders managed to find refuge in Austria. For years, Kun would guide from Vienna what remained of the Hungarian Communist Party, or at least one of its factions. After outliving his welcome in the Austrian capital, he moved to Moscow, where he became a top official of the Communist International (Comintern) and a hard-line Stalinist, only to fall victim to Stalin's purges.

The assessment of the revolutions of 1918–19 is often as colorful as the events themselves. Denounced and decried by the leaders of the subsequent regimes, historians followed suit. Even after 1948, under a regime that claimed to be socialist, the perception of the 133 days of the Hungarian Soviet Republic of 1919 had its ups and downs; it was alternately rejected, overlooked, and hailed as a heroic episode of Hungarian history. In contrast, the liberal democratic regime that immediately preceded the Soviet Republic, less subject to the vagaries of ideological considerations, was viewed in an increasingly positive light; not so the counterrevolution that followed, also referred to as the period of conservative consolidation. The label "conservative" is appropriate enough, implying, among other things, that the structure of Hungarian society had hardly changed at all. In other words, the aristocracy and the gentry continued to function as the ruling classes, while workers and peasants remained without political power, often without the franchise.

The fall of Kun's republic was followed by weeks of chaos. In August 1919, with the backing of the Romanian army occupying Budapest, a government emerged, headed by István Friedrich (1883–1951). In the ensuing weeks, some seventy thousand so-called collaborators were arrested and five thousand were killed in the course of pogrom-like reprisals organized by officers of the counterrevolutionary detachments. The term "pogrom" is not inappropriate, because the leadership of Kun's Republic of Councils, among the many victims of the white terror, was disproportionately Jewish, or of Jewish background. The luckier ones, including Kun, philosopher György Lukács, and many Socialist leaders, sympathizers, and prominent intellectuals, succeeded in crossing the border, mainly into more progressive Austria.

While the Allies, represented by the mission of Sir George Russel Clerk (1874–1959), were intent on promoting to power a moderate coalition or democratic socialist government, Admiral Horthy and a Christian National Unity Party emerged dominant. All that Allied pressure could accomplish was to persuade the new leaders to legalize the Social Democratic Party; the conservative parties had a stranglehold on Hungarian politics.

In December 1919 the peacemakers in Paris recognized this new government in Budapest. Official recognition allowed the peacemakers to conclude their discussions of punishment to be meted out to Hungary, in the framework of what became known as the Treaty of Trianon. As with the Versailles treaty for the likewise defeated Germany, the country most directly concerned was not invited to take part in the negotiations. In June 1920 the Hungarian delegation, which had been sequestered in Paris for several months to keep it from access to the French public, signed the treaty.

Trianon saw the loss of 70 percent of the territory of the Kingdom of Hungary and 60 percent of the total population, including 28 percent of all

Hungarian speakers. The army was restricted in size to thirty thousand officers and men, leaving little opportunity for revenge or reconquest. The treaty also left Hungary isolated and in dire economic straits.

Economically, the natural resources, especially the ores and the mines, now lay outside the country, while much of the industry, including heavy industry, remained within. The Hungarian plains, still within rump Hungary (as many now called the state), had always been the most productive agricultural region, but the level of their production depended on exports, rendered difficult by the growing antagonism of the neighboring states.

The neighboring countries, known as the "successor states," were not blind to Hungarian resentment of the treaty's provisions and desire for revenge. Within two years after the war, Czechoslovakia, Romania, and Yugoslavia signed treaties among themselves and with France, forming the Little Entente to secure themselves and one another against any attempts at Hungarian revisionism.

Indeed, revision of the Treaty of Trianon became the principal preoccupation, if not obsession, of all Hungarian governments until near the end of World War II, and it affected all social groups, even those who had little at stake, materially speaking, in the outcome. The slogan, rhyming rather lamely in Hungarian and printed over miniature maps of Hungary pasted on the doorways to apartments of ordinary citizens, was "Mutilated Hungary is no country, Greater Hungary is paradise" (*Csonka Magyarország nem ország, Nagy-Magyarország mennyország*). No Hungarian government or politician had a chance of success if advocating patience or reason, even at polls that were often manipulated or controlled outright by the government. Whatever his personal conviction, even Count István Bethlen projected the image of a chauvinist, a sly statesman from Transylvania, biding his time for the opportune moment to break Hungary's isolation through the right alliance or wage the right war to regain territory. In fact, the all-pervasive feeling of injustice distracted the attention of much of the working class and the landless peasantry from their economic woes.

Although the white terror of the post-Kun period was eventually superseded, under the leadership of Bethlen (who served as prime minister from 1921 to 1931), by a regime that aimed at respectability in the eyes of the Western powers, there was no resurgence of communism or socialism. The conservatives even signed a secret pact with socialist leaders who remained in Hungary. In addition to enhancing the image of the Hungarian regime in the eyes of the governments of France, Germany, or even Austria, where Social Democrats were in or near power, the pact served to reconcile the labor unions, which had by and large supported Kun's ill-fated republic. But then, the working class was no longer a force to be feared by the conservatives. It remained demoralized and disorganized by the failure of the Bolshevik Revolution in Hungary, by the bloody reprisals, and eventually by the infighting within the leadership of the Hungarian Communist Party in exile and the Comintern in Moscow. Moreover, economic conditions had improved sufficiently by the second half of the 1920s to have a positive impact on wages and the standard of living, before the world crisis of 1929 at any rate.

Likewise, the condition of the peasantry did not improve much. In 1935, 30 percent of the arable land was still owned by large landowners, who may be defined as those with property over 1,000 holds (1 hold = 1.42 acres). With a few exceptions, this land was in the hands of 526 aristocratic families. Most of the land (52 percent) was divided into parcels of 10–100 holds. The remainder, about 20 percent of the arable land, was held in parcels of fewer than 10 holds, insufficient to maintain a family regardless of the crop cultivated or of soil quality.

The agrarian proletariat formed the largest group of peasants, some one million families, with numerous children. Among them were the servants and other hired hands on the large estates, the agricultural laborers and migrant workers, seasonally employed, and the owners of parcels of one or two holds who also had to sell their labor to survive, a predicament eloquently described in the work of poet Gyula Illyés (1902–83), "The People of the Puszta" ("Puszták népe," 1936).

Next to the aristocracy, a class of capitalists, numbering about five hundred, held controlling interests in the banks and industry. Although their religious affiliation was not always evident, it is clear that many of these families were of Jewish background (albeit several had been knighted in the period of the Dual Monarchy). Consequently in Hungary, as elsewhere, anti-Semitism was often the product of a paradox; while Jews were excoriated for having engineered and led the anticapitalist Bolshevik revolution, they were at the same time stereotyped as arch-capitalist exploiters. Jewish dominance was real in one respect: the children of the Jewish middle-class enrolled at Hungarian universities in disproportionate numbers, to the point where one-half of all lawyers and almost one-half of all physicians in the country were of Jewish background.

One outcome of the anti-Semitic feelings aroused or rekindled in 1919 was the introduction of the *numerus clausus,* legislation aimed at limiting the number of Jewish students who could be admitted to Hungarian universities. It was not until 1938, however, that further legislation was introduced discriminating against the Jewish population.

As regards welfare, there was steady progress, even if Hungarian society could not keep pace with Western industrialized nations. Although declining, infant mortality rates in 1941 were still over 19 percent. It was due partly to this high mortality that the population of rump Hungary grew so slowly, from about 8 million in 1920 to 9.3 million in 1941. Emigration and the high death rate were better than compensated for by the influx of immigrants—Hungarians moving in from neighboring lands. By 1941, about one-fifth of the population lived in the capital city, while one-half was still involved in agricultural production.

In 1931 Bethlen, aware that the world economic depression could not be overcome overnight, and having lost the trust of the regent, Admiral Horthy, resigned. Although he expected to return to power shortly, the internal and international situation became increasingly unfavorable.

After a transition regime headed by Prime Minister Gyula Károlyi (1871–1947), who enjoyed the confidence of both Horthy and Bethlen, it was the turn of Gyula Gömbös (1886–1936), an army officer who had distinguished himself in the counterrevolution of 1919, to direct the nation's fortunes. Despite certain commitments made at the time of his appointment, he leaned toward fascist totalitarianism, intent on transforming Hungary into a "corporatist" state on the Italian model, perhaps more for the sake of overcoming the Great Depression than to gain personal power. Gömbös earned the dubious distinction of being the first foreign statesman to pay an official visit to Adolf Hitler (1889–1945), in June 1933. Economically, Hungary's drift

toward fascism was beneficial. The ill effects of the Depression were overcome; Italy, and especially Germany, were willing to serve as unlimited markets for Hungarian agricultural exports. Politically, the drift to the right would prove disastrous.

In the elections of 1935, the Party of National Unity, no longer led by Bethlen, made substantial headway. However, so too did the extreme rightwing forces—even though not all of them were willing to back Gömbös, whose regime they deplored as insufficiently fascist. Yet it was not until Gömbös fell terminally ill in 1936 and died that he was replaced.

The implicit mission of the next prime minister, Kálmán Darányi (1886–1939), was to steer the country away from the totalitarian course adopted or advocated by Gömbös. But to appease the right-wing forces and ward off further pressure from Nazi Germany, Darányi adopted policies increasingly similar to those of Gömbös.

The *Anschluss* (German annexation of Austria) in March 1938 sealed the fate of Hungary. It provided an added impetus to the radical right, especially the faction under the leadership of Ferenc Szálasi (1897–1946), whose movement was variously known as the Arrow Cross or the Hungarist Movement. Its obsession with anti-Semitism notwithstanding, the radical right owed much of its success to certain populist stands. Although Darányi had authorized the arrest of Szálasi on two occasions, he was now ready to deal with the Arrow Cross, guaranteeing them a certain number of seats in parliament. Darányi was also instrumental in passing the "first anti-Jewish law," limiting the number of Jews who could practice in certain professions.

In May 1938 Darányi was replaced by Béla Imrédy (1891–1946). Although Imrédy was chosen, as was Darányi before him, primarily with the hope that he would be able to reverse the rightward drift of Hungary's foreign and domestic policies, he simply followed the same course as Darányi.

In September 1938 the Czechoslovak crisis led to the Munich Pact, which turned over the Sudetenland to Germany. The agreement also stipulated direct negotiations between the Hungarian and Czechoslovak governments regarding Hungary's territorial claims. While the Czechoslovak government at first refused to surrender further territories, the Vienna Award of November 1938 forced it to hand over areas along the border with a predominantly Hungarian population. Unlike the Sudetenland, this award was made without the participation or sanction of France and the United Kingdom; it had been dictated solely by Germany and Italy.

Once again, the fate of Hungary seemed sealed. While the Hungarian government could not refuse the gift—lest it cease to be the government—neither could it overlook the fact that the gift was sponsored by two fascist powers. Imrédy's cabinet seemed inclined to make concessions beyond even what the German government expected; in gratitude for the award, Imrédy granted legal recognition to the Volksbund, the right-wing organization of the German ethnic group in Hungary, signed the Anti-Comintern Pact, and withdrew Hungary from the League of Nations.

For the moment, conservative forces in Hungary were able to intervene to stop the drift toward the extreme right; Horthy was persuaded to act against Imrédy when presented with documentation revealing the latter's part-Jewish ancestry. Leadership of the country was handed to Count Pál Teleki (1879–1941).

World War II

With the outbreak of World War II in Europe in September 1939, Hungarian domestic affairs became largely a function of events beyond the border of the state, and Hungarian foreign affairs were caught in the squeeze between domestic pressures for further territorial revisions and avoiding participation in the war. In a letter to Hitler, Teleki made it clear that Hungary would not participate in the campaign against Poland "out of moral considerations." In fact, large numbers of Polish officers and other refugees escaped from their occupied country by way of Hungary.

Despite German indignation over Hungarian "ingratitude" in the matter of Poland, on August 30, 1940, Germany and Italy sponsored another territorial revision, the so-called Second Vienna Award, which resulted in the return of about half of Transylvania from Romania. The award proved generous to the Hungarian side, since the Hungarian population of Transylvania amounted to no more than 27 percent. Although it was made at Romania's expense, at least Romania had the prospect of territorial compensation in Bessarabia on the expected defeat of the Soviet Union. In the case of Hungary, the promulgation of the Second Vienna Award merely created further obliga-

tions; Hungary had sold its soul to satisfy its irredentist yearnings.

The showdown came with Germany's attack on Yugoslavia. While the Hungarian government had signed a treaty of "permanent peace and eternal friendship" with Yugoslavia in December 1940, only four months later, in March 1941, it was asked to collaborate in the invasion and occupation of that country. The regent, and the Hungarian government in general, acceded to the German request. The day after the Hungarian government caved in to the German demands, thereby breaking its word, Teleki committed suicide. His suicide note, addressed to Horthy, stated: "we are becoming despoilers of corpses! The most contemptible of nations." The gesture was not without impact: a chair will be reserved at the peace talks, commented Winston Churchill (1874–1965), for Hungary.

If history were a series of moral judgments, it might be noted, as an extenuating circumstance, that the power of Nazi Germany was now at its height, and perhaps no more than a handful of people in Eastern Europe suspected that Germany would lose the war, let alone be forced to surrender unconditionally.

The German invasion of the Soviet Union was launched on June 22, 1941. Four days later, the Hungarian government, now under prime minister László Bárdossy (1890–1946), decided to join the fray. The circumstances leading to Hungarian participation in the war are the subject of heated debates to this day. The German government did not solicit Hungarian participation, in order to avoid Hungarian requests for the return of further territories. German documents indicate, however, that though no explicit request was made, any Hungarian assistance would be most welcome and the Hungarian chief of the general staff was eager to oblige.

On June 26, unidentified aircraft dropped bombs on the city of Kosice, then part of Hungary. Kosice was near the Soviet border; moreover, an unexploded bomb and fragments of others indicated that these were manufactured in the Soviet Union. This evidence was accepted by Bárdossy at face value, and he was able to persuade the regent to consider the assault an act of war. Hungarian bombers were immediately sent to strike Soviet territory, and the next day some forty thousand Hungarian troops crossed the border into the USSR.

On December 6, 1941, Great Britain finally declared war on Hungary, as it had threatened to do since the Yugoslav affair; a few days later, Bárdossy informed the American ambassador in Budapest that "a state of war existed" between Hungary and the United States. By that time, however, the German offensive on the eastern front had bogged down, without reaching Moscow or capturing Leningrad. A small minority of Hungarian political personalities, including conservative and pro-Western politicians, could now see the writing on the wall.

In March 1942 Bárdossy was dismissed, ostensibly for health reasons, and replaced by Miklós Kállay (1887–1967). One of Kállay's tasks, although never explicitly stated, was to extricate Hungary from its hasty decision to join the war effort. The urgency of this task became evident in January 1943. The tide of the war was about to turn at the battle of Stalingrad, and that battle had further immediacy for the Hungarian government, because the Soviet pincer movement launched to encircle the German Fifth Army in Stalingrad broke through the flanks guarded by troops belonging to the Axis partners—Italians, Romanians, and Hungarians. The Hungarian Second Army, ill equipped and demoralized, perished in the snow.

The Hungarian government persuaded the German high command to allow the withdrawal of what little remained of that army. It accepted another mission, however—antipartisan operations in the rear of the eastern front. In the meantime, the Hungarian Ministry of Foreign Affairs engaged in a secret, elaborate and, as it turned out, futile effort to contact the Western allies with peace feelers. Hungarian emissaries met British and American agents in Portugal, Switzerland, Turkey, and elsewhere. While these efforts remained hidden from the Hungarian public, including the pro-Nazi forces, they were almost immediately detected by German intelligence.

Although the British government was willing to accept Hungary's conditional surrender, to enter into effect the moment Allied troops reached the borders of the country, the other Allied governments were not interested in concluding a separate armistice, lest they antagonize the already suspicious Soviet leader, Stalin (1879–1953). The logical solution would have been to include the Soviet Union in the negotiations, but the Hungarian efforts were conducted by individuals (including the regent) who were as anti-Soviet as they were anti-Nazi. Thus, when in late winter 1944, units of the Red Army were approaching the Carpathians—while the Western allies were bogged down in southern Italy—the situation turned from desperate to hopeless, especially after Hitler decided to send German troops to occupy Hungary.

The German occupation was carried out on March 19. Perhaps because Hitler overestimated Horthy's prestige among his own people, the regent was tricked into leaving the country to visit with Hitler two days before the planned invasion. Hitler succeeded in browbeating Horthy into remaining at his post, while appointing the former ambassador to Berlin, the reliably pro-German Döme Sztójay (1883–1946), to replace Kállay as prime minister. Thus, unlike what happened in Poland or the Protectorate of Bohemia and Moravia, the semblance of Hungarian sovereignty was preserved. The ultimate cost would be no less high.

Only in the summer of 1944 did Horthy recover his senses. By then the Hungarian army had been fully mobilized, Hungarian industry and other resources expropriated or loaned (with no prospect of repayment) for the German war effort, and Hungarian Jews deported by the hundreds of thousands to the death camps of Poland. Only the Jews of Budapest, collected in the ghetto or in special houses designated as "yellow," remained. At this juncture, Horthy, with the help of loyal troops, asserted himself, ordering units of the army to occupy their own capital city, thus preventing the mass deportation of the remaining Jews.

On August 23, Hungary's arch-rival, Romania, surrendered to the Red Army, without suffering dire consequences. Still, the Hungarian government, now in the hands of prime minister Géza Lakatos (1890–1967), hesitated to contact the Soviets. Finally, a secret mission was dispatched to Moscow in the first half of October, and on October 15 the regent announced a coup against the German occupation force. Although there was armed confrontation between German and Hungarian troops in the Castle District of Budapest, the next day Horthy was already in German custody; the coup had failed.

For the next two–three months, parts of Hungary, including the capital, were under the control of the extreme right-wing Arrow Cross party, led by Szálasi, who had been appointed by the regent to head the government before Horthy's deportation. (Horthy was acting under duress as his only surviving son had just been abducted by the German SS.) But the regime had become irrelevant, except for those tens of thousands of Jewish and other last-minute victims who could not be saved by diplomatic intervention or by well-meaning fellow Hungarians.

At the time of Horthy's attempt to bail out of the war on October 15, the Red Army had already reached the outskirts of Debrecen, in eastern Hungary. The regent's radio message was ambiguous from the start; at any rate, his orders were promptly countermanded by the chief of the general staff, and Hungarian troops continued to fight their rearguard action alongside the Germans in retreat from their debacle in the USSR. The siege of Budapest, fought by Soviet and German forces, lasted two and a half months. Even after that, western Hungary was almost the last piece of foreign territory that remained in Nazi German hands. Nevertheless, the Soviet Union wasted no time in setting up a provisional Hungarian government in Debrecen, headed by one of Horthy's trusted generals who had changed sides during the coup attempt.

The "Socialist" Regime: 1945–90

The Germans' last-ditch military effort to hold the advancing Soviet armies at bay had left Hungary, especially the capital city, in shambles. As the survivors scrambled from their cellars, they faced a city where practically no building was left undamaged (27 percent had been destroyed) and all six bridges across the Danube had been blown up. Despite reconstruction efforts, the pockmarks left by bullets on the less severely damaged buildings were to remain for decades, mingling with the marks left by the subsequent shootout in 1956. The country had lost 40 percent of its national wealth, five times the amount of its GNP of 1938, and half a million Hungarian citizens were detained in the Soviet Union as prisoners of war for several years to come.

The terms of the armistice required Hungary to pay reparations in kind to the Soviet Union, hampering the recovery of Hungarian industry. Nevertheless, the economy did recover. And a land reform was to benefit 650,000 landless or nearly landless peasants, at least until collectivization was launched a few years later.

Soviet military and political officials exercised enough authority to keep Western representatives out or to render them ineffective, perhaps in keeping with the infamous "percentages deal" negotiated in Moscow between Churchill and Stalin in the fall of 1944, which gave the Soviets and the West each a fifty-fifty share of influence in the country, revised a few days later in favor of predominant Soviet influence. Nevertheless, between 1945 and 1948, Hungary enjoyed a multiparty system, the results at the polls indicating that political democracy prevailed for the time being. While the Communist Party obtained 17 percent of the votes in 1945, the Smallholders Party emerged as the absolute winner, with 57 percent. Both the prime minister and the president of the coalition cabinet represented the Smallholders; nevertheless, the Communist Party retained, among others, the key posts of Ministry of the Interior, which included the police, secret and otherwise, and Ministry of Agriculture, which was to carry out and receive credit for land reform.

The peace treaty, signed in 1947, did not alter relations among the Soviet Union, Hungary, and its neighbors. The terms of Trianon were simply confirmed, with the additional loss of a few square kilometers along the Danube, opposite Bratislava, to Czechoslovakia. The Red Army, while technically no longer an occupation force, nevertheless stayed in Hungary, where it would remain for the next forty-three years. To safeguard its presence and to create a cordon sanitaire (buffer zone) between itself and the West, the Soviet Union had to ensure the loyalty of Hungary and other East Central European nations.

Although elections held in 1947 still did not result in a victory for the united front of the Communist and Socialist Parties, the pressure was on. The pattern of takeover in Hungary was similar to that which occurred in much of the rest of East Central Europe. In 1947 the election results were significantly altered when the political police announced that a "plot against the republic" had been uncovered. The general secretary of the Smallholders Party was arrested and Ferenc Nagy (1903–79), the prime minister from the same party, on a visit to Switzerland, was persuaded not to return. While the leaders of the Smallholders resigned, went into exile, or were arrested one by one, the coalition was soon reduced to the Socialist and Communist Parties, and the two parties merged in June 1948 to become the Hungarian Workers Party (drawing a precedent from the Kun regime of 1919). By the time of the elections of 1949, there was no opposition left.

H In Hungary, as elsewhere in East Central Europe, purges became the order of the day, reminiscent of the more encompassing purges in the Soviet Union from 1936 to 1938; here too, ironically, the victims were usually prominent members of the Communist Party. The charges against them were almost entirely trumped up. Moreover, they followed the pattern of the Soviet trials of a decade earlier, except for the fresh charge of "Titoism"— support for the Yugoslav leader's anti-Soviet challenges, or of contacts with the "renegade" Tito (1892–1980); even here, however, little credible evidence was ever presented. In 1949 the most prominent victim of the purges in Hungary was László Rajk (1909–49), a veteran of the Spanish Civil War of the 1930s who, unlike Mátyás Rákosi (1892–1971) and other Communist leaders, had remained in Hungary, at great risk, even during the worst period of German occupation, rather than sitting out the war in Moscow. Other victims, such as Imre Nagy (1896–1958) and János Kádár (1912–89), while tortured, were spared.

As in the Soviet Union, the party in Hungary also purged the rank and file who were considered insufficiently committed to the cause; this resulted in a significant decline in the party's rosters. The period was also one of mass deportations, as a consequence of which some seven hundred thousand members of the urban middle class were exiled to villages or work camps in the countryside.

Economically as well as politically, Hungary adopted the Stalinist model; heavy industry was emphasized, while the production of consumer goods was relegated to an insignificant part of overall production. Productivity was promoted not by material incentives but by so-called moral ones, including the introduction of the Soviet Stakhanovite system, which set quotas (usually unrealistic) and rewarded production by the piece.

The death of Stalin in 1953, the efforts at reconciliation with Tito on the part of the new Soviet leadership, and Premier Nikita Khrushchev's (1894–1971) denunciation of Stalin at the Twentieth Party Congress of the Soviet Union in 1956 (although guarded and "secret") had a dramatic impact on Hungary and the other countries of East Central Europe, contributing in the case of Hungary to the great uprising of 1956 and the subsequent Soviet invasion that highlighted so dramatically the reality of an Iron Curtain.

The events of 1956 in Hungary were a sequel to the East German strikes of 1953 and the confrontation with Soviet tanks in Berlin, as well as to unrest in Poland earlier in 1956. The death of Stalin shook the position of the hard-line Communist leadership everywhere, including Hungary.

Although Hungarian leader Rákosi retained at least some of his positions and influence until 1956, his rival within the party, Imre Nagy, who had already served as prime minister once in 1953, enjoyed far greater appeal. This appeal was based in part on the expectation of greater independence from Moscow, which, under the circumstances, could be favorably interpreted by the public as veiled nationalism.

International events also seemed to favor greater independence. Late in 1955, the Soviet government endorsed the resolutions of the Bandung conference of nonaligned nations, which renounced colonialism. The Soviet Union relinquished its hold on part of Austria and signed the Belgrade declaration, intimating the possibility of recognition of other East Central European nations as true partners. The door appeared to be open for genuine change in Hungary.

Writers and university students in Budapest took the lead in demanding freedoms, especially freedom of the press, while the figures and events of 1848 functioned as powerful symbols. A key event was the rehabilitation of the executed Rajk and his reburial in October, his coffin escorted by a quarter of a million mourners. On October 23, another symbolic episode took place, as students and others marched to the statue of Józef Bem, the Polish general who had fought against the Russians in 1830 and for Hungarian independence in 1848. Later that day, the crowd marched to Kossuth Square in front of the parliament building, where they were addressed by Nagy. The first act of violence was armed confrontation at the radio station.

While some fighting involved Soviet troops stationed in Hungary, for a few days the Soviet government hesitated and units of the Red Army were withdrawn from the country. On November 1, Nagy announced over the radio that the Hungarian government might go so far as to withdraw from the Warsaw Pact, the East European system of military alliance set up as a counterpoise to the West's North Atlantic Treaty Organization (NATO). While Hungarians contemplated their future, the Soviet decision to invade Hungary had already been reached.

Moscow's decision to intervene was made on the last day of October. The threat of a Hungary prepared to follow its own path, guided by nationalism, warranted armed intervention on the part of a Soviet Union bent on preserving its buffer zone and its hold on the region. Its decision was inadvertently aided by the distraction created by the British and French attack on Egypt during the Suez crisis, likewise an act of imperialism.

The first half of November witnessed heavy street fighting in Budapest between Soviet tanks and Hungarian patriots, called freedom fighters; but once it became clear that the West would not intervene, the outcome was no longer in doubt. Nagy, who had initially sought refuge inside the Yugoslav embassy, was arrested the moment he left, tried secretly, and executed a year later. János Kádár, who at first appeared to side with the revolutionaries, was now given power by the Soviets, and was to hold on to it for the next thirty years.

Over the next few weeks, some two hundred thousand citizens managed to cross the Hungarian-Austrian border to the West, joining the already extensive Hungarian diaspora across the world. Over thirty thousand of them were admitted by special legislation to the United States. Even Switzerland, with its policy of refusing immigrants, admitted several tens of thousands.

Meanwhile, the Kádár regime consolidated itself in much the same manner as the conservative, counterrevolutionary regime had done a generation earlier: gradual liberalization, amnesty for political prisoners within a few years, abrogating the most obnoxious measures introduced under Rákosi, improving the standard of living, and obtaining aid from the Soviet Union—a reversal of the pre-1956 process. The ballast of Stalinism, or at least its most oppressive features, was discarded.

Progress was also achieved through the collectivization of land. Unlike the Rákosi method, which, while not as draconian as Stalin had been in the early 1930s, resorted to force and alienated much of the peasantry, this time economic incentives were used. Moreover, peasants were allowed to retain private plots of about 2.5 acres (one hectare) that competed effectively with collectivized farms in terms of productivity. Hungary once again became a country of agricultural exports, with diversified production.

At the beginning of 1968, the New Economic Mechanism (NEM), reminiscent of the New Economic Policy (NEP) initiated under Lenin in the early 1920s, was introduced. It was designed to reward productivity, reduce central planning, and give the market an important role in economic transactions. It also became a model for reform in the so-called socialist countries of East Central Europe, with varying degrees of success. In Hungary itself, the results of the NEM were promising. By the late 1970s, real wage and consumption levels of the population had tripled compared with the period before 1956. The growth in agricultural production was double the world average.

As regards social changes, Hungary was no longer a predominantly agricultural country; the rural population had shrunk to no more than 20 percent. Income gaps were significantly reduced; unskilled workers earned two-thirds as much as the average manager, while skilled workers earned only slightly less than the average engineer. The educational level increased comparably; by the 1970s, about 50 percent of all secondary-school students went on to obtain their high school diploma, for which standards were traditionally high.

The state socialist regime introduced in 1948 affected women more than other population categories. Between 1930 and 1975, the workforce increased by 1.3 million, 93 percent of which was attributable to women. Women became wage earners, especially after 1948, as a result of the policy of full employment but also to offset the inadequacy of the average salary to maintain a family. While almost 100 percent of men were in the labor market by 1980, women participated in the economy at the rate of 71 percent. Encouraging women to work outside the home was in line with the Marxist-Leninist rhetoric on women's emancipation, but it also placed an extremely heavy burden on most women, since the total number of hours they worked—inside and outside the home—far exceeded the totals for men. Moreover, women had limited access to training and were normally assigned to unskilled or semiskilled jobs, while the wage differential—theoretically nonexistent—remained significant. Although the number of women in leadership positions doubled between 1960 and 1980, women still remained a minority on that level.

In the 1960s, however, a welfare state was gradually introduced. The establishment and proliferation of free or low-cost nursery schools and kindergartens was among the provisions of this state, although the demand for such services continued to outpace the supply. At the same time,

H mothers were granted extensive, fully paid maternity leave and eventually received tax benefits for the cost of child care. In addition to socialist theory and the labor requirements of the economy, welfare measures and policies affecting women were also influenced by the low birthrate in Hungary (at times the lowest in the world) and the on-and-off natalist campaigns of the government. Although the principle of "control over your own body" was recognized, at times access to abortion was restricted.

The early 1970s was a period of boom, at least until the oil crisis of 1973; since Hungary produced little oil, its trade deficit increased rapidly, as did its international debt, reaching the equivalent of eight billion dollars by 1978. In little over a decade, the huge foreign debt was to trigger the collapse of the regime.

By the 1980s, the Kádár regime, as well as the rule of the Hungarian Workers Party, was among the most liberal in Eastern Europe. There was no institutionalized censorship other than self-censorship and, in fact, even self-censorship was limited mainly to one taboo subject, criticism of the Soviet Union. What could not get printed in official or semiofficial papers was printed in the tolerated "underground" press called, as it was in the Soviet Union, samizdat. At the same time, there was a resurgence of nationalism or, more exactly, manifestations of concern for the fate of the Hungarian minority populations living in neighboring lands, especially Transylvania.

Throughout the 1980s, internationalist solidarity among the nations of East Central Europe, let alone Comecon—the program of economic division of labor and production among the "community" of East Central European nations under Soviet tutelage—was falling by the wayside. The Soviet Union had held East Central Europe together as part of its sphere of influence. Now the Soviet Union itself was undergoing glasnost (openness). Along with the political crisis, its own international debt and its socioeconomic crisis compelled it to become introverted and relinquish its sphere. New pressures had begun to divide the Soviet bloc; cracks in the facade of socialist solidarity grew ever wider with increased liberalization.

Kádár resigned in 1986 and died three years later. His successors, however, could not or did not wish to halt political liberalization. In February 1989 a multiparty system was legalized, as the Communist Party surrendered its privileged role. The party line with regard to the revolution of 1956, hitherto dubbed a "counterrevolution," was abandoned, and Imre Nagy was rehabilitated and reburied under ceremonial circumstances.

Perhaps the key event in the downfall of the so-called socialist regime, like many of the other socialist states in other parts of East Central Europe, was the decision taken by the Hungarian government to allow masses of refugees from the German Democratic Republic to transit through Hungary on their way to the West. Even before it was torn down, the Berlin Wall had become a futile barrier.

Except for the brief experiment of 1945–47, Western-style democracy had never been practiced in Hungary; thus, the first elections, held in 1990, may be considered a landmark. The victorious party, the Hungarian Democratic Forum, represented conservative forces that had been marginalized during the state socialist regime. Their program included an appeal to nationalist sentiment in the guise of advocating protection for Hungarian minorities in neighboring countries. Their economic program included privatization and allowing more scope for market forces.

"Freedom" and "democracy" did not, however, create instant positive effects. Since the "lawful revolution" of 1989–90, the status of women, for example, has suffered setbacks. Although unemployment in Hungary, unlike other areas in East Central Europe, has affected men more than women, the decline in living standards has affected everyone but a privileged few. The ratio of women deputies in parliament has dropped drastically; in the 1990 elections only 9 percent of the candidates were women, and an even smaller percentage got elected. Women are no longer guaranteed their jobs while on childcare leave. In the name of liberalism and a free press, prostitution and pornography, outlawed under the socialist regime, have become mainstays of the country's domestic and export services.

It did not take long for the new regime to squander its popularity. The play of the market, far from resolving the economic crisis of the 1980s, made matters worse, and the economic crisis turned into a socioeconomic one. The pace of privatization had to be slowed. The party comprising former Socialist and Communist forces gained a clear victory in the ensuing elections of 1994 and set up a coalition cabinet with the participation of liberals. While nationalism was de-emphasized and the new regime attempted to cultivate good relations with neighboring countries, its economic policies did not significantly differ from those of the former conservative regime.

In 1998, with the victory of the Alliance of Young Democrats—some of whom had aged considerably since the party was formed—the pendulum had swung the other way. It seems that right-wing and left-wing regimes or, better said, right-of-center and left-of-center politics and economics alternate in power. As with developments in other countries of the former Soviet bloc, it would be presumptuous to summarize or assess Hungarian history since 1990, the year of the introduction of pluralism in politics. Whatever might be said about the past five or ten years could easily be negated by the unfolding of the next five or ten. And whatever seems important at this moment may well pale into insignificance in the near future.

Mario D. Fenyo

Further reading

Augustinos, Gerasimos. *The National Idea in Eastern Europe.* Lexington, Massachusetts, 1996.

Barany, George. *Stephen Széchenyi and the Awakening of Hungarian Nationalism, 1791–1841.* Princeton, New Jersey, 1968.

Berend, Iván T. and György Ránki. *The European Periphery and Industrialization, 1780–1914.* Cambridge, Massachusetts, 1982.

Borsányi, György. *The Life of a Communist Revolutionary, Béla Kun.* New York, 1993.

Crampton, R.J. *Eastern Europe in the Twentieth Century.* London, 1994.

Deak, Istvan. *The Lawful Revolution: Louis Kossuth and the Hungarians, 1848–1849.* New York, 1979.

Eterovich, Francis H. and Christopher Spalatin, eds. *Croatia—Land, People, Culture.* Toronto, 1964.

Fenyo, Mario D. *Hitler, Horthy and Hungary.* New Haven, Connecticut, 1972.

———. *Literature and Politics.* Philadelphia, 1986.

Georgescu, Vlad. *The Romanians: A History.* Columbus, Ohio, 1991.

Janos, Andrew C. *The Politics of Backwardness in Hungary: 1825–1945.* Princeton, New Jersey, 1982.

Király, Béla, Peter Pastor, and Ivan Sanders, eds. *Essays on World War I: Total War and Peacemaking: A Case Study on Trianon.* New York, 1982.

Kohn, Hans. *The Habsburg Empire, 1804–1918.* New York, 1961.

Lukacs, John. *Budapest 1900: A Historical Portrait of a City and Its Culture.* New York, 1988.

Macartney, C.A. *October Fifteenth: A History of Modern Hungary,* 2 vols. Edinburgh, 1956.

Magyarorszag Története, 10 vols.; vol. 6 (1848–90), ed. by Endre Kovacs; vol. 7 (1890–18), ed. by Peter Hanak; vol. 8 (1918–45), ed. by György Ránki; vol. 9 (from liberation to the present), ed. by Dezső Nemes. Budapest, 1978.

Romsics, Ignác. *István Bethlen: A Conservative Statesman of Hungary, 1874–1946.* New York, 1995.

Sakmyster, Thomas L. *The Admiral on Horseback.* New York, 1994.

Sugar, Peter F., Peter Hanak, and Tibor Frank, eds. *A History of Hungary.* Bloomington, Indiana, 1990.

Sugar, Peter F. and Ivo J. Lederer, eds. *Nationalism in Eastern Europe.* Seattle, 1969.

See also Endre Ady; Agriculture; Ivo Andrić; *Anschluss;* Anti-Comintern Pact; Gyula Andrássy, Sr.; Architecture; Arrow Cross; *Ausgleich;* Mihály Babits; Alexander Bach; Béla Balázs; Nicolae Bălcescu; Banking; László Bárdossy; George Barițiu; Simion Bărnuțiu; Béla Bartók; Lajos Batthyány; Józef Bem; Berlin Wall; Antonín Bernolak; István Bethlen; Blaj; Censorship; Winston Churchill; Cinema; Collectivization; Comecon; Comintern; Communist Party of Hungary; Congress of Vienna; Croatian Military Frontier; Crownlands of St. Stephen; Kálmán Darányi; Ferenc Deák; De-Stalinization; Ernő Dohnányi; Dual Monarchy; Dualism; Economic Development in Hungary; Education; Emigration; József Eötvös; Ethnic Minorities; Franz Ferdinand; Ljudevit Gaj; Glasnost and Perestroika; Gyula Gömbös; Artur Görgey; Great Depression; Great Powers; Habsburg Empire; Ion Heliade Rădulescu; Johann Herder; Adolf Hitler; Holy Alliance; *Honvéd;* Miklós Horthy; Hungarian Art; Hungarian Culture; Hungarian Émigrés; Hungarian Language; Hungarian Literature; Hungarian War for Independence; Hungarian Revolution of 1956; Hungarian Soviet Republic; Avram Iancu; Gyula Illyés; Illyrian Movement; Béla Imrédy; Industrialization; Intelligentsia; Iron Curtain; Irredentism; Janissaries; Oszkár Jászi; Josip Jelačić; János Kádár; Mikló Kállay; Mihály Károlyi; Ferenc Kazinczy; Károly Khuen-Héderváry; Zoltán Kodály;

H Ján Kollár; Lajos Kossuth; Béla Kun; Labor; Law; Lenin; György Lukács; Magyarization; Károly Mannheim; Media; Munich Pact; Ferenc Nagy; Imre Nagy; Napoléon; Nationalism; Neoabsolutism; NEM; János von Neumann; Nicholas I; Nonaligned Movement; *Numerus Clausus; Nyugat;* Ottoman Empire; Pan-Slavism; Paris Peace Conference; Peasants; Percentages Agreement; Sándor Petőfi; Philosophy; Privatization; Protectorate of Bohemia and Moravia; Railroads; László Rajk; Mátyás Rákosi; Red Army; Revisionism; Revolutions of 1848; Revolutions of 1989; Right-Radicalism; Romanticism; Stalin; Ľudovít Štúr; Sudeten Crisis; Ferenc Szálasi; István Széchenyi; Albert Szent-Györgyi; Leo Szilárd; *Szlachta;* Döme Sztójay; Pál Teleki; Edward Teller; István Tisza; Kálmán Tisza; Tito; Trade Unionism; Transylvania; Trianon, Treaty of; Vienna Awards; Mihály Vörösmarty; Warsaw Pact; White Terror; Women in Hungary; World War I; World War II

Hurban-Vajanský, Svetozár (1847–1916)

Slovak writer, political journalist, and editor. Hurban-Vajanský belonged to a generation of Slovak intellectuals at a time when all attempts to reach national rights within Hungary had failed and Magyarization (the spreading of Hungarian language and culture) seemed to threaten the very existence of Slovaks as a separate nation. All his activities were permeated by a perception that mighty Russia would liberate the oppressed Slavonic peoples.

Hurban-Vajanský began his career with a book of poetry, *Tatry a more* (*The Tatry Mountains and the Sea,* 1879), considered the starting point for realism in Slovak poetry as well as for a new verse structure. As a prose writer, Hurban-Vajanský authored hundreds of novels, short stories, travel sketches, and the like. His most representative novels included *Suchá ratolesť* (*A Faded Branch,* 1884) and *Letiace tiene* (*Flying Shadows,* 1883). His prose evoked various aspects of Slovak society as he ideally envisioned it, trying to identify Slovak aspects in the by-then almost completely Magyarized gentry, worrying about a Magyarized intelligentsia and the consequences of crass capitalism.

His novel *Kotlín* (1901) is a critique of the young liberal generation, pupils of Czech philosopher Tomáš G. Masaryk (1850–1937), a group that criticized Hurban-Vajanský's generation for conservativism, Russophilism, and political passivity, and demanded more Czech- or generally Western-oriented Slovak politics.

Hurban-Vajanský was especially important as a journalist and editor. For several years, he was editor of two main Slovak periodicals: the daily *Národnie noviny* (*The National Journal*) and the monthly review *Slovenské pohľady* (*Slovak Views*). In their pages he skillfully and sharply defended the Slovaks against Magyarization.

Ľubomír Ďurovič

Further reading

Čepan, Oskar. "Vajanského významotvorný princíp." *Slovenská literatúra* 14 (1967): 167–92.

Matuška, Alexander. *Vajanský prozaik.* Bratislava, 1946.

Petrus, Pavol. *Svetozár Hurban Vajanský.* Bratislava, 1978.

See also Magyarization; Tomáš G. Masaryk; Press; Slovak Literature

Husák, Gustáv (1913–91)

Slovak Communist who returned Czechoslovakia to orthodox Marxism after the Prague Spring, the liberal period in Communist Czechoslovakia during the spring and summer of 1968. Husák was born near Bratislava. Trained in law and an ardent Slovak nationalist and Marxist, he joined the Czechoslovak Communist Party in 1933. During the wartime Slovak Republic, he was repeatedly jailed for illegal Communist activities. In 1943 he joined the covert Slovak National Council, which staged a violent revolt against the clerico-fascist government in the fall of 1944. When the uprising failed, he fled to the Soviet Union, returning to liberated Czechoslovakia in 1945.

In postwar Czechoslovakia, Husák held important party and government posts. But in 1951, as a prominent "national Communist," he was accused of treason and sabotage and sentenced to life imprisonment in 1954. He was amnestied in 1960 and fully rehabilitated in 1963. In the 1960s he joined the Prague Spring reformers who sought to humanize and de-Sovietize Czechoslovak communism, but when Warsaw Pact forces invaded the country on August 20, 1968, Husák renounced the reformers. With Soviet support, he became Communist Party secretary in April 1969, as well as president of Czechoslovakia in May 1975. He rapidly "normalized" the country into an obedient puppet of Moscow, harshly repressing dissidents such as Charter 77 and Soviet troops were stationed on Czechoslovak soil. However, Husák did permit the planned Czech-Slovak federalization in 1969. Stubbornly opposed to the Communist reform movement of the 1980s, he was replaced as party secretary in December 1987, and as president in December 1989 during the Velvet Revolution which toppled the Communist regime. He died on November 18, 1991.

Joseph Frederick Zacek

Further reading

Husák, Gustáv. *Speeches and Writings.* New York, 1986.

Kusin, Vladimir V. *From Dubček to Charter 77: A Study of "Normalization" in Czechoslovakia, 1968–1978.* New York, 1978.

See also Charter 77; Communist Party of Czechoslovakia; Prague Spring; Slovak Republic; Warsaw Pact

Hviezdoslav, Pavol O. (1849–1921)

Slovak poet of national and social themes. The third major poet of the modern Slovak language definitively codified in the 1850s, Hviezdoslav was inspired by his predecessor Andrej Sládkovič (1820–72) to drop his early Magyar versifying, and he became the first Slovak poet to achieve international notice and to produce fine translations of major Western European poetry (Shakespeare [1564–1616], Goethe [1749–1832], Hugo [1802–85], Dante [1265–1321]). His talents encompassed epic, lyrical, and dramatic texts. Hviezdoslav's verse epics ranged from short allegories, biblical (*Agar,* 1883, and *Ráchel,* 1891), or folkloric (*Na Luciu* [*On St. Lucy's Day*], 1904), to monumental elegies of the corrupt, dying aristocracy (*Ežo Vlkolinský,* 1890, and *Gábor Vlkolinský,* 1901) and paeans to earthy peasant heroism (*Hájnikova žena* [*The Woodsman's Wife*], 1884–86). The blank-verse drama *Herodes a Herodias* (*Herod and Herodias,* 1909) shows Parnassian (which emphasized metrical form) historical and moral exaltation. Hviezdoslav returned to lyrics in a cycle of thirty-two *Krvavé sonety* (*Bloody Sonnets,* 1914), condemning the world war but passionately hoping for social justice for the Slavs in the coming peace and defending himself against the charge of treason for his Slovak and Czechoslovak aspirations. Much of his work allegorizes the Slovaks' unhappy position in Austria-Hungary. Hviezdoslav's involved diction and complex prosody lessen his accessibility for modern readers, but his historical significance is uncontested.

Norma L. Rudinsky and Michal Gáfrik

Further reading

Hviezdoslav, Pavol O. *Bloody Sonnets,* trans. by Jaroslav Vajda, intro. by Karol Štrmen. Scranton, Pennsylvania, 1950.

———. *Spisy P. O. Hviezdoslava v 12 zväzkoch,* ed. by Ján Brezina and Andrej Kostolný. Martin, Slovakia, 1951–57.

Turčány, Viliam. "Hviezdoslav a Shakespeare." *Slovenská literatúra* 11 (1963): 193–251.

See also Slovak Literature

I

Iancu, Avram (1824–72)

Transylvanian-born Romanian who led the armed resistance to the Hungarians in Transylvania during the revolution of 1848–49. The son of well-off peasants, Iancu studied law at the secondary school in Cluj (Hungarian, Kolozsvár) from 1841 to 1847. After working briefly with the provincial treasury in Sibiu, he was engaged by the provincial court in Tîrgu Mureş. As the leader of the Romanian patriots in that city, he helped organize the Romanian National Committee to defend Romanian rights. Relations with the Hungarians over Romanian rights in Transylvania worsened, and at an assembly in Blaj in September 1848, the people were called to arms. Iancu became the leader of the suprisingly successful Romanian military resistance to the Hungarians. While allied with the Austrian imperial forces, he controlled Transylvania's Western Mountains and was popularly titled "King of the Mountains." He received peace overtures from the Hungarian government sceptically but eventually declared his troops' neutrality after Hungary approved a liberal nationality statute in July 1849. Owing to this fact, as well as to his stubborn defense of the mountaineers' social interests, the victorious Austrians offered him only a mediocre decoration, which he refused. Arrested and abused by local authorities in 1852, he became mentally deranged and never again played a public role. Romanians considered him a hero and a martyr.

James P. Niessen

Further reading

Dragomir, Silviu. *Avram Iancu.* Bucharest, 1965.

Pascu, Stefan. *Avram Iancu: Viaţa şi faptele unui erou şi martir.* Bucharest, 1972.

Ranca, Ioan. *Avram Iancu: Documente şi bibliografie.* Bucharest, 1974.

Teodor, Pompiliu. *Avram Iancu în memoralistica.* Cluj, Romania, 1972.

See also Blaj; Hungarian War for Independence; Revolutions of 1848

Iaşi

Historic capital of Moldavia. Situated 8 miles (13.5 km) from the border with Moldova on the shores of the Bahlui River, Iaşi was settled in the seventh century. By the fourteenth century, it served as a military outpost and customs station on trade routes. The city gradually succeeded Suceava as the capital of Moldavia in the sixteenth century as ruling families established their primary residence in the more economically prosperous area of Iaşi.

As the Moldavian capital, Iaşi was the site of many historic events. In 1792 the Treaty of Iaşi recognized Russian acquisition of the lands between the Bug and Dniester Rivers and redrew the Russian border tangent to Moldavia. In January 1859 Moldavians hoping to unify the Danubian Principalities into one state unanimously elected Alexandru Ioan Cuza (1820–73) to rule Moldavia. Elections soon followed in Bucharest, confirming Cuza's reign over Wallachia too. The de facto unification of the two territories by the double election of Cuza was a precursor to the formation of the independent Romanian national state. In 1860 the oldest university in Romania, named after Cuza, was founded in Iaşi. The city also served as the headquarters of the Romanian government beginning in December 1916 during World War I after the king and his ministers were forced to evacuate Bucharest by invading Austro-Hungarian and German forces.

The city is presently the capital of the district of Iaşi with a population of approximately 340,000. Agricultural products, metal and leather goods, furniture, and candles are manufactured there.

Tanya L.K. Dunlap

Further reading

Cihodaru, Constantin and Gheorge Platon, eds. *Istoria Oraşului Iaşi,* vol. 1. Iaşi, 1980.

Giurescu, Constantin C. and Dinu C. Giurescu. *Istoria Românilor.* Bucharest, 1975.

See also Alexandru Ioan Cuza; Danubian Principalities; Moldavia

Ignatiev, Nikolai Pavlovich, Count (1832–1908)

One of the most controversial Russian diplomats of the nineteenth century, whose activities had a profound effect on Eastern Europe. Ignatiev's career began at the Congress of Paris in 1856, which ended the Crimean War (1853–56). In 1858 he concluded a successful friendship and trade mission with Bukhara in Central Asia. In 1860 he negotiated the highly advantageous Treaty of Peking, in which China recognized Russia's control of all lands west of the Amur River and those between the Ussuri River and the Pacific. Thereby Russia emerged as a Pacific power with its base in Vladivostok.

Ignatiev was appointed head of the Foreign Office Asiatic Department, which included the Ottoman Empire. In 1864 he was designated ambassador to Constantinople (Istanbul), one of Russia's most important posts. It was here that he gained international attention, principally because of his close association with Pan-Slavism. Ignatiev was a Russian nationalist who sought to exploit Pan-Slav sentiment on behalf of the tsar. Although he fought to preserve unity within the Orthodox Church, he could not forestall the split between the Ecumenical Patriarchate in Constantinople and the Bulgarians, which led to the creation of the Bulgarian Exarchate (an independent Bulgarian Orthodox Church) in 1870–72.

During the Balkan crisis of 1875–78, Ignatiev first championed the Serbs and then the Bulgarians. Following the Russo-Turkish War of 1877–78, which, in part, he fostered, Ignatiev was the architect of the Treaty of San Stefano, which created the Pan-Slavic Greater Bulgaria. The treaty included Bulgaria and all the Macedonian lands, which drastically weakened the Ottoman Empire in the Balkans and gave Russia predominant influence there by outflanking the strategic Turkish Straits—the Bosphorus and the Dardanelles. Led by Great Britain, Austria-Hungary, and Germany, Russia was compelled at the Congress of Berlin in 1878 to accept the partition of Greater Bulgaria, an act seen as a humiliating defeat for Russia generally and Ignatiev personally. He was recalled as ambassador and his influence in official circles waned quickly, even though he held several other administrative posts until the mid-1880s.

Charles Jelavich

Further reading

Jelavich, Charles and Barbara Jelavich. *The Establishment of the Balkan National States, 1804–1920.* Seattle, Washington, 1977.

See also Congress of Berlin; Eastern Question; Exarchate; Pan-Slavism; Patriarchate; Russo-Turkish War of 1877–78; San Stefano, Treaty of

Ilarion (1812–75)

Bulgarian patriot and most outspoken religious leader in the struggle for an independent Bulgarian church. He was born Ilarion Stoyanovitch Mikhailovski. In September 1858 Ilarion was consecrated bishop of St. Stefan's Church in Constantinople and took the name Makariopolsky. Since the 1820s, the leaders of the Bulgarian national movement had been demanding religious autonomy, and this eventually grew into a movement for an autocephalous Bulgarian Orthodox Church. This was opposed by the Ecumenical Patriarchate in Constantinople, which had jurisdiction over most of the Orthodox peoples of the Ottoman Balkans. On Easter Sunday 1860, Bishop Ilarion celebrated the liturgy in St. Stefan's Church but omitted the Greek Patriarch's name. This act represented the symbolic break with the Ecumenical Patriarchate on the part of the Bulgarians and had a tremendous impact in Bulgaria as numerous priests followed his example. The Bulgarians no longer recognized the patriarch as their supreme religious leader.

Bishop Ilarion and his supporters were subsequently excommunicated by the patriarch. Nevertheless, Ilarion's action represented an important step toward ecclesiastical independence and national self-identity. This conflict was essentially political rather than religious, for it was a clash of two opposing nationalisms, Bulgarian and Greek. Hence, the 1860s saw a bitter nationalist struggle under the guise of an ecclesiastical issue. Ilarion played a crucial role in this struggle and in the establishment of an autonomous Bulgarian Orthodox Church—the Exarchate—which was formally decreed by the Ottoman authorities in 1870, although it was not created until February 1872.

Mark Biondich

Further reading
MacDermott, Mercia. *A History of Bulgaria, 1393–1885*. London, 1962.
Sirakov, Stan'o. *Ilarion Makariopolski*. Sofia, 1973.

See also Exarchate; Patriarchate

Iliescu, Ion (1930–)
Former Romanian Communist Party official demoted by Nicolae Ceauşescu (1918–89) in 1971, and later president of Romania, from Ceauşescu's overthrow in 1989 until 1996. Born to a Communist family, Iliescu studied in Moscow in the early 1950s and then returned to Bucharest, where he worked with youth organizations, including the Union of Communist Youth (UCY). From 1956 to 1960, he was president of the National Student Association. During the 1960s, he worked at the party's Central Committee, and in 1967–71 he headed the UCY. He became a Central Committee secretary in February 1971 and traveled to China and North Korea with the Ceauşescus in June—a trip followed by Romanian emulation of the Asian communist cultural revolutions and personality cults. He lost his post in the Secretariat in July 1971 after having disagreed with Ceauşescu.

Thereafter he was relegated to party posts in Timiş and Iaşi counties, at the Ministry for Water Supply, and as head of a technical publishing house. Although approached during the 1980s by various conspirators trying to overthrow Ceau-

şescu, he never committed himself sufficiently to warrant arrest. In December 1989 he played a major role in establishing the post-Ceauşescu government and emerged as its leader. Elected president in national elections in May 1990, he was reelected in September 1992 but lost to Emil Constantinescu (1939–) in 1996.

Mary Ellen Fischer

Further reading
Behr, Edward. *Kiss the Hand You Cannot Bite: The Rise and Fall of the Ceauşescus*. New York, 1991.
Nelson, Daniel N., ed. *Romania after Tyranny*. Boulder, Colorado, 1992.
Ratesh, Nestor. *Romania: The Entangled Revolution*. New York, 1991.

See also Elena Ceauşescu; Nicolae Ceauşescu; Communist Party of Romania

Ilinden Uprising (1903)
Unsuccessful revolt for Macedonian autonomy, launched by the Internal Macedonian Revolutionary Organization (IMRO) in the Monastir region of Macedonia on August 2–15, 1903 (Saint Elijah's Day, or *Ilinden* in Slavonic). The revolt is also called the Ilinden-Preobrazhenski Uprising after the revolt spread to the Adrianople area of Macedonia on August 6–19 (Transfiguration Day, or *Preobrazhenski*).

IMRO'S nationalistic aim of autonomy for Macedonia's Slavic Christians precipitated the poorly conceived and ill-fated rebellion, with most fighting occurring in the Monastir, Adrianople, and Salonika regions of Ottoman Macedonia. Despite the insurgents' mobility and some initial successes, Ottoman forces used superior manpower and firepower to crush the uprising. IMRO's cause was further doomed when Bulgaria failed to provide expected military aid. With IMRO insurgents demoralized and retreating, Ottoman reprisals victimized villages, homes, crops, women, children, and other noncombatants in regions that had cooperated with the rebel bands.

Although it failed, the Ilinden revolt prompted Russian and Habsburg diplomatic intervention. Franz Joseph (1830–1916) and Nicholas II (1868–1918) met at Mürzsteg and proposed reforms for Macedonia: Ottoman police to be placed under

I foreign control, victims of the uprising to receive financial compensation, and administrative boundaries to be delineated along ethnic lines. These and subsequent reform efforts, however, did not resolve the Macedonian question. The province remained badly governed and volatile, while the issue continued to bedevil Balkan and Ottoman politics.

The Ilinden debacle discredited and fragmented IMRO, which never regained its former cohesion and unity. Bulgaria's claim to Macedonia was severely undermined by that state's non-intervention and by the flight of Macedonian Bulgars. Sectarian conflict between Christians and Muslims, as well as increasingly frequent ethnic clashes among Serb, Greek, Bulgarian, and Macedonian armed bands, made the Macedonian question all the more explosive on the eve of the Balkan Wars (1912–13).

Theophilus C. Prousis

Further reading

Crampton, Richard. *Bulgaria, 1878–1918: A History.* Boulder, Colorado, 1983.
Dakin, Douglas. *The Greek Struggle for Macedonia, 1897–1913.* Thessaloniki, 1966.
Jelavich, Barbara. *History of the Balkans: Twentieth Century.* New York, 1983.
Perry, Duncan. *The Politics of Terror: The Macedonian Liberation Movements, 1893–1903.* Durham, North Carolina, 1988.
Poulton, Hugh. *Who Are the Macedonians?* Bloomington, Indiana, 1995.

See also Balkan Wars; Franz Joseph; IMRO; Macedonia; Mürzsteg Agreement; Nicholas II

Illyés, Gyula (1902–83)

Hungarian poet, prose writer, dramatist, member of the populist writers' group, editor of the literary journal *Nyugat* (*West*, later renamed *Magyar Csillag* [*Hungarian Star*]), and, after 1945, editor of the literary journal *Válasz* (*Answer*). Illyés was born in 1902 on a large estate in western Hungary to parents who were servants for aristocratic families. With great difficulty he managed to acquire a secondary education, and because of his minor role in the upheavals of 1919 was forced into exile by the regime of Admiral Horthy (1868–1957). After spending four years in Paris, he returned to Hungary imbued with the spirit of French surrealism. By the end of the 1920s, he was a recognized poet, having won the admiration and recognition of Mihály Babits (1883–1941), chief editor of *Nyugat*. Before he died in April 1983, Illyés had become a celebrated national poet, decorated with honors from both home and abroad.

Illyés's poetry is characterized by his concern for the survival of his nation and the intolerable living conditions of the peasant class, conditions he himself experienced firsthand. He saw his role as a poet of the community, a spokesman for the underdog, the disenfranchised, and the exploited. His approach to these issues underwent a stylistic evolution from his early youthful poems reflecting the influence of the French avant-garde, to a more mature, realistic, simple, orderly, straightforward presentation in later years. His first volumes of poetry, *Nehéz föld* (*Heavy Earth,* 1928), and *Sarjúrendek* (*Swath of Aftermath,* 1930), captured in free verse the peasants' suppressed anger. His affinity for narrative poetry is evident in *Ifjúság* (*Youth,* 1932) and *Hősökről beszélek* (*I Speak of Heroes,* 1933). One of his most significant prose works, *Puszták népe* (*The People of the Puszta,* 1936), an autobiographical and sociological study, described the daily life of farm workers, while his *Petőfi* (1936) remains the best biography of the nineteenth-century national poet-hero, whom he saw as the embodiment of his own revolutionary ideals. Illyés also published historical dramas, folk comedies, travel books, and volumes of essays. Since the 1950s, his writings increasingly intimated a pessimism and disillusionment at the lessening prospects of social progress and the limitations of personal freedom by totalitarian government.

Katherine Gyékényesi Gatto

Further reading

Basa, Enikő M., spec. ed. *Hungarian Literature.* Whitestone, New York, 1993.
Czigány, Lóránt. *The Oxford History of Hungarian Literature.* Oxford, 1984.
Klaniczay, Tibor, ed. *A History of Hungarian Literature.* Budapest, 1982.
Reményi, Joseph. *Hungarian Writers and Literature: Modern Novelists, Critics, and Poets.* New Brunswick, New Jersey, 1964.

See also Mihály Babits; Miklós Horthy; Hungarian Literature; *Nyugat;* Sandor Petrőfi

Illyrian Movement

Name used for the Croat national revival, usually dated 1835–48. The political and cultural Illyrian Movement advocated traditional Croatian political privileges, cultural unity of all South Slavs, and adoption of a standard literary norm for Croatian based on the štokavian dialect spoken among both Catholic and Orthodox South Slavs. Most of those associated with the movement, like its leader, Ljudevit Gaj (1809–72), were Croats of social strata lower than that of the nobility, which alone possessed political rights in pre-1848 Croatia-Slavonia through the noble diet (Sabor). While the Illyrians' personal political views spanned a wide spectrum, before the Revolutions of 1848 they all collaborated with sympathetic noblemen and, after 1845, with the Hungarian Conservatives. In self-defense against opponents among the nobility, the Illyrians organized an Illyrian Party in 1841, under Gaj's slogan "May God preserve the Hungarian Constitution, the Croatian Kingdom, and the Illyrian Nationality." In 1843, after Emperor Ferdinand (1793–1875) banned the use of the term "Illyrian," the party became the National Party and ultimately in 1847 dominated the last traditional Sabor, which made the newly standardized language official in Croatia-Slavonia.

Although now considered Croat national awakeners, Gaj and other Illyrians were under the influence of Slovak reformer Ján Kollár's (1793–1852) ideas of Slavic reciprocity and spoke initially of the nation to which they belonged as much wider than Croatia. The entity was the Slavic nation and later the Illyrian nation, not initially Croatia. The term "Illyrian" harkened back to the Roman province of Illyria and to Napoléon's (1769–1821) short-lived Illyrian Provinces (1809–15) but also to an early modern tradition among educated, primarily clerical South Slavs, both Catholic and Orthodox, which referred to the dominant Slavic language of the whole Balkans as Illyrian. Gaj consciously chose the term to transcend narrower regional, ethnic, and religious identities. With a few notable exceptions, however, Illyrianism appealed mostly to inhabitants of Croatia and Slavonia and to educated Catholics, primarily clergy, in Dalmatia and Bosnia. However, Illyrians were responsible for the ultimate choice as the basis of literary Croatian of the štokavian dialect spoken in Slavonia, Bosnia, and Dalmatia, rather than the more geographically restricted čakavian, spoken primarily on the coast of Dalmatia, or kajkavian, the dialect of Zagreb and its hinterland.

Illyrian literature, strongly influenced by European romanticism, consists primarily of patriotic prose and poetry, both lyric and epic, much of which appeared in Gaj's newspaper *Danica* (*The Morning Star*). Illyrian literature's patriotic themes remained true to notions of Slavic reciprocity. Ivan Mažuranić's (1814–90) *Smrt Smail-age Čengića* (*The Death of Smail-Aga Ćengić,* 1846), for example, which is generally acknowledged as the best Illyrian work, deals with warfare between Orthodox Montenegrins and Muslim South Slavs.

James P. Krokar

Further reading

Banac, Ivo. "Main Trends in the Croat Language Question," in *Aspects of the Slavic Language Question,* vol. 1, *Church Slavonic—South Slavic—West Slavic,* ed. by Riccardo Picchio and Harvey Goldblatt. New Haven, Connecticut, 1984.

Despalatović, Elinor Murray. *Ljudevit Gaj and the Illyrian Movement.* Boulder, Colorado, 1975.

Djilas, Aleksa. "The Illyrianist Movement and the Logic of the Yugoslav Idea." *South Slav Journal* 10 (1987): 46–54.

Šidak, Jaroslav. "Hrvatski narodni preporod—Ideje i problemi," in *Studije iz hrvatske povijesti 19 stoljeća.* Zagreb, 1973.

Vucinich, Wayne. "Croatian Illyrism: Its Background and Genesis," in *Intellectual and Social Developments in the Habsburg Empire from Maria Theresa to World War I,* ed. by Stanley B. Winters and Joseph Held. Boulder, Colorado, 1975.

See also Croatian Literature; Ljudevit Gaj; Ján Kollár; Ivan Mažuranić; Napoléon; Revolutions of 1848; Romanticism; Serbo-Croatian Language

Imrédy, Béla (1891–1946)

Hungarian economist, bank official, and politician. After completing law school, Imrédy began his career in the Ministry of Finance. From 1932 to 1935, he was minister of finance, after which he was appointed president of the Hungarian National Bank. In March 1938 he rejoined the cabinet and became prime minister two months later. Up to the time of the Munich conference, called because of German claims regarding the Sudetenland of Czechoslovakia, Imrédy favored a pro-British orientation in Hungary's foreign policy; after it, he placed his money on the Germans. Under his administration, Hungary joined the Anti-Comintern Pact (with Berlin and Rome) and passed anti-Jewish legislation. In February 1939 Imrédy felt compelled to resign after his opponents produced evidence of his own part-Jewish ancestry. He then quit the Government Party and founded the Party of Hungarian Renewal, which followed a right-radical agenda. Imrédy returned to the limelight of wartime politics after the German occupation of Hungary, when he became minister in charge of economic affairs (May–August 1944). After the war, he was convicted of war crimes and executed.

N.F. Dreisziger

Further reading

Tilkovsky, Loránd. "The Late Interwar Years and World War II," in Peter F. Sugar et al., eds. *A History of Hungary.* Bloomington, Indiana, 1990.

See also Anti-Comintern Pact; Right Radicalism

IMRO (Internal Macedonian Revolutionary Organization)

Common and, after 1912, official name of the Macedonian national liberation organization. In English it is usually referred to either as IMRO, or MRO (Macedonian Revolutionary Organization).

IMRO was founded in Salonika on November 3, 1893. In the spring of 1896 the Congress of IMRO declared its governing principle: achievement of full political autonomy for Macedonia and the province of Adrianople through internal revolution. Its members were primarily composed of Macedonian Christians. The Central Committee, chosen at this congress, controlled the hierarchically established regional, district, and local committees, as well as the organization's armed units. Despite the opposition of a number of influential leaders, a congress held in Salonika in 1903 decided to launch an armed rebellion in Macedonia. The Ilinden-Preobraženski Uprising began on August 2, 1903. But members of the Supremist Movement, an organization controlled by the Bulgarian government with the principal goal of

annexing Macedonia to Bulgaria, had infiltrated and weakened IMRO; moreover, the Bulgarian state and church were hostile to it, the Ottoman regime was persecuting and arresting its followers, the Great Powers rejected revolutionary activities, and Serbia and Greece wanted to reduce its growing influence. Under such unfavorable circumstances, the rebel army, composed mainly of scattered, ill-equipped, outnumbered Macedonian peasant units, could not really succeed. Despite the initial successes, mainly in Bitola (Monastir) province, the rebellion was suppressed, and the Macedonian population suffered from Turkish reprisals. The Macedonian revolutionary organization became disorganized and its manpower wasted.

After the uprising, the organization split into two factions. At its Rila Congress in 1905, the so-called left wing of the organization advocated full liberation of Macedonia from Turkish rule, democratization and decentralization of the movement, and rejection of external, mainly Bulgarian, influences and armed bands; the right wing sided with the Supremists, who looked to coordination with Bulgaria and a Greater Bulgaria policy. In the period after the Young Turk Revolution of 1908, IMRO's leadership dissolved the armed units and organized a legal political and national movement by forming the People's Federal Party. Dissatisfied with the progress of the reforms in the Ottoman Empire, a number of former IMRO followers reestablished a Central Committee in Sofia in 1911 and proceeded with terrorist activities in Macedonia.

After the Balkan Wars (1912–13) and World War I, Serbia, Bulgaria, and Greece partitioned Macedonia against the will of the Macedonian population. Bulgaria, dissatisfied with the terms of the partition, supported the Supremist IMRO; this organization claimed to fight for the independence of the whole of Macedonia, organized a parallel legal and military power in the Bulgarian part of Macedonia (Pirin Macedonia), started to eliminate its ideological opponents, sent armed bands into the Serbian (Vardar) and Greek (Aegean) parts of Macedonia, and played an important role in internal Bulgarian political struggles. In 1924, in Vienna, the leadership of the organization accepted the May Manifesto, which called for the unification of all Macedonian liberation organizations, for an independent Macedonia in its geographic and ethnic boundaries, as well as for cutting off all connections with the Sofia government. As a result, Bulgarian military circles killed its leader. In the aftermath, internal struggles in the organization developed, while the general policy of the organization remained unchanged. On May 19, 1934, the new Bulgarian military government prohibited the work of IMRO, and members who had avoided arrest were forced to continue their activity in emigration by supporting fascist movements.

In 1925, also in Vienna, pro-Communist–oriented Macedonians, who remained loyal to the May Manifesto, organized an independent Macedonian liberation organization. It became known as IMRO-United, and its main goal became the struggle for the unification and liberation of Macedonia with the support of the Comintern (Communist International). It survived until 1936.

Aleksandar Panev

Further reading

Bogoev, Ksente and Manol Pandevski, eds. *A Hundred Years on from the Founding of I.M.R.O. (VMRO) and Ninety Years on from the Ilinden Uprising, Symposium, October 21–23, 1993.* Skopje, 1994.

Katardžiev, Ivan. *Sto godini od formiranjeto na VMRO: Sto godini revolucionerna tradicija.* Skopje, Macedonia, 1993.

———. *Vreme na zreenje: Makedonskoto nacionalno prasanje megju dvete svetski vojni 1919–1930),* 2 vols. Skopje, 1977.

Perry, Duncan. *The Politics of Terror: The Macedonian Revolutionary Movements 1893—1903.* Durham, North Carolina, 1988.

See also Alexander I Karadjordjević; Balkan Wars; Comintern; Ilinden Uprising; Young Turks

Independent State of Croatia *See* Ustaša

Industrialization

Industry did not develop to any significant extent in East Central Europe until the last three decades of the nineteenth century. Generally, the farther south and east the region, the later the economies industrialized.

The historic Czech lands, along with the Habsburg Empire's capital of Vienna, were among the first areas in the region to industrialize. The protectionist policies of Austrian empress Maria Theresa (1717–80) and Joseph II (1741–90) promoted glass and textile factories, as well as mining. The nobility also played an important role in industry's earliest stages, especially in Bohemia and Moravia. Industry did not expand as rapidly as it had in the English economy but grew in a more gradual, protracted manner. The empire contained a sufficient number of craftsmen and could afford to hire English mechanics, but it lacked the commercial ties and abundant natural resources that spurred German and French industrial growth. As such, industrialization progressed only piecemeal at first, while outmoded laws and bureaucratic red tape hindered the pace of expansion. Some of the ruling landed aristocracy deliberately wanted a slower pace of industrial expansion; the Viennese government and the Hungarian nobility remained suspicious of large-scale production because of its threatening political and social consequences. Nonetheless, the flood of cheap English textiles into the region following the Napoleonic Wars forced existing enterprises in Bohemia to mechanize and create more efficient, modern factories. Industrialization accelerated after competition, the crushing defeat of Austria in the Austro-Prussian War of 1866, and the *Ausgleich* (Compromise) of 1867, which created the Dual Monarchy of Austria-Hungary, made it politically possible.

Industrial advances in the machine, chemical, paper, and electrical industries accelerated in the last three decades of the nineteenth century and peaked during the first decade of the twentieth. The availability of coal in Bohemia and oil in Polish Galicia provided the raw materials that fueled industrial progress. The Czech lands attracted the overwhelming majority of heavy industry as well as thriving breweries and sugar refineries. By World War I, about 70 percent of the Austrian half of the Dual Monarchy found its home in Bohemia and Moravia.

In the Hungarian half of the empire, a small middle class, outdated laws, and heavy tax burdens combined to impede growth. Only when the Hungarian state moved in and heavily subsidized an industrial infrastructure did factories begin to boom. Mechanization in agriculture and expansion of roads, bridges, and railroads stimulated the iron and machine industries. In addition, more food sources fostered the rapid expansion of food-processing industries. Nevertheless, some enterprises continued to rely on artisan production late into the nineteenth century.

Capital for Hungarian industrialization came primarily from foreign sources, mainly Viennese and other European financial institutions. The greatest concentration of Hungarian industry developed in Budapest, and secondarily, in northern Hungary (Slovakia). Most Hungarian industries aimed at producing for domestic consumption; milling was the only substantial export industry, spurred by the invention of the rolling mill, which could process the bountiful Hungarian grain harvests. Between 1866 and 1873, Hungarian production grew 18 percent annually, largely owing to the fact of a high rate of reinvestment from profits (50 percent). By the end of the century, a domestic industry in textiles, machinery, paper, and leather goods even displaced many of the Austrian and Czech products that had dominated the Hungarian market.

Russian Poland industrialized during the 1870s as Russian markets opened up with the abolition of customs and the construction of railroads. Textiles, food processing, and some heavy industries predominated in the western regions. Industrial production rose ninefold in three decades. Thus, by the turn of the century, a structural transformation of the economies of Austria-Hungary and Polish territories had definitely occurred.

Such was less the case in the Balkan countries, where the declining Ottoman Empire did little to promote industrialization. Bulgaria and Serbia saw little growth in their industrial sectors until the years just prior to World War I. On the other hand, Romania showed slightly higher levels of output because of foreign investment in its lucrative petroleum industry. Most of the crude was exported, placing Romania in fifth place among world oil producers. Oil-generated wealth heated up the Romanian economy and led to a threefold spurt in production in the iron, machine, and timber industries by 1914.

In general, most of East Central Europe experienced only the beginnings of industrialization by World War I. Unlike the classical English model, food processing rather than textiles was the leading manufacture, and foreign, not domestic, capital provided the financing. Although substantial economic changes had occurred, most of these countries continued to remain agrarian and dependent on agricultural exports to a more developed Western Europe. Moreover, the Great Depression retarded growth even further.

World War II wreaked damage on much of the industrial sector. After the war, Soviet forces extracted huge reparations payments of industrial materials from the lands occupied by the Red Army. Central planning also began, first with two- and three-year plans, followed by the Soviet-style Five-Year Plans. These emphasized investment in heavy industry at the expense of the agricultural sector and consumer goods. Marxist ideology dictated the expansion of the energy and metallurgical industries. Massive steel works were erected throughout the Soviet bloc: the Lenin Plant in Nowa Huta and the Bierut Complex near Czestochowa, Poland; the Gottwald Steel Works in Moravia and the huge steel plant in Košice, Slovakia; Dunapentele and Csepel in Hungary; huge expansions near Hunedoara in Romania; and the giant Kremikovtsi complex outside Sofia, Bulgaria.

The grandiose plans created new jobs but diverted investment from the more practical production of chemicals and plastics. In addition, the emphasis on quantity rather than quality made Eastern Europe's products less competitive in the world market. Soviet dominance tied the region's economies to Moscow via the Council for Mutual Economic Assistance (CMEA), which determined where individual countries would allocate investment and what products would be traded within the socialist bloc. Only Yugoslavia (and later Romania and Albania) opted for their own industrial planning, yet with hardly more success than that of their neighbors.

Despite this regimentation, substantial economic growth did occur, which improved the standard of living for most people, and consumer goods started to become more available by the 1960s. Still, planners realized that decentralization would be required to continue to increase productivity. Hungary's and Czechoslovakia's initial plans were thwarted by Soviet-led invasions in 1956 and 1968, respectively. However, Hungary introduced the "new economic model" during the 1960s, which gave industrial managers more latitude and provided for profit incentives. Industrial output and exports rose substantially at first in Hungary, but central authorities choked off what might have been a more buoyant expansion.

By the 1980s, nearly all the economies of the region had stagnated, falling behind the technological advances of the West. At the same time, people's expectations had been raised and countries such as Poland could satisfy consumer demand only through extensive borrowing. The failure of the Soviet economic system contributed to the discontent that eventually toppled the various Communist governments in 1989.

New challenges for East Central European industry require the building of an infrastructure to compete in the modern world. Domestic and foreign investment are leading to a rebuilding of the factories, roads, and telecommunications systems, and to the hope of integration into the European Union.

Michael J. Kopanic, Jr.

Further reading
Berend, Iván T. and György Ránki. *Economic Development in East-Central Europe in the 19th and 20th Centuries.* New York, 1974.
————. *The European Periphery and Industrialization 1780–1914.* Cambridge, 1982.
Good, David F. *The Economic Rise of the Habsburg Empire, 1750–1914.* Berkeley, California, 1984.
Kaser, M.C. and E.A. Radice, eds. *The Economic History of Eastern Europe 1919–1975,* 3 vols. Oxford, 1985–86.
Komlos, John. *The Habsburg Monarchy as a Customs Union.* Princeton, New Jersey, 1983.
Lampe, John R. and Marvin R. Jackson. *Balkan Economic History, 1550–1950.* Bloomington, Indiana, 1982.

See also Banking; Comecon; Economic Development in Albania; Economic Development in Bulgaria; Economic Development in Czechoslovakia; Economic Development in Hungary; Economic Development in Poland; Economic Development in Romania; Economic Development in Yugoslavia; Great Depression; Labor; Law; NEM; Privatization; Railroads; Self-Management; SovRoms

Intelligentsia

Social class defined not by economic status but by predilection for sociopolitical ideologies, alienation from existing reality, and commitment to radical change. Its origins in Eastern Europe reach back to the years after Waterloo (1815), when intellectual activists enlisted a quasi-religious nationalism in their peoples' struggle for cultural renewal and political liberation. Representative was Adam Mickiewicz (1798–1855), the poet who proclaimed the stateless Polish people to be the "Christ of the Nations" and hence the soon-to-be-risen savior of oppressed peoples everywhere. Others, like Czech historian František Palacký (1798–1876), spoke in less messianic terms but with almost equal fervor of a coming national revival. So influential did they and like-minded members of the intelligentsia become that British historian Lewis Namier (1888–1960) scarcely exaggerated when he described the national uprisings of 1848–49 as a "revolution of the intellectuals."

After 1849, the nationalism of the intelligentsia assumed an increasingly exclusive and political character. "Young Czechs" adopted more militant tactics than Palacký and the "Old Czechs" were willing to countenance; Polish natural scientist Roman Dmowski (1864–1939) updated Mickiewicz with an all but total disregard for other nations; ideological defenders of Hungary's Magyarization policies sneered at the more charitable outlook of István Széchenyi (1791–1860) and József Eötvös (1813–71). To be sure, some members of the intelligentsia eschewed chauvinism, in part at least because of their allegiance to democracy, both political and social. Czech philosopher Tomáš G. Masaryk (1850–1937) and Hungarian poet Endre Ady (1877–1919) believed that respect for other peoples and advocacy of sociopolitical reform could be reconciled with fidelity to one's own nation, because both nationalism and democracy emphasized the importance of human association.

In the aftermath of the Great War and the creation, or re-creation, of what purported to be "nation-states," the East European intelligentsia concentrated its ire on the authoritarian social and political policies that, with the exception of President Masaryk's Czechoslovak democracy, the new governments pursued. That experience, when placed alongside the horrors of Hitler's (1889–1945) Reich and World War II, prompted many of its members to ally themselves with the Communists after 1945. One who did, the later repentant Czesław Miłosz (1911–), recalled that intellectuals, having gazed into the abyss of nihilism, thought they had discovered in communism a faith and a set of values by which to live. Their service to the postwar Communist regimes remains the darkest chapter in their collective history.

Before long, however, some began to entertain second thoughts. One of Yugoslav dictator

I Jozef Broz Tito's chief lieutenants, Milovan Djilas (1911–95), broke ranks with Tito (1892–1980) and, with the publication abroad of *The New Class: An Analysis of the Communist System* (1957), established himself as the paradigmatic "dissident," or Marxist humanist. Only a year earlier, agitation by conscience-stricken Communist intellectuals in Hungary helped trigger a violent revolution, the suppression of which occasioned new defections from official communism. Polish philosopher Leszek Kolakowski (1927–), for example, began to question *diamat* (dialectical materialism) and to explore other traditions of thought. Expelled from the party, he chose a life in exile.

So too did Czech novelist Milan Kundera (1929–), though only after he abandoned all hope of a new Prague Spring, the reform movement that Warsaw Pact forces crushed in 1968. Even the disciples of renowned Marxist theoretician György Lukács (1885–1971)—Ferenc Fehér (1933–94), Ágnes Heller (1929–), and György Márkus (1934–)—left Hungary because of irreconcilable conflicts with the government of János Kádár (1912–89). And though the neo-Marxist philosophers associated with the Yugoslav journal *Praxis* elected to remain in their homeland, they eventually had to suspend publication. In the end, almost every one of these former Communists abandoned the effort to revise Marxism, convinced, finally, that "Marxist humanism" was a contradiction in terms; in its stead they began to campaign for "radical" democracy.

Not all dissidents were ex-Communists, of course. Some, like Czech playwright Václav Havel (1936–), never succumbed to the totalitarian temptation, but the persecution to which they were subjected drove them into the ranks of semiorganized dissidence. Havel first caught the attention of the world when he and other intellectuals, including distinguished philosopher Jan Patočka (1907–77), issued Charter 77 (1977) in a vain attempt to prod the government into obeying its own laws. It would take years, mounting economic crises, and the appearance on the historical scene of Soviet leader Mikhail Gorbachev (1931–) before the dissidents' moment arrived. When it did, in 1989, their victory was capped by Havel's election as the democratic president of Czechoslovakia.

Lee Congdon

Further reading

Djilas, Milovan. *The New Class: An Analysis of the Communist System.* New York, 1985.

Masaryk, Tomáš G. *The Meaning of Czech History,* ed. by René Wellek and trans. by Peter Kussi. Chapel Hill, North Carolina, 1974.

Milosz, Czeslaw. *The Captive Mind,* trans. by Jane Zielonko. New York, 1951.

Namier, Lewis. *1848: The Revolution of the Intellectuals.* Garden City, New York, 1964.

Riese, Hans-Peter, ed. *Since the Prague Spring: Charter '77 and the Struggle for Human Rights in Czechoslovakia.* New York, 1979.

See also Endre Ady; Charter 77; Milovan Djilas; Roman Dmowski; József Eötvös; Václav Havel; Milan Kundera; György Lukács; Magyarization; Tomáš Masaryk; Adam Mickiewicz; Czesław Miłosz; Old Czechs; František Palacký; Prague Spring; István Széchenyi; Young Czechs

Ioanna (1907–79)

Queen of Bulgaria. The wife of Boris III (1894–1943), Ioanna (Giovanna) was born in 1907 in Rome, the daughter of Victor Emmanuel III of Italy (1869–1947). Ioanna married Boris on October 25, 1930, and acquiesced in his conviction to baptize their children in the Orthodox Church. She was well educated, an excellent linguist, and something of a cosmopolitan. When not at work, Boris spent all his free time with Ioanna. She kept out of state affairs and, from what is known, rarely discussed politics with her husband. Her interests and time were given to her family, the arts, and various charities. Ioanna remained a devoted wife, companion, and supporter of her husband until his untimely and suspicious death in 1943. After a Communist-conducted plebiscite outlawed the monarchy in 1946, she and her two children were given forty-eight hours to leave Bulgaria. They first traveled to Egypt and then settled in Spain, where the Bulgarian royal family presently resides.

David Cassens

Further reading

Groueff, Stephane. *Crown of Thorns: The Reign of King Boris III of Bulgaria, 1918–1943.* Lanham, Maryland, 1987.

Kazasov, Dimo. *Burni godini 1918–1944.* Sofia, 1949.

Miller, Marshall Lee. *Bulgaria during World War II.* Stanford, California, 1975.

See also Boris III

Ionescu, Eugen (1912–94)

Romanian-born playwright. Born in Slatina in 1912, Ionescu wrote poetry and criticism in Romanian and became one of the leaders of avant-garde theater in France after World War II. His plays bring into focus that language may lose meaning and be transformed into a sequence of sounds that hide egoistic and even mad purposes. The Romanian cultural milieu put its imprint on his work in different ways; in fact, he started by writing in Romanian, and his protest against self-sufficiency and routine uttered in the volume *Nu* (*No,* 1934) provoked a lively discussion in the literary press. The Romanian language is used frequently in his later plays, such as *The Lesson,* while the fascist movement in Romania inspired one of his greatest plays, *Rhinoceros.* Moreover, the conflict between automatism and clear thought, between illusion and a keen perception of reality, may have come to his mind through the plays of Romanian playwright and satirist I.L. Caragiale (1852–1912). Ionescu was inspired by Caragiale, who discovered with delight the mechanism of talking without thinking. Ionescu established a clear difference between cold reasoning and dreaming; we often utter slogans instead of thinking and dreaming: "The man whose spirit feeds with dreams may recapture the archetypes," a statement that is in tune with the thinking of Mircea Eliade (1907–86), Constantin Noica (1909–87), Mircea Vulcănescu (1904–52), and other outstanding scholars from interwar Romania. *Rhinoceros,* in which the British actor Laurence Olivier (1907–89) performed, and *Exit the King* met with international success. *The Chairs* and *Jacques or Obedience,* as well as *Victim of Duty,* go far behind analysis of verbal rhythm and raise the question that haunts us of the relationship between order and freedom. Ionescu died in Paris in 1994.

Alexandru Duţu

Further reading
Cleynen-Serghiev, Ecaterina. *La Jeunesse littéraire d'Eugène Ionesco.* Paris, 1993.

Ionesco, Marie-France, ed. *Non.* Paris, 1986.
Paleologu, Alexandru. *Spiritul şi litera,* Bucharest, 1970.

See also Ion Luca Caragiale; Mircea Eliade; Romanian Literature; Theater

Ionescu, Nae (1888–1940)

Romanian philosopher, journalist, politician, and sinister mentor of a generation of radical nationalist and ultra-Orthodox youth. Educated at the Universities of Bucharest, Göttingen, and Munich, where he received a doctorate in 1919, Ionescu was the founder of Romanian existentialism (*triarism*). He taught logic and metaphysics at the University of Bucharest and edited the extremist newspaper *Cuvântul* (*The Word*).

Ionescu's penchant for self-dramatization, his nihilistic style, and his undeniable success in gathering a passionate student following created a personal and ideological mythos that continues to influence Romanian ideas to the present despite his scanty published writings, persistent repudiation of the philosophical system, and deliberately vague and paradoxical nature of his work. His thought, which contained elements of German philosophers Hegel (1770–1831), Dilthey (1833–1911), and Spengler (1880–1936), as well as French writers Péguy (1873–1914) and Gide (1869–1951), lauded relativism, experiences, and the collective, and stressed the superiority of action-oriented "life" over mere contemplation. His devoted disciples included such luminaries as philosophers Mircea Eliade (1907–86), Emil Cioran (1911–95), Constantin Noica (1909–87), and Mircea Vulcănescu (1904–52).

In politics, he was at first a collaborator of Carol II (1893–1953), but by the mid-1930s, he became associated with Romania's leading right-radical movement, the Legion of the Archangel Michael (commonly known as the Legionary Movement, or the Iron Guard). He lost his teaching position in 1938 and died in March 1940, shortly before the Legionaries came to power.

Paul E. Michelson

Further reading
Eliade, Mircea. *Autobiography,* 2 vols. San Francisco, 1981–88.

I

Hitchins, Keith. *Rumania 1866–1947.* New York, 1994.

See also Carol II; Mircea Eliade; Iron Guard; Philosophy; Right Radicalism

Ionescu, Take (Dumitru G.) (1858–1922)

Romanian jurist, journalist, politician, and statesman. Born to a family of upwardly mobile shopkeepers in Ploeşti, Ionescu studied law in Paris, married an Englishwoman, and entered Romanian political life as a liberal and a journalist. He wrote for a number of Romanian and foreign newspapers, stressing the necessity and inevitability of Romanian national unification. Disillusioned by the Liberals' rejection of reform, he became a Conservative in 1885 and served as minister of education in two turn-of-the-century governments. In that capacity, he introduced drastic educational reform designed to spread literacy in rural areas.

In 1908 Ionescu founded the centrist Democratic Conservative Party, which attracted many of the foremost cultural and academic Romanians into its ranks. He was the leading figure in the Conservative government of Titu Maiorescu (1840–1917) from 1912 to 1913.

Ionescu wrote voluminously on foreign affairs, and in the Maiorescu government he played the central role in Romania's policy during the Balkan Wars of 1912–13. An advocate of Romania's joining World War I on the side of the Entente, Ionescu left Romania in mid-1918 to organize pro-Romanian activities in France, Britain, and Italy. Ion I.C. Brătianu (1864–1927), Romanian prime minister, excluded him, however, from Romania's delegation to the Paris Peace Conference in 1919.

Ionescu served as foreign minister in 1920–21 in the government of General Alexandru Averescu (1859–1938), overseeing the formation of the Little Entente, the alliance of Romania, Czechoslovakia, and the Kingdom of Serbs, Croats, and Slovenes (Yugoslavia), and establishing an alliance with Poland. Ionescu was briefly prime minister again (December 1921–January 1922) before his death from typhoid fever in Italy.

Walter M. Bacon Jr.

Further reading

Netea, Vasile. *Take Ionescu.* Bucharest, 1971.
Xeni, Constantin. *Take Ionescu.* Bucharest, n.d.

See also Alexandru Averescu; Balkan Wars; Ion I.C. Brătianu; Little Entente; Titu Maiorescu

Ionian Islands

Archipelago extending from the Albanian coast to the southern tip of the Peloponnisus that consists of seven major islands: Corfu, Paxos, Leucas, Ithaca, Cephalonia, Zacynthus, and Cythera. In the lush valleys and lowlands among the low limestone hills on the islands, a traditional cultivation (olives, currants, and grapes) is practiced together with a more limited distribution of specialty crops (grain, cotton, tobacco, and citrus fruit). Tourism, especially on Corfu, is focused on the beaches as well as the complex historical and cultural tradition of the islands.

Located at the juncture of the Adriatic and the Mediterranean Seas, the islands retained their political and strategic importance during the nineteenth and twentieth centuries. France, which ended the long Venetian occupation of the islands at the beginning of the nineteenth century, contended for their control with Russia, the Ottoman Empire, and Great Britain. A British protectorate (1815–64) preceded their annexation by Greece. During World War I, Corfu was the seat of the Serbian government-in-exile and the site of the Corfu Declaration, which formed the basis for the creation of Yugoslavia. During World War II, Cephalonia, which controls access to the Gulf of Patras, was occupied by Axis forces.

Albert M. Tosches

Further reading

Baedeker's Mediterranean Islands. Englewood Cliffs, New Jersey.
Diem, Aubrey. *Western Europe: A Geographical Analysis.* New York, 1979.
Freeman, E.A. and J.B. Bury. *Historical Geography of Europe.* Chicago, 1974.

See also Corfu Declaration

Iorga, Nicolae (1871–1940)

Romanian historian and politician. Born a lawyer's son in Botoşani, Iorga early displayed the intelligence and linguistic talents that would characterize his future scholarship. He graduated with a degree in history and literature from Iaşi University. In 1890 he began four years of study and travel in Italy, Paris (where he received a diploma in history), and Leipzig, where he took a doctorate in 1893. During this period, Iorga visited European archives, copying documents relevant to Romanian history, which resulted in thirty-six volumes of historical documentation. Named to the chair of world history at the University of Bucharest (1894), he remained there as professor or rector until his death. His enormous bibliography includes 1,003 books, 12,755 articles, and 4,963 reviews (many of these are newspaper articles, translations, or reprints with minor changes). Although he is sometimes charged with lacking originality in historical methodology and philosophy, Iorga authored works of substantial scholarship including the archival documentation ten-volume *History of the Romanians* (1936–1939), and five-volume *History of the Ottoman Empire* (1906–13).

Iorga also pursued careers as journalist, editor, and politician. He first came to national attention in 1906 while leading a demonstration protesting French-language plays at the National Theater. In 1907 he was elected to parliament, and in 1910 he cofounded the nationalist National-Democratic Party. After the war, he served as president of the Council of Ministers, prime minister, minister of education and religion, and minister of state. On the night of November 27–28, 1940, he was murdered by members of the Iron Guard, the Romanian right-radical/fascist organization, in apparent revenge for his opposition to their activities and his associations with Carol II (1893–1953).

Iorga's enduring significance rests in having defined the Romanian national tradition: the Romanian peasant in a unified, patriarchal village society. He insisted this tradition was fundamental to Romanian identity and that from it sprang a uniform national psychology that was manifested throughout Romanian culture. He rejected European developmental models as being inappropriate for Romania. He regarded capitalism, national minorities, industry, and the urban experience with deep suspicion, warning that their contact with Romanian culture might dilute or destroy important components of the peasant/village tradition. Iorga's formulation of the Romanian national tradition, albeit at times unsystematic and inconsistent, gave an intellectual base for Romanian pride and confidence but sometimes at the risk of intellectual isolation and xenophobia.

Ernest H. Latham Jr.

Further reading

Nagy-Talavera, Nicholas M. *Nicolae Iorga: A Biography.* Iaşi, 1996.

Oldson, William O. *The Historical and Nationalistic Thought of Nicolae Iorga.* Boulder, Colorado, 1973.

Theodorescu, B. *Bibliografia istorică şi literară a lui N. Iorga 1890–1934.* Bucharest, 1935.

———. *Bibliografia politică, socială şi economică a lui N. Iorga 1890–1934.* Bucharest, 1937.

See also Carol II; Iron Guard; Peasants

Iron Curtain

Term that represented the political and military division between the Soviet Union and the Western Allies during the period of the Cold War. The term "Iron Curtain" came to prominence when employed by former British Prime Minister Winston Churchill (1874–1965) in a speech delivered on March 5, 1946, in Fulton, Missouri. Titled "The Sinews of Peace," the speech served as the first authoritative public declaration of the political and ideological division within post–World War II Europe, while stressing the need for a firm stance against Soviet aggression. Churchill tried to impress on his American audience that Soviet expansionism and Communist infiltration, as evidenced at the time in Eastern Europe, Greece, and Iran, threatened the security and liberty of Western democracy. To face these new political realities, Churchill advocated a common foreign policy for the West based on effective international organization and a fraternal alliance between England and the United States. Choosing his words carefully and using vivid imagery, Churchill declared that, "From Stettin in the Baltic to Trieste in the Adriatic, an iron curtain has descended across the continent." For future generations, "Iron Curtain" would become a widely used catch phrase representing the Cold War and conditions in Soviet-dominated Eastern Europe. The speech caused a sensation around the world, with Western journalists critical of its militant tone and Moscow denouncing it as warmongering. Although not considered the cause of the Cold War, the Iron Curtain speech galvanized American public opinion regarding Soviet conduct and reoriented Western foreign policy.

Conrad Jarzebowski

I

Further reading

Churchill, Winston S. *His Complete Speeches, 1897–1963,* ed. by Robert Rhodes James. New York, 1974.

Gorodetsky, Gabriel. "The Origins of the Cold War: Stalin, Churchill and the Formation of the Grand Alliance." *Russian Review,* 47 (1988).

Harbutt, Fraser J. *The Iron Curtain: Churchill, America and the Origins of the Cold War.* New York, 1986.

See also Berlin Wall; Cold War; Winston Churchill; Revolutions of 1989

Iron Gates

Gorge in the southern Carpathian Mountains, near the town of Orşova, that separates the Middle from the Lower Danubian Plain at its 942.5 kilometer mark. At the beginning of the gorge, the Danube is about 1.2 miles (2 km) wide, while at its middle point, its width is less than 495 feet (150 m). The riverbed was regulated first by the Romans and later, in the eighteenth century, by the Habsburg Empire, though passage of the river continued to be extremely difficult. In 1950 the Iron Gates Administration was set up between Yugoslavia and Romania to maintain passage and, until 1972, collect fees.

In 1970 the Danube Commission, the regulatory agency for the waterway, decided that all Danubian states would participate financially in the construction of a dam to facilitate navigation on the Danube River's most treacherous stretch. In 1972 Romania and Yugoslavia erected the largest lake wall, navigation, and hydroelectrical system on the Danube. The lake wall is 4,217 feet (1,278 m) long, 185 feet (56 m) high, and 165 feet (50 m) wide to accommodate a road connecting Belgrade and Bucharest. The 446-foot-long (135 m) artificial lake stretches all the way to Belgrade, allowing 6,000-ton sea vessels to reach the capital of Yugoslavia. The hydroelectric system is the second largest in Europe and the world's tenth in power production. Two power plants, with a capacity of 1,050 megawatts each, produce annually about 13.5 billion kilowatt-hours of electricity. Navigation channels are constructed at both ends of the lake wall. Construction of the system has increased the cargo capacity of the Iron Gates fourfold: from 12 to 48 million tons per year.

Boian Koulov

Further reading

Doikov V. and L. Botev. *Dunav i dunavskiya voden pat.* Sofia, 1980.

Glovnia, M., St. Stavrev, and B. Balevski. *Evropa, Asia—geografska hristomatia.* Sofia, 1978.

Gratsianskii, A. *Priroda Yugoslavii.* Moscow, 1955.

See also Danube Question; Danube River

Iron Guard (Legion of the Archangel Michael)

Romanian nationalist-fascist movement. The Iron Guard, a direct-action group within the Legion of the Archangel Michael, is the more familiar term for both organizations and a variety of other of the legion's offshoots.

As a law student at the University of Iaşi in the early 1920s, Corneliu Zelea Codreanu (1899–1938) became a leader of anticommunist and anti-Semitic students. In 1927 Codreanu and a few colleagues established the Legion of the Archangel Michael, a disciplined, hierarchically structured, religiously inspired movement (*mişcare*) for national spiritual renewal. Codreanu became the legion's "captain" and the focus of a personality cult. The legion's incorporation of the mysticism of the Romanian Orthodox Church defines its difference from other integral nationalist (fascist) movements of the interwar period. The religious fervor that attracted early recruits, mostly students and peasants but also a number of young Orthodox clergy, also inspired members' aspiration for martyrdom, their charitable work with poor peasants and, later, industrial workers, their devotion to ceremony, and their belief in the nontemporal and exclusive nature of the nation. Legionaries rejected materialism, abhorred equally communism and capitalism, and pledged to purify Romania's thoroughly corrupt political system. Among the legion's anti-Enlightenment intellectual admirers were Nae Ionescu (1888–1940) and his students (including Ion Mircea Eliade [1907–86] and Emil Cioran [1911–95]) of the Bucharest school of philosophy. Codreanu's compendium of legionary ideals and behavior, *Pentru Legionari* (*For My Legionaries*), became the movement's scripture.

The legion distrusted Western democracy, resorting to direct action (such as assassination) when it wished to make a political statement. That did not prevent legionaries, under various party labels, from running in elections and being elected to national and local offices.

From 1930 on, virtually all Romanian governments vainly sought to outlaw the legion. Still, membership increased and its social base expanded in the 1930s. While many legionaries were imprisoned for acts of violence against their enemies and "foreigners" (especially Jews), it was only after their 1937 display of electoral strength (nearly 16 percent of the vote for the legion's All for the Fatherland Party) that Carol II (1893–1953) had Codreanu arrested, imprisoned, and murdered (May–November 1938). A struggle ensued for the legion's leadership and the violently inclined Horia Sima (1903/1908–93) emerged victorious in June 1940. The legion participated in the National Legionary State, a quasi-fascist government (September 1940–January 1941), during which time it committed some of its worst atrocities. General Ion Antonescu (1882–1946) excluded the legionaries from his government in January 1941 and sent the leadership either into exile or to prison. A core group of legionaries remained active in the Romanian exile community through the 1990s.

Walter M. Bacon Jr.

Further reading

Codreanu, Corneliu Zelea. *For My Legionaries.* Madrid, 1976.
Heinen, Armin. *Die Legion "Erzengel Michael" in Rumänien.* Munich, 1986.
Nagy-Talavera, Nicholas M. *The Green Shirts and Others.* Stanford, California, 1970.
Palaghiță, Ştefan. *Istoria Mişcării Legionare.* Bucharest, 1993.
Webster, Alexander. *The Romanian Legionary Movement.* Pittsburgh, Pennsylvania, 1986.

See also Ion Antonescu; Carol II; Corneliu Codreanu; Mircea Eliade; Nae Ionescu; National Legionary State; Right Radicalism; Horia Sima

Irredentism

State politics claiming territories that belong to other, mainly neighboring, states, on the basis of historic, linguistic, or ethnic affiliation, as well as the tendency on the part of national minorities to separate their territories and to unite with their national centers. Irredentism emerges with the formation of national, semi-independent, or independent states.

As a result of frequent migrations, as well as colonization performed by the Byzantine, Ottoman, and Austrian Empires, the population in the Balkans became ethnically and religiously mixed. During the nineteenth century, when the modern Balkan states appeared (Serbia, 1830; Greece, 1833; Romania, 1856; Bulgaria, 1878; Albania, 1913), they began to conduct irredentist policies toward the regions of the weakened Ottoman and Austrian Empires. With the *Načertanje (Outline)* of Ilija Garašanin (1812–74), Serbia set the goal of uniting all Serbs (and eventually all South Slavs) who lived in Serbia, Bosnia and Hercegovina, Vojvodina, Kosovo, and Macedonia. Similarly, the Greek independent state adopted the *megali idea* (great idea), seeking the restoration of the Byzantine Empire and focusing its irredentist politics mainly on Thessaly, Crete, Asia Minor, Northern Epirus, and Macedonia. Romanian politicians likewise used lands inhabited by ethnic Romanians (Transylvania, Bessarabia, Bukovina, Dobrudja) as an effective political tool. The semi-independent principality of Bulgaria embraced the idea that all the territories in which the Bulgarian Exarchate—the independent Bulgarian Orthodox Church—operated (Eastern Rumelia, Macedonia, Thrace) had to be incorporated in one national state. Albania looked toward the territories in Kosovo and Macedonia that contained a sizable Albanian population.

The Great Powers, influenced by the strategic importance of the region, often found themselves involved in Balkan affairs, supporting different Balkan states' irredentist claims. Numerous wars (Serbo-Turkish of 1876–77; Russo-Turkish of 1877–78; Bulgarian-Serb of 1885; Balkan of 1912–13) were the result of this Balkan entanglement and helped produce the incessant suffering of the population and drastic changes in the ethnic structure. Balkan antagonisms contributed to the outbreak of World War I and to the continued tension and instability in the region up to the present day.

Macedonia serves as an ideal case study for the problems wrought by irredentism, becoming the clashing point of Balkan states' irredentist politics. Bulgaria conducted its propaganda and sent armed bands into Macedonia through various state-sponsored "Macedonian" organizations and its church, the Exarchate. The Greek independent state directed its irredentism through the Patriarchate of Constantinople and its ecclesiastical schools, as well as through various irredentist organizations, that is, the Ethniki Etairia (National Society) and the Macedonian Committee, which were founded in 1894 and 1904, respectively. These organizations formed armed bands and sent them to Macedonia to promote Greek irredentist claims. Serbia started to organize its propaganda in Macedonia more intensively after 1903. Especially active in Kosovo and Macedonia were the Circle of Serbian Sisters and the Society for the Collection of Aid. Serbia also organized armed bands and sent them to Macedonia to promote Serbian interests and to reduce Bulgarian influence. These Bulgarian, Greek, and Serbian bands were joined by Albanian and Vlach irregulars. Greece, Serbia, and Bulgaria partitioned Macedonia after the Second Balkan War (1913).

After World War I, irredentist claims exacerbated tensions throughout the interwar period. In East Central Europe, the Treaty of Trianon, which saw Hungary lose most of its prewar territory to its neighbors (Romania, Yugoslavia, Czechoslovakia), made Hungary's desires to "reclaim" its lost territories an obsession that often diverted the country's attention from its real needs. Hungarian irredentism in turn brought a counterreaction by its neighbors, who formed the Little Entente with the express purpose of controlling Hungary's territorial aspirations. Poland and Czechoslovakia each claimed the Teschen region. Germans in the Sudentenland region of Czechoslovakia looked to ally themselves with a resurgent Germany. Poland was also beset by the claims of Germany over the so-called Polish Corridor and the city of Danzig (Gdańsk). Serbia achieved Garašanin's *Načertanje* with the formation of the Kingdom of Serbs, Croats, and Slovenes, but this future Yugoslavia would be an ethnically troubled state. Romania became Greater Romania with the additions of Bessarabia, Transylvania, Bukovina, and the Dobrudja, but these lands were also claimed by its neighbors. Bulgaria, an ally of the defeated Central Powers, continued its irredentist politics mainly toward the Serbian (Vardar) and Greek (Aegean) parts of Macedonia in the interwar years.

After World War II, the nature of the Communist takeover—including its emphasis on internationalism—did lead to a suppression of irredentist activities. Nevertheless, Albanian irredentism erupted in the Yugoslav autonomous province of Kosovo. In 1981 the Yugoslav army was sent to suppress Albanian demonstrations there. The tensions in Kosovo, now part of Serbia, have continued to the present day. Finally, after the expulsion of Yugoslavia from the Cominform, the Communist propaganda organization, in 1948, Communist Bulgaria resumed its prewar irredentist claims toward the newly formed Macedonian Republic, which was one of the republics in the Yugoslav federation.

Aleksandar Panev

Further reading

Jelavich, Barbara. *The History of the Balkans,* 2 vols. Cambridge, 1981.

MacKenzie, David. "Serbia as Piedmont and the Yugoslav Idea." *East European Quarterly* 28 (Summer 1994).

Perry, Duncan. *The Politics of Terror: The Macedonian Revolutionary Movements 1893–1903.* Durham, North Carolina, 1988.

Pollo, Stefanaq and Arben Puto, eds. *Histoire de l'Albanie des origines à nos jours.* Lyon, 1974.

Skendi, Stavro. *The Albanian National Awakening 1878–1912,* 3 vols. Princeton, New Jersey, 1967.

Veremis, Thanos. *Greece's Balkan Entanglement.* Athens, 1995.

See also Balkan Wars; Bessarabian Question; Bosnia-Hercegovina; Bulgarian–Serb War of 1885; Dobrudja; Easter Question; Eastern Rumelia; Ethnic Minorities; Ethniki Etairia; Exarchate; Ilija Garašanin; Great Powers; Greater Romania; IMRO; Kosovo; Little Entente; Macedonia; *Načertanije*; Patriarchate; Polish Corridor; Revisionism; Russo-Turkish War of 1877–78; Sudeten Crisis; Teschen; Transylvanian Dispute; Trianon, Treaty of; Vojvodina.

Islam

A monotheistic world religion whose adherents include inhabitants of southeastern Europe. Islam originated in Arabia with the leadership and preaching of the Prophet Muhammad (570–632). Islam teaches respect for "the people of the book," that is, Jews with the Torah and Christians with the Gospel. It accepts the biblical prophets from Abraham and Moses to Elijah and Jesus, but it also continues the prophetic line with the Prophet Muhammad, who is the "seal of the prophets." The revelations that the Prophet Muhammad, received from God in Arabic were written down and make up the Qur'an, the holy book of Islam. The Prophet Muhammad is revered but not worshipped; thus comparisons of the place of Jesus in Christianity with that of the Prophet Muhammad in Islam are incorrect. It therefore follows that it is incorrect to refer to the religion as "Muhammadan." Rather, the correct name for the religion, "Islam," denotes submission to God, and a "Muslim" is one who has submitted to God.

Tenets and practices of Islam reflect the strong monotheism of the faith and the importance of the community in the life of believers. The central tenets are often referred to as the "five pillars": attesting to the Oneness of God and the prophethood of Muhammad, prayer, almsgiving, fasting, and pilgrimage. There is belief in a Day of Judgment and an afterlife. Reflecting the importance of the community, the Islamic calendar begins not with the first revelation or the birth of the Prophet but with the founding of the community of Believers. Besides the Qur'an, there is also hadith, the sayings and accounts of the Prophet. These two sources include moral teachings and practical prescriptions on community life; they serve as the bases of the different schools of Islamic law.

There are two major divisions in Islam whose basic difference centers on who should be the successors to the Prophet. The largest group, the Sunni, accept the first four caliphs, three of whom were companions of the Prophet but not related by blood. The other, smaller group, the Shi'a, hold that the successors should come from the family of the Prophet, beginning with his son-in-law and cousin, Ali (597–660), and followed by his descendants. Besides these two major divisions, there also grew in Islam Sufi or mystical fraternities. These Sufi orders became organized in the thirteenth and fourteenth centuries and spread across the Islamic world. They often provided the missionaries for Islam, and they continue today in Muslim societies, where they offer more personal expression of love of God that complements the profound transcendence of God in other aspects of Islam.

Islam spread to southeastern Europe with the entrance of Ottoman armies in the fourteenth and fifteenth centuries, often accompanied by Sufi missionaries. Conversion to Islam was gradual. Most converts came from Bosnia and Albania, where neither Roman Catholicism nor Eastern Orthodoxy had established a strong presence. The Ottoman Empire did not force conversion except with boys levied for the special military corps, the Janissaries. However, there were economic incentives for local people to convert, namely, non-Muslims had to pay an extra tax, and to those who converted an array of administrative and military positions were open. Turks from Anatolia, both colonists and former soldiers, also settled in southeastern Europe, thereby adding to the Muslim populations. Most of these Muslims were Sunni, but some tribesmen also settled in Bulgaria, whose practices resemble those of the Shia Muslims.

As the Ottoman Empire declined, many Muslims emigrated from southeastern Europe. But the Muslims in Albania, who achieved a popular majority, and those in Bosnia stayed. Muslims who remained in Bulgaria, Macedonia, and Greece lived mostly in rural areas. The local practices that distinguish Muslims from their non-Muslim neighbors today include use of Muslim names, circumcision of boys, dietary restrictions on pork, a relatively more conservative family structure, and burial in Muslim cemeteries. Muslims also celebrate the main holidays of the Breaking of the Fast at the end of the thirty-day fast of Ramadan, and the Sacrifice Holiday to commemorate Abraham's willingness to sacrifice his son Ismael. The sharing of sweets like baklava and the drinking of Turkish coffee, along with the high value placed on hospitality, reflect the Ottoman cultural past, but they are especially pronounced among Muslim peoples.

The call to prayer is broadcast from mosques five times a day, with the Friday noon prayer the time for a sermon. But attendance at a mosque is not required; other lifetime community and familial practices define Muslim communities. As with all religions, Islam's members vary from those who are secularized, particularly in Bosnian cities, to those for whom religion is the center of their lives and the foundation of their identity. The main Sufi groups in southeastern Europe—the Bektashi, Halveti, Mevlevi, Naqshibandi, Kadiri, Rifa'i, Sa'di, and Melami—include many devout Muslims who gather privately and practice their distinctive ways of praising God.

During the nineteenth century nationalist movements in southeastern Europe, except that in Albania, arose among Christians. In their ideologies there was no place for Muslims. In the twentieth century, Communist regimes have opposed all religions, although several have been particularly hard on Islam. Communist Albania even declared itself an atheist state in 1967 and subsequently destroyed mosques and prohibited all religious observance. Bulgaria campaigned in the early 1970s and 1980s to force Muslims to change their names to Bulgarian ones, and punished families who circumcised their sons. Since the early 1990s, Albania and Bulgaria have rescinded such policies.

Far less subtle policies against Muslim identity have been followed by ultranationalist Serb and Croat groups in Bosnia since the spring of 1992. Over one thousand mosques, including centuries-old ones (the Colored Mosque in Foca, the Ferhadiye Mosque in Banja Luka), cemeteries, and libraries of documents of Bosnia's Islamic past were deliberately destroyed in the first year of fighting. Muslims were forced from their homes in ways to discourage their ever returning. Besides cultural and human loss, these actions have added a religious dimension to what had been a largely secularized Muslim identity and undermined Bosnia's longtime intercommunal tolerance.

Frances Trix

Further reading

Izetbegovic, 'Alija' Ali. *Islam Between East and West.* Indianapolis, 1989.
Popovic, Alexandre. *L'Islam balkanique: Les musulmans du sud-est européen dans la période post-ottomane.* Berlin, 1986.
Schimmel, Annemarie. *Islam: An Introduction.* Albany, New York, 1992.
Voll, John Obert. *Islam: Continuity and Change in the Modern World.* Boulder, Colorado, 1982.

See also Janissaries; Muslims; Ottoman Empire

Islaz Proclamation

Wallachian call for reforms during the Revolutions of 1848. The revolution that began in Paris in February 1848 sparked a revolutionary groundswell in Wallachia culminating in the issuance of a twenty-one-point reform program at the Danube town of Islaz on June 21, 1848. Read by writer Ion Heliade Rădulescu (1802–72), the proclamation called for an end to both the Russian protectorate over Wallachia and the regime based on the Organic Statutes (which governed the principality). Every ethnic Romanian was declared to be a member of the "nation" with equal rights—the freedoms of speech, press, and assembly. It also called for expanded education, equal taxation, peasant emancipation (with indemnification for owners), and granting the franchise to all citizens.

Following the issuance of the proclamation, revolutionaries set up a provisional government and adopted a new flag inscribed with the motto *Dreptate—Frăţie* (Justice—Brotherhood) in blue, yellow, and red. Despite the initial euphoria that followed the proclamation, the government was beset with problems. Internal disagreements among its members over measures contained in the proclamation (notably regarding the peasants), as well as growing concern by Russia and the Porte over developments in the region, would soon bring about its downfall. Although the government attempted to reassure the Ottomans of Wallachia's loyalty, Ottoman troops entered the principality on September 25, 1848, with Russian troops following suit two days later. The ensuing Convention of Balta Liman (May 1849) reestablished Ottoman and Russian control over the Romanian Principalities.

Richard Frucht

Further reading

Hitchins, Keith. *The Romanians 1777–1866.* Oxford, 1996.
Jelavich, Barbara. *History of the Balkans,* vol. 1, *The Eighteenth and Nineteenth Centuries.* Cambridge, 1983.
———. *Russia and the Formation of the Romanian National State 1821–1878.* Cambridge, 1984.

See also Balta Liman, Convention of; Danubian Principalities; Ion Heliade Rădulescu; Organic Statutes; Revolutions of 1848

Istria

Peninsula located in the north Adriatic Sea and the westernmost part of the Republic of Croatia. It is bordered by Slovenia to the north, the Croatian mainland and the Kvarner Gulf to the east, the Adriatic Sea to the south, and the Gulf of Venice to the west. It covers an area of more than 1,500 square miles (4,166 sq km).

The Dinaric Alps form the northern periphery of the region. Limestone karst terrain is characteristic of the region and slopes downward toward the south. The coastal plain features a very irregular shoreline with deep natural harbors. The peninsula has a Mediterranean-type climate with hot summers and cool winters. The area receives approximately 50 inches (127 cm) of precipitation per year, most during the winter months. The natural vegetation of the region is of the mixed forest variety.

A booming tourist industry has developed on the peninsula, its mild climate and ancient Roman ruins helping to attract tourists from many parts of Europe. Two principal highways, on either side of the peninsula, facilitate travel. These north-south highways converge on Pula, the largest city in the region—a major seaport of Croatia and a ship-building center. In addition to tourism and ship-building, the area supports agriculture and mining, especially of bauxite.

William B. Kory

Further reading

Bertić, Ivan. *Veliki geografski atlas Jugoslavije.* Zagreb, 1987.

Izetbegović, Alija (c. 1925–)

President of Bosnia-Hercegovina, a constituent republic of Yugoslavia, in 1990, who remained as president when Bosnia-Hercegovina declared independence in 1992. Izetbegović was born to a Muslim Slav family in Bosanski Samac, a town in northern Bosnia. After World War II, he became a lawyer and also wrote various works about the plight of Yugoslavia's Muslim community. The Yugoslav Communist regime imprisoned him for three years during the late 1940s because of his advocacy of greater religious freedom. He was jailed again in 1983 after publishing his book *Islam between East and West* (1982), which the government deemed "Islamic propaganda." He was released in 1988.

Izetbegović then became a leader of the Muslim-oriented Party of Democratic Action, which dominated the Bosnian elections of November 1990. After Slovenia and Croatia seceded from Yugoslavia in 1991, the Izetbegović government determined that Bosnia-Hercegovina could not remain part of a Serb-dominated rump Yugoslavia. On March 1, 1992, a majority of the Bosnian public supported a referendum on independence, and two days later Izetbegović proclaimed the republic's independence.

The Bosnian government soon found itself at war with the Bosnian Serbs who did not support an independent Bosnian state dominated by ethnic rivals.

Izetbegović traveled around the world to gain support for the fledgling Bosnian state and to publicize evidence that Serbian forces had committed atrocities against Muslims. In December 1995 Izetbegović, along with the presidents of Croatia and Serbia, signed the Dayton Peace Accords, intended to end the warfare in Bosnia. Izetbegović became the first chairman of the three-member Bosnian presidency (established by the Dayton Accords) when his Party of Democratic Action won a plurality of the vote in the September 1996 Bosnian election.

Paul D. Lensink

Further reading

Cohen, Lenard J. *Broken Bonds: Yugoslavia's Disintegration and Balkan Politics in Transition,* 2d ed. Boulder, Colorado, 1995.

Woodward, Susan L. *Balkan Tragedy: Chaos and Dissolution after the Cold War.* Washington, D.C., 1995.

See also Birth of the Republic of Bosnia-Hercegovina; Muslims

J

Jagiellonian University

Historically the most significant center of higher education in the Polish lands. Founded on the model of the academies in Bologna and Padua in 1364 by King Kazimierz the Great (1310–70), and refounded with more extensive financial backing by King Władysław Jagiełło (c. 1351–1434) in 1400, the university was the thirty-sixth such institution in Europe and the second university in Central Europe after Charles University in Prague. At its inception, the Jagiellonian University was intended as a home for legal studies and the education of state officials, rather than as a theological center. The latter was added only after Kazimierz's death, when the Jagiellonians remodeled the school along the lines of the most famous theological school in Europe, the Sorbonne. The subsequent history of the university reflects both the vicissitudes of the history of the Polish state and the main currents of European educational development.

The high point of the university came in the fifteenth century, when it was a center of the humanist tradition and of Aristotelian philosophy. It was an international institution, drawing faculty and students from throughout Europe during the fifteenth and sixteenth centuries. With the onset of the Reformation and the Counter-Reformation, however, the academy struggled to maintain its independence from the growing power of the Jesuits and lost much of its international appeal. During the seventeenth century, the Jagiellonian University failed to keep pace with European developments in education, except in the field of mathematics.

A fundamental reform of the educational system in the entire Polish Commonwealth was instituted in the 1780s. The university benefited tremendously from these reforms, becoming a center of Enlightenment ideas. With the partitions of Poland at the end of the century, however, the Jagiellonian University once again became a backwater. Germanized throughout much of the nineteenth century, the university then benefited from the relative mildness of Austrian rule and was Polonized in 1870, thus beginning the next period of flowering. Under the leadership of such respected scholars as Józef Szujski (1835–83) and Michał Bobrzyński (1849–1935), history; Stanisław Tarnowski (1837–1917), literature; Ludwik Gumplowicz (1838–1909), sociology; and Karol Estreicher (1827–1905), literature and librarianship, the Jagiellonian University rose to great heights and played an important role in the furtherance of a Polish national consciousness until the outbreak of World War I.

During the interwar years, the university served as a model for new Polish academies and universities, supplying both curricular frameworks and individual faculty. The arts continued to be the centerpiece of scholarship, although the natural sciences did not lag far behind. The history of the institution during the German occupation of Poland is a dark one. On November 6, 1939, a number of university scholars were invited to a meeting with Nazi German authorities; 183 were arrested and sent to Sachsenhausen concentration camp, near Berlin. In addition, 123 more academics were killed during the war. Clandestine activity against the German occupiers began in 1942.

After the war, the university vied with a number of other institutions of higher learning in the People's Republic of Poland. It continues to be a premier center for the study of history and literature, and most recently has begun projects and institutes focusing on the study of the Jews in Poland.

Peter Wozniak

Further reading

Bieniarzówna, Janina and Jan Małecki. *Dzieje Krakowa*. Kraków, 1979.

Klimaszewski, Bolesław, ed. *An Outline History of Polish Culture*. Warsaw, 1984.

Wroczyński, Ryszard. *Dzieje Oświaty Polskiej*, 2 vols. Warsaw, 1987.

See also Michał Bobrzyński; Charles University; Higher Education

Jakšić, Đura (1832–78)

Painter and writer, the greatest representative of Serbian romanticism and one of the most talented painters in nineteenth-century Serbian art. Jakšić studied drawing in Budapest (1847) and Vienna (1851), but owing to illness he did not enter the School of Art; instead, he copied works of old masters. Several of his works from this period have been preserved (*Montenegrins Fighting the Turks, Virgin with Christ*), already revealing romantic features and elements of his individual style: dynamic composition, strong dark and light contrasts, and an inclination toward Dutch painter Rembrandt (1606–69) and the Flemish Rubens (1577–40).

The next period began with his studies at the Munich School of Art (1853) and ended with his second visit to Vienna (1861). In the meantime, he worked as a schoolteacher in Serbia (1854–57). Although frequently misunderstood and ridiculed, and often having to move, he still produced several portraits, compositions, and icons that represent the backbone of Serbian romantic painting (*Girl in Blue; Girl with a Lute; Sacrifice of Abraham; Torch Procession through the Stambol Gate*).

After a year of studying in Vienna, he returned to Serbia in 1862, never to leave again, working mainly as a schoolteacher. Although he had become more active as a poet, he nevertheless produced his best paintings during this last period

(*The Murder of Karadjordje; Uprising of Montenegrins; The Principal Ćirić; The Schoolmistress Živka Protić; Prince Michael on His Deathbed; St. George on Horseback; Prince Milan Obrenović; Rest after a Battle; Takovo Uprising*).

Svetlana Rakić

Further reading

Jovanović, Miodrag. *Srpsko slikarstvo u doba romantizma 1848–1878*. Novi Sad, Yugoslavia, 1976.

Kusovac, Nikola. *Đura Jakšić*. Kragujevac, Yugoslavia, 1974.

Medaković, Dejan. "Đura Jakšić, vrhunac srpskog romantizma," *Srpska umetnost u 19. veku*. Belgrade, 1981.

See also Serbian Art

Janáček, Leoš (1854–1928)

Czech composer best known for his expressive operas and interest in folk music. Janáček's career was closely associated with Brno and the Moravian countryside. He entered the Prague Organ School in 1874 and wrote his first compositions for choir. He later studied at the conservatories in Leipzig and Vienna but returned to Brno to cultivate Czech cultural life, especially with the Beseda Brneňská Choir and Brno Organ School. Janáček received an honorary doctorate from Masaryk University in Brno in 1925.

Janáček's nationalism leaned toward social, humanitarian Slavism, with an eastern orientation. His eclectic musical style was somewhat influenced by Antonín Dvořák (1841–1904) and Russian music. He sought the autonomy of Moravian music and particularly studied speech inflections, rather than quoting folk songs in his music. The best known of his operas, *Jenůfa* (1904), is an expressionistic work on a folk story that Janáček related to the death of his daughter. Better known internationally than his operas are his instrumental works, such as the orchestral rhapsody *Taras Bulba* (1918) and the two string quartets. A chamber music style is evident in the orchestration of his mature works. Among his last compositions is the *Glagolitic Mass,* a setting of the old Slavic text. In addition to musical compositions, Janáček wrote musicological essays, autobiographical sketches, letters, and texts for vocal works.

William Smialek

Further reading

Hollander, Hans. *Leoš Janáček: His Life and Work*, trans. by Paul Hamburger. New York, 1963.

Tyrrell, John. *Janáček's Operas: A Documentary Account.* Princeton, New Jersey, 1992.

Vogel, Jaroslav. *Leoš Janáček: A Biography,* rev. ed. by Karel Janovický. New York, 1981.

See also Antonín Dvořák; Folk Music; Music

Janissaries

Elite Ottoman military corps. Drawing from the example of earlier Islamic rulers, the Ottoman sultans used slaves to fill the ranks of the empire's administrative and military establishments. Through the *devshirme,* or child levy, beginning around the end of the fourteenth century, children were taken from their subject Christian parents by the Ottoman authorities, converted to Islam, and trained to serve the sultan and his state. Many of these slaves made up the sultan's principal infantry formation—the Janissary corps. This body of dedicated and fanatic convert soldiers became Europe's most feared fighting force and was responsible for the virtually uninterrupted succession of victories that Ottoman armies enjoyed up to the seventeenth century.

All the same, gradual changes in the character and composition of the Janissary corps began to reduce its effectiveness. In the sixteenth century the formerly celibate Janissaries won permission to marry, raise families, and, subsequently, enroll their sons in the corps. Concurrently, to supplement their meager military salaries, the Janissaries were allowed to engage in commerce. These new privileges set into motion a process of change that in less than a century transformed the Janissaries from the most feared and professional unit of the Ottoman army into a bloated and widely dispersed militia of city traders and artisans. This deterioration was magnified by the influx of civilians who bribed their way into the corps to gain the privileges enjoyed by the Janissaries, such as tax exemption and monopolies over certain commercial guilds. The *devshirme* system, which had formerly filled the Janissary ranks, was rendered unnecessary and abandoned altogether after 1763. No longer a force of fanatic converts and professional soldiers willing to risk their lives for Islam and the sultan, by the seventeenth century, the Janissaries had become a privileged and self-perpetuating class concerned only with their own prosperity and advancement, who often preyed on the civilian population in the Balkans.

Interested more in their immunities and privileges than their duties, the Janissaries rapidly degenerated as a military force. By the 1820s, for example, although they numbered more than one hundred thousand, only two thousand of their ranks were professionally trained and fit for active duty. Nonetheless, they retained their weapons and thus remained the largest armed group in the empire. Their arms, privileged commercial position, and intense conservatism made the Janissaries the principal obstacle to Ottoman attempts to reform the state and modernize the military. Moreover, because of their military power and prestige, the Janissaries had become an increasingly independent political force that often interfered in the government and sometimes overthrew the sultan. Finally, after a number of unsuccessful efforts by previous sultans, reformist Mahmud II (1785–1839) destroyed the Janissary corps in a military confrontation in Constantinople in 1826.

Alexandros K. Kyrou

Further reading

Goodwin, Godfrey. *The Janissaries.* London, 1994.

Palmer, J.A.B. "The Origins of the Janissaries." *Bulletin of the Rylands Library* 35 (1953): 448–91.

See also Mahmud II; Ottoman Empire

Janša, Janez (1958–)

Slovene politician. Janša, who has a degree in military science from the University of Ljubljana, first attracted world attention when he was arrested in 1988 for writing articles critical of the federal Yugoslav government's controversial military policies. The uproar that followed his conviction and sentencing acted as a catalyst in the Slovene movement toward secession and the creation of an independent state.

In 1990 Janša was named defense minister of Slovenia. In this position he moved to reorganize the Slovene Territorial Defense Forces and to lay the foundations for the army of today's independent Slovenia. Janša sought to "depoliticize" the army by making sure that Slovene soldiers served under Slovene (rather than Serb) officers. His actions in this regard reflected the widespread sentiment among Slovenes that they were paying for a disproportionate share of Yugoslavia's defense budget and that their soldiers should be allowed to serve within their republic, instead of being dispatched to other regions of the country.

When the Yugoslav People's Army moved to crush the secession of Slovenia in June 1991, Janša's forces carried out a successful guerrilla campaign against federal troops. After independence, Janša continued in his position as minister of defense until March 1994, when his ministry was accused of interfering in civilian affairs. Although originally a member of the Slovene Democratic Alliance, Janša later joined the Social Democratic Party of Slovenia.

John K. Cox

Further reading

Cohen, Lenard J. *Broken Bonds: The Disintegration of Yugoslavia,* 2d ed. Boulder, Colorado, 1995.

Janša, Janez. *Na svoji strani: Zbornik.* Ljubljana, 1988.

———. *Okopi: Pot slovenske države, 1991–1994.* Ljubljana, 1994.

———. *Premiki: Nastajanje in obramba slovenske države, 1988–1992,* 2d ed. Ljubljana, 1992.

See also Slovenia, Birth of the Republic of

Jancsó, Miklós (1921–)

Hungarian film director. Jancsó graduated from the Budapest Academy of Dramatic and Cinematographic Art in 1950. His explorations of historical topics serve as a background to his aesthetic experiments with the cinematic form. Some of his features—especially *Csillagosok katonák (The Red and the White,* 1967) and *Szegénylegények (The Roundup,* 1965)—are considered masterpieces by many critics. He worked abroad for some time during the 1970s and 1980s and occasionally works as a theater director. Jancsó's other feature films include *Oldás és kötés (Cantata,* 1962); *Csend és káltás (Silence and Cry,* 1968); *La Pacifista (The Pacifist,* 1970); *Roma rivuole Cesare (Rome Wants Another Caesar,* 1973); *A zsarnok szíve (The Tyrant's Head,* 1981); *L'Aube (The Dawn,* 1985); and *Kék Duna Keringö (The Blue Danube,* 1991).

Dina Iordanova

Further reading

Biró, Yvette. *Miklós Jancsó.* Paris, 1977.

Petrie, Graham. "History Must Answer to Man," in *The Contemporary Hungarian Cinema.* Budapest, 1978, 20–106.

———. "Miklós Jancsó: Decline and Fall?" in *Politics, Art and Commitment in the East European Cinema.* New York, 1983, 189–210.

See also Cinema

January Uprising (1863)

One in a series of failed eighteenth- and nineteenth-century Polish revolts against Russian domination. The January Uprising (*Powstania Styczniowa*) followed several years of increased tension between the Congress Kingdom's Poles and their Russian masters. After the November Uprising (1830–31), Russia clamped down on Poland, but the death of anti-Polish Nicholas I (1796–1855), Russia's defeat in the Crimean War (1853–56), and the looming emancipation of the Russian serfs persuaded the tsarist government to relax its grip. Consequently, repressed discontent surfaced; however, Polish leadership was badly divided between moderates (Whites) and radicals (Reds).

The Whites' leader, Andrzej Zamoyski (1800–1874), a prominent aristocrat who advocated gradual emancipation for Poland's peasantry, established the Agricultural Society. His urban, bourgeois counterpart, financier Leopold Kronenberg (1812–78), led the Warsaw-based City Delegation. The Reds, a leaderless hodgepodge composed chiefly of students and young Polish officers in the Russian army, demanded independence for Poland and the peasantry's immediate emancipation.

Alexander Wielopolski (1803–77), a wealthy, intelligent, fiercely independent nobleman who sought both socioeconomic reform and greater autonomy, belonged to neither Whites nor Reds. As the situation in Poland deteriorated, Alexander II (1818–81) turned to Wielopolski, who introduced major administrative and educational reforms. However, Wielopolski's brusque manner and determination to crush the Reds isolated him from Polish society. Meanwhile, Russia's customary brutality in dealing with Polish dissent inflamed the Poles.

When Wielopolski decided to emasculate the Reds by conscripting a large number of young Poles, he provoked open revolt. In January 1863 the Reds proclaimed a Provisional National Government. Hopelessly outmatched, the Reds fought a guerrilla war for sixteen months before the revolution died out. Appeals to the West for aid fell on deaf ears.

Like the failed November Uprising in 1830, the January Uprising was a catastrophe for Poland. In addition to great physical destruction, the Kingdom of Poland lost its special status and became just another province in the Russian Empire.

Frank W. Thackeray

Further reading

Davies, Norman. *God's Playground: A History of Poland,* 2 vols. New York, 1982.

Gieysztor, Aleksander et al. *History of Poland,* 2d ed. Warsaw, 1979.

Kieniewicz, Stefan. *The Emancipation of the Polish Peasantry.* Chicago, 1969.

Leslie, R.F. *Reform and Insurrection in Russian Poland, 1856–1865.* London, 1963.

Wandycz, Piotr S. *The Lands of Partitioned Poland, 1795–1918.* Seattle, Washington, 1974.

See also Alexander II; Leopold Kronenberg; November Uprising; Polish Congress Kingdom; Alexander Wielopolski; Andrzej Zamoyski

Jaruzelski, Wojciech (1923–)

Polish military officer, and political leader during the 1980s. Deported to the Soviet Union during World War II, Jaruzelski entered the Polish army organized by Soviet forces. From 1945 to 1960, Jaruzelski held a number of teaching positions at military schools of higher education. In 1965 he advanced to the post of vice minister of national defense, holding this position until 1968. From 1968 to 1983, he served as minister of national defense. While maintaining his national defense portfolio, Jaruzelski became prime minister (1981–85). In June 1981 he was named first party secretary of the Polish United Workers' Party, a position held until 1989. Declaring a "state of war" (martial law) on December 13, 1981, during the unrest associated with the Solidarity trade union movement, Jaruzelski ruled Poland from 1981 to 1983 as chairman of the Military Council of National Salvation (WRON). Incurring widespread criticism at home and abroad, Jaruzelski, having failed to "normalize" Communist rule in Poland, played a key role in bringing about a negotiated end of communism by initiating the Round Table (1989) between the Polish regime and Solidarity. Elected president of People's Poland in 1989 and then serving as the first president of the Third Polish Republic, Jaruzelski retired from public life in 1990.

Peter Lavelle

Further reading

Kaminski, Bartlomiej. *The Collapse of State Socialism: The Case of Poland.* Princeton, New Jersey, 1991.

Staar, Richard F. *Communist Regimes in Eastern Europe.* Stanford, California, 1988.

Staniszkis, Jadwiga. *The Dynamics of the Breakthrough in Eastern Europe: The Polish Experience.* Berkeley, California, 1991.

See also Revolutions of 1989; Solidarity

Jászi, Oszkár (1875–1957)

Sociologist, politician, university professor, and the leading figure of bourgeois radicalism in Hungary. Jászi became the right-hand man of Mihály Károlyi (1875–1955), Hungary's premier during the revolution of 1918 (which followed the collapse of Austria-Hungary at the end of World War I). His views on relations with ethnic "minorities" proved more progressive than those of most Hungarian politicians of his age.

Jászi studied in Budapest, France, and the United Kingdom. Upon graduation, he took a position in the civil service but was soon appointed to a chair in government at the University of Kolozsvár in 1911. He married writer Anna Lesznai (1885–1966).

Jászi was a founder and general secretary of the Society of the Social Sciences and director of the Free School, intended to provide informal higher education to factory workers. He also founded and edited the progressive journal of the social sciences, *Huszadik Század* (*Twentieth Century*), and became chairperson of the National Bourgeois Radical Party—all endeavors that manifested his basic concern for social justice in Hungary.

At the time of the October 1918 revolution, Jászi was appointed minister of nationalities without portfolio in Károlyi's cabinet, since he had been one of the few to advocate autonomy for the ethnic groups of Hungary. For the same reason—the acceptability of his attitudes to Western

J advocates of self-determination—he was appointed chair of the Council on Foreign Relations. In late 1918 he negotiated the armistice agreement with the Allies at Belgrade and traveled to Arad in an attempt to negotiate the fate of Transylvania with Romanian leaders.

Upon the proclamation of the Hungarian Soviet Republic in 1919 led by Béla Kun (1886–1938), Jászi went into exile, first to Vienna. He was active as editor in chief of *Bécsi Magyar Ujság* (*Hungarian Daily of Vienna*), castigating first the Communists, then the perpetrators of the white terror, the antisocialist reaction to the short-lived Communist republic. In 1924 he was invited for a conference tour to the United States and, the following year, he was appointed professor of sociology at Oberlin College in Ohio, where he remained until his death.

In his writings and political practice, Jászi devoted much attention to democratization, the struggle against large landowners, and the issue of minorities, advocating an "Eastern Switzerland"—autonomy for the main ethnic groups—as a way of preserving the multinational Hungarian state. His best-known work is *Dissolution of the Habsburg Monarchy* (1929).

Mario D. Fenyo

Further reading

Hajdu, Tibor. *Az 1918-as magyarországi polgári demokratikus forradalom.* Budapest, 1968.

Jászi, Oszkár. *Revolution and Counter-Revolution in Hungary.* New York, 1969.

———. *A Monarchia jövöje.* Facsimile reprint of the 1918 edition, Budapest, 1988.

Litván, György, ed. *Homage to Danubia.* Lanham, Maryland, 1995.

See also Ethnic Minorities; Hungarian Soviet Republic; Mihály Károlyi; Béla Kun; Transylvanian Dispute; White Terror

Jelačić, Josip (1801–59)

Nineteenth-century Habsburg military figure and *ban* (governor) of Croatia (1848–59). Born into a military family in the Croatian Military Frontier garrison town of Petrovaradin and educated at the Theresianum in Vienna, Jelačić served in Galicia, Vienna, the Military Frontier, Italy, and Dalmatia before becoming colonel of the Frontier's Glina Regiment in 1841. On March 23, 1848, in the early days of the Revolutions of 1848, Habsburg Emperor Ferdinand (1793–1875) appointed Jelačić *ban* of Croatia as well as military commander in both Croatia and the Military Frontier. A revolutionary assembly in Zagreb also proclaimed Jelačić *ban* on March 25, the day on which he learned of his royal appointment. The revolutionary Hungarian government, which claimed authority over Croatia and which Ferdinand had already recognized, objected to these acts of which it had no prior knowledge. On September 11, 1848, after numerous intrigues at the court, Jelačić led an invading army into Hungary, inaugurating the armed struggle between military forces loyal to the revolutionary Hungarian government and those loyal to the imperial court. Despite Jelačić's losses, the court in early October named him supreme commander of all imperial forces in Hungary. Then, shortly thereafter, it subordinated him to Alfred Windischgrätz (1787–1862). Jelačić remained Croatian *ban* during the remainder of the revolution and through the period of reaction that followed in the 1850s.

Historians, particularly those writing in German and Hungarian, frequently portray Jelačić as a reactionary. Croatian historiography shows him in a more sympathetic light, pointing out that he was both a loyal military officer and—even before the revolution—an adherent of an Austroslav (the aim of which was to achieve equality for the empire's Slavic peoples) and federalist reorganization of the Habsburg monarchy. Although opposed to many of the policies implemented by the court after 1849, as a loyal military officer he remained at his post as *ban,* contributing to his reputation as a reactionary.

James P. Krokar

Further reading

Deak, Istvan. *The Lawful Revolution: Louis Kossuth and the Hungarians, 1848–1849.* New York, 1979.

Hartley, M. *The Man Who Saved Austria: The Life and Times of Baron Jellačić [sic].* London, 1912.

Rothenberg, Gunther E. "Jelačić, the Croatian Military Border, and the Intervention against Hungary in 1848." *Austrian History Yearbook* 1 (1965): 45–73.

Šidak, Jaroslav. *Studije iz hrvatske povijesti za revolucije 1848–49.* Zagreb, 1979.

See also Austroslavism; Croatian Military Frontier; Hungarian War for Independence; Revolutions of 1848; Alfred Windischgrätz

Jewish Bund

First Jewish Socialist Party created in October 1897 in Vilna (Polish, Wilno; Lithuanian, Vilnius). The Bund fought for the betterment of the general political conditions in the Russian Empire, for civil rights, and for national-cultural autonomy for the Jews in Russia. The party claimed to speak for the entire Jewish proletariat, opposed Zionism, supported the Yiddish language, and developed a concept of "hereness" ("being here," as opposed to immigration and Zionism) as an important part of its ideology.

The Bund was preceded by Jewish socialist propaganda circles, workers' mutual assistance funds, and clandestine Jewish socialist groups active in the Lithuanian-Belorussian provinces of Russia. Thirteen representatives of those groups met at a secret convention and founded the Bund. In 1898 it helped to organize the Russian Social Democratic Labor Party. During 1898–1902 and 1906–12, the Bund was an autonomous and important part of the Russian party. However, Jewish leaders disagreed with the Bolsheviks on the question of nationality rights and strongly opposed Lenin's (1870–1914) concept of a highly centralized party and state. After the split in the Russian Social Democratic Party, the Bund cooperated with the Mensheviks, one of the two main branches of Russian socialism. The Bund organized strikes and protests against tsarist oppression, established self-defense groups to protect Jews during pogroms, and fought against anti-Jewish boycotts and anti-Semitism. The party was especially active and played an important role during the Revolution of 1905 in Russia. After its failure, the Bund went through a crisis but regained its strength before World War I. In 1917 the Bund had about forty thousand members and supported the government of Alexander Kerensky (1881–1970). After the Bolsheviks seized control in Russia, a minority of the Bundists joined the Communist parties of Ukraine and Russia, and a majority became victims of Soviet persecution.

During the German occupation of Russian Poland in World War I, Polish Bundists created a separate party. After the war, Poland became the main center of the Bund; small party organizations also existed in Romania, Lithuania, Belgium, France, and the United States. The Bund joined the Socialist International, worked closely with the Polish Socialist Party, and became a powerful political force especially in the towns of central and northeastern Poland. The Bund opposed communism, the *Sanacja* regime (the government created by Józef Piłsudski [1867–1935] in 1926), Zionism, and Jewish clericalism. The party developed impressive educational activities, cultural and sport organizations, and the youth movement Zukunft. In the last Polish pre–World War II local elections, the Bund proved to be the strongest Jewish group in many towns. After the outbreak of war, many Bund leaders left Poland, most of them for America. One of them, Samuel Zygelbojm (1895–1943), joined the Polish National Committee in London in 1942 and tried to persuade the Great Powers to help Polish Jews. When his plan failed, he committed suicide in May 1943. The Bund was active in the anti-German resistance in occupied Poland and played a great role in the Jewish Fighting Organization (Żydowska Organizacja Bojowa—ŻOB) during the Warsaw Ghetto Uprising of spring 1943. Most Bund members perished during the war, but after, the party was rebuilt in Poland. In 1948 the Bund was forced to join the Polish United Workers Party and ceased to exist. Small branches survived in the United States and Western Europe.

Piotr Wróbel

Further reading

Encyclopedia Judaica, vol. 4. Jerusalem, 1971, 1497–1507.

Johnpoll, B. *The Politics of Futility: The General Jewish Workers' Bund of Poland, 1917–1943.* Ithaca, New York, 1967.

Tomicki, J. "The General Union of Jewish Workers (Bund) in Poland, 1918–1938." *Acta Poloniae Historica* 45 (1982).

See also Józef Piłsudski; Pogrom; *Sanacja;* Warsaw Ghetto.

Jews

It is assumed that Jews penetrated into Eastern Europe during the First Exile after the fall of Jerusalem in 586 B.C. In the fourth century B.C. Jews settled in the Greek colonies in the Crimea and in the Black Sea littoral and then migrated to the valleys of the Volga, Don, and Dnieper. After the

J Roman conquest of Erez Israel, the Jewish settlement in Europe grew constantly. When the Romans crushed a Jewish uprising and destroyed the Temple in A.D. 70, Jews were deported to various Roman provinces, including Eastern Europe (especially Panonia and Greece). The Jewish position in the Roman Empire deteriorated after its Christianization. Between the fifth and eighth centuries, waves of religious fanaticism pushed Jews in Byzantium north to Central and Eastern Europe. In about A.D. 740 the Khazar Kaganate on the Volga and Dnieper converted to Judaism and attracted Jewish newcomers. An important Jewish center was established in Kiev, the Khazarian border stronghold. After the conquest of Khazaria by Rus, the Khazarian Jews moved northward. Simultaneously, Eastern Europe was reached by Jews from the West. The Radanites, Jewish merchants from France, established numerous Jewish communities along the trade route from Western Europe to the Caspian region, especially in southern Poland, Bohemia, and the Danube valley.

A mass migration of Jews to Eastern Europe began after the beginning of the Crusades and the onslaught on the Jews in France and the Rhineland in 1096. In 1290 Jews were expelled from England and in 1306 from France. Yiddish-speaking Ashkenazic Jews moved to Poland, Austria, Hungary, Bohemia, and Moravia. In Poland, which became the main cultural center of the Ashkenazim (German Jews and their descendants) during the next nine centuries, Jews received privileges, became a separate estate, developed a unique self-government known as the Council of the Four Lands, and enjoyed wide cultural autonomy. After the 1569 union of Poland and Lithuania and the establishment of the Polish-Lithuanian Commonwealth, its eastern lands were colonized by a new wave of Jewish settlers. Between 1569 and 1648, the Jewish community in Ukraine rose to 120,000. Jews acted as the middlemen of Polish nobles and were perceived as the immediate overlords of the peasants. Therefore, Jews became one of the main victims of a number of insurrections in the seventeenth and eighteenth centuries. After 1648, the Jewish position in the Commonwealth deteriorated constantly. In 1764 the Council of the Four Lands was abolished and a wave of Jews emigrated back to Western Europe.

In 1492 Jews were expelled from Spain, in 1497 from Portugal, and in 1542 from the Kingdom of Naples. About 300,000 Jews left the Iberian Peninsula during the fifteenth and sixteenth centuries. A wave of Sephardic Jews moved to the Ottoman Empire, including its large southern European part. The Balkans, with such communities as Salonika and Sarajevo, became the great center of the Latino-speaking Sephardim (Jews often identified as being from the Iberian Peninsula and North Africa).

By the end of the eighteenth century, after the partitions of the Polish-Lithuanian Commonwealth, its Jews became subjects of Prussia, Austria, or Russia, whose governments were unprepared to deal with masses of Jews. In 1785 there were about 70,000 Jews in Bohemia, Moravia, and Silesia, and about 80,000 in the vast Hungarian Kingdom, but no Jews lived in Austria proper; Leopold I (1640–1705) had banished them from Vienna in 1669 and two years later from the whole of Lower Austria. Simultaneously, in 1785 there were about 215,000 Jews (almost 9 percent of the entire population) in newly acquired Galicia. The Austrian authorities started several experiments dealing with Jews and treated them badly, which was especially harmful because Galicia was one of the poorest and most backward provinces of the empire. Eventually, the 1867 Austrian constitution granted the Habsburg Jews equal rights. In 1900 over two million Jews lived in the Austro-Hungarian Empire, including 831,000 in Hungary, 811,000 in Galicia, 157,000 in Lower Austria, 92,000 in Bohemia, and 44,000 in Moravia.

Before the partitions of the Polish-Lithuanian Commonwealth, the Jewish population of Prussia was not numerous. In 1573 the Hohenzollerns exiled their Jews, after which only a very limited number of Jewish families were admitted into the country. After the partitions, about 67,000 Polish Jews became subjects of Prussia. Its authorities began to assimilate the Jews and use them to germanize the Polish territories. By the mid-nineteenth century, most Prussian Jews considered themselves Germans of Mosaic faith. In 1869 they received equal rights.

A majority of the 750,000 Jews living in the Polish-Lithuanian Commonwealth in the eighteenth century were incorporated into the Russian Empire. The Jews had been expelled from Muscovy by the end of the fifteenth century, and the administration of Catherine the Great (1729–96) did not know how to deal with masses of Jews. After an unsuccessful attempt to integrate them with the Russian merchant class, the Jews were concentrated in the Pale of Settlement, established in western Russia in 1791. During the nineteenth century, anti-Jewish persecutions and restrictions continued to increase, culminating in the 1880s after the assassination of Alexander II (1818–81). The Jews of Russia received equal rights for the first time after the Russian Revolution of 1917. The tradition of persecution pushed many Jews into revolutionary movements and stimulated the emergence of Zionism and emigration to America and Western Europe. Mass emigration also took place in Galicia and Romania, where about 265,000 Jews lived by the end of the nineteenth century. In the late eighteenth century Jewish emancipation started and a new type of Jew appeared in Western Europe. In Russia, Galicia, Romania, and Hungary only a small segment of the Jewish population reformed their religion and everyday life. A majority of *Ostjuden* (Eastern Jews) remained in the shtetl (little Jewish community), spoke exclusively Yiddish, wore traditional garb, and stuck to Orthodoxy. Poverty, lack of opportunities, and oppression forced about three million Eastern European Jews to emigrate. Steady birthrates kept the total Jewish population level of over five million unchanged, and Jews constituted the third-largest ethnic group (after Ukrainians and Poles) in the Central European countries between Russia and Germany proper.

Developments unfavorable to the Jews accelerated during World War I. The war stimulated anti-Semitism and curtailed the economic means of Eastern European Jews. During the war and a series of local postwar military conflicts, about 250,000 Eastern European Jews were killed, especially during pogroms in the Ukraine. Hundreds of thousands were deported and otherwise uprooted. The war broke up the unity of *Ostjuden*. Half of them landed in the Soviet Union where they were recognized initially as a separate nation but soon subjected to accelerated acculturation. The other half found themselves in several newly established states inhabited mostly by a nationalistically oriented population. Throughout the interwar period, conflicts between Jews and local populations grew steadily. Anti-Jewish legislation and the Great Depression pauperized a large segment of the Jewish population. Before World War II, about 3.3 million Jews lived in Poland, 3 million in the Soviet Union, 900,000 in Romania, 400,000 in Hungary, 360,000 in Czechoslovakia, 75,000 in Yugoslavia, and 50,000 in Bulgaria.

During World War II, Nazi Germany, with the help of segments of the East European population it controlled, carried out a systematic extermination of the Jews. Approximately six million European Jews were murdered during the Holocaust, mostly in Eastern Europe. Its Ashkenazi civilization disappeared. By 1946, about 120,000 Jews remained in Poland, 55,000 in Czechoslovakia, 200,000 in Hungary, 300,000 in Romania, 10,000 in Yugoslavia, and 46,000 in Bulgaria. Threatened by Stalinist anti-Semitic policies, most of them emigrated eventually to Israel and the West. In 1969 about 15,000 Jews lived in Poland, 14,000 in Czechoslovakia, 7,000 in Bulgaria, 7,000 in Yugoslavia, 80,000 in Hungary, and 100,000 in Romania. About 2.6 million Jews lived in the entire Soviet Union; however, in the 1970s a mass Jewish emigration began. Between 1970 and 1980, 250,000 Jews emigrated from the Soviet Union. After severe restrictions in the early 1980s, emigration picked up again in the last years of the decade.

Piotr Wróbel

Further reading

Baron, S. *Social and Religious History of the Jews,* 18 vols. New York, 1952–78.

Die Habsburgermonarchie 1848–1918, vol. 3, *Die Völker des Reiches,* pt. 2, ed. by A. Wandruschka and P. Urbanitsch. Vienna, 1980.

Dubnov, S. *History of the Jews in Russia and Poland from the Earliest Times until the Present Day,* 3 vols. Philadelphia, 1916–20.

Encyclopedia Judaica, vol. 6. Jerusalem, 1971, 966–77, and vol. 13, 709–89.

Encyclopedia of Ukraine, vol. 2, ed. by V. Kubijovyć. Toronto, 1988, 385–93.

Haumann, H. *Geschichte der Ostjuden.* Munich, 1990.

Lerski, G. and H. Lerski. *Jewish-Polish Coexistence, 1772–1939: A Topical Bibliography.* Westport, Connecticut, 1986.

Mendelsohn, E. *The Jews of East Central Europe between the World Wars.* Bloomington, Indiana, 1983.

Shaw, S.J. *The Jews of the Ottoman Empire and the Turkish Republic.* New York, 1991.

See also Auschwitz; Emigration; Ethnic Minorities; Holocaust; Jewish Bund; Judaism; Numerus Clausus; Pale of Settlement; Pogrom; Warsaw Ghetto

Jirásek, Alois (1851–1930)

Prolific Czech writer. A member of an old Silesian family, Jirásek graduated from Charles University in Prague in 1874. From 1874 to 1909, he taught high school, first in Litomyšl then in Prague. Influenced by the romantic movement, he wrote numerous plays, poems, and short stories, publishing his first work in 1874. His fame, however, stems from his popular historic novels. The majority of these simply written, highly detailed, realistic, and nationalistic pieces, based on historical research, span the fifteenth to eighteenth centuries and cover the Hussite Wars (1400s) in works such as *Mezi proudy* (*Between the Currents,* 3 vols., 1891), *Proti všem* (*Against All the World,* 1894), and *Bratrstvo* (*Brotherhood,* 3 vols, 1900–1909); the decline of the Czech nation after the Battle of White Mountain in 1618, in *Temno* (*Darkness,* 1915); and the Czech national revival, in *F.L. Věk* (5 vols., 1890–1907).

During World War I, Jirásek became the first writer to sign, in May 1917, the "Manifesto of Czech Writers," an appeal to Czech deputies in the Vienna parliament to defend Czech national interests. His action spurred more than two hundred other authors to do likewise. On April 13, 1918, he read aloud before a large demonstration in Prague the "Czechoslovak National Oath," demanding self-determination for Czechs and Slovaks. After the creation of Czechoslovakia, he became a member of the provisional national assembly. From 1920 to 1925, he represented the National Democratic Party in the Senate before retiring from public life. He remains one of the greatest Czech writers of the late-nineteenth and early-twentieth centuries.

Gregory C. Ference

Further reading

Hýsek, Miroslav, ed. *Alois Jirásek.* Prague, 1921.
Janáčková, Jaroslava. *Alois Jirásek.* Prague, 1987.
Voborník, Jan. *Alois Jirásek.* Prague, 1901.

See also Czech Literature

John Paul II (1920–)

Polish-born Roman Catholic pope. Born Karol Wojtyła on May 18, 1920, in Wadowice, Poland, John Paul II studied theater, literature, and philology before he was forced to resign from these ambitions with the advent of World War II. He worked for a time as a common laborer in a factory and collaborated with the Polish resistance fighting German occupation. Under the protection of the archbishop of Kraków, Wojtyła studied to be a Catholic priest during the war and was ordained in 1946. He moved quickly through the church's hierarchy. He was consecrated bishop in 1958, named as archbishop of Kraków in 1964, and made a cardinal in 1967. Apart from being a cleric, Wojtyła was a respected playwright, writer of poetry, and lecturer of ethics at the Catholic University of Lublin. As a contributor to the documents of the Second Vatican Council, he gained world attention as a capable theologian. Speaking out against violations of human and civil rights in Poland in the 1970s, Wojtyła openly defended such organizations as the dissident group KOR (Workers' Defense Committee). Elected pope in 1978 (taking the name John Paul II after his three immediate predecessors), Wojtyła not only became the first Polish pontiff but the first pope from a Communist-bloc country. A supporter of the Solidarity trade union movement, John Paul II became, along with Lech Wałęsa (1943–), the Solidarity leader, a living symbol of the Poles' attachment to Catholicism and their European heritage. Before the events of 1989, he made three trips to Poland (1979, 1983, 1987) and is believed to have played a supporting role in the Round Table talks of 1989, ending Communist rule in Poland. As a Slav, John Paul II took a strong interest in the "silenced" churches of Eastern Europe and the former Soviet Union.

Peter Lavelle

Further reading

John Paul II. *Crossing the Threshold of Hope.* New York, 1994.
Micewski, Andrzej. *Cardinal Wyszyński.* New York, 1984.
Schimmelpfennnig, Bernhard. *The Papacy,* trans. by James Sievert. New York, 1993.

See also Catholicism; KOR; Revolutions of 1989; Lech Wałęsa

Jókai, Mór (1825–1904)

Hungarian novelist, poet, humorist, and creator of romantic prose. Jókai was born into a provincial, landowning family of the lesser nobility. His father was a respected and wealthy lawyer, and Jókai was designated to follow in his footsteps. But instead, after receiving a law diploma, he embarked on a career as a writer. Along with poet Sándor Petőfi (1823–49), he quickly became one of the youthful, intellectual leaders of the uprising against the Habsburgs in 1848. Forced into hiding after the defeat of the Hungarians in the Revolution of 1848–49, he was granted amnesty by the emperor, through the intercession of his wife, Róza Benke Laborfalvi (1817–86), whom he had married in 1848, the foremost Hungarian actress of the time. After settling in Budapest, he dedicated the next decade to producing his most famous novels. He also spent time in jail for some of his more liberal views. With time, his political stance became more moderate and conciliatory toward the Habsburgs. He retired from political life in the 1880s.

In his early writings, Jókai was greatly influenced by the French romantics, but he later evolved to create his own brand of romanticism. He did not attempt to depict reality but rather created his own world in which good and evil do battle and good always prevails. His heroes are either angels or devils. A dreamer and idealist, Jókai imagined how it should be and not how it is, but he could not resolve the problems of humankind. His secondary characters were drawn from the folk and thus he was able to add much humor to his literary portraits. His novels can be divided into four types: the novel of incident or anecdote; the novel of heroism; the novel of personal confession; and the novel of adventure. The mastery of detail, creation of atmosphere, fresh and natural dialogue, precise and limpid evocation of times and places, and boundless creative imagination are the hallmarks of his writing, and helped to make him one of the legendary figures of nineteenth-century Hungarian literature. His most famous works include: *Erdély aranykora* (*Erdely's Golden Age*, 1852); *Kárpáthy Zoltán* (1854); *Az új földesúr* (*The New Landlord,* 1863); *A kőszívü ember fiai* (*The Baron's Sons,* 1869); *Fekete gyémántok* (*Black Diamonds,* 1870); *Aranyember* (*The Golden Man,* 1873); and *A lőcsei fehér asszony* (*The White Woman from Lőcse,* 1885).

Katherine Gyékényesi Gatto

Further reading

Czigány, Lóránt. *The Oxford History of Hungarian Literature.* Oxford, 1984.
Hegedüs, Géza. *A magyar irodalom arcképcsarnoka.* Budapest, 1976.
Klaniczay, Tibor, ed. *A History of Hungarian Literature.* Budapest, 1982.
Nemeskürty, István. *Diák, Írj Magyar Éneket: A Magyar Irodalom Története,* 2 vols. Budapest, 1985.

See also Hungarian Literature; Hungarian War for Independence; Sándor Petőfi; Revolutions of 1848

Jószef, Attila (1905–37)

Hungarian interwar poet. József was born in Budapest, the son of a soap factory worker who emigrated to America when the boy was only three, leaving the family in dire poverty. His mother, a washerwoman, died of uterine cancer in 1919. With the help of his brother-in-law, he finished secondary school and attended Szeged University but never completed his studies.

While only seventeen, he published his first volume of poetry, *Szépség koldusa* (*Beggar of Beauty,* 1922), followed by *Nem én kiáltok* (*It's Not Me Shouting: It's the Earth Rumbling,* 1924). He lived in Paris and Vienna, before returning to Budapest University in 1927. He published his third volume of poetry, *Nincsen apám, se anyám* (*Fatherless and Motherless*) in 1929. In the 1920s he was influenced by the music of Béla Bartók (1881–1945) and Zoltán Kodály (1882–1967) and the rediscovery of Hungarian folk motifs, later by the "proletarian" poetry of European Communist movements.

During the economic crisis brought on by the Great Depression of the 1930s, he joined the underground Communist Party, and although he later severed his ties, he sympathized with Marxism and the working classes until the end of his life. *Döntsd a tőkét, ne sivánkozz!* (*Fell the Tree-Trunks!*) (1930), an eager expectation of coming revolution, dates from this period. In Hungarian, the word *"tőke"* can also mean "capitalism," and thus the title can also be interpreted as *"Fell Capitalism."*

Although beset by personal woes, he wrote his great intellectual poems in the years that followed: "Külvárosi éj" (Night in the Slums, 1932), "Medvetánc" ("Bear's Dance," 1934), and "Nagyon fáj" ("It Hurts a Lot," 1936). His last years were blighted with psychosis, and in 1937 he committed suicide by hurling himself in front of a train at a resort near Lake Balaton.

Mártha Pereszlényi-Pintér

J

Further reading
Czigány, Loránt. *The Oxford History of Hungarian Literature*. Oxford, 1984.
Klaniczay, Tibor, ed. *A History of Hungarian Literature*. Budapest, 1982.
Klaniczay, Tibor, József Sauder, and Miklós Szabolcsi. *A History of Hungarian Literature*. Budapest, 1964.
Molnár, August J. *Hungarian Writers and Literature by Joseph Reményi*. New Brunswick, New Jersey, 1964.

See also Béla Bartók; Hungarian Literature; Zoltán Kodály

Jovanović, Dragoljub (1895–1977)

Serb left agrarian leader and university professor. Born in eastern Serbia near the Bulgarian border, Jovanović served in the Serbian army in World War I. Before the war's end, he was sent to study in Paris, where he obtained a doctorate. He later became a professor of sociology at Belgrade University. Politically active, Jovanović was a member of the opposition during the 1920s and was highly critical of the monarchy and Serbian nationalism. After publishing a newspaper viewed as antistate, he was placed under house arrest for a year. In the 1930s he was a close collaborator of Croatian Peasant Party leader Vladko Maček (1879–1964), and along with several other Serbian parties was part of the United Opposition electoral bloc. He also wrote extensively on agrarian problems.

On the eve of World War II, he was convinced that Yugoslavia could not avoid involvement in the conflict and advised his followers to align themselves with the Communists (at that time an illegal party). Although he remained in Belgrade during the war, Jovanović was rewarded by the Communists with a seat in parliament.

When, as a deputy, he openly criticized collectivization of agriculture, Jovanović was stripped of his seat, arrested, and given a prison term lasting eight years. While in prison, he wrote his memoirs on toilet paper and afterward had them typed and deposited in archives. It was a bitter pill when his strongest supporters told him that he had made a mistake in cooperating with the Communists. When released from prison, he published two volumes (in 1973 and 1975) that he called "Medallions," picture portraits of 102 dead contemporaries and his relations with them. To the end, he remained committed to the Yugoslav state, but he had some inner doubts. One indication of this was his decision (along with that of his devoted wife) in the 1971 census to declare themselves "Serbs." In all previous censuses they had declared themselves "Yugoslavs."

Alex N. Dragnich

Further reading
Jovanović, Dragoljub. *Ljudi, Ljudi: Medaljoni 56 umrilih savremenika*, vol. 1. Belgrade, 1973.
———. *Ljudi, Ljudi: Medaljoni 46 umrilih savremenika*, vol. 2. Belgrade, 1975.

See also Collectivization; Vladko Maček

Jovanović, Slobodan (1869–1958)

Serbia's greatest historian. The principal works by Jovanović, a professor at Belgrade University, concerned the reigns of Milan (1854–1901) and Alexander Obrenović (1876–1903); each encompassed three volumes. He also wrote briefer studies dealing with the reigns of Miloš (1780–1860) and Mihailo Obrenović (1823–68). In addition, Jovanović authored books on political ideas and systems, as well as the standard work on the constitutional law of interwar Yugoslavia. Curiously, however, he never wrote about the reign of the Karadjordjevićes. His writing style was greatly admired, and even intellectuals not friendly to him agreed that if he had written in a major European language he would have been rated with historians such as Englishman Arnold Toynbee (1889–1975).

Jovanović avoided association with political movements or parties until 1939, when it became evident that the Croats were about to gain an autonomous unit in which over one million ethnic Serbs would reside. At that time, the Serbian Culture Club was formed and, although Jovanović was not its driving force, he became its president. He defended his actions as necessary because Serbian educational and cultural organizations that were once strong, notably in Bosnia-Hercegovina and the Vojvodina, had been neglected and therefore something needed to be done.

In 1941 Jovanović became vice president in the Yugoslav government following the overthrow of the cabinet that had signed a pact with Hitler (1889–1945). After the government was forced to flee abroad ahead of the subsequent German invasion of Yugoslavia, he served the government-in-exile in London in several capacities, including that of prime minister. After the war, he was tried in absentia, convicted by a Communist court in Belgrade, and given a twenty-year prison sentence. Remaining in London, where he died, Jovanović wrote several brief but insightful monographs (in Serbian) under the general title *My Contemporaries,* published in Canada in 1962. These concerned famous men in Serbia, such as Serbian leader Nikola Pašić (1845–1926). After the death of Tito (1892–1980), Jovanović's collected works were published in Belgrade.

Alex N. Dragnich

Further reading

Djordjević, Dimitrije. "Historians in Politics: Slobodan Jovanović," in *Historians in Politics,* ed. by Walter Laquer and George Mosse. London, 1974, 253–74.

Dragnich, Alex N. *The Development of Parliamentary Government in Serbia.* Boulder, Colorado, 1978.

See also Adolf Hitler; Tito

Judaism

Monotheistic religion professed by the Jews, also Jewish philosophy and civilization. The word "Judaism" (*Judaismos*) was used first by Greek-speaking Jews about 100 B.C. to distinguish their religion from Hellenism. The definition of Judaism and its essence is difficult. Twelfth-century philosopher Maimonides (1135–1204) classified thirteen principles of the Jewish faith, including belief in the following: the existence of God; God's unity; that God is incorporeal; that God is eternal; that God alone is to be worshipped; prophecy; that Moses is the greatest of the prophets; that the Torah is divine; that the Torah is unchanging; that God knows the thoughts and deeds of humans; that God rewards the righteous and punishes the wicked; the coming of the Messiah; the resurrection of the dead. Later philosophers and theologians discussed and reduced Maimonides' principles in many ways, but most of them considered the three following ideas to be the core of Judaism: belief in God; belief in God's revelation of the Torah to Israel; belief in Israel as the people that lives by the Torah in obedience to God.

During its development, Judaism has undergone many phases and absorbed multiple influences. It began in the Nomadic Period (ca. 2000–1600 B.C.), when, according to the Bible, patriarch Abraham, the founding father of Judaism, recognized the spiritual nature of the one and only God. Under Moses (ca. 1500 B.C.), Judaism evolved into the exclusive worship of Yahweh. After the settlement in Canaan, Judaism became a religion of an agricultural people and absorbed many influences from its neighbors. Further changes took place during the Babylonian Exile. After the Jews returned from Babylon, during the Pre-Rabbinical Age, the Torah, the sacred Scripture and foundation of Judaism, was created and the Jewish religion was challenged by rich Persian and Greek civilizations. Judaism further developed during the Rabbinical Period, which lasted until the sixth century, and during the Middle Ages, when the greatest codes of Jewish law and sophisticated theological theses were written. The Middle Ages, in terms of Jewish civilization, ended by the eighteenth century, when the Period of Transformation started. Many Jews from Central and Eastern Europe embraced Haskalah, the Jewish Enlightenment. Others supported the new mystical movement of Hasidism. Judaism has been split into several groups including, besides the members of Haskalah and Hasidism, the supporters of Orthodoxy, Neo-Orthodoxy, Conservative Judaism, and Reform Judaism.

The Jews have lived in Central and Eastern Europe since the beginning of the Diaspora, but initially this subcontinent did not play a special role in the development of Judaism. In the sixteenth century Poland became the world center of Jewish studies and the Ashkenazi civilization (Jews from northern Europe). Several important schools were established and some were active until World War II. The lands of the Polish-Lithuanian Commonwealth were the cradle of Hasidism, a religious movement attached to Zionism, a bulwark of Orthodoxy, and an outpost of Haskalah. In 1846 the L'vov Deutsch Jüdisches Bethaus became the first Reform synagogue of Eastern Europe. The most important Hasidic dynasties of America and Israel have their roots in Eastern Europe. After the exile of the Jews from Spain in 1492, a wave of Sephardim (Jews from the Iberian Peninsula) arrived in the Balkans and created one of the world centers of Sephardic civilization. In several towns of southeastern Europe, such as Zagreb and Sarajevo, three Jewish religious communities existed simultaneously: Sephardic, Orthodox Ashkenazic,

J

and Reform Ashkenazic. An important and long chapter in the history of the transformation of Judaism took place in Eastern and Central Europe.

Piotr Wróbel

Further reading

Encyclopedia Judaica, vol. 8. Jerusalem, 1971, 383–97.

Marmur, Dow. *On Being a Jew: A Reform Perspective.* Toronto, 1994.

Roth, Leon. *Judaism. A Portrait.* London, 1960.

See also Jews

Jungmann, Josef (1773–1847)

Czech pedagogue, linguist, poet, and translator who gave his name to the second generation of the Czech national renaissance during the nineteenth century. Jungmann rose from humble origins through intellectual ability to a career in teaching, first at the gymnasium in Litoměřice (1799), then after 1815 in Prague. As a student he published poetry, in which his translations (including those of Schiller [1759–1805], Goethe [1749–1832], Chateaubriand [1768–1848], and Milton [1608–84]) were more important than his original works. Jungmann demanded that in the Czech lands Czech be used for all forms of cultural and scientific expression, contributing compilatory works on the language (1820) and Czech literary history (1825). Jungmann realized that the Czech used in the Bohemian Brethren's sixteenth-century Bible of Kralice and the humanists required further development, above all in vocabulary, to be capable of what he demanded. To this end, he was instrumental in establishing the cultural foundation Matice česká (Czech Foundation) (1831). His greatest contribution was his Czech-German dictionary (1834–39), which stabilized modern literary Czech.

Through his activities and encouragement he influenced an entire generation of patriots, including Pavel Josef Šafárik (1793–1861), František Palacký (1798–1876), Václav Hanka (1791–1861), Milota Zdirad Polák (1788–1856), Antonín Marek (1785–1877), Ján Kollár (1793–1852), and Jan Ladislav Čelakovský (1799–1852). Educated in the spirit of the Enlightenment, Jungmann was influenced by romantic attitudes and his patriotism was also colored by consciousness of Slavic links, in which he always expressed warm sympathy for the Russians. His overwhelming emphasis on the language led him to articulate an ethnolinguistic concept of "nation" in articles in 1806. This linguistic focus remained characteristic of the Czech national renascence, to which Jungmann contributed so much.

Hugh Agnew

Further reading

Dolanský, Julius. *Jungmannův odkaz: Z dějin české slovesnosti.* Prague, 1948.

Jedlička, Alois, Vladimír Barnet, Bohuslav Havránek, and Václav Křístek. *Slovanské spisovné jazyky v době obrození: Sborník věnovaný Universitou Karlovou k 200. výročí narození Josefa Jungmanna.* Prague, 1974.

Vodička, Felix. *Počátky krásné prozy novočeské: přispěvek k literárním dějinám doby Jungmannovy.* Jinočany, 1994, reprint of 1948 ed.

Zelený, Vácslav. *Život Josefa Jungmanna.* Prague, 1873.

See also Ján Kollár; František Palacký; Romanticism; Pavel Josef Šafárik

Junimea

Romanian cultural and literary association. Junimea (Youth) developed from a series of lectures at the Bank of Iaşi, initiated in 1863 by critic, academic, and politician Titu Maiorescu (1840–1917). By April 1864, a group of five young Moldavian academics and intellectuals, German-educated like Maiorescu but also from the Moldavian upper class, agreed to meet for witty conversation in one another's homes following the lectures. Although Maiorescu was the leading personality of Junimea, the society had no formal structure beyond the annual meeting and banquet. Despite such lighthearted mottos as "Whoever wishes, enters; whoever can, remains" and "First friendship, then literature," Junimea was a serious intellectual society whose members were severely critical of one another's lectures, essays, plays, poetry, and translations. The society also sponsored promising students for study abroad, such as historian A.D. Xenopol (1840–1920) who was sent to Berlin.

Convorbiri literare (*Literary Conversations,* 1867), Junimea's unofficial monthly, edited for twenty-eight years by Iacob Negruzzi (1842–

1932), spread the society's influence throughout Romania. The periodical soon attracted contributions from such major Romanian writers as Vasile Alecsandri (c. 1818–90), Ion Creangă (1837–89), Mihai Eminescu (1850–89), Ion Luca Caragiale (1852–1912), and Ioan Slavici (1848–1925). No less important for future Romanian culture, however, were essays by Maiorescu urging that Romanian culture replace the nationalist romanticism of the 1848 revolution in the Romanian lands with a more conservative, evolutionary, and Romanian-specific approach. Cautioning against "forms without substance," he criticized efforts to establish cultural institutions before Romanian culture had developed sufficiently to require such forms. By emphasizing Romanian rather than foreign solutions, the rigorously cosmopolitan members of Junimea ironically gave early voice to the traditionalist rather than the international approach and thus helped define what has remained a major dichotomy in Romanian intellectual life.

Although Junimea was overwhelmingly conservative in outlook, it avoided mixing politics with its cultural agenda. Yet some leading members like Petre Carp (1837–1918) and Maiorescu did ultimately pursue successful political careers as moderate conservatives. By the time Negruzzi and *Convorbiri literare* had followed Maiorescu to Bucharest in 1885, Junimea had accomplished its important work in establishing standards and directions for Romanian culture.

Ernest H. Latham Jr.

Further reading

Hiemstra, Paul A. *Alexandru D. Xenopol and the Development of Romanian Historiography.* New York, 1987.

Hitchins, Keith. *Rumania: 1866–1947.* Oxford, 1994.

Ornea, Z. *Junimea si junimismul,* 2d rev. ed. Bucharest, 1978.

Zub, Alexandru. *Junimea: Implicatii istoriografice, 1864–1885.* Iaşi, 1976.

See also Ion Luca Caragiale; Petre Carp; Ion Creangă; Mihai Eminescu; Titu Maiorescu; Romanticism; Alexandru D. Xenopol

K

Kádár, János (1912–89)

Prime minister of Hungary. Born to working-class parents, as a young man Kádár (who was born János Czermanik but adopted the code name Kádár when he became a revolutionary) took part in workers' strikes and joined the small Communist movement in Hungary. Imprisoned under the regime of Admiral Horthy (1868–1957), the Hungarian regent, he held various political posts after World War II, in the Hungarian People's Republic, before being imprisoned again during the purges of the (Mátyás) Rákosi (1892–1971) era of the late 1940s and early 1950s.

On October 25, 1956, during the first stage of the Hungarian Revolution against Soviet domination, Kádár and Imre Nagy (1896–1958), with approval from the Soviet leadership, became joint leaders of Hungary. Kádár, who was seen by some at the time as a centrist figure, was ambivalent about the revolution. When it became apparent that Moscow was prepared to crush the Hungarian insurgents, Kádár fled Budapest and offered to cooperate with the Soviets. He returned under Soviet escort on November 4, charged with leading a Soviet-sponsored regime that would end the "counterrevolution." As prime minister of the new government, Kádár employed harsh measures to reestablish the primacy of the Communist Party. The chief leaders of the revolution, including Nagy, were executed, and many more were imprisoned. Because of these repressive steps in the late 1950s and his willingness to cooperate with the Soviet Union, Kádár was despised by many Hungarians as a traitor.

In the 1960s, however, Kádár slowly regained a degree of popularity. He made it clear that he had no intention of returning to the policies of the Stalinist era, and he showed a certain tolerance of non-Communists by insisting that "all those who are not against us are for us." Moreover, he was willing to experiment with economic reforms. The New Economic Mechanism (NEM), introduced in the late 1960s, shifted the focus from heavy industry to the consumer sector and introduced a degree of private enterprise and increased trade with the West. Because the economic reforms were accompanied by a degree of political liberalization, Hungary was regarded by the early 1980s as the least rigid and most Western-oriented of the Soviet satellite countries. Later in the 1980s, however, when the desire for fundamental changes grew throughout the Communist world, Kádár was seen by Hungarian dissidents as a hindrance to fundamental reform. In 1988 he was forced by the reform wing of the Hungarian Communist Party to relinquish power. Kádár died in 1989, the year in which Communist regimes were toppled throughout Eastern Europe.

Judith Fai-Podlipnik and Thomas Sakmyster

Further reading

Held, Joseph. "Hungary on a Fixed Course: An Outline of Hungarian History," in Joseph Held, ed., *The Columbia History of Eastern Europe in the Twentieth Century.* New York, 1992.

Hoensch, Jorg K. *A History of Modern Hungary.* New York, 1988.

Molnar, Miklós. *From Béla Kun to János Kádár: Seventy Years of Hungarian Communism.* New York, 1990.

Sugar, Peter, Peter Hanak, and Tibor Frank. *A History of Hungary.* Bloomington, Indiana, 1990.

K *See also* Hungarian Communist Party; Hungarian Revolution of 1956; Imre Nagy; NEM; Mátyás Rákosi

Kafka, Franz (1883–1924)

Czech Jewish author. Kafka, who spoke both Czech and German, lived most of his life in Prague, where he studied law, received a doctorate of law in June 1906, and worked as an insurance inspector from 1908 until his early retirement in 1922, two years before his death from tuberculosis.

Kafka wrote three novels, all incomplete and published posthumously: *Der Prozess* (*The Trial,* 1925), *Das Schloss* (*The Castle,* 1927), and *Amerika* (1927). In addition, Kafka wrote numerous stories, many of which were also published posthumously. Among his most widely acclaimed stories are "Die Verwandlung" (The Metamorphosis, 1915), "Das Urteil" (The Judgment, 1916), "In der Strafkolonie" (In the Penal Colony, 1919), "Ein Landarzt" (A Country Doctor, 1919), and "Ein Hungerkünstler" (A Hunger Artist, 1924).

As a writer, Kafka is known for his intensely personal narratives, typically depicting individuals thrust into extraordinary, often bizarre circumstances that defy comprehension and consign the protagonist to a hopeless fate. The protagonist of Kafka's most widely acclaimed story, "The Metamorphosis," for example, discovers one morning that he has been transformed into an insect, later to be shunned by his family and to die a lonely death. Kafka's writings have received diverse critical interpretations, but his commentators generally agree that they express the alienation of the individual in the complexities and absurdities of modern life. Another of Kafka's enduring themes is the ambiguity of personal guilt, a theme clearly motivated by his own persistent sense of unworthiness that plagued him throughout his life. This theme is central to *The Trial,* in which the protagonist, Joseph K., is arrested for a charge he does not understand and tried by judicial proceedings that bewilder and frustrate him, finally to be executed by a band of anonymous assassins.

Kafka's work marked a watershed for fiction in Europe and America. His themes of the estrangement and absurdity of human life have been echoed in the work of many of the most prominent writers of the post–World War II era.

Richard Field

Further reading

Bloom, Harold, ed. *Franz Kafka.* New York, 1986.
Brod, Max. *Franz Kafka,* trans. by G. Humphreys-Roberts and Richard Winston. New York, 1960.
Hayman, Ronald. *Kafka: A Biography.* New York, 1980.
Pawel, Ernst. *The Nightmare of Reason: A Life of Franz Kafka.* New York, 1984.
Wagenbach, Klaus. *Franz Kafka: Eine Biographie seiner Jugend, 1883–1912.* Bern, 1958.

See also Czech Literature

Kállay, Miklós (1887–1967)

Prime minister of Hungary (1942–44) who attempted to extricate Hungary from World War II and sign a peace agreement with the Western allies. Kállay was the son of a distinguished aristocratic family who could afford to send him to study abroad. Nevertheless, he obtained a doctorate in law from the University of Budapest. He held administrative posts in the provinces and became undersecretary of commerce in 1929–30. He was elected to parliament in 1931 and became minister of agriculture in the right-wing cabinet of Gyula Gömbös (1886–1936) from 1932 to 1935.

On March 9, 1942, the conservative Kállay was appointed prime minister by Miklós Horthy (1868–1957), regent of Hungary, to replace László Bárdossy (1890–1946), who was largely responsible for committing Hungary to the campaign against the Soviet Union and for a state of war with the Western Allies as well. Kállay's implied mission, judging from the attitude of the regent and his advisers, was to undo the damage done by Hungary's wartime ties to Berlin; he represented the Anglophile forces, which disapproved of the pro-German and especially the pro-Nazi orientation. Although he favored continued Hungarian military activity on the eastern front—the Second Hungarian Army was dispatched to the front after Kállay took over—he promoted secret contacts with the Western powers and tempered anti-Semitic and right-wing radical measures inside Hungary.

Kállay's policy of "two steps to the right, two steps to the left" was bound to fail, however; he would not consider dealing with the Soviet Union, and he was unable and unwilling to carry out the stipulations of the Western powers, who insisted on unconditional surrender, nor could he keep these negotiations secret from German intelligence. German troops occupied the country in March 1944, partly because of their distrust of the Hungarian government, and of Kállay in particular. He was arrested by the Gestapo and detained in a concentration camp. After the war, he settled in Italy then resettled in the United States in 1951. There, in 1954, he published *Hungarian Premier: A Personal Account of a Nation's Struggle in World War II*, which, like most such memoirs, is bent on self-justification.

Mario D. Fenyo

Further reading

Fenyo, Mario D. *Hitler, Horthy and Hungary*. New Haven, Connecticut, 1971.
Ránki, György. *Emlékiratok és valóság*. Budapest, 1964.

See also László Bárdossy; Gyula Gömbös; Miklós Horthy

Karadžić, Vuk Stefanović (1787–1864)

Linguist, ethnographer, historian, philologist, folklorist, and father of the Serbo-Croatian literary language. Born in Tršić, a village near Serbia's western border with Bosnia, Vuk won acclaim for his learning and knowledge. In 1808 he became one of the first pupils of Serbian pedagogue Dositej Obradović (c. 1739–1811) at the newly opened Velika škola (gymnasium). In 1813 Vuk wrote an article about the fall of Karadjordje's Serbia (Black George [1768–1817], leader of the first revolt against Ottoman rule), which caught the attention of an imperial censor, Slovene philologist and father of Slavic linguistics, Jernej Kopitar (1780–1844). At Kopitar's urging, Vuk published two volumes of Serbian folk songs and poetry in 1814 and 1815 (*Mala prostonarodna slavenoserbska pesmarica* [*Little Songbook of the Slavic-Serbian Common People*]) and *Narodna Srbska pesmarica* (*National Serb Songbook*) and in 1814 published *Pismenica serbskog jezika,* a Serbian grammar. Continuing his linguistic work, in 1818 Vuk published his groundbreaking and monumental *Srpski rječnik,* the first Serbo-Croatian dictionary, with 26,270 words and a new grammar and orthography. In it, Vuk insisted that all written forms follow the pronunciation of the people, a break with the prevailing educational practices in Orthodox monasteries. It constituted a major reform of written Serbian, which hitherto used an orthography with Russian, Church Slavonic, and Serbian elements. The dictionary met with great success among Europe's educated circles, causing Vuk to turn entirely to issues of literary, grammatical, and linguistic reform.

Vuk vigorously defended his grammatical and orthographic reforms through a series of articles in journals and newspapers. He also traveled extensively throughout the Serbian and Croatian regions of the Habsburg Empire, collecting folk sayings, customs, songs, stories, and legends, while continuing his efforts at literary reform.

In 1848 he traveled to Prague, where he participated in the Slavic Congress (called during the revolutions of 1848 in the Habsburg lands). A year later, he published a second, enlarged edition of folk sayings and ethnographic material. In March 1850 Vuk met in Vienna with a group of Croatian and Slovenian philologists and writers—including Croatian poet Ivan Mažuranić (1814–90)—in an attempt to regulate literary affairs among the South Slavs. All were strongly influenced by the Illyrian Movement, the Croatian national revival, and viewed the Serbs, Croats, and Slovenes as one people. Conscious of the need for a single people to have a single language, they decided to adopt one orthography and dialect as the literary standard. At this meeting, Vuk successfully pressed for the adoption of the Western Serbian dialect (štokavian/jekavian), which had been used by Croatian Renaissance authors in Dubrovnik, throughout much of Bosnia-Hercegovina, and in most of the popular songs in the Serbo-Croatian–speaking areas of the Balkans. The Literary Agreement that emerged from this meeting called for one common literature and one literary language, written in two alphabets—the Cyrillic and the Latin—which were to share equal status. This agreement formed the basis for the modern Serbo-Croatian literary language, the literature of the Yugoslav movement, and the principle of linguistic unity that prevailed in the twentieth-century Yugoslav state.

By the end of his life, Vuk had published over twenty books and dozens of articles covering modern Serbian history, biography, grammatical reform and orthography, dictionaries, and ethnographic collections. In addition, a number of his works were published posthumously.

James M.B. Lyon

K

Further reading
Duncan Wilson. *The Life and Times of Vuk Stefanović Karadžić, 1787–1864: Literacy, Literature, and National Independence in Serbia.* Ann Arbor, Michigan, 1986.

See also Folklore; Illyrian Movement; Jernej Kopitar; Ivan Mažuranić; Dositej Obradović; Prague Slav Congress; Revolutions of 1848; Serbo-Croatian Language

Karavelov, Petko Stoichev (1843–1903)

Bulgarian politician and statesman. After studying in Bulgaria and Greece, Karavelov went to Russia for further education. Enrolling in Moscow University in 1861, he eventually graduated from its faculty of law. He remained in Russia until the outbreak of the Russo-Turkish War of 1877–78, when he returned to Bulgaria with the Russian army.

After Bulgaria's liberation, Karavelov became a delegate to the nation's organizing Constitutional Convention (1878). He then served briefly as president of the first constituent National Assembly (October 21–November 24, 1879). Soon he became an editor of the newspaper *Tselokupna Bulgariya* (*Bulgaria in Its Entirety*) and leader of the Liberal Party, a position he held from 1879 to 1883. On January 13, 1880, he married Ekaterina Peneva (1860–1947), a Russian-educated Bulgarian poet and writer who became an outstanding advocate for women's causes. He served briefly as minister of finance, and from November 28, 1880, to April 27, 1881, also as prime minister. When his government was overthrown in 1881, he fled to Plovdiv, in Eastern Rumelia, where he obtained a teaching position in the men's gymnasium. He remained there until constitutional government was reestablished in Bulgaria.

In the elections of 1884, the Liberal Party again came to power, and once more Karavelov became prime minister and minister of finance, holding the posts from 1884 to 1886. But after Stefan Stambolov (1854–95) became prime minister in 1877, Karavelov was arrested on political grounds and imprisoned for several months. He was arrested again in 1891 for conspiracy in the murder of Khristo Belchev (1857–91), a cabinet minister. Apparently innocent of the charge, Karavelov nevertheless was convicted and given a long prison term but was freed in the general amnesty of 1894. Again he became a member of the National Assembly, and in 1896 founded the Democratic Party and became its president. For a third time, in 1901 he was given the prime ministership but held the post only briefly, resigning in December of the same year, partly for reasons of health. He died in Sofia thirteen months later.

John Georgeoff

Further reading
Drenkova, Fani, comp. and ed. *Kato antichna tragediia: Sudbata na Ekaterina Karavelova i neinoto semeistvo v pisma, dnevnitsi, fotografii.* Sofia, 1984.
Georgov, Iv. *Zhivot i deinost na Petko Karavelov.* Sofia, 1946.
Kozhuykharov, K. *Petko Karavelov.* Sofia, 1968.
Peev, P. *Petko Karavelov.* Sofia, 1946.
Statelova, Elena, comp. and ed. *Spomeni za Petko Karavelov.* Sofia, 1991.

See also Russo-Turkish War of 1877–78; Stefan Stambolov

Kardelj, Edvard (1910–79)

Slovene Communist theoretician and politician. Kardelj held numerous positions in the Yugoslav Communist Party (later, the League of Communists of Yugoslavia, or LCY) and in the country's post–World War II governments. He also functioned in many ways as the official theoretician of the LCY. He oversaw the drafting of several of the country's constitutions and provided the revisionist Marxist justifications for President Tito's (1892–1980) policies.

Most of Kardelj's theoretical works dealt with domestic politics and economics. He designed Yugoslavia's variant of workers' self-management, which later was rechristened "self-managing socialism." He also wrote on the foreign policy of nonalignment, which one could call Yugoslavia's *Südpolitik* ("Policy toward the South"), dealing with countries of the developing world. Kardelj claimed that this *Südpolitik* was an external reflection of the country's internal system, based as it was on the supposedly effective combination of socially owned property, self-managing enterprises, and a federal solution to the country's nationality problems.

Two unresolved ambiguities trouble Kardelj's legacy today. The first is that he never adequately resolved the tension between maintenance of the federal party's "leading role" in society and the right of enterprises and individuals to act according to their own interests or consciences. The second ambiguity turns on his conflicting views of nationalism, which he began to elaborate in his 1939 work *Razvoi slovenskega narodnega vprašanja* (*The Development of the Slovene National Question*). On the one hand, nationalism could be divisive and exploitative, but on the other, it could serve as the vehicle for building socialist consciousness within certain ethnic communities. His furtherance of the Slovene nation within the Yugoslav federation contributed to some extent to the independence of Slovenia in the 1990s, although his economic theories can justifiably be regarded as having failed.

John K. Cox

Further reading

Basom, Kenneth E. "Class and Nation in Slovenia: Edvard Kardelj versus Josip Vidmar." *East European Quarterly,* 26, no. 2 (1992): 209–18.

Kardelj, Edvard. *Reminiscences: The Struggle for the Recognition and Independence of the New Yugoslavia, 1944–1957.* London, 1982.

———. *Yugoslavia in International Relations and the Non-aligned Movement.* Belgrade, 1979.

Rogel, Carole. "The Education of a Slovene Marxist, 1924–1934." *Slovene Studies* 11, no. 1–2 (1989): 177–84.

Šetinc, Franc. *Misel in delo Edvarda Kardelja.* Ljubljana, 1979.

See also Communist Party of Yugoslavia; Non-aligned Movement; Self-Management; Tito

Károlyi, Count Mihály (1875–1955)

Hungarian statesman, politician, and diplomat. Károlyi was the scion of one of the wealthiest families in Hungary. He was first elected to parliament in 1905 as an independent but soon joined the opposition Independence Party. Although he favored dropping out of the 1879 Dual Alliance between Austria-Hungary and Germany, in August 1914 he supported Austria-Hungary's entrance into World War I. By 1916, however, he turned against the war and founded the Károlyi Party. His platform called for a personal union, universal and secret ballot, land reforms, and a separate peace. Károlyi also supported autonomy for nationalities within integral Hungary.

On October 24, 1918, a revolutionary National Council, headed by Károlyi, was formed. It demanded power, and on October 31, 1918, Emperor-King Charles (1887–1922), who soon after abdicated, named Károlyi as premier. Károlyi's left-of-center coalition introduced liberal democratic reforms, including land reforms, which began with the division of Károlyi's own estates. On January 11, 1919, Károlyi resigned and became the president of the short-lived People's Republic, which collapsed on March 21, 1919, as a result of the territorial demands of the Allied victors in the world war.

Since he did not support the Soviet Republic, led by Béla Kun (1886–1938), that followed, he left for exile in the West in June 1919. In the interwar years he opposed the regime of the regent, Miklós Horthy (1868–1957), which charged him with wartime treason and confiscated his wealth. During World War II, he attempted to form a government-in-exile in London but received no Allied backing. He returned to Hungary in May 1946 and was appointed ambassador to France in 1947. In response to the Communist purges, he resigned his post in 1949 and remained in France.

Peter Pastor

Further reading

Hajdu, Tibor. *Károlyi Mihály.* Budapest, 1978.

Károlyi, Catherine. *A Life Together: The Memoirs of Catherine Károlyi.* London, 1966.

Károlyi, Mihály. *Károlyi Mihály levelezése I. 1905–1920,* ed. by György Litván. Budapest, 1978.

———. *Károlyi Mihály levelezése II. 1921–1925,* ed. by Tibor Hajdu. Budapest, 1990.

———. *Károlyi Mihály levelezése III. 1925–1930,* ed. by Tibor Hajdu. Budapest, 1991.

Károlyi, Michael. *Memoirs of Michael Karolyi: Faith without Illusion.* New York, 1957.

See also Charles I; Dual Alliance; Miklós Horthy; Hungarian Soviet Republic; Béla Kun

Kasprowicz, Jan (1860–1926)

Polish poet, playwright, and translator. Although Kasprowicz came from a poor, uneducated peasant family, in 1909 he became a professor of comparative literature at Lwów University. His first original poems, a collection of forty sonnets, *Z chałupy* (*From the Cottage,* 1891), were attempts to create "naturalistic verse" by combining images

K of Polish peasant life with religious motifs and formal experiments. These "versified essays" were softened by Kasprowicz's great love of nature, which is present in all his work. His most famous works were written after 1892 with a collection of symbolic poems, *Krzak dzikiej róży* (*A Wild Rosebush,* 1898), and free-verse hymns, *Ginącemu światu* (*To the Perishing World,* 1902) and *Salve Regina* (1902). The hymns united medieval millenarianism and apocalyptic visions of the dying world and civilization with accusations of God, the creator of the world and universal evil. The relationship between good and evil as well as the role of God in the contemporary world is resolved in Kasprowicz's later collections of poetry resembling "meditation in verse" (*Księga ubogich* [*Book of the Poor,* 1916]; *Mój świat* [*My World,* 1926]). These tonic-quatrains suggest final reconciliation with God and humbleness toward God's rule in the spirit of St. Francis. Kasprowicz also wrote a volume of ironic poems-in-prose, *O bohaterskim koniu i walącym się domie* (*On a Heroic Horse and on a Tumble-Down House,* 1906), which harshly judges modern civilization.

Katarzyna Zechenter

Further reading

Górski, Konrad. *Jan Kasprowicz—Studia.* Warsaw, 1977.

Lipski, Jan Józef. *Twórczość Jana Kasprowicza,* vols. 1–2. Warsaw, 1967–75.

Miłosz, Czesław. *The History of Polish Literature.* Berkeley, California, 1983.

See also Polish Literature

Katowice

Industrial and administrative center, the capital city of the province (*voivod*) of Katowice, in southwestern Poland. The densely populated province has an area of 2,412 square miles (6,700 sq km) and a population of just under four million. The city of Katowice is situated 40 miles (64 km) west of Kraków on a tributary of the Oder River in south-central Poland.

Katowice is a major rail junction and a cultural center as well, with several technical schools and colleges specialized in art, music, and economics. The city's population has been rather stable, growing from 351,300 in 1979 to 366,900 by the end of 1989.

Coal mining began in the region in the 1860s, and the German village of Katowice (German, Kattowitz) was incorporated as a city in 1867. The Katowice region became part of Poland in 1921 with the partition of Upper Silesia, and remained so except during Nazi German occupation (1939–45), when the Germans drew on and expanded the industrial resources of the city and region to aid in the war effort. The city was called Stalinogrod between 1953 and 1956.

The city of Katowice developed, along with several surrounding towns, into Poland's largest urban agglomeration. The coal deposits in the province are Poland's largest and among the most extensive in Europe. Besides coal, the region produces coking coal, electrical energy, steel, and all of Poland's zinc, lead, and silver. The Huta Katowice metal complex was one of Poland's major development projects of the 1970s. In addition to mining and metals, the city produces chemicals, textiles, heavy machinery, and pharmaceutical products.

The Upper Silesian coal basin in Katowice is the most polluted area in Eastern Europe, and the district is especially affected by sewage, dust, and gases (notably sulfur dioxide emissions) from the local mining and metallurgical operations. The consequences of the environmental degradation in the region—especially due to heavy metals in the atmosphere—are Poland's highest infant mortality rates (up to 52 percent in one region in 1989); birth defects and childhood illnesses; respiratory diseases; and a lowered life expectancy for adults throughout the region.

Barbara VanDrasek

Further reading

Curtis, Glenn E., ed. *Poland: A Country Study.* Washington, D.C., 1994.

Hoffman, George W., ed. *Europe in the 1990s: A Geographic Analysis,* 6th ed. New York, 1990.

Rostowski, Jacek. "The Decay of Socialism and the Growth of Private Enterprise in Poland," *Soviet Studies* 41, no. 2 (April 1989): 194–215.

See also Environment; Health; Industrialization

Katyn Forest

Site of the massacre of fifteen thousand Polish reserve officers during World War II. Following the Soviet alliance with the Allies in 1941, questions arose about the fate of thousands of Polish officers missing since the defeat of Poland by Germany and the USSR in 1939. During its attack on Poland in September 1939, the Soviet Red Army, then allied with the Germans, captured more than two hundred thousand Polish soldiers and placed them in camps. Months after their capture, outside communication with the officers ceased.

In April 1943 a German radio station reported the discovery, in the Katyn Forest (near Smolensk, in the western Soviet Union), of mass graves containing the remains of thousands of Polish officers. The Polish government-in-exile confronted Stalin (1879–1953) about the incident; the Soviet leader denied responsibility for the atrocity and blamed the Nazis for the murders.

The gravesite revealed much evidence (verified by one international commission) that pointed to Soviet guilt, despite Soviet claims that the officers had been murdered by the Germans in the winter of 1941. The bodies were clad in summer uniforms. The hands of numerous victims were tied behind their backs with Russian-made ropes. Moreover, the executioners had used German revolvers originating from Gutave Genschow and Company, which exported weapons to the Soviet Union and the Baltic nations. In spite of this incriminating evidence, the subject of the massacre remained closed for years and the issue left a deep scar in Polish-Soviet relations.

Although most of the incriminating evidence pointed to the Soviets, Moscow did not own up to the heinous deed until 1989; after forty-six years, the Soviet government under Mikhail Gorbachev (1931–) admitted responsibility for the massacre.

Judith Fai-Podlipnik

Further reading

Davies, Norman. *God's Playground: A History of Poland,* vol. 2. New York, 1982.

Korbonski, Andrzej. "Poland: 1918–1990," in Joseph Held, ed., *The Columbia History of Eastern Europe in the Twentieth Century.* New York, 1992

Leslie, Roy F. *A History of Poland since 1863.* Cambridge, 1992.

Zawodny, Janusz. *Death in the Forest.* Notre Dame, Indiana, 1962.

See also Mikhail Gorbachev; Red Army; Stalin; World War II

Kazasov, Dimo (1886–1980)

Bulgarian politician. Kazasov came from a family of teachers, entered the same profession, and rose to the position of secretary of the teachers union. He later graduated from law school and plunged into politics and journalism. In 1902 he joined the Social Democratic Party and in 1919 became a member of its Central Committee and editor of its paper, *Narod (Nation).* On June 9, 1923, he plotted the overthrow of the government of Aleksandur Stamboliiski (1879–1923) with Aleksandur Tsankov (1879–1959), but under party pressure he left the government in 1924. In 1925 he published the account of his part in the plot, for which he was expelled from the Social Democratic Party. He formed his own group and in 1927 organized Zveno, made up of some of his confederates of June 9, 1923, with whom he plotted the overthrow of the democratic government of the National Bloc on May 19, 1934. In this, they were outmaneuvered by King Boris (1894–1943), who then established his personal regime. Kazasov served briefly as ambassador to Yugoslavia, which had subsidized Zveno. During the war, he and his associates of 1923 and 1934 joined the Communist-led Fatherland Front (a coalition of left and center political parties) and the pro-Soviet resistance, and on September 9, 1944, under the protection of the Soviet Red Army, overthrew the government made up of the Bulgarian Agrarian National Union, the Democratic Party, and the People's Party. This coup established the Communist regime in Bulgaria. Kazasov served it first as minister of information. After his retirement, he practiced journalism.

Spas T. Raikin

Further reading

Grigorov, Boyan. *Ot suglashatelstvo kum zalez: Sotsialdemokraticheskata partiva v Bulgaria, 9 iuni 1923–19 Mai 1934.* Sofia, 1980.

Kazasov, Dimo. *Burni godini.* Sofia, 1949.

———. *V tumninite na zagovora.* Sofia, 1925.

———. *"Zveno" bez grim.* Sofia, 1936.

Kumanov, Milen. *Politicheski partii, organizatsii i dvizhenia v Bulgaria i tekhnite lideri.* Sofia, 1991.

See also Bulgarian Agrarian National Union; Boris III; Communist Party of Bulgaria; Fatherland Front; Red Army; Aleksandur Stamboliiski; Aleksandur Tsankov; Zveno

Kazinczy, Ferenc (1759–1831)

Cultural organizer, essayist, translator, and chief motivator of Hungary's early-nineteenth-century language reform movement. Born into a family of Protestant landed gentry, Kazinczy studied art, the classics, and languages. In 1775 he published a geography handbook of Hungary, and his 1776 translation of *Der Amerikaner* (*The American*) brought him into contact with the author, György Bessenyei (1747–1811), the leader of Hungary's literary revival. A Freemason (pseudonym: Orpheus), he held a number of county positions, translated the great European works, and founded literary reviews.

In 1794 Kazinczy was arrested for his political activities. First condemned to death, he ended up serving 2,387 days in prison. Imprisonment changed him from an educated county official set to create refined taste through translation into a leader of a national cultural movement. After starting a family and settling at Széphalom (Fair Hill), he depended on his small state for meager support while he devoted his life to cultural activities.

A prolific letter writer, Kazinczy corresponded with a wide variety of intellectuals. His letters contained a wealth of advice and criticism. Writers came to respect his opinion, and he became the "enlightened despot" of Hungary's cultural life. Aside from his journals and prison diaries, his sentimental writings are of little interest. More important were his translations, which revealed clear ideas about language as a vehicle for sophisticated communication. He fought obsolete language conventions and introduced new ones in close accordance with the spirit of Hungarian. As such, the Hungarian language reform movement succeeded in opening doors to European ideas and in creating a suitable medium for transmitting them to readers.

By the 1820s, romanticism came to replace classicism, and young writers such as Mihály Vörösmarty (1800–55) rejected Kazinczy's cosmopolitan outlook as anachronistic in the nationalist revival of the time.

András Boros-Kazai

Further reading

A History of Hungarian Literature, ed. by Tibor Klaniczay. Budapest, 1982, 127–30.

Czigány, Lóránt. *The Oxford History of Hungarian Literature.* Oxford, 1984.

See also Freemasonry; Hungarian Language; Romanticism; Mihály Vörösmarty

Khitov (Hitov), Panayot (1830–1918)

Bulgarian revolutionary and one of the founders of the Bulgarian *haiduk* (resistance) movement in the struggles for liberation from the Ottomans. Born in Sliven, Khitov was a descendant of a prominent local leader assassinated by the Turks. He began his underground activities at the age of twelve. Failing in small-business adventures, he joined the *cheta* (armed band) of legendary hero Hadji Dimitar (1837–68) as a flag bearer. Although illiterate until late in his life, Khitov rose to the highest ranks of the revolutionary movement and led numerous incursions of his *cheta* into Bulgaria from bases in Serbia and Romania. He impressed his contemporaries with his burning love for fatherland, great natural intellect, ingenious strategy, simple eloquence, fearless bravery, directness, pride, manly appearance, and conduct. No man in Bulgaria was feared more by the Turks than Khitov. He established close ties with Serbian cabinet ministers, used Serbia as a staging area for his forays into Bulgaria, received a pension from Belgrade, and married a Serbian woman. His failure to deliver Serbian help, however, for the failed April insurrection in 1876 in Bulgaria and the Serbian anti-Bulgarian policies during the Russo-Turkish War of 1877–78, especially after the Congress of Berlin, where Austria-Hungary backed Serbia's claim to occupy Bulgarian territories, discredited Khitov among the new leaders of his country, and he vanished from the political stage after 1878.

Spas T. Raikin

Further reading

"Donesenie, na I[van] Krilov do N[ikolai] P[avlovich] Ignatiev za P[anayot] Khitov, Septemvri 5, 1875," in Akop A. Oulounyan, "Novi dokumenti za revoliutrionnata Deinost na . . . P. Khitov." *Istoricheski pregled,* 25, no. 5. Sofia, 1969, 86–87.

Khitov, Panayot. *Spomeni ot khaidutstvoto.* Sofia, 1975.

Mitev, Yono. *Istoria na aprilskoto vustanie, 1876,* vol. 1. Sofia, 1986.

Raikin, Spas T. "Osvobozhdenieto na Bulgaria," in *Politicheski problemi pred bulgarskata obshtestvenost v chuzhbina,* vol. 1. Sofia, 1993.

See also April Uprising; *Cheta;* Congress of Berlin; *Haiduk;* Russo-Turkish War of 1877–78

Khuen-Héderváry, Count Károly (1849–1918)

Hungarian politician and official, *ban* (governor) of Croatia, and twice prime minister of Hungary. Born into a Hungarian noble family holding estates in Croatia, Khuen-Héderváry entered a career in state service. Following serious Croatian national disturbances in 1883, Khuen-Héderváry was appointed *ban,* a position he held until 1903. He maintained order and Hungarian interests in the kingdom through a combination of electoral manipulation, restriction of opposition political activity, and concessions to the Serbian minority. During his administration, the radical nationalist Party of Right gained in strength among Croats.

In the Hungarian constitutional and political struggles of the early twentieth century, Khuen-Héderváry sided with Count István Tisza (1861–1918) in seeking to uphold the constitutional structure established in the *Ausgleich* (Compromise) of 1867, which established the Dual Monarchy of Austria-Hungary, and resisted calls for the use of Hungarian as a language of command in the imperial army. Khuen-Héderváry joined Tisza in establishing the Party of National Work in 1910 and opposed the constitutional demands of the opposition Independence Party in his terms as prime minister in 1903 and again from 1910 to 1912.

Philip Pajakowski

Further reading

Jelavich, Charles. "The Croatian Problem in the Habsburg Empire in the Nineteenth Century," *Austrian History Yearbook* 3 (1967): 83–115.

Kann, Robert A. and Zdeněk V. David. *The Peoples of the Eastern Habsburg Lands, 1526–1918.* Seattle, Washington, 1984.

Vermes, Gabor. *István Tisza: The Liberal Vision and Conservative Statecraft of a Magyar Nationalist.* New York, 1985.

See also Ausgleich; Dual Monarchy; István Tisza

Kieślowski, Krzysztof (1941–1996)

Polish film director and screenwriter. Kieślowski studied film at the Film Academy in Łódź. In his early career he directed numerous short features, television dramas, and documentaries, the best known of which is *From the Night Porter's Point of View* (1977). Kieślowski began directing feature films in the mid-1970s. In 1988 he made the television series *The Decalogue,* two episodes of which were adapted for the wide screen and received international acclaim. In the 1990s Kieślowski worked mostly in international coproductions. In the early stages of his career he was interested primarily in political and moral issues. Gradually he lost interest in sociopolitical considerations and began to devote his attention entirely to exploring the existential-ethical aspects of human experience. His features include *Blizna* (*The Scar,* 1976); *Amator* (*Camera Buff,* 1979); *Przypadek* (*Blind Chance,* 1981); *Bez Konca* (*No End,* 1984); *Krótki film o zabijaniu* (*A Short Film about Killing,* 1988); *Krótki film o milosci* (*A Short Film about Love,* 1988); *Podwójne Zycie Weroniki* (*The Double Life of Veronique,* 1991); *Trois Couleurs* (*Three Colors*): *Bleu* (*Blue,* 1993); *Blanc* (*White,* 1994); and *Rouge* (*Red,* 1994).

Dina Iordanova

Further reading

Stok, Danusia, ed. *Kieslowski on Kieslowski.* London, 1993.

See also Cinema

Kingdom of Serbs, Croats, and Slovenes (Serbo-Croatian, *Kraljevstvo Srba, Hrvata i Slovenaca*)

Official name of the "Triune" Kingdom of Yugoslavia, the "first Yugoslavia," between 1918 and 1929, named for the three principal South Slavic (Yugoslav) peoples who made up the vast majority of the country's population.

On July 20, 1917, Serbian Prime Minister Nikola Pašić (1845–1926) and Ante Trumbić (1868–1938), leader of the Yugoslav Committee (in exile), representing Austria-Hungary's South Slavs, signed the vaguely worded Corfu Declaration, calling for the postwar union of Serbs, Croats, and Slovenes in a single democratic, constitutional state, under the Serbian House of Karadjordjević.

In accordance with this agreement, and with the concurrence of the Yugoslav National Council meeting in Zagreb at war's end, the former Habsburg lands populated principally by South Slavs (Slovenia, Croatia-Dalmatia, and Bosnia-Hercegovina) joined with the Kingdom of Serbia (already enlarged by the absorption of Montenegro and the Hungarian Vojvodina) to form the "Kingdom of Serbs, Croats, and Slovenes," officially proclaimed on December 1, 1918. The new country's borders were officially confirmed by the Treaties of St. Germain (1919), Trianon (1920), Neuilly (1920), and Rapallo (1920). The kingdom had a population of some twelve million. More than seven hundred thousand Yugoslavs lived outside the borders of the new state; approximately two million non-Yugoslavs lived within them.

The country's first head of state was Serbia's aged king, Peter I Karadjordjević (1844–1921). Peter's son Alexander (1888–1934), who had served as prince regent of Serbia since 1914, formally succeeded his father on August 16, 1921. The first common cabinet, representing all major regions and ethnic groups, was formed on December 20, 1918.

The kingdom was plagued with numerous problems from the outset, in particular prickly relations between Serbs and Croats, the two largest Yugoslav national groups. Many Serbs thought of the kingdom as an extension of prewar Serbia, which provided the new country's capital, ruling house, and highest-ranking military and police officials. Many Croats resented what they perceived to be Serb high-handedness in the structuring of the new country. Most of the kingdom's political parties developed along ethnic lines.

An interim Yugoslav parliament began functioning in March 1919, but elections for a Constituent Assembly did not take place until November 1920, after the frontiers of the new state had been agreed upon. Seven months later, on June 28, 1921 (St. Vitus's Day, or Vidovdan), a constitution was finally adopted, providing for a centralized, rather than a federal, governmental system. Although Serbian Radical Party leader Pašić, the dominant political figure of the new kingdom in its early years, had managed to win the support of many Slovenes and Bosnian Muslims for his centralist political program, Stjepan Radić (1871–1928), leader of the Croat Republican Peasant Party (CRPP), led a spirited opposition to the new state and its constitution. Croatian deputies refused to take their seats in the Yugoslav parliament in Belgrade, while Radić courted favor with certain anti-Yugoslav elements abroad. Finally, in 1925, a compromise was reached, the CRPP dropped the designation "republican" from its name, and the

mercurial Radić entered the government for a while. In August 1928, however, Radić and several other Croatian deputies were shot on the floor of the Skupština parliament; Radić died from his wounds shortly thereafter. In an attempt to restore political order and contain national hostilities, King Alexander established a royal dictatorship on January 6, 1929, dissolving parliament, abolishing the Vidovdan constitution, banning political parties, curtailing freedoms of speech, press, and association, and dividing the country into nine administrative units called *banovine*. On October 3, 1929, he formally changed the country's name to "Yugoslavia." Two years later the kingdom received a new constitution.

John D. Treadway

Further reading

Djilas, Aleksa. *The Contested Country: Yugoslav Unity and Communist Revolution, 1919–1953.* Cambridge, Massachusetts, 1991.

Dragnich, Alexander. *The First Yugoslavia: The Search for a Viable Political System.* Stanford, California, 1983.

Lampe, John R. *Yugoslavia as History: Twice There Was a Country.* Cambridge, 1996.

See also Alexander I Karadjordjević; Corfu Declaration; Neuilly, Treaty of; Nikola Pašić; Peter Karadjordjević; Stjepan Radić; St. Germain, Treaty of; Skupština; Trianon, Treaty of; Triune Kingdom; Ante Trumbić; Vidovdan Constitution; Yugoslav Committee

Kiselev, Count Pavel Dimitrievic (1788–1863)

Enlightened Russian general, statesman, and diplomat who helped draft Romania's first constitution and became president of the principalities of Moldavia and Wallachia during the period of Russian occupation (1828–34). With wisdom and tact, Kiselev endeavored to make the constitutions (one for each principality) acceptable to prince, *boiar,* assembly, and the population at large. As a general who distinguished himself during the Napoleonic Wars, he had a special interest in the new military and sanitary establishments, fought against the extraterritorial privileges of foreign residents, and attempted (without success) to persuade the *boiar* assemblies to tackle peasant reform. Following the resignation of Prince Alexandru

Ghica (r. 1834–42) in 1842, he seriously considered becoming a candidate for the Wallachian throne, and although he withdrew his name, he continued serving as consultant to *boiars* and princes. As Russian ambassador to France during the Crimean War (1853–56), he continued to support Romania's cause. For all these reasons he was among the few Russians whose death was mourned by the Romanian nation, and as a tribute one of Bucharest's most elegant streets (originally built by him) was named in his honor.

Radu Florescu

Further reading

Filitti, Ion C. *Les Principautés roumaines sous l'occupation russe 1824–1834.* Paris. 1904.

Florescu, Radu R. "British Reactions to the Russian Regime in the Danubian Principalities." *Journal of Central European Affairs* 22, no. 1 (April 1962): 27–42.

———. *The Struggle against Russia in the Roumanian Principalities 1821–1834,* Munich, 1962.

See also *Boiars;* Crimean War; Danubian Principalities

Klaipéda

The third-largest city and an important Baltic port in Lithuania (203,000 population). Klaipéda (German, Memel) was founded by Teutonic Knights in 1252 on the site of an old fishing village and became a Hanseatic port town located on the northern end of the Kurisches Haff, where the shallow bay is connected by a narrow strait with the Baltic Sea. An especially dredged channel permits seagoing ships to reach the modern, highly mechanized port facilities rebuilt after almost complete destruction at the end of World War II. The Kurisch spit, in places two miles wide, covered by a planted forest, protects the port and the city from western winds. A pine forest protects the city from the north.

Before World War I, the German port Memel (as part of Germany's Polish territories), with its sawmills and plywood and pulp factories, exported raw timber, wood products, grain, and flax, the main products of its hinterland in Russia. It imported rice for its small rice mill, coal, and raw materials for a fertilizer plant.

Lithuania seized the city in 1923. The sawmills and the timber industry, having lost their supply of raw materials in the east, declined, and exports were dominated by agricultural products. The scope of imports broadened by the addition of many industrial products and raw materials for textile industries.

After World War II, the industrial profile of Klaipéda broadened considerably with the addition of new textiles, food processing, woodworking, and paper plants. The city's industrial production is 6.3 percent of total Lithuanian industrial output. The modern port acquired a shipyard and other ship repair facilities. Klaipéda became the home port of the Lithuanian fishing fleet, which counts some 170 modern trawlers and several ship factories.

The townscape of the old city is typically medieval: narrow streets, closely built brick houses, and the market with the Town Hall. It is full of old commercial stores and industrial warehouses. The new industries are located on the very southern end of the shore strip.

Abraham Melezin

Further reading

Lithuanian Department of Statistics. *Lithuania in Figures.* Vilnius, 1994.

Tarvidas, S.S. and A.B. Basalikas. *Lithuania.* Moscow, 1967, 224–31.

Klofáč, Václav Jaroslav (1868–1942)

Czech radical nationalist journalist, politician, and first Czechoslovak minister of defense. Klofáč was the most influential radical nationalist Czech politician in the Habsburg monarchy and an important leader of the First Czechoslovak Republic. Born in Německý/Havlíčkův Brod, Klofáč modeled his public life after Czech national leader Karel Havlíček (1821–56), striving to continue the work of national awakening and the realization of civil liberties through his journalism and public activities.

Klofáč began his political life as a student in Prague in the late 1880s. Like many of his young colleagues, Klofáč was dissatisfied with both Young Czech party moderation and what he felt were the antinational activities of Czech Social Democrats. In 1898 he quit his job as an editor at *Národní listy* (*National Gazette*) to found the Czech National Socialist Party. Elected to the imperial parliament for the first time in 1901, Klofáč was the most outspoken and most eloquent

K Czech radical nationalist and antimilitarist, and the most consistent supporter of women's rights in the parliament.

His opposition to the Habsburg government and his close identification with the South Slav movement resulted in his treason trial and death sentence in 1915. Amnestied in 1917, Klofáč played an important part in the creation of the First Czechoslovak Republic, served as defense minister in the new state's first two governments, and later was vice chairman and chairman of the Senate. Klofáč and his party were the most loyal supporters of President Tomáš G. Masaryk (1850–1937).

T. Mills Kelly

Further reading

Garver, Bruce. "Václav Klofáč and the Czechoslovak National Socialist Party," in *The Czech and Slovak Experience,* ed. by John Morison. New York, 1991.

Klofáč, Václav. "Třicet pět let práce a bojů," *Májovy List Národních Socialistů.* Prague, 1932.

Šantrůček, Bohuslav. *Václav Klofáč (1868–1928): Pohledy do života a díla.* Prague, 1928.

See also Karel Havlíček; Tomáš G. Masaryk; Young Czechs

Kodály, Zoltán (1882–1967)

Hungarian composer and ethnomusicologist. Immersed in the study of languages and law, Kodály decided relatively late in life to become a musician. His attention soon focused on Hungarian folk music, which—with Béla Bartók (1881–1945)—he began to collect on a large scale. Among the many influences he absorbed, French composer Debussy's (1862–1918) is the most obvious. In time, however, he developed an idiom steeped in Hungarian folk music, which usually provided the thematic material in his works, conveying a sense of natural affinity. His most significant original composition, eventually renamed *Psalmus Hungaricus,* made him a national icon.

Kodály's Sonata for unaccompanied cello is a significant addition to the repertoire, and his choral works (many a capella) are especially noteworthy. For many years, he taught composition at the Liszt Academy in Budapest. Kodály's output is a model of folk music–based composition on the highest level. His insistence on introducing rudimentary music education at an early age, and in every school, created a worldwide following in time. A man of few words and of rigid professional standards, he brought up generations of disciples. Through them, he began to advocate the value of sight singing, accurate intonation, and swimming. After World War II, with fellow composer Ernő Dohnányi's (1877–1960) departure and Bartók's death, Kodály assumed a position of power not conceivable for a musician in a Western democracy.

Balint Vazsonyi

Further reading

Eösze, László. *Zoltán Kodály—His Life and Work.* London, 1962.

Young, Percy. *Zoltán Kodály.* London, 1964.

See also Béla Bartók; Ernő Dohnányi; Folk Music; Music

Kogălniceanu, Mihail (1817–1891)

Romanian political reformer, jurist, journalist, statesman, and historian. After studying in Iaşi, France, and Berlin, where he attended the lectures of German historian Leopold von Ranke (1795–1886), Kogălniceanu became an adviser to the prince of Moldavia in 1838. He published a historical journal, *Arhiva românească (Romanian Archives),* between 1840 and 1845, and three volumes of the most important Romanian chronicles. As a professor in Iaşi, in 1843 he delivered an inaugural lecture that established the national mission of Romanian historiography. After a period in prison for his political activity, he joined other Romanian activists in Paris from 1846 to 1848. Although he returned to Moldavia, he was soon forced to flee to Austrian Bukovina after publishing a political pamphlet. There, he composed a draft constitution and revolutionary program on behalf of the defeat of the "Moldavian Revolutionary Committee." He returned to Moldavia after the defeat of the revolution of 1848 in Moldavia and agitated for the unification of the Danubian Principalities, especially through a newspaper he founded in 1855, *Steaua Dunării (Star of the Danube).* After the dual election of Alexandru Ioan Cuza (1820–73) as prince of Moldavia and Wallachia in 1859, Kogălniceanu became a leader of the liberal faction in Romanian politics. Becoming the United Principalities' prime minister in

1863, he carried out the expropriation of monastic estates, land reforms, and a law on the armed forces and one on public instruction, before resigning in 1865. Thereafter he was politically prominent for many more years. As foreign minister between 1876 and 1880, he signed the convention with Russia against the Turks, proclaimed the country's independence in the Romanian parliament during the victorious war in 1878, represented Romania at the Congress of Berlin, and protested Russian annexation of southern Bessarabia following the Russo-Turkish War of 1877–78.

James P. Niessen

Further reading

Kogălniceanu, Mihail, *Opere,* 5 vols. Bucharest, 1974–89.

Zub, Alexandru. *Mihail Kogălniceanu 1871–1891. Bibliografie.* Bucharest, 1971.

———. *Mihail Kogălniceanu: Un fondateur de la Roumanie moderne.* Bucharest, 1978.

See also Congress of Berlin; Alexandru Ioan Cuza; Danubian Principalities; Revolutions of 1848; Russo-Turkish War of 1877–78; United Principalities

Kolarov, Vasil Petrov (1877–1950)

Bulgarian Communist politician. Born into a family of artisans in Shumen, Kolarov initially became a schoolteacher. Later, he studied law in Switzerland and returned to practice law in his hometown in 1900. There he became an early member of the Bulgarian Social Democratic Party. In 1903 he joined the Narrow Socialist Party led by Dimitur Blagoev (1856–1924). From 1913 to 1919, Kolarov represented that party in the Bulgarian Subranie (parliament). In 1919 Kolarov joined the new Bulgarian Communist Party and represented it in the Subranie. The same year he became the secretary-general of the Bulgarian Communist Party, playing a major role in instigating an attempted Communist uprising in Bulgaria in September 1923. After its failure, Kolarov fled Bulgaria for Berlin, where he worked for the Comintern (Communist International), and served as the formal leader of the Bulgarian Communist Party until 1934. Following the trial of Georgi Dimitrov (1882–1949), the Bulgarian Communist leader, after the Reichstag fire in Berlin, Kolarov left Berlin for Moscow, where he spent the years of World War II. He returned to Bulgaria in 1945

and became acting president of the new Bulgarian republic the next year. He later served as prime minister and foreign minister, and in 1949 presided over the judicial murder of Traicho Kostov (1847–1949), a fellow Communist accused of spying for the West. After the death of his close associate Dimitrov that same year, Kolarov became president of the state and head of the Politburo of the Bulgarian Communist Party. He held these posts until his death in Sofia on January 23, 1950.

Richard C. Hall

Further reading

Bell, John D. *The Bulgarian Communist Party from Blagoev to Zhivkov.* Stanford, California, 1986.

Kolarov, Vasil. *Spomeni.* Sofia, 1968.

Rothschild, Joseph. *The Communist Party of Bulgaria.* New York, 1959.

See also Dimitur Blagoev; Comintern; Communist Party of Bulgaria; Georgi Dimitrov; Traicho Kostov; Subranie

Kollár, Ján (1793–1852)

Slovak Lutheran minister in Budapest, leading personality of the Slovak and Czech national awakening, and originator of the idea of Slavonic literary mutuality. Inspired by the German post-Napoleonic movement for political unification, Kollár launched the idea of Slavonic literary mutuality (*O literárnej vzájemnosti mezi kmeny a nářečími slavskými* [*About the Literary Mutuality between the Slavonic Tribes and Dialects,* 1836]). He conceived all the Slavonic peoples and their "dialects" as parts of one huge Slavonic nation (*národ*) and one Slavonic language. There would be four highly developed "book printing" dialects: Russian, Polish, Czechoslovak, and Illyrian; every educated Slav would have to understand and buy books in these four. Kollár himself was a legalist with no political intentions, but he advocated an atmosphere of proximity and mutual solidarity among Slavonic peoples.

Kollár expressed these ideas most efficiently in his poetry. In the spirit of early romanticism he combined personal love poetry with pathetic verses of pathos about the fates of the Slavs. His famous poem "Slávy dcera" ("The Daughter of Sláva") was composed by the addition of new parts to his *Básně* (*Poems,* 1821), and reached its final shape in 1832.

K

Since Kollár considered popular poetry as the deepest expression of a people's mind, he collected Slovak popular songs. His collection *Národnie Zpievanky* (*People's Songs*, 1834–35) provided an important impetus for the codification of a Slovak literary language different from Czech. Kollár, however, was an ardent defender of the existent common literary language for Slovaks and Czechs, that of the Kralice Bible, which had been used by Slovaks since the 1600s and referred to by them as *"řeč československá,"* or simply *"slovenčina."* He urged the Czechs, without success, to adapt this language to the commonly spoken Slovak, while, at the same time, harshly condemning the new Slovak literary language (*Hlasové o potřebě jednoty spisovného jazyka pro Čechy, Moravany a Slováky* [*Voices about the Necessity of One Common Literary Language for Czechs, Moravians and Slovaks,* 1846]).

Ľubomír Ďurovič

Further reading

Brock, Peter. *The Slovak National Awakening: An Essay in the Intellectual History of East Central Europe.* Toronto, 1976.

Kimball, Stanley B. *The Austro-Slav Revival: A Study of Nineteenth-Century Literary Foundations.* Philadelphia, 1973.

Mráz, Andrej. *Ján Kollár.* Bratislava, 1952.

Slovanská vzájemnost 1836–1936. Sborník prací k 100. výročí rozpravy Jana Kollára o slovanské vzájemnosti. Prague, 1936.

Várossová, Elena. "Európske zdroje a súvislosti filozofie dejín Jána Kollára." *Filozofia* 38, no. 5 (1983): 601–14.

See also Romanticism; Slovak Literature

Kolowrat-Liebsteinsky, Count Anton (1778–1861)

Habsburg official. Born in Prague of an aristocratic family, Kolowrat undertook a career in the imperial civil service that led to his appointment as governor (*Oberstburggraf*) of Bohemia in 1810. In 1826 Francis I (1768–1835) named Kolowrat to the State Council, where he was chief of the political and financial departments. Noted for his efforts on behalf of the development of Czech culture and his strenuous attempts to balance the imperial budget, Kolowrat emerged as the chief rival of Chancellor Clemens von Metternich (1773–1859). The mutual jealousy of Metternich and Kolowrat sharpened after the death of Francis I in 1835, when both men served as permanent members of the State Conference, which acted as a regency for the mentally incompetent Ferdinand I (1793–1875). The resulting paralysis of the State Conference and stagnation of the imperial government ended with the resignation of Metternich in March 1848 and the brief service of Kolowrat as president of the first constitutional ministry. He resigned in April 1848, however, and returned to his estates.

Philip Pajakowski

Further reading

Herzog, Elizabeth. "Graf Franz Anton Kolowrat-Liebsteinsky: Seine politische Tätigkeit in Wien 1826–1848." Ph.D. diss., University of Vienna, 1968.

Sked, Alan. *The Decline and Fall of the Habsburg Empire, 1815–1918.* London, 1989.

Walter, Friedrich. "Franz Anton Graf Kolowrat-Liebsteinsky." *Neue österreichische Biografie* 15 (1963): 25–33.

See also Clemens von Metternich; Revolutions of 1848

Kopitar, Jernej (1780–1844)

Slovene philologist and founder of Slavic linguistics, who helped introduce Europe to the languages and cultures of the Slavs. Kopitar was educated in Ljubljana (German, Laibach), where in his formative years he was greatly influenced by Slovene Enlightenment writers, and in Vienna, where after 1810 he was censor of Slavic, modern Greek, and later Romanian books. He attained academic renown and high position in the imperial capital and was widely acclaimed by his European contemporaries.

Kopitar wrote the first scientifically researched grammar of the Slovene language (*Grammatik der slawischen Sprache in Krain, Kärnten und Steyermark,* 1808), using data from the vernacular spoken in three Slovene-inhabited duchies of Austria. He focused on the peasant idiom, which he believed was alone still pure. Kopitar is also noted for his Pannonian (or kajkavian) theory, which embodied a kind of pan-Slovenism. It held that the Slovenes and those Croats who shared the kajkavian dialect had the same Pannonian ancestors;

that Pannonia (western Hungary) was the original homeland of the Slavs; and that its language was the basis of Old Church Slavonic. Kopitar lost potential Croat support for his theory to Illyrism, the intellectual movement that accepted štokavian as the basis for a Serbo-Croat literary language; and he alienated from his cause those Slovene intellectuals, such as romantic poet Francè Prešeren (1880–49), who were developing a modern secular Slovene literary language, which Kopitar denigrated and, in his official capacity, censored.

Kopitar's Pannonian theory fortified his conservative political inclination—Austroslavism—which attempted ideologically to link traditional institutions: the Catholic Church, the Austrian Empire, and its numerically dominant Slavic peoples (who were Western and used the Latin alphabet). He urged, but did not really convince, Austria to make Vienna a center of Slavic learning and culture, the purpose being to counterbalance the might of Slavic Orthodox Russia, which he regarded as backward. Along these lines, hoping to lure the Balkan Orthodox Serbs away from Russian influence and into Austria's embrace, Kopitar embarked on an association with Serb writer Vuk Karadžić (1787–1864). Their famous collaboration, although failing to forward the cause of Austroslavism, produced a grammar and a dictionary of the Serb vernacular language, a translation of the Bible, and a spectacular collection of Serbian oral folk poetry.

Carole Rogel

Further reading

Papers in Slavic Philology II: To Honor Jernej Kopitar 1780–1980. Ann Arbor, Michigan, 1982.
Pogačnik, Jože. *Bartholomaus Kopitar: Leben und Werk.* Munich, 1978.

See also Austroslavism; Vuk Karadžić; Francè Prešeren; Serbo-Croatian Language; Slovene Language

KOR

Polish dissident group (1976–81). KOR (Komitet Obrony Robotników [Workers' Defense Committee]) announced its establishment with the publication of "An Appeal to Society and State" as an independent social group on September 23, 1976 (although its actual activities began on July 17, 1976), in Warsaw as a circle of individuals of various political and social orientations all voicing their opposition to the regime's repression of workers' strikes and demonstrations against sudden price increases of June 1976. KOR did not have a political program or any specific ideological orientation. Its primary goals were to assist in providing legal council to those tried for participating in strikes, financial aid to victims' families, to inform public opinion of these events bypassing state censorship, and to demand an amnesty for all those wrongfully persecuted by the state.

KOR transformed itself into KSS-"KOR" (Committee of Social Support) on September 29, 1977. The committee expanded its activities to the protection of civil and human rights. This involved informing Polish society and international public opinion of illegal acts committed by the Polish regime against citizens' rights. This was done through organizing petitions, collecting signatures for letters of protest, hunger strikes, and the establishment of independent publishing networks.

Peter Lavelle

Further reading

Bernhard, Michael. *The Origins of Democratization in Poland: Workers, Intellectuals, and Oppositional Politics, 1976–1980.* New York, 1993.
Lipski, Jan Jozef. *KOR: A History of the Workers' Defense Committee in Poland, 1976–1981.* Berkeley, California, 1985.
Michnik, Adam. "KOR i Solidarność." *Zeszyty Historyczne,* no. 74 (1985).
Zuzowski, Robert. "KOR and the Transformation of Politics in the 1970s." *Politics* 21, no. 2 (1986).

Korošec, Anton (1872–1940)

Slovene politician. Born in Videm ob Sčavnici in Slovenia, Korošec was educated in Maribor. A Catholic priest and a prominent member of the Slovenian National Party, he actively participated in the regional parliaments in Austria-Hungary. As president of the Yugoslav Club in the Austrian Reichsrat (parliament), he propagated the further federalization of the Habsburg monarchy and promoted greater autonomy for Slovenian-speaking regions. In 1918 he became deputy prime minister of the first government of the Kingdom of Serbs, Croats, and Slovenes and later held several ministerial posts in various Yugoslav governments. Although inclined to compromise, Korošec was a strenuous supporter of Slovenian autonomy throughout his political career. In the late 1930s he particularly supported a right-wing organization of Slovenian nationalists, Straža v Viharju (Guardian in the Storm).

Željan E. Šuster

Further reading
Enciklopedija Jugoslavije. Zagreb, 1980.
Mala Enciklopedija. Belgrade, 1978.

See also Kingdom of Serbs, Croats, and Slovenes

Kőrösi Csoma, Sándor (1784–1842)

Explorer, historian, linguist, and student of Eastern medicine. Kőrösi Csoma left his home in Transylvania for Asia, searching for traces of Magyar tribes believed to have been lost before the conquest of Hungary in the ninth century. Unsuccessful at first, he traveled three times to Tibet, where he spent more than five years living as a monk. During this period, he produced the world's first Tibetan dictionary, featuring over forty thousand words (*Essay towards a Dictionary Tibetan and English,* 1834), along with a grammar book (*A Grammar of the Tibetan Language in English,* 1834). In the 1830s he became the first English translator of the *"rGyud bZhi"* (*Gyüshi/Gushi*), or *The Four Tantras,* otherwise known as *Medical Codices,* the principal work on Tibetan medicine. Although not a doctor, he understood, synthesized, and explained a healing system difficult for the Western mind to grasp. This system integrated mind, spirit, body, and basic balances. On his fourth voyage to Tibet, while attempting to track information about the Yougar, a people possibly related to the Magyars, he was struck with malaria and died and was buried in Darjeeling, India. Here, his grave is marked by a monument co-erected in 1910 by the Hungarian Academy of Sciences, the Transylvanian village of Csomakőrös, and the Asiatic Society of Bengal.

Mártha Pereszlényi-Pintér

Further reading
Csoma de Kőrös, Alexander. *Collected Works of Alexander Csoma de Kőrös: Tibetan Studies,* ed. by E. Denison Ross. New Delhi, 1991.
Galántha-Hermann, Judith. "Alexander Csoma de Kőrös and the Evolution of the Traditional Tibetan Medicine," *Lectures and Papers in Hungarian Studies* 8 (1994).

Sisa, Stephen. *The Spirit of Hungary: A Panorama of Hungarian History and Culture,* 2d ed. Toronto, 1990.
Wagner, Francis S. *Hungarian Contributions to World Civilization.* Center Square, Pennsylvania, 1977.

Kościuszko, Tadeusz (1746–1817)

Military leader in the American War for Independence, leader of the 1794 uprising in Poland, and a symbol of Polish independence and egalitarian principles. As such a symbol after the partitions of Poland in the late 1700s, Napoléon (1769–1821) and Alexander I (1777–1825) attempted to use him as an ally for their ends. While Kościuszko did not trust Napoléon, he believed that Alexander's liberalism offered a basis for Russo-Polish understanding. In 1814 Kościuszko met Alexander in Paris and again, in 1815, at Braunau, near Vienna. Before agreeing to cooperate, Kościuszko asked for agreement from the Russian emperor on three points: that Polish peasants abroad (primarily in Napoléon's armies) be considered free when they returned to Poland; that Poland be given a free constitution, modeled on that of England; and that a system of education for the peasantry be established by the government so that serfdom could be abolished within a decade. Alexander did not respond to Kościuszko's letter and never met with him again. The Polish leader's price was too high, interfering with Alexander's own views.

Kościuszko left France and settled in Switzerland, where he became interested in new educational theories and tried to persuade Polish authorities to introduce them. He also freed his own serfs on the family estate, Siechnowicze, shortly before his death.

The legend of Kościuszko never died. His body was transported to Kraków in 1818 and buried at the Wawel Castle. Outside Kraków, an earthen mound was raised in his memory, with soil from every part of Poland. Numerous political movements, particularly on the left, attempted to associate his name with their causes, such as the first Polish military unit established in the Soviet Union during World War II, the Kościuszko Infantry Division.

John Stanley

Further reading
Haiman, Miecislaus. *Kościuszko: Leader and Exile.* New York, 1946.

Szyndler, Bartlomiej. *Tadeusz Kościuszko 1746–1817*. Warsaw, 1991.

See also Alexander I; Napoléon; Peasants

Košice

Second-largest city in Slovakia (population 260,000 in 1989) and capital of East Slovakia province. Founded in the thirteenth century as a trading town on a route across the mountains to Poland, most of Košice's early development was attributed to Hungarians, who referred to the city as Kassa, and Jews. It was the second-largest city in the Hungarian Empire during the Middle Ages, and was even the capital of Hungary for a brief time after the fall of Buda to the Turks. Košice was incorporated into the Czechoslovak state in 1919 but reverted to Hungary after the Vienna Award in 1940.

Nestled in the southeast corner of Slovakia, Košice is much closer to the border with Ukraine than to Bratislava, Slovakia's capital. As a result of this distance and the mountainous interior of Slovakia, much of the city's livelihood has been oriented eastward toward Ukraine and other parts of the former Soviet Union, to which it is well connected via road and rail networks.

Natural conditions contributed to a strong agricultural base for the region, which encompasses the Hornad, Torysa, and Olšava Rivers. The city lies within the Košice basin, a triangular region of highly fertile soils that widens to the south approaching the Hungarian border. However, the city's economy greatly changed during the Communist period. Košice became a significant industrial center in the 1960s with the building of the East Slovak Steel Works (VSZ). The city was second only to Ostrava in terms of steel output in the country. This rapid economic growth in turn stimulated population growth. From a total of approximately fifty thousand in the 1960s, Košice grew to become one of the most populous and ethnically diverse cities in Czechoslovakia, attracting sizable numbers of Czechs, Hungarians, Ukrainians, Ruthenians, and others.

Russell L. Ivy

Further reading
Berentsen, William, ed. *Europe in the 1990s: A Geographical Analysis,* 7th ed. Chicago, 1997.

Pounds, Norman J. G. *Eastern Europe.* Chicago, 1969.
Rugg, Dean. *Eastern Europe.* London, 1985.
UNIDO, *Czechoslovakia: Industrial Transformation and Regeneration.* Oxford, 1992.

See also Industrialization; Vienna Awards

Kosovo

Predominantly Albanian region of Yugoslavia. Across the northeastern boundary of Albania lies a compact region of complex topography that forms an administrative region of Yugoslavia, nearly encircled by Montenegro, Serbia, and Macedonia. It forms the core of a historic territory characterized by conflicting ethnic and political claims of Albanians and Serbs.

A primary goal of Serbia during the nineteenth century was the acquisition of Kosovo as national territory. The mineral wealth of the region and its proximity to the Adriatic Sea across northern Albania were of great economic and strategic value. More important, Kosovo represented hallowed ground for the Serbs. It was there, on a plain near the Serbian-Bulgarian boundary, that the Serbian army suffered a catastrophic defeat at the hands of the Ottoman Turks in June 1389. The battle became an important part of Serbian folklore. The day of the disaster became the Serbian national holiday, and as such the territory of Kosovo became synonymous with the fate of the Serbian nation.

Albanians predominated in Kosovo (Albanian, Kosova) in the 1800s, and the proportion has steadily increased during the twentieth century. By 1981, nearly 80 percent of its 1.6 million inhabitants were Albanian. Kosovo also represents the center of modern Albanian nationalism. Major uprisings against the Ottoman authority took place in Kosovo during the late-nineteenth and early-twentieth centuries. The League of Prizren (1878), the first national manifestation by the Albanians, was organized in opposition to the partitioning of Albanian ethnic territory by the Congress of Berlin (1878).

Under Ottoman administration the *vilayet* (province) of Kosovo was predominantly Albanian and included the Sanjak of Novi Pazar and part of western Macedonia, in addition to the present territory of Kosovo province. Serb and Yugoslav policy after 1918 sought to disrupt the Albanian ethnic character of the region by administrative division, forced migration, and colonization by Serbs and Montenegrins. The creation of the Kosovo-Metohija Autonomous Region after World War II recognized the Albanian character of Kosovo, though the economic and political condition of the population did not effectively improve until after 1963. Kosovo obtained its own constitution in 1974 when it was designated a "Socialist Autonomous Province." Although improvements in the social and economic condition of the population followed, the development gap with other regions of Yugoslavia widened and a movement for greater autonomy in regional affairs increased after the death of Tito (1892–1980). The subsequent Serb reaction has included imposition of direct political and economic control, dismantling of political and cultural institutions, and encouragement of Albanian emigration and Serb colonization. Constitutional provisions for regional autonomy were revoked in 1989, leading to increased tensions in the 1990s. Serb crackdowns on the Albanian population led ultimately to a brutal war in 1999 during which NATO bombed Yugoslavia while the Serbs expelled some one million Albanians from the province. Eventually, Yugoslavia withdrew its forces from Kosovo and NATO troops took on the role of peacekeepers in the province.

Albert M. Tosches

Further reading

Pipa, Arshi and Sami Repishti, eds. *Studies on Kosova.* New York, 1984.

Prifti, Peter R. "Minority Politics: The Albanians in Yugoslavia." *Balkanistica,* 2 (1975): 7–30.

Tosches, Albert M. "The Albanian Lands: Continuity and Change in a Buffer Region," in John Chay and Thomas E. Ross, eds. *Buffer States in World Politics.* Boulder, Colorado, 1986.

See also Congress of Berlin; League of Prizren; Sanjak of Novi Pazar; Tito

Kossuth, Ferenc (1841–1914)

Hungarian engineer and politician. The oldest son of Lajos Kossuth (1802–94), Ferenc grew up with his father in exile. After completing his studies in Britain, he worked as an engineer and won European recognition for his work on bridges, railroads, and tunnels. In 1894, with the death of Lajos, he

accompanied his father's body to Budapest and settled in Hungary. The name Kossuth had a magical effect and enthusiastic crowds acclaimed Ferenc on his first tour of the country. He was quickly elected to parliament and became one of the leaders of the Independence Party. These "Forty-Eighters" claimed to stand for the politics of Lajos Kossuth and of the 1848 revolution, but their saber rattling was as different from the deeds of 1848 as Ferenc proved to be from his father. Cautious and preferring aristocratic company, he lacked his father's insight and charisma. As minister of transportation from 1906 to 1910, Kossuth renewed the custom and trade agreement with Austria without securing significant concessions. When the 1910 elections swept the Independence Party from power, the more radical elements of the party defected. Kossuth, already quite ill, remained as a leader of the renamed "Independence and Forty-Eighter Party." He died in 1914, unmourned by contemporaries for his failure to live up to the Kossuth name.

Robert Nemes

Further reading

Bödy, Pál. *Hungarian Statesmen of Destiny 1860–1960.* Boulder, Colorado, 1989.

Jászi, Oskár. "Kossuth Ferenc (1841–1914)." *Huszadik Század* 15 (1914): 793–806.

Sugar, Peter. "An Underrated Event: The Hungarian Constitutional Crisis of 1905–1906," *East European Quarterly* 15 (1981): 281–306.

See also Lajos Kossuth; Revolutions of 1848

Kossuth, Lajos (1802–94)

Leader of Hungary's struggle for independence. Kossuth was born in Monok in northeastern Hungary. Like many sons of poor nobles, he studied law and returned to his native county to work in the local administration. While attending the national diet in Pressburg (Hungarian, Poszony; Slovak, Bratislava) in 1832, Kossuth began publishing its proceedings. Cleverly written in the form of letters to avoid censorship, the *Dietal Reports* openly supported the liberal cause. They also attracted the attention of Vienna, and when Kossuth began to write a similar account of the county assemblies, he was arrested, imprisoned, and sentenced to four years for subversion.

A popular hero on release from prison, Kossuth became editor of the newspaper *Pesti Hirlap* (*Pest News*) in 1841, and his witty, wide-ranging editorials swiftly made it the most important newspaper in Hungary. Kossuth later turned his energies to a variety of economic associations, which provided another platform for his increasingly radical ideas. In 1847 Pest County elected Kossuth to the diet, where he soon became leader of the liberal opposition. When news of the 1848 revolution in Paris reached Hungary, Kossuth seized the initiative and called for immediate and fundamental changes in his country. His demands served as the basis for the April Laws, transforming Hungary into a constitutional monarchy, freeing the peasants of feudal dues and services, and establishing civil rights. As minister of finance in the new government under Lajos Batthyány (1806–49), Kossuth called on parliament to raise two hundred thousand troops to defend Hungary and later issued banknotes to pay for the troops. In September, parliament put executive power in the hands of the National Defense Committee with Kossuth at its head. Barnstorming the country, Kossuth worked tirelessly to organize a Hungarian army (*Honvéd*), which drove back the Habsburg forces in the spring of 1849.

On Kossuth's advice, on April 14, 1849, parliament approved Hungary's declaration of independence, dethroning the House of Habsburg-Lorraine. Independence, however, was short-lived. When the intervention of two hundred thousand Russian troops made defeat inevitable, Kossuth handed over power to General Artur Görgey (1818–1916), commander of the Hungarian armies, and fled to the Ottoman Empire.

Kossuth spent almost half his life in exile, never abandoning his dream of an independent Hungary. In 1850–51 his speeches charmed English and American audiences but won no official support. When Austria went to war against France and Italy in 1859, Kossuth won Napoléon III's (1808–73) backing, but Napoléon's sudden peace with Austria foiled his plans. He became increasingly isolated and could not stop Hungary from coming to terms with its old enemy, Vienna. Kossuth died in 1894 in Turin, Italy. He was buried in Budapest amid national mourning, a symbol both of the quest for independence and of a modernizing, liberal Hungary.

Robert Nemes

Further reading

Deák, István. *The Lawful Revolution: Louis Kossuth and the Hungarians 1848–1849.* New York, 1979.

Haraszti, Éva. *Kossuth as an English Journalist.* Boulder, Colorado, 1990.

Komlos, John. *Kossuth in America, 1851–1852.* Buffalo, New York, 1973.

Spira, György. "Kossuth and Posterity," in *Études Historiques Hongroises.* Budapest, 1980.

Szabad, György. *Kossuth politikai pályája ismert és ismeretlen megnyilatkozásai tükrében.* Budapest, 1977.

See also Lajos Batthyány; Artur Görgey; *Honvéd*; Hungarian War for Independence; Napoléon III; Revolutions of 1848

Kostov, Traicho (1897–1949)

Bulgarian Communist. Kostov was born and educated in Sofia and served in World War I in the officers reserve corps. In 1920 he joined the Communist Party and in 1923 was co-opted to work in its Central Committee. Arrested in 1924, he tried to commit suicide by jumping from the fourth floor of police headquarters but survived and was in jail until 1929. During the 1930s, he traveled back and forth between Moscow and Sofia, working for the Comintern (Communist Interntional) and managing the affairs of the Bulgarian Communist Party. When Germany attacked the Soviet Union in 1941, he drafted the party manifesto calling for resistance to the government and the Germans. He was arrested in 1942 and escaped execution thanks to the intervention of a friend in the royal palace. Released from jail on September 7, 1944, he assumed the duties of party political secretary and for all practical purposes ran the government. It was Kostov who charted the transformation of Bulgaria from a capitalist to a socialist state. Unfortunately he ran afoul of Stalin (1879–1953). He concealed from his Soviet colleagues the prices of Bulgarian goods sold on the international market and was personally exposed and denounced by Stalin. A campaign for his expulsion from the party was initiated by future Communist leader Todor Zhivkov (1914–98); this led to his arrest, trial, and execution in December 1949. He was accused of spying for the British and the United States, but he denied all charges. The party, to which he had devoted his life, murdered him on trumped-up charges. Later, like many other such purge victims, he was halfheartedly rehabilitated.

Spas T. Raikin

Further reading
Bell, John D. *The Bulgarian Communist Party from Blagoev to Zhivkov.* Stanford, California, 1986.
Kostov, Traicho. *Izbrani suchinenia.* Sofia, 1978.
Semerdjiev, Peter. *Sudebnii protses Traicho Kostova v Bolgarii, 7–12 dekabria, 1949.* Jerusalem, 1980.
The Trial of Traicho Kostov and His Group. Sofia, 1949.

See also Comintern; Communist Party of Bulgaria; Stalin; Todor Zhivkov

Kovács, Imre (1913–80)

Hungarian writer and politician. Kovács, a member of the populist writers' movement, was a radical representative of peasant democracy and a founding member of the revolutionary 1937 March Front, which demanded democratic political rights and land reform. Active in political life in the short-lived democratic period after World War II, he was forced to flee his country in 1947 after the Communist takeover. He became a seminal figure in the emigrant community in the United States, publishing several works on Hungary, but never achieved his aim to return to active political life in his homeland.

Kovács spent his early life among employees on a large estate but was placed in an orphan home at the age of nine. Hard work and ability enabled him to enter secondary school, and from 1932 he studied economics in Budapest. He was one of the authors of the study *The Declining Village,* which attracted nationwide attention. For his sociographic work, *The Silent Revolution* (1937), which delineated the misery of agrarian laborers, he was sentenced to three months in prison and expelled from the university. In 1939 he helped found the National Peasant Party and later took part in the resistance movement against the occupying Germans. He was secretary-general of the National Peasant Party from 1945 until his escape in 1947. In the United States he worked with the Free Europe Committee until 1951 and again from 1954 until 1969. He became a prominent figure among Hungarian exiles as publishing editor of *Magyarországi Hírek* (*News of Hungary*) from 1963 and senior editor of *Uj Látóhatár* (*New Horizon*) from 1958 to 1972.

Deborah S. Cornelius

Further reading
Kovács, Imre. *A néma forradalom.* Budapest, 1937.
————. *Facts about Hungary.* New York, 1958.
László, Péter, ed. *Új Magyar Irodalmi Lexikon.* Budapest, 1994, 1117.
Tibor, Huszár. *Beszélgetések.* Budapest, 1983, 62–209.

See also Agrarian Parties; Hungarian Émigrés

Krajina

Military frontier province of the Habsburg Empire situated across southern Croatia facing territories held by the Ottoman Empire. The Krajina (Serbo-Croatian, borderland) extended from the Adriatic coast in the vicinity of Senj eastward to the end of the Iron Gates Gorge. When abolished in 1881 the Krajina had an area of 7,300 square miles (20,280 sq km) and a population of 855,000.

In 1578 the Habsburg emperor, facing the advance of Ottoman troops up the Balkan Peninsula, created a special Military Frontier from lands expropriated from the Croatian nobility in the mostly depopulated Croatian and Slavonian territories remaining to him. He allotted these, free of feudal obligations, to soldier-peasants who agreed to lifetime service in Habsburg forces along the border. In 1699, after the Turks were driven south of the Sava and Danube Rivers, the Military Frontier was extended eastward to include additional Croatian and Slavonian lands and the Vojvodina east of Slavonia.

The Krajina was administratively divided into eleven territorial regiments, each further subdivided into twelve companies. More than 40 percent of those settling in the province were Serbian refugees from Ottoman domination. Many Croatians and Germans also colonized the region. Settlers were noted for their direct loyalty to the Habsburg emperor, resisting pressures from Croatian nationalists during the uprising of 1848 and the separatist agitation in World War I. The 1878 Austro-Hungarian occupation of Bosnia-Hercegovina ended the rationale for a military frontier, and it was formally dissolved three years later.

Anti-Croatian sentiments remained manifest in the Krajina during World War II and also after the fall of communism in 1990. In 1995 virtually all Serbian families fled or were expelled from the Krajina in the face of a Croatian military advance against their self-proclaimed separatist government.

Thomas M. Poulsen

Further reading

Bertić, Ivan. *Veliki geografski atlas Jugoslavije.* Zagreb, 1987.

Clissold, Stephen, ed. *A Short History of Yugoslavia: From Early Times to 1966.* Cambridge, 1968.

Valentić, Mirko. "Vojna Krajina," *Enciklopedija Jugoslavije,* vol. 8. Zagreb, 1971.

See also Croatian Military Frontier

Kraków

The third-largest city in Poland, situated in the Vistula River basin, at the foot of the Carpathian Mountains. Kraków, along with Leipzig and Budapest, is an anchor of the industrial triangle of East Central Europe. The city is situated on the upper Vistula River and serves as a major rail hub for Warsaw, Prague, Berlin, and Vienna.

The former Hanseatic League city was under Austrian rule from 1795 to 1918, except for a brief period from 1809 to 1815, when it was part of the Grand Duchy of Warsaw, and from 1815 to 1846, when it became, along with its surrounding province, an independent republic. It was returned to Poland in 1918 but was occupied by the Germans during World War II.

After the war, there was rapid industrialization in the region. The city's population in 1949 was 312,300 and by 1960 had risen to 481,300; industrial employment rose from 35,500 to 87,300 in the same period. By 1989, the total population in the city had reached 748,400. An increasing surplus of labor from Poland's rural areas fed urban growth.

Kraków's character changed from a cultural and intellectual center to an industrial city with the development of the industrial suburb of Nowa Huta (New Foundry) just east of the city center, based on the huge Huta Lenina (Lenin Metal Works) iron and steel plant. This development tied Kraków more closely to the vast industrial complex development of the coalfield to its west. The Lenin Metal Works was the principal element in Kraków's industrialization, absorbing the majority of investment outlays for Kraków's industry from 1950 to 1975.

The development of Nowa Huta took investment away from the infrastructure of the older parts of Kraków. Between 1950 and 1968, nearly half the new apartments built in Kraków were in the industrial suburb; from 1950 to 1957, 70 percent of new units were reserved for laborers of the Lenin Metal Works. The location of the metalworks east of the city changed Kraków's historic concentric form to a new axis of east-west development, along the valley of the Vistula. The local environment was increasingly degraded as the metalworks expanded. In the 1960s some limits were placed on industrial agglomeration in Upper Silesia; an agricultural and forest zone west of the city was meant to protect it from industrial air and water pollution.

Kraków's fate as an industrial city with an underdeveloped urban infrastructure was reversed somewhat through the late 1960s and 1970s. There was a brief surge of investment in scientific and cultural institutions and activities around the six hundredth anniversary of Jagellonian University in 1964, and through the 1970s other higher-level service activities, higher-technology industries, and some tourism and historic preservation developed. Presently, the city's center is undergoing major renewal.

Barbara VanDrasek

Further reading

Curtis, Glenn E., ed. *Poland: A Country Study.* Washington, D.C., 1994.

Held, Joseph. *Dictionary of East European History since 1945.* Westport, Connecticut, 1994.

Hoffman, George W., ed. *Europe in the 1990s: A Geographic Analysis,* 6th ed. New York, 1990.

See also Duchy of Warsaw; Environment; Industrialization; Jagellonian University; Republic of Kraków

Kramář, Karel (1860–1937)

Czech politician and statesman. Kramář was the foremost Czech politician in pre-1914 Austria-Hungary and the arch-conservative opponent of President Tomáš G. Masaryk (1851–1937) in the Czechoslovak Republic. He was born in Vysoké nad Jizerou into a middle-class family. After studying in Prague, Berlin, and Paris, he gave up

K pursuing an academic career to enter politics as a Realist and Young Czech in 1890 with Masaryk and Josef Kaizl (1854–1901). He was elected a deputy to the Austrian parliament in 1891 and to the Bohemian diet in 1894.

Upon Kaizl's death, Kramář became the principal Young Czech spokesman. He advocated restoration of the historic rights of the Bohemian kingdom and civil and linguistic equality for the Czechs and other Austrian Slavs. He urged an Austro-Russian rapprochement to block imperial Germany's expansion to the East. In 1907 he turned the Young Czech Party toward a centrist "positive policy" and supported the Austrian universal suffrage reform. An ardent Czech nationalist and Russophile, he propagated Slavic cultural and economic cooperation at neo-Slav congresses in Prague (1908) and Sofia (1910).

He broke with Austria in August 1914. For participating in a secret Czech movement against Austria's war effort, he was arrested, tried by a military court, and in 1916 sentenced to death. Emperor Charles I (1887–1922) commuted his sentence to twenty years' imprisonment and granted him amnesty in 1917. After Austria's collapse in October 1918, Kramář became prime minister of Czechoslovakia and in 1919 headed its delegation to the Paris Peace Conference. His calls for Allied military intervention to overthrow the Bolshevik regime in Russia were opposed by Masaryk and Foreign Minister Edvard Beneš (1884–1948) and rejected by the Allies. Masaryk dismissed Kramář from office in 1919 when his National Democratic Party fared poorly in municipal elections.

Kramář remained influential in Czechoslovakia as a deputy in parliament and a member of the committee that set the legislative agenda, as head of his party and author of articles and books on public affairs, and as a crony of powerful businessmen and politicians, but he was a peripheral figure. His prescient warnings against Beneš's one-sided dependence for the country's security on France and the League of Nations against a resurgent Germany were ignored. In a final foray in parliamentary elections of 1935, he formed an extreme right-wing coalition against the Masaryk-Beneš *Hrad* ("Castle group") but to no avail.

Stanley B. Winters

Further reading

Herman, Karel and Zdeněk Sládek. *Slovanská politika Karla Kramáře.* Prague, 1971.

Sís, Vladimír. *Karel Kramář 1860–1930.* Prague, 1930.

Winters, Stanley B. "Kramář, Kaizl, and the Hegemony of the Young Czech Party, 1891–1901," in *The Czech Renascence of the Nineteenth Century: Essays in Honour of Otakar Odložilík,* ed. by Peter Brock and H. Gordon Skilling. Toronto, 1970, 282–314.

———. "T.G. Masaryk and Karel Kramář: Long Years of Friendship and Rivalry," in *T.G. Masaryk (1850–1937): Thinker and Politician,* ed. by Stanley B. Winters. London, 1990, 153–90.

See also Edvard Beneš; Charles I; *Hrad;* League of Nations; Tomáš G. Masaryk; Neo-Slavism; Paris Peace Conference; Young Czechs

Kraszewski, Józef Ignacy (1812–87)

Polish novelist, historian, literary critic, newspaper editor, and educator. Born in Warsaw, Kraszewski was educated at the University of Wilno. He spent two years in prison after the 1830 uprising against the Russians; for the next two decades he managed his family estates, while also publishing a literary-scholarly journal, *Athenaeum* (1841–51). He was superintendent of schools in Żytomierz from 1853 to 1858; from 1860 he edited the Warsaw *Gazeta codzienna* (*Daily Gazette*). After another failed uprising in 1863, he was banished from Warsaw and settled in Germany. In 1883 he was arrested in Berlin on charges of treason, convicted, spent more than a year in jail, and fled to Switzerland when released on bail. He died in Geneva.

Kraszewski was probably Poland's most prolific writer, having produced literally hundreds of historical novels as well as many writings in other genres. His hastily written novels are usually long, convoluted, and colorful; he was more concerned with educating his readers about contemporary social issues or Polish history than with aesthetic questions. One series of novels dealt with the peasantry; another with the landed gentry; a third with the 1863 uprising against Russian domination. His most famous and ambitious undertaking was his attempt to encapsulate the history of Poland, starting with prehistoric times, in a series of twenty-nine novels in seventy-six volumes, written from 1876 until his death in 1887. Two of these, which deal with the period of the eighteenth-century Saxon dynasty, are widely accepted as his most accomplished works: *Hrabina Cosel* (1874) and

Brühl (1875). Today, Kraszewski is more revered than read.

Madeline G. Levine

Further reading

Danek, Wincenty. *Józef Ignacy Kraszewski: Zarys biograficzny.* Warsaw, 1976.

See also January Uprising; November Uprising; Polish Literature

Kreditanstalt

The first modern commercial bank in Austria, founded in 1855. Formally titled the K.k. privilegierte österreichische Creditanstalt für Handel und Gewerbe, the Kreditanstalt was created by a group of financiers led by the Rothschild family. It opened with sixty million gulden of share capital and invested heavily in railroads during the heady days of railroad expansion in the 1850s. Following the economic crisis of 1857, the Kreditanstalt expanded its business from railroads into other branches of industry. It engaged in a wide range of lending to industry, from short-term discount loans to longer-term credit and direct purchase of company shares. It also participated in government loans.

Losses from the stock market crash of 1873 caused the bank to shy away from risky industrial loans until the 1890s, when the Kreditanstalt began to take on the features of a German-style universal bank, helping private firms reorganize as joint-stock companies. This led to a close, symbiotic relationship between the bank and the industries in which it invested, as bank officials served on the boards of directors of companies in which it had an interest. The Kreditanstalt was tied closely with the major Austrian firms in agricultural industries, textile manufacture, machine building, paper and chemicals, mining and metallurgy, transportation, building materials, and electrical and gas works. The Kreditanstalt established branch offices throughout the Habsburg monarchy to take advantage of business opportunities in other regions, although its main office remained in Vienna.

After World War I, the Kreditanstalt lost its branch offices and industrial partners outside the Austrian republic. It had invested heavily in Austrian war bonds, and its financial position was eroded by the inflation of the early 1920s. The bank's position was saved by foreign, particularly British, investment and by mergers with other financial institutions in Austria. The Kreditanstalt continued to invest in industrial concerns, particularly in southeastern Europe, and it nearly collapsed in 1931 during the Great Depression but was saved by Austrian government intervention. It merged with the Wiener Bankverein in 1934, and the joint institution was renamed the Kreditanstalt-Bankverein.

After the *Anschluss* (annexation) of Austria by Germany in 1938, the Kreditanstalt became an important component in the Nazi financial system. It was nationalized by the Austrian government following World War II and currently is owned jointly by public and private interests.

Catherine Albrecht

Further reading

Creditanstalt-Bankverein. *Ein Jahrhundert Creditanstalt-Bankverein.* Vienna, 1957.

März, Eduard. *Austrian Banking and Financial Policy: Creditanstalt at a Turning Point, 1913–1923,* trans. by Charles Kessler. London, 1985.

———. *Österreichische Industrie- und Bankpolitik in der Zeit Franz Josefs I: Am Beispiel der k.k. priv. österreichischen Credit-Anstalt für Handel und Gewerbe.* Vienna, 1968.

Stiefel, Dieter. *Finanzdiplomatie und Weltwirtschaftskrise: Die Krise der Credit-Anstalt für Handel und Gewerbe, 1931.* Frankfurt, 1989.

Teichová, Alice. "Creditanstalt," in Peter Newman et al., eds. *The New Palgrave Dictionary of Money and Finance,* vol. 1. London, 1992, 517–19.

See also *Anschluss;* Banking; Great Depression; Industrialization; Railroads

Kremsier/Kroměříž Parliament (October 1848–March 1849)

Austrian constitutional assembly, relocated from Vienna to the Moravian archbishop's palace in Kremsier (Czech, Kroměříž) following the capital's recapture by the imperial army in October 1848. A constitutional draft was produced but never implemented. This draft has been viewed as the Habsburg monarchy's last best opportunity to solve its nationality problems.

The delegates assembled in Kremsier were charged with producing a liberal constitution for the monarchy that would guarantee the rights of all citizens and rationalize and modernize the administration of the multinational state. A product of

K intense negotiation and sincere attempts at compromise, the constitutional draft made all citizens equal before the law and included a bill of rights. Titles of nobility were to be abolished and the Catholic Church disestablished. The emperor was to retain control over foreign policy and the military, and his sanction was required for all laws, although a veto could be overridden. Most significant, however, was the assembly's attempt to deal with the national question. The final draft read: "All peoples of the Empire are equal in rights. Each people has an inviolable right to preserve and cultivate its nationality in general and its language in particular." However, there was little consensus over who would be granted the authority to enforce these rights. German delegates argued for a strong central authority while Poles and Czechs held out for decentralization based on the historic provinces. The final compromise created a bicameral legislature with a federal house that included six delegates from each province and a lower house with 360 members elected by direct, although not universal, manhood suffrage. Each local commune was given broad administrative independence, thereby providing a check on the power of the provincial governments and a virtual guarantee of minority rights.

This promising constitution was never adopted. The imperial government prorogued the assembly on March 4, 1849, and imposed its own centralizing constitution.

T. Mills Kelly

Further reading

Kann, Robert A. *The Multi-national Empire,* vol. 2. New York, 1950.

Macartney, C.A. *The Habsburg Empire 1790–1914.* New York, 1969.

Robertson, Priscilla. *Revolutions of 1848: A Social History.* Princeton, New Jersey, 1952.

See also Revolutions of 1848

Kretzulescu, Nicolae (1812–1900)

Romanian medical doctor, scholar, politician, and prime minister. A member of a family of Romanian *boiars* from Wallachia, Kretzulescu became a public servant in 1832, working at the court of appeals before leaving for Paris in 1834, where he studied medicine and completed a doctorate in 1839. He returned to Romania in 1840, where he practiced medicine and opened a surgical school in Bucharest. In 1843 he published the first anatomy book in the Romanian language.

Inspired by the liberal ideas of the time, Kretzulescu took part in the revolutionary movement in Wallachia in 1848, serving as a member of the committee to draft a new constitution. After the collapse of the revolution, he fled to Paris and Constantinople, returning to Wallachia in 1850. Kretzulescu held several administrative posts in Wallachia, serving as minister of finance in 1857–58. A promoter of the union of Moldavia and Wallachia and close collaborator of Prince Alexandru Ioan Cuza (1820–73), Kretzulescu held several important administrative posts during Cuza's reign, twice serving as prime minister (1862–63 and 1865–66). He helped achieve the administrative and political union of the principalities, including the organization of academic and cultural institutions.

Briefly detained after the abdication of Cuza in 1866, Kretzulescu reentered political life shortly thereafter, becoming a member of parliament and holding several cabinet posts. He also served as Romania's diplomatic representative to Berlin, Rome, Paris, and St. Petersburg. In 1888 he withdrew from political life to become president of the Romanian Academy.

Kurt W. Treptow

Further reading

Barbu, G. *Nicolae Kretzulescu.* Bucharest, 1964.

Iszak, Samuil. *Nicolae Kretzulescu, inițiatorul învățământului medical românesc.* Bucharest, 1957.

Parhon, C.I. *Viața și activitatea doctorului Nicolae Kretzulescu.* Bucharest, 1944.

Trancuași, Grigore, *Nicolae Kretzulescu ca simbol al emanciparii noastre economice.* Bucharest, 1936.

Xenopol, A.D., *N. Kretzulescu. Viața și faptele lui, 1812–1900.* Bucharest, 1915.

See also *Boiars*; Alexandru Ioan Cuza; Revolutions of 1848; United Principalities

Krleža, Miroslav (1893–1981)

Leading Croatian novelist of the twentieth century and an important figure on the political scene of socialist Yugoslavia. Krleža's writing was characterized by a forceful style and a tendency to take aggressive stands on social and political issues. Most of his famous works originated in the interwar period. Although he continued to write after 1945, he spent much of his time in his positions as president of the Yugoslav Writers' Union, vice president of the Yugoslav Academy of Sciences and Arts, and director of the Croatian Institute of Lexicography.

While many of Krleža's most famous works in translation are novels, he was also active in most other genres, including short stories, poetry, drama, travel literature, and essays on political, historical, and cultural themes. Viewed as a whole, his œuvre evinces the author's tendencies toward socialism and Yugoslavism. Equally striking is his skillful and detailed evocation of Croatian life in the waning years of the Habsburg Empire and in the unified South Slav state (Yugoslavia) created after World War I. A good example of this kind of work is the psychological novel *Povratak Filipa Latinovicza* (*The Return of Filip Latinovicz*, 1932), which can be viewed as a critique of provincial, bourgeois life. Other well-known works with political and historical overtones include the multivolume novels *Banket u Blitvi* (*Banquet in Blitva*, 1938–62) and *Zastave* (*Banners*, 1967).

John K. Cox

Further reading

Bogert, Ralph Baker. *The Writer as Naysayer: Miroslav Krleža and the Aesthetic of Interwar Central Europe.* Columbus, Ohio, 1991.

Čengić, Eneš. *Krleža.* Zagreb, 1982.

Kadić, Ante. "Life and Works of Miroslav Krleža" and "Krleža on Križanić—from History to Legend," in *Essays in South Slavic Literature.* New Haven, Connecticut, 1988, 119–34, 135–42.

See also Yugoslav Literature; Yugoslavism

Kronenberg, Leopold (1812–78)

Financier, industrialist, and political and economic activist. Kronenberg was born into a wealthy Warsaw Jewish family. After completing his education in Hamburg and Berlin, he returned to Warsaw in 1832 to take charge of the family banking firm and later became involved in such industries as tobacco, railroads, sugar refining, and newspapers, as well as participating in politics and various philanthropic activities. The basis of his fortune, estimated eventually at twenty million rubles, making him the richest man in the kingdom, was his early lease from the state tobacco monopoly. Within a matter of years, Kronenberg branched out into agricultural processing, trade, and banking. His association with Warsaw financial circles led to the establishment of the Commercial Bank in Warsaw in 1870, with a branch in St. Petersburg. Kronenberg's cooperation with the landed gentry also led to his becoming a partner in the Warsaw Steam Navigation Company in 1848, directed by Andrzej Zamoyski (1800–1874). By the mid-1850s, he began his involvement with railroad building, which eventually led to his direct influence over four of the six major rail lines in the state.

Kronenberg's fortune served as the base for his later social and political activities. By the 1850s, his contacts with Zamoyski and Polish statesman Alexander Wielopolski (1803–77) inspired him to support a program of organic work in the spirit of economic and social reform. As one of his tools to this end, Kronenberg bought the newspaper *Gazeta codzienna* (*Daily Gazette*) in 1859, which he placed under the editorship of Józef I. Kraszewski (1812–87). Among the positions advocated in the paper were equal rights for Jews (though he himself had converted to Evangelical Reform upon his marriage in 1845) and municipal self-government.

Politically moderate to conservative, as the tide of revolution began to rise at the beginning of the 1860s, Kronenberg attempted to steer a moderate course. Although he aided the 1863 Polish uprising against the Russians financially, his more moderate approach met with violent attacks in the "red" press.

Kronenberg gradually withdrew from business while remaining active in many philanthropic activities. He contributed to the creation of the *Agricultural Encyclopedia* and in 1875 established a business school in Warsaw. In 1868 he achieved hereditary nobility in the Kingdom of Poland. He withdrew from active life in 1876, dying after a long illness in 1878.

Robert A. Berry

Further reading

Kołodziejszyk, Ryszard. *Portret warszawskiego milionera.* Warsaw, 1968.

See also Banking; January Uprising; Jews; Polish Congress Kingdom; Alexander Wielopolski; Andrzej Zamoyski

K

Kučan, Milan (1941–)

First elected president of Slovenia in April 1990, when the republic was still part of Yugoslavia. Kučan joined the League of Communists of Slovenia in 1958 and earned a law degree from the University of Ljubljana in 1963. He spent much of his early career working in the Communist Party bureaucracy that controlled the Yugoslav state. In 1986, after a period working in the Yugoslav federal government, Kučan took over the leadership of the League of Communists of Slovenia.

In the late 1980s, when Slovenia emerged at the forefront of democratic change in Yugoslavia, Kučan himself became an advocate of democratic reform and a defender of Slovene national interests. In January 1990 Kučan and his fellow Slovene Communists walked out of a special Congress of the League of Communists of Yugoslavia (LCY)—intended to resolve the country's growing national disputes—because Slovene proposals aimed at transforming Yugoslavia into a confederation of states were not considered. This action signaled an end to the forty-five-year rule of the unified LCY.

Although a non-Communist coalition won a majority of seats in the Slovene parliament in the elections of May 1990, Kučan, now leader of the Party of Democratic Renewal (formerly the Communist Party), was elected president. Many Slovenes regarded him as a moderate figure who could help smooth Slovenia's transition to independence, democracy, and a market economy. Kučan did help lead the republic to independence in 1991, and he won reelection by direct popular vote in December 1992.

Paul D. Lensink

Kuchuk Kainardji, Treaty of (1774)

Treaty between tsarist Russia and the Ottoman Empire in July 1774, which ended Ottoman dominance in the Black Sea and granted Russia the right to speak for Orthodox Christians in the Ottoman Empire, a provision that would have profound repercussions on nineteenth-century Balkan affairs. Russia gained part of the Crimean peninsula and eventually annexed all of it in 1783. Russia also acquired territory along the Black Sea coast between the Bug and Dnieper Rivers. The treaty also granted Russian merchant vessels free navigation of the Black Sea and the Turkish Straits leading to the Mediterranean Sea. By far the most significant parts of the treaty were articles eight and fourteen. Under article eight, the Ottoman government promised to protect Orthodox Christian populations and their churches within the Ottoman domain, and also granted to ministers of the Russian government the right to protect the interests of their official church building in the Ottoman capital, Constantinople. Article fourteen granted the right to the Russian government to construct an Orthodox Church in the Galata district of Constantinople, and reiterated the point that this building would always be under the protection of Russian officials. By these stipulations, Russia gained entry into Ottoman internal affairs because the Ottoman government had given its formal endorsement that the tsarist government could speak on behalf of the Orthodox peoples under Turkish rule. Russian officials subsequently invoked these provisions of the treaty as the basis for Russian intervention against the Ottomans until Russia's defeat in the Crimean War (1853–56) negated the treaty in 1856.

Jonathan A. Grant

Further reading

Benderly Jill and Evan Kraft. *Independent Slovenia: Origins, Movements, Prospects.* New York, 1995.

Cohen, Lenard J. *Broken Bonds: Yugoslavia's Disintegration and Balkan Politics in Transition,* 2d ed. Boulder, Colorado, 1995.

Woodward, Susan L. *Balkan Tragedy: Chaos and Dissolution after the Cold War.* Washington, D.C., 1995.

Further reading

De Madariaga, Isabel. *Russia in the Age of Catherine the Great.* New Haven, Connecticut, 1981.

Goldfrank, David M. "Policy Traditions and the Menshikov Mission of 1853," in *Imperial Russian Foreign Policy,* ed. by Hugh Ragsdale. Cambridge, Massachusetts, 1993, 119–58.

Jelavich, Barbara. *History of the Balkans: Eighteenth and Nineteenth Centuries.* Cambridge, 1983.

See also Communist Party of Yugoslavia; Slovenia, Birth of the Republic of

See also Crimean War; Eastern Question; Orthodoxy; Ottoman Empire; Paris; Treaty of; Russia

Kulturkampf

"Cultural war," in the 1870s between the Kingdom of Prussia in Germany and the Catholic Church. At a time of general European hostility toward Catholic clerics, the Prussian government attempted to destroy the Catholic Church in Prussia. Although the government campaign failed and was dropped after less than a decade, the alienation of both German and Polish Catholics from the Prussian state was never fully overcome.

German unification in 1871, which occurred under Protestant leadership, produced a Protestant majority population in the new German Empire. In response, the Vatican encouraged Catholics to organize their own political party, the Center Party, to defend Catholic rights. As both chancellor of Germany and head of government in Prussia, the largest of the German states, Otto von Bismarck (1815–98) viewed the Center as "an enemy of the Empire in its tendency, even if not in all its members." Prussia sought to establish government control over the organizational foundations of the Catholic Church—the parish priests and the Catholic school system.

The church refused to submit to new regulations. By 1876, the Prussian government had deported disobedient priests from some 1,400 parishes, one-third of the total in Prussia. Catholics rallied to the Center Party, which gained significantly in the elections of 1874. Bismarck then used the accession of Leo XIII (1810–1903) in 1878 as an opportunity to break off the conflict by ceasing to enforce the new church regulations, most of which were repealed in the 1880s. German Catholics remained deeply resentful of government suspicions of their loyalty. In the eastern provinces of Prussia, the Kulturkampf further increased the dislike of German rule among the overwhelmingly Catholic Polish population.

Robert Mark Spaulding

Further reading

Gall, Lothar. *Bismarck, the White Revolutionary,* trans. by J.A. Underwood. Boston, 1990.

Pflanze, Otto. *Bismarck and the Development of Germany,* 3 vols. Princeton, New Jersey, 1990.

Trzeciakowski, Lech. *The Kulturkampf in Prussian Poland,* trans. by Katarzyna Kretkowska. New York, 1990.

See also Otto von Bismarck; Germany; Prussia

Kun, Béla (1886–1938)

Publicist, founder of the Hungarian Communist Party, and Comintern leader. Son of a district notary, Kun joined the Social Democratic Party in 1902 and by 1913 was a midlevel official. He was captured on the Russian front in 1916. After the 1917 February revolution, he joined the Social Democratic then the Bolshevik organization in Tomsk. On March 24, 1918, he set up the Hungarian Section of the Russian Communist Party.

Kun was a contributor to *Pravda,* the Soviet Communist Party paper, and was a commander of internationalists in the Russian Civil War. On November 4, 1918, he founded the Communist Party of Hungary in Moscow and did the same later that month in Budapest. When on March 21, 1919, Allied exactions forced the collapse of the liberal democratic regime of Count Mihály Károlyi (1875–1955), the Communists and the Socialists formed a fusion government and promulgated the Soviet Republic. Kun became commissar of foreign affairs and de facto government leader. He was expected to fight for Hungary's integrity with help from Soviet Russia. However, he quickly lost the goodwill of Hungary's majority because of his excessive zeal to destroy religion, nationalize capital, and collectivize agriculture. The anti-Semitic agitation of the counterrevolutionaries also contributed to his fall, and of the Soviet Republic's, which received no help from Russia and could not withstand Czechoslovak and Romanian offensives.

On August 1, 1919, the "Commune" collapsed and Kun fled to Vienna. In the middle of 1920 he went to Russia and was a leader of the bloody repression in the Crimea. From his Moscow exile, he headed the outlawed Communist Party in Hungary. In 1921 he became a member of the Executive Committee of the Comintern (Communist International) and stayed on until 1936. His leadership also caused a split in the Hungarian party.

In spite of his obvious incompetence, he remained in the good graces of his Soviet masters. In the early 1930s he had his Hungarian opponents in Russia arrested. Nevertheless, his political decline started in 1935. He was jailed in June 1937 on trumped up charges, and was tried and executed on August 29, 1938.

Peter Pastor

K

Further reading

Borsányi, György. *The Life of a Communist Revolutionary, Béla Kun.* Highland Lakes, New Jersey, 1993.

Kovrig, Bennett. *Communism in Hungary: From Kun to Kádár.* Stanford, California, 1979.

Molnár, Miklós. *From Béla Kun to János Kádár: Seventy Years of Hungarian Communism.* New York, 1990.

Pastor, Peter, ed. *Revolutions and Interventions in Hungary and Its Neighbor States, 1918–1919.* Highland Lakes, New Jersey, 1988.

Tökés, Rudolf. *Béla Kun and the Hungarian Soviet Republic: The Origins and the Role of the Communist Party of Hungary in the Revolutions of 1918–1919.* New York, 1967.

See also Comintern; Communist Party of Hungary; Hungarian Soviet Republic; Mihály Károlyi

Kundera, Milan (1929–)

Czech writer. Kundera, nominated for the Nobel Prize in literature in 1988, is one of the most important novelists of the twentieth century. Kundera has also written poetry (three books in the 1950s), plays, a collection of essays, as well as numerous critical articles. Kundera, the son of a famous pianist, was born in Brno. Having joined the Communist Party after World War II (1947), he was expelled in 1950, automatically reinstated in 1956 at the time of the political thaw in the Soviet Union, only to be expelled again in 1970. He studied music at Charles University in Prague and film at the Prague Academy of Arts. He taught at the Film Faculty of the Academy of Arts in the 1960s, during the exhilarating period of Czech New Wave film. At this time, he joined the editorial board of *Literarní noviny* (*Literary Gazette*), and in 1968 his novel *The Joke* won the Czechoslovak Writers Union prize. In 1970, as a result of the Soviet-led Warsaw Pact invasion of Czechoslovakia in 1968 and the ensuing political and cultural repression, Kundera lost his job and his traveling privileges, and his books were removed from libraries. In 1975 he and his wife settled in France, where he taught at the University of Rennes, and later at the École des Hautes Études en Sciences Sociales in Paris. Kundera's novels after 1973 were first published in French, and his collection of essays *L'Art du roman* (1986) was written in French. He was not published in his native land until after the Velvet Revolution of 1989, which brought an end to Communist rule in Czechoslovakia. Kundera's reputation as a novelist is international; he has won prizes in France, Austria, and Germany and lectured all over the world.

Sophisticated humor, apparent lightheartedness, and irony characterize Kundera's prose. His novels have largely been read and evaluated on two levels, one political and social, the other universal and existential. On the political level, his works are read as an indictment of communism in Eastern Europe, while on a universal level, they question the nature of human existence. His plots are complex and tightly woven. Major themes include helplessness and lack of control over one's own destiny, often exemplified by erotic episodes in characters' lives. The individual becomes the object, not the subject, of history, with external factors determining much, if not all, of human behavior. The result in Kundera's fiction is farce, yet farce that is generally sympathetic to these human-puppets, not cruel. Kundera's works include the collection of stories, *Směšné lásky* (*Laughable Loves,* 1974) and the novels *Žert* (*The Joke,* 1967), *Život je jinde* (*Life Is Elsewhere,* 1973), *Valčík na rozloučenou* (*The Farewell Party,* 1976), *Kniha smíchu a zapomnění* (*The Book of Laughter and Forgetting,* 1979), *Nesnesitelná lehkost bytí* (*The Unbearable Lightness of Being,* 1984), *Nesmrtelnost* (*Immortality,* 1990), and *La Lenteur* (1994).

Ann Marie Basom

Further reading

Banerjee, Maria Němcová. *Terminal Paradox: The Novels of Milan Kundera.* New York, 1990.

Chvatík, Květoslav. *Svět románů Milana Kundery.* Brno, 1994.

Misurella, Fred. *Understanding Milan Kundera: Public Events, Private Affairs.* Columbia, South Carolina, 1993.

See also Cinema; Czech Literature; Prague Spring; Velvet Revolution

Kusturica, Emir (1954–)

Yugoslav film director. Dubbed the "Balkan Fellini," Kusturica is the most celebrated director of the Balkans. He was born in Sarajevo to a well-placed Yugoslav family of Muslim descent and graduated from the Prague Film Institute (FAMU). All his features have enjoyed wide international acclaim. Kusturica won the Golden Palm at Cannes twice (1985 and 1995), the Golden Lion in Venice (1981), and the Best Director award at Cannes (1989). His best work has been devoted to exploring the specifics of the Balkan mentality. Until the breakup of Yugoslavia, he taught at the film school in his native town. Since 1990, he has worked abroad (in the United States and France), and occasionally in Serbia (the latter a controversial decision that has been discussed internationally). He insists on being considered a "Yugoslav." His features include *Sjecas li se Dolly Bell? (Do You Remember Dolly Bell?* 1981); *Otac na sluzbenom putu (When Father Was Away on Business,* 1985); *Dom za vesanje (Time of the Gypsies,* 1989); *Arizona Dream* (1992); and *Underground* (1995).

Dina Iordanova

Further reading

Binder, David. "A Bosnia Movie Maker Laments the Death of the Yugoslav Nation (Emir Kusturica)," *New York Times,* October 25, 1992, E7.

See also Cinema

Kvaternik, Eugen (1825–71)

Croatian revolutionary and politician. The son of a history professor, Kvaternik was born in Zagreb and studied theology and law. He briefly practiced as an attorney but lost the right to practice law in 1857 because of his political opinions. He then emigrated to Russia, where he adopted Russian citizenship and hoped to find support for his native land among the Russian Slavophiles, the group that held Russia to be culturally and morally superior to the West. When the tsar proved uninterested in Croatia, he left Russia for Western Europe, where he advocated the liberation of Croatia from Habsburg control. He promoted the possibility of rebellion in Croatia in cooperation with other revolutionary movements and actively sought, though failed to receive, political support from Italy and France.

Kvaternik returned to Croatia only after a general political amnesty in 1867. Although he received permission to practice law again, his more important work was to promote the cause of Croatia in a series of publications that generally supported the political goals of the Party of Rights (*Stranka prava*). Especially important to Kvaternik's thought was that the territorial fragmentation of Croatia must be overcome by any means possible, including the exercise of violence. Although he collaborated with his fellow Croatian nationalist Ante Starčević (1823–96), the two eventually disagreed on several issues, including the course to take in practical politics.

The Rakovica rebellion, which Kvaternik organized, began on October 8, 1871, when Kvaternik marched on Rakovica with a small band of men who seized the local police station and announced the formation of a new government that would guarantee equality of citizens and liberation from foreign oppression. Kvaternik and his supporters then set about to raise local villages in revolt. On the second day, the rebellion stalled because the local Serbs refused to join the movement; the inhabitants of Bosnia also did not rise in revolt. On October 10, Habsburg army units surrounded the rebels and defeated them the following day. The leaders of the revolt were unceremoniously placed in a joint grave, but Kvaternik and the Rakovica rebellion became an important rallying point for Croatian nationalists after 1871.

Sarah A. Kent

Further reading

Gross, Mirjana. *Povijest pravaške ideologije.* Zagreb, 1983.

Šišić, Ferdo. *Kvaternik (Rakovička buna).* Zagreb, 1926.

See also Slavophilism; Ante Starčević

L

Labor

In the late nineteenth and early twentieth centuries the population of East Central Europe grew at a rate that far outpaced that of Western Europe. The number of industrial and agrarian laborers increased as the region gradually shifted toward mechanized agriculture on large estates, the factory system, and large-scale production. At the same time, increasingly obsolete methods of farming and handicrafts persisted as modernization spread unevenly. Specifics varied widely from region to region, but industrialization affected most people's lives, even if indirectly. With the exception of the Czech lands, pockets of industrial labor surrounded by a sea of peasants practicing age-old methods of farming was a characteristic pattern throughout the region.

A rural proletariat and an underemployed and impoverished group of smallholders emerged after most peasants were freed from serfdom following the 1848 revolutions and after the abolition of serfdom in Congress Poland in 1861. Given only a very small portion of the land, the peasants found freedom to be no panacea to their daily struggle to make ends meet. They often had to rent land and/or work as day laborers for thirteen to seventeen hours on aristocratic estates. Others migrated to different parts of the Habsburg Empire, especially to the larger cities or emigrated overseas in order to earn enough to support their families. Laborers found opportunities for self-betterment to be somewhat limited because the economic expansion could not keep pace with the rapid rise in the population.

In parts of the Balkans, life for laborers was often worse than elsewhere in East Central Europe, often resembling feudal conditions. Many peasants did not even have the freedom to move. Until 1908, in Bosnia-Hercegovinia, a hereditary laborer was bound to uphold a lease and paid one-third of his earnings to his landlords. Most peasants lived at near subsistence level and continued to do so even after land reform following World War I.

The predominance of impoverished peasants should not belie the fact that in terms of percentage, the industrial labor force rose rapidly, particularly in the Austrian lands and in parts of Hungary and partitioned Poland. For example, from 1898 to 1913, the number of workers employed in Hungarian industry jumped from 226,000 to over 417,000. In Congress Poland, 250,000 laborers found work in industry. But only in highly industrialized Bohemia and Moravia did more laborers work in industry than in agriculture.

In contrast, the Balkans remained far more backward. The 1905 Serbian census showed only 16,000 workers employed in 470 factories, or about 7 percent of the population. Likewise Bulgaria in 1911 counted 15,886 workers in 345 industries.

Although World War I temporarily relieved the demographic crunch, prewar social patterns for labor continued to persist in the newly independent and reconstituted states. In 1920, 65 percent of the region's 81 million people still depended upon agriculture for their livelihood, and in the Balkans the proportion was 80 percent. Land reform divided up some of the huge estates but in many cases only created more smallholders.

Excluding farm laborers, only 14 percent of labor received wages from employment in industrial enterprises. Not until 1922 did some of the countries begin to see incremental increases in industrial employment. Population growth though still exceeded what the industrial sector could absorb. Czechoslovakia was again the exception; only 28 percent worked at farming in 1928.

Rising social discontent predominated among the laboring class in the interwar period. Since productivity was generally lower than in Western Europe, wages were relatively low and working conditions poor in most places. The social unrest that had appeared in the postwar recession reignited discontent as the Great Depression took its toll on everyone. With the example of the Soviet Union, some workers joined or many more at least sympathized with revolutionary political movements in their search for a better tomorrow. The inability to provide labor with a decent wage undermined the legitimacy of democracy and paved the way for more authoritarian regimes in the 1930s.

During World War II, satellite and occupied countries were forced to provide slave labor or migrant workers for work at munitions factories in Germany and at home. While the war stimulated economies and eliminated unemployment, it also ended any independent voice for workers. Laborers in factories and agriculture were regimented in a way hitherto unseen.

After the war, the new Communist regimes sought to build a base of support among labor by engineering a massive expansion of the industrial working class. Based on the Soviet model of five-year plans, the Communists promoted heavy industry and recruited portions of the agricultural population to work in newly established factories both in the cities and in the countryside. Reconstruction ensured plenty of blue-collar work. Full employment was guaranteed in a region that had experienced chronic unemployment and underemployment before the war. The influx of young, inexperienced workers from rural areas and the recruitment of women into the workplace provided a measure of social mobility in addition to educational opportunities and a new system of social security unknown before. Rural laborers who had always flirted with subsistence-level poverty at least could enjoy the security of a job and a gradually rising income. The social welfare state also propped up the Moscow-sponsored governments, which needed the acquiescence of the working class to maintain at least an outward stamp of legitimacy.

Because most countries in the region had started from such a low base, labor saw a continual rise in its standard of living for over thirty years after the war. Blue-collar workers also enjoyed the fact that they earned as much if not more than many professional and white-collar workers. Nonetheless, the standard of living did not match the pace of improvement in Western Europe. While powerless to effectuate meaningful change, workers expressed their rising discontent through informal means such as slowdowns at the workplace, high rates of absenteeism, and cynicism about promises of a workers' paradise. Worker participation in official activities and organizations diminished. As economic growth slowed, demands for more and better consumer goods mushroomed.

With the exception of Poland, labor discontent never reached a point where it threatened to overturn the regimes. But the Communists never again commanded the kind of loyalty they attained during the early postwar period. When Communist governments began to topple in 1989, this disaffection among labor was apparent. In no country did workers rise to defend the tottering regime.

In the 1990s labor experienced both the positive and the negative consequences of an increasingly free marketplace. Unemployment soared, although with uneven results. Double-digit joblessness existed in most countries. While wages rose for some categories of skilled workers, especially those who worked in private businesses, real wages after inflation for unskilled workers dropped by 25 percent or more in most countries. In addition, social benefits gradually diminished for economic reasons. In the former Yugoslavia, war all but totally disrupted the labor market and social services. The challenge for the entire region became one of competing in an increasingly global economy. Low wages and a highly skilled workforce in the northern tier provided a potential for the future. The more agricultural regions, however, especially in the south and east, faced more formidable obstacles.

Michael J. Kopanic Jr.

Further reading

Berend, Iván T. and György Ránki. *Economic Development in East-Central Europe in the 19th and 20th Centuries.* New York, 1974.
———. *The European Periphery and Industrialization 1780–1914.* Cambridge, 1982.

Good, David F. *The Economic Rise of the Habsburg Empire, 1750–1914.* Berkeley, California, 1984.

Hitchins, Keith, ed. *Studies in East European Social History.* Leiden, Netherlands, 1981.

Kaser, M.C. and E.A. Radice, eds. *The Economic History of Eastern Europe 1919–1975,* 3 vols. Oxford, 1985–86.

Teichova, Alice. *The Czechoslovak Economy, 1918–1980.* New York, 1978.

Tipton, Frank B. and Robert Aldrich. *An Economic and Social History of Europe, 1890–1939.* Baltimore, Maryland, 1987.

———. *An Economic and Social History of Europe, 1939 to the Present.* Baltimore, Maryland, 1987.

See also Agriculture; Emigration; Great Depression; Industrialization; Peasants; Revolutions of 1848; Revolutions of 1989; Solidarity; Trade Unionism

Lake Balaton

Lake located southwest of Budapest in western Hungary. The largest lake in Central Europe, Balaton's surface area is 230 square miles (590 sq km); however, this 48-mile-long (77 km) body of water reaches only 35 feet (11 m) at its deepest point and is only 8 miles (13 km) at its widest.

Lake Balaton is a relic of the Pleistocene Age, when the Pannonian basin (centered in modern-day Hungary) formed an inland sea. The lake's depression is formed by a down-dropped block located between two parallel southwest-northeast–trending faults. The area remains geologically active, as evidenced by geothermal activity and hot springs. Water temperature in summer rises to the upper 70° F (middle 20° C), though in winter the lake freezes. It provides habitat for unique bird life and vegetation.

Lake Balaton is Hungary's principal tourist area; each summer sun seekers from all parts of the country and beyond flock to its shores. An almost continuous string of resorts spans its southern shore, and many Hungarians have second homes there. All this activity, though, has resulted in severe pollution. Besides tourism, the Balaton region is known for wines produced on the volcanic soils found to the north.

Darrick Danta

Further reading

Bernát, Tivadar, ed. *An Economic Geography of Hungary.* Budapest, 1985.

Bora, Gyula. "Environmental Management in the Lake Balaton Region," in Paul A. Compton and Márton Pécsi, eds. *Environmental Management: British and Hungarian Case Studies.* Budapest, 1984, 91–108.

Enyedi, György. *Hungary: An Economic Geography.* Boulder, Colorado, 1976.

Webster's New Geographical Dictionary. Springfield, Massachusetts, 1984.

Lake Ohrid

Southeastern European lake. Situated at an altitude of over 2,000 feet (660 m) and occupying a deep tectonic basin along the southern portion of the Albanian-Macedonian boundary, Lake Ohrid is one of the oldest and deepest European lakes. With a surface area of more than 200 square miles (555 sq km), Lake Ohrid is smaller than in its geological past but retains a huge volume of water, owing to depths often exceeding 500 feet (165 m). Supplied by an area of 2,000 square miles (5,550 sq km) and by springs fed by underground channels from nearby Lake Prespa, it is drained northward by the Black Drin. Steep mountain slopes rise from the shores, though alluvial plains stretch along the northern and southern edges.

About one-third of Lake Ohrid, together with one-half of its shoreline, lies in Albania, where it is known as Lake Ohër or Pogradec. Delimitation of the boundary after World War I, while partitioning the lowland zones between the Slav and Albanian populations, left a substantial number of Albanians in Yugoslav Macedonia. This incongruence of the ethnic and international boundary complicates regional politics, since Macedonians retain an intimate cultural and historic association with the town and district of Ohrid.

Albert M. Tosches

Further reading

Letcher, Piers. *Yugoslavia: Mountain Walks and Historical Sites.* Bucks, United Kingdom, 1989.

Pounds, Norman J.G. *Eastern Europe.* Chicago, 1969.

Zickel, Raymond and Walter R. Iwaskiw. *Albania: A Country Study.* Washington, D.C., 1994.

L

Lake Scutari

Southeastern European lake. A portion of the southwestern boundary between Albania and Montenegro divides the depression occupied by the largest lake in southeastern Europe. Most of Lake Scutari is in Montenegro with the southern end in Albania. Although only slightly larger than Lake Ohrid on the average, Lake Scutari (Albanian, Shkodra; Serbian, Skadar) differs significantly in three respects: the average altitude is much lower, resulting in a higher mean temperature of the surface waters; it is extremely shallow, with an average depth of 20 feet (6.1 m), resulting in considerable areas of marsh and swamp; and it is subject to great fluctuations, resulting in an increase of 50 percent in surface area during seasonal periods of flood. The principal tributary, the Moraca, enters the northern side of the lake from Montenegro, while the Bunë (Serbian, Boyana) drains the lake southward to the Adriatic and allows access to the town of Shkodra by barge and shallow-draught vessels.

Numerous species of fish support the major economic activity of the region. Despite the attractiveness of the physical environment, the potential for tourism is little developed in this border region, which remains largely isolated and difficult to access.

Albert M. Tosches

Further reading

Albania. Nagel's Encyclopedia-Guide. Geneva, 1990.

Letcher, Piers. *Yugoslavia: Mountain Walks and Historic Sites.* Bucks, United Kingdom, 1989.

Pounds, Norman J.G. *Eastern Europe.* Chicago, 1969.

See also Lake Ohrid

Lausanne, Treaty of (1923)

Revised peace settlement signed in July 1923 between the victorious World War I Allies and Turkey. The Treaty of Lausanne was necessitated by Greece's postwar military debacle in Anatolia and Kemal Atatürk's (1881–1938) successful repudiation of the Sèvres treaty (1920). In the treaty, Turkey gained Smyrna, Eastern Thrace, and the islands of Imbros and Tenedos from Greece. Lands of the short-lived independent Armenia and autonomous Kurdistan were returned to Turkey. Italy's control of the Dodecanese and Britain's annexation of Cyprus were confirmed. Capitulations were abolished, and no reparations were imposed. The demilitarized Straits were administered by an international commission with a Turkish chairman. A compulsory exchange of minorities (400,000 Turks and 1.3 million Greeks) left Greece and Turkey more homogeneous ethnically, although Greek Christians and Turkish Muslims continued to reside respectively in Istanbul and Western Thrace.

Lausanne affirmed Turkey's territorial integrity, political sovereignty, and economic independence. The treaty marked the demise of the *megale idea* (great idea), the Greek nationalist dream of uniting Anatolian Greeks in an enlarged Greek state. Greek communities, some dating as far back as Homeric times, were forcibly uprooted from Asia Minor, but their relocation in Macedonia Hellenized that embattled multi-ethnic region.

Theophilus C. Prousis

Further reading

Davison, Roderic. *Essays in Ottoman and Turkish History, 1774–1923.* Austin, Texas, 1990.

Howard, Harry. *The Partition of Turkey: A Diplomatic History, 1913–1923.* Norman, Oklahoma, 1931.

Jelavich, Barbara. *History of the Balkans: Twentieth Century.* New York, 1983.

Pentzopoulos, Dimitri. *The Balkan Exchange of Minorities and Its Impact on Greece.* Paris, 1962.

Psomiades, Harry. *The Eastern Question: The Last Phase.* Thessaloniki, 1968.

Shaw, Stanford. *History of the Ottoman Empire and Modern Turkey,* vol. 2. New York, 1977.

See also Capitulations; Sèvres, Treaty of

Lavrenov, Tsanko Ivanov (1896–1978)

Bulgarian artist. In his search for a distinct national style, Lavrenov became the leader of Bulgarian primitivism. A self-taught painter, Lavrenov was born in Plovdiv and demonstrated his talent in graphics and woodcuts as a student in the St. Augustin French high school. Reared as a Catholic, Lavrenov was fascinated by Orthodox icon painting. He spent several months in Vienna in 1920–21, where he encountered German expressionism and entered the Kunstgewerbeschule. His studies were interrupted, and after a tour of Italy (1925), Lavrenov settled in Plovdiv, where he produced his best work. He discovered a new technique to ground his canvas: by covering it with a mixture of oil and chalk to provide an uneven surface for his brush strokes. A primitive charm imbues his paintings of urban scenes, many from old Plovdiv and Turnovo. He replaced conventional perspective with overlapping, and, by combining bold flat colors with decorative architectural elements, he created stylized images reminiscent of folk and applied art. The emotional intensity of his early work betrays his indebtedness to expressionism, as demonstrated by his *Nightmare* and *The Mourners*. Prompted by trips to Orthodox monasteries in Greece (1935–36) and Macedonia (1940–42), Lavrenov created his *Monasteries Cycle*. Since nationalism was on the rise, he began his cycle *Visions from Ancient Bulgaria* (1938–47), based more on legend than fact.

Lavrenov moved to Sofia in 1940, where he continued his iconlike depiction of old Bulgarian towns. After 1944, he included socialist themes as his subjects: *The Construction of Beglika Dam* (1956), *The Batak Dam* (1971). These paintings earned Lavrenov the Dimitrov Order (1968), the Dimitrov Prize (1969), and the titles "People's Artist" (1963) and "Hero of Socialist Labor" (1969).

Milka T. Bliznakov

Further reading
Delchev, Boris. *Tsanko Lavrenov.* Sofia, 1968.
Kotsev, I. *Tsanko Lavrenov.* Sofia, 1972.

See also Bulgarian Art

Law and Codification
Codification of law involves the process of collecting and arranging systematically, usually by subject, the laws of a state or country, or the rules and regulations covering a particular area or a subject of law or practice. The product may be called a code, a revised code, or a revised statute. A constitution, on the other hand, is the fundamental law of a state establishing the character of its government and the basic principles to which its internal life is to be conformed, as well as regulating, distributing, or limiting the functions of its different departments, and prescribing the extent and the exercise of sovereign powers. In essence, it is a charter of government deriving its whole authority from the governed.

Behind these definitions lie two thousand years of history and successive changes in the social and legal structure of societies: the *Pax Romana* of the Roman Empire; the feudal period of the Middle Ages; the emergence of the Third Estate, the bourgeoisie, with the simultaneous rise of the merchant class and its political organization into city-states; the American, French, and Russian Revolutions; and finally the arrival of the welfare state. This long sequence of events is described in the language of the law as the progress from "status to contract," or the gradual progress of society from a strict status-controlled social system to the legal recognition of individual freedom of contracting.

The forces that molded these changes were political, economic, and intellectual. Political forces were behind the events that discarded the notion of the divine rights of kings; political forces helped to bring about a governmental system founded on the social contract, the validity of which depended on the agreement between the government and the governed, while the progress of political organization molded the tangible aspects of such agreement into the popular representation of parliamentary democracy. On the other hand, economic forces controlled the long period of the predominantly agrarian economy of a landholding aristocracy, which was broken only by the technical inventions of the Industrial Revolution that opened avenues to the unlimited economic possibilities of nineteenth-century laissez-faire capitalism. It equally opened the doors to an emerging and ever-growing working class that, of necessity, had to change agrarian serfdom into industrial bondage, a situation that was created under the new guise of contractual freedom. It was not until the middle of the twentieth century that the welfare state produced the legal framework for protective labor-related legislation.

Yet, none of these developments might have come to pass without the driving impetus of the third force: the awesome power of human thought that elaborated theories on the strength of which the modern structures of the rule of law (*Rechtsstaat*) were erected. The results, among others, were the social contract, the separation of powers, the supremacy of parliament, and the establishment of the inalienable rights and freedoms of the individual. The force of these ideas unleashed the

American and French Revolutions, which, in turn, have changed our world.

The idea of codification, that is, the collection and publication of laws in a written form, arises whenever a great variety of laws and customs, often at variance with one another, make legal uniformity and security desirable. Three names conspicuously stand out in this process: Justinian (483–565), Napoléon (1769–1821), and Stalin (1879–1953). The life span of their codes lasted 1,500, 200, and 50 years, respectively.

In 533 Justinian ordered the systematic collection of all the laws that ruled over the Roman Empire. This legislation became the foundation of the civil law system that was subsequently adopted throughout Europe and Latin America. Even though the countries of the common law system have never officially adopted the Roman rules, these strongly influenced the decisions of the courts of the Royal Chancery since its judges were members of the Church of Rome and were also trained in Roman law. The *Code Napoléon* was promulgated in 1804, and, owing to the logic, efficiency, and timeliness of its rules, became a model for modern codification. Stalin's constitution was issued in 1936 and was intended to mark the first effort in the transitional period from socialism to communism. At the end of World War II, as the countries of Central and Eastern Europe fell into the Soviet orbit, they came under the rule of the Stalin constitution.

No history of European codification is complete without at least a brief reference to the *Lex Mercatoria* (the medieval Law Merchant). This particular field of law was originally a separate body of commercial rules that came to exist side by side with the civil laws of individual nations. It arose in the fairs of the tenth century and expanded by the thirteenth century into an independent body of its own supported by uniform mercantile customs and administered under uniform rules by separate merchant courts. It was a law made by the medieval merchant for the medieval merchant. Its principal organization, the Hansa, was established in Germany, from where it spread throughout Europe, with the center of its lawmaking and administrative activities in Lübeck (present-day Germany). The rules were uniform and covered substance as well as procedure: equity, bona fides, and fairness on the one hand; summariness, speed, and efficiency on the other. The emphasis was on fact, not law; the judges and the jury were merchants—indeed, the commercial courts were off limits to lawyers since their presence meant "embroilment in legal technicalities."

But the monumental achievement of the *Law Merchant* was the elaboration of rules that in time came to be called private international law, that particular field of law that deals with individual controversies between parties of different nationalities. It was perhaps the perfect working of the Law Merchant that made the codification of commercial law unnecessary until the end of the seventeenth century.

Over the next centuries lawmaking followed in the footsteps of history. The creation of new national states by the Congress of Vienna on the ruins of the Napoleonic Empire led to the rise of nationalism all over Europe, which, in turn, led to the desire for national codes. The leading models became the French (1804), the Austrian (1811), and the German (1900) civil codes; each was drafted by scholars influenced by the leading philosophies of their time: the natural law of the Age of Reason, the supremacy of positive (enacted) law, and the evolving idea of the public interest. Three nations exemplify these developments: Poland, the Czech Republic, and Hungary—each arising from different ethnic backgrounds, possessing different languages, traditions, and laws, and each an outstanding example of the European legal scene: the unity in diversity.

In Poland the first official codification was the *Statut Laskiego* of 1506; it contained the earlier constitutions and enactments of the Sejm (parliament). The laws showed elements of Roman and canon law; French influence was added to these in later years. Poland's first modern constitution was promulgated on May 3, 1791. Inspired by the ideas of the French Revolution, it became the model for Poland's future codifications. For the time being, however, it brought upon the country two geographic partitions, in addition to the one suffered earlier in 1772, the partitions of 1793 and 1795. When the Congress of Vienna convened in 1815, it ended Poland's existence as a separate country. Its territory was divided among Austria, Prussia, and Russia, with two exceptions, the Grand Duchy of Warsaw and the Republic of Kraków. The congress completed the fourth partition, leaving the Duchy of Warsaw and the Republic of Kraków in the Polish domain but under the sovereignty of Russia. It created an Austrian Poland and a Prussian Poland, and incorporated Lithuania-Ruthenia into the Russian Empire. This remained the status quo until the end of World War I, when Poland regained its independence. One of the consequences of the partitions was that Poland was governed for almost two hundred years by the laws of each partitioning power. On the other hand, this situation turned later to Poland's advantage when the time came to establish its own national legal system. The next twenty years of independence were marked by intensive codifying activities: a new constitution was promulgated on March 17, 1921 (the March Constitution), that established the Republic of Poland with a bicameral legislature (Sejm) and a comprehensive catalog of civil rights. A newly created codification commission successfully adapted foreign legislation to the needs of Polish society and secured the passage of various laws destined to bring the country a unified legal system. These included the commercial code, the penal code and penal procedure code, the law on obligations, the law on negotiable instruments, and the law on private international law, among others.

Poland's independence ended in September 1939 with the German invasion and Poland's subsequent incorporation into the Soviet orbit as one of the "People's Democracies." This situation came to an end in June 1989, when, as a result of the "bloodless revolution," the first free elections in forty years were held and a majority of the Solidarity trade union representatives was sent to the new Polish parliament.

The new legislature now faced the complex task of coordinating the new legislation with laws that had been enacted under three different political and economic systems. An interesting aspect of the legislators' approach was their pragmatism that helped to apply, even during the periods of "ideological purity," such parts of the old laws as were not explicitly repealed. The Supreme Court upheld this practice and even recently sections of the old commercial code are applied to regulate enterprises that are organized as changeovers in the new free-market economy.

Since 1989 a flurry of laws have been promulgated. Among these are the constitution (first drafted in 1952 and amended 1989 and 1990), called the "Little Constitution"; amendments to the civil (1990), judicial (1991), and commercial codes (1991); and various laws regulating foreign investments, trade, unfair competition, and joint ventures.

The earliest traces of Czech law date to the ninth century, when the two main groups of the original settlers—Czechs and Slovaks—lived under the rules of customary law. Collections of law began to be published in 1400: "On the Czech Law"; the "Institutions of the Kingdom of Bohemia" in 1410; and the "Constitutions of King Vladislav" in 1500. During these centuries, the Kingdom of Bohemia was slowly absorbed by Habsburg rule within the Holy Roman Empire, and the first Habsburg Code of Emperor Maximilian II (1527–76) became the governing law of the country. This absorption meant the subordination of national laws to the Roman legal system as it was "received" at the time in Austria, and these developments culminated with the publication in 1627 of the *Erneuerte Landesordnung* (Revised Laws of the State), under which the Bohemian crown, hitherto elective, became a Habsburg hereditary possession. Under this legislation, Bohemia was an integral part of Austria, and Slovakia was annexed to Hungary. The Austrian incorporation was followed by increased Habsburg domination after the Czech defeat in the battle of the White Mountain in 1620, and this situation continued for the next four hundred years. Nevertheless, the Czech provinces successfully retained their national identity, but Austrian rule over the Czech and Slovak lands dominated the area of law. Due to the intensive Austrian codification efforts in the nineteenth century, Bohemia became the recipient of a series of new laws that served as models for future codifications. These included the civil code (1811), the code of civil procedure, the criminal code and the criminal procedure code, and the commercial code. Such Slovak regions as were under Hungarian authority did not participate in this development.

With the dissolution of the Austro-Hungarian monarchy at the end of World War I, a constitution promulgated in 1920 established the Czech Democratic Republic, built on the separation of powers, respect for human rights, and freedom of ethnic minorities. During the interwar years, Czechoslovakia became a bastion of democracy in Central Europe and a center of banking, industry, culture, and the arts. Codification, however, proceeded slowly, owing mainly to the country's ethnic divisions. For example, the Austrian commercial code of 1863 remained in force and the civil code progressed only in stages. Slovakia continued to follow Hungarian laws.

After World War II—during which parts of the country had been annexed by Germany—Czechoslovakia attempted to renew efforts at democratic codification. However, the Soviet takeover in 1948 transformed the country into the usual Communist Party–controlled dictatorship. The new constitution of 1948 abolished the enforcement of all former legislation that "ran counter to the professed goals of the popular democracies." This constitution was replaced in 1960, and again in 1968, the last reform declaring a federative statehood for Czecho-Slovakia. Other codifications followed, aiming at the country's social and political conformity with the USSR. A civil code was enacted in 1950 along the model of the 1922 Soviet code that was already obsolete at the time of its enactment. It was replaced with a new code in 1960 that was amended in 1981. New codes passed in the 1960s included a criminal code, family code, labor code, and code on private international law. In the 1980s important modifications (especially in the economic codes) appeared, doubtless under the influence of perestroika (restructuring), which opened new contacts with the West.

After Czechoslovakia regained its independence in the Velvet Revolution of 1989, a new constitution was adopted on December 16, 1992, establishing the Czech Republic as a sovereign, unified, and democratic law-abiding state, built on the separation of powers and the respect for the rights and freedoms of its citizens. Legislative powers are vested in the bicameral parliament, while judicial powers are exercised by an independent judiciary. The president of the republic is head of state, elected for a term of five years. The president may not be elected for more than two consecutive terms. Another act of constitutional order is the Charter of Fundamental Rights and Freedoms of January 9, 1991; it recalls in its preamble "the bitter experience gained at times when human rights and fundamental freedoms had been suppressed in our country." Another constitutional act followed in February 1991, establishing the Constitutional Court. Other important laws included new labor (1992), commercial (1991–92), civil (reformed in 1992), and business codes. In 1992 the federal structure of Czechoslovakia was dissolved by a popular referendum, and the separate Czech Republic and Slovak Republic were established.

In Hungary, the Romans left behind their language and their law. The future, however, divided this legacy. Even though Latin became the lingua franca of the Hungarian upper and middle classes, and the official language of the legislature, the administration, and the courts was Latin until 1844, the Hungarian legal system resisted Roman influence and, contrary to what occurred in the countries of Western Europe, Roman law was never officially "received." Another feature of Hungarian law that set it apart from the civil law countries was its resistance to accepting a written constitution and a codified body of civil law. This fact vested the jurisprudence of the Hungarian courts with the force of ruling precedents. In this respect Hungarian law was similar to the British common law; like the British Magna Carta, the Hungarian Golden Bull of 1222 declared the freedoms of the nobility as well as its right to resist the king, while István Werbőczy's (1458–1541) *Tripartitum Opus Iuris . . . Regni Hungariae* fulfilled the same purpose as Henry Bracton's (d. 1268) thirteenth-century work, "On the Laws and Customs of England." The *Tripartitum* was essentially the Restatement of the Hungarian feudal system and its jurisprudence. It became for the next four hundred years a bulwark of national unity during the years of Turkish occupation and the ensuing centuries of Habsburg hegemony. Also, as a less fortunate consequence, in its strict adherence to feudal principles, especially in the social-class system and the laws on landed property, the *Tripartitum* was a hindrance to progress. It propounded Werbőczy's doctrine on the Holy Hungarian Crown that remained a feature of Hungarian constitutional law until 1946. It was a combination of the organic and the ideal concept of the crown, first, as a physical object composed of the bodies of all its subjects and, second, as the ideal proof of true national sovereignty.

The turning point in Hungarian law was the Revolution of 1848. The new Hungarian parliament repealed all feudal legislation, together with the privileges of the nobility; it enacted the freedoms of the individual, of the press, association, and religion. In short, all the achievements of the French Revolution of 1789 became part of Hungarian law. Even after the suppression of the Hungarian Revolution in 1849, the social transformation of Hungary from feudalism toward an industrialized and commercially developing capitalism continued its course. Ironically though, this movement was supported by the imposition of Austrian legislation that had adapted itself sooner to the arising needs of the Industrial Revolution. Since Hungarian courts had to apply Austrian law, the Hungarian legislature had to follow. All feudal remnants of land ownership were abolished and a national Office of Land Registry was created for keeping track of lands that might pass into private ownership. The adaptation of Hungarian legislation to the Austrian laws continued even after the decree of December 31, 1851, abolished the rule of the Austrian civil code. A National Judicial Conference (*Országbírói Értekezlet*) was established for the coordination of Austrian and Hungarian laws, and its rulings became binding on the courts. This situation, clearly temporary, ended with the promulgation of Act XII of 1867, which laid down the details of the *Ausgleich* (Compromise) between the two countries and established the Austro-Hungarian monarchy. This particular political structure was built on the personal union of the two countries: the Austrian emperor was equally the crowned Hungarian king, but each country had independent legislatures, administrations, and courts. In common were the Ministries of Foreign Affairs and Defense, and the Treasury that financed them. The ministries were responsible to two delegations appointed by their national parliaments, with a membership of sixty each.

This period lasted until the end of World War I and was one of the most successful decades in Hungarian history. The increase in wealth and of the diversity of professional occupations brought a corresponding need for new legislation. This was carried ahead on three levels: codification; single, specialized laws; and the jurisprudence of the courts. It included the code of commerce (1875), the code of civil procedure (1911), the criminal code (1878), and the code of criminal procedure (1896). Laws were also introduced in the fields of commerce and industry, as well as in the new area of social legislation.

The Austro-Hungarian monarchy came to an end with its defeat in World War I. In the political and economic chaos that followed the stringent impositions of the Trianon peace treaty (1920), the intellectual Left of the country looked to the Soviet model. Under the leadership of Mihály Károlyi (1875–1955) and Béla Kun (1886–1938), a manifesto was issued that proclaimed the "Dictatorship of the Proletariat" under the governmental form of a "Council Republic." The principal aim was the abolition of feudal landownership and the separation of church and state. For the rest, the achievements of the 1848 revolution controlled. This brief interlude, called the "October Revolution" (October 1918–May 1920), was brought to an end through the armed intervention of the Allies, assisted by Hungary's neighboring countries, newly created or enlarged under the Paris peace treaties (1919–20) that did not favor harboring a Soviet-style enclave in their midst. A temporary government was formed based on a nationwide election, and under Law No. 1 of 1920 a regent appointed in the person of Miklós Horthy (1868–1957). His powers as head of state were fairly limited, however: liability to parliament and limited veto power over bills (but no power of signature). Since there was no legal continuity between the new regime and the old monarchic structure, it was considered as a temporary legal interregnum. It lasted until the end of World War II.

Although Hungary's recovery in the interwar period was dramatic, and literature, the sciences, and the arts flourished, the country did not shed its feudal past. Church and state were not separated and no land reform emerged. Moreover, codification of the law was slow; the last Draft of the Civil Code (1928) (showing German and Swiss influence) came to be used by the courts as the authoritative source of private law until 1959. Further legislation appeared on limited liability companies (1930), mortgages (1927), authors' rights (1921), and unfair competition (1933, as amended). There were also signs of social legislation: a National Institute of Social Insurance was established that was one of the first of its kind in Europe, followed a few years later by the Institute of Private Employees' Insurance; further legislation covered workmen's compensation in mining, industry, and agriculture. A law on children's education was enacted in 1938.

However, the legislative process ground to a halt in the late 1930s because of Nazi Germany's imposed alliance with Hungary. The country's only possible reaction was passive resistance. For example, the "Jewish Law" (Act No. IV/1939) took almost three years to pass and was not strictly enforced until 1944, when German troops overthrew the Hungarian government.

The nation celebrated the end of the war and its regained independence with intensive legislative activities. In August 1945 a new electoral law was published as a basis for the election of the temporary National Assembly. This was followed by Law No. I/1946 on Hungary's new form of

L government. In essence, the act contained Hungary's first written constitution. Hungary became a republic built on the separation of powers; its citizens were guaranteed all fundamental rights and freedoms. The final text of the constitution was promulgated by the second parliament of 1949 (Act No. XX/1949), one year after the Communist takeover of the country in the summer of 1948. The original text was substituted by a new document followed the pattern of those of the other popular democracies. Nevertheless, between 1945 and 1947, several laws were passed that were not repealed, covering the separation of church and state (1947), land reform (1945), equal protection of women (1946), and marital property (1946).

The events of the Hungarian Revolution of 1956 and the subsequent Soviet crackdown had an unexpected consequence: the relaxation of Soviet-imposed restrictions on freedom. As such, a number of new laws were enacted that were closer to Hungary's interwar traditions than to its Communist-imposed principles. The most important legislation is the Hungarian civil code, Hungary's first written code in this field. It was promulgated by Act IV/1959 (later revised and amended by Act IV/1977 and Act XXV/1988). The revisions incorporated the changing policies of government: the move toward free-market economy and the freedom of assembly and association. Three new codes also deserve mention: the family code, the code of private international law, and the company law. The family code was adopted in 1952, followed by two important revisions, Law No. I/1974 and Law No. IV/1986. An interesting feature of the code was the legislative acknowledgment of the law-making functions of the Supreme Court. The code laid down new regulations on the protection of marriage and the family, the equal status of husband and wife, and the added importance of the interest of the children. The code on private international law (conflict of laws) (Act No, XIII/1979) contained the latest and most liberal rules in this field. It stressed the *international* nature of transactions that assures the recognition of foreign decisions and foreign laws; it admits equally the validity of the parties' autonomy in choosing the applicable law. The law on economic associations (Act No, VI/1988), called the Company Act, represented a bold departure from the incompetent state control that dominated the outdated theories of centralized economy. The code is listed as a product of postliberation, even though it was drafted in the mid-1980s "to have it ready by the time it is needed!" The model was the commercial code of 1875, drafted at the height of capitalist economy, but the new code merged traditional rules with the arising needs of a more socially oriented economy. Thus, the old taboo of Communist economy—private profit—was discarded and new forms of economic association were added. For instance, the traditional forms of stock corporation, limited-liability companies, and business partnerships were enlarged by new economic cooperatives and savings or building partnerships. In these associations, private profit and free individual disposal are the rule; however, liability for losses lies with the community of the partnership.

The foundation of all the reforms is the constitution of 1989, which established the Hungarian republic and laid down the necessary dispositions for the rule of law. The future will show whether the country will be able to develop the proper ways and means by which the continued working of this rule can be implemented. For the time being, the efforts directed toward Hungary's admission into the European Union have met with success.

Vera Bolgár

Further reading

Black, Henry Campbell. *Black's Law Dictionary,* 6th ed. St. Paul, Minnesota, 1990.

Csizmadia, A., K. Asztalos Kovács, and L. Magyar. *Állam és Jogtörténet.* Budapest, 1972.

Lasok, D., ed. *The Polish Civil Code,* trans. by. Z. Negbi, in *18 Law in Eastern Europe.* Leiden, 1975.

Palmer, Alan. *The Lands Between: A History of East Central Europe since the Congress of Vienna.* London, 1970.

Rácz, B. and I. Kukorelli. "The Second Generation: Post-Communist Elections in Hungary in 1994." *Europe–Asia Studies,* no. 2. (1995).

Reynolds, Thomas A. and Arturo A. Flores, eds. *Foreign Law: Current Sources of Codes and Legislation in Jurisdictions of the World,* AALL Publications Series No. 33 (1989–).

See also Congress of Vienna; Duchy of Warsaw; Family; Miklós Horthy; Hungarian Revolution of 1956; Hungarian Soviet Republic; Mihály Károlyi; Béla Kun; Labor; Nationalism; Paris Peace Conferences; Press; Privatization; Republic of Kraków; Revolutions of 1989; Sejm; Solidarity; Trianon, Treaty of; Velvet Revolution

League of Nations

First major worldwide organization formed to preserve peace through international cooperation. The League of Nations was established January 20, 1920, and dissolved April 18, 1946. Its primary responsibilities were to resolve conflicts between states and improve human welfare. Czechoslovakia, Poland, Romania, and Yugoslavia were charter members, and Albania (1920), Bulgaria (1920), and Hungary (1922) were quickly admitted. However, Hungary (1939) and Romania (1940) later withdrew their membership, and Albania (1939) left when annexed by Italy.

The league's legacy in Eastern Europe was mixed. The organization had both successes and failures in resolving conflicts between states. It administered the Free City of Danzig (Gdańsk), the ethnically German city tied to Poland after World War I, which remained a source of conflict between Poland and Germany throughout the interwar period, and settled the disposition of Upper Silesia between Germany and Poland in 1922. Although it acquiesced to Poland's acquisition of Lithuanian territory in 1923, the league did make peace between the two states in 1927. Albania was protected by the league when threatened by Yugoslavia, Greece, and Italy in 1921, but the league did not act when Italy annexed Albania in 1939. The league was also able to prevent a war between Bulgaria and Greece over a border dispute.

The league had mixed results regarding its mandate to improve human welfare. Hungary's economy, damaged by the loss of territory after World War I, was rescued by a loan through the league in 1923. But petitions from the minorities received little real attention. By the late 1930s, the League of Nations was moribund, powerless to act against aggressors. As such, when threatened neither Czechoslovakia nor Poland appealed to the league for protection from Nazi Germany.

Jo Ellen Kerksiek

Further reading

Scott, George. *The Rise and Fall of the League of Nations.* New York, 1973.

Walters, F.P. *A History of the League of Nations.* New York, 1952.

See also Ethnic Minorities; Gdańsk; Silesian Question

League of Prizren

First major nationalistic manifestation by Albanians. The Treaty of San Stefano of March 1878 (which concluded the Russo-Turkish War of 1877–78) assigned lands to Serbia and Montenegro that Albanians believed to be theirs. The Great Powers subsequently convened the Congress of Berlin in June 1878 to revise the treaty, which many considered too favorable to Russia. In response, Albanian leaders met at Prizren (in Kosovo) beginning on June 10, at first with the blessing of the Turks. Initially, most of the delegates were landowning beys from the north, though Abdul Frashëri (1839–92), one of the few delegates from the south, became a moving spirit of the league.

In his opening speech, Frashëri suggested sending a protest against any attempted partition to the Congress of Berlin and the Ottoman Empire. The Albanians proclaimed their unity and threatened to use force in the event of any cession of territory. The league set up committees throughout Albania to recruit and indoctrinate men, but centralized control always remained elusive. In the south, the league organized a force to resist Greek demands for Thessaly and Epirus. Eventually Greece received only a small amount of territory from the Albanians.

In 1880 the Albanians drove the Montenegrins out of two northern towns. Later, when the league refused to turn over Ulcinj to Montenegro, the Great Powers pressured the Ottoman government to make the league submit. A Turkish army arrived in the region and forced the Albanians to relinquish Ulcinj in November 1880.

The other main objective of the League of Prizren was to obtain autonomous status for Albania within the Ottoman Empire. Frashëri had been working tirelessly for autonomy. While many members of the league agreed with him in principle, few were willing to take action until the Turkish army moved against Ulcinj. At a meeting at Dibër, the league passed a resolution calling for autonomy. It insisted that the four *vilayets* (provinces) with Albanian inhabitants be united into one Albanian province. It also demanded that Albanian officials be selected to run the province and an Albanian militia be mustered to defend it. Finally, they demanded that the language of administration be Albanian.

When the Ottoman government refused to consider their demand for autonomy, the Albanians resorted to armed resistance. The league declared itself the provisional government of Albania and took control over most of Kosovo, Skoplje, Dibër, and other areas. But by spring, the Turkish army had begun to reassert control. Prizren fell on April 20, 1881. By the summer, the Turks had regained their authority over the northern region and suppressed the autonomy movement in the south.

Despite its suppression, the league succeeded in saving Albanian territory and gave the Albanians their first national organization and objectives. The movement stimulated Albanian nationalism and was the first great step toward Albanian independence.

Gregory J. Pano

Further reading

Skendi, Stavro. *The Albanian National Awakening, 1872–1912.* Princeton, New Jersey, 1967.

———. "Beginnings of Albanian Nationalist and Autonomous Trends: The Albanian League (1878–1881)." *American Slavic and East European Review* 12 (1953): 219–32.

Stavrianos, Leften S. *The Balkans since 1453.* New York, 1958.

See also Congress of Berlin; Abdul Frashëri; Great Powers; Nationalism; San Stefano, Treaty of

Lednicki, Aleksander Robertovich (1866–1934)

Prominent Polish lawyer and liberal politician. Born into the Polish *szlachta* (gentry), Lednicki was educated in his youth at a Russian gymnasium in Minsk. He later attended Moscow University, but after student disturbances in 1887 he transferred to the Demidovskii Lyceum in Yaroslavl, where he obtained a law degree in 1889. Lednicki returned to Moscow, where he established a flourishing legal practice, using his wealth and reputation to further his political career in Russia and Poland. He was a founding member of two liberal parties: the Progressive-Democratic Union, created in Warsaw in late 1904, and the Constitutional Democratic Party (Kadets), founded in Moscow in October 1905.

Lednicki was elected to the First Duma in 1906, representing the Minsk district. He created two Duma factions to further the cause of autonomy: the Group of Deputies from the Western Regions, or Territorialists, and the more inclusive Parliamentary Fraction of the Union of Autono-

mists. Lednicki's parliamentary career in Russia ended with the tsar's dismissal of the First Duma.

With the formation of the provisional government after the tsar's abdication in 1917, Lednicki was co-opted by his Russian colleagues to help formulate a decree of Polish independence. He served in the provisional government as president of the Liquidation Commission, a body established to sever legal ties between Russia and the Polish Kingdom.

After the Bolshevik coup, Lednicki served briefly as representative in Russia for the Polish Regency Council, but he never played a major political role in independent Poland. He committed suicide in 1934.

Andrew Kier Wise

Further reading

Lednicki, Waclaw. *Pamietniki,* 2 vols. London, 1963–67.

Wise, Andrew Kier. "Aleksander Lednicki: Polish Patriot and Russian Liberationist." Ph.D. diss., University of Virginia, 1996.

See also Duma; *Szlachta*

Legion of the Archangel Michael *See* Iron Guard

Lelewel, Joachim (1786–1861)

Polish historian and political activist. Descended from a Polonicized German family, Lelewel studied at Wilno University, where he eventually joined the faculty as professor of history. The university's Russian authorities dismissed Lelewel in 1824 for supporting student secret societies, and he returned to Warsaw, where he joined the Patriotic Society in 1825. In 1829 he was elected to the Sejm (parliament), where he resolutely defended Poland's liberal constitution.

Although Lelewel mildly encouraged the conspirators who launched the November Uprising in 1830 against the Russians, he did not participate in the revolution's initial stages. As the revolution gathered steam, however, Lelewel, president of the Patriotic Society, emerged as a leader of its left wing. He advocated social as well as political change, but he proved too indecisive and contemplative.

With the revolution's failure, Lelewel fled first to Paris and then, in 1833, to Brussels. In exile he continued to represent Polish radicalism. He either headed or played an active role in the Polish National Committee, the United Polish Emigration, and Young Poland, all of which had contacts with the Italian Carbonari and other European revolutionary movements.

Lelewel's attachment to Polish nationalism and his belief in the primacy of the common man complemented his historical findings. The first Polish historian to employ modern research methods, Lelewel reflected in his studies the romanticism of his times. According to Lelewel, the essence of the Polish nation was the peasantry, who had lived in a sort of idyllic Slavic democracy before the corrupting elements of monarch, nobility, and church intervened.

Frank W. Thackeray

Further reading

Kukiel, Marian. "Lelewel, Mickiewicz, and the Underground Movements of the European Revolution (1816–1833)." *Polish Review* 5 (1959): 59–76.

Mocha, Frank. "The Karamzin-Lelewel Controversy." *Slavic Review* 31 (1972): 592–610.

Skurnowicz, Joan S. *Romantic Nationalism and Liberalism: Joachim Lelewel and the Polish National Idea.* Boulder, Colorado, 1981.

See also November Uprising; Romanticism Young Poland

Lenin, Vladimir Ilyich (1870–1924)

Founder of the Bolshevik Party and leader of the Soviet government from its inception to his death. Lenin was the third child of Ilya Nikolaevich Ulyanov (1831–86), a provincial school inspector who had attained noble status, and Maria Alexandrovna Ulyanov (1835–1916). His older brother, Aleksandr (1866–87), was executed for participation in a plot of the radical group People's Will to kill the tsar. This event greatly affected Lenin, who would combine his brother's populism with Marxism to create his own unique ideology. Lenin's revolutionary activities resulted in his expulsion from Kazan University, but he later gained a law degree from St. Petersburg University in 1891.

Lenin was arrested and exiled to Siberia in 1897. He left Russia in 1900, living mainly abroad until 1917. His first great contribution to Marxist doctrine was his publication in 1902 of *What Is to Be Done?,* which called for the creation of an elite, highly centralized, and well-disciplined party of professional revolutionaries. This was the blueprint for the Bolshevik Party.

Lenin was a Marxist ideologue, and he believed the revolution in Russia would be fueled by class antagonisms. He was also a pragmatist and sought to enlist the dissatisfied national minorities of the Russian Empire as allies in the struggle against tsarism. He later sought to reconcile nationalism and proletarian internationalism. Fearing isolation, he supported the short-lived Communist regime in Hungary in 1919 under Béla Kun (1886–1938), which was created during the turbulent period following Austria-Hungary's defeat in World War I. Lenin also advocated the Red Army's invasion of Poland in 1920, hoping to precipitate a social revolution.

Lenin was shot by a Socialist Revolutionary terrorist in 1918. He was soon able to resume his government duties, but his health was permanently affected. After a series of strokes, he died in January 1924 at the age of fifty-three.

Andrew Kier Wise

Further reading

Lenin, V. I. *Polnoe sobranie sochinenii,* 55 vols. Moscow, 1958–65.

Volkogonov, Dmitri. *Lenin: A New Biography,* trans. and ed. by Harold Shukman. New York, 1994.

See also Hungarian Soviet Republic; Béla Kun; Marxism; Polish-Soviet War; Red Army

Levski, Vasil (1837–73)

Bulgarian revolutionary. Born in Karlovo to a member of the painters' guild, Levski (whose real name was Vasil Ivanov Kûnchev) studied in Karlovo and Stara Zagora. In 1859 he became a monk and two years later he became a deacon, thereby earning one of his nicknames, Diakona. He participated in the First Bulgarian Legion, a paramilitary force composed of émigré Bulgarians trained and prepared in Belgrade to aid Serbian forces attempting to oust the Turks from their nearby garrison, in 1862. There he acquired his best-known alias—Levski (lionlike)—for a heroic leap he made during a skirmish. From 1864 to 1868, he taught in various schools. In 1867 he was standard bearer for Panayot Khitov's (1830–1918) *cheta* (armed band) and together with other members of that *cheta* joined the Second Bulgarian Legion in Belgrade (1867–68).

In Romania he was involved with émigré organizations that were willing to fund his efforts to tour the Bulgarian lands in the winter of 1868 to gauge support for a potential uprising. He completed a second tour in May 1869 and unsuccessfully tried to convince the émigrés of the efficacy of an organization within their homeland. With Liuben Karavelov (c. 1834–79), in 1869 he established the Bulgarian Revolutionary Central Committee (BRCC), aimed at promoting an uprising. Beginning in 1870, he worked primarily within the Bulgarian territories to organize revolutionary cells. In 1872 he was recognized as the Apostola (apostle) of freedom (a reference to his religious training and his revolutionary new direction in life) for Bulgaria, Thrace, and Macedonia by the BRCC and given a mandate to represent the committee in these regions and foment revolutionary activity. However, he was betrayed and captured near Lovech in 1872. Tried and sentenced to death, he was hanged in Sofia.

Mari A. Firkatian

Further reading

Genchev, N. *Vasil Levski.* Sofia, 1987.

Kosev, D. "BRTsK v Bukuresht, Vasil Levski i vûtreshnata revoliutsionna organizatsiia!" *Istoricheski Pregled,* no. 3 (1973).

Macdermott, Mercia. *The Apostle of Freedom.* Sofia, 1977.

Undzhiev, Ivan. *Vasil Levski: Biografiia.* Sofia, 1980.

See also Cheta; Panayot Khitov

Liapchev, Andrei (1866–1933)

Bulgarian interwar politician. Born in Macedonia, Liapchev became involved in the events leading to the unification of Eastern Rumelia and the principality of Bulgaria in 1885. A member of the Macedonian revolutionary movement, he kept his ties to it until his death. In the 1890s he joined the Democratic Party of Petko Karavelov (1843–1903), and served for many years as a member of the National Assembly. Liapchev led the Bulgarian delegation to sign the Salonika Front armistice in 1918, which ended Bulgarian participation in World War I (despite the fact that it was, in his words, "the tombstone" of his native Macedonia). In 1923 he split from the Democratic Party and joined the plot that overthrew the Agrarian regime of Aleksandur Stamboliiski (1879–1923). In 1926 he succeeded Aleksandur Tsankov (1879–1959) as prime minister, but in 1931 his coalition government was ousted in national elections by the National Bloc, led by his former associates in the Democratic Party, Aleksandur Malinov (1867–1938) and Nikola Mushanov (1872–1951). He emerged as a moderate among extremists on the right and the left, propounding the philosophy of governing "gently and kindly" (*So krotse, so blago*). He paved the way for the restoration of constitutional democratic order in the country and laid the foundations for national reconciliation after the turbulent and bloody events of 1923–25. In foreign policy he tilted the balance toward Italy and closely cooperated with the forces of IMRO (Internal Macedonian Revolutionary Organization), which sought the creation of an independent Macedonia.

Spas T. Raikin

Further reading

Dimitrov, Ilcho. *Bulgaro-italianski politicheski otnoshenia, 1922–1943.* Sofia, 1976.

Kossev, Dimitur et al. *Istoria na Bulgaria,* vol. 2. Sofia, 1955.

Kumanov, Milen. *Politicheski partii, organizatsii i dvizhenia v Bulgaria i tekhnite lideri—1879–1949.* Sofia, 1991.

See also Eastern Rumelia; IMRO; Petko Karavelov; Aleksandur Malinov; Nikola Mushanov; Salonika Front; Aleksandur Stamboliiski

Liberalism

Throughout the nineteenth and most of the twentieth centuries, political realities as well as social and economic conditions in Eastern Europe precluded any possibility for the establishment of liberalism as a viable doctrine. Stemming from the Enlightenment, liberalism's major principles included written constitutions; broad, if not universal, suffrage; political control in the hands of the middle class; equality before the law; abolition of serfdom; and anticlerical views. Divided, at first, among four autocracies (Russian, Habsburg, Ottoman, and Prussian/German), whose vested interests and power structures generally ensured the rapid containment of liberal tendencies among their subject peoples, liberalism could show sparks of life only at times of internal crisis among the monarchies, generally brought about by revolutionary actions. By the midnineteenth century, the growth of nationalism further clouded the picture. While an individual nationalism might proclaim the principles of liberalism for itself, simultaneously it attempted to prevent rival nationalisms among minority populations from the free exercise of liberal principles for themselves, suborning in fact the doctrine itself. In the patchwork quilt of nationalities struggling to establish their identities at the expense of neighbors, liberalism could lead to chaos.

Liberalism, thus, in Eastern Europe is the story of a doctrine that from time to time attempted to rise from adversity and that, before being restrained, left a mark on the political field and established precedents for the future. It is a story of principles compromised often by nationalism, of initiatives repressed often by force, or of a doctrine struggling to take root in soil unprepared for it. Among Eastern Europeans, those who possessed a greater political awareness and who could feel their bondage more acutely as a result were the first to attempt, even in circumscribed means, to implement liberal principles, that is, Poles, Czechs, and Hungarians.

One of the earliest manifestations of liberalism was the Polish Third of May Constitution of 1791. Essentially an attempt to dismantle the feudal system to prevent the state's dismemberment, it failed owing to the opposition of Russia, Austria, and Prussia, and led to the second partition of Poland. Inspired by the American and French Revolutions, the Kościuszko (1746–1817) rising of 1794 also embodied liberal concepts, especially equality for the peasantry, but fell to Russian military power and consequently led to the disappearance of Poland in the third partition.

The Napoleonic Wars injected liberal elements into the region through the establishment of the Illyrian state on the Adriatic Sea and the Grand Duchy of Warsaw on Polish territory, both of which embodied many of the principles of the French revolutionary liberal movement. Illyria did not survive Napoléon (1769–1821), though seeds were sown for the future in the Balkans. As a result of the Congress of Vienna, the Grand Duchy was transformed into the Congress Kingdom of Poland, a state based on many liberal principles. Although it was a separate state, its constitutional monarch was the Russian tsar Alexander I (1777–1825). A mutual antipathy and Great Russian chauvinism soon led to restrictions on Polish rights, intensified strongly after the failed 1825

uprising in St. Petersburg led by the Decembrists, a loosely knit group opposed to the tsarist autocracy, and the coming to power of Nicholas I (1796–1855), an arch-reactionary who hated the Poles. Increasing repression and rising tensions culminated in the November Uprising of 1830–31, an attempt to reestablish Polish independence and a state imbued with liberal principles. Lacking outside support, the Poles quickly succumbed to Russian military might. Thousands emigrated to avoid capture and punishment. The vast majority of refugees settled in France, where, under the political leadership of such individuals as Joachim Lelewel (1786–1861) and organizations such as the Polish Democratic Society, the émigrés kept alive hopes for an independent Poland and the concepts of liberalism as the basis of a future state.

Not until the Revolutions of 1848 could liberalism again come to the forefront. The rising in Vienna and German actions toward unification inspired activities in Eastern Europe based on liberal ideas. The Prague Slav Congress of 1848, led by František Palacký (1798–1876), had as a goal the restructuring of the Habsburg state on a constitutional basis, giving equality to the Slavic populations of the monarchy. Following the suppression of the Congress, the government proposed a convention at Kremsier (Czech, Kroměříž), to draft a constitution for the Habsburg state based on liberal principles. In a narrower sense, the Hungarian Revolution of 1848–49, led by Lajos Kossuth (1802–94), also espoused liberalism in the sense of gaining liberties for the Hungarians in the empire. But the Hungarians were unwilling to grant these same liberties to their own minorities. The strength of reactionary forces and the military, however, proved too powerful for liberalism to establish itself in the Habsburg lands.

In the Balkans, the midnineteenth century saw the growth of nationalism, but little in the way of liberalism. A plan introduced into the region by František Zach (1807–92), based on an idea of Prince Adam Czartoryski (1770–1861), projected the establishment of a Yugoslavia based on federative principles and liberal elements. Yet this concept was co-opted by Serbian prime minister Ilija Garašanin (1812–74), rewritten, and transformed into the *Načertanije,* which guided Serbia's foreign policy prior to World War I.

The Polish January Uprising of 1863 was the last revolutionary action to implement liberal ideas through force. The Austro-Hungarian *Ausgleich*

L (Compromise) of 1867, which created the Dual Monarchy of Austria-Hungary, demonstrated the tendency to gain liberal concessions for one's national group at the expense of others. The neglect that the Hungarians showed their minorities led the Croats to demand a similar arrangement for themselves in the *Nagodba* of 1868.

By the late nineteenth century, changing social and economic conditions transformed the area and opened new possibilities for political activity. Industrialization, the growth of cities and the working class, greater educational opportunities, and the rise of a larger middle class drove political changes. Both Germany and Austria-Hungary established parliaments, though with very circumscribed powers. Political parties developed, some legal and others illegal, and agitation for liberal reforms increased. Though their numbers were small and the chances of significant reform were almost nonexistent, groups such as the Young Czechs and the Croat Peasant Party in the Habsburg parliaments were able to advocate openly for liberal reform. After the establishment of the Duma in Russia in 1905, even Poles could hope that liberalization would occur. Yet the grip of the autocracies remained too strong for the moment.

World War I opened new possibilities. The actions of such people as Ignacy Paderewski (1867–1941) and Józef Piłsudski (1867–1935) for Poland, Tomáš G. Masaryk (1850–1937) and Edvard Beneš (1884–1948) for Czechoslovakia, and others led to the dissolution of the old monarchies at the end of the war and their replacement by newly independent states. Adopting liberalism, all these new states embodied the concepts of constitutionalism, equality, universal suffrage, and political control in the hands of the middle class, though few were willing to concede rights to their minorities or to face the problems of peasant landlessness and land reform. Soon the social, economic, and political problems they faced proved to be overwhelming so that, with the sole exception of Czechoslovakia, all of them quickly turned to dictatorships and abandoned liberalism.

The cataclysmic events of World War II and the subsequent Communist takeover of the region precluded any attempts to establish liberal regimes with, again, the exception of pre-1948 Czechoslovakia. Yet the desire to create modern, democratic, liberal states did not die, and the next forty years witnessed vain attempts to overthrow tyranny. Uprisings—in East Germany in 1953, in Poland and Hungary in 1956—demonstrated that the people rejected totalitarianism. The Prague Spring of 1968, the short-lived period of reform in Czechoslovakia, was a genuine attempt to temper communism with liberal features. Later the popular demonstrations that led to the overthrow of Władysław Gomułka (1905–82) in Poland in 1970, the "goulash" communism of János Kádár (1912–89) in Hungary, and the establishment of the Charter 77 human rights movement in Czechoslovakia proved that liberalism, as an aspiration, still lived.

Prior to the overthrow of communism, however, only the rise of Solidarity, the Polish trade union, in 1980 achieved any success. Centered in the shipyards and industrial plants of Gdańsk, the movement, advised by many of the leading liberal intellectuals of Poland, soon spread throughout the country and almost succeeded in toppling the Communist regime. Only the fear of Soviet invasion and the declaration of martial law prevented its immediate success. Repressed but not destroyed, embodying the basic concepts of liberalism, the Solidarity movement continued to exist and provided a framework that helped topple communism throughout Eastern Europe in 1989.

Robert A. Berry

Further reading

Davies, Norman. *God's Playground: A History of Poland,* vol. 2. New York, 1982.

Held, Joseph, ed. *The Columbia History of Eastern Europe in the Twentieth Century.* New York, 1992.

Johnson, Lonnie R. *Central Europe: Enemies, Neighbors, Friends.* New York, 1996.

Wandycz, Piotr. *The Price of Freedom: A History of East Central Europe from the Middle Ages to the Present.* London, 1992.

See also *Ausgleich;* Edvard Beneš; Charter 77; Adam Czartoryski; Duchy of Warsaw; Duma; Ethnic Minorities; Ilija Garašanin; Władysław Gomułka; Hungarian Revolution of 1956; Hungarian War for Independence; Illyrian Movement; January Uprising; János Kádár; Thaddeus Kościuszko; Lajos Kossuth, Kremsier; Kroměříž Parliament; Law; Joachim Lelewel; Tomaš Masaryk; *Načertanije; Nagodba;* Napoléon; Nationalism;

Lidice

Czech mining community near Prague, destroyed as an act of Nazi reprisal for the assassination of Reinhard Heydrich (1904–42), acting Reich protector of Bohemia and Moravia, by two Czechoslovak commandos dispatched from London. The decision to demolish Lidice was made by Adolf Hitler (1889–1945) after Heydrich's funeral in Berlin on June 9, 1942. The locality was selected quite arbitrarily. The Führer ordered his troops to shoot the entire adult male population, deport all women to concentration camps, and send all children to educational institutions. The community was to be razed to the ground and its name obliterated. The slaughter of all 199 males over the age of fifteen took place on June 10. Of the 196 women, 144 survived and returned after the war. Of the more than 100 children who were one year or older, only 17 were repatriated after 1945. A few had been placed in foster homes in the Reich. The rest had been gassed in Chelmno, Poland, in 1942.

The international impact of the officially announced massacre of innocent people strengthened greatly the position of the Czechoslovak government-in-exile in London. On August 5, the British cabinet repudiated the 1938 Munich Pact (which had turned the Sudetenland over to Germany). Numerous protests took place across Great Britain, the United States, and Latin America. In July 1942 the Illinois town of Stern Park Gardens adopted the name Lidice, an act later followed by other communities in Mexico, Brazil, and Panama.

Radomír V. Luža

Further reading
Bradley, John. *Lidice: Sacrificial Village.* New York, 1962.

Hutak, Jakob B. *With Blood and With Iron: The Lidice Story.* London, 1957.

Konopka, Vladimír. *Zde stávaly Lidice.* Prague, 1962.

Ministry of the Interior. *Lidice: Čin krvavého teroru i porušení zákonů a základních lidských práv.* Prague, 1946.

See also Reinhard Heydrich; Adolf Hitler; Munich Pact; Protectorate of Bohemia and Moravia

Limanowski, Bolesław (1835–1935)

Polish socialist. After arrest and exile at the hands of the Russian authorities and similar treatment by Habsburg officials because of his conspiratorial activities, Limanowski lived as an émigré from 1878 to 1916 in Switzerland and France, where he became the seminal figure in the creation of a modern socialist movement in the Polish lands. Limanowski enunciated and developed the concept of patriotic socialism in the Polish context. As the first systematic Polish socialist theoretician, he posited an inextricable link between the Poles' desire for independence and the perceived need for social emancipation.

Limanowski helped found the Polish Socialist Party in 1892, when he chaired its first congress, held in Paris. He established himself in the European socialist milieu as a committed proponent of Polish independence and tireless critic of the internationalist faction in the Polish working-class movement. During the period leading up to World War I and then during the war, the grand old man of the Polish Left supported his fellow socialist Józef Piłsudski's insurrectionary program. From 1922 to 1935, Limanowski served in the Polish Senate. Following the coup of May 1926 that brought Piłsudski (1867–1935) to power, Limanowski—like many of his comrades in the Polish Socialist Party—increasingly adopted a hostile attitude toward the new government. Already during his lifetime, Limanowski enjoyed the status of a legendary figure, symbolizing the Polish nation's struggle for liberation and democracy.

Limanowski was also an accomplished historian; his works devoted to Polish history—particularly to the period after the final partition in 1795—constituted pioneering contributions rich in printed and archival sources. In the Prussian and Russian partitions, an entire generation of Polish high school students secretly learned Polish history from Limanowski's writings.

William Lee Blackwood

Further reading
Cottam, Kazimiera Janina. *Bolesław Limanowski, 1835–1935: A Study in Socialism and Nationalism.* Boulder, Colorado, 1978.

L

See also May Coup; Józef Piłsudski; Socialism

Liszt, Franz (Ferenc) (1811–86)

Internationally renowned virtuoso pianist and composer of Hungarian birth. Liszt's musical gifts and fragmented personal life resulted in his recognition as a mythic romantic figure. He studied piano and began composing at an early age. In 1821 his family left Hungary for Vienna, where Liszt continued his study with the noted teachers Carl Czerny (1791–1857) and Antonio Salieri (1750–1825). He was influenced by Hector Berlioz (1803–69), Frédéric Chopin (1810–49), and Niccolò Paganini (1782–1840) to build a virtuosic command of piano technique and travel as a performer. His personal life included relationships with George Sand (1804–76), Countess Marie d'Agoult (1805–76), Cosima von Bülow (1837–1930), and Princess Carolyne von Sayn-Wittgenstein (1819–87). As a pianist, he used his instrument to full advantage, exploring its coloristic and orchestral possibilities.

During his career, Liszt instituted the piano recital as a concert format and transcribed numerous works of other composers. In 1842 he was appointed court music conductor in Weimar. From 1869 to 1884, he spent part of the year in Budapest, and in 1875 became the president of the Hungarian Music Academy there.

Although Liszt's piano music is today the most popular of his works, his creativity made the symphonic poem (for example, *Mazeppa,* 1856) a standard resource of orchestral music. Particular structural features of Liszt's music are the reliance on cyclic form and thematic transformation. He exhibited his musical nationalism in such works as the Hungarian Rhapsodies, which built on Hungarian, Romanian, and Gypsy melodies.

William Smialek

Further reading

Saffle, Michael. *Franz Liszt: A Guide to Research.* New York, 1991.

Walker, Alan. *Franz Liszt,* 2 vols. Ithaca, New York, 1983, 1989.

Watson, Derek. *Liszt.* New York, 1989.

See also Music

Little Entente

Interwar alliance among Czechoslovakia, Romania, and Yugoslavia. So named by the Hungarian newspaper *Pesti Hirlap* (*Pest News*) on February 21, 1920, the Little Entente was originally based on bilateral conventions of defensive alliance between Czechoslovakia and Yugoslavia (officially, the Kingdom of Serbs, Croats, and Slovenes) of August 14, 1920, between Czechoslovakia and Romania of April 23, 1921, and Romania and Yugoslavia of June 7, 1921. These accords provided for mutual assistance in the event of a Hungarian (or Bulgarian, in the Romanian-Yugoslav accord) aggression. France at first viewed the Little Entente with reservations, but it shortly extended its blessing to the group. Attempts at establishing a common front between the Little Entente and Poland did not survive the early 1920s.

In 1923 a secret tripartite military accord was signed, later replaced in 1931 by a military convention. In 1929 the original bilateral accords were unified and henceforth automatically prolongated. Official statements to the effect that the Little Entente had outgrown its original anti-Hungarian thrust and became an instrument of collaboration in Central Europe sounded hollow. Attempts at economic cooperation announced since the 1920s produced little result in view of the divergent interests of the members.

Hitler's (1889–1945) coming to power in Germany hastened the announcement on February 16, 1934, in Geneva of the Organizational Pact of the Little Entente. It endowed the grouping with a Permanent Council of Foreign Ministers, an Economic Council, and a Secretariat based in Geneva. Claims that the bloc had now forged a common foreign policy were exaggerated, but the Little Entente could better perform as a diplomatic instrument at the League of Nations.

The pact did not extend the obligations of mutual defense against an attack by a great power, and the efforts in 1936 of Edvard Beneš (1884–1948) of Czechoslovakia and Nicolae Titulescu (1882–1941) of Romania to transform the Little Entente into a single defensive bloc against any aggression and allied with France failed. Overprotected from inside and underprotected from outside, the Little Entente was a dead letter by 1937. At its last session on August 21, 1938, it went full circle by authorizing Hungarian rearmament.

Piotr S. Wandycz

Further reading

Ádám, Magda. *The Little Entente and France 1920–1929.* Budapest, 1993.

Campus, Eliza. *The Little Entente and the Balkan Entente*. Bucharest, 1978.

Wandycz, Piotr S. "The Little Entente: Sixty Years Later." *Slavonic and East European Review* 59, no. 4 (October 1981).

See also Edvard Beneš; Adolf Hitler; League of Nations; Nicolae Titulescu

Ljubljana

Capital city and principal industrial center of Slovenia. Ljubljana is situated in the basin of the Ljubljanica River, a tributary of the Sava. It lies at the intersection of the principal route from Vienna to the Dalmatian coast and the ancient route from the Pannonian (Hungarian) basin through the Ljubljana "Gate" to the northern Adriatic. Ljubljana's population has reached 250,000, with an additional 50,000 in suburban areas.

Illyrians founded on the site of Ljubljana a settlement they named Emona, which Romans later fortified and made the headquarters of a legion. As Roman authority waned, the Ljubljana basin became a zone of contention among Slavs, Magyars, and Germans. In the tenth century it came under Germanic control as part of the Carniola (Croatian, Kranj) Mark (marchland). Ljubljana's first documentary mention was in 1144 under its German name, Laibach. Its Slavic name, Luwigana, was recorded two years later. The Habsburgs acquired the settlement in 1335 and later made it the center of their Carniola province.

Napoléon (1769–1821) designated Ljubljana the capital of his short-lived Illyrian Provinces (1809–13), providing the spark for later development of the Slovenian national identity. A monument to the general stands in the city. In 1918 Ljubljana became the capital of secessionist Slovenia, which immediately became a component of the Kingdom of Serbs, Croats, and Slovenes (after 1929, Yugoslavia).

Ljubljana became an industrial center of textiles, tobacco, and sugar production during the nineteenth century, financed initially by English investment. During the Communist era, it developed a wide range of industrial production, including hydroelectric turbines and electrical goods.

Among notable features of the city are its medieval fortress on a hill above the old town and a number of seventeenth- and eighteenth-century baroque buildings that survived a devastating earthquake in 1895.

Thomas M. Poulsen

Further reading

Bertić, Ivan. *Veliki geografski atlas Jugoslavije.* Zagreb, 1987.

Hamilton, F.E. Ian. *Yugoslavia: Patterns of Economic Activity.* New York, 1968.

Pavić, Radovan and Nikola Stražičić. *Ekonomska Geografija Jugoslavije,* 3rd ed. Zagreb, 1970.

See also Kingdom of Serbs, Croats, and Slovenes; Napoléon

Ljubljana Declaration of 1912

Declaration creating the Croat-Slovene Party of Right. The October 20, 1912, meeting in Ljubljana formalized the merger of the Slovene People's Party and the Croatian Party of Right, two conservative Catholic parties. The Slovene clericals accepted the idea of a Croat-Slovene nation and adopted the Croatian party's position on the historical right of the Croatian state to autonomy within Austria-Hungary. Since the Slovenes had no similar historical claims, the new party somewhat awkwardly added demographically based Slovene demands for a unified Slovenia (transcending the several provinces into which the Slovenes were dispersed) to the Croatian claims.

It was largely the Frankists, the right wing of the Croatian party, who successfully opposed including the term "Serbs" in the declaration. The Frankists often denied the existence of a distinct Serb identity, viewing them rather as Orthodox Croats. This deliberate omission was likely designed to appeal to Archduke Franz Ferdinand (1863–1914), who was often associated with the idea of trialism (the organization of the Habsburg Empire into Austrian, Hungarian, and Slavic units). The archduke was more interested in weakening Hungary than in granting recognition and autonomy to the Serbian population of the empire.

Ivan Šušteršič (1863–1925), who together with Mile Starčević (1862–1917) presided over the meeting, supported Vienna's foreign policy of opposition to the Balkan League, the alliance of

L Balkan states against the Turks. Owing to popular support for the league and its war against the Ottoman Empire, however, the Ljubljana Declaration expressed loyalty to the monarchy but not to its anti-league stance.

By March 1913, a permanent split between the followers of Starčević and the anti-Serbian Frankists made the new party practically unworkable. Slovene leaders were also divided over differing interpretations of the declaration, especially how to incorporate Serbs into any trialistic agreement. The union therefore dissolved in May 1914, testimony to the extreme difficulty of Slovene and Croat conservatives in reconciling loyalty to the Habsburg Empire with rising nationalist and broader South Slav sentiments.

Kenneth E. Basom

Further reading

Kann, Robert A. *The Multinational Empire: Nationalism and National Reform in the Habsburg Monarchy, 1848–1918,* vol. 1, *Empire and Nationalities.* New York, 1950.

Rogel, Carol. *The Slovenes and Yugoslavism, 1890–1914.* Boulder Colorado, 1977.

See also Balkan League; Frankovici; Franz Ferdinand; Trialism

Locarno Pacts

Peace agreements initialed at Locarno, Switzerland, on October 16, 1925, and signed in London on December 1, 1925, which mutually guaranteed peace in Western Europe. The most significant of the Locarno treaties reaffirmed the borders between France and Germany and Belgium and Germany, and these borders were guaranteed by Britain and Italy. This dispelled suspicion and hostility following World War I, with former enemies pledging themselves to peace. Other Locarno agreements institutionalized arbitration as a means to settle any future disputes involving Germany and France, Belgium, Poland, and Czechoslovakia, further reducing postwar tensions. In addition, France signed treaties of mutual assistance in case of a German attack with Poland and Czechoslovakia. Finally, the Locarno agreements included a diplomatic communication to the Germans reminding them of the League of Nations sanctions to be used should Germany break these peace pledges.

By signing the Locarno treaties, Germany renounced the use of force to alter its western boundaries, agreed to submit to arbitration any questions involving its eastern boundaries, and generally agreed to settle conflicts by pacific means, in the "Spirit of Locarno." However, Germany did not renounce the use of force concerning its eastern frontiers. Moreover, although Britain and France agreed to protect the western boundaries delineated by the pact, Britain did not commit itself to fighting to defend the eastern boundaries (which included Poland and Czechoslovakia). This later helped lead to German aggression in East Central Europe that precipitated the outbreak of World War II.

As a result of Germany's renunciation of force in the west, France gave up much of its coercive power over Germany. Germany joined the League of Nations in September 1926 and was given a permanent Council seat. The Nobel Peace Prize was awarded in 1926 to Britain's Austen Chamberlain (1863–1937), France's Aristide Briand (1862–1932), and Germany's Gustave Stresemann (1878–1929) for securing the Locarno agreements.

Barbara Peterson

Further reading

Cienciala, Anna M. *From Versailles to Locarno: Keys to Polish Foreign Policy, 1919–1925.* Lawrence, Kansas, 1984.

Eyck, Erich. *A History of the Weimar Republic,* 2 vols., trans. by Harlan P. Hanson and Robert G.L. Waite. Cambridge, Massachusetts, 1962–63.

Jacobson, Jon. *Locarno Diplomacy: Germany and the West, 1925–1929.* Princeton, New Jersey, 1972.

Wandycz, Piotr Stefan. *The Twilight of French Eastern Alliances, 1926–1936: French-Czechoslovak-Polish Relations from Locarno to the Remilitarization of the Rhineland.* Princeton, New Jersey, 1988.

See also Franco-Czechoslovak Alliance; League of Nations

Łódź

Industrial city located 75 miles (121 km) southwest of Warsaw. Łódź is Poland's second-largest city and the capital of Łódź province in central

Poland. The city sits on high ground between the Oder and Vistula drainage basins, 12 miles (20 km) southeast of the center of Poland. In 1968 the city's population was 749,000; by the end of 1989, Łódź had grown to 851,700.

In 1816 Łódź became part of Congress Poland, under Russian rule, and in 1830 was made part of the Russian Empire. During this period, industrial development began in the region. Łódź was selected by the government to become a planned textile center, producing cotton, wool, and silk. The population of Łódź grew from 799 in 1820 to 4,343 in 1830, and to 50,000 by 1850, when trade barriers with Russia were lifted. While under Russian rule, the city supplied all the Russian Empire and thus grew into one of the world's largest textile producers. When the city passed to Poland in 1918, however, its access to the Russian market was ended.

There was a major migration out of Saxony and Bohemia in the 1830s and 1840s; many of the migrants went to Łódź. In the latter half of the nineteenth century Łódź was a major destination of Jewish migration; during this period, over 60 percent of the city's registered nonlocal natives were Jewish.

The urban portion of Łódź province includes approximately four hundred industrial estates; it thus earned the label the "Polish Manchester." Łódź remains Poland's most important textile center; in 1985 over half of the city's two hundred thousand industrial employees still worked in the textile manufacturing sector, constituting about 28 percent of Polish textile industry employment.

Barbara VanDrasek

Further reading

Held, Joseph. *Dictionary of East European History since 1945.* Westport, Connecticut, 1994.

Hoerder, Dirk and Inge Blank. *Roots of the Transplanted,* vol. 1, *Late 19th Century East Central and Southeastern Europe.* Boulder, Colorado, 1994.

Hoffman, George W., ed. *Europe in the 1990s: A Geographic Analysis,* 6th ed. New York, 1990.

Paczka, Stanislaw and Raymond Riley. "Łódź Textiles in the New Polish Economic Order." *Geography* 7, pt. 4, no. 337 (October 1992): 361–63.

Turnock, David. *Eastern Europe: An Historical Geography 1815–1945.* New York, 1989.

See also Industrialization; Polish Congress Kingdom

London Pact (1915)

Secret agreement signed on April 26, 1915, between Italy and the three Entente Powers: Great Britain, France, and Russia. By the terms of the treaty, Italy was promised the southern Tyrol, Trieste, Gorizia, Istria, and a large segment of Dalmatia, all parts of the Austro-Hungarian Empire; it was also promised the Albanian port city of Vlorë, a protectorate over Albania, the Dodecanese islands, Libya, and a share in the war indemnity. In return, Italy pledged to enter the war against the Central Powers (Germany, Austria-Hungary, and the Ottoman Empire) within thirty days of signing the treaty. Italy declared war against Austria-Hungary on May 23, 1915, but did not declare war against Germany until the following year.

The treaty, which was published by the Bolsheviks in 1918, became a matter of considerable controversy, particularly since its terms violated the principle of national self-determination. Although some of the regions promised to Italy contained Italian-speaking populations, most of the areas concerned had non-Italian majorities. For example, Istria had large Croat and Slovene populations, whereas Dalmatia and Vlorë were overwhelmingly Croat and Albanian, respectively. After the entry of the United States into the war in 1917 and because of the impact of Woodrow Wilson's (1856–1924) Fourteen Points, which enunciated the right of national self-determination, the terms of the treaty were never implemented, causing considerable consternation in Italian nationalist and political circles.

Mark Biondich

Further reading

Calder, Kenneth J. *Britain and the Origins of the New Europe, 1914–1918.* Cambridge, 1976.

Fest, Wilfried. *Peace or Partition: The Habsburg Monarchy and British Policy, 1914–1918.* London, 1978.

Grenville, J.A.S. *Major International Treaties, 1914–1973: A History and Guide with Texts,* 2d ed. London, 1974.

May, A.J. "Seton-Watson and the Treaty of London." *Journal of Modern History* 29, no. 1 (1957): 42–47.

Zeman, Z.A.B. *A Diplomatic History of World War I.* London, 1971.

See also Fourteen Points; Woodrow Wilson

Lublin

City in eastern Poland (340,000 population). Lublin was known since the eleventh century as a defensive burg located on a high ground in the fork of the Bystrzyca and Czechówka Rivers. It controlled the crossroads of trade routes from Kraków to Vilnius and from Ruthenia to Mazowsze. Its charter dates from 1317. It was known as a trade center frequented by multiethnic merchants (Greeks, Armenians, and Jews). Designation as a voievodeship (provincial) seat in 1474, the Lublin Union (1569), which created the Polish-Lithuanian state, and the Catholic bishopric (1805) contributed to its vitality and growth. The railroad link with Warsaw (1877) attracted many tanneries and some metalworking industries.

In 1918 Lublin was the seat of the first Polish government. The Catholic University was founded the same year. The interwar years attracted additional industries including an airplane plant (Plage & Laśkiewicz). During World War II, the Jewish population of Lublin was exterminated (its prewar population of 38,937 represented 34.7 percent of the city's inhabitants); they were replaced by migrations from overpopulated rural areas. After liberation by the Soviet army in July 1944, Lublin became the seat of the temporary government of Poland (until the end of January 1945).

Presently, Lublin is a large industrial center with a truck assembly plant, and metal, construction, chemical, food-processing, tobacco-processing, and garment industries. Its cultural profile broadened by the addition of a second university, medical, agricultural, polytechnical colleges, specialized research institutes, and other cultural institutions.

Abraham Melezin

Further reading

Janiszewski, Michal. *Geograficzne warunki powstawania miast polskich.* Lublin, 1991, 111–13.

Mileska, M.I. and Olendzki, W., eds. *Słownik Geograficzno—Krajoznawczy Polski.* Warsaw, 1994, 358–60.

See also Lublin Committee

Lublin Committee (1944–45)

Polish provisional government at the end of World War II. The Polish Committee of National Liberation (Lublin Committee) was formed on July 22, 1944, as a result of the merger of the Polish Worker's Party and the Union of Polish Patriots in the city of Lublin. The fifteen-member committee was Moscow-oriented and was to be a counter-balance to the Polish government-in-exile in London. The chairman of the committee took on the role of "provisional executive authority" after its "July Manifesto," which agreed to changes in Poland's eastern border, promised agrarian reform, and fostered cooperation with the Soviet Union and the Red Army. Stalin (1879–1953) saw the committee as the nucleus of a new Polish government. Committee officials declared themselves the provisional government of Poland on December 31, 1944, although Moscow gave it immediate recognition; the West withheld recognition until after the Yalta conference in 1945. The dispute over the future of the Polish government, which began with the question of the Lublin Committee's authority, is considered by many to be a major factor in the coming of the Cold War.

David Stefancic

Further reading

Dziewanowski, M.K. *The Communist Party of Poland: An Outline History.* Cambridge, 1976.

Polonsky A. and B. Drukier. *The Beginnings of Communist Rule in Poland.* London, 1979.

deWeydenthal, Jan. *The Communists of Poland.* Stanford, California, 1978.

See also Cold War; Communist Party of Poland; Red Army; Stalin; Yalta

Luca, Vasile (1898–1952)

Romanian Communist. Luca was born in Transylvania and was active in Communist Party politics in Romania in the interwar period. He spent most of World War II in the Soviet Union, returning to Romania in 1944. He was one of the leading figures in the Romanian Communist Party, and is usually identified with the Muscovite wing of the party, that is, those members of the party trained in Moscow. He was appointed in 1947 as finance minister. Luca was critical of the role that the Romanian Communist Party played in the coup that overthrew the regime of Ion Antonescu (1882–1946) on August 23, 1944. He believed it would have been better had the coup not taken place at all, since it slowed down the transition to communism in Romania. He was purged in 1952 along with other key Muscovites in the party and sentenced to life in prison. Among other things, he was accused of right-wing deviationism, a traditional charge in purges throughout the Soviet Union and Eastern Europe, as well as sabotaging economic reform in Romania while he was finance minister. His purge should be seen within the context of the Romanian Communist Party's version of de-Stalinization, which allowed Gheorghe Gheorghiu-Dej (1901–65) to consolidate his power against the Soviet antiparty group.

Robert Weiner

Further reading

Fischer, Mary Ellen. *Nicolae Ceauşescu: A Study in Political Leadership.* Boulder, Colorado, 1989.

Fischer-Galati, Stephen. *Twentieth Century Rumania.* New York, 1991.

Held, Joseph. *Dictionary of East European History Since 1945.* Westport, Connecticut, 1994.

Ionescu, Ghita. *Communism in Rumania.* Westport, Connecticut, 1976.

Roberts, Henry L. *Rumania.* New Haven, Connecticut, 1951.

See also Ion Antonescu; Communist Party of Romania; De-Stalinization; Gheorghe Gheorghiu-Dej

Luchian, Ştefan (1868–1916)

Romanian painter. Born in northern Moldavia, Luchian moved with his family to Bucharest in 1873. After graduating from the School of Fine Arts in 1879, Luchian studied at the Fine Arts Academy in Munich and the Julian Academy in Paris. Although he inherited a significant legacy after his mother's death in 1883, he soon squandered it, forcing a decline into poverty that characterized the remainder of his life. He was also plagued by a degenerative spinal disorder that left him housebound by 1911; his brushes had to be tied to his arms for him to paint at all.

Throughout his life, Luchian eschewed association with the Romanian artistic establishment, preferring to exhibit by himself or at small exhibits of like-minded artists. In 1896 he contributed fifteen paintings to the Exhibit of Independent Artists, a milestone in the Romanian movement away from sterile academicism. Luchian's work did not fit into any of the contemporary schools. He acknowledged the early influence of Nicolae Grigorescu (1838–1907), the founder of modern Romanian painting, who is alleged to have exclaimed at Luchian's exhibit at the Romanian Athenaeum in 1904 "I have found my successor at last." Other early influences came from Degas (1834–1917), Manet (1832–1883), the impressionists, and the symbolists. Luchian drew extensively on Romanian landscapes and subjects, frequently reflecting a melancholic affection for them in dark pastels. Many of his works display a deep concern for the rural and urban poor. The critical realism in his poignant treatments of Bucharest slums and the violent Romanian Peasant Revolt of 1907 attracted the attention of Marxist critics, who saw in these works a precursor of socialist realism. Later in his life, Luchian turned to still lifes that he interpreted with broad brush strokes and a strong use of color.

Ernest H. Latham Jr.

Further reading

Drăguţ, Vasile. *Luchian,* 2d ed. Bucharest, 1963.

Jianu, Ionel and Petru Comarnescu. *Ştefan Luchian.* Bucharest, 1956.

Lassaigne, Jacques. *Ştefan Luchian.* Bucharest, 1994.

See also Nicolae Grigorescu; Romanian Art; Romanian Peasant Revolt of 1907

Lukács, György (1885–1971)

Hungarian philosopher. Lukács (often referred to as George Lukács) is ranked as one of the eminent philosophers of the twentieth century, even by those who reject his line of thought for ideological reasons. Whether written in German, Hungarian, or Russian, his works, including those on aesthetics and the sociology of literature, have had a major impact on ideas in the twentieth century, through the intermediary of analysts, reviewers, and other philosophers. Aspects of his thought have been the focus of approximately 150 monographs in diverse languages.

Born in Budapest, Lukács came from a well-to-do family; his father was president of a bank and, although of Jewish background, was knighted in 1899. In 1902 Lukács enrolled at the Faculty of Law and Government of the University of Budapest but received his doctorate in 1906 from the University of Kolozsvár. He continued his studies in Berlin and Heidelberg. In 1909 he obtained another doctorate, and his dissertation was published (in 1911) as *A modern dráma fejlödésének története* (*The History of the Evolution of Modern Drama*). In the 1930s he worked on the manuscript of *Der junge Hegel* (*The Young Hegel*), which also earned him a doctorate in philosophy from the University of Moscow.

Early in life, Lukács founded, along with others, the Thália Society, whose mission was to present plays for the benefit (not necessarily the edification) of the factory workers of Budapest.

Lukács wrote reviews for the periodical *Nyugat* (*West*), some of which were reprinted in a volume entitle *A lélek és a formák* (1910). He also published in the progressive review of the social sciences, *Huszadik szazad* (*Twentieth Century*), including several essays on the poet Endre Ady (1877–1919).

Lukács moved to Heidelberg, where he interacted with the circle of German historian and philosopher Max Weber (1864–1920) and began to systematize his views on aesthetics. In 1914 he published *Die Theorie des Romans*, originally intended as an introduction to a monograph on Dostoievsky (1821–81). Unlike his German friends and professors, he opposed World War I. He returned to Hungary frequently, where he eventually organized the Sunday Circle, a discussion group that included some of the greatest philosophical and critical minds of Hungary in the period (Béla Balázs [1884–1949], Arnold Hauser [1892–1978], and Károly Mannheim [1893–1947], among others).

Lukács increasingly turned to Marxism, reading the works of revolutionaries such as Rosa Luxemburg (1871–1919). He was one of the first to join the Communist Party of Hungary. During the turmoil of 1918 and 1919, he was one of the editors of *Vörös Ujság* (*Red Paper*) and held various posts during the short-lived Soviet regime (the Republic of Councils) led by Béla Kun (1886–1938), including that of commissar for education. Shortly after the fall of the socialist republic, he managed to escape to Vienna, where he continued to function on the Central Committee of the party, now in exile.

In 1929 Lukács moved to the Soviet Union with his family, where he worked with the Marx-Engels-Lenin Institute, and on the staff of the literary review *Lityeraturnii krityik* (*Literary Criticism*). Unlike many of his comrades and compatriots, he survived the purges. In the same period

he wrote *The Historical Novel*, first published in Russian.

After World War II, he returned to Budapest and was given a chair at the university in Budapest. In 1949, during the height of Stalinism, he became involved in polemics once again. During the days of the Hungarian Revolution of 1956, he headed the Ministry of Popular Culture in the cabinet of Imre Nagy (1896–1958). From 1957 to 1967, he lived in semiretirement, shunned by the regime. Nevertheless, he published his essays on aesthetics in *Die Eigenart des Ästetischen*, in 1963. In 1967 he was readmitted to the party.

Mario D. Fenyo

Further reading

Arato, Andrew and Paul Breines. *The Young Lukács and the Origins of Western Marxism*. New York, 1979.

Congdon, Lee. *Young Lukács*, Chapel Hill, North Carolina, 1983.

Gluck, Mary. *Georg Lukács and His Generation, 1900–1918*. Cambridge, Massachusetts, 1985.

Goldmann, Lucien. *Lukács and Heidegger*. London, 1977.

Heller, Agnes, ed. *Lukács Reappraised*. New York, 1983.

Kadarkay, Arpad. *Georg Lukács: Life, Thought, and Politics*. Cambridge, Massachusetts, 1991.

Löwy, Michel. *Georg Lukács—from Romanticism to Bolshevism*. London, 1979.

See also Endre Ady; Béla Balázs; Communist Party of Hungary; Hungarian Revolution of 1956; Hungarian Soviet Republic; Béla Kun; Rosa Luxemburg; Károly Mannheim; Marxism; Imre Nagy; *Nyugat;* Philosophy

Łukasiński, Walerian (1786–1868)

Polish military officer, Freemason, conspirator, and revolutionary "martyr." Born into a gentry family in Warsaw, Łukasiński entered the infantry in 1807 and advanced rapidly. Like many other Poles in the Congress Kingdom, Łukasiński advocated Polish nationalism in all sections of the partitioned country and the restoration of a Polish state. His motivations, influenced probably by his ties to Freemasonry and by the emergence of secret societies throughout Europe, led him and several close companions to establish a new secret

Masonic lodge, the National Freemasonry, on May 3, 1819. Łukasiński personally wrote the rules of the lodge and the ceremonies. His desire to maintain strict control over its activities soon led, however, to doctrinal differences and a split with the leadership in Pose (Polish, Poznań). An attempt to heal the split led to the creation of a new (although short-lived) secret organization in May 1821, the Patriotic Society.

In 1821 Grand Duke Constantine (1779–1831) demanded sureties from Łukasiński concerning the actions of the National Freemasonry (which had already dissolved). Still not satisfied and suspicious, Constantine maneuvered to remove Łukasiński from active military duty. The major's fate was sealed, however, in October 1822, when a commission of inquiry obtained a description of the ceremonies of the National Freemasonry, in Łukasiński's hand, that embodied the concept of the restoration of a Polish state.

Constantine ordered his arrest and Łukasiński was imprisoned in Warsaw, never to be freed. Subsequent investigations led to a sentence of seven years' imprisonment. A later death sentence was commuted to fourteen years' solitary confinement in irons. Despite his imprisonment, St. Petersburg considered Łukasiński to be an instigator of the November 1830 insurrection against tsarist rule. He was sent to Schlosselberg Castle, and placed in solitary confinement, his name and origin known only to the commandant. In 1862 he moved to a more open cell, received reading and writing materials, and wrote his *Memoirs* in 1863. He died in prison in 1868 and was buried in an unmarked grave. His family, which had made numerous attempts to secure his release, was not informed of his death until 1876.

Robert A. Berry

Further reading

Wandycz, Piotr. *The Lands of Partitioned Poland, 1795–1918*. Seattle, Washington, 1974.

See also Constantine; Freemasonry; November Uprising; Polish Congress Kingdom

Lupescu, Elena (Magda) (1899–1977)

Royal mistress of Carol II of Romania (1893–1953). The daughter of Nicolae Lupescu (née Grünberg) (n.d.) and Elizei Falk (n.d.), Magda Lupescu attended Pitar Moş, a fashionable finishing school for girls in Bucharest. She married at the age of sixteen and later divorced. An intelligent, attractive, and charming woman with a strong personality and driving ambition, she met Crown Prince Carol of Romania in 1925. Their relationship proved to be scandalous. Not long after, Carol abandoned his rights to the throne, his wife (Helen [1896–1982]), and his son (Michael [1921–]) so he could live abroad with her.

In June 1930 Carol returned to Romania and seized the throne. Shortly afterward, Lupescu returned. In part because she was Jewish, she was sharply attacked by opposition political groups, which helped to weaken the king's popularity. Nevertheless, the two were inseparable. As the royal mistress, Lupescu had a powerful influence over the king, and this resulted in her being dubbed a twentieth-century Madame de Pompadour. In September 1940 she fled Romania with Carol when he was forced to give up the throne. They finally married in 1947 in Brazil. Shortly after, they moved to Estoril, Portugal, where Carol died in 1953. She lived in Estoril until her death in 1977.

Paul D. Quinlan

Further reading

Moats, Alice-Leone. *Lupescu.* New York, 1955.
Quinlan, Paul D. *The Playboy King: Carol II of Romania.* Westport, Connecticut, 1995.

See also Carol II; Michael

Lusatia

Region in present-day Germany between the Oder and Elbe Rivers. Lusatia was initially populated by a Slavic group known as the Lusatians—or Sorbs, as the Germans referred to them. Throughout history, Lusatia shifted among Prussian, German, Polish, and Bohemian hands. During the nineteenth century, the area was subjected to intensive "Germanization," with the result that the Slavic group became a regional minority. Extensive deposits of brown coal brought industry as well as numerous Germans to work in the factories. The intermarriage of Lusatians with Germans also played a hand in the decline of Lusatian culture in favor of a German one. However, as part of Communist East Germany, the group was permitted to maintain their own language and culture. Some

L Lusatian place-names survive. In fact, the mountains of northern Bohemia (part of the Sudeten Mountains) are sometimes referred to as the Lusatian Mountains.

Russell L. Ivy

Further reading
Berentsen, William, ed. *Europe in the 1990s: A Geographical Analysis,* 7th ed. Chicago, 1997.
Pounds, Norman J.G. *Eastern Europe.* Chicago, 1969.
Rugg, Dean. *Eastern Europe.* London, 1985.
UNIDO. *Czechoslovakia: Industrial Transformation and Regeneration.* Oxford, 1992.

See also Germanization; Lusatian Sorbs

Lusatian Sorbs

Residual West Slavic people in eastern Germany. With the demise of Polabian in the early nineteenth century, Sorbian became the last remnant of the Wendish language group, whose speakers formerly extended over much of today's eastern Germany and western Poland. There are two distinct dialects: Upper Sorbian centers upon Bautzen, Lower Sorbian upon Cottbus. The heavily rural population has a colorful tradition of peasant culture and folk customs, but the long-term prospects for an independent Sorbian identity now appear poor.

The Congress of Vienna awarded most of Lusatia to the kingdom of Prussia in 1815, leaving only a fifth of the Sorbian population within Saxony. In the decades that followed, official pressure to Germanize increased, particularly in Prussia. Previously, isolation and rural poverty had permitted Sorbian survival, but now industrialization increased the German presence. The expansion of German schools added to the assimilatory pressure. Nevertheless, a Sorbian cultural movement, directly influenced by the Czech national revival, began to emerge in Saxony by the 1840s. This movement remained small.

With Germany's defeat in World War I, Sorbian leaders established a National Council in Bautzen and asked the Paris Peace Conference to assign Lusatia to Czechoslovakia, or at least to guarantee autonomy within Germany. This effort failed. In general, the Sorbs fared only slightly better under the Weimar Republic (1919–33) than under the German Empire, while official pressure increased greatly under the Nazis. Administrative measures brought Sorbian cultural life to a virtual halt by 1937, although later Nazi plans for a more forcible Germanization were never implemented. The arrival of German refugees and expellees after the war further tipped the ethnic balance.

The German Democratic Republic had a mixed impact on the Sorbs. Although the Sorbs were officially recognized and protected, many of the regime's policies adversely affected them. Especially harmful was the exploitation of Lusatia's extensive brown coal deposits, begun in the 1950s and accomplished by the importation of German labor and the demolition of entire villages. The chief Sorbian organization, the Domowina, which had resisted the Nazis, quietly subordinated itself to the Communists. Sorbian schools were reopened, but their number fell from 140 in the early 1950s to 61 by 1974, and most of those had only minimal Sorbian instruction.

The number of Sorbian speakers in 1815 was approximately 250,000. By 1989, the number lay between 60,000 and 80,000. The heaviest assimilation took place in Lower Lusatia, while the Catholic Sorbian minority in the Bautzen-Kamenz-Hoyerswerda triangle held its own (numbering perhaps 15,000 in 1989).

Todd Huebner

Further reading
Geschichte der Sorben: Gesamtdarstellung, 4 vols. Bautzen, Germany, 1974–79.
Oschlies, Wolf. *Die Sorben: Slawisches Volk im Osten Deutschlands.* Bonn, 1990.
Stone, Gerald. *The Smallest Slavonic Nation: The Sorbs of Lusatia.* London, 1972.

See also Congress of Vienna; Germanization

Luxemburg, Rosa (1871–1919)

Polish-born Marxist revolutionary. A severe critic of any attempt to revise Marxism, Luxemburg was active in Social Democratic politics in Poland as well as being active in the German Social Democratic Party from 1898 onward. In *Industrial Development of Poland* (1898) she argued against Polish nationalism, detailing the lack of an economic basis for an independent nation. Her commitment to socialist democracy brought Luxemburg into conflict with Lenin (1870–1924) and the Russian Bolsheviks, whom she severely criticized for their elite party structure and repressive behavior during the Russian Revolution.

Within Germany, she quickly became the leading theoretician of the revolutionary Left, and in "Reform or Revolution" (1899) she attacked those who contended socialism could develop gradually within capitalist society. Her faith in the common people led Luxemburg to see them as the engine of social change. With the outbreak of World War I in 1914, she moved to organize an antiwar group that became known as the Spartakusbund (Spartacus League). Although imprisoned by the government, she continued her antiwar writing, most notably, her *Junius Pamphlet,* which decried the betrayal of pro-war socialists. In 1918 Luxemburg, along with Karl Liebknecht (1873–1919), Clara Zetkin (1857–1933), and Franz Mehring (1846–1919), established the German Communist Party. During street fighting in Berlin in January 1919, she was arrested by right-wing soldiers and brutally murdered.

William A. Pelz

Further reading

Frölich, Paul. *Rosa Luxemburg: Ideas in Action.* London, 1972.

Howard, Dick, ed. *Selected Political Writings of Rosa Luxemburg.* New York, 1971.

Nettl, J.P. *Rosa Luxemburg,* 2 vols. London, 1966.

Waters, Mary-Alice, ed. *Rosa Luxemburg Speaks.* New York, 1970.

See also Lenin; Marxism; Socialism

L'vov

Largest city of northwestern Ukraine (675,000 population). L'vov (Polish, L'wów; Ukrainian, L'viv; German, Lemberg) was founded about 1256 as a fortress and soon became the seat of the Halicz dukes. It was annexed by Poland in 1340. Its strategic location on the divide between the Bug and the Dniester Rivers at the banks of the Peltev River (presently canalized within the city) controlled the intersection of trade routes from Kiev Rus and the Black Sea to Poland and Ruthenia. It played an important defensive role during the Tar-

tar raids and the Cossack uprisings in the seventeenth century.

Annexed by Austria in 1772, L'vov became the seat of the Galician Sejm (diet) and an important commercial, industrial, and cultural center. When incorporated into Poland in 1919 (despite Ukrainian claims and armed resistance), the city had diverse industries ranging from iron foundries, machinery, and metal shops through automobile assembly plants, to tanneries and textiles. Large international fairs reflected the city's position in commerce. L'vov was the seat of four archbishoprics: Roman, Greek, Armenian-Catholic, and Orthodox. The University, founded in 1656, the Polytechnic (1923), several scientific institutes, and numerous Polish, Jewish, and Ukrainian cultural institutions marked the city's growth.

L'vov was annexed by the Soviet Union during World War II and after the war Poland ceded the city to the Soviet Union in July 1945. Postwar L'vov's industrial profile expanded by the addition of new industries (electrical, electronics, precise instruments, chemical), but its commercial standing declined. The prewar multiethnic composition of its population, after extermination of the Jewish population (in 1931 it had been 99,595—31.9 percent of the city's population) and postwar emigration of Poles, changed to predominantly Ukrainian, and it became an important Ukrainian cultural center. In addition to the university, the city acquired several specialized colleges and scientific institutes, new theaters, and museums. Although L'vov grew by the incorporation of suburban settlements, the majority of cultural institutions and historic monuments are located in the center, which is framed by several parks.

Abraham Melezin

Further reading

Chubatyi, M. "The 700th Anniversary of the City L'viv (1252–1952)." *Ukrainian Quarterly* 9: 242–53.

Kalesnik, S.V., et al., eds. *Sovietskii Soyuz, Ukraina.* Moscow, 1969, 202–8.

Maliszewski, E. and B. Olszewica. *Podręczny Słownik Geograficzny,* vol. 1. Warsaw, 1928–29, 700.

M

Macedonia (Geography)

Newly independent Balkan state between Greece, Albania, Yugoslavia (Serbia), and Bulgaria. Macedonia has an area of 10,000 square miles (27,780 sq km), or 40 percent of historic Macedonian territory. It consists of the Vardar Macedonia section allotted to Serbia in 1913 after the Balkan Wars (1912–13), contrasting with Bulgaria's Pirin Macedonia and Greece's Aegean Macedonia.

Vardar Macedonia is situated between the high Šar Planina and Pindus ranges on the Albanian border to the west and the foothills of Bulgaria's Rhodope Massif to the east. Its terrain is often characterized as a checkerboard of mountain blocks divided by basins and river valleys. Elevations range from 2,000 to 6,000 feet (610–1,830 m). The Vardar River flowing southward through the state, its headwaters joined with Serbia's northward-flowing Morava River, has served as a principal route between Mediterranean Europe and Central Europe since prehistoric times.

The climate of Macedonia represents a transition between Mediterranean and continental regimes. Winters are significantly colder than coastal regions and receive the bulk of the 20 inches (50 cm) of annual precipitation; summers are hot and dry. Vegetation is relatively sparse, reflecting centuries of denudation. Where forests are present, lower slopes tend to be of drought-resistant oaks and higher elevations are characterized by beech woods.

The population of Macedonia numbers approximately two million, of whom two-thirds are Slavic-speaking Macedonians, one-fifth are Albanians, 4 percent are Turks, and 2 percent are Gypsies. Albanians are concentrated along the western border with Albania and in Skopje, the capital city. The Macedonian language is closer to Bulgarian speech than to Serbo-Croatian.

Macedonia has one of the weakest economies in Europe, with more than 20 percent of the population engaged in farming. Another 5 percent works abroad, including more than a quarter of the population living adjacent to the Greek border. Some 40 percent of the land is cultivated, with about half in grains and the rest in cotton, tobacco, tomatoes, and red peppers. Cattle raising is significant on steeper slopes, and minor areas are devoted to orchards and vineyards. Industry is primarily food processing and textiles. There is some mining and processing of lignite, chrome, and copper.

Thomas M. Poulsen

Further reading

Bertić, Ivan. *Veliki geografski atlas Jugoslavije.* Zagreb, 1987.

Clissold, Stephen, ed. *A Short History of Yugoslavia: From Early Times to 1966.* Cambridge, 1968.

Wilkinson, H. R. *Maps and Politics: A Review of the Ethnographic Cartography of Macedonia.* Liverpool, 1951.

See also Agriculture; Balkan Wars; Macedonia (History); Macedonian Language; Skopje

Macedonia (History)

Modern Macedonia encompasses roughly the region situated between the Šar and Osogov Mountains in the north, the Bistrica River and the Aegean Sea in the south, the Rhodope Mountains and the lower portion of the Mesta River in the

M east, and the Korab, Jablanica, Galičica, Grammos, and Pindus Mountains in the west. Since the Middle Ages, Macedonia has been inhabited by a predominantly (Slav) Christian population. From the second half of the fourteenth century until 1912, Macedonia was under Turkish rule as an integral part of the Ottoman Empire.

After the Congress of Berlin in 1878, the Slavic-speaking population of the region intensified their struggle for national liberation. On August 2, 1903, led by the Internal Macedonian Revolutionary Organization (IMRO), they rose in the Ilinden-Preobraženski Uprising, with the goal of achieving autonomy for Macedonia. The Great Powers disapproved of revolutionary activities, however, while Bulgaria, Serbia, and Greece, intent on partitioning Macedonia, carried on their own nationalist propaganda among the Macedonian population. The main Macedonian revolutionary body comprised scattered, ill-equipped, and outnumbered peasant units. Therefore, despite some initial successes, mainly in Bitola (Monastir) province, the rebellion failed. The Macedonian population in turn suffered from Turkish reprisals. About five thousand civilians were killed and seventy thousand people were left homeless.

After this rebellion, the Ottomans, pressured by Russia and Austria-Hungary, initiated financial and juridical reforms in Macedonia. But Bulgaria, Serbia, Greece, and Montenegro concluded secret treaties among themselves providing for the expulsion of Turkey from the Balkans. On October 18, 1912, they attacked Turkey. In the First Balkan War (1912–13), Bulgaria, Serbia, Greece, and Montenegro seized virtually all the Turkish Balkan provinces. After the war, however, Serbia and Bulgaria quarreled over the partition of Macedonia. In addition, Greece and Serbia wanted to have a common border. Unable to find a peaceful solution to the territorial disputes, Serbia, Greece, and Montenegro, on one side, and Bulgaria, on the other, fought the Second Balkan War (1913). Turkey and Romania also took part in the war by attacking Bulgaria. Bulgaria was decisively defeated and compelled to sign the Treaty of Bucharest in 1913.

As a result of the Second Balkan War, Serbia gained 39 percent of Macedonian territory. It is bounded by the Šar and Osogov mountains in the north; Lake Ohrid, the Demir Kapija Pass, and the Belasica Mountain in the south; the Albanian highlands in the west; and the Maleševo and Ogražden Mountains in the east, and is commonly known as Vardar (Yugoslav) Macedonia. Greece seized 51 percent of Macedonia, mainly the area south of the Serbian possession to the lower River Mesta in the east, which is known as Aegean Macedonia. Bulgaria obtained the remaining 10 percent of the territory, known as Pirin Macedonia.

Serbia, Greece, and Bulgaria immediately began to change the ethnic structure of their regions, declaring the inhabitants of Macedonia Serbs, Greeks, and Bulgarians, respectively. They declared and sought the assimilation of Macedonians by force. The Turkish population began to migrate to Turkey. Bulgaria and Greece, as well as Greece and Turkey, also concluded treaties for the exchange of minorities. Consequently, part of the Macedonian Slav population left Aegean Macedonia, and the Greeks expelled from Turkey were mainly settled in Macedonia.

During World War II, Macedonians in all three parts of Macedonia rose against the fascist occupation. This uprising had the attributes of a national liberation movement. On August 2, 1944, the antifascist Assembly of National Liberation of Macedonia proclaimed the establishment of a Macedonian People's Republic, later renamed the Socialist Republic of Macedonia, on the territory of Vardar (Yugoslav) Macedonia, as an equal partner in Democratic Federal Yugoslavia. With the collapse of the Yugoslav federation, on September 8, 1991, the Socialist Republic of Macedonia declared full independence.

Meanwhile, as a result of previous Greek oppression, the Macedonian Slav population in Aegean (Greek) Macedonia backed the Communist side in the Greek Civil War (1946–49). After the defeat of the Communists, great numbers of Macedonians were compelled to emigrate, thereby dramatically altering the ethnic structure of Greek Macedonia.

Aleksandar Panev

Further reading

Apostolski, Mihailo, Dančo Zografski et al., eds. *Istorija na makedonskiot narod,* 3 vols. Skopje, 1969.

Jelavich, Barbara. *The History of the Balkans,* 2 vols. Cambridge, 1983.

Koledarov, Petar. *Imeto Makedonija v istoričeskata geografiia.* Sofia, 1985.

Palmer, Stephen and Robert R. King. *Yugoslav Communism and the Macedonian Question.* Hamden, Connecticut, 1971.

Poulton, Hugh. *Who Are the Macedonians?* Bloomington, Indiana, 1995.

See also Balkan Wars; Bucharest, Treaty of (1913); Congress of Berlin; Ethnic Minorities; Great Powers; Greek Civil War; IMRO; Ilinden Uprising

Macedonian Language

South Slavic language in the Slavic group of the Indo-European family, whose closest relatives are Serbian and Bulgarian. Ancient Macedonian is a dead Indo-European language of uncertain affiliation and may or may not have been closely related to Greek. Modern Macedonian is descended from the dialects spoken by those Slavic tribes that settled during the sixth and seventh centuries on the territory of geographic Macedonia (defined by Mount Olympus, the Pindus range, the southern and western shores of Lakes Prespa and Ohrid, Mounts Šar, Osogovo, Rila, and Dospat to the Mesta River).

The modern Macedonian literary language, which is the official language of the Republic of Macedonia, is based on the dialects of that country's west central region, roughly defined by the towns of Veles, Prilep, Bitola, and Kičevo, although elements from other dialects were also incorporated. This language is also taught in schools through grade four in the Prespa region of southeastern Albania. Official Bulgarian policy treats Macedonian as a dialect of Bulgarian, which is comparable to claiming Norwegian is a dialect of Danish. In Greece, Macedonian has never been permitted in any form of public or private discourse, although it continues to be spoken in parts of Greek Macedonia.

During the nineteenth and early twentieth centuries, as the modern Bulgarian and Serbian literary languages took shape, Macedonians also attempted to create a literary language based on their speech, as seen in texts such as Gjorgji Pulevski's (1838–94) trilingual dictionary published in 1875 and Krste Misirkov's (1874–1926) *Za makedonckite raboti* (*On Macedonian Matters,* 1903). Because of political factors, however, Macedonian did not receive official recognition and thus did not begin to achieve codification until 1944 in what was then Yugoslav Macedonia. Macedonian was taught as a minority language in Bulgarian Macedonia from 1946 to 1948. Attempts were also made to open Macedonian schools in Greek Macedonia in the nineteenth century and during the Greek civil war in the 1940s.

Macedonian shares many features with the non-Slavic Balkan languages with which it has been in contact over the centuries. The following characteristics are unique to literary Macedonian, as opposed to other Slavic literary languages: the sounds /ḱ/ and /ǵ/, which have a dorso-palatal articulation; three definite articles, in -t-, -n-, and -v-, such as *knigata* (the book), *knigava* (this here book), *knigana* (that there book); a series of perfect tenses using the auxiliary *ima* (have) and the neuter verbal adjective, such as *imam dojdeno* (I have come); obligatory pronouns agreeing with definite direct and all indirect objects, such as *mu go dadov molivot na momčeto* (I gave the pencil to the boy); and specific words such as *bara* (seek), *saka* (want, like), *zbor* (word).

Victor A. Friedman

Further reading

Friedman, Victor A. "Macedonian," in *The Slavonic Languages,* ed. by B. Comrie and G. Corbett. London, 1993, 249–305.

———. "The Sociolinguistics of Literary Macedonian." *International Journal of the Sociology of Language* 52 (1985): 31–57.

Ilievski, Petar. "The Position of the Ancient Macedonian Language and the Modern Name *Makedonski.*" *Balkanistica* 10 (1997): 227–40.

Lunt, Horace. "On Macedonian Language and Nationalism." *Slavic Review* 45 (1986): 729–34.

Macedonian Literature

Literary achievements in the Macedonian language shared the fate of the Macedonian people and became the expression of that fate—subjection under Ottoman rule, forced assimilation in the new Balkan states, and nonrecognition as an independent entity. Only as late as 1945, with the final liberation of Vardar (Yugoslav) Macedonia, did the necessary conditions arise for the creation of literature in the Macedonian language.

The first literary attempts to write in the popular speech appeared at the beginning of the nineteenth century. These works became the foundation of the modern Macedonian language and literature. During the first half of the nineteenth century, Joakim Krčovski (d. 1820) and Kiril Peičinović (1770–1845) wrote mainly religious and didactic prose works in the popular vernacular. In the second half of the nineteenth century, however, secular works appeared. Konstantin Miladinov (1830–62), a poet, and his brother Dimitar (1810–62) collected and published folk literature, while Jordan Hadžikonstantinov (1820–82), Raiko Žinzifov (1839–77), and Grigor Prličev (1830–93) contributed to the process of Macedonian national awakening with their prose works and poems. They raised a number of important national and social issues, especially the problem of the Macedonian literary language.

At the beginning of the twentieth century, the struggle for national liberation, as well as the social circumstances of the population, became dominant themes in Macedonian literature. In 1903, in his work *Za makedonckite raboti (On Macedonian Matters)*, Krste P. Misirkov (1874–1926) declared that the most significant task of the national liberation movement had become the standardization and establishment of the Macedonian literary language. In the period before World War II, Vojdan Černodrinski (1875–1951), Marko Cepenkov (1829–1920), Nikola Kirov-Majski (1880–1962), Vasil Iljoski (1902–), and Risto Krle (1900–1975) wrote plays about the social circumstances of the population. Writing in this period, Kočo Racin (1908–43) became the founder of modern Macedonian poetry.

Macedonian literature after World War II has produced five generations of poets, prose writers, and dramatists. In the first generation, Blaže Koneski (1921–93) wrote the first grammar of standard Macedonian and the first history of the Macedonian language, as well as a number of poems and short stories; in addition, Aco Šopov (1923–82) and Slavko Janevski (1920–), with their poems and prose writings, introduced modern European literary trends. In the second generation, Mateja Matevski (1929–) wrote in the style of the modern Mediterranean lyrical genre, while Gane Todorovski (1929–) embraced themes from everyday life. The third generation, represented by Vlado Urošević (1934–), Petar T. Boškovski (1936–), Petre M. Andreevski (1934–), Radovan Pavlovski (1937–), Jovan Kotevski (1932–), and Slobodan Mickovič (1935–), was in closer contact with world literary trends. In the 1960s a dispute developed between the first generation, which favored realism, and the second and third generations, which became more inclined to modernism. In the fourth generation, its representatives—Bogomil Gjuzel (1939–), Atanas Vangelov (1946–), Eftim Kletnikov (1946–), Sande Stojčevski (1948–), Katica Kiulafkova (1951–), and Goran Stefanovski (1952–)—developed authentic and individual literary styles. The youngest, the fifth generation, is following the trend toward post-modernism.

Aleksandar Panev

Further reading

Drugovats, Miodrag. *Contemporary Macedonian Writers.* Skopje, 1976.

———. *Istorija na makedonskata kniževnost 20 vek.* Skopje, 1990.

Konevski, Blaže. *Makedonskiot 19 vek: jazični i kniževno—istoriski prilozi.* Skopje, 1986.

Stalev, Georgi. *Poslednite sto godini makedonska kniževnost.* Skopje, 1994.

Todorovski, Gane. *Makedonskata Literatura 19—20 vek,* Skopje, 1993.

See also Folklore; Macedonian Language

Maček, Vladko (1879–1964)

Croatian political leader in interwar Yugoslavia. Maček headed the Hrvatska Seljačka Stranka (HSS, Croatian Peasant Party), the most important Croatian political party, from the death by assassination of Stjepan Radić (1871–1928) in August 1928 through World War II.

After King Alexander (1888–1934) established his royal dictatorship on January 6, 1929, Maček spent time under house arrest and in prison. When political parties were able to operate again under the regency of Prince Paul (1893–1976), Maček led the HSS through its most successful years (1935–39). The HSS became a broad-based party with support in urban as well as rural areas. It headed a network of cooperatives (Gospodarsko društvo) and an active cultural organization (Seljačka sloga), and had its own militia to protect party members at elections.

Maček finally found a solution to the "Croatian question," which had plagued Yugoslavia since its foundation. After an initial attempt in the early 1920s to find outside support for an independent Croatian peasant republic, Radić and then Maček sought a solution within the Yugoslav kingdom. This involved a basic revision of the Yugoslav constitution, and finally materialized in the *Sporazum* of August 26, 1939, which Maček negotiated with Prime Minister Dragiša Cvetković (1893–1969). This agreement established a semiautonomous

Maps

Central and Southeastern Europe: 1815

BALTIC SEA

ANHALT

PRUSSIA

Copenhagen

Gdańsk

Vilnius

Lida

Minsk

Mogilev

Gomel

Berlin

Poznań

Warsaw

CONGRESS

POLAND

RUSSIA

THURINGIA

SAXONY

Wrocław

Lutsk

Kiev

Kraków

L'vov

Vinnitsa

Prague

BOHEMIA

GALICIA

Nürnberg

BAVARIA

Brno

Košice

Dnester River

BESSARABIA

Odessa

Danube River

Vienna

AUSTRIAN EMPIRE

Buda Pest

Debrecen

Iaşi

MOLDAVIA

Graz

Lake Balaton

HUNGARY

Cluj-Napoca

Galaţi

Sava River

Drava River

Pécs

Mures River

TRANSYLVANIA

Brăila

VENETIA

Venice

Zagreb

CROATIA-SLAVONIA

Belgrade

WALLACHIA

Bucharest

Constanţa

PAPAL

STATES

DALMATIA

BOSNIA

SERBIA

Vidin

Ruse

Varna

BLACK
SEA

ADRIATIC SEA

Sarajevo

OTTOMAN

Sofia

Burgas

Dubrovnik

Lake Scutari

Lake Ohrid

Skopje

Plovdiv

EMPIRE

Istanbul

Rome

KINGDOM

OF

THE

Naples

TYRRHENIAN SEA

TWO SICILIES

Xanthi

AEGEAN
SEA

N

| 0 | 50 | 100 | 150 | 200 | 250 | 300 Miles |

| 0 | 100 | 200 | 300 | 400 Kilometers |

Albania

ADRIATIC

SEA

ALBANIA

ITALY

YUGOSLAVIA

MONTE-NEGRO

KOSOVO

Dubrovnik

Lake Scutari

Shkodër

Skopje

MACEDONIA

Tirana

Lake Ohrid

Vlorë

GREECE

0	20	40	60	80	100 Miles		
0	40	80	120	160 Kilometers			

N

Cities and Towns

⬢ 1,000,000 and over ⊙ 50,000 to 500,000

◎ 500,000 to 1,000,000 • 0 to 50,000

★ national capital

Bulgaria

ROMANIA

Bucharest

Constanţa

DOBRUDJA (DOBRUDJA)

Vidin

Ruse

Varna

Pleven

YUGOSLAVIA

Niš

BULGARIA

STARA PLANINA

Burgas

BLACK

SEA

Sofia

Plovdiv

Rhodope Mts.

Skopje

MACE-DONIA

GREECE

TURKEY

Marmara Denizi

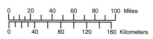

0	20	40	60	80	100 Miles		
0	40	80	120	160 Kilometers			

N

Cities and Towns

⬢ 1,000,000 and over ⊙ 50,000 to 500,000

◎ 500,000 to 1,000,000 • 0 to 50,000

★ national capital

Czech and Slovak Lands

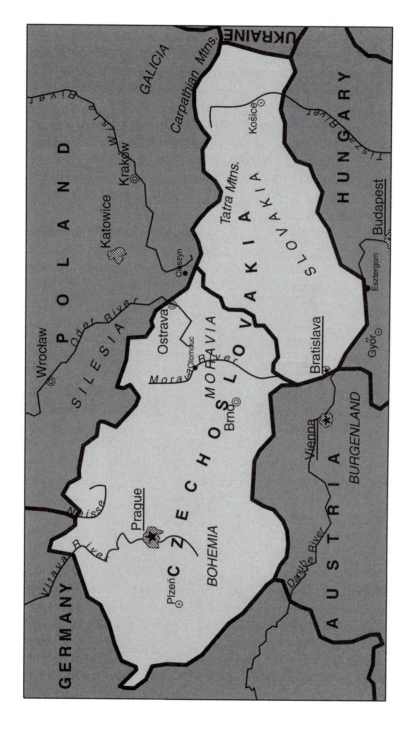

GERMANY

POLAND

Wrocław

SILESIA

Meisse

Vltava River

Prague

Plzeň

C Z E C H O S L O V A K I A

BOHEMIA

Oder River

Katowice

Kraków

Wisła River

GALICIA

Cieszyn

Ostrava

Olomouc

Morava River

Brno

MORAVIA

Carpathian Mtns.

Tatra Mtns.

S L O V A K I A

Košice

UKRAINE

Vienna

BURGENLAND

Danube River

AUSTRIA

Bratislava

Győr

Esztergom

Budapest

HUNGARY

Tisza River

N

0   20   40   60   80   100 Miles

0   40   80   120   160 Kilometers

Cities and Towns

🌐 1,000,000 and over   ⊙ 50,000 to 500,000

◎ 500,000 to 1,000,000   • 0 to 50,000

★ national capital

Czechoslovakia: 1920–1938

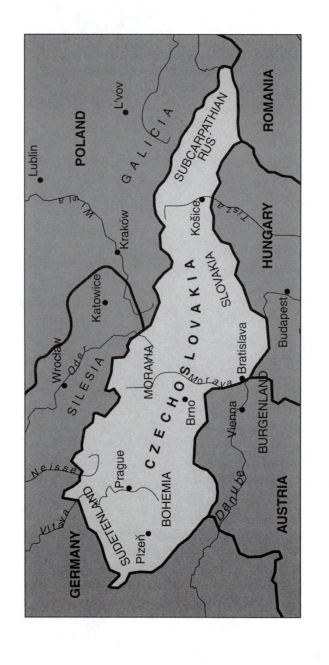

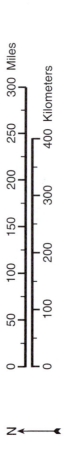

Austria-Hungary: 1867–1918

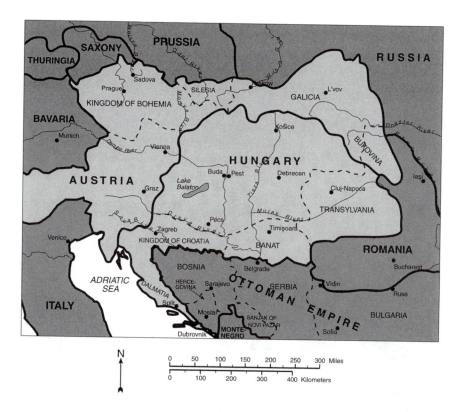

Hungary

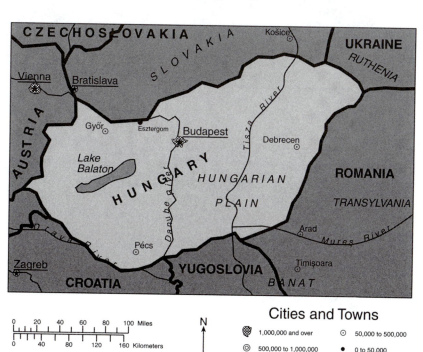

Cities and Towns

- 1,000,000 and over
- 500,000 to 1,000,000
- 50,000 to 500,000
- 0 to 50,000
- ★ national capital

Trianon Hungary: 1920

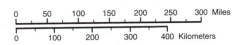

| 0 | 50 | 100 | 150 | 200 | 250 | 300 | Miles |
| 0 | 100 | 200 | 300 | 400 | Kilometers |

N

Pre-1918 Kingdom of Hungary

Trianon Hungary, 1920

Post–World War I East-Central Europe

BALTIC SEA

LITHUANIA
Vilnius

GERMANY

Copenhagen
Gdańsk
POMERANIA
Mogilev
Minsk

Hamburg

G E R M A N Y
Berlin
P O L A N D
Bug River
Poznań
Warsaw
Gomel

LUSATIA
Lublin
SOVIET
UNION
Kiev

Wrocław
SILESIA
Oder River
Elbe River
Neisse R.

SUDETENLAND
Prague
Katowice
Kraków
G A L I C I A
L'vov

Nürnberg
Plzeň
BOHEMIA
C Z E C H O S L O V A K I A
Brno
Morava River
Tatras Mtns.
Carpathian Mtns.
Košice

Danube River
Vienna
Bratislava
Dniester River
Prut River

BURGENLAND
Budapest
Tisza River
Debrecen
Iaşi
Chişinău
Odessa

AUSTRIA
Graz
Lake Balaton
H U N G A R Y
Szeged
Cluj-Napoca
TRANSYLVANIA
Mureş River
R O M A N I A

Drava River
Ljubljana
Zagreb
Trieste
Rijeka
Venice
Sava River
B A N A T
Timişoara
Belgrade
Bucharest
Constanţa
DOBRUDJA
BLACK SEA

Firenze
ITALY
Rome
A D R I A T I C   S E A
Dinaric Mtns.
Split
Sarajevo
KINGDOM OF SERBS, CROATS AND SLOVENES
Niš
Ruse
Varna

Dubrovnik
Kotor
Lake Scutari
Skopje
Sofia
BULGARIA
Plovdiv
Rhodope Mts.
Istanbul

Naples
Bari
Tirana
Lake Ohrid
ALBANIA
GREECE
Xanthi
Bursa
TURKEY

TYRRHENIAN SEA
AEGEAN SEA

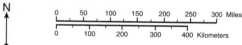

N

| 0 | 50 | 100 | 150 | 200 | 250 | 300 Miles |

| 0 | 100 | 200 | 300 | 400 Kilometers |

East-Central Europe During World War II

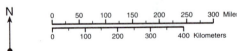

East-Central Europe: 1945–1989

BALTIC SEA

Copenhagen

Gdańsk

POMERANIA

Vilnius

Minsk

EAST

Berlin

GERMANY

LUSATIA

P O L A N D

Poznań

Warsaw

U. S. S. R

Kiev

Wrocław

S I L E S I A

Lutsk

Kraków

G A L I C I A

L'vov

Prague

Nürnberg

C Z E C H O S L O V A K I A

Carpathian Mtns.

BOHEMIA

MORAVIA

Tatra Mtns.

BUKOVINA

MOLDOVA

WEST

Brno

Košice

RUTHENIA

BESSARABIA

GERMANY

Danube River

Vienna

Bratislava

AUSTRIA

BURGENLAND

Budapest

Debrecen

Iaşi

Chişinău Odessa

Lake Balaton

HUNGARY

HUNGARIAN PLAIN

Cluj-Napoca

MOLDAVIA

TRANSYLVANIA

ROMANIA

SLOVENIA

Ljubljana

Zagreb

Drava River

Timişoara

Mureş River

Venice

Trieste

B A N A T

CROATIA

Sava River

Y U G O S L A V I A

Belgrade

Bucharest

Constanţa

Zadar

BOSNIA-HERCEGOVINA

SERBIA

DOBRUDJA

Ruse

Varna

Split

Dinaric Mtns.

Sarajevo

Niš

STARA PLANINA

BULGARIA

Rome

ADRIATIC SEA

Dubrovnik

MONTENEGRO

Lake Scutari

Skopje

Sofia

Rhodope Mts.

Istanbul

Naples

MACEDONIA

Tirana

Lake Ohrid

ALBANIA

G R E E C E

AEGEAN SEA

TURKEY

TYRRHENIAN SEA

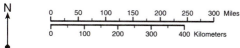

N

0   50   100   150   200   250   300 Miles

0   100   200   300   400 Kilometers

The Partitions of Poland, 1772–1795

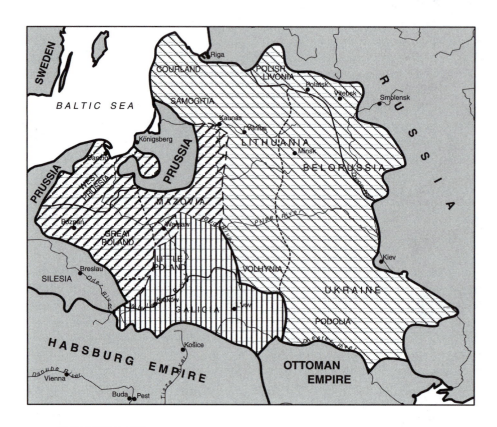

Border of Poland in 1771

Border of Poland following the First Partition, 1772

- - - - - - Border of Poland following the Second Partition, 1793

– – – – Central European Borders after the Third Partition, 1795

Polish Lands taken by Russia

Polish Lands taken by Prussia

Polish Lands taken by the Habsburg Empire

N

| 0 | 50 | 100 | 150 | 200 | 250 | 300 Miles |
| 0 | 100 | 200 | 300 | 400 Kilometers |

Poland

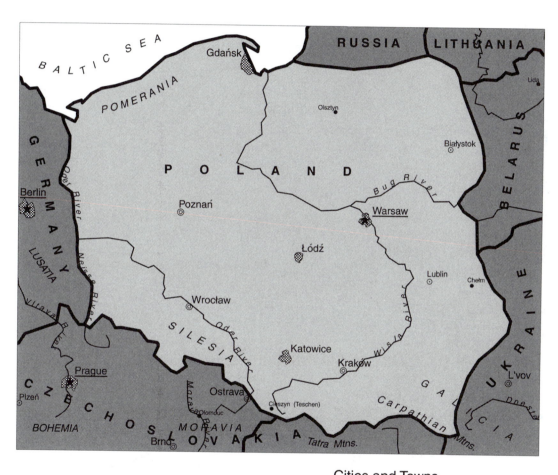

BALTIC SEA

RUSSIA   LITHUANIA

Gdańsk

POMERANIA

Lida

Olsztyn

P O L A N D

Białystok

GERMANY

Oder River

Berlin

Bug River

Poznań

Warsaw

BELARUS

LUSATIA

Neisse River

Łódź

Vltava River

Lublin

Chełm

Wrocław

S I L E S I A

Oder River

Wisla River

UKRAINE

Katowice

L'vov

Prague

Kraków

G A L I C I A

Plzeň

CZECHOSLOVAKIA

Ostrava

Cieszyn (Teschen)

Dniestr

Carpathian

BOHEMIA

Olomuc

MORAVIA

Mtns.

Brno

Tatra Mtns.

0 20 40 60 80 100 Miles

0   40   80   120   160 Kilometers

N

Cities and Towns

1,000,000 and over   ⊙ 50,000 to 500,000

◎ 500,000 to 1,000,000   • 0 to 50,000

★ national capital

Romania

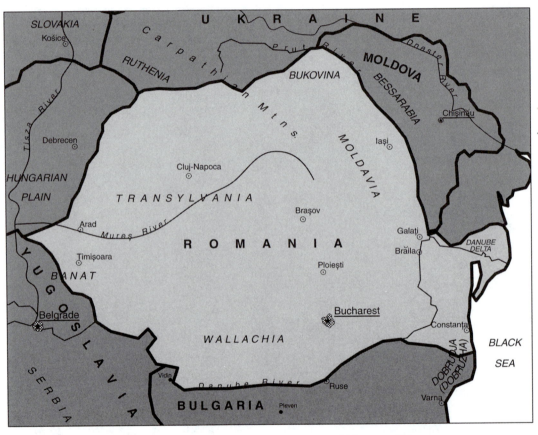

SLOVAKIA

Košice

Carpathian

RUTHENIA

U K R A I N E

Prut River

Dnaster River

MOLDOVA

BUKOVINA

BESSARABIA

Chișinău

Debrecen

Tisza River

Iași

MOLDAVIA

HUNGARIAN
PLAIN

Cluj-Napoca

T R A N S Y L V A N I A

Mtns.

Brașov

Arad

Mureș River

R O M A N I A

Galați

DANUBE
DELTA

Timișoara

BANAT

Brăila

Ploiești

YUGOSLAVIA

Belgrade

Bucharest

Constanța

BLACK

SEA

WALLACHIA

SERBIA

Vidin

Danube River

Ruse

DOBRUJA
(DOBRUDJA)

Varna

BULGARIA

Pleven

Cities and Towns

1,000,000 and over

50,000 to 500,000

500,000 to 1,000,000

0 to 50,000

national capital

| 0 | 20 | 40 | 60 | 80 | 100 Miles |

| 0 | 40 | 80 | 120 | 160 Kilometers |

N

Yugoslavia

AUSTRIA · Graz
Lake Balaton
HUNGARY
HUNGARIAN PLAIN
Cluj-Napoca
TRANSYLVANIA
Drava River
Szeged
Arad
Mures River
Timișoara
Sava River
Ljubljana
SLOVENIA
Zagreb
Pécs
Tisza River
BANAT
ROMANIA
Trieste
Flume
ISTRIA
CROATIA
Novi Sad
Belgrade
BOSNIA AND HERCEGOVINA
Danube River
YUGOSLAVIA
SERBIA
Morava River
Vidin
Sarajevo
A D R I A T I C   S E A
Split
DINARIC MTNS
DALMATIA
Dubrovnik
MONTENEGRO
Titograd
Nis
KOSOVO
Priština
Sofia
BULGARIA
Lake Scutari
Skopje
Blagoevgrad
I T A L Y
Naples
Bari
MACEDONIA
Vardar River
Tirana
Lake Ohrid
ALBANIA
GREECE

0 20 40 60 80 100 Miles
0 40 80 120 160 Kilometers

N

Cities and Towns

⬤ 1,000,000 and over   ⊙ 50,000 to 500,000
◎ 500,000 to 1,000,000   • 0 to 50,000
★ national capital

Yugoslavia: 1921–1941

Croatian *Banovina* (province) within the Kingdom of Yugoslavia, and Maček became vice president of the Cvetković government. Maček did not join the government-in-exile when war broke out. He stayed in Croatia and instructed the HSS not to cooperate with the German and Italian invaders, the Ustaša, the Croatian ultranationalist organization, or later the Communists.

Elinor Murray Despalatović

Further reading

Boban, Ljubo. *Maček i politika Hrvatske Seljačke Stranke 1928/1941,* 2 vols. Zagreb, 1974.

Hoptner, J.B. *Yugoslavia in Crisis, 1934–1941.* New York, 1962.

Maček, Vladko. *In the Struggle for Freedom.* University Park, Pennsylvania, 1957.

Radelić, Zdenko. *Hrvatska Seljačka Stranka 1941–1950.* Zagreb, 1996.

See also Alexander I Karadjordjević; Dragiša Cvetković; Paul Karadjordjević; Stjepan Radić; *Sporazum* of 1939; Ustaša

Mácha, Karel Hynek (1810–36)

Greatest Czech romantic poet. Mácha grew up in a working-class area of Prague and completed a degree in law at Charles University. While studying, he became actively involved in the literary and theatrical circles of his time, where his gray, red-lined cloak reinforced his image as a romantic dandy. He was an avid reader forced to rely on what he could borrow. Fluent in German and Polish, Mácha was influenced by the romantic writers of those traditions, as well as by Lord Byron (1788–1824) and Sir Walter Scott (1771–1832). Among his theater acquaintances, he met Leonora (Lori) Šomková (n.d.), with whom he began a tumultuous relationship. Attracted to castle ruins and mountains, which provided the settings for many of his works, Mácha spent days walking the Czech countryside exploring such romantic and picturesque locales, as well as visiting graveyards and places of execution. According to legend, Mácha took ill as a result of having helped extinguish a town fire; however, as the onset of his illness occurred two weeks after the fire, a direct connection seems unlikely. He died of a sudden and violent illness just days before the date he had set to marry Lori. Although he was buried in Litoměřice, his body was exhumed and moved to Prague at the beginning of the German occupation of the Sudetenland in 1938.

Mácha's writings were not well received by critics during his lifetime. Most attacked his work for lack of national content, the driving force of Czech romanticism at the beginning of the nineteenth century. Mácha, by contrast, focused on the inner world, producing metaphysical contemplations on life, love, death, and the isolation of the human soul. While he wrote both prose and lyric poetry, he is best known for his epic-lyric masterpiece *Máj* (May, 1836). *Máj,* characterized by erotic nature imagery, expresses obsessive love, jealousy, violence, hatred, and despair. The genius of Mácha's poetic creation rests in his mastery of linguistic and sound effects and in his metric innovations. Much of the subtlety and musicality of his verse is virtually impossible to convey in translation. Thematically Mácha's œuvre centers on love (violent passions), specifically the inability to attain ideal love, and on death (dark forces), depicted as eternal nothingness. The contrast between nature—beautiful, eternal, unconcerned—and the tragic destinies of mortal men and women creates much of the pathos of Mácha's poetic world.

The reevaluation of Mácha's verse began in the late 1850s, when a new generation of Czech poets initiated a literary movement centered around a journal named for *Máj.*

Ann Marie Basom

Further reading

Jakobson, Roman. "Towards a Description of Mácha's Verse," in *Selected Writings,* 2d ed. The Hague, 1971–87, vol. 5, 433–85.

Mácha, Karel Hynek. *May,* trans. by Hugh Hamilton McGoverne. London, 1949.

Součková, Milada. "The Romantic Waste-Land: K.H. Mácha," in *The Czech Romantics.* The Hague, 1958, 38–86.

Wellek, René. "Mácha and English Literature," in *Essays on Czech Literature.* The Hague, 1963, 148–78.

See also Czech Literature; Romanticism

Madgearu, Virgil (1887–1940)

Leading economic theorist of Romania's National Peasant Party. Madgearu served in the National Peasant governments between 1929 and 1933, and

M was assassinated in 1940 by the Iron Guard, the Romanian nationalist-fascist organization. He believed that the future of Romania's economic development lay with small peasant agricultural holdings, which in the long run would turn out to be more efficient than large-scale capitalist farming enterprises. He was also influenced by Constantin Dobrogeanu-Gherea's (1855–1920) concept of *neoiobăgia,* or neoserfdom, which argued that the Romanian system was based on a hybrid mixture of bourgeois-liberal reforms and neofeudal economic conditions, because he also believed that Western institutional political forms were not suited to the particular substantive socioeconomic conditions that existed in Romania. Although he opposed the type of industrialization advocated for Romania by the National Liberals, and believed that the penetration of foreign capital had resulted in the exploitation of the Romanian economy, he supported the integration of Romania into the world economy. Madgearu believed that Romania's foreign economic policy should be based on the notion of international economic cooperation so that Romania would not be isolated from the world economy, and he favored a reduction of Romanian tariffs as part of this program. Although he supported the creation of an agrarian state consisting of smallholder peasants, he also recognized the need for the development of industry in Romania.

Robert Weiner

Further reading

Fischer-Galati, Stephen. *Twentieth Century Rumania.* New York, 1991.

Hitchins, Keith. *Rumania: 1866–1947.* Oxford, 1994.

Ionescu, Ghita. *Communism in Rumania.* Westport, Connecticut, 1976.

Madgearu, Virgil. *Rumania's New Economic Policy.* London, 1930.

Roberts, Henry L. *Rumania.* New Haven, Connecticut, 1951.

See also Agrarian Parties; Constantin Dobrogeanu-Gherea; Peasants

Magyarization

Process of turning members of non-Magyar (non-Hungarian) minorities into Magyars through spreading or imposing the Hungarian language and culture. Already the diets of 1790–91, 1792, 1807, 1825–27, and 1830 aimed at securing a role for the Hungarian language—along with Latin—in public life. Further legal, political, and social pressures for Magyarization during the 1830s and 1840s culminated in the 1844 law that made Hungarian the official language in the Kingdom of Hungary. However, Magyarization was not simply a matter of legislation, because Hungarian newspapers, journals, clubs, schools, and churches were also involved in promoting it.

The principal advocates of Magyarization were the liberals, who believed that, by becoming a Magyar, a person would enjoy the fruits of a liberal heritage and superior culture. Opposition came primarily from the Croats, and, to a lesser extent, from the Slovaks. Slovak Ján Kollár (1793–1852), for example, wrote a famous pamphlet in 1833 entitled "Sollen wir Magyaren werden?" ("Should We Become Magyars?"), which attacked the notion of Magyarization. Not surprisingly, the 1848–49 Hungarian War for Independence (during the Revolutions of 1848) witnessed armed conflict between Hungarian troops and Croatian, Romanian, and Serbian insurgents.

Following Hungary's defeat in 1849, political life was not restored until 1861. Then and in subsequent years, the effort to set Austro-Hungarian relations on a new course pushed the issue of Magyarization to the background.

Austro-Hungarian relations were settled by the *Ausgleich* (Compromise) of 1867, which elevated Hungary to equal status with Austria within the empire. The 1868 Law of Nationalities recognized all citizens of the country as members of the Hungarian political nation. But within that framework, each ethnic minority obtained the right to use its own language and develop its own autonomy in the educational and religious spheres.

Defying both the spirit and the letter of this law, Hungarian governments embarked on a policy of Magyarization. Hardest hit were the Slovaks, who were accused of involvement in anti-Hungarian "Pan-Slav" conspiracies. The 1879 educational law made the teaching of Hungarian obligatory even in non-Hungarian schools. This direction was reinforced by a series of subsequent laws in 1883, 1891, and 1893. Romanian opponents of this trend sent a memorandum to Franz Joseph (1830–1916) in 1892 protesting these acts. Three years later, Romanian, Serbian, and Slovak representatives held a joint conference of protest in Budapest. Although political activism by these minorities accelerated in the early twentieth century, efforts at Magyarization did not abate. The 1907 educational law reinforced the dominance of Hungarian as a language of instruction in all schools. This dominance remained in force until the dissolution of Austria-Hungary in 1918.

Although Magyarization was partially successful in larger towns, especially Budapest, primarily among Germans, Jews, and the Slovak middle class, it could not penetrate large blocs of ethnic minorities. Consequently, Magyarization failed to reach its final goal, an ethnically homogeneous Hungary.

Gabor Vermes

Further reading
Kann, Robert A. *The Peoples of the Eastern Habsburg Lands 1526–1918.* Seattle, Washington, 1984.

See also *Ausgleich;* Ethnic Minorities; Franz Joseph; Hungarian War for Independence; Ján Kollár; Hungarian Language; Nationality Law of 1868; Pan-Slavism; Revolutions of 1848

Mahmud II (1785–1839)
Ottoman sultan. Mahmud II ascended to the throne of the Ottoman Empire in the midst of a period of rebellion and terror that culminated in the murder of his predecessors, Selim III (r. 1789–1807/1808) and Mustafa IV (r. 1807–08). Confronted by an unruly and conservative military and imperial disintegration at the hands of defiant local governors, Mahmud committed his reign to strengthening the central government and revitalizing the Ottoman system to safeguard its survival. Early in his rule, he seems to have realized, at least in principle, that for reforms to be successful they had to encompass all Ottoman institutions and society, that the only way that reformed institutions could operate was through the destruction of the ones they were replacing, and that changes had to be carefully planned and support assured before they were attempted.

Toward that end, and after careful preparation, Mahmud attacked the janissaries, the formerly elite Ottoman military corps, in Constantinople in June 1826, thus destroying the chief obstacle to reform in the Ottoman state. He also abolished the increasingly unreliable military fief system and proceeded to establish a new army modeled on European lines and under his direct control. In contrast to his dramatic transformation of the military, Mahmud's administrative reforms were negligible. In fact, once he implemented them as policy, it would appear that his sole concern was to strengthen his army to subdue his enemies, both external and internal.

Ironically, concurrent with his reformist rule, the empire experienced serious defeats and losses of territory. Bessarabia was ceded to Russia in 1812; by 1815 Serbia was virtually autonomous; and in 1821 the Greek revolution broke out. Furthermore, the Ottomans were defeated in the Russo-Turkish War of 1828–29, and Mahmud was forced to accept Greek independence in 1830. Despite his military defeats, and although his official attempts to improve the position of his Christian subjects failed, Mahmud succeeded in asserting the authority of the central government that made possible the reform movement of the following decades, and thus he forestalled the process of Ottoman recession from the Balkans.

Alexandros K. Kyrou

Further reading
Lalor, Bernard A. *Politics and Reform of Sultan Mahmud II, 1826–1839.* n.p., 1975.

See also Greek Revolution; Janissaries; Ottoman Empire; Russo-Turkish War of 1828–29; *Tanzimat*

Maiorescu, Titu L. (1840–1917)
Romanian critic, politician, and academic. Born in Craiova, the son of a school teacher and revolutionary, Maiorescu received a doctorate of philosophy (1859) at Giessen and diplomas in literature (1860) and law (1861) in Paris. He became headmaster at the National Lyceum in Iaşi (1862) and then at the University of Iaşi professor of history (1862–71). He played a major role in founding the Junimea Society (1863), the Romanian literary and cultural association, and published frequently in the associated periodical *Convorbiri literare (Literary Conversations)*. Maiorescu thus gained a national reputation as a major cultural arbiter. He became a founding member of the Romanian Academic Society, which later became the Romanian Academy in 1879.

In 1871 he was elected to parliament. A successful politician in the Conservative and

M Constitutional Parties, serving as foreign minister (1910–13) and concomitantly as president of the Council of Ministers (1912–13), Maiorescu made a no less important contribution to Romania as a commentator on the national culture. At a time when the adoption of the Latin alphabet for the Romanian language occasioned various orthographic experiments and considerable linguistic controversy, Maiorescu resolutely opposed artificialities that highlighted Latinity at the expense of spoken Romanian or attempts to impose on Romanian a German-style compounding and word order. He urged a national culture that was free of unnecessary imports and pretensions. Maiorescu gave important support to Romanian intellectuals who met his high standards, defending Ion Luca Caragiale (1852–1912), the national playwright, against charges of immorality, and encouraging Mihai Eminescu (1850–89), the national poet, whose first poetry collection Maiorescu published in 1884.

Ernest H. Latham Jr.

Further reading

Hitchins, Keith. *Rumania: 1866–1947.* Oxford, 1994.

Lovinescu, Eugen. *Maiorescu,* 2d ed. Bucharest, 1972.

Ornea, Z. *Viaţa lui Titu Maiorescu.* Bucharest, 1986–87.

See also Ion Luca Caragiale; Mihai Eminescu; Junimea; Romanian Culture; Romanian Language

Makavejev, Dušan (1932–)

Serbian film director. Makavejev graduated with a degree in psychology from the University of Belgrade. He began as an amateur filmmaker in the 1950s. In the 1960s he worked on a number of documentaries before making his first feature film in 1965. His work typically includes nontraditional narrative structures, the use of documentary archival material, and collage-type intercutting of clips from various motion pictures. He has demonstrated a preoccupation with issues of sexuality and ideology in the social context. His internationally acclaimed feature *WR: Mysteries of the Organism* (1971) caused a controversy in Yugoslavia. Working in exile since 1971, he has directed several international feature coproductions and the autobiographical documentary *Hole in the Soul* in 1994. His other feature films include *Covek nije tica* (*Man Is Not a Bird,* 1965); *Ljubavni slucaj ili tragedija sluzbenice PTT* (*Love Affair or the Case of the Missing Switchboard Operator,* 1967); *Nevinost bez zastite* (*Innocence Unprotected,* 1968); *Sweet Movie* (1975); *Montenegro* (1981); *The Coca-Cola Kid* (1985); *Manifesto* (1988); and *Gorilla Bathes at Noon* (1992).

Dina Iordanova

Further reading

Goulding, Daniel. "Makavejev," in *Five Filmmakers.* Bloomington, Indiana, 1994, 209–64.

See also Cinema

Malczewski, Jacek (1854–1929)

Polish painter. Malczewski studied at the School of Fine Art in Kraków under (among others) painter Jan Matejko (1838–93), and attended the École des Beaux-Arts in Paris. He became a professor at the Academy of Fine Art in Kraków (1897–1900, 1912–21). His career began with the painting of country scenes. In the period from 1882 to 1895 he concentrated on patriotic issues related to the downfall of the 1863 January Uprising against Russian domination. The scenes of Polish martyrdom used a dark range of colors, following the rules of traditional realism. Around 1890, Malczewski turned to symbolism and changed style. Figures from fairylands and dreams appeared on his canvases next to real ones expressing the truths of human and national existence, life and death. Employing bold brush strokes, luminous color, and shimmering light to expose abundant human bodies, Malczewski created a vibrant art, employing a realistic manner of expression while representing allegorical and symbolic content. Its pulsating energies emanate from tensions between the intellectual and the emotional. His most notable works are *Introdukcja* (*Introduction,* 1890), *Melancholia* (*Melancholy,* 1890–94), *Błędne koło* (*Vicious Circle,* 1895–97), *Zatruta studnia* (*Poisoned Well*), *Thanatos,* and *Śmierć Ellenai* (*Death of Ellenai*). He is the author of excellent portraits and self-portraits painted against the landscape background.

Marta Tobolczyk

Further reading

Jakimowicz, A. *Jacek Malczewski i jego epoka.* Warsaw, 1970.

Ławniczakowa, A. *Jacek Malczewski*. Warsaw, 1976.

Olszewski, Andrzej. *A History of Polish Art 1890–1980*. Warsaw, 1988.

Polish Painting in Ewa and Wojtek Fibak Collection. Warsaw, 1992.

Suchodolski, Bogdan. *History of Polish Culture*. Warsaw, 1986.

See also January Uprising; Jan Matejko; Polish Art

Malinov, Aleksandur (1867–1938)

Bulgarian politician who established the Democratic Party as a pillar of democracy. Born in Bessarabia in a Bulgarian refugee family, Malinov studied law in Kiev. He joined the Democratic Party of Petko Karavelov (1843–1903), became his deputy, and in 1903, after Karavelov's sudden death, succeeded him as head of the party. On January 16, 1908, he formed the government and on September 22, the same year, proclaimed the independence of Bulgaria. In 1915 he opposed King Ferdinand's (1868–1948) involvement of the country on the side of Germany in World War I. In 1918 Malinov was called to power to extricate Bulgaria from the losing side. He failed in this task, and on September 29 Bulgaria surrendered to the victorious allies at the Salonika Front, the Allied southern front. In 1922 he was arrested and charged with having continued the war. He was freed after the overthrow of the Agrarian government of Aleksandur Stamboliiski (1879–1923) on June 9, 1923. Having refused to join the coup, he led the democratic opposition forces and, after an electoral victory in 1931, formed his third government. Unable to withstand the pressures over Macedonia, he yielded the premiership to his deputy Nikola Mushanov (1872–1951). After the overthrow of Mushanov and his National Bloc on May 19, 1934, and the establishment of the personal regime of King Boris (1894–1943), he resumed leadership of the democratic forces. During the electoral campaign of 1938, while addressing a political rally of the opposition, Malinov collapsed on the stage and died.

Spas T. Raikin

Further reading

Georgiev, Velichko. *Bourzhoaznite i drebnobourzhoaznite partii v Bulgaria, 1934–1939*. Sofia, 1971.

Kumanov, Milen. *Politicheski partii, organizatsii i dvizhenia v Bulgaria i tekhnite lideri*. Sofia, 1991.

Malinov, Aleksandur. *Stranichki ot nashata nova politicheska istoria spomeni*. Sofia, 1938.

Nikolova, V. *Problemi na politicheskata istoria na Bulgaria, 1878–1944*. Sofia, 1979.

See also Boris III; Ferdinand; Nikola Mushanov; Salonika Front; Aleksandur Stamboliiski

Malypetr, Jan (1873–1947)

Prime minister in the First Czechoslovak Republic. The son of an estate owner, Malypetr entered Czech politics in 1900 as an Agrarian, was elected to the party's executive committee in 1906, and was closely allied to its leader, Antonín Švehla (1873–1933). In 1918 he became a deputy in the Czechoslovak National Assembly and was elected to the chairmanship of the Republican (formerly Agrarian) Party. He served as interior minister (1922–25) in Švehla's first government and was then chairman of the Chamber of Deputies (1925–32). Malypetr led three governments. His first (1932–34) varied little from that of the previous government under František Udržal (1868–1938). As prime minister, Malypetr also administered the Ministry of Supplies until 1933, when it was disbanded. His two governments in 1935 consisted of parties ranging from the Socialists to the conservative National Democrats in the so-called Wide Coalition. Although a moderate Republican and a supporter of the *Hrad,* the informal group around the president, Malypetr did not raise the ire of conservative Republicans as did Udržal. Unlike his predecessor, Malypetr took steps to prime the economy through currency devaluation, public works, the grain monopoly, and other measures. He had little success in contending with the demands of Konrad Henlein's (1898–1945) Sudeten German Party and Andrej Hlinka's (1864–1938) Slovak People's party (although Malypetr considered bringing Slovak Populists into his third cabinet). He resigned as prime minister and again chaired the Chamber of Deputies from 1935 until he retired in 1939. In 1946 Malypetr was charged with collaborating with the Germans but was acquitted.

Daniel E. Miller

Further reading

Harna, Josef and Vlastislav Lacina. "Základní problémy vývoje agrárního politického hnutí v Československu v letech 1918–1939," *Sborník historický* 24 (1987): 87–126.

Lacina, Vlastislav. *Velká hospodářská krize v Československu, 1929–1934.* Prague, 1984.

See also Agrarian Parties; Andrej Hlinka; *Hrad;* Konrad Henlein; Antonín Švehla; František Udržal

Mánes, Josef (1820–71)

Czech artist and painter, and a founder of the Czech national art movement. Mánes was born in Prague, where he received his early artistic training at the hands of his father, Antonín Mánes (1784–1843), also a well-known Czech artist. He began his studies in the Prague Art Academy in 1835, and studied further in Munich (1844–46). A journey to Silesia, Moravia, and Kraków greatly influenced his artistic work. Events during the Revolutions of 1848 also played a large role in his activities. In 1849 he paid his first visit to the castle of Count Bedřich Sylva-Tarouca (1816–81) in Moravia, a place to which he was drawn for the next two decades. A later, second trip to Moravia, Silesia, and Slovakia, combined with an 1867 journey to Moscow, reinforced and strengthened his Pan-Slav feelings.

Mánes was the first Czech painter of the nineteenth century to create a purely national Czech art. His work was based on the traditions of the Prague Art Academy. The Munich period strengthened his tendency toward drawing. The all-German environment in which he worked influenced his nationalistic and pro-Slavic feelings. His stays in Moravia, Silesia, Slovakia, and Poland also spurred his creative output as he documented not only various folk costumes but also ethnographic types situated in the countryside. Mánes demonstrated a strong sensualism as seen in his portraits of women, of which his *Josefina* is an exceptionally good example. His mastery of detail shows in his drawings of plants, flowers, and trees. Illustrations and landscapes clearly show his patriotic feelings.

Mánes's best-known work is perhaps the *Zodiac* and the portraits of life in a Czech village, which are to be seen on the Astrological Clock on the Old Town City Hall in Prague (1865–66). He is considered to have laid the foundations for the so-called generation of the National Theater, those artists whose work decorated that building later. His significance is also demonstrated by the fact that young artists in Prague who established the Association of Czech Graphic Artists, with the goal of supporting modern art, named their organization after him.

Dagmar Berry

Further reading
Josef Mánes: Katalog jubilejní výstavy. Prague.

See also Czech and Slovak Art; Pan-Slavism; Revolutions of 1848

Maniu, Iuliu (1873–1953)

Romanian prime minister, agrarian leader, and perhaps Romania's best-known champion of democratic government. Maniu was born in Simleul Silvaniei, Transylvania, when it was part of the Austro-Hungarian Empire. He became a leading spokesman for self-determination for Romanians in Transylvania and a leader of the National Party. Maniu was influential in bringing about the unification of Transylvania with Romania at the end of World War I, and in 1926 he helped to establish the National Peasant Party and became its president. He served as Romania's prime minister three times between 1928 and 1933. Known for his personal probity and strength of character, he became an outspoken opponent of Carol II (1893–1953) and his mistress, Elena (Magda) Lupescu (1899–1977). Indeed, Maniu was always at his best when in opposition.

Although he opposed Marshall Ion Antonescu's (1882–1946) military dictatorship, Maniu supported Romania's entry into World War II on the side of the Axis powers to recover Bessarabia and Northern Bukovina from the Soviet Union. Later, however, he tried unsuccessfully to work out an arrangement with the United States and England whereby Romania would change sides and be able to escape Soviet occupation and restore the country's prewar frontiers. During the postwar period, he helped to lead the fight for democracy in the country and was a constant thorn in the side of the Soviet-installed minority Communist regime. He was finally silenced by the Communists in 1947 when charged with treason and sentenced to prison for life, where he would die.

Paul D. Quinlan

Further reading
Mușat, Mircea and Ion Ardeleanu. *România dupa Marea Unire, 1918–1933.* Bucharest, 1986.

———. *România dupa Marea Unire, noiembrie 1933–septembrie 1940*. Bucharest, 1988.

Quinlan, Paul D. *Clash over Romania: British and American Policies toward Romania, 1938–1947*. Los Angeles, 1977.

———. *The Playboy King: Carol II of Romania*. Westport, Connecticut, 1995.

See also Agrarian Parties; Ion Antonescu; Bessarabian Question; Carol II; Elena Lupescu

Mannheim, Károly (1893–1947)

Sociologist known for his exposition of a "sociology of knowledge" and advocacy of democratic social planning. Born in Hungary to a family of assimilated Jews, Mannheim studied philosophy and participated actively in the literary-philosophic circle that gathered around noted Hungarian philosopher György Lukács (1885–1971) during World War I. After the fall of Hungary's postwar Soviet Republic in 1919, he emigrated to Germany, where he taught sociology at the universities of Heidelberg and Frankfurt. With the publication of *Ideology and Utopia* (1929), he established himself firmly as the leading proponent of an interpretive—as opposed to reductive—method that regarded ideas in their social context. By exposing the limited character of world view, he hoped not to engender cynicism and nihilism but to prepare the way for a synthesis—a less one-sided, more comprehensive outlook.

When Adolf Hitler (1889–1945) assumed power in 1933, Mannheim moved to England, where he lectured at the London School of Economics and the University of London's Institute of Education. Badly shaken by the Weimar Republic's collapse and fearful of the social chaos toward which he believed mass democracies gravitated, he searched for a "third way" that would synthesize a too anarchic laissez-faire liberalism and a too brutal totalitarianism, freedom, and planning. Such a way, he concluded, could be found by allowing for democratically monitored planning and by directing education toward social control. Just as he had in Germany, Mannheim identified "uprooted" and socially unattached intellectuals like himself as those best situated to recognize the pressing need for synthesis in a divided world.

Lee Congdon

Further reading

Congdon, Lee. *Exile and Social Thought: Hungarian Intellectuals in Germany and Austria, 1919–1933*. Princeton, New Jersey, 1991.

Kettler, David, and Volker Meja. *Karl Mannheim and the Crisis of Liberalism: The Secret of These New Times*. New Brunswick, New Jersey, 1995.

Simonds, A. P. *Karl Mannheim's Sociology of Knowledge*. Oxford, 1978.

See also Hungarian Soviet Republic; György Lukács

Manuscripts, The (Czech)

Two celebrated "medieval" literary fragments important to the growth of Czech national consciousness but generally considered to be nineteenth-century forgeries. The Queens Court (*Králové Dvůr—RK*) and Green Mountain (*Zelená Hora—RZ*) manuscripts were "discovered" in 1817 and 1818, respectively, by an eminent Czech philologist, Václav Hanka (1791–1861). Allegedly dating from the thirteenth and the ninth or tenth centuries, respectively, the parchments included fragments of lyric-epic poems and songs and part of the historical "Judgment of Libuše," all in archaic Czech. Aesthetically impressive and testifying to advanced and unique cultural and legal conditions among the Czechs in murky antiquity, the "Manuscripts" (*RKZ*) were seized upon enthusiastically by Czech scholars, artists, and the lay public as a boost to national self-esteem during the Czech National Revival. Despite suspicions voiced by credible domestic and foreign (especially German) critics that the documents were recent forgeries, leading Czech intellectual and cultural figures, such as historian František Palacký (1798–1876), vigorously defended their authenticity and incorporated them into their own works. Nevertheless, in 1886 a multidisciplinary team of experts assembled by Tomáš G. Masaryk (1850–1937), the future president of Czechoslovakia, subjected the "Manuscripts" to intensive internal and external criticism and convincingly established them as modern forgeries, probably the creation of Hanka and several associates. But this did not end the "Battle of the Manuscripts." They still enjoy a multitude of patriotic supporters all over the world, and the controversy has been kept alive by an unending stream of new editions, translations, detailed technical analyses, and polemics.

Joseph Frederick Zacek

M

Further reading

Bartoš, F. *Rukopisy královédvorský a zelenohorský.* Prague, 1946.

Otruba, Mojmír, ed. *Rukopisy královédvorský a zelenohorský: Dnešní stav poznání,* 2 vols. Prague, 1969.

See also Tomáš G. Masaryk; František Palacký

Mărăşti-Mărăşeşti-Oituz (July–August 1917)

Three bitterly fought battles in the summer of 1917 between the Russo-Romanian armies and those of the Central Powers for the control of Moldavia. The Battle of Mărăşti began on July 24 as part of a summer offensive on the eastern front. The Romanian Second and Russian Fourth Armies initially routed the enemy forces but were unable to exploit this success when Russian revolutionary agitation forced cancellation of operations on other fronts. Hoping to take advantage of the situation and occupy Moldavia, the last enclave of Romanian resistance, the Austro-German commands launched twin offensives of their own at Mărăşeşti and Oituz. In the Battle of Mărăşeşti (August 6–27) some Russian units stood and fought but many disintegrated when attacked, forcing the Romanians to bear the burden of the fighting. Fortunately, recently reorganized Romanian divisions were available and the Romanian First Army under General Erimea Grigorescu (1863–1919) fought the enemy to a standstill, albeit with heavy losses. Simultaneously at Oituz, the Romanian Second Army under General Alexandru Averescu (1859–1938) likewise withstood violent and prolonged enemy assaults. The heroic Romanian resistance, praised by ally and enemy alike, saved Romania's independence in World War I and marked the emergence of the Romanian army as a respected fighting force.

Glenn E. Torrey

Further reading

Alexandrescu, Vasile. *Romania in World War I.* Bucharest, 1985.

Cupsa, Ion. *Mărăşeşti 1917.* Bucharest, 1957.

Mărăşti-Mărăşeşti-Ortuz. Documente militare. Bucharest, 1977.

România în anii primul razboi mondial, vol. 2. Bucharest, 1987.

Torrey, Glenn E. "The Redemption of an Army: The Romanian Campaign of 1917." *War and Society* 12 (October 1994): 23–42.

See also Alexandru Averescu; World War I

Marghiloman, Alexandru I. (1854–1925)

Romanian politician and prime minister. The son of a wealthy landowner, Marghiloman was educated in Paris as a lawyer before entering politics in 1884. Marghiloman's unusual intelligence, organizational ability, capacity for hard work, and skill in parliamentary debate made him an effective cabinet minister in many Conservative governments from 1885 to 1914. With the retirement of party chief Titu Maiorescu (1840–1917) in 1914, Marghiloman assumed leadership of the Conservative Party. Although he shared in the nationalist desire to annex Transylvania, he opposed Romania's decision to attack Austria-Hungary in August 1916 because he could not conceive of Germany losing the war. Remaining in occupied Bucharest following the ensuing Romanian defeat by the Central Powers, he was called by King Ferdinand (1865–1927) to head the government when the Russian Revolution forced Romania to sue for peace in 1918. Marghiloman was forced to accept the harsh terms of the Treaty of Bucharest (May 1918), but he saved the dynasty and the army, and even annexed Bessarabia in April 1918. Although he was widely discredited by his actions vis-à-vis the Central Powers, the consequences of these actions qualify him as one of the creators of postwar Greater Romania, the postwar unification of the Romanian lands.

Glenn E. Torrey

Further reading

Bulei, Ion. *Sistem politic al României moderne: Partidul Conservator.* Bucharest, 1987.

Marghiloman, Alexandru. *Note Politice 1897–1924,* 5 vols. Bucharest, 1927.

Torrey, Glenn E. "Alexandru Marghiloman of Romania," in Béla Király, ed., *East European War Leaders: Civilian and Military.* Boulder, Colorado, 1988, 95–114.

See also Bucharest, Treaty of (1918); Ferdinand; Greater Romania; Titu Maiorescu

Marie (1875–1938)

Queen of Romania. The English-born granddaughter of Queen Victoria (1819–1901) and Alexander II (1818–81) of Russia, Marie was married at seventeen to Crown Prince Ferdinand (1865–1927) of Romania. Charismatic and free-spirited, Marie verbally dominated her slow-thinking and uninspiring husband. But although both pursued numerous affairs outside the marriage, by middle age they had achieved a measure of friendship and mutual respect.

Ferdinand's accession to the throne on October 10, 1914, provided a wider stage for Marie's talents. While her influence on Romania's realignment from the Central Powers to the Entente during World War I has been exaggerated, she did encourage her husband to acquiesce to Prime Minister Ion I.C. Brătianu's (1864–1927) decision for war in 1916, even though it meant Ferdinand had to turn his back on his Hohenzollern relatives. It was in Romania's darkest days of defeat (1916–18) that Marie had her finest hour. Tirelessly, she visited her subjects at the front, in hospitals, in villages, bringing compassion and hope. She became and remained immensely popular with the Romanian people. When the government finally found it necessary to sue for peace in 1918, she schemed to continue the struggle to the bitter end. Queen of a Greater Romania following Romania's eventual victory in the war and the incorporation of Transylvania, Bessarabia, and Bukovina, she basked in the world's limelight. But her public career virtually ended with Ferdinand's death in 1927. Her son, Carol II (1893–1953), jealous of his own image, did his best to undermine hers. She died unhappy and feeling rejected at the age of sixty-two.

Glenn E. Torrey

Further reading

Elsberry, Terence. *Marie of Romania.* New York, 1972.

Marie, Queen of Romania. *The Story of My Life.* New York, 1962.

Pakula, Hannah. *The Last Romantic.* New York, 1984.

See also Ion I.C. Brătianu; Carol II; Ferdinand; Greater Romania

Marie Louise (1870–99)

Wife of Tsar Ferdinand (1861–1948) and the first queen of modern Bulgaria. Marie Louise was selected to marry the new Bulgarian monarch by his strong-willed and Russophobe prime minister, Stefan Stambolov (1854–95) and Emperor Franz Joseph (1830–1916) of Austria. The marriage was essentially an arranged political match. Marie Louise was the daughter of Robert, duke of Bourbon-Parma (n.d.), and was considered an attractive, intelligent, and gifted woman. Quiet, timid, and nervous, she was deeply religious and a devout Roman Catholic. She married Ferdinand on April 6, 1893, with the stipulation that all their children be reared in the Roman Catholic faith. This decision caused consternation among most members of the Bulgarian parliament (Subranie) and the imperial Russian government. However, there was little indignation among the Bulgarian people, who, in fact, welcomed the marriage. On January 30, 1894, Marie Louise gave birth to a son, the first heir to a reigning Bulgarian monarch in over five hundred years. National rejoicing erupted when it was learned that the heir was to be named Boris (1894–1943), the name of one of Bulgaria's greatest medieval tsars. After the birth of their son, the relationship between Marie Louise and Ferdinand soured. The two were never really compatible, and the marriage remained only a political convenience. In ill health for some time, Marie Louise died in 1899.

David Cassens

Further reading

Constant, Stephen. *Foxy Ferdinand: Tsar of Bulgaria.* New York, 1980.

Crampton, Richard J. *Bulgaria 1878–1918: A History.* Boulder, Colorado, 1983.

Perry, Duncan M. *Stefan Stambolov and the Emergence of Modern Bulgaria 1870–1895.* Durham, North Carolina, 1993.

See also Boris III; Ferdinand; Franz Joseph; Stefan Stambolov

Maritsa Valley

Valley of the largest river in the Balkan Peninsula, surrounded by the Rila and Rhodope Mountains to the south and the Balkan Mountains (Stara Planina) and Sredna Gora Mountain to the north. The 1,764-feet-long (534.6 m) river springs from the Upper Marichino Lake in Bulgaria and flows into the Aegean Sea. Generally, it follows an east-southeastern direction through the Thracian lowland. After leaving Bulgarian territory, it serves as the boundary between Greece and Turkey.

M Approximately one hundred tributaries flow into the valley. Although severe floods have occurred, water flow decreases in times of summer droughts. Currently, the Maritsa bed is regulated to reduce risks of flooding.

Coniferous and deciduous forests cover approximately 40 percent of the valley. In the Upper Thracian valley the alluvial soil is used for vegetable and grape growing. The waters of the Maritsa and its tributaries have historically been used for irrigation and energy production purposes. Several hydroelectric cascades have been built in the Upper Thracian lowland. The most important towns in the valley are Svilengrad (in Bulgaria), Edirne (in Turkey), and Didimotihon and Suflion (in Greece).

Boian Koulov

Further reading

Bogorov, I. *Niakolko denia rashodka po Balgarskite mesta.* Bucharest, 1868, 22.

Bulgarian Academy of Sciences. *Entsiklopedia Bulgaria,* vol. 4. Sofia, 1984.

Marković, Svetozar (1846–75)

Serbian revolutionary democrat and father of Balkan socialist journalism. Marković was born in Zaječar, Serbia, and studied engineering in Belgrade, St. Petersburg, and Zurich. During these stays, he was particularly influenced by the Russian revolutionary democrats, especially N.G. Chernyshevsky (1828–89) and the teachings of Karl Marx (1818–83) and Friedrich Engels (1820–95).

After returning to Serbia in 1870, Marković propagated a socialism permeated with utopian ideas. Like Chernyshevsky, who insisted that by modernizing the *obschina* (commune) Russia could proceed directly from its existing semifeudalism to socialism, Marković believed that by rehabilitating and modernizing the *zadruga* (communal extended family), Serbia could skip capitalism and establish a socialist society. However, he departed from Chernyshevsky by refusing to advocate the violent overthrow of the existing government in Serbia because, in his view, the conditions were much more favorable than those in Russia for the peaceful legal establishment of a new society. He believed that the enlightened Serbian intelligentsia would lead the nation to the creation of the new society based on the collectivism of the *zadruga.*

In numerous works, he dealt with problems and issues facing Serbia. He attacked the government, particularly the bureaucratic system in Serbia, and demanded its destruction. He also criticized the liberals and their idea of Great Serbia. In *Srbija na istoku* (*Serbia in the East,* 1872), he insisted that the complete liberation of the oppressed Balkan Slavs had to be followed by their union based on democratic federalism, which was the only way to ensure freedom in the Balkans.

On June 1, 1871, Marković began publishing *Radenik* (*The Worker*), the first socialist newspaper in the Balkans. However, its publication lasted only until May 1872. Because of his writings against the government, Marković was imprisoned in 1874, which made his already poor health from tuberculosis worse. He died in Trieste at the age of twenty-eight.

Milenko Karanovich

Further reading

Čubrilović, Vasa. *Istorija političke misli u Srbiji 19 veka.* Belgrade, 1958.

Djordjević, Miroslav. *Politički pogledi Svetozara Markovića.* Sarajevo, 1952.

Masleša, Veselin. "Svetozar Marković" in *Dela* 3. Sarajevo, 1956, 12–100.

McClellan, Woodford. *Svetozar Marković and the Origin of Balkan Socialism.* Princeton, New Jersey, 1964.

Skerlić, Jovan. *Svetozar Marković: Njegov život, rad i ideje.* Belgrade, 1922.

See also Greater Serbia; Socialism; *Zadruga*

Marshall Plan

Post–World War II economic recovery program that further divided East and West. After World War II, the United States had few options available in Eastern Europe. Although President Harry S Truman (1884–1972) first believed that the United States could continue to influence decisions in Eastern Europe, by late 1945 detailed reports from the region left little doubt that Soviet domination of the region was inevitable. The vague pronouncements of the 1945 Yalta conference may have fed American idealism, but reality, driven in part by the political backlash of anticommunism led by the Republican Party, brought a policy of containment. This included the Truman Doctrine, the creation of the North Atlantic Treaty Organization (NATO), and the promulgation of the Marshall Plan. The latter, announced in 1947 and organized and directed by Secretary of State George C. Marshall (1880–1959), was designed to defuse the appeal of the Communist parties of Western Europe and aid the recovery of the Continent in general. Although Czechoslovakia and Poland at first indicated a willingness to participate in the program, the plan's stipulations made it virtually impossible for Soviet-style governments and economies to receive assistance. Moscow's renunciation of the program as American imperialism therefore not only precluded Polish and Czechoslovak participation but also deepened the Cold War's divisions, and guaranteed that Eastern Europe's economic future lay with Moscow.

Richard Frucht

Further reading

Davis, Lynn Etheridge. *The Cold War Begins: Soviet-American Conflict over Eastern Europe.* Princeton, New Jersey, 1974.

Hammond, Thomas T. *The Anatomy of Communist Takeovers.* New Haven, Connecticut, 1975.

See also Cold War; Truman Doctrine; Yalta

Martin Declaration (*Martinská Deklarácia*)

Name conventionally given to the "Declaration of the Slovak Nation," issued in Turčiansky Svätý Martin (a town now called simply Martin) on October 30, 1918. When World War I broke out, the Slovak National Party, which claimed to represent the Slovak people, declared its loyalty to the Austro-Hungarian monarchy and suspended its activities for the duration of the hostilities. However, Slovak political life revived during the final months of the war, when the Habsburg Empire—buffeted by the competing ideologies of the Russian Revolution and the American crusade for democracy—began to disintegrate. Matúš Dula (1846–1926), chairman of the Slovak National Party, called a general meeting of the party for October 30, 1918, in Martin, the principal Slovak cultural and political center since the nineteenth century. A total of 106 delegates came to the meeting, elected a twelve-member Slovak National Council, and issued the Martin Declaration. It announced the Slovak intention to break with Hungary and unite with the Czechs in a new Czecho-Slovak state: "The Slovak Nation is a part of the Czecho-Slovak

Nation, united in language and in the history of its culture." The delegates were informed about the peace notes exchanged between Vienna and Washington but had not yet heard of the declaration of Czechoslovak independence, issued by the Czech National Committee in Prague on October 28, 1918, in an effort to prevent Vienna from obtaining peace terms and saving the integrity of the empire. In issuing the Martin Declaration, therefore, the Slovak leaders were not prompted by Prague but acted on their own.

The Slovak National Council attempted to administer Slovakia but was dispersed by Hungarian troops, which occupied Martin on November 15. Although Martin was soon taken by Czech troops, Vavro Šrobár (1867–1950), the minister sent by the government in Prague to administer Slovakia, did not believe that Slovakia was ready for autonomy. He dissolved the Slovak National Council in January 1919 and integrated Slovakia into the centralist system instituted by the provisional Czechoslovak National Assembly in Prague.

Victor S. Mamatey

Further reading

Grečo, Martin. *Martinská deklarácia.* Turčiansky Svätý Martin, Slovakia, 1947.

Hronský, Marián, *Slovansko na rázcestí 1918.* Košice, Slovakia, 1976.

See also Vavro Šrobár

Marxism

Political philosophy that focuses on the struggle between conflicting social classes over control of the economy. Karl Marx (1818–83) never used the term "Marxism" to describe his work and even rejected the idea that his theories represented an all-encompassing worldview. After his death, and particularly during the period of the Second International, however, many members of the socialist movement began to consider Marx's ideas a comprehensive theory. Notable in this regard were Russia's Georgy Plekhanov (1856–1918) and Germany's Karl Kautsky (1854–1938), both of whom stressed the universal nature of Marxism. Had he lived during this time, Marx may well have repeated his statement, "all I know is that I am not a Marxist," which was originally prompted by the overly zealous actions of some of his French followers.

M Although a complex theory with many nuances, Marxism may be summarized as having certain key tenets. Marx saw society being shaped by the mode of production, or the manner in which goods and services were produced. Thus, for instance, societies, such as ancient Rome and Greece, which depended on slave labor, could be analyzed as examples of the slave mode of production. Furthermore, all human history was the history of struggle between opposing classes defined by their position within the economy. In modern times, this class conflict was between the bourgeoisie, or capitalists, who owned the means of production, and the proletariat, or workers, who were forced by economic necessity to labor for others. Marx argued that if workers gained control of the means of production, the unfairness and exploitation of past history could be replaced with a more equal and humane social order that he called "socialism."

Beginning in the late nineteenth century, Marxism was to become the official doctrine of the majority of European socialist parties. Given their differences in political tradition and economic development, these various parties naturally interpreted Marxism in different ways. Nations with the possibility of democratic reform tended to have socialist movements that emphasized the desirability of working within the political system, while autocratic nations tended to spawn more revolutionary-oriented movements. In virtually all countries, factions within the socialist movement interpreted Marxism in distinct ways.

In Russia, Lenin (1870–1924) saw Marxism as the combination of three intellectual developments from three separate lands. From France, Marxism drew the concept of socialism as a political project. The methodology of dialectics was seen as the product of German philosophy, especially the writings of Hegel (1770–1831), while Marxism's economic theories, particularly the labor theory of value, were credited to England. All the conflicting interpretations of Marxism underscored the centrality of the working class to future revolutionary developments. For more moderate European socialists, this often took the form of emphasizing the growing voting power of labor and the enhanced strength of trade unions. In Russia, Lenin was faced with a proletariat that represented only a small percentage of the population. Therefore, he developed the idea of a new type of party to represent the labor movement while bas-

ing itself on Marxism as an all-powerful worldview. After Lenin's death, Stalin (1879–1953) turned this conception into a type of state religion where Marxism ceased to be a theory and became instead official orthodoxy.

In Eastern Europe, Marxism was popular among sections of the urban working class from the nineteenth century onward. After World War I, there were important Marxist-oriented parties and groups in most all of Eastern Europe. During the worldwide depression of the 1930s, Marxism seemed to offer a solution to the brutality of the business cycle. In addition, the rise of fascism and the conquest of Eastern European nations by Nazi Germany caused Marxism to be seen as a theory of resistance. The appeal of Marxism faded for many in the post–World War II world as it became identified with the Soviet Union, whose armies had occupied most of Eastern Europe by the end of the war. In Czechoslovakia, for example, Marxism was extremely popular immediately after the war, only to become discredited as the ideology of Soviet occupation, particularly after the 1968 invasion of that nation by Warsaw Pact forces.

Despite its reduction to a static doctrine in most of Eastern Europe and the lands of the former Soviet Union, Marxism has continued to enjoy popularity throughout the twentieth century. This may well be due to the variety of interpretations that differing radical intellectuals have been able to render on the theory. Further, it may be a result of the compelling critique Marx made of existing social and economic relations under capitalism.

William A. Pelz

Further reading

Bottomore, Tom et al. *A Dictionary of Marxist Thought.* Oxford, 1991.
Callinicos, Alex. *The Revolutionary Ideas of Marx.* London, 1983.
Lichtheim, George. *Marxism: An Historical and Critical Study.* New York, 1982.
Mandel, Ernest. *The Place of Marxism in History.* Atlantic Highlands, New Jersey, 1993.
McLellan, David. *Karl Marx: His Life and Thought.* New York, 1973.

See also Communist Party of Albania; Communist Party of Bulgaria; Communist Party of Czechoslovakia; Communist Party of Hungary; Communist Party of Poland; Communist Party of Romania; Communist Party of Yugoslavia; Lenin; Socialism; Stalin; Trade Unions; Warsaw Pact

Masaryk, Jan (1886–1948)

Czechoslovak statesman and foreign minister before, during, and after World War II. The son of Tomáš G. Masaryk (1850–1937) and his American wife, Charlotte Garrigue (1850–1923), Masaryk left Austria-Hungary in 1907 for the United States. There, among other jobs, he worked as an ironworker and as a pianist in a movie theater, while studying part-time. In World War I he served in a Hungarian regiment. After the creation of an independent Czechoslovakia in 1918, Masaryk went into the foreign service, serving as chargé d'affaires in Washington, D.C., and as his legation's chancellor in London. In 1921 he became secretary to the foreign minister, Edvard Beneš (1884–1948). He became ambassador to London in 1925 and remained there until September 1938, when he resigned in protest over the Munich Pact, which turned over the Sudetenland to Nazi Germany. In July 1940 Masaryk was named foreign minister in Beneš's government-in-exile. In 1945 Masaryk accompanied Beneš to Moscow and later led the Czechoslovak delegation to the founding of the United Nations in San Francisco. Unfortunately, Soviet foreign minister Vyacheslav Molotov (1890–1986) had made it clear that Czech support was to be expected. When Stalin (1879–1953) insisted that Czechoslovakia refuse participation in the Marshall Plan, Masaryk lamented: "I went to Moscow a free minister, and I am coming back a servant of Stalin."

After the Communist takeover in 1948, Masaryk joined the government of Klement Gottwald (1896–1953) as foreign minster. However, two weeks later he was found dead under the windows of his Černín Palace apartment. The Communists quickly announced that he had committed suicide, but many of his friends believed that he had been murdered by the secret police.

Peter Hruby

Further reading

Davenport, Marcia. *Too Strong for Fantasy.* New York, 1968.

Kettner, Petr and I.M. Jedlička. *Proč zemřel Jan Masaryk?* Prague, 1990.

Lockhart, Sir R.H. Bruce. *Jan Masaryk: A Personal Memoir.* New York, 1951.

Sterling, Claire. *The Masaryk Case.* New York, 1968.

Zeman, Zbyněk A.B. *The Masaryks: The Making of Czechoslovakia.* New York, 1976.

See also Edvard Beneš; Charlotte Garrigue; Klement Gottwald; Marshall Plan; Tomáš G. Masaryk; Vyacheslav Molotov; Munich Pact; Stalin

Masaryk, Tomáš Garrigue (1850–1937)

Philosopher, statesman, and founder and first president of Czechoslovakia (1918–35). The son of a coachman on imperial estates in southern Moravia, Masaryk worked his way through secondary schools to the University of Vienna, where he obtained a doctorate in history in 1876 and a docentship in 1879. In 1882 he moved to the Czech University of Prague, where he soon became a central figure in intellectual and political circles. Not only did he establish a considerable reputation in the fields of sociology (he was an authority on suicide) and philosophy, he also became interested in contemporary Czech politics, which he analyzed against the background of Czech history in such works as *Česká otázka* (*Czech Question,* 1895) and *Naše nynější krise* (*Our Present Crisis,* 1895), as well as studies of Czech historical figures such as theologian Jan Hus (1370–1415), historian František Palacký (1798–1876), and Czech national leader Karel Havlíček (1821–56). He concluded that Czech spiritual development followed—and at times even preceded—the general development of Western societies. If Czech history had differed somewhat from that of other nations, it was in its accent on religion, especially the postulates of the Czech Reformation of the fifteenth century. He argued that these ideals not only gave meaning to Czech history but that they should also advise and guide Czech politics of the present and future.

His initial forays into politics proved to be a failure. He was elected to the Bohemian and Austrian parliaments on the ticket of the Young Czechs in 1891, but resigned two years later over differences with the party's leadership. Although he later founded and led two parties of his own between 1900 and 1914, they both remained small and irrelevant. Yet the outbreak of war in 1914 catapulted Masaryk into the position of national leader and international figure. He had previously supported the continued existence of the Habsburg monarchy (if it could be transformed into a federation of free nations), but he became convinced that only the dissolution of the empire could bring freedom. Leaving Prague in late 1914, he organized a Czechoslovak National Council in Paris

M and London aimed at creating a republic common to Czechs and Slovaks. By the late summer of 1918, his council, aided by support from Czech and Slovak emigrants in Allied countries and the military legions organized from among Czech and Slovak deserters from the Austro-Hungarian forces, was recognized as a provisional government of the Czechoslovak republic.

Following the capitulation of Austria-Hungary and the proclamation of the Czechoslovak republic on October 28, 1918, Masaryk was elected president. The popular "President-Liberator" would be reelected in 1922, 1927, and 1934. However, he did not have a direct role in governing the country. The republic's constitution, based on the French model, assigned the president only a ceremonial role as head of state. But to the point he could influence the politics of the state he founded, he did so successfully, as he relentlessly admonished political parties and the general public to work together for the consolidation and preservation of their state. Because of old age and illness, he resigned in 1935 and died two years later.

Josef Anderle

Further reading

Čapek, Milíč and Karel Hrubý, eds. *T.G. Masaryk in Perspective: Comments and Criticism.* Washington, D.C., 1981.

Herban, Jan. *T.G. Masaryk,* 3 vols. Prague, 1926–27.

Korbel, Josef. *Twentieth Century Czechoslovakia.* New York, 1977.

Masaryk, Thomas G. *The Making of a State.* Prague, 1927.

———. *President Masaryk Tells His Story.* Prague, 1934.

Szporluk, Roman. *The Political Thought of Thomas G. Masaryk.* Boulder, Colorado, 1981.

Winters, Stanley B., Robert B. Pynsent, and Harry Hanak, eds. *T.G. Masaryk (1850–1937),* 3 vols. London, 1989–90.

See also Edvard Beneš; Charlotte Garrigue; Czech Mafia; Karel Havlíček; Národni Výbor; František Palacký; Philosophy; Young Czechs

Matejko, Jan (1838–93)

Polish painter and Poland's most outstanding creator of historical and battle scenes. Matejko was born in Kraków and studied art there and in Munich and Vienna. Several visits to France and other countries completed his comprehensive international experience. Matejko nevertheless created his own way of expression. His huge, expressive canvases were realistic in their composition and detail while providing a baroque exuberance, theatricality, and emotion.

Matejko's creative activity took place while Poland was under foreign rule. Thus, his paintings carried a mission to preserve the national identity. The early works *Stańczyk* (1862), *Kazanie Skargi* (*The Sermon of Skarga,* 1864), and *Reytan* (1867) were critical accusations of the past. His later paintings *Batory pod Pskowem* (*Bathory at Pskov,* 1872), *Bitwa pod Grunwaldem* (*Battle at Grunwald,* 1879), and *Hołd pruski* (*Prussian Homage,* 1882) glorified the nation's historic military victories. His work is significant for both artistic and documentary values. The cycle of drawings *Poczet królów i książąt polskich* (*Body of Polish Kings and Princes*), which included portraits of all national rulers, was preceded by a precise historical study. His outstanding achievements were the murals in St. Mary's Church in Kraków (1889–91). Matejko received numerous international awards and was a member of many foreign art academies. As a professor and (after 1873) as head of the Kraków School of Fine Art, he taught many prominent Polish painters.

Marta Tobolczyk

Further reading

Krawczyk, J. *Matejko i historia.* Warsaw, 1990.

Malinowski, Jerzy and Krystyna Sroczyńska. *Matejko: Obrazy olejne.* Warsaw, 1993.

Michałowski, J.M. *Jan Matejko.* Warsaw, 1979.

Sroczyńska, Krystyna. *Matejko: Obrazy olejne. Catalogue.* Warsaw, 1993.

Suchodolski, Bogdan. *A History of Polish Culture.* Warsaw, 1986.

See also Polish Art

Matica Hrvatska

Oldest existing Croat cultural institution, which furthered literary and intellectual endeavor in the Croat lands more than any other organization. Founded in Zagreb as the Matica Ilirska (Illyrian Foundation) in February 1842, the society formally changed its name to Matica Hrvatska (Croat Foundation) in November 1874.

The Matica originated within the organizational framework of the Illyrian Reading Club, established in Zagreb in 1838 by Count Janko Drašković (1770–1856), who also acted as the Matica's first president from 1842 to 1850. Its founders were all proponents of the Illyrian Movement, which represented the initial stage of the Croat national awakening. In the 1840s Croatia was increasingly threatened by attempts at Magyarization. The Matica was established in an attempt to counteract these pressures in the realm of culture by spreading the use of the "Illyrian" (Croatian) language. It was modeled after similar foundations among the Czechs and the Serbs. As a national cultural society, its main purpose was to publish educational and literary works, both books and journals, in Croatian. To this end, it published works from the sixteenth and seventeenth centuries, such as Ivan Gundulić's (1589–1638) epic *Osman* in 1844, which were written in the national language, as well as works by contemporary writers, linguists, and poets. It also published translated editions of Western classics. The Matica was originally organized around two committees: the Literary-Artistic and the Economic. The former determined which works were to be published and also organized cultural exhibitions, whereas the latter looked after finances. The Matica was funded through membership dues and the financial contributions of patriots. Its activities were not limited exclusively to publishing, for it also organized artistic and historical exhibitions. The Matica continues to play an important role in Croat cultural life.

Mark Biondich

Further reading
Ravlić, Jakša. *Matica Hrvatska 1842–1962.* Zagreb, 1963.

See also Illyrian Movement; Magyarization

Matica Slovenská

Institution to promote Slovak culture. Historically, the Matica slovenská has symbolized Slovak national identity. Founded in 1863, the Matica slovenská originated as a cultural society to foster Slovak literature and fine arts. Although Emperor Franz Joseph (1830–1916) donated one thousand florin to launch the effort, the society relied on membership subscriptions. The organization, which was located in Turčiansky Svätý Martin, held its first formal meeting on August 4, 1863; the 984 members elected Bishop Stefan Moyses (1797–1869) president. Slovak Protestants, however, remained the driving force behind the institute's expanding array of literary, cultural, and educational activities. It established a library, museum, and publishing house. The institute translated literary works and published folklore, poetry, and historical materials in Slovak. It advanced education by printing school books and assisting Slovak students. In 1875 the Matica slovenská fell victim to the Hungarian government's renewed Magyarization policy. Charging it with promoting "Pan-Slavism," the government closed the institute, seized its assets, and shipped the library to Budapest.

In 1919, following the creation of Czechoslovakia, the Matica slovenská was revived. With the facility at Martin reopened, the institute resumed its publishing, educational, and cultural activities. It also established local branches. In the mid-1950s, under Communist rule, the Matica slovenská's operations were curtailed; it was made a state institution and functioned essentially as a library and repository. During the 1960s and 1970s, its cultural functions enjoyed a rebirth. After 1989, in the newly constituted Czech and Slovak Federative Republic, the Matica slovenská's activities included promoting Slovak culture and Slovak political independence.

June Granatir Alexander

Further reading
Berta, John. "The Matica Slovenská and Its Role in Slovak Cultural Development, 1919 to 1939." Ph.D. diss., State University of New York at Binghampton, 1983.
Haviar, Štefan and Ivan Kučma. *V pamäti národa: Kniha o Matici slovenskej.* Martin, Slovakia, 1988.
Národná svetlica: Výber dokumentov k dejinám Matice slovenskej, comp. by Michal Eliáš and Vojtech Šarluška. Martin, Slovakia, 1988.

See also Franz Joseph; Magyarization; Pan-Slavism; Slovak Culture

May Coup (1926)

Coup launched by Marshal Józef Piłsudski on May 12, 1926, which effectively ended a period

M of parliamentary government in Poland and ushered in an era of authoritarian rule. Piłsudski (1867–1935), recognized as the founder of the Polish state and army, served as commander in chief of the armed forces (1918–21) and as head of state (1918–22). By 1923, however, he had resigned his remaining military positions and entered into a self-imposed exile at his estate outside Warsaw. The formation of a center-right government, the members of which (Piłsudski believed) were morally responsible for the assassination of newly elected President Gabriel Narutowicz (1865–1922), was the foremost cause of his withdrawal from public life.

Piłsudski remained politically active, demanding that the military high command be organized so that it would be free from parliamentary control. The legislature's refusal to adopt this measure, the instability of successive governments, and Poland's growing international isolation appeared to push the state toward crisis. Such an atmosphere inspired the widespread perception, in the spring of 1926, that only the marshal could save the country.

Supported by a number of detachments, Piłsudski marched on Warsaw on May 12. Following a dramatic confrontation on the Poniatowski Bridge between Piłsudski and President Stanisław Wojciechowski (1869–1953), three days of street fighting ensued. Railroad workers affiliated with the Socialists refused to transport troops loyal to the government to the capital. To avoid civil war, Wojciechowski and the government resigned on May 14.

Even though Piłsudski refused the position of president, the May Coup made him the leader of Poland for the rest of his life. He took firm command of the army and exercised political control by installing ministers who implemented his intentions and policies.

Piłsudski's coup is one of the more contentious aspects of the historiography of interwar Poland. Sympathetic scholars argue that he acted to extract the state from economic and political crisis, and to remove the army, which he considered to be the sole guarantor of the state's existence, from the instable influence of parliamentary politics. Others suggest that Piłsudski himself was partially responsible for the crisis situation and that his action was above all a grab for power.

Robert M. Ponichtera

Further reading

Garlicki, Andrzej. *Przewrót majowy.* Warsaw, 1987.
Jędrzejewicz, Wacław. *Piłsudski: A Life for Poland.* New York, 1982.
Przewrót majowy 1926 w relacjach i dokumentach, ed. by Eugeniusz Kozłowski. Warsaw, 1987.
Roos, Hans. *A History of Modern Poland,* trans. by J.R. Foster. New York, 1966.
Rothschild, Joseph. *Piłsudski's Coup d'Etat.* New York, 1966.

See also Józef Piłsudski; Stanisław Wojciechowski

Mažuranić, Ivan (1814–90)

Croatian literary figure and politician, and the first commoner to serve as *ban* (governor) of Habsburg Croatia (1873–80). Born in Novi Vinodol and educated in both Croatia and Hungary, Mažuranić participated actively in the Illyrian Movement—the political and cultural movement that advocated Croatian rights, the cultural unity of all South Slavs, and the adoption of a standard literary norm for Croatian. He is the author of what is usually considered the best Illyrian work, *Smrt Smail-age Čengića* (*The Death of Smail-Aga Čengić,* 1846), an epic glorification of religious warfare between Christian Montenegrins and Muslim Slavs. In addition, the prolific Mažuranić wrote historical and philological works; translated from Latin, Greek, Italian, Czech, and Russian; coauthored a "German-Illyrian Dictionary"; and served for fourteen years (1858–72) as president of Matica Hrvatska, the principal Croatian cultural organization. Although a lifelong advocate of Yugoslavism and a signer with the Serbian language reformer Vuk Karadžić (1787–1864) of the abortive Literary Agreement (1850), which advocated a common literary language for Croats and Serbs, Mažuranić and Karadžić differed over the basis for such a common language. While the latter wished to build solely on the peasant language, Mažuranić espoused a codification that built on the Renaissance and early modern literature of the Dalmatian coast, as well as on contemporary peasant speech.

Considered a radical in the Revolution of 1848 because of his call for the equality of all nationalities in Hungary, Mažuranić later embarked on a career in the Habsburg bureaucracy. As court chancellor for Croatia in the 1860s, he headed the Independent National Party, which advocated Croatian cooperation with Habsburg constitutional experiments. As *ban* after the 1873 revision of the *Nagodba* (the legal arrangement that regulated the position of Croatia within Austria-Hungary) and now a member of the National Party, Mažuranić oversaw an extensive liberal reform program, affecting in particular civil liberties, the judiciary, and education. He also faced the refugee and political crisis caused by the Bosnian uprising of 1875, the opposition of both the Catholic Church and many Serbs to greater secularization of the schools, and increasing Hungarian pressure on Croatian autonomy. Resigning in 1880, he went into political opposition.

James P. Krokar

Further reading

Barac, Antun. *Mažuranić*. Zagreb, 1945.

Krokar, James P. "Liberal Reform in Croatia, 1872–75: The Beginnings of Modern Croatia under Ban Ivan Mažuranić." Ph.D. diss., Indiana University, 1980.

Šidak, Jaroslav. "Ivan Mažuranić kao političar," in *Studije iz hrvatske povijesti XIX stoljeća.* Zagreb, 1973.

Živančević, Milorad. "Ivan Mažuranić." *Rad JAZU 333* (1963): 31–237.

See also Croatian Literature; Illyrian Movement; Vuk Karadžić; Matica Hrvatska; *Nagodba;* Revolutions of 1848; Serbo-Croatian Language; Yugoslavism

Media

During the Communist period, the means of mass communication were owned and run by the state. Media were seen mostly as propaganda tools, and censorship was widely practiced. Governments in Eastern Europe were able to exercise almost full control over the information environment. Censorship institutions in different countries were organized in different ways—from clearly identified censorship in Poland to loosely structured, but no less efficient, self-regulation in Hungary.

Since 1989, most print and some broadcast media have been privatized. The new owners are usually either recently established political parties or business organizations. Today there is international investment in the media of all East European countries, but it is predominantly concentrated in Hungary and the Czech Republic. Foreign invest-

ments originate mostly from Germany, the United Kingdom, France, Italy, and the United States.

All East European countries are working on passing new legislation to regulate the media, ownership issues, issues of media content, journalistic standards, and copyright problems. Legislative efforts are in different stages in various countries, and changes involving media legislation and deregulation are evolving.

In studies of international news flows, Eastern Europe is usually referred to as the Second World, a designation identifying countries under Communist control. In the past, the major sources of international information for East European countries have been the Soviet agency, TASS, and occasionally the Western Big Four (Reuters, Presse-France, United Press International, and Associated Press). National news agencies have operated as well: ATSH (Albania); BTA (Bulgaria); CTK (Czechoslovakia); MTI (Hungary); PAP (Poland); Agerpres (Romania); and Tanjug (Yugoslavia).

The major newspapers during the Communist period were traditionally the daily official publications of the Communist party in power: *Zeri i Populit* (Albania); *Rabotnichesko Delo* (Bulgaria); *Rudé Právo* (Czecholsovakia); *Népszabadság* (Hungary); *Trybuna Ludu* (Poland); *Scînteia* (Romania); and *Politica* (Yugoslavia). After 1989, a large number of newspapers have appeared that reflect a much wider spectrum of ideas and interests. Among the most popular are *Rilindja Demokratika* (Albania); *Duma Demokratsia* (Bulgaria); *Lidovi Noviny* (Czech Republic); *Slobodna Dalmacija* (Croatia); *Magyar Hírlap* (Hungary); *Tygodnik Powszechny, Zycie Warszawy,* and *Rzeczpospolita* (Poland); *România Libera* (Romania); *Národná Obroda* (Slovakia); and *Politika* and *Naša Borba* (Yugoslavia). Since 1989, a number of English-language newspapers have appeared, such as the *Prague Post* (Czech Republic), *Warsaw Voice* (Poland), and the *Budapest Sun* (Hungary). Today newspapers operate in a situation of almost constant newsprint shortage, and often access to newsprint becomes a political issue. A large variety of weeklies and magazines are also available. Various scholarly journals are published, mostly in the national language. Publishing houses that were once run by the state are now in the process of privatization. The state-run system of distribution of print materials is no longer in place, and new alternative distribution agencies have appeared only

M gradually. Some publications in the former Yugoslavia have continued to exist despite difficult conditions, and newspapers such as *Oslobodjenie* in Bosnia have received international recognition.

In each country in Eastern Europe there has been usually one or two national radio channels. Before 1989, radio was a state monopoly run by the government. During the Communist period, a number of Western organizations engaged in cross-border broadcasting in the languages of the East European countries, although their broadcast operations were usually jammed. These were Radio Free Europe; the Voice of America; Deutsche Welle, Radio France International; and the British Broadcasting Company. Most of these operations continued broadcasting after 1989, since their emissions are no longer jammed. In 1994 Radio Free Europe was transformed into the Open Media Research Institute and moved its headquarters to Prague and Budapest. Since 1989, private radio broadcasters have appeared in all East European countries. Licenses have been granted and bandwidths have been allocated mostly to private radio stations that operate locally.

Television broadcasting became a feature of the media landscape in the 1950s. Television networks were entirely controlled by the state until 1989. Most of the East European countries participated in the Organisation Intérnationale de Radio et Télévision, an international broadcasting organization dissolved in 1992. Since 1989, owing to its significance as a major national medium, television has remained more or less under government control. In some countries, new private television companies have been launched and function successfully (such as Nova TV in the Czech Republic), while in other cases governments have delayed passing the relevant legislation, and private television stations have been licensed on an arbitrary basis (Hungary, Bulgaria). As a result of globalization and deregulation, as well as the introduction of new technologies, international channels now are received in the broadcast space of Eastern Europe.

The region's telecommunications infrastructure is fairly obsolete and needs basic renovation. Major Western companies are under contract to modernize the telephone systems, as well as to introduce other telecommunications services. New features have been computers and the access for more people to electronic means of communication.

Alternative media practices have always been very important for the cultural traditions of East European countries, especially when the central government suppressed freedom of speech. The most prominent examples of dissent included Poland's Solidarity newspaper, *Gazeta Wyborcza*, edited by Adam Michnik (1946–), the typewritten samizdat (underground) publications in Czechoslovakia, run by writers like Václav Havel (1936–), and the broadcasts of Belgrade TV Studio B.

In most East European countries communication science is still considered a part of journalism education. Only in the 1990s has communication started to develop as a recognized scholarly discipline. There has been a concerted effort to improve journalism education, especially in Poland, Slovenia, and Hungary. Many major international agencies have participated in programs aimed at creating and establishing new standards for running the media in a democratic way.

Dina Iordanova

Further reading

Becker, Jorg and Tamas Szecsko, eds. *Europe Speaks to Europe: International Information Flows between Eastern and Western Europe.* New York, 1989.

Contarnine, Claude, ed. *Media in Eastern and Western Europe: Shared Problems, Shared Solutions?* Manchester, 1991.

Dennis, Everette E. and Jon Vanden Heuvel. *Emerging Voices: East European Media in Transition: A Report of the Gannett Foundation Task Force on Press Freedom in Eastern Europe.* New York, 1990.

Goban-Klas, Tomasz. *The Orchestration of the Media: The Politics of Mass Communications in Communist Poland and the Aftermath.* Boulder, Colorado, 1994.

Gross, Peter. *Mass Media in Revolution and National Development: The Romanian Laboratory.* Iowa City, Iowa, 1996.

Haraszti, M. *The Velvet Prison: Artists under State Socialism.* New York, 1987.

Hester, Al and L. Earle Reybold, eds. *Revolutions for Freedom: The Mass Media in Eastern and Central Europe.* Athens, Georgia, 1991.

Hester, Al, L. Earle Reybold, and Kimberly Conger, eds. *The Post-Communist Press in Eastern and Central Europe: New Studies.* Athens, Georgia, 1992.

HPaletz, David, Karol Jakubowicz, and Pavao Novosel, eds. *Glasnost and After: Media and Change in Central and Eastern Europe.* Cresskill, New Jersey, 1995.

Thompson, Mark. *Forging War: The Media in Serbia, Croatia, and Bosnia-Hercegovina.* New York, 1994.

See also Censorship; Miklós Haraszti; Václav Havel; Law; Adam Michnik; Press; Privatization

Mediterranean Agreements

Two multilateral agreements of 1887 designed to prevent any extension of Russian power into the eastern Mediterranean basin. Britain and Italy exchanged notes on February 12, 1887, agreeing to joint consultation to preserve the status quo in the Mediterranean, including the Aegean and Black Seas. Some months later, Austria-Hungary and Spain joined the agreement. The continuing decline of the Ottoman Empire inspired a second agreement, framed as a treaty among Britain, Italy, and Austria-Hungary and signed on December 12, 1887. This treaty foresaw joint action to prevent Russian encroachment in the Balkans and/or the Near East in the event that the Turks surrendered their rights or positions in those areas. The two agreements were important pieces in Britain's long struggle in the late nineteenth century to contain Russian expansion in the Balkans, the Near East, and Central Asia.

Robert Mark Spaulding

Further reading

Bridge, F.R. *The Great Powers and the European States System, 1815–1914.* New York, 1980.

———. *The Habsburg Monarchy among the Great Powers, 1815–1918.* New York, 1990.

Jelavich, Barbara. *A Century of Russian Foreign Policy, 1814–1914.* Philadelphia, 1964.

See also Eastern Question

Mendel, Johann (Gregor) (1822–84)

Austrian monk who formulated the basic laws of heredity. Mendel was born in Austrian Silesia, now part of the Czech Republic. After two years of study at the Philosophical Institute in Olmütz (Czech, Olomouc), he joined the Augustinian monastery in Brünn (Czech, Brno) and took the religious name Gregor. The monastery was a center of learning, especially in science, and Mendel was sent to Vienna for more advanced study. Upon returning, from 1856 to 1864, he bred, planted, observed, sorted, and counted nearly thirty thousand plants, most of them the edible pea *Pisum sativum.* By carefully recording the traits of successive generations—such as smooth pea vs. wrinkled pea or tall plant vs. short plant—he deduced what are now called the law of segregation and the law of independent assortment. Mendel also noted that some inherited factors, what we now call "genes," act in a "dominant" role and others in a "recessive" role. These findings on inheritance form the basis for the modern science of genetics.

His results were presented to the Natural Sciences Society of Brünn in 1865 and published soon after, but his work remained virtually unknown for thirty-five years. Around 1900, the same findings were announced independently by three scientists, each of whom learned of Mendel's experiments and gave him proper credit.

Mendel was elected abbot of the monastery in 1868, effectively ending his research. However, he remained the top authority on meteorology in the area around Brünn.

Mark Sand

Further reading

Gillispie, Charles Coulston, ed. *Dictionary of Scientific Biography,* vol. 9. New York, 1976.

Orel, Vâtéezslav. *Mendel.* Oxford. 1984.

Porter, Roy, ed. *The Biographical Dictionary of Scientists,* 2d ed. New York, 1994.

Měšťanská Beseda (Burghers' Club)

First social club of the Czech wealthy and educated middle class in Prague. After the first application of thirty Prague citizens for the founding of a club, signed on November 12, 1844, was rejected by the municipal authorities, a new action taken by ninety others on January 21, 1845, was more successful. The governorship of Bohemia approved the foundation of the Burghers' Club on July 18, 1845. According to legal restrictions, the club was a nonpolitical organization devoted to the education and entertainment of its members. Its public activities began on January 31, 1846. Although the group's slogan, Equality and Concord, expressed the main interests of the Czech middle class (in competition with the more influential German

M bourgeoisie in Bohemia), the club was strictly bilingual during its first two decades, and it embraced, besides Czech speakers, German-speaking sympathizers with Czech national endeavors. A reading hall provided members with Austrian and foreign newspapers, books, and journals. Lectures, concerts, and dancing parties supported social communication among the Czechs in Prague.

Only proprietors and people of higher education with the right of domicile in Prague could become members of the club; the lower social classes had no access. In March/April 1848 the Měšťanská Beseda was the principal place for the signing of two petitions to the government in Vienna and for the reading of the letter of historian František Palacký (1798–1876) declining the participation of the Czechs in the German National Assembly. The club was a model for similar organizations throughout Bohemia, such as Chrudim in 1847, Příbram in 1849, Rakovník in 1850, and Plzeň, Mladá Boleslav, and Tábor in 1862. In the 1860s the name "Měšťanská Beseda" became connected with the upper stratum of the Czech middle class, while artisans and other opponents of the notables established other associations in many Czech towns under the name of Občanská Beseda (Citizens' Club).

Jiří Kořalka

Further reading

Cohen, Gary B. *The Politics of Ethnic Survival: Germans in Prague, 1861–1914.* Princeton, New Jersey, 1981.

Pech, Stanley Z. *The Czech Revolution of 1848.* Chapel Hill, North Carolina, 1969.

Schwarz, František V. *Památník Besedy Měšťanské na oslavu padesátileté činnosti spolku 1845/6 až 1895/6.* Prague, 1896.

Stompe, Alois. *Devadesát let Besedy Měšťanské v Praze.* Prague, 1936.

Tobolka, Zdeněk V., ed. *Karla Havlíčka Borovského Politické spisy,* vol. 1, Prague, 1900.

See also František Palacký

Meštrović, Ivan (1883–1962)

Most important Yugoslav sculptor in the twentieth century and one of few who immediately gained international fame. Meštrović was educated in Vienna (1901–5). Most of his early works deal with symbolical subjects (*A Thinker, Passion,* and *The Well of Life,* his first masterpiece under Rodin's [1840–1917] influence). Meštrović's support of South Slavic political unification is evident in his choice of subjects at the turn of the century, particularly in his famous *Kosovo Cycle* (Paris, 1907) which deals with themes from Serbian heroic history (*Banović Strahinja, Miloš Obilić, Big Widow,* and *Marko the Prince*).

During World War I, he turned toward reliefs in wood with religious subjects. By the end of the war, more cheerful themes emerged in his work (feminine figures with musical instruments). In the interwar period he worked on large public monuments in Yugoslavia (the mausoleum of the Račić family in Cavtat; the Avala mausoleum; and monuments of Marko Marulić [1450–1524], Grgur Ninski [d. c. 928], and Josip Juraj Strossmayer [1815–1905]) and a number of sensual female nudes. These works reveal classical features, inspired by Michelangelo (1475–1564).

Meštrović left Yugoslavia in 1942 and came to America in 1947, where he took up teaching in Syracuse, New York, and South Bend, Indiana. During this period, he worked on biblical subjects and portraits.

In all, Meštrović made almost one thousand sculptures, mostly in stone or wood. He also worked as an architect and near the end of his life as a painter and writer. One of the founders of modern Croatian sculpture, he strongly influenced his contemporaries Frano Kršinić (1897–1982) and Antun Augustinčić (1900–1979). Most of his works are in galleries in the Croatian cities of Split, Zagreb, and Vrpolje.

Svetlana Rakić

Further reading

Adamec, Ana. *Ivan Meštrović 1883–1962.* Belgrade, 1984.

Barbić, Vesna. *Atelje Meštrović.* Zagreb, 1973.

Ivančić, Jasna. *Građa za bibliografiju Ivana Meštrovića od 1899–1993.* Zagreb, 1993.

Kečkemet, Duško. *Ivan Meštrović.* Belgrade, 1983.

See also Croatian Art

Mészáros, Marta (1931–)

Hungarian film director. Born in Budapest, Mészáros was raised and educated in the Soviet

Union. After a career as a documentary filmmaker, she made her first feature film in 1968. She has been interested in exploring the problems of women in contemporary society. Though celebrated as a feminist filmmaker, she prefers not to make a public commitment to feminist causes. Mészáros has made some of her films in France and Canada. Her autobiographical *Diary Trilogy* is a reflection on personal issues of adolescence and coming-of-age in the time of Stalinism. Her feature films include *Eltdvozott nap* (*The Girl,* 1968); *Holdudvar* (*Binding Sentiments,* 1969); *Szabad lélegzet* (*Riddance,* 1973); *Orökbefogadás* (*Adoption,* 1975); *Kilenc hónap* (*Nine Months,* 1979); *Ok ketten* (*The Two of Them/Women,* 1977); *Olyan, mint otthon* (*Just Like at Home,* 1978); *Utközben* (*On the move,* 1979); *Orökség* (*The Heiresses,* 1980); *Mother and Daughter/Anna* (1981); *Délibábok országa* (*Land of Miracles,* 1983); *Napló gyermekeimnek* (*Diary for My Children,* 1982); *Napó szerelmeimnek* (*Diary for My Loves,* 1987); *Piroska és a farkas* (*Bye-Bye Red Riding Hood,* 1989); *Napló apámnak, anyámnak* (*Diary for My Father and Mother,* 1990); and *A magzat* (*Fetus,* 1993).

Dina Iordanova

Further reading

Portuges, Catherine. *Screen Memories: The Hungarian Cinema of Marta Mészáros.* Bloomington, Indiana, 1993.

See also Cinema

Metternich-Winneburg, Prince Clemens Wenzel Lothar von (1773–1859)

Habsburg statesman whose conservative policies toward domestic politics and foreign affairs had a long-lasting impact on the development of Central and Eastern Europe. A native of the Rhineland, Metternich entered the Habsburg diplomatic service in 1801 and quickly rose to prominence, becoming foreign minister of the Austrian Empire in 1809. In 1821 he was given the additional title of house, court, and state chancellor. Metternich's first diplomatic triumph occurred in 1813, when he succeeded in extricating the Austrian Empire from a burdensome and dangerous alliance with Napoléon (1769–1821) and, subsequently, maneuvering the empire to a leading role in the anti-Napoleonic, allied coalition. A milestone in his

career was the Congress of Vienna of 1814–15, at which, through skillful diplomacy, he greatly enhanced the prestige of the empire as a leading Great Power and as a dominating force in Central and East Central Europe. Most noteworthy in this regard was Metternich's role in checking Russia's plan for the complete absorption of Poland and in attaining for Austria a leading position in the newly created German Confederation. At the height of his career, he became one of the most influential advisers to the Habsburg emperor, Francis I (1768–1835), as well as Europe's leading international statesman. He was forced to resign on the outbreak of the Revolutions in 1848.

While Metternich often proved pragmatic and flexible in his conduct of politics and diplomacy, he nonetheless remained an implacable foe of the French Revolution and all that he believed emanated from it. Throughout his long career, he set himself against liberalism, constitutionalism, and nationalism. Within the Austrian Empire, he sponsored active police surveillance and censorship that aimed at stifling all challenges to the absolutist Habsburg regime. Abroad, he focused his considerable prestige and influence on buttressing and coordinating the conservative policies of Europe's reigning monarchs and in maintaining international peace, a condition he deemed essential both for the welfare of the exhausted and vulnerable Habsburg realm and for the survival of the general conservative, monarchical order established throughout Europe after 1815.

Lawrence J. Flockerzie

Further reading

Billinger, Robert D., Jr. *Metternich and the German Question: States' Rights and Federal Duties, 1820–1834.* Newark, New Jersey, 1991.

Guillaume de Bertier de Sauvigny. *Metternich: Staatsmann und Diplomat für Österreich und den Frieden.* Gernsbach, Germany, 1988.

Kraehe, Enno E. *Metternich's German Policy,* 2 vols. Princeton, New Jersey, 1963 and 1983.

Schroeder, Paul W. *Metternich's Diplomacy at Its Zenith, 1820–1823.* Austin, Texas, 1962.

Sked, Alan. "The Metternich System, 1815–48," in Alan Sked, ed. *Europe's Balance of Power, 1814–1848.* London, 1977, 98–121.

See also Congress of Vienna; Habsburg Empire; Napoléon; Revolutions of 1848

M

Michael (1921–)

Former king of Romania. After the death of his grandfather, King Ferdinand (1865–1927), in July 1927, the young Prince Michael assumed the throne under a regency. Michael's father, Prince Carol (1893–1953), had earlier renounced his claim to the throne and fled with his mistress to Paris. But in June 1930 Carol returned to Bucharest and, supported by most political parties, assumed the throne as Carol II.

After a decade-long reign marked by scandal and ineptitude, Carol I abdicated in favor of Michael in September 1940. The new king's powers were immediately curtailed by the wartime authoritarian leader, Marshal Ion Antonescu (1882–1946), who took the title Conducătorul (Supreme Leader) and allied Romania with Nazi Germany. On August 23, 1944, Michael led a coup against the regime, arrested Antonescu, and switched Romania's allegiance to the Allies.

After the war, the king proved to be a thorn in the side of Romania's Communists and an impediment to full Soviet domination. His trip to London for the wedding of Princess Elizabeth (his second cousin) in November 1947 allowed leaders of the Romanian Communist Party to formulate plans for his elimination. Shortly after his return, Romania was declared a "people's republic" and Michael was forced to abdicate on December 30, 1947, and flee abroad with the royal family. After traveling widely in Europe and America, he worked as a pilot and eventually settled in Versoix, Switzerland, with his wife and five daughters. Since 1947, Michael has been allowed to return to Romania only once, for two days in April 1992.

Charles King

Further reading

Ciobanu, Mircea. *Convorbiri cu Mihai I al Romîniei.* Bucharest, 1991.

Ionescu, Ghita. *Communism in Romania, 1944–1962.* Oxford, 1964.

See also Ion Antonescu; Carol II; Ferdinand

Michnik, Adam (1946–)

Polish political activist and dissident. As a student studying history at the University of Warsaw, Michnik organized a group of radical socialists known as the Commandos, who criticized the Communist Party. Arrested and detained for two months in 1964, Michnik went on to play a prominent role in the student movement at the University of Warsaw protesting the government's education and cultural polices in 1968. He joined the dissident group KOR in 1977. Author of *The Church, the Left, and Dialogue* (1975), and the essay "New Evolutionism" (1976), Michnik established himself not only as a major figure critiquing communism in Poland but also as a political thinker recognized worldwide. A lecturer for the unofficial "Flying University," one of the institutions of Polish dissidence in the 1970s that offered courses in subjects considered to be taboo by the authorities, Michnik became an adviser for the Solidarity trade union movement in 1980. With the imposition of martial law on December 13, 1981, he was interned, tried, and sentenced in 1984 with other union activists for political crimes against the Polish state. Amnestied later that year, Michnik continued to speak out against the regime. A member of the Polish Round Table negotiations ending Communist rule in Poland, he later became a critic of Solidarity leader and earlier Polish President Lech Wałęsa (1943–). Michnik was elected to the Sejm (Polish parliament) in 1989.

Peter Lavelle

Further reading

Michnik, Adam. *The Church and the Left.* Chicago, 1993.

———. *Letters from Prison and Other Essays.* Berkeley, California, 1985.

———. "The New Evolutionsim." *Survey* 21, no. 4 (1976).

———. *Szanse polskiej demokracji.* London, 1984.

———. "What We Want to Do and What We Can Do." *Telos* 47 (1981).

See also Communist Party of Poland; Flying University; KOR; Solidarity; Lech Wałęsa

Mickiewicz, Adam Bernard (1798–1855)

Poland's national poet. Like many other important Poles, Mickiewicz belonged to the impoverished nobility that lived in Poland's eastern borderlands. He attended Wilno University, but his involvement with student secret societies led to his arrest and deportation in 1824 to Russia, where poet Alexander Pushkin (1799–1837) befriended him.

Mickiewicz's first works, *Poetry I* (1822) and *Poetry II* (1823), abandoned the conventional classical form, substituting instead a romantic foundation for Polish belles lettres. His *Crimean Sonnets* (1826) emphasized feelings and emotion, and *Konrad Wallenrod* (1828) exalted patriotism as the supreme virtue.

Leaving Russia in 1829, Mickiewicz traveled to Western Europe but did not participate in the November Uprising in 1830 against the Russians. However, he joined the Polish émigrés from that struggle, settling in Paris in 1832. In that year he wrote *Books of the Polish Nation and the Polish Pilgrims,* which drew a conscious parallel between the fate of Jesus Christ and that of the Polish nation. This sense of Polish messianism, which hinted at the resurrection of a morally pure and sanctified Polish nation after a cruel and unjust death, also surfaced in *Dziady* (1833). In 1834 Mickiewicz wrote his masterpiece, *Pan Tadeusz,* an epic poem describing gentry life in rural Lithuania on the eve of Napoléon's (1769–1821) invasion of Russia in 1812.

With *Pan Tadeusz,* Mickiewicz's most productive years ended. In 1839 he was appointed professor of Roman literature at the University of Lausanne. He returned to Paris in 1840 to assume the chair of Slavonic literature at the Collège de France, but he soon fell under the spell of Polish mystic Andrzej Towiański (1799–1878). Although personally close to the moderate Prince Adam Czartoryski (1770–1861), Mickiewicz enthusiastically supported the Revolutions of 1848. After failing to raise a Polish legion for the Italian revolution that year, he edited *La Tribune des Peuples,* a radical newspaper. With the onset of the Crimean War (1853–56), Mickiewicz went to the Ottoman Empire to raise a Polish force to fight against Russia. In the midst of his efforts, he died in Constantinople.

Frank W. Thackeray

Further reading

Dernałowicz, Maria. *Adam Mickiewicz,* trans. by Halina Filipowicz. Warsaw, 1981.

Kridl, Manfred, ed. *Adam Mickiewicz, Poet of Poland.* New York, 1951.

Lednicki, Wacław, ed. *Adam Mickiewicz in World Literature.* Berkeley, California, 1956.

Weintraub, Wiktor. *The Poetry of Adam Mickiewicz.* Leiden, 1954.

Welsh, David. *Adam Mickiewicz.* New York, 1966.

See also Crimean War; Adam Czartoryski; November Uprising; Polish Émigrés; Polish Literature; Revolutions of 1848

Mieroslawski, Ludwik (1814–78)

Polish revolutionary and historian. Born in France of a Polish military officer, Mieroslawski played a major role as a leader and inspiration in Poland's struggle for independence throughout most of the nineteenth century. A participant in the failed Polish November Uprising of 1830 against Russian domination, Mieroslawski was later forced to leave Poland for France to join other Polish revolutionaries in exile. From 1834 he was a member of the Mlada Polska (Young Poland) literary group and in 1843 a leading figure in the Towarzystwo Demokratyczne Polskie (Polish Democratic Society). Arrested in Prussian-occupied Poland and sentenced to death by the Prussians for planning a general uprising in 1846, Mieroslawski was later freed as events unfolded in Berlin during the Revolutions of 1848. Not being able to directly help his Polish compatriots in partitioned Poland, Mieroslawski, like many other Poles in exile, participated in the Sicilian and Palatinate movements for independence after 1848. His revolutionary activities served as an inspiration and authority for many Poles participating in the failed uprising of January 1863 against the Russians. Not only a revolutionary, Mieroslawski was a prolific writer of Polish history (especially on the November insurrection), military strategy, and politics.

Peter Lavelle

Further reading

Tyrowicz, M. *Towarzystwo Demokratyczne Polskie: Przywodcy i kadry czlowkowskie 1832–1863.* Warsaw, 1964.

Zychowski, M. *Ludwik Mieroslawski.* Warsaw, 1963.

See also January Uprising; November Uprising; Revolutions of 1848; Young Poland

Mihailo Obrenović (1823–68)

Serbian monarch (1860–68) whose ambition was to rid the Balkans of the Turkish presence, promote domestic tranquility and modernization, and maintain absolute monarchical rule. Although he technically succeeded to the throne with the abdication

M of his father, Miloš (1780–1860) in 1838, Mihailo was forced to flee in 1842 when Alexander Karadjordjević (1806–85) became prince. He came to the throne following his father's brief return in 1859 and death in 1860.

Mihailo rid Serbia of whatever Turkish authority remained but was unsuccessful in his wider ambition of a general Balkan uprising. Domestically, he took great strides to end the discord with Karajordjević partisans. Surprised by Serbia's poverty, the backwardness of its agriculture, and the low cultural level of the people, he made modest gains in introducing the rule of law and in improving the economy. Mihailo did not believe that the mostly illiterate Serbs were prepared for democratic government. Historians agree that his greatest achievement was the creation of a national army.

Mihailo's troubles multiplied in the last three years of his reign, highlighted by his wife's affair with a foreigner and their agreement to divorce. Although she was of Hungarian background and a Roman Catholic, and she had never been accepted by the Orthodox Serbs, divorce in patriarchal Serbia was difficult to fathom by the population. Nevertheless, Mihailo's ministers would have accepted it as a personal matter, but Mihailo's determination to marry a teenage second cousin, an act regarded as incest by the canons of the Serbian Orthodox faith, lost him the services of his leading ministers. A carefully hatched plot to kill him succeeded in 1868, but Obrenović partisans in the army were able to save the throne for the dynasty, even though Mihailo had no children.

A person of vision and broad horizons, Mihailo gave unstintingly of his personal fortune. More reserved and formal than his father, he introduced pomp and ceremony at the court. European-educated, Mihailo built the opera house in Belgrade (which still stands). In the words of historian Slobodan Jovanović (1869–1958), Mihailo "was just, honest, noble; he had a high awareness of duty, much principle and steadfastness, patriotism. But he lacked a certain intellectual capacity that was required and he was indecisive." Yet of all of Serbia's rulers, the only one with a prominent statue in Belgrade is Mihailo.

Alex N. Dragnich

Further reading

Dragnich, Alex N. *The Development of Parliamentary Government in Serbia.* Boulder, Colorado, 1978.

Jovanović, Slobodan. *Druga vlada Miloša i Mihaila 1858–1868.* Belgrade, 1923.
Petrovich, Michael B. *A History of Modern Serbia,* 2 vols. New York, 1976.

See also Alexander Karadjordjević; Slobodan Jovanović; Miloš Obrenović

Mihailović, Dragoljub (Draža) (1893–1946)

Serbian military and nationalist leader of underground Serbian military forces during World War II. Mihailović is one of the most controversial figures in recent European history. From his headquarters at Ravna Gora, Colonel Mihailović organized remnants of the Yugoslav Royal Army after the German invasion in the spring of 1941. These bands bore the name "Chetniks," a term that evoked strong connotations of freedom fighters, especially in earlier struggles against the Ottoman Turks. However, at issue was whom they held to be their chief foe: the Axis or domestic Communists.

At first, Mihailović, who had been promoted to general and then minister of war by the government-in-exile in London, enjoyed Allied support. But by the end of 1943, the British and Americans had elected to support Tito (1892–1980), leader of the antifascist Partisans.

Cooperation had broken down between the Partisans and the Chetniks early in the war over ideological and tactical issues. Mihailović supported a restoration of the prewar Yugoslav government, based on the Serbian ruling family of Karadjordjević. Thus, he fought both the Communist-led Partisans of Tito and the Axis occupiers. After the war, the socialist government executed Mihailović as part of its bloody settling of accounts with nationalist forces suspected of being unsympathetic to socialism and federalism.

John K. Cox

Further reading

Committee for a Fair Trial for General Draža Mihailovich. *Commission of Inquiry. Patriot or Traitor. The Case of General Mihailovich. Proceedings and Report of the Commission of Inquiry of the Committee for Fair Trial for Draja Mihailovich.* Stanford, California, 1978.
Karchmar, Lucien. *Draža Mihailović and the Rise of the Chetnik Movement, 1941–1942.* New York, 1987.

Roberts, Walter. *Tito, Mihailović, and the Allies, 1941–1945*. Durham, North Carolina, 1987.

See also Antifascism; Chetniks; Tito

Mihalache, Ion (1882–1963)

Leader of the Romanian National Peasant Party. After World War I, Mihalache served as minister of agriculture. He also served in the cabinet of the National Peasant government, and in subsequent governments in other positions such as minister of the interior. He was arrested by the Communists in 1947 on charges of espionage and perished in prison in 1963. Mihalache believed that to end the exploitation of the peasantry by the rich oligarchy, it was necessary for the peasants to organize their own political party. He felt that the peasants should be recognized as a major force in society, and that the primary emphasis in Romanian economic development should be on agriculture, not industry. Consequently, he was critical of the manner in which the Liberals had attempted to pursue a policy of national industrialization. He argued that Romanian agriculture would be more productive if it revolved around small farms and cooperatives.

Robert Weiner

Further reading

Fischer-Galati, Stephen. *Twentieth Century Rumania*. New York, 1991.

Hitchins, Keith. *Rumania: 1866–1947*. Oxford, 1994.

Roberts, Henry L. *Rumania*. New Haven, Connecticut, 1951.

See also Agrarian Parties

Mikhailov, Ivan (1896–1990)

Leader of the Internal Macedonian Revolutionary Organization (IMRO). Mikhailov was born in Novo Selo, near Shtip, Macedonia, and grew up in a family involved in the activities of IMRO. He studied in Turkish, Bulgarian, and Serbian schools and ended up as a law student in Sofia, where he founded a Macedonian Student Association. In 1920 he became the private secretary and most trusted aide to Todor Aleksandrov (1881–1924), IMRO's leader. After the assassination of the latter on August 31, 1924, he seized power in the organization and held its reins until his death in 1990. A man of iron will, strong disposition, and fiercely anticommunist sentiments, he pursued with ruthless determination the cause of IMRO—the creation of a free and independent Macedonia as a Switzerland in the Balkans, made up of the ethnically Bulgarian Slavic population and other minorities, and sharing equal rights in a secular state. He curried no favor in Sofia, Belgrade, or Athens but found support from Mussolini's (1883–1945) Italy. His first act as leader was to avenge the death of Aleksandrov and purge the organization of traitors. The streets of Sofia were turned into a shooting gallery, as over one thousand revolutionaries were killed. After a coup in Sofia of May 19, 1934, led by pro-Yugoslav forces, he sought refuge in Turkey, moved to Poland, and spent the war years in Croatia. In 1944 the Germans offered to make him president of an independent Macedonia, but he declined, pointing out that their war was already lost. After the war, he settled in Italy and died in Rome.

Spas T. Raikin

Further reading

Bregalnishki (Iv. Mikhailov). *Po trunlivia put na mekedonskoto osvoboditelno dvizhenie*. Sofia, 1939.

Mikhailov, Ivan. *Macedonia: A Switzerland in the Balkans*. St. Louis, Missouri, 1950.

———. *Spomeni*, vols. 1–4. Louvain, Belgium, 1958, 1965, 1967, 1973.

See also Todor Aleksandrov; IMRO

Mikołajczyk, Stanisław (1901–66)

Premier of the Polish government-in-exile (1943–44). During the interwar period, Mikołajczyk was an active member of the Polish Peasant Party and Sejm (parliament). In 1939, at the beginning of World War II, he fled to England, where he participated in the government-in exile under General Władysław Sikorski (1881–1943). When Sikorski died in a plane crash in 1943, Mikołajczyk became the leader of the government.

Lacking the stature of Sikorski, Mikołajczyk struggled to maintain the authority of the government-in exile—especially given Moscow's opposition to its role in the future Polish state. As such, Mikołajczyk protested the decision made at the 1943 Tehran conference to alter Poland's eastern and western borders, for he felt that his nation would then be dependent on the Soviet Union.

M Though he claimed that the Allies had no authority to delineate such a boundary—only he and the Polish parliament had the right to sign this resolution—the Allies ignored his protests.

In 1945 Mikołajczyk returned to Poland and assumed the post of deputy premier in the new coalition government. Seen by many as the symbol of anti-Soviet opposition, he pressed for free elections. He nevertheless had little room to act. During fraudulent elections held in 1947, the Communists won the majority of seats in parliament. Fearing for his life, Mikołajczyk fled from Poland and his supporters suffered under subsequent Communist persecution.

Judith Fai-Podlipnik

Further reading

Bogdan, Henry and Istvan Fehervary, eds. *From Warsaw to Sofia: A History of Eastern Europe.* Santa Fe, New Mexico, 1989.

Korbonski, Andrzej. "Poland 1918–1990," in Joseph Held, ed. *The Columbia History of Eastern Europe in the Twentieth Century.* New York, 1992.

Mikołajczyk, Stanisław. *The Rape of Poland: The Pattern of Soviet Domination.* London, 1948.

See also Sejm; Władisław Sikorski

Milan Obrenović (1854–1901)

Serbian prince and later, after 1882, king, whose reign was characterized by a long but losing struggle with the overwhelmingly popular Radical Party. The fourteen-year-old grandnephew of Prince Mihailo (1823–68), Milan was brought to the throne on the latter's death. After a four-year regency, Milan ruled in accordance with the moderate precepts of the regency until about 1878. The next decade was characterized by rearguard actions against the Radical Party; difficulties with his wife, Natalie (1859–1941), whom he divorced; a scandalous private life; a disastrous war with Bulgaria, at which time he proclaimed himself king; and abdication in favor of thirteen-year-old son Alexander (1876–1903) after facilitating the adoption of one of the most democratic constitutions in Europe.

Milan's abdication was only pro forma; for more than a decade thereafter he continued to intervene in Serbia's politics. In large part, he wanted to protect his minor son from the influence of certain elements, especially from his ex-wife, but also from Radical Party leaders. The government at one point forced Natalie to leave Serbia, but she kept coming back. Milan himself spent a great deal of time abroad; he liked to gamble and he liked women. At one point, he planned to marry the wife of his private secretary, but when she got a divorce three years later, he was no longer interested. Because of his lifestyle, he accumulated enormous debts. He was able to obtain substantial sums from the government, and indirectly from Russia, on the condition that he stay out of Serbia, agree to forgo rights as a member of the Obrenović dynasty, and even renounce his Serbian citizenship. As soon as the money was gone, he reneged on his promises and returned to Serbia. When he failed to get more money from the government, he decided on a more radical course. He engineered a coup in April 1893 by his son Alexander, who proclaimed himself of age (although he was then only seventeen), and dismissed the regency. Milan even became commandant of Serbia's armed forces. As such, he was almost a state within a state. Even cabinet ministers did not dare to discuss the army budget or other military matters.

A definitive break between father and son came in 1900, when Alexander told his father that he planned to marry a widow ten years his senior. In many circles she was regarded as a woman of questionable virtue. Milan resigned as commandant and told his son that if he were to go through with "this impulsive act," he would be the first to greet the government that would overthrow him. The following year Milan died abroad, a grieving and dejected "old" man who had not yet reached his forty-seventh birthday.

Alex N. Dragnich

Further reading

Dragnich, Alex N. *The Development of Parliamentary Government in Serbia.* Boulder, Colorado, 1978.

Jovanović, Slobodan. *Vlada Milana Obrenovića,* 3 vols. Belgrade, 1934.

Petrovich, Michael B. *A History of Modern Serbia,* 2 vols. New York, 1976.

See also Bulgarian–Serb War of 1885; Alexander Obrenović; Mihailo Obrenović

Military League

Clandestine (and sometimes semilegal) political organization of Bulgarian army officers. In

October 1919 a group of army officers in Sofia founded the Military League (Voenen Suiuz) as an organization allegedly "far away from and outside politics." This move was triggered by the imminent signing of the Treaty of Neuilly, which imposed severe military restrictions on Bulgaria after World War I. From 1919 to 1923, the Bulgarian army was reduced from 80,000 soldiers and 3,975 officers to 20,000 soldiers and 1,650 officers. Accordingly, the Military League's statutes highlighted the need to preserve the Bulgarian officers corps, with the secondary aim of protecting the country from what was perceived as Bolshevism. Led by a nine-member standing committee (which included prominent officers like Kimon Georgiev [1882–1969] and Damian Velchev [1883–1954]), the new organization tried to establish cells in every army unit. By 1920, the Military League claimed to have some 1,700 members. In October of that year, however, the organization was officially dissolved by the Agrarian government of Aleksandur Stamboliiski (1879–1923). Nevertheless, the Military League managed to survive underground and in November 1921 successfully reorganized itself—this time as a secret and accordingly small organization of some two hundred members. In early 1922 Ivan Vulkov (1875–1962) became its new leader, and among his three deputies were Georgiev and Velchev. The Military League now became the spearhead of radical opposition to Stamboliiski's Agrarian rule. At the same time, the league became part of a pan-opposition coalition called the Konstitutsionen blok (Constitutional Bloc), which was also supported by Boris III (1894–1943). The successful, bloody coup against Stamboliiski on June 9, 1923, was in fact the work of the league.

Under the new conservative-nationalist coalition government led by Aleksandur Tsankov (1879–1959), with three members of the Military League in the cabinet (including Vulkov as Minister of National Defense), the semilegal officers' organization became an extralegal instrument to suppress Agrarians, Communists, and other opposition groups. In the summer of 1923 the Military League and the government jointly set up the so-called Convent, a secret body empowered to carry out executions, assassinations, and other terrorist actions against political opponents. The league's close collaboration with the rightist new government coalition, as well as with the Internal Macedonian Revolutionary Organization (IMRO), which sought autonomy for Macedonia, and with Fascist Italy, led to the emergence of a struggle within the group. Beginning in 1925, the league was divided into a right wing around Vulkov and a radical faction around Velchev. With Vulkov sent away as ambassador to Rome in early 1929, Velchev reorganized the faction-ridden organization on a strictly conspiratorial basis. The Military League now became decidedly antimonarchist, anti-IMRO, anti-Mussolini, and pro–South Slav. The Spy Affair of 1930—a conspiracy by IMRO against an army officer—mobilized Velchev's followers, who teamed up with opposition intellectuals favoring authoritarian solutions to the country's problems. However, although Velchev carried out a successful coup in May 1934, he and the other antimonarchists in the league were pushed aside in January 1935, and on April 21, 1935, the tsar regained political control over the country by removing the league from power. Split into several rival factions, the league lost its influence and collapsed.

Stefan Troebst

Further reading

Georgiev, Velichko. "Formirane na organizatsionnata sistema, programata i taktikata na Voenniia suiuz (1918–1920)." *Izvestiia na Bulgarskoto istorichesko druzhestvo* 32 (1978): 173–203.

———. *Narodniiat sgovor 1921–1923.* Sofia, 1989.

Whetstine, B.J. "Bulgarian Interwar Politics and the Military Solution: The *Coup d'Etats* of 1923 and 1934." *Bulgarian Historical Review* 16, no. 3 (1988): 81–90.

See also Boris III; Kimon Georgiev; IMRO; Neuilly, Treaty of; Aleksandur Stamboliiski; Aleksandur Tsankov; Damian Velchev; Ivan Vulkov

Millet

Basic system of Ottoman social organization. A *millet* (nation) was a group of people considered a legal-administrative unit by the Ottomans. In accordance with Islamic principles, the Ottoman Empire, in both its administrative and social forms, was organized on the *millet* system. In other words, the empire's subjects were administered by units organized on the basis of religion rather than nationality or locality. Although the number of *millets* changed over the course of the empire's history, at the most, a total of six non-Islamic *millets*

M existed alongside the Muslim community. In order of numerical importance, they were the Orthodox, Gregorian Armenian, Jewish, Roman Armenian, Roman Catholic, and Protestant. Christians and Jews were regarded as "people of the Book," and were thus afforded relative, but arbitrary, tolerance by the Ottomans. Muslims, however, maintained a superior position in the empire, while non-Muslims were subjected to restrictive laws and discriminatory taxation, including the *devshirme* (tax in children).

The Orthodox *millet,* which presided over most of the Balkan peoples, was administered by the patriarch of Constantinople. As head of the Orthodox *millet,* the patriarch was a high official of the Ottoman government, and was responsible to the sultan for the behavior and loyalty of his population. The patriarch was also responsible to the sultan for tax collection. In exchange, the patriarch enjoyed full jurisdiction over a wide range of civic and commercial matters. The *millet* system thus preserved a measure of nominal self-government for the subject Christians. Nevertheless, although theoretically it was understood that the Orthodox *millet* would be administered by the patriarch with a holy synod composed of his metropolitans, in reality, and increasingly after the seventeenth century, the sultan maintained a strong degree of direct control over the Orthodox establishment.

Despite its close connections with the Ottoman state, the Orthodox Church, paradoxically, functioned as the central formal institution in the perpetuation of Christian exclusiveness and eventually in the furtherance of national identity. Indeed, given the Greeks' dominant position in the Patriarchate, Greek cultural hegemony expanded throughout the Balkans, often prompting significant resentment among non-Greeks. As a result, religion, or at least ecclesiastical independence, became inexorably linked with national identity and the subsequent struggles for national independence among the Balkan peoples in the nineteenth century and beyond.

Alexandros K. Kyrou

Further reading

Pantazopoulos, N.J. *Church and Law in the Balkan Peninsula during the Ottoman Rule.* Thessaloniki, 1967.
Papadopoullos, Theodore H. *Studies and Documents Relating to the History of the Greek Church and People under Turkish Domination.* Brussels, 1952.
Runciman, Steven. *The Great Church in Captivity: A Study of the Patriarchate of Constantinople from the Eve of the Turkish Conquest to the Greek War of Independence.* Cambridge, 1968.

See also Muslims; Ottoman Empire; Orthodoxy; Patriarchate

Milošević, Slobodan (1941–)

Serbian politician and president. Milošević studied law at the University of Belgrade and held various offices in the Yugoslav Communist Party (League of Communists) and in the municipal administration of Belgrade. He rose to political power in Serbia in the mid- to late 1980s as the popularity and constitutional resilience of Yugoslavia were waning in the midst of the economic and ethnic turmoil in Yugoslavia after the death of longtime leader Josip Broz Tito (1892–1980). Milošević became head of the Serbian League of Communists in 1987 then head of the Serbian government. He presided over the recentralization of Serbia, in which the former autonomous republics of overwhelmingly Albanian Kosovo and partially Hungarian Vojvodina were reintegrated into Serbia proper against their will.

Through a series of mass meetings and speeches, Milošević drew great attention to and played on the fears and ambitions of Serbs living in several of the republics of the former Yugoslavia. After Tito's death, many Serbs were encouraged by Milošević to think that the federal structure of the state robbed them of their supposedly rightful, dominant position in the country. Thus, through a series of mass rallies, Milošević helped foment popular demands for a greater Serbia or a continued Yugoslavia that would contain all Serbs. Milošević remained in power through struggles with domestic rivals, enormous tensions and war with neighboring Croatia, and economic and military sanctions in place by the West since 1991 for his part in the disastrous Bosnian war. In 1997 he became the president of the rump Republic of Yugoslavia, which consists of Serbia and Montenegro and continued to use ethnic tensions in Kosovo to galvanize Serbian nationalism.

John K. Cox

Further reading

Bennett, Christopher. *Yugoslavia's Bloody Collapse: Causes, Course and Consequences.* New York, 1995

Djilas, Aleksa. "A Profile of Slobodan Milošević." *Foreign Affairs* 72 (Summer 1993): 81–96.

Glenny, Misha. *The Fall of Yugoslavia: The Third Balkan War,* rev. and updated ed. New York, 1994.

Magaš, Branka. *The Destruction of Yugoslavia: Tracking the Breakup, 1980–92.* New York, 1993.

Milošević, Slobodan. *Godine raspleta,* 4th ed. Belgrade, 1989.

Woodward, Susan L. *Balkan Tragedy: Chaos and Dissolution after the Cold War.* Washington, D.C., 1995.

See also Communist Party of Yugoslavia; Greater Serbia; Kosovo; Serbia and the Breakup of Yugoslavia; Tito; Vojvodina

Miloš Obrenović (1780–1860)

Leader of the first successful Serbian revolt against the Ottoman Turks in 1815. Miloš succeeded in getting the Turks to accept Serbia's autonomy and to recognize him as hereditary prince of Serbia. Miloš realized that full autonomy was not possible, and, although he was illiterate, he was politically shrewd, managing to manipulate the Turkish *paša* (governor), largely with money, so as to substitute a good deal of Serbian authority in place of the Turkish. He also enlarged Serbia's area significantly.

Domestically, his authority was crude and primitive. Although he was ruthless toward his enemies, in fairness Miloš faced difficult problems such as outlaws. He viewed the people as children who needed a firm hand at the top. He did not permit the rise of an aristocracy, however, operating on the principle that vacated Ottoman lands should be given to those who tilled the soil. Although he sought men of loyalty, he transferred a good deal of administrative and judicial authority to the national elders, who subsequently turned against him.

His opponents, having become favorites of the sultan, got the latter to create a National Council, which was to share power with Miloš. Under the sultan's constitution for Serbia (1838), Miloš appointed its members but could not remove them.

They became a self-perpetuating oligarchy that was to rule Serbia for the next twenty years. Miloš abdicated in 1839. His son Mihailo (1823–68) succeeded him but was forced to flee Serbia in 1842. In the same year, council members convinced the Turks to recognize Alexander Karadjordjević (1806–85), son of Karadjorje (Black George) (1768–1817), leader of the 1804 revolt against the Turks, as hereditary prince of Serbia.

After the oligarchy was ousted by a popular parliament in 1858, the latter brought Miloš back as prince, but he died within less than two years. Initially he was popular, but it was soon evident that he had not learned much in the intervening years. The legendary hero demonstrated his opportunism by seemingly changing his politics from day to day. The appearance of his son Mihailo was welcomed by many.

Alex N. Dragnich

Further reading

Dragnich, Alex N. *The Development of Parliamentary Government in Serbia.* Boulder, Colorado, 1978.

Jovanović, Slobodan. *Druga vlada Miloša i Mihaila, 1858–1868.* Belgrade, 1923.

Petrovich, Michael B. *A History of Modern Serbia,* 2 vols. New York, 1976.

See also Alexander Karadjordjević; Black George; Mihailo Obrenović

Miłosz, Czesław (1911–)

Polish poet, writer, essayist, literary critic, and 1980 Noble Prize winner. Miłosz's early poems in *Trzy zimy* (*Three Winters,* 1936) present the world through a catastrophic lens. In 1951 Miłosz, who worked as a cultural attaché, requested political asylum in Paris and two years later published his famous study about the interdependence between a totalitarian state and the intellectuals who supported it (*Zniewolony umysł* [*The Captive Mind,* 1953]). Consequently, for the next thirty years his writings were banned in Poland. He published in France and then in the United States (*Traktat poetycki* [*Treatise on Poetry,* 1957]; *Miasto bez imienia* [*City without Name,* 1969]; *Kroniki* [*Chronicles,* 1987]). At the core of Miłosz's writing lies an ethical dilemma: detachment from life that might be morally unacceptable but is necessary for description, and full participation in reality that precludes writing about it. Miłosz rejects preoccupation with aestheticism in the name of poetry's moral obligation (*Traktat moralny* [*Treatise on Morals,* 1948]). His poetry is emotionally restrained, intellectual yet sensual, metaphorically dense, contemplative, often prophetic, and it unites various literary traditions. Miłosz's latest poetry moves toward acceptance of the world as the poetic persona reaches *apokatastasis,* the state of equilibrium absent from his earlier poems.

Although primarily a poet, Miłosz wrote several novels, including *Dolina Issy* (*The Valley of the Issa,* 1955) and *Rodzinna Europa* (*Native Realm,* 1959), the latter an autobiography of an East European who attempts to explain his "otherness" to the Western reader. These works reveal Miłosz's roots in his native Lithuania and explain the point of view of an outsider speaking with many voices.

Katarzyna Zechenter

Further reading

Czarnecka, Ewa and Aleksander Fuit. *Conversations with Czesław Miłosz,* trans. by Richard Lourie. San Diego, California, 1987.
Czesław Miłosz: An International Bibliography 1930–1980. Ann Arbor, Michigan, 1983.
Fiut, Aleksander. *The Eternal Moment: The Poetry of Czesław Miłosz,* trans. by Theodosia S. Robertson. Berkeley, California, 1990.
Możejko, Edward, ed. *Between Anxiety and Hope: The Poetry and Writing of Czesław Miłosz.* Edmonton, Alberta, 1988.
Nathan, Leonard and Arthur Quinn. *The Poet's Work: An Introduction to Czesław Miłosz.* Cambridge, Massachusetts, 1991.

See also Polish Literature

Mindszenty, Jószef (1899–1975)

Roman Catholic cardinal of Hungary (1945–75). Cardinal Mindszenty was one of the most influential and respected opponents of communism in Hungary. He opposed the Hungarian Stalinist regime, supported the Hungarian Revolution of 1956, and for nearly twenty years lived in protective custody in the U.S. Embassy in Budapest. Mindszenty's political leanings began when, as a young priest, he spoke out against the short-lived Communist government of Béla Kun (1886–1938) in 1919, and was imprisoned. After his release, he became the bishop of Vesprém and a member of the Smallholders Party. During World War II, Mindszenty opposed the Hungarian fascists and spoke out against the deportation of Jews—activities that resulted in his imprisonment again.

After World War II, Mindszenty became the Hungarian Primate and was in the forefront of the struggle against the Communist Party. He particularly opposed the takeover of the schools. In 1949 the secret police arrested him, tortured him, and arranged a show trial at which he was forced to confess to crimes of espionage and conspiracy against the state. He was imprisoned until the outbreak of revolution in Hungary against the Soviets in 1956. Mindszenty gave cautious support to the revolution and urged that bloodshed be avoided. When Soviet tanks rolled into Budapest in November, Mindszenty gained refuge at the U.S. Embassy, where he remained for the next twenty years. In 1974 the Hungarian government reached a rapprochement with the Vatican, and Mindszenty was permitted to go into exile in the West. He remained a staunch opponent of the Hungarian Communist government until his death in 1975.

Judith Fai-Podlipnik

Further reading

Hoensch, Jorg K. *A History of Modern Hungary.* New York, 1988.
Mindszenty, József Cardinal. *Memoirs: József Cardinal Mindszenty.* New York, 1974.
Sugar, Peter, Peter Hanak, and Tibor Frank. *A History of Hungary.* Bloomington, Indiana, 1990.

See also Catholicism; Hungarian Revolution of 1956; Hungarian Soviet Republic; Béla Kun

Mitteleuropa

"Middle Europe." As a geographic term, *Mitteleuropa* corresponded approximately to the English "Central Europe." As a political and economic term, *Mitteleuropa* denoted a sought-after but never-realized central European area under German economic and/or political hegemony. Among German-speaking geographers, *Mitteleuropa* generally includes the territory of present-day Germany, Austria, Switzerland, Poland, Czechoslovakia, Hungary, and Romania. Some definitions also include Belgium, Luxembourg, northeastern France, and the northern portions of Italy and Yugoslavia. The area has no clear physical or cultural borders.

German nationalists used *Mitteleuropa* as an economic and political term from the mid-nineteenth century through 1945. In the 1840s economist Friedrich List (1789–1846) used the term to describe an economically integrated area in Central Europe protected by tariffs from foreign, chiefly British, industrial competition. In the 1850s Austrian Minister of Trade Karl Ludwig Bruck (1798–1860) used the term for a planned customs union of the German states, the Austrian Empire, and at least some parts of Italy.

During World War I, *Mitteleuropa* became a broadly popular concept and a central, if vague, German war aim. In 1915 political theorist Friedrich Naumann (1860–1919) produced a widely read and influential book titled *Mitteleuropa*. In it, Naumann envisioned a German-dominated economic union of Germany, Austria-Hungary, and some annexed territory. In the 1920s German nationalists retained *Mitteleuropa* as a goal, hoping for German economic dominance over the small successor states to the old Austro-Hungarian Empire. After 1933, the more radical Nazi goal of conquering extensive Lebensraum (living space) in Eastern Europe eclipsed the older goals of *Mitteleuropa*. After 1945, the term dropped out of active political vocabulary, and in contrast, remains current as a geographic expression.

Robert Mark Spaulding

Further reading

Naumann, Friedrich. *Central Europe,* trans. by Christabel M. Meredith. New York, 1917.

See also Germanization; Pan-Germanism

Mochnacki, Maurycy (1803–34)

Polish publicist, revolutionary, and historian of the November Uprising. Born in Bojaniec, Mochnacki received his early education at home. After moving to Warsaw in 1819, he became an active member of a secret organization that sought freedom for Poland. After enrolling in the Faculty of Law at Warsaw University in 1820, he soon turned from legal studies to pursue literature and philosophy. His defiant spirit and membership in secret organizations led to his arrest in December 1823. While in prison, he seemingly recanted his radical views, presenting himself as a model of a law-abiding citizen.

After release from prison in July 1824,

Mochnacki began a literary career, writing for numerous papers and journals throughout the 1820s. During the 1820s, his career as publicist and literary critic flourished. As a literary critic, his writings on romanticism stated that one of its main tasks was to awaken the national consciousness of the Poles. Mochnacki's other work as a publicist advocated a national and social revolution in Poland, including the emancipation of the peasantry, but his writing revealed no coherent program of action.

By 1830, Mochnacki was thoroughly enmeshed in the revolutionary movement and in plotting an uprising. With the outbreak of the November insurrection against the Russians, Mochnacki approached historian Joachim Lelewel (1786–1861) to take the leadership of the movement, feeling that the revolutionaries should seize power themselves. He proposed granting civil rights and equality to the peasantry. Although Mochnacki aspired to leadership in the provisional government, he was rebuffed strongly. In his writing he now began to turn against the revolutionary leaders, accusing them of ineptitude, while still advocating the struggle for Polish independence.

In November 1831 Mochnacki arrived in Paris. Failing once again to achieve leadership among the Polish émigrés, he continued his writing, returning to advocacy of a social revolution in Poland that would give equality to the peasantry.

Mochnacki's legacy is mixed. He was a revolutionary who lacked a clear-cut program and whose aspirations for leadership were constantly thwarted, but his work on the uprising, never completed, remained, despite its serious flaws of historical writing, as an inspiration to succeeding generations of Polish patriots and revolutionaries.

Robert A. Berry

Further reading

Kucharzewski, Jan. *Maurycy Mochnacki.* Kraków, 1910.

See also Joachim Lelewel; November Uprising; Peasants; Polish Émigrés; Romanticism

Moldavia

Romanian principality. Geographically, Moldavia is roughly defined as the area extending between the eastern Carpathians, the Dniester River, and the Danube. It is one of three geographic and

M political areas (along with Wallachia and Transylvania) that are, though not fully, integrated into present-day Romania. Moldavia was settled, or, at least, politically organized, somewhat later than the other two, with much of its population, especially its political leadership, coming originally from Transylvania. In the middle of the fourteenth century it emerged as an independent principality. From 1387 to the midfifteenth century, it was a vassal state of Poland but subject to repeated invasion by the Ottoman Turks. Acceptance of Turkish sovereignty with a guaranteed respect for domestic political autonomy and for the Orthodox Church seemed the best available solution, and Moldavia became part of the Ottoman Empire in 1512. A strong demographic eastward expansion was reflected in the shift of the capital in 1564 from Suceava in the north to Iaşi in the east. Moldavia prospered under Ottoman rule, but there were stirrings of discontent and in 1711 Prince Dimitrie Cantemir (1673–1723) joined the invading armies of Peter the Great (1672–1725). The Russians were defeated and from then on the Turks did not trust any native princes. There followed the difficult so-called Phanariot period, when the rulers were Greek princes chosen by Constantinople. Greek rule and Greek control of Romanian churches and monasteries were resented for both economic and cultural reasons. Meanwhile, Russia and Austria combined to push back the Ottoman Empire. They were gradually successful, but Moldavia paid a heavy price. In 1775 Austria "liberated" the northern part of Moldavia, transforming it into the Austrian dukedom of Bukovina, while Russia "liberated" the eastern part of Moldavia (Bessarabia) in 1812. Still, truncated to almost half its area, Moldavia awoke intellectually after the French Revolution. A new spirit of nationalism led to demands for joining with Wallachia to create a united Romania. Such a union was implemented in 1862 and international recognition and full independence for the resulting state of Romania were achieved in the Treaty of Berlin in 1878.

Ladis K.D. Kristof

Further reading

Magocsi, Paul Robert. *Historical Atlas of East Central Europe.* Seattle, Washington, 1993.
România: Atlas istoric-geografic. Bucharest, 1996.

See also Congress of Berlin; Danubian Principalities; Iaşi; Phanariots; Transylvania; Wallachia

Moldova, Birth of the Republic of

Successor state to the Moldovan Soviet Socialist Republic (MSSR) and generally known in the West by its Russian name, "Moldavia." Before its declaration of independence on August 27, 1991, Moldova was one of the fifteen constituent republics of the Soviet Union. It covers 12,130 square miles (33,700 sq km) and has a population of 4.3 million, of which 65 percent are ethnic Romanians/Moldovans, 14 percent Ukrainians, 13 percent Russians, 4 percent Gagauzi (Orthodox Christian Turks), and 2 percent Bulgarians.

Moldova is divided into two regions by the Dniester River: the Bessarabia region on the western, or right, bank and the Transnistria region on the eastern, or left, bank. Before the creation of the MSSR on August 14, 1940, Bessarabia was a part of the kingdom of Romania, while Transnistria existed as part of the Moldovan Autonomous Soviet Socialist Republic (MASSR), created inside Soviet Ukraine on October 12, 1924. In June 1940 the Soviet Union forcibly annexed Bessarabia, apportioned areas in the north and south to Ukraine, and fused the remaining region with part of Transnistria to form the new MSSR. As justification for the annexation, the Soviets argued that the majority population in Bessarabia and Transnistria represented a distinct ethnic group—Moldovans. Romanian authorities, however, held that Moldovans were simply a subgroup of the Romanian nation. To buttress their argument, the Soviets mandated that the Moldovan "language" be written in the Cyrillic alphabet, even though there was little to distinguish it from Romanian (written in the Latin alphabet).

In mid-1988 Moldovan intellectuals began to argue for a return to the Latin alphabet and a recognition that Moldovans and Romanians formed part of a single Pan-Romanian nation. In May 1989 local opposition forces organized the Popular Front of Moldova to press these demands. Despite the intransigence of the Communist Party of Moldova, on August 31, 1989, the local parliament passed new laws making "Moldovan" the MSSR's official language, returning it to the Latin alphabet, and implicitly recognizing its unity with Romanian.

Fearing that the Popular Front's cultural reforms would lead to their forced Romanianization, pro-Russian groups in Transnistria declared an independent Transnistrian Moldovan Republic on September 2, 1990. Another separatist state—

the Republic of Gagauzia—was also formed by the Turkic-speaking Gagauzi in southern Moldova on August 19, 1990.

Charles King

Further reading

Crowther, William. "The Politics of Ethno-National Mobilization: Nationalism and Reform in Soviet Moldavia." *Russian Review* 50 (April 1990): 183–202.

Dima, Nicholas. *From Moldavia to Moldova: The Soviet-Romanian Territorial Dispute.* Boulder, Colorado, 1991.

King, Charles. *Post-Soviet Moldova: A Borderland in Transition.* London, 1995.

Vartichan, K. *Moldavskaia Sovetskaia Sotsialisticheskaia Respublika.* Kishinev, 1979.

See also Bessarabian Question; Transnistria

Molnár, Ferenc (1878–1952)

Hungarian-born playwright, journalist, and author of novels and short stories. Born into an upper-middle-class Budapest environment, Molnár first entered journalism before becoming a celebrated playwright abroad as well as in Hungary, noted for his "well-made plays" and theatricality. For example, in *Játék a kastélyban* (*The Play's the Thing,* 1926), the subject matter itself is the making of a play for the theater. In 1940 he emigrated to the United States.

Molnár's short stories and humorous sketches often center on exposing human foibles in a witty yet sophisticated manner. Plays such as *A hattyú* (*The Swan,* 1920), *Harmónia* (*Harmony,* 1923), and *Olympia* (1928) satirize the outmoded Budapest aristocracy and upper bourgeoisie. He also writes with a sympathetic, if somewhat sentimental view of the underclass, as in his most popular novel, *A Pál-utcai fiúk* (*The Paul Street Boys,* 1907), originally written for adolescents and later made into a film. The work is a poignant portrayal of working-class childhood.

Molnár's first dramatic and possibly most popular success, *Liliom* (*Lily,* 1909), eventually became an American musical film and theatrical success, *Carousel,* albeit with a change of geographical location. The "magical" plot of the play has been compared to Hungarian folk tales. The main character, a bad-tempered fellow, mistreats his wife, holds up a factory, and eventually com-

mits suicide. After sixteen years, the celestial police allow him to visit Earth to make amends, but once again, he shows himself to be a bully. However, his wife explains to their daughter that when we truly love, we love even those who mistreat us.

Molnár's female characters generally have instinctual psychological advantages over the males, who often fall victim to their own jealousy. In *A testőr* (*The Guardsman,* 1910), an actor tests his wife's fidelity by pretending to be an officer of the guards, but in the dénouement, the wife pretends only to be playing a part. Herein lies Molnár's main forte, the exploration of the relationship between playacting and reality.

Mártha Pereszlényi-Pintér

Further reading

Czigány, Lóránt. *The Oxford History of Hungarian Literature.* Oxford, 1984.

Klaniczay, Tibor, ed. *A History of Hungarian Literature.* Budapest, 1982.

Klaniczay, Tibor, József Sauder, and Miklós Szabolcsi. *A History of Hungarian Literature.* Budapest, 1964.

Molnár, August J. *Hungarian Writers and Literature by Joseph Reményi.* New Brunswick, New Jersey, 1964.

See also Hungarian Literature; Theater

Molotov, Vyacheslav Mikhailovich (1890–1986)

Soviet political leader and foreign minister. V.M. Skriabin was born into a middle-class family in Kukarka. In 1906 he took the pseudonym Molotov (hammer). With Josef Stalin (1879–1953), he established the Bolshevik newspaper *Pravda* (*Truth*) in 1912. In October 1917 he served on the Petrograd Soviet's Military-Revolutionary Committee, which was used as the vehicle for launching the October Revolution. Molotov became a full member of the Central Committee in 1921 and the Politburo in 1926 (a position he held until 1952, and again from 1953 to 1957). During the Communist Party succession struggles of the 1920s, he was a staunch supporter of Stalin, leading the collectivization campaign in the early 1930s. Together with Stalin, he countersigned many of the death lists during the Great Purges that eradicated much of the Communist hierarchy. A bureaucrat rather than an intellectual, Molotov served as chairman of the Council of People's Commissars (premier) from 1930 to 1941 and also as commissar (later minister) of foreign affairs from 1939 to 1949 and again from 1953 to 1956. He negotiated the Nazi-Soviet Pact, which paved the way for the division of Poland in 1939. Molotov also served as deputy chairman of the State Committee of Defense during World War II. He was in charge of tank production and, with secret police chief Lavrenty Beria (1899–1953), the Soviet program to develop an atomic bomb. He attended the conferences at Tehran, Yalta, and Potsdam that helped determine the fate of postwar Eastern Europe. In these various capacities, Molotov functioned as Stalin's second-in-command, but by the end of World War II, he had been eclipsed in Stalin's council by others. Nonetheless, Molotov represented the Soviet Union at the 1945 San Francisco conference at which the United Nations was founded. He frequently spoke for the USSR at the United Nations, and he attended most of the major international conferences of the early Cold War era. To the Western public, Molotov seemed to embody Soviet tough-mindedness and hostility. In 1948 Stalin forced him to divorce his wife, who was then arrested and exiled on charges of "Zionist connections." Denounced at the Nineteenth Party Congress in 1952, Molotov was saved from being purged by Stalin's death in 1953. Molotov unsuccessfully opposed Khrushchev's (1894–1971) rise to power, as well as his more moderate foreign and domestic policies, especially the de-Stalinization campaign. Ousted from the Politburo in 1957, he was sent as ambassador to Outer Mongolia. He was deprived of his party membership in 1962 (restored in 1984) and forced into retirement. His memoirlike interviews, published in 1991, are an unrepentant defense of his actions as Stalin's henchman.

Teddy J. Uldricks

Further reading

Chuev, Felix. *Molotov Remembers: Inside Kremlin Politics, Conversations with Felix Chuev.* Chicago, 1993.

Lih, Lars T. et al., eds. *Stalin's Letters to Molotov, 1925–1936.* New Haven, Connecticut, 1995.

Medvedev, Roy. *All Stalin's Men: Six Who Carried Out the Bloody Policies.* Garden City, New York, 1984.

Miner, Steven M. "His Master's Voice: Viacheslav Mikhailovich Molotov as Stalin's Foreign Commissar," in *The Diplomats, 1939–1979,* ed. by Gordon A. Craig and Francis L. Loewenheim. Princeton, New Jersey, 65–100.

Watson, Derek. *Molotov and Soviet Government: Sovnarkom, 1930–41.* New York, 1996.

See also Cold War; Collectivization; De-Stalinization; Molotov-Ribbentrop Pact; Potsdam Conference; Stalin; Yalta

Molotov-Ribbentrop Pact

Nonaggression pact signed August 23, 1939, by the Soviet Union and Nazi Germany, variously referred to as the Nazi-Soviet Pact, Hitler-Stalin Pact, Russo-German Nonaggression Treaty. Each power promised not to attack the other or support any third party that might attack one of the signatories. This treaty contained no escape clause invalidating the agreement if either signatory should attack a third party, because Stalin (1879–1953) knew that Hitler (1889–1945) would soon invade Poland. A Secret Additional Protocol divided Eastern Europe into Soviet and German spheres of interest. Moscow would dominate Finland, Estonia, Latvia, eastern Poland, and Bessarabia, while Germany would control the remainder of Eastern Europe. A supplementary Frontier and Friendship treaty of September 28 and an additional protocol of December 15 transferred Lithuania to Moscow's sphere of influence, while Germany acquired a larger share of Poland.

Beginning in late 1933, Stalin attempted to build a coalition with Britain, France, and other powers to prevent or, if necessary, defeat German aggression. This policy, known as collective security, failed because British and French leaders hoped to appease Hitler rather than fight him, and because they strongly distrusted the USSR. Aware that war would soon break out, pressured by Japanese probes in the Soviet Far East, and fearful that the Western leaders were trying to deflect German aggression toward the USSR, Stalin reversed himself and opted for an agreement with Berlin. Hitler, too, reversed his strongly anti-Soviet position because increasing Western resistance to German aggression by 1939 made him anxious to secure his eastern flank by insuring Soviet neutrality. Some historians believe that collective security was never more than a ploy by Stalin to woo Hitler into an aggressive alliance with the USSR.

During the period of the pact, the Soviet Union fought the Winter War against Finland and absorbed small parts of that country, plus all three Baltic states, eastern Poland, Bessarabia, and northern Bukovina. The pact freed Hitler to fight in the west without fear of attack from the east and allowed Germany to circumvent the Allied blockade by procuring many strategic commodities from the Soviet Union. Hitler broke the pact when Germany invaded the USSR on June 22, 1941.

Teddy J. Uldricks

Further reading

Roberts, Geoffrey. *The Soviet Union and the Origins of the Second World War.* London, 1995.

Russian Federation, Ministry of Foreign Affairs. *Dokumenty vneshnei politiki, 1939 god,* 2 vols. Moscow, 1992.

Sontag, Raymond J. and James S. Beddie, eds. *Nazi-Soviet Relations, 1939–1941.* New York, 1948.

Uldricks, Teddy J. "Evolving Soviet Views of the Nazi-Soviet Pact," in *Labyrinth of Nationalism, Complexities of Diplomacy,* ed. by Richard Frucht. Columbus, Ohio, 1992.

Weinberg, Gerhard. *Germany and the Soviet Union, 1939–1941.* Leiden, 1954.

See also Barbarossa; Collective Security; Adolf Hitler; Nazi–Polish War; Vyacheslav Molotov; Stalin

Montenegro (Geography)

Smallest of the six republics united after World War I to create the new nation of Yugoslavia. On April 27, 1992, after four of the six republics had left the union and declared themselves independent nations, Montenegro, with Serbia, formed a new state, the Federal Republic of Yugoslavia. Montenegro covers an area of approximately 5,500 square miles (15,280 sq km), making up about one-fifth of Yugoslavia's land area. Approximately 600,000 people reside in Montenegro. Of this total, nearly two-thirds are Montenegrins, 90,000 are Muslims, 40,000 are Albanians, and the rest are Serbs and other minorities.

Montenegro is bordered by Serbia on the northeast, Albania on the southeast, Bosnia-Hercegovina on the northwest, and the Adriatic Sea on the southwest. The Dinaric Alps cover most of this isolated, mountainous region. The mountains are characterized by karst rocky terrain, with the highest peaks reaching over 8,000 feet (2,042 m) in elevation. The area's principal river, the Moraca, empties into Lake Scutari, which lies on the border with Albania.

Montenegrins are historically and ethnically close to the Serbs. Both are predominantly Orthodox Christians and share common traditions and customs. Once part of the Serbian Empire, the region was later ruled by local bishops who were able to maintain the nation's autonomy during the Ottoman occupation. Under its present union with Serbia, the region continues to enjoy a large degree of autonomy and is governed from its capital city, Podgorica (formerly Titograd).

William B. Kory

Further reading

Bertić, Ivan. *Veliki geografski atlas Jugoslavije.* Zagreb, 1987.

Boehm, Christopher. *Montenegrin Social Organization and Values.* New York, 1983.

Glenny, Misha. *The Fall of Yugoslavia: The Third Balkan War.* New York, 1993.

See also Dinaric Alps

Montenegro (History)

The Latinized name of *Crna Gora* (Black Mountain), Montenegro is a diamond-shaped mountainous region in southwestern Yugoslavia bounded by Bosnia-Hercegovina to the northwest, Serbia to the northeast, the Adriatic Sea to the southwest, and Albania to the southeast. During the Middle Ages, the territory of what became Montenegro formed part of the medieval Serbian Empire of Tsar Dušan (c. 1308–55). After its disintegration, Zeta, Montenegro's immediate predecessor, emerged as an independent political unit. In the wake of the Battle of Kosovo in 1389, in which the Ottomans defeated Serbia, many Serbs found refuge in Montenegro's rugged mountains.

Until the middle of the nineteenth century, landlocked Montenegro was a theocracy, ruled by an elected prince-bishop (*vladika*). After the election of Danilo I (c. 1670–1735) in 1696, succession was generally restricted to members of Danilo's family, the house of Petrović (subsequently Petrović Njegoš). Since Orthodox bishops are celibate, the mantle of religious and temporal authority usually passed from uncle to nephew or grand-nephew.

M Throughout the nineteenth and early twentieth centuries, Montenegro's rulers attempted to rein in the land's unruly tribes and clans, introduce the trappings of modern statehood, and secure additional territory—principally at the expense of the traditional Ottoman enemy, which Montenegro fought in 1819–21, 1828–29, 1852–53, 1858, 1862, 1876–78, and 1912–13.

In the 1790s Vladika Petar I (1747–1830) issued the first written law codes and introduced a rudimentary central court. With the acquisition of the Brda region, Montenegro doubled in size. In 1799 Petar secured fleeting Ottoman recognition of Montenegrin independence and in 1813, during the Napoleonic Wars, gained temporary control of Kotor and a stretch of Adriatic coast. The Congress of Vienna (1814–15) reassigned Kotor to Austrian control, however, and Montenegro remained landlocked until 1878.

Petar I was succeeded by his nephew Rade (1813–51), who ruled as Petar II. Known worldwide simply as Njegoš, a poet of extraordinary power, he organized the country's first police force and created a senate composed of clan notables. Danilo I (1826–60), Njegoš's nephew and successor, separated the offices of prince and bishop (retaining the former for himself), reorganized the army, issued a new law code in 1855, and secured a modest territorial gain after defeating the Turks at the Battle of Grahovo in 1858.

Danilo was succeeded by his nephew Nicholas I (1860–1918), the last ruler of the Petrović Njegoš line, who issued Montenegro's first constitution in 1905 and five years later became the country's only king.

By the terms of the Treaty of Berlin (1878), Montenegro gained international recognition of its independence and doubled in size, acquiring Bar, an important foothold on the Adriatic. Additional coastal land around Ulcinj was acquired in 1880.

In 1912–13 Montenegro fought alongside Serbia in the First and Second Balkan Wars. In 1913 Montenegro occupied Scutari in northern Albania against the wishes of the Great Powers. Although forced to evacuate Scutari, Montenegro nonetheless almost doubled in size as a result of the wars—its third such territorial expansion since the 1790s. Serbia and Montenegro divided the Sanjak of Novi Pazar between them, in the process acquiring a common frontier. This facilitated even closer Serbo-Montenegrin ties, including the possibility of union.

Standing by its Serbian ally, Montenegro declared war on the Habsburg Empire in early August 1914. Toward the end of 1915, however, an Austro-German army invaded Serbia and Montenegro, overrunning both in a matter of weeks, and forcing Montenegro to negotiate a separate peace. The country was occupied by Austro-Hungarian forces until war's end.

In the fall of 1918 Serbian troops entered the territory of Montenegro. In November 1918 the Podgorica Skupština (assembly) formally ended the Petrović Njegoš dynasty and proclaimed Montenegro's union with Serbia in the new Kingdom of Serbs, Croats, and Slovenes. Opponents of the union, the *zelenaši* (greens), many of whom sought the restoration of King Nicholas (whose claims were supported by Italy), fought the *bjelaši* (whites) in a short-lived civil war.

In elections for the Yugoslav Constituent Assembly in 1920, Communist candidates won 38 percent of the vote in Montenegro—a measure of widespread popular discontent as well as the region's traditional Russophilism. Throughout the life of the "First Yugoslavia," Montenegro was a stronghold of rural communism. With the introduction of royalist authoritarian rule in 1929, Montenegro (augmented by additional territory to the west and east) became the Banovina of Zeta, one of the nine regional units into which Yugoslavia was divided.

In the wake of Yugoslavia's invasion and partition by Nazi Germany, Italy, Hungary, and Bulgaria in 1941, Italy assumed administrative responsibility for Montenegro. After transferring those parts of Montenegro populated by ethnic Albanians to its Albanian colony, Rome attempted to resurrect an "independent" Montenegrin kingdom under Italian protection. Armed resistance began on July 13, 1941, with the Communists, drawing on considerable local support, playing a major role. The mountainous land was the site of intense fighting between fascist and antifascist forces, as well as between the Communist-led Partisans (whose leadership included the Montenegrin Milovan Djilas [1911–95]) and various Chetnik resistance groups. In 1943 German troops replaced Italian units as a harassed occupation force. By the end of 1944, the Partisans were in control of most of the country. During the conflict, many Montenegrin towns, most notably Podgorica, were seriously damaged by Allied bombing.

After the war, Montenegro became one of the six constituent republics of the Federal People's Republic of Yugoslavia, which became the Socialist Federative Republic of Yugoslavia after 1963. Podgorica (renamed Titograd) was rebuilt and served as the new republic's capital.

During the Tito-Stalin dispute of the late 1940s, a large number of Montenegrin Communists were arrested and imprisoned as pro-Soviet "Cominformists." On the other hand, throughout the life of Communist Yugoslavia, a disproportionate number of military officers, police officials, and party bureaucrats were ethnic Montenegrins. Under the Communists, financial investment in Montenegro far exceeded the national average, but efforts to produce a thriving economy by developing local industry, building a modern transportation infrastructure, and, later, promoting tourism fell short of the mark.

On the eve of Communist Yugoslavia's collapse, Montenegrin political life mirrored developments in Belgrade, where Slobodan Milošević (1941–), head of Serbia's Communist Party, had enveloped himself in the cloak of Serb nationalism. In 1988–89 a Milošević-engineered "antibureaucratic revolution" replaced the Montenegrin Communist Party leadership. Following Serbia's example, the League of Communists of Montenegro changed its name, becoming the Democratic Party of Socialists. Multiparty elections held in 1990 confirmed the former Communists in power.

With the disintegration of Yugoslavia, Montenegro joined Serbia in 1992 as one of two republics making up what was styled the Federal Republic of Yugoslavia. The same year, Titograd reverted to its former name of Podgorica. Montenegrin "volunteers" participated in the shelling of Dubrovnik and attacks on Croatian coastal towns; others fought in neighboring Bosnia-Hercegovina. During the four-year-long conflict, Montenegro was tarred with the same brush of international opprobrium as Milošević-led Serbia and subjected to international sanctions that further weakened the republic's already feeble economy. Initially supportive of Milošević, who had strong familial ties to Montenegro, the Montenegrin government began to distance itself from Belgrade, with some members of the political opposition calling for total separation from Yugoslavia.

John D. Treadway

Further reading

Stevenson, Francis Seymour. *A History of Montenegro.* London, 1912; reprint New York, 1971.

Thompson, Mark. *A Paper House: The Ending of Yugoslavia.* New York, 1992.

Treadway, John D. *The Falcon and the Eagle: Montenegro and Austria-Hungary, 1908–1914.* West Lafayette, Indiana, 1983.

See also Anti-Fascism; Balkan Wars; Chetniks; Congress of Berlin; Congress of Vienna; Danilo I Petrović Njegoš; Milovan Djilas; Great Powers; Kingdom of Serbs, Croats, and Slovenes; Slobodan Milošević; Montenegro (Geography); Nicholas I of Montenegro; Orthodoxy; Petar I Petrović Njegoš; Petar II Petrović Njegoš; Sanjak of Novi Pazar; Tito–Stalin Split

Morava River

Serbian river. Entering the Danube from the south, this river of central Serbia, with its western and southern branches, drains a region of considerable agricultural value. The unified Morava is formed by the confluence of the Western and Southern Morava channels near the town of Stalac. The Western Morava rises close to the regional boundary with Montenegro and drains a succession of small basins occupied by several agricultural villages and some larger centers (Čačak, Kraljevo, and Kruševac). Similarly, from a source north of Skopje, the Southern Morava flows through a series of gorges and narrow defiles to link the basins occupied by Vranje, Leskovac, and Niš. As a unified stream, the Morava meanders through a flat and often marshy floodplain and enters the Danube a short distance below Smederevo.

The modified Mediterranean climate of the upper (southern) Morava valley allows for the production of specialized crops (fruit, tobacco, rice, and cotton). As the lower Morava valley merges with the Hungarian basin, maize and wheat are the dominant crops, while livestock production (swine, cattle, sheep) has also been an important traditional activity. Irrigation needs, together with an increased susceptibility to flooding and erosion in the lower Morava, have made drainage control and soil- and water-management development priorities in recent years.

Albert M. Tosches

M

Further reading

Hamilton, F.E. Ian. *Yugoslavia: Patterns of Economic Activity.* New York, 1968.

Hoffmann, George W. *Regional Development Strategy in Southeast Europe.* New York, 1972.

Pounds, Norman J.G. *Eastern Europe.* Chicago, 1969.

Moravia

Central region of the Czechoslovak (now Czech) Republic. Most of Moravia's history has been closely aligned with that of Bohemia. The latter was incorporated into the Great Moravian Empire in the ninth century, and, after the fall of the empire, both Bohemia and Moravia were under Austrian rule. Along with Slovakia, the two made up the Czechoslovak state after 1918. Of the three units of Czechoslovakia, Moravia is culturally closer to Bohemia, but the region has adopted some Slovak elements as well.

Moravia is made up of four distinct physical regions: the Brno uplands to the west; the Moravian Plain through the central part of the region; the Moravian Gate to the north along the border with Poland; and the Chriby, an outlier of the Carpathian Mountains bordering Slovakia. The Moravian Gate (connected with the Silesian Corridor of Poland) is one of the more densely populated parts of Europe.

Moravia was a significant contributor to the economy of the Czechoslovak state. It is a successful farming region, particularly important as a producer of wheat and sugar beets, which thrive in Moravia's rich, fertile soil. However, its greatest contributions have been industrial. The great mineral resources of the north gave rise to a very large smelting complex and related industries in the north Moravian Gate. Moravia supplied resources to industrial areas in Bohemia and Slovakia.

Brno, which serves as the regional capital and largest city of Moravia, dates to 1091. Slavs have inhabited the city since the fifth century. Located in south-central Moravia where the Svitava and Svratka Rivers meet, Brno has been an important economic center for Czechoslovakia. Its geographic position made it an important industrial and trading center within the nation. Other urban centers include Ostrava, the industrial giant of the north, and Olomouc, on the Morava River.

Russell L. Ivy

Further reading

Berentsen, William, ed. *Europe in the 1990s: A Geographical Analysis,* 7th ed. Chicago, 1997.

Pounds, Norman J.G. *Eastern Europe.* Chicago, 1969.

Rugg, Dean. *Eastern Europe.* London, 1985.

UNIDO. *Czechoslovakia: Industrial Transformation and Regeneration.* Oxford, 1992.

See also Brno; Olomouc; Ostrava; Silesia

Moravianism

A political and cultural movement to achieve a specific identity among the inhabitants of Moravia within Czech society and/or in relations between the Czechs and other Western Slavs, particularly the Slovaks. The Margravate of Moravia originated at the end of the twelfth century as a constituent part of the Bohemian crown. Henceforth, Moravia had its own administration and later its own estates, diet, and court of law. At the end of the eighteenth century, the consciousness of territorial patriotism—Moravianism—played an important role among Moravia's aristocrats and intellectuals. This consciousness defended the identity of Moravia and its inhabitants not only against Austrian centralism but also against efforts to unite the Czechs of Bohemia, Moravia, and Austrian Silesia into one nation. An attempt (after 1830) to create the Moravian language as a connecting link between Czech and Slovak was completely unsuccessful, rejected even by Moravian-born Czech national leaders such as František Palacký (1798–1876).

As late as the revolutionary spring of 1848, the Moravian diet rejected any political union with Bohemia. Cooperation among Czech deputies from Bohemia and Moravia, however, was established in the Austrian parliament a few months later. During the 1860s, Czech national consciousness prevailed among representatives of the Moravian Czechs (although they did not submit entirely to the leadership of Prague). Neither the Austrian authorities nor the Germans of Moravia wanted to consider the "Slavic speaking" Moravians as "Czechs," and they accentuated the differences between Czechs in Moravia and Bohemia (such as a more intensive Catholic faith and a less developed ethnic antagonism between Czechs and Germans in Moravia). Over the past century, the attempt to revive some kind of ethnic Moravianism has represented little more than the assertion of a regional identity within Czech society.

Jiří Kořalka

Further reading

Glassl, Horst. *Der Mährische Ausgleich.* Munich, 1967.

Hýsek, Miroslav. "Dějiny tzv. moravského separatismu." *Časopis Matice moravské* 33 (1909): 24–51, 146–72.

Malíř, Jiří. "Morava na předělu (K formování národního vědomí na Moravě v letech 1848–1871." *Časopis Matice moravské* 109 (1990): 345–63.

Mezník, Jaroslav. "History of the Czech Nation in Moravia (Outline of the Development of National Consciousness in Moravia up to the mid-19th Century)." *Independent Historiography in Czechoslovakia* 2 (Berlin, 1985): 91–146.

Trapl, Miloslav. *České národní obrození na Moravě v době předbřeznové a v revolučních letech 1848–1849.* Brno, 1977.

See also Moravia; František Palacký; Revolutions of 1848

Mucha, Alfons (1860–1939)

Czech painter, illustrator, and graphic artist. Mucha began his professional career in Vienna. From 1881 to 1883, he worked as a portrait artist in Mikulov. Later he studied in Munich. In 1888 Mucha departed for Paris, where he attended the Académie Julian. His artwork from this period includes a number of illustrations for books, magazines, bookplates, labels, and posters. His 1895 poster for the Renaissance Theater, announcing the *Gismonde* show starring Sarah Bernhardt (1844–1923), transformed him into a famous and sought-after artist. Bernhardt signed an exclusive six-year contract with him. Following this, at the World Exposition in Paris in 1900, Mucha received a silver medal and membership in the French Legion of Honor.

Mucha taught for a time at the Académie Colarossi and later established his own school. In 1904 he left for the United States and taught in Chicago, New York, and Philadelphia. It was during this period that he had the idea for creating a series of monumental paintings he called the *Slavic épopée,* which was to be a series of twenty paintings portraying the history of the Slavs. He completed this work in 1928. The paintings are now housed in the castle of Moravský Krumlov in the Czech Republic.

Mucha's celebrated posters and illustrations exemplify the Art Nouveau style. His work, which included designs and illustrations for calendars, menus, books, periodicals, postcards, and, above all, posters earned him the reputation of being one of the most outstanding and influential graphic artists in Europe. His work not only popularized Art Nouveau but brought poster art to a high level of recognition as a distinct art form.

Dagmar Berry

Further reading

Mucha, Jiří. *Alphonse Mucha, His Life and Art.* New York, 1967.

Reade, Brian. *Art Nouveau and Alphonse Mucha.* London, 1963.

See also Czech and Slovak Art

Münchengrätz Convention (1833)

Strengthening of the Holy Alliance, the post-Napoleonic alliance of conservative powers in Europe. In September 1833 Austrian Chancellor Clemens von Metternich (1773–1859) and Russian Foreign Minister Karl Nesselrode (1780–1862) held negotiations to revitalize the Holy Alliance, which had suffered because of Russian support for Greek independence and suppression of the 1830 Polish uprising. The talks resulted in two conventions signed on September 18 and 19, 1833, with Prussia adhering a month later with the Berlin Convention. In September 1835 the signatories reaffirmed the convention.

The accords supported the integrity of the Ottoman Empire, but the two powers agreed to cooperate to maintain the balance of power in the region if it collapsed despite their efforts. Austria and Russia mutually guaranteed their Polish territory and agreed to settle differences over the area arising from the 1830 rebellion. They also agreed to support each other and any ruler who requested aid against revolutionary activity. Furthermore, Nicholas I (1796–1855) verbally recognized the right of Archduke Ferdinand (1793–1875) to the Austrian throne if a succession crisis arose in the Habsburg Empire.

Metternich wanted to secure British and French consent for the arrangement, but Russia disapproved. The convention, nonetheless, reaffirmed the conservative Holy Alliance for another twenty years, during which Austria and Russia cooperated closely in foreign affairs and exchanged intelligence on revolutionary movements in Europe. Nicholas I became a firm supporter of the agreement, and it served as the basis for Russian intervention in Hungary in 1849 (during the revolution of 1848–49), while he unsuccessfully attempted to use it to secure Austrian aid in the Crimean War (1853–56).

Gregory C. Ference

Further reading

Martens, F. *Recueil des traités et conventions conclus par la Russie avec les puissances étrangers, publié d'ordre du ministere des affaires étrangèes. Traités avec l'Autriche (1815–49)*. St. Petersburg, 1878.

See also Crimean War; Eastern Question; Holy Alliance; Hungarian War for Independence; Clemens von Metternich; Nicholas I; November Uprising; Revolutions of 1848

Munich Pact (1938)

International agreement revising the boundaries of Czechoslovakia. Following Germany's annexation of Austria in March 1938, Adolf Hitler (1889–1945) turned his attention to Czechoslovakia's heavily German region known as the Sudetenland. Czechoslovak President Edvard Beneš (1884–1948) was unwilling to consider demands for autonomy from Sudeten German leaders such as Konrad Henlein (1898–1945). Hitler's insistence on the right to "protect" fellow Germans in the Sudetenland became more aggressive in April 1938. French Premier Édouard Daladier (1884–1970) and British Prime Minister Neville Chamberlain (1869–1940) agreed to resolve the crisis by putting pressure on Beneš to make concessions. Daladier had hoped for a firm guarantee of British support in the event of difficulties with Hitler, since France had signed a mutual defensive alliance with Czechoslovakia in 1924.

In late August 1938 Chamberlain decided to meet with Hitler personally if all other avenues for resolving the crisis failed. Following an incendiary speech by Hitler on September 12 and subsequent unrest in the Sudetenland, Chamberlain met with Hitler at Berchtesgaden on September 15. Hitler promised to take no military action over the next few days; Chamberlain left convinced that Hitler was seeking a peaceful solution to the crisis. (In fact, Hitler was planning to invade.) Great Britain and France, accordingly, drafted a compromise that provided for the cession of part of the Sudetenland, and Beneš, under intense pressure, agreed to support the compromise.

In a meeting with Chamberlain at Bad Godesberg on September 23, Hitler not only rejected the compromise but demanded the evacuation of all Czechs from the Sudetenland by September 28, that Polish and Hungarian claims to Czech territory be satisfied, and that the Sudetenland itself be annexed without delay. After Beneš categorically rejected the Godesberg demands, Hitler demanded Czech acceptance by 2:00 P.M. on September 28. On the 27th, the British informed Hitler that if France felt compelled to support Czechoslovakia, Great Britain would support them as well. Hitler proposed continuing negotiations, and Chamberlain asked Italian dictator Benito Mussolini (1883–1945) to participate. The result was the Munich conference (September 29, 1938), to which the Czechs were not invited and in which Hitler gained most of his Godesberg demands. German troops occupied the Sudetenland on October 1, Poland gained the province of Teschen in Moravia, and parts of Slovakia and Ruthenia were granted to Hungary.

Daniel D. Trifan

Further reading

Adamthwaite, Anthony. *France and the Coming of World War II*. London, 1977.
Latynski, Maya, ed. *Reappraising the Munich Pact: Continental Perspectives*. Washington, D.C., 1992.
Taylor, Telford. *Munich: The Price of Peace*. Garden City, New York, 1979.

See also *Anschluss;* Edvard Beneš; Neville Chamberlain; Adolf Hitler; Konrad Henlein; Protectorate of Bohemia and Moravia; Sudeten Crisis; Sudetenland

Munkácsy, Mihály (1844–1900)

Hungarian painter. Among Hungarian painters living abroad, the name synonymous with world fame was Munkácsy. His uncomplicated beginnings—he was a joiner's apprentice—were colored by the good will of local artists who recognized his talent early.

With important patronage he forged his way through the academies of Vienna, Munich, and Düsseldorf. In his early period his style was compassionate and free of sentimentality, with a breadth and solidity of forms and the drama of light. He belonged spiritually to a generation that prided itself on a Magyar identity. In his successful early masterpiece—painted with romantic pathos—*The Last Day of a Condemned Man* (1872–73), he was still using some of the melancholic genre inherited from the German bourgeois style. However, he already had created a more progressive, fresh view of the contemporary Magyar peasant, which won him a gold medal in the Paris Salon of 1870.

After 1881, Munkácsy's style took a different direction. His colors, with broad tonal variations, usually built around dramatic themes and psychological overtones, captured the attention of the public. The last twenty-five years of his life were years of recognition and fame, when paintings such as *Blind Milton Dictates the Paradise Lost* (gold medal winner of the Salon of 1878), *Pawnshop* (1877), *Christ before Pilate* (1873–74, widely exhibited throughout Europe and America), and *Golgotha* (1882) were placed on display in such places as the Lennox Library and the Metropolitan Museum in New York City and in Wannamaker's Department stores in Philadelphia.

During the last years of his life, a definite decline in his artistic achievements was observed. Some of his canvases, such as *Ecce Homo* (1884), are darkened as a result of the asphalt technique (employment of bitumen to darken parts of the canvas) of the Düsseldorf School. Still, frescoes in the entrance hall of the Kunsthistorisches Museum in Vienna and his influence on painters such as Hungarian József Rippl-Ronai (1861–1927), German Max Liebermann (1847–1935), and Frenchmen such as Jean Jacques Henner (1829–1905) are testimonies to the vigor and the talent that remain his hallmark.

George Tivadar Radân

Further reading

Lyka, K. *Michael von Munkácsy.* Vienna, 1925.
Vegvary, L. *Michael Munkácsy: Katalog der Gemälde und Zeichnungen.* Budapest, 1958.
——. "Tépéscsinálok," in *Müvészettörténeti Tanulmányok.* Budapest, 1954, 291–320.

See also Hungarian Art

Mureş River

Transylvanian river. The Mureş (in antiquity, Marisus; Hungarian, Maros) springs at an altitude of 2,833 feet (850 m) in the Hasmaşul Mare mountain range on the western slope of the Carpathians near the city of Gheorgheni, then flows west through the middle of Transylvania for about 420 miles (700 km). After forming the Romanian-Hungarian boundary for 24 miles (40 km), it enters Hungary and 29 miles (48 km) farther west flows into the Tisza at the edge of the city of Szeged. Its drainage basin covers 10,716 square miles (29,767 sq km), nine-tenths of which are in Romania. After meandering through such smaller cities as Reghin and Târgu Mureş, it flows through the heart of Transylvania—the city of Alba Iulia—built on the ruins of Apulum, the capital of Roman Dacia. Throughout this portion of its flow, and for another 30 miles (50 km) until it reaches the city of Deva, the Mureş is heavily nourished on both sides by numerous affluents. Below Deva it receives only a few streams on the right side. The waters of the Mureş have been used for centuries to float logs downstream and for fishing. Today there is a great emphasis on the aesthetic and touristic values offered by this river, and the Romanian government plans to prevent its flooding, which has recently caused great damage (for example in 1970).

Ladis K.D. Kristof

Further reading

Magocsi, Paul Robert. *Historical Atlas of East Central Europe.* Seattle, Washington, 1993.
România: Atlas istoric-geographic. Bucharest, 1996.

Mürzsteg Agreement (1903)

Accord between Austria-Hungary and Russia concerning the Balkans. Franz Joseph (1830–1916) and Nicholas II (1868–1918) met in a hunting lodge in Styria to discuss the maintenance of peace in the Balkans following the unsuccessful Internal Macedonian Revolutionary Organization–led Ilinden Uprising in Macedonia (to gain Macedonian autonomy) in August 1903. The two rulers agreed

M

to keep the Balkans "on ice" by reaffirming the status quo established earlier in the Austro-Russian Balkan Agreement of 1897. The Austro-Hungarian and Russian foreign ministers worked out a reform program, signed on October 3, 1903, that called for the Turkish inspector-general of Macedonia to be assisted and advised by both a Russian and an Austrian civil agent, the judicial system to be restructured, financial compensation to be paid to victims of the uprising, and the gendarmerie to be reformed. The gendarmerie, technically under Ottoman control, would be run by European officers under the command of a foreign general and responsible for restoring order in Macedonia. To facilitate the process, the three Macedonian *vilayets* (provinces) of Kosovo, Monastir, and Salonika were divided into six districts, with Austria-Hungary responsible for Kosovo, France for Seres, Great Britain for Dranca, Italy for Monastir, and Russia for Salonika. Furthermore, the agreement provided for the restructuring of districts according to ethnicity after the restoration of peace.

Although the Turks objected to the plan, the sultan accepted it on November 24 after pressure from the Great Powers, who were hopeful that it would calm the region. It quickly became apparent, however, that the agreement would do little to solve the problems in Macedonia.

Gregory C. Ference

Further reading

Adolphe de Plason de la Woestyne. *Recueil des traités et conventions conclus par l'Autriche-Hongrie avec les puissances étrangèrs.* Vienna, 1908.

See also Eastern Question; Franz Joseph; Great Powers; Ilinden Uprising; IMRO; Macedonia; Nicholas II

Mushanov, Nikola (1872–1951)

Bulgarian democratic politician. Mushanov studied law in France before entering politics. In the 1890s he joined the Democratic Party of Petko Karavelov (1843–1903) and rose to a leadership position under Aleksandur Malinov (1867–1938). Repeatedly elected to the National Assembly, he served in a variety of positions in the cabinets led by his party. Like Malinov, he divorced himself from the plot that overthrew the Agrarian regime

of Aleksandur Stamboliiski (1879–1923) on June 9, 1923. Mushanov succeeded Malinov as premier in 1931.

Mushanov consistently upheld with dignity the principles of democracy in Bulgarian politics and the national ideals of the Bulgarian people in international affairs. He emerged as the most formidable opponent of the personal regime of King Boris (1894–1943) and Bulgaria's orientation toward Germany in the 1930s. Likewise, he categorically refused to support the Communist resistance movement during World War II. On September 2, 1944, he joined with the Agrarian Party of Dimitur Gichev (1893–1964) in a last effort to save Bulgaria from Soviet occupation, but the government was overthrown, basically by the same people who had made the coups of 1923 and 1934. He was arrested and tried as a war criminal by a "people's court," but his life was spared. He attempted to resume political activities in 1946, but to no avail. Imprisoned and then freed again, he died at home in 1951.

Spas T. Raikin

Further reading

Dimitrov, Ilcho. *Bourzhoaznata opozitsia v Bulgaria, 1939–1944.* Sofia, 1969.

Georgiev, Velichko. *Bourzhoaznite drebnobourzhoaznite partii v Bulgaria, 1934–1939.* Sofia, 1971.

Kossev, Dimitur et al. *Istoria na Bulgaria,* vol. 2. Sofia, 1955.

Kumanov, Milen. *Politicheski partii, organizatsii i dvizhenia v Bulgaria i tekhnite lideri.* Sofia, 1991.

See also Boris III; Dimitur Gichev; Aleksandur Malinov; Aleksandur Stamboliiski

Music

After 1815, the peoples of Eastern Europe absorbed themselves in national renewal and the quest for independence. Cultural activities supported political agendas, and among the arts, music had its special place in nineteenth-century nationalism. The collaboration of music and text in genres such as art song and opera usually provided the most explicit means of promoting an indigenous consciousness, and in many regions public performances had to be strictly controlled to minimize unrest against the ruling authorities.

Instrumental music conveyed national themes as a more abstract message, relying on folk melodies and dance rhythms for local flavor. Political developments coupled with social change in Eastern Europe to further influence musical performance and composition. With a population shift to the cities, musical activities previously supported at country estates and monastic centers were transformed into public performances in the region's urban centers. Consequently, audiences came to represent more of the middle class. The travel and exchange of musicians, along with crosscurrents of Pan-Slavist thought, which emphasized the unity of the Slavic peoples, stimulated common developments during the nineteenth century (unlike the latter half of the twentieth century, when Soviet domination of cultural life enforced a certain uniformity and socialist realism). Music in Eastern Europe is characterized as an extension eastward of Western European musical culture as it connected with local involvement by virtuoso performers, performing ensembles, publishing, and music education. As musicians and composers struggled with their identity vis-à-vis German hegemony in musical thought, the resulting music has become an important facet of the independent identity of each nation.

Music among the South Slavs in the nineteenth century initially concentrated on choral music, patriotic songs, and marches to support the awakened national consciousness. A reliance on folk sources is seen in the singspiel-like productions of Slovene Davorin Jenko (1835–1914) and the choral compositions of Stevan Stojanovic-Mokranjac (1856–1914). In the twentieth century, the first Serbian operas were *Na Uranku* (*At Dawn*, 1903) by Stanislav Binički (1872–1942) and *Knez Ivo od Semberije* (*Prince Ivo of Semberija*, 1911). Vatroslav Lisinski (1819–54) created *Ljubav i zloba* (*Love and Malice*, 1845), the first opera from Croatia. The development of Bulgarian musical life waited until the end of Turkish occupation in 1878. Emanuil Manolov (1860–1902) was a prominent composer of military band music and vocal works.

In the first half of the twentieth century, South Slav composers strove to maintain a national style while conforming to European musical traditions. Prominent names include Georgi Athanassov (1882–1931), Nikolao Athanassov (1886–1969), Panayot Pipkov (1871–1942), Jakov Gotovac (1895–1982), Josip Slavenski (1896–1955), Pantcho Vladigerov (1899–1978), and Matija Bravničar (1897–1977).

The leading musical figure in Romania was George Enescu (1881–1955), who was known as a violinist and a composer. While Enesco championed the development of young Romanian composers, others devoted themselves to collecting folk songs. Romanian composers such as Alfred Alessandrescu (1893–1959) and Mihail Jora (1891–1971) often studied abroad.

In Hungary, recruiting dances called *verbunkos* were the focus of the national musical idiom and, as such, became the foundation of operas and symphonies. Ferenc Erkel (1810–93) was an opera composer who infused his works with folk melodies. The most famous Hungarian musician of the period, Ferenc (Franz) Liszt (1811–86), expressed his roots in works such as the Hungarian Rhapsodies. Later, Béla Bartók (1881–1945) and Zoltán Kodály (1882–1967) came to stand among the greatest composers of the twentieth century. Both collected Hungarian folk songs to use in their serious compositions. Bartók especially was interested in the modes and other scales of Magyar music. Kodály has a special place in the history of music education. The most avant-garde school is represented by György Ligeti (1923–).

The Czechs began to revive their language and cultural history at the beginning of the nineteenth century. Although the composers of Bohemia and Moravia drew on folk sources, as in the manner of other Slavic peoples, Czech history before the Habsburg reign (before 1526) was another source of inspiration for national renewal. Bedřich Smetana (1824–84), often hailed as the figurehead of nineteenth-century Czech nationalism in music, used references such as the early-fifteenth-century Hussite chorale *Ktož jsú Boží bojovnice* (*Ye Who Are Warriors of God*) in his music. This and other historical melodies are found in other composers' works as well. The most noted Czech work of the period is Smetana's *Prodaná nevěsta* (*The Bartered Bride*, 1866). Antonín Dvořák (1841–1904) also chose national subjects for program music and opera. The melodic ease of his music often derives from folk music and popular dance rhythms, as evidenced by his *Slavonic Dances*. In the twentieth century, Leoš Janáček (1854–1928) concentrated on the inflections of Moravian peasant speech and song. His opera *Jenůfa* (1904) recounts a tragic peasant story in an expressionistic style. Bohuslav Martinů (1890–1959) worked mostly outside of Czechoslovakia, but his music also conveys a strong Czech feeling.

M The leaders of musical life in early-nineteenth-century Poland were Karol Kurpiński (1785–1857) and Józef Elsner (1769–1854), who became the teacher of Frédéric Chopin (1810–49). The blossoming cultural life of Polish cities such as Warsaw in the early part of the century was stalled by political events, notably the 1830 November Uprising against Russian rule. The promising young pianist Chopin settled in Paris to compose short pieces on Polish dances like the mazurka and the polonaise, leaving lesser-known composers to develop both private and public musical life. A broad interest in opera was satisfied by Stanisław Moniuszko (1819–72), who composed the national opera *Halka* (1858).

Pianist-statesman Ignacy Paderewski (1860–1941) and composer Karol Szymanowski (1882–1937) gave international exposure to Polish music in the early twentieth century. In the period following World War II, Polish music became quite progressive but still drew on national history and folk themes for inspiration. The festival of contemporary music, Warsaw Autumn, was created in 1956 and became a forum for the avant-garde works of such Polish artists as Witold Lutosławski (1913–1994), Krzystof Penderecki (1933–), Henryk Górecki (1933–), and Tadeusz Baird (1928–81).

William Smialek

Further reading

Černý, Jaromír et al. *Hudba v českých dějinách.* Prague, 1983.

Cvetko, Dragotin. *Musikgeschichte der Südslawen.* Kassel, 1975.

Helm, Eugene, "Music in Yugoslavia." *Musical Quarterly* 51 (1965): 215–24.

Ochlewski, Tadeusz, ed. *Dzieje muzyki polskiej w zarysie.* Warsaw, 1977.

See also Béla Bartók; Frédéric Chopin; Dance; Antonín Dvořák; George Enescu; Folklife; Folk Music; Leoš Janáček; Zoltán Kodály; Franz (Ferenc) Liszt; Nationalism; November Uprising; Ignacy Paderewski; Pan-Slavism; Bedřich Smetana; Theater

Muslims

Adherents to Islam, and one of the six "nations" of former Yugoslavia. While Muslims live principally in Asia and North Africa, there have long been Muslim communities in Europe as well. In Eastern Europe, Islam entered with Ottoman armies and Turkic peoples in the fourteenth and fifteenth centuries. There was a gradual conversion of local people to Islam, particularly in the regions of Bosnia and Albania, where neither Roman Catholicism nor Eastern Orthodoxy had established a strong presence. Islam was tolerant of local practices and was well preached. Further, it offered economic and cultural incentives to conversion in the form of fewer taxes, administrative and military opportunities for Muslims, and links with the vibrant culture and society of Istanbul.

Today in Eastern Europe, Muslims live principally in three regions: Bosnia, Bulgaria, and Albania and the surrounding Albanian-populated regions of Serbia and Macedonia. There are also many Muslims in European Turkey, between Bulgaria and the Bosphorus. All but one of the major Muslim communities in southeastern Europe are local European peoples who converted to Islam during Ottoman rule. Thus the Bosnians and the Bulgarian Pomaks are Slavs, and the Albanians are a European people. The one exception are the Turkish communities of Bulgaria that originated with colonists from Anatolia who began settling there in the fourteenth century.

There are also smaller Muslim communities in southeastern Europe: the Slavic Muslims in the Sanjak of Novi Pazar in southwestern Serbia and in Montenegro; the Slavic Muslims in Macedonia; small ethnic Turkish communities in Macedonia and Serbia; remnants of Turkic communities in Romania; and the Roma (Gypsies) in Bulgaria, Macedonia, Albania, Serbia, and Bosnia, most of whom are Muslim.

The political power and cultural contributions of Muslims in southeastern Europe were greatest before the advent of nationalist movements in the nineteenth and twentieth centuries. For example, in the sixteenth and seventeenth centuries, when the Ottoman Empire was strong, all major cities with their markets, mosques, *medreses* (Muslim religious schools), and scholars were cultural centers for the region. Nine Bosnian Muslims rose to be grand viziers, the highest administrative office in the empire, with three from the Sokullu family. Twenty-one grand viziers were of Albanian origin, with several from the Köprülü family.

In contrast, in the nineteenth and twentieth centuries Muslims in southeastern Europe were largely reduced to mistrusted and disparate minority groups. Most local nationalist movements had no place for Muslims. Not only were Muslims associated with the Ottomans, against whom the nationalists fought for power, but many nationalist ideologies were associated with particular forms of Christianity: Orthodoxy for Serbs, Bulgarians, Romanians, and Greeks; Catholicism for Croats and Slovenes. Muslims of Slavic background were viewed as traitors and those of Turkish background, no matter how many centuries they had been in southeastern Europe, were outsiders. (The exception was Albania, where Muslims led the nationalist movement, advancing an ideology that downplayed religious differences.) The subsequent rise of Communist regimes in Eastern Europe, most of which were antireligious, further undercut Muslim peoples who continued to see Islam as a source of their identity.

While the political place of Muslims in southeastern Europe in the nineteenth and twentieth centuries has been problematic, they have continued to contribute to their societies in different ways. In Bulgaria, Muslims are essential to agricultural production. Throughout the region, Muslims contributed culturally, introducing and preserving Ottoman ways: foods, including sweets like baklava and *kadaif, dolmas* (vegetables stuffed with rice), skewered meats and pilafs, pungent coffee, and *helva* for mourning; distinctive musical instruments, musical genres, poetic forms, and dances; the value placed on hospitality, and a tolerance for people of different faiths with an expectation that city life involves living with people of other faiths. This Ottoman legacy is most strongly preserved among Albanians and Bosnians.

Many Muslims emigrated from the region over the past two centuries in response to the changing political and social climate. Indeed, emigration has been a constant from the late nineteenth century throughout the twentieth. The Muslim communities in Romania and in northern Serbia have all but disappeared. The Muslim communities in Greece are greatly reduced. Policies after World War I by the Serbian government for the Kosovo region of Serbia, and by the Bulgarian government, were designed to encourage landowning Muslims to leave. Many did depart, particularly to Turkey.

In Bulgaria the Communist government worked to eradicate Muslim identity. It made circumcision, a practice common to Muslims, illegal. It conducted campaigns to force local Muslims to give up their "muslim" names, first in 1971–73 among the Pomaks, the Slavic Bulgarian-speaking Muslims in southern Bulgaria, and then from 1984 to 1989, with the Turks living in the northeastern and southern Bulgaria.

The situation of Muslims in Macedonia, Serbia, and Montenegro is clouded by their governments' hostility to the largely Muslim Albanians there. The ruling Slavic nationalist regimes are distrustful of Albanians, with their higher birth rate and proximity to Albania. In the late 1990s, the situation became especially tense in Kosovo, the southernmost region of Serbia that in the fourteenth century was the center of the Serbian state but now is 90 percent Albanian. As for Macedonia and Montenegro, they are concerned that their non-Albanian Muslims will allow themselves to be swallowed up in the larger Albanian Muslim community, and that their Albanian Muslims will seek to be annexed by Albania.

Unlike the Muslims in most parts of southeastern Europe who are minorities, Muslims in Albania are in the majority, with 70 percent of the population according to censuses conducted during the first half of the twentieth century. In Albania, however, the Communist regime that ruled from 1944 to 1991 opposed all religions. In 1967 Albania declared itself an atheist state, and the earlier antireligious practices were carried to extremes with the destruction of mosques and other houses of worship, and severe punishments imposed for public and private practice of religion. Since 1991, the practice of religion in Albania has again become legal. Many of the current Albanian leaders are from formerly Muslim families, but it will take time before local Muslim religious leaders are again trained. Meanwhile, acute economic problems overshadow questions of religion.

Bosnia also represents an exception to the general picture of minority status for Muslim communities in southeastern Europe in the last two centuries. In the 1992 census, Bosnian Muslims were actually an ethnic majority, with 44 percent of the population, the rest split among Bosnian Serbs, Bosnian Croats, and other smaller groups. Historically, Bosnia, which had been a center of Ottoman culture, was occupied by the Habsburg Empire in 1878. Some prominent Muslims emigrated to Ottoman lands, but most did not. On the whole, the Austrians treated the Bosnian Muslims well, seeing them as a balance to Serbian nationalists. But

M in the continuing nationalist movements of Serbia and Croatia, the Muslims had no clear place. During the two world wars, all peoples of Bosnia, Serbia, and Croatia suffered. After World War II, Bosnian Muslims again did not fit into the categories of Yugoslav "nationalities." Nevertheless, they slowly gained status under Tito (1892–1980), moving from having to declare themselves in 1948 as "Muslim/Serbian" or "Muslim/Croatian" or "Muslim/nationality undefined," to 1953, when all categories of "Muslim" were abolished, but "Yugoslav/nationality undefined" was allowed; to 1968, when they were given the opportunity to declare themselves "Muslim in the ethnic sense."

In 1971 the new census category "Muslim" was accorded equal status to that of the five other "nations" of Yugoslavia—Serb, Croat, Slovene, Montenegrin, and Macedonian. (But Muslims not of Bosnian origin were not to use the new category.) Throughout the 1970s, a time of revival in many parts of the Islamic world, many mosques were built in Bosnia and Bosnians went on pilgrimage to Mecca. After World War II, the number of intermarriages increased in urban centers of Bosnia, and much secularism among Muslims occurred. The choice of Sarajevo for the Winter Olympic Games in 1984 gave international recognition to the remarkably tolerant and cosmopolitan nature of the Bosnian capital.

Yet within Bosnia, religious Muslims were alarmed by the trials of alleged Muslim nationalists in 1984, and threatened by the rise of Serbian and Croatian nationalism in the 1980s. Such nationalists had no place for Muslims or those of mixed marriages in territories they sought. As Yugoslavia unraveled along nationalistic lines in the early 1990s, Muslims in Bosnia, Serbia, Montenegro, and Macedonia found themselves in a precarious position.

The fighting that began in Bosnia in 1992 brought the destruction of hundreds of mosques, architectural treasures like the Bridge of Mostar, the Ferhadiye Mosque of Banja Luka, and even the Oriental Institute in Sarajevo, which had preserved thousands of documents of the Ottoman history of Bosnia. Sarajevo itself was besieged by Bosnian Serbs for over three years, with great ensuing destruction. Not only Muslim landmarks but also Muslim people were targeted and forced from their homes. By the end of the first two years of the war, two hundred thousand Bosnians had died and two million more had become refugees.

Later in the decade, tensions in Kosovo led to bloodshed as Serb military and paramilitary units cracked down on the Muslim Albanian population and Albanian guerrillas (the Kosovo Liberation Army) struck back. In 1999 NATO (the North Atlantic Treaty Organization) launched a series of air attacks on Yugoslavia in an attempt to force Belgrade to cease what the West saw as a policy of "ethnic cleansing." After weeks of relentless bombardment, the Yugoslav army withdrew from Kosovo and was replaced by a multinational force that included troops from the United States, Russia, Great Britain, France, Germany, and Italy. The more than one million Kosovar Albanians expelled by the Serbs began returning to their homes under the protection of NATO.

Frances Trix

Further reading

Kappler, Andras, Gerhard Simon, and Georg Brunner, eds. *Muslim Communities Reemerge: Political Perspectives on Nationality, Politics, and Opposition in the Former Soviet Union and Yugoslavia.* Durham, North Carolina, 1994.

Karpat, Kemal. *The Turks of Bulgaria: The History, Culture and Political Fate of a Minority.* Istanbul, 1990.

Pinson, Mark, ed. *The Muslims of Bosnia-Herzegovina: Their Historic Development from the Middle Ages to the Dissolution of Yugoslavia.* Cambridge, Massachusetts, 1994.

Popovic, Alexandre. *L'Islam balkanique: Les musulmans du sud-est européen dans la période post-ottomane.* Berlin, 1986.

Poulton, Hugh. *The Balkans: Minorities and States in Conflict.* London, 1991.

See also Bosnia-Hercegovina, Birth of the Republic of; Emigration; Ethnic Minorities; Gypsies; Islam; Kosovo; Orthodoxy; Ottoman Empire; Pomaks; Sanjak of Novi Pazar; Tito

N

Načertanije

Secret plan for the unification of Serbia drafted in 1844 by Ilija Garašanin (1812–74), Serbia's minister of interior, for Prince Alexander Karadjordjević (1806–85). After its public disclosure in 1906, it became the subject of conflicting interpretations—was it a Greater Serbia program or Yugoslav? The *Načertanije* was based on a plan drafted by František Zach (1807–92), a Czech who was a close associate of Adam Czartoryski (1770–1861), a former Russian foreign minister. The plan envisaged the liberation and unification of the South Slavs, who then would help liberate Poland from Austrian and Russian domination. Approximately 90 percent of the material in the *Načertanije* was incorporated verbatim from Zach's plan. It called for Serbia to complete its "sacred historic" mission, begun by Tsar Dušan (c. 1308–55) in the fourteenth century, of uniting the Serbian nation. The major emphasis was in preparing the inhabitants of Bosnia-Hercegovina, Montenegro, and northern Albania for union with Serbia. Zach, however, had stressed that Serbia would not be successful unless it included the Croats and accepted them as equals, which Garašanin excluded in his program. Hence, those who have denied its Yugoslav orientation have pointed to the systematic exclusion of the term "Yugoslav" found in Zach's plan. For example, when Zach employed "Yugoslav," Garašanin wrote "Serbian"; or when Zach asserted that Serbia must "be the nucleus of the future South Slav empire," Garašanin substituted "future Serbian empire." In addition, one entire section on Serbia's relations with the Croats, which stressed that they were "one and the same people," who spoke the same language written in two scripts, was deleted. Hence, these scholars assert that the *Načertanije* was a Greater Serbian program, not a Yugoslav one.

Charles Jelavich

Further reading

Hehn, Paul N. "The Origins of Modern Pan-Serbism: The 1844 Načertanije of Ilija Garašanin, an Analysis and Translation." *East European Quarterly* 9, no. 2 (1975): 153–71.

Jelavich, Charles. "Garašanin's Načertanije und das grosserbische Programm." *Südostforschungen* 27 (1968): 153–71.

MacKenzie, David. *Ilija Garašanin: Balkan Bismarck.* Boulder, Colorado, 1985.

See also Adam Czartoryski; Ilija Garašanin; Greater Serbia

Nagodba

Legal arrangement (English, compromise; German, *Ausgleich*) that regulated the constitutional position of Croatia (officially the Kingdom of Dalmatia, Croatia, and Slavonia) within the Habsburg monarchy, 1867–1918. After the Austro-Hungarian *Ausgleich* (Compromise) of 1867, which created the Dual Monarchy of Austria-Hungary, delegations from the Hungarian Parliament and the Croatian Sabor negotiated the *Nagodba,* which was later adopted by both legislatures as Croatian Law 1 of 1868 and Hungarian Law 30 of 1868. Revisions of the agreement, usually minor, took place in 1873, 1880, 1881, 1889, 1891, and 1906. The *Nagodba* granted Croatia autonomy over internal affairs (primarily policing), justice, and

Neducational and religious matters. It also made Croatian the official language within the kingdom. At the head of the autonomous government in Zagreb stood the *ban* (governor), with the Sabor acting as the autonomous legislature. To regulate matters common to Croatia and the rest of Hungary, Croatia was guaranteed representation in both houses of the Hungarian Parliament, while a Croatian minister without portfolio served in the Hungarian cabinet. Financial and economic matters, including taxation, were considered common to Hungary and Croatia and thus de facto under the control of the Hungarian government in Budapest. The *Nagodba* also guaranteed Croatian representation in the Hungarian delegation that met with the Austrian delegation to regulate matters common to the entire Habsburg monarchy.

Despite Croatia's official name, Dalmatia remained part of the Austrian half of the Dual Monarchy and thus de facto was not subject to the terms of the *Nagodba*. In the first (1868) version of the *Nagodba,* the Hungarian government had undertaken to facilitate the incorporation into autonomous Croatia of the Military Frontier, but this was not fully accomplished until 1881. In the original negotiations, the Croatian and Hungarian delegations had also been unable to agree on the status of the port city of Rijeka (Italian, Fiume), so Franz Joseph (1830–1916), by royal rescript, established it as a separate entity under the Hungarian crown, as it had been in the eighteenth century.

Throughout the Dualist period, Croat nationalist parties consistently but unsuccessfully advocated greater financial autonomy for Croatia, as well as the incorporation of both Rijeka and Dalmatia into the autonomous kingdom. Hungarian and Croatian nationalists also polemicized over whether, under the terms of the *Nagodba,* Croatia was an integral part of the Hungarian state or showed attributes of a separate state.

James P. Krokar

Further reading

Čulinović, Ferdo. *Državnopravna historija jugoslavenskih zemalja 19. i 20. vijeka,* 3d. ed. Zagreb, 1961.

Krestić, Vasilije. *Hrvatsko-ugarska nagodba 1868. godine.* Belgrade, 1969.

Pallua, Emilio. "A Survey of the Constitutional History of the Kingdom of Dalmatia, Croatia, and Slavonia." *Canadian-American Slavic Studies* 24 (1990): 129–54.

Šarinić, Josip. *Nagodbena Hrvatska: Postanak i osnove ustavne organizacije.* Zagreb, 1972.

See also *Ausgleich;* Croatian Military Frontier; Dual Monarchy; Dualism; Franz Joseph; Rijeka; Sabor

Nagy, Ferenc (1903–79)

Hungarian agriculturist, politician, and later one of the leaders of the Hungarian emigration. Descended from a Calvinist small-peasant family, Nagy worked on the lands of his parents as a farmer, finishing only six classes of elementary school. During the 1920s, he began to publish articles dealing with the life of the peasants. Together with others, in 1930 he founded the Független Kisgazdapárt (Independent Smallholders Party) and served as its general secretary from 1930 to 1945. He also became the principal editor of its weekly paper, *Független Kisgazda* (*Independent Smallholder*). In 1939 he was elected to parliament. Nagy was one of the founders of the Magyar Parasztszövetség (League of Hungarian Peasants). Following the occupation of Hungary by German troops in World War II, he was arrested on April 12, 1944. The Gestapo set him free six months later, but only after the intervention of the Hungarian government. Following the coup d'état of October 15, 1944, which brought to power the right-radical Arrow Cross, led by Ferenc Szálasi (1891–1945), he went underground.

In 1945 Nagy began to reorganize the activity of the Independent Smallholders Party and the League of Hungarian Peasants, eventually becoming president of both. He also began to hold important state positions, including president of the Provisional National Assembly. In 1946 he became the prime minister of Hungary. However, on June 2, 1947, under the pressure from the Hungarian Communist Party, he resigned while on vacation in Switzerland. On the following day he was excluded from his party and on October 7, 1947, deprived of his Hungarian citizenship. He settled in the United States and worked as a farmer in Herndon, Virginia, joining in the activities of the Hungarian emigration movement. Nagy was elected president of the Emigrant Organization of the Hungarian Peasant League and served as editor of the *Parasztszövetségi Értesítő* (*Bulletin of the Peasant League*). In 1954 he took part in the founding of the Assembly of Captive Nations, an organization made up of representatives of states that had fallen to communism. In 1957 he received an honorary doctorate from the University of California at Berkeley. In 1970 he retired from political activity. Nagy died in 1979, just before a planned return to Hungary.

Pál Péter Tóth

Further reading

Nagy, Ferenc. *The Struggle behind the Iron Curtain.* New York, 1948.

Vida, István. *Politikus pályák.* Budapest, 1984.

See also Agrarian Parites; Arrow Cross; Hungarian Émigrés; Peasants; Ferenc Szálasi

Nagy, Imre (1896–1958)

Hungarian Communist leader. Unlike most of the individuals who would become prominent leaders of the Hungarian Communist Party, Nagy came from a peasant background. He became a Communist while a prisoner of war in Russia during World War I. During the 1920s, he was active in radical left-wing activities in Hungary. In 1928 he fled the country and during the 1930s was an exile in the Soviet Union, where he was regarded as an expert in agricultural policy. At the end of World War II, Nagy emerged as one of the more important figures in the Hungarian Communist Party, in part because of support from the Soviet leadership. In the postwar Hungarian government, Nagy held several posts, including minister of agriculture. He supervised the introduction of extensive land reform but clashed with Mátyás Rákosi (1892–1971), head of the regime, over the pace of collectivization. In the late 1940s Nagy became a victim of Rákosi's purges and was forced to withdraw from political activity.

During the process of de-Stalinization after 1953, Nagy's stature rose rapidly. Under pressure from Moscow, Rákosi was forced to yield his title of prime minister to Nagy, who was regarded as a moderate who would correct the errors that had been made during the Stalinist period. Nagy initiated the June Program, in which he condemned Rákosi's policies, shifted the economic focus from heavy to light industry, and ended forced collectivization. Less than two years later, however, Rákosi was able to oust Nagy and thwart the reforms. When revolution against Soviet domination broke out in Hungary in October 1956, one of the key demands of the revolutionaries was the return to power of Nagy, who now became prime minister once again. Swept along by the powerful revolutionary currents, Nagy soon approved the introduction of a multiparty system and the withdrawal of Hungary from the Warsaw Pact, the Soviet-led military alliance. These changes were unacceptable to the Soviet Union. When Soviet tanks rolled into Budapest on November 4, 1956, Nagy found temporary refuge in the Yugoslav Embassy. He remained there until 1958, when he was persuaded to leave by the government of János Kádár (1912–89). Despite the assurances that had been given, the KGB promptly arrested him. He was tried secretly and executed.

In the two decades after Nagy's death he remained a revered figure in Hungary. One of the key events in the dismantling of the Communist regime in 1989 was the rehabilitation and reburial of Nagy, who was eulogized as a martyr and a great Hungarian statesman.

Judith Fai-Podlipnik and Thomas Sakmyster

Further reading

Body, Paul. *Hungarian Statesmen of Destiny, 1860–1960.* Highland Lakes, New Jersey, 1989.

Dombach, Alajos. *The Secret Trial of Imre Nagy.* Westport, Connecticut, 1994.

Hoensch, Jorg K. *A History of Modern Hungary.* New York, 1988.

Molnar, Miklós. *From Béla Kun to János Kádár: Seventy Years of Hungarian Communism.* New York, 1990.

Sugar, Peter, Peter Hanak, and Tibor Frank. *A History of Hungary.* Bloomington, Indiana, 1990.

See also Collectivization; De-Stalinization; Communist Party of Hungary; Hungarian Revolution of 1956; János Kádár; Mátyás Rákosi; Warsaw Pact

Napoléon I (Napoléon Bonaparte) (1769–1821)

Emperor of the French, whose wars of conquest introduced liberal reforms and the ideals of nationalism to East Central Europe. From 1804 to 1814, Napoléon Bonaparte established a French Empire encompassing most of Continental Europe. His conquests dramatically shifted the balance of power on the continent. A Corsican by birth, Napoléon received his education from a French military school in Brienne and the Military Academy in

Paris. In 1785 he became an artillery officer. After the French Revolution broke out in 1789, Napoléon served in the republican army and rose to command French revolutionary forces. In 1799 he seized power as first consul and later proclaimed himself emperor in 1804.

In 1807 Napoléon extended his control over Europe with the Treaties of Tilsit. The peace achieved on July 7, 1807 established a truce between the Ottoman Empire and Russia, which had sent troops to seize Wallachia and Moldavia in 1806. The truce lasted until 1812, when Alexander I (1777–1825) withdrew his troops from his southern front to fight against Napoléon. Tilsit also prevented Russia from aiding Serbian revolutionaries, thereby allowing the Ottomans to suppress the Serbian revolt. The subsequent July 9 Treaty of Tilsit ceded eastern Prussian territory to the newly created Duchy of Warsaw, an independent state with a liberal constitution patterned after the French.

Later, French consolidation of the Illyrian Provinces (Slovenia and Croatia) in 1809 exposed the population there to new ideas, foreshadowing the later Illyrian Movement (the Croatian national revival). French nationalism fostered by Napoléon's campaigns also inspired Greek nationalist movements.

Napoléon's power waned with his disastrous 1812 invasion of Russia. In 1814 the Continental powers invaded and defeated France. After the Battle of Waterloo in 1815, Napoléon was exiled to St. Helena, where he remained until his death in 1821.

Tanya L.K. Dunlap

Further reading

Durant, Will and Ariel Durant. *The Age of Napoléon: A History of European Civilization from 1789 to 1815.* New York, 1975.

Jelavich, Barbara. *History of the Balkans: Eighteenth and Nineteenth Centuries.* Cambridge, 1983.

See also Alexander I; Duchy of Warsaw; Greek Revolution; Illyrian Movement; Nationalism

Napoléon III (Louis Napoléon) (1808–73)

French emperor and advocate of national movements in East Central Europe. After living in Switzerland and Italy, Charles Louis Napoléon Bonaparte attempted twice to overthrow French king Louis Philippe (1773–1850), for which he was condemned to life imprisonment. Escaping to London in 1846, he returned to France after the Revolution of 1848 and became president on December 10, 1848. Three years later, he dissolved the National Assembly and within another year was proclaimed the French Emperor, Napoléon III.

Even before Napoléon's ascension to power, European nationalists had emigrated to Paris to study, establish contacts, and attempt to sway French policy toward the goal of aiding nationalist movements. After his rise, they were increasingly attracted by the emperor's interest in the principle of nationality and his desire to extend and maintain France's continental position.

Napoléon's influence peaked during the settlement of the Crimean War (1853–56), when the question of Romanian nationalism proved an obstacle to peace. As the spokesperson for the national movement, the emperor led those sustaining the small state. The resulting stalemate enabled Romanians unilaterally to unify the provinces of Moldavia and Wallachia. Later, however, Napoléon III proved to be more cautious in his approach. In exchange for Hungarian support in the 1859 Italian uprising (which led to Italian unification), the emperor promised to aid their struggle for independence. However, he yielded to British and Russian pressure and signed an armistice with Vienna, abandoning both movements. When Polish nationalists revolted in the early 1860s, he sympathized with the insurrection but could only suggest a general European conference out of fear of jeopardizing relations with Alexander II (1818–81). In each situation, Napoléon endorsed the national cause but refused to risk war. He increased French influence, especially among nationalists, but rarely moved beyond words of encouragement.

In July 1870 Louis Napoléon declared war on Prussia. A month later, after a crushing defeat at Sedan, he was forced to abdicate.

Tanya L.K. Dunlap

Further reading

Campbell, John C. *French Influence and the Rise of Romanian Nationalism.* New York, 1941.

Mange, Alice Edyth. *The Near Eastern Policy of the Emperor Napoléon III.* Urbana, Illinois, 1940.

Szabad, Gy. *Hungarian Political Trends between the Revolution and the Compromise (1849–1867).* Budapest, 1977.

See also Alexander II; Crimean War; Nationalism; January Uprising; Paris, Treaty of; United Principalities

Národní Výbor

National Committee, known also as the Prague National Committee, Czech National Committee, and Czechoslovak National Committee. Formed in July 1918 in Prague, the National Committee grew out of escalating popular support for establishing an independent Czech-Slovak state. It originally comprised thirty-eight members selected by seven Czech political parties; representation was proportionally based on party strength in the 1911 Austrian Reichsrat (parliament) election. The committee supported the Czechoslovak National Council in Paris and its program to achieve an independent Czech-Slovak nation. On October 28, 1918, following an announcement by the Czechoslovak National Council abroad, the National Committee in Prague also proclaimed independence for Czechoslovakia. For two weeks after this formal declaration, the National Committee served as Czechoslovakia's provisional government. It aggressively took measures to maintain public order in both Slovakia and the Czech lands. The committee declared all prewar Austrian and Hungarian laws still operative and placed all administrative and judicial bodies under its authority. Although the committee included no Slovak representatives, it appointed a temporary government for Slovakia. Through decree, it addressed the volatile issue of land reform. Finally, on November 13, 1918, the committee imposed a provisional constitution that established a national assembly and executive branch to govern the country until a permanent constitution could be formulated. On November 14, 1918, the National Committee was subsumed into the Revolutionary National Assembly, an appointed 256-member body. The National Committee oversaw a peaceful transition to independence that helped provide Czechoslovakia with stability and a responsible government by the time the Paris Peace Conference opened in January 1919.

June Granatir Alexander

Further reading

Beneš, Václav L. "Czechoslovak Democracy and Its Problems, 1918," in *A History of the Czechoslovak Republic, 1918–1948,* ed. by Victor S. Mamatey and Radomír Luža. Princeton, New Jersey, 1973, 39–98.

See also Paris Peace Conference

Nationalism

Among historians of Eastern Europe, where historically multinational empires have dominated, a common view used to be that nations were perennial entities that might go dormant but then inevitably "awaken" and struggle to emerge from under imperial oppression to independence. A newer conception considers nations to be primarily a modern phenomenon brought into being by concerted social, cultural, and intellectual effort under particular favorable economic and political circumstances; in this view, nationalism—as well as nations—is a highly contingent phenomenon that appears on the scene only given certain conditions, developments, and political movements. The French and Industrial Revolutions are generally agreed to have brought about the conditions necessary for the emergence of modern nationalism, and not just for the awakening of dormant but preexisting nations. However, for Eastern Europe the French and Industrial Revolutions were distant; while their reverberations reached the area, they did so belatedly and in attenuated ways.

A useful means of analyzing the nationalist movements in Eastern Europe is through Miroslav Hroch's three-staged model—academic, cultural, and political. In the academic phase a small number of scholars research the history, language, literature, and folklore of their people, writing their findings as grammars, dictionaries, ethnographies, folklore anthologies, and histories. These help define the nation and thus become foundation stones of embryonic nationalist movements. In the cultural phase a larger number of cultural activists propagate the ideas of these pioneers more broadly by means of the press, books, schools, reading clubs, and other cultural institutions. The third and final stage is political; the nationalist program expressed by political parties ceases to be merely academic or cultural but aims at bringing into being a full-fledged political and economic unit based on the culturally defined nation.

Until recently, scholarship on nationalism focused on the broad dichotomy between the "good" political and civic types of nationalism prevalent in Western Europe and the "bad" ethnic and collectivist nationalism, predominant in Germany and Eastern Europe, where imperial powers had interfered with the formation of centralized,

N modern, ethnically homogeneous nation-states. As nation and state did not often coincide in Central and Eastern Europe, the concept of nationality that emerged there in the eighteenth century stressed the primacy of linguistic community. This dichotomy between Eastern and Western European types of nationalism is no longer universally accepted.

Some Eastern European nationalisms, most notably the Polish, originated as political nationalism during the Enlightenment, very much in line with rationalist thinking on popular sovereignty, limited government, and constitutionalism. Before the partitions of the late eighteenth century, Poland had been a great power and a multiethnic commonwealth practicing noble democracy. One could be ethnically Polish, Lithuanian, Ruthenian, or Belorussian and be considered Polish if one belonged to the political nation, that is, the nobility. The Polish nation thus did not begin by being submerged in an imperial state dominated by another nation—the classic scenario for the emergence of Eastern ethnic nationalism—but very much as a politically defined entity. The partitions, which reduced, and finally, in 1795, eliminated independent Poland (until 1918), challenged the earlier, political concept of the nation; as a Polish state no longer existed, Poles lived as minorities in the Russian, Prussian (later German), and Habsburg Empires. Romantic nationalism harbored by the Polish nobility and intelligentsia in the early nineteenth century led them into cultural pursuits in search of the unique Polish, or broader—Slavic—soul. Most of Poland's nineteenth-century nationalists aspired to the restoration of the multinational commonwealth within its old frontiers, not recognizing fully—or often at all—the problem of the non-Polish, mostly peasant, populations of the Eastern borderlands whose national consciousness was in the process of formation as well.

Ethnic nationalism emerged in Poland in the late nineteenth century after the failure of the romantic nationalist ideology and activity to make good on restoring a Polish state. The new ethnic nationalism signaled a turn away from the noble pedigree of the earlier political Polish nationalism toward the Polish peasant, and a decisive shift toward the nation-state ideal. Along with this came chauvinism and anti-Semitism. Ethnic nationalism carried the day in the multiethnic Poland resurrected after World War I, roughly one-third of whose citizens were non-Poles. The smaller Poland that emerged from World War II and the Holocaust

is ethnically homogeneous. Nationalism continued to play a role in the People's Republic of Poland—as elsewhere in the Soviet bloc—in spite of the official socialist ideology, and it helped bring down the socialist regime.

Hungarian and Croatian nationalisms, like that of the Poles, were rooted in the consciousness of medieval noble privileges and early independent statehood. Hungary was multiethnic; it included Germans, Romanians, Slovenes, Serbs, Ruthenians, Slovaks, Greeks, Armenians, and Jews, as well as the autonomous Croats. Modern Hungarian nationalism thus came into conflict with the evolving sentiments of the other, non-Magyar nations developing their own national movements at roughly the same time. Although non-Magyars outnumbered them, many patriotic Magyars believed that the coinhabiting nationalities could be assimilated if offered individual civil and political rights. These conflicting goals and strategies came to a head during the Revolutions of 1848, in which the Habsburg Empire survived partly by dividing and conquering its nationalities. In 1867, however, a historic compromise (*Ausgleich*) was reached between Budapest and Vienna. The *Ausgleich* satisfied to a large extent Hungarian national aspirations at the expense of those of the other nationalities in the Hungarian half of Austria-Hungary.

After 1918, a broad national consensus developed around the goal of revising the Trianon treaty to regain territories lost as a result of World War I. With Hungary's shrinking to less than half its former area, the country became ethnically homogeneous. On the other hand, millions of ethnic Hungarians now found themselves living as minorities in the surrounding states of Romania, Czechoslovakia, and Yugoslavia nurturing irredentism. Other changes occurred as well. Following the nineteenth-century assimilationist tradition, to which the Jewish population had responded enthusiastically, significant levels of organized anti-Semitism surfaced for the first time in interwar Hungary.

Unlike the modern nationalisms of Poland and Hungary, which were grounded in the memory of medieval and early modern statehood and a continuous tradition of noble privileges, other Eastern European nationalisms arose among "nonhistoric" nations and relied on other features of these peoples' collective experience with peasant, clerical, and even bourgeois traditions, and classes playing a more significant role than the nobility. Serbian, Albanian, Bulgarian, Romanian, and Czech nationalisms constitute variations on this pattern.

The Balkans have been the site of a number of peasant-based nationalist movements that were frequently in conflict with one another, as well as being internally fragmented. This stemmed from the overwhelming proportion of peasants and insignificance of a true noble class. Native aristocracies and monarchs were largely eliminated along with independent statehood by the Ottoman conquest of the region.

In Bosnia and Albania, where many conversions to Islam took place, an Ottomanized landed elite emerged. Under the Ottoman *millet* system, the social organization system in the empire, clerical authorities were left intact and assumed the leadership of their peoples. The nationalist intelligentsia often emerged from the ranks of the clergy and prosperous peasants, and cultural references in the process of nationalist mobilization were mostly to peasant oral literature—including heroic historical epics of resistance to foreign incursions—and peasant folk art. Before the Ottoman conquest, Albanians were split religiously between Catholicism in the north and Orthodoxy in the south; the conquest enhanced this fragmentation by the conversion of 70 percent of Albania's population to Islam. The religious division was reinforced by dialectal differences between north and south, and, in the nineteenth century, by schools teaching in the Turkish, Greek, and Italian languages. Nationalism emerged later than in other parts of the Balkans in part because of the multidimensional disunity of the Albanians. As late as 1902, Ottoman authorities suppressed Albanian language schools. Interest in early Albanian history, mythology, and folklore accompanied the rise of Albanian national consciousness as elsewhere. Aware of their neighbors' aspirations for Albanian territories, many Albanian nationalists wished to preserve the Ottoman Empire. In 1913 Albania achieved formal independence but for decades battled Italians, Greeks, and Yugoslavs who claimed parts of Albania. That situation in part led to the isolationist policy later pursued by the Albanian Communist regime.

Romanian nationalism had something of a state tradition because the principalities of Moldavia and Wallachia were able to maintain a large degree of autonomy under the Ottomans. Early nationalism aimed at independence from Ottoman suzerainty and deposing the eighteenth-century Greek Phanariot princes, the latter viewed with suspicion by native elites. Even with the end of Phanariot rule in 1821, foreign—especially Russian—domination remained a major factor shaping Romanian nationalism. In the 1848 revolutions Wallachian and Moldavian rebels aimed at eliminating both Ottoman suzerainty and the Russian protectorate. Moldavians also demanded the union of the two principalities.

Union in 1859, obtaining a foreign prince in 1866, independence from Ottoman overlordship in 1878, and the transformation of the principalities into a kingdom in 1881 laid the groundwork for the creation of modern Romania. Yet Romanian nationalists continued to be concerned with keeping foreign influences at bay and with limiting Jewish privileges and naturalization. Nationalist arguments against Jewish rights focused on fear of economic competition and on the limited extent of Jewish assimilation to Romanian culture, particularly in Moldavia, where the majority of Romanian Jewry dwelled. Here, as elsewhere, there was also a social side to anti-Semitic nationalism. The Jews' traditional roles as traders, money lenders, and estate managers made them the frequent object of peasant and landlord hatred. Romanian nationalists, like many other East European ones, incorporated anti-Semitism into their program; they resented the European powers that, with the exception of Russia, attempted to force Romania to abide by European standards of tolerance, despite their own mixed record. Economic competition with more advanced Western countries, and local, particularly liberal, elites' interest in fostering and in keeping Romanian industry, mining, and oil profits for themselves was also grist for Romanian nationalism expressed by the passage of high protectionist tariffs.

Of the three main regional Romanian groups outside of the principalities—Bessarabians, Bukovinians, and Transylvanians—the last were the most important. In the eighteenth century the Transylvanian Latinist School that emerged chiefly among the Romanian Uniate clergy—Orthodox clerics who had accepted the religious union with Rome in 1700—began emphasizing Romanians' Roman origins. Considering the Romanians heirs of the Romans who conquered and colonized Dacia in the second century, they believed that the Romans had exterminated the indigenous Dacians. Thus, they claimed precedence over the Magyars who arrived in the area in the ninth or tenth century. Such arguments were intended to help Romanians gain rights equal to those of the accepted nations and confessions of Transylvania: Magyars, Saxons, and Szeklers, Roman Catholics, Calvinists, Lutherans, and Unitarians. Although their pleas met with limited success, they marked a new stage in the national movement of Transylvanian Romanians, who began demanding rights for the entire ethnic group regardless of confession. This tendency deepened with advancing secularism and an aggressive Magyar national policy in the nineteenth century. The Romanian national movement's leadership increasingly passed from clerical to secular intellectuals. Although in 1848 Romanian nationalists initially accepted the Magyar revolutionaries' goals of ending feudalism and gaining bourgeois freedoms, they opposed the union of Transylvania with Hungary, as the latter did not recognize Romanian autonomy. Hungarians and Romanians both lost in the process, as the Habsburgs could play the two against each other and reestablish imperial stability.

That scenario applied equally to the other minority nationalisms within Hungary.

Slovaks and Croats similarly came to define their goals at odds with the Hungarians' after the latter refused to recognize their national aspirations in 1848. Anti-Hungarian animosities continued to mount and paved the way for the secession of Hungary's non-Magyar populations in 1918 when offers of federalism were finally made.

The Czech intelligentsia and urbanizing lower classes—many from peasant backgrounds—formed the base of the Czech revival in the eighteenth and nineteenth centuries. Like medieval Poland and Hungary, the medieval Czech lands—Bohemia and Moravia—had been ethnically mixed, largely populated by Czechs and Germans. The presence of these two groups gave rise to polarization and to an early development of Czech protonationalism. Jan Hus's (1370–1415) religious reforms, his consequent martyrdom, and the Hussite movement fostered the development of the Czech language and, more generally, a Czech national consciousness. However, the Czech nobility, language, and culture and the Hussite tradition were all suppressed after the defeat of the Bohemian estates at the Battle of White Mountain in 1620.

The Czech national renascence began in the late eighteenth century, stimulated in part by increased capitalist production and urbanization. The Czech language that had been relegated to rural parish schools and private use among the lower classes began to reappear in publications, theaters, and other institutions of culture. Throughout the nineteenth century, Czechs from lower-middle-class and peasant backgrounds intensified their literary activities and aspired to linguistic and political rights equal to those of the Germans. They hoped for national rights within the political framework of the Habsburg Empire, which they regarded as the best guarantee for the small Czech nation.

It was only World War I that made an independent Czech (and Slovak) state a possibility. Although Czechs and Slovaks had once been part of the early medieval Great Moravian Empire, they had shared little in over one thousand years. The Slovaks had evolved mainly in the framework of the Hungarian state. A Czechoslovak identity was found only among small groups of educated Czechs and Slovaks before World War I. Post–World War I Czechoslovakia was a highly multiethnic state with a large, disgruntled German minority. The Czechoslovak nation was brand-new, and many Slovaks, perceiving themselves to be separate from Czechs but patronized by them, rejected the concept. German and Slovak nationalisms, manipulated by Nazi Germany in the 1930s, helped bring down the most democratic of the Habsburg successor states. That manipulation was not the only ingredient in Slovak anti-Czech nationalism, however, a fact obvious in light of the secession of Slovakia from Czechoslovakia in 1993.

Most Eastern European nationalisms were complex hybrids, exhibiting different ideological features in succession, and even, at times, simultaneously. During the interwar period, the region was made up largely of newly configured states whose leaders championed the nation-state model. All Eastern European nationalisms were predominantly ethnic and integral in orientation, despite the fact that political boundaries did not correspond to ethnic frontiers. Federalism, which had been the dream of many, was now associated with the defunct Habsburg Empire and with the newly Communist Soviet Union. It no longer enjoyed much prestige among peoples constituting majorities in their own states. Nevertheless, there were still large numbers of minority populations incorporated no longer in empires but in countries that visualized themselves as nation-states. Moreover, some of the "state-owning" nations, like the Czechoslovaks and the Yugoslavs, were newly joined and lacked age-old bonds. Even the more homogeneous Poles and Romanians discovered the negative force of regionalism. Integral nationalism had particular appeal among aspiring native elites who wished to overcome regionalism and to displace the previously dominant elites—of alien ethnicity—left over from before the war.

Despite Marxist claims that communism would inaugurate a profoundly internationalist order, after 1945 nationalism continued to haunt Eastern Europe in the shape of internecine ethnic tensions, irredentist conflicts, and nationalist resistance to Soviet domination. Whether Communist leaders like Romania's Nicolae Ceauşescu (1918–89) manipulated nationalist traditions duplicitously merely to legitimize an otherwise unpopular regime, or whether he was pulled into nationalist rhetoric by intellectuals and institutions—that the regime wanted to co-opt—a nationalist socialist synthesis emerged, most obviously in Romania but elsewhere in the Eastern Bloc as well.

Nationalism also played a part in the dismantling of communism in Eastern Europe. In the post-Communist period, given tremendous economic difficulties and scarcities, nationalism has remained a major ideological and political option particularly on the right of the political spectrum.

Irina Livezeanu

Further reading

Gellner, Ernest. *Nations and Nationalism.* Ithaca, New York, 1983.

Hitchins, Keith. *The Rumanian National Movement in Transylvania, 1780–1849.* Cambridge, Massachusetts, 1969.

Hobsbawm, E.J. *Nations and Nationalism since 1780: Programme, Myth, Reality,* 2d ed. Cambridge, 1991.

Hroch, Miroslav. *Social Preconditions of National Revival in Europe.* Cambridge, 1991.

Jelavich, Charles and Barbara Jelavich. *The Establishment of the Balkan National States, 1804–1920.* Seattle, Washington, 1977.

Livezeanu, Irina. *Cultural Politics in Greater Romania: Regionalism, Nation Building, and Ethnic Struggle, 1918–1930.* Ithaca, New York, 1995.

Sugar, Peter F. and Ivo John Lederer, eds. *Nationalism in Eastern Europe.* Seattle, Washington, 1986.

Teich, Mikuláš and Roy Porter, eds. *The National Question in Europe in Historical Context.* Cambridge, 1993.

Verdery, Katherine. *National Ideology under Socialism: Identity and Cultural Politics in Ceauşescu's Romania.* Berkeley, California, 1991.

Walicki, Andrzej. *The Enlightenment and the Birth of Modern Nationhood: Polish Political Thought from Noble Republicanism to Tadeusz Kosciuszko.* Notre Dame, Indiana, 1989.

See also *Ausgleich;* Nicolae Ceauşescu; Eastern Question; Ethnic Minorities; Folklife; Folklore; Folk Music; Greater Romania; Greater Serbia; Holocaust; Intelligentsia; Irredentism; Magyarization; *Millet;* Phanariots; Polish Question; Revolutions of 1848; Trianon, Treaty of; Transylvanian Dispute; Uniate Church; United Principalities

Nationality Law of 1868

Hungary's liberal attempt to meet the demands of its nationalities through legislation. Hungary was a multinational state, and through the turn of the century national minorities—Romanians, Germans, Slovaks, Croats, Serbs, and others—made up a majority of the population. The Hungarian government issued a nationality law during the last months of the Revolution of 1848–49, but it came too late to make a difference. The neoabsolutist regime of the 1850s and 1860s (which reflected post-1848 centralization) treated all groups equally. In negotiations leading to the *Ausgleich* (Compromise) of 1867, which created the Dual Monarchy of Austria-Hungary, Franz Joseph (1830–1916) insisted on a new Hungarian-Croatian agreement and a fair settlement for the other nationalities. The *Nagodba* of 1868, the "minicompromise," gave the Croats political autonomy within Hungary, granting them their own government and parliament, and making Croatian the language of public life in Croatia. The Nationality Law of 1868 allowed the free use of national languages in secondary schools, local government, and churches, while making Hungarian the exclusive language of the central government, parliament, higher courts, and the university. In keeping with nineteenth-century liberalism, the law refused the nationalities' calls for political autonomy. "In Hungary," said Ferenc Deák (1803–76), architect of the *Ausgleich,* "there is only one political nation: the unitary, indivisible Hungarian nation."

On balance, the law was progressive for its time, especially in comparison with neighboring Russia or the states of southeastern Europe. Unfortunately, it lacked teeth, and when subsequent Hungarian governments ignored both its letter and its spirit, the nationalities had no legal remedy. The *Lex Apponyi* of 1907, which mandated the teaching of Hungarian in elementary schools, reflected the growing intolerance in Hungary toward the nationalities.

Robert Nemes

Further reading

Body, Paul. *József Eötvös and the Modernization of Hungary, 1840–1870.* New York, 1985.

Glatz, Ferenc, ed. *Hungarians and Their Neighbors in Modern Times, 1867–1959.* Boulder, Colorado, 1995.

Hanák, Péter. *Die nationale Frage in der Österreichisch-Ungarischen Monarchie, 1900–1918.* Budapest, 1966.

See also *Ausgleich;* Ferenc Deák; Dualism; Ethnic Minorities; Franz Joseph; *Nagodba;* Magyarization; Neoabsolutism; Revolutions of 1848

National Legionary State

Romanian quasi-fascist government (September 14, 1940–January 22, 1941 [de facto]; February 14, 1941 [de jure]). In the aftermath of the cession of Bessarabia and Bukovina to the Soviet Union (June 1940) and the Vienna Award's transfer of northern Transylvania to Hungary (August 1940), Carol II (1893–1953) was first obliged to call on popular General Ion Antonescu (1882–1946) to form a new government and then to abdicate. After leaders of the traditional parties declined to become members of a government that would include members of the Iron Guard, the Romanian nationalist-fascist organization, Antonescu proclaimed the National Legionary State, in which he would wield virtually unrestricted authority (as the Conducator [leader]) with members of the Legion of the Archangel Michael (the Iron Guard) holding important governmental positions. The legion's leader, Horia Sima (1903/1908–1993), became deputy prime minister. The legion was the only legal political movement.

The regime collapsed for a number of reasons: the incompatibility of Antonescu's authoritarian conservatism with the Guard's radical anticapitalism; the social disruption caused by the Guard's

revenge murders of their enemies, including Professors Nicolae Iorga (1871–1940) and Virgil Madgearu (1887–1940); the farce of the "Romanianization Commissions," which looted foreign (that is, Jewish) property, which often ended up enriching corrupt Guard supporters, exacerbating already profound economic disquiet; the Guard's attempt to infiltrate the military and the police; and, Germany's support for Antonescu. A bungled Guardist coup attempt (January 20–22, 1941) led to the end of the regime.

Walter M. Bacon Jr.

Further reading

Heinen, Armin. *Die Legion "Erzengel Michael" in Rumänien.* Munich, 1986.

Nagy-Talavera, Nicholas M. *The Green Shirts and Others.* Stanford, California, 1970.

Palaghiţă, Ştefan. *Istoria Mişcării Legionare.* Bucharest, 1993.

See also Ion Antonescu; Carol II; Nicolae Iorga; Iron Guard; Virgil Madgearu; Right Radicalism; Horia Sima; Vienna Awards

Nazi–Polish War (September 1939)

German conquest of western and central Poland, the first armed engagement of World War II in Europe. As soon as Germany and the Soviet Union signed a nonaggression treaty on August 23, 1939, in which the two countries agreed to divide Poland, the Germans made final preparations for an invasion of Poland. As a pretext for hostilities, the SS staged a phony raid by "Polish soldiers," who were actually concentration camp inmates dressed in Polish uniforms and shot by the SS on the border post at Gliwice on the night of August 31. At 4:45 A.M. on September 1, German armies crossed the Polish frontier.

The German forces were organized in two groups: Army Group North (630,000 men) attacking southeast from East Prussia, and Army Group South (886,000 men) attacking northeast from Slovakia and Silesia. Since the Poles had deployed their army (about one million men) in linear formation along the border, the overall German objective was a giant encirclement, with the two army groups meeting at Warsaw.

German bombers and dive-bombers severely damaged Polish airfields, rail lines, and communications facilities on September 1; German infantry, led by armored units, penetrated the Polish lines within forty-eight hours. Effective Polish resistance ended on September 19 (although some units held out until October 5). The Germans lost about 14,000 killed or missing and 30,000 wounded; the Poles lost about 66,000 killed or missing, 200,000 wounded, and 694,000 taken prisoner.

Daniel D. Trifan

Further reading

Bethell, Nicholas W. *The War Hitler Won: The Fall of Poland, September 1939.* New York, 1973.

Citino, Robert M. *The Evolution of Blitzkrieg Tactics.* Westport, Connecticut, 1987.

Littlejohn, David. *Foreign Legions of the Third Reich.* San Jose, California, 1987.

Read, Anthony. *The Deadly Embrace: Hitler, Stalin and the Nazi-Soviet Pact.* New York, 1989.

See also Generalgouvernement; Molotov-Ribbentrop Pact; World War II

Neisse River

Left tributary of the Oder River. The Neisse has headwaters at the altitude of 2,559 feet (780 m) on the southwestern slopes of the Iser range in the western Sudeten in the Czech Republic. It is 156.4 miles (251 km) long, and its watershed covers 1,659 square miles (4,297 sq km). First it flows northwest in a trough between the Iser and Lausitz (Vrchovina Lužicka) ranges, fed by numerous mountain streams. Near Zittau, where the Czech, German, and Polish boundaries meet, the river turns northward and for 123 miles (198 km) constitutes the German-Polish boundary.

The river breaks through several uplands, and its upper course near Zittau crosses the Zittau-Turoszów brown coal basin, the source of considerable water pollution throughout the entire length. The slope of the river's upper course is about 10 percent, but only 0.7 percent in the lower part where the river valley is relatively wide, having natural levees 6.5–10 feet (2–3 m) high, but the flood stage reaches over 16 feet (4.9m), mainly caused by the impervious bedrock along the upper course. The average water discharge in the lower part is 1,060 cubic feet/second (30 cu m/sec).

The river is navigable downstream only from Gubin. There are few large towns along its course, the most important being Liberec in the Czech Republic; Zittau, Görlitz, Forst, and Guben in Germany; and Zgorzelec and Gubin in Poland.

Abraham Melezin

Further reading

Mileska, M.I. and W. Olendzki, eds. *Słownik Geograficzno—Krajoznawczy Polski.* Warsaw, 1994, 462–63.

NEM (New Economic Mechanism)

Hungarian economic restructuring plan. As a result of the failure of previous economic policies and the rapid deterioration of the trade balance, the Hungarian economy was restructured in 1968. The plan offered on January 1, 1968, was called the New Economic Mechanism (*Új gazdasági mechanizmus*). The major innovation was the elimination of detailed planning by the central government. The NEM applied to both the industrial and the agricultural sectors. With the reduction of central planning, the aim was to rely on price policy to influence enterprise activity. The NEM's major goals were to improve the efficiency of the economy through the process of price and foreign exchange controls and to gradually bring in line world market and domestic prices.

Initially four price categories were created: goods with fixed prices; goods with prices that could fluctuate between preset limits; goods that had ceiling prices; and goods that had no price regulation at all. To avoid inflation, subsidies continued to play a role in the prices of staple goods and basic services. As an incentive for enterprises to become profitable, they were allowed to keep 50 percent of their profits. The retained profits were to be divided by a set formula into four funds: reserve fund, welfare fund, investment fund, and profit-sharing fund. Workers were also classified into three categories: top managers, middle managers, and employees. The income of top and middle managers was tied directly to the profitability of the firm. To prevent the unemployment rate from creeping up, the average wage level of firms was regulated.

In agriculture the emphasis was placed on modernization. The authorities forgave much of the agricultural debt burden, and producer prices were raised. Compulsory targets were eliminated, save one (sown acreage for bread grain). Seed and machinery could be purchased and outputs could

N be sold on the market. Limitation on private livestock was removed.

A new foreign exchange policy was also instituted, with the foreign exchange rate to be calculated as the ratio of exports, valued at wholesale prices, and the foreign exchange received for them.

In 1973 the reform process was halted because of a new political regime and the oil crisis brought on by war in the Middle East. It was thought that by going back to centralization the Hungarian economy would be insulated from the economic upheavals caused by it.

Susan Glanz

Further reading

Balassa, Bela A. *Reforming the New Economic Mechanism in Hungary,* World Bank Staff Working Papers, no. 534. Washington, D.C., 1982.

Friss, István. *Reform of the Economic Mechanism in Hungary.* Budapest, 1971.

Hungary, Economic Developments and Reform (A World Bank Country Study). Washington, D.C., 1984.

Knight, Peter T. *Economic Decisionmaking Structures and Processes in Hungary: The Dilemmas of Decentralization.* World Bank Staff Working Papers, no. 648. Washington, D.C., 1984.

Swain, Nigel. *Hungary: The Rise and Fall of Feasible Socialism.* London, 1992.

See also Economic Development in Hungary

Němcová, Božena (1820–62)

Czech writer and a founder of modern Czech prose. Born Barbora Panková, Němcová possessed charm, natural talent, and social engagement that enabled her to meet many Czech cultural figures. Influenced by them, she first began writing poems but later devoted herself to prose. Drawing much of her inspiration from Czech folklore and folk stories, she wrote *Národní báchorky a pověsti* (*National Tales and Legends,* 1857) and *Slovenské pohádky a pověsti* (*Slovak Fairy Tales and Legends*). During the 1850s she began to concentrate on short stories in which she stressed the moral values of the country people (*Baruška* [1853], *Rozárka* [1854], *Karla* [1854], *Diva Bara* [1856]). Her best and most noted work—*Babička* (*Grandmother,* 1855)—gained great popularity and remains a centerpiece of Czech literature. The character of the grandmother—a simple countrywoman—embodies an ideal of human wisdom and vital harmony. One of Němcová's interests was education, which she saw as a device for liberation, especially of women, from prejudices and bourgeois ideas. An ideal village school where education is based on goodness, love, and noble principles is described in her story "Pan učitel" (The Teacher, 1860). Most of her works were printed in magazines, and her collected works were published for the first time posthumously in 1862–63.

Petra Orálková

Further reading

Malá Československá Encyklopedie. Prague, 1986.

See also Czech Literature

Nemes Nagy, Ágnes (1922–91)

Hungarian poet and literary translator, considered by many to be the finest woman writer of the century. Born in Budapest, Nemes Nagy received a teaching diploma from the University of Budapest in 1944 in the disciplines of Hungarian, Latin, and art history. She was a regular contributor to the pedagogical magazine *Köznevelés* (*Public Education*) and later joined the editorial staff of *Újhold* (*New Moon*), a literary journal. From 1953 to 1957, she taught at the Petőfi Gymnasium, later devoting herself entirely to writing. Nemes Nagy was not a prolific writer but rather a selective, precise, deep-thinking poet. Her verse exhibits intelligence and deep passion, although it has also been criticized for being obscure at times. The subjects of her lyrical meditations are the experience of existence, the ultimate reasons for objects, the crisis of modern civilization, and the responsibilities of the individual. Her important collections include *Kettős világban* (*Dual World,* 1946); *Száraz villám* (*Dry Lightning,* 1957); *A lovak és az angyalok* (*The Horses and the Angels,* 1969); and *Között* (*Between,* 1981). She published two volumes of essays and a study in 1984 of poet Mihály Babits (1883–1941). Nemes Nagy was also acclaimed for her translations of the works of Racine (1639–99), Molière (1622–73), Corneille (1606–84), Cocteau (1889–1963), Brecht (1898–1956), and the poems of Rilke (1875–1926), Saint-John Perse (1887–1975), and other classical and modern poets.

Katherine Gyékényesi Gatto

Further reading

Czigány, Lóránt. *The Oxford History of Hungarian Literature*. Oxford, 1984.

Nemes Nagy, Ágnes. *Between: Selected Poems*, trans. by Hugh Maxton. Dublin, 1988.

Tezla, Albert. *Hungarian Authors: A Bibliographical Handbook*. Cambridge, Massachusetts, 1970.

Vajda, Miklós, ed. *Modern Hungarian Poetry*. New York, 1977.

See also Mihály Babits; Hungarian Literature

Neoabsolutism

Name given to the government of imperial Austria from 1851 to 1859, when a new emperor, Franz Joseph (1830–1916), overhauled the entire administrative structure of the state in response to the defeated liberal demands of the Revolutions of 1848. The new governing style was characterized by a strongly centralized administration, a strengthened bureaucracy and police force, and active participation by the government in social and economic development. Franz Joseph revamped central state organs and increased the size of the bureaucracy so that the state would be able to take the leading role in the reconstitution of society.

The government was given the appellation "neoabsolutism" because of the amount of power concentrated in the hands of the emperor. The de facto beginning of Austrian neoabsolutism may be traced to March 1849. In that month the government dissolved a constituent assembly created in July 1848 and charged with the task of drawing up a constitution for the Habsburg lands. In place of that abortive document, the government imposed its own, so-called March Constitution. The emperor used this constitution over the next few months to carry out the administrative restructuring of the empire. "Constitutional reform" had come to mean organizational overhaul, not acceptance of liberal ideas. By December 1851, this "sham constitutionalism" was dropped. Franz Joseph promulgated the Sylvester Patent, squelching the March Constitution and establishing the political, administrative, and judicial organization of the empire.

With this nonrepresentative governmental structure in place, the government pursued an active policy intended to create a Habsburg nationality through the bureaucracy and the educational system for strengthening the state and weakening the centrifugal tendencies of growing nationalisms. Under the new system, the government regulated church-state relations in a new concordat with the Vatican, completely restructured the educational system, unified the monarchy economically by abolishing internal tariffs, and improved the infrastructure, especially through the development of a rail network.

Competing philosophies of government represented by the various ministers, and the tendency for all issues of importance to devolve upon the emperor himself for the final decision, were structural weaknesses in the neoabsolutist system. In the end, however, the system fell in response to foreign policy defeats. The Crimean War (1853–56), the unification of the Danubian Principalities (1859), and the Austro-Sardinian war (1859), and a growing internal debt combined to weaken both the financial and the military establishments. In March 1860 the emperor bowed to the inevitable, dismissed his ministers, and called for an advisory council to suggest ways to reorganize the state. Neoabsolutism was dead and the monarchy entered a period of experimentation with new administrative and governmental structures.

Peter Wozniak

Further reading

Beller, Steven. *Francis Joseph*. London, 1996.

Boyer, John. *Political Radicalism in Late Imperial Vienna*. Chicago, 1981.

Brandt, Harm-Hinrich. *Der österreichische Neoabsolutismus: Staatsfinanzen und Politik 1848–1860,* 2 vols. Göttingen, 1978.

Macartney, C.A. *The Habsburg Monarchy 1790–1918*. London, 1968.

Redlich, Joseph. *Das österreichische Staats- und Reichsproblem*. Leipzig, 1920.

Sked, Alan. *The Decline and Fall of the Habsburg Empire 1815–1918*. London, 1989.

See also Alexander Bach; Crimean War; Franz Joseph; Nationalism; Revolutions of 1848

Neo-Slavism

A short-lived movement for economic and cultural cooperation by East European Slavs before World War I. Neo-Slavism combined the idea of Slav ethnolinguistic affinity with innovative proposals for

N economic and cultural cooperation among middle-class Slav elites in the decade before 1914. Neo-Slavs adapted nineteenth-century Austroslavism, which sought equality for Slavic groups within the Habsburg Empire, to fit challenging turn-of-the-century circumstances. These included Pan-German violence in the Badeni language reform crisis of 1897, which resulted from ordinances that stipulated the use of the Czech language in government agencies in Bohemia and Moravia, that threatened Slav progress toward civil equality and national autonomy within the Habsburg Empire; rising demand by Slav businessmen and professionals for new markets and investment opportunities in Eastern and Western Europe; and an Austro-Russian détente in the Balkans that gave hope the two powers might ally to block Germany's expansion—the Drang nach Osten—eastward.

Neo-Slavism broke with Russian Pan-Slavism by asserting the equality of all Slav groups, large or small, and by eschewing overtly political aims. As a movement, it emerged after reforms arising from the Russian Revolution of 1905 facilitated joint efforts between Russians and other Slavs, and when the Austrian suffrage reform of 1907 created a potential Slav majority in the Reichsrat (parliament).

The Czechs, with an exposed position in the Germanic cultural orbit, were anxious to secure allies. Karel Kramář (1860–1937), spokesman for the Young Czech Party and chairman of the Slav Committee of the Czech National Council, provided much of the ideological justification and organizational know-how for the movement. Representatives of all Slavs except Ukrainians and Galician Poles participated at one time or another in neo-Slav meetings. The high point was the Neo-Slav Congress of June 1908 in Prague, which commemorated the Slav Congress of 1848 in that city. Delegates proposed a Slav investment bank headquartered in Moscow with branches in other Slav lands, an exhibition of Slav industry and culture, Slav gymnastics, journalism, tourism, and scientific and technical exchanges. These proposals were discussed at the second Neo-Slav Congress held in Sofia in July 1910, but were only partially implemented because of unexpected setbacks.

Austria's annexation of Bosnia and Hercegovina in October 1908 and Russia's renewed oppression in Congress Poland dashed hopes for cooperation by those two powers. A Slav majority in the Reichsrat never materialized. Disputes within neo-Slavism between moderate and extreme nationalists, Austroslavs and Panslavs, and liberals and conservatives further weakened it. The neo-Slavs correctly saw the need to strengthen Slav institutions and enterprises to compete with the Germans, but their movement lacked the unity, mass support, and peace required for its consolidation.

Stanley B. Winters

Further reading

Bradley, J.F.N. "Czech Pan-Slavism before the First World War." *Slavonic and East European Review* 40 (1961–62): 185–202.

Godina, Irena Gantar. *Neoslavizm in Slovenci.* Ljubljana, 1994.

Herman, Karel. "Novoslovanství a česká buržoasie," in *Kapitoly z dějin vzájemných vztahů národů ČSR a SSSR,* 2 vols. Prague, 1958, vol. 1, 235–310.

Vyšný, Paul. *Neo-Slavism and the Czechs, 1898–1914.* Cambridge, 1977.

See also Austroslavism; Karel Kramář; Pan-Germanism; Pan-Slavism; Polish Congress Kingdom; Prague Slav Congress; Young Czechs

Neruda, Jan (1834–91)

Czech writer and journalist. A native of Prague, Neruda was the most important Czech literary figure of the second half of the nineteenth century. The center of the Máj (May) group, a younger generation of writers who in 1860 organized around the journal *Máj,* Neruda guided their promotion of literary and critical realism. Czech literature turned its attention to social and political problems during this period, and writers championed internationalism and cosmopolitanism. Criticism grew in importance, and Neruda, an accomplished literary, dramatic, and art critic, was at the forefront of this movement. He was best known as a journalist and, specifically, as a feuilletonist whose purpose was to educate readers morally and politically to arm them for the struggle for the preservation of the Czech nation. In this he continued the work of the Czech revivalists, dedicating his talents to the service of the national reawakening. Neruda's belief that the national spirit could be preserved in drama, art, and literature was reflected in the many journals he edited, especially *Obrazy života* (*Pictures of Life*) and *Rodinná kronika* (*Family Chronicle*).

In addition to his journalistic work, Neruda wrote four collections of stories, including the collection *Povídky malostranské* (*Tales of Malá Strana,* 1878), best characterized as vignettes, realistic portrayals of everyday life approached with humor and sympathy. Neruda's stories, like his journalism, reflected his ardent patriotism and his cult of the everyday. Neruda the poet is now considered greater than Neruda the feuilletonist, although he was not considered a great poet during his life, when his journalism overshadowed his poetic work. As a poet, Neruda was noted for spiritual intensity heightened by a concise and economic style. His books of verse include *Knihy veršů* (*Books of Verse,* 1867), *Písně kosmické* (*Cosmic Songs,* 1878), *Balady a romance* (*Ballads and Romances,* 1883), and *Prosté motivy* (*Simple Themes,* 1883).

Ann Marie Basom

Further reading
Novák, Arne. *Czech Literature,* trans. by Peter Kussi, ed. by William E. Harkins. Ann Arbor, Michigan, 1976.
———. *Jan Neruda.* 3 vols. Prague, 1920.
Pražák, Albert. "První období činnosti Jana Nerudy" a "Druhé období činnosti Jana Nerudy," in *Literatura česká devatenáctého století. Dílu třetího část druhá.* Prague, 1907, 271–412, 486–598.

See also Czech Literature

Neuilly, Treaty of (1919)

Treaty signed on November 27, 1919, that ended the state of war (World War I) between Bulgaria and the principal Allied and associated powers. Under the provisions of the treaty, Bulgaria ceded western Thrace, its only outlet to the Aegean Sea, to the Allies (who subsequently, at the San Remo Conference of 1920, transferred it to Greece), southern Dobrudja, a strip of the Black Sea coastline and Bulgaria's richest wheat-growing area, to Romania, and the small enclaves of Strumica and Tsaribrod to Serbia. The Allies undertook to provide Bulgaria with an economic outlet to the Aegean Sea, though this promise was never fulfilled. The size of the army was limited to twenty-thousand volunteers, and Bulgaria was forbidden

to have aircraft or submarines. All existing surpluses of armaments, munitions, and war matériel were to be surrendered to the Allies within three months of the treaty. War reparations in the amount of 2.25 billion gold francs were also assessed, to be paid out from 1920 to 1957 in half-yearly installments. The Kingdom of Serbs, Croats, and Slovenes was to receive 50,000 tons of coal a year for five years in compensation for war damage to its coal mines; in addition, Bulgaria was to deliver to its former Balkan enemies 70,825 head of livestock. All Bulgarian nationals over eighteen years of age resident in the territories ceded by Bulgaria to Greece, Romania, and the Kingdom of Serbs, Croats, and Slovenes were entitled to opt for Bulgarian citizenship, while Serbs, Croats, Slovenes, Romanians, and Greeks resident in Bulgaria were given a similar right to opt for their former nationality. An Inter-Allied Commission of three members (from Britain, France, and Italy) was established to monitor Bulgaria's compliance with the treaty provisions; the commission's seat was to be in Sofia, and its members were to enjoy diplomatic immunity.

The economic hardships that Bulgaria underwent as a result of the treaty were compounded by an influx of refugees from Thrace and Macedonia. The consequent economic and political disorganization of the country produced a rising wave of political unrest, which culminated in the June 1923 coup that overthrew the government of Aleksandur Stamboliiski (1879–1923) and an abortive Communist-led uprising against the government in September 1923.

Richard Tempest

Further reading
Dnevikut na Mikhail Sarafov za skliuchvaneto na mirniia dogovor v N'oii prez 1919 g, in *Izvestiia na Institute na Bulgarska Istoriia.* vols. 3–4, 1957.
Dokumenti za dogovora v N'oii. Sofia, 1919.
Genov, G.P. *Bulgaria and the Treaty of Neuilly,* vols. 1–2. Sofia, 1935.
Kamburov, G. "Teritorialnite i voennite klauzi na N'oiiskiia dogovor i tiakhnoto izpulnenie." *Voennoistoricheki sbornik* 5 (1969).
Kesiakov, B.D. *Prinos kum diplomaticheskata istoriia na Bulgaria,* vols. 2–3. Sofia, 1926.

See also Dobrudja; Paris Peace Conference; Aleksandur Stamboliiski

N

Neumann, János (1903–57)

Hungarian-born mathematician and scientist. After Albert Einstein (1879–1955), many consider Neumann (John von Neumann) the greatest mathematician of the twentieth century. He studied chemistry in Zurich and obtained a Ph.D. in mathematics in 1927 in Budapest. In Germany, Neumann authored a technical paper in 1928 that, while using mathematical terminology, systematized the role of chance in games. Neumann's theory was later applied to economics with the publication of *Theory of Games and Economic Behavior* (1944).

Neumann eventually emigrated to the United States, where he worked on the theory of sets, fluid mechanics, and quantum mechanics. His monograph, *Mathematical Foundations of Quantum Mechanics* (1932), has remained a standard treatise on the subject. In 1945 he was appointed director of the Electronic Computer Project at the Institute for Advanced Study in Princeton, New Jersey. He is therefore considered by many the "father of the computer."

During World War II, he took part in the development of the atomic bomb, along with three other scientists of Hungarian origin, Leo Szilárd (1898–1964), Eugene Wigner (1902–95), and Edward Teller (1908–). They became members of the Manhattan Project, for producing atomic weapons. Neumann's contributions, particularly at Los Alamos, New Mexico, included work on the implosion theory, suggesting the use of explosive lenses to direct explosive waves toward the center of bomb material. His scientific work also influenced the design of missiles.

Neumann was presented the prestigious Fermi Award, and he was appointed a member of the U.S. Atomic Energy Commission.

Mártha Pereszlényi-Pintér

Further reading

Fermi, Laura. *Illustrious Immigrants: The Intellectual Migration from Europe, 1930–41,* 2d ed. Chicago, 1971.

Sisa, Stephen. *The Spirit of Hungary: A Panorama of Hungarian History and Culture.* Toronto, 1990.

Wagner, Francis S. *Hungarian Contributions to World Civilization.* Center Square, Pennsylvania, 1977.

See also Leo Szilárd; Edward Teller

Nicholas I (1796–1855)

Tsar of Russia, called the "gendarme of Europe" because of his efforts to preserve order and suppress revolution. Nicholas often turned to armed force to buttress the monarchs of Europe when they were threatened by internal uprisings. Shortly after coming to power in 1825, Nicholas achieved a dominant position for Russia in the Danubian Principalities after the victory over the Ottomans in the Russo-Turkish War of 1828–29 and secured by the Treaty of Adrianople, which gave Russia control of the mouth of the Danube River. Russian administrative reforms in the principalities resulted in the creation of the organic statutes that established parallel institutions in Wallachia (1831) and Moldavia (1832) with an eye to the unification of the territories in the future. Russian reforms thus contributed to Romanian state formation, and Russian troops withdrew in 1834.

Nicholas relied on the Russian army to put down a number of revolutionary disturbances both within his realm and abroad. The first instance in Eastern Europe occurred in Poland in 1830–31. The Poles had deposed the Romanov dynasty and declared the Polish throne vacant. Russian troops succeeded in crushing the revolt, and Nicholas suspended the Polish constitution and abolished the Polish army, both of which had existed since 1815 as part of the Congress Kingdom of Poland. The Polish leaders of the uprising fled abroad. In 1848–49, when revolutionary disturbances sprang up throughout Europe, Nicholas again acted militarily to prop up the old order. He dispatched Russian troops to the Danubian Principalities, Transylvania, and Hungary to aid in the suppression of revolutions there.

By the beginning of the 1850s, Russia under Nicholas was at the zenith of its power. The tsar had overseen the quashing of revolutions throughout East Central Europe and had managed to prevent the disintegration of the Ottoman Empire. However, Nicholas lost Russian gains with his entrance into the Crimean War (1853–56). Nicholas died while the war was in progress, and it fell to his son Alexander II (1818–81) to make peace.

Jonathan A. Grant

Further reading

Jelavich, Barbara. *Russia and the Formation of the Romanian National State, 1821–1878.* Cambridge, 1984.

———. *Russia's Balkan Entanglements, 1806–1914.* Cambridge, 1991.

Lincoln, W. Bruce. *Nicholas I, Emperor and Autocrat of all the Russias.* Bloomington, Indiana, 1980.

Roberts, Ian W. *Nicholas I and the Russian Intervention in Hungary.* New York, 1991.

See also Adrianople, Treaty of; Alexander II; Crimean War; Danubian Principalities; Eastern Question; November Uprising; Organic Statutes; Polish Congress Kingdom; Polish Question; Revolutions of 1848; Russo-Turkish War of 1828–29

Nicholas II (1868–1918)

Last tsar of Russia. During the first portion of his reign, Nicholas continued Alexander III's (1845–94) policy of Russification in Poland, which caused resentment among the Poles and led to a revolutionary outbreak against Russian rule 1904–7. The initial spark for the unrest in tsarist Poland was a protest in Warsaw on November 13, 1904, against the Russo-Japanese War. As the government's position weakened, Nicholas issued an Edict of Religious Toleration that marked the first moderation in St. Petersburg's policy of Russification. It was followed in June 1905 by a decree that allowed bilingualism in public elementary and secondary schools. These measures however did not pacify the Polish provinces, and Nicholas vacillated between offering more reforms and reimposing sterner rule. In August 1905 he declared martial law in Warsaw in an attempt to suppress Polish demands for home rule. Martial law remained in force until 1909.

As a result of Russia's defeat in the war with Japan, Nicholas turned his attention to a more active policy in Eastern Europe and the Balkans in an attempt to restore Russia's tarnished image, and this increased tensions with Austria, Russia's main rival in the Balkans. Russia attempted to orchestrate the creation of a league of Balkan states to counter Austria, but the potential coalition broke away from Russian control as Bulgaria, Serbia, and Greece first waged war against the Ottoman Empire in the First Balkan War of 1912 and then fought against one another in the Second Balkan War during 1913. Nicholas furthermore alienated Bulgaria and Serbia by opposing their expansionist aims. To salvage Russian credibility and to keep Serbia in the Russian fold, Nicholas felt obligated to support Serbia during its next conflict with Austria. As a result, Russia mobilized for war against Austria when the latter threatened Serbia in the summer of 1914, an action that helped spark World War I.

Jonathan A. Grant

Further reading

Blobaum, Robert E. *Rewolucja: Russian Poland, 1904–1907.* Ithaca, New York, 1995.

Lieven, D.C.B. *Russia and the Origins of World War I.* New York, 1983.

McDonald, David MacLaren. *United Government and Foreign Policy in Russia, 1900–1914.* Cambridge, Massachusetts, 1992.

Mosely, Philip E. *Russian Diplomacy and Eastern Europe, 1914–1917.* New York, 1963.

See also Alexander III; Balkan Wars; Duma; Eastern Question; Polish Question; Russification

Nicholas I of Montenegro (1841–1921)

Last ruler of the Petrović Njegoš line in Montenegro. Known as the "father-in-law of Europe" (two daughters married future kings of Serbia and Italy, while two others married Russian grand dukes), Nicholas was remarkably successful in arranging strategic marital unions for his numerous offspring. In addition, he was a writer of some note, perhaps best known for his drama *Balkanska carica* (*Empress of the Balkans*), first performed in Cetinje in 1884.

Lauded by some foreign observers and Montenegrins alike as a great patriot, Nicholas was reviled by others as an unenlightened despot. Building on his predecessors' close ties to the Russian court and church, Nicholas relied heavily on the tsar's military and financial support. In 1862, and again in 1876–78, he fought the Turks, both times in support of revolts in neighboring Hercegovina. In 1878, with the signing of the Treaty of Berlin, which ended the Russo-Turkish War of 1877–78, Nicholas became *vladika* (prince-bishop) of an independent Montenegro. In 1905 he granted the country its first constitution, and in 1910 he became its first and last king. In 1912–13 Nicholas directed Montenegro in joining Serbia in the Balkan Wars. As a result of his military actions, Montenegro virtually doubled in size.

Nicholas stood by Serbia during the summer crisis of 1914, declaring war on the Habsburg

N Empire in early August. However, when an Austro-German army overran Montenegro in late 1915, the king and his entourage escaped first to Italy, then to France, where Nicholas hoped an Allied victory would restore him to his throne. On November 26, 1918, the Podgorica Skupština (assembly) formally deposed Nicholas and the Petrović Njegoš dynasty, however, proclaiming Montenegro's union with Serbia in the new Kingdom of Serbs, Croats, and Slovenes. On October 1, 1989, Nicholas's remains, along with those of his wife and two daughters, were reinterred in Cetinje amid great ceremony.

John D. Treadway

Further reading

Stevenson, Francis Seymour. *A History of Montenegro.* London, 1912; reprint New York, 1971.

Treadway, John D. *The Falcon and the Eagle: Montenegro and Austria-Hungary, 1908–1914.* West Lafayette, Indiana, 1983.

See also Balkan Wars; Congress of Berlin; Kingdom of Serbs, Croats, and Slovenes; Russo-Turkish War of 1877–78

Ninčić, Momčilo (1876–1949).

Serbian politician, statesman, and writer. Born in Jagodina, Ninčić finished gymnasium (high school) in Belgrade and graduated from law school in Paris in 1899. On his return to Serbia, he became secretary of the Ministry of Finance and professor at the University of Belgrade Law School. As a representative of the Radical Party, he became a member of parliament in 1912.

Ninčić's political career was varied. He was minister of finance (1915–17), minister of justice (1917–18), minister of trade and construction (1920), and minister of foreign affairs (1922–26). During his tenure as minister of finance, the first budget was designed and monetary unification was accomplished in the Kingdom of Serbs, Croats, and Slovenes. On March 27, 1941, Ninčić again was named minister of foreign affairs. After the German invasion of Yugoslavia in April 1941, he emigrated to London, where he retained his ministerial post in the government of Slobodan Jovanović (1869–1958) in 1941–42. He died in exile in Lausanne.

Apart from his successful political career, Ninčić was also a prolific writer, the author of numerous essays and monographs on the history of Serbia and on Serbian finances. Between 1920 and 1926, he was director of the political and literary weekly *Novi život* (*New Life*). His works include *Carinski savez Srbije i Bugarske* (*Serbian and Bulgarian Customs Union,* 1904), *Naše valutno pitanje* (*Our Currency Question,* 1920), and *La Crise bosniaque 1908–1909 et les grandes puissances européennes,* vols. 1–2 (1937).

Željan E. Šuster

Further reading

Enciklopedija Jugoslavije. Zagreb, 1980.
Mala Enciklopedija. Belgrade, 1978.

See also Slobodan Jovanović

Niš

City in eastern Serbia, approximately 130 miles (217 km) southeast of Belgrade. Niš is only 50 miles (83 km) from the Bulgarian border and 100 miles (166 km) from Sofia, the capital of Bulgaria. The city was built along the shores of the Nišava River near its confluence with the Morava. Niš contains an important railroad crossing, along with a major highway that runs through the city connecting Belgrade in the north with Athens, Greece, in the south.

The region around Niš is dominated by the Morava depression with its many tectonic basins. The tectonic forces helped create a natural corridor connecting the plains north of the city to the Macedonian Massif in the southeast. From early days, the city served as an important center along a principal route from Central Europe to the Aegean Sea.

Niš has a long and rich history. It was occupied by the Celts in 300 B.C.; destroyed by Attila the Hun in the fifth century; rebuilt and occupied by the Byzantines, Bulgarians, and Serbs; and for over five hundred years was ruled by the Turks. The Serbs finally liberated the city in 1877. Niš has an outstanding university medical center specializing in the treatment of cardiovascular diseases.

William B. Kory

Further reading

Bertić, Ivan. *Veliki geografski atlas Jugoslavije.* Zagreb, 1987.

Niš, Convention of (1923)

Convention signed on March 23, 1923, which marked an important step in the normalization of relations between Bulgaria and the Kingdom of Serbs, Croats, and Slovenes (later, Yugoslavia) during Aleksandur Stamboliiski's (1879–1923) term of office as Bulgaria's prime minister. After assuming power in 1919, Stamboliiski's government embarked on a policy of rapprochement with Belgrade, seeking to win its support for the creation of a Balkan federation and for Bulgaria's efforts to gain an outlet to the Aegean Sea. But the Yugoslavs would agree to an improvement in relations only if Stamboliiski took decisive steps to suppress the Internal Macedonian Revolutionary Organization (IMRO), the Macedonian terrorist organization whose members had been mounting raids into Yugoslav territory from the Petrich district. During his November 1922 visit to Belgrade, Stamboliiski denounced IMRO and soon thereafter Yugoslav and Bulgarian delegations met in the Serbian town of Niš for talks on the Macedonian issue. The resulting convention of Niš provided for joint measures designed to guarantee cross-border security and to prevent the movement of IMRO insurgents from Bulgaria into Yugoslavia and back. In April the Bulgarian government declared IMRO illegal; its publications were closed down, its leaders interned, and its Petrich haven occupied by government troops. IMRO's response was to join the anti-Agrarian conspiracy that led to the coup of June 9, 1923. A month later, Stamboliiski was murdered by a group of Macedonian extremists, who first sliced off his ears and then cut off "the hands that had signed the Niš agreement." The new government of Aleksandur Tsankov (1879–1959) declared that it would respect the terms of the convention but in fact failed to do so.

Richard Tempest

Further reading

Crampton, Richard J. *A Short History of Modern Bulgaria.* Cambridge, 1987.

Kumanov, M. "Nishkata spogodba ot 1923 godina." *Vekovete,* 1972, book 5.

See also IMRO; Macedonia; Aleksandur Stamboliiski; Aleksandur Tsankov

Noli, Fan S. (1882–1965)

Albanian intellectual, cleric, and democrat. Noli was born in a small town inhabited by numerous Albanians in the province of Edrenese, Greece. After completing his education, he went to Egypt, where he taught Greek. There he met and worked with numerous Albanian nationalist leaders in exile.

No other leading Albanian intellectual gave as much to his country and to the Albanian national movement as Noli. Although Noli received a Ph.D. late in life from Harvard University, his encyclopedic knowledge of history, politics, diplomacy, religion, music, and culture made him a unique personality in Albanian history.

In his early twenties, Noli wrote many articles dealing with Albanian politics and history that were published in *Drita* (*The Light*), an Albanian weekly published in Sofia, Bulgaria. Especially noteworthy was his translation and publication into Greek of the influential book by Sami Frashëri (1850–1904) entitled *Albania: What Has It Been, What It Is, and What It Will Be.*

Noli emigrated to the United States in 1906 and resided in Boston most of his life. There he founded the Albanian Orthodox Church. Until that time, all Albanians of the Orthodox faith belonged to the Greek Orthodox Church. In 1908 Noli became a priest and later a bishop.

In 1918 Noli returned to Albania. Between 1920 and 1921, he represented Albania at the League of Nations in Geneva. While there, he vigoriously defended Albania's national interests.

Noli was elected to the first freely elected democratic Albanian parliament in 1921 and in 1924 became the premier of the short-lived Albanian Democratic government. When the government was overthrown by Ahmed Zogu (1895–1961) in 1925, Noli went into exile first in Europe and later in the United States, remaining in the latter until his death in 1965.

While in America, he published an Albanian weekly, *Dielli* (*The Sun*), and a magazine, *Adriatic.* From 1932 to 1950, Noli translated the works of literary giants such as Shakespeare (1564–1616), Cervantes (1547–1616), and Henrik Ibsen (1828–1906) into Albanian. He also researched and wrote on the life of the fifteenth-century Albanian national hero Skanderbeg (1405–68), who kept Albania free of Ottoman domination for twenty-five years. Noli was also well known for his research on world music and he composed a rhapsody in English for Skanderbeg.

In post-Communist Albania, numerous schools, factories, foundations, streets, and a university have been renamed in his honor.

Mirvet S. Muca

Further reading
Historia e Shqiperisë, vols 1–3. Tirana.

See also League of Nations; Ahmed Zogu

Nonaligned Movement

International organization devoted to anticolonialism and peaceful coexistence. During the first years following the outbreak of the Cold War, the leaders of Yugoslavia and India, Josip Broz Tito (1892–1980) and Jawaharlal Nehru (1889–1964), respectively, started to popularize the idea of peaceful coexistence among nations. This concept bitterly opposed the division of the world into two opposing blocs and tried to provide an alternate way of protecting the interests of developing countries. Yugoslavia and India were later joined by Egypt, Indonesia, and a number of other, primarily Third World countries. Together they formed the Organization of Non-Aligned Countries. The founding principles of the organization and the nonaligned movement were peaceful coexistence, the struggle for independence, and the fight against colonialism. The first conference of the organization was held in Belgrade, Yugoslavia, September 1–6, 1961, with the participation of twenty-five member countries and three other countries as observers. The movement rapidly grew and conferences of the organization were regularly held (Lusaka, Algiers, Colombo, Havana, Belgrade, Harare, and Cairo). Strict adherence to the principles of nonalignment generated both positive and negative effects for Yugoslavia. While it facilitated emancipation from the Communist bloc, reliance on Third World countries separated Yugoslavia from the Balkans and Europe, toward which it historically and naturally gravitated. The movement began to weaken in the 1980s owing to the rapidly changing relationship between the two superpowers. The outbreak of a major war between two member countries, Iraq and Iran, further corrupted the organization, especially since it was unable to arrange a prompt settlement. Since the collapse of communism, dismantlement of the Soviet bloc, and the violent breakup of Yugoslavia, the movement has lost its rationale. Presently, the Organization of Non-Aligned Countries is merely an assembly of developing countries with little political significance in world affairs.

Željan E. Šuster

Further reading
Nord, L. *Nonalignment and Socialism: Yugoslav Foreign Policy in Theory and Practice.* Stockholm, 1973.
Rubinstein, A.Z. *Yugoslavian and Nonaligned World.* Princeton, New Jersey, 1970.
Singleton, Fred. *A Short History of the Yugoslav People.* Cambridge, 1985.

See also Cold War; Tito

November Uprising (*Powstanie Listopadowe*) (1830–31)

Failed Polish nationalist revolt. On November 29, 1830, in Warsaw, an ill-prepared group of soldiers and civilians launched what was supposed to be a coordinated attack on the Belvedere Palace to capture Grand Duke Constantine (1779–1831), the commander in chief of the Russian army in Poland, disarm the Russian garrison, and seize the arsenal. This resulted from several catalysts: the revolutions in France and Belgium earlier that year; the general Polish discontent under Russian rule, as manifested in the proliferation of secret societies; the fact that mobilization orders for the army, ostensibly to fight against France, had already been published; and the knowledge that the police had compiled lists of conspirators and would probably soon move to make arrests.

From the beginning, everything went wrong for the conspirators; none of their objectives were attained. They were themselves not united. Some believed an armed rising should strive for complete independence, others that the aim should be simply to defend the rights guaranteed to the Poles under their constitution. Lacking any clear immediate plan of action to implement once the uprising had begun, a stalemate soon ensued. The rebels held the town, but the Russian garrison was still intact.

Prince Ksawery Lubecki (1778–1846), head of the Administrative Council, agreed to try to end the insurrection and to reach some accommodation with the tsar. In effect, political leadership had passed into the hands of those opposed to the insurrection and who wanted to avoid confrontation. By December 4, a provisional government had come into being. Essentially conservative, it included Lubecki, Prince Adam Czartoryski (1770–1861), General Józef Chłopicki (1771–1854), as well as the more leftist Julian Niemcewicz (1758–1841) and Joachim Lelewel (1786–1861). Soon Chłopicki assumed all formal authority as dictator.

The Poles found that Russian tsar Nicholas I (1796–1855) had no intention of negotiating but desired instead to crush the Congress Kingdom. To this end, he ordered General Ivan Diebitsch (1785–1831) to organize a punitive expedition of 120,000. In Warsaw, Chłopicki reluctantly began a military buildup, but he lacked any enthusiasm for resistance. He resigned on January 7, 1831. His replacement, as commander in chief, was Prince Michał Radziwiłł (1778–1850). On January 25, the Sejm (diet) voted to dethrone Nicholas, and on January 30 a new government, headed by Czartoryski, was formed.

Czartoryski faced the task of fighting the war and gaining support for the Poles. Militarily the Poles were well armed and well trained, and they were fighting on their own soil. For a time, the Polish army fought well and inflicted serious casualties on Diebitsch's army. However, the new Polish commander, General Jan Skrzynecki (1787–1860), lacked initiative and allowed the Russians to regroup. On May 26, this failure led to a crushing Polish defeat at Ostrołęka. This marked the beginning of the end militarily for the Poles.

On September 6, the assault against Warsaw began. It lasted two days and the city capitulated at midnight on September 7–8. Although the Poles were far from defeated militarily, they had lost the will to fight and the last resistance crumbled at Zamość on October 21, 1831.

The forming of the Czartoryski government in January signaled a different direction in Polish political activity. Czartoryski realized that the Poles had no chance of success without the support of the Great Powers. Owing to their shares of the spoils of partition, neither Prussia nor Austria would provide any aid to the kingdom. Although the Poles elicited sympathy from individual government officials and significant personages in both France and Great Britain, neither government was willing to commit itself to a cause whose probable outcome was war with Russia. The failure of the military led to riots in Warsaw in August and the replacement of the government by the military dictatorship of General Jan Krukowiecki (1772–1850), who was captured at the fall of Warsaw.

Given the general conditions, the Polish uprising was an unnecessary occurrence. Political and economic conditions were relatively good; Poles had some degree of autonomy in the Congress Kingdom and were better off than their fellow Poles in Prussia or Austria. Hotheaded revolutionaries, combined with Nicholas's antipathy toward the Poles and inept Polish military leadership, provided a recipe for disaster. Thousands of Poles now fled the country to become part of the great emigration.

Robert A. Berry

Further reading

Davies, Norman. *God's Playground: A History of Poland,* vol. 2. New York, 1982.

Wandycz, Piotr. *The Lands of Partitioned Poland, 1795–1918.* Seattle, Washington, 1974.

See also Józef Chłopicki; Constantine; Adam Czartoryski; Prince Ksawery Drucki-Lubecki; Joachim Lelewel; Nicholas I; Polish Congress Kingdom; Polish Émigrés

Novotný, Antonín (1904–75)

First secretary of the Communist Party of Czechoslovakia (KSČ) (1953–68) and state president (1957–68). Novotný was born in a worker's family in an industrial suburb of Prague. He received only a basic education. He joined the KSČ at the age of seventeen and became a paid party worker in 1929 after the party was "bolshevized" (brought under the Soviet model) by pressure from the Comintern (Communist International). When the KSČ was declared illegal after the Munich conference (at which Czechoslovakia was forced to turn over the Sudetenland to Nazi Germany) in 1938, Novotný held the rank of regional party secretary in Hodonín, Moravia. From 1941 to 1945, he was a prisoner in the Nazi concentration camp of Mauthausen. A member of the KSČ Central Committee since 1946, Novotný benefited from the purge of the party old guard in 1951–54. He became first secretary of the Central Committee of the KSČ in 1953, replacing the executed Rudolf Slánský (1901–52). In 1957 he also took over the office of the state president. Novotný was removed from both these offices during the Prague Spring of 1968, the short-lived period of liberalization.

During the last years of his life, even after the Soviet invasion in August 1968, he remained politically inactive. Novotný's rise in the early 1950s resulted from the abnormal political circumstances of that time, when his lack of education and mediocre personality became political assets. He was a conservative Stalinist and he opposed reforms until his fall, which he confirms in his unpublished memoirs. But for years he also resisted Soviet demands to station Soviet troops permanently in Czechoslovakia.

Jiří Hochman

Further reading

Dubček, Alexander. *Hope Dies Last.* New York, 1992.
Rupnik, Jacques. *Histoire du Parti Communiste Tchécoslovaque.* Paris, 1981.
Skilling, Gordon H. *Czechoslovakia's Interrupted Revolution.* Princeton, New Jersey, 1976.
Suda, Zdeněk L. *Zealots and Rebels, A History of the Ruling Communist Party of Czechoslovakia.* Stanford, California, 1980.

See also Communist Party of Czechoslovakia; Munich Pact; Prague Spring; Rudolf Slánský

Nowicki, Maciej (1910–50)

Polish architect and eminent representative of modern architecture. Nowicki studied architecture at the Department of Architecture at Warsaw University of Technology (1928–36). Before World War II, he designed the Polish pavilion at the World Exhibition in New York (1939) and a tourist hotel in Augustów, and codesigned the seat of the provincial government in Łódź. His practice also embraced interior design and applied art (poster and illustration). After the war, he worked on several projects for Warsaw, including the original spatial concept for the rebuilding of the downtown. In 1945 Nowicki went to the United States as a consultant to the Polish consulate; later, as a Polish representative to the commission of the United Nations, he participated in the design of the United Nations complex in New York City. In 1948 he was appointed a professor and chairman of the School of Architecture at North Carolina State University at Raleigh. Nowicki gained international fame for his design of the Dorton Arena (also called the Paraboleum Center because of its geometric design) in Raleigh, completed after his sudden death in a plane crash in 1950. The experimental structural system employed in this pavilion was based on balance between crossed concrete arches (90 feet [27.5 m] high and 300 feet [91 m] wide), working as compressed elements, and the roof suspended on steel ropes. Other projects included the codesign of Brandeis University in Waltham, Massachusetts, and the unrealized master plan and chief buildings for the new city of Chandigarh, India. Nowicki's innovations, particularly in the use of reinforced concrete and shell roofs, supported the idea of aesthetic expression through exposure of structural elements.

Marta Tobolczyk

Further reading

Barucki, Tadeusz. *Maciej Nowicki.* Warsaw, 1986.
Mumford Lewis. *Architecture as a Home for Man.* New York, 1975, 63–101.
———. "Matthew Nowicki." *Architectural Record* 6, 7, 8, 9 (1954).
———. *Roots of Contemporary American Architecture.* New York, 1972.
Starczewski, Jerzy A. "Arena Nowickiego." *Architektura* 1 (1984): 8–9.
Wood, Ernest. "A Radical Settles Down in Raleigh, NC." *AIA Journal* 9 (1980): 54–61.

See also Architecture; Polish Art

Numerus Clausus

First anti-Jewish measure in modern Hungarian history, promulgated by the National Assembly as Act XXV of 1920. The law was the result of a unique combination of factors. The basis for it was provided by the overcrowding of the educated professions and by the overrepresentation of Jews among intellectuals. Tensions caused by this correlation were aggravated and highlighted by the prominent role of leftist intellectuals of Jewish origin in the revolutions of 1918–19 that followed in the wake of Austria-Hungary's defeated in World War I, especially in the Communist one. During the months following the collapse of the Hungarian Soviet Republic led by Béla Kun (1886–1938), several thousand educated refugees from the disannexed territories intensified these concerns.

Before the war, Jews represented about 30 percent of the student body, whereas their proportion in the total population hardly reached 6 percent. Now the *numerus clausus* law decreed that the "proportion of students belonging to the various races and nationalities living in the country correspond to the proportion of those races and nationalities in the population of the country or at least reach nine-tenths of that proportion." The act was passed by the National Assembly on September 22, 1920, with a vote of 55 for and 7 against; only a third of the deputies were present at the vote. Moderate deputies presumably decided to stay away.

The introduction of the system of limited enrollments to higher education was a severe blow to the educational advancement of the young Jewish population. Their proportion in the student body decreased to 8 percent by the end of the 1920s.

The act was modified in 1928 (Act XIV of 1928). As a result of this new amendment, the proportion of Jews in the student population increased to 12 percent by the early 1930s, twice that stipulated by the original law. In spite of this mitigation, the *numerus clausus* law preserved its discriminative character, and young Jews who were high school graduates continued to leave Hungary.

Ignác Romsics

Further reading

Katzburg, Nathaniel. *Hungary and the Jews: Policy and Legislation 1920–1943*. Jerusalem, 1981.

Kovács, Mária M. *Liberal Professions and Illiberal Politics: Hungary from the Habsburgs to the Holocaust.* New York, 1994.

Térffy, Gyula, ed. *Magyar Törvénytár 1920*. Budapest, 1921, 145–46.

See also Hungarian Soviet Republic; Béla Kun; Jews

Nyugat

Hungarian literary periodical, founded in 1908 and published until 1941. The title, meaning "Occident," or "West," embodied the very program of the magazine, a bow to Western culture or civilization and, indirectly, to modernization. Its circulation never exceeded four thousand; yet *Nyugat* had a literary and political impact that cannot be measured in numbers. It carried translations from and reviews of works that appeared in France, Germany, Austria, and, to a lesser extent, the United Kingdom, but it was the spirit of the Hungarian writers who contributed to it that gave it a Western, liberal, progressive outlook.

Although the periodical was literary, in the Eastern European context where culture and politics are not easily distinguished it inevitably acquired a political significance. The journal was financed by members of the upper bourgeoisie, especially in its heyday between 1908 and 1918, when the political clout of that stratum, confronting the power of the landed arsitrocracy, was still minimal. While the politics of the writers who contributed to the journal ranged from conservative to socialist, the periodical itself was consistently regarded as pro-democratic and liberal, in an age when neither democracy nor liberalism was the order of the day. Its political impact can be measured by the attempts at censorship on the part of the government and by the unabated attacks from right-wing and conservative circles.

The journal's history may be divided into three or four periods, corresponding to the regimes or the political climate: after its golden age came the brief period of the revolutions, in late 1918 and 1919, when many of its contributors, socialist or not, were persuaded to serve the revolutionary governments; the period of the counterrevolution, or conservative consolidation, from 1919 to 1931; and the period of the drift to the right, from 1931 to 1941. The periodical ceased publication before the full impact of National Socialism on Hungary.

The founders of the magazine, Pál Ignotus (1901–), Ernö Osvát (n.d.), and Miksa Fenyö (1877–1972), showed good taste and critical acumen in selecting contributions. While all three were of Jewish background, most of the prominent contributors to the journal were not. *Nyugat* helped promote Endre Ady (1877–1919), who became the foremost Hungarian poet and, who received a regular, if modest, stipend. It also promoted the career of Zsigmond Móricz (1879–1942), an outstanding Hungarian novelist and short-story writer, and of poet Mihály Babits (1883–1941), noted for his Catholicism. While Ady died in 1919, Móricz, Babits, and others eventually took over the editorship of the periodical.

Mario D. Fenyo

Further reading

Fenyo, Mario. *Literature and Political Change.* Philadelphia, 1986.

Fenyö, Miksa. *Följegyzések és levelek a Nyugatról,* ed. by Erzsébet Vezér. Budapest, 1975.

Horvath, Zoltan. *Die Jahrhundertwende in Ungarn.* Berlin, 1966.

See also Endre Ady; Mihály Babits; Censorship

Obradović, Dositej (Dimitrije) (c. 1739–1811)

Pedagogue, author, man of letters, and father of modern Serbian education. Born into a family of Serbian craftsmen in the town of Čakovo, Obradović entered a Serbian Orthodox monastery in 1757, where he took the name Dositej. In 1760 he left the monastery and began traveling through the Balkan Peninsula observing folk customs, sayings, and traditions. Obradović's first primer, *Bukvica,* used a mixed Russian Church Slavonic orthography; it circulated widely in manuscript form throughout Dalmatia. Using ideas of the Enlightenment gathered through numerous trips from the 1760s to the 1780s throughout the Balkans and Central Europe, Obradović began to form an educational program for the Serbian people, creating an outline for national education based on the ideas of Hobbes (1588–1679), Locke (1632–1704), and Rousseau (1712–78). Obradović expounded his ideas in a number of works in which he argued not only for educational reforms but also for social change.

After the first Serbian insurrection against Turkish rule (led by Karadjordje Petrović [Black George], 1768–1817), Obradović traveled to Serbia, where he spent the last years of his life (1807–11) attempting to introduce Enlightenment ideas into what had been an illiterate Ottoman backwater. In August 1808 he founded Serbia's first school in a Turkish home in Belgrade (*Velika škola*). Among his pupils was Vuk Stefanović Karadžić (1787–1869), soon to gain fame as a literary and linguistic reformer. Two years later, he founded Serbia's first seminary. As Serbia's first minister of education, his insistence that education be made available across a wide spectrum of society in the common language provoked opposition from the Serbian Orthodox Church. He served on Karadjordje's governing council until his death in 1811. Obradović's importance is due to his creation of an Enlightenment educational system for Serbia, which acted as a forerunner to Karadžić's linguistic and orthographic reforms, as well as his role as the father of Serbian prose literature.

James M.B. Lyon

Further reading

The Life and Adventures of Dimitrije Obradović, Who as a Monk Was Given the Name Dositej, Written and Published by Himself, trans. by George Rapall Noyes. Berkeley, California, 1953.

See also Black George; Vuk Karadžić

Obreshkov, Bencho (1899–1970)

Bulgarian artist. A promoter of modern art, especially expressionism, Obreshkov was noted in Western Europe and famed in Bulgaria. Obreshkov began his art education at the Sofia Art Academy (1918–20) and made the capital his permanent residence. A student at the Dresden Art Academy during the 1920s, Obreshkov continued his studies in Paris (1926–27) with sculptor Antome Bourdelle (1861–1929), and participated in avant-garde exhibitions. Back in Sofia, Obreshkov was renowned for his expressive portraits and landscapes. He continued to travel and exhibit abroad: Dresden (1934), Paris (1937), Athens (1938), Munich (1947), Moscow (1955). He was an active member of the

Native Art Society and a founding member of the progressive Society of New Artists in 1931. He became its president in 1937 and exhibited with the group until it was abolished in 1944. During World War II, over 350 of his paintings were destroyed. Obreshkov did not change his postimpressionist quest to conform to the official style of socialist realism. Consequently, he was ostracized and neglected. He died in 1970 after a long illness.

Milka T. Bliznakov

Further reading
Krustev, K. *Bencho Obreshkov.* Sofia, 1981.

See also Bulgarian Art

Obretenov, Georgi Tihov (c. 1849–76)

Bulgarian revolutionary activist and martyr. Obretenov was born in Ruse into a merchant family prominent in the revolutionary movement. Along with his brother Nikola (1849–1939), Georgi became involved in revolutionary activity at an early age. He attended school in Ruse and later worked in his family business in the Dobrudja. In 1870 Obretenov entered a military academy in Odessa, Russia. Five years later, he returned to Ruse to participate in the growing revolutionary movement and promptly joined a revolutionary band in the Turnovo region. In 1875 he went to Romania, where, together with his brother Nikola and Stefan Stambolov (1854–95), he became a member of the Gyurgevo Committee. This organization made plans and preparations for a new uprising to take place in Bulgaria the next year. They assigned Obretenov to the Sliven region. After arriving in Sliven in February 1876, he carried out revolutionary activities and served as a military instructor. While he was organizing revolutionary bands, Ottoman authorities arrested him but soon afterward released him. Obretenov then joined another revolutionary band. In a battle near the village of Rakovo in the Sliven region, Ottoman forces killed him on May 10, 1876.

Richard C. Hall

Further reading
Gandev, Hristo. *Aprilskoto vŭstanie 1876,* 2d ed. Sofia, 1976.
Macdermott, Mercia. *A History of Bulgaria 1393–1885.* London, 1962.

Mitev, Iono. *Istoriia na Aprilskoto vŭstanie 1876,* vol. 2, *Obiaviavane, boina deistviia i potushvane na vŭstanieto.* Sofia, 1988.

See also April Uprising; Gyurgevo Committee; Nikola Obretenov; Stefan Stambolov

Obretenov, Nikola Tihov (1849–1939)

Bulgarian revolutionary activist. Obretenov was born in Ruse into a merchant family that was prominent in revolutionary activities. He became a schoolteacher in the Dobrudja and later in Ruse. With his mother, Baba Tonka Obretenova (n.d.), he and his brothers were active in the revolutionary movement in his hometown. In 1875 he participated in the meeting of Khristo Botev's (1848–76) Bulgarian Central Revolutionary Committee in Romania. In 1876 he returned to Romania, where (together with his younger brother Georgi Obretenov [c. 1849–76] and Stefan Stambolov [1854–95]) he participated in the Gyurgevo Committee, the Bulgarian revolutionary organization. The committee assigned him to carry out revolutionary preparations in the Vratsa region in northwestern Bulgaria. Thwarted in his activities by Ottoman vigilance, he returned once again to Romania. There he enlisted in the revolutionary band of his friend Khristo Botev and participated in Botev's quixotic attempt to liberate Bulgaria from Ottoman rule in the April Uprising of 1876. After Botev's death, Obretenov was captured by the Ottomans. Although the latter tried Obretenov and sentenced him to death, they failed to execute him and later freed him in a general amnesty after the liberation of Bulgaria. In an attempt to restore the San Stefano borders of Bulgaria (briefly created after the Russo-Turkish War of 1877–78 but later revised at the Congress of Berlin), Obretenov participated in a failed uprising in 1878–79 in eastern Macedonia. A close associate of his revolutionary comrade Stambolov, Obretenov later served as a district administrator and in the national Subranie (parliament). He died in Ruse on October 10, 1939.

Richard C. Hall

Further reading
Macdermott, Mercia. *A History of Bulgaria 1393–1885.* London, 1962.
Obretenov, Nikola. *Spomeni za Bŭlgarskite vŭstaniya.* Sofia, 1942.

Perry, Duncan. *Stefan Stambolov and the Emergence of Modern Bulgaria 1870–1895*. Durham, North Carolina, 1993.

See also April Uprising; Khristo Botev; Gyurgevo Committee; Georgi Obretenov; San Stefano, Treaty of; Stefan Stambolov

October Diploma (1860)

Habsburg imperial decree of 1860 that marked the beginning of a process of constitutional experimentation in the monarchy. Issued as the result of a crisis in state finances and serious political unrest in Hungary following the Habsburg defeat in the Italian war of 1859, the diploma called for the expansion of the imperial council (Reichsrat) into a representative assembly. The Reichsrat, to be constituted of delegates of the provincial diets, assumed the power to advise the emperor on internal matters affecting the entire empire and, especially, to approve taxation. Proposed by conservative Hungarian aristocrats, the diploma assigned substantial powers to the provincial assemblies and thus tended toward the decentralization of state authority. Opposed by German liberals for this tendency and for the relative neglect of the urban populace in ensuing electoral schemes for the diets, the diploma also failed to satisfy the desires for self-government of the Hungarian nationalists and Czech and Polish political leaders. The diploma thus failed to relieve political unrest in the empire, and, despite its proclamation as an "eternal and irrevocable" document, it was substantially revised by the February Patent of 1861.

Philip Pajakowski

Further reading

Brandt, Harm-Hinrich. "Parlamentarismus als staatliches Integrationsproblem: Die Habsburger Monarchie," in Adolf M. Birke and Kurt Klixen, eds., *Deutscher und Britischer Parlamentarismus/British and German Parliamentarism*. Munich, 1985.

Goldinger, Walter. "Von Solferino bis zum Oktoberdiplom," in *Mitteilungen des österreichischen Staatsarchivs* 3 (1950): 106–26.

Macartney, C.A. *The Habsburg Empire, 1790–1918*. London, 1969.

See also February Patent

Oder River

One of the principal rivers of the North German Plain, and the second-largest river emptying into the Baltic Sea (after the Vistula). The Oder (Polish, Odra) is one of four large, navigable European waterways (along with the Rhine, Weser, and Elbe Rivers) flowing south to north across the Northern German Lowlands. The Seine-Oder core of mainland Europe forms the most dense pattern of canals and navigable rivers in the world.

The Oder flows in a general south to north direction 564 miles (907 km) from the Oder Mountains of the northern Czech Republic, through the Upper Silesian industrial districts. The Oder's drainage basin encompasses an area of 46,000 square miles (119,140 sq km). It is connected to the Ems River by the Mittelland (Midland) Canal, built in 1938; this water system provides direct connections between the Oder, Vistula, Rhine, and Ruhr Rivers, and Berlin. The Oder's chief tributaries are the Western Neisse and Warta Rivers.

After World War II, the Oder and the Western Neisse (the Oder's main tributary) became Poland's western boundary; this was established at the Potsdam conference in 1945 and recognized by East Germany in 1950 and by West Germany in 1970 as the Oder-Neisse Line. Poland gained the former German ports of Stettin (Szczecin) and Danzig (Gdańsk), and the Upper Silesian industrial area and surrounding rich farmlands.

The river flows into the Baltic at the Szczecin Lagoon through three channels: the Peene, Swine, and Dievenow. The river divides the Baltic coast into two distinct stretches. To the west, the German coastline is drowned, with many bays, gulfs, and islands, and no deep natural harbor. To the east, the Polish Baltic coast is flat and sandy, with long sand bars. The Polish section has the excellent ports of Szczecin (at the Oder's mouth) and Gdańsk.

Barbara VanDrasek

Further reading

Davies, Norman. *God's Playground: A History of Poland*, vol. 2, *1795 to the Present*. New York, 1984.

Hoffman, George W., ed. *Europe in the 1990s: A Geographic Analysis*, 6th ed. New York, 1990.

Turnock, David. *Eastern Europe: An Historical Geography 1815–1945*. New York, 1989.

See also Gdańsk; Potsdam Conference

Old Czechs

Nineteenth-century Czech political party. After the establishment of constitutional government in the Habsburg monarchy by the October Diploma of 1860 and the February Patent of 1861, Czechs resurrected the "National Party" (*Národní strana*) of the 1848 revolutionary period. By 1863, two factions had emerged within the party: the relatively more conservative Old Czechs (*Staročeši*)—who represented the urban intelligentsia and the upper middle class—and the more civil libertarian, anticlerical, and tactically more radical Young Czechs (*Mladočeši*).

Until the early 1870s, the Old Czechs were led by the most venerable Czechs of the mid-nineteenth century: František Palacký (1798–1876) and Jan Evangelista Purkyně (1787–1869), an internationally renowned physiologist.

Curial voting in elections to the diets of Bohemia and Moravia gave disproportionately larger representation to men of property and education, and especially to large landowners. Consequently, to realize their legislative agenda, the Old Czechs initiated cooperation with the Conservative Great Landowners. Together with the Young Czechs, the Old Czechs succeeded in the 1860s in establishing new institutions in Bohemia and Moravia: self-government (*samosprava*) elected by three-class suffrage; fraternal and benevolent associations such as the *sokols* (gymnastic clubs); corporate enterprises; producers' and consumers' cooperatives; and free, compulsory, universal, state-supported primary educations. They also helped pass laws to protect property rights, introduce civil marriage, and ease censorship and restrictions on political organizations and public assembly.

In December 1874 the Young Czechs split from the Old Czechs in defiance of the latter's policy of passive resistance and boycott of the Reichsrat (parliament) and provincial diets after the refusal of the Habsburgs to grant the Czechs internal independence comparable to that given the Hungarians in the *Ausgleich* (Compromise) of 1867 (which created the Dual Monarchy of Austria-Hungary). In 1878 the Old Czechs abandoned passive resistance and began to work with the Young Czechs toward fulfillment of a mutual national agenda.

From 1874 to 1914, the Old Czechs remained relatively stronger in Moravia than in more populous, industrialized, and urbanized Bohemia, where the Young Czechs supplanted them as the dominant Czech party during the 1890s. In both provinces, the gradual extension of male suffrage strengthened the Young Czechs more than the Old Czechs and facilitated the emergence of mass political parties, notably the Czechoslavonic Social Democrats (1878) and the Czech Agrarians (1889).

Although the Old Czechs lost their dominance to the Young Czechs, they remained an influential party in Czech academic, intellectual, and, to a lesser extent, commercial circles. But their continued belief that men of education and wealth could best determine public policy precluded their winning many votes after the introduction of universal male suffrage in elections to the lower house of the Reichsrat in 1905.

Bruce M. Garver

Further reading

Garver, Bruce M. *The Young Czech Party 1874–1901 and the Emergence of a Multi-party System*. New Haven, Connecticut, 1978.

Sak, Robert. *Rieger: Příběh Čecha devatenáctého věku*. Semily, Czech Republic, 1993.

Zacek, Joseph F. *Palacký: The Historian as Scholar and Nationalist*. The Hague, 1970.

See also *Ausgleich;* February Patent; Curial System; Dual Monarchy; October Diploma; František Palacký; Revolutions of 1848; *Sokol;* Young Czechs

Olmütz, Punktation of (1850)

Diplomatic agreement signed November 30, 1850, between Austria and Prussia. The agreement marked the failure of plans for a union of German states under Prussian leadership initiated in the wake of the Revolutions of 1848. After King Frederick William IV (1795–1851) refused the offer of the crown of a united Germany by the Frankfurt Assembly in 1849, the Prussian government proposed a conservative inner German union under Prussian leadership as part of a greater Central European confederation including the Habsburg Empire. Austria rejected the plan and gained the support of several of the middle German states, including Bavaria. Russia's Nicholas I (1796–1855) joined the Habsburgs in opposition to the proposal. The military intervention of both Prussia and Bavaria in Electoral Hesse brought a crisis between the German states. When Austria issued an ultimatum to Prussia demanding the evacuation of Hesse, the Prussian government relented. At Olmütz, Prussia agreed to abandon its plans for a union, demobilize its army, and meet with the other German governments to discuss the status of the Germanic Confederation, which was soon reconstituted in the form established in 1815. Long regarded as a humiliation for Prussia, the Olmütz Punktation fueled Prussian resentment toward Austria.

Philip Pajakowski

Further reading

Burian, Peter. "Die olmützer Punktation von 1850 und die deutsche Frage." *Geschichte in Wissenschaft und Unterricht* 25 (1974): 668–76.

Jelavich, Barbara. *The Habsburg Empire in European Affairs, 1814–1918.* Hamden, Connecticut, 1975.

Langer, William L. *Political and Social Upheaval, 1832–1852.* New York, 1969.

See also Nicholas I; Revolutions of 1848

Olomouc

Economic and historic ecclesiastical city on the Morava River in the north-central part of Moravia, the Czech Republic. Founded in 1050, Olomouc (German, Olmütz) has been the site of a Roman Catholic bishopric since 1063. Following its destruction in the Thirty Years' War (1618–48), the city's relative importance waned within Moravia, which has since been dominated by Brno to the south. However, Olomouc (population 107,000 in 1990) remains an important religious and economic center in the newly created Czech Republic.

Olomouc has been the site of a number of dramatic events in Central European history. In 1242 the Mongols were defeated here. Swedish forces destroyed the city in 1642. Thereafter, Olomouc's prior stature as a Moravian urban center ebbed. The city was rebuilt in the eighteenth century as an Austrian fortress on the frontier with Prussia, whose forces unsuccessfully besieged it in 1758. In 1850 Prussia suffered a political humiliation in Olomouc when a treaty signed there dissolved the Prussian-led German Union and reestablished the (short-lived) German Confederation.

Modern Olomouc is a trade, manufacturing, and cultural center. Major manufactured products include food products (especially confectionery), steel, machinery, and appliances. The city is the site of Palacký University and contains numerous notable historic buildings, including its cathedral and town hall. The oft-frequented pilgrimage church of Svatý Kopeček is also nearby.

William H. Berentsen

Further reading

Pounds, N.J.G. *Eastern Europe.* London, 1969.

See also Olmütz, Punktation of

Orange Guard

Party militia of the Bulgarian Agrarian National Union (BANU), a key Bulgarian political and social movement of the twentieth century. The Orange Guard—named for BANU's party color—was founded in October 1919. It was designed to meet an imminent threat to the government caused by a string of Communist-led strikes. The guard's members were recruited from among BANU's rural party cells (*druzhbi*) and were initially equipped with clubs. In December 1919, during a countrywide strike by transport workers partly organized by the Communist Party, some ten thousand Orange Guardists were mobilized and dispatched to Sofia and other towns. In security matters, the government increasingly relied on the Orange Guard instead of the disloyal police force and the equally anti-BANU army.

By 1921, the conservative, nationalist, and Macedonian opposition began to challenge the government's authority, and on October 22, 1921, the Internal Macedonian Revolutionary Organization (IMRO), which sought an autonomous Macedonian state, assassinated BANU's minister of war. During 1922, the various opposition forces united in a Constitutional Bloc (*Konstitutsionen blok*) in preparation for a coup d'état. BANU responded by increasing the number of Orange Guardists, supplying them with firearms, and establishing cavalry units. On October 31, 1922, BANU's Standing Committee issued a confidential decree to transform the Orange Guard into a professional paramilitary Agrarian National Guard (*Zemedelska narodna gvardiia*) under the command of Minister of the Interior Raiko Daskalov (1886–1923). This step was the immediate consequence of a serious confrontation between Orange Guardists and opposition demonstrators at Turnovo on

September 16–17, 1923, and of the temporary occupation of the town of Nevrokop by IMRO on October 16, 1922. When IMRO occupied another Bulgarian town, Kiustendil, on December 4, 1922, fifteen thousand Orange Guardists were mobilized. Instead of fighting IMRO, however, they looted the premises of opposition parties and newspapers in Sofia. In May 1923, when tensions between the government and the opposition reached a head, the Orange Guard was reorganized. It was divided into urban and rural cells, each with a so-called combat kernel (*boino iadro*) of one hundred men led by active or reserve officers loyal to the government. When the Military League, the political organization of Bulgarian army officers, staged a long-planned coup during the night of June 8–9, 1923, on behalf of the conservative-nationalist opposition bloc, neither the combat kernels in the province nor the six hundred Orange Guardists located at a Sofia garrison were able to safeguard BANU's rule. Within a week, all attempts at resistance by small Orange Guard units throughout the country were broken by the army and IMRO.

Stefan Troebst

Further reading

Bell, John D. *Peasants in Power: Alexander Stamboliski and the Bulgarian Agrarian National Union, 1899–1923.* Princeton, New Jersey, 1977.

Petrova, Dimitrina. *Samostoiatelnoto upravlenie na BZNS 1920–1923.* Sofia, 1988.

Radulov, Stefan. *Upravlenieto na BZNS i bulgarskata burzhoaziia.* Sofia, 1981.

See also Bulgarian Agrarian National Union; IMRO; Military League

Organic Statutes

Documents established in Eastern Europe to establish local self-government. In Romania, for example, the Organic Statute (*Règlement Organique*) was drafted in St. Petersburg by a committee of *boiars* under the presidency of Count Pavel Dimitrievich Kiselev (1788–1863) between 1829 and 1834. It was the first written constitution in Moldavia and Wallachia, lasting from 1834 to 1859—interrupted only by the Wallachian Republic (May/June 1848) during the Revolutions of 1848. These constitutions (although the term was avoided) established the principle of separation of powers, majority rule, budgetary control by the legislature, promotion by merit, educational systems, national militias, health services, and habeas corpus. There were plans for local government, reform of taxation, liberation of serfs and slaves, and social reform, all of which remained inoperative. Though liberal in theory, the regime in fact reinforced *boiar* privileges and the franchise was restricted to the upper class. The Organic Statute also represented a device for perpetuating Russian control, which superimposed itself on the nominal sovereignty of the sultan. Effective power was exercised by two Russian proconsuls, one in Iaşi, the other in Bucharest (who pitted the elected prince against the *boiar* assemblies). With a Russian army on the Prut River and other contingents manning the quarantine stations on the Danube on the pretext of preventing plague epidemics from Bulgaria, the consuls exercised considerable power to keep prince and *boiars* under control. The Russians were less successful in persuading a new generation of *boiars* to study in Moscow or St. Petersburg (most of the new generation preferred Paris). Nor did the protecting power succeed in isolating the intelligentsia from Western ideology by censorship and other sanctions. Nevertheless, in spite of such flaws, the Organic Statute laid the foundation for the establishment of a modern Romanian government, and by way of the uniformity of institutions adopted in each principality, it helped pave the way for the union of the two principalities in 1859.

Radu Florescu

Further reading

Filitti, Ion C. *Domniile române sub regulamentul organic, 1834–1848.* Bucharest, 1915.

Florescu, Radu R. *The Struggle against Russia in the Romanian Principalities, 1821–1854.* Munich, 1962.

Oţetea, Andrei, "Geneza regulamentului organic," in *Studii şi Articole de Istorii.* Bucharest, 1957.

See also Boiars; Intelligentsia; Count Pavel Kiselev; Revolutions of 1848

Orthodoxy

The Eastern Orthodox Church, the dominant religion in southeastern Europe and Russia, believes that it is the sole depository and authentic preserver of the Christian faith, maintaining a living continuity from the age of the apostles to the present. This reverence for ancient tradition is based on the word *"orthodoxia"* as the right, true, and correct Christian faith and worship, and is expressed in the importance of the Bible, the Nicene Creed, the decrees of the Seven Ecumenical Councils, and the writings of the church fathers. This belief also includes doctrine, church government and canon law, worship, and art forms, particularly the importance of icons. Believing that this ageless inheritance has been transmitted without change from the past, the Orthodox Church feels compelled to pass on an unaltered tradition to the future.

While the Bible for Orthodoxy is the supreme expression of God's revelation to humanity, it is regarded as the product of the church and emanates from tradition. It includes the Old Testament, ten Deutero-Canonical books, and the New Testament. Incorporated in all religious services or read at home, Orthodoxy regards the Bible as a verbal icon of God.

The Nicene Creed summarizes the faith of the Orthodox Church that God is revealed in Jesus Christ, who appeared in time and space to redeem all humanity and reconcile them with God. Orthodox believers hold that the church becomes the source of grace and the means of salvation and through participation in mysteries, reading the Bible, and practicing a life of prayer they come to live in Christ and become one with him. Of the mysteries of faith, the dogma of the Trinity is central to Orthodoxy. The oneness of Father, Son, and Holy Spirit is a mystery of unity in diversity and diversity in unity in which each is distinguished from the other two by personal characteristics, yet all sharing the same essence. Orthodoxy rejects the Western addition of the *filioque* clause, which implies that the Holy Spirit proceeds from the Father and the Son, distorting Christian theology by establishing differences within the Trinity.

The Orthodox Church accepts the doctrinal definitions of the Seven Ecumenical Councils, held from A.D. 325 to 787 as infallible. These defined the human and divine nature of Jesus, adopted the Nicene Creed, and affirmed the importance and role of icons in Orthodox belief and practice. The decisions of subsequent local councils and statements of individual bishops can possess a secondary importance.

The Orthodox attitude to religion is essentially a liturgical approach in which doctrine is understood or presented in divine worship. While the church has not accepted a specific number of mysteries by a formal decree, the seven most important are baptism, chrismation, holy communion, repentance and confession, marriage, a service for the healing of the sick, and ordination or holy orders. Those who are ordained—deacons, priests, and bishops—perpetuate an apostolic ministry and in celebrating the sacraments are links in an unbroken line of succession from Jesus and the apostles to the present. The most frequently performed mystery is the Divine Liturgy, or Eucharist. It is regarded as a reenactment of the Last Supper as a messianic meal in which Jesus unites himself with his disciples and all subsequent Orthodox Christians to create a fellowship that extends from Earth allowing devout worshippers to glimpse a celestial kingdom.

The patristic writings of the church fathers are regarded as living witness to Orthodox tradition, and while not equal to the authority of the Ecumenical Councils, continue to guide Orthodoxy and be a living affirmation of faith. Special recognition is shared by the three great hierarchs, Gregory of Nazianzus (329–390), Basil the Great (330–375), and John Chrysostom (354–407). There is also the recognition that patristic literature may continue to evolve with new writings that can become doctrinal statements.

Orthodox art is most clearly expressed in reverence for icons, or holy images, two-dimensional religious paintings of Jesus, the Virgin Mary, saints, and scenes from the life of Christ and the church. Unique to Orthodoxy and prominent in worship, churches, and processions, they are a vital dimension of Orthodox tradition. Regarded as reflections of heavenly archetypes, they become windows through which God is revealed to humanity. Some are regarded as miracle-working, and special feasts commemorating their healing skills have been instituted.

Finally, an ancient monastic tradition, with an emphasis on prayer, contemplation, and an austere lifestyle, is preserved throughout the Orthodox world. The most ancient communities are on Mount Sinai in Egypt and Mount Athos in northern Greece.

Since the fall of communism, there has been a startling increase in the number of men and women professing monastic vows and the construction of new monasteries and convents, particularly in Romania and Russia.

George R. Ursul

O

Further reading

Florovsky, Georges. *Georges Florovsky: Russian Intellectual and Orthodox Churchman, The Collected Works,* 14 vols. New York, 1987.

Harakas, Stanley. *The Orthodox Church: 455 Questions and Answers.* Minneapolis, Minnesota, 1987.

Ware, Timothy Kallistos. *The Orthodox Church.* New York, 1963

See also Exarchate; Patriarchate; Uniate Church

Orzeszkowa, Eliza (1841–1910)

Polish writer, publicist, and social and women's activist. Much of Orzeszkowa's writing was shaped by her active participation in the failed January Uprising of 1863 against the Russians. Luckily, she escaped imprisonment, and when her husband was exiled to Siberia she did not follow him, as was customary, but divorced him in 1869. These two events—the uprising and an unhappy marriage—repeatedly appeared in her later writings. The setting for the majority of Orzeszkowa's novels was the period after the fall of the January Uprising, which is never mentioned openly because of tsarist censorship.

As a positivist, Orzeszkowa was influenced by the evolutionist ideas of English philosopher Herbert Spencer (1820–1903) and the writings of British economist John Stuart Mill (1806–73). She emphasized the struggle against social and cultural prejudice. In *Marta* (1873), a young widow unsuccessfully struggles to support her daughter. In *Meir Ezofowicz* (1878), a young Jew rebels against his milieu. In *Nad Niemnem* (*On the Banks of the Niemen,* 1888), an impoverished upper-class woman decides to marry against her social class to be useful to her community.

As a writer, Orzeszkowa felt responsible for the moral improvement of society (which she viewed as an organism) and stressed the importance of education, the struggle for social justice, and equal rights for women and Jews. She was a spiritual leader of the women's movement, supported divorce, and emphasized the importance of the intelligentsia and women in a modern society. The characters in her novels were often average people (described by an omniscient narrator) whose lives are presented either as an example to follow (*Silny Samson* [*Strong Samson,* 1877]) or as a warning (*Dziurdziowie* [*The Dziurdzio Family,* 1885]).

Katarzyna Zechenter

Further reading

Jankowski, Edmund. *Eliza Orzeszkowa.* Warsaw, 1973.

Miłosz, Czesław. *The History of Polish Literature.* Berkeley, California, 1983.

Raman, Jan, ed. *W świecie Elizy Orzeszkowej.* Kraków, 1990.

Welsh, David J. "Two Talkative Authors: Orzeszkowa and George Eliot." *Polish Review* 1 (1965).

See also January Uprising; Polish Literature; Positivism; Women in Poland

Ostpolitik

"Opening to the East," which became West German policy in 1969. After the Soviet-led invasion by Warsaw Pact countries into Czechoslovakia in 1968, Western statesmen realized that Kremlin leaders were willing to risk a war to protect the borders of their empire in Central Europe. The policy of trying to isolate East Germany had not worked, and the Communist government in East Berlin was recognized by many countries. When Social Democratic leader Willy Brandt (1913–92) became German federal chancellor in October 1969, he fulfilled his election promise that he would achieve reconciliation with West Germany's eastern neighbors since the hope of unification of the two German states seemed illusory.

West German businessmen were eager to enlarge trade and investments; Soviet leaders hoped finally to get recognition of their exclusive sphere of influence in Eastern Europe and official acceptance of the Oder-Neisse frontier between Germany and Poland. The Soviet–West German treaty of August 1970 recognized the existing borders. Four months later, it was explicitly confirmed by the Treaty of Warsaw between Poland and the Federal Republic of Germany (West Germany). One year later, the difficult problem of the status of Berlin was amicably settled, and in 1973 both German states became members of the United Nations. After 1974, *Ostpolitik* was continued by Chancellor Helmut Schmidt (1918–).

The Soviet aim to achieve recognition of the new balance of power was acknowledged in

August 1975 by the Helsinki Declaration. Its so-called Basket Three, guaranteeing respect for a whole range of human rights, however, would prove to be very important for future changes in the Soviet empire.

Brandt's *Ostpolitik* accepted the power status quo but opened gates to cultural, economic, and even political rapprochement of divided German populations, breaking from the inside the solidity of the Soviet bloc.

Peter Hruby

Further reading

Birnbaum, Karl E. *East and West Germany: A Modus Vivendi.* Lexington, Massachusetts, 1973.

Pittman, Avril. *From Ostpolitik to Reunification: West German–Soviet Relations since 1974.* New York, 1992.

Wettig, Gerhard. *Community and Conflict in the Socialist Camp.* New York, 1975.

Ostrava

Industrial city of Moravia, located in the Czech Republic near the Polish border along the Oder River. With a population of 290,000 in 1989, Ostrava owes its origin mainly to the industrial and commercial growth of the nineteenth century, which is strongly reflected in the city's haphazard settlement and an architecture that mixes block housing and factories. Missing is the large and impressive core (city center) dating back to the Middle Ages so prominent in most Czech cities. German and Polish cultural imprints, however, still exist in the city, reflecting the ethnic diversity (less presently than before World War II) of the region.

Ostrava (also known as Moravská Ostrava) grew to be the major industrial city of northern Moravia, and was one of a string of cities that developed around an extensive coalfield that stretches from eastern Germany to southern Poland and northern Czechoslovakia. This "black country" (so named because of the coal) supported a sizable industrial growth in the Upper Silesian district and beyond. Ostrava was a major supplier of coal throughout the Habsburg Empire, supporting industrial growth at Plzeň, Prague, and other centers. It was the major pig iron– and steel-producing city of Czechoslovakia and played a prominent role (as a supplier of coal) in the development of the large East Slovak Steelworks (VSZ) in Košice. Other industries associated with the Ostrava industrial complex include mechanical and chemical engineering.

Russell L. Ivy

Further reading

Berentsen, William, ed. *Europe in the 1990s: A Geographical Analysis,* 7th ed. Chicago, 1997.

Pounds, N.J.G. *Eastern Europe.* Chicago, 1969.

Rugg, Dean. *Eastern Europe.* London, 1985.

UNIDO. *Czechoslovakia: Industrial Transformation and Regeneration.* Oxford, 1992.

See also Industrialization

Ottoman Empire

Multinational Islamic empire centered in the Balkans, Asia Minor, and much of the Near East, from the fourteenth to the early twentieth centuries. The Ottoman dynasty was founded around 1300 by Turkish *gazis,* or fighters for the faith of Islam, in northwestern Anatolia along the receding borders of the Byzantine Empire. Taking advantage of internecine conflict within the already weakened and much reduced Byzantine state, the Ottomans crossed the Dardanelles into Europe in 1354 and established a stronghold in the Gallipoli peninsula. From this base, the Ottomans rapidly expanded into the Balkans. Disunited and in varying states of decline, the Balkan kingdoms fell to the growing military and organizational prowess of the Ottomans, whose warrior elite was motivated by territorial expansion as the chief means of acquisition and enrichment, as well as its religious mission to destroy the infidel Christians.

Encouraged by their own zeal and emboldened by the obvious weakness of their enemies, the Ottoman Turks secured a dazzling series of victories and conquests in southeastern Europe. By 1361, virtually the whole of Thrace had been overrun, and ten years later the Ottomans added Macedonia to their realm, making their sultanate the most powerful state in the central Balkans. The Ottomans' successes against the Balkan kingdoms escalated following the Turks' strategic victory at the Battle of Kosovo in June 1389, which signaled the destruction of the last major organized resistance to Turkish expansion in the Balkans and paved the way for the subsequent conquest of the northern and southern Balkans. The crowning achievement in the process of Ottoman expansion, as well as the definite subjugation of the Balkan peoples, was the fall of the great imperial Byzantine city of Constantinople to the armies of Sultan Mehmed II (1432–81) in May 1453. Although pockets of resistance in Albania, Montenegro, and the Peloponnisus continued to harass the Ottomans, the Turks were now clearly masters of the Balkans.

The pace of Ottoman conquest reached its peak and began to slow in the sixteenth century concurrent with the reign of Sultan Suleiman I (1494–1566). At the center of the Ottoman system, and affecting virtually every area of the subject Balkan peoples' lives, was the institution known as the *millet*. The *millet,* or nation, reflected the Ottomans' emphasis on religion as the critical determinant in the organization of their administration. In short, through the *millet* the empire's subjects were administered by units organized on the basis of faith, while ignoring both nationality and geography. Consistent with this view, the empire's Orthodox Christian subjects, predominant in the Balkans, were placed under the administration of the Patriarch of Constantinople. Under this system of government, in exchange for its loyalty to, and support of, the sultan, each *millet* was allowed to maintain its own traditional laws and internal administrative organization under the direction of its religious leaders, who now functioned as both civil and religious authorities. Although it assigned permanent inferiority to non-Muslim groups, the *millet* system did in fact hold out the promise of limited self-government and nominal autonomy to its subject Christians. Indeed, the *millet* system, when coupled with a strong centralized government, sometimes contributed to improvements in the material welfare of much of the Balkan population during the early stages of Ottoman administration.

The relative tolerance enjoyed by the Balkan peoples under early Ottoman rule began to decline as the empire weakened. Taking advantage of a succession of feeble sultans and the attendant loss of strength of the central imperial government, Muslim landowning and bureaucratic elites in the provinces assumed more, and increasing, importance. While these groups expanded their influence and enriched themselves rather than serving an ever-weakening and distant central authority's administrative and security needs, governmental efficiency was gradually overwhelmed and replaced by corruption and self-interest. Ability, which had once characterized the Ottoman system, no longer determined advancement; instead, posts were granted to favorites or increasingly sold as investments to profiteers who, in turn, employed their offices to extort, unlawfully tax, and otherwise fleece local subjects. Meanwhile, the Ottoman military—the elite Janissaries and the feudal cavalry—fearing reform that would jeopardize its interests, and succumbing to the corrupting influences of the civil administration, began to deteriorate and grow unreliable. Finally, provincial governors, in concert with local bureaucrats, Janissaries, and police, also ignored the authority of the sultan.

This long process of decline was both marked and stimulated by a shift of power from the sultan and his central government to the provincial governors and their local administrators. As governors accumulated wealth, power, and often independent armed forces, many in their ranks began to establish virtual fiefdoms within the empire against the sultan's authority and will. In fact, by the late eighteenth and early nineteenth centuries, certain provincial governors, such as Ali Pasha of Yannina (c. 1750–1822), were able to exercise virtually independent power. As the tension between the central and provincial authorities increased, and as government corruption and consequent abuse and exploitation of the subject peoples reached epidemic proportions, conditions in the Balkans deteriorated to desperation. Adding to the growing misery of the empire's subjects, the troubling conditions born of political decline were magnified by changes in the land tenure system beginning in the sixteenth century, which, by the early eighteenth century, effectively reduced the Balkan peasant to the status of a serf.

Given their increasing impoverishment, abuse at the hands of corrupt administrators, and the unreliability of the empire's official institutions to protect them from injustice and violence, peasant discontent eventually led to revolt in the Balkans. The first significant revolt of this kind broke out in Serbia in 1804 and would eventually lead to the concession and establishment of autonomy for a small portion of the Serbian lands. In 1821, however, a much larger revolt with far more serious implications and consequences erupted within the empire's Greek lands. Although certain elite segments of the Greek population enjoyed significant influence within the empire by virtue of their preponderant numbers in the Orthodox Church hierarchy and hence disproportionate power within the Orthodox *millet,* the empire's Greeks were also its first group to be significantly affected by the ideas of nationalism, which were, of course, anathema to a multinational empire that suppressed or ignored the rights of the group.

In addition to injecting nationalism into the Balkan political landscape, the Greek Revolution also sparked the direct involvement of the Great Powers in the region. Although the Great Powers had become increasingly involved in the Balkans once Ottoman strength and territory began to recede in the late seventeenth century, their involvement now took on an even more decisive role. The formal precedent for, if not the actual source of, Great Power involvement was the 1774 Treaty of Kuchuk Kainardji, which, according to Russian claims, gave St. Petersburg the right to protect the interests of the Ottoman Empire's Orthodox Christians. Pursuant to that claim, in both concert and competition with Britain and France, and propelled by naval actions within the Ottomans, Russia intervened in the Balkan conflict. The resulting Russo-Turkish War of 1828–29 ended in defeat for the Ottoman Empire. By 1832 an independent Greek kingdom had been established and Serbian autonomy had been recognized. Nationalism began to spread to the other Balkan subject peoples. Moreover, the pattern of Great Power involvement, specifically Russian intervention in the growing national independence movements, in the Balkans during the remainder of the nineteenth century and into the early twentieth century was now a regular fixture of power politics in southeastern Europe.

In an effort to preserve the Ottoman Empire and protect it from growing internal threats, the Ottoman sultans introduced a program of major domestic reforms, the *tanzimat* (reorganization). Toward that goal, Sultan Mahmud II (1785–1839) succeeded in asserting the authority of the central government and thus forestalled the process of Ottoman recession from the Balkans. Ultimately, the reform movement reached its climax during the reign of Sultan Abdul Hamid II (1842–1909), who in December 1876 promulgated the first Ottoman constitution. However, his experiments with reform soon ended, and his reign was to be marked by a series of military and diplomatic disasters, as well as domestic instability. After a mas-

sive revolt in the Bulgarian and Serbian lands beginning in 1875 and a subsequent war with Russia in 1877–78, Abdul Hamid dismissed the Ottoman parliament and suspended the Ottoman constitution in 1878. Thereafter, he ruled as an autocrat assisted by a system of secret police, arbitrary state brutality, and severe censorship. Despite Abdul Hamid's austere efforts to hold the empire together, the Ottomans were forced to endure the loss of significant territories to the Habsburg Empire, as well as to the emergence of a constellation of fully independent successor states—Bulgaria, Romania, Serbia, Greece, and Montenegro.

Discontent with Abdul Hamid's despotic rule, as well as the continued decline of the empire and resentment against foreign intervention in the Balkans, aroused considerable Ottoman Turkish opposition. Inspired by intellectuals and politicians who had been forced to emigrate owing to Abdul Hamid's repression, the growing opposition groups gradually united into a loosely formed coalition known as the Young Turks. Members of one of the Young Turk groups, the Committee of Union and Progress, led a military revolt in Ottoman Macedonia that forced Abdul Hamid to restore the parliament in 1908, and, after a short-lived counterrevolution, forced him from power altogether in 1909.

Despite their official commitment to the principles of constitutional parliamentarianism, once in power the Young Turks, as architects of a nationalist policy of Turkification that further alienated the Balkan Christians remaining under Ottoman rule, proved to be even more oppressive than Abdul Hamid. Furthermore, the foreign relations of the Ottoman Empire under the Young Turks led to disaster. The two Balkan Wars nearly completed the destruction of the Ottoman Empire in Europe. In the First Balkan War (October 1912–May 1913), the Ottomans lost all of their lands in the Balkans, excluding Constantinople and its environs, to a powerful military alliance made up of Bulgaria, Greece, Montenegro, and Serbia. In the Second Balkan War (June–July 1913), fought between Bulgaria and its former allies, including Romania, the Ottomans intervened against Bulgaria and recovered Eastern Thrace. For all practical purposes, however, the Balkan Wars brought an end to the Ottoman Empire as a Balkan power. As if to hasten the empire's dissolution, the Young Turks' greatest foreign policy miscalculation came in October 1914 when the Ottoman

O Empire entered World War I on the side of the Central Powers. The Ottoman Empire's defeat, humiliating peace, partition, and foreign occupation following its collapse in 1918 led to the emergence of the Turkish nationalist republic in its place in the early 1920s. The rule of the Ottoman Empire's last sultan ended in 1924.

Alexandros K. Kyrou

Further reading

Jelavich, Barbara. *History of the Balkans,* 2 vols. Cambridge, 1983.

Jelavich, Charles and Barbara Jelavich. *The Establishment of the Balkan National States, 1804–1920.* Seattle, Washington, 1977.

Lewis, Bernard. *The Emergence of Modern Turkey.* London, 1961.

Runciman, Steven. *The Great Church in Captivity: A Study of the Patriarchate of Constantinople from the Eve of the Turkish Conquest to the Greek War of Independence.* Cambridge, 1968.

Shaw, Stanford J. *History of the Ottoman Empire and Modern Turkey,* 2 vols. Cambridge, 1977.

Stavrianos, L.S. *The Balkans since 1453.* New York, 1958.

Sugar, Peter F. *Southeastern Europe under Ottoman Rule, 1354–1804.* Seattle, Washington, 1977.

See also Abdul Hamid II; Ali Pasha; Balkan Wars; Constantinople/Istanbul; Eastern Question; Great Powers; Greek Revolution; Islam; Janissaries; Kosovo; Kuchuk Kainardji, Treaty of; Lausanne, Treaty of; Mahmud II; *Millet;* Nationalism; Orthodoxy; Patriarchate; Porte; Russo-Turkish War of 1828–29; Russo-Turkish War of 1877–78; Serbo-Turkish War of 1876; Sèvres, Treaty of; *Tanzimat;* Young Turks

P

Paderewski, Ignacy Jan (1860–1941)

Polish pianist, composer, statesman, philanthropist, and patriot. From 1872 to 1878, Paderewski studied piano at the Warsaw Conservatory; from 1881 to 1883, composition in Berlin; and from 1884 to 1887, piano in Vienna. In 1887 he began giving concerts in western Europe. In 1890 he gave his first concert in the United States at New York's Carnegie Hall, which initiated a concert tour in North America. Paderewski also gave concerts in South Africa, South America, Australia, and New Zealand. During World War I, Paderewski organized an assistance committee in Switzerland for the Polish victims of the war and for the Polish Victims Relief Fund in London; he also participated in organizing Polish voluntary military troops in the United States.

As prime minister and minister of foreign affairs of the republic of Poland (1919), Paderewski signed the Versailles treaty, which ended World War I. From 1920 to 1921, he represented Poland in the League of Nations. After the outbreak of World War II in Europe in 1939, Paderewski launched a campaign in the United States to gain help for Poland. During 1940–41, he presided over the State Council of the Polish government-in-exile.

Paderewski spent a large portion of his resources on philanthropic purposes. In 1896 he set up a foundation in the United States for young composers. Two years later, he founded two competitions in Warsaw (for music and drama). And in 1910 he helped erect a monument in Kraków commemorating the quincentenary of the Polish victory over the Teutonic Knights at Grunwald in 1410.

Paderewski's compositional output (seventeen opus numbers and several unnumbered works) includes numerous piano miniatures, Violin Sonata op. 13, Piano Concerto op. 17, the opera *Manru* op. 20, Symphony op. 24, Fantasie Polonaise op. 19 for piano and orchestra, and vocal compositions.

Jolanta T. Pękacz

Further reading

Drozdowski, M.M. *Ignacy Jan Paderewski: A Political Biography.* Warsaw, 1981.

Paderewski, I.J. and M. Lawton. *The Paderewski Memoirs (1939).* New York, 1980.

Przybylski, H. *Między muzyką a polityką.* Katowice, Poland, 1992.

Zamoyski, A. *Paderewski.* London, 1982.

See also League of Nations; Music; Paris Peace Conference

Paisii of Hilendar (Paisii Khilendarski) (1722–73)

Bulgarian monk and historian and first great figure of the Bulgarian Renaissance. Born in the trading town of Bansko, Paisii (his given name is unknown) received little formal schooling. At the age of twenty-three, he traveled to Mount Athos in Greece and entered the Hilendar monastery, where his elder brother was abbot. The monasteries at Mount Athos were centers of South Slavic culture and maintained contacts throughout the Eastern Orthodox lands. Paisii used the monastery library to improve his education. The monks were fond of debating historical, cultural, and religious topics,

P and Paisii took part in these at times heated exchanges. His Greek and Serbian brethren, whose lands were already experiencing a national revival, claimed that Bulgaria had no past. Paisii resolved to prove them wrong and around 1760 began work on a history of his country. In 1761 he went to the Serbian town of Karlovac, where he visited the patriarchal library. That summer he returned to the Hilendar monastery but was forced to move to the Zograf monastery because of "great troubles and dissensions" among the monks. There, he completed his *Istoriia Slavianobolgarskaia (A Slavonic-Bulgarian History,* 1762), the first full-length treatment of the subject. He later traveled to the village of Kotel and met the young priest Stoiko Vladislavov (1739–1813), future bishop Sofronii of Vratsa, who copied out the *History* and placed it in his church for the edification of his parishioners.

The *History* is written in vernacularized Church Slavonic; the style, as befits the author's purpose, is direct and vigorous. It contains elements of the chronicle (the story of the Flood and the division of the earth among Noah's sons, the providential view of history), the hagiography (the brief characterizations of the Bulgarian saints and the account of the deeds of Saints Cyril [d. 869] and Methodius [d. 884]), and the scholarly treatise. Paisii was primarily a polemicist, and his *History* is full of factual mistakes and patriotic exaggerations. He eulogizes "the great sovereigns who ruled wisely," extols the glories of Bulgaria's past, and declares that the Bulgarians were the first Slavic people to convert to Christianity and to acquire a written language. He blames the Byzantines for the Turkish conquest of Bulgaria. Indeed, the *History* had a strong anti-Greek bias, which was due to Paisii's opposition to the Hellenization of the Bulgarian church and his resentment of the fashion for all things Greek among educated Bulgarians. Despite its flaws, the *History* is one of Bulgaria's fundamental national texts. Every Bulgarian schoolchild is taught the lines: "O reckless and foolish one! Wherefore art thou ashamed to call thyself Bulgarian? Or did not the Bulgars possess a kingdom and a state? Be thou not deluded, Bulgarian, but know thine own origin and tongue."

Richard Tempest

Further reading

Khilendarski, Paisii. *Istoriia Slavianobolgarskaia, 1762,* vols. 1–2. Sofia, 1972.

Kulman, D. "Studien zum Griechenbild in der Literatur der bulgarischen Wiedergeburt. I: Paisij Chilendarski." *Die Welt der Slaven: Halbjahresschrift für Slavistik* 14 (1969).

MacDermott, Mercia. *A History of Modern Bulgaria.* New York, 1962.

Niederhauser, E. "The Historian and the National Movement: The Case of Paisi, Rajic, and Lelewel." *Studia Slavica Academiae Scientiarum Hungaricae* 25 (1979).

Picchio, R. "Gli Annali del Baronio—Skarga e la Storia di Paisij Hilendarski." *Ricerche Slavistiche* 3 (1954).

Velchev, Velcho. *Paissi of Hilendar: Father of the Bulgarian Enlightenment.* Sofia, 1981.

See also Orthodoxy; Sofronii Vrachanski

Palacký, František (1798–1876)

Czech historian-statesman and leader of the Czech National Revival of the nineteenth century. Palacký was born to a Moravian peasant family. He studied at the renowned Evangelical lyceum in Pressburg in Hungary (now Bratislava in the Slovak Republic), leaving it for Prague in 1823 with an excellent education and a fervent desire to revive the Czechs' moribund national consciousness. His lifelong dedication to the linguistic, cultural, and political awakening of the Czechs earned him the title Father of the Czech Nation.

In 1827 the Bohemian Estates commissioned Palacký to write a scholarly history of Bohemia and Moravia. The classic *Dějiny národu českého (History of the Czech Nation,* 1848–67) became his chief intellectual preoccupation. The rigorous scientific method and exhaustive archival research embodied in it made him the founder of modern Czech historiography. Focused on the Hussite Revolution of the fifteenth century, the *History* also promulgated a proud philosophy of Czech history: the Czechs' historical mission was to defend political and religious freedom, most often against attacks by Germans.

In the failed Revolution of 1848, Palacký was the Czechs' chief political spokesman, unsuccessfully championing the idea of Austroslavism, the movement to gain equality for the Habsburg Empire's Slavic peoples, and advocating the federalization of the Habsburg monarchy. He returned to political activity after 1860 and was involved in all major negotiations between the Czechs and

Vienna. He and his son-in-law, František Ladislav Rieger (1818–1903), were the leaders of the National Party (Old Czechs), which was committed to the defense of Bohemia's historic state rights (*Staatsrecht*) and supported a Czech boycott of the imperial diet in protest. Toward the end of his life, disillusioned about the future of the Czechs in the Habsburg Empire, Palacký counseled them to cultivate "moral superiority" over their enemies and to wait patiently for the opportunity to regain their independence. He died on May 26, 1876.

Joseph Frederick Zacek

Further reading

Morava, Georg J. *Franz Palacký: Eine frühe Vision von Mitteleuropa.* Vienna, 1990.

Pekař, Josef. *Fr. Palacký.* Prague, 1912.

Zacek, Joseph F. *Palacký: The Historian as Scholar and Nationalist.* The Hague, 1970.

See also Austroslavism; Old Czechs; Prague Slav Congress; Revolutions of 1848; František L. Rieger

Pale of Settlement

Territory in western Russia in which Jews were forced to live. Established by Catherine the Great (1729–96) after the partitions of the Polish-Lithuanian Commonwealth, the Pale of Settlement was created to solve "the Jewish problem in Russia." The Jews had been expelled from Muscovy by the end of the fifteenth century and Catherine's administration did not know how to deal with masses of Jews who had been incorporated into Russia together with the former Polish lands. The eastern border of the Pale, similar to the eastern border of Poland, was changed several times. The Congress Kingdom of Poland was not officially included within the Pale but in practice, after 1868, became part of it. During the reign of Alexander II (1855–81), permission to live outside the Pale was granted only to Jewish professionals and former soldiers of Nicholas I (1796–1855). After the assassination of Alexander II, during a period of political reaction, the Jews were expelled from the countryside and many towns and their rights were drastically limited. By the end of the nineteenth century, the Pale covered about 386,100 square miles (one million sq km) and was inhabited by 4,899,300 Jews, constituting 11.6 percent of the entire local population and 94 percent of the total Russian Jewish population. The Pale was abolished de facto in August 1915 and legally in February 1917.

Piotr Wróbel

Further reading

Baron, Salo W. *The Russian Jew under Tsars and Soviets.* New York, 1976.

Encyclopedia Judaica, vol. 13. Jerusalem, 1971, 24–28.

Klier, John D. "The Ambiguous Legal Status of Russian Jewry in the Reign of Catherine II." *Slavic Review* 35, no. 3 (September 1976): 506–17.

Rowland, Richard H. "Geographical Patterns of the Jewish Population in the Pale of Settlement in Late Nineteenth Century Russia." *Jewish Social Studies* 48, no. 3–4 (Summer–Fall 1986): 209–34.

See also Alexander II; Jews; Nicholas I; Polish Congress Kingdom

Pan-Germanism

Nineteenth-century concept formed in reaction to Pan-Slavism in Russia. Originally, Pan-Germanism indicated belief in the existence of some common root consciousness among all Germans and all Germanic peoples. By 1914, Pan-Germanism signaled extreme German nationalism and a program of territorial expansion for Germany, with strong anti-Semitic tones. Under the Nazis, Pan-Germanism meant belief in a Germanic "race" with some common racial characteristics among all Germanic peoples and a belief in the natural superiority of the Germanic race above all others.

The original vague concept of Pan-Germanism was transformed into an active political program by the Pan-German League, founded in 1894 with the participation of Alfred Hugenberg (1865–1951), chief director of the huge Krupp iron works. The league promoted nationalist feelings within Germany, strengthened German identity in Germans living abroad, and urged aggressive policies for advancing German interests abroad. The league found support among industrialists, merchants, and professionals but most particularly among university professors, secondary school teachers, and students.

During World War I, the Pan-German League advocated the most extreme German war aims. In early 1915 the league drafted a widely supported

P memorandum that cited large territorial annexations in Belgium, France, Luxembourg, Poland, and Russia. Pan-German insistence on these demands through 1918 prevented Germany from reaching a negotiated peace. In the 1920s Pan-Germans loudly rejected German Foreign Minister Gustav Stresemann's (1878–1929) attempts at cooperation with the Western Allies.

In the early 1920s Adolf Hitler (1889–1945) met several times with Heinrich Class (1868–1953), the long-serving leader of the Pan-German League. Many Pan-German demands also appeared in the Nazi Party program of 1920 and in the programs of other radical right parties. By 1930, the Pan-German League had allied itself with the rising Nazi Party, both groups appearing together at demonstrations. After 1933, the Nazis radicalized traditional Pan-Germanism by merging their racial view of the world with older Pan-German concepts and demands. Many Nazi organizations advanced racially updated, Pan-German views, particularly the Alldeutsche Verband (All-German Union).

Robert Mark Spaulding

Further reading

Chickering, Roger. *We Men Who Feel Most German: A Cultural Study of the Pan-German League.* Boston, 1984.

Craig, Gordon. *Germany 1866–1945.* Oxford, 1978.

Jarausch, Konrad Hugo. *Students, Society, and Politics in Imperial Germany: The Rise of Academic Illiberalism.* Princeton, New Jersey, 1982.

See also Germanization; Hakata; Adolf Hitler; Pan-Slavism; Right Radicalism

Pan-Slavism

A varied, largely ill-defined, and poorly coordinated effort among the Slavic-speaking peoples of Europe, mostly in the nineteenth century, by which they affirmed their cultural closeness and sometimes expressed a desire for political association. The most important precursor of Pan-Slavism is generally considered to be Juraj Križanić (1618–83), a Croatian Jesuit who advocated one unified Slavic nation with a universal Slavic language (which he himself devised) and a Uniate Christian religion in a single state ruled by the Russian tsar. Pan-Slavism proper, however, began in the early nineteenth century with the Western and South Slavs. Living under foreign hegemony, they sought cultural and political strength through expressions of Slavic "racial" solidarity, in demonstrations of Slavic cultural reciprocity, and in visions of future Russian diplomatic and military assistance that would help to free them. Despite European (especially German) suspicions that it was Russian-instigated and directed, Pan-Slavism attracted little Russian interest and no official support until the 1860s. Events such as the Crimean War (1853–56), the 1867 Austro-Hungarian *Ausgleich* (Compromise), which created the Dual Monarchy of Austria-Hungary, and the unification of Germany prompted Russian politicians to try to exploit the movement for their country's own political ends. Pan-Slavism was reinterpreted as Pan-Russianism and used as a front for Russian imperialism, especially during the Russo-Turkish War of 1877–78. A philosophical rationale for Russian Pan-Slavism was supplied by the beliefs of the Slavophiles, especially as they were presented in the book *Russia and Europe* (1869) by Nikolai Yakovlevich Danilevsky (1822–85). Danilevsky extolled the superiority of Slavic culture over German-Latin civilization and proclaimed Russia's historic destiny to liberate other Slavs from foreign rule and unite them for the inevitable confrontation with the West. Non-Russian Pan-Slavism made a brief, unsuccessful reappearance as neo-Slavism, a Czech-led movement for Slavic cultural and economic cooperation in the decade before World War I. Pan-Slavism as a whole essentially disappeared after World War I, though the Soviet Union attempted to use some of its ideas and slogans for its own benefit in World War II and immediately afterward. A well-integrated, successful Pan-Slavic movement was doomed from the start by the differing, sometimes contradictory desires and purposes, cultural characteristics, and historic orientations of the various Slavic peoples. It left behind only a literary and aesthetic residue—the record of a long series of Slavic congresses, from Prague in 1848 to Belgrade in 1946, and a wealth of manifestos and polemics, scholarly studies, and cultural creations.

Joseph Frederick Zacek

Further reading

Fadner, Frank L. *Seventy Years of Pan-Slavism in Russia: Karazin to Danilevskii, 1800–1870.* Washington, D.C., 1962.

Kohn, Hans. *Pan-Slavism, Its History and Ideology,* 2d rev. ed. New York, 1960.

Milojković-Djurić, Jelena. *Pan-Slavism and National Identity in Russia and the Balkans, 1830–1880: Images of the Self and Others.* Boulder, Colorado, 1994.

See also *Ausgleich;* Austroslavism; Crimean War; Dual Monarchy; Neo-Slavism; Prague Slav Congress; Russo-Turkish War of 1877–78; Slavophilism; Uniate Church

Landau, Jacob. *Pan-Turkism: From Irredentism to Cooperation.* Bloomington, Indiana, 1995.
———. *Pan-Turkism in Turkey: A Study of Turkish Irredentism.* Hamden, Connecticut, 1981.
Lewis, Bernard. *The Emergence of Modern Turkey.* London, 1961.
Shaw, Stanford. *History of the Ottoman Empire and Modern Turkey,* 2 vols. New York, 1976–77.

See also Nationalism; Pan-Slavism

Panturanianism

Grandiose nationalistic ideal of Turkish expansionists who desired a Turanian state extending from the Danube River to the Pacific Ocean and encompassing Turkic and Finno-Ugric speakers. Panturanianism was designed in reaction to Pan-Slavism, Panhellenism, Balkan nationalism, unsuccessful Ottoman reforms, and failure of Ottomanism as a secular ideology.

"Turan," an ancient Iranian name for the Central Asian homeland of northern Iranians, was mistakenly used by Turkish nationalists in Russia and Turkey to designate Turkic lands of Central Asia, Siberia, and Mongolia. These visionaries adopted "Turanian" for Turks, Mongols, Finns, Hungarians, and other Turkic and Finno-Ugric speakers, and Panturanianism was the movement for a politically unified Turan embracing a broad swathe of territory in Europe and Asia. As an ethnic and linguistic classification, Turanian has long been disproved, but as a political concept Panturanianism retained appeal until the formation of Kemalist Turkey after World War I.

Panturanianism inspired Panturkism, a cultural and political movement focusing on Turkic speakers of Turkey, Central Asia, and Transcaucasia and disseminated in writings by thinkers like Ziya Gokalp (1876–1924). After the failure of Panturkic schemes in the Caucasus and Central Asia during World War I, Turkish secular nationalism found a more viable and pragmatic approach in Mustafa Kemal Atatürk's (1881–1938) notion of a Turkish national fatherland in Anatolia.

Theophilus C. Prousis

Further reading

Arnakis, George. "Turanism: An Aspect of Turkish Nationalism." *Balkan Studies* 1 (1960): 19–32.
Gokalp, Ziya. *The Principles of Turkism.* Leiden, Netherlands, 1968.

Paris, Treaty of (1856)

Agreement officially ending the Crimean War. The peace conference, attended by representatives of Austria, France, Great Britain, the Ottoman Empire, Russia, and Sardinia, opened on February 25, 1856. The powers permitted Prussian delegates to attend only those sessions regarding revision of the 1841 Straits accord (which governed the Turkish Straits), which Prussia had signed. Because the Vienna Four Points, which spelled out the stipulations Russia had to accept for ending the Crimean War (1853–56), served as the basis of the treaty and had already been agreed upon, the negotiations focused on interpretation and implementation of its provisions.

Among its clauses, the treaty called for Russia and Turkey to neutralize and demilitarize the Black Sea, closing it to all warships but opening it to the maritime traffic of all countries. Russia lost its protectorate over Serbia and the Danubian Principalities (Moldavia and Wallachia), to be replaced by a European guarantee. Russia evacuated Turkish territory occupied in the Caucasus region, while the allies restored Russian territory they occupied. Russia returned to Moldavia the southern three districts of Bessarabia, which it had seized in 1812. With Russia removed from the mouth of the Danube River, the treaty created a commission, composed of the countries through which the river flowed, to oversee administration of the Danube. A European Great Power guarantee replaced Russia's right to protect the Christians of the Ottoman Empire. The powers also agreed not to interfere in Turkish internal affairs, recognized the integrity of the Ottoman Empire, and permitted it to become a member of the concert of Europe. The powers signed the treaty on March 30, 1856.

Although not a harsh treaty, Russia tried during the next fourteen years to revise it as it

P signified its decline as a power. Specifically, it resented the clauses relating to the demilitarization of the Black Sea as an affront to its sovereignty. In 1870, in the midst of the Franco-Prussian War, Russia renounced these sections of the treaty.

Gregory C. Ference

Further reading

Hurst, Michael, ed. *Key Treaties for the Great Powers 1814–1914,* 2 vols. New York, 1972.

See also Bessarabian Question; Crimean War; Danube Question; Eastern Question; Great Powers; Napoléon III; United Principalities

Paris Peace Conference (1919)

Conference of Allied and Associated Powers following World War I (January 18, 1919, to January 20, 1920). As a result of the war, a number of independent states emerged, reemerged, or expanded out of the ruins of the Austro-Hungarian, German, and Russian Empires. It was up to the principal peacemakers—President Woodrow Wilson (1856–1924), Prime Minister David Lloyd George (1863–1945), and Premier Georges Clemenceau (1841–1929)—to give the final shape to the new East Central Europe through the Treaties of Versailles (with Germany), St. Germain (with Austria), Trianon (with Hungary), and Neuilly (with Bulgaria).

The pivotal Treaty of Versailles was signed on June 28, 1919, after bitter debates among the Allied Big Three (United States, Great Britain, and France). France wanted a peace that would prevent German resurgence; Britain strove for an eventual reintegration of Germany; and the United States occupied a middle-of-the-road position. The Germans bitterly opposed Polish territorial demands, and the Allies compromised by making Danzig (Polish, Gdańsk) a free city, and by instituting plebiscites in East Prussia (Allenstein-Olsztyn and Marienwerder-Kwidzyń) in 1920 and in Upper Silesia in 1921. The former were won by the Germans, the latter—preceded and followed by armed uprisings—led to a division of the area. The Germans particularly objected to Poland's access to the Baltic and popularized the term "corridor" for the land separating East Prussia from the rest of Germany. The peacemakers reserved to themselves the right to draw Polish borders in the east, but were unable to do so. The German-Czech bor-

der remained the same as the prewar frontier with Austria, which meant that some three million of the so-called Sudeten Germans became citizens of Czechoslovakia.

Minority protection and certain economic clauses were drawn up in a separate treaty with Poland on June 28, 1919, which served as a model for other similar accords.

The Treaty of St. Germain of September 10, 1919, concerned exclusively East Central Europe, disposing of the territories of the Austrian part of the former Dual Monarchy. The new ethnic Austrian republic was forbidden to join Germany, but its borders raised little controversy except for the regions ceded to Italy. In the case of Slovenia (now part of the Kingdom of Serbs, Croats, and Slovenes), a plebiscite in Klagenfurt resulted in an Austrian victory. There were also changes in the border with Hungary. Major disputes arose over the assignment of lands no longer contiguous to Austria: Galicia (ceded to the Allies), in whose eastern part Poles battled Ukrainians; Teschen (Polish, Cieszyn; Czech Těšín), where Poles opposed Czechs; or Bukovina, which went to Romania.

The Treaty of Trianon was delayed until June 4, 1920, when, after the fall of Béla Kun's (1886–1938) Soviet republic in Hungary (created during the turbulent period following Austria-Hungary's defeat in the war), the peacemakers recognized the new Hungarian government with which they were willing to sign the peace. Reduced to its ethnic core and refused requests for plebiscites in contested areas (except in Sopron), Hungary lost Slovakia and Carpatho-Ruthenia to Czechoslovakia; Croatia, Vojvodina, the Banat, and Transylvania to the Kingdom of Serbs, Croats, and Slovenes and to Romania. The total loss amounted to over two-thirds of Hungary's prewar territory and three-fifths of its population. Almost every third ethnic Magyar now lived outside the boundaries of Hungary. Partial disarmament clauses and reparations completed this treaty, which the Hungarians regarded as a national disaster.

The Treaty of Neuilly, signed on November 27, 1919, deprived Bulgaria of access to the Aegean Sea by transferring Western Thrace to Greece, originally to facilitate Greek plans of eastern expansion. Small territorial rectifications to the advantage of the Kingdom of Serbs, Croats, and Slovenes, reparations, and a reduction of the size of the army also figured in the treaty.

The work of the Paris Peace Conference has been subject to bitter criticism not only by the defeated nations but also by others, such as British economist John Maynard Keynes (1883–1946). Arguments about the "balkanization" of Europe mingled with nostalgia for the Austro-Hungarian monarchy. The peace settlement was also said to contain germs of World War II. Although the settlement in East Central Europe included many iniquities and inconsistencies, it is not easy to point to a workable alternative. Many of the borders (Poland excepted) have survived to the present day.

Piotr S. Wandycz

Further reading

Deák, Francis. *Hungary at the Paris Peace Conference.* New York, 1942.

Lederer, Ivo J. *Yugoslavia at the Paris Peace Conference.* New Haven, Connecticut, 1963.

Lundgreen-Nielsen, Kay. *The Polish Problem at the Paris Peace Conference.* Odense, 1979.

Perman, D. The Shaping of the Czechoslovak State. Leiden, Netherlands, 1962.

Spector, Sherman D. *Romania and the Paris Peace Conference.* New York, 1962.

See also Banat; Dual Monarchy; East Prussia; Ethnic Minorities; Fourteen Points; Galicia; Gdańsk; Greater Romania; Hungarian Soviet Republic; Kingdom of Serbs, Croats, and Slovenes; Béla Kun; League of Nations; Neuilly, Treaty of; Polish Corridor; St. Germain, Treaty of; Silesian Question; Subcarpathian Rus'; Sudetenland; Teschen; Transylvanian Question; Trianon, Treaty of; Vojvodina; Woodrow Wilson

Partisans *See* **Antifascism**

Pašić, Nikola (1845–1926)

Serbian leader and founder of the Serbian Radical Party in 1881, whose initial constituency was the peasantry. Born in Zaječar, Pašić served as prime minister from 1891 to 1892, and minster to St. Petersburg from 1893 to 1895. After the Karadjordjević dynasty replaced the Obrenović in 1903, Pašić was Serbia's prime minister from 1904 to 1918, except for three brief interludes. His singular goal, to unite the Serbian nation, he pursued during the Bosnian crisis of 1908–9, the two Balkan Wars (1912–13), and World War I. It was not until after the assassination of Franz Ferdinand (1863–1914) in Sarajevo on June 28, 1914, that Pašić publicly committed himself to the unification of the Serbs, Croats, and Slovenes. After Serbia's defeat in 1915 and the overthrow of the Romanov dynasty in Russia, which supported Serbia, Pašić was compelled to negotiate with the Yugoslav Committee, composed of exiled South Slav leaders of the Austro-Hungarian Empire. It led to the Corfu Pact of 1917, which culminated in the formation of the Kingdom of Serbs, Croats, and Slovenes on December 1, 1918.

Pašić was revered, especially by the peasants, as the wise leader whose age, taciturn demeanor, and white beard seemed to symbolize the millennium of Serbia's history and its struggle for freedom and independence. In the eyes of many foreigners, however, Pašić embodied Balkan deception, intrigue, and traits of "Orientalism."

In 1919–20 Pašić was the government's chief negotiator at the Paris Peace Conference, which established the new state's frontiers. In 1921 he was again appointed prime minister, a post he held with one brief exception to 1926. He was largely responsible for the adoption of the 1921 centralized Vidovdan Constitution, which was modeled on the Serbian constitution of 1903. It assured the supremacy of the Serbs in the kingdom, a goal on which he would not compromise. The Croats and others charged that Pašić's aim now was to create a Greater Serbia within the cloak of a South Slav kingdom. As a result, the kingdom was engulfed in perpetual conflicts between centralists and federalists, which contributed to political instability throughout the interwar decades. In April 1926 Pašić resigned, largely because of corruption charges against his son. Eight months later, he died.

Charles Jelavich

Further reading

Banac, Ivo. *The National Question in Yugoslavia: Origins, History, Politics.* Ithaca, New York, 1984.

Dragnich, Alex N. *Serbia, Nikola Pašić and Yugoslavia.* New Brunswick, New Jersey, 1974.

Stanković, Djordje Dj. *Nikola Pašić i Jugoslovensko Pitanje,* 2 vols. Belgrade, 1985.

See also Balkan Wars; Corfu Declaration; Franz Ferdinand; Greater Serbia; Kingdom of Serbs,

P Croats, and Slovenes; Paris Peace Conference; Vidovdan Constitution; Yugoslav Committee; World War I

Sugar, Peter. *Southeastern Europe under Ottoman Rule, 1354–1804.* Seattle, Washington, 1977.

See also Ali Pasha; *Haiduks;* Janissaries; Porte

Pasvanoglu (1758–1807)

Ottoman bandit and warlord who defied the sultan's directives and established an independent realm in Bulgaria from 1799 to 1807. Pasvanoglu was a rebellious pasha who, with his illustrious contemporary Ali Pasha of Yannina (c. 1750–1822), weakened the Ottoman Empire.

Pasvanoglu Osman Pasha, whose father was executed by the Porte, fought with the Ottoman army against Russia in 1787 then became a notorious bandit in the town of Vidin on the Danube. Supported by brigands, outlaws, and unruly Janissaries (formerly elite Turkish soldiers), Pasvanoglu carved out a personal domain in northwestern Bulgaria where local Muslims and Christians paid heavy taxes but lived in relative security and protection. Pasvanoglu conducted devastating raids in Ottoman-ruled Serbia and Wallachia, repudiated Ottoman officialdom, and rallied Janissary opposition to Sultan Selim III's military and administrative reforms. Selim (1761–1808) recognized the warlord's authority in 1799 only because he needed Pasvanoglu's military aid in the war against France. Until his death in 1807, the independent pasha continued to resist Ottoman reform measures.

Pasvanoglu's rebelliousness demonstrated the breakdown of Ottoman rule in the Balkans, posed a dangerous precedent for the Porte, and accelerated breakaway movements by powerful local lords, both Muslim and Christian. By rejecting the sultan's authority and exacerbating unrest, Pasvanoglu's example inspired local uprisings and independence struggles in the Balkans during the nineteenth century.

Theophilus C. Prousis

Further reading

Jelavich, Barbara. *History of the Balkans: Eighteenth and Nineteenth Centuries.* New York, 1983.

Shaw, Stanford. *Between Old and New: The Ottoman Empire under Sultan Selim III, 1789–1807.* Cambridge, Massachusetts, 1971.

Stavrianos, Leften. *The Balkans since 1453.* New York, 1958.

Pătrăşcanu, Lucreţiu (1900–1954)

Leading Romanian Communist intellectual and minister of justice, 1944–48. Born in Bacău, Pătrăşcanu was the son of a writer and professor. He graduated from the Law Faculty at the University of Bucharest in 1922 and received a doctorate from the University of Leipzig. He published several important works analyzing Romania's political economy, and was the intellectual leader of the Romanian Communist movement in the 1930s, frequently defending Communists in court. Following the overthrow of Marshall Antonescu (1882–1946), Romania's wartime leader, in 1944, he became the first Romanian Communist to hold a high government office, as minister of justice. He organized a coalition government called the United Workers' Front, which included members of the National Peasants, Liberals, Social Democrats, and Communists. He competed with Gheorghe Gheorghiu-Dej (1901–65) for party leadership and lost. Pătrăşcanu was not elected to the party Central Committee in 1945, and by 1946, Gheorghiu-Dej attacked him as a revisionist. He was jailed in February 1948 on the charge of being a Titoist (deviationist) and remained in prison for six years. Tried in April 1954 on charges of being a national deviationist and for conspiring with American agents, he was found guilty and executed on April 17. Nicolae Ceauşescu (1918–89), Gheorghiu-Dej's successor, rehabilitated Pătrăşcanu on April 22, 1968, in the process accusing Gheorghiu-Dej of abuse of power in Pătrăşcanu's trial and execution.

Joseph F. Harrington

Further reading

Fischer, Mary Ellen. *Nicolae Ceauşescu: A Study in Political Leadership.* Boulder, Colorado, 1989.

Fischer-Galati, Stephen. *The New Rumania: From People's Democracy to Socialist Republic.* Cambridge, Massachusetts, 1967.

Wolff, Robert Lee. *The Balkans in Our Times.* New York, 1967.

See also Ion Antonescu; Nicolae Ceauşescu; Communist Party of Romania; Gheorghe Gheorghiu-Dej

Patriarchate

Name given to autocephalous, or self-governing, Eastern Orthodox Churches, the Patriarchate was an established order of precedence, confirmed by the Council of Chalcedon (A.D. 451)—which originally included Rome, Constantinople, Alexandria, and Antioch, the most important cities in the Roman Empire at that time, and Jerusalem—all claiming to have been founded by a disciple of Jesus. Located in areas subsequently subjected to Muslim rule, the churches have declined in membership and importance. Later, national patriarchates were established in the Balkans and Russia. Orthodox followers believe that the pope occupies a special place of honor, but they reject any claim of papal infallibility and authority over the whole Christian Church. The Patriarchate of Constantinople (Istanbul) is also known as the Ecumenical Patriarchate and serves as the symbolic head of the worldwide Eastern Orthodox Church, which contains more than one hundred million members.

The Ecumenical Patriarchate was established after the transfer of the capital of the Roman Empire by Emperor Constantine the Great (c. 288–337) in the fourth century to Byzantium (later called Constantinople), an ancient Greek colony on the Bosphorus. The emperors wanted to provide an organization for the growing Christian Church with the title of bishop of New Rome to parallel that of the state. From 325 to 1453, seven ecumenical councils, held under patriarchal direction, defined theology and established liturgical and ecclesiastical practices. During this period, the church fathers produced important theological writings, missionaries extended the Orthodox faith with great success to Russia, and monastic life flourished. However, it was also an age of caesaropapism, in which secular rulers dominated ecclesiastical matters, constantly interfering in church life, often including the replacement of patriarchs according to the whim of the emperor.

In 1204 Constantinople was sacked and desecrated by Crusaders en route to Palestine. While the Greeks later recovered their capital, the ancient city ultimately fell to the Ottoman Turks in 1453. Originally tolerant of the Patriarchate, which received generous concessions from the conqueror Mehmed II (the Conqueror, 1429–81), as time passed, increasing Turkish interference in the life of the church created an atmosphere of intrigue and servility. The Patriarchate tenaciously maintained Orthodox teaching and practice, and while a few of the patriarchs proved unworthy and even corrupt, others rejected temptation and were imprisoned, exiled, or executed for resisting court demands.

Long before Constantinople fell, both Bulgaria (927) and Serbia (1346) had established independent patriarchates. Revulsion that the Ecumenical Patriarchate should be subjected to Turkish domination led to the foundation of self-governing patriarchates in Russia (1589) and Romania (1925). Subjected to decades of Communist rule following the Russian Revolution and World War II, these patriarchates suffered persecution and martyrdom. Since 1989, they have experienced a reawakening and are attempting to reassert their traditional role in the lives of their respective countries. As the Ecumenical Patriarchate has lost its historic significance, with only a few thousand aging Greeks in Istanbul constituting a local congregation, it is only in the national and not the apostolic patriarchates that the Orthodox Church looks to the future.

George Ursul

Further reading

Runciman, Steven. *The Great Church in Captivity.* Cambridge, 1968.

Ware, Timothy. *The Orthodox Church.* New York, 1963.

See also Exarchate; Orthodoxy

Pauker, Ana (1893–1960)

Romanian Communist leader and foreign minister. Born in Bessarabia, Ana Rabinsohn became a revolutionary and joined the Romanian Social Democratic Party in 1915. She married Marcel Pauker (1896–1938) in 1921, and they had three children. In 1922 she joined with a majority of her party comrades to form the Communist Party of Romania and adhere to the revolutionary goals of the Soviet-led Comintern (Communist International). As a member of the Central Committee, she led numerous efforts to overthrow the government in Bucharest. Following several arrests and imprisonments, she went to Moscow, where she became a member of the Romanian Foreign Bureau of the Comintern. The Soviets wanted Pauker and her group to return to Romania following Germany's defeat in World War II, assume leadership of the Romanian Communist Party, and

P insure its loyalty to Moscow. She returned to Romania in August 1944 and initially played a greater role in the reconstruction of the Romanian Communist Party than was played by the so-called native Romanians led by Gheorghe Gheorghiu-Dej (1901–65). The party grew to over two hundred thousand members in one year, and in November 1947 Pauker became Romania's foreign minister. A year later, she became a member of the Central Committee of the communist Romanian Workers Party. During the next four years, her popularity waned. Her identification with Stalin (1879–1953) and her Jewish origin worked against her in Gheorghiu-Dej's efforts to establish a national Communist regime. Purged in May 1952, Pauker lived in obscurity until her death in 1960.

Joseph F. Harrington

Further reading

Ionescu, Ghita. *Communism in Romania, 1944–1962.* New York, 1964.

See also Comintern; Communist Party of Romania; Gheorghe Gheorghiu-Dej; Stalin

Paul Karadjordjević (1893–1976)

Yugoslav prince and regent (1934–41). Born in St. Petersburg, Russia, and educated at Oxford, England, Paul was the first cousin of King Alexander (1888–1934), whose eldest son, Peter (1923–70), was eleven when the king was assassinated in 1934. Made first regent by Alexander's will, Paul was an Anglophile and an art expert who had little interest in politics and had not been briefed by Alexander on his potential duties. As regent, he now faced two major problems: the need to seek domestic peace through an agreement with the Croats while attempting to preserve Yugoslavia's neutrality in World War II.

After four years in which his ministers failed to find a solution to the festering problem of strained relations with the Croats, Paul undertook to do so himself. He was aware of constitutional impediments to basic changes while the heir was still a minor, but through his new prime minister, he concluded in August 1939 an agreement (*sporazum*) with the Croats, giving them considerable autonomy in the Croatian region of the country. Other projected constitutional changes were postponed by the outbreak of World War II.

Although pressured by Hitler (1889–1945) to have Yugoslavia join the Tripartite Pact (Germany, Italy, and Japan), which Bulgaria, Hungary, and Romania had signed, Paul managed to delay a decision for nearly two years. In the end, on March 27, 1941, Yugoslavia signed a watered down version of the pact, which guaranteed Yugoslav neutrality. Two days later, however, generals in the Yugoslav armed forces, partially inspired by British agents, overthrew Paul and his government and declared Peter II to be of age. Although the new government declared that it would adhere to previous treaties, Hitler was not satisfied and on April 6, 1941, struck a military blow that soon ended the first Yugoslavia.

England's "friend" Paul left Yugoslavia and remained in British custody in South Africa during the war. After the war, he lived in Paris until his death.

Alex N. Dragnich

Further reading

Balfour, Neil and Sally Mackay. *Paul of Yugoslavia: Britain's Maligned Friend.* London, 1980.

Dragnich, Alex N. *The First Yugoslavia: Search for a Viable Political System.* Stanford, California, 1983.

Hoptner, J. B. *Yugoslavia in Crisis, 1934–1941.* New York, 1962.

See also Alexander I Karadjordjević; Axis; Adolf Hitler; Peter II Karadjordjević; *Sporazum*

Pavelić, Ante (1889–1959)

Founder of the Croatian Ustaša state and vehement opponent of the first Yugoslavia. A leader of the Croatian Party of Rights, Pavelić condemned Croatia's union with Serbia in 1918 as illegal. His ideal, as he wrote many times, was the creation of an independent Croatian state from the Drava River to the Adriatic Sea. Given Croat hopes for autonomy within Yugoslavia, Pavelić counted few supporters in the early 1920s.

The intransigence of the Serbian centrist regime and the 1929 royal dictatorship of King Alexander (1888–1934)—which forbade all national political parties—improved Pavelić's prospects. While other Croat and Slovene politicians protested or went to prison, Pavelić sought opportunity in Yugoslavia's unfriendly neighbors. With help from Italy's Mussolini (1883–1945), who coveted the Yugoslav Adriatic, he founded the Ustaša (Insurrection) movement in late 1929. Committed to Croatian independence through violence against Yugoslavia, members of the Ustaša were implicated in terrorist acts throughout the 1930s, including Alexander's murder in October 1934.

By April 1941, success seemed imminent. After the Axis occupation of Yugoslavia, Mussolini made Pavelić *poglavnik* (leader) of an "independent" Croatian state, albeit with large territorial concessions to Italy. However, violent clashes with Partisan and Chetnik (Serb guerrilla) forces, persecution of non-Croatian nationalities, and obvious Axis sponsorship all contributed to its demise.

After the Ustaša collapse in 1945, Pavelić escaped to Argentina, where he wrote several books and pamphlets. Forced to flee that country following an assassination attempt, the *poglavnik* died stateless in Madrid in 1959.

Brigit Farley

Further reading

Banac, Ivo. *The National Question in Yugoslavia.* New Haven, Connecticut, 1984.

Krizman, Bogdan. *Ante Pavelić i Ustaše.* Zagreb, 1978.

Maček, Vladko. *In the Struggle for Freedom.* University Park, Pennsylvania, 1957.

Pavelić, Ante. *Putem hrvatskog državnog prava: Članci, gorovi, izjave.* Buenos Aires, 1977.

See also Alexander I Karadjordjević; Antifascism; Chetniks; Ustaša

PAX

Catholic secular organization centered in Warsaw and sponsored by the government of the Polish People's Republic. PAX was born in 1945 and centered around the weekly *Dziś i Jutro* (*Today and Tomorrow*) and the newspaper *Tygodnik Powszechny* (*Universal Weekly*). Another publication, *Kierunki* (*Directions*) began in 1956. The most important founding members included Bolesław Piasecki (1914–79), Ryszard Reiff (1923–), Witold Bieńkowski (n.d.), Jerzy Hagmajer (n.d.), and Zygmunt Przetakiewicz (n.d.). The group took the name PAX in 1947 and was registered as an official organization in 1952.

In contrast to the Catholic Church hierarchy and other Catholic lay organizations, PAX took the position of working with the regime. This decision reflected the thinking of Piasecki, unquestionably the major figure behind the movement. Driven by intense ambition, Piasecki hoped that PAX would become the major intermediary between the Communist regime and a society that was overwhelmingly Catholic. Such a course led to frequent clashes with the episcopate, including an official injunction to Catholics to avoid having any dealings with PAX. This in turn caused factionalization within the organization. Subsequent developments showed that the regime was willing to use PAX as a tool against the church but in no way ever intended to extend real power to the organization.

PAX was allowed to have representatives in the Polish parliament. It also functioned as an economic entity, enjoying the sponsorship of the state in such enterprises as Veritas (religious objects and books) and Inco (an umbrella organization comprising various enterprises). In these organizations, Piasecki employed many individuals who had been dispossessed by the Communist system and who subsequently were fiercely loyal to their employer.

Peter Wozniak

Further reading

Blit, Lucjan. *The Eastern Pretender: Bolesław Piasecki, His Life and Times.* London, 1965.

Czubiński, Antoni. *Dzieje Najnowsze Polski 1949–1989.* Poznan, 1989.

Dudek, Antoni and Grzegorz Pytel. *Bolesław Piasecki, Próba biografii politycznej.* London, 1990.

Micewski, Andrzej. *Cardinal Wyszyński: A Biography.* San Diego, 1984.

Raina, Peter. *Political Opposition in Poland 1954–1977.* London, 1978.

See also Catholicism; Bolesław Piasecki

Peace of Riga (1921)

Series of treaties, signed March 18, 1921, formally ending the Polish-Soviet War of 1919–20. These agreements established borders among the Russian, Ukrainian, and Belorussian Socialist Republics and Poland. The signing of the agreements followed the armistice ending military hostilities between the belligerents on October 12, 1920. The treaty recognized Polish sovereignty over parts of the western Ukraine and Belorussia as well as Polish recognition of Ukraine and Belorus as independent and sovereign states. The timing of these agreements was significant; the forces of the Soviet Red Army, still absorbed in the Russian Civil War, could not afford to continue military operations on the former western border of the Russian Empire, while the Poles, exhausted after two years of war, domestic reconstruction, and tepid Allied support, were forced to turn their attention to conflicts brewing on their western border with Germany, specifically the conflict over Silesia. This peace also codified an earlier agreement between Soviets and Poles concerning the repatriation of populations between the signators. Other provisions of the agreement involved the return to Poland of works of art and other cultural treasures lost to tsarist Russia during the time of the Polish partitions and the award of thirty million gold rubles.

Peter Lavelle

Further reading

Misiunas, R., and D. Taageper. *The Baltic States: Year of Independence.* Notre Dame, Indiana, 1959.

Tarulis, A. N. *Soviet Foreign Policy toward the Baltic States 1918–1940.* Notre Dame, Indiana, 1965.

Wandycz, Piotr. *Soviet Russia and Poland: 1917–1921.* Cambridge, Massachusetts, 1969.

Watt, Richard M. *Bitter Glory: Poland and Its Fate 1918–1939.* New York, 1979.

See also Polish-Soviet War; Red Army

Peasant Revolts

Armed rebellions against real or perceived oppressors, often occurring as local phenomena with limited ideological justification or practical planning. Anthropologists place peasant uprisings in a spectrum of "everyday forms of peasant resistance," extending from murder, riot, and arson to vandalism, theft, poaching, tax evasion, gossip, and a simple failure to cooperate with authorities. Peasant revolts should be distinguished from national revolutions and planned coups, even those in which peasants take part. Peasant revolts often lead to reforms, but the goals of participants are not described readily in political terms. Some East European peasant revolts are associated with important events; most had no lasting impact.

Beginning in the 1500s, Eastern Europe experienced peasant revolts during the waning of feudalism. Similar uprisings persisted into the nineteenth and early twentieth centuries wherever economic and social change disrupted traditional rural life. Economic hardship was an underlying cause, but bad harvests, real or rumored changes in taxation, disenchantment with government promises, or imitation of nearby uprisings could trigger specific outbursts. Landlords and their proxies were common targets, and mobs often attacked Jewish merchants and estate agents because of their role in commercial life.

The Serbian Revolution of 1804 against the Turks was not a true peasant revolt, led as it was by village leaders (*knezes*), bandits (*haiduks*), and wealthy traders. However, the war that followed triggered peasant revolts in neighboring Bosnia, Macedonia, and Bulgaria between 1807 and 1809.

The "Cholera Uprising" of 1831 in Hungary followed an epidemic, thanks to rumors that landlords and Jews were poisoning the rural population. The ensuing violence created support for social reformer István Szechényi (1791–1860), and was a factor in the abolition of serfdom in 1848.

In Poland, a peasant revolt broke out in 1846 during an insurrection in Kraków and Galicia by nationalist Polish nobles. The conspirators expected support from co-nationals among the peasantry, but the latter saw the nobles only as landlords. Peasant attacks on estates helped defeat the revolutionaries.

Bulgaria experienced waves of peasant unrest in 1835–37, 1841–43, and 1847–53. The failure of Ottoman reform programs was a recurring cause. By the 1840s, Balkan revolutionaries of peasant origin were deliberately provoking or exploiting peasant uprisings. The Bosnian crisis of 1875–78 began as a peasant revolt in Hercegovina; revolutionaries and the European Great Powers then used the unrest to further their own political plans. During the crisis, uprisings took place in Bulgaria in 1875 and 1876, both of them the result of conspiracies. These episodes fall outside the narrowest definition of peasant revolts.

Romania experienced Eastern Europe's last important peasant revolt, after the expansion of commercial agriculture placed severe burdens on Romanian peasants. Outbursts against speculators and absentee landlords during 1888–89 failed to produce meaningful reforms. A larger revolt broke out in 1907. This "jacquerie" spread from Moldavia to Wallachia; starting with anti-Semitic rioting, it grew into assaults on big estates. The government needed artillery and 120,000 troops to end the revolt, and 10,000 people were killed. Significant reforms followed within the year.

After World War I, peasant resistance took other forms. Meaningful land reform addressed one recurring source of grievances. The growth of mass agrarian parties channeled dissatisfaction into politics and helped secure rural improvements. Finally, the decline in rural isolation removed a fundamental precondition for true peasant revolts, as traditional peasants completed their transition into modern society.

Steven W. Sowards

Further reading

Eidelberg, Philip Gabriel. *The Great Rumanian Peasant Revolt of 1907: Origins of a Modern Jacquerie.* Leiden, Netherlands, 1974.

Scott, James C. "Everyday Forms of Resistance," in *Everyday Forms of Peasant Resistance,* ed. by Forrest D. Colburn. Armonk, New York, 1989, 3–33.

Simons, Thomas W., Jr. "The Peasant Revolt of 1846 in Galicia: Recent Polish Historiography." *Slavic Review* 30 (1971): 795–817.

See also Agrarian Parties; Great Powers; *Haiduks;* Peasants; Pogrom; Romanian Peasant Revolt of 1907; István Szechényi

Peasants

Historically, most residents of Eastern Europe have been peasants. Peasants are rural dwellers engaged in agriculture, who follow traditional ways of life centered on the household and occupy a subordinate position within a larger society. Anthropologist Alfred Kroeber in 1923 defined peasants as "part societies with part cultures." In other words, peasant life takes place in association with and subordinate to landlords, priests, merchants, tax collectors, and other government officials. The modern history of Eastern European peasantry is a story of change in the relationship between peasants and the rest of society.

Peasant life is characterized by rural residence and an economy based on subsistence agriculture, supplemented by small-scale crop sales to provide cash for taxes, rents, and a few essential purchases. Both economic and social roles revolve around the family, and to a smaller extent the village. Belief systems and ways of living derive from tradition, and change is regarded with suspicion. Peasants are socially, economically, and politically subordinate to other classes; in particular, peasants depend on landlords or the state for access to farmland. Peasants live beside other rural groups, including landless laborers, tenant farmers, migrant herders, and artisans, with whom they share some but not all interests.

In the nineteenth century, peasants made up the vast majority of Eastern Europe's population, except in industrialized Bohemia. In the 1930s, 60 percent of employed persons still worked in agriculture, and for the Balkan states this figure was closer to 75 percent. Most Eastern Europeans continued to earn their living from agriculture through the 1940s. Despite state-sponsored industrial growth, urban dwellers were the minority in Albania, Yugoslavia, and Romania even into the early 1980s. Urban workers often retained ties to their native villages. Yugoslav "peasant urbanites" owned village land as a hedge against hard times or commuted to work from rural homes. Peasant farms remain important parts of Yugoslav and Polish society.

The family was the center of peasant life. In Poland and the Habsburg domains, a household consisted of a married couple and their children, who maintained ties to relatives in the village or parish. In the Balkans, the *zadruga* (communal household) united two or more related nuclear families in joint ownership and management of land, tools, livestock, and crops. The typical *zadruga* had ten to fifteen members. By pooling labor, the *zadruga* could accommodate lengthy absence by some members engaged in war, trade, or herding. The headman handled the external affairs of the family, while the headwoman managed domestic matters such as food production. During the late 1800s, changes in inheritance patterns and the attractions of commercial agriculture reduced the number of *zadruge,* as land was divided among nuclear families.

The village was another key element in peasant life. Villages were not only geographic locations but administrative units. In some places taxes were assessed on villages as a whole. Some land, especially pasture and woodland, was exploited in common by all villagers. Under communism, villages became the basis for collective cooperatives.

P Peasantry is not synonymous with serfdom, but emancipation from feudal obligations is a major element in the history of Eastern Europe's peasants. During the century preceding World War I, new legal and commercial institutions gradually replaced practices inherited from medieval serfdom. Before reform, peasants owed a variety of dues in cash, kind, and labor. While peasants could not be evicted from their land, neither could they leave voluntarily. Landlords had legal authority over local villagers. The growth of commercial agriculture led to "second serfdom," an expansion of labor and monetary dues. By the late 1700s, many peasants were delivering one-fourth to one-half of their harvest to landlords and performing two to three days' labor per week (*robota*) on the landlord's personal holdings. Peasants owed additional taxes to the state, and sometimes to the church.

The abolition of feudal obligations took place in piecemeal fashion. During the 1700s, many contributions in kind were converted into monetary payments, as absolutist regimes rationalized taxation and landlords converted to farming for profit. In the Habsburg monarchy, legal change began with the "Serfdom Patent" of 1781 and ended during the Revolutions of 1848, when the imperial regime adopted emancipation to outbid revolutionary challengers for peasant loyalties. In partitioned Poland, some aspects of serfdom were abolished in 1807 in the Prussian-ruled districts and the Duchy of Warsaw. Galicia shared in the Habsburg legislation of 1848. The 1861 emancipation of Russian serfs covered eastern Poland.

In the Balkans, serfdom existed in a modified form thanks to the Ottoman system of land tenure. Public officials and feudal cavalry lived on the income from land granted by the sultan, but these fiefs could not be inherited and fiefholders had no jurisdictional rights over their peasants. During the period of Ottoman decline, many fiefs were converted illegally into private holdings (*chiftliks*). Peasants lost historic protections and paid increased taxes. Abuses helped cause the national revolutions of the 1800s. Greek, Serbian, and Bulgarian peasants benefited from the expulsion of Ottoman landlords, the confiscation of large estates, and the redistribution of land. Virtual serfdom persisted in Turkish-ruled Bosnia, Albania, and Macedonia into the early twentieth century.

In Romania, a local aristocracy evolved from village leaders. This new *boiar* class claimed prime village lands and estates expropriated from Greek Orthodox monasteries. Personal bondage was abolished in the 1700s, but in the 1800s "neoserfdom" increased rents and labor obligations. The 1864 Agrarian Reform Law abolished dues in labor and kind but replaced them with cash payments. Meaningful reform took place only in the twentieth century.

The end of serfdom generally included a division of lands that favored landlords. Peasants gained title to roughly one-third of former estates but lost access to common pastures and woodlands. Landlords secured the best plots and received compensation paid for by the peasantry. Such settlements left peasants land-poor and in debt, while landlords gained the flexibility to pursue commercial enterprises.

After World War II, the Communist regimes tried to convert peasants into a rural proletariat through collectivization. Collective farms were never popular; in Poland and Yugoslavia, resistance forced a return to private farms in the 1950s. The revolutions of 1989 implied a restoration of private property and with it the continuation of peasant life.

Steven W. Sowards

Further reading

Halpern, Joel M. and Barbara Kerewsky-Halpern. *A Serbian Village in Historical Perspective.* Prospect Heights, Illinois, 1986.

Mintz, Sidney W. "A Note on the Definition of Peasantries." *Journal of Peasant Studies* 1 (1973): 91–106.

Simić, Andrei. *The Peasant Urbanites: A Study of Rural-Urban Mobility in Serbia.* New York, 1973.

Thomas, William I. and Florian Znaniecki. *The Polish Peasant in Europe and America,* 2 vols. New York, 1927.

Verdery, Katherine. *Transylvanian Villagers: Three Centuries of Political, Economic, and Ethnic Change.* Berkeley, California, 1983.

See also Agriculture; Agrarian Parties; *Boiars; Chiftlik;* Collectivization; Duchy of Warsaw; Folklife; Folklore; Peasant Revolts; Revolutions of 1848; Revolutions of 1989; *Timar; Zadruga*

Pécs

Hungarian city. Pécs is a relatively large city (1990 population 170,039) and capital of Baranya County, located 122 miles (198 km) south of

Budapest below the Mecsek Hills. Pécs was originally a Roman settlement called Sophianae and King Stephen (c. 975–1038) founded a bishopric there in 1009. The town grew during the Middle Ages, when it was known as Quinque Ecclesiae (Five Steeples), as an important trade route to Constantinople. Pécs also developed as an important center of architecture and later as a center of learning after the first university in Hungary was founded there in 1367. The city was fortified after the Mongol invasion of 1241, but the walls were no match for the Turks in 1543. Pécs became an important center of Ottoman administration during their 150 years of occupation; they built several mosques in the city, one of which, located on the central square and later converted to a church, is the largest such structure still standing in Hungary. After the expulsion of the Turks in 1686, Pécs was virtually depopulated. However, the city quickly recovered, spurred by coal mining in the surrounding hills, development of an important porcelain industry, and repair of the eleventh-century cathedral. For a time composer Franz Liszt (1811–86) worked in Pécs.

Today, Pécs is a major university, religious, and museum town of Hungary. Its many art and sculpture galleries, and fine examples of Art Nouveau buildings, make the city one of the most attractive in Hungary.

Darrick Danta

Further reading

Fügedi, Erik. *Castle and Society in Medieval Hungary (1000–1437)*. Budapest, 1986.

Gutkind, E. A. *International History of City Development*, vol. 7: *Urban Development in East-Central Europe: Poland, Czechoslovakia, and Hungary*. New York, 1972.

Hanák, Péter, ed. *One Thousand Years: A Concise History of Hungary*. Budapest, 1988.

Webster's New Geographical Dictionary. Springfield, Massachusetts, 1984.

See also Franz Liszt

Pekař, Josef (1870–1937)

Twentieth-century Czech historian. Pekař was a pioneer in Czech history, often challenging many of the conventions of his colleagues. While at the time controversial, his views, such as those in his *Smysl českých dějin* (*The Meaning of Czech History,* 1929), focused attention on the very nature of the Czech people and nation. He concentrated much of his attention on the Middle Ages and early modern period. Rather than merely following the trappings of nationalism, in his examinations of the Hussite and Thirty Years Wars, he painted pictures of events not as others might wish to see them but rather as they took place. His refusal to be shackled by generally accepted nationalistic scholarship allowed him to argue in *Bílá Hora: Její příčiny a následky* (*White Mountain: Its Causes and Consequences,* 1921), for example, that the Battle of White Mountain (1620), one of the seminal events in the nation's history and one in which Habsburg armies effectively destroyed all hope for an independent Czech land for nearly three centuries, was more complex than the traditionally viewed "age of darkness." He also was a leading figure in modern Czech social and economic history. His histories and commentaries, albeit controversial, forced a maturation in modern Czech historiography. Among his most important works were *Nejstarší kronica česka* (*The Oldest Czech Chronicle,* 1903); *Svatý Václav* (*Saint Wenceslas,* 2d ed., 1932); and *Žižka a jeho doba* (*Žižka and His Times,* 4 vols., 1927–33).

Josef Anderle

Further reading

Hanzal, Josef. *Josef Pekař*. Prague, 1992.

Kalista, Zdeněk, *Josef Pekař*. Prague, parts 1–2, 1941; part 3, 1994.

Percentages Agreement

Agreement signed on October 9, 1944, between British Prime Minister Winston Churchill (1874–1965) and Soviet leader Josef Stalin (1879–1953) dividing interests in southeastern Europe. At the 1943 Teheran conference, called to discuss wartime policy among the Allies, Stalin made it clear that his principal war aim was to insure that Germany would never again be able to threaten the Soviet Union. He did not inform his allies, however, that to achieve this goal he intended to create a buffer zone on the country's western border. In December 1943 President Edvard Beneš (1884–1948) of Czechoslovakia signed a pact of friendship between the Soviet Union and his country, much to the consternation of the United States and Great Britain. In May 1944 elements of the Red Army moved into Romania and Bulgaria, setting up "friendly" governments, all without American or British consent.

With these developments, Churchill began having doubts about the future of Europe. With Germany in ruins, Moscow would clearly dominate Eastern Europe; but the Soviet Union was bearing the lion's share of the Allied military effort against the Germans, and Churchill was in no position to question or challenge Stalin's motives.

Following Allied successes in the West, Churchill finally felt in a position to face Stalin. Acting alone and fully aware of the consequences of his actions, Churchill went to Moscow in October 1944. On a half-sheet of paper, Churchill wrote the following percentages, suggesting the amount of influence the Soviet Union and Great Britain should exert in each country following the war: Romania (90 percent Soviet, 10 percent British); Bulgaria (75 percent Soviet, 25 percent British); Hungary (initially 50 percent for each, this was later changed to 60 percent Soviet and 40 percent British); Yugoslavia (50 percent Soviet and 50 percent British); and Greece (10 percent Soviet and 90 percent British). Interestingly, Stalin approved and appeared to have gone to great lengths to honor the Percentages Agreement. For example, he refused to help the Communist insurgency in Greece; moreover, he advised Tito (1892–1980) to move slowly in Yugoslavia. Given the realities of the coming Cold War, however, the percentages agreed on proved to be meaningless.

Joel D. Benson

Further reading

Bullock, Alan. *Hitler and Stalin.* New York, 1992.
Churchill, Winston. *Triumph and Tragedy.* Boston, 1953.

See also Edvard Beneš; Winston Churchill; Cold War; Greek Civl War; Red Army; Stalin; Tito

Petar I (Peter) Petrović Njegoš (1747–1830)

Prince-bishop (*vladika*) of Montenegro. Petar succeeded his uncle, Sava (c. 1700–1781), as the ruler of Montenegro in 1782 and was formally consecrated as bishop in 1784. At the end of the eighteenth century, Montenegrin warriors fought the Turks on several occasions, in 1796 defeating Kara Mahmud (1742–96), the *pašha* of Scutari, at the Battle of Krusi. As a result, the Brda region to the northeast of "old" Montenegro joined the country, effectively doubling Montenegro's size. During this period Montenegro received its first written law codes (the *Stega* of 1796 and the *Zakonik opći crnogorski i brdski* in 1798) and a rudimentary central court (*Kuluk*) in 1798. In 1799 Petar secured fleeting recognition of Montenegrin independence by the Ottoman sultan, Selim III (1761–1808). During the Napoleonic Wars, Montenegrins joined the Russians in attacking French-held Dubrovnik (Ragusa) in 1806; the following year the Treaty of Tilsit obliged Russia to yield control of the neighboring Bay of Kotor to France. In 1813 Petar's troops assisted the British in forcing a French withdrawal from the area, whereupon he made Kotor his capital. The Congress of Vienna (1814–15) gave the town and the strategic Bay of Kotor to Austria, and Montenegro remained landlocked for six more decades. Petar fought two more wars against the Turks in 1819–21 and 1828–29 before dying at the age of eighty-one. He wrote *Kratka istorija Crne Gore* (*Short History of Montenegro,* published posthumously in 1835) and numerous other didactic works. He was canonized during the reign of his nephew and successor, Petar II (1813–51).

John D. Treadway

Further reading

Lekić, Dušan. *Spoljna politika Petra I Petrovića Njegoša, 1784–1830.* Cetinje, Montenegro, 1950.
Pejović, Djoko. *Crna Gora u doba Petra I i Petra II—Osnivanje države i uslovi njenog razvitka.* Belgrade, 1981.
Petar I. Popović. *Crna Gora u doba Petra I.* Belgrade, 1951.

See also Congress of Vienna; Montenegro; Petar II Petrović Njegoš

Petar (Peter) II Petrović Njegoš (1813–51)

Last prince-bishop (*vladika*) of Montenegro, and celebrated poet. Also known by his given name, Rade, or, worldwide, simply as Njegoš, Petar succeeded his uncle, Petar I (1747–1830), in 1830. In 1833 he made the first of two trips to Russia, where he was formally ordained as Orthodox bishop of Montenegro. En route, he met twice with Serb pedagogue Vuk Stefanović Karadžić (1787–1864), who encouraged the young *vladika's* remarkable literary talents.

During his reign, Petar sought to modernize his rugged mountain land. He built roads and schools where few had existed previously, organized the first Montenegrin police to enforce public order and collect taxes, and imported the country's first printing press in modern times. In an attempt to end tribal feuding, he created a senate (*Praviteljstvujšči senat crnogorski i brdski*) composed of twelve representatives from various Montenegrin clans.

Enjoying Russian diplomatic and financial support, he fought the Ottomans on several occasions but secured no permanent territorial gain at Turkey's expense. During the Revolutions of 1848–49, the Croatian *ban* (governor), Josip Jelačić (1801–59) declined his offer of support in Croatia's struggle with Hungary. At the same time, his hopes of inducing Serbia to join forces with Montenegro in liberating neighboring Bosnia-Hercegovina from Turkish rule came to naught.

An author and poet of unusual power, his three most famous works are *Luča mikrokozma* (*Ray of Microcosm*, 1845), *Gorski vjenac* (*The Mountain Wreath*, 1847), and *Lažni car Šćepan Mali* (*The False Tsar Stephen the Small*, 1847). *Gorski vjenac*, his magnum opus, is widely regarded as the crowning glory of Serbian literature.

Petar II died of tuberculosis at the age of thirty-eight and was succeeded by his nephew, Danilo (1826–60), who secularized the Montenegrin state. Petar's mausoleum atop Mount Lovćen is a Montenegrin national shrine.

John D. Treadway

Further reading

Djilas, Milovan. *Njegoš: Poet, Prince, Bishop.* New York, 1966.

Milović, Jevto M. *Petar II Petrović Njegoš u svom vremenu.* Titograd, Yugoslavia, 1984.

Njegoš, P.P. *The Mountain Wreath,* trans. and ed. by Vasa D. Mihailovich. Irvine, California, 1986.

See also Danilo I Petrović Njegoš; Josip Jelačić; Vuk Karadžić; Petar I Petrović Njegoš; Revolutions of 1848; Serbian Literature to 1918

Peter II Karadjordjević (1923–70)

King of Yugoslavia. Peter was born to great expectations in 1923. His ties to the British royal family augured well for the future ruler of a multinational country. Despite auspicious beginnings, opposition to the centrist organization of the state soon robbed Peter of his youth. In October 1934 assassins—Croatian and Macedonian terrorists—murdered his father, King Alexander (1888–1934), in France. Because the new king was only eleven, his uncle, Prince Paul, became his regent. Peter could only watch as Yugoslavia drifted away from its Little Entente allies (Romania and Czechoslovakia) into the Axis orbit.

In March 1941 he was proclaimed king after a coup d'état in Belgrade. The subsequent Axis invasion, however, forced Peter to flee to London, where he established a government-in-exile with Chetnik leader Draža Mihailović as commander in chief of the Yugoslav army. Recognizing that his future depended on a victory by the Chetniks, the loosely organized Serbian guerrilla forces, the king spent much time lobbying Britain and the United States on behalf of his government and Mihailović. In the end, however, Tito's Partisan military successes won the Allies' allegiance.

The Partisan victory cost Peter his inheritance. With Tito (1892–1980) in firm control, a constituent assembly refused to permit the king's return in November 1945. Afterward, Peter lived the life of so many stateless monarchs, making appearances in Serbian émigré communities and dabbling in public relations. He died in 1970, never having returned to Yugoslavia.

Brigit Farley

Further reading

Karadjordjević, Peter II of Yugoslavia. *A King's Heritage.* New York, 1954.

———. "Unconquerable: A Review of the Historic Visit to the United States and Canada Which Was Made during June and July, 1942, by His Majesty King Peter II, King of Yugoslavia." New York Public Library Pamphlet.

Krizman, Bogdan. *Jugoslavenske vlade u izbjeglištvu 1941–1943.* Zagreb, 1981.

Tomasevich, Joso. *The Chetniks: War and Revolution in Yugoslavia, 1941–1945.* Stanford, California, 1975.

See also Alexander I Karadjordjević; Paul Karadjordjević; Antifascism; Axis; Chetniks; Dragoljub Mihailović; IMRO; Little Entente; Tito

Peter Karadjordjević (1844–1921)

King of Serbia (1903–21). Grandson of the leader of the first revolt against the Turks in 1804, Peter was a model constitutional monarch who stayed above political battles, which were resolved by popularly elected leaders. He was brought to the throne by the Skupština (parliament) after the assassination of Alexander Obrenović (1876–1903), who had no heirs. He ended his effective reign in 1914, when he transferred royal powers to his second son, Alexander (1888–1934).

Most of Peter's early life was spent outside Serbia and much of his mature life in Switzerland. Peter was educated abroad, where he translated into Serbian the essay of British economist John Stuart Mill (1806–73), *On Liberty* (1859), writing the preface in the spirit of democracy. During the Franco-Prussian War of 1870, he fought in the French army and was wounded. In 1876 he fought under an assumed name in the Serbian uprising against the Turks in Bosnia-Hercegovina.

With the Radical Party—with Nikola Pašić (1845–1926) as prime minister—in power during nearly all of his reign, Peter questioned some of the proposals but, in the end, approved them all. This involved such critical questions as the fate of the conspirators who ended the Obrenović dynasty; emancipating Serbia from dependence on Austria-Hungary, a situation that had led to the tariff (pig) war (1906–11); priority of civil authority in areas liberated in the Balkan Wars (1912–13); and abdication of his eldest son, Prince George (1887–1972).

The latter was a touchy personal issue. Peter sought to educate George on the proper role of a constitutional monarch, telling him specifically that political power rested in the hands of the people's elected leaders. In the end, George's haughty behavior toward the essence of a parliamentary system, his unconstitutional attempt to communicate directly with the Skupština, and embarrassing personal acts led Peter to accept the cabinet's recommendation that George be asked to abdicate in favor of his second son, Alexander.

Peter's role as king earned the love and respect of the people, who were also impressed by his modest and frugal way of life.

Alex N. Dragnich

Further reading

Dragnich, Alex N. *Serbia, Nikola Pašić, and Yugoslavia.* New Brunswick, New Jersey, 1974.
Petrovich, Michael B. *A History of Modern Serbia*, 2 vols. New York, 1976.
Živojinović, Dragoljub. *Petar Karadjordjević: Život i delo: U izgnanstvu 1844–1903.* Belgrade, 1988.

See also Alexander I Karadjordjević; Alexander Obrenović; Balkan Wars; Black George; Nikola Pašić; Pig War; Serbo-Turkish War of 1876; Skupština

Pětka

"The Five," an extraparliamentary committee that guided Czechoslovak politics in the 1920s. The impending Communist–Social Democratic split in the autumn of 1920 threatened the Socialist and Republican (Agrarian) or Red-Green Coalition (1919–20). To weather the crisis, the leaders from five major parties—Social Democrats, National Socialists, Republicans, Czech Populists, and National Democrats—decided that Jan Černý (1874–1959) would become premier and interior minister in a nonpolitical cabinet. Agreeing on the suggestion of Republican Antonín Švehla (1873–1933), the leaders of the five parties met as the *Pětka* to set policy for Černý's government and insure the passage of legislation. The original members of the *Pětka* consisted of Švehla, Social Democrat Rudolf Bechyně (1881–1948), National Socialist Jiří Stříbrný (1880–1955), Czech Populist Jan Šrámek (1870–1956), and National Democrat Alois Rašín (1867–1923).

The *Pětka* survived in various forms over the years to limit interparty bickering. When Edvard Beneš (1884–1948) replaced Černý as prime minister in 1921, he resented the interference of *Pětka*, which strained his already tense relations with the *Pětka* leaders. During Švehla's first government (1922–1925), the *Pětka* temporarily had less importance, since all its members were in the cabinet. It became "The Six" (*Šestka*) when the Party of Business and Commerce entered Švehla's second cabinet (1925–26), and it disintegrated with the government. For some time, Švehla's third government (1926–29) had the support of eight parties—National Democrats, Czech Populists, Slovak Populists, German Christian Socialists, Business and Commerce, German Agrarians, Hungarian Nationalists, and Republicans—so they formed a Committee of Eight (*Osmička*). The name remained even after the Hungarian Nationalists withdrew from the coalition in 1927. With the Wide Coalition of 1929 and the second government of František Udržal (1868–1938), extra-parliamentary committees ceased.

The party leaders intended the *Pětka* to avert political disarray, but they became accustomed to rule by oligarchy. As a result, the left and the *Hrad*, the informal political group around the president, eventually criticized the *Pětka* as undemocratic. Despite the controversy, the *Pětka* exemplified the interparty cooperation that accompanied coalition building and policy setting in Czechoslovakia between the wars.

Daniel E. Miller

Further reading

Broklová, Eva. *Československá demokracie: Politický systém ČSR, 1918–1938.* Prague, 1992.

Mencl, Vojtěch and Jarmila Menclová. "Náčrt podstaty a vývoje vrcholné sféry předmnichovské československé mocensko-politické struktury." *Československý časopis historický* 16 (1968): 341–64.

Peroutka, Ferdinand. *Budování státu: Československá politika v letech popřevratových,* 6 vols. Prague, 1934–36. See esp. "Pětka," vol. 4, 2,158–73.

See also Edvard Beneš; Jan Černý; *Hrad;* Alois Rašín; Jan Šrámek; Jiří Stříbrný; Antonín Švehla; František Udržal

Petkov, Dimitur Nikolov (1858–1907)

Bulgarian politician and journalist. Petkov was born in the village of Bashkioi, where he enrolled in the local school. In 1874 he emigrated to Romania. During the Russo-Turkish War of 1877–78, he returned to Bulgaria and fought as a volunteer in the Russian army. Seriously wounded at the battle for the mountain peak St. Nikola (now called Shipka), he lost his hand. Later he became one of the leaders of the People's Liberal Party (the so-called Stambolovists, named for its leader Stefan Stambolov [1854–95]). During Stambolov's regime, Petkov served in a number of capacities, including mayor of Sofia (1887–93), minister of public affairs (1893–94), and chairman of the Regular National Assemblies. He was also editor and publisher of the newspapers *Svirka* (*Whistle*), *Narodno Subranie* (*National Assembly*), *Nezavisimost* (*Independence*), as well as one of the editors of *Novi era* (*New Era*), *Nezavisima Bulgariia* (*Independent Bulgaria*), and *Svoboda* (*Freedom*).

Petkov later served as minister of internal affairs (1903–6) and prime minister (October 1906–February 1907). In his economic policy he supported the growth of the national capital, while his foreign policy was directed toward close association with Austria-Hungary and Germany. In 1907 Petkov was killed by a political enemy. His two sons, who were ardent democrats and progressive thinkers, were also later killed—Petko D. Petkov (1891–1924) by Aleksandur Tsankov's (1879–1959) regime in 1924, and Nikola D. Petkov (1893–1947) by the Communists in 1947.

Yana Hashamova

Further reading

Bozhilov, Ivan, Vera Mutafchieva, and Konstantin Kosev. *Istoria na Bulgariia.* Sofia, 1993.

"Petkov, Dimitur Nikolov," in *Entsiklopediia. Bulgariia.* Sofia, 1978.

Sazdov, Dimitur, Milcho Lalkov, and Trendafil Mitev. *Istoriia na tretata bulgarska durzhava (1878–1944).* Sofia, 1933.

See also Petko Dimitrov Petkov; Russo-Turkish War of 1877–78; Stefan Stambolov; Aleksandur Tsankov

Petkov, Nikola (1893–1947)

Leader of the Bulgarian Peasant Party. Petkov was born into a prominent Bulgarian family long accustomed to tragedy; both his father and brother had been assassinated for political activities. Petkov emerged as a leader of the Agrarians in the 1930s, becoming a member of parliament on the eve of World War II. One of the first Agrarian leaders to cooperate with the Communist-sponsored illegal Fatherland Front (the coalition of left and center parties) after 1942, Petkov joined the resulting Fatherland Front government as minister without portfolio after the successful September 9, 1944, revolution. Along with Agrarian leader G.M. Dimitrov (1903–72), Petkov was instrumental in convening a unity Congress of the Bulgarian Agrarian National Union (BANU) in October 1944, and he succeeded Dimitrov as general secretary in early 1945. Disturbed by Communist efforts to subvert postwar elections, Petkov defied Fatherland Front policy by calling for postponement of those elections. In May 1945 a rapidly convened conference of the BANU elected a new ruling committee, and Petkov was forced to form his own faction of the Agrarian movement. In August 1945 he resigned from the government and the following year led an opposition bloc in parliamentary elections that garnered over 20 percent of the votes despite fraud and violence. Upon approval of the Bulgarian Peace Treaty in 1947, official pressure on Petkov and his followers increased. Exactly one day after the U.S. Senate ratified the peace agreement, Petkov was arrested and his followers subsequently expelled from parliament. He was convicted of treason and hanged in the fall of 1947.

Michael Boll

Further reading

Bell, John D. *The Bulgarian Communist Party from Blagoev to Zhivkov.* Stanford, California, 1977.

Boll, Michael M. *Cold War in the Balkans: American Foreign Policy and the Emergence of Communist Bulgaria, 1943–1947.* Lexington, Kentucky, 1984.

Oren, Nissan. *Bulgarian Communism: The Road to Power.* New York, 1971.

See also Agrarian Parties; Bulgarian Agrarian National Union; Fatherland Front

Petkov, Petko Dimitrov (1891–1924)

Bulgarian politician, diplomat, and active member of the Bulgarian Agrarian National Union (BANU—BZNS). Petkov was the son of Dimitur Petkov (1858–1907), a leading Bulgarian journalist and politician, and the brother of Nikola Petkov (1893–1947), also an ardent democrat. Petkov graduated with degrees in law, political science, and diplomacy from the Sorbonne in 1912. He fought as a volunteer in the two Balkan Wars (1912–13) and served as an officer in World War I. After the war, which was a national catastrophe for Bulgaria, crippling worker strikes brought the BANU to power as Aleksandur Stamboliiski (1879–1923) formed an independent Agrarian government. From 1920 to 1922 Petkov was a diplomat in Paris. At the end of 1922 he returned to Bulgaria and became director of the political department at the Ministry for Foreign Affairs. He geared all his efforts as a diplomat and a leading politician toward improving Bulgaria's image abroad and to correct the unfavorable Treaty of Neuilly, the punishing document that followed Bulgaria's defeat in World War I. On June 9, 1923,

after a military coup, Petkov was arrested, only to be released two months later. As a member of the National Assembly (1923–27), he continued to work for the reestablishment of the Agrarian Union. At the same time, Petkov served as editor of the newspaper *Agrarian Defense.* He also wrote in French and in 1921 published two political texts, *Voinik na mira* (*A Soldier of Peace*) and *Politikata na Bulgariia vchera i dnes* (*The Politics of Bulgaria Yesterday and Today*). He was killed on a Sofia street by political enemies in 1924.

Yana Hashamova

Further reading

Bozhilov, Ivan, Vera Mutafchieva, and Konstantin Kosev. *Istoria na Bulgariia.* Sofia, 1993.

Kosev, Konstantin. *Istoria na Bulgariia.* Sofia, 1993.

"Petkov, Petko Dimitrov," in *Entsiklopediia. Bulgariia.* Sofia, 1978.

Sazdov, Dimitur, Milcho Lalkov, and Trendafil Mitev. *Istoriia na tretata bulgarska durzhava (1878–1944).* Sofia, 1933.

See also Balkan Wars; Bulgarian Agrarian National Union; Neuilly, Treaty of; Dimitur Petkov; Aleksandur Stamboliiski

Petőfi, Sándor (1823–1849)

Hungary's greatest lyric poet in the nineteenth century. Of Slavic background (family name: Petrovics), the young Petőfi never completed his formal education. Although he was attracted to the theater, he failed as an itinerant actor and for want of a better job enlisted in the army, but was forced out because of ill health.

Petőfi's literary career began when a leading journal, *Athenaeum,* printed one of his poems in May 1842. Six months later, a second poem appeared over the signature Sándor Petőfi. The new name marked a new era in his life. With the help of the prince of Hungarian literary romanticism, Mihály Vörösmarty (1800–1855), a volume of Petőfi's verses appeared in November 1844. At the same time, he became editor of a popular cultural periodical in Pest (*Pesti Divatlapok* [*Pest Fashion*]), as well as a chief organizer of a circle of radical intellectuals who gathered regularly in the Café Pilvax.

Together with his close friend János Arany (1817–82), whose poetic career paralleled his, Petőfi championed the elevation of the idiom of the "common people," that is, the peasantry, to the rank of the literary language. No Hungarian writer accomplished this with greater spontaneity, grace, or success. Indeed, with the *œuvres* of Petőfi and Arany there began in Hungarian literature a period known as popular and national classicism.

Petőfi's lyrics immortalized the natural beauty of Hungary's Great Plain, its vegetation and fauna, its rivers, inns, draw wells and, above all, its colorful, self-confident people. Inspired by the rhythm and imagery of the folk song, Petőfi achieved remarkable depths in his love poems, which culminated in verses dedicated to his wife, Julia Szendrey (1828–68). Political passion, love of liberty, and ardent Magyar patriotism were other elements of Petőfi's lyre. An admirer of French revolutionary ideas, he looked forward to an age "when all can equally take from the horn of plenty, and when all shall be equally seated at the table of rights, and the sunlight of morality shineth through the windows of every home." Not surprisingly, Petőfi became one of the leaders of the revolutionary youth as the events of 1848 began to unfold. His poem *Nemzeti Dal* (*National Song*), which became the anthem of the Revolution of 1848–49, was the first piece printed without the censor's approval on a free press.

During the Hungarian revolution, Petőfi was a member of the Radical Left, critical of the government and even of Lajos Kossuth (1802–94), the leader of the revolution. He also participated in the final phase of the armed struggle in Transylvania against the invading Russians as adjutant of Polish General József Bem (1794–1850). Last seen on July 31, 1849, before the battle near Segesvár (Romanian, Sighişoara), he was probably killed by Cossacks. For decades, the Hungarian public refused to accept the poet's death as final. Indeed, Petőfi became an enduring symbol of Hungary's fight for freedom and independence.

George Barany

Further reading

Basa, Enikő Molnár. *Sándor Petőfi.* Boston, 1980.
Czigány, Lóránt. *The Oxford History of Hungarian Literature.* Oxford, 1984, 179–97.
Jones, D. Mervyn. *Five Hungarian Writers.* Oxford, 1966, 229–89.
Petőfi, Sándor. *Petőfi Sándor Összes Művei,* vols. 1–7. Budapest, 1951–64.

See also József Bem; Great Hungarian Plain; Hungarian Literature; Hungarian War for Independence; Lajos Kossuth; Revolutions of 1848; Mihály Vörösmarty

Phanariots (Fanariots)

Wealthy Greek merchants who derived their name from the Phanar (lighthouse) section of Constantinople. These families (Sutu, Callimachi, Mavrocordato, Ypsilantis, etc.) governed Moldavia and Wallachia from 1711 to 1821, held the title of prince (*hospodar,* or governor), and as foreigners acquired an unsavory reputation. They began settling in the Romanian Principalities during the late sixteenth century and intermarried with Romanian *boiars*. They were initially appointed because of Turkish dismay at the lack of loyalty of native princes, who often became tools of Russian or Austrian imperialism, thus contributing to foreign occupations and loss of territory. The most glaring instance was the loss of Bessarabia to Russia in 1812. Since sultans or viziers sold these positions (*hospodariates*) to the highest bidder, considerable sums were expended by families who considered the title "prince" the greatest reward within the Greek bureaucracy, while the distance of Bucharest and Iaşi from Constantinople ensured relative security from arrest and confiscation of property, should they lose favor. A Phanariot prince would average seven years of rule, and upon removal he could flee elsewhere to enjoy his gains. Since making money was an incentive, once established on their thrones the Phanariots sold every office at their disposal to recoup the expense (usually bribes) of obtaining the office, thus systematizing corruption. Recent research, however, has revealed that some (especially the early) Phanariots were enlightened men who helped introduce Western culture, codified laws, and founded the academies of higher learning in both capitals, with Greek as the language of instruction.

Radu Florescu

Further reading

Constantiniu, Florin. "Quelques aspects de la politique agraire des phanariotes." *Revue roumaine d'histoire* 4, no. 4 (1965): 667–80.
Jewsbury, George F. *The Russian Annexation of Bessarabia 1774–1828.* Boulder, Colorado, 1976.
Sturdza, Mihail. *Grandes familles de Grèce, d'Albanie et de Constantinople.* Paris, 1983.

See also Bessarabian Question; *Boiars*

P

Philhellinism

Broad term used to mean love and admiration of things Greek. During the latter part of the eighteenth century and the first three decades of the nineteenth, philhellenism acquired a specific focus among European admirers of antiquity who visited the Greek lands: the liberation of the Greeks from Ottoman rule and their cultural renascence through the imitation of their classical progenitors. Furthermore, the emancipation of an oppressed people was in consonance with the liberal humanistic ideas of social justice and progress of the Enlightenment. During its first phase (1770–1821), philhellenism was primarily a literary theme in the writings of romantic Hellenists and travelers to the Ottoman dominions. It was during the Greek War of Independence (1821–30) that philhellenism became a militant movement actively engaged in the success of the Greek insurrection and arguably one of the first instances of the *"littérature engagée"* (literature of engagement). The death of English poet Lord Byron (1788–1824) in Missolonghi on April 19, 1824, was the quintessential expression of this translation of romantic energy into action. European philhellenes wielded their influence trying to change the stance of their governments whose initial reaction to the Greek revolt had been one of suspicion and even hostility. There was a humanitarian, philanthropic philhellenism promoted through the numerous Greek committees in European and American cities; a religious philhellenism espousing the cause of Christians against Muslims; a liberal philhellenism proclaiming human rights; and, above all, a romantic artistic and literary philhellenism, which inspired such literary figures as Byron, Percy Shelley (1792–1822), and Victor Hugo (1802–85), and French painter Eugène Delacroix (1798–1863). The philhellenes saw their efforts rewarded when on October 20, 1827, the combined fleets of France, Russia, and England destroyed the Egyptian-Ottoman fleet at the Bay of Navarino, a victory that ensured Greek independence.

Olga Augustinos

Further reading

Augustinos, Olga. *French Odysseys: Greece in French Travel Literature from the Renaissance to the Romantic Era.* Baltimore, 1994.

Dakin, Douglas. *British and American Philhellenes.* Thessaloníki, 1955.

Larrabee, Stephen A. *Hellas Observed: The American Experience of Greece.* New York, 1957.

St. Clair, William. *That Greece Might Still Be Free.* Oxford, 1972.

Woodhouse, C. M. *The Philhellenes.* Cranbury, New Jersey, 1971.

See also Greek Revolution; Romanticism

Philosophy

Engagement in the philosophical discourse by East European intellectuals was dramatically influenced by geographic, political, and social/cultural differences. Those regions not under Turkish domination maintained an uneven continuity with the philosophical movements in Western Europe; whereas their neighbors awaited their respective liberations to engage or reengage in the philosophical dialogue. Inevitably, German philosophers Immanuel Kant (1724–1804) and Georg W.F. Hegel (1770–1831) profoundly influenced the thinkers of Eastern Europe. German idealism, especially Hegel's concept of the dialectic and "spirit of a people," provided a format for appropriation and regionalization by various East European intellectuals. Romanticism and the scientific movements, especially British empiricism, also contributed to the philosophical landscape. Amid these influences and developments, pockets of Catholic scholasticism criticized the various forms of modernism. Subsequently and upon these foundations, interest emerged in Edmund Husserl's (1859–1938) phenomenology, Auguste Comte's (1798–1857) and the Vienna Circle's positivism, and logic. Each of these movements attempted to secure knowledge and truth by its respective methodological focus on irreducible phenomenon, scientific facts, and logical truths and analysis. Finally, all of these and other varied and nuanced systems and movements became rivaled and often eclipsed by the various forms of Marxism.

Albania

Albania was unable to establish a significant participation in the Western philosophical discourse, owing to domination by the Turks from the fourteenth century until 1912. In addition, the brief period of independence until 1939 did not provide sufficient stability needed for the cultivation of a philosophical tradition. The triumph of the Communists further neutralized any genuine philosophical development.

Enver Hoxha's (1908–85) Communist regime, driven by its social and political goals, provided a constrained stability that enabled a weak semblance of "philosophical" thought. It attempted to create a "philosophical" anthropology of the *new man*—a polemical extension of socialist doctrine that had little appeal to the philosophical traditions. Cultural advances in literature became the only safe arena for the expansion of intellectual ideas.

Albania's cultural revolution of 1966 led to the removal of the classics of the Western tradition and the further isolation of the country from philosophical discourse. This isolation and rigid control of thought by the central government left Albania the least philosophically developed region in Eastern Europe.

Bulgaria

With the end of Turkish domination in 1878, Bulgaria awakened to its ancient religious/philosophical traditions, which had been suppressed from the fourteenth century. The University of Sofia quickly became the center for philosophical interests, and the study of the history of philosophy, encouraged by Ivan Georgeoff (1862–1936) during the last decades of the nineteenth century, nurtured the nascent Bulgarian revitalization.

During the first decades of the twentieth century, Dimitur Michaltchev (n.d.) defended the German-inspired conception of philosophy as the fundamental science, rejected metaphysics, and argued for a form of classic empiricism. He rejected the ethics of duty, replacing it with an ethics of disinterested love. In addition to pure philosophy, literature and literary criticism experienced a promising influence from this awakening of the philosophical tradition with writers like Krŭsto Krŭstev (1866–1919) and Pencho Slaveikov (1866–1912).

Prior to the Communist era, Dimitur Blagoev (1855–1924), a Russian-trained socialist, lent his voice to the growing philosophical discourse in Bulgaria, while ironically helping to pave the way for the postwar Marxism that was to bring an end to the budding diversity of thought. The most influential and articulate Communist was the president of the Academy of Science and an aesthetician, Todor Pavlov (n.d.). In concert with the party line, Pavlov conceived art to be a function of the development of dialectical materialism and the communist social agenda—a formalization of the Stalinist theory of social realism. Not surprisingly, controversies and debates surfaced between Pavlov and the non-Marxists, but the political realities increasingly reduced the room for philosophical divergence. Eventually, the scientific propensities of Michaltchev and the Marxism of Pavlov found an interesting synthesis in philosopher-politician Todor Zhivkov (1911–98), who saw science as a generative instrument that could be utilized in restructuring the intellectual sphere and thereby assist in the transformation of society.

Czechoslovakia

The rich philosophical heritages of Bohemia, Moravia, and Slovakia provided a sophisticated and stable basis for the nineteenth-century revitalization that exhibited regional developments directly connected to the cultivation of the indigenous traditions and languages, as well as a strong sense of philosophy's role in social reformation.

In the early nineteenth century Bernard Bolzano (1781–1848) attempted an elucidation of fundamental truths independent of language and human beings, thereby giving credence to his rational interpretation of Catholicism. However, during the first half of the century, Hegel remained the dominant intellectual force in Bohemia. The works on aesthetics and history by František Palacký (1798–1876) cultivated sensitivity toward cultural identity in his presentation of history. Palacký's involvement in Czech political life created a model for future philosophers to be engaged in the liberation of the people and the vitalization of the national spirit. In Slovakia, Ľudovít Štúr (1815–56) rallied interest in the uniqueness of the Slovak language and culture by making use of Hegel's doctrine of national spirit. In the latter half of the century, Hegelianism subsided and was replaced by other German thinkers and a growing interest in English science and philosophy under the leadership of the Czech Josef Durdik (1837–1902). This transformation characterized the growing understanding that the philosophical enterprise was demarcated by its rigorous scientific methodology rather than by Hegelian-like cosmological or historical pronouncements.

In the twentieth century the scientific climate encouraged by Durdik was transformed into positivism under František Krejčí (1858–1934) and Tomáš G. Masaryk (1850–1937). Masaryk

P envisioned positivism (and philosophy in general) as a practical tool to change the world. Although he later rejected positivism, owing to his devout religiosity, Masaryk retained the social purpose of philosophy. At the same time, literature felt the impact of the existentialist themes of absurdity, dread, and alienation with the writings of Franz Kafka (1883–1924).

These developments, interrupted by the Nazi German occupation of Czechoslovakia, became truncated with the Communist takeover. After 1948, the official hardline attitude toward all positions other than Marxist-Leninism made open discussion of philosophical issues problematic if not impossible. However, during this period, underground cells of intellectuals continued to maintain contacts with other philosophers from the rest of Europe, exhibiting bursts of intellectual activity especially in the Prague Spring, the liberal reform period in 1968. But with the Soviet-led invasion, philosophers retreated again to the shadows, where they continued to nurture the social and political intellectual life of Czechoslovakia, while remaining engaged in the struggle for human rights and dignity.

Hungary

In Hungary, a promising medieval philosophical tradition that had been interrupted by the wars with the Turks eventually became divided into the Catholic western regions and Protestant Transylvania. Typically, the rise in national pride in the nineteenth century led to a demand for a vernacular philosophical language and eventually a Hungarian philosophy. This was met by the emergence of the philosophy of harmony and the ascendancy of German, especially Kantian, thought. Philosophy was viewed as a practical tool for the achievement of this balancing of thought, action, world, person, and deity. The philosophy of harmony, while not providing a systematic philosophy, attempted an integration of various components of Hungarian social-cultural experience and existence, thus forming the rudiments of a national or regional philosophy. Some of the principal proponents of this school were János Hetényi (1786–1853), Gusztáv Szontágh (1793–1853), and Samuel Köteles (1790–1831).

Suspicious of this "regionalization" of the philosophical enterprise, János Erdélyi (1814–68) criticized the philosophy of harmony's concept of a national philosophy as insufficiently universal

and subject to emotionalism. On the other hand, he believed that the structure of Hegel's dialectical concept of history would be an appropriate framework for the development of Hungarian philosophizing. Károly Kerkápoly (1824–1891), Erdélyi's student, attempted to strengthen this conceptualization by vindicating Hegel's analyses through a detailed study of history.

As the debates over the philosophy of harmony raged, a revival of scholasticism occurred. The strong Catholic traditions in western Hungary, struggling against various strains of "modern thought," attempted various syntheses of Thomas Aquinas (1225–74) and contemporary strands of thought. The eclectic character of much of the neoscholastic thinkers can also be found in the writings of Imre Pauer (1854–1950), who best represented the brief but intense interest in Comte and positivism that occurred at the end of the nineteenth century. Akos Pauler (1876–1933), a student of Pauer, eventually rejected positivism and came to the defense of metaphysics. He identified his reductive methodology, the rational movement from *that which is given* to that which is presupposed by the *given,* as a contemporary version of the Platonic dialectic.

In the twentieth century Hegelian Menyhert (Melchior) Palágyi (1859–1924), who spent most of his career in Germany, developed a psychological/epistemological critique of positivistic scientific theories that founded all knowledge on "scientific fact." On the opposite end of the philosophical spectrum, he criticized Husserl's phenomenological search for "ideal essences" as the ultimate foundation for knowledge. Palágyi introduced a characteristically Hegelian polar distinction between mechanical processes (public and visible) and vital processes (mental and invisible) claiming the mutual nonreducibility. Nevertheless, interest in phenomenology developed and can be seen in the works of émigré Wilhelm (Vilmos) Szilasi (1889–1966) in his attempt to reconcile Kant, Husserl, and Martin Heidegger (1889–1976). Language and philosophy as a way to *eudæmonia* (happiness) played center stage in his development of thought.

With the eventual rise of communism, the pluralism of this dynamic period of philosophical inquiry disappeared from the public arena with the exception of György Lukács (1885–1971). Originally concerned with aesthetics, Lukács eventually focused on a Hegelian criticism of Soviet orthodoxy, recognizing that Marx's theory of history and economics was best understood within the Hegelian dialectical processes. While creating difficulties with the authorities, Lukács's work provided limited room for philosophical exploration within Hungary, and a popular resource for Western European Marxists.

Poland

Poland, among all of its Eastern European neighbors, enjoyed the most sustained connection with the Western philosophical tradition, enabling it to develop a sophisticated internal philosophical discourse. The foundation that medieval and Renaissance thinkers built included the full range of philosophical issues and paradigms. The Enlightenment of the mid–eighteenth century introduced an eclectic assimilation of modern thinkers with a committed emphasis on the freedom of rational inquiry.

As the intellectual ferment of the Enlightenment, with its firm conviction in the rational project, took hold on Polish thought, empiricism and logic occupied a greater place on center stage. Jan Śniadecki (1757–1830), a mathematician and scientist, became a focal point of the critiques of speculative metaphysics, and assisted in molding the Polish philosophical temperament in the style of the British empiricists, foreshadowing themes of positivism. Voices against the Enlightenment, such as Józef K. Szaniawski (1765–1843), sought restraints on the believed omnipotence of the rational project and cultivated Kantian thought with its structural limitations on knowledge. Consequently, many of the anti-Enlightenment forces became associated with the conservative "Throne and Altar" movement, an alliance that supported the established order. Critiques of the Enlightenment also developed from the nonconservative romantic movement with its celebration of feeling and intuition.

Between 1830 and 1863, Polish intellectual life was captivated by a metaphysical speculative movement called messianism, which focused on the fate of Poland. This movement became a prophetic philosophy of history expressing what it perceived to be the spirit of the nation—an announcing of a new age of justice and freedom in a new political state. The Messiah was understood differently by various members of the movement, ranging from a specific person, the Polish people, to philosophy itself. Messianists such as

Józef Maria Hoene-Wroński (1778–1853), August Cieszkowski (1815–94), and Józef Kremer (1806–75) believed that philosophy ought to change the world.

The optimism of messianism, however, was crushed with the failure of the 1863 uprising against the Russians, and the intellectual climate quickly turned to positivism. Polish thinkers adopted the methodological patterns associated with positivism but broadened it to include social issues that messianism had attempted to address. In place of romanticism, it proposed a rigorous and slow reconstruction of society through piecemeal action on the economic, education, and social fronts. Julian Ochorowicz (1850–1917) and Adam Mahrburg (1855–1913) exemplified this positivistic trend. Positivism was not, however, alone on the philosophical stage. Neoscholastic thinkers, existentialists, and various metaphysicians criticized positivism. There also appeared, prior to World War I, representatives of the emerging socialist movements.

The most creative period of Polish philosophy occurred between the two world wars with the development of logic. Under the tutelage of Kazimierz Twardowski (1866–1938), scholars convinced of the connection of philosophy to science committed themselves to methodological rigor and unambiguous thought and expression. Twardowski's Platonic theory of the reality of logical objects not only profoundly shaped the face of Polish philosophy but influenced Husserl's phenomenological search for "ideal essences" and the critical realism of Moritz Schlick (1882–1936). Thus, Twardowski's influence was extended through the continent via the phenomenological and positivist movements. The Lwów School (later Warsaw School), which grew around Twardowski, emphasized logic and semantics, while rejecting logical positivism. Independently of Twardowski, at the University of Kraków, other thinkers such as Leon Chwistek (1884–1944) developed their own analysis of logic and science. They applied the rigors of logical analysis to art, the natural sciences, and mathematics.

After 1939, the Nazi German attempt to destroy Polish culture and independent thought forced the philosophical enterprise and teaching underground. After 1945, the Communist leadership encouraged the focusing of philosophical debate around Soviet-style dialectical materialism. Adam Schaff (1913–) became the principal

P representative of this period, and all other types of "content" philosophizing became silenced. Logic, being "content free," remained largely untouched by these political machinations.

After 1956, a thawing of the monolithic control of philosophical discourse began. Poland's strong Catholic heritage supported a reemergence of the metaphysics of Aquinas with contemporary applications to logic, law, and existentialism, and produced personalist/existential thinkers like Karol Wojtyła (1920–), who later became Pope John Paul II. While Marxism-Leninism remained the officially preferred doctrine, Marxism became transformed by nonorthodox thinkers like Leszek Kołakowski (1927–), creating an increasingly diverse tableau of philosophical thought.

Romania

While a few intellectual-political leaders attempted to elevate the intellectual life of Romania, its domination by the Turks and the competing tendencies of mystical theology and folklore encouraged by the clergy impeded the development of a substantial and durable foundation for philosophical thought before the 1800s. During the nineteenth century, Western influences began to penetrate the Romanian lands through the works of various historians and romantic literary figures. Titu Maiorescu (1840–1917) became the father of Romanian aesthetics, while Vasile Conta (1845–82), Romania's first original philosopher, established a materialist school of thought based on his concept of the rhythmic pattern of waves as universally constituting matter.

By far the most creative and original philosophical work was accomplished in the twentieth century by Constantin Rădulescu-Motru (1886–1954) and his student Nae Ionescu (1890–1940). Rădulescu-Motru's philosophy of energetic personalism attempted an integration of biology and psychology, conceiving the human personality to be the highest form of cosmic energy. Ionescu, revitalizing interest in metaphysics and the philosophy of religion, stressed the integration of theoretical conceptualization of human experience with the appreciation of the artifacts of that experience.

Romania's complex political position during the interwar period and the development of domestic fascism did little to facilitate the maturation of philosophical thought. In spite of these political and cultural difficulties, however, some heroic contributions to Romanian philosophy were made. With an emphasis similar to Ionescu's philosopher-poet Lucian Blaga (1899–1962) attempted to integrate the religious and folkloric tendencies of the Romanian tradition with systematic Western thought, producing the most complete and complex system of thought. Blaga's work elevated Romanian folklore and traditions to worthy objects of speculation and reflection, thereby assisting in the development of Romania's intellectual self-awareness and pride.

With the ascendancy of communism and Romania's hardline orthodoxy, philosophical thought was driven underground or disguised in the form of literature. Despite this repressive climate, Romanian thought achieved some moments of grandeur, especially when the Romanian intellect was reflecting on its own cultural moorings, folklore, and traditions.

Yugoslavia

Philosophical discourse in Yugoslavia was built on the scholastic foundation established by Byzantine influences in Serbia and Catholic influences in Croatia and Slovenia. On the shoulders of scholastics, humanists, and thinkers of the Enlightenment, a rich and diverse intellectual tradition developed.

In the early 1800s, amid growing interests in German thought, Petar Petrović Nejegoš (1813–51), prince-poet of Montenegro, focused attention on human suffering, struggle, and freedom. His Platonic dualism conceived human struggle as the consequence of the cosmic struggle between two co-eternal realities: God and matter. This focusing on the human struggle eventually matured into Svetozar Marković's (1846–75) activistic philosophy. Marković, influenced by Marx (1818–83), French materialism, and Russian revolutionaries, developed a scientific atheism that postulated that a spiritual revolution via art was a necessary prerequisite to the social-political-economic revolution. The spirit of this activistic philosophy, an identifying feature of Yugoslavian philosophy, stressed education and science as tools for social change.

A variety of other philosophical theories appeared in the late nineteenth and early twentieth centuries. Among the most significant were the theory of universal evolution of Božidar Knežević (1862–1905) and the empirical metaphysics of Branislav Petronievć (1873–1954). Yugoslav positivism was best represented by Dragiša Djurić

(1871–1941). A peculiar form of irrationalism also developed among some Serbs as they attempted to blend pragmatism, intuitionism with Pan-Slavism, and Orthodox Christianity.

In nineteenth-century Croatia, early interests in materialism, evolutionary theories, and existentialism were broadened by Franjo Marković's (1845–1914) ethical theory and Albert Bazala's (1877–1947) popularization of a voluntary activistic philosophy with its "education is revolutionary" thesis. In the twentieth century various thinkers developed different strands of the philosophical discourse, ranging from meta-analysis of philosophical methods, existentialism, Marxist epistemology, and neoscholasticism. In Slovenia, neoscholasticism and positivism dominated the philosophical landscape.

Throughout Yugoslavia, the activistic tendencies of philosophical thought matured into revolutionary spirit stressing praxis over theory. This spirit nurtured the interests in Marxism as well as fears concerning it. Prior to World War II, a great deal of creativity and originality arose from the Marxist camp with thinkers like Marković and Dimitrije Tucović (1881–1914), who had major influence on political organizations.

After World War II, official dogma rejected non-Marxist ideologies and proclaimed Marxism the final truth. However, Tito's (1892–1980) split with Stalin (1879–1953) in 1948 fueled the drive toward greater intellectual pluralism. Thus, in spite of the initial dogmatism, some non-Marxists continued in their academic positions through this period, and Yugoslavia did not suffer a complete break in intellectual continuity. Significant among them was phenomenologist Vladimir Filipović (1906–84). After the political break with Stalin and official rejection of monolithic Marxist-Leninism, the intellectual space was created for a rethinking of the humanistic Marx. Philosophy was seen as playing a fundamental and critical (rather than dogmatic) role in every aspect of society's self-reflection and action. In this more tolerant climate, discussions flourished between Marxist and non-Marxist existentialists and positivists, between Marxist-Leninist purists and Marxists who wanted to adapt Marxism in light of contemporary science. This phase of Yugoslav thought was penetrated by an optimism that sought practical ways to change the social structures and thereby change historical reality.

James Eiswert

Further reading

Bŭnkov, Angel Iliev. *History of Philosophy in Bulgaria,* trans. by Vezko Izmirliev. Sofia, 1975.

Duţu, Alexandru. *Romanian Humanists and European Culture.* Bucharest, 1977.

Gluck, Mary. *Georg Lukács and His Generation, 1900–1918.* Cambridge, Massachusetts, 1985.

Gruenwald, Oskar. *The Yugoslav Search for Man: Marxist Humanism in Contemporary Yugoslavia.* South Hadley, Massachusetts, 1983.

Hitchins, Keith. *Studies on Romanian National Consciousness.* Pelham, New York, 1983.

Jordan, Z. A. *Philosophy and Ideology: The Development of Philosophy and Marxism-Leninism in Poland since World War II.* Dordrecht, Netherlands, 1963.

Logoreci, Anton. *The Albanians: Europe's Forgotten Survivors.* Boulder, Colorado, 1978.

Philosophy and Culture: Studies from Hungary, ed. by József Lukács and Ferenc Tokei. Budapest, 1983.

Schmidt-Hartmann, Eva. *Thomas G. Masaryk's Realism: Origins of a Czech Political Concept.* Munich, 1984.

Skendi, Stavro. *The Albanian National Awakening, 1878–1912.* Princeton, New Jersey, 1967.

See also Dimitur Blagoev; Catholicism; August Cieszkowski; Folklore; Intelligentsia; Nae Ionescu; January Uprising; John Paul II; Franz Kafka; György Lukács; Titu Maoirescu; Svetozar Marković; Marxism; Tomáš Masaryk; František Palacký; Pan-Slavism; Petar II Petrović Nejegoš; Polish Logic; Positivism; Prague Spring; Romanticism; Socialism; Ľudovít Štúr; Kazimierz Twardowski; Todor Zhivkov

Piasecki, Bolesław (1914–79)

One of the most curious figures in twentieth-century Polish politics, and one of the founders of interwar Polish fascism who later came to work with the Communist regime as the organizer of the Catholic lay movement PAX. Born near Radom, by the late 1920s, Piasecki had been attracted to the right-wing nationalist movement headed by Roman Dmowski (1864–1939). The latter's death was a blow to the coherence of the national movement, which soon broke into a number of different groupings. In 1934, after a spell in the infamous Bereza prison, Piasecki founded his own fascist association, known as the Falanga, espousing an antiliberal, anti-Communist, and extremely anti-Semitic program. Piasecki believed that fascism was the wave of the future in Europe, looking as he did to the successes of other youth groups such as the Italian Balilla, the Hitler Jugend, the Spanish Falanga, and the Soviet Komsomol.

Arrested by the Gestapo in October 1939 after Germany's occupation of Poland, Piasecki was saved by the personal intervention of Italian leader Mussolini (1883–1945). He joined the Polish underground and fought in the resistance. His first wife died fighting the Germans in 1944. When later arrested by the Soviet secret police, Piasecki's luck held and he was once more saved by personal intervention. He dropped his anti-Communist stance and began his long career as a Communist gadfly against the Polish Catholic Church.

The nature of Piasecki's association with the Communist regime in Poland was one of a tool or weapon to be used by the authorities against the hierarchy of the Catholic Church. For his part, Piasecki hoped that he could make himself indispensable to the regime by developing a Catholic brand of socialism. As the leader of PAX, Piasecki attempted to place himself at the head of a secular Catholic movement dedicated to working with the regime in the building of a new Poland. His publication house was often used by the Communist Party as a platform for blasting the episcopate and other opposition Catholic figures.

Piasecki himself amassed a considerable fortune and commanded a loyal following among members of PAX. His authoritarian style, however, alienated others and PAX was often plagued with factionalism.

Peter Wozniak

Further reading

Blit, Lucjan. *The Eastern Pretender: Bolesław Piasecki: His Life and Times.* London, 1965.

Bromke, Adam. "From Falanga to PAX," *Survey* 39 (1961): 29–40.

Dudek, Antoni and Grzegorz Pytel. *Bolesław Piasecki: Próba biografii politycznej.* London, 1990.

Wasiutyński, Wojciech. *Czwarte Pokolenie: Szkice z dziejów nacjonalizmu polskiego.* London, 1982.

See also Communist Party of Poland; Roman Dmowski; PAX; Right Radicalism

Pig War (1906–11)

Trade war between Serbia and Austria-Hungary. The provisions of the Treaty of San Stefano (March 1878), which ended the fighting in the Russo-Turkish War of 1877–78, prompted Serbia's Prince Milan Obrenović (1854–1901) and Foreign Minister Jovan Ristić (1831–99) to approach the Austro-Hungarian foreign minister, Count Gyula Andrássy, Sr. (1823–90), to secure Austrian backing for Serbian territorial claims at the Congress of Berlin (July 1878). Austria readily agreed to Serbia's plea by setting out several conditions, including a general economic agreement between the two countries. The treaty of April 24, 1880, led to Serbia's extensive economic and political dependence on Austria-Hungary. By the beginning of the twentieth century, this dependence became a major impediment to further Serbian economic development and political emancipation.

The assassination of the last Obrenović (Alexander [1876–1903]) on May 24, 1903, and the subsequent dynastic change in Serbia marked the beginning of a new era in Austro-Serbian relations. The new Serbian government introduced sweeping economic reforms intended to stabilize domestic finances, to reorganize foreign trade, and consequently to free Serbia from its heavy dependence on Austria-Hungary. A new tariff system was introduced in 1904, while a trade treaty with the Ottoman Empire and a customs union treaty with Bulgaria were concluded the following year. Austria-Hungary became discontent with Serbia's decision to modernize its army by placing an order with the French firm of Schneider Creusot rather than with the Austro-Hungarian Škoda arms works, which Austria perceived as a direct challenge to its vital interests in the Balkans. Anxious to show Europe that Serbia lay in its power and to prevent the economic emancipation of Serbia, Austria-Hungary closed its borders to Serbia's exports in January 1906. When the ensuing negotiations broke down, a tariff war between the two countries erupted. Contrary to Austro-Hungarian expectations, Serbia greatly benefited from what became popularly known as the Pig War (live hogs were the principal Serbian export). During the tariff war (1906–11), Austria-Hungary's share in Serbia's foreign trade decreased from more than 50 percent to less than 20 percent, while the composition of Serbia's exports improved by changing from live animals to processed meat and grains.

The structural changes in the foreign trade sector were also accompanied by the increased presence of French and British capital in Serbia's economy and the rapid industrial development of the country. The number of industrial enterprises increased from 93 in 1904 to 428 in 1910. The tariff war and the annexation of Bosnia-Hercegovina in 1908 were rooted in Austro-Hungarian determination to control Serbia economically and politically. The economic and political emancipation of Serbia that resulted directly from the tariff war prompted Austria-Hungary to resort to more belligerent ways of settling future disputes.

Željan E. Šuster

Further reading

Đorđević, D. *Carinski rat Austro-Ugarske i Srbije 1906–1911.* Belgrade, 1962.

Petrovich, Michael B. *A History of Modern Serbia 1804–1918.* New York, 1976.

Šuster, Željan E. *Historical Dictionary of the Federal Republic of Yugoslavia.* Metuchen, New Jersey, 1997.

———. "Serbia's Economic Relations with the West before World War I." *Serbian Studies,* no. 2 (Fall 1993).

See also Alexander Obrenović; Gyula Andrássy, Sr.; Congress of Berlin; Economic Development in Yugoslavia; Industrialization; Milan Obrenović; Jovan Ristić; Russo-Turkish War of 1877–78; San Stefano, Treaty of; Škoda

Piłsudski, Józef (1867–1935)

Polish revolutionary, statesman, and founder of modern Poland. Piłsudski was born in Zulow, in the Russian part of Poland, in 1867. As a very young boy, he developed a hatred for Russian imperialism. While studying medicine at Kharkov University, he came in contact with socialist circles, and in 1887 he was arrested for his association with a plot to kill Alexander III (1845–94), the same plot that cost Lenin's (1870–1924) brother his life. Piłsudski was sentenced to five years in Siberia, where he became even more attracted to socialism. On his return, he joined the newly formed Polish Socialist Party (PPS) and became editor of a clandestine newspaper, *Robotnik* (*Worker*). He became one of the most prominent leaders of the party.

Following the 1905 revolution, which saw unrest throughout Russia, Piłsudski began to move further away from social reform and closer to the concept of armed struggle to free Poland—always his paramount objective. To this end, he formed the Bojowki (fighting squads) and in 1908 the Union for Military Action, an underground paramilitary organization. In 1910 Austrian officials agreed to let him legally form Riflemen's Unions (Strelcy), which were used to train officer cadres for a future Polish army.

When World War I began, Piłsudski formed the Polish Legions to fight for Polish independence against Russia. The legions were loosely associated with the Austrian army, which created friction between the two forces whose goals were often at odds. Piłsudski was arrested and the legions disbanded when they refused to take an oath of loyalty to the German and Austrian governments. As a result, Piłsudski became a martyr, fighting for Polish independence against all the partitioning powers.

After Germany's collapse, Piłsudski returned to Warsaw on November 10, 1918, as a national hero and was named head of state. He devoted himself to defending the new Polish state against the advancing Red Army. Piłsudski envisioned a confederation of Central European countries from the Baltic to the Black Sea with Poland at its center. The coalition was to defend itself against a resurgent Germany and/or Russia. His attempts to create this confederation brought Poland into direct conflict with Soviet Russia in 1919. The Polish-Soviet War (1919–21) ended in defeat for the Red Army but a Poland too weak to press its advantage. The Treaty of Riga, which ended the conflict, was a compromise that killed the confederation plan.

Piłsudski remained in politics until the assassination of Poland's first elected president in 1922. He retired out of disgust for politics but by 1926 felt the need to return. With the Polish government on the verge of collapse, Piłsudski led a coup d'état that put him in complete control of Poland from 1926 until 1935.

Piłsudski's new government was called *Sanacja* (Sanitation), and was meant to cleanse the state of partisan politics. He left the day-to-day functioning of the government to his associates (referred to as the Colonels) and devoted his time to diplomacy, trying to balance Poland between the

P Soviet Union and a resurgent Germany. Until his death in 1935, he also kept control over the army to build it up to the task of a dual defense against Poland's totalitarian neighbors.

David Stefancic

Further reading

Dziewanawski, M. K. *Joseph Piłsudski: A European Federalist.* Stanford, California, 1969.

Garlicki, A. *Jozef Piłsudski.* London, 1990.

Jedczejewicz, W. *Piłsudski: A Life for Poland.* New York, 1982.

Piłsudski, J. *Memoires of a Polish Revolutionary and Soldier.* London, 1931.

Reddaway, W. F. *Marshall Piłsudski.* London, 1939.

See also Alexander III; May Coup; Peace of Riga; Polish Legions; Polish-Soviet War; Red Army; *Sanacja;* Warsaw, Battle of

Pittsburgh Agreement (*Pittsburgská Dohoda*)

Programmatic agreement between Czech and Slovak organizations in the United States, concluded in Pittsburgh on May 30, 1918. As in the earlier Cleveland agreement (October 22, 1915), the Czech and Slovak organizations pledged in the Pittsburgh agreement to work for "the union of the Czechs and Slovaks in an independent state," in which Slovakia would have "its own administration, its own diet, and its own courts," but left "the detailed provisions for the organization of the Czecho-Slovak state to the liberated Czechs and Slovaks and their accredited representatives" to decide. What gave the Pittsburgh agreement special significance was that it was drafted in the presence and with the assistance of Toáš G. Masaryk (1850–1937), chairman of the exile Czechoslovak National Council of Paris, and that he signed its final calligraphic copy in Washington on November 14, 1918—the day the provisional Czechoslovak National Assembly elected him first president of Czechoslovakia.

Father Andrej Hlinka (1864–1938), leader of the autonomist Slovak People's Party, believed that the Pittsburgh agreement guaranteed Slovakia's autonomy. The provisional National Assembly refused to recognize it, however, whereupon Hlinka went to the Paris Peace Conference and sought international recognition of Slovakia's autonomy, analogous to that accorded Subcarpathian Rus' (Ruthenia) in the Treaty of St. Germain (September 10, 1919). He had no more success in Paris than he had had in Prague, however. On his return to Slovakia, he was arrested, accused of treason, and imprisoned.

The provisional National Assembly had declared that all agreements and commitments made by Masaryk and the Paris National Council during the war were binding on the Czechoslovak government. When the assembly prepared to draft Czechoslovakia's constitution, Prime Minister Vlastimil Tusar (1880–1924) asked Masaryk to pronounce himself on the validity of the Pittsburgh agreement. The president replied (February 5, 1920) that it was an agreement between Czechs and Slovaks in the United States, who were mostly American citizens and, consequently, had no right—indeed, had no wish—to determine the internal structure of the Czechoslovak state.

The provisional National Assembly went on to draft a French-style, highly centralist constitution, which postulated the existence of a single Czechoslovak nation, wiped out the distinction between the historical Czech lands (Bohemia, Moravia, and Silesia), and failed to recognize Slovakia as a distinct province. After the constitution's proclamation (February 29, 1920), Masaryk's attitude was that as a constitutional president it was his duty to uphold the constitution and that of all the citizens of the republic to respect it—nothing could be changed in it. The weakness of this argument was that the provisional National Assembly had not been elected but appointed and its authority to draft a permanent constitution was doubtful. The national minorities—notably, the Germans in the Czech lands and the Hungarians in Slovakia—were excluded from it. Numerically and politically, the Slovak people—let alone all of Slovakia—were not fairly represented in it.

Hlinka continued to agitate for Slovakia's autonomy on the basis of the Pittsburgh agreement. His last public act (June 4, 1938) was to display the calligraphic copy of the agreement, which a delegation of the Slovak League of America, the political/cultural organization comprising affiliated Slovak societies and Americans of Slovak ancestry, had brought to Slovakia, to a crowd of cheering supporters in Bratislava and pledged continued support for it.

Victor S. Mamatey

Further reading

Čulen, Konstantín. *Pittsburghská dohoda.* Bratislava, 1937.

Minar, Imrich. *Americkí Slováci a Slovensko, 1880–1980.* Bratislava, 1994.

See also Ethnic Minorities; Andrej Hlinka; Tomáš G. Masaryk; Paris Peace Conference; St. Germain, Treaty of; Slovak League of America; Subcarpathian Rus'; Vlastimil Tusar

Pleven

Former district center in north-central Bulgaria near the Vit River, a tributary of the Danube. Pleven's name is derived from *"pleva,"* a kind of grass. At one time a Thracian and Roman settlement, Pleven became an important commercial center with a large cattle market after the fifteenth century. The town became famous during the Russo-Turkish War of 1877–78, when for over five months Russian and allied Romanian troops were engaged in bitter battles against the Turkish army. The fall of this key fortress of the Ottoman Empire was one of the decisive victories of the conflict.

Pleven has a temperate continental climate with cold winters (temperatures in January average 29° F (–1.7° C]), and hot summers (July temperatures average 75° F [23.6° C]). The average annual precipitation is 24 inches (60 cm). There are several springs and thermal mineral waters.

The first industrial enterprises were set up after 1900, mainly grain mills, oil presses, tobacco processing, and textile plants. Pleven (population of 130,812 in 1994) has become one of the most industrialized towns in Bulgaria, with machine building (forklift trucks) and metallurgy, petroleum processing and chemical industry, and food processing, among others. Agriculture is well developed, especially traditional grape growing. Pleven is also a center of higher education and research. In 1840 the first women's civil school in Bulgaria was opened in Pleven.

Boian Koulov

Further reading

Broi na naselenieto po oblasti, obshtini i naseleni mesta. Resultati ot prebroyavaneto na naselenieto, vol. 3. Sofia, 1994.

Bulgaria, 1983, vol. 1. 656–59.

Bulgarian Academy of Sciences. *Entsiklopedia Bulgaria,* vol. 5, Sofia, 1986.

Vasil, Mikov. *Proizhod i Znachenie na Imenata na Nashite Gradove, Sela, Reki, Planini i Mesta.* Sofia, 1943.

See also Pleven, Battle of; Russo-Turkish War of 1877–78

Pleven, Battle of

Important battle in the Russo-Turkish War of 1877–78 that represented a serious, if temporary, defeat of the Russian army in its campaign against Ottoman forces. In July 1877 the Russo-Turkish War entered its third month, with the Russians seemingly on their way to a speedy victory and possible occupation of the Ottoman capital, Constantinople. An unexpectedly successful Ottoman stand at Pleven, under the leadership of Osman Pasha (1832–1900), however, stopped the Russian juggernaut in mid-July. Having beaten back one Russian attack, the Ottoman armies repulsed two more in late July and September. In October General E.I. Todleben (1818–84) organized a blockade of Pleven. Ottoman forces attempted to break out of the encirclement on December 10–11 but were forced to capitulate after sustaining heavy casualties.

The fall of Pleven became a turning point in the war. Although the Russian armies needed just over a month to reach Adrianople, a city within striking distance of Constantinople, the delay at Pleven imposed on them altered the course of the conflict and the subsequent peace treaties. Talk of quick victories and conquests stopped. Reversing its previous position, the Russian government was compelled to request military assistance from Serbia and Romania. Those states' participation in the war helped them make a convincing case for territorial concessions and independence in the San Stefano and Berlin treaties.

The battle of Pleven also resurrected Great Britain's flagging support for the Ottoman Empire. British interests there remained the same—preventing Russian hegemony in the area near the Turkish Straits—but its policy toward the Ottomans had suffered from the publicity surrounding the "Bulgarian horrors"—accounts of Ottoman atrocities against Bulgarian rebels in 1876. In the wake of the Ottoman defense at Pleven, London

P repeatedly reasserted its determination that the Ottoman Empire be preserved.

Brigit Farley

Further reading
Anderson, M. S. *The Eastern Question 1774–1923.* New York, 1966.
Herbert, W. V. *The Defense of Pleven, by One Who Took Part in It. 1877.* London, 1895.
Sumner, B. H. *Russia and the Balkans 1870–1880.* London, 1937.

See also Bulgarian Massacres; Congress of Berlin; Russo-Turkish War of 1877–78; San Stefano, Treaty of

Ploughman's Front

Romanian political party (1933–48). Founded in 1933 in the Hunedoara district in Transylvania and led by Petru Groza (1884–1958), the Ploughman's Front appealed to the poorer peasantry by calling for a drastic reduction of peasant debt, increased taxation of great wealth, and exemption from taxation and assurance of free medical and legal assistance for peasants with fewer than 12.5 acres (five hectares) of land. While it remained antifascist, the party had little influence on Romanian politics until it became part of the Communist-organized National Democratic Front on October 12, 1944. The Ploughman's Front maintained its autonomy, gained support in the provinces, and was bolstered by the appointment of Groza as premier in March 1945. The front held its first congress on June 24–27, 1945. Most of the representatives were poor peasants who wanted to strengthen the individual small landholder and revitalize the village cooperatives. In February 1947 a joint meeting of the Politburo of the Communist Party and the Executive Committee of the Ploughman's Front decided that the front would work with the Party and be the organization to represent the working peasantry. In preparation for the 1948 elections, the Ploughman's Front joined the Communist-sponsored Popular Democratic Front and, although victorious, the party lost its identify. Its members became part of the Romanian Workers' Party, which in 1965 became the Romanian Communist Party.

Joseph F. Harrington

Further reading
Hitchins, Keith. *Rumania, 1866–1947.* Oxford, 1994.
Quinlan, Paul. *Clash over Romania: British and American Policies toward Romania, 1938–1947.* Los Angeles, 1977.
Wolff, Robert Lee. *The Balkans in Our Times.* New York, 1967.

See also Agrarian Parties; Communist Party of Romania; Petru Groza; Peasants

Plovdiv

Bulgarian economic and cultural center in the Maritsa valley of upper Thrace about 100 miles (167 km) east of Sofia. Its ancient core, Trimontium, is situated on easily defended granite hills that rise 400 feet (121 m) above the river plain. The modern city has expanded across lands on both sides of the Maritsa River. For most of its history Plovdiv was known as Philippopolis, for Philip II of Macedon (382–336 B.C.), who made the ancient Thracian settlement his capital after capturing it in 342 B.C. Bulgaria officially adopted the city's present name only after World War I. Plovdiv served as capital of Thrace for most of its subsequent history, which saw repeated ravages from barbarian tribes and Crusaders. In the thirteenth century it became a center of Bogomil Christianity, a faith persecuted by both Orthodox and Roman Catholic religious bodies. Philippopolis remained a fortified center after falling to the Ottoman Empire in 1364. Beginning in 1878 it served as capital of the short-lived Ottoman autonomous province of Eastern Rumelia until that entity was absorbed by the Bulgarian state in 1885. Bulgaria officially designated Plovdiv a historic district in 1956.

Plovdiv (population 385,000) is second only to Sofia in industrial development. It is the foremost Bulgarian textile center and is noted also for food and tobacco processing and the production of electronic goods. It has a university and other higher educational institutions. It is also the site of a biennial trade fair.

Thomas M. Poulsen

Further reading
Iordanov, Tanko, ed. *Geografiia na Bŭlgaria.* Sofia, 1981.
Penkov, Ignat and Todor Khristov. *Ikonomicheska Geografiia na Bŭlgariia,* 2d ed. Sofia, 1965.

Zakhariev, Ivan. Dobri Bradistilov, and Petŭr Popov. *Ikonomichesko Raionirane na N.R. Bŭlgariia.* Sofia, 1963.

See also Bogomilism; Eastern Rumelia

Plzeň

Cultural, administrative, and commercial center of western Bohemia. Plzeň (German, Pilsen) is located approximately 55 miles (91 km) southwest of Prague in the Czech Republic. Plzeň (population 175,000 in 1989) began to prosper in the Middle Ages as an important stop on a trade route between Prague and Nuremberg, and was also a major contributor to the wealth of the Habsburg Empire. The city has had a long history of German influence.

Located in a plateau region in Bohemia amid the Berounka Uplands, the Plzeň area is a rich agricultural district producing barley, wheat, oats, sugar beets, and hops used in the brewing of beer since 1295. The famous Pilsner-Urquell brewery, which produces about 40 million gallons (151 million liters) of beer per year, opened in 1842 and regularly supplied an average of 10 percent of Czechoslovakia's exports by value.

Plzeň is a major contributor to the industrial economy of Bohemia, especially known for mechanical engineering, machinery production, steel, armaments, ceramics, and paper, in addition to the breweries. The famous Škoda steelworks is located in the city and has been the heart of the Czechoslovak economy. The high level of industrial buildup has made Plzeň one of the most polluted cities in the country.

Russell L. Ivy

Further reading

Berentsen, William, ed. *Europe in the 1990s: A Geographical Analysis,* 7th ed. Chicago, 1997.
Pounds, N.J.G. *Eastern Europe.* Chicago, 1969.
Rugg, Dean. *Eastern Europe.* London, 1985.
UNIDO. *Czechoslovakia: Industrial Transformation and Regeneration.* Oxford, 1992.

See also Environment; Škoda

Podolacy

Term used to identify a bloc of Polish landowning nobility from the eastern region of Galicia who exercised considerable influence over both local and imperial politics from about 1860 to 1914. Their significance stemmed from Austria's failure in wars and from the need to find some counterweights to the Hungarians following the *Ausgleich* (Compromise) of 1867, which created the Dual Monarchy of Austria-Hungary.

Beginning in the 1850s, Vienna found it necessary to effect some compromises and to make concessions to various groups within the monarchy to retain control. None were better at gaining concessions than the Poles in Galicia, territorially Austria's largest province as well as one of the most backward. Led by Count Agenor Gołuchowski (1812–75), viceroy of Galicia, conservative aristocrats began to press Vienna for concessions that would guarantee them a high degree of autonomy within Galicia and preserve their control over the Ukrainian peasantry, who constituted the majority population in eastern Galicia. In return, the Poles would pledge their loyalty to the regime in Vienna. The first steps for the Poles' success in their quest for autonomy were visible in Gołuchowski's provisions in the October Diploma (1860) for granting separate legal and administrative institutions to Galicia. Although modified in the February Patent (1861), the fight was far from over, and as a result of the *Ausgleich,* Galicia gradually gained virtual autonomy. A local elective legislature and provincial executive with limited competency, as well as provisions for the use of Polish as the administrative and legal language, the creation of a Ministry for Galician Affairs in the imperial government, and a separate school board were proof by 1873 of the political strength of the Podolacy.

For the next forty years, the Podolacy gave general unswerving support to the imperial government in Vienna while simultaneously maintaining political (as well as economic and social) control in Galicia. Much of this success was due to the peculiar electoral system of voting by *curias* (groups of voters organized by social or income status), which allowed a small number of landowners to exert political control in the provincial sejm (diet), and by the preponderance of the Podolacy in the Polish Circle in the Austrian Reichsrat (parliament), where they served as a counterweight to other national groups and/or liberals in their support of imperial policies.

By the 1890s, in the face of economic, social, and political changes arising from the growth of industrialization, the influence of the Podolacy began to wane. By 1902, Roman Dmowski's (1864–1939) National League, in trying to establish a political base throughout partitioned Poland, was able to gain some support from the Podolacy because of its heavy emphasis on Polish nationalism. A few years later, the National Democrats' anti-Ukrainian views also struck sympathetic chords among the Podolacy. However, in imperial elections in 1911 the Podolacy and their allies, campaigning on an essentially anti-Ukrainian and anti-Jewish platform, were defeated even in their former stronghold of eastern Galicia, effectively ending their four-decade political influence.

Robert A. Berry

Further reading

Kieniewicz, Stefan. *Historia Polski 1795–1918.* Warsaw, 1969.

Wandycz, Piotr. *The Lands of Partitioned Poland, 1795–1918.* Seattle, Washington, 1974.

See also *Ausgleich;* Curial System; Roman Dmowski; February Patent; Galicia; Agenor Gołuchowski; October Diploma; Sejm

Pogány, József (1886–1938)

Hungarian Communist. Born into a lower-middle-class Jewish family, Pogány pursued a career as a journalist. He was active in the Social Democratic Party but in 1919 joined the Communists and held several key political and military offices during Hungary's short-lived Soviet republic that followed in the wake of Austria-Hungary's defeat in World War I. Because he had written a play about Napoléon Bonaparte (1769–1821), Pogány became known as the Red Napoléon. He fled Hungary when the government of Béla Kun (1886–1938) collapsed and traveled to Moscow to offer his services to the world Communist movement.

After several missions on behalf of the Comintern (Communist International), Pogány was dispatched in 1922 to the United States to help organize the Hungarian Communists in New York. He quickly acclimated himself to American society and, because of his forceful personality and prestige as a veteran European Communist, he soon became a dominant figure in the American Communist Party. Using the pseudonym "John Pepper," he played a key role in formulating strategy and applying Marxist principles to problems

in the United States. During the 1920s, he published more than a dozen pamphlets and short books, some of which remain classics of the genre.

Pogány/Pepper had a flair for intrigue and opportunism that enabled him to survive the factionalism endemic in both the Hungarian and American Communist parties. But over the years he accumulated too many enemies; in 1929 he was censured by the Comintern and demoted to a minor position in a Soviet planning office. He was arrested and executed in 1938, one of the many foreign Communists who fell victim to the purges initiated by Stalin (1879–1953).

Thomas Sakmyster

Further reading

Sylvers, Malcom. "Pogány/Pepper: Un représentant du Komintern auprès du parti communiste des États-Unis," *Cahiers d'Histoire de l'Institut de Recherches Marxistes* 28 (1987): 119–31.

Varga, Lajos, ed. *Pogány József válgatott írásai.* Budapest, 1987.

See also Comintern; Hungarian Communist Party; Hungarian Soviet Republic; Béla Kun; Stalin

Pogrom

In Russian, Polish, and some other Slavic languages, a term meaning devastation, massacre, or violent action against a group of people who form a religious, racial, or national minority. Since the 1880s, the term "pogrom" is usually applied to attacks on Jews and, since 1905, it has been used in English. In modern history, pogroms also took place in Germany, Austria, the Balkans, Africa, and Asia, but those in Russia were the most numerous and savage. The first wave of pogroms followed the assassination of Alexander II (1818–81) in March 1881 and lasted until the summer of 1882, although isolated attacks continued to take place in 1883 and 1884. Provoked by rumors that Jews killed the tsar and perpetrated by the proletariat and peasants, pogroms were used by the authorities to relieve political tension. Concentrated in the Ukraine and limited mostly to looting and beating, pogroms fostered mass Jewish emigration and the birth of national and Zionist movements. During the second wave of pogroms, 1903–6, Russian authorities and reactionary societies known as the Black Hundreds used the attacks to transform the workers' movement and the 1905 revolution into an anti-Jewish campaign. About 800 Jews were killed in about 680 pogroms, mostly in the Pale of Settlement, a territory created by Catherine the Great (1729–96) after the partitions of Poland to solve "the Jewish problem in Russia." The Jews built self-defense organizations, became more politically active, and emigrated in greater numbers. The third wave started with World War I. Russian and Austrian armies persecuted and robbed the Jews of eastern Poland and Galicia. During 1917–21, about 60,000 Jews were killed in 887 major and 349 minor pogroms mostly in Ukraine by soldiers of the disintegrating tsarist army, the Red Army, Ukrainian army, White Russian armies, and peasant bands. During one of the largest pogroms in Proskurov on February 15, 1919, about 1,700 Jews were killed during a few hours. In 1918–19 eight pogroms took place in the territories controlled by Polish armies. About 100 Jews lost their lives. During the interwar period, several small outbreaks occurred in East Central Europe, where large pogroms recurred during World War II, especially in the Ukraine and Romania. After the war, several pogroms took place in Poland, Czechoslovakia, and Hungary.

Piotr Wróbel

Further reading

Encyclopedia Judaica, vol. 13. Jerusalem, 1971, 694–701.

Klier, John D. and Shlomo Lambroza. *Pogroms: Anti-Jewish Violence in Modern Russian History.* Cambridge, 1992.

Morgenthau, Henry. *All in a Life-Time.* Garden City, New York, 1923.

See also Alexander II; Emigration; Ethnic Minorities; Jews; Pale of Settlement

Poland (Geography)

The compact territory of 120,727 square miles (312,683 sq km) located in Central Europe on the watersheds of the Vistula (Wisła) and the Oder (Odra) Rivers. Poland's southern borders (778 miles [1,252 km]) rest on the arch of the Carpathian and the Sudeten Mountains; the northern border runs for 308.8 miles (497 km) along the Baltic Sea; the western boundary with Germany (283.2 miles [455.8 km]) runs along the Neisse (Nysa Łużycka) and the Oder Rivers; the eastern boundaries (820 miles [1,319 km]) with Ukraine, Belarus, and Russia, partially along the Bug River, enclose almost the entire basin of the Vistula River and, essentially, the Polish ethnic territory.

The relief of Poland, molded by continental glaciers, is arranged zonally. A narrow belt of littoral lowlands borders the Pomeranian and Mazurian lakelands, where the hills of terminal moraines reach over 1,000 feet (300 m). The adjoining Polish Great Lowlands—the western Wielkopolska-Kujavy and the eastern Mazowsze-Podlasie—are formed of ever older obliterated morainic remnants. The low uplands alternate with broad fluvioglacial valleys and sandy and gravel depositions left by the waters of the melting glaciers.

The southeastern uplands—the Małopolska Plateau (Polonia Minor)—an important historical region between the Vistula and Pilitsa Rivers and the sharp escarpment, the Cracovian Jura, have a pronounced relief and higher elevations; the western Kraków-Częstochowa and the eastern Kielce-Sandomierz uplands average 1,300–1,500 feet (396–457 m), and the old Paleozoic Holy Cross Mountains rise over 2,000 feet (600 m).

West of the Cracovian Jura extends the small but economically important Silesian Upland, underlain by carboniferous formations. It gradually lowers westward toward the Lower Silesian Lowland situated between the Trzebnica Hills (840 feet [256 m]) and the Sudeten Piedmont, the strongly peneplainized remnants of the outer ridges of the Sudeten Mountains, where the monadnocks reach over 2,300 feet (700 m).

The outer western zone is occupied by the Sudeten Mountains, with a mature rolling landscape and altitudes over 3,500 feet (1,080 m). The Moravian Gate separates it from the young folded Alpine arch of the Carpathians known in Poland as the Beskids. Erosion since the Tertiary era created sharp mountain edges that strongly contrast with the adjacent plains of the Carpathian Piedmont. The higher part of the Beskids is in the west. Here, also thrusting somewhat southward, is the small area of the highest Beskids ranges, the Tatra Mountains.

The Beskids ranges gradually lower to the Carpathian Piedmont, which adjoins the zone of subcarpathian depressions. The largest is the triangular Sandomierz Lowland between the Vistula and San Rivers. The Lublin plateau, located between the Vistula and Bug Rivers, has higher elevations in its southern portion, called Roztocze, but in the north it gradually merges with the Podlasie Lowland.

Poland has a transitional climate from humid continental with warm summers in the east, to marine west coast with slightly cooler summers in the west. Summer temperatures (62–65° F [16.5–18.5° C]) change from north to south, but those of winter (27.5–30° F [minus 4.5–minus 1° C]) from east to west, indicating the influence of the Atlantic. Precipitation, 19.5–47 inches (50–120 cm) from plains to mountains, respectively, has a summer maximum. In most cases it is adequate for agricultural purposes. The snow cover lasts from fewer than 50 days in the Silesian Lowland to over 90 days in the northeast and up to 150–200 days in the mountains. The growing season lasts 225 days in the Silesian Lowland but only 160 days in the Mazurian Lakeland.

The main Polish rivers—the Vistula (678 miles [1,092 km]) and the Oder (441 miles [715 km])—have one-sidedly developed watersheds. The length of usable waterways is 4,290 miles (6,907 km), of which 3,000 miles (4,800 km), or 67 percent of them, are navigable, mostly by barge. Poland has 9,000 small lakes, the majority of which are of postglacial origin. The largest, Śniardwy in the Mazurian Lakeland, covers 22.75 square miles (63 sq km).

Soils, predominantly podzolic or weakly podzolized in the plains and lake regions, are interspersed with bog, heavy loam, and sandy patches. The Lower Silesia, the Malopolska, the Lublin plateau and the Carpathian, and the Sudeten Piedmonts have also loess and rendzina soils. With good husbandry, Polish soils can provide acceptable crops. Soil erosion is not a problem. Forest, mostly mixed, occupies 22 percent of Polish territory. The largest complexes are in the west.

Poland has a variety of mineral resources, but in uneven quantities. The Silesian reserves of coal are estimated at 70 billion tons and Poland mines over 225 million metric tons annually. There are also large reserves of lignite and brown coal. Lately discovered and old sources of natural gas produce about 5.2 billion cubic meters annually (55–56 percent of consumption). Reserves of sulfur, zinc, and copper are sufficient, but iron ore has a low metal content and its supply may last for a decade only; therefore large imports are required to supply the Polish steel industry.

The population of Poland, 38.4 million (1990), evolved from pre–World War II multi-ethnic to homogeneous, following demographic upheavals during and immediately after the war. The loss of eastern territories, the extermination of Poland's Jewish population (estimated 3.35 million in 1939), war losses, forcible transfers, and migrations reduced the share of minorities from at least 34 percent in 1931 to about 1 percent recently. The high natural increase in the population of postwar years (18 per thousand in 1957) resulted in a young population: 25 percent is under the age of 15 and only 10 percent is over 65 years. Recently, the natural increase dropped because of sharply decreased birth and increased death rates. Life expectancy is 67 years for males and 76 for females, and there is still a considerable imbalance between males and females as a result of war losses among the male population.

The urban population constitutes 60 percent (as compared with 27.2 percent in 1931) of the total population. Since the normalization of postwar population movements, Poland has a negative migration balance: immigration of 334,900 and emigration of 1,093,600 persons in 1957–1990. It indicates a considerable drain on Polish human resources.

Abraham Melezin

Further reading

Główny Urzad Statystyczny. *Mały Rocznik Statystyczny.* Warsaw, 1939–88.

Lencewicz, Stanisław and Kondracki Jerzy. *Geografia Fizyczna Polski.* Warsaw, 1964.

Population Reference Bureau. *1992 World Population Sheet.* Washington D.C., 1992.

SOPEMI. *Trends in International Migration,* Paris, 1992, 106.

See also Białystok; Bug River; Chelm; Curzon Line; Emigration; Environment; Galicia; Gdańsk; Katowice; Kraków; Łódź; Lublin; L'vov; Neisse River; Oder River; Pomerania; Poznań; Silesia; Vilnius; Vistula River; Warsaw; Wielkopolska

Poland (History)

Poland to 1815

In many textbooks on modern European history, Poland first appears at the time of the partitions (1772–95), though in the period 1410–1648 Poland was the leading power in East Central Europe. It had a well-developed parliamentary system, participated in the Renaissance, and was an exemplar of religious toleration in the period of Europe's religious wars (1500s–1600s). Poland's decline is explained generally in terms of "anarchy," often attributed to the "selfishness" of its nobles, as exemplified by the *Liberum Veto,* whereby one deputy's opposition to a piece of legislation could dissolve the Sejm (parliament). At the same time, the military power of its neighbors—Prussia, Russia, and Austria—and their predatory designs on Poland are generally allotted secondary importance.

Monarchical power eroded in Poland as magnate power grew, especially after 1648, when crown and country were bankrupted by constant wars. The Swedish War of 1655–60, accompanied by famine and plague, ruined the towns and killed at least one-third of the population. After the reign of John III, Sobieski (1629–96), who saved Vienna from the Turks in 1683, came the "Saxon Kings," Augustus II (1670–1733) and Augustus III (1697–1763). Elected with Russian and Austrian money, they did nothing to strengthen Poland. On the contrary, after the Great Northern War (1700–1721), the country became, in effect, a Russian protectorate.

Catherine the Great of Russia (1729–96) decided to partition Poland with Austria and Prussia. After the first partition of 1772, a group of educated, enlightened Poles banded together under the leadership of Stanisław Augustus Poniatowski (1732–98), the last king of Poland to reform education and government. They drew up an enlightened constitution, ratified by the Sejm on May 3, 1791. It was the second written constitution in the world and the first in Europe. Fearing that a rejuvenated Poland would try to regain its lands, Russia and Prussia partitioned the country again in 1793. Thaddeus Kościuszko (1746–1817), a hero of the American Revolution, raised the standard of revolt in the spring of 1794 and appealed to the peasants for support. He could not, however, defeat Russia and Prussia who (along with Austria) partitioned Poland for the third time in 1795. The final partition was signed in St. Petersburg in January 1797; the three powers agreed that the name of Poland should never be mentioned again.

In that same year, however, Polish legions were formed in Lombardy (Italy) by Napoléon (1769–1821). Led by General Jan Henryk Dąbrowski (1755–1818), they began their marching song with the words "Poland has not yet perished as long as we're alive"; this song later became the Polish national anthem. Poles went on to fight in Napoléon's armies throughout Europe and as far away as Haiti–Santo Domingo. They formed about a quarter of the Grande Armée, which invaded Russia in 1812. Meanwhile, Napoléon created the Grand Duchy of Warsaw (1807), which expanded with Polish victories to include Galicia (Austrian Poland, 1809). Although the Grand Duchy was a French protectorate, it was, in fact, a small Polish state.

1815–64

At the Congress of Vienna (1815), the Polish question almost led to war between the victors. Alexander I of Russia (1777–1825), advised by Prince Adam Jerzy Czartoryski (1770–1861), his erstwhile friend and former foreign minister, proposed the union of all former Polish territories in a kingdom under the Russian crown. Prussia and Austria, however, refused to give up their Polish lands, while England's foreign secretary, Robert Stewart, Viscount Castlereagh (1769–1822), made secret treaties with France and Austria to thwart Alexander's plan. Thus, the final outcome of the Congress of Vienna was Congress Poland, also known as Russian Poland, while Austria and Prussia retained the two other parts of the country. The congress also created the Republic of Kraków, which was, in fact, an independent city-state.

In Prussian Poland—named the Grand Duchy of Posen (Polish, Poznań)—Polish institutions were generally respected, but in Austrian Galicia, Poles faced repression and Germanization. In Congress Poland, whose sovereign was Alexander I, king of Poland and emperor of Russia, the Poles had a constitution with a two-chamber legislature and their own administration, army, and educational system. The viceroy, General Józef Zajączek (1752–1826), a veteran of the Kościuszko uprising of 1794 and the Napoleonic Wars, obeyed the directives of the commander in chief of the Polish army, Grand Duke Constantine (1779–1831), a brother of Alexander I and Nicholas I. Although the kingdom achieved significant economic development, especially the textile industry, the political system depended on the tsar. As Alexander became more conservative, repression grew, especially censorship and the secret police. This led to secret societies among both students and military cadets. The situation worsened still further in December 1825 when Alexander died and was succeeded by his brother, Nicholas I (1796–1855).

In 1830 revolutions swept through Europe. In Warsaw, military cadets conspired against their

P brutal commander, Grand Duke Constantine. The conspirators' fear of discovery and the tsar's announced plan to march on Belgium to help repress a revolt there combined to produce a cadet revolt in Warsaw on November 29, 1830. After Constantine fled, a new government emerged, led by Czartoryski, who tried to negotiate with Nicholas. The tsar's insistence on unconditional surrender radicalized the insurgents and led to his official dethronement by the revolutionaries in Warsaw on January 25, 1831.

The small Polish army gained a few victories over the Russians but could not defeat a large, well-armed Russian army, which outnumbered it by ten to one. No aid came from France and Britain, even though they had helped the Greeks win independence from the Turks in 1829. Nevertheless, the 1830–31 Polish revolt against Russia strengthened Polish national consciousness. Most Poles judged the defeat as due more to military and political mistakes than to Russian military might, believing that if the insurrectionary leadership had abolished serfdom, this would have produced the mass army needed to defeat the Russians. (However, the Poles had no arms factories to produce weapons.)

Russian repression was brutal. Besides executions, thousands of gentry families were deported to Siberia from eastern Poland and replaced by Russians. The former kingdom was placed in the hands of Field Marshal Ivan Fyodorevich Pashkevich (1782–1856), who sacked Warsaw's eastern suburb of Praga and massacred its inhabitants, including many Jews. He ruled Russian Poland as viceroy until his death.

In Prussian Poland, the office of viceroy (Statthalter) was abolished and the Polish gentry lost the right of electing the province captains (Landräte). German became the official language, and the new governor (Oberpräsident) of Poznania, Edward Flottwell (1786–1865), followed a policy of assimilating the region to Prussia.

From 1831 to 1864, Polish political thought and thus the struggle for independence were represented by the Great Emigration (the elite who fled after the November Uprising of 1830 failed), most of whose members lived in France. The two main political groups were the Conservatives, led by Czartoryski, and the Polish Democratic Society. Czartoryski, who resided in the Hôtel Lambert on the Ile St. Louis in Paris, sought to regain Polish independence with the support of France and

Britain. He expected them to become involved in a war with Russia, since both opposed Russian expansion into the Balkans at the expense of the Ottoman Empire. Finally, Czartoryski and his followers supported moderate agrarian reform through gradual commutation of peasant labor dues into money rents.

The Polish Democratic Society, on the other hand, consisted mainly of former officers. Their ideologue was historian Joachim Lelewel (1798–1855), who blamed the Polish nobles for destroying what he called ancient, Polish democracy, thus causing the demise of Poland. The Democrats planned to regain Polish independence through a "War of the Peoples" that would abolish European monarchies, including the partitioners of Poland. Some also advocated the abolition of serfdom without compensation. In their Poitiers Manifesto (1839), they called for a War of the Peoples and favored changing labor dues to money payments. In 1840 they established a tightly organized leadership at Versailles, known as the Centralization (*Centralizacja*), to direct all revolutionary activities in Poland.

Paris also became the center of Polish artistic life. The three great Polish romantic poets lived there: Adam Mickiewicz (1798–1855), Zygmunt Krasiński (1812–59), and Juliusz Słowacki (1809–49). In addition, Polish romantic composer and pianist Frédéric Chopin (1810–49) lived in France after 1830 and died in Paris.

The Democrats inspired and tried to lead uprisings in Poland. In 1846, when hunger and unrest swept across Europe, members of the Polish Democratic Society in Prussian Poland plotted a national revolt. They were denounced, arrested, and imprisoned in Berlin, but their trial publicized their cause. In Galicia, insurgent leaders proclaimed an uprising and the abolition of serfdom on February 18, 1846. The Austrian authorities, however, told the peasants that their lords opposed the "good" emperor's desire to free them and offered rewards for captured or dead nobles. What ensued was the "Galician slaughter" of nobles by peasants. In the Republic of Kraków, where peasants were more prosperous and enlightened, democratic nobles led by philosopher Edward Dembowski (1822–46) and his cousin, also a philosopher, Henryk Kamieński (1814–65), succeeded in winning their support. But they were soon defeated by Austrian troops.

In 1848 revolution again swept through

Europe, beginning with the February revolution in Paris. The Poles organized a National Committee in Poznań, which raised a small army, as well as national councils and national guards in Kraków and Lwów (Ukrainian, L'viv; German, Lemberg; Russian, L'vov). In Lwów, twelve thousand signed a petition to the emperor on March 19, demanding guarantees for Polish national rights and the abolition of serfdom. The two national councils also appealed to Polish nobles to give up serfdom voluntarily on Easter Sunday. A Polish delegation went to Vienna in early April to present these demands to the emperor; they also demanded autonomy for Galicia.

The Austrian government in Vienna tottered, but its governor in Galicia proclaimed that peasant emancipation would take place on Easter Saturday, a day earlier than planned by Polish revolutionaries. Thus, he undercut the Polish national movement, and the peasants of Galicia were free several months earlier than in the rest of the Austrian Empire. The Austrian government however soon reestablished its hold over Galicia. It also defeated Italian rebels—helped by Polish émigrés including Mickiewicz—and the Hungarians, whose armies were led at times by two Polish generals, Henryk Dembiński (1791–1850) and Józef Bem (1794–1850).

In Prussian Poland, the Prussian government feared Russian intervention against the new "democratic" government in Berlin, so it tolerated the Polish National Committee, which demanded autonomy in the Grand Duchy. When Russia did not move, however, the Prussian government offered autonomy only for a small part of the duchy. The small Polish army, led by Ludwik Mierosławski (1814–78) and supported by some peasants, briefly fought the Prussians, but the uprising collapsed on May 9, 1848.

The Revolutions of 1848 marked a turning point in the development of Polish national consciousness, just as of other peoples of Eastern Europe. The Galician Poles and Ukrainians clashed over Galicia at the Slavic Congress in Prague, which discussed how to transform the Habsburg Empire into a federation of nations. At this time, Poles and Czechs also clashed over the Duchy of Teschen (Polish, Cieszyn; Czech, Těšín), claimed by the former on ethnic and the latter on historical grounds. Andrzej Cinciała (1825–91), Jerzy Cienciała (1834–1913), and Paweł Stalmach (1824–91) worked to develop Polish national con-

sciousness in this region. The same development took place in Upper Silesia. Here, most of the population east of the Oder River was Polish-speaking and Catholic, forming the lower class of peasants and workers. The impetus to national consciousness came with the restoration of Polish as the language of religious education in the schools in 1848, because German Catholic bishops expected this to produce good Polish Catholics, while Prussian officials expected loyal Prussian citizens. Polish educator Józef Lompa (1797–1863) and later political leader Wojciech Korfanty (1873–1939) worked successfully to strengthen Polish national consciousness in the region, a process greatly aided by industrialization, which added the class-economic factor to the existing religious and linguistic divisions between Poles and Germans.

The Crimean War (1853–56) seemed to offer another chance to regain Polish freedom. Mickiewicz went to Istanbul to organize a Polish-Jewish legion but died there, presumably of infection. Polish cavalry units, paid by Queen Victoria of Great Britain (1819–1901), served in the Ottoman army. Unfortunately for the Poles, although France and Britain defeated Russia, they accepted the promises of Alexander II (1818–81) to treat the Poles well.

Alexander II did, indeed, liberalize Russian policy toward Poland. He released many Polish exiles from Siberia and, in 1856 he also allowed the establishment of a Medical Academy and a School of Fine Arts in Warsaw. This drew Polish students from Russian universities, many of them inspired by national-revolutionary ideas. In Russian Poland, Count Andrzej Zamoyski (1800–1874), president of the Agricultural Association—which became a surrogate parliament—seemed a natural leader of nationalist sentiment. He was a moderate but always feared being judged as pro-Russian; he therefore demanded the restoration of Poland's old eastern territories. This popular demand in Poland could not be granted by a Russian tsar.

Liberalization, the influx of students from Russia, and the unification of a large part of Italy with the help of Napoléon III of France (1808–73), all combined to produce high expectations in Russian Poland. Patriotic demonstrations took place in Warsaw and Vilna (Polish, Wilno; Lithuanian, Vilnius). After Russian troops fired on a Warsaw crowd, killing five people in late February 1861, Marquess Aleksander Wielopolski

P (1803–77) emerged as the key figure with a program of obtaining limited concessions from Russia. Once Alexander II had approved his limited reform program, however, Wielopolski alienated Polish opinion by dissolving the popular Agricultural Association and the Warsaw National Guard—which included both Poles and Jews. When this was followed by the killing of one hundred demonstrators by Russian troops on April 8, 1862, he was blamed, even though he had tried to stop the shooting at the risk of his own life. He became even more hated when, in the summer of that year, he ordered the execution of three young Polish workmen who tried to assassinate liberal Grand Duke Constantine Nikolaevich (1827–92), the younger brother of Alexander II, who had been appointed viceroy in Russian Poland (1862–64).

The uprising of 1863—led by the radicals, or "Reds"—was sparked by Wielopolski's use of select conscription into the Russian army to eliminate revolutionary leaders all over Russian Poland. This led to the Red National Committee's decision to begin the revolt on January 22, 1863. Its manifesto declared that all citizens were free, regardless of religion or national descent. All peasants were declared owners of the land they worked, and landless peasants who joined the revolt were promised land. Landlords were to be indemnified from state funds. Separate manifestos were issued appealing to Ruthenians (Ukrainians), Belorussians, and Jews to join the Poles.

The insurrection—really a guerrilla war that included fighting in the old eastern provinces, especially Lithuania—lasted until May 1864. Again, no help came from the West, though Napoléon III had hinted at possible aid. Once again, Poles had taken up arms to fight for independence, and once again, they had failed, even though more Polish peasants had participated in the fighting than ever before. Women from gentry families also played their part. As in 1830–31, one or two exceptional women took part in the fighting, but the vast majority who participated acted as couriers and/or nursed the wounded. Russian repressions were severe, particularly in the old eastern provinces, whence some fifty thousand Polish gentry families were deported to Siberia and their land given to Russians. A policy of comprehensive Russification was implemented in Russian Poland, now called "The Vistula Land." Russian liberals, alienated by the uprising, supported these repressive measures.

1864–1914

The years from 1864 to 1890 are known as the era of Polish positivism. Its best-known exponents were historian, journalist, and literary critic Aleksander Świętochowski (1849–1938) and novelists Eliza Orzeszkowa (1841–1910) and Bolesław Prus (pen name of Aleksander Głowacki, 1847–1912). They propagandized the idea of "organic work," that is, economic development and education, as well as the emancipation of women and Jews. At the same time, a conservative movement in Galicia was led by the Kraków School of historians, the most famous of whom was Michał Bobrzyński (1849–1935). They attributed the decline and fall of old Poland to the lack of strong central power—in their eyes, an original sin—and condemned the insurrections far more strongly than the Warsaw positivists. Both groups gradually embraced the doctrine of "triple loyalism"—loyalty to each partitioning power, postponing independence to the dim and distant future.

The decades before World War I witnessed varying degrees of economic development in the three parts of Poland, as well as a struggle to preserve Polish national identity in Russian and Prussian Poland. The textile industry of Russian Poland grew significantly, spurred by an expanding Russian market, until tariff barriers arose to protect domestic Russian textiles. The iron and steel industry also expanded. The value of industrial production grew almost tenfold between 1864 and 1892, and the number of industrial workers almost doubled from 80,000 to 150,000, 90 percent of whom worked in the textile industry. At the same time, however, the number of landless peasants increased fourfold between 1870 and 1891, and the birthrate grew by 100 percent from 1850 to 1900. Since industry could not absorb these people, there was a massive emigration, mostly to the United States. An estimated four million people emigrated from all Polish lands to the United States between 1885 and 1914 alone.

Between 1864 and 1914, the Jewish population grew to form about 14 percent of the total population of Polish lands, though it was much larger in the cities of Russian and Austrian Poland. By 1900, Jews made up about 33 percent of the population of Warsaw, while forming 80 percent and more in the small market towns of East Galicia (western Ukraine), Volhynia, Belorussia, and Lithuania. The period also witnessed the growth of anti-Semitism. While this appeared all over Europe, it was relatively new in Poland. Here, it was based less on religious grounds than on economic competition between the Jews and a rising Polish middle class.

In Prussian and Russian Poland, Poles faced forcible Germanization and Russification. In 1871 German Chancellor Otto von Bismarck (1815–98), began a policy of intensive Germanization in Prussian Poland. In the schools, German lay teachers replaced Poles, and Polish Catholic clergy were banned from their parishes because the Vatican refused to comply with German educational regulations. Furthermore, German settlers were brought in to strengthen the German element vis-à-vis the Polish majority. Thus, the Poles had to fight for their language, their priests, and their land, which united them in the face of the enemy. This union led to successful Polish resistance to German colonization and German legal obstructions to Polish farmers' use of their land. Finally, Polish children won sympathy in the West by their 1904–7 protest strikes against the use of German to teach religion in the schools.

In Russian Poland after 1864—as in former eastern Poland annexed to Russia after 1831—no Polish schools were allowed. At the same time, boys had to attend Russian high schools to escape conscription into the Russian army. Women in Polish noble/gentry and middle-class families fought to preserve Polish identity by teaching their children the language, literature, and history of the country. In so doing, they risked prison or severe financial penalties. Future Polish soldier and statesman Józef Piłsudski (1867–1935), born into a Polish gentry family in Lithuania, often recalled how he had learned Polish history, literature, and patriotism at his mother's knee. The positivists encouraged educated young people to teach peasant children how to read and write in Polish, and also to give them a general knowledge of Polish history and literature. Maria Skłodowska-Curie (1867–1934), later the codiscoverer of radium with her husband, Pierre Curie (1859–1906), did this kind of voluntary teaching when she worked as a governess in a gentry family, before leaving to study in Paris. Women studied in flying universities, secret university seminars; some also played an active role in the Polish Socialist Party, mainly as couriers carrying illegal literature—and sometimes even ammunition—hung from the belt under their voluminous skirts.

Austrian Poland (Galicia) obtained home rule in 1868 as a reward for the Polish nobles' declaration of loyalty to Emperor Franz Joseph (1830–1916) after Austria's defeat by Prussia in 1866. At this time, the emperor made his peace with the Hungarian nobles by creating the Dual Monarchy (Austria-Hungary) and granting extensive self-government to the Poles in Galicia. Between 1868 and 1914, Galicia served as the center of Polish culture and political thought. Education was in Polish, though the curriculum was established in Vienna. Polish schools grew in number, and peasant literacy increased. The Jagiellonian University in Kraków and the University of Lwów were Polonized, and the Polish Academy of Sciences (Polska Akademia Umiejętności, PAU) was established in Kraków in 1873. The provincial Sejm, dominated by Polish nobles, sat in Lwów. Polish deputies sat in the Austrian parliament in Vienna, and Poles were prominent in the imperial government.

Galicia was not, however, a homogenous Polish province, for east of the river San the majority of the population was Ukrainian. Most were peasants and belonged to the Uniate or Ukrainian Catholic Church, an Eastern, Slavonic rite church attached to Rome, while most of the Poles were landlords or officials and were Roman Catholic, that is, of the Western (Latin) rite. In these circumstances, Ukrainian national consciousness was strongly anti-Polish—as was Lithuanian national consciousness, although most Lithuanians were Roman Catholic. Unlike the Lithuanians and the Ukrainians under Russian rule, however, the Ukrainians of East Galicia were encouraged by the Austrian government to develop their language and culture. The Ukrainian intelligentsia dreamed of a Ukrainian crownland in Austria as the first step to an independent Ukraine encompassing both Russian Ukraine and a large part of Galicia—a program opposed by the Poles. Poverty led to a wave of emigration from Galicia, just as it did from Polish lands under Russian rule.

Jews in Galicia more than doubled their numbers in the period from 1857 to 1890, where they accounted for 50–75 percent of the urban population. They also owned 16.2 percent of the land. After the emancipation of the Jews in the Austrian Empire in 1867, many educated Galician Jews opted for a Polish national identity—along with conversion to Roman Catholicism. Most of the Jewish population, however, was Orthodox and

P lived in Jewish villages (shtetls), and in Jewish urban districts, rejecting assimilation. Many Jews emigrated to Germany and Austria-Hungary, but most Jewish emigrants sought a new life in the United States.

This period also witnessed the development of political parties and the spread of national consciousness among workers and peasants. The political parties or movements that developed at this time were to be active in Polish political life, both in independent Poland and in World War II, and some survived the Communist era to reemerge in new parties after 1989.

By the late 1880s, a new generation had matured in Russian Poland. Some young people listened to an older, adamant fighter for freedom, Zygmunt "T.T. Jeż" Miłkowski (1824–1915), who established the "Polish League" in Switzerland in 1887. Its goal was an independent, democratic, federal Poland, and Miłkowski created a "national treasury" for this purpose. He established contact with Zygmunt Balicki (1858–1916), originally a Socialist, who went on to organize a secret Polish student society known as Zet. The league movement was soon taken over by a young, politically minded science student at the Russian University of Warsaw, Roman Dmowski (1864–1939), who established the National Democratic movement and set himself the goal of developing a modern, ruthless, and exclusively Polish national consciousness. He aimed to establish an ethnically homogeneous Poland, with the assimilation of other nationalities—except for the Jews, whom he judged as unassimilable, loyal to the partitioning powers, and an obstacle to the development of a Polish middle class. On May 3, 1891, the centenary of the May constitution of 1791, National Democratic students staged the first public demonstration in Warsaw since 1864. They expressed the feelings of a large part of the young generation, not only those in the National Democratic movement.

Peasant parties also began to form in the 1890s. The Peasant Party Union of Galicia, founded in 1893, was soon dwarfed by the Polish Populist Party, founded in 1894. The most famous peasant politician, Wincenty Witos (1874–1945), became the leader of the right-wing peasant party, Piast, in 1913, and also dreamed of an independent Poland. Witos was a deputy to the Galician Sejm in 1900–1914, to the Austrian Reichstag (parliament) in Vienna in 1911–18, and to the Polish Sejm in 1919–30. The peasant parties, however, did not play as great a role in Polish politics as did the National Democratic and Polish Socialist Parties.

A tiny socialist movement began in Russian Poland in the early 1880s. Ludwik Waryński (1856–89), who had absorbed socialist ideas at Russian universities, founded the first Polish socialist party, Proletariat, in Warsaw in 1882. He and his followers put socialism above independence. They were arrested in September 1883 and condemned to sixteen years of hard labor. Although Waryński died six years later in prison in St. Petersburg, Proletariat ideas were taken up by Rosa Luxemburg (1871–1918), who came from an assimilated Jewish family in Russian Poland. She condemned nationalism as a "bourgeois" idea and also claimed that an independent Poland could not survive because it would lose its Russian markets. Though better known for her activity in the German Social Democratic Party, in 1893 she was also a cofounder of the Social Democratic Party of the Kingdom of Poland, renamed in 1900 the Social Democracy of the Kingdom of Poland and Lithuania (Socjaldemokracja Królestwa Polskiego i Litwy, SDKPiL). Feliks Dzierżyński (1877–1926)—generally known as the first head of the Cheka, the Soviet secret police, established in December 1917—became its key leader in 1899. The SDKPiL was always a small party, except for the revolutionary period of 1905–7, and declined after 1907 because of its opposition to Polish independence. On December 18, 1918, it united with the left wing of the Polish Socialist Party to form the Communist Workers Party of Poland (Komunistyczna Partia Robotnicza Polski, KPRP), renamed the Communist Party of Poland (Komunistyczna Partia Polski, KPP) in 1925. This party also had few members because it opposed independent Poland as a "bourgeois-capitalist state."

The strongest socialist party in Poland was the Polish Socialist Party (PPS), founded in Paris in 1892 with the goal of an independent, socialist Poland. Józef Piłsudski soon emerged as its key leader. Raised by a patriotic mother, Piłsudski attended a Russian high school in Vilna, then a preponderantly Polish-speaking city with a large Jewish community. He was arrested in 1887 with his older brother, who was betrayed by a member of his conspiratorial, Russian, student group, which tried to assassinate Alexander III (1845–94). Piłsudski spent five years in Siberia, where he met other Polish exiles and Russian revolutionaries, read a great deal, and became a Socialist. He came to believe that Poland must be both independent and socialist and viewed Russia as Poland's principal enemy.

After joining the PPS, Piłsudski wrote, edited, and printed a paper called *Robotnik* (*The Worker*). Arrested with his wife in 1900, he was imprisoned in the Warsaw citadel, where he feigned madness. Transferred to a mental hospital in St. Petersburg, he escaped with the help of a Polish doctor and settled in Kraków, making forays into Russian Poland. With the outbreak of the Russo-Japanese War (1904–5), he traveled to Japan via Western Europe and the United States, arriving in Tokyo in July 1904. He tried but failed to persuade the Japanese government to form a Polish legion out of Polish prisoners of war and, more important, to finance a Polish uprising that would force the Russian army to divert troops from the Far East to Russian Poland. In Tokyo, he met Dmowski, whose goal ironically was to persuade the Japanese not to support a Polish uprising against Russia. Ultimately, the Japanese gave Piłsudski only some financial help for the military training of Polish students studying at European universities.

The decisive break between Piłsudski and Dmowski came during the Russian Revolution of 1905, which sparked workers' revolts in Russian Poland. While the PPS fought Russian troops and police, Dmowski's National Democratic workers tried to prevent strikes and even battled PPS units. The split became even deeper after 1906, when Russia became a semiconstitutional monarchy with an elected legislature, the Duma. Given this development and the increasing polarization between the Triple Entente of Britain, France, and Russia on the one hand (1907), and the Triple Alliance—also known as the Central Powers—of Germany, Austria-Hungary, and Italy on the other, Dmowski decided that Poland's future lay with Russia. Like Czartoryski in the Napoleonic Wars, he believed that Polish cooperation with Russia, and the expected Entente victory over the Central Powers, would lead to the unification of all Polish lands under the Russian crown, then to autonomy, and finally to independence.

Not surprisingly, Piłsudski drew different conclusions from both the revolution and the international crises that followed. In 1906 he formed the "Revolutionary Fraction" in the PPS with the goal of fighting for Polish independence, while the PPS Left followed the "internationalist" line with

the goal of an international, socialist revolution—which drew it nearer to the SDKPiL. Piłsudski offered intelligence services to the Austro-Hungarian General Staff, in return for which Vienna allowed him to form riflemen's associations in Galicia. These provided military training to Polish students, whom Piłsudski viewed as the cadres of a future Polish army. In February 1914 he foresaw a world war in which the Central Powers would first defeat Russia and then be defeated by France, Britain, and the United States. This would lead to the rebirth of Poland.

World War I and the Rebirth of Poland

The outbreak of World War I in August 1914 found Poles divided physically among the three powers in whose armies they had to serve, and politically among three proposed solutions for a future Poland: Dmowski's project of uniting all Polish lands under the Russian crown; the Austro-Polish project of uniting Austrian Poland with Russian Poland in an Austrian crownland; and Piłsudski's project of building up a Polish armed force on the side of Austria and Germany against Russia. Of the three, Piłsudski at first seemed to have the least chance of success, for though he managed to organize a Polish legion in the Austrian army, he found little support at first in Russian Poland, where he had hoped to start an insurrection.

While secretly assuring the French and British governments that his soldiers would never fight against them, Piłsudski offered military cooperation to Germany and Austria in return for increasing Polish control of public life in Polish lands. He met with limited success. Even the Manifesto of the Two Emperors (Wilhelm II [1859–1941] of Germany and Franz Joseph of Austria-Hungary) of November 5, 1916, which put the Polish question on the international agenda, was disappointing. It promised a future self-governing Polish kingdom made up of former Russian territories, whose frontiers were to be decided later. The kingdom would be closely associated with the Central Powers and its army organized according to a common agreement. The goal of this manifesto was, of course, to gain the Polish manpower of Russian Poland for the German and Austrian armies. The Germans created a Polish Provisional State Council in Warsaw (Tymczasowa Rada Stanu) in December 1916, with departments of finance, political affairs, interior, education, and religion. Though the council had a purely advisory function, Piłsudski joined it as chairman of the Military Commission. The Germans, however, were disappointed with the small Polish military recruitment into the Polish army (Polnische Werhmacht). At the same time, the German High Command drew up secret plans for annexing a strip of Polish land bordering on Prussian Poland and expelling the population, and for making Russian Poland an agricultural colony. They also planned to award the cities of Wilno, Grodno, and Minsk to a satellite Lithuania.

The first Russian Revolution of March 1917 and the entry of the United States into the war in April 1917 both had a great impact on the Polish question. In fact, already on January 22, 1917, President Woodrow Wilson (1856–1924) declared that statesmen everywhere agreed there should be an independent Poland. Then there were declarations from the new Russia. The Petrograd Soviet issued an appeal to the Poles on March 28, 1917, recognizing their right to national self-determination and independence. On March 30, the Provisional Government declared itself in favor of an independent Polish state made up of all preponderantly Polish lands (that is, an ethnic Poland). However, it left frontier delimitation to the future Russian Constituent Assembly and spoke of a permanent alliance between the two countries.

Piłsudski now concluded that the Poles should no longer fight for the Central Powers. He refused to swear an oath of loyalty in arms to Germany and was followed in this by most of the First and Third Brigades of the Polish Legion, which were then dissolved. Piłsudski was arrested and interned in Germany, which made him a national hero. Also, his secret Polish Military Organization (Polska Organizacja Wojskowa) continued to develop underground in Poland.

Meanwhile, Dmowski and the National Democrats at first supported Russia. The August 1914 Manifesto of Grand Duke Nicholas Nikolaevich (1856–1929), the commander in chief of the Russian armies, had promised the Poles the union of their lands and free national development under the Russian crown, but this did not lead to any concrete agreements. Furthermore, the brutal treatment of Poles in East Galicia by the Russian military commander there in 1915–16 ended most Polish support for the Russian solution. In 1916 Dmowski moved his activities to the West. Immediately after the first Russian Revolution, he presented a memorandum to the British and American governments, proposing a large Poland, but found no encouragement. As for the French government, it signed a secret agreement with St. Petersburg just before the March revolution, giving it a free hand in establishing the postwar Polish-Russian border in return for a free hand in establishing the future Franco-German border.

In June 1917 French President Raymond Poincaré (1860–1934) authorized the creation of a Polish army in France, though at first subordinated to a Russian commander. In mid-August 1917 Dmowski established the Polish National Committee (Polski Komitet Narodowy) in Lausanne, Switzerland, and moved it to Paris a week later. Made up mostly of National Democrats, it was soon recognized by France as representing Poland, and was recognized as such by Britain, Italy, and the United States in late 1917. The Western powers did not, however, support the frontiers Dmowski proposed for a large Poland. They still hoped for a negotiated peace with Germany, or at least Austria-Hungary, and respected the interests of their Russian ally.

The situation began to change with the peace negotiations between the Central Powers and the new Bolshevik government of Lenin (1870–1924). During the negotiations in Brest-Litovsk (December 1917–March 1918), the Bolsheviks propagandized their goals of national self-determination and peace without annexations or reparations. They hoped to provoke working-class revolutions in Germany and Austria-Hungary and mutinies in their armies. Up to that time, the goal of keeping Bolshevik Russia in the war led British Prime Minister David Lloyd George (1863–1945) on January 5, 1918, to proclaim the war goal of an independent Poland consisting of all Poles who wished to belong to it. A few days later, on January 17, Wilson proclaimed his famous Fourteen Points, the thirteenth of which specified an independent Polish state made up of indisputably Polish populations with a free and assured access to the sea, and guaranteed by international covenant.

The signing of the Treaty of Brest-Litovsk on March 3, 1918, between the Central Powers and Bolshevik Russia took Russia out of the war and freed the hands of the Western powers regarding Poland. At the same time, the Central Powers' treaty with the Ukrajińska Rada (Ukrainian Council), handing the mixed Polish-Ukrainian district of Kholm (Chełm) to the Ukraine, destroyed the remnants of Polish support for the Austro-Polish solution. Finally, on June 3, 1918, after the collapse of hopes for a separate peace with Austria-Hungary, an Inter-Allied Conference at Versailles declared that an independent Poland, with free access to the sea, was necessary for a just and lasting peace. The war in the West finally ended with the defeat of Germany, signaled by the signing of the armistice on November 11, 1918.

Piłsudski was released by the new, Socialist-led German government established on November 9, 1914. Arriving in Warsaw the next day, he was received as a national hero. The Regency Council (a surrogate Polish government created by the Germans in October 1917) handed over its powers to him, while the Socialist government formed in Lublin under Ignacy Daszyński (1866–1936) on November 7 dissolved itself. Piłsudski assumed the title of Head of State and became commander in chief of Poland's armed forces. A Socialist government was formed under Jędrzej Moraczewski (1870–1944), which implemented many Socialist laws, such as the eight-hour day, health insurance, and free school education. Piłsudski was not a dictator but wielded executive power until the Constituent Assembly elected a president. In January 1919 Polish pianist Ignacy Jan Paderewski (1860–1941), who had propagandized the Polish cause in the United States, became prime minister. This led to allied recognition of the Polish government.

Meanwhile, however, the country was under siege. The Ukrainians seized the predominantly Polish city of Lwów on November 1, 1918. Heavy fighting followed and the Ukrainians were forced out of the city. A brief Polish-German war flared up in Prussian Poland in early 1919, but the Germans gave up in the face of a French threat to invade Germany in the west. In the southeast, Polish troops continued to fight the Ukrainians in East Galicia. They also skirmished with Red Army units in February 1919, which marked the beginning of the Polish-Soviet War. Meanwhile, the country was devastated by war, hunger, and disease. Herbert Hoover's (1874–1964) American Relief Administration helped save many lives.

One of the most difficult problems at the Paris Peace Conference of 1919 was the determination of the Polish-German border. The Poles demanded Prussian Poland (Poznania), Polish Pomerania (later known in the West as the Polish Corridor), the port city of Danzig (Gdańsk), the southern part of East Prussia, and Upper Silesia east of the Oder

River. Except for Danzig, which was predominantly German-speaking, the other territories were predominantly Polish. In the east, the Poles demanded a frontier roughly equivalent to that of the second partition (1793), where they formed a significant minority. The eastern frontier was not, however, settled by the Paris Peace Conference, which no Russian government attended. Furthermore, after the peace of Brest-Litovsk, the Western powers supported the Whites against the Reds in the Russian Civil War (May 1918–January 1921), and thus favored White territorial claims.

In the west, France favored Polish demands on Germany, while Britain generally opposed them. Ultimately, Lloyd George forced through a compromise solution for Danzig/Gdańsk, which became a free city under the protection of the League of Nations. Poland was assured the free use of the port and the conduct of the city's foreign relations, as well as cultural-educational rights for the Polish minority. Polish Pomerania (the Polish Corridor), however, was awarded to Poland since it was predominantly Polish. The British also forced a compromise on Upper Silesia, which had been awarded to Poland in the draft peace treaty. The Versailles treaty stipulated that a plebiscite be held there in two years. Both sides used this period to propagandize the population. The plebiscite, held in March 1921, yielded a large German majority. But this was due to German "outvoters," born in Upper Silesia though resident in Germany, who merely came in to vote and returned home. Without them, the resident German vote in the territory was only 54 percent, and this mainly in the towns; east of the Oder River the countryside was predominantly Polish-speaking. The British and Italian governments favored awarding the entire region to Germany. Therefore Polish Silesians rose up for the second time in May 1921 to prevent this. Ultimately, the British and French governments passed the problem on to the League of Nations, whose special commission awarded the industrial center, along with the rural areas, to Poland in October 1921.

The settlements in Danzig and Upper Silesia were never accepted by Germany, which always claimed they were unjust. In fact, they were patched together by the Allies, mostly on British initiative, as compromises between Polish and German claims. Nevertheless, Poland needed Danzig as a port more than Germany (it ranked only fifth among German ports in 1914), and it

P also needed the Upper Silesian coal and iron/steel industry more than Germany, which possessed the Ruhr basin. These were not convincing arguments for the Germans, however. Their constant protests greatly influenced British and, to some extent, American opinion. Many came to accept the view that once Germany recovered its Great Power status it would also regain its former Polish territories.

Poland's eastern borders were decided by Polish victories over the Red Army in 1920. The Polish-Soviet War, in abeyance since a skirmish in February 1919, revived in late April 1920. At that time, after receiving intelligence reports of Red Army concentrations in the Ukraine directed against Poland, Piłsudski arranged the signing of an alliance and military convention with the anti-Bolshevik Ukrainian leader Semyon Petlyura (1879–1926), who, in return for Polish help, recognized Polish possession of East Galicia. Piłsudski then led the Polish army and Petlyura forces into Ukraine. His aim was not to annex the country but to establish it as an independent state allied to Poland. But there was no Ukrainian uprising in support of the Petlyura government, while the Ukrainians of East Galicia rejected the treaty that left them in Poland.

In June the Red Army counterattacked and drove the Poles back to the gates of Warsaw. On July 2, its commander, Mikhail N. Tukhachevsky (1893–1937), called on his soldiers to march over the corpse of Poland to Berlin. The Soviet government rejected the July 12 Western offer of an armistice on the Curzon Line, named after British Foreign Secretary Lord Curzon (1859–1925). It approximated the eastern border of ethnic Poland and also left East Galicia on the Russian side. Lenin rejected this because the Soviet aim was to "help sovietize Poland." Likewise, the peace conditions the Soviets offered the Poles in early August were designed to make Poland a Soviet state controlled by Moscow. Piłsudski, however, launched a daring counterattack in mid-August from a point south of Warsaw. He defeated Tukhachevsky's army group, first at the Battle of the Vistula (Warsaw), then in September, at the Battle of the Nemen River in Lithuania. The Russian armies in the south were also thrown back. It should also be noted that there were women's units in the Polish army in 1919–20, though women served mainly in support positions.

The Polish victory saved not only Polish independence but also that of the newly established Baltic states, especially Lithuania. The Polish-Soviet border was finally established by the Treaty of Riga on March 23, 1921, far to the east of the Curzon Line. Poland also gained the city and region of Wilno (Vilna). It had been held by Polish troops from April 1919 to July 1920, and was taken again by them in late October 1920, while Polish-Lithuanian negotiations were being conducted with the aid of the League of Nations—a source of Lithuanian resentment down to the present. The city and the surrounding region joined Poland in 1922 after a plebiscite, which was boycotted by Lithuanians, who were a small minority in the region at the time.

Although the Western powers reluctantly recognized the Polish eastern frontier in March 1923, they never approved of it; Lithuania also refused to recognize the Polish possession of Wilno. There were, therefore, no diplomatic communications or postal relations between the two countries until March 1938, when Poland forced their reestablishment.

Interwar Poland: The Second Republic

Interwar Poland, called the Second Republic—the successor of the first republic partitioned in 1772–95—existed from November 1918 to September 1939, when it fell victim to joint German-Soviet aggression. Much was accomplished in these short twenty-one years. The country, devastated in World War I, was rapidly rebuilt, its legal system unified, its economy integrated, and its railroad system greatly expanded. Free and compulsory education almost ended illiteracy by 1939. Social services, including health and housing, reached a high level in the towns. Although agricultural reform was slow, the percentage of land in large estates was reduced by almost half, from 35 percent in 1919 to 18 percent in 1939.

Although industrialization was hampered by lack of adequate foreign capital investment, there were nevertheless two signal economic achievements. First, there was the development of the port city of Gdynia in the Polish Corridor, some 20 miles (33 km) west of Danzig/Gdańsk. Gdynia grew from a fishing village into a city of some 150,000 with the largest annual turnover (tonnage) on the Baltic Sea in 1939. It shared Polish seaborne trade with Danzig/Gdańsk. Second, the Central Industrial District (Centralny Okręg Przemysłowy, COP) was developed in the fork of the Vistula and San Rivers. This was the only government-planned and financed economic region in interwar East Central Europe. The goal was to develop an industrial center away from the German frontier, for Germany was expected to seize Upper Silesia if there was a war. At the same time, COP was designed to end massive unemployment in the region. Begun in 1936 and slated for completion in 1942, its development was cut short by the war, but it served as the base for the industrial region developed after World War II. Both achievements owed much to Eugeniusz Kwiatkowski (1888–1974), minister of trade and industry in 1926–30, also deputy premier and treasury minister in 1935–39.

Poland was not a multinational state like Czechoslovakia and Yugoslavia. Nevertheless, out of a population estimated at 35 million in 1939, one-third were minorities. The largest of these were Ukrainians, estimated at about five million (maximum), followed by about three million Jews and about one million Belorussians. At that time, there were also some 760,000 Germans, plus 139,000 Russians, 98,000 Czechs, 84,000 Lithuanians, and some 700,000 others. The Polish constitutions of 1923 and 1935 recognized equal rights for all Polish citizens. As in most East European states, however, implementation was uneven at best. Only the Germans, backed by the German government, fully enjoyed these rights.

Germany helped finance extreme nationalist Ukrainian groups in East Galicia. In 1919–1921 David Lloyd George pushed for Ukrainian autonomy, though mostly with an eye to facilitating its eventual absorption into Soviet Russia, with which he wanted good trade relations. Fear of Soviet domination and memories of bitter fighting combined to produce a Polish refusal to implement Ukrainian autonomy. The Ukrainians, who had fought the Poles in 1918–19, rejected autonomy, although some demanded it later. Polish opinion, however, both in East Galicia and in Poland as a whole, rejected it. Most Ukrainians were never reconciled to Polish rule, though this was not equivalent to mass support for the extreme nationalists who, in 1930, launched attacks on Polish landlords and farmers, killing many and burning their property. In the fall of that year, Piłsudski sent in troops to "pacify" the region. The violence which exploded into mass murders of Poles by special units of the Ukranian Insurrectionary Army (UPA) in Polesie and Volhynia, 1943–44. In 1947, Polish and Soviet forces cooperated under Moscow orders to deport some 200,000 Ukrainians from Southeast to Northwest Poland in "Operation Vistula" (Akcja Wista), so as to deprive UPA units from fighting Soviet and Polish authorities of local support. On May 21 1997, the presidents of Poland and Ukraine signed a declaration expressing sorrow for both tragic events and hope for good relations in the future.

Unlike the assimilated Jews of Hungary, Germany, Austria, Western Europe, and America, only about 5 percent of Jews in interwar Poland were assimilated. Most lived in Jewish villages or traditionally Jewish districts in towns. Although the Polish census of 1931 gave the Jewish population of Lwów and Wilno as below 10 percent, it likely neared 20–30 percent, while they accounted for about 30 percent of the population of Warsaw, and the small market towns in eastern Poland were predominantly Jewish. The Jews used their own languages (Yiddish and Hebrew), had their own religious schools (though children had to attend regular Polish schools), and their own political parties, newspapers, literature, and theater. While they experienced several pogroms in 1918–1920, notably in Lwów (where seventy-two were killed), and later suffered from intermittent outbursts of anti-Semitism, there was no anti-Semitic policy or legislation in Poland as there was in Germany or Italy. There were, however, extralegal restrictions on admission to certain university schools (medicine) and to universities in general. Jews were also excluded from some professional associations. At the same time, the assimilated 5 percent of Jews formed about 25 percent of the Polish intelligentsia, who were especially prominent in the legal and medical professions, and produced some leading figures in Polish literature. The Polish government pressed Great Britain for expanded immigration quotas for Polish Jews to British-ruled Palestine. When this proved impossible, the government cooperated with the New Zionist Organization (NZO), led by Ze'ev (Vladimir) Jabotinsky (1880–1940), who admired Piłsudski and wanted to build military cadres to fight for a Jewish state in Palestine. He founded the Haganah (Jewish Self-Defense Organization) there in 1920, and some of the NZO fighters trained in Poland helped win the establishment of Israel in 1948.

Independence gave many new opportunities to women. They obtained the right to vote and equal civil rights. Most uneducated women still worked on the land, in factories, or as domestic servants,

P and most educated women still worked as teachers. However, increasing numbers obtained doctoral degrees in all branches of knowledge, especially in the humanities. (Yet there was only one female full professor of history—at the Stefan Batory University in Wilno.) There were also women doctors, dentists, journalists, and a few lawyers and architects. Female traffic police appeared in Warsaw. While not visible in public life, women established and ran all kinds of social organizations, including many to help the underprivileged.

In politics, the Second Polish Republic conformed to the pattern of all interwar East Central European governments—except Czechoslovakia—by starting out as a parliamentary democracy but changing later to an authoritarian government. Like other states in the region, Poland adopted a French-style constitution with a figurehead president and a multiparty system with proportional representation. This led to frequently changing coalition governments, accompanied by wholesale changes in the civil service. Political passions sometimes reached extremes, the worst being exemplified by Eligiusz Niewiadomski (1869–1923), an art historian and fanatical National Democrat. He assassinated the first president of Poland, Gabriel Narutowicz (1865–1922), whose election in parliament was assured by the votes of minority deputies, including Jews. The assassin and many others saw this election as a "betrayal" of Poland, but most Poles condemned the deed.

From 1923 to 1926, Piłsudski was absent from the political scene, having retired from his post of army inspector general in protest against the use of political criteria in military appointments. In early May 1926, however, he decided to intervene against the government created on May 10, made up of the National Democrats and the Peasant Party and headed by Witos as premier. This led to a general political crisis, with the PPS and the left-wing Peasant Party opposing the new government, and to fears of a right-wing dictatorship. Piłsudski decided to organize a military demonstration to help President Stanisław Wojciechowski (1869–1953) create a new government in which he could participate. Unfortunately, Wojciechowski was absent from Warsaw, so they could not meet. Piłsudski then ordered some of his loyal troops to march on Warsaw. Wojciechowski returned to the capital and proclaimed Piłsudski's action illegal, but left-wing parties called on the government to resign.

When Wojciechowski and Piłsudski finally met on the Poniatowski Bridge, the former refused to yield. Fighting broke out, most of it uncoordinated, between troops loyal to Piłsudski and those loyal to the government. The government called for reinforcements from the Poznań area, but their trains were prevented from reaching Warsaw by socialist railwaymen. On the afternoon of May 13, the government resigned. Before it was all over, 379 people were killed, about half of them civilians who had been in the line of fire.

Despite strong, popular pressure, Piłsudski refused to run for president. Contrary to many Western history textbooks, he did not assume dictatorial powers. In the new government, headed by Kazimierz Bartel (1882–1941), he held the post of war minister, along with the post of inspector general of the armed forces—both of which he kept until he died. He served as premier in 1926 and 1928, and managed to expand the power of the presidency. His old friend and follower Ignacy Mościcki (1867–1946) was elected to this post in 1926 and held it until September 1939.

In June 1937 a new movement, the Center-Left Bloc (Centrolew), organized mass demonstrations in Kraków and Lwów calling for the resignation of the government. The demonstrations were broken up by police and their leaders were arrested. Piłsudski became premier again in late August, dissolved parliament, and decreed new elections. The leaders of the Center-Left Bloc were imprisoned, but in the public trial that followed, the government lost face because it could not make a convincing case that they had conspired to overthrow it by force. Ultimately, some politicians were jailed, while others went into exile.

From 1930 to 1937, the Non-Party Bloc of Cooperation with the Government (Bezpartyjny Blok Współpracy z Rzadem, BBWR) dominated parliament, while Piłsudski devoted himself to military matters and major foreign policy issues. In April 1935 his followers managed to pass an authoritarian constitution vesting great powers in the presidency. A new electoral law passed the same year allowed local committees of government supporters to approve deputies standing for parliament. The new presidency was tailored for Piłsudski, but he died of cancer on May 12, 1935. He was deeply mourned by the nation and buried in the Wawel Castle in Kraków, the resting place of Polish kings and famous Poles.

From Piłsudski's death to the outbreak of World War II, Poland was governed by authoritarian governments made up of his followers, but they were not military juntas. Several ministers were reserve officers but did not represent a specific military constituency. Although a new progovernment party, the Camp of National Unity (Obóz Zjednoczenia Narodowego, OZON), dominated parliament after 1937, traditional political parties continued to exist, each with its own press. The latter was limited not by prepublication censorship but by the government's use—and misuse—of the law of libel. Also, the electoral law did not apply to municipal elections, most of which were won by opposition parties in November 1938. Thus, the Polish government system was authoritarian but not fascist. The only fascist organization in interwar Poland, Falanga, was an offshoot of the National Democratic party led by Boleslaw Piasecki (1915–79). Finally, as in all East Central European states (except Czechoslovakia), the Communist Party was illegal. It had never enjoyed a strong following in Poland however, and most of its leaders, who had taken refuge in the Soviet Union, were executed in the Stalin purges of 1936–38; the party itself was dissolved by the Comintern (Communist International) in 1938 on false charges of having been infiltrated by Polish police agents.

In foreign policy, Piłsudski aligned Poland with France, signing an alliance and secret military convention in Paris in March 1921. But both France and Britain soon adopted a policy of conciliating Germany. This was exemplified by the Locarno treaties, (1925) in which Berlin recognized Germany's frontiers with France and Belgium—guaranteed by Britain and Italy—but not those with Poland and Czechoslovakia. France signed mutual assistance treaties with these two countries at Locarno, but its aid was now dependent on the League of Nations, thus undercutting previous, automatic French obligations.

Polish relations with Germany and Russia were cool at best, since each power made it clear that it did not accept the frontiers established in 1919–21. Nevertheless, when Moscow showed interest in better relations, Poland signed a nonaggression pact with the USSR in 1932. After Hitler (1889–1945) came to power in Germany, Piłsudski initiated negotiations that led to a Polish-German Declaration of Nonaggression of January 26, 1934, and balanced it in July of the same year by renewing and extending the Polish-Soviet Pact for ten years. Piłsudski thus inaugurated the policy of "equilibrium," that is, good relations with each of Poland's powerful neighbors but alliance with neither. This policy was continued by his disciple Col. Józef Beck (1894–1944), foreign minister from 1932 to 1939, who shared Piłsudski's belief that alliance with either Great Power would make Poland its satellite and that, in any case, alliance with one would provoke an attack on Poland by the other. Neither Piłsudski nor Beck believed that France would stand up to Hitler without British support, or that Britain would support France in fighting for the independence of Austria or Czechoslovakia. At the same time, therefore, as Beck tried to avoid a clash with Germany, he worked hard to improve and tighten relations with Britain. In this he was unsuccessful until March 1939. Meanwhile, he used the Austrian crisis of March 1938, which resulted in the German annexation (Anschluss) of Austria, to force the Lithuanian government to establish normal relations with Poland. The goal was to create an alliance between Poland and the Baltic states, backed by Britain, against German and Soviet expansion in the region. But Britain showed no interest in this project.

During the Czechoslovak (Sudeten) crisis of 1938, Beck assumed that France and Britain would give in to Hitler's demands while the USSR would make threatening noises but would not help Czechoslovakia. He therefore followed a policy of raising Polish demands to the preponderantly Polish-speaking part of western Teschen Silesia (Polish, Zaolzie)—seized by the Czechs in January 1919 and awarded to Czechoslovakia by the Western powers in July 1920. At the same time, he tried to sell Polish "neutrality" to Berlin in return for official German recognition of the Polish-German frontier and the Free City of Danzig. As he told the Polish cabinet, however, if France and Britain decided to fight Germany over Czechoslovakia, Poland would have to change its policy for it could never be on Germany's side in a European war. But if, as he foresaw, the Western powers abandoned Czechoslovakia, Poland would act to regain Zaolzie, with its Polish population and its economic wealth (coking coal and a steel mill). Eleven hours after the Czechoslovak government's acceptance of the Munich diktat on September 30, which turned over the Sudetenland to Hitler, the Polish government issued an ultimatum to Prague demanding the cession of Zaolzie, which was united with Poland.

P This did not make Poland an ally of Hitler. Beck rejected German proposals that Poland return Danzig to Germany and create a German "corridor through the Polish Corridor" to allow extraterritorial German communications with Danzig and East Prussia in return for official German recognition of the Polish-German frontier. He did not take up the German proposal that Poland join the Anti-Comintern Pact and hints of compensation for Poland in the Ukraine, but kept the door open to negotiations on improving German communications through the Corridor. Thus, although Beck rejected German demands, he did not indicate he was averse to further talks. In January 1935, however, the Polish cabinet decided that any concessions to Germany would lead to more demands and finally to the loss of Polish independence. Therefore, the government expressly rejected the German proposals on March 25, six days before accepting the British guarantee of Polish independence. This guarantee was announced officially in parliament by Prime Minister Neville Chamberlain (1869–1949) on March 31 1939, and was joined by Poland's ally France.

Beck believed the guarantee would deter Hitler from aggression and allow a reasonable compromise with Germany. He did not realize, however, that the British government was ready to sanction Hitler's demands on Poland, provided he obtained them through peaceful negotiations with the latter. At the same time, the British government tried to construct an anti-German bloc in the Balkans— Romania, Yugoslavia, Greece—linked to Poland. This bloc—more bluff than reality—was to prevent German domination of this region and, through Greece, of the eastern Mediterranean. Britain also tried to obtain Soviet assurances of aid for Poland and Romania, as well as the Baltic states, and therefore entered into negotiations for an alliance with Moscow, but Stalin played Britain off against Germany. After the signature of the Nazi-Soviet Nonaggression Pact on the night of August 23–24 (plus a secret protocol including the partition of Poland), the British government signed a treaty of mutual assistance with Poland on August 25.

World War II

Germany attacked Poland on September 1, 1939. When, on the demand of France and Britain, Hitler failed to withdraw his troops from Poland by the deadlines set for September 3, the two powers declared war on Germany.

According to a military agreement between the French and Polish General Staffs signed on May 17, 1939, the French had committed themselves to launching a major offensive against Germany in the west within fifteen days of a German attack on Poland—but they made no such plans. Since the French and British General Staffs had already agreed on a purely defensive war in the west if Germany attacked Poland, the French goal was to boost Polish morale and encourage Poland to fight as long as possible to gain time for France. Thus Poland was left to fight Germany alone. Even so, Warsaw withstood a brutal siege from land and air for three weeks. In fact, the Polish-German War lasted thirty-five days, or about the same amount of time as the British and French struggle with Germany in France in May–June 1940. The Poles suffered great losses but gained precious time for their Western allies by delaying the German attack in the west.

Meanwhile, the Red Army entered eastern Poland on September 17, proclaiming the "liberation" of its Ukrainian and Belorussian brothers. There were a few minor battles, but most Polish troops in the region did not resist, and the Soviets took about three hundred thousand prisoners. Upon hearing of the Soviet attack, the Polish government, having already reached the Polish-Romanian frontier, decided to cross it. They expected to proceed to France and organize a new Polish army. Indeed, the head of the French military mission and the French ambassador both advised Beck and commander in chief Marshal Edward Śmigły-Rydz (1886–1941) to do so. But the Romanian government under German pressure, interned the key members of the Polish government. The French government, which greatly disliked Beck, Śmigły-Rydz, and "Piłsudskiite" officers in general, did not make a great effort to secure their release. Instead, it helped a pro-French opposition leader, General Władysław Sikorski (1881–1943), to reach France and become the premier of a new Polish government in Paris on September 30. He became commander in chief of Polish armed forces in November that year.

The Polish army in France reached a total of eighty thousand men—three-quarters of whom had escaped from Romanian and Hungarian internment camps. The unexpected collapse of France in June 1940, however, and the ensuing chaos meant that only some twenty thousand reached Britain. Sikorski and his government took up residence in London, and Polish pilots contributed significantly to winning the Battle of Britain, where, in September 1940, they constituted 20 percent of Royal Air Force pilots.

Throughout the war, German-occupied Poland suffered a reign of terror. Many prominent people were arrested as "hostages" and promptly shot. Universities and schools were closed. The entire faculty of the Jagiellonian University, including instructors and teaching assistants, were arrested on the first day of the school year and deported to the Dachau concentration camp in Germany. Many died there, but others were released owing to interventions, mostly from Italy. Over two million Poles were used as forced labor in Germany. During the winter of 1939–40, one million were forcibly deported from the western territories annexed by Germany to the General gouvernement, or occupied Poland. There Poles lived on inadequate rations, as most food was requisitioned for Germany. Furthermore, up to one hundred Poles were executed for every German killed.

Jews had to wear a yellow star and were forced into ghettos. In the summer of 1942 deportations to the death camps—Bełżec, Majdanek, Treblinka, and Auschwitz-Birkenau (Oświęcim)—began. The penalty for helping Jews was death, so most Poles were passive, fearing for their lives and their families. Some blackmailed hidden Jews, but others helped them through a special organization named Żegota. Financed by the underground authorities with money parachuted into Poland from England, Żegota forged documents and hid and fed Jews. The underground also forbade cooperating with the Germans in any way, mandating the death penalty for betraying Jews. The Polish government-in-exile and Jewish leaders appealed vainly for Allied air strikes against German towns and railroad lines to stop transports to German extermination camps. At war's end, the total number of survivors was around two hundred thousand, out of a prewar population of nearly three million Jews. The vast majority of survivors eventually left Poland for Palestine and the United States.

The Polish resistance movement was unique in Europe in that it included not only a military force—the Home Army (Armia Krajowa, AK), which numbered some four hundred thousand in 1944—but also an underground state (Polskie Państwo Podziemnne). Headed by a delegate of the Polish government-in-exile, this state was governed by a council representing the five key interwar opposition parties. There were regional government delegates, embryonic ministries, and an underground educational system extending from elementary school through doctoral programs. There was also an extensive and varied underground press representing all shades of political opinion as well as the arts. This underground state existed in an atmosphere of terror, including street roundups by occupying German forces and public executions that Polish citizens were forced to watch. The Home Army sabotaged industrial production and supply trains to the eastern front. Although its key action was to be an uprising against the Germans as they retreated from Poland, from 1943 onward it fought pitched battles, tying down several German divisions. Home Army soldiers depended on the help of peasant farmers, who often suffered massive retaliation; the Germans burned some three hundred Polish villages, massacring their inhabitants. At the end of the war, approximately three million ethnic Poles were dead, only 644,000 of whom died as a direct result of military activities.

In Soviet-occupied Poland, separated from the Generalgouvernement by the "Ribbentrop-Molotov Line" of September 28, 1939 (which replaced the original line of August 23, and approximated the postwar Polish-Soviet frontier of 1945), the terror was, if anything, even worse. After initial "list killings" of prominent local leaders, Soviet authorities sponsored the establishment of local government committees made up of the poorest elements, whom they set against Polish landowners and the middle class. In late October Soviet authorities carried out rigged elections, each district with one list of approved candidates, to the National Assemblies (Soviets) of Western Belorussia and Ukraine. These assemblies then petitioned the Supreme Soviet of the USSR to unite their territories with the Soviet Belorussian and Ukrainian republics, petitions granted on November 1 and 2, 1939, respectively. All persons living in these territories at the time became Soviet citizens, subject to Soviet law.

Some 1.5 million people were deported in three great waves in 1940–41, among them an estimated 52 percent ethnic Poles. These individuals, labeled "hostile elements" by the Soviet authorities, included Polish veterans settled as farmers in eastern Poland, landowners, administrators, lawyers, doctors, teachers, police, and Roman Catholic priests. In addition, they deported educated

Ukrainians and Uniate priests, Jewish merchants and shopkeepers, and middle and prosperous farmers of all nationalities. These deportees and their families were transported in packed cattle cars to labor camps in Siberia, or to collective farms in the Caucasus, Trans-Caucasus, and Soviet Central Asia. By the time of Germany's attack on the USSR on June 22, 1941, the Soviets had killed some 450,000 Poles in eastern Poland, while at least 300,000 Polish deportees died in the USSR.

Hitler's attack on the USSR demoted the Poles from the rank of Britain's number-one ally to a problematic second, and third after the U.S. entered the war. The British government pressed Sikorski to resume relations with Moscow, to which he had no objection, having always favored good relations with the Soviet Union. In any case, he wanted to save as many Poles there as possible to raise a large Polish army. He also feared that refusal to normalize relations with Moscow would open the way to a Soviet-controlled national committee and army, along with a possible break in Anglo-Polish relations. He therefore signed an agreement with the Soviet ambassador in London, Ivan M. Maisky (1884–1975), on July 30, 1941. This stipulated the annulment of the 1939 German-Soviet agreements regarding Poland; reestablished relations; provided for mutual cooperation in the war with Germany and the release of Poles interned in the USSR; and the raising a Polish army there. In view of radically different demands by each side regarding their common frontier—the Soviets wanted an "ethnic" Poland in order to keep their 1939–41 gains, while the Poles wanted the restoration of the Riga frontier of 1921—this issue was left temporarily in abeyance.

Stalin's concessions to the Poles were short-lived, however. Polish, British, as well as Soviet documents available to date indicate that the Soviet dictator's goal was a Soviet-dominated Poland with ethnic borders in the east and large accessions of German territory in the west. As the war progressed, Stalin became more and more insistent that the Polish government-in-exile formally agree to give up former eastern Poland. At the same time, he prepared an embryonic government of his own in the USSR and supported an underground Polish Workers Party (Polska Partia Robotnicza, PPR) in German-occupied Poland. With its program formulated in the fall of 1941, their leaders, chosen in Moscow, were then parachuted from a Soviet plane over Warsaw at the end of December of that year.

In late April 1943 Stalin broke off official relations between the two governments. Two weeks earlier, on April 13, the Germans had announced the discovery of the corpses of thousands of Polish officers in the Katyn Forest, near Smolensk, claiming they had been murdered by the Soviets. The Polish government had in the past vainly queried Soviet authorities about some fifteen thousand missing officers, cadets, police, and others, but was always told that all had been released. Now, under great pressure from the Polish army—evacuated in 1942 by General Władysław Anders (1892–1970) to the Middle East, and then included in Britain's Eighth Army as the Second Polish Corps—as well as from the victims' families in Poland, the government requested an inquiry by the International Red Cross. Coincidentally, the German government made the same request. Stalin broke off relations with the London Poles, accusing them of cooperating with the Germans. He then unveiled the Union of Polish Patriots in the USSR (Związek Patriotów Polskich w ZSRR, ZPP) headed by Polish writer Wanda Wasilewska (1904–64), who was by then a member of the Soviet Communist Party and a Soviet citizen. The ZPP had, in fact, been created in early February, and the first number of its paper, *Wolna Polska* (*Free Poland*) appeared on March 1, 1943. In late spring recruitment began for a new, Communist-led Polish army commanded by pro-Soviet colonel (soon general) Zygmunt Berling (1896–1980). Owing to the dearth of Polish officers, most of the field officers were Russians—though many had Polish family names—but the political officers were Polish Communists.

For almost half a century, all Soviet governments blamed the Germans for the Katyn and other associated massacres (Mednoe near Tver, and in Kharkov). In April 1990, however, Soviet President Mikhail Gorbachev (1931–) admitted Soviet guilt, and two years later Russian President Boris Yeltsin (1932–) gave the Polish government copies of a large number of documents on the massacres of the Polish officers and others held in three special camps: Kozielsk and Ostashkov in Belorussia, and Starobelsk in the Ukraine, also Soviet prisons. By this time, Russian and Polish archival research uncovered details on their transportation to and the location of their executions. The shooting of these "enemies of the USSR" was proposed to the Politbureau by NKVD (secret police) chief Lavrenty P. Beria (1899–1953) and approved the same day. The victims—10 percent of whom were Polish Jews—were shot in batches by special NKVD details in April–June 1940. Several thousand others were shot in NKVD prisons in Belorussia and Ukraine. The total number of Polish prisoners murdered at this time was 21,857.

Even without knowing the details of the massacres, British officials believed the Soviets guilty but blamed the Poles for the break in relations with Moscow. Although Winston Churchill (1874–1965) strove to restore relations, Stalin's demand for the 1939–41 Polish-Soviet frontier proved an insuperable obstacle for the Poles. The British government, for its part, agreed with Stalin. It had always believed that this frontier should be based on the Curzon Line of 1920—which meant that the USSR would keep almost all of former eastern Poland. While both Sikorski—killed in an air crash off Gibraltar on July 4, 1943—and his successor, leader of the Polish Peasant Party in exile, Stanisław Mikołajczyk (1901–66), privately agreed that Poland should give up these territories except for the mostly Polish cities of Lwów and Wilno, they could not say so publicly, let alone give the government's official assent. Polish public opinion was (except for a small minority of Communists and sympathizers) adamantly opposed to giving up this land, and above all, Wilno and Lwów. In any case, the government had no constitutional power to do this. Churchill, however, believed that territorial concessions would make Stalin accept a truly independent Polish government headed by Mikołajczyk and his Peasant Party—the largest in Poland. He also believed such a government to be in Britain's interest. At the Tehran conference of the Big Three (November 28–December 2, 1943), he proposed to Stalin that Poland "be moved west, like a soldier taking three steps left close," that is, give up eastern Poland to the USSR and gain German territory in the west instead. Stalin approved; after all, he had proposed this to Foreign Secretary Anthony Eden (1897–1977) in December 1941. U.S. President Franklin D. Roosevelt (1882–1945) agreed but told Stalin he could not do so publicly because he needed Polish-American votes in the upcoming presidential election of 1944. In this way, Poland's future borders were decided—with details to be worked out later—without the assent of its government and people.

In late August 1944 Mikołajczyk's cabinet—with the Polish Socialist Party dissenting—went as far as it could by implicitly agreeing to give up most of eastern Poland. In a memorandum to the British government, it stated that Poland must retain Wilno, Lwów, and the adjoining oilfields, and that the parliament would determine Polish frontiers after the war. By this time, however, Stalin had created an embryonic government dependent on him, the Polish Committee of National Liberation (Polski Komitet Wyzwolenia Narodowego, PKWN)—allegedly created in Poland but actually in Moscow on July 21, 1944—which took up residence in Lublin. The Home Army rose up against the Germans in Warsaw on August 1 but received no Soviet help, even though the Red Army stood on the eastern bank of the Vistula River and liberated the eastern suburb of Praga in mid-September. Instead, the Red Army watched as the Germans systematically destroyed Warsaw, building by building. Stalin also rejected Anglo-American appeals to allow planes to land behind Soviet lines after dropping supplies to the Warsaw insurgents, except for one American relief flight in mid-September. At the same time, the NKVD was arresting officials of the underground state as well as shooting and/or deporting Home Army officers while forcing the rank and file into the Communist-led Polish army. The Warsaw Uprising ended after sixty-three days on October 2. Stalin had achieved his aim, for the Home Army and the underground administration could no longer oppose the Polish Committee of National Liberation.

At the Yalta conference in February 1945, Churchill and Roosevelt formally agreed to Stalin's demand for a Polish-Soviet frontier approximating the Curzon Line and to compensate Poland with German territory. There was disagreement on whether the southern part of the Polish-German frontier should follow the western Neisse (Polish, Nysa) River—as Stalin and the Polish Communists demanded—thus giving Poland all of Upper Silesia, or the eastern Neisse line, as Western leaders proposed. The three leaders agreed, however, to a Soviet-proposed procedure for establishing a democratic Polish provisional government. A commission was set up consisting of Soviet Foreign Minister Vyacheslav M. Molotov (1890–1986), U.S. Ambassador to the USSR, W. Averell Harriman (1891–1986), and British Ambassador to the USSR Sir Archibald Clark-Kerr (1882–1951). They were to invite selected Polish politicians from Poland and the West to Moscow for consultations on forming the new provisional government, which was then to

P hold free elections for parliament and thus produce a new, democratic government.

Molotov stalled the commission's work by opposing candidates unwelcome to Moscow. Also, in March 1945 the NKVD used a ruse to arrest key Polish political leaders, along with the last Home Army commander. They were promised a trip to London to consult the Polish government before flying to Moscow for meetings on the new government. Instead, they were flown directly to Moscow, imprisoned, and pressured to confess to "crimes" against the Red Army. The trial of the sixteen leaders was held in Moscow in June 1945, at the same time that Mikołajczyk—who had resigned as premier of the government-in-exile in November 1944—negotiated with members of the Soviet-recognized provisional government on forming a new one. On June 21, just as Mikołajczyk agreed to accept the post of deputy premier and minister of agriculture, the trial ended with relatively mild sentences, at least by Soviet standards. (Three of the Polish leaders, however, died in prison in unclear circumstances.)

Mikołajczyk and his supporters received only four out of twenty-four cabinet seats but accepted this disparity in the belief that the Western powers would insist on truly free elections in Poland, which would be won by the Peasant Party. The new provisional government was formally established on June 28. It was recognized by France on June 29, followed by Great Britain and the United States on July 5, 1945. At the Potsdam conference (July 28–August 2, 1945), the Polish delegation, which included Mikołajczyk, managed to persuade the Western leaders to place German territories east of the Oder–Western Neisse line under Polish administration and deport the German population west under Allied supervision. The Potsdam decision did not mean official recognition of the new Polish-German frontier, for this was reserved for the final peace treaty with a united Germany. Nevertheless, by allowing the deportation of the Germans, the Allies indicated that they saw the settlement as final. In return, the Polish delegation promised to hold free elections as soon as possible.

Many Polish women participated actively in the resistance movement during the war. The most dangerous work was that of Home Army couriers, who ensured contact between regional resistance leaders and headquarters in Warsaw. Many of them were killed in the line of duty, or tortured or shot in German prisons. Some risked their lives working for the Żegota organization to save Jews. Many served as couriers and nurses during the Warsaw Uprising. In the Polish army in the west, women served in auxiliary units, while a handful of pilots ferried planes from the United States to Britain. In the Polish army attached to the Red Army, women served as nurses with frontline troops as well as in auxiliary units.

Communist Poland 1945–89

Pseudo-Democracy, Stalinism, and Revolt: 1945–56

The elections to which Mikołajczyk and his party, as well as the majority of Poles, pinned their hopes did not take place until January 1947. In the meanwhile, fighting continued in parts of Poland between, on the one hand, many Home Army and other veterans who feared accepting an amnesty, and Polish security troops, on the other. The Polish Workers Party (PPR) blamed the fighting on the Peasant Party, whose members were constantly harassed, arrested, and even killed. The PPR organized a "referendum" in June 1946 entitled Three Times Yes! (*Trzy razy tak!*), asking voters whether they supported the abolition of the Senate, the new economic system initiated by the land reform, the nationalization of key branches of the economy, which would be enshrined in the future constitution, and whether they wanted the new western frontiers to be permanent. Mikołajczyk and his party stood for no on the first question, expecting massive support and thus a clear defeat for the PPR. The PPR, however, destroyed the negative ballots and proclaimed victory.

Mikołajczyk still hoped for Western support, but on September 6, 1946, U.S. Secretary of State James F. Byrnes (1879–1972) made a speech in Stuttgart, stating that the United States did not view Poland's western frontiers as final. While this was in keeping with the Potsdam decisions, the PPR and Moscow saw it as an indication that Washington had lost interest in Poland. Harassment of the Peasant Party increased. Mass arrests preceded the elections of January 1947, and their results were clearly rigged. Many Peasant Party members were in prison and the party was listed as winning only 10 percent of the vote. In October Mikołajczyk escaped to the West, followed by some party leaders who also feared for their lives.

In March 1947 President Harry S Truman (1884–1972) offered American aid to all governments requesting it to defend themselves against communism, a policy that came to be known as the Truman Doctrine. In June Secretary of State George C. Marshall (1880–1959) offered U.S. aid for postwar economic reconstruction to all European countries, including the Soviet bloc through the Marshall Plan. Stalin ordered the Polish and Czechoslovak governments to reject it and in October 1947 established the Cominform (Communist Information Bureau) to act as a watchdog over all Communist parties.

As the Cold War unfolded, Stalin consolidated his hold on the region's Communist parties. There were widespread purges on the Soviet model, with torture, forced confessions, and rigged trials. Although Władysław Gomułka (1905–1982), head of the PPR from November 1943, escaped trial, he was forced to resign. He was then arrested, imprisoned, and later kept under house arrest until 1955. Many of his followers were imprisoned as well. While party purges took place in all Soviet bloc countries, in Poland the terror touched many non-Communists as well. Thousands of amnestied Home Army veterans, as well as veterans of Polish armed forces in the West, were arrested. They were tortured to confess either that they were former German agents or had spied for the Western powers. Many died under torture or lack of medical care, or were executed. The Roman Catholic Church was also attacked. The Polish primate, Cardinal Stefan Wyszyński (1901–81), was arrested in late September 1953 after protesting repressive government policy toward the church. He was interned in monasteries and convents until his release in late October 1956. There was no full-scale war against the church on the Soviet model, however, because it enjoyed the strong support of the vast majority of the population. The government's support of the "Polish National Catholic Church"—an organization that actually began in the United States in the late nineteenth century—also failed to weaken the Roman Catholic Church in Poland.

In December 1948 the PPS was forcibly united with the PPR to produce the Polish United Workers Party (Polska Zjednoczona Partia Robotnicza, PZPR). The new leaders proceeded to industrialize the country at breakneck speed, regardless of cost. There was also an attempt to collectivize agriculture, but peasant resistance was so strong that party leaders feared a civil war. They chose, therefore, to proceed slowly on the assumption that industrialization would draw people off the land, gradually eliminating private farmers. Meanwhile, the latter had to deliver quotas to the state at low prices, which produced endemic food shortages. At the same time, industrial workers endured bad work and living conditions—especially crowded housing—instead of the prosperity promised by party leaders.

The Gomułka Era: 1956–70

At the Twentieth Party Congress in February 1956, the first secretary of the Soviet Communist Party, Nikita S. Khrushchev (1894–1971), launched an attack on Stalin and Stalinism. While the text of the speech became known in Polish party circles, it had little impact on Polish workers, who were already restless. On June 28, 1956, when their delegates failed to return on time from negotiations with the government in Warsaw, workers in Poznań demonstrated in the streets for "bread and freedom." They destroyed police files and party offices but were crushed by Polish security police and Soviet-driven tank units from a nearby training center. Party leaders realized that a change of leadership was needed to avoid civil war, and thus Soviet military intervention. The party's Central Committee met on October 19 to elect Gomułka as first secretary. (He had been released from internment in April 1955 and reinstated in the party in July 1956.) On that day, however, Khrushchev landed in Warsaw with a group of close political and military advisers. At the same time, Soviet troops massed on Poland's eastern and western borders; two Soviet divisions began to move from Legnica toward Warsaw, and Soviet warships stood off the Polish coast. In view of this threat, armed Polish workers in Warsaw stood guard over leaders who might be arrested, while the Polish army showed determination to fight Soviet troops if they intervened.

Khrushchev ranted at Gomułka but finally agreed to his reelection. Chinese Communist leaders also exerted pressure on Moscow to allow some liberalization in Poland. It seems that Khrushchev backed off partly because he wished to avoid armed confrontation and partly because Gomułka convinced him that he would be loyal to Moscow—provided he had some leeway at home. To the Poles as well as to the outside world, however, Gomułka looked like a Polish David who had vanquished the Soviet Goliath. His public speech on October 22, in which he sharply criticized the political and economic excesses and errors of the Stalinist period in Poland, was cheered by half a million people. Gomułka dismissed most Soviet advisers and army officers, including the commander in chief of the Polish armed forces, the Polish-born but Soviet-raised Marshal Konstantin Rokossovsky (1896–1968). He relaxed party control over the media, as well as over academe and the press. He also allowed peasants to leave collective farms, which they did in droves. He released Cardinal Wyszyński from internment in late October 1956, and allowed the teaching of religion in schools in return for the church's support of the party-government and its policies, but he did so only because he needed the church's cooperation. He also allowed more than one approved candidate to run for election in any constituency.

Gomułka's honeymoon with the Polish people began to ebb in 1959–60, when signs of economic stagnation became visible. The leadership rejected the advice of Polish economists to shift investments away from raw material production, especially coal, and into the chemical industry, decentralize the economy, allow management to decide production according to market demand, and permit more private enterprise.

Moreover, church-state relations worsened when the government ended religion lessons in the schools in 1959. They were moved to "catechism points" in churches or parish buildings, which children could attend only after school. In 1966 the government celebrated Poland's one thousandth anniversary as a state, while the church celebrated the anniversary of the country's conversion to Christianity from Rome. The government refused to grant the pope a visa to visit Poland's national shrine at the monastery of Jasna Góra, Częstochowa. When Polish bishops wrote an open letter to their German brother bishops proposing mutual forgiveness for past wrongs, the government accused them of treason.

Meanwhile, the intelligentsia, especially writers, were frustrated by increasing restrictions. In 1964 a group of thirty-four intellectuals signed an open letter to the government protesting censorship. The text was broadcast by the Polish section of Radio Free Europe, a U.S.-supported radio station in Munich, Germany. That same year, two graduate history students at Warsaw University, Jacek Kuroń (1934–) and Karol Modzelewski (1937–), the latter the son of the first postwar foreign minister and a signatory of the letter of the thirty-four, sent an open letter to the party authorities at the university. They accused the party of being a ruling bureaucracy that ruthlessly exploited workers and called for a real workers' revolution and government through workers' councils. They also called for free trade unions, freedom of the press, and free cultural and scientific activity. This letter was also broadcast by Radio Free Europe and published in the West. Its authors were arrested and jailed. Likewise, philosopher Leszek Kołakowski (1927–) came under attack when he contrasted the humanist writings of the young Karl Marx (1818–83) with the dogmatism of the Polish party and claimed that democracy could evolve under socialism. In 1966 he was expelled from the party and left Poland for the West in 1968.

The Arab-Israeli War of 1967 sparked another crisis. When Polish intellectuals celebrated the Israeli victory, Gomułka alleged that this was a "Zionist plot." He was no anti-Semite—his wife was Jewish—but he was infuriated by the open rejoicing at the Israeli victory. The result was a widespread purge of Jewish Poles from academic, managerial, and media positions. Consequently, Poland was deprived of several thousand gifted Jewish Poles, most of whom emigrated, and Poland's image as an anti-Semitic country was confirmed once again.

In March 1968 student demonstrations demanding the abolition of censorship and the establishment of democracy erupted at universities all over the country. The students protested the closing down of Mickiewicz's anti-Russian play, *Forefathers' Eve,* and demanded the abolition of censorship—which had already disappeared in Czechoslovakia's Prague Spring, the Czechoslovak reform period. The government sent security police dressed as workers to the universities. If allowed in by the administration, they beat up students and some professors as well.

In late 1970 Poland's international situation greatly improved. Khrushchev's successor, Leonid Brezhnev (1906–82), initiated a policy of détente with the West, beginning with the signing of a Soviet–West German treaty of friendship and cooperation on August 12, 1970, whereby West Germany recognized all postwar borders, including the Polish-German border (the Oder-Neisse line). The Moscow treaty led to the "Warsaw Treaty," signed by the West German and Polish governments on December 7, 1970, whereby West Germany recognized the Polish-German frontier.

In Communist Poland, workers and peasants were encouraged and helped to seek social advancement through higher education. The political goal was the creation of a new intelligentsia loyal to the regime. However, the policy was a great benefit to the entire nation, even though for most of the period young people of peasant and working-class backgrounds were favored over others—who were at first disbarred from higher education because of the "wrong" social origin. The policy introduced large numbers of women doctors, dentists, lawyers, university professors, and even engineers, but they rarely attained leadership positions either in the professions or in politics. Furthermore, most working women had to run the household as well as work outside the home, and this was a heavy burden, especially given the lack of labor-saving devices and the need to stand in line every day to buy food. Some educated women were active in dissident organizations and the Solidarity trade union movement, and some, particularly writers and artists, were active in the underground literary movement during the 1980s.

Gomułka's reign came to an abrupt end when he decided to raise the prices of basic goods to reduce price subsidies, which accounted for one-third of the state budget. The government announced these measures without any warning on December 13, 1970, when it also canceled the "thirteenth month" salary payment, the customary Christmas bonus for key industrial workers. This provoked a massive protest by shipyard workers in the port cities of Gdańsk, Elbląg, Gdynia, and Szczecin. In Gdańsk, the initiative was taken by the strike committee of the Lenin Shipyard, one of whose members was a young electrician named Lech Wałęsa (1943–). After a bloody clash with police, the workers agreed to go back to work. Party leaders, however, viewed them as "counter-revolutionaries" and sent regular and riot troops against them. (Some of the troops were told they would defend the port cities against a German invasion.) There was a massacre in Gdynia and clashes in other port cities. An Interfactory Strike Committee was formed in Szczecin, which drew up a list of twenty-one demands, including free trade unions.

Gomułka asked for Soviet support, but Moscow advised resolving the crisis without the use of armed force. Gomułka was then forced to resign for "health reasons" (he did have a bad heart) and was succeeded by Edward Gierek (1913–), the popular and ambitious party boss of Upper Silesia. Gierek took over the party leadership on December 20, 1970, and called off the troops.

The Gierek Era: 1970–80

Despite the change of leadership, more strikes broke out in January 1971, including one at the Warski Shipyard in Szczecin. Its workers demanded not only the cancellation of the price increases but also free elections to party and trade union posts. They invited Gierek and the prime minister to come and talk with them. Indeed, a top-level party-government delegation went to Szczecin, where Gierek said he was a worker himself and appealed to the workers to "help him save Poland and socialism." They agreed and he found the same favorable reception in Gdańsk. When more strikes broke out elsewhere, Gierek rescinded the price increases and calm was restored.

A new era of liberalization set in with party discussions reported in the media, which were also encouraged to report on social ills. Furthermore, Gierek courted intellectuals by liberalizing censorship in humanities and social sciences publications. Also, the government allowed the collection of funds to rebuild the Royal Castle in Warsaw, which had been destroyed by the Germans in World War II. The PZPR had previously opposed this as a symbol of anti-Russian sentiment.

Gierek seemed to favor some economic reform. He set out to replace outdated machinery with Western imports and purchased Western consumer goods, both with the aid of Western credits and loans, mostly from West Germany. He also obtained credits from the United States and the USSR. By 1971–73, Poland's industrial rate of growth ranked third in the world and living standards rose appreciably. People could purchase washing machines, refrigerators, TV sets, and even cheap cars. At the same time, joint ventures began, including the production of Italian Fiat cars and West German Grundig tape recorders. Such products, manufactured with Western parts by cheap but skilled Polish labor, were to be marketed in the West to pay off credits and loans.

The 1973 oil crisis, however, raised oil prices and led to a recession in the West, which meant reduced markets for Polish goods. At the same time, a series of poor harvests reduced Polish agricultural exports. These factors, plus the lack of economic reform, resulted in economic stagnation and food

P shortages, which grew worse as the government exported more and more processed foods for hard currency to pay off high interest rates on its loans.

In this situation, the government again decided to reduce price subsidies for basic products, especially meat. On June 24, 1976, Premier Piotr Jaroszewicz (1909–92) announced huge price hikes (69 percent for meat; 100 percent for sugar; 35 percent for butter and cheese). Furthermore, he made a bad situation worse by stating that workers had been consulted and agreed to the prices. In fact, only party workers were consulted, and strikes erupted the next day. In Radom, 60 miles (100 km) south of Warsaw, workers broke into the local party building and distributed the goods from the special shop for party members. There was also some looting in town. Worker protests occurred elsewhere as well. The government immediately rescinded the price increases but used club-swinging riot police to punish the workers. Some were killed, while many were badly injured and/or fired.

The beatings of workers sparked indignation throughout the country. A group of dissident intellectuals organized a Committee for the Defense of Workers (Komitet Obrony Robotników, KOR). KOR raised money at home and abroad for the families of dead, injured, and fired workers, as well as for the legal defense of those put on trial. Its first manifesto appeared in September. A similar, more conservative organization, the Movement for the Defense of the Rights of Man and Citizen (Ruch Obrony Praw Czlowieka i Obywatela, ROPCIO) came into being in March 1977. The Association for Academic Courses (Towarzystwo Kursów Naukowych, TKN) was established in 1978, in which university professors and instructors conducted seminars on subjects distorted by the party line (history, philosophy) or not taught at all (sociology). Seminars were held in private apartments, on the model of the "flying universities" of Russian Poland and underground classes during the German occupation. TKN legal experts also instructed peasants with private farms on their legal rights.

KOR, ROPCIO, and TKN authors signed all their published materials, often listing their addresses and telephone numbers. This began an underground publication boom, including not only newspapers and periodicals but also books. The dissidents took their stand on the rights of free speech and association enshrined in the 1952 Polish constitution—though they had not been respected—and on the Helsinki Declaration on Human Rights, which Soviet-bloc governments had signed in August 1975 in return for Western recognition of the postwar frontiers of the USSR and Eastern European countries.

The activities of the dissident organizations were supported by the Catholic Church, whose leader, Cardinal Wyszyński, had spoken out, after the crushing of the December 1970 strikes, in defense of workers' rights as well as for freedom of conscience. In March 1976, following a protest by Polish intellectuals against the draft constitution, Wyszyński demanded the establishment of free trade unions, an independent judiciary and civil service, as well as free elections to parliament. He also demanded recognition of the "indispensable human rights of all Poles."

On October 16, 1978, the cardinal and bishop of Kraków, Karol Wojtyła (1920–), was elected pope, the first non-Italian elected since the sixteenth century and the first Pole. The country erupted with joy and the government had to welcome the election of "a great son of Poland." The pope's first visit to his homeland, in June 1979, was a triumph for both the church and dissidents. Millions flocked to see him; they cheered when he said they had the right to have God in their lives and freedom of conscience. The police were powerless and this experience broke "the barrier of fear," paving the way to the events of August 1980.

It was the economic crisis, however, that lit the powder keg. In the late 1970s goods were scarce, so shortages and waiting in line became a daily experience. Electric power cuts idled factories for hours and reduced household consumption. At any one time, 50 percent of rolling stock and public transport was idle for lack of spare parts. The national health service deteriorated to the point where it was hazardous for an ordinary citizen to stay in the hospital, while ill-paid doctors and nurses often demanded "gifts" in order to provide their services. Despite increased construction, people had to wait an average of seven to ten years for an apartment in government-built housing, while a cooperative apartment required a large down payment. At the same time, high party and government officials enjoyed excellent housing, shops, clinics and hospitals, imported medications, and luxury vacation resorts. On a more modest level, similar perks were enjoyed by army and police officers.

Solidarity: August 1980–December 1981

Popular discontent was already high when Premier Edward Babiuch (1927–) announced price increases for meat and other basic products on July 1, 1980. Uncoordinated strikes broke out immediately all over Poland. Government officials settled one after another by promising wage increases. In mid-July, however, the city of Lublin witnessed a coordinated strike by all state enterprises. Although Deputy Premier Mieczysław Jagielski (1924–) reached an agreement with the strikers, Lublin was the harbinger of things to come. Meanwhile, Radio Free Europe was informing the people of the strikes, while KOR acted as an information exchange for the whole country.

In mid-August a strike broke out in the Lenin Shipyard in Gdańsk, where some workers had been killed in the strikes of December 1970. The strikers wanted the reinstatement of a female crane operator who had been fired for political reasons, and they also demanded wage hikes to equal the price raise. The director told the workers that she could return and that Warsaw had agreed to a pay raise. Wałęsa, who came in by climbing the shipyard wall, could not stop the workers from going back to work, but they listened to delegates from other state enterprises who urged they all stand together. All agreed to from a Provisional Coordinating Commission (Tymczasowa Komisja Koordynacyjna, TKK) as well as an Interfactory Strike Committee (Międzyfabryczny Komitet Strajkowy, MKS). Local intellectuals offered their services as advisers, while others arrived from Warsaw.

The government reacted by cutting off all telephone, telegraph, road, and rail communications with Gdańsk and then offered negotiations. The strikers agreed, provided communications were restored, and they were.

After some difficult negotiations, Wałęsa and Jagielski signed an agreement on August 31, 1980, entitled "The 21 Points" (a similar agreement was signed in Szczecin on August 30). Most of these dealt with wages, work conditions, health insurance and facilities, vacations, and the like, but the core was political: the right to strike and to form free trade unions; a law defining censorship; the freeing of all political prisoners; and free access to the media for both the church (Sunday mass) and the free trade union. The name Solidarity (Solidarność) and its logo first appeared in the strike bulletin during the negotiations.

Moscow did not intervene in Poland owing in part to its involvement in Afghanistan, which began in late December 1979 and led to tension with the United States. There was also tension in Europe for, after the placing of new Soviet SS-20 missiles in the western USSR and some bloc states, the European members of NATO requested the installation of new, medium-range U.S. missiles on their soil. Thus, armed Soviet intervention in Poland might have sparked an armed clash on the Continent. Finally, Soviet and Polish leaders viewed concessions to Solidarity as a means of gaining time to regroup and crush the movement.

Gierek was forced to resign in September 1980—again, for health reasons—and was replaced by Stanisław Kania (1927–), a member of the Central Committee, formerly in charge of security. The PZPR disintegrated; at least one-third of its three million members joined Solidarity, while many others demanded the democratization of the party. At the same time, Solidarity membership grew to ten million out of a labor force of eighteen million. Private peasant farmers also formed their own union, "Rural Solidarity" (which did not receive official recognition until May 1981).

Solidarity chapters sprang up everywhere, while all professional associations, including the police, elected their own leaderships. Self-government, the goal of most Poles, began to make inroads in industry and other state enterprises. Censorship of the media almost disappeared, and much previously banned or new material that formerly would have been unacceptable was published. In December 1980 a monument was unveiled in Gdańsk in memory of the shipyard workers killed ten years earlier. At its base were carved the words of a poem by a Polish poet in exile, Czesław Miłosz (1913–), who won the Nobel Prize in literature that year and visited Poland.

Storm clouds, however, were gathering over Poland. In December 1980 Soviet troops carried out maneuvers near the Polish frontier and Soviet warships anchored off the coast. It seems that Moscow was exerting psychological pressure on the Polish party leadership and the population as a whole but the U.S. warned th Soviets against armed intervention. In March 1981 some Solidarity leaders were beaten by police in Bydgoszcz, and a general strike was narrowly averted through negotiations between Deputy Premier Mieczysław

Rakowski (1926–) and Wałęsa. At this time, Warsaw Pact maneuvers took place in Poland and at one point all airports were closed, apparently to install Russian air controllers. In May an attempt was made by a Turkish terrorist to assassinate the pope, possibly with the support of the Bulgarian secret police on orders from Moscow. At the end of the month, Cardinal Wyszyński died of cancer. It is clear now that if the pope had died too, this would have had a most demoralizing effect on Solidarity.

In October General Wojciech Jaruzelski (1923–)—defense minister since 1968 and premier since February 1981—became first secretary of the party, thus concentrating all power in his hands. By this time, enthusiasm for Solidarity was waning because of worsening food shortages. At the Solidarity congress held in Sopot in September 1981, Wałęsa barely won enough votes for reelection as chairman. Soviet warships stood off the coast and Soviet marines carried out landing exercises.

In November talks took place between Solidarity and church leaders on one side, and the government-party leadership headed by Jaruzelski on the other. They ended in a stalemate, since the party would not even consider a "partnership" among church, Solidarity, and the authorities. In early December Solidarity leaders met in Radom. Some radicals spoke of overthrowing the government, while more moderate members wanted Solidarity to field its own candidates in the elections due in February 1982. Their victory, however, would mean a vote of no confidence in the government. Wałęsa opposed both proposals. The room in which they met was bugged and the government obtained recordings of some of the discussions, using them later to "prove" that Solidarity leaders were plotting to overthrow the government and socialism by force.

The Soviets pressured Jaruzelski to crush Solidarity. By mid-December, the situation was very tense. Solidarity planned widespread demonstrations on December 17, the anniversary of the 1970 massacres in the port cities. Soviet troops concentrated in Belorussia, while several East German and Czechoslovak divisions were also ready to move. Polish scholars disagree whether Jaruzelski imposed martial law on the night of December 12–13, 1981, because he believed that otherwise the situation would get out of hand during the Solidarity demonstrations planned for a few days later,

and thus provoke a Warsaw Pact invasion, or whether he acted mainly to save his own power and communism in Poland; perhaps it was both. The imposition of martial law caught the country completely by surprise. All telephone, telegraph, road, and rail communications were cut instantly, making any coordinated resistance impossible. Five thousand Solidarity leaders were immediately arrested and interned, including Wałęsa. Troops surrounded factories, mines, and shipyards, while riot police moved in to break up Solidarity sit-ins. The only significant clash occurred in the Wujek coal mine in Katowice, where riot police shot some miners, who in turn killed a few policemen. The miners then went down the mine to await the outbreak of a general strike but gave up two weeks later. Loss of life was small under the circumstances, amounting to some fifty dead.

The Jaruzelski Era: 1982–89
From 1982 to 1989, Jaruzelski attempted to stabilize the situation and carry out economic reforms. But another Poland existed underground with its own press and even forays into government-controlled radio and television. Many interned Solidarity members were released in 1982, including Wałęsa, who was freed in November. He was awarded the Nobel Peace Prize a year later for advocating peaceful means of struggle and as a symbol of world sympathy for Solidarity. His wife went to Oslo to collect it, since Wałęsa feared he would not be allowed to return home. In June 1983 the pope visited Poland and pressed for lifting martial law; this was done a month later, but the government continued to repress all dissent. In October 1984 the country was shocked by the brutal murder of a much-loved priest, Father Jerzy Popieluszko (1947–1984), whose "Fatherland masses" and support for Solidarity had drawn crowds to his Warsaw church. At the trial that followed, a security police captain took all the blame, but it was clear that orders had come from above.

Economic reforms brought hardship without positive results. Prices rose about 500 percent in January 1982, while wages were indexed up only to 60 percent of price increases. State enterprises were supposed to become self-governing and self-sufficient. Most of this, however, remained on paper, for the government avoided closing down unproductive enterprises for fear of social unrest. As for prices, some were set by the market, but basic products were regulated. In Poland, as elsewhere in the Soviet bloc, there was no successful compromise between a planned, state-run economy and a free market.

The turning point in Polish political and economic affairs can be traced to the election of Mikhail Gorbachev as first secretary of the Soviet Communist Party in March 1985, and especially to the launching of his twin policies of *glasnost* (openness) and *perestroika* (restructuring) two years later. In 1987–88 Polish authorities and (separately) Solidarity leaders, as well as party and nonparty intellectuals, discussed various ways to make the transition from a command to a free market economy.

At this time, some four hundred newspapers and periodicals of all kinds were published underground, and there were also several book publishing companies. Many writers, artists, playwrights, and actors boycotted state employment and lived in this independent society, which the government harassed but largely tolerated. Indeed, it relaxed censorship controls to compete with it. This society also had church support, so many exhibits and performances took place in parish buildings. Finally, the pope, who visited Poland in June 1987, openly urged the government to recognize the agreements of August 1980 (Workers' Solidarity) and those of 1981 (Rural Solidarity). He spoke of the need for truth, freedom, political pluralism, self-government, and protection of the environment.

In the spring of 1988 a wave of strikes swept across Poland, including Gdańsk, where workers of the Lenin Shipyard again came out into the streets and demanded the reestablishment of Solidarity. Wałęsa joined the Gdańsk demonstrations. There were mass demonstrations all over the country both on May Day (May 1), a labor holiday, and on May 3, in honor of the constitution of May 3, 1791, a symbol of opposition.

Consultations took place between the PZPR leadership and Gorbachev, in which the Soviet leader apparently advised negotiations with Wałęsa. Gorbachev seems to have assumed that a controlled liberalization of the political-economic system in Soviet-bloc countries would both avert bloody clashes and preserve Communist rule, without endangering Soviet détente with the United States.

It is not surprising, therefore, that after Wałęsa had persuaded the leaders of more strikes in August to return to work, exploratory talks began on August 31, 1988, between Wałęsa and his advisers on one side and Minister of the Interior General Czesław Kiszczak (1925–) on the other. Church representatives were also present. The talks at first yielded no result because the authorities proposed not a partnership with the church and Solidarity but a Communist-dominated coalition. It is unclear whether this reflected the views of hard-liners in the Polish party or advice from Moscow, or perhaps both. In any event, someone in the party leadership suggested a television debate between the leader of the government-controlled trade union, Alfred Miodowicz (1929–), and Wałęsa, expecting the latter to prove ineffective in a studio setting without a cheering audience. Wałęsa, however, was the winner. He made an excellent impression on millions of viewers, many of whom saw him for the first time.

The Collapse of Communism

In January 1989 Premier Mieczysław Rakowski (1926–) declared that the government was ready to consider relegalizing Solidarity—if Wałęsa guaranteed there would be no strikes for the next two years. Although Wałęsa made no such commitment, "Round Table" talks began in February between the government-party delegation led by General Kiszczak and the Solidarity delegation led by Wałęsa. Kiszczak first tried to persuade the Solidarity group to join the government. When Wałęsa refused, the details of an agreement were hammered out in long negotiations, which lasted until April 6, when a series of agreements was signed. Solidarity was reinstated and Rural Solidarity was relegalized by a separate law. Political pluralism was recognized, as reflected in free associations. There was to be freedom of speech and real access to the media for different political groups. There would be democratic elections, the courts would be independent, and there was to be responsible local government. State power was to be clearly divided among the legislative, executive, and judicial branches, and a National Council of the Judiciary was to guard judicial independence.

The key agreements on social and economic policy stated that investment was to be diverted from defense, heavy industry, and raw materials to consumer goods and services. Strict savings were to balance the budget in three years. Most important, the entire economy was to operate on free-market principles. Price hikes, however, were to be offset by indexing wages up to 80 percent of prices.

P Elections to parliament, now again a bicameral assembly, were to be held in May–June 1989. The 460-seat lower house (Sejm) was to be the supreme authority. The 100-seat Senate was to have veto power, which could be overturned by a two-thirds majority in the Sejm. The Communists tried to safeguard their hold on power through an agreement that Solidarity candidates could freely contest only 35 percent of the lower house, while 65 percent of the seats were to go to the PZPR and its satellites—chiefly the United Peasant Party and the Democratic Party. Elections to the Senate, however, would be unrestricted. The next parliamentary elections, scheduled for 1993, were to be completely free. Furthermore, the Round Table agreements reestablished the office of president, who was to have absolute authority in foreign policy and defense, and also veto power over the Sejm, which could be overturned by a two-thirds vote. He would also have the power to introduce, in case of a threat to national security or a natural disaster, a three-month state of emergency, renewable only once for another three months, subject to agreement by Sejm and Senate. He could dissolve the Sejm and call for new elections if it took more than three months to agree on a new government, or if the Sejm threatened presidential prerogatives. The first president—clearly Jaruzelski—was to be elected by the two houses of parliament, but at the end of his six-year term, there was to be a popular election. The Sejm approved the agreements on April 7. Solidarity was relegalized on April 17 and Rural Solidarity three days later. U.S. President George Bush (1924–) hailed the Polish reforms as concrete steps requiring active U.S. support and promised this would be forthcoming.

With the election date set for June 4, Solidarity leaders had only two months' time to prepare but used it well. Local Solidarity committees worked in every electoral district. Poles abroad contributed money. Wałęsa confirmed Solidarity candidates by posing with them for photographs, which was very important because election rules did not allow ballots to specify candidates' political affiliation. The Communists expected to win because they had the organization and the money; they were shocked by the results. Although Solidarity candidates could run for only 35 percent of the seats in the Sejm, people crossed out Communist candidates' names on the ballot papers. Only three former ministers were elected in the first round, while eleven government members who ran on the uncontested "national list" failed to win the requisite 50 percent of the vote. Solidarity won 99 out of the 100 seats of the Senate. Wałęsa nevertheless honored the Round Table agreements by agreeing to a second round of elections for the 33 vacant Sejm seats on the national list. In the second round, however, held on June 18, only 32 percent of the electors bothered to vote, as compared with 62 percent in the first.

The Polish elections—eclipsed in the Western media by the tragic massacre of students in Tienanmen Square, Beijing—opened the way to the collapse of communism in Poland and the rest of Eastern Europe. Jaruzelski was elected president on July 19 by the 540 members of parliament—by 270 votes against 233 (with 34 abstentions), obtaining only one vote over the number required for election. Ten days later, he resigned as head of the PZPR, to be followed in that post by Rakovski. On August 17, the former PZPR satellites, the Peasant Party and the Democratic Party, joined in a coalition with the Civic Club, the Solidarity group in parliament. When one Communist premier after another—Rakowski and Kiszczak—failed to form a new government, Jaruzelski consulted Wałęsa. The latter, having refused the Civic Club's proposal to become premier, submitted to Jaruzelski the names of three Solidarity candidates, including Catholic-Solidarity adviser and journalist Tadeusz Mazowiecki (1927–).

After a stormy debate in the PZPR Central Committee on August 19, and after Gorbachev had allegedly advised Rakowski that the party participate in a new coalition government under a Solidarity leader, Jaruzelski nominated Mazowiecki as premier. The Sejm approved the nomination on August 24 by 378 votes to 4 (with 41 abstentions). The Soviet press commented that the new government was "an internal Polish affair"; the Hungarian government welcomed it; Czechoslovak leaders ignored it; and Romanian dictator Nicolae Ceauşescu (1918–89) lobbied unsuccessfully for armed intervention by the Warsaw Pact. After arduous negotiations, Mazowiecki announced the formation of a new government on September 12. It was the first preponderantly non-Communist government in the Soviet bloc, and led the way for the collapse of Communist governments in the rest of Eastern Europe.

Anna M. Cienciala

Further reading

Abramsky, Chimen, Maciej Jachimczyk, and Antony Polonsky, eds. *The Jews in Poland.* Oxford, 1986.

Ash, Timothy Garton. *The Polish Revolution: Solidarity.* New York, 1984.

Cienciala, Anna M. *Poland and the Western Powers 1938–1939: A Study in the Interdependence of Eastern and Western Europe.* London, 1968.

Cienciala, Anna M. and Titus Komarnicki. *From Versailles to Locarno: Keys to Polish Foreign Policy, 1919–1923.* Lawrence, Kansas, 1984.

Curry, Jane Leftwich and Luba Fajfer, eds. *Poland's Permanent Revolution: Peoples vs. Elites, 1956–1990.* Washington, D.C., 1996.

Davies, Norman. *God's Playground: A History of Poland,* 2 vols. New York, 1982.

Garlinski, Jozef. *Poland in the Second World War.* New York, 1985.

Jaworski, Rudolf and Bianka Pietrow-Ennker, eds. *Women in Polish Society.* Boulder, Colorado, 1992.

Kersten, Krystyna. *The Establishment of Communist Rule in Poland, 1943–1947.* Berkeley, California, 1991.

Landau, Zbigniew and Jerzy Tomaszewski. *The Polish Economy in the Twentieth Century,* trans. by Wojciech Roszkowski. New York, 1985.

Lerski, George J., with Piotr Wróbel and Richard J. Kozicki. *Historical Dictionary of Poland, 966–1945.* Westport, Connecticut, 1996.

Leslie, R. F., ed. *The History of Poland since 1863.* Cambridge, 1980.

Michnik, Adam. *Letters from Prison and Other Essays.* Berkeley, California, 1985.

Pogonowski, Iwo. *Poland: A Historical Atlas.* New York, 1987.

Polonsky, Antony. *Politics in Independent Poland 1921–1939: The Crisis of Constitutional Government.* Oxford, 1972.

Raina, Peter. *Political Opposition in Poland, 1954–1977.* London, 1978.

Rothschild, Joseph. *East Central Europe between the Two World Wars.* Seattle, Washington, 1974.

Wandycz, Piotr S. *The Lands of Partitioned Poland, 1795–1918.* Seattle, Washington, 1974.

See also Agrarian Parties; Agriculture; Alexander I; Alexander II; Alexander III; *Anschluss;* Anti-Comintern Pact; Armia Krajowa; Auschwitz; Zygmunt Balicki; Józef Beck; Józef Bem; Michał Bobrzyński; Brest-Litovsk, Treaty of; Brezhnev Doctrine; Carpatho-Rusyns; Catholicism; Censorship; Frédéric Chopin; Winston Churchill; Cinema; Cold War; Collectivization; Comecon; Cominform; Comintern, Communist Party of Poland; Congress of Vienna; Constantine; Crimean War; Marie Curie; Curzon Line; Adam Czartoryski; Duchy of Warsaw; Ignacy Daszyński; Edward Dembowski; De-Stalinization; Roman Dmowski; Duma; Feliks Dzierzyński; Economic Development in Poland; Education; Emigration; Ethnic Minorities; Family; Flying University; Fourteen Points; Franz Joseph; Freemasonry; Galicia; Gdańsk; Generalgouvernement; Germanization; Edward Gierek; *Glasnost* and *Perestroika;* Władysław Gomułka; Mikhail Gorbachev; Habsburg Empire; Hakata; Adolf Hitler; Hôtel Lambert; Holocaust; Hungarian War for Independence; Industrialization; Intelligentsia; Jagiellonian University; January Uprising; Wojciech Jaruzelski; Jews; John Paul II; Katyn Forest; KOR; Thaddeus Kościuszko; Kraków; Kulturkampf; Law; League of Nations; Joachim Lelewel; Lenin; Liberalism; Locarno; Lublin Committee; Rosa Luxemburg; L'vov; Marshall Plan; May Coup; Media; Adam Mickiewicz; Ludwik Mieroslawski; Stanisław Mikołajczyk; Cresław Miłosz; Vyacheslav Molotov; Molotov-Ribbentrop Pact; Munich Pact; Napoléon; Nationalism; Nazi-Polish War; Nicholas I; November Uprising; Eliza Orzeszkowa; *Ostpolitik;* Ignacy Jan Paderewski; Paris Peace Conference; Peace of Riga; Peasants; Bolesław Piasecki; Józef Piłsudski; Pogrom; Polish Art; Polish Congress Kingdom; Polish Corridor; Polish Culture; Polish Émigrés; Polish Language; Polish League; Polish Legions; Polish Literature; Polish Question; Polish-Soviet War; Positivism; Potsdam Conference; Poznań; Prague Slav Congress; Prague Spring; Press; Bolesław Prus; Prussia; Red Army; Republic of Kraków; Revolutions of 1989; Konstantin Rokossovsky; Russia; Russification; *Sanacja;* Sejm; Władysław Sikorski; Silesian Question; Juliusz Słowacki; Solidarity; Soviet Union; Stalin; Sudeten Crisis; Aleksander Świętochowski; Teschen; Trade Unionism; Truman Doctrine; Mikhail Tukhachevsky; Uniate Church; Upper Silesian Uprisings; Vilna Dispute; Lech Wałęsa; Warsaw, Battle of; Warsaw Pact; Warsaw Uprising; Aleksander Wielopolski; Woodrow Wilson; Wincenty Witos; Stanisław Wojciechowski; Women in Poland; World War I; World War II; Stefan Wyszyński; Yalta Andrzej Zamoyski; Zet

Polányi, Károly (1886–1964)

Economic sociologist-anthropologist who anathematized market economies and championed a democratic, quasi-religious socialism. Born in Vienna but reared in Hungary by a gifted family of assimilated Jews, Polányi read for the bar and presided over the Galileo Circle, a radical student organization dedicated to the advance of science and the reform of society. In 1919, after having served as a cavalry officer in World War I, he left what was then Soviet Hungary for Austria, where he earned a living as an economic and political commentator. Impressed by the socialist experiments in "Red Vienna," as the city was often called, he took an active part in the contemporary debate over the possibility of a "socialist accounting" without benefit of market guidance.

In 1933, when he could no longer support his family in Austria, Polányi emigrated to England, where he joined the Christian Left and exhibited a growing sympathy for Soviet economic—though not political—policies. While teaching university extension and Workers' Educational Association classes, he began to plan his most celebrated work, *The Great Transformation* (1944). The transformation in question was the changeover from a market economy that subjected human beings to its impersonal operation to a planned economy that subordinated itself to the needs of the community.

In 1947 Polányi accepted a visiting professorship at New York's Columbia University, where he continued to teach until 1953. During his last years, he directed scholarly investigations of primitive and archaic economies in a systematic attempt to show that market economy was an historical anomaly.

Lee Congdon

Further reading

Congdon, Lee. *Exile and Social Thought: Hungarian Intellectuals in Germany and Austria, 1919–1933*. Princeton, New Jersey, 1991.

McRobbie, Kenneth, ed. *Humanity, Society, and Commitment: On Karl Polanyi*. Montreal, 1994.

Polanyi-Levitt, Kari, ed. *The Life and Work of Karl Polanyi*. Montreal, 1990.

See also Hungarian Soviet Republic

Polish Art

The leading trends of Western culture have been reflected in the development of Polish art and architecture. In the nineteenth century ties with such cultural centers as Paris, Munich, and Vienna were strongly established. The intention of Polish art, however, was to produce its own national image. It was manifested mainly by the transposition of folk motives, the representation of Polish landscape, and in themes of the national history. The emphasis on patriotic issues was primarily due to Poland's loss of independence in 1795 with the final partition.

At the beginning of the nineteenth century, romanticism succeeded classicism in Poland. In the fine arts, this new trend was represented by paintings of Piotr Michałowski (1800–1855), a master of portraits and battle scenes such as *Somosierra* (1837). In Artur Grottger's (1837–67) work romantic passion appeared in a graphic cycle that commemorated the fight of the 1863 January Uprising, the failed attempt to overthrow Russian domination. The great portrait painter of that era was Henryk Rodakowski (1823–1894), whose art combined elements of classical realism with romantic expression.

The romantic trend in architecture, manifested mainly in historic styles, was represented by architects Piotr Aigner (1746–1827), who designed the park of Isabella Czartoryski in Puławy (1798–1806); H. Marconi (1792–1863); and Franciszek M. Lanci (1799–1875).

By the end of the nineteenth century, Polish art was characterized by realism and naturalism. Jan Matejko (1838–93), generally considered the greatest Polish painter, was a master of historic and battle scenes. He documented important events of the Polish past with an excellent sense of realistic expression and historic precision. His most notable works were *Bitwa pod Grunwaldem* (*Battle at Grunwald*, 1879) and *Hold pruski* (*Prussian Homage*, 1882). Henryk Siemiradzki (1843–1902) represented academic classicism. Aleksander Gierymski (1850–1901) and Józef Chełmoński (1849–1914) realistically painted scenes of country and city life of lower classes, while Juliusz Kossak (1824–99) was famous as a painter of horses.

In the period known as "Young Poland" (1890–1918), in which Kraków served as the nation's cultural center, Polish painting reached its apex. Polish artistic expression followed three general movements of Western art: secession (Art Nouveau), symbolism, and impressionism. Stanisław Wyspiański (1869–1907) was the most prominent painter of the era. His greatest achievements were the wall paintings (1896) and the stained glass windows (1897–1902) in the St. Francis Church in Kraków, done in the Art Nouveau style. The other great secession-style artist was Józef Mehoffer (1868–1946), who received first prize in the international competition for the glass windows for the Fribourg (Switzerland) Collegiate Church in 1895. Symbolism was strongly marked in the paintings of Jacek Malczewski (1854–1929), Witold Wojtkiewicz (1879–1909), and Ferdynand Ruszczyc (1870–1936). Impressionism was evident in works of Aleksander Gierymski (1850–1901), Józef Pankiewicz (1866–1940), Władysław Podkowiński (1866–95), Jan Stanisławski (1860–1907), and Olga Boznańska (1865–1940). The great landscape painters Leon Wyczółkowski (1852–1936) and Julian Fałat (1853–1929) created their individual styles of expression, which combined realistic representation with the impressionistic use of natural light effects. The outstanding portrait painter was Konrad Krzyżanowski (1872–1922). Władysław Ślewiński (1854–1918), associated with the school of Pont-Aven led by French painter Paul Gauguin (1848–93), painted synthetic compositions applying lush color and large flat areas. The great sculptors were Wacław Szymanowski (1859–1930) and Xawery Dunikowski (1875–1964).

At the end of the nineteenth century, Polish architecture was dominated by historic revivals (J.P. Dziekoński [1844–1927] and S. Szyller [1857–1933]). Secession appeared in Poland about 1900 with the work of architects Mikołaj Tołwiński (1857–1924) and Franciszek Mączyński (1847–1947). Stanisław Witkiewicz (1851–1915), inspired by the vernacular building of the Zakopane region, created the so-called Zakopiański style aimed at Polish national expression in architecture. The modern movement was represented mainly by Czesław Przybylski (1880–1936) and Jan Heurich (1873–1925).

After World War I—when Poland regained its independence—new postrevolutionary movements in the Soviet Union and the West significantly affected the development of Polish art and architecture. Numerous artistic associations were established devoted to such European trends as constructivism, cubism, and postimpressionism. Formism was a movement (1917–22) referring to cubism, futurism, and expressionism, and was primarily concerned with abstraction rather than life-like representation. Its leaders were Zbigniew (1885–1958) and Andrzej Pronaszko (1888–1961), Tytus Czyżewski (1880–1945), Leon Chwistek (1884–1944), and Stanisław Ignacy Witkiewicz (pseudonym: Witkacy, [1885–1939]). The abstract compositions of Katarzyna Kobro (1898–1950), Henryk Berlewi (1899–1967), Władysław Strzemiński (1893–1952), and Henryk Stażewski (1894–1988) followed Russian constructivism. The fascination with color, as influenced by French postimpressionism, was evident in the works of Jan Cybis (1897–1972). The outstanding sculptors of the era were August Zamoyski (1893–1970) and Edward Wittig (1879–1941).

In architecture the most avant-garde group was Praesens (1926–30), led by architects Barbara (1899–1980) and Stanisław Brukalski (1894–1967), Bohdan Lachert (1900–1987), Józef Szanajca (1902–39), Helena (1900–1982) and Szymon Syrkus (1893–1964), and artists Henryc Stażewski (1894–1988) and Mieczysław Szczuka (1898–1927). Following the German Bauhaus school, it propagated functionalism and constructivism, formulated social goals, and sought the integration of architecture with other disciplines of art.

From 1949 to 1955, Polish art was dominated by socialist realism. The pro-Stalin doctrine of the time required artists to use monumental forms and realistic representation for glorification of the worker class. New ways of abstract expression were explored only after 1955. Contemporary painters who attained international recognition include Stażewski, Tadeusz Brzozowski (1918–), Jerzy Nowosielski (1923–), Konstanty Mackiewicz (1894–1985), Jerzy Duda Gracz (1941–), and Zdzisław Beksiński (1929–). The tapestry and sculpture of Magdalena Abakanowicz (1930–), and the posters of Jan Lenica (1928–), Henryk Tomaszewski (1914–), and Jan Młodożeniec (1929–) also became well known. Władysław Hasior (1928–) and Gustaw Zemła (1931–) were the foremost Polish sculptors of the post–World War II generation.

Polish book illustration also is held in high regard for excellence. The creators of the contemporary school of illustration in Poland are Jan Marcin Szancer (1902–73), Olga Siemaszko (1914–), Józef Wilkoń (1933–), Janusz Stanny (1932–), and Maria Mackiewicz (1927–).

The leading contemporary architects are Bohdan Pniewski (1897–1965); Maciej Nowicki

(1910–50); Marek Leykam (1908–83); Jerzy Hryniewiecki (1908–88); Jan Bogusławski (1910–82); Hanna (1920–96) and Kazimierz Wejchert (1912–93), and Maciej Krasiński (1923–).

Marta Tobolczyk

Further reading

Dobrowolski, Tadeusz. *Nowoczesne malarstwo polskie 1764–1963*, vols. 1–3. Wrocław, 1964.

Juszczak, Wiesław and Maria Liczbińska. *Malarstwo polskie: Modernizm*. Warsaw, 1977.

Olszewski, Andrzej. *A History of Polish Art 1890–1980*. Warsaw, 1988.

Polish Painting in the Ewa and Wojtek Fibak Collection. Warsaw, 1992.

Pollakówna, Joanna. *Malarstwo polskie między wojnami 1918–1939*. Warsaw, 1982.

Suchodolski, Bogdan. *A History of Polish Culture*. Warsaw, 1986.

See also Magdalena Abakanowicz; Architecture; Folklife; January Uprising; Kraków; Jacek Malczewski; Jan Matejko; Maciej Nowicki; Polish Culture; Romaticism; Stanisław Ignacy Witkiewicz; Stanisław Wyspiański; Young Poland

Polish Congress Kingdom

Quasi-independent Polish kingdom established at the Congress of Vienna (1815) and extinguished after the 1863 January Uprising against the Russians. At the insistence of Tsar Alexander I (1777–1825), in 1815 the delegates at the Congress of Vienna resurrected a rump Kingdom of Poland, sometimes called the Congress Kingdom. Comprising 46,080 square miles (128,000 sq km), with a population of approximately 3.3 million, the Congress Kingdom included the heartland of prepartition Poland. The kingdom had a constitution and a Sejm, or legislature, but it was tied to the autocratic Russian Empire by its king, who was also the Russian tsar.

From its inception, the Congress Kingdom led a precarious existence. Not only was Alexander uncomfortable with his constitutional role, but the tsar also selected Constantine (1779–1831), his ill-tempered brother, to head the kingdom's army, and named N.N. Novosiltsov (1761–1836), a cynical and corrupt Russian statesman, as his imperial commissioner. Prince Adam Czartoryski (1770–1861), a popular Polish nobleman and Alexander's former confidant, was pushed aside.

Difficulties marked the kingdom's first years. Much to Alexander's displeasure, some members of the Sejm took the constitution seriously. Other Poles wanted to recover former Polish lands to the east that were now part of the Russian Empire. Romantically inspired youths joined illegal secret societies. A near fatal budgetary crisis gripped the kingdom; however, it was solved in 1821 with the appointment of Prince Ksawery Drucki-Lubecki (1778–1846) as treasury minister. Drucki-Lubecki straightened out the kingdom's finances and initiated an ambitious economic expansion.

Alexander's death in 1825 brought the reactionary Polonophobe Nicholas I (1796–1855) to the throne, and Poland drifted into revolution in 1830. The November Uprising failed miserably. Russia enjoyed an overwhelming military advantage; the Polish leadership was hopelessly fragmented; the Polish peasantry remained mired in ignorance and servitude; and appeals for international support failed. With the revolution's defeat, the tsar suspended the constitution and the most capable Poles fled the country.

For the next twenty-five years, the kingdom was politically inert, although village priests promoted a sense of Polish national consciousness. There was some economic progress, and the concept of organic work, the idea that Poles should concentrate on economic and cultural development rather than pursue impossible political dreams, gained ground.

Nicholas's death in 1855, Russia's defeat in the Crimean War (1853–56), and the onset of emancipation for the serfs led Russia to loosen its grip on Poland. Long-repressed tensions now surfaced, and in 1863 revolution swept Poland once again. For virtually the same reasons, the January Uprising proved as futile as the November one had been. This time, however, the victorious Russians destroyed the Congress Kingdom, folding it into the Russian Empire as the Vistula province.

Frank W. Thackeray

Further reading

Davies, Norman. *God's Playground: A History of Poland*, 2 vols. New York, 1982.

Gieysztor, Aleksander, et al. *History of Poland*, 2d ed. Warsaw, 1979.

Thackeray, Frank W. *Antecedents of Revolution*. Boulder, Colorado, 1980.

Wandycz, Piotr S. *The Lands of Partitioned Poland, 1795–1918*. Seattle, Washington, 1974.

Zawadzki, W. H. *A Man of Honour.* Oxford, 1993.

See also Alexander I; Congress of Vienna; Constantine; Crimean War; Adam Czartoryski; Ksawery Drucki-Lubecki; January Uprising; Nicholas I; November Uprising; Sejm

Polish Corridor

Territory ceded to Poland by Germany on January 10, 1920, as required by the Treaty of Versailles. The Polish Corridor encompassed most of the German province of West Prussia (Pomorze), with an area of 6,300 square miles (17,200 sq km) and a population of 935,000. The number of ethnic Germans was over 175,000 in 1921 but declined considerably thereafter under Polish pressure.

The creation of the corridor stemmed from point thirteen of Woodrow Wilson's (1856–1924) Fourteen Points, which called for Poland's free and secure access to the sea. The long, narrow strip of land divided the German province of East Prussia from Germany proper, although Poland was required to provide unhindered and duty-free transportation across the corridor. The dispute between Germany and Poland over the area was a contentious issue in interwar European diplomacy and one of the immediate causes of World War II.

Poles considered the corridor a reassertion of their sovereignty over historic lands and economic viability through access to the Baltic Sea. Germans were outraged at the separation of East Prussia, an area closely associated with the grandeur of the German past; further, the creation of the corridor was presented by the Allies as a fait accompli with no possibility of a plebiscite, which Germany thought would have resulted in a vote to remain under its sovereignty. The Allies considered this historical justice, since the area had been taken from Poland with the Prussian partition of 1772 and was a step to support the new Polish state. The result poisoned German-Polish relations. In Germany, revision of the eastern borders provided the only common cause of all political parties. In Poland, German threats and fear of a fifth column among the German minority planted a sense of defensiveness in the new republic's national consciousness. On March 21, 1939, Hitler (1889–1945) demanded the return of Danzig (Gdańsk), a free city in the corridor, and construction of an extraterritorial transit corridor in exchange for recognition of the borders and a twenty-five-year nonaggression pact. Poland rejected the offer on March 26. Shortly thereafter, on April 11, Hitler approved Operation White—the invasion of Poland.

James Glapa-Grossklag

Further reading

Blanke, Richard. *Orphans of Versailles: The Germans in Western Poland, 1918–1939.* Lexington, Kentucky, 1993.

Morrow, Ian F.D. *The Peace Settlement in the German Polish Borderlands.* London, 1936.

Riekhoff, Harold von. *German-Polish Relations, 1918–1933.* Baltimore, Maryland, 1971.

See also Józef Beck; East Prussia; Fourteen Points; Gdańsk; Adolf Hitler; Nazi-Polish War; Paris Peace Conference; Woodrow Wilson

Polish Culture

In many ways, Polish culture in the nineteenth and twentieth centuries parallels its historic past. A nation with a deep cultural tradition reflected in education, literature, and the arts, Poland witnessed a significant impact on culture with the partitions among Prussia, Russia, and Austria in the late 1700s. This national trauma caused a reorientation of culture, often around patriotic and historic issues.

Romanticism in Poland, which stressed the nation's historic mission, reached its highest artistic expression in the fields of literature and music. Romanticism in literature (1822–63) manifested ideas of freedom, independence, the solidarity of nations, and the cult of youth. It favored the attitude of protest and the devotion of life in struggle. The most outstanding literary masters of this era were Adam Mickiewicz (1798–1855), Juliusz Słowacki (1809–49), Cyprian Kamil Norwid (1821–83), and Zygmunt Krasiński (1812–59). In 1831, after the downfall of the November Uprising aimed at overthrowing Russian domination, many writers emigrated to France, Switzerland, and Italy, where they produced their best compositions. The most significant works of Mickiewicz were *Dziady* (*Forefathers,* 1833) and the national epic poem, *Pan Tadeusz* (*Master Thaddeus,* 1834). *Kordian* (1834), written by Słowacki, ranks among the greatest masterpieces of Polish drama. Other great figures of the era included Polish comedist Aleksander Fredro (1793–1876) and novelist Józef Ignacy Kraszewski (1812–87).

P Romanticism in art was best represented by the portraits and battle scenes of Piotr Michałowski (1800–1855). It also appeared in the genre scenes of Artur Grottger (1837–67). Architects Piotr Aigner (1756–1841) and Henryk Marconi (1792–1863) expressed the romantic trend in architecture.

The highest achievement of Polish romanticism, however, was found in the music of Frédéric Chopin (1810–49), regarded by many as the greatest of all composers for the piano. Stanisław Moniuszko (1819–72) created the Polish national opera.

With the failure of the January Uprising of 1863, also aimed against Russian domination, romanticism as a doctrine leading to bravado in the national fight became ineffective. National activists and writers led by Aleksander Świętochowski (1849–1938) and Bolesław Prus (pseudonym of Aleksander Głowacki [1847–1912]) now turned to positivism, the philosophical movement that dominated Polish intellectual life until the 1890s. They developed positivist concepts introduced abroad by Auguste Comte (1798–1857), John Stuart Mill (1806–73), and Herbert Spencer (1820–1903). The literature of this period (chiefly prose and journalism) was characterized by political realism and dealt with national and social problems. It propagated rational attitudes and manifested such ideas as the comprehensive economic and cultural development of Polish society and the education of the masses. The positivistic utopian doctrine turned later into critical realism and naturalism.

Prus wrote short stories depicting the plight of the lower classes and novels dealing with social and patriotic issues. His *Lalka* (*The Doll*, 1890) is regarded as a masterpiece of Polish realism. The other eminent representatives of that era were writers Eliza Orzeszkowa (1841–1910) and Maria Konopnicka (1842–1910), the latter an author of patriotic lyrics and short stories depicting social injustice. Henryk Sienkiewicz (1846–1916), a novelist, was the first Polish writer to receive the Nobel Prize in literature (in 1905 for *Quo Vadis*).

The art of the second half of the nineteenth century was characterized by realism and naturalism, following trends in Western Europe. Jan Matejko (1838–93), widely considered the greatest Polish painter, was a master of historical and battle scenes. Aleksander Gierymski (1850–1901) and Józef Chełmoński (1849–1914) painted scenes of country and city life. Juliusz Kossak (1824–99) attained fame as a painter of horses.

Of the many theaters that developed in Poland, the Old Theater in Kraków, which flourished during the period 1865–85, was considered the greatest.

The years from 1890 to 1918, called the period of Young Poland, were dominated by trends related to European modernism. Literature expressed feelings of the decline of traditional middle-class values and cultural decadence. It was characterized by symbolism, turning for inspiration to national folklore and romantic revival. The chief figures of this trend were novelist and playwright Stanisław Przybyszewski (1868–1927) and poets Kazimierz-Przerwa Tetmajer (1865–1940) and Jan Kasprowicz (1860–1926). Władysław Reymont (1867–1925) received the 1924 Nobel prize for the novel *Chłopi* (*The Peasants*, 4 vols., 1904–09). Stefan Żeromski (1864–1925), considered the greatest writer of modern Polish prose, emphasized ideas of social and patriotic mission. Stanisław Wyspiański (1869–1907) was the most prominent dramatist and painter of the era of Young Poland.

At the turn of the century, Polish painting reached its apex. Artistic expression followed the trends in Western art—Art Nouveau (secession), symbolism, and impressionism—while reflecting a distinctive Polish identity. Wyspiański and Józef Mehoffer (1869–1946) created unique paintings and stained-glass windows in Art Nouveau style. The paintings of Jacek Malczewski (1854–1929) represented symbolism. Impressionism was evident in works of Józef Pankiewicz (1866–1940), Władysław Podkowiński (1866–1895), and Olga Boznańska (1865–1940).

The great sculptors of this period were Wacław Szymanowski (1859–1930) and Xawery Dunikowski (1875–1964). Stanisław Witkiewicz (1851–1915) sought Polish national expression in architecture. In music, the foremost composer was Karol Szymanowski (1882–1937).

After World War I, Poland regained its independence. Culture, liberated from its patriotic mission, developed trends associated with new European movements. The most prominent poets of the time after World War I were Leopold Staff (1878–1957), Julian Przyboś (1901–70), Maria Pawlikowska-Jasnorzewska (1891–1945), and Konstanty Ildefons Gałczyński (1905–53).

Among the many eminent prose writers of

the interwar and postwar period were Jarosław Iwaszkiewicz (1894–1980), Maria Dąbrowska (1889–1965), Zofia Nałkowska (1884–1954), and Witold Gombrowicz (1904–69). Dramatist Stanisław I. Witkiewicz (pseudonym, Witkacy [1885–1939]) developed a unique style of expression. The most significant contemporary literary figures include Jerzy Andrzejewski (1909–83), Tadeusz Różewicz (1921–), Stanisław Lem (1921–), and Leon Kruczkowski (1900–1962). Poets Czesław Miłosz (1911–) and Wisława Szymborska (1923–) won the Nobel Prize in literature in 1980 and 1996, respectively.

Polish theater in the interwar period was held in high regard throughout Europe. From 1945 to 1989, all theaters were state-supported, which permitted the establishment of about seventy permanent dramatic teams. Internationally recognized was the vanguard theater, Cricot 2, founded in 1956 by Tadeusz Kantor (1915–90), who was also an eminent painter.

Contemporary Polish art achieved the highest international recognition in painting (Henryk Stażewski [1894–1988], Władysław Strzemiński [1893–1952], Zbigniew Makowski [1930–], Jerzy Duda Gracz [1941–], and Zdzisław Beksiński [1929–]), in poster design (Jan Lenica [1928–], Henryk Tomaszewski [1914–], and Jan Młodożeniec [1929–]), and in tapestry and sculpture (Magdalena Abakanowicz [1930–]).

Polish designers associated with the vanguard group Praesens (1926–30) creatively participated in the international modern movement in architecture. The leading contemporary architects were Bohdan Pniewski (1897–1965); Bohdan Lachert (1900–1987); Maciej Nowicki (1910–1950), designer of Dorton Arena in Raleigh, North Carolina, Marek Leykam (1908–1983), and Jerzy Hryniewiecki (1908–88).

Composers Krzysztof Penderecki (1933–), Henryk Mikołaj Górecki (1933–), and Witold Lutosławski (1913–94) attained international fame, as did filmmakers Roman Polański (1933–), Andrzej Wajda (1926–), Krzysztof Zanussi (1939–), and Krzysztof Kieślowski (1941–96).

Marta Tobolczyk

Further reading

Bogucka, Maria. *Dzieje Kultury polskiej do 1918 roku*. Wrocław, 1987.

Kridl, M. *A Survey of Polish Literature and Culture*. New York, 1967.

Language Bridges Quarterly.

Milosz, Czeslaw. *The History of Polish Literature*. New York, 1969.

Polish Review.

Suchodolski, Bogdan. *A History of Polish Culture*. Warsaw, 1986.

See also Magdalena Abakanowicz; Architecture; Frédéric Chopin; Cinema; Witold Gombrowicz; Jan Kasprowicz; Krzysztof Kieślowski; Józef Kraszewski; Jacek Malczewski; Jan Matejko; Adam Mickiewicz; Czesław Miłosz; Maciej Nowicki; Eliza Orzeszkowa; Polish Art; Polish Literature; Positivism; Bolesław Prus; Romanticism; Henryk Sienkiewicz; Juliusz Słowacki; Aleksander Świętochowski; Wisława Szymborska; Theatre; Andrzej Wajda; Stanisław Wyspiański; Young Poland; Stefan Żeromski

Polish Émigrés

Successive waves of emigration over the past two centuries have created the largest diaspora of East European peoples in the world. The partitions of Poland meant that emigration figures generally were included with those of Russia, Austria, and Prussia/Germany, so no reliable figures exist. Estimates, however, indicate that the number of émigrés and those of Polish descent currently living abroad range between fifteen and twenty million, the largest group being in the United States.

Two different types of emigration can be identified: political and economic. Political emigration began with the partitions and came in several discrete waves following the Poles' defeats in their struggles for liberty after 1795, 1831, 1846–48, 1864, 1905, and 1944, and again in the Communist era after 1956 and 1968. Emigration of those seeking economic betterment began as a trickle in the 1840s that, by the turn of the century, became a veritable flood. Between 1885 and 1914, for example, figures indicate that at least 1.5 million Poles came to the United States alone.

Quantitative and qualitative differences mark the two categories of emigrants. Those who left for economic reasons were a much larger group. Typically they began as migrant laborers moving from impoverished regions of eastern Poland to the more developed regions to the west, primarily Germany. They performed seasonal and heavy physical labor, often wintering back home. Over time many journeyed farther, settled, and assimilated.

P Following the American Civil War, rapid advances in transportation and communications drew many Poles across the Atlantic. Arriving via New York, Boston, and other eastern ports, they quickly spread along the coast to Baltimore, and westward through New York, Pennsylvania, Ohio, Michigan, Indiana, and Illinois, where their labor became a major component in America's growth, both in industry and through the prosperous farming communities they established. Even today, Chicago probably has the highest concentration of ethnic Poles outside Warsaw. At times, whole communities would emigrate and reestablish themselves as ethnic enclaves, such as Panna Maria in Texas.

Most of these emigrants were peasants, craftsmen, and miners. They were poor, illiterate, and had little ethnic awareness. Theirs was a deliberate act, leaving their homeland to escape poverty and oppression. Many retained minimal contacts with their homeland through family ties and the retention of some ethnic foods, holiday traditions, and religion. Though they often continued to speak their dialects and initially their children mostly married within the ethnic community, these emigrants and their offspring quickly assimilated into the new society. Some even went so far as to change their names to avoid ridicule or persecution. At present, their descendants retain, at best, a vague sense of Polishness rooted in ethnic foods, religion, and some social customs. Most of the economic émigrés came to the United States, but significant diaspora communities exist in Canada, Britain, France, Germany, Australia, and Brazil.

Political émigrés were very different. This group, composed of defeated soldiers and political and intellectual leaders escaping incarceration or death, was much smaller in number, generally highly educated, and from the social elite. They brought their ideals with them and sought not economic betterment but rather the opportunity to pursue the cause of Polish liberty in their adopted countries. The majority settled in France, though post–World War II political émigrés have tended toward Britain. Few brought families, especially the soldiers. They pursued a political agenda and only gradually, much more slowly than the economic émigrés, did they assimilate. Some never did.

No greater example of political emigration exists than the Great Emigration (*Wielka Emigracja*), which followed the failure of the 1830–31 Uprising against the Russians. Many of Poland's greatest political and cultural figures were among this group, including Prince Adam Czartoryski (1770–1861), Joachim Lelewel (1786–1861), Adam Mickiewicz (1798–1855), and Frédéric Chopin (1810–49). They brought Polish culture with them, enhanced it, and made it part of European culture as they nurtured and strengthened the sense of Polish nationalism through their actions.

Characteristically, these individuals brought their political baggage with them and continued to fight old battles on new territory, unable to establish unity to pursue their greater goal. In the Great Emigration, Czartoryski's Hôtel Lambert, the center of Polish political émigré activities, conservatively inclined, opposed Lelewel and the Polish Democratic Society's concept for a more democratically oriented state. Similarly, prior to World War I, followers of Roman Dmowski's (1864–1939) National Camp struggled against those of Józef Piłsudski's (1867–1935) Independence Camp for domination of Poland's political future. During World War II, Polish Communists systematically undermined the London government-in-exile. Even following the war, especially in Britain, émigré factions continued what were by then meaningless political quarrels rooted in the prewar era.

The social and cultural gap between the two types of emigrations, their differing goals, as well as the political factionalism prevalent among the cultural and intellectual émigré elite have cumulatively kept Poles from exercising the political power their sheer numbers would indicate they possess. The greatest contributions of the émigrés, therefore, have come on an individual basis, often in the spheres of arts and culture. A few of the best known are Marie Skłodowska-Curie (1867–1934, physics); Ignacy Paderewski (1860–1941, music); Wacław Nijinsky (c. 1889–1950, dance); Joseph Conrad (1857–1924, literature); Sir Lewis Namier (1880–1960, history); Jacob Bronowski (1908–76, philosophy of science); and Samuel Goldwyn (1882–1974, film). The contribution of Polish émigrés to science, culture, the arts, politics, and even sports has been varied and remarkable.

Robert A. Berry

Further reading

Davies, Norman. *God's Playground: A History of Poland,* vol. 2. New York, 1982.

Wandycz, Piotr. *The Lands of Partitioned Poland, 1795–1918.* Seattle, Washington, 1974.

See also Frédéric Chopin; Joseph Conrad; Marie Curie; Adam Czartoryski; Roman Dmowski; Emigration; Hôtel Lambert; Joachim Lelewel; Adam Mickiewicz; November Uprising; Ignacy Paderewski; Józef Piłsudski

Polish Language

Polish is spoken by approximately thirty-eight million people in Poland and by several million others elsewhere. The sixth most widely spoken language in Europe after English, German, French, Italian, and Spanish, it belongs to the Lechitic group (Pomeranian, Slovincian, Polabian, and Kashubian) of the West Slavic languages (Czech, Slovak, Upper and Lower Sorbian) in the Indo-European language family. Characteristics that differentiate Polish from Czech include fixed penultimate stress, loss of quantity distinctions, no syllabic r or l, and the preservation of nasal vowels. Kashubian, spoken by some 150,000 people, is often classified as a dialect of Polish.

The earliest written records include the Papal Bull of Gniezno (1136), whose Latin text contains many Polish toponyms and proper names, the "Bogurodzica," a Polish religious hymn found in a copy of 1408, and the *Kazania Świętokrzyskie,* a mid-fourteenth-century collection of sermons translated from Latin. The literary language, based on linguistic features from Wielkopolska (northwest Poland) and Małopolska (southwest Poland), dates from the sixteenth century and competed with Latin for the following two centuries. Czech provided loan words and served as a cultural and linguistic model from 966—when Moravian missionaries introduced Christianity to Poland—until the sixteenth century. Polish also has borrowings from Latin, German, Ukrainian, French, Italian, and English.

There are five oral vowels in Polish spelled (a, e, i [y], and u [spelled u and ó]) and two nasal vowels (/ē/, ę and /õ/, ą). The thirty-three consonants may be divided into palatalized and nonpalatalized labials (p, p', b, b', f, f', v, v', [w, wi], m, m'), dentals (t, d, s, z, c, dz, n), alveolars (š, ž, č, dž, l, r spelled sz, ż and rz, cz, dż, l, r, respectively), palatals (ś, ź, ć, dź, ń, j), and velars (k, g, x, spelled ch and h, and w, spelled ł). The palatals are spelled si, zi, dzi, ni before vowels other than /i/; the /i/ is spelled y after nonpalatals. Nasal vowels decompose into a vowel and a nasal consonant before other consonants (except w), and voiced consonants are devoiced at the end of the word, such as *ząb* "tooth" [*zomp*].

Polish is an inflected language with markers for gender, number, animacy, and case in the nominal system and for person, number, gender, tense, mood, conjugation class, and aspect in the verbal system. There are seven cases in the singular, and the nominative is substituted for the vocative in the plural. The masculine singular is further differentiated by animacy, and the masculine plural has a personal/nonpersonal distinction (a uniquely Polish feature) manifested in grammatical endings and agreement, such as *stare psy siedziały* (old dogs were sitting) vs. *starzy siąsiedzi siedzieli* (old neighbors were sitting). The verbal system distinguishes person and number in all tenses and in the conditional, as well as gender and masculine personal forms in the past tense, the conditional, and in the imperfective future. Unprefixed verbs tend to be imperfective, while prefixed ones are often perfective or derived imperfectives, such as *pisać* (to write), *napisać,* perfective, *zapisać* (to note down), perfective, *zapisywać,* derived imperfective. Motion verbs have a determinate vs. indeterminate opposition in addition to aspect.

The five major dialect areas are Wielkopolska, Małopolska, Mazowsze, Śląsk (Silesia), and Kaszuby. *Mazurzenie,* the pronunciation of š, ž, č, and dž as s, z, c, and dz, characterizes the central dialects but not the standard language.

Christina Y. Bethin

Further reading

Brooks, Maria Zagorska. *Polish Reference Grammar.* The Hague, 1975.

Klemensiewicz, Zenon. *Historia języka polskiego,* 3 vols. Warsaw, 1961–72.

Rothstein, Robert A. "Polish," in *The Slavonic Languages,* ed. by Bernard Comrie and Greville G. Corbett. London, 1993, 686–758.

Stone, Gerald. "Polish," in *The World's Major Languages,* ed. by Bernard Comrie. London, 1987, 348–66.

Szober, Stanisław. *Gramatyka języka polskiego,* 10th ed. Warsaw, 1968.

See also Slavic Languages

Polish League

Late-nineteenth-century Polish political organization. The Polish League was founded in 1887 in Geneva, largely on the initiative of exiled Polish political activist Col. Zygmunt Miłkowski (1824–1915). A conspiratorial group, the league embraced Polish nationalism, advocated restoration of an independent Poland, and urged reunification of the Polish lands then under tripartite foreign rule (Habsburg, German, and Russian). In many ways, the league drew on the traditions of the Polish insurrections of the earlier decades of the century. In 1893 a circle of league activists, including Roman Dmowski (1864–1939) and Zygmunt Balicki (1858–1916), denouncing the society's purported liberal and Masonic leanings, gained control of the group and transformed it into the National League, espousing a platform of integral nationalism. Within a few years, the National League had evolved into the National Democratic political movement and its various offshoots. The principal historical significance of the Polish League resides in its status as a forerunner of National Democracy, the leading Polish political party of the nationalist right in the modern era.

Neal A. Pease

Further reading

Davies, Norman. *God's Playground: A History of Poland,* vol 2. New York, 1982.

See also Zygmunt Balicki; Roman Dmowski; Freemasonry

Polish Legions

Polish volunteers who fought for the Central Powers against Russia during World War I, numbering twenty thousand in three brigades. Emerging from Józef Piłsudski's (1867–1935) prewar Riflemen's Clubs in Galicia, and later renamed Polish Auxiliary Corps, the legions were closely identified with Piłsudski's movement for an independent Poland. The legions were established on August 16, 1914, by the Polish Supreme National Committee in Kraków, and authorized by the Austrian high command as a separate force on August 27, 1914. While the Polish language was used, legionaires swore an Austrian loyalty oath and were first commanded by Austrian officers of Polish origin. Piłsudski was relegated to commanding the First Brigade. They were disbanded in July 1917 after refusing integration into German forces.

On August 6, 1914, Piłsudski led his irregular Riflemen across the Galician border into Russian Poland to liberate the town of Kielce. While the liberation was short-lived, action by an independent Polish force was received enthusiastically as a symbol of Polish self-reliance. Three days later, the Riflemen were constituted as the Polish Legions. Like Piłsudski, they were more successful in rousing morale and strengthening the Polish diplomatic hand than in military endeavors. The legions fought on the eastern front, seeing significant action at Rokitno (June 1915), Kostiuchnowka (July 1916), and Styre and Stochod (July–August 1916). The Central Powers realized that while the legions weakened the enemy, they also bolstered Polish claims to independence. In April 1917 the Germans absorbed the legions into the German-controlled Polish Armed Forces and demanded that the legionnaires swear an oath of loyalty. At that point, Piłsudski demonstrated his determination to prepare for a Polish state independent of the Central Powers. He refused the new oath and requested the same of the legionnaires, even though he had given up command of the First Brigade in October 1916. The legions were dissolved in July 1917, and the majority, who refused to join either the Austrians or the new Polish army under German command, were interned.

James Glapa-Grossklag

Further reading

Davies, Norman. *God's Playground: A History of Poland,* vol. 2. New York, 1982.

Garlicki, Andrzej. *Geneza Legionów.* Warsaw, 1964.

Wandycz, Piotr. *The Lands of Partitioned Poland, 1795–1918.* Seattle, Washington, 1975.

See also Józef Piłsudski; World War I

Polish Literature

Poland's loss of independence in 1795 altered the course of Polish literature for the next two centuries. In partitioned Poland, literature assumed a position of moral and political leadership, owing to the lack of autonomous Polish organizations. After a brief period of emulating Western ideas, Polish romanticism (1822–64) created messianism, a movement that equated the suffering of partitioned Poland with that of the crucified Christ. Messianism professed the resurrection of a free Poland but at the same time saw Poland's suffering as necessary to save Europe—hence the motto For Your Freedom and Ours.

The failure of the November Uprising of 1831 against the Russians forced many poets into exile and consequently created a division between literature written in Poland and that written abroad, a division that persisted until the 1980s. Three Polish romantic poets—Adam Mickiewicz (1798–1855), Juliusz Słowacki (1809–49), and Zygmunt Krasiński (1812–59)—became spiritual leaders of the nation. Their work united romantic sensibility and created the influential persona of a man who sacrifices not for love but for country (as in Mickiewicz's *Forefather's Eve: Part III*). An émigré was thus not an exile but a pilgrim in search of the Holy Land—free Poland—which in turn would free the world. The writers who stayed in the country popularized romantic ideas in prose; Józef Ignacy Kraszewski (1812–87) wrote several hundred historically accurate novels that enjoyed great popularity and, at the same time, taught Polish history.

The failure of the later January Uprising in 1863, which ended hopes for Polish independence, coincided with the Western influence of scientism, utilitarianism, and anticlericalism, and shifted the stress to social and economic issues. The press, especially the journals *Przegląd Tygodniowy* (*Weekly Review*) and *Kraj* (*The Country*), and prose, especially short narrative forms, were initially the major means of propagating the ideas of positivism aimed at improving the lower classes, equal rights for women and Jews (Eliza Orzeszkowa [1841–1910]), education of society (Maria Konopnicka [1842–1910]), and "the work at the foundations of a nation," among peasants (Bolesław Prus [1847–1912]). A poor but talented child, a backward village, factory life, and immigrants became favorite topics of positivist short stories and novels. Unlike romanticism, which preferred poetry, positivism especially valued prose because of its usefulness and tendentiousness, such as Orzeszkowa's *Martha* (1873).

After the 1880s, the stress shifted from social issues to existential problems of protagonists who struggled to find the right approach to the changing world (seen in works such as Prus's *The Doll* [1890]). Literature still enjoyed a special status of preserving the national spirit in the face of hard-

ships and increasing Russification, as seen in the enormous popularity of historical novels by Henryk Sienkiewicz (1846–1916), which brought him the Nobel Prize in literature in 1905. A special role was seen for the intelligentsia (Stefan Żeromski [1864–1925]), which was supposed to carry out the improvement of the nation.

The period between 1890 and 1918 is usually called Young Poland. It was characterized by a reaction against positivism and by a variety of artistic ideas, including symbolism, expressionism, and naturalism. Unlike positivism, Young Poland freed literature from patriotic and national themes and proclaimed "free art" and "universalism." Young Poland was indebted to Polish romanticism (this period is often called neoromanticism) and rediscovered dramas by romantic poet Juliusz Słowacki and the poetry of Cyprian Kamil Norwid (1821–83). Literary life blossomed mostly in Kraków, which enjoyed more political freedom than other parts of occupied Poland. This can be seen in the journal *Życie* (*Life*), the cabaret Zielony Balonik (Green Balloon), and Stanisław Wyspiański's (1869–1907) "total theatre." Władysław Reymont's (1867–1925) novel, *Chłopi* (*Peasants,* 1904–9), which united naturalism and symbolism, earned him the Nobel Prize in literature (1924).

The end of World War I brought Poland independence and a multitude of new ideas. The literary scene was dominated by various poetic groups. The initial euphoria was marked by the creation of groups such as Skamander, which called for optimism and vitalism. Another literary group, Kraków Avant-garde, was fascinated with "city, mass, machine" and urbanization, and stressed the semantic density of poetry, epitomized in the work of T. Peiper (1891–1969). Disillusionment in the 1930s brought the Second Avant-Garde, with its apocalyptic visions of the future; this was best seen in the writings of Czesław Miłosz (1911–). Stanisław Ignacy Witkiewicz (1885–1939) created his theory of pure form in theater, while Bruno Schulz (1892–1942) created a new world of visions in his two collections of short stories. The psychological novels of Zofia Nałkowska (1884–1954) and especially those of Maria Kuncewiczowa (1899–1989) explored the realm of womanhood.

After World War II, Poland found itself in a situation resembling its plight during the nineteenth century, with a division between literature written by Poles at home and by émigrés. The

P short-lived period of socialist realism after the war, which followed the artistic dictates of the Soviet Union and its leader Josef Stalin (1879–1953), did not bring any major works in Poland, though major works were written abroad. In Paris, Miłosz wrote his famous *Zniewolony umysł* (*The Captive Mind*, 1953). In Argentina, Witold Gombrowicz (1904–69) created his "inter-human theatre," in which one always creates oneself through others' eyes. In Italy, Gustaw Herling-Grudziński (1919–) wrote *Inny świat* (*The Other World*), one of the most compelling accounts of concentration camps in the Soviet Union.

In Poland, many poets "debuted" for the second time in 1956 during the political thaw after Stalin's death. This included Zbigniew Herbert (1924–) and Wisława Szymborska (1923–). Others, like Tadeusz Różewicz (1921–), who witnessed unspeakable horrors during World War II, struggled with its inheritance.

During the 1970s, writers came increasingly to criticize the regime, thanks to the emergence of an independent press and many underground publishing houses, such as Kultura (Culture) in Paris. These changes allowed for grotesque visions of corroding communism in Tadeusz Konwicki's (1924–) fiction. Lost lands, the lost people of pre-war Poland, and their cultures emerged in novels by Julian Stryjkowski (1905–95), Tadeusz Konwicki (1926–), and Paweł Huelle (1957–). In theater, Sławomir Mrożek (1930–) invented his version of the theatre of absurd, Tadeusz Kantor (1915–90) expanded the boundaries of theater with his Cricot-2 (theatre of memory), while Jerzy Grotowski (1933–) invented "poor theatre" with his Laboratory Theatre.

Katarzyna Zechenter

Further reading

Carpenter, Bogdana. *The Poetic Avant-garde in Poland*. Seattle, Washington, 1983.

Czerwinski, E. J., ed. *Dictionary of Polish Literature*. Westport, Connecticut, 1994.

Gerould, Daniel. ed., *Twentieth-Century Polish Avant-Garde Drama*. Ithaca, New York, 1977.

Levine, Madeline G. *Contemporary Polish Poetry 1925–1975*. Boston, 1981.

Miłosz, Czesław. *The History of Polish Literature*. Berkeley, California, 1983.

See also De-Stalinization; Witold Gombrowicz; Zbigniew Herbert; Intelligentsia; January Uprising; Adam Mickiewicz; Czesław Miłosz; November Uprising; Eliza Orzeszkowa; Polish Culture; Polish Émigrés Positivism; Press; Bolesław Prus; Romanticism; Russification; Bruno Schulz; Henryk Sienkiewicz; Juliusz Słowacki; Stalin; Wisława Szymborska; Theater; Stanisław Witkiewicz; Stanisław Wyspiański; Young Poland; Stefan Żeromski; Zhdanovshchina

Polish Logic

Major intellectual current focusing on methodological and propaedeutical concerns that dominated successive generations of Polish intellectual life. Between the world wars (1918–39), Poland experienced an intense and sophisticated development in the study of logic, a natural outgrowth of the interest in positivism that had been prevalent since the Polish uprising of 1863 against the Russians. This progressive development sought the philosophical relevance of symbolic logic, cultivated an interest in semantics, and finally explored practical applications of the analytic tools to philosophy. The central figure in the cultivation of logical studies was Kazimierz Twardowski (1866–1938), who was joined by many students motivated by his interest in methodological rigor, as well as clarity of thought and expression. Centered first in Lwów and later in Warsaw, Twardowski's school was opposed to all forms of irrationalism and dogmatism, emphasizing the continuity of philosophy and science.

Later, Kazimierz Ajdukiewicz (1890–1963) and Alfred Tarski (1902–83) dominated the landscape. Ajdukiewicz concentrated on the influence of language on knowledge, and stressed that science contains a priori elements embedded in the language that science presupposes. He argued that the progress of the empirical sciences may demand a modification of these provisionally taken a priori elements. In the domain of semantics, Tarski attempted to develop an understanding between expressions and their denoted objects. By his expansion of scientific language beyond the mere syntactical, he laid the foundation for metalanguages that could bridge the gap between various languages and extralinguistic objects. Jan Łukasiewicz (1878–1956) also made significant contributions to the logic of propositions with his introduction of the principle of trivalence and its associated truth tables, replacing the traditional bivalent true/false.

In Warsaw, Stanisław Leśniewski (1886–1939) and Tadeusz Kotarbiński (1886–1981) developed logic as an autonomous discipline in conjunction with the Warsaw School of Mathematics. Writing first in natural language and subsequently formalized logical expressions, Leśniewski contributed to the development of a foundation for mathematics as well as an ontology. Besides his developments in the semantics of concretism, Kotarbiński extended his interest to practical philosophy and the achievement of happiness.

James Eiswert

Further reading

Philosophical Logic in Poland, ed. by Jan Woleânski. Boston, 1994.

Simons, Peter. Philosophy and Logic in Central Europe from Bolzano to Tarski: Selected Essays. Boston, 1992.

See also Kazimierz Ajdukiewicz; January Uprising; Philosophy; Alfred Tarski; Kazimierz Twardowski

Polish Question

A complex of issues touching on general European diplomatic history and the internal affairs of the three "partitioning" empires: tsarist Russia, Prussia (and its successor, imperial Germany), and the Habsburg Empire. The Polish Question first arose with the dismemberment of the Polish Commonwealth at the end of the eighteenth century. It then functioned as a common denominator in the formulation of foreign policy for these powers until World War I. The question was not fully resolved until 1946, with the creation of the Polish People's Republic, remaining a highly explosive and delicate issue that vexed Europe's diplomats.

In its narrow, diplomatic sense, the Polish Question concerned the disposition of the Polish lands throughout the nineteenth and part of the twentieth century. Over that span of time, a truly independent Polish state existed only briefly (1918–39). For the rest of the period, the Polish lands were constituent parts of the three great neighboring states, which came to regard their Polish population as nothing more than another ethnic minority. Nonetheless, from the Congress of Vienna (1815) through the Treaty of Versailles (1919–20), and on to the December 1970 legit-imization of Poland's western boundary with the Federal Republic of Germany, the Polish Question continually emerged as an issue affecting European statesmen. In 1815, for example, coupled with disagreements about how to treat defeated Saxony, the Polish Question led to great strains among the victorious allied coalition against Napoléon (1769–1821). During 1848–49, the fate of Polish lands and Polish patriots was discussed from London to Istanbul. At the end of World War I, the constitution of a free and independent Poland was enshrined in President Woodrow Wilson's (1856–1924) Fourteen Points. The subsequent fighting over the frontiers of the new state illustrated both the depth of nationalist feeling and the complexity of defining legitimate borders in Eastern Europe. Again at the end of World War II, border issues were crucial, as Stalin (1879–1953) forcibly pushed Poland westward while absorbing some "traditional" Polish eastern lands.

While clearly an issue that made its presence felt often on the diplomatic chessboard, the Polish Question was never of fundamental importance to the Great Powers. It was, rather, a tool to be used by diplomats and often a mirror that reflected other strains in the relations among the more powerful European states. Many historians now agree that, although the Polish Question generated a tremendous number of diplomatic memoranda and a mountain of secondary literature, its actual influence on political as well as socioeconomic developments within the Polish lands was negligible.

A broader definition of the Polish Question should also include a discussion of the domestic problems posed by the partitions for Russia, Austria, and Germany. The histories of each of the provinces during the nineteenth century reflect the varied policies of the different regimes. The great, though futile, insurrections of 1830 and 1863 against Russian domination led to fundamental changes in the political fate of Poles in each of the partitions. Similarly, events during the 1905 revolution in Russia (and its Polish lands) reflected the new, modernizing structure of society at large. Each of these events had its effect not only on Poles but on the governments of each of the partitioning states. In this sense, the Polish Question had become an integral part of the internal developments of the region as a whole.

Peter Wozniak

P

Further reading

Davies, Norman. *God's Playground: A History of Poland,* vol. 2, *1795 to the Present.* New York, 1982.

Dziewanowski, M. K. *Poland in the 20th Century.* New York, 1977.

Leslie, Robert F. *The Polish Question.* London, 1964.

See also Congress of Vienna; Fourteen Points; Great Powers; Habsburg Empire; January Uprising; Napoléon; November Uprising; Paris Peace Conference; Polish-Soviet War; Prussia; Revolutions of 1848; Russia; Stalin; Woodrow Wilson

Polish–Soviet War (1919–21)

Military conflict between Poland and the Soviet Union. The end of World War I, combined with the Russian Revolution and general chaos in Eastern Europe, produced an immediate outbreak of major war between the Second Polish Republic and the Soviet regime in their infancy. In a sense, the struggle represented a renewal of the centuries-old rivalry between Poland and Russia for control of the intervening borderlands. More immediate causes of war were the hopes of Józef Piłsudski (1867–1935), the Polish chief of state and commander in chief, to secure his country's future by constructing a large, Polish-led East European confederation at Russian expense, and on the Soviet side, the Bolsheviks' efforts to retain the lands of the former tsardom and, later, to export their revolution westward to the vulnerable, war-torn regions of East Central Europe. Contrary to durable legend, Poland received little aid or encouragement from the Allied powers, and the campaign bore no marks of a Western-sponsored crusade against communism.

The first armed clashes between Polish and Soviet units occurred in 1919, upon the withdrawal of German forces after their defeat in the world war. Attempts by the Allies to mediate the dispute on the basis of the so-called Curzon Line were, in effect, rejected by both combatants. A joint offensive of Polish and sympathetic Ukrainian forces reached Kiev in May 1920, but at that point a Red Army counterthrust seized the initiative and carried the fighting onto Polish territory. The Soviet advance threatened the existence of the Polish republic, and the Bolshevik military and political leadership openly forecast the spread of their revolution into Germany and beyond.

In August 1920 Polish forces under Piłsudski's command unexpectedly checked the Red Army offensive before Warsaw, and the tide of battle changed yet again. The Poles won a series of victories and took back much territory before the Soviets sued for peace in October 1920. A formal peace settlement was reached in the Treaty of Riga of March 1921.

The last great war of horse cavalry in Europe, the Polish-Soviet conflict produced a variety of significant results. Poland got the better of the fighting and in so doing preserved the independence of the country. It has been argued that its efforts delayed the Soviet engulfment of Central Europe by a quarter century. The Battle of Warsaw, often described as the "miracle on the Vistula," has been termed one of the decisive military engagements of modern history. At the same time, some commentators note that the Polish military victory was not sufficiently complete to achieve a permanent weakening of Soviet strength and may, in fact, have increased the determination of the Soviet leadership to reclaim a sphere of influence in Central and Eastern Europe.

Neal A. Pease

Further reading

Davies, Norman. *White Eagle, Red Star.* London, 1972.

Dziewanowski, M. K. *Joseph Pilsudski.* Stanford, California, 1969.

Piłsudski, Józef, *Rok 1920.* Łódź, 1989.

Wandycz, Piotr S. *Soviet-Polish Relations, 1917–1921.* Cambridge, Massachusetts, 1969.

See also Curzon Line; Józef Piłsudski; Peace of Riga; Red Army; Mikhail Tukhachevsky; Warsaw, Battle of

Pomaks

Most common name given to indigenous Orthodox Bulgarians who converted to Islam during the five-hundred-year period of Ottoman rule in the regions of southeastern Europe inhabited by Bulgarians. Other names used to identify non-Muslim converts to Islam in various areas of southeastern Europe included ahryanins, apovniks, mŭrvaks, poganiks, and torbeshes.

The term *pomak* (helper) is derived from the Bulgarian Slavic word *pomagach,* used by

Orthodox Bulgarians to describe their sentiments regarding those who apostatized their Christian faith to join the ranks of the dominant religious-cultural segment of Ottoman Turkish society. In the eyes of their fellow Christian Bulgarians, the converts were "helpers" of the Muslim Turkish ruling establishment, and, in the context of the Ottoman *millet* system, which officially recognized differences among groups of people solely on the basis of religion, the converts were considered "Turks."

Pomaks accepted all the dogmatic precepts of Islam but tended to modify Islamic rules regarding such matters as dress and cuisine by retaining much of their ethnically Slavic traditions. Most significantly, they continued using their native Slavic Bulgarian language rather than adopting the Turkish tongue spoken by the Ottoman ruling establishment or by the Muslim ethnic Turks settled in lands inhabited by the empire's Bulgarian subjects.

The majority of pomaks were concentrated in the Rhodope Mountains region of what today is south-central Bulgaria. Past Bulgarian nationalist historiography attributed this fact to the massed forced conversion of Orthodox Rhodope Bulgarians during the middle of the seventeenth century, as a subsidiary consequence of mustering Ottoman troops from the central Balkans for use in Crete during an extended war against the Venetians (1645–70). This interpretation of pomak origins is disputed today by many Bulgarian and Western scholars, who trace the Rhodope and other Bulgarian conversions to social-political factors inherent in the system of Ottoman rule itself.

Dennis P. Hupchick

Further reading

Hupchick, Dennis P. *The Bulgarians in the Seventeenth Century: Slavic Orthodox Society and Culture under Ottoman Rule.* Jefferson, North Carolina, 1993.

Kosev, Dimitŭr et al., eds. *Istoriia na Bŭlgariia,* vol. 4. Sofia, 1983.

Shishkov, S. N. *Pomatsite v trite bŭlgarski oblasti: Trakiia, Makedoniia, i Miziia.* Plovdiv, Bulgaria, 1914.

See also Islam; *Millet;* Muslims; Rhodope Mountains

Pomerania

Former Prussian province (along with Brandenburg and Upper and Lower Silesia) straddling the border between eastern Germany and western Poland, and stretching north to south from the Baltic Sea to the Notec and Warta Rivers. Pomerania (from a Slavic root, Pomorze, meaning "along the coast") is a low-lying, poorly drained sandy coastal plain, formed from sediments deposited by the sea. Much of the region is covered by pine forests and swamps and is dotted by many glacial lakes that, along with the seacoast beaches, provide recreational opportunities and an economic base for tourism.

The physical geography of the coastline was shaped by the rising waters of the Baltic Sea as the Scandinavian glacier retreated. The coast is different on either side of the Oder River; to the west the shore is irregular and broken with several islands; on the Polish side, to the east, it becomes more regular and smooth. The area slopes gently to the northwest; glacial moraines are significant here, reaching more than 800 feet (242 m) in height in some places. Near Gdańsk, glacial deposits are over 450 feet (136 m) thick.

Pomerania, along with Silesia and East Prussia, was a German homeland for six centuries. Eastern (Farther) Pomerania (German, Hinterpommern) in Poland stretches over 300 miles (500 km) from the Baltic's Pomeranian Bay at the mouth of the Oder River to the Vistula delta on the Gulf of Gdańsk, and includes the provinces of Gdańsk and Bydgoszcz. Polish Pomerania has an area of 5,899 square miles (16,386 sq km). Products of the area include rye, oats, sugar beets, barley, potatoes, wheat, and some cattle. The region was Polish until the partition of Poland in 1772, when it came under Prussian control. In the latter nineteenth century Pomerania (except for the district of Dzieldowo) was incorporated into the German administrative area of West Prussia. After World War I, it was returned to Poland and remained in Polish hands except for the German occupation during World War II. Hither (Western) Pomerania (German, Vorpommern) ranges from Stralsun in Germany to Szczecin in Poland, an area about 30 miles (50 km) wide. It became part of East Germany after World War II.

Since World War II, under Polish control Gdańsk has been rebuilt and repopulated and its coastal port economy is well integrated with that of Gdynia. The division of labor between the two

P cities leaves most passenger traffic to Gdynia, while Gdańsk remains an industrial port, serving the timber and food-processing industries, and the export of Upper Silesian coal. Shipbuilding is important in Szczecin (German, Stettin), as well as in the German cities of Stralsund and Greifswald.

Barbara VanDrasek

Further reading

Curtis, Glenn E., ed. *Poland: A Country Study.* Washington, D.C., 1994.

Davies, Norman. *God's Playground: A History of Poland,* vol. 2, *1795 to the Present.* New York, 1982.

Gottmann, Jean. *A Geography of Europe,* 3d ed. New York, 1962.

See also Gdańsk; Oder River

Porte

Short for Sublime Porte, the personal residence of the Ottoman grand vizier (prime minister) and official headquarters of Ottoman government in Constantinople/Istanbul. The term "Sublime Porte" was used in Europe in much the same way as the Court of St. James is used for the British government. In 1654 Sultan Mehmed IV (1642–93) presented the grand vizier with a building that served as the vizier's official residence and government office, a move that marked the gradual transfer of political authority away from the imperial palace. The grand vizierate was increasingly recognized as the Ottoman government's nerve center, known as Bab-i Ali, High Gate, or Sublime Porte. The use of terms like "gate," "door," and "threshold" for the seat of government was an ancient one in the Middle East.

During centralizing reforms of the *Tanzimat* era in the nineteenth century, the Porte acquired greater administrative and executive authority and became the center of an expanding secular bureaucracy that tried to keep the empire together. The grand vizier directed the Porte's network of offices and departments, such as Ministries of Internal and Foreign Affairs, Council of Ministers, and Council of State. The Porte also became the focus of European diplomatic intrigue and rivalry associated with the Eastern Question.

Theophilus C. Prousis

Further reading

Anderson, M. S. *The Eastern Question, 1774–1923.* London, 1966.

Findley, Carter. *Bureaucratic Reform in the Ottoman Empire: The Sublime Porte, 1789–1922.* Princeton, New Jersey, 1980.

Shaw, Stanford. *History of the Ottoman Empire and Modern Turkey,* 2 vols. New York, 1976–77.

See also Eastern Question; Ottoman Empire; *Tanzimat*

Positivism

Diverse collection of thinkers and schools sharing a firm belief in the power of scientific methodology that had a profound effect on East Central European intellectual developments. In general, positivists agree that facts are the valid objects of knowledge; science is the only valid generator of truth claims about facts; and philosophy is the general science that seeks the principles of all the regional sciences (physics, biology, etc.), and it applies those principles to all domains of human life and organization. Positivism is traditionally divided into three camps or schools: social positivism, evolutionary positivism, and critical positivism. Social positivists, following the spirit of Auguste Comte (1789–1857) and John Stuart Mill (1806–73), applied the positivistic creeds to social and cultural phenomena. Evolutionary positivists, influenced by Herbert Spencer (1820–1903) and Wilhem Wundt (1832–1920), attempted a unification of physical, psychological, and social phenomena. Inspired by Ernst Mach (1838–1916), critical positivists interpreted scientific law as cognitive constructions rather than objective realities. Critical positivism can be further divided into neopositivism and logical positivism. Neopositivists, influenced by Bertrand Russell (1872–1970) and the later Ludwig Wittgenstein (1889–1951), focused on linguistic issues of meaning and syntax, while the logical positivists, inspired by Rudolf Carnap (1891–1970) and the early Wittgenstein, accepted a correspondence between reality and language that could be verified. The impact of these schools on Eastern Europe varied in direct proportion to each region's philosophical traditions and openness to Western thought.

In Poland, the antiromantic climate after the failure of the 1863 uprising against the Russians became fertile ground for Polish positivism. Influenced by the social positivists, Julian Ochorowicz (1850–1917) focused on the practical applications of scientific methodology to human social, political, economic, and legal institutions with a firm commitment to the progress of humanity through the application of that methodology. This progress was achieved through slow "organic work," a sober empiricism, and a distrust of all metaphysics. Marxism, with its shared interests in the practical application of the scientific paradigm to social concerns, eventually absorbed or eclipsed the social positivist thought of Ochorowicz.

In contradistinction, critical positivism, or empiriocriticism, refashioned the positivists' notion of scientific law as an epistemic construct for cognitive efficiency, rather than a relation between facts. The rise of Polish logic reflected the developments in critical positivism known as neopositivism, with its emphasis on language, logic, and the clarification of meaning. Many Polish logicians kept in close contact with the logical positivists of the Vienna Circle (the major European center for positivism) but rejected many of their tenets. Logical positivism, which also arose from critical positivism, maintained a one-to-one correspondence between atomic fact and elementary experience, and the verification principle as the ultimate principle of scientific methodology. Alfred Tarski's (1902–83) work on semantics had a major influence on the Vienna Circle. Tarski encouraged its members to loosen the restrictive views concerning language and truth that eventually led to a break with others in the movement and its splintering.

In Czechoslovakia and Yugoslavia, evolutionary positivism was best represented by František Krejčí (1858–1934). Krejčí's acceptance of Wundt's double aspect theory underwrote his attempt to show that all progress is a variation of biological evolutionary processes enfolding from a primordial substance (matter/energy)—the centerpiece of evolutionary positivism. Evolutionary positivism produced both materialistic and spiritualistic/idealistic interpretations, as well as attempts to unify the two.

Although Tomáš G. Masaryk (1850–1937), Czech philosopher and statesman, initially espoused positivism, he eventually became disillusioned with it. Nevertheless, Masaryk's early writings influenced a small group of positivists in Yugoslavia. In Serbia, Svetozar Marković (1846–75) adapted evolutionary positivism into an activist anthropological philosophy providing an agenda for social change; in Slovenia, Dragiša Djurić (1871–1941) attempted to resolve the tension between the two forms of evolutionary positivism.

Positivism, like all forms of philosophy in Czechoslovakia, was interrupted by the German invasion of 1939 and later became absorbed by the official Marxist positions. However, after the break with dogmatic Stalinism in Yugoslavia, various forms of positivism joined with existentialism to provide a counterpoint to Marxism.

James Eiswert

Further reading

Blejwas, Stanislaus A. *Realism in Polish Politics: Warsaw Positivism and National Survival in Nineteenth Century Poland.* New Haven, Connecticut, 1984

Scharff, Robert C. *Comte after Positivism.* New York, 1995.

Simon, Walter Michael. *European Positivism in the Nineteenth Century: An Essay in Intellectual History.* Ithaca, New York, 1963.

See also January Uprising; Svetozar Marković; Marxism; Thomáš G. Masaryk; Philosophy; Polish Logic; Alfred Tarski

Potsdam Conference

Final meeting of the Big Three to resolve post–World War II differences. From July 17 to August 2, 1945, representatives from Great Britain, the United States, and the Soviet Union met at Potsdam, outside Berlin, to resolve outstanding issues generated by World War II. Winston Churchill (1874–1965) and Harry S Truman (1884–1972) demanded that the Soviets adhere to the Yalta Declaration of Liberated Europe, which called for free elections in Hungary, Romania, and Bulgaria, as the criterion for awarding diplomatic recognition to the former Axis states. Conversely, the Soviets viewed the already existing governments there as legitimate. In an attempt to break the stalemate, the delegates agreed to send the Balkan issue to the newly formed Council of Foreign Ministers, which had responsibility for drafting treaties with the former Axis satellite states.

The council began its meetings on September 11, 1945, and completed its work in January 1947, with treaties signed at a Paris Peace Conference on February 10, 1947. In return for promises of free elections, Great Britain and the United States agreed to sign peace treaties awarding diplomatic recognition to the three Balkan states. Specifically, the Bulgarian treaty restored the borders of January 1, 1941, which included Southern Dobrudja (Dobruzha); the Hungarian treaty restored the boundaries of January 1, 1938, marking the loss of Transylvania to Romania, Eastern Slovakia and the area opposite Bratislava to Czechoslovakia, and Ruthenia to the Soviet Union. The Romanian treaty confirmed the loss of Northern Bukovina and Bessarabia to the Soviet Union, the cession of Southern Dobrudja to Bulgaria, and the restoration of Transylvania from Hungary. Since there was no Austrian peace treaty and Soviet troops occupied Austria, Moscow received the right to station troops in Hungary and Romania in a line of communication between the Soviet Union and Austria. This situation remained until 1958, three years after an Austrian peace treaty.

Joseph F. Harrington

Further reading

Foreign Relations of the United States: The Conference of Berlin (The Potsdam Conference) 1945, 2 vols. Washington, D.C., 1960.

Harrington, Joseph and Bruce Courtney. *Tweaking the Nose of the Russians: Fifty Years of American-Romanian Relations, 1940–1990.* Boulder, Colorado, 1991.

Wheeler-Bennett, John W. and Anthony Nicholls. *The Semblance of Peace: The Political Settlement After the Second World War.* New York, 1972.

See also Bessarabian Question; Winston Churchill; Dobrudja; Subcarpathian Rus'; Transylvanian Dispute; Yalta

Poznań

One of Poland's largest commercial and industrial cities and capital of the province of Poznań. Poznań (German, Posen) is located 190 miles (300 km) west of Warsaw on a broad fertile plain of the Warta River. The population of Poznań in 1960 was 390,000; in 1971, 476,300; and by the end of 1989, the city had grown to 588,700.

Poznań was a Hanseatic trading center during the Middle Ages—one of Poland's oldest—and the traditional capital of western Poland. Poznania was annexed to Prussia after the Congress of Vienna in 1815, then became part of independent Poland after World War I. The majority of Germans in Poland resided in the regions of Poznania, Pomerania, and Silesia, before large-scale emigration from these regions between the two world wars.

Most of the ethnic Germans expelled from south and central Yugoslavia were resettled in the Polish area occupied by the Nazis in 1939, especially in Poznania. To accommodate this influx, the Nazis expelled many Polish and Jewish residents of this area. After wartime occupation, Poznań was liberated by the Soviets and returned to Poland in 1945. The battle to free the city took two arduous months, however, so much was left in ruins; more than half of the city was destroyed, including 80 percent of the historic old center.

After the war, the city was rebuilt as an important industrial and engineering center by the Polish government. The first Polish factory that produced machinery was built in Poznań. The local economy is diverse, based on mills, breweries, rubber, ceramics and pottery making, agricultural machinery, metallurgy, and finishing of consumer goods. Its proximity to rich lignite deposits in the area provides energy and raw materials for chemical manufacture. The city is an important rail junction.

Since 1929, Poznań has been the site of some of the largest international fairs in Europe and is also home to the Adam Mickiewicz University and to many technical and scientific institutions.

Barbara VanDrasek

Further reading

Curtis, Glenn E., ed. *Poland: A Country Study.* Washington, D.C., 1994.

Held, Joseph. *Dictionary of East European History since 1945.* Westport, Connecticut, 1994.

Hoffman, George W. ed. *Europe in the 1990s: A Geographic Analysis,* 6th ed. New York, 1990.

Turnock, David. *Eastern Europe: An Historical Geography 1815–1945.* New York, 1989.

See also Congress of Vienna

Pozsgay, Imre (1933–)

Hungary's best-known Communist-Populist reform politician. Born into a peasant family, Pozsgay was educated as a teacher and studied Marxism-Leninism at Moscow's Lenin Institute in the 1950s. From 1957 to 1965, he was a functionary (and after 1965–68 secretary) of the Bács-Kiskun county committee of the country's Communist Party. In 1969 he was put in charge of the Central Committee's press department. Between 1971 and 1975, he was also the managing editor of the party journal, *Társadalmi Szemle* (*Review of Society*). During the 1970s and 1980s, he served in numerous important government and party posts.

Along with Rezső Nyers (1923–), Pozsgay was the most outspoken representative of the party's reform wing. His broad appeal was largely due to his ability to discuss Hungary's specific problems in an erudite and straightforward manner, and to his courage in breaking with dogma. For example, he was the first party figure to refer to the events of 1956 as a "revolution," rejecting the official pro-Soviet label of "counterrevolution." After the party's 1989 reorganization as the Hungarian Socialist Party, he served as its vice president but soon broke with it. In 1997 he resurfaced as an influential figure in the Magyar Democratic Forum.

András Boros-Kazai

Further reading

Banac, Ivo, ed. *Eastern Europe in Revolution.* Ithaca, New York, 1992.

Bozóki, András, A. Köröséy, and G. Schöpflin, eds. *Post-Communist Transition: Emerging Pluralism in Hungary.* New York, 1992.

East, Roger. *Revolutions in Eastern Europe.* New York, 1992.

Poszgay, Imre. *1989: Politikus-Pálya a pártállamban és a rendszerváltásban.* Budapest, 1993.

———. *Demokrácia és kultúra.* Budapest, 1980.

———. *Esélyünk a reform.* Budapest, 1988.

———. *Szocialista társadalom és humanizmus.* Budapest, 1978.

See also Communist Party of Hungary

Prague

One of Central Europe's greatest cities and capital of the Czech Republic. Prague (Czech, Praha) has a prominent role in the histories of the Holy Roman and Habsburg Empires, Czechoslovakia, and the Czech Republic. Prague (population 1,215,000 in 1990) is a major center of industry, administration, culture, and tourism.

Prague has been occupied since Paleolithic times, because it offers a crossing over the Vltava River. The modern settlement emerged in the ninth century. In the thirteenth century Prague became the Bohemian capital, and in the fourteenth through sixteenth centuries it served as one of the royal residences for the Holy Roman Empire. From 1526 until 1918, when it became the capital of Czechoslovakia, Prague was a provincial capital of the Habsburg Empire.

Prague has frequently been the site of civil rebellion. Protests and uprisings related to the Reformation occurred in Prague, notably those led by the martyr Jan Hus (c. 1370–1415) and his Hussite followers. In 1618 such a revolt was a major factor in the outbreak of the Thirty Years' War (1618–48); in 1620 Protestant forces were defeated in battle at the nearby White Mountain. Civil uprisings also took place during the Revolutions of 1848 and again in May 1945, shortly before Soviet troops replaced the German occupiers. In 1968, during the so-called Prague Spring, a rejection of some aspects of Communist rule led to an invasion by Warsaw Pact forces. In 1989 demonstrations on Wenceslaus Square successfully forced the Communists from power in what was called the Velvet Revolution.

Fittingly, post-Communist Czechoslovakia's first leader was writer Václav Havel (1936–). Prague is a major center of European culture; it is closely associated with the lives of Mozart (1756–91), Bedřich Smetana (1824–84), Antonín Dvořák (1841–1904), Leoš Janáček (1854–1928), Rainer Maria Rilke (1875–1926), and Franz Kafka (1883–1924). The city is the site of many musical and theatrical institutions, as well as Charles University (founded in 1348), other educational institutions, and seats of power of both Roman Catholic and Orthodox archbishops.

Prague's economic role grew rapidly during the eighteenth and nineteenth centuries. It is a major rail and highway junction and the terminus of shipping on the Vltava. A wide variety of heavy industrial and consumer-oriented manufactured goods are produced. Tourism soared after 1989, and Prague is now one of Europe's most popular tourist destinations. Both its site in a deep valley of the Vltava and its store of architectural treasures dating back to medieval times account for the city's beauty, which has been enhanced by recent investment to refurbish its buildings. However, planners have long worked to preserve the city's numerous

P extensive historic areas. Thus, for example, expansion of manufacturing and housing during the socialist era took place on its margins. Prague, "City of 100 Spires," is especially noted for its castle (Hradčany), which rises impressively above the Vltava and the Charles Bridge.

William H. Berentsen

Further reading

Magocsi, Paul Robert. *Historical Atlas of East Central Europe.* Seattle, Washington, 1993.

Mellor, R.E.H. *Eastern Europe.* London, 1975.

Wechsberg, J. *Prague: The Mystical City.* New York, 1971.

See also Architecture; Charles University; Czech Culture; Antonín Dvořák; Václav Havel; Leoš Janáček; Franz Kafka; Prague Spring; Prague Slav Congress; Revolutions of 1848; Bedřich Smetana; Velvet Revolution; Vltava River

Prague Slav Congress (May 1848–June 1848)

Assembly of 341 Slavic delegates—mostly from the Habsburg monarchy—during the Revolutions of 1848 intended to promote political cooperation among the Slavs of East Central Europe to counter rising German and Magyar nationalism. Leading members of the Czech liberal middle class believed that the Slavs were threatened on all sides by Germans, Magyars, and Russians and that only in a strong Habsburg monarchy would they be safe. The clearest exposition of this belief is the letter from Czech historian František Palacký (1798–1876) in rejecting the *Grossdeutsche* ("big" German) program of the Frankfort Parliament, in which he said: "If the Austrian Empire had not already existed for centuries, one would have to make all speed, in the interest of Europe and humanity itself, to create it."

The Congress's agenda focused on Slav reciprocity and imperial reorganization. The greatest difficulty faced by the delegates was reconciling the position of the liberals who initiated the congress with that of their more radical counterparts on the question of imperial reorganization. The Czech liberals and their allies argued for a federal reorganization plan based on the historic crownlands. The more radical proposals came from delegates who did not have a crownland to call their own, most notably the Slovenes and Ruthenes, who demanded reorganization along ethnic lines.

The congress also experienced difficulty over how to resolve the Polish question. Polish delegates from Austria and Prussia refrained from calling openly for a reconstituted Polish state, but their desire could not be hidden completely. Rather than demanding the independence of Galicia, which would seriously weaken Austria, the Poles promoted a Pan Slavic unity that was not based on existing political entities.

Despite these differences, the Austroslav vision of the Czech liberals prevailed. The congress issued two manifestoes, the first of which was an address to the emperor requesting a reorganization of the Slavic parts of the monarchy on the basis of the existing crownlands. Concessions to Slovene and Ruthene demands included the call for a single administration for the Slovenes; Galicia was to remain unified, but the Ruthenian language was to be elevated to an equal status with Polish. The second manifesto was a proclamation to the Slav peoples of Europe, which affirmed the idea of Slav solidarity, and demanded equality with Germans and Magyars in the monarchy and a reorganization of the state into a federation of nationalities. That this last demand was not spelled out in detail is an indication of the congress's difficulty in reconciling the various historic and ethnic programs promoted at the congress.

Despite its lack of concrete results, the congress made major strides toward strengthening the political characteristics of Slavic national consciousness, and it defined the middle ground in the upcoming debates over ethnic versus political nationalism. The congress was closed in June when martial law was imposed on Prague by the Austrian army under Field Marshall Windischgrätz (1787–1862).

T. Mills Kelly

Further reading

Hantsch, Hugo. "Pan-Slavism, Austro-Slavism, Neo-Slavism: The All-Slav Congresses and the Nationality Problems of Austria-Hungary." *Austrian History Yearbook* 1 (1965): 23–37.

"Letter Sent by František Palacký to Frankfurt." *Slavonic and East European Review* 26, no. 67 (April 1948): 303–6.

"Manifesto of the First Slavonic Congress of the Nations of Europe," trans. by William Beardmore. *Slavonic and East European Review* 26, no. 67 (April 1948): 309–13.

Orton, Lawrence D. *The Prague Slav Congress of 1848.* Boulder, Colorado, 1978.

Zacek, Joseph. *Palacký: The Historian as Scholar and Nationalist.* The Hague, 1970.

See also Austroslavism; Carpatho-Rusyns; František Palacký; Pan-Slavism; Polish Question; Revolutions of 1848; Alfred Windischgrätz

Prague Spring

Period of openness and free expression in Czechoslovakia during the spring and summer of 1968. This thaw in the formerly Stalinist satellite capped a gradual push from within the Communist Party for economic reforms and party democratization. After free public speech produced demands for an independent foreign policy, Soviet-led Warsaw Pact armies forced an end to the Czechoslovak experiment in August 1968.

After sustained economic stagnation in the 1950s and early 1960s, many members of the Czechoslovak Communist Party began quietly calling for economic reforms. In 1963 an intra-party debate began, with economist Ota Šík (1919–) calling for a return of market forces to the highly centralized Czechoslovak economy. Though hard-liners such as party leader Antonín Novotný (1904–75) managed to block reforms from 1963 to 1967, debate continued, with reformers insisting that democratization of the party accompany economic liberalization.

Demands for reform intensified and became public when Czech writers openly criticized Stalinism and the Novotný regime at the 1967 Congress of the Union of Czechoslovak Writers. Reformers in the party seemed to have the upper hand. When Soviet Premier Leonid Brezhnev (1906–82) showed little support for Novotný in a December visit, the party Central Committee forced him to step down in favor of Slovak Alexander Dubček (1921–92). Though not previously known as a reformer, Dubček assumed the reform mantle soon after his elevation to party secretary on January 5, 1968. His slogan Socialism with a Human Face became a rallying cry of the Prague Spring.

As the country buzzed with its newfound freedom of expression, the Central Committee produced in April a so-called Action Program, a manifesto for economic and political reform. As the season changed with the melting snow and the melting dictatorship, speech flowed freely in public forums and independent newspapers. Dubček and the Central Committee quickly found themselves losing control of the reform debate. The most popular plan saw publication in June of the "2,000 Words Manifesto," written by nonparty intellectuals, workers, and students. It implied that all reforms should be approved by the people, not just the Communist Party. And it hinted that Czechoslovakia should be free to follow a foreign policy independent of the Soviet Union.

These signs, ominous for bloc unity, turned the previously noncommittal Brezhnev against the Czechoslovak reforms. While hastily removing Dubček and other reform leaders to Moscow, the Soviets led their Warsaw Pact allies in an invasion of Czechoslovakia on August 20. Czechs offered only symbolic resistance to the five hundred thousand invading troops. Unarmed protesters placed flowers in tank gun barrels and berated the foreign troops for carrying out an immoral invasion. But ultimately force prevailed, and the Soviet Union installed a new, collaborationist government under Gustáv Husák (1913–91).

The repression of Prague Spring was not the first postwar Soviet intervention in East Central Europe, as Soviet forces had put down a revolution in Budapest twelve years earlier. But it proved to be particularly embarrassing to Communists around the world. The Soviet Union had destroyed earnest and well-intentioned reforms coming from within a fraternal Communist Party. Throughout Europe, Communists who had generally accepted even the harsh show trials of the Stalinist period lost faith in Soviet leadership. The destruction of "socialism with a human face" in Czechoslovakia was a blow against socialist idealism in general. After 1968, Soviet communism would survive only through threat of force and inertia, and few could any longer envision a socialist utopia.

Eagle A. Glassheim

Further reading

Korbel, Josef. *Twentieth Century Czechoslovakia.* New York, 1977.

Renner, Hans. *A History of Czechoslovakia since 1945.* New York, 1989.

P

Skilling, Gordon. *Czechoslovakia's Interrupted Revolution.* Princeton, New Jersey, 1976.

See also Brezhnev Doctrine; Communist Party of Czechoslovakia; Alexander Dubček; Gustáv Husák; Antonín Novotný; Warsaw Pact

Preradović, Petar (1818–72)

Principal representative of romanticism in Croatian poetry. The son of a noncommissioned officer, Preradović received eight years of military training in the Austrian town of Wiener Neustadt. There, in 1834, he started writing verse in German (for example, "An mein Vaterland," three sonnets, 1843). Later he became an ardent Croatian patriot and Pan-Slavist, joining the movement that promoted unity among Slavs. As a lieutenant, he lived in various garrisons of the Habsburg Empire; although he felt unhappy and out of place in the military, he made a career in the army and attained the rank of major general. His poetic activity, now exclusively in Croatian, unfolded during his stay in the military harbor town of Zadar, where he published in the newly launched magazine *Zora dalmatinska* (*Dalmatian Dawn*). He became a propagandist of the Illyrian (South Slavic) idea. His first collection of poems, *Prvenci* (*Firstlings*), was published in Zadar in 1846. After participating in skirmishes and battles with Italian insurgents, he settled in 1859 in Zagreb, where he published his second volume, *Nove pjesme* (*New Poems*, 1851). His name was mentioned as the future *ban* (governor) of Croatia in 1870 but he fell seriously ill. At the same time, he turned to mysticism and spiritism, as expressed in his epic *Prvi ljudi* (*The First Humans,* 1862). After his death he was buried in Vienna, but in 1879 his remains were transferred to Zagreb.

His other literary achievements include the poem "Putnik" (The Traveler), the (almost finished) drama on the hero of South Slavic folk epics *Marko Kraljevič* (1847), and the polemical essay "Jezik južnoslavski" (The South Slavic Language, 1844).

Thomas Eekman

Further reading

Frangeš, Ivo. "Poezija Petra Preradovića." *Kolo* 6, no. 4, Zagreb (1968): 467–73.
Haler, Albert. "O poeziji Petra Preradovića," in *Srpski književni glasnik.* Belgrade, 1928.
Ravlić, Jakša. "Preradović u Zadru," in *Radovi.* Zadar, 1959.
Živančević, Milorad. "Petar Preradović." *Povijest hrvatske književnosti* 4, Zagreb (1975): 125–36.
———. "Preradović juče i danas," in *Letopis Matice Srpske.* Novi Sad, Yugoslavia, 1968.

See also Croatian Literature to 1918; Illyrian Movement; Pan-Slavism; Romanticism

Prešeren, Francè (1800–1849)

Leading Slovene romantic poet and defender of "Slovene-ness" against pressures to assimilate. Of a peasant family, educated with a degree in law—although it brought little professional advantage owing partly to his liberal political leanings—Prešeren wrote poetry that matched that of the greatest European romantics. His poems reveal a breadth of influences from classical writings to those of European contemporaries. They employ the themes of the time: unrequited love, grief, nostalgia for home and nation, the bitterness of fate, and the call of death. One of his best-known poems is the poignant epic *Krst pri Savici* (*Baptism at the Savica,* 1836), in which he laments the eighth-century defeat of a Slovene pagan leader who hesitatingly accepts the conqueror's Christian religion (persuaded by a woman, his love), but thereby brings his people into the Western cultural world, saving them from extinction. Prešeren's collected poetry was first published only in 1847, two years before his early death.

In the first half of the nineteenth century, Prešeren and other Slovene intellectuals debated how to prevent the Germanization of their culture. Two issues were primary. One, dealing with how the Slovene language should be developed, pitted Jernej Kopitar (1780–1844), who favored the folk idiom, against Prešeren, who believed a modern, secular literary language must be developed to battle Germanization where its impact was greatest—in the towns. The second related to Illyriansm (or cultural Yugoslavism), whose advocates felt Slovenes had a better chance of surviving Germanizing pressures if they threw in their lot with other South Slavs by adopting a common literary language. Prešeren, in debates with noted Slovene Illyrianst Stanko Vraz (1810–51), dismissed Illyrianism as just another kind of assimilation. Prešeren's position on both issues prevailed. Hence

Illyriansm was rejected and a modern Slovene literary language was thereafter consciously nurtured. In independent Slovenia (1991) verses of Prešeren's *Zdravljica* (*A Toast,* 1848), set to music, are now the national anthem, and Prešeren Day (February 8), when prizes are awarded for national excellence, is a national cultural holiday.

Carole Rogel

Further reading
Cooper, Henry R., Jr. *Francè Prešeren.* Boston, 1981.
Paternu, Boris. *Francè Prešeren.* Bled, Slovenia, 1994.

See also Germanization; Illyrian Movement; Jernej Kopitar; Slovene Language; Slovene Literature; Yugoslavism

Press

Newspapers and magazines have played a significant part in the national, political, and economic development of the various East European countries. Initially published for the educated classes, during the twentieth century the press came to serve a mass population. Only when television's entertainment role gained increasing importance in the declining years of communism did the press lose its preeminent role in public discourse.

The local-language press of Eastern Europe was developed by nations that were part of multinational empires, usually in subordinate positions. Newspapers therefore helped create the imagined communities of modern nations and also reflected their growth. They developed as national political institutions devoted to fostering national goals in politics, economics, and culture.

The first local-language newspaper in the region appears to have been *Merkuriusz Polski Ordynaryjny* (*Polish Common Messenger*), which first appeared in Kraków in 1661, but until the nineteenth century there were few newspapers in Eastern Europe and they had tiny circulations. Beginning in the mid-1840s, newspapers in East Central Europe became increasingly politicized. They were subjected to various licensing and censorship controls. As late as 1894, even the most widely read and respected Czech paper, *Národní listy* (*National News*), sold only fourteen thousand copies. In the early twentieth century a few urban, sensational, nonpolitical, large-circulation dailies for Czechs, Poles, and Hungarians began to be hawked on the streets. The profits sometimes helped support political parties. Journalism often served as a way station for individuals more interested in being writers and politicians. Political, social, and economic backwardness delayed the development of the press in southeastern Europe. In Albania, for example, the first domestically produced paper appeared only in 1910.

The political role of newspapers intensified with independence at the end of World War I. The unifying national function of journalism was taken over by the press of state minorities. The chief journalistic value was political allegiance. Mass-circulation commercial city newspapers, such as *Illustrowany Kurier Codzienny* (*Illustrated Daily Courier*), continued to grow in importance in East Central Europe and developed in Romania, while illiteracy and economic backwardness kept the press in the hands of a minority in the rest of southeastern Europe. Except for Czechoslovakia, regimes in Eastern Europe used threats, rewards, and financial backing to try to control the press.

During World War II, many newspapers were shut down and others subjected to severe censorship. Underground newspapers sprang up to help opponents of the ruling regimes promote their causes. As many as two thousand such papers existed in Poland, and more than three thousand five hundred in Yugoslavia.

The basic function of the press during the Communist period was mobilization. In order to ensure that the press would not stray too far from its role, a series of controls was employed, including censorship, self-censorship, threats, rewards, and guidance. Communist parties were the dominant force, but the party presence was not monolithic. The main party organs were newspapers of record, providing official political roadmaps for party officials and other readers who needed to be informed. Newspapers such as *Trybuna Ludu* (*Tribune of the People*) in Poland, *Rudé právo* (*Red Truth*) in Czechoslovakia, and *Scînteia* (*Spark*) in Romania generally had the largest circulations in their respective countries. Problems of particular concern to one audience were given considerable attention in the appropriate publication, and less attention elsewhere. Newspapers aimed at young people tended to be more open. The Communist regimes created a mass reading public in Eastern Europe. In some countries, the press provided a significant source of income for the ruling parties.

Despite outward similarities in press policy, there was an enormous difference in the roles and functions of the mass media in the various countries under communism. Where they were more liberal, as in Poland, Hungary, and Yugoslavia, there was a national subtext as well as a significant element of entertainment. Newspapers and magazines were generally the most visible part of the liberalizing forces in Poland in 1956 and 1980–81, in Hungary in 1956, and in Czechoslovakia in 1968, because reformers used the media to convey their own liberal goals, thereby helping awaken the mass public to the possibilities of political change. The reforms of the Prague Spring, the liberal period in Czechoslovakia during the spring and summer of 1968, were presaged in the Slovak press, given almost free rein by Alexander Dubček (1921–92) after he became head of the party in Slovakia in 1963. There was almost always some room for journalists to expand the boundaries of public discussion under Communist rule, especially in Poland and Yugoslavia. The press in Tito's (1892–1980) Yugoslavia was a vigorous promoter of nationalism and openness. Every reform movement made freedom of the press an important goal. Every ruling regime, however, sought to maintain control of the press in order to guarantee that its messages would be distributed throughout the public and to prevent competing messages from destroying the party's monopoly. Although there were exceptions, the party messages in the press in the late Communist period increasingly diverged from reality, thus contributing to the declining faith of the public in Communist rule. Regimes responded in various ways. In Poland, the newspapers in the period after the government's martial law declaration in December 1981 produced Eastern Europe's most informative press, but Poles gave it little credit since alongside it thrived hundreds of vibrant underground newspapers that the regime could not quash. Most notable was *Tygodnik Mazowsze* (*Mazovian Weekly*). In Hungary, the press continued to grow more open so that there was virtually no sharp demarcation line when communism ended. Even in Czechoslovakia, the press became more open in the 1980s, particularly in Slovakia, where national themes became more visible. In Yugoslavia, the post-Tito press turned increasingly nationalist, reflecting the opportunist politicians who played nationalist chords to appeal to a population increasingly disenchanted with communism. Only in Romania and Albania did the press remain under tight dictatorial control right up to the end of Communist rule.

Owen V. Johnson

Further reading

Buzek, Antony. *How the Communist Press Works.* New York, 1964.

Curry, Jane Leftwich. *Poland's Journalists: Professionalism and Politics.* New York, 1990.

Johnson, Owen V. "Bibliography of Russian and East European Journalism," *International Communication Bulletin* 24:1–2 (Spring 1989): 13–27.

Kaplan, Frank L. *Winter into Spring 1963–1968.* Boulder, Colorado, 1977.

Kosary, Domokos. *The Press during the Hungarian Revolution of 1848–1849.* Boulder, Colorado, 1986.

Robinson, Gertrude J. *Tito's Maverick Media.* Urbana, Illinois, 1977.

See also Censorship; Alexander Dubček; Hungarian Revolution of 1956; Media; Nationalism; Prague Spring; Tito

Pribičević, Svetozar (1875–1936)

Serbian interwar political figure. Born in Austria-Hungary and a member of the Croato-Serb Coalition in Zagreb, Pribičević became a key figure in interwar Yugoslav politics. As leader of the newly formed Democratic Party, he assisted Radical Party leader Nikola Pašić (1845–1926) in writing the nation's first constitution in 1921 and became minister of interior in the latter's cabinet. As an expert on Croatia, he formulated early administration policy for that and other regions. He believed that Croats respected only a firm hand. However, after harsh policies against the Croatian Peasant Party's leaders failed to bear fruit, Pašić and King Alexander (1888–1934) succeeded in reaching agreement with the Croats in 1925. When that accord soon began to unravel, Pribičević reached agreement with the Croats in November 1927 to form the Peasant-Independent Democratic Coalition, from which he continued to fight Alexander and Serbian leaders until his death in 1936 in Czechoslovakia.

During his turbulent political career, Pribičević radically changed directions. He began as a worshiper of monarchy and a champion of unitarism, yet later became a republican and a federalist. Both friend and foe viewed this change as a disastrous element in frustrating Yugoslavia's struggle for a viable political system.

Alex N. Dragnich

Further reading

Dragnich, Alex N. *The First Yugoslavia: Search for a Viable Political System*. Stanford, California, 1983.

See also Alexander I Karadjordjević; Nikola Pašić; Vidovdan Constitution

Princip, Gavrilo (1894–1918)

Bosnian Serb nationalist and member of the Young Bosnia (Mlada Bosna) revolutionary movement. Expelled from school in Bosnia because of his revolutionary activities, Princip continued his education in Belgrade, where he came into contact with the Serbian nationalist organization Union or Death (Ujedinjenje ili smrt), commonly known as the Black Hand (Crna Ruka). On June 28, 1914, the 525th anniversary of the Battle of Kosovo (in which the Serbs were defeated by the Ottomans), he fired the shots that killed Archduke Franz Ferdinand (1863–1914), the Austro-Hungarian heir presumptive, and his wife, Sophie Chotek (1868–1914). The ensuing crisis led to the outbreak of World War I. A minor under Austro-Hungarian law at the time of the assassination (he was not quite twenty), he received the maximum sentence of twenty years' imprisonment in his murder trial held in Sarajevo. While in prison in Theresienstadt, he lost an arm to tuberculosis before succumbing to the disease six months before the end of the war.

John D. Treadway

Further reading

Dedijer, Vladimir. *The Road to Sarajevo*. London, 1967.

Ljubibratić, Dragoslav. *Mlada Bosna i Sarajevski atentat*. Sarajevo, 1964.

See also Apis; Black Hand; Franz Ferdinand; World War I

Privatization

Economic liberalization in the formerly Communist countries of Eastern Europe following the collapse of communism. Among the changes brought about by events of the late 1980s, none proved to be more ticklish than that of economic reform, especially privatization. Until the end of 1992, the Czech lands, to cite one example, were still a part of the Czechoslovak Federation, which consisted, since 1969, of the Czech Socialist Republic and the Slovak Socialist Republic. The adjectives in both names were dropped early in 1990. Departure from planned economy toward the market system started shortly after the fall of the Communist regime in November 1989. Legal framework for privatization was gradually established at both the federal and the republican level. The federal assembly voted a law on free enterprise in April 1990; a law on "small privatization" (encompassing smaller economic units) in October 1990; and a law on "large privatization" (affecting most large enterprises) in January 1991. Specific tasks in the field of privatization were then carried out by the national legislatures and governments. In the Czech Republic, this process was more conceptual and faster than in Slovakia. A Czech Ministry of Privatization and a Ministry for the Administration of National Property and Its Privatization were created after the elections in June 1992. A Fund of National Property was also established and entrusted with the execution of approved privatization projects. An overall concept of privatization was prepared, consisting of restitution, reestablishment of municipal property, "small privatization," transformation of existing cooperatives into corporate economic entities, "large privatization," voucher privatization (*kuponová privatizace*), and foreign capital participation. Restitution covered properties nationalized between 1948 and 1959, and it was largely accomplished by the end of 1991. Enterprises nationalized between 1945 and February 1948 were not subject to restitution, namely, because the early post–World War II nationalization was carried out by democratically elected bodies and legal processes. In 1990 municipalities were granted independent status with responsibility for government; previously state-owned properties within their jurisdiction were transferred to them. The goals of "small privatization" were attained by the end of 1993, with over 22,000 units sold to individuals in public auctions. "Large privatization" was carried out in two stages, the first of which started in October 1991 and was accomplished at the end of 1993. The second stage began in 1993 with the goal of completion by the first months of

1996. The institutions created for the purpose of administering the privatization process were abolished after the June 1996 elections. The most specific and innovative feature of the Czech privatization was the use of vouchers (*kupónové knížky*). All citizens eighteen years of age and older were offered the opportunity to buy—for a nominal price of about $35—a set of investment coupons for the purchase of shares. About 80 percent of qualified citizens took part in the first round, and almost 90 percent in the second. Assets worth some $15 billion were thus distributed among Czech citizens. Most of them entrusted their vouchers to various investment funds that had been established for that purpose. The Czech government created a favorable environment for foreign investors, and by the end of 1994, external investments in the Czech Republic reached the total value of more than $4 billion. Some assets were excluded from privatization, namely, property of state organs and institutions including courts, schools, postal services, railroads, oil and gas pipelines, public television channels, and most health-care facilities. Nor did privatization apply to the Czech News Agency and such treasures as the National Theater and National Museum. The most sensitive part of privatization has been the complex of largest enterprises, including mines, that employed hundreds of thousands of people. Most of them still remained, directly or indirectly, owned by the state. While obviously successful in its fundamental purpose—introduction of a full-scale market economy—the Czech privatization process was also criticized as a wasteful giveaway of large parts of national property. Debates on this subject among experts are far from over.

Jiří Hochman

Further reading

Center for Voucher Privatization. *Voucher Privatization in Facts and Figures*. Prague, 1994.

Czech National Bank. *Annual Reports 1993* and *1994*. Prague, 1993, 1994.

Statistical Yearbooks of the Czech Republic 1993, 1994, 1995. Prague, 1994, 1995, 1996.

See also Czech Republic, Birth of; Law

Protectorate of Bohemia and Moravia

Czech "autonomous" territory under Nazi occupation, 1939–45. On March 15, 1939—one day after Slovakia seceded from the short-lived Czecho-Slovak Second Republic—Nazi Germany seized those portions of Bohemia and Moravia it had not already acquired by the Munich Pact in 1938. Entering the country at the nominal request of President Emil Hácha (1872–1945), the Germans declared a protectorate. Hitler (1889–1945) allowed Hácha to remain as formal head of state but appointed Konstantin von Neurath (1873–1956), a former German foreign minister, as Reich protector. When Neurath proved ineffectual, his more ruthless subordinate, State Secretary (and Higher SS and Police Leader) Karl Hermann Frank (1898–1946), quickly took real power into his own hands. In September 1941 Frank managed to oust von Neurath, although he failed in his bid to succeed him. Instead, Hitler appointed Reinhard Heydrich (1904–42), the feared head of the Reich Security Main Office (RSHA), as acting Reich protector. On May 27, 1942, commandos acting on the orders of the Czechoslovak government-in-exile fatally wounded Heydrich in an ambush. Heydrich's successors were mere figureheads, and real power again fell to Frank, who retained it until the German defeat in 1945.

Although German "protection" ostensibly involved control only over foreign policy and defense, leaving domestic affairs in Czech hands, the Germans allowed the Czechs little meaningful autonomy. Nevertheless, it was more than most other occupied peoples enjoyed, and Czech leaders were painfully aware that they had something to lose. German policy in the protectorate derived above all from the territory's strategic importance. In the long term the Nazis planned to assimilate "racially valuable" elements of the population and to expel or kill the remainder, but in the short term they considered the Czech economy too important to the war effort to permit such disruption. Although they deported the Jews to death camps in Poland, the Germans sought to keep the Czechs productive and quiescent through bribery and intimidation. Frank and Heydrich both calculated that they could induce ordinary Czechs to work by allowing them a tolerable standard of living, while quelling their will to resist through judicious applications of terror.

Czech attempts to play a double game with the Nazis, similar to the one they had played with the Habsburgs in World War I, were doomed to failure. The Gestapo efficiently infiltrated and neutralized resistance groups. Prime Minister Alois Eliáš (1890–1942), who maintained covert contact with London, was convicted of treason in 1941. The Germans retaliated for the assassination of Heydrich in 1942 with a brief but intense wave of repression that included the execution of Eliáš and the destruction of the villages of Lidice and Ležáky. The protectorate was profoundly quiet thereafter, until the Czechs finally took up arms to expel the Germans in the Prague Uprising of May 1945.

Judged by the brutal standard the Nazis set elsewhere in the region, the German regime in the protectorate was relatively mild (always excepting its murder of the Jews). It was nevertheless deeply humiliating to the Czechs, who would not easily forgive the ease with which the Germans had cowed and manipulated them.

Todd Huebner

Further reading

Brandes, Detlef. *Die Tschechen unter deutschem Protektorat,* 2 vols. Munich, 1969–75.

Grant Duff, Sheila. *A German Protectorate: The Czechs under Nazi Rule.* London, 1942.

MacDonald, Callum and Jan Kaplan. *Prague in the Shadow of the Swastika: A History of the German Occupation, 1939–1945.* London, 1995.

Mastny, Vojtech. *The Czechs under Nazi Rule: The Failure of National Resistance, 1939–1942.* New York, 1971.

See also Alois Eliáš; Karl Hermann Frank; Emil Hácha; Reinhard Heydrich; Adolf Hitler; Lidice; Munich Pact; Slovak Republic

Protestantism

Protestantism includes a variety of movements often said to have originated with Martin Luther's (1483–1546) nailing of ninety-five theses to the doors of the Wittenburg Cathedral in 1517. However, it was Czech theologian Jan Hus (1370–1415), drawing on the writings of English reformer John Wycliff (c. 1328–84), who presaged Luther's break with the Roman Catholic Church. Many of Hus's critiques—including the pope's infallibility and an emphasis on the vernacular—later become fundamental aspects of the Protestant Reformation. Hus, who emphasized the authority of Scripture over the church hierarchy, was invited to defend his view at the Council of Constance in 1414 but was arrested, tried as a heretic, and burned at the stake.

Foundational to Luther's understanding of Christianity was the acceptance of the priesthood of all believers, a doctrine that undermined the priestly and hierarchical system of Roman Catholicism. Related to this was an emphasis on justification by faith alone and an insistence on Scripture as the sole norm of faith, thereby rejecting the Catholic claims to tradition as a distinct source of faith. On these points, most other Protestants would agree.

Luther himself retained two of the seven Catholic sacraments (baptism and the Eucharist, or Lord's Supper) and in some ways kept the flavor of the Roman liturgy though insisting on its translation into the language of the people. Generally Luther kept many practices from Catholicism on the basis of the claim that such practices, even if not mentioned in Scripture, could be adopted by Christians if they were not detrimental to faith.

By contrast, John Calvin (1509–64), who agreed with Luther in most respects, rejected this latter claim, arguing that no practice should be accepted except what is found in Scripture itself. This is the view of the Reformed tradition, and more particularly of the Presbyterian churches, which argued for a system of elected elders, or presbyters, to direct the internal affairs of the Christian community. Calvin and his colleague Huldrych Zwingli (1484–1531) emphasized the doctrines of God's absolute sovereignty, the absolute depravity and wickedness of humanity, and the belief in the predestination of the elect to heaven and the wicked to hell. An important modification of these beliefs within the Reformed tradition came with the thought of James Arminius (1560–1609), which emphasized the importance of free will in salvation, and therefore the denial of the strict predestinationism of Calvin.

A third important mainstream of Reformation thought was the Anabaptist tradition, which united around the importance of faith in baptism. Anabaptists reject infant baptism, insisting instead on the biblical practice of immersion. The relative independence of each Anabaptist community and the rejection of any close relations with the state are typical of this movement.

Sometimes classified with Protestants is the Anglican Church, which was initially a nationalization of the Catholic Church in England by

Henry VIII (1491–1547). One important break from Anglicanism was Methodism, which began as a reformation by John Wesley (1703–91) of the English church, and strongly emphasized religious enthusiasm and preaching.

One form of Protestantism that downplayed sacramentalism altogether in favor of an emphasis on the "inner light" of the spirit was the Society of Friends, or Quakers, founded by George Fox (1624–91).

One final form of Protestantism was Unitarianism, whose doctrines were first sketched by Michael Servetus (1511–53) in 1531. Unitarianism claimed in particular that many of the traditional doctrines of Christianity, most notably the Trinity and the belief that Jesus was God, could not be found in Scripture.

During the sixteenth century, Protestantism made incursions into East Central Europe, most notably in the Czech lands (Lutheranism) and eastern Hungary (Calvinism). However, Vienna's defeat of the Czech nobility at the Battle of White Mountain (1620) and the Habsburg conquest of Hungary in the late seventeenth century effectively witnessed the reconversion of these lands to Catholicism.

Presently, the Czech and Slovak Republics are home to significant groups of the Brethren, who are part of the Anabaptist tradition, as well as to Lutherans in the Slovak community. There is a strong minority presence of Lutherans, Calvinists, and Baptists in Hungary. In addition, there are small communities of Lutherans, Calvinists, and Baptists (among others) in Romania. Protestantism made few inroads in Albania, Yugoslavia, Bulgaria, and Poland. Since the fall of communism, numerous Protestant denominations have sent missions to Eastern Europe.

Eugene F. Bales

Further reading

Dillenberger, John and Claude Welch. *Protestant Christianity, Interpreted through Its Development.* New York, 1954.

Johnson, Lonnie R. *Central Europe: Enemies, Neighbors, Friends.* New York, 1996.

McGrath, Alister E. *Reformation Thought: An Introduction.* New York, 1988.

McNeill, John T. *The History and Character of Calvinism.* Oxford, 1954.

Ozment, Steven E. *Protestants: The Birth of a Revolution.* New York, 1993.

Williams, George Huntson. *The Radical Reformation.* Kirksville, Missouri, 1992.

See also Catholicism

Prus, Bolesław (1847–1912)

Polish novelist and journalist. Writing under the pseudonym Bolesław Prus, Aleksandr Głowacki was the finest novelist to emerge from the novel-rich period dominated by Polish positivism. His bitter experience in the unsuccessful 1863 uprising against the Russians (he was wounded and imprisoned) and his subsequent studies in science and mathematics linked him early on with the positivists and their anti-romantic orientation. Their notion of the writer's pragmatic service, rather than messianic mission, also dominated his long career (his famous *Weekly Chronicles* appeared for forty years) and his social activism (for example, his cofounding of the Philanthropic Fund for Writers and Journalists). One of the few Polish writers to make a living from his work in this period, he showed deep concern for the professional and financial plight of his colleagues. Prus's feuilletons and short stories at once engage and educate readers with their humor, compassion, and incisive social commentary. Most of Prus's novels focus on topical subjects, and some—*Emancypantki* (*Emancipated Women,* 1894) and *Dzieci* (*Children,* 1907), trained on a new generation of Polish revolutionaries—are marred by tendentiousness and facile judgments. Yet his best works—*Placówka* (*The Outpost,* 1886), *Lalka* (*The Doll,* 1890), and *Faraon* (*Pharaoh,* 1897)—build impressively on his acute observations of Polish society and delineate far richer and more ambiguous social portraits than the positivists would approve. *The Outpost,* set in a Polish village, exposes both the tenacity and the hobbling conservatism of its peasant protagonist Ślimak. *The Doll,* which portrays Warsaw with an insider's detailed appreciation, explicitly challenges positivism through the tragic romanticism of its hero, a scientist-turned-revolutionary-turned-businessman. A historical novel based in ancient Egypt, *Pharaoh* nonetheless conveys fascinating insights into the mechanisms of both historic and contemporary state power. These novels as well as his feuilletons ensure Prus's reputation as a beloved classic of Polish literature, a reputation analogous to that of Dickens (1812–70) in England and Balzac (1799–1850) in France.

Beth Holmgren

Further reading

Kasparek, Christopher. "Prus's *Pharaoh*: The Creation of a Historical Novel." *Polish Review* 39, no. 1 (1994): 45–50.

Kulczycka-Saloni, Janina. *Boleslaw Prus,* rev. and enlarged ed. Warsaw, 1967.

Miłosz, Czesław. *The History of Polish Literature,* 2d ed. Berkeley, California, 1980, 291–303.

Szweykowski, Zygmunt. *Twórczość Bolesława Prusa,* 2d ed. Warsaw, 1972.

Welsh, David. "Realism in Prus's Novel *Lalka.*" *Polish Review* 8, no. 4 (1964): 33–38.

See also January Uprising; Polish Literature; Positivism

Prussia

From the eleventh to the twentieth centuries, "Prussia" was the name, successively, of a coastal area at the southeast corner of the Baltic Sea, a duchy (1466–1701), a kingdom spreading across northern Germany (1701–1918) that dominated the German Empire (1871–1918), and the largest state in Germany after 1918. After World War II, the victorious Allied powers abolished the state of Prussia in 1947.

In the tenth century a Baltic-speaking people called the Prussians (or Porussi or Borussi) inhabited the Baltic coast between the Vistula and Niemen Rivers. In 1226 the Polish prince, Conrad of Mazovia (c. 1191–1247), invited the Knights of the Teutonic Order into Polish territory for a campaign against the non-Christian Prussians. By 1400 the largely German Teutonic Order had acquired territory along the Baltic coast from the Vistula northward to the Gulf of Finland, establishing the Baltic littoral as a major avenue of German expansion into Eastern Europe for centuries to come. In 1466 the knights accepted Polish sovereignty over their remaining possessions between the Vistula and the Niemen, which became known as ducal Prussia.

In 1618 control of the duchy passed into the hands of John Sigismund Hohenzollern (1572–1619), who was already ruler (elector) of a medium-sized German territory, Brandenburg. After 1700, the name "Prussia" came to designate all the Hohenzollern family territories, including holdings in north Germany as far west as the Rhine River. The Hohenzollerns militarized Prussian society by creating a large army and giving the nobility (Junkers) absolute control over their peasants and soldiers.

Prussia participated in the three partitions of Poland (1772, 1793, and 1795), acquiring both territory and a Catholic Polish minority population in largely Protestant German Prussia. From the eighteenth to the twentieth centuries, preventing a revival of any Polish state became a central point of Prussian policy. Problems with the Polish population in Prussia grew as a result of the Kulturkampf ("struggle for culture"), which attacked the power of the Catholic Church and the 1872 ban on Polish as a language of instruction in the schools. As part of a later policy of Germanization, the Prussian parliament passed a law in 1908 allowing the expropriation of large Polish estates for the settlement of German farmers.

After World War I, the Versailles treaty transferred some of West Prussia to the reestablished Polish state. This created the Polish Corridor, which separated East Prussia from the remainder of Prussia and Germany, an arrangement that had historic roots in the fifteenth-century position of ducal Prussia within Poland. The vast majority of the German population never reconciled itself to this separation of territory and population. The Nazis used German minority issues in the corridor as their excuse for invading Poland to start World War II in Europe. Because of its militaristic traditions, Prussia was abolished in 1947 by the Allied coalition that defeated Germany.

Robert Mark Spaulding

Further reading

Carsten, F. L. *A History of the Prussian Junkers.* Brookfield, Vermont, 1989.

———. *The Origins of Prussia.* Oxford, 1954.

Koch, H. W. *A History of Prussia.* New York, 1978.

See also Otto von Bismarck; East Prussia; Germanization; Germany; Kulturkampf; Nazi-Polish War; Pan-Germanism; Paris Peace Conference; Polish Corridor

Prut River

Important river in Eastern Europe. In Roman times called the Pyretus or Pirtos (also Porata) River, the Prut springs in the Cernogora Mountains (Eastern Carpathians) of western Ukraine and flows, first east then south, for 572 miles (953 km) until it reaches the Danube east of the Romanian city of Galaţi. Emerging from the sub-Carpathian hills, it passes the Ukrainian (formerly Romanian) city of Chernivtsi and, after forming very briefly the Romanian-Ukrainian border, for 420 miles (700 km) serves as the boundary between Romania and Moldova. Its relatively important tributaries on the right (western) side are the Tsheremosh in Ukraine and the Baseul, Jijia, Pruteţul, and Elanul Rivers in Romania. There are no tributaries of any significance on the left (eastern) side. The water level fluctuates substantially according to season. The average yearly water debit when it reaches the Danube is 3,200 cubic feet (86 cu m) per second. Historically (until World War II), the Prut played a role in the exploitation of forests, with rafts of logs being brought from as far as the Carpathians down to the Danube and then to the Black Sea. Today the only industrial exploitation of the river takes place at Stanca-Costeşti, where, through a joint Romanian-Moldovan effort, a lake was created that supplies water to neighboring towns and for agricultural irrigation. Politically, ever since 1812, when Russia annexed Bessarabia—the eastern part (between the Prut and Dniester Rivers) of the historic Principality of Moldavia—the boundary on the Prut became for Romanians the symbol, and reality, of Russian expansionist tendencies.

Ladis K.D. Kristof

Further reading

Magocsi, Paul Robert. *Historical Atlas of East Central Europe.* Seattle, Washington, 1993.

România: Atlas istoric-geographic. Bucharest, 1996.

See also Bessarabian Question; Moldavia, Republic of

R

Račić, Josip (1885–1908)

One of the founders of modern Croatian art. Račić learned lithography and took drawing classes from Oton Iveković (1869–1939) in Zagreb (1903). Afterward, he traveled to Vienna, Munich, and Berlin. The most important part of his education was a course with Anton Ažbe (1862–1905) in Munich (1904). The attention he paid to volume is apparent even in the paintings from this period. Familiar with contemporary trends that he saw at exhibitions in Munich and Berlin, and an admirer of Velásquez (1599–1660), Rembrandt (1606–69), and Manet (1832–83), Račić quickly developed an idiosyncratic style. Between 1904 and 1906, he painted his well-known *Old Man with a Cane, A Female Portrait,* and *Ljuba the Gipsy.*

At the Munich School of Art, Račić founded the Kroatische Schule (Croatian School) in 1905 with Vladimir Becić (1886–1954), Oskar Herman (1886–1974), and Miroslav Kraljević (1885–1913). The following summer he spent in Zagreb, drawing cartoons for the satiric paper *Koprive* (*Nettles*). His last months were spent in Paris, where he was found dead in a hotel room.

The Paris landscapes, his best-known paintings, follow basic principles of impressionism and postimpressionism. Račić produced his best work while in Paris: portraits, self-portraits, paintings of parks, banks of the Seine, cafés (*Pont des Arts, Boulevard, Luxembourg Park, Cafe on a Boulevard, Place d'Étoile, On the Seine*). Some of these works are watercolors.

Svetlana Rakić

Further reading

Gagro, Božidar. *Slikarstvo minhenskog kruga.* Zagreb, 1973.

Novak-Oštrić, Vesna. *Josip Račić.* Zagreb, 1971.

Uskoković, Jelena. "Kratka kronika posthumne sudbine slikarstva Josipa Račića," in *Josip Račić—Miroslav Kraljević 1885–1985.* Zagreb, 1985.

See also Croatian Art

Rački, Franjo (1828–94)

Nineteenth-century Croatian churchman, historian, and politician. Educated in Croatia and Vienna and ordained in 1852, Rački earned a doctorate in theology and taught church history and canon law for two years (1855–57) at the diocesan seminary in Senj, Croatia. Appointed a canon of that diocese in 1857, he spent 1857–60 in Rome, where he devoted himself to historical studies. After repeated unsuccessful attempts by patrons to name him a canon of the archdiocese of Zagreb, his close friend Bishop Josip J. Strossmayer of Djakovo (1815–1905) appointed him a canon in his own diocese in 1877.

Rački began publishing articles on South Slavic church history as early as 1851, but his stay in Rome was crucial for introducing him to the modern source-based historical methodology. On his return, he introduced these methods among the Croats, who consider him the founder of modern critical Croatian historiography. In 1864 he was a cofounder of the first scholarly journal in Croatia, *Književnik* (*The Writer*). He also served as the first president of the Yugoslav Academy of Arts and Sciences (JAZU) in Zagreb from 1866 to 1886.

His writings dealt primarily with medieval South Slavic history, but he also edited important collections of primary sources for the medieval and early modern periods.

First entering politics in 1860 as a representative in the Croatian Sabor (diet), Rački was a close collaborator of Bishop Strossmayer. Like him, Rački forcefully advocated Yugoslavism (the cultural and political concept advocating the unity of South Slavs) and the cooperation of Croats and Serbs. His published correspondence with Strossmayer is itself a major primary source for nineteenth-century Croatian history.

James P. Krokar

Further reading

Antoljak, Stjepan. *Hrvatska historiografija do 1918*, vol. 2. Zagreb, 1992.

Smičiklas, Tade. *Život i djela dra. Franje Račkoga.* Zagreb, 1895.

Zagorsky, Vladimir. *François Rački et la renaissance scientifique et politique de la Croatie, 1828–1894.* Paris, 1909.

See also *Sabor;* Bishop Josip J. Strossmayer; Yugoslavism

Radić, Stjepan (1871–1928)

Croatian leader and founder (together with his brother, Antun [1868–1919]) of the Croatian People's Peasant Party in 1904, which became the dominant political party in interwar Croatia. Radić's basic premise was that the peasants were the repository of Croatian nationhood, culture, and social justice. He defended Croatian states rights and before 1914 supported an autonomous federal South Slav unit within the Habsburg Empire. In November 1918 he spoke strongly against the unification of Croatia with Serbia, which did not guarantee Croatia's historic and territorial integrity. After 1918, Radić became the uncompromising champion of Croatian autonomy within a federalized Yugoslav state (which he wanted modeled on the United States), believing this would eventually lead to an independent Croatian republic. Using popular slogans and oratorical skills, he was able to galvanize the newly enfranchised peasants in the 1920 elections to the Constituent Assembly. His party boycotted the assembly that adopted the centralized Vidovdan Constitution of 1921. Thereafter, Radić, whose political base had been in Croatia-Slavonia, expanded his influence in Dalmatia and among the Croats in Bosnia-Hercegovina. In 1923–24 Radić unsuccessfully sought British and French support for the Croatian cause, although he found Moscow more receptive to his pleas. In 1925 he reversed himself, accepted the Vidovdan Constitution and the Karadjordjević dynasty, and even entered Nikola Pašić's (1845–1926) government as minister of education. However, he quickly found himself again at odds with the regime. He now joined Svetozar Pribičević (1875–1936), who had been the personification of centralism but who had also become disillusioned with Belgrade, to form the Peasant Democratic Coalition, which championed federalism. Radić's unpredictable behavior, seemingly uncompromising positions, and frequent "political somersaults" caused him to be described as the "enfant terrible" by foreign diplomats and to be despised by most Serbs. On June 20, 1928, during a stormy parliamentary session, Radić was shot by a Montenegrin deputy. He died six weeks later, leaving a legacy of unanimous Croatian opposition to the Belgrade regime.

Charles Jelavich

Further reading

Banac, Ivo. *The National Question in Yugoslavia: Origins, History, Politics.* Ithaca, New York, 1984.

Gazi, Stjepan. "Stjepan Radić: His Life and Political Activities (1871–1928)." *Journal of Croatian Studies* 14–15 (1973–74): 13–73.

Tomasevich, Jozo. *Peasants, Politics and Economic Change in Yugoslavia.* Stanford, California, 1955.

See also Nikola Pašić; Peasants; Svetozar Pribičević; Vidovdan Constitution

Radlinský, Andrej (1817–79)

Catholic priest, editor, and Slovak cultural nationalist. Born in Dolný Kubín, Radlinský studied theology in Bratislava, Trnava, and Vienna. In 1841 he was ordained to the priesthood and received a doctorate. A Catholic and grandnephew of Anton Bernolák (1762–1813), Radlinský supported *bernolákovčina*—the literary Slovak developed by his granduncle; but he was also committed to establishing a single Slovak literary language. In 1851 he attended the Bratislava conference between "Bernolákovites" and Protestant adherents of *štúrovčina,* a literary language developed in the 1840s. Radlinský is credited with unifying Catholics and swaying them to accept a compromise codification, *opravená slovenčina* (revised Slovak), that became the basis of modern Slovak. Between 1848 and 1880, he founded or served as an editor of at least eight serial publications. He became a charter member of the Slovak cultural institution Matica slovenská and, in 1869, organized the Spolok Sv. Vojtecha (St. Adalbert Society), dedicated to publishing Catholic religious and educational literature.

Radlinský labored unsuccessfully to persuade the government to recognize Slovak as the administrative language in northern Hungary and to permit Slovak schools. Seeking cultural autonomy for Slovaks, he circulated petitions and authored memoranda. After 1869, Radlinský's activities centered almost exclusively on the translating and publishing functions of the Spolok Sv. Vojtecha. He also edited the society's official organ, *Katolícky noviny* (*Catholic News*). He died in Kúty, where he was pastor.

June Granatir Alexander

Further reading

Šteller, Ferdinand. *Andrej Radlinský: jeho život a boj za práva národa slovensko.* Trnava, Slovakia, 1934.

See also Anton Bernolák; Catholicism; Matica slovenská; Slovak Language

Radomir Rebellion (1918)

Bulgarian uprising in September 1918, alternately referred to as the Radomir Rebellion or the Radomir Republic. The movement, sparked by a mutiny of troops at the Bulgarian army headquarters in Kiustendil, was localized at the village of Radomir, a short distance from Sofia. Their aims were largely a demand for an end to Bulgaria's involvement in World War I and an accounting of those responsible for Bulgaria's decision to join the Central Powers. The government released from prison Raiko Daskalov (1886–1923), a leading Agrarian politician, and Aleksandur Stamboliiski (1879–1923), leader of the Bulgarian Agrarian National Union, in an attempt to quell the mutiny. Instead, Daskalov became the leader of the rebellion. It is unclear whether Stamboliiski gave

his permission to attempt some type of protest action against the government. On September 27, Daskalov declared a republic, named himself commander in chief, and threatened to march on Sofia if the government did not relinquish power. Stamboliiski at first distanced himself from the movement, although he was named president of the self-proclaimed republic. Later, when the government would not believe his protestation of noninvolvement, he supported the effort. The rebellious troops moved on the capitol and launched an attack. The poorly organized rebellion was suppressed by loyal troops supported by German and Macedonian soldiers. The government retook Radomir on October 2. Casualties were high, with as many as ten thousand wounded and three thousand dead. The main objective of the rebellion, an end to Bulgaria's involvement in World War I, was accomplished with the signing of the armistice in Salonika on September 29 and King Ferdinand's (1861–1948) abdication and departure from Bulgaria on October 3; with that, support for the uprising rapidly dissipated.

Mari A. Firkatian

Further reading

Bozhilov, Iv. et al. *Istoriia na Bûlgariia.* Sofia, 1993.
Crampton, Richard J. *Bulgaria 1878–1918: A History.* New York, 1983.
Lalkov, Milcho et al. *Istoriia na tretata Bûlgarska dûrzhava 1878–1944.* Sofia, 1993.

See also Bulgarian Agrarian National Union; Ferdinand; Aleksandur Stamboliiski; World War I

Radoslavov, Vasil Hristov (1854–1929)

Bulgarian politician and leader of the Liberal Party. A German-trained lawyer, Radoslavov became a follower of Petko Karavelov (1843–1903), leader of Bulgaria's anti-Russian Liberal Party. On June 29, 1884, Karavelov named Radoslavov minister of justice, and on August 16, 1886, Radoslavov succeeded him as prime minister. On June 28, 1887, he was forced to give way to his inner-party rival Stefan Stambolov (1854–95). Only after Stambolov's dramatic fall in May 1894 did Radoslavov come back. From 1894 to 1900, he held several cabinet posts and on July 4, 1913, again became prime minister. He managed to overcome the country's precarious international and financial situation by rhetorically advocating a policy of neutrality, while at the same time opening secret negotiations with Russia, Great Britain, France, and Germany over the territorial "price" of this neutrality. On the basis of far-reaching promises by Berlin, Radoslavov signed an agreement with the Central Powers on September 6, 1915, and subsequently attacked Serbia on October 14, 1915. On September 1, 1916, Radoslavov's government joined Austria-Hungary and Germany in declaring war on Romania. In the summer of 1918, however, the territorial issue of the Dobrudja's future resulted in a sharp controversy between Radoslavov and his German-Austrian allies; as a result, he resigned on June 21, 1918. During the country's military collapse of September 1918, he sought refuge in Germany, where he later settled owing to efforts of the new Agrarian government at Sofia to bring him to trial as the principal culprit for Bulgaria's "national catastrophes" of 1913 and 1918: defeat in the Second Balkan War and World War I. In early 1923 Radoslavov was sentenced in absentia by a Bulgarian court to life imprisonment. Shortly after being pardoned in May 1929, he died in his German exile.

Stefan Troebst

Further reading

Friedrich, Wolfgang-Uwe. *Bulgarien und die Mächte 1913–1915.* Stuttgart, 1985.

Radoslawoff, Vasil. *Bulgarien und die Weltkrise.* Berlin, 1923.

See also Balkan Wars; Dobrudja; Petko Karavelov; Stefan Stambolov; World War I

Railroads

Prior to the railroad era, travel in central and southeastern Europe was cumbersome, limited to navigable rivers and dirt roads. Strongly advocated by liberals and progressives, railroads were looked on as the catalyst for national unity and economic well-being. Friedrich List (1789–1846), a German economist, wrote tracts urging that railroads be built throughout central Europe to circumvent narrow dynastic interests and facilitate unity in German-populated areas. Identical arguments were advanced by other national leaders, such as František Palacký (1798–1876) in Bohemia and Lajos Kossuth (1802–94) in Hungary. Conversely, the shortsightedness of Ottoman sultan Abdul Hamid II (1842–1918) limited the extent of railroad construction in the southern Balkans. One example of a railroad built for nationalist as well as economic reasons was the Sud- und Nord-Deutsche Verbindungsbahn (South- and North-German Railroad Company), which connected Vienna with the Sudetenland, Prussia (Silesia), and Saxony. Gradually, the railroad era spread throughout Eastern Europe from north to south: Russia (1836), Hungary (1846), Romania (1869), the Ottoman Empire (1866), and Serbia (1881).

Initially, the railroads were privately owned and operated, except for certain unprofitable lines built for political or strategic reasons; but as governments realized the importance of railroads, especially for military purposes, the lines became increasingly subjected to state control, culminating in nationalization, in most cases, after World War I.

Railroads not only improved communications in Eastern Europe but they helped to inaugurate the Industrial Revolution in each country. Supply needs for the lines, such as rails, ties, rolling stock, engines, and buildings, created permanent employment opportunities, both on the lines themselves and in manufacturing and related service industries. This led to the growth of cities, with railroad stations replacing town squares as centers of life. Railroad workers, subject to long hours and low pay, were heavily influenced by socialism and quickly swelled the ranks of the region's socialist parties, greatly helping labor parties win more elections.

Most lines in eastern Europe were built to standard gauge 41 (1435 mm). However, significant exceptions were those in Russian-ruled lands, which used a wider gauge, 51 (1524 mm), while many lines in mountainous areas used narrower gauges. For Russia, the gauge difference was viewed as a military necessity, even though it also hampered trade and commerce.

Following the collapse of communism, attempts at reprivatization are being studied or undertaken. Despite some retrenchment in employment and mileage, railroads continue to be the major means of transportation for freight and passengers throughout eastern Europe.

John A. Fink

Further reading

Dunlavy, Colleen. *Politics and Industrialization: Early Railroads in the United States and Prussia.* Princeton, New Jersey, 1993.

Janes World Railways. London, published annually.
Richards, Jeffrey and John MacKenzie. *Transportation: A Social History.* New York, 1986.

See also Abdul Hamid II; Industrialization; Lajos Kossuth; František Palacký; Privatization

Rajk, László (1909–49)

Communist revolutionary and politician. Rajk became a member of the illegal Hungarian Communist Youth Alliance (KIMSZ) and the Hungarian Communist Party (KMP) in 1931. While at the university, he was active in organizing students. Facing possible prosecution for his activities in 1935, he was ordered by the party to emigrate and in 1937 was sent as a Comintern (Communist International) volunteer to fight in the Spanish Civil War. He was party secretary of a unit of the Hungarian battalion, and was wounded in mid-1938. From the spring of 1939 until 1941, he was interned in France and was able to return to Hungary only following a brief labor stint in Germany.

In Hungary he was interned again, but in 1944 the Communist underground managed to free him with forged documents. During his brief freedom, he became secretary of the Central Committee of the newly reorganized—although still illegal—Communist Party. He was rearrested in December 1944 but was saved from court-martial and possible execution by his brother, who was a state secretary of the Hungarian fascist Arrow Cross government.

Following the liberation of Hungary by Soviet troops in April 1945, Rajk became a member of the Communist Party's Central Committee, which then elected him to the Politburo and to the Secretariat. He also became the secretary of the Budapest Area Committee, the most powerful regional party group. In November 1945 he was elected to parliament from the party list.

On March 20, 1946, Rajk was appointed to head the Ministry of Interior, which he transformed into a Communist Party tool. In 1946–47 Rajk initiated the disbanding of 1,500 civic organizations, including the Scouts, and the purging of the Smallholders, the largest party in the governing coalition. By 1948, the one-party Communist state was firmly established with the active support of Rajk's ministry. In August 1948 a personality clash with the chief of the political police led to Rajk's transfer to head the Ministry of Foreign Affairs.

On May 30, 1949, Rajk was arrested on trumped-up charges of being a spy, and his show trial took place September 16–24, 1949. He and his "co-conspirators" were found guilty. He was executed on October 15. Following the February 1956 Twentieth Party Congress in Moscow—in which Stalin's (1879–1953) crimes were denounced by Soviet leader Nikita Khrushchev (1894–1971)—Hungarian leaders had the Supreme Court rehabilitate some of their victims, including Rajk. On October 6, 1956, his remains were ceremoniously reburied before one hundred thousand mourners. As a victim, his name became a symbol of the crimes of communism and contributed to the outbreak of the Hungarian Revolution of October 23, 1956.

Peter Pastor

Further reading

Sipos, Peter. "Rajk László," in *Politikuspályák,* ed. by Ilona Sánta. Budapest, 1984.
Soltész, István, ed. *Rajk-dosszié.* Budapest, 1989.
Stéphane, Roger. *Rue László Rajk, une tragédie hongroise.* Paris, 1991.
Strassenreiter, Erzsébet. *Rajk László.* Budapest, 1974.
Szász, Béla. *Volunteers for the Gallows: Anatomy of a Show-Trial.* New York, 1972.

See also Arrow Cross; Comintern; Communist Party of Hungary; De-Stalinization; Hungarian Revolution of 1956; Stalin

Rákosi, Mátyás (1892–1971)

Hungarian Communist Party leader. Rákosi became an adherent of Marxism-Leninism while a prisoner of war in Russia during World War I. In 1918 he became a founding member of the Hungarian Communist Party. In 1919 he returned to Hungary and participated in the short-lived Soviet Republic—led by Béla Kun (1886–1938)—which was established during the chaotic period following Austria-Hungary's defeat in the war. After the collapse of the regime, Rákosi returned to the Soviet Union. In 1924 the Comintern (Communist International) sent him back to Hungary to establish an underground Communist movement. He was quickly captured, however, and sentenced to a long prison term. In 1940, as part of an agreement between Budapest and Moscow, Rákosi was freed and returned to the Soviet Union.

R

At the end of World War II, Rákosi returned once again to Hungary, where he led the Communist Party in the struggle to gain political primacy. Using a strategy of attrition that he called "salami politics," Rákosi was able to establish a Communist dictatorship by 1948. Under his regime, the country experienced intensive Stalinization, including forced collectivization, nationalization of all businesses, banning of any private enterprises, heavy industrialization, show trials, and the use of terror to suppress all opposition. These oppressive policies produced widespread discontent. During the period of de-Stalinization after Stalin's (1879–1953) death, reform-minded Communists in Moscow and Budapest moved against the hard-liner Rákosi, hoping to replace him with Imre Nagy (1896–1958). Although Rákosi proved resilient, his authority was slowly undermined, especially when the Soviet leadership sought a rapprochement with Tito (1892–1980), the leader of Yugoslavia. In 1955 Rákosi was finally ousted but permitted to retire to the Soviet Union, where he died in 1971. The revolution that broke out in Hungary in 1956 against Soviet domination was a reflection of the disaffection of the Hungarian people, who had endured the years of harsh oppression under Rákosi. Later Communist governments conceded that many mistakes had been made during the "Rákosi era."

Judith Fai-Podlipnik and Thomas Sakmyster

Further reading

Hoensch, Jorg K. *A History of Modern Hungary.* New York, 1988.

Kovrig, Bennett. *Communism in Hungary: From Kun to Kádár.* Stanford, California, 1979.

Molnar, Miklós. *From Béla Kun to János Kádár: Seventy Years of Hungarian Communism.* New York, 1990.

Sugar, Peter, Peter Hanak, and Tibor Frank. *A History of Hungary.* Bloomington, Indiana, 1990.

See also Collectivization; De-Stalinization; Hungarian Communist Party; Hungarian Revolution of 1956; Hungarian Soviet Republic; Imre Nagy; Industrialization; Tito

Rakovski, Christian Georgevich (1873–1941)

Balkan socialist leader and Soviet diplomat. Born in Bulgaria, Rakovski became a Romanian citizen after his family settled near Constanţa in 1880. He studied in Bulgaria, where he became a Marxist. Later, he studied in France, where he completed a doctorate in medicine with a thesis on criminality and degeneracy from a Marxist viewpoint. In 1905 he began to devote himself to reviving the floundering socialist movement in Romania. A close friend of Bolshevik revolutionary Leon Trotsky (1879–1940), Rakovski became the most famous Balkan socialist leader during the pre–World War I era. Active in the socialist press, he lent financial assistance to Trotsky's activities. Imprisoned in Romania after that country entered the war in 1916, Rakovski was freed in 1917 and left for Russia, where he joined the Bolsheviks. In January 1919 Lenin (1870–1924) appointed Rakovski to head the Provisional Ukrainian Government. In that position, he worked to consolidate Soviet power in the Ukraine.

After his dismissal by Stalin (1879–1953) in 1923 as head of the Ukrainian government, Rakovski became the Soviet representative to London (1923–25) and Paris (1925–27). In that capacity, his work to improve relations with the West led to recognition of the Soviet Union by both Great Britain and France in 1924. In 1927 Stalin recalled Rakovski to the Soviet Union as he began to purge the opposition centered around Trotsky. In March 1938 Rakovski was condemned for treason and in October 1941 executed on Stalin's orders.

Kurt W. Treptow

Further reading

Constantinescu-Iaşi, Petru. "Din viaţa frămîntatoare a unui vechi luptător socialist. Cîteva date inedite," in *Anuarul institutului de istorie şi arheologie "A.D. Xenopol."* Iaşi, Romania, 1972.

Conte, Francis. *Christian Rakovski (1873–1941): A Political Biography.* Boulder, Colorado, 1989.

———. *Un Révolutionnaire-diplomate: Christian Rakovski. L'Union Soviétique et l'Europe (1922–1941).* Paris, 1978.

Iacoş, Ion. *Cristian Racovski: Scrieri social-politice (1900–1916).* Bucharest, 1977.

See also Lenin; Stalin

Rakovski, Georgi Stoikov (1821–67)

Bulgarian activist who planned various unsuccessful efforts for revolt and liberation for his country from Ottoman rule. Born in Kotel to moderately well-off parents, Rakovski received a broad education. In 1841 he took part in an unsuccessful revolt in the Danube port city of Brăila, which landed him in prison. Back in Kotel, he became the center of controversy when he incited the local youth to insubordination and revolt. He and his father were jailed in Constantinople. After this sobering experience, he attempted to live an unobtrusive life first by practicing law then by becoming involved in various unsuccessful business ventures.

During the Crimean War (1853–56), he decided to become a spy for the Russians. After this escapade, he spent considerable time in the Russian Empire, where he sought work as a teacher and wrote various liberation plans. In 1860 he began an extended association with the Serbian government. In Belgrade he was allowed to publish his newspaper, *Dunavski Lebed* (*Danubian Swan*). He was charged with the organization of the First Bulgarian Legion, a paramilitary force composed of émigré Bulgarians trained and prepared to aid Serbian forces in their attempt to oust the Turks from their garrison in the vicinity of Belgrade.

His next association was with the Romanians. In Bucharest he began to publish two newspapers, each in rapid succession, *Viitorul* (*The Future*) and *Branitel* (*Defender*). During this period, he also attempted to head the *cheta* movement (small bands of revolutionaries), which was expanding in the 1860s. He died in 1867, a decade before Bulgaria would gain its independence.

Mari A. Firkatian

Further reading

Arnaudov, Mikhail P. *G.S. Rakovski: Zhivot, delo, idei.* Sofia, 1969.

Borshukov, Georgi. "Zhurnalistikata na G.S. Rakovski: Ot nai-rannite proiavi na Rakovski kato publitsist i zhurnalist do kraia na vestnik *Bûlgarska Dnevnitsa.*" *Godshnik na Sofiiskia Universitet* 57, no. 1 (Sofia 1963): 203–334.

Dimitrov, M., D. Kosev, et al. *Georgi Stoikov Rakovski: Vûzgledi, deinost i zhivot,* vol. 1. Sofia, 1964.

Firkatian, Mari. *The Forest Traveler: Georgi Stoikov Rakovski and Bulgarian Nationalism.* Baltimore, Maryland 1996.

Petrov, Bobi. *Biografiia na Georgi Stoikov Rakovski.* Sofia, 1910.

Traikov, Veselin. *Georgi Stoikov Rakovski: Biografia.* Sofia, 1974.

See also *Cheta;* Crimean War

Ranković, Aleksandar (1909–83)

Yugoslav Communist and head of the Department for the Protection of the People (UDBa), or the secret police. Ranković was born into the family of a tailor's apprentice living in Serbia's heartland, Šumadija. He first joined the Yugoslav Communist Youth organization and then became a member of the Communist Party of Yugoslavia in 1928. Under the dictatorship of King Alexander (1888–1934), Ranković and other Communists were arrested and imprisoned at Sremska Mitrovica. There, he became identified with Montenegrin Communist Petko Miletić-Sepo (1897–1939), who preached militant radicalism and anti-intellectualism. Allied with Miletić, Ranković learned firsthand the effectiveness of terror and intimidation in settling ideological disputes. In 1940 Ranković became a member of the Politburo and remained there until 1966.

After World War II, Ranković administered the UDBa and held various top positions in the Serbian party organization and government. He grew into a consummate political operator and became a defender of the highly centralized vision of Yugoslav communism. When reforms in the 1960s undermined party control and decentralized economic decision making, Ranković emerged as a key critic because of his fear that these reforms would hurt Serbia. His opponents mounted an investigation against him that uncovered a wide range of unethical practices, including mistreatment of Albanians in Kosovo, smuggling, and surveillance of Tito (1892–1980). In 1966 Tito purged the secret police and removed Ranković from his positions in the government and party. Until his death in 1983, Ranković remained the champion for Serbian nationalist groups, particularly on the issue of Kosovo.

Melissa Bokovoy

Further reading

Sekulić, Zoran. *Pad i ćutnja Aleksandra Rankovića.* Belgrade, 1989.

See also Communist Party of Yugoslavia; Kosovo; Tito

Rapacki, Adam (1909–70)

Polish minister for foreign affairs (1956–68). Born into an intelligentsia family, Rapacki attended the Main School for Economics in Warsaw in the 1920s and 1930s and received a master's of economics in 1938. He served as a second lieutenant in the Polish army and was captured during the German invasion in September 1939; he spent the rest of the war as a prisoner of war. Upon his return to Poland, he joined the economic planning commission in Łódź and became active in the Polish Socialist Party. In 1948, he was elected to the central committee of the newly formed Polish United Workers Party. He held various government positions, from minister of higher schools to foreign minister. As foreign minister under Władysław Gomułka (1905–82), he tried to pave a more independent foreign policy from that of Moscow; an example was his attempt to establish a nuclear-free zone in central Europe to include Poland, Czechoslovakia, East Germany, and West Germany. The nuclear-free plan eventually became known as the Rapacki Plan. He also tried to play the role of mediator during the Vietnam War. Yet, by the mid-1960s, Polish foreign policy slipped back under Moscow's control. Rapacki resigned as foreign minister in 1968, refusing to take part in the government's anti-Jewish demonstrations. He died two years later.

David Stefancic

Further reading

Liczmanski, Riszard. *Adam Rapacki.* Warsaw, 1984.
Ozinga, James. *The Rapacki Plan.* Jefferson, North Carolina, 1989.
Stefancic, David. "The Rapacki Plan: A Case Study in East European Diplomacy." *East European Quarterly* 21, no 4 (1988): 401–12.

See also Władysław Gomułka

Rašín, Alois (1867–1923)

Czechoslovak National Democrat and finance minister. Although initially active in the Czech Progressive movement, Rašín won election to the Austrian Reichsrat (parliament) in 1911 as a representative of the Young Czechs. A leading member of the Czech Mafia, the secret Czech committee that promoted independence from Austria-Hungary during World War I, he was sentenced to death for treason in 1916. Amnestied a year later, Rašín immediately resumed his anti-Austrian activities. He was the most forceful of the "Men of October 28," who led the overthrow of Habsburg rule in Prague in 1918.

Rašín was also the strongest personality in the new Czechoslovak National Democratic party, which he later represented in the *Pětka,* an extra-parliamentary committee that guided Czech politics in the 1920s. An uncompromising nationalist, Rašín opposed accommodation with the German minority. He was finance minister from November 1918 to June 1919, and again from October 1922 until his death in February 1923. Despite his brief tenure, Rašín made a lasting impact as minister, establishing and stabilizing the country's currency. Closely associated with banking interests, Rašín pursued a strong currency (the crown) through fiscal austerity and deflation. His harsh policies and abrasive personality earned him enemies across the political spectrum. His murder by a young anarchist—the only political assassination in interwar Czechoslovakia—provoked adoption of the Law for the Protection of the Republic, which restricted civil liberties, in March 1923.

Todd Huebner

Further reading

Hoch, Karel. *Alois Rašín: Jeho zivot, dílo a doba.* Prague, 1934.
Lacina, Vlastislav. *Alois Rašín.* Prague, 1992.
Peroutka, Ferdinand. *Budování státu,* 3d ed., 4 vols. Brno, 1991, vol. 2, 486–97.

See also Banking; Czech Mafia; *Pětka;* Young Czechs

Red Army

Army of the Soviet Union that fought against Poland in the aftermath of the Russian Revolution of 1917 and that retook Eastern Europe in 1941–45, thereby establishing Moscow's domination of the region during the Cold War. The Soviet Red Army was formed by the Bolshevik Party in the immediate aftermath of the October Revolution of 1917. The Red Army, commanded by Leon Trotsky (1879–1940) and utilizing superb officers such as Mikhail Tukhachevsky (1893–1937), emerged victorious in the civil war of 1918–20. One principal factor was ideological conformity in the ranks, a product of Trotsky's system of "political education" for the troops. As a "people's army," the Red Army was organized on the model of equality, with no fixed system of ranks until 1935, when it was reorganized by Josef Stalin (1879–1953).

Stalin installed a typically European rank system, from private to field marshal.

As the Russian civil war was ending in the spring of 1920, Soviet Russia was invaded by Poland, which sought a more favorable boundary in the Ukraine. The Red Army counterattacked under Tukhachevsky, driving deep into Poland and threatening Warsaw. The Polish capital did not fall, however, and renewed Polish advances drove back the Soviet forces. In the Treaty of Riga, Poland regained territory inhabited by approximately four million Ukrainians and one million Belorussians.

The Red Army's command structure was decimated during Stalin's great purges of 1936–39. Approximately 70 percent of all officers of the rank of major and above were shot in 1937 and 1938, more than forty-three thousand officers in all, including most of the Red Army's most skillful and experienced commanders (including Tukhachevsky). The deleterious effects of the purges on the effectiveness of the Red Army was graphically illustrated by its poor performance in the Soviet-Finnish War of 1939–40. As a result, Stalin greatly limited the authority of political officers and improved equipment and training.

In June 1941 the Red Army faced the fury of the Nazi invasion of the USSR. The forward Soviet positions were quickly overrun, and Hitler (1889–1945) believed that the war would end in a matter of weeks. Despite enormous losses, however, the Red Army stopped the Germans at Leningrad and managed to halt their drive on Moscow in early December 1941. The Germans resumed their offensive in June 1942, advancing to the Volga River at Stalingrad. The Germans made every effort to capture the city in November but were held off by fierce Soviet counterattacks organized by General Georgi K. Zhukov (1896–1974). In January 1943 the German Sixth Army was enveloped by Zhukov's troops and forced to surrender on February 2. Following its victory at Stalingrad, the Red Army began an enormous linear offensive sweeping westward that would last until the end of the war.

In August 1944 the Red Army moved rapidly into Romania and Poland. Romania surrendered on August 23, and Bucharest was occupied on the 31st. Bulgaria surrendered on August 26, and within three weeks the Red Army entered Sofia. From Bulgaria and Romania, units advanced into Yugoslavia, taking Belgrade on October 19. The Red Army now converged on Hungary from three sides, entering Budapest on February 14, 1945.

As Soviet forces swept into Poland, units of the clandestine Polish Home Army (Armia Krajowa) mounted a fierce uprising against the Germans in Warsaw on August 1, 1944. Within three days, much of Warsaw was controlled by the Home Army, but the Germans sent in SS reinforcements who leveled most of what remained of the city and deported most of the remaining civilians. The Red Army did virtually nothing to aid the Home Army in its struggle, remaining instead on the far side of the Vistula until December. While the Soviets claimed they needed to reorganize and refit their troops, a more likely explanation was that since the Home Army supported the anti-Communist Polish government-in-exile in London, Stalin decided to let the Germans finish off the Home Army. The Red Army finally entered Warsaw on January 17, 1945, and took Kraków two days later. Although, German resistance in northwest Poland continued until April, the Red Army continued to advance into Austria and Czechoslovakia, taking most of the latter by late April.

In postwar Europe, the Red Army was the mainstay of the Warsaw Pact. The pact, formed in May 1955, established a joint military command structure and a standing commission to coordinate foreign policy. All the countries entered by the Red Army in 1944–45 except Austria were included in the organization. Politically and militarily, the Warsaw Pact was dominated by the Soviet Union, and Soviet security concerns were periodically invoked to justify intervention by Warsaw Pact forces, as in Hungary in 1956 and in Czechoslovakia in 1968. The Red Army remained the largest conventional military force in Europe, at well over four million men in peacetime, until the dissolution of the Soviet Union in December 1991.

Daniel D. Trifan

Further reading

Dunn, Walter S. *Hitler's Nemesis: The Red Army, 1930–1945*. Westport, Connecticut, 1994.

Moynihan, Brian. *Claws of the Bear*. Boston, 1989.

Von Hagen, Mark. *Soldiers in the Proletarian Dictatorship*. Ithaca, New York, 1990.

See also Armia Krajowa; Barbarossa; Cold War; Hungarian Revolution of 1956; Peace of Riga; Polish-Soviet War; Prague Spring; Mikhail

Tukhachevsky; Warsaw, Battle of; Warsaw Pact; Warsaw Uprising; World War II

Reinsurance Treaty (1887)

German-Russian agreement that replaced the collapsed Three Emperors' League (Dreikaiserbund) and played a central role in German Chancellor Otto von Bismarck's policy of maintaining good political relations with Russia. In the treaty, the two powers pledged each other neutrality in war unless Germany attacked France or Russia attacked Austria-Hungary. By these terms, Germany could abandon neutrality and actively defend Austria-Hungary if the German government viewed Russia as the aggressor in a Russian-Austrian conflict. In this way, Bismarck (1815–98) sought to deter any reckless Russian moves against Austria-Hungary and maintain peace in Eastern Europe.

After Bismarck's dismissal in 1890, the German government chose not to renew the treaty in the belief that it did nothing to protect Germany from the greatest danger: a two-front war against France and Russia. Instead, Germany sought, but did not find, an alliance with Britain. Russia responded by forming an alliance with France, thus undoing much of Bismarck's diplomacy and dramatically worsening Germany's international position.

Robert Mark Spaulding

Further reading

Bridge, F. R. *The Great Powers and the European States System, 1815–1914.* New York, 1980.

Jelavich, Barbara. *A Century of Russian Foreign Policy, 1814–1914.* Philadelphia, 1964.

Kennan, George. *The Decline of Bismarck's European Order.* Princeton, New Jersey, 1979.

See also Otto von Bismarck; Three Emperors' League

Republic of Kraków

Short-lived, nineteenth-century independent Polish city-state. In discussions among the peacemakers at the Congress of Vienna in 1815, the territorial disposition of the Polish city of Kraków arose. The conferees eventually agreed to a compromise solution and established Kraków as a free city, or republic, under the joint protection of Austria, Prussia, and Russia, the three countries that had partitioned Poland at the end of the eighteenth century.

The republic consisted of Kraków and its environs—totaling 419 square miles (1,164 sq km) with an 1815 population of 88,000 that grew to 120,000 by 1827. Its creators demanded that the republic be "strictly neutral." The republic had a constitution, and an assembly and senate chosen by fairly broad suffrage. The president of the senate had full executive authority; however, real power rested with resident commissioners representing the three partitioning states. Although Kraków itself was an urban center with an ancient university, most of the republic's citizens lived in the countryside. The republic was fairly prosperous, owing in large measure to its status as a free-trade zone. The decision to convert its peasants from labor service to rents further modernized the economy.

Despite the partitioning powers' opposition, the republic—influenced by the quasi-independent Congress Kingdom's proximity—became a center for Polish patriots. During the November Uprising in 1830 against the Russians, many of the republic's citizens supported the insurgents, thereby outraging the partitioning powers.

In 1832 Austria temporarily occupied the republic. In 1833 the republic's liberties were greatly curtailed, and in that year's Münchengrätz Agreement the partitioning powers secretly decided to destroy the republic when the opportunity arose. In 1836 Austrian troops occupied the republic once again, this time remaining until 1840. During the occupation, the republic's independence was further restricted. In 1846 the republic erupted in revolution. When the revolution failed, Austria annexed it with the approval of Prussia and Russia.

Frank W. Thackeray

Further reading

Davies, Norman. *God's Playground: A History of Poland,* 2 vols. New York, 1982.

Kieniewicz, Stefan. "The Free State of Cracow, 1815–1846." *Slavonic and East European Review* 26 (1947–48): 64–89.

Wandycz, Piotr S. *The Lands of Partitioned Poland, 1795–1918.* Seattle, Washington, 1974.

See also Congress of Vienna; Münchengrätz Convention; November Uprising; Polish Congress Kingdom

Revisionism

The determination of those European states dissatisfied with the Versailles peace settlements to effect changes. Near the close of World War I, most combatants believed that the peace treaties would be based on U.S. President Woodrow Wilson's (1856–1924) calls for self-determination among peoples in the Habsburg Empire and an equitable settlement devoid of punitive measures. In fact, however, the Versailles settlements reflected British and French determination that the Central Powers be punished and the Allies rewarded.

The Versailles treaty forced moral and financial responsibility for the war on Germany, limited its armed forces, and awarded crucial German economic areas to the reconstituted state of Poland. Germany's allies—Bulgaria and the Habsburg successor states of Austria and Hungary—fared no better in the component settlements. The Treaty of St. Germain left Austria an impoverished, landlocked state with just six million inhabitants. Former Austrian territories were awarded to Allied associates Yugoslavia, Italy, and Czechoslovakia. By the terms of the Treaty of Trianon, Hungary paid reparations, submitted to limitations in its armed forces, and watched as ethnic Hungarian territories were awarded to Czechoslovakia, Yugoslavia, and Romania. Bulgaria lost territories to Yugoslavia and Greece in the Treaty of Neuilly and accepted the imposition of reparations and reductions in its armed forces. Among the victor states, Italy also felt aggrieved because it did not receive all the territories promised by the Allies in the 1915 Treaty of London.

Often the settlements mocked both Wilsonian principles and simple justice; for example, the Sudetenland was given to Czechoslovakia even though its population was overwhelmingly German. Furthermore, the principle of self-determination became largely a tool of the victors. Thus, when Austrian citizens expressed their wish to join Germany, Allied peacemakers denied them, refusing to sanction a huge German presence in Central Europe.

The obvious injustices inflicted on the "vanquished" states during the peacemaking left them determined to revise the settlements. A Hungarian official spoke for most of his countrymen when he declared that the sole goal of his country's foreign policy was to eliminate injustices and inequalities in post-Versailles Europe. In the short term,

prospects for change appeared slim, but revisionist sentiments nonetheless took their toll. They cost Danubian Europe a chance at peaceful economic integration; the vanquished states scuttled plans for a Danubian federation because they believed it would prevent any territorial adjustments. Revisionism also poisoned the political development of the victor states. In Yugoslavia, the security concerns born of proximity with vanquished neighbors reinforced the ruling Serbs' decision to reject demands for autonomy from Croats and Slovenes. As subsequent struggles with Croat dissidents attested, however, federalism was the sine qua non of a peaceful Yugoslavia.

With the rise of Nazism in Germany, revisionism became a dynamic force. Adolf Hitler (1889–1945) used the perceived inequities of the peace settlements as cover in the early stages of his diplomatic revolution. He rearmed Germany, annexed Austria, and demanded the incorporation of the Sudeten Germans all in the name of righting Versailles-imposed wrongs. Moreover, he rewarded fellow revisionists in Hungary and Bulgaria with territories originally awarded by the peacemakers to Yugoslavia and Romania in the so-called Vienna Awards of 1941. In conjunction with Italy, which had subsidized terrorist attacks against Yugoslavia, Hitler also helped establish an independent Croatian state in the Yugoslav lands.

By 1941, revisionism and its proponents had effected a complete, if short-lived, revision of the Versailles order in Europe.

Brigit Farley

Further reading

Duroselle, Jean B. *La Décadence (1932–39)*. Paris, 1979.

MacCartney, C.A. and A.W. Palmer. *Independent Eastern Europe*. New York, 1966.

Wandycz, Piotr. *The Twilight of France's Eastern Alliances, 1936–1939*. Princeton, New Jersey, 1988.

Weinberg, Gerhard L. *The Foreign Policy of Hitler's Germany: Diplomatic Revolution in Europe, 1933–1936*. Chicago, 1970.

See also *Anschluss;* Fourteen Points; Adolf Hitler; London Pact; Munich Pact; Neuilly, Treaty of; Paris Peace Conference; St. Germain, Treaty of; Sudeten Crisis; Trianon, Treaty of; Vienna Awards; Woodrow Wilson

R Revolutions of 1848

Revolutions that swept through Europe in 1848–49. The Revolutions of 1848 in East Central Europe date from the uprising in Vienna on March 13, 1848, to the suspension of the Austrian constitution at the end of 1850; geographically, they comprised all the lands of the Habsburg Monarchy, the Polish areas of Prussia, and within the Ottoman Empire only the Danubian Principalities.

Famine, debt, liberal opposition, and events in Western Europe led to the revolutions. While the political centrality of Vienna was decisive in one sense, Hungary was the home of the strongest political opposition. Two weeks before the revolution began in Vienna, news of an uprising in Paris enabled opposition leader Lajos Kossuth (1802–94) to gain the support of the diet's lower house for a program of liberal and national reforms. Kossuth's speech of February 29 was translated into German and stiffened the demands of the Lower Austrian diet and radical students. By the time Kossuth's delegation arrived in Vienna on March 15 to present its demands to the court, Viennese students, artisans, and burghers had forced the resignation of Prince Metternich (1774–1859), the Austrian chancellor, while in Pest, in Hungary, a group of intellectuals led by Sándor Petőfi (1823–49) forced the Viceregal Council to grant the abolition of censorship and the recognition of a Committee of Public Safety. The Hungarian diet retained political leadership of the country but used the upheaval in Pest and the countryside in support of its demands. The diet enacted what came to be known as the April Laws, which the court, in its weakened position, proceeded to ratify. Hungary gained a virtually independent parliamentary government that included its own foreign minister. The leaders of Hungary's national minorities (Slavs, Germans, and Romanians) at first welcomed the April Laws for the press freedom and the emancipation of the peasants they granted. However, many soon began to oppose the new government, claiming oppression of their linguistic rights and autonomy by Hungarians.

Strains were felt throughout the Habsburg Empire. At the end of March, Germans of the Austro-Bohemian lands, as well as elsewhere in the German Confederation, elected deputies to a German constituent assembly in Frankfurt. Meanwhile, the Czechs, under historian František Palacký (1798–1876), convened a Slavic Congress in June in Prague, as a counterweight to Frankfurt. Although the congress could not agree on details, in its concluding manifesto it called for just treatment of Slavs living abroad and a federal reorganization of the Habsburg realm. The Bohemian diet was itself divided between Czechs and Germans, unable to provide a base for true national autonomy such as the Hungarians had obtained. But to the south, Italian uprisings expelled the Habsburg forces from most of Lombardy and Venetia.

In Vienna, a student-controlled committee forced a nominally liberal government to hold elections for an Austrian parliament under universal manhood suffrage with deputies from throughout the empire (except the Hungarian and Italian lands). The court stood by uneasily, first in Vienna, then in Innsbruck, then again in Vienna, then in Olmütz, sanctioning the acts of its governments but also supporting the military adversaries of the revolutionaries. Its decree of March 20, promising an end to peasants manorial obligations, proved to be its first effective counterattack, as it undermined the solidarity of the countryside with the Vienna radicals. Imperial forces under General Alfred Windischgrätz (1787–1862) suppressed a Czech uprising in Prague in the aftermath of the Prague Slav Congress, bombarding the city with artillery, and in July Italian troops were defeated at Custoza, effectively recovering Lombardy for Austria.

In September the revolutionary assembly in Vienna enacted a law providing for immediate peasant emancipation, thereby going further than the decree of March. However, when Vienna resisted the use of its garrison against the Hungarian government in October and called on the countryside to support it, the revolutionaries were forced to capitulate to Windischgrätz.

By this time, the democratic movement in the Danubian Principalities had been subdued. Events in France had a powerful influence here because of the strong affinity for that country among many writers and *boiars*. After popular assemblies in Moldavia demanded political and social reforms in April 1848, however, the prince, Barbu Ştirbei (1799–1869), expelled the leading liberals from the country. In Wallachia, liberals gained greater social support and controlled the government from June to September, before being overthrown by Russian and Turkish troops.

Hungary's "lawful revolution" from March to September 1848 enacted many social and constitutional reforms, but it could not overcome the contradiction between the country's independence and its place in imperial military and foreign policy. Victorious against the revolutions elsewhere, the court's military supporters moved against Hungary at the end of the summer, and the moderate members of the Hungarian government resigned. Kossuth became virtual dictator, and through his inspiring leadership and organizational ability led a successful military resistance. At the height of this success in April 1849, the Hungarian parliament voted to dethrone the Habsburg dynasty. However, Russian intervention on the side of the Austrians made the Hungarian surrender in August 1849 inevitable. Romanian, Serbian, and Croatian resistance to the Hungarian government, strengthened by nationalist strivings, class differences, and Austrian support, played a subsidiary role in the Hungarian defeat.

Compared to the repression that ensued in Hungary, counterrevolution in Austria was more gradual. The accession of Franz Joseph (1830–1916) to the throne and Felix von Schwarzenberg (1801–52) as chief minister in December 1848 signified a government committed to both imperial unity and modernization. The Austrian parliament met until April 1849 in Kremsier/Kroměříž, working on a federal constitution for the Austrian lands that would have combined liberal freedoms and municipal autonomy. The emperor and Schwarzenberg instead dissolved the parliament and decreed a centralist constitution for the entire empire. Even that was not put into effect, and the Sylvester Decree at the end of 1850 established unitary absolute rule.

In the end, the most significant and lasting impact of the Revolutions of 1848 was on the emancipation of the peasants; the achievement of liberal freedoms and national autonomy were less extensive and also abortive, but set the agenda for demands during succeeding decades.

James P. Niessen

Further reading

Bodea, Cornelia. *The Roumanians Struggle for Unification, 1834–1849*. Bucharest, 1970.

Deak, Istvan. *A Lawful Revolution: Louis Kossuth and the Hungarians, 1848–1849*. New York, 1979.

Jaworski, Rudolf and Robert Luft, eds. *1848/49: Revolutionen in Ostmitteleuropa*. Munich, 1996.

Pech, Stanley Z. *The Czech Revolution of 1848*. Chapel Hill, North Carolina, 1969.

Robertson, Priscilla. *Revolutions of 1848: A Social History*. Princeton, New Jersey, 1952.

See also Jósef Bem; *Boiars;* Franz Joseph; Habsburg Empire; Hungarian War for Independence; Lajos Kossuth; Kremsier/Kroměříž Parliament; Clemens von Metternich; Neo-Absolutism; František Palacký; Peasants; Sándor Petőfi; Prague Slav Congress; Felix von Schwarzenberg; Barbu Ştirbei; Alfred Windischgrätz

Revolutions of 1989

Fall of the Soviet bloc. In 1989 the Communist regimes of six Eastern European countries suddenly and unexpectedly collapsed. Soviet leader Mikhail Gorbachev (1931–) opened the door to this collapse after coming to power in 1985 by calling for "new thinking" in Soviet foreign policy and pursuing a policy of creating a "common European home." Two countries in Eastern Europe were particularly well situated to take advantage of this opening. In Poland, General Wojciech Jaruzelski (1923–), who had imposed martial law in 1981, had concluded that he would have to accommodate his ruling party to Solidarity, the trade union movement, which represented civil society. After a roundtable discussion, the two sides agreed to an election in which 65 percent of the seats in the Sejm (parliament) would go to the Communist list, while the remainder would be elected openly. The roundtable also formed a senate, the election to which was open. To the surprise of everyone, Solidarity won every contested seat but one in the June election. By September, Solidarity used this victory to work out an arrangement whereby Jaruzelski remained president and a non-Communist government led by Tadeusz Mazowiecki (1927–) took power.

Meanwhile, in Hungary, where economic reforms had created a more open society in the 1980s, reformers took over leadership of the Communist Party. Inspired in part by the Polish example but seeking also to calm a vigorous underground opposition, the Hungarian party sponsored a roundtable discussion that led to a referendum in November. Again to everyone's surprise, the government lost the referendum and was forced to put off elections until 1990. By that time, the Communist Party had declined so much in authority that a right-center coalition won and formed a non-Communist government.

R In March 1989 reform Communists abolished Hungarian border restrictions, and in August vacationing East Germans in Hungary began escaping into Austria in large numbers. The German Democratic Republic, led by Erich Honecker (1912–94), vigorously protested, but to no avail. Opponents of the Honecker regime began demonstrating weekly, first in Leipzig and then throughout East Germany. On November 4, one million persons demonstrated in East Berlin. In trying to determine what to do, the East German Politburo decided to ease travel restrictions, but a botched announcement led to thousands of persons converging on the Berlin Wall in the evening of November 9–10. When guards began letting them through, hundreds of thousands of people from East and West Berlin gathered to cheer the breaching of that infamous barrier between East and West. Honecker's government collapsed, and within a year East Germany joined West Germany in a unified German state on Western terms.

The day after the collapse of the Berlin Wall, Todor Zhivkov (1911–98), ruler of Bulgaria for thirty-five years, resigned, beginning a process of reform that brought a non-Communist president and government to power in 1990.

A week later, rioting between students and the police in Prague led to strikes and protests throughout Czechoslovakia. Hundreds of thousands of people gathered nightly in Wenceslas Square in the center of Prague to jangle their keychains and shout "This is it!" and "Now is the time!" Within six weeks, the seemingly entrenched government had collapsed and Václav Havel (1936–)—leader of Charter 77, the Czech human rights organization, and Czechoslovakia's most famous dissident—became president.

The final domino to collapse was Romania. There elements in the Romanian Communist Party opposed to the rule of Nicolae Ceauşescu (1918–89) took advantage of a spontaneous rebellion in Timişoara to overthrow and kill the dictator and his wife, Elena (c. 1919–89). The National Liberation Front led by those elements took power almost immediately.

Gorbachev opened the space in which the Revolutions of 1989 could occur, but it was the East Europeans themselves who took advantage of the opportunity. American foreign policy had little to do with the 1989 events, despite much trumpeting to the contrary. The elevation of Havel, a playwright and philosopher, from prison to the Hradčany Castle, the seat of the presidency, symbolized the enormous moral strength oppositionists enjoyed in comparison with the intellectual and ethical hollowness of the "real existing socialism" that they replaced.

Gale Stokes

Further reading

Glenny, Misha. *The Rebirth of History: Eastern Europe in the Age of Democracy.* New York, 1990.

Stokes, Gale. *The Walls Came Tumbling Down: The Collapse of Communism in Eastern Europe.* Oxford, 1993.

See also Berlin Wall; Nicolae Ceauşescu; Charter 77; Mikhail Gorbachev; Václav Havel; Wojciech Jaruzelski; Sejm; Solidarity; Velvet Revolution; Todor Zhivkov

Rhodope Mountains

Dominant topographic feature of Bulgaria. The Rhodope Mountains consist primarily of ancient, resistant crystalline rocks and constitute the highest European region between the Caucasus and the Alps. Musala (formerly called Stalin Peak) reaches an elevation of 9,600 feet (2,909 m). A dozen other peaks rise more than 8,000 feet (2,424 m). The Rhodopes lie south and west of the Maritsa River, occupying a triangular area of 35,000 square miles (97,220 sq km) that extends into northern Greece. Their west-to-east dimension is about 150 miles (250 km).

The Rhodope Mountains receive from 40 inches (102 cm) of precipitation on their western slopes to 25 inches (64 cm) in their eastern reaches. They are covered with snow from September to May. Forests constitute the principal natural resource. Some lead and zinc are also found. Rivers have cut deep gorges, several of which have been harnessed for hydroelectric installations.

The mountains have been a significant refuge area for many centuries. Vlachs and Greeks sought haven in the Rhodopes during the periods of barbarian incursions. Slavic Bulgarians similarly found sanctuary in the mountains from invaders. In the tenth century they founded Rila Monastery at an elevation of 3,800 feet (1,152 m). Subsequently, Ottoman forces were reluctant to advance into the mountains. During the twentieth century, the Rhodope Mountains have become a significant destination for European tourists.

Thomas M. Poulsen

Further reading

Gerasimov, I.P. and Zh.S. Gŭlŭbov. *Geografiia na bŭl-gariya,* vol. 1, *fizicheska geografiia.* Sofia, 1966.

Iordanov, Tanko, ed. *Geografiia na Bŭlgaria.* Sofia, 1981.

Valev, E. B. *Bolgariya: Ekonomiko-geografich-eskaya kharakteristika,* 2d ed., Moscow, 1957.

Rieger, František L. (1818–1903)

Important and popular Czech nationalist and politician and one of the leaders of the nineteenth-century Czech National Revival. Rieger was born to a comfortable miller's family. Trained as a lawyer, he became a prominent member of the younger generation of Czech "national awakeners" in Prague in the 1840s. In the Revolution of 1848, he joined Czech historian František Palacký (1798–1876) and other Czech liberal political figures in proposing Austroslavism, a movement that sought equality for the Habsburg Empire's Slavic peoples, and urging imperial federalization. When the revolution failed, he went into voluntary exile in France and Great Britain.

In 1851 Rieger returned to Prague and continued his many activities on behalf of Czech culture, including the realization of a Czech national theater, the first scholarly Czech encyclopedia, and the first Czech political daily newspaper. In 1853 he married Palacký's daughter, Marie (n.d.), cementing an already firm friendship with the Czech historian. In the 1860s and 1870s the two men shared leadership of the National Party (Old Czechs), a liberal-conservative alliance devoted to the defense of the historic state rights of Bohemia. Although repeatedly elected a deputy to the Bohemian and imperial diets until he left politics about 1890, till 1879 Rieger advocated passive resistance and a parliamentary boycott by the Czechs. After that, he approved limited cooperation with the Viennese government but also continued to mobilize a Czech defense against the monarchy's Magyars and Germans and maintained strong ties with the ruling circles of France and Russia. In 1897 he was raised to noble rank by the emperor. He died on March 3, 1903.

Joseph Frederick Zacek

Further reading

Pech, Stanley Z. "The Role of František L. Rieger in Nineteenth Century Czech Political Development." Ph.D. diss., 1955.

See also Austroslavism; Czech Culture; Old Czechs; František Palacký; Revolutions of 1848

Right Radicalism

Ultraright movements whose greatest impact occurred during the interwar period. Right Radicalism had a myriad of roots: defeat and dismemberment in Hungary; fear of communism in Poland and Romania; ethnic tensions throughout East Central Europe; irredentism and nationalism; anti-Semitism; and economic tensions brought on by destruction of previous economic ties within the former Habsburg Empire and by the Great Depression.

After World War I, the countries of the region adopted democratic systems of government, but they lacked the preconditions for a working democracy (with the exception of Bohemia). When the Great Depression discredited liberal economics, political liberalism's discredit followed. During the interwar period, much of this area was part of the French alliance system. During the 1930s, however, France was powerless in the face of the Depression and determined Nazi-Fascist aggression. After the occupation of the Rhineland by Hitler (1889–1945) in 1936, the West's policy of appeasement, and the Munich Pact in 1938, which gave the Sudetenland to Hitler, an "Axis Rainbow" rose over East Central Europe. Nazism and fascism seemed to many as an invincible wave of the future.

In most of the countries of the region, the appeals of fascism were present. Yet often the right-radical movements adopted and adapted only fascist trappings. While they pleased Berlin and Rome and ended the cumbersome parliamentary institutions in their respective countries, there was little ardor behind these theatrical fascist displays. Only in Hungary and Romania did fascist movements exist with genuine mass support.

Hungary and Romania

Hungary lost World War I and in the subsequent Treaty of Trianon two-thirds of its territory. Exposed to Communist misrule briefly in 1919, a counterrevolution, the legacy of Trianon, Romanian military intervention, and economic hardships, Hungary had the conditions for the rise of fascism. From the counterrevolution, a vague ideology, the *"Szegedi-Gondolat"* (Szeged Idea) emerged, representing a mixture of anticommunism (equated with violent anti-Semitism), irredentism, revision of the peace treaties, and vague "social reform." The Szeged Idea became the basis of Hungarian fascism. However, the followers of the Szeged Idea, under Gyula Gömbös (1886–1936) and later Béla Imrédy (1891–1946) evolved, with their numerous allies—such as the Hungarian National-Socialist Party—into a Bourgeois-Fascist group not interested in reform but grabbing Jewish properties and positions. The most popular fascist movement thus became Ferenc Szálasi's (1891–1946) Arrow Cross, a grassroots movement that the bourgeois fascists fought with police methods and imprisonments.

Unlike Hungary, Romania emerged victorious from the war, realized its national unity, greatly increased its territory, carried out sweeping agrarian reform, adapted a democratic constitution, and was rich in resources. But reality had little to do with this otherwise fortunate state of affairs. The problems bequeathed by history and economic underdevelopment as well as unresolved questions of regional differences and ethnic tensions created in Romania a radicalism on the right instead of the left, and politics took a decidedly rightward turn. The fascist trappings of Carol II (1893–1953), the Goga-Cuzists (followers of fascist poet Octavian Goga [1881–1938] and professor Alexander Cuza [1857–1947]), and the Antonescu regime (although Marshall Ion Antonescu [1892–1946] himself was no fascist) followed similar patterns. On the other hand, the Iron Guard of Corneliu Codreanu (1898–1938)— the Legionaries—represented genuine right radicalism, like the Arrow Cross in Hungary. In fact, more Legionaries were imprisoned and killed than Communists in the struggle with the authorities, even though the latter also called themselves fascist.

Both the Arrow Cross and the Legionaries were anti-Semitic, as were the followers of the Szeged Idea and the Goga-Cuzists. In Hungary, 90 percent of Jews had been assimilated successfully, but as in Austria and Germany, they were turned into scapegoats for the lost war. Most of the numerous Romanian Jews were unassimilated. The Arrow Cross was based mainly on workers, while the Legionaries tried to mobilize the peasants (who made up 80 percent of the Romanian population). The desire to help the lower classes is in both cases beyond doubt. The Legionaries were the nemesis of the ruling classes, protesting against what they considered the careless, rapid Westernization of Romania. The Goga-Cuzists and the Imrédist-Fascist bourgeoisie of Hungary were interested mainly in Jewish property and positions, not reform. It was the Imrédist conservatives who, in the spring of 1944, a few weeks before the fall of Nazism in Hungary, delivered the Hungarian Jews to Auschwitz in a particularly horrendous fashion, where about half a million of them perished.

The Legionaries were destroyed by Antonescu in January 1941, ironically, the first Nazi movement to fall at a time when Nazi power reached its zenith in the region. But at the beginning of the German campaign against the USSR in June 1941, grave anti-Jewish excesses occurred in Bessarabia and Bukovina, and tens of thousands of Jews perished. Yet the majority of Jews in Romania were not touched. When in 1942 the Germans wanted to start mass deportations to assembly-line killing centers in the death camps of Poland, Queen Helen (1891–1982), King Michael (1921–), and Antonescu stopped them.

Czechoslovakia and Yugoslavia

The creation of the multinational states of Czechoslovakia and Yugoslavia reflected Wilsonian idealism embodied in Woodrow Wilson's (1851–1924) Fourteen Points issued during World War I; but these ideals also reflected the nineteenth century. Badly shaken by twentieth-century realities, both states were beset by problems.

In the Czech part of Czechoslovakia, democracy was a national ideology, the economy was well-enough developed to support democracy, and the leader, Tomáš G. Masaryk (1850–1937) was a dedicated democrat and humanist. While he was alive, his name alone was enough to reduce to insignificance any fascist movement.

Underdeveloped Slovakia was different. The Slovaks were disappointed by Czech supremacy, and in Slovakia only the Lutheran minority had liberal traditions. The Catholic (and majority) Church had authoritarian, anti-Semitic traditions. These tendencies coalesced during the Depression around Father Andrej Hlinka (1864–1938) into a conservative clerical-fascism, fearing a "Jewish-Communist menace." After the fall of Czechoslovakia in 1939 to the Germans, Slovakia became an "independent" Nazi satellite, as Josef Tiso (1887–1947), Vojtech Tuka (1880–1946), and others established a clerical-fascist government. Stringent anti-Jewish measures were enacted, and by 1942 the Nazi's Final Solution was put into effect there.

In Yugoslavia, the *Jugoslovenske Misao* (Yugoslav Idea) fared badly. Fascism was not strong in Serbia, Montenegro, or Bosnia except in Bosnia's Croat-inhabited areas. Similarly, although Slovene leader Father Anton Korošec (1872–1940) leaned toward fascism, the Slovene people did not. However, Croat discontent with Serbian centralizing attempts made Croatia fertile ground for the radical right, especially after the Depression hit. Supported by Italian dictator Benito Mussolini (1882–1945) and Hungarians, Croatian fascists rose. Their organization, the Ustaša, was a conservative, clerical-fascist movement that professed violent anti-Semitism. Under their leader (*poglavnik*), Ante Pavelić (1889–1959), they specialized in terrorism; in 1934 they murdered King Alexander (1888–1934).

In 1941 Yugoslavia resisted Hitler bravely. After the country fell to the German army, the Nazis established an Ustaša-led, clerical-fascist government under Pavelić and began an extermination campaign against Serbs and Jews. Often Catholic priests were the leaders of this campaign. Between 500,000 and 800,000 people perished in the ethnic civil war, a precursor of the tragedy that was to follow the collapse of Yugoslavia in the 1990s.

Bulgaria

Bulgaria was defeated in World War I. After internal upheavals, the Internal Macedonian Revolutionary Organization (IMRO)—which sought the creation of an independent Macedonia—terrorized the country until 1934. The ruling class was anti-Communist, but Bulgarians were also profoundly pro-Russian. During the 1930s, Boris III (1894–1943) established a royal dictatorship with fascist trappings, but he lacked popular support. Although he sided (for the sake of revising the post–World War I Treaty of Neuilly) with Hitler, no Bulgarian Jew was delivered to the Nazis.

Poland

After 120 years of foreign domination, in 1919 Poland regained its independence, but the country was situated between two predators: Germany and the USSR. Poland was still underdeveloped, with pressing economic problems. There were 3.5 million Jews, as well as millions of Ukrainians and White Russians, Lithuanians, and Germans, within the nation's borders. And there was the danger that those who had partitioned Poland three times in the past might do it again (which, in fact, they did in 1939 with the Molotov-Ribbentrop Pact). Communism inspired by the national enemy (Russia) was tantamount to treason in this Catholic country. But the democratic constitution did not work. Józef Piłsudski (1867–1935) established an authoritarian regime in 1926, and until his death in 1935 held Poland together, despite the Depression and the rise of Germany and the Soviet Union. After Piłsudski, fascist tendencies appeared. Seceding from the National Democratic Party, the National Radicals (NA-RA) had a Nazi program, complete with anti-Semitic hooliganism. The governing "Colonels" who succeeded Piłsudski competed with them, forming the totalitarian Party of National Will (*Ozon*). Anti-Jewish violence also rose, even though the majority of Poles wanted democracy. Fascist tendencies never rallied the Polish masses, however, and the bitter experiences after 1939 were not propitious for fascism either. After the German conquest of Poland in 1939, the country and its people were subjected to the most repressive occupation in Eastern Europe.

Nicholas M. Nagy-Talavera

Further reading

Heinen, Armin. *Die Legion "Erzengel Michael" in Rumänien: Soziale Bewegung und Politische Organisation.* Munich, 1986.

Nagy-Talavera, Nicholas M. *The Green Shirts and the Others.* Stanford, California, 1970.

Seton-Watson, Hugh. *Eastern Europe between the Wars, 1918–1941,* 2d ed. Cambridge, 1946.

Weber, Eugen. *Varieties of Fascism: Doctrines of Revolution in the Twentieth Century.* Princeton, New Jersey. 1964.

See also Alexander I Karadjordjević; Ion Antonescu; Arrow Cross; Aushwitz; Boris III; Carol II; Corneliu Codreanu; Fourteen Points; Octavian Goga; Great Depression; Andrej Hlinka; Béla Imrédy; IMRO; Iron Guard; Irredentism; Jews; Anton Korošec; Tomáš G. Masaryk; Michael; Molotov-Ribbentago Pact; Munich Pact; National Legionary State; Neuilly, Treaty of; Ante Pavelić; Peasants; Józef Piłsudski; Revisionism; Horia Sima; Ferenc Szálasi; Josef Tiso; Trianon, Treaty of; Vojtech Tuka; Ustaša; Woodrow Wilson

R

Rijeka (Fiume)

Principal port and third-largest city of Croatia. In both the Croatian and the Italian languages Rijeka's name reflects its site, where the Rječina (Italian, Fiumara) River enters Rijeka Bay. Rijeka is backed by the Gorski Kotar Mountains and is the Mediterranean port closest to the Pannonian (Hungarian) Plain. The city has a population of 160,000.

Rijeka was known in Roman times as Tharstaticum, and a fragment of its Roman wall still stands. In the fifteenth century the settlement was acquired by the Habsburgs, who in 1599 proclaimed it a free city and later, in 1719, a free port. Many eighteenth-century buildings still stand. In 1779 the Habsburgs declared Rijeka an autonomous city under the crown of Hungary, although it lay more than 100 miles (166 km) from the lands of the Hungarian Kingdom. Its eastern suburb of Sušak, fortified in the Middle Ages by the Frankopan family, was recognized as part of the Kingdom of Croatia.

Although the Western allies during World War I originally had assigned Rijeka to a future Croatian state, Italian poet and adventurer Gabriele D'Annunzio (1863–1938) declared the city to be an inalienable part of Italy, and with three hundred supporters he seized it in 1919. Rijeka remained a source of contention between Italy and the Kingdom of Serbs, Croats, and Slovenes for several years until its assignment to Italy by a 1924 treaty between the two states. The treaty confirmed Sušak as part of Croatia, however. Rijeka became part of Yugoslavia in 1945, and a large part of its Italian population emigrated to Italy.

In addition to its port activities, Rijeka is important for shipbuilding and as a tourism transit point to the eastern Adriatic Coast. Each year the community sponsors the festival Melodies of Istria and the Kvarner Gulf.

Thomas M. Poulsen

Further reading

Bertić, Ivan. *Veliki geografski atlas Jugoslavije.* Zagreb, 1987.

Lijepa naša Hrvatska, ed. by Boris Zdunić. Zagreb, 1991.

Pavić, Radovan and Nikola Stražičić. *Ekonomska geografija Jugoslavije,* 3d ed. Zagreb, 1970.

See also Gabriele D'Annunzio

Ristić, Jovan (1831–99)

Serbian politician-statesman who played a leading role in guiding Serbia to the path of a parliamentary democracy. Born in central Serbia, Ristić lost his father at an early age and his family was left in poverty. He was aided by neighbors in obtaining schooling, and his achievements led the government in 1849 to send him to study in Berlin and Heidelberg; he earned a doctorate at the latter. After two subsequent years at the Sorbonne in Paris, he began his government career upon his return to Serbia in 1854.

In 1861 Ristić was sent as Serbia's minister to Istanbul, a position he held until 1867. There, he guided negotiations that led the Porte to give up fortresses in Serbia. In 1868 Ristić became a member of the royal regency for the young Prince Milan (1854–1901). Although only thirty-eight, Ristić was by far the most experienced member of the regency and soon became its driving force. He played the key role in the drafting and adoption of the constitution of 1869, the first written by Serbia. Subsequently, he headed several cabinets as prime minister. In that capacity, he stated the classic defense of ministerial responsibility. From 1872 to 1880, he spent much of the time as either prime minister or minister of foreign affairs, and served as Serbia's delegate at the Congress of Berlin, where he succeeded in getting some territorial revisions in Serbia's favor as well as de jure international recognition of Serbia as an independent state. Following the decision of King Milan to abdicate in 1887, Ristić aided in drafting a more democratic constitution and became the moving force in a new royal regency, a position he held until its overthrow in 1893.

Ristić wrote about Serbian politics and produced several important works dealing with the nation's foreign policy. Although he also wrote personal accounts of the two regencies, the manuscript dealing with the second one was lost during World War I as the government withdrew across Albania in the winter of 1915.

Alex N. Dragnich

Further reading

Dragnich, Alex N. *The Development of Parliamentary Government in Serbia.* Boulder, Colorado, 1978.

———. "Jovan Ristić and Serbia's Struggle for Independence and Democracy." *Serbian Studies* 5 (Spring 1990): 57–66.

Petrovich, Michael B. *A History of Modern Serbia,* 2 vols. New York, 1976.

See also Congress of Berlin; Milan Obrenović

Robert College

Turkish university with American ties. Robert College was founded in Constantinople (later, Istanbul) through the philanthropy of Christopher Rheinlander Robert (1802–78), a New York merchant of French Huguenot descent. The college opened in 1863 as an all-male institution. It was formally incorporated the following year by an act of the New York State Legislature as one of the institutions forming the University of the State of New York. This legal arrangement, which has continued to the present, permits its graduates to attend schools of higher education in the United States on a par with any of the institutions of the state university system of New York.

Established as a nondenominational Protestant institution, the college aimed to provide an outstanding secular education and, at the same time, to develop solid moral and spiritual values in its students. The school became noted early for providing students with an education comparable to that of similar institutions in the United States.

From the beginning, young men of all nationalities and faiths were admitted to the college, although Bulgarians, Armenians, and Greeks predominated. Many of its graduates became outstanding in business and the professions. Its Bulgarian graduates in particular were also very influential in bringing about the Bulgarian national reawakening in the late nineteenth century and in the subsequent political development of their country. However, with the formation of national states and the disintegration of the Ottoman Empire in the late nineteenth and early twentieth centuries, the nature of the student body changed. Today, the majority of students are Turkish.

In 1912 the college opened a School of Engineering, providing the first civil engineering curriculum in the then Ottoman Empire. Three additional schools were added in 1958, one each in business administration, science, and foreign languages. The college also had a six-year preparatory school. That same year, the American College for Girls, which had been in existence since 1871, and Robert College formed a legal merger under the name of the Trustees of Robert College of Istanbul. However, it was not until 1971 that the two schools were actually combined as a coeducational institution. In that same year, as a result of Turkish government policies, the degree-granting part of Robert College and its facilities was transferred to Turkish administration, leaving only the preparatory school under American auspices.

John Georgeoff

Further reading

Robert College of Istanbul. *Robert College: On the Threshold of the 21st Century.* New York and Istanbul, n.d.

Trustees of Robert College of Istanbul. *Robert College of Istanbul: Challenge of a New Century.* New York, 1992.

———. *Robert College of Istanbul: Report of Annual Giving in the United States, July 1, 1993–June 30, 1994.* New York, n.d.

Washburn, George. *Fifty Years in Constantinople.* Boston, 1909.

See also Higher Education

Robeva, Neshka Stefanova (1946–)

Head coach of the Bulgarian national team of rhythmic gymnastics. Robeva was born in Ruse. She attended the Secondary School of Choreography and completed the National Sports Academy with a specialization in rhythmic gymnastics in 1974. She competed in many world and European championships of rhythmic gymnastics (Copenhagen, 1967; Varna, 1969; Havana, 1971). In 1974 Robeva became an assistant professor at the National Sports Academy as well as a coach of the national team of rhythmic gymnastics. In 1978 she was appointed its head coach. The beginning of her triumph as a coach was at the European championship in Amsterdam in 1980. Since then, the Bulgarian team and school in rhythmic gymnastics has been recognized as among the best in technique and artistic qualities in the world. After the games in Barcelona in 1992, which were considered a failure for the Bulgarian team, Robeva requested a release from her position. In 1994 she was asked to return to the team as its head coach until the next Olympic games in Atlanta. Robeva became a member of the Bulgarian Communist Party (later Bulgarian Socialist Party) in 1982. As a member of

R parliament, she was active in an environmental movement known as the Ruse Committee. In 1990 she was elected as a representative of the Bulgarian Socialist Party in the VII Great National Assembly. However, in 1991 she withdrew from parliament.

Yana Hashamova

Further reading

Nozharova, Silvia. *Biografichna spravka: Neshka Stefanova Robeva.* Sofia, 1995.

Todorova, Sofia, ed. *Deputatite, VII Veliko Narodno Subranie, 10–17 iuni 1990.* Sofia, 1991.

See also Communist Party of Bulgaria; Women in Bulgaria

Rokossovsky, Konstantin (1896–1968)

Polish-born Soviet military officer. Born in Russian Poland, Rokossovsky was evacuated to Russia during World War I and participated in the Russian Revolution and the civil war on the side of the Bolsheviks in the Red Guards and the Red Army, respectively. A victim of the purges of the 1930s in which Soviet dictator Stalin (1879–1953) decimated the Soviet officer corps, Rokossovsky was imprisoned from 1937 to 1940. Released in 1941, he became a frontline officer holding the rank of general. A participant in the Battles of Moscow, Stalingrad, and Kursk during World War II as well as military operations in Poland, he later was sent to Poland by Stalin to command the Polish armed forces (1945–49). Named a marshal of the Polish military in 1949, Rokossovsky became a member of the Central Committee in the same year, a member of the Politburo in 1950, and a deputy premier in 1952. During Poland's political crisis of October 1956, brought on by widespread riots against the Soviets, Rokossovsky is widely believed to have been the guarantor of Soviet interests in Poland. However, with the return of Władysław Gomułka (1905–82) and the beginnings of de-Stalinization, Rokossovsky was expelled from the Politburo in October 1956. He returned to the Soviet Union in November of the same year and finished his career as deputy minister of national defense of the USSR.

Peter Lavelle

Further reading

Bialkowski, Wieslaw. *Rokossovsky: Na Ile Polak?* Warsaw, 1994.

Dziewanowski, M.K. *The Communist Party of Poland,* 2d ed. Cambridge, Massachusetts, 1976.

Kersten, Krystyna. *Narodziny Systemu Wladzy Polska, 1943–1948.* Paris, 1986.

Toranska, Teresa. *"Them": Stalin's Polish Puppets.* New York, 1987.

See also De-Stalinization; Władysław Gomułka; Red Army

Romania (Geography)

Medium-sized European country of 85,300 square miles (237,000 sq km) located in southeastern Europe between the 43rd and 48th parallels and the 20th and 29th meridians. Romania is surrounded by its former province of Bessarabia (Moldova) to the east, Ukraine to the north and east, Hungary to the West, Yugoslavia to the southwest, and Bulgaria to the south. It also borders the Black Sea. Because of this location, Romania serves as a link between Europe and Asia Minor, as well as between Europe and southern Russia.

Romania's nature is almost equally divided among forested mountains, green hills and plateaus, fertile valleys, and flatlands. The Carpathian Mountains make an arch in the middle of the country, enclosing within it the Transylvanian plateau. The mountains reach over 8,250 feet (2,500 m) in altitude and are generally covered by forests and high meadows. Around the Carpathians are gentle piedmonts covered by pastures, orchards, and vineyards. The southeastern region of the country is one of the largest, most fertile plains of Europe. Approximately 43 percent of Romania is made up of arable land, 20 percent is meadows and pastures, and 24 percent is covered by forests. This is the largest forested area in Europe, and many claim that the Romanian woodlands are critical for the environmental health of the continent.

The climate of Romania is temperate with four distinct seasons. Winters are cold and windy, particularly in the east. Springs are short and capricious. Summers are hot but dry. Autumns are long, stable, and pleasant. The rich natural vegetation reflects the climate and the landforms. From the Black Sea littoral to the highest mountain peaks, the vegetation types change from submediterranean to subarctic. With only 2.3 percent of Europe's area, Romania has 40 percent of its floristic diversity. The amount of annual precipitation varies from adequate in the mountains, to moderate around them, to poor in the plains. The southern and eastern parts of Romania are prone to droughts. However, the mountains receive enough precipitation in the form of snow and rain to supply a multitude of rivers. These rather small rivers drain into the Danube, which flows for 645 miles (1,075 km) through Romania.

Romania is divided into forty counties (*judeţe*), but people continue to refer to its historical provinces and to identify with them locally. They are Moldova (Moldavia), Muntenia and Oltenia (Wallachia), Transylvania, Banat, and Dobrudja (Romanian, Dobrogea, or Transdanubia). Romania has about 23 million inhabitants, 90 percent of whom are ethnic Romanians. The most important minorities are Hungarians, about 7.2 percent, then Gypsies, Germans, and other small groups.

Most Romanians are Eastern Orthodox, but some are Eastern Catholics. Life expectancy is about seventy years and adult literacy is 98 percent. About half the population is in the labor force, with some 38 percent engaged in industry, 28 percent in agriculture, and 34 percent in services. Slightly over 50 percent of the population live in urban areas. But many of these people moved to characterless, look-alike cities built in recent decades following the forced collectivization of the land and the planned industrialization of the country.

Romania is endowed with timber, oil, natural gas, salt, coal, and minerals. Its best resource, however, is agriculture, which is far from properly developed. Nevertheless, Romania is a leading producer of corn, wheat, meat, vegetables, sunflower seeds, fruits, grapes, and wines. Under the Communist regime, Romania made efforts to build industry, especially metallurgy, machine building, chemicals, petroleum refineries, food processing, and others. Yet those efforts impoverished the people, neglected the country's infrastructure, created enormous ecological problems, and produced dubious results. Like most of Europe, Romania is energy-deficient. Its oil reserves are declining and most of its coal resources are of low quality. The building of several hydroelectric power plants—especially on the Danube—has helped to alleviate the problem. But nuclear plants at Cernavoda are supposed to make Romania self-sufficient.

The largest city in Romania is its capital, Bucharest. Before World War II, Bucharest had about one million inhabitants and was a vibrant city known as the Paris of the East. Currently, it has two million inhabitants, but it has been overbuilt and has lost most of its charm. Other large cities, with 300,000–350,000 people are the provincial centers of Constanţa, Iaşi, Cluj-Napoca, Timişoara, and Craiova. These are followed by some ten other cities with 200,000–300,000 inhabitants. Other important cities include Braşov, Arad, Oradea, Bacau, Brăila, and Galaţi.

Despite its potential, the tourist industry in Romania is largely untapped. The Carpathian resorts are beautiful year-around; the Black Sea littoral is hot and sunny in summer; the Danube delta is unique in Europe; and the culture, such as the Romanian monasteries, is unique.

Nicholas Dima

Further reading

Enciclopedia Geografică a României. Bucharest, 1982.
Geografia României. Bucharest, 1983.
Romania: A Country Study. Washington, D.C., 1991.
The World Factbook. Washington, D.C., 1994.

See also Banat; Bessarabian Question; Black Sea; Braşov; Bucharest; Bukovina; Carpathian Mountains; Cluj-Napoca; Constanţa; Danube Delta; Danube River; Dobrudja; Environment; Iaşi; Industrialization; Moldavia; Systematization; Timişoara; Transdanubia; Transnistria; Transylvania; Wallachia

Romania (History)

The Romanian Lands Before the Nineteenth Century

The Danubian-Carpathian region inhabited by the Romanian people has had a long, complex, and disputed past. In antiquity, the area was initially the domain of the Geto-Dacians (first mentioned by Herodotus [c. 484–c. 425 B.C.), whom the Romanians consider their precursors. The Dacians were formidable enough under Burebista (c. 70–44 B.C.) to hinder Roman expansion north of the Danube in the first century B.C. A successor, Decebal (c. A.D. 87–106), whose kingdom was centered in present-day Transylvania, was able to resist Emperor Trajan's (c. A.D. 53–117) political and military pressure for nearly five years before the Romans destroyed his forces and created the new imperial province of Dacia.

R Roman occupation and colonization of Dacia lasted until A.D. 271, a period that saw the introduction of Christianity into the region along with a substantial number of Roman colonists. After the withdrawal of the Roman administration south of the Danube in 271, a Latinized population remained; Romanians today regard this mixed Daco-Roman group as the basis for subsequent Romanian ethnogenesis.

Romanian development from the fourth to the twelfth centuries is shrouded by the lack of direct written materials and clouded by nationalistic controversies. There is no question that the Romanian language emerged in the Carpathian/Balkan region by the ninth century with a Latinate lexicology and grammatical structure. And by the ninth century, Romanian political formations appear to have existed both north and south of the Danube.

In Transylvania (the bulk of the former Dacia), this development was short-circuited by the Magyar conquest of the Pannonian Plain and the establishment of a Christian Hungarian kingdom in A.D. 1000. By the end of the twelfth century, Transylvania had been incorporated into the Hungarian Kingdom, though it was the only province of medieval Hungary with enough autonomy to be recognized as a principality (*voievodate*).

East and south of the Carpathians the medieval Romanian principalities of Wallachia (ca. 1310) and Moldavia (ca. 1359) emerged partly as a result of the weakening of Magyar influence and partly because of the decline of Mongol-Tatar power to the north. The principalities were under continuous pressure from Hungary and Poland; these threats diminished only in the face of even greater menace from the Ottoman Empire and Russia. This prevented the formation of a single Romanian state and also impeded development.

Some medieval Romanian princes nevertheless had notable accomplishments despite their limited resources and precarious geographical situation. Mircea the Old (r. 1386–1418) expanded Wallachia's borders to the Black Sea by including the Dobrudja in his realm. He was also a significant leader in anti-Ottoman military campaigns. Alexandru the Good (r. 1400–32) was able to resist Ottoman incursions and strengthen the foundations of the Moldavian state. Ştefan the Great (r. 1457–1504), Moldavia's greatest prince, not only defeated the Turks repeatedly in battle but built numerous churches and monastic foundations that

produced a distinctive Moldavian architecture and culture.

Ottoman pressure, however, proved too great to resist, especially after the fall of Constantinople in 1453 and the destruction of the Hungarian Kingdom at Mohács in 1526. Moldavia and Wallachia came under Turkish suzerainty in the sixteenth century. In 1541 Transylvania became an autonomous principality under Ottoman rule. Unfortunately for the majority Romanian population, political arrangements in Transylvania recognized the rights and religious faiths of only the three "historic nations"—Magyars, Saxons, and Szeklers.

From the modern Romanian national point of view, the career of Michael the Brave (1558–1601) was a signal event. As Wallachian prince (1593–1601), he led a renewed anti-Ottoman movement. He also managed to become prince of Transylvania (1599–1601) and then Moldavia (1600–1601), thereby briefly uniting all three Romanian principalities.

The Ottoman Empire tightened its control over Moldavia and Wallachia in the seventeenth century while it was losing Hungary and Transylvania. A quartet of Romanian princes distinguished themselves, nevertheless, in these turbulent times. Under Matei Basarab (r. 1632–54), Wallachia experienced a cultural renaissance and a great expansion of monastic foundations. His contemporary in Moldavia, Vasile Lupu (r. 1634–53), was also a significant patron of education, the arts, and the church. Wallachia's Constantin Brîncoveanu (r. 1688–1714) was a skilled diplomat and cultural leader (church builder, founder of schools and presses, patron of a baroque synthesis of Western and Eastern art known as the Brîncovan style). His relatively long reign brought stability and development to Wallachia. Moldavia at the same time was experiencing economic and demographic decline. Its one shining light was Prince Dimitrie Cantemir (1673–1723), now recognized as the greatest Romanian scholar of medieval times.

Cantemir came to the throne as part of an Ottoman effort to ensure its position north of the Danube. However, when the Russo-Turkish War of 1711 broke out, Cantemir cast his lot with Peter the Great (1672–1725). With the defeat of Russian and Moldavian forces, Cantemir went into Russian exile. The Moldavian throne was given to a Greek prince from the Phanar district in Istanbul who brought the principality under much more direct Ottoman control. Thus began the Phanariot age in Moldavia. Although Brîncoveanu had remained neutral, he was deposed and executed in 1714. In 1716 a Phanariot prince was also installed on the Wallachian throne.

The Phanariot period lasted until 1821. Though it represented a further consolidation of Ottoman rule over the principalities, it was neither an annexation nor a conversion of the area into an Ottoman province, as had happened south of the Danube. The principalities' continued autonomy was rightly seen by Constantinople as a militarily and economically stronger solution than incorporation into the empire.

The era of the Phanariots is often regarded as a bleak epoch in Romanian development, but this view is misleading in a number of respects. Romanian political and cultural traditions continued in ways quite different from those of Serbian, Bulgarian, and Greek regions absorbed into the Ottoman Empire. Second, there was considerable modernization during the eighteenth century in administration, finance, agriculture and agrarian relations, justice, culture, and the church—which set the stage for developments in the nineteenth century. Finally, Ottoman control slowed the imperial expansion of Austria and Russia into the area.

On the other hand, many Phanariot princes were rapacious, attempting to recoup as quickly as possible the money used to obtain their thrones. The Ottomans also profited financially from a rapid turnover in princes as well as from escalating tribute demands. These factors and repeated Austro-Turkish-Russian wars and occupations impoverished the principalities and led to significant annexations of Wallachian and Moldavian territories: Oltenia temporarily by Austria between 1719 and 1739; Bukovina by Austria in 1775; and Bessarabia by Russia in 1812. And through the Treaty of Kuchuk Kainardji (1774), Russia assumed a protectorate over Wallachia and Moldavia. Still, the principalities managed to avoid the fate of Poland, which at this same time was swallowed up entirely.

The eighteenth century in Transylvania laid the basis for the Romanian cultural awakening. In 1691 the Habsburgs incorporated the principality into the Austrian Empire but retained the "three nations" regime, which ignored the Romanian majority. In 1699 the union of the Orthodox Church in Transylvania with the Roman Catholic Church was proclaimed by Leopold I (1655–1735). Though the Uniates, as they were called, gained some religious rights, they constituted less than a third of the Romanian population and, as the Habsburgs intended, drove a wedge between Romanians west and east of the Carpathians.

Ironically, the link to Rome (where many of the Uniate elite were sent to be educated) became the means by which the principal cultural concepts and ideals that led to Romanian national revival were developed. A Uniate episcopal residence, established in Blaj in 1737, became the center of the Transylvanian School, promoters of Romanian culture and language, the Daco-Roman theory and historical continuity, and political awareness. Among the leaders of this Transylvanian Enlightenment were Samuil Micu (1745–1806), George Şincai (1754–1816), and Petru Maior (1761–1821).

Toward the end of the century, the reformist era created by Joseph II (1741–90) sparked two significant political movements among the Romanians. In 1784 Vasile Nicola Ursu, better known as Horea (1730–85), led an antifeudal uprising of Romanian peasants that was brutally repressed. In 1791 Romanian self-awareness was further manifested when Uniate scholars sent a memorial to Leopold II (1747–92) arguing for Romanian rights. This and a subsequent memorial in 1792 were ignored and soon overshadowed in the repressive aftermath of the French Revolution.

Romania, 1815–1914

The Romanian lands at the beginning of the nineteenth century were divided into several political entities, none of which was independent. In the Black Sea region were the two landlocked Romanian principalities of Moldavia and Wallachia, which had been under Ottoman Empire authority since the early sixteenth century but retained their identities and a semblance of autonomy. Turkish control had been tempered since 1774 by a Russian protectorate, though it was not always clear that this arrangement was favorable to Romanian development.

Several other areas also had large Romanian populations. Between the Prut and the Nistru Rivers was the eastern half of Moldavia, now usually called Bessarabia, which had been seized by Russia in 1812. Another portion of Moldavia in the north, usually called the Bukovina, had been annexed by Austria in 1775. To the east of

R Wallachia, between the Danube and the Black Sea and under Turkish control, was the Dobrudja, an area of widely mixed populations. In addition, several zones on the left bank of the Danube in Wallachia were held by the Turks as military reservations.

Across the Carpathian Mountains lay four areas with substantial Romanian populations: Transylvania; the Banat in the southwest, inhabited by Romanians, Hungarians, Germans, and a significant Serb population; and two mixed Magyar and Romanian areas, the eastern Hungarian lands (the Partium), mostly plains areas that had been under direct Hungarian rule for a long time, and the Maramureş in the north.

At the beginning of the nineteenth century, Russia, the Habsburg monarchy, and the Ottoman Empire for centuries had dominated the lands inhabited by Romanians. Yet by 1918, the three empires were gone and a Romanian national state had emerged. Romanian development had become part of European evolution generally and was greatly influenced by the West from the Napoleonic era onward. This development was closely related to the balance-of-power considerations of the dominant empires. On the other hand, Romanian national leaders in the nineteenth century took considerable initiative in pursuing their own ends, often achieving their objectives via clever faits accomplis in the face of Great Power opposition.

The precise nature of this resurgence has been disputed because it includes social, economic, cultural, political, and developmental dimensions; the last three were by far the most important motive forces. The key was the penetration of the Western European industrial, political, and cultural revolutions into southeastern Europe. The fact that the order in which these revolutions took place in the East was the opposite of that in the West is one reason for the contrast in the evolution of Eastern and Western Europe. (The first to unfold in the West, the Industrial Revolution, did not really reach Romania until well into the twentieth century, while the first to manifest itself in the East was the cultural, followed shortly thereafter by the political.)

The cultural revolution associated with the Enlightenment and romanticism made its appearance in southeastern Europe relatively quickly; however, it was considerably transformed by filtering into the Romanian lands through Central Europe. This altered its force even though it retained its basically European character. Ideas—especially cultural ones—became the primary force for modernization. The Romanian awakening was a direct result of the work of the Transylvanian School along with the decline of Greek cultural and religious domination in Moldavia and Wallachia. In Moldavia, Metropolitan Veniamin Costache (1768–1846) and Gheorghe Asachi (1788–1869) were leading figures. In Wallachia, Gheorghe Lazăr (1779–1823), a Transylvanian by birth and education, became head of a new school at St. Sava in which Romanian replaced Greek as the language of instruction and courses on Romanian national history were taught for the first time.

Political change was also in the air. In 1821 the Phanariot era ended with the armed uprising associated with Tudor Vladimirescu (1780–1821). Ironically, the fall of the Phanariots was triggered by an attempt to launch a Greek national revolution in the Ottoman Empire beginning with an incursion into Moldavian territory by Greek forces gathered in Russia. Though this began a chain of events that led a decade later to Greek independence, it was a failure in the principalities, where little sympathy for the Greek cause existed, and resulted in the restoration of indigenous Romanian rulers to the thrones of the principalities in 1822.

One major problem for the Romanians was continued Russian movement into the Balkans. The Russo-Turkish clash over Greek independence led to tsarist occupation of both principalities and a reaffirmation of the Russian protectorate. The Ottoman presence on the left bank of the Danube was ended, and much-needed reforms were implemented by the Russian governor, Count Pavel Kiselev (1788–1872). This was followed in 1834 by the opening of a new developmental period, with Romanian princes now operating under the principalities' first constitutions—the Russian-designed Organic Statutes—an odd combination of liberal and reactionary principles.

Russian domination of Bessarabia also intensified. Chişinău was declared the capital in 1818, and a relatively liberal reorganization of the province ensued. After 1825, the reactionary regime of Nicholas I (1796–1855) began to modify the autonomy of Bessarabia. Russo-Turkish conflicts increasingly disrupted the area, which served as a staging point for Russian forces invading the Balkans. Finally, in 1827 the autonomous status of Bessarabia was abrogated and forceful Russification began. Russians were appointed to most administrative positions, the Russian language was made official, and a policy of colonization, especially by Germans and Russians, was encouraged. Thereafter, the Romanian population encountered repression, exile, and a gradual loss of national identity.

The political and cultural movement begun in the 1820s continued in the 1830s and 1840s. The leading figure in Wallachia was Ion Heliade Rădulescu (1802–72), a pupil of Gheorghe Lazăr. Heliade was a teacher, editor, journalist, and literary leader. Important historical and cultural journals also appeared, including several in the 1840s under Moldavian historian Mihail Kogălniceanu (1817–91), and one jointly edited by the Transylvanian August Treboniu Laurian (1810–81) and Wallachian Nicolae Bălcescu (1819–52).

Meanwhile, the national awakening was also having its effects on the Romanians of the Habsburg monarchy. Those of Transylvania and the Banat were the most active, as befitted their direct contact with the Transylvanian School of the eighteenth century. For the most part, Transylvanian political and cultural life was linked to the two national churches, the Romanian Orthodox and the Greek Catholic, or Uniate, but gradually a generation of lay intellectuals and activists also appeared. The most prominent leaders were Uniate cleric and scholar Timotei Cipariu (1805–87), Orthodox bishop Andrei Şaguna (1809–73), and journalist and historian George Bariţiu (1812–93). Similar development occurred in the Banat. In Bukovina, national development was more modest. A few ethnic Romanians (such as the Hurmuzachis) were major landholders and had local influence. Cultural stirrings began to be felt, but it wasn't until 1848 that significant manifestations of the Bukovinian Romanians were seen.

All this substantial effort not only invigorated national culture and sparked a publishing and educational boom; it also produced a younger generation that was both increasingly aware of its heritage and desirous to affirm itself politically as well as culturally. Largely educated abroad, they called for greater democratization of domestic political life and for the founding of modern political institutions. Russia's retrograde influence on the activity of the native princes in Wallachia and Moldavia accelerated the growth of social, political, and cultural activism in the Romanian lands. The peasantry became increasingly dissatisfied and restive.

In the decades preceding the Revolutions of 1848, the development of national consciousness was one of transition from the Enlightenment to the more romantic revolutionary spirit. This encompassed a diversity of forms and activities ranging from conflicts within the Moldavian and Wallachian assemblies to secret revolutionary societies modeled on the Freemasons and Carbonari societies in Western Europe. In addition, during these years, contacts and cooperation among students and intellectuals from all Romanian areas increased, especially young Romanians studying in Paris—including Ion C. Brătianu (1821–91), his brother Dumitru (1818–92), C.A. Rosetti (1816–85), Bălcescu, Kogălniceanu, and Ion Ghica (1816–97). Although such movements were typical of Europe as a whole in the 1840s, unification, independence, and national identity were specific problems of the Romanian lands.

When the Revolutions of 1848 broke out in Europe, the Romanian lands were also involved. Because they were divided, the events of the Romanian 1848 took various courses. However, events in the Romanian lands were not merely a reaction or response to European developments but the product of local circumstances and factors as well.

In Moldavia, the revolution never really got off the ground. An incipient revolt in Moldavia in March was easily suppressed with Russian support. A number of Moldavian exiles—including Kogălniceanu, poet Vasile Alecsandri (1818–90), Alecu Russo (1819–59), and Costache Negri (1812–76)—subsequently had an important impact on national development in Bukovina and Transylvania. While in exile, they also produced a statement (written by Kogălniceanu) on "The Wishes of the National Party in Moldavia," which summarized the core demands of the emerging Romanian national movement: end of the Regulament system, based on the Organic Statutes, and the Russian protectorate; internal autonomy; civil and political liberties; abolition of serfdom and class privilege; and union of Moldavia and Wallachia.

In Wallachia, a full-fledged revolution broke out in June 1848 under the leadership of Heliade Rădulescu, Bălcescu, the Brătianu brothers, the Golescu brothers (Nicolae [1810–77], Ştefan [1809–74], Alexandru C. [1818–73], and Radu [1814–82]), Ghica, Rosetti, Al. G. Golescu (1814–81), George Magheru (1802–80), and Christian

R Tell (1807–84), among others. Unlike the Moldavians, the Wallachians were able to plan and execute a successful uprising because of a more active conspiratorial tradition, the radical positions of many of the Wallachian leaders, and the weaknesses of the ruling prince. Their revolutionary élan was also greater since many of them had actually witnessed and participated in the French Revolution of February 1848 and then hurried back to Wallachia to do likewise.

In Wallachia, Prince Bibescu (1804–73) and his Russian mentors were caught completely unawares when on June 9 the revolutionaries gathered at Islaz in the south, issued a manifesto, and set up a provisional government. They soon took over Craiova, the principal city in Oltenia, and on June 11 were able to force the prince to sanction the revolutionary program and to name a second provisional government. Bibescu abdicated two days later.

The provisional government survived two counterrevolutionary coup attempts in July but did not gain support abroad. The implementation of reforms proceeded much too slowly, revealing insurmountable differences among various factions of the revolutionary leadership, especially concerning land reform. In late September the Ottoman Empire denounced the provisional regime as "a rebellion springing from the spirit of communism," and its troops occupied Bucharest despite fierce resistance. Three days later, Russian troops also entered Wallachia and the revolution was virtually over. Exile followed for most of the Wallachian 1848ers.

In Transylvania, the events of 1848 were much more dramatic and prolonged, partly because they overlapped with the Hungarian Revolution of 1848–49 and events in the Habsburg lands. The adoption by the Transylvanian diet in 1842 of a law stipulating the gradual introduction of Hungarian as the official language of the country had galvanized Romanian intellectuals, who came to fear the eventual denationalization of their people. Although the language law was never put into effect, it deepened Romanian mistrust of the Magyars, propelled ever larger numbers of them into nationalist activities, and politicized the hitherto largely culturally oriented Romanian national movement.

As the events of 1848 unfolded, the Transylvanian Romanians organized a series of national meetings, the most important of which was held at Blaj on May 3–5, 1848, where perhaps forty thousand gathered to support a wide ranging political and social program enunciated by Simion Bărnuţiu (1808–64). His main contention was that a union of Transylvania with Hungary meant the eventual destruction of the Romanian nation. In Bărnuţiu's view, without national freedom, individual freedom would have no meaning. Thus, the former had to be maintained at all costs.

The Blaj meeting established a Romanian National Committee under the chairmanship of Bishop Şaguna. Similar meetings took place in the Banat, where Romanians under Eftimie Murgu (1805–70) set up their own army and administration. The stage was now set for pursuit by the Romanians of self-determination and civil war.

The principal aim of the Magyar elite was to remove Transylvania from the control of the Habsburg authorities and unify it with the Hungarian Kingdom. In general, the liberal principles proclaimed by the Magyar revolutionaries did not include national rights for the Romanians and other minorities. When the Magyar-dominated diet of Transylvania proclaimed union with Hungary on May 17, conflict between Romanians and Hungarians of Transylvania was assured.

In early September another assembly was convened at Blaj. This time some sixty thousand armed and militant peasants participated. The meeting rejected union with Hungary and demanded the abolition of serfdom and the election of a truly representative Transylvanian diet (one that included all national groups). Bărnuţiu became president of a Committee of Pacification, a kind of Romanian provisional government, and a Romanian people's army was established under the leadership of Avram Iancu (1824–72).

Bloody fighting ensued. The Romanians' army was provided weapons by the Habsburgs, who promised recognition of Romanian national aims and committed large forces of their own to the Transylvanian front. Though the Magyars had gained the upper hand by 1849, they were never able to defeat Iancu's legions in the Apuseni Mountains. The tide turned against the Hungarians with the intervention of the Russians in June 1849. Efforts at reconciliation between Romanians and Magyars and the formation of an anti-Habsburg coalition in mid-1849 were unavailing. The Hungarian army capitulated to the Russians in August 1849, effectively ending the 1848 uprisings.

For the Romanians, the Revolutions of 1848 were a crucial turning point. The short-run consequences for Romanians were slight. The failures in Moldavia, Wallachia, and Transylvania were not surprising, given the inexperience, circumstances, lack of preparation, and scant resources at their disposal. However, although the status quo ante bellum was apparently restored in all three cases, this was deceptive. Within a decade, Moldavia and Wallachia managed to obtain European support for their autonomy, which in turn led to the union of the principalities in 1859–61 and the appearance of the modern Romanian national state.

Russian and Ottoman occupation lasted from 1848 to 1851. The new prince of Moldavia, Grigore Ghica (1807–57), supported the ideas of the Romanian 1848, which gave further impetus to the reform and unionist movement. The ruler of Wallachia, Barbu Ştirbei (1799–1869), was hostile toward 1848 but continued cultural development that fostered reformist/unionist ideas as well.

The next key event in the advancement of the Romanian national cause came not from revolutionary politics but from another turn in Great Power conflict—the Crimean War (1853–56). The principalities were occupied at various times by Russia, Austria, and the Ottoman Empire but then freed entirely from the Russian protectorate and vaulted onto the agenda of the European powers. Through the Treaty of Paris (1856), Romanians were given a voice in the future status of their principalities and even regained from the defeated Russians three southern Bessarabian counties along the Danube.

Romanian national leaders in Moldavia and Wallachia now accelerated their efforts to promote the union of Moldavia and Wallachia. A central committee was formed in the spring of 1857 to coordinate activity between the two principalities. They executed several clever maneuvers to achieve union despite Great Power reticence and internal anti-unionist opposition. The Moldavian unionists led by Kogălniceanu, among others, played the conservative claimants off against one another and on January 5, 1859, unanimously elected Alexandru Ioan Cuza (1820–73) as prince of Moldavia. The Wallachian unionists—led by Ion Brătianu, Rosetti, Vasile Boerescu (1830–83), among others—resorted to street demonstrations and mass protests to intimidate the anti-unionist majority in Bucharest. On January 24, 1859, the Wallachian assembly also unanimously elected Cuza.

The Great Powers were peeved, but since the double election of Cuza did not violate the letter of the 1858 Convention of Paris, which now constituted the administrative statute of the principalities, the Romanian fait accompli was allowed to stand. In September 1859 the representatives of the guaranteeing powers agreed to recognize the double election of Cuza, though they insisted that it would apply only for the duration of his reign.

Cuza embodied the liberal revolutionary spirit of 1848, and his election also became a symbol of the Romanian elite's desire for unity. The problem of developing a national identity had achieved its first major political resolution.

Though it lasted only seven years, Prince Cuza's reign fell into three distinct periods: 1859–62, during which the prince tried to convert a de facto personal union into de jure union; 1862–64, during which he futilely pursued agrarian reform; and 1864–66, during which Cuza tried to resolve political and social conflict through an authoritarian solution.

Cuza's reign began the truly autonomous internal development of Romania. Modernization became a principal objective, with reforms pursued in the economic, educational, cultural, and social sectors. Legitimating the new system and achieving a satisfactory participation in it now constituted the primary agenda of the Romanian elite.

Cuza's election provided Romanians with a single ruler for the first time in the modern era along with real autonomy, but administrative unification of the principalities became a reality only two years later. The cumbersome system of the Paris Convention led to chaos and stalemate; between 1859 and 1862 there were fifteen separate cabinets, while most unionwide legislative actions died in conference; only six joint laws were enacted in the entire period.

Cuza turned to diplomatic channels to resolve the problem and, with the tacit support of France, brought the United Romanian Principalities into official existence on December 4, 1861, with the capital in Bucharest. The assemblies of Moldavia and Wallachia were reconvened in January 1862 as a single national assembly.

The establishment of definitive union in 1861 was a noteworthy success for Cuza, but ironically, it increased internal political turmoil. During the struggle for union, the diversity of aims among Romanian political leaders was generally obscured. Once the basic international arrangements established the new Romanian state, these divisions came to the fore. The new system did not alter the electoral regime established by the Convention of 1858 nor any of its mandates for social reform. This guaranteed conflict, since the system ensured a parliamentary majority automatically opposed to reform. The electorate established by the Paris convention was an exceedingly narrow body of fewer than four thousand voters. The vast majority of the population, mainly peasants, simply did not count. Though occasionally their interests and demands were given lip service, the peasant majority had virtually no role in Romanian politics in the nineteenth century.

Real political power during Cuza's reign was in the hands of perhaps no more than several dozen individuals. Because of this, no actual political parties formed in Romania before World War I, only groupings, factions, and personality cliques. There was a general division between those who had not participated in the events of 1848 and those who had. The former believed that the statute established at Paris was satisfactory, with the possible exception of not providing complete union or a foreign prince. They were generally referred to as conservatives. The latter saw the Paris system merely as a stepping stone to an expanded and independent Romania. Generally referred to as liberals, they favored, to varying degrees, social reforms and the introduction of constitutional institutions.

Cuza was basically a moderate liberal. He and his closest associates, such as Kogălniceanu, were nationalist activists from Moldavia who favored agrarian reform but otherwise advocated moderation. He was opposed by the conservatives, who regarded him as an upstart whose election was something of an accident and, in any event, an event not to be taken seriously. The conservatives followed a largely obstructionist policy toward the prince and his reform ideas. They did not organize, had no platform, and had no powerful press organ, but they did have a parliamentary majority. Their principal figures were Wallachian Barbu Catargiu (1807–62) and Moldavian Lascăr Catargiu (1823–99).

More surprisingly, Cuza was also opposed by liberal nationalists from Wallachia under the leadership of Ion Brătianu and Rosetti. They were more organized than any other group—*Romînul (The Romanian)*, Romania's most widely circulated newspaper, was their press organ, and they attempted to create a rudimentary party organization—but they had little support outside Wallachia or in rural areas. They were civil libertarians, modernizers, and nationalists who never tired of raising the issue of irredenta in Transylvania and elsewhere. Their main complaint was that the prince preferred to seek counsel and support elsewhere.

Between 1859 and 1863, Cuza introduced a series of reforms such as measures to develop the army, create a new fiscal system, establish a modern university system, and modernize the legal system. But he eventually realized that the electoral problem had to be resolved if agrarian and other social reforms were to be achieved. In October 1863 he formed a new government headed by Kogălniceanu to push this agenda. When the assembly refused in May 1864 to consider their wide-ranging land reform proposal, Cuza dismissed the parliament and established by plebiscite an authoritarian regime. The Great Powers acceded to the coup and Cuza's reform program was unilaterally implemented.

In the nineteenth century the replacement of tradition-based agrarian relationships enforced by custom, informal agreement, and quasi-legal contracts had cheated the peasantry and led to abuses and exaggerated claims by landholders now converted into proprietors. Cuza's reform abolished all feudal dues and restrictions on the personal liberties of the peasant, provided varying amounts of land for over five hundred thousand peasants, and compensated landholders. However, the well-intentioned reform was ill-conceived and hastily executed, allowing considerable evasion and fraud in implementation. The fiscal provisions turned out to be harmful to the peasant, and the problem of fragmenting already small plots seems to have been ignored. Thus the long-term impact of this reform on the modernization of agriculture and the well-being of the peasantry was problematic.

Though Cuza carried out other significant reforms, by 1865 he had a falling out with Kogălniceanu, budget deficits surged, and his corrupt inner circle (camarilla) acquired increasing influence. His reforms liberalized and modernized, as was evident after 1866. On the other hand, the methods used fostered an unhealthy centralization of state power, accustomed Romanian political culture to administrative manipulations of the system, and legitimized authoritarian, oligarchical governance. In the end, a coup—organized and orchestrated by liberals and conservatives and supported by key elements of the army—forced Cuza's abdication on February 11, 1866. A provisional ruling council undertook to bring a foreign prince to the throne.

In May 1866 Prince Karl of Hohenzollern-Sigmaringen (1839–1914) assumed the Romanian throne as Prince Carol. His reign, the longest in the history of the Romanians, fell into four periods: 1866–71, a time of constitutional development, conflict, and crisis; 1871–81, an era of consolidation, the gaining of independence and territorial expansion to the Black Sea, and the establishment of the Romanian Kingdom in 1881; 1881–1907, a period of maturation and growing self-confidence culminating in the celebration in 1906 of the fortieth anniversary of Carol's rule; and 1907–14, when the great peasant uprising of 1907 showed the tentative nature of much Romanian progress. Throughout, the developmental problems of national identity, creating a lasting and legitimated system, and regulating participation in that system continued to be a focus of the Romanian elite. The problems of modernizing the state bureaucracy and the creation and distribution of wealth in a backward economy remained critical.

The most lasting achievements of the Romanians continued to take place in nonpolitical contexts. These years saw the flowering of modern Romanian civilization with the appearance of its national poet, Mihai Eminescu (1850–89); classic storyteller, Ion Creangă (1837–89); principal dramatist, Ion Caragiale (1852–1912); leading musical luminary George Enescu (1881–1955); and one of the pioneers of modern art, Constantin Brancuşi (1876–1957). The Romanian Academy was created in 1866 and the universities of Iaşi (1862) and Bucharest (1864) began to achieve a much higher level of respectability and prominence. Romanian cultural life was led by the Junimea society, founded in Iaşi in 1863 and dominated by Titu Maiorescu (1840–1917). Their journal, *Convorbiri Literare* (*Literary Conversations*), became Romania's premier literary publication. Even more salutary was Junimea's withering attacks on mediocrity and superficiality. It was no accident that Eminescu, Creangă, Caragiale, and others first blossomed and prospered in the atmosphere created by the Junimists.

Romanian women played only a small direct role in politics in the nineteenth century. In fact, Romanian society remains patriarchal even today. Women did not have a vote under the constitution of 1866, and a women's suffrage movement was virtually nonexistent. Even in cultural affairs, they had little prominence. Maria Rosetti (1819–93), wife of C.A. Rosetti, was a writer, courageous participant in the Wallachian revolution of 1848, and political collaborator with her husband. Queen Elisabeta (1843–1916), wife of Carol I and an enthusiastic patron of the arts, achieved notoriety in Europe as a writer under the pen name Carmen Sylva. Another literary figure of note was Dora d'Istria (Elena Ghica [1828–88]), widely known outside Romania for her studies of folk poetry and southeast European social, religious, and cultural life.

The process of national development fostered fierce debate over the questions "Who are we? Where have we come from? And where are we going?" as Romanians continued to be obsessed with their "becoming." The precariousness of the Romanian national situation—located at the crossroads of southeastern Europe, surrounded by expansionistic empires—contributed to an activist "philosopher-patriot" mentality and a "historicizing" of Romanian civilization, in which history making and history studying were inextricably bound up with each other. Romanian historiography rose to the next level, producing in this era one of the giants of modern scholarship, historian-politician Nicolae Iorga (1871–1940).

Economic growth remained at modest levels. The pervasive assumption that the state needed to dominate this development was a major hindrance. The Romanian elite pursued economic policies designed to solidify its share of oligarchical power. Patronage was perpetuated in the economy and the politics that stifled entrepreneurial growth, increased the disequilibrium of Romanian economic development, and created a system rife with inefficiencies. Market liberalism, an important precondition for the expansion of political liberty and the creation of a modern civic society, did not exist. Indeed, much of what was positive in Romanian economic development occurred in spite of rather than because of governmental policies and actions. At the same time, many sectors of the economy that could have promoted capital formation and essential entrepreneurial activity became state monopolies or protected fiefdoms. Agriculture, the primary component of the pre–World War I economy in a society that was 82

R percent rural in 1912, was neglected and even impeded by official policies. Industrial development was largely related to agriculture, with 49 percent of production related to food processing in 1914. The major growth sector was in oil and petroleum, which accounted for 29 percent of industrial production in 1914, growing from 12,000 metric tons in 1870 to 1.8 million in 1913. Another area of substantial development was in communications, with a dramatic expansion in the road and rail networks.

Politically, the constitution of 1866 provided for a representative system that was relatively more open than those of Romania's imperial neighbors and had many promising features. However, the establishment of a centrally controlled, French-style bureaucratic regime of prefects, subprefects, and mayors gave the government leverage over most political matters, including elections. The compatibility of strong, honest civic traditions with such a centralized regime is questionable; the consequences of this Romanian centralist tradition have still to be fully understood. Moreover, political groupings continued to be factions or quasi-kinship groups organized around personalities and patron-client relationships rather than ideas, ideologies, or programs. As under Cuza, "liberal" and "conservative" continued to identify temperamental dispositions and personal loyalties. Participation in political life was limited to less than 1 percent of the population, and electoral fraud became the norm. Controlled elections, coupled with the restricted size of the ruling group, made the creation of permanent organizational structures and communities of interests unnecessary. The election results depended on who was governing rather than on determining who would govern.

Another consequence of all this was that entrepreneurial endeavor tended to be channeled into politics rather than into more productive outlets, while the career objective of too many Romanians was to become a government functionary. By 1900, some 2 percent of the population were employed as state functionaries, compared with 3 percent in industry. These problems and trends, linked primarily to the twin developmental crises of participation and bureaucratization, contributed to modern Eastern Europe's bloodiest peasant uprising in 1907. Nevertheless, by 1914, the process of Romanian development had produced a relatively stable political entity where none had previously existed.

Between 1866 and 1871, Carol faced the same chaotic conflicts and political infighting that had characterized Cuza's reign. Cabinets followed one another in rapid succession. Carol made the cardinal error of acquiescing in the institutionalization of electoral fraud. His effort between 1867 and 1868 to collaborate with Romania's most capable modernizers, the Wallachian liberal faction under Brătianu and Rosetti, foundered on external opposition, internal machinations, and a flare-up of anti-Semitic agitation. The result was Carol's near abdication in 1871.

This was followed by a coalescing of the political system between 1871 and 1877, which culminated in the achievement of national independence in 1877–78. From 1871 to 1876, the Conservatives, under Catargiu, a traditionalist landholder, were in power. But with the outbreak of a new crisis in Bosnia and Hercegovina in June 1875, Carol believed that Romania had a chance to achieve full independence. This course conservative Catargiu was reluctant to pursue. In mid-1876 Brătianu returned to power as the prince's most trustworthy and able collaborator.

Romanian political leaders understood that independence could be achieved only through a cunning diplomatic game coupled with a favorable international context. When the Russians entered the war on the grounds of protecting the Orthodox Christian peoples of the Balkans, the Romanians knew their opportunity had arrived. In 1877 a Russo-Romanian military convention was signed in which Russia agreed to recognize and defend the territorial integrity and rights of Romania in exchange for assistance in their war against the Turks.

In May 1877 Romanians proclaimed their independence. Their armed participation in subsequent battles in the Balkans was critical in the defeat of the Ottoman Empire, at the cost of some ten thousand men killed in action. However, the Russians ignored their ally in the peace negotiations and eventually forced the Romanians to give up southern Bessarabia in exchange for the bulk of the Dobrudja and the Danube delta, both of which had been under Ottoman control. The 1878 Congress of Berlin recognized the independence of Romania, but this was made contingent on changing the constitution of 1866 to allow Jewish citizenship.

The period after 1878 was one of consolidation and internal development. It saw the entrenchment of a nationalist-liberal oligarchy under Brătianu. In 1880 the monarchy's continuity was strengthened with the selection of Ferdinand of Hohenzollern (1865–1927), the childless Carol's nephew, as heir to the throne. A year later, in 1881, Carol I was proclaimed the first king. This step, meant to stress Romania's political maturity and underline its potential role as a factor of stability in southeastern Europe, also solidified Carol's throne.

Brătianu's long ministry became more and more autocratic in the 1880s, and he came to be called the "Vizier" in light of his increasingly personal rule. Though he "allowed" a minor broadening of the franchise in 1884, the essentials of the oligarchical system of 1866 were preserved. As a result, between 1884 and 1914, no government ever lost an election. Brătianu's attention was increasingly devoted to furthering Romanian modernization as a means of cementing the hold of his group on the levers of political and economic power.

Eventually a United Opposition was formed, composed of conservatives led by Catargiu, liberals led by the prime minister's own brother Dumitru, as well as some of the young liberals that had been Brătianu's protégés, such as Take Ionescu (1858–1922). Carol finally became convinced his own position would be weakened if Brătianu remained. When peasant unrest resulted in violence in 1888, the king brought an end to the "vizieriate."

This led to the inauguration of a rotational system of governance between 1888 and 1914 in which power alternated between the Conservatives and the National-Liberals. Between 1888 and 1895, Carol tried various conservative combinations. The dominant influence on all these cabinets was P.P. Carp (1837–1919), whose Junimist ideas formed the basis for much of what was attempted between 1889 and 1895. Perhaps their most important action came in 1895 with a mining law that promoted foreign investment and created opportunities for the exploitation of Romania's mineral wealth. Liberal cabinets between 1895 and 1899 accomplished little except for notable school reforms.

Though other political groups existed besides the two major factions, their leading members were often co-opted into the ruling groups and usually disappeared. At the end of the nineteenth century, Constantin Dobrescu-Argeş (1859–1903),

Vasile M. Kogălniceanu (1863–1941), and Ion Mihalache (1882–1963) tried to found a peasant party. They engaged in worthy educational activity and spoke out courageously but had limited impact because, in the end, peasants did not have the vote. In 1893 a Romanian Social Democratic Workers' Party appeared, but in 1899 they self-destructed when their principal leaders joined the liberals in the belief that plausible reform could be channeled only through the existing system.

Between 1899 and 1903, various Romanian governments were paralyzed by economic crises. An oversupply of government functionaries, costly public works projects, and bureaucratic meddling in the economy combined to produce huge debts and economic chaos. Local credit bank legislation (1903) and a village cooperative law (1904) reflected ideas popular among reformist liberals but affected few peasants.

While the Conservatives were in office in 1906, elaborate celebrations were staged to recognize Carol's forty years on the throne. This self-satisfied manifestation convinced the Romanian elite that all was well. While Romania's neighbors frequently experienced peasant revolts, political violence, and other Balkan-style upheaval, Romania appeared to be a model of social harmony, peaceful development, and orderly political change.

These illusions were painfully exploded in 1907 when a relatively peaceful peasant protest escalated into massive violence. The Liberals were hastily called to take over and ruthlessly repress the uprising. The full costs of the 1907 revolt have never been revealed, but thousands were killed, the myth of an exemplary Romania was shattered, and the image of a docile Romanian peasantry was demolished.

Legislation in 1907–8 to benefit the peasants, including a new law on agricultural contracts, a law establishing a rural credit bank to facilitate peasant land purchases and leases, and a law abolishing lease trusts were steps forward, but the younger Liberals, led by Ion I.C. Brătianu (1864–1927), realized the impotence of these half-measures.

In 1910 the Conservatives returned to power and accomplished little, but, on their watch, the Balkan Wars (1912–13) erupted in 1912. When the Bulgarians launched a preemptive attack on Serbia and Greece in 1913, the Romanians joined the counterattack on Bulgaria. Romania received as compensation the southern Dobrudja, but since the territory in question had never been part of a Romanian state and its population was mostly non-Romanian, there was a sense that Romania's involvement was a bit devious. And, ironically, when Romanian peasant soldiers saw how poorly their material situation compared with that of the supposedly more backward Bulgarians, they returned home convinced that it was time for political and agrarian reform.

In May a constituent assembly was elected to revise the constitution to give land and the franchise to the peasants, but the outbreak of World War I temporarily ended this process.

Meanwhile, on the other side of the Carpathians, cultural activism also continued to be a major emphasis. For the Transylvanian Romanians, the post-1848 era was one of major disappointments. They were infuriated to find themselves receiving as a reward from the Habsburgs the same thing that the Magyars received as punishment: absolutist rule from Vienna between 1849 and 1860. A window of hope was opened after 1860, when Franz Joseph (1830–1916) proclaimed a constitution that granted a degree of autonomy to Transylvania and political rights to the Romanian population.

In 1861 the Transylvanian Association for the Literature and Culture of the Romanian People (ASTRA) was founded as part of this new engagement of the Romanians in Transylvanian public life. It promoted cultural literacy, education, publications, conferences, museums, libraries, and other programs to foster cultural ties among Romanians throughout Transylvania. As a result of the Diet of Sibiu of 1863–64, the Romanians won legal and religious equality for the first time. And in 1864 the Romanian Orthodox Church was raised to a metropolitanate.

However, the emperor effectively ended the autonomy of Transylvania in 1866, and in early 1867 he agreed to the creation of a dualist state, Austria-Hungary. Transylvania was incorporated into Hungary and the laws of 1863 were voided. Another consequence was the beginning of a systematic policy of forced assimilation of the other nationalities by the Hungarian authorities. Among other measures, Hungarian became the official language, personal names and place-names were Magyarized, electoral laws were manipulated to favor Hungarians, Romanian schools were slowly Magyarized, and administrative and legal harassment of Romanians became common.

After 1867, the Romanian political elite in Transylvania was divided between those who favored passivism—withdrawal from political life and nonrecognition of the dualist state—and those who favored activism, hoping to expand and defend the rights of Romanians through the existing system, calling for participation in political life, and using parliamentary means to promote and defend the rights of the Romanian nation. In 1869 the passivists led in the founding of the Romanian National Party of Transylvania, which called for the basics of the 1848 program, but it was quickly suppressed by the Hungarian authorities. In 1881 Romanians throughout the monarchy united to form the Romanian National Party of Transylvania, the Banat, and Hungary. Though the passivist program continued, the Romanians of the Banat and Hungary were allowed to participate in the Parliament in Budapest.

The first Romanian daily newspaper in Transylvania, *Tribuna,* edited by Ioan Slavici (1848–1925), appeared in 1884. It became a major voice of Romanian nationalism and increased militancy. Its writers spearheaded the 1892 Memorandum Movement, designed to gain support from the emperor for Romanian rights. But Franz Joseph refused even to accept the petition; this was the last memorial addressed to the emperor by the Romanians. The 1893 trial of its signatories was a public relations fiasco for the Hungarians, providing a European-wide forum for Ion Raţiu (1828–1902) and others, and energizing the Romanian national movement. Raţiu's statement that "the existence of a people cannot be discussed, only affirmed" became the watchword for Transylvanian Romanians up to the collapse of the Habsburg monarchy. By 1905, the Romanians were sufficiently radicalized to pursue an activist program. Cooperation with other non-Magyar nationalities was encouraged to resist Magyarization and promote national self-determination.

On the other hand, the post-1848 period saw a number of gains for the Romanians in Bukovina. The imperial constitution of March 4, 1849 granted Bukovina autonomy. The province became a duchy and remained directly subordinate to Vienna until 1918. In 1862 the Society for Romanian Culture and Literature was established in Bukovina, and in 1875 a department of Romanian language and literature was created at the University of Cernăuţi. The Putna celebration in 1871, which attracted cultural leaders from all the

Romanian lands, became a rallying point for Romanian nationalists. The Orthodox Church played a major role in defending Romanian culture and rights in Bukovina, though colonization and immigration from Habsburg Galicia resulted in considerable denationalization by 1914.

Romania and World War I

The outbreak of World War I posed a dilemma for Romania. There was no question that Romanian national interests lay with the defeat of the Habsburg Empire. On the other hand, Romania had had an alliance with Austria-Hungary, Germany, and Italy since 1883. Carol hoped that Romania would join the Central Powers, but his prime minister, Ion I.C. Brătianu, and others, both liberal and conservative, argued successfully that the treaty was purely defensive in nature. Romania therefore remained neutral in 1914. This decision gave the country time to prepare politically, diplomatically, and militarily for war. Carol's death and the accession to the throne in late 1914 of his nephew King Ferdinand (1865–1927) and his English consort Marie (1875–1938) furthered solidified this position.

Between 1914 and 1916, Brătianu sought to preserve Romania's freedom of action in an extremely dangerous situation, recognizing that the nation's very existence might be in question. He rapidly accelerated Romanian preparations for war, especially since the Second Balkan War (1913) had shown how unprepared Romania was militarily. The political and military conventions between Romania and the Entente (Britain, France, Russia, and Italy) were finally signed in August 1916. The Allies recognized Romania's rights over Transylvania, the Banat, and Bukovina, and promised official recognition for the union of these territories with the Romanian Kingdom at the postwar peace conference (in which Romania would participate as an equal partner). Ten days later, a crown council convened by Ferdinand declared war, and Romanian troops crossed the Carpathians into Transylvania.

Initial success soon turned to disaster as German and Austro-Hungarian armies embarked on massive counteroffensives that resulted in the German occupation of Bucharest in December. Three-quarters of the territory of the Romanian Kingdom fell under enemy control and the government was forced to retreat to Iaşi.

Despite these defeats, Romanian participation on the Allied side significantly changed the geo-political situation of the war. The Central Powers' general position was weakened as forces were drawn to the Eastern Front. And despite the debacle, Romanians continued to fight.

At the beginning of 1917, the Romanians, assisted by a French military mission under General Henri Berthelot (1861–1931), rebuilt their army in time to blunt a concentrated German effort to take the remainder of Romanian territory. In the battles of Mărăşti, Mărăşeşti, and Oituz (July-August 1917), Romanian soldiers fought valiantly. Battling the Germans to a standstill, they saved the Romanian Kingdom, redeemed Romanians in the eyes of their allies, and halted the last German offensive in this sector. A major role in stiffening Romanian resolve was played by Queen Marie.

The Russian revolution in November 1917 and Lenin's (1870–1924) decision to pursue peace created new dangers for Romania, particularly after the Russians signed an armistice with the Central Powers. The Entente demand that Romania continue armed resistance was clearly untenable. Brătianu was replaced as prime minister by General Alexandru Averescu (1859–1938) and then by Alexandru Marghiloman (1854–1925) in the futile hope that they could strike a better deal with the Germans. The Peace of Bucharest in May 1918 dealt a severe blow to Romania's territorial integrity and sovereignty, and effectively knocked Romania out of the war.

The collapse of the Bulgarian front in September 1918 allowed the Romanians to reenter the war on November 10. The next day, the Germans signed an armistice ending the war, and on December 1, the king and queen reentered the capital at the head of Romania's battered but victorious army. On the same day, a Romanian national assembly in Transylvania proclaimed the union of Transylvania and the Banat with the Romanian Kingdom.

Throughout the war the Romanians actively promoted the unification of all the Romanian lands and asserted the legitimacy of Romania's territorial claims. Such efforts were supported by numerous Romanian associations, societies, and individuals inside and outside the country. These efforts were rewarded in 1918.

The first Romanian land to be reunited with the kingdom was Bessarabia. In early 1918 the Bessarabian assembly (Sfatul Ţării) declared independence from Russia and then voted for a federal union with the Romanian Kingdom. Meanwhile,

R in the fall of 1918, when the Entente had come to favor breaking up the Austro-Hungarian Empire, Romanian leaders in Bukovina began to push for self-determination. A Romanian national council was established; on November 28 it voted for the unification with the Romanian Kingdom. In Transylvania, the Romanian National Party was reactivated at the end of September 1918 and soon began to organize local and regional national councils. In November it called for a Grand National Assembly in Alba Iulia to bring about union with the Romanian Kingdom. On December 1, 1918, some 1,200 delegates and tens of thousands of others from throughout Transylvania converged on Alba Iulia to declare the unification of Transylvania with Romania in the name of "all Romanians of Transylvania, Banat, and Hungary."

On December 12, Brătianu triumphantly resumed the Romanian prime ministership (his cabinet was the first to include members from all the Romanian lands), and on December 24, Ferdinand promulgated the Union of Transylvania and the Romanian Kingdom. From the ashes of near fatal defeat in 1916–17, Greater Romania had emerged.

Romania in the Interwar Period

The national state that earlier patriotic enthusiasts had only faintly imagined now entered the interwar epoch with a territory of 105,300 square miles (295,000 sq km) and sixteen million people, ranking tenth and eighth, respectively, in size in the new Europe. For the Romanian generation that matured in the 1920s, the era offered great promise in which Romanian culture would know its fullest flowering.

The transition years immediately following the war were a trying period of adjustment and recuperation. The creation of Greater Romania opened new horizons, but the disorder and destruction of war, coupled with all the changes that needed to be implemented in the significantly expanded state, made for difficult material and financial conditions. The presence of substantial national minorities (more than 28 percent of the population) also presented difficulties.

Escalating change, hard times, and national insecurities fostered continuation of the highly centralized administrative methods of the old Romanian Kingdom. Promises of local autonomy made to Transylvanians and Bessarabians were soon jettisoned. An almost pathological fixation on "national unity" allowed those who wanted or benefited from the imposition of a centralized administration to maintain control.

Important reforms were implemented after the war. A political party system began to appear, though parties were still far too centered around personalities and kinship/patronage. For the first time the peasantry became a substantial factor in the political life of the country with the introduction of universal manhood suffrage and comprehensive agrarian reform. A new constitution adopted in 1923 formalized these changes.

The enfranchising of the peasantry had exactly the result feared by prewar Romanian conservatives: the latter virtually disappeared as a political force. On the other hand, it did not result in a truly representative or honest parliamentary system. The major interwar parties were the National-Liberal Party, led by Brătianu; the People's Party, led by General Averescu, which gradually disintegrated after 1927; the Peasant Party, led by Mihalache, which merged with the Romanian National Party in 1926; the Romanian National Party, led by Iuliu Maniu (1873–1953); the National-Peasant Party, formed in 1926 and led by Maniu, Mihalache, and Alexandru Vaida-Voevod (1872–1950); the Social Democratic Party; a minuscule Romanian Communist Party, almost always led by ethnic minorities and banned after 1924; the anti-Semitic National Christian Party, led by Octavian Goga (1881–1938) and A.C. Cuza (1857–1947); and the radical nationalist Legion of the Archangel Michael, led by Corneliu Codreanu (1899–1938).

Between 1919 and 1927, a plethora of parties and personalities produced fragmented parliaments, though the National-Liberals generally had the upper hand. In part, this was because Brătianu had the unstinting support of Ferdinand and Marie until the monarch's death in 1927.

Under the aegis of the Liberals, a uniform monetary system was established (1919), more substantial agrarian reform was begun, and a relentless struggle was waged for Romanian interests at the Paris Peace Conference. In 1919 Romanian troops also occupied Budapest, helping to end the short-lived Hungarian Soviet Republic that had formed during the tumultuous period after World War I. However, when Brătianu was unable to obtain acceptable terms at Paris regarding Romanian demands for territory, he resigned in protest.

The elections of 1919 were designed to produce a National-Liberal landslide and impress the delegates from the Great Powers in Paris. The result, however, was a hopelessly divided parliament that highlighted the divergent interests of the various Romanian lands: the National-Liberals and the new Peasant Party had their main support in the old kingdom, the Romanian National Party won the upper hand in Transylvania and the west, while the Bessarabian Peasant Party and the Democratic-Union Party in Bukovina emerged as the strongest in these areas. In 1919 Ferdinand called to power a coalition cabinet. Agrarian reform proceeded, union of the new provinces with the kingdom was finalized (December 1919), and the peace treaties with Austria and Bulgaria were signed. In 1920, when the powers also recognized the union of Romania and Bessarabia, Averescu became prime minister.

Almost the first action of the new government was to dissolve the parliament and hold new elections, which not surprisingly produced a majority for Averescu's People's Party. Agrarian and financial reforms were the primary issues, along with continued measures to integrate the various provinces. Though some 66 percent of the large landholdings were broken up, the agrarian reform's restrictions on mortgages and its tendency to fragment already tiny holdings thwarted the creation of a real smallholder class. Averescu's finance minister, Nicolae Titulescu (1882–1941), one of interwar Romania's outstanding leaders, president of the League of Nations (1930 and 1931), and foreign minister for much of the period between 1927 and 1936, produced the first organized budget in 1921. In foreign affairs, Take Ionescu played an important role in the formation of the Little Entente (1920–21)—an alliance of Romania, Czechoslovakia, and Yugoslavia—and the 1920 signing of the Treaty of Trianon (with Hungary) and the Treaty of Paris, which affirmed Romania's right to incorporate Bessarabia.

Brătianu returned to the helm in January 1922, dissolved the legislature, and illegally replaced it with a constituent assembly in which his party held over 60 percent of the seats. With the external and internal situation somewhat solidified, the National-Liberals were now in a position to implement their own vision of Romania's future. This was to be codified in the constitution of 1923, in their political-economic program under the slogan *Prin noi înşine* (By and Through Ourselves Alone), and in ruthlessly laying to rest any federalist aspirations and promises. Such acts culminated in the pomp and ceremony of October 15, 1922, when Ferdinand and Marie were officially crowned as rulers of "all Romanians" in Alba Iulia.

The 1923 constitution had many democratizing elements, but these were overshadowed by overcentralization, a subtle shift to a more collective/statist/national world view, and electoral fraud. In addition, the religious provisions of the 1923 statute clearly discriminated against all but the two "national cults." In 1925 the Orthodox Church was raised to a patriarchate (under Miron Cristea [1868–1939]). In 1926 the Liberals implemented a new electoral law that gave half the seats in parliament to the majority party if it had 40 percent of the vote, the other half being distributed proportionally among all parties with at least 2 percent. This ensured continued corruption of elections without substantially reducing instability (only two of the ten interwar parliaments actually completed their terms of office). Though the Peasant Party and the Romanian National Party both denounced the 1923 constitution as "absolutistic," imposed by fraud and force, and without legitimacy, when they took control of the government in 1928 they did little to change it.

The new constitution's interventionist tendencies were a reflection of the protectionist ideology promoted by the National-Liberals. Much of Romania's mineral wealth was nationalized, though the stock was often held by the party's supporters (the National-Liberals directly controlled the National Bank, the Romanian Bank, the Mine Credit Bank, and numerous other major companies). Various industries were proclaimed to be of national interest and placed under government control, particularly metallurgy and petroleum. In addition, a number of other areas were or now became state monopolies, such as the railroads and the post-telegraph-telephones. Numerous industries required that 60 percent of the capital as well as management be Romanian. These actions concentrated the wealth of the country in the hands of the political elite and perpetuated Romania's backwardness.

On the international level, Romania was plagued after 1922 by the "Hungarian Optants" issue, the claim that Magyar landowners who had opted for Hungarian citizenship after 1918 had been treated unfairly in the agrarian reform. Though that was not the case, the matter allowed

Hungarian revisionists to attack the postwar settlement. Relationships with the Soviet Union remained poor, especially after September 1924, when Soviet agents attempted to proclaim a "Soviet republic" at Tatar-Bunar in Bessarabia, and December 1924, when the Romanian Communist Party was permanently banned.

Opposition to the Brătianu regime was varied. The National Party discussed fusion with several old-kingdom parties, eventually unifying with the Peasant Party in 1926. A student-led anti-Semitic movement beginning in 1922 shut down several universities; it was these demonstrations that propelled Corneliu Codreanu into the limelight. In 1924, he shot and killed the police prefect of Iaşi; his subsequent acquittal showed how rapidly extremism was taking hold.

A crisis was reached in 1925–26, when Brătianu and Ferdinand accepted Crown Prince Carol's (1893–1953) renunciation of the throne because he wished to remain in exile with his mistress, Elena Lupescu (1899–1977). In October 1926 it was found that Ferdinand had cancer. This sparked a debate over the proposed regency, projected to last at least a decade with the prospect of extending National-Liberal domination of Romania indefinitely. When Ferdinand died in July 1927, Brătianu was left the de facto ruler of Romania since the new king, Mihai (Michael, 1921–), was only six years old. Ironically, Brătianu died shortly thereafter, on November 24.

In the face of National-Liberal schemes, Iuliu Maniu's National-Peasant Party now slowly gained the upper hand. Because of the uncertainty arising from the deaths of Ferdinand and Brătianu, Romania's external financial situation grew precarious; it worsened when Maniu announced that his party would not stand behind any new loans made by a government it regarded as illegitimate. At the same time, Carol began to campaign abroad for the overthrow of the regency, and a number of his agents were arrested for complicity in these schemes.

Maniu and the National-Peasant Party were now called to power by the regency. The party was by all odds the most popular in Romania, and its popularity was confirmed in December 1928 by a relatively honest election. The National-Peasant Party won 78 percent of the vote (to 7 percent for the National-Liberals). Maniu, renowned for his honesty, was ably seconded by Virgil Madgearu (1887–1940), the ideologist of "peasantism," a program designed to promote Romanian development by strengthening agriculture through cooperatives and financial incentives, and fostering free markets (including open foreign investments). These initiatives, coupled with a democratically elected regime and Maniu's incorruptible leadership, could have led to substantial economic progress for all levels of society. Unfortunately, the Great Depression was just around the corner. Ensuing economic difficulties were particularly severe for agricultural countries such as Romania, further spurring social discontent. The same conditions undermined a well-taken but unsuccessful attempt in 1929 to introduce considerable local autonomy into administrative organization. The crisis would soon lead to Europe's 1930s "era of tyrannies," dictatorships, and war.

On June 6, 1930, Carol illegally flew into Romania. Maniu resigned but did not protest or take steps to prevent Carol's restoration. Two days later, Carol II took the throne. His first cabinet was headed by Maniu, on the understanding that Carol's mistress would not come back to Romania. Carol's bad faith was revealed in August 1930, when Lupescu returned to Bucharest. She soon became a member of Carol's personal clique of intellectuals, industrialists, and mountebanks, the so-called camarilla that dominated Romanian political and economic life between 1930 and 1940, mostly behind the scenes. Maniu resigned without revealing the real reasons for his rupture with the king. Corrupting the Romanian system and undermining the constitution of 1923 came to be the principal objectives of Carol II. Maniu's failure to take a public stand here would eventually prove to be a grave mistake.

Carol was content for the time being for the National-Peasant Party to take the blame for rapidly escalating public debt, reductions in the salaries of bureaucrats and army officers, plummeting standards of living for the peasant majority, and repression of strikes and other manifestations of discontent and despair. Then in 1931, Carol launched a two-week-long attempt to set up a "nonparty" government of "national union," a thinly disguised effort at taking more control into his own hands.

A government of "technicians" was appointed in April 1931 under Nicolae Iorga, the king's former tutor, who had for years been decrying political parties. The Iorga government lasted just a year and accomplished little. And while the economic situation worsened on all fronts and government revenues fell by a third between 1930 and 1932, expenditures for the royal household rose conspicuously. Iorga resigned, ironically informing Carol that government without the support of a strong party was impossible. The National-Peasant Party returned to power.

The fall of the cabinet of technicians was a gesture of no confidence in the king, since it was his creation. Carol, however, took the lesson to be that the existing parties—more than sixteen, many of them foes of parliamentary democracy—needed to be further emasculated before a royal takeover.

Madgearu, as minister of finance, and the National-Peasants embarked on policies to restore protectionism to Romanian markets. These ill-advised tariffs and restrictions not only did not solve Romania's problems; they created new opportunities for illicit behavior on the part of the elite. The king and his camarilla were the principal benefactors, but much of the resulting scandals tainted the National-Peasants and their scrupulous leader, Maniu.

In January 1933 Maniu resigned for the last time, publicly declaring his differences with the king, but it was too late. Romania now suspended payment on external debts, implemented further protectionist measures, and carried out another round of salary reductions for state workers. The largest interwar strike, at the Grivița railroad workshops in January–February 1933, led to the declaration of a state of siege, several deaths, and hundreds of arrests. Possibly alarmed by such worker unrest and Communist agitation, the new National-Liberal prime minister, Vaida-Voevod, publicly declared his sympathy for the Legionaries and their anti-Semitic, anti-Communist platform.

In November 1933 Vaida's government collapsed. Carol now turned to the National-Liberal Party, which had been in opposition since 1930 because of its stance against the return of Carol. Ion G. Duca (1879–1933), the party's energetic head since 1930, became prime minister. The traditional dissolving of parliament followed Duca's installation. So, too, did a massive campaign against the Legionaries, whose party, the Iron Guard, was dissolved. The influence of the movement, subtly and not so subtly encouraged by individuals like Vaida and even Carol himself, had grown to the point of fielding candidacies in sixty-eight of the seventy-one counties.

On December 29, a Legionary death squad assassinated the prime minister, whose elimination was fortuitous for the king because Duca had opposed authoritarian politics and was a leader of the National-Liberal old guard. Now Carol could promote opportunistic young liberals such as Gheorghe Tătărescu (1886–1957), whom he appointed as prime minister without consulting National-Liberal Party leaders.

For all its dubious start, the Tătărescu government lasted nearly four years, benefiting from a partial recovery of the economy that began in 1933. Though its interventionist policies hampered economic improvement, and other legislation led to cartels in some industries, industrial output by 1938 was more than double what it had been in 1923. Economic improvement, in turn, augmented government revenues. One positive step was an April 1934 law that liquidated and refinanced agricultural debt, successfully relieving the peasants' financial burden and discontent. On the other hand, civil liberties continued to erode along with political freedoms. The state of siege imposed after Duca's assassination continued for four years; parliament ceded part of its prerogatives to the government "to deal with urgent problems"; and the use of arbitrary decrees was considerably expanded. Tătărescu also connived with Carol to support the Legionaries, ceasing repressive measures against them and even providing facilities for their 1936 student congress in Tîrgu-Mureș. The king hoped to use the legion to establish authoritarian personal rule; it is not clear what Tătărescu had in mind.

In international affairs, 1934 saw the establishment of the Balkan Entente, an alliance with Greece, Turkey, and Yugoslavia, as well as the reopening of diplomatic relations with the USSR. Hitler's (1889–1945) coming to power in Germany and the signing of a revisionist accord among Italy, Hungary, and Austria were clouds on the horizon. In 1936 Titulescu negotiated a nonaggression pact with the Soviet Union, but Carol was now ready to dispense with Romania's most internationally known political figure. A cabinet reshuffle in August 1936 excluded Titulescu.

By 1937, the king was ready to try an even more radical tactic. He proposed to Codreanu that an authoritarian state be established with the Legion in support of the monarchy. He badly mistook the intentions of Codreanu and the Legion, whose revivalistic Orthodoxy, anticapitalism, and moral reformism had little in common with Romania's amoral, plutocratic monarch and his Jewish mistress.

In November 1937 Tătărescu carried out new elections. The government, for all its traditional electoral advantages, however, received only 36 percent of the vote. The National-Peasant Party got 20 percent, the Legionaries 16 percent, and the extremist anti-Semitic National-Christian Party 9 percent. This humiliation forced Tătărescu to resign.

The king responded with his own surprise, calling to power the National-Christian Party, headed by Goga and Cuza. Given the extremism of these two rabid nationalists and the scant support for them in the legislature and the country, Carol may have called them to office precisely to discredit what remained of the parliamentary regime. In its brief tenure in office, the Goga-Cuza cabinet set a new low for demagoguery, especially anti-Semitic. Goga ruled mostly by decree and concentrated on Romania's alleged "Jewish problem." Laws implementing *numerus clausus* (numerical limits) in various areas, suspension of major daily newspapers for being Jewish, reexamination of citizenship granted to Jews after World War I, and similar measures were quickly passed. Goga also proposed aligning Romanian foreign policy with that of Germany and Italy.

Elections were called for March 1938, and Goga began to discuss with Codreanu a new electoral pact, this time among radical nationalist, anti-Semitic, pro-German parties. The disorder created by Goga's ill-conceived and executed measures, coupled with the general incompetence of the cabinet, provided Carol with the opening he needed. On February 10, he forced Goga to resign and on February 11 declared a state of siege and proclaimed a royal dictatorship.

Carol moved swiftly to cement his powers. By the end of February, a new constitution had been adopted by 99 percent in a public referendum, political parties were abolished, and a unitary National Renaissance Front was established. Steps were taken to establish a quasi-corporatist state. The Legionaries were suppressed while Codreanu was accused of treason and slander and sentenced to ten years in prison in May 1938; in November he and a number of his associates were murdered by the government. When the Legionaries retaliated the following year by assassinating the prime minister, Carol ordered further mass arrests and some 250 Legionary leaders were summarily executed. This left the Legion under the ineffective leadership of second-raters, such as Horia Sima (1907–93).

As Carol attempted to zigzag internationally, he soon found himself out of his depth in dealings with Hitler and Stalin (1879–1953). The appeasement of Germany, the dismemberment of Czechoslovakia in 1938, and the collapse of the Versailles/League of Nations system in 1939 in the wake of the Nazi-Soviet Pact left Carol (and Romania) fewer and fewer options. In 1940 the king released the surviving members of the Legion and transformed the National Renaissance Front into a "totalitarian" Party of the Nation; and on June 28, the day after the USSR demanded that Romania cede Bessarabia and Northern Bukovina, he included Sima in the government. Anti-Semitic legislation and royal decrees now drastically altered the legal status of Jews in Romania, eliminating them from public positions and the armed forces, and prohibiting intermarriage. Meanwhile, Hitler demanded further territorial concessions by Romania to Hungary (northern Transylvania) and Bulgaria (the southern Dobrudja) in the Vienna Awards.

This sounded the death knell of Carol's rule. The king summoned Ion Antonescu (1882–1946) in a desperate move to save his throne. Antonescu instead demanded Carol's abdication, which occurred on September 6, 1940. Mihai (now nineteen) was installed for the second time as king, and Antonescu was named leader of the state based on the Legionary movement and ideology.

The National Legionary State (1940–41) was an uneasy partnership between Antonescu and the military on the one hand, and the Legionary movement under Sima—seconded by the Gestapo (which had patronized them while in German exile). Although Antonescu wanted to prepare for war and end corruption, the Legionaries wanted to settle accounts, purge the country and its institutions, and conduct a revolution. The Legionaries also controlled the Ministry of the Interior and the police, and on November 26–27, 1940, they killed some sixty-five Carolist leaders being held at Jilava Prison. Death squads also brutally murdered Iorga and Madgearu. In January 1941 Antonescu and the Legionaries arrived at an impasse; the Legionaries decided to attempt a complete takeover. Antonescu had the far better hand, including the support of Hitler, for whom a stable Romanian army was now more important than any kind of ideological revolution. The marshall crushed the revolt and many Legionaries fled into German exile once more as the National Legionary State was replaced by a military dictatorship gearing up for war with the USSR.

Women played a much more significant role in interwar Romania than previously. The constitution of 1923 provided universal suffrage for men (already in effect since 1918), but not for women. Article 6 promised that additional statutes would outline political rights for women but this remained a dead letter. The suffrage movement became more active but was ineffectual; women did not get the vote until 1946. Yet for the first time, women wielded significant political power. Queen Marie was a dominant political player between 1914 and 1927, probably more so than her husband, Ferdinand. Her influence was well earned by her wartime activities. Elena Lupescu was a major power broker in the 1930s and doubtless contributed a good deal to Carol II's failures.

Women were also much more active in cultural life than previously. Elena Văcărescu (1866–1947), who lived mostly in exile after a thwarted romance with then Crown Prince Ferdinand, was well known in Parisian literary circles and between the wars functioned as a kind of Romanian cultural ambassador to France and Switzerland. Hortensia Papadat-Bengescu (1876–1955), a novelist, was more typical. She raised a family, then later became a successful writer. Marta Bibescu (1888/1890–1973), whose reputation was made primarily in France, was another influential writer.

World War II

In June 1941 Antonescu enthusiastically joined in the German attack on the Soviet Union. He was, however, no Germanophile or Nazi sympathizer, as is often assumed. His objectives were limited to regaining the territories seized by the Soviets in 1940 and reducing as much as possible future Soviet threats to Romania. In December 1941 he summarized his position: "I am the ally of the Reich against Russia; I am neutral between Great Britain and Germany; and I am for the Americans against the Japanese." Romanian options in 1940–41 were narrow, but since Antonescu was not a democrat by conviction or inclination, and since he believed until October 1942 that victory by Hitler was likely, he pursued an alliance with Germany.

Though Romanian troops pushed far into the Soviet Union and administered territories beyond the Nistru River (especially so-called Transnistria), Romania did not annex them. Nevertheless, this brought Romanians deeper into the Holocaust than might otherwise have been the case. Officially sponsored genocide was limited under Antonescu, and the majority of Romanian Jewry exterminated during the war was not under Romanian jurisdiction. On the other hand, Antonescu believed that Jews had collaborated with the Soviet occupation in 1940, and he shrugged off reports of violence against them in territories under his control. During the first eighteen months of Romania's involvement in the war, the Antonescu regime was responsible for pogroms in Iaşi, Bukovina, Bessarabia, and elsewhere, as well as brutal deportations of Jews to Transnistria in the winter of 1941–42. Some 120,000 people died as a result. But after late 1942, the Romanian dictatorship actually rejected the Nazis' Final Solution and saved almost all of the remaining Jews in Romania.

After the Axis debacle at Stalingrad in 1942–43, Antonescu sought to leave the war, though, because he always regarded the Soviet Union as the primary threat to Romania's independence, he proceeded circumspectly. Hitler's occupation of a wavering Hungary in March 1944 was another motive for caution. Antonescu's principal hope was that Maniu, as leader of the democratic opposition, might arrive at some kind of agreement with the Western Allies. However, both the British and the Americans regarded Romania's future principally as a Russian concern. Meanwhile, Mihai and the Romanian opposition began to take steps to oust Antonescu. With Soviet troops already on Romanian territory, Mihai had Antonescu arrested on August 23, 1944, told the Germans they had fifteen days to evacuate Romanian territory, and informed the Romanian people that Romania had left the war.

German troops in Romania then went on the offensive and Romania counterattacked, eventually capturing 56,000 Germans and suffering 5,000 fatalities. Romania now joined the Allies, seriously undermining Germany's strategic position and contributing significantly to the Allied victory. By the time the war ended, some 540,000 Romanian troops had fought on the Allied side in the liberation of Romanian national territory (October 1944), Hungary, Czechoslovakia, and

R Austria, suffering 168,000 casualties (ranking fourth in number of Allied troops and third in number of casualties).

Unfortunately for the Romanians, they were not recognized as a cobelligerent, and the Soviet Union delayed the armistice with Romania until mid-September 1944 while occupying a substantial part of the country and seizing vast quantities of war booty. In October 1944 Romania's postwar fate was sealed when Winston Churchill (1874–1965) made the percentages agreement with Stalin that placed Romania 90 percent in the Soviet sphere.

Communist Romania, 1944–89

Romanian history under communism falls into three main periods: 1944–47, a transition that ended the Europeanizing process in Romania that had begun in the eighteenth century; 1947–65, the era of Gheorghe Gheorghiu-Dej's (1901–65) leadership, which led to the Stalinization of Romanian culture and civilization (through the "building of socialist society") and a wrenching turn away from Europe; and 1965–89, when Romania was dominated by Nicolae Ceauşescu (1918–89), when the Communist Party co-opted Romanian nationalism to create its own neo-Stalinist solution to the problems of late-twentieth-century Leninist regimes. In official Marxist historiography, this latter era was divided into two parts—1965–69, during which socialist society in Romania was said to have been "consolidated," an event signaled by the change in the name of the country to the Socialist Republic of Romania. This was followed after 1969 by the phase of the "multilaterally developed socialist society." In the 1980s the entire Ceauşescu period came to be referred to as the "Epoch of Gold" and the "Era of Ceauşescu."

The Communist seizure of power in southeastern Europe after the war entailed the establishment of so-called people's democracies, through the adaptation and application of the Stalinist model to the states of the region. This process was facilitated in Romania by the discrediting of pre-Communist regimes and parties, by the events of World War II, and by the Red Army's occupation of the country. Under normal circumstances, the insignificant and vastly unpopular Romanian Communist Party shouldn't even have had a share in political power after World War II, let alone sweep its rivals from the field.

The process of Sovietization was achieved in three stages: establishment of a coalition government, followed by a bogus coalition government, culminating in a monolithic Communist-managed regime. In the first stage (1944–45), the coalition was genuine enough, but its power was circumscribed by the presence of the Red Army (which did not leave Romania until 1958), by Communist control over the ministries of interior, propaganda or information, and education, as well as the general staffs of the army. Non-Communists were allowed to hold the prime ministership and other high-visibility portfolios, such as foreign affairs, but the levers of power were in Soviet-directed hands, particularly those of Gheorghiu-Dej, chosen as party secretary in 1945, and Ana Pauker (1893–1960), a longtime instrument of Stalin's Comintern (Communist International) apparatus in Moscow.

These faithful minions of the Kremlin oversaw the disbanding of Romania's military, police, and other armed units at home, carried out forced and arbitrary "repatriations" and deportations, and organized frequent provocations, frame-ups, and other "incidents" that provided pretexts for Soviet intervention and undermined the authority of the government. They assumed a stranglehold over Romanian economic life (joint Soviet-Romanian firms were established in 1945, ostensibly to pay the Soviets for war damages, but the real function of these SovRoms, which functioned until 1954, was to bleed the Romanian economy), took control of the broadcast media and the trade unions, and split non-Communist political groups by co-opting their less principled members with official appointments.

The Soviet Union then forced a transition to a bogus coalition that was clearly Communist-dominated and controlled. King Mihai was obliged to appoint Communist sympathizer and toady Petru Groza (1884–1958) as prime minister in March 1945 under the guise of giving power to the National Democratic Front, a mélange of Communists, fellow travelers, opportunists, and former fascists. The moving of some ten thousand Soviet troops and NKVD (Soviet secret police) forces into Bucharest at the end of February 1945 clinched the transition.

The major opposition parties were now sidelined or subverted, their newspapers unable to circulate, their gatherings often broken up by ruffians while police authorities stood by. The coalition stage lasted from spring of 1945 to the autumn of 1947. A feeble Western attempt to make the Groza regime more representative failed. Show trials in 1946, which resulted in the execution of Antonescu and several of his associates, also sent a stark message to potential opponents. In November 1946 managed elections produced a landslide for the Communist bloc. By 1947, the stage was set for the elimination of any pretense of coalition and the proclamation of the success of "people's democracy." All open opposition parties were squelched and their leaders fled or were arrested, exiled, or executed. On December 30, 1947, Mihai was forced to abdicate and Romania was formally declared a People's Republic.

Many have subsequently argued that there could have been another outcome to this depressing story if the West had been more informed or more principled or if non-Communist Romanian leaders had been less compromised or more decisive. This is an illusion. As U.S. President Franklin Roosevelt (1882–1945) noted to Churchill in March 1945, "Romania is not a good place for a test case. There were two reasons for that: (1) The Russians have been in undisputed control from the beginning and (2) [w]ith Romania lying athwart the Russian lines of communications it is moreover difficult to contest . . . their action."

Between 1947 and 1965, the essentials of modern Romanian civil society were systematically attacked and destroyed. The Soviet model provided a rough blueprint to follow. Romania's traditional peasant society was transformed by two waves of forced collectivization (1948–53, and 1958–62). Some eighty thousand Romanians perished during the implementation.

At the same time, education and the arts were Stalinized and any vestiges of pluralism suppressed. From 1948 to 1965, Leonte Răutu (1910–93) was virtual dictator of Romanian culture, transforming Romanian writers, intellectuals, and academicians into propagandists and fostering a semiliterate class of *culturnicii* (culturocrats) whose baneful effects continue to the present. Though there were exceptions, many pre-1947 intellectuals fell over one another to collaborate with the new regime. More significantly, the rest of the pre-Communist generation of Romanian intellectuals was systematically exterminated or marginalized after 1950. Many would die in the numerous Romanian concentration camps; untold others died doing forced labor on the Danube canal

project, designed more to humiliate and destroy human life than to produce economic benefits.

Religious groups were similarly persecuted, ranging from recalcitrant Orthodox priests to the entire hierarchy of the Greek Catholic (Uniate) Church (which was forcefully "reunited" with the Orthodox Church in 1948), to Roman Catholics said to be under the control of foreign forces, to evangelical Protestants whose religious fervor was unsuitable in a totalitarian society.

Though there was some partisan resistance after 1947, Romania's relative isolation, lack of a forceful resistance tradition, and ruthless Communist leadership all made for less opposition to the regime than elsewhere in Eastern Europe. After the failure of the Hungarian Revolution in 1956, passivity and mere survival became even more the order of the day.

For all its advantages, the Romanian Communist Party (RCP) suffered from enormous handicaps when it assumed control of Romania. These made it one of the least flexible and least reformable ruling parties in the Soviet bloc. First, in contrast to many other Eastern European Communist parties, the tiny RCP had been of no significance in the previous political life of the country. Second, it had virtually no notable thinkers. The party's intellectual poverty not only contributed to a continuing sense of inferiority but also gave birth to ludicrous posturing by party leaders whose alleged thoughts were collected and widely circulated. This lack of a Communist intelligentsia also crippled post 1947 Romanian academic and cultural development as key positions had to be filled by mediocrities. Third, the RCP was characterized from its inception in the 1920s by the kind of tribalization and personalization that typified Stalin's Soviet system in the 1930s and 1940s. Indeed, the history of the RCP in power is the story of personalities (Pauker, Dej, Ceauşescu), patronage, and clientage, backed by monolithic support from an extensive party apparatus (nomenclature) and implacable, extensive security forces (Securitate). Finally, the RCP was dominated prior to 1944 by non-Romanians, primarily Hungarians and Jews; between 1924 and 1944, not a single ethnic Romanian headed the party. This accounts in part for the party's lack of resonance in Romanian life. Communism itself was generally viewed as something inherently un-Romanian.

Thus, the Romanian party was always insecure, antidemocratic, intolerant of critical Marxism,

R and invariably lacking in substantive intellectual and popular support. This inferiority complex helps to explain why the RCP remained Stalinist and why its leadership in the 1980s shrilly promoted increasingly inane programs.

After 1944, two groups of Communists came to power, one close to Gheorghe Gheorghiu-Dej, Stalin's choice as party leader—including Chivu Stoica (b. 1908), Emil Bodnaraş (1904–76), Teohari Georgescu (b. 1908), and Ceauşescu—who had spent the war in Romanian prisons, and another led by Ana Pauker—including Vasile Luca (1898–1960) and Răutu—all of whom had spent the war in Moscow. Also briefly influential in 1944–46 was Lucreţiu Pătrăşcanu (1900–54), who was part of neither group but had contacts with Dej. Because of his relative independence and suspected national Communist leanings, Pătrăşcanu was purged from the party in 1948 and later executed by Dej in 1954.

Pauker was probably the dominant figure between 1944 and 1950; thereafter the more colorless but equally ruthless Gheorghiu-Dej not only assumed control but in 1952 purged Pauker, Luca, and Georgescu from the leadership. The fact that Dej always played his cards carefully and was neither Jewish (as was Pauker) nor an intellectual (he capitalized on his past as a railroad worker) put him in Stalin's good graces during the Soviet dictator's final, obsessively anti-Semitic years.

Stalin's death in 1953 created problems for the RCP, especially when Soviet Premier Nikita Khrushchev (1894–1971) initiated a thaw in the system. The RCP was far too weak to loosen the reins. Instead, between 1953 and 1964, it hit upon a successful survival policy: pseudo–de-Stalinization. When Khrushchev began openly to modify the Stalinist system in 1956, Dej's mastery of Leninist maneuver (intrigue, patronage, and cold-blooded settling of accounts) paid off. He capitalized on Khrushchev's own sloganeering and difficulties to construct a new basis for the RCP's continuing exercise of power. In 1956 he gained Khrushchev's gratitude for Romanian assistance in putting down the Hungarian uprising. And in 1958 the Soviet leader agreed to the withdrawal of Soviet troops from Romania and ending the compulsory study of Russian—policies that were not so much de-Stalinization as de-Russification.

The irony of the RCP's pseudo–de-Stalinization is that between 1958 and 1965, Dej utilized Khrushchev's acceptance of Titoism (allowing local variations and interpretations of Marxism-Leninism) not only to bolster the Stalinist system in Romania but also to derail Khrushchev's plans for economic integration of Eastern Europe and to lessen Soviet influence in the region. The key event was the April 1964 Declaration of the RCP, which laid out the Romanian position on relations among socialist states. This enabled the Romanians to have it both ways: a rigid Stalinist system and development model internally coupled with an often autonomous foreign policy that assured minimal Soviet intervention in party affairs. When Gheorghiu-Dej died in 1965, pseudo–de-Stalinization had set the stage for the RCP to create a version of Marxism-Leninism-Stalinism that was much less dependent on the vagaries of Soviet leadership changes.

With Gheorghiu-Dej's death, Nicolae Ceauşescu became head of the party. He was initially perceived as something of a reformer, at least in light of his refusal to collaborate in the Soviet-led invasion of Czechoslovakia in 1968 and his pursuit of foreign policy openings to West Germany, Israel, and the United States. His stand on Czechoslovakia even led many younger Romanians to join the party. Yet they failed to see that he rejected the USSR's interventionism but not its Stalinism. Socialist society in Romania was "consolidated" in 1965–69; thereafter Ceauşescu could move on to "building a multilaterally developed socialist society" whose grim outlines became apparent in the 1980s.

The refashioning of the Romanian nationalist ethos into a Romanian national communism contributed to Romania's misleading positive international image. Thus, the release from prison and even eventual return to their posts of many pre-1947 academics and others was due not to de-Stalinization but to the party's need to revive Romanian nationalism culturally. Between 1964 and 1971, the Romanian leadership transformed the regime from a Soviet copy into "national Stalinism." A fitting irony was that Gheorghiu-Dej became the scapegoat for any previous party failings.

Ceauşescu had at the same time consolidated his own power, laying the groundwork for the next transformation. In 1971, he and his wife, Elena (c. 1919–89), paid a visit to North Korea and China. These despotic regimes with their cult of personality inspired a Romanian-style cultural revolution based on escalating doses of national Stalinism.

This was made easier because Romania had never really de-Stalinized, and was solidified from 1971 onward, when Elena Ceaușescu began her rise to second place in the Romanian hierarchy. She eventually came to control academic and cultural life, and in 1980 she became first vice premier.

The regime renewed cultural and political vigilance and pursued a personality cult adulating both Ceaușescus; both were acclaimed as "world-renowned" thinkers and leaders, and an entire industry was devoted to their works and singing their praises. Elena's assertiveness as a supposedly renowned scientist was reflected in further pursuit of costly, Stalinist developmental projects, such as steel, petrochemical, and machine-building industries. Declining world demand in these sectors in the 1980s, coupled with the uncompetitive quality of Romanian production and the need to supply these industries with imported raw materials, led to an economic disaster that increasingly swamped Romanian planners in the late 1980s.

From a political point of view, women played a much larger role under communism in Romania than ever before. Both Ana Pauker and Elena Ceaușescu were co-rulers of the Romanian state and wielded massive power. Communist propaganda often emphasized the superiority of such societies for allegedly promoting the equality of women, and more women were indeed involved in political and governmental organizations; the number of women in the party's Central Committee and in parliament increased to around 30 percent, and there seems to have been a goal to increase women's membership in the party to 50 percent, though this power was only pro forma.

On the other hand, the lot of women in Communist Romania generally deteriorated as the regime attempted to push more of them into the workforce while compelling them to have more children. Women's health certainly took a backseat to the goals of the party. Realization of this may have accounted for the presence of more and more women in what little public antiregime protest existed in Romania in the 1980s.

The End of Communism in Romania

When the decentralist, pro-market trends of the 1980s led to Mikhail Gorbachev's (1931–) accession to power in the Soviet Union and his campaigns for *perestroika* (restructuring) and *glasnost* (openness), the writing was on the wall. Ceaușescu, acutely aware of this, accelerated the national Stalinization process after 1985. This included the promotion of a megalomaniacal personality cult; demolition of much of the center of Bucharest, including numerous churches; plans to finish off what remained of independent peasant life through a ruthless "systematization" scheme that would raze hundreds of villages and move their populations to "agro-industrial centers"; increased pro-natalist efforts including compulsory gynecological examinations and taxes on families with too few children; a "scientific nutrition program" backed up by severe rationing that specified the optimum number of calories and proteins for each citizen (not surprisingly, a quantity considerably lower than previously thought); and a draconian scheme to liquidate Romania's massive foreign debt accumulated by its Stalinist developmental program.

Interestingly, the Ceaușescu regime was not toppled by the kinds of events and factors that undermined regimes elsewhere in the Communist bloc. There was no apparent intellectual disillusionment with socialism or calls for a new social contract between regime and people (as in Poland and Czechoslovakia) because there were no major Romanian socialist thinkers. There were no noteworthy movements for a civil society (such as the church, the Solidarity trade union, the anti-politics movements, and the roundtables in Poland, Czechoslovakia, Hungary, and even Bulgaria) because Ceaușescu's Securitate had suppressed most of this. There wasn't even a political reform movement disguised as ecological activism (as in Bulgaria and Czechoslovakia). There had been strikes in the Jiu Valley in 1977 and in Brașov in 1987. A number of people spoke out against the regime from time to time, but they were usually imprisoned, exiled, or otherwise silenced.

Ceaușescu had been rumored for years to be in failing health, but in the fall of 1989 he appeared to be healthier than ever, delivering a seven-hour speech to the Fourteenth Romanian Communist Party Congress in mid-November that "unanimously" reelected him party secretary-general. However, Gorbachev's experimentation had cut the ground out from under neo-Stalinist regimes in Eastern Europe by 1989. Romanians, who were generally well informed about what was going on elsewhere because of Radio Free Europe, the BBC, and the Voice of America, began to ask themselves, "If not here, why? If not now, when?" and finally and most important, "If not me, who?"

R

What precipitated the Romanian 1989 was the refusal of Pastor László Tökés (1952–) to leave his church in Timişoara. A vigil in his support on December 15 became a mass protest on December 16 and then defiance of the regime. Attempts to suppress the protest failed. In the meantime, rebellion spread to Bucharest on December 21, where Ceauşescu was hooted down as he described the Timişoara events as having been led by hooligans and foreign intelligence agents. When the army refused to open fire the next day on the crowds that flooded into the streets, the Ceauşescus fled and a provisional government was proclaimed. Three days later, the unlamented Ceauşescus were executed by a military firing squad after a swift trial. The Socialist Republic of Romania was no more.

Paul E. Michelson

Further reading

Bobango, Gerald J. *The Emergence of the Romanian National State.* Boulder, Colorado, 1979.

Bodea, Cornelia. *The Romanians' Struggle for Unification, 1834–1849.* Bucharest, 1970.

Deletant, Dennis. *Ceauşescu and the Securitate: Coercion and Dissent in Romania, 1865–1989.* London, 1995.

Fischer, Mary Ellen. *Nicolae Ceauşescu: A Study in Political Leadership.* Boulder, Colorado, 1989.

Fisher-Galati, Stephen. *Twentieth Century Rumania,* 2d ed. New York, 1991.

Georgescu, Vlad. *The Romanians: A History.* Columbus, Ohio, 1991.

Giurescu, Constantin C., ed. *Chronological History of Romania,* 2d ed. Bucharest, 1974.

Hitchins, Keith. *The Romanians, 1774–1866.* Oxford, 1996.

————. *Rumania, 1866–1947.* Oxford, 1994.

Ionescu, Ghita. *Communism in Rumania, 1944–1962.* London, 1964.

Jelavich, Barbara. *Russia and the Formation of the Romanian National State, 1821–1878.* Cambridge, 1984.

Kellogg, Frederick. *The Road to Romanian Independence.* West Lafayette, Indiana, 1995.

King, Robert R. *A History of the Romanian Communist Party.* Stanford, California, 1980.

Livezeanu, Irina. *Cultural Politics in Greater Romania: Regionalism, Nation-Building, and Ethnic Struggle, 1918–1930.* Ithaca, New York, 1995.

Michelson, Paul E. *Romanian Politics, 1859–1871: From Prince Cuza to Prince Carol.* Iaşi, 1998.

Roberts, Henry L. *Rumania: Political Problems of an Agrarian State.* New Haven, Connecticut, 1951.

Seton-Watson, R. W. *A History of the Roumanians from Roman Times to the Completion of Union.* Cambridge, 1934.

Shafir, Michael. *Romania: Politics, Economy, and Society. Political Stagnation and Simulated Change.* Boulder, Colorado, 1985.

Treptow, Kurt, ed. *A History of Romania,* 3d ed. Iaşi, 1997.

Treptow, Kurt and Marcel Popa. *Historical Dictionary of Romania.* Lanham, Maryland, 1996.

Verdery, Katherine. *National Ideology under Socialism: Identity and Cultural Politics in Ceauşescu's Romania.* Berkeley, California, 1991.

Watts, Larry L. *Romanian Cassandra: Ion Antonescu and the Struggle for Reform.* Boulder, Colorado, 1993.

See also Agrarian Parties; Agriculture; Alba Iulia; Ion Antonescu; Alexandru Averescu; Nicolae Bălcescu; Balkan Entente; Balkan Wars; Banat; George Bariţiu; Simion Bărnuţiu; Bessarabian Question; Gheorge Bibescu; Blaj; Emil Bodnaraş; *Boiars;* Constantin Brancuşi; Ion Brătianu; Ion I.C. Brătianu; Bucharest, Treaty of (1918); Bukovina; Ion Caragiale; Carol I; Carol II; Lascăr Catargiu; Elena Ceauşescu; Nicolae Ceauşescu; Winston Churchill; Communist Party of Romania; Corneliu Codreanu; Collectivization; Comecon; Comintern; Congress of Berlin; Ion Creangă; Miron Cristea; Alexandru Ioan Cuza; Danube Question; Danubian Principalities; De-Stalinization; Dobrudja; Eastern Question; Economic Development in Romania; Elisabeth; George Enescu; Ethnic Minorities; Ferdinand; Franz Joseph; Freemasonry; Gheorghe Gheorghiu-Dej; Ion Ghica; Glasnost/Perestroika; Octavian Goga; Golescu Family; Mikhail Gorbachev; Great Depression; Great Powers; Greater Romania; Greek Revolution; Petru Groza; Habsburg Empire; Ion Heliade Radulescu; Holocaust; Hungarian Soviet Republic; Hungarian War for Independence; Hungarian Revolution of 1956; Avram Iancu; Nae Ionescu; Take Ionescu; Nicolae Iorga; Irredentism; Iron Guard; Islaz Proclamation; Junimea; Count Pavel Kiselev; Mihail Kogălniceanu; Kuchuk Kainardji, Treaty of; Little Entente; Vasile Luca; Elena Lupescu; Virgil Madgearu; Magyarization; Titu Maiorescu; Iuliu Maniu; Mărăşti-Mărăşeşti-Oituz; Alexandru Marghiloman; Marie; Media; Michael; Ion

Mihalache; Molotov-Ribbentrop Pact; Nationalism; National Legionary State; Neoabsolutism; Nicholas I; Organic Statutes; Orthodoxy; Ottoman Empire; Paris, Treaty of; Lucreţiu Pătrăşcanu; Ana Pauker; Peasants; Percentages Agreement; Phanariots; Pogrom; Press; Railroads; Red Army; Revolutions of 1848; Revolutions of 1989; Romanian Art; Romanian Culture; Romanian Language; Romanian Literature; Romanian Peasant Revolt of 1907; Romanticism; C.A. Rosetti; Russia; Russification; Russo-Turkish War of 1877–78; Andrei Şaguna; Saxons; Securitate; Horia Sima; Sovietization; SovRoms; Stalin; Barbu Ştirbei; Sturdza Family; Systematization; Székely; Gheorghe Tătărescu; Nicolae Titulescu; Transnistria; Transylvania; Transylvanian Question; Trianon, Treaty of; Uniate Church; United Principalities; Vienna Awards; Vlachs; Tudor Vladimirescu; Women in Romania; World War I; World War II

Romanian Art

Romanian art reflects Romania's position at the crossroads of Europe. Thus, Transylvania in the west experienced Romanesque, Gothic, and Baroque influences reinforced by its large Hungarian and German communities. Moldavia, to the north and east, was subjected to influences from Russia, Ukraine, and even Islamic Central Asia. Wallachia, to the south, was influenced by the Byzantine-Mediterranean lands, the Ottoman-Arabic world, as well as Serbia and Bulgaria. Such influences became important components in the rich, variegated, complex, and tenacious Romanian folk art and contributed to the regional differences of design, form, coloration, and even materials. Prominent in Romanian folk traditions are painted icons on wood and glass, cloth and leather embroidery, weaving and rug making, ceramics, wood carving, and metalwork. The exchanges between the folk art of Romania and its neighbors are especially obvious in icons and designs on painted Easter eggs.

Formal Romanian art began during the medieval period under the influence of Byzantine traditions. It centered on religion and eschewed sculpture, landscapes, and portraits (save for those traditionally painted inside Orthodox churches). The first great period dates from the reign of Stephen the Great of Moldavia (c. 1438–1504). Stephen erected over thirty churches in the Mol-

davian style, which combined Byzantine, Gothic, and traditional Moldavian elements and, when perfected, revealed balance, proportion, and unity of design. Following Stephen's death, frescoes were painted in many of these churches. The exterior frescoes at Voroneţ and Neamţ—as well as those at Humor, Arbore, Suceviţa, Rîşca, and Moldoviţa—are major monuments of medieval art, famous for their sweeping narration and vitality of color.

In the early modern age Wallachia experienced an artistic flowering associated with Constantin Brâncoveanu (1654–1714). Although the so-called Brâncoveanu style predated its namesake and continued to flourish after his death, the prosperity of his time provided the resources to construct the Kreţulescu and Stavropoleos churches in Bucharest and the monasteries at Hurezu and Văcăreşti (the latter destroyed by the Communist regime in the 1980s). Architecture displayed many influences, including prominent loggias with exterior stairs adopted from Italy, squat and spiraling columns, and Gothic as well as oriental arches. At the turn of the twentieth century, the Brâncoveanu style would be revisited by Ion Mincu (1852–1912), Nicolae Ghica-Budeşti (1869–1943), and Grigore (1851–1927) and Cristofi Cerchez (1872–1955) and modified. Known as the national style, it enjoys a prominent place in Romanian architecture and design.

Romanian painting in the early nineteenth century abandoned its former religious constraints and began experimenting with portraiture and landscapes. Nicolae Polcovnicul (1788–1842) was the first Romanian to address secular portrait painting. Important influences were also imported by itinerant painters from Italy and the Habsburg lands. At the same time, artists such as Ion Negulici (1812–51), the watercolorist Carol Popp de Szathmary (1812–88), and Gheorghe Tattarescu (1820–94) began to study abroad, usually in Vienna, Rome, Munich, or Paris. There they came under political as well as artistic influences, and many participated in the Revolution of 1848 in the Romanian Principalities.

During the second half of the nineteenth century, the Romanian national school of painting emerged. Its first representative was Theodor Aman (1831–91), a founder and director of the School of Fine Arts in Bucharest, who painted academic historical scenes, as well as romantic, idealistic portraits of contemporary Romanian life.

Nicolae Grigorescu (1838–1907), frequently identified as Romania's national artist, was deeply influenced by French impressionists and landscape artists. His paintings provide a vision of rural and pastoral life in vibrant colors. Working as a field artist during the Russo-Turkish War of 1877–78, he produced battle paintings that remain national icons, as well as portraits of ordinary soldiers. The third prominent figure of the national school was Ion Andreescu (1851–82), who in his brief life focused on still lifes and landscapes rendered with darker tones than those of his predecessors and a profound identification with the emotional meaning of his subjects. The division of a landscape into a clearly differentiated foreground, middle distance, and wide, luminous sky is a particular characteristic of his work.

Ştefan Luchian (1868–1916) bridged the national school and the art of the twentieth century. Despite a crippling spinal disorder and poverty, his paintings reflect great internal strength. His poignant self-portraits and pictures of rural and urban poverty stand in contrast to his landscapes and still lifes of flowers painted in life-affirming colors.

Modern Romanian sculpture dates from Karl Stork (1826–87), a self-taught artisan. His sons Carol (1854–1926) and Frederic (1872–1942) were also prominent sculptors. Cornel Medrea (1888–1964) attracted international attention for his control of mass and form in his nudes and portraits, as did Dimitire Paciurea (1873–1932) and Ion Jalea (1887–1983) for their representations of allegorical and mythological creatures. However, Romania's greatest sculptor and arguably the most influential sculptor of the twentieth century was Constantin Brancuşi (1876–1957). His simplified, reductionist visions in metal, stone, and wood eliminated the individual, specific, and superficial to grasp what has been described as the platonic essence of his subjects. Although he lived in Paris after 1904, Brancuşi maintained close ties with Romania and on several occasions utilized themes inspired by Romanian folk design. In 1937 he assembled at Tîrgu Jiu (near his birthplace) a monumental complex: *Endless Column, Gate of the Kiss,* and *Table of Silence.*

During the interwar period, many Romanian artists studied abroad and foreign influences circulated freely within the country. An artists' colony grew up around the retreat of Queen Marie (1875–1938) at Balcic on the Black Sea coast, highlighting seascapes and oriental themes such as mosques and native Turks and Tatars. Among the leading figures of the period were Gheorghe Petraşcu (1872–1942), Theodor Pallady (1871–1956), Nicolae Tonitza (1886–1940), Camil Ressu (1880–1962), and Iosif Iser (1881–1958).

World War II and the subsequent forty-five years of Communist rule isolated Romanian art from direct contact with developments elsewhere. Immediately after the war, artists were forced to conform to the precepts of socialist realism. In the early 1960s this requirement was lifted and artists began to experiment with new styles and less ideological subjects. Nevertheless, homage to the regime remained a vital ingredient in successful careers. Totalitarian society did not make Romania an attractive place for foreign artists to visit, and severe limits on studying abroad further reduced the opportunities for inspiration and exchange.

Ernest H. Latham Jr.

Further reading

Cebuc, Alexandru. *The National Gallery.* Bucharest, 1984.

Drăguţ, Vasile and Vasile Florea. *Romanian Art.* Bucharest, 1984.

Drăguţ, Vasile et al. *Romanian Painting.* Bucharest, 1977.

Oprescu, George. *Peasant Art in Roumania.* London, 1929.

Sinigalia, Tereza-Irene. "Romania." *The Dictionary of Art,* vol. 26. New York, 1996.

See also Architecture; Constantin Brancuşi; Victor Brauner; Folklife; Nicolae Grigorescu; Ştefan Luchian; Marie; Russo-Turkish War of 1877–78; Ion Tuculescu

Romanian Culture

Romanians see their culture as a synthesis of the indigenous Thracian Geto-Dacians with the Romans, who conquered Dacia in A.D. 107. While the Dacian contributions to Romanian culture are disputed, the reverse is not: the Latinity of the Romanian language, Christianity, and a consciousness of the relationship as preserved in the name "Romania." The fall of the Roman Empire, the barbarian invasions, and the paucity of reliable sources permit no clear vision of culture in this area for the next millennium. Only in the mid–

fourteenth century, with the establishment of independent Romanian principalities in Wallachia and Moldavia, does a Romanian culture come into focus. In the following century it experienced its first great flowering in the Moldavia of Stephen the Great (c. 1438–1504), whose reign was marked by impressive military victories. As well as building fortresses and citadels throughout Moldavia, Stephen also erected nearly thirty churches and monasteries in the emerging Moldavian style, including Neamţ, Putna, and Voroneţ, one of Moldavia's most highly regarded painted churches, whose exterior was covered in frescoes in 1547. He also commissioned murals, illuminated manuscripts, religious embroideries, and silverware. In 1517 Wallachian prince Neagoe Besarab (r. 1512–21) built a cathedral at Curtea de Argeş whose spiral towers remain a major statement of Romanian architecture. Equally important was the emergence early in the sixteenth century in Transylvania of written Romanian, which appeared first in manuscripts; by 1560, printed materials were produced in Braşov.

The brief unification in 1600 of Wallachia, Moldavia, and Transylvania under Michael the Brave (1557–1601) foreshadowed the future Romanian cultural space. While the ensuing disunity meant political weakness, which challenged Romanian leaders for the next three centuries, there were important benefits for Romanian culture. Transylvania from the west experienced Austrian and Hungarian influences; Moldavia from the east, Slavic influences; Wallachia from the south, Mediterranean and Ottoman influences. These cultural currents bore fruit in the reign of Wallachian prince Constantin Brâncoveanu (1654–1714). The Brâncoveanu style is typified by the palaces of Potlogi and Mogoşoaia, the Kreţulescu and Stavropoleos churches, and the monasteries of Hurezu and Văcăreşti (the latter destroyed on the orders of Romanian dictator Nicolae Ceauşescu [1918–89] in the mid-1980s). The style displayed many influences, prominent loggias with exterior stairs adopted from Renaissance Italy, squat and spiraling columns, and Gothic as well as oriental arches. At the end of the nineteenth century, architect Ion Mincu (1852–1912) modified the Brâncoveanu style to modern requirements; the result, known as the national style, has enjoyed a prominent place in Romanian arts ever since.

The modern era of Romanian culture began in 1822, when native princes replaced the Pha-nariots—Greek rulers appointed by the Ottomans—in Wallachia and Moldavia. The most visible change was the evolution from the Cyrillic to the Latin alphabet, completed by the time of the Romanian war for independence (during the Russo-Turkish War of 1877–78), although linguistic and orthographic controversies continued throughout the twentieth century. Romanticism focused Romanian culture on its roots in pastoral and peasant life. In 1852–53 writer Vasile Alecsandri (1819–90) examined this focus in his collected folk songs and ballads, including the *Mioriţa,* an account of a shepherd's calm acceptance of violent death and his resulting integration with the surrounding nature. Despite its relative brevity and the absence of martial heroics, the ballad is for Romanians what early, defining epics are for other peoples. Only in the twentieth century did Romanian culture develop an urban experience; thus the culture at every level continues to take inspiration from and to relate to the particularly large, rich legacy of folk traditions, designs, and music.

With unification of the Romanian Principalities in 1859, Romanian culture began its golden age, characterized by the work of national poet Mihai Eminescu (1850–89), national playwright Ion Luca Caragiale (1852–1912), and Ion Creangă (1839–89), whose fables exemplify the relationship of the culture to the national peasant tradition, as do the stories of Ioan Slavici (1838–1925). In the fine arts, no less important were painters Ion Andreescu (1851–82), Theodor Aman (1831–91), and, preeminently, Nicolae Grigorescu (1838–1907), whose paintings and sketches of the war for independence and Turkish prisoners are particularly poignant. In 1888 the great cultural center in Bucharest, the Romanian Atheneum, was completed and soon became a symbol of the city and the period's cultural accomplishments. Here in the great auditorium Romania's foremost composer, George Enescu (1881–1955) conducted the premier of his Romanian Rhapsodies, op. 9, in 1903.

After World War I, Romania entered upon its cultural silver age. The war had doubled the country's area and population at the expense of its neighbors, and the culture of this interwar Greater Romania must be seen against a backdrop of resentful minorities and disputed frontiers. Additionally, the culture began to display a dichotomy with roots deep in the Romanian past. On the one hand were the internationalists led by literary critic

Eugen Lovinescu (1881–1943), who held that although Romanian culture had much to offer, it had much to gain from contacts with the outside world. Some, like composer Enescu and sculptor Constantin Brancuşi (1876–1957), moved effortlessly between Romania and the larger world, hailed by both. Others, like dadaist poet Tristan Tzara (1896–1963) and playwright Eugen Ionescu (1912–94), settled permanently outside Romania. On the other hand were the nativists. A more complex phenomenon, they included those whose vision of Romanian realities focused almost exclusively on peasant and village life. Historian Nicolae Iorga (1871–1940) and novelist Mihail Sadoveanu (1880–1961) spoke for this vision. There were also those who rejected Western attitudes and values. Lucian Blaga (1895–1961) and the editor of the philosophic journal *Gîndirea* (*Thought*), Nichifor Crainic (1889–1972), were leaders of this group. A third group centered around Nae Ionescu (1890–1940), a charismatic philosophy professor whose influence reached to historian of religion Mircea Eliade (1907–86) and philosopher Emil Cioran (1911–95). This group embraced an existential irrationalism, corporatism, and nationalism often manifested as strident xenophobia. Coming from this group were the intellectual supporters of the extreme right, including the anti-Semitic Romanian fascists, the Iron Guard. These categories were never rigid, however; individuals selected among the ideas and moved among the groups. Some major figures, such as writer Gala Galaction (1879–1961) and poets Ion Barbu (1895–1961) and Tudor Arghezi (1880–1967), do not fit comfortably in any category.

World War II and subsequent Communist rule meant for Romanian culture five decades of ideological conformity that was only occasionally relieved, mainly in aesthetic criticism and the performing arts. Threatened by the secret police (Securitate), whose prisons destroyed the lives of some of Romania's finest minds, many fled the country. Socialist realism and pervasive censorship silenced others. Some, such as Sadoveanu, compromised with the Communists and thus earned the Lenin Prize and the contempt of many Romanians. Others, like theologian Nicolae Steinhardt (1912–89), uncompromisingly served prison sentences but failed to catch the attention of the West and thus did not reach the moral stature of Czech playwright Václav Havel (1936–) or the founder of the Solidarity trade union movement in Poland, Lech Wałęsa (1943–). Simultaneously, the popular folk culture was exploited and forced to support the regime.

The December revolution of 1989 overthrew the tyranny but left Romanian culture the difficult tasks of understanding what had happened and preparing for the transition ahead. Thus, the attention of Romanian intellectuals since 1989 has focused more on economics, history, and political science than on the arts and humanities.

Ernest H. Latham Jr.

Further reading

Calinescu, G. *History of Romanian Literature.* Rome, 1988.

Dragut, Vasile and Vasile Florea. *Romanian Art.* Bucharest, 1984.

Enachescu-Cantemir, Alexandrina. *Popular Roumanian Dress.* Craiova, Romania, 1939.

Giurchescu, Anca, with Sunni Bloland. *Romanian Traditional Dance.* Costa Mesa, California, 1995.

Livezeanu, Irina. *Cultural Politics in Greater Romania: Regionalism, Nation Building, and Ethnic Struggle, 1918–1930.* Ithaca, New York, 1995.

Rumania: Painted Churches of Moldavia. Greenwich, Connecticut, 1962.

Verdery, Katherine. *National Ideology under Socialism: Identity and Cultural Politics in Ceauşescu's Romania.* Berkeley, California, 1991.

See also Architecture; Tudor Arghezi; Constantin Brancuşi; Ion Luca Caragiale; Nicolae Ceauşescu; Censorship; Ion Creangă; Dance; Mihai Eminescu; George Enescu; Folklife; Folklore; Folk Music; Greater Romania; Nicolae Grigorescu; Václav Havel; Eugen Ionescu; Nae Ionescu; Nicolae Iorga; Iron Guard; Junimea; Nationalism; Phanariots; Revolutions of 1989; Romanian Art; Romanian Language; Romanian Literature; Romanticism; Mihail Sadoveanu; Securitate; United Principalities; Lech Wałęsa

Romanian Émigrés

Modern Romanian political emigration dates from the eighteenth century, when the corruption of and onerous taxation levied by the Phanariot rulers (wealthy Greeks appointed by the Ottomans as princes) caused many peasants to find refuge in Romanian villages across the Carpathians in

Transylvania. It was not until the first half of the nineteenth century, however, that a sociopolitical emigration emerged. With the failure of the Revolution of 1848, Romanian revolutionaries from Moldavia escaped westward, generally to Transylvania and Bukovina, while those of Wallachia went to France, Austria, and Italy. With a general amnesty in 1857, exiles were free to return.

Only in the last quarter of the nineteenth century did a small emigration begin from the Romanian lands to the United States. Though a few were from Romania itself, most were Romanians from the Austro-Hungarian Empire, especially from central and western Transylvania. Émigrés were motivated by the economic opportunities they understood awaited them in the New World, while many were threatened by Magyarization. Because U.S. immigration and census authorities identified individuals by their state of origin, accurate statistics for the nationality of immigrants from the Habsburg Empire are not available. Those from Romania were so identified, although they were in many cases Jews or other minorities. Romanians from the Habsburg Empire were frequently identified as Hungarians or Austrians, those few from Bessarabia as Russians. There were roughly 85,000 ethnic Romanians in the United States in 1920, many of whom were unskilled, younger men who had settled in the industrial areas of New York, Illinois, Pennsylvania, and Ohio, but only temporarily; many intended to return to Romania, and by 1925 over 60 percent had.

A second, major emigration from Romania westward following World War I continued through the second half of the century. This consisted of individuals fleeing the violence and upheavals of the war or the Communist oppression that followed. Unlike the earlier emigration, many elected to remain in Europe. Among these were dissident poet Paul Goma (1935–) and the historian Vlad Georgescu (1937–88), who was the head of the Romanian Service of Radio Free Europe in Munich at the time of his death. Another difference between earlier and later patterns of emigration was that the latter frequently included persons of considerable education; for example, historian of religion at the University of Chicago Mircea Eliade (1907–86), playwright Eugen Ionescu (1912–94), and 1974 Nobel laureate in medicine at Yale, George Palade (1912–). In the 1990 U.S. census, 365,544 persons indicated they were of Romanian ethnic origin, the largest number in New York State.

The national minorities of Romania also suffered severely from the upheavals of the twentieth century. A comparison of the disputed censuses of the Hungarians in 1910 and the Romanians in 1930 shows a loss of 371,176 (or 20.6 percent) of the Hungarian population in the formerly Hungarian-ruled area of Romania. The decline reflects losses in World War I as well as the return to Hungary of administrators, officials, and military personnel. Of the 355,972 Jews who survived the Holocaust and were living in Romania in 1945, only 8,955 identified themselves as Jews in the 1992 Romanian census, the decline largely resulting from emigration to Palestine/Israel, Western Europe, and North America. The 1930 Romanian census counted some 342,000 Germans living in Transylvania, Bukovina, and the Banat; the 1992 census recorded 119,462 Germans throughout Romania. Many thousands of Germans were deported eastward by the Soviet occupying army after 1944; thousands more emigrated as opportunities presented themselves during the Communist era, generally going to the Federal Republic of Germany.

Since the Revolution of 1989, many Romanians who before were unable to emigrate have taken advantage of their new freedom to do so, especially youths seeking greater economic opportunities.

Ernest H. Latham Jr.

Further reading

Bobango, Gerald. "Romanians," in *Harvard Encyclopedia of American Ethnic Groups.* Cambridge, Massachusetts, 1980, 879–85.

Braham, Randolph, ed. *The Tragedy of Romanian Jewry.* New York, 1994.

Calafeteanu, Ion, ed. *Emigrarea populaţiei evreieşti din România în anii 1940–1944.* Bucharest, 1993.

Cristea, Mihaela. *Experienţa iniţiatica a exilului.* Bucharest, 1994.

Metes, Stefan. *Emigrări romaneşti din Transilvania în secolele XIII–XX.* Bucharest, 1971.

Wertsman, Vladimir. *The Romanians in America 1748–1974.* Dobbs Ferry, New York, 1975.

See also Mircea Eliade; Emigration; Paul Goma; Holocaust; Eugen Ionescu; Magyarization; Phanariots; Revolutions of 1848; Revolutions of 1989

R

Romanian Language

Romanian is an Eastern Romance language that today is spoken by over twenty million people, primarily in Romania, although dialects of Romanian can be found in the territories of Moldova, Ukraine, Hungary, Bulgaria, and the former Yugoslavia. Referred to by linguists as Daco-Romanian, Romanian divides into six distinct regional dialects. During the nineteenth century, two of these dialects, Muntenian and Oltenian (taken together to form Wallachian), as well as the speech of the capital city of Bucharest, were chosen as the basis for the literary standard.

Romanian is descended from Latin, the language of communication in Dacia during the Roman occupation of the first half of the first millennium. The descendants of the Romanized population, the Vlachs, were shepherds who spoke a language that was Romance yet no longer Latin. The Vlachs were placed by various historians in the late eleventh century in Moldavia; from the second half of the twelfth century south of the southern Carpathian Mountains; and in the mid–thirteenth century in Muntenia. They and the language they spoke survived in this area, despite several large-scale invasions.

Romanian is written today in a thirty-character Latin alphabet. While its lexicon is overwhelmingly Latin, a certain pre-Latin (most likely Thracian) vocabulary has survived in some one hundred primarily pastoral terms. Romanian has been influenced by the Slavic, Greek, Turkish, and French languages, and its contemporary Latin-like grammar distinguishes it significantly from the better-known Western Romance languages such as Spanish, French, and Portuguese. The grammar presents a thirty-two-member phonemic system with seven vowels, three diphthongs, and twenty-two consonants, among which its high-mid vowels (orthographic î and â) are unique to Romance. It has a robust morphology that displays a case system distinguishing nominative-accusative and genitive-dative paradigms in the substantive, a post-posed definite article, and a rich set of pronouns for address. Its syntactic system is characterized by a subject-verb-object word order. A number of its grammatical features have led linguists to characterize Romanian, together with Bulgarian, Macedonian, and Albanian as a *sprachbund*—a group of languages displaying typological similarities, ostensibly owing to their geographic contiguity.

Donald L. Dyer

Further reading

Agard, Frederick B. *Structural Sketch of Rumanian.* Baltimore, Maryland, 1958.

Deletant, Dennis. *Colloquial Romanian.* London, 1983.

du Nay, André. *The Early History of the Romanian Language.* Lake Bluff, Illinois, 1977.

Mallinson, Graham. "Rumanian," in *The World's Major Languages,* ed. by Bernard Comrie. Oxford, 1990.

Rosetti, Alexandru. *Istoria limbii române de la origni pînă în secolul al XVII-lea.* Bucharest, 1979.

Ştefănescu-Drăgăneşti, Virgiliu and Martin Murrell. *Romanian.* London, 1970.

See also Vlachs

Romanian Literature

Written Romanian appeared late and so too did Romanian literature. The first text extant is a letter to Braşov Mayor Benckner (n.d.) in 1521. Not surprisingly, the first literature betrayed Byzantine and religious dominance, as seen in the historical *Chronicle of Stephen the Great* (written in the late fifteenth century) and Gavril Protul's (n.d.) sixteenth-century *Life of St. Nifon: Chronicles of Macarie, Eftimie, and Azarie.* Also notable was *The Teachings of Neagoe Basarab to His Son Theodosius* (1520), written not in Romanian but rather in Old Church Slavonic.

The first Romanian language texts were religious translations from Slavonic and Greek, the Schei, Voroneţ, and Hurmuzaki Psalters, and the Voroneţ Codex (all from the sixteenth century).

The verse translation *The Psalter* (1673) saw the inception of Romanian cultivated poetry. Prose began with Nicolaus Olahus (1493–1568) during the sixteenth century and continued in the writings of the seventeenth-eighteenth century chroniclers Miron Costin (1633–91), Ion Neculce (c. 1672–1745), Grigore Ureche (c. 1590–1647), Constantin Cantacuzino (1650–1716), and Radu Popescu (c. 1650–1729). Olahus expounded on the unity and common origin of the Romanian people.

Dimitrie Cantemir (1673–1723), a prince of Moldavia, was the dominant intellect of his era, and, in many respects, the founder of modern Romanian writing and culture. His *Description of Moldavia* (1714) and *History of the Ottoman Empire* (1714–16), both written in Latin, and his masterpiece, *Hieroglyphical History* (1705), in Romanian, propelled Romanian literature onto the world scene.

Later in the 1700s (and early 1800s), the so-called Transylvanian School marked the transition to the modern age. Samuil Micu-Clain (1745–1806), Gheorghe Şincai (1754–1816), and Petru Maior (1760–1821) militated for the rights of Transylvanian Romanians and further promulgated the Latinity of the people and their language.

Noteworthy too was Transylvanian Ioan Budai-Deleanu's (c. 1763–1820) mock-heroic epic *Ţiganiada* (1812) involving the Gypsies and the lyric poetry represented by the Văcărescu family (in Wallachia), Costache Conachi (1778–1849), and Gh. Asachi (1788–1869), the latter two both from Moldavia.

Modern Romanian literature, following Tudor Vladimirescu's (1780–1821) failed uprising against the Turks in 1821, increasingly was dominated by foreign influences, particularly French. *Dacia literară* (*Literary Dacia,* 1840), edited by Mihail Kogălniceanu (1817–91) and inspired by Romanian history, set the ideological tone with writers from the 1848 revolution such as Ion Heliade Rădulescu (1802–72), Nicolae Bălcescu (1819–52), and Alecu Russo (1819–59). It also published Costache Negruzzi's (1808–68) novella *Alexandru Lăpuşneanu.*

Post-1848 literature was dominated by the novellas of Alexandru Odobescu (1834–95), Nicolae Filimon's (n.d.) *Ciocoii vechi şi noi* (*Upstarts Old and Young,* 1863), the first Romanian novel, and the prodigious output of Bogdan Petriceicu-Hasdeu (1838–1907), a historian, man of letters, and philologist (*Etymologicum magnum Romaniae*). Important poets included Grigore Alexandrescu (1810–85), Dimitrie Bolintineanu (1819–72), and, above all, Vasile Alecsandri (1818–90).

It was in the literary society Junimea, founded by Titu Maiorescu (1840–1917) in 1863, that Romanian literature reached its apogee with dramatist Ion Luca Caragiale (1852–1912), folk writer Ion Creangă (1839–89), novelist Ioan Slavici (1848–1925), and, most important, romantic and philosophical poet Mihai Eminescu (1850–89).

In poetry, the late nineteenth and early twentieth centuries witnessed a consolidation of the national tradition in the works of Gheorghe Coşbuc (1866–1918) and Octavian Goga (1881–1938), as well as innovators like Symbolist Alexandru Macedonski (1854–1920). The novel was well represented by Duiliu Zamfirescu (1858–1922) and historical drama by Barbu Ştefănescu-Delavrancea (1858–1918). The journal *Contemporanul* (*Contemporary*), edited by Constantin Dobrogeanu-Gherea (1855–1920), promoted realistic literature on social themes. At the turn of the century, literary life was marked by conflict between *Samănatorism* and *Poporanism,* the former movement advocating (under distinguished historian Nicolae Iorga [1871–1940]) literature of idealized rural experience, while the latter, promoted by writers like Constantin Stere (1865–1936) and Garabet Ibrăileanu (1871–1936), stressed a harsher literature of social inspiration through the journal *Viaţa Românească* (*Romanian Life*).

The interwar period was marked by a clash over the direction of Romanian culture. Eugen Lovinescu's (1881–1943) *Sburătorul* movement advocated synchronization with Western culture. This conception, however, clashed with a strong movement toward traditionalism and orthodoxy promoted by Nichifor Crainic's (1889–1972) review *Gândirea* (*Thought*). This literary clash mirrored the debate in Romanian society itself over the nation's past and future. The interwar years also saw the emergence of world-class Romanian poets such as Tudor Arghezi (1880–1967), Ion Barbu (1895–1961), Gheorghe Bacovia (1881–1957), Ion Pillat (1895–1945), Emil Botta (1911–77), V. Voiculescu (1884–1963), and Lucian Blaga (1895–1961); novelists Mateiu Caragiale (1885–1936), Hortensia Papadat-Bengescu (1876–1955), Camil Petrescu (1894–1957), Liviu Rebreanu (1885–1944), and especially Mihail Sadoveanu (1880–1961); and critics Gheorghe Călinescu (1899–1965), Tudor Vianu (1897–1964), and Lovinescu.

A brief outburst of creative activity after World War II was quickly suppressed by the Communists. The protagonists included writers Gellu Naum (1915–), Dimitrie Stelaru (1917–71), Constant Tonegaru (1919–52), Geo. Dumitrescu (1920–), Ion Negoiţescu (1921–91), Adrian Marino (1921–), Pavel Chihaia (1922–), Mihail Crama (1923–94), and Ion Caraion (1923–86).

Political émigrés also achieved fame, notably Emil Cioran (1911–95), Mircea Eliade (1907–86), Eugen Ionescu (1912–94), and dissident Paul Goma (1935–). Others included Aron Cotruş (1891–1961), Vintilă Horia (1915–95), Zahu Pană

R (1925–), Toma Pavel (1941–), Gelu Ionescu (1941–), and Sanda Golopenţia-Eretescu (1942–).

Despite the tight control of literature and the arts under the Communist regime, there were some bright spots in Romanian writing, with poets such as Mircea Ivănescu (1931–), Ileana Mălăncioiu (1940–), Marin Sorescu (1936–96), Nichita Stănescu (1933–83), Cezar Baltag (1937–), Ana Blandiana (1942–), Ioan Alexandru (1941–), Mircea Dinescu (1950–), and Denisa Comănescu (1954–); novelists like Radu Petrescu (1927–82), Marin Preda (1922–80), and the most widely translated Romanian writer, Zaharia Stancu (1902–74); essayists and critics such as Nicolae Manolescu (1939–), Marino, Ion Negoţescu (1921–91), Constantin Noica (1908–87), Octavian Paler (1923–), N. Steinhardt (1916–88), and Eugen Simion (1933–).

The 1980s produced a number of outstanding poets, including Liviu Ioan Stoiciu (1950–), Traian T. Coşovei (1954–), Florin Iaru (1954–), Ion Stratan (1955–), Mircea Cărtărescu (1956–), Mariana Marin (1956–), Romulus Bucu (1956–), and Bogdan Ghiu (1958–), among others.

Charles M. Carlton and Ştefan Stoenescu

Further reading

Academia Republicii Socialiste România. *Dicţionarul literaturii române de la origini pînă la 1900.* Bucharest, 1979.

G. Călinescu. *Istoria literaturii române de la origini pînă în prezent,* 2d ed., Bucharest, 1982.

See also Tudor Arghezi; Nicolae Bălcescu; Ion Caragiale; Ion Creangă; Constantin Dobrogeanu-Gherea; Mircea Eliade; Mihai Eminescu; Octavian Goga; Paul Goma; Ion Heliade Rădulescu; Eugen Ionescu; Nicolae Iorga; Junimea; Mihail Kogălniceanu; Titu Maiorescu; Revolutions of 1848; Romanian Culture; Mihail Sadoveanu; Constantin Stere; Tudor Vladimirescu

Romanian Peasant Revolt of 1907

Violent peasant uprising. High taxes, drought, and absentee landlords compounded the inadequacy of peasant landholdings in Romania. Firms leased land from the owners and employed managers who recouped the investments through high rents. Beginning February 21, 1907, peasants in northern Moldavia held mass meetings and prepared petitions. Forceful occupation of estates, then attacks on the property of leaseholders (*arendaşi*) and merchants in the towns began March 13. Jews served as the object of much of the violence; some Orthodox priests presented the conflict as one between Christians and their Jewish oppressors. The peasants' root motivation was economic, however, and they clashed with army troops seeking to protect private property.

In late March the revolt spread to Wallachia. Peasant activity was less spontaneous there and more strongly influenced by teachers and clergy who read the calls for reform of Vasile Kogălniceanu (1863–1941), author of a pamphlet entitled "Catre săteni" (To the Villagers). Their newspaper, *Gazeta ţaranilor* (*Peasants' Gazette*) inflamed sentiments with its accounts of events in Moldavia. Attacks on property in Wallachia became more intense, and the military crackdown was more severe than in Moldavia. A new Liberal government took power and directed the army to take drastic repressive measures throughout the country. By mid-April, the villages were quiet again, but the death toll numbered more than eleven thousand, mostly peasants.

The immediate legislative impact of the revolt—a law on agricultural contracts and the creation of a rural credit bank—was less than reformists had sought. But the revolt increased awareness of the peasant question and led eventually to land reform in 1921.

James P. Niessen

Further reading

Documente privind marea răscoală ţaranilor din 1907, 5 vols. Bucharest, 1977–78.

Eidelberg, Philip G. *The Great Rumanian Peasant Revolt of 1907: Origins of a Modern Jacquerie.* Leiden, Netherlands, 1974.

Ilincioiu, Ion, ed. *The Great Romanian Peasant Revolt of 1907.* Bucharest, 1991.

Rebreanu, Liviu. *The Uprising* (a novel). London, 1964.

See also Jews; Peasant Revolts; Peasants

Romanticism

Early-nineteenth-century literary and cultural movement. Romanticism provoked a mutation in artistic and intellectual life throughout Europe. In the eastern part of the continent, it adopted Western forms, while Western writers began to discover the poetry from Central and southeastern Europe and the works of Polish and Russian writers. The romantic period covers a time span of changes in which social, political, and cultural structures were replaced by new ones. Literary historians have proposed several phases, but they agree that representative works of Central and southeastern European romanticism were produced in the first half of the nineteenth century.

Subjective attitudes replaced the prevailing rationalistic approach as artists pretended they were called on to create a new mythology and a new world view. The new literature not only contested the old one but also tried to destroy its basis by stressing the roles of creativity and originality. The deep change may be easily noticed in southeastern cultures where modern literature made a dramatic start.

The sudden diversification of written culture was not only a consequence of the evolution of national consciousness, or the intensification of relations with Western literatures, but even more of the transformation of the structure of traditional cultures and of their value systems. Romanticism was a unique case of the general transformations that occurred in all European literatures. Comparisons can be easily made between English and Russian poets Coleridge (1772–1834) and Pushkin (1799–1837); German and Slovak poets Schiller (1759–1805) and Ján Kollár (1793–1852); and French and Romanian poets Lamartine (1790–1869) and Ion Heliade Rădulescu (1802–72). While Eastern writers translated and adapted Western works (Rădulescu is a good example), Goethe (1749–1832) showed interest in Vuk Karadžić's (1787–1864) collection of popular poetry. English and German translators published versions of Romanian poetry, for example, in widely circulated languages.

Romanticism was strictly connected to populism and modernism in Eastern Europe. Leaders of intellectual life pretended everywhere that the eighteenth century had been a "dark age." Writers were called on to renew the form and the content of artistic expressions. The "true" and "pure" source of literature was to be found in "popular" works that kept unaltered the "spirit" of the "nation." Intellectuals collected verses that were sung in villages and composed poems that resembled "popular" creations. As such, for example, "Miorița," a poem with a pastoral topic in which a shepherd accepts death as a form of marriage,

became the most representative work of Romanian culture. In their search for "popular" works, romantic authors confused popular with oral literature and contributed (mostly unconsciously) to the secularization of southeastern European cultures, which, on a higher level, had developed thanks to the efforts of the clergy. (This populist trend remains alive in southeastern European and Russian cultures.) Modernization furthermore implied the formation of new cultural structures, a continuous contact with other literatures, the creation of works that met the Western standard, and literary forms that had not existed before.

All leaders of the literary movement initiated the collection of outstanding works, literary associations or societies, and literary journals meant to offer support for the development of literary expression. The press was often connected to learned societies founded at the beginning of the nineteenth century. Along with the press, the theater encouraged the literary movement and the formation of new artistic tastes. Intellectuals initiated publishing programs meant to familiarize the public with both new and ancient writers. Romanians and Greeks, for example, collaborated within the framework of a Greek-Dacian Society, while others worked alone. Scholars published translations of romantic works, like those of Byron (1788–1824), Hugo (1802–85), and Schiller, and of classics that had not yet circulated in southeastern European cultures, like Dante (1265–1321), Shakespeare (1564–1616), and Cervantes (1547–1616).

The new original works that appeared in the Eastern European cultures combined romantic with classical features. Southeastern European poets resembled the family of Spanish and Italian writers who produced a patriotic, political, practical romanticism—the result of a long tradition of coexistence between classical and romantic elements in their national character. Print culture, which had developed the subjectivity of writers and readers in the West, progressed slowly into southeastern European cultures, while the traditional world view was not modified radically; both these aspects may account for the mixture that may be found in the works of Romanians Alecu Russo (1819–59) and Vasile Alecsandri (1821–90); of Bulgarians Khristo Botev (1848–76) and Ivan Vazov (1850–1921); or of Serbs Sima Milutinovic (1791–1847) and Đura Jakšić (1832–78), to name but a few. Works of southeastern European literatures offer the opportunity to perceive more clearly

R

the emergence of the imagination as a creative power that became a watershed in the history of world literature: on one side a traditional literature, on the other, belles lettres. The blend of romanticism and patriotic feeling, or nationalism, is characteristic of this movement in Central and southeastern Europe.

Alexandru Duţu

Further reading

Duţu, Alexandru. *European Intellectual Movements and Modernization of Romanian Culture.* Bucharest, 1981.
———. "The Individuation of the Imaginary Universe and the Reconstruction of Literary Periods," in *Comparative Literary History as Discourse.* Bern, 1992, 175–95.
Lord, Albert B. "Nationalism and the Muses in Balkan Slavic Literature in the Modern Period," in *The Balkans in Transition,* ed. by Charles Jelavich and Barbara Jelavich. Berkeley, California, 1963, 258–96.
Nemoianu, Virgil. *The Taming of Romanticism.* Cambridge, Massachusetts, 1984

See also Khristo Botev; Ion Heliade Rădulescu; Đura Jakšić; Vuk Karadžić; Ján Kollár; Nationalism; Press; Theater; Ivan Vazov

Rosetti, C.A. (1816–85)

Romanian radical liberal politician and journalist. Rosetti owned a publishing house in Bucharest and edited *Românul* (*The Romanian*), the most widely circulated publication in the country. When the Revolution of 1848 broke out, Rosetti began to champion a radical social and economic program in *Pruncul Român* (*Romanian Infant*) patterned in many respects after the ideas of French socialist Louis Blanc (1811–82). Like Blanc, he looked to organize labor along the lines of associations and workshops.

After the failure of the revolution, Rosetti went to France, where he became a propagandist for the Romanian cause. There he became an ally of Ion C. Brătianu (1821–91). A representative of the spirit of the generation of 1848, the term given to the young intellectuals who helped promote Romanian autonomy in 1856, Rosetti remained committed to the ideals of independence, the naming of a foreign prince for a united Romania, economic expansion, and a constitutional monarchy.

Although he at first moved to create a broad coalition of support behind Alexandru Ioan Cuza (1820–73) after the latter became prince of the United Principalities, Rosetti later broke with Cuza and became one of the leading conspirators in Cuza's overthrow and the subsequent naming of Carol of Hohenzollern-Sigmaringen (1839–1914) to the throne. Under Carol, Rosetti served as minister of religion and education. With Brătianu, he set out to create a broad-based political party, the National Liberals. In 1877 he was one of the leading supporters of Romanian intervention in the Russo-Turkish War of 1877–78. By 1884, a year before his death, Rosetti's radical agenda, which sought greater agrarian reform and a broadened franchise, led to a break with Brătianu.

Richard Frucht

Further reading

Bucur, Marin. *C.A. Rosetti: Mesianismşi Donquijotism Revoluţionar.* Bucharest, 1970.
Hitchins, Keith. *The Romanians 1774–1866.* Oxford, 1996.
———. *Rumania 1866–1947.* Oxford, 1994.
Jelavich, Barbara. *History of the Balkans,* vol. 1, *The Eighteenth and Nineteenth Centuries.* Cambridge, 1983.

See also Ion C. Brătianu; Carol I; Alexandru Ioan Cuza; Generation of 1848; Revolutions of 1848; Russo-Turkish War of 1877–78; United Principalities

Ruse

Bulgaria's principal river port. Ruse is located 300 miles (500 km) upstream from the mouth of the Danube River on terraces fronting the bluffs of Bulgaria's Danubian Upland Plain. In 1954 a 1.5 mile (2.5 km)–long bridge was constructed across the river to the Romanian town of Giurgiu.

A settlement has existed at the site of Ruse since the second century B.C. Romans constructed a major naval base there. Beginning in the sixth century A.D., the town was devastated by marauding Goths, Huns, and Crusaders. Ottoman authorities rebuilt and fortified the town in the fourteenth century, renaming it Roustchuk. The defensive walls were dismantled in 1878 following Bulgarian independence under terms of the Treaty of Berlin.

Ruse's modern development began in 1866, when the Ottoman Empire's first railroad connected it with the port of Varna, on the Black Sea. Ruse subsequently became a hub of railroads and highways. Its modern port facilities were completed in 1975.

Ruse (population 195,000) serves as a cultural and economic center for the productive, densely inhabited farm regions that lie about it on both sides of the Danube. It has Bulgaria's largest agricultural machinery plant and is noted for food processing and fertilizer production.

Thomas M. Poulsen

Further reading

Iordanov, Tanko, ed. *Geografiia na Bŭlgaria*. Sofia, 1981.
Penkov, Ignat and Todor Khristov. *Ikonomicheska Geografiia na Bŭlgariia*, 2d ed. Sofia, 1965.
Zakhariev, Ivan, Dobri Bradistilov, and Petŭr Popov. *Ikonomichesko Raionirane na N.R. Bŭlgariia*. Sofia, 1963.

See also Congress of Berlin; Railroads

Russia

Russia shared two important ethnolinguistic and cultural traits with many of the peoples of Eastern Europe. Russian is a Slavic language and thus is related to Bulgarian, Serbo-Croatian, Czech, Slovak, Slovene, and Polish. In addition to the linguistic affiliations, tsarist Russia was also officially an Orthodox Christian country, and in this respect it held a common faith with the peoples of Bulgaria, Romania, Serbia, Montenegro, Macedonia, and Greece. These filial ties of language and religion served as key elements in forging bonds between Russia and Eastern Europe both culturally and politically.

Tsarist Russia's political connections to Eastern Europe originated in the Russian Empire's foreign policy and military victories of the late eighteenth century under Empress Catherine the Great (1729–96). Under Catherine, Russia annexed the Khanate of the Crimean Tatars and thereby extended control over the Black Sea steppe all the way to the Crimean peninsula. As a result, Russia became a power on the Black Sea, and tsarist foreign policy acquired a long-term interest in the affairs of neighboring territories along the Black Sea coast, and especially the Romanian and Bulgarian lands, which were subject to Ottoman Turkish rule. Russian interest in these areas was based largely on the bonds of a shared religion, namely, Orthodox Christianity of the Eastern rite. After defeating the Turks, Russia gained the right, through the Treaty of Kuchuk Kainardji (1774), to act as the protector of the Orthodox Christians within the Ottoman realm. This right subsequently served as the basis for Russian claims to intervene in Ottoman affairs until the Crimean War (1853–56).

In addition to this southern expansion, Russia also advanced westward during Catherine's reign as she worked in concert with the monarchs of Austria and Prussia to partition Poland. In this way, Russia gained Polish territory as a western buffer, and an independent Poland ceased to exist. The years of the Napoleonic Wars witnessed the brief reconstitution of the Duchy of Warsaw as a pro-French state, but the Vienna peace settlement of 1815 recognized a Congress Kingdom of Poland with the Russian tsar as its king, and in one form or another Russian rule over Poland would last until 1914.

The period from 1815 to 1853 marked the high point in tsarist prestige and power in Eastern Europe, and during the first half of the nineteenth century, Russia's ties to coreligionists in Eastern Europe remained the most important element in Russian policy. Russian policy focused on the adjacent Romanian territories and their Orthodox Christian populations. After its victory in the Russo-Turkish War of 1828–29, Russia gained the right to administer the Romanian principalities of Moldavia and Wallachia, although technically these areas remained subject to Ottoman rule. Russia continued to base its claims as the protecting power in the Danubian Principalities on the basis of religious oversight granted under Kuchuk Kainardji. However, economic interests also played a role in the tsarist attitude toward Eastern Europe. In particular the grain trade on the Black Sea played a significant part in Russia's export trade. By the 1830s and 1840s, Russia was exporting vast quantities of grain through the port of Odessa. The Russian stake in this growing trade was in turn dependent on the status of the Bosphorus and Dardanelles straits; Russian statesmen sought to keep the straits open to merchant ships so that Russia's grain trade would not be hindered.

Beginning in the 1850s, the emphasis of Russian interest in Eastern Europe changed from

R the religious basis to a Slavic one. In the years following the Crimean War, a Russian Pan-Slavic ideology developed that emphasized the existence of a common bond of language among Slavic peoples and strong similar cultural traditions. The Pan-Slavists believed that this common culture would inevitably yield to political unity among all Slavs. Moreover, since Russia stood as the sole independent Slavic country in the world, Pan-Slavists expected that the mission of bringing about the Pan-Slavic political union would naturally fall to Russia. In this way, Pan-Slavist thought combined cultural and political goals. As part of their cultural program, Russian Pan-Slavs established Slavic benevolent societies to educate their fellow Slavs outside Russia. In spite of the calls to action from Russian Pan-Slavists, the tsarist government never officially endorsed the Pan-Slav ideology and did not eagerly respond to Pan-Slavic pleas for Russia to liberate its brother Slavs from Austrian or Turkish rule. Nevertheless, Russia did fight the Russo-Turkish War of 1877–78 with the aim of liberating Balkan Slavs from Ottoman rule.

During the reigns of the last two tsars, Alexander III (1845–94) and Nicholas II (1868–1918), Russian policies toward Eastern Europe became more complicated. Within the boundaries of the Russian Empire, the government pursued an official policy of Russification in tsarist Poland. To counter the force of Polish nationalism, Russification policies sought to control and limit institutional expressions of Polish identity. To that end, the government prohibited the use of the Polish language in administration and in social organizations. Discontent generated by Russification, which came into the open while Russia was engaged in the Russo-Japanese War (1904–5), led tsarist authorities to proclaim martial law in Poland, which lasted until 1909.

In foreign relations, Russia's connections to Eastern Europe were complicated because the newly independent Balkan states followed their own foreign policies, and these were often in conflict with one another. Tsarist statesmen attempted to coordinate the alignment of Balkan states into a pro-Russian bloc that could serve as a diplomatic check on Austria-Hungary in the region. Russia fostered the creation of the Balkan League of Bulgaria, Serbia, and Greece. However, these countries ultimately fought amongst themselves in the Second Balkan War in 1913. Thus, Russia was forced to choose sides, and ultimately tsarist policy supported Serbia when that country confronted war with Austria-Hungary in 1914. As a result, Russia fought on Serbia's side in World War I against a German-Austrian alliance. The war went badly for Russia. In 1915 German forces drove the Russian army from Poland. Further military setbacks ultimately contributed to the collapse of the tsarist empire in 1917 and paved the way for an independent Poland after the war.

Jonathan A. Grant

Further reading

Geyer, Dietrich. *Russian Imperialism: The Interaction of Domestic and Foreign Policy, 1860–1914.* New Haven, Connecticut, 1987.

Jelavich, Barbara. *Russia's Balkan Entanglements, 1806–1914.* Cambridge, 1991.

Milojkovic-Djuric, Jelena. *Pan-Slavism and National Identity in Russia and the Balkans 1830–1880: Images of Self and Others.* Boulder, Colorado, 1994.

Ragsdale, Hugh. *Imperial Russian Foreign Policy.* Cambridge, 1993.

Seton-Watson, Hugh. *The Decline of Imperial Russia, 1855–1914.* New York, 1965.

See also Alexander I; Alexander II; Alexander III; Balkan League; Balkan Wars; Brusilor Offensive; Congress of Berlin; Congress of Vienna; Crimean War; Danube Question; Danubian Principalities; Duchy of Warsaw; Eastern Question; January Uprising; Kuchuk Kainardji, Treaty of; Nicholas I; Nicholas II; November Uprising; Organic Statutes; Orthodoxy; Pan-Slavism; Polish Congress Kingdom; Polish Question; Russification; Russophobia; Russo-Turkish War of 1828–29; Russo-Turkish War of 1877–78; World War I

Russification

Process of promoting Russian culture among the non-Russian population of the tsarist empire. In 1815 Romanians, Lithuanians, Latvians, Estonians, and Poles lived in the Russian Empire's western borderlands. This ethnic, religious, linguistic, and cultural diversity prompted Alexander I (1777–1825) to suspend Russification in hopes of gaining the goodwill of the local nobility, in part because the Russian government lacked the determination, money, and manpower to unify its vast empire. While Estonia and Latvia prospered as centers of Russian industry and trade and

Vilna remained a leading center of Jewish culture and scholarship, Poland's new constitution gave it considerable domestic autonomy and cultural freedom.

Administrative Russification resumed following the Polish insurrection of 1830–31. Nicholas I (1796–1855) made Poland an integral part of the Russian Empire in 1832. Customs were abolished and Polish universities closed. In this period the Roman Catholic Church gained a "halo of martyrdom" and became a rallying point for Polish nationalism. The best-educated and most dynamic leaders of the Polish nobility were either killed or driven into exile. In Lithuania, Russian officials acted even more energetically. The Polish nobility and Roman Catholic clergy were removed from positions of influence; Russian became the official language; Russian laws and courts were introduced; and Russian landowners took over the land. In Latvia and Estonia, Russification was primarily cultural and religious. In the 1830s Russian became the language of instruction in secondary schools, and Estonian and Latvian peasants converting to Russian Orthodoxy were promised lands of their own.

The policy of Russification abated after the 1848 revolutions in the Baltic provinces and after the Crimean War in Congress Poland. Polish shows of support for France and Britain during the Crimean War, however, destroyed Russian moderates' goodwill toward Poland. Following the 1863–64 Polish insurrection, Poles were considered traitors to the Russian Empire, and Russification resumed. Poland was renamed "Vistulaland" (after the Vistula River) and ruled as another Russian province, with complete administrative and governmental fusion beginning in 1867. Russians were sent to fill the bureaucracy, a land reform unfavorable to the gentry was enacted, the property of the Roman Catholic Church was confiscated, and the clergy were put on the state payroll. The church and Polish education were placed under the control of Russian ministries. Russian became the official language in the Polish lands under Moscow's control. Russification was harsh as well in Lithuania, where the aristocracy was identified with the Polish uprisings of 1830 and 1863. The nobility's estates were divided among local peasants and Russian settlers, and aggressive Orthodox evangelization resumed. The study of Lithuanian was repressed and the Russian educational system imposed. Alexander II's (1818–81) administrative and cultural Russification, though, brought about the emergence of new national elites demanding separate national and cultural rights.

After 1881, Konstantin Pobedonostsev (1827–1907), one of Alexander's principal advisers, began a policy of forcible evangelization supported by the bureaucracy and the military, which helped stimulate the Baltic revolutions of 1905. Although some concessions were won, they were short of full self-determination as suggested by the Russian Social-Democrats in 1906. In Russian Poland, Russification slowed down after 1905 and Polish was again permitted to be taught in the schools.

In 1914 Józef Piłsudski's (1867–1935) legions rose to fight the Russians, demonstrating that a century of Russian domination had been unable to undo local institutions, customs, and cultures.

Alice-Catherine Carls

Further reading

Longworth, Philip. *The Making of Eastern Europe.* New York, 1992.
Pobog-Malinowski, Wladyslaw. *Najnowsza historia polityczna Polski, 1864–1945,* vol. 1, *1864–1914.* London, 1961.
Thaden, E. C. *Russification in the Baltic Provinces and Finland, 1855–1914.* Princeton, New Jersey, 1981.

See also Alexander I; Alexander II; Crimean War; January Uprising; Nicholas I; November Uprising; Józef Piłsudski; Polish Congress Kingdom; Polish Legions.

Russophobia

Anti-Russian sentiment and opposition to perceived Russian expansionism. Opposition to the tsarist regime between 1815 and 1918 was most prevalent in Russian Poland, where Poles established a parallel society and participated in three major insurrections against Russian domination. Russified Polish bureaucrats supported Russia, but the peasants fought the Russians and the landlords. The Polish gentry supported national independence and Western ideas of social and economic change. Anti-Russian attitudes in turn led to intensified nationalist sentiment. Such national consciousness was epitomized in Poland by romantic artists such as Frédéric Chopin (1810–49) and Adam

Mickiewicz (1798–1855). In all Russian-occupied territories, religion and nationalism formed a symbiotic relationship, and the Catholic Church encouraged the study of national languages in the schools.

Triggered by Alexander II's (1818–81) emancipation of the serfs (1861), the Polish insurrection of 1863 led to repression by Russia. The Polish Catholic Church led the fight against the Russification of education, while the intelligentsia, Jewish townsmen, and the urban middle class led the fight toward independence. After 1890, a pragmatic nationalism developed around two political parties based in Austrian Galicia. The National Democrats moved toward cooperation with the Russian government after 1905 to secure a solution from within. The Polish Socialists on the other hand engaged in terrorist actions in Russian Poland and organized the Polish Legions as the war drew close. Clashes with the tsarist state intensified after 1905.

Even in areas not directly controlled by Moscow, intense anti-Russian feelings were pervasive in most of Eastern Europe. In Hungary, for example, Russia's intervention in the Revolution of 1848–49 on the side of the Habsburgs led to enduring hatred for the tsarist regime. The Russian annexation of southern Bessarabia in 1878, despite assurances that it had no such aspirations, likewise angered Romanians.

The legacy of distrust of Russia and its designs on the region did not abate with the demise of the tsarist empire, even though during the interwar years (1918–39), some in the new countries of East Central Europe experienced a revival of sympathy for Russian culture, especially the newly created Communist parties. Hostility toward the Soviet Union therefore quickly resurfaced after 1945 despite attempts by the new regimes to create a socialist elite from working-class origin. For peasants and workers, opposition to Stalinism and neo-Stalinism was economically and religiously motivated, while the restriction of personal liberty and human rights turned the intelligentsia into dissidents. Directly after World War II, Yugoslav and Albanian Communists were the most pro-Soviet of the Eastern European bloc; however, both would break with Moscow later (Belgrade in 1948 and Tirana in 1961). Bulgarians were traditionally pro-Russian, and their country became a full-fledged Soviet satellite. In Hungary and Yugoslavia, which

practiced "socialism with a human face," the Communist regimes gained legitimacy.

From philosophical revisionism to economic revolts, from dissidence to a parallel society, from samizdats (underground publications) to emigration, however, the failure of the Soviet model in time became visible at all levels. The rejection of Soviet culture signified a deep attachment to religion and nationalism and continued affinity for Western values and traditions. With each generation, the demands for greater freedom from Soviet domination grew more insistent. The 1956 generation fought for non-Soviet Communist renewal and the 1968 generation for a more humane brand of socialism. The 1989 generation fought cynicism, corruption, shortages, and falling living standards. By 1977 in Czechoslovakia, and by 1980 in Poland, workers, intellectuals, the church, and students were united in opposition to the regime. Dissidence climaxed with the creation of Solidarity (Solidarność), the Polish trade union, ultimately helping to lead to the demise of the Soviet bloc.

Alice-Catherine Carls

Further reading

Bialer, Seweryn. *The Soviet Paradox: External Expansion, Internal Decline.* New York, 1986.

Brzezinski, Zbigniew. *The Soviet Bloc: Unity and Conflict.* New York, 1991.

Simon, Jeffrey. *Cohesion and Dissension in Eastern Europe: Six Crises.* New York, 1983.

Swain, Geoffrey and Nigel Swain. *Eastern Europe since 1945.* New York, 1993.

Tökés, Rudolf L., ed. *Opposition in Eastern Europe.* Baltimore, Maryland, 1979.

Walters, E. Garrison. *The Other Europe: Eastern Europe to 1945.* Syracuse, New York, 1988.

See also Bessarabian Question; Frédéric Chopin; Galicia; Hungarian War for Independence; Intelligentsia; January Uprising; Adam Mickiewcz; Nationalism; November Uprising; Polish Legions; Prauge Spring; Revolutions of 1848; Revolutions of 1989; Russification; Solidarity; Sovietization; Tito-Stalin Split

Russo-Turkish War of 1828–29

One of a number of conflicts between the Russian and the Ottoman Empires in the nineteenth century, which first raised the specter of a total Ottoman collapse in Europe. The war was born of complications surrounding a Greek revolt against Ottoman rule. In the chaos of the revolt, Ottoman forces occupied the Danubian Principalities, kidnapped Serbian diplomats, and interfered with Russian shipping in the Black Sea. Meanwhile, Ottoman atrocities against Greek Orthodox Christians, including the murder of the patriarch and thousands of Orthodox believers in April 1822, disturbed Alexander I (1777–1825). Because of his well-known aversion to revolution however, the tsar declined to intervene.

Alexander's successor, Nicholas I (1796–1855), soon found himself dealing with the Greek question. Ottoman-Greek hostilities had aroused public indignation in Russia. As it became clear that Russia and the other Great Powers would have to intervene to save the Greeks, in the summer of 1826 British representatives traveled to St. Petersburg to discuss the Greek situation. These meetings produced the London Convention, which called for autonomy for the Greeks within the Ottoman lands and freedom from interference in overseas commerce.

The Ottoman government rejected the convention. This led to the October 1827 confrontation in Navarino Bay (off the Greek coast), in which a joint Russian, British, and French squadron sank the entire Ottoman fleet. The Ottomans responded with a call for a holy war against Russia; hostilities commenced in April 1828.

The first few months went well for the Russians. Nicholas, commanding the army himself, counted on a quick victory. When that did not occur, shortages, heat, and disease took their toll, forcing the Russian army into a retreat to winter quarters. With a new commander and the coming of spring, Russian forces retook lost ground and marched steadily toward Constantinople, stopping at Adrianople.

The weeks preceding the peace negotiations revealed what would become a familiar drama: Russian armies poised to expel the Ottomans from their southeastern European possessions, the other powers determined to prevent this, by force if necessary. Austria and Great Britain especially opposed a Russian takeover of the Ottoman lands; the former feared the impact on its South Slavs, while the latter was concerned about the consequences for its overseas possessions. Despite the obvious opportunities Russia's position presented, Nicholas was unwilling to antagonize either power and risk a wider conflict. He therefore accepted the recommendation of a special commission charged with determining Russia's next move vis-à-vis the Ottomans. The Russian government would not destroy the Ottoman Empire but instead attempt to exercise predominant influence there. The Treaty of Adrianople, which formally ended the war, reflected the commission's advice.

The war helped make Greek independence possible in the 1830 Treaty of London. It also exposed Ottoman weaknesses and British and French fears of Russian influence in the area. British and French apprehension, Russian interests in the Balkans, and Ottoman decline would prove to be a dangerous combination in successive conflicts and crises throughout the nineteenth and early twentieth centuries.

Brigit Farley

Further reading

Anderson, M.S. *The Eastern Question 1774–1923.* New York, 1966.

Dakin, Douglas. *The Greek Struggle for Independence, 1821–1833.* London, 1973.

Lincoln, W. Bruce, *Nicholas I, Emperor and Autocrat of All the Russias.* Bloomington, Indiana, 1978.

Jelavich, Barbara. *St. Petersburg and Moscow: Tsarist and Soviet Foreign Policy, 1814–1974.* Bloomington, Indiana, 1974.

Jelavich, Charles and Barbara Jelavich. *The Establishment of the Balkan National States, 1804–1920.* Seattle, Washington, 1977.

See also Adrianople, Treaty of; Alexander I; Danubian Principalities; Eastern Question; Great Powers; Greek Revolution; Nicholas I; Ottoman Empire

Russo-Turkish War of 1877–78

Fourth major Turkish-Russian war of the nineteenth century. The Russo-Turkish War of 1877–78 marked the failure of the Great Powers to resolve successfully the general Balkan crisis of 1875–76. It also reprised the disagreement among the Great Powers over control of the declining Ottoman Empire and paved the way for several fateful developments in the Balkans, in particular Austria-Hungary's occupation of Bosnia-Hercegovina.

The war followed two years of negotiations intended to settle the future of Bosnia-Hercegovina and the Bulgarian lands, both of which had seen rebellions against Ottoman rule in 1875–76. Russian, Austro-Hungarian, and German representatives had presented the Ottomans with various plans for reform, only to have them rejected. In a show of its traditional support for the integrity of the Ottoman Empire, the British government urged the Turks to resist such demands.

Negotiations proved fruitless and Alexander II (1818–81) prepared for war. To secure the cooperation of Austria-Hungary, the Russian government promised support for that country's occupation of Bosnia-Hercegovina and pledged not to create a large Bulgaria. In April 1877 the tsar personally led the Russian army into battle against the Ottomans. Despite Russia's agreements with Austria-Hungary, at least one member of the tsar's general staff had big plans for the campaign, declaring the army's objective "the full, irrevocable decision of the Eastern Question and the unconditional destruction of Turkish rule in the Balkans."

Taking advantage of Ottoman weakness and disorganization, the Russian armies recorded impressive early advances in Asia and the Balkans, reaching the Danube River at the end of June. By early July, however, problems with supply lines, a shortage of rank-and-file soldiers, and confusion between leaders in the field and diplomats in St. Petersburg began to take their toll. At the same time, Ottoman forces had regrouped and repulsed a Russian attack on the town of Pleven in northern Bulgaria. They were to achieve the same success against two subsequent attacks, after which the Russians' advance halted. Only in December 1877 did Russia's superior strength begin to overcome the Ottomans and drive the army on toward the Ottoman capital of Constantinople. The British government warned against the seizure of that city by dispatching its fleet to the Turkish Straits.

The tsar did not order the march on Constantinople that some of his advisers anticipated. The denouement of the war proved controversial nonetheless, because the initial settlement took no account of the prewar agreements with Austria-Hungary. The Treaty of San Stefano stipulated the creation of a large Bulgarian state and failed to acknowledge Austria-Hungary's right to occupy Bosnia-Hercegovina.

In the face of determined opposition from Austria-Hungary and Great Britain, the Russians were obliged to abandon the San Stefano negotiations and leave the peacemaking to the Congress of Berlin, which decided the future of the new Bulgaria and its neighbors, and authorized Austria-Hungary's occupation of Bosnia-Hercegovina.

Brigit Farley

Further reading

Anderson, M.S. *The Eastern Question 1774–1923.* New York, 1966.

Jelavich, Charles and Barbara Jelavich. *The Establishment of the Balkan National States, 1804–1920.* Seattle, Washington, 1977.

Jelavich, Barbara. *St. Petersburg and Moscow: Russian and Soviet Foreign Policy, 1814–1974.* Bloomington, Indiana, 1974.

Sumner, B. H. *Russia and the Balkans 1870–1880.* London, 1937.

See also Alexander II; Congress of Berlin; Eastern Question; Great Powers; Pleven, Battle of; San Stefano, Treaty of

S

Sabin, Albert Bruce (1906–93)

Virologist, known chiefly for his live-virus polio vaccine. Sabin was born in Białystok, in Russian Poland, and at the age of fifteen moved with his family to the United States. After two years at the New York University (NYU) dental school, he dropped out and began pursuing a medical degree, obtaining an M.D. in 1931 at the NYU College of Medicine.

Sabin immediately entered into virology research, especially the quest for a polio vaccine, while the disease was reaching epidemic proportions in the United States. During World War II, he served in the U.S. Army Medical Corps and was stationed with American troops in the western Pacific. While there, he developed vaccines for dengue fever and several other viral diseases.

After the war, Sabin continued his polio research at the University of Cincinnati. He and Jonas Salk (1914–95) were the most prominent figures in the sometimes-public race for a polio vaccine. Salk got there first, in 1953, with an injected killed-virus vaccine that was put into wide distribution in 1955.

Sabin doubted the long-term safety and effectiveness of such a vaccine and finally produced his live, but weakened, virus version in 1956. The first large-scale test was in the Soviet Union in 1957; by the early 1960s, it was the dominant vaccine in use. Its administration by mouth and longer-lasting immunity made it more popular with both doctors and patients. The two vaccines virtually eliminated polio from the Western Hemisphere.

Mark Sand

Further reading

McMurray, Emily J., ed. *Notable Twentieth-Century Scientists,* vol 4. Detroit, 1995.

Porter, Roy, ed. *The Biographical Dictionary of Scientists,* 2d ed. New York, 1994.

Shorter, Edward. *The Health Century.* Garden City, New York, 1987.

Sabor

Croatian diet or parliament. One of the main institutions that demonstrated the historic continuity of the Croatian nation, the Croatian Sabor originated in regional assemblies of notables that advised the king or his representative, performed judicial and administrative functions, and levied taxes. Into the early modern period, Croatia and Slavonia had their own assemblies. After 1557, these two diets usually convened as one body.

Over the course of the eighteenth century, Habsburg absolutism progressively eroded the independence of the Sabor. In addition, during the disturbances at the end of the reign of Joseph II (1741–90), the Sabor itself reassigned some powers to the Croatian representatives in the Hungarian diet. During the nationalist revival of the 1840s, the drive toward Croatian independence began to reassert itself, and in 1848 the Sabor emerged briefly as a body with a majority of elected representatives. The diet fell into disuse during the period of neoabsolutism (1850s), was revived briefly during the constitutional experiments of the 1860s, but began regular sessions only after the conclusion of the *Nagodba* (Compromise) in 1868, the legal arrangement that regulated Croatia's constitutional position within

S Austria-Hungary. Until the demise of the Habsburg monarchy, the Sabor was a unicameral diet composed of elected representatives and so-called virilists, or nobles.

During the tenure of Viceroy Ivan Mažuranić (1814–90) in the 1870s, representatives to the Sabor enacted much important legislation, especially in such fields as education. At the end of the nineteenth century, however, Count Károly Khuen-Hédérváry (1849–1918) rigidly controlled the Croatian Sabor. The ruling National Party altered the Sabor's rules to facilitate suspension of members of the opposition and passed a new electoral law in 1888, which redesigned and decreased the number of electoral districts. Until 1910, when a new electoral reform was enacted, less than 2 percent of the population voted.

In the first Yugoslav state, the Croatian parliament was completely eclipsed by the Skupština in Belgrade. After 1945, the Sabor was revived as the legislative body of the Socialist Republic of Croatia within Yugoslavia. Before the first free, post–World War II elections in April 1990, the Communist Party of Croatia, confident of electoral victory, constructed an electoral system that guaranteed approximately two-thirds of the seats in the tricameral Sabor to the party that won the largest number of votes.

Sarah A. Kent

Further reading

Beuc, Ivan. *Povijest institutcija državne vlasti u Hrvatskoj (1527–1945).* Zagreb, 1969.

Šidak, Jaroslav. "Sabor," *Encikolopedija Jugoslavije,* vol. 7. Zagreb, 1968.

See also Croatia, Birth of the Republic of; Count Károly Khuen-Hédérváry; Ivan Mažuranić; *Nagodba;* Neoabsolutism; Skupština

Sadoveanu, Mihail (1880–1961)

Romanian writer and one of the greatest prose writers of the first half of the twentieth century. Born in Pașcani, Sadoveanu was a prolific author who contributed to various journals, including *Sămănătorul,* which exalted the patriarchal life of the village and the virtues of the peasant, and *Viața Românescă (Romanian Life),* which proposed similar topics in a more thoughtful social perspective. He combined keen analysis of the peasants' way of life with a study of history; the world of the past was set in contrast to the abuses that destroyed the system of solidarities still maintained by the peasants. Historical novels, such as *Zodia Cancerlui (The Sign of Cancer,* 1929), *Nunta Domniței Ruxandra (The Wedding of Princess Ruxandra,* 1932), and *Frații Jderi (The Brothers Jderi,* 1935–42), alternated with depictions of societies where nothing happened, such as *Locul unde nu s-a întâmplat nimic (The Place Where Nothing Happened,* 1933). Sadoveanu modernized old versions of "popular books" that recommended wisdom as the supreme virtue; this wisdom, however, did not prevent him from writing an uninspired piece of communistic propaganda, *Mitrea cocor (The Crane's Womb,* 1949), the story of a peasant illuminated by the "great" Soviet experience. Sadoveanu was at his best in *Baltagul (The Axe,* 1930), in which a widow tries to avenge the death of her husband killed by other shepherds (a topic taken from the old Romanian poem "Miorița"), and in *Creanga de aur (Branch of Gold,* 1933), in which initiation and wisdom form the core of the narration. A reality discovered behind everyday life leads the reader into a world of intense spirituality where eternal principles guide those who wish to transcend treachery, misery, and the deceiving appeals of passion. Sadoveanu's work may be read as an attempt to recapture the tradition of Romanian culture at a moment in which architects renovated old monuments and thinkers inquired about new forms of expression. He died in Bucharest in 1961.

Alexandru Duțu

Further reading

Brezianu, Andrei. "The Unknown Gate: 'Ochi de urs' by M. Sadoveanu and 'The Bear' by William Faulkner." *Synthesis* 7 (1980): 121–30.

Manolescu, Nicolae. *Sadoveanu sau utopia cărții.* Bucharest, 1976.

Paleologu, Alexandru. *Treptele lumii sau calea către sine a lui Mihail Sadoveanu.* Bucharest, 1978.

Sadoveanu, Mihail. *Opere,* 12 vols., Bucharest.

See also Romanian Literature

Šafárik, Pavel Jozef (1795–1861)

Slovak/Czech scholar, and pioneer of Slavonic comparative philology and ethnography. Beginning with his lyceum studies, Šafárik was an enthusiastic advocate for the mutuality of Slavonic peoples. His first work was a book of poetry, *Tatranská musa s lyrou slovanskou (A Muse from Tatry with a Slavonic Lyre,* 1814), but later he was active only as a scholar in the area of Slavonic philology, ethnography, and history. He became the friend of Ján Kollár (1793–1852), the proponent of Slavic literary mutuality, and František Palacký (1798–1876), the Czech historian with whom he collaborated throughout his life.

As a teacher in Novi Sad, Šafárik became acquainted also with the languages and literatures of the Balkan Slavs. With this knowledge and his abiding idea of only one Slavonic nation (*národ*), he wrote his pioneering work, *Geschichte der slawischen Sprache und Literatur nach allen Mundarten (The History of the Slavonic Language and Literature in All [Its] Dialects,* 1826), the first systematic description of all Slavonic languages and literatures. Šafárik divided the Slavs into southeastern and northwestern groups. The first consists of Russians, *"Slawoserben griechischen Ritus"* (Orthodox Balkan Slavs), *"katholische Slawoserben und Kroaten"* (Dalmatians, Bosnians, Slavonians, and Croats) and *"Winden"* (Slavs in Carinthia, western Hungary). To the second group belong the Czechs, Slovaks, Poles, and *"Sorben und Wenden in den Lausitzen"* (Sorbs).

On Palacký's initiative, Šafárik moved to Prague in 1833. There he wrote his other famous works: *Slovanské starožitnosti (Slavonic Antiquities,* 1837), the prehistory of the Slavonic peoples, and *Slovanský národopis (Slavonic Ethnography,* 1842), with an ethnographical map of the Slavs. Those three systematic works remained fundamental during the entire century to comparative Slavonic studies. Šafárik was the foremost authority on these issues by maintaining strict scholarly methods, while never succumbing to fantastic Slavophile assertions.

Ľubomír Ďurovič

Further reading

Brock, Peter. *The Slovak National Awakening: An Essay in the Intellectual History of East Central Europe.* Toronto, 1976.

Brock, Peter and H. Gordon Skilling, eds. *The Czech Renascence of the Nineteenth Century: Essays Presented to Otakar Odložilík.* Toronto, 1970.

Hrozienčik, Jozef, ed. *Odkaz P.J. Šafárika.* Bratislava, 1963.

Novotný, J. *Pavel Josef Šafárik.* Prague, 1971.

Tibenský, Ján. *Pavol Jozef Šafárik.* Bratislava, 1975.

See also Ján Kollár; František Palacký; Slavic Languages

Şaguna, Bishop Andrei (1808–73)

Outstanding Romanian religious leader in the nineteenth century. Şaguna dominated Transylvanian Romanian politics between his appointment as vicar of the Orthodox Diocese of Transylvania in 1846 and his death as metropolitan in 1873. Born Anastasiu Şaguna in Miskolc in 1808, the son of a Vlach merchant who had settled in Hungary, he studied law at the university in Pest before entering the Serbian Orthodox seminary at Vršac in 1829. After his appointment as a seminary professor, he took the monastic name Andrei, and between 1842 and 1846 directed two Serbian monasteries in southern Hungary. In the latter year he became vicar, then bishop two years later.

Despite many years in Hungarian and Serbian institutions, he proved an energetic advocate of Romanian cultural and political interests during the Revolutions of 1848–49 and subsequent decades. He consistently paired his advocacy with loyalty to the Habsburg dynasty; this explains his collaboration with the Hungarian government in 1848, then his resistance to it. Though he championed the alliance with the Austrian government in 1861–65, he reluctantly accepted the *Ausgleich* (Compromise) of 1867 between Vienna and the Hungarians (which established the Dual Monarchy of Austria-Hungary) once it was decided. Romanian rivals and opponents accused him of subservience to the central government.

Şaguna concentrated his efforts on his church. He expanded the diocesan seminary's curriculum from six months to three years, placed schools in every parish, and founded three high schools. He also established a diocesan publishing house and the Transylvanian Romanians' second most important newspaper. His greatest achievements were ecclesiastic independence from the Serbs (the metropolitanate) and a church constitution providing for lay participation in governance.

James P. Niessen

Further reading

Hitchins, Keith. *Orthodoxy and Nationality: Andreiu Şaguna and the Rumanians of Transylvania, 1846–1873.* Cambridge, Massachusetts, 1977.

Puşcariu, Ilarion. *Metropolia românilor ortodocşi din Ungaria şi Transilvania: Studiu istoric despre reînființarea metropoliei, dempreuna cu o colecțiune de acte.* Sibiu, Romania, 1900.

Tulbure, Gheorghe. *Mitropolitul Șaguna: Opera literară, scrisori pastorale, circulari școlare, diverse.* Sibiu, 1938.

See also *Ausgleich;* Dual Monarchy; Revolutions of 1848

Salonika Front (1915–18)

Efforts to pressure the Central Powers in the region around the port of Salonika and southern Macedonia from 1915 to 1918, which led to the end of World War I. As Bulgaria prepared to attack Serbia in October 1915, the Entente sent troops to Salonika in hopes of persuading Bulgaria, Greece, and Romania to remain neutral or to enter the war on its side. Although they arrived too late to prevent the fall of Serbia, Entente forces did manage to take up positions that allowed elements of the Serbian army to withdraw safely through southern Macedonia. By early 1916, the Entente had constructed a fortified line around Salonika from the Gulf of Orfano on the east, to the Ionian Sea on the west, with 150,000 troops. In May 1916 the Serbian army arrived from Corfu, along with additional French, British, Russian, and Italian troops.

In August 1916 the Entente planned an offensive to distract Bulgarian attention from Romania, which was about to enter the war. Anticipating this, Bulgaria attacked Serbian forces on August 17. Fierce fighting followed over the next three months, as both sides attempted to exploit weaknesses in the other's lines. By early December, Entente forces had pushed back the Central Powers some 24 miles (40 km) north of their original lines. Losses were heavy and quiet reigned for much of 1917 as both sides struggled to replace losses.

Removed from its population base, the Serbian army relied heavily on South Slavic volunteers from North and South America, Australia, Italy, and Habsburg prisoners of war. These arrived in sufficient number to form an entire volunteer division (16,000 men). In June 1917 Greece's King Constantine (1868–1923) abdicated and Greek troops now joined the British, French, Serbian, Italian, Albanian, and Russian forces along the front.

On September 15, 1918, the Entente launched an offensive, and within three days the Serbian army penetrated more than 30 miles (50 km) behind enemy lines. By September 29—the day Bulgaria's army capitulated—the Entente had taken most of Macedonia, and the Serbian army reached the Bulgarian border. Austro-Hungarian and German forces began a rapid withdrawal northward to defend the vital Belgrade-Sofia rail line. By October 7, the Serbian army had pushed some 120 miles (200 km) ahead of the other Entente forces and bypassed the German defensive positions at Niš. They continued to press the attack, and the Serbian army liberated Belgrade on November 1, 1918. The rapid collapse of the Salonika Front and the successful Entente breakout forced both Austria-Hungary and Bulgaria to capitulate. Cut off from Turkey and left without allies, Germany sued for peace.

James M.B. Lyon

Further reading

Mann, Arthur James. *The Salonika Front.* London, 1920.
Packer, Charles. *Return to Salonika.* London, 1964.

See also World War I

Sanacja

Polish reform government created in 1926. Following the 1926 coup d'état that brought him to power in Poland, Józef Piłsudski (1867–1935) formed a regime that was a combination of personal military dictatorship and centralized authoritarian oligarchy. The government became known by its nickname *"sanacja"* (sanitation). The objectives of the government were to rid the state of the excesses of party politics that resulted from the constitution of 1921, introduce a moral cleansing of public life, and improve economic conditions. Through strengthening executive powers, an authoritarian government was created that became dominated by the military. Piłsudski did not believe this to be a dictatorship but described his approach as "directed democracy."

The *sanacja* was formalized by the creation of the Nonpartisan Bloc for the Cooperation with the Government (BBWR) in 1928, an umbrella organization for small groups and political parties that supported the Piłsudski government. It had no clear political program except for strengthening the government and was meant to be the embodiment of apoliticism. However, it was never very successful and was disbanded in 1935.

David Stefancic

Further reading

Polonsky, Anthony. *Politics of Independent Poland.* London, 1971.

Rothschild, Joseph. *Piłsudski's Coup d'Etat.* New York, 1966.

Wynot, Edward. *Polish Politics in Transition.* Athens, Georgia, 1974.

See also May Coup; Józef Piłsudski

Sanjak (Sandžak) of Novi Pazar

Mountainous area bordering Serbia and Montenegro inhabited by Serbian Orthodox and Slavic and Albanian Muslims. The region gained prominence in the nineteenth century in the Treaty of Berlin (1878). However, its importance predates that to the fifteenth century, when the region was incorporated into the Ottoman Empire. Novi Pazar became the seat of a *sanjak,* an administrative unit, and a thriving commercial center, which by the seventeenth century made it one of the most important cities in the Balkans. In the eighteenth century the Sanjak suffered as a result of the Austro-Turkish conflicts that caused many Serbs to flee the region. In the nineteenth century the Sanjak regained its importance as a trading center, second only to Sarajevo in the area. For a brief period the British even had a vice consul stationed there. By the mid–nineteenth century, the local Ottoman officials had come to rule the area arbitrarily; this led to unrest, at times created anarchy, and finally contributed to the social and economic turmoil among the Christians that helped precipitate the Balkan crisis of 1875–78.

The Treaty of Berlin awarded the Sanjak to Austria-Hungary to administer so as to prevent the establishment of a common frontier between Serbia and Montenegro, thereby forestalling Serbia's access to the Adriatic Sea through Montenegro. Vienna also expected it would facilitate the empire's expansion toward the Aegean Sea through Macedonia.

In 1909 Vienna relinquished control of the Sanjak to Constantinople following the Ottoman Empire's recognition of Austria's annexation of Bosnia-Hercegovina. Four years later, in the Balkan Wars (1912–13), Serbs and Montenegrins seized and divided the Sanjak, thereby establishing their present frontier.

During the interwar era and later under Tito (1892–1980), the Muslims of the Sanjak often endured social, religious and human rights abuses.

Charles Jelavich

Further reading

Jelavich, Barbara. *History of the Balkans,* 2 vols. Cambridge, 1983.

See also Balkan Wars; Congress of Berlin; Eastern Question; Muslims; Tito

San Stefano, Treaty of (1878)

Agreement that marked the end of the Russo-Turkish War of 1877–78. Although it never took effect, the Treaty of San Stefano influenced the course of Balkan history well into the twentieth century. The treaty was intended to settle all questions related to the Balkan crisis of 1875–78: the Bosnia-Hercegovinian and Bulgarian uprisings, as well as the military action taken by Serbia, Greece, and Montenegro against the Ottomans. It reflected the sentiments of Pan-Slavic elements in the Russian foreign ministry, who believed that a greater Bulgaria would be a reliable friend to Russia in southeastern Europe. Accordingly, the treaty provided for a large Bulgarian state to be composed of the remnants of the Ottoman Empire in Europe, namely, Bulgaria proper, Eastern Rumelia, and Macedonia. It also granted independence to Greece, Serbia, and Montenegro, and assured Russia certain acquisitions in Central Asia.

The agreement outraged the Habsburgs, because it made no provision for their occupation of Bosnia-Hercegovina, a matter on which they had agreed with Russia prior to the war. It revived the British conviction that Russia sought to dominate the ex-Ottoman lands and possibly launch an attack on Constantinople. It also upset representatives of neighboring Balkan countries since the proposed Bulgarian state would dwarf their own.

This multitude of objections forced Russian representatives to withdraw the treaty and agree to a renegotiation at the Congress of Berlin. The Berlin agreement substantially modified San Stefano; it provided for the Austro-Hungarian occupation of Bosnia-Hercegovina, granted independence to Serbia and Montenegro, and reduced the size of the Bulgarian state. The large Bulgaria of San Stefano was divided into three parts. The first was a small, autonomous Bulgaria proper. A

S Christian governor would administer Eastern Rumelia, which remained under nominal Ottoman control. The third section, Macedonia, reverted to Ottoman rule.

The division of the large Bulgarian state gave the San Stefano treaty its continuing importance in Balkan affairs. Bulgarians refused to abandon the vision of the Bulgaria outlined therein. It became the source of Bulgarian irredentism as the recovery of the San Stefano territories, particularly Macedonia, served as the linchpin of Bulgarian foreign policy between the state's foundation and World War I. After that conflict, Bulgarian nationalists continued to agitate for the acquisition of Macedonia and became a destabilizing element in interwar Bulgaria.

Brigit Farley

Further reading

Anderson, M.S. *The Eastern Question 1774–1923.* New York, 1966.

Bell, John D. *Peasants in Power: Alexander Stamboliski and the Bulgarian Agrarian National Union, 1899–1923.* Princeton, New Jersey, 1977.

Jelavich, Barbara. *St. Petersburg and Moscow: Tsarist and Soviet Foreign Policy, 1814–1974.* Bloomington, Indiana, 1974.

Jelavich, Charles and Barbara Jelavich. *The Establishment of the Balkan National States, 1804–1920.* Seattle, Washington, 1977.

See also Congress of Berlin; Eastern Rumelia; Irredentism; Macedonia (Montenegro); Pan-Slavism; Russo-Turkish War of 1877–78

Sarajevo

Capital city of Bosnia-Hercegovina, located in the mountainous region of Bosnia. In 1991 its population numbered over 300,000 inhabitants.

The Ottoman sultans made Sarajevo the capital of Bosnia during their occupation, and it remained the capital of the region during the Austro-Hungarian Empire. The assassination of the Austrian heir apparent, Archduke Franz Ferdinand (1863–1914), in the city on June 28, 1914, helped trigger World War I. After the war, the city remained a regional capital in the new nation of Yugoslavia.

The climate of the region is continental, with hot summers and cold winters. Sarajevo was the site of the 1984 Winter Olympics. In preparation for that event, a new sports stadium, new apart- ment houses, and numerous other buildings were built. The city residents helped defray part of the cost of these improvements by donating a portion of their income for the project. The city served as the cultural and economic center of the region. Its workers were employed in steel manufacturing, weaving, and tobacco production, as well as in a myriad of other smaller enterprises.

In 1991 approximately half of Bosnia's population was Muslim, and Sarajevo, with the majority of its residents being of the Islamic faith, was the religious core of the country. The city was also the seat for a Roman Catholic bishop and an Orthodox metropolitan.

In April 1992 Sarajevo became the capital city of the newly reorganized Republic of Bosnia-Hercegovina, a new nation with a Muslim plurality carved out of former Yugoslavia. Besieged by Serb forces during the subsequent conflict, the city suffered great devastation and loss of population.

William B. Kory

Further reading

Bertić, Ivan. *Veliki geografski atlas Jugoslavije.* Zagreb, 1987.

MacKenzie, Lewis. *Peacekeeper: The Road to Sarajevo.* Vancouver, 1993.

Malcolm, Noel. *Bosnia: A Short History.* New York, 1994.

See also Bosnia-Hercegovina; Bosnia-Hercegovina, Birth of the Republic of; Franz Ferdinand; Islam; Muslims; World War I

Sava River

River in the Balkans. The Sava River has its source in the Savica waterfall located in the Julian Alps in eastern Slovenia, near the borders of Austria and Italy. The river flows in an easterly direction for over 500 miles (833 km), separating the mountainous region to its south from the plain and hilly area to its north. It empties into the Danube River.

Three capital cities—Ljubljana, Slovenia; Zagreb, Croatia; and Belgrade, Serbia—have been built on the shores of the Sava River. Belgrade is situated at the confluence of the Sava and Danube Rivers.

The Sava's principal tributaries, all flowing from the mountainous region of the south, include the Kupa, Una, Vrbas, Bosna, and Drina. These tributaries provide the Sava with much of its water volume. Part of the Sava River forms a border between Croatia to the north and Bosnia-Hercegovina to the south.

The Sava flows through a broad fertile valley enriching the soil and providing the region with grain, fruit, cattle, and other foodstuffs. It is navigable for over half of its length and serves as an avenue for transporting agricultural products, timber, and some metallic ores.

William B. Kory

Further reading

Bertić, Ivan. *Veliki geografski atlas Jugoslavije.* Zagreb, 1987.

Saxons

Ethnic Germans of East Central Europe. The two principal Saxon groups of Eastern Europe are the settlers in eastern Hungary (currently Romania), the Transylvanian Saxons, and those in northern Hungary (modern Slovakia), the Saxons of Zips/Szepesség/Spiš. The Saxons settled in Transylvania in the twelfth century; privileges granted in 1224 were subsequently extended to most of the Saxon region known later as Siebenbürgen. Their wealth and study in German universities enabled Saxons to maintain German identity despite a growing population of non-Germans. Owing to their contacts with Germany, Saxons of both communities became Lutherans. Their attitude toward Austrian rule (established in the sixteenth and seventeenth centuries) and Hungarian nationalism was complex: their sympathy for the dynasty and the antifeudalism of Habsburg monarch Joseph II (1741–90) and Hungarian reformers clashed with anxiety over threats to their autonomy. Some Saxons sought to work with the Hungarian government, while others favored solidarity with Hungary's disaffected minorities. After 1918, the anti-Hungarian faction asserted leadership, but in the late 1930s, the forces favoring cooperation with Nazi Germany triumphed. Drafted into the German SS, Saxons suffered war losses, deportation to the Soviet Union, and expropriations; many Transylvanian survivors emigrated, while many others were expelled.

Transylvanian Saxons numbered roughly 186,000 in 1966. Pessimism about their future in Romania increased Saxons' desire to emigrate, and successive West German governments made its facilitation a keystone of policy toward Roma-

nia. From 1968, annual emigration rose steadily, becoming a mass phenomenon in the 1980s. Fewer than 10,000 Saxons remain in Romania today.

James P. Niessen

Further reading

Die Siebenbürger Sachsen in den Jahren 1848–1918. Cologne, 1988.

Geschichte der Deutschen auf dem Gebiete Rumäniens, Erster Band: 12. Jahrhundert bis 1848. Bucharest, 1979.

Heinz, Herman. *Bücherkunde zur Volks- und Heimatforschung der Siebenbürger Sachsen.* Munich, 1960.

See also Emigration; Ethnic Minorities

Schönerer, Georg von (1842–1921)

Radical Austrian political leader. The son of an ennobled railroad builder and administrator, Schönerer seemingly was destined for a career as a liberal politician representing his rural district. Instead, the radical Schönerer broke with Austrian liberalism in the 1870s and moved to the left within the context of the stirring of mass politics among Germans and other peoples of the empire, which was ultimately to spell the empire's doom. Schönerer developed a program to appeal to the disaffected in the liberal economy of the time, particularly artisans and the petit bourgeoisie. His Linz Program (1882) emphasized democracy, social reform, and German nationalism. He introduced a strident tone and raucous behavior to the politics of the time that disrupted the old order and had widespread appeal among the disaffected, although he never succeeded in fostering a truly mass movement.

As time went on, he became increasingly radical, going beyond even what some of his adherents supported. He seemed to exploit every disruptive force in the empire and built an ideological structure composed largely of negatives: anti-Slavism, anticapitalism, antisocialism, anti-Catholicism, and, most important, Pan-Germanism and anti-Semitism, which anticipated two major themes of Adolf Hitler (1889–1945), a later admirer. In the end, it was not his words but his deeds that brought him down. Convicted of a break-in at the editorial offices of a "Jewish" newspaper, the *Neues Wiener Tageblatt* (*New Vienna Daily Paper*), he was sent to jail, lost his title of nobility, and had his political rights suspended for five years. He never recovered but disappeared into obscurity, leaving behind a legacy that would resonate terribly in the coming century.

Ronald Smelser

Further reading

Pulzer, Peter. *The Rise of Political Antisemitism in Germany and Austria.* New York, 1974.

Whiteside, Andrew Gladding. *The Socialism of Fools: Georg von Schönerer and Austrian Pan-Germanism.* Berkeley, California, 1975.

See also Adolf Hitler; Pan-Germanism

Schulz, Bruno (1892–1942)

Polish writer, painter, and critic. Schulz was an art teacher in the provincial town of Drohobycz in Galicia. He was gifted with extraordinary imagination, which made his two slim volumes of short stories an exceptional accomplishment of Polish literature: *Sklepy cynamonowe* (*Cinnamon Shops,* 1934) and *Sanatorium pod klepsydrą* (*The Sanatorium under the Sign of the Hourglass,* 1937). Schulz's literary career began late (1934) and ended tragically on November 19, 1942, when he was killed by the occupying Germans, despite several attempts by the Polish underground to rescue him.

Schulz's stories are rooted in his private world and his private mythology. They are narrated in the first person and united by the protagonist (Joseph), who closely resembles the author himself—the son of a Jewish shopkeeper. The narrator's unusual adventures, which are a re-creation of Schulz's biography, take place in a town resembling Drohobycz. The town becomes transformed into a magical and phantasmagorical reality where everyday objects are presented as a medium for entering the spiritual world. The narrator describes the "dawn of childhood" using the language of myths and parables where nothing is ever final and everything can always be transformed. The time is no longer linear—events take place beyond time or on "the branch-lines of time, somewhat illegal and suspect" while the narrator searches for the primal meaning of the word (the myth of the book) or the essence of seasons (the myth of spring). Plot in Schulz's stories is secondary, unlike the ever-present characters, who are transformed into beings of mythical stature: the narrator, the narrator's father ("the incorrigible improviser"), mother, and Adela, the servant girl.

Katarzyna Zechenter

Further reading

Brown, Russell. "Bruno Schulz and World Literature." *Slavic and East European Journal* 2 (1990).

———. *Myths and Relatives: Seven Essays on Bruno Schulz.* Munich, 1991.

Kuprel, Diana. "Errant Events on the Branch Tracks of Time: Bruno Schulz and Mythical Consciousness." *Slavic and East European Journal* 1 (1996).

Letters and Drawings of Bruno Schulz, with Selected Prose, ed. by Jerzy Ficowski, trans. by Walter Arndt and Victoria Nelson. New York, 1988.

Polish Review. Special Schulz Issue. 2, 1991.

See also Polish Literature

Schwarzenberg, Prince Felix zu (1800–1852)

Influential adviser to Emperor Franz Joseph (1830–1916), who, in his dual capacity as minister-president and foreign minister from 1848 to 1852 is credited with reviving the foreign and domestic power of the Habsburg dynasty in the wake of the Revolutions of 1848–49. A staunch conservative and monarchist, Schwarzenberg worked energetically to bring about the final defeat of rebellious forces within the empire and to neutralize the liberal, federalist constitution of the Kremsier Reichstag, an elected diet that he summarily dismissed on March 7, 1849. As an alternative to the popular sovereignty asserted by the Kremsier constitution, Schwarzenberg promoted a postrevolutionary program that combined a strong, centralized monarchy with limited concessions to popular will, such as guaranteed civil rights and an elected, albeit restricted, parliament. This program, most clearly articulated in the stillborn Stadion constitution of March 4, 1849, was passed over by Franz Joseph, who fashioned his own, authoritarian, absolutist ruling instrument in the so-called Sylvester Patent of December 31, 1851.

In foreign affairs, Schwarzenberg attempted to regain the empire's predominant role in Central Europe that had been threatened with the suspension of the German Confederation by the revolutionary Frankfurt Parliament and by Prussia's bid for leadership in Germany. At the conferences of Olmütz and Dresden during 1850–51, Schwarzenberg succeeded in reviving the old German Confederation, with Austria once again ensconced in its presidency, a move that restored the prerevolutionary status quo and served to check, temporarily, Prussia's hegemonic ambitions in Germany. Some contend that Schwarzenberg's ultimate goal was far more ambitious—the creation of a vast, Central European union merging the German Confederation with the Habsburg realm. Schwarzenberg's sudden death from a heart attack on April 5, 1852, deprived the empire of a resolute and intelligent leader for the postrevolutionary era.

Lawrence J. Flockerzie

Further reading

Austensen, Roy A. "Felix Schwarzenberg: Realpolitiker or Metternichian? The Evidence of the Dresden Conference." *Mitteilungen des Österreichischen Staatsarchiv* 30 (1977): 97–118.

Heller, Eduard. *Fürst Felix zu Schwarzenberg: Mitteleuropas Vorkämpfer.* Vienna, 1933.

Schwarzenberg, Adolph. *Prince Felix zu Schwarzenberg, Prime Minister of Austria 1848–1852.* New York, 1946.

Walter, Friedrich. "Fürst Felix Schwarzenberg im Lichte seiner Innenpolitik." *Virtute Fideque, Festschrift für Otto von Habsburg zum fünfzigsten Geburtstag.* Vienna (1965): 180–89.

See also Franz Joseph; Kremsier; Kroměříž Parliament; Olmütz, Punktation of; Revolutions of 1848

Securitate

Romanian secret police (variously, the General Directorate, or Department, or Council of State Security). The pre-Communist Romanian secret police, the *siguranţa,* was established shortly after the Great Romanian Peasant Revolt of 1907 to gather information on, infiltrate, disrupt, and suppress "subversive" groups. It and its successors were formally subordinated to the Ministry of Internal Affairs. During the interwar period, the *siguranţa* targeted both Communists and the Iron Guard, the Romanian nationalist-fascist organization.

After the imposition of Communist rule, Soviet NKVD (later, KGB) "counselors" created the General Directorate of People's Security, the first incarnation of the *securitate.* Class enemies, prewar intellectuals and professionals, peasants reluctant to become members of collective farms, and even suspect members of the Romanian Workers (Communist) Party elite became victims of the *securitate's* special courts, prisons, and slave labor camps. Under Alexandru Draghici (1913–), in one role or another in charge of state security from 1952 to 1967, the *securitate* exercised broad autonomy.

Under the regime of Nicolae Ceauşescu (1918–89), the *securitate* enforced political conformity by creating the impression of omnipresence. While dissidents were suppressed in the traditional way, general acquiescence was achieved by engineered paranoia. *Securişti* (*securitate* personnel) were also engaged in foreign operations. During the Romanian "revolution" of 1989, some *securişti* sided with the National Salvation Front, which overthrew the regime, while others, especially members of Ceauşescu's personal guard, were among the last defenders of it.

From 1990 to 1997 the post-Communist successor institution, the Romanian Intelligence Service, and its director, Virgil Măgureanu (1940–), were suspected of political skullduggery and widespread corruption. Reform of the institution was undertaken in 1997.

Walter M. Bacon Jr.

Further reading

Deletant, Dennis. *Ceauşescu and the Securitate.* Armonk, New York, 1995.

See also Nicolae Ceauşescu; Communist Party of Romania; Iron Guard; Revolutions of 1989; Romanian Peasant Revolt of 1907

Seifert, Jaroslav (1901–86)

Czech poet, journalist, editor, and writer. Deeply influenced by his surroundings while growing up in Žižkov, a working-class district in Prague, Seifert found revolutionary ideas attractive and joined the Communist Party. He began his career as a journalist and became a founding member of Devětsil, an avant-garde Czech literary group. Devětsil's first program of "proletariat poetry"

S was reflected in Seifert's *Město v slzách* (*City in Tears,* 1921) and *Samá Láska* (*All the Love,* 1923), where he portrayed his dreams and images of revolution.

A change toward poetism—a Czech movement that viewed the world in lyrical terms—in Devětsil's program resonated in Seifert's next two collections, *Na vlnách T.S.F.* (*On the Waves of Wirelesss Telegraphy,* 1925) and *Slavík zpívá špatně* (*The Nightingale Sings Poorly,* 1926), which celebrated the ecstasy of life and fantasy. The impact of free-ranging images on Czech authors is also readily apparent in these works.

Nostalgic memories and family motifs with a touch of irony characterize the third stage of Siefert's poetic development. During the 1930s, he shifted from modern lyricism to the poetry of personal confession in *Jablko z klína* (*The Apple from the Lap,* 1933) and *Ruce venušiny* (*Hands of Venus,* 1936), noticing beauty in ordinary reality. Melodic, songlike structures with frequent repetitions and changes in rhythm represent other classic examples of his work.

After World War II, Seifert's stage of personal lyricism ended with *Maminka* (*Mommy,* 1954), often perceived as an example of Czech soft poetics. Highly melodic and rhythmical, the poems emphasize the details of everyday life. Owing to his open public disregard for official ideology, as well as health difficulties, Seifert ceased publishing for ten years. In the 1960s, with *Koncert na Ostrově* (*Concert on the Island,* 1965) and *Halleyova kometa* (*Halley's Comet,* 1967), Seifert returned to previous stages and styles. Most of his later work was censured or had to be published abroad. In *Morový sloup* (*Plague Column,* 1981) he expressed a strong reaction to the Soviet invasion of Czechoslovakia in 1968. Seifert's last work, *Všechny krásy světa* (*All the Beauties of the World,* 1981), was first published in Canada and Germany, and then in its censored version in Prague. Seifert was awarded the Nobel Prize in literature in 1984, the first Czech to receive the award.

Lucie Zacharová

Further reading
Machala, Lubomír and Eduard Petru. *Panorama české literatury.* Olomouc, Czech Republic, 1994.

See also Czech Literature

Sejm

Polish national assembly. In the nineteenth and twentieth centuries, there was no continuous parliamentary tradition as Poland had lost its independence. However, those Sejms that did exist permitted the development of a modern parliamentary tradition and served as a training ground for future parliamentarians. The Sejms of this period are those of the Congress Kingdom (1815–31), Galicia (1861–1918), the Second Republic (1919–39), and People's Poland (1947–89).

The Sejm of the Congress Kingdom was established by the 1815 constitution given to Poland by the Russian tsar Alexander I (1777–1825), as promised at the Congress of Vienna. It was bicameral, consisting of a senate and a house of representatives. Contrary to the constitution, the Sejm was called only four times (1818, 1820, 1825, 1830). In 1820 the Sejm rejected two pieces of legislation and, in response, Alexander I abolished public debates at the next session (1825), which was also closed to the leaders of the opposition. The Sejm met for the last time on December 18, 1830, and served as the Polish legislature during the November Uprising against the Russians. This last session lasted until the end of the uprising in 1831, after which Nicholas I (1796–1855) abolished the constitution and the kingdom.

The Sejm of the Kingdom of Galicia and Lodomeria was a provincial legislature within the Austrian Empire. It was established in 1861 and met until 1918 in Lwów (Ukrainian, L'viv; German, Lemberg). Its jurisdiction included culture, public works, education, and local government. However, its decisions had to be approved by the Austrian emperor. As a result of electoral laws, the Galician Sejm was dominated by the most conservative elements of the landed aristocracy.

The first Sejm of the Second Republic was initially unicameral. It proclaimed the 1921 constitution, which established a parliamentary democracy similar to that of France. This legislature was bicameral, composed of a Sejm—the lower house—and a senate. The legislature had power over the executive—which was established from parliament's own ranks—and the judiciary, which was responsible to parliament. The senate had the power to review and reject laws passed by the Sejm. However, a simple majority in the Sejm could overturn the senate's decision.

Until 1930, no party had a majority in the Sejm. The Second Republic therefore saw numerous governments, although the personalities and parties within the various government often remained the same, providing stability. After Józef Piłsudski's (1867–1935) coup d'état in 1926, the president acquired the power to issue decrees with the force of law. When parliamentary leaders rejected Piłsudski's rule, the legislature was dissolved and new elections were held. Piłsudski's supporters won a majority in 1930, but in an election marked by violence and illegality on the government's part. From this date, Poland's Sejm became a mere sideshow to Piłsudski and his successors. The opposition boycotted the elections in 1935 and 1938 in protest. After the German occupation of Poland in 1939, the members of the Sejm met in London, giving legitimacy to the Polish government-in-exile.

The Sejm in People's Poland was formed after the elections of 1947. This initial constituent assembly, dominated by the Left, drafted a temporary working constitution in 1947 and the formal Constitution of the Polish People's Republic in 1952. The 1952 elections, held under the new constitution, were for a unicameral legislature of 425 deputies. Given the conditions prevailing in Stalinist Poland, a majority of seats were captured by the Communist Polish United Workers Party.

Subsequent elections were mere window dressing for Communist rule, which always resulted in a solid majority for the Communists, despite their increasing unpopularity among the vast majority of Poles. Although non-Communist parties and groups were represented, the Sejm itself had little authority, real power being vested in the Central Committee of the Polish United Workers Party and its leaders.

John Stanley

Further reading

Czapliński, W. "The Polish *Sejm.*" *Acta Poloniae Historica* 22 (1970): 180–92.

Groth, Alexander J. *People's Poland: Government and Politics.* San Francisco, 1972.

Historia Sejmu Polskiego: t. 2, cz. 1, *W dobie rozbiorów* and t. 2, cz. 2, II *Rzeczypospolita*, Warsaw, 1989.

Polonsky, Anthony. *Politics in Independent Poland, 1921–39.* London, 1971.

Wandycz, Piotr. "The Poles in the Austrian Empire." *Austrian History Yearbook* 3, no. 2 (1967): 261–86.

See also Alexander I; Congress of Vienna; Nicholas I; November Uprising; Józef Piłsudski; Polish Congress Kingdom

Self-Management in Yugoslavia

Economic model in post–World War II Yugoslavia. The disruption caused by the Cominform (Communist Information Bureau) blockade of Yugoslavia following the breakdown in relations between Belgrade and Moscow in 1948 forced Yugoslav policymakers to reschedule the timing of the First Five-Year Plan and to find a longer-term alternative to the Soviet-type command economy. The leading theoreticians in Yugoslavia's Communist Party, Boris Kidrič (1912–53) and Edvard Kardelj (1910–79), propagated the idea of the free association of workers who would manage their own affairs (self-management). Although they initially claimed that this idea was to be found in orthodox Marxism, the intellectual origins of self-management are to be found in anarchosyndicalism. The entire concept relied on the vaguely defined idea of social property, which differs from both private and state property. Although officially proclaimed as owners of the factories, workers enjoyed only severely limited property rights since those rights did not include free disposition of the physical assets they used. Such assets belonged both to the workers and to society as a whole. Along with this dichotomy, workers' participation in the decision-making process was shadowed by the monopoly of power of the League of Communists of Yugoslavia (official name of the Communist Party). Although the introduction of self-management in June 1950 initially spurred the growth of the Yugoslav economy, the intrinsic weaknesses of the model produced disastrous long-run effects. In the absence of market signals, the voluntarism associated with local self-government directly led to growing autarky in the Yugoslav economy. The increasing economic and political isolationism of the Yugoslav republics from one another in part resulted in the demise of Yugoslavia as constituted under Tito (1892–1980).

Željan E. Šuster

Further reading

Horvat, B. *The Yugoslav Economic System.* White Plains, New York, 1976.

Sirc, Lj. *The Yugoslav Economy under Self-Management.* London, 1979.

Vanek, J. *The Economics of Workers' Management.* London, 1972.

See also Cominform; Communist Party of Yugoslavia; Economic Development in Yugoslavia; Edvard Kardelj; Tito

Šenoa, August (1838–1891)

Greatest Croatian novelist of the nineteenth century. Šenoa grew up in Zagreb in a middle-class family of Czech-German origin. He was gripped by the patriotic movement that arose among young Croatians during the period of "neoabsolutism" of the 1850s—the conservative era initiated in the Habsburg Empire following the Revolutions of 1848. After two years at the Zagreb Law Academy, he continued his studies in Prague, where he lived from 1859 to 1865. He never finished his law studies but instead became an active journalist and litterateur. After moving to Vienna, he edited the periodicals *Glasonoša* (*The Herald*) and *Slawische Blätter* (*Slavic Leaves*). In his programmatic article "Naša književnost" ("Our Literature," 1865), he called the struggle to lift and educate the masses of the highest importance, and he attempted to write in a language accessible to broad layers of the Croatian population. Born into a home where only German was spoken, he became the father of modern Croatian literature. First, he published poems and short stories of an ideological character. He was the director of the Zagreb Theater from 1868 to 1871, and editor in chief of the literary and social magazine *Vijenac* (*The Wreath*).

In the novellas and novels published in the years 1874–81 (including the historical novel *Kletva* [*The Cursed*], dictated on his deathbed), he painted crucial episodes of the Croatian past in great and colorful detail. The five novels that made him into a central figure in Croatian literature were *Zlatarovo zlato* (*The Goldsmith's Gold,* 1871), depicting the struggle between the nobility and the commonalty in feudal times; *Čuvaj se senjske ruke* (*Beware of the Hand of Senj,* 1875), focusing on the pirate harbor Senj; *Seljačka buna* (*Peasant Uprising,* 1877); *Diogenes* (1878); and *Prosjak Luka* (*The Beggar Luka,* 1879).

Thomas Eekman

Further reading

Barac, Antun. *August Šenoa, Studija.* Zagreb, 1926.

Frangeš, Ivo. "August Šenoa." *Povijest hrvatske književnosti* 4, Zagreb (1975): 339–55.

Ježić, S. "Život i djelo Augusta Šenoe," in A. Šenoa, *Sabrana djela,* vol. 20. Zagreb, 1964.

Malby, Maria B. "August Šenoa," in *Dictionary of Literary Biography,* vol. 147: *South Slavic Writers before World War II.* Detroit, 1995, 212–21.

Živančević, M. "Literatura o A. Šenoi," in *Godišnjak* 17 of the Philosophy Department. Novi Sad, Yugoslavia (1974): 221–46.

See also Croatian Literature to 1918; Neoabsolutism; Revolutions of 1848

Serbia (and the Breakup of Yugoslavia)

State that emerged in the wake of the breakup of Yugoslavia. As the Communist Party (after 1952 the League of Communists of Yugoslavia, LCY) succeeded the Serb-dominated government-in-exile in 1945, the Serbs' privileged position in the political nation ended. Communists divided the LCY and the Yugoslav government into six national republics (Serbia, Croatia, Bosnia-Hercegovina, Slovenia, Macedonia, and Montenegro) and two autonomous provinces (Kosovo and Vojvodina) within Serbia, representing Albanian and Magyar national minorities, respectively.

In the 1960s and 1970s, however, political power in the LCY began to devolve to the republics, and the federal government attempted to quash Serb and Croat "ultranationalism." The intolerance for Serb nationalism was illustrated by the fall from power of Alesksander Ranković (1909–83), one of Tito's (1892–1980) closest aides. In addition, the 1974 constitution gave the autonomous provinces political equality with the republics, setting the context for the reemergence of Serb nationalism.

In the 1980s hyperinflation, declining wages, and plummeting living standards overwhelmed the federal government. Communist parties in the republics increasingly turned to nationalist explanations for their decline. In Serbia, this shifting political climate was illustrated by the infamous 1986 memorandum of the Serbian Academy of Arts and Sciences, which claimed the Serbs had been the chief victim of Communist rule. In particular, the academy cited equality of the autonomous provinces with the republics and Albanian control of Kosovo (the site of the medieval Serbian state and the Serbian Orthodox patriarchate) as evidence of Communist oppression of Serbs.

In the context of discredited communism, Serbian political leaders drew on nationalism to mobilize mass support for a Serb-dominated state. Between 1989 and 1991, Serb leaders tried to recentralize Yugoslavia by nullifying large parts of the 1974 constitution, while Croat and Slovene leaders sought further decentralization. In 1990 irreconcilable differences brought about the dissolution of the LCY and the election of nationalist presidents in each republic. Further, Serbia unilaterally stripped Kosovo and Vojvodina of their autonomy, suspended their parliaments, and imposed martial law in Kosovo, giving Serbia control over four of eight votes in the Yugoslav presidency (Montenegro always voted with Serbia).

In 1991 Serbian President Slobodan Milošević (1941–) claimed that Serbs' rights could be protected only by a Serbian government. With reform under the Yugoslav presidency effectively stymied, Slovenia and Croatia announced plans to secede if the stalemate continued. In June 1991 Croatia and Slovenia declared their independence, followed months later by Bosnia-Hercegovina and Macedonia. These breakaway movements were met by Serb-dominated Yugoslav army tanks. With the international recognition of Slovenia, Croatia, and Bosnia-Hercegovina by January 1992, the disintegration of Yugoslavia was de facto complete, leaving Serbia as a separate entity.

Katherine McCarthy

Further reading

Cohen, Lenard J. *Broken Bonds: Yugoslavia's Disintegration and Balkan Politics in Transition,* 2d ed. Boulder, Colorado, 1995.

Sekelj, Laslo. *Yugoslavia: The Process of Disintegration.* Boulder, Colorado, 1993.

Silber, Laura and Allan Little. *Yugoslavia: Death of a Nation.* New York, 1996.

See also Bosnia-Hercegovina, Birth of the Republic of; Communist Party of Yugoslavia; Croatia, Birth of the Republic of; Kosovo; Macedonia (History); Slobodan Milošević; Montenegro (History); Nationalism; Aleksandar Ranković; Slovenia, Birth of the Republic of; Tito

old kingdom with a rich history dating back to the eighth century. Montenegro and Serbia remain the only republics of Yugoslavia. Serbia is bordered by Hungary in the north, and, proceeding in a clockwise direction, by Romania, Bulgaria, Macedonia, Albania, Montenegro, Bosnia-Hercegovina, and Croatia.

The northern part of the country is characterized by a fertile alluvial plain. This is the major agricultural region of the nation, with the Tisa River flowing through it to the south and emptying into the Danube River near the capital city of Belgrade. Novi Sad and Subotica are the major cities in the region.

The southeastern part of Serbia consists of gently rolling plains washed by the Morava River. The river flows north and empties into the Danube east of Belgrade. The region is noted for both agriculture and industry, with Niš being the largest city in the area.

The southwest is covered by the majestic Dinaric Alps. These rugged mountains are characterized by their karst formations, reaching altitudes of nearly 9,000 feet (2,070 m). At the border with Albania, the ranges are made of limestone or sandstone with some good pasturelands. Sheep and goats graze on the slopes.

Serbia has approximately ten million inhabitants, of whom ethnic Serbs number fewer than seven million. The rest of the population is made up of minorities, including Hungarians in the north, Croats in the northwest, Muslims in the east, and Albanians in the south. Over two million ethnic Serbs live outside the boundaries of Serbia. In 1991 nearly 1.5 million lived in Bosnia-Hercegovina, half a million in Croatia, with others constituting smaller minorities in the surrounding countries.

William B. Kory

Further reading

Bertić, Ivan. *Veliki geografski atlas Jugoslavije.* Zagreb, 1987.

Cohen, Lenard J. *Broken Bonds: The Disintegration of Yugoslavia.* Boulder, Colorado, 1993.

See also Belgrade; Dinaric Alps; Montenegro (Geography); Niš

Serbia (Geography)

Independent state prior to World War I and one of the republics that made up Yugoslavia. Serbia is an

Serbian Art

At the beginning of the nineteenth century, trends in European art that had culminated several decades earlier were still important for Serbian artists. Thus, classicism dominated the first half of the nineteenth century. Its early representatives were Arsen Teodorović (1767–1826) and Pavel Đurković (1772–1832), painters of portraits and iconostases, two dominant subjects of Serbian classicism. Uroš Knežević (1811–76) was famous for his portraits, while Dimitrije Avramović (1815–55)—apart from being a prolific portraitist—was the author of several well-known iconostases in Belgrade, Topola, and Vrdnik.

Major representatives of romanticism in the third quarter of the nineteenth century were Novak Radonić (1826–90) and Đura Jakšić (1832–78), the leading artist of the period. Another talented artist, Stevan Todorović (1832–1925), painted several iconostases in Belgrade, together with a whole gallery of portraits of Serbian middle-class citizens from the second half of the nineteenth century. Portraits remained the main theme in Serbian romanticism.

Academic realism characterized Serbian art in the last quarter of the century, its best representative Đorđe Krstić (1851–1907). The closing phase of the period belonged to two prominent academic realists, Uroš Predić (1857–1953), who painted iconostases, portraits, and historical compositions, and Paja Jovanović (1859–1957), who produced portraits and scenes of peasant life from Serbia and Albania. Both were typical representatives of the Vienna School.

Twentieth-century trends began with plein air paintings and the first signs of impressionism, visible in the works of Marko Murat (1864–1944), Mališa Glišić (1885–1915), and Đorđe Mihailović (1875–1919). The friction between academic realism and impressionism, tradition and modernism characterized the period before World War I. The most prominent modernist of this period was Nadežda Petrović (1873–1915), who opposed conservative ideas. With her expressionist paintings, which belonged to the fauvist movement, Serbian art reached a level with contemporary European art for the first time. Impressionism reached its peak in the works of Kosta Milićević (1877–1920) and Milan Milovanović (1876–1946), who went on to produce their best paintings during World War I, when Milićević worked in Greece and Milovanović in Italy and France.

After the war, Serbian art embraced modernism completely. The work of French painter Paul Cézanne (1839–1906) strongly influenced Serbian painting in the second and third decade, as visible in the works of Petar Dobrović (1890–1942), Jovan Bijelić (1886–1964), and Milo Milunović (1897–1967), who later turned to expressionism. Cubist influences marked the end of the third decade, serving as a starting point for another group of talented painters—Sava Šumanović (1896–1942), Milan Konjović (1898–1993), and Zora Petrović (1894–1962). However, these artists soon abandoned the strict geometry of cubism and joined the fauvist movement.

Plasticity and volume rather than color and drawing were generally more important in the interwar period. But in the years immediately preceding World War II, Serbian painters turned toward expressionsm and surrealism, using vivid colors and sometimes exploring contemporary social themes. Vividly colored expressionist paintings in the tradition of Nadežda Petrović represent some of the best examples of modern Serbian art: dramatic Bosnian and Belgrade landscapes by Bijelić; ecstatic Vojvodina landscapes by Konjović; Dalmatian landscapes and pictures of Dubrovnik by Dobrović; and calm Srem landscapes by Šumanović.

The abstract art of Petar Lubarda (1907–74) and Stojan Ćelić (1925–92), the surrealism of Dado Đurić (1933–), and the poetic sensualism of Mladen Srbinović (1925–) and Nedeljko Gvozdenović (1902–88) characterize Serbian art after World War II.

The development of Serbian sculpture began only in the twentieth century. The most important artists from the first half of the century were Sreten Stojanović (1898–1960) (psychological portraits and monumental sculptures), Petar Palavičini (1887–1958) (female nudes in stone or bronze), and Rista Stijović (1894–1974) (rustic treatment of the female body in wood). Younger representatives of the post–World War II generation, such as Jovan Soldatović (1920–) and Nandor Glid (1924–97), strove toward dramatic expression of more abstract forms.

Svetlana Rakić

Further reading

Medaković, Dejan. *Srpska umetnost u 19 veku.* Belgrade, 1981.

———. *Srpski slikari 18–20 veka: Likovi i dela.* Novi Sad, 1968.

Trifunović, Lazar. *Od impresionizma do enformela: Studije i članci o umetnosti.* Belgrade, 1982.

——. *Srpsko slikarstvo 1900–1950.* Belgrade, 1973.

See also Đura Jakšić; Romanticism

Serbian Culture

The reigns of Stefan Nemanja (1166–96), who established the territorial basis of the future Serbian kingdom and united the Serbian people for the first time, and his son Stefan Nemanjić (1196–1227), who obtained the title of king from the pope in 1217 and made the Serbian church autonomous, set the stage for future Serbian cultural developments. Numerous churches and monasteries, which became inspirational to later generations, were built. These included Hilendar (built in 1293), Studenica (1196), Gračanica (1314), Žiča (ca. 1215), Sopoćani (1265), and Mileševa (1235), all of which reflected Byzantine, Greek, and Italian influences.

During the medieval period, Serbs also produced three kinds of paintings: frescoes, *ikonopsis* (icon) painting on a wooden board, and painting on parchment or paper, especially in books written by hand. Like its architecture, Serbian painting was influenced by Byzantine, Greek, Venetian, and Italian schools of painting.

Literature was not as rich as painting and architecture. Most works had religious characteristics and were written in the Church Slavonic language. *Miroslavljevo jevandjelje* (*Miroslav's Gospel,* twelfth century) was one of the first preserved manuscripts. Translations of church books and biographies of Serbian rulers were the most numerous. For example, St. Sava, the first head of the Serbian church, in 1208 wrote a book about his father, Stefan Nemanja, entitled *Život gospodina Simeona* (*The Life of Mr. Simeon*).

The medieval Serbian state reached its zenith under Stefan Dušan (c. 1308–55). During his reign, church architecture flourished, monasteries became centers of learning, and literature reflected national unity. Great popular epics emerged that were exclusively and peculiarly Serbian.

Although Serbia ceased to exist as an independent state after the Turkish conquest in 1459, cultural activities continued. Folk literature flourished, particularly epic ballads. Those epics, usually divided into nine cycles, present a fascinating picture of the Serbian people from medieval times to the nineteenth century.

After 1830, when Serbia became an autonomous state, an intensive political, economic, social, and cultural development began. From 1838 to 1858, numerous schools, lyceums, and cultural institutions opened, and promising young Serbs were sent to Western European universities to continue their education. For such cultural progress Serbia had to thank educated Serbs from Vojvodina, who had greater opportunities for advancement. The first Serbian gymnasium (high school) was opened in Sremski Karlovci in 1791. A cultural literary society, the Matica Srbska, was founded in 1826. And in 1791 the first Serbian newspaper was printed in Vienna.

The most influential Serbian intellectuals in the first half of the nineteenth century were Dositej Obradović (1742–1811) and Vuk Stefanović Karadžić (1787–1864). Obradović created both a modern Serbian literary language and a modern Serbian literature. He wrote on secular topics in the unaffected spoken language of his countrymen. With his work in Serbia from 1806 to 1811, he started the nation's cultural development and served as Serbia's first secretary of education. Karadžić was the greatest reformer of the Serbian language and orthography, a collector of folk songs, and an ethnographer, historian, and writer. He published a collection of Serbian folk songs, a grammar, and a dictionary; translated the New Testament into Serbian (1847); and introduced phonetic reforms into the old Cyrillic alphabet.

Petar Petrović Njegoš (1813–51) was one of the greatest South Slavic writers. A poet, philosopher, bishop, and prince of Montenegro, Njegoš wrote in the spirit of the national poetry. In works such as *Gorski vjenac* (*The Mountain Wreath,* 1847), he gave an epopee of life in Montenegro, his life experience, and his view of the world. Among Serbian romantic writers influenced by European romanticism was Branko Radičević (1826–53), the first Serbian poet who wrote in the *narodni* (people's) language. Other scholars included geographer Jovan Cvijić (1865–1927), astronomer Milutin Milanković (1879–1958), and the greatest Serbian literary critic, Jovan Skerlić (1877–1914).

Music in Serbia also began to develop at the end of the nineteenth century. Musical creations were primarily oriented toward chorales, solo songs, and stage works. Foundations for professional and nationally oriented music were laid by composer, pianist, and conductor Kornelije

Stanković (1831–65). The dominant figure in Serbian music was Stevan Stojanović-Mokranjac (1856–1914). His *Petnaest rukoveti* (*Fifteen Songs*), chorale compositions written from 1883 to 1909, were based on folk music from Serbia, Kosovo, Montenegro, Macedonia, and Bosnia.

Although Serbian art was greatly influenced by general European trends, in the 1860s Biedermeier style from Austria came to dominate Serbian artistic circles. Its most important representatives were Katarina Ivanović (1811–82), Dimitrije Avramović (1815–55), and Jovan Popović (1810–64). Realist painters Uroš Predić (1857–1953), Paja Jovanović (1859–1957), and Dimitrije Petković (1791–1852), all educated in Vienna, enjoyed great popularity and esteem. During the last quarter of the nineteenth century, three artists marked the beginning of Serbian sculpture: Petar Ubavkić (1852–1910), Djordje Jovanović (1861–1953), and Simeon Roksandić (1874–1943).

After World War I, the cultural life of the Serbs continued to flourish. The Opera House in Belgrade was completed in 1920, and a theater in Niš was formed in 1922. The Belgrade Philharmonic was established in 1923. The Academy of Music was created in 1937. Modern architecture began in Belgrade in the 1930s thanks to the work of Milan Zloković (1898–1965). Writers followed several literary directions. Modernism, surrealism, and socialist realism were the most prominent art forms. Serbian art dealt mainly with the study of forms, and this period (1918–1941) can be considered the most dynamic in the genesis of Serbian modern art. Noteworthy artists included Jovan Bijelić (1888–1964), Milan Konjović (1898–1993), Ivan Radović (1894–1973), Sava Šumanović (1896–1942), and Zora Petrović (1894–1962).

Sculpture continued to develop slowly. After 1920, an avant-garde trend in the form of geometrized synthetic forms appeared. Exceptional works included *Portrait of a Friend* by Sreten Stanojević (1898–1960), *Rastko Petrović* by Petar Plavični (1891–1945), and *The Virgin* by Dušan Jovanović Djukin (1891–1945).

After World War II, the Communist regime encouraged socialist realism. Political pressure for cultural conformity diminished only in the 1960s, and creativity, greatly influenced by the West, blossomed again. Of the many who received international recognition, none stands out more than Ivo Andrić (1892–1975), who was awarded the Nobel Prize in literature in 1961 for works dealing with the history of Bosnia, especially *Travnička hronika* (*The Travnik Chronicle,* or *Bosnian Story*) and *Na Drini ćuprija* (*The Bridge on the Drina,* 1945).

Milenko Karanovich

Further reading

Bogdanović, Dimitrije. *Istorija stare srpske književnosti.* Belgrade, 1980.

Derok, Aleksandar. *Monumentalna i dekorativna arhitektura u srednjovekovnoj Srbiji.* Belgrade, 1962.

Istorija srpske kulture. Gornii Milanovac, 1994.

Karanovich, Milenko. *The Development of Education in Serbia and Emergence of Its Intelligentsia, 1838–1858.* Boulder, Colorado, 1995.

Koljevic, Svetozar. *The Epic in the Making.* Oxford, 1980.

Kostić, Mita. *Dositej Obradović u istorijskoj perspektivi XVIII i XIX veka.* Belgrade, 1952.

Protić, Miodrag B. *Srpsko slikarstvo XX veka,* 2 vols. Belgrade, 1970.

See also Ivo Andrić; Architecture; Education; Folklife; Folklore; Folk Music; Vuk Karadžić; Dositej Obradović; Petar II Petrović Njegŏs Romanticism; Serbian Art; Serbian Literature; Yugoslav Literature

Serbian Émigrés

Voluntary or forced migrations of Serbs in the early modern and modern periods occurred in six major waves, the first in 1690. After defeating the Turks outside Vienna in 1683, the Austrian army advanced as far south as Kosovo, in the south of present-day Yugoslavia. Serbs joined the Austrians hoping to liberate their country and reestablish their independent state. However, after the Turks halted the offensive, as many as one hundred thousand Serbs, led by Patriarch Arsenije III Čarnojević (1633–1706), migrated to Hungary. Although Holy Roman Emperor Leopold I (1640–1705)—who viewed the Serbs as excellent soldiers of value to Austria in future wars against the Turks—promulgated a charter in 1690 promising to respect their Orthodox faith and guaranteeing them the right to elect their own patriarch, his promise was not long observed. Difficult economic, social, and religious conditions in Hungary forced a large number of Serbs to migrate to Russia and the Ukraine between 1751 and 1753, the second mass migration of Serbs.

The third major wave—primarily from Habsburg territories—occurred at the end of the nineteenth and the beginning of the twentieth centuries. Most Serbs under Austro-Hungarian rule were peasants who owned small plots of poor land or who were landless and made their living as hired agricultural workers. Facing difficult economic conditions at home, many Serbs also did not wish to serve in the Habsburg army. In addition to various European countries, their destinations were overseas countries, notably the United States.

Serbs also emigrated from Montenegro, the district of Kosovo, and Macedonia, where economic conditions were even poorer than in the Habsburg Empire. In Montenegro, for example, 90 percent of the population were peasants who could not produce enough food for themselves. Since many could not find additional employment, they had few options but to emigrate.

The economic picture in Serbia, which gained autonomy in 1830 and became an independent state in 1878, was often better than in other areas in which Serbs lived. The Ottoman feudal system was abolished after 1830 and capitalism began to penetrate slowly into Serbia's agricultural society. Although Prince Mihailo Obrenović (1823–68) issued a law in 1865 stating that the last five acres (two hectares) of a peasant's land and everything that was needed to till it, as well as all necessary food for his family, could not be sold for unpaid debts either by the peasant or by his creditor, this law was not strictly observed. As a result, many peasants became landless and were unable to support their families. Therefore, many emigrated, mainly to the United States. Yet the number of emigrants from Serbia was not as great as from Montenegro and the Serb-populated provinces under Austro-Hungarian rule.

After World War I, Serbian emigration decreased considerably, owing primarily to agrarian reform of 1919 in the Kingdom of Serbs, Croats, and Slovenes, the general improvement of economic conditions, and the United States Quota Acts of 1921, 1924, and 1929, which severely curtailed immigration from Eastern Europe. However, World War II produced a fourth wave of emigration that continued for a decade after the war. Most émigrés were former Yugoslav army officers and soldiers, former prisoners of war in Germany, and members of political groups that opposed the Communist regime in Yugoslavia. Their principal destinations were Australia, the United States, Argentina, the United Kingdom, and Canada. A decade later, a fifth wave followed as thousands of Serbs went to Western Europe, particularly to Germany, as temporary workers. This time, a large number of them stayed permanently.

The final wave of Serb emigration began at the end of the 1980s, brought on by the dissolution of Yugoslavia, national and religious tensions, political uncertainties, and economic difficulties. A large number of young, educated Serbs departed, many for the United States and Canada. This intellectual drain will have negative consequences for Serbia for the foreseeable future.

Among the many distinguished Serb émigrés, the three most admired are Nikola Tesla (1856–1943), Michael Idvorsky Pupin (1858–1935), and Bogdan Maglić (1934–). Tesla, who after studying in Graz and Prague emigrated to the United States in 1884, was the inventor of more than seven hundred patented electrical devices. His greatest discovery was the high-frequency alternating current, including the high-frequency resonant transformer, or Tesla coil. Pupin also owed his fame to his work in electricity, notably in telephone and telegraph systems and X rays. Besides such inventions as electrical wave propagation, multiplex telegraphy, electrical resonance, secondary X-ray radiation, and short-exposure X-ray photography, his greatest invention was the Pupin's Coils, which greatly extended the range of long-distance telephone calls. Maglić, a Serbian-American physicist, came to the United States in 1956. He was trained as a physicist in Yugoslavia, England, and the United States, and his most important discoveries include the sonic spark chamber, missing-mass spectrometer, and aneutronic energy process.

Milenko Karanovich

Further reading

Colakovic, Branko M. *Yugoslav Migrations to America.* San Francisco, 1973.

Gakovich, Robert P. and Milan M. Radovich. *Serbs in the United States and Canada: A Comprenhensive Bibliography.* Minneapolis, 1976.

Grečić, Vladimir, ed. *Seoba Srba nekad i sad.* Belgrade, 1990.

Grečić, Vladimir and Marko Lopušina. *Svi Srbi sveta.* Belgrade, 1994.

Karanovich, Milenko. "Causes of Serbian Immigration to the United States." *Balkan Studies* 31, no. 1 (1990): 131–63.

S

Petrovich, Michael B. *A History of Modern Serbia, 1804–1918,* 2 vols. New York, 1976.

Petrovich, Michael B. and Joel Halpern. "Serbs," in *Harvard Encyclopedia of American Ethnic Groups.* Cambridge, Massachusetts, 1980: 916–26.

See also Agriculture; Economic Development in Yugoslavia; Emigration; Kingdom of Serbs, Croats, and Slovenes; Mihailo Obrenović; Peasants

Serbian Language
see **Serbo-Croatian Language**

Serbian Literature to 1918

The modern period in Serbia was marked by a national revival beginning in the early nineteenth century. The standardization of a literary language and the development of a national literature became hallmarks of nineteenth-century Serbian culture. Modern Serbian literature generally proceeded from collections of oral literature through romanticism, realism, and modernism.

Serbian literature during the early nineteenth century included collections of oral poetry, as well as epic and lyric poetry imitating by oral tradition. Serbian folklorist and grammarian Vuk Karadžić (1787–1864) published his first collection of oral poetry in 1814; it was followed by many others that inspired generations of writers. Karadžić also standardized the grammar and orthography of the vernacular, thus laying the foundations for the modern literary language. The first romantic Serbian poet of the revival was Sima Milutinović-Sarajlija (1791–1847), who collected oral epics and published poetry based on that style. Montenegrin poet-bishop Petar Petrović Njegoš (1813–51) is esteemed as the greatest of all Serbian poets. His masterpiece, *Gorski vijenac* (*The Mountain Wreath,* 1847), is a dramatic epic poem that narrates the intense strife between Christians and Muslims in Montenegro. The primary genre during the middle decades of the nineteenth century was lyric poetry, thus forming the core of the romantic period. Branko Radičević (1824–53) is considered the most profound Serbian romantic poet. Other important poets were Đura Jakšić (1833–78), an impassioned lyric poet, and Jovan Jovanović-Zmaj (1833–1904), an influential lyricist.

Prose became the primary medium of expression in the late nineteenth century as realism permeated the Serbian literary scene. Realism was promoted by Svetozar Marković (1846–75), who was instrumental in the critical reappraisal of Serbian romanticism that took place in the late 1860s. Influenced by Russian critics, Marković was also the founder of Serbian socialism. Village realism emerged as the portrayal of the rural patriarchal order confronted by the economic and social transitions of the late nineteenth century became central concerns in literature. Writing in the 1870s and 1880s, Milovan Glišić (1847–1908) and Laza Lazarević (1851–90) were among the most representative writers of short, realist fiction. Dominating the 1890s, Stevan Sremac (1855–1906) and Simo Matavulj (1852–1908) were the first major novelists. Vojislav Ilić (1862–94) was the most important lyric poet of the period.

The end of the nineteenth and the beginning of the twentieth centuries saw the emergence of modernism in Serbian literature as an intensification of Western influence—particularly French—took place. Lyric poetry dominated. Jovan Dučić (1874–1943) sought to emulate Western models, while Milan Rakić (1876–1938) introduced decadence and pessimism in his verse, topics that flourished in the decade preceding World War I. Literary criticism also developed at the turn of the century, with writers such as Bogdan Popović (1863–1944) and Jovan Skerlić (1877–1914). At the same time, ethical and national subjects found expression in the literature of poet Aleksa Šantić (1868–1924)—who rejected the aesthetic convictions of his modernist contemporaries—and Borisav Stanković (1876–1927), considered the most important Serbian prose writer of the early twentieth century. Stanković's *Nečista krv* (*Tainted Blood,* 1911) is a powerful psychological novel depicting the clash between old and new in village life. Satire and comedy were best represented by Radoje Domanović (1873–1908)—who excelled in allegorical short stories—and Branislav Nušić (1864–1938), a prolific author of humorous prose and drama.

With the emergence of Yugoslavia after World War I, Serbian literature became part of a new, larger entity.

Margaret H. Beissinger

Further reading
Barac, Antun. *A History of Yugoslav Literature.* Ann Arbor, Michigan, 1976.

Lord, Albert B. *The Singer of Tales.* Cambridge, Massachusetts, 1960.

Wilson, Duncan. *The Life and Times of Vuk Stefanović Karadžić, 1787–1864: Literacy, Literature, and National Independence in Serbia.* Ann Arbor, Michigan, 1970.

See also Đura Jakšić; Vuk Karadžić; Svetozar Marković; Petar II Petrović Njegoš; Romanticism; Serbian Culture; Borisav Stanković; Yugoslav Literature

Serbian Revolt (1804)

see **Black George**

Serbo-Croatian Language

Serbo-Croatian is a South Slavic language spoken in Serbia, Croatia, Bosnia-Hercegovina, and Montenegro. It is divided into three main dialects, based on the word for "what" ("*kaj*," "*ča*," and "*što*"). In northern Croatia the dialect is called kajkavian; čakavian is heard in Istria, though it is disappearing. However, most speakers employ the štokavian dialect, which is composed of two main subdialects, Serbian and Croatian. Pronunciation differences between the subdialects focus on the quality of the vowels *e* and *je* (or *ije*). In most of Serbia, ekavian (otherwise known as Serbian, or the Eastern variant) is dominant; elsewhere, jekavian (or ijekavian) is spoken—that is, Croatian, or the Western variant. A third minor subdialect (ikavian) is heard in parts of Dalmatia. Certain regional distinctions in lexicon also distinguish the subdialects. Finally, Serbian is generally written in Cyrillic, while Croatian is rendered in the Latin alphabet, reflecting historical Eastern Orthodox and Roman Catholic orientations, respectively.

Modern Serbo-Croatian emerged as a standardized literary language in the first half of the nineteenth century. The written language in Serbia had been a hybrid form (known as Slaveno-Serbian) based on Russian Church Slavonic, adopted in the late seventeenth century. Serbian folklorist and language reformer Vuk Karadžić (1787–1864) turned to the štokavian dialect spoken in Hercegovina to establish a vernacular literary language and normalize the orthography. At the same time, concerned by the lack of linguistic unity owing to the diversity of dialects in Croa-

tia, grammarian and leader of the Croatian national revival, Ljudevit Gaj (1809–72), also advocated the adoption of the Hercegovinian štokavian dialect as the literary language. A single standard literary language was thus embraced by both Serbs and Croats.

Throughout the nineteenth and twentieth centuries, the degree to which Serbo-Croatian was seen as a homogeneous language has varied. This has reflected, more than anything else, social and political sentiment. In the fervor of the Pan-Slavic movements of the nineteenth century, as well as following the creation of Yugoslavia after World War I, linguistic similarities were emphasized, thus underscoring national unity. By contrast, conflicts among various ethnic groups have also found expression in professed differences in the language, such as in the years leading to the breakup of Yugoslavia. From a linguistic point of view, however, Serbo-Croatian is a unified language with insignificant differences.

Margaret H. Beissinger

Further reading

Browne, Wayles. "Serbo-Croat," in *The Slavonic Languages,* ed. by Bernard Comrie and Greville G. Corbett. London, 1993.

Ivić, Pavle. *Dijalektologija srpskohrvatskog jezika,* 2d ed. Novi Sad, Yugoslavia, 1985.

Magner, Thomas. *Introduction to the Croatian and Serbian Language,* rev. ed. University Park, Pennsylvania, 1991.

See also Ljudevit Gaj; Vuk Karadžić; Pan-Slavism

Serbo-Turkish War of 1876

Conflict from July to October 1876 between Serbia and Montenegro on one side and the Ottoman Empire on the other. In July 1875 Christians in Turkish-ruled Bosnia and Hercegovina revolted against Ottoman rule. Soon Serbia and Montenegro sent volunteers to aid the insurgents. Strong public sentiment for war developed in Serbia, whose ruler, Prince Milan Obrenović (1854–1901), favored peace but could not control the popular movement. In Russia, Pan-Slavs fostered a public movement to assist the insurgents in the name of Slavic and Orthodox solidarity. However, the Russian government cooperated with European powers seeking a peaceful solution. The dispatch to Belgrade in April 1876 of retired

S Russian general M.G. Cherniaev (1828–98), an ardent Pan-Slav, heightened bellicosity in Serbia. Soon after, Prince Milan reluctantly restored the pro-war cabinet to power and named Cherniaev a Serbian citizen and commander of its eastern armies.

On June 16, 1876, Serbia and Montenegro concluded a military alliance, and on June 30 declared war and invaded Ottoman territory. In a manifesto, Cherniaev appealed for a general Balkan insurrection, hoping Pan-Slav agitation would draw Russia into the war. Roughly five thousand Russian volunteers went to Serbia and some three thousand fought in Cherniaev's army. The Serbian armies of poorly trained peasants and primitive homemade cannon were no match for the Ottomans, and General Cherniaev proved to be an inept strategist. After a truce was concluded on August 23, Cherniaev's army proclaimed Serbia an independent kingdom, but Prince Milan wisely refused the crown. When fighting resumed, Serbo-Russian forces were badly defeated at Djunis on October 29, 1876, and the road to Belgrade lay open. Responding to Prince Milan's desperate appeal to save Serbia, Russia's foreign minister issued an ultimatum threatening war unless the Turks halted, which they did. The war cost Serbia some five thousand dead and temporarily undermined Serbian-Russian relations. However, it helped provoke a Russo-Turkish War in 1877 during which Serbia—allied with Russia—gained territory and independence. The Serbo-Turkish War of 1876 was part of an anti-Turkish Balkan movement for independence that proved partially successful with Russia's aid.

David MacKenzie

Further reading

MacKenzie, David. *The Lion of Tashkent: The Career of General M.G. Cherniaev.* Athens, Georgia, 1974.

———. *The Serbs and Russian Pan-Slavism, 1875–1878.* Ithaca, New York, 1967.

Petrovich, Michael B. *A History of Modern Serbia 1804–1918,* 2 vols., New York, 1976.

Sumner, B. H. *Russia and the Balkans, 1870–1880.* Oxford, 1937.

See also Milan Obrenovic; Pan-Slavism; Russo-Turkish War of 1877–78.

Seton-Watson, Robert W. (1879–1951)

Most knowledgeable and influential of the various British scholars of Eastern Europe during the first half of the twentieth century, who, in many respects, brought Eastern Europe to the attention of the West. Educated at Oxford, Seton-Watson spent postgraduate years at the universities of Berlin, Paris, and Vienna, where he began an active publicist's career in the early 1900s. His books *The Future of Austria-Hungary* (1907) and *Racial Problems in Hungary* (1908) brought him to the attention of both scholars and politicians by virtue of their incisive and uncompromising portrayal of the Habsburg monarchy's dilemma in dealing with its subject nationalities.

With the outbreak of World War I, Seton-Watson became the unofficial contact in London for the various Austro-Hungarian nationality groups attempting to persuade the Allied governments to support their respective independence movements. In 1916 he founded the influential monthly *New Europe,* editing it until its demise in 1920. In its pages he and his colleague Henry W. Steed (1887–1975), foreign editor of the London *Times,* published the views of the nationality leaders, particularly those of Tomáš Masaryk (1850–1937), the postwar Czech president, who was Seton-Watson's close collaborator. Seton-Watson continued his scholarly career after the close of World War I, being appointed Masaryk Professor of Central European History at the University of London (1922), and joint editor of the newly founded *Slavonic Review,* a post he held until 1949. During World War II, he was active in the Political Intelligence branch of the Foreign Office, with particular interests in Eastern European affairs. In 1945 he was made professor of history at Oxford, where he taught until illness forced his retirement in 1949.

Besides the two works mentioned above, Seton-Watson's most important publications were *The Balkans, Italy, and the Adriatic* (1915), an attempt to dissuade the London government from signing the ill-fated Treaty of London, which handed over the upper Adriatic to Italy; *Sarajevo* (1926); *A History of the Czechs and Slovaks* (1943); and *A History of the Roumanians* (1934), the first extensive English language history of Romania and a reply to the revisionists in Hungary. Throughout his life, he was a staunch believer in the necessity of national self-determination, both for international peace and for beneficial evolution of society at large.

Philip J. Adler

Further reading

Seton-Watson, Hugh, ed. *Robert W. Seton-Watson and the Yugoslavs: Correspondence.* London, 1986.

See also London Pact; Tomáš Masaryk

Sèvres, Treaty of (1920)

World War I peace settlement (August 1920) imposed on Turkey by the victorious Allies but never implemented. The treaty's punitive terms stripped Ottoman Turkey of non-Turkish lands. Syria, Palestine, and Mesopotamia became English and French mandates. Independent Armenia and autonomous Kurdistan were recognized. Greece gained Eastern Thrace, the strategic islands of Imbros and Tenedos, and a five-year administration of the Smyrna region, after which a plebiscite would determine that area's political future. Italy retained possession of Rhodes and the Dodecanese, France and Italy received Anatolian spheres of influence, and the Turkish Straits were demilitarized and internationalized. Turkey had to accept a reduced army of fifty thousand and restored capitulations, long a symbol of subservience to the West.

The treaty provoked resentment and sparked Mustafa Kemal's Turkish War for Independence. Kemal's nationalist drive rejected Sèvres, defeated Greek forces near Ankara, and expelled Greek troops from Smyrna. Kemal (1881–1938) also used deft diplomacy, reaching an accord with the Soviet Union that stabilized Anatolia's eastern frontier and negotiating France's and Italy's evacuation from Anatolia in exchange for economic concessions. The Kemalist military and political triumph produced a more favorable peace settlement for Turkey, the Lausanne Treaty (1923).

Theophilus C. Prousis

Further reading

Anderson, M.S. *The Eastern Question, 1774–1923.* London, 1966.

Helmreich, Paul. *From Paris to Sèvres: The Partition of the Ottoman Empire at the Peace Conference of 1919–1920.* Columbus, Ohio, 1974.

Howard, Harry. *The Partition of Turkey: A Diplomatic History, 1913–1923.* Norman, Oklahoma, 1931.

Jelavich, Barbara. *History of the Balkans: Twentieth Century.* New York, 1983.

Shaw, Stanford. *History of the Ottoman Empire and Modern Turkey,* vol. 2. New York, 1977.

See also Capitulations; Lausanne, Treaty of; Paris Peace Conference

Sidor, Karol (1901–53)

Slovak autonomist newspaperman, politician, and diplomat. Sidor was born and raised in Ružomberok, the Slovak Catholic stronghold of Father Andrej Hlinka (1864–1938). When he completed his secondary education, he joined the staff of Hlinka's Slovak People's party's organ, *Slovák,* rising to the position of editor in chief. In 1935 he was elected deputy to the Czechoslovak National Assembly in Prague, in which he continued to clamor for Slovak autonomy on the basis of the Pittsburgh agreement, the 1918 programmatic agreement between Czech and Slovak organizations in the United States that provided for a union of Czechs and Slovaks in which the latter would maintain a significant degree of local autonomy. Sidor was the founder and organizer of the party's uniformed Hlinka Guards. His inspiration was not Hitler (1889–1945) and national socialism or Mussolini (1883–1945) and fascism, however, but Austrian Chancellor Engelbert Dollfuss (1892–1934) and conservative Catholic authoritarianism. In foreign policy, he advocated an orientation toward Catholic Poland. During the Munich crisis, when the breakup of Czechoslovakia was feared, Sidor went to the Polish legation in Prague and suggested Polish annexation of Slovakia. When the breakup of Czechoslovakia did occur in March 1939, Sidor was chairman of the provincial autonomous Slovak government. As such, he firmly rejected the demand of German agents that he declare Slovakia's independence. Consequently, he became persona non grata to Germany and lost the leadership of the Slovak People's Party and of the German-sponsored Slovak state to Father Jozef Tiso (1887–1947). He spent World War II as Slovak minister to the Vatican. After the war, he went into exile and died in Canada. A prolific writer on political matters, Sidor was the author of—among other books—*Andrej Hlinka* (1934); *Slovenská politika* na pôde pražského snemu, 1918–1938 (Slovak Politics in the Prague Parliament, 1918–1938, 1943); Moje poznámky k historickým dňom (My Notes about the Historical Days, 1971), Sidor's notes on the events of March 1939; and Šest rokov pri Vatikáne (Six Years at the Vatican, 1947).

Victor S. Mamatey

Further reading

Hoensch, Jörg N. "The Slovak Republic, 1939–1945," in Victor S. Mamatey and Radomír Luža, eds., A History of the Czechoslovak Republic 1918–1948. Princeton, New Jersey, 1973.

See also Andrej Hlinka; Munich Pact; Pittsburgh Agreement; Slovak Republic; Sudeten Crisis; Jozef Tiso

Sienkiewicz, Henryk (1846–1916)

Polish novelist and short story writer, and first Polish winner of the Nobel Prize in Literature (1905). Sienkiewicz was born in Wola Okrzejska of a country gentry family. He studied history, literature, and philology at the University of Warsaw but left in 1871 without a degree. He began writing critical articles in 1869 showing the influence of positivism, a popular philosophy of the day emphasizing scientific progress, and his first novel, Na marne (In Vain), appeared in 1872, while his first short stories, Stary sluga (The Old Servant) followed in 1875 and Hania (Hannah) in 1878. From 1876 to 1878, he traveled in the United States as a special correspondent of the Gazeta Polska (Polish Gazette) and lived in Anaheim, California, as a member of an unsuccessful socialist colony, before returning to his country via Italy and France. Despite his early liberalism, in his later years Sienkiewicz was an extremely conservative, ardently Roman Catholic follower of the Polish aristocratic tradition.

After his American hegira, he published a number of successful short stories including "Janko muzykant" (Yanko, the Musician, 1879), "Latarnik" (The Lighthouse Keeper, 1882), and "Bartek zwycięzca" (Bartek the Conqueror, 1882). For five years (1882–87), he was co-editor of the daily Słowo (Word), and in 1883 the newspaper began publishing his great trilogy, Ogniem i mieczem (With Fire and Sword, 1884), Potop (The Deluge, 1886), and Pan Wolodyjowski (Mr. Wolodyjowski, 1887–88). Set at the end of the sev-

enteenth century, the trilogy describes in a vibrant epic style the valiant Polish defenses against the invading Cossacks, Swedes, Tartars, and Turks. Turning to contemporary life for his material, Sienkiewicz published Bez dogmatu (Without Dogma) in 1891 and Rodzina Polanieckich (The Polaniecki Family) in 1895. His widely translated Quo Vadis? (Whither Goest Thou? 1896), a historical novel set in Rome during Nero's (37–68) reign, brought him international fame. In 1900, to celebrate his three decades as a writer, he received a small estate near Kielce, where he lived until the outbreak of World War I. During the war, he promoted the cause of Polish independence and organized relief for Polish war victims. He died in Switzerland in 1916, and in 1926 his remains were moved to the Warsaw cathedral.

Edward Bojarski

Further reading

Czerwinski, E.J., ed. Dictionary of Polish Literature. Westport, Connecticut, 1994.
Miłosz, Czesław. The History of Polish Literature. Berkeley, California, 1983.

See also Polish Literature; Positivism

Sikorski, Władysław (1881–1943)

Polish statesman, soldier, and military writer. Born in Galicia, Sikorski headed the War Department of the Polish Supreme National Council during World War I and in 1918 was appointed chief of staff of the Polish army in Galicia and Silesia. In 1920 he commanded the Fifth Army in the Battle of Warsaw, the turning point in the Polish-Soviet War (1919–21) and the outstanding Polish military victory of the modern era. He served the Polish republic in 1921 as chief of the general staff and in 1922 was appointed prime minister after the assassination of President Gabriel Narutowicz (1865–1922). From 1924 to 1925, Sikorski was minister of military affairs, but after the coup d'état of Józef Piłsudski (1887–1935), with whom relations were strained, he was demoted. He spent the next years writing on military history and strategy, and opposing Piłsudski's regime. Following the German invasion in September 1939, he went to Paris, where he was appointed prime minister, minister of war, and commander in chief of the Polish armed forces. After the fall of France in 1940, he led the Polish government-in-exile from London. In 1941 he signed the Polish-Soviet Pact, which allowed the formation of a Polish army in the Soviet Union. Once the mass graves containing the bodies of thousands of Polish officers were discovered at Katyn in 1943, however, relations with Moscow were broken. He died in an airplane crash at Gibraltar on July 4, 1943. First interred in England, Sikorski's remains were returned to Poland and reburied in Wawel Castle in Kraków on September 17, 1993.

James Glapa-Grossklag

Further reading

Korpalska, Walentyna. *Władysław Eugeniusz Sikorski: Biografia polityczna.* Wrocław, 1981.

Sword, Keith, ed. *Sikorski: Soldier and Statesman.* London, 1990.

Terry, Sarah Meiklejohn. *Poland's Place in Europe: General Sikorski and the Origins of the Oder-Neisse Line, 1939–1943.* Princeton, New Jersey, 1983.

See also Battle of Warsaw; Katyn Forest; Józef Piłsudski; Polish-Soviet War; Nazi-Polish War; Warsaw, Battle of

Silesia

Historic industrial region that has been the object of international conflict for centuries. Most of Silesia is in Poland, but a small western area is in Germany, and a coal and industrial area around Ostrava is within the Czech Republic. Silesia is rich in raw materials, on which heavy manufacturing developed by the late eighteenth century. Lower Silesia (on the lower reaches of the Oder River) is an agricultural region with several industrial nodes, notably Wrocław (German, Breslau). Upper Silesia is underlain by a vast coal field, and, drawing especially on this resource, has developed into one of Europe's most important heavy industrial regions. Important urban centers include Katowice and Opole, but numerous smaller towns display a high concentration of urban-industrial development as well as high levels of air and water pollution. Silesia has numerous industrial resources besides coal, including lead and zinc ores.

Originally Polish territory, Silesia was controlled by Bohemia for most of the period between 1335 and 1526. From 1526 to 1742, it was within the Habsburg Empire, but most of Silesia was later incorporated into Prussia, which won and defended it during three mid-eighteenth century wars with Austria. Most of Silesia was in Prussia and then Germany until 1945, when it was reincorporated into Poland, though portions of Upper Silesia were awarded to Poland and smaller areas to Czechoslovakia after a plebiscite in 1921.

Owing to immigration, Silesia for centuries had a mixture of ethnic and religious groups. In most areas Poles and Germans dominated, though Czechs are numerous in several small areas. Germans came as skilled workers beginning in the thirteenth century; many of their descendants fled during World War II, and about three million were expelled after its end. In the 1990s a reemergent German minority began reorganizing politically.

The painful post-Communist economic transition within Poland has yet to be fully felt in Silesia, where large, relatively inefficient state-owned firms continue to operate with heavy subsidies and large workforces.

William H. Berentsen

Further reading

Hartshorne, R. "Geographic and Political Boundaries in Upper Silesia." *Annals of the Association of American Geographers* 25 (1933): 195ff.

Pounds, N.J.G. *An Historical Geography of Europe 1800–1914.* Cambridge, 1985.

See also Environment; Industrialization; Katowice; Ostrava; Silesian Question; Upper Silesian Uprisings; Wrocław

Silesian Question

Diplomatic squabbles and fighting among Poland, Germany, and Czechoslovakia at the end of World War I over the territorial division of the rich and prosperous province of Silesia. Silesia is the site of the largest coal deposits in continental Europe and also contains significant deposits of zinc. It may be divided topographically into Upper and Lower halves along the upper and middle Oder (Polish, Odra) river basin. The area served as a bone of contention and a prize for various states since the early medieval period. Inhabited primarily by Slavs from the ninth century, Silesia passed from Czech to Polish rule in the tenth century. The native Polish dynasty (Piast) encouraged German immigration to the province. In the fourteenth century, Silesia left Polish control and became part of the Holy Roman Empire, where it stayed until

S wrested from the Habsburgs by Frederick the Great (1712–86) in 1748. The new Prussian government developed mining and manufacturing in the area. Silesia remained in German control until the end of World War I. By the middle of the nineteenth century, Lower Silesia had become almost purely German, while Upper Silesia retained a mixed German-Polish population. Generally, most of the urban centers were distinctly German in character, while many agricultural districts were clearly Polish. A sizable portion of the miners and unskilled industrial workers were Poles.

At the end of World War I, each of the neighboring states advanced claims to part or all of the province. It was impossible to draw borders in the area in a manner that would have satisfied both ethnic groups. Upper Silesia proved particularly problematic. After two uprisings (August 1919 and August 1920) by Poles over the territorial settlement of the region reached at Versailles, an intense propaganda campaign by Germans and Poles, and a plebiscite (March 20, 1921), the disposition of the province was resolved, but in a manner acceptable to neither Germans nor Poles. Both countries were deeply committed to gaining as much of the province as possible or at least defending their conationals. In the plebiscite, 479,359 voted for incorporation into Poland, 707,605 for Germany. According to voting eligibility terms, people who had been born in the province but no longer lived there were eligible to vote. The result was that roughly 10,000 such "emigrants" voted from the Polish side, and more than 200,000 on the German. Dissatisfaction with the outcome led to a third, particularly bloody armed uprising on the night of May 2, 1921. Lasting until July, the uprising affected the position of the Allies in determining a final drawing of frontiers. In a compromise signed on May 15, 1922, and supervised by the League of Nations, Polish and German diplomats awarded Poland roughly 30 percent of the total area, 46 percent of the population, but three-quarters of the coal mines and nearly two-thirds of the steelworks. A small area including the city of Cieszyn (German, Teschen; Czech, Těšín) was awarded to Czechoslovakia. The final decision left approximately 625,000 Poles in Germany (Lower Silesia) and 260,000 Germans in Poland (Upper Silesia). Anger over the situation in Silesia festered in Warsaw, Berlin, and Prague throughout the interwar years and contributed to the difficult state of relations among these states.

Peter Wozniak

Further reading

Cienciala, Anna. *From Versailles to Locarno: Keys to Polish Foreign Policy, 1919–25.* Lawrence, Kansas, 1984.

Garlicki, Andrzej. *Pierwsze lata Drugiej Rzeczypospolitej.* Warsaw, 1989.

Temperley, H.W.V., ed. *A History of the Peace Conference of Paris,* vol. 6. London, 1924.

See also League of Nations; Paris Peace Conference; Silesia; Teschen; Upper Silesian Uprisings

Sima, Horia (1903 or 1908–93)

Romanian fascist leader. Born in Făgăraş in Hungarian-ruled Transylvania, Sima studied philosophy at the University of Bucharest under Nae Ionescu (1888–1940) and became an activist in Corneliu Zelea Codreanu's (1899–1938) Legion of the Archangel Michael (Iron Guard), the Romanian nationalist-fascist organization. As early as 1931, Sima was numbered among prominent legionaries and was soon after named leader of the movement in the Banat.

Sima was affiliated with the more extreme, violent wing of the legion and, after the murder of Codreanu and the deaths or imprisonments of other legionary leaders (1938–40), he first fled to Germany and then took over the legion's leadership by discrediting or eliminating more senior candidates.

In June 1940 Sima agreed to collaborate with Carol II (1893–1953), the chief architect of the repression of the legion, briefly serving in the cabinets of Gheorghe Tătărescu (1886–1957) and Ion Gigurtu (1886–1959). Three months later, Sima became deputy prime minister of the National Legionary State, in which General Ion Antonescu (1882–1946) was "Leader." Conflicts between Sima's fascism and Antonescu's authoritarian conservatism led to a failed legionary rebellion (January 21–23, 1941) and Sima was forced into exile in Germany. After the August 1944 overthrow of Antonescu, he formed the Nazi-backed government-in-exile (in Vienna). He remained active in the exile movement for more than three decades and died in Bavaria in 1993.

Walter M. Bacon Jr.

Further reading

Heinen, Armin. *Die Legion "Erzengel Michael" in Rumänien.* Munich, 1986.

Hillgruber, Andreas. *Hitler, König und Marschall Antonescu.* Wiesbaden, Germany, 1954.

Nagy-Talavera, Nicholas M. *The Green Shirts and Others.* Stanford, California, 1970.

Sima, Horia. *Destinée du nationalisme.* Paris, 1951.

See also Ion Antonescu; Carol II; Corneliu Codreanu; Nae Ionescu; Iron Guard; National Legionary State; Right Radicalism; Gheorghe Tătărescu

Simeon II (1937–)

Child tsar of Bulgaria who succeeded his deceased father, Boris III, to the throne in 1943, and was subsequently expelled from Bulgaria by the new Communist government in 1946. Simeon was born on June 16, 1937, son of Boris III of the House of Saxe-Coburg-Gotha (1894–1943) and Tsarina Ioanna (1907–), daughter of King Victor Emmanuel III of Italy (1869–1947). At age six, Simeon became Tsar Simeon II, after his father's fatal heart attack on August 28, 1943. Boris's brother, Prince Kiril (b. 1895), accompanied by two high-ranking Bulgarian officials, immediately instituted a regency and ruled in Simeon's name. In September 1946 the Communist-led government presided over a referendum that abolished the monarchy and proclaimed Bulgaria a people's republic. Within days, the government exiled Simeon and his mother and sister from Bulgaria. The family made its way to Alexandria, Egypt, via Istanbul and in 1951 accepted the invitation of Francisco Franco (1892–1975) to move to Spain. In 1955, at the age of eighteen, Simeon was formally proclaimed Tsar of Bulgaria in accordance with the 1879 Turnovo Constitution. He purchased a mansion in suburban Madrid, began a career in business, and, in 1962, married Margarita Gomez-Acebo (n.d.), a Spanish aristocrat. With the collapse of the Communist government in 1989, Simeon initially vowed not to return to Bulgaria as anything but tsar and advocated the restoration of a constitutional monarchy. In 1996 he did visit Bulgaria, but as a private citizen holding a Bulgarian passport in the name of Simeon Saks-Koburgski.

Gregory L. Bruess

Further reading

Crampton, R. J. *A Short History of Modern Bulgaria.* Cambridge, 1987.

McIntyre, Robert J. *Bulgaria: Politics, Economics and Society.* London, 1988.

See also Boris III; Ioanna; Turnovo Constitution

Singer, Isaac Bashevis (1904–91)

Polish-born novelist, short story writer, journalist, and Nobel laureate in literature in 1978. Singer left his native Poland for America in 1935, following his novelist brother, I.J. Singer (1893–1944). For more than four decades, he published stories and sketches in the New York Yiddish-language daily, *The Forward.* Singer wrote in Yiddish, the language of the destroyed culture that gave rise to his fictional universe; English translations, beginning with Saul Bellow's 1953 rendering of "Gimpel the Fool," offered him a wider readership.

All his novels except *Satan in Goray* (1935) were written in America, and the overwhelming majority of his short stories and novels are set in the lost world of Polish Jewry. Singer is bent on recapturing that world, alternately pursuing it through magical fantasies and old-fashioned realistic narratives. Demonism, madness, bizarre erotic urges, and the strange enthrallment of bewitched lovers are recurrent motifs. Many of his Yiddish readers found these themes shocking and particularly inappropriate for a Jewish writer after the Holocaust. Forbidden sexual desire is also important in the novels, where it is inextricably intertwined with the heroes' search for an authentic Jewish identity located somewhere between the opposing poles of strict orthodox religiosity and militant secularism. Singer's other major works include *The Family Moskat* (1950), *The Magician of Lublin* (1960), *In My Father's Court* (a memoir, 1966), *The Manor* (1967), *Enemies: A Love Story* (1972), and *Shosha* (1978); also the short story collections, *Gimpel the Fool* (1957), *The Spinoza of Market Street* (1961), and *A Crown of Feathers* (1973).

Madeline G. Levine

Further reading

Biltezky, Israel Ch. *God, Jew, Satan in the Works of Isaac Bashevis Singer.* Lanham, Maryland, 1995.

Farrell, Grace, ed. *Critical Essays on Isaac Bashevis Singer.* New York, 1996.

Gibbons, Frances Vargas. *Transgression and Self-Punishment in Isaac Bashevis Singer's Searches.*

Twentieth-Century American Jewish Writers 6. New York, 1995.

Miller, David Neal. *Fear of Fiction: Narrative Strategies in the Works of Isaac Bashevis Singer.* Albany, New York, 1985.

See also Holocaust; Jews; Polish Literature

Škoda

Main machine-tool, defense, and automobile manufacturing company in Czechoslovakia. The Škoda works were founded in Plzeň (Pilsen) in 1859 by the Waldstein family and were taken over by Emil Škoda (1839–1900) in 1869. Škoda remained privately owned until 1899, when it was converted to a joint-stock company with the aid of the Kreditanstalt bank in Vienna. The Škoda works manufactured most of the large guns used by the Austrian army and navy during World War I.

After the war, the Škoda works lost both their ties with Viennese creditors and the orders of the Habsburg government for military equipment. Despite some agitation for nationalizing the firm, Škoda received an infusion of cash from the French firm of Schneider in 1919, which enabled it to continue to expand. The acquisition of a majority of Škoda shares by Schneider was controversial, although supported by the Czechoslovak government and the Živnostenská Banka in Prague.

During the interwar years, the Škoda works expanded the range of products it manufactured by acquiring and merging with other firms, such as the automobile manufacturer Laurin and Klement of Mladá Boleslav in 1925. Škoda also expanded internationally, founding branches or purchasing existing companies in Poland, Yugoslavia, Bulgaria, Romania, Turkey, and other countries. It produced munitions, light tanks and armored personnel carriers, and large field and mountain guns used by the Nazis during World War II. In addition, Škoda was known for its airplanes, locomotives, specialized machinery, automobiles, and street and bridge construction. The firm employed 37,000 workers in 1930, though this figure dropped sharply during the Depression before rising to 32,000 in 1938 and 78,000 in 1945.

With the dismemberment of Czechoslovakia in March 1939, the Škoda works were taken over by the Nazi government and managed as part of Hermann Göring Reichswerke. Škoda was nationalized after the war and renamed the V.I. Lenin works by the Communist government. The firm's automobile manufacturing was privatized after 1989 through an arrangement with Volkswagen of Germany.

Catherine Albrecht

Further reading

"Emil Ritter von Škoda (1839–1900)," in Josef Mentschl and Gustav Otruba, *Österreichische Industrielle und Bankiers.* Vienna, 1965, 158–61.

Hauner, M. "Military Budgets and the Armaments Industry," in M.C. Kaser and E.A. Radice, eds., *The Economic History of Eastern Europe, 1919–1975,* vol. 2, *Interwar Policies, the War and Reconstruction.* London, 1986, 49–116.

Jíša, Václav. *Škodovy závody, 1859–1919.* Prague, 1965.

Jíša, Václav and Alois Vaněk. *Škodovy závody, 1918–1938: Příspěvek k dějinám závodů V.I. Lenina v Plzni.* Prague, 1962.

See also Economic Development in Czechoslovakia; Great Depression; Industrialization; Kreditanstalt

Skopje

Capital and regional center of Vardar Macedonia, and one of the most populous cities of the central Balkans. Situated on the upper Vardar River, Skopje lies near the upper valley of the Morava where the two valleys join to form the Vardar-Morava Corridor, a natural route linking the Danube River to the Mediterranean. It commands access to major lowlands, such as the Polog Depression and Kosovo Polje to the west, and an extensive basin to the south and southeast approaches the valley of the Struma with its access to western Thrace. These situational advantages are in contrast to its location on a major geological fault line that extends northwest to Banja Luka in Bosnia.

Skopje continued to be a major military and administrative center of the Ottoman Empire as the capital of the Kosovo *vilayet* (province) in the late nineteenth century. The city was long a major trading center on Balkan caravan routes from Sofia and Salonika, and its commercial importance increased after 1874 with the completion of the railroad from Salonika to Mitrovica, which passed through Skopje and was later extended to Belgrade in 1888. In this agricultural marketing center, the population grew from 20,000 in 1910 to 87,654 in 1948. Notwithstanding a devastating earthquake in 1963, the development of Skopje as an industrial center after 1945 has led to rapid growth over the past forty years; between 1948 and 1971 the population nearly quadrupled and now exceeds 500,000. In addition to Macedonian Slavs, the population includes substantial numbers of Albanians and Turks as well as Rom (Gypsies) and Vlachs.

Though largely rebuilt as a Western city after a 1963 earthquake, Skopje retains much from the Ottoman period or has restored certain areas, including the old Turkish bazaar with its mosques and open-air markets, the huge caravanserai (Kursumli Ham) and Daut Pasha's Bath, the Skopje Fortress, and the Church of Sveti Spas.

Albert M. Tosches

Further reading

Hamilton, F.E. Ian. *Yugoslavia: Patterns of Economic Activity.* New York, 1968.

Hoffman, George W., ed. *Eastern Europe: Essays in Geographical Problems.* New York, 1970.

Letcher, Piers. *Yugoslavia: Mountain Walks and Historical Sites.* Geneva, 1989.

Pounds, Norman J.G. *Eastern Europe.* Chicago, 1969.

See also Gypsies; Macedonia; Vlachs

Skupština

Serbian and Yugoslav assembly or parliament. The historical roots of the Skupština were found in the medieval Serbian state and peasant clan assemblies, which came to an end under Turkish rule. Irregular, popular gatherings recommenced when Serbia began its revolt in 1804. The institutionalization of the Skupština occurred gradually and with many reversals over the course of the nineteenth century. In the power struggle among the prince, the state council, and the popular assembly, the latter was consistently the weakest. One notable exception was the St. Andrew's Assembly of 1858, which removed both the prince and the council. Parliamentary norms such as annual sessions, ministerial responsibility to parliament, the power of the purse, and parliamentary immunity were not fully secured in the nineteenth century. The constitution of 1888 represented a victory for parliamentary government and made Serbia one of the most democratic states in Europe. Although the 1890s found the assembly again subservient to the crown, the constitution of 1903 restored the Skupština as the representative of the sovereign will of the people. In the decade before World War I, parliamentary supremacy was an accomplished fact in Serbia.

With the creation of Yugoslavia in 1918, the Skupština in Belgrade became the seat of the national parliament. The 1921 Vidovdan Constitution created a unicameral parliament of 315 deputies elected for a four-year term on the basis of proportional representation. The parliamentary era of interwar Yugoslavia (December 1918 to December 1928) was a period of unsuccessful governance. Skupština sessions witnessed obstructionist party tactics, political paralysis, boycotts, inflammatory rhetoric, personal insults, and murder. No single Skupština survived its entire four-year mandate. In response to the political chaos, King Alexander (1888–1934) suspended the constitution, dismissed parliament, and established a royal dictatorship in 1929. The subsequent Alexandrine Constitution of 1931 (which lasted until World War II) substantially downgraded the authority of the Skupština and turned Yugoslavia into a constitutional monarchy.

During the Communist era, the Skupština was organizationally restructured with each constitutional change. Its final form had two houses—the Federal Chamber and the Chamber of Republics and Provinces—the latter of which was more politically significant. By 1974, however, the balance of power had shifted to political bodies in the republics and provinces. In preparation for multiparty elections in 1990, the Serbian Socialist Party created a republican Skupština with one house and 250 seats. The electoral method required the winning candidate to receive a majority vote within two rounds.

Robert Hislope

Further reading

Burg, Steven L. *Conflict and Cohesion in Socialist Yugoslavia: Political Decision Making since 1966.* Princeton, New Jersey, 1983.

Dragnich, Alex N. *The Development of Parliamentary Government in Serbia.* New York, 1978.

———. *The First Yugoslavia: Search for a Viable Political System.* Stanford, California, 1983.

Rothschild, Joseph. *East Central Europe between the Two World Wars.* Seattle, Washington, 1974.

Seroka, Jim and Radoš Smiljković. *Political Organizations in Socialist Yugoslavia.* Durham, North Carolina, 1986.

See also Alexander I Karadjordjević; Vidovdan Constitution

Škvorecký, Josef (1924–)

Czech writer. Škvorecký's witty semiautobiographical novels on political and cultural developments during his life in Czechoslovakia and, after 1969, in North America made him popular both at home and abroad. His first novel, *Zbabělci* (*The Cowards,* 1948), had to wait ten years to be published in Prague; it would be quickly banned. The major novel concerning the events surrounding the Soviet-led invasion that ended the Prague Spring, the short-lived period of reform in 1968, *Mirákl* (*The Miracle Game,* 1972), continued the author's sad and skeptical deflation of historical legends.

While in Prague, Škvorecký studied English and American literature, which he taught later, as a Canadian citizen, at the University of Toronto. He also lectured on his other loves—film and creative writing. With his wife, Zdena Salivarová (1933–), Škvorecký founded Sixty-Eight Publishers in Toronto, and helped to publish hundreds of books by Czechoslovak writers who could not be published in their own country.

Škvorecký's other works include *The Bass Saxophone* (1977), *Miss Silver's Past* (1980), *The Republic of Whores* (in Czech, 1980; in English, 1993), *The End of the Nylon Age* (1967), *Dvořák in Love* (1986), a personal history of Czechoslovak film (*All the Bright Young Men and Women* [1971]), as well as a series of detective stories and numerous literary essays and reviews.

Peter Hruby

Further reading

Jungman, Milan. *O Josefu Škvoreckém.* Prague, 1993.

Solecki, Sam, ed. *The Achievement of Josef Škvorecký.* Toronto, 1994.

———. *Prague Blues: The Fiction of Josef Škvorecký.* Toronto, 1990.

Trensky, Paul. *The Fiction of Josef Škvorecký.* Boston, 1991.

See also Cinema; Czech Literature; Prague Spring

Slánský, Rudolf Salzmann (1901–52)

One of the founders of the Czechoslovak Communist Party and the most prominent Czechoslovak "national Communist" to be purged on Stalin's (1879–1953) orders. Slánský was born in Pilsen, Bohemia, to a Czech-Jewish middle-class family. After World War I, he started a business career in Prague and joined the new Czechoslovak Communist Party in 1921. He rose rapidly in the party's hierarchy, from editor of its newspaper, *Rudé Právo* (*Red Right*), to member of its presidium and politburo in 1929, to Communist deputy in the Czechoslovak National Assembly from 1935 to 1937. He spent World War II directing the Czech broadcasts of Radio Moscow and helping to organize Czechoslovak military units and partisan groups. In 1944 he was sent to assist the unsuccessful Slovak National Uprising against the fascists.

After the war, Slánský became secretary general of the Czechoslovak Communist Party. In February 1948 he helped execute the bloodless Communist seizure of power, becoming a vice premier in the new government. In November 1951, however, he was arrested and charged with organizing a "Titoist" and "Zionist" conspiracy to overthrow the Communist regime with British and American assistance. After a year of physical and psychological mistreatment, he and his codefendants admitted their guilt in a garish show trial and were sentenced to death. Slánský was hanged on December 3, 1952, his body cremated, and the ashes scattered on an icy winter road. In the 1960s he was exonerated of his alleged crimes, legally rehabilitated, and restored to Czechoslovak citizenship.

Joseph Frederick Zacek

Further reading

Kaplan, Karel. *Report on the Murder of the General Secretary.* London, 1990.

Pelikán, Jiří, ed. *The Czechoslovak Political Trials, 1950–1954.* Stanford, California, 1970.

Slánská, Josefa. *Report on My Husband.* New York, 1969.

See also Communist Party of Czechoslovakia; Stalin

Slaveikov, Petko Rachov (1827–95)

Bulgarian teacher and writer. Born in a craftsman's home in Turnovo, Slaveikov took his mother's family name, Slaveiski. After studying at Turnovo, Drianovo, Triavna, and the Preobrazhenski Monastery, he took a job as teacher in Turnovo in 1843. In 1864 Slaveikov moved to Constantinople and worked as a translator of the Bible with Protestant missionaries. He continued to teach as well as serve as the editor of *Gaida* (*Bagpipe,* 1863–67), *Makedoniia* (*Macedonia,* 1866–72), *Pchelitsa* (*Bee,* 1871), and *Ruzhitsa* (*Hollyhock,* 1871), among others. He also participated in the publication of nearly every Bulgarian newspaper and magazine in Constantinople.

In 1874 Slaveikov moved to Adrianople and then to Stara Zagora, where he supported himself by teaching. He was arrested during the April Uprising, the failed 1876 revolt in Bulgaria, but was later released. During the Russo-Turkish War of 1877–78, he served as a translator for the Russian army and was a member of a reconnaissance detachment. After the liberation of Bulgaria, he led the Liberal Party and began publication of a new newspaper, *Tselokupna Bûlgariia* (*All Bulgaria*). He was named minister of education in 1880 and then minister of internal affairs from 1880 to 1881. Between 1880 and 1888, he produced five more newspapers.

Slaveikov's literary contributions were prodigious. He wrote poetry, romantic fiction, and satire. He also contributed to the development of Bulgarian folklore and the development of literature for children.

Mari A. Firkatian

Further reading

Baeva, Sonia. *Petko Slaveikov: Zhivot i tvorchestvo, 1827–1870.* Sofia, 1968.

Gulubov, K. *Petko Slaveikov, zhivot, deinost, tvorchestvo.* Sofia, 1970.

Kosev, Dimitur. *Petko Rachev Slaveikov: Obshtestvena i politicheska deinost.* Sofia, 1996.

Slaveikova, Sv. *Petko R. Slaveikov, biografichen ocherk.* Sofia, 1959.

Topalov, K. *P.R. Slaveikov, zhivot i tvorchestvo.* Sofia, 1979.

See also April Uprising; Bulgarian Literature; Folklore; Russo-Turkish War of 1877–78

Slavic Languages

The Slavic ("Slavonic" in British usage) languages are a branch of the Indo-European family and within it are related most closely to the Baltic languages, Lithuanian and Latvian. On the basis of shared innovations and archaisms, Slavic itself divides into three groups: East, South, and West, although some features are distributed along other lines, such as geographically central versus geographically peripheral. The literary languages in each group, with number of speakers, are East: Russian (150 million), Ukrainian (45 million), and Belorussian (9 million); South: Bulgarian (9 million), Macedonian (2 million), Serbo-Croatian (17 million), and Slovenian (2 million); West: Slovak (5 million), Czech (10 million), Upper and Lower Sorbian (in eastern Germany, with perhaps only 60,000 remaining, almost all bilingual with German), and Polish (35 million). Serbo-Croatian, only five years ago a single language with at least three variants (Serbian, Croatian, and Bosnian) showing no greater difference from one another than American, Australian, and British English, is being split apart as a result of deliberate nationalistic efforts to produce three separate languages from the variants.

Slavic languages with predominantly Catholic speakers (Polish, Czech, Slovak, Slovenian, Croatian) use the Latin alphabet with diacritic signs or letter combinations to render certain sounds (such as č or cz to render English "ch"). The Cyrillic alphabet, which in general has a separate letter for each sound, is used where the population is primarily Orthodox: Serbian, Macedonian, Bulgarian, Ukrainian, Belorussian, and Russian.

The Slavic languages in general are highly inflected, with three genders and six or seven case forms for nouns, adjectives, and pronouns. Nouns have at least three different types of declension, and in some languages more. Verbs are inflected for person and number (also for gender in certain forms in some Slavic languages). They show aspect (which says something about the nature of the action, such as completed or iterative) as well as tense. The details of aspect and the number and use of tenses vary from language to language, but the principles are essentially the same in all Slavic languages.

Slavic writing began in the second half of the ninth century A.D. with the mission of Saints Cyril (d. 869) and Methodius (d. 884) to Moravia; the earliest surviving manuscripts (tenth and eleventh centuries, primarily representing a Bulgarian dialect of Common Slavic) make up the corpus of

Old Church Slavonic. Church Slavonic continued to serve as a common literary language among the Orthodox Slavs throughout the Middle Ages.

In connection with romanticism and nationalism, many of the modern Slavic literary languages developed in the nineteenth century: Belorussian, Bulgarian, Serbo-Croatian, Slovak, Slovenian, and Ukrainian. In some cases this involved rejecting a more archaic written language that had become very different from the spoken version. Czech was revived in the same century, but the literary language was frozen into a form dating from the late sixteenth century, which has resulted in a great difference between the modern colloquial Czech language and the formal literary language. Although there were attempts to use Macedonian dialects in writing in the nineteenth century, it took form as a literary language only in the twentieth century. Polish and Russian both evolved without such a sharp break, reaching their modern form in the first part of the nineteenth century.

The Slavic languages have had great influence on one another at various times, especially in the area of vocabulary, where much conscious borrowing took place in the nineteenth century as a part of building the modern literary languages. French provided not only vocabulary but also models for syntactic constructions and word formation. German has also had a very strong influence, particularly on Czech and Slovenian. English has of course become the most influential language in recent times.

Charles E. Gribble

Further reading

Comrie, Bernard and Greville G. Corbett, eds. *The Slavonic Languages.* London, 1993.
Schenker, Alexander M. and Edward Stankiewicz, eds. *The Slavic Literary Languages,* New Haven, Connecticut, 1980.

See also Bulgarian Language; Czech Language; Macedonian Language; Nationalism; Polish Language; Romanticism; Serbo-Croatian Language; Slovak Language; Slovene Language

Slavonia

Region in northeast Croatia. Slavonia is located east of Zagreb and is bounded by the Drava River in the north and the Sava River in the south. Vojvodina, the northern area of Yugoslavia, forms its eastern border. Bosnia-Hercegovina lies to the south, across the Sava River. Forming part of the Pannonian (Hungarian) Plain, Slavonia is characterized by its fertile and gently rolling terrain. The rich soil provides the region with a variety of agricultural products, including grain and potatoes. The area is also noted for its plush forests and renowned mineral springs. The flatlands of central Slavonia give way to the Kozara Mountains across the border to the south in Bosnia-Hercegovina.

Slavonia is the most densely populated region in Croatia. Osijek, on the Drava River, is the largest city in the region. Vinkovci and Vukovar, near the Yugoslav border, are its other major cities. Although these cities had a majority Croat population in 1991, they were flanked by dozens of villages with a predominantly Serbian population. Throughout the region, the majority of people are Croatian, with Serbs making up about one-fourth of the total population. The latter reside primarily in eastern Slavonia, although they also form pockets in the central part of the region. There are also Hungarian minorities in the area. The large German community of eastern Slavonia had either evacuated or were expelled shortly after World War II.

William B. Kory

Further reading

Bertić, Ivan. *Veliki geografski atlas Jugoslavije.* Zagreb, 1987.

Slavophilism

Major ideology that flourished in Russia in the mid-nineteenth century. Its spokesmen, an informal group of intellectuals, mostly writers and philosophers residing in Moscow, included Aleksei Khomiakov (1804–60), Konstantin (1817–60) and Ivan (1823–86) Aksakov, Ivan (1806–56) and Piotr (1808–56) Kireyevskii, and Yurii Samarin (1819–76). The Slavophiles were diametrically opposed to the rival group of so-called Westernizers, such as Aleksandr Herzen (1812–70), who criticized Russia's backwardness and advocated rapid, wholesale imitation of the civilization of Western Europe. Instead, they saw Russia as politically, religiously, culturally, and morally superior to the West (which they considered corrupt, anarchic, and disintegrating). Drawing on contemporary romantic and idealistic currents, they denounced Western materialism, rationalism, and individualism and eulogized Russia's rural society, autocratic government, and Orthodox Christian church. They believed that these embodied exemplary qualities once characteristic of all the Slavs but had been preserved best by the Russians in such traditional institutions as the *zemsky sobor* (assembly) and the *mir* (communal organization). These qualities, such as love, peace, harmony, simplicity, and voluntary cooperation, were clustered about the central Slavophile tenet, Khomiakov's *sobornost* (organic integration, unity in multiplicity). The Slavophiles believed that Russia's historic mission was to reassimilate all the scattered Slavic peoples into a single community under Russian rule, and then to lead them in bringing the redemptive Slavic virtues to a spiritually bankrupt West. Though politically conservative and religiously Orthodox, the Slavophiles were not merely uncritical apologists for the Russian status quo; for example, they advocated freedom of conscience, speech, and the press, and opposed the death penalty and serfdom. Many of the Slavophile beliefs found their way into Pan-Slavism and other all-Slavic movements and programs that originated elsewhere.

Joseph Frederick Zacek

Further reading

Riasanovsky, Nicholas V. *Russia and the West in the Teaching of the Slavophiles: A Study of Romantic Ideology.* Cambridge, Massachusetts, 1952.

Walicki, Andrzej. *The Slavophile Controversy: History of a Conservative Utopia in Nineteenth-Century Russian Thought.* Oxford, 1975.

See also Orthodoxy; Pan-Slavism; Romanticism

Slavs

Largest ethnic and linguistic group in Europe. The Slavs reside chiefly in east central, eastern, and southeastern Europe, and north Asia to the Pacific Ocean. They are generally subdivided into West (Czechs, Poles, Slovaks), East (Belarusians, Russians, Ukrainians), and South (Bosnians, Bulgarians, Croats, Macedonians, Montenegrins, Serbs, Slovenes) Slavs; they speak distinct but related Slavic languages, belonging to the Indo-European family.

From a central location north of the great Pripet Marshes, the Slavs migrated in great numbers westward and southward into the present-day Czech Republic and Slovakia, and the Balkan Peninsula, and east and north along the Dnieper River between the fifth and eighth centuries. They originally spoke a common language, Proto-Slavic, but geographic distances now separating Slavic tribes produced increasing cultural and linguistic differentiation among them. The Slavs' first state organizations emerged after these migrations. Their medieval states included Bohemia, Moravia, Poland, Kievan Rus', Bosnia, Bulgaria, Croatia, and Serbia.

In the ninth and tenth centuries the Slavs converted to Christianity. The rulers of Bulgaria, Serbia, and Kiev, for example, adopted the Byzantine rite from Constantinople, while those of Croatia, Bohemia, and Poland accepted the Latin rite from Rome. These different religious orientations led to the adoption of the Glagolithic alphabet (later replaced by the Cyrillic) by the Byzantine rite Slavs and the Latin alphabet by the Latin rite Slavs. The Church Schism of 1054 created a formal denominational divide in eastern Europe and subsequently produced even more profound cultural and political divisions among the Slavs.

Between 1237 and 1240, the thriving Kievan state was destroyed by the Mongols, and the Eastern Slavs fell under their domination for about two centuries. By the 1460s, the Balkan Peninsula was captured by the Ottoman Turks, beginning Ottoman control over the Balkan Slavs for approximately five centuries. The Turks introduced Islam into the Balkans, further complicating the religious and cultural landscape there. The Mongols and the Ottomans contributed to separating those Slavs they dominated from western European intellectual and cultural movements such as the Renaissance and humanism. The Czechs and Poles, however, were exposed to these currents. By 1795, the Polish-Lithuanian Commonwealth, a dominant state in eastern Europe in the sixteenth and early seventeenth centuries, was itself partitioned by Russia, Prussia, and Austria, all of which grew to political and military prominence in the seventeenth and eighteenth centuries. Thus, by the late eighteenth century, the Slavs lived in one of these three empires or in the Ottoman Empire. Of these large, multinational empires, only Russia was a Slavic state. By now, too, economic contacts and migrations had interspersed large numbers of Germans and Jews among the Slavs and smaller numbers of Greeks, Tatars, Armenians, and others.

During the last two centuries, the drive for political sovereignty and economic progress initiated by the French and Industrial Revolutions has most shaped the Slavs. In the nineteenth century minority Slavic and non-Slavic (such as Lithuanians, Magyars, and Romanians) peoples in the four eastern European empires redefined themselves along cultural lines and developed strong national movements to emancipate themselves from these empires. Pan-Slavism, a mid-nineteenth century intellectual movement calling for Slavs to unite under Russia, had little practical appeal. With the collapse of the eastern European empires in the wake of World War I, independent Slavic and non-Slavic states arose in eastern Europe; and the 1917 Bolshevik Revolution transformed imperial Russia into the Soviet Union. From 1917 (1944–45 for the eastern European states) to the collapse of communism between 1989 and 1991, most non-Russian Slavs were under direct or implicit Soviet political and military control. During this time, each Slavic nation, including the Russians, continued its self-definition in relation to ethnic minorities living in its midst, particularly Jews; neighboring Slavic and non-Slavic nations and states; and western European nations and states, especially Germany. Violence and persecution (such as the post–World War I civil wars, World War II, and the Stalinist purges and Communist Party repressions) frequently accompanied these processes of definition.

Konrad Sadkowski

Further reading

Dvornik, Francis. *The Slavs in European History and Civilization.* New Brunswick, New Jersey, 1962.

Longworth, Philip. *The Making of Eastern Europe.* New York, 1994.

Obolensky, Dimitri. *The Byzantine Commonwealth: Eastern Europe, 500–1453.* New York, 1971.

Riasanovsky, Nicholas V. *A History of Russia,* 5th ed. New York, 1993.

Wandycz, Piotr S. *The Price of Freedom: A History of East-Central Europe from the Middle Ages to the Present.* New York, 1991.

See also Islam; Nationalism; Pan-Slavism; Slavic Languages

Slovak Culture

Although predominantly Roman Catholic, the Slovak populace has historically included a significant Protestant, primarily Lutheran, minority. This Roman Catholicism and Protestantism links Slovaks to western European society and distinguishes them from Orthodox Christian Slavs. Literary Slovak employs the Latin alphabet. A cultural minority in a multinational empire, Slovaks cultivated a folk culture based on local traditions and honeycombed with regional variations. The Slovak language has three distinct dialects (western, central, and eastern). Religion, folk traditions, and a historical struggle to establish a national identity have fashioned Slovak culture.

The development of Slovak culture and its unique characteristics reflect a millennium of Hungarian domination. A people loosely identified by their Slavic language, Slovaks constructed local cultures rooted in a peasant past, grounded in mystic traditions, and affixed to the Christian calendar. Diverse folk customs celebrated local historical events or patron saints. Distinct folk costumes could indicate locale, marital status, and religion. Folk handicrafts, music, and cuisine also reflected regional variations characteristic of Slovak culture. Without a nationally conscious intelligentsia, Slovak high culture lagged until the early nineteenth century. Threats of cultural annihilation through Magyarization, a policy of forced assimilation, led to standardizing the central Slovak dialect as the literary language. This codification, achieved by 1852, established Slovak as a linguistically distinct language. Competing and lasting ideas about Slovak national identity emerged during the early nineteenth century Slovak cultural awakening. Literary works promoted a Slavic identity and advanced the "Czechoslovak" idea that linguistically and culturally Slovaks and Czechs constituted one people. An opposing national theme affirmed Slovak linguistic and cultural distinctiveness and sought to legitimize this claim, in part, by creating a national past. Events and personages of the ninth century—Cyril (d. 869) and Methodius (d. 884) and their Christianization of the Slavs; the Great Moravian Empire and its last ruler, Svätopluk (d. 894)—were introduced both as Slovak history and as symbols of Slovak cultural distinctiveness.

Magyarization retarded subsequent Slovak literary, cultural, and educational developments. While Slovak belles lettres were suppressed, Slovak folk arts and traditions in all their regional variations continued to flourish. The historic tension between the "Czechoslovak" idea and Slovak cultural distinctiveness surfaced after the creation of Czechoslovakia and took on political overtones that generated a renewed struggle for a Slovak national identity. The twentieth century witnessed a reassertion of the ninth-century symbols of Slovakia's past, even as traditional folk arts, customs, and themes filtered into Slovak high culture.

Communist ideology had a stultifying effect on Slovak culture and cultural development. With a few notable exceptions, Slovak literary and artistic works reflected accepted ideological themes. The Slovak folk heritage, however, experienced a reinvigoration during the latter decades of Communist rule. Slovak traditional folk arts and handicrafts thrived as they reinforced the traditionally unique characteristics of Slovak culture. With Slovak independence, the historical trend of identifying with Western culture while reinforcing a folk heritage and asserting a distinct Slovak national identity continues.

June Granatir Alexander

Further reading

Garver, Bruce. "The Czechoslovak Tradition," in *Czechoslovakia: The Heritage of Ages Past, Essays in Memory of Josef Korbel*, ed. by Hans Brisch and Ivan Volgyes. Boulder, Colorado, 1979, 25–56.

Mistrík, Jozef, comp. *Slovakistické Štúdie*. Martin, Slovakia, 1985.

Seton-Watson, R.W., ed. *Slovakia Then and Now: A Political Survey.* London, 1931.

Slovensko Dejiny. Bratislava, 1978.

See also Czech and Slovak Art; Folklife; Folklore; Folk Music; Magyarization; Matica slovenská; Slovak Language; Slovak League of America; Slovak Literature; Slovak Republic, Birth of the; Ľudovít V. Štúr

Slovak Émigrés

Slovakia has had two waves of émigrés in the last century. The first group fled their homeland in the Kingdom of Hungary before World War I because they opposed the Magyarization policies of the government. The second cohort appeared in the West after World War II ended the Slovaks' first attempt at national independence (1939–45). Both groups championed the right of the Slovaks to self-determination.

Among the Slovak political émigrés who followed about half a million of their working-class compatriots to the United States before 1914, two stand out. Peter V. Rovnianek (1867–1933) was expelled from the Budapest Roman Catholic seminary in 1887 for his Slovak nationalism and emigrated to the United States in 1888. There he founded the fraternal National Slovak Society (1890) and cofounded the political Slovak League of America (1907), as well as half a dozen Slovak American newspapers. Because of business failures, he died penniless in California. A younger contemporary of Rovnianek, Štefan Osuský (1889–1974), was expelled from the Bratislava gymnasium in 1906 for his Slovak nationalism and quickly made his way to Chicago. He was partly responsible for the 1915 Cleveland Agreement between American Czechs and Slovaks regarding the creation of the new Czecho-Slovak Republic, and in 1916 he was sent to Europe as one of two delegates of the Slovak League to participate in the liberation movement. After the war he was named Czechoslovak minister to France. During World War II, he moved back to the United States, where he died in exile.

After World War II, a second major wave of political émigrés left Slovakia. The most important was Karol Sidor (1901–53), former Slovak ambassador to the Vatican, who founded the Slovak National Council Abroad in 1948 to carry on the struggle for Slovak independence, but died in Montreal before his dream came true. Next in importance was Ferdinand Ďurčanský (1906–74), former minister of foreign affairs of the Slovak Republic. Ďurčanský fled into exile in 1945 and quickly founded the Slovak Action Committee, a rival to Sidor's SNCA. He was a cofounder of the Slovak World Congress in 1970 but died in Munich shortly thereafter. Meanwhile, the former editor in chief of the daily *Slovák,* the official organ of the ruling Slovak's People's Party in the Slovak Republic, Jozef Paučo (1914–75), also went into exile in 1945. He eventually made his way to the United States, where he became executive secretary of the Slovak League of America and editor of the weekly *Slovák v Amerike* (*The Slovak in America*) until his death in Middletown, Pennsylvania in 1975.

Three other political émigrés also deserve mention. After the war, Jozef Kirschbaum (1913–), former secretary-general of the Slovak People's Party in 1940 and subsequently chargé d'affaires

S for the Slovak Republic in Switzerland, emigrated to Canada and, among academic and other pursuits, became a cofounder of the Slovak World Congress. In 1948 Kirschbaum was joined in exile by Jozef Mikuš (1909–), former chargé d'affaires of the Slovak Republic in Spain, who had been persecuted by the postwar Czechoslovak government. Mikuš made his way to Washington, D.C., in 1952, where he became chief of the press office of the Slovak League of America. Also a cofounder of the Slovak World Congress, Mikuš, like Kirschbaum, published many books and articles championing the right of the Slovaks to their national independence. In 1961 Jozef Staško (1917–) joined Kirschbaum and Mikuš in exile. A former member of the postwar Czechoslovak parliament, he was the only one who voted against the confirmation of Edvard Beneš (1884–1948) as postwar president of Czechoslovakia and spent six years in jail as a result. In 1961 Staško managed to escape to the West and settled in New York City, where he worked as a librarian and political activist.

M. Mark Stolarik

Further reading

Encyklopédia slovenska, 6 vols. Bratislava, 1977–82.
Literárny almanach Slováka v Amerika, 1967. Middletown, Pennsylvania, 1966, 115–249.
Paučo, Jozef, *Slovenskí prekopníci v Amerike.* Cleveland, Ohio, 1972.

See also Edvard Beneš, Magyarization; Karol Sidor; Slovak League of America; Slovak Republic

Slovakia (Geography)

Eastern province of Czechoslovakia and, since 1992, the Slovak Republic. Slovakia is a mountainous and primarily rural region. The High Tatras of northern Slovakia, with peaks over 8,500 feet (2,590 m) high, and the Low Tatras of central Slovakia form part of the Carpathians. The southern margins of the region are part of the Great Hungarian Plain. The complex physiography has proven to be a transportation barrier within Slovakia itself, and between Slovakia and the Czech lands.

The Slavic peoples of Slovakia speak a language closely related to Czech and have a long history of ties with Bohemia and Moravia. As early as the ninth century, Slovakia was part of the Great Moravian Empire. During the tenth century, Slovakia came under Hungarian rule and remained so until 1918, when the Slovaks were once again joined with the Bohemians and Moravians to form Czechoslovakia.

The relatively thin and scattered population of Slovakia (some five million) live mainly in valleys separated by ridges that run to the Hungarian Plain. The Danube River, which forms part of the southern boundary between Slovakia and Hungary, and the Váh River (Slovakia's longest), which cuts through the north central part of the country, are the two most widely known. However, many lesser rivers cut through the mountains.

Bratislava is the capital and largest city of Slovakia. It is located in the southwest corner of the country, across the Danube River from Vienna; only 35 miles (58.5 km) separate the two cities. Bratislava, known to Hungarians as Pozsony (having served as Hungary's capital from 1536 to 1784) and as Pressburg to Germans, has been inhabited since 400 B.C. Slavs migrated to the city in the fifth and sixth centuries. Bratislava experienced rapid growth after World War II, as exemplified by the Communist-style architecture that dominates the cityscape.

Slovakia initially supplied industrial Bohemia with raw materials and food supplies, but the Communist years brought a very different economic role to the country. Czechoslovak planning policy geared new industrial development away from Bohemia in favor of Slovakia in an attempt to balance economic development. Heavy industries such as metallurgy and armaments eventually dominated the Slovak economy.

Russell L. Ivy

Further reading

Berentsen, William, ed. *Europe in the 1990s: A Geographical Analysis,* 7th ed. Chicago, 1997.
Pounds, Norman J.G. *Eastern Europe.* Chicago, 1969.
Rugg, Dean. *Eastern Europe.* London, 1985.
UNIDO. *Czechoslovakia: Industrial Transformation and Regeneration.* Oxford, 1992.

See also Bratislava; Carpathian Mountains; Great Hungarian Plain; Industrialization; Tatra Mountains

Slovak Language

One of the Western Slavic languages, now spoken by five million people in the territory of the Slovak Republic. Typologically, it is very similar to

Czech, with which it has had a long common development. Slovak is a national language, existing as a literary, or standard speech (*spisovná reč*), and dialects. Standard Slovak, codified in grammar and lexicon, and used in literature, mass media, schools, and wherever formal speech is expected, exists also in its colloquial form (*hovorová slovenčina*), which is defined more loosely as a spoken norm for everyday use. Geographically, three dialects still exist—western, central, and eastern—although the differences between them are slowly disappearing and an interdialect is coming into existence.

In the ninth and the beginning of the tenth centuries, Slovakia shared its history with Bohemia and Moravia. The missionaries Cyril (d. 869) and Methodius (d. 884) had a significant impact on the region, especially linguistically. The Old Slavonic language, together with the Cyrillic script, played an important part in the rise of Slovak.

At the end of the tenth century, Slovakia became a territory of Hungary, and the Slovak language, separated from Czech, remained for centuries in spoken form only, while Latin took over the role of the region's literary language. In the fifteenth century Czech returned to Slovakia as the speech of people of the Protestant, evangelic church. During the following two centuries, however, Czech was often "Slovakized." The nineteenth century witnessed a significant move toward establishing a genuine Slovak literary language. In the development of its central dialect, Slovak had to contend with Hungarian, which authorities used in all official transactions. Only with the end of World War I and the rise of Czechoslovakia was the Slovak language able to develop unimpeded.

The phonology of standard Slovak is represented by five short simple vocalic phonemes and their long counterparts, by four diphthongs (and the rather specific [uo]), and twenty-six consonants. Using the modern Latin alphabet, its written form is able to recall all the phonemes with the maximum possible correspondence between phonemes and graphemes. Its morphology, although less robust than that of Czech, displays a six-case declension and a five-class conjugation, indicating such grammatical categories as gender, number, person, tense, aspect, voice, and mood. Its predominant synthetic character allows for a relatively loose word order; modifications of meaning are expressed within the words themselves. Many derivational morphemes add to the possibility of extending its vocabulary.

Stanislav Kavka

Further reading

Blanár, V. and M. Majtan. *Historický slovník slovenského jazyka*. Bratislava, 1991.

Krajčovič, R. *Dějiny spisovnej slovenčiny*. Bratislava, 1992.

———. *Vyvin slovenského jazyka a dialektologia*. Bratislava, 1988.

Oravec, J. *Súčasný slovenský spisovný jazyk: Morfologia*. Bratislava, 1987.

Pauliny, E. *Slovenská gramatika*. Bratislava, 1981.

Pravidlá slovenského pravopisu. Bratislava, 1991.

Slovník slovenského jazyka. Bratislava, 1959.

See also Czech Language

Slovak League of America

A political/cultural organization comprising affiliated Slovak societies and Americans of Slovak ancestry. Organized in 1907, the league resulted from a meeting of Slovak journalists and fraternal society representatives in Pittsburgh. Concerned primarily with politics in the Slovak homeland, the league aimed to expose and counter the Hungarian government's Magyarization policies. It also provided financial assistance to Slovak nationalists and newspapers in Hungary. During World War I, it supported the creation of a unified, independent Czech and Slovak nation. In October 1915 the Slovak League and the Bohemian National Alliance jointly issued the Cleveland Agreement, calling for a federal state with autonomy for Slovakia. In May 1918 league officials convinced Tomáš Masaryk (1850–1937), Czech philosopher and statesman, to draft and sign the Pittsburgh Agreement, which called for an independent Czech and Slovak state in which the Slovaks would have an independent administration, diet, and courts. The league opposed Czechoslovakia's 1920 centrist constitution. During the 1920s and 1930s, it backed Andrej Hlinka's (1864–1938) Peoples Party and platform, demanding implementation of the Pittsburgh Agreement. The league endorsed the Slovak Republic (1939–1945), created by the Nazi German dismemberment of Czechoslovakia, and opposed the reestablishment of a unified Czechoslovakia. After World War II, the league defended the wartime Slovak Republic and officially adopted

S the policy that Slovakia should become an independent nation, a stand it maintained until Slovak independence in 1993.

League positions regarding the Slovak homeland divided Slovak Americans, and, consequently, Protestant and nondenominational societies withdrew their affiliation. Thus, while the Slovak League ostensibly remained nonsectarian, Slovak Catholic organizations became its sole institutional affiliates. The Slovak League also evolved into a cultural organization. By the 1960s, it had developed programs to preserve a Slovak cultural heritage in the United States.

June Granatir Alexander

Further reading

Mikuš, Joseph A. "The Slovak League of America: A Historical Survey," trans. by Sister M. Martina Tybor, in *Slovaks in America: A Bicentennial Study,* comp. by Joseph C. Krajsa et al. Middletown, Pennsylvania, 1978, 39–56.

Paučo, Joseph. ed. *Sixty Years of the Slovak League of America.* Middletown, Pennsylvania, 1967.

See also Andrej Hlinka; Magyarization; Tomáš Masaryk; Pittsburgh Agreement; Slovak Republic

Slovak Literature

Slovak literature may be construed as the body of texts in any version of Slovak before and after its definitive codification during the 1850s, as well as in early Slovakized versions of Czech. This linguistic variety was illustrated in 1824–39 by Ján Kollár's (1793–1852) *Slávy dcera* (*Daughter of Sláva*) in a form of Czech and Ján Hollý's (1785–1849) epics in West Slovak as codified by Anton Bernolák (1762–1813) in the late 1780s. Modern literature exploded into being with a maturity explainable only by the extraordinary vitality of the preceding versions of the language.

The poetic romanticism of Janko Kráľ (1822–76) and Andrej Sládkovič (1820–72), celebrating folk life rebelliously and harmoniously in turn, preceded Pavol Hviezdoslav's (1849–1921) national Parnassicism (a movement that emphasized metrical form while minimizing emotion as poetic material) and S.M. Hurban-Vajanský's (1847–1916) nationalist realism. The earliest collection of a woman poet was Ľudmila Podjavorinská's (1872–1951) in 1895, but other women had an outlet in national magazines. The European *moderne* found a distinguished advocate in Ivan Krasko (1876–1958), whose melodic, intensely introspective lyrics in *Nox et solitudo* (*Night and Solitude,* 1909) and *Verše* (*Verses,* 1912) broke with prior social poetry. The great loss in Krasko's ensuing silence was minimized by his powerful effect on E. B. Lukáč (1900–1979), Ján Smrek (1898–1982), Valentín Beniak (1894–1973), Ladislav Novomeský (1904–76), Catholic modernists, and the Trnava school. Surrealism, represented by Vladimír Reisel (1919–) and Štefan Žáry (1918–), died out with the advent of imitative, didactic socialist realism. The latter could not prevent the emergence of major philosophical lyricists Milan Rúfus (1928–), who echoed folk genres in his ecological meditations, and Lýdia Vadkerti-Gavorníková (1932–), nor the persistence of Maša Haľamová's (1908–95) lyrical intimacy.

Fiction developed within the national awakening and prevailing European realism. Novelists Vajanský, Terézia Vansová (1857–1942), and Elena Maróthy-Šoltésová (1855–1939) created middle-class families active against the current of Magyarization, the promotion of Hungarian language and culture, while Martin Bencúr Kukučín (1860–1928) and Božena Slančíkova Timrava (1867–1951) ironized similar characters, the latter naturalistically delineating also the peasant class. In the 1930s and 1940s expressionism culminated in Milo Urban's (1904–82) *Živý bič* (*The Living Scourge,* 1927); Jozef C. Hronský's (1896–1960) *Chlieb* (*Bread,* 1931), *Jozef Mak* (1933), *Pisár Gráč* (*Grac the Clerk,* 1940), and *Andreas Búr Majster* (*Andreas Bur, Master Craftsman,* 1948); Ladislav Jégé's (1866–1940) historical novels; and most pessimistically, Gejza Vámoš's (1901–56) *Atómy boha* (*The Atoms of God,* 1928) and *Odlomená haluz* (*The Broken-off Branch,* 1934). After World War II, the officially established socialist realism was elastic enough to allow (often with severe penalties) far more valuable experimentalism and neomodernism both thematically and formally, notably, Alfonz Bednár's (1914–89) *Sklený vrch* (*The Glass Peak,* 1954) and *Hodiny a minúty* (*Hours and Minutes,* 1956); Dominik Tatarka's (1913–89) *Démon súhlasu* (*The Demon of Conformism,* 1956); Ladislav Mňačko's (1919–93) *Oneskorené reportáže* (*Delayed Reports,* 1964) and *Ako chutí moc* (*The Taste of Power,* 1967); Ján Johanides's (1934–) *Sukromie* (*Privacy,* 1963) and *Podstata kameňolomu* (*Stone Quarry Essence,* 1965); Vincent Šikula's (1936–) three-volume *Majstri* (*Master*

Craftsmen, 1976–79); Ladislav Ballek's (1941–) *Pomocník* (*The Assistant,* 1977) and *Agáty* (*Black Locust Trees,* 1981); and Johanides's historical *Marek koniar a uhorský pápež* (*Mark the Groom and the Hungarian Pope,* 1983).

Drama has been less prominent, though amateur theater prospered in the national awakening with Ján Chalupka's (1791–1871) comedies. After Ivan Stodola's (1888–1977) penetrating social commentary and Július Barč-Ivan's (1909–53) original expressionistic drama in the 1930s and 1940s, Peter Karvaš's (1920–) intellectual parables satirized first fascism then Stalinism before he was censored in favor of the positive heroes of socialist realism.

Norma L. Rudinsky

Further reading

Dejiny slovenskej literatúry, 5 vols. Bratislava, 1958–84.

Encyklopédia slovenských spisovateľov, 2 vols. Bratislava, 1984.

Pynsent, Robert B., ed. *Modern Slovak Fiction.* London, 1989.

Rudinsky, Norma L., ed. *Slovakia,* vol. 30. West Patterson, New Jersey, 1982–83.

See also Anton Bernolák; Pavol Hviezdoslav; Svetozár Hurban-Vajansky; Ján Kollár; Magyarization; Romanticism; Slovak Culture

Slovak Republic (1939–45)

Quasi-independent state during World War II. The Slovak Republic was proclaimed on March 14, 1939, under pressure from Adolf Hitler (1889–1945) in conjunction with his efforts to destroy Czechoslovakia, the Czech parts of which German forces occupied one day later. The Slovak Republic was established as a one-party state, dominated by the Slovak People's Party and its leader, Jozef Tiso (1887–1947), who served first as its president, then ultimately as its *vodca,* or führer. It remained closely tied to Nazi Germany throughout its existence, with its foreign policy, military, and economy closely coordinated with Germany's. Domestically, the Slovak Republic was characterized by a battle between two political factions—the relatively moderate faction led by Tiso and the radical one led by Prime Minister Vojtech Tuka (1880–1946) and Interior Minister Alexander Mach (1902–80), both zealous supporters of Nazi Germany. Nazi policy was to support Tiso, while using Tuka and Mach to insure that Tiso toed the Nazi line. Germany intervened from time to time in Slovak politics to maintain this balance.

The economy of the Slovak Republic was relatively good, and Slovakia experienced significant industrial development under its auspices. Culturally, the Roman Catholic Church, of which Tiso was a priest, held a favored position, and Slovak nationalism was ardently supported by the state. The Slovak Republic took part in the Holocaust, sending approximately fifty-five thousand Jews to Nazi death camps. In late summer 1944, Communists and Democrats staged an armed uprising against the regime, which Germany crushed. Henceforth, Slovakia was totally under the control of the Nazis. Germany's collapse brought the end of the Slovak Republic. Tiso and other leaders fled to Austria, where they were arrested by the Americans and repatriated to postwar Czechoslovakia, where they stood trial as war criminals. Tiso was executed in April 1947 after a politically motivated show trial.

Among the legacies of the Slovak Republic was that it convinced Slovaks they were capable of self-government; it gave a number of Slovaks experience in the administrative, economic, and professional realms. It was also the first independent national state that Slovaks had ever had. At the same time, the experience tainted Slovaks with the stigma of collaboration with Nazi Germany in its war effort and in the Holocaust. Defenders of the Slovak Republic and its regime point to the limited choices available to Slovaks at the time and argue that collaboration with Nazi Germany was the price Slovaks had to pay for survival. Others have questioned just how limited Slovak options were, or whether the price Slovak leaders paid was too high.

James Felak

Further reading

Hoensch, Jörg K. "The Slovak Republic: 1939–1945," in Victor S. Mamatey and Radomír Luža, *A History of the Czechoslovak Republic 1918–1948.* Princeton, New Jersey, 1973, 271–95.

Jelinek, Yeshayahu. *The Parish Republic: Hlinka's Slovak People's Party, 1939–1945.* Boulder, Colorado, 1976.

See also Adolf Hitler; Holocaust; Jozef Tiso; Vojtech Tuka

Slovak Republic, Birth of (1993)

Independent state created in 1993. The Slovak Republic became independent on January 1, 1993, much to the surprise of most Western observers. Shortly after the Velvet Revolution of November 1989, which overthrew Communist rule in the Czechoslovak Socialist Republic, divisions between Czechs and Slovaks, which the Communists had suppressed, began to surface. Once the process of dismantling communism began in earnest in January 1990, newly elected president Václav Havel (1936–) suggested that the name of the republic be changed simply by dropping the word "Socialist" from it. Slovak deputies in the federal parliament countered on March 29 with the demand that Czecho-Slovakia be spelled with the hyphen, as had been the case in 1918–20. Czech deputies refused, arguing that the hyphen reminded them of the hated post-Munich Czecho-Slovakia (1938–39). They reached a compromise on April 11, 1990, whereby they renamed the state into the Czech and Slovak Federal Republic, although the Czechs kept using the old name, Czechoslovakia, while the Slovaks spelled it Czecho-Slovakia. This "hyphen war" continued for the next two years as a visible sign of the inability of Czechs and Slovaks to agree on their political future.

Meanwhile, the two sides disagreed on their economic future. The federal finance minister, Václav Klaus (1941–), an admirer of U.S. economist Milton Friedman's (1912–) conservative capitalist theories, wished to transform the Czechoslovak economy quickly from socialism to capitalism. Slovak leaders, led by Premier Vladimír Mečiar (1942–), on the other hand, wished to proceed slowly with the economic transformation because Slovakia had the heavy, smokestack industries, while the Czech lands had largely the light, finishing ones. Mečiar felt that Klaus's rush into capitalism would hurt the Slovaks more than the Czechs. Indeed, in 1990, owing to the closing of Slovak branch plants by Czech managers and a hasty decree by President Havel that the heavy arms industry of Slovakia would be immediately shut down, Slovak unemployment shot up to 18 percent, while Czechs had only 4 percent unemployment.

In June 1992 Czech voters elected Klaus as their new premier, while Slovaks returned Mečiar to power. These two ideologically and ethnically different leaders met on July 22–23 in a last-ditch effort to save the federation, but by then it was too late. In the previous two years, Czech and Slovak leaders had met six times to try to resolve their differences but could not do so. On July 17, 1992, the Slovak parliament declared the sovereignty of Slovakia. Klaus and Mečiar concluded that Czechs and Slovaks had irreconcilable differences, and, therefore, should dissolve the union. They instructed the federal parliament to do so, and it agreed on November 22, 1992. Thus, on January 1, 1993, the independent Czech and Slovak Republics appeared on the map of Europe.

M. Mark Stolarik

Further reading

Kirschbaum, Stanislav J. "Czechoslovakia: The Creation, Federalization and Dissolution of a Nation-State." *Regional Politics & Policy* 3 (Spring 1993): 69–95.

Pick, Otto. "Eastern Europe II: Czechoslovakia's Divisions." *The World Today* 48 (May 1992): 83–85.

Švec, Milan. "Czechoslovakia's Velvet Divorce." *Current History* (November 1992): 376–80.

See also Czech Republic, Birth of; Václav Havel; Munich Pact; Velvet Revolution

Slovene Art

In Slovene areas, baroque sacral and secular portrait painting dominated the first half of the nineteenth century. The most important portrait painters were Josip Tominc (1790–1866), Matevž Langus (1792–1855), and Mihael Stroy (1803–71). Anton Karinger (1829–90) was a representative of romantic landscape painting. Landscapes and portraits by Ivan Franke (1841–1927), and particularly paintings with religious themes, landscapes, and portraits by Janez (1850–89) and Jurij (1855–90) Šubica, heralded the realism of the second half of the nineteenth century.

Major representatives of Slovene impressionism in the early twentieth century were Rihard Jakopič (1869–1943), Matija Jama (1872–1947), Ivan Grohar (1867–1911), and Matej Sternen (1870–1949), who were educated in Munich in the school of Anton Ažbe (1862–1905). These painters brought the first international recognition to Slovene art. France Pavlovec (1897–1959), the most important landscape painter from the interwar period, also worked under the impressionist influence. In the 1930s the brothers France (1895–1960) and Tone (1900–1975) Kralj with their wall paintings and scenes from peasant life represented new expressionist trends that replaced those of impressionism after World War I. The major exponent of the interwar generation, Gojmir Anton Kos (1896–1970), began to paint portraits in an expressionist manner, and then turned toward historical themes and landscapes. His best works are still lifes done in a cubist manner after World War II. The second most important name in Slovene modern art is Božidar Jakac (1899–1989), who was famous for his portraits, landscapes, and illustrations. Jakac was the founder of the well-known modern Slovene school of print. As an artist, Jakac combined classical printing techniques with lyrical expressionism.

After just a few years of post–World War II socialist realism, Slovene art departed from realism in general, and through abstract painting and strong colors approached structuralism and art informel, or lyrical abstraction, a movement in European painting that flourished in the 1950s as a parallel to abstract expressionism in the United States. However, none of these trends prevailed but instead coexisted alongside one another. This shift was introduced by a generation of painters born just before World War I: Maksim Sedej (1909–75), Stane Kregar (1905–73), Gabrijel Stupica (1913–90), and Marij Pregelj (1913–67). Postwar Slovene art is especially important for its prints. Works by Pregelj, Sedej, Riko Debenjak (1908–87), Miha Maleš (1903–87), Janez Bernik (1933–), and Marjan Pogačnik (1920–), all of them disciples of Jakac and under his strong artistic influence, soon gained international recognition for the Slovene school of print.

The internationally renowned group of painters IRWIN was particularly active in the 1980s. Their art is based on recognizing ontological differences between East and West, in both ideological and political terms.

The mid-twentieth century marked a turning point in the development of Slovene sculpture, as it finally departed from the realism of the previous epoch and turned toward contemporary Western European trends. Printer and sculptor Janez Boljka (1931–) was among the first to show this new direction in his monumental epic works made of iron, as well as Slavko Tihec (1928–), who worked with welded wire and sheets of metal, and Peter Černe (1931–), who combined wood and metal in his abstract, voluminous compositions.

Svetlana Rakić

Further reading

Ambrožič, Katarina. *Wege zur Moderne und die Azbe-Schule in München.* Recklinghausen, Germany, 1988.

Gržinić, Marina, "Neue Slowenische Kunst (NSK): The Art Groups Laibach, IRWIN, and Noordung Cosmokinetical Theater Cabinet—New Strategies in the Nineties," *Slovene Studies* 15, nos. 1–2 (1993): 5–16.

Menase, Lev. *Art Treasures of Slovenia.* Belgrade, 1981.

Slovene Culture

Slovenes settled in their current location in central Europe during the sixth century, but for almost their entire history they were part of some larger political or state unit. The Franks gained control of the Slovene lands in the ninth century, though by the fifteenth century most Slovene lands fell under the domination of the Habsburg monarchy, where they remained until 1918. Early in their history in east central Europe, the Slovenes were enserfed by primarily German feudal nobles and became a dependent people with no intellectual or ruling class. As part of the greater culture of Western Christendom during the medieval period, the Slovenes enjoyed little national expression, and the Slovene language was relegated to peasant idiom.

The seeds of a distinct Slovene cultural identity in the modern sense did not emerge until the sixteenth century, when Protestant reformers began to produce religious texts in Slovene to support the Reformation movement. Primož Trubar (1508–86), a Slovene Protestant preacher and scholar, published the first catechism in Slovene in 1551 and an elementary grammar of the Slovene language in 1552. The greatest achievement of the period was a Slovene translation of the Bible by Jurij Dalmatin (1547–89), printed in 1584. The same year, Adam Bohorič (1520–98) completed the first comprehensive grammar of the Slovene language. The first Slovene publishing house was established in 1575, and over fifty books were published in Slovene during the second half of that century. This expansion of literary activity laid the groundwork for further development of culture and the creation of a linguistic standard. The Catholic Counter-Reformation, which swept the Habsburg Empire, slowed progress toward the use of Slovene for two hundred years, however.

The Enlightenment, as well as economic expansion in the eighteenth century, gave Slovene culture a new boost. Reforms in the Habsburg Empire, carried out during the reigns of Maria Theresa (1717–80) and Joseph II (1741–90), emancipated the peasants and made primary school attendance mandatory. At the same time, a stronger emphasis on Germanization generated corresponding stronger resistance among some Slovenes, who began to develop a true national consciousness in response. The position of the Slovene lands along important trade routes aided the development of a Slovene middle class in the eighteenth century. This nascent middle class refused to assimilate into the German cultural mainstream and began to assert a Slovene identity. In 1768 the monk Marko Pohlin (1735–1801) wrote the *Krajnska gramatika* (*Carniolan Grammar*), which is regarded as one of the first real expressions of national awareness among the Slovenes. The first Slovene newspaper was published in 1797 by Valentin Vodnik (1758–1819), himself a popular poet and grammarian. In 1789 Anton Linhart (1756–1795), a playwright and historian of Slovenes and the South Slavs, wrote the first drama in Slovene.

Napoléon's advancing armies also helped to spread Enlightenment ideas and the concept of modern nationalism into central Europe. When Napoléon (1769–1821) defeated the Habsburgs, he established the Illyrian provinces (1809–13), which comprised the southern half of the Slovenian lands, parts of Croatia and Dalmatia, with Ljubljana as the capital. The French encouraged the use of Slovene in schools and Slovene, along with French, was used as an official language.

Although Austria regained control of Slovene lands in 1813, the Slovene cultural awakening continued to gain strength. The Slovene intellectuals of the early nineteenth century were influenced by romanticism, particularly as it emphasized the ideal of nationhood, and they sought to identify the Slovene national spirit by studying language, history, and folklore. The linguist Jernej Kopitar (1780–1844), who worked as a librarian and censor in the imperial library in Vienna, played a fundamental role when he identified Slovene as a distinct South Slavic language in his Slovene grammar, published in 1808. Slovene literary and cultural development reached a peak with Francè Prešeren (1800–1849), a Slovene romantic poet who used national themes and who drew inspiration from the oral folk tradition of Slovene peasants. Although not widely read at the time, Prešeren established the basis for modern Slovene secular literature. His poem *Zdravlica* (*The Toast*) is now independent Slovenia's national anthem.

In the 1830s and 1840s some South Slav intellectuals began discussing the idea of Illyrianism, which advocated the establishment of a common idiom for all South Slav peoples and the creation of a South Slav political unit within the Habsburg Empire. Illyrianism, however, never generated much of a following among Slovene intellectuals, who instead concentrated on what they believed was their own distinct culture and language. Slovene intellectuals created the Slovenes' first national political program in 1848 when they called for the Slovene lands of the Habsburg Empire to be joined into one administrative unit and also demanded that Slovene, rather than German, be used in schools and administration. These ideas were never realized because the 1848 national revolutions that erupted throughout Europe were ultimately crushed by the forces of conservative reaction.

In the second half of the nineteenth century romanticism in Slovene culture gave way to realism. Slovene literary development reached another peak with the realist novelist and playwright Ivan Cankar (1876–1918). Cankar's often satiric stories dealt with poverty as well as problems of social justice. He also wrote about the Slovene national problem and the struggle against Austrian domination. His best known work, *Hlapec Jernej in njegova pravica* (*The Servant Jernej and His Rights*, 1907) tells the story of a poor farmhand who toils all his life for one master, but is wrongfully dismissed and left penniless. The farmhand seeks justice from officials all the way up to the emperor in Vienna, but never finds it and is killed after he burns down his master's house. The story supposedly helped to inspire a push for land reform in east central Europe.

With the destruction of the Habsburg Empire in World War I, the Slovenes opted to become part of the Kingdom of Serbs, Croats, and Slovenes established in 1918. While some Slovenes argued for political and cultural integration with other South Slavs, most Slovene intellectuals considered Yugoslavia a means to preserve Slovene cultural identity rather than have it subsumed into a larger South Slav or Yugoslav identity. They asserted that the South Slav nations could band together for political reasons without necessarily forming a single culture. Between the two world wars, Yugoslavia did enable the Slovenes to establish several important cultural institutions. The University of Ljubljana was created in 1919 and schools in Slovenia were completely Slovenized. The Slovenes also established two professional theaters, a state academy of music with a theater school, and eventually an academy of arts and sciences.

In the second Yugoslavia created at the end of World War II, the ruling Communist Party initially followed the Soviet model and insisted that culture adhere to socialist realism. However, this changed after Tito (1892–1980) broke with Stalin (1879–1953) in 1948. The Communist Party ended direct control over cultural activities and allowed for the relative cultural autonomy of Yugoslavia's nationalities. The autonomy provided for freedom of choice in style and form, but strictly limited themes that were considered anti-regime, anti-Communist, or anti-Yugoslav.

The most notable Slovene writer of the twentieth century is Edvard Kočbek (1904–81), whose work marks the beginning of both modern Slovene poetry and prose. Kočbek's literary work and life testified to the fundamental conflict between the ideal of communism and the alienation of life under Communist rule. He initially cooperated with the Communist Party and attempted to resolve Christianity with the principles of communist revolution. He even rose to a high-ranking position in postwar leadership, but was suspended in 1952 for writing stories that contradicted official Communist historiography.

One of the main constants throughout Slovene cultural history has been the promotion and maintenance of Slovene national identity. For much of its history, the Slovene nation has been the target of integration, assimilation, and denationalization. Centuries of domination sharpened the Slovene desire for free national development. Since the late eighteenth century, resistance to centralizing influences and ethnolinguistic assimilation have been key components of Slovene intellectual tradition. This tradition continued to influence Slovene culture during the Yugoslav era. In the 1980s, when the Yugoslav system began to fracture, some members of Yugoslavia's ruling Communist Party argued for increased centralization in the fields of culture, education, and science. Slovene cultural figures and intellectuals responded by arguing that Slovenia needed to protect its culture and identity,

if necessary by seceding from Yugoslavia. Their struggle for greater Slovene autonomy ultimately culminated in the nation gaining independence in 1991.

Paul D. Lensink

Further reading

Benderly, Jill and Evan Kraft, eds. *Independent Slovenia: Origins, Movements, Prospects.* New York, 1994.

Cooper, Henry. *Francè Prešeren.* New York, 1980.

"The Voices of the Slovene Nation," in *Nationalities Papers,* vol. 30, no. 1, Spring 1993.

Zgodovina Slovencev. Ljubljana, 1979.

See also Ivan Cankar; Communist Party of Yugoslavia; Folklore; Illyrian Movement; Kingdom of Serbs, Croats, and Slovenes; Jernej Kopitar; Napoléon; Francè Prešeren; Revolutions of 1848; Romanticism; Slovene Art; Slovene Language; Slovene Literature; Slovenia, Birth of the Republic of; Tito; Tito-Stalin Split

Slovene Émigrés

The Slovenes did not have an independent state until 1991. From the fifteenth century to the end of World War I, the territories inhabited by Slovenes were under the control of the Habsburg monarchy. From 1918 to 1991, most Slovene lands were part of the kingdom of Yugoslavia and then post–World War II socialist Yugoslavia, although significant Slovene minorities continued to live in neighboring Italy and Austria. Slovenes did not begin to emigrate in large numbers until the late nineteenth century, when economic and political changes also prompted other national minorities in Eastern Europe to leave primarily for North America. The Slovenes who emigrated at this time generally were poorer peasants in search of better economic opportunities. The major waves of Slovene emigration occurred between 1880 and 1914, 1919 and 1923, and 1949 and 1956. World War I disrupted the flow of emigration in 1914, although the end of the war led to a new surge. Restrictive immigration laws passed by the U.S. Congress in the early 1920s limited the number who could settle in the United States. Thousands of Slovenes also left Yugoslavia after the Communist takeover in 1945, primarily for political reasons. The vast majority of Slovenes who emigrated from their homeland settled in the United States, but significant numbers also went to Canada, South America, and Australia.

Reliable data on how many Slovenes left their native territories and on how many stayed abroad are scarce. U.S. and Canadian census and immigration records often listed Slovenes as Austrians, Germans, Yugoslavs, or Croats. Available data indicate that approximately 550,000 Slovenes emigrated permanently in the century prior to 1945. Before 1880, only a few thousand Slovene immigrants were in the United States, but in the three ensuing decades their numbers increased rapidly. Like other East European immigrant groups, Slovenes established a pattern of chain migration where individuals would send back for family members or neighbors, thereby establishing new communities composed of people from the same or neighboring villages. Although Slovenes settled in cities and towns throughout North America, the largest and best-known center of Slovene immigration was Cleveland, Ohio.

Some of the first Slovenes to come to North America were Roman Catholic priests, who frequently served as missionaries to the Indian tribes of Michigan, Minnesota, and the Dakotas. The most prominent missionary priest was Reverend Frederick Baraga (1797–1868), who arrived in the United States in 1831 and remained for the rest of his life. Baraga County in Michigan is named after him. Many Slovene priests who came as missionaries also began to minister to Slovene settlers, particularly in the copper and iron mines of Michigan and Minnesota. Joseph Buh (1833–1922), another Slovene priest, arrived in 1864 and established the first Slovene-language newspaper in the United States, *Amerikanski Slovenec* (*American Slovene*), which first appeared in Chicago in 1891.

Several Slovene Americans became distinguished intellectual and cultural figures, establishing reputations beyond the Slovene community. Louis Adamic (1899–1951), who migrated to the United States in 1913, became a popular author in the 1930s and 1940s. He wrote seventeen books and hundreds of articles, many dealing with the themes of immigrant life in America. One of his best-known works is *Laughing in the Jungle: The Autobiography of an Immigrant in America*. Frank Sakser (1859–1937), another notable Slovene American, came to the United States in 1892 and settled in New York, where he founded the newspaper *Glas Naroda* (*Voice of the People*), which was published until 1963. Sakser also established a travel agency and the Frank Sakser State Bank. Karl Mauser (1918–77), a Catholic writer, is probably the best-known post–World War II Slovene immigrant. Many Slovene women immigrants such as Katka Zupančič (1889–1967), writer and dramatist, also became leading cultural figures in their new communities.

As with other groups of immigrants, most first-generation Slovenes retained the culture and ethnic identity they acquired from their homeland, but subsequent generations have, to some extent, lost a cohesive sense of Slovene identity and proficiency in the Slovene language. The impact of mixed marriages has also reduced the sense of Slovene identity among immigrants. Except for a brief period after World War II, no substantial wave of Slovene emigration has occurred since the early 1920s. As a result, the connection many foreign-born ethnic Slovenes have with their Slovene heritage has declined.

Paul D. Lensink

Further reading

Adamic, Louis. *Laughing in the Jungle: The Autobiography of an Immigrant in America*. New York, 1969.
Gobetz, Giles Edward. *Adjustment and Assimilation of Slovenian Refugees*. New York, 1980.
Govorchin, Gerald G. *Americans from Yugoslavia*. Gainesville, Florida, 1961.

See also Emigration

Slovene Language

Official language of Slovenia. Slovene, or Slovenian as it is also known, is spoken by approximately two million people in Slovenia and adjoining regions of Italy, Austria, and Hungary, and by about four hundred thousand émigrés, mostly in the United States, Canada, Australia, and Argentina. Slovene is a South Slavic language, most closely related to the kajkavian dialects of Serbo-Croatian; there is some mutual intelligibility with standard Serbo-Croatian, which assisted the limited but noticeable influence of that language on Slovene during their coexistence from 1920 to 1990. Several features give Slovene a distinctive flavor, particularly the dual number (special endings when two people or objects are referred to), several other archaic grammatical endings, and a vocabulary that combines archaic words and terms with loanwords from Italian, German, and other languages.

Slavs first settled in the region of today's Slovenia in the sixth century. Since the early Middle Ages the Slovene lands were controlled by speakers of Italian, German, and Hungarian. Slovene was spoken in nonformal contexts, and urban populations were largely bilingual. Consequently, marked dialect differentiation developed; today there is some lack of mutual comprehension. Also, there were few medieval writings in Slovene. In the sixteenth century, however, a written form of the language was developed by Protestant writers and some fifty books were printed. Further development of literary Slovene was essentially postponed by the Counter-Reformation; after 1768, and especially during the nineteenth century, there was intense discussion of the form the literary language should take. Crucial questions had to be resolved, particularly the choice of dialect base, the alphabet, the amount to which the sixteenth-century language should be used as a model, and the relative value of borrowed elements from other Slavic and from non-Slavic sources. Although relative agreement was reached in most areas, the "language question" has always been a matter for interested public debate. Also, the threat of centralist Yugoslav policies was symbolized during the 1980s by the imposition of Serbo-Croatian in key areas of usage, and this aspect of the language question played a role in the movement toward independence.

Slovene speakers in neighboring countries have for social, political, and above all economic reasons undergone much assimilation since the mid-nineteenth century, and especially during the period from 1920 to 1945. As such, their numbers have decreased significantly.

Tom Priestly

Further reading

Derbyshire, William W. *A Basic Reference Grammar of Slovene.* Columbus, Ohio, 1993.

Lencek, Rado L. *The Structure and History of the Slovene Language.* Columbus, Ohio, 1982.

Priestly, Tom M.S. "Slovene," in B. Comrie and G. Corbett, eds., *The Slavonic Languages.* London, 1993, 388–451.

See also Serbo-Croatian Language; Slavic Languages; Slovenia, Birth of the Republic of

Slovene Literature

Scholars have usually considered the history of Slovene literature broadly, applying to it the term *slovstvo* (writings). Thus, the earliest recorded examples of religious writings, the *Freising Fragments* (972–1039), and other medieval, Reformation, and baroque texts are part of Slovene literature. The oral folk tradition contained themes that later entered written literature. A prominent example is the ballad "Lepa Vida," which in its earliest version recounts a girl's abduction and death. The ballad has reverberated through many Slovene writers' works during the nine hundred years since its appearance.

Translations from the Old and New Testaments by Primož Trubar (1508–86) between 1550 and 1582 and Jurij Dalmatin (1547–89) in 1584 were milestones in the formation of a literary language. Theologians and educators dominated Slovene letters in the seventeenth and eighteenth centuries, until Enlightenment ideas inspired creative use of the written language as well as the collection of folk poetry. Two literary figures of the Enlightenment generation were poet Valentin Vodnik (1758–1819) and dramatist and historian Anton Tomaž Linhart (1756–95). Linguists such as Jernej Kopitar (1780–1844) led the younger generation of Enlightenment writers, dealing with questions relevant to Slovene national aspirations and relations with other Slavs.

Slovene writers have participated in European, and later American, intellectual and religious trends, but it is not possible to speak of creative movements in Slovene letters during each historical period. There is but one Slovene romantic poet, Francè Prešeren (1800–1849), who revealed the young literary language's potential and became the first Slovene poet recognized both at home and abroad. He wrote in a variety of romantic forms. The narrative poem "Krst pri Savici" (Baptism on the Sava) is his best-known extended work. Like some of his successors, he was more inclined to Romance than Germanic literary models. He resembled romantic poets in other cultures in that modernists at the century's end revived his reputation.

Poets of the so-called Slovene *Moderna* (1899–1918) redirected readers' attention to verse with their innovative forms and intimate themes. Slovene poetry, best represented by Josip Stritar (1836–1923), Simon Gregorčič (1844–1906), and especially Simon Jenko (1835–69), had paled in

S interest after Prešeren. The contemporaneous appearance of Ivan Cankar (1876–1918), Dragotin Kette (1876–99), Josip Murn Aleksandrov (1879–1901), and Oton Župančič (1878–1949) was dramatic. Kette, Murn, and Župančič used primarily natural (as opposed to urban) imagery, distinguishing them from modernists in other cultures. Their poetic innovations and psychological and metaphysical themes marked a major literary shift. Slovene poetry became increasingly more diverse following the *Moderna*. Conventional forms and conservative use of tropes characterize the work of the contemplative Alojz Gradnik (1882–1967). The lyrics of Miran Jarc (1900–1942) and Srečko Kosovells (1904–26) are representative of expressionism in Slovene literature. Roman Catholicism's ethos was influential among a number of writers after World War I, including symbolist poet Anton Vodnik (1901–65). Božo Vodušek's (1905–) art exemplifies the extent of diversification in Slovene poetry by its unique form and intense rationality.

Edvard Kocbek's (1904–81) poetry of the 1930s combines realistic depiction and metaphysical themes. Following World War II, he used a more proselike style. Kocbek's philosophic reflections and mastery of verse made him Slovenia's leading poet. Cene Vipotnik (1914–72) and Jože Udovič (1912–) continued the symbolist tradition. Udovič inclined toward greater introspection; other poets reflected on the lyrical subject's alienation and fate. In their own ways, such poets as Janez Menart (1929–), Dane Zajc (1929–), Veno Taufer (1933–), Gregor Strniša (1930–), and Niko Grafenauer (1940–) explored existential questions in their art. Tomaž Šalamun (1941–) took this thematic tendency to its extreme in his highly experimental poetry of the 1960s.

Slovene poetry has been more renowned than prose, both at home and abroad. Therefore, the lessening of literature's prestige during Slovenia's move to independence in the 1980s made older poets' social satire and existential themes appear superfluous. Minimalism in expression and withdrawal into the lyric self became new features of poetry.

Modern narrative prose began in the late 1850s with Fran Levstik's (1831–87) story "Martin Krpan" (1858) and programmatic travelogue, *Popotovanje iz Litije do Cateža* (*A Trip from Litija to Catež*, 1858), followed in 1866 by Josip Jurcic's (1844–81) novel-length *Deseti brat* (*The Tenth*

Brother). A key idea in all three works was that literature should draw on the folk's life and, in turn, help improve it. This program contradicted the romantic viewpoint of Prešeren and others and proved largely infertile, although writers such as Fran Saleški Finžgar (1871–1962) adopted it with success.

Writers such as Janko Kersnik (1852–97) and Ivan Tavčar (1851–1923) excelled in the 1870s and 1880s in brief descriptions of rural life, and wrote lengthier works about the intelligentsia (Kersnik) and historical topics (Tavčar).

The versatile Ivan Cankar employed symbolic and poetic prose and a variety of genres, including social satire, autobiography, and lyrical sketches. Cankar's modernist works appeared in Slovene literature before realist or naturalist prose fully matured.

The development of realist prose continued between the world wars. There was also another upsurge in popular literature about rural life. Thus, traditional tendencies in prose paralleled expressionist, futurist, and symbolist poetry. Leading prose writers of the 1920s to the 1950s were France Bevk (1890–1970), Ciril Kosmač (1910–), Juš Kozak (1892–1964), Miško Kranjec (1908–83), Lovro Kuhar (Prežihov Voranc, 1893–1950), Boris Pahor (1913–), Ivan Pregelj (1883–1960), and Alojz Rebula (1924–). These writers' outlooks diverged markedly but they shared a preference for realist treatment of social and moral themes. The next generation of prose writers (such as Vladimir Kavčič [1932–], Rudi Seligo [1935–], and Dominik Smole [1929–]) used more complex styles of narration.

Slovene postmodern writers have adopted more straightforward realistic styles, reduced overt psychological exploration, and increased ambiguity.

Timothy Pogacar

Further reading

Bernik, Francè. *Slowenische Literatur im europaischen Kontext: Vortrage und Abhandlung zur Slavistik,* vol. 22. Munich, 1993.

Pogačnik, Jože. *Twentieth-Century Slovene Literature,* trans. by Anne Čeh. Ljubljana, 1989.

Slodnjak, Anton and Joze Pogačnik. *Slovensko slovstvo: Ob tisočletnici Brižisnkih spomenikov.* Ljubljana, 1968.

Slovene Studies: Journal of the Society for Slovene Studies.

See also Ivan Cankar; Jernej Kopitar; Francè Prešeren; Slovenia; Birth of the Republic of; Oton Župančič

Slovenia, Birth of the Republic of (1991)

Central European state with a relatively homogeneous population of two million that until mid-1991 was a constituent republic of the Socialist Federal Republic of Yugoslavia. South Slavic and Roman Catholic, Slovenia's inhabitants, whose political tradition dates to the state of Karantania in the seventh century, have lived in the eastern Alps since the sixth century. Slovene lands belonged to the Holy Roman Empire and were original crownlands of the Habsburg domain. Protestantism (although brief) produced the first printed Slovene books, including a primer, a grammar, and a translation of the Bible (1584). In 1848 the Slovenes, after three-quarters of a century of national cultural activity, drafted their first political program: United Slovenia. It called for a federal ethnic unit within Austria where the language of administration and education would be Slovene. Ever conscious of their small numbers, Slovenes felt independence would not be to their advantage. Most worked, however, for closer association with other Habsburg South Slavs (Yugoslavs), hoping to gain leverage within the Austro-Hungarian state.

After World War I and Austria's collapse, most Slovenes were included in the new Yugoslav kingdom; after World War II they were part of Tito's Yugoslavia. In both Yugoslavias, the Slovenes, now living in a Balkan state, remained loyal yet always supported federalism against Belgrade's centralism. In the 1980s, for the first time, Slovenes began seriously considering independence. Tito (1892–1980), who had somehow balanced diverse national and political forces, had died; the economy was in decline, racked by rampant inflation and out-of-control foreign debt; and centralism was being dangerously charged with Great Serbism. The international situation—the collapse of communism in the Soviet Union and its bloc and the imminence of European unity in 1992—convinced Slovenes that they must pressure Belgrade to liberalize or, failing that, get out of the association. Slovene intellectuals, such as those associated with *Nova revija* (*New Review*), after 1987 wrote about new options; new political groupings emerged and were legalized at the end of 1989; even the Slovene Communists, whose delegation walked out of a national congress in Belgrade in January 1990 precipitating the collapse of the League of Communists of Yugoslavia, liberalized. In April 1990 multiparty elections in Slovenia brought the center-right to power, an accomplishment of Demos, the coalition of parties whose aim was to defeat the Communists. In December Slovenes held a successful referendum on independence, giving notice that they would implement it six months hence, if Belgrade refused to rejuvenate federalism or establish a confederation. On June 25, 1991, the Slovenes (together with the Croats) declared independence and in the ensuing ten-day war effectively fended off Yugoslav National Army forces. Today Slovenes consider themselves, again, a part of Central Europe.

Carole Rogel

Further reading

Benderley, Jill and Evan Kraft, eds. *Independent Slovenia: Origins, Movements, Prospects.* New York, 1994.

Rogel, Carole. "Slovenia's Independence: A Reversal of History." *Problems of Communism* vol. 40 (July–August 1991): 34–40.

See also Communist Party of Yugoslavia; Tito

Slovenia (Geography)

Former region of the Habsburg Empire prior to World War I and Yugoslavia after 1918. Slovenia is bordered by Italy to the west, Austria to the north, Hungary to the northeast, and Croatia to the south and east. It has an area of 7,819 square miles (20,600 sq km). Approximately 10 miles (17 km) of Slovenia's coastline extends along the northeastern shore of the Adriatic Sea.

The northern region of Slovenia is part of the Alpine system, with the highest area ranging between 8,000 and 9,000 feet (2,042–2,075 m) in elevation. To the south, the foothills give way to the gentle rolling hills of the Pannonian (Hungarian) Plain and, in the southwest, to the coastal lowlands of the Adriatic. The Sava River, cutting the nation roughly in half, runs in an easterly direction through some rich agricultural lands. Almost half of Slovenia is covered by mixed forest, but the coastal plain has a Mediterranean-type climate.

Unlike other former republics of Yugoslavia, Slovenia has a homogeneous population. Of the

S nation's nearly two million people, over 90 percent are ethnic Slovenes. The infant mortality rate in the nation is a low seven deaths per one thousand births, and the literacy rate is over 90 percent. Its capital city, Ljubljana, with nearly one-third of a million inhabitants, is located in the center of the country.

With the breakup of the Habsburg Empire at the end of World War I, Slovenia gradually emerged as the most Westernized republic in the newly created nation of Yugoslavia. After six centuries of Austrian rule, the Slovene language survived. The peasant population continued to use the language during foreign occupations, and the Roman Catholic clergy helped preserve it.

Independent Slovenia is a member of the United Nations and has been virtually untouched by the armed conflict raging in other regions of former Yugoslavia. It maintains good relations with its neighbors and a solid economy based on livestock and agricultural crops (wheat and potatoes), minerals (coal and mercury), and industry (textiles and steel).

William B. Kory

Further reading

Benderly, Jill and Evan Kraft, eds. *Independent Slovenia.* New York, 1994.

Bertić, Ivan. *Veliki geografski atlas Jugoslavije.* Zagreb, 1987.

See also Ljubljana; Slovenia, Birth of the Republic of

Słowacki, Juliusz (1809–49)

Polish poet and playwright. The adored only son of a well-read mother, Słowacki was raised and educated in Wilno. He was introduced early to Polish, English, and French literature. He worked in Warsaw briefly but was sent to London in 1831 as a courier for the Polish insurrectionary movement. His early writings show the influence of Shakespeare (1564–1616), Scott (1771–1832), Schiller (1759–1805), and Byron (1788–1824); later, he also found inspiration in Calderón (1600–1681), Dante (1265–1321), and the Bible. Słowacki's greatest contributions to Polish literature were his dramas in verse, the mystical-satirical-prophetic prose poem *Anhelli* (1838), the brilliant digressive-narrative poem *Beniowski* (1841), the idiosyncratic historiosophical poem *Król Duch (King*

Spirit, 1845–48), and his letters to his mother, to whom he confided everything he felt, observed, and planned to write. Słowacki's adult life was lived in exile, mainly in Switzerland and France; he died in Paris.

Like his fellow poet Adam Mickiewicz (1798–1855), whose attention he craved, Słowacki was obsessed with the Polish cause. In his dramas *Kordian* (1834), the satiric *Fantazy* (1841), and *Sen Srebrny Salomei* (*The Silver Dream of Salomea,* 1844), in *Anhelli* and *Król Duch,* and other works, he put forward his critique of the Polish gentry as unfit to lead the "angelic soul" of the Polish people, and his theory of progress as inevitably the product of spiritually cleansing cataclysmic events. Słowacki's mature verse is rich in symbolism, color, and sound; the vitality of the poetry and the mystical blending of the real and the fantastic prefigures the symbolist poetry of the late nineteenth and early twentieth centuries. Dismissed in their time, his mystical works were rediscovered in the 1890s to great acclaim.

Madeline G. Levine

Further reading

Dernalowicz, Maria. *Juliusz Słowacki.* Warsaw, 1987.

Piwińska, Marta. *Juliusz Słowacki od duchów.* Warsaw, 1992.

Weiss, Tomasz. *Romantyczny genealogia polskiego modernizmu: Rekonesans.* Warsaw, 1974.

See also Adam Mickiewicz; Polish Literature

Smetana, Bedřich (1824–84)

Czech composer and founder of the Czech national school of music. Smetana was involved with music from his earliest childhood; his first known composition dates from 1832. Smetana's strongest artistic influence was Franz Liszt (1811–86). In 1843 Smetana arrived in Prague with the intention of becoming a musician. As the political situation in the 1840s polarized, he found himself involved in the pro-democratic and pro-Slavic movements. Following the defeat of the 1848 revolution, Smetana briefly left Prague, fearing persecution for his political activities. During this period his interest in public welfare became a dominant characteristic in his work. He began to lean toward the concept of Czech nationalism, which became more evident in his compositions. His admiration for the music of Liszt also led to personal contact between the two and a series of correspondence and meetings that lasted for years.

In 1856 Smetana left for Göteborg, Sweden, to take up conducting and teaching duties. He remained in Sweden until 1859 and there produced one of his better-known works, a symphonic poem, *Hakon Jarl,* which had as one of its dominant themes the victory of truth over oppression. After his return to Prague, he remained there until 1876, when he moved to Jabkenice to live with his daughter's family. In 1884 he was admitted to a mental institution and died shortly thereafter.

Smetana left a large body of compositions ranging from polkas to operas and symphonic poems. Among his operas are *Braniboři v Čechách* (*Brandenburgers in Bohemia,* 1866), *Prodaná nevěsta* (*The Bartered Bride,* 1866), and *Dalibor* (1868), which clearly showed his radical nationalistic sentiments. Other operas included *Libuše* (1872), *Dvě vdovy* (*Two Widows,* 1874), *Hubička* (*The Kiss,* 1876), *Tajemství* (*The Secret,* 1878), and *Čertova stěna* (*Devil's Wall,*1882). His most famous composition was his cycle of symphonic poems *Má vlast* (*My Country,* 1874–79). The cycle consists of several parts, including *Vypehrad, Vltava,* and *Šárka* composed in 1874–75, *Z českých luhů a hájů* (From Czech Meadows and Forests) composed in 1875, *Tábor* (1878), and *Blaník* (1879). The work, which premiered in 1882, is considered the piece that most typifies the Czech nationalist movement in music.

Dagmar Berry

Further reading

Československá vlastivěda, díl IX—umění, svazek 3. Prague, 1971.
Mahler, Zdeněk. *Nekamenujte proroky.* Prague, 1989.
Očadlík, Mirko. *Svet Orchestru.* Prague, 1995.

See also Franz Liszt; Music; Revolutions of 1848

Socialism

Political philosophy that maintains society should be based on the social, economic, and political equality of all its members. One of the first recorded uses of the term "socialist" was by French theologian Vinet (1797–1847) in 1831 in an article where he utilized it as an antonym to "individualism." The general idea of a collectivist society may be traced back to the ancient world, as some scholars would regard early Christian communities as socialistic. More recently, socialism has been associated with the radical movement that grew up in the wake of the 1848 revolutions in Europe.

This modern form of socialism was based on the belief that exploitation, poverty, war, racism, and a host of other human ills were a result of the acquisitive nature of capitalism. Therefore, if the capitalist system could be transformed, the world would likewise change for the better. To this end, socialists of almost all types believed in the nationalization of the basic means of production and transportation. The idea was to establish a society where production would be for use rather than profit.

Even if there was some general agreement as to the ultimate goal, the socialist movement was divided into many different factions. Many, often called "reformists" or "gradualists," argued that, particularly in Eastern Europe, society would have to go through a stage of complete capitalist transformation that would eliminate all feudal institutions. Only then would it be possible to achieve socialism. Others, typically called "revolutionary socialists," saw Eastern European society as able to skip the stage of capitalist development and move into socialism by means of a worker's party supported by the mass of the peasantry.

Up until at least World War I, socialism was generally seen as the world view of the various labor-oriented movements that had developed within industrialized nations. With the 1917 Russian Revolution, the term became associated with the type of society that was being constructed in the USSR. That transformation was strengthened by the rise of Stalin (1879–1953), who claimed socialism was being built in the Soviet Union while any movement that was not pro-Soviet was antisocialist. This meant that every expansion of the Soviet model was accompanied by the proclamation of the triumph of socialism. Thus, the establishment of pro-Soviet governments in Eastern Europe after World War II was seen as a victory for socialism.

Although there were certainly pro-Soviet socialists in Eastern Europe, there were also a large number of socialists who saw their goals as having little to do with the USSR. These socialists sought to develop an independent type of socialism that fit within their nation's traditions. Often these Eastern European socialists had ideological

S and even organizational ties to the social democratic parties of Western Europe, while some smaller groups looked to the ideals of Leon Trotsky (1879–1940) and the Left Opposition, which had opposed Stalin in the 1920s in the Soviet Union. These socialists were brutally suppressed after 1945 first by the Soviet occupation authorities and later by the pro-Moscow regimes. Eastern European governments engaged in a number of purges in which Communist party members were often arrested if suspected of sympathy for—or mere contact with—anti-Soviet socialists.

The matter of the Soviet Union divided many scholars. Some accepted that the Soviet Union represented a socialist society, while others fiercely maintained that the USSR had betrayed socialism since the time of Stalin. In fact, many intellectuals have even argued that a form of capitalism was restored in the Soviet Union in the 1930s. Therefore, the term "socialism" is often used differently by different people. Sometimes it refers to the labor parties of industrialized capitalist nations, while other times it is employed as a description of Soviet-style society. This controversial and confusing debate has become further clouded by developments since the collapse of the Soviet Union. Since then, many movements of formerly pro-Soviet parties now claim to have returned to their previous, pre-Stalinist socialist beliefs.

William A. Pelz

Further reading

Caute, David. *The Left in Europe since 1789.* New York, 1971.

Lindemann, Albert S. *A History of European Socialism.* New Haven, Connecticut, 1983.

Steenson, Gary P. *After Marx, before Lenin: Marxism and Socialist Working-Class Parties in Europe, 1884–1914.* Pittsburgh, Pennsylvania, 1991.

Sweezy, Paul M. *Post-Revolutionary Society.* New York, 1980.

See also Marxism; Revolutions of 1848; Revolutions of 1989; Stalin; Soviet Union; Trade Unionism

Sofia

Capital city and leading industrial center of Bulgaria. Sofia is located in the enclosed basin of the Isker River between the Stara Planina (Balkan) and Rhodope Mountain complexes. The basin lies at an elevation of 1,800 feet (545 m) and is backed by Mt. Vitosha, which rises to an altitude of 7,000 feet (2,121 m). Sofia's population by the 1990s was estimated at 1,150,000.

The city has prospered since Roman times because of its strategic location on the ancient road from Belgrade to Constantinople. Sofia became part of the first Bulgarian Kingdom in 809. It was then called Sredec (Center) from its medial position in the Balkan Peninsula. However, the Bulgarian capital was located in the mountain city of Pliska in the eastern Stara Planina Mountains. Its present name, derived from the large church of St. Sophia, has been used since the fourteenth century.

Ottoman forces captured Sofia in 1382 and made it the headquarters of the *beglerbeg* (governor general) of Rumelia, which embraced virtually all the Balkan Peninsula. Following a sixteenth-century uprising, most Bulgars were forced to leave the city. The town then assumed an oriental appearance, recording in 1553 some eleven large mosques and more than one hundred smaller ones. It was at this time that many Turks, Greeks, and Armenians came to live in Sofia, as well as Sephardic Jews from Salonika who had settled there after expulsion from Spain in 1492.

Sofia was captured by Russian troops in 1877 and soon was named the capital of newly independent Bulgaria. At that time the city had barely twenty-one thousand inhabitants, but Bulgarian leaders saw its location as central to their envisioned greater Bulgarian state. However, the Great Powers denied Macedonia to Bulgaria, and their capital city since that time has been located within 35 miles (58 km) of the Yugoslav (Serbian) border.

In addition to its governmental role, Sofia has developed a wide range of cultural functions that include a university, the Bulgarian Academy of Sciences, the national library, and a number of museums. Sofia also has become the most significant industrial city in Bulgaria, in part because of the nearby brown coal and the development of major hydroelectric complexes.

Thomas M. Poulsen

Further reading

Iordanov, Tanko, ed. *Geografiia na Bŭlgaria.* Sofia, 1981.

Valev, E.B. *Bolgariya: Ekonomiko-geograficheskaya kharakteristika,* 2d ed. Moscow, 1957.

Sofronii Vrachanski, Bishop (1739–1813)

Important figure of the early Bulgarian national revival, distinguished for his efforts in spreading Bulgarian Slavic literacy as a writer, teacher, and cultural-political activist, and for his nationalist church and political activities. Born Stoiko Vladislavov in Kotel, he was ordained a priest in 1762. In 1765 he met Paisii Hilendarski (1722–73), author of the nationalistically important *Istoriia slavenobolgarskiaia* (*Slaveno-Bulgarian History,* 1762), became his student and disciple, and made two of the earliest copies of that writer's work (in 1765 and 1781). He thereafter tirelessly promoted anti-Greek sentiment and literacy in the Bulgarian vernacular language in all of his educational and liturgical activities; this resulted in his near constant harassment by Greek ecclesiastical and Turkish civil authorities. Ordained a bishop and appointed to the seat of Vratsa in 1794, he took the ecclesiastical name Sofronii. He soon was forced to flee to Wallachia because of disturbances in the area, and took up residence in Bucharest in 1803. There he remained until his death in 1813, conducting Bulgarian literary and nationalist activity, and serving as a political spokesperson for the Bulgarians to the Russians during the Russo-Turkish War of 1806–12.

During his Wallachian exile, Sofronii compiled a Bulgarian language anthology, *Ispovedanie pravoslavniia veri khristiianskiia* (*A Confession of Orthodox Faith,* 1805), which included his autobiography, *Zhitie i stradaniia greshnogo Sofroniia* (*The Life and Suffering of Sinful Sofronii,* 1804), and published the first printed book in modern Bulgarian, *Kiriakodromion* (*Sunday Book,* 1806), and a translation of a German cultural-political work, *Teator politikon* (*Political Theater,* 1809).

Dennis P. Hupchick

Further reading

Arnaudov, Mihail. *Sofronii Vrachanski, 1739–1813.* Sofia, 1943.

Clarke, James F. *Bible Societies, American Missionaries, and the National Revival of Bulgaria.* New York, 1971.

Genchev, Nikolai. *Bŭlgarsko vŭzrazhdane,* 3d ed. Sofia, 1988.

Kosev, Dimitŭr et al., eds. *Istoriia na Bŭlgariia,* vol. 5. Sofia, 1985.

See also Paissii of Hilendar

Sokol

Slavic gymnastic club. Founded in Prague in 1862 on the model of the older German Turnverein, the gymnastic club Sokol soon developed a spirit and style that were peculiarly Czech. Wearing the red shirts of Italian revolutionary Garibaldi's (1807–82) legions in their uniforms and adopting the falcon (*sokol*) as their symbol in a reference to South Slav folk heroes, the organization became a major force in the Czech national movement, counting over 150,000 adherents in more than one thousand clubs by 1912. The foundations for this success were laid by the Prague Sokol's gymnastic director, Miroslav Tyrš (1832–84), who created the organization's gymnastic and national program, and its president, Jindřich Fügner (1822–65), a wealthy businessman who supported the club in its early years. The Czech organization inspired the creation of similar movements among Slovenes, Poles, Croats, Russians, Serbs, Slovaks, and Ruthenes, both in Eastern Europe and in the vast Slavic diaspora beyond. A high point of Sokol life was the Slet, a gymnastic festival lasting several days that culminated in a mass calisthenic display featuring hundreds of members from various clubs performing together in a show of solidarity. Efforts to use gymnastics to promote Slavic solidarity were less effective, despite ventures such as the Federation of Slavic Sokols, created in 1908. While the Sokol organizations flourished in the new national states of interwar Eastern Europe, they suffered persecution and dissolution at the hands of the Nazi and Communist regimes that succeeded them and survived only in exile until the 1989 revolutions allowed for their revival in their homelands.

Claire E. Nolte

Further reading

Blecking, Diethelm, ed. *Die slawische Sokolbewegung: Beiträge zur Geschichte von Sport und Nationalismus in Osteuropa.* Dortmund, 1991.

Havlíček, Věnceslav. *The Sokol Festival,* trans. by R. Finlayson-Samsourová. Prague, 1948.

Jandásek, Ladislav. "The Sokol Movement in Czechoslovakia." *Slavonic and East European Review* (July 1932): 65–80.

Macháček, Fridolin. "The Sokol Movement: Its Contribution to Gymnastics." *Slavonic and East European Review* 17 (1938–39): 73–90.

Toufar, F.A. *Sokol, the Czechoslovak National Gymnastic Organisation.* London, 1941.

Solidarity

Polish trade union and social movement. Established as the Independent Self-governing Trade Union (NSZZ) "Solidarity" (Solidarność) on August 31, 1980, and officially registered on October 10, 1980, with the signing of the Gdańsk Agreement at the Lenin Shipyard between a government commission and the Interfactory Strike Committee under the leadership of Lech Wałęsa (1943–), Solidarity was a result of workers' strikes protesting the sudden and drastic price increases of the same month. The advent of the Solidarity union had its antecedents in workers' protests in 1970 and 1976. Structured both on a regional and a centralized basis during its first legal period of existence (October 30, 1980–October 8, 1982), the union had over 9.5 million members. This period was marked by almost endless confrontation with the Communist regime over issues of economic reform, the role of unions in a Communist economy, and social reforms. A year after the union's establishment, a National Delegate Conference clarified union structures, elected a new leadership, and announced economic goals. Solidarity's public activities came to an end with the internment of its leadership and the imposition of martial law by General Wojciech Jaruzelski (1923–) on December 13, 1981. Under martial law, union structures went underground. The Jaruzelski regime, failing to "normalize" Polish society, entered into a dialogue with Solidarity resulting in the "Round Table" talks in 1989 that led to the end of Communist rule in Poland. The union's most important political achievement was the appointment of Tadeusz Mazowiecki (1927–) as prime minister in 1989, heading a Solidarity government.

Peter Lavelle

Further reading

Ash, Timothy G. *The Polish Revolution: Solidarity.* New York, 1985.

Holzer, Jerzy. *"Solidarność" 1980–1981.* Paris, 1984.

Holzer, Jerzy and Krzysztof Leski. *Solidarność w podziemiu.* Łódź, 1990.

Laba, Roman. *The Roots of Solidarity.* Princeton, New Jersey, 1991.

Staniszkis, Jadwiga. *Poland's Self-Limiting Revolution.* Princeton, New Jersey, 1984.

Sovietization

Process of transforming the countries behind the Iron Curtain into models of the Soviet Union. The post-1945 Sovietization of Eastern Europe was a gradual assimilation of local political, socioeconomic, and cultural patterns into Soviet standards, accompanied by the severing of ties with "bourgeois" Western values and traditions. Stalin (1879–1953) used "salami tactics" (isolation and neutralization of opposition forces) to impose Communist rule, purge opponents, persecute prewar political activists, and establish Soviet-style systems. The redistribution of land and collectivization of the 1950s disrupted traditional farming patterns. The churches, especially the Roman Catholic Church, were persecuted. The economy was socialized, and close trade relations with the Soviet Union were built. Cultural patterns were disrupted in the areas of education, ideology, and art. Russian became a mandatory foreign language in the schools, textbooks were rewritten, and the chairs of philosophy, sociology, and history at the universities were closely monitored to promote official Soviet interpretations. Marxism-Leninism was taught to the people, and the young were registered in Communist youth organizations. Atheistic and folklore elements were emphasized in art, which was made to conform to the canons of socialist realism. "Palaces of Culture," massive Stalinist architectural edifices, sprang up in Eastern European capitals. The 1948 world congress of Intellectuals for Peace espoused the anti-Western, antibourgeois ideology of the day and established socialist realism as the dominant dogma.

Terror and mass violence consolidated Communist regimes, and the secret police, in collaboration with the Soviet security network, declared war on the old ruling classes. This period, which lasted until Stalin's death in 1953, affected mostly Czechoslovakia, Bulgaria, and Hungary. In 1951 Stalin prompted local Communist leaders to nationalize Eastern European communism to achieve a legitimate "socialist patriotism." Following Stalin's death, however, de-Stalinization led to popular revolts in East Germany, Poland, and Hungary, followed by repression and subsequent re-Stalinization. The economic dimension of the discontent was symbolized by the building of the Berlin Wall in 1961, which was meant to stem the flow of East German emigration to the West.

During the 1960s and 1970s, the regime of Leonid Brezhnev (1906–82) allowed limited autonomy in the region, but attempts to contain the floodgates of opposition were reflected in dissident trials and expulsions from the party. This more subtle use of terror was unable to stop the emergence of samizdat (underground) publications, growing political activism in Poland, or the moral authority of the churches of various confession. By the late 1970s, the economic failure of Sovietization was apparent. Unpopular leaders (János Kádár [1912–89] in Hungary and Gustáv Husák [1913–91] in Czechoslovakia, among others) compounded popular irritation. The drying up of Western credits precipitated a systemic crisis whose most dramatic response was the emergence of Solidarity (Solidarność), the Polish trade union. In the end, communism never became identified with national historic traditions, and the forcible Sovietization of Eastern Europe ended in 1989 with the dissolution of the Soviet bloc.

Alice-Catherine Carls

Further reading

Adelman, Jonathan R., ed. *Terror and Communist Politics: The Role of the Secret Police in Communist States.* Boulder, Colorado, 1984.

Held, Joseph, ed. *The Columbia History of Eastern Europe in the Twentieth Century.* New York, 1992.

Longworth, Philip. *The Making of Eastern Europe.* New York, 1992.

Walters, E. Garrison. *The Other Europe: Eastern Europe to 1945.* Syracuse, New York, 1988.

See also Berlin Wall; Brezhnev Doctrine; Collectivization; De-Stalinization; Gustáv Husák; Iron Curtain; János Kádár; Revolutions of 1989; Solidarity; Stalin; Zhdanovshchina

Soviet Union

After World War I, war-torn Europe offered hopes and opportunities for the fledgling Bolshevik government that came to power in Russia in 1917. Between 1919 and 1921 the Bolsheviks supported the Hungarian revolution led by Béla Kun (1886–1938), founded the Comintern (Communist International), went to war against Poland (Polish-Soviet War), and recaptured Belorussia and the Ukraine. Lenin (1870–1924) hoped to use the Comintern to "Sovietize" Hungary, Czechoslovakia, Romania, and Lithuania. When this failed, the Soviet Union signed peace treaties with the Baltic countries and Poland. Many East European Communists in turn came to Moscow. But Stalin (1879–1953) distrusted such "outsiders." As such, he dissolved the Polish Communist Party and executed its Central Committee in 1937. Similarly, Hungarian, Latvian, Lithuanian, Polish, Romanian, Estonian, and Yugoslav Communist leaders who had sought asylum in Moscow in the 1930s were purged as well.

By the 1930s, Stalin began to fear a resurgent Germany. Despite initial efforts to use the international arena, Stalin's attempts to enforce collective security agreements against fascism with Czechoslovakia and the Baltics in 1935 never materialized. Instead, Soviet interests seemed to him better served by an alliance with Hitler (1889–1945). In September 1939 the USSR invaded eastern Poland and incorporated it into the Soviet Union under the provisions of the Nazi-Soviet Nonaggression Treaty. The Baltic countries in turn were annexed in 1940. Thousands of Balts were executed; 1.5 million Poles were deported to the USSR; and fifteen thousand Polish officers were massacred by the Soviet secret police apparatus at Katyn Forest. After standing idle on the opposite banks of the Vistula during the Warsaw Uprising of August 1944 until the Germans could systematically destroy the city, the Red Army liberated Warsaw as well as the Balkans and the Baltics later in 1944 and moved into Hungary, Czechoslovakia, and Poland in 1945. Several million people in the Baltic area, eastern Poland, and Bessarabia were now forcibly incorporated into the Soviet state. Poland's borders were pushed hundreds of miles westward, creating a flood of refugees.

With Eastern Europe essential to Soviet great power status, the USSR quickly moved to integrate the region. Revolutionary propaganda, political and economic integration, and the military occupation of Eastern Europe provided powerful backing for local Communist takeovers. The installation of Moscow-backed coalition regimes, trumped-up elections, purges, and show trials secured Moscow's gradual control between 1945 and 1949. To fend off rising tensions with the West, the Soviets refused participation in the

S Marshall Plan, created the Cominform (Communist propaganda organ) in 1947, intervened in Czechoslovakia in February 1948, blockaded Berlin (1948–49), and implemented terror against all perceived enemies of the state. Its economic and military alliances, Comecon (1949) and the Warsaw Pact (1954), respectively, finished cementing the Soviet bloc.

Dissent quickly appeared, however. Yugoslavia broke with the Kremlin in 1948 and pursued an independent path toward socialism. Albania too broke with Moscow, while Romania pursued its own foreign and economic agenda. Soviet failure to control Eastern Europe was highlighted by the 1956 Polish and Hungarian revolts that were prompted in part by Soviet premier Nikita Khrushchev's (1894–1971) denunciation that year of Stalin's crimes of the 1930s. Polish leaders narrowly avoided Soviet intervention and won limited political concessions, whereas repression was swift and cruel in Hungary, where Soviet tanks rolled in the streets of Budapest. The building of the Berlin Wall in 1961 further exemplified the lack of Communist legitimacy. Under the modicum of autonomy granted by Leonid Brezhnev (1906–82), a reform movement took shape in Czechoslovakia during the 1960s, leading to the Prague Spring, which ended with the Soviet occupation of Czechoslovakia in August 1968. Following this intervention, the Brezhnev Doctrine was crafted to justify intervention in stray socialist countries.

Soviet ambivalence toward economic reform and Eastern Europe's growing economic dependence on the West created a predicament for both Eastern European and Soviet leaders. Soviet hegemony remained precarious, especially in view of growing Polish anti-Communist sentiment. To ward off change, Brezhnev called for a European-wide security summit to obtain Western recognition for the Soviet position in Central and Eastern Europe. West Germany's *Ostpolitik* (Policy toward the East) opened a decade of détente. Several treaties with the Soviet Union and Poland between 1970 and 1973 were followed by the Helsinki Accords of 1975, which recognized the "actually existing socialism" and confirmed existing borders. Follow-up meetings of the Conference on Security and Cooperation in Europe (CSCE) gave considerable leverage to Eastern European dissidents, particularly in the area of human rights.

Worsening economic conditions spurred watershed changes at the end of the 1970s. Char-ter 77 united Czech intellectuals in the fight for freedoms and reforms. Following Pope John Paul II's (1920–) visit to Poland, strikes broke out in Gdańsk and the Solidarity trade union was born in August 1980. The economic recession of the 1980s left most Eastern European regimes critically vulnerable and tested Soviet commitment to preserve its empire. Solidarity was outlawed in December 1981 and martial law imposed, but Soviet intervention was avoided.

Mikhail Gorbachev's (1931–) policy of retrenchment highlighted the negative effect of Eastern European developments on Soviet economic and political troubles. Once again, the Kremlin was recommending reform. Fearing economic collapse, Czechoslovakia, Bulgaria, East Germany, and Romania demurred. Yet Poland, where martial law was lifted in 1984, and Hungary, long a proponent of economic reform, seized the momentum. In 1989 the Berlin Wall, symbol of Eastern Europe's isolation, fell, and the nations of the region were no longer under the Soviet yoke.

Alice-Catherine Carls

Further reading

Bialer, Seweryn. *The Soviet Paradox: External Expansion, Internal Decline.* New York, 1986.
Longworth, Philip. *The Making of Eastern Europe.* New York, 1992.
Stokes, Gale, ed. *From Stalinism to Pluralism: A Documentary History of Eastern Europe since 1945.* New York, 1991.
Swain, Geoffrey and Nigel Swain. *Eastern Europe since 1945.* New York, 1993.

See also Berlin Wall; Brezhnev Doctrine; Charter 77; Cold War; Collective Security; Comecon; Cominform; Comintern; Conference on Security and Cooperaton in Europe; De-Stalinization; Glasnost and Perestroika; Mikhail Gorbachev; Adolf Hitler; Hungarian Revolution of 1956; Hungarian Soviet Republic; John Paul II; Katyn Forest; Béla Kun; Lenin; Marshall Plan; Molotov-Ribbentrop Pact; *Ostpolitik;* Polish-Soviet War; Prague Spring; Red Army; Revolutions of 1989; Russia; Solidarity; Sovietization; SovRoms; Stalin; Warsaw Pact; Warsaw Uprising

SovRoms

Soviet-Romanian joint stock companies, symbolic of Soviet economic domination of Eastern Europe following World War II. On May 8, 1945, the Soviets signed a five-year economic collaboration accord with Romania enabling Moscow to establish SovRoms, or joint enterprises, in nearly every sector of the Romanian economy. The SovRoms had preferential status including lower tax rates than other foreign companies, foreign exchange privileges, and premiums on exports and imports. The Soviet contribution to the joint enterprises frequently was materials seized as reparations in Romania. For example, for SovRom Petrol, the Soviets contributed eleven confiscated German firms as their share of assets, while the Romanians had to surrender control over a similiar number of Romanian-owned companies. By 1949, SovRoms controlled all oil equipment and prospecting and the natural gas, coal, metal, timber, aviation, and chemical industries. Further, SovRom Construcţie controlled all construction, while SovRom Asiguare and SovRom Bank provided similar controls over insurance and banking. By 1952, additional SovRoms controlled all naval and maritime traffic and uranium exploration. The death of Stalin (1879–1953) and the subsequent changes in the Soviet Union produced an agreement with the Soviets on March 31, 1954, to end all SovRoms. Fourteen of sixteen were discontinued in 1954, and the remaining two in 1956.

Joseph F. Harrington

Further reading

Fischer-Galati, Stephen. *The New Rumania: From People's Democracy to Socialist Republic.* Cambridge, Massachusetts, 1967.

Jowitt, Kenneth. *Revolutionary Breakthroughs and National Development: The Case of Romania, 1944–1965.* Berkeley, California, 1971.

Wolff, Robert Lee. *The Balkans in Our Times.* New York, 1967.

See also Economic Development in Romania; Industrialization

Split

Croatian seaport resort situated on the Adriatic Sea. Split is located approximately 150 miles (250 km) south of Zagreb and 90 miles (150 km) west of Sarajevo. The city is built on a peninsula along the Split Channel and serves as an important economic, cultural, and trade center of Croatia. Sitting along a narrow strip of coastal plain in southern Croatia, the area has a mild Mediterranean-type climate. The high karst of the Dinaric Alps rises to the north of the city. This limestone region, where most of the drainage flows in underground channels, has a dry and barren surface. Very few streams flow on the surface, and the topography is uneven. There are a number of underground caves scattered in the region.

The Dalmatian Islands off the coast, along with the city of Split and the surrounding area, were once the ancient Greek Kingdom of Dalmatia. Roman Emperor Diocletian (245–313) lived in the city in the early fourth century, and his palace, where he is buried, still stands in the middle of the city. Split is a modern city with wide boulevards, massive apartment buildings, shopping areas, museums, and restaurants. A huge stadium built in 1979 to host the Mediterranean Games is now used primarily for soccer matches, a passion among the city's inhabitants.

William B. Kory

Further reading

Bertić, Ivan. *Veliki geografski atlas Jugoslavije.* Zagreb, 1987.

See also Dinaric Mountains

Sporazum of 1939

Agreement between Vladko Maček (1879–1964), head of the Croatian Peasant Party, and Dragiša Cvetković (1893–1969), Yugoslav prime minister, that finally solved the Croatian quest for autonomy in the Kingdom of Yugoslavia. The *Sporazum,* concluded on August 26, 1939, established the Croatian *Banovina* (province), which included Croatia, most of Slavonia, Dalmatia from Rijeka to below Dubrovnik, and a small section of Bosnia-Hercegovina. The Croatian *Banovina* had its own parliament (Sabor) and its own government headed by the *ban* (governor), who was appointed by the regent. The *Banovina* was responsible for its own justice, internal affairs, education, social policy, agriculture, forestry and mining, commerce, industry, finance, construction, and public health. The royal government controlled foreign affairs, foreign trade, defense, transportation, and communications. The *Sporazum* gave Croatia more autonomy than it had received in the *Nagodba* (Compromise) with

S Hungary of 1868, which defined Croatia's constitutional position within Austria-Hungary.

Regent Paul (1893–1976) chose Croatian Peasant Party member Ivan Šubašić (1892–1955) as *ban*. The Croatian *Banovina* included 26 percent of the territory and 29 percent of the population of the Kingdom of Yugoslavia; 75 percent of its inhabitants were Roman Catholic (Croat), 19 percent Orthodox (Serb), and 4 percent Muslim. The *Sporazum* was supposed to be the first step in the revision of the unitarist Yugoslav constitution, with the Slovenes and Serbs next in line for their own national *banovine*. No additional *banovine* were created before World War II.

The expansion of fascist Italy and Nazi Germany in the late 1930s had strengthened the Croatian Peasant Party's negotiating position with the Serb-dominated government, and Maček openly explored the various alternatives. The *Sporazum* was certainly preferable to the Serbs than the creation of a rump national state such as Slovakia. In addition, the United Opposition led by Maček made a strong showing in the 1938 elections.

Maček became vice president of a new coalition government headed by Cvetković, which stayed in power until it was overthrown by a military coup on March 26–27, 1941. Axis troops invaded a week and a half later, and the first Yugoslavia disappeared from the map.

Elinor Murray Despalatović

Further reading

Banske Vlast, Banovine Hrvatske. *Godišnjak 1939– 26. VIII–1940.*

Boban, Ljubo. *Maček i politika Hrvatske Seljačke Stranke 1928/1941,* 2 vols. Zagreb, 1974.

Dragnich, Alex N. *The First Yugoslavia: Search for a Viable Political System.* Stanford, California, 1983.

Lampe, John. *Yugoslavia as History: Twice There Was a Country.* New York, 1996.

Maček, Vladko. *In the Struggle for Freedom.* University Park, Pennsylvania, 1957.

See also Dragiša Cvetković; Vladko Maček; *Nagodba;* Paul Karadjordjević

Šrámek, Jan (1870–1956)

Czechoslovak Catholic politician and cabinet minister. A priest of modest origins, Šrámek founded the Moravian-Silesian Christian Social Party in 1899. He was elected to the Moravian diet in 1906, and to the Austrian Reichsrat (parliament) in 1907. Šrámek and his party remained loyal to the Habsburgs during World War I, supporting the creation of an independent Czechoslovakia only when the downfall of the monarchy became unavoidable. He united the various contentious Czech Catholic parties into a single Czechoslovak People's Party in 1919. Past Catholic support for Austria-Hungary made this new organization unpopular in the early years of the republic, but Šrámek foresaw its long-term electoral potential and made his party an essential component in the Czechoslovak political system. One result of this success was that Šrámek sat in twelve out of thirteen cabinets between 1921 and 1938. He also represented the party in the *Pětka,* the extraparliamentary committee that guided Czech politics in the 1920s.

Šrámek was premier of the Czechoslovak government-in-exile from 1940 to 1945. After the war, he remained deputy premier and resumed leadership of the People's Party. Although doubting the wisdom of the move, he joined the collective resignation of democratic ministers that inadvertently facilitated the Communist seizure of power in February 1948. Apprehended while attempting to flee the country, he was held without trial until his death.

Todd Huebner

Further reading

Peroutka, Ferdinand. *Budování státu,* 3d ed., 4 vols. Brno, 1991, vol. 1, 390–93.

Tobolka, Zdeněk. *Politické dějiny československého národa od r. 1848 až do dnešní doby,* 4 vols. Prague, 1932–37, vol. 3, no. 2, 109–10.

See also *Pětka*

Šrobár, Vavro (1867–1950)

Slovak agrarian leader who, like many Protestants, strongly advanced Czech and Slovak unity. Šrobár studied medicine in Prague and was close to Tomáš G. Masaryk (1850–1937), the future Czechoslovak president who influenced him and others to establish the journal *Hlas* (*Voice*) in 1897. As a doctor in Ružomberok, Slovakia, Šrobár was active in rural cooperatives and entered the Hungarian parliament in 1906 for the Slovak National Party. During World War I, he maintained contacts with the

Czech Mafia, the secret Czech political committee that promoted independence from Austria-Hungary, and was in Prague in October 1918 to help create Czechoslovakia.

Šrobár served as a deputy (1918–25) and senator (1925–35) in the Czechoslovak National Assembly. In 1922 he merged his Slovak National and Farmers' Party with the Republicans, and he remained influential in Slovak party affairs until Milan Hodža (1878–1944) supplanted him in 1929. In the government (1918–1919) of Karel Kramář (1860–1937) and the first government (1919–20) of Vlastimil Tusar (1880–1924), Šrobár served as minister of health and minister for Slovakia, and in the early 1920s he headed the ministries of health and education and national culture.

During World War II, Šrobár was active in the Slovak resistance, becoming the non-Communist cochairman of the Slovak National Council that led the Slovak National Uprising against the Germans in 1944. As the war ended, he helped establish the Democratic Party, which attracted many former Slovak Republicans, but he left it to form the Slovak Freedom Party in 1946, after the Democrats concluded an electoral union with the Catholics, many of whom had supported Jozef Tiso (1887–1947), the Slovak nationalist activist. In 1945–46 Šrobár served in the two cabinets of Zdeněk Fierlinger (1891–1976) as finance minister. Under the Communists, he was minister for the unification of laws in the second government of Klement Gottwald (1896–1953) in 1948 and under Antonín Zápatocký (1884–1957) from 1948 until his death in 1950.

Daniel E. Miller

Further reading

Šrobár, Vavro. *Z môjho života*. Prague, 1946.

See also Agrarian Parties; Czech Mafia; Klement Gottwald; Milan Hodža; Karel Kramář; Tomáš G. Masaryk; Jozef Tiso; Vlastimil Tusar

Stalin, Josef (1879–1953)

Leader of the Soviet Union after the death of Lenin (1870–1924) who exerted Communist control over Eastern Europe after World War II. Before World War II, Stalin's goals in Eastern Europe were two-fold: controlling Eastern European Communist parties and protecting the Soviet Union from fascist aggression. The first goal made him purge thousands of Yugoslav, Hungarian, Bulgarian, and Polish Communists in the 1930s. The second led to a 1935 nonaggression pact with Czechoslovakia and a 1941 nonaggression pact with Yugoslavia. Neither, however, was honored. Stalin then bought a reprieve through the Nazi-Soviet Non-Aggression Treaty of August 23, 1939. With the Soviet invasion of Poland in September 1939 and the annexation of the Baltic States and the "Moldavian Republic" in 1940, Stalin achieved a third goal: he restored the nineteenth-century Russian Empire.

Securing Eastern Europe as a buffer zone against the West was Stalin's main goal. To that end, he destroyed the social elites who took refuge or lived in his zone in 1940. Thousands of Balts were executed, close to two million Poles and other minorities were deported to Siberia and Soviet Central Asia, and fifteen thousand Polish officers were murdered in the Katyn Forest. At the wartime Moscow conferences in 1943–44, Stalin insisted that the Soviet Union retain a significant zone of influence in Eastern Europe, and at the Yalta conference in February 1945 he promised free elections in exchange for the recognition of Moscow-sponsored Communist regimes in the territories liberated by the Red Army.

Stalin's checkered postwar policy still puzzles historians. To some, he was initially indifferent to the form of East European governments as long as they were reliable allies of the Soviet Union. Not believing that Eastern Europeans could become Communist, he made them pay reparations before Soviet influence in the region would wane, as seen in the economic exploitation of Germany, Poland, Romania, and Yugoslavia between 1944 and 1948. He began to "Sovietize" Eastern Europe in 1947 only because of the danger of losing the region to the Marshall Plan. To others, the takeover of Eastern Europe was part of a grand scheme, and Stalin's Yalta promises were calculated deceptions. Stalin's plans included elimination of national elites during the war and grooming of local Communists in Moscow; installation of coalition governments supported by Moscow in 1944–46; falsification of elections; and creation of Soviet-like governmental systems in 1948–49 and crushing of resistance through purges and show trials.

To further his control over Eastern Europe, Stalin paired countries saddled with historical antagonisms in treaties of friendship and economic cooperation: Poland and Czechoslovakia,

Romania and Hungary, Yugoslavia and Bulgaria, Yugoslavia and Albania. He imposed a reign of terror between 1949 and 1953, persecuting all political, cultural, social, and religious institutions not affiliated with local Communist parties. In the end, the break with Yugoslavia and the blockade of Berlin in 1948–49 weakened Stalin's hand and worsened the Cold War. Fifty years of Stalinism in Eastern Europe have left a legacy of cruelty, oppression, and missed opportunities.

Alice-Catherine Carls

Further reading

Adams, Arthur E. *Stalin and His Times*. Hinsdale, Illinois, 1972.

Conquest, Robert. *Stalin, Breaker of Nations*. New York, 1991.

Deutscher, Isaac. *Stalin: A Political Biography*. Oxford, 1953.

Laqueur, Walter. *Stalin: The Glasnost Revelations*. New York, 1990.

Volkogonov, Dmitri. *Stalin: Triumph and Tragedy*. New York, 1992.

See also Cold War; De-Stalinization; Katyn Forest; Lenin; Marshall Plan; Molotov-Ribbentrop Pact; Red Army; Sovietization; Soviet Union; SovRoms; Tito-Stalin Split; Yalta; Zhdanovshchina

Stamboliiski, Aleksandur (1879–1923)

Agrarian leader and Bulgarian prime minister. Stamboliiski was born in Slavovitsa, near Pazardzhik, into a peasant family. He briefly studied agriculture in Germany and became an ardent advocate of peasants' rights. In 1903 he was appointed editor of *Zemledelsko zname* (*Agrarian Banner*), the newspaper of the Bulgarian Agrarian National Union (BZNS). He rose to become the organization's leader and chief theorist, tagging militarism and the monarchy as the prime enemies of peasant welfare. He was elected to parliament in 1908 and became party chief in 1911. He opposed Bulgaria's entry into the Balkan Wars (1912–13). Bulgaria's defeat in 1913 in the Second Balkan War brought dissolution of parliament and rigged elections, and the BZNS vote was reduced. When in 1915 King Ferdinand (1861–1948) committed Bulgaria to World War I on the side of Germany, Stamboliiski, a vocal opponent of this decision, was imprisoned. Bulgaria lost in 1918 and Stamboliiski was freed to maintain order among the troops while the government sought armistice terms. He thereupon headed a failed revolt.

Postwar disillusionment gave the BZNS an election victory in 1919 and Stamboliiski became prime minister. A pragmatist, Stamboliiski was not interested in irredentist dreams of acquiring Macedonia, a prominent feature of national politics. Rather, his program was directed at reform at home and peaceful relations with neighbors. His government instituted land and legal reform, and also increased the amount of compulsory education, instituted a progressive income tax, and established a compulsory labor service. Stamboliiski was a founder of the Green International, the organization of agrarian political parties. The political/military establishment worked against this authoritarian, plainspoken, and antiurban prime minister, and his own party was divided, with some leaders corrupted by power. Stamboliiski moved against the ardently nationalistic Internal Macedonian Revolutionary Organization (IMRO), which had been regenerated in 1920. He believed in the need for a Balkan Federation and to this end negotiated the Treaty of Niš with the newly created Kingdom of Serbs, Croats, and Slovenes to cooperate on halting IMRO cross-border provocations. In the end, Stamboliiski's numerous enemies brought him down. In 1923 he was assassinated by a loose coalition of IMRO adherents and political opponents. The Communists, his only potential allies, failed to come to his aid. His murder cut short a promising beginning to Bulgarian postwar recovery.

Duncan M. Perry

Further reading

Bell, John D. *Peasants in Power: Alexander Stamboliski and the Bulgarian Agrarian National Union, 1899–1923*. Princeton, New Jersey, 1977.

Khristov, Khristo et. al., eds. *Aleksandûr Stamboliiski: Zhivot, delo, zaveti*. Sofia, 1980.

See also Agrarian Parties; Balkan Wars; Bulgarian Agrarian National Union; Green International; IMRO; Irredentism; Kingdom of Serbs, Croats, and Slovenes; Macedonia; Niš, Convention of

Stambolov, Stefan (1854–95)

Bulgarian revolutionary, regent, and prime minister. Stambolov was born in Tûrnovo, the son of an innkeeper. Entering a Russian seminary in 1870, he was expelled as a revolutionary four years later. He became a teacher in Bulgaria, although this vocation served merely as cover for revolutionary activity. Stambolov took part in the ill-fated April Uprising of 1876 against Turkish rule and came to national attention as a Liberal Party deputy in the 1879 parliament. He opposed the policies of Bulgaria's young prince, Alexander of Battenburg (1857–93), who abrogated Bulgaria's constitution in 1881, but rose to defend him when the constitution was restored in 1883. In 1885 Eastern Rumelia, an Ottoman Bulgarian province contiguous to Bulgaria and created by the 1878 Congress of Berlin, declared union with Bulgaria. Russia, until then Bulgaria's patron, withdrew its officers, who had commanded the Bulgarian military, while Serbia, already infuriated by the expansion of its neighbor, sought to take advantage of Bulgaria's vulnerability by declaring war. Although Bulgaria repelled its enemies, Russophile Bulgarian officers abducted Alexander and forced his abdication. It was Stambolov who roused the Bulgarian citizenry to the prince's defense and assured his return, only to have him abdicate again, this time of his own volition after failing to reconcile with Russian tsar Alexander III (1845–94).

The self-reliant Stambolov held the country together during the subsequent regency (1886–87), fending off Russian attempts to control affairs. He recruited the next prince, Ferdinand of Saxe-Coburg-Gotha (1861–1948), who took the throne in 1887 and appointed Stambolov prime minister. The two were to become bitter enemies, however. Stambolov implemented a foreign policy that looked away from Russia and toward Istanbul, London, and Vienna. He launched a policy aimed at acquiring Macedonia through gradual and peaceful penetration using as his vehicles the Bulgarian Exarchate Church and education. While in office, he was instrumental in modernizing Sofia, improving the national rail system, and increasing the number of schools. Stambolov's program brought economic stability and security to Bulgaria.

Stambolov slipped from being Bulgaria's most popular figure at the outset of the regency to being a roundly hated personality by the end of his career. He stepped down in 1894 and was brutally murdered on the streets of Sofia in 1895 by Macedonian revolutionaries whose organization he had suppressed. He was little mourned at the time, and with his death Ferdinand took firm control and reversed Stambolov's policies regarding Russia and Macedonia.

Duncan M. Perry

Further reading

Beaman, A. Hulme. *M. Stambuloff.* New York, 1895.

Pantev, Andrei, ed. *Stefan Stambolov v spomenii na sûvremennitsi.* Sofia, 1992.

Perry, Duncan M. *Stefan Stambolov and the Emergence of Modern Bulgaria, 1870–1895.* Durham, North Carolina, 1993.

See also Alexander III; Alexander of Battenberg; April Uprising; Bulgarian-Serb War of 1885; Congress of Berlin; Eastern Rumelia; Exarchate; Ferdinand; IMRO; Macedonia

Stanković, Borisav (1876–1927)

Serb writer, realist, naturalist, poet, storyteller, psychologist, sociologist, and linguist. Stanković was born in Vranje, a small town in southern Serbia, and was raised by his grandmother, once a well-to-do woman who had fallen on hard times. Stanković's descriptions of her pride, which expressed itself in the pretense that everything was as before, are some of the most memorable descriptions in Serbian prose, from both the social and the psychological point of view.

A sensitive child who later developed into an unhappy, brooding man with a difficult disposition, Stanković observed everything, especially the gossip and stories about people who lived their own lives apart from the tightly knit community bound by patriarchal ethics and mores. This, combined with what he heard and saw in his family, inspired the themes in most of his works, especially his most famous novel, *Nečista krv* (*Tainted Blood*), written in 1910.

As a boy, he was drawn to literature. He wrote poetry and read his poems aloud, but as soon as someone criticized them, he retreated into himself. Thinking that others plotted against him, he burned all his poems. This gave rise to the idea in his stories that everyday reality represents in the eyes of his heroes merely plots against them. This thought left him embittered throughout his life.

Neither his education at the Law Faculty at the University of Belgrade nor his year abroad had any apparent impact on him or on his writings. Stanković remained loyal to the environment of his native Vranje, which, at the end of the nineteenth century, was undergoing a social and cultural metamorphosis after centuries of Ottoman rule. None of his characters traveled outside of Serbia, nor did his female characters know about Western fashions, furniture, or ways of life. In Vranje, according to Stanković, everyone was unhappy.

There are few dialogues in Stanković's works. Instead, his pages are full of lyrical descriptions of nature, the town, holiday and wedding celebrations, and sensual and complicated human interrelationships. Sofka, the heroine in *Nečista krv*, like many of his other characters, is a tragic victim of patriarchal conventions and established mores. His heroes are women and men who live life to the extreme; they love to possess, to hold as their own, to enjoy, and to indulge. Regardless of their ethnic or social position, they all yearn for *ono* (it), the unobtainable in life. To most of them, this "it" is nothing but a dream, causing tragic collisions of emotions.

Ruzica Popovitch

Further reading

Dučić, Jovan. "Borisav Stanković." *Sabrana djela*, vol. 4. Sarajevo, 1969, 71–98.

Jovičić, Vladimir. *Umetnost Bore Stankovića*. Belgrade, 1972.

Simonović, Rista. *Život i književno delo Borisava Stankovića*, vol. 1. Belgrade, 1968.

Vlatković, Dragoljub. "Borisav Stanković," in *100 najznamenitijih Srba*. Belgrade, 1993, 474–79.

See also Serbian Literature to 1918

Starčević, Ante (1823–96)

Croatian nationalist. Born in the village of Žitnik in the Lika region of Croatia, Starčević founded the Party of Rights, a political party that fought for Croat state rights, in 1861. In collaboration with his associate Eugen Kvaternik (1825–71), he formed an integral Croat national ideology that rested on historic states' rights and the notion of a Croat "political nation."

Initially Starčević argued that all South Slavs, excluding the Bulgars, were Croats, since only the latter had managed to preserve the continuity of their states' rights from the medieval era. Although Starčević eventually recognized the existence of a Serbian "political nation" in Serbia proper, he continued to regard all South Slavs on the territory of

his concept of Greater Croatia, which encompassed modern-day Croatia, Bosnia-Hercegovina, and Slovenia, as "Croats," regardless of their faith. His Party of Rights was the main Croat opposition party in the late 1870s and 1880s and opposed both the *Ausgleich* (Compromise) of 1867, which established the Dual Monarchy of Austria-Hungary, and the Croat-Hungarian *Nagodba* (Agreement) of 1868, which regulated Croatia's constitutional status within the Hungarian half of the empire, which he believed to be a violation of Croat states' rights. He considered Croatia to be an independent state linked to the rest of the monarchy only through the person of the monarch. Starčević's significance lies not only in his articulation of an integral Croat national ideology but also in his views that shaped a generation of Croat youth and intellectuals, in Croatia proper and in Dalmatia, Istria, and Bosnia-Hercegovina. Although his party split in two on the eve of his death, the different factions of the states' rights movement that he founded commanded a considerable following in Croat political and intellectual circles until 1918.

Mark Biondich

Further reading

Gross, Mirjana. *Povijest pravaške ideologije*. Zagreb, 1973, 1–309.

Horvat, Josip. *Ante Starčević: Kulturno-povjesna slika*. Zagreb, 1940.

Starčević, Ante. *Politički spisi*, comp. by Tomislav Ladan. Zagreb, 1971, 7–75.

See also *Ausgleich;* Eugen Kvaternik; *Nagodba*

Štefánik, Milan Rastislav (1880–1919)

Slovak astronomer, soldier, diplomat, and the third member of Czechoslovakia's liberation triumvirate (Masaryk-Beneš-Štefánik). A son of a Lutheran minister in the village of Košariská, Štefánik received a good education, first in Hungary and then at the Czech University in Prague. He earned a Ph.D. in astronomy at the latter in 1904, then emigrated to France, where he became a French citizen in 1912. He conducted research in astronomy, meteorology, and climatology in France, North Africa, the Pacific Islands, and South America. During World War I, he joined the French army air force and rose from private to general, flying missions on the western and Balkan fronts.

In December 1915 Štefánik joined Tomáš G. Masaryk (1850–1937) and Edvard Beneš (1884–1948) in launching the Czechoslovak movement for independence by forming volunteer "legions" to fight with Allied armies. To divide the labor in the Czechoslovak movement, the French-educated Beneš remaining in Paris to run the movement's headquarters there; Masaryk went to London to promote the cause; and Štefánik became the movement's troubleshooter. As a French officer, he could travel freely between Allied countries on his mission to organize the Czechoslovak legions and recruit volunteers for them among Czech and Slovak emigrants and prisoners of war in Allied countries. This mission took him in 1916 to Russia, in 1917 to the United States, and in 1918 to Italy.

The outbreak of conflict between the Soviet government and the legion while in that country led Štefánik to travel, in September 1918, through the United States and Japan to Siberia. He returned to Paris in March 1919 to ask Allied leaders assembled for the Paris Peace Conference for help in transporting the Czech legion home to the newly created Czechoslovakia. In April he went to Italy to expedite the return home of the Czech legion there, as it was needed to defend Slovakia against an invasion by the Hungarian Red Army of the government of Béla Kun (1886–1938). Štefánik decided to precede it on May 4, 1919, when he flew from Padua to Slovakia. Tragically, his plane crashed and he perished on the threshold of his liberated country, at Vajnory near Bratislava. He was buried on the Bradlo, a hill overlooking his native Košariská. A magnificent mausoleum marks his tomb.

Victor S. Mamatey

Further reading

Juríček, Ján et al. *Milan Rastislav Štefánik, July 21, 1918–May 4, 1919.* New York, 1980.

Rajchl, Rostislav. *Štefánikova pařížská léta.* Prague, 1937.

———. *Štefánik: Voják a diplomat.* Prague, 1948.

See also Edvard Beneš; Czechoslovak Legion; Hungarian Soviet Republic; Béla Kun; Tomáš G. Masaryk; Paris Peace Conference

Stere, Constantin (1865–1936)

Romanian intellectual and promoter of agrarian populism (*poporanism*). From a *boiar* family in Bessarabia (then part of Russia), Stere became a member of the radical antitsarist Russian movement, Narodnaya Volya (People's Will). Stere's philosophy was in part derived from the Russian *narodniki* (peasant populist) movement, as well as from the realities of economic conditions within Romania itself. He believed that the Marxist model of bourgeois and proletariat did not account for the peasants, who fell into neither group. After spending eight years in Siberian exile, Stere crossed into Romania with his family.

Writing in the journal *Viaţa românească* (*Romanian Life*), which he founded in 1906, Stere did not envision the rise of Romanian industrialization because the prerequisites of capitalism, including free enterprise and foreign markets, were unlikely to develop. Progress would instead come from the Romanian people and their peasant background. It therefore was imperative to improve their lot. This view differed dramatically from other Romanian socialists, who adhered to more doctrinaire Marxist views. Although one of the founders of the Social Democrats, Stere broke with the party. For him, the true Romanian ideal remained in the village, not the factory. Only in the former could one escape the fragmentation of the modern world. Land reform was thus of paramount importance. Industry should be devoted more to household crafts and be aimed at internal consumption, which could utilize peasant labor during the nongrowing winter months.

After World War I, the *poporanism* of Stere was eclipsed by the principles of peasantism advocated by Virgil Madgearu (1887–1940), which saw agrarian Romania as a unique entity between socialism and Western capitalism. Nevertheless, Stere remained influential within Romanian intellectual and political circles.

Richard Frucht

Further reading

Hitchins, Keith. *Rumania 1866–1947.* Oxford, 1994.

Roberts, Henry L. *Rumania: Political Problems of an Agrarian State.* New Haven, Connecticut, 1951.

See also Virgil Madgearu; Marxism; Peasants; Socialism

St. Germain, Treaty of (1919)

Treaty signed by the victorious Allies and defeated Austria at the end of World War I. The Treaty of

S St. Germain's 13 chapters and 381 articles mainly replicated the provisions of the Treaty of Versailles, signed a short time earlier with Germany; but some paragraphs pertained exclusively to Austria, which was recognized by the Allies as the legal successor to the majority of the German-speaking portions of the former Habsburg Empire. The chief controversies centered on the questions of *Anschluss* (annexation) to Germany and the loss of South Tirol and part of Carinthia to the Italians and the Yugoslavs, respectively. *Anschluss* was expressly prohibited by article 88. South Tirol remained with Italy (despite its Austro-German majority), but the question of Carinthia was eventually decided in Vienna's favor by a plebiscite supervised by the Allies. As for the rest of the former Austrian half of the monarchy, St. Germain simply recognized that there was no prospect of reversing their current independence as successor states (those created out of the former Habsburg Empire). The three million German speakers in Bohemia-Moravia were incorporated into the new Czechoslovakia, joining the quarter-million now under Italian sovereignty. Other provisions of the treaty handed over the entire navy (military and commercial) of former Austria-Hungary to the successor states; established a maximum of thirty thousand troops in the military; and in article 177 replicated the "war guilt" clause previously applied to Germany. Reparations were stated to be an Austrian responsibility, not fixed by the Peace Commission but left—as were many complex financial and citizenship questions—to bilateral negotiations between Austria and the respective successor entities. Most of these questions were resolved in the period from 1920 to 1923.

A draft form was presented to the Austrian delegation on July 20, 1919, after which slight revision followed in response to Austrian protests against various articles, with the final signing ceremonies on September 10 of that year.

Philip J. Adler

Further reading

Temperley, H.W.V. *A History of the Peace Conference of Paris.* London, 1920.

See also *Ausgleich;* Paris Peace Conference

Ştirbei, Barbu (1799–1869)

Prince (*hospodar*) of Wallachia. The brother of Gheorghe Bibescu (1804–73), Ştirbei (who took his name from his mother) was educated in Paris. In 1842 Bibescu named him minister of the interior in Wallachia. Following the signing of the Convention of Balta Liman in 1849, which restored order in the Romanian Principalities following the suppression of the Revolution of 1848, Ştirbei was chosen to serve for a seven-year term as prince of Wallachia by the Russians and the Ottomans. An able conservative administrator viewed with favor by St. Petersburg, Ştirbei received little support from either his fellow *boiars* or the exiled members of the "generation of 1848" (Romanian intellectuals), whom he despised. Ştirbei promoted an economic agenda, including the reduction of foreign debt, a land law that increased the days of labor owed by the peasants but that also limited expectations of what could be demanded for a day's work, and a plan to expand education beyond schools for the chosen few. His promotion of medical and technical training was especially noteworthy.

Russia's occupation of Bucharest in 1853, prior to the formal outbreak of the Crimean War (1853–56), caused Ştirbei to leave for Vienna. He returned in October 1854 and began to work for autonomy from Ottoman control. With the signing of the Treaty of Paris in 1856, the Porte blocked Ştirbei's reappointment to the throne.

Richard Frucht

Further reading

Hitchins, Keith. *The Romanians 1774–1866.* Oxford, 1996.

Jelavich, Barbara. *History of the Balkans,* vol. 1, *The Eighteenth and Nineteenth Centuries.* Cambridge, 1983.

———. *Russia and the Formation of the Romanian National State 1821–1878.* Cambridge, 1984.

See also Balta Liman, Convention of; Gheorghe Bibescu; *Boiars;* Crimean War; Danubian Principalities; Generation of 1848; Paris, Treaty of; Revolutions of 1848

Stoilov, Konstantin (1850–1901)

Bulgarian statesman. Born in Plovdiv, Stoilov graduated from the American-supported Robert College, located in Constantinople, in 1871. He later received a doctor of law degree from Heidelberg University. A fluent speaker of English, French, and German, Stoilov became Prince Alexander of Battenberg's personal secretary and adviser. He later served in several ministries during the reign of Prince Alexander (1857–93) and was named prime minister on May 30, 1894. Stoilov dreamed of creating an "enlightened administration," or, as he liked to say, "a second Belgium in the Balkans." Loyal to those he served, Stoilov faithfully did the ruler's bidding. Neither a Russophile nor a Russophobe, Stoilov was a diplomat who sought to better the political life of Bulgaria. Although cultured, urbane, and well mannered, he gave the impression of being weak and aristocratic.

David Cassens

Further reading

Constant, Stephen. *Foxy Ferdinand: Tsar of Bulgaria*. New York, 1980.

Nikolova, Veska. *Narodnata partiia i burzhoaznata demokratsiia i kabinet na Konstantin Stoilov, 1894–1899*. Sofia, 1986.

Perry, Duncan M. *Stefan Stambolov and the Emergence of Modern Bulgaria 1870–1985*. Durham, North Carolina, 1993.

Stanev, Nikola. *Istoriia na nova Bulgariia, 1878–1928*. Sofia, 1929.

See also Alexander of Battenberg; Robert College

Stojadinović, Milan (1888–1961)

Serbian interwar politician and member of the Serbian Radical Party. Stojadinović served as minister of finance in a succession of cabinets from December 1922 to June 1935, beginning his tenure when the Kingdom of Serbs, Croats, and Slovenes was a democracy, through King Alexander's (1888–1934) dictatorship (established January 6, 1929) and the king's assassination in 1934.

Stojadinović became prime minister and foreign minister under the regent, Prince Paul (1893–1976), Alexander's cousin (King Alexander's son Peter [1923–70] was still a minor). Stojadinović formed his first cabinet in June 1935 and remained in office until February 1939. He founded a new government party—the Yugoslav Radical Union—with Slovene clerical leader Anton Korošec (1872–1940) and Bosnian Muslim leader Mehmed Spaho

(1883–1939). Under Stojadinović, opposition political leaders were released from prison and their political parties came to life once again, yet his government remained authoritarian and by 1938 began to adopt some of the external trappings of fascism, although not its ideology.

Stojadinović was a unitarist; he refused to consider revision of the 1931 constitution and was unable to come to a settlement with the Croats, the major source of internal disunity in the kingdom. Stojadinović led his country through the worst of the Depression, a weakening French alliance, Italian fascist and Nazi German expansion, appeasement by the Western powers, and the approach of World War II.

Elinor Murray Despalatović

Further reading

Čulinović, Ferdo. *Jugoslavija izmedju dva rata,* 2 vols. Zagreb, 1961.

Dragnich, Alex N. *The First Yugoslavia: Search for a Viable Political System*. Stanford, California, 1983.

Hoptner, J. B. *Yugoslavia in Crisis, 1931–1941*. New York, 1962.

Lampe, John R. *Yugoslavia as History: Twice There Was a Country*. New York, 1996.

Stojadinović, Milan M. *Ni rat ni pakt: Jugoslavija izmedju dva rata*. Buenos Aires, 1963.

See also Alexander I Karadjordjević; Kingdom of Serbs, Croats, and Slovenes; Anton Korošec; Paul Kardjordjević; Peter II Karadjordjević

Stojałowski, Stanisław (1845–1911)

Roman Catholic priest who organized Polish peasants into an independent political force in Austrian Galicia in the late nineteenth century using Catholic social thought and activities as a foundation for his work. Stojałowski was born in Zniesienie near Lwów and was educated in a Jesuit seminary. From 1872 to 1873, he resided in Belgium, where he came into contact with the social Catholic movement. He then took up social Catholic organizing in the impoverished Galician countryside. In 1875 Stojałowski purchased and began to edit *Wieniec* (*Wreath*) and *Pszczółka* (*Honey Bee*). These publications became key instruments in Polish peasant politics, and their success led to a great expansion of the Polish peasant press. In 1892 Stojałowski founded the Peasant Party, the first Polish peasant political party independent of landlord influence. The party espoused national and Catholic goals. By 1895, however, Stojałowski broke with the party over a conflict about its Christian character. That same year, he founded the Christian Peasant Party, the first Polish political party with a social Catholic program. By 1908—after years of conflict with the Catholic hierarchy, conservative landowners, and state authorities, as well as after achieving some success in extending his social and political activities to workers—Stojałowski began to cultivate contacts with the National Democrats. By 1909, he helped forge an alliance between the National Democrats and the Christian Peasant Party, uniting parliamentary members in the National Popular Union. In 1911 he transferred control over *Wieniec* and *Pszczółka* to the National Democratic Party. Stojałowski died on October 23, 1911, in Kraków.

Konrad Sadkowski

Further reading

Strzeszewski, Czesław, ed. *Historia katolicyzmu społecznego w Polsce, 1832–1939.* Warsaw, 1981.

Szaflik, Józef Ryszard. *O rząd chłopskich dusz.* Warsaw, 1976.

Wandycz, Piotr S. *The Lands of Partitioned Poland, 1795–1918.* Seattle, Washington, 1974.

Wielka encyklopedia powszechna PWN, vol. 11 (Ster-Urz). Warsaw, 1968.

Wyczawski, Ks. Hieronim E., ed. *Słownik polskich teologów katolickich,* vol. 4. Warsaw, 1983.

See also Agrarian Parties

Stoyanov, Zakhari (1850–89)

Bulgarian revolutionary and writer. Zakhari Stoyanov Dzhedev was born in 1850 in the village of Medven. He studied in the local cell schools of Ottoman Bulgaria and later spent four years as a shepherd in southern Dobrudja. At the age of nineteen, he left the flocks and went to Varna seeking more schooling. He later ventured to Ruse, where he became a member of the Bulgarian cultural organization Zora (Dawn). There he became friends with members of the Secret Bulgarian Revolutionary Committee, including Nikola Obretenov (1849–1939), Vasil Levski (1837–73),

Father Matei Preobrazhenski (1828–75), and other Bulgarian freedom fighters.

During the Bulgarian uprising of 1876 against Turkish rule, Stoyanov was the assistant of Stefan Stambolov (1854–95), who had been designated leader of the uprising. In 1876 Stoyanov was asked to lead an uprising in the Rhodope Mountain region. After its failure, he was arrested by the Turks but was miraculously released a few months later. Following the Russo-Turkish War of 1877–78, he moved to Ruse, where he published his first work, "Znaesh li koi sme" (Do You Know Who We Are) in the newspaper *Nezavisimost* (*Independence*). He began writing regularly for the newspaper *Rabotnik* (*The Worker*) and in 1882 published *Razkaz iz bulgarskiya zhivot* (*A Story from Bulgarian Life*), which expressed his strong antimonarchist tendencies.

Stoyanov's writings are essential sources for the study of the Bulgarian liberation from the Turks and the union of Eastern Rumelia and Bulgaria in 1895. He was an original personality and probably the most colorful artistic figure of the 1880s, combining the perception of a historian and the artistry of a popular novelist. Philosophically he was a follower of Bulgarian writer and revolutionary Khristo Botev (1848–76), hating the superstitions and the social inequities of peasant Bulgaria.

In 1884 he joined the movement to free Macedonia from Turkish rule and also began publishing his own newspaper, *Borba* (*The Struggle*), which expressly called for the unification of Eastern Rumelia and the Princedom of Bulgaria, regions separated by the Congress of Berlin in 1878. In 1888 Stoyanov was elected president of the Bulgarian National Assembly and in August 1889 traveled to Paris as a representative of the government. However, on the way he became seriously ill and died in France in November 1889.

David Cassens

Further reading

Crampton, Richard J. *Bulgaria 1878–1918: A History.* Boulder, Colorado, 1983.

Perry, Duncan M. *Stefan Stambolov and the Emergence of Modern Bulgaria 1870–1895.* Durham, North Carolina, 1993.

Stanev, Nikola. *Istoriia na nova Bulgariia, 1878–1928.* Sofia, 1929.

See also April Uprising; Khristo Botev; Congress of Berlin; Eastern Rumelia; Vasil Levski; Macedonia; Nikola Obretenov; Russo-Turkish War of 1877–78

Stříbrný, Jiří (1880–1955)

Czechoslovak cabinet minister and radical. Stříbrný was an early member of the Czech National Social party and one of its leading publicists. Elected to the Austrian Reichsrat (parliament) in 1911, he was partisan and brash but not ideological. In 1917 Stříbrný took the lead in reviving the National Social party, which the Austrian police had cowed through arrests at the outset of World War I. In 1918 he became one of the "Men of October 28," who led the overthrow of the Habsburg monarchy in Prague.

Stříbrný held various cabinet posts for the now renamed Czechoslovak Socialist Party, which he also represented in the *Pětka,* an extraparliamentary committee that guided Czech politics in the 1920s. He was twice forced from office by minor scandals. After a bitter power struggle with rivals Václav Klofáč (1868–1942) and Edvard Beneš (1884–1948), Stříbrný was expelled from the party in 1926. He then moved sharply to the right, toward fascism, founding a Party of Slavic National Socialists in 1927, which he reorganized as the National League in 1930. Unable to attract significant electoral support, Stříbrný remained a political gadfly, noisy but ineffectual. Despite his retirement from public life during the German occupation of World War II, the postwar authorities settled old scores in 1947 by sentencing Stříbrný to life in prison for "acts against the republic."

Todd Huebner

Further reading

Kelly, David. *The Czech Fascist Movement, 1922–1942.* Boulder, Colorado, 1995.
Tobolka, Zdeněk. *Politické dějiny československého národa od r. 1848 až do dnešní doby,* 4 vols. Prague, 1932–37, vol. 4, 264.

See also Edvard Benep; Václav Klofáh; Pftka

Strossmayer, Bishop Josip Juraj (1815–1905)

Croatian Catholic clergyman, cultural patron, and politician. Of humble origins, Strossmayer was educated in Djakovo, Pest, and Vienna. Ordained in 1838, he earned a doctorate in religion in 1842 with a dissertation on church unity. He served as a chaplain in Petrovaradin (1840–42) and taught at the Djakovo seminary (1842–47). Moving to Vienna in 1847 as a court chaplain, he briefly taught canon law at Vienna University. Named bishop of Djakovo in Slavonia in November 1849, Strossmayer served there until his death.

As bishop, Strossmayer had jurisdiction over Catholics in Bosnia and Hercegovina until the Habsburg annexation in 1878 and was also apostolic vicar for Serbia (1851–96). He was a lifelong proponent of Catholic-Orthodox religious reconciliation and a firm supporter of the Croatian-language Glagolitic liturgy based on the ancient Slavic alphabet), which he envisioned as a bridge to reconciliation between Catholic and Orthodox. At the First Vatican Council, Strossmayer vociferously opposed the promulgation of the doctrine of papal infallibility and in 1872 was the last bishop to submit to the council decree.

Strossmayer used the extensive income from his bishopric to endow Croatian, other Balkan, and Habsburg Slav cultural institutions and to aid individuals. He constructed a neo-Gothic cathedral in the city of Djakovo and financially supported a number of educational initiatives there, including until 1874 the education of Franciscan clergy for Bosnia. He led the fund-raising for the establishment of Zagreb University, was the main benefactor of the Yugoslav Academy in Zagreb, and contributed his own art collection to the academy to establish a national art museum. He was a benefactor of Rome's College of St. Jerome, which educated Balkan Slavs as Catholic priests. He also financially supported the collection and publication of historical documents about the Croats and other South Slavs.

Strossmayer's political activity was grounded in Croatian realities but embraced wider Habsburg and Balkan perspectives. Along with his close confidant Franjo Rački (1828–94), Strossmayer was the principal proponent of Yugoslavism and of the equality of Balkan Slavs in general and Croats and Serbs in particular. He was especially active politically from 1860 to 1873, when he was the single most prominent individual within the Croatian National Party. During the era of Habsburg constitutional experimentation in the 1860s, Strossmayer advocated a federalized monarchy, the seeking of a modus vivendi with the Magyars, and a distrust of Viennese centralism. In the face of the

S *Ausgleich* (Compromise) of 1867, which created the Dual Monarchy of Austria-Hungary, he at first remained a firm federalist and opponent of dualism. He even established clandestine contacts with Prince Mihailo of Serbia (1823–68), although his ultimate purpose in doing so remains in dispute. Reluctantly reconciling himself with dualism, Strossmayer was one of the Croatian negotiators during the first revision of the *Nagodba,* the legal arrangement governing the constitutional position of Croatia within Austria-Hungary, in 1872. Disappointment with the terms of that renegotiation led to his withdrawal from active political life, but he remained involved behind the scenes for another two decades.

James P. Krokar

Further reading

Bukowski, James B. "Bishop Strossmayer's Political Career, 1860–1873." Ph.D. diss., Indiana University, 1972.

Kadić, Ante. "Bishop Strossmayer and the First Vatican Council." *Slavonic and East European Review* 49 (1971): 382–409.

Okey, Robin. "Austro-Hungarian Diplomacy and the Campaign for a Slavonic Liturgy in the Catholic Church, 1881–1914," *Slavonic and East European Review* 70 (1992): 258–83.

Sivrić, Ivo. *Bishop J.G. Strossmayer: New Light on Vatican I.* Chicago, 1975.

Slovak, Charles J. III. "J.J. Strossmayer as a Balkan Bishop." *Balkan Studies* 18 (1977): 121–44.

See also *Ausgleich;* Dual Monarchy; Dualism; Mihailo Obrenović; *Nagodba;* Franjo Rački; Yugoslavism

Štúr, Ľudovít (1815–56)

Political leader of the Slovak national movement and codifier of the contemporary Slovak literary language. As a student at the Lutheran lyceum in Bratislava, Štúr organized a literary society and edited poetry in the spirit of Slovak national awakening and of the political struggle against Magyarization. Later, after studies in Germany, where he was influenced by German philosopher Johann Herder (1744–1803), he returned to the same lyceum, where he formed around him the kernel of the Slovak national and literary movement of the 1840s (the national society Tatrín).

Štúr's most important step was the codification of a new Slovak literary language, based on the idiom of the central Slovak urban intelligentsia. Štúr himself wrote both the motivation for this reform (*Nárečja slovenskuo . . .* [*The Slovak Dialect or Why It Is Necessary to Write in This Dialect,* 1844]) and an outstanding theoretical grammar of the new standard language (*Nauka reči slovenskej* [*The Doctrine of the Slovak Language,* 1844]). The reform consisted in introducing Slovak phonology and morphology but did not touch the lexicon, especially the cultural layer of the old common language. In this way, his reform guaranteed the continued mutual comprehensibility of Czech and Slovak.

As a political leader, Štúr argued for the removal of the feudal system in Hungary and started a modern democratic daily, *Slovenskje národňje novini* (*The Slovak National Journal*), with the literary supplement *Orol tatránski* (*The Tatry Eagle*). His movement stimulated different forms of popular education, economical cooperation, abstinence activities, and the like.

When in 1848 the Magyars rose against Habsburg Austria, Štúr and his fellows organized a military struggle against them on the Habsburg side. In connection with this struggle, Slovak national emblems (flag, coat of arms) were instituted, and Štúr stated that the Slovaks would separate from Hungary if the Magyars continued their politics of assimilation.

In the atmosphere of political reaction after the revolution, in a deep personal depression, Štúr dreamed about a visionary common future for all Slavonic peoples, converted to Orthodoxy in a mighty Russian state (*Slavjanstvo i mir buduščago* [*The Slavs and the World of the Future,* 1867]).

Ľubomír Ďurovič

Further reading

Auty, Robert. "The Evolution of Literary Slovak," in *Transactions of the Philological Society.* Oxford, 1953, 143–60.

Bombík, Svetoslav. *"Das Slawenthum . . .* ako Štúrovo odmietnutie Západu," in *Ľudovít Štúr, Slovanstvo a svet budúcnosti.* Bratislava, 1993, 7–22.

Brock, Peter. *The Slovak National Awakening: An Essay in the Intellectual History of East Central Europe.* Toronto, 1976.

Ďurovič, Ĺubomír, "Slovak," in *The Slavic Literary Languages: Formation and Development*. New Haven, Connecticut, 1980, 211–28.

Ĺudovít Štúr: Život a dielo 1815–1856. Bratislava, 1956.

See also Johann Herder; Magyarization; Revolutions of 1848; Slovak Language

Sturdza Family

One of the foremost *boiar* families of Moldavia, whose members played a leading role in the making of modern Romania. Although the Sturdza family can be traced back to the fifteenth century, the first Sturdza to use that surname was a governor of the fortress of Hotin who led a conspiracy against the prince of Moldavia, Alexandru Lapuşneanu (r. 1552–61; 1564–68). Another Sturdza, Ilie (n.d.), was elected prince of Moldavia in the seventeenth century, but declined the honor in favor of a Transylvanian knighthood. The first Sturdza who occupied the Moldavian throne was Ioniţa Sandu (r. 1822–28), the first native prince after a century of Greek (Phanariot) rule. (He was later dismissed by the Russian administration and exiled to Bessarabia.) Other Sturdzas served Russia, including helping St. Petersburg in drawing up the Holy Alliance, the post-Napoleonic union of conservative monarchs in Europe. A controversial Sturdza was Prince Mihai (1795–1888), who helped draft the Organic Statute (1829–34) that governed the Danubian Principalities until 1859, then ruled Moldavia under Russian control (1834–49). His administration was considered to be enlightened; he founded an academy in Iaşi, endowed schools, and organized the militia. Although opposed to Russian interference in Moldavia, he refused to side with the Moldavian revolutionaries in 1848 and died in exile as an honorary citizen of Baden. The best-known Sturdza was Prince Dimitrie A. Sturdza (1833–1914), leader of the Liberal Party in Romania after 1892. Prime minister four times, one of the founders of the Romanian Academy, an author, and an astute financier, Sturdza weakened his reputation by retreating from his early policy in support of the Romanian majority in Transylvania and his reactionary stance during the peasant revolt of 1907.

Radu Florescu

Further reading

Gorovei, Stefan Sorin. "Sturdzeştii." *Magazin istoric* 1 (1994): 7.

Popisteanu, Christian and Matei Sorin. *Sturdzeştii din cronica unei familii istorice*. Bucharest, 1995.

Prousis, Theophilus C. "Alexandru Sturdza: A Russian Conservative Response to the Greek Revolution." *East European Quarterly* 26, no. 1 (1992): 309–44.

Strempel, Gabriel Dimitrie. "A. Sturdza-Academia-cel dintaiu centru de cultura naţională." *Magazin istoric* 1 (1993): 16.

Sturdza, Alexandru A. *Le Regne de Michel Stourdza*. Paris, 1907.

Torrey, Glenn. "When Treason Was a Crime: The Case of Colonel Alexandru Sturdza of Romania." *Emporia State Research Studies* 39, no. 1 (1992): 30.

See also Boiars; Danubian Principalities; Holy Alliance; Organic Statutes; Phanariots; Romanian Peasant Revolt of 1907

Subcarpathian Rus'

Historic name for a territory that between 1919 and 1939 comprised a province (Czech, Podkarpatská Rus) at the far eastern end of Czechoslovakia (Ruthenia). Since 1945, it has been known as the Transcarpathian oblast of Ukraine and is bordered in the west and northwest by Slovakia and a small strip of Poland, and in the south by Hungary and Romania.

Subcarpathian Rus' covers 4,600 square miles (12,800 sq km) and is located for the most part within the north-central slopes and foothills of the Carpathian Mountains. The crests of the mountains are on average between 3,000 and 5,600 feet (1,100–1,700 m), with the highest peaks in the far southeast. Several passes allow communication with the historic region of Galicia and the rest of Ukraine to the north. The most natural direction of geographic and human communication, however, is southward via seven rivers (Uzh, Latorytsia, Borzhava, Rika, Tereblia, Teresva, and Black Tysa) that flow into the Tisza (Ukrainian, Tysa) River and on into the Hungarian Plain.

Roughly two-thirds of Subcarpathian Rus' is composed of mountainous terrain, about half of which, in turn, is covered by forest. The remaining one-third of the territory along its south-central and southeastern border is a flat lowland that is basically an extension of the Hungarian Plain beyond the southern (left) bank of the Tisza River.

Before the twentieth century, over 90 percent of the people of Subcarpathian Rus' lived in about 450 villages with on average between 300 and 600 inhabitants. They were primarily small-scale subsistence farmers, although in the higher mountainous regions livestock raising and forest work predominated. There were no cities, and on the eve of World War I the largest towns (Uzhgorod and Mukachevo) had at most 17,000 inhabitants. By 1921, the total population of Subcarpathian Rus' was over 604,000 people of various national or ethnic backgrounds: Rusyns (62.3 percent), Magyars (17.3 percent), Jews (15.3 percent), Romanians (1.8 percent), and Germans (1.7 percent).

The size and composition of the population have changed significantly during the second half of the twentieth century. There are 1.2 million inhabitants (1989), nearly one-third of whom work in factories and other urban jobs made possible by industrialization that was introduced by the Soviet regime after World War II. The formerly large Jewish population (ca. 100,000 in 1930) was almost entirely decimated by the Germans in 1944, while in the decades that followed nearly 200,000 Ukrainians (most especially from Galicia) and Russians immigrated from other parts of the Soviet Union to Subcarpathian Rus'. Most of the newcomers settled in the region's towns and cities. Presently, the indigenous Rusyn inhabitants, together with the post–World War II immigration of Ukrainians, make up 77.9 percent of the population, Magyars (12.4 percent), Russians (3.9 percent), Romanians (2.3 percent), followed by Rom/Gypsies, Slovaks, Germans, and Jews (together 3.2 percent).

Paul Robert Magocsi

Further reading

Anuchin, V. A. *Geografiia Sovetskogo Zakarpat'ia.* Moscow, 1956.

Istoriia mist i sil Ukraïns'koï RSR: Zakarpats'ka oblast'. Kiev, 1969.

Mousset, Jean. *Les villes de la Russie subcarpatique, 1919–1938.* Paris, 1938.

See also Carpatho-Rusyns; Uzhgorod

Sŭbranie

Bulgarian National Assembly (parliament). The *Sŭbranie,* the representative body in Bulgarian politics since the liberation of 1878, exists in two forms: an ordinary *Sŭbranie* and a Grand National *Sŭbranie.* The Bulgarians adopted this division from the Serbian Constitution of 1869. According to the Turnovo Constitution of 1878, the ordinary *Sŭbranie* was a unicameral body elected by universal manhood suffrage in the proportion of one member per every ten thousand inhabitants. It possessed legislative and budgetary powers, and its executive functions were held by a Council of Ministers. The monarch had the right to prolong or dissolve the ordinary *Sŭbranie* and the right to convoke it. The *Sŭbranie* had the authority to initiate legislation and to amend bills proposed by the government. The Grand National Assembly had twice as many members as the ordinary *Sŭbranie.* The monarch could convoke it to amend the constitution or to approve the cession of exchange of territory. The personal regime of Tsar Ferdinand (1861–1948), the Zveno regime (the sociopolitical organization that believed the party system was detrimental to the interests of the nation), and the royal dictatorship of Boris III (1894–1943) limited to some degree the powers of the *Sŭbranie* but never entirely circumscribed them. The Dimitrov Constitution, adopted in 1947, retained the same basic structure but provided for a four hundred–member ordinary *Sŭbranie* elected for a five-year term from a single list of candidates. It also gave women the right to vote. Yet the powers of the *Sŭbranie* were subordinate to the authority of the Bulgarian Communist Party. After the collapse of communism in Bulgaria in 1989, multiparty elections for a Grand National Assembly took place in June 1990. In August 1990 this body in turn elected Zheliu Zhelev (1935–) president and approved a new constitution. The July 1991 constitution provided for a 240-seat ordinary *Sŭbranie,* with all candidates elected on a proportional basis. The first elections for the post-Communist *Sŭbranie* took place in October 1991.

Richard C. Hall

Further reading

Black, C.E. *The Establishment of Constitutional Government in Bulgaria.* Princeton, New Jersey, 1943.

Dellin, L.A.D., ed. *East Central Europe under the Communists: Bulgaria.* New York, 1957.

East, Roger. *Revolutions in Eastern Europe.* London, 1992.

See also Boris III; Ferdinand; Communist Party of Bulgaria; Turnovo Constitution; Zheliu Zhelev; Zveno

Suceava

City of almost one hundred thousand inhabitants and the most important economic (trade and manufacturing), cultural (university, historical museums), religious (monastery that attracts pilgrims), and administrative center in northeastern Romania, known as the province of Bukovina. Suceava stands on a plateau (elevation 1,133 feet [340 m]) above the Suceava River and existed for many centuries as a settlement before documents mention it as a town in 1388. A century later it became the capital of the Principality of Moldavia and was equipped with powerful fortifications. During the high point of its development in the fifteenth and sixteenth centuries, it was a commercial center on a European scale with many foreigners visiting and settling there. Its international trade was largely in the hands of Armenians, who built several churches and monasteries. After 1564, when the capital of the principality was moved to Iaşi, a slow decline began in the city's overall importance. In 1775 the Austrian Empire annexed the northern part of the Principality of Moldavia and named it Bukovina. By this act, Suceava was cut off from its historic and economic roots and became merely the administrative center of a district, while the Austrian authorities built a customs wall in its backyard. When Suceava rejoined Romania in 1918, it did not regain its previous status because the Austrians had built up Cernăuţi (Ukrainian, Chernovtsy) as the major cultural and economic center of Bukovina. After World War II, the Soviet Union annexed the northern part of Bukovina and Suceava was again stultified by an impenetrable boundary in its vicinity. This may slowly change with northern Bukovina and Chernovtsy in the hands of an independent Ukraine.

Ladis K.D. Kristof

Further reading

Ionescu, Grigore. *Istoria Arhitecturii în Romînia.* Bucharest, 1963.
Magocsi, Paul Robert. *Historical Atlas of East Central Europe.* Seattle, Washington, 1993.

Popp, N. et al. *Judeţul Suceava.* Bucharest, n.d.
România: Atlas istoric-geographic. Bucharest, 1996.

See also Bukovina

Sudeten Crisis (1938)

Dispute that precipitated the Munich Pact. After World War I, the newly constituted state of Czechoslovakia found within its borders a German minority numbering in excess of three million people (in a total of fourteen million). This minority was concentrated along a border region, the Sudeten Mountains. The Sudeten Germans, who had been the overlords during the imperial era of Austria-Hungary, were a recalcitrant minority in a country dominated by peoples whom until recently they had themselves dominated. This was the crux of the Sudeten problem. Only reluctantly did the German population accept its minority position during the relatively prosperous 1920s. With the onset of the Great Depression during the 1930s, however, much of this population, which suffered disproportionately in the economic crisis, became radicalized. The rise of Adolf Hitler (1889–1945) in Germany, another consequence of the Depression, only encouraged a radicalized Sudeten German populace that saw in the German Nazi regime at least support for their ethnic autonomy and for some the future agent of their liberation from Czech rule. This range of desires crystallized politically after 1933 in the Sudeten German Party of Konrad Henlein (1898–1945), which soon won the allegiance and vote of a majority of the Sudeten Germans.

In 1938, when an increasingly confident Hitler turned his attention to Czechoslovakia, the Sudeten problem ripened into the Sudeten crisis. Using an allegedly persecuted Sudeten German minority as his pretext, Hitler brought Europe to the brink of war in the fall of 1938 over the issue of whether this minority should be detached from Czechoslovakia and made part of Germany. This was accomplished at the Munich conference in September 1938, when Italy, Germany, France, and England agreed to the partition of Czechoslovakia. Yet far from creating "peace in our time," as proclaimed by British Prime Minister Neville Chamberlain (1869–1940), the Munich "settlement" was merely a prelude to the complete dismemberment of Czechoslovakia in March 1939 and a major step toward war in September of that year.

Ronald Smelser

Further reading
Campbell, F. Gregory. *Confrontation in Central Europe: Weimar Germany and Czechoslovakia.* Chicago, 1975.
Luža, Radomír. *The Transfer of the Sudeten Germans: A Study of Czech-German Relations, 1933–1962.* New York, 1964.
Smelser, Ronald. *The Sudeten Problem: Volkstumspolitik and the Formulation of Nazi Foreign Policy, 1933–1938.* Middletown, Connecticut, 1975.

See also Neville Chamberlain; Great Depression; Konrad Henlein; Adolf Hitler; Munich Pact; Sudetenland

Sudetenland

Coal-rich region in north-central Moravia and northern and western Bohemia. The Sudetenland had a historic role in the prelude to World War II, culminating in the Western Allies' appeasement of Adolf Hitler (1889–1945) by pressuring Czechoslovakia to cede the territory to the Third Reich.

Sudetenland derives its name from the Sudetes, or Sudeten, Mountains in Moravia, but by tradition also includes regions in Bohemia immediately south of the Erzgebirge (Ore Mountains). These areas were settled in the Middle Ages by Germans whom Bohemian rulers encouraged because they valued their labor skills. By the mid-1930s, over two million Germans lived in the region, constituting a substantial majority of its population. Though the Sudeten Germans' relationship with the politically dominant Czechs was not always harmonious, relative peace prevailed until economic problems and the rise of German nationalism in the 1930s created tensions. In the mid-1930s a Sudeten German Nazi party led by Konrad Henlein (1898–1945) achieved political success by pressuring Czechoslovakia for ever greater concessions and autonomy for the region. Hitler used the heated political atmosphere to demand annexation of the Sudetenland into Germany. In September 1938 French and British officials met with German leaders in Munich and agreed that Czechoslovakia had to relinquish the territory. The territorial transfer weakened the Czechoslovak state, which Germany soon thereafter dismembered and partially absorbed.

William H. Berentsen

Further reading
Pounds, N.J.G. *Eastern Europe.* London, 1969.
Smelser, Ronald M. *The Sudeten Problem: Volkstumspolitik and the Formulation of Nazi Policy, Foreign 1933–1938.* Middletown, Connecticut, 1975.

See also Konrad Henlein; Adolf Hitler; Munich Pact; Sudeten Crisis

Švehla, Antonín (1873–1933)

Czechoslovak agrarian, politician, and prime minister. Švehla, a farmer near Prague, joined the Czech Agrarian Party when it began in 1896. He was among the founders of the Central Union of Sugar Beet Growers and other groups that transformed the Agrarian Party into a mass organization. Švehla entered the Agrarian Party leadership (1902), was elected to the Bohemian diet (1908), and served as his party's chairman from 1909 until his death.

During World War I, Švehla encouraged collaboration among all Czech parties and the Czech Mafia, the secret political organization that promoted independence from Austria-Hungary. Like many Czechs, he originally desired a constitutional restructuring of the monarchy but abandoned these hopes in mid-1917. Švehla was one of the "men of 28 October" who led the revolution in Prague that formed the First Czechoslovak Republic (1918–38).

In 1922 the Czech Agrarians merged with the Slovak National and Farmers' Party to create the Republican Party of Agriculturalists and Small Farmers, the strongest party in the National Assembly during most of the interwar years. Although the Republicans had a powerful conservative wing, Švehla preserved his party's unity and moderate course by including conservatives in leading party and government positions and achieving consensus on policies. After 1918, this "master of compromise" held the interests of the Czechoslovak state paramount, using the strength and position of his party at the center of the political spectrum to build governing coalitions and insure cooperation among parties, including the Sudeten German parties, and the *Hrad,* the unofficial political group around the president.

Švehla participated in every government between 1918 and 1929. He was interior minister in a broad coalition under Karel Kramář (1918–19). During that time, he was involved in the committee that wrote the constitution. He also negotiated a land reform with the socialists to benefit farmers and peasants, ease land hunger, and guarantee stability. During the Social Democratic–Communist split in 1920–21, Švehla established and ran the *Pětka,* the extraparliamentary committee that led Czechoslovak politics in the 1920s, to guide a cabinet of nonpolitical experts. He headed two cabinets in the broad All-National Coalition (1922–25 and 1925–26) and one in the center-right Gentlemen's Coalition (1926–29), which for the first time included Sudeten German parties. Švehla suffered from diabetes and was ill from December 1927 until he resigned as prime minister in 1929. Afterward, he had little influence on his party or the country. Moderate Republicans continued as prime ministers until the Munich crisis (in which Czechoslovakia was forced to turn over the Sudetenland to Nazi Germany), but conservatives dominated the party.

Daniel E. Miller

Further reading

Dostál, Vladimír. *Antonín Švehla: Profil československého státníka.* New York, 1989.

Miller, Daniel E. "Antonín Švehla: Master of Compromise." *East Central Europe* 17 (1990): 179–94.

Paleček, Antonín. "The Good Genius of Czechoslovak Democracy: Masaryk, Beneš, or Švehla?" *East European Quarterly* 8 (1969): 213–34.

See also Agrarian Parties; Czech Mafia; *Hrad; Karel Kramář; Munich Pact; Pětka;* Sudeten Crisis

Svoboda, Ludvík (1895–1979)

Czechoslovak general, minister of national defense, and president. Born in Hroznatín in southwest Moravia, Svoboda grew up on a small farm and attended a two-year agricultural school. He fought bravely for the independence of Czechoslovakia when he joined the Czechoslovak Legion in Russia, returning home as a captain and enlisting in the army in 1922. In March 1939, during the German occupation, he served as battalion commander in the city of Kroměříž. As a member of the military resistance, Svoboda secretly crossed the Czechoslovak-Polish border on June 5, 1939, becoming commanding officer of the Czechoslovak military unit in Poland and retreating with his men to the Soviet Union. After the German invasion of the USSR, Svoboda became combat commander of the First Czechoslovak Battalion, which gradually grew into a brigade and army corps. Svoboda was promoted to brigadier in 1943. An admirer of the Red Army and a patriotic soldier, he found himself drawn closer to the Communists. He concealed his wartime membership in the Communist Party and was appointed minister of national defense as a nonparty expert in April 1945. In August of that year he was made army general.

A figurehead, Svoboda was never fully trusted by Communist hard-liners. On the express wish of Josef Stalin (1879–1953), Svoboda was abruptly dismissed from government in September 1951. After a brief detention in November 1952, he was made an accountant at the agricultural cooperative of his village. During his 1954 visit to Prague, Soviet premier Nikita Khrushchev (1894–1971) intervened on behalf of Svoboda. Svoboda was rehabilitated and became the head of the Military Academy of Klement Gottwald in Prague, then retired in 1959. A popular, patriotic military figure, he was elected president of the republic on March 30, 1968, and in August became a Communist Party Presidium member. Ineffective, weak, politically naive, and uncomfortable with the party hard-liners who were creeping back into power but unwilling to challenge them, Svoboda wasted his reputation with his acquiescence to Soviet demands at the Moscow negotiations in the wake of the August 1968 Warsaw Pact invasion of Czechoslovakia; he accepted passively the "normalization" process that eradicated all traces of the Prague Spring reforms. The party leadership banned the publication of the second volume of his memoirs in 1972. By 1975 the gravely ill Svoboda was relieved, against his wishes, of his presidential duties before the end of his term.

Radomír V. Luža

S

Further reading

Kadlec, Vladimír. *Podivné konce našich presidentů.* Hradec Králové, Czech Republic, 1991.

Kaplan, Karel. *Mocní a bezmocní.* Toronto, 1989.

Svoboda, Ludvík. *Cestami života,* vol. 1, Prague, 1971; vol. 2, Prague, 1992.

Vališ, Zdeněk. "Ludvík Svoboda (Druhá světová válka)." *Historie a vojenství* 39, no. 6 (1990): 134–51.

See also Communist Party of Czechoslovakia; Czechoslovak Legion; Prague Spring; Red Army; Stalin

Świętochowski, Aleksander (1849–1938)

Polish journalist, playwright, short-story writer, novelist, social historian, philosopher, and essayist. Through his articles and columns in large-circulation newspapers in the 1870s, Świętochowski emerged as the leading theorist and spokesman of the Warsaw positivist school. From 1881 he edited *Prawda* (*Truth*), a weekly devoted to popularizing the tenets of positivism and to inculcating in its readers the habits of rational thought. An often scathing polemicist, Świętochowski gave vent to his outspoken critiques of the power of the Catholic Church and the mystique of the *szlachta,* or Polish gentry, in his weekly column, "Liberum veto," published under the pen name Poseł Prawdy (Ambassador of Truth). Although as a positivist he championed capitalism as a necessary stage of social and economic development and was adamantly antisocialist, he considered capitalism a destructive, demoralizing social force. He placed his main hopes for society on compulsory education based on secular, scientific principles.

Over the course of a writing career that spanned six decades, Świętochowski wielded his pen with one grand purpose in mind: to give voice to his rationalist critique of everything that threatened Polish society's secular, progressive, Western-style development. To this end he wrote a dozen or so unstageable dramas of ideas (mostly in the 1870s and 1880s), then took to writing heavily tendentious prose fiction. His most ambitious drama, *Duchy* (*Spirits,* 1895–1909), is a play in six parts that attempts to recapitulate the development of humankind, with emphasis on the roles played by extraordinary individuals. There is a general consensus that his most important works are his "Liberum veto" feuilletons and his monumental ethnographic study, *Historia chłopów polskich* (*The History of the Polish Peasants,* 1925–28).

Madeline G. Levine

Further reading

Brykalska, Maria. *Aleksander Świętochowski: Biografia,* 2 vols. Warsaw, 1987.

See also Polish Literature; Positivism; *Szlachta*

Syrový, Jan (1888–1970)

Czechoslovak general and prime minister. When World War I broke out, Syrový was working as an architect in Russian Poland. Although an Austro-Hungarian reserve officer, he joined the Russian-led Czech Družina, the forerunner of the Czechoslovak Legion, in September 1914, as a common soldier. He received a commission in May 1915 but lost an eye in 1917. As the legion grew following the Russian Revolution of 1917, Syrový rose rapidly to the rank of general. Along with General Radola Gajda (1892–1948), he led the revolt of the legion against the Bolsheviks in May 1918. In August Syrový became commander of all Czechoslovak troops in Russia.

After his return home, Syrový held various high commands in the new Czechoslovak army. He served briefly as minister of national defense in 1926. At the height of the Munich crisis in September 1938, brought on by German demands regarding the Sudetenland, President Edvard Beneš (1884–1948) appointed him prime minister. Rejecting calls for a military dictatorship, the popular general had to announce the Czechoslovak capitulation to the public. In December he resigned as prime minister but continued to serve as minister of national defense until shortly after the German occupation in March 1939. After the war, Syrový was scapegoated and condemned to prison; he was released in 1960.

Todd Huebner

Further reading

Československo: Biografie, 3 vols. Prague, 1936–41.

See also Edvard Beneš; Czechoslovak Legion; Radola Gajda; Munich Pact; Sudeten Crisis

Systematization

A scheme imposed in Romania by President Nicolae Ceaușescu (1918–89) to reorganize urban and rural spaces in accordance with his ideas of rational land use. Begun in the 1960s and intensified in the 1970s, the program initially tried to bring industry, higher standards of living, and cultural facilities to outlying and previously disadvantaged regions. By the 1980s, however, systematization meant destroying selected villages and urban sectors and forcibly concentrating residents into modern high-rise apartments on the sites of their former homes to become good socialist citizens. Areas not chosen for such treatment often were simply razed, the land put to other uses, and the residents resettled elsewhere.

The original idea had promise—to distribute the jobs and social amenities of economic development more evenly—but it was distorted into a revolutionary scheme to transform the entire country in accordance with Ceauşescu's ideological priorities. Ethnic minorities, especially Hungarians and Germans, were singled out for harsh treatment and their homes and churches destroyed. Romanians also suffered, however, and in Bucharest large areas of the old city including homes, churches, and cultural monuments were razed to create grandiose modern apartment buildings. Ceauşescu took a personal interest in the process, and although local resistance blocked systematization in some areas of the country, places the president frequented—particularly central Bucharest—were devastated.

Mary Ellen Fischer

Further reading

Giurescu, Dinu C. *The Razing of Romania's Past.* New York, 1989.

See also Nicolae Ceauşescu; Ethnic Minorities

Szabó, Dezső (1879–1945)

Hungarian novelist, essayist, short-story writer, and publicist, who during the interwar years was the sage of Hungarian populism. Szabó began his career as a secondary-school teacher in 1906, and soon after that also as an essayist. A devotee of avant-garde poet Endre Ady (1877–1919), Szabó initially published in the progressive literary and sociological periodicals *Nyugat* (*West*) and *Huszadik Század* (*Twentieth Century*). Later, however, he switched to a conservative-nationalist-populist course. In 1918 he moved to Budapest to partake in the revolution and to devote himself to

writing. Although a social reformer and protester by inclination, Szabó was disappointed by the Revolutions of 1918–19 that followed in the wake of Austria-Hungary's defeat in World War I, and especially with the Red terror connected with the short-lived Communist regime (1919) led by Béla Kun (1886–1938). He gave vent to his displeasure in the novel *Az elsodort falu* (*The Village That Was Swept Away,* 1919), which for a while placed him at the very pinnacle of popularity in postrevolutionary Hungary. During the 1920s, he tried his hand at editing his own periodicals (*Auróra, Élet és Irodalom,* and *Kritikai Füzetek*), but lived mostly off his writing. He also held regular public meetings and lectures in some of the main cafés of Budapest (Centrál, Philadelphia, and Abázia), and began to assemble a group of devoted followers for whom he was the "Master" and the "Sage of the Nation." For a while, he moved to the right by playing around with ideas of "Hungarian racial purity," "ethnic collectivism," and anti-Semitism, but by the 1930s, he reversed himself and turned his fulminations against Nazism, notions of German racial superiority, and the pro-German elements in Hungarian society. In the early 1920s Hungary's conservative political leaders idealized Szabó, but his relationship with the regime of Admiral Miklós Horthy (1868–1957), the Hungarian regent, soon deteriorated, partly because of his social radicalism that emphasized the need to uplift the Hungarian peasants, and partly because of his rejection of the alliance with Hitler's (1889–1945) Germany. Starting in 1934, Szabó gave vent to his social and political views in a series of pamphlets entitled *Ludas Mátyás Füzetek* (*Essays by Matthias Goose,* 80 parts, 1934–42). Some of the best of these essays were published separately under the title *Egész látóhatár* (*The Whole Horizon,* 3 vols., 1939), which soon became the bible of his supporters. Having lost some of his popularity during World War II, Szabó died as a lonely eccentric during the siege of Budapest in early 1945.

Steven Béla Várdy

Further reading

András, Emmerich. *The Rise and Development in Hungary of the So-called "Popular [Populist] Movement," 1920–1956.* Vienna, 1974.

Borbándi, Gyula. *Der ungarische Populismus.* Munich, 1976.

Gati, Charles G. "The Populist Current in Hungarian Politics." Ph.D. diss., Indiana University, 1965.

Gömbös, Gyula. *Szabó Dezső,* 2d ed. Munich, 1969.
Nagy, Péter. *Szabó Dezső,* 2d ed. Budapest, 1979.

See also Endre Ady; Miklós Horthy; Hungarian Literature; Hungarian Soviet Republic; Béla Kun; Nyugat

Szabó, István (1938–)

Hungarian film director. Szabó studied at the Academy of Dramatic and Cinematographic Art in Budapest. Internationally acclaimed for his work, he received the Golden Palm Award at Cannes for his 1982 film, *Mephisto.* During the 1960s and 1970s, he made a number of short features and two documentaries. His films often explore twentieth-century issues of central European consciousness and historical identity. His best-known features are *Father* (1966), a tale of coming-of-age during Stalinist times, and the movies of his 1980s "Central European trilogy." His other feature films include *Álmodozások kora* (*The Age of Daydreaming,* 1964); *Szerelmes film* (*Love Film,* 1970); *Tüzoltó utca 25* (*25 Fireman Street,* 1973); *Budapesti mesék* (*Budapest Tales,* 1976); *Bizalom* (*Confidence,* 1979); *Redl ezredes* (*Colonel Redl,* 1984); *Hanussen* (1988); *Meeting Venus* (1991); and *Dear Emma, Sweet Böbe* (1993).

Dina Iordanova

Further reading
Paul, David. "Szabó," in *Five Filmmakers.* Bloomington, Indiana, 1994, 156–209.

See also Cinema

Szálasi, Ferenc (1891–1946)

Founder, ideologue, and *pártvezető* (party leader) of the Arrow Cross Party, and after October 1944 *nemzetvezető* (leader of the nation). Szálasi was born in 1891 in Kassa (Slovak, Košice); his father was of Armenian ancestry from Transylvania and his mother was of Ruthenian ancestry. An officer during World War I, after the war Szálasi continued to serve as an officer, and in 1925 he joined the General Staff. He also joined a radical-right secret society and dabbled early in political writing, attracting the interest of Hungarian rightist and future prime minister Gyula Gömbös (1886–1936).

The coming of the Depression shocked him. Guided by the Bible, the writings of Karl Marx (1818–83), Leon Trotsky (1879–1940), V.I. Lenin (1870–1924), and others, and the influence of a clairvoyant (Szálasi had definite eccentricities and psychological dysfunctions), he developed his ideology—"Hungarism." Its originality (it was not an imitation of Nazism), inimitable language (when Szálasi was reproached for his chaotic style, he answered: "God too created the world out of chaos!"), and inflexibility were striking. He believed in Christianity (but Szálasi's Christ was not Jewish), and church and state were to be separated.

Since Szálasi espoused the cause of the masses and had plenty of support, the government imprisoned him in 1938. He was freed in the fall of 1940. During World War II, Szálasi was suspicious of the Germans (who likewise detested him). Moreover, he opposed Jewish deportations in 1944. But his patent sincerity and interest in the common Hungarian's fate continued to garner him mass support.

In October 1944 the Germans—having little alternative, given concerns over the continued loyalty of the Hungarian government—offered Szálasi power. Szálasi delivered Hungary to destructive German rearguard action. There were no systematic deportations to Auschwitz (as in the spring of 1944) but tens of thousands of Jews died while Szálasi retreated into his fantasies. In 1945 the Americans arrested him, and, after he was returned to Hungary, he was hanged in 1946.

Nicholas M. Nagy-Talavera

Further reading
Kékessy, Rudolf. *Vádak és valóság.* Budapest, 1941.
Nagy-Talavera, Nicholas M. *The Green Shirts and the Others.* Stanford, California, 1970.
Szálasi, Ferenc. *Út és cél.* Budapest, 1936.

See also Arrow Cross; Auschwitz; Gyula Gömbös; Right Radicalism

Széchenyi, Count István (1791–1860)

Hungarian statesman and economic reformer. The youngest son of Count Ferenc Széchenyi (1754–1820), founder of the Hungarian National Museum, István served in the Habsburg army and distinguished himself in the last phase of the Napoleonic Wars. Following repeated trips to the German lands, France, and England, the latter a country whose institutions inspired him for the rest of his life, Széchenyi traveled in Italy, the Balkans, and Asia Minor, always comparing the Ottoman world with the West and wondering about the backward state of his fatherland.

To encourage capitalistic entrepreneurship among the nobility, he attacked—in *Hitel* (*Credit,* 1830), *Világ* (*Light,* 1831), and *Stádium* (*Stage,* 1833)—Hungary's feudal institutions, serfdom, and backward transportation and economic systems. In *Stádium,* Széchenyi supported "the civil existence of all inhabitants of Hungary," specifically referring to the kingdom's nine million underprivileged, Magyars and non-Magyars alike. He proposed a moderate economic and progressive social program aimed at Hungary's gradual transformation under the political leadership of the aristocracy and within the Habsburg monarchy. He initiated construction of the first permanent bridge over the Danube connecting the twin cities of Buda and Pest; this Chain Bridge, named after Széchenyi, became a symbol, even during his lifetime, of the principle requiring all citizens to contribute to major national enterprises, because the toll charges to cross it had to be paid by noble and nonnoble alike. He also established the Hungarian Academy of Sciences with an offer to donate one year's income from his estates.

As a member of the upper chamber of the diet, Széchenyi was the first to speak in the Magyar language, though at the time the diet's official language was Latin. He supported legislation granting equal rights to Protestants, which had been opposed by the Court and the Catholic clergy. He also had friendly ties with the leaders of the liberal opposition in the diet, including Ferenc Deák (1803–76). But the rise of Lajos Kossuth (1802–94), a new star among a younger, more radical group of liberals, caused Széchenyi to join forces with the conservatives after the diet of 1839–40. Széchenyi, whom Kossuth earlier labeled the greatest Magyar, launched a violent diatribe entitled *A kelet népe* (*People of the Orient,* 1841) against the newspaper *Pesti Hirlap* (*Pest News*) and its editor Kossuth, accusing him of leading the nation into revolution and ruin. Széchenyi also criticized Kossuth's protectionist economic initiatives. In addition, he sharply condemned the policy of forcible Magyarization of non-Magyars.

Despite his fear of revolution, Széchenyi accepted the portfolio of transportation and public works in the first independent Hungarian government formed in April 1848 by Count Lajos Batthyány (1806–49). However, the pressures of the revolutionary changes, and fear of the consequences of the military conflict with Austria, caused him to suffer a nervous breakdown. He was taken to an asylum in Döbling near Vienna in September 1848, where he remained for the rest of his life.

Not until his last four years did Széchenyi resume writing his private diaries. One of his writings, *Blick* (1859), a biting satire on the neoabsolutist regime of Baron Alexander Bach (1813–93), was printed in London anonymously. After copies of the book were smuggled back to Austria, police authorities began to suspect the existence of a wider plot, especially when it was discovered that Széchenyi was the author. Afraid he would have to face the disgrace of a public trial, Széchenyi shot himself on Easter Sunday on April 8, 1860. Public opinion in Hungary saw in his suicide an act of patriotic protest against Vienna's absolutism.

George Barany

Further reading

Barany, George. *Stephen Széchenyi and the Awakening of Hungarian Nationalism, 1791–1841.* Princeton, New Jersey, 1968.

Hungarian Historical Association. *Gróf Széchenyi István Összes Munkái,* 12 vols. Budapest, 1921–39 (published in *Fontes Historiae Hungaricae Aevi Recentioris,* this series has remained incomplete).

Kosáry, Domokos. *Széchenyi Döblingben.* Budapest, 1981.

Spira, György. *A Hungarian Count in the Revolution of 1848.* Budapest, 1974.

———, ed. *Széchenyi István válogatott müvei,* 3 vols. Budapest, 1991.

See also Alexander Bach; Lajos Batthyány; Ferenc Deák; Lajos Kossuth; Magyarization; Neoabsolutism

Székely (Székelyek)

Designation given to Hungarians who settled in the eastern corner of the Carpathian basin within Transylvania. Today the Székely population constitutes anywhere between one-third and two-fifths of the Hungarian population in Romania, located mainly in the counties of Sovata (Szováta), Harghita (Hargita), and Mureş (Maros). In this region they form an island of eight hundred thousand in the geographic center of modern Romania.

Historians have frequently disputed the origin of the Székely population. In the legendary version they are the remnant of the Huns, who escaped to their present homeland after the collapse of Attila's (d. 453) empire. Other historians have linked them to the Avars, or "late Avars." However, it is clear that with the establishment of the Hungarian Kingdom under István I (St. Stephen [c. 975–1038]) in 1000–1038, they were already given a role as the defenders of the eastern marches against barbarian incursions, especially from the Petchenegs and Cumans. While their earliest settlements were probably a little farther west, by the tenth or eleventh centuries they located in their present homeland. Although in the interwar period some Romanian historians made a half-hearted effort to show that the Székely were not Hungarians, and some census takers tried to separate the Székely population from the Hungarians to reduce their overall percentage of the population, those efforts have been discredited both by their intentions and by responsible scholarship.

Romania attempted to dilute the Székely character of eastern Transylvania by the settlement of Romanians from the Regat (Wallachia and Moldavia) in the Székely cities. While it has reduced the overall Hungarian character in the region, it has not eliminated the desire of the Székely population for local political autonomy. In fact, such autonomy was granted to them in 1952 to show the world that "proletarian internationalism" was well on its way to solving nationality conflicts. However, this autonomy (for what was called the Maghiar Autonomous Region) was short-lived, serving mainly a symbolic objective. By 1962, the Romanian government gerrymandered the region and diluted both its ethnic and its symbolic significance. In that year it became the Mureş-Maghiar Autonomous Region. Finally, in 1968 Romanian leader Nicolae Ceauşescu (1918–89) eliminated the autonomous region and replaced it with three counties directly subordinated to the central administration in Bucharest. Because of their compact settlement pattern, the Székely population has been able to provide the Hungarians of Transylvania with their foremost cultural and political leaders.

Andrew Ludanyi

Further reading

Barta, Gábor, István Bóna, Béla Köpeczi, et al. *History of Transylvania,* trans. by Adrienne Chambers-Makkai et al. Budapest, 1994.

Jancsó, Benedek. *The Székelys: A Historical and Ethnographical Essay.* Budapest, 1921.

Malonyay, Dezsö. *A magyar nép müvészete: A székelyföldi, a csángó és a torockói magyar nép müvészete,* vol. 3. Budapest, 1909.

See also Nicolae Ceauşescu; Ethnic Minorities

Szekfű, Gyula (1883–1955)

Hungary's greatest historian. Educated at the intellectually exclusive Eötvös College of the University of Budapest, for two decades after his graduation while also teaching at his alma mater, he was employed at the National Museum, National Archives, Austrian National Archives, and Hungarian Ministry of Foreign Affairs. In 1925 he was appointed to the chair of modern Hungarian history in Budapest.

During the interwar years, Szekfű was allied with conservative prime minister Count István Bethlen (1874–1947), and served as the founding editor of the influential *Magyar Szemle* (*Hungarian Review*) from 1927 to 1944. By the late 1930s, his distaste for Adolf Hitler (1889–1945) forced him to break with his earlier pro-German orientation. In 1938 he resigned his editorship of the *Hungarian Review* and became an outspoken opponent of Hungary's rightward turn. After Germany occupied Hungary in 1944, Szekfű went underground. After the war, he served as Hungary's ambassador to the USSR (1946–48), and then as a member of parliament (1953–55).

Through much of his scholarly life, Szekfű was an opponent of provincialism. He viewed his nation's history from a European perspective, was more critical of it than was customary in those days, and also assessed the role of the Habsburgs more favorably. This embroiled him in many controversies, especially when dealing with such revered personalities as the Transylvanian princes Ferenc Rákóczi (1676–1735) and Gábor Bethlen (1580–1629).

Szekfű's magnum opus is the eight-volume *Magyar történet* (*Hungarian History,* 1928–33), coauthored with noted medievalist Bálint Hóman (1885–1951). He wrote in the spirit of "Europeanism" with the tools of the then fashionable *Geistesgeschichte,* which rejected the role of "laws and objective reality" and emphasized the significance of ideas and "creative spirituality." Szekfű's view in this synthesis came to shape Hungarian historical thinking for the next several decades.

In addition to *Hungarian History,* Szekfű's most influential works were his *Három nemzedék* (*Three Generations,* 1920) and its sequel, *Három nemzedék és ami utána következik* (*Three Generations and Its Aftermath,* 1934), in which he presented a moving and personal analysis of the ills of Hungarian society that led to his nation's downfall at Trianon, the post–World War I peace treaty that forced Hungary to relinquish two-thirds of its prewar territory. He broke with some of his views during World War II but only grudgingly, and only when seeing the world embroiled in the "new barbarism" represented by Nazism. He expressed his disenchantment in his *Valahol utat vesztettünk* (*We Lost Our Way Somewhere,* 1942–43). Yet he never accepted the new social order or adjusted to the requirements of Marxist historiography. Although he died disillusioned, his intellectual prowess never left him.

Steven Béla Várdy

Further reading

Epstein, Irene Raab. *Gyula Szekfű.* New York, 1987.
Várdy, Steven Béla. *Clio's Art in Hungary and in Hungarian-America.* New York, 1985.
———. *Modern Hungarian Historiography.* New York, 1976.

See also István Bethlen; Bálint Hóman; Trianon, Treaty of

Szentgyörgyi, Albert (1893–1986)

Hungarian Nobel laureate in medicine. Szentgyörgyi studied at Budapest and later at Cambridge University (1927, 1929) and at the Mayo Foundation in Rochester, Minnesota (1928), where he was the first to isolate hexuronic acid, later known as ascorbic acid, or Vitamin C, from plant juices and adrenal gland extracts. He taught medical chemistry at Szeged University in Hungary from 1931 to 1945 and was awarded the 1937 Nobel Prize in physiology and medicine for his work on biological combustion. From 1945 to 1947, he was a professor of biochemistry at Budapest University, and in 1947 he emigrated to the United States, where he was named director of muscle research at the Marine Biological Laboratory at Woods Hole, Massachusetts. There he conducted investigations into the biochemistry of muscular action and the causes of cell division, respiration, oxidation, and so on. Among his many books and articles in English, German, and Hungarian are *On Oxidation, Fermentation, Vitamins, Health, and Disease* (1940), *Chemical Physiology of Contractions in Body and Heart Muscle* (1953), and *Introduction to a Submolecular Biology* (1960).

Mártha Pereszlényi-Pintér

Further reading

Sisa, Stephen. *The Spirit of Hungary: A Panorama of Hungarian History and Culture,* 2d ed. Toronto, 1990.
Wagner, Francis S. *Hungarian Contributions to World Civilization.* Center Square, Pennsylvania, 1977.

Szilárd, Leo (1898–1964)

Hungarian-born pioneer in physics and biophysics. After serving in the Habsburg army in World War I, Szilárd transferred from the Budapest Institute of Technology to the Technische Hochschule in Berlin. There he studied under Albert Einstein (1879–1955), Max Planck (1858–1947), and Max von Laue (1879–1960). Szilárd received a doctoral degree under the supervision of von Laue before emigrating to England and the United States. He studied nuclear reactions and was the first to realize that the neutron was the key particle to sustaining a nuclear chain reaction.

When nuclear fission was demonstrated to produce neutrons, Szilárd was again the first with an important realization—that a sustained chain reaction could release enough energy to produce a devastating explosion. He and Eugene Wigner (1902–95) convinced Einstein to urge President Franklin Roosevelt (1882–1945) to develop a fission-based bomb before the Germans could produce one; this led to the formation of the Manhattan Project, on which Szilárd served. With Enrico Fermi (1901–54), he created the first self-sustaining controlled nuclear reaction in December 1942 at the University of Chicago.

When the atomic bomb was made in 1945, Szilárd argued for a demonstration of its power

S rather than using it to cause major destruction. Afterward, he worked tirelessly for arms control and peace. His later scientific work was in biology, on the processes of aging and memory.

Mark Sand

Further reading

Gillispie, Charles Coulston, ed. *Dictionary of Scientific Biography,* vol. 13. New York, 1976.

McMurray, Emily J., ed. *Notable Twentieth-Century Scientists,* vol. 4. Detroit, 1995.

Szlachta

Gentry or nobility in Poland. In the Polish Commonwealth, which existed until 1795, the *szlachta* included all those of noble birth who had the right to vote in elections for the king and to participate in local assemblies, as well as to sit in the national parliament, the Sejm. The Polish gentry or nobility thus considered themselves to be synonymous with the Polish nation.

Poland had proportionately one of the largest nobilities in Europe, equaling 10 percent of the population. It was sizable because the child of every noble was also a noble, like other European nobilities, but unlike that of England, where only the firstborn was noble. However, 60 percent of the gentry had little or no property and were thus dependent on the magnates (large, noble landholders). The vast majority of peasants were the property of noble families until emancipation in the nineteenth century.

While the *szlachta* monopolized the local assemblies, there was no separate corporate organization of the Polish nobility. The king had the right to create nobles but he used it sparingly, particularly in modern times. Although the monopoly on land ownership was formally abolished by the Duchy of Warsaw's constitution (1807), the nobility continued to control most landholdings until the twentieth century. By this same constitution, the nobility were subject to the courts as were all other subjects and had to pay taxes on their estates.

The Polish nobleman, however, was not a gentleman farmer or a professional agricultural manager but the lord of the manor who was to be freed from agricultural duties by his peasants so that he could serve the nation. Most noblemen served Poland in the army or in the government. After the extinction of the Kingdom of Poland in 1831, they served the same role either in exile or within the partitioning empires.

By the eighteenth century, the nobility had four distinct strata: the magnates, the middle nobility (*zamożna szlachta*), the minor nobility (*szlachta zagradowa*), and the landless gentry. This division continued into the twentieth century, although the number of landless gentry increased. While the magnates represented Poland's aristocracy, the middle nobility held estates large enough to maintain a comfortable lifestyle. Their political vision was generally limited to their own region. The *szlachta zagradowa* owned land but worked on it themselves. Often there was little but a title and sword to differentiate this group from their peasant neighbors. The landless nobility were usually poor and consequently eager for social change. Once centralized government was introduced in the nineteenth century, the landless gentry found positions in the ministries, departments, and courts. They also dominated the professions and consequently were sometimes called the "Polish third estate." The majority of the intelligentsia was of gentry origin.

According to the census of 1810 in the Duchy of Warsaw, the magnates represented 3.7 percent of the nobility and the middle nobility 31 percent, while 11.1 percent of the rural *szlachta* worked for other nobles. As Poland was a rural society until after World War II, most of the gentry—60 percent—lived in the country.

The partitioning powers—Austria, Prussia, and Russia—recognized the Polish nobility and incorporated it into their own institutions. However, by the late nineteenth century, the nobility's new basis was wealth, not blood. Already in the Duchy of Warsaw, nobles who did not own land could not vote in the local assemblies.

Peasant emancipation in the nineteenth century was a further blow to the nobles' role in Polish society. In Austria and Prussia, peasant emancipation was carried out so as to disturb as little as possible the nobles' position. However, in Russian-ruled Poland, emancipation was used as a tool to reduce the influence of the *szlachta,* whom St. Petersburg saw as the soul of Polish resistance to Russian rule.

World War I, interwar land reform, and the Great Depression struck at the great estates, leading to their division or bankruptcy. Although the nobility's landholdings declined over the nineteenth and twentieth centuries, this class continued to set the tone for Polish society. In fact, such noble traditions as hand kissing have survived as Polish custom long after they disappeared elsewhere in Europe. While picturesque, these noble traditions are also sometimes considered to have restrained many Poles from participating in commerce and led to the low status assigned to earning money in traditional Polish culture.

John Stanley

Further reading

Jedlicki, Jerzy. "Szlachta," in *Przemiany społeczne w Królestwie Polskim 1815–1864*. Wrocław, 1974.

Kieniewicz, Stefan. *The Emancipation of the Polish Peasantry*. Chicago, 1969.

Leśkiewiczowa, Janina, ed. *Ziemianstwo polskie 1795–1945*. Warsaw, 1985.

Tazbir, Jan. *Tradycje szlacheckie w kulturze polskim*. Warsaw, 1976.

Żarnowski, Janusz. *Społeczeństwo Drugiej Rzeczy-pospolitej 1918–1939*. Warsaw, 1973.

See also Duchy of Warsaw; Great Depression; Intelligentsia; Peasants; Polish Congress Kingdom; Sejm

Sztójay, Döme (1883–1946)

Leading military and political figure in Hungary before and during World War II. Born into a Serbian-Hungarian family with the name Sztojakovich, Sztójay embarked on a military career and later in the 1920s adopted the more Magyar-sounding name Sztójay. He rose quickly in the Hungarian General Staff, specializing in counter-intelligence. In the early 1930s he served as Hungary's military attaché in Berlin, and gained a reputation as a strong admirer of Adolf Hitler (1889–1945) and Nazi Germany. From 1935 to 1944, he was Hungary's chief diplomatic representative to Germany. So ardent was his advocacy of a pro-German orientation for Hungary that his critics sarcastically called him the best ambassador Germany had in Hungary.

When Hitler ordered the occupation of Hungary in 1944, Sztójay became prime minister of the puppet government. During his tenure, the deportation of most of Hungary's Jews took place. Sztójay was not himself a fanatical anti-Semite, but he was indifferent to the fate of the Jews because he believed Hungary's future could be secured only in full cooperation with Nazi Germany. His government took steps to intensify the military struggle against advancing Soviet troops. In August 1944 the Hungarian regent, Admiral Miklós Horthy (1868–1957), dismissed Sztójay and initiated efforts to withdraw from the war. At a postwar trial in Budapest, Sztójay was convicted of war crimes and executed.

Thomas Sakmyster

Further reading

Macartney, C. A. *October Fifteenth: A History of Modern Hungary. 1929–1945*. Edinburgh, 1961.

Sakmyster, Thomas. "A Hungarian Diplomat in Nazi Berlin: Döme Sztójay," in *Hungarian History/World History*, ed. by György Ránki. Budapest, 1985, 295–305.

Szöllösi-Janze, Margit. *Die Pfeilkreuzlerbewegung in Ungarn*. Munich, 1989.

See also Adolf Hitler; Holocaust; Miklós Horthy

Szymborska, Wisława (1923–)

Polish poet, literary critic, and 1996 Nobel Prize recipient. Szymborska's entire literary output of fewer than two hundred poems constitutes one of the most important achievements of contemporary poetry. Her debut as a poet took place in 1957 (*Wołanie do Yeti* [*Calling Out to Yeti*]), even though she had earlier published two volumes of political poems that she eventually repudiated. *Yeti* reveals typical features of Szymborska's mature style: first, the attitude of amazement and wonderment toward the phenomenon of the world and toward human existence; second, curiosity and humanity toward others; and third, seriousness intertwined with playfulness and irony. Despite their deceptive simplicity, Szymborska's poems constitute complex "miniature philosophical treatises" in which she asks questions rather than answers them: "Sól" (Salt, 1962); "Sto pociech" (A Million Laughs, a Bright Hope, 1967); "Wszelki wypadek" (There but for the Grace, 1972); "Wielka liczba" (A Great Number, 1976); "Ludzie na moście" (People on a Bridge, 1986). Her poems often begin with a description of an "insignificant" event or a common belief, which by means of asking "naive questions" and subtle irony become transformed into concise and universal comments on the human condition. Her poems make frequent use of neologisms, wordplay, free verse as well as metrically

S regular verse, allusions, phonetic correspondences, polyphony, and brilliant use of *pointe* (a short, witty conclusion that often challenges the reader's beliefs). Unlike many contemporary Polish writers, Szymborska is neither overtly political nor autobiographical, although she is concrete and situational.

Katarzyna Zechenter

Further reading

Carpenter, Bogdana. "The Importance of the Unimportant." *World Literature Today* 1 (1997).

Barańczak, Stanisław. "The Szymborska Phenomenon." *Salmagundi* 103 (1994).

Kryński, Magnus J. and Robert A. Maguire, trans. *Sounds, Feelings, Thoughts: Seventy Poems by Wisława Szymborska,* Princeton, New Jersey, 1981.

Levine, Madeline G. *Contemporary Polish Poetry 1925–1975.* Boston, 1981.

The Mature Laurel: Essays on Modern Polish Poetry, ed. by Adam Czerniawski. Chester Springs, Pennsylvania, 1991.

See also Polish Literature

T

Taaffe, Count Eduard (1833–95)

Austrian official and twice minister-president. Having held a number of high administrative posts between 1867 and 1879, including minister of the interior, minister of defense, minister-president, and governor of Tirol, Taaffe attained greatest notoriety for his management of the Austrian government as interior minister and minister-president from 1879 to 1891. A conservative aristocrat who had been a boyhood friend of Emperor Franz Joseph (1830–1916), Taaffe regarded himself primarily as a servant of the monarch. Governing with the support of the Iron Ring Coalition, which included German conservative, Czech, and Polish delegates in the Reichsrat (parliament), Taaffe displaced the previously dominant German Liberals and redirected Austrian politics from issues of constitutional structure and parliamentary development to a "muddling through" focused on the negotiation of concessions to national and social interest groups. Under his government, concessions to Slavic national demands included the division of the University of Prague into Czech and German faculties and the Streymayr Ordinances (1880), which extended the official use of Czech in Bohemia and Moravia.

Taaffe attempted to overcome persistent political problems by manipulating the qualifications for electoral participation. To weaken the German Liberals, he extended the suffrage by lowering the requisite yearly taxation payment to five gulden in 1882. Faced with intensifying national and social conflict in his last years in office, he moved to expand the suffrage to include nearly all adult men in 1893. He thereby lost the support of his conservative parliamentary allies and fell from power.

Philip Pajakowski

Further reading

Beck, Georg. "Die Personlichkeit des Grafen Eduard Taaffe." Ph.D. diss., University of Vienna, 1949.

Jenks, William A. *Austria under the Iron Ring, 1879–1893.* Charlottesville, Virginia, 1965.

Skedl, Arthur, ed. *Der politische Nachlass des Grafen Eduard Taaffe.* Vienna, 1923.

See also Franz Joseph

Tanzimat

Reform era in the Ottoman Empire from 1839 to 1876 (the reigns of Abdul Mejid [1839–61] and Abdul Aziz [1861–76]), continuing and amplifying the reforms begun by Mahmud II (1785–1839). Strengthening the armed forces had been Mahmud's priority, and he controlled the reforms. The *tanzimat* (reorganization) was guided by three leading statesmen in the civil bureaucracy: Mustafa Reshid Pasha (1800–1858), Ali Pasha (1815–71), and Fuad Pasha (1815–69). The reforms they initiated were seen as a challenge to the traditional order. They and their supporters sought to strengthen the administrative, fiscal, and military power of the central government. In the process, they also hoped to create a greater sense of common loyalty (*Osmanlilik* [Ottomanism]) among the empire's ethnically diverse subjects by promoting civic equality. The imperial decrees, Hatt-i Sherif (1839) and Hatt-i Hümayun of Gülhane (1856), and the constitution issued in 1876 exemplified the latter goal. Both practical needs and a broad ideal necessitated changes in administration and education. The Vilayet Law of 1864 reorganized provincial government. *Sanjaks,* heretofore the administrative units within which the *timars* (land-holdings) were grouped, were reorganized into *vilayets* (provinces) varying in size. Governors (*vali*) and lesser officials were appointed from Istanbul. The work of Midhat Pasha (1822–84) in Bulgaria illustrates how the new system could be effective. Councils made up of appointed and elected representatives were established to advise the officials. In areas where non-Muslims resided, they also served on the councils. Better-trained administrators and informed subjects required educational reforms. *Tanzimat* officials left primary schooling to the respective religious communities. Secular secondary schools, however, were expanded in the 1850s and opened to students of all faiths. An institution of higher learning embracing European pedagogy was established in Istanbul in the late 1860s. Also the Ottoman Council of State, created in 1868, drew up an ambitious plan to reorganize state educational institutions and make them competitive with schools operated by the Christian communities. The imperial decrees of 1839 and 1856 set out basic principles intended to assure the equality of all subjects, ensure their security, and promote economic development. Christians in the Balkans, however, saw reform as ending discrimination against them while maintaining their separate identities through their confessional communities, the *millets*. *Tanzimat* officials encouraged reform of the *millets* in the early 1860s to separate secular from religious functions, but they continued to recognize their validity. The *millets* served Christians as the focus of a growing national identity. From the 1840s to the 1870s, legal reforms in commercial, civil, and criminal law were introduced. Borrowing from European jurisprudence, codes and courts were established alongside the *Shari'ah,* Islamic religious law. Like these reforms, the constitution promulgated in 1876 did not accomplish much and was quickly suspended by Abdul Hamid II (1842–1909). Following on the efforts in the 1820s and 1830s to build, train, and equip a European-style army, reorganizations were undertaken in 1842 and 1869 to create a conscript army able to keep abreast of new developments in Europe. Lack of financial resources, however, hampered efforts at military modernization. The *tanzimat* reforms produced mixed results because of contradictory views among and within the groups involved and the difficulty of applying foreign ideas to the traditional order. Ottoman civil and military bureaucrats sought to secure their own interests while serving the state, European diplomats represented their countries and Christian clients in the empire, and Christians, especially in the Balkans, sought economic and social advancement but espoused ethnically defined politics.

Gerasimos Augustinos

Further reading
Augustinos, Gerasimos. *The Greeks of Asia Minor.* Kent, Ohio, 1992.
Berkes, Niyazi. *The Development of Secularism in Turkey.* Montreal, 1964.
Davison, Roderic H. *Reform in the Ottoman Empire 1856–1876.* Princeton, New Jersey, 1963.
Findley, Carter V. *Bureaucratic Reform in the Ottoman Empire.* Princeton, New Jersey, 1980.
Lewis, Bernard. *The Emergence of Modern Turkey.* London, 1961,

See also Abdul Hamid II; *Millet;* Ottoman Empire; *Timar*

Tarski, Alfred (1902–83)
Member of the Warsaw School of Logic and major contributor to meta-mathematics and semantics. Trained under the tutelage of Kazimierz Twardowski (1866–1938), Tarski earned the title of cofounder (with David Hilbert [1862–1943]) of meta-mathematics for his early work in mathematics and especially meta-mathematics, a branch of logic that investigates formal mathematical theories. In this area, Tarski attempted to describe an axiomatic theory of formal systems that would be universal in that all formal systems could be analyzed within this theory. His flexible use of set theory, which separated him from others working in the field, provided a basis for his subsequent work in semantics.

Building on his work in meta-mathematics, Tarski in the 1930s developed his semantic method that focused on an articulation of the relationship between expressions and their denoted objects. His ultimate goal was to provide an adequate and correct definition of the expression "a true sentence." Hence, his semantic endeavors placed him squarely in the center of the perennial philosophical issue of the relationship between language and reality and the establishment of criteria for the true proposition. By developing the concept of a "model" (a formal, ordered description of a set of propositions in terms of its constant predicates and relations), Tarski was able to divide propositions into two sets, the true and the false. Further considerations led him to state that the set of (number of) sentences that are true in a given model are not definable in that model.

James Eiswert

Further reading

Tarski, Alfred. *Introduction to Logic and to the Methodology of the Deductive Sciences,* ed. by Jan Tarski, 4th ed. New York, 1994.
———. *Logic, Semantics, Meta-Mathematics: Papers from 1923 to 1938,* trans. by J.H. Woodger, ed. by John Corcoran, 2d ed. Indianapolis, Indiana, 1983.

See also Philosophy; Kazimierz Twardowski

Tătărescu, Gheorghe (1886–1957)

A leader of Romania's National Liberal Party and prime minister. Tătărescu, widely regarded as an opportunist, was appointed prime minister by Carol II (1893–1953) following the assassination of his predecessor, Ion Duca (1879–1933). The first period during which he was prime minister (1934–37) was followed by the introduction of King Carol's royal dictatorship. During this period, he was viewed as indulgent toward the Iron Guard, the Romanian nationalist-fascist organization, and as harsh in dealing with Romanian Communists. Tătărescu led the Liberal Party to defeat in the general elections in 1937, then formed his own faction of the party during World War II. He served as vice prime minister and foreign minister in the Communist regime led by Petru Groza (1884–1958) in 1945. But as foreign minister, in an effort to advance the Liberal agenda, he was critical of the economic policies of the Communist regime. The Communists also viewed the Foreign Ministry as a haven for anti-Communist elements. Consequently, Tătărescu was forced out as foreign minister in 1947.

Robert Weiner

Further reading

Fischer-Galati, Stephen. *Twentieth Century Rumania.* New York, 1991.
Hitchins, Keith. *Rumania: 1866–1947.* Oxford, 1994.
Ionescu, Ghita. *Communism in Rumania.* Westport, Connecticut, 1976.
Roberts, Henry L. *Rumania.* New York, 1951.

See also Carol II; Petru Groza; Iron Guard

Tatra Mountains

Highest part of the western Carpathian Mountains. The Tatras were elevated during the Alpine orogenic process in the Upper Cretaceous period. They cover 276 square miles (715 sq km) in two national parks in Poland (23 percent) and Slovakia. The eastern sector is divided into High and Lower Tatra. The rugged and jagged peaks tower over the low-lying floors of the surrounding basins and traversing deep river valleys: the Orava and Podhale basins from west and north; the Vah with the Orava Rivers, and the Dunajec (Dounaiets) with the Poprad Rivers, in Slovakia and Poland, respectively.

The igneous and metamorphic core of the mountains is mantled by sedimentary Trias-Cretaceous and Tertiary (Neocen) limestones and dolomites. Karst phenomena—underground streams and caves—appear on the northern slopes. The weathering of dolomite rocks created odd forms bearing several local names (monks, funnels).

Several ponds of postglacial origin are well-known tourist attractions for their emerald to deep blue waters: Morskie Oko (The Sea Eye), Czarny Staw (The Black Pond), and Wielki Staw (The Great Pond).

The five altitudinal climatic-vegetational zones have a characteristic temperature lapse rate. Snow cover lasts from September to May. Vegetation ranges from mixed forest to coniferous to high-altitude dwarf vegetation beyond which are Alpine meadows, called hale (hahleh), on gentle slopes.

Abraham Melezin

Further reading

Lencewicz, Stanisław. *Geografia Fizyczna Polski,* 3d ed. Warsaw, 1955.
Passendorfer, Edward. *Jak Powstały Tatry.* Warsaw, 1952.

Teleki, Count László (1811–61)

Writer, politician, diplomat, and member of the Hungarian Academy of Sciences. Teleki was born in Pest, where he received degrees from Pest University, then continued his studies in Berlin. He began his career as a poet and drama-writer and in the course of his trips abroad, came in touch with Victor Hugo (1802–85), whose influence was clearly discernible in his works. His most significant drama, *The Minion,* was published in 1841. At the age of twenty-five, he was elected a member of the Hungarian Academy of Sciences and was also elected to the Transylvanian diet. He took a serious interest in politics in 1841, and participated in the reform-oriented sessions of the Hungarian diet in the years before the Revolution of 1848–49. In 1844 he became the vice president of the Society for the Protection of Hungarian Products, which had been created to support home industries. Under the influence of Lajos Kossuth (1802–94), his political attitude became increasingly more radical. He became a liberal representative from County Pest, demanding the independence of Hungary from the Habsburg monarchy. Although he did not accept a ministerial position in the independent Hungarian government, in September 1848 he became the Hungarian envoy to France. Following the defeat of the Hungarian revolution, he remained in Paris. In his absence, he was sentenced to death and even executed in effigy. While serving as Hungarian envoy (and also during his twelve years in exile), Teleki did his best to obtain the assistance of the French government and other circles to promote Hungarian independence. His book dealing with the Hungarian War for Independence, *La Hongrie aux peuples civilisés,* was published in France in 1849, and later also in English, German, and finally Hungarian. In 1860 Saxon police captured him and delivered him to the Austrian government. Emperor Franz Joseph (1830–1916) released him with the stipulation that he could not leave the territories of Hungary and Austria, that he break his connections with the foreign enemies of Austria, and that he not take part in politics. Teleki later received an invitation in the form of a royal letter to the upper house of the parliament. He was elected as a representative of the upper house and became the leader of the opposition. He was accused of breach of faith for his political views and committed suicide on May 8, 1861.

Pál Péter Tóth

Further reading

Chassin, Ch. L. *Ladislas Téleky.* Paris, 1851.

Szabad, György. *Miért halt meg Teleki László?* Budapest, 1985.

Szinnyei, József. *Magyar írók élete és munkái,* vol. 13. Budapest, 1984.

Horváth, Zoltán. *Teleki, László 1811–1861,* vols 1–2. Budapest, 1964.

See also Franz Joseph; Hungarian War for Independence; Lajos Kossuth; Revolutions of 1848

Teleki, Pál (1879–1941)

Hungarian scholar and statesman, and descendant of a historic Transylvanian family. After receiving a doctorate in 1903, Teleki began his university teaching career as a geographer. He traveled widely in Europe and elsewhere and in 1905 he was elected to parliament. In the postrevolutionary governments of 1919–21 (following the tumultuous period after World War I that gripped Hungary in 1918–19), he held several portfolios before becoming prime minister. After leaving office, he continued to be active in academic and public life. Teleki was a lifelong promoter of the scouting movement and held prominent positions in national and international academic organizations. He was a persistent advocate of the revision of the postwar territorial settlement and was the founder of the Hungarian League for Revision, which opposed the 1920 Treaty of Trianon formalizing those revisions.

Early in 1939, he again became prime minister. The second Teleki administration's agenda was ambitious; it strove to gather in more of the lands that Hungary had lost after World War I, tried to appease Nazi Germany, and struggled to maintain Hungarian neutrality. Under Teleki, Hungary regained Subcarpathia Rus' (Ruthenia) through military action and northern Transylvania through arbitration by Germany and Italy (the Vienna Award). However, the price paid for such gains was substantial: the Germans were given nearly unrestricted access to Hungarian resources, and Hungary joined the Tripartite Pact (Germany, Italy, Japan). Furthermore, the government extended restrictions on Jews and granted extensive privileges to the country's German minority. Sometimes the Teleki government refused to comply with German wishes. In September 1939, for example, it denied permission for German troops to move against southeastern Poland through Hungarian territory and, in fact, opened Hungary's borders to Polish refugees. When late in 1940 rumors of Hitler's (1889–1945) planned invasion of the Soviet Union reached Budapest, Teleki sought to bolster Hungarian neutrality through closer relations with Yugoslavia and the Soviet Union. When, during the Yugoslav crisis of early spring 1941, it became evident these policies would fail and Teleki could not keep Hungary from becoming involved in Hitler's invasion of Yugoslavia, he committed suicide.

N.F. Dreisziger

Further reading
Tilkovszky, Loránt. *Pál Teleki, 1879–1941: A Biographical Sketch.* Budapest, 1974.

See also Revisionism; Subcarpathian Rus'; Transylvanian Dispute; Trianon, Treaty of; Vienna Awards

Teller, Edward (1908–)

Hungarian-born physicist who is considered the father of the hydrogen bomb. Teller studied at several universities in Germany, earning a doctorate in 1930 at the University of Leipzig; his work with Werner Heisenberg (1901–76) led to a dissertation on using quantum mechanics to calculate energy levels in a hydrogen molecule. After working in Copenhagen and London, he moved in 1935 to George Washington University in Washington, D.C.

The outbreak of war in Europe and the discovery of nuclear fission in the late 1930s pushed the U.S. government to form the Manhattan Project to build a fission-based atomic bomb. Teller was involved from the beginning, but after a time convinced project director J. Robert Oppenheimer (1904–67) to allow him to work on a more powerful hydrogen fusion bomb, or "super." When dropping the fission bomb on Japan ended World War II, interest in the H-bomb faded. It was revived after the Soviet Union tested a fission bomb in 1949, and Teller was put in charge of H-bomb development. A successful test of the "super" was held in November 1952.

Teller increasingly became caught up in political matters and Cold War rhetoric. In 1983 he was the primary scientific voice that convinced U.S. President Ronald Reagan (1911–) to propose the national missile shield known as the Strategic Defense Initiative.

Mark Sand

Further reading
Blumberg, Stanley A. and Louis G. Panos. *Edward Teller: Giant of the Golden Age of Physics.* New York, 1990.
McMurray, Emily J., ed. *Notable Twentieth-Century Scientists,* vol. 4. Detroit, 1995.
Porter, Roy, ed. *The Biographical Dictionary of Scientists,* 2d ed. New York, 1994.

See also Cold War; Hungarian Émigrés

Teschen

Oft-disputed industrial town and region on the Polish, Czech, and Slovak borders, now divided between Poland and the Czech Republic. Frequent political maneuvering and military action to control the coal, iron ore, iron, and steel production of this region epitomizes the historic, destructive territorial conflicts among great and small powers in the region.

Originally the duchy of Teschen (Polish, Cieszn; Czech, Těšín) was part of Polish Silesia, but it was subsequently ruled by Bohemia (1335–1526) and the Habsburgs (1526–1919). It was part of only small areas of Silesia retained within the Austrian Empire after 1742, when most of the region was seized by Prussia. After World War I, Poland occupied and claimed all of Teschen and its strategic economic resources and rail network; Czechoslovakia claimed it on grounds of historical precedence. In 1920 the Conference of Ambassadors, which implemented the conditions of the Versailles treaty, divided the region without holding a planned plebiscite, giving the town of Teschen and the eastern part of the region to Poland and the more valuable western areas with the major coal, industrial, and rail resources to Czechoslovakia. Poland was unhappy and the territorial dispute soured Polish-Czechoslovak relations in the interwar period. After Czechoslovakia was weakened by the loss of the Sudetenland to Germany in 1938, Poland reoccupied all the region, which was soon thereafter incorporated into the Third Reich. In 1945 the Soviet Union interceded in the dispute and forced acceptance of the 1920 boundaries, which remain in effect.

William H. Berentsen

Further reading
Bowman, I. *The New World: Problems in Political Geography,* 4th ed. Chicago, 1928.

Theter

A number of common experiences have shaped the development of theater in Eastern Europe. Some of these have been pan-European, while others were specific to the various cultures that were for centuries within the Austrian or Ottoman Empires and then later members of the Soviet bloc. The romanticism and cultural nationalism that developed after the French Revolution and a continuing ferment against entrenched power informed nineteenth-century Eastern European theater. In the twentieth century, the two world wars and their aftermaths, the establishment of Communist governments in the region, and the hegemony of the Soviet Union over most of the countries critically affected all aspects of theatrical life and creation.

Within both the Habsburg and the Ottoman Empires, dramatic performances existed in two general contexts—urban and rural. Most of the urban areas were part of an international network of theater exchange and influence. In large and small cities—particularly in the Habsburg holdings in Czechoslovakia, Hungary, Poland (divided among Austria, Prussia, and Russia), Croatia, and Slovenia, and also in the northern Ottoman areas of Romania and Serbia—German, French, Italian, and other touring companies performed, bringing new plays, new ideas, and new stage practices to local audiences and theater practitioners. In addition, permanent German-language theaters and companies had been established throughout the Habsburg Empire. Influences from the rest of Europe were less common in Ottoman-held Bulgaria, Albania, Bosnia, and Macedonia.

In rural areas, traditions of peasant drama continued to thrive as they had for centuries. Such works included seasonal dramas, popular puppet shows, and a Romanian Orthodox Church pageant incorporating pagan traditional elements such as the *Călușari* dance. The peasant genres were important not only in themselves but also because they provided models and thematic material for the urban playwrights who sought to rediscover their peasant roots and to promote the cause of peasant liberation.

An important component in the development of national theaters was the presentation of plays in local languages. While some of the populations had been producing such work earlier, it was during the nineteenth century, and as a central factor in the various national revival movements, that vernacular literature and drama came to the fore. The Czechs, for example, date their Czech-language drama from the Middle Ages; however, their culture was nearly obliterated under seventeenth- and eighteenth-century Habsburg rule, and it was in the late eighteenth and nineteenth centuries that Czech language drama gained renewed energy and motivation. Bulgaria went through a similar process under the Turks; its literary language nearly disappeared but was revived in the nineteenth century and was used in drama and other literature. The first plays in Hungarian and Polish appeared in the late eighteenth century; the first in Romanian in 1819; and in Albanian in 1874. Yugoslavia's diverse language groups, including Croats, Serbs, and Slovenes, developed their own literatures and dramas also mainly during the nineteenth century. As East European drama developed in this era, its content addressed major political and social concerns of the day. Through their art, practitioners engaged directly in the struggles to achieve liberation both of the national groups from imperial domination and of the peasantry from their serfdom. The consequent growing interest in the "people," in cultural roots, and in nationalism led to the introduction of peasant characters and themes into urban theater contexts—and even the adaptation of traditional peasant dramatic forms. At the same time that national dramatic literatures were developing, foreign plays were also being produced in translation, and Eastern European theater was following the various trends of European theater in general. Thus drama in the region went through periods of romanticism, realism, naturalism, and so on.

Eastern European theater in the twentieth century was interrupted and buffeted by wars, foreign occupations, and various kinds of repression. After World War II, the Communist takeover of the entire region was both beneficial and detrimental to theater development. On the one hand, theater was now officially encouraged and underwritten by the government. The price for such support and security, however, was the burden of creating according to party dictates. This meant thematic material in line with Communist policy and rendered in the style of socialist realism. The strictures were particularly rigid under Stalin (1879–1953), easing only when he was no longer in control. Thus, after Yugoslavia broke with the Soviet Union in 1948, that country enjoyed free expression in all its arts, and it was artists rather than politicians who determined artistic and administrative policy. Stalin's death led to greater freedom elsewhere—except in Albania, where repression deepened as that country became the most fanatical Communist regime.

In the twentieth century, Eastern European theater became a vital force in the international arena, contributing to developments in both form and content. For example, Czech dramatist Karel Čapek (1890–1938) wrote innovative theater pieces on the evils of war, technological regimentation, and political oppression. His *RUR* (1921), which pitted robots against humans, became an international success in the 1920s and 1930s. Another important Czech dramatist, Václav Havel (1936–) also wrote on political matters—targeting the repressive Communist regime under which he lived. His works first appeared internationally in the 1960s. Havel was imprisoned on a number of occasions but remained a moral force in the country. In 1989 he was elected president of the post-Communist government. Other notable Czech theater artists include designer Josef Svoboda (1920–), who worked at the Czech National Theater and also for theater and opera houses around the world. One of the most important forces in twentieth-century theater has been Polish director Jerzy Grotowski (1933–), known for his experimental laboratory theater (established in Opole in 1959 and moved to Wrocław in 1965). Its tours of the West in the 1960s irrevocably altered the conception of theater and the actor's role in it. Grotowski's *Towards a Poor Theater* (1968), an anthology on his theory and method, disseminated his approach even further. It elaborated the idea of theater that relied solely on the expressive art of the actor, eliminating scenery, elaborate costumes, lighting, and sound effects. Grotowski's innovations in the aesthetics of theater, actor training, and staging formats and practices have had a profound significance internationally.

Other artists—dramatists, directors, designers, and actors—have also had an impact internationally. Exchange has been frequent between Eastern European countries—particularly Czechoslovakia, Poland, Hungary, and Yugoslavia—and the West. Plays are translated and performed; directors, designers, and teachers work outside their own theaters and countries; and companies perform all over the world. An array of theater practitioners meet at international conferences and festivals to explore and share works and ideas. By the end of the twentieth century, Eastern European theater had become a major player in the world arena.

Nancy Lee Ruyter

Further reading

Banham, Martin, ed. *The Cambridge Guide to World Theatre.* Cambridge, 1988.
The Drama Review (formerly *Tulane Drama Review*).
Hartnoll, Phyllis. *The Oxford Companion to the Theatre,* 4th ed. Oxford, 1983.
Kullman, Colby H. and William C. Young. *Theatre Companies of the World.* New York, 1986.
Performing Arts Journal.

See also Karel Čapek; Dance; Václav Havel; Eugene Ionescu; Nationalism; Stalin; Zhdanovshchina

Thrace

Historic region of the southeastern Balkan Peninsula. The territory embraced by the term has varied greatly. At different times the accepted northern boundary has been the Danube River, the Balkan (Stara Planina) Mountains, or the Bulgarian boundary with Greece. Generally Thrace has been thought of as the region south and east of the Rhodope Mountains to the Aegean Sea.

Thrace was made a Roman province in A.D. 46 and became part of the eastern Byzantine Empire in 395. The Ottoman Empire incorporated all of Thrace after 1453. Although the Maritsa valley region of Upper Thrace was inhabited principally by Bulgarians, it became the core of the short-lived Ottoman autonomous province of Eastern Rumelia after Bulgaria became independent in 1878. After the 1885 merger of Eastern Rumelia with Bulgaria, the term "Thrace" came to be applied only to the Aegean Sea strip of Southern Thrace. Thrace was partitioned politically following the two Balkan Wars (1912–13) and World War I. Since present boundaries were fixed in 1923, approximately two-thirds of the region has been in Bulgaria, one-quarter in Greece, and one-tenth in Turkey.

The Bulgarian section of Thrace embraces the densely populated Maritsa Valley. The ancient town of Plovdiv is its regional center. The fertile land produces high yields of Turkish tobacco, corn (maize), rice, and grapes for wine. Peppers, essential oils, and peanuts are also produced. Some 60 percent of farmland is irrigated because summers

T tend to be dry. Thrace also has significant industrial development based particularly on local coal supplies.

Thomas M. Poulsen

Further reading

Macdermott, Mercia. *A History of Bulgaria, 1393–1885*. London, 1962.

See also Balkan Wars; Eastern Rumelia; Maritsa Valley; Plovdiv

Three Emperors' League (Dreikaiserbund)

International political understanding of the 1870s and 1880s among Germany, Austria-Hungary, and Russia. The league existed as a series of agreements negotiated by German Chancellor Otto von Bismarck (1815–98) with the two other powers. Its purpose was to maintain peace in Eastern Europe and, for Germany, to prevent France from allying with either Austria-Hungary or Russia.

In September 1872 William I (1797–1888) of Germany, Franz Joseph (1830–1916) of Austria-Hungary, and Alexander II (1818–81) of Russia met in Berlin. In May and June 1873 the three governments pledged themselves to a vague agreement for monarchical cooperation against subversive political forces.

In 1881 Bismarck negotiated a more formal alliance among the three powers, sometimes referred to as the "second" Three Emperors' League. This provided for joint consultation on Turkish territorial changes in the Balkans and promised benevolent neutrality if one of the three powers went to war with a fourth power, except Turkey. That agreement was renewed in 1884, but it lapsed in 1887 because of tensions between Russia and Austria-Hungary in the Balkans.

Robert Mark Spaulding

Further reading

Bridge, F. R. *The Great Powers and the European States System, 1815–1914*. New York, 1980.

Kennan, George. *The Decline of Bismarck's European Order*. Princeton, New Jersey, 1979.

Jelavich, Barbara. *A Century of Russian Foreign Policy, 1814–1914*. Philadelphia, 1964.

Pflanze, Otto. *Bismarck and the Development of Germany,* 3 vols. Princeton, New Jersey, 1990.

See also Eastern Question; Otto von Bismarck

Timar

Ottoman landholding system used in the Balkans. As the Ottoman Empire expanded into southeastern Europe during the fifteenth century, the *timar* became a basic institution linking the peasant subjects (*reaya*), the military class (*sipahi*), and wealth from cultivated land. The state granted the spearhead of the Ottoman military, the cavalrymen (*sipahi*), nonheritable rights to an estate and the villagers who cultivated the land. In return for providing military service, the *sipahi* was entitled to a share of the revenues in kind paid by peasants to the state. All agricultural land belonged to the state as crownland (*miri*), but the peasant enjoyed usufruct over the produce and hereditary rights to cultivate the land. The peasant's house, livestock, orchard or garden, and perhaps a shop were his own property. Peasant obligations included the tithe, a head tax (in the Balkans, a household tax), irregular taxes, and a small tax on livestock. The *sipahi* acted as the state's representative, enforcing its laws on the peasants and managing the *timar* property. The *sipahi* equipped himself with armor and horse for military service and, depending on the amount of income the *timar* produced, was required to provide additional armed horsemen for the army. In the Balkans, Christians who had held fiefs before the Ottoman conquest could receive a *timar* if they agreed to serve the sultan and later became Muslims. The majority of the *timar* holders, however, were slaves of the sultan. When it functioned as intended, the *timar* system provided security for the *reaya* and armed warriors for the sultan's military. But the system was subject to abuse as nonmilitary individuals bribed provincial officials to acquire a *timar*. Also pressure mounted on the government to conquer new lands to provide *timars* as non-*sipahi* warriors competed with the *sipahi* class for *timars* in the Balkans. By the seventeenth century, with the development in Europe of modern armies based on infantry, the *sipahi* class became obsolete. Fewer *sipahi* were willing to offer military service. Moreover, the *timars,* based on a fixed income, were economically obsolete. The system deteriorated as many *timars* were converted to private property and acquired by *reaya*, while the Ottoman government, trying to meet its fiscal needs, turned to leasing state land. This led to the emergence of large private farms, the *chiftliks*. Some *timars* remained, mostly in Anatolia, and were finally revoked by Sultan Mahmud II (1785–1839) in 1831.

Gerasimos Augustinos

Further reading

Beldiceanu, Nicoara. *Le Timar dans l'etat ottoman: Début XIVe–début XVIe siècle.* Wiesbaden, 1980.

Inalcik, Halil. *The Ottoman Empire.* London, 1973.

McGowan, Bruce. *Economic Life in Ottoman Europe: Taxation, Trade, and the Struggle for Land, 1600–1800.* Cambridge, 1981.

Sugar, Peter. *Southeastern Europe under Ottoman Rule 1354–1804.* Seattle, Washington, 1977.

See also Chiftlik; Mahmud II; Ottoman Empire; Peasants

Timişoara

Romanian city. Timişoara (German, Temeschwar; Hungarian, Temesvar; Serbian, Timisvar) is spread over 20 square miles (114 sq km) in a rich agricultural area irrigated from the river Bega close to the border with Serbia. It now has almost three hundred thousand inhabitants, the great majority of them Romanians but with a substantial Hungarian minority, some Gypsies, a few Serbs, and the remnants of a previously large, almost dominant, group of German settlers. From a city reflecting primarily the needs and production of the surrounding agricultural areas, it has developed in recent decades into an industrial center with an emphasis on light and consumer industry. But it continues to cultivate its image as a technologically progressive, well-maintained, pleasant place to live, with many educational establishments (a university and research institutes with twenty thousand students) and several cultural institutions.

Historically, Timişoara was on the border where Europe (primarily Austria) and the Ottoman Empire and their respective civilizations confronted each other. First recorded in documents in 1266 as Castrus Timisiensis, Timişoara appears on a map dated 1339 and is later mentioned in the context of anti-Ottoman struggles. Bloody conflicts notwithstanding, a Turkish scribe recorded in 1660 that during the era of Ottoman occupation Timişoara was an important town of twelve thousand inhabitants, four hundred shops, many schools, and a Muslim university. But by the middle of the eighteenth century, Timişoara was in Austrian hands. In 1867, after the *Ausgleich* (Compromise) that formed the Dual Monarchy of Austria-Hungary, the Hungarians took jurisdiction over the city. In 1918 it was incorporated into Greater Romania, the unified Romanian state created after World War I. In December 1989 Timişoara attracted worldwide attention by starting a revolution that unseated the dictatorial Communist regime of Nicolae Ceauşescu (1918–89).

Ladis K.D. Kristof

Further reading

Ardelean, Victor and Ion Zăvoianu. *Judeţul Timiş.* Bucharest, 1979.

Ionescu, Grigore. *Istoria Arhitecturii în Romînia.* Bucharest, 1963.

Magocsi, Paul Robert. *Historical Atlas of East Central Europe.* Seattle, Washington, 1993.

România: Atlas istoric-geographic. Bucharest, 1996.

See also Ausgleich; Nicolae Ceauşescu; Dual Monarchy; Greater Romania

Tirana

Capital and largest city of Albania and its principal industrial and commercial center. Inland from the central coast and on the edge of the coastal lowland, Tirana (Albania, Tiranë) is located on the Tirana River at the head of the basin of the river Ishm. Connection to the port of Durrës on the coast is short and manageable, but the Dajti Massif to the east and the Krraba Highlands to the southeast make communication difficult in those directions.

Until it became the national capital in 1920, Tirana remained a small and unimportant town. In 1923 it had a population of only 11,000. Owing largely to its increasing administrative functions, its population grew to 25,000 by 1938; by 1945, it had 60,000 inhabitants and was the largest town in Albania. The expansion of industry and government functions after 1945 brought about rapid growth, reaching a population of 157,000 in 1964. Continued industrial growth, resulting in the concentration of almost half of Albania's light industry and more than half of the metallurgical industry in Tirana, contributed to increase the population to 226,000 (1987), nearly equal to the total of Durrës, Shkodra, and Elbasan combined.

Before the 1930s, the urban landscape was similar to that of most Turkish provincial towns, with a central bazaar surrounded by narrow streets and neighborhoods centering on local mosques. A plan for a grand urban center, surrounded by broad avenues lined with public buildings, was

T initiated under Italian supervision. Resumed and elaborated in 1952–56, it resulted in the completion of Skanderbeg Square as the city focus. The equestrian statue of Skanderbeg (1405–68) (1968), the Albanian hero who fought the forces of the Ottoman Turks, on the south side faces the high-rise Tirana Hotel (1979) and is flanked by the Palace of Culture (1966) to the east and the National Historical Museum to the west. In stark contrast is the nearby glass-and-steel pyramid of the Enver Hoxha (1908–85) Memorial (1988), the monument to the Communist leader. While much of the Turkish and oriental character of the center has disappeared, including the old bazaar, some structures have been preserved, as in the case of the Mosque of Etem Bey with its adjoining clock tower.

Albert M. Tosches

Further reading

Albania, Nagel's Encyclopedia—Guide. Geneva, 1990.

Mellor, Roy E.H. *Eastern Europe.* New York, 1975.

Osborne, R.H. *East Central Europe.* New York, 1967.

Pounds, Norman J.G. *Eastern Europe.* Chicago, 1969.

See also*:* Enver Hoxha

Tiso, Jozef (1887–1947)

Roman Catholic priest, Slovak nationalist activist, and president of the pro-Nazi Slovak Republic that existed from 1939 to 1945. Tiso was born of humble origins in Vel'ká Bytča in northwest Slovakia in 1887. He studied theology at the Pazmaneum in Vienna, after which he was ordained in 1910. After holding a series of church positions, he became pastor in Bánovce nad Bebravou in 1924, an office he held until 1945. Though not an active Slovak nationalist before 1918, he joined the Catholic and nationalist Slovak People's Party (SSP) after World War I, engaging in its organizational and propaganda work. He was a parliamentarian from 1925 to 1938 and Czechoslovakia's minister of health from 1927 to 1929. In the 1930s, as the SSP's ideologist and primary negotiator, he was the party's most influential member after Andrej Hlinka (1864–1938), whom he succeeded as party chairman in August 1938. Tiso was the chief Slovak political leader during the period of Nazi German domination, serving as prime minister of autonomous Slovakia from October 1938 to March 1939, prime minister of the Slovak Republic from March 1939 to October 1939, and that republic's president from October 1939 until its collapse in the spring of 1945. After his regime's demise, Tiso fled to Austria and was eventually imprisoned by American forces. He was extradited to Czechoslovakia in 1946, tried for war crimes, and executed on April 18, 1947. As the head of a state closely allied with Nazi Germany that sent 55,000 Jews to Nazi death camps but that represented the first (and until 1993 the only) independent Slovak state, Tiso remains a figure of historical controversy.

James Felak

Further reading

Čulen, Konštantín. *Po Svätoplukovi druhá naša hlava (Život Dr. Jozefa Tisu).* Bratislava, 1992.

Hoensch, Jörg K. "The Slovak Republic, 1939–1945," in Victor S. Mamatey and Radomír Luža, *A History of the Czechoslovak Republic 1918–1948.* Princeton, New Jersey, 1973.

Jelinek, Yeshayahu. *The Parish Republic: Hlinka's Slovak People's Party, 1939–1945.* Boulder, Colorado, 1976.

Sutherland, Anthony X. *Dr. Jozef Tiso and Modern Slovakia.* Cleveland, Ohio, 1978.

Rašla, Anton and Ernest Žabkay. *Proces s dr. J. Tisom, Spomienky.* Bratislava, 1990.

See also Andrej Hlinka; Slovak Republic

Tisza, Count István (1861–1918)

Hungarian politician and prime minister (1903–05; 1913–17). The son of Kálmán Tisza (1830–1902), István Tisza was born in Pest. He entered parliament in 1886 as a member of the Liberal Party. He represented those in that party who most uncompromisingly defended the 1867 *Ausgleich* (Compromise) that created the Dual Monarchy of Austria-Hungary. He also strongly repudiated the opposition's constant filibustering, which, in his opinion, both paralyzed legislation and undermined the Hungarian parliament's reputation. In 1897 the title of count was conferred on him through his uncle, who had himself been awarded this rank only in 1883 and had no direct heirs. While prime minister between 1903 and 1905, Tisza's destruction of the tactic of filibustering caused such resentment that in the 1905 election his Liberal Party suffered a devastating defeat. Tisza was vindicated in 1910, as the resurrected Liberal Party, renamed the Party of National Work, won a landslide election. In 1912 Tisza became speaker of parliament, where he instituted new strict rules of parliamentary procedure. In 1913 he was appointed prime minister again. In late June/early July 1914, following the murder of Archduke Franz Ferdinand (1863–1914) in Sarajevo, Tisza played a solitary role among the monarchy's leading politicians in attempting to avert the outbreak of a world war. By mid-July, he succumbed to German pressure and gave his consent to the dispatch of an ultimatum to Serbia that ultimately led to the outbreak of hostilities. Until his dismissal by King Charles (1887–1922) in 1917, Tisza was undisputedly the monarchy's most prominent statesman and war leader. On October 31, 1918, following the outbreak of a revolution in Budapest, he was murdered by soldiers who held him responsible for the war.

Gabor Vermes

Further reading

Erenyi, Gustav. *Graf Stefan Tisza, ein Staatsman und Martyrer.* Vienna, 1935.

Hegedüs, Lóránt. *Két Andrássy és Két Tisza.* Budapest, 1941.

Herczeg, Ferenc. *Graf Stefan Tisza.* Vienna, 1926.

Pölöskei, Ferenc. *Tisza István.* Budapest, 1985.

Vermes, Gabor. *Istvan Tisza: The Liberal Vision and Conservative Statecraft of a Magyar Nationalist.* Boulder, Colorado, 1985.

See also *Ausgleich;* Charles; Dual Monarchy; Franz Ferdinand; Kálmán Tisza

Tisza, Kálmán (1830–1902)

Hungarian politician and prime minister (1875–90). Born in Geszt, Tisza served as a minor government official during the 1848–49 Hungarian War for Independence against Austria during the Revolutions of 1848. After the Hungarian defeat, he left the country but returned in the early 1850s. He participated in the affairs of the Calvinist Church and became the leader of a Calvinist protest movement against Vienna's severe curtailment of Protestant religious autonomy. Tisza was elected to parliament in 1861, where he joined Count László Teleki's (1811–61) intransigently nationalistic Resolution Party. In the 1865 parlia-

ment, Tisza represented the same policy line, but by then, his party was called "Left-of-Center." The party accepted the 1867 *Ausgleich* (Compromise) between Austria and Hungary, which created the Dual Monarchy, only with reservations that aimed at securing a larger measure of independence for Hungary. From 1867 to 1875, Tisza was the principal leader of the opposition, until, in 1875, his Left-of-Center fused with the Deák Party to become the Liberal Party, and Tisza was appointed prime minister. He evidently realized the futility of attempting to revise the Compromise substantially to Hungary's advantage. His administration was characterized by the promotion of industrial and urban development on the one hand and by the sanctioning of the country's antiquated social system as well as the process of Magyarization on the other. Strong resistance to certain military bills prompted his resignation in 1890. Tisza continued to play some role in behind-the-scenes politics until his death on March 22, 1902.

Gabor Vermes

Further reading

Ábrányi, Kornél. *Tisza Kálmán; Politikai Élet és Jellemrajz.* Budapest, 1878.

Gottas, Friedrich. *Ungarn im Zeitalter des Hochliberalismus (1875–1890).* Vienna, 1976.

Hegedüs, Lóránt. *Két Andrássy és Két Tisza.* Budapest, 1941.

See also *Ausgleich;* Dual Monarchy; Hungarian War for Independence; Magyarization; Revolutions of 1848

Tisza River

Second most important river of Hungary. The Tisza flows north-south through the eastern half of the country draining the Great Hungarian Plain (*Nagy Alföld*). Major tributaries include the Bodrog, Sajó, Zagyva, Körös, and Maros Rivers. Throughout most of its course, the river drops only one–two inches per mile (two–three cm per km); consequently, stream flow was characterized by wide meander loops, frequent course changes, and twice-yearly floods during early spring and early summer, which would often inundate up to two million hectares and keep large sections of land in swamplike condition for much of the year. A major flood in 1879, which caused considerable damage to the city of Szeged, prompted authorities to begin to regulate stream flow on the Tisza. Projects carried out especially during the post–World War II period included construction of levees, channels, dams, and canals. These efforts have reduced the stream's course through Hungary to 370 miles (600 km), two-thirds of its former length; they have also greatly reduced flooding, allowed former marshy or permanently flooded land to be drained, and provided irrigation water to some half million hectares. The Tisza now is regulated along its entire Hungarian section and is navigable as far as the Ukraine border.

Darrick Danta

Further reading

Bernát, Tivadar, ed. *An Economic Geography of Hungary.* Budapest, 1985.

Enyedi, György. *Hungary: An Economic Geography.* Boulder, Colorado, 1976.

Webster's New Geographical Dictionary. Springfield, Massachusetts, 1984.

See also Great Hungarian Plain

Tito, Josip Broz (1892–1980)

Yugoslav guerrilla fighter, revolutionary, and Communist head of state. Tito was born into a Croatian-Slovene family in the Habsburg Empire. After leaving Croatia to earn money as a metalworker and then fighting in World War I, he became head of the Yugoslav Communist Party. During the interwar period, the party was closely linked to Moscow. The massive purges initiated by Stalin (1879–1953) in the 1930s claimed the lives of dozens of Yugoslav Communists, including the two general secretaries who preceded Tito. Since it was common for promising young Communists to spend time studying and training in the USSR, Tito visited Moscow three times in the 1930s. Stalin probably reasoned that as a non-Serb Tito would be more successful at implementing a new strategy aimed at fomenting nationalist discontent in the multiethnic but Serb-dominated Yugoslavia.

Tito led a successful resistance against the German and Italian occupiers of Yugoslavia during World War II, consistently tying down enemy units in the bitter Partisan struggle. After the war, he became president of socialist Yugoslavia.

By the late 1940s, Tito had begun to steer his country along an independent socialist course after bitter public and private disputes with Stalin.

Owing to his strong personality, autocratic style of leadership, war record, and ability to promote Yugoslavia's interests in the United Nations and other world forums, Tito charted certain political successes. He managed, for example, to improve Yugoslavia's standard of living and to avoid major bloodshed caused by ethnic disputes. Many argue that the foreign policy of nonalignment, sponsored by Tito and given its theoretical basis by theoretician Edvard Kardelj (1910–79), also brought a degree of world media attention and domestic stability to the country.

But Tito also failed in many crucial areas. Instead of building a stable, democratic system that might have survived his death, he enshrined his own cult of personality and the institutions of the Communist Party and the army as the pillars of the political system. Instead of airing the nationalist grievances generated since the creation of Yugoslavia in 1918, Tito pursued contradictory national policies and demanded obeisance to the concepts of "brotherhood and unity." This slogan meant to emphasize the cooperation of the various Yugoslav "nations." Six of these (Serbs, Croats, Bosnians [at that time largely a regional designation, but today roughly equivalent to the Muslims of Bosnia], Slovenes, Macedonians, and Montenegrins) had their own republics, most of which became independent during the breakup of Yugoslavia in the 1990s. There were many other national groups, or nationalities, not large enough to warrant their own republics. These included Albanians, Hungarians, Italians, Gypsies, and Turks. Believing in "brotherhood and unity" was vital for Yugoslavia, in large part because it implied a common sense of purpose despite the country's diversity. It also implied (falsely) that the rivalries and bloodshed among the peoples of Yugoslavia, especially during World War II, had been overcome. While espousing unity, Tito actually devolved much of the day-to-day governance of the country to the republican level. Republics had their own languages, their own territorial defense forces, and even their own Communist parties. This gave groups like the Slovenes, Croats, and Macedonians practice in self-governance and a sense of self-confidence that would aid them in the secession movements during the 1990s. He also purged the party periodically of younger, more liberal, and more practical leaders who could have had a positive impact on the region after his death.

John K. Cox

Further reading

Auty, Phyllis. *Tito: A Biography.* New York, 1970.

Djilas, Milovan. *Tito: The Story from Inside.* New York, 1980.

Tito, Josip Broz. *The Essential Tito,* ed. by Henry M. Christman. New York, 1970.

———. *Non-Alignment: The Conscience and Future of Mankind.* Belgrade, 1979.

West, Richard. *Tito and the Rise and Fall of Yugoslavia.* London, 1994.

See also Antifascism; Communist Party of Yugoslavia; Milovan Djilas; Edvard Kardelj; Non-aligned Movement; Tito-Stalin Split; World War II

Tito-Stalin Split

Permanent break between Josip Broz Tito (1892–1980) and Josef Stalin (1879–1953). On June 28, 1948, members of the Soviet-led organization of Communist states known as the Cominform expelled their erstwhile ally Yugoslavia from the organization and from the fold of international communism. The resolution outlining the action charged that Yugoslavia's leaders had betrayed international communism and seceded from the united front against imperialism. Stalin demanded that the Yugoslavs give up their nationalist position and return to internationalism. The Cominform action prompted a permanent break between Yugoslavia and the Soviet bloc that was symbolized and personified by the two leaders involved, Tito and Stalin. Although the Cominform blamed the Yugoslavs for taking a "nationalist" position, the core reason for the split was the question of whether Tito or Stalin would control the destiny of Yugoslavia.

When the Yugoslavs did not react favorably to Stalin's demands, the Cominform instituted an economic and military blockade against Yugoslavia intended to force Tito and his colleagues to abandon power. To offset Soviet-bloc economic and military pressure, the Yugoslav Communists ultimately looked to the West for help. President Truman (1884–1972) determined it would be in U.S. interests to aid Yugoslavia because it might encourage other regimes to break from the Soviet bloc. During the period from 1949 to 1955, the Yugoslavs received—primarily from the United States—approximately $1.2 billion in military and economic assistance, only a small fraction of which was to be repaid. This aid made it possible for the Yugoslavs to undertake an ambitious program of economic development and at the same time to maintain one of the largest military forces in Europe. Tito found that he could deal with the United States with minimal interference in Yugoslavia's internal affairs as long as Yugoslavia maintained its independent position.

The Tito-Stalin split also prompted Yugoslav Communists to rethink traditional Stalinist policies. The Yugoslavs wanted to remain faithful to Marxism but also to develop policies that would justify their break with Stalin. They concluded that Soviet communism was flawed because of its highly centralized and burdensome bureaucracy. To distance themselves from Soviet practice and to create an alternative communism, they passed a major reform called the Basic Law on the Management of State Economic Enterprises by Workers' Collectives. This was the first step in what eventually led to decentralized planning, the removal of the Communist Party from direct control of economic activity, and the introduction of self-management into all areas of society. The reforms served Tito's international purposes not only by providing an ideological foundation for Yugoslavia's split from the Soviet bloc but also by demonstrating to the West that Yugoslavia had a more open system than other Communist states.

The Tito-Stalin split also influenced events in the rest of the Communist world. To insure that no more "Titoists" emerged in Eastern Europe, Stalin initiated a massive purge in Cominform countries. Hundreds of alleged Titoists were tried and executed in the early 1950s. Even so, the split marked an end to the Soviet Union's absolute control over the world Communist movement. Yugoslavia would later serve as an example to Poles and Hungarians during their uprisings in 1956 and for China's independent path.

Most significantly, the split between Tito and Stalin set the stage for a dramatic shift in the course of postwar Yugoslav history. Tito and his associates successfully resisted Stalin and the Cominform and turned the break to their advantage. Yugoslavia became one of the more economically successful Eastern European countries, and Tito also gained considerable international influence because of his unique position as an independent Communist leader.

Paul D. Lensink

Further reading

Banac, Ivo. *With Stalin Against Tito: Cominformist Splits in Yugoslav Communism*. Ithaca, New York, 1988.

Dedijer, Vladimir. *The Battle Stalin Lost: Memoirs of Yugoslavia, 1948–1953*. New York, 1970.

Johnson, A. Ross. *The Transformation of Communist Ideology: The Yugoslav Case, 1949–1953*. Cambridge, Massachusetts, 1972.

Vucinich, Wayne S., ed. *At the Brink of War and Peace: The Tito-Stalin Split in Historic Perspective*. New York, 1982.

See also Cominform; Communist Party of Yugoslavia; Self-Management; Stalin; Tito

Titulescu, Nicolae (1882–1941)

Romanian jurist and statesman. Born to a landowning family near Craiova, Titulescu studied law at the University of Paris. Returning to Romania, he was appointed professor of law at the University of Iaşi (1905) and Bucharest (1910). A brilliant lecturer, Titulescu also wrote incisively on how effective law had to reflect the dynamics of socioeconomic reality. He joined the Conservative Democratic Party of Take Ionescu (1858–1922) and was elected to parliament in 1912. A convinced supporter of the Entente during World War I, Titulescu left Romania in mid-1918 to assist Ionescu's efforts aimed at gaining support for national unification in Western capitals.

In the government of General Alexandru Averescu (1859–1938), Titulescu served as minister of finance (1920–21), introducing Romania's first progressive taxation system. Later appointed minister to the Court of Saint James (1922–27, 1928–32) and permanent delegate at the League of Nations (1920–36), Titulescu championed the cause of the sovereign equality and territorial integrity of the successor states. During the 1920s, he successfully defended the Romanian position in the Optants Dispute over Hungarian citizens' property rights in recently integrated Transylvania. He renegotiated Romania's Western war debt and twice served as president of the League Assembly (1930–31).

Titulescu briefly served as foreign minister in the last government of Ion I.C. Brătianu (1864–1927), and his most productive statesmanship occurred during his second tenure as foreign minister (1932–36). He initiated the institutionaliza-

tion of the Little Entente (1933), the alliance among Romania, Czechoslovakia, and Yugoslavia, and was among the founders of the Balkan Entente (1934), the regional pact among Romania, Greece, Turkey, and Yugoslavia. His attempts to create wider security communities and to strengthen the league's authority ultimately failed. Carol II (1893–1953) dismissed Titulescu in August 1936 shortly after he had initialed a draft defensive pact with Soviet foreign minister Maxim Litvinov (1876–1951), which would have recognized Romanian sovereignty in Bessarabia.

Titulescu also wrote voluminously on international relations theory, emphasizing the indivisible and dynamic character of peace and the necessity of institutions and laws to maintain it. He died in exile in France in 1941.

Walter M. Bacon Jr.

Further reading

de Launay, Jacques. *Titulescu et l'Europe*. Nyon, France, 1976.

Macovescu, George, ed. *Nicolae Titulescu: Documente Diplomatice*. Bucharest, 1967.

Netea, Vasile. *Nicolae Titulescu*. Bucharest, 1969.

Oprea, Ion. *Nicolae Titulescu*. Bucharest, 1966.

Titulescu, Nicolae. *Romania's Foreign Policy (1937)*. Bucharest, 1994.

See also Balkan Entente; Ion I.C. Brătianu; Carol II; League of Nations; Little Entente; Take Ionescu

Tomasevich, Joso (1908–94)

Yugoslav historian. Tomasevich had the rare fortune to become both a participant in and a scholar of twentieth-century Yugoslav history. A native of Dalmatia, he began his career as a finance expert at the Yugoslav National Bank, observing developments in the country's economic life firsthand. After receiving a Rockefeller grant in 1938 for research at Harvard University, Tomasevich came to the United States. He eventually moved to California and launched a teaching and writing career at San Francisco State University.

Tomasevich wrote two books of importance to English-speaking students of Yugoslavia. The first, *Peasants, Politics, and Economic Change in Yugoslavia*, although dated, covers economic and political events in great detail and explains particularly well the interplay of politics and economics in Yugoslavia's shifting international alignment in the 1930s. In the second, *The Chetniks: War and Revolution in Yugoslavia, 1941–1945,* Tomasevich shifted his focus to wartime Yugoslavia and the Serbian monarchist resistance led by Draža Mihailović (1893–1946). The work is a comprehensive history of the Chetniks (loosely organized World War II Serbian guerrilla fighters) and their origins, strategy, and relations with other groups in war-torn Yugoslavia. It makes the essential point that for those Yugoslavs who resisted the Axis powers, World War II concerned as much the future of the country as the expulsion of the invaders.

At the time of his death in 1994, Tomasevich had completed a history of the Croatian and Serbian puppet governments. He did not live long enough to begin the third volume of what he obviously intended as a trilogy—a history of Tito (1892–1980) and the Partisans.

Brigit Farley

Further reading

Tomasevich, Joso. *The Chetniks: War and Revolution in Yugoslavia, 1941–45.* Stanford, California, 1975.

———. *Peasants, Politics, and Economic Change in Yugoslavia.* Stanford, California, 1955.

Vucinich, Alexander. "Joso Tomasevich: 1908–1994." *Slavic Review* 54, no. 1 (Spring 1995): 257–58.

See also Antifascism; Chetniks; Dragoljub Mihailović; Tito

Toptani, Esad Pasha (1863–1920)

One of the many figures that sought power in the chaotic years following Albania's 1912 declaration of independence. From a large landowning family in central Albania, Toptani is considered by Albanian historians to be an antinational figure because of his willingness to collaborate with Serbia to obtain power. Immediately following independence, Toptani competed with the provisional government of Ismail Bey Kemal (1844–1919) and established his own government in Durrës. With the arrival of William of Wied (1876–1945) as monarch in March 1914, Toptani secured positions in Wied's first cabinet as minister of war and of interior. Wied, much to his discredit, was forced to rely extensively on Toptani, whose loyalty to Albania's first sovereign was extremely superficial.

Later convinced that Toptani was a traitor, Wied removed him and Toptani took refuge abroad.

Toptani's exile was brief. The First World War and Wied's departure brought new opportunities, and with the aid of Serbia and Italy he gained control over most of central Albania in 1915. In 1916 he was forced to retreat, alongside Serbian forces, in the face of advancing Austro-Hungarian troops. Outside Albania, he acted as a kind of president-in-exile, surrounded by his loyal supporters and holding court in Salonika, Greece. After the war, Toptani hoped to secure his position as ruler of Albania and attended the 1919 Paris Peace Conference, but he was no longer taken seriously by the Great Powers. He was assassinated by a young Albanian idealist on June 13, 1920, in front of Paris's Hotel Continental.

Robert C. Austin

Further reading

Fischer, Bernd J. *King Zog and the Struggle for Stability in Albania.* Boulder, Colorado, 1984.

Swire, J. *Albania—The Rise of a Kingdom.* New York, 1971.

See also Paris Peace Conference; William of Wied

Tosks

Southern Albanian group. In southern Albania, northern and western Greece, and southern Italy and Sicily, historical differences in social and political development, as well as language, have differentiated the ethnic Albanian populations of these regions from those to the north of the river Shkumbin.

Tosk dialects have fewer speakers but are more widespread than those of northern Albanian (Geg). Southern Tosk is spoken in the Berat and Vlorë regions while Laberisht (regions of Gjirokastër and Himarë) and Çamerisht (Sarandë region) are also identified in adjacent regions of northern and western Greece. The Italo-Albanians of southern Italy and Sicily mostly use the Arberisht dialect. A unified Tosk dialect replaced Geg as the literary standard among Albanians after 1972.

Proximity and greater accessibility of the lowland of southern Albania to Ottoman control had a major impact on the social and political development of the Tosks. Because the population was grouped in small villages on the large landholdings of Muslims, most aspects of the tribal organization and functional autonomy characteristic of the north disappeared. However, the less isolated Tosks had greater exposure to Greek culture and, in southern Italy and Sicily, maintained and elaborated on the literary and cultural traditions that would support the development of Albanian nationalism in the late nineteenth century.

Efforts of the Tosk minority to create the conditions of a modern society were frustrated under the interwar regime of Ahmed Zogu (Zog I) (1895–1961), which based its power on the support of the tribal and clan leaders in the north. After World War II, under the regime of Communist leader Enver Hoxha (1908–85), a Tosk, the situation was substantially reversed, with Tosks dominating the higher organs of the economy and government.

Albert M. Tosches

Further reading

Huld, Martin E. *Basic Albanian Etymologies.* Columbus, Ohio, 1984.

Jaques, Edwin E. *The Albanians: An Ethnic History from Prehistoric Times to the Present.* Jefferson, North Carolina, 1995.

Pano, Nicholas C. *The People's Republic of Albania.* Baltimore, Maryland, 1968.

Skendi, Stavro. *The Albanian National Awakening: 1878–1912.* Princeton, New Jersey, 1967.

Zickel, Raymond and Walter R. Iwasshiw, eds. *Albania: A Country Study.* Washington, D.C., 1992.

See also Albanian Culture; Albanian Language; Gegs; Enver Hoxha; Muslims; Ahmed Zogu

Trade Unionism

Before World War I, most of East Central Europe had little experience with trade unionism because of the one-sided predominance of agriculture in the economies. Workers generally accounted for no more than 5 percent of the population, and only 10 percent of those were unionized. The exceptions included a few industrialized cities and the Czech regions of Bohemia and Moravia, where 39 percent of population earned its living in industry by 1914.

As a pattern, trade unions grew out of workers' self-help, educational, and crafts societies during the early phases of industrialization in the latter half of the nineteenth century. Unions developed first in the Austrian half of the Habsburg monarchy and Prussian Poland based on the German model after the governments passed laws between 1867 and 1870 expanding the right to organize. More restrictive laws and less industrialization in Hungary and Russian Poland inhibited growth there until the first decade of the twentieth century. Likewise, few unions formed in southeastern Europe before 1914, and those that did remained relatively weak. Most unionized workers lived in a small number of towns, worked in certain industries (textile, leather working, metal, and tobacco), and union organization structures lacked stability and remained parochial in concerns. In Hungary, attempts to organize rural laborers met with only modest success.

When workers first organized, few differences existed between social democratic parties and trade unions, but those became more pronounced by the early twentieth century. Once the trade unions had established themselves, the Catholic Church, fearing the loss of workers to atheistic socialism, fostered the growth of Christian Socialist trade unions to provide labor with another option to seek livable wages and improved working conditions.

Trade unions also played an important cultural and social role in the region. Typically trade unions built "workers' homes" that housed libraries for members and were equipped with their own restaurants. They also sponsored various lectures, concerts, theatrical events, sporting matches, and other forms of entertainment and games. Trade unions sought to make workers totally involved in their organization.

Trade unions throughout the region suffered the same negative effects common throughout Europe from the 1921 split of the world socialist movement into left and right wings, that is, the struggle between Communist and Social Democratic wings. The latter tended to view unions more as economic vehicles to improve workers' living standards, while the Communists envisioned the unions as instruments to carry on the class political conflict and increase worker involvement in radical organizations. The bitter rift over political differences, combined with the failure of general strikes and a weakened industrial sector in many regions, led to a decline in union membership. Although the decline was less pronounced and unions had more freedoms in Czechoslovakia and Poland, heightened government suppression in countries such as Bulgaria, Yugoslavia, Romania, and Hungary diminished trade union numbers in the early 1920s. The Great Depression dealt yet another heavy blow to union membership and union finances.

The authoritarian regimes of the 1930s generally outlawed existing trade unions and placed workers under one state-controlled umbrella organization. Although their primary purpose was to increase labor productivity and discipline, state-controlled unions did provide some forum for workers to press forward their own social and economic interests.

The establishment of Communist governments after the war led to a boom in trade union growth. Since the Communists viewed themselves as the vanguard of the workers, they sought to control those organizations closest to workers, in particular the factory councils and trade unions. Communists aggressively sought leadership positions in unions and spearheaded calls for the nationalization of large private enterprises after the war. Trade union representatives began to play a more active political role, served on land reform committees and political screening committees, worked in people's courts, and even became involved in the armed forces. Communists also insisted on labor unity, albeit under their leadership.

Once the Communists seized power, independent labor unions were banned and workers were compelled to join the Communist unions. Central trade union councils were set up in all the "people's democracies" to ensure conformity with the Communist party line. The trade unions' role now stressed achievement of higher work norms and production goals set by the party hierarchy.

In Yugoslavia, the introduction of workers' self-management after 1948 somewhat modified the emphasis on self-sacrifice and merely raising production. While remaining a bulwark of the Communist Party, Yugoslav trade unions served as advisers and oversaw self-management in the enterprises. They also negotiated workers' grievances and sought to improve social amenities such as housing and an assured supply of basic food staples. However, unions usually sided with management in disputes over wages or investment allocation in enterprises.

After Stalin's (1879–1953) death, trade unions became increasingly discredited as workers began to take seriously the Communist claim that their states were actually workers' states run for the benefit of the laboring class. During the revolu-

tions that erupted in Poland and Hungary in 1956, workers' councils demanded a larger role in self-government at their enterprises. As a result, union representatives obtained broader supervisory roles and worked with government agencies; however, power still remained in the hands of the central council, which was subservient to the party apparatus. In Albania, Bulgaria, and Romania, few if any reforms took hold until after the 1989 revolutions.

Czechoslovakia conformed to this pattern until the mid-1960s, when trade unions acquired more autonomy and even the right to strike. Once the Warsaw Pact invasion of 1968 ended the Prague Spring—Czechoslovakia's short-lived liberal period—trade unions were purged of "counterrevolutionary" elements and the newly formed workers council were eliminated. The new regime increased social benefits as a carrot to quell labor dissatisfaction but retained tight control over union leadership.

Trade unions began to receive more attention from most regimes after the Solidarity trade union movement in Poland successfully garnered concessions from the government. While in the short run it led to repression of dissent in most East European countries, in the long run the appearance of Solidarity and the politicization of Polish unions forced governments to pay more attention to trade union economic demands, although the insistence on strict party control remained a fact in all countries except Poland. Changes took place gradually and unevenly during the 1980s, but there was a gradual increase in rank-and-file activism. Union members began to seek a more participatory role in addressing matters such as working conditions, pollution, benefits, and other social issues.

The events of 1989 led workers to join in the broader sociopolitical movement for change. The old Communist trade unions quickly disintegrated, and in 1990 union members proceeded to found their own independent organizations. A vast re-education program took place, and trade unions sought the help of their Western counterparts to cope with the difficult transition to a free-market economy. They played an important role in safeguarding the interests of labor through collective bargaining, negotiating minimum wages, coordinating strike activities, and other practices traditionally associated with trade unions worldwide. However, the rapid rise of smaller private-sector businesses has contributed to a decline in union membership, and hence a gradual diminution of the power of organized labor.

Michael J. Kopanic Jr.

Further reading

Campbell, Joan, ed. *European Labor Unions*. Westport, Connecticut, 1992.

Caranfil, Andrew G. "Labor," in *Romania*, ed. by Stephen Fischer-Galati. New York, 1957, 248–69.

Gross, Feliks. *The Polish Worker: A Study of a Social Stratum*. New York, 1945.

Kabos, Erno and Andras Zsilak, eds. *Studies in the History of the Hungarian Trade Union Movement*. Budapest, 1977.

Kopanic, Michael J. Jr. *Industrial Trade Unions in Slovakia*. Ann Arbor, Michigan, 1986.

McDermott, Kevin. *The Czech Red Unions, 1918–1929: A Study of Their Relations with the Communist Party and the Moscow Internationals*. Boulder, Colorado, 1988.

Pravda, Alex and Blair A. Ruble, eds. *Trade Unions in Communist States*. Boston, 1986.

Triska, Jan F. and Charles Gati, eds. *Blue-Collar Workers in Eastern Europe*. London, 1981.

See also Great Depression; Hungarian Revolution of 1956; Industrialization; Labor; Prague Spring; Revolutions of 1989; Self-Management in Yugoslavia; Solidarity; Warsaw Pact

Transdanubia

Romanian province located in the eastern part of the country between the Danube and the Black Sea. The Dobrudja (Romanian, Dobrogea) is one of the smallest Romanian provinces, having an area of 5,580 square miles (15,500 sq km) and close to one million inhabitants.

Historically, this region belonged to Wallachia in the Middle Ages, was later occupied by the Ottoman Empire, and was returned to Romania in 1878. During the Turkish occupation, the two Romanian principalities developed the Danube ports of Brăila and Galaţi for their international trade. The recuperation of the Dobrudja allowed modern Romania to establish a direct maritime link with the world. In 1895 Romania built the longest bridge in Europe at the time over the Danube and later transformed Constanţa into one of the largest harbors of Europe.

The northern part of the Dobrudja is covered by the Danube delta and by the Razelm lakes complex. South of the delta, the region is covered by hills and plateaus that descend in altitude from about 1,320 feet (400 m) to about 330 feet (100 m) toward Bulgaria.

Vegetation varies from submediterranean plants in the south to temperate forests in the north. Despite its arid nature, the province is famous for its grapes, orchards, and wineries. It is also noted for its high-quality sheep furs and wool.

The importance of the region for Romania, however, is its location by the sea. Constanţa is Romania's principal link with the rest of the world. It is now the second-largest Romanian city and an industrial center. The shipyards of Constanţa are also known for their capacity, and the completion of the Danube–Black Sea Canal adds a new dimension to its importance and perspective. This 38.5 mile (64 km) canal leaves the Danube at Cernavoda, where Romanian nuclear power plants are being built, crosses the province, and reaches the Black Sea through two arms located north and south of Constanţa.

Tulcea, a small city located to the north, is the gateway for visiting the delta, and Constanţa is the gateway for the littoral. Other tourist attractions are beautiful vineyards on terraced hills, as well as many remains of ancient Greek cities and Roman archaeology.

Nicholas Dima

Further reading

Brătescu, C. "Pământul Dobrogei," in *Dobrogea*. Bucharest, 1928.

Enciclopedia Geografică a României. Bucharest, 1982.

Geografia României. Bucharest, 1983.

See also Constanţa; Danube Delta; Dobrudja

Transnistria

Region of Moldova where tensions flared after the dissolution of the Soviet Union. In 1990 the Trans-Dniester region declared itself independent, fought a bloody war against Moldova, and became a hotbed of frustrated Russian Communists.

By early Soviet estimates, when Bessarabia united with Romania in 1918, there were five hundred thousand Romanians on the left bank of the Dniester River. Accordingly, Moscow organized a Moldovan Autonomous Republic in 1924. In July 1940, when the USSR again annexed Bessarabia, it gave new boundaries to the newly named Moldovan Soviet Socialist Republic. Most of the land of the former autonomous republic was returned to Ukraine, while a sliver of land along the left bank of the Dniester was given to the new Moldovan Republic. The region is a strip of some 2,340 square miles (6,500 sq km) and accounts for one-eighth of Moldova's territory. It is a flat, rich land that produces a large share of Moldova's agricultural output.

During decades of Soviet domination, the Soviets built heavy industry in the region and brought in many Russians and Ukrainians, thereby changing the ethnic balance. The last Soviet census, of 1989, indicates that Moldovans were still the largest ethnic group but no longer a majority except in rural areas. The region had some eight hundred thousand inhabitants, of whom 41 percent were Moldovans (Romanians), 31 percent Ukrainians, and 22 percent Russians. The capital (and only major city), Tiraspol, had 182,000 inhabitants, was highly Russified, and was the region's political and industrial center. In the past, when Moscow was poised for future expansion, Tiraspol was an important military and strategic outpost, but this significance is now lost.

The region poses a dilemma for the countries of the area. Should Moldova decide to reunite with Romania, the region would either go to Ukraine or continue its attempts to become independent. Either way, it would remain a source of frustration, defying easy solution.

Nicholas Dima

Further reading

Dima, Nicholas. *From Moldavia to Moldova: The Soviet-Romanian Territorial Dispute.* Boulder, Colorado, 1991.

Matei, Valeriu, ed. *Pactul Molotov-Ribbentrop şi Consecinţele lui pentru Basarabia.* Kishinev, 1991.

Nedelciuc, Vasile. *The Republic of Moldova.* Kishinev, 1992.

See also Bessarabian Question; Moldova, Birth of the Republic of

Transylvania

Region of Romania meaning "the land across the forest." In many ways Transylvania is the heart of Romania. From this plateau, the Romanians descended east and south of the Carpathians at the beginning of the second millennium, founding the principalities of Moldova (Moldavia) and Wallachia and reclaiming their ancestors' land.

Transylvania, with an area of 22,320 square miles (62,000 sq km), is an intra-Carpathian depression of about 120 miles by 90 miles (200 km by 150 km). While the northwestern part of this plateau reaches up to 3,300 feet (1,000 m) in altitude, the central lands descend to about 1,320–1,650 feet (400–500 m), and the southern area rises again in altitude to about 3,300 feet (1,000 m). The Carpathian Mountains, which surround Transylvania, reach 6,600 feet (2,000 m) in the north and east, 8,250 feet (2,500 m) in the south, but only 4,950–5,940 feet (1,500–1,800 m) in the west.

By formation, the Western Carpathians and the lowlands near the border with Hungary do not belong to the Transylvanian plateau, but through generalization they came to be considered as part of the same province. These western smaller mountains are crossed by many rivers and passes, and it is through this area that the Hungarians entered Romania during the tenth century, advancing gradually eastward and settling mostly in the lower areas of Transylvania.

In 1992 the population of Transylvania was 4.6 million (73 percent of whom are Romanian and 24 percent Hungarian). The Hungarian population formed a majority in Harghita and Covasna counties, located in the middle of Romania. The other counties, including those near Hungary, were inhabited by ethnic Romanian majorities. Since the Middle Ages, Transylvania also had a strong German community that was instrumental in developing the region, but this community declined rapidly during and after World War II. Although only a few thousand Germans remain, their heritage is present in many places.

Transylvania is a rich region endowed with a variety of landforms, good agricultural land, timber, pastures, as well as natural gas, salt, and minerals. It is also one of the most developed regions in Romania, with a better infrastructure, industry, good schools and universities, and many cities. The largest city, Cluj-Napoca, with over three hundred thousand inhabitants, contains a prestigious university and impressive art monuments. Although industrialized in recent decades, the city continues to be an important cultural center. Târgu Mureş is a mixed Romanian/Hungarian city and the cultural center of Hungarians in Romania. Braşov and Sibiu were predominantly German cities, and their architecture reflects this past. Baia Mare, Satu Mare, and Oradea, located in the western part of the province, have become large industrial centers.

Transylvania has many tourist attractions, including ski resorts, thermal spas, rustic villages, and Bran Castle, with its legends of Dracula. It is also noted for its folk art, especially the unique wooden churches in the northern part of the region.

Nicholas Dima

Further reading

Enciclopedia Geografică a României. Bucharest, 1982.

Geografia României. Bucharest, 1983.

Lehrer, M. *Transylvania: History and Reality.* Silver Spring, Maryland, 1987.

See also Braşov; Carpathian Mountains; Cluj/Napoca; Transylvanian Dispute

Transylvanian Dispute

Geographic area contested and claimed by Romanians and Hungarians. Transylvania is the northwestern region of present-day Romania, and the easternmost province of the former Kingdom of Hungary. The latin designation "Transylvania," first used in Hungarian medieval documents, means "land beyond the forest." The Hungarian popular reference to this region is *"Erdély,"* which means "forested" or "forest-covered land." This name has also been adopted by the Romanians, although with an altered spelling, *"Ardeal."* In contrast, the Saxon German name for the region was Siebenbürgen, "the land of seven castles."

Transylvania is situated in the southeastern corner of the Carpathian basin and has 7.5 million inhabitants (1991), of whom two million are Hungarians while Gypsies, Serbs, Germans, Jews, Armenians, Ruthenes, and Bulgarians constitute the other minorities that share the territory with the present Romanian majority.

Until World War I, Transylvania was ruled by Hungarians either as an autonomous region of the crownlands of St. Stephen or as the domain of the Habsburg monarchy. After the war, the Treaty of Trianon (1920) transferred this territory, as well as the neighboring western and northern regions of the Banat, Crişana (Hungarian, Körös Vidék), and Satu-Mare (Hungarian, Szatmár) to Romania. Ever since, these areas, as well as historic Transylvania, are considered together as Transylvania.

The region has been under dispute between Romania and Hungary for most of the twentieth century. Hungary regained control over northern Transylvania in 1940 via an agreement (the Vienna Award) imposed by the Axis powers on their lesser allies. This was reversed in the 1947 Paris Peace Treaty, which reestablished the Trianon borders.

The dispute over the region can be summarized in terms of ethnographic, demographic, historical, and legal arguments. The ethnographic argument is that the Romanians claim to be the descendants of the original, autochthonous Dacian settlers of this region, while the Hungarians settled in this area 1,100 years ago. Hungarians argue that present-day Romanians are not the descendants of the Dacians, because the claimed relationship is not based on concrete archaeological, linguistic, or historical documentation.

This raises the merits of the Romanian and Hungarian historical arguments. Romanian historians contend that the Dacians established a viable political system under the rulers Burebista (first century B.C.) and Decebalus (first century A.D.). This realm was located roughly in the region of present-day Transylvania. However, Romans under Emperor Trajan (c. A.D. 51–117) defeated the Dacians in A.D. 106 and incorporated the province into the empire until A.D. 271. Under the pressure of barbarian invasions, the Romans then withdrew their legions from the area. But Romanian historians contend that the 165 years of the Roman presence in this region led to the intermarriage of Roman legionnaires and widowed Dacians to produce a new people who became the ancestors of present-day Romanians. This, Romanian historians contend, is substantiated by the Latin-based romance language spoken by Romanians today.

Hungarian historians concede that Dacia existed and that it was under Roman control from A.D. 106 to 271. Yet they reject the argument that present-day Romanians are the product of this "Dacian-Roman synthesis." They argue that the Roman withdrawal was complete and that the archaeological evidence indicates that the region was from this time onward inhabited by other peoples, not the remnants of Dacians or Romans. They point out that the Goths, Huns, Gepids, and Avars controlled the region in rapid succession between 271 and 896, when the Hungarians arrived. They also contend that when the Hungarians arrived in the region they encountered only a sparse Slavic population under Bulgarian control. Furthermore, they argue that the first documented instances of a "Vlach" (Romanian) presence in southern Transylvania can be traced on the basis of Hungarian royal documents back to the early thirteenth century. Thus, they contend, Romanians are the "late comers," not the Hungarians.

Romanian historians argue that written evidence is lacking because their ancestors had to withdraw to the mountains to survive the successive invasions by the barbarians. As conditions improved, they again descended to the valleys and became a visible and significant history-shaping force. Therefore, they argue, their presence in the region was uninterrupted.

This leads to the demographic argument. Romanians claim that they compose an absolute majority in Transylvania and therefore the region should be part of Romania. Hungarians again concede that this has been the case since the eighteenth century. But they argue that Hungarians were the state-forming people who built the cities (together with the Saxon Germans) and provided the legal foundations and political leadership for Transylvania until 1918–20. Until the disaster at Mohács in 1526, when the forces of the Ottoman Turks destroyed the Hungarian army (including much of its nobility), they claim that two-thirds of the Transylvanian population was still Hungarian and that the Vlachs (Romanians) and Saxon Germans together made up only the remaining third. Moreover, the war against the Ottoman Turks decimated the Hungarian population of the lowlands and the river valleys between 1526 and 1686. These vacated lands were then filled by Serb, Swabian German, Vlach, and other immigrants who came in at the invitation of the Habsburg monarchs of the realm. It is this, Hungarians argue, that has changed the demographic profile of the region. Furthermore, if only the ethnic profile

counts, Hungarians contend that the division of the region according to the Vienna Award (1940) reflected a more equitable solution than that of Trianon two decades earlier.

Finally, the legal argument relates to two issues: state continuity and rights. In this context, Hungarians argue that Transylvania was an integral part of the Hungarian kingdom from the reign of St. Stephen (c. 975–1038) to 1918–20. There were interruptions in this relationship, as when Transylvania became an independent principality following the collapse at Mohács. However, the independent Transylvanian principality was always governed by Hungarian princes as a crownland of the Hungarian kingdom. Even under Habsburg rule from 1691 to 1867, the legal structure depended on the Hungarian nobility and the Székely and the Saxon German communities.

Romanian historians reject this as a class-based governance that oppressed and exploited the Romanian majority of the region. They argue that "Romanian countries" existed from the time of Burebista and Decebalus. Foreign conquest simply forced them underground. However, these "Romanian countries" were able to unite for the first time (since A.D. 271) under the reign of Michael the Brave (1557–1601). Although this unity among Transylvania, Moldavia, and Wallachia lasted less than a year, it set the precedent for the "national unification" that took place in 1918–20.

The final legal argument relates to the present. Hungarians now concede that Romania controls Transylvania both de facto and de jure. But they argue that the two million Hungarians in Transylvania should have their rights recognized as a coequal nation with the Romanians and they should have their cultural and educational rights protected with the free use of Hungarian in public discourse and the right to self-government and autonomy in those parts of Romania where they compose an absolute or relative majority of the population. This is rejected by Romanians, who claim that Romania is a unitary state and the treatment of minorities within its borders is a domestic problem. In other words, Hungarians in the present Romanian state should assimilate and become Romanian nationals, not just Romanian citizens of Hungarian nationality. As is true of other such regional/ethnic disputes in Eastern Europe, there is little middle ground between the two sides.

Andrew Ludanyi

Further reading

Barta, Gábor, István Bóna, Béla Köpeczi, et al. *History of Transylvania,* trans. by Adrienne Chambers-Makkai, György Donga, et al. Budapest, 1994.

Cadzow, John, Andrew Ludanyi, and Louis J. Elteto, eds. *Transylvania: The Roots of Ethnic Conflict.* Kent, Ohio, 1983.

Cornish, Louis C. *Transylvania: The Land beyond the Forest.* Philadelphia, 1947.

Foisel, John. *Saxons through Seventeen Centuries: A History of the Transylvanian Saxons.* Cleveland, Ohio, 1936.

Illyes, Elemér. *National Minorities in Romania: Change in Transylvania.* Boulder, Colorado, 1983.

Pascu, Ştefan. *A History of Tranylvania,* trans. by D. Robert Ladd. Detroit, Michigan, 1982.

Peter, Laszlo, ed. *Historians and the History of Transylvania.* New York, 1992.

See also Crownlands of St. Stephen; Ethnic Minorities; Irredentism; Revisionism; Saxons; Székely; Transylvania; Trianon, Treaty of; Vienna Awards; Vlachs

Trialism

Political concept to change Austro-Hungarian dualism by adding a third group to the division of authority. From its origins in 1526–27, the Habsburg monarchy was composed of three basic historical parts: the Austrian hereditary lands, the Kingdom of Bohemia, and the Kingdom of Hungary. The acquisition of large territories formerly under Ottoman rule in 1699, of Lombardy in 1714, of Polish Galicia in 1772, and of Venetia, Istria, and Dalmatia in 1797 increased the heterogeneity of the realm. More than the other territories, Hungary was in a position to preserve its ancient self-administration and legal system. Thus, Austro-Hungarian dualism had a long prehistory before 1867. At the same time, different economic and political conditions in the other parts of the multinational empire provoked several attempts at changing dualism into trialism. There were four diverse types, or models, of trialism proposed for the empire between 1815 and 1918, according to the regional or ethnic character of the third party involved.

Austro-Hungaro-North-Italian trialism between 1815 and 1848 existed only as a matter of fact, without constitutional act. Neither Hungary nor the Lombardo-Venetian Kingdom belonged to the so-called Theresian state core of the Habsburg monarchy (which included the Austrian hereditary lands with Carniola and Trieste, as well as the lands of the Bohemian crown). The Austrian civil code of 1811, as well as other important laws, were in effect in the Austrian and Bohemian lands (along with Galicia), whereas Hungary and the north Italian provinces had a legal system of their own. Their self-government was limited, but their different position was symbolized by the leading role of secondary members of the dynasty in their administration.

Austro-Hungaro-Bohemian trialism was the political goal of the Czech national movement immediately following the proclamation of dualism through the *Ausgleich* (Compromise) of 1867 (which created the Dual Monarchy of Austria-Hungary). Czech leaders insisted that the rights of the Kingdom of Bohemia were not inferior to those of Hungary. Mass protest movements were organized against the Austro-Hungarian *Ausgleich* and against the new constitution of the non-Hungarian lands of the empire. By a rescript of September 12, 1871, Emperor Franz Joseph (1830–1916) renewed his promise to be crowned as king of Bohemia. In the absence of German deputies, the Bohemian diet answered this rescript with the so-called Fundamental Articles of October 10, 1871, which called for some kind of subdualism through a largely autonomous Bohemia. The bill of the same date for protection of nationalities was a well-balanced project aimed at adjusting the relationship between the two ethnic groups in the region. The Bohemian compromise failed, however, because of strong opposition by the chancellor, Count Friedrich von Beust (1809–86), the Germans of Bohemia, and the Hungarian government, as well as the negative attitudes of both Germany and Russia.

Austro-Hungaro-South-Slav trialism was a favorite of several members of the circle of counselors to Archduke Franz Ferdinand (1863–1914), heir to the Austrian throne. To break down the dominant position of Hungary in the Dual Monarchy, the Archduke's advisers considered the possibility of uniting Croatia, Dalmatia, and the recently annexed Bosnia-Hercegovina in a complex Catholic-dominated South Slav territory. But the archduke preferred merely to change the status of Hungary to that of any other province and wished for a strong, centralized Austria rather than any trialistic experiment.

Austro-Hungaro-Polish trialism appeared to be one of Austria's aims during World War I. This was supported by influential Polish politicians who were aware that the situation of the Poles under Austrian rule was significantly better than under Russia or Germany. Under circumstances of front-line successes in May–July 1915, political negotiations were held suggesting the granting of a subdualism to the Austrian and Russian parts of Poland. In return, the German government decided in November 1916 to proclaim a much smaller Polish state dependent on Germany.

Jiří Kořalka

Further reading

Batowski, Henryk. "Die Drei Trialismen." *Österreichische Osthefte* 7 (1965): 265–74.

———. "Trialismus, Subdualismus oder Personalunion: Zum Problem der österreichisch-polnischen Lösung (1914–1918)." *Studia Austro-Polonica* 1 (1978): 7–19.

Kann, Robert A. *The Multinational Empire: Nationalism and National Reform in the Habsburg Monarchy, 1848–1918,* 2 vols. New York, 1950.

Kazbunda, Karel. "Pokusy rakouské vlády o české vyrovnání." *Český časopis historický* 27 (1921): 94–134, 353–412.

———. "Ke zmaru českého vyrovnání." *Český časopis historický* 37 (1931): 512–73.

Rath, R. John. *The Provisional Austrian Regime in Lombardo-Venetia.* Austin, Texas, 1969.

Wierer, Rudolf. "Das böhmische Staatsrecht und der Ausgleichsversuch des Ministeriums Hohenwart-Schäffle." *Bohemia* 4 (1963): 54–173.

See also *Ausgleich;* Friedrich von Beust; Dualism; Dual Monarchy; Franz Ferdinand; Franz Joseph; Law and certification

Trianon, Treaty of (1920)

Peace treaty between the victorious powers of World War I and Hungary signed on June 4, 1920, at the Trianon Palace in Versailles, France. Among the treaty's provisions, 290 of its 364 clauses were the same as the ones given to Germany and Austria. Considered by many to be the harshest of the treaties dictated to the defeated states, Trianon reduced Hungary's territory from 101,520 to 33,500 square miles (282,000 to 93,000 sq km), and its population from 18.2 million to 7.9 million. Since the new borders were not drawn to overlap ethnic frontiers, 3.3 million Hungarians found themselves in neighboring states. To protect the minorities, the treaty also included the minority clause that gave them the same collective rights the dominant nationality enjoyed. Hungary's armed force was set at 35,000, with no heavy armaments or air force. A universal draft was abolished, and Hungary was required to pay reparation for war damages.

The Hungarian government accepted the peace terms under duress, and at the precise moment the treaty was signed, Hungarian church bells tolled and all traffic and work stopped for ten minutes. Parliament ratified the treaty on November 15, 1920.

Because the peace treaty included the Covenant of the League of Nations, the United States, which never joined the league, refused to sign it. On August 29, 1921, the two countries signed a separate peace treaty in Budapest.

The consequence of the Trianon treaty was economic hardship, exacerbated by the influx of 426,000 refugees from the successor states of the Austro-Hungarian Empire. The shock to Hungary's collective national psyche was a constant factor in Hungarian politics during the interwar period and led to the governments' revisionist policies through diplomacy and ultimately the use of force.

Peter Pastor

Further reading

Deak, Francis. *Hungary at the Paris Peace Conference.* New York, 1942

Király, Béla K., Peter Pastor, and Ivan Sanders, eds. *Essays on World War I: A Case Study on Trianon.* Highland Lakes, New Jersey, 1982.

Király, Béla K. and László Veszprémy, eds. *Trianon and East Central Europe: Antecedents and Repercussions.* Highland Lakes, New Jersey, 1995.

Mócsy, István I. *The Effects of World War I. The Uprooted: Hungarian Refugees and Their Impact on Hungary's Domestic Politics, 1918–1921.* Highland Lakes, New Jersey, 1983.

Ormos, Mária. *From Padua to the Trianon.* Highland Lakes, New Jersey, 1990.

See also Ethnic Minorities; Revisionism; Transylvanian Dispute; Vienna Awards

Trieste

City in northeast Italy, situated on the northern shore of the Adriatic Sea. Trieste lies just a few miles west of the border with Slovenia and is easily accessed by superhighways from east and west. It is the largest seaport on the Adriatic. A huge lighthouse was built in 1927 at the north end of the harbor to commemorate those lost at sea.

Since 1719, the city has been a free port where no customs duty is charged on imported or exported goods. Many nations use this service. Nearly one-third of Austria's overseas traffic, for example, goes through Trieste.

Celts and Illyrians were the early inhabitants of the city, before the Romans made it their center for trade. Over the centuries, a mixture of diverse peoples and ideas provided an atmosphere of tolerance for the inhabitants of the city. Trieste served as a refuge for political exiles and artists. One of its famous residents was James Joyce (1882–1941), the Irish writer who lived in the city for a few years before World War I. After World War I, the city was annexed by Italy following a quarrel with the new Yugoslav state.

After World War II, the United Nations took over the administration of Trieste from Italy. U.S. and British troops occupied the city and an area to the north, while Yugoslav forces occupied the Istrian Peninsula south of the city.

The Mediterranean climate, with hot dry summers and mild rainy winters, along with beautiful rugged terrain, brings many visitors from other parts of Europe to the city.

William B. Kory

Further reading

Magocsi, Paul Robert. *Historical Atlas of East Central Europe.* Seattle, Washington, 1993.

See also Trieste Affair

Trieste Affair

Italian-Yugoslav border dispute between 1941 and 1954 involving nationalist and Cold War politics. Italy and Yugoslavia claimed the region and its major city, Trieste. After World War II, the Great Powers divided the region into three sections. Italy received the smaller, western part and Yugoslavia the larger eastern territory. In 1947 Trieste, its hinterland, and northwest Istria became a United Nations protectorate known as the Free Territory of Trieste (FTT). The FTT itself was divided into two zones. Anglo-American forces controlled Zone A (Trieste and its surroundings) and Yugoslavia occupied Zone B (northwestern Istria). Yugoslavia and Italy maintained their claims on the area until 1954.

Before 1918, Austria controlled Trieste, which was its only port and a center of Italian irredentism. While the city of Trieste was ethnically Italian, its surroundings were Slovene and Croatian. In 1919 the Italian and Yugoslav governments both claimed this region, but Italy was allowed to annex Trieste, Istria, and parts of Dalmatia. In 1945 the Yugoslav government renewed its claim to the area, arguing that its interests should be honored because it had allied with Western forces against Axis troops, fought the fascist Italian regime, and suffered under Italian occupation.

The Trieste Affair also exacerbated the deterioration of Yugoslav-Soviet relations. Until 1947 the Soviet Union backed Yugoslav claims to the FTT, while Britain and the United States supported Italy. The Soviet decision to drop support of Yugoslav claims added to strained relations between Tito (1892–1980) and Stalin (1879–1953). The resulting Tito-Stalin split in June 1948 created the first opportunity for Western penetration into the Soviet bloc.

Diplomatic fumbling over the issue of Trieste fueled Yugoslav distrust of its post-1948 allies in the Cold War. In 1948 the British and American governments declared in favor of returning the FTT to Italy. In 1952 Anglo-American forces ignored Yugoslav proposals for compromise and turned the civil administration of Zone A over to Italy. In 1953 Britain and the United States began to return military control of Trieste to Italy, leaving the fate of northwest Istria ambiguous. Immediately, the Italian government claimed Zone B. Tito dispatched troops to the FTT frontier and requested a hearing at the UN Security Council. Ultimately, direct negotiations between Italy and Yugoslavia resolved the affair. Italy obtained control of Trieste city, while Yugoslavia absorbed Zone B and two small strips of Zone A, gained access to the port of Trieste, and received a tripartite credit to develop a Yugoslav port at Koper in western Istria.

Katherine McCarthy

Further reading

Novak, Bogdan. *Trieste, 1941–1954: The Ethnic, Political, and Ideological Struggle.* Chicago, 1970.

Rusinow, Dennison. *Italy's Austrian Heritage, 1919–1946*. Oxford, 1969.

Unger, Leonard and Kristina Segulja. *The Trieste Negotiations*. Washington, D.C., 1977.

See also Cold War; Irredentism; Stalin; Tito; Tito-Stalin Split; Trieste

Triune Kingdom

Term referring to the historic Croatian lands known as Croatia, Slavonia, and Dalmatia. These lands are associated with early Croatian settlements in southeastern Europe and constituted a political entity during the reign of Croatian ruler Zvonimir (r. 1075–1089). Croats have always claimed them on the basis of historic rights.

A series of events broke the unity of these lands after Croatia's union with Hungary in 1102. However, the idea of reconstituting the kingdom revived in the nineteenth century, when Croats began pressing for changes in their status within the Habsburg Empire. During the Revolutions of 1848, for example, Croat representatives demanded the reunion of Dalmatia with Croatia and Slavonia in the interest of autonomy within the monarchy. Following the annexation of Bosnia-Hercegovina by Austria-Hungary in 1878, Croatian nationalists such as Ante Starčević (1823–96) sought the lands of the Triune Kingdom plus Bosnia-Hercegovina as part of their political programs.

With the formation of the first Yugoslavia in 1918, Croats believed that in the federal arrangement they envisioned, the lands of the Triune Kingdom would surely be under their jurisdiction. As with other matters, such as the continued existence of their Sabor (legislature), they were disappointed. The 1921 Vidovdan Constitution divided the country into numerous oblasts, or districts, with no regard for the unity of the Croatian lands. The state reorganization connected with the dictatorship of King Alexander (1888–1934) did nothing to restore that unity.

Following World War II, the Communist government of Josip Broz Tito (1892–1980) placed Croatia, Slavonia, and Dalmatia under Croatian administrative jurisdiction, thereby reuniting the lands. After the breakup of Yugoslavia, independent Croatia claimed the lands, though they have suffered incursions in the conflict that followed.

Brigit Farley

Further reading

Banac, Ivo. *The National Question in Yugoslavia*. Ithaca, New York, 1984.

Clissold, Stephen. *A Short History of Yugoslavia*. Cambridge, 1966.

Jelavich, Charles and Barbara Jelavich. *The Habsburg Monarchy: Toward a Multinational Empire of National States?* New York, 1959.

Jelavich, Barbara. *History of the Balkans*, 2 vols. Cambridge, 1983.

Rothenberg, Gunther E. *The Military Frontier in Croatia, 1740–1881: A Study of an Imperial Institution*. Chicago, 1966.

See also Alexander I Karadjordjević; Croatia, Birth of the Republic of; Revolutions of 1848; Sabor; Ante Starčević; Tito; Vidovdan Constitution

Truman Doctrine

U.S. policy to contain the spread of communism. Prompted by the British government's notice of February 21, 1947, that it could no longer supply economic and military aid to Greece and Turkey, President Harry S Truman (1884–1972), fearful of a successful Communist coup in the area, asked Congress on March 12 for financial aid for Greece and Turkey to assist them in their struggle against communism. America had watched the Soviets gain control of Eastern Europe in the immediate post–World War II period. Consequently, Truman's ideological argument quickly won congressional approval by May 9 to appropriate $250 million for Greece and $150 million for Turkey. These funds became available through the Marshall Plan.

The Truman Doctrine accepted the containment recommendations of George Kennan (1904–), which essentially drew a line between the so-called free world and the Communist world. To some, the Truman Doctrine was a response to Soviet aggression; to others, it was a stimulus that forced the Soviets to secure control of Eastern Europe and intensify their influence in Western Europe.

Joseph F. Harrington

Further reading

Gaddis, John Lewis. *Strategies of Containment: A Critical Appraisal of Postwar American National Security Policy*. New York, 1982.

Harrington, Joseph and Bruce Courtney. *Tweaking the Nose of the Russians: Fifty Years of*

T

American-Romanian Relations, 1940–1990. Boulder, Colorado, 1991.

Wheeler-Bennett, John W. and Anthony Nicholls. *The Semblance of Peace: The Political Settlement after World War II.* New York, 1972.

See also Cold War; Greek Civil War; Marshall Plan

Trumbić, Ante (1868–1938)

Croatian politician and promoter of a federal Yugoslavia. A lifelong supporter of Yugoslavism (unity among the South Slavs), Trumbić began his career as a lawyer and politician in Habsburg Dalmatia. He believed that South Slavic solidarity was preferable to Austrian or Hungarian rule at the turn of the century. To this end, he became an active participant in the Croato-Serb coalition in 1905, which promoted the concept of Yugoslavism.

Following the outbreak of World War I, Trumbić founded the Yugoslav Committee, which sought the union of Habsburg South Slavs with Serbia and Montenegro on an equal basis in an independent state. With Nikola Pašić (1845–1926), he negotiated the 1917 Corfu Declaration, the blueprint for the first Yugoslavia, and became the country's first foreign minister in 1919.

Trumbić always insisted that union among Serbs, Croats, and Slovenes guarantee equal rights for each group. As the constituent assembly debated state organization in 1921, he argued forcefully for decentralized rule, even suggesting that the state be named "United Kingdom of Yugoslavia," rather than the "Kingdom of Serbs, Croats, and Slovenes." Aided by the Croat delegates' boycott, the Serbian majority managed to impose centralism in the Vidovdan Constitution (1921). But Trumbić continued his campaign, working actively in the Croatian Union and the Croatian Peasant Party. He also traveled abroad to warn Yugoslavia's allies of the dangers posed by Serbian rule to the state's future.

After the imposition of a royal dictatorship by King Alexander (1888–1934) in 1929, Trumbić again raised the federalist banner, demanding in the so-called *Punctacije* declaration a reorganization of the state along lines of national equality. After Alexander's murder in 1934, Peter II's (1923–70) regent, Prince Paul (1893–1976), proved unwilling to make major changes.

Trumbić remained committed to his conception of the ideal Yugoslav state until his death in 1938. Shortly before the end, however, he spoke darkly of separatism and war, as if anticipating that his legacy would be the unfulfilled promise of Yugoslavism and Yugoslavia.

Brigit Farley

Further reading

Krizman, Bogdan. "Trumbićeva misija u inozemstvu uoći proglašenije šestojanuarske diktature." *Historijski pregled,* no. 3 (July–August 1962): 176–202.

Paulova, Milada. *Jugoslavenski odbor.* Zagreb, 1925.

Pavelić, Ante Smith. *Dr. Ante Trumbić: Problemi hrvatsko-srpskih odnosa.* Munich, 1959.

See also Alexander I Karadjordjević; Corfu Declaration; Nikola Pašić; Paul Karadjordjević; Peter II Karadjordjević; Kingdom of Serbs, Croats, and Slovenes; Vidovdan Constitution; Yugoslav Committee; Yugoslavism

Tsankov, Aleksandur Tsalov (1879–1959)

Bulgarian politician. Tsankov graduated high school in Ruse and then completed studies in law and finance at Sofia University. He joined the Bulgarian Workers' Social Democratic Party at the end of the nineteenth century, collaborating on the editing and publication of the party's organ, *Novo vreme* (*New Times*), with Dimitur Blagoev (1856–1924). When the party fragmented in 1903, he joined with the Socialists. In 1907 he broke completely with that party and concentrated on teaching at Sofia University, rising to the rank of professor of political economics.

After World War I, Tsankov became one of the leading organizers of the political group National Accord and became its secretary in 1921. He later assumed leadership of the group and took an active role in the preparation and execution of the June 1923 coup that overthrew the government of Aleksandur Stamboliiski (1879–1923).

During the 1920s and early 1930s, Tsankov served in a number of capacities, including minister of education and president of the National Assembly. In May 1932 he created a political party called Democratic Accord. From the beginning of 1933, he attempted to mold this party on the Nazi model by renaming it the National Socialist Movement. The coup carried out by the Zveno group, the organization comprising individuals who believed the party system was detrimental to the interests of the nation, in May 1934 preempted any plans Tsankov may have had of obtaining power. Although his party was banned, he continued to carry out some political activity and sided with Nazi Germany rather than with the "rightist" political parties of Bulgaria. Shortly before the fall of Bulgaria to Soviet troops in 1944, he left the country and resided in Austria for a time. There, he headed a Nazi-supported émigré government that he left to move to Argentina at the end of the 1940s.

Mari A. Firkatian

Further reading

Kazasov, Dimo. *Political Bulgaria between 1913 and 1944.* Sofia, 1945.
Politicheski partii, organizatsii i upravleniia v Bûlgariia (1879–1944). Sofia, 1983.
Politicheski partii, organizatsii i dvizheniia v Bûlgaria i tehnite lideri 1879–1949. Sofia, 1991.
Radev, Simeon. *Stroitelite na sûvremenna Bûlgariia,* 2 vols. Sofia, 1911.

See also Dimitur Blagoev; Aleksandur Stamboliiski; Zveno

Tsankov, Dragan Kiriakov (Dimitr Gikov) (1828–1911)

Bulgarian writer and activist. Born to a merchant's family in Svishtov, Tsankov studied first in his hometown before attending the Odessa Seminary and the Kiev High School. In 1848 he moved to Romania, where he became a teacher. Two years later, he moved to Vienna, where he lived with his brother and learned the printing trade. He also bought a printing press that he later moved to Constantinople. By 1855, he was established in the Ottoman capital as a publisher and teacher. From 1858 to 1863, he edited the newspaper *Bûlgaria.* He used this forum to expound on his ideas regarding the rectitude of Bulgarians converting to the Uniate rite. (The Uniate Church comprised formerly Orthodox Christians who accepted union with Roman Catholicism.) He actively promoted the opening of Uniate schools, an effort that culminated in 1860 with an open letter to the Vatican to accept him and the followers under the pope's spiritual guidance. Between 1864 and 1873, he worked in Svishtov, Ruse, and Niš in various capacities for the Ottoman administration as well as a teacher of French. He returned to Con-

stantinople, where he continued to be active in publishing.

After the 1876 April Uprising against the Turks, he was charged by the Bulgarian Exarchate (Bulgarian Orthodox Church) to make the rounds of European capitals to gauge the opinion of the powers vis-à-vis the Bulgarian situation and to draw attention to the plight of Bulgarians under Ottoman rule. He participated in the Russo-Turkish War of 1877–78, and after the peace was appointed vice governor of Svishtov, Turnovo, and Ruse. He was subsequently elected to the constituent assembly and participated in the creation of the Turnovo Constitution. He became one of the leaders of the Liberal Party and later the Progressive Liberal Party. He also held several ministerial posts. However, his Russophile position kept him under police surveillance, and after an unsuccessful coup against Prince Alexander of Battenberg (1857–93), Tsankov emigrated. He returned only after Stefan Stambolov (1854–95), the prime minister, fell from power in 1894. Tsankov was elected as a representative to the National Assembly and later was president of that body from 1902 to 1903.

Mari A. Firkatian

Further reading

Dragan Tsankov (biograficheski belezhki), in *100g. narodno chitalishte "Zora."* Sofia, 1967, 37–49.
Kiril, patriarh bûlgarski: Katolicheskata propaganda sred bûlgarite prez vtorata polovina na XIX vek 1859–1865. Sofia, 1962, 106–12.
Kovacheva, M. *Dragan Tsankov obshtestvenik, politik i diplomat do 1878.* Sofia, 1982.
Popova, P. *Edin zhurnalist pred sûda na istoriata, Dragan Tsankov* in *Vûrhove na bûlgarskata zhurnalistika,* vol. 1. Sofia, 1976, 295–319.

See also Alexander of Battenberg; April Uprising; Exarchate; Russo-Turkish War of 1877–78; Stefan Stambolov; Turnovo Constitution; Uniate Church

Tuculescu, Ion (1910–62)

Romanian abstract painter. Tuculescu began painting at the age of fifteen, later studying at the Faculty of Natural Sciences (1928–36) in Bucharest. In conjunction with a lifelong scientific career, he regularly opened one-man shows in the late 1930s and throughout the 1940s. His artistic origins appear to have been influenced by Van Gogh (1853–90); the paintings of his first art shows were primarily landscapes of a violent and rather tormented nature, full of unleashed lyricism. This can be seen in his Greek and Black Sea landscapes, or the series of "Rape fields." In 1947 Tuculescu entered a folklore period, in which he explored the expressionist features of the decorative signs to be found in Romanian archaic folk art, arriving at a mystical interpretation of their symbolic contents. From 1957 until his death in 1962, Tuculescu created works of the "totemic periods": large canvases that stylized the pantheistic world of his previous art up to more geometric, abstract compositions. With the coming of the Communist regime, he retired from public life; only in 1956 did he open a show in his own apartment. After his death, a retrospective, organized in 1965 at the National Museum of Art, finally brought him recognition, and his works have been exhibited throughout Romania and the West. A permanent museum dedicated to his work was opened in 1973 in his birthplace, Craiova.

Magda Carneci

Further reading

Baconsky, A. E. *Ion Tuculescu*. Bucharest, 1972.
Carneci, Magda. *Ion Tuculescu*. Bucharest, 1984.
Davidescu, Catalin. *Ion Tuculescu*. Craiova, 1988.
Iftodi, Eugenia. *Close to Tuculescu*. Bucharest, 1996.
Vlasiu, Ion. *Ion Tuculescu*. Bucharest, 1966.

See also Folklore; Romanian Art

Tudjman, Franjo (1922–1999)

President of the Republic of Croatia. After fighting as a Partisan against the fascists in World War II, Tudjman worked in the Yugoslav Defense Ministry and on the General Staff until 1961. At that time, he was made director of the Institute for the History of the Workers' Movement in Croatia. In 1967 he lost his academic positions owing to his activism in support of the Croatian (as opposed to the Serbo-Croatian) language and was twice imprisoned for his activities. As Serbia escalated its anti-Croatian rhetoric in the late 1980s Tudjman emerged as the political leader of the Republic of Croatia in its declaration for independence from Yugoslavia in 1991. He and his party, the Croatian Democratic Alliance (Hrvatska Demokratska Zajednica), espousing a Croatian nationalist platform, have remained in power and have played important roles in negotiations with the United Nations, the North Atlantic Treaty Organization, and the United States.

Tudjman, who earned a Ph.D in history, is the author of numerous books, including *Bespuća povijesne zbiljnosti* (*Wilderness of Historical Reality,* 1989), which sparked controversy for its treatment of anti-Semitism and genocide during World War II. One of the revisions of this book was released in English as *Horrors of War: Historical Reality and Philosophy* (1996). Among his other works are *Nationalism in Contemporary Europe* (1981) and *Hrvatska u monarhističkoi Jugoslaviji, 1918–1941* (*Croatia in Royal Yugoslavia, 1918–1941,* 1993).

John K. Cox

Further reading

Butković, Davor and Dubravko Grakalić. *Prilozi za političku biografiju Dr. Franje Tudjmana Predsjednika Republike Hrvatske.* Zagreb, 1991.
Lenard J. Cohen. *Broken Bonds: The Disintegration of Yugoslavia,* 2d ed. Boulder, Colorado, 1995.
Misha Glenny. *The Fall of Yugoslavia: The Third Balkan War,* rev. ed. New York, 1994.
Woodward, Susan L. *Balkan Tragedy: Chaos and Dissolution after the Cold War.* Washington, D.C., 1995.

See also Croatia, Birth of the Republic of; Serbia and the Breakup of Yugoslavia

Tuka, Vojtech (1880–1946)

Legal scholar, fascist activist, and war criminal prominent in interwar and wartime Slovak politics. Born in 1880 in Piarg in central Slovakia, Tuka was a law professor at the university in Bratislava from 1914 to 1919. Though remaining in Slovakia after 1918, Tuka, as a Magyarized Slovak, maintained sympathy for Hungary and bitterly opposed the new Czechoslovakia. Losing his university position, Tuka made a career in the nationalist Slovak People's Party as editor of its daily newspaper from 1921 to 1929, parliamentarian from 1925 to 1929, and close adviser to party chairman, Andrej Hlinka (1864–1938). Throughout the 1920s, he kept close contact with Hungarian irredentists and Central European fascists, and organized the Rodobrana, a nationalist paramilitary organization. Soon after arguing in a January 1928 article that Czechoslovak law would become void in Slovakia on the republic's tenth anniversary, Tuka was convicted of treason and imprisoned. Amnestied in 1937, he returned to political life after the Munich Pact, which saw Czechoslovakia lose the Sudetenland to Germany. During the wartime Slovak Republic, he served as prime minister and foreign minister. As leader of the radical right wing of Slovak politics, he was the chief rival of the more moderate President Jozef Tiso (1887–1947). An avid supporter of Hitler's (1889–1945) Germany, Nazi ideology, and deportation of Slovakia's Jews to German death camps, Tuka was tried, condemned as a war criminal, and executed in the summer of 1946.

James Felak

Further reading
Československý biografický slovník. Prague, 1992.

Hoensch, Jörg K. *Der ungarische Revisionismus und die Zerschlagung der Tschechoslowakei.* Tübingen, Germany, 1967.

Jelinek, Yeshayahu. *The Parish Republic.* Boulder, Colorado, 1976.

Kramer, Juraj. *Iredenta a separatizmus v slovenskej politike.* Bratislava, 1957.

See also Adolf Hitler; Andrej Hlinka; Irredentism; Munich Pact; Right Radicalism; Slovak Republic; Jozef Tiso

Tukhachevsky, Mikhail Nikolayevich (1893–1937)

Marshal of the Soviet Union. One of the Soviet Union's most talented and innovative military officers, Tukhachevsky was wounded during World War I and taken prisoner by the Germans in February 1915. He remained in captivity until the fall of 1917, when he returned to Russia just before the October Revolution. He joined the Red Army early in 1918, and in May 1920 Tukhachevsky was ordered to direct operations against an invading Polish army in the western Russia. Within two weeks, Tukhachevsky had checked the Polish advance, then counterattacked vigorously, pushing the Poles back more than 400 miles (666 km) to defensive positions around Warsaw. The Russians failed to take Warsaw, and Tukhachevsky criticized the political commander of the sector, Josef Stalin (1879–1953), for failing to send reinforcements. This act, along with his frequent warnings to Stalin concerning German military preparations in the mid-1930s, would cost Tukhachevsky dearly.

Stalin distrusted Tukhachevsky's independence of thought, and at the beginning of Stalin's purge of the Red Army, Tukhachevsky and seven other high-ranking officers were arrested, brutally interrogated, and shot by firing squad in June 1937.

Tukhachevsky's principal contribution to military theory was his concept of deep operations, designed in the early 1930s, which combined armored-mechanized units, tactical aviation, and airborne units. This conception is more sophisticated than the German blitzkrieg, since it can be used for defense as well as for offense.

Daniel D. Trifan

Further reading
Shukman, Harold, ed. *Stalin's Generals.* New York, 1993.

See also Polish-Soviet War; Red Army; Stalin; Warsaw, Battle of

Turks

Ethnically Turkic-speaking Islamic peoples who settled in various urban and rural locales of southeastern Europe as a consequence of the Ottoman conquest of the region. The Turks originally entered southeastern Europe in the mid-thirteenth century as the military forces of the Ottoman state in northwestern Anatolia, which hired them out to contending parties in the endemic civil and foreign wars fought among the Orthodox Christian states of Byzantium, Serbia, and Bulgaria. In the mid–fourteenth century the Ottoman Turks entered southeastern Europe to stay. Over the course of the following two centuries, the Ottoman hold on most of the Balkans solidified into a powerful imperial state, and the Turkish cavalry forces (*sipahis*) settled on the land in a pseudofeudal system of support. Over time, most of the landed *sipahis* gravitated to local urban centers for their primary residences, where a significant number of Turkish-speaking Ottoman civil-military administrative, commercial, and religious elements were concentrated. These urban Turks constituted the most numerous segment of the Turkish ethnic presence in Ottoman-controlled southeastern Europe during the period of Ottoman rule.

In certain areas of southeastern Europe—especially in the Bulgarian and Macedonian lands—the numbers of urban Turks were augmented by widespread settlements of Turkish-speaking peoples in the countryside. The most common among these rural Turkish settlers were *yürüks,* pastoral Anatolian Turkic tribes who were colonized in the Bulgarian areas of southeastern Europe by the Ottoman authorities in the fifteenth century. These colonists, as well as other Turkic settlers, were organized by the Ottoman authorities into loose military formations and considered irregular auxiliary military forces supporting the regular landed cavalry and slave standing infantry and cavalry formations.

Beginning in the seventeenth century, Ottoman power in southeastern Europe commenced to decline. Along with that development, the original military and administrative characteristics of the Turkish ethnic presence gradually were transformed into more mundane channels. By the close of the eighteenth century, the numerous urban Turks primarily were involved in social-economic affairs or religious matters, although urban administrative, judicial, and penal responsibilities remained exclusively in their hands. Rural Turks lived in villages (either exclusively Turkish or of mixed Turk and non-Turk inhabitants) and pursued traditional agricultural activities. A few pursued religious functions.

The Serb and Greek wars of independence (1804–30 and 1821–31, respectively), the Russo-Turkish War of 1877–78, and the Balkan Wars (1912–13) resulted in mass emigrations of ethnic Turks from the newly independent states created out of the former Ottoman Empire in southeastern Europe. By the late twentieth century, significant numbers of ethnic Turks could be found only in Bulgaria, Macedonia, and northeastern Greece, where they provided the pretext for nationalist anti-Turk sentiment in the 1950s, 1980s, and 1990s.

Dennis P. Hupchick

Further reading

Inalcik, Halil. *The Ottoman Empire: The Classical Age, 1300–1600,* trans. by Norman Itzkowitz and Colin Imber. London, 1973.

McCarthy, Justin. *Death and Exile: The Ethnic Cleansing of Ottoman Muslims.* Princeton, New Jersey, 1996.

Shaw, Stanford J. *History of the Ottoman Empire and Modern Turkey,* vol. 1. Cambridge, 1976.

Sugar, Peter F. *Southeastern Europe under Ottoman Rule, 1354–1804.* Seattle, Washington, 1977.

See also Balkan Wars; Greek Revolution; Muslims; Ottoman Empire; Russo-Turkish War of 1828–29; Russo-Turkish War of 1877–78

Turnovo

Former district center in north-central Bulgaria. Since 1965, its name, derived from the Slavic *"traneto"* (thorn bush), has been called Veliko Turnovo. Turnovo is a crossing point of the Sofia-Varna (west-east) and Ruse-Kurjali (north-south) roads.

The earliest discovered settlement in Turnovo dates from the Neolite period. In the thirteenth century B.C., Thracians settled the area until it was turned into a fortress by the Romans. From the twelfth to fourteenth centuries, Turnovo served as the capital of the Second Bulgarian Kingdom. Western and Byzantine sources referred to it as "Magna civitas Trinov" (Great City of Trinov) and the "Second after Constantinople."

Turnovo, with a population of 67,540 in 1994, is one of the most picturesque towns in Bulgaria. It is situated in the northern foothills of the Balkan ranges on the Yantra River. The town is an ancient center of learning. In the twelfth to fourteenth centuries its renowned School of Arts and Letters influenced all southeastern Europe. It currently has two universities.

The city is located about 726 feet (220 m) above sea level and has a temperate continental climate; (the average annual temperature is 53° F (11.5° C) with below Bulgaria's average precipitation of 27 inches (67.5 cm).

Industrialization began in 1861 but lagged until the 1950s. Currently, the economy is dominated by machine building (hoist engines, metal-processing machines, television and radio sets, and electronics), wood-processing and furniture plants, plastic and rubber goods, food processing, and large textile (cotton and silk fabrics) and child apparel factories. It is a rich agricultural center specializing in grains, animal breeding, vegetables, and fruits.

Boian Koulov

Further reading

Bulgarian Academy of Sciences. *Entsiklopedia Bulgaria,* vol. 1. Sofia, 1981.

National Statistical Institute. *Broi na naselenieto po oblasti, obshtini i naseleni mesta (okonchatelni danni): Resultati ot prebroyavaneto na naselenieto,* vol. 3. Sofia, 1994.

Vasil, Mikov. *Proizhod i Znachenie na Imenata na Nashite Gradove, Sela, Reki, Planini i Mesta.* Sofia, 1943.

See also Turnovo Constitution

Turnovo Constitution

Constitution of the Principality, Kingdom, and People's Republic of Bulgaria from April 16, 1879, to December 4, 1947. According to article 4 of the Treaty of Berlin of July 1, 1878, an Organic Statute for the new Principality of Bulgaria had to be worked out. This was done by a constituent assembly of 231 elected and nominated notables, which convened on February 10, 1879, in the northeast Bulgarian town of Turnovo. On April 16, 1879, after prolonged debates between Conservatives and Liberals, the Organic Statute was proclaimed under the name Turnovo Constitution. It constituted Bulgaria as a constitutional monarchy with the prince and the parliament balancing each other. As early as April 27, 1881, however, Bulgaria's first monarch, Alexander I of Battenberg (1857–93), suspended the constitution and introduced personal rule. Constitutional government was reestablished only on September 6, 1883. Alexander's successor, Prince (later King) Ferdinand I of Saxony-Coburg-Gotha (1861–1948), also strove to strengthen royal power unilaterally. In 1911 his most important success in this regard was to change article 17 to get a free hand for secret negotiations with foreign powers without having to inform the parliament. During the reign of Boris III (1894–1943), the radical Bulgarian Agrarian National Union (BANU) government planned to change the Turnovo Constitution. In April 1923 Prime Minister Aleksandur Stamboliiski (1879–1923) proposed drastically limiting royal prerogatives, establishing a second chamber, and introducing what he called "economic democracy." The conservative-nationalist coup of June 9, 1923, however put an end to those plans. In May 1934 the constitution again was suspended, parliament was dissolved, and political parties forbidden. Boris, who on April 21, 1935, regained his former political influence, did not immediately reestablish the constitution. Instead, he used the situation to implement his personal rule in the form of a "Parliamentary autocracy"—with parliament, but without parties. Only in 1937, after having firmly consolidated his dominant position, did he put the constitution into force again.

On December 4, 1947—a year after the abolition of the monarchy—the Communist-dominated parliament replaced the Turnovo Constitution with one designed for a "people's democracy," colloquially named after Georgi Dimitrov (1882–1949), Bulgaria's Communist leader.

Stefan Troebst

Further reading
Black, Cyril E. *The Establishment of Constitutional Government in Bulgaria.* Princeton, New Jersey, 1943.

"Turnovska konstitutsiia," in Veska Nikolova and Milen Kumanov, eds., *Kratuk istoricheski spravochnik*, vol. 3, *Bulgariia.* Sofia, 1983, 389–91.

See also Alexander of Battenberg; Boris III; Bulgarian Agrarian National Union; Communist Party of Bulgaria; Congress of Berlin; Georgi Dimitrov; Aleksandur Stamboliiski

Tusar, Vlastimil (1880–1924)

Czechoslovak Social Democrat and prime minister. Tusar became involved in the Social Democratic movement as a young shop assistant in Prague. He moved to Brno in 1903, where he worked as a newspaper editor. In 1911 he was elected to the Austrian Reichsrat (parliament). Tusar was a careful, pragmatic politician. During World War I, he initially supported the Habsburg monarchy and worked closely with his pro-Austrian colleague Bohumír Šmeral (1880–1941). As the war turned against the Central Powers, however, Tusar switched allegiance and supported Czechoslovak independence. After Austria-Hungary collapsed, Tusar became the Czechoslovak representative in Vienna, where he proved himself to be an able diplomat. In July 1919 he became prime minister, heading a "Red-Green" (Socialist-Agrarian) coalition. This coalition survived the first parliamentary elections in April 1920, but pressures within the Social Democratic Party forced the cabinet to resign in September. Tusar led the right wing of his party in a campaign against the left, led by Šmeral. After an ugly internal struggle, Tusar forced the left wing to secede and establish an independent Communist Party in 1921. Despite failing health, Tusar accepted a final diplomatic assignment, as Czechoslovak minister to Berlin (1921–24). Tusar was among the most moderate Czech politicians of his day on the national question, but his tenuous political position as prime minister prevented him from reaching out openly to the Sudeten Germans.

Todd Huebner

Further reading
Peroutka, Ferdinand. *Budování státu,* 3d ed., 4 vols. Brno, 1991, vol. 3, 1,268–80.

Twardowski, Kazimierz (1866–1938)

Principal catalyst in the development of the Polish logical tradition. In the spirit of his Viennese teacher Franz Brentano (1838–1917), Twardowski sought to establish a rigorous scientific methodology for philosophy and thereby eliminate the excesses of speculative thought that went beyond the parameters of justification and induced terminological ambiguities. While metaphysics itself remained a possible form of inquiry, the methodological constraints that Twardowski sought would clearly define the boundaries of justifiable expressions, beyond which the philosopher should not speak.

Hovering between the dangers of unguarded speculation and skepticism, Twardowski developed his theory of "cognitive objects" that were not reducible to the content of psychological or mental states. Twardowski's antipsychologism had a significant influence on Edmund Husserl (1859–1938), founder of phenomenology, and Moritz Schlick (1882–1936), a major force of the positivism of the Vienna Circle (the major center for positivism), and subsequently twentieth-century philosophy. Building on this base, Twardowski remolded the face of Polish philosophy. Focusing on methodological precision, he developed a theory of logic and its objects that attempted to avoid both Platonic idealism and psychological reductionism. His logical work became the cornerstone for subsequent Polish thinkers such as Kazimierz Ajdukiewicz (1890–1963), Alfred Tarski (1902–83), Jan Łukasiewicz (1878–1956), Stanisław Leśniewski (1886–1939), and Tadeusz Kotarbiński (1886–1981).

In addition to his research, Twardowski also established the Polish Philosophical Society in 1904 and a quarterly journal in 1911. He became editor of *Studia Philosophica* (*Philosophical Studies*), publishing articles by Polish thinkers in foreign languages.

James Eiswert

Further reading
Ingarden, Roman. "The Scientific Activity of Kazimierz Twardowski." *Studia Philosophica* 3 (1948): 17–30.
Twardowski, Kazimierz. *On the Content and Object of Presentations: A Psychological Investigation,* trans. by R. Grossmann. The Hague, 1977.

See also Kazimierz Ajdukiewicz; Philosophy; Positivism; Alfred Tarski

Tyrš, Miroslav (1832–84)

Founder of the Czech gymnastic society Sokol, art critic, and historian. Best known for his work in the Sokol, the Czech nationalist gymnastic society, Tyrš was born Friedrich Emanuel Tirsch and adopted a Czech identity as a young man. As gymnastic director (*náčelník*) of the Prague Sokol from its founding in 1862 until shortly before his death in 1884, he defined the club's gymnastic and national mission in a series of essays and speeches that became required reading throughout the movement. Using the exercises and apparatus of the older German gymnastic society, the Turnverein, Tyrš attempted to create a peculiarly Slavic gymnastic system for the Sokol, which he described in *Základové tělocviku* (*The Fundamentals of Gymnastics,* 1873). He constructed his Sokol ideology out of traditions of Czech nationalism, an idealized view of classical Greek culture, and contemporary notions of popular Darwinism. These values informed his work in art history and criticism as well, which he began in 1872. Considered the pioneer of Czech art criticism, he wrote for newspapers and journals, served on artistic juries, and lectured at both the Prague Technical College and the University, where he was named professor extraordinarius of art history in 1883. His career in art was cut short by his premature death at age fifty-two.

Claire E. Nolte

Further reading
Dvořáková, Zora. *Miroslav Tyrš: Prohry a vítězství.* Prague, 1989.

Jandásek, Ladislav. "The Founder of the Sokols: Miroslav Tyrš." *Slavonic and East European Review* (April 1932): 572–87.

Nolte, Claire. "Art in the Service of the Nation: Miroslav Tyrš as Art Historian and Critic." *Bohemia: Zeitschrift für Geschichte und Kultur der böhmischen Länder* 34, no. 1 (1993): 47–62.

See also Gymnastic Societies; Sokol

U

Udržal, František (1868–1938)

Czechoslovak Agrarian and prime minister. Udržal, a small estate owner, was involved in the creation of the Czech Agrarian Party in the late nineteenth century. He was close to the party's chairman, Antonín Švehla (1873–1933), and others who broadened its representation to include not only estate owners and wealthy farmers but also small farmers and peasants. Udržal was among the founders of the Central Union of Sugar Beet Growers, a lobby that launched the careers of many Agrarians around Švehla. Udržal was a deputy in the Austrian Reichsrat (parliament) from 1897 to 1918, first as a Young Czech, then as an independent, and from 1907 as an Agrarian. After World War I, he served in the Czechoslovak National Assembly as a deputy (1918–35) and a senator (1935–37) for the Republican Party, the new name of the Agrarian Party. Udržal, like Švehla and Jan Malypetr (1873–1947), was among the Republicans who were close to President Tomáš Masaryk (1850–1937) and his supporters in the *Hrad,* the informal group around the president. Udržal was minister of defense (1921–22) in the government of Edvard Beneš (1884–1948), Švehla's first government (1922–25), and Švehla's third government (1926–29). He replaced Švehla as prime minister and formed two cabinets (1929 and 1929–32). Udržal's governments were no more creative than others in the West at combating the Great Depression; they economized rather than increasing spending to stimulate the economy. Not only was he attacked for his economic policies, Udržal was also assailed by conservative Republicans for his cooperation with the *Hrad.* In 1932 he resigned, and in 1935 he entered the Senate, often considered a repository for politicians whose careers were near an end.

Daniel E. Miller

Further reading

Čada, Václav. "Politika republikánské strany na počátku velké hospodářské krize." *Československý časopis historický* 22 (1974): 329–60.

Pasák, Tomáš. "K politickému pozadí krize vlády Františka Udržala roku 1932." *Československý časopis historický* 11 (1963): 165–93.

Uhlíř, Dušan. "Konec vlády panské koalice a republikánská strana v roce 1929." *Československý časopis historický* 18 (1970): 551–92.

See also Agrarian Parties; Edvard Beneš; Great Depression; *Hrad;* Jan Malypetr; Tomáš G. Masaryk; Antonín Švehla; Young Czechs

Uniate Church

Church (also often called Byzantine Catholic or Greek Catholic) comprising of formerly Orthodox Christians who accept union with Roman Catholicism by compromising a few important tenets of Orthodox dogma.

One of the consequences of the Great Schism (1054), which divided medieval Christianity into Roman Catholic and Orthodox halves, was the Catholic Church's attempts to gain ecclesiastical authority over Orthodox communities in Europe. The first opportunity to do so arose at the Council of Florence (1439), when Byzantine Emperor John VIII Palaiologos (r. 1425–48) and Orthodox Patriarch of Constantinople Joseph II (r. 1416–39)

U agreed to a union of the churches, on terms dictated by the Catholics, in a vain attempt to win Western assistance against the Ottoman threat to Byzantium in the Balkans. Although the union floundered on the resistance of most Orthodox clergy and the majority of Byzantium's Orthodox subjects, its terms served as a model for subsequent efforts.

In return for retaining most Orthodox dogma, rituals, and customs, those Orthodox involved were obliged to compromise four dogmatic beliefs: acceptance of the pope as ecclesiastically sovereign, instead of collective leadership through ecumenical councils alone; acceptance of the Roman Catholic *filioque* clause in the Nicene Creed, which defined the Third Person (Holy Spirit) of the Trinity (the Christian godhead) as proceeding from *both* the Father *and* the Son (Christ), rather than from the Father alone; the use of unleavened bread in the sacrament of Holy Communion, instead of leavened bread; and acceptance of the unique Roman Catholic belief in purgatory.

The Florentine model was used in 1596 when, through the Union of Brest, Polish King Sigismund III Vasa (1587–1632) attempted to reduce the number of potentially pro-Russian Orthodox Ukrainian and Belorussian subjects in his kingdom. It was also followed within the Habsburg Empire, where numerous Orthodox Carpatho-Ruthenians (Union of Uzhgorod, 1648) and Transylvanian Romanians (Union of Alba Iulia, 1697) were constrained to acknowledge religious union with Rome. While such unionist attempts were never entirely successful, most of those Orthodox who did consent remained true to their decision, and Uniate religious affiliation came to constitute an important component in their ethnonational self-identities.

Dennis P. Hupchick

Further reading

Halecki, Oskar. *From Florence to Brest (1439–1596)*. Rome, 1958.

Hitchins, Keith. *The Rumanian National Movement in Transylvania, 1780–1849*. Cambridge, Massachusetts, 1969.

Hofmann, G. *Epistolæ pontificiæ, ad Councilium Florentinum spectantes*, 3 vols. Rome, 1941–46.

Pelesz, J. *Geschichte der Union der ruthenischen Kirche mit Rom*, 2 vols. Würzburg, Germany, 1881.

See also Catholicism; Orthodoxy

United Principalities

Forerunner of the Romanian nation. The 1856 Treaty of Paris, which concluded the Crimean War (1853–56), abolished the Russian protectorate over the Romanian Principalities of Moldavia and Wallachia and replaced it with a seven-power guarantee that prohibited any power from acting without the remaining signatory powers' consent. The treaty failed to stipulate the reorganization of the principalities, but representatives agreed to consult the Romanians' wishes. Instead, the Great Powers allowed freely elected assemblies temporarily to govern the principalities.

When the Moldavian interim government issued the initial electoral lists in June 1857, ensuring a victory by separatists who opposed a union with Wallachia, France, Prussia, Piedmont, and Russia protested, but elections nevertheless took place. Moldavian unionists refused to vote and separatists won overwhelmingly. Because the results appeared unrepresentative, an international crisis ensued, forcing new elections to be held. Both principalities brought unionists to power and the assemblies were dissolved.

After resolving conflicts at a conference in Paris in May 1858, the Great Powers signed a convention in August granting limited independence to each principality, including a national assembly and an elected prince. Moldavian liberals elected an unknown *boiar*, Alexandru Ioan Cuza (1820–73), on January 17, 1859. In Wallachia, liberals and conservatives unanimously chose Cuza as well. An April 1859 meeting of the Great Powers abruptly ended with the outbreak of war between Austria and Sardinia. The Ottomans were forced to recognize the union of the principalities during Cuza's reign.

Faced with challenges of coordinating two assemblies and two administrations, Cuza presented plans to unify the principalities' legislatures and administrations, but he received little support. Not until the Romanian assemblies decided to discuss the peasant question in April 1861 did the Great Powers recognize a looming crisis. In 1861 they granted Cuza permission to unite the ministries and assemblies for his reign. These actions established the framework for a viable Romanian state.

Tanya L.K. Dunlap

Further reading

East, William. *The Union of Moldavia and Wallachia, 1859*. Cambridge, 1929.

Jelavich, Barbara. *Russia and the Formation of the Romanian National State.* Cambridge, 1977.

Riker, Thad W. *The Making of Roumania: A Study of an International Problem, 1856–1866.* London, 1931.

See also Alexandru Ioan Cuza; Danubian Principalities; Eastern Question; Great Powers; Napoléon III; Paris, Treaty of

Upper Silesian Uprisings (1919–21)

Armed actions by Polish inhabitants of Upper Silesia in the aftermath of World War I to secede from Germany and join the newly re-created Polish state. Three armed struggles determined the fate of Upper Silesia, an area in which the Polish national liberation movement rapidly developed in the first decades of the twentieth century. The first uprising (August 16–23, 1919) was a reaction to the decision of the Entente powers, included in the Treaty of Versailles, to determine the boundaries of the region by plebiscite. Polish patriots, believing that the judgment was unfavorable for their side, resolved to join Poland by force of arms. Yet German regular army forces defeated the Poles, and German reprisals forced many insurgents to flee into Polish territory. The second clash (August 18–25, 1920) was launched in response to an influx of German paramilitary groups and increased political activism in the area, which the Poles took as a sign that the Germans were attempting to influence the outcome of the plebiscite. Polish forces gained control of a substantial area before the Entente powers intervened to bring the uprising to a close. The plebiscite was held on March 20, 1921. The results of the vote showed that the Poles had done well in industrial areas to the east but poorly in the rural regions to the west, which they also claimed were predominantly Polish. As both sides squabbled over the outcome, Polish patriots launched the third Silesian uprising on the night of May 2–3, an action that lasted until July 5. The situation was not resolved until the Entente powers agreed to partition the area in October 1921, leaving the major industrial areas under Polish control but assigning more than half the disputed territory to Germany.

Robert M. Ponichtera

Further reading

Anusiewicz, Marian and Mieczysław Wrzosek. *Kronika powstań śląskich, 1919–1921.* Warsaw, 1980.

Blanke, Richard. *Orphans of Versailles: The Germans in Western Poland, 1918–1939.* Lexington, Kentucky, 1993.

Cienciala, Anna M. and Titus Komarnicki. *From Versailles to Locarno: Keys to Polish Foreign Policy 1919–1925.* Lawrence, Kansas, 1984.

Ryżewski, Wacław. "Die polnischen Nationalaufstände, 1918–1921," in *Historia Militaris Polonica.* Warsaw, 1974, 66–94.

———. *Trzecie Powstanie Śląskie, 1921.* Warsaw, 1977.

Ustaša

Croatian ultranationalist organization. Croatian politician Ante Pavelić (1889–1959) founded the Ustaša (Insurgent) movement in 1929 with the support of Italian fascist leader Benito Mussolini (1883–1945). The Ustaša promoted extreme Croatian nationalism, demanded the creation of independent Croatian state, and espoused the use of violence to achieve political objectives.

During the 1930s, many members of the Ustaša, including Pavelić, lived and trained in camps in Italy. They had little political influence in Yugoslavia until the German army invaded the country in April 1941. At that time, Hitler (1871–1945) agreed to Mussolini's proposal to install Pavelić as the leader of an Ustaša-controlled Croatian puppet state. On April 10, 1941, the day the German army entered the Croatian capital, Zagreb, the Ustaša proclaimed the Independent State of Croatia (Nezavisna Država Hrvatske, or NDH). In reality, the NDH was neither independent nor a real state because it was subservient to Germany and Italy and lacked international legitimacy. Although Pavelić and the Ustaša did not enjoy widespread political support in Croatia, many Croats, including prominent figures such as the leader of the Croatian Peasant Party, Vladko Maček (1879–1964), and the archbishop of Zagreb, Alojzije Stepinac (1898–1960), reacted passively to the Ustaša takeover because they were sympathetic to the cause of Croatian independence.

The NDH encompassed nearly all of present-day Croatia and Bosnia-Hercegovina. Of its approximately 6.5 million inhabitants only 3.4 million were Croats. Nearly two million were Serbs who adhered to the Orthodox faith, 700,000 were Muslims, and another half million were of some other non-Croat origin. Pavelić and his associates were virulently anti-Serb, and they viewed the large Serbian minority as a threat to the state. The regime developed three primary methods to eliminate the Serbian population of the NDH: extermination, expulsion, or conversion to Catholicism. Although estimates vary widely, it is likely that Ustaša forces slaughtered at least 350,000 Serbs during the war. The Ustaša regime forced equal numbers of Serbs to convert to Catholicism or to flee to Serbia. Ustaša fanatics also murdered many Jews, Gypsies, and anti-Ustaša Croats.

The Ustaša's extremism and brutality encouraged many inhabitants of the NDH to join the Communist-led Partisan resistance or the Serbian Chetnik guerrillas. When Partisan forces began to push the Germans from Yugoslavia in 1945, many Ustaša supporters fled to Austria to escape reprisals and to surrender to the British army. However, the British, in accordance with wartime agreements, turned these individuals back to the newly established Communist-led government in Yugoslavia. Thousands of alleged Ustaša supporters were executed or imprisoned by the new regime. Nonetheless, several high-ranking Ustaša leaders, including Pavelić, escaped to North and South America.

Paul D. Lensink

Further reading

Hory, Ladislaus and Martin Broszat. *Der kroatische Ustascha-Staat, 1941–1945*. Stuttgart, 1964.

Jelić-Butić, Fikreta. *Ustaše i Nezavisna Država Hrvatska, 1941–1945*. Zagreb, 1977.

Krizman, Bogdan. *Ante Pavelić i ustaša*. Zagreb, 1978.

Tanner, Marcus. *Croatia: A Nation Forged in War*. New Haven, Connecticut, 1997.

See also Antifascism; Chetniks; Adolf Hitler; Vladko Maček; Ante Pavelić

Uzhgorod

Major city and capital of Ukraine's westernmost oblast and Transcarpathian region (also called Subcarpathian Rus'). Uzhgorod (population 117,000 in 1989) dominates a region whose ethnic diversity and shifting boundaries typify the "Shatter Belt" stereotype often used to describe East Central and southeastern Europe. Numerous ethnic groups populate the historically poor region, the most numerous being the Carpatho-Rusyns, or Ruthenians, people descended from Ukrainians who migrated across the Carpathians. Other ethnic groups either once or now numerous among the populace are Jews, Hungarians, Ukrainians, Russians, Czechs, Slovaks, Romanians, and Gypsies.

Uzhgorod was founded on the Uzh River at the southwestern foot of the central Carpathians' strategic Uzhok Pass in the ninth century. Originally part of Kievan Rus', from the eleventh century until 1919 it was within the Hungarian and Austro-Hungarian Empires. Émigré political pressure helped place it within Czechoslovakia in 1919; from 1938 to 1944, it was reincorporated into Hungary; but after World War II it was ceded back to Czechoslovakia, which transferred it to Ukraine (then in the Soviet Union). Soviet control of the Uzhok Pass gave it a foothold on the Hungarian Plain, useful to the Soviet military during operations in Hungary in 1956 and Czechoslovakia in 1968.

Uzhgorod itself is a key highway and rail junction, has a small, diversified manufacturing base, and is an administrative, educational, and cultural center.

William H. Berentsen

Further reading

Pounds, N.J.G. *Eastern Europe*. London, 1969.
Rónai, A. *Atlas of Central Europe*. Budapest, 1993.

See also Carpatho-Rusyns; Subcarpathian Rus'

Uzunov, Dechko (1899–1986)

Bulgarian artist. During his long, highly productive life, Uzunov explored a range of painting techniques, styles, and subject matter. Between the wars, he was well known for his expressionist portraits of Ivan Tutev (1922), Nikola Liliev (1924), and Nikolai Masalitinov (1931), among others. After World War II, Uzunov embraced the bucolic genre and produced large canvases with political content: *Farewell* (1948), *Harvest* (1952), and, of course, a portrait of Georgi Dimitrov (1969), Bulgarian Communist leader (1882–1949). His later work became symbolic and abstract, yet retained the emotional intensity that characterized his earlier artistic creations. He was also prominent in the applied arts: wall frescoes in several churches and private houses, in the Sofia Courthouse (1932–42), and in the Palace of Culture (1981); stained glass windows in the National Bank (1939) and Sofia University (1980s).

Uzunov began studying art (1919) at the Sofia Art Academy, but in the early 1920s transferred to the Munich Art Academy, the center of German expressionism. Back in Sofia, Uzunov was appointed professor at the Art Academy (1932) and became its president (1945–51). He was awarded numerous distinctions and titles: "Artist of Merit" (1952), Laureate of "Dimitrov Prize" (1962), "People's Artist" (1963), "Hero of Socialist Labor" (1967), and the order "Georgi Dimitrov" (1969).

Milka T. Bliznakov

Further reading

Balkanski, Nenko. *Dechko Uzunov.* Sofia, 1956.
Voeikova, Irina. *Dechko Uzunov.* Moscow, 1989.

See also Bulgarian Art

V

Varna

Maritime port and industrial center of northeastern Bulgaria. Varna is located on the Black Sea coast at the edge of the Dobrudja plateau. The city occupies the site of Odessus, a Greek colony founded in 572 B.C. Remains of a Roman tower and baths are present. Documents establish the continuous employment of the name "Varna" since the seventh century A.D. After capture by the Ottomans in the fourteenth century, it served primarily as a fortified defensive outpost. British and French troops used Varna as an embarcation port during the Crimean War (1853–56). The city experienced rapid growth after a British-built railroad linked it with the Danube River port of Ruse in 1866. Its maritime activity expanded rapidly after Bulgarian independence in 1878, only to fall behind Burgas during the early twentieth century. The slowing reflected the loss to Romania of Varna's primary hinterland of Dobrudja (Dobruzha) as a consequence of the Balkan Wars (1912–1913). Varna regained its leading position after the World War II return of Southern Dobrudja. The port city was known as Stalin from 1949 to 1956.

Varna (estimated population 320,000) particularly benefited from the 1979 establishment of train ferry service with the port of Odessa. This permitted wide-gauge Soviet rail cars to enter Bulgaria directly, bypassing the rather poorly constructed standard-gauge tracks across Romania. Varna is also noted for shipbuilding and flour milling. Since the 1950s, it has been the center of the notable Golden Sands beach resort complex.

Thomas M. Poulsen

Further reading

Iordanov, Tanko, ed. *Geografiia na Bŭlgaria.* Sofia, 1981.

Penkov, Ignat and Todor Khristov. *Ikonomicheska Geografiia na Bŭlgariia,* 2d ed., Sofia, 1965.

Zakhariev, Ivan, Dobri Bradistilov, and Petŭr Popov. *Ikonomichesko Raionirane na N.R. Bŭlgariia.* Sofia, 1963.

See also Balkan Wars; Dobrudja

Vazov, Ivan (1850–1921)

Bulgarian poet, prose writer, and statesman. The son of a well-to-do merchant family in Sopot, Vazov started writing verse at the age of fourteen. His status as Bulgaria's national poet is similar to that of Adam Mickiewicz (1798–1855) in Poland and Sándor Petőfi (1823–49) in Hungary. His artistic range was immense. He wrote novels, stories, memoirs, plays, travelogues, ballads, narrative poems, lyrical verse, and patriotic encomia, and was a prolific journalist. He expanded the vocabulary and literary possibilities of the Bulgarian language. His work is an encyclopedia of Bulgarian life, covering Bulgarian history from the coming of the Bulgars to the country's defeat in World War I, and describes every class of society and every human type. His wide-ranging knowledge of world literature, refracted through his works, enriched Bulgarian letters in form, style, and content. In Vazov, three principal and frequently antagonistic elements in his nation's culture—orientation toward Russia, orientation toward the West, and innate individualism of the

V Bulgarian peasant—were happily and productively reconciled.

After the defeat of the April 1876 uprising against the Turks, which he described in his memoir *Neotdavna* (*Recent Times*, 1881), Vazov fled to Bucharest, where he published his first two books, the verse collections *Priaporets i gusla* (*The Banner and the Rebec*, 1876), which contained his rebel poetry, and *Tagite na Balgaria* (*The Sorrows of Bulgaria*, 1877), a lament for the insurgents' defeat. Vazov's appointment as district judge in the town of Berkovitsa (1879–80) introduced him to Bulgarian provincial life, which he depicted in the short novel *Mitrofan* (1881), the long poem *Zagorka* (1881), and the comedy *Mikhalaki Chorbadzhi* (1882). After resigning his judgeship, he went to Plovdiv, where he experienced his most productive periods of literary activity. Between 1880 and 1884, he published several verse anthologies, the drama *Ruska* (1883), the short novel *Chichovtsi* (*Uncles*, 1885), which described preliberation Bulgaria, and the patriotic poem *Epopeia na zabravenite*, I (1881) and II (1884) (*The Epopee of the Forgotten Ones*), which became one of his country's national texts. He also edited the daily *Narodnii glas* (*The People's Voice*, 1881–81) and the journal *Nauka* (*Science*, 1880–84).

In the mid-1880s, Vazov was forced into exile by Stefan Stambolov (1854–95), Bulgaria's prime minister. In Russia, he began work on his prose masterpiece, the novel *Pod igoto* (*Under the Yoke*, 1889–90), which describes preliberation Bulgaria and the 1876 uprising and is based, in part, on his own childhood reminiscences. In 1889 he returned to Bulgaria, where he edited the journal *Dennitsa* (1890–92), in which he published the anti-Stambolov story "Tamen geroi" (The Dark Hero). By the early twentieth century, he was increasingly drawn to the theater and turned several of his prose works into plays, including *Pod igoto* (1913). His achievements as a writer and patriot were rewarded with the title "People's Poet," which he received on October 24, 1920.

Richard Tempest

Further reading

Anthology of Bulgarian Poetry, trans. by Peter Tempest. Sofia, 1980.

Endler, D. "Neue Beitrage zur Vazov—Forschung," *Zeitschrift für Slawistik* 16 (1971).

Gesemann, Wolfgang. *Die Romankunst Ivan Vazovs*. Munich, 1966.

Moser, Charles A. "National Renown and International Reputation: The Case of Ivan Vazov." *Slavic and East European Journal* 23 (1979).

Shishmanov, D. *A Survey of Bulgarian Literature*. Sofia, 1932.

Shishmanov, Ivan. *Ivan Vazov: Spomeni i dokumenti*. Sofia, 1937.

See also April Uprising; Bulgarian Literature; Adam Mickiewicz; Sándor Petőfi; Stefan Stambolov

Velchev, Damian (1883–1954)

Bulgarian political figure who played a key role in the revolutions of 1923, 1934, and 1944. Velchev entered political life as a co-conspirator in the successful 1923 coup against the government of Aleksandur Stamboliiski (1879–1923), and occupied the position of commandant of the Bulgarian Military College from 1923 to 1928. Associated with the Zveno group, which functioned as the political front of the Military League, the political organization of army officers, Velchev played a prominent role in the subsequent May 1934 coup that brought fellow Zveno adherent Kimon Georgiev (1882–1969) to power as prime minister. Dissension within the Military League over Velchev's continuing influence led to exile in Yugoslavia in 1935. The following year, Velchev was sentenced to death for an abortive coup attempt, a sentence commuted to life in prison, where he remained until 1940.

In 1942 Velchev again entered political life, pledging support to the newly formed Fatherland Front, a coalition of center and left parties dominated by the Communists, in its struggle for political power. Velchev later became war minister in the Fatherland Front cabinet led by his old ally Georgiev. Despite a seeming willingness to accommodate to new political realities, Velchev retained his first loyalty to his military comrades despite Communist demands for a new order. Following the end of World War II, he attempted to resist growing Communist penetration of the military. In 1946 power over the military was transferred from the war ministry to the Fatherland Front cabinet as a whole. That same year, Velchev resigned and became ambassador to Switzerland. With the Communist Party now firmly in power, Velchev resigned this post too and ended his political career once again in exile.

Michael Boll

Further reading

Bell, John D. *The Bulgarian Communist Party from Blagoev to Zhivkov.* Stanford, California, 1977.

Crampton, R.J. *A Short History of Modern Bulgaria.* Cambridge, 1987.

Oren, Nissan. *Bulgarian Communism: The Road to Power.* New York, 1971.

See also Communist Party of Bulgaria; Fatherland Front; Kimon Georgiev; Military League; Aleksandur Stamboliiski; Zveno

Velics, László (1890–1952)

Hungarian diplomat. Born in Dresden, Velics entered the foreign service of the Austro-Hungarian Empire in 1913. After the collapse of the empire in 1918, Velics stayed at his Budapest post during the turbulent period of revolution and counter-revolution in 1918–19. However, the decision to stay during both the democratic and the Communist revolutions hindered his later career. During the 1920s and 1930s, he served in various positions including representative to the League of Nations and ambassador to Greece.

When war broke out between Italy and Greece in 1940, Velics represented Italian interests. He also organized an international protest against the deportation of foreign Jews in Greece and appealed on humanitarian grounds to the occupation authorities (as well as to the Greek government) on behalf of the persecuted.

Velics was involved with the pro-Allied opposition in Hungary and was considered a potential peace negotiator in 1943 when his name surfaced during negotiations with the Americans. When Velics returned to Athens in late 1944, his representation of Hungary was purely private; the embassy had, in effect, ceased to function in October 1944. A year later, he decided to return to Hungary.

When Velics confronted a de-Nazification committee in Budapest in 1946, the Communists were determined to deny his professional credentials. Although he resigned from the foreign service, he was soon reappointed as ambassador to Rome in 1947. In 1949, however, Communist Foreign Minister László Rajk (1909–49) recalled him. In February 1953 Velics died alone and forgotten in a remote village in northern Hungary.

Peter I. Hidas

Further reading

Hidas, Peter I. "A View from the Embassy: László Velics and Occupied Greece," in *Eastern Europe and the West,* ed. by John Morison. New York, 1992, 102–28.

See also Hungarian Soviet Republic; League of Nations; László Rajk

Velvet Revolution

Series of nonviolent student and popular protests in Czechoslovakia in November and December 1989, followed by the resignation of the Communist government and election of a non-Communist government under the presidency of dissident Václav Havel (1936–). The revolution of 1989 in Czechoslovakia earned the title "Velvet" because of its nonviolent nature and the rapid and smooth transition to power of the newly formed opposition bloc, Civic Forum. Student protests on November 17 began the disintegration of the old regime.

The students first gathered near Vyšehrad, the legendary seat of early Czech kings, to commemorate the fiftieth anniversary of the shooting of Czech student Jan Opletal (n.d.) by Nazi occupation forces. After a series of emotional speeches, the students began a procession toward Wenceslas Square, home to the equestrian statue of the revered Saint Wenceslas. The symbolism of the event was not lost on the Communist police, who brutally ended the march with truncheons just short of the square.

This excessive police reaction sparked a strike and more demonstrations by students, who were soon joined by actors and intellectuals. In a country that had long looked to its intellectuals as mythologized leaders, the strikes gained widespread support. On November 19, an opposition group called Civic Forum coalesced around a core of Charter 77 dissidents, the most notable of whom was playwright Havel. Together with students, the Forum engineered a successful nationwide general strike for November 27th.

Faced with widespread popular dissatisfaction and lacking support from Mikhail Gorbachev's (1931–) Soviet Union, the beleaguered Communists agreed on December 10 to a transfer of power and free elections. On December 29, the still-Communist National Assembly elected Havel the first post-Communist president of Czechoslovakia.

Eagle Glassheim

V

Further reading

Ash, Timothy Garton. *The Magic Lantern.* New York, 1993.

Banac, Ivo, ed. *Eastern Europe in Revolution.* Ithaca, New York, 1992.

Holy, Ladislav. *The Little Czech and the Great Czech Nation.* Cambridge, 1996.

Kavan, Zdeněk and Bernard Wheaton. *The Velvet Revolution: Czechoslovakia 1988–1991.* Boulder, Colorado, 1992.

See also Charter 77; Civic Forum; Mikhail Gorbachev; Václav Havel; Revolutions of 1989

Vidin

Former district center in northwest Bulgaria. Its Roman name, Bononia, was changed by the Slavs to Badin and under Greek influence became Vidin. According to folklore, the name originated from that of Bulgarian Queen Vida (n.d.), who built its fortress in the Middle Ages. Sections of this fortification and other historical monuments serve as tourist attractions.

Vidin is one of the oldest towns on the Danube River. In its surroundings, the remains of two-thousand-year-old settlements have been discovered. In the thirteenth and fourteenth centuries the town was often the center of independent feudal principalities.

Vidin, with a population of 62,691 (1994), has an altitude of 122 feet (37 m) above sea level and a temperate continental climate with relatively cold winters (the average January temperature is 29° F [–1.6° C]), and hot summers (average July temperatures reach 73° F [23° C]). Precipitation is lower than the average for the country.

Local industry is characterized by chemicals (polyamide fibers and pneumatic tires), textiles and apparel, food (tobacco processing, cigarette production, fruit and vegetable canning), machine building (irrigation pumps and cutting instruments), porcelain and ceramics, timber processing, and furniture manufacturing. Vidin is also the center of a rich agricultural region specializing in grain and forage production, as well as vegetables, fruits, and livestock (mainly cattle and pigs).

A railroad, airport, and port on the Danube link the town to the rest of the country and a car/bus ferry links it to Calafat, Romania.

Boian Koulov

Further reading

Broi na naselenieto po oblasti, obshtini i naseleni mesta (okonchatelni danni): Resultati ot prebroyavaneto na naselenieto, vol. 3. Sofia, 1994.

Bulgaria, 1983, vol. 1, 656–59.

Vasil, Mikov. *Proizhod i Znachenie na Imenata na Nashite Gradove, Sela, Reki, Planini i Mesta.* Sofia, 1943.

Vidovdan Constitution

Unofficial name of the constitution adopted for the Kingdom of Serbs, Croats, and Slovenes on June 28, 1921. The constitution remained in force until King Alexander (1888–1934) abrogated it in January 1929. Since it was enacted on the feast day of Saint Vitus, it became known as the Vidovdan (Saint Vitus Day) Constitution. June 28 is also the anniversary of the 1389 Serbian defeat at Kosovo Polje at the hands of the Ottoman Turks; as such, this constitution was sometimes viewed as Serbia's ultimate triumph over its long history of subjection to foreign rule.

The Radicals and the Democrats were the major parties favoring its passage. The Yugoslav Muslim Organization was persuaded to support it in return for preserving the territorial integrity of Bosnia-Hercegovina and providing compensation to landowners for land taken in the course of land reform. Delegates of the Communist Party of Yugoslavia and the Croatian Republican Peasant Party either refused to attend or walked out of the Constituent Assembly that proceeded to pass the document. These delegates, combined with other abstentions and the 35 delegates who voted against the proposed constitution, came close to equaling the 223 who voted for it (210 votes were needed for passage), and indicated the high level of opposition to this constitution's centralism. It was largely based on Serbia's constitution, and most of the non-Serb parties opposed it.

The Croatian Republican Peasant Party of Stjepan Radić (1871–1928) became the leading opposition party demanding revision of the constitution. Although it won fifty seats in the November 1919 elections for the Constituent Assembly, it boycotted the assembly to protest the government's decision that the new constitution would be passed by half the total number of deputies plus one, rather than by a majority within each ethnic group.

Under the Vidovdan Constitution, the king held considerable legislative and executive powers. His approval was required for legislation to become valid; the king also appointed state officials and was commander of the armed forces. The government was responsible to both the parliament (Skupština) and the king. The legislature was unicameral. The largest administrative districts (*oblasti*) were kept relatively small (from 100,000 to 800,000 inhabitants each). Larger historical regions (Croatia, Dalmatia, and Vojvodina) received no autonomy, and the districts were forbidden to combine into regions. District assemblies were generally weak in relation to the government officials appointed by the king, although in some cases these bodies developed revenue sources independent of the central government.

Kenneth E. Basom

Further reading

Banac, Ivo. *The National Question in Yugoslavia: Origins, History, Politics.* Ithaca, New York, 1984.
Lampe, John R. *Yugoslavia as History: Twice There Was a Country.* New York, 1996.
Pavlowitch, Stevan K. *Yugoslavia.* New York, 1971.

See also Alexander I Karadjordjević; Kingdom of Serbs, Croats, and Slovenes; Stejpan Radić; Skupština

Vienna Awards

Territorial adjustments in Eastern Europe before and during World War II. The first Vienna Award took place in November 1938. Hungarians demanded territorial concessions from Czechoslovakia in the wake of the Munich Pact and Czechoslovakia's loss of the Sudetenland to Germany and mobilized its forces. Arbitration by Germany and Italy resulted in the cession of 12,000 square miles (33,300 sq km) of southern Slovakia and Carpatho-Ukraine (Ruthenia) to Hungary with a population of approximately one million (80 percent of whom were Magyars).

The second Vienna Award involved the partition of Transylvania by Germany in 1940. In June 1940 the Soviet Union forced Romania to cede Bessarabia and Northern Bukovina. Perceiving Romania to be diplomatically isolated, Hungary demanded Transylvania, while Bulgaria claimed northern Dobrudja (Dobruzha). On July 1, Romania installed a pro-Axis government that appealed to Germany for support and sought a German guarantee of Romania's frontiers and military cooperation between the countries. Eager for access to Romania's natural resources but concerned about the need to maintain Hungarian and Bulgarian loyalty to the Axis, Hitler (1889–1945) stipulated that the Hungarian and Bulgarian demands be negotiated before any other steps were taken. Romania quickly agreed to surrender northern Dobrudja to Bulgaria, but talks with the Hungarians about Transylvania broke down. When Hungarian and Soviet armies massed on the Romanian border, Hitler feared damage to Romanian oilfields or Soviet seizure of them. He therefore ordered the partition of Transylvania in such a way as to leave both Hungary and Romania dissatisfied and dependent on Germany for redress, as well as to bring the Hungarian borders close enough to Romanian oilfields to enable Germany to protect them. Faced with the threat of war by an Axis-supported Hungary and lured by a guarantee of the new frontiers, the Romanians acquiesced. When Romanians learned that they had lost 15,207 square miles (42,243 sq km) of land and 2.6 million inhabitants (about half of them Romanian) to Hungary, the crisis brought down the government. Carol II (1893–1953) was forced to abdicate, and Ion Antonescu (1882–1946) became premier with unlimited powers.

Joseph M. McCarthy

Further reading

Hillgruber, Andreas. *Hitler, König Carol und Marschall Antonescu: Die deutsch-rumänischen Beziehungen, 1938–1944.* Wiesbaden, 1954.
Hitchins, Keith. *Rumania 1866–1947.* Oxford, 1994.
Lukacs, John. *The Great Powers and Eastern Europe.* New York, 1953.
Manoilescu, Mihail. *Dictatul de la Viena: Memorii, iulie–august 1940.* Bucharest, 1991.

See also Ion Antonescu; Carol II; Dobrudja; Munich Pact; Revisionism; Transylvanian Dispute

Village Explorers

Movement among Hungarian youth, closely linked with the Populist (*népi*) Movement, to bring about reform and national renewal through examination of agrarian conditions. The village explorers aimed to influence public opinion on behalf of the politically powerless agrarian population through objective scientific research, or sociography, documenting what they considered the hopeless conditions of the countryside. In the 1930s the situation of the Hungarian agrarian population was acknowledged to be the gravest problem facing Hungarian society. In a country still dominated by large estates, the majority of the peasantry were landless laborers or poor peasants, dependent on seasonal labor for their livelihood. The young intellectuals believed that only radical agrarian reform and a revolutionary reorganization of society could lead to the renewal of the nation.

Taking their model from the village exploring of minority youth of the late 1920s, who turned to the peasantry in search of their national identity, numerous groups experimented with village research in the early 1930s. The most significant, the Szeged Youth, the Protestant Pro Christo Students, and Young Hungary, all produced collective and/or individual sociographic publications documenting the decline of village life. The numerous publications that appeared from 1936 to 1938 (including *Pro Christo: Kemse, the Sinking Village,* Zoltán Szabó's [1912–84] *The Situation at Tard,* Imre Kovács's [1913–80] *The Silent Revolution,* and Ferenc Erdei's [1910–71] *Shifting Sands*) exerted a major impact on public opinion, preparing the way for radical land reform after World War II.

Deborah S. Cornelius

Further reading

Borbándi, Gyula. *Der ungarische Populismus.* Mainz, Germany, 1976.

Némedi, Dénes. *A népi szociográfia 1930–1938.* Budapest, 1985.

See also Hungarian Populist Movement; Imre Kovács; Peasants

Vilna Dispute

Prolonged rivalry between Poland and Lithuania for possession of the city of Vilna and its environs. The emergence of separate, independent Polish and Lithuanian states after World War I gave rise to mutually exclusive claims to custody of Vilna (Russian, Vilna; Polish, Wilno; Lithuanian, Vilnius), formerly a metropolis of the joint Polish-Lithuanian Commonwealth. Poland appealed for the city, primarily populated by Poles and Jews, on the grounds of nationality and history, while Lithuania regarded Vilna as its natural capital. The fact that Józef Piłsudski (1867–1935), leader and commander in chief of the interwar Polish republic in its formative years, was a native of the region played more than an incidental role in determining its fate.

The city changed hands repeatedly during the two years that followed the end of World War I, shifting among Polish, Lithuanian, and Soviet control in response to the shifting tides of the Russian Revolution and local warfare. In October 1920, at the inspiration of Piłsudski, Polish forces under the command of Gen. Lucjan Żeligowski (1865–1947) captured the city and its vicinity, reconstituting it as "Central Lithuania" under Polish influence. Poland annexed the region in 1922 following a local plebiscite boycotted by resident Lithuanians, and Vilna remained a part of Poland for the remainder of the interwar era.

Although Poland's acquisition of Vilna received formal international recognition in 1923, Lithuania never accepted the loss of the city. The issue poisoned relations between the two countries, which remained in chronic hostility; normal diplomatic relations were not established until 1938, and then only as a consequence of a Polish ultimatum. Following its conquest of eastern Poland in the opening campaign of World War II, the Soviet Union "restored" Vilna to Lithuania in 1939, only to take it back the next year by forcible incorporation of all the Baltic states into the USSR. With the reassertion of Lithuanian independence on the collapse of the Soviet Union, Poland renounced its claim to present-day Vilnius, but the status of the Polish minority within Lithuania remains a source of potential bilateral friction.

Neal A. Pease

Further reading

Senn, Alfred A. *The Great Powers, Lithuania and the Vilna Question, 1920–1928.* Leiden, Netherlands, 1966.

Sierpowski, Stanisław. *Piłsudski w Genewie.* Poznań, 1990.

See also Józef Pilsudski; Vilnius

Vilnius

Largest city (584,000 population) and historical capital of Lithuania. Vilnius (Polish, Wilno; Russian, Vilna) is located in a picturesque valley surrounded by forested hills at the confluence of the Neris and the Vilnele Rivers. It was founded by Grand Duke Gediminas (n.d.) in 1323. The town around his castle started to grow only after the defeat of the Teutonic Knights by Polish-Lithuanian forces in 1410. It spread south and west of the castle hill along the main thoroughfares on the relatively flat terraces of the Neris.

The layout of the old town around the market, with its maze of narrow streets and passages, was conditioned by the town walls completed in 1522. Only one gate remains standing presently, housing a chapel with the venerated icon of Madonna (*Ostra Brama,* The Pointed Gate). The many architecturally notable churches (from Gothic to baroque to neoclassical) and palatial residences were built in the seventeenth and eighteenth centuries. A Jesuit Academy (later the university) was founded in 1578 by King Stephen Báthory (1533–86).

Long a part of the Polish-Lithuanian state, Vilnius was annexed by Russia after the last partition of Poland (1795). It started to grow after the construction of the St. Petersburg–Warsaw railroad (1860) and thrived mainly on transit trade. There were few industries, mainly timber, wood processing, furs, and some tanneries. Little improvement occurred in the interwar years, because the city became cut off from its natural hinterland by politically impervious boundaries after it was formally annexed by Poland in 1922, despite Lithuanian protestations.

Vilnius (Wilno), an important center of Polish and Jewish culture, was all but destroyed during and after World War II. Its Jewish population (55,006—28.2 percent of the city's total in 1931) was exterminated by the Nazis and a large part of the Polish population opted for Poland and emigrated. The present Polish share in Vilnius's population is only 19 percent versus 65.0 percent in 1931, and that of Jews only 1.6 percent.

Postwar Vilnius attracted many diverse industries: machine-tool, electrotechnical, electronic, paper and pulp, building materials, pharmaceutical, food processing, and garment and footwear. In 1993 these accounted for 11.2 percent of the total industrial production of Lithuania. Vilnius also became the most important Lithuanian cultural center, with a university, five other specialized colleges, several research institutes, the Lithuanian Academy of Sciences, numerous museums and theaters, and several libraries with over fourteen million books total.

Abraham Melezin

Further reading

Limanowski, Mieczysław. "Wilno," *Congrès International de Géographie.* Warsaw, 1934.
Medonis, Arolfas. *Vilnius.* Vilnius, 1972.
Remer, Jerzy. *Wilno.* Wrocław, 1990.

See also Jews; Vilna Dispute

Vistula River

Poland's principal inland waterway and the largest river of the Baltic Sea drainage basin. The Vistula (Polish, Wisła) winds 679 miles (1,092 km) south to north through Poland, across the lowland of the North European Plain. The Vistula originates 15 miles (25 km) south of Bielsko-Biała in the mountains of Galicia in southern Poland, and forms the nation's largest drainage system, with 85 percent of its area of 75,100 square miles (194,500 sq km) lying within Polish territory. The Vistula empties into the Baltic Sea near Gdańsk and enters the sea through a delta estuary whose channels have shifted greatly over time. The river's principal tributaries are the Dunajec, San, Wieprz, Bug, and Pilica Rivers. Fed chiefly by snow and rain, the Vistula floods in spring and fall and freezes from one to four months during winter. Great seasonal fluctuations in water level constitute a navigational hazard.

The Vistula is connected with the Oder River by the Bydgoszcz Canal, and to the inland waterways of Belarus, Ukraine, and Russia through the Narew and Bug Rivers and the Dnieper-Bug Canal. In its lower course, from Toruń to the Baltic Sea, the river is fully improved for navigation. The city of Kraków sits on the Vistula River, as do Warsaw and Sandomierz. Much of the river serves tourism, recreation, and health resorts.

The Vistula basin is thought to be the original home of the Polish people. The Vistula was economically important through the end of the eighteenth century and the partitions of Poland. Not much effort was made between the world wars to improve navigation on the river. After World

V

War II, a prewar scheme was revived to develop a central industrial district at the confluence of the Vistula and San Rivers, to take advantage of water transport and the position of the confluence halfway between Kraków and Warsaw.

The river carries two million tons of sediment annually. It is heavily polluted in its lower stretches owing to hydroelectric plants, municipal and industrial wastewater, and agricultural runoff. By the late 1970s, it was estimated that the river was so polluted that only 40 percent of its total length was suitable for industrial use. The upper reaches of the Vistula, however, remain relatively unspoiled, and the river supports over forty different kinds of fish.

Barbara VanDrasek

Further reading

Curtis, Glenn E., ed. *Poland: A Country Study.* Washington, D.C., 1994.

Gottmann, Jean. *A Geography of Europe,* 3d ed. New York, 1962.

Hoffman, George W., ed. *Europe in the 1990s: A Geographic Analysis,* 6th ed. New York, 1990.

Turnock, David. *Eastern Europe: An Historical Geography 1815–1945.* New York, 1989.

See also Environment

Vlachs

Balkan ethnic group. There are three historical meanings to the term "Vlach": Romance-speaking people living east of the Italians and the Germans; a subset living south of the Danube River; and shepherds. The Old German word denoted Romanized inhabitants of the Roman Empire; the reference to the Vlachs is plentiful in Byzantine sources following the first Balkan reference in 976. Their location in these documents corresponds to the ancient Via Egnatia that crossed the Balkans and to other areas that long remained within the empire.

Vlachs were soon found north of the Danube. The first of these settlers were Romance speakers, but their successors were Slavs. Further east, a compact Romanian people emerged. In modern times, Hungarians and Germans often used the term pejoratively, reinforcing Romanians' rejection of it for themselves.

The predominant usage of "Vlach" is for speakers of a dialect related to Romanian living south of the Danube. They have been multilingual and mobile, and their political identity has been equally flexible. Mostly shepherds, they also thrived as merchants in towns like Ragusa/Dubrovnik, in Dalmatia, and Moscopole, in current southern Albania. As the Vlachs' economic vitality declined, national education imperiled their linguistic survival. Linguistic patriots founded a few Vlach schools, but independent Romania's support for Balkan Vlachs was subordinate to its claims on neighboring territories. By contrast, the Vlachs' areas of concentration were dispersed and far from Romania. Vlach is the preferred language for perhaps fifty thousand persons today, with nearly two-thirds of these residing in Greece.

James P. Niessen

Further reading

Peyfuss, Max. *Die aromunische Frage.* Vienna, 1974.

Wace, A. and N. Thompson. *The Nomads of the Balkans.* London, 1914.

Winnifrigh, T.J. *The Vlachs: The History of a Balkan People.* New York, 1987.

Vladimirescu, Tudor (1780–1821)

Social crusader and champion of Romanian national rights who led the revolution of 1821 in the Romanian lands against Greek Phanariot rule. Born in Vladimir of lower *boiar* rank, Vladimirescu served in the military and headed three thousand irregular soldiers (*panduri*) under Russian command in the Russo-Turkish war of 1806–12. In 1815 he had contacts with the Filiki Etairia (Friendly Society), which aimed at the liberation of Greece from Turkish rule. When Prince Alexandros Ypsilantis (1792–1828) crossed into Moldavia from Russia in 1821 and appealed to the Moldo-Wallachians to rise against the Turks, Vladimirescu was expected to answer his call. Instead, Vladimirescu, whose sympathies lay with the peasants oppressed by the Phanariot regime, marched at the head of his irregular troops into his native Oltenia and appealed to peasants and *boiars* to rid the country of Phanariot rule. Counting on Russian support, Vladimirescu then marched on to Bucharest and for a short period tried to negotiate with Ypsilantis. Alexander I's (1777–1825) denunciation of both revolutionary leaders hastened a confrontation. Ypsilantis denounced Vladimirescu as a traitor to the Etairia and released all soldiers from their oath of allegiance. Vladimirescu then withdrew to his stronghold in Oltenia and appealed to all "good" Romanians to rise against the Greeks. Arrested by one of his own captains, he was executed at Tîrgovişte as a traitor after a mock trial. Following the defeat of Ypsilantis, Vladimirescu's pro-Turkish stance led to the reestablishment of native rule in the Romanian Principalities in 1822.

Radu Florescu

Further reading
Berindei, Dan. *L'Année révolutionnaire 1821 dans les pays roumains.* Bucharest, 1973.
Oţetea, Andrei. *Tudor Vladimirescu şi mişcarea eterista în ţarile române.* Bucharest, 1945.
———. *Tudor Vladimirescu şi revoluţia din 1821.* Bucharest, 1971.
Panait, Ioana Christache. *Oraşul Bucharest şi răscoala poporului din 1821.* Bucharest, 1960.

See also *Boiars;* Danubian Principalities; Filiki Etairia; Greek Revolution; Phanariots; Alexandros Ypsilantis

Vlahov, Dimitar Janakiev (1878–1953)
Macedonian intellectual, Ottoman parliamentarian, Bulgarian official and diplomat, Comintern functionary, and Yugoslav politician. Vlahov studied chemistry in Germany and Switzerland before becoming a teacher in Salonika in 1903. At the same time, he became a member of the Central Committee of the Internal Macedonian Revolutionary Organization (IMRO), which was devoted to the creation of an autonomous Macedonia. In the wake of IMRO's 1903 Ilinden Uprising against Ottoman authorities, he was briefly arrested. However, as a pro-Ottoman Macedonian autonomist with socialist ideas, Vlahov was elected to the Young Turk parliament in 1908. After the Second Balkan War (1913), the new Greek authorities in Salonika expelled him to Bulgaria. During World War I, he served first as Bulgarian military district commander in Vardar Macedonia and Kosovo, then as the representative of the army's Directorate for Economic Affairs and Public Planning in Istanbul, Kiev, and Odessa. After the war, as Bulgarian consul and trade attaché in Vienna, Vlahov negotiated an agreement between the rival factions of the Macedonian movement and the Soviet-led Comintern (Communist International). But when

he published the contents of the agreement in the summer of 1924, the two most important Macedonian signatories, Todor Aleksandrov (1881–1924) and Aleksandur Protogerov (1867–1928), denounced it. As a result, Vlahov was dismissed from the Bulgarian foreign service. Staying on in Vienna as a political émigré, he became a Comintern representative in the Balkans. After living in Berlin and Paris, he emigrated to the Soviet Union in 1935, where he was employed at the Comintern's International Agrarian Institute in Moscow. He barely escaped Stalin's (1879–1953) purges of the late 1930s, thanks to energetic intervention by Comintern leader Georgi Dimitrov (1882–1949). In 1941 he became a leading disseminator of Soviet war propaganda in the Balkans (especially in Greece). On November 23, 1943, Vlahov was elected vice president of Tito's all-Yugoslav partisan parliament, AVNOJ. In October 1944 he left the Soviet Union and returned to Vardar Macedonia. Having been a member of the Bulgarian Communist Party from 1925 to 1944, he now joined the Communist Party of Yugoslavia. However, as a "Moscow Communist," Vlahov had been a proponent of a Greater Macedonia, that is, the Vardar (Yugoslav) part plus Bulgarian Prin Macedonia and Greek Aegean Macedonia; he thus soon clashed with the dominant faction in Skopje, who favored intra-Yugoslav consolidation. As a consequence, Tito (1892–1980) "promoted" Vlahov to vice president of the Yugoslav parliament in 1946 and transferred him to Belgrade, where he would never regain political influence.

Stefan Troebst

Further reading
Adanir, Fikret. "Makedonya sorunu ve Dimitar Vlahof'un anilarinda II. Mesrutiyet." *Birikim* 9 (November 1975): 14–26.
Vlahov, Dimitar. *Memoari.* Skopje, 1970.

See also Todor Aleksandrov; Balkan Wars; Comintern; Communist Party of Bulgaria; Georgi Dimitrov; Ilinden Uprising; IMRO; Tito; Young Turks

Vltava River
Shallow river that flows northward through the Bohemian plateau where the incision of the river has brought on base-level erosion. Also known as the Moldau, the Vltava is joined by the Berounka, Elbe, and Labe Rivers near Prague, and cuts through

the Czech capital. A series of islands (such as Kampa Island) lie in the middle of the convergence of these rivers and have been important in the early settlement and protection of Prague. Today the river houses several dams and large hydroelectric projects that supply power to Bohemia's industrial regions.

Russell L. Ivy

Further reading

Berentsen, William, ed. *Europe in the 1990s: A Geographical Analysis,* 7th ed. Chicago, 1997.

Pounds, Norman J.G. *Eastern Europe.* Chicago, 1969.

Rugg, Dean. *Eastern Europe.* London, 1985.

UNIDO. *Czechoslovakia: Industrial Transformation and Regeneration.* Oxford, 1992.

Vojvodina

Fertile agricultural region of Serbia on the Panonian (Hungarian) Plain, north of the Danube River and its western tributary, the Sava. The Vojvodina has an area of 8,000 square miles (22,200 sq km) and a population of 2,250,000, representing a quarter of Serbia's inhabitants. Conventionally the Vojvodina is divided into three regions: the Banat, lying between the Tisa River and the Carpathians; Bačka, between the Danube and Tisa Rivers; and Srem, between the Danube and Sava Rivers. Novi Sad is the capital.

The land is mainly a rolling plains area, although the Fruška Gora Mountains in the southwest rise to an elevation of 1,700 feet (510 m) above sea level. The climate is continental, with January temperatures generally just below freezing and July averages reaching 85° F (29° C). Rainfall ranges from 18 to 30 inches (46–72 cm) annually. The excellent climate, combined with rich black earth (chernozem) soils, has resulted in three-quarters of the territory being cultivated. Wheat and other grains constitute the principal crops, but the Vojvodina is also noted for the production of sugar beets, cattle, and swine.

The Vojvodina is home to many ethic groups, reflecting Habsburg resettlement of a virtually empty land after Ottoman troops were expelled during the seventeenth and eighteenth centuries. Before the 1991 secessions of republics from Yugoslavia, Serbs constituted about half the Vojvodina population, Hungarians one-quarter, Croats 7 per-cent, and Slovaks 4 percent. In more recent times, many Hungarians and Croats have fled abroad, their abandoned homes being taken over by Serbian refugees from Croatia and Bosnia. Many Germans formerly lived in the Vojvodina. During the World War II German occupation of Serbia, they established their own self-governing territory. All were expelled at the end of the war, their lands being taken over mainly by Serbian migrants from the hills of southern Serbia and Bosnia.

Thomas M. Poulsen

Further reading

Bertić, Ivan. *Veliki geografski atlas Jugoslavije.* Zagreb, 1987.

Clissold, Stephen, ed. *A Short History of Yugoslavia: From Early Times to 1966.* Cambridge, 1968.

Pounds, Norman J.G. *Eastern Europe.* London, 1969.

Volov, Panaiot Vichev (c. 1850–76)

Bulgarian revolutionary and one of the organizers and leaders of the April Uprising of 1876, in which Bulgarian nationals fought for the liberation and separation of the country from the Ottoman Empire. Volov was born into a middle-class family in Shumen. He completed the Dobri Voinikov secondary school in Shumen, one of the best Bulgarian schools at the time. Volov continued his education abroad, from 1869 to 1873 studying in the South Slavic Boarding School in Ukraine. In 1873 he returned to Shumen, where he was appointed a teacher and the principal of the Voinikov school. Active in all social, cultural, and political affairs, Volov was soon elected leader of the Shumen Revolutionary Committee, an organization aimed at fomenting Bulgarian independence. In 1875 he was jailed for several months for his political involvement. After his release from prison, he emigrated to Bucharest. There he participated in every meeting of the Bulgarian Revolutionary Central Committee. Volov returned to Bulgaria in the beginning of 1876 together with Georgi Benkovski (1841/44–1876) and other revolutionaries and began their feverish preparation for the April Uprising against the Turks. Volov fought as the leader of his band in the northern part of the region. After the uprising's defeat, he tried to return to Romania but he was betrayed and died while attempting to escape.

Yana Hashamova

Further reading

Stoyanoff, Zachary. *Pages from the Autobiography of a Bulgarian Insurgent,* trans. by M.W. Potter. London, 1913.

Dzhumaliev, Georgi. *Panaiot Vichev Volov: Bibliografska spravka.* Shumen, Bulgaria, 1971.

"Volov, Panaiot Vichev," in *Entsiklopediia: Bulgariia.* Sofia, 1978.

See also April Uprising

Vörösmarty, Mihály (1800–1855)

Considered the greatest of the Hungarian romantic poets, as well as an epic writer, dramatist, translator, and literary critic. Of noble origin and the son of an impoverished estate steward, Vörösmarty obtained a university degree in Pest, and also served as a tutor, particularly on the estate of the Perczel family in Tolna County. There he allied himself with the anti-Austrian movement. His yearning for national independence, along with his hopeless love for Etelka, sister of one of his pupils, inspired him to write a romantic national epic, *Zalán futása* (*The Flight of Zalán,* 1825), set in the time of the Magyar conquest of Hungary in the ninth century. He combined national heroism and epic battle scenes with idyllic love.

In 1828 he left the Perczel estate, moved to Pest, and became editor of the then most prominent periodical, *Tudományos Gyüjtemény* (*The Learned Collection*). He thus became the first Hungarian poet to live off his own literary work.

His dramatic poem, *Csongor és Tünde* (*Csongor and Tünde,* 1831), which recounts the love of a Hungarian prince, Csongor, for a fairy girl, Tünde, has often been compared to Shakespeare's (1564–1616) *A Midsummer Night's Dream.* He also wrote ballad-style narrative poems, such as *Szép Ilonka* (*Fair Ilonka,* 1833). His political activism reappeared in 1836 with his lyrical poem, *Szózat* (*Appeal*), which after Ferenc Kölcsei's (1790–1838) *Hymnus* (*Hymn,* 1823), is considered the second national anthem of Hungary. During the 1830s and 1840s, Vörösmarty turned to playwriting.

In his early forties, Vörösmarty fell in love with, and eventually married, Laura Csajághy (n.d.), more than twenty years his junior. His romantic poems, such as "A szomjú" (Thirst) and "Laurához" (To Laura), express longing and desire that the poet hopes his beloved will return.

As a result of the 1848–49 revolution in Hungary, Vörösmarty was forced into hiding in Pest, where he became beset with financial and other worries. In his last lyrical poem, *A vén cigány* (*The Old Gypsy,* 1854), he casts himself in the role of an old gypsy violinist, hallucinating about disasters befalling humankind, yet his realization of the "eternal struggle" is a confident reaffirmation of life.

Mártha Pereszlényi-Pintér

Further reading

Czigány, Loránt. *The Oxford History of Hungarian Literature.* Oxford, 1984.

Klaniczay, Tibor, ed. *A History of Hungarian Literature.* Budapest, 1982.

Klaniczay, Tibor, József Sauder, and Miklós Szabolcsi. *A History of Hungarian Literature.* Budapest, 1964.

Molnár, August J. *Hungarian Writers and Literature by Joseph Reményi.* New Brunswick, New Jersey, 1964.

See also Hungarian Literature; Hungarian War for Independence; Revolutions of 1848; Romanticism

Vulchanov, Rangel (1928–)

Bulgarian film director. One of the most distinguished figures of Bulgarian cinema, Vulchanov has a very lyrical cinematic style. With his magical realism, Vulchanov, who also worked in Czechoslovakia during the 1960s, made a significant contribution to the cinematic treatment of the Balkans in both imagery and narrative. His feature films include *Na malkia ostrov* (*On the Small Island,* 1958); *Parviyat urok* (*First Lesson,* 1960); *Slantseto i syankata* (*The Sun and the Shadow,* 1962); *Inspektorat i noshta* (*The Inspector and the Night,* 1963); *Valtschitsata* (*The She-wolf,* 1965); *Ezop* (*Aezop,* 1970); *Litseto zad maskata* (*The Face behind the Mask,* 1970); *Shans* (*Chance,* 1970); *Byagstvo v Ropotamo* (*Escape to Ropotamo,* 1973); *Sledovatelyat i gorata* (*The Inspector and the Forest,* 1975); *S lyubov i nezhnost* (*With Love and Tenderness,* 1978); *Lachenite obuvki na neznayniya voyn* (*The Patent Leather Shoes of the Unknown Soldier,* 1979); *Posledni zhelania* (*Last Wishes,* 1983); *Zakade patuvate?* (*Where Are You Going?,* 1986); *A sega nakade?* (*Now, Where To?,* 1988); *Nemirnata ptica lyubov* (*The Mischievous Bird of Love,*

V

1990); and *Fatalna nezhnost* (*Fatal Tenderness*, 1992).

Dina Iordanova

Further reading

Holloway, Ronald. *The Bulgarian Cinema*. London and Toronto, 1984.

See also Cinema

Vulkov, Ivan (1875–1962)

Bulgarian general. Vulkov received his military training in Sofia and St. Petersburg. After graduation, he became an instructor at the military school in Sofia and during the Balkan Wars (1912–13) and World War I served in various capacities as a general in the Bulgarian army. After the Great War, he became director of Bulgaria's Cartographic Institute in Sofia, a position he held from 1919 to 1923. In 1919 he also helped found and led the Military League, a secret, right-wing nationalist organization composed mostly of active and reserve army officers. On June 9, 1923, the Military League participated in the overthrow of Bulgaria's Agrarian government and the assassination of the prime minister, Aleksandur Stamboliiski (1879–1923). Vulkov is regarded as one of the architects of the coup and the repressions that followed.

Vulkov became minister of war in 1923 and served in this capacity until 1929. He then was appointed minister plenipotentiary to Rome, a position he held until his retirement in 1934. He was arrested after the Communists came to power and was condemned to death for his part in the coup d'état of 1923 and for the repressions that followed. Because of his advanced age, his life was spared, and his sentence was commuted to life in prison, where he died sometime during 1962.

John Georgeoff

Further reading

Dimitriev, Radko. *Treta armiia v Balkanskata voina.* Sofia, 1922.

Grishina, R. P. *Vozniknovenie fashizma v Bolgarii, 1919–1925.* Moscow, 1976.

Kazasav, Dimo. *Burni godini, 1918–1944.* Sofia, 1944.

Naumov, Georgi Gavrilov. *Atentatut v katedralata "Sv. Nedelia." 16 april 1925 g.* Sofia, 1989.

Stoichev, Ivan K. *Stroiteli i voini vozhdove na bulgarskata voiska, 1879–1941.* Sofia, 1941.

Vulkov, Ivan. *Iztochniia sektor pri blokadata i atakata na Odrinskata krepost'.* Sofia, 1913.

See also Balkan Wars; Military League; Aleksandur Stamboliiski

W

Wajda, Andrzej (1926–)

Polish film director and screenwriter. The best known of contemporary Polish filmmakers, Wajda received training in painting and film. His filmmaking career began with the postwar trilogy *A Generation, Canal,* and *Ashes and Diamonds,* films that brought him prominence. An extremely productive director, he has directed more than thirty feature films. He has also worked actively in theater. Wajda's other feature films include *Lotna* (1959); *Niewinni Czarodzieje* (*Innocent Sorcerers,* 1960); *Samson* (1961); *Sibirska Ledi Magbet* (*Fury Is a Woman,* 1962); *L'Amour a vingt ans* (*Love at Twenty,* 1962); *Popioły* (Ashes, 1965); *Gates to Paradise* (1967); *Wszystko na Sprzedaz* (*Everything for Sale,* 1968); *Połowanie na muchy* (*Hunting Flies,* 1969); *Krajobraz po Bitwie* (*Landscape after Battle,* 1970); *Brzezina* (*Birch Wood,* 1970); *Wesełe* (*The Wedding,* 1972); *Ziemia Obiecana* (*The Promised Land,* 1976); *Smuga Cienia* (*The Shadow Line,* 1976); *Człowiek z Marmuru* (*Man of Marble,* 1976); *Bez Znieczulenia* (*Without Anesthesia,* 1978); *Panny z Wiłka* (*The Maids of Wilko,* 1979); *Dyrygent* (*The Conductor,* 1980); *Człowiek z Zełaza* (*Man of Iron,* 1981); *Danton* (1983); *A Love in Germany* (1984); *Kronika Wypadków Milosnych* (*Chronicle of Amorous Accidents,* 1986); *Korczak* (1990); *Pierscionek z orlem w koronie* (*The Horsehair Ring,* 1993); and *Holly Week* (1996).

Dina Iordanova

Further reading

Eagle, Herbert. "Andrezej Wajda: Film Language and the Artist's Truth," in *Cross Currents: A Yearbook of Central European Culture.* Ann Arbor, Michigan, 1982, 333–53.
Falkowska, Janina. *The Political Films of Andrzej Wajda.* Providence, Rhode Island, 1996.
Michalek, Boleslaw. *The Cinema of Andrzej Wajda.* London, 1973.

See also Cinema

Wałęsa, Lech (1943–)

Polish political activist, Solidarity union leader, and president of post-Communist Poland. A worker at the Lenin Shipyard in Gdańsk, Wałęsa was a member of the strike committee established in December 1970 to protest sudden government price increases. Fired from the Lenin Shipyard in 1976 for antiregime agitation, Wałęsa collaborated with KOR, the Polish dissident group. Arrested repeatedly and harassed by the authorities for his political activities, Wałęsa became the charismatic figure to whom shipyard workers turned during strikes in August 1980. As chairman of the strike committee, Wałęsa signed an agreement with the regime establishing the Independent Self-Governing Trade Union "Solidarity" (Solidarność). He was elected chairman of Solidarity in September 1981 and interned with the imposition of martial law by the regime of Wojciech Jaruzelski (1923–) on December 13, 1981. Nevertheless, Wałęsa not only remained officially head of the Solidarity union and social movement but also became the individual whom Poles (as well as much of the rest of the world) identified as the person symbolizing the determination of the Polish nation to combat Communist rule. A recipient of the Nobel Peace Prize in 1983, Wałęsa continued to represent the union during its underground period until the Jaruzelski regime began to search for a way out of the political stalemate brought about with the union's delegalization. He returned to public life in 1988 with a television debate with the head of the regime-supported trade union, and played a key role in the Polish "Round Table" negotiations. He was later elected president of a non-Communist Poland in 1990, but was defeated in his bid for reelection in 1995.

Peter Lavelle

Further reading

Ash, Timothy G. *The Magic Latern.* New York, 1990.
———. *The Polish Revolution: Solidarity.* New York, 1985.
Ost, David J. *Solidarity and the Politics of Anti-Politics.* Philadelphia, 1990.
Wałęsa, Lech. *A Way of Hope.* New York, 1987.

See also Wojciech Jaruzelski; KOR; Solidarity; Trade Unionism

Wallachia

Oldest Romanian principality founded, according to tradition, by Prince Litovoi (r. 1290–1310) toward the end of the thirteenth century (the dates have varied from 1273 to 1377), by a descent to the Danubian plain from the plateau of Transylvania, along the right bank of the Olt River. Though the precise succession of events leading to the formation of Wallachia is undocumented, it was an attempt by a number of leaders of the Romanian population of southern Transylvania to escape from Hungarian control. By 1324, the Basarab family had succeeded in establishing its authority in that region by force of arms. The precise boundaries of the new state, however, were not well defined. It probably comprised the territories between the Carpathian Mountains, the Danube, and the Banat. Along the Danube, the boundary extended from the Iron Gates at Turnu Severin to the port of Brăila. Nevertheless, judging by the oldest capitals Argeş, Cîmpuling, and Tîrgovişte (1430), the center of power hugged the Carpathians. Bucharest, first mentioned in a document by Vlad Ţepeş (Dracula) (1431–76) in 1451, served intermittently as the capital from the sixteenth century. The term "Vlach" (Wallachen) denotes Latin-speaking peoples. From the Germans it was transmitted to the Slavs and Greeks with the same meaning, whereas in Transylvania the term Vlach of Olah in Hungarian meant "serfs." The Romanians themselves preferred the term Muntenia ("land of the mountains," derived from the word *munte* [mountain]) or *"Ţara Românească"* (Romanian land). In time, the rulers of Wallachia extended their sway over other districts in Transylvania, Bessarabia (the term derives from the ruling family, Basarab), Kilia, and Lower Moldavia.

Initially independent, confronted by the Ottoman incursion in Eastern Europe, the Wallachian princes were compelled to sign certain treaties (the original were never found) known as "capitulations," the most famous of which dated to 1415 during the rule of Mircea the Old (r. 1386–1418). These reduced the status of the principality to vassal and tributary state, though, unlike other Balkan provinces, a native regime and an autonomous church survived, Wallachia was never reduced to the status of a *pashalik* (administrative district), and no Turks had the right of settling on Romanian soil. The nature of the relationship with the Ottomans from that point onward depended on the personality of the prince and his military valor. Indeed, in many instances Wallachian princes could be considered totally independent—briefly, under Vlad Ţepeş and during the period of Michael the Brave (1557–1601)—that is, when the Turks were defeated. In the latter case, the prince, during a brief period, achieved the unity of all Romanian lands (Wallachia, Moldavia, Transylvania) at the close of his reign. The nonobservance of the capitulations and the increasing flirtation of princes with the Habsburg emperors and Russian tsars led to the reduction of Wallachia's autonomy. The eighteenth century led to the appointment of Greek princes of the Phanar (known as Phanariots), a name derived from the lighthouse section of Constantinople where they lived. Traditionally considered the "black period in Romanian history," the era has been found by historians of late to have produced a few remarkably enlightened men who helped Wallachia's progression to a modern state. Following the Greek revolution of 1821, when many Phanariots were enrolled in the Filiki Etairia, the secret cultural and political group, the Turks decided to reestablish native rulers in 1822–28. There followed a Russian protectorate, the *Règlement Organique* (Organic Statute) (1834–54), which virtually superimposed itself on Turkish suzerainty and lasted to the Crimean War (1853–56) save for the three months of revolutionary rule during the Revolutions of 1848. The election of Alexandru Ioan Cuza (1820–73), which created the United Principalities (Moldavia and Wallachia), ended Wallachia's existence as a separate state. While the newly elected Prince Cuza was Moldavian, the capital was moved to Bucharest and the first institution in the country to be united (the military) was left to a Wallachian: General Ion Emanoil Florescu (1819–93).

Radu Florescu

Further reading

Florescu, Radu R. and Raymond T. McNally. *Dracula, Prince of Many Faces: His Life and Times.* Boston, 1989.

Giurescu, Constantin C. and Dinu C. Giurescu. *Istoria Românilor din cele mai veche timpuri pînă astăzi.* Bucharest, 1975.

România: Atlas istoric-geografic. Bucharest, 1996.

Sugar, Peter F. *Southeastern Europe under Ottoman Rule, 1354–1804.* Seattle, Washington, 1977.

See also Banat; Bucharest; Capitulations; Carpathian Mountains; Crimean War; Alexandru Ioan Cuza; Filiki Etairia; Greek Revolution; Moldavia; Organic Statutes; Phanariots; Revolutions of 1848; Transylvania; United Principalities; Vlachs

Wallenberg, Raoul (b. 1912)

Swedish diplomat credited with saving tens of thousands of Jewish lives in Budapest during World War II. Born into a distinguished family of bankers, diplomats, and officers, Wallenberg studied architecture in the United States but then took up banking and international trade. His interest in the fate of Europe's Jews was stimulated during his 1936 professional stay in Haifa. In July 1944, on the recommendation of the Swedish branch of the World Jewish Council and the U.S. War Refugee Board, the Swedish Foreign Ministry sent him to Budapest to protect the city's two hundred thousand Jewish inhabitants.

Special detachments under Adolf Eichmann (1906–62), the head of the Gestapo's Jewish section, were already rounding up Jewish citizens of German-occupied Hungary. When Wallenberg arrived in Budapest, the deportations of Jews were halted in response to international outrage and appeals made by statesmen from various countries.

One successful strategy employed by Wallenberg was to issue provisional Swedish passports to Jews who had family or business ties in Sweden. He was granted broad authority for making arrangements and channeling money to cover the operation's expenses. Following the failed attempt by Hungary's regent, Miklós Horthy (1868–1957), to take the country out of the war and the subsequent takeover by the Arrow Cross, the right-radical party, Wallenberg exhibited tireless dedication, inventiveness, and courage in accomplishing his task. He issued thousands of protective passports and plucked Jews from the marching columns and trains that were to take them to the death camps of Poland. In cooperation with other legations, he also established thirty-one safe houses in Budapest where some fifteen thousand individuals found refuge from Arrow Cross detachments roaming the streets. As the Soviet army approached Budapest, SS and Arrow Cross fanatics planned to blow up the ghettos. Wallenberg was instrumental in foiling these plans, thus saving some one hundred thousand lives.

While negotiating with Red Army authorities concerning the care of the ghettos' liberated inhabitants, Wallenberg aroused the distrust of Soviet military intelligence, which already suspected the Swedes of spying for Germany. Notwithstanding his diplomatic status and the fact that Sweden represented Soviet affairs vis-à-vis Germany, on January 17, 1945, Wallenberg disappeared after last having been seen guarded by Red Army soldiers. His fate remains unclear, but according to most indications he died in Soviet captivity.

András Boros-Kazai

Further reading

Anger, Per. *With Raoul Wallenberg in Budapest.* New York, 1981.

Fogelman, Eva. *Conscience and Courage: Rescuers of Jews during the Holocaust.* New York, 1994.

Marton, Kati. *Wallenberg: Missing Hero.* New York, 1982.

Werbell, F.E. and Clarke, T. *Lost Hero: The Mystery of Raoul Wallenberg.* New York, 1982.

See also Arrow Cross; Holocaust; Red Army

Warsaw

Capital of Poland (1,650,200 population). Warsaw (Polish, Warszawa) was first mentioned in 1241 as a settlement around a castle on the high left bank of the Vistula (Wisła) River at the junction of two land routes and a river crossing. Located at the center of the Mazovian Lowland, the settlement grew in the wake of economic, political, and social developments in Poland, particularly the development of trade routes along and on the Vistula, the designation of the Old City (Stare Miasto) as the seat of the Sejm (diet) in 1569, the royal election in 1573, and finally as the capital in 1596.

The influx of population caused expansion northward along the high escarpment. The first bridge across the river (1568–73) increased accessibility to the city and spurred further growth. By the end of the seventeenth century, Warsaw had become the largest city in Poland, the center of trade and manufacturing.

In the second half of the nineteenth century, Warsaw expanded along both the escarpment and westward along the newly built Viennese Railroad, but the right-bank suburb, Praga, grew at a slower pace. In independent Poland (after 1918), Warsaw became the nation's most important manufacturing, commercial, and cultural center, and the population reached an estimated 1.3 million in 1939. Its diversified industries accounted for 13.8 percent of all employment in manufacturing in Poland. Warsaw had several institutions of higher learning and numerous cultural institutions, historical monuments, and palatial buildings.

World War II caused severe population loss and an enormous amount of physical destruction. The Jewish population (more than 350,000, approximately 30 percent of the city's inhabitants in the 1930s) was annihilated, and after the uprising in 1944 the city's physical plant was 84 percent destroyed by the Germans, particularly the historical Stare Miasto and the residential and industrial districts on the left bank. Its population declined to 479,000 in 1946. Postwar reconstruction restored all historical sites to the original architectural plans and gradually revived the economic and cultural significance of the city.

Warsaw is a leader in electronics, pharmaceuticals, precision tools, and optics. Metal working, machinery, transportation, polygraphic, and garment industries also play an important role in the economy. Warsaw is the largest transportation hub in the country, with seven railroad lines, five highways, and an international airport. It remained the most important cultural and scientific center in the country, with the Polish Academy of Sciences (PAN, with several research institutes), fourteen institutions of higher learning, numerous libraries, museums, and theaters, and cultural events.

Abraham Melezin

Further reading

Dawson, A. "Warsaw—An Example of City Structure in Free-Market and Planned Socialist Environment." *Tijdschrift voor Economische en Sociale Geografie* 62 (1971): 104–13.

Dziewoński, K. "Zagadnienia Geografii Warszawy." *Czasopismo Geograficzne* 40, no. 2 (1969): 249–56.

Janiszewski, M. *Geograficzne Warunki Powstawania Miast Polskich.* Lublin, 1991, 149–51.

See also Sejm; Warsaw Ghetto; Warsaw Uprising

Warsaw, Battle of

Also known as "the Miracle on the Vistula," a battle that determined the outcome of the Polish-Soviet War (1919–20) in favor of the Poles. In an effort to stave off impending defeat, Polish forces under the command of General Józef Piłsudski (1867–1935) struck Red Army forces in a dramatic, and in the opinion of many military historians, unorthodox counteroffensive on August 13, 1920. Five Polish divisions struck the Red Army with the aim of disrupting the continued Soviet advance toward Warsaw and to force a Soviet retreat. From August 16–18, units of the Polish Second Army advanced over 200 miles (333 km) eastward, effectively neutralizing the earlier Soviet offensive and brought about a complete Soviet route. Soviet forces, under the command of General Mikhail Tukhachevsky (1893–1937), suffered the loss of 65,000 prisoners, 231 guns, and well over 1,000 machine guns. The battle crippled the newly formed Soviet regime's aim of exporting its Bolshevik revolution to Western Europe, especially Germany. Moreover, the establishment of an independent Polish republic was assured, with the determination of the new Polish-Soviet border advantageous to the Poles.

Peter Lavelle

Further reading

Davies, Norman. *God's Playground: A History of Poland,* vol. 2. New York, 1982.

Komarnicki, Titus. *Rebirth of the Polish Republic: A Study in the Diplomatic History of Europe 1914–1920.* London, 1957.

Rothschild, Joseph. *East-Central Europe between the Two World Wars.* Seattle, Washington, 1974.

Watt, Richard M. *Bitter Glory: Poland and Its Fate 1918–1939.* New York, 1979.

See also Józef Piłsudski; Polish-Soviet War; Red Army; Mikhail Tukhachevsky

Warsaw Ghetto

Warsaw district in which the occupying Germans gathered Jews from the city and neighboring towns in 1940. On the eve of World War II, more than 370,000 Jews (nearly 30 percent of the city's population) lived in Warsaw, the second-largest Jewish community in the world. After Warsaw surrendered to the Germans in September 1939, the Jews were subjected to discrimination and oppression. In early 1940 the Germans started organizing a ghetto in Warsaw. Between April and August 1940, a 11.5 foot (3.5 m) high wall was erected around the northeast district of Warsaw, where the Jewish population prevailed before the war. Over one hundred thousand Poles were evacuated from this district and replaced by Jews transferred from other parts of the city and other towns. On November 16, 1940, the "Jewish quarter" (Jüdische Wohnbezirk) was sealed off with 396,000 Jews, over 30 percent of Warsaw's population, concentrated on a small area of 73 streets (out of 1,800 streets of the city). The ghetto was administered by the Judenrat (Jewish Council), which carried out German instructions and orders. The leaders of Warsaw's Jewish community tried to make ghetto life bearable. Various societies were engaged in welfare, mutual help, clandestine education, and cultural life. Yet the conditions grew steadily worse. The Germans tried to cut off the ghetto from the outside "Aryan" world. Jews found outside without permission were executed. Growing numbers of ghetto Jews were sent to labor camps. The Germans established a daily caloric quota that led to starvation; by mid-1942, over one hundred thousand people had died in the ghetto. But new Jewish deportees from Poland and Germany were constantly moved to Warsaw, the largest ghetto in Europe, including 445,000 individuals in March 1941.

The ghetto became a transitional phase leading to the Final Solution. Various forms of resistance were organized in the ghetto. Smuggling of food and illegal economic activities became an everyday occupation of a large segment of the walled-in population. A clandestine press was established, and prewar Jewish political parties secretly resumed their activities. In March 1942 leaders of the Jewish youth movements made their first attempt to create a self-defense organization. On July 22, 1942, the Germans began to deport the ghetto's inhabitants. Before September 6, a majority of the ghetto population had been taken to the Treblinka extermination camp. Only about sixty thousand Jews remained in the ghetto, divided into three small areas isolated and reshaped into a labor camp. During the deportation, the Jewish Fighting Organization (Żydowska Organizacja Bojowa, ŻOB) was created. When the Germans started a new deportation on January 18, 1943, the ŻOB and the Jewish Military Union (Żydowski Związek Wojskowy) answered with armed resistance. The Germans halted the deportation and started a final liquidation of the ghetto on April 19, 1943. The Jewish underground revolted. German special forces crushed it by systematically burning the entire ghetto. On May 16, 1943, the Great Synagogue was ordered destroyed and it was announced that "The Jewish quarter of Warsaw no longer exists." In fact, the last small and isolated groups of Jews survived in the ruins of the ghetto until the 1944 Warsaw Uprising.

Piotr Wróbel

Further reading

Ainsztein, R. *The Warsaw Ghetto Revolt.* New York, 1979.

Edelman, M. *The Ghetto Fights.* New York, 1946.

Encyclopedia of the Holocaust, ed. by Israel Gutman, vol. 4. New York, 1990, 1,598–1,632.

See also Holocaust; Jews; Warsaw Uprising

Warsaw Pact

Alliance of eight nations in Eastern Europe, headed by the Soviet Union. Following the defeat of Nazi Germany and its allies in May 1945, the Soviet Union proceeded to install Communist governments in territories "liberated" from the Germans by the Red Army. By 1948, all Eastern Europe was under Communist administration, with the exception of Greece. With the admission of the Federal Republic of Germany (West Germany) to the North Atlantic Treaty Organization (NATO) in the Paris Agreements of October 23, 1954, the Soviet Union decided to formalize its alliance system. A conference was held at Warsaw in May 1955, with representatives from the Soviet Union, Poland, Czechoslovakia, Hungary, Romania, Bulgaria, Albania, and the German Democratic Republic; on May 14 the conferees signed the Warsaw Treaty of Friendship, Cooperation, and Mutual Assistance. The Warsaw agreement provided for a joint military command, a standing commission to coordinate foreign policy, and a secretariat composed of representatives of all the participating nations. The headquarters for these joint bodies would be located in the Soviet Union. The ostensible purpose of the treaty was to formalize mutual assistance provisions among the member states.

Despite its formal status, the Warsaw Treaty fundamentally continued existing Soviet military policy in the region, although it granted a new legitimacy for the presence of Soviet military units on the territory of its neighbors.

Although Soviet domination of the Warsaw Pact was never in question, Soviet relations with member states did not always proceed smoothly. Soviet military units intervened in Poland and Hungary in 1956; the Romanians proved to be the most difficult of allies; and Albania formally withdrew from the pact in 1968.

The Soviets utilized the provisions of the Warsaw Pact to mount a multinational invasion of Czechoslovakia in 1968 to suppress the Prague Spring, the short-lived liberal reform period. The collapse of nearly all the Communist regimes in Europe in 1989 caused the Warsaw Pact to disintegrate by the end of that year.

Daniel D. Trifan

Further reading

Eyal, Jonathan. *The Warsaw Pact and the Balkans: Moscow's Southern Flank.* New York, 1989.

Holden, Gerard. *The Warsaw Pact: Soviet Security and Bloc Politics.* Cambridge, Massachusetts, 1989.

Remington, Robin A. *The Warsaw Pact.* Cambridge, Massachusetts, 1971.

See also Hungarian Revolution of 1956; Prague Spring; Revolutions of 1989

Warsaw Uprising (August–October 1944)

Ill-fated uprising by the Polish underground army against the Nazis. On August 1, 1944, the Polish Home Army (Armia Krajowa, AK) launched an uprising against German forces in Warsaw. Over the course of the next sixty-three days, the Nazis crushed the insurrection, deported or executed almost the entire population of Warsaw, and left the city in ruins.

In 1944 the advance of the Red Army into Poland seemed to signal an end to the German occupation. With reports of Soviet tanks nearing Warsaw, the AK command issued orders to commence operations ("Tempest") against the Germans.

The plan to seize Warsaw was poorly timed and organized. Polish forces were ill-prepared and ill-equipped to take on the Wehrmacht. Nevertheless, on August 1, the AK (as well as many citizens of Warsaw) struck. The battle raged for two months. Poorly armed, the insurgents faced crack German units who advanced through the city leveling it block by block. Although in September the Red Army approached the banks of the Vistula River, only a few kilometers from Warsaw, they did not advance to aid the insurgents. Short of ammunition and with little chance of obtaining needed food and supplies, the Home Army surrendered to the Germans in October.

Over two hundred thousand Poles died in the uprising. The city's remaining population was deported, many to concentration camps or to forced labor. Hitler (1889–1953) in turn ordered Warsaw razed. When the Red Army entered Warsaw in January, they found only rubble.

Judith Fai-Podlipnik

Further reading

Bogdan, Henry and Istvan Fehervary, ed. *From Warsaw to Sophia: A History of Eastern Europe.* Santa Fe, New Mexico, 1989.

Ciechanowski, Jan. *The Warsaw Rising of 1944.* New York, 1974.

Davies, Norman. *God's Playground: A History of Poland,* vol. 2. New York, 1982.

Komorowski, Tadeusz. *The Secret Army.* New York, 1951.

Korbonski, Andrzej. "Poland: 1918–1990," in Joseph Held, ed., *The Columbia History of Eastern Europe in the Twentieth Century.* New York, 1992.

Leslie, Roy F. *A History of Poland since 1863.* Cambridge, 1980.

See also Armia Krajowa; Adolf Hitler; Red Army

White Terror

Retribution that followed the collapse of the Hungarian Soviet Republic—the short-lived regime led by Béla Kun (1886–1938) that took power during the chaotic period after World War I—on August 1, 1919. Its victims were supporters of the Soviet government, or of the liberal democratic regime that preceded it. Jews especially fell prey to the lawlessness, regardless of political convictions.

The terror began as the Romanian army occupied Budapest and the Great Hungarian Plain. Captured Soviet leaders were tortured and often executed, while Red Army soldiers were interned. The government that took power in Hungary by a coup used a 1912 state of emergency law to suspend habeas corpus and the right of appeal. Commissars of the Soviet regime were executed and lesser officials imprisoned. Public servants who remained at their posts during the 133-day Soviet rule were fired or were forced to retire. Admiral Miklós Horthy's (1868–1957) National Army, which was organized to fight the "reds" (although it saw no action), also joined the terror campaign. Officers' units engaged in acts of mass murder and in anti-Semitic pogroms. Their actions "against civilians" were proscribed by the minister of defense only in June 1920.

It is estimated that from August to November 1919, between 1,500 and 5,000 people were killed. Another 60,000 were imprisoned or sent to internment camps. The terror abated because of Allied pressure and consolidation of the counterrevolutionary Horthy regime. The last internment camp was closed in 1924. A consequence of the terror was the mass emigration of about 100,000 Hungarians, including many outstanding members of the intellectual elite.

Peter Pastor

Further reading

Congdon, Lee. *Exile and Social Thought: Hungarian Intellectuals in Germany and Austria 1919–1933.* Princeton, New Jersey, 1991.

Hollós, Ervin, and Vera Lajtai. *Horthy Miklós a fehérek vezére.* Budapest, 1985.

Romsics, Ignác. *Ellenforradalom és konszolidáció.* Budapest, 1982.

Szabó, Agnes and Ervin Pamlényi, eds. *A határban a halál kaszál: Fejezetek Prónay Pál feljegyzéseiböl.* Budapest, 1963.

See also Communist Party of Hungary; Hungarian Émigrés; Hungarian Soviet Republic; Miklós Horthy; Béla Kun

Wielkopolska

Oldest historical region of Poland (Polonia Maior, the Older Poland) and the cradle of the Polish nation. Wielkopolska accounts for 13.6 percent of Poland's area—encompassing 16,413 square miles (42,510 sq km)—and 11.7 percent of its population (4.5 million). It occupies the lowest part of the Polish lowlands where several broad fluvio-glacial valleys alternate with low, little undulating uplands built of morainic materials. Low morainic hills diversify the central and southern parts. Numerous lakes in glacial depressions and elongated troughs often arranged in the north-south string pattern are found in the northeastern part, called Kujawy (Kouiavih).

The climate, transitional from maritime to continental, has warm summers (64° F [18° C]) and mild winters (36° F [2° C]). Precipitation is fewer than 20 inches (51 cm) annually with a summer maximum. The vegetative period is 170–180 days in the north and east, and 210–217 days in the south and west.

Soils are podzolic, often sandy. Intensive husbandry created a surplus grain production, the foundation of a strong food industry, but the region is poorly endowed with mineral resources. The most important is brown coal, used to generate electricity and for export. There is also salt and gypsum.

Although approximately 17 percent of the population perished during World War II, postwar industrialization contributed considerably to the growth of the urban population, presently almost double its prewar share (34.9 percent in 1931).

Wielkopolska is divided into six *voievodeship*s (provinces)—Poznań, Piła, Kalisz, Leszno, Konin, and Bydgoszcz. The largest cities are Poznań and Bydgoszcz. Poznań (590,000 population) is one of the oldest cities in Poland and was the capital until the twelfth century. It originated in the ninth century on Tum (Toum) Island, which facilitated the crossing of the Warta River. The location attracted several trade routes from Silesia and Germany leading north and east. It grew mainly on the left bank of the Warta River around the so-called Old Town (Stare Miasto). Poznań is an important cultural and industrial center and a considerable transportation hub. Bydgoszcz (370,000 population) grew up at a convenient dry crossing across a broad and marshy fluvio-glacial valley. Its growth started after the completion of the canal, which joined the systems of the Vistula and the Warta Rivers (1774). It became an important transportation and industrial center.

Abraham Melezin

Further reading

Lencewicz, Stanisław and Jerzy Kondracki. *Geografia Fizyczna Polski.* Warsaw, 1964, 213–27.
Zajchowska, Stanisława. *Województwo Poznańskie.* Warsaw, 1959, 38, 43–46.

See also Industrialization; Poznán

Wielopolski, Count Aleksander (1803–77)

Conservative Polish statesman and advocate of cooperation with Russia at the time of the January Insurrection in 1863 against Russian domination. Wielopolski was born into the impoverished Polish nobility. After studying in Germany, he participated in the 1830 November Uprising against the Russians, an experience that soured him on both armed insurrection and the belief that foreign governments would help the Poles.

In 1846 Wielopolski wrote an open letter to Clemens von Metternich (1773–1859), the Austrian chancellor, blaming Austria for the bloody peasant revolt in Austrian-controlled Galicia. He concluded that accommodation with Russia would best serve Polish interests. Wielopolski's pro-Russian sentiments favorably impressed the tsarist authorities. However, Wielopolski represented only himself and not Polish opinion. His unpopularity was partly due to his benign view of Russia and partly due to his personality. He was an arrogant, iron-willed, self-contained man who said of his fellow countrymen that it might be possible to do something for them but nothing could be done with them.

As Russo-Polish tensions rose in 1861, Alexander II (1818–81) appointed Wielopolski de facto prime minister of Poland. He could now pursue his policy of cooperating with Russia to gain greater autonomy for Poland. But the Russians expected him to dampen revolutionary sentiments, and the dual undertaking of reform and repression proved unworkable.

Wielopolski reformed the education system, emancipated Polish Jews, revitalized local self-government, Polonicized the bureaucracy, and ended serfdom by converting labor dues to compulsory rents. Despite these accomplishments, Wielopolski remained unpopular. He vigorously suppressed would-be Polish revolutionaries, and his decision to draft those who supported the dissident movement sparked an armed uprising in January 1863 that Russia brutally crushed. The uprising also led to Wielopolski's departure from government in July 1863. After the defeat of the Polish insurrectionaries, Russia rescinded Wielopolski's reforms. Wielopolski eventually migrated to Saxony, where he died.

Frank W. Thackeray

Further reading

Davies, Norman. *God's Playground: A History of Poland,* 2 vols. New York, 1982.
Rosevare, Irena M. "Wielopolski's Reforms and Their Failure before the Uprising of 1863." *Antemurale* 15 (1971): 87–214.
Wandycz, Piotr S. *The Lands of Partitioned Poland, 1795–1918.* Seattle, Washington, 1974.

See also Alexander II; January Uprising; Prince Clemens von Metternich; November Uprising

William of Wied (1876–1945)

Albanian monarch. In the aftermath of Albania's independence proclamation in November 1912, the Great Powers undertook to provide the legal foundation for the new state and determined that the country would be a hereditary monarchy. After reviewing a long list of potential candidates, the powers offered the throne to William of Wied and he accepted the offer in February 1914. Wied's selection was not easy, owing to the competing foreign interests in the country, but he did meet the demands of many Albanian patriots, especially Ismail Bey Kemal (1844–1919), who envisioned the creation of a "European" Albania and thus hoped for a monarch from Western Europe.

Wied, a member of a Prussian noble family, was the nephew of Queen Elisabeth of Romania

(1843–1916) and grand nephew of German Emperor Wilhelm I (1797–1888). Along with his wife and family, he arrived in Albania in March 7, 1914, completely unprepared for the difficult task that lay ahead. Setting up a government in the coastal town of Durrës, he was forced to rely on Albanians of very suspect credentials, especially Esad Pasha Toptani (1863–1920), who was both war and interior minister in Wied's first cabinet. In the first few months of his rule he was unable to establish control over little more than a portion of central Albania, and fighting raged in the country between various factions. Moreover, the intrigues of Albania's neighbors made his rule difficult as Italy, Serbia, and Greece fomented opposition to his government. Despite Toptani's removal, the coming of World War I and ongoing confusion ensured Wied's failure. He left Albania on September 3, 1914, without formally abdicating and never returned.

Robert C. Austin

Further reading

Fitzherbert, M. *The Man Who Was Greenmantle: Biography of Aubrey Herbert.* London, 1983.

Skendi, Stavro. *The Political Evolution of Albania.* New York, 1954.

Swire, Joseph. *Albania—The Rise of a Kingdom.* New York, 1971.

See also Esad Pasha Toptani

Wilson, Thomas Woodrow (1856–1924)

Twenty-eighth president of the United States (1913–21), called the godfather of the new nations of East Central Europe—Poland, Czechoslovakia, Greater Romania, and Yugoslavia—that came into existence in 1918 on the ruins of the Habsburg and Russian Empires. The accolade is well deserved, although his contribution to their establishment was an accidental by-product of his policies rather than one of desired aims. He had no personal or sentimental interest in these nations.

When World War I broke out in Europe, Wilson admonished Americans to remain neutral and impartial. He looked askance at efforts by European immigrant groups ("hyphenated Americans") to promote the cause of their countrymen in Europe as prejudicial to American neutrality. In 1916 he was reelected to the presidency on a neutralist platform ("He kept us out of the war!"). The best way to keep America out of the war was to induce the belligerents to make peace. He made a bid to mediate peace between the warring camps in an address to the U.S. Senate on January 22, 1917, and suggested that the United States would guarantee it—provided it was based on principles acceptable to the American people. He included among them the principle of national self-determination. As an example, he cited that there should be "a united, independent, and autonomous Poland," which ineradicably inscribed it on the list of questions to be taken up at the peace conference.

Although Wilson asked Congress to declare war on Germany in April 1917, he did not recommend war against Austria-Hungary, hoping to isolate Germany by inducing Austria to conclude a separate peace. When that failed, on December 4, 1917, Wilson asked for war against Austria, but hastened to add that he did not wish to destroy the Austro-Hungarian Empire. In his Fourteen Points issued on January 8, 1918, he again called for the creation of an independent Polish state with free and secure access to the sea (Point 13), but recommended only "the freest opportunity for autonomous development" for the peoples of Austria-Hungary (Point 10).

In May 1918, when the secret Allied negotiations with Vienna for a separate peace finally collapsed, Wilson was ready to give stronger encouragement to Czechoslovaks and Yugoslavs. In a declaration on May 29 and a more explicit one on June 28, Secretary of State Robert Lansing (1864–1928) announced that their aspirations to freedom from Austria-Hungary had the support of the U.S. government. When Vienna attempted to renew negotiations in October, the president replied that he had committed himself to the Czechoslovaks and the Yugoslavs and that, therefore, it had to negotiate with them, not with him. So encouraged, the Czech National Committee in Prague issued a declaration of Czechoslovak independence on October 28, and the Yugoslav National Council in Zagreb issued one on Yugoslav independence on October 29. Romanian aspirations to national unification were recognized by the United States at the Paris Peace Conference.

Victor S. Mamatey

Further reading

Gerson, Louis L. *Woodrow Wilson and the Rebirth of Poland, 1914–1920.* New Haven, Connecticut, 1953.

Mamatey, Victor S. *The United States and East Central Europe, 1914–1918: A Study in Wilsonian Diplomacy and Propaganda.* Princeton, New Jersey, 1957.

See also Fourteen Points; Paris Peace Conference

Windischgrätz, Prince Alfred Candid Ferdinand zu (1787–1862)

Bohemian aristocrat, politician/general, conservative's conservative, and the man most responsible for the collapse of the Revolutions of 1848 in Prague and Vienna. Commissioned a lieutenant in the Habsburg army in 1804, Windischgrätz achieved the rank of field marshal in 1833, and was commanding general of Bohemia when revolution swept through the Habsburg domains in 1848.

On his own initiative, Windischgrätz moved against the revolutionaries in Prague on June 12. During six days of fighting, imperial forces under Windischgrätz put down the revolutionary movement in the Bohemian capital, although at great personal loss to their commander, whose wife was killed during the fighting. That Windischgrätz's loyalty was to his class and dynasty, not to any one of the national groups in the empire, is shown in his subsequent actions against the revolutionary government in Vienna. On October 28, he launched his assault on the city. Three days and several thousand casualties later, Windischgrätz controlled the capital and proclaimed martial law.

In collusion with Field Marshall Josef Radetzky (1766–1858), General Josip Jelačić (1801–59), and Prince Felix zu Schwarzenberg (1800–1852); Windischgrätz engineered the abdication of Emperor Ferdinand (1793–1875) and the elevation of the eighteen-year-old Franz Joseph (1830–1916) to the imperial throne. But after a series of military failures in Hungary, Windischgrätz was relieved of his command by the new emperor on April 14, 1849. After his dismissal, Windischgrätz continued to serve the dynasty. His last important commission was as envoy to Prussia during the monarchy's war with France and Sardinia-Piedmont in 1859.

T. Mills Kelly

Further reading

Müller, Paul. *Feldmarschall Fürst Windischgrätz. Revolution und Gegenrevolution in Österreich.* Vienna, 1934.

Polišenský, Josef. *Aristocrats and the Crowd in the Revolutionary Year 1848.* Albany, New York, 1980.
Redlich, Joseph. *Emperor Francis Joseph of Austria.* New York, 1929.

See also Franz Joseph; Josip Jelačić; Prague Slav Congress; Revolutions of 1848; Felix zu Schwarzenberg

Witkiewicz, Stanisław Ignacy (1885–1939)

Polish writer, playwright, philosopher, and painter (pseud., Witkacy). Witkiewicz was essentially a philosopher whose novels, plays, and essays, as well as his extraordinary life (study of art, a scientific expedition to Australia, an officer in the Russian white army, military service as a red commissar) were means of expressing his ideas. He believed that contemporary civilization was approaching the end of religion, philosophy, and art. The future revolution, Witkiewicz believed, might bring humanity more material prosperity, but at the same time it would destroy all metaphysical strivings and ontological searchings. Witkiewicz's plays (*Kurka wodna* [*Water Hen,* 1921]; *W małym dworku* [*In a Small Country House,* 1921]; and *Szewcy* [*The Shoemakers,* 1931–34]) were written according to his theory of "pure form," in which the goal of art is to win complete freedom of formal elements to bring the viewer to a state of "metaphysical feeling of the strangeness of existence." He is often seen as a precursor of the theater of the absurd.

Although Witkiewicz rejected realism and naturalism and did not consider the novel an art form, he wrote several novels: *Pożegnanie jesieni* (*Farewell to Autumn,* 1927) and *Nienasycenie* (*Insatiability,* 1930). In the catastrophic world of *Insatiability,* metaphysical anxiety is wiped out by mysterious pills that change individuals into happy, empty beings, succumbing to the rules of a totalitarian ministry of the mechanization of culture. Seeing the Soviet attack on Poland in September 1939 as a fulfillment of his own prophecies, Witkiewicz committed suicide.

Katarzyna Zechenter

Further reading

Gerould, Daniel. *Witkacy: Stanisław Ignacy Witkiewicz as an Imaginative Writer.* Seattle, Washington, 1981.

Le Théatre en Pologne: The Theatre in Poland. Special Witkiewicz Issues: no. 3 (1970), no. 6–7 (1978).

Polish Review. Special Witkiewicz Issue 18, no. 1–2 (1973).

The Witkiewicz Reader, ed. by Daniel Gerould. Evanston, Illinois, 1992.

See also Polish Literature

Witos, Wincenty (1874–1945)

Polish political figure. Born a peasant in the Austrian zone of partitioned Poland, Witos educated himself and entered the Polish agrarian political movement. He served briefly as minister without portfolio in one of the formative governments of the newly independent Second Polish Republic in 1918.

Witos was the most significant agrarian politician of interwar Poland. From 1918 to 1931, he acted as leader of the moderate Polish Peasant Party (*Piast*) and headed its parliamentary delegation. He served twice as prime minister, in 1920–21 and 1923. Asked to form a third government in May 1926, he was in effect unseated by the coup d'état that installed Józef Piłsudski (1867–1935) in power. Witos became a vocal antagonist of the Piłsudski regime and was instrumental in forming the so-called Center-Left opposition faction. He was arrested, imprisoned, and tried in 1930–31. In 1933 he went into exile, returning clandestinely in 1939, shortly before the outbreak of World War II.

During the war, the German occupation regime attempted unsuccessfully to procure his services as a collaborator, imprisoned him in 1939–41, and kept him under house arrest for the balance of the conflict. At war's end he planned to resume political activity and was selected to resume leadership of the Polish Peasant Party, but he died in 1945 after a period of declining health. His lengthy, posthumously published memoirs are a useful source for modern Polish political history.

Neal A. Pease

Further reading

Witos, Wincenty. *Moje wspomnienia.* Warsaw, 1981.
Zakrzewski, Andrzej. *Wincenty Witos.* Warsaw, 1977.

See also Agrarian May Coup Parties; Józef Piłsudski

Wojciechowski, Stanisław (1869–1953)

Second president of the Second Polish Republic. Wojciechowski began his political career in the 1890s, when, as a student, he participated in the conspiratorial Union of Polish Youth (Zet). He expanded his activities beyond the confines of the intelligentsia to include the working class, and subsequently became one of the founders of the Polish Socialist Party. Until 1905, he worked closely with Józef Piłsudski (1867–1935), the future Polish leader. He abandoned the socialist movement after opponents of independent statehood temporarily gained the upper hand in the Polish Socialist Party. In 1906 Wojciechowski emerged as a pioneering figure in the cooperative movement in the Russian partition (the part of Poland under Russian control). During World War I, he gravitated toward the national democratic line, accepting the view that Germany posed the greatest threat to Polish interests. From 1919 to 1920, Wojciechowski served as minister of internal affairs. By this point, his political affiliation lay with the strongest peasant party in the second republic (*Piast*), whose support proved instrumental in his election to the presidency.

Wojciechowski's tenure as president lasted from 1922, when he was elected following the assassination of the first president of the republic, Gabriel Narutowicz (1865–1922), until May 1926, when he resigned in the wake of Piłsudski's coup d'état. During a dramatic confrontation with Piłsudski on a Warsaw bridge in the midst of the coup, Wojciechowski demanded that the marshal recognize his authority as head of state and commander in chief of the armed forces. Wojciechowski's subsequent resignation symbolized the widespread determination to avoid a debilitating civil war and the international risks such an internal conflict would have entailed.

William Lee Blackwood

Further reading

Ajnenkiel, Andrzej, ed. *Prezydenci Polski.* Warsaw, 1991.
Kto był kim w Drugiej Rzeczypospolitej. Warsaw, 1994.
Wojciechowski, Stanisław. *Wspomnienia, orędzia, artykuły.* Warsaw, 1995.

See also May Coup; Józef Piłsudski; Zet

Women in Albania

In 1912 Albanians were still subjects of the Ottoman Empire. Over 70 percent of them were Muslim, the rest Greek Orthodox or Roman Catholic. The place of women remained under the patriarch of the extended family or under the head of the household, and social restrictions on them were legitimized by Turkish laws and local customary codes upheld by Albanian Muslim and Christian religious authorities. In the country's poorest mountain districts, women were little more than commodities exchanged by in-laws. One American missionary school in the 1890s briefly provided some education for Albanian girls in their own language. A decade of war and political turmoil between 1915 and 1925 led to basic educational opportunities under Ahmed Bey Zogu (1895–1961), who proclaimed himself king (King Zog) in 1929 in a country still ruled by Muslim families. However, professional training for women before the country was invaded by Italian forces under Benito Mussolini (1883–1945) in 1939 came more as the result of emigration than nationhood.

Centuries-long traditions in the country were radically affected by the events of 1939–66: annexation by Italy, German occupation, centralized Communist control under Enver Hoxha (1908–85), creation of a Soviet-style educational system and a university open to women, and outlawing of all religion. Women who left their families to fight in World War II became the first to benefit from government policies directed at them. Industrialization and modernization of Europe's poorest country were impossible, it was argued, without the integration of half the population into the expanding labor pool. For the next two decades, in spite of enormous societal problems and long-standing prejudices, Albanian women for the first time entered the professional and managerial elite, owing to their educational background and work experience as well as their political reliability, not family connections, as had been the case immediately following the war and the later break between Tirana and Belgrade. Government control from above remained in place, but by the mid-1980s new professional opportunities for many thousands of educated women had nevertheless become a reality.

The political upheavals that followed the forty-year rule of Albania's first Communist leader, Hoxha, led to the arrest of his wife and his hand-picked successor and eventually brought down women as well as men who had risen to prominence between 1965 and 1985. It remains to be seen, after the 1990s introduced a decade marked by economic and political revolution, just how long the present generation of young, ambitious, well-educated Albanian women will take advantage of the absence of restrictive traditional and totalitarian controls and continue to benefit from new opportunities such as Humphrey and Fulbright fellowships to travel, study, and work abroad. The answer, in part, will depend on the so-called "ex-Communists" who have managed to retain their jobs and positions of authority, as it once depended on ex-Ottoman officials in King Zog's Albania.

John Kolsti

Further reading

Kolsti, John. "From Courtyard to Cabinet: The Political Emergence of Albanian Women," in *Women, State, and Party in Eastern Europe,* ed. by Sharon L. Wolchik and Alfred G. Meyer. Durham, North Carolina, 1985.

Marmullaku, Ramadan. *Albania and the Albanians.* London, 1975.

Prifti, Peter. *Socialist Albania since 1944.* Cambridge, Massachusetts, 1978.

Vickery, Miranda. *The Albanians: A Modern History.* London, 1995.

See also Family; Enver Hoxha; Muslims; Ahmed Zogu

Women in Bulgaria

Women first came into prominence in Bulgarian history during the years of Ottoman rule (1396–1878), when some of them, such as Raina Knyaginya (n.d.) and Baba Tonka (n.d.), became involved in the struggle for national liberation. Although women have been active participants in all facets of Bulgarian life since 1878, few were committed to purely feminist causes, even though by the early years of the twentieth century, Ekaterina Karavelova (b. 1860) started women's groups and was an outspoken feminist. Throughout the centuries, Bulgarian society has preserved a patriarchal attitude toward women, in particular to those who have lived in the traditional setting of villages. In many ways that did not change until the Communist era.

Many women entered the labor force during the 1950s and 1960s, when a mass migration to the cities occurred. In 1990 women constituted 46.4 percent of the total labor force. Women were granted equal access to education and were allowed to practice various professional occupations. Under the Communists, women were employed in some traditional fields such as child-care, primary education, health care, clerical work, and weaving. More women than ever were employed in nontraditional fields such as construction and heavy industry. For example, while the percentage of women majoring in engineering was 26.4 percent in 1960, by 1980 it had reached 38.9 percent. At the same time, in some nontraditional professional fields very few women have been visible—only one woman aviator and one woman orchestra conductor. Although professionally active, women were underrepresented at the executive and decision-making levels

The average Bulgarian woman is married and has two children. The birth rate, however, has been steadily falling since the mid-1970s, and the rate of population growth in the country has been declining since the 1980s. Various forms of contraception are in use, but abortion is still the main form of birth control. The number of divorces stands at 30 percent.

The transitional period from communism (after 1990) has affected women in several ways: social benefits such as provisions for paid and unpaid maternity leave have disappeared, while health-care and day-care arrangements have worsened. Unemployment among women has grown faster than among men.

Women are rarely appointed to prominent political positions. Traditionally, the Bulgarian cabinet included one or two women who carried the portfolios of social care, health, or culture. During the period of Communist rule, only two women were ever members of the Politburo—Tsola Dragoicheva (1898–1993), an active member of the antifascist resistance movement, and Liudmila Zhivkova (1940–81), daughter of Bulgarian president Todor Zhivkov (1911–98), who became minister of culture. The percentage of women in the Bulgarian parliament traditionally has also been low. The ratio of women and men elected to legislative bodies is 1:4. In post-Communist times occasionally women have been elected leaders of some of the new parties. Poet Blaga Dimitrova (1922–) was a vice president for two years (1991–92).

During the period 1944–90, there was only one official organization of women in Bulgaria—the Movement of Bulgarian Women—and it was supervised by the Communist Party. It formally included all women but had no connection with grassroots activism. Since 1990, various women's organizations and women's caucuses of the newly established parties have come into being. Many Bulgarian women have joined international organizations, and women's studies courses are offered at some universities. Issues of importance to women in the West, such as sexual harassment, violence against women, and access to nontraditional occupations, gradually have become issues for Bulgarian women, who still face patriarchal attitudes.

Women of prominence include poets Dora Gabe (1888–1983), Elissaveta Bagryana (1893–1991), and Blaga Dimitrova; writers Anna Kamenova (1894–1982), Yana Yazova (1912–74), Fani Popova-Mutafova (1902–77), and Vera Mutafchieva (1929–); film director Binka Zhelyazkova (1923–); opera singers Raina Kabaivanska (1934–) and Anna Tomova-Sintova (n.d.); pop singers Lili Ivanova (n.d.) and Bogdana Karadotcheva (n.d.); and athletes Iliana Raeva (1963–), Maria Gigova (n.d.), Lili Ignatova (n.d.), Stefka Kostadinova (n.d.); and Neshka Robeva (1946–), head coach of the Bulgarian rhythmic gymnastics team and later a prominent member of parliament.

Dina Iordanova

Further reading

Panova, Rossitsa, Raina Gavrilova, and Cornelia Merdzanska. "Thinking Gender: Bulgarian Women's Impossibilities," in *Gender Politics and Post-Communism,* ed. by N. Funk and M. Mueller. New York, 1993, 15–22.

Petrova, Dimitrina. "The Winding Road to Emancipation in Bulgaria," in *Gender Politics and Post-Communism,* ed. by N. Funk and M. Mueller. New York, 1993, 22–30.

Todorova, Maria. "The Bulgarian Case: Women's Issues or Feminist Issues?" *Gender Politics and Post-Communism,* ed. by N. Funk and M. Mueller. New York, 1993, 30–39.

See also Communist Party of Bulgaria; Family; Neshka Robeva; Liudmila Zhivkova

Women in Czechoslovakia

Public roles for Czech and Slovak women steadily increased over the course of the nineteenth and twentieth centuries, initially in Bohemia, and later in Moravia and Slovakia. During the nineteenth century, the majority of Czech and Slovak women lived in rural environments and worked in their own homes or engaged in domestic work. Upper-middle-class women participated in charity and church-related activities.

The Revolution of 1848 marked the first major political event in which Czech women played significant public roles. Nationalist newspapers urged women to devote themselves to patriotic work, and women participated in the June uprising in Prague. Young women helped build and defend the barricades, and five of the forty-three dead were women. The first recorded political meeting of Czech women took place during the events of 1848 and led to the formation of the nationalist women's organization, Spolek Slovanek (Club of Slavic Women). The activist women in 1848 did not seek political emancipation or suffrage but argued for improvements in education for women. A leading figure from the 1848 era was Božena Němcová (1820–62), a poet and novelist who devoted her writing career to highlighting Czech women's roles in preserving the nation's language and culture. The conservative reaction that followed the 1848 revolution retarded the fledgling nationalist-oriented women's movement in the Czech lands. The Kremsier/Kroměříž Parliament of 1849 passed the Law of Association which banned all political activity of women and explicitly excluded them from suffrage.

Following the downfall of the conservative Habsburg government of Alexander Bach (1813–93) in 1860, both nationalist and women's organizations in the Czech lands experienced a resurgence. Slovak women, in the more reactionary and less economically developed Hungarian half of the empire, did not have as many opportunities to become publicly active. Most Czech women's voluntary associations were centered in Prague. Women's and girls' education was the primary concern of activist women in the late nineteenth century. Arguing that educated women could better contribute to the national cause, organizations such as Minerva, headed by journalist and novelist Eliška Krásnohorská (1847–1926), led the movement for girls' academic high schools (*gymnasia*) and women's access to universities and medical schools. The first girls' gymnasium opened in Prague in 1890.

At the turn of the century, women's rights became an issue that distinguished new political parties from the more conservative Old Czechs. The Young Czech Party and Tomáš Masaryk's Realist Party supported women's suffrage. Masaryk (1850–1937) became a leading spokesmen in Prague for women's rights, and his American wife, Charlotte Garrigue Masaryk (1850–1923), became involved in women's politics and translated into Czech *Vindication of the Rights of Women* by English author and feminist Mary Wollstonecraft (1759–1797).

When Czechoslovakia became independent in 1918, the new state immediately extended suffrage to women. Women also took advantage of increased educational opportunities. In the 1920s full-time female students made up 24.7 percent of Prague's Charles University, 17.5 percent of Brno's Masaryk University, and 12.5 percent of Bratislava's Komensky University. Women entered professions in increasing numbers, and especially made contributions in the fields of literature, journalism, education, performing arts, and social services. Yet few women held managerial posts in commerce and industry.

Social welfare and public health legislation in the early 1920s benefited women and Czechoslovak families. The eight-hour working day was established to strengthen the working-class family, and new laws regulated labor by women, who made up 34 percent of the industrial workforce. The state also subsidized low-income housing, established national unemployment insurance, and broadened and extended health and accident insurance for industrial, agricultural, and domestic workers. By 1930, only 34 percent of the population remained in agriculture, and female as well as general literacy was nearly universal.

Although many women were politically active during the interwar period, few held elected or appointed political offices. No woman held a cabinet post, and representation in parliament was low. In 1924 only 4.1 percent of the representatives in the lower house of parliament were women; in 1930 the number dropped to 3.3 percent. The economic upheavals of the Great Depression retarded the progress of women. Layoffs affected a higher percentage though not larger numbers of women than men, and the state cut back many social services.

During the Communist period, the concerns of Czechoslovak women shifted. Since state ideology emphasized that women were to contribute to the national labor force and to give birth to future generations of workers, women became increasingly concerned with balancing work and family obligations. Women received gynecological and other medical care within the national health care system, and Czechoslovakia had the lowest infant mortality rate among East bloc countries, at 16.8 per 1,000 live births in 1981. The state granted a 22–26 week maternity leave and paid new mothers 75–90 percent of their income for eighteen weeks and 40–60 percent for an additional four weeks. The state also provided a system of nurseries and day-care centers. Abortion was legalized in 1957, but women had to appear before a regional commission to petition for the procedure. Abortion became the most common form of contraception, since periodic shortages of consumer goods including birth control pills and intrauterine devices made these methods unreliable. Prenatal and postnatal care was provided free by the state.

During the 1970s and 1980s, intellectual women and female artists became involved in the human rights and dissident movements. Women constituted 21 percent of the signatories of Charter 77, the organization that reported on human rights violations in Czechoslovakia, and were well represented among the leadership of the organization. After 1980, there was almost always a woman among the three official spokespersons of Charter 77. Women's rights were a priority to Charter 77, which decried women's economic dependence and relatively lower wages. For example, women were the majority of doctors in Czechoslovakia, but the relative wage of this career fell significantly compared with male-dominated occupations. Individual Czechoslovak women, including singer Marta Kubišová (1930–) and writer Eva Kantůrková (1930–), made contributions in the sphere of human and women's rights.

Cynthia Paces

Further reading

Pech, Stanley Z. *The Czech Revolution of 1848.* Chapel Hill, North Carolina, 1969.

Volet-Jeanneret, Helena. *La Femme bourgeoise á Prague 1860–1895: De la philanthropic á la emancipation.* Geneva, 1988.

Wolchik, Sharon L. and Alfred G. Meyer, eds. *Women, State, and Party in Eastern Europe.* Durham, North Carolina, 1985.

Yedlin, Tova, ed. *Women in Eastern Europe and the Soviet Union.* New York, 1980.

See also Alexander Bach; Charter 77; Education; Charlotte Garrigue; Family; Great Depression; Kremsier/Kroměříž Parliament; Tomáš Masaryk; Božena Němcová; Old Czechs; Revolutions of 1848; Young Czechs

Women in Hungary

Women in Hungary have played a significant role in the country's history and cultural life, although their influence was often exerted indirectly. Some legal protection, including the right to control property, was always guaranteed, but custom assigned the home, child rearing, and cultural pursuits or patronage as their particular spheres. Still a series of "great ladies" punctuate Hungarian history: Sarolt (c. 954–c. 997), mother of Stephen I (St. Stephen, c. 975–1038), brought the allegiance of Transylvania to her son's realm; Katica (Klára) Dobo (sixteenth century) led the women of Eger to repulse the Turkish attack; and Ilona Zrinyi (1643–1703) not only instilled patriotism in her son Ferenc Rákoczi II (1676–1735), who led a war of liberation against the Habsburgs in the early 1700s, but also defended the last independent bastion of the country for several months against the Habsburg forces. Zsuzsanna Lorántffy (c. 1600–1660) was a patron of schools and printing presses during the Reformation. In literature, Lea Ráskai (sixteenth century) and Kata Szidnónia Petrőczi (1662–1708) were important early writers, while Kata Bethlen (1700–1759) contributed to the development of Hungarian prose and the memoir.

The primary preserve of women, however, remained that of transmitters of culture, patrons of arts and learning, founders of schools, and providers of medical care. Teréz Brunszvik (1775–1861) campaigned for equality of opportunity, established schools for the daughters of the nobility, and set up the first kindergartens as early as the 1820s. She considered education for the peasantry and lower classes to be a means of raising their economic status and thus advancing the development

W of the country, so she set up schools for domestic servants also. She was not alone; by the 1840s, a movement to make education available to village girls also took hold, leading to a coeducational school system in the country. Women also took the lead in organizing hospitals and relief to the poor. Most of these activities were the culmination and institutionalization of the work that had been carried out by aristocratic women, particularly in the sixteenth and seventeenth centuries.

The feminist movement began in Hungary at the turn of the century and at first followed the Western European model. It was led by aristocratic and middle-class women such as Countess Blanka Teleki (1806–62). Their goal of political and legal equality led to women receiving the vote in 1920. Events following World War I, however, caused Hungarian women to turn toward more conservative, national values. In the political climate of the 1920s, they concentrated on ensuring that women would continue to be admitted to the universities rather than more radical political goals. Their chief argument again was that educated women were the only guarantee of a cultured future for the nation. In this they were successful; by the 1930s, women were accepted in most highly qualified occupations, including medicine.

The Communist era ushered in contradictions and reversed gains of the earlier years. Although all jobs and positions were open to women in theory, and in fact all were expected to work, the occupations dominated by women paid less than so-called male occupations. While visible at all levels, including politics and the bureaucracy, women did not rise to leading positions or assume real power. Even in education and social work they tended to be in supportive positions. Furthermore, since they were still considered the primary caretakers and chiefly responsible for the household, women were doubly taxed by their ostensible right to work outside the home. Unlike in the past, even educated women could not have domestic help and modern innovations largely did not exist.

Gender divisions and expectations also resulted in women being less involved in opposition politics before 1989 than men. In the environmental and peace groups, however, they did make an impact. A group of young women was largely responsible, for example, for the initial moves against construction of a Danube dam. Dialogue groups and the *"klub"* movement united women at various universities and in the major cities.

Currently two main types of groups offer organized options to women: Women Entrepreneurs and the Feminist Network. The former is closer to Western feminist models as it seeks to achieve equality for women in the masculine world; the latter seeks to change the terms of the debate. The Feminist Network does not exclude men but seeks to represent women's interests and give them a voice in Hungarian society, politics, and cultural life. In charting new paths, urban, more educated women sought to be relieved of some of the burdens of work outside the house and to gain greater influence within the family.

Enikő Molnár Basa

Further reading

Corrin, Chris. *Magyar Women: Hungarian Women's Lives, 1960s–1900s.* New York, 1994.

Eberhardt, Eva. *Women of Hungary.* Brussels, 1991.

Kovács, Mária M. "The Politics of Emancipation in Hungary," in *Women in History—Women's History: Central and Eastern European Perspectives.* Budapest, 1994, 81–85.

Orosz, Lajos, ed. *A Magyar nőnevelés úttörői.* Budapest, 1962.

Takács, Sándor. *Magyarország nagyasszonyai,* 2 vols. Budapest, 1990 (reprint of 1911 ed.).

See also Education; Family

Women in Poland

Women's roles and positions in the family and society in Poland are changing from the patriarchal patterns (division of labor combined with high status in the family) to legal equality (1918) linked (after 1945) with required wage employment, and continuing division of labor.

In the nineteenth century the majority of the Polish population inhabited villages. Rural women prepared necessities for their families, took care of the children, worked as farm laborers, performed different agricultural operations, and cared for the animals. Most of them were illiterate. For those women, little has changed. At present, most rural women still work on family farms while providing child care and performing housekeeping chores. Long hours of hard work contribute to an outflow of young rural women to the cities.

An underdeveloped economy and loss of national independence (1795) aimed the urban women's movements (also the gentry and nobility) toward preserving national culture and the Polish language, and promoting education and Catholicism. Some were active in combat or underground operations, in struggles for national independence as soldiers, such as Emilia Plater (1803–31), couriers, and nurses—trends continued during the two world wars and in the activities of the Solidarity trade union movement (1980–89). The nineteenth century offered limited opportunities for women's education. Some traveled abroad to acquire professional skills, for example, Marie Skłodowska-Curie (1867–1934). Among writers focusing on the "woman's question" were Klementyna Tańska Hoffmanowa (1798–1845); Narcyza Żmichowska (1819–76); Eliza Orzeszkowa (1841–1910); Bolesław Prus (1847–1912); and Zofia Nałkowska (1884–1954).

At the end of the nineteenth century, 75 percent of working women were occupied in domestic services, small business, and clothing and textiles. With the coming of Polish national independence in 1918, women obtained equality of civil rights. In 1921 women in nonagricultural occupations accounted for 28.7 percent of all employees; by 1931 that figure had risen to only 30.8 percent. These figures increased when married women's employment became an economic necessity and a social norm under socialism. In 1950, in the newly socialized economy, women constituted 30.6 percent of all employees; by 1989, that had risen to 46.7 percent, most of them married, with children.

To assure present and future workers' health and qualifications, socialist legislation guaranteed equality for all, full-time employment, free health care and education, and protection for working mothers. Legal abortion was introduced in 1956. Low wages were supplemented by state-subsidized prices, services, health care, and education, as well as allowances for working mothers and (some) for couples. Legally decreed equality did not encourage special interest groups or provide formal platforms for the disenchanted. The only significant official organization for women was the League of Women, a government agency that specialized in solving family-employment conflicts.

In practice, education and employment were gender-segregated, coinciding with the division of labor and with accepting women's family roles as their primary functions. Women selected education (women—comprehensive; men—vocational and technical) and jobs that allowed them to perform their family and occupational roles simultaneously. Men avoided housekeeping and childcare chores. In spite of employed women's higher level of education than men's, the socialist system did not encourage men to share family roles.

Urban women worked in jobs related to child care and housekeeping as their primary labor environment (production of food, textiles and clothing, lower-level positions in education, health care, clerical jobs, and light industries). They were employed in low-profit, low-priority branches of the economy, in menial jobs. Their wages constituted approximately 60–70 percent of men's salaries. This was rationalized by stereotypes of women's special predisposition for specific jobs and their supposed mental and physical limitations in such areas as technical skills and leadership. This resulted in a feminization of occupations, with lower salaries, low positions, and limited career advancement. Women were considered less reliable and more expensive (allowances, maternal leave of absence) employees. They seldom occupied managerial and executive positions, while hiring and promotion practices gave priority to male workers. Women were also involved in "two-shift" jobs, with less afterwork time and leisure than men. Moreover, they became party activists primarily through nominations and quotas. A linkage between executives and party activism was manifested in management positions acquired through party nominations. Women's issues were not included in the Communist Party program, nor were they featured by Solidarity, the 1980s workers' organization, an oversight that still exists in the post-Communist period.

Barbara Łobodzińska

Further reading

Janicka, Krystyna. "Women and Men in the Socio-Occupational Structure: Similarities and Differences." *Polish Sociological Review* 109, no. 1 (1995): 73–94.

Łobodzińska, Barbara. "Love as a Factor in Marital Decisions in Contemporary Poland." *Journal of Comparative Family Studies* 6, no. 1 (1975): 56–73.

————. "Education and Employment of Women in Contemporary Poland." *Journal of Women in Culture and Society* 3, no. 3 (1978): 688–97.

————. "Divorce in Poland: Its Legislation, Distribution and Social Context." *Journal of Marriage and the Family* 45, no. 4 (1983): 927–42.

————. "Urban and Rural Working Women in Poland Today: Between Social Change and Social Conflict," in *Research in the Interweave of Social Roles,* vol. 3, ed. by Helena Z. Lopata and Joseph F. Pleck. Greenwich, Connecticut, 1983: 3–33.

Reske, Irena. "Factors Defining Preferences for Certain Occupations by Women and Occupational Segregation," in *Cross-Currents: East-West, Dialogues on Women and Work,* ed. by Mary Ellen Brown and Michał Rozbicki. Bloomington, Indiana, 1991, 43–52.

Sołołowska, Magdalena. "Some Reflections on the Different Attitudes on Men and Women Towards Work." *International Labour Review* 92, no. 1 (June 1965): 35–50.

Strykowska, Maria. "Women in Management in Poland." *Women's Studies International Forum* 18, no. 1 (January–February 1995): 9–12.

See also Marie Curie; Family; Eliza Orzeszkowa; Bolesław Prus; Solidarity

Women in Romania

Women have been a silent majority in Romanian history. Most of their achievements are not noted in the grand historical narratives—women did not lead armies, have direct access to political power, or even lead independent economic transactions. However, in indirect ways in these areas and through their direct impact on family education, social relations, and culture, Romanian women constitute a significant voice in their country's past.

During the premodern period in Romanian history, women's social roles were confined to the household, as producers in a subsistence family economy and as wives and mothers. They worked side by side with men, performing similar tasks in agriculture and engaging in local artifact production and trade. However, women were not able to gain authority in the local community beyond their nurturing roles in the family. They could not own property, take part in elders' councils, or make any public substantive decisions. The Orthodox Church—the spiritual leader and, in many ways, the highest local social authority—reinforced a patriarchal world view of the present and afterlife.

It was in times of crisis that women received public recognition for their talents and abilities. Names like Queen Marie (1875–1938), wife of King Ferdinand (1865–1927), or Ecaterina Teodoroiu (1895–1918), a sublieutenant in World War I, became symbols of women's assets as potential diplomats, politicians, or military leaders. These individuals served as role models for other Romanian women aspiring to public recognition. However, they also helped to reinforce women's "proper" place in the home, as these individuals' exceptional achievements were identified with their nurturing qualities.

Women who fought for civil and political rights for their gender have not found their way into the history books. Since the 1840s, women like Maria Rosetti (1819–93), a "forty-eighter" liberal (for her activities in the generation of the Revolution of 1848), lobbied on behalf of women's civil rights. After World War I, when women were active both in the war and on the home front, individuals such as Calypso Botez (n.d.) and Elena Meissner (n.d.) turned toward suffrage rights as their main goal. However, these educated, middle-class women were little concerned with the great majority of peasant women and were easily marginalized in the political arena. Elena (Magda) Lupescu (1899–1977), mistress of Carol II (1893–1953), remains the only woman whose name is familiar to all who study interwar Romanian history. Unfortunately, she also became the symbol of corruption and of the limited, often negative impact women had on the public sphere.

Women gained full political rights only in 1945, an empty achievement in a system where political leaders paid only lip service to constitutional democratic practices. The evolution of women's position in Romanian society during the 1945–89 period was marked by an increase in the "double burden"—working full-time while remaining responsible for most household and parenting obligations, as was true in all Soviet-bloc countries. Many scholars give this period little credit for improving women's position in society. Nonetheless, under the Communist regime women gained access to more education and economic power than ever before.

An issue that dominated the discourse over women's position in Communist Romania was birth control legislation. The 1967 anti-abortion decree placed women's bodies under state surveillance, from forced gynecological checkups to public displays of pregnant women. This legislation had an impact on every family—through unwanted pregnancies, health problems resulting from illegal abortions, or even imprisonment for those caught performing such operations. Thus, legalization of abortion on demand was among the first measures passed after Communist leader Nicolae Ceauşescu's (1918–89) execution in December 1989.

Since 1989, women have paid a higher price than men for their country's transition toward a democratic political system and a free-market economy. Their access to public office has been hampered by a debilitating symbol of female ruthlessness and unreliability—the "Elena Ceauşescu syndrome." Stories of Elena Ceauşescu's (c. 1919–89) role behind the scenes during the twenty-five years of her husband's dictatorial reign have pinned on her responsibility for some of the most horrendous policies of the regime. In addition, women have had less access to the means of accumulating capital and fewer connections with trading partners abroad. Furthermore, they make up over 60 percent of the unemployed but less than 5 percent of the political leadership. Nonetheless, many women have awakened to a new consciousness of their self-worth. Presently, over four hundred nongovernmental organizations work with improving women's position in their communities and the larger social fabric.

Maria Bucur

Further reading

Câncea, Paraschiva. *Mişcarea pentru emanciparea femeii în România.* Bucharest, 1976.

Einhorn, Barbara. *Cinderella Goes to Market: Citizenship, Gender, and Women's Movement in East Central Europe.* London, 1993.

Funk, Nanette and Magda Mueller, eds. *Gender Politics and Post-Communism: Reflections from Eastern Europe and the Former Soviet Union.* New York, 1993.

Kligman, Gail. "The Politics of Reproduction in Ceauşescu's Romania: A Case Study in Political Rule." *East European Politics and Societies* 6, no. 3 (1992): 364–418.

See also Carol II; Elena Ceauşescu; Nicolae Ceauşescu; Family; Ferdinand; Health; Magda Lupescu; Marie; Orthodoxy

Women in Yugoslavia

Regardless of their respective ethnic group, Yugoslav women have always led difficult lives. They sent their sons and husbands to defend the country while they stayed home, worked in the fields, and took care of those who remained behind. They were expected to be as tough and brave as their men and capable of taking over and running the household without a male head. A hardworking woman who sacrificed for the benefit of her family was highly respected in her community for being *"pravi muškarac"* (a real man). On the other hand, in times of relative peace, most women were treated as second-class citizens, without any rights except to obey and serve their husbands. The position of women was particularly hard in the areas ruled by the Turks, while in areas dominated by Austria, women's emancipation through education began to take root in the late-eighteenth and especially mid–nineteenth centuries.

In the northern parts of what would become Yugoslavia, the first educated professional women appeared in the second half of the nineteenth century, thanks to the activities of early feminists such as Draga Dejanović (1840–71) in Vojvodina, whose basically patriotic intentions were aimed at the improvement of women's position through education and equal employment opportunity. Among the women who gained prominence in the mid–nineteenth century, were, for example Katarina Ivanović (1811–82), the first Serbian woman painter; Mina Vukomanović-Karadžić (1828–94), a translator of Serbian folk songs in German; and poet, Milica Stojadinović-Srpkinja (1830–77). By the mid-1890s, many women were making contributions, including Jelena Dimitrijević (1862–1945) and Danica Bandić-Telečkova (1871–1950) in literature; Croatian writer Camilla Luzerna (1868–1963), who wrote poems, plays, and essays both in Croatian and in German; and Isidora Sekulić (1887–1958), one of the most outstanding women authors in Yugoslavia.

By the 1870s, women also achieved recognition in some other "male" fields: in higher education, Katarina Milovuk (1844–1909); in medicine, Draga Ljočić (1855–1937), the first woman physician in Serbia and the Balkans; in ethnography, Savka Subotić (1834–1918); in the performing arts, Jovanka Stojković (1855–92), a student of Franz Liszt (1811–86) and an accomplished pianist; and opera singer Milka Trnina (1863–1914) in Zagreb.

WThere were also women among the political activists, literary critics, and translators.

While the early feminists cannot be denied their initial successes in emancipating Yugoslav women, they came mainly from the affluent classes and their goals, at first, did not include the acquisition of political rights for women. When social democratic parties and labor organizations began to form in the Yugoslav lands, their leaders urged women, especially those from the working classes, to unite with workingmen in the struggle for equality and social and political justice. Eventually, however, separate sections for women were formed within each party. Women were thus partially segregated and their activities directed toward supporting the workers' movement led by the men, rather than being men's equal partners. These women were indoctrinated by socialist and, later, communist ideology. They immediately dissociated themselves from "bourgeois" feminists, because the feminists fought against men for the interests of upper-class women alone, within an otherwise unjust social system. By definition, feminists were the enemies of working-class women, who had revolutionary ambitions and wanted to fight together with men, for a new ideal social system in which everyone would have equal rights.

The division and disunity between feminists and social democrats weakened the women's movement in former Yugoslav territories, and continued to hamper women's efforts in the struggle for equal rights even after World War I, when the first Yugoslavia was created. Bourgeois feminist organizations resumed their activities in the early postwar years and became more political after women in Great Britain and the United States obtained their suffrage rights. These political activities abruptly died out, as the new Yugoslav assembly failed to give suffrage rights to women.

In the first Yugoslavia, women had no political and legal rights. They were treated as minors incapable of making any decisions concerning their own lives. Abortions were illegal except when the woman's life was endangered. The Serbian proverb describing women as having "long hair, but short intelligence" was still popular and often quoted to justify exclusion of women from political life and decision-making bodies. Even though many women from all walks of life obtained a college education and the highest degrees at Yugoslav universities and abroad, they still had difficulty in getting highly paid jobs, in being promoted, and in breaking into traditionally male professions, such as law and banking, and into any executive, decision-making positions. While a thin layer of urbanites and intellectuals, at least publicly, expressed progressive views about the place and role of women in society, it was still generally considered that a woman's place was in the home. The talents and creativity of the majority of Yugoslav women remained concentrated on cultural endeavors (education, literature, theater, arts, opera) and on work in various philanthropic and charitable societies that supported orphanages, halfway houses for poor mothers with children, and educational institutions for lower-class women.

Women who wanted to remain involved in political activities after World War I eventually joined the Communist Party and were forced to go underground in the 1930s, when the party became illegal. Like many other Yugoslavs, they too were opposed to the growing threat of fascism, but they also saw the struggle for the so-called democratization of Yugoslavia under Communist rule as the only way to secure a bright future. In 1941, when the Germans occupied Yugoslavia, these women joined Tito's (1892–1980) Partisans. They came out of the war believing that the new regime would change everything, that women would finally obtain total equality with men, and that their joint struggle would be crowned by women's inclusion in all aspects of life of the new Communist state.

Yugoslav women's rights did indeed improve, but their position in society did not. Legally, women received all they were promised by the Communist Party and its leaders in the 1930s, including the right to vote. The Anti-fascist Front of Women of Yugoslavia, founded during World War II as a branch of the Tito's National Liberation Front, was an organization aimed at helping women integrate in the new, postwar Communist society and assume an active role in it. It was expected that women would work side by side with men to rebuild the war-torn country and that they would contribute their fair share to the new economic, cultural, and political order in Communist Yugoslavia. In the first postwar local elections, many women were put on the ballot and elected to various local committees, but they gained equality de jure only in the first constitution of the Federal People's Republic of Yugoslavia (1946). All privileges based on ownership and all forms of political inequality were abolished. Women were given the right to vote, and it was proclaimed that the position of every citizen in the new society would depend solely on his or her own labor. This was supposed to bring about the end of the patriarchal way of life in which the man, who owned the land, was the master, while the woman was expected to be his servant and the mother of his children. Nothing, of course, was further from the truth. Most women had to work outside the home and also take care of the home and the family, but their wages were too low to enable them to pay for decent childcare. While the state provided free childcare centers, they were overcrowded and understaffed, so that many parents soon decided that it was safer to keep their children at home. The institution of grandmothers as full-time babysitters became an indispensable arrangement while raising children. Women, tired after the day's work, had to cook the meals for the next day. They also had to wash the family laundry, iron their husband's and their children's clothes, clean, dust, and buy food, just as in the old days, except that then domestic chores had been the woman's only duties. Moreover, for many years most Yugoslav women did not have modern ranges, dishwashers, washing machines, or dryers; there was no central heating and no hot water tanks, and in winter, wood and coal had to be used to heat the kitchen stove and those in other rooms.

There were, however, some benefits in the new order. Women did gain the freedom to decide whether they wanted to bear a child. Abortions were legalized and performed safely by doctors in hospitals. The costs were covered by medical insurance provided by the state. After childbirth, the woman stayed in the hospital as long as was necessary. All expenses were covered by government insurance. Women were also entitled to up to six months' leave for each childbirth. Their jobs and wages were secure during the leave. The employer could neither fire them nor hire someone else in their place. Women were also protected by law from physically hard jobs in the workplace. They could vote and be elected, but most of the offices to which women were elected were of local rather than state or federal importance. Prominent women in high political positions were few and far between. In the new state, with free education, many women obtained the highest education and excelled in all professions, although key positions in institutions of higher education, factories, enter-

prises, and businesses were held mostly by men. Careers suffered because of multiple obligations in the office and at home. Once again, talented and ambitious Yugoslav women achieved the most in the cultural and educational spheres, which allowed for relatively flexible work schedules, rather than in politics and business.

Despite the problems, many Yugoslav women made their mark. Significantly more women have become high achievers since 1945. Their skills and professional reputations allow them today to compete successfully in international job markets. As a result, a number of them have left Yugoslavia and live as immigrants, permanent residents, or long-term visitors in the United States and in European and Asian countries. Their fields of expertise range from the humanities and social sciences to medicine, engineering, architecture, arts, and even sports.

Biljana Šljivić-Šimšić

Further reading

Drakulić, Slavenka. "Women and the New Democracy in the Former Yugoslavia," in *Gender Politics and Post-Communism: Reflections from Eastern Europe and the Former Soviet Union,* ed. by Nanette Funk and Magda Mueller. New York, 1993, 123–30.

Duhaček, Daša. "Women's Time in the Former Yugoslavia," in *Gender Politics and Post-Communism: Reflections from Eastern Europe and the Former Soviet Union,* ed. by Nanette Funk and Magda Mueller. New York, 1993, 131–37.

Lukić, Jasmina. "Women-Centered Narratives in Contemporary Serbian and Croatian Literatures," in *Engendering Slavic Literatures,* ed. by Pamela Chester and Sibelan Forrester. Bloomington, Indiana, 1996, 223–43.

Milić, Andjelka, "Women and Nationalism in the Former Yugoslavia," in *Gender Politics and Post-Communism: Reflections from Eastern Europe and the Former Soviet Union,* ed. by Nanette Funk and Magda Mueller. New York, 1993, 109–22.

Šljivić-Šimšić, Biljana. "The Beginnings of the Feminist Movement in Nineteenth-Century Serbia." *Serbian Studies* 3, no. 1–2 (Fall–Spring 1984–85): 35–51.

———. "The 'Modest Violets,' Their Varieties and Antipodes in Nineteenth Century Serbian Literature." *Serbian Studies* 1, no. 4 (Spring 1982): 93–116.

———. "The Woman in Serbian Folk Proverbs: On the Material Collected by Vuk St. Karadžić." *Serbian Studies* 1, no. 1 (Spring 1980): 41–50.

See also Antifascism; Communist Party of Yugoslavia; Education; Family; Tito; Zadruga

World War I (1914–18)

In 1914 three great empires dominated Eastern Europe: the German, the Russian, and the Austro-Hungarian. An important, if not preeminent, reason for their going to war in 1914 was to preserve or extend their influence in this geographic area, especially in the Balkans, long a trouble spot for Europe's Great Powers. Austro-Hungarian leaders had reached a consensus that Greater Serbian nationalism posed a mortal threat to their multinational empire. In St. Petersburg, the conviction ruled that Russia's image as the protector of the South Slavs and, indeed, its reputation as a Great Power would be compromised if it failed, as in 1908–09, to react to Austria's humiliation of Serbia in the wake of the assassination of Archduke Franz Ferdinand (1863–1914) in Sarajevo in June 1914. Germany's interests in Eastern Europe were less direct, but it was determined to support its Austrian ally and to prevent expansion of Russian influence.

But as the fighting unfolded, and with all the states of the region caught up in the conflict, a war over Great Power interests in eastern Europe was increasingly challenged by a new conflict: a war of national liberation on behalf of the various ethnic groups under alien domination. Both the Central Powers and the Allies, anxious to improve their chances of victory, did not hesitate to stimulate the aspirations of these peoples. Secret treaties encouraged the creation of a Greater Serbia, a Greater Bulgaria, and a Greater Romania, that is, enlarged states. But perhaps even more decisive in transforming the conflict in eastern Europe into a war of national liberation was the encouragement of destabilizing movements within these three doomed empires. The Central Powers from the beginning of the war supported separatist and revolutionary elements within the Russian Empire. The Allied powers did the same for the Austro-Hungarian Empire. Although internal agitation in the latter was muted until the later stages of the war, émigré nationalists, especially Czech and South Slav, were active abroad and eventually succeeded in getting Allied recognition for all or part of their programs.

The Allies soon came to regret the far-reaching commitments made by secret treaties and émigré agendas, often in contradiction to one another and certainly without reasoned consideration of their consequences. But when the Allies sought to back away from these commitments, the chaos that attended the end of the war gave the peoples of Eastern Europe opportunities to realize their fulfillment anyway. With or without the sanction of the victorious powers and sometimes with force of arms, many of the former subjects of these three now defunct empires achieved their independence. Finland, Estonia, Latvia, Lithuania, Poland, Czechoslovakia, and Yugoslavia (the Kingdom of Serbs, Croats, and Slovenes) were restored or newly created. Romania emerged greatly enlarged. Unfortunately, unresolved conflicts festered between many of these new nations themselves. To these problems were added the resentments of the defeated nations, especially Germany, Soviet Russia, Hungary, and Bulgaria. To an extent no one had imagined, World War I dramatically transformed eastern Europe. Whether these results are judged positively or negatively and despite all that has happened since, World War I remains the great determining event for the modern history of the area.

Glenn E. Torrey

Further reading

Seton-Watson, Hugh and Christopher Seton-Watson. *The Making of a New Europe.* Seattle, Washington, 1981.

Stone, Norman. *The Eastern Front 1914–1917.* New York, 1975.

Sukiennicki, Wiktor. *East Central Europe during World War I: From Foreign Domination to National Independence.* Boulder, Colorado, 1984.

See also Czech Mafia; Franz Ferdinand; Great Powers; Greater Romania; Greater Serbia; Nationalism; Paris Peace Conference; Pittsburgh Agreement; Polish Legions; Yugoslav Committee

World War II (1939–45)

The origins of World War II can be traced to the Paris Peace Conferences following World War I, which not only redrew the map of Eastern Europe but in large part laid the foundation for the rise of Adolf Hitler (1889–1945) and National Socialism in Germany. Although the treaties created a number of new nation-states in Central and Eastern Europe based on the concept of self-determination, many ethnic and national boundaries remained contentious. In March 1938 the *Anschluss* saw Germany annex Austria. Hitler next began complaining that the 3.5 million Germans living in the Sudetenland were being abused by the Czechoslovak government. When Czechoslovak president Edvard Beneš (1884–1948) refused to grant autonomy to the Sudeten Germans, the Western powers feared a general war, and at the Munich conference (September 1938), agreed to turn over the German-speaking areas of the Sudetenland to Germany. In March 1939 German troops abruptly annexed the rest of Czechoslovakia. When Hitler began to assert that the German minority in Poland was being repressed by the Polish government, France and Britain finally abandoned their policy of appeasement and guaranteed the independence of Poland, Romania, Greece, and Turkey.

Forced to reassess his original goals, Hitler signed a nonaggression pact with the Soviet Union in August 1939. Soviet Premier Josef Stalin (1879–1953) was convinced that he would eventually have to face the German war machine, but he hoped to postpone this as long as possible. In a secret clause to this treaty, Hitler also agreed to Stalin's demands for the Baltic states, eastern Poland, and Bessarabia. With this agreement, German and Soviet troops conquered and partitioned Poland in the autumn of 1939. In 1940 German forces seized Denmark and Norway, smashed through the Low Countries, and captured France in a mere six weeks.

Romania, Hungary, and Yugoslavia now signed treaties of friendship with Germany. In the spring of 1941, a Serbian coup deposed the Yugoslav regent, pro-German Prince Paul (1893–1976), replacing him with the seventeen-year-old anti-German King Peter (1923–70). When Peter openly repudiated the Nazi alliance, German troops invaded the Balkans, taking control of both Yugoslavia and Greece. This effectively delayed the attack on the Soviet Union until June 22. Although three million German troops caught the Red Army by surprise and by late fall had advanced to Leningrad and the outskirts of Moscow, by December, the Red Army, aided by the Russian winter, finally brought the German advance to a halt.

Despite the setback, Hitler was still confident of victory. By August 1942, German troops, aided by forces from Hungary and Romania, were fighting in the streets of Stalingrad, while other German units raced toward the oil fields of the Caucasus. The Battle of Stalingrad, however, signaled a reversal of German fortunes in Europe. After penetrating the German flanks guarded by Romanian, Hungarian, and Italian troops, in February 1943 Soviet forces destroyed the German Sixth Army. At the same time, German troops were bogged down in Yugoslavia in a bitter struggle with Tito's (1892–1980) Partisans.

With the change in the tide of war, the need for tighter coordination among the Allies became apparent, leading to the Tehran Conference. Meeting at Tehran for the first time in November and December 1943, Stalin, Franklin Roosevelt (1882–1945), and Winston Churchill (1874–1965) reached no final decisions, but the conference did engender a feeling of cooperation and optimism.

Stalin, however, was determined to create a buffer zone on the USSR's western border to prevent Germany from ever again threatening the Soviet Union. In December 1943 Beneš signed a treaty of friendship with the Soviet Union, and in the spring of 1944 the Red Army established "friendly" governments in Romania and Bulgaria. Concerned that Eastern Europe was exchanging German for Soviet control, Churchill faced Stalin in Moscow in October 1944, where the two leaders concluded the Percentages Agreement, laying the foundation for the postwar division of Europe by the Iron Curtain.

By January 1945, Soviet troops had entered Warsaw and embarked on one final push, penetrating deep into Germany itself. This was the situation when Stalin, Roosevelt, and Churchill met for the second and last time at Yalta. The question of Poland dominated the conference, as Stalin had already installed a new puppet government in Lublin, in opposition to the Polish government-in-exile in London. A Declaration of Liberated Europe was issued in which the three powers agreed to establish governments in liberated areas that were responsible to the people and democratic in nature. Obviously this did not happen in Eastern Europe, but the Western democracies were in no position to oppose the Red Army. The Yalta conference also agreed to divide postwar Germany into four zones of occupation, laying the groundwork for the later separation of Germany into two states and heralding the start of the Cold War.

Joel D. Benson

Further reading

Bullock, Alan. *Hitler and Stalin.* New York, 1992

Keegan, John. *The Second World War.* New York, 1989.

Taylor, A.J.P. *The Origins of World War II.* New York, 1962.

Weinberg, Gerhard L. *A World at Arms: A Global History of World War II.* Cambridge, Massachusetts, 1994.

Wright, Gordon. *The Ordeal of Total War, 1939–1945.* New York, 1968.

See also *Anschluss;* Antifacism; Auschwitz; Barbarossa; Winston Churchill; Generalgouvernement; Reinhard Heydrich; Adolf Hitler; Holocaust; Katyn Forest; Lidice; Lublin Committee; Molotov-Ribbentrop Pact; Munich Pact; Nazi-Polish War; Percentages Agreement; Red Army; Stalin; Sudeten Crisis; Tito; Vienna Awards; Warsaw Uprising; Yalta

Wrocław

Largest city of Lower Silesia (637,000 population) and the seat of a voievodeship (province). Wrocław (German, Breslau) originated in the tenth century on Tum (Toum) Island, one of several in the channel of the Oder River. The highly defensive settlement at the river crossing attracted several local and international routes. The old Amber Route ran through Wrocław. Originally the capital of a principality ruled by the Silesian branch of the Polish Piast dynasty, the town passed successively to Bohemia (1335), the Habsburg Empire (1526), Prussia (1742), and Poland (1945).

After destruction by the Mongols (1241), several fires, and the ravages of the Black Death epidemic (1349), Wrocław began unabated growth, mainly on the left river bank, facilitated by surrounding fertile soils that supplied agricultural products for the growing population and trade. In the nineteenth century the coming of railroads (1842) and proximity to Upper Silesia contributed to the development of major industries and commerce.

Wrocław was largely destroyed during World War II because of stubborn German resistance to the advancing Red Army, but the postwar reconstruction of its physical plant returned the city to its previous significance. Presently its industries include nonferrous metal, machinery, building and repair of railroad cars, textiles, garment manufacturing, polygraphic, food processing, and modern electrotechnical and electronics. Wrocław is a transportation hub, with eleven railroad lines, a river port with a river shipyard, numerous bus lines, and an airport.

The city is also a major cultural center. Its university and several colleges are known as centers of applied sciences. Several Gothic and baroque monuments (the cathedral, several churches, the town hall, numerous palaces housing the university, and various museums), six theaters, a concert hall, various cultural service institutions, and the largest zoo in Poland are spread throughout the city.

Abraham Melezin

Further reading

Janiszewski, Michał. *Geograficzne warunki powstawania miast polskich.* Lublin, 1991, 153–55.

Kaczmarczyk Z., M. Suchocki, and Z. Wojciechowski, eds. *The Lands of the Older Poland,* I, part 2. Wrocław, 1949.

Wyspiański, Stanisław (1869–1907)

Polish painter, dramatist, poet, and reformer of theater. Wyspiański studied at the Kraków School of Fine Arts under Jan Matejko (1838–93), at the Jagiellonian University in Kraków, and abroad, mainly in Paris. He became the most eminent artist and playwright of the Young Poland era (a movement often associated with modernism and decadence), and one of the greatest, most innovative, versatile personalities in the history of Polish culture. His activities included painting, drawing, pastel, scenography, stained glass, murals, interior design, book illustration, furniture, and fabric design. His style of artistic expression combined realism with features typical of Art Nouveau, characterized by the employment of flowing lines, stylized plants, contoured flat surfaces of vivid color (in painting and stained glass), and decorative use of folklore motifs. However, elements of expressionism, modernism, and symbolism are also evident in his *œuvre*. Among his most outstanding works are the wall painting (1896) and stained-glass windows (1897–1902) in the St. Francis Church in Kraków. Expressiveness and dynamism distinguish the stained glass with the God-Father representation. Wyspiański attained fame for poetic pastel drawings of children, his wife, and self-portraits rendered with subtle though expressive curved lines. This collection of pictures includes the cycle *Macierzyństwo* (*Maternity,* 1905).

Wyspiański's achievements as a dramatist were also significant for Polish literature. His plays, usually symbolic, confront contemporary situations with a mystical vision of the Polish past, and referred to the great romantic literature. *Wesele* (*The Wedding,* 1901), ranks among the best national dramas. His other notable works are *Warszawianka* (*Varsovienne,* 1898), *Wyzwolenie* (*Liberation,* 1903), and *Noc Listopadowa* (*November Night,* 1904).

Marta Tobolczyk

Further reading
Hutnikiewicz, Artur. *Młoda Polska.* Warsaw, 1995.
Leksykon malarstwa. Warsaw, 1995.
Suchodolski, Bogdan. *A History of Polish Culture.* Warsaw, 1986.
Wałek, Janusz, *Świat Wyspiańskiego.* Warsaw, 1994.

See also Folklore; Jan Matejko; Polish Art; Polish Culture; Polish Literature; Young Poland

Wyszyński, Stefan (1901–81)

Roman Catholic primate of Poland. In January 1953 Bishop Wyszyński became a cardinal. With the purpose of normalizing the tense relationship between the church and Poland's Communist authorities, Cardinal Wyszyński signed, in the name of the Polish Episcopate, an agreement with the state (1950) better defining the church's legal standing in Poland. This agreement, failing to protect the church, prompted the Episcopate to issue a memorandum entitled "Non possumus" (May 8, 1953), defending the church and society. The regime's response to this act was to arrest Wyszyński on September 25, 1953, and intern him for three years. On October 26, 1956, as part of the events related to the first steps of de-Stalinization of the Polish United Workers Party, he was released and returned to his former position. With his return, a new agreement with the state was signed in November 1956 recognizing the church's independent status within Poland. Considered by many Poles as the most important accomplishment of Wyszyński's life was the program "Wielka Nowenna" (Great Novena), which celebrated a thousand years of Polish Catholism. Wyszyński, popularly known as the "Cardinal of a thousand years," is also remembered for his support of Karol Wojtyła (later Pope John Paul II [1920–]) and his patronization of Solidarity, the Polish trade union movement.

Peter Lavelle

Further reading
Micewski, Andrzej. *Cardinal Wyszyński.* New York, 1984.
Michnik, Adam. *The Church and the Left.* Chicago, 1993.
Wyszyński, Stefen Cardinal. *A Freedom Within.* New York, 1983.

See also Catholicism; De-Stalinization; John Paul II; Solidarity

Xenopol, Alexandru D. (1847–1920)

Romanian historian. Born near Iaşi, Xenopol was the son of an immigrant schoolmaster. Xenopol received doctorates (1871) in law from Berlin and philosophy from Giessen. At the four hundredth anniversary celebration of Putna Monastery in 1871, Xenopol came to national attention by delivering the prize speech, an impassioned urging of Romanian unity. In Iaşi, he became a public prosecutor, history instructor at the Academic Institute, and recording secretary of the Junimea Society, the Romanian cultural and literary association. However, his seriousness contrasted with Junimea's traditionally lighthearted style. This contributed to his break with the society in 1878.

Xenopol's first historical monograph, the two-volume *History of Russian-Turkish Relations 1711–1877* (1880), identified Russia as Romania's most threatening enemy, a recurring theme in his writing. In 1888 he published the first of six annual volumes of *History of Romanians from Trajan's Dacia,* his great patriotic synthesis of Romanian history to 1859; two additional volumes covered the reign of Prince Alexandru Ioan Cuza (1820–73), the first prince of the United Principalities of Moldavia and Wallachia. After an appointment as professor, he became rector of the University of Iaşi in 1898. Among many other honors, he was elected to the Romanian Academy (1893) and to be a corresponding member of the French Institute (1900).

Xenopol argued for a scientific history studying unique events, not natural categories, and making observations about reality, not general laws. He viewed historical reality as the product of four principles: constant factors such as climate and race; historical conditions, the specific contexts of an event; historical series, the sequence of events that result from the interaction of constant factors and historical conditions; and historical forces that produce and define the historicity of a series of events. Echoing contemporary scientific thought, he identified evolution as such a force of history, refining the material into the organic and ultimately the spiritual. Both his Romanian history and his philosophy were challenged during his lifetime by younger historians, including his former student and most famous Romanian historian, Nicolae Iorga (1871–1940), who distanced themselves from Xenopol's enthusiasms and conclusions.

Ernest H. Latham Jr.

Further reading

Hiemstra, Paul A. *Alexandru D. Xenopol and the Development of Romanian Historiography.* New York, 1987.

Hitchins, Keith. *Rumania: 1866–1947.* Oxford, 1994.

Michelson, Paul E. "Themes in Modern and Contemporary Romanian Historiography," in *East European History,* ed. by Stanislav J. Kirschbaum. Columbus, Ohio, 1988, 27–40.

Zub, Alexandru. *A. D. Xenopol: Biobibliografie.* Bucharest, 1973.

See also Alexandru Ioan Cuza; Nicolae Iorga; Junimea; United Principalities

Xoxe, Koci (1911–49)

Albanian Communist. Born in Greece, Xoxe went to work in his father's shop as an artisan after

X completing five years of elementary school. In 1931 he became a member of a workers' association, Puna (Work), which had just been formed in the city of Korçë. Four years later, he became the secretary of the organization and was arrested twice for organizing workers.

When the Italians occupied Albania in April 1939, Xoxe actively participated in organizing Albanians against the foreign occupiers. He was arrested three times as an antifascist, spending a year in jail.

Xoxe became one of the founders of the Communist Party of Albania and became a member of its Provisional Central Committee. At the first conference of the party, he was elected a member of the Politburo and organizational secretary of the party. During World War II, Xoxe was named to the General Staff of the army and, at the Congress of Permet, held on May 24, 1944, he became a member of the Anti-Fascist Council.

After the war, Xoxe became vice premier and minister in charge of internal security. During the late 1940s, he was given the military title of lieutenant general. His other duties included general director for security and defense; vice president of the Democratic Front of Albania; and special prosecutor for so-called war criminals. However, he soon began to have major differences with Albanian Communist leader Enver Hoxha (1908–85), and this led him to criticize Hoxha for being anti-Yugoslav and pro-Soviet.

At the Eleventh Plenum of the party's Central Committee held in June 1948, and at the First Party Congress held in November of the same year, Xoxe was condemned as a traitor to both the party and the Albanian people. In 1949 he was executed. In the late 1950s Tito (1892–1980) and Khrushchev (1894–1971) both tried to rehabilitate Xoxe but to no avail.

Mirvet S. Muca

Further reading

Dilo, Jani. *The Communist Party Leadership in Albania.* Washington, D.C., 1961.

Enver Hoxha and Ramiz Alia's Speech at the Plenum of the Central Committee of the Albanian Party of Labor. Tirana, 1964.

Prifti, Peter. *Socialist Albania since 1944.* Cambridge, Massachusetts, 1978.

Secretariat Inostranik Poslova (Secretariat of Foreign Affairs). *The White Book.* Belgrade, 1949.

See also Communist Party of Albania; Enver Hoxha; Tito

Y

Yalta Conference

Meeting of the Big Three Allied leaders—U.S. President Franklin Roosevelt (1882–1945), British Prime Minister Winston Churchill (1874–1965), and Soviet Premier Josef Stalin (1879–1953) on the Crimean peninsula in the USSR on February 4–11, 1945. The Yalta conference marked the high point of cooperation among the wartime Allies. They coordinated strategy for the final defeat of Germany and issued the Crimea Declaration (or Declaration on Liberated Europe), which reaffirmed the principles of the Atlantic Charter and the Casablanca Conference. Protracted negotiations produced agreements on a number of key issues: the Allies would divide defeated Germany into four occupation zones, including one for France; the USSR would receive substantial reparations from Germany and its allies as compensation for massive war damage; the Western powers recognized the Soviet-backed government of Poland (the "Lublin Poles," though with the addition of "democratic elements" from Poland and some Western-backed "London" Poles) and Stalin promised to facilitate free elections there; the Soviet Union promised to enter the war against Japan after the final defeat of Germany and would receive control over the Kurile Islands, the southern half of Sakhalin Island, the Manchurian Railway (jointly with China), and the strategic ports of Darien and Port Arthur; and the Allies would create a new United Nations to foster peace in the postwar world. The Big Three also confirmed their earlier agreement that Allied citizens liberated from Axis control be returned to their respective homelands. This provision would later obligate Western governments forcibly to repatriate Soviet citizens to the USSR against their will.

At the time, the outcome of this conference seemed a major success for American policy. Roosevelt had secured the three most important items to him: the United Nations, Soviet participation in the Pacific war, and Stalin's promise to establish democratic governments in Poland and elsewhere in liberated Eastern Europe. Stalin was unable to secure his goal of an even more westward relocation of the German-Polish border or for an exorbitant level of reparations from Germany. Some historians and politicians have accused Roosevelt of "selling out" Eastern Europe to Stalin. Yet, with the Red Army in actual occupation of most of Eastern European countries and the American administration and public unwilling to precipitate a new war over these issues, Roosevelt had little leverage. Moreover, such criticism presupposes the collapse of the Grand Alliance and the onset of the Cold War—events that were not foregone conclusions at Yalta.

Teddy J. Uldricks

Further Reading

Buhite, Russell D. *Decisions at Yalta: An Appraisal of Summit Diplomacy.* Wilmington, Delaware, 1986.

Clemens, Diane Shaver. *Yalta.* London, 1970.

Mastny, Vojtech. *Russia's Road to the Cold War.* New York, 1979.

U.S. Department of State. *Foreign Relations of the United States: The Conferences at Malta and Yalta, 1945.* Washington, D.C., 1955.

Yergin, Daniel. *Shattered Peace: The Origins of the Cold War and the National Security State.* Boston, 1977.

See also Winston Churchill; Cold War; Lublin Committee; Red Army; Stalin

Young Czechs

Dominant Czech political party in the late nineteenth and early twentieth centuries. The Young Czechs (*Mladočeši*) emerged as a faction within the Czech National Party in 1863 and established themselves as an independent National Liberal Party in 1874 as advocates of Czech national autonomy, civil liberties, and economic development. Although they differed little in age with their more conservative counterparts, the Old Czechs, the Young Czechs reflected a broader spectrum of Czech society and advocated a more radical defense of Czech national rights.

In December 1874 the Young Czechs split from the Old Czechs over the latter's policy of passive resistance and boycott in light of the Czechs' failure to obtain "internal independence" comparable to that given the Hungarians in the *Ausgleich* (Compromise) of 1867, which created the Dual Monarchy of Austria-Hungary. Four years later, the two rejoined to work toward the creation of a mutual national agenda. The Young Czechs emerged as the dominant Czech political party in the Austrian Reichsrat (parliament) in 1891, in which they appealed to public resentment of the Old Czechs for having compromised the administrative unity of Bohemia by making an agreement with German liberals to dampen the nationality conflict and retard political democratization. More stridently patriotic than the Old Czechs, the Young Czechs typically attracted more Czech voters in more populous, industrialized, and urban Bohemia than in Moravia, especially with the extension of male suffrage to taxpayers who paid "five gulden" or more in property taxes. As such, they became the leading Czech party in the Bohemian diet after the elections of 1895.

In cooperation with the Conservative Great Landowners and other parties, the Young Czechs in 1897 persuaded Minster President Kazimierz Badeni (1846–1909) to issue ordinances making the Czech language the equal of German in all operations of the civil government in Bohemia and Moravia. But German riots against these ordinances forced Franz Joseph (1830–1916) to cancel them and dismiss Badeni. The subsequent Young Czech loss of electoral support accelerated the emergence of a multiparty system of nine Czech political parties by the turn of the century.

Although the Young Czechs lacked leaders of the stature of Old Czechs such as historian František Palacký (1798–1876) and physiologist Jan Evangelista Purkyně (1787–1869), or later Czech statesmen such as Tomáš G. Masaryk (1850–1937), their leaders typically were public spirited and highly respected professionals and businessmen. Notable were Emanuel Engel (1844–1907), physician, poet, and longtime party chairman; František Tilšer (1825–1913), professor of mathematics at the Prague Polytechnic Institute who was an outspoken critic of Habsburg policies and an outspoken advocate of civil liberties; and the brothers Edvard (1827–1907) and Julius Grégr (1831–96). Edvard, a physician and former student of Tilšer, and Julius, for thirty years editor of *Národní listy* (*National News*), were the principal spokesmen for the party's radical and anticlerical wing, opposed to cooperation with the Conservative Great Landowners.

With the introduction of universal male suffrage in 1905 to elections to the lower house of the Reichsrat, the Young Czechs ceased to be the leading Czech political party. They lost most of their rural constituency to the Czech Agrarian Party and most lower-middle-class voters to the Czech National Socialist Party. Both these parties adopted Young Czech anticlericalism and advocacy of greater Czech national autonomy. Among their leaders were many former Young Czechs. The Young Czech moderates, whose spokesmen included Karel Kramář (1860–1937) and Alois Rašín (1867–1923), made party policy until the outbreak of World War I. Though the Young Czechs made no further gains in enlarging Czech national autonomy or in advancing civil liberties, they did protect the work of Czech self-governmental institutions in districts and communes. Apologists for the Habsburg monarchy have often caricatured the Young Czechs as nationalistic radicals bent on obstructing paternalistic authoritarian rule and have thereby overlooked the successful Czech promotion of economic development and self-governmental responsibility. Marxist historians have also downplayed Young Czech advocacy of individual liberty and freedom of the press by suggesting that "bourgeois" class interests conditioned these and other Young Czech goals.

Bruce M. Garver

Further Reading

Garver, Bruce M. *The Young Czech Party 1874–1901 and the Emergence of a Multi-Party System.* New Haven, Connecticut, 1978.

Malíř, Iiří. *Od spolků k moderním politickým stranám: Vývoj politických stran na Moravě v letech 1848–1914.* Brno, 1996.

Urban, Otto. *Česká společnost, 1848–1918.* Prague, 1982.

Zacek, Joseph F. *Palacký: The Historian as Scholar and Nationalist.* The Hague, 1970.

See also *Ausgleich;* Kazimierz Badeni; Dual Monarchy; Edvard Grégr; Julius Grégr; Karel Kramář; Tomáš G. Masaryk; Old Czechs; František Palacký; Alois Rašín

Young Poland

Primarily a literary movement among a generation of young Polish writers at the fin de siècle that rebelled against recognized forms of art and literature and was often associated with modernism and decadence. Paralleling the Young German and Young Scandinavian movements, these writers may be considered the founders of modern Polish literature. The movement was shaped both by influences from abroad and by native traditions. In 1887 Zenon Przesmycki (1861–1944) edited the Warsaw journal *Życie* (*Life*), publishing the writings of Poe (1809–49), Baudelaire (1821–67), Swinburne (1837–1909), and others. To the young readers and contributors to *Życie,* the political philosophy of positivism, which emphasized scientific methodology, seemed a defeat; thus they returned to certain aspects of the romantic tradition to the extent that some scholars even speak of neo-romanticism rather than Young Poland.

The foremost figure of the early days of Young Poland was Stanisław Przybyszewski (1868–1927), who took over the editorship of *Życie* and moved it to Kraków. With their emphasis on sexuality and psychological drama, Przybyszewski's writings ignored convention and set the tone for the growing movement. All aspects of literature were affected: poetry (Kazimierz Tetmajer [1865–1940], Jan Kasprowicz [1860–1926], Bolesław Leśmian [1878–1937], and Leopold

Staff [1878–1957]); drama (Stanisław Wyspiański [1869–1907]); prose (Stefan Żeromski [1864–1925], Władysław Reymont [1867–1925]); and criticism (Stanisław Brzozowski [1878–1911]).

In terms of social origin, the Young Poland movement reflected the changes sweeping Polish society at the end of the nineteenth century. Especially among the poets was an increasing prominence of youths from peasant or Jewish backgrounds, rather than from the traditional intelligentsia. Women such as actress Gabriela Zaspolska (1857–1921) and portrait painter Olga Boznańska (1865–1940) also made important contributions to the movement.

Peter Wozniak

Further Reading

Klimaszewski, Bolesław, ed. *An Outline History of Polish Culture.* Warsaw, 1984.

Miłosz, Czesław. *The History of Polish Literature.* Berkeley, California, 1969.

See also Jan Kasprowicz; Polish Literature; Positivism; Stanisław Wyspiański; Stefan Żeromski

Young Turks

Ottoman Turkish nationalists and state reformers. Consisting of many opposition groups formed within and without the Ottoman Empire during much of the reign of Sultan Abdul Hamid II (1842–1918), these various movements came together in a loose-knit coalition commonly known as the Young Turks. The Young Turks came from different backgrounds and expressed their opposition in different ways, but generally they shared the common goals of constitutionalism, Ottomanism, and an end to absolutist rule. Although they were divided on the extent to which Ottoman political and social systems required change, they agreed that major reforms were needed to save the empire from collapse.

While exiled intellectuals debated the nature of yet unrealized reforms, within the empire itself one particular Young Turk organization, the Committee of Union and Progress (CUP), penetrated state institutions, making inroads into the Ottoman army. A number of secret military societies emerged to support the CUP's agenda, including the Society of Liberty, first organized in 1905 as the Fatherland Society by the young officer Mustafa Kemal (later Kemal Atatürk, 1881–1938).

Within a few years, the Society of Liberty established significant influence in the Third Army Corps stationed in Ottoman Macedonia. Discontent had been growing for some time among the officers of the Third Corps, who had witnessed the failure of Abdul Hamid's regime to restore order in Macedonia, where Bulgarian, Greek, and Serb bands continued to operate in defiance of Ottoman authority. Nonetheless, the Young Turk officers did not wish to launch a violent revolution. Instead, their chief goal was to compel the sultan to restore the constitution. Nevertheless, a spontaneous revolt broke out in June 1908 when the Young Turks learned that the sultan's secret police had discovered their organization.

The Third Corps marched on Constantinople and forced Abdul Hamid to agree to the demands of the CUP in July 1908. Thereafter, the Young Turks, in concert with the military, exercised power over the state. Once in control of the state, the Young Turks abandoned their principles of freedom and equality in favor of Turkish hegemony. At any rate, they were unsuccessful in their efforts to reform and save the empire. Increasing nationalism and Turkification policies alienated and antagonized the empire's non-Muslim populations. Finally, their military unpreparedness and poor leadership led to the defeat and collapse of the empire in the First Balkan War (1912–13) and World War I (1914–18), respectively. Still, the Young Turks did establish the official foundations of Turkish national identity and the Turkish republic, which emerged as the successor of the Ottoman Empire in the 1920s.

Alexandros K. Kyrou

Further Reading

Hanioglu, M. Sukru. *The Young Turks in Opposition.* New York, 1995.
Ramsaur, Ernest E., Jr. *The Young Turks: Prelude to the Revolt of 1908.* Beirut, 1965.

See also Abdul Hamid II; Balkan Wars; Macedonia; Ottoman Empire; World War I

Ypsilantis, Alexandros Konstantinos (1792–1828)

Greek officer in the Russian army who precipitated the Greek War for Independence when he launched an unsuccessful armed invasion of the Danubian Principalities in March 1821. Ypsilantis was born in the Phanar (Greek) district of Constantinople in 1792. His father was the Ottoman-appointed *hospodar* (governor) of Wallachia when he provided assistance to the Serbian revolt of 1804, an act that led to his deposition and flight to Russia in 1806. In Russia, young Alexandros graduated from the prestigious Household Cavalry of the Imperial Guards in 1810, fought in the Napoleonic Wars with distinction, became aide-de-camp to Alexander I (1777–1825) in 1816, and, at the age of twenty-five, rose to the rank of major general. In April 1820 Ypsilantis accepted the leadership of the Filiki Etairia (Society of Friends), the radical Greek secret society in Odessa dedicated to the violent liberation of Greece from Ottoman rule. Ypsilantis's campaign to liberate Greece began on March 6, 1821, when he led an armed insurrection in Moldavia with naive expectations of support from the Russian military, Serbs, Bulgarians, and Romanians. Unfortunately, Russia condemned the incursion while the indigenous Romanian and Bulgarian populations greeted Ypsilantis's calls to "fight for the motherland" with apathy. With all lost, Ypsilantis fled to Austria, where he was imprisoned until 1827. He died in Vienna on January 31, 1828.

Gregory L. Bruess

Further Reading

Clogg, Richard. *A Short History of Modern Greece,* 2d ed. Cambridge, 1986.
Dakin, Douglas. *The Struggle for Greek Independence, 1821–1833.* London, 1973.
Prousis, Theophilus C. *Russian Society and the Greek Revolution.* DeKalb, Illinois, 1994.

See also Alexander I; Filiki Etairia; Greek Revolution; Tudor Vladimirescu.

Yugoslav Committee

Committee organized during World War I to promote Yugoslav unity. The Yugoslav Committee, a key player in the birth of Yugoslavia, was the creation of Ante Trumbić (1868–1938) and other South Slavs in the Habsburg monarchy. Unhappy with Austrian and Hungarian rule, they had supported political unity among the South Slav peoples. With the outbreak of World War I, Trumbić resolved to seek union with Serbia and Montenegro in a South Slav state. Fleeing abroad to Italy then Britain, he founded the Yugoslav Committee in May 1915 to promote his vision of Yugoslavia—an equal partnership for all the state's peoples.

The Yugoslav Committee found agreement with the Serbs difficult despite their common goal. It feared that Serbia—one of the first independent states in the Balkans—would claim the leading role in the new entity or abandon the Yugoslav idea for purely Serbian goals, such as the acquisition of Bosnia-Hercegovina. Following the disclosure of the Treaty of London in April 1915, which granted Italy territorial concessions in the region in return for Rome's entrance into the war, Serbian prime minister Nikola Pašić (1845–1926) outraged committee members when he conceded historic Croatian territory to satisfy Italy's predominant interest in the Adriatic. Still, without some formal arrangement with Serbia, the committee could not achieve its objective, for its members were citizens of Austria-Hungary, an enemy power.

By June 1917, circumstances favored the committee. Following serious military and diplomatic setbacks, Pašić suddenly found agreement with representatives of the Habsburg lands useful and summoned Trumbić to Corfu for talks. The result was the Corfu Declaration, a plan for the future Yugoslavia. This document met the committee's requirements insofar as it stipulated equality of flags, religion, and language; the question of state organization was to be resolved later.

Despite this public show of unity, the Yugoslav Committee worried that Pašić might yet abandon the Habsburg Slavs or quietly craft a Serbian-dominated state. It therefore lobbied the Allies for recognition as an allied power, hoping to force Serbia to agree to the committee's conditions prior to formal union. Despite the help of prominent European friends such as British scholar R.W. Seton-Watson (1879–1951), the committee's efforts were unavailing. Both Serbia and Italy opposed recognition; unlike the Czechs and the Poles, the committee had no military successes with which to buttress its claim.

Ultimately, the chaos attending the collapse of the monarchy decided the terms of the union of Habsburg Serbs, Croats, and Slovenes with Serbia in December 1918. Yet the wisdom of the committee's vision—a federal Yugoslavia—would be reaffirmed repeatedly in the destructive strife produced by Serbian centrist rule.

Brigit Farley

Further Reading

Haumant, Emile. *La Formation de l'Yougoslavie.* Paris, 1930.

Paulova, Milada. *Jugoslavenski odbor.* Zagreb, 1925.

Pavelić, Ante Smith. *Dr. Ante Trumbić: Problemi hrvatsko-srpskih odnosa.* Munich, 1959.

Šepić, Dragovan. *Supilo diplomat: Rad Frana Supila u emigraciji, 1914–1917 godina.* Zagreb, 1961.

Stokes, Gale. "The Role of the Yugoslav Committee," in *The Creation of Yugoslavia, 1914–1919,* ed. by Dmitrije Djordjević and Stephen Fischer-Galati. Santa Barbara, California, 1980.

See also Corfu, Declaration of; Nikola Pašić; R.W. Seton-Watson; Ante Trumbić

Yugoslav Congress

Meeting held on May 6, 1915, in Niš, Serbia, which represents a controversial milestone in the creation of the first Yugoslavia. It marked one of the first instances of formal cooperation between the Serbian government and representatives of South Slavic peoples from the Habsburg monarchy, some of whom had formed the Yugoslav Committee.

The congress convened in Niš following the premature disclosure of the Treaty of London, in which the Allied nations intended to buy Italy's entrance into World War I with promises of territorial concessions in the peacemaking. Because some of the concessions involved the transfer of historically South Slav lands to Italy, both Serbian and Habsburg South Slav leaders became alarmed and decided to make a show of solidarity.

Several thousand people attended the Niš meeting, including residents of Serbia, Habsburg émigrés, and official representatives of Serbia and the Habsburg South Slavs. They heard Yugoslav Committee member Franjo Supilo (1870–1917) proclaim his support for the unity of all Yugoslav peoples, echoing the sentiments the Serbian leadership had expressed in December 1914. At the close of the meeting, attendees drafted a resolution in which they declared the South Slavic peoples one nation and promised to work together for a united Yugoslav state.

The congress remains a little-known but significant moment for those interested in the history of the first Yugoslavia. On the one hand, it refutes claims that the Serbian government was uninterested in the creation of Yugoslavia; the Niš meeting proceeded with the support of the Serbian government. At the same time, the resolution produced by the congress left the erroneous impression of complete agreement between Serbia and the Habsburg South Slavs regarding the future of the Yugoslav state. In fact, the common purpose expressed at the Niš meeting concerned only the necessity of creating a state. Questions of organization, ethnic composition, and borders were two years away from serious discussion in 1915. Once on the table, these issues would provoke acrimonious disagreements up to and long after the birth of Yugoslavia in December 1918.

Brigit Farley

Further Reading

Čulinović, Ferdo. *Historija od osnutka zajedničke države do danas.* Zagreb, 1968.

Petrovich, Michael Boro. *A History of Modern Serbia,* vol. 2. New York, 1976.

Pisarev, Iurii. *Serbiia i Chernogoriia v pervoi mirovoi voine.* Moscow, 1968.

Šišić, Ferdo, ed. *Dokumenti o postanku Kraljevine Srba, Hrvata i Slovenaca 1914–1919.* Zagreb, 1920.

See also Yugoslav Committee

Yugoslavia (Geography)

Balkan state that extended from Austria to Greece for seven decades during the twentieth century but that, since 1991, has been confined to the more limited territory of Serbia and Montenegro.

The Kingdom of Serbs, Croats, and Slovenes was formed in November 1918, at the end of World War I, as a state for South Slavic–speaking peoples. It was composed of parts of the former Austro-Hungarian Empire (Carniola, Croatia-Slavonia, Vojvodina, Dalmatia, Bosnia-Hercegovina) plus Serbia and Montenegro, which had won independence from the Ottoman Empire during the nineteenth century. Agreement to establish the new entity had been formulated two years earlier at a meeting of Serbian, Croatian, and Slovenian representatives on the Greek island of Corfu, where the Serbian government and army had found refuge after being driven from the mainland by combined Austrian, German, and Bulgarian forces.

The Serb-Croat-Slovene kingdom embraced an area of 96,000 square miles (266,670 sq km) with a population of 12,500,000. Disagreements among the component national groups began soon after its formation, particularly between Roman Catholic Croats, who had a Central European cultural heritage, and Eastern Orthodox Serbs, whose traditions derived from the Byzantine and Ottoman Empires. Croats, who accounted for approximately one-quarter of the population, initially perceived the new state as an association of equal partners who had become free of past imperial tyrannies; Serbs, numbering 40 percent, saw the entity as a greater Serbian territory earned by Serbian victory during World War I.

Ethnic conflicts between Croats and Serbs culminated in 1928 with the assassination in parliament of leaders of the Croatian Peasant Party. During ensuing months, the king, who was from the Serbian royal dynasty, established a personal dictatorship and abolished as entities Croatia, Serbia, and the other component historic provinces, replacing them with administrative territories named after river basins and other natural features. He also renamed the state "Yugoslavia." These efforts did not stifle Croatian nationalism, however, and the king himself was assassinated in Marseilles in 1934 by agents of the Ustaša. Confronted with continuing Croatian demands for self-government, the regime in 1939 reached agreement to establish a Croatian *banovina* (province) that joined the former Croatian territories of Hungary with Austria's former province of Dalmatia.

Germany, Italy, Hungary, and Bulgaria invaded Yugoslavia in April 1941, during World War II, and dismembered it. Germany annexed northern Slovenia, Italy attached southern Slovenia and parts of coastal Croatia, Hungary gained adjacent border territories, and Bulgaria acquired south Serbia (Macedonia). Croatia was allowed to become an independent state allied to Germany and enlarged by Bosnia-Hercegovina and portions of the Serbian Vojvodina. Italy established a protectorate over Montenegro. Italian-controlled Albania annexed significant territories from Serbia and Montenegro. What remained of Serbia had the status of German-occupied territory under a puppet administration for civil affairs.

The fighting forces of Josip Broz Tito (1892–1980), called Partisans, liberated nearly all the Yugoslav lands by the end of World War II. In 1945 Tito's regime reconstituted Yugoslavia as a socialist federal republic, and subsequent treaties added nearly 3,000 square miles (8,330 sq km) of former

Italian territory on the Istrian peninsula and adjacent to the city of Trieste. Tito defied attempts by the Soviet Union to dominate Yugoslavia in 1948 and successfully maintained an independent stance in political and economic affairs.

To minimize ethnic frictions within the federal republic, Tito adopted the Soviet model of establishing "republics" that were "national in form, socialist in content." In addition to separate internal republics for Serbs, Croats, Slovenes, and Montenegrins, Macedonians for the first time received recognition as a distinctive nation with a right to their own republic. A sixth republic was created for the mixed Serb, Croat, and Muslim population living in the historic province of Bosnia-Hercegovina.

Ethnic rivalries continued to plague Yugoslavia throughout the postwar period. In June 1991, at a time of general collapse of Communist regimes in Eastern Europe, Slovenia and Croatia declared their independence from the Yugoslav federation. Macedonia separated in September and Bosnia-Hercegovina in October. Serbia and Montenegro continued to identify themselves as parts of Yugoslavia and established a new federal constitution in April 1992. Their combined areas and populations represented barely 40 percent of previous Yugoslav totals.

Thomas M. Poulsen

Further reading

Bertić, Ivan. *Veliki geografski atlas Jugoslavije.* Zagreb, 1987.

Clissold, Stephen, ed. *A Short History of Yugoslavia: From Early Times to 1966.* Cambridge, 1968.

Djordjević, Dimitrije, ed. *The Creation of Yugoslavia, 1914–18.* Oxford, 1980.

See also Antifascism; Banat; Belgrade; Bosnia-Hercegovina; Corfu Declaration; Croatia; Dalmatia; Krajina; Kingdom of Serbs, Croats, and Slovenes; Ljubljana; Macedonia; Montenegro; Sarajevo; Serbia; Slovenia; Tito; Vojvodina; Zagreb

Yugoslavia (and the South Slavic Lands) (History)

In 1800 a state of Yugoslavia could not be found on any map. What could be found were its component lands: Slovenia, Dalmatia, Croatia, Slavonia, the Military Frontier, Vojvodina, Bosnia-Hercegovina, Serbia, Montenegro, Kosovo, and Macedonia. In 1800 each of these territories was under the control of either the Habsburg monarchy or the Ottoman Empire. The Habsburg monarch directly ruled the territories of Slovenia (composed of Carniola and parts of Styria), Istria, and Carinthia; Dalmatia; the Croatian Military Frontier; and Vojvodina, composed of the western part of the Banat of Temesvar, most of Bačka, and a small part of Baranja. Croatia and Slavonia, with certain autonomous provincial institutions, were a part of the Hungarian crown lands. Bosnia-Hercegovina, Serbia, Montenegro, Kosovo, and Macedonia were under Ottoman rule. When these lands were joined together in 1918 to form the first Yugoslav state, the ethnic heterogeneity, geographical and economic diversity, and cultural, religious, and historical complexity were its most striking features.

The South Slavic Lands before 1800

During the sixth century, the barbarian invasions associated with the breakup of the Roman Empire greatly affected the Balkan Peninsula. One group of Indo-Europeans, the Slavs, combined sedentary agriculture with raiding expeditions and penetrated into the Balkan region. Little is known of early distinctions among the various Slavic tribes, but the differences were soon accentuated by religious, cultural, and regional experiences.

While the population gradually became Slavic-speaking and Christian, each tribe developed differently. The Slovenes and Croats of the north and west came under Western Christendom's influence; the Serbs were influenced by Byzantium and Eastern Orthodoxy. The language of the Slovenes differed from the language spoken by the Serbs and Croats. The Croats (and the Slovenes) adopted the Latin alphabet and the Serbs the Cyrillic. Variations in vocabulary, syntax, and dialect came to exist within the Serbo-Croatian language. By the end of the ninth century, the basis had been laid for contemporary Yugoslavia's complex ethnic mosaic. It would be difficult to say that at this point there existed a simple division between "Western Slovenes and Croats" and "Eastern Serbs"; cultural, linguistic, religious, and imperial borders remained too much in flux.

Beginning in the mid–seventh century, the Slavic tribes of the peninsula experienced periods of political independence and expansion. The Slovenes were part of the short-lived Slavonic empire of Samo (r. 627–658). In 748 they

Y submitted to Frankish Emperor Charlemagne (c. 742–814) and remained under some form of Germanic rule until 1918. An independent state of Croatia existed from the tenth to the twelfth centuries. In 1102 the Croatian nobility of the Triune Kingdom, that is, the kingdoms of Dalmatia, Croatia, and Slavonia, recognized the Hungarian king as their monarch. Croatia and Slavonia remained a constituent part of Hungary until 1918. Dalmatia, the original center of the Croatian medieval kingdom, was a contested coastal region throughout its history. Beginning in the sixth century, it was to be controlled by various empires—Byzantine, Hungarian, Turk, and for a short time Napoleonic. Venetian control, which lasted from 1420 to 1797, was the most significant. In 1815 Dalmatia came under Habsburg control.

Under the Serbian Nemanija dynasty in the twelfth century, the Serbian tribes built a substantial medieval Serbian state. At its height of power and influence in 1345 under Tsar Stefan Dušan (c. 1308–55), the Serbian state included much of today's Serbia, Macedonia, Albania, Montenegro, and northern Greece. Shortly after Dušan's death in 1355, the empire broke apart into smaller kingdoms and principalities that were unable to withstand the expanding Ottoman Empire. A coalition of Serbian armies met defeat at the hands of the Ottoman army at Kosovo in 1389. The Ottoman Turks were now established in the southern part of the Balkan Peninsula. Serbia, Macedonia, and Bosnia fell under Turkish rule in 1463 and Hercegovina in 1481. The small Serbian polity of Zeta, later called Montenegro, succumbed to the Turks at the end of the fifteenth century.

At the time of the Ottoman conquest, Slavs belonging to three religious groups inhabited Bosnia and Hercegovina: Catholic Slavs, Orthodox Slavs, and adherents of the medieval Bosnian Church. Within a century, large numbers of the inhabitants had converted to Islam. These converts came from all social classes and religious groups and appeared to be drawn to Islam because it was the vital, dynamic faith of conquerors.

Not all Slavs converted to Islam, and the religious mix of Bosnia and Hercegovina consisted of Muslims, Catholics, and Orthodox Christians; the Bosnian Church disappeared. By the nineteenth century, adherents of each faith, regardless of ancestry, identified with a particular nationality: Catholics as Croats, Orthodox Christians as Serbs, and Muslims as Bosnian Muslims.

The Ottoman conquest of southeastern Europe provoked massive movements of peoples, mostly from the south to the north. Many Serbs and Croats crossed the Danube to seek safety and security in Hungarian and Habsburg lands. Large numbers of Serbs settled in the Vojvodina, which the Hungarians considered to be an integral part of their state. This group of Serbs, known as *prečani* (those from across the river), played a pivotal role in the Serbian cultural and national movements during the nineteenth and twentieth centuries. Wherever the borders of the Ottoman and Habsburg Empires came into contact, a great mixing of populations took place.

A distinct area that emerged as a result of Ottoman expansion was the Croatian Military Frontier. Established in the sixteenth century by the Habsburgs, it consisted of a narrow belt of land that stretched from the northern Dalmatian coastline, along northern Bosnia-Hercegovina, to Belgrade. The Habsburgs invited fleeing Serbs to settle as free peasants and in return the new settlers were to defend the Habsburg frontier against Turkish incursions. In the eighteenth century, the Habsburgs created a similar Military Frontier in the Banat, which became a continuation of the Croatian Military Frontier.

The South Slav Lands 1815–1918

During the nineteenth century, the forces of nationalism, liberalism, industrialization, secularization, and social mobilization buffeted the lands of the South Slavs and began to undermine the foundations of the multinational, agrarian, and autocratic empires of the Ottomans and the Habsburgs. To understand the creation of the state of Yugoslavia in 1918 is to understand the process of decay and disintegration of both the Habsburg and the Ottoman states, and the political, social, and economic development of the South Slavs.

At the beginning of the nineteenth century, the vast majority of South Slav inhabitants were peasants. Even with this fact, the peasant communities and the economic and social conditions under which they lived varied considerably. A small minority of South Slavs, predominately Croats and Muslims of South Slavic origin, lived in towns and cities and could be classified as artisans, merchants, bureaucrats, professionals, or members of the nobility.

The social and economic position of Christian peasants, both Orthodox and Catholic, under

Ottoman control varied over time and place. During the fifteenth and sixteenth centuries, the Ottoman system of land tenure rested on the state's ownership of almost all lands and on the sultan's grants of land to selected cavalry officers, or *sipahi.* For this grant of land, or *timar,* officers had to provide military or administrative services to the Ottoman state. These nonhereditary grants were closely regulated. Peasants worked the land for a fixed set of dues, owed no personal services to the *sipahi,* and, most important, were not bound to the soil. The *timar* system differed greatly from other European land tenure systems; Orthodox Christians were not serfs bound to the land or to a lord.

During the seventeenth century, the Porte's authority over the *timar* system eroded. Steadily during this century and the next, local Ottoman officials (*ayans*) began to acquire large blocks of land by acquiring leases from peasants, exploiting their position as tax collector, or using force. These land estates, or *chiftliks,* were found mostly in Macedonia and Bulgaria, predominating along well-traveled waterways or in cultivated valleys. The average holding varied between fifteen and thirty acres (six to twelve hectares). The creation of these *chiftliks* altered the economic, social, and political structures of the South Slav lands south of the Danube.

The *ayans* increased their control over the countryside at the expense of the Porte. In Serbia, control of the area fell to the Janissaries, who originally had been enslaved infantrymen of the sultan but by the late seventeenth century had moved beyond the sultan's control. The peasants who found themselves outside the Porte's control faced increased labor and in-kind dues, as well as violence. They were now at the mercy of the Muslim provincial elites. Some peasants responded to these changes by fleeing into more mountainous and remote regions. They supported themselves by raising livestock and had more control over the land. These communities often organized themselves around an extended family commune, or *zadruga.* Similar communal structures were also found throughout the South Slavic lands.

The classic South Slav *zadruga* was composed of a two- or three-generation family traced through the male line. It was a social and economic unit based on joint ownership of land and implements, producing and consuming goods collectively, the common organization of agricultural tasks, and a parallel organization of women's tasks.

The *zadruga* was bound together by blood, life, goods, and work. The head of the household (*domaćin*), in cooperation with other male members, directed the activities of the *zadruga.* The *domaćin* also represented his family to the outside authorities.

Women were subordinate to men in this socioeconomic structure. They could not be members of the *zadruga,* nor could they inherit *zadruga* property. In Serbia, the inheritance pattern was altered in 1844 when women could inherit *zadruga* property in the form of a money inheritance. When daughters married, they lived in their husbands' *zadruga* and assumed the lowest status in the household. Women's labor, however, was essential for the survival of the household. They not only worked within the home, which was exclusively the women's sphere, but they also worked with the men in the fields and took care of the animals. As industrialization and the money economy penetrated into the region, the *zadruga* became obsolete.

In Serbia, the industrial and agricultural sectors grew during the nineteenth century. This was due in part to the new market opportunities for Serbian livestock traders in the Habsburg monarchy. In addition, Serbia's formal recognition as a self-administrated principality in 1830 spurred new growth in both agriculture and industry.

Between 1815 and 1833, the Ottoman land tenure system in Serbia gave way to peasant ownership of the land. Adhering to the principle that the land belongs to those who till it, Serbian prince Miloš Obrenović (1780–1860) introduced the Homestead Act of 1836. This act decreed that a house and a small plot of land with two oxen and a cow were deemed essential and could not be taken away from the peasant family. Legislation in 1860–61 and 1873 strengthened this minimum. The *zadruga* disappeared as a consequence of these individual smallholdings.

With land reform, the need for cash to pay taxes, and the increased demand for imported goods, the Serbian economy evolved from an agrarian to a cash basis. Agricultural cultivation of wheat, a crop grown for in-kind payment because it was the primary product for the Ottoman markets, gave way to livestock raising (especially hogs), and cash crops such as cotton, tobacco, corn, and grapes.

The state did little for its peasantry and agriculture. Agricultural credit was difficult to obtain.

The rising costs of building a modern infrastructure—roads, railroads, the army, and public administration—burdened the peasantry. In addition, the population explosion in Serbia between 1878 and 1910, from 1.3 million to 2.9 million, worsened the land-population ratio. By 1914, Serbia was a country of small and dwarf landowners with 58 percent of the peasants holding five hectares (12.5 acres) or fewer. Unlike other South Slavs, there was very little Serbian emigration overseas.

Urbanization and industrialization in Serbia grew at a slower rate than in the Habsburg lands. In 1834 Serbia's capital, Belgrade, had only eighteen thousand inhabitants and the urban population was only 6.5 percent of the total. The urban population grew to 10 percent in the 1870s and peaked to 14 percent before 1914. Muslims made up half the population in Belgrade; Serbs and other Christian groups made up the other half in 1834. As Ottoman control waned during the nineteenth century, Serbianization of the cities took place.

Agricultural activities for pre-1914 Serbia accounted for nearly 80 percent of gross output. Prior to Serbian independence in 1878, industrial development was minimal. After 1878, its industrial development was built around processing agricultural raw materials. Tobacco processing, flour mills, and meatpacking made up more than 70 percent of Serbia's industrial output by 1910; brewing, textiles, sugar refining, wood processing, and construction materials made up the rest. The bulk of these operations was financed by foreign capital and entrepreneurs, as Serbia was slow to develop its own banking and credit institutions. At the time of union with the other South Slavs in 1918, Serbia's industries accounted for only 13 percent of the new state's industrial base. The other ex-Ottoman lands of Macedonia and Montenegro accounted for less than 2 percent. Bosnia-Hercegovina contributed 7 percent, with most of its industrialization taking place after Austria-Hungary gained administrative control over the region in 1878.

In Macedonia, the land tenure system rested upon the *chiftlik* system until the end of the First Balkan War (1912–13). During the nineteenth century, this system accounted for over 90 percent of agricultural land. Turks and Albanians held ownership of the *chiftliks* with Macedonian and Greek peasants farming the holdings. Over three-fourths of the peasants' production went to the landlord and the local tax collector. In 1903 the Macedonian peasantry rallied around its nationalist movement, the Internal Macedonian Revolutionary Organization (IMRO) and revolted against Ottoman rule. The Porte summarily crushed the revolt. As a result, the second wave of Macedonian and Greek peasant emigration began. Roughly one hundred thousand left between 1890 and 1903, and two hundred thousand emigrated between 1903 and 1914.

The land tenure system in Bosnia-Hercegovina resembled that of Macedonia. The rural landlord was a native South Slav Muslim and the majority of peasants were Orthodox or Catholic. The burden on these peasants was exorbitant, with over 40 percent of their income going for taxes.

During the nineteenth century, peasant revolts were aimed at bettering economic conditions. Local Muslim landlords often disregarded the Porte's authority to regulate peasant taxes and labor dues. Peasant revolts broke out in 1857–58 and 1861–62. The most significant of these revolts came in July 1875 after a bad harvest the year before. The revolt first broke out in Hercegovina and then Bosnia, swept into Serbia and Montenegro, then spread into the international realm. The Treaty of Berlin (1878) settled both the local and the international conflicts. Austria-Hungary was granted the right to occupy and administer Bosnia-Hercegovina.

The Joint Ministry of Finance for the Austro-Hungarian Empire administered these lands. The administrator of these regions, Benjamin Kállay (1839–1903), attempted to foster economic growth, improve sanitation, reduce lawlessness, build roads and railroads, and establish schools. He introduced tobacco and potato plantations and sugar-beet production. Livestock raising, especially cattle, was improved. The success of these innovations was thwarted largely because of Hungarian and Habsburg political bickering.

In 1908, with the formal annexation of Bosnia-Hercegovina by Austria-Hungary, a reform of the land tenure system was decreed. The peasants were to become freeholders and not leaseholders. But there was little time for these reforms to succeed. By 1914, Austrian rule had left Bosnia-Hercegovina little in the way of a modern infrastructure. The Austrians had improved roads and built railroads, but there was little industrial base or banking industry.

The population of Bosnia-Hercegovnia at the time of Austrian occupation is estimated at one million to 1.4 million. Of this population, 38 percent were Muslim, 42 percent were Orthodox, 18 percent were Roman Catholic, and .25 percent were Jewish. No group had or ever has had a majority.

The economic and social conditions of the South Slavs under the Habsburg monarchy were as varied as those found in the Ottoman Empire. Like their counterparts in the Ottoman Empire, the majority of Croats, Serbs, and Slovenes were peasants, but they lived under a system of land tenure comparable to the European feudal system.

In Civil Croatia and Slavonia, the Hungarian nobility predominated. They held estates granted to them by the crown, along with the services of the peasants, who were mostly Croatian. The formal abolition of serfdom in this region did not occur until 1848. The Croatian Military Frontier possessed a different land tenure system. The Habsburgs recruited Croatian, German, Hungarian, and Serbian peasants to serve as military border guards. More than 80 percent of the Frontier's population were Serbs and Croats. Austria assumed direct control of this area and granted land to peasants in return for military obligations. The Habsburgs demilitarized this area in 1873 and unified it with the other parts of Croatia-Slavonia in 1881. The ethnic patchwork of this borderland survived until the late twentieth century.

The industrial and agricultural sectors of the economy grew during the second half of the nineteenth century in Croatia and Slavonia as a result of the abolition of serfdom; the development of railroads, canals, and roads; and the penetration of the money economy. Agricultural production shifted from animal husbandry to crop agriculture. After 1880, the area under field crops such as grains, potatoes, legumes, vegetables, as well as vineyards and orchards expanded, a result of a steadily growing population and production for both the domestic and the foreign market.

Industrial growth started earliest in Vojvodina and then in Croatia-Slavonia. The primary industries were in food and agricultural raw materials processing, especially lumber. Foreign capital and entrepreneurs financed the bulk of mining operations. Production was often for export, not the domestic market. The great portion of industrial labor was half industrial and half agricultural. Industry employed less than 10 percent of the work force prior to 1914.

During the second half of the nineteenth century, population and urban areas grew. In 1850 the population in Croatia-Slavonia was 1.6 million; by 1914, it had grown to 2.7 million. In 1880 peasants still accounted for 84 percent of the population, and this percentage fell to 79 percent in 1910. Croatian population figures were influenced by migrations. Austria and Hungary sponsored migrations of Germans and Hungarians into Croatia-Slavonia. In 1840 Croats and Serbs were 98.4 percent of the population, in 1910 87.1 percent. Overseas emigration also impacted these populations. Between 1899 and 1913, 400,000 to 450,000 people left Croatia-Slavonia.

Dalmatia was assigned to Austria in 1814–15 by the Congress of Vienna. The Austrians found a largely Croatian peasant population and an urban commercial and professional middle class that was Italian in culture. Under the Austrians, the Dalmatian peasantry continued to farm the land under sharecropping arrangements and feudal customs. Most landlords insisted on the cultivation of grapevines, olives, and some grains. Dalmatia's integration into the Austrian economy lessened the commercial importance of Dalmatia's ports. Between 1840 and 1910, Dalmatia's population grew from 399,000 to 646,000. This growth contributed to the severity of Dalmatia's land tenure conditions. Some of Dalmatia's population sought relief in fishing, the merchant marine, and overseas emigration.

In Slovenia, which was a hereditary Habsburg land, similar feudal structures existed but the nobility was predominately German. However, the mountainous terrain, unlike the plains of Slavonia and parts of Civil Croatia, were not conducive to large agriculture estates. Instead, the Slovenian agrarian economy rested on forest holdings and on pastureland for grazing livestock, especially sheep. This base encouraged the development of a household textile industry that spurred the proto-industrialization of Slovenia.

During the early nineteenth century, rural Slovenian entrepreneurs migrated to the towns and cities and joined the German urban population in advancing manufacturing. Slovenia's industrial base also developed as a result of large deposits of iron ore and coal found in its mountains, and timber farmed from its forests. Railroad construction in the 1840s prompted the opening of several ironworks and wood processing. By the second half of the nineteenth century, Slovenia was the

Y most industrially advanced of the future Yugoslav lands.

The urbanization of Slovenia, as well as Croatia-Slovenia, proceeded much more quickly than in the Ottoman lands. Until 1800, the composition of most towns was non-Slavic and numbered only in the thousands. Slavicization of the towns took place during the nineteenth century. At the end of the nineteenth century, Ljubljana had a population of 30,000, Zagreb 61,000. Between 1857 and 1910, Slovenia's population grew from 1.1 million to 1.3 million. In 1880, 83 percent of the population lived off the land; by 1910, this total had fallen to 67 percent.

Nation and State

There are two general types of nationalism in the South Slav lands: the nationalism of individual nations and a common South Slav, or Yugoslav, nationalism. The roots of these two types of nationalism are found in the intellectual, cultural, and political circumstances of late-eighteenth- and early-nineteenth-century Europe.

The ideas and ideals of the French Revolution glorified the notion of a people united against the absolutism of kings and the tyranny of foreign oppressors. In addition, a new breed of intellectuals began to explore the roots of a group's identity and purpose. These nationalist writers, poets, philologists, folklorists, and publicists began to concern themselves with history, language, and literature to shape an identity beyond empire, monarchy, and religion. The feelings of solidarity against Austrian, Hungarian, and Ottoman rule also gained prominence.

Croatian, Serbian, and Slovene nationalisms have their roots during and in the Enlightenment, after the French Revolution, and the Napoleonic Wars. Macedonian, Montenegrin, Bosnian Muslim, and Albanian nationalisms are of more recent origin. The primary objective of these nationalisms was the defense and promotion of their special aims as individual nations without regard to the interests of the other South Slav nations and often at their expense. However, a different form of nationalism, Yugoslavism, also arose.

The First Yugoslavism: Illyrianism

Yugoslav nationalism, or Yugoslavism, is the belief in the ethnic, linguistic, and cultural unity of the South Slavs, support for their unification, and/or belief that the South Slavs are or should become one nation. The modern roots of Yugoslavism are primarily found in the historical experiences of the Croats. The centralization pressures of Habsburg Emperor Joseph II's (1741–90) reforms, the pressures of an emerging Hungarian nationalism, and Napoléon's (1769–1821) 1809 unification of Croatia, Dalmatia, Slavonia, and parts of Slovenia-Istria and Trieste into the "Illyrian" provinces spurred the Illyrian Movement of the 1830s and 1840s.

Dominated by Ljudevit Gaj (1809–72), a Croat, the Illyrian Movement promoted the linguistic and cultural unification of South Slavs. Politically, Illyrianism's immediate goal was the unification of the South Slavs of the Habsburg Empire. This meant an orientation toward Central Europe. However, the Revolutions of 1848–49 brought the Illyrian Movement to an end when the desired autonomy did not materialize.

This movement did have support among educated Habsburg Serbs, but it was not received with equal enthusiasm in Serbia. By the 1830s, the Serbs were engaged in their own nation-building projects. Yet this idea of close linguistic and cultural ties and cooperation among South Slavs continued to develop throughout the nineteenth century, albeit in a changed form.

Yugoslavism: Strossmayer and Rački

After 1848, two opposing political and national currents developed. One emphasized Croatian nationalism, while the second was an expansion of the Illyrian idea. This new movement, Yugoslavism (*jugoslavenstvo*), was promoted by two Croatian Catholic clerics, Josip Juraj Strossmayer (1815–1905) and Franjo Rački (1828–94).

Under Strossmayer and Rački, Yugoslavism sought the joining together of all South Slavs both within and without the monarchy. As Catholics, these two clerics addressed not only the issues of political, linguistic, and cultural unity but also sought to reconcile Catholic Croats and Orthodox Serbs. To further their goals, Rački and Strossmayer promoted the establishment of an Academy of Arts that bore the name "Yugoslav" rather than "Croatian." The Yugoslav Academy of Arts and Sciences provided an outlet for all South Slavic publications.

Strossmayer's overtures to the Serbian government were rebuffed. The Serbs were more interested in alliances that targeted Ottoman, not Habsburg, lands. Interest in Yugoslavism remained confined to the liberal and middle-class elements of urban Croatian society during the latter part of the nineteenth century. In fact, the Yugoslav idea was now competing with the more strident nationalisms of the individual nations of the South Slavs.

Croatian Nationalism 1848–68

The Revolutions of 1848–49 not only helped to foster a redefinition of the Illyrian Movement but also sowed the seeds of a Croatian nationalism that demanded at first a semi-independent, self-ruled Greater Croatia within the Austrian Empire; it later demanded Croatian independence. Autonomy appeared to be within the reach of the Croats in 1848–49, but their hopes were dashed when the Croats were denied self-rule after the Habsburgs regained control of their empire in 1849. The disappointment over the ill-fated autonomy coupled with the emergence of neoabsolutism and harsh Germanization under the new young emperor, Franz Joseph (1830–1916), dissuaded many Croats of the possibility of a reconfigured empire. Soon after, a new current of Croatian nationalism emerged under the direction of Ante Starčević (1823–96) and Eugen Kvaternik (1825–71).

Starčević was the first Croat leader to break with the idea of South Slav unity. Frustrated by the Croats' lack of progress in uniting Croatian lands and the Serbs' lack of interest, this former Illyrian advocated an independent Croatian state. In 1861 Starčević (with Kvaternik) founded the Party of Rights (that is, states' rights), which espoused an integral Croat nationalism and opposed cooperation with Austria and Hungary. Their platform did not recognize the existence of any other South Slavic nations besides Bulgarians. Starčević disparaged the history and culture of other Slavs and reserved his harshest criticism for the Serbs, whom he described as an "unclean race." His plan was to incorporate these people into a future Greater Croatia, including Bosnia. Two other political groups, the Magyarones and the Independent National Party, sought solutions in cooperation with other national groups; the Party of Rights did not.

Croatian Nationalism, 1868–1914

The *Ausgleich* (Compromise) of 1867, which created the Dual Monarchy (Austria-Hungary), dealt a serious blow to Croatian autonomy. In 1868 the Croats negotiated an administrative agreement with the Hungarians. On the surface, the compromise (*Nagodba*) appeared to give the Croats a large degree of autonomy. Croatia was to have its own assembly (Sabor); Croatian was to be the official language; the Croatian flag was to fly beside the Hungarian; and Croatian-elected representatives were to be sent to the parliament in Budapest. However, the Hungarians still controlled appointment of the governor (*ban*) and finances. The extremely limited franchise for the Sabor, as well as the manipulation of the election process by various *bans,* ensured that the Sabor was dominated by the conservative nobility. Count Khuen-Héderváry (1849–1918), *ban* from 1883 to 1903, initiated a strict policy of Magyarization, that is, promotion of Hungarian culture, laws, and language. In hope of further weakening Croatian opposition, he also played Serbs and Croats against each other by favoring Serbs in education, politics, the civil service, and the professions.

From 1868 until the outbreak of World War I, the conflict with Hungarian authorities dominated Croatian political life. However, Croatian nationalists were still divided over the issue of how best to achieve Croatian independence. The answer to this question grew murkier when Bosnia-Hercegovina came under Habsburg control in 1878. Not only did Croatian nationalists claim this area for Croatia, but the Serbs in Serbia proper also believed that Bosnia-Hercegovina should be part of their state.

During the 1880s, Croats supported Starčević's Party of Rights, which advocated an independent Croatia; it was also clearly anti-Serb. In 1894 a group headed by Josip Frank (1844–1911) splintered from the Party of Rights. This party, the Pure Party of Rights, fought for a Croatian part to the Dual Monarchy. This "trialist" solution would include the Triune Kingdom and Bosnia-Hercegovina; Croatia's status would be equal to that of Austria and Hungary. It provided a place for Catholic Slovenes but not Orthodox Serbs. During this period, Yugoslavism as a political program all but disappeared. It reappeared only when its goals proved useful in thwarting Austrian and Hungarian hegemony in the region.

Yugoslavism: The Croato-Serb Coalition, 1905–14

In December 1905 two Croatian parties, the Party of Croatian Rights and the Croatian Progressive Party, and the Serbian parties of the empire, the Serbian Independent Party and the Serbian People's Radical Party, formed the Croato-Serb

Coalition. Under the tutelage of two Dalmatian politicians, Ante Trumbić (1868–1938) and Franjo Supilo (1870–1917), this coalition represented a new generation of Croatian and Habsburg Serb politicians who believed their fortunes would be best served by returning to the Yugoslav idea.

The greatest contribution of this group was to put an end to the Serb-Croat feuding that had prevented the South Slavs from uniting against Budapest and winning greater rights for both Serbs and Croats in the monarchy. The coalition ended Budapest's divide-and-rule policy and stood for cooperation among all the South Slavs within the empire. The Croato-Serb Coalition dominated Croatian politics until 1918. Other parties at this time endorsed different programs. The newly founded Croatian Peasant Party (1904) and its leaders, Stjepan (1871–1928) and Ante (1868–1919) Radić, supported the union of the South Slavs of the monarchy. The Pure Party of Rights continued to support trialism.

Slovene Nationalism, 1800–1914

In 1800 the Slovenes were the smallest of the Slavic national groups in the Habsburg Empire, and this demographic position limited their call for political autonomy. Nineteenth-century Slovenian nationalists focused primarily on cultural autonomy.

The development of a coherent Slovene culture and identity began in the late eighteenth century. Joseph II, in an attempt to "enlighten" his subjects, encouraged translation of educational materials into Slovenian despite his general Germanizing policy. The new Slovenian middle class began to send their sons to study in Vienna and Paris, centers of the Enlightenment. Bent on examining their own culture, many began to write in Slovenian rather than in German and explore Slovenia's past. Anton Linhart's (1756–95) *An Attempt at a History of Carniolan and Other South Slavs in Austria* depicted Slovenians for the first time as a single people. In 1797 Father Valentin Vodnik (1758–1819) founded the first Slovenian newspaper. His newspaper, poetry, and most famous poem, "Zadovoljni Kranjac" (The Satisfied Carniolan), were important catalysts for modern Slovenian literature.

The Slovenian national movement first became politicized during French administration of Slovenia, Croatia, and Dalmatia between 1809 and 1813. Slovenian intellectuals approved of the French policies of issuing decrees in the Slovenian language, appointing Slovene administrators, and establishing Slovenian schools for both boys and girls. The Slovenes' brief experience in the Illyrian Provinces furthered the cause of not only a Slovene identity but also an identity common to Slovenes, Croats, and Serbs.

Austria regained control over the Illyrian Provinces in 1813 and rescinded the French reforms. Between 1813 and 1848, the Austrians confined Slovenian energies to the cultural sphere. However, revolution and war once again politicized the Slovenian national movement. Ljubljana, like other Habsburg cities, erupted in 1848. The demonstrators called for constitutional limits on the monarch. In Slovenia, the first political platforms to call for an autonomous "Unified Slovenia" were drafted. In addition, other platforms demanded unification of the Habsburg South Slavs into a state linked with Austria or Germany. By 1849, Austria reasserted itself, and the Slovenes had to withdraw their calls for autonomy.

The *Ausgleich* secured the supremacy of the Austro-Germans in Austria and the Hungarians in Hungary. Slovene reaction to the reconfigured empire varied. In the late 1860s the Slovenian middle class and intellectuals agitated for a united Slovenia. This Slovenia was to be composed of Carniola and the Slovene areas of Carinthia, Styria, and Istria. In addition, they wanted Slovene to be the administrative and educational language. Very little came of these demands as the Austro-Germans united in maintaining German primacy in their half of the monarchy. This meant constructing the Vienna-Trieste railroad, which brought Austro-German capital, goods, and entrepreneurs into Slovenia. This railroad and the accompanying industrial development strengthened the German element in Slovenia.

In 1882 the Slovenes obtained a majority in the diet of Carniola and in the Ljubljana town council. Vienna granted the use of Slovene in schools and local administration where the population was heavily Slovene. With these concessions and favorable economic growth, the Slovenes adapted to life within the monarchy. Beginning in the 1880s, Slovene political life was dominated by the Clerical Party. Superbly organized, this party concentrated on the economic, educational, and social welfare of Slovene peasants, workers, and craftspeople. The Slovene Liberal Party and the Social Democrats also developed at this time but with much smaller constituencies. Prior to 1914, none of the Slovene political parties wanted the elimination of the imperial system or direct union of the Slovenes with a South Slav state. The Slovenes remained convinced that the key to their autonomy was to remain within the reconfigured Habsburg Empire. Of all the South Slavs, the Slovenes remained the most loyal to the monarchy.

Serbia, 1804–78

Unlike the Croats in the Habsburg monarchy, the Serbs in the Ottoman Empire were a much more homogeneous group. In contrast to Croats who spoke several dialects, most Serbs spoke the štokavian dialect. Vuk Karadžić (1787–1864), a Serbian linguist, provided important points of unity for Serbs by collecting Serbian epic poetry, proverbs, and folk tales, compiling a dictionary, and arguing that anyone speaking štokavian was a Serb, even the štokavian-speaking Catholic Croats and Bosnian Muslims. Karadžić's efforts facilitated interaction among Serbian peasants and intellectuals alike, but his argument that Croats and Muslims were essentially Serbs, from a linguistic point of view, undercut his role as an advocate of South Slav unity.

While Karadžić advocated a cultural basis for unity, most Serbs found themselves united primarily by Eastern Orthodoxy and the Serbian Orthodox Church. During the medieval Serbian kingdom, the church had strong links to the state and the Nemanija dynasty. Under the Ottomans, the Serbian Orthodox Church and its patriarch controlled the civil sphere. The church acquired legal powers to sanction marriage, divorce, and inheritance, as well as assessing and collecting taxes due to the Ottoman state. Concomitant with this civil authority went certain police powers that even included a patriarchal jail in Constantinople. Thus, language and religion became two cornerstones of a Serbian national identity. A third element, Serbian experience under Ottoman rule, became more important with the anti-Ottoman uprisings of 1804 and 1815.

The first uprising, in 1804, was led by Karadjordje "Black George" Petrović (1768–1817), a livestock merchant with military experience gained from fighting the Turks. The Serbs rebelled against the tyranny of the Janissaries who ruled Serbia in the name of the sultan but who, in reality, obeyed few orders from Constantinople. When the sultan refused to support the Serbs in their struggle against the renegade Turks, the uprising became a war of independence. The Serbs captured Belgrade in 1806, and their revolt lasted until 1813, when the Ottomans regained control of Belgrade and conducted severe reprisals against the population. The first revolt came to an end, but the continued reprisals and violence in the countryside provoked a second revolt in 1815, this time under Miloš Obrenović (1780–1860).

With the Napoleonic Wars coming to an end, the Ottoman government did not want a major uprising. Obrenović was willing to negotiate, and the Russians supported the Orthodox Serbs. The Porte therefore granted the Serbs limited autonomy that allowed Serbs to administer the state and have a Serbian *knez* (prince) as head of the new government. However, the head of the new government was not Karadjordje, who had fled Serbia for southern Hungary in 1813, but Miloš. Fearing Karadjordje's return, Obrenović had him murdered and his head sent to the sultan as a sign of Serbian loyalty to the Porte. From this time forward, the two families contended for leadership of the Serbian state. Miloš and his heirs ruled Serbia from 1815 to 1903, with the exception of the seventeen-year rule of Alexander Karadjordjević (1806–85), Karadjordje's son, between 1842 and 1859.

Between 1815 and 1878, Serbia evolved from a Turkish province with limited autonomy to an independent sovereign state. Like that of many of its neighbors, Serbia's political life was dominated by constitutional, national, and dynastic issues.

In the 1830s the Porte redefined Serbia's status, recognizing it as a principality under Serbian control, with Miloš as hereditary prince. In 1838 the Porte issued an administrative statute, the so-called Turkish Constitution, which placed the power of government in the hands of a council of seventeen appointed by the prince. The ruler and council shared legislative functions, but in reality the council held the real power in Serbian political life. The constitutional oligarchy and its supporters, the Constitutionalists, remained in control until 1859. This assemblage of notables, bureaucrats, merchants, and those opposed to the despotic Miloš forced the resignation of first Miloš himself then his son, Mihailo (1823–68). In 1842 they placed Alexander Karadjordjević on the throne. Alexander ruled until 1859, when first Miloš then Mihailo returned to power.

Under Mihailo and his cousin Milan (1854–1901), Serbia wrested itself from Ottoman control.

Y Ottoman troops left Serbian territory in 1867 and Mihailo created a regular army for eventual battle with the Ottomans for independence. The opportunity came in 1876, when the Serbs joined in a widespread revolt against Ottoman rule in the Balkans. Serbia and Montenegro did not gain the advantage until Russia, Romania, and Bulgarian rebels joined the fray to defeat the Turks. The Treaty of Berlin (1878) recognized Serbia and Montenegro as sovereign states and added territory to both. It also granted Austria-Hungary the occupation of Bosnia-Hercegovina and the Sanjak of Novi Pazar, areas coveted by Serbian nationalists. Russia's conduct during the negotiations alienated Serbia because of its support for an enlarged Bulgarian state at the expense of Serbia. Prince Milan became disillusioned with Russia and fearful of the newly created autonomous Bulgaria. He cast Serbia's fortunes with Austria-Hungary, and Serbia's foreign policy until 1903 remained tied to Vienna.

During the 1860s, modern political institutions emerged in Serbia as the oligarchy's power was restricted and transferred to a representative assembly, the Skupština. The prince still played a key role because of his right to appoint a quarter of the Skupština's delegates. This constitution included statements on the equality of all citizens; property rights; freedom of speech, religion, and the press; and the right to petition. In the 1870s the Liberals were the dominant political party, sometimes with challenges from the Progressives. Both these parties drew from the same ideological base, classic nineteenth-century liberalism.

In contrast, another party, the Serbian Radical Party, had its roots in populist, socialist, and anarchist currents of the 1870s. The Radicals promoted the establishment of a parliament elected by universal manhood suffrage, self-administration of districts, direct and progressive taxation, free compulsory education, and a volunteer militia instead of recruitment by force. By 1888, the Radicals had become the dominant party in Serbian politics, only to be eclipsed for a time by the Obrenović dynasty.

While in power, the Radicals hoped that they could expand civil liberties, give more power to the parliament, strengthen local government, provide secret elections, and extend the suffrage to all taxpayers. However, these achievements, codified in a new constitution in 1888, were overshadowed by the domestic affairs of the Obrenović dynasty.

Milan abdicated in 1889 in favor of his son, Alexander (1876–1903).

Alexander was widely unpopular in Serbia because of his arbitrary rule, which included suspension of the 1888 constitution in favor of the 1869 constitution, scandalous personal affairs, and his position favoring Austria-Hungary. In 1903 a group of young army officers brutally murdered Alexander and his wife. Peter Karadjordjević (1844–1921), who knew of the conspiracy, returned from exile to take the throne.

Peter restored the constitution of 1888 and embarked on a foreign policy that turned Serbia away from the Dual Monarchy toward Russia. The Radical Party reemerged and held control of the government from 1906 to 1918. That party, and its leader, Nikola Pašić (1845–1926), supported Peter's foreign policy. Serbia began disengaging from Austria-Hungary's hegemonic financial and tariff practices. In 1905 Serbia and Bulgaria negotiated a customs agreement that eventually resulted in virtual economic union by 1917. Vienna regarded this agreement as hostile to its position in the Balkans and placed a punitive tariff on livestock from Serbia. The "Pig War," so named because hogs were Serbia's most important export, lasted until 1911. This tariff war, along with Peter's and Pašić's connections to Russia, broke Serbia's tight political, economic, and military ties with Austria-Hungary. Serbia now looked to Russia for direction.

Serbian Nationalism, 1833–1914

The years between 1833 and 1878 saw the strengthening of Serbian state and constitutional structures at the expense of Ottoman rule but no territorial acquisitions. Nevertheless, Serbia's political elite and intelligentsia formulated a foreign policy that viewed Serbia as the leader of Serbian and South Slav unification. Like other European nationalists, they equated unification with expansion. In 1844 Ilija Garašanin (1812–74), a Constitutionalist, articulated this view in a secret document, the *Načertanije* (Outline).

Garašanin argued that Serbia's first goal should be complete independence of Serbia from the Ottoman Empire. In addition, he warned of the possibility of another Great Power replacing the Ottomans. The second goal called for the unification of all lands considered Serbian and Orthodox. The lands that fell under this vague description were Vojvodina, Bosnia, Hercegovina, Montenegro,

Kosovo, and northern Albania. He felt the interests of all South Slavs were those of the Serbian state, and South Slav unification was simply an extension of Serbian unification and its state. The basic tenets of the *Načertanije* continued to dominate Serbia's foreign policy in the nineteenth and early twentieth centuries.

During the second half of the nineteenth century, Serbian nationalists to varying degree sought to limit and extinguish the Habsburg and Ottoman presence in the Balkans. This aim was closely connected to their concern of Serbia's gaining the preeminent position in a reconfigured peninsula, much as Prussia had done in the new Germany. With the crowning of Peter Karadjordjević and his policies aimed at loosing Serbia's ties with the Habsburg Empire, Serbian nationalists within and without Serbia proper were emboldened. In the years between 1903 and 1914, a strong emphasis was placed on Serbian expansion. This not only meant the annexation of land still under Ottoman control but also an increased concern over the fate of the Habsburg South Slavs. But the imperial powers would not leave the peninsula without a fight.

The End of Habsburg and Ottoman Rule

In 1908 Austria-Hungary formally annexed Bosnia-Hercegovina. This action frustrated Serbian designs on these lands and precipitated an international crisis. Serbia mobilized its army but under pressure from the Russians, who were pressured by the Germans, backed down. This crisis revealed Russia's weakened position in the Balkans, Serbia's dependence on St. Petersburg for expansion, and Austria-Hungary's determination to maintain its position. On the surface, Belgrade maintained strict official propriety in its relations with Vienna. Behind the scenes, some Serbian government and military factions, as well as clandestine organizations, plotted to limit Habsburg and Ottoman influence in the Balkans.

Serbia's opportunity came in October 1912 when it joined Bulgaria, Greece, Montenegro, and Albanian rebels in ousting the Ottomans from the peninsula. During the First Balkan War, Serbia captured western Macedonia and Kosovo and moved rapidly through Albanian lands to the Adriatic. Austria-Hungary as well as Italy opposed a Serbian outlet to the sea. The Treaty of London (1913) barred Serbia from access to the Adriatic but sought to compensate Serbia and Greece with

the lion's share of Macedonia at the expense of Bulgaria. A conflict erupted immediately over Macedonia. The Second Balkan War began in June 1913. This time Serbia, Montenegro, Greece, Romania, and Turkey joined to defeat Bulgaria in six weeks. The Treaty of Bucharest (August 1913) awarded Serbia the northern portion of Macedonia and half of the Sanjak of Novi Pazar. Greece received southern Macedonian lands, the port of Thessaloníki (Salonika), and part of Epirus. Montenegro was awarded the other half of Novi Pazar. However, Serbia was blocked from the Adriatic by the creation of an Albanian state. Austria's maneuvering during the negotiations to block Serbia from the sea further alienated Serbia and its Great Power supporter, Russia.

Before 1914, Serbian national sentiment had intensified both inside and outside Serbia, and expansionist, nationalist groups flourished. A group of Serbian army officers, headed by the chief of intelligence of the army, Colonel Dragutin Dimitrijević (Apis) (1876–1917), formed the secret organization Ujedinjenje ili Smrt! (Union or Death!), commonly known as the Black Hand. This group's aim was the "unification of Serbdom," and its militancy was matched by "the revolutionary youth."

This revolutionary youth could be found among the Serbs, Croats, and some Bosnian Muslims of the Habsburg monarchy. Their politics lacked any ideological direction, and they were populist, anarchist, and socialist. The most renowned of these groups was Young Bosnia, an organization of young Croats, Serbs, and Muslims in Bosnia-Hercegovina who opposed the oppressive measures of the Austro-Hungarian regime. The assassin of the Habsburg heir, Archduke Franz Ferdinand, was a member of Young Bosnia.

On June 28, 1914, Gavrilo Princip (1894–1918), a member of Young Bosnia, shot and killed Franz Ferdinand (1863–1914) and his wife, Sophia (1868–1914) in Sarajevo. Austria-Hungary, suspecting Serbian government complicity, used the assassination as an excuse to go to war. On July 28, Austria-Hungary declared war on Serbia. Historians have since determined that while Pašić's government can be exonerated of the charge of direct involvement, the Black Hand and Dimitrijević cannot be, for the Black Hand armed and trained the assassin. Within a few weeks, the Central Powers—Germany, Austria-Hungary, and the Ottoman Empire—were at war with the Triple

Y Entente of Britain, Russia, and France. World War I prepared the way for the emergence of the first Yugoslav state.

World War I

During the war, Serbia was buffeted on both sides by the Habsburgs and the Bulgarians, who joined the Central Powers in 1915. Resolutely refusing to surrender, Serbia withstood both the military onslaught and a deadly typhus epidemic, but at the cost of 450,000 casualities. In the fall of 1914 the Serbian government articulated its war aims in the Niš Declaration, which endorsed the unification of Serbs and Croats in one state. The unanswered question was whether Serbia came to the new state as the liberator of the South Slavs or as an equal partner.

Many South Slavs in the Dual Monarchy fought for the empire, but for a reconfigured one. During the war, some Slovene and Croat representatives continued to participate in parliamentary life but argued for trialism. However, a number of prominent South Slavs fled abroad and formed the Yugoslav Committee in November 1914. This committee and its leaders, Trumbić and Supilo, were committed to the unification of the South Slavs in a single state. At this time, the Entente Powers did not support the dissolution of the Habsburg monarchy, even though they were willing to use territories along the Dalmatian coast to entice the Italians to enter the war on their side. In April 1915 the Entente and Italy signed the secret Treaty of London to this effect.

The Treaty of London, as well as Serbia's precarious position in the war, brought the Yugoslav Committee and the Serbian government, now in exile on the island of Corfu, closer together. In July 1917 the Serbian government under Pašić and the Yugoslav Committee signed the Corfu Declaration, calling for creation of a Serb-Croat-Slovene state, which was to be a constitutional monarchy under the Karadjordjević dynasty. The declaration guaranteed equality of language, culture, and religion of the three constituent peoples—Serbs, Croats, and Slovenes. But the document did not specify whether the new state was to adopt a federal or a unitary constitution.

As Habsburg authority disintegrated in October 1918, a group of Slovene, Croat, and Serb politicians from the monarchy formed the National Council of the Slovenes, Croats, and Serbs. Its leaders—Slovene Anton Korošec (1872–1940),

Croat Ante Pavelić (1889–1959), and Serb Svetozar Pribičević (1875–1936)—called for a free South Slav state, which the Croatian Sabor endorsed. The Sabor declared Croatia an independent state on October 29. The Sabor then proceeded to pass a motion advocating the unification of Croatia with Serbia and Montenegro. On December 1, 1918, the Serbian prince-regent, Alexander Karadjordjević, proclaimed the establishment of the Kingdom of Serbs, Croats, and Slovenes.

1918–1945: The First Yugoslavia

The first tasks of the newly independent kingdom were formal recognition of its existence, establishment of its international borders, and adopting a constitution.

At the peace table, the new kingdom had to settle border disputes with six of its seven neighbors: Italy, Austria, Albania, Bulgaria, Hungary, and Romania. The occupation of key areas by the Serbian army gained the new kingdom an advantage in these disputes except with Italy. The Italians demanded full implementation of the Treaty of London, and most of its claims were recognized, though many of the areas had large Slavic majorities. Italy received Istria, an independent Rijeka, the city of Zadar, and some Dalmatian islands. This settlement poisoned Yugoslav-Italian relations between the wars.

The battles at the peace table were matched by the battles waged over the constitution for the new kingdom. Leading up to the elections for the Constituent Assembly in November 1920, political parties that represented ethnic, regional, and religious interests debated the merits of centralism versus federalism. The Democratic Party of Pribičević, which elected ninety-two members to the assembly, represented Serbs who lived mostly outside Serbia and supported centralism. The Serbian Radical Party of Pašić, which elected ninety-one members, drew its constituency from the Serbian peasantry and also essentially campaigned for its tradition of a centralized, unitary state.

In opposition to these two Serbian parties was Radić's renamed Croatian Republican Peasant Party, which won fifty seats. Radić mobilized the Croatian peasantry, which was now a powerful force in electoral politics, owing to universal male suffrage. (Women did not receive the right to vote until 1945.) Radić and his candidates campaigned for some sort of loose federation or confederation; they would not accept centralism.

Maneuvering between the centralist Serbs and the federalist Croats were the Slovenes, represented by the People's Party with twenty-seven deputies, and the Muslims of Bosnia-Hercegovina, represented by the Yugoslav Muslim Organization with twenty-four deputies. The smaller Slavic nationalities—Montenegrins, Macedonians, and non-Slavic peoples (Albanians and the Hungarians)—received no constitutional recognition and exerted little influence over the decision-making process.

Taking advantage of the social and political upheaval in the South Slav lands were the Communists. Throughout 1919, they helped to organize labor actions and strikes. In November 1920 they drew on their links with trade unions and youth organizations to elect fifty-nine deputies to the assembly. The following month the government outlawed all Communist activity, and in 1921 the assembly denied the Communist delegates their seats. The Communists were driven underground and operated illegally throughout the interwar period.

The constitution for the Kingdom of Serbs, Croats, and Slovenes was adopted on the Serbian national holiday Vidovdan, the feast of St. Vitus (June 28, 1921). The Vidovdan Constitution, a replica of the 1903 Serbian constitution, rejected a federalist solution in favor of a unitary system. The constitution established a parliamentary democracy and provided individual liberties, but allowed little room for regional and local initiative and autonomy. This centralist solution had all but been ensured when the anticentralist factions boycotted or left the assembly. Croatian Republican Peasant Party delegates had refused to send delegates to Belgrade, and the Slovene People's Party and the Communists left the assembly when they realized a centralist constitution was inevitable. Out of the 419 delegates, 161 did not vote.

Bitter conflicts between Serbs and Croats over the unitary nature of the state plagued the interwar kingdom. The Vidovdan Constitution guaranteed Serbia the preeminent position in the new state and pushed the Croats into the position of revisionists. Government after government refused to reopen the constitutional question or increase Croatia's autonomy. The Croats boycotted the parliament until 1925.

In 1925 Radić and the Croatian Peasant Party agreed to recognize the constitution and the Karadjordjević dynasty. For a year, the Croatian Peasant Party was part of a coalition government with Pašić's Radicals. This coalition failed and Radić sought out another of his former adversaries, Pribičević and his party, the Independent Democrats, to form a Peasant-Independent bloc in parliament. This bloc was made possible by Pribičević's rejection of centralism, which he believed not only worked against the Croats but also against the Serbs in Croatia. The Independent-Peasant bloc proved to be the most effective opposition to centralism until 1941.

In June 1928 parliamentary politics turned violent. Radić and two other Croatian deputies were shot on the floor of the Skupština by a Montenegrin deputy belonging to the Serbian Radical Party. The two Croatian deputies died immediately, and Radić died in August. This violence highlighted the system's failure to achieve interethnic cooperation and political legitimacy.

After several attempts to reconcile Serbs and Croats, King Alexander dissolved parliament, suspended the constitution, abolished religious and ethnically based parties, and initiated a royal dictatorship in January 1929. Between 1929 and 1934, Alexander renamed the country the "Kingdom of Yugoslavia," reorganized the state into nine *banovine* (districts) that ignored traditional, historical, and ethnic boundaries and increased the power of the king and the central authorities. Alexander's newly reconfigured state was still dominated by Serbs.

Opposition continued to exist. In the "Zagreb Resolution," the Peasant-Independent bloc denounced the changes and called for a federal system. Less moderate opposition also appeared. The radical Croatian Ustaša and the Internal Macedonian Revolutionary Organization (IMRO) preferred violent confrontation to parliamentary discourse. These two organizations, with the help of the Hungarians and Italians who had territorial claims against the kingdom, planned the assassination of King Alexander. On October 9, 1934, they succeeded.

Grief for the king, who was murdered in Marseilles, was genuinely expressed by Serbs and Croats alike. His son, Peter II (1923–70), was too young to ascend the throne, so Alexander's cousin, Prince Paul (1893–1976), created a three-man regency. Paul, while continuing to rule with the 1931 constitution, made gestures toward opposition groups. The leader of the Croatian Peasant Party after Radić's death, Vladko Maček (1879–1964),

Y was released from prison. Elections held in 1935, despite voting fraud, revealed an emboldened opposition. The Croatian deputies boycotted the Skupština, but the new prime minister, a young Serbian Radical, Milan Stojadinović (1888–1961), persuaded the Slovene and Muslim party leaders to join his government.

Stojadinović, in his three years as prime minister, refused to weaken the authoritarian system or address the Croatian question. Stojadinović faced increasing militancy among Croatian separatists and Communist-inspired student protests. In addition, his support among Serbian nationalists suffered when he negotiated an agreement with the Vatican that gave the Catholic Church equal footing with the Orthodox Church. The Serbian-dominated Skupština refused to recognize it, and relations with the Croats further deteriorated when Stojadinović abandoned this concordat in early 1938.

Displeasure over Stojadinović's handling of the concordat was reflected in the Skupština elections of December 1938. Maček's opposition bloc, composed of the Croatian Peasant Party, the Independent Democrats, the Democrats, the Serbian Agrarian Party, and the Radical Party, won 44.9 percent of the vote. While the biased electoral system gave the opposition only 67 of the 373 seats, Stojadinović suffered a moral defeat. Recognizing this election as a vote of no confidence, Prince Paul asked Dragiša Cvetković (1893–1969) to form a government in February 1939. Both the domestic and the international situation forced Cvetković's government to negotiate with Maček and the Croatian Republican Peasant Party.

On August 26, 1939, the Belgrade government signed the *Sporazum* (Understanding) with the Croats. Negotiated by Maček, this agreement granted the Croats their own *banovina,* made up of the Savska and Primorska provinces. The *Sporazum* gave Croatia almost complete autonomy. It was to have its own parliament and a governor appointed by the monarch. Belgrade would control only foreign affairs, foreign trade, defense, transportation, and communications. Maček and four other Peasant Party leaders joined Cvetković's government, and Ivan Šubašić (1892–1955) was appointed governor.

This step toward federalism, instead of satisfying the Croats, only fueled greater expectations for devolution. Maček and the Croats viewed the *Sporazum* as a step toward independence. The other nationalities within the kingdom wanted similar concessions.

Parliamentary instability, corruption, and the Serb-Croat conflict prevented the new state from developing either political legitimacy or socioeconomic stability and often plunged the government into legislative paralysis. Significant social or economic legislation stalled in the Skupština or met with implementation problems. Promises of reconstruction, economic development, and agrarian reform remained unfulfilled during the interwar period.

The most pressing problems facing the new kingdom in 1918 were peasant discontent and rural overpopulation. To rectify the land problem, the provisional government in 1919 passed a major land reform bill. The state expropriated large estates between 747 and 1,245 acres (300–500 hectares) and distributed the land to peasant families. This law also initiated a program of colonization that moved Serbian, Montenegrin, and Croatian war veterans into Macedonia and Vojvodina. The purpose of the colonization was to dilute the indigenous populations in those areas because non-Slavic Germans, Hungarians, and Albanians were supposedly not to be trusted. Between 1920 and 1938, 6.2 million acres (2.5 million hectares) were distributed among 637,328 families.

Interwar Yugoslavia was to remain predominately a country of smallholders and faced the problem of rural overpopulation. There were a total of 36.1 million acres (14.5 million hectares) of arable land; 18.9 million acres (7.6 million hectares) were cultivated by 2.2 million peasant families. By the early 1930s, land reform had done little to alleviate rural overpopulation. In 1931, 10.6 million people, or 76.5 percent of the population, were still engaged in agriculture, while 11 percent, or 1.5 million, made their living from industry, handicrafts, and mining. There were regional differences as well. In the northernmost *banovina,* Drava (Slovenia), only 60.3 percent were peasants, while in the *banovina* Vrbas (northwestern Bosnia) 88.2 percent were engaged in agriculture. Interwar governments never succeeded in decreasing agricultural overpopulation, peasant indebtedness, and illiteracy. Industrialization was not developing fast enough to siphon off excess population.

Industrialization in the interwar state was hampered by a weak internal market, few capital resources, an unskilled labor force, a small entrepreneurial class, and a helter-skelter transportation network designed for Hungarian, Habsburg, and Ottoman markets. Interwar governments pursued economic policies that hoped to create a strong internal market, which would in turn drive capital formation. Before 1914, most domestic industrial and manufactured goods had been exported. After 1918, industrial exports fell because Hungarian and Austrian markets were lost. New markets had to be found, but this was not an easy task because of the high protective tariffs of many European countries during the interwar period. Manufactured goods were now confined to domestic sales. As a result of these trends, agricultural processing fell off significantly. Growth in flour milling, meatpacking, and leather processing remained below prewar levels until 1929.

Until the mid-1930s, interwar governments followed an economic policy of import substitution and high customs tariffs to spur industrial growth. But these policies were ill conceived. There was little real infrastructure, and the country had too little market and technical expertise to forgo importing machinery, expertise, and finished goods. In addition, no significant tax policy was ever devised to foster capital accumulation. Instead, the government borrowed money at high interest rates that was difficult to repay. Once the loans were obtained, they went to enlarging the state bureaucracy and to pet projects of politicians and business leaders.

Some industries did expand. Above-average growth was recorded in cement production, timber and paper processing, and sugar refining. Mining and metallurgy also saw growth. However, this expansion was due primarily to foreign capital and to high prices at the expense of the consumer. What domestic capital existed was often invested in urban construction. Between 50 and 60 percent of domestic capital formation went to housing.

During the mid-1930s, Stojadinović's government pushed for local processing of minerals and ore and for developing manufacturing industries based on processing and finishing materials found in Yugoslavia. For the textile industry, the government imported machinery and workers from Poland and Czechoslovakia. Under government stimulation, cement plants and furniture factories began to process asphalt and timber resources. Under Stojadinović, manufacturing increased but it was based on foreign capital and agreements with foreign governments. Despite some successes, interwar governments were unable to sustain consistent economic growth. Yugoslavia in 1939 remained one of the poorest countries in Europe.

Throughout the interwar period, the majority of Yugoslav women, like their male counterparts, lived and made their livelihoods in the countryside. Yet unlike their fathers, brothers, husbands, and sons, women made few economic or political gains during the interwar period. While the Yugoslav constitution of 1921 granted male suffrage, it did not extend the same right to women or alter women's legal status. The kingdom continued relegating women to the position of minors, dependent on male family members. In addition, women were not allowed to run for public office or to serve in government positions. During the interwar period, many urban middle-class women fought for economic and political rights.

Women's socioeconomic position during the interwar period also remained below the gains made by men. Girls were required to attend school for only four years, half the requirement for boys. In rural areas, officials tended not to enforce mandatory schooling for boys or girls. The 1931 census revealed that 32.2 percent of the male population and 54.4 percent of the female were illiterate. In the primarily Muslim communities in Macedonia, Serbia, Kosovo, and Bosnia-Hercegovina, female illiteracy was reported to be as high as 85 to 90 percent.

During the interwar period, women represented between 20 and 30 percent of the industrial workforce. Most women worked in domestic service or in the textile, clothing, or tobacco industries. As in other countries, women's wages were lower than men's, ranging from as little as 5 percent to as much as 36 percent. In the countryside, industrialization and disintegration of the *zadruga* had reduced the extended family to a single-family household. With their husbands, sons, and fathers looking for work in the cities, women assumed a greater variety and burden of tasks. By 1939, one out of five agricultural households was headed by a woman.

World War II
During the interwar period, Yugoslavia allied itself with countries that wished to keep the Versailles treaty intact. Czechoslovakia, Romania, and Yugoslavia, through a series of treaties signed in the early 1920s, formed the Little Entente, established

to defend against countries with territorial claims against each signatory. Bulgaria, Italy, Hungary, and later Germany all wished to revise the peace settlements and looked to gain territory from their neighbors. France was the only major European power that actively supported the Little Entente against these revisionists. France itself stood to lose in any modification of Versailles. Thus, Europe was divided diplomatically into two camps: status quo states and revisionist states. Two months before his death in October 1934, Alexander tried to strengthen Yugoslavia's position vis-à-vis the revisionist Italians and Bulgarians by signing a mutual defense agreement with Romania, Greece, and Turkey. This agreement was known as the Balkan Entente.

During the 1930s, the Kingdom of Yugoslavia began to doubt the sincerity of France's and Britain's support. Both states refused to censure Italy for its part in Alexander's murder. In addition, Prince Paul became wary of France's commitment to the Little Entente as Nazi Germany grew in power and influence and the French did nothing. The weakening of French influence and resolve pushed the Yugoslavs into making a series of agreements with their revisionist neighbors. Between 1937 and 1941, the kingdom undertook agreements that reversed its alliance system. By 1941, it had only to sign a pact with Nazi Germany to complete the circle.

On March 25, 1941, the government of Cvetković and Maček signed the Tripartite Pact, which militarily allied Yugoslavia with Nazi Germany, Italy, Japan, Hungary, Slovakia, and Romania. The pact was directed against the United States and Great Britain. Cvetković felt that this pact was necessary to protect the kingdom from its revisionist neighbors. However, pro-Western sentiments were running high, and on learning of the pact, a group of pro-Western Serb military officers executed a coup d'état in the name of the young king, Peter II, on March 27, 1941.

The new government of General Dušan Simović (1882–1962) had a difficult time winning the confidence of Maček and the Croats. Despite assurances from Simović that his government would honor the pact with Germany, Hitler (1889–1945) ordered air attacks on Belgrade and a land offensive to commence on April 6. Axis forces from Italy, Albania, Bulgaria, Romania, and Hungary entered the country and defeated the Yugoslav army in eleven days.

Representatives of the royal Yugoslav government surrendered on April 17, 1941. Several days earlier, Peter II and members of the government had fled into exile. All governmental authority was now in the hands of the kingdom's detractors and conquerors.

Under its occupiers, Yugoslavia did not remain a single multinational state. Instead, it fell victim to irredentist envy, militaristic demands, and interwar nationalistic aims. Italy, Germany, Bulgaria, Hungary, and Albania all received parts of the newly defeated kingdom. Italy and Germany divided Slovenia between them; Italy annexed large parts of Dalmatia and some islands in the Adriatic and controlled Kosovo-Metohija through its puppet state in Albania. The Croatian fascist Ustaša, headed by Pavelić, proclaimed an independent state of Croatia, and under Nazi patronage incorporated large areas of Bosnia-Hercegovina. Germany and Bulgaria administered parts of Serbia and Macedonia either directly or through collaborators.

In early April, before the kingdom's surrender, the Axis powers tried to persuade Croatia's most influential political party and the primary representative of Croatian nationalism, the Croatian Peasant Party and its leader Maček, to establish an independent state of Croatia and to ally the new state with the Axis. Maček refused. As a result, the Axis turned to the Ustaša, which had been politically insignificant, to proclaim an independent state and to preside over its development. The Ustaša proclaimed the Nezavisna Država Hrvatske (Independent State of Croatia, NDH) on April 10. Maček issued a statement calling on Croats to cooperate with the new government. The Ustaša came to power with the support of Germany and Italy and in the political vacuum left by the exit of the Croatian Peasant Party. Maček would spend the majority of the war under house arrest.

The Ustaša shared the cult of the state with the fascist and Nazi movements and used the instruments of the state to promulgate a new vision of the Croatian nation. It viewed the new state as a bulwark of Western civilization against the Serbs, one that was to be racially pure Croat. From 1941 to 1945, Pavelić's regime instituted a campaign to rid the new Croatian state of its two million Serbs. The policies of the Independent State of Croatia directed at the Serbs within their newly expanded territory were threefold: expulsion of Serbs from Croatia and Bosnia-Hercegovina; conversion of

Orthodox Serbs to Catholicism; internment of Serbs in concentration camps. The extreme violence used to carrying out these policies resulted in the death or disappearance of over three hundred thousand Serbs as well as Gypsies and Jews. The number of Serbs who died within the territory administered by the Independent State of Croatia is disputed today, yet even the Germans were appalled by the Ustaša violence, and warned that it would ignite resistance. Italy reoccupied areas of Hercegovina to halt the Ustaša slaughter there.

The rump of Serbia was occupied by the Germans, but local collaborators under the direction of General Milan Nedić (1877–1946) administered the state. However, the German authorities never trusted Nedić and kept military control by working with Dimitrije Ljotić (1891–1945), a Serb fascist, and his Serbian Volunteer Corps. The Germans supplied and maintained this force of approximately 3,600 men.

The German occupation of northern Slovenia brought terror, bloodshed, the erasing of Slovenian culture, and resettlement. Slovenes were forced to vacate their farms and houses and move to Serbia. German colonists moved into the vacant homes. In areas occupied by Italians, Hungarians, and Albanians, Jews and Serbs suffered violence at the hands of the occupiers and many Serbs fled into Serbia. In Macedonia, many welcomed Bulgarian forces. Macedonians hoped they would receive autonomy, but instead they suffered a brutal Bulgarianization campaign. The Italians tried to install a puppet regime in Montenegro, but the Montenegrins ruined these plans with an uprising, remaining outside the Italians' grasp and contributing a high percentage of both Chetnik and Partisan soldiers.

Amid this chaos, a number of resistance movements emerged. Serbs within the Royal Army gathered around General Staff Colonel Draža Mihailović (1893–1946). This group of Yugoslav officers, noncommissioned officers, soldiers, and policemen adopted the name Chetnik Detachments of the Yugoslav Army and fled to the mountains of northern Bosnia after the rapid collapse of the royal army in April 1941. Moving southward into Serbia, the Chetniks tapped into the resistance in the south and soon had units in Serbia, Montenegro, and regions of the Independent State of Croatia where the Serb population fought against the policies of the Croatian state.

Primarily a Greater Serbian group with anti-Croatian and anti-Communist sentiments, the Chetniks pledged allegiance to the government-in-exile and sought to reinstall the monarchy after the war. Until December 1943, the Allies fully supported the Yugoslav government-in-exile, Mihailović, and the Chetniks.

The absence of a central unifying authority was crucial to the development of the Communist Partisan movement. With the monarchy gone and the country dismembered, the Communists activated their small but well-organized party. Headed by Josip Broz Tito (1892–1980), son of a Croatian-Slovenian peasant family, the Communist Party called on their membership of twelve thousand, which had been rebuilt after years of police repression, internal conflict, and the Stalinist purges of the 1930s, and the thirteen thousand members of the Communist Youth Organization to wage war against the invaders. In July 1941, a few weeks after the German attack on the Soviet Union, the Communist-led Partisans, with some Chetnik support, launched a series of armed actions against the occupiers. Having taken the Germans by surprise, the Partisans held parts of western Serbia around Užice for several months.

In response to the resistance from Chetniks and Partisans, the Germans used a tactic that they had employed elsewhere in their occupied areas to discourage attacks on German soldiers; for every German soldier killed, one hundred citizens would be killed. On October 21, 1941, German army units killed seven thousand men and boys in Kragujevac in retaliation for an attack on German soldiers. The Chetniks' response was to order their forces not to engage the Germans. Mihailović feared their activities would place too many Serb lives in jeopardy. Tito believed that the Germans' actions would bring more people into the Partisan movement for protection and revenge. He disregarded the German threat and continued overt resistance and guerrilla warfare.

In September 1941 Tito and Mihailović met to coordinate Chetnik and Partisan resistance efforts. This cooperation was short-lived because of their differences in strategy and visions for the postwar world. Their different reactions to Kragujevac sealed the fate of the alliance. In late October Partisans and Chetniks parted ways. Throughout the war, both resistance groups, when possible, waged war against each other, sometimes collaborating with the occupiers to do so.

Y Until December 1943, the Allied governments supported the royal government-in-exile and the Chetniks in the war for Yugoslavia. However, during the summer and fall of 1943, the Partisans' fortunes changed. They survived a German offensive designed to end their resistance, and they took advantage of Italy's surrender in September 1943. The Partisans captured Italian arms and gained control of coastal territory. Recognizing the Partisans' resolve to engage the Germans, the Allies at the December 1943 conference in Tehran decided to support the Partisans and supply them with weapons and war matériel. A month later, Britain stopped supplying the Chetniks and withdrew its liaison officers from Mihailović's headquarters. In February 1944 the first Soviet advisers reached the Partisans.

As the war drew to a close, the Allies accepted that the Partisans had a political edge over any opponent. Britain encouraged King Peter to negotiate with the Partisans and to abandon his pro-Chetnik government. On June 1, 1944, Peter appointed Šubašić as the head of the government-in-exile and agreed to remain outside Yugoslavia until the end of the war. Šubašić, the former *ban* of Croatia, accepted the resolutions of the second AVNOJ (the Partisans' Anti-Fascist Council) conference. In mid-June, Šubašić traveled to the island of Vis, where Partisan headquarters had been relocated after an unsuccessful German raid in May, and signed an agreement with Tito whereby members of Šubašić's government should join Tito's provisional government.

All enemy armies had left or been driven out of the country by spring 1945. In October 1944 the Soviet Red Army had aided the Partisans in liberating the northern part of Yugoslavia and Belgrade but left no troops behind. The Partisans and the Western allies were left to defeat the remaining occupiers and domestic foes. On March 7, 1945, the united governments of Šubašić and Tito took control of Yugoslavia. Šubašić was appointed foreign minister and Tito prime minister. Only two other members of the government-in-exile served in the provisional government. In reality, the Communists and their supporters controlled it.

During 1945, the Communists positioned themselves to be the sole heirs to the Kingdom of Yugoslavia. They accomplished this by prohibiting suspected fascist sympathizers from serving in the Provisional Assembly, harassing non-Communist politicians and rivals, and controlling the election process in November. Some opponents were also treated to farcical trials and brutal punishments such as confiscation of capital, internment in labor camps, imprisonment, and even death. In the elections of November 1945, the Communists' candidates won 90 percent of the vote. The newly elected Skupština renamed the kingdom the Federal People's Republic of Yugoslavia, and the Karadjordjević dynasty and monarchy were abolished. The Communists would rule Yugoslavia until 1991.

1945–1989: Communist Yugoslavia

The vision for the new Yugoslavia was laid out in the constitution of 1946, Yugoslavia's third in thirty years, modeled on the Soviet Constitution of 1936. This document created a federalist state with six federal units: Slovenia, Croatia, Bosnia-Hercegovina, Serbia, Montenegro, and Macedonia. In an effort to lessen Serbian influence, Vojvodina and Kosovo were given autonomous status within Serbia. The constitution spoke of "brotherhood and unity" and promised a better world based on social equality. Despite the establishment of a Federal Assembly (Skupština) and other federal and democratic structures, Yugoslavia was not democratic or federal. This new federalism and socioeconomic system was ruled over by the highly centralized Yugoslav Communist Party. Formal politics were dominated by the party and its inner party elite. Party and state were inextricably linked.

World War II had claimed 1.1 million people, or 10.8 percent of Yugoslavia's prewar population. In addition, the war had decimated the industrial and agricultural sectors of the economy. At the end of the war, for the whole of Yugoslavia, the total industrial output was 32–35 percent of its 1938 level. Textile production had fallen to 30–40 percent of its prewar level, food processing to 40–50 percent, and metal industries to 15–20 percent. In addition, transportation networks in some areas were completely destroyed. The total cost of the devastation and destruction wrought by the four years of fighting were industry—$3,060,800,858; private and public buildings—$130,834,678; and agriculture—$388,801,000. This destruction compounded the past inadequacies in industrial and agricultural production and the shortage of capital, equipment, and modern industrial practices in the interwar period. The Yugoslav Communists now had to wrestle with the consequences of war and the task of building the "new" Yugoslavia.

The Communist government embarked on its reconstruction and modernization campaign armed with the Soviet model of economic development. For the first several years, the Communists copied Soviet-type economic planning to become a modern industrial power. In 1946 the Skupština nationalized industries of federal importance, banking, and transportation. By 1948, the Communists had nationalized the industrial and service sectors. In 1947 they adopted a five-year plan that focused on the development of heavy industry, the exploitation of domestic raw materials, and the economic development of the poorer, rural regions. Missing from this plan was the collectivization of agriculture. The Communists treaded more warily in the countryside because of their wartime alliance with the peasantry and their need for agricultural surplus.

In August 1945 the Skupština approved the Law on Agrarian Reform and Colonization. This law redistributed to the peasantry all confiscated land from banks, religious institutions, absentee landlords, large landowners, and the expelled German minority in Vojvodina. Half of the 3.73 million acres (1.5 million hectares) went to the peasants; the other half was reserved for state-owned agricultural institutions. The Communists postponed any decision about collectivization until 1949. Instead, they required peasants to sell their produce at below-market prices and to tie themselves to a variety of state-run cooperatives and agricultural stations. In 1949 the Communists attempted to form peasant work cooperatives, the Yugoslav collective farm. But peasant resistance and the Communists' changing domestic and international fortunes forced the government to abandon this endeavor in 1951. Communist peasant policies were not without victims. Tens of thousands were forced to give up land, property, and possessions, and were sent to prison or killed.

Separate Road to Socialism

Between 1941 and 1948, Tito and his party many times adopted positions and policies contrary to the Soviets and their interests. Yugoslav Communists implemented a brand of national communism following practices that met specific country conditions and interests but did not necessarily serve the interests of the world Communist movement (i.e., the Soviets). Such practices were tolerated until 1947 when Stalin (1879–1953) feared that Soviet control of Eastern Europe was slipping. In

September the Soviets sponsored the creation of the Communist Information Bureau (Cominform) to coordinate information and propaganda among Communist parties. The headquarters was to be in Belgrade. On the surface, the Yugoslavs appeared to be Stalin's staunchest ally. Yet Stalin resented Yugoslavia's drive for independence and saw Tito and his supporters as a threat to his efforts to create a Soviet-dominated Eastern Europe.

In 1948 Tito and Stalin clashed over Tito's aggressive, independent foreign policy initiatives. Beginning in 1945, Tito had defied Soviet counsel in disputes over Trieste, the Greek civil war, and a proposed federation of Balkan states. These policies flew in the face of Stalin, who did not want a polycentric Communist world. Tito challenged Soviet monocentrism and thus had to be removed from power. Stalin initiated the break when he expelled the Yugoslav Communist Party from the Cominform on June 28, 1948. But the Yugoslav party rallied around Tito and refused to remove him and his supporters from power. Yugoslavia survived the political and economic ostracism of the Soviets and their allies. Beginning in 1949, the Yugoslav Communists began to experiment with their own brand of socialism.

The break with the Soviets was not without consequences for the Yugoslavs. In 1949 Yugoslavia stood isolated and had to contend with a Soviet-led embargo, dwindling food supplies, an ill-planned collectivization drive, a centrally planned economy whose fortunes had been tied to the other economies of the Soviet bloc, and possible Soviet military intervention. As realists, the Yugoslav Communists began to rethink both their ideological and international positions.

In late 1949 the Yugoslavs went on an ideological counterattack. They scaled back the drive to form peasant work cooperatives and began to form workers' councils in state enterprises. These actions signaled a shift away from Stalinist socioeconomic policies. The Yugoslav Communists claimed that these changes rested on the writings of Karl Marx (1818–83), which Stalin had perverted. In June 1950 the Skupština passed the Basic Law on the Management of State Economic Enterprises and Higher Economic Associations by the Working Collectives. This law and several others addressed the relationship of workers to their workplace and the state. Known as workers' self-management, the system was based on transferring the means of production from state to social control. In theory, workers were entrusted with management responsibilities in the form of workers' councils. These councils, made up of workers, set production goals and supervised finances. However, state-appointed directors could veto council decisions. To emphasize their "separate road to socialism" and their break with Stalinist ways, the Yugoslavs renamed their party the League of Communists of Yugoslavia (LCY) in 1952.

Despite these changes, the Communists retained political control over the state. They removed themselves from government and economic activity but rejected political pluralism. The party was to lead society through persuasion and education. Intraparty debate would determine the proper policies, and once agreed upon there could be no dissent. When dissent appeared, as it did in Miljovan Djilas's (1911–95) critique of the bureaucratism and elitism of the League of Communists, it was stifled.

In September 1949 Yugoslavia and the United States forged a relationship based on realpolitik, the politics of the practical. The United States loaned the Yugoslav government $620 million and gained political and ideological advantage; they aided Yugoslavia in the interest of dividing the Soviet bloc. Yugoslavia's ties with the West remained the cornerstone of Tito's foreign policy until Stalin's death in 1953. After 1953, Tito and Stalin's successors' normalized relations between the two countries.

Tito's successful maneuvering between East and West propelled him into making alliances with the newly independent states of the colonial world. In 1956 Tito and the leaders of India and Egypt issued a declaration condemning the bipolar world. Five years later, fifty-one nonaligned states met in Belgrade to formulate strategies that would allow them to create a third bloc. The nonaligned movement denounced colonialism, condemned apartheid, and ordered a halt to military actions against liberation movements. Nonalignment remained the basis of Yugoslavia's foreign policy into the 1980s.

The political and economic reforms of the 1950s had been half-measures designed to restore order at home and promote Yugoslavia's ideological vision abroad. The economy and state institutions stood in between central planning institutions and hybrid market mechanisms. At the beginning of the 1960s, the consequences of these reforms were seen in industrial inefficiency; highly politi-cized investment decisions; bickering among republican and local governments over prestigious infrastructure projects; deep regional differences in income, productivity, social services, and development; and the 1962 recession. Nationalist sentiments reemerged as a result of the different standards of living among the republics, usually along a north-south divide.

The Yugoslavs adopted both a new federal constitution and new republican constitutions in 1963 to harmonize their reforms of the last decade. In these constitutions, the concept of self-management was expanded into the social realm. Local councils were established for education, culture, welfare, public health, and administration. Conditions for holding office were changed; except for Tito, no official could hold both a party and a governmental office.

During the early 1960s, two groups concerned with economic policy emerged within the party. The reformers or liberals were led by Croat Vladimir Bakarić (1912–) and Slovene Edvard Kardelj (1910–79), and advocated decentralization in investment and industrial decision making. The drive was for investment based on efficiency and productivity. These policies benefited the wealthier republics of Croatia and Slovenia. Conservatives in the party, mostly from Serbia and Montenegro, favored centralization and targeting the less developed regions for investment. At the Eighth Party Congress in December 1964, the liberals' reforms were adopted. Not only did the reformers succeed in moving important economic institutions from the federal to the republican level, but concurrently, their staunchest critic, Aleksandar Ranković (1909–83), head of the security police, was also removed from power in 1966.

The economic and political reforms of the mid-1960s revealed deep divisions within the party and outside it. The economic reforms had benefited the wealthier northern republics over the southern republics. The tightening of credit and the rationalization of investment policy spurred unemployment and left the underdeveloped regions undercapitalized. The party was also divided within itself. The reformers wanted power transferred to the republics, and the "localists" wanted power devolved even further into regional and local organizations. Both these factions bumped up against an unchanged bureaucracy reluctant to implement any reform. The problems of economic stagnation, unemployment, declining real wages, inflation, balance-of-payments deficits, and a falling currency remained unsolved, adding to political discontent.

The loosening of party controls over the economy and politics also permeated the social realm. During the 1960s, universities and newspapers became centers of dissent for critics of the Yugoslav experiment. In 1964 a number of intellectuals in Zagreb and Belgrade began the journal *Praxis*, whose articles used unorthodox interpretations of Marx to critique social and political conditions in Yugoslavia. The *Praxis* circle also lent support to the Belgrade student demonstrations in June 1968. The students demanded better living conditions, guaranteed employment after graduation, elimination of police brutality, and an end to social inequality. Tito expressed sympathy for the students' demands and some of them were met.

The party dealt with this type of societal discontent with a measured response. The most sensitive issue, however, the national question, had not yet been confronted. In 1969 the Ninth Congress of the LCY met to address the configuration of the party. This congress affirmed that the League of Communists of Yugoslavia now comprised eight parties—one for each republic, and one for Kosovo and Vojvodina. This decision was made in the wake of the riots in Kosovo.

During the protests, Albanians, who made up 90 percent of Kosovo's population, demanded that Kosovo have republican status, the right to secede, and an Albanian university. Scores of Albanians were arrested, and a purge of the party undertaken.

The social and nationalist unrest in Serbia and Kosovo spread into Croatia, where intellectuals and party leaders had been revisiting past discriminations and complaining of discriminatory economic practices. The grievances ranged from denying the validity of Serbo-Croatian as a historical language and promoting the Croatian language's distinctiveness, to discontent over the placement of many banking and industrial headquarters in Belgrade and the leveling of disproportionate taxes on Croatia for the federal budget and the development fund. Between 1969 and 1972, the nationalist forces were led in the League of Communists of Croatia by Miko Tripalo (1926–), Pero Pirker (n.d.), and Savka Dabčević-Kučar (1923–), and outside the party by the cultural institution Matica Hrvatska (Croatian Home).

In November 1971 the nationalist paper *Hrvatski tjednik* (*Croatian Weekly*) published a proposal from Matica Hrvatska for a new Croatian constitution. This proposal sought autonomy for Croatia, the right to secede, and a Croatian territorial army. A month later, Tito intervened decisively and put an end to the "Croatian Spring." The Croatian party and government was purged of its nationalists and liberals. Over four hundred people were dismissed or resigned from their jobs. Matica Hrvatska was closed and its leaders, including the future president of Croatia, Franjo Tudjman (1922–), were arrested.

This crackdown signaled the end of an era that had allowed liberal forces greater latitude within the party and in society. Tito called for tightening discipline within the party and backed this up by dismissing the reformist party leaders of Serbia, Slovenia, Macedonia, and Vojvodina. He now equated liberal reformers with nationalists. In addition, the party silenced the media, arrested dissidents, pressured universities to root out subversive elements, and gained control over the domain of culture. Democratic centralism within the party and Tito's leading role were affirmed by the Tenth Party Congress in May 1974. However, the federal basis of the state was left untouched. The new constitution of 1974 enshrined the decentralization reforms of the last decade. Despite the threat of nationalist sentiments, the constitution shifted considerable power to the six republics and the two autonomous provinces of Vojvodina and Kosovo. Such reforms encouraged the growth of regional bureaucracies and strengthened the power of the republican leagues of Communists.

The 1974 constitution also divided the country's ethnic groups into two categories: Yugoslav nations whose traditional homeland lay within the country and main nationalities whose traditional homeland lay outside the country. The Yugoslav nations were Croats, Serbs, Slovenes, Montenegrins, Macedonians, and Muslim Slavs. The main nationalities were Albanians, Bulgars, Czechs, Hungarians, Italians, Romanians, Ruthenians, Slovaks, Turks, and Ukrainians. This constitution elevated Muslims Slavs to nation status, while denying the same status to Albanians.

After World War II, the Yugoslav population grew from 15.7 million in 1948 to 22.4 million in 1981. According to the census of 1981, Serbs made up 36.3 percent of the population, or 8.14 million people; Croats, 19.8 percent or 4.42 million; Muslim Slavs, 8.9 percent, or 2 million; Slovenes, 7.8 percent, or 1.75 million; Albanians,

7.7 percent, or 1.73 million; Macedonians, 6.0 percent, or 1.33 million; Montenegrins, 2.6 percent, or 579,023; and Hungarians, 1.9 percent, or 426,866. About 1.2 million people, or 5.4 percent, declared themselves ethnic Yugoslavs. The census of 1981 provides a complex view of Yugoslavia's ethnic diversity.

In Bosnia-Hercegovina, the most ethnically diverse republic with a population of 4.12 million, Muslim Slavs made up 39.5 percent of the population; Serbs, 32 percent; Croats, 18.4 percent; and Yugoslavs, 7.9 percent. In Croatia, with a population of 4.6 million, Croats made up 75.1 percent of the population; Serbs, 11.5 percent; and Yugoslavs, 8.2 percent. In Kosovo, with a population of 1.58 million, 77.4 percent were Albanians; Serbs, 13.2 percent; Muslim Slavs, 3.7 percent; and Montenegrins, 1.7 percent. In Macedonia, with a population of 1.91 million, Macedonians made up 67 percent; Albanians, 19.8 percent; Serbs and Muslims Slavs at 2 percent each. In Montenegro, with a population of 584,310, Montenegrins made up 68.5 percent; Muslim Slavs, 13.4 percent; Albanians, 6.3 percent; Yugoslavs, 5.3 percent; and Serbs 3.3 percent. In Serbia proper, with a population of 5.69 million, Serbs made up 85.4 percent of the population; Yugoslavs, 4.8 percent; and Muslim Slavs, 2.7 percent. In Slovenia, the most homogeneous of the republics with a population of 1.89 million, Slovenes made up 90.5 percent; Croats and Serbs, 2.9 and 2.2 percent, respectively; and Yugoslavs, 1.4 percent. In Vojvodina, with a population of 2 million, Serbs made up 54.4 percent; Hungarians, 19 percent; Yugoslavs, 8.2 percent; Croats, 5.4 percent; and Montenegrins, 2.1 percent.

Between 1945 and 1980, Yugoslavia was transformed from an agrarian country into a modern, industrial state. Industrialization and urbanization radically changed the country's socioeconomic structures. The agricultural population shrank from 67.1 percent in 1948 to 16.7 by 1981, and the number of workers grew from one million, or 15 percent of the population in 1948, to over seven million, or over 50 percent by 1981. Yugoslavs were not only employed in industrial and service sectors at home, but by 1981, over one million Yugoslavs worked abroad. In addition, the urban populations grew 80 percent, and by 1981 over a third of Yugoslavs lived in urban centers.

Between 1948 and 1960, Yugoslav industry grew at the rate of 10.7 percent. This growth was fueled by an investment policy largely based on borrowed resources and at the expense of the agricultural sector and consumers. The combined growth and foreign borrowing fueled inflation and trade deficits. The rapid economic growth of the 1950s also widened the income gap between the poorest region, Kosovo, and the richest, Slovenia. Beginning in 1961, industrial policy focused on narrowing the income gap by investing in the underdeveloped economies of Montenegro and Macedonia. This meant that Croatia and Slovenia had to contribute more to the national investment fund. Despite heavy investment in the poorer regions, the gap in per capita income widened further. The national per capital income in Yugoslavia rose from $375 in 1955 to $750 in 1970. Slovenes still enjoyed the highest income at $1,000 to the Kosovars' $200.

Yugoslavia's economic difficulties continued during the 1970s, with economic growth fueled by foreign loans and investments. However, these loans did little to expand export production. Instead, the government diverted much of the money to workers in the form of pay raises to increase their standard of living or wasted money on projects with more political than economic significance. By the end of the 1970s, Yugoslavia was servicing a debt of over $18 billion, a third of its gross national project.

The 1946 Yugoslav constitution granted women the right to vote, as well as guaranteeing political and economic equality with men. The constitution also gave women access to education, employment, social welfare programs, health care, and political office. Even with these guarantees, women did not win full equality in the job market or advancement into high political office. By the 1980s, women were represented in low-level political management positions, but their numbers dwindled toward the top.

Economically, women were highly visible in the economy immediately after World War II. In 1948, 48 percent of industrial workers were women, concentrated primarily in textile, paper, tobacco, and handicrafts manufacturing. Yet women were still relegated to the same lower-paying and lower-skilled jobs that they had had before the war. As more males entered the workforce, women's employment dropped to around 25 percent. This number rose and then fluctuated between 30 and 40 percent in the 1970s and 1980s. The participation of women in the workforce varied dramatically according to the region. Slovene women made up 43.9 percent of the workforce; in Kosovo, women made up only 20 percent. By the late 1980s, Yugoslav women worked primarily in the social welfare fields, public services and administration, retail and catering, and elementary education.

Politically, women could be found in the lower levels of government, but not in the higher offices of the federal legislative and executive branches. In addition, by the mid-1980s, female membership in the League of Communists fell to only 16 percent. Despite a falloff of women's involvement in politics, Yugoslavia during the 1980s became home to one of the strongest feminist movements in Eastern Europe. Feminists, mostly academics and journalists, brought attention to the unfulfilled promises made by the party to women.

Yugoslavia after Tito, 1980–91

Tito died on May 4, 1980, and the new collective leadership had to deal with the last years of his legacy: increasing unemployment, balance-of-trade deficits, plummeting economic growth, serious food shortages, and national conflict. In the 1980s economic discontent mingled with the pent-up resentment of Yugoslavia's nationalities.

Throughout the 1980s, the Yugoslav government tried to stabilize the economy through a series of austerity programs that devalued the currency, froze prices and wages, rationed energy, and abandoned development programs. Despite these efforts, gross national product plummeted, efficiency dropped, real income went down, and investment declined. As Yugoslavs saw their standard of living fall, popular discontent grew, confidence in the government declined, and the number of strikes and demonstrations grew. In 1988 an estimated four million Yugoslavs took to the streets to express their dissatisfaction with the country's economic and political leaders.

Moreover, after 1974, Tito presided over a highly divided, complex, and complicated federation. With his death, republican parties turned away from the increasingly ineffectual and weak central party and governmental structures and began to promote and assert their own republican interests. During the 1980s, the Slovenian and Croatian parties fought for greater autonomy, especially in economic decisions; the Serbian party supported a stronger federal government. In addition, Albanians in Kosovo began to campaign for greater autonomy and possible republic status,

and the Slavic Muslims of Bosnia-Hercegovina asserted a distinct Bosnian Muslim nationhood.

Ethnic conflict in the shape of republican and party politics erupted in March 1981 when Albanian students demonstrated for better living conditions at the University of Priština. This protest touched a nerve within Albanian society and soon Kosovo was awash in demands for republican status and anti-Serb slogans. The Serbs of Kosovo countered with claims of discrimination, terror, and "genocide" owing to their numerical inferiority, and they looked to the Serbian Communists for help. The revolt was eventually put down by the Yugoslav People's Army, but ethnic relations in Kosovo continued to deteriorate in the 1980s.

The Albanians' demand for republic status highlighted one of the major grievances that the League of Communists of Serbia had against Tito's Yugoslavia—the stripping away of Kosovo and Vojvodina from their control. The Serbs were embittered not only because of this decentralization, but also because Kosovo, having been the center of the Serbian medieval kingdom, held a special place in Serbian history, and Serbs were being denied access to their culture and history. The Albanians grew more embittered during the 1980s as Serbian authorities, who controlled the police, intimidated, threatened, beat, and even killed Albanian protesters and leaders.

Throughout the 1980s, the League of Communists of Yugoslavia continued to lose control over the republican and provincial parties. Slovenia and Croatia balked at having to support the rising costs of the police action in Kosovo, which essentially maintained Serbian control over the Albanian population. Slovenia was also the center of a large number of official and unofficial non-Communist political groups that championed such issues as pacifism, nuclear disarmament, ecology, feminism, and gay and lesbian rights. Slovenian politicians and activists felt that Serbs were obstacles to political and socioeconomic reform. The moderate wing within the League of Communists of Croatia attempted to mediate the increasingly tense Serb-Slovene dispute.

In 1987 Slobodan Milošević (1941–) used the explosive issue of Kosovo and the plight of its Serbian and Montenegrin populations to drive the Titoists out of the Serbian League of Communists and to assume the top leadership position. Once in power, Milošević aroused mass support around the idea that Serbia had been discriminated against in

Tito's Yugoslavia and that it was time to reassert control over its two autonomous provinces, Kosovo and Vojvodina. In 1988 Milošević removed political rivals from Vojvodina and Kosovo, and his supporters orchestrated numerous demonstrations to legitimize his actions. With these tactics, along with his control over the media, in March 1989 Milošević had the Serbian parliament pass a new constitution that eliminated the autonomous status of Kosovo and Vojvodina. The constitutional changes and the installation of a pro-Milošević government in Montenegro gave Milošević control over four of the eight seats in the collective presidency. He appeared poised to recentralize federal political institutions under greater Serbian control.

Milošević's nationalist platform and his destabilization of Yugoslavia was weakly resisted by both federal and republican Communist politicians. By 1989, most seemed unwilling to defend Tito's Yugoslavia any longer. The Slovene and Croatian Communist parties legalized opposition parties and initiated multiparty elections. In late 1989 non-Communist political parties began forming and readying themselves for the elections of 1990. Adding to the volatile mix, the Slovene parliament in October adopted an amendment to its constitution giving itself the right to secede. When parties calling for the secession of Croatia and Slovenia from Yugoslavia won the elections in early spring 1990, Tito's Yugoslavia had come to an end.

Melissa Bokovoy

Further reading

Banac, Ivo. *The National Question in Yugoslavia: Origins, History, Politics.* Ithaca, New York, 1984.

Dedijer, Vladimir et al. *History of Yugoslavia.* New York, 1974.

Djilas, Aleksa. *The Contested Country: Yugoslav Unity and Communist Revolution, 1919–1953.* Cambridge, Massachusetts, 1991.

Fine, John V.A., Jr. *The Bosnian Church: A New Interpretation.* Boulder, Colorado, 1975.

Jackson, Marvin and John Lampe. *Balkan Economic History 1550–1950.* Bloomington, Indiana, 1982.

Jancar-Webster, Barbara. *Women and Revolution in Yugoslavia.* Denver, Colorado, 1990.

Jelavich, Barbara. *History of the Balkans,* 2 vols. Cambridge, 1983.

Lampe, John. *Yugoslavia: Twice a Country.* Cambridge, 1997.

Petrovich, Michael Boro. *A History of Modern Serbia, 1804–1918,* 2 vols. New York, 1976.

Rusinow, Dennison. *The Yugoslav Experiment, 1948–1974.* Berkeley, California, 1977.

Tomasevich, Jozo. *Peasants, Politics, and Economic Change in Yugoslavia.* Stanford, California, 1955.

See also Agrarian Parties; Agriculture; Alexander Karadjordjević; Alexander I Karadjordjević; Alexander Obrenović; Antifascism; Apis; *Ausgleich;* Axis; Balkan Entente; Balkan Wars; Belgrade; Black George; Black Hand; Bosnia-Hercegovina; Bosnia-Hercegovina, Birth of the Republic of; Chetniks; *Chiftlik;* Collectivization; Cominform; Communist Party of Yugoslavia; Congress of Berlin; Congress of Vienna; Corfu Declaration; Croatia; Croatia, Birth of the Republic of; Croatian Art; Croatian Culture; Croatian Émigrés; Croatian Literature to 1918; Croatian Military Frontier; Croatian Spring; Dragiša Cvetković; Dalmatia; Miljovan Djilas; Dual Monarchy; Economic Development in Yugoslavia; Emigration; Folklife; Folklore; Josip Frank; Frankovici; Franz Ferdinand; Franz Joseph; Ludjevit Gaj; Ilia Garašanin; Greater Serbia; Greek Civil War; Adolf Hitler; Illyrian Movement; IMRO; Industrialization; Irredentism; Islam; Alija Izetbegović; Janissaries; Vuk Karadžić; Edvard Kardelj; Károly Khuen-Héderváry; Kingdom of Serbs, Croats, and Slovenes; Anton Korošec; Kosovo; Eugen Kvaternik; Labor; Little Entente; London Pact; Ljubljana; Macedonia; Vladko Maček; Magyarization; Matica Hrvatska; Mihailo Obrenović; Draža Mihailović; Milan Obrenović; *Millet;* Miloš Obrenović; Slobodan Milošević; Montenegro; Muslims; *Načertanije;* Nationalism; Neoabsolutism; Nonaligned Movement; Orthodoxy; Paris Peace Conference; Paul Karadjordjević; Ante Pavelić; Peasants; Petar I Petrović Njegoš; Petar II Petrović Njegoš; Peter Karadjordjević; Peter II Karadjordjević; Pig War; Porte; Svetozar Pribičević; Gavrilo Princip; Franjo Rački; Railroads; Aleksander Ranković; Red Army; Revolutions of 1848; Right Radicalism; Sabor; Sanjak of Novi Pazar; Self-Management in Yugoslavia; Serbia; Serbia and the Break-up of Yugoslavia; Serbian Art; Serbian Culture; Serbian Émigrés; Serbian Literature to 1918; Serbo-Croatian Language; Serbo-Turkish War of 1876; Skupština; Slavonia; Slavs; Slovene Art; Slovene Culture; Slovene Émigrés; Slovene Language;

Slovene Literature; Slovenia; Slovenia, Birth of the Republic of; *Sporazum;* Stalin; Ante Starčević; Milan Stojadinović; Bishop Josip Juraj Strossmayer; *Timar;* Tito; Tito-Stalin Split; Trialism; Triune Kingdom; Ante Trumbić; Franjo Tudjman; Ustaša; Vidovdan Constitution; Vojvodina; Women in Yugoslavia; World War I; World War II; Yugoslav Literature; Yugoslavism; *Zadruga*

Yugoslavism

Cultural and political concept advocating the unity of South Slavs. The word "Yugoslavism" first appeared in print in 1860 as the title of a newspaper article urging South Slavic cultural unity written by Croat historian and politician Franjo Rački (1828–94). The "Yug-*"* (transliterated into English from "jug-") at the root of the term means "south" in all the South Slavic languages. Yet despite the call for unity, Yugoslavism's goals and bases of support have varied considerably since this first appearance.

A major area of discord among adherents of Yugoslavism has been which groups should be united as Yugoslavs. Some, primarily nineteenth-century, Yugoslavists advocated the unity of all southeastern European Slavs, including Bulgarians. The narrowest conceptions of Yugoslavism have advocated unity solely between Croats and Serbs. Since the creation of a Yugoslav state in 1918, both "Yugoslavism" and "Yugoslav" have seldom included Bulgars.

Two very different Yugoslavist concepts have also existed historically about the cultural relationship between the Yugoslav group and its subgroups. One, called "integral Yugoslavism," or "Yugoslavist unitarism," by scholars, posited a Yugoslav nation that would replace more particular identities like Croat, Slovene, or Serb, often described by the word *"pleme"* (tribe) . The other recognized existing ethnic or national identities as subunits within a broader Yugoslav group.

Yugoslavism's political goals have also varied historically. Before World War I, its advocates differed over whether unity should be restricted to South Slavs within the Habsburg Empire or extend to those beyond its borders. Those who favored expansion split in turn over whether the enlarged Yugoslav unit should be part of or separate from the Habsburg monarchy. After the creation of a Yugoslav state in 1918, political differences among advocates of Yugoslavism paralleled differences in the cultural sphere. Those who favored integral Yugoslavism tended to favor a centralized Yugoslav state; those who advocated a continuance of earlier national identities favored a federalized state.

Varieties of Yugoslavism also differed considerably between the nineteenth and twentieth centuries in their base of support. Before 1918, Yugoslavism found its greatest support among the South Slavs within the Habsburg monarchy, particularly intellectuals. The first proponents of Yugoslavism were Croats—Bishop Josip Juraj Strossmayer (1815–1905) and his close collaborator Rački, respectively the patron and first president of the Yugoslav Academy of Arts and Sciences founded in Zagreb in 1866. A Yugoslav orientation also characterized the Croatian National Party (1860s–1880s), many educated Habsburg South Slav youth after 1903, the political parties of the Croato-Serb coalition (Croatia's dominant post-1903 political grouping), and the émigré Yugoslav Committee during World War I.

The creation of the Kingdom of Serbs, Croats, and Slovenes in 1918 (after 1929, Yugoslavia), with the capital in Belgrade, the former capital of Serbia, marked a shift in the meaning of and social base for Yugoslavism. It now came to be associated with the maintenance of the existing state, which in the interwar period in particular depended on a largely ethnically Serb state apparatus. King Alexander (1888–1934) and many interwar Belgrade intellectuals advocated varieties of integral Yugoslavism.

The World War II Partisan slogan Brotherhood and Unity attempted to promote Yugoslavism as a way to unite under one overarching identity peoples who would also retain their separate national identities. With the exception of the period from 1953 until 1962, when it promoted an integral Yugoslavism, the League of Communists of Yugoslavia (Communist Party of Yugoslavia) officially held to this wartime concept of Yugoslavism while at the same time conceiving all nationalisms in Marxist terms as a type of "false consciousness."

James P. Krokar

Further reading

Banac, Ivo. *The National Question in Yugoslavia: Origins, History, Politics.* Ithaca, New York, 1984.

Cohen, Lenard J. "The Evolution of the Yugoslav Idea: 1830–1980," in *Broken Bonds: Yugoslavia's*

Disintegration and Balkan Politics in Transition, 2d ed. Boulder, Colorado, 1995.

Djilas, Aleksa. *The Contested Country: Yugoslav Unity and Communist Revolution, 1919–1953.* Cambridge, Massachusetts, 1991.

Rogel, Carol. *The Slovenes and Yugoslavism, 1890–1914.* Boulder, Colorado, 1977.

Rusinow, Denison. "The Yugoslav Peoples," in Peter F. Sugar, ed. *Eastern European Nationalism in the Twentieth Century.* Washington, D.C., 1995.

Southeastern Europe 1, pt. 2 (1974): 119–212. Special Edition: "Yugoslavism."

See also Alexander I Karadjordjević; Antifascism; Communist Party of Yugoslavia; Kingdom of Serbs, Croats, and Slovenes; Franjo Rački; Bishop Josip Juraj Strossmayer; Yugoslav Committee

Yugoslav Literature

The formation of the modern state of Yugoslavia in 1918 resulted in a rich and varied literary culture. Standing at the crossroads between East and West and fed by the experiences of varied ethnic groups, literature in Yugoslavia from 1918 to 1989 was a perpetual contemplation on the regional, multiethnic, and foreign—factors that critically shaped twentieth-century Yugoslav character. Yugoslav literature has generally followed a modernist direction, evolving through periods of realism, romanticism, and finally postmodernism.

After World War I, Yugoslav literature reflected a "new" modernism, with an urbane style and more universal themes, albeit within the context of native concerns. Surrealism was embraced by Serbian writers, while expressionism was introduced in Croatia and Slovenia. Outstanding modernist poets of interwar Yugoslavia include Oton Župančić (1878–1949) from Slovenia and Miloš Crnjanski (b. 1893) from Serbia. A figure with strong leftist leanings, Miroslav Krleža (1893–1981), was the most prominent and prolific interwar writer from Croatia. His most celebrated works include the novel *Povratak Filipa Latinovicza* (*The Return of Philip Latinovicz,* 1932) depicting a disillusioned hero's search for identity. Ivo Andrić (1892–1975), whose writing reflects historical and realist tendencies, is considered the greatest Yugoslav novelist. He published short stories before World War II, but his most acclaimed works were three novels, all published in 1945. His *Na Drini ćuprija* (*The Bridge on the Drina*)—awarded the Nobel Prize in literature in 1961—is a masterfully constructed chronicle of the complex and colorful life and lore of his native Bosnia. Branko Ćopić (1915–1984) also described Bosnia in his psychological fiction.

Immediately following World War II, Yugoslavia entered a short period of censorship and government control of the arts. Socialist realism centered on war novels, such as by the Serb Dobrica Ćosić (1921–). After Tito's (1892–1980) break with Stalin (1879–1953) in 1948, the cultural climate relaxed, and by the mid-1950s literature was rejuvenated. Much of the provincialism that dominated earlier works was supplanted by more cosmopolitan writing that mirrored Western trends and style. Prominent in the postwar generation of poets were Serbs Vasko Popa (1922–) and Desanka Maksimović (b. 1898). Major fiction writers included Oskar Davičo (1909–), who reflected Serbian surrealism in his original novel *Pesma* (*The Poem,* 1952), and Bosnian Meša Selimović (1910–82), whose prose was psychological. Vjekoslav Kaleb (n.d.) was an important Croat writer during the 1950s; Montenegrin Miodrag Bulatović (1930–) excelled in popular short fiction. Slavko Janevski (n.d.) wrote the first novel in literary Macedonian in 1953.

Experimental writing was widespread throughout the 1960s and 1970s. Originally from Montenegro, Borisav Pekić (1930–93) won a major Yugoslav prize for literature in 1964 for his *Vreme, čuda* (*The Time of Miracles*). Danilo Kiš (1935–89), a Serb who began writing in the 1960s, was an internationally recognized postmodernist; his innovative novel *Grobnica za Borisa Davidoviča* (*A Tomb for Boris Davidovich*) was published in 1976. Throughout the 1980s, writers continued to challenge boundaries of genre and style. Serb poet Milorad Pavić (1929–) won international acclaim for his postmodernist novel *Hazarski rečnik* (*Dictionary of the Khazars,* 1988). Also embracing postmodernism in her prose, Croat Dubravka Ugrešić (1949–) achieved recognition in the 1980s as a significant feminist writer.

Margaret H. Beissinger

Further reading
Eekman, Thomas. *Thirty Years of Yugoslav Literature: 1945–1975.* Ann Arbor, Michigan, 1978.

Hawkesworth, Celia. *Ivo Andrić: Bridge between East and West.* London, 1984.

Kadić, Ante. *Contemporary Croatian Literature*. The Hague, 1960.

———. *Contemporary Serbian Literature*. The Hague, 1964.

Lukić, Sveta. *Contemporary Yugoslav Literature: A Sociological Approach*. Urbana, Illinois, 1972.

See also Ivo Andric; Censorship; Dobrica Cosic; Croatian Literature to 1918; Miroslav Krleza; Macedonian Literature; Serbian Literature to 1918; Slovene Literature; Tito-Stalin Split; Oton Zupanhic

Yugov, Anton Tanev (1904–91)

Bulgarian Communist and prime minister. Yugov was born on August 5, 1904, in Karasuli in Macedonia. He moved to Plovdiv and worked there in the tobacco industry. In 1928 he joined the Bulgarian Communist Party and organized tobacco workers during the 1930s, rising to a position of some prominence within the party. His adopted hometown of Plovdiv served as his power base. After the German attack on the Soviet Union in June 1941, Yugov became a member of the party's Central Military Commission, which carried out resistance activities against Germany's Bulgarian ally. He became minister of the interior in the Fatherland Front, the coalition of left and center parties, when it seized control in Bulgaria in September 1944. Yugov utilized this position to consolidate Communist power ruthlessly in Bulgaria. He joined the Politburo in 1945. Owing to "lack of vigilance," however, Yugov lost his position as minster of the interior in 1949. He retained his position in the Politburo, however, and by 1956, in something of a comeback, became prime minister. After a prolonged power struggle, Todor Zhivkov (1911–98), Bulgarian Communist leader, with the support of Soviet Premier Nikita Khrushchev (1894–1971), ousted Yugov in 1962 from his government and party positions because of "gross violations of socialist legality." In 1984 Yugov was rehabilitated in yet another comeback and made a "hero of socialist labor."

Richard C. Hall

Further reading

Bell, John D. *The Bulgarian Communist Party from Blagoev to Zhivkov*. Stanford, California, 1986.

Brown, J.F. *Bulgaria under Communist Rule*. New York, 1970.

Oren, Nissen. *Revolution Administered: Agrarianism and Communism in Bulgaria*. Baltimore, Maryland, 1973.

See also Communist Party of Bulgaria; Fatherland Front; Todor Zhivkov

Z

Zadruga

Communal extended family found historically in the Balkans, primarily but not solely among South Slavs and Albanians. Such families might be extended either through multiple generations or through a group of siblings, usually male, and their descendants. Adoptive kinship was also possible. Family members lived in proximity to one another, usually in one house or household compound, not only sharing agricultural and domestic work but also eating together. Heads of such families were usually the eldest male, but on rare occasions were women, usually mature widows; *zadruge* had and sometimes exercised the right to choose the most capable family member as head. The head of the *zadruga* could neither unilaterally dispose of the assets of the family nor make decisions regarding its future without consulting other men within the family. Habsburg legal codes recognized the *zadruga* itself, not its head, as a legal person.

Widespread in the nineteenth century, *zadruge* have gradually disappeared. In the north-western Balkans they were gradually dissolving by the mid–nineteenth century, and they persisted into the mid–twentieth mainly in south-central regions. Rising taxation, the penetration of a money economy into the countryside, and the adoption of modern legal codes all encouraged the dissolution of *zadruge*. Scholars disagree about the origin of this family type, some tracing it to the Middle Ages and others to the social dislocations and uncertainty of the post-medieval era of warfare between the Ottoman and Habsburg empires.

Written scholarly descriptions of *zadruge* date from the late eighteenth century (1776 and 1783). The word *"zadruga,"* however, is more than likely a neologism, which first appeared in Vuk Karadžić's (1787–1864) Serbian dictionary of 1818 and corresponded to the German term *"Hauskommunion"* (house commune), used in the 1807 Austrian legal code devised for the Military Frontier. Peasants themselves used various other terms for such families; these terms varied from region to region and frequently corresponded to the local word meaning "house."

James P. Krokar

Further reading

Byrnes, Robert F., ed. *Communal Families in the Balkans: The Zadruga.* Notre Dame, Indiana, 1976.

Erlich, Vera St. *Family in Transition: A Study of 300 Yugoslav Villages.* Princeton, New Jersey, 1966.

Halpern, Joel M. and Barbara Kerewsky Halpern. *A Serbian Village in Historical Perspective.* New York, 1972.

Hammel, Eugene A. "The Zadruga as Process," in *Household and Family in Past Time,* ed. by Peter Laslett. Cambridge, 1972.

Todorova, Maria N. *Balkan Family Structure and the European Pattern: Demographic Developments in Ottoman Bulgaria.* Washington, D.C., 1993.

See also Croatian Military Frontier; Vuk Karadžić; Peasants

Zagreb

Capital city and chief industrial center of the Republic of Croatia. Zagreb is situated at the intersection of the shortest routes from Western Europe to the Middle East and from East Central Europe

Z to the Mediterranean Sea. It has a population of 850,000.

Illyrians early established a settlement at Zagreb's site on low hills overlooking the Sava River floodplain to the south. In Roman times it became a recognized municipality called Andautonia. The present city has its roots in the competing medieval towns of Kaptol and Gradec (Grič), which were joined together formally only in 1850.

Kaptol is first mentioned as seat of a bishop in 1094. It became a wealthy community through ownership of extensive farming lands in the Sava River valley. Gradec was proclaimed a free city in 1242 by a golden bull of King Bela IV (1206–70). Its success derived from profitable handicraft industries and trade, including an annual fair. The twin cities were separated by a stream known appropriately as Bloody Creek.

Zagreb's dominance was assured during the mid–nineteenth century when it became the junction of east-west and north-south railroads in the Austro-Hungarian Empire. At this time, Donji Grad appeared, a third major section of the city, on drained and levee-protected land on the northern half of the Sava River floodplain. After World War II, a fourth section, Novi Zagreb (New Zagreb), was constructed south of the Sava River.

Zagreb's industry is diversified, with more than two hundred major enterprises producing a wide range of goods, from steam generators to petrochemicals. Particularly significant is the production of electrical goods. Zagreb's important trade functions are reflected in its continuing annual trade fair, which began in 1909. It maintains an active trade with other areas by railroad, barge, and air transport.

A number of medieval structures still stand in Zagreb, including several defensive towers and sections of walls. Particularly noteworthy are the twelfth-century cathedral in Kaptol and the thirteenth-century stone entrance gate to Gradec.

Thomas M. Poulsen

Further reading

Hamilton, F.E. Ian. *Yugoslavia: Patterns of Economic Activity.* New York, 1968.

Lijepa naša Hrvatska., ed. by Boris Zdunić. Zagreb, 1991.

Pavić, Radovan and Nikola Stražičić. *Ekonomska geografija Jugoslavije,* 3d ed. Zagreb, 1970.

Zakhariev Stoianov, Vasil (1895–1971)

Bulgarian artist. Born in Samokov, a town noted for its wood carvers, Zakhariev was a leading engraver and a popular illustrator of children's books. As a student at Sofia Art Academy, Zakhariev joined the Contemporary Art Society, but when the Native Art Society was formed in 1919 he became one of its founding members and later its president.

After teaching in his native Samokov, Zakhariev departed for Leipzig to study at the Academy of Graphic Art (1922–24), where he encountered the revival of primitivism in art and the philosophy of Friedrich Nietzsche (1844–1900). On his return, Zakhariev was appointed lecturer (1924), adjunct professor (1929), and professor (1934) of decorative art and graphics at the art academy. In his lithographs and graphics on wood or linoleum, Zakhariev balanced traditional icon and contemporary expressionist techniques. His themes emanated from the Bulgarian heritage (churches, monasteries, village life, and folk tales) as seen in his *Rila Monastery* (1935), *Rila Shepherds* (1932), *Raspberry Pickers* (1932), and *Marincho Binbelov the Terrifying* (1935). Zakhariev exhibited his work extensively in Europe and the United States (Los Angeles, 1934; Chicago, 1937; New York, 1938). A scholar of nineteenth-century Bulgarian applied art, he was involved in historic preservation and tried to keep the crafts alive.

The Communist regime dismissed him from his professorship in1944. His research on icons was published in East Germany but neglected at home. Zakhariev was finally named "Artist of Merit" (1971), shortly before his death in Sofia.

Milka T. Bliznakov

Further reading

Sventila, Vladimir. *Vasil Zakhariev,* Sofia, 1972.

Tomov, Evtim. *Vasil Zakhariev.* Sofia, 1954.

See also Bulgarian Art

Zamoyski, Count Andrzej (1800–1874)

Agrarian reformer and Polish conservative political activist during the January Uprising of 1863 against the Russians. The Zamoyskis were among the richest and most important families in Poland. Zamoyski entered the Kingdom of Poland's administration after completing his studies in Western Europe. During the November Uprising of 1830, aimed at ending Russian domination, he went to Vienna to secure support for the revolutionaries; when the uprising failed, Zamoyski retired to his family estates.

Zamoyski showed a keen interest in agrarian reform. He was one of the first landlords to shift his peasants from compulsory labor service (corvée) to rents, and beginning in 1842 he held annual meetings at his residence, Klemensów, which brought together Polish landowners to discuss modern agricultural techniques. Zamoyski, a leader of the conservative reform movement, founded the Agricultural Society in 1858 to accelerate the modernization of Poland's rural economy. However, the society veered away from Zamoyski's goals and soon became enmeshed in that era's tumultuous political events.

As tensions between Russians and Poles mounted, Zamoyski tried to steer a middle course. He recommended extensive reforms, especially in the economic sphere, but he rejected calls for revolution. His moderate position, characteristic of the moderates (Whites) at the time of the January Insurrection, proved untenable. As the Russian authorities resorted to violence and brutality, the Polish revolutionaries, or Reds, captured public opinion.

The Agricultural Society was closed in April 1861, and several months later the Russian viceroy, Grand Duke Constantine (1827–92), summoned Zamoyski for an interview. When Zamoyski raised the explosive issues of a Polish constitution and army, and the status of the "western *gubernias,*" or prepartition Poland's eastern lands that Russia had annexed, an angry tsar ordered him to St. Petersburg. Subsequently, Alexander II (1818–81) sent Zamoyski into exile abroad, but he later returned to Kraków, where he died.

Frank W. Thackeray

Further reading

Grabski, Władysław. *Historia Towarzystwa Rolniczego,* 2 vols. Warsaw, 1904.

Kieniewicz, Stefan. *Między Ugodą a Rewolucją: Andrzej Zamoyski w Latach 1861–1862.* Warsaw, 1962.

Wandycz, Piotr S. *The Lands of Partitioned Poland, 1795–1918.* Seattle, Washington, 1974.

See also Alexander II; January Insurrection; November Uprising; Peasants

Żeromski, Stefan (1864–1925)

Polish novelist, playwright, and short-story writer. Żeromski was born into an impoverished noble family after the failed January Uprising of 1863 against the Russians (which became one of the pivotal points of his work). His autobiographical *Syzyfowe prace* (*Sisyphean Labors,* 1898) depicts high school students' resistance to Russification in a small Polish town, Kielce. *Ludzie bezdomni* (*Homeless People,* 1899) analyzes the struggle between the right to one's happiness and moral responsibility toward society as the protagonist, Dr. Judym, sacrifices his love to help the poor. An epic novel, *Popioły* (*The Ashes,* 1903), juxtaposes the glory of war with its cruelty, the need for national freedom with the means of acquiring it, and the passion of love with the destruction it causes. Żeromski's masterpiece, *Wierna rzeka* (*The Faithful River,* 1912), is a tragic love story during the January Uprising that parallels the fate of partitioned Poland. *Przedwiośnie* (*Before Spring,* 1924) brings the realization that the newly independent Poland was unable to fulfill its promise of social justice.

Żeromski was a passionate moralist. He saw literature as a moral duty toward Polish society and a carrier and a tool for shaping national consciousness. His passion and bravery to touch on controversial aspects of Polish history earned him the labels "conscience of the nation" and "insatiable heart." His style reflects the passionate and moralistic nature of his work; it is at the same time naturalistic and realistic, expressionistic, and lyrical although at times sentimental. He was instrumental in creating the ethos of the Polish intelligentsia and their moral role in educating and improving society, which to some degree is still alive in contemporary Poland.

Katarzyna Zechenter

Further reading

Czerwiński, Edward Joseph, ed. *Dictionary of Polish Literature.* Westport, Connecticut, 1994.

Hutnikiewicz, Artur. *Żeromski.* Warsaw, 1987.

Miłosz, Czesław. *The History of Polish Literature.* Berkeley, California, 1983.

See also Intelligentsia; January Uprising; Polish Literature; Russification

Zet

Secret organization dedicated to the resurrection of an independent Polish state. Following Masonic forms of organization, Zet (Union of Polish Youth) was founded in Warsaw in November 1886 by émigré democrat and novelist Zygmunt Miłkowski (1824–1915) and publicist Zygmunt Balicki (1858–1916). Membership was drawn at first chiefly from university students within Poland and abroad who wished to elevate the consciousness of the Polish masses through education. Since popular education in the Polish language was illegal in the Kingdom of Poland, Zet members were active in an underground network of secret schools, from the primary to the university level. As such, they were largely responsible for the spread of literacy among the peasants and for advocating a greater role for women in schooling.

Over the course of its existence, Zet was often rent by division. In 1888 it subordinated itself to the Polish League. That organization, founded in Switzerland in response to increasing Germanization policies in the Prussian partition, was dedicated to uniting all elements actively working toward a free Poland, regardless of political orientation. By 1893, however, the league had taken on a decidedly nationalist tone under the leadership of Roman Dmowski (1864–1939), Jan Popławski (1854–1908), and Balicki, who had begun to distance himself from his earlier socialist ideology. The league moved its central committee to Warsaw and was renamed the National League. The leadership then proceeded to tighten the organization's discipline. As a result of these changes, which fit uncomfortably with the leftist leanings of many Zet members, Zet ended its association with the league and functioned independently until 1897. It reentered the National League fold, only to secede once again in 1909 when the league attempted an abortive policy of reconciliation with the tsarist government.

Along with other nationalist organizations, Zet represented the disenchantment of the new generation of Polish youth with the older generation's philosophy of positivism. Polish youth demanded a more active approach to the Polish question, that is, the disposition of the Polish lands. Thus, Zet members were active in the Russian Revolution of 1905 by organizing school strikes. Nonetheless, differences regarding tactics led to factionalism and eventual splits and subgroupings within Zet. For example, many members retained their association with the National Democrats, the nationalistic party that had grown out of the National League in 1897, even after Zet had seceded from the league. Further, in 1909 an independent Zet was formed in Lwów, some of whose adherents later participated in the Polish Legions, volunteers who fought for the Central Powers against Russia during World War I. In the interwar years, many Zet members supported Józef Piłsudski's (1867–1935) government while others found themselves in opposition. After the marshall's death, Zet once again split along right and left lines. During the German occupation in World War II, Zet members were active in the resistance and in organizations dedicated to the rebuilding of the state.

Peter Wozniak

Further reading

Blobaum, Robert. *Rewolucja: Russian Poland, 1904–1907.* Ithaca, New York, 1995.

Gieysztor, Aleksander et al., eds. *History of Poland.* Warsaw, 1979.

Sienkiewicz, Witold. *Mały Słownik Historii Polski.* Warsaw, 1991.

Wandycz, Piotr. *The Lands of Partitioned Poland 1795–1918.* Seattle, Washington, 1974.

See also Zygmunt Balicki; Roman Dmowski; Freemasonry; Germanization; Nationalism; Józef Piłsudski; Polish League; Polish Legions; Polish Question; Positivism

Zhdanovshchina

Cultural and ideological purge in the Soviet Union and Eastern Europe led by Stalin's key adviser between 1945 and 1948, Andrei Zhdanov (1896–1948), aimed at eradicating anti-Soviet influences and fighting American imperialism. The creation of the Cominform, the Communist propaganda organization, in September 1947 marked its opening salvo. The Zhdanovshchina cut Poland and Czechoslovakia off from the Marshall Plan and shaped Soviet Cold War policies that outlasted the Leningrad party secretary's career. Yugoslavia and Bulgaria were the most affected by it, Poland and Czechoslovakia, less so. As non-Slav nations, Romania and Hungary were of little interest to Zhdanov.

Zhdanov used Pan-Slav doctrines to reinforce ties between Russia and the Balkan Slavs. Moscow's wartime scheme to create a Yugoslav-Bulgarian federation gave way to a larger, independent project of a Yugoslav-Bulgarian-Romanian-Albanian-Greek federation led by Yugoslavia's Tito (1892–1980), Bulgaria's Georgi Dimitrov (1882–1949), and Zhdanov. Stalin (1879–1953) could not tolerate this challenge to his authority, and during the winter of 1947–48, he decided to confront Tito. The crisis led to Yugoslavia's expulsion from the Cominform in June 1948 and the disgrace and death of Zhdanov in August 1948 and of Dimitrov in 1949.

The Zhdanovshchina also affected reparations and Eastern European economic reconstruction after World War II. Skeptical about the ability of the people's democracies installed by the USSR to be economically separated from the West, some in the Kremlin (led by Georgi Malenkov [1902–88]) backed the rapid exploitation of Poland and Czechoslovakia, while the "Zhdanovites" favored reconstruction in the belief that Eastern Europe could be rapidly Sovietized. In 1946 East Germany became a testing ground for both factions, with Zhdanov favoring the creation of a separate East German state. Some historians consider the Berlin blockade of 1948–49 as the Zhdanovites' last stand.

Alice-Catherine Carls

Further reading

Brzezinski, Zbigniew. *The Soviet Bloc: Unity and Conflict.* New York, 1991.

Fejtö, François. *Histoire des démocraties populaires: L'ère de Staline, 1945–1952,* 2 vols. Paris, 1952.

Ra'anon, Gavrial D. *International Policy Formation in the USSR: Factional Debates during the Zhdanovshchina.* Hamden, Connecticut, 1983.

See also Cominform; Georgi Dimitrov; Pan-Slavism; Stalin; Tito; Tito-Stalin Split

Zhelev, Zheliu Mitev (1935–)

President of Bulgaria. Born in Veselinovo, Zhelev graduated with a degree in philosophy from Sofia University in 1958. Shortly thereafter he became a member of the Bulgarian Communist Party (1960). In 1961 Zhelev started his graduate program in the Department of Dialectical and Historical Materialism. His dissertation analyzed and questioned Lenin's (1870–1924) definition of materialism, putting Zhelev at odds with the ideology of the party. He was expelled from both the Bulgarian Communist Party and the university. Zhelev spent six years with his wife in exile in a small village. In 1972 he returned to Sofia with a new dissertation that he was able to defend in 1974 despite some obstacles, then became a researcher at the Institute of Culture. At the end of the 1980s, Zhelev became one of the organizers of the first dissident groups in Bulgaria (Club for Glasnost and Perestroika, Ruse Committee, and Ecoglasnost). In June 1989 he was fired from his position at the institute for dissident activity. In 1989 a group of dissidents formed the Union of Democratic Forces and Zhelev was appointed its leader. In the VII Great National Assembly (June 1990) he was elected as a representative for the Union of Democratic Forces. On August 1, 1990, the Great Assembly elected him president of the republic. In the next presidential election (1992) Zhelev was the first president directly elected by the people of Bulgaria. He has received numerous international titles and awards. His works include *Fashizmut* (*Fascism,* 1982), *Realnoto fizichesko prostranstvo* (*Real Physical Extension,* 1989), *Chovekut i negovite lichnosti* (*Man and His Personality,* 1991), *Relatsionna teoriia na lichnostta* (*Relation Theory of Personality,* 1993), *Inteligentsiia i politika* (*The Intelligentsia and Politics,* 1995), and *Fizicheskoto prostranstvo* (*Physical Extension,* 1995).

Yana Hashamova

Further reading

Ginev, Dimitri. "Kriticheski komentar kum edno metodologichesko nachinanie," in *Godishnik na Sofiiskiia universitet Sv. Kliment Okhridski,* Center of Culture, vol. 84, 1991, 171–83.

Nozharova, Silvia. *Biografichna spravka: Zheliu Mitev Zhelev.* Sofia, 1995.

Todorova, Sofia, ed. *Deputatite, VII Veliko Narodno Subranie,* June 10–17, 1990. Sofia, 1991.

See also Communist Party of Bulgaria

Zhivkov, Todor (1911–98)

Bulgarian Communist leader. Zhivkov was a printer when he joined the Bulgarian Communist Party (BCP) in 1932, and was elected secretary of the local party organization. During World War II, he served as a member of the Sofia district committee of the BCP. From 1943 to 1944, as a Central Committee representative, Zhivkov organized the

Z underground antifascist struggle in the Botevgrad region of Bulgaria. In July 1944 he became deputy commander of the First Revolution Operational Zone, centered around Sofia.

Following the 1944 political takeover by the Fatherland Front coalition of center and left political parties, Zhivkov rose quickly through the party ranks. After Stalin's (1879–1953) death, with Soviet support he received the highest party post. Zhivkov held the prime minister's position from 1962 until 1971. After the adoption of the 1971 constitution, he acquired the highest state post— state council chairman. On his initiative, Bulgaria faithfully followed the Soviet developmental model and maintained close political and economic relations with the Soviet Union.

The economic downturn in 1984, coupled with the policy of pushing forcible name changes on the Turkish population of the country and a cooling in relations with Moscow, signaled the end of his political career. Zhivkov launched his own reform campaign but received neither external nor internal support. On November 10, 1989, BCP reformers deposed him.

In 1990 Zhivkov was placed under house arrest and in 1992 he was sentenced to seven years in prison on charges of embezzlement. However, he was exempted from serving the sentence on medical grounds and was kept under house arrest. In 1996 the High Court overturned the verdict and in September 1997 his house arrest was ended. Although Zhivkov did not return to politics, he enjoyed new popularity because of widespread disillusionment in the country after the failure of the reforms of the early 1990s.

Boian Koulov

Further reading
Delev, P. et al. *Istoria na Bulgaria.* Sofia, 1996.

See also Communist Party of Bulgaria; Fatherland Front; Turks

Zhivkova, Liudmila (1942–81)
Bulgarian state and Communist Party leader, as well as a student of history and art. In 1965 Zhivkova graduated from Sofia University with a degree in contemporary Balkan history. After studying for a year at Oxford University, she obtained a doctorate in 1971. In 1974 she became senior researcher in the Balkanistics Institute of the Bulgarian Academy of Sciences. In 1979 she became Doctor Honoris Causa of Tokai University in Japan and in 1980 received the Large Cross for Service to the Italian Republic.

As the daughter of Bulgarian state and Communist Party leader Todor Zhivkov (1911–98), her career advanced rapidly. In 1975 she became minister of culture and the next year a member of the Central Committee of the Bulgarian Communist Party. In 1979, two years before her death, she was elected to the Politburo, the highest managing body of the party.

Among Zhivkova's primary achievements was opening up Bulgarian culture to the West. She initiated multiple programs, including "Leonardo da Vinci," "Lenin," and "1300 Years of the Establishment of the Bulgarian State"—all intended to publicize Bulgarian culture around the world and to introduce Bulgarians to other cultures. In 1979 Zhivkova was instrumental in organizing the UNESCO-sponsored International Children's Assembly, Banner of Peace. She died at the age of thirty-nine from injuries sustained in a car wreck amid preparations for the celebrations of the 1,300th anniversary of the foundation of the Bulgarian state.

Boian Koulov

Further reading
Entsiklopedia na izobrasitelnite izkustva, vol. 1. Sofia, 1980.
Lyudmila Zhivkova—zhivot i delo, 1942–1981. Letopis. Sofia, 1987.

See also Bulgarina Culture; Communist Party of Bulgaria; Women in Bulgaria; Todor Zhivkov

Živković, Petar (1879–1947)
Serbian general and politician. Born in Negotin, Živković graduated from the Military Academy in Belgrade. As a young officer, he actively participated in the assassination of King Alexander Obrenović (1876–1903) on May 29, 1903. In 1911 Živković formed an organization called Bela Ruka (White Hand), consisting of officers loyal to Crown Prince Alexander Karadjordjević and was a counterpart to Crna Ruka (Black Hand), the secret organization led by Colonel Dragutin Dimitrijević (Apis) (1876–1917), which sought to liberate and unite all Serbs by any means. In 1917 Živković became the commander of the King's

Guard and played a prominent role in organizing the trial of Apis in Salonika. After Apis's execution, Živković took an active part in a purge of members of the Black Hand from the Serbian army.

After January 6, 1929, in the period of King Alexander's (1888–1934) personal dictatorship, Živković became prime minister and minister of internal affairs. After Alexander's assassination in 1934, Živković held the post of defense minister in various Yugoslav governments. In April 1941 he emigrated to London, where he served in the government-in-exile in 1943. During the 1946 trial of General Dragoljub Mihailović (1893–1946), leader of Serbian military forces during World War II, Živković was charged with treason and sentenced to death in absentia. He died in exile in Paris.

Željan E. Šuster

Further reading
Enciklopedija Jugoslavije. Zagreb, 1980.
Mala Enciklopedija. Belgrade, 1978.

See also Alexander I Karadjordjević; Alexander Obrenović; Apis; Black Hand; Dragoljub Mihailović

Zogu, Ahmed Bey (1895–1961)

Political leader and self-proclaimed king of Albania. Zogu was born into a leading landowning family of the Mati clan in central Albania. He served as a delegate to the nationalistic Congress of Lushnjë in 1920, which protested the proposed partition of Albania and organized a new Albanian government. As interior minister in this government, he took measures to stabilize Albania's internal situation. After some political maneuvering, Zogu was named prime minister in 1922. Although his party won a majority in general elections in 1923, allegedly through underhanded means, popular discontent resulted in his ouster in a revolution in June 1924. A liberal and reformist government was established under Orthodox Bishop Fan S. Noli (1882–1965), while Zogu fled to Yugoslavia. There, Zogu organized an armed force that, with Yugoslavia's assistance, returned him to Albania in December. With his return, parliamentary government and political parties in Albania came to an end. Zogu allied himself with the landowners to enhance his power. In 1925 he proclaimed himself president of an Albanian republic. In foreign policy, Zogu abandoned Yugoslavia, looking instead to an accommodation with Italy in 1926. Italy provided economic and military aid but came increasingly to dominate Albania.

In 1928 Zogu made the republic into a monarchy and proclaimed himself King Zog I. During the Zog era, despite some attempts at modernization, Albania remained backward and poor. Yet he did make some progress by centralizing and establishing a semblance of order in the country. The response to the increasingly authoritarian nature of the regime and to the growing ties with Italy was a series of revolts and an attempt on Zog's life in 1931. All opposition was dealt with severely. Beginning in 1933, Zog did all that circumstances allowed to lessen Albania's dependence on Italy, but within a few years he returned to the fold. In 1939 he again resisted and Italy answered by invading Albania on April 7, 1939. Zog fled the country with his new wife and his newborn son. He never returned and died in exile in France in 1961.

Gregory J. Pano

Further reading
Fischer, Bernd. *King Zog and the Struggle for Stability in Albania.* Boulder, Colorado, 1984.
Logoreci, Anton. *The Albanians, Europe's Forgotten Survivors.* Boulder, Colorado, 1977.
Swire, Joseph. *Albania—The Rise of a Kingdom.* New York, 1971.
———. *King Zog's Albania.* London, 1937.

See also Congress of Lushnjë; Fan S. Noli

Županćić, Oton (1878–1949)

One of the greatest poets in modern Slovene literature. Županćič studied history and geography in Vienna. In 1913 he became city archivist of Ljubljana and was also manager of the National Theater in Ljubljana from 1920 until his death. Two factors were of decisive importance for his growth as a poet: his friendship with poets Ivan Cankar (1876–1918), Josip Murn-Aleksandrov (1879–1901), and Dragotin Kette (1876–1899), who formed the Slovene *moderna* (modernism) with their new ways of expression, and his stay in Vienna, where he became acquainted with the new European trends in poetry and art (symbolism, impressionism, decadence). In Vienna he wrote his first volume of poetry, *Čaša opojnosti* (*Goblet of Intoxication,*

Z

1899). More mature was his next collection, *Čez plan* (*Across the Plain,* 1904). He developed into a major figure in Slovene letters, possessing a superior command of the language, while balancing emotion and reason, with an ultimate belief in the integrity of the individual and the community.

His third book of verse, *Samogovori* (*Soliloquies,* 1908), had a more homogeneous theme: the relation of the poet and the fatherland, the poet and humankind. With this book, Župančič became less self-centered and more conscious of the national, social, and political responsibility of the poet. The fate of his homeland was even more central in *V zarje Vidove* (*The Dawn of St. Vid's Day,* 1920). In 1924 his lyrical drama in verse, *Veronika Deseniška,* appeared. In 1945 *Zimzelen pod snegom* (*Evergreen Snowbound*) reflected his reactions to World War II. Župančič became a member of the Slovene Academy of Art and Sciences in 1939. After World War II, he was elected a delegate to the Slovene parliament and a member of the presidium. He also received an honorary doctorate from Ljubljana University.

Thomas Eekman

Further reading

Cooper, Henry R. Jr. "Župančič and Whitman." *South East Europe* vol. 9 (1982): 14–59.

Cronia, A. *Ottone Župančič.* Rome, 1928.

Mahnić, J. *Oton Župančič.* Maribor, Slovenia, 1955.

Pogacar, Timothy. "Oton Župančič," in *Dictionary of Literary Biography,* vol. 147, *South Slavic Writers before World War II.* Detroit, 1995, 284–91.

Vidmar, Josip. *Studija o Otonu Župančiču.* Ljubljana, 1935.

See also Ivan Cankar; Slovene Literature

Zveno

Bulgarian sociopolitical organization (1927–49) founded by individuals who believed that the political party system—and the special interests it represented—was detrimental to the nation. The two main organizers of Zveno (Link) were Dimo Kazasov (1886–1980) and Kimon Georgiev (1882–1969). From 1927 to 1934, the group remained largely aloof from politics; members already enrolled in political parties were encouraged to remain and effect change from within.

The group was small and elite in its makeup until 1934, when it split. Kazasov and his supporters for a time joined the National Socialist movement with Aleksandur Tsankov (1879–1959). Georgiev and the rest remained independent and eventually joined the Military League, the clandestine (although sometimes semilegal) political organization of Bulgarian officers, in the coup of May 19, 1934, that overthrew the government of Aleksandur Malinov (1867–1938). The authoritarian nature of the group, along with monarchist elements among its membership, made it a suitable ally for the army. The Zvenari (members of Zveno) felt that they had a mandate to create a "supraparty authority" that would rid the country of politicians and create a state-controlled economy. In foreign policy, they supported rapprochement with Yugoslavia and France, which engendered controlling the Internal Macedonian Revolutionary Organization (IMRO), the revolutionary organization that supported creation of an autonomous Macedonia. Diplomatic relations with the Soviet Union led to trade talks and an exchange of diplomatic personnel. In January 1935 the Zvenari had an opportunity to apply their unique principles with the appointment of Georgiev to head the government. The Turnovo Constitution (established in 1879) was abolished, political parties were suppressed, and strict censorship was introduced. At this juncture, the group put into action its credo of government by a nonpartisan elite; however, this led to the very state of affairs that the Zvenari claimed to abhor—an insular political elite ruling from above with no base of support.

By 1939, Zveno's membership was split between various groups. During World War II, coalitions were attempted with the Communists, the left, Agrarians, and the Social Democrats in the Fatherland Front—the coalition of political organizations that seized power in 1944. Between October 1944 and February 1949, the organization metamorphosed into the National Union Zveno. They, along with the remaining "independent" parties, were subsumed into the Fatherland Front and then disbanded.

Mari A. Firkatian

Further reading

Bozhilov, Iv. et al. *Istoriia na Bŭlgariia.* Sofia, 1993.

Georgiev, V. *Burzhoaznite i drebnoburzhoaznite partii v Bŭlgariia 1934–1939.* Sofia, 1971.

———. "Ideite i politicheskite pozitsii na 'Zveno' prez vtorata svetovna voina," in *Pûrvi kongres na Bûlgarskoto istorichesko druzhestvo 27–30 ian. 1970,* vol. 1. Sofia, 1972.

Lalkov, Milclio et al. *Istoriia na tretata Bûlgarska dûrzhava 1878–1944.* Sofia, 1993.

See also Fatherland Front; Kimon Georgiev; IMRO; Dimo Kazasov; Military League; Aleksandur Tsankov; Turnovo Constitution

Index

revival style, 619
romantic trend, 618
See also specific countries
Arch of Triumph, 87
Ardeal, 804
arendaşi, 698
Argeş, 838
Arghezi, Tudor, **38**, 694, 697
Arhiva românească (Romanian Archives), 422
Árkay, Aladár, 36
Armenia, 727
Armenians, in Transylvania, 804
Armia Krajowa (Home Army), **38–39**, 605, 608, 609, 655
    Warsaw uprising, 842
Arminius, James, 643
Árpád, 337, 349
Arrabona, 314
Arrow Cross, **39**, 47, 364, 366–367, 662
    founder of, 778
art
    academic realism, 720
    Art Nouveau, 181, 183, 336, 511, 619, 622, 860
    asphalt technique, 513
    avant-garde, 169, 337, 543–544, 722
    Bauhaus, 337
    Biedermeier, 168–169
    book illustration, 511, 619, 900
    under communism, 16, 107, 109, 113
    Easter eggs, 691
    etchings, 223
    folk art, 107
    folk-based, 107, 182, 223, 812
    formism, 619
    historic scenes, 169, 181, 335, 486, 618, 622, 692, 745
    Hungarian impressionism, 336
    iconostases, 720
    icons, 108, 691, 721, 831
    illuminated manuscripts, 108, 170
    landscapes, 107, 336, 463, 692, 720, 744–745
    Moderna, 170, 171
    modernism, 169, 176, 182, 720
    monumental works, 1, 17, 107, 511, 745
    multicolored Zagred school, 169
    murals, 17, 107
    Nagybánya school, 336, 337
    nationalistic, 181–182, 336, 445, 478
    plein air method, 169, 176, 312
    Pont-Aven school, 619
    primitivism, 444–445
    as propaganda, 17
    realism, 618, 622, 744–745
    religious art, 108, 170, 549
    romanticism, 335, 396, 618, 622, 720
    sculpture, 1, 80, 169, 181, 492, 619, 622, 623
    secession-style, 169, 619–620
    Slavic épopée, 511
    socialist realism, 16, 17, 113, 169, 182, 619
    surrealism, 83–84, 720
    tapestry, 1, 107
    totemic period works, 812
    Zakopiański style, 619
    See also individual countries and specific art forms and
        styles; specific artists by name
Art Nouveau style
    architecture, 36
    art, 181, 183, 336, 511, 860
    stained glass, 619, 622, 860
Asachi, Gheorghe, 670, 697
Asen, Ivan, 92
Asen, Peter, 92
Ashes and Diamonds, 137
Ashkenazic Jews, 402, 407
Asia Minor, 389

Askenazy, Szymon, **39–40**
Asparuch, 92
Assembly of Captive Nations, 520–521
Assembly of National Liberation of Macedonia, 470
Association for Academic Courses, 612
Atanassov, John V., 111
Atatürk, Kemal, 236, 444, 559, 867
Athanassov, Georgi, 515
Athanassov, Nikolao, 515
atheist state, Albania as, 19, 334–335, 392
Athenaeum, 432, 574
Atntim I, exarch of Bulgaria, 94
atomic bomb, development of, 534, 781, 789
ATSH, 489
Attila the Hun, 536, 780
Audience, The (Havel), 322
August, Frederick, 231
Augustinčić, Antun, 169
August, Prince of Saxe-Coburg-Gotha, 267
Augustus II, king of Poland, 591
Augustus III, king of Poland, 591
Auróra, 777
Auschwitz, **40**, 331, 605, 662
Ausgleich (Compromise), 28, 34, **41**, 46, 67, 317–318
    architect of, 218
    Cisleithania/Transleithania, 139–140, 317–318
    and Croats, 877
    dualism, 229
    Dual Monarchy, 229–230
    and Hungarian War for Independence, 345–347, 354–357
Auslandsdeutsche, 289–290
Auslands-Organisation, 289
Aussenpolitisches Amt der NSDAP, 289
Austerlitz, Battle of, 22, 85
Austria
    and Albania, 10
    Anschluss, 30, 128, 228, 364, 859
    banking, 433
    Danubian Principalities, 216
    education, 251–252
    and Germany, 30, 328
    Kremsier/Kroměříž Parliament, **433–434**
    neoabsolutism, 531
    and Ottoman Empire, 70
    and Prussia, 60, 67, 301, 546–547
    and Slovenia, 746
Austria-Hungary
    Ausgleich (Compromise), 28, 34, 41, 46, 67, 139–140
    Austroslavism, 41–42
    capital city, 88
    and Croatia, 519–520, 877
    Dual Monarchy, 28, 34, 41, 46, 67, 229–230
    ethnic minorities, 122
    Franz Ferdinand assassination, 33, 52, 63, 77, 278, 308, 360
    and Germany, 228, 792
    last king, 128–129
    and Paris Peace Conference, 560
    and Russia, 88–89, 513, 513–514
    and Serbia, 250, 582–583
    trialism, 806–807
    World War I, 85–86, 128–129, 881–882
    and Yugoslav lands, 874–876, 880–882
Austrian Empire. *See* Habsburg Empire
Austrian National Bank, 54
Austrian Nazi Party, 30
Austria Poland. *See* Galicia
Austro-Hungarian Bank, 54
Austro-Prussian War of 1866, 60, 67, 301
Austro-Russian Balkan Agreement, 514
Austro-Sardinian War, 46, 531
Austroslavism, **41–42**, 323, 400, 425
Austro-Turkish War of 1788–90, 70
Avala Film, 139

Bulgarian National Assembly, 772
Bulgarian National Committee, 110
Bulgarian National Front, 110
Bulgarian Nationalist Socialist Party, 100
Bulgarian Opera Society, 109
Bulgarian Orthodox Chruch. *See* Exarchate
Bulgarian Peace Treaty, 574
Bulgarian Peasant Party, 573
Bulgarian Principality, 134
Bulgarians
    in Moldova, 504
    in Transylvania, 804
Bulgarian Secret Central Revolutionary Committee, 34, 95,
    237, 315, 454
Bulgarian-Serb War of 1885, 26, 96–97, **114**, 389
Bulgarian Social Democratic Party, 71, 148, 266, 423
Bulgarian Socialist Party, 104
Bulgarian Workers' Party, 100, 148
Bulgarian Workers' Social Democratic Party (BWSDP)
    (Narrow Socialists), 148, 222
Bulgars
    in Albania, 9
    in Bulgaria, 92
Bûlgarski knizhitsi (Bulgarian Letters), 74
Bûlgarski Orel (Bulgarian Eagle), 74
Bull of Gniezno, 625
Bülow, Cosima von, 458
Bund, **401**
Bund der Auslandsdeutscher, 289
Burebista, 667, 804
Burgas, 91, **114**
Burgenland, **114–115**, 140
Bürgerschulen, 252
Burmov, Tudor, 96
Burza (Tempest), Operation, 38, 842
Bush, George, 616
Butrint, 18
Buzuku, Gjon, 21
Bydgoszcz, 631, 843, 844
Byrnes, James F., 608
Byron, Lord George, 576
Byzantine chant, 108
Byzantine Church. *See* Uniate Church
Byzantine Empire
    and Albania, 8
    and Bulgaria, 92–93, 108
    and Thrace, 791
Byzantium, 563

čakavian dialect, 725
Čalfa, Marián, 151
Călinescu, Gheorghe, 697
Calvinists, 644
Calvin, John, 643
Camp of Great Poland, 224
Camp of National Unity, 603
Cankar, Ivan, **117**, 746, 750
Cantacuzino, Constantin, 696
Cantemir, Dimitrie, 696
Cantemir, Dimitrie, prince of Moldavia, 668
Čapek-Chod, Karel Matěj, 187
Čapek, Josef, 117, 181, 183
Čapek, Karel, **117–118**, 187, 198, 791
capitulations, **118–119**, 838
Caragiale, Ion Luca, **119**, 385, 409, 476, 675, 693, 697
Caragiale, Mateiu, 697
Caraion, Ion, 697
Carinthia, 766
Carnap, Rudolf, 632
Carniola, 870
Carniola Mark, 459
Carniolan Agricultural Society, 72
Čarnojević, Arsenije III, Patriarch, 722

Carol I, king of Romania, 81, **119–120**, 124, 255, 268, 675,
    677, 682
Carol II, king of Romania, 32, 101, **120**, 142, 297, 465, 481,
    494, 662, 682, 684
Carousel, 505
Carpathian Mountains, 89, 90, **121**, 589
Carpatho-Rusyns, **121–122**, 197
    in Transylvania, 804
Carpatho-Ukranians, 123
Carp, Petre P., **120–121**, 409, 677
Cărtărescu, Mircea, 698
Castle Hill (Várhegy), 261
Castlereagh, Viscount, 591
Castle, The (Kafka), 412
Castrus Timisiensis, 793
Catargiu, Barbu, 674
Catargiu, Lascăr, **124**, 674, 676
Catharism, 74
Catherine the Great, queen of Russia, 402–403, 557, 589, 591,
    701
Catholicism, **124–125**
    Albania, 9, 12
    Balkan region, 52
    Bosnia, 77
    and communism, 609, 610
    and Czechs, 191
    and education, 252, 593
    Hungary, 261–262, 502
    and Kulturkampf, 437
    PAX, 565
    Poland, 125, 593, 595, 609, 703, 861
    and Russification, 703, 704
    Slovakia, 738, 743
    and Solidarity, 296
    and Uniate Church, 819–820
Catholic University, 328
"Catre săteni" ("To the Villagers"), 698
Căuşari dance, 790
*Causes of the Hungarian State's Preservation and
    Constitutional Liberty, The* (Andrássy), 28
caviar, 214
Cavour, Camilio de, 347
Ceauşescu, Elena, **125–126**, 253, 660, 688–689, 855
Ceauşescu, Nicolae, **126**
    and communist party, 156–157, 377
    destruction of historic places, 693
    destruction of villages, 37
    execution of, 126, 660, 690
    intellectual protest of, 298
    nationalism of, 253, 527, 686
    regime of, 126, 688–689
    secret police under, 126, 715
    systemization, 776–777
    women's status under, 854–855
Čech, Svatopluk, 187
Čelakovský, František Ladislav, 186
Čelakovský, Jan Ladislav, 408
Ćelić, Stojan, 720
Celts
    in Belgrade area, 60–61
    in Bratslava, 82
    in Hungary, 314
    in Moravia, 85
    in Serbia, 536
censorship, 21, **127**, 188, 298, 370
Center-Left Bloc (Centrolew), 602, 847
Center Party, 437
Central Industrial District, Poland, 600–601
Centralization, 592
Central Powers. *See* Triple Alliance
Central Union of Sugar Beet Growers, 774, 819
Cepenkov, Marko, 472
Cephalonia, 386

Dual Monarchy, **229–230**
    establishment of, 28, 34, 41, 46, 67, 218, 229–230
    Hungary under, 357–360
    See also Austria-Hungary
Dubček, Alexander, 151, 185, 204–207, 221, **230**, 637
Dubrovačka trilogija (Dubrovnik Trilogy) (Vojnović), 173
Dubrovnik, 93, **230–231**
Duca, Ion G., 683, 787
duchik, 109
Duchy (Spirits) (Świętochowski), 776
Duchy of Warsaw, **231–232**
Dučić, Jovan, 724
Duke Bluebeard's Castle, 47, 57
Dukhnovych, Aleksander, 122
Dula, Matúš, 483
Duma, **232–233**
Duma Demokratsia, 489
Duma na bûlgarskite emigranti (The Word of Bulgarian Émigrés), 79
Dumitrescu, Geo., 697
Dunapentele, 382
Dunaújváros, **233**
Dunavska Zora (Danubian Dawn), 79
Dunavski Lebed (Danubian Swan), 653
Dunikowski, Xawery, 619, 622
Durčanský, Ferdinand, 739
Durdik, Josef, 577
Đuric, Dado, 720
Durrës, 7, 8, 11, 13, 160
Dušan, Stefan, tsar of Serbian Empire, 8, 507, 721, 872
Dušek, František X., 183
Dužan, Džamonja, 169
Dvořák, Antonin, 183, 194, **233–234**, 515, 635
dvoransko kolo, 212
Dyulgerov, Georgi, 139
Dziady (Forefathers) (Mickiewicz), 495, 621
Dzieje Polski w zarysie (Survey of Polish History) (Bobrzyński), 72–73
Dziekoński, J.P., 619
Dziennik (Diary) (Gombrowicz), 299
Dzierzynski, Feliks Edmundovich, 154, **234**, 596
Dzierzynski Square, 35
Dziś i Jutro (Today and Tomorrow), 565

Easter Article, 41, 218
Easter eggs, 691
Eastern Orthodox Church
    Albania, 9, 12, 21
    Balkan region, 52
    break of 1054, 124
    Bulgaria, 80, 91, 92, 93, 94, 108
    Romania, 667
    See also orthodoxy
Eastern question, 35, 88–89, **235–236**
    and Balkan Wars, 52–53
    and Congress of Berlin, 159, 236
    and Congress of Vienna, 161
    meaning of, 52
    and Porte, 632
Eastern Rumelia, 26, 96, 114, **236–237**
    capital city, 237
    geography, 236–237
    history, 237
East Germany, 143, 145, 291
    Berlin Wall, 64–65, 757
East Prussia, **235**
    Paris Peace Conference decision, 560
    World War I, 235
    World War II, 235
East Slovak Steel Works, 427
Ecce Homo, 513
Eckhardt, Tibor, **237**
Ecoglasnost, 903

economic crisis
    Poland, 303, 611–614
    Serbia, 718–719
economic development. *See* Industrialization; specific countries
Ecumenical Council of Churches, 205
Ecumenical Councils, 549
Ecumenical Patriarchate, 563
Eden, Anthony, 607
education, **251–253**
    chitalishte (reading room), 108, 133–134
    Enlightenment educational system, 543
    higher education, 327–328
    Hungarian folk high school movement, 340
    Jewish schools, 601
    journalism education, 490
    Muslim schools, 516
    of women, 848, 850, 851–852, 856, 885
    See also specific countries
Egész Iátóhatár (The Whole Horizon) (Szabó), 777
Egoizm narodowy wobec etyki (National Egoism in Relation to Ethics) (Balicki), 49
Egry, József, 337
Ehrenroth, Casimir, 96
Eichmann, Adolf, 839
1867 Compromise, The (Andrássy), 28
Einsatzgruppen, 329, 331
Einstein, Albert, 781
ekevian, 725
Ekzarkh, 112
Elbasan, 7, 17, 20
Elbe River, pollution problem, 259
Elek, Judit, 138
Eleonore von Reuss-Kostritz, queen of Bulgaria, **253–254**
Élet és Irodalom, 777
Eliade, Mircea, 87, **254**, 385, 388, 694, 695, 697
Eliáš, Alois, 201, **254–255**, 643
Elin Pelin, **255**
Elisabeth (Carmen Sylva), queen of Romania, 255–256, 675
Elsner, Józef, 135, 516
emigration, **256–257**
    See also émigrés subentry of specific coutries
Eminescu, Mihai, 165, **257–258**, 409, 476, 675, 693, 697
Emona, 459
empiricism, 579
Endless Column, 80, 692
Endlösung, 331
energetic personalism, 580
Enescu, George, 256, **258**, 515, 675, 693, 694
Engel, Emanuel, 866
Engels, Friedrich, 482
Enlightenment, 183, 579, 746, 749
Enos-Media line, 52
Entente Powers, 306–307, 597
environmental movement, 666, 903
environmental problems, **258–260**
    Bohemia, 75
    Bulgaria, 103–104
    Danube delta, 214–215
    Hungary, 443
    Poland, 416, 832
Enyédi, Ildikó, 138
Eötvös, Baron József, 229, **260–261**, 342, 359, 383
epics
    Croatia, 170, 173, 487
    Czechoslovakia, 186, 226, 473
    haiduk, 319–320
    Hungarian, 341–342
    Poland, 495
    Serbia, 721, 724
    Slovenia, 638
Epidaurus, 231
Epiros, 27
Epirus, 11, 13, 263, 451

Ignatiev, Nikolai Pavlovich, Count, 264, **376**
Ignatova, Lili, 849
Ignotus, Pál, 541
ikavian dialect, 725
Ikonomov, Georgi, 315
Ilarion, **376–377**
Ilić, Vojislav, 724
Iliescu, Ion, 298, **377**
Ilinden uprising, 110, **377–378**, 380
Ilirske narodne novine (Illyrian National Newspaper), 284
Iljoski, Vasil, 472
illuminated manuscripts, 108, 170
Illustrowany Kurier Codzienny (Illustrated Daily Courier), 639
Illyés, Gyula, 342, 343, 363, **378**
Illyrian movement, **379**
    and Croatian literature, 172–173, 352
    focus of, 170, 352, 488
    leader of, 170, 172, 283–284, 876
Illyrian Party, 284
Illyrian Provinces, 459
Illyrian Reading Club, 487
Illyrians
    and Albanians, 8, 18, 20
    in Bosnia, 77
    in Croatia, 170, 900
    in Slovenia, 459
Imperial Council, 60
Imrédy, Béla, 364, **379–380**
IMRO (Internal Macedonian Revolutionary Organization), 22, 25, 71, 97, 98, 100–101, **380–381**, 537, 762
    Ilinden uprising, 377–378, 470
    leader of, 497
incompleteness theorem, 296
Independence Party, 428
Independent Democrats, 883
Independent National Party, 488–489, 877
Independent Self-governing Trade Union (NSZZ). *See* Solidarity
Independent Smallholders' Party, 30–31, 47, 237, 367, 520
Independent State of Croatia, 886–887
India, and Gypsies, 314
Indo-European languages
    Albanian, 52
    ancient Macedonian, 471
    Poland, 625
industrialization, **381–383**
    and banking, 54–55
    and environmental problems, 259–260
    and Great Depression, 304
    and labor force, 441–442
    and mass production, 58
    and Soviet Union, 382
    See also specific countries
influenza panepidemic, 323
Information Bureau of the Communist and Workers Parties. *See* Cominform
Institut für Auslandsbeziehungen, 290
intelligencia, **383–384**
    Albania, 537
    Carpatho-Rusyns, 122
    Czechoslovakia, 118, 383–384
    Hungary, 383
    Poland, 48–49, 383, 384, 610, 612
    Romania, 287
    Transylvanian, 56
    Ukranian, 595
Inter-Allied Conference, 599
Interfactory Strike Committee, 611, 613
Internal Macedonian Revolutionary Organization. *See* IMRO (Internal Macedonian Revolutionary Organization)
International Agrarian Bureau, 310
International Agrarian Bureau Bulletin, 310
International Children's Assembly, Banner of Peace, 904

International Control Commission, 11
International Monetary Fund, 251
International Peasant Union, 310
International Romani Union, 315
International Style, architecture, 36–37
International Women's Day, 103
Ioanna, queen of Bulgaria, 76, **384**, 731
Ionescu, Eugen, 87, **385**, 580, 694, 695, 697
Ionescu, Gelu, 698
Ionescu, Nae, 254, **385**, 388, 694
Ionescu, Take (Dumitru G.), **386**, 677
Ionian Islands, **386**
Iorga, Nicolae, **386–387**, 528, 675, 682–683, 684, 694, 697
Iosif I, Exarch, 264
Iosifova, Anna, 107
Iovkov, Iordan, 113
Iron Curtain, 136, 142, 308, **387**
    and Sovietization, 756–757
Iron Gates, 61, 121, 216, **388**, 838
Iron Guard (Legion of the Archangel Michael), 4, 33, 142, 254, 385, **388–389**, 528, 662, 730
Iron Ring, 129, 785
irrationalism, 581
irredentism, **389–390**
    Besserabian question, 65–66
    groups involved, 389
    Transylvania, 120
    wars related to, 389
IRWIN group, 745
Iser, Iosif, 692
Iskra (Spark), 133
Islam, **390–392**
    See also Muslims
island settlements, 263
Islaz Proclamation, 48, 53, 68, 325, **392**
Ismael, 391
Ispovedanie pravoslavniia veri khristiianskiia (A Confession of Orthodox Faith) (Sofronii), 755
Israel, Jewish emigration to, 403
Istanbul. *See* Constantinople/Istanbul
Istoriia slavenobolgarskiaia (Slaveno-Bulgarian History) (Sofronii), 755
Istoriia Slavianobolgarskaia (A Slavonic-Bulgarian History) (Paisii of Hilendar), 557
Istoriia slavianobolgarskaia (History of the Bulgarian Slavs) (Hilendarski), 112
Istria, 11, 167, **392–393**, 882
d'Istria, Dora, 675
István a király (Stephen the King), 338
Italo-Turkish War of 1911, 50
Italy
    and Albania, 8, 10, 11, 12–13, 19, 238
    Albanians in, 799
    Anti-Comintern Pact, 31
    in Axis, 31, 42–43, 101
    Ethiopian invasion, 13, 42
    fascism. *See* Mussolini, Benito
    as Great Power, 307
    and Libya, 50, 99
    and London Pact, 461
    London Pact, 461
    and Montenegro, 508
    and Ottoman Empire, 50
    unification, 593
    World War I, 461
    World War II, 31, 42–43, 101
    and Yugoslavia, 214, 808
Ithaca, 386
Ivalo, 107
Ivan Alexander, emperor of Bulgaria, 93
Ivănescu, Mircea, 698
Ivanova, Lili, 849
Ivanović, Katarina, 722, 855

Luchian, ştefan, **463**, 692
Lukáč, E.B., 742
Lukács, György, 48, 359, 362, 384, **463–464**, 578–579
Lukanov, Andrei, 104
Łukasiewicz, Jan, 6, 628, 816
Łukasiński, Walerian, 39, 280, **464–465**
Lumir, 187
Lumírovci, 187
Lupescu, Elena (Magda), 120, **465**, 478, 682, 685, 854
Lupescu, Nicolae, 465
Lupu, Vasile, prince of Moldavia, 668
Lusatia, **465–466**
Lusatian Sorbs, 465, **466**
Lushnjë, Congress of, 11, 12
Lutherans, 644, 713
Luther, Martin, 643
Lutosławski, Witold, 516, 623
Luwigana, 459
Luxemburg, Rosa, 154, 234, 464, **466–467**, 596
Luxemburgs, 191
Luzerna, Camilla, 855
L'vov, 287, **467**
L'vov Deutsch Jüdisches Bethaus, 407
Lwów, 595, 601, 607

Macedonia, 249, **469–472**
  as Balkan country, 52
  and Bulgaria, 53, 91, 94, 97, 100–101, 110
  capital city, 469, 732–733
  communism, 470
  émigrés, 257
  ethnic minorities, 378, 389, 390, 469, 516, 814, 892
  geography, 469
  history, 50, 52–53, 94, 95, 99, 390, 469–470, 874
  independence movement, 22, 25, 71, 97, 98, 100–101, 377–378, 380–381, 470
  irredentism, 389–390
  language, 20, 111, 469, 471
  literature, 471–472
  and Ottoman Empire, 470, 551, 553
  political parties. *See* political parties; individual parties by name
  religion, 470
  World War II, 887
Macedonian Committee, 390
Macedonian Question, 264
Macedonian Student Association, 497
Macedonski, Alexandru, 697
Maček, Vladko, 172, 179, 406, **472–473**, 759–760, 883
MacGahan, Januarius A., 95, 113
Mácha, Karel Hynek, 186, 194, **473**
Machar, Josef, 187
Machatý, Gustav, 137
Mach, Ernst, 632
Macierzyństwo (Maternity), 860
Mackiewicz, Konstanty, 619
Mackiewicz, Maria, 619
Mączyński, Franciszek, 619
Madách, Imre, 342
Madarász, Victor, 335
Madgearu, Virgil, **473–474**, 528, 682, 683, 684
mafia, Czech, 189, 196
MAFILM, 176
Magazinul istoric pentru Dacia (Historic Magazine for Dacia), 48
Magheru, George, 671
Maghiar Autonomous Region, 780
Magic Lantern, 322
Maglić, Bogdan, 723
Măgureanu, Virgil, 715
Magyar Csillag (Hungarian Star), 378
Magyar Democratic Forum, 635

Magyar Hirlap, 489
magyarization, **474–475**
  focus of, 34, 252, 877
  and Slovakia, 195, 351, 372, 738–739
Magyarones, 877
Magyarország 1514-ben (Hungary in 1514) (Eötvös), 260
Magyarországi Hirek (News of Hungary), 430
Magyars, 41, 191, 192, 314, 348, 526
  and *Ausgleich*, 317–318
  origin, 337, 426
Magyar Szemle (Hungarian Review) (Szekfű), 780
Magyar történet (Hungarian History) (Szekfű and Hóman), 332, 780
Mahrburg, Adam, 579
Mahumud II, Ottoman sultan, 27, 94, 397, **475**, 553, 792
Măiastra, 80
Maimonides, 407
Maiorescu, Titu L., 120, 386, 408, **475–476**, 580, 675, 697
Maior, Petru, 669, 697
Maisky, Ivan M., 606
Maitreyi (Eliade), 254
Majális, 336
Majdanek, 331, 605
Máj group, 187, 532
Máj (May) journal, 186, 187
Máj (May) (Mácha), 473
Major, Štefan, 141
Majstri (Master Craftsmen) (Šikula), 742
Makavejev, Dušan, 138, 139, **476**
Makedoniia (Macedonia), 735
Makedonska tribuna (Macedonian Tribune), 111
Makk, Karoly, 137, 139
Makovecz, Imre, 37
Makowski, Zbigniew, 623
Maksimović, Desanka, 896
Mălăcioiu, Ileana, 698
Malczewski, Jacek, **476**, 619
Malenkov, Georgi, 903
Maleš, Miha, 745
Maléter, Pál, 153
Malinov, Aleksandur, **477**
Mallý, Gustáv, 182
Malobabic, Rade, 70
Małopolska dialect, 625
W malym dwarku (In a Small Country House) (Witkiewicz), 846
Malypetr, Jan, **477**, 819
Maminka (Mommy) (Seifert), 716
Manchukuo, 31
Manchuria, 31
Mánes, Antonín, 181, 478
Mánes, Josef, 181, 182, 183, 194, **478**
Manhattan Project, 781, 789
Manichaeanism, 74
Manifesto of Czech Writers, 404
Manifesto of the Two Emperors, 597
Man of Iron, 138
Maniu, Iuliu, 4, **478**, 680, 682–683, 685
Mannheim, Károly, 359, 464, **479**
Manolescu, Nicolae, 698
Manolov, Emanuil, 109, 515
Manuscripts, The (Czech), **479**
Mărăsti, Battle of, 42, 480
Mărăşti-Mărăşeşti-Oituz, **480**
March Constitution, 531
March Front movement, 343, 430
Marconi, H., 618, 622
Marek, Antonín, 408
Margaret Islands, 88
Marghiloman, Alexandru I., 42, 87, **480**, 679
Mariánské Lázně, 75
Maria Theresa, empress of Austria, 191, 350, 351, 359

Nehru, Jawaharlal, 538
Neisse River, **529**
Nemanja, Stefan, 721
Nemanjić, Stefan, 721
Neman River, Battle of, 600
Němcová, Božena, 186–187, 194, **530**, 850
Nemec, Jan, 138
Nemes, Nagy, Ágnes, **530–531**
Németh, László, 343
Nemiri (Anxieties) (Andrić), 29
NEM (New Economic Mechanism), 368, 411, **529–530**
Nemzeti Dal (National Song) (Petőfi), 575
Nenshkodra, 7
neoabsolutism, 356, **531**
neoclassical style, architecture, 35
neoiobăgia. See neoserfdom
neoserfdom, 225, 474, 568
Neo-Slav Congress, 42, 532
Neo-Slavism, **531–532**
Népi movement, 342–343, **342–343**
Népszabadság, 489
Neruda, Jan, 187, 194, **532–533**
Neshev, Ivan, 107
Nesselrode, Karl, 511
Neues Wiener Tageblatt (New Vienna Daily Paper), 713
Neuilly, Treaty of, 22, 100, 226, 420, **533**, 560
Neumann, János (John von Neumann), 359, 534, **534**
Neumann, Stanislav, 187
Neurath, Konstantin von, 200, 642
New Class: An Analysis of the Communist System (Djilas), 384
New Economic Mechanism. *See* NEM (New Economic Mechanism)
New Economic Policy (NEP), 369
New Europe, 726
New Party, Hungary, 54
newspapers. *See* Press; individual countries; specific newspapers by name
New Zionist Organization, 601
Nezavisima Bulgariia (Independent Bulgaria), 573
Nezavisimost (Independence), 79, 573, 768
Nezval, Vitěslav, 187
Nicene Creed, 549, 820
Nicholas I of Montenegro, 508, **535–536**
Nicholas I, tsar of Russia, 134, 165–166, 180, 346, **534**, 703, 705
Nicholas II, tsar of Russia, 24, 76, 513, **535**, 702
Nicolaaescu, Sergiu, 139
Niederösterreichische Escomptegesellschaft, 54
Niemcewicz, Julian, 539
Nienasycenie (Insatiability) (Witkiewicz), 846
Niewiadomski, Eligiusz, 602
Nijinski, Wacław, 624
Nikolaevich, Grand Duke Constantine, 594
Nikolaevich, Nicholas, 598
Ninčič, Momčilo, **536**
Niš, 8, **536**
Niš, Convention of, **537**
Niš Declaration, 882
Njegos. *See* Petar II (Peter) Petrović Njegoš
Noica, Constantin, 385, 698
Noli, Fan S., 12, 17, 18, 21, 238, **537**, 905
nonaligned movement, **538**
Nonpartisan Bloc for the Cooperation with the Government, 710
Non-Party Bloc of Cooperation with the Government, 602
North Atlantic Treaty Organization (NATO)
    and Bulgaria, 104
    creation of, 482–483
    intervention in Kosovo crisis, 518
    and West Germany, 842
Northern Bukovina, 33, 120
Northern Epirus, 389

Norwid, Cyprian Kamil, 621, 627
Novak, Vjenčeslav, 173
Nova revija (New Review), 751
Nova TV, 490
November Uprising (Powstanie Listopadowe), 64, 134, 162, 398, 455, **538–539**
Novi Beograd, 61
Novice, 72
Novi era (New Era), 573
Novine Horvatzke (Croatian News), 283, 284
Novi Pazar. *See* Sanjak of Novi Pazar
Novomeský, Ladislav, 742
Novosil'tov, N.N., 180, 620
Novotný, Antonín, 151, 204, 205, 221, **539–540**
Novotný, Otakar, 36
Novo vreme (New Times), 810
Nowa Huta (New Foundry), 431
Nowicki, Maciej, **540**, 619, 623
Nowosielski, Jerzy, 619
NS-Lehrerbund, 289
numerus clausus, 364, **540–541**, 684
Nušić, Branislav, 724
Nyers, Rezső, 635
Nyirség, 306
Nyolcak (the Eights), 336
Nyugat (West), 3, 45, 336, 342, 359, 378, 464, **541**
Nyugtalanság völgye (The Valley of Unrest) (Babits), 45

Občanská Beseda (Citizens' Club), 492
Oberstburggraf, 424
oblasti, 829
Obradović, Dositej (Dimitrije), 413, **543**, 721
Obrana národa (Nation's Defense), 255
Obrazopisov, Nikola, 106
Obrenović, Alexander, king of Serbia, **25–26**, 249–250, 498, 880
Obrenović, Mihailo, 50, 501, 723, 879
Obrenović, Milan, king of Serbia, 25, 96, 114, **498**, 664, 880
Obrenović, Miloš, 24, 26, 70, 269, 284, 873, 879
Obrenović, Natalie, 498
Obreshkov, Bencho, **543–544**
Obretenov, Baba Tonka, 544
Obretenov, Georgi Tihov, 315, **544**
Obretenov, Nikola Tihov, **544**
obschina, 482
O'Buda, 88
Obycejny zivot (An Ordinary Life) (Capek), 118
Ochab, Edward, 155
Ochorowicz, Julian, 579, 633
October Diploma, 267, **545**, 546
October Manifesto, 232
October Patent, 298
October Revolution, 449, 505
Oder River, **545**, 590
Odessa, 329, 701
Odobescu, Alexandru, 697
"O făcile de Paşte" ("An Easter Torch") (Caragiale), 119
Ogniem i mieczem (With Fire and Sword) (Sienkiewicz), 728
Ohmann, Bedřich, 36
Ohrid, 92
oil production, 248, 249
Oituz, Battle of, 42
Ojcze Nasz (Our Father) (Cieszkowski), 136
Oláh, George, 340
Olahus, Nicolaus, 696
Olbracht, Ivan, 188
Old Church Bulgarian (Slavonic), 92, 93, 112, 185, 226, 721, 735–736
Old Czechs, 194, 311, **546**
Old Man with a Cane, 647
Old Slovenes, 72
Old Theater, 622

People's Party, 42, 680, 681, 760, 883
People's Republic of Albania, 14
People's Republic of Czechoslovakia, 203
People's Republic of Hungary, 415
People's Republic of Romania, 687
People's Will, 453
Pepper, John, 588
Percentages Agreement, 136, **569–570**, 686
perestroika. See glasnost and *perestroika*
Persian Gulf War, 104
Perushtitsa, 35
Pesma (The Poem) (Davičo), 896
Pest, 88, 353
Pesti Divatlapok (Pest Fashion), 574
Pesti Hirlap (Pest News), 345, 354, 429
Pesti Magyar Külkereskedelmi Bank, 243
Petar I (Peter) Petrović Njegoš, prince-bishop of Montenegro,
   508, **570**
Petar II (Peter) Petrović Njegoš, prince-bishop of Montenegro,
   508, **570–571**, 580, 721, 724
Petchenegs, 780
Peter, tsar of Bulgaria, 92
Peter the Great, tsar of Russia, 504
Peter Karadjordjević, king of Serbia, 33, 420, 564, **571–572**,
   880–881
Peter II Karadjordjević, king of Yugoslavia, 25, **571**
pětka, 4, 197, **572–573**, 775
Petkov, Dimitur Nikolov, **573**
Petković, Dimitrije, 722
Petkov, Nikola, 102, 294, **573–574**
Petkov, Petko Dimitrov, 573, **574**
Petlyura, Semyon, 600
Petnaest rukoveti (Fifteen Songs), 722
Petőczi, Kata Szidnónia, 851
Petőfi (Illyés), 378
Petőfi, Sándor, 176, 221, 297, 337, 342, 353, 354, 356,
   574–575
Petorka (Five), 294
Petrașcu, Gheorghe, 692
Petrescu, Camil, 697
Petrescu, Radu, 698
Petriceicu-Hasdeu, Bogdan, 697
Petronievič, Branislav, 580
Petrova, Sultana, 98
Petrović, Aleksandar, 139
Petrović, Karadjordje. *See* Black George
Petrović, Nadežda, 720
Petrović, Zora, 720, 722
Petrov, Nikola, 107
Petrov, Racho, 97, 98
Petrov, Valeri, 113
Pfaff, Ferenc, 36
Phanariots (Fanariots), 75, 268–269, 504, 525, **575**, 694
   in Romania, 668–669, 693, 838
phenomenology, 578, 581
Philanthropic Fund for Writers and Journalists, 644
Philharmonic Society, 16
philhellinism, **576**
Philip II, of Macedonia, 92
philosophy/philosophers, **576–581**
   communism, effects on, 579–580
   dualism, 580
   empiricism, 579
   energetic personalism, 580
   of Enlightenment, 579
   folklore based, 580
   Hegelianism, 577, 578–579
   on human diversity, 326
   irrationalism, 581
   logic, 579
   Marxism, 577, 580, 581
   materialism, 580, 581
   messianism, 579

metaphysics, 579, 580
new man concept, 577
phenomenology, 578, 581
philosophy of harmony, 578
Polish logic, 628
positivism, 577–578, 579, 581, 622
Romanian existentialism, 385
theory of universal evolution, 580
See also specific countries
Piasecki, Bolesław, 565, **581–582**, 603
Piast, 4, 596
Pig War, 250, **582–583**, 880
Pilinszky, János, 342
Pillat, Ion, 697
Piłsudski, Józef, **583–584**
   interwar period, 602
   May Coup, 224, 302, 303, 487–488, 717
   Polish Legions, 59, 583, 628
   and Polish Socialist Party, 596–597
   Polish unification plan/World War I, 583, 597–600
Pindus Mountains, 7
Pintilie, Lucian, 138, 139
Pipa, Arshi, 20
Pipkov, Panayot, 515
Pirin, 91
Pirin Macedonia, 470
Pirinski, Georgi, 110, 111
Pirker, Pero, 891
Pita, Dan, 139
Pittsburgh Agreement (Pittsburgská Dohoda), 196, **584**
Placówka (The Outpost) (Prus), 644
Planck, Max, 781
Plater, Emilia, 853
plays and playwrights
   Bulgaria, 113
   Croatia, 170, 173
   Czechoslovakia, 118, 187–188, 322
   Hungary, 505
   Poland, 299, 326, 610, 776, 846, 861
   Romania, 119, 385, 693, 694
   Slovakia, 743
   Slovenia, 117
   See also theater
Plečnik, Jože, 37
plein air method, 169, 176, 312
Plekhanov, Georgy, 483
Pleven, 91, 95, **585**
Pleven, Battle of, **585–586**
Ploče, 77
Ploughman's Front, 313
Plovdiv, 34, 91, 95, 96, 237
pluralistic franchise concept, 28
Plzeň, 75
Pniewski, Bohdan, 619
Pobedonostsev, Konstantin, 703
Podgorica, 507, 508
Podídky z druhé kapsy (Tales from the Other Pocket) (Capek),
   118
Pod Igoto (Under the Yoke) (Vazov), 113, 826
Podjavorinská, Ludmila, 742
Podkowiński, Władysław, 619
Pod manastirskata loza (Under the Monastery Grapevine)
   (Pelin), 255
Podobe iz sanj (Dream Visions) (Cankar), 117
Podolia, 122
poetry
   Bulgaria, 79, 112–113, 292, 825–826
   Croatia, 170, 171, 173, 638
   Czechoslovakia, 186, 187, 473, 532–533, 715–716
   Hungary, 2–3, 45, 338, 341, 342, 378, 405, 415–416, 530,
      574–575, 835
   Macedonia, 472
   Montenegro, 570–571

and Germany, 656, 792
as Great Power, 307–308
history, 701–702
and Japan, 232, 535, 597, 702
Mediterranean Agreements, 491
and Napoléon I, 22–23, 64
nationalism, 702–703, 736–737
and Ottoman Empire, 2, 23, 53, 65, 436, 585–586, 701, 704–706
pogrom, 588–589
and Poland, 134, 398–399, 535, 565–566, 603, 620, 703
religion, 701
and Romania, 679–680
Russification, 702–703
russophobia, 703–704
Slavophilism, 737
World War I, 84, 86–87
See also Soviet Union
Russian Civil War, 84, 599
Russian Communist Party Hungarian Section, 152
Russian Poland. *See* Polish Congress Kingdom
Russian Polish National Committee, 49
Russian Social Democratic Labor Party, 401
Russification, **702–703**
of Poland, 24, 535, 594, 595
Russo, Alecu, 671, 697, 699
Russo-German Nonaggression Treaty. *See* Molotov-Ribbentrop Pact
Russo-Japanese War, 232, 535, 597, 702
Russophile movement, categorization of Russian, 123
Russophobia, **703–704**
Russo-Turkish War of 1806–12, 65
treaty, 65
Russo-Turkish War of 1828–29, 553, **704–705**
treaty, 2
Russo-Turkish War of 1877–78, 18, 23, 26, 64, 89, 113, 227, 264, 389, 585–586, **705–706**
Battle of Pleven, 585–586
treaty, 2, 9, 77, 89, 95, 114, 159, 711–712
Rusynophiles, 123
Rusyns, 121–123
Carpatho-Rusyns, 121–123
Ruszczyc, Ferdynand, 619
Ruthenes. *See* Carpatho-Rusyns
Ruzhitsa (Hollyhock), 735
Rzeczpospolita, 489

Sabin, Albert Bruce, **707**
Sabor, 346, **707–708**
Sachsenhausen, 395
sacraments, Catholicism, 125
Sacrifice Holiday, 391
Sa'di, 391
Sadoveanu, Mihail, 694, 697
Šafařík, Pavel Jozef, 186, 193, 283, 408, **708–709**
Şaguna, Bishop Andrei, 671, **709**
St. Andrew's Assembly, 733
St. Cyril, 92, 112, 122, 185, 186, 735, 738, 741
St. Elijah's Day uprising, 98
St. Francis Church, 860
St. Germain, Treaty of, 420, 560, 584, **765–766**
St. Mary's Church, 486
St. Methodius, 92, 112, 122, 185, 186, 735, 738, 741
St. Sava, 721
St. Stefan's Church, 376
St. Stephen, king of Hungary, 261, 314, 569, 780, 805
Crownlands of, 140, **175**, 349
rock opera, 338
St. Stephen's Day, 354
St. Theodore icon, 108
St. Wenceslas, 181
Sakhalin Island, 865

Sakser, Frank, 748
salami tactics, of Stalin, 756
Šalamun, Tomaž, 750
Šalda, František Xaver, 187
Salieri, Antonio, 458
Salivarová, Zdena, 188
Salk, Jonas, 707
Sallai, Imre, 152
Salogótarján Coal Mines, 135
Salonika, 52, 402, 514
Salonika Front, 25, 33, 70, 100, **710**
Salve Regina (Kasprowicz), 416
Samănatorism, 697
Sămănătorul, 708
Samarin, Yurii, 736
samizdat, 176, 370, 490
Samogovori (Soliloquies), 906
Samokov Apprentices School, 106
Samo, Slavonic empire, 871
Samuil, tsar of Bulgaria, 92
Sanacja, 401, 583–584, **710**
Sanatorium pod klepsydrą (The Sanatorium under the Sign of the Hourglass) (Schultz), 714
Sandanski, Jane, 97
Sand, George, 135, 458
Sandoveanu, Mihail, **708**
Sandu, Ioniţa, 771
sanjak, 711, 785
Sanjak (Sandžak) of Novi Pazar, 53, 89, 159, 427, 508, 711, **711**
ethnic minorities, 516
history, 711, 881
San Stefano, Treaty of, 9, 77, 89, 95, 114, 159, 301, **711–712**
Šantić, Aleksa, 724
Saracens, 314
Sarajevo, **712**
ethnic conflicts, 518
Franz Ferdinand assassination, 63, 77, 278, 858
Jews in, 402, 407
Serb capital, 79
Sarajevo (Seton-Watson), 726
Sarandë, 7, 18
Sarolt, mother of St. Stephen, 851
Satan in Goray (Singer), 731
Sava River, 215, **712–713**
Savćicsl, Vladimir, 750
Saxons, 288, 526, 591, 805
Sayn-Wittgenstein, Carolyne von, 458
Sburătorul movement, 697
Schaff, Adam, 579–580
Schäffle, Albert, 330
Schatz, Boris, 106
Scheinpflugová, Olga, 118
Schei Psalter, 696
Schlick, Moritz, 579, 816
Schlosselberg Castle, 465
Schmerling, Anton Ritter von, 60, 177, 267
Schmidt, Helmut, 550
Schoenberg, Arnold, 57
Schönerer, Georg von, **713–714**
Schulz, Bruno, 627, **714**
Schuschnigg, Kurt von, 30
Schuyler, Eugene, 113
Schwarzenberg, Prince Felix zu, prince of Austria, 46, 59, **714–715**, 846
science, theories/discoveries, 177–178, 491, 534, 707, 723, 781
science fiction, 118, 164–165, 187–188
Scientific Review, 220
Scînteia, 489
Scînteia (Spark), 489, 639
scouting movement, 788
Scouts, 651

AQUINAS COLLEGE LIBRARY

3 5060 00138 907 4

WITHDRAWN